standard catalog of
WORLD PAPER MONEY

Volume Two – General Issues to 1960
Eighth Edition
Based on the original works of Albert Pick

Colin R. Bruce II
Senior Editor

Neil Shafer
Technical Editor

George S. Cuhaj
Coordinating Editor

Special Contributors
Milt Blackburn, William G. Henderson, Dr. Maurice Kolosky
Kenneth MacKenzie, John T. Martin, William McNatt, Tom Michael
Tony Pisciotta, Robert Wilhite, Christof Zelbweger

It is the glorious prerogative of the empire of knowlege, that what it gains it never loses. On the contrary, it increases by the multiple of its own power: all its ends becomes means: all its attainments help to new conquests. – *Daniel Webster.*

krause publications

Published in the United States by Krause Publications, Inc.
700 E. State Street, Iola, WI 54990
Telephone: 715-445-2214 • FAX: 715-445-4087
E-mail: www.krause.com

Library of Congress Catalog Card Number: 80-081510
International Standard Book Number: 0-87341-469-1

Printed in the United States of America

TABLE OF CONTENTS

ACKNOWLEDGEMENTS

The contributions to this catalog have been many and varied, and to recognize them all would be a volume in itself. Accordingly, we wish to acknowledge these invaluable collectors, scholars and dealers in the world paper money field, both past and present, for their specific contributions to this work through the submission of notes for illustration, improved descriptive information and market valuations.

Esko Ahlroth
Jan Alexandersson
Walter D. Allan
Paulo Almeida
Milan Alusic
Carl A. Anderson
Dr. Jorge E. Arbelaez
Efrain Archilla Diez
Brian Asquith
Norman Athy
David August
Keith Austin
William L. S. Barrett
Richard Bates
Adriaan C. F. Beck
Richard Becker
Michel Becuwe
Dr. Anton Belcev
Yasha Beresiner
Wolfgang Bertsch
Milt Blackburn
Gilles Blançon
Ed Bohannon
Joseph E. Boling
Wilfried A. Bracke
Jean Bricaud
Dr. Alejandro Brill
Robert Brooks
Weldon D. Burson
Lance K. Campbell
David Carlson
Arthur D. Cohen
George Conrad
Scott E. Cordry
Guido Crapanzano
Jehangir B. Dalal
Howard A. Daniel III
Paul Davis
A. A. C. de Albergaria Pinheiro
Ricardo de Leon Tallavas

Richard G. Doty
Duane D. Douglas
Vladimir Duic
Dundar Numismatik
Wilhelm Eglseer
Esko Ekman
Jack G. Fischer
Guvendik Fisekcioglu
George A. Fisher, Jr.
Mark Fox
Ian Fraser
W. A. Frick
Gary Ganguillet
Brian Giese
Arcelio Gomez-Prada
Bernardo Gonzales-White
Lee Gordon
John S. Haas
Agus Halim
Flemming Lyngbeck Hansen
Len Harsel
Dr. James A. Haxby
William G. Henderson
Melvin P. Hennisch
Dick Herman
David Hollander
Anton Holt
Nicolae Hridan
Louis Hudson
Mikhail Istomin
Dr. Norman Jacobs
Walter Jellum
William M. Judd
Alex Kaglyan
Olaf Kiener
Josef Klaus
John M. Kleeberg
Tristan Kolm
Michael Kvasnica
George Lill III

Claire Lobel
L.K. Loimaranta
Dennis Luck
Alan Luedeking
Ma Tok Wo
Kenneth MacKenzie
Ranko Mandic
Ian A. Marshall
John T. Martin
Arthur C. Matz
Leo May
A.L.T. McCammon
William McNatt
Donald Medcalf
Lazar Mishev
Howard Mitchell
Ernest J. Montgomery
Tanju Mutlu
Colin Narbeth
George S. Notarpole
Son Xuan Nguyen
Andrew Oberbillig
Geoffrey P. Oldham
Julian Papenfus
Frank Passic
Antonio E. Pedraza
Juan Pena
William H. Pheatt
Albert Pick
Tony Pisciotta
Rick Ponterio
Michel Prieur
Yahya J. Qureshi
Nazir Rahemtulla
Beate Rauch
Jerome H. Remick
Ron Richardson
Rudolph Richter
Duane C. Riel
Peter Robin
William M. Rosenblum

O.E. Royer
Alan Sadd
Karl Saethre
Michael Schöne
Hartmut Schoenawa
Carlton "Fred" Schwan
Robert Schwartz
Timothy R. G. Sear
Christian Selvais
Joel Shafer
Alex Shagin
Brian A. Silsbee
Ladislav Sin
Arlie Slabaugh
George Slusarczuk
Bruce W. Smith
Gary Snover
Jimmie C. Steelman
Mel Steinberg
Tim Steiner
Zeljko Stojanovic
Roger B. Stolberg
Mark Strumpf
Imre Szatmari
Steven Tan
David Tang
Reiny Tetting
Mike Tiitus
S.P. Ting
Gunther Toleti
Anthony Tumonis
Jan Vandersande
Dr. Karel Vanka
James Warmus
Igor Victorov-Orlov
A. Wang
Stewart Westdal
Yu Chien Hua
Joseph Zaffern
Christof Zellweger

INSTITUTIONS AND PUBLICATIONS

American Numismatic Association   American Numismatic Society   International Bank Note Society   Smithsonian Institute

The Stateman's Year-Book, 1995-96.
133rd Edition
by Brian Hunter, editor, The Stateman's Year-Book Office, The Macmillan Press Ltd., 4-6 Crinan Street, London N1 9SQ, England.
(Statistical and Historical Annual of the States of the World).

INTRODUCTION

Welcome to this eighth edition of the *Standard Catalog of World Paper Money, General Issues - 1650 to 1960*. The first change previous users of this series will notice is that the listings end with 1960. This was done to better keep pace with the ever increasing 'modern' listings and keep current in major price fluctuations by splitting off issues since 1961 into their own annual volume - the *Standard Catalog of World Paper Money, Modern Issues - 1961 to present.*

The second change users familiar with the Standard Catalog series will notice is the format of the listings. The maps, introductions and listings of rulers, monetary system and the like are all here, but in slightly larger typesizes, hopefully making it easier to read. In addition to the larger typesize for the listings, they are structured with the catalog number and denomination listings on a separate line from that of the date, descriptive, and price information giving more space for all fields of information. Finally, extensive variety revision has been added when it has been noted within the collecting community to affect prices. These varieties could be as basic as the addition of listings for the availability of specimens or proofs; or extensive runs of signature combinations or dates where there have been increased interest and value changes for short print runs.

For the ease of identification, notes are listed under their historic country name (British Honduras is no longer hidden within Belize). Notes of a particular bank are listed in release date order, and then grouped in ascending denomination order. In the cases of countries where more than one issuing authority is in effect at a single time, follow the bank headings in the listings and it will become apparent if that country's listing is by date or alphabetical by issuing authority. In the cases where a country has changed from a kingdom to a republic all the banknotes of the kingdom's era would be listed before that of the republic's.

Catalog numbers have become the hobby's shorthand for listing a banknote in an inventory booklet or dealer advertisement. Catalog numbers in this book have been extensively changed within many countries in order to retain a consecutive system that most people have become comfortable with. It will cause many to look at their collections again and compare listings to update catalog numbers and varieties; but at the same time, those collectors should be pleasantly surprised at the current market valuation listings.

A review of paper money collecting

Paper money collecting is undoubtedly nearly as old as paper money itself, this segment of the numismatic hobby did not begin to reach a popularity approaching that of coin collecting until the latter half of the 1970's. While coins and paper money are alike in that both served as legal obligations to facilitate commerce, long-time paper money enthusiasts know the similarity ends there.

Coins were historically guaranteed by the intrinsic value of their metallic content - at least until recent years when virtually all circulating coins have become little more than legal tender tokens, containing little or no precious metal - while paper money possesses a value only when it is accepted for debts or converted into bullion or precious metals. With many note issues, this conversion privilege was limited and ultimately negated by the imposition of redemption cutoff dates.

Such conditions made collecting of bank notes a risky business, particularly with notes possessing a high face value. This is why in most instances, except where issued were withdrawn shortly after release or became virtually worthless due to hyper-inflation, early high denomination notes are extremely difficult to locate, especially in choice to uncirculated grades of preservation.

The development of widespread collector interest in paper money of most nations were long inhibited by a near total absence of adequate documentary literature. No more than three and a half decades ago collectors could refer to only a few catalogs and dealer price lists of limited scope, most of which were incomplete and difficult to acquire, or they could build their own knowledge through personal collecting pursuits and contact with fellow collectors.

This situation was somewhat corrected over the past 30 years with a number of special catalogs covering the more popular collected countries. Still, many areas remained uncataloged, and no single volume existed which provided comprehensive, detailed, illustrated listings of issues from all countries of the world.

The early catalogs authored by Albert Pick chronicled issues of Europe and the Americas and were assembled as stepping stones to the ultimate objective which became reality with publication of the first *Standard Catalog of World Paper Money* in 1975. That work provided collectors with near complete listings and up-to-date valuations of all recorded government note issues of the 20th century, incorporating Pick's previously unpublished manuscripts on Africa, Asia and Oceiana, plus many earlier issues.

This completely revised and updated eight edition presents a substantial extension of the cataloging effort initiated in 1975 and revised in succeeding editions. As the most comprehensive world paper money reference ever assembled, it fully documents the many and varied legal tender paper currency issued circulated by nearly 300 past and current governments of the world from 1650 to 1960.

Falling within the scope of this General Issues volume are all legal tender issues circulated under the auspices of recognized national governments and their banking agents, including notes which enjoyed wide circulating in their respective countries. Exceptions are the multitudinous notes of the German states and cities, especially those of the World War I and postwar period to 1923, and the vast category of Chinese local issues and similar limited-circulation issues of other countries.

An Invitation

Users of this catalog may find a helpful adjunct is the *Bank Note Reporter,* the only monthly newspaper devoted exclusively to North American and world paper money. Each issue presents up-to-date news, feature articles and information - including appearances of the *World Paper Money Update* on the latest world paper money releases and discoveries. Listings in these presentations are all keyed to the Standard Catalog numbering system utilized in this catalog. All purchasers of this catalog are invited to subscribe to the *Bank Note Reporter*. Requests for a sample copy should be addressed to *Bank Note Reporter*, 700 East State Street, Iola, WI, 54990-0001.

INDEX

COUNTRIES

BANKS

Collecting Paper Money

*"To kill a person needs no knife . . .
a piece of paper that is written
. . . or printed on suffices."*

by Albert Pick
Translated by E. Sheridan

**Germany, 2 Groschen,
siege note of Kolberg, 1807**

France, 3 Livres, siege note, Mainz 1793

With this observation the Chinese, as the inventors of paper, wished to emphasize the great need for responsibility in dealing with this material.

There is hardly any application of paper qualified to such a degree as paper money in providing that it is within man's power to have it be a benefit or a curse to mankind. On the one hand, lack of credit and a shortage of legal tender have been overcome by issues of paper money to serve trade and industry commensurate with economic development; yet on the other hand, the immense increase in the volume of paper money in inflationary periods has been the cause of economic and personal catastrophes. The many issues of paper money retaining their full value were mostly destroyed after redemption and have largely faded from the memory of man. The paper money originating during times of inflation and then becoming worthless has outlived the period, since it was no longer redeemable, and it acts as a constant reminder of the period of monetary devaluation.

Thus, paper money is considered by many people around the world as legal tender with an inglorious tradition. As negatively as periods of inflation influence the opinion of a superficial observer of the history of paper money, these relics of a monetary devaluation have positively influenced the collecting of paper money.

Frequently, the hope of a later redemption may have contributed toward placing the old notes in safekeeping. Later on, attempts were made to complete the series of notes and in this manner the first collections may have originated; perhaps even as early as the time of the French Revolution, when in addition to the French assignats and the "mandats Territoriaux," the regional issues of "Billets de confiance" were in circulation. In the United States, too, there was a very early opportunity to collect paper money as the Colonial and Continental bills, notes of the Confederate States and the numerous notes, rich in design, of the many 19th century banks became worthless as a circulating medium.

In our own time, an ever increasing number of persons come into contact with foreign currencies through international travel – and even war. A particularly pleasing note is retained as a souvenir and not infrequently becomes the cornerstone of a bank note collection. Here, it is a feature of the bank note that because of its relatively large surface (compared with a coin or postage stamp) it offers space for many motifs and frequently impresses the viewer with the quality of its printing on high-grade paper. The catalogs published in recent years provide the necessary reference tools for building a collection, and thus it is small wonder that the number of paper money collectors is steadily on the increase.

Particularly for the novice collectors not yet fully acquainted with the collecting sphere, hints are given regarding the different types of paper money, various avenues of collecting, historical backgrounds and the possibilities for building a specialized collection.

Government Paper Money

—Bank Notes—

Emergency Money

For some would-be collectors, the lack of knowledge and the means for easy orientation in a hobby causes a decline in interest and often ends in a short-lived participation. Conversely, an interested person can become a real collector if he is aided in acquainting himself with his new hobby and in finding the right way to develop a meaningful collection.

The collector of paper money should know from the start which items belong to his collecting sphere and what paper money represents.

In contrast to coins, which in the past represented money of intrinsic value guaranteed by virtue of the material in which they were struck, paper money is money of no intrinsic value; it is printed paper without material value.

Today, in common hobby parlance, we categorize as paper money all forms of money made of paper or printed on a paper-like material. Only a few decades ago, the term paper money, as applied to government issues, stood in contrast to other monetary forms of paper such as bank notes. Whereas the government paper money had to be considered general legal tender because the government was obliged to accept the notes at face value

Italy, 500 Lire

Italy 1000 Lire, Banca d'Italia

**Germany, 2 Mark, Emergency money
note of Bielschowitz, 1914**

**Germany, Emergency money
note of Bremen, 1922**

France, 5000 Francs, Banque de France, 1944

New Zealand, 2 Dollars with bird

Indonesia, 100 Rupiah with flowers, 1959

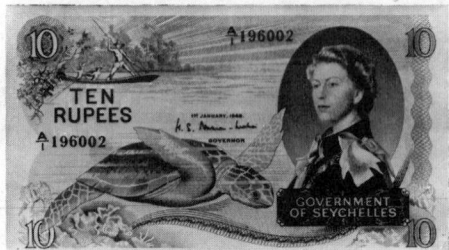

Seychelles, 10 Rupees with sea turtles

in payments to itself, in the case of the bank note, the issuing bank promises to redeem it at any time at its face value for legal tender. Still, in former times as well as today, it was difficult to recognize what was government paper money and what was bank notes.

There are many examples in the history of paper money of the adoption of bank notes by the government. Especially in times of distress, if the government had overtaxed a bank for its purposes, the bank's notes were declared government paper money (e.g. Spain, 1794, the notes of the Banco de San Carlos, and Austria, 1866). The opposite situation was less frequent; i.e., a bank adopting government paper money and making it into bank notes, yet there are also examples of this (Oldenburg, 1869). In our time, however, the difference between government paper money and the bank note is generally no longer discernible. This often involves differences contingent only on tradition or the organization of the government or banking authority which are of no consideration when using the notes as legal tender.

Differentiating between government paper money and the bank note remains for the paper money collector a purely theoretical consideration. In practice, few collectors exclude one or the other from their collecting except in rare instances.

In addition to the government paper money and the bank note, there is also a third kind of paper money, the emergency money. This form of substitute currency was issued to overcome a shortage or lack of government legal tender (for example, in times of distress, as a substitute for coins which have disappeared from circulation). Sometimes issued by authority of the official government or other competent authorizing body, but also frequently issued without such authority, these emergency issues may have been officially prohibited or tacitly tolerated, and accepted on a par with the legal tender issues they replaced, if only in a small district. Among the best known of such issues are the "notgeld," a familiar expression even to non-German speaking collectors for the emergency paper money issues of Austria and Germany circa 1914-1923. In fact, the term is being increasingly applied to many other emergency issues as well.

General Collection - Specialized Collection

A bank note collection does not always develop in a straight line direction. The interest in paper money is in many cases of a general nature and thus the individual collects everything he encounters. The general collection thus formed often does not please the collector as his interest matures. He may then select those collecting spheres that interest him most and will either dispose of all other notes not fitting those spheres or add to his collection only those notes which fit into his newly specialized collection. The sooner he can decide the limits of his collecting interests, the sooner he can concentrate on building his collection.

Thematic Collection

The creation of general paper money collections will increasingly become a matter only for the museums. The majority of private collectors can occupy themselves only with specialized spheres for financial reasons or lack of time, and even within these spheres the rare pieces may remain generally unobtainable for them. Thus, collectors are increasingly turning their attention to the aesthetic qualities of paper money. The idea of thematic collecting is becoming quite strong. The underlying causes for this are not only the financial considerations and the inability to acquire the rarest pieces, but also in the pleasure obtained from the beauty of individual notes.

Over the last decade a number of countries have stimulated interest in collecting bank notes by designs with definite motifs. Thus, indigenous birds are depicted on the different values of the Reserve Bank of New Zealand. In the Seychelles and a number of African states, notes show illustrations of animals. Representations of flowers are present on the Israeli notes of 1955 and the 1959 Indonesian currency. According to his choice of subject, the taste of the collector is not always adequate for building a collection which will find general recognition. With more ambitious themes, he is obliged to acquire some basic knowledge about the topic he has chosen. The wealth of motifs is inexhaustible, so that possibilities offer themselves even for very special themes.

Varieties

Even in the consideration of varieties, opinions of collectors differ. One collector is content to acquire one note of each basic type, and will ignore minor differences; another is interested in watermark varieties, various dates of issue, serial numbers, sheet marks, signatures, printers, color varieties and other differences within a type. It is by no means easy for a collector to determine what he will include along these lines and what he will leave out. The differences of material value in the one collecting sphere, and which frequently occur in varying combinations, can be of no consequence for another collecting sphere. A few examples will show that general guidelines, applying to all areas of paper money collecting, are impossible.

In the case of German Reichsbank notes from 1883-1914, the few dates varieties which delimit the different issues are included by almost all collectors. On the other hand, all date varieties are not even considered by the most specialized collectors of Belgian notes since the notes bear the date of the day of printing. In this instance collectors are usually satisfied with one note of each year. In areas such as Scottish, Italian and Romanian notes, there are also numerous date varieties and collectors who specialize in them. On United States paper money there are only year dates, sometimes followed by a letter suffix. This year date, as a rule, changes only when the type of note changes; while the letter following the year date moves forward by one if the signature change.

Example: $1 Silver Certificate
1928-D, signature Julian/Woodin
1928-E, Julian/Morgenthau
1934, Julian/Morgenthau

The notes dated 1928 have the Treasury seal on the left, those with 1934, on the right. On U.S. notes the year date hardly permits the date of issue to be determined, a better clue being taken from the suffix letter, or better still, the signatures.

Signature varieties are practically unknown for some countries, such as with German Reichsbank notes. Other countries, however, change note signatures with any change in officials (France, Belgium, Great Britain, several South American countries and others). Since these changes in signature are also important in determining the date of issue (such as with modern British notes which carry no date), these different signatures are of interest to all collectors. A change of signature in notes issued at the same time was already known on assignats of the 18th century. It is still found today with notes of the Scandinavian countries and Switzerland, where a signature

China 1 Kuan, Ming–Dynasty, 14th century

Netherlands, 20 Stuiver, Cardboard coin of the City of Leyden, 1574

Sweden, 10 Daler silver, Stockholms Banco, 1666, one of the oldest European banknotes

often does not change over lengthy periods (such as that of the bank president). Only the specialized collectors will deal with these changing signatures and they, too, must content themselves with the lower values.

Since variations in serial numbers, printers and colors do not occur too often in paper money, they are often included in a collection. Such things as prefix and suffix letters with serial numbers and sheet marks or plate numbers, on the other hand, may interest only specialized collectors, and then only when the bank note material is correspondingly plentiful.

History of Paper Money

In the 13th century, the famous Venetian, Marco Polo, undertook a journey to China. His records of this journey contain the first Western reports regarding the production and the use of paper money, a currency still incomprehensible for European conditions of that time, due to its lack of intrinsic worth. His contemporaries did not give credence to Marco Polo's report. Only much later were his accounts actually verified in the form of Chinese notes of the 14th century (Ming Dynasty) produced in the same manner. Today, such bluish-tinted notes are found in many of the larger collections, and it is now known that they were not the oldest notes, but stood at the end of a development which began already in the 7th century A.D. The Chinese, who called paper money "flying money" because of its light weight and ability to circulate over a wide area, had a well organized bank note clearing system as early as the 10th century.

Along with the first bank notes, the first counterfeiters also made their appearance. Numerous files still in existence provide information regarding the fight waged by the Chinese against these forgers.

The first European paper money is of much more recent origin. It was emergency money issued in 1483 by the Spaniards during the siege by the Moors. Since up to the present day not a single one of these notes has been discovered, it may be assumed that they were all destroyed after their redemption. In contrast to this, the cardboard coins produced in 1574 by the beleaguered citizens of Leyden are preserved in various denominations. The cities of Leyden and Middelburg were lacking silver for the striking of coins during the siege by the Spaniards, so they took as a material the covers of Catholic parish registers. The cardboard coins may indeed be described as the oldest preserved European money consisting of paper, but on the other hand, they are not true paper money.

Only 300 years after Marco Polo's account of Chinese paper money, the Stockholms Banco in Sweden issued the first European bank notes for circulation. The cause for the issuing of these notes was the devaluation of the copper plate money introduced in 1644. In the search for a legal tender for a transition period, Johann Palmstruch suggested the issue of so-called "Kreditivsedlar." In 1661 the first notes were issued made out in Riksdaler specie and Daler silver. It is assumed that this involved forms where the denomination and currency were inserted in handwriting. More is known about the second issue which occurred in 1662-1664. In this instance the denomination was imprinted. In 1666 the third, considerably augmented, issue was ordered. Of these notes for 10, 25, 50 and 100 Daler silver, approximately 60 specimens have been preserved.

At this time, the so-called Goldsmith Notes were already known in England. The transactions of the English goldsmiths also included brokerage and money changing. When King Charles I demanded a part of the ready money for himself, deposited by merchants in the Tower or in the office of the Chief Cashier of the government, the merchants went in search of new depositories and discovered these in the vaults of the goldsmiths. With this deposited money, the goldsmiths began speculating and were thus also able to pay interest. Withdrawal periods were laid down for deposits yielding interest, those not yielding interest being repaid on demand. The goldsmiths thus became bankers, issuing notes in respect to the deposits which, as required, were made out to the bearer without an indication of name. For the purpose of facilitating the redemption of parts of the deposited money, possibly for third parties, the notes were even issued in smaller denominations in round sums, and these notes can be considered forerunners of bank notes.

The desire for an independent credit institution was strengthened when some goldsmiths went bankrupt on the king's refusal to discharge some debts which fell due. In 1694 the Bank of England was founded, and its first notes were similar to the notes of the goldsmiths. Acts of Parliament strengthened the special position of the Bank, and merchants increasingly came to realize that support of the Bank provided them backing in time of crisis; thus the Bank of England succeeded in obtaining a firm foundation.

In Scotland, one year later than in England, a central bank, the Bank of Scotland, was also founded. In Norway, then a Danish province, the issue of

Great Britain, 1 Pound, Bank of England, 1818

Denmark, 1 Mark, 1713

For the purpose of restoring confidence in the currency, it was decided to abolish the assignats and to issue a new type of paper money, the "Mandats Territoriaux." At a conversion ratio of 30 to 1, "Promesses des Mandats Territoriaux" were initially issued for the assignats to be converted. The actual mandats were later issued only in small quantities. Even this new kind of paper money was unable to put a brake on inflation, though. Within a few weeks the value of the mandats dropped by 95 percent. By November, 1796, all notes were declared worthless.

After the disappearance of the assignats and mandats, a number of note-issuing banks originated. Their notes, however, circulated only in small quantities. Out of one of these banks, the "Caisse des Comptes Courants," the Bank of France was founded in 1800, due mainly to the influence of Napoleon.

In other European countries, too, attempts were made in the 18th century to eliminate the financial difficulties of the government by issuing paper money. In Russia, the Assignation Bank was established in 1768. Its paper money was widely accepted. However, when the government began circulating ever increasing quantities of notes during the second war against the Turks (1787-1792), confidence waned and the notes lost value. Since that time Russia has continued to issue government paper money in an uninterrupted sequence.

The Austrian Wars of Succession and the battles under Maria Theresia with Frederick the Great had encumbered the Austrian government heavily with debts. At that time, attention was turned to the issue of paper money. The "Banco del Giro," founded in 1703, was originally supposed to issue obligations for circulation, but confidence in this bank was found wanting, so the plan was quickly abandoned. Only when administration of the bank was transferred to the city of Vienna and the name changed to "Wiener Stadt-Banco" did the mistrust disappear.

In 1759 the first provisional paper money issue came about. It was superceded by the true government paper money in 1762. Initially these notes, termed "Bancozettel" (Bank Scrip), were popular, but when government indebtedness continually rose because of wars, and various new issues in ever-greater quantities became necessary, the notes lost value. The war with

Poland, 10 Groszy, 1974

Norway, 25 Rixdaler, Thor Mohlen, 1695

non-interest bearing notes occurred in the same year on the initiative of the merchant Thor Mohlen. In Denmark itself, King Frederick IV had paper money produced 18 years later, in 1713, during the Nordic Wars.

The poor financial position of France forced King Louis XIV to carry out a "reformation" of the coins in circulation. In 1703 he ordered coins to be withdrawn, overstamped, and then reissued at a higher rate. Receipts were issued for the withdrawn coins and this so-called coin scrip was declared legal tender.

The continued indebtedness of the government persisted even after the king's death, and it was therefore not astonishing that the Scotsman John Law's ideas for the restoration of the government finances were gladly seized upon. Law wished to increase circulation of money by issuing bank notes and promoting credit. In 1716 he received permission for founding the Banque Generale which issued "Ecus" (Taler) in the form of notes. In 1718 the bank was taken over by the government. With the notes later made out to "Livres Tournois" and the shares of the two colonial companies "Compagnie des Indes" and "Compagnie D'Occident," Law indulged in a dangerous financial and stock exchange scheme which resulted in 1720 in a tremendous catastrophe. The bank was closed and Law had to leave France, abandoning his assets.

This was not to remain the only French experiment with paper money in the 18th century. France's ever-unfavorable financial position deteriorated still further through the revolution. The receding revenues of the government faced increased demands in the face of burgeoning expenditures. In accordance with a plan worked out by Tallyrand, the first assignats were issued in 1790, for which confiscated Church property was to serve as security. Notes of the first issue bore interest, while the later issues did not.

For relieving the shortage of small change, many towns and municipalities issued so-called "Billets de confiance," of which a few thousand types were in circulation. The government, too, was not printing assignats in small denominations. Simultaneously the issues of higher value were continually being increased.

The Royal Assignats were substituted at the inception of the Republic by new issues which were themselves superceded in 1795, upon the introduction of the metric system, by assignats of Franc currency. On January 1, 1796, over 27 million Livres in assignats were in circulation, the value of which merely amounted to one-half of one percent of the face value.

France, 1000 Livres, Banque Royale (of the time of John Law), 1719

France produced the peak of indebtedness and the government found itself incapable of continuing to redeem the notes. Only a monetary reform could prevent national bankruptcy. Thus, it was decided in 1811 to issue "Redemption Notes," which could be converted at the ratio of 1:5 for the old Banco scrip.

Soon the value of these new notes also dropped and they were followed in 1813 by another kind of paper money, the "Anticipation Notes" (anticipatory of future taxes). The end of the Napoleonic Wars gave rise to a new hope for a peaceful economic development and a stable currency. In 1816 the "Austrian National Scrip Bank" was established to create legal tender of stable value with its notes.

The first German money of paper material was the issue of the previously mentioned cardboard coins in the Dutch towns of Leyden and Middelburg in 1574. Whereas these were emergency money, the "Banco Scrip" issued in 1705 by the Elector Johann Wilhelm can be considered the first real paper money in Germany. The Elector had founded the "Banco di gyro d'affrancatione," whose notes were in fact made out to individual names, but were transferable.

In Ansbach-Bayreuth the "Hochfurstlich Brandenburgische Muntz-Banco" made out so-called "Banco-Billets" (Bank Scrip) by the middle of the 18th century. However, in exactly the same manner as the interest-bearing bank notes of the "Hochfurstlich Brandenburg-Anspach-Bayreuthische Hof-Banco," founded in 1780, they remained of little importance in the way of a legal tender.

The fear of monetary devaluation by the introduction of paper money was too deeply rooted in Germany. Until the end of the 18th century and partly until the middle of the 19th century such issues were planned but decisions postponed.

USA, 20 Dollars, Georgia, Bank of Commerce, 1857

Germany, 1 Taler, Saxony, 1855

USA, 15Shillings, New Jersey, 1776

Germany, 5 Taler, Prussia, 1806

In Prussia the first notes were issued by the "Konigliche Giro-und Lehn-bank" founded in 1765. The notes, in denominations of Pound-Banco, however, remained of little importance in circulation. Only those notes issued from 1820 onwards gained any importance. The bank name was changed to "Preussische Bank" in 1847, from which the Reichsbank originated in 1876.

Of greater importance at the beginning of the 19th century was the Prussian government paper money, the "Tresorscheine" (bank-safe notes).

In Bavaria, attempts were made at the end of the 18th and the beginning of the 19th century to create an issue of government paper money by issuing diverse monetary substitutes. Government indebtedness was therefore not less than in countries with paper money issues.

It was the time of peace following the Napoleonic Wars that brought a slow financial recovery. But the lack of credit and shortage of legal tender, due to the favorable development of trade, was not eliminated until 1835, when the Bayerische Hypotheken-und Wechselbank was founded. This institution in subsequent years issued notes of 10 and 100 Gulden and remained the only Bavarian central bank until the foundation of the German Reich.

At the beginning of the 19th century, paper money remained unpopular in Germany. A change occurred after 1848, when some German states felt the need to produce their own paper money to protect themselves against notes of smaller states whose issue quantities far exceeded the circulation requirements of their own areas. The larger states could then prohibit the circulation of these notes within their boundaries. The decisive step on the way toward centralization of banks in Germany occurred in 1875 with the new Bank Act and the foundation of the Reichsbank. The last four banks retained their issuing rights up to 1935.

In Italy the banking system developed earlier than in all other European countries. Deposit receipts and promissory notes made out by the banks existing as early as the Middle Ages, such as the "Casa di St. Giorgio," in Genoa, the "Banco di Sant' Ambrogio" in Milan and the "Banco di Rialto" in Venice, were transferable with an endorsement. These notes can be considered forerunners of modern bank notes. Real bank notes, however, were first issued in the middle of the 18th century in the Kingdom of Sardinia. Subsequently came the notes of the "Sacro Monte della Pieta di Roma" and those of the "Banco di Santo Spirito di Roma."

In Poland, issues of paper money first appeared during the 18th century. Rebels under the leadership of Kosciuszko issued various kinds of notes in 1794. With the crushing of the rebellion, paper money issues also ceased. Only in the Duchy of Warsaw, created by Napoleon (personal union with the Kingdom of Saxony), did paper money circulate again, so-called currency notes resembling Saxon currency tickets in their design.

It might be expected that paper money became known in America much later than in Europe. But exactly like in Europe, North America became acquainted with money of no intrinsic value in the 1600s.

The inadequate supply of coins in Canada under French colonial administration led to a chronic lack of legal tender. In order to at least ensure the soldiers' pay, the Canadians resorted to self-help and utilized quartered playing cards, to which the treasurer's seal and signatures of the Governor and Administrator were added, as paper currency. In 1685 the first money of this nature was circulated. It was the intention to withdraw these emer-

Italy, 7 Scudi, Banco di Santo Spirito di Roma, 1786

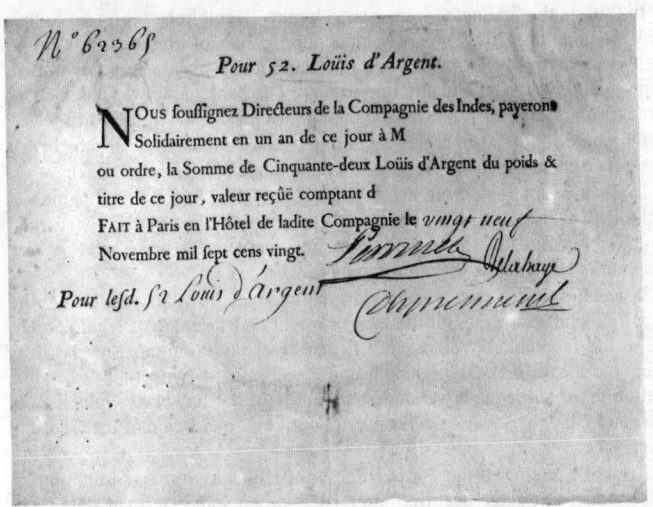

France, 52 Louis d' Argent, Compagnie des Indies, Banque Royale
(of the time of John Law), 1720

France, 5 Sous, Billet de confiance,
St. Gaudens, 1972

France, 4000 Livres, Assignat, 1792

France, 2000 Francs, Assignat, 1794

France, 10 Livres (of the time of John Law), 1720

France, 5 Livres, Royal Assignat, 1791

France, 3 Livres, Billet de Confiance, Marseille, 1792

gency items of legal tender immediately after adequate coin supplies arrived, but this did not happen. Further issues which included half or whole cards followed, gaining circulation throughout the whole of the colony. The money remained valid until 1718/19 when the governor had it withdrawn from circulation and prohibited further issues.

In 1729, new issues of this strange money were recorded and from then on circulated in ever increasing quantities. When the British took over the Canadian territories in 1759, more than 14 million Livres of such notes were in circulation. Because the French government refused to redeem the notes, the value of playing card money dropped considerably until an agreement was finally reached for its redemption.

In 1690, the Colony of Massachusetts lacked the necessary metallic currency to pay its soldiers returning from Canada and this led to the production of the Colonial Bills of Credit. A few years later other colonies, such as Connecticut, New Hampshire, New Jersey, New York, Pennsylvania, Rhode Island and South Carolina followed with similar issues. It was believed that an increase in the paper money would foster general prosperity, thus great quantities of new notes were constantly being created. Benjamin Franklin was also of this opinion, as may be seen from his treatise "A Modeste Inquiry Into the Nature and Necessity of a Paper Money." All attempts by the British government to bring the devaluation of paper money to an end at the beginning of the 18th century failed, and thus, America with its Colonial bills encountered the same experience France had with its John Law notes: they became completely worthless.

After the battle of Lexington in 1775, a new attempt was made to issue paper money in the form of Continental bills issued by order of the Continental Congress. After being in circulation for just a year, the notes had already lost some of their value. By 1777, ten dollars in Continental bills was worth only one silver dollar. In 1780, one silver dollar fetched 75 of the Continental currency. By 1781, the ratio was 1000 to 1. George Washington at the time observed in a letter that a wagon full of notes was just sufficient for purchasing a wagon full of provisions.

Liberal laws in the 19th century allowed an almost incalculable number of private note-issuing banks to form, many of which circulated worthless, sometimes fraudulent note issues. So-called "wildcat banks" established their offices in such remote areas - where there were more wildcats than people - as to make redemption of their notes virtually impossible. In the New England states, by contrast, the introduction of severe penalties against swindlers and the rise of an effective clearing house system allowed a solid banking system to develop.

Due to the Civil War, the currency confusion which existed in time of peace was further compounded, particularly as the Confederate States of America and its constituent states began issuing notes which quickly became worthless. However, it was also during the Civil War that the first United States government paper money originated, the beginning of an unbroken string of notes which remain legal tender to this day.

The American bills of the last century, rich in design and well printed, are popular with collectors today, abroad as well as in the U.S.

In most of the civilized world the development towards centralizing the bank note system took place during the second half of the 19th century or in the first decades of the 20th century. Central banks were established which ousted the private or local banks issuing notes, or at least considerably limited their influence on circulating paper money issues.

Until a few years ago, paper money could be described as the most modern form of currency, but we are today on the threshold of a new development. The system of payment by check, some two decades ago common only in business, is increasingly gaining in importance. The use of checks in the private sector has today become a matter of course. Just beyond is the use of the credit card and other electronic fund transfers which may someday create a moneyless society. The development of money from the pre-coin era to the days of coin as the dominant legal tender to the paper money which ousted the coin is again about to begin a new era.

Collecting Early Note Issues

Within the scope of a general collection, a collector attempting to acquire notes from the beginnings of the history of paper money will soon discover that he will hardly be in a position, due to the lack of available and affordable material, to form a review of the early history of paper money with the individual specimens he has purchased.

The oldest bank note obtainable is the Chinese Ming note. This note is indeed rare, but it is still feasible today to acquire it. The Leyden cardboard coins, too, considered to be the earliest European form of money made of paper, are still obtainable. Considerably more difficult, if not impossible, is the situation regarding the Swedish notes of the 17th century, the early Bank of England notes, the Norwegian Thor Mohlen notes and the French coin scrip. These notes are all firmly entrenched in museums and other major collections. The few specimens occasionally placed on the market fetch very high prices. Only a modicum of good fortune, along with strong financial standing, can assist in building a collection of these early notes.

It looks a little more favorable for the collector with regard to John Law notes. Of the 1720 issues (January and July), the 10 Livres note is still procurable. More difficult, though, is the 100 Livres note. The 50 and 1000 Livres of 1720 and the notes of 1719 are offered only rarely and at high prices.

French assignats and mandats of 1792-1794 are still relatively easy to obtain today, and with a great deal of endurance and collector's skill, it is possible to assemble a specialized collection.

Of the "Billets de Confiance" orginating from the same period, notes of the different local authorities and towns, there are several thousands. These notes may indeed represent the oldest group of emergency money notes. With a lot of patience a collector may gather a small collection of some 100 notes of this description during the course of several years, if he is able to build on a collection bought from French collectors.

1 Fun

2 Fun

Japan, Hansatsu (clean or local notes)

Austria, 10 Gulden (form), 1762

Apart from those already mentioned, not many European notes remain from the 18th century which are within the reach of the collector.

In Poland the treasury notes in denominations of 5 and 10 Groszy, 4, 5, 10 and 25 Zloty, issued in 1794 during the Kosciuszko uprising, are obtainable. The other denominations, 1, 50 and 100 Zloty, are rare, with the 500 and 1000 Zloty practically unobtainable. The Taler notes of the Duchy of Warsaw, reminiscent of Saxony currency tickets, are also still procurable. Danish notes of 1792 until the beginning of the 19th century belong to the already expensive class of old notes from that country still on the market. Equally, Swedish and Norwegian notes of the 18th century are still obtainable. The same applies to the latter as to the Danish notes, being highly popular in Scandinavia and therefore achieving correspondingly high prices.

The old Russian notes appearing in private collections generally originate from the beginning of the 19th century. Older notes are very rare and are found only as singles in key collections.

American Colonial and Continental bills issued at the end of the 18th century can be purchased without difficulty, even though prices for such notes rose considerably in the U.S. during the 1976 Bicentennial celebration.

Among older non-European notes, mention should be made of the Japanese "Hansatsu" or "Shisatsu." These narrow, bookmark-like and thematically rich notes were issued by the many different Daimios (territorial

Austria, 10 Kreuzer,
Emergency money note,
Marienthal (Bohemia), 1848

Italy, 50 Lire, Torino, 1765

Portugal, 10 Milreis, 1799

rulers) and impress the Western collector as exotic. There are many thousands of these notes available relatively cheaply. They are hard to attribute, but perhaps a Japanese collector or dealer can help.

Of the first Austrian issues through 1796, none of the original notes are offered. The low denominations of the 1800 and 1806 issues, on the other hand, are still plentiful and inexpensive today. Among the numerous other Austrian issues of the 19th century there are partly decorative notes available at a favorable price.

Among collectors of national German notes, the number of whom is rising steadily, many are now attempting to obtain German notes issued before 1871. Such old German notes, including issues of private banks in Mark currency up to 1914, can be acquired in only a few pieces. The systematic building of this type of collection is no longer feasible today.

The difficulty in procuring bank notes from the beginnings of paper money history may stimulate collectors to acquire at least some singles which are then given prominent display as very noteworthy showpieces, independently of the building of the rest of the collection.

Counterfeiters

The battle against counterfeiters pervades the entire history of paper money. The Chinese occupied themselves with protection against counterfeits by enforcing strict regulations. Forgers were given the death penalty, and the informer received a reward along with the property of the criminal. The essential aids in the battle against counterfeiting were, and remain, the finesse in printing techniques and paper manufacture, in connection with which the watermark and, during the last century, the printing of the guilloches, play a special part.

The recognition of old notes as counterfeits generally requires great experience on the part of the collector. The lack of means of comparison renders recognition difficult and frequently such notes are in a collection for many years before they are recognized. This discovery is not as painful for a paper money collector as it would be for collectors of other objects, since the value of a contemporary counterfeit bank note is little less than the original in many cases. With common notes, the counterfeit may well be worth more than the original.

Collectors of paper money differentiate between counterfeiting and alteration. A counterfeit note is false in all its parts; whereas an altered note originated from a genuine note. If, for example, an overprint has been added later, or the denomination was raised on a genuine note, then it is termed an alteration.

Most counterfeiters fail because of special types of processing machines which are not available for their use in imitating genuine production methods. Even professional qualifications and artistic abilities will not suffice for coping with the sophisticated security techniques employed by prominent bank note printers, especially with modern paper money.

If, however, such counterfeits were carried out at the instigation of the government or official authorities, then the possibility existed for achieving so-called "perfect" counterfeits. The two best-known examples in this respect are found in the last century and during World War II.

After Napoleon's entry into Vienna, he ordered the printing blocks for the Austrian Banco Scrip to be imitated, and notes, distinguishable from originals only by paper tint, to be printed in Paris. Despite the ban pronounced after his marriage to Princess Marie Louise on issuing the notes,

such counterfeits did enter circulation. Russian ruble notes, too, were forged on Napoleon's instructions.

With the greatest bank note forgery of all time, known under the code of "Operation Bernhard," the press, radio and television have repeatedly occupied themselves with the postwar period, particularly since such counterfeit notes were subsequently discovered in Lake Toplitz, Austria. Books have also been written on this subject. The German Security Service prepared counterfeit Bank of England notes during World War II after careful preparatory work in laboratories hidden in concentration camps. The finest machinery and specifically produced watermarked paper were used by experts and inmates of the camps. These notes, circulated via neutral foreign countries (the payment to the spy "Cicero" became known especially), were so identical to the genuine notes that the Bank of England was compelled to withdraw the subject issue from circulation.

There are also notes which were imitated to the detriment of collectors. After the issuing of the first notgeld notes in 1914, the number of notgeld collectors began increasingly steadily during subsequent years. The high demand for these first issues prompted some local authorities and other issuing offices to produce reprints of these sometimes primitively printed notes. In contrast to the rare originals, these reprints are generally considerably cheaper.

The numerous fancy issues of notgeld, intended for the collector in the period 1920-1922, also belong here.

Particularly easy is the counterfeiting of overprinting on notes. The stamp "Fezzan," on the 5-Franc note of the Banque de l'Afrique Occidentale, is an example of such a forgery and can be differentiated only with difficulty from the original stamp.

Falsification of a Russian 25 Rubles note of 1807 (by Napoleon's Army)

Germany, Alteration to 100 Mark of a genuine 20 Mark note, issued by Allies Military administration authority

Brazil, Alteration of a genuine 10 Milreis note to 100 Milreis

Germany, Falsification of an English 50 Pound note (World War II)

HOW TO USE THIS CATALOG

Catalog listings consist of all regular and provisional notes attaining wide circulation in their respective countries for the period covered. Notes have been listed under the historical country name. Thus British Honduras is not under Belize, Dahomey is not under Benin, and so on, as had been the case in past catalogs. Where catalog numbers have changed, and you will find extensive renumbering in this edition, the old catalog numbers appear in parentheses directly below the new number. The listings continue to be regrouped by issue range rather than by denomination, and a slight change in the listing format should make the Bank name, Issue dates as well as catalog numbers and denominations easier to locate. These changes have been made to make the catalog as easy to use as possible for you.

The editors and publisher make no claim to absolute completeness, just as they acknowledge that some errors and pricing inequities will appear. Correspondence is invited with interested persons who have notes previously unlisted or who have information to enhance the presentation of existing listings in succeeding editions of this catalog. To receive a printed errata sheet, please return the bound in reply postcard found in this volume.

Catalog Format

Listings proceed generally according to the following sequence: Country, Geographic or Political chronology, Bank Name, sometimes alphabetically or by date of first note issue. Release within the bank, most often in date order, but sometimes by printer first.

Catalog number — The basic reference number at the beginning of each listing for each note. For this General Issues volume the regular listing require no prefix letters except when an 'A' or 'B' appear within the catalog number. (Military and Regional prefixes are explained later in this section.)

Denomination — the value as shown on the note, as western numerals. When denominations are only spelled out, then a conversion chart is usually supplied in that section.

Date — the actual issue date as printed on the note; in day-month-year order. Where more than one date appears on a note, only the latest is used. Where the note has no date, the designation ND is used, followed by a year date in parentheses when it is known. If a note is date by the law or decree of authorization, then these dates appear with a L or D and are italicized.

Descriptions of the note are broken up into one or more items as follows:

Color — the main color(s) of the face, and the underprint are given first. If the color of the back is different, then they follow the face design description.

Face Design — The identification and location of the main design elements if known. Back color follows only if different than the face color. Back design elements identified if known.

If design elements and or signatures are the same for an issue group then they are printed only once at the heading of the issue, and apply for the group that follows.

Printer — often a local printer has the name shown in full. Abbreviations are used for the most prolific printers. Refer to the list of printer abbreviations elsewhere in this introduction. In these listings the use of the term imprint referees to the logo or the printer's name as usually appearing in the bottom frame or below in the margin of the note.

Valuations — are generally given under the grade headings of Good, Fine and Extremely Fine for early notes; and Very Good, Very Fine and Uncirculated for the later issues. Listings which do not follow these two patterns are clearly indicated. Unc followed by a price is used usually for specimens and proofs when lower grade headings are used for a particular series of issued notes.

A word about renumbering

For this eighth edition, there has been extensive reordering and renumbering of many major countries and sporadic renumbering of smaller sections of many other countries. This will give all an opportunity to look at their collections again, as well as the descriptions and prices and enjoy the changes made in this edition all the more. Sure, you could complain about changing the numbers on your labels, but I don't think you'll complain about the improvement in most prices.

As the cataloging of paper money has matured with more information being shared the editors have endeavored to be as accurate as possible. To ease the task of renumbering, in most cases the previous edition's catalog number appears in parentheses immediately underneath the current number where changes have been made. In addition, an information line noting a catalog renumbering appears at the start of the country's listing.

Catalog prefix or suffix letters

A catalog number preceded by a capital 'A' indicated the incorporation of an earlier listing as required by type or date; a capital letter following the catalog number usually shows the addition of a later issue. Both may indicate newly discovered lower or higher denominations to a series. Listings of notes for regional circulation are distinguished from regular national issues with the prefix letter 'R'; military issues use a 'M' prefix; foreign exchange certificates are assigned a 'FX' prefix. Varieties, specific date or signature listings are shown with small letters 'a' following a number within their respective entries. Some standard variety letters include: 'p' for proof notes, 'r' for remainder notes, 's' for specimen notes and 'x' for errors.

Denominations

The denomination as indicated on many notes issued by a string on countries stretching from the eastern Orient, through western Asia and on across northern Africa often appear only in unfamiliar non-Western numeral styles. Within the listings which follow, however, denominations are always indicated in Western numerals.

A comprehensive chart keying Western numerals to their non-Western counterparts is included elsewhere in this introduction as an aid to the identification of note types. This compilation features not only the basic numeral systems such as Arabic, Japanese and Indian; but also the more restricted systems such as Burmese, Ethiopian, Siamese, Tibetan, Hebrew, Mongolian and Korean, plus other localized variations which have been applied to some paper money issues.

In consulting the numeral systems chart to determine the denomination of a note, one should remember that the actual numerals styles employed in any given area, or at a particular time, may vary significantly from these basic representations. Such variations can be deceptive to the untrained eye, just as variations from Western numeral styles can prove deceptive to individuals not acquainted with the particular style employed.

Dates and Date Listing Policy

In previous editions of this work it was the goal to provide a sampling of the many date varieties that were believed to exist. In recent times, as particular dates (and usually signature combinations) were known to be scarcer, that particular series was expanded to include listings of individual dates. At times this idea has been fully incorporated, but with some series it is not practicable, especially when just about every day in a given month could have been an issue date for the notes.

Accordingly, where it seems justifiable that date spans can be realistically filled with individual dates, this has been done. In order to accommodate the many new dates, the idea of providing small letters to break them up into narrower spans of years has been used. Within these small letter date spans, the aim has been to include no more than five of six dates. If it appears that there are too many dates for a series, with no major differences in value, then a general inclusive date span is used (beginning and ending) and individual dates within this span are not shown.

For those notes showing only a general date span, the only important dates become those that expand the range of years, months or days; earlier or later. But even they would have no major value change.

Because a specific date is not listed does not necessarily mean it is rare. It may be just that it has not been reported. Those date varieties which are known to be scarcer are cataloged separately. Newly reported dates in a wide variety of listings are constantly being reported. This indicates that research into the whole area is very active, and a steady flow of new dates are fully expected upon publication of this edition.

Abbreviations

Certain abbreviations have been adopted for words occurring frequently in note descriptions. Following is a list of these:

#	—	number (catalog or serial)
bldg.	—	building
ctr.	—	center
dk.	—	dark
FV	—	face value
Gen.	—	General
govt.	—	government
Kg.	—	king
l.	—	left
lg.	—	large
lt.	—	light
m/c	—	multicolored
ND	—	no date
ovpt.	—	overprint
portr.	—	portrait
Qn.	—	queen
r.	—	right
sign.	—	signature or signatures
sm.	—	small
unpt.	—	underprint (background printing)
wmk.	—	watermark
w/	—	with
w/o	—	without

Valuations

Valuations are given for most notes in three grades. Earlier issues are usually priced in the grade headings of Good, Fine and Extremely Fine; later issues take the grade headings of Very Good, Very Fine and Uncirculated. While it is true that some early notes cannot be priced in Extremely Fine and some later notes have no premium value in Very Good, it is felt that this coverage provides the best uniformity of value data to the collecting community. There are exceptional cases where headings are adjusted for either single notes of a series which really needs special treatment. We have endeavored to print the Grade Headings often for ease of reference.

Valuations are determined generally from a consensus of individuals submitting prices for evaluation. Some notes have NO pricing, but this does not necessarily mean they are expensive or even rare; but it shows that no pricing information was forthcoming. A number of notes have a 'Rare' designation, and no values. Such notes are generally not available on the market, and when they do appear the price is a matter between buyer and seller. No book can provide guidance in these instances except to indicate they are rare.

Valuations used in this book are based on the IBNS grading standards and are stated in U.S. Dollars. They serve only as aids in evaluating paper money since actual market conditions throughout the world wide collector community is constantly changing. In addition, particularly choice examples of many issues listed may bring higher premiums to values listed.

Unless otherwise presented, values are given for types only, without regard for date or signature. In a number of instances there could be dates or signature varieties worth a substantial premium over the listed value.

FV (for Face Value) is used as a price designation on older but still redeemable legal tender notes in lower conditions. FV may appear in one or both condition columns before Uncirculated, depending on the relative age and availability of the note in question.

Collection care

The proper preservation of a collection should be of paramount importance to all in the hobby - dealers, collectors and scholars. Only a person who was housed notes in a manner giving pleasure to himself and others will keep alive the pleasure of collecting for future generations. The same applies to the way of housing as to the choice of the collecting specialty: it is chiefly a questions of what most pleases the individual collector.

Arrangement and sorting of a collection is most certainly a basic requirement. Storing the notes in safe paper envelopes such as those used in the philatelic trade for stamps and boxes should, perhaps, be considered only when building a new section of a collection; for accommodating varieties or for reasons of saving space when the collection has grown quickly.

The grouping of notes on large sheets and fixing them into position with photo corners had been a method practiced for many years. The collector could arrange the notes to his own taste, identify and otherwise embellish them. Difficulties arise in the accommodation of supplements and the exchanging of notes for examples in better condition, since even slight differences in the format will necessitate detaching and most likely remaking a whole page.

Most paper money collections are probably housed in some form of plastic-pocketed album which are today manufactured in many different sizes and styles to accommodate many types of world paper money.

Because of the number of bank note collectors has grown continually over the past twenty-five years, some specialty manufacturers of albums have developed a paper money selection. The notes, housed in clear plastic pockets, individually or in groups, can be viewed and exchanged without difficulty. These albums are not cheap, but the notes displayed in this manner do make a lasting impression on the viewer. A large collection will hardly be accommodated in its entirety in this manner, thus many collectors limit themselves to partial areas or especially valuable notes which are displayed thus. A word of concern: certain types of plastic and all vinyl used for housing notes may cause notes to become brittle over time, or cause a irreversible and harmful transfer of oils from the vinyl onto the bank notes.

The high demands which stamp collectors make on their products cannot be transferred to the paper money collecting fraternity. A postage stamp is intended for only a single use, then it is relegated to a collection. With paper money, it is nearly impossible to acquire uncirculated specimens from a number of countries due to export laws or just because of internal bank procedures. Bends from excessive counting, or even staple holes are commonplace. Once acquiring a circulated note, the collector must endeavor to maintain its state of preservation.

The face that there is a classification and value difference between notes with greater use or even damage is a matter of course. It is part of the opinion and personal taste of the individual collector to decide what he will consider worthy of collecting and what will pay for such items.

For the purposed of strengthening and mending torn paper money, under no circumstances should one use plain cellophane tape or a similar material. These tapes warp easily, with sealing marks forming at the edges, and the tape frequently discolors. Only with the greatest of difficulty (and often not at all) can these tapes be removed, and damage to the note or the printing is almost unavoidable. The best material for mending tears is an archival tape recommended for the treatment and repair of documents.

There are collectors who, with great skill, remove unsightly spots, repair badly damaged notes, replace missing pieces and otherwise restore or clean a note. Before venturing to tackle such work, one should first experiment with cheap duplicates and not endanger a collection piece. Really difficult work of this nature should be left to the experienced restorer. There is also the question of morality of tampering with a note to improve its condition, either by repairing, starching, ironing, pressing or other methods to possibly deceive a potential future buyer. Such a question must, in the final analysis, be left to the individual collector.

COMPANION CATALOGS

Volume I - Specialized Issues
Volume III - Modern Issues, 1960-present

The Companion Catalogs in the Standard Catalog of World Paper Money series include a volume on Specialized Issues of the world - listed are those banknotes which were issued on a limited circulation basis rather than the nationally-franchised note issues detailed in this work. The Specialized volume is currently in its 7th edition, and it is updated periodically. The Modern issues, 1961 - present, catalogs national notes issued since 1961. It is an annual publication released in the spring of each year. Inquiries on the availability of both these volumes are invited to contact Book Department, Krause Publications, 700 East State Street, Iola, WI 54990-0001 or you may call 1-800-258-0929 or www.krause.com.

IBNS
GRADING STANDARDS
FOR
WORLD PAPER MONEY

The following introduction and Grading Guide is the result of work prepared under the guidance of the Grading Committee of the International Bank Note Society (IBNS.) It has been adopted as the official grading standards of that society.

Introduction

Grading is the most controversial component of paper money collecting today. Small differences in grade can mean significant differences in value. The process of grading is so subjective and dependent on external influences such as lighting, that even a very experienced individual may well grade the same note differently on separate occasions.

To facilitate communication between sellers and buyers, it is essential that grading terms and their meanings be as standardized and as widely used as possible. This standardization should reflect common usage as much as practicable. One difficulty with grading is that even the actual grades themselves are not used everywhere by everyone. For example, in Europe the grade 'About Uncirculated' (AU) is not in general use, yet in North America it is widespread. The European term 'Good VF' may roughly correspond to what individuals in North America call 'Extremely Fine' (EF).

The grades and definitions as set forth below cannot reconcile all the various systems and grading terminology variants. Rather, the attempt is made here to try and diminish the controversy with some common-sense grades and definitions that aim to give more precise meaning to the grading language of paper money.

How to look at a banknote

In order to ascertain the grade of a note, it is essential to examine it out of a holder and under a good light. Move the note around so that light bounces off at different angles. Try holding it up obliquely so that the not is almost even with your eye as you look up at the light. Hard-to-see folds or slight creases will show up under such examination. Some individuals also lightly feel along the surface of the note to detect creasing.

Cleaning, Washing, Pressing of Banknotes

a) Cleaning, washing or pressing paper money is generally harmful and reduced both the grade and the value of a note. At the very least, a washed or pressed note may loose its original sheen and its surface may become lifeless and dull. The defects a note had, such as folds and creases, may not necessarily be completely eliminated and their telltale marks can be detected under a good light. Carelessly washed notes may also have white streaks where the folds or creases were (or still are).

b) Processing of a note which started out as Extremely Fine will automatically reduce it at least one full grade.

Language	January	February	March	April	May	June	July	August	September	October	November	December
English	January	February	March	April	May	June	July	August	September	October	November	December
Albanian	Kallnuer	Fruer	Mars	Prill	Maj	Qershuer	Korrik	Gusht	Shtatuer	Tetuer	Nanduer	Dhetuer
Czech	Leden	Unor	Brezen	Duben	Kveten	Cerven	Cervenec	Srpen	Zari	Rijen	listopad	Prosinec
Danish	Januar	Februar	Maart	April	Maj	Juni	Juli	August	September	Oktober	November	December
Dutch	Januari	Februari	Maart	April	Mei	Juni	Juli	Augustus	September	Oktober	November	December
Estonian	Jaanuar	Veebruar	Marts	Aprill	Mai	Juuni	Juuli	August	September	Oktoober	November	Detsember
French	Janvier	Fevrier	Mars	Avril	Mai	Juin	Jillet	Aout	Septembre	Octobre	Novembre	Decembre
Finnish	Tammikuu	Helmikuu	Maaliskuu	Huhtikuu	Toukokuu	Kesakuu	Heinakuu	Elokuu	Syyskuu	Lokakuu	Marraskuu	Joulukuu
German	Januar	Februar	Marz	April	Mai	juni	Juli	August	September	Oktober	November	Dezember
Hungarian	Januar	Februar	Marcius	Aprilis	Majus	Junius	Julius	Augusztus	Szeptember	Oktober	November	December
Indonesian	Djanuari	Februari	Maret	April	Mai	Djuni	Djuli	Augustus	September	Oktober	November	Desember
Italian	Gennaio	Fabbraio	Marzo	Aprile	Maggio	Giugno	Luglio	Agosto	Settembre	Ottobre	Novembre	Dicembre
Lithuanian	Sausis	Vasaris	Kovas	Balandis	Geguzis	Birzelis	Liepos	Rugpiutis	Rugsejis	Spalis	Lapkritis	Gruodis
Norwegian	Januar	Februar	Mars	April	Mai	juni	Juli	August	September	Oktober	November	Desember
Polish	Styczen	Luty	Marzec	Kwiecien	Maj	Cerwiec	Lipiec	Sierpien	Wrzesien	Pazdziernik	Listopad	Grudzien
Portuguese	Janerio	Fevereiro	Marco	Abril	Maio	Junho	Julho	Agosto	Setembro	Outubro	Novembro	Dezembro
Romanian	Ianuarie	Februarie	Martie	Aprilie	Mai	Iunie	Iulie	August	Septembrie	Octombrie	Noiembrie	Decembrie
Croatian	Sijecanj	Veljaca	Ozujak	Travanj	Svibanj	Lipanj	Srpanj	Kolovoz	Rujan	Listopad	Studeni	Prosinac
Spanish	Enero	Febrero	Marzo	Abril	Mayo	Junio	Julio	Agosto	Septiembre	Octubre	Noviembre	Diciembre
Swedish	Januari	Februari	Mars	April	Maj	Juni	Juli	Augusti	September	Oktober	November	December
Turkish	Ocak	Subat	Mart	Nisan	Mayis	Haziran	Temmuz	Agustos	Eylul	Ekim	Kasim	Aralik
Arabic-New (condensed)	يناير	فبراير	مارس	ابريل	مايو	يونيو	يوليو	اغسطس	سبتمبر	اكتوبر	نوفمبر	ديسمبر
(extended)	كانون الثاني	شباط	آذار	نيسان	أيار	حزيران	تموز	آب	أيلول	تشرين الأول	تشرين الثاني	كانون الأول
Persian (Solar)	فروردین	اردیبهشت	خرداد	تیر	مرداد	شهریور	مهر	آبان	آذر	دی	بهمن	اسفند
(Lunar)	محرم	صفر	ربيع الأول	ربيع الثاني	جمادى الأولى	جمادى الآخرة	رجب	شعبان	رمضان	شوال	ذو القعدة	ذو الحجة
Chinese	一月	二月	三月	四月	五月	六月	七月	八月	九月	十月	十一月	十二月
Japanese	一月	二月	三月	四月	五月	六月	七月	八月	九月	十月	十一月	十二月
Greek	Ιανουαριος	Φεβρουαριος	Μαρτιος	Απριλιος	Μαιος	Ιουνιος	Ιουλιος	Αυγουστος	Σεπτεμβριος	Οκτωβριος	Νοεμβριος	Δεκεμβριος
Russian	ЯНВАРЬ	ФЕВРАЛЬ	МАРТ	АПРЕЛЬ	МАЙ	ИЮНЬ	ИЮЛЬ	АВГУСТ	СЕНТЯБРЬ	ОКТЯБРЬ	НОЯБРЬ	ДЕКАБРЬ
Serbian	Јануар	Фебруар	Март	Април	Мај	Јун	Јул	Август	Септембар	Октобар	Новембар	Децембар
Yiddish	יאנואר	פעברואר	מערץ	אפריל	מאי	יוני	יולי	אויגוסט	סעפטעמבער	אקטאבער	נאוועמבער	דעצעמבער
Hebrew (Israeli)	ינואר	פברואר	מרץ	אפריל	מאי	יוני	יולי	אוגוסט	ספטמבר	אוקטובר	נובמבר	דצמבר

Note: Word spellings and configurations as represented on actual notes may vary significantly from those shown on this chart.

Unnatural Defects

Glue, tape or pencil marks may sometimes be successfully removed. While such removal will leave a cleaned surface, it will improve the overall appearance of the note without concealing any of its defects. Under such circumstances, the grade of that note may also be improved.

The words "pinholes", "staple holes", "trimmed", "writing on face", "tape marks" etc. should always be added to the description of a note. It is realized that certain countries routinely staple their notes together in groups before issue. In such cases, the description can include a comment such as "usual staple holes" or something similar. After all, not everyone knows that certain notes cannot be found otherwise.

The major point of this section is that one cannot lower the overall grade of a note with defects simply because of the defects. The price will reflect the lowered worth of a defective note, but the description must always include the specific defects.

The Term *Uncirculated*

The word *Uncirculated* is used in this grading guide only as a qualitive measurement of the appearance of a note. It has nothing at all to do with whether or not an issuer has actually released the note to circulation. Thus, the term About Uncirculated is justified and acceptable because so many notes that have never seen hand to hand use have been mishandled so that they are available at best in AU condition. Either a note is uncirculated in condition or it is not; there can be no degrees of uncirculated. Highlights or defects in color, centering and the like may be included in a description but the fact that a note is or is not in uncirculated condition should not be a disputable point.

GRADING GUIDE —
Definitions of Terms

UNCIRCULATED: A perfectly preserved note, never mishandled by the issuing authority, a bank teller, the public or a collector.

Paper is clean and firm, without discoloration. Corners are sharp and square, witout any evidence of roudning. (Rounded corners are often a tell-tale sign of a cleaned or "doctored" note.)

An uncirculated note will have its original, natural sheen.

NOTE: Some note issuers are most often avaialble with slight eveidence of very light counting folds which do not "break" the paper. Also, French-printed notes usually have a slight ripple in the paper. Many collectors and dealers refer to such notes as AU-UNC.

ABOUT UNCIRCULATED: A virtually perfect note, with some minor handling. May show very slight evidence of bank counting folds at a corner or one light fold through the center, but not both. An AU note cannot be creased, a crease being a hard fold which has usually "broken" the surface of the note.

Paper is clean and bright with original sheen. Corners are not rounded.

NOTE: Europeans will refer to an About Uncirculated or AU note as "EF-Unc" or as just "EF". The Extremely Fine note described below will often be referred to as "GVF" or "Good Very Fine".

EXTREMELY FINE: A very attractive note, with light handling. May have a maximum of three light folds or one strong crease.

Paper is clean and bright with original sheen. Corners may show only the slightest evidence of rounding. There may also be the slightest sign of wear where a fold meets the edge.

VERY FINE: An attractive note, but with more evidence of handling and wear. May have several folds both vertically and horizontally.

Paper may have minimal dirt, or possible color smudging. Paper itself is still relatively crisp and not floppy.

There are no tears into the border area, although the edges do show slight wear. Corners also show wear but not full rounding.

FINE: A note which shows considerable circulation, with many folds, creases and wrinkling.

Paper is not excessively dirty but may have some softness.

Edges may show much handling, with minor tears in the border area. Tears may not extend into the design. There will be no center hole because of excessive folding.

Colors are clear but not very bright. A staple hole or two would not be considered unusual wear in a Fine note. Overall appearance is still on the desirable side.

VERY GOOD: A well used note, abused but still intact.

Corners may have much wear and rounding, tiny nicks, tears may extend into the design, some discoloration may be present, staining may have occurred, and a small hole may sometimes be seen at center from excessive folding.

Staple and pinholes are usually present, and the note itself is quite limp but NO pieces of the note can be missing. A note in VG condition may still have an overall not unattractive appearance.

GOOD: A well worn and heavily used note. Normal damage from prolonged circulation will include strong multiple folds and creases, stains, pinholes and/or staple holes, dirt, discoloration, edge tears, center hole, rounded corners and an overall unattractive appearance. No large pieces of the note may be missing. Graffiti is commonly seen on notes in G condition.

FAIR: A totally limp, dirty and very well used note. Larger pieces may be half torn off or missing besides the defects mentioned under the Good category. Tears will be larger, obscured portions of the note will be bigger.

POOR: A "rag" with severe damage because of wear, staining, pieces missing, graffiti, larger holes. May have tape holding pieces of the note together. Trimming may have taken place to remove rough edges. A Poor note is desirable only as a "filler" or when such a note is the only one known of that particular issue.

STANDARD INTERNATIONAL GRADING TERMINOLOGY AND ABBREVIATIONS

U.S. and ENGLISH SPEAKING LANDS	UNCIRCULATED	EXTREMELY FINE	VERY FINE	FINE	VERY GOOD	GOOD	POOR
Abbreviation	UNC	EF or XF	VF	FF	VG	G	PR
BRAZIL	(1) DW	(3) S	(5) MBC	(7) BC	(8)	(9) R	UTGeG
DENMARK	O	O1	1+	1	1÷	2	3
FINLAND	0	01	1+	1	1?	2	3
FRANCE	NEUF	SUP	TTB or TB	TB or TB	B	TBC	BC
GERMANY	KFR	II / VZGL	III / SS	IV / S	V / S.g.E.	VI / G.e.	G.e.s.
ITALY	FdS	SPL	BB	MB	B	M	—
JAPAN	未 使 用	極美品	美品	並品	—	—	—
NETHERLANDS	FDC	Pr.	Z.F.	Fr.	Z.g.	G	—
NORWAY	0	01	1+	1	1÷	2	3
PORTUGAL	Novo	Soberbo	Muito bo	—	—	—	—
SPAIN	Lujo	SC, IC or EBC	MBC	BC	—	RC	MC
SWEDEN	0	01	1+	1	1?	2	—

BRAZIL

FE	— Flor de Estampa
S	— Soberba
MBC	— Muito Bem Conservada
BC	— Bem Conservada
R	— Regular
UTGeG	— Um Tanto Gasto e Gasto

DENMARK

O	— Uncirkuleret
01	— Meget Paent Eksemplar
1+	— Paent Eksemplar
1	— Acceptabelt Eksemplar
1	—Noget Slidt Eksemplar
2	— Darlight Eksemplar
3	— Meget Darlight Eskemplar

FINLAND

00	— Kiitolyonti
0	— Lyontiveres
01	— Erittain Hyva
1+	— Hyva
1?	— Keikko
3	— Huono

FRANCE

NEUF	— New
SUP	— Superbe
TTB	— Tres Tres Beau
TB	— Tres Beau
B	— Beau
TBC	— Tres Bien Conserve
BC	— Bien Conserve

GERMANY

VZGL	— Vorzüglich
SS	— Sehr schön
S	— Schön
S.g.E.	— Sehr gut erhalten
G.e.	— Gut erhalten
G.e.S.	— Gering erhalten Schlect

ITALY

Fds	— Fior di Stampa
SPL	— Splendid
BB	— Bellissimo
MB	— Molto Bello
B	— Bello
M	— Mediocre

JAPAN

未 使 用	— Mishiyo
極美品	— Goku Bihin
美品	— Bihin
並品	— Futuhin

NETHERLANDS

Pr.	— Prachtig
Z.F.	— Zeer Fraai
Fr.	— Fraai
Z.g.	— Zeer Goed
G	— Good

NORWAY

0	— Usirkuleret eks
01	— Meget pent eks
1+	— Pent eks
1	— Fullgodt eks
1-	— Ikke Fullgodt eks
2	— Darlig eks

SPAIN

EBC	— Extraordinariamente Bien Conservada
SC	— Sin Circular
IC	— Incirculante
MBC	— Muy Bien Conservada
BC	— Bien Conservada
RC	— Regular Conservada
MC	— Mala Conservada

SWEDEN

0	— Ocirkulerat
01	— Mycket Vackert
1+	— Vackert
1	— Fullgott
1?	— Ej Fullgott
2	— Dalight

Foreign Exchange Table

The latest foreign exchange fixed rates below apply to trade with banks in the country of origin. The left column shows the number of units per U.S. dollar at the official rate. The right column shows the number of units per dollar at the free market rate.

Country	Official #/$	Market #/$
Afghanistan (Afghan)	4,750	5,300
Albania (Lek)	102.50	–
Algeria (Dinar)	55.489	66.00
Andorra uses French Franc and Spanish Peseta		
Angola (Readjust Kwanza)	201,994	–
Anguilla uses E.C. Dollar	2.70	–
Antigua uses E.C. Dollar	2.70	–
Argentina (New Peso)	.9998	–
Armenia (Dram)	420.00	–
Aruba (Florin)	1.79	–
Australia (Dollar)	1.2726	–
Austria (Schilling)	10.635	–
Azerbaijan (Manat)	4,230	–
Bahamas (Dollar)	1.00	–
Bahrain Is. (Dinar)	.377	–
Bangladesh (Taka)	42.61	43.00
Barbados (Dollar)	2.01	–
Belarus (Ruble)	11,500	–
Belgium (Franc)	31.13	–
Belize (Dollar)	2.00	2.00
Benin uses CFA Franc West	510.57	–
Bermuda (Dollar)	1.00	–
Bhutan (Ngultrum)	35.74	39.00
Bolivia (Boliviano)	5.18	–
Bosnia-Herzegovina (New Dinar)	141.00	–
Botswana (Pula)	3.629	–
British Virgin Islands uses U.S. Dollar	1.00	–
Brazil (Real)	1.034	–
Brunei/Ringgit	1.39	–
Bulgaria (Lev)	248.71	–
Burkina Faso uses CFA Fr. West	510.57	–
Burma (Kyat)	5.81	110.00
Burundi (Franc)	216.31	–
Cambodia (Riel)	2,300	–
Cameron uses CFA Fr. Central	510.57	–
Canada (Dollar)	1.3301	–
Cape Verde (Escudo)	82.97	91.00
Cayman Is. (Dollar)	0.8282	–
Central African Rep.	510.57	–
CFA Franc Central	510.57	–
CFA Franc West	510.57	–
CFP Franc	92.83	–
Chad uses CFA Franc Central	510.57	–
Chile (Peso)	417.95	–
China, P.R. (Renminbi Yuan)	8.297	–
Colombia (Peso)	1,000.75	–
Comoros (Franc)	382.93	–
Congo uses CFA Franc Central	510.57	–
Cook Islands (Dollar)	1.47	–
Costa Rica (Colon)	216.5	–
Croatia (Kuna)	5.371	–
Cuba (Peso)	20.00	35.00
Cyprus (Pound)	.4611	–
Czech Republic (Koruna)	26.909	–
Denmark (Krona)	5.81	–
Djibouti (Franc)	165.00	–
Dominica uses E.C. Dollar	2.70	–
Dom. Rep. (Peso)	13.78	–
East Caribbean (Dollar)	2.70	–
Ecuador (Sucre)	3,365.00	–
Egypt (Pound)	3.3928	–
El Salvador (Colon)	8.75	–
England (Sterling Pound)	.6050	–
Equatorial Guinea uses CFA Franc Central	510.57	–
Eritrea, see Ethiopia		
Estonia (Kroon)	12.06	–
Ethiopia (Birr)	6.231	7.25
European Currency Unit	.7869	–
Falkland Is. (Pound)	.6050	–
Faroe Islands (Krona)	5.811	–
Fiji Islands (Dollar)	1.39	–
Finland (Markka)	4.5625	–
France (Franc)	5.1057	–
French Polynesia uses CFP Franc	92.83	–
Gabon (CFA Franc)	510.57	–
Gambia (Dalasi)	10.04	–
Georgia/Lari	1.30	–
Germany (Mark)	1.5103	–
Ghana (Cedi)	1,723.50	–
Gibraltar (Pound)	.6050	–
Greece (Drachma)	238.39	–
Greenland uses Danish Krona		
Grenada uses E.C. Dollar	2.70	–
Guatemala (Quetzal)	6.039	–
Guernsey uses Sterling Pound	.6050	–
Guinea-Bissau (Peso)	23,418	–
Guinea Conakry (Franc)	1,000.00	–
Guyana (Dollar)	140.30	–
Haiti (Gourde)	15.271	–
Honduras (Lempira)	12.70	–
Hong Kong (Dollar)	7.732	–
Hungary (Forint)	159.21	–
Iceland (Krona)	66.22	–
India (Rupee)	35.739	–
Indonesia (Rupiah)	2,333.5	–
Iran (Rial)	3,000	5,000
Iraq (Dinar)	.31	1,200
Ireland (Eire) (Punt)	.6046	–
Isle of Man uses Sterling Pound	.6050	–
Israel (New Sheqalim)	3.2438	–
Italy (Lira)	1,521.25	–
Ivory Coast uses CFA Fr. West	510.57	–
Jamaica (Dollar)	34.00	38.00
Japan (Yen)	111.96	–
Jersey (Sterling Pound)	.6050	–
Jordan (Dinar)	.709	–
Kazakhstan (Tenge)	65.00	–
Kenya (Shilling)	55.75	–
Kiribati uses Australian Dollar		
Korea-PDR (Won)	2.15	–
Korea-Rep. (Won)	829.0	–
Kuwait (Dinar)	.299	–
Kyrgyzstan (Som)	11.05	–
Laos (Kip)	920.00	–
Latvia (Lat)	.55	–
Lebanon (Pound)	1,551.00	–
Lesotho (Maloti)	4.685	–
Liberia/Dollar "JJ"	1.00	30.00
"Liberty"	–	49.00
Libya (Dinar)	.3555	1.00
Liechtenstein uses Swiss Franc		
Lithuania (Litas)	4.00	–
Luxembourg (Franc)	31.13	–
Macao (Pataca)	7.988	–
Macedonia (New Denar)	40.298	–
Madagascar (Franc)	3,950	–
Malawi (Kwacha)	15.325	16.50
Malaysia (Ringgit)	2.521	–
Maldives (Rufiya)	11.77	–
Mali uses CFA Franc West	510.57	–
Malta (Lira)	.3565	–
Marshall Islands uses U.S. Dollar		
Mauritania (Ouguiya)	138.92	140.00
Mauritius (Rupee)	20.205	–
Mexico (Peso)	7.925	–
Moldova (Leu)	4.55	–
Monaco uses French Franc		
Mongolia (Tugrik)	466.67	–
Montenegro uses Yugo New Dinar		
Montserrat uses E.C. Dollar	2.70	–
Morocco (Dirham)	8.675	–
Mozambique (Metical)	11,140.5	–
Myanmar (Burma) (Kyat)	5.81	110.00
Namibia (Rand)	4.685	–
Nauru uses Australian Dollar		
Nepal (Rupee)	56.775	–
Netherlands (Gulden)	1.6937	–
Netherlands Antilles (Gulden)	1.79	–
New Caledonia uses CFP Franc		
New Zealand (Dollar)	1.4085	–
Nicaragua (Cordoba Oro)	8.775	–
Niger uses CFA Franc West	510.57	–
Nigeria (Naira)	79.00	–
Northern Ireland uses Sterling Pound	.6050	–
Norway (Krone)	6.346	–
Oman (Rial)	.385	–
Pakistan (Rupee)	40.22	–
Palau uses U.S. Dollar		
Panama (Balboa) uses U.S. Dollar		
Papua-New Guinea (Kina)	1.3395	–
Paraguay (Guarani)	2,100	–
Peru (Nuevos Soles)	2.589	–
Philippines (Peso)	26.255	–
Poland (Zloty)	2.8105	–
Portugal (Escudo)	155.875	–
Qatar (Riyal)	3.639	–
Romania (Leu)	3,450	–
Russia (Ruble)	5,458	–
Rwanda (Franc)	323.85	–
St. Helena (Pound)	.6050	–
St. Kitts uses E.C. Dollar	2.70	–
St. Lucia uses E.C. Dollar	2.70	–
St. Vincent uses E.C. Dollar	2.70	–
San Marino uses Italian Lira		
Sao Tome e Principe (Dobra)	2,385.13	–
Saudi Arabia (Riyal)	3.7504	–
Scotland uses Sterling Pound	.6050	–
Senegal uses CFA Franc West	510.57	–
Seychelles (Rupee)	5.0008	–
Sierra Leone (Leone)	750	–
Singapore (Dollar)	1.3985	–
Slovakia (Sk. Koruna)	30.937	–
Slovenia (Tolar)	137.88	–
Solomon Is. (Dollar)	3.6063	–
Somalia (Shillin)	2,620	12,000
Somaliland (Somali Shillin)	N/A	100
South Africa (Rand)	4.685	–
Spain (Peseta)	127.14	–
Sri Lanka (Rupee)	57.05	–
Sudan (Dinar)	146	980.00
Surinam (Guilder)	410.00	–
Swaziland (Lilangeni)	4.685	–
Sweden (Krona)	6.6255	–
Switzerland (Franc)	1.2733	–
Syria (Pound)	41.95	–
Taiwan (NT Dollar)	27.24	–
Tajikistan uses Russian Ruble		
Tanzania (Shilling)	602.50	–
Thailand (Baht)	25.475	–
Togo uses CFA Franc West	510.57	–
Tonga (Pa'anga)	1.2141	–
Transdniestra (New Ruble)	N/A	30,000
Trinidad & Tobago (Dollar)	6.045	–
Tunisia (Dinar)	.9725	–
Turkey (Lira)	97,479.00	–
Turkmenistan (Manat)	195	–
Turks & Caicos uses U.S. Dollar		
Tuvalu uses Australian Dollar		
Uganda (Shilling)	1,096	–
Ukraine (Hryvnia)	1.844	–
United Arab Emirates (Dirham)	3.672	–
Uruguay (Peso Uruguayo)	8.51	–
Uzbekistan (Som)	24.00	40.00
Vanuatu (Vatu)	111.31	–
Vatican City uses Italian Lira		
Venezuela (Bolivar)	471.51	–
Vietnam (Dong)	11,030	–
Western Samoa (Tala)	2.4295	–
Yemen Rial	130.00	145.00
Yugoslavia (Novikh Dinar)	5.034	–
Zaire (Nouveaux Zaire)	29,226.5	–
Zambia (Kwacha)	1,275.00	–
Zimbabwe (Dollar)	10.665	–

DATING

Determining the date of issue of a note is a basic consideration of attribution. As the reading of dates is subject not only to the vagaries of numeric styling, but to variations in dating roots caused by the observation of differing religious eras or regal periods from country to country, making this determination can sometimes be quite difficult. Most countries outside the North Africa and Oriental spheres rely on Western date numerals and the Christian (AD) reckoning, although in a few instances note dating has been tied to the year of a reign or government.

Countries of the Arabic sphere generally date their issues to the Muslim calendar which commenced on July 16, 622 AD when the prophet Mohammed fled from Mecca to Medina. As this calendar is reckoned by the lunar year of 354 days, it is a year 3.03% shorter than the Christian year. A conversion formula requires you to subtract the percent from the AH date, and then add 621 to gain the AD date.

The Muslim calendar is not always based on the lunar year (AH), however, causing some confusion. Afghanistan and Iran (Persia) used a calendar based on a solar year (SH) introduced around 1920. These dates can be converted to AD by simply adding 621. In 1976 Iran implemented a solar calendar based on the founding of the Iranian monarchy in 559 BC. The first year observed on this new system was 2535(MS) which commenced on March 20, 1976.

Several different eras of reckoning, including the Christian (AD) and Muslim (AH) have been used to date paper money of the Indian subcontinent. The two basic systems are the Vikrama Samvat (VS) era which dates from October 18, 58 BC, and the Saka (SE) era the origin of which is reckoned from March 3, 78 AD. Dating according to both eras appear on notes of several native states and countries of the area.

Thailand (Siam) has observed three different eras for dating. The most predominant is the Buddhist (BE) era which originates in 543 BC. Next is the Bangkok or Ratanakosind-sok (RS) era dating from 1781 AD (and consist of only 3 numerals), followed by the Chula-Sakarat (CS) era which date from 638 AD, with the latter also observed in Burma.

Other calendars include that of the Ethiopian (EE) era which commenced 7 years, 8 months after AD dating, and that of the Hebrew nation which commenced on October 7, 3761 BC. Korea claims a dating from 2333 BC which is acknowledged on some issues.

The following table indicates the years dating from the various eras which correspond to 1997 by the Christian (AD) calendar reckoning. It must be remembered that there are overlaps between the eras in some instances:

Christian Era (AD)	—	1997
Mohammedan era (AH)	—	AH1418
Solar year (SH)	—	SH1376
Monarchic Solar era (MS)	—	MS2556
Vikrama Samvat era (VS)	—	SE2054
Saka era (SE)	—	Saka 1919
Buddhist era (BE)	—	BE2540
Bangkok era (RS)	—	RS216
Chula-Sakarat era (CS)	—	CS1359
Ethiopian era (EE)	—	EE1989
Jewish era	—	5757
Korean era	—	4330

Paper money of Oriental origin - principally Japan, Korea, China, Turkestan and Tibet generally date to the year of the government, dynastic, regnal or cyclical eras, with the dates indicated in Oriental characters which usually read from right to left. In recent years, however, some dating has been according to the Christina calendar and in western numerals reading from left to right.

More detailed guides to the application of the less prevalent dating systems than those described, and others of strictly local nature, along with the numeral designations employed are presented in conjunction with the appropriate listings.

Some notes carry dating according to both the locally observed and Christian eras. This is particularly true in the Arabic sphere, where the Muslim date may be indicated in Arabic numerals and the Christian date in western numerals.

In general the date actually carried on a given paper money issue is indicated. Notes issued by special Law or Decree will have a L or D preceding the date. Dates listed within parentheses are dates of issue which may differ from the date appearing on the note, but which is documented by other means. Undated notes are listed with ND, followed by a year when the year of actual issue is known.

Timing differentials between the 354 day Muslim and the 365 day Christian year cause situations whereby notes bearing dates of both eras have two date combinations that may overlap from one or the other calendar system.

China – Republic 9th year, 1st month, 15th day (15.1.1920), read r. to l.

Thailand (Siam) – 1 December 2456

Poland – 28 February 1919

Israel – 1973, 5733

Egypt – 1967 December 2

Korea – 4288 (1955)

Afghanistan – Solar year 1356

Indonesia – January 1950

Russia – 1 October 1920

Greece – 5 March 1943

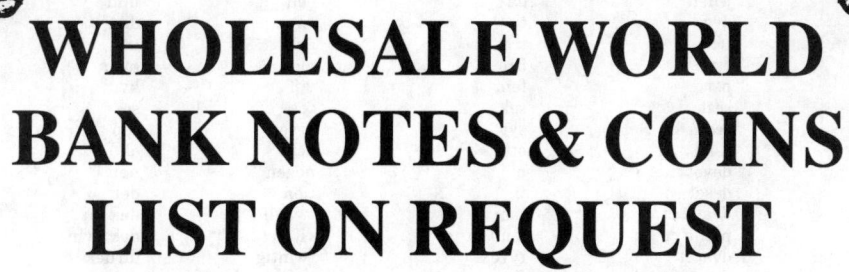

A Guide To International Numerics

	ENGLISH	CZECH	DANISH	DUTCH	ESPERANTO	FRENCH
1/4	one-quarter	jeden-ctvrt	én kvart	een-kwart	unu-kvar' ono	un-quart
1/2	one-half	jeden-polovicni or pul	én halv	een-half	unu-du'one	un-demi
1	one	jeden	én	een	unu	un
2	two	dve	to	twee	du	deux
3	three	tri	tre	drie	tri	trois
4	four	ctyri	fire	vier	kvar	quatre
5	five	pet	fem	vijf	kvin	cinq
6	six	sest	seks	zes	ses	six
7	seven	sedm	syv	zeven	sep	sept
8	eight	osm	otte	acht	ok	huit
9	nine	devet	ni	negen	nau	neuf
10	ten	deset	ti	tien	dek	dix
12	twelve	dvaná ct	tolv	twaalf	dek du	douze
15	fifteen	patná ct	femten	vijftien	dek kvin	quinze
20	twenty	dvacet	tyve	twintig	du'dek	vingt
24	twenty-four	dvacet-ctyri	fire og tyve	twintig-vier	du'dek kvar	vingt-quatre
25	twenty-five	dvacet-pet	fem og tyve	twintig-vijf	du'dek kvin	vingt-cinq
30	thirty	tricet	tredive	dertig	tri'dek	trente
40	forty	ctyricet	fyrre	veertig	kvar'dek	quarante
50	fifty	padesát	halytreds	vijftig	kvin'dek	cinquante
60	sixty	sedesát	tres	zestig	ses'dek	soizante
70	seventy	sedmdesát	halvfjerds	zeventig	sep'dek	soizante-dix
80	eighty	osemdesát	firs	tachtig	ok'dek	quatre-vingt
90	ninety	devadesát	halvfems	negentig	nau'dek	quatre-vingt-dix
100	one hunded	jedno sto	et hundrede	een-honderd	unu-cento	un-cent
1000	thousand	tisí c	tusind	duizend	mil	mille

	GERMAN	HUNGARIAN	INDONESIAN	ITALIAN	NORWEGIAN	POLISH
1/4	einvertel	egy-negyed	satu-suku	uno-quarto	en-fjerdedel	jeden-c wierc
1/2	einhalb	egy-fél	satu-setengah	uno-mezzo	en-halv	jeden-polowa
1	ein	egy	satu	uno	en	jeden
2	zwei	kettö	dua	due	to	dwa
3	drei	három	tiga	tre	tre	trzy
4	vier	négy	empat	quattro	fire	cztery
5	fünf	öt	lima	cinque	fem	piec´
6	sechs	hat	enam	sei	seks	szes´ c´
7	sieben	hét	tudjuh	sette	sju	siedem
8	acht	nyolc	delapan	otto	atte	osiem
9	neun	kilenc	sembilan	nove	ni	dziewiec´
10	zehn	tí z	sepuluh	dieci	ti	dziesiec´
12	zwolf	tizenketto	dua belas	dodici	tolv	dwanas´ cie
15	fünfzehn	tizenöt	lima belas	quindici	femten	pietnas´ cie
20	zwanzig	húsz	dua puluh	venti	tjue or tyve	dwadzies´ cia
24	vierundzwanzig	húsz-négy	dua puluh-empat	venti-quattro	tjue-fire or tyve-fire	dwadzies´ cia-cztery
25	fünfundzwanzig	húsz-öt	dua-puluh-lima	venti-cinque	tjue-fem or tyve-fem	dwadzies´ cia-piec
30	dreissig	harminc	tigapuluh	trenta	tredve	trzydzies´ ci
40	vierzig	negyven	empat puluh	quaranta	forti	czterdries´ ci
50	fünfzig	otven	lima puluh	cinquanta	femti	piec´ dziesiat
60	sechzig	hatvan	enam puluh	sessanta	seksti	szes´ c´ dziesiat
70	siebzig	hetven	tudjuh pulu	settanta	sytti	siedemdziesiat
80	achtzig	nyolvan	delapan puluh	ottanta	atti	osiemdziesiat
90	neuzig	kilencven	sembilan puluh	novanta	nitty	dziewiec´ dziesiat
100	ein hundert	egy-száz	seratus	uno-cento	en-hundre	jeden-sto
1000	tausend	ezer	seribu	mille	tusen	tysiac

	PORTUGUESE	ROMANIAN	SERBO-CROATIAN	SPANISH	SWEDISH	TURKISH
1/4	um-quarto	un-sfert	jedan-ceturtina	uno-cuarto	en-fjärdedel	bir-ceyrek
1/2	un-meio	o-jumatate	jedan-polovina	uno-medio	en-hälft	bir-yarim
1	um	un	jedan	uno	en	bir
2	dois	doi	dva	dos	tva	iki
3	três	trei	tri	tres	tre	üc
4	quatro	patru	cetiri	cuatro	fyra	dört
5	cinco	cinci	pet	cinco	fem	bes
6	seis	sase	sest	seis	sex	alti
7	sete	sapte	sedam	siete	sju	yedi
8	oito	opt	osam	ocho	atta	sekiz
9	nove	noua	devet	nueve	nio	dokuz
10	dez	zece	deset	diez	tio	on
12	doze	doisprezece	dvanaest	doce	tolv	on iki
15	quinze	cincisprezece	petnaest	quince	femton	on bes
20	vinte	douazeci	dvadset	veinte	tjugu	yirmi
24	vinte-quatro	douazeci-patru	dvadesel-cetiri	veinte-cuarto	tjugu-fyra	yirmi-dört
25	vinte-cinco	douazeci-cinci	dvadeset-pet	veinte-cinco	tjugu-fem	yirmi-bes
30	trinta	treizeci	trideset	treinta	trettio	otuz
40	quarenta	patruzeci	cetrdeset	cuarenta	fyrtio	kirk
50	cinqüenta	cincizeci	padeset	cincuenta	femtio	elli
60	sessenta	saizeci	sezdeset	sesenta	sextio	altmis
70	setenta	saptezeci	sedamdeset	setenta	sjuttio	yetmis
80	oitenta	optzeci	osamdeset	ochenta	attio	seksen
90	noventa	novazeci	devedeset	noventa	nittio	doksan
100	un-cem	o-suta	jedan-sto	uno-ciente	en-hundra	bir-yüz
1000	mil	mie	hiljada	mil	tusen	bin

SPECIMEN NOTES

To familiarize private banks, central banks, law enforcement agencies and treasuries around the world with newly issued currency, many issuing authorities provide special 'Specimen' examples of their notes. Specimens are actual bank notes, complete with consecutive or all zero serial numbers, proper signatures and bearing an overprint or pin-hole perforation of the word SPECIMEN, sometimes in English, or in the language of the nation of issue or choice of the printing firm.

Some countries have made specimen notes available to collectors. These include Cuba, Czechoslovakia, Poland and Slovakia. Aside from these collector issues, specimen notes usually command higher prices than regular issue notes of the same type, even though there are far fewer collectors of specimens. In some cases notably older issues in high denominations, specimens may be the only form of such notes available to collectors today. Specimen notes are not legal tender or redeemable, thus have no real 'face value' which also is indicated on some examples.

The most unusual form of specimens were produced by the firm of Waterlow and Sons Ltd. They printed the notes with a company seal, and very often printed them in several different color combinations in addition to the regularly approved colors. These were intended to be mounted in salesman's sample books. Generally these are not included in the scope of this catalog.

Some examples of how the word SPECIMEN is represented in other languages or on notes of other countries follow:

AMOSTRA: Brazil
COMPIONE: Italy
CONTOH: Malaysia
EKSEMPLAAR: South Africa
ESPÉCIME: Portugal and Colonies
ESPECIMEN: Various Spanish-speaking nations
GIAY MAU: Vietnam
MINTA: Hungary
MODELO: Brazil
MODEL: Albania
MUSTER: Austria, Germany
MUESTRA: Various Spanish-speaking nations
NUMUNEDIR GECMEZ: Turkey
ORNEKTIR GECMEZ: Turkey
ОБРАЗЕЦ or **ОБРАЗЕЦЪ:** Bulgaria, Russia
PARAUGS: Latvia
PROFTRYK: Sweden
SPEZIMEN: Switzerland
UZORAK: Croatia
VZOREC: Slovenia
WZOR: Poland
ЗАГВАР: Mongolia

نموذج or ـنموذـح : Arabic

نمونه : Persian

نمونه : Pakistan

דוגמא : Israel

แบบบ๋ำ : Laos

Specimen of face of a Taiwan Bank year 53 (1964) dated note with perforated ancient Chinese seal script characters.

Specimen of a Bermuda Monetary Authority 1978 dated note with punched normal serial numbers having been created at a later date for sale to collectors.

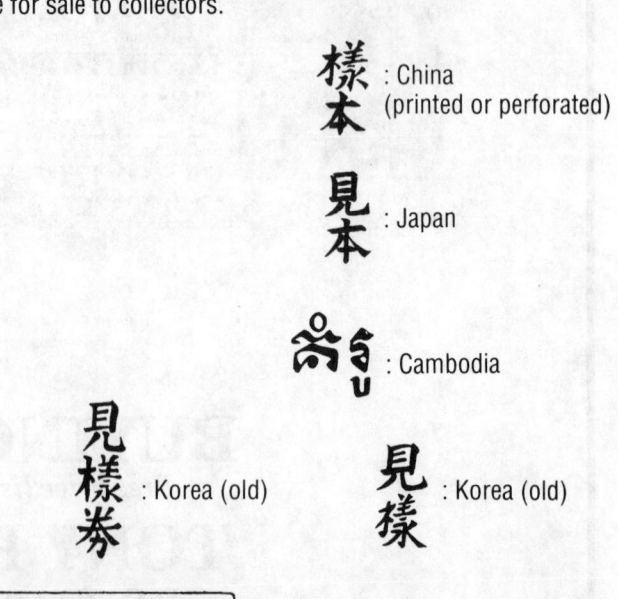

樣本 : China (printed or perforated)

見本 : Japan

: Cambodia

見樣券 : Korea (old)

見樣 : Korea (old)

견본 : Korea (new)

HEJIRA DATE
CONVERSION CHART
HEJIRA DATE CHART

HEJIRA (Hijra, Hegira), the name of the Mohammedan era (A.H. = Anno Hegirae) dates back to the Christian year 622 when Mohammed "fled" from Mecca, escaping to Medina to avoid persecution from the Koreish tribesmen. Based on a lunar year the Mohammedan year is 11 days shorter.

* = Leap Year (Christian Calendar)

AH Hejira	AD Christian Date
1010	1601, July 2
1011	1602, June 21
1012	1603, June 11
1013	1604, May 30
1014	1605, May 19
1015	1606, May 19
1016	1607, May 9
1017	1608, April 28
1018	1609, April 6
1019	1610, March 26
1020	1611, March 16
1021	1612, March 4
1022	1613, February 21
1023	1614, February 11
1024	1615, January 31
1025	1616, January 20
1026	1617, January 9
1027	1617, December 29
1028	1618, December 19
1029	1619, December 8
1030	1620, November 26
1031	1621, November 16
1032	1622, November 5
1033	1623, October 25
1034	1624, October 14
1035	1625, October 3
1036	1626, September 22
1037	1627, September 12
1038	1628, August 31
1039	1629, August 21
1040	1630, July 10
1041	1631, July 30
1042	1632, July 19
1043	1633, July 8
1044	1634, June 27
1045	1635, June 17
1046	1636, June 5
1047	1637, May 26
1048	1638, May 15
1049	1639, May 4
1050	1640, April 23
1051	1641, April 12
1052	1642, April 1
1053	1643, March 22
1054	1644, March 10
1055	1645, February 27
1056	1646, February 17
1057	1647, February 6
1058	1648, January 27
1059	1649, January 15
1060	1650, January 4
1061	1650, December 25
1062	1651, December 14
1063	1652, December 2
1064	1653, November 22
1065	1654, November 11
1066	1655, October 31
1067	1656, October 20
1068	1657, October 9
1069	1658, September 29
1070	1659, September 18
1071	1660, September 6
1072	1661, August 27
1073	1662, August 16
1074	1663, August 5
1075	1664, July 25
1076	1665, July 14
1077	1666, July 4
1078	1667, June 23
1079	1668, June 11
1080	1669, June 1
1081	1670, May 21
1082	1671, May 10
1083	1672, April 29
1084	1673, April 18
1085	1674, April 7
1086	1675, March 28
1087	1676, March 16*
1088	1677, March 6
1089	1678, February 23
1090	1679, February 12
1091	1680, February 2*
1092	1681, January 21
1093	1682, January 10
1094	1682, December 31
1095	1683, December 20
1096	1684, December 8*
1097	1685, November 28
1098	1686, November 17
1099	1687, November 7
1100	1688, October 26*
1101	1689, October 15
1102	1690, October 5

AH Hejira	AD Christian Date
1103	1691, September 24
1104	1692, September 12*
1105	1693, September 2
1106	1694, August 22
1107	1695, August 12
1108	1696, July 31*
1109	1697, July 20
1110	1698, July 10
1111	1699, June 29
1112	1700, June 18
1113	1701, June 8
1114	1702, May 28
1115	1703, May 17
1116	1704, May 6*
1117	1705, April 25
1118	1706, April 15
1119	1707, April 4
1120	1708, March 23*
1121	1709, March 18
1122	1710, March 2
1123	1711, February 19
1124	1712, February 9*
1125	1713, January 28
1126	1714, January 17
1127	1715, January 7
1128	1715, December 27
1129	1716, December 16*
1130	1717, December 5
1131	1718, November 24
1132	1719, November 14
1133	1720, November 2*
1134	1721, October 22
1135	1722, October 12
1136	1723, October 1
1137	1724, September 29*
1138	1725, September 9
1139	1726, August 29
1140	1727, August 19
1141	1728, August 7*
1142	1729, July 27
1143	1730, July 17
1144	1731, July 6
1145	1732, June 24*
1146	1733, June 14
1147	1734, June 3
1148	1735, May 24
1149	1736, May 12*
1150	1737, May 1
1151	1738, April 21
1152	1739, April 10
1153	1740, March 29*
1154	1741, March 19
1155	1742, March 8
1156	1743, February 25
1157	1744, February 15*
1158	1745, February 3
1159	1746, January 24
1160	1747, January 13
1161	1748, January 2
1162	1748, December 22*
1163	1749, December 11
1164	1750, November 30
1165	1751, November 20
1166	1752, November 8*
1167	1753, October 29
1168	1754, October 18
1169	1755, October 7
1170	1756, September 26*
1171	1757, September 15
1172	1758, September 4
1173	1759, August 25
1174	1760, August 13*
1175	1761, August 2
1176	1762, July 28
1177	1763, July 12
1178	1764, July 1*
1179	1765, June 20
1180	1766, June 9
1181	1767, May 30
1182	1768, May 18*
1183	1769, May 7
1184	1770, April 27
1185	1771, April 16
1186	1772, April 4*
1187	1773, March 25
1188	1774, March 14
1189	1775, March 4
1190	1776, February 21*
1191	1777, February 9
1192	1778, January 30
1193	1779, January 19
1194	1780, January 8*
1195	1780, December 28*
1196	1781, December 17
1197	1782, December 7
1198	1783, November 26
1199	1784, November 14*
1200	1785, November 4
1201	1786, October 24
1202	1787, October 13
1203	1788, October 2*
1204	1789, September 21
1205	1790, September 10
1206	1791, August 31
1207	1792, August 19*
1208	1793, August 9

AH Hejira	AD Christian Date
1209	1794, July 29
1210	1795, July 18
1211	1796, July 7*
1212	1797, June 26
1213	1798, June 15
1214	1799, June 5
1215	1800, May 25
1216	1801, May 14
1217	1802, May 4
1218	1803, April 23
1219	1804, April 12*
1220	1805, April 1
1221	1806, March 21
1222	1807, March 11
1223	1808, February 28*
1224	1809, February 16
1225	1810, February 6
1226	1811, January 26
1227	1812, January 16*
1228	1813, January 4
1229	1813, December 24
1230	1814, December 14
1231	1815, December 3
1232	1816, November 21*
1233	1817, November 11
1234	1818, October 31
1235	1819, October 20
1236	1820, October 9*
1237	1821, September 28
1238	1822, September 18
1239	1823, September 7
1240	1824, August 26*
1241	1825, August 16
1242	1826, August 5
1243	1827, July 25
1244	1828, July 14*
1245	1829, July 3
1246	1830, June 22
1247	1831, June 12
1248	1832, May 31*
1249	1833, May 21
1250	1834, May 10
1251	1835, April 29
1252	1836, April 18*
1253	1837, April 7
1254	1838, March 27
1255	1839, March 17
1256	1840, March 5*
1257	1841, February 23
1258	1842, February 12
1259	1843, February 1
1260	1844, January 22*
1261	1845, January 10
1262	1845, December 30
1263	1846, December 20
1264	1847, December 9
1265	1848, November 27*
1266	1849, November 17
1267	1850, November 6
1268	1851, October 27
1269	1852, October 15*
1270	1853, October 4
1271	1854, September 24
1272	1855, September 13
1273	1856, September 1*
1274	1857, August 22
1275	1858, August 11
1276	1859, July 31
1277	1860, July 20*
1278	1861, July 9
1279	1862, June 29
1280	1863, June 18
1281	1864, June 6*
1282	1865, May 27
1283	1866, May 16
1284	1867, May 5
1285	1868, April 24*
1286	1869, April 13
1287	1870, April 3
1288	1871, March 23
1289	1872, March 11*
1290	1873, March 1
1291	1874, February 18
1292	1875, February 7
1293	1876, January 28*
1294	1877, January 16
1295	1878, January 5
1296	1878, December 26
1297	1879, December 15
1298	1880, December 4*
1299	1881, November 23
1300	1882, November 12
1301	1883, November 2
1302	1884, October 21*
1303	1885, October 10
1304	1886, September 30
1305	1887, September 19
1306	1888, September 7*
1307	1889, August 28
1308	1890, August 17
1309	1891, August 7
1310	1892, July 26*
1311	1893, July 15
1312	1894, July 5
1313	1895, June 24
1314	1896, June 12*

AH Hejira	AD Christian Date
1315	1897, June 2
1316	1898, May 22
1317	1899, May 12
1318	1900, May 1
1319	1901, April 20
1320	1902, April 10
1321	1903, March 30
1322	1904, March 18*
1323	1905, March 8
1324	1906, February 25
1325	1907, February 14
1326	1908, February 4*
1327	1909, January 23
1328	1910, January 13
1329	1911, January 2
1330	1911, December 22
1331	1912, December 11*
1332	1913, November 30
1333	1914, November 19
1334	1915, November 9
1335	1916, October 28*
1336	1917, October 17
1337	1918, October 7
1338	1919, September 26
1339	1920, September 15*
1340	1921, September 4
1341	1922, August 24
1342	1923, August 14
1343	1924, August 2*
1344	1925, July 22
1345	1926, July 12
1346	1927, July 1
1347	1928, June 20*
1348	1929, June 9
1349	1930, May 29
1350	1931, May 19
1351	1932, May 7*
1352	1933, April 26
1353	1934, April 16
1354	1935, April 5
1355	1936, March 24*
1356	1937, March 14
1357	1938, March 3
1358	1939, February 21
1359	1940, February 10*
1360	1941, January 29
1361	1942, January 19
1362	1943, January 8
1363	1943, December 28
1364	1944, December 17*
1365	1945, December 6
1366	1946, November 25
1367	1947, November 15
1368	1948, November 3*
1369	1949, October 24
1370	1950, October 13
1371	1951, October 2
1372	1952, September 21*
1373	1953, September 10
1374	1954, August 30
1375	1955, August 20
1376	1956, August 8*
1377	1957, July 29
1378	1958, July 18
1379	1959, July 7
1380	1960, June 25*
1381	1961, June 14
1382	1962, June 4
1383	1963, May 25
1384	1964, May 13*
1385	1965, May 2
1386	1966, April 22
1387	1967, April 11
1388	1968, March 31*
1389	1969, March 20
1390	1970, March 9
1391	1971, February 27
1392	1972, February 16*
1393	1973, February 4
1394	1974, January 25
1395	1975, January 14
1396	1976, January 3*
1397	1976, December 23*
1398	1977, December 12
1399	1978, December 2
1400	1979, November 21
1401	1980, November 9*
1402	1981, October 30
1403	1982, October 19
1404	1983, October 8
1405	1984, September 27*
1406	1985, September 16
1407	1986, September 6
1408	1987, August 26
1409	1988, August 14*
1410	1989, August 3
1411	1990, July 24
1412	1991, July 13
1413	1992, July 2*
1414	1993, June 21
1415	1994, June 10
1416	1995, May 31
1417	1996, May 19*
1418	1997, May 9
1419	1998, April 28
1420	1999, April 17
1421	2000, April 6*

BANKNOTE PRINTERS

Printers' names, abbreviations or monograms will usually appear as part of the frame design or below it on face and/or back. In some instances the engravers name may also appear in a similar location on a note. The following abbreviations identify printers for many of the notes listed in this volume:

ABNC .... American Bank Note Company (USA)
BABN(C) .... British American Bank Note Co., Ltd. (Canada)
B&S .... Bouligny & Schmidt (Mexico)
BEPP .... Bureau of Engraving & Printing, Peking (China)
BF .... Banque de France (France)
BFL .... Barclay & Fry Ltd. (England)
BWC .... Bradbury, Wilkinson & Co. (England)
CABB .... Compania Americana de Billetes de Banco (ABNC)
CBC .... Columbian Banknote Co. (USA)
CBNC .... Canadian Bank Note Company (Canada)
CCBB .... Compania Columbiana de Billetes de Banco (CBC)
CdM- .... Casa da Moeda (Brazil)
CdM- .... Casa de Moneda (Argentina, Chile, etc.)
CHB .... Chung Hua Book Co. (China)
CMN .... Casa de Moneda de la Nacion (Argentina)
CMPA .... Commercial Press (China)
CNBB .... Compania Nacional de Billetes de Banco (NBNC)
CONB .... Continental Bank Note Company (USA)
CPF .... Central Printing Factory (China)
CSABB .... Compania Sud/Americana de Billetes de Banco
.... (Argentina)
CS&E .... Charles Skipper & East (England)
DLR .... De La Rue (England)
DTB .... Dah Tung Book Co., and Ta Tung Printing (China)
E&C .... Evans & Cogwell (CSA)
EAW .... E. A. Wright (USA)
FLBN .... Franklin-Lee Bank Note Company (USA)
FNMT .... Fabrica Nacional de Moneda y Timbre (Spain)
G&D .... Giesecke & Devrient (Germany)
HBNC .... Hamilton Bank Note Company (USA)
HKB .... Hong Kong Banknote (Hong Kong)
HKP .... Hong Kong Printing Press (Hong Kong)
H&L .... Hoyer & Ludwig, Richmond, Virginia (CSA)
HLBNC .... Homer Lee Bank Note Co. (USA)
H&S .... Harrison & Sons Ltd. (England)
IBB .... Imprenta de Billetes-Bogota (Columbia)
IBSFB .... Imprenta de Billetes-Santa Fe de Bogota (Columbia)
IBNC .... International Bank Note Company (USA)
JBNC .... Jeffries Bank Note Company (USA)
JEZ .... Johan Enschede en Zonen (Netherlands)
K&B .... Keatinge & Ball (CSA)
KBNC .... Kendall Bank Note Company, New York (USA)
LN .... Litografia Nacional (Columbia)
NAL .... Nissen & Arnold (England)
NBNC .... National Bank Note Company (USA)
OCV .... Officina Carte-Valori (Italy)
ODBI .... Officina Della Banca D'Italia (Italy)
OFZ .... Orell Fussli, Zurich (Switzerland)
P&B .... Perkins & Bacon (England)
PBC .... Perkins, Bacon & Co. (England)
PB&P .... Perkins, Bacon & Petch (England)
SBNC .... Security Banknote Company (USA)
TDLR .... Thomas De La Rue (England)
UPC .... Union Printing Co. (China)
UPP .... Union Publishers & Printers Fed. Inc. (China)
USBNC .... United States Banknote Corp. (USA)
WDBN .... Western District Banknote Fed. Inc.
W&S .... Waterlow & Sons Ltd. (England)
WPCo .... Watson Printing Co. (China)
WWS .... W. W. Sprague & Co. Ltd. (England)

International Bank Note Society

The International Bank Note Society (IBNS) was formed in 1961 to promote the collecting of world paper money. A membership in excess of 2,000 in over 100 nations around the globe draw on the services of the Society in advancing their knowledge and collections.

The benefits of Society membership include the quarterly IBNS Journal, a magazine featuring learned writings on the notes of the world, their history, artistry and technical background. Additionally each member receives a directory which lists the membership by name as well as geographic location. Collector specialties are also given. A newsletter is published, to announce events in a timely fashion, as well a semi-annual auctions of bank notes. Finally, an attribution service is offered by the society for persons with paper money they could not identify.

One of the greatest benefits of IBNS membership is the facility for correspondence with other members around the world, for purposes of exchanging notes, information and assistance with research projects.

Application for Membership in the INTERNATIONAL BANK NOTE SOCIETY

Name _____
         Last   First   Initial

Street _____

_____
City   Province or State

_____
Country   Postal Code

Type of Membership:
Individual: ❑ $17.50 per year
Junior (Ages 11-17): ❑ $9.00 per year
Family (includes children under 18): ❑ $22.50 per year

Payment in US Dollars payable to IBNS.

Check ❑   Other ❑   Money Order ❑

Do you wish your name and address to appear in our Membership Directory?   Yes ❑ No ❑

Collecting Interest _____

_____

_____

Mail to: Milan Alusic
           P.O. Box 1642
           Racine, Wisconsin
           U.S.A. 53401

AFGHANISTAN

The Islamic Republic of Afghanistan, which occupies a mountainous region of Southwest Asia, has an area of 250,000 sq. mi. (647,497 sq. km.) and a population of 16.6 million. Presently about a fourth of the total population reside mostly in Pakistan in exile as refugees. Capital: Kabul. It is bordered by Iran, Pakistan, Russia, and Peoples Republic of China's Sinkiang Province. Agriculture and herding are the principal industries; textile mills and cement factories are recent additions to the industrial sector. Cotton, wool, fruits, nuts, sheepskin coats and hand-woven carpets are exported but foreign trade has been interrupted since 1979.

Because of its strategic position astride the ancient land route to India, Afghanistan - formerly known as Aryana and Khorasan - was conquered by Darius I, Alexander the Great, various Scythian tribes, the Arabs, the Turks, Genghis Khan, Tamerlane, the Mughals, the Persians, and in more recent times by Great Britain.

It was a powerful empire under the Kushans, Hephthalites, Ghaznavids and Ghorids. The name Afghanistan, "Land of the Afghans," came into use in the eighteenth and ninteenth to describe the realm of the Afghan kings. Previously this mountainous region was the eastern most frontier of the Iranian world, with strong cultural influences from the Turks and Mongols to the north and India to the south.

The first Afghan king, Ahmad Shah Abdali, founder of the Durrani dynasty, established his rule at Qandahar in 1747. He conquered large territories in India and eastern Iran, which were lost by his grandson Zaman Shah. A new family, the Barakzays, drove the Durrani king out of Kabul, the capital, in 1819, but the Durranis were not eliminated completely until 1858. Further conflicts among the Barakzays prevented full unity until the reign of 'Abd al-Rahman in 1880. In 1929 the last Barakzay was Saqao, "Son of the Water-Carrier," who ruled as Habib Allah for less than a year before he was defeated by Muhammad Nadir Shah, a relative of the Barakzays. The last king, Muhammad Zahir, became a constitutional, though still autocratic, monarch in 1964. In 1973 a coup d'etat displaced him and created the Republic of Afghanistan. A subsequent military coup established the pro-Soviet Democratic Republic of Afghanistan in 1978. Mounting resistance in the countryside and violence within the government led to the Soviet invasion of late 1979 and the installation of Babrak Kamal as prime minister. A brutal civil war ensued, which continues to the present, even after soviet forces withdrew in 1989 and Kamal's government was defeated in 1992. Various militant Islamic movements have had control on and off since. Troops of President Rabbani regained possession of Kabul in March, 1995.

RULERS:
Amanullah, SH1298-1307/1919-1929AD
Habibullah Ghazi (rebel, known as Baccha-i-Saqao) SH1347-1348/1929AD
Muhammad Nadir Shah, SH1310-1312/1929-1933AD
Muhammad Zahir Shah, SH1312-1352/1933-1973AD

MONETARY SYSTEM:
1 Rupee = 100 Paise to 1925
1 Amani = 20 Afghani 1925-
1 Afghani = 100 Pul

KINGDOM - PRE-REBELLION

TREASURY

1919-20 ISSUES

#1-5 are encountered w/ and w/o counterfoils at l. Add 20% to market valuations indicated for unissued examples of these notes complete w/counterfoil.

	1 RUPEE	VG	VF	UNC
1	SH1298-99. Green. Uniface. Coin-like design at r. ctr. Back: Seal.			
	a. SH1298 (1919). Red serial #.	4.00	15.00	50.00
	b. SH1299 (1920). Red or black serial #.	2.00	7.00	25.00

1A	1 RUPEE	VG	VF	UNC
	SH1299 (1920). Brown. Coin-like design at r. ctr. Uniface. W/o serial #. Color trial (?). 1 known. Back: W/o seal.	—	—	—

2	5 RUPEES	VG	VF	UNC
	ND; SH1298-99. Black on brownish pink unpt. Arms at top ctr. Date on design at l. and r. ctr. Uniface. Back: Green, purple and tan. Seal.			
	a. SH1298 (1919).	5.00	17.50	40.00
	b. SH1299 (1920).	3.00	7.50	25.00
3	DELETED.			

4	50 RUPEES	VG	VF	UNC
	SH1298 (1919). Black on green unpt. Arms at top ctr. Uniface.	6.00	20.00	50.00

5	100 RUPEES	VG	VF	UNC
	SH1299 (1920). Green and gray. Arms at top ctr. Uniface.	5.00	12.00	40.00

1926-28 ISSUES

#6 and #8-10 back w/French text, w/o additional handstamps. For similar notes w/handstamps see #11-13.

6	5 AFGHANIS	VG	VF	UNC
	ND. Lt. brown and gray on pink and lt. green unpt. Arms at top ctr. Back: Greenish gray.	3.00	7.50	30.00

7	**5 AFGHANIS**	VG	VF	UNC
	SH1305 (1926). Dk. red. Arms at upper corners.			
	a. Back: Green, purple and tan. Toughra at ctr.	20.00	40.00	70.00
	b. Uniface. Back: Lilac.	12.00	20.00	35.00

8	**10 AFGHANIS**	VG	VF	UNC
	ND. Brown w/tan border. Back: Green. W/French text at l.	1.00	5.00	20.00

9	**10 AFGHANIS**	VG	VF	UNC
	SH1307 (1928). Black and orange w/green border. Back: Brown w/French text at l.			
	a. W/o wmk.	8.00	20.00	65.00
	b. Wmk: Small squares.	15.00	40.00	100.00

10	**50 AFGHANIS**	VG	VF	UNC
	SH1307 (1928). Green, and red w/lt. brown unpt. W/ and w/o serial #. Back: Green.			
	a. W/o wmk.	3.00	8.00	20.00
	b. Wmk: Small squares.	5.00	20.00	50.00

1928 REBELLION
BACCHA I SAQAO
1928 AFGHANI ISSUE
#11-13 face w/1 validation handstamp and 3 different handstamps on back, one having the date SH1307 (1928).

11	**5 AFGHANIS**	GOOD	FINE	XF
	SH1307 (1928). Lt. brown and gray on pink and lt. green unpt. Arms at top ctr. and handstamps. Back: Greenish gray.	5.00	15.00	60.00

12	**10 AFGHANIS**	GOOD	FINE	XF
	SH1307 (1928). Brown w/tan border. Handstamps. Back: Green w/French text at l.	4.00	12.00	35.00
13	**50 AFGHANIS**	3.00	10.00	25.00
	SH1307 (1928). Green, and red w/lt. brown unpt. W/ and w/o serial # and handstamps. Back: Green.			

1928 RUPEE ISSUE

14	**1 RUPEE**	GOOD	FINE	XF
	ND (1928-29). Green on yellow unpt. Uniface printing w/French text at l.			
	a. W/o additional handstamps.	10.00	30.00	60.00
	b. W/additional handstamps similar to #11-13.	13.00	35.00	70.00

KINGDOM - POST REBELLION
MINISTRY OF FINANCE
1936 ISSUES
#15-20 dates SH1315 (1936) w/face in Pashtu and back in Farsi languages. Block letters and serial #.

#	Denomination	Good	Fine	XF
15	**2 Afghanis** SH1315 (1936). Blue and m/c. Arms at top ctr. Back: Monument at ctr.	4.00	12.00	35.00
16	**5 Afghanis** SH1315 (1936). Lilac and m/c	10.00	35.00	90.00
16A	**5 Afghanis** SH1315 (1936). Green and m/c.	10.00	35.00	90.00
17	**10 Afghanis** SH1315 (1936). Dk. brown and m/c.	15.00	55.00	120.00
18	**20 Afghanis** SH1315 (1936). Red-brown and m/c.	35.00	90.00	250.00

#	Denomination	VG	VF	UNC
21	**2 Afghanis** SH1318 (1939). Brown and m/c.	1.00	3.00	9.00

#	Denomination	Good	Fine	XF
19	**50 Afghanis** SH1315 (1936). Blue and m/c.	50.00	175.00	500.00
20	**100 Afghanis** SH1315 (1936). Violet and m/c.	75.00	250.00	750.00

ND Issue

#	Denomination	Good	Fine	XF
16B	**5 Afghanis** ND. Green and m/c.	10.00	35.00	90.00
17A	**10 Afghanis** ND. Dk. brown and m/c.	15.00	55.00	120.00
18A	**20 Afghanis** ND. Red-brown and m/c.	35.00	90.00	250.00
19A	**50 Afghanis** ND. Blue and m/c.	50.00	175.00	500.00

#	Denomination	VG	VF	UNC
22	**5 Afghanis** SH1318 (1939). Green and m/c.	1.00	3.00	8.50
23	**10 Afghanis** SH1318; 1325. Dk. red.			
	a. SH1318 (1939).	3.50	7.50	20.00
	b. SH1325 (1946).	5.00	12.50	35.00
24	**20 Afghanis** SH1318; 1325. Violet and m/c.			
	a. SH1318 (1939).	60.00	165.00	—
	b. SH1325 (1946).	75.00	200.00	—

#	Denomination	VG	VF	UNC
25	**50 Afghanis** SH1318; 1325. Blue and m/c.			
	a. SH1318 (1939).	7.50	15.00	45.00
	b. SH1325 (1946).	9.00	30.00	75.00
26	**100 Afghanis** SH1318; 1325. Dk. green and m/c.			
	a. SH1318 (1939).	10.00	25.00	65.00
	b. SH1325 (1946).	15.00	40.00	120.00
27	**500 Afghanis** SH1318 (1939). Lilac and m/c.	50.00	145.00	285.00
27A	**1000 Afghanis** SH1318 (1939). Brown, green and m/c.	60.00	225.00	575.00

#	Denomination	Good	Fine	XF
20A	**100 Afghanis** ND. Violet and m/c.	75.00	250.00	750.00

BANK OF AFGHANISTAN

1939 Issue
#21-27A Kg. Muhammad Zahir. W/o imprint.

1948-51 Issues
#28-36 Kg. Muhammad Zahir. W/o imprint. Sign. varieties.

#	Denomination	VG	VF	UNC
28	**2 Afghanis** SH1327 (1948). Black, blue and m/c. Back: Black.	.75	2.00	5.00

29	**5 AFGHANIS**	VG	VF	UNC
	SH1327 (1948). Green and m/c. Back: Green.	.75	2.00	7.00
30	**10 AFGHANIS**			
	SH1327-36. Greenish brown m/c.			
	a. SH1327 (1948).	3.00	10.00	22.50
	b. SH1330 (1951).	2.00	6.00	14.00
	c. SH1333 (1954).	2.00	9.00	27.50
	d. SH1336 (1957).	1.25	4.00	10.00
30A	**10 AFGHANIS**			
	SH1327 (1948). Brown and m/c. Sign. 3 sign. varieties.	2.00	5.00	12.00
31	**20 AFGHANIS**			
	SH1327-36. Blue and m/c.			
	a. SH1327 (1948).	2.50	7.50	22.50
	b. SH1330 (1951).	2.00	7.00	18.50
	c. SH1333 (1954).	2.00	9.00	27.50
	d. SH1336 (1957).	2.00	6.00	15.00
32	**50 AFGHANIS**			
	SH1327 (1948). Green and m/c.	4.00	10.00	25.00

33	**50 AFGHANIS**	VG	VF	UNC
	Brown and m/c.			
	a. SH1330 (1951).	5.00	15.00	35.00
	b. SH1333 (1954).	6.00	17.50	45.00
	c. SH1336 (1957).	5.00	15.00	35.00

34	**100 AFGHANIS**	VG	VF	UNC
	SH1327-36. Purple and m/c.			
	a. SH1327 (1948).	5.00	12.00	40.00
	b. SH1330 (1951).	4.00	10.00	35.00
	c. SH1333 (1954).	4.00	10.00	35.00
	d. SH1336 (1957).	3.00	8.00	30.00
35	**500 AFGHANIS**			
	SH1327; 1336. Blue and green.			
	a. SH1327 (1948).	20.00	45.00	150.00
	b. SH1333 (1954).	20.00	50.00	175.00
	c. SH1336 (1957).	17.50	40.00	125.00
36	**1000 AFGHANIS**			
	SH1327 (1948). Brown.	35.00	100.00	300.00

ALBANIA

The Republic of Albania, a Balkan republic bounded by the rump Yugoslav state of Montenegro and Serbia, Macedonia, Greece and the Adriatic Sea, has an area of 11,100 sq. mi. (28,748 sq. km.) and a population of 3.3 million. Capital: Tirana. The country is predominantly agricultural, although recent progress has been made in the manufacturing and mining sectors. Petroleum, chrome, iron, copper, cotton textiles, tobacco and wood products are exported.

Since it had been part of the Greek and Roman Empires, little is known of the early history of Albania. After the disintegration of the Roman Empire, Albania was overrun by Goths, Byzantines, Venetians and Turks. Skanderberg, the national hero, resisted the Turks and established an independent Albania in 1443, but in 1468 the country again fell to the Turks and remained part of the Ottoman Empire for more than 400 years.

Independence was re-established by revolt in 1912, and the present borders established in 1913 by a conference of European powers which, in 1914, placed Prince William of Wied on the throne; popular discontent forced his abdication within months. In 1920, following World War I occupancy by several nations, a republic was set up. Ahmet Zogu seized the presidency in 1925, and in 1928 proclaimed himself king with the title of Zog I. King Zog fled when Italy occupied Albania in 1939 and enthroned King Victor Emanuel of Italy. Upon the surrender of Italy to the Allies in 1943, German troops occupied the country. They withdrew in 1944, and communist partisans seized power, naming Gen. Enver Hoxha provisionaly president. In 1946, following a victory by the communist front in the 1945 elections, a new constitution modeled on that of the USSR was adopted. In accordance with the constitution of Dec. 28, 1976, the official name of Albania was changed from the People's Republic of Albania to the People's Socialist Republic of Albania. A general strike by trade unions in 1991 forced the communist government to resign. A new government was elected in Mar. 1992.

RULERS:
Ahmet Zogu-King Zog 1, 1928-1939
Vittorio Emanuele III (Italy), 1939-1943

MONETARY SYSTEM:
1 Lek = 100 Quindar Lecu
1 Franga (Franka) Ari = 1 Lek = 100 Qindar Ari to 1946
1 Lek = 100 Qindarka 1948-

NOTE: Certain listings encompassing issues circulated by various bank and regional authorities are contained in Volume 1.

KINGDOM

BANKA KOMBËTARE E SHQIPNIS

BANCA NAZIONALE D'ALBANIA

1925-26 ISSUES

1	**5 LEK / 1 FRANK AR**	GOOD	FINE	XF
	ND (1925). Brown on green, gray and pink unpt. Eagle on shield at lower ctr. Printer: Printer: Richter & Co, Naples.			
	a. Issued note.	325.00	950.00	1800.
	s. Specimen	—	Unc	300.00

2	**5 FRANKA ARI**	GOOD	FINE	XF
	ND (1926). Dk. green on m/c unpt. Portr. boy's head at r. Back: Purple. Bridge at ctr. Sign. 2 sign. varieties.			
	a. Issued note.	5.00	20.00	75.00
	s. Specimen.	—	Unc	100.00

3	**20 FRANKA ARI**	GOOD	FINE	XF
	ND (1926). Dk. blue on m/c unpt. Portr. youth's head at l.			
	a. Issued note.	4.00	20.00	85.00
	s. Specimen.	—	Unc	100.00

4	**100 FRANKA ARI** ND (1926). Lilac on m/c unpt. Pres. A. Zogu at r. Back green and purple; valley and mountains at ctr.	GOOD	FINE	XF
	a. Issued note.	100.00	350.00	1000.
	s. Specimen.	—	Unc	225.00

ITALIAN OCCUPATION - WWII

BANKA KOMBËTARE E SHQIPNIS

BANCA NAZIONALE D'ALBANIA

1939 PROVISIONAL ISSUE

5	**100 FRANKA ARI** ND (1939). Lilac. Pres. A. Zogu at r. Back green and purple; valley and mountains at ctr. Ovpt: Lg. black double headed eagle at r. on face.	GOOD 300.00	FINE 900.00	XF 1750.

1939 ISSUE

6	**5 FRANGA** ND (1939). Green-blue. Wmk: Head of Victor Emanuel III.	GOOD 1.50	FINE 5.00	XF 25.00

7	**20 FRANGA** ND (1939). Green. Reclining Roma at bottom ctr., wolf w/Romulus and Remus at r. Printer: ODBI.	GOOD 2.00	FINE 7.00	XF 30.00

GERMAN OCCUPATION - WWII

BANKA KOMBËTARE E SHQIPNIS

1944 ISSUE

8	**100 FRANGA** ND (1944). Lilac-brown. Peasant woman seated on sheaves w/sickle and sheaves at r. Printer: ODBI.	GOOD 4.00	FINE 15.00	XF 60.00

9	**2 LEK** ND (1944). Violet on brown unpt. Male bust at r., crowned arms at l. ctr. Crowned double-headed eagle at l. on back.	GOOD 4.00	FINE 15.00	XF 40.00

10	**5 LEK** ND (1944). Blue on yellow unpt. Double-headed eagle at bottom ctr. Back: Crowned arms at l., female bust at r. Printer: ODBI.	GOOD 2.00	FINE 7.50	XF 27.50
11	**10 LEK** ND (1944). Red on brown unpt. Double-headed eagle at bottom ctr. Back: Crowned arms at l., female at r. Printer: ODBI.	2.00	7.00	22.50

PEOPLES REPUBLIC

BANKA E SHTETIT SHQIPTAR

1945 PROVISIONAL ISSUE

#11A-14 new bank name and double headed eagle in rectangular ovpt. on earlier issues of the Banka Kombëtare e Shqipnis.

11A	**10 LEK** ND (1945). Red on brown unpt. Double-headed eagle at bottom ctr. Crowned arms at l., female bust at r. on back Ovpt. on #11.	GOOD 100.00	FINE 500.00	XF —

12	**20 FRANKA ARI** ND (1945). Dk. blue on m/c unpt. Portr. youth's head at l. Ovpt. on #11.	GOOD	FINE	XF
	a. Prefix A-E.	15.00	90.00	—
	b. Prefix F-J.	10.00	50.00	250.00
13	**20 FRANGA** ND (1945). Green. Reclining Roma at bottom ctr., wolf w/Romulus and Remus at r. Ovpt. on #7.	12.50	50.00	150.00

14	**100 FRANGA** ND (1945). Lilac-brown. Peasant woman seated on sheaves w/sickle and sheaves at r. Ovpt. on #8.	GOOD 15.00	FINE 70.00	XF 200.00

1945 ISSUE

#15-18A Skanderbeg at l.

15	**1 FRANGA** 1.5.1945.	VG 10.00	VF 40.00	UNC 100.00

		VG	VF	UNC
18A	**500 FRANGA**	15.00	50.00	150.00
	1.5.1945. Brown and blue.			

1947 ISSUE
#19-23 soldier w/rifle at r.

		VG	VF	UNC
19	**10 LEKE**	1.75	6.00	20.00
	1947. Green on brown unpt.			

		VG	VF	UNC
16	**5 FRANGA**	1.75	6.00	17.50
	1.5.1945. Green, blue and brown.			

		VG	VF	UNC
20	**50 LEKE**	2.50	10.00	30.00
	1947. Brown on green unpt.			

		VG	VF	UNC
17	**20 FRANGA**	2.50	8.00	20.00
	1.5.1945. Blue and brown.			

		VG	VF	UNC
21	**100 LEKE**	5.00	25.00	75.00
	1947. Violet.			

		VG	VF	UNC
18	**100 FRANGA**	3.00	10.00	25.00
	1.5.1945. Reddish brown.			

		VG	VF	UNC
22	**500 LEKE**	8.50	35.00	95.00
	1947. Brown on violet unpt. at r.			

23	1000 LEKE	VG	VF	UNC
	1947. Dk. brown on lt. blue unpt.	8.00	40.00	150.00

1949 ISSUE

24	10 LEKE	VG	VF	UNC
	1949. Red, blue and green. Arms at ctr. Arms at r. on back	1.00	4.00	10.00
25	50 LEKE			
	1949. Violet on green unpt. Skanderbeg at r. Arms at ctr., soldier at r. on back.	1.50	5.00	12.00

26	100 LEKE	VG	VF	UNC
	1949. Green. Soldier at l., arms at upper ctr. r.	2.50	7.00	15.00

27B	100 LEKE	GOOD	FINE	XF
	ND. Blue and dull red on lt. green and lt. yellow-orange unpt. Steel workers at l., steel mill at ctr. Oil well derricks at l. ctr., arms at upper r. on back. Specimen.	—	75.00	165.00
27	500 LEKE	VG	VF	UNC
	1949. Brown-violet. Peasant woman w/sheaf of wheat at l., arms at r. on back.	3.50	10.00	25.00

27A	1000 LEKE	VG	VF	UNC
	1949. Violet on m/c unpt. Portr. Skanberbeg at l., oil well derricks at r. Arms at l., miner w/jackhammer at r. on back.	4.00	10.00	40.00

1957 ISSUE
#28-32 wmk: *BSHSH* within outlines, repeated.

28	10 LEKE	VG	VF	UNC
	1957. Red, blue and green. Arms at ctr. repeated.			
	a. Issued note.	.25	.75	2.00
	s. Specimen ovpt: *MODEL*.	—	—	6.00

29	50 LEKE	VG	VF	UNC
	1957. Violet on green unpt. Skanderbeg at r. Arms ctr., soldier at r. on back.			
	a. Issued note.	.35	1.25	4.00
	s. Specimen ovpt: *MODEL*.	—	—	7.00

30	100 LEKE	VG	VF	UNC
	1957. Green. Soldier at l., arms at upper r. ctr.			
	a. Issued note.	.50	1.75	5.00
	s. Specimen ovpt: *MODEL*.	—	—	8.00

31 500 LEKE

1957. Brown-violet. Back: Peasant woman w/sheaf of wheat at l., arms at r.

		VG	VF	UNC
a.	Issued note.	1.00	3.00	9.00
s.	Specimen ovpt: *MODEL*.	—	—	9.00

32 1000 LEKE

1957. Violet on m/c unpt. Portr. Skanderbeg at l., oil well derricks at r. Back: Arms at l., miner w/jackhammer at r. repeated.

		VG	VF	UNC
a.	Issued note.	1.25	4.00	12.00
s.	Specimen ovpt: *MODEL*.	—	—	10.00

FOREIGN EXCHANGE CERTIFICATES

BANKA E SHTETIT SHQIPTAR

1953 ISSUE

		VG	VF	UNC
FX4	**1 LEK**	—	—	35.00
	1953. Brown and red on m/c unpt. Arms at r. Back brown-orange and purple on yellow unpt.; bank seal at ctr.			
FX5	**5 LEK**	—	—	35.00
	1953. Green and red on m/c unpt. Arms at r. Back green and purple on m/c unpt.; bank seal at ctr.			
FX6	**10 LEK**	—	—	35.00
	1953. Purple and red on m/c unpt. Arms at r. Back purple on m/c unpt.; bank seal at ctr.			
FX7	**50 LEK**	—	—	35.00
	1953. Black and red on yellow unpt. Arms at r. Back green on orange and yellow unpt.; bank seal at ctr.			
FX8	**100 LEK**	—	—	40.00
	1953. Brown, purple and red on yellow unpt. Arms at r. Back purple on red and yellow unpt.; bank seal at ctr.			
FX9	**500 LEK**	—	—	50.00
	1953. Grayish green and red on m/c unpt. Arms at r. Back red on yellow unpt.; bank seal at ctr.			

1956 ISSUE

		VG	VF	UNC
FX10	**1/2 LEK**	30.00	90.00	175.00
	1956. Gray on red-orange unpt. Arms at r. Back pale purple and m/c; bank seal at ctr.			

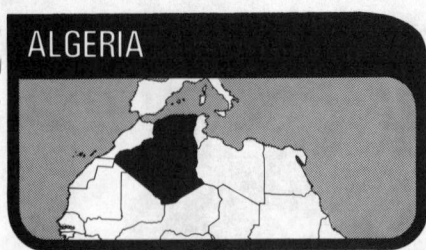

The Democratic and Popular Republic of Algeria, a North African country fronting on the Mediterranean Sea between Tunisia and Morocco, has an area of 919,595 sq. mi. (2,381,741 sq. km.) and a population of 25.3 million. Capital: Algiers (Alger). Most of the country's working population is engaged in agriculture although a recent industrial diversification, financed by oil revenues, is making steady progress. Wines, fruits, iron and zinc ores, phosphates, tobacco products, liquified natural gas, and petroleum are exported.

Algiers, the capital and chief seaport of Algeria, was the site of Phoenician and Roman settlements before the present Moslem city was founded about 950. Nominally part of the sultanate of Tlemcen, Algiers had a large measure of independence under the amirs of its own. In 1492 the Jews and Moors who had been expelled from Spain settled in Algiers and enjoyed an increasing influence until the imposition of Turkish control in 1518. For the following three centuries Algiers was the headquarters of the notorious Barbary pirates. The French took Algiers in 1830, and after a long and wearisome war completed the conquest of Algeria and annexed it to France, 1848. Following the armistice signed by France and Nazi Germany on June 22, 1940, Algeria fell under Vichy Government control until liberated by the Allied invasion forces under the command of Gen. Dwight D. Eisenhower on Nov. 8, 1942. The inability to obtain equal rights with Frenchmen led to an organized revolt which began on Nov. 1, 1954 and lasted until a ceasefire was signed on July 1, 1962. Independence was proclaimed on July 5, 1962, following a self-determination referendum.

RULERS:
French to 1962

MONETARY SYSTEM:
1 Franc = 100 Centimes to 1960
1 Nouveau Franc = 100 Old Francs, 1960-64
1 Dinar = 100 Centimes, 1964-

FRENCH INFLUENCE

BANQUE DE L'ALGÉRIE

ALGER (ALGIERS) BRANCH

1852 ISSUE

#1-4 held in reserve.

#5 and 6 allegorical male w/ship's rudder and mast w/sail at l., allegorical male w/trident and anchor at r., ancient galleys at upper l. and r.

		GOOD	FINE	XF
5	**500 FRANCS**	—	—	—
	ca. 1852-60. Blue. "France" greeting Arab between 2 reclining women at bottom ctr. Proof.			
6	**1000 FRANCS**	—	—	—
	ca. 1852-60. Blue. Medallic caduceus between 2 reclining women at bottom ctr.			

1861 ISSUE

#7-9 held in reserve.

#10 and 11 allegorical male w/ship's rudder and mast w/sail at l., allegorical male w/trident and anchor at r., caduceus between 2 cornucopiae at top ctr.

10	**100 FRANCS**	—	—	—
	ca. 1861-68. Blue. Ancient galley between 2 reclining women at bottom ctr. Proof.			
11	**500 FRANCS**	—	—	—
	ca. 1861-68. Blue. Frame for date w/*ALGER* between 2 reclining women at bottom ctr.			

1868-77 ISSUE

#12 held in reserve.

NOTE: For 1000 Francs on 100 Francs 1892, ovpt: *BANQUE DE L'ALGÉRIE* on remainders of Banque de France type (#22b), see Tunisia #31.

13	**5 FRANCS**	375.00	—	—
(2)	31.5.1873. Blue. Mercury at l., peasant at r.			

14 (6A)	**10 FRANCS** 10.2.1871; 15.5.1871; 20.11.1871. Blue. Head at l. and r.	**GOOD** —	**FINE** Rare	**XF** —
15 (7)	**20 FRANCS** 1873; 22.10.1874; 2.8.1877; 24.8.1887; 27.10.1892. Blue. Mercury at l., Hercules at r.	500.00	1000.	2000.
16 (12A)	**25 FRANCS** 15.10.1870; 15.10.1872. Blue. Standing figure at l. and r., head at lower ctr.	—	Rare	—
17 (13)	**50 FRANCS** 1873; 21.6.1877. Blue. Cherubs at lower l. and r., woman's head at bottom ctr. 4 medallic heads on oval band design on back.	500.00	1000.	2000.
18 (17)	**100 FRANCS** 1874; 1883; 1887; 1892. Blue. Boy w/oar and hammer at l., boy w/shovel and sickle at r., woman's head between snakes at bottom ctr.	500.00	1200.	2500.
19 (21)	**500 FRANCS** 1874. Blue. Fortuna at l., Mercury at r. 2 boys seated at bottom.	—	Rare	—
20 (27)	**1000 FRANCS** 1875. Blue. Woman w/oar at l., blacksmith at r., 2 boys w/lion at bottom.	—	Rare	—

BONE BRANCH

1868-77 ISSUE

#21-24 held in reserve.

#25 and 27 ovpt: *BONE* and *SUCCURSALE DE BONE.*

25	**50 FRANCS** 14.4.1868. Blue.	—	Rare	—

27 (A8)	**100 FRANCS** 9.8.1877. Blue. Boy w/oar and hammer at l., boy w/shovel and sickle at r., woman's head between snakes at bottom ctr. Punched hole cancelled, ovpt: *ANNULÉ.*	**GOOD** —	**FINE** Rare	**XF** —

CONSTANTINE BRANCH

1868-77 ISSUE

#28-33, 35-37, 39 held in reserve.

#34, 38 and 40 ovpt: *SUCCURSALE DE CONSTANTINE.*

34 (A6B)	**50 FRANCS** 20.9.1870. Blue.	—	Rare	—

38 (A10B)	**500 FRANCS** 4.10.1870; 16.11.1870. Blue. Allegorical male w/ship's rudder and mast w/sail at l., allegorical male w/trident and anchor at r., caduceus between 2 cornucopiae at top ctr., frame for date w/*ALGER* between 2 reclining women at bottom ctr. Punched hole cancelled, ovpt: *ANNULÉ.*	**GOOD** —	**FINE** Rare	**XF** —
40 (A11B)	**1000 FRANCS** 18.5.1869. Blue.	—	Rare	—

ORAN BRANCH

1861 ISSUE

#41-44, 47-48, 50 held in reserve.

#45, 46 and 49 ovpt: *SUCCURSALE D'ORAN.*

45 (A5C)	**50 FRANCS** 26.7.1864; 26.10.1864. Blue.	**GOOD** —	**FINE** Rare	**XF** —

46 (A7C)	**100 FRANCS** 26.10.1861; 8.4.1864; 26.11.1867. Blue. Allegorical male w/ship's rudder and mast w/sail at l., allegorical male w/trident and anchor at r., caduceus between 2 cornucopiae at top ctr., ancient galley between 2 reclining women at bottom ctr. Punched hole cancelled, ovpt: *ANNULÉ.*	**GOOD** —	**FINE** Rare	**XF** —

49 (A11C)	**1000 FRANCS** 11.8.1868. Blue. Allegorical male w/ship's rudder and mast w/sail at l., allegorical male w/trident and anchor at r., ancient galleys at upper l. and r., medallic caduceus between 2 reclining women at ctr. Punched hold cancelled, ovpt: *ANNULÉ.*	**GOOD** —	**FINE** Rare	**XF** —

W/O BRANCH

1903-12 ISSUE

#50-70 held in reserve for Philippeville and Tlemcen branches, from which no notes are currently known.

#71-76 like #13, 15, 17-20 but w/o *ALGER* or any branch name ovpt.

71 (2B)	**5 FRANCS**	**VG**	**VF**	**UNC**
	1912-25. Blue. Mercury seated at l., peasant seated at r. Facing lion's head at top, medallic head of Mercury at l. and Alexander the Great at r. on back.			
	a. 12.6.1912; 23.11.1914.	20.00	80.00	250.00
	b. 1.8.1916-17.3.1925.	15.00	60.00	200.00
72 (8)	**20 FRANCS**			
	July 1903; May 1910. Blue. Mercury at l., Hercules at r.	250.00	500.00	—

73 (14)	**50 FRANCS**	**GOOD**	**FINE**	**XF**
	2.3.1904; 15-29.4.1910. Blue. Cherubs at lower l. and r., woman's head at bottom ctr. 4 medallic heads on oval band design on back.	100.00	300.00	600.00
74 (18)	**100 FRANCS**			
	6.3.1907; 18.9.1911; 6.10.1911; 9.10.1911. Blue. Boy w/oar and hammer at l., boy w/shovel and sickle at r., woman's head between snakes at bottom ctr.	65.00	175.00	500.00

75 (22)	**500 FRANCS**	**GOOD**	**FINE**	**XF**
	1903-24. Blue. Fortuna at l., Mercury at r., 2 boys seated at bottom.			
	a. 1903; 15.5.1909.	125.00	350.00	800.00
	b. 1918; 22.2.1924.	75.00	200.00	550.00
	s. Specimen. 33.5.3091 (sic).	—	Unc	750.00
76 (28)	**1000 FRANCS**			
	1903-24. Blue. Woman w/oar at l., blacksmith at r., 2 boys w/lion at bottom.			
	a. 1903; 1909.	300.00	600.00	1500.
	b. 25.11.1918; 5.1.1924; 16.4.1924; 7.5.1924.	100.00	250.00	650.00

1913-26 ISSUES

77 (3)	**5 FRANCS**	**VG**	**VF**	**UNC**
	1924-41. Red, blue and m/c. Girl w/kerchief at r.			
	a. Serial # at upper ctr. 1924-8.1.1941.	.25	2.00	17.50
	b. W/o serial #. 24.1.1941-25.9.1941.	.25	2.00	17.50

78 (9)	**20 FRANCS**	**VG**	**VF**	**UNC**
	1914-42. Purple on blue unpt. Girl at r. 166 x 105mm. 4 sign. varieties.			
	a. 1914-21.	100.00	200.00	350.00
	b. 17.6.1924-32.	2.00	25.00	100.00
	c. 1933-13.3.1942.	1.00	6.00	50.00
79 (14A)	**50 FRANCS**	**GOOD**	**FINE**	**XF**
	11.9.1913; 17.9.1913. Violet. Mosque at r., aerial view of city of Algiers at bottom ctr. Child picking fruit from tree, woman seated at ctr. on back.	300.00	600.00	

80 (15)	**50 FRANCS**	**VG**	**VF**	**UNC**
	1920-38. Green. Like #79. 3 sign. varieties.			
	a. Issued note.	50.00	100.00	200.00
	s. Specimen. 1.2.9124 (sic).	—	—	225.00
81 (19)	**100 FRANCS**			
	1921-38. Purple and brown on blue unpt. 2 boys at l., Arab w/camel at r.			
	a. 22.9.1921.	60.00	200.00	—
	b. 1.5.1928-20.10.1938.	30.00	100.00	150.00

82 (23)	**500 FRANCS**	**VG**	**VF**	**UNC**
	28.6.1926; 21.9.1938. Green and blue-violet on m/c unpt. Girl's head at l., woman w/torch and youth at r. 2 women w/jugs at ctr. on back.	40.00	150.00	500.00

			VG	VF	UNC
87 (16B)	**50 FRANCS** 27.7.1942-1.3.1945. M/c. Veiled woman and man w/red fez at r. City w/ruins of amphitheatre in background on back. Wmk: *BANQUE DE L'ALGÉRIE.*		1.25	8.00	45.00
88 (20B)	**100 FRANCS** 27.3.1942-2.11.1942. M/c. Algerian w/turban at l. Plowing w/oxen at ctr. on back. Wmk: *BANQUE DE L'ALGÉRIE.*		1.00	8.00	45.00
89 (30B)	**1000 FRANCS** 17.8.1942; 6.11.1942. M/c. French colonial family and field work. Wmk: *BANQUE DE L'ALGÉRIE.*		35.00	150.00	325.00

			VG	VF	UNC
83 (29)	**1000 FRANCS** 28.6.1926-15.9.1939. Brown-violet. Woman w/sword and child at l. Algerian woman w/child at r. "France" seated w/arm on shoulder of seated Arab woman at upper ctr. on back.				
	a. Issued note.		100.00	300.00	700.00
	s. Specimen. ND.		—	—	650.00

1938-39 ISSUE

			VG	VF	UNC
84 (16)	**50 FRANCS** 1938-42. M/c. Veiled woman and man w/red fez at r. City w/ruins of amphitheatre in background on back. Wmk: Head.		.75	5.00	35.00

			VG	VF	UNC
85 (20)	**100 FRANCS** 1939-45 M/c. Algerian w/turban at l. Wmk: Head. 14.12.1939-2.2.1942; 20.6.1945.		1.50	9.00	50.00

VICHY GOVERNMENT

BANQUE DE L'ALGÉRIE

1941 ISSUE
NOTE: For #86 w/*TRESOR* ovpt., see France #47.

			VG	VF	UNC
86 (30A)	**1000 FRANCS** 2.1.1941-3.11.1942. M/c. French colonial family and field work. Wmk: Head.		15.00	75.00	225.00

1942 ISSUE
NOTE: For #32 w/ovpt. *TRESOR*, see France #48.

			VG	VF	UNC
90 (32)	**5000 FRANCS** 1942. Blue and pink. Young Algerian woman at l., woman w/torch and shield at r. 2 women w/jugs at ctr. on back. Wmk: Ornamental design and head.				
	a. Issued note. 20.2.1942; 9.4.1942; 18.5.1942; 17.8.1942; 22.8.1942.		200.00	500.00	1000.
	s. Specimen. 9.4.1942; 26.6.1942.		—	—	650.00

ALLIED OCCUPATION

BANQUE DE L'ALGÉRIE

1942-43 ISSUE
NOTE: For #24 w/ovpt. *TRESOR*, see France #46.

			VG	VF	UNC
91 (4)	**5 FRANCS** 16.11.1942. Green. Facing woman at r. on back.		.25	1.50	6.50
92 (10)	**20 FRANCS** 1942-45. Purple on blue unpt. Like #9 but 122 x90 mm w/wmk: *BANQUE de l'ALGÉRIE.*				
	a. Sign. titles: *Inspecteur General* and *Caissier Principal.* 11.11.1942-30.5.1944.		.50	3.00	32.50
	b. Sign. titles: *Caissier Principal* and *Secretaire General.* 29.11.1944; 2.2.1945; 3.4.1945; 7.5.1945.		.50	4.50	35.00
93 (24)	**500 FRANCS** 29.3.1943-23.12.1943. Blue and green. 2 boys at l., Bedouin w/camel at r.		10.00	75.00	225.00

1944-45 ISSUE

94 (5)	5 FRANCS	VG	VF	UNC
	1944. Red, blue and m/c. Girl w/kerchief at r.			
	a. Sign. titles: *Inspecteur Gal.* and *Caissier Pal.* 8.2.1944.	.25	1.00	7.00
	b. Sign. titles: *Secret. Gen.* and *Caissier Principal.* 2.10.1944.	.25	1.00	6.50

95 (25)	500 FRANCS	VG	VF	UNC
	15.9.1944. Violet. 2 boys at l., Bedouin w/camel at l.	10.00	75.00	225.00
96 (30A)	1000 FRANCS			
	23.5.1945; 23.3.1949. M/c. Woman at l., sailing ship at r. Farmers at l., woman w/Liberty at r. on back.	—	—	2000.

FRENCH INFLUENCE - POST WWII

REGION ECONOMIQUE D'ALGÉRIE

1944 FIRST ISSUE
Law 31.1.1944

#97-99 fig trees at ctr., palm tree at l. and r., 8 coat-of-arms in border on back.

This series was exchangeable until 1.3.1949.

97 (103)	50 CENTIMES	VG	VF	UNC
	L.1944. Red.			
	a. Block letter: C; C1-C4.	.35	1.50	7.50
	b. Block letter: F; F1.	.75	3.00	15.00
98 (99)	1 FRANC			
	L.1944. Blue to dk blue.			
	a. Block letter: B; B1-B4.	.35	1.50	7.50
	b. Block letter: E; E1.	.75	3.00	15.00
99 (101)	2 FRANCS			
	L.1944. Dk. green to olive-black.			
	a. Block letter: A; A1-A3.	.50	2.00	10.00
	b. Block letter: D; D1; D2.	1.00	4.00	20.00

1944 SECOND ISSUE
#98-102 fig trees at ctr., palm tree at l. and r. Ovpt: *2eT.* 8 coat-of-arms in border on back.

100 (98)	50 CENTIMES	VG	VF	UNC
	L.1944. Orange to red. Ovpt: Block letter: I; I1-I4.	.40	1.75	8.50
101 (100)	1 FRANC			
	L.1944. Blue to dk blue. Ovpt: Block letter: H; H1-H4.	.40	1.75	8.50
102 (108)	2 FRANCS			
	L.1944. Dk. green. Ovpt: Block letter: G; G1-G3.	.50	2.25	11.50

BANQUE DE L'ALGÉRIE

1946-48 ISSUE

103 (42)	20 FRANCS	VG	VF	UNC
	4.6.1948. Green. Ornamental design.	1.00	4.50	35.00
104 (31)	1000 FRANCS			
	9.12.1946; 7.2.1947; 18.9.1947; 4.11.1947; 18.11.1947. Brown and yellow. Isis at r.	150.00	300.00	500.00
105 (33)	5000 FRANCS			
	1946; 7.10.1949. M/c. Pythian Apollo at l.	35.00	150.00	450.00

BANQUE DE L'ALGÉRIE ET DE LA TUNISIE
For 50 FRANCS type of 1946 (3.2.1949) see Tunisia #13.

For 100 FRANCS type of 1946 see Tunisia #17.

For 500 FRANCS type of 1946 see Tunisia #21 and 22.

For 1000 FRANCS type of 1950 see Tunisia #27.

For 5000 FRANCS type of 1950 see Tunisia #29.

1949-55 ISSUE

106 (40)	500 FRANCS	VG	VF	UNC
	15.6.1950-8.8.1956. Green and m/c. Ram at ctr., Bacchus at r.	20.00	85.00	275.00
107 (41)	1000 FRANCS			
	1949-58. Brown and yellow. Iris at r.			
	a. 13.10.1949; 22.11.1949; 8.3.1950; 6.7.1950; 14.12.1950.	17.50	85.00	250.00
	b. 17.4.1953-14.2.1958.	15.00	75.00	225.00
108 (42)	5000 FRANCS			
	25.11.1949; 2.2.1950; 15.5.1951. M/c. Pythian Apollo at l., penal code blacked out at bottom ctr.	25.00	100.00	300.00
109 (42A)	5000 FRANCS			
	1949-56. M/c. Pythian Apollo at l., penal code shows at bottom ctr.			
	a. 7.10.1949; 8.11.1949; 31.7.1950; 15.5.1951; 6.11.1951; 12.11.1951.	24.00	100.00	300.00
	b. 20.3.1953; 22.6.1953; 21.6.1955; 1.12.1955; 11.12.1955; 4.1.1956.	24.00	85.00	250.00
110 (43)	10,000 FRANCS			
	10.2.1955-17.6.1957. Blue and m/c. Seagulls w/city of Algiers in background.	25.00	125.00	350.00

1956 PROVISIONAL ISSUE

111 (44)	5 NF ON 500 FRANCS	VG	VF	UNC
	29.10.1956; 2.11.1956; 13.11.1956. Green and m/c. Ovpt. on #109.	75.00	175.00	400.00
112 (45)	10 NF ON 1000 FRANCS			
	13.5.1958; 27.5.1958; 22.7.1958; 23.7.1958. Brown and yellow. Ovpt. on #110.	75.00	175.00	400.00

113 (46)	50 NF ON 5000 FRANCS			
	27.2.1956. M/c. Ovpt on #99.	135.00	350.00	800.00

114	100 NF ON 10,000 FRANCS	VG	VF	UNC
(46A)	22.1.1958-14.3.1958. Blue and m/c. Ovpt. on #113.	150.00	375.00	750.00

BANQUE DE L'ALGÉRIE (RESUMED)

1956-58 ISSUE

115	100 FRANCS			
(20A)	ND. M/c. Like #101. (Not issued).	—	—	1500.

116	500 FRANCS	VG	VF	UNC
(25A)	8.2.1956; 17.5.1956. M/c. Head at r. (Not issued).	—	—	1500.

117	500 FRANCS	VG	VF	UNC
(26)	2.1.1958-22.4.1958. Blue-green and m/c. 2 vultures perched on rock. Native objects and sheep on back.	15.00	75.00	250.00

1959 PROVISIONAL ISSUE

118	5 NOUVEAUX FRANCS			
(47)	1959. Green and m/c. Ram at bottom ctr., Bacchus at r.	10.00	60.00	150.00
	a. 31.7.1959; 18.12.1959.	10.00	70.00	200.00
	s. Specimen. 31.7.1959.	—	—	160.00
119	10 NOUVEAUX FRANCS			
(48)	1959-61. Brown and yellow. Isis at l.			
	a. 31.7.1959-2.6.1961.	15.00	85.00	210.00
	s. Specimen. 31.7.1959.	—	—	165.00
120	50 NOUVEAUX FRANCS			
(49)	1959. M/c. Pythian Apollo at r.			
	a. 31.7.1959; 18.12.1959.	35.00	125.00	325.00
	s. Specimen. 31.7.1959.	—	—	250.00
121	100 NOUVEAUX FRANCS			
(50)	1959-61. Blue and m/c. Seagulls w/city of Algiers in background.			
	a. 31.7.1959; 18.12.1959.	65.00	175.00	350.00
	b. 3.6.1960; 25.11.1960; 10.2.1961; 29.9.1961.	22.50	75.00	225.00
	s. Specimen. 31.7.1959.	—	—	175.00

ANDORRA

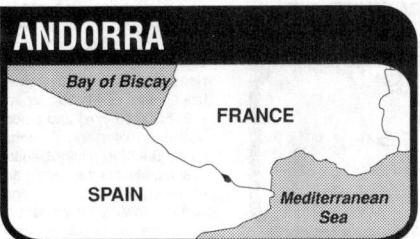

Andorra (Principal d' Andorra), previously an autonomous co-principality that became a sovereign nation with a constitution in May 1993. It is situated on the southern slopes of the Pyreness Mountains between France and Spain, has an area of 175 sq. mi. (453 sq. km.) and a population of 56,000. Capital: Andorra la Vella. Tourism is the chief source of income. Timber, cattle and derivatives, and furniture are exported.

According to tradition, the independence of Andorra derives from a charter Charlemagne granted the people of Andorra in 806 in recognition of their help in battling the Moors. An agreement between the Court of Foix (France) and the Bishop of Seo de Urgel (Spanish) in 1278 to recognize each other as Co-Princes of Andorra gave the state what has been its politcal form and territorial extent continously to the present day. Over the years, the title on the French side passed to the Kings of Navarre, then to the Kings of France, and is now held by the President of France. In 1806, Napoleon declared Andorra a republic, but today it is referred to as a principality.

During the Spanish Civil War, there was an issue of emergency money in the Catalan language.

MONETARY SYSTEM:
1 Pesseta (Catalan) = 100 Centims

1936 SPANISH CIVIL WAR

CONSELL GENERAL DE LES VALLS D'ANDORRA

DECRET NO. 112 - 1936 FIRST ISSUE
#1-9 arms at top ctr.

1	1 PESSETA	VG	VF	UNC
	19.12.1936. Blue.	20.00	55.00	145.00
2	2 PESSETES			
	19.12.1936. Blue.	25.00	65.00	175.00

3	5 PESSETES	VG	VF	UNC
	19.12.1936. Blue.	35.00	95.00	225.00
4	10 PESSETES			
	19.12.1936. Blue.	60.00	125.00	300.00
5	50 CENTIMS			
	19.12.1936. Brown.	6.00	15.00	60.00

1936 SECOND ISSUE

6	1 PESSETA			
	19.12.1936. Brown.	6.00	20.00	75.00
7	2 PESSETES			
	19.12.1936. Brown.	25.00	65.00	175.00
8	5 PESSETES			
	19.12.1936. Brown.	35.00	95.00	225.00

9	10 PESSETES	VG	VF	UNC
	19.12.1936. Brown.	60.00	125.00	300.00

The Peoples Republic of Angola, a country on the west coast of southern Africa bounded by Zaïre, Zambia and Namibia (South-West Africa), has an area of 481,354 sq. mi. (1,246,700 sq. km.) and a population of 10.4 million, predominantly Bantu in origin. Capital: Luanda. Most of the people are engaged in subsistence agriculture. However, important oil and mineral deposits make Angola potentially one of the richest countries in Africa. Iron and diamonds are exported.

Angola was discovered by Portuguese navigator Diogo Cao in 1482. Portuguese settlers arrived in 1491, and established Angola as a major slaving center which sent about 3 million slaves to the New World.

A revolt against Portuguese rule, characterized by guerrilla warfare, began in 1961 and continued until 1974, when a new regime in Portugal offered independence. The independence movement was actively supported by three groups, the National Front, based in Zaïre, the Soviet-backed Popular Movement, and the moderate National Union. Independence was proclaimed on Nov. 11, 1975.

RULERS:
Portuguese to 1975

MONETARY SYSTEM:
1 Milreis = 1000 Reis = 20 Macutas to 1911
100 Centavos - 1 Escudo, 1911
1 Escudo = 1 Milreis
100 Centavos = 1 Escudo, 1954-77
1 Kwanza = 100 Lwei, 1977-95
1 Kwanza Reajustado = 1,000 "old" Kwanzas, 1995-

STEAMSHIP SEALS

Type I	Type II	Type III
LOANDA	LISBOA	C,C,A

Colonias, Commercio, Agricultura.

PORTUGUESE INFLUENCE

JUNTA DA FAZENDA PUBLICA DA PROVINCIA D'ANGOLA

1861 ISSUE
#1-4 arms at top ctr., legend ends:...*D'ANGOLA*. Various date and sign. varieties.

		GOOD	FINE	XF
1	**1000 REIS** 1.7.1861; 13.9.1867.	—	—	—
2	**2000 REIS** 1.7.1861. Red.	—	—	—
3	**5000 REIS** 1861.	—	—	—
4	**20,000 REIS** 1861.	—	—	—

1877-84 ISSUE
#5-9 arms at top ctr., legend ends:...*DE ANGOLA*. Various date and sign. varieties.

5	**1000 REIS** 1.10.1884. Gray unpt.	—	—	—
6	**2000 REIS**	—	—	—
7	**5000 REIS**	—	—	—
8	**10,000 REIS**	—	—	—

		GOOD	FINE	XF
9	**20,000 REIS** 1.10.1877. Blue unpt.	—	—	—

BANCO NACIONAL ULTRAMARINO

1865 ISSUE
#10-12 sailing ship at top ctr. *Succursal* (Branch) *em LOANDA*. Various date and sign varieties.

10	**5000 REIS** 1865.	—	—	—

		GOOD	FINE	XF
11	**10,000 REIS** 7.7.1865.	—	—	—
12	**20,000 REIS** 1865.	—	—	—

1876-77 ISSUE
#13-15 sailing ship at top ctr. Various date and sign. varieties.

13	**1000 REIS** 1876.	—	—	—

		GOOD	FINE	XF
14	**2000 REIS** 1.6.1877.	—	—	—
15	**2500 REIS** 1876.	—	—	—

1878-90 ISSUE
#16-20 sailing ship at top ctr. Various date and sign. varieties.

16	**1000 REIS** 1878-90.	—	—	—

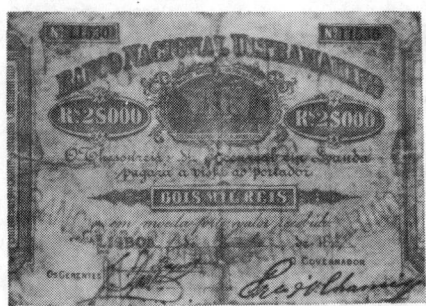

#		GOOD	FINE	XF
17	**2000 REIS** 21.3.1888. Green.			

#		GOOD	FINE	XF
18	**5000 REIS** 1878-90.			
	a. Issued note.	—	—	—
	b. W/2 oval handstamps: *Cobre 1896*. (-old date 30.6.1880).	—	—	—
19	**10,000 REIS** 1878-90.	—	—	—
20	**20,000 REIS** 28.1.1890. Gray-green.	—	—	—

1892 EMERGENCY ISSUE

Issued because of small change shortages. Redeemed in 1905.

#20A-20C crowned arms at upper ctr.

#		GOOD	FINE	XF
20A	**100 REIS** 1892; 1893; 1895. Black on red-brown unpt.	—	—	—
20B	**200 REIS** 1892; 1893; 1895. Red on green unpt.	—	—	—
20C	**500 REIS** 1892; 1893; 1895. Blue on ivory unpt.	—	—	—

1897-1905 ISSUE

#21-24 various date and sign. varieties.

#		GOOD	FINE	XF
21	**1000 REIS** 2.1.1897. Green. Native w/bow and arrow at l., ship at top ctr.	—	—	—

#		GOOD	FINE	XF
22	**2500 REIS** 20.2.1901. Gray-blue. Sailing ship at l., landscape at ctr.	—	—	—
23	**5000 REIS** 2.1.1897. Violet. Native woman seated, sailing ship at ctr r.	—	—	—
24	**10,000 REIS** 20.2.1905. Lilac. Female seated at l., sailing s hip at ctr., Mercury at r.	—	—	—

1909 PROVISIONAL ISSUE

#		GOOD	FINE	XF
25 (29)	**2500 REIS** 1.3.1909. Red. Ovpt: *Pagavel na Filial de Loanda* on St. Thomas and Prince #8.	—	—	—
26 (32)	**5 MIL REIS** 1.3.1909. Ovpt: *Pagavel na Filial de Benguela* on St. Thomas and Prince #9.	—	—	—

1909 REGULAR ISSUES

#27-38 ovpt: *LOANDA* Printer: BWC.

#29-38 portr. Vasco da Gama at l., arms at upper ctr., steamship seal below. Seated allegorical women looking out at ships on back.

NOTE: For provisional 2500 Reis see #25, for provisional 5 Mil Reis see #26.

#		GOOD	FINE	XF
27 (25)	**1000 REIS** 1.3.1909. Green and yellow unpt. Steamship seal Type I.	80.00	200.00	—
28 (26)	**1000 REIS** 1.3.1909. Green and yellow unpt. Steamship seal Type III.	85.00	225.00	—
29 (27)	**2500 REIS** 1.3.1909. Black on m/c unpt. Steamship seal Type I.	100.00	350.00	—
30 (28)	**2500 REIS** 1.3.1909. Black on m/c unpt. Steamship seal Type III.	125.00	375.00	—
31 (30)	**5 MIL REIS** 1.3.1909. Black on m/c unpt. Steamship seal Type I.	150.00	450.00	—
32 (31)	**5 MIL REIS** 1.3.1909. Black on m/c. Steamship seal Type III.	100.00	450.00	—
33	**10 MIL REIS** 1.3.1909. Black on m/c unpt. Steamship seal Type I.	175.00	650.00	—
34	**10 MIL REIS** 1.3.1909. Black on m/c unpt. Steamship seal Type III.	175.00	700.00	—

#		GOOD	FINE	XF
35	**20 MIL REIS** 1.3.1909. Black on m/c unpt. Steamship seal Type I.	200.00	725.00	—
36	**20 MIL REIS** 1.3.1909. Black on m/c unpt. Steamship seal Type III.	200.00	725.00	—
37	**50 MIL REIS** 1.3.1909. Black-green on m/c unpt. Steamship seal Type I.	250.00	950.00	—
38	**50 MIL REIS** 1.3.1909. Black-green on m/c unpt. Steamship seal Type III.	250.00	900.00	—

1914 ISSUES

#39-46 arms at r., steamship seal at lower ctr. Printer: BWC.

#		GOOD	FINE	XF
41	*DELETED.* See #40.			
44	*DELETED.* See #43.			
39	**10 CENTAVOS** 5.11.1914. Violet. Steamship seal Type II.	7.00	30.00	80.00

#		GOOD	FINE	XF
40	**10 CENTAVOS** 5.11.1914. Violet. Steamship seal Type III.			
	a. Black ovpt: *LOANDA* 18mm long; sans-serif letters.	7.00	25.00	70.00
	b. Black ovpt: *LOANDA* 28mm long; letters w/serifs.	6.00	20.00	65.00

42 20 CENTAVOS
5.11.1914. Blue. Steamship seal Type II.

	GOOD	FINE	XF
	5.00	22.50	75.00

43 20 CENTAVOS
5.11.1914. Blue. Steamship seal Type III.

	GOOD	FINE	XF
a. *LOANDA* 18mm long; sans-serif letters.	3.00	15.00	50.00
b. *LOANDA* 23mm long; letters w/serifs.	5.00	17.50	60.00

45 50 CENTAVOS
5.11.1914. Green. Steamship seal Type II.

	5.00	25.00	85.00

46 50 CENTAVOS
5.11.1914. Green. Steamship seal Type III.

	GOOD	FINE	XF
a. *LOANDA* 18mm long; sans-serif letters.	3.00	15.00	60.00
b. *LOANDA* 28mm long; letters w/serifs.	5.00	17.50	60.00

1914 PROVISIONAL ISSUES

#47 and 48 printer: BWC.

47 50 CENTAVOS
5.11.1914. Green. *Pagavel na Filial de Loanda* at r. on St. Thomas and Prince #18.

	35.00	200.00	400.00

48 50 CENTAVOS
5.11.1914. Green. Steamship seal Type II w/ovpt: *LOANDA* over *S. THOME* on St. Thomas Thomas and Prince #18.

	50.00	225.00	500.00

1918 ISSUE

49 5 CENTAVOS
19.4.1918. Gray-green on yellow unpt. Steamship seal Type II at r. Back: Sailing ship at ctr.

	GOOD	FINE	XF
	10.00	30.00	100.00

50 20 CENTAVOS
19.4.1918. Brown on yellow-orange unpt.

	30.00	100.00	300.00

1920 ISSUE

#51-53 ovpt: *ANGOLA*.

NOTE: #54 is the so-called "Porto Issue" as the notes were printed there.

51 10 CENTAVOS
1.1.1920. Red. Ship at l. and r.

	30.00	100.00	300.00

52 20 CENTAVOS
1.1.1920. Green. Angels at l. and r.

	50.00	125.00	400.00

53 50 CENTAVOS
1.1.1920. Blue. Mercury at l., allegory at r.

	30.00	100.00	300.00

54 50 ESCUDOS
1.1.1920. Blue on lt. green unpt. Arms at upper ctr. Back: Brown on gold unpt. Lake and trees at ctr.

	GOOD	FINE	XF
	—	—	—

1921 ISSUE

#55-61 portr. Francisco de Oliveira Chamico at l., arms at bottom ctr., steamship seal at r. Back like #27-38.

#57-61 printer: BWC.

55 1 ESCUDO
1.1.1921. Green. at r. Steamship seal Type III. Printer: BWC.

	VG	VF	UNC
	2.00	20.00	100.00

56 2.50 ESCUDOS
1.1.1921. Blue. steamship at r. Steamship seal Type III. Printer: TDLR.

	20.00	75.00	275.00

57 5 ESCUDOS
1.1.1921. Dk. green. steamship at r. Steamship seal Type III.

	12.50	75.00	225.00

58 10 ESCUDOS
1.1.1921. Brown. steamship at r. Steamship seal Type III.

	45.00	150.00	450.00

59 20 ESCUDOS
1.1.1921. Blue. steamship at r. Steamship seal Type III.

	VG	VF	UNC
	45.00	150.00	500.00

60 50 ESCUDOS
1.1.1921. Lt. Brown. steamship at r. Steamship seal Type II.

	150.00	475.00	—

61 100 ESCUDOS
1.1.1921. Green. steamship at r. Steamship seal Type III.

	250.00	700.00	—

REPUBLICA PORTUGUESA - ANGOLA

1921 ISSUE

62 50 CENTAVOS
1921. Gray on lt. brown unpt. Woman plowing at l. ctr., arms at lower r.

	VG	VF	UNC
	5.00	20.00	90.00

1923 ISSUE

63 50 CENTAVOS
1923. Brown w/red text at ctr. Dock scene at l., woman seated holding wreath at r. Back: Explorers at shoreline.

	VG	VF	UNC
	4.00	15.00	70.00

PROVINCIA DE ANGOLA - JUNTA DA MOEDA

DECREE NO. 12.124 OF 14.8.1926

#64-66 sign. varieties. Printer: TDLR.

		VG	VF	UNC
64	**1 ANGOLAR** *D.1926.* Green. Portr. Diogo Cao at lower l. Back: Head of antelope at ctr.	5.00	25.00	95.00

		VG	VF	UNC
65	**2 1/2 ANGOLARES** *D.1926.* Purple. Portr. Paulo Dias de Novaes at lower l. Back: Rhinoceros at ctr.	7.00	65.00	200.00

		VG	VF	UNC
66	**5 ANGOLARES** *D.1926.* Brown. Portr. Paulo Dias de Novaes at l. Back: Elephant at ctr. Arms in circular design at lower l.	25.00	150.00	350.00

		VG	VF	UNC
67	**10 ANGOLARES** *D.1926.* Blue. 2 people weaving and spinning at l. ctr. Back: Lion at ctr.	35.00	175.00	550.00

PROVINCIA DE ANGOLA - GOVERNO GERAL DE ANGOLA

DECREE NO. 31.942 OF 28.3.1942

#68 and 69 printer: TDLR.

		VG	VF	UNC
68	**1 ANGOLAR** *D.1942.* Green. Portr. Diogo Cao at lower l. Back: Head of antelope at ctr.	1.50	12.50	60.00

		VG	VF	UNC
69	**2 1/2 ANGOLARES** *D.1942.* Purple. Portr. Paulo Dias de Novaes at lower l. Rhinoceros at ctr. on back.	2.00	20.00	90.00

DECREE NO. 37.086 OF 6.10.1948 COMMEMORATIVE ISSUE

300th Anniversary Restoration of Angola to Portuguese Rule 1648-1948.

#70 and 71 printer: TDLR.

		VG	VF	UNC
70	**1 ANGOLAR** *D.1948.* Green. Landing boat, seamen and sailing ships at l. ctr. Back: Animal head at ctr.	7.50	35.00	120.00

		VG	VF	UNC
71	**2 1/2 ANGOLARES** *D.1948.* Purple. Bombardment of fortress. Back: Rhinoceros at ctr.	10.00	50.00	185.00

BANCO DE ANGOLA

1927 ISSUE

#72-76 portr. Salvador Correia at ctr. or at l. Sign. title varieties. Printer: TDLR.

		GOOD	FINE	XF
72	**20 ANGOLARES** 1.6.1927. Red on blue unpt. Jungle river. Back: Hippo at ctr.	55.00	250.00	600.00
73	**20 ANGOLARES** 1.6.1927. Dk. brown on green unpt. Jungle river. Back: Hippo at ctr.	55.00	250.00	600.00

74	50 ANGOLARES	GOOD	FINE	XF
	1.6.1927. Purple on rose unpt. Waterfall. Back: Leopard.	125.00	450.00	825.00
74A	50 ANGOLARES			
	1.6.1927. Purple on green unpt. Waterfall. Back: Brown-violet. Leopard.	125.00	450.00	750.00

75	100 ANGOLARES	GOOD	FINE	XF
	1.6.1927. Green on blue unpt. Flamingos. Back: Crocodile.	175.00	550.00	—

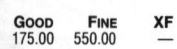

76	500 ANGOLARES	GOOD	FINE	XF
	1.6.1927. Blue on green unpt. Shoreline with palm trees. Back: Eagle.			
	a. Issued note.	—	—	—
	s. Specimen.	—	—	1500.

1944-46 ISSUE
#79-82 printer: TDLR.

77	5 ANGOLARES	VG	VF	UNC
(81)	1.1.1947. Brown on yellow unpt. 3 men at l., Portr. Gen. Carmona at r. Back: Green. 2 women at l., small monument at r. W&S.	6.00	30.00	95.00

78	10 ANGOLARES	VG	VF	UNC
(82)	D.14.8.1946 (1.6.1947). Dk. blue and dk. brown. Portr. Padre A. Barroso at r., children at l. Back: Dk. blue. *Treaty of Simalambuco, 1885.*	7.50	60.00	190.00

79	20 ANGOLARES	VG	VF	UNC
(77)	1.12.1944. Lilac. Portr. Correia at r., fortress at ctr. Back: *W/Reconquest of Luanda, 1648.*	18.50	50.00	175.00
80	50 ANGOLARES			
(78)	1.10.1944. Green. Portr. Pereira at r. Back: *W/Founding of Benguela, 1617.*	25.00	125.00	350.00
81	100 ANGOLARES			
(80)	2.12.1946. Blue. Portr. Sousa Coutinho at r. Back: Explorers and Africans.	30.00	150.00	450.00
82	1000 ANGOLARES			
(79)	1.6.1944. Carmine, blue and m/c. Portr. Joao II at r. Back: Purple. Return of Diogo Cao, 1489.			
	a. Issued note.	—	—	—
	s. Specimen.	—	—	1350.

1951-52 ISSUE

83	20 ANGOLARES			
	1.3.1951. Lilac. Portr. Correia at r., fortress at ctr. Back: *W/Reconquest of Luanda, 1648.* TDLR.	8.50	70.00	225.00
84	50 ANGOLARES			
	1.3.1951. Green. Portr. Pereira at r. Back: *W/Founding of Benuela, 1617.*	20.00	85.00	325.00
85	100 ANGOLARES			
	1.3.1951. Red-brown and deep blue. Portr. Sousa Coutinho at r. Back: Explorers and Africans.	30.00	125.00	450.00

86	1000 ANGOLARES	VG	VF	UNC
	1.3.1952. Carmine. Portr. Joao II at r. Back: Purple. Return of Diogo Cao, 1489. TDLR.			
	a. Issued note.	—	—	—
	s. Specimen.	—	—	1200.

1956 ISSUE
#87-91 sign. varieties. Printer: TDLR.

87	20 ESCUDOS	VG	VF	UNC
	15.8.1956. Lilac on m/c. Portr. Porto at r., dock at l. Back: Red-brown. Gazelle running.	1.50	4.00	15.00

88	50 ESCUDOS	VG	VF	UNC
	15.8.1956. Green on m/c. Portr. H. de Carvalho at r., airport at l. Back: Various animals at waterhole.	2.00	9.00	45.00

89   100 ESCUDOS
15.8.1956. Blue on m/c unpt. Portr. S. Pinto at r., Salazar Bridge at l.
Back: Purple. Elephants at waterhole.

VG	VF	UNC
3.00	20.00	100.00

90   500 ESCUDOS
15.8.1956. Orange. Portr. R. Ivens at l., Port of Luanda at ctr. Back: 2
rhinoceros

VG	VF	UNC
12.50	65.00	260.00

91   1000 ESCUDOS
15.8.1956. Brown. Portr. B. Capelo at r., dam at l. ctr. Back: Herd at
ctr.

VG	VF	UNC
22.50	110.00	400.00

ARGENTINA

The Argentine Republic, located in southern South America, as an area of 1,068,301 sq. mi. (2,766,889 sq. km.) and a population of 32.6 million. Capital: Buenos Aires. Its varied topography ranges from the subtropical lowlands of the north to the towering Andean Mountains in the west and the windswept Patagonian steppe in the south. The rolling, fertile pampas of central Argentina are ideal for agriculture and grazing, and support most of the republic's population. Meat packing, flour milling, textiles, sugar refining and dairy products are the principal industries. Oil is found in Patagonia, but most of the mineral requirements must be imported.

Argentina was discovered in 1516 by the Spanish navigator Juan de Solis. A permagnent Spanish colony was established at Buenos Aires in 1580, but the colony developed slowly. When Napoleon conquered Spain, the Argentines set up their own government in the nane of the Spanish king on May 25, 1810. Independence was formally declaired on July 9, 1816.

MONETARY SYSTEM:
   1 Peso (m/n) = 100 Centavos to 1970
   1 New Peso (Ley 18.188) = 100 Old Pesos (m/n), 1970-1983
   1 Peso Argentino = 10,000 Pesos, (Ley 18.188) 1983-1985
   1 Austral = 100 Centavos, 1985-1992
   1 Peso = 10,000 Australes, 1992-
   1 Peso = 8 Reales = 100 Centavos

NOTE: The listing encompassing issues circulated by various bank and regional authorities are contained in Volume 1.

REPUBLIC

BANCO NACIONAL

1883 FIRST ISSUE
#1-4 printer: R. Lange, Buenos Aires. Sign. varieties.

1   5 CENTAVOS
1.1.1884. Black on gray unpt. Avellanda at l., arms at upper r. ctr.
Back: Green.

GOOD	FINE	XF
5.00	15.00	40.00

2   10 CENTAVOS
1.1.1884. Black on pink and yellow unpt. Arms at lower l., portr.
Sarmiento at r. Back: Brown. Liberty head at l.

GOOD	FINE	XF
7.50	20.00	60.00

3   20 CENTAVOS
1.1.1884. Black on green unpt. Mitre at upper ctr., arms below. Back:
Orange.

GOOD	FINE	XF
6.00	17.50	50.00

3A   20 CENTAVOS   Good   Fine   XF
1.1.1884. Black on blue unpt. Arms at l., Mitre at ctr. Back: Blue. Arms   10.00   30.00   85.00
at ctr.

4   50 CENTAVOS   Good   Fine   XF
1.1.1884. Black on grayish-brown unpt. Portr. Urquiza at ctr., arms   8.00   30.00   85.00
below. Back: Brown. Women at ctr.

1883 SECOND ISSUE
#5-8 printer: ABNC. 3 sign. varietes.

5   5 CENTAVOS   Good   Fine   XF
1.1.1884. Black on brown and yellow unpt . Avellanda at l., arms at r.   1.00   4.00   8.50
Back: Brown. Helmeted Athena at ctr.

6   10 CENTAVOS   Good   Fine   XF
1.1.1884. Black on green unpt. Portr. Sarmiento at l., arms at r. 2   1.00   4.00   8.50
serial # varieties. Back: Green. Gaucho hunting ostriches at ctr.
Printer: ABNC.

7   20 CENTAVOS   Good   Fine   XF
1.1.1884. Arms at l., portr. Mitre at r.
a. Black on lt. reddish-brown unpt. 2 serial # varieties. Back: Brown.   1.75   5.00   12.00
Steer's head at ctr.
b. Black w.o unpt. Series P.

8   50 CENTAVOS   Good   Fine   XF
1.1.1884. Black on brown unpt. Arms at lower l., portr. Urquiza at r.   3.00   8.00   25.00
Back: Red-brown. 3 girls at ctr.

BANCO DE LA NACIÓN ARGENTINA

1891 ISSUE
Ley No. 2707 del 21 de Agosto de 1890
#209-212A Printer: CSABB, Buenos Aires.

209   5 CENTAVOS   Good   Fine   XF
1.11.1891. Black on blue unpt. Arms at l., Avellaneda at r. Back: Gray   1.00   3.00   6.50
to blue-green. Helmeted Athena at ctr. Sign. 5 varieties.

210   10 CENTAVOS   Good   Fine   XF
1.11.1891. Black on brown unpt. Arms at l., portr. Samiento at r.   1.00   3.00   7.50
Back: Brown. Gaucho on horseback at ctr. Sign. 5 varieties.

211   20 CENTAVOS   Good   Fine   XF
1.11.1891. Black on green unpt. Portr. Mitre at l., arms at r. Back:
Green. Steer's head at ctr.
a. Inspector.../President...   3.00   8.00   25.00
b. Sign. 4 varieties. Sindico/Presidente...   1.00   3.00   6.50

212   50 CENTAVOS
1.1.1891. Lt. ochre and black. Urquiza at l., arms at r. CINCUENTA   8.00   15.00   60.00
unpt. Back: Brown. 3 girls at ctr. Sign. 2 varieties.

212A   50 CENTAVOS   Good   Fine   XF
1.11.1891. Lt. ochre and black. Urquiza at l., arms at r. 50 in unpt.   1.00   4.00   10.00
Back: Brown. 3 girls at ctr. Sign. 2 varieties.

1892 ISSUE
Ley No. 2822 del 29 Septembre de 1891 Printer: CSABB, Buenos Aires. 3 sign varieties.

213   5 CENTAVOS   Good   Fine   XF
1.5.1892. Black on blue unpt. Arms at l., Avellaneda at r. Back: Gray to   1.00   4.00   9.00
blue-green. Helmeted Athena at ctr. Sign. 5 varieties.

214	**10 Centavos**	GOOD	FINE	XF
	1.5.1892. Black on brown unpt. Arms at l., portr. Sarmiento at r. Back: Brown. Gaucho on horseback at ctr. Sign. 5 varieties.	1.00	4.00	9.00
215	**20 Centavos**			
	1.5.1892. Black on green unpt. Portr. Mitre at l., arms at r. Back: Green. Steer's head at ctr.	1.00	4.00	10.00
216	**50 Centavos**			
	1.5.1892. Lt. ochre and black unpt: *CINCUENTA*. Urquiza at l., arms at r. *50* in unpt. Back: Brown. 3 girls at ctr. Sign. 2 varieties.	1.50	5.00	12.50

1895 First Issue
Ley No. 3062 del 8 de Enero de 1894
#218-227 sign. varieties. Printer: CSABB, Buenos Aires.

218	**1 Peso**	GOOD	FINE	XF
	1.1.1895. Black on green and brown Portr. Adm. Brown at l., arms at ctr., women w/lyre at r. Back: Green. Arms at ctr. Ovpt: Rectangular *Ley 20.9.1897*.			
	a. Issued note.	6.00	20.00	75.00
	b. Remainder perforated: *SIN VALOR*.	—	Unc	75.00

222	**20 Pesos**	GOOD	FINE	XF
	1.1.1895. Black on lt. green and lt. orange unpt. Seated woman writing at l., arms at upper ctr., Arenales at r. Back: Green. Liberty w/cap at ctr.			
	a. Issued note.	150.00	400.00	—
	b. Remainder perforated: *SIN VALOR*.	—	Unc	400.00

219	**2 Pesos**	GOOD	FINE	XF
	1.1.1895. Black on lt. brown and green unpt. Child w/flag at l., Alvear at r.			
	a. Issued note.	75.00	200.00	—
	b. Remainder perforated: *SIN VALOR*.	—	Unc	325.00

220	**5 Pesos**	GOOD	FINE	XF
	1.1.1895. Black on pink and green unpt. Dragon at l., arms at upper ctr., portr. V. Sarsfield at r. Back: Slate blue. Sailing ships at ctr.			
	a. Issued note.	50.00	100.00	—
	b. Remainder perforated: *SIN VALOR*.	—	Unc	175.00

223	**50 Pesos**	GOOD	FINE	XF
	1.1.1895. Ship at l., Pueyrredon at right.			
	a. Issued note.	500.00	—	—
	b. Remainder perforated: *SIN VALOR*.	—	Unc	500.00

224	**100 Pesos**	GOOD	FINE	XF
	1.1.1895. Portr. Moreno and child at l.			
	a. Issued note.	—	Rare	—
	b. Remainder perforated: *SIN VALOR*.	—	Rare	—

221	**10 Pesos**	GOOD	FINE	XF
	1.1.1895. Black on yellow-brown unpt. Woman and monument at l., arms at upper ctr., Arenales at r. Back: Brown. Ornamental design.			
	a. Issued note.	100.00	300.00	—
	b. Remainder perforated: *SIN VALOR*.	—	Unc	350.00

225	**200 Pesos**	GOOD	FINE	XF
	1.1.1895. Portr. Rivadavia at r., reclining female w/sheep at l.			
	a. Issued note.	—	Rare	—
	b. Remainder perforated: *SIN VALOR*.	—	Rare	—

226   500 PESOS

	Good	Fine	XF
1.1.1895. Portr. Belgrano and angel w/globe at l.			
a. Issued note.	—	Rare	—
b. Remainder perforated: *SIN VALOR*.	—	Rare	—

227   1000 PESOS

	Good	Fine	XF
1.1.1895. Portr. San Martin, seated woman and child.			
a. Issued note.	—	Rare	—
b. Remainder perforated: *SIN VALOR*.	—	Rare	—

1895 SECOND ISSUE
Ley No. 2070 del 21 de Augusto de 1890
#228-230 printer: BWC.

228   5 CENTAVOS

	Good	Fine	XF
19.7.1895. Black on red unpt. Arms at l., portr. Sarmiento at r. Back: Red. Liberty at ctr.	1.50	6.50	17.50

229   20 CENTAVOS

	Good	Fine	XF
19.7.1895. Black on green unpt. Portr. Mitre at l., arms at r. Back: Green. Helmeted woman at ctr.	2.00	8.50	22.50

230   50 CENTAVOS

	Good	Fine	XF
19.7.1895. Black on brown unpt. Arms at l., portr. Urquiza at r. Back: Brown. Columbus at ctr. Sign. 3 varieties.	2.50	12.50	40.00

CAJA DE CONVERSION

1899 ISSUE
Ley de 20 Septiembre de 1897

WATERMARK VARIETIES		
Wmk. A: PE of *PESO*	**Wmk. B:** PE of *PESO*	**Wmk. C:** Pe of *PESO*

#231-233 woman seated w/torch (Progreso motif) at l., 7-digit red serial # w/special code prefix and suffix.

231   50 CENTAVOS

	Good	Fine	XF
ND (1899-1900). Gray-blue. W/o unpt.	40.00	100.00	250.00

232   1 PESO

	Good	Fine	XF
ND (1899-1903). Gray-blue-pink. W/o unpt.	45.00	110.00	260.00

233   100 PESOS

	Good	Fine	XF
ND (1899-1902). Blue and green. W/o unpt.	200.00	500.00	1200.

1900 ISSUE
#234-241 Liberty (Progreso) w/torch l., 7 digit red serial # w/prefix letter and special code suffix.

234   50 CENTAVOS

	Good	Fine	XF
ND (1900-02). Gray-blue. 130 x 67mm.	50.00	120.00	250.00

235   1 PESO

	Good	Fine	XF
ND (1900-02). Gray-blue. 150 x 77mm.	45.00	110.00	120.00

236   5 PESOS

	Good	Fine	XF
ND (1900-02). Blue, yellow and pink. 170 x 87mm.	60.00	150.00	275.00

237   10 PESOS

	Good	Fine	XF
ND (1900-02). Blue and gray. 190 x 97mm.	70.00	160.00	300.00

238   50 PESOS

	Good	Fine	XF
ND (1900-02). Pinkish-blue and gray. 195 x 100 mm.	100.00	220.00	440.00

239   100 PESOS

	Good	Fine	XF
ND (1900-02). Blue, yellow and green. 200 x 107 mm.	150.00	300.00	600.00

240   500 PESOS

	Good	Fine	XF
ND (1900-02). Blue and yellow. 210 x 117 mm.	400.00	800.00	1600.

241   1000 PESOS

	Good	Fine	XF
ND (1900-02). Pinkish-blue and violet. 220 x 127 mm.	—	Rare	—

1902-05 ISSUE
#236A-241A reduced size.

236A   5 PESOS

	Good	Fine	XF
ND (1903-06). 144 x 72mm.	60.00	150.00	300.00

237A	10 PESOS	GOOD	FINE	XF
	ND (1903-06). 158 x 77mm.	60.00	150.00	300.00
238A	50 PESOS			
	ND (1903-06). 173 x 83mm.	70.00	160.00	350.00
239A	100 PESOS			
	ND (1902-06). 180 x 88mm.	100.00	200.00	400.00
240A	500 PESOS			
	ND (1903-06). 188 x 93mm.	110.00	225.00	500.00
241A	1000 PESOS			
	ND (1905-08). 196 x 98mm.	—	Rare	—

1906-07 ISSUE
#235B-239B w/7-digit red serial # w/special code prefix and suffix letter.

235B	1 PESO			
	ND (1906-08). 130 x 65mm.	50.00	100.00	250.00
236B	5 PESOS			
	ND (1907-08). 144 x 71mm.	70.00	140.00	300.00
237B	10 PESOS			
	ND (1906-08). 158 x 77mm.	50.00	100.00	250.00
238B	50 PESOS			
	ND (1906-08). 172 x 83mm.	Reported Not Confirmed		
239B	100 PESOS			
	ND (1906-08). 180 x 88mm.	Reported Not Confirmed		

1908-23 ISSUES
#242-249 Liberty (Progreso) w/torch at l., w/*RA* monogram at upper l. 8-digit serial #. Major wmk. varieties. Many sign. varieties.

242	50 CENTAVOS	VG	VF	UNC
	ND (1918). Blue on green unpt. Printed *RA* monogram and *50 CENTAVOS* in lt. green.	.75	2.25	7.50
242A	50 CENTAVOS			
	ND (1922). Blue on green unpt. Wmk: *RA* monogram and *50 CENTAVOS*.	.75	2.25	7.50
243	1 PESO			
	ND (1908-35). Blue on pink paper. Back: Green. 130 x 65mm. *RA* monogram.			
	a. Wmk: A. ND (1908-25).	1.00	5.00	20.00
	b. Wmk: B. ND (1925-32).	.75	3.00	8.00
	c. Wmk: C. ND (1932-35).	.50	1.50	3.50
244	5 PESOS			
	ND (1908-35). Blue. Back: Dk. red. 144 x 71mm.			
	a. Wmk: A. ND (1908-25).	3.00	10.00	30.00
	b. Wmk: B. ND (1925-32).	2.00	8.00	17.00
	c. Wmk: C. ND (1932-35).	1.00	4.00	15.00
245	10 PESOS			
	ND (1908-35). Blue. Back: Green. 158 x 77mm.			
	a. Wmk: A. ND (1908-25).	2.00	8.00	17.00
	b. Wmk: B. ND (1925-32).	2.00	8.00	17.00
	c. Wmk: C w/Gen. San Martin at upper l. ND (1933-35).	1.00	3.00	8.00
246	50 PESOS			
	ND (1908-35). Blue. 172 x 83mm.			
	a. Wmk: A. ND (1908-25).	10.00	35.00	75.00
	b. Wmk: B. ND (1925-32).	8.00	30.00	70.00
	c. Gen. San Martin at upper l. Wmk: C. ND (1932-35).	7.00	25.00	60.00

247	100 PESOS	VG	VF	UNC
	ND (1908-35). Blue on aqua unpt. Back: Olive. 180 x 88mm.			
	a. Wmk: A. ND (1908-25).	25.00	60.00	120.00
	b. Wmk: B. ND (1925-32).	15.00	40.00	90.00
248	500 PESOS			
	ND (1923-35). Blue on blue paper. Back: Brownish-purple. 188 x 93mm.			
	a. Wmk: A. ND (1923-25).	40.00	100.00	250.00
	b. Wmk: B. ND (1925-30).	40.00	100.00	250.00
	c. Gen. San Martin at upper l. Wmk: C. ND (1932-35).	20.00	50.00	110.00

249	1000 PESOS	VG	VF	UNC
	ND (1923-35). Blue on aqua unpt. Back: Red. 196 x 98mm.			
	a. Wmk: A. ND (1923-25).	60.00	125.00	300.00
	b. Wmk: B. ND (1925-32).	60.00	125.00	300.00
	c. Gen. San Martin at upper l. Wmk: C. ND (1932-35).	30.00	65.00	175.00

BANCO CENTRAL
Signature Titles:
A - *GERENTE GENERAL*
B - *SUBGERENTE GENERAL*
C - *GERENTE GENERAL* and *PRESIDENTE*
D - *SUBGERENTE GENERAL* and *VICE-PRESIDENTE*
E - *SUBGERENTE GENERAL* and *PRESIDENTE*

ART. 36 - LEY 12.155 (FIRST ISSUE)
#250-252 Liberty (Progreso) w/torch at l. Many sign. varieties. Notes have Banco Central designation just above signs. at bottom.

249A	1 PESO	VG	VF	UNC
	ND. Dp. brown-orange. Head of Republica at ctr. Uniface face proof w/o sign., serial # or wmk.	—	—	10.00

249B	5 PESOS	VG	VF	UNC
	ND. Blue-black. Head of Republica at r. Uniface face proof w/o sign., serial # or wmk.	—	—	10.00

ART. 36 - LEY 12.155 (SECOND ISSUE)

250	50 CENTAVOS	VG	VF	UNC
	ND (1943). Blue. Sign. 5 sign. varieties. 2 wmk. varieties.			
	a. Sign. titles: A in blue.	1.00	3.00	8.00
	b. Sign. titles: B in blue.	1.00	3.00	8.00
	c. Sign. titles: A in black.	.60	1.75	5.00
251A	1 PESO			
	ND (1935). Blue on pink paper. Sign. 8 sign. varieties.			
	a. Sign. titles: A in blue.	.50	1.50	4.00
	b. *SUB* added in black to sign. titles A in blue.	.60	1.75	5.00
	c. Sign. titles: B in black.	.60	1.75	5.00
	d. Sign. titles A in black.	.60	1.75	5.00
252	5 PESOS			
	ND (1935). Blue. Sign. 5 sign. varieties.			
	a. Sign. titles: A in blue.	1.25	3.50	10.00
	b. Sign. titles: B in blue.	2.50	7.00	20.00
	c. Sign. titles: A in black.	1.00	3.00	8.00

1935 - LEY NO. 12.155 DE 28 DE MARZO DE 1935
#253-255 lg. heading: *El Banco Central*. Liberty (Progreso) w/torch at l. Wmk: San Martin.

253	10 PESOS			
	L.1935 (1936). Blue. Back: Green.. 2 sign. varieties.	4.00	12.50	35.00
254	50 PESOS			
	L.1935 (1936). Blue.	11.50	35.00	100.00

			VG	VF	UNC
255	100 PESOS		10.00	30.00	80.00
	L.1935 (1936). Blue on green unpt. Back: Gray.				

1948 - LEY NO. 12.962 DEL 27 DE MARZO DE 1947

#256-258 Liberty (Progreso) w/torch at l. Printer: CMN.

			VG	VF	UNC
256	50 CENTAVOS		.35	1.00	3.00
	L.1947 (1948). Blue. Sign. 2 sign. varieties.				

			VG	VF	UNC
257	1 PESO		.50	1.50	4.00
	L.1947 (1948). Blue. Back: Green. Sign. 2 sign. varieties. Pink.				
258	5 PESOS		.65	1.85	5.00
	L.1947 (1948). Blue. Back: Lt. red.				

1950 - LEY NO. 12.962 DEL 27 DE MARZO DE 1947

Replacement notes: R prefix.

			VG	VF	UNC
261	50 CENTAVOS				
	L.1947 (1950). Brown. Head of Republica at l. Back: Green. Open book of constitution at ctr.				
	a. Garrasi at lower r., letter A.		.25	1.00	3.00
	b. W/o Garrasi at lower r., letter A.		.25	1.00	3.00

1952 COMMEMORATIVE ISSUE

#263, Declaration of Economic Independence (#264 regular issue) w/dates: 1816-1947.
Replacement notes: R prefix.

			VG	VF	UNC
263	1 PESO		.25	1.00	3.00
	ND (1952). Brown, violet and blue. Justice holding sword and scale at ctr. Back: "1816-1947" at top. Sign. 2 sign. varieties.				

1951 - LEYES NOS. 12.962 Y 13.571

#262-264 regular and commemorative notes. Printer: CMN.
#270-274 Portr. Gen. San Martin in uniform at r. Sign. varieties, also in red or black.
Replacement notes: R prefix.

			VG	VF	UNC
262	50 CENTAVOS		.25	1.00	3.00
	ND (1951). Brown. Head of Republica at l. Regular issue. Letter B. Sign. 2 sign. varieties.				

			VG	VF	UNC
259	1 PESO		.35	1.50	4.00
	ND (1951). Blue on pink paper. Back: Green.				

			VG	VF	UNC
264	1 PESO				
	ND (1956). Brown, violet and blue. Justice holding sword and scale at ctr. Sign. 2 sign. varieties. Regular issue.				
	a. 1 w/o dk. line in upper part.		.25	1.00	3.00
	b. 1 w/dk. line in upper part.		.25	1.00	3.00
260	5 PESOS				
	ND (1951). Blue. Back: Back lt. red. Sign. 6 sign. varieties.				
	a. Wmk: A, red serial #.		.50	2.00	6.00
	b. Wmk: B, red serial #.		.50	2.00	6.00
	c. Wmk: C, red serial #.		.50	2.00	6.00
	d. Wmk: C, black serial #.		.35	1.50	6.00
	x. Error w/Leyes Nos. 19.962 y 13.571.		1.00	4.00	12.50

			VG	VF	UNC
270	10 PESOS				
	ND. Red. Back: Meeting scene Sign. 9 sign. varieties.				
	a. Sign. titles: C.		.40	1.25	4.00
	b. Sign. titles: D.		.40	1.25	4.00
	c. Sign. titles: E.		.25	1.00	3.00
271	50 PESOS				
	ND. Green. 3 serial # varieties. Series A-C unpt. Series D w/o unpt. Back: Army in mountains Sign. 14 sign. varieties in red or Sign. black.				
	a. Sign. titles: C.		.50	2.00	6.00
	b. Sign. titles: D.		.20	1.25	20.00
	c. Sign. titles: E.		.60	2.25	7.00
	d. Back: Litho. Sign. titles: E.		.25	1.00	3.00
272	100 PESOS				
	ND. Brown. Back: Spanish and Indians Sign. 10 sign. varieties. 2 serial # varieties. Series A-D w/gray unpt. Series D w/o unpt.				
	a. Sign. titles: C.		.50	2.00	6.00
	b. Sign. titles: D.		1.25	5.00	15.00
	c. Sign. titles: E.		.50	2.00	6.00
273	500 PESOS				
	ND. Blue. Back: Banco Central Sign. 6 sign. varieties. 3 serial # varieties in red or black.				
	a. Sign. titles: C.		2.50	10.00	30.00
	b. Sign. titles: E.		3.25	13.50	40.00
274	1000 PESOS				
	ND. Violet. Back: Sailing ship Sign. 9 sign. varieties. 3 serial # varieties in red or black.				
	a. Sign. titles: C.		1.25	5.00	15.00
	b. Sign. titles: D.		1.25	5.00	15.00
	c. Sign. titles: E.		1.00	4.00	12.00

1943 - LEY NO. 12.155 DE 28 DE MARZO DE 1935

#265-269 Portr. Gen. San Martin in uniform at r. Sign. varieties.
Replacement notes: R prefix.

265	**10 Pesos**	**VG**	**VF**	**UNC**
	L.1935 (1943). Red. Some wmk. varieties. Back: Meeting scene. Sign. 9 varieties. Wmk: Large or small head of Gen. Belgrano.			
	a. Sign. Red sign.	2.50	10.00	30.00
	b. Sign. Black sign. w/sign. titles C.	.60	1.75	5.00
	c. Sign. Red sign. w/sign. titles E.	2.00	8.00	25.00
266	**50 Pesos**			
	L.1935 (1943). Green. Back: Army in mountains. Sign. 7 varieties.			
	a. Sign. Green sign.	4.00	16.00	50.00
	b. Sign. Black sign.	1.75	7.00	20.00
267	**100 Pesos**			
	L.1935 (1943). Brown. Back: Spanish and Indians. Sign. 7 varieties.			
	a. Sign. Brown sign. w/sign. titles E.	3.50	14.00	40.00
	b. Sign. Black sign. w/sign. titles C.	1.75	7.00	20.00

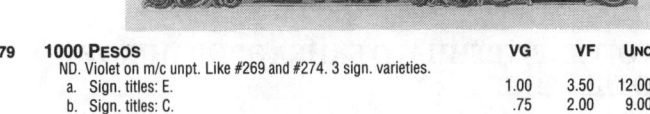

267A	**100 Pesos**	**VG**	**VF**	**UNC**
	L.1935. Purple and violet on pale green and orange unpt. Back: Spanish and Indians. Uniface face proof w/o sign., serial # or wmk.	—	—	10.00

277	**100 Pesos**	**VG**	**VF**	**UNC**
	ND. Brown on m/c unpt. 2 sign. varieties.	.40	1.65	5.00

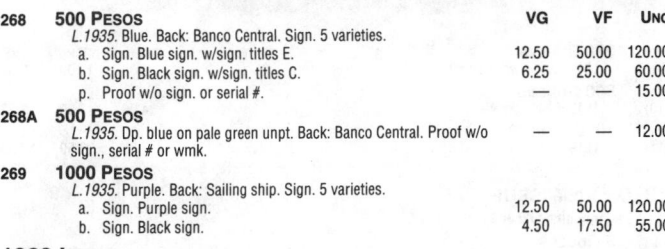

268	**500 Pesos**	**VG**	**VF**	**UNC**
	L.1935. Blue. Back: Banco Central. Sign. 5 varieties.			
	a. Sign. Blue sign. w/sign. titles E.	12.50	50.00	120.00
	b. Sign. Black sign. w/sign. titles C.	6.25	25.00	60.00
	p. Proof w/o sign. or serial #.	—	—	15.00
268A	**500 Pesos**			
	L.1935. Dp. blue on pale green unpt. Back: Banco Central. Proof w/o sign., serial # or wmk.	—	—	12.00
269	**1000 Pesos**			
	L.1935. Purple. Back: Sailing ship. Sign. 5 varieties.			
	a. Sign. Purple sign.	12.50	50.00	120.00
	b. Sign. Black sign.	4.50	17.50	55.00

279	**1000 Pesos**	**VG**	**VF**	**UNC**
	ND. Violet on m/c unpt. Like #269 and #274. 3 sign. varieties.			
	a. Sign. titles: E.	1.00	3.50	12.00
	b. Sign. titles: C.	.75	2.00	9.00

1960 Issue

W/o Ley

#275-277, 279-280 Gen. San Martin in uniform at r. Sign. varieties.

Replacement notes: *R* prefix.

275	**5 Pesos**	**VG**	**VF**	**UNC**
	ND (1960). Brown on yellow unpt. People gathering before bldg. on back. Printer: CMN.			
	a. Sign. titles: D.	.30	1.35	5.00
	b. Sign. titles: C.	.75	3.25	10.00
	c. Sign. titles: E.	.40	1.65	5.00

276	**50 Pesos**	**VG**	**VF**	**UNC**
	ND. Green on m/c unpt.	.40	1.65	5.00

68 ARMENIA

The Republic of Armenia (formerly Armenian S.S.R.) is bounded in the north by Georgia, to the east by Azerbaijan and to the south and west by Turkey and Iran. It has an area of 11,490 sq. mi. (29,800 sq. km) and a population of 3.3 million. Capital: Yerevan. Agriculture including cotton, vineyards and orchards, hydroelectricity, chemicals - primarily synthetic rubber and fertilizers, and vast mineral deposits of copper, zinc and aluminum and production of steel and paper are major industries.

The earliest history of Armenia records continuous struggles with expanding Babylonia and later Assyria. In the sixth century B.C. it was called Armina. Later under the Persian empire it enjoyed the position of a vassal state. Conquered by Macedonia, it later defeated the Seleucids and Greater Armenia was founded under the Artaxis dynasty. Christianity was established in 303 A.D. which led to religious wars with the Persians and Romans who divided it into two zones of influence. The Arabs succeeded the Persian Empire of the Sassanids which later allowed the Armenian princes to conclude a treaty in 653 A.D. In 862 A.D. Ashot V was recognized as the "prince of princes" and established a throne recognized by Baghdad and Constantinople in 886 A.D. The Seljuks overran the whole country and united with Kurdistan which eventually ran the new government. In 1240 A.D. onward the Mongols occupied almost all of western Asia until their downfall in 1375 A.D. when various Kurdish, Armenian and Turkoman independent principalities arose. After the defeat of the Persians in 1516 A.D. the Ottoman Turks gradually took control over a period of some 40 years, with Kurdish tribes settling within Armenian lands. In 1605 A.D. the Persians moved thousands of Armenians as far as India developing prosperous colonies. Persia and the Ottoman Turks were again at war, with the Ottomans once again prevailing. The Ottomans later gave absolute civil authority to a Christian bishop allowing them free enjoyment of their religion and traditions.

Russia occupied Armenia in 1801 until the Russo-Turkish war of 1878. British intervention excluded either side from remaining although the Armenians remained more loyal to the Ottoman Turks, but in 1894 the Ottoman Turks sent in an expeditionary force of Kurds fearing a revolutionary movement. Large massacres were followed by retaliations, then amnesty was proclaimed which led right into WW I and once again occupation by Russian forces in 1916. After the Russian revolution the Georgians, Armenians and Azerbaijanis formed the short lived Transcaucasian Federal Republic on Sept. 20, 1917 which broke up into three independent republics on May 26, 1918. Communism developed and in Sept. 1920 the Turks attacked the Armenian Republic; the Russians soon followed suit from Azerbaijan routing the Turks. On Nov. 29, 1920 Armenia was proclaimed a Soviet Socialist Republic. On March 12, 1922, Armenia, Georgia and Azerbaijan were combined to form the Transcaucasian Soviet Federated Socialist republic, which on Dec. 30, 1922, became a part of U.S.S.R. On Dec. 5, 1936, the Transcaucasian federation was dissolved and Armenia became a constituent republic of the U.S.S.R. A new constitution was adopted in April 1978. Elections took place on May 20, 1990. The Supreme Soviet adopted a declaration of sovereignty in Aug. 1991, voting to unite Armenia with Nagorno-Karabakh. This newly constituted "Republic of Armenia" became fully independent by popular vote in Sept. 1991. It became a member of the CIS in Dec.1991.

Fighting between Christians in Armenia and Muslim forces of Azerbaijan escalated in 1992 and continued through early 1994. Each country claimed the Nagorno-Karabakh, an Armenian ethnic enclave, in Azerbaijan. A temporary cease-fire was announced in May, 1994.

MONETARY SYSTEM:
1 Ruble = 100 Kopeks

NOTE: For later issues of the Armenian Socialist Soviet Republic refer to Volume 1, Russia-Transcaucasia, and for current issues of the new Republic refer to Volume 3.

AUTONOMOUS REPUBLIC

ГОЈУДАРЈТВЕННАГО БАНКА ЭРИВАНЈКОЕ ОТДѢЛЕНIЕ

GOVERNMENT BANK, YEREVAN BRANCH

1919 FIRST ISSUE
#1-29 date on face: АВГУЧТЬ (August) 1919. Many color shades.
#1-18 w/date 15 НОЯБРЯ (November) 1919 on back.
#1-13 w/o Armenian text at upper l. and r.

		Good	Fine	XF
1 (12)	**5 RUBLES** 1919. Black on blue unpt.	3.00	10.00	25.00
2 (13)	**10 RUBLES** 1919. Black on pink unpt.			
	a. Issued note.	2.50	8.00	20.00
	x. Misprint w/text inverted.	4.50	14.00	35.00
3 (5)	**25 RUBLES** 1919. Dk. gray. Value numerals in middle and 4 corners.			
	a. Issued note.	10.00	30.00	75.00
	x. Error printed in brown.	22.00	65.00	165.00

		Good	Fine	XF
4 (6)	**50 RUBLES** 1919. Green. Value numerals in middle and 4 corners.	16.50	50.00	125.00

		Good	Fine	XF
5 (1)	**100 RUBLES** 1919. Green. Plain value numerals in black.	5.00	16.00	40.00
6 (2)	**250 RUBLES** 1919. Orange. Like #5.	5.00	16.00	40.00
7 (3)	**500 RUBLES** 1919. Blue. Like #5.	5.00	16.00	40.00
8 (4)	**1000 RUBLES** 1919. Lilac. Like #5.	5.00	16.00	40.00

1919 SECOND ISSUE
#9-13 w/ornamental numerals of value.

		Good	Fine	XF
9 (7)	**50 RUBLES** 1919. Green. Ornamental value numerals.	4.00	12.00	30.00
10 (8)	**100 RUBLES** 1919. Lt. green. Like #9.			
	a. Issued note.	4.00	12.00	30.00
	x. Error printed in yellow.	7.00	22.00	55.00

		Good	Fine	XF
11 (9)	**250 RUBLES** 1919. Lt. brown. Like #9.	4.00	13.00	32.50
12 (10)	**500 RUBLES** 1919. Blue. Like #9.	4.00	13.00	32.50
13 (11)	**1000 RUBLES** 1919. Lilac. Like #9.	7.50	22.50	55.00

1920 FIRST ISSUE
#14-18 w/Armenian text at upper l. and r.

		Good	Fine	XF
14	**5 RUBLES** 1919 (1920). Gray-blue.			
	a. Issued note.	2.25	7.00	17.50
	x. Misprint w/text: ГОЧУДАРЧТВЕНАГО.	2.25	7.00	15.00
	y. Misprint w/text on back.	5.00	16.00	40.00

		Good	Fine	XF
15	**10 RUBLES** 1919 (1920). Pink-brown.			
	a. Issued note.	2.25	7.00	17.50
	x. Misprint w/text: ГОЧУДАРЧТВЕНАГО.	3.00	9.00	22.50
	y. Misprint w/unpt. inverted.	3.00	9.00	22.50
	z. Misprint w/text: ДЕЕЧЯТЬ.	4.50	13.50	27.50
16	**25 RUBLES** 1919 (1920). Brown.			
	a. Issued note.	2.25	7.00	17.50
	x. Misprint w/text: ГОЧУДАРЧТВЕНАГО.	3.00	9.00	22.50
	y. Misprint w/text: ДВАДЦАШЬ.	4.00	12.00	30.00

17	**50 RUBLES**	GOOD	FINE	XF
	1919 (1920). Black on turquoise unpt.			
	a. Issued note.	2.25	7.00	17.50
	x. Misprint w/text on back.	3.00	9.00	22.50
	y. Misprint w/text on back inverted.	3.00	9.00	22.50
	z. Misprint w/text: ГОЧУДАРЧТВЕНАГО.	2.25	7.00	17.50
18	**100 RUBLES**			
	1919 (1920). Black on yellow-green unpt.			
	a. Issued note.	2.25	7.00	17.50
	x. Misprint w/text on back.	2.25	7.00	17.50
	y. Misprint w/text on back inverted.	4.00	12.00	30.00
	z. Misprint w/text: МИНЧТЕРЧТВОМЪ.	4.00	12.00	30.00

1920 SECOND ISSUE
#19-29 w/date 15 ЯНВАРЯ (January) 1920 on back.

19	**25 RUBLES**	GOOD	FINE	XF
	1919 (1920). Gray-brown. Sign. stamped on back.			
	a. Issued note.	4.00	13.00	32.50
	x. Misprint w/text on back.	6.50	20.00	50.00
	y. Misprint w/text on back inverted.	6.50	20.00	50.00
20	**25 RUBLES**			
	1919 (1920). Brown. Sign. on back in facsimile print.			
	a. Issued note.	4.00	13.00	32.50
	x. Misprint w/text on back.	4.00	13.00	32.50
	y. Misprint w/unpt. inverted.	4.00	13.00	32.50

21	**50 RUBLES**	GOOD	FINE	XF
	1919 (1920). Green-blue.	4.00	13.00	32.50
22	**100 RUBLES**			
	1919 (1920). Lt. green.	3.00	9.00	22.50
23	**250 RUBLES**			
	1919 (1920). Pink. Sign. stamped on back.			
	a. Issued note.	3.00	9.00	22.50
	x. Misprint w/text: ПЯТЬДЕЧТЯЪ.	4.00	13.00	32.50
	y. Misprint w/text on back inverted.	3.00	9.00	22.50
24	**250 RUBLES**			
	1919 (1920). Yellow-brown. Numerals of value in black. Sign. on back in facsimile print.	4.50	14.00	35.00
25	**250 RUBLES**			
	1919 (1920). Yellow-brown. Like #24 but numerals of value in lt. blue.	7.50	22.50	55.00

26	**500 RUBLES**	GOOD	FINE	XF
	1919 (1920). Lt. blue to gray-blue.			
	a. Issued note.	4.00	13.00	32.50
	x. Misprint w/unpt. inverted.	6.50	20.00	50.00
27	**1000 RUBLES**			
	1919 (1920). Black.			
	a. Lt. violet unpt.	3.00	9.00	22.50
	b. Orange-brown unpt.	3.00	9.00	22.50
	c. Pink unpt. White paper.	3.00	9.00	22.50
	d. Pink unpt. Wmk. buff paper.	3.00	9.00	22.50
	x. Misprint w/text on back.	3.00	9.00	22.50
	y. Misprint w/unpt. inverted.	3.00	9.00	22.50
28	**5000 RUBLES**			
	1919 (1920). Black.			
	a. Gray unpt.	4.50	14.00	35.00
	b. Lt. purple unpt. White paper.	6.50	20.00	50.00
	c. Lt. purple unpt. Wmk. buff paper.	4.50	14.00	35.00
	x. Misprint w/unpt. inverted.	8.00	24.00	60.00

29	**10,000 RUBLES**	GOOD	FINE	XF
	1919 (1920). Green. Sign. stamped on back.			
	a. Issued note.	3.00	9.00	22.50
	x. Misprint w/numerals of value reversed.	6.50	20.00	50.00
	y. Misprint w/text on back.	6.50	20.00	50.00
	z. Misprint w/margin text from top to bottom at l.	4.50	14.00	35.00

1920 THIRD ISSUE
#30-32 printer: W&S.

30	**50 RUBLES**	GOOD	FINE	XF
	1919 (1920). Brown on orange unpt. Facing dragons at l. and r.	4.00	10.00	25.00

31	**100 RUBLES**	GOOD	FINE	XF
	1919 (1920). Green on orange and yellow unpt. Landscape w/mountains. Eagle at ctr. on back.	5.00	13.50	32.50

32	**250 RUBLES**	GOOD	FINE	XF
	1919 (1920). Violet on green and yellow unpt. woman spinning at l. on back.	6.00	17.50	45.00

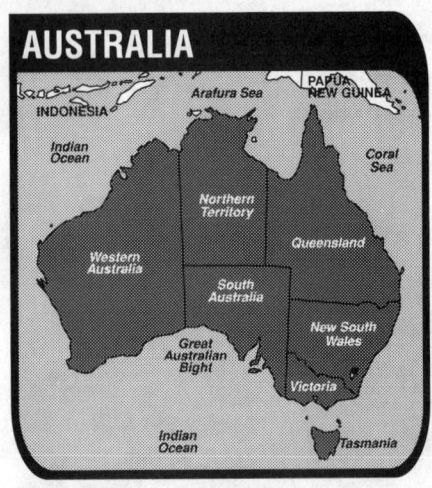

AUSTRALIA

The Commonwealth of Australia, the smallest continent and largest island in the world, is located south of Indonesia between the Indian and Pacific oceans. It has an area of 2,967,909 sq. mi. (7,686,849 sq. km.) and a population of 16.8 million. Capital: Canberra. Due to its early and sustained isolation, Australia is the habitat of such curious and unique fauna as the kangaroo, koala bear, platypus, wombat and barking lizard. The continent possesses extensive mineral deposits, the most important of which are gold, coal, silver, nickel, uranium, lead and zinc. Livestock raising, mining and manufacturing are the principal industries. Chief exports are wool, meat, wheat, iron ore, coal and nonferrous metals.

The first whites to see Australia probably were Portuguese and Spanish navigators of the late 16th century. In 1770, Captain James Cook explored the east coast and annexed it for Great Britain. The Colony of New South Wales was founded by Captain Arthur Phillip on Jan. 26, 1788, a date now celebrated as Australia Day. Dates of creation of six colonies that now comprise the states of the Australian Commonwealth are: New South Wales, 1823; Tasmania, 1825; Western Australia, 1838; South Australia, 1842; Victoria, 1851; Queensland, 1859. A constitution providing for federation of the colonies was approved by the British Parliament in 1900; the Commonwealth of Australia came into being in 1901. Australia passed the Statute of Westminster Adoption Act on Oct. 9, 1942, which officially established Australia's complete autonomy in external and internal affairs, thereby formalizing a situation that had existed for years.

During WWII Australia was the primary supply and staging area for Allied forces in the South Pacific Theatre. Japan had included Australia in its failed plan of the Co-prosperity Sphere of occupied areas.

Australia is a member of the Commonwealth of Nations. The Queen of England is Chief of State.

Australia's currency system was from pounds - shillings - pence to a decimal system of dollars and cents on Feb.14, 1966.

RULERS:
British

MONETARY SYSTEM:
1 Shilling = 12 Pence
1 Pound = 20 Shillings to 1966
1 Dollar = 100 Cents, 1966-

COMMONWEALTH

GOVERNMENT TREASURY

#A72-195 ovpt: *AUSTRALIAN NOTE/Payable in Gold Coin at the/Commonwealth Treasury/at the seat of Government w/3 serial # on unissued notes of 17 different private banks.*

1910 AUSTRALIAN BANK OF COMMERCE - SYDNEY, N.S.W. OVPT. ISSUE

		GOOD	FINE	XF
A72	**1 POUND** ND (1910).	2500.	5000.	—
A73	**5 POUNDS** ND (1910).	—	—	—
A74	**10 POUNDS** ND (1910).	—	—	—
A75	**50 POUNDS** ND (1910).	—	—	—

1910 BANK OF ADELAIDE OVPT. ISSUE

A76	**1 POUND** ND (1910).	2100.	4200.	—
A77	**5 POUNDS** ND (1910).	1800.	3600.	—

A78	**10 POUNDS** ND (1910).	—	—	—
A79	**20 POUNDS** ND (1910).	—	—	—
A80	**50 POUNDS** ND (1910).	—	—	—

1910 BANK OF AUSTRALASIA - SYDNEY, N.S.W. OVPT. ISSUE

A81	**1 POUND** ND (1910).	1600.	4200.	—
A82	**10 POUNDS** ND (1910).	—	—	—
A83A	**10 POUNDS** ND (1910). Ovpt. on Brisbane, Queensland issue.	3300.	6600.	—
A83	**50 POUNDS** ND (1910).	—	—	—

1910 BANK OF AUSTRALASIA - ADELAIDE, SO. AUSTRALIA OVPT. ISSUE

A84	**1 POUND** ND (1910).	—	—	—
A85	**10 POUNDS** ND (1910).	—	—	—
A86	**50 POUNDS** ND (1910).	—	—	—

1910 BANK OF AUSTRALASIA - HOBART, TASMANIA OVPT. ISSUE

A87	**1 POUND** ND (1910).	2100.	4200.	—
A88	**5 POUNDS** ND (1910).	—	—	—
A89	**10 POUNDS** ND (1910).	3300.	6500.	—
A90	**50 POUNDS** ND (1910).	—	—	—

1910 BANK OF AUSTRALASIA - MELBOURNE, VICTORIA OVPT. ISSUE

A91	**1 POUND** ND (1910).	—	—	—
A92	**10 POUNDS** ND (1910).	—	—	—
A93	**50 POUNDS** ND (1910).	—	—	—
A94	**100 POUNDS** ND (1910).	—	—	—

1910 BANK OF AUSTRALASIA - PERTH, WESTERN AUSTRALIA OVPT. ISSUE

A95	**1 POUND** ND (1910).	1800.	3600.	—
A96	**5 POUNDS** ND (1910).	—	—	—
A97	**10 POUNDS** ND (1910).	3500.	7000.	—

1910 BANK OF N.S.W. - SYDNEY, N.S.W. OVPT. ISSUE

A98	**1 POUND** ND (1910). Ovpt. on Sydney.	2400.	4800.	—
A99	**1 POUND** ND (1910). Ovpt. on half finis hed form w/o city.	2400.	4800.	—
A100	**5 POUNDS** ND (1910).	—	—	—
A101	**10 POUNDS** ND (1910).	3500.	7000.	—
A102	**20 POUNDS** ND (1910).	—	—	—
A103	**50 POUNDS** ND (1910).	—	—	—
A104	**100 POUNDS** ND (1910).	—	—	—

1910 BANK OF N.S.W. - ADELAIDE, SO. AUSTRALIA OVPT. ISSUE

A105	**10 POUNDS** ND (1910).	—	—	—
A106	**20 POUNDS** ND (1910).	—	—	—
A107	**50 POUNDS** ND (1910).	—	—	—
A108	**100 POUNDS** ND (1910).	—	—	—

1910 BANK OF N.S.W. - MELBOURNE, VICTORIA OVPT. ISSUE

A109	**10 POUNDS** ND (1910).	—	—	—
A110	**20 POUNDS** ND (1910).	—	—	—
A111	**50 POUNDS** ND (1910).	—	—	—
A112	**100 POUNDS** ND (1910).	—	—	—

1910 BANK OF N.S.W. - PERTH, WESTERN AUSTRALIA OVPT. ISSUE

A113	**20 POUNDS** ND (1910).	—	—	—

1910 BANK OF VICTORIA OVPT. ISSUE

		Good	FINE	XF
A114	1 POUND ND (1910).	2100.	4200.	—
A115	5 POUNDS ND (1910).	—	—	—
A116	10 POUNDS ND (1910).			
	a. Ovpt. on Adelaide.	—	—	—
	b. Ovpt. on Melbourne.	—	—	—
	c. Ovpt. on Perth.	3500.	7000.	—
	d. Ovpt. on Sydney.	—	—	—
A117	20 POUNDS ND (1910).			
A118	50 POUNDS ND (1910).	—	—	—

1910 CITY BANK OF SYDNEY OVPT. ISSUE

A119	1 POUND ND (1910).			
A120	5 POUNDS ND (1910).	—	—	—
A121	10 POUNDS ND (1910).	—	—	—
A122	20 POUNDS ND (1910).	—	—	—
A123	50 POUNDS ND (1910).	—	—	—

1910 COMMERCIAL BANK OF AUSTRALIA OVPT. ISSUE

A126	1 POUND ND (1910).			
	a. Ovpt. on Melbourne.	1800.	3600.	—
	b. Ovpt. on Perth.	1800.	3600.	—
A127	5 POUNDS ND (1910). Ovpt. on Hobart.	2000.	4000.	—

1910 COMMERCIAL BANK OF TASMANIA OVPT. ISSUE

A132	1 POUND ND (1910).			
	a. Ovpt. on Hobart.	2100.	4200.	—
	b. Ovpt. on Launceston.	2100.	4200.	—
A133	5 POUNDS ND (1910). Ovpt. on Launceston .	—	—	—
A134	10 POUNDS ND (1910). Ovpt. on Hobart.	—	—	—
A135	20 POUNDS ND (1910).	—	—	—

1910 COMMERCIAL BANKING CO. OF SYDNEY OVPT. ISSUE

		Good	FINE	XF
A136	1 POUND ND (1910).	1800.	3600.	—
A137	5 POUNDS ND (1910).	—	—	—
A138	10 POUNDS ND (1910).	—	—	—

1910 ENG, SCT, & AUS, BK - SYDNEY, N.S.W. OVPT. ISSUE

		Good	FINE	XF
A139	1 POUND ND (1910).	—	—	—
A140	5 POUNDS ND (1910).	—	—	—
A141	50 POUNDS ND (1910).	—	—	—

1910 ENG, SCT, & AUS, BK - ADELAIDE, SO. AUSTRALIA OVPT. ISSUE

		Good	FINE	XF
A142	1 POUND ND (1910-old date 1.9.1891).	—	—	—
A143	5 POUNDS ND (1910).	—	—	—
A144	10 POUNDS ND (1910).	—	—	—
A145	20 POUNDS ND (1910).	—	—	—
A146	50 POUNDS ND (1910).	—	—	—

1910 ENG, SCT, & AUS, BK - MELBOURNE, VICTORIA OVPT. ISSUE

A147	1 POUND ND (1910).	2700.	5400.	—
A148	5 POUNDS ND (1910).	—	—	—
A149	10 POUNDS ND (1910).	—	—	—
A150	20 POUNDS ND (1910).	—	—	—
A151	50 POUNDS ND (1910).	—	—	—

1910 LDN BK OF AUSTRALIA - SYDNEY, N.S.W. OVPT. ISSUE

A152	10 POUNDS ND (1910).	—	—	—
A153	50 POUNDS ND (1910).	—	—	—
A154	100 POUNDS ND (1910).	—	—	—

1910 LDN BK OF AUSTRALIA - ADELAIDE, SO. AUSTRALIA OVPT. ISSUE

A155	1 POUND ND (1910).	—	—	—
A156	10 POUNDS ND (1910).	—	—	—
A157	50 POUNDS ND (1910).	—	—	—
A158	100 POUNDS ND (1910).	—	—	—

1910 LDN BK OF AUSTRALIA - MELBOURNE, VICTORIA OVPT. ISSUE

A159	1 POUND ND (1910).	GOOD 1800.	FINE 3600.	XF
A160	5 POUNDS ND (1910).	2700.	5400.	11000.
A161	10 POUNDS ND (1910).	—	—	—
A162	50 POUNDS ND (1910).	—	—	—
A163	100 POUNDS ND (1910).	—	—	—

1910 N.B. OF AUSTRALASIA - SYDNEY, N.S.W. OVPT. ISSUE

A164	1 POUND ND (1910).	—	—	—
A165	5 POUNDS ND (1910).	—	—	—
A166	50 POUNDS ND (1910).	—	—	—

1910 N.B. OF AUSTRALASIA - ADELAIDE, SO. AUSTRALIA OVPT. ISSUE

A167	1 POUND ND (1910).	—	—	—
A168	5 POUNDS ND (1910).	—	—	—
A168A	10 POUNDS ND (1910).	2700.	5400.	—
A169	20 POUNDS ND (1910).	—	—	—
A170	50 POUNDS ND (1910).	—	—	—

1910 N.B. OF AUSTRALASIA - VICTORIA, MELBOURNE OVPT. ISSUE

A171	1 POUND ND (1910).	GOOD 1800.	FINE 3600.	XF
A172	5 POUNDS ND (1910).	2100.	4200.	—
A173	10 POUNDS ND (1910).	—	—	—
A174	20 POUNDS ND (1910).	3300.	6600.	—
A175	50 POUNDS ND (1910).	—	—	—
A176	100 POUNDS ND (1910).	—	—	—

1910 N.B. OF AUSTRALASIA - PERTH, WESTERN AUSTRALIA OVPT. ISSUE

A177	1 POUND ND (1910).	—	—	—
A178	5 POUNDS ND (1910).	—	—	—
A179	10 POUNDS ND (1910).	2200.	4400.	—
A180	20 POUNDS ND (1910).	4300.	8600.	—

1910 QUEENSLAND GOVERNMENT OVPT. ISSUE

| A181 | 1 POUND
ND (1910). Ovpt. on Brisbane. | 1800. | 3600. | — |
| A182 | 5 POUNDS
ND (1910). Ovpt. on Brisbane. | 2100. | 4200. | — |

1910 ROYAL BANK OF AUSTRALIA OVPT. ISSUE

| A183 | 1 POUND
ND (1910).
a. Ovpt. on Melbourne.
b. Ovpt. on Sydney. |

2700.
2700. |

5400.
5400. |

—
— |

1910 UNION BANK OVPT. ISSUE

A188	1 POUND ND (1910). a. Ovpt. on Adelaide. b. Ovpt. on Melbourne. c. Ovpt. on Perth.	GOOD — — —	FINE — — —	XF — — —
A189	5 POUNDS ND (1910). a. Ovpt. on Adelaide. b. Ovpt. on Hobart. c. Ovpt. on Melbourne. d. Ovpt. on Perth. e. Ovpt. on Sydney.	 — — — — —	 — — — — —	 — — — — —
A190	10 POUNDS ND (1910). a. Ovpt. on Adelaide. b. Ovpt. on Hobart. c. Ovpt. on Perth. d. Ovpt. on Sydney.	 — — — —	 — — — —	 — — — —
A191	20 POUNDS ND (1910). a. Ovpt. on Adelaide. b. Ovpt. on Hobart. c. Ovpt. on Melbourne. d. Ovpt. on Perth. e. Ovpt. on Sydney.	 — — 5400. — —	 — — — — —	 — — — — —
A192	50 POUNDS ND (1910). a. Ovpt. on Adelaide. b. Ovpt. on Melbourne.	 — —	 — —	 — —

1910 WESTERN AUSTRALIAN BANK OVPT. ISSUE

A193	1 POUND ND (1910).	2400.	4800.	—
A194	5 POUNDS ND (1910).	—	—	—
A195	10 POUNDS ND (1910).	—	—	—

COMMONWEALTH OF AUSTRALIA, TREASURY NOTES

1913 FIRST ISSUE

NOTE:#1B: Because of the shortage of currency created by WWI, old plates from the English, Scottish & Australian Bank Ltd. were used for a special printing of 1,300,000 notes.

NOTE: #2A was issued primarily for interbank transactions only, but a few were released to the public.

1	5 SHILLINGS ND (ca. 1916). Black on green unpt. Portr. Kg. George V at l. Back green. a. Sign. C. J. Cerutty and J. R. Collins. (Not issued). s1. Specimen w/o sign. s2. W/violet handstamp: *Specimen*. Sign. C. J. Cerutty and J. R. Collins. (Not issued).	GOOD — — —	FINE — — —	XF — — —
1A	10 SHILLINGS ND (1913). Dk. blue on m/c unpt. Arms at l. Red serial #. Goulburn Weir (Victoria) at ctr on back. Sign. J. R. Collins and G. T. Allen.	1200.	3500.	7000.
1B	1 POUND ND (1914-15 -old date 1.9.1894). Pale blue and pink. Allegorical woman w/anchor standing at l., arms at r. A reprint of the English, Scottish & Australian Bank Limited superscribed: *AUSTRALIAN NOTE* w/text. Sign. J. R. Collins and G. T. Allen. a. Serial # prefix and suffix *A*. b. Serial # prefix and suffix *B*.	 — 1000.	 Rare 2500.	 — 5000.
2	1 POUND ND (1913-14). Black text on blue, orange and m/c unpt. *Australian Note* at top. Sign. J. R. Collins and G. T. Allen. a. W/*No.* by serial #. b. W/o *No.* by serial #.	 2750. 3000.	 6500. 7000.	 13,000. 14,500.
2A	1000 POUNDS ND (1914-24). Lt. blue. Arms at bottom ctr. Flock of Merino sheep (Bungaree, S.A.) at ctr. a. Sign. J. R. Collins and G. T. Allen (1914). b. Sign. J. Kell and J. R. Collins (1924).	 — —	 — —	 — —

1913 SECOND ISSUE

3	**10 SHILLINGS**	**GOOD**	**FINE**	**XF**
	ND (1914-18). Dk. blue on m/c unpt. Arms at l. Goulburn Weir (Victoria) at ctr. on back. Black serial #. *HALF SOVEREIGN* in borders.			
	a. Sign. J. R. Collins and G. T. Allen (1914).	300.00	850.00	3500.
	b. Sign. C. J. Cerutty and J. R. Collins (1918).	150.00	350.00	2100.

4	**1 POUND**			
	ND (1913-18). Dk. blue on m/c unpt. Crowned arms at ctr. Mine workers at ctr. on back.			
	a. Sign. J. R. Collins and G. T. Allen (1914).	300.00	800.00	2500.
	b. Sign. C. J. Cerutty and J. R. Collins (1918).	125.00	300.00	1000.

4A	**5 POUNDS**			
	ND (1913). Dk. blue on m/c unpt. Arms at l. River landscape (Hawkesbury) at ctr. w/o mosaic unpt. of 5's on back.	2250.	6500.	14,000.

5	**5 POUNDS**			
	ND (1913-18). Dk. blue on m/c unpt. Arms at l. Back: River landscape (Hawkesbury) at ctr. w/mosaic unpt. of 5's.			
	a. Sign. J. R. Collins and G. T. Allen (1913). 2 serial # varieties.	450.00	1650.	4500.
	b. Sign. C. J. Cerutty and J. R. Collins (1918).	250.00	800.00	2400.

6	**10 POUNDS**			
	ND (1913-18). Dk. blue on m/c unpt. Arms at bottom ctr. Back: Horse drawn wagons loaded w/sacks of grain (Narwonah, N.S.W.) at ctr.			
	a. Sign. J. R. Collins and G. T. Allen (1913).	4000.	10,000.	—
	b. Sign. C. J. Cerutty and J. R. Collins (1918). 2 serial # varieties.	2000.	6000.	12,500.

7	**20 POUNDS**			
	ND (1914-18). Dk. blue on m/c unpt. Arms at l. Back: Lumberjacks cutting a tree at ctr. (Bruny Isle, Tasmania).			
	a. Sign. J. R. Collins and G. T. Allen (1914).	3500.	8000.	19,000.
	b. Sign. C. J. Cerutty and J. R. Collins (1918).	3000.	6500.	15,500.

8	**50 POUNDS**	**VG**	**VF**	**UNC**
	ND (1914-18). Blue on m/c unpt. Arms at top ctr. Back: Flock of Merino sheep (Bungaree, S. A.) at ctr.			
	a. Sign. J. R. Collins and G. T. Allen (1914).	—	—	—
	b. Sign. C. J. Cerutty and J. R. Collins (1918).	1700.	5000.	13,500.

9	**100 POUNDS**	**GOOD**	**FINE**	**XF**
	ND (1914-18). Blue on m/c unpt. Arms at l. Back: Upper Yarra River (Victoria) at l. ctr., Leura Falls (N.S.W.) at ctr. r.			
	a. Sign. J. R. Collins and G. T. Allen (1914).	6000.	13,500.	—
	b. Sign. C. J. Cerutty and J. R. Collins (1918).	3500.	10,000.	20,000.

COMMONWEALTH BANK OF AUSTRALIA

1923-25 ISSUE

#10-14 portr. Kg. George V at r., arms at l. w/title: *CHAIRMAN OF DIRECTORS NOTE ISSUE DEPT./COMMONWEALTH BANK OF AUSTRALIA* below l. sign.

10	**1/2 SOVEREIGN**	**VG**	**VF**	**UNC**
	ND (1923). Dk. brown and brown on m/c unpt. Ovpt: *HALF SOVEREIGN*. Goulburn Weir (Victoria) at ctr on back. Sign. D. Miller and J. R. Collins.	350.00	1200.	4000.

11	**1 POUND**	**VG**	**VF**	**UNC**
	ND (1923). Dk. olive-green on m/c unpt. Capt. Cook's Landing at Botany Bay at ctr. on back. Sign. D. Miller and J. R. Collins. Printer: T. S. Harrison.			
	a. Serial # prefix H; J; K.	1000.	2500.	6000.
	b. Fractional serial # prefix.	250.00	700.00	2500.

12	**1 POUND**			
	ND (1923). Dk. olive-green on m/c unpt. Capt. Cook's landing at Botany Bay at ctr. on back. Sign. D. Miller and J. R. Collins.			
	a. Serial # prefix J; K.	3000.	6500.	—
	b. Fractional serial # prefix.	200.00	600.00	1700.

13	**5 POUNDS**	**VG**	**VF**	**UNC**
	ND (1924-27). Deep blue on m/c unpt. River landscape (Hawkesbury) at ctr. on back.			
	a. Sign. J. Kell and J. R. Collins (1924).	350.00	1250.	3500.
	b. Sign. J. Kell and J. Heathershaw (1927).	500.00	1750.	4500.
	c. Sign. Sign. E. C. Riddle and J. Heathershaw (1927).	3000.	7500.	—

14	**10 POUNDS**			
	ND (1925). Dp. red on m/c unpt. Horse drawn wagons loaded w/sacks of grain at lower ctr. on back. Proof w/o sign.	—	Unc	10,000.

1926-27 ISSUE

#15-19 portr. Kg. George V at r., arms at l. w/title: *GOVERNOR/COMMONWEALTH BANK OF AUSTRALIA* below lower l. sign.

15	**1/2 SOVEREIGN**	**VG**	**VF**	**UNC**
	ND (1926-33). Dk. brown and brown on m/c unpt. Goulburn Weir (Victoria) at ctr. on back.			
	a. Sign. J. Kell and J. R. Collins (1926).	225.00	800.00	2400.
	b. Sign. J. Kell and J. Heathershaw (1927).	350.00	950.00	3500.
	c. Sign. E. C. Riddle and J. Heathershaw (1927).	125.00	400.00	1200.
	d. Sign. E. C. Riddle and H. J. Sheehan (1933).	325.00	900.00	2400.

16	**1 POUND**			
	ND (1926-32). Dk. olive-green on m/c unpt. W/o imprint. Capt. Cook's landing at Botany Bay at ctr. on back.			
	a. Sign. J. Kell and J. R. Collins (1926).	120.00	350.00	1700.
	b. Sign. J. Kell and J. Heathershaw (1927).	100.00	325.00	2000.
	c. Sign. E. C. Riddle and J. Heathershaw (1927).	30.00	100.00	400.00
	d. Sign. E. C. Riddle and H. J. Sheehan (1932).	65.00	300.00	1800.

17	**5 POUNDS**	**VG**	**VF**	**UNC**
	ND (1927-32). Dp. blue on m/c unpt. River landscape (Hawkesbury) at ctr. at back.			
	a. Sign. J. Kell and J. Heathershaw (1927).	650.00	2200.	5500.
	b. Sign. E. C. Riddle and J. Heathershaw (1928).	200.00	750.00	2500.
	c. Sign. E. C. Riddle and H. J. Sheehan (1932).	400.00	1000.	4000.

18	**10 POUNDS**			
	ND (1925-33). Dp. red on m/c unpt. Horse drawn wagons loaded w/sacks of grain (Narwonah, N.S.W.) at ctr. at back.			
	a. Sign. J. Kell and J. R. Collins (1925).	1750.	4500.	12,000.
	b. Sign. E. C. Riddle and J. Heathershaw (1925).	650.00	2000.	5000.
	c. Sign. E. C. Riddle and H. J. Sheehan (1933).	3000.	8000.	18,500.

1933-34 ISSUES

#19-24 Sign. E. C. Riddle and H. J. Sheehan. Wmk: Edward (VIII), Prince of Wales.

19	**10 SHILLINGS**	**VG**	**VF**	**UNC**
	ND (1933). Brown on m/c unpt. Portr. Kg. George V at r. Allegorical manufacturers at ctr., lg. *1/2* at l. on back.	350.00	900.00	4000.
20	**10 SHILLINGS**			
	ND (1934). Brown on m/c unpt. Red ovpt: *TEN SHILLINGS* in margins on #19.	150.00	400.00	1400.
21	**10 SHILLINGS**			
	ND (1936-39). Orange on m/c unpt. Reduced size from #19 and #20. Allegorical manufacturers at ctr., lg. *10/-* at l. on back.	85.00	250.00	750.00
22	**1 POUND**			
	ND (1933-38). Dk. green on m/c unpt. Portr. Kg. George V at r. Shepherds w/sheep at ctr. on back.	30.00	70.00	375.00

23	**5 POUNDS**	**VG**	**VF**	**UNC**
	ND (1933-39). Dp. Blue on m/c unpt. Portr. Kg. George V at l. Dock workers w/sacks, bales and barrels at upper l. on back.	150.00	450.00	1600.
24	**10 POUNDS**			
	ND (1934-39). Dp. red on m/c unpt. Portr. Kg. George V at ctr. Group symbolizing agriculture at upper r. on back.	175.00	600.00	1800.

1938-40 ISSUE

#25-28B wmk: Captain Cook.

NOTE: #28A and 28B were intended for interbank use during WWII only. All but a few specimens were destroyed in 1958.

24A	**5 SHILLINGS**	**VG**	**VF**	**UNC**
	ND (1946). Black on red-brown unpt. Portr. Kg. George VI at ctr. Back red-brown; Australian crown coin design at ctr. Sign. H. T. Armitage and S. G. McFarlane. (Not issued).	—	—	—
25	**10 SHILLINGS**			
	ND (1939-52). Orange on m/c unpt. Portr. Kg. George VI at r. Back: Allegorical manufacturers at ctr., lg *10/* at l.			
	a. Orange sign. H. J. Sheehan and S. G. McFarlane (1939).	5.00	30.00	250.00
	b. Black sign. H. T. Armitage and S. G. McFarlane (1942).	2.50	15.00	90.00
	c. Black sign. H. C. Coombs and G. P. N. Watt (1949).	3.50	20.00	150.00
	d. Black sign. H. C. Coombs and R. Wilson (1952).	3.50	20.00	150.00

26	**1 POUND**	**VG**	**VF**	**UNC**
	ND (1938-52). Dk. green on m/c unpt. Portr. Kg. George VI at r. Shepherds w/sheep at ctr. on back.			
	a. Green sign. H. J. Sheehan and S. G. McFarlane (1938).	5.00	20.00	200.00
	b. Black sign. H. T. Armitage and S. G. McFarlane (1942).	2.50	10.00	90.00
	c. Black sign. H. C. Coombs and G. P. N. Watt (1949).	5.00	15.00	100.00
	d. Black sign. H. C. Coombs and R. Wilson (1952).	4.00	14.00	90.00

27	**5 POUNDS**	**VG**	**VF**	**UNC**
	ND (1939-52). Dp. blue on m/c unpt. Portr. Kg. George VI at l. Workers w/sacks, bales and barrels at upper l. on back.			
	a. Blue sign. H. J. Sheehan and S. G. McFarlane (1939).	20.00	55.00	700.00
	b. Black sign. H. T. Armitage and S. G. McFarlane (1941).	15.00	40.00	250.00
	c. Black sign. H. C. Coombs and G. P. N. Watt (1949).	15.00	45.00	400.00
	d. Black sign. H. C. Coombs and R. Wilson (1952).	12.00	35.00	250.00

28	**10 POUNDS**	**VG**	**VF**	**UNC**
	ND (1940-52). Dp. red on m/c unpt. Portr. Kg. George VI at bottom ctr. Group symbolizing agriculture at upper r. on back.			
	a. Red sign. H. J. Sheehan and S. G. McFarlane (1940).	45.00	250.00	1750.
	b. Black sign. H. T. Armitage and S. G. McFarlane (1942).	30.00	90.00	450.00
	c. Black sign. H. C. Coombs and G. P. N. Watt (1949).	30.00	100.00	525.00
	d. Black sign. H. C. Coombs and R. Wilson (1952).	50.00	300.00	1500.
28A	**50 POUNDS**			
	ND (1939). Purple on m/c unpt. Portr. Kg. George VI. Sign. H. T. Armitage and S. G. McFarlane. Specimen.	—	—	—

28B	**100 POUNDS**	**VG**	**VF**	**UNC**
	ND (1939). Brown on m/c unpt. Portr. Kg. George VI. Sign. H. J. Sheehan and S. G. McFarlane. Specimen.			

1953-54 ISSUE

#29-32 sign. H. C. Coombs and R. Wilson. w/title: *GOVERNOR/COMMONWEALTH BANK OF AUSTRALIA* below lower l. sign. Wmk: Captain Cook.

29	**10 SHILLINGS**	**VG**	**VF**	**UNC**
	ND (1954-60). Dk. brown on m/c unpt. Portr. M. Flinders at r. Parliament in Canberra at l. ctr. on back.	2.00	6.00	30.00

30	**1 POUND** ND (1953-60). Dk. green on m/c unpt. Medallic portr. Qn. Elizabeth II at r. Facing medallic portr. C. Sturt and H. Hume on back.	2.00	6.00	30.00
31	**5 POUNDS** ND (1954-59). Blue on m/c unpt. Portr. Sir J. Franklin at r. Sheep and agricultural products between bull and cow's head on back.	8.00	20.00	80.00
32	**10 POUNDS** ND (1954-59). Red and black on m/c unpt. Portr. Gov. Phillip at l. Symbols of science and industry at ctr., allegorical woman kneeling w/compass at r. on back.	20.00	40.00	225.00

COMMONWEALTH OF AUSTRALIA

RESERVE BANK

1960-61 ISSUE
#33-36 w/title: *GOVERNOR/RESERVE BANK OF AUSTRALIA* below lower l. sign.

		VG	VF	UNC
35	**5 POUNDS** ND (1960-65). Blue. Sir J. Franklin at r. Cattle, sheep and agricultural products on back. Sign. H. C. Coombs and R. Wilson.	10.00	22.50	75.00
36	**10 POUNDS** ND (1960-65). Red. Gov. Philip at l. Symbols of science and industry on back. Sign. H. C. Coombs and R. Wilson.	20.00	35.00	190.00

AUSTRIA

The Republic of Austria (Oesterreich), a parliamentary democracy located in mountainous central Europe, has an area of 32,374 sq. mi. (83,849 sq. km.) and a population of 8 million. Capital: Vienna. Austria is primarily an industrial country. Machinery, iron and steel, textiles, yarns and timber are exported.

The territories later to be known as Austria were overrun in pre-Roman times by various tribes, including the Celts. Upon the fall of the Roman Empire, the country became a margravate of Charlemagne's Empire. Ottokar, King of Bohemia, gained possession in 1252, only to lose the territory to Rudolf of Habsburg in 1276. Thereafter, until World War I, the story of Austria was that of the ruling Habsburgs, German emperors from 1438-1806. From 1815-1867 it was a member of the "Deutsche Bund" (German Union).

During World War I, the Austro-Hungarian Empire was one of the Central Powers with Germany, Bulgaria and Turkey. At the end of the war, the Empire was dissolved and Austria established as an independent republic. In March 1938, Austria was incorporated into Hitler's short-lived German Third Reich. Allied forces of both East and West liberated Austria in April 1945, and subsequently divided it into four zones of military occupation. On May 15, 1955, the four powers formally recognized Austria as a "sovereign," independent democratic state.

RULERS:
Maria Theresa, 1740-1780
Joseph II, jointly with his Mother, 1765-1780 alone, 1780-1790
Leopold II, 1790-1792
Franz II (I), 1792-1835 (as Franz II, 1792-1806) (as Franz I, 1806-1835)
Ferdinand I, 1835-1848
Franz Joseph, 1848-1916
Karl I, 1916-1918

MONETARY SYSTEM:
1 Gulden = 60 Kreuzer, 1754-1857
1 Gulden = (Florin) = 100 Kreuzer, 1857-1892
1 Krone = 100 Heller, 1892-1924
1 Schilling (= 10,000 Kronen) = 100 Groschen, 1924-38; 1945-

NOTE: This section has been renumbered.

KINGDOM

NOTE: Corresponding to the following listings through the 1840's there existed so-called "Formulare" w/o seal, sign. or serial # destined to be displayed in various banking houses. These are included in many collections. Market value of "Formulare" is shown in each respective section.

WIENER STADT BANCO

1759 ISSUE
Zettel (note).

NOTE: Market value for "Formulare" #A1 and #A2 is $500.00.

#A11, 50 Gulden

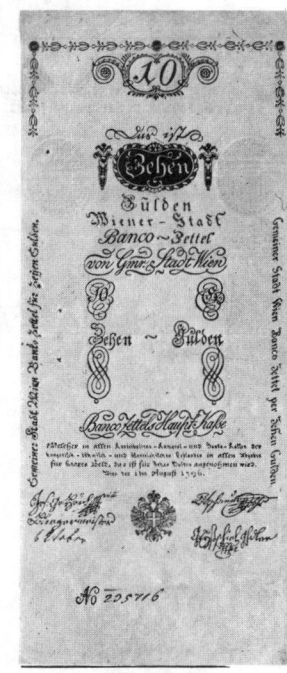

#A23, 10 Gulden

		GOOD	FINE	XF
A1	**10 GULDEN** 1.11.1759.	—	—	—
A2	**20 GULDEN** 1.11.1759.	—	—	—

1762 ISSUE

NOTE: Market value for "Formulare" #A3 is $500.00.

		GOOD	FINE	XF
A3	5 GULDEN	—	—	—
	1.7.1762.			
A4	10 GULDEN	—	—	—
	1.7.1762.			
A5	20 GULDEN	—	—	—
	1.7.1762.			
A6	50 GULDEN	—	—	—
	1.7.1762.			
A7	100 GULDEN	—	—	—
	1.7.1762.			

1771 ISSUE

A8	5 GULDEN	—	—	—
	1.7.1771.			
A9	10 GULDEN	—	—	—
	1.7.1771.			
A10	20 GULDEN	—	—	—
	1.7.1771.			
A11	50 GULDEN	—	—	—
	1.7.1771.			
A12	100 GULDEN	—	—	—
	1.7.1771.			
A13	500 GULDEN	—	—	—
	1.7.1771.			
A14	1000 GULDEN	—	—	—
	1.7.1771.			

1784 ISSUE

A15	5 GULDEN	—	—	—
	1.11.1784.			
A16	10 GULDEN	—	—	—
	1.11.1784.			
A17	25 GULDEN	—	—	—
	1.11.1784.			
A18	50 GULDEN	—	—	—
	1.11.1784.			
A19	100 GULDEN	—	—	—
	1.11.1784.			
A20	500 GULDEN	—	—	—
	1.11.1784.			
A21	1000 GULDEN	—	—	—
	1.11.1784.			

1796 ISSUE

A22	5 GULDEN	—	—	—
	1.8.1796.			
A23	10 GULDEN	—	—	—
	1.8.1796.			
A24	25 GULDEN	—	—	—
	1.8.1796.			
A25	50 GULDEN	—	—	—
	1.8.1796.			
A26	100 GULDEN	—	—	—
	1.8.1796.			
A27	500 GULDEN	—	—	—
	1.8.1796.			
A28	1000 GULDEN	—	—	—
	1.8.1796.			

1800 ISSUE

NOTE: #A31-A37 exist as forgeries printed in France during the reign of Napoleon (often on blue paper). These are valued about the same as originals.

NOTE: Market value for "Formulare" #A33-A35 is $35.00.

#A29, 1 Gulden

#A30, 2 Gulden

		GOOD	FINE	XF
A29	1 GULDEN	4.00	9.00	30.00
	1.1.1800.			
A30	2 GULDEN	5.00	10.00	35.00
	1.1.1800.			

#A31, 5 Gulden

#A32, 10 Gulden

		GOOD	FINE	XF
A31	5 GULDEN	6.00	12.00	50.00
	1.1.1800.			
A32	10 GULDEN	8.50	18.50	65.00
	1.1.1800.			

#A33, 25 Gulden

#A35, 100 Gulden

		GOOD	FINE	XF
A33	25 GULDEN	17.50	40.00	100.00
	1.1.1800.			
A34	50 GULDEN	50.00	200.00	—
	1.1.1800.			
A35	100 GULDEN	37.50	150.00	—
	1.1.1800.			
A36	500 GULDEN	—	Rare	—
	1.1.1800.			
A37	1000 GULDEN	—	Rare	—
	1.1.1800.			

1806 ISSUE

NOTE: Market value for "Formulare" #A38-A43 is $20.00.

#A38, 5 Gulden

#A39, 10 Gulden

A38	5 GULDEN	GOOD	FINE	XF
	1.6.1806.	6.00	15.00	50.00
A39	10 GULDEN			
	1.6.1806.	8.50	18.50	55.00

#A40, 25 Gulden   #A41, 50 Gulden

A40	25 GULDEN	GOOD	FINE	XF
	1.6.1806.	17.50	50.00	110.00
A41	50 GULDEN			
	1.6.1806.	25.00	75.00	150.00

A42	100 GULDEN	GOOD	FINE	XF
	1.6.1806.	30.00	85.00	225.00
A43	500 GULDEN			
	1.6.1806.	—	Rare	—

PRIVILEGIRTE VEREINIGTE EINLÖSUNGS UND TILGUNGS DEPUTATION

1811 ISSUE
Einlösungs - Scheine (Demand Notes)

NOTE: Market value for "Formulare" #A44-A49 is $30.00.

A44	1 GULDEN	GOOD	FINE	XF
	1.3.1811.	12.00	25.00	50.00
A45	2 GULDEN			
	1.3.1811.	17.50	40.00	80.00
A46	5 GULDEN			
	1.3.1811.	35.00	70.00	200.00

A47	10 GULDEN	GOOD	FINE	XF
	1.3.1811.	55.00	110.00	350.00
A48	20 GULDEN			
	1.3.1811.	225.00	425.00	1000.
A49	100 GULDEN			
	1.3.1811.	400.00	650.00	—

1813 ISSUE
Anticipations - Scheine (Anticipation Notes)

NOTE: Market value for "Formulare" #A50-A53 is $25.00.

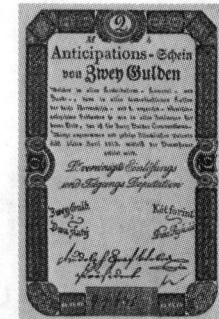

A50	2 GULDEN	GOOD	FINE	XF
	16.4.1813.	12.00	25.00	60.00

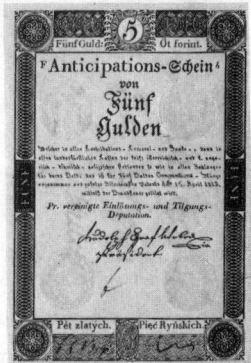

A51	5 GULDEN	GOOD	FINE	XF
	16.4.1813.	20.00	50.00	150.00
A52	10 GULDEN			
	16.4.1813.	200.00	—	—
A53	20 GULDEN			
	16.4.1813.	450.00	—	—

OESTERREICHISCHE NATIONAL ZETTEL BANK

1816 ISSUE
NOTE: Market value for "Formulare" #A54-A60 is $20.00.

A54	5 GULDEN	GOOD	FINE	XF
	1.7.1816.	75.00	225.00	450.00
A55	10 GULDEN			
	1.7.1816.	200.00	450.00	1000.
A56	25 GULDEN			
	1.7.1816.	—	—	—
A57	50 GULDEN			
	1.7.1816.	—	—	—
A58	100 GULDEN			
	1.7.1816.	—	—	—
A59	500 GULDEN			
	1.7.1816.	—	—	—
A60	1000 GULDEN			
	1.7.1816.	—	—	—

PRIVILEGIRTE OESTERREICHISCHE NATIONAL-BANK

1825 ISSUE

NOTE: Market value for "Formulare" #A61-A67 is $30.00.

		GOOD	FINE	XF
A61	**5 GULDEN** 23.6.1825.	30.00	85.00	185.00
A62	**10 GULDEN** 23.6.1825.	60.00	135.00	285.00
A63	**25 GULDEN** 23.6.1825.	—	—	—

		GOOD	FINE	XF
A64	**50 GULDEN** 23.6.1825.	—	—	—
A65	**100 GULDEN** 23.6.1825.	—	—	—
A66	**500 GULDEN** 23.6.1825.	—	—	—

		GOOD	FINE	XF
A67	**1000 GULDEN** 23.6.1825.	—	—	—

1833-34 ISSUE

		GOOD	FINE	XF
A68	**5 GULDEN** 9.12.1833.	25.00	75.00	175.00
A69	**10 GULDEN** 8.12.1834.	40.00	125.00	275.00

1841 ISSUE

NOTE: Market value for "Formulare" #A70-A74 is $30.00.

		GOOD	FINE	XF
A70	**5 GULDEN** 1.1.1841. Profile of Austria at top ctr., arms between cherubs below.	20.00	60.00	150.00
A71	**10 GULDEN** 1.1.1841. Austria at top ctr.	25.00	75.00	175.00
A72	**50 GULDEN** 1.1.1841. Eleven female heads (Pomona) at top ctr.	—	—	—
A73	**100 GULDEN** 1.1.1841. Eleven female heads (Pomona) at top ctr.	—	—	—

		GOOD	FINE	XF
A74	**1000 GULDEN** 1.1.1841. Eleven female heads (Pomona) at top ctr., 2 heads of Austria facing below, allegorical woman standing at l. and r.	—	—	—

1847 ISSUE

		GOOD	FINE	XF
A75	**5 GULDEN** 1.1.1847. Atlas and Minerva at l., Austria at r.	20.00	60.00	130.00
A76	**10 GULDEN** 1.1.1847. Atlas and Minerva at l., Austria at r.	25.00	75.00	175.00

		GOOD	FINE	XF
A77	**100 GULDEN** 1.1.1847. Austria at l., Atlas and Minerva at r., crowned shield at top ctr., arms below.	250.00	600.00	1200.
A78	**1000 GULDEN** 1.1.1847. Austria at lower l. and r., Atlas and Minerva at l. and r.			

1848 ISSUE

		GOOD	FINE	XF
A79	**1 GULDEN** 1.5.1848. Uniface.	22.50	50.00	75.00
A80	**2 GULDEN** 1.5.1848. Uniface.	25.00	55.00	85.00

1848-54 ISSUE

		GOOD	FINE	XF
A81	**1 GULDEN** 1.7.1848. Austria at top ctr., arms below at bottom	10.00	20.00	45.00

		GOOD	FINE	XF
A82	**2 GULDEN** 1.7.1848. Atlas and Minerva at l., Austria at r., arms at bottom ctr.	15.00	30.00	60.00
A83	**10 GULDEN** 1.7.1854. Austria at l., Atlas and Minerva at r.	50.00	150.00	250.00

1858 ISSUE

		GOOD	FINE	XF
A84	**1 GULDEN** 1.1.1858. Black and red. Austria at top ctr., arms at bottom.	5.00	10.00	25.00
A85	**10 GULDEN** 1.1.1858. Black and red. Man w/genius on pedestal at l. and r., Austria w/lion below.	35.00	100.00	250.00

		GOOD	FINE	XF
A86	**100 GULDEN** 1.3.1858. Black and red. Austria at l., arms between 2 cherubs at top ctr., god of the river Danube at r.	175.00	450.00	1000.
A87	**1000 GULDEN** 1.3.1858. Black and red. Woman symbolizing power at l., w/symbol of abundance.			

1859-63 ISSUE

		GOOD	FINE	XF
A88	**5 GULDEN** 1.5.1859. Black and red. Austria at top ctr., Imperial eagle at bottom	12.50	40.00	100.00

		GOOD	FINE	XF
A89	**10 GULDEN** 15.1.1863. Black and red. Shepherd, miner and peasant.	30.00	70.00	150.00

		GOOD	FINE	XF
A90	**100 GULDEN** 15.1.1863. Black and green. 2 cherubs w/coins at left supported arms at bottom ctr., 2 cherubs w/sword, book and purse at r.	150.00	375.00	850.00

K.K. HAUPTMÜNZAMT

MÜNZSCHEINE
Münzschein (Coin Notes).

1849 ISSUE

 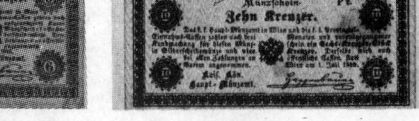

#A91, 6 Kreuzer   #A92, 10 Kreuzer

		GOOD	FINE	XF
A91	**6 KREUZER** 1.7.1849. Black on green unpt. Arms at ctr.	1.25	2.50	6.00
A92	**10 GULDEN** 1.7.1849. Black. Arms at ctr.			
	a. Rose unpt.	2.00	4.00	7.50
	b. Lt. blue unpt.	2.00	4.00	7.50

1860 ISSUE

		GOOD	FINE	XF
A93	**10 KREUZER** 1.11.1860. Black on lt. brown unpt. of waves. 87 x 38mm.			
	a. Plain edges.	1.50	3.00	6.50
	b. Serrated edges. White wmk. paper.	1.50	3.00	6.50

		GOOD	FINE	XF
A94	**10 KREUZER** 1.11.1860. Black on lt. brown unpt. Back: Green. *Oest.* at bottom l., *Wahr.* at r. 87 x 39mm.	1.50	3.00	7.00

		GOOD	FINE	XF
A95	**10 KREUZER** 1.11.1860. Black on green unpt. *10* at bottom l. and r. 55 x 37mm.	1.50	3.00	7.00

K.u.K. STAATS-CENTRAL-CASSA

CASSA-ANWEISUNGEN

All "Cassa-Anweisungen" were interest bearing notes except #A96. Most of them exist only as "Formulare" which give general design characteristics.

1848 ISSUE

		GOOD	FINE	XF
A96	30 GULDEN 1.9.1848.	—	—	—
A97	60 GULDEN 1.9.1848.			
A98	90 GULDEN 1.9.1848.			
A99	300 GULDEN 1.9.1848.			
A100	600 GULDEN 1.9.1848.			
A101	900 GULDEN 1.9.1848.			

1849 FIRST ISSUE

A102	10 GULDEN 1.1.1849.	—	—	—

		GOOD	FINE	XF
A103	25 GULDEN 1.1.1849.	—	—	—
A104	50 GULDEN 1.1.1849.	—	—	—
A105	100 GULDEN 1.1.1849.	—	—	—
A106	500 GULDEN 1.1.1849.	—	—	—
A107	1000 GULDEN 1.1.1849.	—	—	—

1849 SECOND ISSUE

A108	5 GULDEN 1.3.1849.			
A109	10 GULDEN 1.3.1849.			
A110	25 GULDEN 1.3.1849.			
A111	50 GULDEN 1.3.1849.			
A112	100 GULDEN 1.3.1849.			
A113	500 GULDEN 1.3.1849.			
A114	1000 GULDEN 1.3.1849.			

1849 THIRD ISSUE

A115	30 GULDEN 1.3.1849.			

		GOOD	FINE	XF
A116	60 GULDEN 1.3.1849.	—	—	—
A117	90 GULDEN 1.3.1849.	—	—	—
A118	300 GULDEN 1.3.1849.	—	—	—
A119	600 GULDEN 1.3.1849.	—	—	—
A120	900 GULDEN 1.3.1849.	—	—	—

1849 FOURTH ISSUE

A121	5 GULDEN 1.7.1849.			
A122	10 GULDEN 1.7.1849.			
A123	25 GULDEN 1.7.1849.			
A124	50 GULDEN 1.7.1849.			
A125	100 GULDEN 1.7.1849.			
A126	500 GULDEN 1.7.1849.			
A127	1000 GULDEN 1.7.1849.			

1850 ISSUE

A128	50 GULDEN 1.1.1850.			
A129	100 GULDEN 1.1.1850.			
A130	500 GULDEN 1.1.1850.			
A131	1000 GULDEN 1.1.1850.			

K.K. STAATS-CENTRAL-CASSE

REICHS-SCHATZSCHEINE

All "Reichs-Schatzscheine" were 3% interest-bearing notes except #A135-A137.

1850 ISSUE

NOTE: Market value for "Formulare" #A132-A134 is $100.00.

A132	100 GULDEN 1.1.1850.			
A133	500 GULDEN 1.1.1850.			
A134	1000 GULDEN 1.1.1850.			

1851 ISSUE

NOTE: Market value for "Formulare" #A135-A137 is $15.00.

		GOOD	FINE	XF
A135	5 GULDEN 1.1.1851. Bearded man w/club at l., helmeted woman at r., arms at bottom ctr.	15.00	45.00	100.00
A136	10 GULDEN 1.1.1851. Floating woman at l., floating warrior at r.	35.00	85.00	200.00

			Good	Fine	XF
A137	**50 Gulden** 1.1.1851. Plowing w/Emperor Joseph II, aide and peasant farmer at bottom.		110.00	275.00	750.00
A138	**100 Gulden** 1.1.1851.		—	—	—
A139	**500 Gulden** 1.1.1851.		—	—	—
A140	**1000 Gulden** 1.1.1851.		—	—	—

1852 Issue

A141	**100 Gulden** 1.1.1852.				
A142	**500 Gulden** 1.1.1852.		—	—	—
A143	**1000 Gulden** 1.1.1852.		—	—	—

1853 First Issue
NOTE: Market value for "Formulare" #A144-A146 is $100.00.

A144	**100 Gulden** 1.1.1853.				
A145	**500 Gulden** 1.1.1853.		—	—	—
A146	**1000 Gulden** 1.1.1853.		—	—	—

1853 Second Issue
NOTE: Market value for "Formulare" #A147-A149 is $100.00.

			Good	Fine	XF
A147	**100 Gulden** 8.10.1853.		—	—	—
A148	**500 Gulden** 8.10.1853.		—	—	—
A149	**1000 Gulden** 8.10.1853.		—	—	—

K.K. Staats-Central-Casse

1866 Issue

			Good	Fine	XF
A150	**1 Gulden** 7.7.1866. Black on green unpt. Woman seated holding gear at lower l., Mercury seated at r. Back: Gray. 10 coats-of-arms in border.		3.00	7.50	20.00

			Good	Fine	XF
A151	**5 Gulden** 1866-67. Black on pink unpt. Woman w/lyre at upper l., elderly man seated at upper r.				
	a. 7.7.1866-18.1.1867. Black serial (block) #.		25.00	65.00	140.00
	b. Red serial (block) #.		7.50	20.00	50.00

			Good	Fine	XF
A152	**50 Gulden** 25.8.1866. Black on green-blue unpt. Warrior w/lion at l., woman w/dragon and book at r.		75.00	200.00	450.00

K.K. Reichs-Central-Cassa

1881-84 Issue
#A153-A156 medallic head of Emperor Franz Joseph at upper ctr.

			Good	Fine	XF
A153 (A154)	**1 Gulden** 1.1.1882. Blue on gray-brown unpt.		2.25	7.00	20.00
A154 (A153)	**5 Gulden** 1.1.1881. Green on gray-brown unpt. Woman w/book at l., woman in armor at r.		10.00	30.00	70.00

			Good	Fine	XF
A155	**50 Gulden** 1.1.1884. Blue on gray-brown unpt. 2 boys at l. and at r.		45.00	140.00	300.00

1888 ISSUE

		GOOD	FINE	XF
A156	**1 GULDEN** 1.7.1888. Blue. Kneeling angel at bottom r. Back: Reversed image except for kneeling angel.	5.00	10.00	30.00

OESTERREICHISCH-UNGARISCHE BANK

AUSTRO-HUNGARIAN BANK

1880 ISSUE
NOTE: The Description refers to the side of the note w/German text.

		GOOD	FINE	XF
1	**10 GULDEN** 1.5.1880. Blue. Women at l. and r.	15.00	40.00	100.00

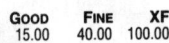

		GOOD	FINE	XF
2	**100 GULDEN** 1.5.1880. Blue. Boy w/sheaf and sickle at l., boy w/book at r.	75.00	160.00	375.00
3	**1000 GULDEN** 1.5.1880. Blue. Child at l. and r.			

1900-02 ISSUE

		GOOD	FINE	XF
4	**10 KRONEN** 31.3.1900. Lilac. Child at l. and r.	10.00	40.00	100.00

		GOOD	FINE	XF
5	**20 KRONEN** 31.3.1900. Red and green unpt. Cherub w/portr. woman over arms at l.	15.00	50.00	150.00

		GOOD	FINE	XF
6	**50 KRONEN** 2.1.1902. Blue on rose unpt. Seated woman at l. and at r., arms at upper ctr.	8.00	25.00	90.00

		GOOD	FINE	XF
7	**100 KRONEN** 2.1.1902. Green on rose unpt. Seated woman w/child at l., blacksmith stands at anvil at r.	70.00	150.00	300.00
8	**1000 KRONEN** 2.1.1902. Blue. Woman at r.			
	a. Gray-green unpt.	1.00	4.00	12.00
	b. Rose unpt. Later issue from Series #1440 on.	.50	2.00	6.00

1904-12 ISSUE

		GOOD	FINE	XF
9	**10 KRONEN** 2.1.1904. Blue-violet on red and green unpt. Princess Rohan at r.	1.50	6.00	15.00

		GOOD	FINE	XF
10	**20 KRONEN** 2.1.1907. Blue on red-brown and green unpt. Arms at upper l., Austria at upper ctr., portr. woman at r.	6.00	15.00	45.00
11	**100 KRONEN** 2.1.1910. Blue. Woman w/flowers at r.	50.00	125.00	250.00

12   100 KRONEN
   2.1.1912. Green on red and blue unpt. Facing portr. woman at r. Back: Profile portr. of woman at upper r.

	GOOD	FINE	XF
	.25	.75	3.00

1913-14 ISSUE

13   20 KRONEN
   2.1.1913. Blue on green and red unpt. Portr. woman at upper l., arms at upper r. Back: Arms at upper l., portr. woman at upper r.

	VG	VF	UNC
	.25	.50	1.50

14   20 KRONEN
   2.1.1913. Blue on green and red unpt. Woman at l. w/*II AUFLAGE* at l. border (2nd issue).

	.25	.50	1.50

15   50 KRONEN
   2.1.1914. Blue and green. Woman at ctr.

	.50	1.50	3.00

1914-15 ISSUE

16   1 KRONE
   5.8.1914. Woman at ctr. Proof. — — —

17   2 KRONEN
   5.8.1914. Portr. girl at upper ctr. Back: Brown-orange on green unpt.

	VG	VF	UNC
a. Thin paper, series A or B. 2 serial # varieties.	2.00	6.00	12.00
b. Heavier paper, series C.	.25	.75	2.00

18   5 KRONEN
   5.8.1914. Red and green. Woman in relief at r. Proof. — — —

19   10 KRONEN
   2.1.1915. Blue and green. Arms at upper l., portr. boy at bottom ctr. Back: Arms at upper l., portr. young man at upper r.

	VG	VF	UNC
	.25	.75	3.50

1916-18 ISSUE
NOTE: For #20 and #21 w/block # over 7000 see Hungary #10 and #11.
NOTE: For #23 w/block # over 3000 see Hungary #12 and 13.
NOTE: For #24 Series A see Hungary #14-16.

20   1 KRONE
   1.12.1916. Red. Woman's head at upper l. and r. Back: Helmeted warrior's bust at ctr. Block #1000-1700.

	VG	VF	UNC
	.10	.20	.40

21   2 KRONEN
   1.3.1917. Red on gray unpt. Woman at l. and r. Block #1000-1600 and Block #A1000-1100. 2 serial # varieties.

	VG	VF	UNC
	.15	.25	.50

22   5 KRONEN
   1.10.1918. Woman at l. and r. Proof.

23   25 KRONEN
   27.10.1918. Blue on gray-brown unpt. Girl at l. Up to block #2000.

	4.00	10.00	22.00

24   200 KRONEN
   27.10.1918. Green on pink unpt. Girl at l. Series B.

	10.00	22.00	45.00

25   10,000 KRONEN
   2.11.1918. Violet. Woman at r.

	10.00	25.00	75.00

KRIEGSDARLEHENSKASSE KASSENSCHEIN

WAR STATE LOAN BANK

1914 ISSUE
#26-28 arms at l., 3 allegorical figures standing at r.

26	**250 KRONEN**	VG	VF	UNC
	26.9.1914. Red and green.	20.00	50.00	175.00
27	**2000 KRONEN**			
	26.9.1914. Green and brown.	25.00	60.00	200.00
28	**10,000 KRONEN**			
	26.9.1914. Lilac and blue.	30.00	70.00	250.00

REPUBLIC

OESTERREICHISCH-UNGARISCHEN BANK
KASSENSCHEIN
1918-19 ISSUE

29	**1000 KRONEN**	GOOD	FINE	XF
(32)	28.10.1918. Green. Uniface.	125.00	250.00	500.00
30	**1000 KRONEN**			
(33)	30.10.1918. Green. Uniface. Like #29.	125.00	250.00	500.00
31	**5000 KRONEN**			
(30)	25.10.1918.	200.00	400.00	800.00
32	**5000 KRONEN**			
(36)	5.2.1919. Olive. Back printed.	125.00	250.00	500.00
33	**10,000 KRONEN**			
(31)	26.10.1918. Back printed.	125.00	250.00	500.00
34	**10,000 KRONEN**			
	4.11.1918. Back printed.	125.00	250.00	500.00
35	**100,000 KRONEN**			
(29)	3.10.1918. Violet and brown. Back printed.	125.00	250.00	500.00
36	**1,000,000 KRONEN**			
(35)	18.11.1918. Red-brown. Uniface.	125.00	250.00	500.00

1921 ISSUE

NOTE: For Treasury notes of various Hungarian branch offices, see Hungary #4-9.

37	**1000 KRONEN**			
	23.12.1921. Green.	52.50	125.00	250.00
38	**5000 KRONEN**			
	23.12.1921. Olive.	87.50	175.00	350.00
39	**10,000 KRONEN**			
	23.12.1921. Blue.	87.50	175.00	350.00
40	**100,000 KRONEN**			
	23.12.1921. Violet.	87.50	175.00	350.00

1920 ISSUE

#41-45 ovpt: *Ausgegeben nach dem 4. Oktober 1920* (issued after October 4, 1920) on Oesterreichisch-Ungarische Bank issues.

#49-66 ovpt: *DEUTSCHÖSTERREICH* on Oesterreichisch-Ungarische Bank issue.

41	**1 KRONE**			
	4.10.1920. Ovpt: Green ovpt. on #20.	5.00	12.50	50.00
42	**2 KRONEN**			
	4.10.1920. Green ovpt. on #21.			
	a. Ovpt: Ovpt. on German side.	6.00	15.00	60.00
	b. Ovpt: Ovpt. on Hungarian side.	18.00	25.00	100.00

43	**10 KRONEN**	GOOD	FINE	XF
	4.10.1920. Red ovpt. on #19.	7.00	17.50	70.00
44	**20 KRONEN**			
	4.10.1920. Red ovpt. on #13.	9.00	22.50	90.00
45	**20 KRONEN**			
	4.10.1920. Red ovpt. on #14.	7.00	17.50	70.00
46	**50 KRONEN**			
	4.10.1920. Red ovpt. on #15.	7.00	17.50	70.00

47	**100 KRONEN**			
	4.10.1920. Red ovpt. on #12.	7.00	17.50	70.00

48	**1000 KRONEN**	GOOD	FINE	XF
	4.10.1920. Red ovpt. on #8.	8.00	20.00	80.00

1919 ISSUE
#49-66 ovpt: *DEUTSCHÖSTERREICH* on Oesterreichisch-Ungarische Bank issues.

49	**1 KRONE**	VG	VF	UNC
	ND (1919). Green ovpt. on #20	.10	.25	.50

50	**2 KRONEN**	VG	VF	UNC
	ND (1919). Green ovpt. on #21.	.15	.25	.50
51	**10 KRONEN**			
	ND (1919). Orange ovpt. on #19.			
	a. Issued note.	.15	.25	.50
	b. W/handstamp: *NOTE ECHT, STEMPEL FALSCH* (note genuine, ovpt. forged).	Reported Not Confirmed		
52	**20 KRONEN**			
	ND (1919). Red ovpt. on #13.	.35	.65	1.25

53	**20 KRONEN**	VG	VF	UNC
	ND (1919). Red ovpt. on #14.			
	a. Issued note.	.15	.25	.75
	b. W/handstamp: *NOTE ECHT, STEMPEL FALSCH* (note genuine, ovpt. forged.)	10.00	20.00	35.00

54 50 KRONEN

		VG	VF	UNC
	ND (1919). Blue and green. Red ovpt. on #15.			
a.	Issued note.	.15	.25	.50
b.	W/handstamp *NOTE ECHT, STEMPEL FALSCH* (note genuine, ovpt. forged.)	10.00	20.00	35.00

55 100 KRONEN

	ND (1919). Green on red and blue unpt. Hungarian text on back. Red ovpt. on #12.			
a.	Issued note.	.15	.25	.50
b.	W/handstamp *NOTE ECHT, STEMPEL FALSCH* (note genuine, ovpt. forged.)	10.00	25.00	50.00
c.	W/handstamp *NOTE ECHT, STEMPEL NICHT KONSTATIERBAR* (note genuine, ovpt. cannot be verified.)	20.00	40.00	70.00

56 100 KRONEN

	ND (1919). Green. Woman at r. German text on.back. Red ovpt.	.15	.25	.50

57 1000 KRONEN

	ND (1919). Hungarian text on back. Red ovpt. on #8b.			
a.	Issued note.	.25	.50	2.00
b.	W/handstamp *NOTE ECHT, STEMPEL FALSCH* (note genuine, ovpt. forged.)	10.00	20.00	35.00
c.	W/handstamp *NOTE ECHT, STEMPEL NICHT KONSTATIERBAR* Reported Not Confirmed (note genuine, ovpt. cannot be verified).			

58 1000 KRONEN

		VG	VF	UNC
	ND (1919). Blue. Red ovpt. on #57, w/additional black ovpt: *ECHT / OESTERREICHISCH-UNGARISCHE BANK / HAUPTANSTALT WIEN.*	15.00	30.00	75.00

59 1000 KRONEN

	ND (1919). Blue. Portr. Woman at r. Like #8 & 57 but w/German text on back and red ovpt.	.50	1.50	6.00

60 1000 KRONEN

	ND (1919). Blue. Portr. Woman at r. Like #8 & 57 but w/ornaments, portr. woman at upper l. and r. on back.	.25	.75	3.00

61 1000 KRONEN

	ND (1919). Blue. Like #60 but w/additional red ovpt: *II AUFLAGE* (2nd issue).	.25	.75	3.00

62 10,000 KRONEN

		VG	VF	UNC
	ND (1919). Violet. Woman at r. Hungarian text on back. Red ovpt. on #25.			
a.	Issued note.	40.00	90.00	175.00
b.	W/handstamp *NOTE ECHT, STEMPEL FALSCH* (note genuine, ovpt. forged).	20.00	45.00	100.00

63 10,000 KRONEN

	ND (1919). Violet. Hungarian text on back. Red ovpt. on #62. W/additional black ovpt: *ECHT. ÖSTERR - UNGAR BANK HAUPTANSTALT WIEN.*	40.00	90.00	175.00

64 10,000 KRONEN

	ND (1919). Purple. Woman at r. German text on back. Red ovpt.	1.00	2.50	6.50

65 10,000 KRONEN

		VG	VF	UNC
	ND (1919). Purple. Woman at r. Red ovpt. Ornaments, portr. eoman at upper l. and r. on back.	.50	1.00	4.00

66 10,000 KRONEN

	ND (1919). Violet. Portr. woman at r. and *II AUFLAGE* (2nd issue) in left margin. Ornaments and portr. woman at upper l. and r. on back.	.50	1.00	5.50

AUSTRIAN GOVERNMENT

1922 FIRST ISSUE

73 1 KRONE

	VG	VF	UNC
2.1.1922. Red. Uniface.	.10	.15	.25

74 2 KRONEN

	VG	VF	UNC
2.1.1922. Red. Uniface. Woman at upper r.	.10	.15	.25

75 10 KRONEN

	VG	VF	UNC
2.1.1922. Blue-violet. Child at r.	.10	.20	.40

76	20 KRONEN	VG	VF	UNC
	2.1.1922. Purple. Bearded man at r.	.10	.20	.40

77	100 KRONEN	VG	VF	UNC
	2.1.1922. Green. Princess Rohan at r.	.10	.20	.50

78	1000 KRONEN	VG	VF	UNC
	2.1.1922. Blue. Woman at r.	.10	.25	.60

79	5000 KRONEN	VG	VF	UNC
	2.1.1922. Green and red-brown. Portr. woman at r.	.75	3.00	9.00
80	50,000 KRONEN			
	2.1.1922. Red-brown and green. Portr. woman at r. 2 serial # varieties.	4.00	12.00	40.00

81	100,000 KRONEN	VG	VF	UNC
	2.1.1922. Blue and green. Portr. woman in floral frame at r.	8.00	45.00	100.00

1922 SECOND ISSUE

82	100,000 KRONEN	VG	VF	UNC
	11.9.1922. Purple.	—	—	—
83	5,000,000 KRONEN			
	11.9.1922. Green.	—	—	—

1922 THIRD ISSUE

84	500,000 KRONEN	VG	VF	UNC
	20.9.1922. Brown-lilac. Portr. woman w/3 children at r.	15.00	80.00	225.00

OESTERREICHISCHE NATIONALBANK

AUSTRIAN NATIONAL BANK

1924 FIRST ISSUE

85	10,000 KRONEN	VG	VF	UNC
	2.1.1924. Violet and green. Girl at upper r.	.75	3.50	9.50
86	1,000,000 KRONEN			
	1.7.1924. Woman at r.	—	—	—

1924 REFORM ISSUE

87	1 SCHILLING ON 10,000 KRONEN	VG	VF	UNC
	2.1.1924. Ovpt. Red ovpt: *Ein Ovpt: Schilling* and *II Ovpt: Auflage* on #85.	.60	2.00	4.50

1925 ISSUE

88	5 SCHILLING	GOOD	FINE	XF
	2.1.1925. Green. Arms at upper l., portr. youth (by painter E. Zwiauer) at upper r.	6.00	30.00	120.00
89	10 SCHILLING			
	2.1.1925. Brown-violet. Man at r.	15.00	50.00	175.00

90	20 SCHILLING	GOOD	FINE	XF
	2.1.1925. Green. Arms at upper l., portr. woman at upper r.	17.50	75.00	225.00
91	100 SCHILLING			
	2.1.1925. Blue and m/c. Woman at r.	25.00	100.00	300.00

92	1000 SCHILLING	GOOD	FINE	XF
	2.1.1925. Blue on green and red-brown unpt. Portr. woman at r.	250.00	600.00	2000.

1927-30 ISSUE

93	5 SCHILLING	VG	VF	UNC
(95)	1.7.1927. Blue on green unpt. Portr. Prof. Dr. H. Brücke w/compasses at l. Back: Terraced mountain iron ore mining near Eisenerz (Steirmark) at top l. ctr.	3.00	10.00	30.00

94	10 SCHILLING	VG	VF	UNC
(93)	3.1.1927. Blue on green and red unpt. Mercury at top. Back: Allegorical female (Harvest) at bottom.	3.00	10.00	50.00
95	20 SCHILLING			
(96)	2.1.1928. Green. Girl at l., farmer at r. Back: Farmer in field	7.00	20.00	50.00

96	50 SCHILLING			
(97)	2.1.1929. Blue on brown-olive. Woman at l., man at r.	45.00	125.00	300.00

97	100 SCHILLING	VG	VF	UNC
(94)	3.1.1927. Violet and green. Allegorical female (Sciences) at r.	10.00	37.50	85.00

98	1000 SCHILLING	VG	VF	UNC
	2.1.1930. Blue-violet on green unpt. Woman w/figure of Athena at upper r. Back: Salzburg in mountains	450.00	1500.	—

1933-36 ISSUE

NOTE: During 1938-45 the following German notes were in circulation: #171, #173, #174, #179-186, #188-190.

99	10 SCHILLING	VG	VF	UNC
	2.1.1933. Blue. Woman in national costume at top. Back: Arms above Grossglockner mountain at top			
	a. Back: Numerals of value in 4 corners on diagonal lines.	3.00	10.00	30.00
	b. Back: Numerals of value in 4 corners on diagonal and vertical lines.	3.00	10.00	30.00
100	50 SCHILLING			
	2.1.1935. Blue-violet on green unpt. Hubert Sterrer as youth at r. Back: Villages of Maria Wörth and Lake Wörth (Wörthersee)	30.00	125.00	300.00

101	100 SCHILLING	VG	VF	UNC
	2.1.1936. Dk. green on m/c unpt. Woman w/Edelweiss at r. (Not issued).	—	350.00	750.00

ALLIED OCCUPATION - WWII

ALLHERTE MILITARBEHORDE

ALLIED MILITARY AUTHORITY

1944 ISSUE

#102-111 issued from 1944 through 29.5.1945. Wmk: "a" printed by Forbes Lithograph Corp. for U.S.B.E.P. and wmk: "b" in England.

102	50 GROSCHEN			
	1944. Red-brown.			
	a. Forbes Lithograph Corp. Wmk: *MILITARY AUTHORITY* (generally w/parts of words, rarely w/parts of words visible).	7.00	17.50	37.50
	b. In England. Wmk: Wavy lines.	.20	.50	2.00
103	1 SCHILLING			
	1944. Blue on green unpt.			
	a. Forbes Lithograph Corp. Wmk: *MILITARY AUTHORITY* (generally w/o parts of words, rarely w/parts of words visible).	.75	2.00	8.00
	b. In England. Wmk: Wavy lines.	.40	1.00	4.00
104	2 SCHILLING			
	1944. Blue.			
	a. Forbes Lithograph Corp. Wmk: *MILITARY AUTHORITY* (generally w/o parts of words, rarely w/parts of words visible).	.75	2.00	8.00
	b. In England. Wmk: Wavy lines.	.40	1.00	4.00

		VG	VF	UNC
105	**5 SCHILLING** 1944. Lilac.	.40	1.00	5.00
106	**10 SCHILLING** 1944. Green.	.40	1.00	6.00
107	**20 SCHILLING** 1944. Blue on violet unpt.	1.25	3.00	8.50
108	**25 SCHILLING** 1944. Brown on lilac unpt.	40.00	85.00	150.00
	a. Issued note.	50.00	75.00	160.00
	r. Replacement w/small "x" to r. of serial #.	250.00	600.00	1000.
109	**50 SCHILLING** 1944. Brown on yellow-brown unpt.	2.00	5.00	12.50
110	**100 SCHILLING** 1944. Green.			
	a. Serial # prefix fraction w/o line.	2.00	5.00	12.50
	b. Serial # prefix fraction w/line.	3.00	7.50	15.00
111	**1000 SCHILLING** 1944. Blue on green and m/c unpt.	50.00	125.00	425.00

RUSSIAN OCCUPATION - WWII

REPUBLIK ÖSTERREICH

1945 ISSUE
Issued (20.12.1945) during the Russian occupation.

		VG	VF	UNC
112	**50 REICHSPFENNING** ND. Brown on orange unpt. Specimen stamped and perforated: *MUSTER.*	—	—	165.00
113	**1 REICHSMARK** ND. Green.			
	a. Space below *1* at l. and *Reichs-/mark* 3mm.	3.00	8.00	20.00
	b. Space below *1* at l. and *Reichs-/mark* 3mm.	3.00	8.00	20.00

REPUBLIC - POST WWII

OESTERREICHISCHE NATIONALBANK

AUSTRIAN NATIONAL BANK

1945 ISSUES

		VG	VF	UNC
114	**10 SCHILLING** 29.5.1945. Blue and violet. 2 serial # varieties. Woman in national costume. Back: Arms above Grossglockner mountain at top	.25	1.00	6.50
115	**10 SCHILLING** 29.5.1945. Blue. Woman in national costume at top. 2 serial # varieties. *ZWEITE AUSGABE* in lower design (2nd issue). Back: Mountains.	2.00	7.50	25.00

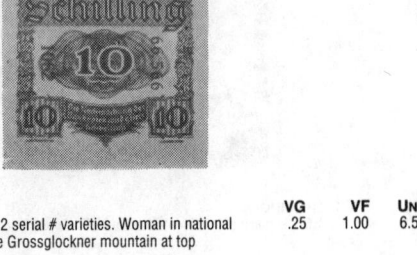

		VG	VF	UNC
116	**20 SCHILLING** 29.5.1945. Blue-green. Girl at l., farmer at r. Many color variations, 2 serial # varieties. Back: Farmer in field	.25	1.00	7.50

		VG	VF	UNC
117	**50 SCHILLING** 29.5.1945. Dk. green on brown unpt. Hubert Sterrer as youth at r. Many color varieties. Back: Bldg. and lake scene	2.50	7.50	30.00

		VG	VF	UNC
118	**100 SCHILLING** 29.5.1945. Blue-violet. Woman (allegory of the sciences) at r. Many color varieties. Back: Academy of Sciences in Vienna at ctr.	.25	1.00	7.50
119	**100 SCHILLING** 29.5.1945. Blue-violet. Woman (allegory of the sciences) at r., w/*ZWEITE AUSGABE* vertically at r. (2nd issue). Many color varieties. Back: Academy of Sciences in Vienna at ctr.	30.00	75.00	200.00

		VG	VF	UNC
120	**1000 SCHILLING** 29.5.1945. Green. Woman w/figure of Athena at upper r. Back: Salzburg in mountains	60.00	150.00	400.00

1945-47 ISSUE

		VG	VF	UNC
121	**5 SCHILLING** 4.9.1945. Blue or violet on gray-green unpt. Many color varieties. Portr. Prof. Dr. H. Brücke w/compass at l. Back: Terraced mountain iron mining near Eisenerz (Steirmark) at top l. ctr.	.50	1.50	10.00

122	10 SCHILLING	VG	VF	UNC
	2.2.1946. Brown and m/c. Portr. woman at upper r. Back: Mint tower in Solbad Hall (Tirol) at top ctr.	.75	3.50	25.00

128	10 SCHILLING	VG	VF	UNC
(129)	2.1.1950. Violet. Bldgs. at lower l. ctr., horseman of the Spanish Royal Riding School at r. Back: Belvedere Castle in Vienna at l. ctr. Ovpt: *2 AUFLAGE* on back (2nd Ovpt: issue).	1.00	2.00	12.50

123	20 SCHILLING	VG	VF	UNC
	2.2.1946. Brown and m/c. Woman at ctr. Back: St. Stephen's church in Vienna at ctr.	2.00	15.00	50.00

124	100 SCHILLING	VG	VF	UNC
	2.1.1947. Dk. green on violet, blue and m/c unpt. Portr. woman in national costume at r. Back: Lilac and green. Mountain scene.	15.00	45.00	150.00
125	1000 SCHILLING			
	1.9.1947. Dk. brown on gray green unpt. Woman w/figure of Athena at upper r., w/*ZWEITE AUSGABE* vertically at l. (2nd issue). Back: Salzburg in mountains	100.00	300.00	600.00

129	20 SCHILLING	VG	VF	UNC
(130)	2.1.1950. Brown on red and blue unpt. Portr. Joseph Haydn at r. Back: Tower at l., cherub playing kettledrum at ctr.			
	a. *OESTERREICHISCHE* in unpt.	1.00	3.00	10.00
	b. Error in bank name *OESTERREICHISCEE* in unpt. (Error visible in second or third line at bottom of unpt. at bottom).	15.00	30.00	65.00

1949-54 ISSUES

126	5 SCHILLING	VG	VF	UNC
(131)	1951. Violet on gray-green. Portr. Prof. Dr. H. Brücke w/compass at l., w/*AUSGABE* in l. margin. Back: Terraced mountain iron mining Eisenerz (Steirmark) at top l. ctr.	1.00	3.00	15.00

127	10 SCHILLING	VG	VF	UNC
(128)	2.1.1950. Violet. Bldgs. at lower l. ctr., horseman of the Spanish Royal Riding School at r. Back: Belvedere Castle in Vienna at l. ctr.	.50	1.50	12.50

130	50 SCHILLING	VG	VF	UNC
(132)	2.1.1951. Lilac and violet on m/c unpt. Portr. J. Prandtauer at r. Back: Woman, cloister at Melk at l.	4.00	15.00	55.00

132	100 SCHILLING	VG	VF	UNC
(127)	3.1.1949. Dk. green on lilac and purple unpt. Cherub at lower l., woman's head at upper r. Back: Olive green and purple; mermaid at l. ctr., Vienna in background. Ovpt: *2 AUFLAGE* at lower l. Ovpt: (2nd issue).	7.00	15.00	40.00

133	100 SCHILLING	VG	VF	UNC
(134)	2.1.1953. Green on m/c unpt. F. Grillparzer at r. Back: Castle Dürnstein	9.00	15.00	40.00

		VG	VF	UNC
134 (133)	**500 SCHILLING** 2.1.1954. Dk. brown on blue and red unpt. Prof. Wagner-Jauregg at r. Back: University of Vienna	45.00	75.00	150.00

		VG	VF	UNC
135	**1000 SCHILLING** 2.1.1954. Blue on m/c unpt. A. Bruckner at r. Back: Bruckner organ at St. Florian	90.00	140.00	250.00

1956-65 ISSUE

		VG	VF	UNC
136	**20 SCHILLING** 2.7.1956. Brown on red-brown and olive unpt. A. von Welsbach at r., arms at l. Maria Rain Church and Karawanken mountains on back.	1.50	7.00	12.00

		VG	VF	UNC
138	**100 SCHILLING** 1.7.1960. Dk. green on violet and m/c unpt. Violin and music at lower l., J. Strauss at r., arms at l. Schönbrunn Castle on back.	5.00	14.00	30.00

AZERBAIJAN

The Republic of Azerbaijan (formerly Azerbaijan S.S.R.) includes the Nakhichevan Autonomous Republic and Nagorno-Karabakh Autonomous Region (which was abolished in 1991). Situated in the eastern area of Transcaucasia, it is bordered in the west by Armenia, in the north by Georgia and Dagestan, to the east by the Caspian Sea and to the south by Iran. It has an area of 33,430 sq. mi. (86,600 sq. km.) and a population of 7.1 million. Capital: Baku. The area is rich in mineral deposits of aluminum, copper, iron, lead, salt and zinc, with oil as its leading industry. Agriculture and livestock follow in importance.

In ancient times home of Scythian tribes and known under the Romans as Albania and to the Arabs as Arran, the country of Azerbaijan formed at the time of its invasion by Seljuk Turks a prosperous state under Persian suzerainty. From the 16th century the country was a theatre of fighting and political rivalry between Turkey, Persia and later Russia. Baku was first annexed to Russia by Czar Peter I in 1723 and remained under Russian rule for 12 years. After the Russian retreat the whole of Azerbaijan north of the Aras River became a khanate under Persian control until Czar Alexander I, after an eight-year war with Persia, annexed it in 1813 to the Russian empire.

Until the Russian Revolution of 1905 there was no political life in Azerbaijan. A Mussavat (Equality) party was formed in 1911 by Mohammed Emin Rasulzade, a former Social Democrat. After the Russian Revolution of March 1917, the party started a campaign for independence, but Baku, the capital, with its mixed population, constituted an alien enclave in the country. While a national Azerbaijani government was established at Gandzha (Elizavetpol), a Communist-controlled council assumed power at Baku with Stepan Shaumian, an Armenian, at its head. The Gandzha government joined first, on Sept. 20, 1917, a Transcaucasian federal republic, but on May 28, 1918, proclaimed the independence of Azerbaijan. On June 4, 1918, at Batum, a peace treaty was signed with Turkey and a Turko-Azerbaijani force started an offensive against Baku, but it was occupied on Aug. 17, 0918 by 1,400 British troops coming by sea from Anzali, Persia. On Sept. 14 the British evacuated Baku, returning to Anzali, and three days later the Azerbaijan government, headed by Fath Ali Khan Khoysky, established itself at Baku.

After the collapse of the Ottoman empire the British returned to Baku, at first ignoring the Azerbaijan government. A general election with universal suffrage for the Azerbaijan constituent assembly took place on Dec. 7, 1918 and out of 120 members there were 84 Mussavat supporters; Ali Marden Topchibashev was elected speaker, and Nasib Usubekov formed a new government. On Jan. 15, 1920, the Allied powers recognized Azerbaijan de facto, but on April 27 of the same year the Red army invaded the country, and a Soviet republic of Azerbaijan was proclaimed the next day. Later it became a member of the Transcaucasian Federation joining the U.S.S.R. on Dec. 30, 1922; it became a self-constituent republic in 1936.

The Azerbaijan Communist party held its first congress at Baku in Feb. 1920. From 1921 to 1925 its first secretary was a Russian, S.M. Kirov, who directed a mass deportation to Siberia of about 120,000 Azerbaijani "nationalist deviationists," among them the country's first two premiers.

In 1990 it adopted a declaration of republican sovereignty, and in Aug. 1991 declared itself formally independent; this action was approved by a vote of referendum in Jan. 1992. It announced its intention of joining the CIS in Dec. 1991, but a parliamentary resolution of Oct. 1992 declined to confirm its involvement. Communist President Mutaibov was relieved of his office in May, 1992. A National Council replaced Mutaibov and on June 7 elected Abulfez Elchibey in the first democratic election in the country's history. Surat Huseynov led a military coup against Elchibey and seized power on June 30, 1993. Huseynov became prime minister with former communist Geidar Aliyev, president.

Fighting commenced between Muslim forces of Azerbaijan and Christian forces of Armenia in 1992 and continued through early 1994. Each fraction claimed the Nagomo-Karabakh, an Armenian ethnic enclave, in Azerbaijan. A cease-fire was declared in May, 1994.

AUTONOMOUS REPUBLIC
Independent from May 26, 1918 to April 30, 1920, when it was conquered by Bolshevik forces.

AZERBAIJAN REPUBLIC

АЗЕРБАИДЖАНСКАЯ РЕСПУБЛИКА

1919 FIRST ISSUE
Many variations of color, paper and serial # are known.

		VG	VF	UNC
1	**25 RUBLES** 1919. Lilac and brown.	1.50	5.00	15.00

2	50 RUBLES	VG	VF	UNC
	1919. Blue-green and brown.	1.75	6.00	18.00

AZERBAIJAN GOVERNMENT
АЭРБАИДЖАНСКОЕ ПРАВИТЕЛЬСТВО

1919 SECOND ISSUE

1919 ISSUE

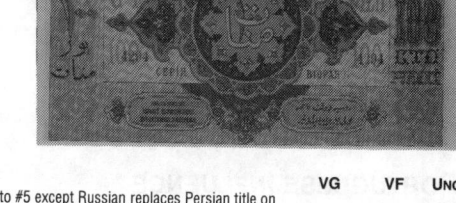

5	100 RUBLES	VG	VF	UNC
	1919. Brown. Similar to #9 except Persian replaces Russian title on face, different Russian title on back.	1.75	6.00	18.00
6	250 RUBLES			
	1919. Lilac, brown and green.			
	a. Issued note.	2.00	6.50	20.00
	p. Green, brown and rose. Proof.	—	—	120.00

9 (3)	100 RUBLES	VG	VF	UNC
	1919. Brown. Similar to #5 except Russian replaces Persian title on face, different Russian title on back.			
	a. W/o series on back.	2.25	7.50	22.50
	b. W/СЕРІЯ (ВТОРАЯ) series on back.	2.25	7.50	22.50

1920 FIRST ISSUE

Issuer name in Arabic and French: Republique d'Azerbaidjan.

NOTE: For note issues as a Socialist Soviet Republic, 1920-23, refer to Volume 1 - Russia/Transcaucasia. The latter series of #7 fall, by rights, in the time of the Soviet Republic of Azerbaijan.

7	500 RUBLES	VG	VF	UNC
	1920. Dk. brown and dull gray-green on lilac and m/c unpt. Series I-LV.	2.25	7.50	22.50

1920 SECOND ISSUE

8	1 RUBLE			
	1920. Unfinished proof print.	—	35.00	70.00

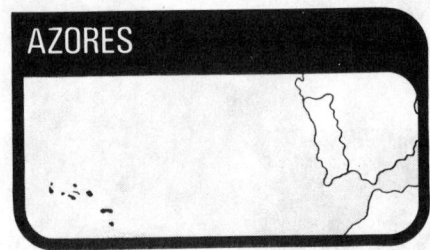

AZORES

The Azores, an archipelago of nine islands of volcanic origin, are located in the Atlantic Ocean 740 miles (1,190 km.) west of Cape de Roca, Portugal. They are under the administration of Portugal, and have an area of 902 sq. mi. (2,336 sq. km.) and a population of 252,000. Principal city: Ponta Delgada. The natives are mainly of Portuguese descent and earn their livelihood by fishing, wine making, basket weaving, and the growing of fruit, grains and sugar cane. Pineapples are the chief item of export. The climate is particularly temperate, making the islands a favorite winter resort.

The Azores were discovered about 1427 by the Portuguese navigator Diago de Silves. Portugal secured the islands in the 15th century and established the first settlement, on Santa Maria, about 1432. From 1580 to 1640 the Azores were subject to Spain.

Angra on Terceira Island became the capital of the captaincy-general of the Azores in 1766 and it was here in 1826 that the constitutionalists set up a pro-Pedro government in opposition to King Miguel in Lisbon. The whole Portuguese fleet attacked Terceira Island and was repelled at Praia, after which Azoreans, Brazilians and British mercenaries defeated Miguel in Portugal. Maria de Gloria, Pedro's daughter, was proclaimed queen of Portugal on Terceira Island in 1828.

A U.S. naval base was established at Ponta Delgada in 1917.

After World War II, the islands acquired a renewed importance as a refueling stop for transatlantic air transport. The United States maintains defense bases in the Azores as part of the collective security program of NATO.

Since 1976 the Azores are an Autonomous Region with a regional government and parliament.

RULERS:
Portuguese

MONETARY SYSTEM:
1 Milreis = 1000 Reis to 1910
1 Escudo = 100 Centavos 1910-

PORTUGUESE INFLUENCE

BANCO DE PORTUGAL

1876-85 ISSUE

#1-3 ovpt: *S. MIGUEL*. Hand dated.

		GOOD	FINE	XF
1	**5 MIL REIS**	—	Rare	—
	1.12.1885. Blue. Standing figure at l. and r., arms at lower ctr. Arms at ctr. on back. Red ovpt.: *PAGAVEL NA AGENCIA DE S. MIGUEL EM MOEDA INSULANA PRATA* on face at lower ctr., on back in each corner.			
2	**10 MIL REIS**	—	Rare	—
	28.1.1878. Blue. Ovpt. on Portugal #20A.			
3	**20 MIL REIS**	—	Rare	—
	30.8.1876. Blue and brown. Portr. of Kg. w/crown above at upper ctr. Back lt. brown.			

1895 ISSUE

#4-7 w/inscription: *Pagavel nos Agencias dos Açôres*.

		GOOD	FINE	XF
4 (A1)	**5 MIL REIS** 1.10.1895. Lt. blue. Allegorical figure at l., arms at upper ctr. Arms at ctr. on back.	—	Rare	—
5 (A2)	**10 MIL REIS** 1.10.1895. Lt. brown. Allegorical figure of Agriculture at l., Commerce at r. Standing figure at l. and r. on back.	—	Rare	—
6 (A3)	**20 MIL REIS** 1.10.1895. Orange. Allegorical figure of Industry at l., Commerce at r. Bakc blue on dk. orange unpt.	—	Rare	—
7 (A4)	**50 MIL REIS** 1.10.1895. Red. Allegorical figure of Industry at l., Commerce at r., arms at lower ctr. Back red and blue; arms at ctr.	—	Rare	—

1905-10 ISSUES

#8-14 ovpt: *MOEDA INSULANA*, w/ or w/o lg. *ACRES* diagonally on face in red between bars of *ACRES* one or more times on face and back. Regular issue Portuguese types and designs are used, though colors may vary. Notes payable in silver (prata) or gold (ouro). This issue circulated unitl 1932.

		GOOD	FINE	XF
8 (1)	**2 1/2 MILREIS PRATA** 30.6.1906; 30.7.1909. Black on orange, blue and olive unpt. Ovpt. on Portugal #8.			
	a. Face w/o diagonal ovpt: *ACORES*.	40.00	100.00	250.00
	b. Face w/red ovpt: *ACORES*.	40.00	100.00	250.00

		GOOD	FINE	XF
9 (2)	**5 MILREIS PRATA** 30.1.1905. Black, green and brown. Ovpt. on Portugal #17.	200.00	400.00	850.00

		GOOD	FINE	XF
10 (3)	**10 MILREIS OURO** 30.1.1905. Blue on lt. green unpt. Like Portugal #21, but different color.	300.00	650.00	1500.

		GOOD	FINE	XF
11 (3A)	**10 MILREIS OURO** 30.1.1905. Brown and yellow. Ovpt. on Portugal #21.	200.00	500.00	1000.

		GOOD	FINE	XF
12 (4)	**10 MILREIS OURO** 30.9.1910. Green on lt. tan unpt. Ovpt. on design type of Portugal #22.	200.00	600.00	1200.

13
(5) **20 MILREIS OURO**
30.1.1905. Brown and lt. red. Ovpt. on Portugal #23.

	GOOD	FINE	XF
	250.00	600.00	1200.

14
(6) **50 MILREIS OURO**
30.1.1905. Blue-gray. Back: Blue on red unpt. Ovpt. on design type of Portugal #28.

	GOOD	FINE	XF
	400.00	1100.	1850.

BAHAMAS

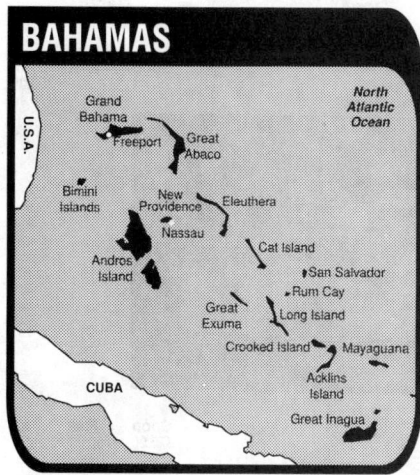

The Commonwealth of The Bahamas is an archipelago of about 3,000 islands, cays and rocks located in the Atlantic Ocean east of Florida and north of Cuba. The total land area of the 800-mile (1.287 km.) long chain of islands is 5,380 sq. mi. (13,935 sq. km.). They have a population of 255,000. Capital: Nassau. The Bahamas imports most of their food and manufactured products and exports cement, refined oil, pulpwood and lobsters. Tourism is the principal industry.

The Bahamas were discovered by Columbus in October, 1492, but Spain made no attempt to settle them. British influence began in 1626 when Charles I granted them to the lord proprietors of Carolina. They continued under British proprietors until 1717, when the civil and military governments were surrendered to the King and the islands designated a British Crown Colony. The Bahamas obtained complete internal self-government under the constitution of Jan. 7, 1964. Full independence was achieved on July 10, 1973. The Bahamas is a member of the Commonwealth of Nations. The Queen of England is Chief of State.

RULERS:
British

MONETARY SYSTEM:
1 Shilling = 12 Pence
1 Pound = 20 Shillings to 1966
1 Dollar = 100 Cents 1966-

BRITISH INFLUENCE

BANK OF NASSAU

ND ISSUE (CA. 1870'S)
#A1-A4A printer: CS&E.

A1 **5 SHILLINGS**
18xx. Red. Portr. Qn. Victoria at upper l. Specimen.

	GOOD	FINE	XF
	—	—	350.00

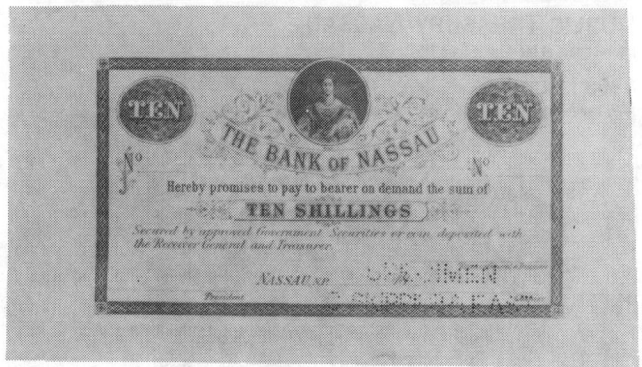

		GOOD	FINE	XF
A2	**10 SHILLINGS** 18xx. Red. Qn. Victoria at top ctr. Specimen.	—	—	350.00
A3	**10 SHILLINGS** 18xx. Blue. Specimen.		—	350.00
A4	**10 SHILLINGS** 18xx. Brown.		—	350.00
A4A	**1 POUND** 18xx. Lt. orange. Qn. Victoria at ctr. Specimen.		—	350.00

1897 ISSUE
#A4B-A7 ship seal at l., portr. man at r. Uniface.

		GOOD	FINE	XF
A4B	**5 SHILLINGS** 18xx. Black.	—	—	350.00

		GOOD	FINE	XF
A5	**5 SHILLINGS** 28.1.1897; 3.4.1902. Blue.	375.00	750.00	1650.

		GOOD	FINE	XF
A7	**1 POUND** 190x. Blue.	450.00	950.00	1850.

1906 ISSUE
#A8-A8B ship seal at l., portr. man at r. Uniface.

		GOOD	FINE	XF
A8	**4 SHILLINGS** 11.5.1906; 22.10.1910; 19.3.1913; 16.4.1913; 21.0.1916. Green.	375.00	800.00	1750.
	Printer: CS&E.			
A8A	**1 POUND** 190x. Black. Back: Red-brown. Unsigned remainder.	—	—	—
A8B	**1 POUND** 190x. Dp. green. Proof.	—	—	—

PUBLIC TREASURY/NASSAU
Interest paid at least until June 1973.

1868 ISSUE
#A9, handwritten dates 1868-1869. Various date and sign. varieties.

		GOOD	FINE	XF
A9	**1 POUND** 4.11.1868. Circular Public Treasury seal at upper l.	—	Rare	—

BAHAMAS GOVERNMENT

1869 ISSUE
#A10 and A11 circular Public Treasury seal at upper l. Printer: Major and Knapp.

		GOOD	FINE	XF
A10	**1 POUND** 1.2.1869. Black on lt. blue unpt.	—	Rare	—

		GOOD	FINE	XF
A11	**5 POUNDS** 1.2.1869; 1.2.1869. Black on red-violet unpt.	—	Rare	—

1919 CURRENCY NOTE ACT
#2-4 donkey cart at l., ship seal at ctr., bushes at r. Printer: CBNC (w/o imprint).

		GOOD	FINE	XF
1	**4 SHILLINGS** L.1919. Ship seal at r. Gov't bldg. on back.	—	Rare	—
2 (1)	**4 SHILLINGS** L.1919. Black on green unpt. Back: Green.			
	a. No serial # prefix. Sign. H. E. W. Grant at l.	125.00	350.00	1250.
	b. Serial # prefix A. Sign. A. C. Burns at l.	100.00	275.00	950.00
3 (2)	**10 SHILLINGS** L.1919. Black on red unpt. Back: Red.			
	a. No serial # prefix. Sign. H. E. W. Grant at l.	250.00	1000.	—
	b. Serial # prefix A. Sign. A. C. Burns at l.	250.00	1000.	—
4 (3)	**1 POUND** L.1919. Black on gray unpt. Back: Black.			
	a. No serial # prefix. Sign. H. E. W. Grant at l.	225.00	850.00	3000.
	b. Serial # prefix A. Sign. A. C. Burns at l.	225.00	800.00	2500.

1919 CURRENCY NOTE ACT (1930)
#5-7 ship seal at l., Kg. George V at r. Printer: W&S. Sign. varieties.

		GOOD	FINE	XF
5	**4 SHILLINGS** L.1919 (1930). Green.	75.00	225.00	850.00

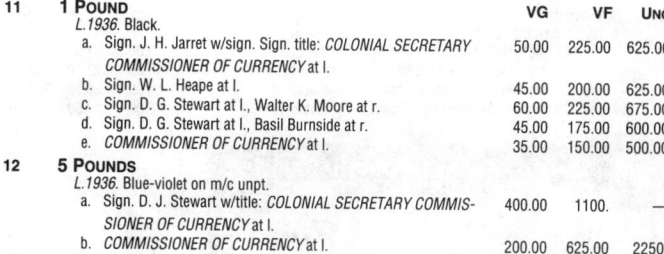

			VG	VF	UNC
11	**1 POUND**				
	L.1936. Black.				
	a. Sign. J. H. Jarret w/sign. Sign. title: *COLONIAL SECRETARY*	50.00	225.00	625.00
	COMMISSIONER OF CURRENCY at l.			
	b. Sign. W. L. Heape at l.	45.00	200.00	625.00
	c. Sign. D. G. Stewart at l., Walter K. Moore at r.	60.00	225.00	675.00
	d. Sign. D. G. Stewart at l., Basil Burnside at r.	45.00	175.00	600.00
	e. *COMMISSIONER OF CURRENCY* at l.	35.00	150.00	500.00
12	**5 POUNDS**				
	L.1936. Blue-violet on m/c unpt.				
	a. Sign. D. J. Stewart w/title: *COLONIAL SECRETARY COMMIS-*	400.00	1100.	—
	SIONER OF CURRENCY at l.			
	b. *COMMISSIONER OF CURRENCY* at l.	200.00	625.00	2250.

		GOOD	FINE	XF
6	**10 SHILLINGS**	175.00	650.00	—
	L.1919 (1930). Red.			

COMMONWEALTH

GOVERNMENT OF THE BAHAMAS
Replacement notes: Z prefix.

1953 ISSUE

		GOOD	FINE	XF
7	**1 POUND**	125.00	350.00	925.00
	L.1919 (1930). Black.			

1936 CURRENCY NOTE ACT
#9-11 ship seal at l., Kg. George VI at r. Sign. varieties. Printer: TDLR.

		VG	VF	UNC
13	**4 SHILLINGS**			
	ND (1953). Green.			
	a. Ctr. sign. H. R. Latreille, Basil Burnside at r.	1.50	15.00	85.00
	b. Ctr. sign. W. H. Sweeting, Basil Burnside at r.	1.00	10.00	65.00
	c. Ctr. sign. W. H. Sweeting, Chas. P. Bethel at r.	1.00	12.50	75.00
	d. Ctr. sign. W. H. Sweeting, George W. K. Roberts at r.	1.00	7.50	45.00

		VG	VF	UNC
9	**4 SHILLINGS**			
	L.1936. Green.			
	a. Sign. J. H. Jarret w/sign. Sign. title: *COLONIAL SECRETARY*	20.00	85.00	450.00
	COMMISSIONER OF CURRENCY at l.			
	b. Sign. W. L. Heape at l.	15.00	60.00	375.00
	c. Sign. D. G. Stewart at l., Walter K. Moore at r.	20.00	75.00	375.00
	d. Sign. D. G. Stewart at l., Basil Burnside at r.	20.00	85.00	400.00
	e. *COMMISSIONER OF CURRENCY* at l.	8.00	40.00	275.00

		VG	VF	UNC
14	**10 SHILLINGS**			
	ND (1953). Red.			
	a. Ctr. sign. H. R. Latreille, Basil Burnside at r.	4.00	25.00	165.00
	b. Ctr. sign. W. H. Sweeting, Basil Burnside at r.	4.00	17.50	125.00
	c. Ctr. sign. W. H. Sweeting, Chas. P. Bethel at r.	4.00	20.00	150.00
	d. Ctr. sign. W. H. Sweeting, George W. K. Roberts at r.	2.00	12.50	90.00

		VG	VF	UNC
10	**10 SHILLINGS**			
	L.1936. Red.			
	a. Sign. J. H. Jarret w/sign. Sign. title: *COLONIAL SECRETARY*	40.00	250.00	625.00
	COMMISSIONER OF CURRENCY at l.			
	b. Sign. W. L. Heape at l.	30.00	225.00	525.00
	c. Sign. O. G. Stewart at l., Walter K. Moore at r.	30.00	225.00	525.00
	d. *COMMISSIONER OF CURRENCY* at l.	20.00	85.00	375.00

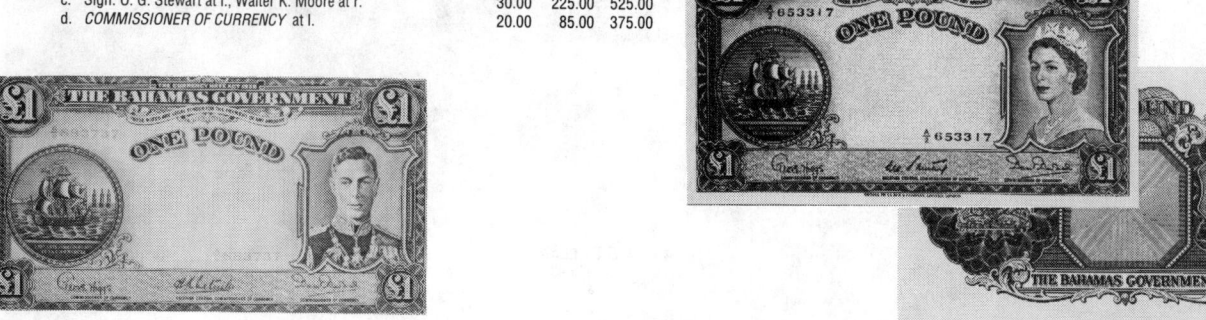

15	**1 POUND**		VG	VF	UNC
	ND (1953). Black.				
	a. Ctr. sign. H. R. Latreille, Basil Burnside at r.		5.00	27.50	285.00
	b. Ctr. sign. W. H. Sweeting, Basil Burnside at r.		5.00	22.50	235.00
	c. Ctr. sign. W. H. Sweeting, Chas. P. Bethel at r.		5.00	28.50	265.00
	d. Ctr. sign. W. H. Sweeting, George W. K. Roberts at r.		3.00	17.50	185.00

16	**5 POUNDS**		VG	VF	UNC
	ND (1953). Blue.				
	a. Ctr. sign. H. R. Latreille, Basil Burnside at r.		—	Rare	—
	b. Ctr. sign. W. H. Sweeting, Basil Burnside at r.		40.00	350.00	1350.
	c. Ctr. sign. W. H. Sweeting, Chas. P. Bethel at r.		50.00	375.00	1500.
	d. Ctr. sign. W. H. Sweeting, George W. K. Roberts at r.		37.50	300.00	1250.

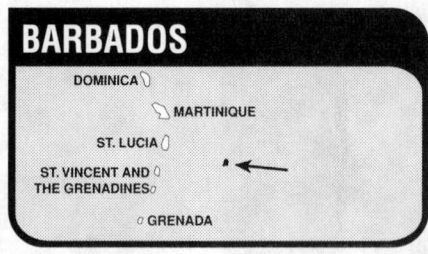

BARBADOS

- DOMINICA
- MARTINIQUE
- ST. LUCIA
- ST. VINCENT AND THE GRENADINES
- GRENADA

Barbados, an independent state within the British Commonwealth, is located in the Windward Islands of the West Indies east of St. Vincent. The coral island has an area of 166 sq. mi. (431 sq. km) and a population of 258,600. Capital: Bridgetown. The economy is based on sugar and tourism. Sugar, petroleum products, molasses and rum are exported.

Barbados was named by the Portuguese who achieved the first landing on the island in 1563. British sailors landed at the site of present-day Holetown in 1624. Barbados was under uninterrupted British control from the time of the first British settlement in 1627 until it obtained independence on Nov. 30, 1966. It is a member of the Commonwealth of Nations. The Queen of England is Chief of State.

Barbados was included in the issues of the British Caribbean Territories - Eastern Group and later the East Caribbean Currency Authority until 1973.

RULERS:
British to 1966

MONETARY SYSTEM:
- 1 Dollar = 100 Cents, 1950-
- 1 British West Indies Dollar = 4 Shillings - 2 Pence
- 5 British West Indies Dollars = 1 Pound - 10 Pence

BRITISH INFLUENCE

GOVERNMENT OF BARBADOS

1915 ISSUE

1	**1 POUND**		GOOD	FINE	XF
	1915-17. (28,000 issued).		—	—	—

1938-43 ISSUE

#2-6 Neptune on seahorse cart at l., Kg. George VI at r. Various dates and sign. varieties. Wmk: 2 horse heads. Printer: BWC.

2	**1 DOLLAR**	VG	VF	UNC
	1938-49. Green, brown-violet and m/c.			
	a. 3.1.1938.	20.00	85.00	475.00
	b. 1.9.1939; 1.12.1939; 1.6.1943.	15.00	80.00	425.00
	c. 1.1.1949.	30.00	100.00	475.00
3	**2 DOLLARS**	GOOD	FINE	XF
	1938-49. Brown and green.			
	a. 3.1.1938.	40.00	150.00	575.00
	b. 1.9.1939; 1.12.1939; 1.6.1943.	35.00	125.00	500.00
	c. 1.1.1949.	50.00	200.00	600.00

4	**5 DOLLARS**	GOOD	FINE	XF
	1939-43. Purple and blue.			
	a. 1.9.1939; 1.12.1939.	50.00	200.00	500.00
	b. 1.6.1943.	40.00	125.00	450.00

Belgian Congo (now the Republic of Zaire), located in the south-central part of Africa, has an area of 905,378 sq. mi. (2,344,920 sq. km.) and a population of 13.6 million. Capital: Leopoldville. The mineral-rich country produces copper, tin, diamonds, gold, zinc, cobalt and uranium. In ancient times the territory comprising the Belgium Congo was occupied by Negrito peoples (Pygmies) pushed into the mountains by Bantu and Nilotic invaders. The interior was first explored by the American correspondent Henry Stanley, who was subsequently commissioned by King Leopold II of Belgium to conclude development treaties with the local chiefs. The Berlin conference of 1885 awarded the area to Leopold, who administered and exploited it as his private property until it was annexed to Belgium in 1907. Belgium received the mandate for the German territories of Ruanda-Urundi as a result of the international treaties after WWI. During WWII Belgian Congolese troops fought on the side of the Allies, notably in Ethiopia. Following the eruption of bloody independence riots in 1959, Belgium granted the Belgian Congo independence as the Republic of the Congo on June 30, 1960.

RULERS:
 Leopold II, 1885-1907
 Belgium, 1907-1960

MONETARY SYSTEM:
 1 Franc = 100 Centimes to 1967

	20 DOLLARS	GOOD	FINE	XF
5	1.6.1943. Pink and green.			
	a. 1.6.1943.	500.00	600.00	2000.
	s. Specimen.	—	Unc	1350.

	100 DOLLARS	GOOD	FINE	XF
6	1.6.1943. Brown and black. (One verified).			
	a. 1.6.1943.	—	Rare	—
	s. Specimen.	—	Unc	2750.

CONGO FREE STATE

ETAT INDEPENDANT DU CONGO

INDEPENDENT STATE OF THE CONGO

1896 ISSUE
#1 and 2 also circulated in Belgium in 1914. Issued in Bruxelles. Printer: W&S.

	10 FRANCS	GOOD	FINE	XF
1	7.2.1896. Child holding cornucopia at ctr. Back: Woman's head at l.			
	a. Issued note.	550.00	900.00	—
	b. Remainder w/o date or sign.	—	—	1600.
	c. As a. Punched hole cancellation.	150.00	300.00	1000.

	100 FRANCS	GOOD	FINE	XF
2	7.2.1896. Brown unpt. Woman seated holding caduceus at l. ctr., lion at upper r. Back: Portr. woman at ctr.			
	a. Issued note.	650.00	1250.	—
	b. Remainder w/o date or sign.	—	—	2000.
	c. As a. Punched hole cancelled.	175.00	350.00	1100.

BELGIAN CONGO

BANQUE DU CONGO BELGE

BANK OF THE BELGIAN CONGO

1914 ISSUE

#3-4C Various date and sign. varieties. Printer: W&S.

#3A *Deleted*

			GOOD	FINE	XF
3	1 FRANC	9.10.1914; 9.1.1920; 2.6.1920. Black on red unpt. Woman seated w/sheaf of grain and wheel at l. *ELISABETHVILLE*.	40.00	100.00	200.00

			GOOD	FINE	XF
3B	1 FRANC	15.10.1914; 15.1.1920; 26.6.1920. Black on red unpt. Woman seated w/sheaf of grain and wheel at l. *MATADI*.	20.00	50.00	125.00
4	5 FRANCS	9.10.1914; 2.3.1920; 2.4.1921; 2.4.1924. Black on blue unpt. Woman seated w/child at l. *ELIZABETHVILLE*. Back: Elephant and hippo at ctr.	30.00	85.00	250.00
4A	5 FRANCS	26.10.1914; 19.2.1919; 3.3.1920; 3.6.1920; 3.4.1921; 3.4.1924. Black on blue unpt. Woman seated w/child at l. *KINSHASA*. Back: Elephant and hippo at ctr.	30.00	85.00	250.00

			GOOD	FINE	XF
4B	5 FRANCS	15.10.1914; 26.3.1920; 26.4.1921. Black on pale blue unpt. Woman seated w/child by beehive at l. *MATADI*. Back: Elephant and hippo at ctr.	20.00	70.00	200.00
4C	5 FRANCS	30.10.1914; 4.4.1921. Black on blue unpt. Woman seated w/child at l. *STANLEYVILLE*. Back: Elephant and hippo at ctr.	20.00	70.00	200.00

1912-37 ISSUE

#8-12 wmk: Elephant's head. Printer BNB (w/o imprint).

			GOOD	FINE	XF
8	5 FRANCS	1924-30. Red, brown and green. Huts, palm trees at l. Back: River steamboat.			
		a. Ovpt: *ELISABETHVILLE*. 2.12.1924; 2.7.1926.	20.00	85.00	300.00
		b. *LEOPOLDVILLE*. 3.12.1924; 3.7.1926.	20.00	85.00	300.00
		c. Ovpt: *MATADI*. 15.10.1924; 26.12.1924; 26.6.1926; 26.7.1926; 21.1.1929.	20.00	85.00	300.00
		d. Ovpt: *STANLEYVILLE*. 4.12.1924; 4.7.1926.	20.00	85.00	300.00
		e. Ovpt: W/o office. 21.1.1929; 4.4.1930.	12.50	50.00	225.00

		GOOD	FINE	XF
9	10 FRANCS			
	10.9.1937. Brown. Market scene. Back: Water bucks, trees at ctr. r.	30.00	100.00	350.00

		GOOD	FINE	XF
10	20 FRANCS			
	1912-37. Green. Portr. Ceres at upper l., woman kneeling w/hammer and anvil, native woman reclining w/elephant tusk at l. Back: Village on the waterfront and canoe.			
	a. Ovpt: *ELISABETHVILLE*. 2.11.1920; 2.10.1925; 2.7.1926; 2.7.1927.	120.00	360.00	900.00
	b. Ovpt: *KINSHASA*. 10.9.1912; 3.5.1914; 3.3.1917; 3.3.1920; 3.11.1920.	135.00	400.00	1000.
	c. Ovpt: *LEOPOLDVILLE*. 3.10.1925; 3.7.1926; 3.7.1927.	135.00	400.00	1000.
	d. Ovpt: *MATADI*. 26.4.1914; 26.3.1920; 26.11.1920; 26.7.1926; 26.6.1927.	135.00	400.00	1000.
	e. Ovpt: *STANLEYVILLE*. 10.9.1912; 4.3.1920; 4.10.1925; 4.7.1926; 4.7.1927.	135.00	400.00	1000.
	f. Ovpt: W/o office. 1.2.1929; 15.9.1937.	40.00	100.00	300.00

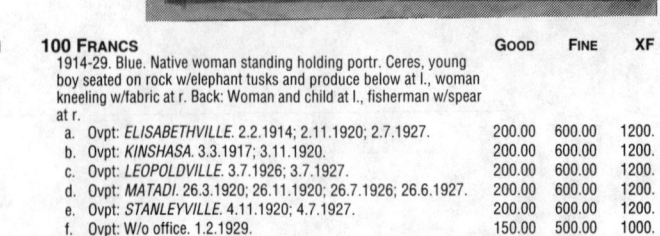

		GOOD	FINE	XF
11	100 FRANCS			
	1914-29. Blue. Native woman standing holding portr. Ceres, young boy seated on rock w/elephant tusks and produce below at l., woman kneeling w/fabric at r. Back: Woman and child at l., fisherman w/spear at r.			
	a. Ovpt: *ELISABETHVILLE*. 2.2.1914; 2.11.1920; 2.7.1927.	200.00	600.00	1200.
	b. Ovpt: *KINSHASA*. 3.3.1917; 3.11.1920.	200.00	600.00	1200.
	c. Ovpt: *LEOPOLDVILLE*. 3.7.1926; 3.7.1927.	200.00	600.00	1200.
	d. Ovpt: *MATADI*. 26.3.1920; 26.11.1920; 26.7.1926; 26.6.1927.	200.00	600.00	1200.
	e. Ovpt: *STANLEYVILLE*. 4.11.1920; 4.7.1927.	200.00	600.00	1200.
	f. Ovpt: W/o office. 1.2.1929.	150.00	500.00	1000.
12	1000 FRANCS			
	ND (1912-26). Brown. Woman seated at l. Back: 2 men and child by woman w/lyre.			
	a. Ovpt: *ELISABETHVILLE*. 21.8.1920.	Reported Not Confirmed		
	b. Ovpt: *KINSHASA*. 3.11.1920.	600.00	1200.	3000.
	c. Ovpt: *LEOPOLDVILLE*.	Reported Not Confirmed		
	d. Ovpt: *MATADI*. 26.11.1920.	600.00	1200.	3000.
	e. Ovpt: *STANLEYVILLE*. 4.11.1920.	1000.	2500.	—

1941-50 ISSUE

#13-19 sign. title varieties.

#14D *Deleted*.

NOTE: #20 is believed to have been used in interbank and real-estate transactions.

13	5 FRANCS	Good	Fine	XF
	10.6.1942. Red on green unpt. Woman seated w/child by beehive at l. Back: Elephant and hippo at ctr. Ovpt: *DEUXIMEME EMISSION-1942.* Printer: W&S.	20.00	100.00	250.00

13A	5 FRANCS	Good	Fine	XF
	1943-47. Blue-gray on orange unpt. Woman seated w/child by beehive at l. Back: Elephant and hippo at ctr.			
	a. Ovpt: *TROISIEM EMISSION-1943.*	10.00	50.00	125.00
	b. 10.8.1943. Ovpt: *QUATRIEME EMISSION-1943.*	5.00	20.00	85.00
	c. 10.3.1944. Ovpt: *CINQUIEME EMISSION-1944.*	4.00	20.00	85.00
	d. 10.4.1947. Ovpt: *SIXIEME EMISSION-1947.*	4.00	20.00	85.00
13B	5 FRANCS			
	18.5.1949; 7.9.1951; 15.2.1952. Blue-gray on orange unpt. Woman seated w/child by beehive at l. Back: Elephant and hippo at ctr. Ovpt: W/o *EMISSION.*	4.00	15.00	50.00
14	10 FRANCS			
	10.12.1941. Green on blue and pink unpt. Dancing Watusi at l. Back: Soldiers on parade at r. Wmk: Hornless antelope. Printer: W&S.	15.00	60.00	200.00
14A	10 FRANCS			
	10.7.1942. Brown on green and pink unpt. Ovpt: *DEUXIEME EMISSION-1942.*	30.00	75.00	200.00

14B	10 FRANCS	Good	Fine	XF
	10.2.1943. Violet on pink unpt. Ovpt: *TROISIEME EMISSION-1943.*	35.00	80.00	225.00
14C	10 FRANCS			
	10.6.1944. Gray-blue on pink unpt. Ovpt: *QUATRIEME EMISSION-1944.*	15.00	30.00	150.00
14E	10 FRANCS			
	11.11.1948; 15.8.1949; 14.3.1952; 12.5.1952. Gray-blue on pink unpt. Ovpt: W/o *EMISSION.*	10.00	30.00	150.00

15	20 FRANCS	Good	Fine	XF
	10.9.1940. Blue. Longboat w/7 oarsmen at l ctr. Back: Working elephant at ctr r. Ovpt: W/o *EMISSION.* Wmk: Elephant's head. Printer: TDLR.	20.00	65.00	225.00
15A	20 FRANCS			
	10.3.1942. Violet. Like #15. Ovpt: *DEUXIEME EMISSION-1942.*	20.00	65.00	225.00
15B	20 FRANCS			
	10.12.1942. Orange. Like #15. Ovpt: *TROISIEME EMISSION-1943.*	20.00	75.00	275.00
15C	20 FRANCS			
	10.3.1943. Orange. Like #15. Ovpt: *QUATRIEME EMISSION-1943.*	20.00	75.00	275.00

15D	20 FRANCS	Good	Fine	XF
	10.5.1944. Orange. Like #15. Ovpt: *CINQUIEME EMISSION-1944.*	20.00	75.00	275.00
15E	20 FRANCS			
	10.4.1946. Blue. Like #15. Ovpt: W/o *EMISSION.*	20.00	65.00	225.00
15F	20 FRANCS			
	10.8.1948. Blue. ctr. Ovpt: *SEPTIEME EMISSION-1948.* Wmk: Elephant's head.	10.00	30.00	150.00
15G	20 FRANCS			
	18.5.1949. Blue. ctr. Ovpt: *HUITIEME EMISSION-1949.* Wmk: Elephant's head.	10.00	30.00	150.00
15H	20 FRANCS			
	11.4.1950. Blue. Like #15. Ovpt: *NEUVIEME EMISSION-1950.*	10.00	30.00	150.00

16	50 FRANCS	Good	Fine	XF
	ND (1941-42); 1943-52. Black on m/c unpt. Woman at r. Back: Leopard at ctr. Printer: ABNC.			
	a. Serial # repeated 5 times. Ovpt: W/o *EMISSION.* Series A.	50.00	150.00	400.00
	b. Serial # repeated 4 times. Ovpt: *EMISSION-1943.*	40.00	120.00	300.00
	c. Ovpt: *EMISSION-1945.* Series D; G.	40.00	120.00	300.00
	d. Ovpt: *EMISSION-1946.* Series E.	40.00	120.00	300.00
	e. Ovpt: *EMISSION-1947.*	40.00	120.00	300.00
	f. Ovpt: *EMISSION-1948.* Series G.	40.00	120.00	300.00
	g. Ovpt: *EMISISON-1950.* Series N.	40.00	120.00	300.00

17	100 FRANCS	Good	Fine	XF
	1944-51. Blue and green. 2 Elephants, palm trees at ctr. Back: Native, 3 oxen at ctr. r. Wmk: Zebra's head. Printer: W&S.			
	a. Ovpt: W/o *EMISSION.* Ovpt: 10.5.1944.	50.00	135.00	350.00
	b. Ovpt: *DEUXIEME EMISSION-1944.* Ovpt: 10.6.1944.	40.00	100.00	300.00
	c. Ovpt: W/o *EMISSION.* 11.3.1946; 10.4.1947.	35.00	90.00	275.00
	d. Ovpt: W/o *EMISSION.* 16.7.1949; 14.9.1949; 13.3.1951; 7.9.1951.	35.00	90.00	275.00

18	500 FRANCS	GOOD	FINE	XF
	ND. (1927-37). Black on m/c unpt. Portr. woman at upper ctr. Back: Elephants bathing at ctr. Ovpt: W/o *EMISSION*. Printer: ABNC.	400.00	1250.	3000.
18A	500 FRANCS			
	ND (1941); 1943; 1945. Brown, yellow and blue. Woman at ctr. Back: Elephants bathing. Printer: ABNC.			
	a. Series 2. Serial # repeated 5 times. Ovpt: W/o *EMISSION*, ND (1941).	350.00	900.00	2000.
	b. Series 3. Ovpt: *EMISSION* 1943.	400.00	1250.	—
	c. Series 4. Ovpt: *EMISSION*-1945.	400.00	1250.	—
	d. Ovpt: *EMISSION*-1946.	Reported Not Confirmed		

19	1000 FRANCS	GOOD	FINE	XF
	1944-47. Brown-black, yellow and blue. 3 Warega fisherman at l. Back: 2 musicians at l. and ctr., portr. youth at r. Wmk: Leopard's head. Printer: W&S.			
	a. 10.5.1944.	350.00	850.00	1750.
	b. 11.2.1946; 10.4.1947.	250.00	600.00	1250.

20	10,000 FRANCS	GOOD	FINE	XF
	10.3.1942. Black and green. Uniface. Wmk: BCB/BBC. Printer: W&S. Specimen.	—	—	3000.

BANQUE CENTRALE DU CONGO BELGE ET DU RUANDA-URUNDI

1952 ISSUE
#21-29 various date and sign. varieties. Designs similar to previous issues.

21	5 FRANCS	VG	VF	UNC
	1.10.1952-15.9.1953. Blue-gray on orange unpt. Woman seated w/child by beehive at l. Back: Elephant and hippo at ctr. Printer: W&S.	5.00	20.00	50.00

22	10 FRANCS	VG	VF	UNC
	1.7.1952-31.8.1952. Gray-blue on pink unpt. Dancing Watusi at l. Back: Soldiers on parade at r. Wmk: Giraffe's head. Printer: W&S.	10.00	25.00	160.00
23	20 FRANCS			
	1.7.1952-1.12.1952. Blue. Longboat w/7 oarsmen at l. ctr. Back: Working elephant at ctr. r. Wmk: Elephant's head. Printer: TDLR.	20.00	75.00	275.00
24	50 FRANCS			
	15.7.1952-15.12.1952. M/c. Woman at r. Back: Leopard at ctr. Printer: ABNC.	40.00	125.00	400.00

25	100 FRANCS	VG	VF	UNC
	1952-54. Blue and green. 2 elephants, palm trees at ctr. Back: Native, 3 oxen at ctr. r. Wmk: Okapi's head. Printer: W&S.			
	a. 1.7.1952-15.11.1953.	60.00	180.00	500.00
	b. 15.12.1954.	50.00	150.00	425.00

1952-53 ISSUE

26	20 FRANCS	VG	VF	UNC
	15.12.1953-15.4.1954. Olive green, yellow on unpt. Woman at l., waterfall in background at ctr. Back: Qn. Astrid laboratory in Leopoldville at ctr., man w/spear at r. Wmk: Elephant's head. Printer: TDLR.	15.00	75.00	300.00

27   50 FRANCS

		VG	VF	UNC
1953-1955. Green on m/c unpt. Portr. woman at l. Back: 2 fisherman w/net at ctr r. Wmk: Leopard's head. Printer: BWC.				
a.	15.11.1953-15.4.1954.	25.00	120.00	550.00
b.	1.1.1955-1.3.1955.	20.00	100.00	500.00

28   500 FRANCS

		GOOD	FINE	XF
15.3.1953-1.1.1955. Violet on orange unpt. Portr. girl at l. Back: Okapi at ctr. Printer: W&S.				
a.	15.3.1953; 15.4.1953.	150.00	350.00	650.00
b.	1.1.1955.	135.00	320.00	600.00

29   1000 FRANCS

1.8.1953-1.4.1955. Blue. Portr. African male at l., boat along river at bottom ctr. Back: Waterbuck drinking at ctr. Wmk: Antelope's head.				
a.	1.8.1953-15.9.1953.	100.00	250.00	550.00
b.	15.2.1955-1.4.1955.	90.00	225.00	500.00

1955-58 ISSUE

30   10 FRANCS

		VG	VF	UNC
1955-59. Gray-blue on blue and orange unpt. Soldier at l. Back: Antelope at r. Wmk: Giraffe's head. Printer: W&S.				
a.	Sign. titles: *LE PREMIER-DIRECTEUR* and *LE GOUVERNEUR.* 1.5.1955-1.6.1955.	2.00	5.00	40.00
b.	Sign. titles: *UN DIRECTEUR* and *LE GOUVERNEUR.* 15.7.1956-1.12.1959.	2.00	5.00	28.50

31   20 FRANCS

	VG	VF	UNC
1.12.1956-1.12.1959. Green on m/c unpt. Young boy at l., reservoir in background at ctr. Back: River landscape at ctr., young girl at r. Wmk: Elephant's head. Printer: TDLR.	3.00	6.00	32.50

32   50 FRANCS

	VG	VF	UNC
1.3.1957-1.10.1959. Red on m/c unpt. Workers at modern weaving machinery at ctr. r. Back: Huts, weaving by hand at l. Leopard's head. Printer: BWC (w/o imprint).	4.00	10.00	55.00

33   100 FRANCS

		VG	VF	UNC
1955-60. Green on m/c unpt. Kg. Leopold II at l. Back: Basket weavers at ctr. Printer: BWC (w/o imprint).				
a.	Sign. titles: *LE GOUVERNEUR* and *LE PREMIER-DIRECTEUR.* Wmk: Elephant's head. 15.1.1955-1.10.1956.	4.00	15.00	75.00
b.	Sign. titles: *LE GOUVERNEUR* and *UN DIRECTEUR.* Wmk: Elephant's head. 1.10.1956-1.1.1960.	4.00	15.00	70.00
c.	1.9.1960. W/o wmk.	4.00	20.00	80.00

34   500 FRANCS

	VG	VF	UNC
1.9.1957-1.9.1959. Brown-violet on m/c unpt. Ships dockside at Leokin wharf at ctr. Back: Africans transporting fruit in boat at ctr. Wmk: Lion's head. Printer: TDLR.	20.00	100.00	300.00

35   1000 FRANCS

	VG	VF	UNC
15.7.1958-1.9.1959. Dp. blue on m/c unpt. Kg. Baudouin at l., aerial view of Leopoldville at lower ctr. Back: Huts at r. Wmk: Waterbuck's head. Printer: BWC (w/o imprint).	20.00	60.00	275.00

The Kingdom of Belgium, a constitutional monarchy in northwest Europe, has an area of 11,779 sq. mi. (30,513 sq. km.) and a population of 10.1 million, chiefly Dutch-speaking Flemish and French-speaking Walloons. Capital: Brussels. Agriculture, dairy farming, and the processing of raw materials for re-export are the principal industries. Beurs voor Diamant in Antwerp is the world's largest diamond trading center. Iron and steel, machinery, motor vehicles, chemicals, textile yarns and fabrics comprise the principal exports.

The Celtic tribe called "Belgae," from which Belgium derived its name, was described by Caesar as the most courageous of all the tribes of Gaul. The Belgae eventually capitulated to Rome and the area remained for centuries as a part of the Roman Empire known as Belgica.

As Rome began its decline, Frankish tribes migrated westward and established the Merovingian, and subsequently, the Carolingian empires. At the death of Charlemagne, Europe was divided among his three sons Karl, Lothar and Ludwig. The eastern part of today's Belgium lay in the Duchy of Lower Lorraine while much of the western parts eventually became the County of Flanders. After further divisions, the area was absorbed into the Duchy of Burgundy from whence it passed into Hapsburg control when Marie of Burgundy married Maximilian of Austria. Phillip I (the Fair), son of Maximilian and Marie, then added Spain to the Hapsburg empire by marrying Johanna, daughter of Ferdinand and Isabella. Charles and Ferdinand, sons of Phillip and Johanna, began the separate Spanish and Austrian lines of the Hapsburg family. The Burgundian lands, along with the northern provinces which make up present day Netherlands, became the Spanish Netherlands. The northern provinces successfully rebelled and broke away from Hapsburg rule in the late 16th century and early 17th century. The southern provinces along with the Duchy of Luxembourg remained under the influence of Spain until the year 1700 when Charles II, last of the Spanish Hapsburg line, died without leaving an heir and the Spanish crown went to the Bourbon family of France. The Spanish Netherlands then reverted to the control of the Austrian line of Hapsburgs and became the Austrian Netherlands. The Austrian Netherlands along with the Bishopric of Liege fell to the French Republic in 1794.

At the Congress of Vienna in 1815 the area was united with the Netherlands but in 1830 independence was gained and the constitutional monarchy of Belgium was established. A large part of the Duchy of Luxembourg was incorporated into Belgium and the first king was Leopold I of Saxe-Coburg-Gotha. It was invaded by the German army in Aug. 1914 and the German forces carried on a devastating occupation of most of the territory until the Armistice. Belgium joined the League of Nations. On May 10, 1940 it was invaded again by Nazi German armies. The Belgian and Allied forces were quickly overwhelmed and were evacuated through Dunkirk. Allied troops reached Belgium again in Sept. 1944. Prince Charles, Count of Flanders assumed King Leopold's responsibilities until his liberation by the U.S. army in Austria on May 8, 1945. From 1920-1940 and since 1944 Eupen-Malmedy went from Germany to Belgium.

RULERS:
Leopold I, 1831-1865
Leopold II, 1865-1909
Albert I, 1909-34
Leopold III, 1934-50
Baudoiun I, 1951-93
Albert II, 1993-

MONETARY SYSTEM:
1 Franc = 100 Centimes
1 Belga = 5 Francs

*** This section has been renumbered. ***

KINGDOM - PRE-WWI

SOCIÉTÉ DE COMMERCE DE BRUXELLES

CA 1810 ISSUE
#1, 2, 4, 7 are held in reserve.

		GOOD	FINE	XF
3 (A1A)	**100 FRANCS** ND. Black. Uniface.	—	—	—
5 (A1B)	**1000 FRANCS** ND. Black. Uniface.	—	Rare	—
6 (A1C)	**1000 FRANCS** ND. Blue. Uniface.	—	Rare	—

SOCIÉTÉ GÉNÉRALE POUR FAVORISER L'INDUSTRIE NATIONALE

1822-26 ISSUES
Various dates from 1826. Sign. varieties.

		GOOD	FINE	XF
8 (A1)	**1/2 FLORIN** 1.10.1826. Uniface.	—	Rare	—
9 (A2)	**1 FLORIN**	Reported Not Confirmed		
10 (A3)	**2 FLORINS**	Reported Not Confirmed		
11 (A4)	**3 FLORINS**	—	Rare	—
12 (A5)	**5 FLORINS**	Reported Not Confirmed		
13 (A6)	**10 FLORINS** Uniface.	—	Rare	—
19 (A6A)	**1000 FLORINS** 1822-30. Uniface.	—	Rare	—

1837-48 ISSUE

		GOOD	FINE	XF
20 (A7)	**5 FRANCS** ND (1848). Uniface.	1000.	2000.	3000.
21 (A8)	**20 FRANCS** ND (1848). Uniface.	—	Rare	—
22 (A9)	**50 FRANCS** 6.2.1837. Uniface.	—	Rare	—
23 (A10)	**100 FRANCS** 6.2.1837. Uniface.	—	Rare	—
24 (A10A)	**500 FRANCS** 6.2.1837. Uniface.	—	Rare	—
25 (A11)	**1000 FRANCS** 6.2.1837. Uniface.	—	Rare	—

BANQUE DE BELGIQUE

1835 ISSUE
NOTE: Denominations of 20, 50, 100, 500 and 1000 Francs are also reported.
#27-31 held in reserve.

		GOOD	FINE	XF
26 (A12)	**5 FRANCS** ND (1835). Uniface.	—	Rare	—

BANQUE DE FLANDRE

GHENT BRANCH

1841 ISSUE
NOTE: Denominations of 25 and 1000 Francs are also reported.

		GOOD	FINE	XF
32 (A12A)	**100 FRANCS** ND (1841). Uniface.	—	Rare	—

		GOOD	FINE	XF
33 (A13)	**250 FRANCS** ND (1841). Uniface.	—	Rare	—

BANQUE LIÈGEOISE ET CAISSE D'ÉPARGNES

LIÈGE BRANCH

1835 ISSUE

NOTE: Denominations of 100, 500 and 1000 Francs are also reported.
#38-40 held in reserve.

		GOOD	FINE	XF
34 (A14)	**5 FRANCS** ND (1835). Yellow.	—	Rare	—
35 (A15)	**10 FRANCS** ND (1835). Yellow.	—	Rare	—
36 (A16)	**25 FRANCS** ND (1835). Green.	—	Rare	—
37 (A17)	**50 FRANCS** ND (1835). Green.	—	Rare	—

BANQUE NATIONALE DE BELGIQUE

1851-56 ISSUES

		GOOD	FINE	XF
41 (A18)	**20 FRANCS** L.5.5.1850. Black. Ceres reclining at lower l., Neptune at lower r. 16 sign. varieties.	—	Rare	—
42 (A28)	**20 FRANCS** L.5.5.1850. (ca.1851-62). Blue on green unpt. Ceres reclining at lower l., Neptune at lower r. 7 sign. varieites.	1250.	2500.	—
43 (A19)	**50 FRANCS** 2.1.1851-4.10.1851. Rose. Cherubs in corners. Back: Pink.	1000.	3000.	—
44 (A20)	**50 FRANCS** 1.6.1852. Blue. Cherubs in 4 corners.	—	Rare	—
45 (A27)	**50 FRANCS** ca.1851-2.1.1862. Blue on green unpt. Cherubs in 4 corners. 5 sign. varieties.	—	Rare	—

		GOOD	FINE	XF
46 (A21)	**100 FRANCS** 2.1.1851-1.6.1852. Cherubs in 4 corners.	—	Rare	—
47 (A26)	**100 FRANCS** 2.1.1856. Blue. Woman seated w/2 lions at bottom ctr.	—	Rare	—
48 (A21A)	**500 FRANCS** 2.1.1851. Blue. Cherubs in 4 corners.	—	Rare	—
49 (A23)	**500 FRANCS** 1.6.1852. Black. 2 allegorical figures at l. (Industry and Trade) and at r. (Liberty and Justice). 3 sign. varieties.	—	Rare	—
50 (A24)	**500 FRANCS** 1.6.1852. Blue. 2 allegorical figures at l. (Industry and Trade) and at r. (Liberty and Justice). 3 sign. varieties.	—	—	—

		GOOD	FINE	XF
51 (A22)	**1000 FRANCS** 2.1.1851-1.6.1852. Black. Cherubs in 4 corners.	—	Rare	—
52 (A25)	**1000 FRANCS** 22.8.1853. Blue. Cherubs in 4 corners. 4 sign. varieties.	—	Rare	—

1869-73 ISSUE

		GOOD	FINE	XF
53 (A29)	**20 FRANCS** 25.1.1869-29.6.1878. Blue. 2 allegorical figures (Agriculture and Cattle Breeding). 4 sign. varieties.	1500.	3000.	—
54 (A32)	**50 FRANCS** 3.4.1871-6.7.1871. Blue. Woman and 2 children at l., child w/crown of laurel leaves at r. Back: Children leaning on cornucopia.	—	Rare	—
55 (A30)	**100 FRANCS** 4.3.1869-14.8.1882. Blue. Seated man at l., woman w/sceptre at r. 5 sign varieties. Back: 2 allegorical figures (Security) at l., (Progress) at r.	—	Rare	—
56 (A33)	**500 FRANCS** 9.5.1873-25.9.1886. Blue on pink unpt. Allegorical figures at l. (Science) and at r. (Art).	—	Rare	—
57 (A31)	**1000 FRANCS** 31.5.1870-2.2.1884. Blue. Neptune at l., and Amphitrite at r. 4 sign. varieties.	—	Rare	—

1875 ISSUE

		GOOD	FINE	XF
58 (A34)	**50 FRANCS** 19.7.1875-30.6.1879. Blue on gray unpt. Woman and 2 children at l., group of children in background. Red Serial #.	—	Rare	—

1879; 1881 ISSUE

		GOOD	FINE	XF
59 (A35)	**20 FRANCS** 8.8.1879-17.10.1892. Blue on gray unpt. 2 allegorical figures (Agriculture and Cattle Breeding). W/o counterfoil. 5 sign. varieties.	400.00	1000.	1800.
60 (A36)	**50 FRANCS** 3.1.1881-23.9.1887. Blue. Women and 2 children at l., modifications in engraving. W/o counterfoil.	1000.	—	—

1883-96 ISSUE

		GOOD	FINE	XF
61 (A37)	**20 FRANCS** 13.12.1892-29.6.1896. Blue on brown unpt. Allegorical figures at l. (Agriculture and Trade) and at r. (Industry).	250.00	550.00	1250.

		VG	VF	UNC
62 (3)	**20 FRANCS** 30.7.1896-30.12.1909. Dk. red and green. Minerva w/lion at l. 3 sign. varieties. Back: Brown. Arms of 30 towns.	30.00	100.00	300.00
63 (4)	**50 FRANCS** 26.9.1887-30.12.1908. Blue and black. Medallic female head and children. 5 sign. varieties.	325.00	1000.	
64 (6)	**100 FRANCS** 5.6.1883-31.7.1905. Blue on lt. brown unpt. Seated man at l., woman w/sceptre at r. 5 sign. varieties. Modifications in engraving and w/o counterfoil. Back: 2 allegorical figures (Security) at l., (Progress) at r. Wmk: Minerva.	400.00	1000.	2000.
65 (11)	**500 FRANCS** 1.1.1887-11.3.1908. Blue and red on gray unpt. 3 sign. varieties. Bank name and denomination in red surrounded by women and small angels.	1000.	2000.	
66 (13)	**1000 FRANCS** 3.1.1884-30.4.1908. Blue and m/c. 4 sign. varieties. Like #73 but slight changes in design.	1350.	2500.	

1905-10 ISSUES

67 (3A)	**20 FRANCS** 3.1.1910-19.7.1920. Red and green. Minerva w/lion at l. 3 sign. varieties. Back: Brown. Arms of 30 towns.	**VG** 3.00	**VF** 12.00	**UNC** 35.00
68 (5)	**50 FRANCS** 1909-26. Dk. green on lt. green and blue unpt. Seated woman (Agriculture) at l. and (Law) at r. Back: Several figures (Intelligence and Industry).			
	a. 1.5.1909-5.2.1914. W/embossed arabesque design on border. 2 sign. varieties.	15.00	65.00	200.00
	b. 1919-1.10.1926. W/o embossed arabesque design on border. 3 sign. varieties.	10.00	30.00	80.00
69 (7)	**100 FRANCS** 31.7.1905-7.3.1906. Blue. Seated man at l., woman w/sceptre at r. 5 sign. varieties. W/brown denomination. Back: 2 allegorical figures (Security) at l., (Progress) at r.	400.00	1000.	—
70 (8)	**100 FRANCS** 15.3.1906-21.12.1908. Brown and black. Quadrigas driven by Ceres at l. and Neptune at r. Back: Green. Women (Sowing) at l. and (Harvesting) at r.	135.00	300.00	700.00

74 (1)	**5 FRANCS** 1914; 1919. Brown and orange. Allegorical figures.	**VG**	**VF**	**UNC**
	a. 1.7.1914.	8.00	40.00	150.00
	b. 25.1.1919. Wmk: *BNB*.	6.00	30.00	120.00
75 (2)	**5 FRANCS** 1914-21. Green and brown. Allegorical figures.			
	a. 1.7.1914.	2.50	12.50	45.00
	b. 27.12.1918-3.1.1921. Wmk: *BNB*.	2.00	10.00	30.00
76 (3B)	**20 FRANCS** 1.9.1914. Red and green. Minerva w/lion at l. Red serial #, date below. Back: Brown. Arms of 30 towns.	200.00	600.00	1200.
77 (5A)	**50 FRANCS** 1.8.1914. Green. W/embossed arabesque design on border. Red serial #.	300.00	900.00	1800.
78 (10)	**100 FRANCS** 1914-16.10.1920. Black and brown. Quadrigas driven by Ceres at l. and Neptune at r. 2 sign varieties. Back: Green. Women (Sowing) at l. and (Harvesting) at r. Medallion and white edges below. Wmk: Minerva.	2.50	10.00	30.00
79 (10A)	**100 FRANCS** 12.9.1914-14.10.1914. Black and brown. W/red serial #. Wmk: Minerva.	1200.	3000.	—

71 (9)	**100 FRANCS** 12.1.1909-1914. Black and brown on pink and pale green unpt. Quadrigas driven by Ceres at l. and Neptune at r. 2 sign. varieties. Back: Green. Women (Sowing) at l. and (Harvesting) at r. Medallion and white edges below and r. embossed arabesque. Wmk: Minerva.	**VG** 6.50	**VF** 16.00	**UNC** 40.00
72 (12)	**500 FRANCS** 1910-25. Blue and green on gray unpt. 4 sign. varieties. Bank name and denomination (only in Francs) in green surrounded by women and small angels.			
	a. 13.10.1910-1914. W/embossed arabesque design on border. 2 sign. varieties.	200.00	500.00	—
	b. 25.1.1919-31.7.1925. W/o embossed arabesque design on border. 3 sign. varieties.	35.00	85.00	200.00

73 (14)	**1000 FRANCS** 3.7.1909-24.1.1921. Green. 3 sign. varieties.	**VG** 275.00	**VF** 900.00	**UNC**
80 (15)	**1000 FRANCS** 17.1.1919-23.3.1919. Brownish-yellow and black. Like #73 but w/o edge printing.	125.00	300.00	700.00

1914 COMPTES COURANT ISSUE

		VG	VF	UNC
81 (16)	**1 FRANC** 27.8.1914. Blue on gray unpt.	4.00	20.00	50.00

		VG	VF	UNC
82 (17)	**2 FRANCS** 27.8.1914. Brown on gray unpt.	10.00	35.00	80.00
83 (18)	**20 FRANCS** 27.8.1914. Blue and brown.	100.00	350.00	750.00
84 (19)	**100 FRANCS** 27.8.1914. Blue on gray unpt.	800.00	2000.	—

		VG	VF	UNC
85 (20)	**1000 FRANCS** 27.8.1914. Wine red.	—	Rare	—

GERMAN OCCUPATION - WWI
SOCIETE GENERALE DE BELGIQUE

1915 ISSUE
#86-91 portr. Qn. Louise-Marie at l.
Notes issued by the bank during the German occupation and after the war carry various printing dates during 1915-18.

		VG	VF	UNC
86 (21)	**1 FRANC** 1.3.1915-29.10.1918. Violet on pink unpt.	3.00	5.00	20.00
87 (22)	**2 FRANCS** 1.4.1915-25.5.1918. Reddish brown on lt. green unpt.	5.00	12.50	30.00
88 (23)	**5 FRANCS** 2.1.1915-14.7.1918. Green on gray unpt. Back: Blue and green.	15.00	50.00	150.00

		VG	VF	UNC
89 (24)	**20 FRANCS** 1.2.1915-11.10.1918. Blue on pink unpt. Portr. P. P. Rubens at l.	75.00	200.00	400.00

		VG	VF	UNC
90 (25)	**100 FRANCS** 26.12.1914-2.9.1918. Brown and green on pink and green unpt. Portr. Qn. Louise-Marie at l.	150.00	450.00	1000.

		VG	VF	UNC
91 (26)	**1000 FRANCS** 18.9.1915-26.10.1918. Brown and green on lt. green unpt. Portr. P. P. Rubens at l.	—	Rare	—

KINGDOM - 1920-44

BANQUE NATIONALE DE BELGIQUE

1920-22 ISSUE
#92-96 denominations in Francs only. Various date and sign. varieties. Conjoined portr. Kg. Albert and Qn. Elisabeth at l.

		VG	VF	UNC
92 (27)	**1 FRANC** 1.3.1920-8.6.1922. Blue. Back: Arms at upper corners and ctr.	1.00	5.00	12.50
93 (28)	**5 FRANCS** 1.4.1922-25.6.1926. Blue. Qn. Elisabeth at l. Back: Seated man looking at factory scene.	1.50	8.00	20.00
94 (29)	**20 FRANCS** 1.6.1921-10.4.1926. Brown on lt. blue and brown unpt. 2 sign varieties.	4.50	17.50	60.00

		VG	VF	UNC
95 (30)	**100 FRANCS** 1.4.1921-2.6.1927. Lilac-brown. 3 sign varieties.	2.00	8.00	25.00

96	**1000 FRANCS**	**VG**	**VF**	**UNC**
(31)	15.6.1922-28.10.1927. Blue on pink unpt. 3 sign varieties.	7.50	30.00	100.00

1926 ISSUE

97	**5 FRANCS**			
(46)	14.6.1926-10.5.1931. Blue on lt. brown unpt. Portr. Kg. Albert and Qn. Elisabeth at l. Back: Seated man looking at factory scene. 2 sign. varieties.	.75	4.00	12.50
98	**20 FRANCS**			
(48)	14.4.1926-27.1.1940. Brown on lt. blue and yellow-green unpt. Portr. Kg. Albert and Qn. Elisabeth at l. 3 sign. varieties.	1.50	8.00	20.00

1927-29 ISSUES

#32-50 denominations in Francs and Belgas. Various date (from 1927) and sign. varieties.

99	**50 FRANCS-10 BELGAS**			
(32)	1.3.1927; 23.3.1927. Green. W/o embossed arabesque design on border. 3 sign. varieties.	50.00	150.00	300.00

100	**50 FRANCS-10 BELGAS**	**VG**	**VF**	**UNC**
(33)	1.9.1927-6.1.1928. Brown on yellow unpt. Peasant woman w/sheaf and 2 horses at l. ctr. Back: Allegorical figure holding sailing ship and large cornucopia.	50.00	150.00	350.00
101	**50 FRANCS-10 BELGAS**			
(34)	1.10.1928-20.4.1935. Green on yellow unpt. Peasant woman w/sheaf and 2 horses at l. ctr. Back: Allegorical figure holding sailing ship and lg. cornucopia. For #34 w/*TRÉSORERIE* ovpt. see #50.	3.00	8.00	16.00

102	**100 FRANCS-20 BELGAS**	**VG**	**VF**	**UNC**
(35)	1.7.1927-2.8.1932. Blue-black on ochre and pale blue unpt. Portraits of Kg. Albert and Qn. Elizabeth at l. Wmk: Kg. Leopold I.	.75	2.50	10.00

103	**500 FRANCS-100 BELGAS**	**VG**	**VF**	**UNC**
(40)	3.1.1927-16.11.1936. Blue and green. Bank name and denomination surrounded by women and small angels. Sign. On face only. 2 sign. varieties.	3.00	15.00	30.00

104	**1000 FRANCS-200 BELGAS**	**VG**	**VF**	**UNC**
(42)	2.4.1928-28.11.1939. Green on m/c unpt. Portr. Kg. Albert and Qn. Elisabeth at l. Sign. On face only. 3 sign. varieties.	2.00	7.50	25.00

105	**10,000 FRANCS-2000 BELGAS**	**VG**	**VF**	**UNC**
(45)	22.11.1929-28.8.1942. Blue on pink unpt. Quadrigas driven by Ceres at l., and Neptune at r., lion at ctr. Back: 2 allegorical figures. 3 sign. varieties.	90.00	180.00	385.00

1933; 1935 ISSUE

#46-50 ovpt: *Trésorerie-Thesaurie.*

106   **50 FRANCS-10 BELGAS**
(50)   20.4.1935-28.4.1947. Dk. green on blackish green on lt. green and orange unpt. Peasant woman w/sheaf and 2 horses at l. ctr. Back: Allegorical figure holding sailing ship and large cornucopia. 6 sign. varieties.

	VG	VF	UNC
	.60	3.00	10.00

107   **100 FRANCS-20 BELGAS**
(36)   1.5.1933-15.9.1943. Gray on lt. brown unpt. Portr. Qn. Elisabeth at l., woman w/crown and fruit at ctr., portr. Kg. Albert at r. French text. 4 sign. varieties.

	VG	VF	UNC
	.50	1.50	9.00

1938 ISSUE

108   **5 FRANCS**
(47)   1.3.1938-11.5.1938. Blue. Portr. Kg. Albert and Qn. Elisabeth at l. Back: Seated man looking at factory scene. 2 sign. varieties.

	VG	VF	UNC
	.60	3.00	10.00

109   **500 FRANCS-100 BELGAS**
(41)   3.2.1938-4.10.1943. Blue and green. Bank name and denomination surrounded by women and small angels. Sign. On both sides. 2 sign. varieties.

	VG	VF	UNC
	2.00	9.00	18.00

1939 ISSUE

110   **1000 FRANCS-200 BELGAS**
(43)   12.12.1939-26.10.1944. Green. Portr. Kg. Albert and Qn. Elisabeth at l. Sign. On both sides. 2 sign. varieties.

	VG	VF	UNC
	1.50	6.00	15.00

1940 ISSUE

111   **20 FRANCS**
(49)   27.1.1940-13.6.1947. Brown on lt. blue and brown unpt. Portr. Kg. Albert and Qn. Elisabeth at l. Date at top ctr. 4 sign. varieties.

	VG	VF	UNC
	1.35	7.00	17.50

1941 ISSUE

112   **100 FRANCS-20 BELGAS**
(37)   17.1.1941-10.9.1943. Gray on lt. brown unpt. Portr. Qn. Elisabeth at l., woman w/crown and fruit at ctr., portr. Kg. Albert at r. W/Flemish text.

	VG	VF	UNC
	.50	1.50	9.00

1944 ISSUE

113   **100 FRANCS-20 BELGAS**
(38)   20.9.1944-4.11.1944. Orange. Portr. Qn. Elisabeth at l., woman w/crown and fruit at ctr., portr. Kg. Albert at r. French text.

	VG	VF	UNC
	3.00	20.00	70.00

114   **100 FRANCS-20 BELGAS**
(39)   20.9.1944-4.11.1944. Orange. Portr. Qn. Elisabeth at l., woman w/crown and fruit at ctr., portr. Kg. Albert at r. W/Flemish text.

	VG	VF	UNC
	4.00	35.00	100.00

115   **1000 FRANCS-200 BELGAS**
(44)   20.9.1944-26.10.1944. Red. Portr. Kg. Albert and Qn. Elisabeth at l. Sign. On both sides.

	VG	VF	UNC
	175.00	450.00	900.00

1948 ISSUE

116   **20 FRANCS**
(49A)   1.9.1948. Brown. Portr. Kg. Albert and Qn. Elisabeth at l., wings at top ctr. Date at top l. 4 sign. varieties.

	VG	VF	UNC
	1.50	8.00	20.00

GERMAN OCCUPATION - WWII

BANQUE D'EMISSION A BRUXELLES

CA 1941 ISSUE

117   **50 FRANCS**
(50A)   ND. Gray-blue on yellow unpt.   Reported Not Confirmed

118   **100 FRANCS**
(50B)   ND. Green.   Reported Not Confirmed

119   **100 FRANCS**
(50C)   ND. Brown.   Reported Not Confirmed

120   **10,000 FRANCS**
(50D)   ND. Blue. Farm woman w/sickle and plants at ctr. Back: 5 standing allegorical female figures under tree. (Not issued).

	VG	VF	UNC
	—	Rare	—

KINGDOM IN EXILE

BANQUE NATIONALE DE BELGIQUE

1943-45 ISSUE

#116 and 117 printer: TDLR (w/o imprint).

#118-120 printer: BWC (w/o imprint).

121 (51)	5 FRANCS-1 BELGA 1.2.1943 (1944). Red on pink and lt. blue unpt.	VG .50	VF 2.50	UNC 7.50

122 (52)	10 FRANCS-2 BELGAS 1.2.1943 (1944). Green on lt. green and lt. pink unpt.	VG .50	VF 2.50	UNC 7.50
123 (53)	100 FRANCS-20 BELGAS 1.2.1943 (1944). Red and green. Qn. Elisabeth at l., woman w/crown and fruit at ctr. Kg. Albert at r. Smaller size.	FV	8.50	25.00

124 (54)	500 FRANCS-100 BELGAS 1.2.1943 (1944). Blue, pink and m/c. Back: Reclining figure.	VG FV	VF 75.00	UNC 150.00
125 (55)	1000 FRANCS-200 BELGAS 1.2.1943 (1944). Brown and violet. Qn. Elisabeth at l., woman w/crown and fruit at ctr. Kg. Albert at r. Back: Reclining figure. Different color and value.	100.00	275.00	550.00

KINGDOM - POST WWII

BANQUE NATIONALE DE BELGIQUE

1944-45 ISSUE

126 (56)	100 FRANCS 3.11.1945-31.12.1950. Brown, pink and yellow. Portr. Leopold I at l., Justice Palace, Brussels at ctr. Back: Mounted troops at ctr. r. 2 sign. varieties.	VG 4.00	VF 12.00	UNC 30.00

127 (59)	500 FRANCS 7.11.1944-1.4.1947. Brown and yellow. Portr. Kg. Leopold II wearing a military cap at l., Antwerp Cathedral at ctr. Congo landscape and boat on back. 2 sign. varieties.	VG 20.00	VF 45.00	UNC 110.00

128 (62)	1000 FRANCS 16.10.1944-1.7.1948. Blue. Portr. Kg. Albert I wearing steel helmet at l., monument at ctr. City view of Veurne on back. 3 sign. varieties.	VG 35.00	VF 70.00	UNC 150.00

1950-52 ISSUE

129 (57)	100 FRANCS 1952-59. Brown on m/c unpt. Kg. Leopold I at l. Back: Fr. Orban.	VG	VF	UNC
	a. Sign. Frère-Pirsoul. 1.8.1952-4.12.1952.	FV	7.50	32.50
	b. Sign. Frère-Vincent. 10.9.1953-30.6.1957.	FV	6.50	30.00
	c. Sign. Ansiaux-Vincent. 1.7.1957-26.2.1959.	FV	5.50	25.00
	s. As a. Specimen.	—	—	—
130 (60)	500 FRANCS 1.4.1952-29.5.1958. Brown and yellow. Kg. Leopold II at l. 4 heads (painting by P. P. Rubens) on back. 3 sign. varieties.			
	a. Issued note.	18.00	35.00	75.00
	s. Specimen.	—	—	—
131 (63)	1000 FRANCS 2.1.1950-28.7.1958. Blue and m/c. Kg. Albert at l. Geeraert and lock scene on back. 3 sign. varieties.			
	a. Issued note.	FV	40.00	70.00
	s. Specimen.	—	—	—

ROYAUME DE BELGIQUE - TRÉSORERIE

KONINKRIJK BELGIE - THESAURIE

1948; 1950 ISSUE

132 **20 FRANCS**
(66)

	VG	VF	UNC
1950; 1956. Lilac, violet and blue. Portr. R. de Lassus at ctr. Portr. P. de Monte at ctr. on back.			
a. Sign. Van Heureck 1.7.1950.	.30	1.25	6.00
b. Sign. Williot 3.4.1956.	.25	.50	4.00

133 **50 FRANCS**
(68)

	VG	VF	UNC
1948; 1956. Yellow, green, violet and m/c. Farm woman w/fruit at l., man planting a tree at r. Farmer w/scythe at l., woman w/sheaf at r. on back. Wmk: Kg. Leopold I.			
a. Sign. Van Heureck 1.6.1948.	.50	1.50	7.00
b. Sign. Williot 3.4.1956.	.25	1.00	4.00

MILITARY OCCUPATION OF GERMANY

ARMEE BELGE - BELGISCH LEGER

MILITARY PAYMENT CERTIFICATES

NOTE: Issued under the authority of the Ministry of Defense for Belgian troops stationed in Germany after World War II.

M1 **1 FRANC**

	GOOD	FINE	XF
1.8.1946. Green and blue.			
a. Serial # prefix A.	3.00	9.00	27.50
b. Serial # prefix B.	4.50	12.00	37.50
s. Specimen.	—	Unc	150.00

M2 **2 FRANCS**

1.8.1946. Green and violet.			
a. Issued note.	3.00	30.00	80.00
s. Specimen.	—	Unc	150.00

M3 **5 FRANCS**

1.8.1946. Green and red.			
a. Serial # prefix A.	3.00	32.50	85.00
b. Serial # prefix B.	3.25	35.00	90.00
s. Specimen.	—	Unc	150.00

M4 **10 FRANCS**

	GOOD	FINE	XF
1.8.1946. Brown and blue.			
a. Issued note.	10.00	50.00	130.00
s. Specimen.	—	Unc	150.00

M5 **20 FRANCS**

1.8.1946. Brown and green			
a. Issued note.	15.00	65.00	200.00
s. Specimen.	—	Unc	150.00

M6 **50 FRANCS**

1.8.1946. Brown and red.			
a. Issued note.	30.00	125.00	325.00
s. Specimen.	—	Unc	300.00

M7 **100 FRANCS**

	GOOD	FINE	XF
1.8.1946. Gray-blue and violet.			
a. Issued note.	100.00	300.00	600.00
s. Specimen.	—	Unc	500.00

M8 **500 FRANCS**

	GOOD	FINE	XF
1.8.1946. Gray-blue and green.			
a. Issued note.	350.00	900.00	—
s. Specimen.	—	Unc	1500.

The Parliamentary British Colony of Bermuda, situated in the western Atlantic Ocean 660 miles (1,062 km.) east of North Carolina, has an area of 20.6 sq. mi. (53 sq. km.) and a population of 60,470. Capital: Hamilton. Concentrated essences, beauty preparations, and cut flowers are exported. Most Bermudians derive their livelihood from tourism.

Bermuda was discovered by Juan de Bermudez, a Spanish navigator, in 1503. British influence dates from 1609 when a group of Virginia-bound British colonists under the command of Sir George Somers was shipwrecked on the islands for 10 months. The islands were settled in 1612 by 60 British colonists from the Virginia Colony and became a crown colony in 1684. Internal autonomy was obtained by the constitution of June 8, 1968.

In February, 1970, Bermuda converted from its former currency, the English pound, to a decimal currency, termed a dollar, which is equal to one U.S. dollar. On July 31, 1972, Bermuda severed its monetary link with the British pound sterling and pegged its dollar to be the same gold value as the U.S. dollar.

RULERS:
British

MONETARY SYSTEM:
1 Shilling = 12 Pence
1 Pound = 20 Shillings, to 1970
1 Dollar = 100 Cents, 1970-

BRITISH INFLUENCE

BERMUDA GOVERNMENT

1914 ISSUE

		GOOD	FINE	XF
1 (2)	**1 POUND** 2.12.1914. Black on green unpt. Arms at l. Back: Green. Printer: ABNC.	750.00	1750.	—

1920-27 COMMEMORATIVE ISSUE
#2 and 3 Portr. Kg. George V at ctr.
#4-5 printer: W&S.

2 (2A)	**2 SHILLINGS 6 PENCE** 1.8.1920. Brown. (Not issued).	—	Rare	—

		GOOD	FINE	XF
3	**5 SHILLINGS** 1920; 1935. Brown and green. Back: Purple. Sailing ship at ctr. Printer: TDLR.			
	a. Sign. title: *RECEIVER GENERAL.* 1.8.1920.	350.00	850.00	2750.
	b. Sign. title: *COLONIAL TREASURER.* ND (1935).	325.00	800.00	2500.

		GOOD	FINE	XF
4	**10 SHILLINGS** 30.9.1927. Red on m/c unpt. Arms at l., harbor at St. George at ctr., Kg. George V at r. Back: Royal crest at ctr.	300.00	750.00	2100.

		VG	VF	UNC
5	**1 POUND** 30.9.1927. Blue on m/c unpt. Arms at l., view of Hamilton at ctr., Kg. George V at r.	300.00	650.00	2500.

1937-41 ISSUES
#6-10 portr. Kg. George VI at upper ctr. Royal crest on back. Printer: BWC.
#11-13 portr. Kg. George VI at r.

6 (8A)	**1 SHILLING** 1.3.1939. M/c. Specimen only.	—	—	—
7 (8B)	**2 SHILLINGS 6 PENCE** 1.3.1939. M/c. Specimen only.	—	—	—

		VG	VF	UNC
8 (6)	**5 SHILLINGS** 12.5.1935. Brown on m/c unpt. Portr. Kg. George VI. Date in bottom ctr. frame under picture of Hamilton harbor. Back: Royal crest.			
	a. Single letter prefix.	15.00	90.00	400.00
	b. Fractional style letter-number prefix.	7.50	40.00	250.00

		VG	VF	UNC
9 (6A)	**10 SHILLINGS** 12.5.1937. Green on m/c unpt. Date in bottom ctr. frame under picture of Gate's Fort in St. George.	275.00	850.00	—
10 (7)	**10 SHILLINGS** 12.5.1937. Red on m/c unpt. Date in bottom ctr. frame under picture of Gate's Fort in St. George.			
	a. Single letter prefix.	35.00	225.00	800.00
	b. Fractional style letter-number prefix.	15.00	100.00	550.00

		GOOD	FINE	XF
11 (8)	**1 POUND** 12.5.1937. Blue on m/c unpt. Portr. Kg. George VI, bridge at l.			
	a. Single letter prefix.	30.00	175.00	—
	b. Fractional style letter-number prefix.	20.00	85.00	450.00

12 (9)	**5 POUNDS** 1.8.1941. Brown on m/c unpt. Portr. Kg. George VI, ship entering Hamilton harbor at l. Back: Brown, pink and green.	**GOOD** 450.00	**FINE** 1500.	**XF** —
13 (9A)	**5 POUNDS** 1.8.1941. Orange on m/c unpt. Portr. Kg. George VI, ship entering Hamilton harbor at l.	350.00	1150.	—

1947 ISSUE

#14 and 15 portr. Kg. George VI at upper ctr. Royal crest on back. Printer: BWC.

14 (10)	**5 SHILLINGS** 17.2.1947. Brown on m/c unpt.	**VG** 10.00	**VF** 50.00	**UNC** 350.00
15 (11)	**10 SHILLINGS** 17.2.1947. Red on m/c unpt. Date at l., Gate's Fort in St. George at bottom ctr.	20.00	85.00	700.00

16 (12)	**1 POUND** 17.2.1947. Blue on m/c unpt. Portr. Kg. George VI in profile at r., bridge at l., date at ctr. above *ONE POUND*.	**VG** 17.50	**VF** 100.00	**UNC** 550.00

17 (12A)	**5 POUNDS** 17.2.1947. Lt. orange on m/c unpt. Portr. Kg. George VI, facing at r., ship entering Hamilton Harbor at l. Back: Lt. orange and green.	**VG** 100.00	**VF** 350.00	**UNC** 1250.

1952-66 ISSUE

#18-22 Printer: BWC.

18 (13)	**5 SHILLINGS** 1952; 1957. Brown on m/c unpt. Portr. Qn. Elizabeth at upper ctr. Hamilton Harbor in frame at bottom ctr.	**VG**	**VF**	**UNC**
	a. 20.10.1952.	3.00	10.00	70.00
	b. 1.5.1957.	2.00	7.50	50.00

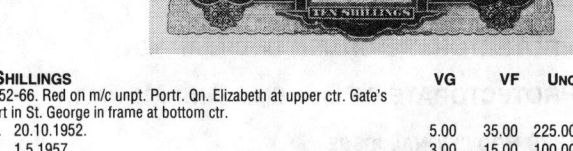

19 (14)	**10 SHILLINGS** 1952-66. Red on m/c unpt. Portr. Qn. Elizabeth at upper ctr. Gate's Fort in St. George in frame at bottom ctr.	**VG**	**VF**	**UNC**
	a. 20.10.1952.	5.00	35.00	225.00
	b. 1.5.1957.	3.00	15.00	100.00
	c. 1.10.1966.	4.00	20.00	225.00

20 (15)	**1 POUND** 1952-66. Blue on m/c unpt. Portr. Qn. Elizabeth at r. Bridge at l.	**VG**	**VF**	**UNC**
	a. 20.10.1952.	7.50	30.00	225.00
	b. 1.5.1957. W/o security strip.	5.00	20.00	225.00
	c. 1.5.1957. W/security strip.	3.50	15.00	185.00
	d. 1.10.1966.	3.00	13.00	140.00
21 (16)	**5 POUNDS** 1952-66. Orange on m/c unpt. Portr. Qn. Elizabeth at r. Ship entering Hamilton Harbor at l.			
	a. 20.10.1952.	25.00	120.00	600.00
	b. 1.5.1957. W/o security strip.	17.50	75.00	450.00
	c. 1.5.1957. W/security strip.	15.00	70.00	425.00
	d. 1.10.1966.	15.00	55.00	375.00

BOHEMIA & MORAVIA

Bohemia, a province in north-west Czechoslovakia, was combined with the majority of Moravia in central Czechoslovakia (excluding parts of north and south Moravia which were joined with Silesia in 1938) to form a German protectorate in March 1939. Toward the end of 1945, the protectorate was dissolved and Bohemia and Moravia once again became part of Czechoslovakia.

MONETARY SYSTEM:
1 Koruna = 10 Haleru

GERMAN OCCUPATION - WWII

PROTEKTORAT BÖHMEN UND MÄHREN

PROTECTORATE OF BOHEMIA AND MORAVIA

1939 PROVISIONAL ISSUE

#1 and 2 state notes w/circular handstamp (usually blurred printing w/larger letters) or machine (usually finer printing w/smaller letters) ovpt: *Protektorat Böhmen and Mähren, Protektorat Cechy a Morava.*

			VG	VF	UNC
1	**1 KORUNA**				
	ND (1939). Blue. Liberty wearing cap at r. Back: Red and blue. Arms at l. Ovpt. on Czechoslovakia #27.				
		a. Handstamp: *Böhmen und Mähren...*	1.50	4.50	12.00
		b. Machine ovpt: *Böhmen und Mähren...*	2.00	5.00	14.00
2	**5 KORUN**				
	ND (1939). Lilac and violet. Portr. J. Jungmann at r. Back: Violet. Woman at l. Ovpt. on Czechoslovakia #28.				
		a. Handstamp: *Böhmen und Mähren...*	2.50	7.50	22.50
		b. Machine ovpt: *Böhmen und Mähren...*	4.00	15.00	40.00

1940 ISSUES

			VG	VF	UNC
3	**1 KORUNA**				
	ND (1940). Brown on blue unpt. Girl at r. Back: Red and blue. Arms at l.				
		a. Issued note.	.40	2.00	5.00
		s. Perforated: *SPECIMEN.*	—	.50	1.50

			VG	VF	UNC
4	**5 KORUN**				
	ND (1940). Green on blue and brown unpt. Woman at r. Back: Violet. Woman at l.				
		a. Issued note.	.50	2.00	8.00
		s. Perforated: *SPECIMEN.*	—	.75	3.00

			VG	VF	UNC
5 (7)	**50 KORUN**				
	12.9.1940. Dk. brown on gray unpt. Woman at r. Back: Green. Arms at l.				
		a. Issued note.	2.00	5.00	20.00
		s. Perforated: *SPECIMEN.*	—	1.50	6.00

			VG	VF	UNC
6 (5)	**100 KORUN**				
	20.8.1940. Blue. View of Prague's Castle and Charles Bridge. Back: Red ctr. w/blue and maroon lettering. W/o *AUFLAGE*				
		a. Issued note.	.50	3.00	9.00
		s. Perforated: *NEPLATNÉ* or *SPECIMEN.*	—	1.00	4.00

			VG	VF	UNC
7 (6)	**100 KORUN**				
	20.8.1940. Blue. View of Prague's Castle and Charles Bridge. Back: Blue ctr. w/blue lettering w/diff. frame at ctr. *II. AUFLAGE* (2nd issue) at l. margin.				
		a. Issued note.	.50	3.00	9.00
		s. Perforated: *SPECIMEN.*	—	1.00	4.00

1942-44 ISSUE

			VG	VF	UNC
8	**10 KORUN**				
	8.7.1942. Brown on lt. orange unpt. Girl at r. 2 serial # varieties. Back: Arms at ctr. in unpt.				
		a. Issued note.	.25	1.50	7.00
		s. Perforated: *NEPLATNÉ* or *SPECIMEN.*	—	1.00	3.00

			VG	VF	UNC
9	**20 KORUN**				
	24.1.1944. Green on lt. green unpt. Fruit across ctr., boy at r. 3 serial # varieties. Back: Arms at ctr. in unpt.				
		a. Issued note.	.50	2.50	8.00
		s. Perforated: *SPECIMEN.*	—	1.00	3.00

			VG	VF	UNC
10	**50 KORUN**				
	25.9.1944. Brownish gray. Wreath at ctr., woman at r. Back: Arms at ctr. in unpt.				
		a. Issued note.	1.00	7.00	30.00
		s. Perforated: *NEPLATNÉ* or *SPECIMEN.*	—	3.00	10.00

NATIONALBANK FÜR BÖHMEN UND MÄHREN
NATIONAL BANK FOR BOHEMIA AND MORAVIA
1942-44 ISSUES

11	500 KORUN	VG	VF	UNC
	24.2.1942. Dk. brown on m/c unpt. Portr. P. Brandl at r. Back: Olive and m/c.			
	a. Issued note.	3.00	8.00	30.00
	s. Perforated: SPECIMEN.	—	2.50	10.00

12	500 KORUN	VG	VF	UNC
	24.2.1942. Dk. brown on m/c unpt. Portr. P. Brandl at r. Back: Olive and m/c. II AUFAGE-II. VYDANI (2nd issue) at l. margin.			
	a. Issued note.	2.00	6.00	25.00
	s. Perforated: SPECIMEN.	—	2.00	10.00

13	1000 KORUN	VG	VF	UNC
	24.10.1942. Dk. green on green and brown unpt. Portr. P. Parler at r.			
	a. Issued note.	4.00	12.00	40.00
	s. Perforated: SPECIMEN.	—	4.00	12.00
14	1000 KORUN			
	24.10.1942. Dk. green. Portr. P. Parler at r. Back: Blue and brown guilloche. II AUFLAGE-II VYDANI (2nd issue) at l. margin.			
	a. Issued note.	2.00	6.00	35.00
	s. Perforated: NEPLATNÉ or SPECIMEN.	—	2.00	10.00
15	1000 KORUN			
	24.10.1942. Dk. green. Portr. P. Parler at r. Back: M/c guilloche. II AUFLAGE-II VYDANI (2nd issue) at l. margin.			
	a. Issued note.	2.00	6.00	35.00
	s. Perforated: SPECIMEN.	—	3.00	10.00
16	5000 KORUN			
	25.10.1943 (-old date 6.7.1920). Brown-violet. Red ovpt: NATIONALBANK FUR BÖHMEN UND MÄHREN on Czechoslovakia #16. Perforated: SPECIMEN.	—	10.00	50.00

17	5000 KORUN	VG	VF	UNC
	24.2.1944. Gray. Portr. H. Wenzel at r. Back: Brown and m/c.			
	a. Issued note.	8.00	27.50	70.00
	s. Perforated: SPECIMEN.	—	8.00	15.00

The Republic of Bolivia, a landlocked country in west central South America, has an area of 424,165 sq. mi. (1,098,581 sq. km.) and a population of 7.6 million. Capitals: La Paz (administrative); Sucre (constitutional). Mining is the principal industry and tin the most important metal. Minerals, petroleum, natural gas, cotton and coffee are exported.

The Incas, who ruled one of the world's greatest dynasties, incorporated the area that is now Bolivia into their empire about 1200AD. Their control was maintained until the Spaniards arrived in 1535 and reduced the predominantly Indian population to slavery. When Napoleon occupied Madrid in 1808 and placed his brother Joseph on the Spanish throne, a fervor of revolutionary activity quickened in Bolivia, culminating with the 1809 proclamation of independence. Sixteen years of struggle ensued before the republic, named for the famed liberator Simon Bolivar, was established on August 6, 1825. Since then, Bolivia has had more than 60 revolutions, 70 presidents and 11 constitutions.

RULERS:
Spanish to 1825

MONETARY SYSTEM:
1 Boliviano = 100 Centesimos (Centavos) to 1965
1 Bolivar = 100 Centavos, 1945-1962
1 Peso Boliviano = 100 Centavos, 1962-1987
1 Boliviano = 100 Centavos, 1987-

NOTE: Certain listings encompassing issues circulated by various bank and regional authorities are contained in Volume 1.

REPUBLIC

TESORERIA DE LA REPÚBLICA DE BOLIVIA

1902 ISSUE
#91-95 intended for circulation in the northwest during the Acre territory conflict with Brazil. Printer: ABNC.

91	50 CENTAVOS	VG	VF	UNC
	29.11.1902. Black on green unpt. Shield w/flags and eagle at ctr. Back: Green. Series E-J.	1.50	5.00	25.00

92	1 BOLIVIANO	VG	VF	UNC
	29.11.1902. Black on brown and olive unpt. Shield w/flags and eagle at l., tropical vegetation at r. Back: Brown. Series F-I; K.	2.00	5.00	25.00
93	5 BOLIVIANOS			
	29.11.1902. Black on pale blue unpt. Shield w/flags and eagle at l., tree on hill at r. Back: Dk. blue.			
	a. Issued note.	—	Rare	—
	r. W/o series. Proof.	100.00	250.00	500.00
94	10 BOLIVIANOS			
	29.11.1902. Black on orange unpt. Shield w/flags and eagle at l., tropical vegetation at r. Back: Orange. Woman's head at ctr.			
	a. Issued note.	—	Rare	—
	r. W/o series. Proof.	75.00	175.00	450.00
95	20 BOLIVIANOS			
	29.11.1902. Black on olive unpt. Tropical trees at l., man tapping tree at r. Back: Olive. Woman's head at ctr.			
	a. Issued note.	—	Rare	—
	r. W/o series. Proof.	150.00	450.00	—

BANCO DE LA NACIÓN BOLIVIANA

PROVISIONAL ISSUE 1911
New bank name ovpt. in red on earlier issues of the Banco Bolivia y Londres. Old date 1.2.190.

96	**1 BOLIVIANO**	GOOD	FINE	XF
	ND (1911).	60.00	200.00	—
97	**5 BOLIVIANOS**			
	ND (1911).	—	—	—
98	**10 BOLIVIANOS**			
	ND (1911).	—	—	—
99	**20 BOLIVIANOS**			
	ND (1911).	—	—	—
100	**50 BOLIVIANOS**			
	ND (1911).	—	—	—
101	**100 BOLIVIANOS**			
	ND (1911).	—	—	—

REGULAR ISSUE 1911
#102,103 and 105-111 arms at ctr. on back. Sign. varieties. Printer: ABNC.

102	**1 BOLIVIANO**	GOOD	FINE	XF
	11.5.1911. Black w/brown, green and purple quilloches at sides. Mercury at ctr. Back: Green. Printer: ABNC.			
	a. Black series letters from A-Z and AA-ZZ (size varieties). AB-AZ.	1.00	3.00	10.00
	b. Red series A1-Z2.	1.00	3.00	10.00

103	**1 BOLIVIANO**	GOOD	FINE	XF
	11.5.1911. Black on green and m/c unpt. Different guilloches at sides. Mercury at ctr. Back: Green. Printer: ABNC. Red series A1-J1.	1.00	3.00	10.00

104	**1 BOLIVIANO**	GOOD	FINE	XF
	11.5.1911. Frame similar to #102 but w/o vignette. At ctr., large wmk. (head of Mercury). Back: Dp. green. Printer: CPM. Series A1-Z1.	50.00	125.00	325.00

105	**5 BOLIVIANOS**	GOOD	FINE	XF
	11.5.1911. Black w/ m/c guilloche. Mercury seated at l. Back: Blue-gray.			
	a. Black series A-Z, Aa-Jj, KK-PP.	1.00	4.00	15.00
	b. Red series QQ-ZZ, A1-D1.	1.00	4.00	15.00

106	**5 BOLIVIANOS**	GOOD	FINE	XF
	11.5.1911. Black on tan and blue unpt. w/different guilloche. Mercury seated at l. Back: Blue-gray. Red series A-E.	1.00	4.00	15.00

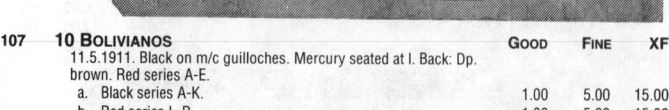

107	**10 BOLIVIANOS**	GOOD	FINE	XF
	11.5.1911. Black on m/c guilloches. Mercury seated at l. Back: Dp. brown. Red series A-E.			
	a. Black series A-K.	1.00	5.00	15.00
	b. Red series L-P.	1.00	5.00	15.00

108	**20 BOLIVIANOS**	GOOD	FINE	XF
	11.5.1911. Black on m/c guilloches. Mercury seated at ctr. Back: Orange. text.			
	a. Issued note. Series A.	200.00	—	—
	p. Back proof.	—	Unc	3000.
109	**20 BOLIVIANOS**			
	11.5.1911. Black on m/c guilloches. Mercury seated at ctr. Back: Orange. BOLIVIANOS in frame. 184 x 89mm. Black series A; B.	5.00	20.00	60.00
109A	**20 BOLIVIANOS**			
	11.5.1911. Black on m/c guilloches. Mercury seated at ctr. Back: Orange. BOLIVIANOS in frame. 184 x 89mm. Red series C; D.	5.00	20.00	60.00
109B	**20 BOLIVIANOS**			
	11.5.1911. Black on m/c different guilloches. Mercury seated at ctr. Back: Orange. BOLIVIANOS in frame. 184 x 89mm. Red series A.	5.00	20.00	60.00

110	**50 BOLIVIANOS**	GOOD	FINE	XF
	11.5.1911. Black on m/c guilloches. Mercury seated at l. Back: Olive. Black series A.	20.00	70.00	150.00

111	100 BOLIVIANOS	GOOD	FINE	XF
	11.5.1911. Black on m/c guilloches. Mercury seated at ctr. Black series A.	12.00	40.00	110.00

BANCO CENTRAL DE BOLIVIA

1929 PROVISIONAL ISSUE

New bank ovpt. (1928) on earlier series of El Banco de la Nación Boliviana. Old date 11.5.1911. Sign varieties.

112	1 BOLIVIANO	GOOD	FINE	XF
	ND (1929). Blue or black ovpt. *BANCO CENTRAL DE BOLIVIA* on #103. Red series from K1-Z4.	.20	1.00	4.00

113	5 BOLIVIANOS	GOOD	FINE	XF
	ND (1929). Blue ovpt. *BANCO CENTRAL DE BOLIVIA* on #106. Red series F-U.	.30	1.50	10.00

114	10 BOLIVIANOS	GOOD	FINE	XF
	ND (1929). Ovpt. on face of #107 but w/different guilloche. Back: Brown-orange. Blue ovpt. *BANCO CENTRAL DE BOLIVIA.* Red series A-H.	.60	3.00	15.00

115	20 BOLIVIANOS	GOOD	FINE	XF
	ND (1929). Blue ovpt. *BANCO CENTRAL DE BOLIVIA* on #109. Red series B-D.	4.00	12.00	60.00

116	50 BOLIVIANOS	GOOD	FINE	XF
	ND (1929). Ovpt. on #110 but w/different guilloche. Blue *BANCO CENTRAL DE BOLIVIA.* Red series A.	4.00	12.00	60.00

117	100 BOLIVIANOS	GOOD	FINE	XF
	ND (1929). Red-violet ovpt. *BANCO CENTRAL DE BOLIVIA.* Red series A.	8.00	20.00	80.00

LAW OF 20.7.1928

#118-127 have arms on back. Printer: ABNC.

#118 and 120-122 portr. S. Bolívar at l., view of Potosíand mountain at r. ctr. Many sign. varieties.

NOTE: The rose unpt. on #125 fades easily; no premium for notes w/o rose unpt.

118	1 BOLIVIANO	VG	VF	UNC
	L.1928. Dp. brown on green, orange and rose unpt. Back: Dp. blue. Arms. Series A-Z; A1-A6.	.20	1.00	5.00

119	1 BOLIVIANO	VG	VF	UNC
	L.1928. Dp. brown. Portr. S. Bolívar at ctr. Back: Dp. blue. Arms. Series A-Z1.	.20	1.00	4.00

120	5 BOLIVIANOS	VG	VF	UNC
	L.1928. Dp. green on blue, brown and rose unpt. Back: Dp. blue. Arms. Series A-M10.	.40	2.00	7.50

121 **10 BOLIVIANOS**
L.1928. Dp. blue on rose, green and lilac unpt. Back: Red. Series A-V4.

	VG	VF	UNC
	.60	3.00	12.50

126 **500 BOLIVIANOS**
L.1928. Olive-green on m/c unpt. Back: Purple.

		VG	VF	UNC
a.	Series A. Hand signed.	60.00	150.00	—
b.	Series A, B. Printed sign.	4.00	20.00	75.00

127 **1000 BOLIVIANOS**
L.1928. Red on green, orange and lilac unpt. Back: Dp. blue-gray. Series A.

		VG	VF	UNC
a.	Hand sign.	60.00	150.00	—
b.	Printed sign.	15.00	75.00	175.00

LAW OF 20.7.1928 SECOND ISSUE

#128-135 arms on back. Printer: W&S.
#128-130 portr. of S. Bolívar at ctr. Sign. varieties.
#131-133 view of Potosí at l. ctr., portr. S. Bolívar at r. Sign. varieties.
#134-135 view of La Paz at l. ctr. Sign. varieties.

122 **20 BOLIVIANOS**
L.1928. Brown on m/c unpt. Back: Green. Series A-Z3.

	VG	VF	UNC
	.80	4.00	15.00

128 **1 BOLIVIANO**
L.1928. Brown. Back: Dp. blue.

		VG	VF	UNC
a.	Ovpt: W/o *EMISION*. Series A-D14.	.10	.50	1.50
b.	Ovpt: *EMISION 1951*. Series E14-Q14.	.60	3.00	10.00
c.	Ovpt: *EMISION 1952*. Series Q14-R16.	.5	.25	.75

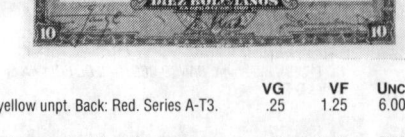

123 **50 BOLIVIANOS**
L.1928. Purple on green, lilac and yellow unpt. Back: Red. Series A-G.

	VG	VF	UNC
	3.00	15.00	50.00

129 **5 BOLIVIANOS**
L.1928. Grayish green. Back: Olive. Series A-R6.

	VG	VF	UNC
	.10	.60	3.00

124 **50 BOLIVIANOS**
L.1928. Purple on green, lilac and yellow unpt. Back: Orange. Series H-Z.

	VG	VF	UNC
	2.00	10.00	35.00

130 **10 BOLIVIANOS**
L.1928. Dp. blue on green and yellow unpt. Back: Red. Series A-T3.

	VG	VF	UNC
	.25	1.25	6.00

131 **20 BOLIVIANOS**
L.1928. Brown on green, lilac and orange unpt. Back: Dp. green. Series A-L6.

	VG	VF	UNC
	.30	1.50	7.50

125 **100 BOLIVIANOS**
L.1928. Blue-black on rose, ochre and green. Back: Dp. brown. Series A-M.

	VG	VF	UNC
	1.75	9.00	37.50

132 50 BOLIVIANOS
L.1928. Purple on green, lilac and yellow unpt. Back: Orange. Series A-H3.

	VG	VF	UNC
	.40	2.00	10.00

133 100 BOLIVIANOS
L.1928. Dk. gray on orange, lilac and rose unpt. Back: Dp. brown. Series A-E2.

	VG	VF	UNC
	2.00	10.00	30.00

134 500 BOLIVIANOS
L.1928. Olive-green on rose and pale yellow-green unpt. Portr. S. Bolívar at r. Back: Purple. Series A-G.

	VG	VF	UNC
	3.00	15.00	45.00

135 1000 BOLIVIANOS
L.1928. Rose on yellow, green and lt. blue unpt. Back: Gray. Series A-D.

	VG	VF	UNC
	5.00	25.00	75.00

DECREE OF 16.3.1942

#136-137 back black on pink, yellow and green unpt., w/arms at ctr. Sign varieties. Series A. Printer: W&S.

136 5000 BOLIVIANOS
D.1942. Red-brown and m/c. Miner at ctr. Back: Dp. greenish gray.

	VG	VF	UNC
	30.00	85.00	225.00

137 10,000 BOLIVIANOS
D.1942. Dp. blue and m/c. Puerta del Sol at ctr. Back: Dp. greenish gray.

	VG	VF	UNC
	30.00	85.00	225.00

LAW OF 20.12.1945

#138-146 Sign. varieties. Printer TDLR.

138 5 BOLIVIANOS
L.1945. Brown on green and sky blue unpt. Portr. S. Bolivar at r., arms at l. Back: Brown. Arms at ctr.

	VG	VF	UNC
a. Ovpt: W/o *EMISION* Series A-Q.	.20	.40	1.00
b. Ovpt: *EMISION 1951* in 1 or Ovpt: 2 lines. Series C; D.	.50	2.00	6.00
c. Ovpt: *EMISION 1952.* Series D.	.25	.75	1.50
d. Ovpt: Remainder w/o ovpt. or sign. Series K; C1.	—	—	1.50

139 10 BOLIVIANOS
L.1945. Blue on rose, brown and sky blue unpt. Portr. A. J. de Sucre at r., arms at l. Back: Dk. olive. W/Potosí scene.

	VG	VF	UNC
a. Ovpt: *EMISION 1951.* Series A.	1.00	3.00	6.50
b. Ovpt: *EMISION 1952.* Series A; B.	.20	.50	1.00
c. Ovpt: W/o *EMISION.* Series C.	.25	.75	3.00
d. Ovpt: Remainder w/o ovpt. or sign. Series R; V; C1.	—	—	1.50

140 20 BOLIVIANOS
L.1945. Brown and m/c. Portr. S. Bolívar at r., arms at l. Back: Dp. red. Obv. and Rev. of 1862 coin and Potosí Mint. Series A-Q.

	VG	VF	UNC
	.20	.40	1.50

141 50 BOLIVIANOS
L.1945. Purple on green and sky blue unpt. Portr. A. J. de Sucre at r. Back: Green. Cows at water hole. Series A-Z; A1-K1.

	VG	VF	UNC
	.25	.75	2.50

142   100 BOLIVIANOS
L.1945. Black and m/c. Portr. S. Bolívar at r., arms at l. Back: Purple. Farmers. Series A-W.

	VG	VF	UNC
	.75	3.00	10.00

143   500 BOLIVIANOS
L.1945. Green on red, lilac and yellow unpt. Portr. A. J. de Sucre at r., arms at l. Back: Orange. Oil well. Series A-C.

	VG	VF	UNC
	1.25	5.00	15.00

144   1000 BOLIVIANOS
L.1945. Red on m/c unpt. Portr. S. Bolivar at r., arms at l. Back: Black. Miners at ctr. Series A-C.

	VG	VF	UNC
	1.75	8.50	25.00

145   5000 BOLIVIANOS
L.1945. Brown and m/c. Portr. A. J. de Sucre at r., arms at l. Back: Blue. Puerta del Sol and llama at l. Series A.

	VG	VF	UNC
	5.00	17.50	55.00

146   10,000 BOLIVIANOS
L.1945. Blue and m/c. Portr. S. Bolívar at r., arms at l. Back: Green. Independence proclamation at l. ctr. Series A.

	VG	VF	UNC
	6.00	25.00	75.00

LAW OF 20.12.1945 SECOND ISSUE
#147-151 altered design or reduced size. Sign. varieties. Printer: TDLR.

147   100 BOLIVIANOS
L.1945. Black and m/c. Portr. G. Villarroel at r. Back: Purple. Oil refinery. Series A-Z; A1-T1.

	VG	VF	UNC
	.15	.40	1.50

148   500 BOLIVIANOS
L.1945. Green and red, blue and orange unpt. Portr. Busch at r. Back: Orange. Miners. Series A-Z; A1-D1.

	VG	VF	UNC
	.50	1.50	7.50

149   1000 BOLIVIANOS
L.1945. Red on green, rose and blue unpt. Portr. Murillo at r. Back: Black. Man w/native horn at ctr. Series A-Z; A1-C1.

	VG	VF	UNC
	.50	1.50	7.50

150   5000 BOLIVIANOS
L.1945. Brown and m/c. Portr. A. J. de Sucre at r., arms at l. Back: Blue. W/Puerta del Sol at ctr. Series A-P.

	VG	VF	UNC
	2.00	8.50	25.00

151	**10,000 BOLIVIANOS**	VG	VF	UNC
	L.1945. Blue and m/c. Flags at ctr., portr. S. Bolívar at r. Back: Green. Independence proclamation at ctr. Series A1-C2.	2.00	8.50	25.00

BRAZIL

The Federative Republic of Brazil, which comprises half the continent of South America, is the only Latin American country deriving its culture and language from Portugal. It has an area of 3,286,470 sq. mi. (8,511,965 sq. km.) and a population of 146 million. Capital: Brasília. The economy of Brazil is as varied and complex as any in the developing world. Agriculture is a mainstay of the economy, although but 4 percent of the area is under cultivation. Known mineral resources are almost unlimited in variety and size of reserves. A large, relatively sophisticated industry ranges from basic steel and chemical production to finished consumer goods. Coffee, cotton, iron ore and cocoa are the chief exports.

Brazil was discovered and claimed for Portugal by Admiral Pedro Alvares Cabral in 1500. Portugal established a settlement in 1532 and proclaimed the area a royal colony in 1549. During the Napoleonic Wars, Dom Joao VI established the seat of Portuguese government in Rio de Janeiro. When he returned to Portugal, his son Dom Pedro I declared Brazil's independence on Sept. 7, 1822, and became emperor of Brazil. The Empire of Brazil was maintained until 1889 when a republic was established. The Federative Republic was established in 1946 by terms of a constitution drawn up by a constituent assembly. Following a coup in 1964 the armed forces retained overall control under a dictatorship until a civilian government was restored on March 15, 1985. The current constitution was adopted in 1988.

RULERS:
Pedro II, 1831-1889

MONETARY SYSTEM:
1 Milreis = 1000 Reis, 1833-1942
1 Cruzeiro = 100 Centavos, 1942-1967
1 Cruzeiro Novo = 1000 Old Cruzeiros, 1967-1985
1 Cruzado = 1000 Cruzeiros Novos, 1986-1989
1 Cruzado Novo = 1000 Cruzados, 1989-1990
1 Cruzeiro = 1 Cruzado Novo, 1990-1993
1 Cruzerio Real (pl. Reals) = 1000 Cruzeiros, 1993-

SIGNATURE VARIETIES

1	CLAUDIONNR S. LEMOS HORÁCIO LAFER	**6**	CLAUDIONNR S. LEMOS LUCAS LOPES
2	CLAUDIONNR S. LEMOS OSWALDO ARANHA	**7**	AFFONSO ALMINO LUCAS LOPES
3	CLAUDIONNR S. LEMOS EUGENIO GUDIN	**8**	SEBASTIÃO P. ALMEIDA CARLOS A. CARRÍLHO
4	CLAUDIONNR S. LEMOS JOSÉ M. WHITAKER	**9**	CLEMENTE MARIANI CARLOS A. CARRÍLHO
5	CLAUDIONNR S. LEMOS JOSÉ MARIA ALKIMIN	**10**	WALTER M. SALLES REGINALDO F. NUNES

PORTUGUESE INFLUENCE

ADMINISTRAÇÃO GERAL DOS DIAMANTES

ROYAL DIAMOND ADMINISTRATION

1771-92 COLONIAL ISSUE
Drafts issued by the Administration to pay successful diamond prospectors. Values of the drafts were filled in by hand for amounts of gold paid for the diamonds. Drafts were exchangeable into coins and circulated at full face value as paper currency.

A101	**VARIOUS AMOUNTS**	GOOD	FINE	XF
	1771-1792. Stubs from draft forms printed in Lisbon.	25.00	50.00	110.00

IMPERIO DO BRASIL

TROCOS DE COBRE
Copper Exchange Notes

LEI DE 3 DE OUTOBRO DE 1833
Notes issued throughout all provincial offices in exchange for debased copper coinage. Names of individual provinces were handwritten on each piece issued. All denominations were reportedly issued by all 18 provinces, though some in small amounts. Almost all were issued in Ceará Province. Values showne are for the most available of each denomination. #A151-A157 arms at l. Uniface. Printed in Rio de Janeiro. Many notes are found w/paper damaged by tannic acid in the early ink used for official hand signatures.

A151	**1 MIL REIS**	GOOD	FINE	XF
	ND. Black.	10.00	30.00	110.00
A152	**2 MIL REIS**			
	ND. Black.	10.00	30.00	110.00
A153	**5 MIL REIS**			
	ND. Black.	10.00	30.00	110.00
A154	**10 MIL REIS**			
	ND. Lt. green.	12.00	35.00	120.00
A155	**20 MIL REIS**			
	ND. Lt. green.	12.00	35.00	120.00

A156	**50 MIL REIS**	GOOD	FINE	XF
	ND. Dk. green.	15.00	40.00	150.00
A157	**100 MIL REIS**			
	ND. Olive.	17.50	50.00	175.00

NO THESOURO NACIONAL

DECRETO DE 1 JUNHO DE 1833 (1835-36) ESTAMPA 1
#A201-A209 black. Arms c rowned at l., decreto at r. Vignettes at upper ctr. Uniface. Printer: PB&P.

A201	**1 MIL REIS**	GOOD	FINE	XF
	D. 1833. Agriculture view at upper ctr.	30.00	90.00	—
A202	**2 MIL REIS**			
	D. 1833. The Arts at upper ctr.	40.00	120.00	—
A203	**5 MIL REIS**			
	D. 1833. Commerce at upper ctr.	60.00	185.00	—
A204	**10 MIL REIS**			
	D. 1833. Dom Pedro II at ctr.	—	—	—
A205	**20 MIL REIS**			
	D. 1833. 2 seated figures (Justice) w/date of Independence of Brazil at upper ctr.	—	—	—
A206	**50 MIL REIS**			
	D. 1833. Allegory of the discovery of Brazil at upper ctr.	—	—	—

A207	**100 MIL REIS**	GOOD	FINE	XF
	D. 1833. Scene of Recife at upper ctr.	—	—	—
A208	**200 MIL REIS**			
	D. 1833. View of Bahia at upper ctr.	—	—	—
A209	**500 MIL REIS**			
	D. 1833. View of Rio de Janeiro at upper ctr.	—	—	—

DECRETO DE 1 JUNHO DE 1833 (1830-44) ESTAMPA 2
#A210-A218 Decree at l., arms at r. Uniface. Printer: PB&P.

A210	**1 MIL REIS**	GOOD	FINE	XF
	D. 1833. Orange. Commerce at upper ctr. Yellow.	30.00	90.00	—
A211	**2 MIL REIS**			
	D. 1833. Orange. Agriculture view at upper ctr.	40.00	120.00	—
A212	**5 MIL REIS**			
	D. 1833. Orange. The arts at upper ctr.	—	—	—
A213	**10 MIL REIS**			
	D. 1833. Blue and sepia. Allegory of the discovery of Brazil at upper ctr.	—	—	—

A214	**20 MIL REIS**	GOOD	FINE	XF
	D. 1833. Blue and sepia. Dom Pedro II at ctr.	—	—	—
A215	**50 MIL REIS**			
	D. 1833. Blue and sepia. 2 seated figures (Justice) w/date of independence of Brazil at upper ctr.	—	—	—
A216	**100 MIL REIS**			
	D. 1833. Green. View of Rio de Janeiro at upper ctr.	—	—	—
A217	**200 MIL REIS**			
	D. 1833. Green. Scene of Recife at upper ctr.	—	—	—
A218	**500 MIL REIS**			
	D. 1833. Green. View of Bahia at upper ctr.	—	—	—

DECRETO DE 1 JUNHO DE 1833 (1843-60) ESTAMPA 3
#A219-A227 Uniface.
#A219-A220 printer: PBC.

A219	**1 MIL REIS**	GOOD	FINE	XF
	D. 1833. Black on blue unpt. Commerce at upper ctr.	15.00	45.00	135.00

A220 **2 MIL REIS**
D. 1833. Black on green unpt. Agriculture view at upper ctr.

	GOOD	FINE	XF
	20.00	60.00	180.00

W/O DECRETO CA. 1850
#A221-A227 printer: PB&P.

A221 **5 MIL REIS**
ND. Royal emblem w/crown at l., agriculture view at upper ctr., arms at r.

	GOOD	FINE	XF
	20.00	60.00	180.00

A222 **10 MIL REIS**
ND. Royal crest at l., 2 seated figures (Justice) w/date of independence at upper ctr., arms at r.

	25.00	75.00	225.00

A223 **20 MIL REIS**
ND. Blue. Royal crest at l., allegory of the discovery of Brazil at upper ctr., arms at r. Yellow.

	GOOD	FINE	XF
	75.00	225.00	—

A224 **50 MIL REIS**
ND. Black on red unpt. Royal crest at l., Dom Pedro II at upper ctr., arms at r.

	—	—	—

A225 **100 MIL REIS**
ND. Arms at l., view of Bahia at upper ctr., royal crest at r.

	—	—	—

A226 **200 MIL REIS**
ND. Arms at l., view of Rio de Janeiro at upper ctr., royal crest at r.

	—	—	—

A227 **500 MIL REIS**
ND. Arms at l., scene of Recife at upper ctr., royal crest at r.

	—	—	—

ESTAMPA 4, 1852-67
#A228-A236 w/o date. Uniface.

A228 **1 MIL REIS**
ND. Black on blue unpt. Portr. Dom Pedro II at l., Justice, Agriculture and Commerce seated at upper ctr., crowned arms at r. Printer: PBC.

	GOOD	FINE	XF
	13.50	40.00	100.00

A229 **2 MIL REIS**
ND. Black on green unpt. Justeice and Truth at upper ctr. Printer: PBC.

	16.50	50.00	125.00

A230 **5 MIL REIS**
ND. Arms at l., 2 seated figures (Justice) w/date of independence at upper ctr., royal emblem w/crown at r. Printer: PB&P.

	20.00	60.00	150.00

A231 **10 MIL REIS**
ND. Black on brown unpt. Agriculture w/Brazilian arms at upper ctr. Back: Most examples of #A231 are counterfeits. Unpt. wording on these forgeries ends in *REIS* at r. instead of *MILas* on genuine notes. forgeries have irregular lettering in imprint. Printer: PBC.

	23.00	70.00	175.00

A232 **20 MIL REIS**
ND. Peace, Agriculture and Science at upper ctr. Printer: PB&P.

	30.00	90.00	225.00

A233 **50 MIL REIS**
ND. Black on blue unpt. Agriculture and Commerece at upper ctr. W/ or w/o *ESTAMPA 4a* on note. Printer: PBC.

	—	—	—

A234 **100 MIL REIS**
ND. Black on purple unpt. Allegrical figures at l. and r., allegory of the descovery of Brazil at upper ctr. Printer: PBC.

	GOOD	FINE	XF

A235 **200 MIL REIS**
ND. Black on purple unpt. Dom Pedro II at upper l. and lower r., arms at lower l. and upper r., 2 seated figures (Justice) w/date of independence at upper ctr., and w/o date of column. Printer: PBC.

	GOOD	FINE	XF

A236 **500 MIL REIS**
ND. Black on green unpt.. Allegorical figures at l. and r., Agriculture, Art and Commerce at ctr. Printer: PBC.

	—	—	—

ESTAMPA 5, 1860-68
#A237-S239 w/o date. Uniface. Printer: PBC.

A237 **5 MIL REIS**
ND. Black on brown unpt. Arms at l., Justice and Commerece w/arms at ctr., Dom Pedro II at r. Printer: PBC.

	GOOD	FINE	XF
	16.50	50.00	125.00

A238 **10 MIL REIS**
ND. Black on purple unpt. Allegorical figures l. and r., Dom Pedro II at upper ctr., arms w/cherubs at lower ctr. Printer: PBC.

	30.00	90.00	225.00

A239 20 MIL REIS

		GOOD	FINE	XF
ND. Black on green unpt. Dom Pedro II at l., Commerce at ctr., arms at r.				
	a. W/o *ESTAMPA.* Series 1-8.	32.50	100.00	250.00
	b. W/*ESTAMPA 5a.* Series 9.	32.50	100.00	250.00

ESTAMPA 6, 1866-70
#A240-A241 w/o date. Uniface. Printer: PBC.

A240 5 MIL REIS

	GOOD	FINE	XF
ND. Black on brown unpt. Commerece, Art and Science w/medallic portr. of Dom Pedro II at ctr.	21.50	65.00	165.00

A241 20 MIL REIS

	GOOD	FINE	XF
ND. Black on green unpt. Allegorical figures at l. and r., Rio de Janeiro harbor at ctr.			

ESTAMPA 1, 1874

A242 500 REIS

	GOOD	FINE	XF
ND (21.12.1874). Black on oragne unpt. Arms at l., Dom Pedro II at ctr., seated woman at r. Back: Orange. Printer: ABNC.	3.50	15.00	75.00

ESTAMPA 2, 1880

A243 500 REIS

		GOOD	FINE	XF
ND (1.9.1880). Black on orange-brown unpt. Woman reclining at l., portr. Dom pedro II at ctr., woman sitting at r. Back: Orange-brown. Printer: ABNC.				
	a. 1 serial #.	3.00	12.50	65.00
	b. 2 serial #.	3.00	12.00	60.00

ESTAMPA 5, 1870-78
#A244-A249 printer: ABNC.

A244 1 MIL REIS

	GOOD	FINE	XF
ND (1870). Black on blue unpt. Dom Pedro II at l., boat, tree and steam train at ctr., arms at r. Back: Blue.	3.50	15.00	75.00

A245 2 MIL REIS

	GOOD	FINE	XF
ND (1870). Black on green unpt. Dom Pedro II at l., arms at ctr., trees at r. Back: Green.	8.00	25.00	100.00

A246 50 MIL REIS

	GOOD	FINE	XF
ND (1874). Black on lt. green and brown unpt. Dom Pedro II at l., abundance at ctr., arms at r. Back: Brown.	12.50	40.00	160.00

A247 100 MIL REIS

		GOOD	FINE	XF
ND (1877). Black on red and green unpt. Arms at l., Dom Pedro II at ctr., woman at r. Back: Orange. Arms at ctr.				
	a. Single serial #.	60.00	250.00	—
	b. 2 serial #.	60.00	250.00	—

A248	**200 MIL REIS**	Good	Fine	XF
	ND (1874). Black on red and blue unpt. Tree at l., Dom Pedro II at ctr., arms at r. Back: Green and black. Seated woman at l. and r.	140.00	425.00	—
A249	**500 MIL REIS**			
	ND (ca.1883). Black on orange and blue unpt. Arms at l., Dom Pedro II at ctr., woman at r. Back: Brown and black. Dom Pedro II at l., arms at r.	—	—	—

ESTAMPA 6, 1869-82
#A250-A254 printer: ABNC.

A250	**1 MIL REIS**	Good	Fine	XF
	ND (1879). Black on green unpt. Arms at l., portr. Dom Pedro II at ctr., seated woman at r. Back: Green.			
	a. 1 serial #.	4.50	22.00	65.00
	b. 2 serial #.	3.50	18.00	55.00

A255	**1 MIL REIS**	Good	Fine	XF
	ND. Black on green unpt. Bldg. and arms at l., portr. Dom Pedro II at r. Back: Black and green. Equestrian statue of D. Pedro I.	5.00	15.00	60.00

A251	**2 MIL REIS**	Good	Fine	XF
	ND (1882). Black on blue unpt. Cherub w/ arms at ., portr. Dom Pedro II at r. ctr. Back: Blue.	6.50	32.50	100.00

A252	**10 MIL REIS**	Good	Fine	XF
	ND (1869). Black on green unpt. Dom Pedro II at l., 2 seated women w/arms at ctr., tree at r. Back: Green.	22.50	90.00	—
A252A	**20 MIL REIS**			
	ND (ca.1868). Black on orange unpt. Allegorical woman w/industrial elements at., Dom Pedro II at ctr. arms at r. Back: Orange.	—	—	—

A253	**50 MIL REIS**	Good	Fine	XF
	ND. Black on orange and yellow unpt. Portr. Dom Pedro II at l., allegorical woman at r. Back: Brown and black. Large bldg. at ctr.	50.00	200.00	—
A254	**200 MIL REIS**			
	ND. Black on blue and yellow unpt. Shoreline scene at l., Dom Pedro II at ctr., arms at r. Back: Black and orange. Scene of the first Mass held in Brazil in ctr.	—	—	—

ESTAMPA 7, 1869-83
#A255-A259 printer: ABNC.

A256	**2 MIL REIS**	Good	Fine	XF
	ND. Black on brown unpt. Portr. Dom Pedro II at l., arms at r. Back: Brown. Arms at l.	8.50	25.00	100.00

A257	**5 MIL REIS**	Good	Fine	XF
	ND (1869). Black on brown unpt. Truth at l., arms at ctr., Dom Pedro II at r. W. or w/o *ESTAMPA 7* on note. Back: Brown.	30.00	90.00	—

A258	**10 MIL REIS**	Good	Fine	XF
	ND (1883). Black on orange and green unpt. Justice w/arms at l., portr. Dom Pedro II at ctr., 2 rams at r. Back: Green. Arms at ctr.	30.00	90.00	—

A259	**20 MIL REIS**	Good	Fine	XF
	ND. Black on gold and green unpt. Portr. Dom Pedro II at l., woman leaning on column w/arms at ctr., seated woman at r. Back: Brown. Arms at ctr.	—	—	—

ESTAMPA 8 CA. 1885
#A260-A263 printer: ABNC.

A260	**2 MIL REIS**	Good	Fine	XF
	ND. Black on brown unpt. Portr. Dom Pedro II at l., church at r. Back: Blue and black. Street scene and Rio de Janeiro Post Office.	6.50	20.00	80.00

		GOOD	FINE	XF
A261	**5 MIL REIS** ND. Black on purple, orange and blue unpt. Woman w/wheat at l., Portr. Dom Pedro II at ctr., man w/sheep at r. Back: Brown. Arms at ctr. 1 or 2 serial #.	26.50	80.00	—

		GOOD	FINE	XF
A262	**10 MIL REIS** ND. Black on green and orange unpt. Portr. Dom Pedro II at l., arms at ctr., standing woman at r. Back: Green. Arms at ctr.	40.00	120.00	—

		GOOD	FINE	XF
A263	**20 MIL REIS** ND. Black on orange and green unpt. 2 women w/arms in column at l., Portr. Dom Pedro II at r. Back: Brown. Arms at l.	45.00	140.00	—

ESTAMPA 9, 1888

		GOOD	FINE	XF
A264	**5 MIL REIS** ND (6.1888). Black on orange and blue unpt. Portr. Dom Pedro II at l., cherub at ctr., Art at r. Back: Brown. Arms at ctr. Printer: ABNC.	17.50	70.00	—

REPUBLIC

REPUBLICA DOS ESTADOS UNIDOSDO BRASIL,

THESOURO NACIONAL

1891-1931 ISSUE
#1-93 w/o date; some individual notes are designated by Estampas…(*E* = printings).

		GOOD	FINE	XF
1	**500 REIS** *E. 3A* (1893). Black on yellow unpt. Woman w/sheep at l., woman at r. Printer: ABNC.			
	a. 1 handwritten sign.	3.00	12.00	35.00
	b. 2 printed sign.	3.50	15.00	45.00

		GOOD	FINE	XF
2	**500 REIS** W/o *Estampa* (1901). Violet on ochre unpt. Liberty at l. Printer: BWC.	4.00	16.00	50.00

		GOOD	FINE	XF
3	**1 MIL REIS** *E. 7A* (1891). Black on green unpt. Imperial Museum at l., child holding caduceus at r. Back: Green. Printer: ABNC.			
	a. Frame 63mm high. 1 handwritten sign.	3.00	13.00	40.00
	b. Frame 65mm high. 2 printed sign.	3.50	15.00	45.00
	c. Back: Frame 60mm high and horizontal bar at ctr. removed. 1 handwritten sign.	3.00	13.00	40.00

		GOOD	FINE	XF
4	**1 MIL REIS** W/o *Estampa* (1902). Blue on ochre unpt. Liberty at top ctr. Printer: BWC.	7.50	30.00	90.00

		GOOD	FINE	XF
5	**1 MIL REIS** *E. 9A* (1918). Black on orange unpt. Imperial Museum at l., child holding caduceus at r. Back: Orange. Printer: ABNC.	5.00	30.00	60.00
6	**1 MIL REIS** *E. 10A* (1919). Blue on m/c unpt. Padre D. A. Feijo at ctr. Printer: ABNC.	4.50	17.50	50.00

		GOOD	FINE	XF
7	**1 MIL REIS** *E. 11A* (1920). Blue on pink unpt. D. Campista at ctr. Printer: CdM (w/o imprint).	4.00	16.50	50.00
8	**1 MIL REIS** *E. 12A* (1921). Blue on olive unpt. D. Campista at ctr. Printer: CdM.	3.50	15.00	45.00
9	**1 MIL REIS** *E. 13A* (1923). Brown on ochre unpt. D. Campista at ctr. Printer: CdM.	4.50	18.50	55.00
10	**2 MIL REIS** *E. 8A* (1890). Ochre unpt. Woman seated w/child at l., bldg. and church at r. Printer: ABNC.			
	a. Small background lettering at top *IMPERIODO BRASIL DOIS MIL REIS*.	4.50	17.50	50.00
	b. Small background lettering at top, only *DOIS MIL REIS*.	4.50	17.50	50.00
11	**2 MIL REIS** *E. 9A* (1900). Lilac and violet unpt. Woman at r. Printer: ABNC.	7.50	30.00	90.00

		GOOD	FINE	XF
12	**2 MIL REIS** W/o *Estampa* (1902). Green on ochre unpt. Liberty a lower r. Printer: BWC.	10.00	40.00	120.00

		GOOD	FINE	XF
13	**2 MIL REIS** *E. 11A* (1918). Red-brown and green unpt. Woman at r. Printer: ABNC.	6.00	25.00	75.00
14	**2 MIL REIS** *E. 12A* (1919). Blue on m/c unpt. Marques de Olinda, P. de Araujo Lima at ctr. Printer: ABNC.	7.50	30.00	90.00
15	**2 MIL REIS** *E. 13A* (1920). Blue on ochre unpt. J. Murtinho at ctr. Printer: CdM (w/o imprint).	7.50	30.00	90.00
16	**2 MIL REIS** *E. 14A* (1921). Blue on olive unpt. J. Murtinho at l. Printer: CdM (w/o imprint).	5.00	20.00	60.00
17	**2 MIL REIS** *E. 15A* (1923). Brown on yellow unpt. J. Murtinho at ctr. Printer: CdM.	5.00	20.00	60.00

		GOOD	FINE	XF
18	**5 MIL REIS** *E. 9A* (1890). Pink and blue unpt. Man at l., woman seated at r. Printer: ABNC.	7.50	30.00	90.00
19	**5 MIL REIS** *E. 10A* (1903). Brown on ochre unpt. Woman seated w/flowers and fruits. Designer: Georges Duval Inv. et del.	7.50	30.00	90.00
20	**5 MIL REIS** *E. 11A* (1907). Sepia. Woman seated w/flowers and fruits. Printer: CdM.	7.50	30.00	90.00
21	**5 MIL REIS** *E. 12A* (1908). Sepia on ochre unpt. Woman seated w/flowers and fruits.	13.50	40.00	120.00

		GOOD	FINE	XF
22	**5 MIL REIS** *E. 13A* (1909). M/c unpt. Woman seated w/laurel wreath and statuette at l. Printer: ABNC.	7.50	30.00	90.00
23	**5 MIL REIS** *E. 14A* (1912). M/c unpt. Woman seated at r. Printer: ABNC. (Not issued).	55.00	65.00	500.00

		GOOD	FINE	XF
24	**5 MIL REIS** *E. 14A* (1913). M/c unpt. B. do rio Branco (foeign minister) at ctr. Printer: ABNC.	6.00	25.00	75.00
25	**5 MIL REIS** *E. 15A* (1918). Claret. Wmk: at l. Printer: CPM.	13.50	40.00	120.00
26	**5 MIL REIS** *E. 16A* (1920). Green on lt. green. Pres. F. de Paula Rodrigues Alves at ctr. Printer: CdM.	8.00	35.00	100.00
27	**5 MIL REIS** *E. 17A* (1922). Brown on green unpt. Pres. F. de Paula Rodrigues Alves at ctr. Printer: CdM.	8.00	35.00	100.00
28	**5 MIL REIS** *E. 18A* (1923). Sepia on yellow unpt. Pres. F. de Paula Rodrigues Alves at ctr. Printer: CdM.	6.00	25.00	75.00

		GOOD	FINE	XF
29	**5 MIL REIS** *E. 19A* (1925). Blue on m/c unpt. B. do Rio Branco (foreign minister) at ctr. Printer: ABNC.			
	a. *BRAZIL.* 1 handwritten sign.	2.00	8.50	35.00
	b. *BRAZIL; Estampa* and serial # together.	1.50	6.00	25.00
	c. *BRASIL; Estampa* and serial # separated.	1.50	6.00	25.00

		GOOD	FINE	XF
30	**10 MIL REIS** *E. 8A* (1892). M/c unpt. Girl w/distaff at l., woman w/wheel at r. Back: Green. Printer: ABNC.	15.00	60.00	180.00
31	**10 MIL REIS** *E. 9A* (1903). Carmine on yellow unpt. Woman w/boy at r.	13.50	40.00	120.00
32	**10 MIL REIS** *E. 10A* (1907). Brown on ochre unpt. Woman w/boy at r. Printer: CdM.	13.50	40.00	120.00
33	**10 MIL REIS** *E. 11A* (1907). Black on red-brown, green and orange unpt. Woman holding law book w/lion at l. Back: Green. Caiza de Amortizacao at cir. Printer: ABNC.	13.50	40.00	120.00
34	**10 MIL REIS** *E. 12A* (1912). M/c unpt. Woman w/eagle at l. Printer: ABNC.	13.50	40.00	120.00
35	**10 MIL REIS** *E. 13A* (1914). Pink and brown unpt. Printer: CPM.	13.50	40.00	120.00
36	**10 MIL REIS** *E. 14A* (1918). Blue on m/c unpt. F. de Campos Slles at cir. Printer: ABNC.	13.50	40.00	120.00
37	**10 MIL REIS** *E. 15A* (1923). Ochre unpt. Woman w/plants at ctr. Printer: CdM.	13.50	40.00	120.00
38	**10 MIL REIS** *E. 16A* (1924). Green. S. Alves Barroso Jr. at ctr. Printer: CdM.	13.50	40.00	120.00

		GOOD	FINE	XF
39	**10 MIL REIS** *E. 17A* (1925). Blue on m/c unpt. Pres. Manuel Ferraz de Campos Salles at ctr. Printer: ABNC.			
	a. *BRAZIL.* 1 handwritten sign.	2.00	8.50	35.00
	b. *BRAZIL.* 2 printed sign.	2.00	8.50	35.00
	c. *BRAZIL; Estampa* and serial # together.	1.50	6.00	25.00
	d. *BRASIL; Estampa* and serial # separated.	1.50	6.00	25.00
40	**20 MIL REIS** *E. 8A* (1892). Orange unpt. 2 women w/cupid at l., women repeating at r. Printer: ABNC.	17.50	75.00	225.00
41	**20 MIL REIS** W/o *Estampa* (1900). Violet on ochre unpt. Woman w/boy at l., woman at r. Back: Pale blue. Arms. BWC.			
	a. Back: W/*NOVEMBRE.*	12.50	50.00	150.00
	b. Back: W/*NOVEMBRO.*	12.50	50.00	150.00
42	**20 MIL REIS** *E. 10A* (1905). Brown on ochre unpt. Boy seated at l., and at r., woman in circle at lower l. Back: Pale blue. Arms.	10.00	40.00	120.00
43	**20 MIL REIS** *E. 11A* (1907). Brown on ochre unpt. Boy seated at l., and at r., woman in circle at lower l. Back: Pale blue. Arms. Printer: CdM.	13.50	55.00	165.00

		GOOD	FINE	XF
44	**20 MIL REIS** *E. 12A* (1909). M/c unpt. Woman seated w/branch at ctr. Printer: ABNC.	12.50	50.00	150.00

45	**20 MIL REIS**	**GOOD**	**FINE**	**XF**
	E. 13A (1912). M/c unpt. Woman reclining at ctr. Printer: ABNC.	12.50	50.00	150.00
46	**20 MIL REIS**			
	E. 14A (1919). Blue on m/c unpt. 1st Pres. M. Manuel Deodoro do Fonseca at ctr. Printer: ABNC.	10.00	40.00	120.00
47	**20 MIL REIS**			
	E. 15A (1923). Brown on yellow unpt. Woman w/child at ctr. Printer: CdM.	12.00	37.00	110.00

48	**20 MIL REIS**	**GOOD**	**FINE**	**XF**
	E. 16A (1931). Blue on m/c unpt. 1st Pres. Manuel Deodoro do Fonseca at ctr. Printer: ABNC.			
	a. *BRAZIL.* 1 handwritten sign.	3.00	12.50	50.00
	b. *BRAZIL.* 2 printed sign.	3.00	12.50	50.00
	c. *BRAZIL; Estampa* and serial # together.	2.50	10.00	40.00
	d. *BRASIL; Estampa* and serial # separated.	2.75	9.00	36.00

49	**50 MIL REIS**	**GOOD**	**FINE**	**XF**
	E. 7A (1893). Yellow unpt. Woman seated w/2 children at l., woman standing with flag at r. Back: Brown and black. First Mass in Brazil at ctr. Printer: ABNC.	15.00	60.00	180.00
50	**50 MIL REIS**			
	W/o *Estampa* (1900). Violet on ochre unpt. Woman seated at l., woman at ctr. Printer: BWC.			
	a. Back: W/*NOVEMBRE.*	15.00	60.00	180.00
	b. Back: W/ *NOEMBRO.*	15.00	60.00	180.00
51	**50 MIL REIS**			
	E. 9A (1906). Brown on green unpt. Boy at l. and at r., woman in circle l. of ctr. Printer: BWC.	15.00	60.00	180.00
52	**50 MIL REIS**			
	E. 10A (1908). Sepia-green and red-brown. Boy at l. and at r., woman in circle l. of ctr. Printer: BWC.	15.00	60.00	180.00
53	**50 MIL REIS**			
	E. 11A (1908). M/c unpt. Steamboat w/sails. Back: Olive. City view, river, mountains at ctr. Printer: ABNC.	15.00	60.00	180.00

54	**50 MIL REIS**	**GOOD**	**FINE**	**XF**
	E. 12A (1912). M/c unpt. Youth seated at r. Printer: ABNC.	12.50	50.00	150.00

55	**50 MIL REIS**	**GOOD**	**FINE**	**XF**
	E. 13A (1915). Ochre unpt. Printer: CPM.			
	a. 1 handwritten sign.	11.50	45.00	135.00
	b. 2 printed sign.	11.50	45.00	135.00
56	**50 MIL REIS**			
	E. 14A (1916). Black and m/c. Woman seated w/sword and flag at l., woman w/wreath at r. Printer: ABNC.	11.50	45.00	135.00
57	**50 MIL REIS**			
	E. 15A (1923). Blue on yellow-green. Woman seated w/scarf at ctr. Printer: CdM.	11.50	45.00	135.00

58	**50 MIL REIS**	**GOOD**	**FINE**	**XF**
	E. 16A (1925). Blue on m/c unpt. Pres. A da Silva Bernardes at cir. Printer: ABNC.	7.50	30.00	90.00
59	**50 MIL REIS**			
	E. 17A (1936). Violet. J. Xavier da Silveira, Jr. at l. Printer: W & S.	5.00	12.00	60.00
60	**100 MIL REIS**			
	E. 6A (1892). M/c unpt. Street scene w/ bldgs. at l., ship at r., woman at ctr. Printer: ABNC.	25.00	100.00	300.00
61	**100 MIL REIS**			
	E. 7A (1897). M/c unpt. Woman seated w/Cupid at r. Printer: ABNC.	25.00	100.00	300.00
62	**100 MIL REIS**			
	W/o *Estampa* (1901). Blue on ochre unpt. Woman w/sickle and Cupid at l. Printer: BWC.	30.00	120.00	360.00
62A	**100 MIL REIS**			
	ND. Blue and pink on tan paper Liberty w/ stars at l. Brown back.	—	—	—

63	**100 MIL REIS**	**GOOD**	**FINE**	**XF**
	E. 9A (1904). Blue and yellow unpt. Woman seated w/2 children reading at ctr.	30.00	120.00	360.00
64	**100 MIL REIS**			
	E. 10A (1907). Carmine on ochre unpt. Woman in circle at lower l.	25.00	100.00	300.00
65	**100 MIL REIS**			
	E. 11A (1909). M/c unpt. Woman seated w/child at l. Printer: ABNC.	25.00	100.00	300.00
66	**100 MIL REIS**			
	E. 12A (1912). M/c unpt. Woman seated w/wreath at l. Printer: ABNC.	22.50	90.00	270.00
67	**100 MIL REIS**			
	E. 13A (1915). Green unpt. Printer: CPM.	22.50	90.00	270.00

68	**100 MIL REIS**	**GOOD**	**FINE**	**XF**
	E. 14A (1919). Blue on m/c unpt. A. Augusto Moreira Pena at ctr. Printer: ABNC.	22.50	90.00	275.00

69 **100 MIL REIS**
E. 15A (1924). Sepia on ochre unpt. R. Barbosa at ctr. Printer: CdM.

	GOOD	FINE	XF
	22.50	90.00	275.00

70 **100 MIL REIS**
E. 16A (1925). Blue on m/c unpt. A. Augusto Moreira Pena at ctr. Printer: ABNC.

	GOOD	FINE	XF
a. *BRAZIL.* 1 handwritten sign.	6.00	25.00	100.00
b. *BRAZIL.* 2 printed sign.	6.00	25.00	100.00
c. *BRAZIL; Estampa* and serial # together.	5.50	22.50	90.00
d. *BRASIL; Estampa* and serial # separated.	5.50	22.50	90.00

71 **100 MIL REIS**
E. 17A (1936). Dk. blue on m/c unpt. A. Santos Dumont at r. Printer: W&S.

	GOOD	FINE	XF
	5.00	20.00	80.00

72 **200 MIL REIS**
E. 7A (1892). M/c unpt. Woman seated at l. and at r., helmsman at ctr. Printer: ABNC. — 32.50 135.00 400.00

73 **200 MIL REIS**
E. 8A (1897). Bicolored unpt. Woman w/child t r. Printer: ABNC. — 32.50 135.00 400.00

74 **200 MIL REIS**
W/o *Estampa* (1901). Violet on ochre unpt. Woman seated w/child at l., woman at ctr. Printer: BWC. — 32.50 135.00 400.00

75 **200 MIL REIS**
E. 10A (1905). Blue on yellow unpt. Ship and coastline at ctr., flanked by 2 women. — 32.50 135.00 400.00

76 **200 MIL REIS**
E. 11A (1908). M/c unpt. Woman and child reading at ctr. Printer: ABNC. — 32.50 135.00 400.00

77 **200 MIL REIS**
E. 12A (1911). M/c unpt. 2 women seated at r. Printer: ABNC. — 32.50 135.00 400.00

78 **200 MIL REIS**
E. 13A (1916). Ochre unpt. Back: Bldg. and plate modifications. Printer: CPM.

	GOOD	FINE	XF
a. 1 handwritten sign.	32.50	135.00	400.00
b. 2 printed sign.	32.50	135.00	400.00

79 **200 MIL REIS**
E. 14A (1919). Blue on m/c unpt. P. Jose de Moraes e Barros at ctr. Printer: ABNC. — 32.50 135.00 400.00

80 **200 MIL REIS**
E. 15A (1922). Sepia on ochre unpt. Woman seated at ctr. Printer: CdM. — 32.50 135.00 400.00

81 **200 MIL REIS**
E. 16A (1925). Blue on m/c unpt. P. Jose de Moraes e Barros at ctr. Printer: ABNC.

	GOOD	FINE	XF
a. *BRAZIL.* 1 handwritten sign.	5.50	22.50	90.00
b. *BRAZIL; Estampa* and serial # together.	5.00	20.00	80.00
c. *BRASIL; Estampa* and serial # separated.	5.00	20.00	80.00

82 **200 MIL REIS**
E. 17A (1936). Red-brown on m/c unpt. J. Saldanha Marinho at r. Printer: W&S. — 5.00 20.00 80.00

83 **500 MIL REIS**
E. 6A (1897). M/c unpt. Woman seated at ctr. flanked by women in circles. Printer: ABNC. — 30.00 120.00 360.00

84 **500 MIL REIS**
W/o *Estampa* (1901). Green on ochre unpt. Woman w/distaff at l., woman at r. Printer: BWC. — 37.50 150.00 450.00

85 **500 MIL REIS**
E. 8A (1904). Red. Woman w/child at l. and r. — 37.50 450.00 375.00

86 **500 MIL REIS**
E. 9A (1908). M/c unpt. Woman w/trumpet and sword at l., woman w/wreath and palm branch at r. Printer: ABNC. — 37.50 150.00 450.00

87 **500 MIL REIS**
E. 10A (1911). M/c unpt. Woman w/wreath at ctr. flanked by Cupids. Printer: ABNC. — 37.50 150.00 450.00

88 **500 MIL REIS**
E. 11A (1917). M/c unpt. Back: Bldg. Printer: CPM. — 37.50 150.00 450.00

89 **500 MIL REIS**
E. 12A (1919). Blue on m/c unpt. J. Bonifacio de Andrade e Silva at ctr. Printer: ABNC. — 37.50 150.00 450.00

90 **500 MIL REIS**
E. 13A (1924). Red. Man seated at ctr. w/train in background. Printer: CdM. — 37.50 150.00 450.00

91 **500 MIL REIS**
E. 14A (1925). Blue on m/c unpt. J. Bonifacio de Andrade e Silva at ctr. Printer: ABNC. — 30.00 125.00 375.00

92 **500 MIL REIS**
E. 15A (1931). Blue on m/c unpt. M. Peixoto at ctr. Printer: ABNC.

	GOOD	FINE	XF
a. *BRAZIL.* 1 handwritten sign.	7.50	30.00	120.00
b. *BRAZIL.* 2 printed sign.	7.50	30.00	120.00
c. *BRASIL; Estampa* and serial # together.	6.00	25.00	100.00
d. *BRASIL; Estampa* and serial # separated.	6.00	25.00	100.00

93	1000 MIL REIS	GOOD	FINE	XF
	E. 1A (1921). Blue on yellow unpt. Woman seated w/sword and Mercury symbol at l. Printer: CdM.	80.00	250.00	750.00

CAIXA DE CONVERSÃO

Closed down in 1920 and later absorbed by the Caixa de Estabilizacão.

1906, ESTAMPA 1

#94-98 printer: W&S.

NOTE: #94-98 are very often encountered as lithographed counterfeits.

94	10 MIL REIS			
	6.12.1906. Brown. Woman w/shield at l., A. Pena at ctr. Back: Bank bldg. at ctr.	6.00	25.00	75.00

95	20 MIL REIS	GOOD	FINE	XF
	6.12.1906. Blue. A. Pena at l., bank bldg. at r. Back: Steam train at ctr.	10.00	40.00	120.00
96	50 MIL REIS			
	6.12.1906. Brown and pink. A. Pena at l., bank bldg. at ctr. Back: 3 allegorical women at ctr.	20.00	80.00	240.00
97	100 MIL REIS			
	6.12.1906. Green and yellow. A. Pena at ctr., bank bldg. at r. Back: Trees at ctr.	25.00	100.00	325.00

98	200 MIL REIS	GOOD	FINE	XF
	6.12.1906. Black, yellow and red. A. Pena at r., bank bldg. at ctr. Back: Allegorical women w/cows, sheaves and farm implements.	30.00	120.00	400.00

1906, ESTAMPA 1A

99	500 MIL REIS	GOOD	FINE	XF
	6.12.1906. Green. Male stanlding at l., A. Pena at r. Back: Bank at lower ctr. Printer: JEZ.	50.00	200.00	700.00
100	1 CONTO DE REIS =1000 MIL REIS			
	6.12.1906. Brown. Winged allegorical male at l., A. Pena at r. Back: Bank at lower ctr. Printer: JEZ.	300.00	1200.	3600.

1910, ESTAMPA 2

101	10 MIL REIS	GOOD	FINE	XF
	31.12.1910. E. 2. Blue. Printer: CPM.	20.00	80.00	240.00
102	50 MIL REIS			
	31.12.1910. E. 2A. Brown. Bldg. at ctr. Back: Purple. Printer: CPM.	—	Rare	—

CAIXA DE ESTABILIZACAO, VALOR RECEBIDO EM OURO

ESTAMPA 1A

#103-109 black on m/c guilloche. Woman at ctr. 6 sign. varieties. Printer: ABNC.

103	10 MIL REIS	GOOD	FINE	XF
	18.12.1926. Back: Dk. brown. Coastal scenery.	7.50	30.00	90.00
104	20 MIL REIS			
	18.12.1926. Back: Red. City and trees at ctr.	10.00	40.00	120.00

105	50 MIL REIS	GOOD	FINE	XF
	18.12.1926. Back: Orange. Cavalry charge at ctr.	25.00	100.00	300.00
106	100 MIL REIS			
	18.12.1926. Back: Green. Bank at ctr.	50.00	150.00	450.00
107	200 MIL REIS			
	18.12.1926. Back: Blue-black. Cavalry and infantry battle scene at ctr.	42.50	175.00	525.00
108	500 MIL REIS			
	18.12.1926. Back: Blue. Naval battle at ctr.	100.00	400.00	1200.
109	1 CONTO DE REIS =1000 MIL REIS			
	18.12.1926. Back: Purple. Mission scene.	150.00	600.00	1800.

1926 ISSUE

#109A-109F Black A CAIXA DE ESTABILISACAO... ovpt. within rectangular frame on Thesouro Nacional notes. 2 printed sign. at lower part of note.

109A	10 MIL REIS	GOOD	FINE	XF
	E. 17A. Series. Ovpt: On #39.	7.50	30.00	90.00
109B	20 MIL REIS			
	E. 16A. Series 10. Ovpt: On #39.	—	—	—

109C	50 MIL REIS	GOOD	FINE	XF
	E. 16A. Series 9, 10. Ovpt: On #58.	7.50	30.00	90.00
109D	100 MIL REIS			
	E. 16A. Series 10. Ovpt: On #70.	15.00	60.00	180.00
109E	200 MIL REIS			
	E. 16A. Series 10. Ovpt: On #81.	12.50	50.00	150.00
109F	500 MIL REIS			
	E. 14A. Series 5. Ovpt: On # 91.	—	—	—

BANCO DO BRASIL

1923 PROVISIONAL ISSUE

110	500 MIL REIS			
	8.1.1923. Blue on yellow unpt. Man seatred w/train in background. Back Brown. Printer: CdM.	—	—	—
110A	1000 MIL REIS=1 CONTO DE REIS			
	E. 1A. ND. Carmine. Ovpt: Diagonal ovpt: NO BANCO DO Ovpt: BRASIL DE ACORDO... Ovpt: on #93.			

LEI N. 4635 A DE 8 DE JANERIODE 1923

#110B-123 printer: ABNC.

#110B-117 have either 1 hand sign. or 2 printed sign.

#110B-113 arms on back.

#118-123 have 2 printed sign only.

NOTE: #110B w/series #279-500 were issued in 1944 as Cruzeiro notes. See #124.

110B	1 MIL REIS	GOOD	FINE	XF
	L. 1923. E. 1A. Green unpt. C. Salles at ctr. Series #1-278	1.00	3.00	12.00

111	2 MIL REIS	GOOD	FINE	XF
	L. 1923. E. 1A. Black on m/c unpt. Portr. P. de Moraes at r.	2.00	7.50	35.00

112	5 MIL REIS	GOOD	FINE	XF
	L. 1923. E. 1A. Black on yellow-green unpt. Portr. B. do Rio Branco at l.	2.00	7.50	40.00
113	5 MIL REIS			
	L. 1923. E. 1A. Black on yellow-green unpt. Portr. B. do Rio Branco at l.	2.00	7.50	40.00

114	10 MIL REIS	GOOD	FINE	XF
	L. 1923. E. 1A. Black on m/c unpt. Portr. S. Vidal at ctr. Back: Orange. Bldg at ctr.	4.00	15.00	60.00

115	10 MIL REIS	GOOD	FINE	XF
	L. 1923. E. 1A. Black on m/c unpt. Portr. R. Alves at ctr. Back: Dk. brown. Bldg at ctr.	3.50	12.50	55.00

116	20 MIL REIS	GOOD	FINE	XF
	L. 1923. E. 1A. Black on m/c unpt. Portr. A. Bernardes at r. Back: Blue. Bldg at ctr.	8.00	30.00	90.00

117	20 MIL REIS	GOOD	FINE	XF
	L. 1923. E. 1A. Black on m/c unpt. Portr. A. Bernardes at r. Back: Brown. Bldg at ctr.	7.00	25.00	75.00

118	50 MIL REIS	GOOD	FINE	XF
	L. 1923. E. 1A. Black on m/c unpt. Portr. D. da Fonseca at l. Back: Brown. Canal at ctr.	20.00	75.00	225.00

119	50 MIL REIS	GOOD	FINE	XF
	L. 1923. E. 1A. Black on m/c unpt. Portr. M. de Olinda at l. Back: Red. Canal at ctr.	22.00	65.00	200.00

120	100 MIL REIS	GOOD	FINE	XF
	L. 1923. E. 1A. Black on m/c unpt. Portr. R. Feijo at ctr. Back: Green. Shoreline at r.	30.00	130.00	300.00
121	200 MIL REIS			
	L. 1923. E. 1A. Black on m/c unpt. Dom Pedro II at r. Back: Black. City and shoreline mountains behind at ctr.	30.00	130.00	300.00

122 (110)	500 MIL REIS	GOOD	FINE	XF
	L. 1923. E. 1A. Blue on yellow unpt. Man seated w/locomotive in background. Back: Brown. Printer: CdM.	—	—	—
122A (122)	500 MIL REIS			
	L. 1923. E. 1A. Black on m/c impt. Portr. J. Bonifacio at l. Back: Dp. orange. City and trees at ctr.	—	—	—
123	1000 MIL REIS=1 CONTO DE REIS			
	L. 1923. E. 1A. Black on m/c unpt. Portr. Dom Pedro I at ctr. Back: Purple. Cavalry charge at ctr.			

1942 CASA DA MOEDA PROVISIONAL ISSUE

#125-131 are 5-500 Mil Reis notes ovpt: *CASA DA MOEDA* and new Cruzeiro denominations in a blue rosette.

Note: The 100 Mil Reis note #82 is also known to exist w/ovpt. although not officially listed, and authenticity is questionable at this time.

125	5 CRUZEIROS ON 5 MIL REIS	GOOD	FINE	XF
	ND (1942). Dk. blue on m.c unpt. Ovpt: on #29b.	2.50	10.00	40.00
126	10 CRUZEIROS ON 10 MIL REIS			
	ND (1942). Dk. blue on m/c unpt. Ovpt: on #39c.	4.00	15.00	65.00

127	20 CRUZEIROS ON 20 MIL REIS	GOOD	FINE	XF
	ND (1942). Dk. blue on m/c unpt. Ovpt: on #48c.	6.00	25.00	100.00

128	50 CRUZEIROS ON 50 MIL REIS	GOOD	FINE	XF
	ND (1942). Violet on m/c unpt. Ovpt: on #59.	40.00	160.00	650.00

129	100 CRUZEIROS ON 100 MIL REIS	GOOD	FINE	XF
	ND (1942). Dk. blue on m/c unpt. Ovpt: on #70c.	18.50	75.00	300.00
130	200 CRUZEIROS ON 200 MIL REIS			
	ND (1942). Dk. blue on m/c unpt. Ovpt: on #81b.	37.50	150.00	600.00
131	500 CRUZEIROS ON 500 MIL REIS			
	ND (1942). Dk. blue on m/c unpt.			
	a. Ovpt: on 92c.	18.50	75.00	300.00
	b. Ovpt: on 92d.	18.50	75.00	300.00

1944 EMERGENCY ISSUE

#131A, 1 Mill Reis of Banco do Brasil w/o ovpt. issued as 1 Cruzeiro.

131A	1 MIL REIS (CRUZEIRO)	GOOD	FINE	XF
(124)	ND (1944). Black on green unpt. Portr. C. Salles at ctr. Series #279-500 Back: Arms.	.50	2.00	8.00

TESOURO NACIONAL, VALOR RECEBIDO

1943-44, W/O ESTAMPA (1A)

#132-141 blue on m/c guilloches, hand-signed across face of note. Printer: ABNC.

132	1 CRUZEIRO	VG	VF	UNC
	ND (1944). Portr. M. de Tamandare at ctr. Back: Blue. Naval school at ctr. Series #1-1000.	.15	.50	2.00
133	2 CRUZEIROS			
	ND (1944). Portr. D. de Caxias at ctr. Back: Gold. Military school at ctr. Series #1-500.	.20	.75	3.00
134	5 CRUZEIROS			
	ND (1943). Portr. B. do Rio Branco at ctr. Back: Brown. "Amazonia" scene. Series #1-500.	1.25	5.00	20.00

135	10 CRUZEIROS	VG	VF	UNC
	ND (1943). Portr. G. Vargas at ctr. Back: Green. Allegorical man w/industrial implements at ctr. Series #1-330.	1.25	5.00	20.00

136	20 CRUZEIROS	VG	VF	UNC
	ND (1943). Portr. D. da Fonseca at ctr. Back: Red. Allegory of the Republic at ctr. Series #1-460.	1.25	5.00	20.00
137	50 CRUZEIROS			
	ND (1943). Portr. Princesa Isabel at ctr. Back: Purple. Allegory of Law at ctr. Series #1-320.	2.50	10.00	40.00
138	100 CRUZEIROS			
	ND (1943). D. Pedro II at ctr. Back: Red-brown. Allegory of National Culture. Series #1-235.	2.50	10.00	40.00

139	200 CRUZEIROS	VG	VF	UNC
	ND (1943). Portr. D. Pedro I at ctr. Back: Olive-green. Battle scene. Series #1-320.	3.75	15.00	60.00
140	500 CRUZEIROS			
	ND (1943). Portr. Joao VI at ctr. Back: Blue-black. Maritime allegory w/ships at ctr. Series #1-160.	11.50	45.00	180.00
141	1000 CRUZEIROS			
	ND (1943). Portr. P. Alvares Cabral at ctr. Back: Orange. Scene of first mass at ctr. Series #1-230.	7.50	30.00	120.00

1949-50, ESTAMPA 2A

#142-149 hand-signed acros face of note. Printer: TDLR.

142	5 CRUZEIROS	VG	VF	UNC
	ND (1950). Brown on m/c unpt. Portr. B. do Rio Branco at ctr. Back: Brown. "Amazonia" scene. Series #1-500.	.50	2.00	8.00
143	10 CRUZEIROS			
	ND (1950). Green on m/c unpt. Portr. G.Vargas at ctr. Back: Green. Allegorical man w/industrial implements at ctr. Series #1-435.	.60	2.50	10.00
144	20 CRUZEIROS			
	ND (1950). Red-brown on m/c unpt. Portr. D. da Fonseca at ctr. Back: Red. Allegory of the Republic at ctr. Series #1-370.	1.25	5.00	20.00

145	50 CRUZEIROS	VG	VF	UNC
	ND (1949). Violet on m/c unpt. Portr. Princesa Isabel at ctr. Back: Purple. Allegory of Law at ctr. Series #1-115.	4.50	17.50	70.00

146	**100 CRUZEIROS**	VG	VF	UNC
	ND (1949). Red on m/c unpt. Portr. D. Pedro II at ctr. Back: Red-brown. Allegory of National Culture. Series #1-115.	6.00	25.00	100.00
147	**200 CRUZEIROS**			
	ND (1949). Green. Portr. D. Pedro I at ctr. Back: Olive-green. Battle scene. Series #1-30.	37.50	150.00	600.00
148	**500 CRUZEIROS**			
	ND (1949). Dk. green. Portr. D. Joao VI at ctr. Back: Blue-black. Maritime allegory w/ships at ctr. Series #1-120.	12.50	50.00	200.00

149	**1000 CRUZEIROS**	VG	VF	UNC
	ND (1949). Orange. Portr. P. Alvares Cabral at ctr. Back: Orange. Scene of first mass at ctr. Series #1-90.	17.50	70.00	280.00

1953-59 W/O ESTAMPA 1A
#150-156 blue on m/c guilloches, 2 printed sign. Printer: ABNC.

150	**1 CRUZEIRO**	VG	VF	UNC
	ND (1954-58). Portr. M. de Tamandare at ctr. Back: Blue. Naval school at ctr.			
	a. Sign. 2. Series #1001-1800.	.5	.20	1.00
	b. Sign. 3. Series #1801-2700.	.5	.20	1.00
	c. Sign. 5. Series #2701-3450.	.5	.20	1.00
	d. Sign. 6. Series #3451-3690.	.5	.20	1.00

151	**2 CRUZEIROS**	VG	VF	UNC
	ND (1954-58). Portr. D. de Caxias at ctr. Back: Gold. Military school at ctr.			
	a. Sign. 2. Series #501-900.	.5	.20	1.00
	b. Sign. 6. Series #901-1135.	.5	.20	1.00

152	**50 CRUZEIROS**	VG	VF	UNC
	ND (1956-59). Portr. Princesa Isabel at ctr. Back: Purple. Allegory of Law at ctr.			
	a. Sign. 5. Series #321-470.	1.00	4.00	20.00
	b. Sign. 6. Series #471-620.	1.00	4.00	20.00
	c. Sign. 7 Series #621-720.	1.25	5.00	25.00
153	**100 CRUZEIROS**			
	ND (1955-59). Portr. D. Pedro II at ctr. Back: Red-brown. Allegory of National Culture.			
	a. Sign. 3. Series #236-435.	.90	4.50	22.50
	b. Sign. 5. Series #436-535.	1.00	5.00	25.00
	c. Sign. 6. Series #536-660.	.90	4.50	22.50
	d. Sign. 7. Series #661-760.	1.35	7.00	35.00

154	**200 CRUZEIROS**	VG	VF	UNC
	ND (1955-59). Portr. D. Pedro I at ctr. Back: Olive-green. Battle scene at ctr.			
	a. Sign. 3. Series #321-520.	1.20	6.00	30.00
	b. Sign. 6. Series #521-620.	2.00	10.00	50.00
	c. Sign. 7. Series #621-670.	7.00	35.00	175.00
155	**500 CRUZEIROS**			
	ND (1953). Portr. D. Joao VI at ctr. Back: Blue-black. Maritime allegory w/ships at ctr. Sign. 1. Series #161-260.	9.00	45.00	225.00
156	**1000 CRUZEIROS**			
	ND (1953-59). Portr. P. Ivares Cabral at ctr. Back: Orange. Scene of first mass at ctr.			
	a. Sign. 1. Series #231-330.	9.00	45.00	225.00
	b. Sign. 3. Series #331-630.	2.50	12.50	65.00
	c. Sign. 4. Series #631-930.	2.00	11.00	55.00
	d. Sign. 6. Series #931-1080.	3.00	15.00	75.00
	e. Sign. 7. Series #1081-1330.	2.25	12.00	60.00

1953-60 ESTAMPA 2A
#157-165 2 printed sign. Printer: TDLR.

157	**2 CRUZEIROS**	VG	VF	UNC
	ND (1955). Turquoise on m/c unpt. Portr. D. de Caxias at ctr. Military school at ctr. Back ochre. Sign. 3. Series #1-230.	.5	.20	1.00
158	**5 CRUZEIROS**			
	ND (1953-59). Brown on m/c unpt. Portr. B. do Rio Branco at ctr. Back: Brown. "Amazonia" scene.			
	a. Sign. 1. Series #501-1000.	.10	.60	3.00
	b. Sign. 3. Series #1001-1300.	.10	.60	3.00
	c. Sign. 5. Series #1301-1800.	.10	.50	2.50
	d. Sign. 6. Series #1801-2050.	.10	.60	3.00
	e. Sign. 7. Series #2051-2301.	.10	.50	2.50

159	**10 CRUZEIROS**	VG	VF	UNC
	ND (1953-60). Green on m/c unpt. Portr. G. Vargas at ctr. Back: Green. Allegorical man w/industrial implements at ctr.			
	a. Sign. 1. Series #436-735.	.10	.50	2.50
	b. Sign. 2. Series #736-1235.	.10	.40	2.00
	c. Sign. 5. Series #1236-1435.	.10	.40	2.00
	d. Sign. 6. Series #1436-1685.	.10	.40	2.00
	e. Sign. 7. Series #1686-1885.	.10	.50	2.50
	6. Sign. 8. Series #1886-2355.	.5	.20	1.00

160	**20 CRUZEIROS**	VG	VF	UNC
	ND (1955-61). Red-brown on m/c unpt. Portr. D. da Fonseca at ctr. Back: Red. Allegory of the Republic at ctr.			
	a. Sign. 3. Series #371-870.	.10	.50	3.00
	b. Sign. 6. Series #871-1175.	.15	.80	4.00
	c. Sign. 7. Series #1176-1225.	.75	4.00	20.00
	d. Sign. 8. Series #1226-1575.	.10	.60	3.00

162 **100 CRUZEIROS**
ND (1960). Red on m/c unpt. Portr. D. Pedro Ii at ctr. Back: Red-brown. Allegory of National Culture. Sign. 8. Series #116-215.

VG	VF	UNC
1.50	2.50	12.50

163 **200 CRUZEIROS**
ND (1960). Olive on m/c unpt. Portr. D. Pedro I at ctr. Back: Olive-green. Battle Scene at ctr. Sign. 8. Series #31-110.

VG	VF	UNC
3.00	7.50	20.00

164 **500 CRUZEIROS**
ND (1955-60). Dk. olive on m/c unpt. Portr. D. Joao VI at ctr. Back: Blue-black. Maritime allegory w/ships at ctr.

	VG	VF	UNC
a. Sign. 3. Series #121-420.	1.25	6.50	32.50
b. Sign. 4. Series #421-720.	1.00	5.00	25.00
c. Sign. 6. Series #721-770.	3.50	17.50	85.00
d. Sign. 8. Series #771-1300.	1.00	5.00	15.00

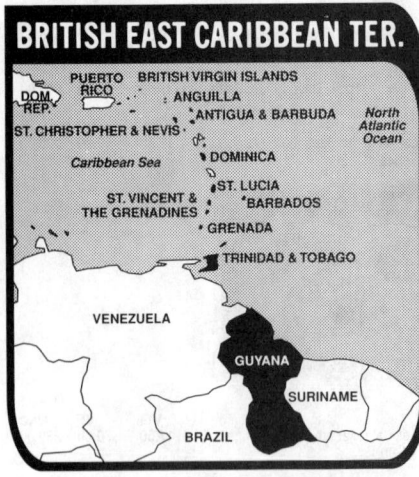

BRITISH EAST CARIBBEAN TER.

The British Caribbean Territories (Eastern Group), a currency board formed in 1950, comprised the British West Indies territories of Trinidad and Tobago; Barbados; the Leeward Islands of Anguilla, Saba, St. Christopher, Nevis and Antigua; the Windward Islands of St. Lucia, Dominica, St. Vincent and Grenada; British Guiana and the British Virgin Islands.

As time progressed, the members of this Eastern Group varied.

For later issues see the East Caribben States, Vol. 3.

RULERS:
British

MONETARY SYSTEM:
1 Dollar = 100 Cents

BRITISH INFLUENCE

BRITISH CARIBBEAN TERRITORIES, EASTERN GROUP

1950-51 ISSUE
#1-6 map at lower l., Portr. Kg. George VI at r. Sign. varieties. Printer: BWC.

		VG	VF	UNC
1	**1 DOLLAR** 28.11.1950; 1.9.1951. Red.	3.50	40.00	165.00
2	**2 DOLLARS** 28.11.1950; 1.9.1951. Blue.	15.00	85.00	550.00

		VG	VF	UNC
3	**5 DOLLARS** 28.11.1950; 1.9.1951. Green.	12.50	80.00	475.00
4	**10 DOLLARS** 28.11.1950; 1.9.1951. Lt. brown.	35.00	185.00	850.00
5	**20 DOLLARS** 28.11.1950; 1.9.1951. Purple.	50.00	250.00	1050.

		VG	VF	UNC
6	**100 DOLLARS** 28.11.1950. Black.	350.00	1000.	—

1953-64 ISSUE
#7-12 map at lower l., portr. Qn. Elizabeth II at r. Printer: BWC.

7 **1 DOLLAR**
1953-64. Red.

	VG	VF	UNC
a. Wmk: Sailing ship. 5.1.1953.	6.00	35.00	150.00
b. Wmk: Qn. Elizabeth II. 1.3.1954-2.1.1957.	3.00	15.00	75.00
c. 2.1.1958-2.1.1964.	1.50	12.00	60.00

8 **2 DOLLARS**
1953-64. Blue.

a. Wmk: Like #7a: 5.1.1953.	20.00	175.00	425.00
b. Wmk: Like #7b: 1.3.1954-1.7.1960.	7.50	35.00	300.00
c. 2.1.1961-2.1.1964.	3.00	15.00	250.00

9 **5 DOLLARS**
1953-64. Green.

	VG	VF	UNC
a. Wmk: Like #7a: 5.1.1953.	22.50	185.00	450.00
b. Wmk: Like #7b: 3.1.1955-2.1.1959.	10.00	35.00	375.00
c. 2.1.1961-2.1.1964.	7.50	25.00	350.00

10 **10 DOLLARS**
1953-64. Brown.

	VG	VF	UNC
a. Wmk: Like #7a: 5.1.1953.	37.50	300.00	1500.
b. Wmk: Like #7b: 3.1.1955-2.1.1959.	20.00	125.00	950.00
c. 2.1.1961; 2.1.1962; 2.1.1964.	15.00	85.00	450.00

11 **20 DOLLARS**
1953-64. Purple.

	VG	VF	UNC
a. Wmk: Like #7a: 5.1.1953.	50.00	400.00	2000.
b. Wmk: Like #7b: 2.1.1957-2.1.1964.	25.00	75.00	1000.

12 **100 DOLLARS**
1953-63. Black.

a. Wmk: Like #7a: 5.1.1953.	375.00	1250.	—
b. Wmk: Like #7b: 1.3.1954; 2.1.1957; 2.1.1963.	225.00	750.00	—

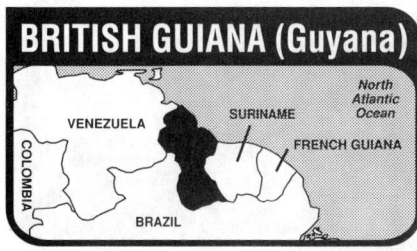

BRITISH GUIANA (Guyana)

The Cooperative Republic of Guyana, (formerly British Guiana) an independent member of the British Commonwealth situated on the northeast coast of South America, has an area of 83,000 sq. mi. (214,969 sq. km.) and a population of 779,000. Capital: Georgetown. The economy is basically agrarian. Sugar, rice and bauxite are exported.

The original area of Guyana, which included present-day Surinam, French Guiana, and parts of Brazil and Venezuela, was sighted by Columbus in 1498. The first European settlement was made late in the 16th century by the Dutch. For the next 150 years, possession alternated between the Dutch and the British, with a short interval of French control. The British exercised de facto control after 1796, although the area, which included the Dutch colonies of Essequebo, Demerary and Berbice, wasn't ceded to them by the Dutch until 1814. From 1803 to 1831, Essequebo and Demerary were administered separately from Berbice. The three colonies were united in the British Crown Colony of British Guiana in 1831. British Guiana won internal self-government in 1952 and full independence, under the traditional name of Guyana, on May 26, 1966.

Notes of the British Caribbean Currency Board circulated from 1950-1965.

RULERS:
British to 1966

MONETARY SYSTEM:
1 Joe = 22 Guilders to 1836
1 Dollar = 4 Shillings 2 Pence, 1837-1965
1 Dollar = 100 Cents, 1966-

DEMERARY AND ESSEQUEBO

COLONIES OF DEMERARY AND ESSEQUEBO

1830s FIRST ISSUE
#A1-A4, ornate *D-E* at upper ctr. (Not issued.)

		GOOD	FINE	XF
A1	**1 JOE OR 22 GUILDERS** 1.5.1830. Black.	—	200.00	485.00
A4	**10 JOES OR 220 GUILDERS** ND (ca. 1830s). Reddish brown.	—	—	650.00

1830s SECOND ISSUE
#B1-B4 black. Woman w/anchor at upper l. W/or w/o counterfoil. (Not issued.)

B1	**1 JOE OF 22 GUILDERS** ND (1830s).	—	200.00	450.00
B2	**2 JOES OF 22 GUILDERS EACH** ND (1830s).	—	—	—
B3	**3 JOES OF 22 GUILDERS EACH** ND (1830s).	—	300.00	500.00
B4	**10 JOES OF 22 GUILDERS EACH** ND (1830s).	—	300.00	500.00

BRITISH INFLUENCE

GOVERNMENT OF BRITISH GUIANA

1916-20 ISSUES
Various date and sign. varieties.
#3-5 Deleted.

1	**1 DOLLAR** 1.8.1916; 2.1.1918. Red-brown. Sailing ship at l. 118 x 63mm.	200.00	500.00	1100.

1A	1 DOLLAR	GOOD	FINE	XF
	1.1.1920; 1.10.1924. Red-brown. Sailing ship at l. Tan or gray paper. 150 x 85mm. Printer: TDLR.	125.00	400.00	900.00
2	2 DOLLARS			
	1.8.1916; 2.1.1918. Blue. Sailing ship at upper ctr. Ship at ctr. on back. 115 x 73mm. Printer: TDLR.	225.00	650.00	1650.

2A	2 DOLLARS	GOOD	FINE	XF
	1.1.1920; 1.10.1924. Blue. Sailing ship at upper ctr. 150 x 85mm. Printer: TDLR.	200.00	600.00	1500.

1929 ISSUE

#6-7 Tucan at l., Kaieteur Falls at ctr., sailing ship seal at r. Kg. George V at ctr. on back. Larger size notes. Printer: W&S.

#8-11 Deleted.

6	1 DOLLAR	GOOD	FINE	XF
	1.1.1929; 1.1.1936. Red.	70.00	325.00	900.00
7	2 DOLLARS			
	1.1.1929; 1.1.1936. Green.	300.00	850.00	—

1937-42 ISSUE

#12-17 Tucan at l., Kaieteur Falls at ctr., sailing ship seal at r. Facing or 3/4 Portr. Kg. George VI at ctr. on back. Reduced size notes. Printer: W&S.

12	1 DOLLAR	GOOD	FINE	XF
	1937-42. Red. 3/4 facing portr. Kg. George VI at ctr. on back.			
	a. 1.6.1937.	15.00	45.00	175.00
	b. 1.10.1938.	10.00	30.00	135.00
	c. 1.1.1942.	5.00	20.00	125.00

13	2 DOLLARS	GOOD	FINE	XF
	1937-42. Green. 3/4 facing portr. Kg. George VI at center on back.			
	a. 1.6.1937.	20.00	80.00	500.00
	b. 1.10.1938.	15.00	70.00	425.00
	c. 1.1.1942.	10.00	50.00	375.00

14	5 DOLLARS	GOOD	FINE	XF
	1938; 1942. Olive. 3/4 facing portr. Kg. George VI at ctr on back.			
	a. 1.10.1938.	35.00	85.00	375.00
	b. 1.1.1942.	20.00	70.00	325.00
15	10 DOLLARS			
	1.1.1942. Blue. Facing portr. Kg. George VI at ctr. on back.	75.00	200.00	550.00
16	20 DOLLARS			
	1.1.1942. Violet. Facing Portr. Kg. George VI at ctr. on back.	185.00	525.00	—
17	100 DOLLARS			
	Like #12. Yellow. Facing Portr. Kg. George VI at ctr. on back.	350.00	1100.	—

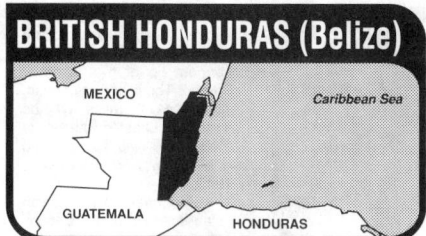

BRITISH HONDURAS (Belize)

The British colony of Belize, formerly British Honduras, a self-governing dependency of the United Kingdom situated in Central America south of Mexico and east and north of Guatemala, has an area of 8,867 sq. mi. (22,965 sq. km.) and a population of 209,000. Capital: Belmopan. Sugar, citrus fruits, chicle and hard woods are exported.

The area, site of the ancient Mayan civilization, was sighted by Columbus in 1502, and settled by shipwrecked English seamen in 1638. British buccaneers settled the former capital of Belize in the 17th century. Britain claimed administrative right over the area after the emancipation of Central America from Spain, and declared it a colony subordinate to Jamaica in 1862. It established as the separate Crown Colony of British Honduras in 1884. The anti-British People's United Party, which attained power in 1954, won a constitution, effective in 1964 which established self-government under a British appointed governor. British Honduras became Belize on June 1, 1973, following the passage of a surprise bill by the Peoples United Party, but the constitutional relationship with Britain remained unchanged.

In Dec. 1975, the U.N. General Assembly adopted a resolution supporting the right of the people of Belize to self-determination, and asking Britain and Guatemala to renew their negotiations on the future of Belize. They obtained independence on Sept. 21, 1981.

Bank notes of the United States circulated freely in British Honduras until 1924.

RULERS:
British

MONETARY SYSTEM:
1 Dollar = 100 Cents

BRITISH HONDURAS
This section has been renumbered

GOVERNMENT OF BRITISH HONDURAS

1894 ISSUE
NOTE: Usually encountered w/various circular city (postal?) handstamps.

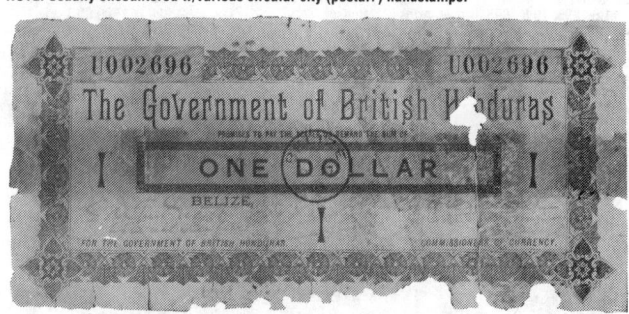

1	**1 DOLLAR**			
(A1)	17.10.1894. Blue. Perforated at l.	—	Rare	—
2	**2 DOLLARS**			
(A2)	1894.	—	Rare	—
3	**5 DOLLARS**			
(A3)	1894.	—	Rare	—
4	**10 DOLLARS**			
(A4)	1894.	—	Rare	—
5	**50 DOLLARS**			
(A5)	1894.	—	Rare	—
6	**100 DOLLARS**			
(A6)	1894.	—	Rare	—

1895 ISSUES
#7-10 arms at top ctr. Printer: TDLR (w/o imprint).

		GOOD	FINE	XF
7	**1 DOLLAR**			
(1)	1.1.1895. Blue and red. Perforated at l. Back: Blue.	725.00	1750.	—
8	**1 DOLLAR**			
(1A)	1.1.1895. Gray and dk. rd. Straight edge at l. Back: Gray.	500.00	1500.	—
9	**1 DOLLAR**			
(1B)	1.5.1912; 1.3.1920.	550.00	1500.	—

		GOOD	FINE	XF
10	**2 DOLLARS**			
(2)	1895-1912. Brown and blue. Back: Brown.			
	a. 1.1.1895. Perforated l. edge.	—	Rare	—
	b. 23.2.1904; 1.5.1912. Straight l. edge.	600.00	1350.	—

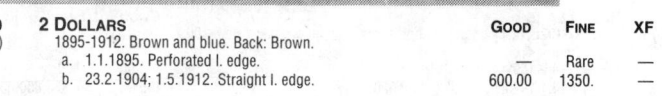

1924 ISSUES
#14-19 arms at top ctr. Printer: TDLR.

14	**1 DOLLAR**			
(1C)	1.5.1924. Blue on brown and green unpt. Back: Blue.	250.00	700.00	1800.
15	**2 DOLLARS**			
(2A)	1.5.1924; 1.10.1928. Brown on green unpt.	350.00	900.00	—

		GOOD	FINE	XF
16	**5 DOLLARS**			
(3)	1.5.1924; 1.10.1928. Green on brown unpt.	600.00	1500.	—

		GOOD	FINE	XF
17	**10 DOLLARS**			
(4)	1.5.1924; 1.10.1928. Purple on green and yellow unpt. Back: purple.	—	Rare	—
18	**50 DOLLARS**			
(5)	1.5.1924; 1.10.1928.	—	Rare	—
19	**100 DOLLARS**			
(6)	1.5.1924; 1.10.1928.	—	Rare	—

1939 ISSUE
#20-23 arms at l., Kg. George VI at r.

		VG	VF	UNC
20	**1 DOLLAR**			
(7)	2.10.1939; 15.4.1942. Blue.	35.00	250.00	1000.
21	**2 DOLLARS**			
(8)	2.10.1939; 15.4.1942. Brown.	60.00	450.00	1500.
22	**5 DOLLARS**	VG	VF	UNC
(9)	2.10.1939; 15.4.1942. Purple.	70.00	600.00	—
23	**10 DOLLARS**	VG	VF	UNC
(10)	2.10.1939; 15.4.1942. Dk. olive-brown.	150.00	650.00	—

1947 ISSUE
#24-27 arms at l., Kg. George VI at r.

24	**1 DOLLAR**			
(7A)	1947-52. Green.			
	a. 30.1.1947.	35.00	275.00	1100.
	b. 1.10.1949; 1.2.1952.	25.00	225.00	900.00
25	**2 DOLLARS**			
(8A)	1947-52. Purple.			
	a. 30.1.1947.	50.00	425.00	1350.
	b. 1.11.1949; 1.2.1952.	50.00	375.00	1250.

		VG	VF	UNC
26	**5 DOLLARS**			
(9A)	1947-52. Red.			
	a. 30.1.1947.	40.00	250.00	800.00
	b. 1.11.1949; 1.2.1952.	25.00	185.00	550.00

27 (10A)	10 DOLLARS 1947-51. Black on m/c unpt.			
	a. 30.1.1947.	65.00	275.00	—
	b. 1.11.1949.	65.00	275.00	—
	c. 1.6.1951.	30.00	175.00	650.00

1952-53 ISSUE
#28-32 arms at l., portr. Qn. Elizabeth II at r.

28 (11)	1 DOLLAR 1952-73. Green.	VG	VF	UNC
	a. 1.2.1952-1.10.1958.	4.00	25.00	125.00
	b. 1.1.1961-1.5.1969.	2.00	10.00	50.00
	c. 1.1.1970-1.1.1973.	1.50	7.00	35.00

29 (12)	2 DOLLARS 1953-73. Purple.	VG	VF	UNC
	a. 15.4.1953-1.10.1958.	7.50	40.00	350.00
	b. 1.10.1960-1.5.1965.	3.00	20.00	100.00
	c. 1.1.1971-1.1.1973.	2.00	15.00	55.00

30 (13)	5 DOLLARS 1953-73. Red.	VG	VF	UNC
	a. 15.4.1953-1.1.1958.	10.00	50.00	325.00
	b. 1.3.1960-1.5.1969.	5.00	30.00	225.00
	c. 1.1.1970-1.1.1973.	4.50	20.00	150.00

31 (14)	10 DOLLARS 1953-73. Black on m/c unpt.	VG	VF	UNC
	a. 15.4.1953-1.10.1958.	15.00	100.00	700.00
	b. 1.5.1965-1.5.1969.	10.00	50.00	500.00
	c. 1.1.1971-1.1.1973.	7.50	35.00	375.00

32 (15)	20 DOLLARS 1952-73. Brown.			
	a. 1.12.1952-1.10.1958.	30.00	150.00	1000.
	b. 1.3.1960-1.5.1969.	20.00	120.00	725.00
	c. 1.1.1971-1.1.1973.	15.00	100.00	650.00

BRITISH NORTH BORNEO

British North Borneo, a former British protectorate and crown colony, occupies the northern tip of the island of Borneo. The island of Labuan, which lies 6 miles off the northwest coast of the island of Borneo, was incorporated with British North Borneo in 1946.

The Portuguese and Spanish established trading relations with Borneo early in the 16th century. Their monopoly was broken by the Dutch and British at the beginning of the 17th century. British North Borneo was administered by the North Borneo Company from 1877 to 1942, and later came under British military control, finally to become a British protectorate. Japan quickly eliminated the British and Dutch forces on Borneo and occupied the entire island during World War II. The island was retaken in 1945, and in July 1946, British North Borneo was made a crown colony. Britain relinquished its sovereignty over the colony in 1963. At that time it joined the Malaysian federation under the name of Sabah.

RULERS:
Japan, 1942-1945
British, 1945-1963

MONETARY SYSTEM:
1 Dollar = 100 Cents

BRITISH INFLUENCE

BRITISH NORTH BORNEO COMPANY

1886-96 ISSUE
#1-8 various date and sign. varieties. Dates partially or completely handwritten or handstamped on partially printed dates, i.e., 18xx, 189x, etc. Printer: Blades, East & Blades Ltd., London.

#29-32 arms at ctr.

1 (A1)	25 CENTS 11.6.1895; 19.8.1895. Brown. Arms at l. Uniface.	GOOD 150.00	FINE 500.00	XF —
2 (A2)	50 CENTS 20.8.1895. Green. Uniface. 176 x 95mm.	160.00	450.00	—

3 (4)	1 DOLLAR 21.3.1886-8.10.1920. Black on red unpt. Mount Kinabalu at upper ctr. Back: Green. 192 x 89mm.	GOOD 125.00	FINE 350.00	XF —
A4	1 DOLLAR 26.2.1920. Black on red unpt. Mount Kinabalu at upper ctr. Green. 200 x 90 mm.	175.00	—	—

4 (6)	5 DOLLARS 189x-1926. Black on green unpt. Arms at upper ctr. Back: Red. 200 x 102mm.	GOOD	FINE	XF
	a. 14.5.189x; 1.10.1901.	300.00	650.00	—
	b. 14.1.1920; 1.12.1922; 7.8.1926.	185.00	450.00	850.00

5	**10 DOLLARS**		GOOD	FINE	XF
(7)	1896-1927. Black on brown unpt. Mount Kinabalu at upper ctr., arms at l. Back: Blue. 215 x 115mm.				
	a. 3.3.1896.		400.00	850.00	—
	b. 13.3.1920; 5.3.1921.		275.00	550.00	—
	c. 1.12.1922; 1.12.1926.		225.00	475.00	—

1900; 1901 ISSUE

7	**25 CENTS**		GOOD	FINE	XF
(1)	1900-13. Dp. red-brown. Arms at l. Uniface. 161 x 82mm.				
	a. 17.10.1900; 1.10.1902; 26.11.1903; 5.10.1907.		135.00	450.00	1150.
	b. 1.1.1912; 13.10.1913; 3.11.1920.		100.00	350.00	850.00
8	**50 CENTS**				
(3)	11.2.1901; 26.11.1902. Green. Arms at l. Uniface. 167 x 50mm.		150.00	500.00	—

1911 ISSUE

10	**50 CENTS**				
(2)	1.7.1911. Dp. brown. Arms at l. Uniface. 174 x 91mm.		140.00	400.00	—

1916-1922 ISSUES

12	**25 CENTS**		GOOD	FINE	XF
(9)	1917-25. Red. Arms at l. Uniface. 173 x 83mm.				
	a. 11.8.1917; 26.3.1919; 9.9.1920. Handstamped dates.		160.00	450.00	—
	b. 1.3.1921. Printed date.		80.00	200.00	650.00
	c. 9.12.1925. Handstamped date.		100.00	350.00	725.00
13	**50 CENTS**				
(3A)	8.11.1918. Black. Arms at l. Uniface. 167 x 50mm.		125.00	350.00	—

14	**50 CENTS**		GOOD	FINE	XF
(10)	1918-29. Green. Arms at l. Printed or handstamped date.				
	a. 26.6.1918; 23.4.1919; 25.2.1920.		175.00	550.00	—
	b. 1.3.1921; 1.6.1929.		90.00	225.00	550.00

15	**1 DOLLAR**		GOOD	FINE	XF
(5)	30.7.1919; 2.1.1922; 2.5.1922. Black on red unpt. Mount Kinabalu at upper ctr. Back: Green. 184 x 82mm.		100.00	225.00	500.00

17	**25 DOLLARS**		GOOD	FINE	XF
(8)	1.12.1922-1.1.1927. Black on green unpt. Mount Kinabalu at upper ctr. Back: Brown. 200 x 123mm.		325.00	800.00	—

1927 ISSUES

19	**1 DOLLAR**				
(11)	1.1.1927. Black on dk. green unpt. Mount Kinabalu at upper ctr. Back: Gray. 205 x 93mm.		175.00	375.00	650.00

20	**1 DOLLAR**		GOOD	FINE	XF
(14)	29.7.1927; 1.1.1930. Black on dk. green unpt. Mount Kinabalu at upper ctr. Back: Gray. 135 x 77mm.		75.00	200.00	450.00
22	**10 DOLLARS**				
(12)	1.1.1927. Black on red-brown unpt. Mount Kinabalu at upper ctr. Back: Blue-green. 205 x 93mm.		250.00	550.00	—
23	**25 DOLLARS**				
(13)	1.1.1927. Black on green. Arms at ctr. Back: Brown. 201 x 126mm.		275.00	600.00	—

1930 ISSUE

25	**50 CENTS**				
(15)	1.1.1930. Green. Arms at l. Back: Green. 129 x 75mm.		55.00	140.00	350.00

1936; 1938 ISSUE

27	**50 CENTS**		GOOD	FINE	XF
(17)	1.1.1938. Olive-green. Arms at l., w/o No. at upper l. 119 x 63mm.		45.00	110.00	275.00

		GOOD	FINE	XF
28 (16)	**1 DOLLAR** 1.1.1936. Black on red unpt. Mount Kinabalu at upper ctr. Back: Black. 123 x 67mm.	22.50	50.00	150.00

1940 ISSUE

		GOOD	FINE	XF
29 (19)	**1 DOLLAR** 1.7.1940. Black on red unpt. 132 x 69mm.	25.00	65.00	225.00

		GOOD	FINE	XF
30 (18)	**5 DOLLARS** 1.1.1940. Black on dk. green unpt. Back: Red. 145 x 76mm.	95.00	250.00	450.00
31 (20)	**10 DOLLARS** 1.7.1940. Black on brown unpt. Arms at ctr. 160 x 82mm.	175.00	375.00	—
32 (21)	**25 DOLLARS** 1.7.1940. Black on green unpt. Arms at ctr. 170 x 98mm.	225.00	600.00	—

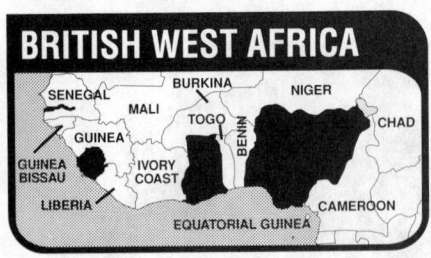

BRITISH WEST AFRICA

British West Africa was an administrative grouping of the four former British West Africa colonies of Gambia. Sierra Leone, Nigeria and Gold Coast (now Ghana). All are now independent republics and members of the British Commonwealth of Nations. These four colonies were supplied with a common currecny by the West African Currency Board from 1907 through 1962.

Also see Gambia, Ghana, Nigeria and Sierra Leone, for related currency and for individual statistics and history.

RULERS:
British to 1952

MONETARY SYSTEM:
1 Shilling = 12 Pence
1 Pound = 20 Shillings

BRITISH INFLUENCE

WEST AFRICAN CURRENCY BOARD

1916-20 ISSUE
#2-5 various date and sign. varieties.

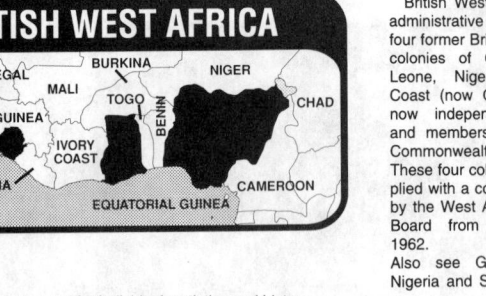

		GOOD	FINE	XF
1	**1 SHILLING** 30.11.1918. Black. Uniface. Paper: Salmon. Coin w/palm tree at lower ctr.			
	a. Issued note.	20.00	70.00	300.00
	s. Specimen.	—	Unc	400.00

		GOOD	FINE	XF
2	**2 SHILLINGS** 1916-18. Blue-gray. Palm tree at ctr. Printer: Printer: W&S.			
	a. 30.6.1916. Uniface.	100.00	250.00	600.00
	b. 30.3.1918. Back: Arabic script.	75.00	175.00	450.00
3 (4)	**5 SHILLINGS** 1.3.1920. Red-brown. (Not issued).	Reported Not Confirmed		
4 (5)	**10 SHILLINGS** 1916-18. Green.			
	a. 31.3.1916. Uniface.	150.00	500.00	1000.00
	b. 30.3.1918. Back: Arabic script.	150.00	500.00	1000.

		GOOD	FINE	XF
5 (7)	**20 SHILLINGS** 1916-18. Black. Red *20* at l. and r.			
	a. 31.3.1916. Uniface.	200.00	650.00	1500.
	b. 30.3.1918. Back: Denomination and Arabic script in black.	150.00	500.00	1250.
	s. Specimen perforated: *SPECIMEN.* 30.3.1918.	—	Unc	1000.

6	100 SHILLINGS = 5 POUNDS	GOOD	FINE	XF
(9)	1.3.1919. Black. Palm tree at lower ctr. (Not issued). Printer: W&S.	—	Rare	—

1928 ISSUE
#7 and 8 printer: W&S.

7	10 SHILLINGS	GOOD	FINE	XF
(6)	1928-48. Green. W/10 at l., palm tree at ctr. 10 at r.			
	a. 2.1.1928-21.7.1930; 14.9.1934.	70.00	225.00	600.00
	b. 4.1.1937-24.12.1948.	15.00	45.00	250.00

سـتـى عشرين

8	20 SHILLINGS	GOOD	FINE	XF
	1928-51. Black and red on lt. green and pink unpt. 20 at l., palm tree at ctr. Back: Denomination and Arabic script in black. 20 at r.			
	a. 2.1.1928-21.7.1930; 14.9.1934.	75.00	200.00	450.00
	b. 4.1.1937-2.7.1951.	10.00	25.00	160.00

1953 ISSUE
#10-12 river scene w/palm trees at l. Printer: W&S.

9	10 SHILLINGS	VG	VF	UNC
(10)	31.3.1953-4.2.1958. Black and green. l. Back: Field workers.	15.00	45.00	250.00
10	20 SHILLINGS			
(11)	31.3.1953-20.1.1957. Black and red. at l. Back: Harvesting.	12.50	35.00	225.00

11	100 SHILLINGS = 5 POUNDS	GOOD	FINE	XF
(12)	1953-54. Blue. at l. Back: Man harvesting.			
	a. 31.3.1953.	50.00	150.00	550.00
	b. 26.4.1954.	50.00	150.00	525.00

The Republic of Bulgaria (formerly the Peoples Republic of Bulgaria), a Balkan country on the Black Sea in southeastern Europe, has an area of 44,365 sq. mi. (110,912 sq. km.) and a population of 8.47 million. Capital: Sofia. Agriculture remains a key component of the economy but industrialization, particularly he-avy industry, has been emphasized since the late 1940's. Machinery, tobacco and cigarettes, wines and spirits, clothing and metals are the chief exports.

The area now occupied by Bulgaria was conquered by the Bulgars, an Asiatic tribe, in the 7th century. Bulgarian kingdoms continued to exist on the peninsula until it came under Turkish rule in 1395. In 1878, after nearly 500 years of Turkish rule, Bulgaria was made a principality under Turkish suzerainty. Union seven years later with Eastern Rumelia created a Balkan state with borders approximating those os present-day Bulgaria. A Bulgarian kingdom fully independent of Turkey was Sept. 22, 1908.

During WWI Bulgaria had been aligned with Germany. After the Armistice certain land concessions were granted to Greece and Romania. In 1934 King Boris III suspended all political parties and established a dictatorial monarchy. In 1938 the military began rearming through the aide of the Anglo-French loan. As WWII developed Bulgaria again supported the Germans but Boris protected their Jewish community. Boris died mysteriously in 1943 and Simeon II became king at the age of six. The country was then ruled by a pro-Nazi regency until it was invaded by Soviet forces in 1944. The monarchy was abolished and Simeon was ousted by plebiscite in 1946 and Bulgaria became a People's Republic in the Soviet pattern. Following demonstrations and a general strike the communist government resigned in Nov. 1990. A new government was elected in Oct. 1991.

RULERS:
Alexander I, 1879-1886
Ferdinand I, as Prince, 1887-1908
Ferdinand I, as King, 1908-1918
Bori III, 1918-1943
Simeon II, 1943-1946

TITLES:
Bulgarian People's Republic: НАРОДНА РЕПУБЛИКА БЪЛГАРИЯ
Bulgarian National Bank: БЪЛГАРСКАТА НАРОДНА БАНКА
State banknote: ЦАРСТО ЪЛГАРИЯ
Cashier's bond: ЦКАЧОБЪ БОВЪ

MONETARY SYSTEM:
1 Lev ЛЕВ = 100 Stotinki ЧТОТИНКИ
Silver Lev = Lev Srebro
Gold Lev = Lev Zlato

* * * This section has been partially renumbered. * * *

KINGDOM
БЪЛГАРСКАТА НАРОДНА БАНКА
BULGARIAN NATIONAL BANK

1885-87 GOLD ISSUE
#A1-A3 printer: ЗПГБ St. Petersburg, Russia. Sign. varieties.
#A1 and A2 arms at upper l.

A1	20 LEVA ZLATO	GOOD	FINE	XF
	1.8.1885. Lt. ochre.	200.00	450.00	—
A2	50 LEVA ZLATO			
	1.8.1885. Lt. green.	300.00	650.00	—

A3   100 LEVA ZLATO
1887. Blue-gray and ochre. Arms at l., woman seated w/child at r.
Back: Blue, pale blue and ochre. Floral spray at ctr.

	GOOD	FINE	XF
	300.00	750.00	—

1890 ND GOLD ISSUE
#A4-A7 printer: BWC. Sign. varieties.

A4   5 LEVA ZLATO
ND (1890). Black on brown unpt. Arms at l. Back: Dk. brown. Farmer plowing with 2 horses at ctr. Like #A6.

	GOOD	FINE	XF
	100.00	385.00	—

A5   10 LEVA ZLATO
ND (1890). Black on blue and ochre. Farm girl carrying roses at l., arms at r. Back: Blue. Shepherd tending flock of sheep at ctr. Like #A7.

	GOOD	FINE	XF
	150.00	475.00	—

1899 ND SILVER ISSUE
#A6 and A7 printer: BWC.

A6   5 LEVA SREBRO
ND (1899). Black on brown unpt. Arms at l. Back: Dk. brown. Farmer plowing w/2 horses. Like #A4.

	GOOD	FINE	XF
	100.00	385.00	—

A7   10 LEVA SREBRO
ND (1899). Black on blue and ochre. Farm girl carrying roses at l., arms at r. Back: Blue. Shepherd tending flock of sheep at ctr. Like #A5.

	GOOD	FINE	XF
	100.00	400.00	—

A8   50 LEVA SREBRO
ND (1899 -old date 1.8.1885). Lt. green. Arms at upper l. *ZLATO* crossed out. Ovpt: *SREBRO* on #A2. Printer: ЗПГБ St. Printer: Petersburg, Russia.

	GOOD	FINE	XF
	250.00	750.00	—

1904-09 ND SILVER ISSUE
#1-6 denomination in *LEVA SREBRO* w/o wmk., various sign. varieties. Printed in St. Petersburg Russia (w/o imprint). Vertical format.

NOTE: #3-6 also exist w/various serbian handstamps (worth 25-50% more).

1   5 LEVA SREBRO
ND (1904). Black on red, gray-green and m/c. Back: Arms w/o inscription at ctr.

	GOOD	FINE	XF
a. Issued note.	8.00	25.00	75.00
s. Specimen.	—	Unc	125.00

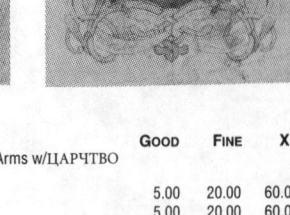

2   5 LEVA SREBRO
ND (1909). Black on green, lilac and m/c. Back: Arms w/ЦАРЧТВО БЪЛГАРИЯ

	GOOD	FINE	XF
a. 2 serial #.	5.00	20.00	60.00
b. 4 serial #.	5.00	20.00	60.00
s. Specimen.	—	Unc	110.00

11	100 LEVA ZLATO	GOOD	FINE	XF
	ND (1906). Black text and arms, edge pink, frame lt. blue. Arms at upper ctr. Back: Arms at l. ctr.			
	a. Issued note.	30.00	85.00	185.00
	s. Specimen.	—	Unc	400.00

3	10 LEVA SREBRO	GOOD	FINE	XF
	ND (1904). Dk. green on m/c. Back: Arms at upper ctr.			
	a. 2 serial #.	5.00	20.00	60.00
	b. 4 serial #.	5.00	20.00	60.00
	s. Specimen.	—	Unc	110.00
4	50 LEVA SREBRO			
	ND (1904). M/c. Back: Arms at center.			
	a. Issued note.	20.00	60.00	200.00
	s. Specimen.	—	Unc	300.00

12	500 LEVA ZLATO	GOOD	FINE	XF
	ND (1907). Black text and arms, edge green, frame pink and green. Arms at upper ctr.			
	a. Issued note.	150.00	250.00	500.00
	s. Specimen.	—	Unc	1000.

1916 КАЧОВ БОНЪ (CASHIER'S BOND) ISSUE
NOTE: #13 also exists w/various Serbian handstamps (worth 25-50% more).

5	100 LEVA SREBRO	GOOD	FINE	XF
	ND (1904). M/c. Arms at upper ctr.			
	a. Issued note.	40.00	125.00	385.00
	s. Specimen.	—	Unc	525.00
6	500 LEVA SREBRO			
	ND (1907). M/c. Back: Arms at upper ctr.			
	a. Issued note.	250.00	450.00	1200.
	s. Specimen.	—	Unc	1850.

13	1000 LEVA ZLATNI	GOOD	FINE	XF
	10.5.1916. Lt. blue-green. Bulgarian printing. Wmk: Cross and curl pattern.			
	a. Issued note.	150.00	400.00	700.00
	s. Specimen.	—	Unc	1000.

1904 ND PROVISIONAL GOLD ISSUE
NOTE: #7 and 8 also exist w/various Serbian handstamps (worth 25-50% more).

7	5 LEVA ZLATO			
	ND (1907). Black on red, gray-green and m/c unpt. Back: W/ЧРЪБО crossed out, arms at ctr. Ovpt: ЗЛАТО	15.00	50.00	150.00
8	10 LEVA ZLATO			
	ND (1907). Dk. green on m/c. Back: W/ЧРЪБО crossed out, arms at ctr. Ovpt: ЗЛАТО at l. and r.	15.00	50.00	150.00

1916 ND SILVER ISSUE
#14-20 printer: RDK (w/o imprint). Wmk: Cross and curl pattern.

NOTE: #14-17 also exist w/various Serbian handstamps (worth 25-50% more).

1904-07 ND GOLD ISSUE
#9-12 by Orlov, denomination in *LEVA ZLATO*, w/o wmk., sign varieties. Horizontal format. Printed in St. Petersburg, Russia (w/o imprint).

NOTE: #9-12 also exist w/various Serbian handstamps (worth 25-50% more).

9	20 LEVA ZLATO			
	ND (1904). Black text and arms, edge pink, frame red and blue. Arms at upper ctr.			
	a. Sign. Black sign.	3.00	15.00	45.00
	b. Sign. Blue sign.	3.00	15.00	45.00
	s. Specimen.	—	Unc	200.00
10	50 LEVA ZLATO	GOOD	FINE	XF
	ND (1907). Black text and arms, edge pink, frame blue and green. Arms at upper ctr.			
	a. Issued note.	10.00	30.00	100.00
	s. Speciman.	—	Unc	275.00

14	**1 LEV SREBRO**	GOOD	FINE	XF
	ND (1916). Black on green and blue unpt. Back: Blue on lilac unpt.			
	a. Issued note.	.50	2.00	7.50
	s. Specimen.	—	Unc	30.00

15	**2 LEVA SREBRO**	GOOD	FINE	XF
	ND (1916). Black on green and pink unpt. Back: Red on tan unpt.			
	a. Issued note.	.75	4.00	10.00
	s. Specimen.	—	Unc	35.00

16	**5 LEVA SREBRO**	GOOD	FINE	XF
	ND (1916). Black on blue and gray unpt. Back: Arms at upper ctr. Off-white paper.			
	a. Issued note.	1.00	5.00	17.50
	s. Specimen.	—	Unc	40.00

17	**10 LEVA SREBRO**	GOOD	FINE	XF
	ND (1916). Black text, edge blue-green, ornament red and lilac. Back: dk. brown on green unpt. Arms at upper ctr.			
	a. Issued note.	1.00	5.00	25.00
	s. Specimen.	—	Unc	45.00

1916 ND GOLD ISSUE

#18-20 wmk: Cross and curl pattern. Printer: RDK (w/o imprint). Horizontal format.

NOTE: #18-20 also exist w/various Serbian handstamps (worth 25-50% more).

18	**20 LEVA ZLATO**	GOOD	FINE	XF
	ND (1916). Black on green unpt. Arms at upper ctr.			
	a. Issued note.	5.00	20.00	50.00
	s. Specimen.	—	Unc	75.00

19	**50 LEVA ZLATO**			
	ND (1916). Black on orange-brown unpt. Arms at upper ctr. Back: brown and blue. Arms at ctr.			
	a. Issued note.	10.00	30.00	120.00
	s. Specimen.	—	Unc	165.00

20	**100 LEVA ZLATO**	GOOD	FINE	XF
	ND (1916). Black text and arms, edge green, ornament blue, lilac and violet. Arms at upper ctr.			
	a. W/o series. Serial # w/o prefix letter.	5.00	20.00	75.00
	b. Serial # w/prefix letter.	3.00	18.00	65.00
	c. As b, w/ ЧЕРИЯ А (Series A) at upper l. and lower r.	70.00	200.00	550.00
	s. As A. Specimen.		Unc	110.00

1917 ND ISSUE

#21-25 printer: G&D, Leipzig. Wmk: БНБ (BNB).

NOTE: #21-25 also exist w/various Serbian handstamps (worth 25-50% more).

21	**5 LEVA SREBRNI**	GOOD	FINE	XF
	ND (1917). Black on olive and lilac Arms at top ctr. Back: lilac on green unpt. Crown at ctr.			
	a. Issued note.	.75	2.00	12.00
	s. Specimen.	—	Unc	50.00

22 10 LEVA ZLATNI

		Good	Fine	XF
ND (1917; 1922). Black on lt. green and pink unpt. Arms at top ctr. Back: green on pink unpt.				
a.	Arms w/supporters w/o flags. 1 prefix letter serial # (1917).	1.00	3.00	17.50
b.	Arms w/supporters w/o flags. 2 prefix letter serial # (1922).	5.00	25.00	70.00
s1.	As a. Specimen.	—	Unc	65.00
s2.	As b. Specimen.	—	Unc	110.00

23 20 LEVA ZLATNI

		Good	Fine	XF
ND (1917). Brown on lt. blue-green and pink unpt. Arms at top ctr. Back: lilac on green unpt. Initals (BNB) in unpt. at ctr.				
a.	Issued note.	1.00	5.00	75.00
s.	Specimen.	—	Unc	75.00

24 50 LEVA ZLATNI

		Good	Fine	XF
ND (1917). Brown on blue, green and salmon unpt. Arms at upper l. Back: Brown on green unpt.				
a.	Serial # begins w/*No.*	3.00	12.00	45.00
b.	Serial # begins w/prefix letter.	2.00	10.00	40.00
s.	Specimen.	—	Unc	90.00

25 100 LEVA ZLATNI

		Good	Fine	XF
ND (1917). Green ochre, purple and pink. Portr. woman w/sheaf at l.				
a.	Issued note.	12.50	35.00	125.00
s.	Specimen.	—	Unc	225.00

1918 TREASURY BOND ISSUE

#27 and 28 red diagonal ovpt. on invalidated state treasury bill issue of 1918.

26 1000 LEVA ZLATNI
(29)

		Good	Fine	XF
ND (1918). Blue-green and tan. Arms at l. Printer: Gebr. Parcus, Munich.				
a.	Issued note.	15.00	50.00	150.00
s.	Specimen.	—	Unc	300.00

1919 TREASURY BOND ISSUE

		Good	Fine	XF
27 **500 LEVA ZLATNI**				
(31) 1919.		—	Rare	—
28 **5000 LEVA ZLATNI**				
(32) 1919.		—	Rare	—

1919 ND PROVISIONAL TREASURY BOND ISSUE

#29 red diagonal ovpt. on invalidated state treasury bill issue of 1918.

		Good	Fine	XF
29 **10,000 LEVA ZLATNI**				
(32A) 1919.		—	Rare	—

1920 ND SILVER ISSUE

#30 and 31 printer: W&S.

30 1 LEV SREBRO
(26)

		Good	Fine	XF
ND (1920). Dk. green and brown. Arms at l., woman at r. Back: Brown. Old Bank bldg. at ctr.				
a.	Issued note.	.50	1.50	10.00
s.	Specimen.	—	Unc	25.00

31 2 LEVA SREBRO
(27)

		Good	Fine	XF
ND (1920). Dk. brown and yellow. Woman at l., arms at r. Back: Lt. green. National Assembly bldg.				
a.	Issued note.	.75	2.00	15.00
s.	Specimen.	—	Unc	30.00

1920 ND TREASURY BOND ISSUE

32 500 LEVA ZLATO
(28A)

		Good	Fine	XF
ND (1920). Black on green and ochre. Portr. man at l., woman at r. Back: Arms at ctr. Ovpt: Specimen.		—	Unc	2000.

33   **1000 Leva Zlatni**

		Good	Fine	XF
	ND (1920). Blue-green and tan. Arms at l. Printer: BWC.			
a.	Issued note.	15.00	50.00	175.00
s.	Specimen.	—	Unc	300.00

1922 Issue
#34-40 arms at ctr. Printer: ABNC.

34   (37)   **5 Leva**

		Good	Fine	XF
	1922. Brown on lt. orange and green unpt. Back: Brown and green. Beehives at ctr.			
a.	Issue note.	1.00	4.00	25.00
s.	Specimen. Ovpt: ОБРАЗЕЦЪ.	—	Unc	40.00

35   (38)   **10 Leva**

		Good	Fine	XF
	1922. Purple on orange and green unpt. Back: Purple and brown. Farm woman w/turkey at ctr.			
a.	Issue note.	1.50	5.00	35.00
s.	Specimen. Ovpt: ОБРАЗЕЦЪ.	—	Unc	55.00

36   (39)   **20 Leva**

		Good	Fine	XF
	1922. Green on blue, lt. green and orange unpt. Back: Orange and olive-gray. Farm women working at ctr.			
a.	Issued note.	4.00	12.50	65.00
s.	Specimen. Ovpt: ОБРАЗЕЦЪ.	—	Unc	100.00

37   (40)   **50 Leva**

		Good	Fine	XF
	1922. Green and m/c. Back: Green. Boy shepherd w/flute at ctr.			
a.	Issued note.	7.50	17.50	85.00
s.	Specimen. Ovpt: ОБРАЗЕЦЪ.	—	Unc	125.00

38   (41)   **100 Leva**

		Good	Fine	XF
	1922. Brown and m/c. Back: Brown. Man plowing w/oxen at ctr.			
a.	Issued note.	20.00	50.00	135.00
s.	Specimen. Ovpt: ОБРАЗЕЦЪ.	—	Unc	200.00

39   (42)   **500 Leva**

		Good	Fine	XF
	1922. Blue and m/c. Back: Blue. Harbor scene.			
a.	Issued note.	30.00	75.00	175.00
s.	Specimen. Ovpt: ОБРАЗЕЦЪ.	—	Unc	250.00

40   (43)   **1000 Leva**

		Good	Fine	XF
	1922. Red-brown, green and pink. Back: Brown. Picking cotton at ctr.			
a.	Issued note.	50.00	150.00	400.00
s.	Specimen. Ovpt: ОБРАЗЕЦЪ.	—	Unc	500.00

1924 Issue

41   (35)   **5000 Leva**

		Good	Fine	XF
	1924. Green, brown-violet and m/c. Arms at l., Portr. Kg. Boris III at r. Back: Man at l.			
a.	Issued note.	125.00	300.00	750.00
s.	Specimen ovpt: ОБРАЗЕЦЪ.	—	Unc	1200.

1924 ND Provisional Treasury Bond Issue

42   (30)   **1000 Leva Zlatni**

		Good	Fine	XF
	ND (1924). Blue-green and tan. Arms at l. Red ovpt. begins: НАЧТОЯЩИПТ КАЧОВ *"This note is only valid within the kingdom"* w/additional red series and serial # at upper l. on #29.	35.00	125.00	350.00

43   (34)   **1000 Leva Zlatni**

		Good	Fine	XF
	ND (1924). Blue-green and tan. Arms at l. Red ovpt. begins: НАЧТОЯЩИПТ КАЧОВ *"This note is only valid within the kingdom"* w/additional red series letter and serial # at upper l. on #33.	35.00	125.00	350.00

1925 Issue
#45-49 Portr. Kg. Boris III at r. Printer: BWC.

45   **50 Leva**

		Good	Fine	XF
	1925. Brown on m/c unpt. Portr. Kg. Boris III at r., arms at l. Back: Blue. Farm women working at ctr.			
a.	Issued note.	5.00	12.00	45.00
s.	Specimen.	—	Unc	65.00

52	**500 LEVA**	GOOD	FINE	XF
	1929. Blue and m/c. arms at l. Back: River canyon.			
	a. Issued note.	15.00	50.00	110.00
	s. Specimen.	—	Unc	150.00
53	**1000 LEVA**			
	1929. Red-brown on lt. green and tan unpt. arms at l. Back: Mountain lake.			
	a. Issued note.	30.00	100.00	275.00
	s. Specimen.	—	Unc	350.00
54	**5000 LEVA**			
	1929. Brown and brown-violet. Arms at l. Back: Monastery.			
	a. Issued note.	100.00	200.00	400.00
	s. Specimen.	—	Unc	500.00

46	**100 LEVA**	GOOD	FINE	XF
	1925. Dk. blue on m/c unpt. Portr. Kg. Boris III at r., arms at l. Back: Dk. Green. People gathered in front of house at ctr.			
	a. Issued note.	6.00	15.00	55.00
	s. Specimen.	—	Unc	75.00
47	**500 LEVA**			
	1925. Dk. green on m/c unpt. Portr. Kg. Boris III at r. Back: Man w/oxen.			
	a. Issued note.	20.00	95.00	200.00
	s. Specimen.	—	Unc	265.00
48	**1000 LEVA**			
	1925. Brown on m/c unpt. Portr. Kg. Boris III at r. Back: Allegorical figure.			
	a. Issued note.	30.00	100.00	300.00
	s. Specimen.	—	Unc	375.00
49	**5000 LEVA**			
	1925. Purple on m/c unpt. Portr. Kg. Boris III at r., arms at l. Back: Aleksandra Nevski Cathedral, Sofia.			
	a. Issued note.	80.00	200.00	400.00
	s. Specimen.	—	Unc	500.00

1938 ISSUE
#55-57 Portr. Kg. Boris III at l. Printer: G&D.

55	**500 LEVA**	GOOD	FINE	XF
	1938. Lilac, brown and green. Arms at r. Back: Sheaf of wheat at r. Wmk: Woman's head.			
	a. Issued note.	15.00	40.00	100.00
	s. Specimen.	—	Unc	110.00
56	**1000 LEVA**			
	1938. Lilac, brown and green. Back: Flowers. Wmk: Child's head.			
	a. Issued note.	20.00	75.00	200.00
	s. Specimen.	—	Unc	220.00
57	**5000 LEVA**			
	1938. Green. Back: New bank bldg.			
	a. Issued note.	75.00	165.00	400.00
	s. Specimen.	—	Unc	440.00

1928 ISSUE

49A	**20 LEVA**	GOOD	FINE	XF
	1925. Ocre and brown. Portr. Kg. Boris III at ctr. Back: Salt-cellars.			
	a. Issued note.	8.00	35.00	120.00
	s. Specimen.	—	Unc	175.00

1929 ISSUE
#50-54 Kg. Boris III at r. Printer: TDLR.

1940 ISSUE
#58 and 59 Portr. Kg. Boris III at r. Printer: RDK.

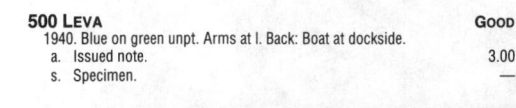

50	**200 LEVA**	GOOD	FINE	XF
	1929. Black on olive and lt. blue unpt. bottom ctr. Back: Green. Old man at ctr. Rampant lion.			
	a. Issued note.	2.00	10.00	35.00
	s. Specimen.	—	Unc	55.00

58	**500 LEVA**	GOOD	FINE	XF
	1940. Blue on green unpt. Arms at l. Back: Boat at dockside.			
	a. Issued note.	3.00	15.00	75.00
	s. Specimen.	—	Unc	85.00

51	**250 LEVA**	GOOD	FINE	XF
	1929. Black and purple on peach unpt. at l. Back: Purple. Aerial view of Tirnovo at ctr.			
	a. Issued note.	5.00	15.00	55.00
	s. Specimen.	—	Unc	85.00

59	**1000 LEVA**	GOOD	FINE	XF
	1940. Red and brown. Back: Man plowing w/oxen.			
	a. Issued note.	5.00	30.00	100.00
	s. Specimen.	—	Unc	120.00

1942 ISSUE

#60-62 Portr. Kg. Boris III at l. Wmk: БНБ (BNB). Printer: G&D.

60	500 LEVA	GOOD	FINE	XF
	1942. Black and blue on green and brown unpt. Back: Woman at r.			
	a. Issued note.	1.50	7.00	30.00
	s. Specimen.	—	Unc	45.00

61	1000 LEVA	GOOD	FINE	XF
	1942. Lt. and dk. brown on orange and blue unpt. Back: Monastery at r.			
	a. Issued note.	2.00	12.00	45.00
	s. Specimen.	—	Unc	65.00
62	5000 LEVA			
	1942. Brown and m/c. Back: National Assembly bldg.			
	a. Issued note.	8.00	40.00	150.00
	s. Specimen.	—	Unc	200.00

1943 ISSUE

#64-67A printer: RDK.

#64-66 young Kg. Simeon II at l., arms at r.

63	20 LEVA	VG	VF	UNC
	1943. Blue-black on lt. red unpt. Year date in lower r. margin. Back: Brown. Arms at l.			
	a. Issued note.	.50	2.50	25.00
	s. Specimen perforated MUSTER.	—	—	60.00

64	200 LEVA	VG	VF	UNC
	1943. Brown and black. Back: View of Tirnovo.			
	a. Issued note.	3.00	10.00	40.00
	s. Specimen perforated MUSTER.	—	—	60.00

65	250 LEVA	VG	VF	UNC
	1943. Green and brown. Back: Man w/oxen.			
	a. Issued note.	3.00	10.00	40.00
	s. Specimen perforated MUSTER.	—	—	60.00
66	500 LEVA			
	1943. Blue on brown unpt. Back: Blue and brown. Boy shepherd w/flute.			
	a. Issued note.	2.50	80.00	35.00
	s. Specimen perforated MUSTER.	—	—	50.00

67	1000 LEVA	VG	VF	UNC
	1943. Dk. red, dk. brown and purple. Portr. Kg. Simeon II at r., arms at l. Back: Nevski Cathedral.			
	a. W/normal serial #. Not issued.	—	—	125.00
	s. Specimen perforated MUSTER.	—	—	150.00

67A	5000 LEVA	VG	VF	UNC
	1943. Brown and red. Portr. Kg. Simeon II at r., arms at l. Back: Orange and green. Rose harvest scene. Specimen perforated: MUSTER.	—	—	1850.

STATE TREASURY

1942 ISSUE

#67B-67F arms at r. (Not issued).

67B	1000 LEVA			
	25.3.1942.	—	—	—
67C	5000 LEVA			
	15.12.1942. Red on blue and pink unpt. Back: Red on green and brown unpt.	—	—	—
67D	10,000 LEVA			
	15.12.1942. Brown on blue and pink unpt.	—	—	—
67E	20,000 LEVA			
	5.12.1942. Gray on green and purple unpt.	—	—	—
67F	50,000 LEVA			
	5.12.1942. Blue on green and purple unpt.	—	—	—

1943 ISSUES

#67G-67J arms at r.

Note: Reportedly used as currency during and after WWII.

		VG	**VF**	**UNC**
67G	**1000 LEVA** 15.1.1943. Orange on lt. blue and ochre unpt. Back: Orange on green unpt.	25.00	50.00	100.00
67H	**1000 LEVA** 25.1.1943. Green on lt. blue and orange unpt. Back: Green on grayish green and ochre unpt.	25.00	50.00	100.00
67I	**1000 LEVA** 15.6.1943. Brownish orange on m/c unpt. Back: Blue on orange and blue unpt.	50.00	100.00	200.00
67K	**1000 LEVA** 15.1.1944. Blue on green and purple.	25.00	50.00	100.00
67J	**5000 LEVA** 15.6.1943. Green on m/c unpt. Back: Blue on orange and blue unpt. (Not issued).	100.00	300.00	500.00

1944 ISSUE
#67K-67N arms at r.
NOTE: Reportedly used as currency during and after WWII.

		VG	**VF**	**UNC**
67L	**1000 LEVA** 5.7.1944. Lt. brown on green and ochre.	25.00	50.00	100.00
67M	**1000 LEVA** 15.11.1944. Ochre on pink and yellow. Back: Dk. brown on lt. blue and ochre.	20.00	40.00	80.00
67N	**5000 LEVA** 15.11.1944. Brown on gray and lt. brown. Back: Orange on lt. blue and ochre.	20.00	40.00	80.00

1944-45 ISSUE
#67O and 67P arms at upper ctr.
NOTE: Reportedly used as currecny during and after WWII.

		VG	**VF**	**UNC**
67O	**1000 LEVA** 5.3.1945. Brown on lt. brown and lt. blue. Back: Green on lt. brown.	15.00	25.00	40.00

		VG	**VF**	**UNC**
67P	**5000 LEVA** 5.3.1945. Purple on yellow and gray. Back: Ochre on lt. brown and yellow.	20.00	35.00	60.00

1946 ISSUE
#66Q and -67R modified arms at upper ctr.
NOTE: Reportedly used as currency after WWII.

		VG	**VF**	**UNC**
67Q	**1000 LEVA** 5.11.1946. Dk. blue on lt. blue and pink.	15.00	25.00	40.00
67R	**5000 LEVA** 5.11.1946. Red on lt. green and pink.	20.00	35.00	60.00

PEOPLES REPUBLIC

БЪЛГАРЧКАТА НАРОДНА БАНКА

BULGARIAN NATIONAL BANK

1947-48 ISSUES

		VG	**VF**	**UNC**
74	**20 LEVA** 1947. Dk. gray on pale blue unpt. Year after imprint. Back: Bank bldg. at ctr.			
	a. Issued note.	.50	2.00	10.00
	s. Specimen.	—	—	15.00

		VG	**VF**	**UNC**
75	**200 LEVA** 1948. Brown. Arms w/9.IX.1944 at l., year date w/printer's name in lower margin. Back: Miner.			
	a. Issued note.	2.00	6.00	20.00
	s. Specimen.	—	—	30.00

		VG	**VF**	**UNC**
76	**250 LEVA** 1948. Green on lt. brown unpt. Arms w/9.IX.1944 at l. Back: Steam passenger train at ctr.			
	a. Issued note.	3.00	12.50	40.00
	s. Specimen.	—	—	55.00

		VG	**VF**	**UNC**
77	**500 LEVA** 1948. Blue-black on brown unpt. Arms w/9.IX.1944 at l. Back: Tobacco harvesting on back.			
	a. Issued note.	2.00	6.00	20.00
	s. Specimen.	—	—	30.00

			VG	VF	UNC
78	**1000 LEVA**				
	1948. Brown on blue unpt. Arms w/9.IX.1944 at l., soldier at r. Back: Tractor and factory scene at lower ctr.				
	a. Normal Serial #. (Not issued).		—	—	50.00
	s. Specimen.		—	—	75.00

1950 ISSUE

			VG	VF	UNC
79	**20 LEVA**				
	1950. Brown on lt. tan unpt. Back: Bank bldg. at ctr.		1.00	4.00	15.00

1951 ISSUE

#83-87A G. Dimitrov at l. on back.

#83-85 wmk: БНБ (BNB) w/hammer and sickle.

#86-87A wmk: hammer and sickle.

			VG	VF	UNC
83	**10 LEVA**				
	1951. Red-brown on m/c unpt. Farm tractor at r.				
	a. Issued note.		—	.10	.25
	s. Specimen.		—	—	6.50

			VG	VF	UNC
84	**25 LEVA**				
	1951. Gray blue on m/c unpt. Railroad construction at ctr.				
	a. Issued note.		—	.10	.25
	s. Specimen.		—	—	6.50

			VG	VF	UNC
85	**50 LEVA**				
	1951. Brown on m/c unpt. Peasant woman w/baskets of roses at ctr.				
	a. Issued note.		—	.10	.25
	s. Specimen.		—	—	6.50

			VG	VF	UNC
86	**100 LEVA**				
	1951. Green and blue on m/c unpt. Woman picking grapes in vineyard.				
	a. Issued note.		—	.10	.25
	s. Specimen.		—	—	6.50

			VG	VF	UNC
87	**200 LEVA**				
	1951. Gray-blue and black on m/c unpt. Farmers harvesting tobacco at ctr.				
	a. Issued note.		—	.10	.30
	s. Specimen.		—	—	6.50
87A	**500 LEVA**				
	1951. Purple and m/c.				
	a. W/normal serial #. (Not issued).		—	—	50.00
	s. Specimen.		—	—	100.00

НАРОДЦА РЕПУБЛИКАБЪЛГАРИА

1951 STATE NOTE ISSUE

#80-82 upright hands holding hammer and sickle on back. Wmk: БНБ (BNB) w/hammer and sickle.

			VG	VF	UNC
80	**1 LEV**				
	1951. Brown on pale olive-green and orange unpt. Arms at l.				
	a. Issued note.		.20	.50	1.75
	s. Specimen.		—	—	6.50
81	**3 LEVA**				
	1951. Dp. olive-green on green and orange unpt. Arms at l.				
	a. Issued note.		—	.10	.25
	s. Specimen.		—	—	6.50
82	**5 LEVA**				
	1951. Blue and green. Arms at l. ctr.				
	a. Issued note.		—	.10	.25
	s. Specimen.		—	—	6.50

RUSSIAN INFLUENCE

БЪЛГАПСКАТА НАРОДНАБАНКА

BULGARIAN NATIONAL BANK

1944-45 ISSUE

#69-73 Russian printing.

68	**20 LEVA**	VG	VF	UNC
	1944. Brown. Year date in lower right margin. Back: Arms at ctr.			
	a. Red serial # w/star. Back: Salmon unpt.	1.00	4.00	20.00
	b. Brown serial # w/o star. Back: Lt. orange unpt.	.75	3.00	15.00
	s. Specimen.	—	—	20.00

69	**200 LEVA**	VG	VF	UNC
	1945. Dk. brown on green and tan unpt. Arms at ctr.			
	a. Issued note.	3.00	12.00	45.00
	s. Specimen.	—	—	45.00

70	**250 LEVA**	VG	VF	UNC
	1945. Green on lt. brown unpt. Arms at upper ctr.			
	a. Issued note.	3.00	12.00	45.00
	s. Specimen.	—	—	45.00

71	**500 LEVA**	VG	VF	UNC
	1945. Blue on m/c unpt. Arms at l. Back: Brown on blue and orange unpt.			
	a. Issued note.	2.50	9.00	40.00
	s. Specimen.	—	—	40.00

72	**1000 LEVA**	VG	VF	UNC
	1945. Brown on lt. blue and salmon unpt. Arms at l. Back: Wine on m/c unpt.			
	a. Issued note.	4.00	15.00	55.00
	s. Specimen.	—	—	55.00
73	**5000 LEVA**			
	1945. Brown on m/c unpt. Arms at upper ctr.			
	a. Issued note.	6.00	30.00	100.00
	s. Specimen.	—	—	100.00

BURMA (Myanmar)

The Socialist Republic of the Union of Myanmar (formally called Burma), a country of Southeast Asia fronting on the Bay of Bengal and the Andaman Sea, has an area of 261,789 sq. mi. (676,522 sq. km.) and a population of 41.5 million. Capital: Rangoon. Myanmar is an agricultural country heavily dependent on its leading product (rice) which embodies two-thirds of the cultivated area and accounts for 40 percent of the value of exports. Petroleum, lead, tin, silver, zinc, nickel, cobalt and precious stones are exported.

The first European to reach Burma, about 1435, was Nicolo Di Conti, a merchant of Venice. During the beginning of the reign of Bodawpaya (1782-1819AD) the kingdom comprised most of the same area as it does today including Arakan which was taken over in 1784-85. The British East India Company, while unsuccessful in its 1612 effort to establish posts along the Bay of Bengal, was enabled by the Anglo Burmese Wars of 1824-86 to expand to the whole of Burma and to secure its annexation to British India. In 1937, Burma was separated from India, becoming a separate British colony with limited self-government. The Japanese occupied Burma in 1942, and on Aug. 1, 1943 Burma became an "independent and sovereign state" under Dr. Ba Maw who was appointed the Adipadi (head of state) which collapsed with the surrender of Japanese forces. Burma became an independent nation outside the British Commonwealth on Jan. 4, 1948, the constitution of 1948 providing for a parliamentary democracy and the nationalization of certain industries. However, political and economic problems persisted, and on March 2, 1962, Gen. Ne Win took over the government, suspended the constitution, installed himself as chief of state, and pursued a socialist program with nationalization of nearly all industry and trade. On Jan. 4, 1974, a new constitution adopted by referendum established Burma as a "socialist republic" under one-party rule. The country name was changed to Union of Myanmar in 1989.

RULERS:
British to 1948
Japanese, 1942-45

MONETARY SYSTEM:
1 Rupee (Kyat) = 10 Mu = 16 Annas (Pe) to 1942, 1945-52
1 Rupee = 100 Cents, 1942-1943
1 Kyat = 100 Pya, 1943-45, 1952-

BRITISH INFLUENCE

GOVERNMENT OF INDIA

RANGOON

1897-1915 ISSUE
#A1-A3 Colonial type, w/4 language panels. Uniface. Ovpt: *RANGOON*.

NOTE: For similar notes from other branch offices see India.

A1	**5 RUPEES**	GOOD	FINE	XF
	1904-05. Black on green unpt.			
	a. Sign. F. Atkinson. 1.6.1904.	75.00	225.00	475.00
	b. Sign. H. J. Brereton. 19.5.1905.	75.00	225.00	475.00

A2	**10 RUPEES**	GOOD	FINE	XF
	1897-1907. Black on green unpt.			
	a. Sign. R. E. Hamilton. 3.4.1897.	150.00	450.00	—
	b. Sign. M. F. Gauntlett. 16.8.1907; 6.9.1907.	100.00	325.00	600.00
A3	**100 RUPEES**			
	1915-22. Black on green unpt.			
	a. Sign. M. M. S. Gubbay. 27.11.1915; 30.11.1915.	—	Rare	—
	b. Sign. H. Denning. 18.8.1922.	—	Rare	—

1911-14 ISSUE
#A4 and A5 Colonial type, w/8 language panels. Uniface. Ovpt: *R. at lower l. and r.*

A4	**5 RUPEES**			
	21.9.1914. Black on red unpt. Sign. M. M. S. Gubbay.	50.00	125.00	300.00

A5	**10 RUPEES**	GOOD	FINE	XF
	1911-18. Black on red unpt.			
	a. Sign. R. W. Gillan. 7.7.1911-30.11.1912.	30.00	80.00	200.00
	b. Sign. H. F. Howard. 2.1.1915.	30.00	80.00	200.00
	c. Sign. M. M. S. Gubbay. 28.3.1916-20.11.1918.	30.00	80.00	200.00

1917 ND PROVISIONAL ISSUE

A6	**2 RUPEES 8 ANNAS**			
	ND (1917). black on green and red-brown unpt. Portr. Kg. George V in octagonal frame at upper l. Ovpt: *R1* on India #2.	50.00	125.00	—

1927 ND PROVISIONAL ISSUE
#A7 and A8 portr. Kg. George V at r. and as wmk. Ovpt: *RANGOON* in lg. or sm. letters.

A7	**50 RUPEES**			
	ND (1927). Lilac and brown. Portr. Kg. George V at r. and as wmk. Ovpt. on India #9. Sign. J. B. Taylor.	125.00	325.00	—

A8	**100 RUPEES**	GOOD	FINE	XF
	ND (1927-37). Violet and green. Portr. Kg. George V at r. and as wmk. Ovpt. on India #10.			
	a. Sign. H. Denning. Ovpt: *RANGOON* in sm. black letters. Series S.	60.00	150.00	400.00
	b. Sign. H. Denning. Ovpt: *RANGOON* in sm. green letters. Series S.	50.00	125.00	500.00
	c. Sign. H. Denning. Ovpt: *RANGOON* in lg. green letters. Series S.	Reported Not Confirmed		
	d. Sign. J. B. Taylor. Ovpt: *RANGOON* in lg. green letters. Series S.	40.00	100.00	325.00
	e. Sign. J. B. Taylor. Ovpt: *RANGOON* in lg. green letters. Series S.	40.00	100.00	325.00
	f. Sign. J. W. Kelly. Ovpt: *RANGOON* in sm. green letters. Series T.	30.00	75.00	250.00

RESERVE BANK OF INDIA

BURMA

1937 ND PROVISIONAL ISSUE
#1-3 portr. Kg. George V at r. and as wmk. Ovpt: *LEGAL TENDER IN BURMA ONLY.*

1	**5 RUPEES**	GOOD	FINE	XF
	ND (1937). Brown-violet on tan unpt. Portr. Kg. George V at r. and as wmk. Ovpt. on India #15. Sign. J. W. Kelly.			
	a. Red ovpt. in margins.	35.00	75.00	200.00
	b. Black ovpt. on face at ctr. and on back at bottom.	35.00	75.00	200.00

2	**10 RUPEES**	GOOD	FINE	XF
	ND (1937). Dk. blue. Portr. Kg. George V at r. and as wmk., palm tree, lake and mountains at ctr. Elephants at ctr. on back. Ovpt. on India #16. Sign. J. W. Kelly.			
	a. Red ovpt. in margins.	30.00	65.00	175.00
	b. Black ovpt. near ctr. on face and back.	30.00	65.00	175.00

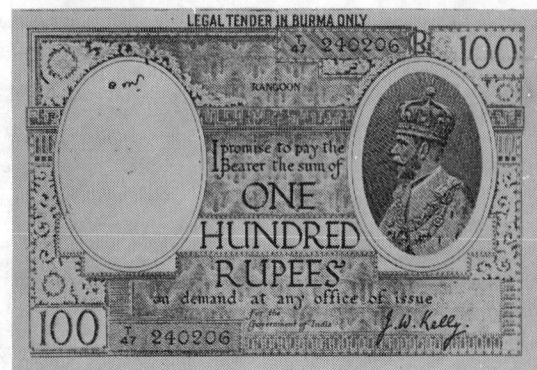

3	**100 RUPEES**	GOOD	FINE	XF
	ND (1937). Portr. Kg. George V at r. and as wmk. Ovpt. on Burma #A8f on face and back in margins. Sign. J. W. Kelly.	—	Rare	—

1938-39 ND ISSUE
#4-8 portr. Kg. George VI and as wmk.

4	5 RUPEES		GOOD	FINE	XF
	ND (1938). Violet and green. Portr. Kg. George VI at r. and as wmk., peacock at ctr. Elephant on back.		1.00	4.00	20.00

5	10 RUPEES		GOOD	FINE	XF
	ND (1938). Green and m/c. Portr. Kg. George VI at r. and as wmk., ox plow and cart at ctr. Dhow on back.		2.00	7.00	30.00

6	100 RUPEES		GOOD	FINE	XF
	ND (1939). Blue and m/c. Portr. Kg. George VI at r. and as wmk., peacock at ctr. Elephant w/logs on back.		50.00	150.00	450.00

7	1000 RUPEES		GOOD	FINE	XF
	ND (1939). Brown and m/c. Portr. Kg. George VI at ctr. and as wmk. Tiger on back.		200.00	500.00	—
8	10,000 RUPEES				
	ND (1939). Green and m/c. Portr. Kg. George VI at ctr. and as wmk. Waterfalls on back.		—	Rare	—

JAPANESE OCCUPATION - WWII

JAPANESE GOVERNMENT

1942-44 ND ISSUE
#9-17 w/B prefix or B/ in block letters.
#13-17 Ananda Temple in Pagan at r.

9	1 CENT		VG	VF	UNC
	ND (1942). Red and lt. blue. Back red.				
	a. Block letters: BA-BP; BR-BZ.		.10	.20	.60
	b. Fractional block letters: B/AA-B/AT.		.10	.25	.75
	s. Specimen ovpt: *Mihon.*		—	—	60.00

10	5 CENTS		VG	VF	UNC
	ND (1942). Violet and lt. green. Back violet.				
	a. Block letters: BA-BU.		.15	.35	1.00
	b. Fractional block letters: B/AB.		.5	.15	.50
	s. Specimen ovpt: *Mihon.*		—	—	70.00

11	10 CENTS		VG	VF	UNC
	ND (1942). Brown and tan. Back brown.				
	a. Block letters: BA-BS; BU-BW; BY-BZ.		.15	.35	1.00
	b. Fractional block letters: B/AA-B/AC.		.25	1.00	4.00
	s. Specimen ovpt: *Mihon.*		—	—	80.00
12	1/4 RUPEE				
	ND (1942). Blue and tan. Back blue.				
	a. Block letters: BA.		.15	.35	1.00
	s. Specimen ovpt: *Mihon.*		—	—	90.00

13	1/2 RUPEE		VG	VF	UNC
	ND (1942). Olive and green. Back olive.				
	a. Block letters: BA-BC.		.20	.65	3.00
	b. Block letters: BD.		.10	.25	.75
	s. Specimen ovpt: *Mihon.*		—	—	100.00

14	1 RUPEE		VG	VF	UNC
	ND (1942). Green and pink. Back green.				
	a. Block letters: BA-Bd closely spaced. Off-white paper.		.25	.75	4.00
	b. Block letters: BD spaced farther apart.		.10	.25	.75
	s. Specimen ovpt: *Mihon.*		—	—	110.00

15	5 RUPEES		VG	VF	UNC
	ND (1942-44). Violet and yellow. Back violet.				
	a. Block letters: BA.		1.00	2.50	7.00
	b. Block letters: BB.		.10	.25	1.00
	s. Specimen ovpt: *Mihon.*		—	—	120.00

16   10 RUPEES
ND (1942-44). Dull red and lt. green. Back dull red.

		VG	VF	UNC
a.	Wmk. Block letters: BA. 8mm wide.	.20	.65	3.00
b.	W/o wmk. Block letters: BA. 6.5mm wide. Silk threads.	.15	.50	2.00
s.	Specimen ovpt: *Mihon*.	—	—	130.00

17   100 RUPEES
ND (1944). Dk. green and gray-violet. Back dk. green.

		VG	VF	UNC
a.	Wmk. Block letters: BA. 7.5mm wide.	.50	1.00	4.00
b.	W/o wmk. Block letters: BA. 6.5mm wide. Silk threads.	.10	.40	1.00
s.	Specimen ovpt: *Mihon*.	—	—	140.00

STATE OF BURMA

BURMA STATE BANK
Instituted by the Japanese with Dr. Ba Maw in charge.

1944 ND ISSUE
#18-21 peacock at l., scene in Mandalay at r. on back. Wmk: Three Burmese characters.

NOTE: A large quantitiy of #19 is reported to exist. This report has not been confirmed.

18   1 KYAT
ND (1944). Blue, pink and violet. Back blue.

		VG	VF	UNC
a.	Block #3; 17; 21; 22; 26; 29.	—	275.00	450.00
s.	Red ovpt: Specimen in script. Block #21.	—	—	4.50

19   5 KYATS
ND (1944). Red, purple and gray-green. Back red, yellow and gray.
Specimens only. Japanese characters *Mihon* (Specimen) ovpt. on
face. Ovpt: Specimen in script on back. Block #0.

		VG	VF	UNC
		—	—	1000.

20   10 KYATS
ND (1944). Green, orange and violet. Back green, pink and blue.

		VG	VF	UNC
a.	Block #0, 1, 23.	—	350.00	600.00
s.	Ovpt: Specimen in script on face and back. Block #0.	—	—	600.00

21   100 KYATS
ND (1944). Orange, blue and lt. green. Back orange, pink and lt. blue.

		VG	VF	UNC
a.	Block #1.	—	175.00	350.00
s1.	Red ovpt: Specimen on face and back. Block #1.	—	—	300.00
s2.	Red Japanese characters. Ovpt: *Mihon* (Specimen) on face only. Block #1.	—	—	400.00

1945 ND ISSUE
#22, printed in Rangoon on unwmk. paper.

22   100 KYATS
Nd (1945). Dk. blue on green unpt. Stylized peacock at lower l., portr.
Ba Maw at upper r. Back blue. Stylized peacock at bottom ctr. Like
#21.

		VG	VF	UNC
a.	Serial # in open box directly below ctr.	—	35.00	100.00
b.	W/o serial #.	—	—	70.00
c.	Sheet of 4.	—	—	

MILITARY

MILITARY ADMINISTRATION OF BURMA

1943 ND PROVISIONAL ISSUE
#23 and 24 prepared in booklet form. Specimens.

23   4 ANNAS
ND (1943). Green. Portr. Kg. George VI at r.

	VG	VF	UNC
	—	—	400.00

24   8 ANNAS
ND (1943). Purple. Portr. Kg. George VI at ctr.

	VG	VF	UNC
	—	—	400.00

1945 ND ISSUE
#25-29 ovpt: *MILITARY ADMINISTRATION OF BURMA. LEGAL TENDER IN BURMA ONLY* on India notes.
#26-29 portr. Kg. George VI at r. and as wmk.

25   1 RUPEE
ND (1945 -old date 1940). Blue-gray on m/c unpt. Coin w/Kg. George
VI at upper r. Coin w/date at upper l. on back. Wmk: Kg. George VI.
Red ovpt. on India #25.

		VG	VF	UNC
a.	W/o lg. *A* after black serial #.	.50	3.00	15.00
b.	Lg. *A* after green serial #.	.25	.75	6.00
s.	As a. Specimen.	—	—	100.00

31   5 RUPEES

	VG	VF	UNC
ND (1947). Brown and green. Portr. Kg. George VI at r. and as wmk. Dk. blue ovpt. on India #18.	2.25	7.00	25.00

26   5 RUPEES
ND (1945). Brown and green. Portr. Kg. George VI at r. and as wmk. Dk. blue ovpt. on India #18.

	VG	VF	UNC
a. Sign. J. B. Taylor.	.75	2.00	15.00
b. Sign. C. D. Deshmukh.	.50	1.50	10.00
s. As a. Specimen.	—	—	120.00

27   10 RUPEES
ND (1945). Blue-violet on olive unpt. Portr. Kg. George VI at r. and as wmk. Back blue. Elephants at ctr. Ovpt. on India #19. Specimen.

	VG	VF	UNC
	—	—	200.00

28   10 RUPEES
ND (1945). Violet on m/c unpt. Portr. Kg. George VI at r. and as wmk. Dhow at ctr. on back. Red ovpt. on India #24. Sign. C. D. Desmukh.

	VG	VF	UNC
	1.00	3.00	17.50

32   10 RUPEES
ND (1947). Blue-violet on olive unpt. Portr. Kg. George VI at r. and as wmk., palm tree, lake and mountains at ctr. Back blue. Elephants at ctr. Red ovpt. on India #24.

	VG	VF	UNC
	2.25	7.00	25.00

33   100 RUPEES
ND (1947). Dk. green on lilac unpt. Portr. Kg. George VI at r. and as wmk. Tiger's head at ctr. on back. Red ovpt. on India #20.

	VG	VF	UNC
	20.00	60.00	165.00

GOVERNMENT OF BURMA

1948 ND ISSUE

#34 and 35 wmk: Peacock. Printer: TDLR.

34   1 RUPEE
ND (1948). Gray, lt. green and pink. Peacock at r. Back gray. Dhows at ctr.

	VG	VF	UNC
	1.00	3.00	10.00

29   100 RUPEES
ND (1945). Dk. green on lilac unpt. Portr. Kg. George VI at r. and as wmk. Tiger's head at ctr. on back. Red ovpt. on India #20.

	VG	VF	UNC
a. Sign. J. B. Taylor.	25.00	75.00	225.00
b. Sign. C. D. Deshmukh.	22.50	70.00	210.00
s. As a. Specimen.	—	—	175.00

STATE OF BURMA - POST WWII

BURMA CURRENCY BOARD

1947 ND PROVISIONAL ISSUE

#30-33 ovpt: *BURMA CURRENCY BOARD, LEGAL TENDER IN BURMA ONLY* **on India notes.**

30   1 RUPEE
ND (1947 -old date 1940). Blue-gray on m/c unpt. Coin w/Kg. George VI at upper r. Coin w/date at upper l. on back. Wmk: Kg. George VI. Red ovpt. on India #25c.

	VG	VF	UNC
	.65	2.00	10.00

35   5 RUPEES
ND (1948). Brown and m/c. Chinze statue at r. Back brown. Woman and spinning wheel.

	VG	VF	UNC
	3.00	10.00	55.00

GOVERNMENT OF THE UNION OF BURMA
Issued by the Burma Currency Board although w/new titles on this issue.

1948-50 ISSUE

36	**10 RUPEES**	VG	VF	UNC
	ND (1949). Blue and m/c. Peacock at r. Back blue. Elephant lifting log at ctr	1.50	5.00	25.00
37	**100 RUPEES**			
	1.1.1948 (1950). Green. Peacock at ctr., head of mythical animal at r. Worker w/oxen on back.	10.00	30.00	100.00

UNION BANK OF BURMA

1953 ND RUPEE ISSUE
#38-41 wmk: Peacock.

38	**1 RUPEE**	VG	VF	UNC
	ND (1953). Gray, lt. green and pink. Similar to #34. Back gray.	.35	.75	1.50

39	**5 RUPEES**	VG	VF	UNC
	ND (1953). Brown and m/c. Similar to #35. Back brown.	1.00	3.50	12.50

CAMBODIA

Cambodia, formerly known as Democratic Kampuchea and the Khmer Republic, a land of paddy fields and forest-clad hills located on the Indo-Chinese peninsula fronting on the Gulf of Thailand, has an area of 69,898 sq. mi. (181,035 sq. km.) and a population of 12 million. Capital: Phnom Penh. Agriculture is the basis of the economy, with rice the chief crop. Native industries include cattle breeding, weaving and rice milling. Rubber, cattle, corn, and timber are exported.

The region was the nucleus of the Khmer empire which flourished from the 5th to the 12th century and attained an excellence in art and architecture still evident in the magnificent ruins at Angkor. The Khmer empire once ruled over much of Southeast Asia, but began to decline in the 13th century as the Thai and Vietnamese invaded the region and attached its territories. At the request of the Cambodian king, a French protectorate attached to Cochin-China was established over the country in 1863, saving it from dissolution, and in 1885, Cambodia was included in the French Union of Indo-China. France established a constitutional monarchy for Cambodia within the French Union in 1949. The 1954 Geneva Convention resulted in full independence for the Kingdom of Cambodia. King Sihanouk abdicated to his father and won the office of Prime Minister.

Prince Sihanouk was toppled by a bloodless coup led by Lon Nol in March of 1970. Sihanouk moved to Peking to head a government-in-exile. On Oct. 9, 1970, Cambodia became the Khmer Republic, and Lon Nol its President. The government of Lon Nol was in turn toppled, April 17, 1975, by the Khmer Rouge insurgents who took control of the government and renamed the country Democratic Kampuchea.

The Khmer Rouge completely eliminated the economy and created a state without money, exchange or barter. Everyone worked for the state and was taken care of by the state. The Vietnamese supported People's Republic of Kampuchea was installed in accordance with the constitution of January 5, 1976. The name of the country was changed from Democratic Cambodia to Democratic Kampuchea, afterwards reverting to Cambodia.

In the early 1990's the UN attempted to supervise a ceasefire and in 1992 Norodom Sihanouk returned as Chief of State.

RULERS:
Norodom Sihanouk, 1941-1955
Norodom Suramarit, 1955-1960
Norodom Sihanouk, (as Chief of State) 1960-1970
Lon Nol, 1970-1975
Pol Pot, 1975-1979
Heng Samrin, 1979-92
Norodom Sihanouk (as Chief of State), 1992-

MONETARY SYSTEM:
1 Riel = 100 Sen to 1975
1 New Riel = 10 Kak = 100 Su, 1975-

SIGNATURE VARIETIES			
GOVERNOR [ ]	CHIEF INSPECTOR [ ]	ADVISOR [ ]	DATE
1			28.10.1955
2			1956
3			1956
4			Late 1961

CAMBODIA - KINGDOM

BANQUE NATIONALE DU CAMBODGE

1955-56 ISSUE

1	**1 RIEL**	VG	VF	UNC
	ND (1955). Blue. Figure "Kinnari" w/raised arms at l. Back blue and brown, w/royal houseboat at l. Like Fr. Indochina #94. Sign. 1. Wmk: Elephant. Printer: TDLR (w/o imprint).	5.00	50.00	150.00

2 5 RIELS
ND (1955). Violet. Sculpture (Bayon head) at l. Royal palace entrance at r. on back. Sign. 1. Wmk: Buddha. Printer: BWC (w/o imprint).

VG	VF	UNC
2.00	10.00	40.00

3 10 RIELS
ND (1955). Brown. Temple of Banteay Srei at r. Back brown and green, central market. Sign. 1. Wmk: Buddha. Printer: TDLR (w/o imprint).

VG	VF	UNC
2.00	10.00	50.00

3A 50 RIELS
ND (1956). M/c. Cambodian w/bamboo water vessels at l. Stupas at Botoum-Waddei on back. Sign. 1. Wmk: Buddha. Printer: BdF (w/o imprint).

VG	VF	UNC
35.00	125.00	500.00

1956 FIRST ISSUE

4 1 RIEL
ND (1956-72). Grayish green on m/c unpt. Boats dockside in port of Phnom-Penh. Royal palace throne room on back. Printer: BW (w/o imprint).

	VG	VF	UNC
a. Sign. 1.	1.00	3.00	15.00
b. Sign. 2; 6; 7; 8; 10; 100.	.15	.25	1.25
c. Sign. 12.	.10	.15	.25

5 20 RIELS
ND (1956-72). Brown. Combine harvester at r. Phnom Penh pagoda on back. Wmk: Buddha. Printer: BWC (w/o imprint).

	VG	VF	UNC
a. Sign. 3; 6; 8; 10.	.25	1.00	5.00
b. Sign. 12.	.15	.25	1.25

7 50 RIELS
ND (1956-72). Blue and orange. Fishermen fishing from boats w/lg. nets in Lake Tonle Sap at l. and r. Back blue and brown; Angkor Wat. Wmk: Buddha. Printer: TDLR (w/o imprint).

	VG	VF	UNC
a. Western numeral in plate block designator. Sign. 3.	1.00	3.00	7.00
b. Cambodian numeral in plate block designator. 5-digit serial #. Sign. 7; 10.	.25	.75	3.00
c. Asb. Sign. 12.	1.00	3.00	7.00
d. Cambodian serial # 6-digits/ Sign. 12.	.10	.20	.35

8 **100 RIELS**   VG   VF   UNC
ND (1956-72). Brown and green on m/c unpt. Statue of Lokecvara at l. Long boat on back. Wmk: Buddha.

		VG	VF	UNC
a.	Imprint: *Giesecke & Devrient Munchen, AG.* Sign. 3; 7; 8; 11.	.50	1.50	8.00
b.	Imprint: *Giesecke & Devrient Munchen.* Sign. 12; 13.	.10	.20	.65

9 **500 RIELS**
ND (1956-70). Green and brown on m/c unpt. Sculpture of 2 royal women dancers "Devatas" at l. 2 dancers in ceremonial costumes on back. Wmk: Buddha. Printer: G&D.

		VG	VF	UNC
a.	Sign. 3; 6.	5.00	20.00	75.00
b.	Sign. 9.	.25	.75	5.00

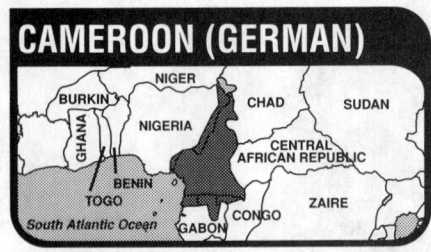

CAMEROON (GERMAN)

The United Republic of Cameroon, located in west-central Africa on the Gulf of Guinea, has an area of 185,568 sq. mi. (475,442 sq. km.) and a population of 12.2 million. Capital: Yaounde. About 90 per cent of the labor force is employed on the land; cash crops account for 80 per cent of the country's export revenue. Cocoa, coffee, aluminum, cotton, rubber and timber are exported.

European contact with what is now the United Republic of Cameroon began in the 16th century with the voyage of Portuguese navigator Fernando Po. The following three centuries saw continuous activity by Spanish, Dutch and British traders and missionaries. The land was spared colonial rule until 1884, when treaties with tribal chiefs brought German domination. After Germany's defeat in WWI, the League of Nations in 1919, divided the Cameroons between Great Britain and France, with larger eastern area going to France. The French and British mandates were converted into United Nations trusteeships in 1946. French Cameroon became the independent Cameroon Republic on Jan. 1, 1960. The federation of East (French) and West (British) Cameroon was established in 1961 when the southern part of British Cameroon voted for reunification with the Cameroon Republic, and the northern part for union with Nigeria.

See also Central African States, French Equatorial Africa and Equatorial African States.

MONETARY SYSTEM:
1 Franc = 100 Centimes

GERMAN KAMERUM

RULERS:
German to 1914

MONETARY SYSTEM:
1 Mark = 100 Pfennig

NOTE: German Reichsbanknoten and Reichskassenscheine circulated freely until 1914.

KAISERLICHES GOUVERNEMENT

TREASURY NOTES

DUALA BRANCH

1914 SCHATZSCHEINE

NOTE: 10 and 20 Mark notes may possibly have been printed but were not issued and later destroyed with no surviving specimens.

1 **5 MARK**   GOOD   FINE   XF
12.8.1914. Blue unpt.

		GOOD	FINE	XF
a.	Issued note.	75.00	250.00	500.00
b.	Cancelled.	60.00	230.00	400.00

2 **50 MARK**   GOOD   FINE   XF
12.8.1914. Gray-brown cardboar d.

		GOOD	FINE	XF
a.	Lt. brown eagle; 2 varieties o f eagles.	25.00	100.00	275.00
b.	Red-brown eagle.	25.00	100.00	275.00
c.	Cancelled.	20.00	80.00	225.00

3	100 MARK	GOOD	FINE	XF
	12.8.1914. Gray-brown cardboar d.			
	a. Blue eagle.	25.00	100.00	275.00
	b. Green-blue eagle.	25.00	60.00	275.00
	c. Cancelled.	20.00	80.00	225.00

FRENCH MANDATE POST WWI

1922 TERRITOIRE DU CAMEROUN

1922 ISSUE

#4 and 5 TC monogram at top ctr., palm fronds at l. and r. on back.

4	50 CENTIMES	VG	VF	UNC
(A1)	ND (1922). Red.	35.00	100.00	275.00
5	1 FRANC			
(A2)	ND (1922). Brown and pink.	45.00	125.00	325.00

CANADA

Jacques Cartier, a French explorer, took possession of Canada for France in 1534, and for more than a century the history of Canada was that of a French colony. Samuel de Champlain helped to establish the first permanent colony in North America in 1604 at Port Royal, Acadia - now Annapolis Royal, Nova Scotia. Four years later he founded the settlement in Quebec.

The British settled along the coast to the south while the French, motivated by a grand design, pushed into the interior. France's plan for a great American empire was to occupy the Mississippi heartland of the country, and from there to press in upon the narrow strip of English coastal settlements from the rear. Inevitably, armed conflict erupted between the French and the British; consequently, Britain acquired Hudson Bay, Newfoundland and Nova Scotia from the French in 1713. British control of the rest of New France was secured in 1763, largely because of James Wolfe's great victory over Montcalm near Quebec in 1759.

During the American Revolution, Canada became a refuge for great numbers of American loyalists, most of whom settled in Ontario, thereby creating an English majority west of the Ottawa River. The ethnic imbalance contravened the effectiveness of the prevailing French type of government, and in 1791 the Constitutional act was passed by the British parliament, dividing Canada at the Ottawa River into two parts, each with its own government: Upper Canada, chiefly English and consisting of the southern section of what is now Ontario; and Lower Canada, chiefly French and consisting principally of the southern section of Quebec. Subsequent revolt by dissidents in both sections caused the British government to pass the Union act, July 23, 1840, which united Lower and Upper Canada (as Canada East and Canada West) to form the Province of Canada, with one council and one assembly in which the two sections had equal numbers.

The union of the two provinces did not encourage political stability; the equal strength of the French and British made the task of government all but impossible. A further change was made with the passage of the British North American act, which took effect on July 1, 1867, and established Canada as the first federal union in the British Empire. Four provinces entered the union at first: Upper Canada as Ontario, Lower Canada as Quebec, Nova Scotia and New Brunswick. The Hudson's Bay Company's territories were acquired in 1869 out of which were formed the provinces of Manitoba, Saskatchewan and Alberta. British Columbia joined in 1871 and Prince Edward Island in 1873. Canada took over the Arctic Archipelago in 1895. In 1949 Newfoundland came into the confederation. Canada is a member of the Commonwealth of Nations. The Queen of England is Chief of State.

RULERS:
 French 1534-1763
 British 1763-

MONETARY SYSTEM:
 French:
 1 Liard = 3 Deniers
 1 Sol = 4 Liards
 1 Livre = 20 Sols
 1 Ecu = 6 Livres
 1 Louis D'or = 4 Ecus
 English:
 1 Pound = 20 Shillings
 Canadian:
 1 Dollar = 100 Cents

PROVINCE OF CANADA

1866 ISSUE

#1-7A black on lt. green unpt. Province of Canada notes w/additional ovpt.

1	1 DOLLAR	GOOD	FINE	XF
	1.10.1866. Samuel de Champlain at lower l., arms at top ctr., flanked by farmer at l., and sailor at r., J. Cartier at lower r.			
	a. Ovpt. PAYABLE AT MONTREAL.	175.00	700.00	1800.
	b. Ovpt. PAYABLE AT TORONTO.	225.00	750.00	2400.
	c. Ovpt. PAYABLE AT ST. JOHN on b.	850.00	2600.	—

2	**2 DOLLARS**	**GOOD**	**FINE**	**XF**
	1.10.1866. Indian woman at lower l., Britannia at top ctr. flanked by a woman w/ agricultural produce at l. and woman playing harp at r., sailor and lion at lower r.			
	a. Ovpt: *PAYABLE AT MONTREAL*.	225.00	1000.	3000.
	b. Ovpt: *PAYABLE AT TORONTO*.	560.00	2000.	—
	c. Ovpt: *PAYABLE AT ST. JOHN* on b.	1000.	3000.	—

3	**5 DOLLARS**	**GOOD**	**FINE**	**XF**
	1.10.1866. Qn. Victoria at l., arms w/lion and woman seated at top ctr., Man-of-War at lower r.			
	a. Ovpt: *PAYABLE AT MONTREAL*.	850.00	3000.	—
	b. Ovpt: *PAYABLE AT TORONTO*.	850.00	3000.	—
	c. Ovpt: *PAYABLE AT HALIFAX*.	1100.	4000.	—
	d. Ovpt: *PAYABLE AT ST. JOHN* on b.	1100.	4000.	—
4	**10 DOLLARS**			
	1.10.1866. Sailors and explorers at l., lion at ctr., beaver at r.			
	a. Ovpt: *PAYABLE AT MONTREAL*.	1500.	6000.	—
	b. Ovpt: *PAYABLE AT TORONTO*. Face proof.	—	Unc	2500.
	c. Ovpt: *PAYABLE AT ST. JOHN* on b.	Reported Not Confirmed		
5	**20 DOLLARS**			
	1.10.1866. Princess of Wales at l., beaver repairing dam at ctr., Prince Consort Albert at r.			
	a. Ovpt: *PAYABLE AT MONTREAL*.	2000.	—	—
	b. Ovpt: *PAYABLE AT TORONTO*.	Reported Not Confirmed		
	c. Ovpt: *PAYABLE AT ST. JOHN* on b.	Reported Not Confirmed		
6	**50 DOLLARS**			
	1.10.1866. Mercury w/map of British America, harbor w/ships and train in background.			
	a. *PAYABLE AT MONTREAL*. Face proof.	—	Rare	—
	b. *PAYABLE AT TORONTO*. Face proof.	—	Unc	2500.
	c. *PAYABLE AT ST. JOHN* on back.	Reported Not Confirmed		
7	**100 DOLLARS**			
	1.10.1866. Qn. Victoria.			
	a. *PAYABLE AT MONTREAL*. Face proof.	—	Unc	2500.
	b. *PAYABLE AT TORONTO*. Face proof.	—	Unc	2500.
7A	**500 DOLLARS**			
	1.10.1866. Provincial arms of Canada flanked by woman w/lion at l. and agricultural produce at r.			
	a. *PAYABLE AT MONTREAL*. Face proof.	—	Unc	2500.
	b. *PAYABLE AT TORONTO*. Face proof.	—	Unc	2500.

DOMINION OF CANADA

FRACTIONAL ISSUES

#8-11 are commonly referred to as "shinplasters."

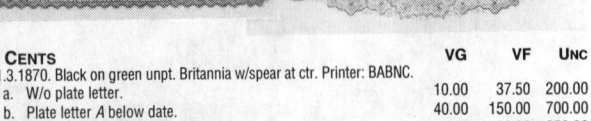

8	**25 CENTS**	**VG**	**VF**	**UNC**
	1.3.1870. Black on green unpt. Britannia w/spear at ctr. Printer: BABNC.			
	a. W/o plate letter.	10.00	37.50	200.00
	b. Plate letter *A* below date.	40.00	150.00	700.00
	c. Plate letter *B* below date.	15.00	50.00	250.00

9	**25 CENTS**	**VG**	**VF**	**UNC**
	2.1.1900. Black on lt. brown unpt. Britannia seated w/shield and trident at r., sailing ship in background. Printer: ABNC.			
	a. Sign. Courtney.	6.00	14.00	50.00
	b. Sign. Boville.	3.50	9.00	40.00
	c. Sign. Saunders.	5.00	10.00	40.00

10	**25 CENTS**	**VG**	**VF**	**UNC**
	2.7.1923. Black on brown unpt. Britannia w/trident at ctr. w/text *AUTHORIZED BY R.S.C. CAP. 31.* across lower l. and r. Sign. Hyndman-Saunders. Printer: CBNC.	14.00	35.00	175.00
11	**25 CENTS**			
	2.7.1923. Like #10 w/o text *AUTHORIZED BY...* but w/letters A-E, H, or J-L at l. of 25. Printer: CBNC.			
	a. Sign. Hyndman-Saunders.	10.00	42.00	225.00
	b. Sign. McCavour-Saunders.	3.50	10.00	45.00
	c. Sign. Campbell-Clark.	4.00	12.00	50.00

1870 ISSUE

#12-16A printer: BABNC.

12	**1 DOLLAR**	**GOOD**	**FINE**	**XF**
	1.7.1870. Black on green unpt. J. Cartier at upper l., reclining woman w/child and globe at ctr.			
	a. *PAYABLE AT MONTREAL* on back.	60.00	200.00	800.00
	b. *PAYABLE AT TORONTO* on back.	70.00	235.00	850.00
	c. Ovpt: *MANITOBA* on face. *PAYABLE AT TORONTO* on back.	2100.	6600.	—
	d. *PAYABLE AT HALIFAX* on back.	525.00	1500.	5500.
	e. *PAYABLE AT ST. JOHN* on back.	525.00	1500.	5500.
	f. *PAYABLE AT VICTORIA* on back.	2100.	6600.	—
	g. Ovpt: *MANITOBA* on face. *PAYABLE AT MONTREAL* on back.	2100.	6600.	—

13	**2 DOLLARS**	**GOOD**	**FINE**	**XF**
	1.7.1870. Black on green unpt. Gen. de Montcalm at lower l., seated Indian chief overlooking steam train at ctr., Gen. J. Wolfe at lower r.			
	a. *PAYABLE AT MONTREAL* on back.	550.00	2000.	6000.
	b. *PAYABLE AT TORONTO* on back.	550.00	2000.	6000.
	c. Ovpt: *MANITOBA* on face. *PAYABLE AT TORONTO* on back.	2500.	—	—
	d. *PAYABLE AT HALIFAX* on back.	1250.	4000.	—
	e. *PAYABLE AT ST. JOHN* on back.	1400.	4500.	—
	f. *PAYABLE AT VICTORIA* on back.	Reported Not Confirmed		
	g. Ovpt: *MANITOBA* on face. *PAYABLE AT TORONTO* on back.	2500.	—	—

1871 ISSUE

14	**500 DOLLARS**			
	1.7.1871. Black on green unpt. Young Qn. Victoria at ctr.			
	a. *PAYABLE AT MONTREAL*. Back proof.	—	Unc	350.00
	b. *PAYABLE AT TORONTO*. Back proof.	—	Unc	350.00
	c. *PAYABLE AT HALIFAX*. Back proof.	—	Unc	425.00
	d. *PAYABLE AT ST. JOHN*. Back proof.	—	Unc	425.00
	e. *PAYABLE AT VICTORIA*. Back proof.	—	Unc	525.00
	f. *PAYABLE AT WINNIPEG*. Back proof.	—	Unc	525.00
	g. *PAYABLE AT CHARLOTTETOWN*. Back proof.	—	Unc	525.00
	h. *OTTAWA* ovpt. Face proof.	—	Unc	2400.
15	**1000 DOLLARS**			
	1.7.1871. Black on green unpt. Canadian arms at ctr. flanked by woman w/lion at l., agricultural produce at r.			
	a. *PAYABLE AT MONTREAL*. Back proof.	—	Unc	350.00
	b. *PAYABLE AT TORONTO*. Back proof.	—	Unc	350.00
	c. *PAYABLE AT HALIFAX*. Back proof.	—	Unc	425.00
	d. *PAYABLE AT ST. JOHN*. Back proof.	—	Unc	425.00
	e. *PAYABLE AT VICTORIA*. Back proof.	—	Unc	525.00
	f. *PAYABLE AT WINNIPEG*. Back proof.	—	Unc	525.00
	g. *PAYABLE AT CHARLOTTETOWN*. Back proof.	—	Unc	525.00
	h. *OTTAWA* ovpt. face proof.	—	Unc	2400.

1872 ISSUE

16   **50 DOLLARS**
1.3.1872. Black on green unpt. Mercury w/map of British America at ctr., harbor w/ships and train in background.
  a. *PAYABLE AT MONTREAL.* Back proof.   —   Unc   350.00
  b. *PAYABLE AT TORONTO.* Back proof.   —   Unc   350.00
  c. Ovpt: *OTTAWA* Face proof.   —   Unc   2400.

16A   **100 DOLLARS**
1.3.1872. Parliament bldg. at ctr.
  a. *PAYABLE AT MONTREAL.* Back proof.   —   Unc   350.00
  b. *PAYABLE AT TORONTO.* Back proof.   —   Unc   350.00
  c. Ovpt: *OTTAWA* Face proof.   —   Unc   2400.

1878 ISSUE

#17-21 printer: BABNC.

17   **1 DOLLAR**
1.6.1878. Black on green unpt. Countess of Dufferin at ctr. Scalloped borders, corners w/o numeral.

	Good	Fine	XF
a. *PAYABLE AT MONTREAL* on back.	52.00	280.00	900.00
b. *PAYABLE AT TORONTO* on back.	52.00	280.00	900.00
c. *PAYABLE AT HALIFAX* on back.	350.00	1000.	3600.
d. *PAYABLE AT ST. JOHN* on back.	350.00	1000.	3600.

18   **1 DOLLAR**
1.6.1878. Like #17 but w/*1* in a circle at the corners.

	Good	Fine	XF
a. W/o series letter; Series A-C. *PAYABLE AT MONTREAL* on back.	20.00	90.00	350.00
b. W/o series letter; Series A. *PAYABLE AT TORONTO* on back.	20.00	90.00	350.00
c. *PAYABLE AT HALIFAX* on back.	350.00	1400.	—
d. *PAYABLE AT ST. JOHN* on back.	350.00	1400.	—

19   **2 DOLLARS**
1.6.1878. Black on green unpt. Earl of Dufferin (Gov. Gen.) at ctr.

	Good	Fine	XF
a. *PAYABLE AT MONTREAL* on back.	250.00	785.00	2800.
b. *PAYABLE AT TORONTO* on back.	250.00	785.00	2800.
c. *PAYABLE AT HALIFAX* on back.	525.00	1750.	—
d. *PAYABLE AT ST. JOHN* on back.	425.00	1250.	—

1882 ISSUE

20   **4 DOLLARS**
1.5.1882. Black on green unpt. Duke of Argyll (Gov. Gen. Marquis of Lorne) at ctr.

	Good	Fine	XF
	85.00	300.00	1500.

1887 ISSUE

21   **2 DOLLARS**
2.7.1887. Black and green. Marchioness and Marquis of Lansdowne (Gov. Gen.) at lower l. and lower r.

	Good	Fine	XF
a. W/o series letter.	120.00	300.00	1400.
b. Series Letter *A.*	210.00	550.00	1750.

1896 BANK LEGAL ISSUE

#21A-21C used in bank transactions only. Printer: BABNC.

21A   **500 DOLLARS**
2.7.1896. Black on peach unpt. Genius at lower l., Marquis of Lorne at ctr., Parliament bldg. tower at lower r. Back blue, seal of Canada at ctr.

	VG	VF	UNC
a. Issued note, cancelled.	—	5000.	—
p1. Face proof.	—	—	5000.
p2. Back proof.	—	—	500.00
s. Specimen.	—	—	5500.

21B   **1000 DOLLARS**
2.7.1896. Black. Qn. Victoria at l. Back deep brown, seal of Canada at ctr.

a. Issued note, cancelled.	—	6500.	—
p1. Face proof.	—	—	5000.
p2. Back proof.	—	—	500.00
s. Specimen.	—	—	5500.

21C   **5000 DOLLARS**
2.7.1896. Black on yellow-orange unpt. J. A. MacDonald at l. Back red-brown, seal of Canada at top ctr.

a. Issued note, cancelled.	—	6500.	—
p1. Face proof.	—	—	5000.
p2. Back proof.	—	—	500.00
s. Specimen.	—	—	5500.

1897-1900 ISSUE

#22-25 printer: ABNC-Ottawa.

22   **1 DOLLAR**
2.7.1897. Black on green unpt. Countess and Earl of Aberdeen (Gov. Gen.) at l. and r., lumberjacks at ctr. Back green, Parliament bldg. at ctr.   70.00   350.00   3500.

24   **1 DOLLAR**
31.3.1898. Like #22 but *ONE's* at l. and r. edge on back curved inward. Sign. Courtney. Series A-D.

	VG	VF	UNC
	35.00	140.00	700.00

24A   **1 DOLLAR**
1.3.1898. Like #24 but *ONE's* at l. and r. edge on back curved outward.

	VG	VF	UNC
a. Sign. Courtney. Series D-K.	28.00	100.00	450.00
b. Sign. Boville. Series L-S.	25.00	75.00	350.00

23   **2 DOLLARS**
2.7.1897. Black on green unpt. Edward, Prince of Wales, at l., boat w/fisherman at ctr. Back red-brown; w/farmers threshing wheat at ctr. Sign. Courtney.   550.00   1500.   —

23A   **2 DOLLARS**
2.7.1897. Like #23 but dk. brown back.

	VG	VF	UNC
a. Sign. Courtney. W/o Series or w/Series A-C.	42.00	150.00	600.00
b. Sign. Boville. Series D-L.	35.00	125.00	475.00

25	4 DOLLARS	VG	VF	UNC
	2.7.1900. Black on green unpt. Countess and Earl of Minto (Gov. Gen.) at l. and r., ship in locks at Sault Ste. Marie (error: view of U.S. side of locks) at ctr. Back green; Parliament bldg. and library at l. ctr.	85.00	350.00	1500.

1901 BANK LEGAL ISSUE

#25A-25B used in bank transactions only. Printer: ABNC-Ottawa.

25A	1000 DOLLARS			
	2.1.1901. Black on green unpt. Lord E. Roberts at l. Back green.			
	a. Issued note, cancelled.	—	6500.	—
	p1. Face proof.	—	—	5000.
	p2. Back proof.	—	—	500.00
	s. Specimen.	—	—	5500.

25B	5000 DOLLARS	VG	VF	UNC
	2.1.1901. Yellow-brown. Qn. Victoria at l. Back brown.			
	a. Issued note, cancelled.	—	7000.	—
	p1. Face proof.	—	—	550.00
	p2. Back proof.	—	—	5500.
	s. Specimen.	—	—	6500.

1902 ISSUES

#26-26A printer: ABNC-Ottawa.

26	4 DOLLARS	VG	VF	UNC
	2.1.1902. Similar to #25 but vignette at ctr. changed to show ship in Canadian side of locks at Sault Ste. Marie, w/4's on top, *Four* on bottom at corners. Parliament bldg. and Library on back.	100.00	365.00	1400.
26A	4 DOLLARS			
	2.1.1902. Like #26 but w/*Four* twice on top, 4's on bottom at corners.	100.00	350.00	1400.

1911-14 ISSUES

#27-32 printer: ABNC-Ottawa.

27	1 DOLLAR	VG	VF	UNC
	3.1.1911. Black on green unpt. Earl (Gov. Gen.) and Countess of Grey at ctr. Back green; Parliament bldg. at ctr.			
	a. Green line above sign. Series A-L.	17.50	55.00	375.00
	b. Black line above sign. Series L-Y.	14.00	50.00	350.00

31	2 DOLLARS	VG	VF	UNC
	2.1.1914. Black on lt. brown and olive unpt. Duke and Duchess of Connaught at l. and r. Back olive-green; 9 provincial shields around Royal arms at ctr.			
	a. Text: *WILL PAY...* curved above ctr. 2. Sign. Boville at r.	35.00	90.00	600.00
	b. Text: *WILL PAY...* straight above ctr. Sign. Boville at r.	35.00	125.00	750.00
	c. W/o seal over r. *TWO*. Sign. Saunders at r.	35.00	90.00	600.00
	d. Black seal over r. *TWO*. Sign. Hyndman-Saunders.	85.00	225.00	1000.
	e. Black seal, w/o *TWO* at r. Sign. Hyndman-Saunders.	35.00	125.00	625.00

30	5 DOLLARS	VG	VF	UNC
	5.1.1912. Black on blue unpt.; steam passenger train *Ocean Limited* in Nova Scotia at ctr. Back blue.			
	a. W/o seal over *FIVE* at r. Sign. Boville at r.	170.00	500.00	2150.
	b. W/o seal over *FIVE* at r. Sign. Boville at r. B after sheet no.	300.00	775.00	2600.
	c. W/o seal over *FIVE* at r. Sign. Boville at r. B before sheet no.	150.00	345.00	1400.
	d. Blue seal over *FIVE* at r. Sign. Hyndman-Boville.	155.00	435.00	1550.
	e. Blue seal over *FIVE* at r. Sign. Hyndman-Saunders.	215.00	600.00	2150.
	f. Blue seal only at r. Sign. Hyndman-Saunders.	130.00	300.00	1300.
	g. Like d. Sign. McCavour-Saunders (Unique).	—	—	—
28	500 DOLLARS			
	3.1.1911. Black on green unpt. Young Qn. Mary at ctr. Back green.			
	a. Issued note.	3500.	—	—
	s. Specimen.	—	—	1000.

29	1000 DOLLARS	VG	VF	UNC
	3.1.1911. Black on blue unpt. Kg. George V at ctr. Back blue.			
	a. Issued note.	3500.	—	—
	s. Specimen.	—	—	1000.

1917 ISSUE

			VG	VF	UNC
32	**1 DOLLAR**				
	17.3.1917. Black on green unpt. Princess Patricia Ramsey (Princess of Connaught) at ctr. W/o seal over r. *ONE*. Back green; Parliament bldg. at ctr.				
	a.	W/*ABNCo.* imprint. Sign. Boville at r.	14.00	50.00	300.00
	b.	W/o *ABNCo.* imprint. Sign. Boville at r.	16.00	55.00	325.00
	c.	W/o *ABNCo.* imprint. Sign. Saunders at r.	14.00	38.00	300.00
	d.	Black seal over right *ONE*. Sign. Hyndman-Saunders.	16.00	55.00	325.00
	e.	W/o *ONE* at r. Sign. Hyndman-Saunders.	16.00	55.00	325.00

1918 BANK LEGAL ISSUES
#32A-32B used in bank transactions only. Printer: ABNC.

			VG	VF	UNC
32A	**5000 DOLLARS**				
	2.1.1918. Black on brown unpt. Qn. Victoria at l. Back yellow-brown.				
	a.	Issued note: Cancelled.	—	6500.	—
	p1.	Face proof.	—	—	5000.
	p2.	Back proof.	—	—	500.00
	s.	Specimen.	—	—	5500.

			VG	VF	UNC
32B	**50,000 DOLLARS**				
	2.1.1918. Black on olive-green unpt. Kg. George V and Qn. Mary at ctr. Back deep olive-green.				
	a.	Issued note: Cancelled.	—	9000.	—
	p1.	Face proof.	—	—	7000.
	p2.	Back proof.	—	—	800.00
	s.	Specimen.	—	—	8500.

1923-25 REGULAR ISSUES
#33-34 printer: CBNC.

			VG	VF	UNC
33	**1 DOLLAR**				
	2.7.1923. Black on green unpt. Kg. George V at ctr., seal at r. Back green; Library of Parliament at ctr.				
	a.	Black seal. Sign. Hyndman-Saunders.	20.00	55.00	325.00
	b.	Black seal. Sign. McCavour-Saunders.	20.00	55.00	350.00
	c.	Blue seal. Sign. McCavour-Saunders.	17.50	50.00	325.00
	d.	Green seal. Sign. McCavour-Saunders.	20.00	55.00	350.00
	e.	Red seal. Sign. McCavour-Saunders.	17.50	50.00	350.00
	f.	Bronze seal. Sign. McCavour-Saunders.	20.00	55.00	325.00
	g.	Lilac seal. Sign. McCavour-Saunders.	85.00	240.00	—
	h.	Black seal. Sign. Campbell-Sellar.	12.00	42.00	250.00
	i.	Lilac seal. Sign. Campbell-Sellar.	120.00	300.00	—
	j.	Black seal. Sign. Campbell-Clark.	10.00	28.00	200.00

			VG	VF	UNC
34	**2 DOLLARS**				
	23.6.1923. Black on olive unpt. Edward, Prince of Wales at ctr. Back olive-green; arms of Canada at ctr.				
	a.	Black seal. Sign. Hyndman-Saunders.	42.00	110.00	550.00
	b.	Black seal. Sign. McCavour-Saunders.	33.00	100.00	500.00
	c.	Blue seal. Sign. McCavour-Saunders.	32.00	85.00	550.00
	d.	Green seal. Sign. McCavour-Saunders.	42.00	100.00	550.00
	e.	Red seal. Sign. McCavour-Saunders.	32.00	85.00	550.00
	f.	Bronze seal. Sign. McCavour-Saunders.	33.00	100.00	500.00
	g.	Black seal. Sign. Campbell-Sellar.	28.00	70.00	450.00
	h.	Blue seal. Sign. Campbell-Sellar.	33.00	100.00	550.00
	i.	Black seal. Sign. Campbell-Clark.	32.00	85.00	450.00

1924 BANK LEGAL ISSUE
#34A-34C used in bank transactions only. Printer: CBNC.

			VG	VF	UNC
34A	**1000 DOLLARS**				
	2.1.1924. Black on green unpt. Lord E. Roberts at l. Back green.				
	a.	Issued note: Cancelled.	—	6500.	—
	p1.	Face proof.	—	—	5000.
	p2.	Back proof.	—	—	500.00
	s.	Specimen.	—	—	5500.
34B	**5000 DOLLARS**				
	2.1.1924. Black on brown unpt. Qn. Victoria at l. Back yellow-brown.				
	a.	Issued note: Cancelled.	—	6500.	—
	p1.	Face proof.	—	—	5000.
	p2.	Back proof.	—	—	500.00
	s.	Specimen.	—	—	5500.
34C	**50,000 DOLLARS**				
	2.1.1924. Black on olive-green unpt. Kg. George V and Qn. Mary at ctr. Back olive-green.				
	a.	Issued note: Cancelled.	—	9000.	—
	p1.	Face proof.	—	—	8500.
	p2.	Back proof.	—	—	800.00
	s.	Specimen.	—	—	9000.

1924-25 REGULAR ISSUE
#35-37 printer: CBNC.

			VG	VF	UNC
35	**5 DOLLARS**				
	26.5.1924. Black on blue unpt. Qn. Mary at ctr. Back blue; East view of Parliament bldgs. at ctr.		250.00	1250.	3750.

36 500 DOLLARS

2.1.1925. Black on blue unpt. Kg. George V at ctr.

	VG	VF	UNC
a. Issued note.	1400.	3850.	—
s. Specimen.	—	—	700.00

37 1000 DOLLARS

2.1.1925. Black and orange. Qn. Mary at ctr.

	VG	VF	UNC
a. Issued note.	1400.	3850.	—
s. Specimen.	—	—	700.00

BANQUE DU CANADA / BANK OF CANADA

1935 ISSUES

#38-57 separate series in English and in French. Allegorical figures on back.
#38-39 printer: CBNC.

38 1 DOLLAR

1935. Black on green unpt. Kg. George V at l. English text. Back green; Agriculture seated at ctr. Series A; B.

VG	VF	UNC
8.50	22.50	125.00

39 1 DOLLAR

1935. Like #38 but French text. Series F.

VG	VF	UNC
10.00	28.00	150.00

40 2 DOLLARS

1935. Black on blue unpt. Qn. Mary at l. English text. Back blue; Mercury standing w/various modes of transportation at ctr.; Series A.

VG	VF	UNC
14.00	35.00	225.00

41 2 DOLLARS

1935. Like #40 but French text. Series F.

VG	VF	UNC
17.50	50.00	375.00

42 5 DOLLARS

1935. Black on orange unpt. Prince of Wales at l. Back orange; Electric Power seated at ctr. English text. Series A.

VG	VF	UNC
21.00	85.00	450.00

43 5 DOLLARS

1935. Like #42 but French text. Series F.

VG	VF	UNC
42.00	100.00	575.00

44 10 DOLLARS

1935. Black on purple unpt. Princess Mary at l. English text. Back purple; Harvest seated at ctr. Series A.

VG	VF	UNC
17.50	50.00	325.00

45 10 DOLLARS

1935. Like #44 but French text. Series F.

VG	VF	UNC
45.00	125.00	650.00

46 20 DOLLARS

1935. Black on rose unpt. Princess Elizabeth at l. English text. Back rose; Agriculture w/farmer at ctr. Printer: CBNC. Series A.

	VG	VF	UNC
a. Large seal.	88.00	260.00	1200.
b. Small seal.	70.00	200.00	1000.

47 20 DOLLARS

1935. Like #46 but French text. Series F.

VG	VF	UNC
140.00	400.00	2000.

1935 COMMEMORATIVE ISSUE

#48 and 49, Silver Jubilee of Accession of George V. Printer: CBNC.

48 25 DOLLARS

6.5.1935. Black on purple unpt. Kg. George V and Qn. Mary at ctr. English text. Back purple; Windsor Castle at ctr. Series A.

VG	VF	UNC
210.00	525.00	2400.

49 25 DOLLARS

6.5.1935. Like #48 but French text. Series F.

VG	VF	UNC
250.00	625.00	2800.

1935 REGULAR ISSUES

#50-57 printer: CBNC.

50	**50 DOLLARS** 1935. Black on brown unpt. Prince George, Duke of York (later Kg. George VI) at l. English text. Back brown; allegorical figure w/modern inventions at ctr. Series A.	140.00	400.00	1950.
51	**50 DOLLARS** 1935. Like #50 but French text. Series F.	175.00	500.00	2750.

		VG	VF	UNC
52	**100 DOLLARS** 1935. Black on dk. brown unpt. Prince Henry, Duke of Gloucester at l. English text. Back dk. brown; Commerece seated w/youth standing at ctr. Series A.	140.00	350.00	1600.
53	**100 DOLLARS** 1935. Like #52 but French text. Series F.	225.00	575.00	2650.
54	**500 DOLLARS** 1935. Black on brown unpt. Sir John A. MacDonald at l. English text. Back brown; Fertility reclining at ctr. Series A.	2100.	3500.	—
55	**500 DOLLARS** 1935. Like #54 but French text. Series F.	3150.	5250.	—
56	**1000 DOLLARS** 1935. Black on olive green unpt. Sir Wilfred Laurier at l. English text. Back olive-green; Security w/shield kneeling w/child at ctr. Series A.	825.00	900.00	1500.
57	**1000 DOLLARS** 1935. Like #56 but French text. Series F.	1000.	1600.	4100.

1937 ISSUE

#58-65 bilingual notes. Allegorical figures on back like #38-47, 50-57.

#58-63 have Kg. George VI at ctr.

NOTE: #58a and some fo #58b (prefixes H/A-J/A) have narrow 9mm signature panels. Some of #58b (prefixes K/A-O/M) and #58c have wide 11mm signature panels.

		VG	VF	UNC
58	**1 DOLLAR** 2.1.1937. Black on green unpt. Back green. Printer: CBNC.			
	a. Sign. Osborne-Towers.	7.50	25.00	95.00
	b. Sign. Gordon-Towers.	2.50	6.50	30.00
	c. Sign. Coyne-Towers.	2.50	6.00	27.00
59	**2 DOLLARS** 2.1.1937. Black on red-brown unpt. Back red-brown. Printer: BABNC.			
	a. Sign. Osborne-Towers.	12.50	50.00	200.00
	b. Sign. Gordon-Towers.	5.00	15.00	55.00
	c. Sign. Coyne-Towers.	5.00	15.00	55.00
60	**5 DOLLARS** 2.1.1937. Black on blue unpt. Back blue. Printer: BABNC.			
	a. Sign. Osborne-Towers.	50.00	125.00	500.00
	b. Sign. Gordon-Towers.	6.00	12.50	60.00
	c. Sign. Coyne-Towers.	6.00	13.50	70.00
61	**10 DOLLARS** 2.1.1937. Black on purple unpt. Back purple. Printer: BABNC.			
	a. Sign. Osborne-Towers.	25.00	70.00	285.00
	b. Sign. Gordon-Towers.	10.00	21.00	65.00
	c. Sign. Coyne-Towers.	10.00	22.00	70.00
62	**20 DOLLARS** 2.1.1937. Black on olive-green unpt. Back olive-green. Printer: CBNC.			
	a. Sign. Osborne-Towers.	55.00	150.00	550.00
	b. Sign. Gordon-Towers.	20.00	27.50	75.00
	c. Sign. Coyne-Towers.	20.00	30.00	85.00
63	**50 DOLLARS** 2.1.1937. Black on orange unpt. Back orange. Printer: CBNC.			
	a. Sign. Osborne-Towers	150.00	550.00	2000.
	b. Sign. Gordon-Towers.	50.00	75.00	200.00
	c. Sign. Coyne-Towers.	50.00	75.00	225.00

		VG	VF	UNC
64	**100 DOLLARS** 2.1.1937. Black on brown unpt. Sir John A. MacDonald at ctr. Back brown. Printer: CBNC.			
	a. Sign. Osborne-Towers.	125.00	300.00	1200.
	b. Sign. Gordon-Towers.	100.00	150.00	300.00
	c. Sign. Coyne-Towers.	100.00	165.00	355.00
65	**1000 DOLLARS** 2.1.1937. Black on rose unpt. Sir Wilfred Laurier at ctr. Back rose. Sign. Osborne-Towers. Printer: CBNC.	1000.	1200.	1700.

BANQUE DU CANADA/BANK OF CANADA

1954 "DEVIL'S HEAD" ISSUE

NOTE:Dates reflect those on the various issues. Dates remain constant even though signatures change.

#66-73 Qn. Elizabeth II at r.

"Devil's face" Retouched

		VG	VF	UNC
66	**1 DOLLAR** 1954. Black on green unpt. "Devil's face" in Qn.'s hairdo. Back green; Western prairie scene. Printer: CBNC.			
	a. Sign. Coyne-Towers.	2.50	5.50	30.00
	b. Sign. Beattie-Coyne.	2.00	5.00	25.00
67	**2 DOLLARS** 1954. Black on red-brown unpt. "Devil's face" in Qn.'s hairdo. Back red-brown; Quebec scenery. Printer: BABNC.			
	a. Sign. Coyne-Towers.	5.00	12.50	65.00
	b. Sign. Beattie-Coyne.	5.00	10.00	55.00

		VG	VF	UNC
68	**5 DOLLARS** 1954. Black on blue unpt. "Devil's face" in Qn.'s hairdo. Back blue; otter falls on the Alaska Highway. Printer: BABNC.			
	a. Sign. Coyne-Towers.	8.50	17.50	75.00
	b. Sign. Beattie-Coyne.	7.50	15.00	65.00
69	**10 DOLLARS** 1954. Black on purple unpt. "Devil's face" in Qn.'s hairdo. Back purple; Mt. Burgess, British Columbia. Printer: BABNC.			
	a. Sign. Coyne-Towers.	15.00	25.00	95.00
	b. Sign. Beattie-Coyne.	12.00	20.00	80.00
70	**20 DOLLARS** 1954. Black on olive green unpt. "Devil's face" in Qn.'s hairdo. Back olive-green; Laurentian Hills in winter. Printer: CBNC.			
	a. Sign. Coyne-Towers.	22.50	45.00	165.00
	b. Sign. Beattie-Coyne.	22.50	40.00	135.00
71	**50 DOLLARS** 1954. Black on orange unpt. "Devil's face" in Qn.'s hairdo. Back orange; Atlantic coastline in Nova Scotia. Printer: CBNC.			
	a. Sign. Coyne-Towers.	55.00	90.00	225.00
	b. Sign. Beattie-Coyne.	55.00	85.00	200.00
72	**100 DOLLARS** 1954. Black on brown unpt. "Devil's face" in Qn.'s hairdo. Back brown; Okanagan Lake, British Columbia. Printer: CBNC.			
	a. Sign. Coyne-Towers.	100.00	145.00	285.00
	b. Sign. Beattie-Coyne.	100.00	150.00	300.00
73	**1000 DOLLARS** 1954. Black on rose unpt. "Devil's face" in Qn.'s hairdo. Back rose; Central Canadian landscape. Sign. Coyne-Towers.	1000.	1200.	1750.

1954 "MODIFIED HAIRSTYLE" ISSUES

#74-83 Qn. Elizabeth II at r. "Devil's face" retouched.

		VG	VF	UNC
74	**1 DOLLAR** 1954. Like #66 but Qn.'s hair in modified style. Printer: CBNC.			
	a. Sign. Beattie-Coyne.	1.25	3.00	12.50
	b. Sign. Beattie-Rasminsky.	1.00	1.50	7.50
75	**1 DOLLAR** 1954. Like #74. Printer: BABNC.			
	a. Sign. Beattie-Coyne.	1.00	2.00	12.50
	b. Sign. Beattie-Rasminsky.	1.00	1.50	5.00
	c. Sign. Bouey-Rasminsky.	1.00	1.50	5.00
	d. Sign. Lawson-Bouey.	1.00	1.50	5.50

76 2 Dollars

	VG	VF	UNC
1954. Like #67 but Qn's hair in modified style. Printer: BABNC.			
a. Sign. Beattie-Coyne.	2.00	5.50	25.00
b. Sign. Beattie-Rasminsky.	2.00	3.50	10.00
c. Sign. Bouey-Rasminsky.	2.00	3.50	11.00
d. Sign. Lawson-Bouey.	2.00	3.00	9.50

77 5 Dollars

	VG	VF	UNC
1954. Like #68 but Qn.'s hair in modified style. Printer: CBNC.			
a. Sign. Beattie-Coyne.	7.50	15.00	45.00
b. Sign. Beattie-Rasminsky.	5.00	7.50	27.50
c. Sign. Bouey-Rasminsky.	5.00	7.50	27.50

78 5 Dollars

	VG	VF	UNC
1954. Like #77. Sign. Beattie-Coyne. Printer: BABNC.	7.50	15.00	45.00

79 10 Dollars

	VG	VF	UNC
1954. Like #69 but Qn.'s hair in modified style. Printer: BABNC.			
a. Sign. Beattie-Coyne.	10.00	12.50	65.00
b. Sign. Beattie-Rasminsky.	10.00	12.50	40.00

80 20 Dollars

	VG	VF	UNC
1954. Like #70 but Qn.'s hair in modified style. Printer: CBNC.			
a. Sign. Beattie-Coyne.	22.50	27.50	100.00
b. Sign. Beattie-Rasminsky.	20.00	25.00	75.00

81 50 Dollars

	VG	VF	UNC
1954. Like #71 but Qn.'s hair in modified style. Printer: CBNC.			
a. Sign. Beattie-Coyne.	50.00	65.00	165.00
b. Sign. Beattie-Rasminsky.	50.00	65.00	150.00
c. Sign. Lawson-Bouey.	50.00	85.00	275.00

82 100 Dollars

	VG	VF	UNC
1954. Like #72 but Qn.'s hair in modified style. Printer: CBNC.			
a. Sign. Beattie-Coyne.	100.00	135.00	250.00
b. Sign. Beattie-Rasminsky.	100.00	125.00	235.00
c. Sign. Lawson-Bouey.	100.00	135.00	250.00

83 1000 Dollars

	VG	VF	UNC
1954. Like #73 but Qn.'s hair in modified style.			
a. Sign. Beattie-Coyne.	1000.	1200.	1750.
b. Sign. Beattie-Rasminsky.	950.00	1100.	1750.
c. Sign. Bouey-Rasminsky.	950.00	1100.	1500.
d. Sign. Lawson-Bouey.	900.00	1050.	1350.
e. Sign. Thiessen-Crow.	950.00	1100.	1500.

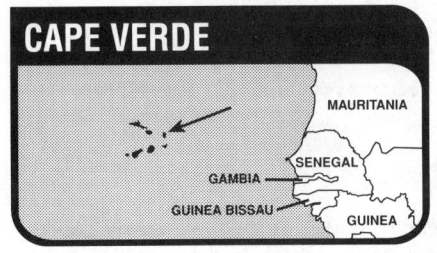

CAPE VERDE

The Republic of Cape Verde, Africa's smallest republic, is located in the Atlantic Ocean, about 370 miles (595 km.) west of Dakar, Senegal off the coast of Africa. The 14-island republic has an area of 1,557 sq. mi. (4,033 sq. km.) and a population of 380,000. Capital: Praia. The refueling of ships and aircraft is the chief economic function of the country. Fishing is important and agriculture is widely practiced, but the Cape Verdes are not self-sufficient in food. Fish products, salt, bananas, coffee, peanuts and shellfish are exported.

The date of discovery of the islands is uncertain. Possibly they were visited by Venetian Captain Alvise Cadamosto in 1456. Portuguese navigator Diogo Gomes claimed them for Portugal in May of 1460. Settlement began two years later. The early importance and wealth of the islands, which caused them to be attacked by Sir Francis Drake and the Dutch, resulted from the monopoly of the Guinea slave trade granted the inhabitants in 1466. Poverty and famine occasioned by frequent periods of severe drought have marked the history of the country since abolition of the slave trade in 1876.

After 500 years of Portuguese rule, the Cape Verdes became independent on July 5, 1975. At the first general election, all seats of the new national assembly were won by the Party for the Independence of Guinea-Bissau and Cape Verde (PAIGC). The PAIGC once had plans to possibly link the two former Portuguese colonies into a common state.

RULERS:
Portuguese to 1975

MONETARY SYSTEM:
1 Mil Reis = 1000 Reis
1 Escudo = 100 Centavos

STEAMSHIP SEALS

Type I	Type II	Type III
S. THIAGO	LISBOA	C, C&A

C, C&A = Colonias, Commercio, Agricultura.

PORTUGUESE INFLUENCE

BANCO NACIONAL ULTRAMARINO

S. THIAGO DE CABO VERDE BRANCH

1897 ISSUE
#1-3 *Agencia de S. Thiago de Cabo Verde.*

			Good	Fine	XF
1	**1 MIL REIS**				
	2.1.1897. Brown. Native man standing w/bow and arrow at l., embossed steamship seal at lower r.		—	—	—
2	**2 1/2 MIL REIS**				
	2.1.1897. Blue. Native woman standing next to embossed steamship seal at lower r.		—	—	—
3	**5 MIL REIS**				
	2.1.1897. Bush at l., embossed steamship seal at lower r.		—	—	—

S. THIAGO BRANCH

1909 ISSUE
#5-9 portr. Vasco da Gama at l. Seated allegorical woman looking out at sailing ships on back. Ovpt: *S. Thiago.* Printer: BWC.

NOTE: For #6b w/rectangular ovpt: *PAGAVEL...... GUINÉ* see Portuguese Guinea #5F.

			Good	Fine	XF
4	**1000 REIS**				
	1.3.1909. Black on green and yellow unpt. Steamship seal at r. *S. Thiago.* ovpt.				
	a. Steamship seal Type I.		65.00	150.00	425.00
	b. Steamship seal Type III.		65.00	150.00	425.00
5	**2500 REIS**				
	1.3.1909. Black on m/c unpt. Sailing ships at r.				
	a. Steamship seal Type I.		85.00	250.00	600.00
	b. Steamship seal Type III.		85.00	250.00	600.00
6	**5 MIL REIS**				
	1.3.1909. Black on m/c unpt. Sailing ships at r.				
	a. Steamship seal Type I.		100.00	300.00	725.00
	b. Steamship seal Type III.		100.00	300.00	725.00
7	**10 MIL REIS**				
	1.3.1909. Black on m/c unpt. Sailing ship at l. and r.				
	a. Steamship seal Type I.		150.00	400.00	950.00
	b. Steamship seal Type III.		150.00	400.00	950.00
8	**20 MIL REIS**				
	1.3.1909. Black on m/c unpt. Vascoda Gama embarking at r., palm fronds at lower l. and r.				
	a. Steamship seal Type I.		175.00	550.00	—
	b. Steamship seal Type III.		175.00	550.00	—
9	**50 MIL REIS**				
	1.3.1909. Black on m/c unpt. Palm trees at l., Vasco da Gama embarking at r.				
	a. Steamship seal Type I.		250.00	850.00	—
	b. Steamship seal Type III.		250.00	850.00	—

1914 PROVISIONAL ISSUE

		Good	Fine	XF
9A	**10 CENTAVOS**			
	5.11.1914. Purple. Arms at r., steamship seal Type II at bottom ctr. Ovpt: *PAGAVEL EM S. TIAGO* on Port. Guinea #6.	100.00	200.00	550.00

1914 REGULAR ISSUES
#10-17 Arms at r., steamship seal at lower ctr. Allegorical woman looking out at sailing ships at ctr. on back. Red ovpt: *S. Tiago.* Printer: BWC.

		Good	Fine	XF
10	**4 CENTAVOS**			
	5.11.1914. Blue-green on m/c unpt. Steamship seal Type III.	12.50	45.00	135.00
11	**5 CENTAVOS**			
	5.11.1914. Rose on m/c unpt. Steamship seal Type I.	12.50	45.00	135.00
11A	**5 CENTAVOS**			
	5.11.1914. Rose on m/c unpt. Steamship seal Type III.	12.50	45.00	135.00

		Good	Fine	XF
11B	**5 CENTAVOS**			
	5.11.1914. Bluish purple on m/c unpt. Steamship seal Type III.	8.00	25.00	100.00
12	**10 CENTAVOS**			
	5.11.1914. Violet on m/c unpt. Steamship seal Type I.	12.50	45.00	135.00
13	**10 CENTAVOS**			
	5.11.1914. Violet on m/c unpt. Steamship seal Type III.	12.50	45.00	135.00
14	**20 CENTAVOS**			
	5.11.1914. Blue on m/c unpt. Steamship seal Type II.	12.50	45.00	145.00
15	**20 CENTAVOS**			
	5.11.1914. Blue on m/c unpt. Steamship seal Type III.	12.50	45.00	135.00

		Good	Fine	XF
16	**50 CENTAVOS**			
	5.11.1914. Green on m/c unpt. Steamship seal Type II.	12.50	45.00	135.00
17	**50 CENTAVOS**			
	5.11.1914. Green on m/c unpt. Steamship seal Type III.	12.50	45.00	135.00

W/O BRANCH

1920 PORTO ISSUE

		Good	Fine	XF
18 (21)	**10 CENTAVOS**			
	1.1.1920. Red. Sailing ship at l. and r.	75.00	200.00	—
19 (21A)	**50 CENTAVOS**			
	1.1.1920. Blue. Mercury at l., ships at lower l., farmer and allegory at r. Back brown. Sailing ship at ctr.	100.00	350.00	—
19A (22)	**50 CENTAVOS**			
	1.1.1920. Dk. blue. Arms at top ctr.	—	Rare	—

1921 PROVISIONAL ISSUE

#20-22A arms at r., steamship seal at lower ctr. Allegorical woman looking out at sailing ships at ctr. on back. Black ovpt: *CABO VERDE*. Various sign. varieties.

			Good	Fine	XF
20 (18)	10 CENTAVOS	ND (1921 - old date 5.11.1914). Violet on m/c unpt. Ovpt. on Mozabique #54. Printer: BWC.	5.00	25.00	110.00
21 (19)	20 CENTAVOS	ND (1921 - old date 5.11.1914). Blue on m/c unpt. Ovpt. on Mozabique #58. Printer: BWC.	25.00	85.00	250.00
22 (20)	50 CENTAVOS	ND (1921 - old date 5.11.1914). Green on m/c unpt. Ovpt. on Mozabique #61. Printer: BWC.	30.00	100.00	275.00
22A (20A)	50 CENTAVOS	ND (1921 - old date 1.1.1921). Green on m/c unpt. Ovpt. on Portuguese Guinea #11.	—	Rare	—

1922 FIRST PROVISIONAL ISSUE

#23-28 ovpt: *Emissao Chamico* in rectangular frame.

			Good	Fine	XF
23	1000 REIS	ND (1922 - old date 1.3.1909). Black on green and yellow unpt. Ovpt. on #4b.	250.00	650.00	—
24	2500 REIS	ND (1922 - old date 1.3.1909). Black on m/c unpt. Ovpt. on #5.	—	Rare	—
25	5 MIL REIS	ND (1922 - old date 1.3.1909). Black on m/c unpt. Ovpt. on #6.	—	Rare	—
26	10 MIL REIS	ND (1922 - old date 1.3.1909). Black on m/c unpt. Ovpt. on #7.	—	Rare	—
27	20 MIL REIS	ND (1922 - old date 1.3.1909). Black on m/c unpt. Ovpt. on #8.	—	Rare	—
28	50 MIL REIS	ND (1922 - old date 1.3.1909). Black on m/c unpt. Ovpt. on #9.	—	Rare	—

1922 SECOND PROVISIONAL ISSUE

#29-31 portr. Oliveira Chamico at l., steamship seal at r., arms at botton ctr. Ovpt: *CABO VERDE* on notes of Portuguese.

			Good	Fine	XF
29	20 ESCUDOS	ND (1922 - old date 1.1.1921). Dk. blue on m/c unpt. Ovpt. on Port. Guinea #16.	250.00	650.00	—

			Good	Fine	XF
30	50 ESCUDOS	ND (1922 - old date 1.1.1921). Blue on m/c unpt. Ovpt. on Port. Guinea #17.	—	Rare	—
31	100 ESCUDOS	ND (1922 - old date 1.1.1921). Brown on m/c unpt. Ovpt. on Port. Guinea #18.	—	Rare	—

CABO VERDE BRANCH

1921 ISSUE

#32-40 portr. Francisco de Oliveira Chamico at l., steamship seal at r., arms at bottom ctr. Allegorical woman looking out at sailing ships at ctr. on back.

			Good	Fine	XF
32	1 ESCUDO	1.1.1921. Green on m/c unpt. Printer: BWC.	7.50	25.00	100.00

			Good	Fine	XF
33	5 ESCUDOS	1.1.1921. Green on m/c unpt. Ovpt. on 1 Escudo #32.	35.00	125.00	425.00
34	5 ESCUDOS	1.1.1921. Black on m/c unpt.	15.00	65.00	325.00
35	10 ESCUDOS	1.1.1921. Brown on m/c unpt.	20.00	100.00	375.00
36	20 ESCUDOS	1.1.1921. Dk. blue on m/c unpt.	45.00	150.00	500.00
37	50 ESCUDOS	1.1.1921. Red on m/c unpt.	85.00	400.00	—
38	100 ESCUDOS	1.1.1921. Violet on m/c unpt.	100.00	575.00	—

1941 ISSUE

#39 and 40 portr. Franciso de Oliveira at l., steamship seal at r., arms at bottom ctr. Allegorical woman looking out at sailing ships at ctr. on back.

			Good	Fine	XF
39	50 ESCUDOS	1.8.1941. Red on m/c unpt.	75.00	350.00	—

			Good	Fine	XF
40	1000 ESCUDOS	1.8.1941. Violet.			
	a.	Issued note.	85.00	500.00	—
	s.	Specimen: punched hole cancelled	—	—	—

1945 ISSUE

#41-46 portr. Bartolome Dias at r., steamship seal at l., arms at upper ctr. Allegorical woman looking out at sailing ships at ctr. on back. Printer: BWC.

		VG	VF	UNC
41	**5 ESCUDOS**	8.00	22.50	85.00
	16.11.1945. Olive-brown.			
42	**10 ESCUDOS**	10.00	35.00	110.00
	16.11.1945. Purple.			

		VG	VF	UNC
43	**20 ESCUDOS**	15.00	100.00	—
	16.11.1945. Green.			
44	**50 ESCUDOS**	25.00	140.00	—
	16.11.1945. Blue.			
45	**100 ESCUDOS**	40.00	225.00	—
	16.11.1945. Red.			
46	**500 ESCUDOS**	150.00	475.00	—
	16.11.1945. Brown and violet.			

1958 ISSUE

Decreto Lei 39221

#47-50 portr. Serpa Pinto at r., sailing ship seal at l. Allegorical woman looking out at sailing ships at ctr. on back. Sign. titles: *O-ADMINISTRADOR* and *VICE- GOVERNADOR*. Printer: BWC.

		VG	VF	UNC
47	**20 ESCUDOS**	1.50	5.00	27.50
	16.6.1958. Green on m/c unpt.			
48	**50 ESCUDOS**	5.00	25.00	125.00
	16.6.1958. Blue on m/c unpt.			

		VG	VF	UNC
49	**100 ESUCDOS**	3.00	10.00	37.50
	16.6.1958. Red on m/c unpt.			
50	**500 ESCUDOS**	15.00	50.00	160.00
	16.6.1958. Brown-violet on m/c unpt.			

SRI LANKA (Ceylon)

Ceylon (later to become the Democratic Socialist Republic of Sri Lanka), situated in the Indian Ocean 18 miles (29 km.) southeast of India, has an area of 25,332 sq. mi. (65,610 sq. km.) and population of 17.25 million. Capital: Colombo. The economy is chiefly agricultural. Tea, coconut products and rubber are exported.

The earliest known inhabitants of Ceylon, the Veddahs, were subjugated by the Sinhalese from northern India in the 6th century BC. Sinhalese rule was maintained until 1498, after which the island was controlled by China for 30 years. The Portuguese came to Ceylon in 1505 and maintained control of the coastal area for 150 years. They were supplanted by the Dutch in 1658, who were in turn supplanted by the British who seized the Dutch colonies in 1796, and made them a Crown Colony in 1802. In 1815, the British conquered the independent Kingdom of Kandy in the central part of the island. Constitutional changes in 1931 and 1946 granted the Ceylonese a measure of autonomy and a parliamentary form of government. Ceylon became a self-governing dominion of the British Commonwealth on February 4, 1948. On May 22, 1972, the Ceylonese adopted a new constitution which declared Ceylon to be the Republic of Sri Lanka - "Resplendent Island." Sri Lanka is a member of the Commonwealth of Nations. The president is Chief of State. The prime minister is Head of Government.

RULERS:
Dutch to 1796
British 1796-1972

MONETARY SYSTEM:
1 Rix Dollar = 48 Stivers
1 Rupee = 100 Cents, ca.1830-

NOTE: Certain listings encompassing issues circulated by various bank and regional authorities are contained in Volume 1.

BRITISH INFLUENCE

GENERAL TREASURY

1870s ISSUE

#1, 2 and 6 held in reserve.

#3-5 Britannia seated at ctr. w/lion and shield, elephant and palm trees in background. Printer: PB&P. (Not issued).

		GOOD	FINE	XF
3 (A35)	**1 POUND**			
	18xx. Like #7.			
	r. Unsigned remainder.	—	—	165.00
	s. Ovpt: *SPECIMEN*.	—	—	475.00

		GOOD	FINE	XF
4 (A36)	**2 POUNDS**			
	18xx. Colombo.			
	r. Unsigned remainder.	—	—	165.00
	s. Ovpt: *SPECIMEN*.	—	—	525.00

5	**5 POUNDS**	GOOD	FINE	XF
(A37)	18xx. Like #7.			
	r. Unsigned remainder.	—	—	165.00
	s. Ovpt: *SPECIMEN*.	—	—	600.00

GOVERNMENT

1809-26 ISSUE

#7 and 8 Britannia seated w/shield and trident at upper l. Uniface.
#9 and 10 held in reserve.

7	**2 RIX DOLLARS**	GOOD	FINE	XF
(A16)	1.11.1826.	—	—	—

8	**5 RIX DOLLARS**	GOOD	FINE	XF
(A17)	1.1.1809; x.2.1809.	—	—	—

1885-99 ISSUE

#9, 10, 13 and 14 held in reserve.

11	**5 RUPEES**	GOOD	FINE	XF
(5)	1885-1925. Black on green unpt. Uniface. 173 x 130mm.			
	a. 1885-1.11.1909.	175.00	375.00	700.00
	b. 20.1.1913-8.12.1919.	75.00	165.00	400.00
	c. 1.9.1922; 1.9.1923; 1.10.1924; 1.10.1925.	50.00	150.00	350.00

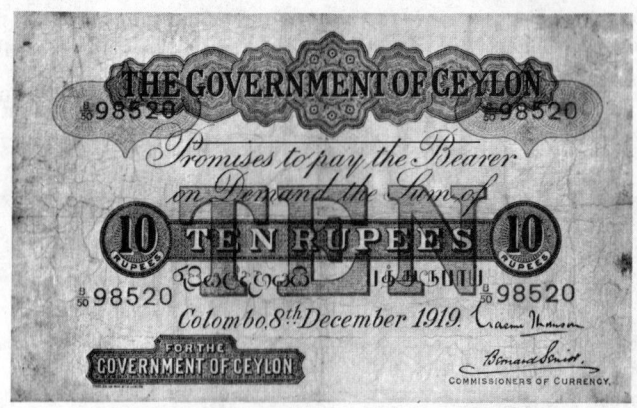

12	**10 RUPEES**	GOOD	FINE	XF
(7)	1894-1926. Black on green unpt. 210 x 127mm. Uniface.			
	a. 1.1.1894; 1.9.1894.	200.00	450.00	850.00
	b. 18.5.1908.	160.00	350.00	675.00
	c. 1.4.1914-1.6.1926.	75.00	225.00	500.00
15	**1000 RUPEES**			
	1.8.1899; 1.4.1915. 234 x 145mm. Uniface.	—	—	—

1914-19 ISSUES

#16-29 w/o pictorial design, different dates, Colombo. Sign. varieties. Printer: TDLR.

16	**1 RUPEE**	GOOD	FINE	XF
(1)	1917-39. Blue on green, gray and lilac unpt. Back blue. Perforated or straight edge at l.			
	a. 1.5.1917-1.10.1924.	3.50	10.00	25.00
	b. 1.10.1925-2.10.1939.	2.50	8.00	20.00
17	**2 RUPEES**			
(2)	1.3.1917. Reddish brown on green and ochre unpt. 2 in circle at l. and r. Uniface.	20.00	85.00	250.00

18	**2 RUPEES**	GOOD	FINE	XF
(3)	10.11.1917; 23.3.1918; 1.10.1921. Black on green unpt. Uniface.	10.00	40.00	135.00

19	**50 RUPEES**	GOOD	FINE	XF
(10)	1.4.1914. Black on green unpt. 233 x 125mm. Uniface.	125.00	350.00	950.00

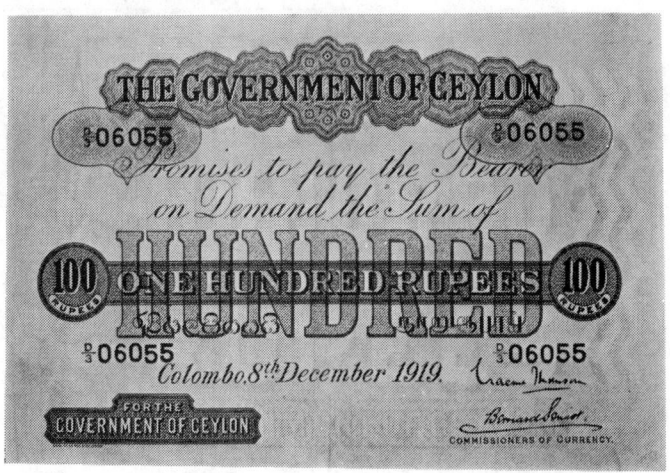

20 (12)	100 RUPEES	GOOD	FINE	XF
	8.12.1919. Black on green unpt. 216 x 145mm. Uniface.	250.00	550.00	1250.

1926-32 ISSUES

21 (4)	2 RUPEES	GOOD	FINE	XF
	1926-39. Black on green and lilac unpt. Back green; palm trees and elephant in central vignette. Perforated or straight edge at l.			
	a. Red serial #, yellow unpt. 1.6.1926; 1.9.1928; 1.7.1929.	5.00	30.00	100.00
	b. Green serial #, dk. green unpt. 10.9.1930-2.10.1939.	3.00	15.00	65.00

22 (5A)	5 RUPEES	GOOD	FINE	XF
	1.12.1925; 1.6.1926; 1.9.1927; 1.9.1928. Black on green and orange unpt. Back like #21. 170 x 130mm.	60.00	125.00	350.00

23 (6)	5 RUPEES	GOOD	FINE	XF
	1.7.1929-2.10.1939. Black on green, orange and lilac unpt. Back like #21. Perforated or straight edge at l. 136 x 88mm.	10.00	30.00	90.00

24 (8)	10 RUPEES	GOOD	FINE	XF
	6.1.1927; 1.9.1928. Black on dull red and yellow-green unpt. Back dull red. Like #21. 198 x 127mm.	70.00	200.00	550.00

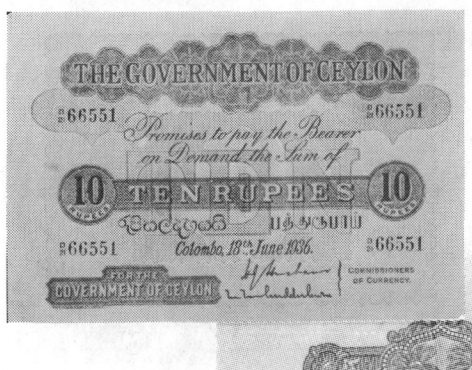

25 (9)	10 RUPEES	GOOD	FINE	XF
	1.7.1929-2.10.1939. Gray on violet and yellow-green unpt. Back brown. 152 x 102mm.	9.00	45.00	135.00
26 (11)	50 RUPEES			
	1932-39. Similar to #25 but reduced size.	60.00	175.00	450.00
27 (13)	100 RUPEES			
	1926-39. Similar to #20 but reduced size.	125.00	350.00	950.00
28 (14)	500 RUPEES			
	1.6.1926. 233 x 145mm.	—	—	—
29 (16)	1000 RUPEES			
	1.7.1929. Similar to #28 but reduced size.	—	—	—

1941 FIRST ISSUE

#30-33 portr. Kg. George VI at l., text at upper ctr. begins *PROMISES TO PAY...* Title on face begins *THE GOVERNMENT...* Wmk: Chinze. Printed in India.

30 (19A)	1 RUPEE	VG	VF	UNC
	1.2.1941. Olive, lilac and blue. Elephant head on back. Perforated or straight l. edge.	2.50	12.50	40.00

31 (19B)	2 RUPEES	VG	VF	UNC
	1.2.1941. Violet on brown, blue and green unpt. Sigiriya Rock on back.	4.00	22.50	85.00

32	5 RUPEES		VG	VF	UNC
(19C)	1.2.1941. Brown on lilac and blue unpt. Thuparama Dagoba on back.		7.50	30.00	125.00

33	10 RUPEES		VG	VF	UNC
(19D)	1.2.1941. Blue and m/c. Back blue on brown and tan unpt.; Temple of the Tooth.		10.00	50.00	200.00

1941 SECOND ISSUE

#34-39 portr. Kg. George VI at l. Text begins: *THIS NOTE IS LEGAL TENDER*... Printed in India.

34	1 RUPEE		VG	VF	UNC
(23)	20.12.1941-1.3.1949. Olive, lilac and blue. Man riding elephant at ctr. on back. Perforated or straight edge at l.		1.00	3.50	15.00

35	2 RUPEES		VG	VF	UNC
(24)	20.12.1941-1.3.1949. Violet and brown on blue and green unpt. Similar to #31. Perforated or straight edge at l.		2.00	8.00	35.00

36	5 RUPEES		VG	VF	UNC
(25)	20.12.1941-1.3.1949. Lilac and brown on green and blue unpt. Similar to #32. Perforated or straight edge at l.		3.50	20.00	60.00

37	50 RUPEES	VG	VF	UNC
(27)	1941-44. Purple on green, blue and brown unpt. Back brown; farmer plowing w/water buffalo in rice paddy.			
	a. Issued note. 4.8.1943; 12.7.1944.	75.00	225.00	650.00
	s. Specimen. 1.9.1941.	—	—	750.00

38	100 RUPEES	VG	VF	UNC
(28)	1941-45. Green on brown and red unpt. Back green and brown; Laxapana Waterfall.			
	a. Issued note. 4.8.1943; 24.6.1945.	55.00	165.00	450.00
	s. Specimen. 1.9.1941.	—	—	525.00

39	1000 RUPEES	VG	VF	UNC
(28A)	1.9.1941. Sailboat at coastline on back. Specimen.	—	—	2500.

1942 FIRST ISSUE

40	25 CENTS	GOOD	FINE	XF
(17)	1.1.1942. Black text on green unpt. Uniface.	7.50	20.00	60.00

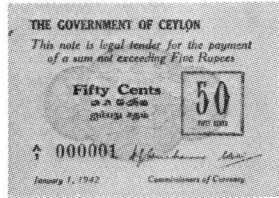

41	50 CENTS	GOOD	FINE	XF
(18)	1.1.1942. Black text on red unpt. Uniface. Like #40.	15.00	37.50	120.00

1942 SECOND ISSUE
#43-46 text begins: *THIS NOTE IS LEGAL TENDER...* Printed in India.

 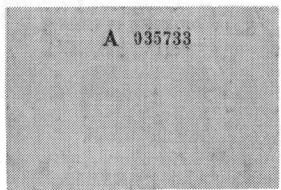

42	5 CENTS	VG	VF	UNC
(19)	1.6.1942. Blue-gray. 2 and 3 cent postal card impressions w/portr. Kg. George VI. Uniface. (Sometimes rouletted down ctr. for ease of separation.)			
	a. Straight edge.	10.00	25.00	55.00
	b. Rouletted 7 (7 dashes per 20mm) edge.	12.50	30.00	90.00

43	10 CENTS	VG	VF	UNC
(20)	1942-43. Blue and m/c. Portr. Kg. George VI at ctr. Serial # on back. Uniface.			
	a. 1.2.1942; 14.7.1942.	1.00	3.00	10.00
	b. 23.12.1943.	1.25	3.50	15.00

44	25 CENTS	VG	VF	UNC
(21)	1942-49. Brown and m/c. Portr. Kg. George VI at ctr. Serial # on back. Uniface.			
	a. 1.2.1942; 14.7.1942.	1.00	4.00	12.50
	b. 7.5.1946; 1.3.1947; 1.6.1948; 1.12.1949.	1.25	5.00	15.00

45	50 CENTS	VG	VF	UNC
(22)	1.2.1942-1.12.1949. Lilac and m/c. Portr. Kg. George VI at l. Serial # on back. Uniface.			
	a. 1.2.1942; 14.7.1942; 7.5.1946; 1.6.1948.	2.00	8.50	30.00
	b. 1.12.1949.	2.25	10.00	35.00

46	10 RUPEES	VG	VF	UNC
(26)	19.9.1942-7.5.1946. Blue and m/c. Portr. Kg. George VI at l. Similar to #33.	7.00	25.00	85.00

CENTRAL BANK OF CEYLON

1951 ISSUE
#47 and 48 portr. Kg. George VI at l. Wmk: Chinze. Printer: BWC.

47	1 RUPEE	VG	VF	UNC
(29)	20.1.1951. Blue on orange and green unpt. Ornate stairway on back.	1.00	5.00	20.00

48	10 RUPEES	VG	VF	UNC
(30)	20.1.1951. Green on violet, brown and blue unpt. Ceremonial figures on back.	3.00	22.50	100.00

1952 ISSUE
#49-53 portr. Qn. Elizabeth II at l. Wmk: Chinze. Printer: BWC.

49	1 RUPEE	VG	VF	UNC
(31)	3.6.1952; 16.10.1954. Similar to #47.	1.00	4.50	18.50

50	2 RUPEES	VG	VF	UNC
(32)	3.6.1952; 16.10.1954. Brown and lilac on blue and green unpt. Pavilion on back.	2.00	8.50	40.00

51 5 RUPEES
(33) 3.6.1952. Purple on blue, green and orange unpt. Standing figure on back.

	VG	VF	UNC
	10.00	35.00	175.00

52 50 RUPEES
(35) 3.6.1952; 12.5.1954. Blue, purple and m/c. Back blue and m/c; ornate stairway.

	VG	VF	UNC
	15.00	65.00	325.00

53 100 RUPEES
(36) 3.6.1952; 16.10.1954. Brown on purple, green and orange unpt. Women in national dress on back.

	VG	VF	UNC
	15.00	75.00	750.00

1953-54 ISSUE

54 5 RUPEES
(33A) 16.10.1954. Orange on aqua, green and brown unpt. Like #51

	VG	VF	UNC
	5.00	18.00	100.00

55 10 RUPEES
(34) 1.7.1953; 16.10.1954. Similar to #48.

	VG	VF	UNC
	3.00	17.50	75.00

1956 ISSUE

56 1 RUPEE
(37) 1956-63. Blue on orange, green and brown unpt. Ornate stairway on back.

	VG	VF	UNC
a. W/o security strip. 30.7.1956-11.9.1959.	.75	2.50	8.50
b. Security strip. 18.8.1960; 29.1.1962; 5.6.1963.	.50	1.75	5.50

57 2 RUPEES
(38) 1956-62. Brown and lilac on blue and green unpt. Pavilion on back.

	VG	VF	UNC
a. W/o security strip. 30.7.1956-11.9.1959.	1.00	3.00	17.50
b. Security strip. 18.8.1960; 29.1.1962.	1.00	2.50	12.50

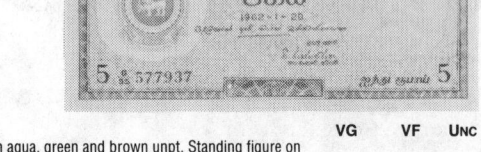

58 5 RUPEES
(39) 1956-62. Orange on aqua, green and brown unpt. Standing figure on back.

	VG	VF	UNC
a. W/o security strip. 30.7.1956; 31.5.1957; 10.6.1958; 1.7.1959	2.00	5.00	22.50
b. Security strip. 18.8.1960; 29.1.1962.	1.00	3.00	20.00

59 10 RUPEES
(40) 1956-63. Green on violet, brown and blue unpt. Ceremonial figures on back.

	VG	VF	UNC
a. W/o security strip. 30.7.1956; 7.11.1958; 11.9.1959.	3.00	8.00	32.50
b. Security strip. 18.8.1960; 7.4.1961; 5.6.1963.	2.00	7.00	25.00

60 50 RUPEES
(41) 30.7.1956; 7.11.1958. Blue and violet on m/c unpt. Ornate stairway on back.

	VG	VF	UNC
	17.50	50.00	200.00

61 100 RUPEES
(42) 24.10.1956. Brown on m/c unpt. 2 women in national costumes on back.

	VG	VF	UNC
	17.50	55.00	250.00

CHILE

The Republic of Chile, a ribbonlike country on the Pacific coast of southern South America, has an area of 292,258 sq. mi. (756,945 sq. km.) and a population of 13.3 million. Capital: Santiago. Historically, the economic base of Chile has been the rich mineral deposits of its northern provinces. Copper, of which Chile has 25 percent of the free world's reserves, has accounted for more than 75 per cent of Chile's export earnings in recent years. Other important exports are iron ore, iodine, fruit and nitrate of soda.

Diego de Almagro was the first Spaniard to attempt to wrest Chile from the Incas and Araucanian tribes, 1536. He failed, and was followed by Pedro de Valdivia, a favorite of Pizarro, who founded Santiago in 1541. When the Napoleonic Wars involved Spain, leaving the constituent parts of the Spanish Empire to their own devices, Chilean patriots formed a national government and proclaimed the country's independence, Sept. 18, 1810. Independence, however, was not secured until Feb. 12, 1818, after a bitter struggle led by Bernardo O'Higgins and San Martin.

MONETARY SYSTEM:
    1 Peso = 100 Centavos
    1 Condor = 10 Pesos to 1960
    1 Escudo = 100 Centesimos, 1960-75
    1 Peso = 100 Escudos, 1975-

REPUBLIC

REPÚBLICA DE CHILE

1880-81 ISSUE
#1-8 w/text: *convertible en oro o plata* (convertible in gold or silver). Text w/law date 10.4.1879 at r. on back. Printer: ABNC.

		GOOD	FINE	XF
1	**1 PESO** 5.4.1881. Black on orange unpt. 2 women seated at l., one holding a caduceus, bldg. at ctr. r., Prat at lower r. Back green. Handstamps Type III and IV.	60.00	150.00	—

		GOOD	FINE	XF
2	**2 PESOS** 3.5.1880-19.2.1881. Black on green unpt. Man in uniform at upper l., village landscape at ctr. r., national arms at lower r. Back brown. Handstamps Type III and IV.	80.00	175.00	—

		GOOD	FINE	XF
3	**5 PESOS** 4.1.1881-12.11.1881. Black on brown unpt. Village landscape at upper l., plumed shield at ctr. r., Gen. R. Freire at lower r. Back red-orange. Handstamps Type III and IV.	20.00	60.00	150.00

		GOOD	FINE	XF
4	**10 PESOS** 4.1.1881-12.11.1881. Black on pink unpt. Towered bridge at upper l., Pres. J.J. Perez at r. Back red-brown. 185 x 80mm. Handstamps Type III and IV.	40.00	100.00	225.00
5	**20 PESOS** ND (ca.1879). Black on brown unpt. Flower girl at l., man at l. ctr., bldg. at r., *VIENTE PESOS* w/o fringe along bottom margin. Back dk. brown. Specimen or proof.	—	—	—
6	**50 PESOS** ND (ca.1879). Black on blue unpt. Man in uniform l., bldg. at ctr., national arms at lower r., w/1 plate letter at upper l. and upper r. Back orange. Specimen or proof.	—	—	—
7	**100 PESOS** 4.1.1881; 26.1.1881; 12.11.1881. Black on orange unpt. B. O'Higgins at lower l., monument at ctr., 2 women seated w/shield at r., w/o double border. Back blue; text w/o border. 183 x 78mm. Handstamps Type III and IV.	90.00	200.00	450.00
8	**1000 PESOS** 12.11.1881. Black on olive unpt. Monument at l., national arms at ctr. r., man at lower r., w/o double border. Back red-brown; text w/o border. Handstamps Type III and IV. Printer: ABNC.	350.00	750.00	1750.

1883-91 ISSUES
#9-10 fractional currency issue. Printer: ABNC.

#11-14 convertible in gold or silver. Text w/law date 10.4.1879 at r. on back. Printer: ABNC.

		GOOD	FINE	XF
9	**20 CENTAVOS** ND (1891). Black on brown unpt. Portr. Liberty at upper l. Back green; arms at ctr. (Not issued).	15.00	30.00	75.00

		GOOD	FINE	XF
10	**50 CENTAVOS** 10.6.1891. Black on green unpt. Portr. Liberty at top ctr. 2 date style varieties. Back brown; arms at ctr.			
	a. Handstamp Type I.	5.00	15.00	60.00
	r. Remainder w/o date, sign. or hand-stamp.	—	—	30.00

		GOOD	FINE	XF
11	**1 PESO** 1883-95. Black on red-orange unpt. Similar to #1 but w/arms at l. and 1's in corners. Back green. Reduced size.			
	a. Handstamps Type III and IV. 17.2.1883.	20.00	55.00	125.00
	r. Handstamps Type I and II. 17.5.1884-1.5.1895.	15.00	45.00	100.00

		GOOD	FINE	XF
12	**2 PESOS** 16.2.1887-1.5.1895. Black on green unpt. Similar to #2 but reduced size. Back brown. Handstamps Type I and II.	25.00	70.00	150.00
13	**100 PESOS** ca.1880-90. Black on orange unpt. Similar to #7 but w/double border on face, single plate letter. Back blue.			
	p. Proof.	—	—	—
	s. Specimen.	—	—	—
14	**1000 PESOS** 18.8.1891. Black on olive unpt. Similar to #8 but w/double border on face, single plate letter. Back dk. red.	325.00	650.00	1500.

1898-1920 ISSUES

#15-28 convertible in gold only.
#16-28 denomination numeral at r. on back.
in #19b.

		GOOD	FINE	XF
15	**1 PESO**			

1898-1919. Black on red-orange unpt. Similar to #11 but further reduced in size. Back dk. green. Printer: ABNC.

		GOOD	FINE	XF
a.	Handstamps Type I and III. 17.11.1898-7.6.1911.	2.00	7.50	25.00
b.	Handstamps Type I and II. 8.11.1911-13.8.1919.	1.00	4.00	12.50

		GOOD	FINE	XF
16	**2 PESOS**	4.00	12.00	30.00

17.11.1898-18.10.1911. Black on green unpt. Similar to #12 but further reduced in size. Handstamps Type I and II. Printer: ABNC.

		GOOD	FINE	XF
17	**2 PESOS**	5.00	15.00	45.00

17.2.1912-26.3.1919. Black on green unpt. Like #16. Handstamps Type I and II. Printer: W&S.

		GOOD	FINE	XF
18	**5 PESOS**			

1899-1918. Black on brown unpt. Similar to #3. Back red-ornage. Printer: W&S.

		GOOD	FINE	XF
a.	Handstamps Type I and III. 3.4.1899-25.4.1906.	10.00	30.00	90.00
b.	Handstamps Type I and II. 21.7.1916-20.6.1918.	8.00	25.00	75.00

		GOOD	FINE	XF
19	**5 PESOS**			

1906-16. Black on brown unpt. Similar to #18 but w/modified guilloches around 5's. and other plate changes. Printer: ABNC.

		GOOD	FINE	XF
a.	Handstamps Type I and III. 23.5.1906-20.1.1911.	10.00	30.00	90.00
b.	Handstamps Type I and II. 2.4.1913-21.7.1916.	10.00	30.00	90.00

		GOOD	FINE	XF
20	**10 PESOS**	30.00	80.00	200.00

6.8.1900-16.6.1905. Black on red-brown unpt. Similar to #4. Handstamps Type I and III. Printer: W&S.

		GOOD	FINE	XF
21	**10 PESOS**			

1906-18. Black on pink unpt. Similar to #20 but w/modified guilloches and other plate changes. Printer: ABNC.

		GOOD	FINE	XF
a.	Handstamps Type I and III. 31.3.1906-23.11.1910.	20.00	50.00	150.00
b.	Handstamps Type I and II. 7.6.1911-20.6.1918.	15.00	45.00	110.00

		GOOD	FINE	XF
22	**20 PESOS**			

1906-14. Black on brown unpt. Similar to #5 but w/fringe around VIENTE PESOS along bottom margin. Back dk. brown. Printer: ABNC.

		GOOD	FINE	XF
a.	Handstamps Type I and III. 31.3.1906; 23.5.1906; 27.8.1907.	15.00	30.00	100.00
b.	Handstamps Type I and II. 13.5.1912-1.8.1914.	10.00	25.00	75.00

23 20 PESOS

	GOOD	FINE	XF
1900-14. Black on red unpt. Similar to #22. Printer: W&S.			
a. Handstamps Type I and III. 31.8.1903; 27.10.1904.	25.00	50.00	125.00
b. Handstamps Type I and II.	20.00	40.00	95.00

24 50 PESOS

	GOOD	FINE	XF
16.12.1899-1.8.1914. Black on blue unpt. Similar to #6. Back orange. Printer: ABNC.			
a. Handstamps Type I and III. To 30.12.1904; 4.3.1905.	35.00	70.00	200.00
b. Handstamps Type I and II. 25.9.1912; 1.8.1914.	30.00	60.00	130.00

25 100 PESOS

	GOOD	FINE	XF
1920. Black on blue and gold unpt. Similar to #13 but w/o *plata*, w/double plate letter. Printer: ABNC.			
a. Handstamps Type I and III.	75.00	150.00	350.00
b. Handstamps Type I and II. 29.3.1920.	60.00	120.00	300.00

26 100 PESOS

	GOOD	FINE	XF
1906-16. Black on blue and red unpt. B. O'Higgins at l., monument at r. Back orange. Printer: ABNC.			
a. Handstamps Type I and III. 23.5.1906.	100.00	200.00	500.00
b. Handstamps Type I and II. 4.3.1912; 31.3.1913; 22.12.1916.	75.00	150.00	350.00

27 500 PESOS

	GOOD	FINE	XF
12.8.1912; 15.5.1917. Black on green and yellow unpt. Man at l. ctr., bldg. at r. Handstamps Type I and II. Back orange. Printer: ABNC.	200.00	400.00	900.00

28 1000 PESOS

	GOOD	FINE	XF
12.8.1912. Similar to #14 but w/o *plata*, w/double plate letter. Back dk. red.	325.00	650.00	1500.

1898 FIRST PROVISIONAL ISSUE

LEI 1054 de 31 de Julio de 1898, EMISION FISCAL

Ovpt. on various unissued notes of private banks and also on notes of the Republic of Chile w/handstamps Type I and III.

#29 ovpt. on Banco de Jose Bunster.

#30-33 ovpt. on Banco Comercial de Chile.

NOTE: Regular commercial bank issues of #29-51 including other denominations w/o ovpt: *EMISION FISCAL* are listed in Volume 1.

29 1 PESO

	GOOD	FINE	XF
17.8.1898. Black on yellow unpt. Ovpt. on #S131.	—	Rare	—

30 1 PESO

	GOOD	FINE	XF
17.8.1898. Black on yellow and pink unpt. Ovpt. on #S151.	—	Rare	—

31 2 PESOS

	GOOD	FINE	XF
17.8.1898. Black on green and pink unpt. Ovpt. on #S152.	—	Rare	—

		GOOD	FINE	XF
32	**10 PESOS** 17.8.1898 (- old date 8.6.1893). Black on green and rose unpt. Ovpt. on #S160.	—	Rare	—
33	**20 PESOS** 1.8.1898.	—	Rare	—

1898 SECOND PROVISIONAL ISSUE
#34 ovpt. on Banco de Concepcion.

		GOOD	FINE	XF
34	**1 PESO** 14.9.1898. Black on green and m/c unpt. Ovpt. on #S176.	—	Rare	—

1898 THIRD PROVISIONAL ISSUE
#35-36 ovpt. on Banco de Curico.

		GOOD	FINE	XF
35	**5 PESOS** 14.9.1898. Black on green and peach unpt. Ovpt. on #S218.	—	Rare	—
36	**20 PESOS** 18.8.1898; 14.9.1898. Black on blue and yellow unpt. Ovpt. on #S220.	—	Rare	—

1898 FOURTH PROVISIONAL ISSUE
#37-39 ovpt. on Banco de Escobar Ossa y Ca. (Supurious issue.)

37	**5 PESOS** 14.9.1898. Black on blue unpt. Ovpt. on #S253.	—	—	—

		GOOD	FINE	XF
38	**10 PESOS** 14.9.1898. Black on brown unpt. Ovpt. on #S254.			

		GOOD	FINE	XF
39	**20 PESOS** 14.9.1898. Black on rose-pink unpt. Ovpt. on #S255.	—	—	—

1898 FIFTH PROVISIONAL ISSUE
#40 ovpt. on Banco de D. Matte y Ca.

		GOOD	FINE	XF
40	**10 PESOS** 1.8.1898. Black on yellow and green unpt. Ovpt. on #S278.	—	Rare	—

1898 SIXTH PROVISIONAL ISSUE
#41 ovpt. on Banco de Matte, Mac-Clure i Ca.

		GOOD	FINE	XF
41	**1 PESO** 14.7.1898. Blue on violet paper. Ovpt. on #S283.	—	Rare	—

1898 Seventh Provisional Issue
#42 ovpt. on Banco de Melipilla.

			Good	**Fine**	**XF**
42	**5 Pesos**		—	Rare	—
	1.8.1898. Black on tan unpt. Ovpt. on #S297.				

1898 Eighth Provisional Issue
#43-44 ovpt. on Banco de Mobiliario.

			Good	**Fine**	**XF**
43	**1 Peso**		—	Rare	—
	17.8.1898. Black on green and gold unpt. Ovpt. on #S306.				

			Good	**Fine**	**XF**
44	**10 Pesos**		—	Rare	—
	14.9.1898. Black. Ovpt. on #S308.				

1898 Ninth Provisional Issue
#45-49 ovpt. on Banco Nacional de Chile, Valpraiso.

			Good	**Fine**	**XF**
45	**1 Peso**		—	Rare	—
	17.8.1898. Black on green and peach unpt. Ovpt. on #S331.				
46	**2 Pesos**		—	Rare	—
	17.8.1898. Black on red-brown and green unpt. Ovpt. on #S332.				
47	**5 Pesos**		—	Rare	—
	1.8.1898. Black on green and orange unpt. Ovpt. on #S333.				
48	**10 Pesos**		—	Rare	—
	17.8.1898. Black on green and brown unpt. Ovpt. on #S334.				
49	**500 Pesos**		—	Rare	—
	1898. Black on green and yellow unpt. Ovpt. on #S338.				

1898 Tenth Provisional Issue
#50 ovpt. on Banco San Fernando.

			Good	**Fine**	**XF**
50	**5 Pesos**		—	Rare	—
	16.5.1899. Black on green unpt. Ovpt. on #S397.				

1898 Eleventh Provisional Issue
#51 ovpt. on Banco de Santiago.

			Good	**Fine**	**XF**
51	**1 Peso**		30.00	125.00	—
	14.9.1898. (- old date 25.2.1896). Black on brown unpt. Ovpt. on #S411.				

1898 Twelfth Provisional Issue
#52-56 ovpt. on Republica de Chile.

52 **1 PESO**
17.8.1898. Ovpt. on #11.

GOOD	FINE	XF
30.00	125.00	—

53 **2 PESOS**
17.8.1898. Ovpt. on #12.

GOOD	FINE	XF
—	Rare	—

54 **5 PESOS**
1.8.1898. Ovpt. on #18.

GOOD	FINE	XF
—	Rare	—

55 **100 PESOS**
1.8.1898. Ovpt. on #25.

	Rare	
—	Rare	—

56 **1000 PESOS**
1.8.1898. Ovpt. on #28.

—	Rare	—

1918-22 REGULAR ISSUES

#57-66 w/handstamps Type I and II.

57 **2 PESOS**
ND. Black on blue and lt. brown unpt. Heading in 1 line. Condor at r.
Back dk. olive; seated woman w/shield at ctr. (Not issued).

58 **2 PESOS**
19.10.1920-30.1.1922. Blue on green and red unpt. Woman seated
w/shield at r. Back on red unpt. Red serial #.

GOOD	FINE	XF
2.00	6.00	35.00

59 **2 PESOS**
1922-25. Blue on yellow unpt. Similar to #39. Back brown w/o unpt.
a. Brown serial #. 5.5.1922.
b. Blue serial #. 20.12.1922-22.9.1925.

2.00	6.00	35.00
2.00	5.00	25.00

60 **5 PESOS**
14.8.1918-2.1.1922. Blue. Woman seated w/shield at l., value at r.
Red serial #.

GOOD	FINE	XF
3.00	10.00	40.00

61 **5 PESOS**
16.8.1922-22.6.1925. Blue on yellow unpt. Like #60. Date in 1 or 2
lines. Blue serial #. 2 sign. varieties.

GOOD	FINE	XF
3.00	10.00	40.00

62 **10 PESOS**
8.11.1918-2.1.1922. Brown on pink unpt. Condor at l., woman seated
w/shield at ctr.

GOOD	FINE	XF
5.00	15.00	60.00

63 **10 PESOS**
31.7.1922-22.6.1925. Brown in green unpt. Like #62. 2 sign. varieties.

GOOD	FINE	XF
3.00	10.00	45.00

64 **20 PESOS**
1919-24. Green on rose unpt. Condor at l., woman seated w/shield at
r.
a. Red serial #. Series A. 21.6.1919-10.6.1920.
b. Blue serial #. Series B. 25.2.1924.

10.00	25.00	80.00
10.00	25.00	80.00

65 **50 PESOS**
26.12.1919-2.2.1921. Blue-green. Woman seated w.shield at l., ships
at r. Back blue.

GOOD	FINE	XF
20.00	50.00	185.00

66 **100 PESOS**
1918-24. Blue on lt. blue paper. Woman seated w/shield at l., 3
women reclining at r. Back brown; woman and globe at ctr.
a. Red unpt. and serial #. Date placement higher or lower.
31.5.1918.
b. Blue unpt. and serial #. 17.7.1923-31.10.1924.

GOOD	FINE	XF
40.00	125.00	350.00
40.00	90.00	250.00

1920-1924 ISSUES

67 **50 PESOS**
7.9.1921. Lt. blue Woman reclining at l. Handstamps Type I and II.

GOOD	FINE	XF
—	—	—

68 **100 PESOS**
7.9.1921. Brown and ochre. Woman at l.

—	—	—

69 **500 PESOS**
19.4.1920; 11.12.1920; 25.4.1921; 2.12.1924. Brown. Woman at l.
Back pale red.

—	—	—

| 70 | **1000 Pesos** 2.12.1924. | **Good** — | **Fine** — | **XF** — |

BANCO CENTRAL DE CHILE

1925 FIRST PROVISIONAL ISSUE

#71-81 ovpt: new bank name, value in condores, *BILLETE PROVISIONAL* and bank validation stamp on República de Chile notes.

71	**5 Pesos = 1/2 Condor** 10.12.1925. Blue on yellow unpt. Woman seated w/shield at l. Ovpt. on #61.	**Good** 2.50	**Fine** 8.00	**XF** 30.00
72	**5 Pesos = 1/2 Condor** 10.12.1925. Dk. blue on lt. blue unpt. Woman seated w/shield at l.	2.50	8.00	30.00
73	**10 Pesos = 1 Condor** 10.12.1925. Brown. Woman seated w/shield at l. Back blue-green.	3.00	10.00	45.00

| 74 | **10 Pesos = 1 Condor** 10.12.1925. Brown on green unpt. Condor at l., seated woman w/shield at ctr. Ovpt. on #63. | **Good** 3.00 | **Fine** 10.00 | **XF** 45.00 |
| 75 | **100 Pesos = 10 Condores** 10.12.1925. Black on blue unpt. Woman seated w/shield at l., 3 women reclining at r. Blue paper. Ovpt. on #66b. | 40.00 | 100.00 | 250.00 |

| 76 | **500 Pesos = 50 Condores** 10.12.1925. Brown on orange unpt. Woman reclining at l., seated w/shield at r. Back blue. | **Good** 60.00 | **Fine** 150.00 | **XF** 350.00 |
| 77 | **1000 Pesos = 100 Condores** 10.12.1925. Dk. brown on violet and yellow unpt. Woman seated w/horns at l., woman seated w/shield at r. Back violet. | 125.00 | 250.00 | 600.00 |

1925 SECOND PROVISIONAL ISSUE

| 78 | **50 Pesos** 10.12.1925. Blue. Similar to #67. Back green. | — | — | — |
| 79 | **100 Pesos** 10.12.1925. Brown. Silimat to #68. Back brown. | — | — | — |

1927-29 BILLETE PROVISIONAL ISSUE

#80-81 Deleted. #82-87 various dates and sign. varieties. W/lg. or sm. serial # varieties. Wmk: BANCO CENTRAL DE CHILE.

| 82 | **5 Pesos = 1/2 Condor** 18.4.1927-2.6.1930. Black on green unpt. Blue paper. Back brown. | **Good** 1.00 | **Fine** 5.00 | **XF** 15.00 |

83	**10 Pesos = 1 Condor** 1927-30. Black on salmon unpt. Yellow paper. Back dk. blue.	**Good**	**Fine**	**XF**
	a. Printer's name in margin. 18.4.1927.	1.00	6.00	17.50
	b. Printer's name in frame. 14.5.1928-2.6.1930.	1.00	5.00	15.00

84	**50 Pesos = 5 Condores** 1927-30. Black on brown unpt. Pink paper. Condor at upper l. Back brown.	**Good**	**Fine**	**XF**
	a. Printer's name in margin. 28.3.1927.	8.00	20.00	55.00
	b. Printer's name in frame. 14.5.1928-2.6.1930.	5.00	15.00	35.00

| 85 | **100 Pesos = 10 Condores** 28.3.1927-2.6.1930. Black on lt. blue and red-brown unpt. Back dk. green. | **Good** 5.00 | **Fine** 15.00 | **XF** 55.00 |
| 86 | **500 Pesos = 50 Condores** 29.1.1929. Green on purple unpt. Condor at upper l. Back red-orange. | 50.00 | 150.00 | 300.00 |

| 87 | **1000 Pesos = 100 Condores** 29.1.1929. Blue on pink and purple unpt. Condor at upper l. Back dk. purple. | **Good** 90.00 | **Fine** 200.00 | **XF** 500.00 |

1932 BILLETE PROVISIONAL ISSUE

88	**1 Pesos = 1/10 Condor** 1932-33. Black frame, blue ctr. w/wide diagonal pink stripe. Back green. 120 x 60mm.	**VG**	**VF**	**UNC**
	a. Tan paper. 12.9.1932.	1.00	3.00	12.50
	b. Peach paper. 7.3.1933.	1.00	3.00	12.50

1942-43 BILLETE PROVISIONAL ISSUES

| 89 | **1 Pesos = 1/10 Condor** 11.2.1942. Like #82 but blue frame. 124 x 62mm. | 1.50 | 4.00 | 10.00 |

90	**1 PESOS = 1/10 CONDOR**	VG	VF	UNC
	3.3.1943. Blue on yellow unpt. 88 x 50mm.			
	a. Back lt. orange; w/A-A.	.50	1.50	4.00
	b. Back violet; w/B-B.	.50	1.50	4.00
	c. Back green; w/C-C.	.50	1.50	4.00
	d. Back red-orange; w/D-D.	.50	1.50	4.00
	e. Back blue; w/E-E. (Not issued).	—	25.00	65.00

1931-42 ISSUES

#91-101 w/o name under portr. Values given in pesos and condors. Various date and sign. varieties.

91	**5 PESOS = 1/2 CONDOR**	VG	VF	UNC
	1932-42. Blue on lt. orange unpt. Portr. B. O'Higgins at r.			
	a. 26.9.1932.	6.00	15.00	30.00
	b. 17.6.1933.	3.00	7.00	15.00
	c. 3.7.1935-8.7.1942.	.75	3.00	7.50

92	**10 PESOS = 1 CONDOR**	VG	VF	UNC
	1931-42. Red-brown on lt. yellow unpt. Portr. Bulnes at r.			
	a. Month in letters. 9.2.1931.	2.50	10.00	30.00
	b. Month in Roman numerals. 29.9.1932.	2.00	8.00	25.00
	c. 7.6.1933; 22.11.1933.	1.00	6.00	20.00
	d. 3.7.1935-8.7.1942.	.75	3.00	10.00

93	**20 PESOS = 2 CONDORES**	VG	VF	UNC
	1939-47. Portr. Capt. Valdivia at ctr. Statue in park w/trees and bldg. at ctr. on back.			
	a. Purple-brown. Back vignette lilac. 22.11.1939.	1.50	4.00	12.50
	b. Brown. Back vignette brown. 2.4.1947; 24.12.1947.	1.25	3.50	10.00

94	**50 PESOS = 5 CONDORES**	VG	VF	UNC
	1932-42. Green. Portr. Pinto at r. Back green on lt. gold unpt. German-style numerals at corners.			
	a. 22.8.1932.	3.00	15.00	40.00
	b. 22.11.1933.	2.50	12.00	30.00
	c. 3.7.1935-8.7.1942.	1.00	8.00	20.00

95	**100 PESOS = 10 CONDORES**	VG	VF	UNC
	7.6.1933-10.3.1937. Red. Portr. Prat at r. Face w/o red unpt.	3.00	20.00	50.00
96	**100 PESOS = 10 CONDORES**			
	19.4.1939-20.1.1943. Face w/red unpt. Dufferent plate from #95.	2.00	10.00	35.00

97	**500 PESOS = 50 CONDORES**	VG	VF	UNC
	7.6.1933; 3.7.1935; 1.4.1936. Black on yellow unpt. Portr Montt at ctr. Back black on brown unpt.; explorer on horseback at l.	6.00	35.00	80.00
98	**500 PESOS = 50 CONDORES**			
	8.7.1942; 18.8.1943. Red-brown. Portr. Montt at ctr. Back grayish-purple; Spainards at l.	5.00	25.00	60.00

99	**1000 PESOS = 100 CONDORES**	VG	VF	UNC
	7.6.1933-18.8.1943. Brown on green unpt. Portr. Blanco at r. Back brown; Spainards at ctr.	25.00	60.00	150.00
100	**5000 PESOS = 500 CONDORES**			
	1.2.1932. Brown on yellow unpt. Portr. M. A. Tocornal at ctr. Lg. *5000* on back.	75.00	225.00	500.00
101	**10,000 PESOS = 1000 CONDORES**			
	1.2.1932. Blue on m/c unpt. Portr. M. Balmaceda at ctr. Lg. *10,000* on back.	—	Rare	—

1940-45 ISSUE

#102-109 dated notes. Name under portr. Various date and sign. varieties.

102	**5 PESOS = 1/2 CONDOR**	VG	VF	UNC
	19.4.1944; 3.7.1946; 30.4.1947. Blue. Like #91.	.50	1.50	4.00

103	**10 Pesos = 1 Condor**	VG	VF	Unc
	18.8.1943-20.11.1946. Red-brown. Like #92.	1.00	2.50	7.50
104	**50 Pesos = 5 Condores**			
	19.1.1944-1.10.1947. Green. Like #94.	1.00	3.00	10.00

105	**100 Pesos = 10 Condores**	VG	VF	Unc
	1943-48. Red. Like #96.			
	a. W/o security thread. 29.5.1943-28.5.1947.	1.00	3.00	10.00
	b. W/security thread. 24.11.1948.	1.00	3.00	10.00
106	**500 Pesos = 50 Condores**			
	28.2.1945. Orange-brown. Similar to #98. Back dk. brown.	6.00	15.00	45.00

107	**1000 Pesos = 100 Condores**	VG	VF	Unc
	28.2.1945; 1.10.1947. Brown on green unpt. Like #99. Back brown.	6.00	20.00	60.00
108	**5000 Pesos = 500 Condores**			
	2.10.1940. Blue. M. A. Tocornal at ctr. Battle scene on back.	25.00	80.00	200.00

109	**10,000 Pesos = 1000 Condores**	VG	VF	Unc
	2.10.1940. Violet on brown unpt. M. Balmaceda at ctr. Military horseman on back.	35.00	100.00	300.00

1947-48 ND Issues

#110-118 name under portr. but w/o date. Sign. varieties, also sm. or lg. size sign. W/or w/o security thread. Wmk: Man in uniform. Printer: Talleres de Especies Valoradas, Santiago, Chile.

110	**5 Pesos = 1/2 Condor**	VG	VF	Unc
	ND (1947-58). Blue. Like #91. Back blue, or blue on pink unpt.	.15	.30	1.50

111	**10 Pesos = 1 Condor**	VG	VF	Unc
	ND (1947-58). Red-brown. Like #92. Back red-brown or dk. brown. 2 block # varieties.	.15	.30	1.50

112	**50 Pesos = 5 Condores**	VG	VF	Unc
	ND (1947-58). Green. Like #94.	.25	1.00	4.00

113	**100 Pesos = 10 Condores**	VG	VF	Unc
	ND (1947-56). Red. Similar to #95. Sm. black seal at ctr. on back.	.50	1.50	7.50
114	**100 Pesos = 10 Condores**			
	ND (1947-58). Red. Face like #113. Different design w/lg. red seal at bottom on back. 2 block # varieties.	.50	1.00	5.00

115	**500 Pesos = 50 Condores**	VG	VF	Unc
	ND (1947-59). Blue. Portr. Montt at ctr. Explorer on horseback on back.	1.00	3.50	15.00

116	**1000 Pesos = 100 Condores**	VG	VF	Unc
	ND (1947-59). Brown. Portr. Encalada at ctr. Founding of Santiago on back.	3.00	8.00	25.00

117	**5000 Pesos = 500 Condores**	VG	VF	Unc
	ND (1947-59). Brown-violet. Portr. M. A. Tocornal at ctr. Smaller size than #100. Battle of Rancagua on back.			
	a. Larger size, printed portion 169 mm horizontally.	3.00	10.00	30.00
	b. Smaller size, printed portion 166 mm.	3.00	10.00	30.00
	c. Larger size resumed, 169 mm.	3.00	10.00	30.00

IMPERIAL CHINESE RAILWAYS

局總路官軌鐵洋北

Pei Yang Tieh Kuei Kuan Lu Tsung Chu

PEIYANG BRANCH 洋北

1895 ISSUE

#A56, handwritten dates exist over printed date. Printer: BFL.
#A57-A58 *Deleted.*

		GOOD	FINE	XF
A56	**1 DOLLAR** 22.4.1895. Blue on orange unpt. Train passing through fortress at ctr. Back red; boat, shoreline w/mountains in background. *(S/M #P34-1).*			
	a. Issued note.	45.00	135.00	400.00
	r. Unsigned remainder.			

SHANGHAI BRANCH 海上

局路鐵外內關海山

Shan Hai Kuan Nei Wai Tieh Lu Chü

1899 ISSUE

#A59-A61 train passing through fortress at ctr. W/o sign.

		GOOD	FINE	XF
A59	**1 DOLLAR** 2.1.1899. Blue on orange unpt. Back red. *(S/M #S13-1).*	18.50	55.00	165.00
A60	**5 DOLLARS** 2.1.1899. Blue on orange unpt. *(S/M #S13-2).*	50.00	150.00	450.00
A61	**10 DOLLARS** 2.1.1899. *(S/M #S13-3).*			
	a. Issued note.	90.00	275.00	825.00
	r. Remainder perforated: *CANCELLED.*	—	Unc	650.00

NINGPO COMMERCIAL BANK, LTD.

行銀明四海上

Shang Hai Szu Ming Yin Hang

1909 ISSUE

#A61A-A61D dragons at upper ctr. on face and back. Chinese printer: TSPC.

		GOOD	FINE	XF
A61A	**1 DOLLAR** 22.1.1909. Gray. *SHANGHAI.* *(S/M #S107-1).*			
	a. Issued note.	50.00	150.00	450.00
	b. *HK* monogram (Hankow)/*SHANGHAI.*	62.50	175.00	525.00
	c. *NP* (Ningpo)/*SHANGHAI.*	75.00	225.00	675.00
	d. *SH* monogram *SHANGHAI.*	100.00	325.00	1000.
A61B	**2 DOLLARS** 22.1.1909. Green and yellow. *SHANGHAI.* *(S/M #S107-2).*	75.00	225.00	675.00
A61C	**5 DOLLARS** 22.1.1909. Black and yellow. *SHANGHAI.* *(S/M #S107-3).*	82.50	250.00	750.00
A61D	**10 DOLLARS** 22.1.1909. Black and brown. *SHANGHAI.* *(S/M #S107-4).*	90.00	275.00	825.00

TA-CH'ING GOVERNMENT BANK

行銀清大

Ta Ch'ing Yin Hang

CHINANFU BRANCH 福南濟

行銀部戶清大

Ta Ch'ing Hu Pu Yin Hang

1906 ISSUE

#A62A-A75A supported arms at upper ctr. on back. Printer: CMPA.

A62	**1 DOLLAR** 1.9.1906. Green and lilac. *(S/M #T10-).*	—	—	—

FENGTIEN BRANCH 天奉

1907 ISSUE

A62A	**50 CENTS** 1907. Purple and blue. Back red. *(S/M #T10-).*	—	—	—

FOOCHOW BRANCH 州福

1906 PROVISIONAL ISSUE

		VG	VF	UNC
A62B	**1 DOLLAR** 1.9.1906. Violet ovpt: 12 Chinese characters across top on #A71D. *(S/M #T10-).*	30.00	90.00	—

HANGCHOW BRANCH 州杭

1906 ISSUE

A63	**1 DOLLAR** 1.9.1906. Ovpt. on #A62. *(S/M #T10-1b).*	—	—	—

HANKOW BRANCH 口漢

1906 ISSUE

A63A	**1 DOLLAR** 1.9.1906. Supported arms at upper ctr. on back. *(S/M #T10-).*	16.00	48.00	—
A64	**5 DOLLARS** 1.9.1906. Blue and orange. Crossed flags at ctr. *(S/M #T10-2a).*	30.00	90.00	—

		VG	VF	UNC
A65	**10 DOLLARS**			
	1.9.1906. Lilac and yellow. Crossed flags at top ctr. (S/M #T10-3a).			
	a. Issued note.	50.00	150.00	—
	r. Unsigned remainder.	—	—	250.00

1907 ISSUE

		VG	VF	UNC
A66	**1 DOLLAR**			
	1.6.1907. Green and lilac. (S/M #T10-10a).			
	a. Issued note.	10.00	30.00	—
	r. Unsigned remainder.	—	—	75.00

HUNAN BRANCH 湖南

1906-07 ISSUE

A66A	**1 DOLLAR**			
	1.9.1906. Ovpt. on #A63A. (S/M #T10-).	—	—	—
A67	**5 DOLLARS**			
	1.6.1907. Blue and orange. Crossed flags at ctr. (S/M #T10-11).	—	—	—
A68	**10 DOLLARS**			
	1.6.1907. Lilac and yellow. Crossed flags at top ctr. (S/M #T10-12).	—	—	—

KAIFONG BRANCH 開封

1906 PROVISIONAL ISSUE

A69	**1 DOLLAR**			
	1.9.1906. Ovpt. on #A72. (S/M #T10-1c).			
	a. Issued note.	—	Rare	—
	r. Unsigned remainder.	—	72.50	135.00

		VG	VF	UNC
A70	**5 DOLLARS**			
	1.9.1906. Ovpt. on #A73. (S/M #T10-2c).			
	a. Issued note.	—	—	—
	r. Unsigned remainder.	—	60.00	150.00
A71	**10 DOLLARS**			
	1.9.1906. Ovpt. on #A74. (S/M #T10-3c).			
	a. Issued note.	—	—	—
	r. Unsigned remainder.	—	75.00	200.00

KALGAN BRANCH 張家口

1906 ISSUE

A71A	**1 DOLLAR**			
	1.9.1906. Dk. green and lilac on yellow unpt. Back blue on brown unpt. (S/M #T10-).	—	—	—

KWANGCHOW (CANTON) BRANCH 廣州

1908 ISSUE

A71B	**1 DOLLAR**			
	1.3.1908. Dk. green and lilac on yellow unpt. Back blue on brown unpt. (S/M #T10-).	40.00	125.00	375.00
A71C	**10 DOLLARS**			
	1.3.1908. Brown and yellow. Crossed flags at top ctr. (S/M #T10-).			

PEKING BRANCH 北京

1906 ISSUE

A71D	**1 DOLLAR**			
	1.9.1906. Supported arms at upper ctr. on back. (S/M #T10).			

SHANGHAI BRANCH 上港

1906 ISSUE

		VG	VF	UNC
A71H	**5 DOLLARS**			
	1.9.1906. Red-violet on green unpt. Similar to #A75A but 9 seal characters at bottom ctr. (S/M #T10-).	—	—	—

1907 ISSUE

A71J	**1 DOLLAR**			
	1.9.1907. (S/M #T10-).	—	—	—

TIENTSIN BRANCH 天津

1906 ISSUE

A72	**1 DOLLAR**			
	1.9.1906. Green and lilac. (S/M #T10-1a).	—	—	—
A73	**5 DOLLARS**			
	1.9.1906. Blue and orange. Crossed flags at ctr. (S/M #T10-2a).	—	—	—
A74	**10 DOLLARS**			
	1.9.1906. Lilac and yellow. Crossed flags at ctr. (S/M #T10-3a).	—	—	—

URGA BRANCH 庫倫

1907 ISSUE

A74A	**1 DOLLAR**			
	1.6.1907. (S/M #T10-).	—	—	—
A74C	**10 DOLLARS**			
	1.6.1907. (S/M #T10-).	—	—	—

1908 ISSUE

A75	**1 DOLLAR**			
	1.3.1908. Green and lilac. (S/M #T10-20).			

A77	5 DOLLARS	VG	VF	UNC
	1.10.1909. Brown on blue and m/c unpt. Gazebo at r. Hillside pagoda, village at ctr. on back. (S/M #T10-31).	32.50	100.00	300.00
A78	10 DOLLARS			
	1.10.1909. Teahouse at r. Great Wall at ctr. on back. (S/M #T10-32).	40.00	125.00	375.00

A78A	50 DOLLARS	VG	VF	UNC
	1.10.1909. Fortified city gates at r. Pagodas atop monastery at ctr. r. on back. (S/M #T10-33).	80.00	250.00	750.00
A78B	100 DOLLARS			
	1.10.1909. Temple of Heaven at r. Teahouse w/gazebos at ctr. on back. (S/M #T10-34).	100.00	300.00	900.00

A75A	5 DOLLARS	VG	VF	UNC
	1.3.1908. Blue and orange. (S/M #T10-).			
A75B	10 DOLLARS	—	—	—
	1.3.1908. (S/M #T10-).	—	—	—

WUHU BRANCH

1906 PROVISIONAL ISSUE

A75E **1 DOLLAR**
1.9.1906. Ovpt. on #A72. (S/M #T10-). — — —

YINGKOW BRANCH 口營

1906 ISSUE

A75J **1 DOLLAR**
1.6.1906. Specimen. Uniface pair. (S/M #T10-). — — —

A75K **5 DOLLARS**
1.6.1906. Specimen. Uniface pair. (S/M #T10-). — — —

A75L **10 DOLLARS**
1.6.1906. Specimen. Uniface pair. (S/M #T10-). — — —

YUNNAN BRANCH 南雲

1906 PROVISIONAL ISSUE

A75P **1 DOLLAR**
1.9.1906. Ovpt. on #A71B. (S/M #T10-). — — —

W/O BRANCH

1909 GENERAL ISSUE

#A76-A78 black text. Portr. Li Hung Chan at l. W/o office of issue or sign. Printer: ABNC (Not issued).

NOTE: See also Bank of China provisional issue #16-18.

A76	1 DOLLAR			
	1.10.1909. Olive-brown on red-orange unpt. Hillside village, railroad at r. Waterfront park at ctr. on back. (S/M #T10-30).	25.00	75.00	225.00

1910 ND ISSUE

#A79-A82 portr. Prince Chun at l., dragon at upper ctr. W/o date, sign. or serial #.

NOTE: Crudely printed souvenir copies exist.

A79	1 DOLLAR	VG	VF	UNC
	ND (1910). Green. Junks at lower r. (S/M #T10-40). (Not issued).	32.50	100.00	300.00
A80	5 DOLLARS			
	ND (1910). Red. Mounted patrol at lower r. (S/M #T10-41). (Not issued).	32.50	100.00	300.00

A81	10 DOLLARS	VG	VF	UNC
	ND (1910). Black. Great Wall at lower r. (S/M #T10-42).			
	a. Issued note.	300.00	900.00	—
	r. Unsigned remainder w/o seal stamps on back.	—	—	250.00

A82	100 DOLLARS	VG	VF	UNC
	ND (1910). Dk. green. Field workers at lower r. (S/M #T10-43). (Not issued).	—	—	—

TA CHING GOVERNMENT BANK, SHANSI 行銀清大西陝

Shan Hsi Ta Ch'ing Yin Hang

NOTE: Prefixing a provincial or city name to that of a bank's name in the heading was not an uncommon practice during the banking days of the Empire.

1911 ISSUE

#A83, A83A, A83H and A83J; facing dragons w/crossed flags at top ctr. Unissued remainders w/ or w/o counterfoils.

NOTE: Beware of remainders missing red validation seal stamps over the serial # in the counterfoil. These were 'created' in recent times for collectors.

A83	1 TAEL			
	ca.1911. Purple on lt. green unpt. Remainder. (S/M #T10-50).	—	—	250.00
A83A	3 TAELS			
	ca.1911. Remainder. (S/M #T10-51).	—	—	325.00

A83H	100 TAELS	VG	VF	UNC
	ca.1909. Purple on lt. green unpt. Remainder. (S/M #T10-54).	—	—	375.00
A83J	1000 TAELS			
	ca.1911. Brown-orange on pale olive-green unpt. Remainder. (S/M #T10-60).	—	—	500.00

REPUBLIC
AGRICULTURAL BANK OF THE FOUR PROVINCES 行銀民農省四

Szu Sheng Nung Min Yin Hang

行銀民農省四贛皖鄂豫

Yü O Huan Kan Szu Sheng Nung Min Yin Hang

This bank was established in 1933 with strong connections to the Chinese nationalist administration and an assigned area of operations in Honan, Hupei, Anhwei and Kiangsi. Two years later, in June 1935, it was reorganized into the Farmers Bank of China and given national bank status. See #451-482. The succeeding bank took over the small existing note issue. This bank was established in 1933 with strong connections to the Chinese nationalist administration and an assigned area of operations in Honan, Hupei, Anhwei and Kiangsi. Two years later, in June 1935, it was reorganized into the Farmers Bank of China and given national bank status. See #451-482. The succeeding bank took over the small existing note issue.

1933 ISSUE

A84	10 CENTS	GOOD	FINE	XF
	ND (1933). Red. Farmer at ctr. Chinese printer: TYPC. (S/M #S110-1).	5.00	12.00	35.00
A84A	20 CENTS			
	1933. Purple and yellow. Back red and green. Chinese printer: TYPC. (S/M #S110-).	—	—	—
A84B	20 CENTS			
	1933. Purple. Back green and yellow. (S/M #S110-).	—	—	—

A85	20 CENTS	GOOD	FINE	XF
	1933. Green and purple. Farmers carrying baskets at r. Chinese printer: CCCA. (S/M #S110-2).			
	a. Issued note.	6.50	20.00	50.00
	b. Remainder w/o sign. or serial #.	—	Unc	50.00

A86	50 CENTS	GOOD	FINE	XF
	ND (1933). Blue. Farmer plowing w/ox at ctr. Farm workers at r. on back. Chinese printer: CCCA. (S/M #S110-3).			
	a. Issued note.	10.00	30.00	75.00
	b. Remainder w/o sign. or serial #.	—	Unc	75.00

A87	1 DOLLAR	GOOD	FINE	XF
	1933. Brown on yellow unpt. Farm workers at l. and r. Back blue and green; farm workers at ctr. Chinese printer: TYPC. (S/M #S110-10).			
	a. Issued note.	13.00	40.00	125.00
	b. Ovpt: SIAN.	15.00	45.00	135.00

1933 PROVISIONAL ISSUE

#A88-A90 joint issue w/Hupeh Provincial Bank. New issuer ovpt. on notes of Hupeh Provincial Bank.

A88	1 DOLLAR	VG	VF	UNC
	ND (1933 - old date 1929). Violet on m/c unpt. Pagoda at r. Ovpt. on #S2104. (S/M #S110-20).	16.50	50.00	
A89	5 DOLLARS			
	ND (1933 - old date 1929). Green on m/c unpt. Pagoda at ctr. Ovpt. on #S2105. (S/M #S110-21).	20.00	60.00	
A90	10 DOLLARS			
	ND (1933 - old date 1929). Red on m/c unpt. Pagoda at l. Ovpt. on #S2106. (S/M #S110-22).	25.00	75.00	

1934 ISSUE

A91A **10 CENTS**
1934. Orange and blue. Back purple and orange. Chinese printer: TYPC. (S/M #S110-).

	GOOD	FINE	XF
	—	—	—

A91B **20 CENTS**
1934. Purple and yellow. Back red and green. Chinese printer: TYPC. (S/M #S110-).

	GOOD	FINE	XF
	—	—	—

A91E **1 DOLLAR**
1.5.1934. Red. Farm workers at upper l. Back green; ox at ctr. Chinese printer: TYPC.

	GOOD	FINE	XF
a. Foochow. (S/M #S110-30a).	10.00	30.00	90.00
b. HANG CHOW. (S/M #S110-30b).	10.00	30.00	90.00
c. Control ovpt: Yu.	10.00	30.00	90.00

AGRICULTURAL AND INDUSTRIAL BANK OF CHINA

中國農工銀行

Chung Kuo Nung Kung Yin Hang

1927 DOLLAR ISSUES
#A92-A108 Printer: BEPP (Peiping or Peking).

A92 **10 CENTS**
1.2.1927. Purple. Bridge over water at ctr.

	GOOD	FINE	XF
a. Peking. (S/M #C287-1a).	2.00	6.00	18.00
b. Tientsin. (S/M #C287-1c).	3.00	9.00	27.50

A93 **10 CENTS**
1.2.1927. Purple. Like #A92 but printer: BEP-Peking.

	GOOD	FINE	XF
a. Peking. (S/M #C287-2).	3.00	9.00	27.50
b. Tientsin (S/M #C287-1b).	3.00	10.00	30.00

A94 **20 CENTS**
1.2.1927. Green. Bridge over water at ctr.

	GOOD	FINE	XF
a. Peking. (S/M #C287-3a).	2.00	6.00	18.00
b. Tientsin. (S/M #C287-3c).	3.00	9.00	27.50

A94A **20 CENTS**
1.2.1927. Green. Like P#A94 but printer: BEP-Peiping.

	GOOD	FINE	XF
a. Peking (S/M #C287-).	2.00	6.00	18.00
b. Tientsin (S/M #C287-3b).	3.00	9.00	27.50

A94B **50 CENTS**
1.2.1927. Orange. Bridge over water at ctr. Back orange. Peking. (S/M #C287-).

	GOOD	FINE	XF
	8.00	25.00	75.00

A95 **1 DOLLAR**
1.9.1927. Brown and m/c. Great Wall at ctr. PEKING. 2 sign. varieties. (S/M #C287-10).

	GOOD	FINE	XF
	10.00	30.00	90.00

A98 **5 DOLLARS**
1.9.1927. Red-orange on m/c unpt. Like #A99. PEKING. (S/M #C287-13).

	GOOD	FINE	XF
	22.50	67.50	200.00

A99 **5 DOLLARS**
1.9.1927. Red and m/c. Sailing ships at ctr.

	GOOD	FINE	XF
a. HANKOW. (S/M #C287-14a).	16.50	50.00	150.00
b. HANKOW, PAYABLE AT CHANGSHA ovpt. (S/M #C287-14b).	20.00	60.00	180.00
s. As b. Specimen.	—	Unc	100.00

A100 **5 DOLLARS**
1.9.1927. Orange and m/c. TIENTSIN. (S/M #C287-15).

	GOOD	FINE	XF
	16.50	50.00	150.00

A101 **5 DOLLARS**
1.9.1927. Green and m/c. Like #A99. SHANGHAI. (S/M #C287-16).

	GOOD	FINE	XF
a. Issued note.	16.50	50.00	150.00
s. Specimen.	—	Unc	100.00

A105	10 DOLLARS	GOOD	FINE	XF
	1.9.1927. Green and m/c. Like #A104.			
	a. SHANGHAI. (S/M #C287-22a).	16.50	50.00	150.00
	b. TIENTSIN. (S/M #C287-22b).	12.00	36.00	110.00
	s. As b. Specimen.	—	Unc	135.00
A106	10 DOLLARS			
	1.9.1927. Brown and m/c. Like #A104. SHANGHAI. (S/M #C287-23).	9.00	28.00	85.00

1927 YUAN ISSUES

A96	1 YUAN			
	1.9.1927. Green and m/c. Like #A95.			
	a. HANKOW. (S/M #C287-11a).	13.50	40.00	120.00
	b. HANKOW, PAYABLE AT CHANGSHA ovpt. (S/M #C287-11b).	20.00	60.00	180.00
A97	1 YUAN			
	1.9.1927. Red and m/c. Like #A95. SHANGHAI. (S/M #C287-12).	11.00	32.50	100.00
A103	10 YUAN			
	1927. PEKING. (S/M #C287-20).	Reported Not Confirmed		
A104	10 YUAN			
	1.9.1927. Purple and m/c. Farm workers at ctr.			
	a. HANKOW. (S/M #C287-21a).	20.00	60.00	180.00
	b. HANKOW, PAYABLE AT CHANGSHA ovpt. (S/M #C287-21b).	22.50	70.00	210.00

1932 ISSUE

#A109-A111 Sign. varieties. Printer: ABNC.

A110	5 YUAN	GOOD	FINE	XF
	1932. Green and m/c. Farmer plowing w/water buffalo at l.			
	a. HANKOW. W/various numerical ovpt.: 11; 21; 22. (S/M #C287-41a).	11.50	35.00	105.00
	b. SHANGHAI. W/various numerical ovpt.: 11-43, etc. (S/M #C287-41b).	7.00	21.50	65.00
	c. PEIPING. (S/M #C287-41c).	7.00	21.50	65.00
	d. HANKOW. Ovpt: PAYABLE AT CHANGSHA. (S/M #C287-41d).	11.50	35.00	105.00

A111	10 YUAN	GOOD	FINE	XF
	1932. Purple and m/c. Farmer plowing w/water buffalo at r.			
	a. HANKOW. W/various numerical ovpt.: 3; 4; 7, etc. (S/M #C287-42a).	20.00	60.00	180.00
	b. SHANGHAI. W/various numerical ovpt.: 33; 40; 43 etc. (S/M #C287-42b).	12.50	40.00	120.00

A107	10 CENTS			
	1.1.1932. Brown and red. Bridge over water at ctr. HANKOW. (S/M #C287-31).	2.50	8.50	24.00
A108	20 CENTS			
	1.1.1932. Yellow. HANKOW. (S/M #C287-31).	3.00	9.00	27.00

A109	1 DOLLAR	GOOD	FINE	XF
	1932. Red and m/c. Farmer plowing w/water buffalo at ctr. SHANGHAI. (S/M #C287-40).			
	a. Issued note.	6.00	19.00	57.00
	b. W/various numerical ovpt.	7.00	21.50	65.00

1934 ISSUE

A112	1 YUAN	GOOD	FINE	XF
	1934. Red and m/c. Farmer plowing w/water buffalo at ctr. Printer: W&S.			
	a. SHANGHAI. (S/M #C287-50a).	5.00	16.00	48.00
	b. PEIPING. (S/M #C287-50b).	5.00	16.00	48.00
	c. W/o place name. (S/M #C287-50c).	4.00	12.00	36.00
	d. TIENTSIN (S/M #C287-50d).	5.00	16.00	48.00

BANK OF AGRICULTURE AND COMMERCE

行銀商農
Nung Shang Yin Hang

1921 ISSUE

#A113-A117D printer: Wu Foong Industrial Development Co. Ltd., Peking.
#A112A-A112C see A114A or A117C, D.

A113	1 YUAN	GOOD	FINE	XF
	Yr.11 (1921). Red-brown and blue. Harvesting grain.			
	a. SHANGHAI. Specimen. (S/M #N23-1).	—	—	—
	b. PEKING. Specimen. (S/M #N23-).	—	—	—
	c. HANKOW. (S/M #N23-).	—	—	—

A114 5 YUAN
Yr. 11 (1921). Gray and m/c. Similar to #A113.

	GOOD	FINE	XF
a. *SHANGHAI*. Specimen. *(S/M #N23-).*	—	—	—
b. *PEKING. (S/M #N23-).*	—	—	—

A114A 5 YUAN
(A112C) ND. (1921) Lilac. Similar to #A117C. Specimen. *(S/M #N23-).*

	—	—	150.00

A115 10 YUAN
Yr. 11 (1921).

	GOOD	FINE	XF
a. *SHANGHAI. (S/M #N23-3).*	13.00	40.00	120.00
b. *PEKING. (S/M #N23-).*	—	—	—

A116 50 YUAN
Yr. 11 (1921). *SHANGHAI. (S/M #N23-).*   Reported Not Confirmed

A117 100 YUAN
Yr. 11 (1921). *SHANGHAI. (S/M #N23-).*   Reported Not Confirmed

1922 DOLLAR ISSUE
#A117A and A117B printer: BEPP.

A117A 1 DOLLAR
1.5.1922. Red and blue. *(S/M #N23-).*   —   —

A117B 5 DOLLARS
1.5.1922. Green and yellow. River scene at center.

	GOOD	FINE	XF
a. *SHANGHAI. (S/M #N23-).*	32.50	100.00	300.00
b. *HANKOW. (S/M #N23-).*	20.00	60.00	180.00

1922 YUAN ISSUE

A117C 1 YUAN
(A112A) 1922. Red. Agricultural workers. *(S/M #N23-).*

s1. Specimen.	—	—	150.00
s2. Specimen perforated: *UNGÜLTIG.*	—	—	150.00

A117D 5 YUAN
(A112B) 1922. Dk. brown and violet. Similar to #A117C. Specimen. *(S/M #N23-).*

	—	—	150.00

1926 ISSUE
#A118-A120 pagoda on hilltop, shoreline at ctr. Printer: ABNC.

A118 1 YUAN
1.12.1926. Brown and m/c. *SHANGHAI. (S/M #N23-10).*

	GOOD	FINE	XF
a. Issued note.	13.00	40.00	120.00
s. Specimens. Uniface face and back.	—	Unc	100.00

A119 5 YUAN
1.12.1926. Green and m/c.

	GOOD	FINE	XF
a. *SHANGHAI.* W/various numerical ovpt: 3; 6; 10; 21. *(S/M #N23-11a).*	13.00	40.00	120.00
b. *CHANGSHA. (S/M #N23-11b).*	15.00	45.00	135.00
c. *HANKOW. (S/M #N23-11c).*	13.00	40.00	120.00
s. As a. Specimens. Uniface face and back.	—	Unc	100.00

A120 10 YUAN
1.12.1926. Purple and blue. *SHANGHAI. (S/M #N23-12).*

	GOOD	FINE	XF
a. Issued note.	15.00	45.00	135.00
s. Specimen. Uniface pair.	—	Unc	125.00

CHINA SILK AND TEA INDUSTRIAL BANK

行銀茶絲國中

Chung Kuo Szu Ch'a Yin Hang

1925 ISSUE
#A120A-A120C harvesting tea at ctr. Weaving at ctr. on back. Printer: BEPP.

A120A 1 DOLLAR
15.8.1925. Blue on m/c unpt.

	GOOD	FINE	XF
a. *PEKING. (S/M #C292-1a).*	10.00	30.00	90.00
b. *TIENTSIN. (S/M #C292-1b).*	10.00	30.00	90.00
c. *CHENGCHOW / PEKING. (S/M #C292-1c).*	10.00	30.00	90.00

A120B 5 DOLLARS

15.8.1925. Orange on m/c unpt.

		GOOD	FINE	XF
a.	PEKING. (S/M #C292-2a).	11.00	32.50	100.00
b.	TIENTSIN. (S/M #C292-2b).	8.50	26.50	80.00
c.	CHENGCHOW / PEKING. (S/M #C292-2c).	11.00	32.50	100.00

A120C 10 DOLLARS

15.8.1925. Green on m/c unpt.

a.	PEKING. (S/M #C292-3a).	14.00	42.50	125.00
b.	TIENTSIN. (S/M #C292-3b).	14.00	42.50	125.00
c.	CHENGCHOW / PEKING. (S/M #C292-3c).	11.50	35.00	105.00

CHINA AND SOUTH SEA BANK, LIMITED   中 南 銀 行

Chung Nan Yin Hang

Established 1921. Though bearing only the China and South Sea Bank's name, all these notes were backed and circulated by a coalition of four major Shanghai banks, of which the issuer was one. These notes achieved wide circulation and acceptance.

1921 ISSUE

#A122-A123A common w/various letter and numerical control ovpt: *SK; SK-b; SK-P; SS, etc.* Printer: ABNC.

A121 1 YUAN

1.10.1921. Blue on m/c unpt. Monument at ctr. Sign. varieties.

		GOOD	FINE	XF
a.	SHANGHAI. Title: CHAIRMAN below sign. on back. (S/M #C295-1a).	10.00	30.00	90.00
b.	SHANGHAI. W/o title: CHAIRMAN below sign. on back. (S/M #C295-1a).	8.00	25.00	75.00
c.	HANKOW. Title: CHAIRMAN below sign. on back. (S/M #295-1b).	10.00	30.00	90.00
d.	TIENTSIN. (S/M #C295-1c).	10.00	30.00	90.00

A122 5 YUAN

1.10.1921. Purple on m/c unpt. Monument at l. Title: *CHAIRMAN* below sign. on back. SHANGHAI. (S/M #C295-2).

	GOOD	FINE	XF
	13.00	40.00	120.00

A123 10 YUAN

1.10.1921. Black and m/c. Monument at r.

		GOOD	FINE	XF
a.	SHANGHAI. (S/M #C295-3a).	20.00	60.00	180.00
b.	TIENTSIN. (S/M #C295-3b).	20.00	60.00	180.00
c.	HANKOW. (S/M #C295-3c).	25.00	75.00	225.00

A123A 50 YUAN

1.10.1921. SHANGHAI. (S/M #C295-4).

—	—	—

1924 ISSUE

#A124 and A125 common w/letter control ovpt: *SK* or *SY*. Printer: ABNC.

A124 5 YUAN

1924. Purple and m/c. Like #A122.

		GOOD	FINE	XF
a.	SHANGHAI. (S/M #C295-10a).	10.00	30.00	90.00
b.	TIENTSIN. (S/M #C295-10b).	10.00	30.00	90.00
c.	HANKOW. (S/M #C295-10c).	11.00	32.50	100.00
d.	AMOY. (S/M #C295-10d).	11.50	35.00	105.00

A125 10 YUAN

1924. Black and m/c. Like #A123.

a.	SHANGHAI. (S/M #C295-11a).	8.00	25.00	75.00
b.	TIENTSIN. (S/M #C295-11b).	11.00	32.50	100.00
c.	HANKOW. (S/M #C295-11c).	11.50	35.00	105.00
d.	AMOY. (S/M #C295-11d).	16.50	50.00	150.00

1927 ISSUE

A126 1 YUAN

1927. Purple and m/c. 3 women's busts over dollar coin at ctr. 2 women's busts over Yuan Shih Kai dollar coin on back. Printer: W&S.

		GOOD	FINE	XF
a.	SHANGHAI. W/various control ovpt. (S/M #C295-20a).	20.00	60.00	180.00
b.	TIENTSIN. (S/M #C295-20b).	11.50	35.00	200.00

A127 5 YUAN

	GOOD	FINE	XF
1927. Red and m/c. Similar to #A124. Printer: ABNC. Also various numerical, letter or Chinese character control ovpt.			
a. HANKOW. (S/M #C295-21b).	16.50	50.00	150.00
b. SHANGHAI. (S/M #C295-21a).	16.50	50.00	150.00

A128 5 YUAN

	GOOD	FINE	XF
1927. Purple and m/c. Similar to #A129. SHANGHAI. Also w/various letter or Chinese character control ovpt. Printer: ABNC. (S/M #C295-22).	16.50	50.00	150.00

A129 10 YUAN

	GOOD	FINE	XF
1927. Brown and red. 2 women's busts at l. and r. Back brown and blue, 3 women's busts at l., ctr. and r. 2 sign. varieties. Printer: W&S. SHANGHAI. Also various letter or Chinese character control ovpt. (S/M #C295-23).	20.00	60.00	180.00

A130 50 YUAN

1927. Purple. Printer: ABNC. (S/M #C295-24).	Reported Not Confirmed

A131 100 YUAN

1927. Red. Printer: ABNC. (S/M #C295-25).	Reported Not Confirmed

1931-32 ISSUE

A132 1 YUAN

	GOOD	FINE	XF
1931. Blue and m/c. Monument at l. Printer: W&S.			
a. SHANGHAI. (S/M	8.00	25.00	75.00
b. TIENTSIN. (S/M #C295-30b).	8.00	25.00	75.00

A133 5 YUAN

	GOOD	FINE	XF
Jan. 1932. Purple and m/c. Control letter ovpt: HK. SHANGHAI. Printer: TDLR. (S/M #C295-40).	16.50	50.00	150.00

COMMERCIAL BANK OF CHINA

中國通商銀行

Chung Kuo T'ung Shang Yin Hang

Formerly the Imperial Bank of China. Earlier issues have been reported to exist w/Republic period ovpts. The issues of the Commercial Bank are also found w/various numerical, letter or Chinese character ovpt.

1913 PROVISIONAL TAEL ISSUE

#A133A-A133B ovpt: COMMERCIAL/IMPERIAL.

A133A 1 TAEL

	GOOD	FINE	XF
ND. (1913-old date 22.1.1898). Red ovpt on #A46. (S/M #C293-).	40.00	120.00	360.00

1913 PROVISIONAL DOLLAR ISSUE

A133B 5 DOLLARS

	GOOD	FINE	XF
ND (1913-old date 16.2.1904). Black and m/c. Ovpt on #A55. (S/M #C293-).	100.00	300.00	900.00

A133C 10 DOLLARS

	GOOD	FINE	XF
ND (1913-old date 16.2.1904). Ovpt on #A55B. (S/M #C293-).	100.00	300.00	900.00

1920 SHANGHAI TAEL ISSUE 上海

#A134-A138 "Confucius" standing at ctr. Medallion supported by 2 lions on back. Printer: ABNC.

		GOOD	FINE	XF
A134	**1 TAEL**			
	15.1.1920. Blue on m/c unpt. Back brown. (S/M #C293-30).			
	a. Issued note.	9.00	28.00	85.00
	p. Proof.	—	Unc	150.00
	s. Specimen.	—	Unc	125.00
A135	**5 TAELS**			
	15.1.1920. Yellow-orange on m/c unpt. Back purple. (S/M #C293-31).			
	a. Issued note.	16.50	50.00	150.00
	p. Proof.	—	Unc	200.00
	s. Specimen.	—	Unc	175.00

		GOOD	FINE	XF
4	**5 DOLLARS**			
	15.1.1920. Yellow and m/c. (S/M #C293-43).	11.50	35.00	105.00
4A	**5 DOLLARS**			
	15.1.1920. Brown and m/c. (S/M #293-).			
	p. Proof.	—	Unc	225.00
	s. Specimen.	—	Unc	200.00

		GOOD	FINE	XF
A136	**10 TAELS**			
	15.1.1920. Purple on m/c unpt. Back brown. (S/M #C293-32).			
	a. Issued note.	22.50	70.00	210.00
	p. Proof.	—	Unc	300.00
	s. Specimen.	—	Unc	250.00
A137	**50 TAELS**			
	15.1.1920. (S/M #C293-33).		Reported Not Confirmed	
A138	**100 TAELS**			
	15.1.1920. (S/M #C293-34).		Reported Not Confirmed	

1920 DOLLAR ISSUES
#1-8 "Worthy" standing at ctr. Medallion supported by 2 lions on back. Printer: ABNC.

		GOOD	FINE	XF
1	**1 DOLLAR**			
	15.1.1920. Black and m/c. (S/M #C293-40).			
	a. Issued note.	11.50	35.00	105.00
	p. Proof.	—	Unc	125.00
	s. Specimen.	—	Unc	100.00
2	**1 DOLLAR**			
	15.1.1920. Blue and m/c. (S/M #C293-41).			
	a. Issued note.	11.50	35.00	105.00
	b. W/character ovpt: Yuan.	13.00	40.00	120.00
	p. Proof.	—	Unc	150.00
	s. Specimen.	—	Unc	125.00

		GOOD	FINE	XF
5	**10 DOLLARS**			
	15.1.1920. Yellow and m/c. (S/M #C293-44).			
	a. Issued note.	15.00	45.00	135.00
	b. W/character ovpt.	13.00	40.00	120.00
	p. Proof.	—	Unc	200.00
	s. Specimen.	—	Unc	175.00
6	**10 DOLLARS**			
	15.1.1920. Red and m/c. (S/M #C293-45).			
	a. Issued note.	16.50	50.00	150.00
	b. W/character ovpt.	15.00	45.00	135.00
	p. Proof.	—	Unc	200.00
	s. Specimen.	—	Unc	175.00
7	**50 DOLLARS**			
	15.1.1920. Blue and m/c. (S/M #C293-46).			
	a. Issued note.	100.00	300.00	—
	p. Proof.	—	Unc	250.00
	s. Specimen.	—	Unc	225.00

		GOOD	FINE	XF
3	**5 DOLLARS**			
	15.1.1920. Purple and m/c. (S/M #C293-42).			
	a. Issued note.	11.50	35.00	105.00
	b. W/character ovpt: Yuan.	13.00	40.00	120.00
	s. Specimen.	—	Unc	150.00

		GOOD	FINE	XF
8	**100 DOLLARS**			
	15.1.1920. Olive-green and m/c. Back purple. (S/M #C293-47).			
	a. Issued note.	125.00	375.00	—
	p. Proof.	—	Unc	300.00
	s. Specimen.	—	Unc	275.00

1926 SHANGHAI ISSUE 上海

#9-10 harbor scene at l., Confucius standing at r. Medallion supported by 2 lions on back. Printer: W&S.

		GOOD	FINE	XF
9	**5 DOLLARS**			
	Jan. 1926. Green and m/c. *(S/M #C293-50).*	6.00	18.00	55.00
10	**10 DOLLARS**			
	Jan. 1926. Brown and m/c. *(S/M #C293-51).*	8.00	25.00	75.00

1929 NATIONAL CURRENCY ISSUE

#11-13 medallion supported by lions at top ctr., Confucius standing at r. Medallion supported by 2 lions on back. W/o printer.

		GOOD	FINE	XF
11	**1 DOLLAR**			
	Jan. 1929. Black and green.			
	a. *SHANGHAI. (S/M #C292-60a).*	5.00	20.00	60.00
	b. *SHANGHAI/AMOY. (S/M #C293-60b).*	5.00	20.00	60.00
	c. *HANKOW. (S/M #C293-60c).*	6.00	25.00	75.00
	d. *AMOY. (S/M #C293-60d).*	7.50	30.00	90.00

1929 SHANGHAI CURRENCY ISSUE

		GOOD	FINE	XF
12	**1 DOLLAR**			
	Jan. 1929. Black and yellow. Similar to #13. *SHANGHAI. (S/M #C293-61).*	4.50	18.00	55.00

		GOOD	FINE	XF
13	**1 DOLLAR**			
	Jan. 1929. Blue and m/c. Back blue and yellow. *SHANGHAI. (S/M #C293-62).*	4.50	18.00	55.00
13A	**1 DOLLAR**			
	1929. Purple. *(S/M #C293-63).*	4.50	18.00	55.00

1932 ISSUE

#14-15 w/ and w/o various Chinese character control ovpt. Printer: W&S.

		GOOD	FINE	XF
14	**5 DOLLARS**			
	June 1932. Purple and m/c. Similar to #9.			
	a. *SHANGHAI. (S/M #C293-70a).*	4.00	16.00	48.00
	b. *AMOY. (S/M #C293-70b).*	5.00	20.00	60.00
15	**10 DOLLARS**			
	June 1932. Red and m/c. Similar to #10. *SHANGHAI. (S/M #C293-71).*	5.00	20.00	60.00

BANK OF CHINA

КИТАЙСКІЙ БАНКЪ

中國銀行
Chung Kuo Yin Hang

中國銀行兌換券
Chung Kuo Yin Hang Tui Huan Ch'üan

1912 PROVISIONAL ISSUE

#16-18 ovpt. new issuer name on Ta Ching Government Bank notes. Sign. varieties.
#19-24 *Deleted.*

		GOOD	FINE	XF
16	**1 DOLLAR**			
	ND (1912 - old date 1.10.1909). Ovpt. on #A76.			
	a. Ovpt: *Chung Kuo* at l. and *Yin Hang* at r. Dated yr. 1. *(S/M #C294-1a).*	16.50	50.00	150.00
	b. *HANKOW. (S/M #C294-1b).*	20.00	60.00	180.00
	c. *HONAN. (S/M #C294-1c).*	20.00	60.00	180.00
	d. *PEKING. (S/M #C294-1d).*	18.00	55.00	165.00
	e. *SHANTUNG. (S/M #C294-1e).*	20.00	60.00	180.00
	f. *SHANTUNG/CHIHLI. (S/M #C294-1f).*	22.50	70.00	210.00
	g. *TIENTSIN* ovpt. in red on #16a. *(S/M #C294-1g).*	20.00	60.00	180.00
	h. *SHANGHAI. (S/M #C294-1h).*	22.50	70.00	210.00
	i. *MANCHURIA (S/M #C294-1i).*	26.50	80.00	240.00
	j. *CHIHLI (S/M #C294-1j).*	26.50	80.00	240.00

			GOOD	FINE	XF
17	**5 DOLLARS** ND (1912 - old date 1.10.1909). Ovpt. on #A77.				
	a.	Ovpt: *Chung Kuo* at l. and *Yin Hang* at r. (S/M #C294-2a).	26.50	80.00	240.00
	b.	HANKOW. (S/M #C294-2b).	32.50	100.00	300.00
	c.	HONAN. (S/M #C294-2c).	32.50	100.00	300.00
	d.	PEKING. (S/M #C294-2d).	26.50	80.00	240.00
	e.	SHANTUNG. (S/M #C294-2e).	32.50	100.00	300.00
	f.	SHANTUNG/CHIHLI. (S/M #C294-2f).).	36.50	110.00	330.00
	g.	TIENTSIN. (S/M #C294-2g).	26.50	80.00	240.00
	h.	TIENTSIN/PEKING. (S/M #C294-2h).	36.50	110.00	330.00
	i.	SHANGHAI. (S/M #C294-2i).	32.50	100.00	300.00
	j.	MANCHURIA. (S/M #C294-2j).	32.50	100.00	300.00
18	**10 DOLLARS** ND (1912 - old date 1.10.1909). Ovpt. on #A78.				
	a.	Ovpt: *Chung Kuo* at l. *Yin Hang* at r. (S/M #C294-3a).	40.00	120.00	360.00
	b.	HANKOW. (S/M #C294-3b).	45.00	140.00	425.00
	c.	HONAN. (S/M #C294-3c).	45.00	140.00	425.00
	d.	PEKING. (S/M #C294-3d).	40.00	120.00	360.00
	e.	SHANTUNG. (S/M #C294-3e).	45.00	140.00	425.00
	f.	SHANTUNG/CHIHLI. (S/M #C294-3f).	50.00	150.00	450.00
	g.	TIENTSIN. (S/M #C294-3g).	40.00	120.00	360.00

1912 ISSUES

#25-27 portr. Emperor Huang-ti at l., rural vignettes similar to #A76-A78 at r. Printer: ABNC.

			GOOD	FINE	XF
25	**1 DOLLAR** 1.6.1912. Dk. green on m/c. unpt.				
	a.	ANHWEI. (S/M #C294-30a).	12.50	50.00	150.00
	b.	CANTON. (S/M #C294-30b).	10.00	40.00	120.00
	c.	CHEFOO. (S/M #C294-30c).	13.50	55.00	165.00
	d.	CHEHKIANG. (S/M #C294-30d).	12.50	50.00	150.00
	e.	FUHKIEN (Fukien). (S/M #C294-30e).	12.50	50.00	150.00
	f.	HANKOW. (S/M #C294-30f).	12.50	50.00	150.00
	g.	HONAN. (S/M #C294-30g).	12.50	50.00	150.00
	h.	KIANGSI. (S/M #C294-30h).	12.50	50.00	150.00
	i.	KIANGSU. (S/M #C294-30i).	13.50	55.00	165.00
	j.	KUEISUI. (S/M #C294-30j).	15.00	60.00	180.00
	k.	KWANGTUNG. Ovpt: *N.B. Payable in subsidiary (silver) coins...* on back. (S/M #C294-30k).	10.00	40.00	120.00
	l.	MANCHURIA. (S/M #C294-30l).	15.00	60.00	180.00
	m.	MUKDEN. (S/M #C294-30m).	12.50	50.00	150.00
	n.	SHANSI. (S/M #C294-30n).	12.50	50.00	150.00
	o.	SHANTUNG. (S/M #C294-30o).	12.50	50.00	150.00
	p.	*Szechuen in Chinese characters in oval frames at l. and r. edge on face. Lg. SZECHUEN below date at bottom ctr. on back.* (S/M #C294-30p).	13.50	55.00	165.00
	q.	*One Dollar in Chinese characters in oval frames at l. and r. edge on face. One Dollar / sm. SZECHUEN below date at bottom ctr. on back.* (S/M #C294-30p).	13.50	55.00	165.00
	r.	THREE EASTERN PROVINCES. (S/M #C294-30q).	15.00	60.00	180.00
	s.	YUNNAN. (S/M #C294-30r).	6.00	25.00	80.00
	t.	SHANGHAI. (S/M #C294-30s).	12.50	50.00	150.00
	u.	TIENTSIN. (S/M #C294-30t).	13.50	55.00	165.00

	v.	КАЛГАНЪ (Kalgan). (S/M #C294-30u).	16.50	66.50	200.00
	w.	PEKING. (S/M #C294-30w).	15.00	60.00	180.00
26	**5 DOLLARS** 1.6.1912. Black on m/c. unpt.		GOOD	FINE	XF
	a.	ANHWEI. (S/M #C294-31a).	18.50	75.00	225.00
	b.	CANTON. (S/M #C294-31b).	10.00	40.00	120.00
	c.	CHEFOO. (S/M #C294-31c).	22.50	90.00	270.00
	d.	CHEHKIANG. (S/M #C294-31d).	22.50	90.00	270.00
	e.	FUHKIEN (Fukien). (S/M #C294-31e).	18.50	75.00	225.00
	f.	HANKOW. (S/M #C294-31f).	22.50	90.00	270.00
	g.	HONAN. (S/M #C294-31g).	18.50	75.00	225.00
	h.	KIANGSI. (S/M #C294-31h).	18.50	75.00	225.00
	i.	KIANGSU. (S/M #C294-31i).	22.50	90.00	270.00
	j.	KUEISUI. (S/M #C294-31j).	25.00	100.00	300.00
	k.	KWANGTUNG. Ovpt. *N.B. Payable in subsidiary (silver) coins....* on back. (S/M #C294-31k).	13.50	55.00	165.00
	l.	MANCHURIA. (S/M #C294-31l).	25.00	100.00	300.00
	m.	MUKDEN. (S/M #C294-31m).	18.50	75.00	225.00
	n.	SHANSI. (S/M #C294-31n).	22.50	90.00	270.00
	o.	SHANTUNG. (S/M #C294-31o).	18.50	75.00	225.00
	p.	SZECHUAN. (S/M #C294-31p).	22.50	90.00	270.00
	q.	THREE EASTERN PROVINCES. (S/M #C294-31q).	25.00	100.00	300.00
	r.	YUNNAN. (S/M #C294-31r).	8.00	32.50	100.00
	s.	KWEICHOW. (S/M #C294-).	25.00	100.00	300.00
	t.	W/o place name. Specimen. (S/M #C294-).	—	Unc	175.00

			GOOD	FINE	XF
27	**10 DOLLARS** 1.6.1912. Deep blue on m/c. unpt.				
	a.	ANHWEI. (S/M #C294-32a).	22.50	90.00	270.00
	b.	CANTON. (S/M #C294-32b).	12.50	50.00	150.00
	c.	CHEFOO. (S/M #C294-32c).	32.50	100.00	300.00
	d.	CHEHKIANG. (S/M #C294-32d).	20.00	80.00	240.00
	e.	FUHKIEN (Fukien). (S/M #C294-32e).	22.50	90.00	270.00
	f.	HANKOW. (S/M #C294-32f).	22.50	90.00	270.00
	g.	HONAN. (S/M #C294-32g).	22.50	90.00	270.00
	h.	KIANGSI. (S/M #C294-32h).	22.50	90.00	270.00
	i.	KIANGSU. (S/M #C294-32i).	25.00	100.00	300.00
	j.	KUEISUI. (S/M #C294-32j).	30.00	120.00	360.00
	k.	KWANGTUNG. Ovpt. *N.B. Payable in subsidiary (silver) coins...* on back. (S/M #C294-32k).	22.00	66.50	200.00
	l.	MANCHURIA. (S/M #C294-32l).	30.00	120.00	360.00
	m.	MUKDEN. (S/M #C294-32m).	22.50	90.00	270.00
	n.	SHANSI. (S/M #C294-32n).	25.00	100.00	300.00
	o.	SHANTUNG. (S/M #C294-32o).	25.00	100.00	300.00
	p.	SZECHUAN. (S/M #C294-32p).	25.00	100.00	300.00
	q.	THREE EASTERN PROVINCES. (S/M #C294-32q).	30.00	120.00	360.00
	r.	YUNNAN. (S/M #C294-32r).	11.50	45.00	135.00
	s.	SHANGHAI. (S/M #C294-32s).	20.00	80.00	240.00
	t.	W/o place name. Specimen. (S/M #C294-).	—	Unc	250.00

1913 PROVISIONAL ISSUE

#29 and 29A ovpt. new bank name on notes of the Provincial Bank of Kwangtung Province.

#28 *Deleted.*

			GOOD	FINE	XF
29	**5 DOLLARS** ND (-old date 1.1.1913). Dk. green on m/c unpt. Ovpt. on #S2398. (S/M #C294-41).		20.00	60.00	180.00
29A	**10 DOLLARS** ND (-old date 1.1.1913). Ovpt. on #S2399. (S/M #C294-42).		26.50	80.00	240.00

1913 REGULAR ISSUE

#30-32B portr. Huang Ti (Yellow Emperor) at l., rural vignettes at r. Printer: ABNC.

30	**1 DOLLAR**	GOOD	FINE	XF
	1.6.1913. Olive and red. Similar to #25.			
	a. CANTON. (S/M #C294-42a).	5.50	22.00	66.00
	b. FUKIEN. (S/M #C294-42b).	8.00	25.00	75.00
	c. SHANTUNG. (S/M #C294-42c).	8.00	25.00	75.00
	d. SHANSI. (S/M #C294-42d).	7.50	30.00	90.00
	e. W/o place name. (S/M #C294-42).	5.50	22.00	66.00
31	**5 DOLLARS**			
	1.6.1913. Black and brown on blue and m/c unpt. Similar to #26.			
	a. CANTON. (S/M #C294-43a).	7.50	30.00	90.00
	b. FUKIEN. (S/M #C294-43b).	8.50	35.00	105.00
	c. SHANTUNG. (S/M #C294-43c).	10.00	40.00	120.00
32	**10 DOLLARS**			
	1.6.1913. Similar to #27.			
	a. CANTON. (S/M #C294-44a).	11.50	45.00	135.00
	b. FUKIEN. (S/M #C294-44b).	12.50	50.00	150.00
	c. SHANTUNG. (S/M #C294-44c).	13.50	55.00	165.00

32A	**50 DOLLARS**	GOOD	FINE	XF
	1.6.1913. Purple on m/c unpt. Lg. bldg. at r. PEKING. Specimen perforated w/Chinese characters. (S/M #C294-45a).	—	Unc	750.00

32B	**100 DOLLARS**	GOOD	FINE	XF
	1.6.1913. Dk. olive-green on m/c unpt. Temple of Heaven at r. PEKING. Specimen perforated w/Chinese characters. (S/M #C294-46a).	—	Unc	750.00

1914 PROVISIONAL ISSUE

32C	**1 DOLLAR**	GOOD	FINE	XF
	1914 (-old date-1.10.1909). Olive-brown on red-orange unpt. Ovpt. on #A76. CHIHLI. (S/M #C294-46).	—		

1914 "YUAN SHIH-KAI" ISSUE

#33-35B black on m/c unpt. Portr. Yuan Shih-kai at ctr. Unsigned remainders w/ or w/o perforated "cancelled" in Chinese characters. Printer: ABNC.

33	**1 YUAN**	VG	VF	UNC
	4.10.1914. Back black. (S/M #294-50).	—	125.00	375.00
34	**5 YUAN**			
	4.10.1914. Back brown. (S/M #294-51).	—	200.00	600.00
35	**10 YUAN**			
	4.10.1914. Back brown. (S/M #294-52).	—	250.00	750.00

35A	**50 YUAN**	VG	VF	UNC
	4.10.1914. Back brown. (S/M #294-53).	—	—	—
35B	**100 YUAN**			
	4.10.1914. Back dk. olive-green. (S/M #C294-54).	—	—	—

1914 "SMALL CHANGE" ISSUE

#36 and 37 Great Wall at ctr. Printer: BEPP.

36	**20 CENTS**			
	1.12.1914. Black on green unpt. Back orange. MANCHURIA. (S/M #C294-60).	15.00	45.00	135.00

	37	50 CENTS		VG	VF	UNC
		1.12.1914. Brown on red unpt. MANCHURIA. (S/M #C294-61).		16.50	50.00	150.00

1915 "HUANG TI" ISSUE

#37A-37C *Deleted.* See #37D-37F.
#37D-37F portr. Emperor Huang Ti at l. Proofs w/o sign. or office of issue. Printer: ABNC.

				VG	VF	UNC
37D	1 DOLLAR					
(37A)	1.7.1915. Green. Back blue and red. Proof. (S/M #C294-62).			—	—	250.00
37E	5 DOLLARS					
(37B)	1.7.1915. Black. Back blue, red and brown. Proof. (S/M #C294-63).			—	—	300.00
37F	10 DOLLARS					
(37C)	1.7.1915. Blue. Back blue, red and brown. Proof. (S/M #C294-64).			—	—	350.00

1917 "TSAO KUAN" ISSUE

#37J-37N Tsao Kuan at l. or r. Proofs w/o sign. or office of issue. Printer: ABNC.

				VG	VF	UNC
37J	1 DOLLAR					
(37D)	1.5.1917. Black on blue, red and purple unpt. Back brown. Proof. (S/M #C294-65).			—	—	500.00
37K	5 DOLLARS					
(37E)	1.5.1917. Black on blue, red and green unpt. Back dk. green. Proof. (S/M #C294-66).			—	—	550.00
37L	10 DOLLARS					
(37F)	1.5.1917. Black on red, blue and ochre unpt. Back red-orange. Proof. (S/M #C294-67).			—	—	600.00

				VG	VF	UNC
37M	50 DOLLARS					
(37G)	1.5.1917. Black on olive-green, red and blue unpt. Back: olive-green. Proof. (S/M #C294-68).			—	—	700.00
37N	100 DOLLARS					
(37H)	1.5.1917. Black on blue, brown and green unpt. Back: blue. Proof. (S/M #C294-69).			—	—	800.00

1917 "TIENTSIN" ISSUE

#38-40 gateways at l. or r. Printer: ABNC.
NOTE: For similar notes dated yr.7//1.5.1917, see 54A and 54C.

	38	1 DOLLAR	VG	VF	UNC
		Yr. 6//1.5.1917. Black on brown, purple and green unpt. Back blue-gray. TIENTSIN. Proof. (S/M #C294-80).	—	—	250.00
	39	5 DOLLARS			
		Yr. 6//1.5.1917. Blue-black on red, blue and brown unpt. TIENTSIN. Proof. (S/M #C294-81).	—	—	250.00
	40	10 DOLLARS			
		Yr. 6//1.5.1917. Black on blue, purple and green unpt. Back deep green. TIENTSIN. Proof. (S/M #C294-82).	—	—	275.00

1917 "SMALL CHANGE" ISSUES

#41-45 printer: BEPP.
45A and 45B *Deleted.* See #58 and 59.

	41	5 CENTS	GOOD	FINE	XF
		1.10.1917. Brown. HARBIN. (S/M #C294-70).	3.75	15.00	45.00

	42	10 CENTS = 1 CHIAO	GOOD	FINE	XF
		1.10.1917. Green. Temple at l. Harbin. (S/M #C294-71).			
		a. HARBIN. (S/M #C294-71).	5.00	20.00	60.00
		b. MANCHURIA. (S/M #C294-).	5.00	20.00	60.00
		r. Remainder, w/o serial #, sign. or place name. (S/M #C294-).	—	Unc	60.00

	43	10 CENTS = 1 CHIAO	GOOD	FINE	XF
		1.10.1917. Bridge at ctr.			
		b. HARBIN. Orange. Exchange clause blocked out on face and back. Ovpt. new exchange clause in Chinese at l. and r. on back. (S/M #C294-72b).	3.00	12.00	36.00
		c. КАЛГАНЪ Kalgan in Chinese at l. and r. Brown. (S/M #C294-72c).	3.00	12.00	36.00
		d. KIANGSI. (S/M #C294-72d).	3.00	12.00	36.00
		e. KUEISUI. Green. (S/M #C294-72e).	4.00	16.50	50.00
		f. MANCHURIA. Orange. (S/M #C294-72f).	3.50	13.50	40.00
		g. PAOTING. Green. (S/M #C294-72g).	3.50	13.50	40.00
		h. SHANSI. Brown. (S/M #C294-72h).	3.00	12.00	36.00
		i. SHANGTUNG. Purple. Back green. (S/M #C294-72i).	3.00	12.00	36.00
		j. TSINGKIANGPU. Red. (S/M #C294-72j).	3.50	13.50	40.00
		k. TSINGTAO. Brown. (S/M #C294-72k).	4.00	16.50	50.00
		l. TSINGTAO/SHANTUNG. (S/M #C294-72l).	3.50	13.50	40.00
		m. Калганъ. KALGAN in Manchu at l., Chinese at r. on face. Green. Back purple; Russian text. (S/M #C294-72m).	4.00	16.50	50.00
		r. Green. Back purple. Remainder, w/o serial #, sign. or place name. (S/M #C294-72a).	—	Unc	45.00

	44	20 CENTS = 2 CHIAO	GOOD	FINE	XF
		1.10.1917. Pagoda on hill at shoreline at ctr.			
		b. HARBIN. Violet. Exchange clause blocked out on face and back. Ovpt. new exchange clause in Chinese at l. and r. on back. (S/M #C294-73b).	6.00	17.50	50.00
		c. КАЛГАНЪ (Kalgan). Black. Back dk. brown. (S/M #C294-73c).	5.00	20.00	60.00
		d. KIANGSI. Red. (S/M #C294-73d).	4.00	16.50	50.00
		e. KUEISUI. Brown. (S/M #C294-73e).	5.00	20.00	60.00
		f. MANCHURIA. (S/M #C294-73f).	4.00	16.50	50.00
		g. PAOTING. Orange. (S/M #C294-73g).	4.00	16.50	50.00
		h. SHANSI. Green. (S/M #C294-73h).	4.00	16.50	50.00
		i. SHANTUNG. (S/M #C294-73i).	4.00	16.50	50.00
		j. TSINGKIANGPU. (S/M #C294-73j).	5.00	20.00	60.00
		k. TSINGTAO. Orange. (S/M #C294-73k).	5.00	20.00	60.00
		l. TSINGTAO/SHANTUNG. (S/M #C294-73l).	5.00	20.00	60.00
		r. Green. Back violet. Remainder w/o serial #, sign. or place name. (S/M #C294-73a).	—	Unc	45.00

		Good	Fine	XF
45	**50 CENTS = 5 CHIAO**			
	1.10.1917. Various colors. Bridge w/bldg. in background at ctr.			
	b. *HARBIN.* Exchange clause blocked out on face and back. Ovpt. new exchange clause in Chinese at l. and r. on back. *(S/M #C294-74b).*	3.50	13.50	40.00
	c. КАЛГАНЪ (Kalgan). *(S/M #C294-74c).*	3.50	13.50	40.00
	d. *KIANGSI. (S/M #C294-74d).*	3.50	13.50	40.00
	e. *KUEISUI. (S/M #C294-74e).*	3.00	12.00	36.00
	f. *MANCHURIA. (S/M #C294-74f).*	4.00	16.50	50.00
	g. *PAOTING. (S/M #C294-74g).*	3.75	15.00	45.00
	h. *SHANSI. (S/M #C294-74h).*	3.75	15.00	45.00
	i. *SHANTUNG. (S/M #C294-74i).*	3.00	12.00	36.00
	j. *TSINGKIANGPU. (S/M #C294-74j).*	3.00	12.00	36.00
	k. *TSINGTAO. (S/M #C294-74k).*	3.75	15.00	45.00
	l. *TSINGTAO/SHANTUNG. (S/M #C294-74l).*	5.00	20.00	60.00
	r. Remainder w/o serial #, sign. or place name. *(S/M #C294-74a).*	—	Unc	30.00

1918 ND ISSUE
#47 *Deleted.* See #50.

		Good	Fine	XF
46	**5 FEN**			
	ND (1918). Blue on red unpt. Chinese printer. *HARBIN. #C294-90).*	3.50	14.00	52.50
46A				
	ND (1918). Blue and red. Printer: BEPP. *HARBIN. (S/M #C294-91).*	3.50	14.00	52.50

1918 ISSUES
#48-54C sign. varieties. Also w/various Chinese character or western numeral or letter control ovpts: D; HS; TF, etc. Printer: ABNC.

#54A and 54C are unusual as the face is dated yr. 7 while the back is dated 1st May 1917. For similar notes dated Yr. 6//1.5.1917 see #38-40.

		Good	Fine	XF
55	**2 TIAO = 98 COPPER COINS**			
	Sept. 1918. Gray-green and orange. Back red. Remainder w/o sign. or serial #. *SHANTUNG. (S/M #C294-).*	—	Unc	100.00
48	**10 CENTS = 1 CHIAO**			
	Sept. 1918. Black and m/c. Temple of Heaven at r. W/bank name also in Russian on back.			
	a. *HARBIN. (S/M #C294-93a).*	3.50	14.00	52.50
	b. *SHANGHAI/HARBIN.* 2 sign. varieties. *(S/M #C294-93b).*	3.75	15.00	45.00
	c. As a. but w/red official 4-Chinese character ovpt. *(S/M #C294-93c).*	5.00	20.00	60.00

		Good	Fine	XF
49	**20 CENTS = 2 CHIAO**			
	Sept. 1918. Black and m/c. Temple of Heaven at l. W/bank name also in Russian on back.			
	a. *HARBIN. (S/M #C294-94a).*	5.00	20.00	60.00
	b. *SHANGHAI/HARBIN. (S/M #C294-94b).*	3.50	14.00	52.50
	c. As a. but red official 4-Chinese character ovpt. *(S/M #C294-94c).*	5.00	20.00	60.00
50	**50 CENTS = 5 CHIAO**			
	Sept. 1918. Green and m/c. Temple of Heaven at l. w/bank name also in Russian on back.			
	a. *HARBIN. (S/M #C294-95a).*	7.50	30.00	90.00
	b. *SHANGHAI/HARBIN. (S/M #C294-95b).*	8.50	35.00	105.00

		Good	Fine	XF
51A	**1 DOLLAR**			
	Sept. 1918. Back orange; similar to #51 but w/bank name also in Russian text. *HARBIN. (S/M #C294-100f).*			
	a. Issued note.	12.50	40.00	120.00
	s. Specimen.	—	Unc	125.00

		Good	Fine	XF
51B	**1 DOLLAR**			
	Sept. 1918. Orange on m/c unpt. 2 bldgs. at r. Back: olive-green. Printer: ABNC. *Shanghai.* Proof. *(S/M #C294-100.5).*	—	Unc	250.00

		Good	Fine	XF
51	**1 DOLLAR OR YUAN**			
	Sept. 1918. Temple of Heaven at ctr. Color, sign. and serial # varieties.			
	a. *AMOY-FUKIEN.* Green on m/c unpt. Back green. *(S/M #C294-100d).*	6.00	18.00	55.00
	b. *ANHWEI.* Back red-orange. *(S/M #C294-100a).*	15.00	45.00	135.00
	c. *CHEFOO-SHANTUNG.* Orange. *(S/M #C294-100-).*	15.00	45.00	135.00
	d. *CHEKIANG.* Orange on m/c unpt. Back dk. green. *(S/M #C294-100q).*	15.00	45.00	135.00
	e. *CHENGTU-SZECHUAN.* Back orange. *(S/M #C294-100q).*	15.00	45.00	135.00
	f. *FUKIEN.* Green. *(S/M #C294-100c).*	15.00	45.00	135.00
	g. *HANKOW.* Green. Back green. *(S/M #C294-100e).*	15.00	45.00	135.00
	h. *KALGAN.* Green. *(S/M #C294-100g).*	15.00	45.00	135.00
	i. *KIANGSI.* Orange on m/c unpt. Back orange. *(S/M #C294-100h).*	18.00	55.00	165.00
	j. *KIANGSU.* Brown. Back brown. *(S/M #C294-100i).*	15.00	45.00	135.00
	k. *PEKING.* Blue-black. Back black. *(S/M #C294-100j).*	15.00	45.00	135.00
	l. *SHANGHAI/PEKING.* Blue-black. Back blue-black. *(S/M #C294-100k).*	11.50	35.00	105.00
	m. *SHANGHAI.* Brown. Back blue. 3 sign varieties. *(S/M #C294-100k).*	4.00	12.00	36.00
	n. *SHANSI.* Back purple. *(S/M #C294-100m).*	18.00	55.00	165.00
	o. *SHANTUNG.* Orange on m/c unpt. Back orange. *(S/M #C294-100n).*	7.00	22.50	67.50
	p. *SZECHUAN.* Back red-orange. *(S/M #C294-100p).*	18.00	55.00	165.00
	q. *TIENTSIN.* Brown. 2 sign. varieties. *(S/M #C294-100r).*	6.50	20.00	60.00
	r. *TIENTSIN/KALGAN.* Green. Back green. *(S/M #C294-100s).*	7.00	22.50	67.50
	s. *TIENTSIN/PEKING.* Blue-black. *(S/M #C294-100-).*	15.00	45.00	135.00
	t. *TSINGTAO.* Back Orange. *(S/M #C294-100-).*	15.00	45.00	135.00
	u. *TSINGTAO/SHANTUNG.* Orange. *(S/M #C294-100-).*	15.00	45.00	135.00
	v. *KIUKIANG. (S/M #C294-100-).*	15.00	45.00	135.00
	w. *SHANTUNG WEIHAIWEI. (S/M #C294-100-).*	20.00	60.00	180.00
	s1. *KIATING/SZECHUAN.* Orange. Specimen. *(S/M #C294-).*	—	Unc	100.00

52A 5 DOLLARS

	GOOD	FINE	XF
Sept. 1918. Back brown; similar to #52 but w/bank name also in Russian text. *HARBIN. (S/M #C294-101f).*			
a. Issued note.	10.00	30.00	90.00
s. Specimen.	—	Unc	150.00

52B 5 DOLLARS

	GOOD	FINE	XF
Sept. 1918. Green on m/c unpt. 2 bldgs. at l. Back brown. *SHANGHAI. (S/M #C294-101.5).*			
a. Issued note.	40.00	125.00	375.00
s. Specimen.	—	Unc	250.00

52 5 DOLLARS OR YUAN

	GOOD	FINE	XF
Sept. 1918. Houses w/Peking pagoda at ctr. Color, sign. and serial # varieties. Local or National Currency.			
a. AMOY-FUKIEN. Purple. (S/M #C294-101d).	5.00	15.00	45.00
b. ANHWEI. Blue-black. Back olive-green. (S/M #C294-101a).	12.00	36.50	110.00
c. CHEKIANG. Green. Back blue. (S/M #C294-101b).	12.00	36.50	110.00
d. CHENGTU-SZECHUAN. Back green. (S/M #C294-101q).	12.00	36.50	110.00
e. FUKIEN. Purple. Back purple. Sign. varieties. (S/M #C294-101c).	12.00	36.50	110.00
f. HANKOW. Back brown. (S/M #C294-101e).	12.00	36.50	110.00
g. KALGAN. Back purple. (S/M #C294-101g).	12.00	36.50	110.00
h. KIANGSI. Back gray-brown. (S/M #C294-101h).	12.00	36.50	110.00
i. KIANGSU. Brown. Back red-orange. (S/M #C294-101i).	5.00	15.00	45.00
j. PEKING. Brown. (S/M #C294-101j).	10.00	30.00	90.00
k. SHANGHAI. Dk. blue. Sign. varieties. (S/M #C294-101k).	6.50	20.00	60.00
l. SHANGHAI/PEKING. Brown. (S/M #C294-101l).	7.50	22.50	67.50
m. SHANSI. Back orange. (S/M #C294-101m).	12.00	36.50	110.00
n. SHANTUNG. Green. Back dk. green. (S/M #C294-101n).	12.00	36.50	110.00
o. SZECHUAN. Back green. (S/M #C94-101p).	12.00	36.50	110.00
p. TIENTSIN. Back orange. Sign. varieities. (S/M #C294-101r).	5.50	17.50	55.00
q. TIENTSIN/KALGAN. (S/M #C294-101s).	15.00	45.00	135.00
r. TIENTSIN/PEKING. Brown. (S/M #C294-101-).	10.00	30.00	90.00
s. TSINGTAO/SHANTUNG. Green. (S/M #C294-100o).	15.00	45.00	135.00

53A 10 DOLLARS

	GOOD	FINE	XF
Sept. 1918. Back blue; similar to #53 but w/bank name also in Russian text. *HARBIN. (S/M #C294-102f).*			
a. Issued note.	20.00	60.00	180.00
s. Specimen.	—	Unc	175.00

53B 10 DOLLARS

	GOOD	FINE	XF
Sept. 1918. Brown on m/c unpt. 2 bldgs. at r. *SHANGHAI.* Specimen. (S/M #C294-102.3).	—	Unc	150.00

53 10 DOLLARS OR YUAN

	GOOD	FINE	XF
Sept. 1918. Various colors. Temple behind trees at ctr. Sign. varieties.			
a. AMOY-FUKIEN. Orange. (S/M #C294-102d).	5.50	16.00	48.00
b. ANHWEI. Back green. (S/M #C294-102a).	16.50	50.00	150.00
c. CHEFOO-SHANTUNG. Brown. (S/M #C294-102-).	16.50	50.00	150.00
d. CHEKIANG. Orange. Back red-brown. (S/M #C294-102b).	16.50	50.00	150.00
e. CHENGTU-SZECHUAN. Back brown. (S/M #C294-102q).	16.50	50.00	150.00
f. FUKIEN. Orange. Back red-orange. Sign. varieties. (S/M #C294-102c).	5.50	16.00	48.00
g. HANKOW. Dk. green. Back purple. (S/M #C294-102e).	16.50	50.00	150.00
h. KALGAN. Back orange. (S/M #C294-102g).	16.50	50.00	150.00
i. KIANGSI. Back blue. (S/M #C294-102h).	16.50	50.00	150.00
j. KIANGSU. Back blue-gray. (S/M #C294-102i).	16.50	50.00	150.00
k. PEKING. Green. (S/M #C294-102j).	16.50	50.00	150.00
l. SHANGHAI/PEKING. Back orange. (S/M #C294-102l).	16.50	50.00	150.00
m. SHANGHAI. Back red-orange. Sign. varieties. (S/M #C294-102k).	13.00	40.00	120.00
n. SHANTUNG. Brown. Back brown. (S/M #C294-102n).	8.00	24.00	72.00
o. SZECHUAN. Back red-brown. (S/M #C294-102p).	20.00	60.00	180.00
p. TIENTSIN. Green. Sign. varieties. (S/M #C294-102r).	5.50	16.00	48.00
q. TIENTSIN/KALGAN. (S/M #C294-102s).	6.50	20.00	60.00
r. TIENTSIN/PEKING. Green. (S/M #C294-102-).	5.50	16.00	48.00
s. TSINGTAU/SHANTUNG. Brown. (S/M #C294-102o).	16.50	50.00	150.00
t. WEIHAWAI-SHANTUNG. (S/M #C294-).	20.00	60.00	180.00
u. SHANSI. Back green. (S/M #C294-102m).	16.50	50.00	150.00

54 50 DOLLARS

	GOOD	FINE	XF
Sept. 1918. Purple on m/c unpt. 2 bldgs. at l. *SHANGHAI.* Proof. (S/M #C294-102.4).	—	Unc	300.00

54A 50 DOLLARS

	GOOD	FINE	XF
Yr. 7//1.5.1917. Black on brown, green and purple unpt. Gateways at l. Back green. *TIENTSIN.* Proof. (S/M #C294-102.5).	—	Unc	600.00

54B 100 DOLLARS

	GOOD	FINE	XF
Sept. 1918. Olive-green on m/c unpt. Back olive-green. *SHANGHAI.* Proof. (S/M #C294-102.5).	—	Unc	450.00

54C	100 DOLLARS	GOOD	FINE	XF
	Yr. 7 1.5.1917. Black on m/c unpt. Gateways at r. Back purple. TIENTSIN. (S/M #C294-103).	200.00	600.00	1200.

1919 ISSUE
#56-61 Printer: BEPP.

56	10 COPPER COINS	GOOD	FINE	XF
	March 1919. Brown. Temple and trees at shoreline at l. Back blue and red. Kiukiang. (S/M #C294-110).	10.00	40.00	120.00
57	50 COPPER COINS			
	March 1919. Violet.			
	a. Kiukiang. (S/M #C294-111a).	4.00	16.50	50.00
	b. Kalgan. (S/M #C294-111b).	4.00	16.50	50.00

58	1 YUAN	GOOD	FINE	XF
	May 1919. Dk. blue-black. Pavilion in park at ctr. Back brown on lt. blue unpt. HARBIN, MANCHURIA. (S/M #C294-120).			
	a. Issued note.	5.50	22.50	67.50
	r. Remainder, w/o serial #, sign. seals, w/ or w/o place name.	—	Unc	50.00

59	5 YUAN	GOOD	FINE	XF
	May 1919. Orange. Pavilion in park at ctr. Back purple on lt. yellow unpt. HARBIN, MANCHURIA. (S/M #C294-121).			
	a. Issued note.	10.00	30.00	125.00
	r. Remainder, w/o serial #, sign. seals or place name.	—	Unc	75.00
60	10 YUAN			
	May 1919. Dk. brown. Back brown on lt. green unpt. HARBIN, MANCHURIA. (S/M #C294-122).			
	a. Issued note.	10.00	25.00	110.00
	r. Remainder, w/o serial #, sign. seals or place name.	—	Unc	80.00

1920 ISSUE

61	100 COPPER COINS			
	1920. Orange. Kiukiang. (S/M #C294-130).		Reported Not Confirmed	

1924 ISSUE

62	10 YUAN	GOOD	FINE	XF
	1924. Purple. Houses and pagoda at shoreline at ctr. 3 sign. varieties. Back brown. Printer: ABNC. Shanghai. (S/M #C294-140).	5.50	22.50	67.50

1925 ISSUES
#62A-65 printer: W&S.

62A	10 CENTS			
	1925. Brown. Chenkiang. (S/M #C294-150).		Reported Not Confirmed	

63	10 CENTS	VG	VF	UNC
	1.7.1925. Brown. Pagoda by house at water's edge. Back blue. 7 sign. varieties. SHANGHAI. (S/M #C294-151).	3.00	9.00	27.50
64	20 CENTS			
	1.7.1925. Dk. blue on olive. Monument of Bull w/bridge in background at top. Back brown. 4 sign. varieties. SHANGHAI. (S/M #C294-152).			
	a. Issued note.	3.00	9.00	27.50
	s. Specimen.	3.00	9.00	27.50
65	50 CENTS			
	1.7.1925. Orange. Stag and man w/beard at top. Back green. SHANGHAI. (S/M #C294-153).			
	a. Issued note.	5.50	16.50	50.00
	s. Specimen.	5.50	16.50	50.00

1925 PROVISIONAL ISSUE
#65A-65C Fengtien-MUKDEN, MANCHURIA office. Printer: ABNC.
#65E and 65F ovpt: Liaoning on face; Promises to pay...Silver dollars... on back.

65A	1 DOLLAR	VG	VF	UNC
	1.7.1925. Green on m/c unpt. Temple of Heaven at ctr. Back olive-green. Proof. (S/M #C294-154).	—	Unc	200.00

65B	5 DOLLARS	VG	VF	UNC
	1.7.1925. Orange on m/c unpt. Temple and Peking pagoda at ctr. Back orange. Proof. (S/M #C294-155).	—	Unc	275.00

65C **10 DOLLARS**
1.7.1925. Blue on m/c unpt. Temple in woods at ctr. Back blue. Proof. *(S/M #C294-156).*

	VG	VF	UNC
	—	Unc	335.00

1925 ND PROVISIONAL ISSUE

#65E and 65F ovpt: *Liaoning on face; Promises to pay... Silver dollars... on back.*

65E **5 DOLLARS**
ND (old date - 1.7.1925). Ovpt. on #65Ba. Specimen. *(S/M #C294-158).*

		Unc	185.00

65F **10 DOLLARS**
ND (old date - 1.7.1925). Ovpt. on #65Ca. Specimen. *(S/M C294-159).*

	VG	VF	UNC
	—	Unc	225.00

1926 ISSUE

66 **5 YUAN**
1926. Black on m/c unpt. Temple and Peking Pagoda on hilltop at ctr. Back green on m/c unpt; bank at ctr. *SHANGHAI.* Printer: ABNC. Also various letter, numeral and Chinese character control ovpt.

		GOOD	FINE	XF
a.	Black sign. (3 varieties). *(S/M #C294-160a).*	3.00	15.00	45.00
b.	Red Sign. (5 varieties). *(S/M #C294-160b/i).*	2.50	12.50	37.50

1930 ISSUE

#67-69 printer: ABNC.

67 **1 DOLLAR**
Oct. 1930. Dk. green on red and m/c unpt. Temple of Heaven at ctr. *AMOY. (S/M #C294-170).*

	GOOD	FINE	XF
	4.00	20.00	60.00

68 **5 DOLLARS**
Oct. 1930. Purple on m/c unpt. Temple and Peking Pagoda at ctr. *AMOY.* 2 sign. varieties. *(S/M #C294-171).*

	GOOD	FINE	XF
	4.00	20.00	60.00

69 **10 DOLLARS**
Oct. 1930. Orange on m/c unpt. Temple behind trees at ctr. *AMOY.* 2 sign varieties. *(S/M #C294-172).*

	GOOD	FINE	XF
	5.00	25.00	75.00

1931 ISSUE

70 **5 YUAN**
Jan. 1931. Orange and black. Temple of Heaven at l., landscape, mountains at r. Bank on back. *TIENTSIN.* Printer: TDLR. *(S/M #C294-180).*

		VG	VF	UNC
a.	Serial # face only.	1.60	6.50	20.00
b.	Serial # face and back.	1.25	5.00	15.00

1934 ISSUE

#71-73 printer: TDLR.

71 **1 YUAN**
Feb. 1934. Yellow-brown. Colonnade, animal figures at ctr. Long stairway on back. *SHANTUNG. (S/M #C294-190).*

	VG	VF	UNC
	2.50	10.00	30.00

71A **1 YUAN**
1934. Red and brown. Farmer plowing w/oxen. *TIENTSIN. (S/M #C294-191).*

	VG	VF	UNC
	7.50	30.00	90.00

72 **5 YUAN**
Feb. 1934. Green. Portico behind trees at ctr. House in rocks on back.

a.	*SHANTUNG. (S/M #C294-192a).*	2.25	9.00	27.50
b.	*TSINGTAU/SHANTUNG. (S/M #C294-192b).*	3.75	15.00	45.00
c.	*CHEFOO/SHANTUNG. (S/M #C294-192c).*	10.00	40.00	120.00
d.	*WEI HAI WEI/SHANTUNG. (S/M #C294-192d).*	10.00	40.00	120.00

72A **5 YUAN**
1934. *TIENTSIN. (S/M #C294-193).*

	3.00	12.50	37.50

73 **10 YUAN**
Oct. 1934. Dk. green. Shepherd, sheep at ctr. Great Wall on back; pavilion at r. *TIENTSIN. (S/M #C294-194).*

	3.50	14.00	42.50

1935 FIRST ISSUE

74	**1 YUAN**	VG	VF	UNC
	1935. Dk. brown. Temple of Heaven at ctr. Back blue; junk 1 Yuan coin at ctr. Printer: W&S. *SHANGHAI*. W/o ovpt. (S/M #C294-200).			
	a. Issued note.	1.25	5.00	15.00
	b. Ovpt: *TN* on face.	1.25	5.00	15.00
	c. Ovpt: *TN* on face and back.	1.25	5.00	15.00

75	**10 YUAN**	VG	VF	UNC
	Jan. 1935. Brown. Temple behind trees at ctr. *SHANTUNG*. Printer: TDLR. (S/M #C294-204).	3.50	14.00	42.50

1935 SECOND ISSUE

#76 and #77 printer: TDLR.

NOTE: The "Bottle Pagoda" structure was erected in Peking as a complimentary gesture towards Tibet.

76	**1 YUAN**	VG	VF	UNC
	March 1935. Brown. Farmer plowing w/horse at l., irrigation system at r. Junk 1 Yuan coin at ctr. on back. *TIENTSIN*. (S/M #C294-201).	1.00	4.00	12.00

77	**5 YUAN**	VG	VF	UNC
	March 1935. Black on m/c unpt. SYS at l., bridge to Bottle Pagoda at r. Back: deep green on pale yellow orange unpt. w/bank bldg. at ctr.			
	a. *SHANGHAI*. (S/M #C294-202).	1.00	4.00	12.00
	b. W/o *SHANGHAI*. (S/M #C294-203).	.75	3.00	9.00

1936 ISSUE

78	**1 YUAN**	VG	VF	UNC
	May 1936. Green on m/c unpt. SYS at l. Back blue; junk 1-Yuan coin at ctr. Printer: TDLR. (S/M #C294-210).	.80	3.25	10.00

1937 ISSUE

#79-81 printer: TDLR.

79	**1 YUAN**	VG	VF	UNC
	1937. Blue. SYS at l. Skyscraper at r. on back. (S/M #C294-220).	.20	.65	2.00

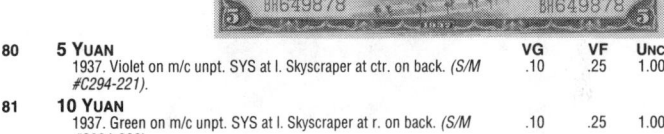

80	**5 YUAN**	VG	VF	UNC
	1937. Violet on m/c unpt. SYS at l. Skyscraper at ctr. on back. (S/M #C294-221).	.10	.25	1.00
81	**10 YUAN**			
	1937. Green on m/c unpt. SYS at l. Skyscraper at r. on back. (S/M #C294-222).	.10	.25	1.00

1939 ISSUE

#81A-81C portr. Liao Chung-kai at l. Bank bldg. at r. on back. Printer: ABNC.

81A	**1 YUAN**	VG	VF	UNC
	1939. Purple on m/c unpt. (S/M #C294-223).			
	a. Unsigned remainder.	50.00	150.00	300.00
	p. Proof.	—	—	250.00

81B	**5 YUAN**	VG	VF	UNC
	1939. Brown and m/c. Proof. (S/M #C294-224).	—	—	250.00
81C	**10 YUAN**			
	1939. Black and m/c. Back blue-gray. Proof. (S/M #C294-225).	—	—	275.00

1940 ISSUE

#84-88 portr. SYS at l., Temple of Heaven at r. on back. Printer: ABNC.

NOTE: #85 w/ovpt: *SHENSI PROVINCE* and *CHUNGKING* have been determined to be modern fantasies.

NOTE: #88 ovpt: *SHENSI PROVINCE* is believed to be a modern fantasy.

			VG	VF	UNC
84	**5 YUAN**				
	1940. Blue on m/c unpt. (S/M #C294-240).		.10	.25	1.00
85	**10 YUAN**				
	1940. Red on m/c unpt.				
		a. Serial # on face. (S/M #C294-241a).	.75	4.00	10.00
		b. Serial # on face and back. (S/M #C294-241b).	.10	.25	1.00
86	**25 YUAN**				
	1940. Green on m/c unpt. (S/M #C294-242).		3.75	15.00	45.00
87	**50 YUAN**				
	1940. Brown on m/c unpt.				
		a. Serial # on face. (S/M #C294-243c).	3.75	15.00	45.00
		b. Serial # on face and on back. (S/M #C294-243d).	3.75	15.00	45.00
		c. Serial # and *CHUNGKING* on face. *CHUNGKING* on back. (S/M #C294-243b).	1.00	3.00	10.00
		d. Serial # and *CHUNGKING* on face. Serial # and *CHUNGKING* on back. (S/M #C294-243b).	1.00	3.00	10.00

			VG	VF	UNC
88	**100 YUAN**				
	1940. Purple on m/c unpt.				
		a. Serial # on face and back. (S/M #C294-244d).	.50	1.75	9.00
		b. Serial # and *Chungking* at l. and r. on face. *CHUNGKING* on back. (S/M #C294-244a).	.35	1.25	6.00
		c. Serial # and *Chungking* at l. and r. on face. Serial # and *CHUNGKING* on back. (S/M #C294-244b).	.25	1.00	4.00

			VG	VF	UNC
82	**10 CENTS**				
	ND (1940). Red. Temple of Heaven at r. Back brown and green. Chinese printer: TTBC. (S/M #C294-230).		.25	.75	3.50

			VG	VF	UNC
83	**20 CENTS**				
	ND (1940). Blue. Great Wall at l. Back green and brown-violet. Chinese printer: TTBC. (S/M #C294-231).		.25	.75	3.50

1941 ISSUE

NOTE: For #93 w/ovpt: *HONG KONG GOVERNMENT* see Hong Kong #317.

			VG	VF	UNC
91	**1 YUAN**				
	1941. Blue on m/c unpt. SYS at top. Celestial Temple at bottom on back. Printer: ABNC. (S/M #C294-260).				
		a. Issued note.	6.00	25.00	100.00
		s. Specimen.	—	—	100.00
92	**5 YUAN**				
	1941. Red on m/c unpt. Like #91. Printer: ABNC. (S/M #C294-261).				
		a. Issued note.	6.00	25.00	100.00
		s. Specimen.	—	—	100.00

			VG	VF	UNC
93	**5 YUAN**				
	1941. Blue on m/c unpt. Temple at r. Gateway at r. on back. Printer: CMPA. (S/M #C294-262).		3.75	15.00	60.00
94	**10 YUAN**				
	1941. Purple on m/c unpt. Similar to #91. Printer: ABNC. (S/M #C294-264).				
		a. Issued note.	6.50	25.00	100.00
		s. Specimen.	—	—	75.00
95	**10 YUAN**				
	1941. Red on m/c unpt. SYS at ctr. Chinese printer: DTBC. (S/M #C294-263).		2.25	9.00	36.00
96	**100 YUAN**				
	1941. Similar to #91. Printer: ABNC. (S/M #C294-265).				
		a. Issued note.	22.50	90.00	225.00
		s. Specimen.	—	—	175.00
97	**500 YUAN**				
	1941. Brown on m/c unpt. Similar to #91. Printer: ABNC. (S/M #C294-266).				
		a. Issued note.	25.00	100.00	250.00
		s. Specimen.	—	—	185.00
89	**10 CENTS**				
	1941. Green. Temple of Heaven at top. Vertical format. (S/M #C294-250).				
		a. Issued note.	3.50	17.50	75.00
		s. Specimen.	—	—	75.00
90	**20 CENTS**				
	1941. Red on yellow and pink unpt. Temple of Heaven at top. Vertical format. (S/M #C294-251).				
		a. Issued note.	3.50	17.50	75.00
		s. Specimen.	—	—	75.00

1942 ISSUE

98 **50 YUAN**
1942. Green and m/c. Steam passenger train at l. Chinese printer: TTBC. *(S/M #C294-270).*

VG	VF	UNC
2.00	7.50	35.00

99 **500 YUAN**
1942. Olive-green and m/c. SYS at l. Printer: ABNC. *(S/M #C294-271).*

VG	VF	UNC
5.00	25.00	100.00

100 **1000 YUAN**
1942. Green and m/c. Like #99. Printer: ABNC. *(S/M #C294-272).*

	VG	VF	UNC
a. Issued note.	7.00	35.00	125.00
s. Specimen.	—	—	135.00

BANK OF COMMUNICATIONS
БАНКЪ оЧТИ СООЩЕНЯ

交通銀行

Chiao T'ung Yin Hang

Formerly the General Bank of Communications. Also see #A13A-A19D.

1912 ISSUE
#102-109 sailing ships dockside by depot and train at bottom ctr.

102 **50 CENTS**
1912. YINGKOW. *(S/M #C126-10).*

GOOD	FINE	XF
32.50	100.00	300.00

104 **1 DOLLAR**
1912. Green and yellow. Back blue and red.

	GOOD	FINE	XF
a. PEKING. *(S/M #C126-20a).*	26.50	80.00	240.00
b. SHANGHAI. *(S/M #C126-20b).*	26.50	80.00	240.00
c. TSINAN *(S/M #C126-20c).*	—	—	—
d. HONAN. Perforated and ovpt: SPECIMEN. *(S/M #C126-).*	—	Unc	200.00

105 **1 DOLLAR**
1.9.1912. Green and m/c. Back blue and green. Specimen. *(S/M #C126-21).*

GOOD	FINE	XF
—	Unc	200.00

103 **100 CENTS**
1912. *(S/M #C126-).*

	GOOD	FINE	XF
a. MUKDEN. *(S/M #C126-11).*	26.50	80.00	240.00
b. CHANGCHUN. *(S/M #C126-).*	26.50	80.00	240.00
c. YINGKOW. *(S/M #C126-).*	26.50	80.00	240.00

107 **5 DOLLARS**
1.9.1912. Blue and m/c. Back brown and green.

	GOOD	FINE	XF
a. CHANGCHUN. Cancelled remainder. *(S/M #C126-24a).*	—	—	120.00
b. HONAN. Perforated and ovpt. SPECIMEN. *(S/M # C126-24b).*	—	Unc	150.00
c. PEKING. *(S/M #C126-23).*	26.50	80.00	240.00
d. YINGKOW. Specimen. *(S/M #C126-22).*	—	Unc	200.00
e. W/o place name. Specimen. *(S/M #C126-24c).*	—	Unc	150.00

106 **500 CENTS**
1.9.1912. Purple and blue on yellow unpt. *Mukden* handstamp. *(S/M #C126-215).*

GOOD	FINE	XF

108 **10 DOLLARS**
1.9.1912. Blue. Crossed flags at top ctr., steam passenger train below. Back brown.

	GOOD	FINE	XF
a. HONAN. Perforated and ovpt. SPECIMEN. *(S/M #C126-25a).*	—	Unc	250.00
b. KALGAN. *(S/M #C126-25b)*	—	—	—
c. TIENTSIN. *(S/M #C126-25c).*	50.00	150.00	450.00
d. W/o place name. Specimen. *(S/M #C126-25d).*	—	Unc	225.00

107A **1000 CENTS**
1.9.1912. Green w/black text. FENGTIEN. *(S/M #C126-).*

109 **100 DOLLARS**
1.9.1912. *(S/M #C126-26).*

GOOD	FINE	XF
75.00	225.00	675.00

1913 ISSUE
#110-111C printer: ABNC. Specimens were also prepared from notes w/normal serial numbers.

110 1 DOLLAR

1.7.1913. Red-orange on m/c unpt. Electric direct current generator at ctr. Sailing ship at ctr. on back.

		GOOD	FINE	XF
a.	CHANGCHUN. Chinese ovpt. on face. English ovpt: *N.B. Payable in subsidiary (silver) coins....* on back. *(S/M #C126-31d)*.	26.50	80.00	240.00
b.	CHUNGKING. Specimen. *(S/M #C126-31d)*.	—	Unc	150.00
c.	HUNAN. *(S/M #C126-31a)*.	26.50	80.00	240.00
d.	Fengtien//MUKDEN. Chinese ovpt. on face. English ovpt: *N.B. This note is exchangeable...* on back. *(S/M #C126-)*.	26.50	80.00	240.00
e.	PUKOW. *(S/M #C126-31e)*.	26.50	80.00	240.00
f.	TIENTSIN. *(S/M #C126-30a)*.	32.50	100.00	300.00
g.	TSITSIHAR. Chinese ovpt. on face. English ovpt.: *N.B. Payable in subsidiary (silver) coins....* on back. Specimen. *(S/M #C126-31f)*.	—	Unc	150.00
h.	YOCHOW/KALGAN. Specimen. *(S/M #C126-31f)*.	—	Unc	150.00
i.	PEKING *(S/M #C126-31g)*.	26.50	80.00	240.00
j.	WUSIH. Specimen. *(S/M #C126-30b)*.	—	Unc	150.00
k.	CHEFOO. *(S/M #C126-31h)*.	—	—	—
l.	LUNGKOW/CHEFOO. *(S/M #C126-30i)*.	26.50	80.00	240.00
m.	HANKOW. *(S/M #C126-30m)*.	26.50	80.00	240.00

111 5 DOLLARS

1.7.1913. Green on m/c unpt. Steam passenger train in ravine at l. Back green; steam passenger train at ctr.

		GOOD	FINE	XF
a.	CHANGCHUN. Chinese ovpt. on face. English ovpt: *N.B. Payable in subsidiary (silver) coins...* on back. Specimen. *(S/M #C126-32b)*.	—	Unc	150.00
b.	CHUNGKING. Specimen. *(S/M #C126-32c)*.	—	Unc	150.00
c.	HUNAN. Specimen. *(S/M #C126-32a)*.	—	Unc	150.00
d.	TIENTSIN. Specimen. *(S/M #C126-32d)*.	—	Unc	150.00
e.	CHEFOO. Specimen. *(S/M #C126-32e)*.	—	Unc	150.00
f.	HANKOW. Specimen. *(S/M #C126-32f)*.	—	Unc	150.00
g.	HONAN. Specimen. *(S/M #C126-32g)*.	—	Unc	150.00
h.	KALGAN. Specimen. *(S/M #C126-32h)*.	—	Unc	150.00
i.	Fengtien//MUKDEN. Chinese ovpt. on face. English ovpt: *N.B. This note is exchangeable...* on back. Specimen. *(S/M #C126-32i)*.	—	Unc	150.00
j.	PEKING. Specimen. *(S/M #C126-32j)*.	—	Unc	150.00
k.	PUKOW. Specimen. *(S/M #C126-32k)*.	—	Unc	150.00
l.	TSITSIHAR. Chinese ovpt. on face. English ovpt: *N.B. Payable in subsidiary (silver) coins...* on back. Specimen. *(S/M #C126-326)*.	—	Unc	150.00
m.	YOCHOW. Specimen. *(S/M #C126-32m)*.	—	Unc	150.00
n.	SHANGHAI. *(S/M #C126-32n)*.	50.00	120.00	250.00

111A 10 DOLLARS

1.7.1913. Purple and m/c. Steam passenger train in ravine at l. Back green; steam passenger train at ctr.

		GOOD	FINE	XF
a.	HUNAN. *(S/M #C126-40a)*.	40.00	120.00	360.00
b.	CHANGCHUN. Chinese ovpt. on face. English ovpt: *N.B. Payable in subsidiary (silver) coins...* on back. *(S/M #C126-40b)*.	—	Unc	150.00
c.	ANHUI. Specimen. *(S/M #C126-40c)*.	—	Unc	150.00
d.	LUNGKOW/CHEFOO. *(S/M #C126-40d)*.	—	Unc	150.00
e.	CHUNGKING. Specimen. *(S/M #126-40e)*.	—	Unc	150.00
f.	Fengtien//MUKDEN. Chinese ovpt. on face. English ovpt: *N.B. this note is exchangeable...* on back. *(S/M #C126-40f)*.	—	Unc	150.00
g.	HANKOW. Specimen. *(S/M #C126-40g)*.	—	Unc	150.00
h.	KALGAN. Specimen. *(S/M #C126-40h)*.	—	Unc	150.00
i.	TIENTSIN. Specimen. *(S/M #C126-40i)*.	—	Unc	150.00
j.	TSITSIHAR. Chinese ovpt. on face. English ovpt: *N.B. Payable in subsidiary (silver) coins...* on back. Specimen. *(S/M #C126-40j)*.	—	Unc	150.00
k.	WUSIH. Specimen. *(S/M #C126-40k)*.	—	Unc	150.00

111B 50 DOLLARS

1.7.1913. Blue and m/c. Steam passenger train at ctr. Back blue; w/Maritime Customs bldg., street car at ctr.

		GOOD	FINE	XF
a.	CHANGCHUN. Chinese ovpt. on face. English ovpt: *N.B. Payable in subsidiary (silver) coins...* on back. Specimen. *(S/M #C126-40.5a)*.	—	Unc	240.00
b.	LUNGKOW/CHEFOO. Specimen. *(S/M #C126-40.5b)*.	—	Unc	240.00
c.	KALGAN. Specimen. *(S/M #C126-40.5c)*.	—	Unc	240.00
d.	FENGTIEN. Specimen. *(S/M #C126-40.5d)*.	—	Unc	240.00
e.	HSUCHOW. *(S/M #C126-40.5e)*.	—	—	—

111C 100 DOLLARS

1.7.1913. Blue and m/c. Ship at dockside, steam train at ctr. Back: blue w/sailing ships at ctr.

		GOOD	FINE	XF
a.	CHANGCHUN. Chinese ovpt. on face. English ovpt: *N.B. Payable in subsidiary (silver) coins...* on back. *(S/M #C126-41b)*.	—	Unc	300.00
b.	Fengtien/MUKDEN. Chinese ovpt. on face. English ovpt: *N.B. This note is exchangeable...* on back. Specimen. *(S/M #C126-41d)*.	—	Unc	300.00
c.	HANKOW. Specimen. *(S/M #C126-41c)*.	—	Unc	300.00
d.	HUNAN. Specimen. *(S/M #C126-41a)*.	—	Unc	300.00
e.	KIANGSU. *(S/M #C126-41e)*.	—	—	—

1914 ISSUE

#112-115 printer: BEPP.

#116-120 printer: ABNC.

NOTE: The original issues have Chinese script signatures while the more common reissues have red Chinese sign. seals on face. All have handwritten English sign. (i.e. *S.M. Tong - T.S. Wong*) on back. Various Western control letter, numeral or Chinese characters are encountered on earlier issues, but rarely on the WWII reissues. In addition, earlier issues w/various banking commercial and private handstamps are encountered and command a small premium.

NOTE: #118q w/ovpt: *KANSU PROVINCE/SHANGHAI* is a modern fabrication.

112	5 FEN	GOOD	FINE	XF
	ND (1914). Green and m/c.			
a.	HARBIN. Specimen. (S/M #C126-50a).	—	Unc	45.00
b.	KALGAN. (S/M #C126-50b).	10.00	30.00	90.00
c.	TAIHEIHO. (S/M #C126-50c).	12.50	35.00	105.00
d.	TULUNNOERH. (S/M #C126-50d).	12.50	35.00	105.00
e.	W/o place name. Specimen. (S/M #C126-50).	—	Unc	37.50

113	1 CHOH (CHIAO)	GOOD	FINE	XF
	ND (1914). Black and red-brown on lt. green unpt.			
a.	HARBIN. (S/M #C126-51d).	5.00	15.00	45.00
b.	KALGAN. (S/M #C126-51e).	5.50	16.00	48.00
c.	SHIHKIACHWANG. (S/M #C126-51a).	6.50	20.00	60.00
d.	TSINGTAU. (S/M #C126-51b).	5.50	16.00	48.00
e.	TULUNNOERH. (S/M #C126-51c).	6.50	20.00	60.00
f.	WEIHAIWEI. (S/M #C126-f).	5.50	16.00	48.00
g.	WEIHAIWEI/HARBIN. (S/M #C126-51g).	5.50	16.00	48.00
h.	W/o place name. Specimen. (S/M #C126-51).	—	Unc	75.00

114	2 CHOH (CHIAO)	GOOD	FINE	XF
	ND (1914). Blue-black and blue-gray on pink unpt. Similar to #113.			
a.	HARBIN. Specimen. (S/M #C126-52c).	—	Unc	75.00
b.	KALGAN. (S/M #C126-52a).	5.00	15.00	45.00
c.	TAIHEIHO. (S/M #C126-52d).	5.00	15.00	45.00
d.	TSINGTAU. (S/M #C126-52e).	5.00	15.00	45.00
e.	TULUNNOERH. (S/M #C126-52f).	5.00	15.00	45.00
f.	WEIHAIWEI/HARBIN. (S/M #C126-52b).	5.00	15.00	45.00
g.	PAOTOW. (S/M #C126-52g).	5.00	15.00	45.00
h.	WEIHAIWEI. (S/M #C126-52h).	5.00	15.00	45.00
i.	W/o place name. Specimen. (S/M #C126-52).	—	Unc	75.00

115	5 CHOH (CHIAO)	GOOD	FINE	XF
	ND (1914). Brown. Similar to #113.			
a.	HARBIN. Specimen. (S/M #C126-53a).	—	Unc	75.00
b.	KALGAN. (S/M #C126-54b).	5.00	15.00	45.00
c.	TSINGTAU. (S/M #C126-54c).	5.00	15.00	45.00
d.	WEIHAIWEI. (S/M #C126-54d).	5.00	15.00	45.00
e.	W/o place name. Specimen. (S/M #C126-54).	—	Unc	75.00

116	1 YUAN	GOOD	FINE	XF
	1.10.1914. Steam passenger train in ravine at ctr. Sailing ship on back. Also w/various ovpt.			
a.	AMOY. (S/M #C126-60).	8.50	26.50	80.00
b.	CHANGCHUN. (S/M #C126-63).	10.00	30.00	90.00
c.	CHEFOO. Dk. brown and m/c. (S/M #C126-61).	10.00	30.00	90.00
d.	CHEKIANG. (S/M #C126-62).	10.00	30.00	90.00
e.	CHUNGKING. Violet and m/c. (S/M #C126-64).	1.50	5.00	15.00
f.	HANKOW. Brown and m/c. (S/M #C126-65).	10.00	30.00	90.00
g.	HONAN. (S/M #C126-66).	10.00	30.00	90.00
h.	KALGAN. Orange and m/c. (S/M #C126-67).	10.00	30.00	90.00
i.	KIANGSU. (S/M #C126-70).	10.00	30.00	90.00
k.	KIUKIANG. Dk. brown and m/c. (S/M #C126-71).	10.00	30.00	90.00
l.	PUKOW. Dk. brown and m/c. (S/M #C126-72).	10.00	30.00	90.00
m.	SHANGHAI. Purple and m/c. (S/M #C126-73).	.30	1.00	3.00
n.	SHANGHAI. Dk. brown and m/c. 2 sign. varieties. (S/M #C126-74).	10.00	30.00	90.00
o.	SHANGHAI. Blue and m/c. (S/M #C126-75).	1.00	3.00	9.00
p.	SHANTUNG. (S/M #C126-76).	1.00	3.00	9.00
q.	SIAN. Violet and m/c. (S/M #C126-77).	10.00	30.00	90.00
r.	TIENTSIN. Purple and m/c. (S/M #C126-78).	1.00	3.00	9.00
s.	TSINGTAO. Dk. brown and m/c. (S/M #C126-79).	10.00	30.00	90.00
t.	SHANGHAI. Violet and m/c. Red control letter P at l. and r. (S/M #C126-73a).	1.65	5.00	15.00
u.	TULUNNOERH. Brown and m/c. Mongol text at l. and r. (S/M #C126-79.6).	—	—	—
v.	W/o place name. Specimen. (S/M #C126-).	—	Unc	50.00

117	5 YUAN	GOOD	FINE	XF
	1.10.1914. Steam passenger train at ctr. Post Office at ctr. on back. Also w/various ovpt.			
a.	AMOY. Dk. brown and m/c. (S/M #C126-80).	3.25	10.00	30.00
b.	CHANGCHUN. (S/M #C126-84).	6.50	20.00	60.00
c.	CHEFOO. (S/M #C126-82).	6.50	20.00	60.00
d.	CHEKIANG. (S/M #C126-83).	6.50	20.00	60.00
e.	CHUNGKING. Dk. brown and m/c. (S/M #C126-85).	1.75	5.50	17.50
f.	FOOCHOW/AMOY. Dk. brown and m/c. (S/M #C126-81).	8.00	25.00	75.00
g.	HANKOW. (S/M #C126-86).	8.00	25.00	75.00
h.	HONAN. Blue-black and m/c. (S/M #C126-87).	8.00	25.00	75.00
i.	KALGAN. Green on m/c unpt. (S/M #C126-88).	9.00	27.50	85.00
k.	KIANGSU. (S/M #C126-90).	8.00	25.00	75.00
l.	KIUKIANG. Blue and m/c. (S/M #C126-91).	9.00	27.50	85.00
m.	PUKOW. (S/M #C126-92).	9.00	27.50	85.00
n.	SHANGHAI. Dk. brown and m/c. Shanghai ovpt. in black w/red sign. seals. (S/M #C126-93a).	—	Unc	2.50
o.	SHANGHAI. Dk. brown and m/c. Shanghai ovpt. and script sign. in blue-black. (S/M #C126-93).	2.00	6.00	30.00
p.	SHANTUNG. Dk. brown and m/c. (S/M #C126-).	2.00	6.50	20.00
q.	SHANTUNG. Blue-black and m/c. (S/M #C126-94).	2.00	6.50	20.00
r.	SIAN. Orange and m/c. (S/M #C126-95).	4.00	12.00	36.00
s.	TIENTSIN. Red and m/c. (S/M #C126-96).	3.25	10.00	30.00
t.	TIENTSIN. Dk. brown and m/c. (S/M #C126-99).	1.00	3.00	10.00
u.	TSINGTAU. Dk. blue and m/c. (S/M #C126-97).	8.00	25.00	75.00
v.	TULUNNOERH. Mongol text at l. and r. (S/M #C126-98).	—	—	—
w.	SHANGHAI. Blue and m/c. (S/M #C126-).	3.25	10.00	30.00
x.	SHANGHAI. Dk. brown and m/c. Red control letter P at l. and r. (S/M #C126-93b).	—	Unc	2.50
y.	SHANGHAI. Black and m/c. (S/M #C126-).	6.00	15.00	85.00

118	10 YUAN	GOOD	FINE	XF
	1.10.1914. Maritime Customs bldg., streetcar at ctr. Ship at dockside, steam passenger train at ctr. on back. Also w/various ovpt.			
a.	AMOY. Blue and m/c. (S/M #C126-100).	2.50	8.00	25.00
b.	AMOY. Red and m/c. (S/M #C126-101).	2.75	8.00	25.00
c.	CHANGCHUN. (S/M #C126-104).	8.00	25.00	75.00
d.	CHEFOO. (S/M #C126-102).	8.00	25.00	75.00
e.	CHEKIANG. (S/M #C126-103).	8.00	25.00	75.00
f.	CHUNGKING. Red and m/c. (S/M #C126-105).	1.25	4.00	12.50
g.	HANKOW. (S/M #C126-106).	8.00	25.00	75.00
h.	HONAN. (S/M #C126-107).	6.50	20.00	60.00
i.	KALGAN. Orange and m/c. (S/M #C126-110).	10.00	30.00	90.00
j.	KALGAN. Green and m/c. (S/M #C126-111).	10.00	30.00	90.00
k.	KANSU. (S/M #C126-109).	12.50	40.00	120.00
l.	KIUKIANG. Green and m/c. (S/M #C126-112).	10.00	30.00	90.00
m.	PUKOW. (S/M #C126-113).	10.00	30.00	90.00
n.	SHANGHAI. Green and m/c. (S/M #C126-114).	3.00	10.00	30.00
o.	SHANGHAI. Red and m/c. Shanghai and sign. in blue-black. (S/M #C126-115).	—	Unc	3.00
p.	SHANGHAI. Red and m/c. Shanghai in black w/red sign. seals. (S/M #C126-115a).	—	Unc	1.50
q.	SHANGHAI. Red and m/c. Shanghai in blue-black w/red sign. seals. (S/M #C126-115b).	—	Unc	1.75
r.	SHANTUNG. Red and m/c. (S/M #C126-116).	1.00	3.00	10.00
s.	SIAN. (S/M #C126-117).	10.00	30.00	90.00
t.	TIENTSIN. Purple and (S/M #C126-120).	1.00	3.00	10.00
u.	SHANGHAI. Red and m/c. Shanghai in black w/red sign. seals and red control letter P at l. and r. (S/M #C126-115a).	—	Unc	3.00

119	50 YUAN	GOOD	FINE	XF
	1.10.1914. Mountain landscape w/2 steam freight trains at ctr. Ships at ctr. on back.			
a.	CHUNGKING. Orange and m/c. (S/M #C126-121).	2.00	6.50	20.00
b.	KALGAN. Orange and m/c. (S/M #C126-122).	12.50	37.50	115.00
c.	SHANGHAI. Orange and m/c. (S/M #C126-123).	2.00	6.50	20.00
d.	TIENTSIN. (S/M #C126-).	10.00	30.00	90.00
e.	KIUKIANG. Orange and m/c. Specimen. (S/M #C126-).	—	Unc	80.00

120	100 YUAN	GOOD	FINE	XF
	1.10.1914. Purple and m/c. Steam passenger train crossing bridge at ctr. Steam passenger train at ctr. on back.			
a.	CHUNGKING. (S/M #C126-124).	3.00	10.00	30.00
b.	KALGAN. (S/M #C126-125).	15.00	45.00	135.00
c.	SHANGHAI. (S/M #C126-126).	2.00	5.00	20.00
d.	TIENTSIN. (S/M #C126-).	8.00	25.00	75.00
e.	KIUKIANG. Specimen. (S/M #C126-).	—	Unc	100.00

1915 ISSUE
#121-122B printer: ABNC.

121	50 CENTS	GOOD	FINE	XF
	1.1.1915. Black. Ship at l. CHANGCHUN. (S/M #C126-).	16.50	50.00	150.00

122	100 CENTS	GOOD	FINE	XF
	1.1.1915. Black. Steam locomotive at r. CHANGCHUN. (S/M #C126-).	13.00	40.00	120.00

122A	500 CENTS	GOOD	FINE	XF
	1.1.1915. Gray. Steam passenger train in mountain pass at l. YINGKOW. Specimen. (S/M #C126-).	—	Unc	100.00

122B	1000 CENTS	GOOD	FINE	XF
	1.1.1915. Gray. Steam passenger train at r. YINGKOW. Specimen. (S/M #C126-).	—	Unc	100.00

1917 ISSUE

123	10 CENTS	GOOD	FINE	XF
	1.8.1917. Orange. CHANGCHUN. (S/M #C126-).	8.00	25.00	75.00

124	20 CENTS	GOOD	FINE	XF
	1.8.1917. Black. River view at ctr. CHANGCHUN. (S/M #C126-).	10.00	30.00	90.00

124A 50 CENTS
1.8.1917. Green. Steam passenger train at ctr. Back green. *MUKDEN.*
Specimen. *(S/M #C126-).*

	GOOD	FINE	XF
	—	Unc	125.00

1919 ISSUE
#125-127 printer: BEPP.

125 1 YUAN
1.7.1919. Blue. Village near mountain at ctr. Back brown and green.
HARBIN. 2 sign. varieties. *(S/M #C126-131).*

	GOOD	FINE	XF
a. Issued note.	8.00	25.00	75.00
r. Remainder w/o serial # or place name.	—	Unc	65.00

126 5 YUAN
1.7.1919. Green. Bridge across brook. Back brown and green.

	GOOD	FINE	XF
a. *HARBIN. (S/M #C126-132).*	11.50	35.00	105.00
b. *TAHEIHO.* Specimen. *(S/M #C126-).*	—	Unc	120.00
r. Remainder w/o place name. *(S/M #C126-).*	—	Unc	75.00

127 10 YUAN
1.7.1919. Pagoda near mountain. Back: brown and orange.

	GOOD	FINE	XF
a. *HARBIN.* Cancelled. *(S/M #C126-133).*	8.00	25.00	75.00
b. *TAHEIHO.* Specimen. *(S/M #C126-).*	—	Unc	100.00

1920 HARBIN ISSUE
#128-130B similar to #116-120 but w/bank name, office of issue and denomination also in Russian text.
Printer: ABNC.

128 1 YUAN
1.12.1920. Black. Similar to #116. Red official 4-Chinese character
ovpt. on face. 2 sign. varieties. *HARBIN. (S/M #C126-140).*

	VG	VF	UNC
	16.50	50.00	150.00

129 5 YUAN
1.12.1920. Similar to #117. Red official 4-Chinese character ovpt. on
face. *HARBIN. (S/M #C126-141).*

	VG	VF	UNC
	23.00	70.00	210.00

130 10 YUAN
1.12.1920. Similar to #118. Red official 4-Chinese character ovpt. on
face. *HARBIN. (S/M #C126-142).*

	VG	VF	UNC
	27.50	82.50	250.00

130A 50 YUAN
1.12.1920. Similar to #119. *HARBIN.* Proof. *(S/M #C126-143).*

	VG	VF	UNC
	—	—	185.00

130B 100 YUAN
1.12.1920. Similar to #120. *HARBIN.* Proof. *(S/M #C126-144).*

	VG	VF	UNC
	—	—	250.00

1923 ISSUE
#131-133 printer: ABNC.

131 **1 DOLLAR**

	VG	VF	UNC
1.1.1923. Orange and m/c. Electric direct current generator at ctr. Sailing ship on back. *FENGTIEN PROVINCE*. Specimen. *(S/M #C126-150)*.	—	—	125.00

132 **5 DOLLARS**

	VG	VF	UNC
1.1.1923. Green and m/c. Steam passenger train at ctr. Steam passenger train at ctr. on back. *FENGTIEN PROVINCE*. Specimen. *(S/M #C126-151)*.	—	—	125.00

133 **10 DOLLARS**

	VG	VF	UNC
1.1.1923. Purple and m/c. Steam passenger train at ctr. Back purple; bank bldg. at ctr. *FENGTIEN PROVINCE*. *(S/M #C126-152)*.	20.00	60.00	180.00

1924 ISSUE
#134-137 printer: W&S.

134 **1 YUAN**

	GOOD	FINE	XF
1.7.1924. Brown. Steam passenger train at ctr. Bank bldg. at ctr. on back. *SHANGHAI*. *(S/M #C126-160)*.	4.00	12.00	36.00

135 **5 YUAN**

	GOOD	FINE	XF
1.7.1924. Black-brown. Steam passenger train at ctr. Bank bldg. at ctr. on back.			
a. KIUKIANG. *(S/M #C126-)*.	12.00	36.00	110.00
b. SHANGHAI. *(S/M #C126-161)*.	5.00	15.00	45.00

136 **10 YUAN**

	GOOD	FINE	XF
1.7.1924. Green. Ship dockside. Steam passenger train at ctr. Back green; bank bldg. at ctr. *SHANGHAI*. *(S/M #C126-162)*.	7.50	22.50	67.50

137 **20 YUAN**

	GOOD	FINE	XF
1.7.1924. Blue. Ship, airplane, steam locomotive and truck at ctr.			
a. SHANGHAI. *(S/M #C126-)*.	55.00	165.00	500.00
s. W/o place name. Specimen. *(S/M #C126-163)*.	—	Unc	350.00

1925 ISSUE
#138-140 printer: BEPP.

138 **10 CENTS**

	GOOD	FINE	XF
1.7.1925. Green. Steamship at ctr.			
a. HARBIN. *(S/M #C126-170a)*.	5.00	20.00	60.00
b. SHANGHAI. *(S/M #C126-)*.	5.50	16.50	50.00
c. TSINGTAU. *(S/M #C126-170b)*.	5.50	16.50	50.00
d. WEIHAIWEI. *(S/M #C126-170c)*.	5.50	16.50	50.00
e. SHIH-KIA CHUANG. *(S/M #C126-)*.	8.00	25.00	75.00

139 **20 CENTS**

	GOOD	FINE	XF
1.7.1925. Orange. Steam passenger train at ctr.			
a. HARBIN. *(S/M #C126-171b)*.	5.50	16.50	50.00
b. SHANGHAI. *(S/M #C126-171a)*.	3.00	10.00	30.00
c. TSINGTAU. *(S/M #C126-)*.	5.50	16.50	50.00
d. WEIHAIWEI. *(S/M #C126-)*.	5.50	16.50	50.00

1927 FIRST ISSUES
#141-143 printer: W&S.

140 **5 CENTS**

	GOOD	FINE	XF
1.1.1927. HARBIN. *(S/M #C126-180)*.	10.00	30.00	90.00

141 **10 CENTS**

	GOOD	FINE	XF
1.1.1927. Blue. Similar to #143. Back lilac-brown.			
a. SHANGHAI. *(S/M #C126-181a)*.	2.50	10.00	30.00
b. TSINGTAU. *(S/M #C126-181b)*.	2.75	11.00	33.00
s. W/o place name. Specimen uniface face and back. *(S/M #C126-181-)*.	—	Unc	45.00

142 **10 CENTS**

	GOOD	FINE	XF
1.1.1927. Red. Similar to #143. Back violet-black. *TSINGTAU* *(S/M #C126-182)*.	3.00	10.00	30.00

143 **20 CENTS**

	GOOD	FINE	XF
1.1.1927. Red-brown. Steamship l., steam locomotive at r. Back blue.			
a. KALGAN. *(S/M #C126-183a)*.	3.25	10.00	30.00
b. SHANGHAI in black. *(S/M #C126-183b)*.	6.50	20.00	60.00
c. SHIHKIACHWANG. *(S/M #C126-183c)*.	8.50	26.50	80.00
d. TSINAN. *(S/M #C126-183d)*.	4.00	12.00	36.00
e. TSINGTAU. *(S/M #C126-183e)*.	4.00	12.00	36.00
f. SHANGHAI in blue. Specimen. Uniface face and back. *(S/M #C126-183b-a)*.	—	Unc	45.00

144 **50 CENTS**

	GOOD	FINE	XF
1.1.1927. HARBIN. *(S/M #C126-184)*.	8.50	26.50	80.00

1927 SECOND ISSUES

#145-147C printer: ABNC.

145 1 YUAN
1.11.1927. Purple and m/c. Steam passenger train in ravine at ctr. *FENGTIEN. (S/M #C126-190).*   8.50 26.50 80.00

145A 1 YUAN	GOOD	FINE	XF
1.11.1927. Similar to #145 but different colors and guilloches. *SHANGHAI.*			
a. Purple and m/c. (S/M #C126-191).	5.50	16.50	50.00
b. Brown and m/c. (S/M #C126-192).	5.50	16.50	50.00
c. Blue and m/c. (S/M #C126-193).	5.50	16.50	50.00

145B 1 YUAN	GOOD	FINE	XF
1.11.1927. Yellow-orange and m/c. Similar to #145 but different guilloches.			
a. *SHANTUNG. (S/M #C126-194).*	5.50	16.50	50.00
b. *CHEFOO/SHANTUNG.* Black Chinese sign. on face and back. (S/M #C126-195).	7.50	21.50	63.50
c. *CHEFOO/SHANTUNG.* Red sign. seals. Black English sign. on back. (S/M #C126-195).	7.50	21.50	63.50
d. *LUNGKOW/SHANTUNG. (S/M #C126-196).*	7.50	21.50	63.50
e. *TSINAN/SHANTUNG. (S/M #C126-197).*	7.50	21.50	63.50
f. *TSINGTAU/SHANTUNG. (S/M #C126-198).*	7.50	21.50	63.50
g. *WEIHAIWEI/SHANTUNG. (S/M #C126-199).*	10.00	30.00	90.00

145C 1 YUAN	GOOD	FINE	XF
1.11.1927. Green and m/c. Similar to #145 but different guilloches. *TIENTSIN. (S/M #C126-200).*	5.50	16.50	50.00

146 5 YUAN
1.11.1927. Brown and m/c. Steam passenger train at ctr. *FENGTIEN. (S/M #C126-201).*   8.00 25.00 75.00

146A 5 YUAN
1.11.1927. Green and m/c. Similar to #146 but different guilloches. *HANKOW. (S/M #C126-202).).*   7.50 20.00 60.00

146B 5 YUAN
1.11.1927. Olive-brown and m/c. Similar to #146 but different guilloches. *SHANGHAI. (S/M #C126-203).*   4.00 10.00 30.00

146C 5 YUAN	GOOD	FINE	XF
1.11.1927. Purple and m/c. Similar to #146 but different guilloches.			
a. *SHANTUNG.* English sign. (S/M #C126-204).	4.00	12.50	37.50
b. *CHEFOO/SHANTUNG. (S/M #C126-210).*	4.00	12.50	37.50
c. *LUNGKOW/SHANTUNG. (S/M #C126-211).*	4.00	12.50	37.50
d. *TSINAN/SHANTUNG. (S/M #C126-212).*	4.00	12.50	37.50
e. *TSINGTAU/SHANTUNG. (S/M #C126-213).*	4.00	12.50	37.50
f. *WEIHAIWEI/SHANTUNG. (S/M #C126-).*	4.00	12.50	37.50
g. *SHANTUNG.* Chinese sign. (S/M #C126-).	4.00	12.50	37.50

146D 5 YUAN
1.11.1927. Orange and m/c. Similar to #146 but different guilloches. *TIENTSIN. (S/M #C126-214).*   6.50 20.00 60.00

147 10 YUAN
1.11.1927. Similar to #A147A but different guilloches. *FENGTIEN. (S/M #C126-220).*   10.00 30.00 90.00

147A 10 YUAN	GOOD	FINE	XF
1.11.1927. Red and m/c. Maritime Customs bldg., street car at ctr. *SHANGHAI. (S/M #C126-221).*	3.00	10.00	30.00

147B 10 YUAN	GOOD	FINE	XF
1.11.1927. Green and m/c. Similar to #147 but different guilloches.			
a. *SHANTUNG.* English sign. (S/M #C126-222).	5.50	16.50	50.00
b. *CHEFOO/SHANTUNG. (S/M #C126-223).*	7.50	21.50	63.50
c. *LUNGKOW/SHANTUNG. (S/M #C126-224).*	7.50	21.50	63.50
d. *TSINAN/SHANTUNG. (S/M #C126-225).*	7.50	21.50	63.50
e. *TSINGTAU/SHANTUNG. (S/M #C126-226).*	5.50	16.50	50.00
f. *WEIHAIWEI/SHANTUNG. (S/M #C126-).*	11.00	33.00	100.00
g. *SHANTUNG.* Chinese sign. (S/M #C126-).	5.50	16.50	50.00

147C 10 YUAN
1.11.1927. Brown and m/c. Similar to #147 but different guilloches.
	GOOD	FINE	XF
a. *TIENTSIN. (S/M #C126-227).*	8.00	25.00	75.00
b. *HANKOW. (S/M #C126-).*	10.00	30.00	90.00

1931 ISSUE

148 1 YUAN
1.1.1931. Red. Steam passenger train at ctr. Back red; houses and pagoda at ctr. Printer: TDLR. *SHANGHAI. (S/M #C126-230).*
	VG	VF	UNC
a. English sign. and red sign. seals printed separately at lower l. and r.	—	—	—
b. Red sign. seals printed separately at lower l. and r.	2.50	7.50	30.00
c. Red sign. seals engraved in frame design at lower l. and r.	.50	1.50	5.50

1935 FIRST PROVISIONAL ISSUE
New issuer ovpt. of 9-Chinese characters and/or English on National Industrial Bank of China notes.

149 1 YUAN
ND (1935-old date 1931). Purple and m/c. Ovpt. on #531c. *(S/M #C126-231).*   12.50   50.00   150.00

150 5 YUAN	VG	VF	UNC
ND (1935-old date 1931). Red and m/c. Black Chinese ovpt. on 532a. *(S/M #C126-232).*	7.50	30.00	90.00

151 10 YUAN	VG	VF	UNC
ND (1935-old date 1931). Green and m/c. Black Chinese ovpt. on #533. *(S/M #C126-233).*	8.00	32.50	100.00

1935 SECOND PROVISIONAL ISSUE

152 1 YUAN	VG	VF	UNC
Nov. 1935 (-old date 1935). Red and m/c. Red Chinese ovpt. Black English ovpt. on back on #534. *(S/M #C126-240).*	7.50	30.00	90.00

1935 REGULAR ISSUE
#153-155 pagoda on hill, shoreline at ctr. on back. Printer: TDLR.

153 1 YUAN	VG	VF	UNC
1935. Purple on green unpt. Steam locomotive at ctr. *(S/M #C126-241).*	.50	2.00	10.00

154 5 YUAN	VG	VF	UNC
1935. Dk. green on pink unpt. Junks at ctr. *(S/M #C126-242).*			
a. Issued note.	.10	.25	1.00
r. Remainder w/o red sign. seals on face at lower l. and r.	.30	1.00	4.00

155 10 YUAN	VG	VF	UNC
1935. Red on yellow-orange unpt. High voltage electric towers at r. Back red. *(S/M #C126-243).*	.15	.45	1.25

1941 ISSUES
#156-162 Nationalist issues w/*CHUNGKING* while those w/o any place name were issued in Japanese controlled areas.

#160-163 printer: ABNC.

156 5 YUAN	VG	VF	UNC
1941. Brown and m/c. Steam passenger train at ctr. Back brown; bank at ctr. Printer: ABNC. *(S/M #C126-252).*	1.00	4.00	15.00

157 5 YUAN	VG	VF	UNC
1941. Brown and m/c. Ship at ctr. Chinese printer: CMPA. *(S/M #C126-#251).*	.35	1.00	3.00

		VG	VF	UNC
158	**10 YUAN**	1.00	5.00	15.00
	1941. Red and m/c. Bldg. w/clock tower at ctr. Back red; dockside scene at ctr. Printer: ABNC. (S/M #C126-253).			

		VG	VF	UNC
162	**100 YUAN**			
	1941. Purple and m/c. Steam passenger train on bridge at ctr. Back purple; steam train at ctr.			
	a. CHUNGKING. (S/M #C126-262b).	1.50	6.00	24.00
	b. W/o place name. (S/M #C126-262a).	.75	3.00	12.00

		VG	VF	UNC
163	**500 YUAN**	32.50	100.00	300.00
	1941. Blue on m/c unpt. Ship at dockside at ctr. Back blue; steam passenger train, high voltage electrical towers across landscape. (S/M #C126-263).			

		VG	VF	UNC
159	**10 YUAN**			
	1941. Brown and m/c. Steam passenger train at ctr. Chinese printer: Dah Tung Book. (S/M #C126-254).			
	a. Serial # face and back.	.25	.75	3.00
	b. Serial # on face only.	.25	.75	3.00
	c. W/o serial # or sign. seals.	.25	.75	3.00
	d. Mismatched serial #.	1.00	3.00	10.00
	e. Cancellation handstamp, serial # on face and back.	.25	.75	3.00
	f. Cancellation handstamp, w/o serial # or sign. seals.	.25	.75	3.00
	g. Cancellation handstamp and mismatched serial #.	1.00	3.00	10.00
	h. Serial # on back only.	.25	.75	2.50
	s. Specimen.	—	Unc	75.00

1942 ISSUE
#164-165 issued under Japanese control. Chinese printer: Ta Tung (Dah Tung) Printing.

		VG	VF	UNC
164	**50 YUAN**			
	1942. Steam passenger train at l. (S/M #C126-270).			
	a. Purple.	3.00	12.00	48.00
	b. Brown-violet.	2.50	10.00	40.00

		VG	VF	UNC
160	**25 YUAN**	9.00	37.50	150.00
	1941. Green and m/c. Electric direct current generator, Zeppelin and plane at ctr. Back green; airplane at ctr. (S/M #C126-260).			

		VG	VF	UNC
161	**50 YUAN**			
	1941. Brown and m/c. 2 railroad trains in a mountain pass. Back brown; ships at ctr.			
	a. CHUNGKING. (S/M #C126-261b).	1.25	5.00	20.00
	b. W/o place name. (S/M #C126-261a).	1.00	4.50	18.00

165	100 YUAN	VG	VF	UNC
	1942. Brown. Steam train at l., ships at r. Large value *100* on back. (S/M #C126-271).	2.25	9.00	36.00

1949 CIRCULATING CASHIER'S CHECKS ISSUE
#165A-165D steam passenger train at upper ctr. on back.

165A	500 YUAN			
	ND (1949). Lt. brown on lt. green. Specimen. (S/M #C126-).	—	Unc	65.00

165B	1000 YUAN	GOOD	FINE	XF
	ND (1949). Green. (S/M #C126-).			
	a. Issued note.	8.00	25.00	75.00
	s. Specimen.	—	Unc	65.00
165C	2000 YUAN			
	ND (1949). Red. (S/M #C126-).			
	a. Issued note.	8.00	25.00	75.00
	s. Specimen.	—	Unc	65.00
165D	5000 YUAN			
	ND (1949). Purple. Specimen. (S/M #C126-).	—	Unc	65.00

166	1000 GOLD YUAN	GOOD	FINE	XF
	ND (1949). Green. Printer: CPF. (S/M #C126-280).	8.00	25.00	75.00

CENTRAL BANK OF CHINA (NATIONAL)

行銀央中
Chung Yan Yin Hang

Established in November 1928 as the primary note issuing agency for the Chinese Nationalist Government in Nanking. Not to be confused with the other Central Bank of China (quasi-national) which was based in Kwangtung Province w/issues dated 1923-27. See #171-192. For other national issues see #193-450.

NOTE: Numerous sign. varieties exist for issues prior to 1940.

1928 (ND) COIN NOTE ISSUE

167	10 COPPERS	VG	VF	UNC
	ND. (1928) Violet and green unpt. Pagoda at l. W/o ovpt.			
	a. Black ovpt: *SHENSI*.	3.75	15.00	45.00
	b. Red Chinese ovpt: *5 Fen* (5 Cents) (Legal tender for circulation in Szechuan Province).	3.75	15.00	45.00

		VG	VF	UNC
	c. Similar to #167b but w/additional black Chinese ovpt: *5 Fen*.	6.00	25.00	75.00

168	20 COPPERS	VG	VF	UNC
	ND. (1928) Dk. blue on red unpt. Pagoda at r.			
	a. Black ovpt: *SHENSI*.	5.00	20.00	60.00
	b. Red ovpt: *1 CHIAO* (10 Cents). Similar to #167b.	3.75	15.00	45.00
	c. Similar to #168b but w/additional Chinese ovpt: *1 Chiao* over *20 Coppers*.	5.00	20.00	60.00

169	50 COPPERS	VG	VF	UNC
	ND. (1928) Lilac-brown on lt. brown. Pagoda at r.			
	a. Black ovpt: *SHENSI*.	6.00	25.00	75.00
	b. Red ovpt: *2 CHIAO 5 FEN* (25 Cents). Similar to #167b and #168b.	6.00	25.00	75.00

1920 PROVISIONAL ISSUE

170	5 DOLLARS	GOOD	FINE	XF
	ND (1928-old date 1.9.1920). Red and m/c. Ovpt. on #541.			
	a. English ovpt. 80mm. on back.	15.00	60.00	180.00
	b. English ovpt. 83mm. on back.	15.00	60.00	180.00

CENTRAL BANK OF CHINA (QUASI-NATIONAL)

行銀央中
Chung Yan Yin Hang

Not to be confused w/the national bank of the same name, this issuer was located in Kwangtung Province. Included are many military issues of the Kuomintang forces during the 1926-27 Northern Expedition.

1923 ISSUE
#171-179B portr. SYS at ctr. Printer: ABNC.

171 1 DOLLAR
1923. Green and m/c. Back blue. English sign.

	Good	Fine	XF
a. English sign.	1.00	4.00	16.00
b. Chinese sign.	1.00	4.00	16.00
c. sign. Ovpt: *HUNAN, KIANGSI & KWANGSI* on back. English	4.50	17.50	70.00
d. Red ovpt: 4-Chinese characters in circles at corners, (Kwangchow) on face. English sign.	10.00	40.00	165.00
e. Ovpt: *Swatow* at l. and r. SWATOW at lower ctr. w/Swatow diagonally at l. and r. on back. English sign.	1.00	4.00	16.00
f. SWATOW. W/circular violet Central Bank handstamp.	1.25	5.00	20.00
g. Red ovpt: *HUPEH, HUNAN, & KWANGSI* on back.	5.50	22.50	90.00
h. Ovpt: *Kwangtung* above portr.	1.50	6.00	24.00
i. Large oval branch office handstamp: *HUNAN, KIANGSI & KWANGSI* also w/Chinese characters on face.	—	—	—
s. Specimen.	—	Unc	75.00

171A 1 DOLLAR
1923. Dk. green and m/c. Back brown.

	Good	Fine	XF
a. *Haikow* at l. and r. *HAI KOW* at lower l. and r. on back. Specimen.	—	Unc	175.00
b. *Kongmoon* at l. and r. *KONG MOON* at lower l. and r. on back. Specimen.	—	Unc	175.00
c. *Meiluck* at l. and r. *MEI LUCK* at lower l. and r. on back. Specimen.	—	Unc	175.00
d. *Pakhoi* at l. and r. *PAK HOI* at lower l. and r. on back. Specimen.	—	Unc	175.00
e. *Suichow* at l. and r. *SUI CHOW* at lower l. and r. on back. Specimen.	—	Unc	175.00
f. *Swatow* at l. and r. *SWATOW* at lower l. and r. on back. Specimen.	—	Unc	175.00

172 1 DOLLAR
1923. Yellow-orange and m/c. Similar to #171. Back black.

	Good	VG	Fine
a. English sign.	1.75	7.50	30.00
b. Chinese sign.	1.75	7.50	30.00
c. Ovpt: *Kwangtung* at l. and r. of portr.	2.75	11.00	45.00
d. 4-Chinese character ovpt: *Kwang-Chung-Tsung-Hang* for Kwangchow head office. Chinese sign.	10.00	40.00	160.00
e. Ovpt: *Kwangchow* and *Kwangtung.*	5.00	20.00	80.00
s. Specimen.	—	Unc	135.00

173 5 DOLLARS
1923. Brown and m/c. SYS at ctr. Back blue.

	Good	VG	Fine
a. English sign.	2.50	10.00	40.00
b. Chinese sign.	2.50	10.00	40.00
c. Ovpt: *HUNAN, KIANGSI & KWANGSI* on back. English sign.	15.00	60.00	240.00
d. 4 character Chinese ovpt: *Kwang-Chung-Tsung-Hang* for Kwangchow head office in circles in corners. English sign.	7.50	30.00	120.00
e. Red ovpt: *HUPEH, HUNAN & KIANGSI* on back.	11.00	45.00	180.00
f. Lg. oval branch office handstamp: *HUNAN, KIANGSI, & KWANGSI* also w/Chinese characters on face.	—	—	—
g. Ovpt: *PAKHOI.*	3.75	15.00	60.00
h. *PAKHOI.* English sign.	3.75	15.00	60.00
s. Specimen.	—	Unc	100.00

174 5 DOLLARS
1923. Red. Similar to #173. Back yellow.

	Good	Fine	XF
a. Chinese and English sign.	3.75	15.00	60.00
b. Ovpt: *Kwangtung* above portr. Chinese and English sign.	3.75	15.00	60.00
c. Ovpt: *Kwangtung* above portr. English sign.	3.75	15.00	60.00
d. 4 character Chinese ovpt: *Kwang-Chung-Tsung-Hang* for Kwanchow head office.	5.50	22.50	90.00
s. Specimen.	—	Unc	150.00

175 5 DOLLARS
1923. Green and m/c. Similar to #174. Back red.

	Good	Fine	XF
a. *Haikow* at l. and r. *KAI KOW* on back. Specimen.	—	Unc	225.00
b. *Kongmoon* at l. and r. *KONG MOON* at l. and r. on back. Specimen.	—	Unc	225.00
c. *Meiluck* at l. and r. *MEI LUCK* at l. and r. on back. Specimen.	—	Unc	225.00
d. *Pakhoi* at l. and r. *PAK HOI* at l. and r. on back. Specimen.	—	Unc	225.00
e. *Suichow* at l. and r. *SUI CHOW* at l. and r. on back. Specimen.	—	Unc	225.00
f. *Swatow* at l. and r. *SWATOW* at l. and r. on back. Specimen.	—	Unc	225.00

176 10 DOLLARS
1923. Brown on m/c unpt. SYS at ctr. Back olive. Printed area is either 157 x 78mm or 152 x 76mm.

	Good	Fine	XF
a. Ovpt: *Kwangtung* in Chinese on face (single black characters at upper l. and r. ctr.), English sign. 152 x 76mm.	.75	2.50	7.50
b. As a. Chinese and English sign. 152 x 76mm.	.75	2.50	7.50
c. As a., 157 x 78mm.	.60	1.75	6.00
d. As b. 157 x 78mm.	.50	1.50	5.00
e. W/o ovpt: *Kwangtung* on face. Chinese sign. 157 x 78mm.	.50	1.50	5.00
s. Specimen.	—	Unc	100.00

176A 10 DOLLARS
1923. Pink and m/c. Similar to #176. Back orange.

	Good	Fine	XF
a. *Haikow* at l. and r. *HAI KOW* on back. Specimen.	—	Unc	300.00
b. *Kongmoon* at l. and r. *KONG MOON* at l. and r. on back. Specimen.	—	Unc	300.00
c. *Meiluck* at l. and r. *MEI LUCK* at l. and r. on back. Specimen.	—	Unc	300.00
d. *Suichow* at l. and r. *SUI CHOW* at l. and r. on back. Specimen.	—	Unc	300.00
e. *Pakhoi* at l. and r. *Pak Hoi* at l. and r. on back. Specimen.	—	Unc	300.00
f. *Swatow* at l. and r. *SWATOW* at l. and r. on back. Specimen.	—	Unc	300.00

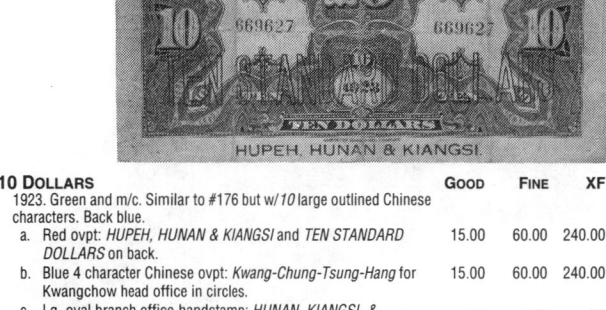

177 10 DOLLARS
1923. Green and m/c. Similar to #176 but w/*10* large outlined Chinese characters. Back blue.

	Good	Fine	XF
a. Red ovpt: *HUPEH, HUNAN & KIANGSI* and *TEN STANDARD DOLLARS* on back.	15.00	60.00	240.00
b. Blue 4 character Chinese ovpt: *Kwang-Chung-Tsung-Hang* for Kwangchow head office in circles.	15.00	60.00	240.00
c. Lg. oval branch office handstamp: *HUNAN, KIANGSI, & KWANGSI* also w/Chinese characters on face.	—	—	—
s. Specimen.	—	Unc	150.00

178 50 DOLLARS
1923. Orange and m/c. Back dk. blue.

	Good	Fine	XF
a. English sign.	13.50	55.00	220.00
b. SWATOW. W/circular violet *Central Bank* handstamp on face.	11.00	45.00	180.00
c. Ovpt: *The Central Bank of China - SWATOW* on face and back.	30.00	120.00	480.00
s. Specimen.	—	Unc	375.00

178A 50 DOLLARS
1923. Green and m/c. Back black.

	Good	Fine	XF
a. *Kongmoon* at l. and r. *KONG MOON* at l. and r. on back. Specimen.	—	Unc	350.00
b. *Suichow* at l. and r. *SUI CHOW* at l. and r. on back. Specimen.	—	Unc	350.00
c. *Swatow* at l. and r. *SWA TOW* at l. and r. on back. Specimen.	—	Unc	850.00

178B 50 DOLLARS
1923. Blue and m/c. Back violet. Specimen.

	Good	Fine	XF
	—	Unc	450.00

179 100 DOLLARS
1923. Brown. Back blue.

	Good	Fine	XF
a. Issued note.	30.00	120.00	480.00
b. Ovpt: *HUNAN, KIANGSI & KWANGSI* on back.	30.00	120.00	480.00
s. Specimen.	—	Unc	500.00

			GOOD	FINE	XF
179A	**100 DOLLARS**		—	Unc	750.00
	1923. Green and m/c. Back red. Specimen.				

1923 COMMEMORATIVE ISSUE
#180 and 180A death of Sun Yat Sen.

			VG	VF	UNC
180	**5 DOLLARS**		120.00	360.00	900.00
(173A)	1923. Brown and m/c. Back blue. Black ovpt. on #173.				
180A	**10 DOLLARS**		150.00	475.00	1200.
(177A)	1923. Green and m/c. Back blue. Black commemorative ovpt. on #177.				

1926 PROVISIONAL ISSUE

			GOOD	FINE	XF
181	**1 DOLLAR**		17.50	70.00	175.00
(179B)	ND (1926). Orange and m/c. Ovpt. on Bank of Kiangsi #S1097.				

1926 ISSUE
#182-184B printer: ABNC.

			GOOD	FINE	XF
182	**1 DOLLAR**				
	1926. Blue on m/c unpt. Portr. SYS at l. Back brown.				
	a. *CHUNGKING* and *ONE YUAN LOCAL CURRENCY...* ovpt. on back.		4.00	15.00	60.00
	b. *FUKIEN.*		3.00	12.50	50.00
	c. *HANKOW.*		10.00	30.00	125.00

			GOOD	FINE	XF
183	**5 DOLLARS**				
	1926. Orange on m/c unpt. Portr. SYS at r. Back dk. green.				
	a. *CHUNGKING* Green ovpt. *FIVE YUAN LOCAL CURRENCY...* on back.		11.00	45.00	180.00
	b. *FUKIEN.*		11.00	45.00	180.00

	c. *HANKOW* w/control letters *TH.*		11.00	45.00	180.00
	d. *HOIKOW.*		11.00	45.00	180.00
	e. *SHANGHAI.*		11.00	45.00	180.00
184	**10 DOLLARS**				
	1926. Red on m/c unpt. Portr. SYS at ctr. Back blue.				
	a. *CHUNGKING. TEN YUAN LOCAL CURRENCY...* ovpt.		7.50	30.00	120.00
	b. *FUKIEN.*		7.50	30.00	120.00
	s. Specimen.		—	Unc	150.00
184A	**50 DOLLARS**				
	1926. Black and m/c. Portr. SYS. Back orange.				
	a. *HANKOW.*		22.50	90.00	360.00
	b. *SHANGHAI.*		22.50	90.00	360.00
	s. Specimen w/o office of issue.		—	Unc	300.00
184B	**100 DOLLARS**				
	1926.				
	p. Proof.		—	Unc	300.00
	s. Specimen.		—	Unc	350.00

1926 MILITARY ISSUE

			GOOD	FINE	XF
185	**1 DOLLAR**				
	1926. Lilac-brown. Sailing ship at l., steamer at r. Back purple; w/large red handstamp.				
	a. Red serial #.		12.50	50.00	150.00
	b. Blue serial #.		12.50	50.00	150.00
	c. Cancelled w/Chinese handstamp.		9.00	35.00	105.00

			GOOD	FINE	XF
186	**5 DOLLARS**				
	1926. Gray-green. Temple at ctr. Back black; w/lg. red handstamp.				
	a. Issued note.		15.00	60.00	180.00
	b. Cancelled w/Chinese handstamp.		15.00	60.00	180.00

187 10 DOLLARS
1926. Brown. Ship at ctr. Back violet; w/lg. red handstamp.

		GOOD	FINE	XF
a.	Issued note.	17.50	75.00	225.00
b.	Cancelled w/Chinese handstamp.	17.50	75.00	225.00

1927 ISSUE
#188 *Deleted*. See #193.
#190 *Deleted*. See #194.

			GOOD	FINE	XF
192	**5 CHIAO = 50 CENTS**				
	1927. Orange. Temple of Heaven at ctr. Printer: CHB.		12.50	50.00	150.00
189	**1 CHIAO = 10 CENTS**				
	1927. Green. Temple of Heaven. Printer: CHB.		17.50	75.00	225.00
191	**2 CHIAO = 20 CENTS**				
	1927. Red. Temple of Heaven. Printer: CHB.		17.50	75.00	225.00

CENTRAL BANK OF CHINA (NATIONAL-CONTINUED)

行銀央中
Chung Yuan Yin Hang.

SIGNATURE/TITLE VARIETIES		
1	GENERAL MANAGER	MANAGER
2	ASST. MANAGER	GENERAL MANAGER
3	ASST. MANAGER	GENERAL MANAGER
4	ASST. MANAGER	GENERAL MANAGER
5	ASST. MANAGER	GENERAL MANAGER
6	ASST. GENERAL MANAGER	GENERAL MANAGER
7	ASST. GENERAL MANAGER	GENERAL MANAGER
8	ASST. GENERAL MANAGER	GENERAL MANAGER
9	ASST. GENERAL MANAGER	GENERAL MANAGER
10	GENERAL MANAGER	GOVERNOR
11	GENERAL MANAGER	GOVERNOR
12	ASST. GENERAL MANAGER	GENERAL MANAGER

1924 ISSUE
#193 and 194 printer: ABNC.

			VG	VF	UNC
193	**1 CHIAO = 10 CENTS**				
	ND (1924). Black on m/c unpt. Back brown and purple; pagoda at l.				
	a.	Sign. 1.	1.00	5.00	15.00
	b.	Sign. 5.	1.00	5.00	15.00
	s.	As a. Specimen.	—	—	35.00

			VG	VF	UNC
194	**2 CHIAO = 20 CENTS**				
	ND (1924). Black on m/c unpt. Pagoda at r. Back green and lilac.				
	a.	Sign. 1.	2.50	10.00	25.00
	b.	Sign. 2.	2.50	10.00	25.00
	c.	Sign. 5.	4.00	15.00	40.00
	s.	Specimen.	—	—	35.00

1928 ISSUE
#195-200A printer: ABNC.
#195-196 also/various control ovpt: symbols, numerals and Chinese characters.
NOTE: #198a-g, 199a-g w/various control ovpt. are considered spurious.

			VG	VF	UNC
195	**1 DOLLAR**				
	1928. Green. Back brown; portr. SYS at l. Serial # on face and back.				
	SHANGHAI.				
	a.	Sign. 2.	2.00	6.00	20.00
	b.	Sign. 3.	1.50	5.00	15.00
	c.	Sign. 5.	.50	2.00	10.00

196	**5 DOLLARS**	VG	VF	UNC
	1928. Olive and m/c. Back red; portr. SYS at r. Serial # on face and back. Black sign. *SHANGHAI*.			
	a. Sign. 2.	3.00	9.00	25.00
	b. Sign. 3.	2.00	6.00	20.00
	c. Sign. 5.	1.00	4.00	12.00
	d. Sign. 8.	2.00	7.50	22.50

Small black sign.   **Large black sign.**

197	**10 DOLLARS**	VG	VF	UNC
	1928. Dk. blue and m/c. Back green; portr. SYS at ctr. *SHANGHAI*.			
	a. Sign. 2.	1.50	5.00	15.00
	b. Sign. 3.	1.00	4.00	12.00
	c. Sign. 4.	1.50	5.00	15.00
	d. Sign. 5a.	.20	.50	1.25
	e. Sign. 5b.	.25	.60	1.50
	f. Sign. 7 in black. Serial # on face and back.	.30	.75	1.75
	g. As f. Serial # on face only.	.20	.50	1.25
	h. Sign. 7 in green as part of plate.	.15	.30	1.00

198	**50 DOLLARS**			
	1928. Orange and m/c. Back blue-gray; portr. SYS at ctr. *SHANGHAI*.			
	a. Sign. 5.	.50	2.00	6.00
	b. Sign. 5. Ovpt: *CHUNGKING/SHANGHAI*.	.75	2.50	7.50
	c. Sign. 6.	.75	2.50	7.50
	d. Sign. 7 in blue.	1.00	3.50	12.50
	e. Sign. 7 in black. Serial # on face and back.	.50	2.00	6.00
	f. As e. Serial # on face only.	.75	2.50	7.50
	g. As e. Sign. thinner, as part of plate.	.50	2.00	6.00

199	**100 DOLLARS**	VG	VF	UNC
	1928. Olive and m/c. Back purple; portr. SYS at ctr. *SHANGHAI*.			
	a. Sign. 5. Serial # on face and back.	1.00	4.00	12.00
	b. As a. Serial # on face only.	1.00	4.00	12.00
	c. As a. Ovpt: *CHUNGKING/SHANGHAI*.	1.00	4.00	12.00
	d. Sign. 6.	1.00	4.00	12.00
	e. Sign. 7. Black.	1.00	4.00	12.00
	f. Sign. 7. Purple as part of plate.	.75	3.00	9.00

1930 ISSUE

200	**5 DOLLARS**	VG	VF	UNC
	1930. Dk. green and m/c. SYS at ctr. Back green; temple at ctr. *SHANGHAI*. Also w/various control ovpt. Printer: ABNC.			
	a. Sign. 2.	2.00	6.00	20.00
	b. Sign. 3.	1.50	5.00	17.50
	c. Sign. 4.	2.00	6.00	20.00
	d. Sign. 5.	.50	1.50	3.50
	e. Sign. 7 in black. Serial # on face and back.	.50	1.50	3.50
	f. Sign. 7 in green as part of plate. Serial # on back only.	.25	.75	2.00

1931 ISSUE

#201 *Deleted*. See #205A.

#202-205A printer: CHB.

202	**10 CENTS = 1 CHIAO**	VG	VF	UNC
	ND (1931). Green. Temple behind trees at l. Back blue and green.	.15	.40	1.25

203	**20 CENTS = 2 CHIAO**	VG	VF	UNC
	ND (1931). Blue. Chu-Shui-Bridge at r. Back aqua, brown and purple.	.25	.75	2.50

204	**25 CENTS**	VG	VF	UNC
	ND (1931). Lilac. P'ai-lou (commemorative archway) at l. Back blue.	2.50	8.00	25.00

205	**50 CENTS**	VG	VF	UNC
	ND (1931). Purple. Temple of Confucius at l. Back brown and blue. Paper and 3 serial # varieties.	3.00	10.00	30.00

210 (211)	1 YUAN	VG	VF	UNC
	1936. Orange and black. Similar to #210 but monument in black at r. Back dk. brown. 135 x 65mm.	3.00	8.00	27.50
211 (212)	1 YUAN			
	1936. Orange on m/c unpt. Vessel at l., SYS at r. Back dk. brown. Confucious, men w/2 horse-drawn carts.			
	a. Sign. 10.	.25	.75	2.00
	b. Sign. 11.	.50	2.00	5.00

205A	1 DOLLAR	VG	VF	UNC
	ND (-old date 1934). Ovpt. on #A112.			
	a. *SHANGHAI.*	22.50	70.00	210.00
	b. *TIENTSIN.*	22.50	70.00	210.00
	c. *PEIPING.*	22.50	70.00	210.00
	d. W/o place name.	13.50	40.00	120.00

1936 "TDLR" ISSUES
#212-214 printer (except #212A): TDLR.
#215 *Deleted.*

1935 REGULAR ISSUE
#205B-205C Portr. SYS at upper ctr. on back. *SZECHUAN.*
#206-208 *CHUNGKING.*

206	1 YUAN			
	1935. Orange and m/c. Ships. Back gray. Printer: CHB.	30.00	120.00	360.00
207	5 YUAN			
	1935. Red and m/c. Portr. SYS at l. Back dk. blue. Printer: BEPP.	25.00	100.00	300.00

208	10 YUAN	VG	VF	UNC
	1935. Green. Portr. SYS at l. Back purple. Printer: BEPP.	20.00	80.00	240.00

212 (213)	1 YUAN	VG	VF	UNC
	1936. Orange and black on m/c unpt. SYS at l. and as wmk. Back brown; gateway and temple behind trees at ctr. Printer: TDLR.			
	a. Sign. 5.	.20	.60	2.00
	b. Sign. 8.	.40	1.25	3.00
	c. Sign. 9.	.15	.50	1.50

205B	10 CENTS	VG	VF	UNC
	ND(1935). Dk. blue. Back violet.	17.50	70.00	210.00
205C	20 CENTS			
	ND(1935). Brown. Back green.	22.50	90.00	270.00

212A (213A)	1 YUAN	VG	VF	UNC
	ND (-old date 1936). Lithograph face like #213. Chinese text on back. (pass for Nanking Military Government).	200.00	450.00	—

1936 "CHB" ISSUES
NOTE: The Tibetan ovpt. occurs on #216-220. Authenticity of this ovpt. on #216 and 220 is questionable.
#209-211 printer: CHB.

209 (210)	1 YUAN	VG	VF	UNC
	1936. Orange on m/c unpt. Wan Ku Chang Ch'un monument at r. Back brown. 2 sign. varieties.	10.00	50.00	150.00

213 (216)	5 YUAN	VG	VF	UNC
	1936. Dk. green and black on m/c unpt. SYS at l. and as wmk. Back olive-green; gateway and temple behind trees at ctr. Printer: TDLR.			
	a. Sign. 5.	.10	.30	.75
	b. Sign. 8.	.40	1.25	3.00
	c. Sign. 9.	.20	.50	1.50

		Large sign.				Small sign.	
			VG	VF	UNC	VF	UNC
220	100 YUAN						

220 100 YUAN
1936. Olive-green and dk. brown on m/c unpt. SYS at l. and as wmk.
Back purple; Palace of China in Peking at ctr. Printer: W&S.
a. Issued note. Sign. 11 in purple. — VG 1.00 — VF 5.00 — UNC 30.00
b. Ovpt: *Chungking* in Chinese at l. and r. and in English at upper ctr. on back. Sign. 10 in black. — 25.00 — —
c. Ovpt: Tibetan character on face and back. Sign. 11 in black. — 60.00 — —

		VG	VF	UNC
214	10 YUAN			
(218)				

214 10 YUAN
(218) 1936. Dk. blue and black on m/c unpt. SYS at l. and as wmk. Back dk.
green, gateway and temple behind trees at ctr. Printer: TDLR.
a. Sign. 5. — .15 — .40 — 1.00
b. Sign. 8. — .40 — 1.25 — 3.00
c. Sign. 9. — .20 — .50 — 1.50

1936 "W&S" ISSUE
#216-221 printer: W&S.

216 1 YUAN
(209) 1936. Orange. SYS at l. Back brown; temple (Palace of China in
Peking). Printer: W&S. 2 serial # varieties.
a. Sign. 5. — .10 — .40 — 1.25
b. Sign. 7. — .15 — .50 — 1.50
c. Sign. 8. — .15 — .50 — 1.50
d. Sign. 9. — .15 — .50 — 1.50
e. Ovpt: Tibetan characters on face and back. Sign. 5; 7-9. — 50.00 — —

		VG	VF	UNC
221	500 YUAN			

221 500 YUAN
1936. Red-brown. SYS at l. Back blue; Palace of China in Peking at ctr.
Printer: W&S.
a. Sign. 11. — 13.00 — 52.50 — 135.00
s. Specimen. — — — 100.00

		VG	VF	UNC
217	5 YUAN			
(214)				

217 5 YUAN
(214) 1936. Green on m/c unpt. SYS at l. Back green; w/temple (Palace of
China in Peking). Printer W&S. 2 serial # varieties
a. Sign. 5. — .10 — .40 — 1.25
b. Sign. 8. — .25 — 1.00 — 3.00
c. Sign. 9. — .15 — .50 — 1.50
d. Ovpt: Tibetan characters on face and back. Sign. 5. — 20.00 — 50.00 — —

1937 ISSUE
#222 and 223 printer: CHB.

		VG	VF	UNC
222	5 YUAN			

222 5 YUAN
1937. Green on m/c unpt. Antique bronze tripod at l., portr. SYS at r.
Back dk. olive-green; Confucius, men w/2 horse-drawn carts. — 8.00 — 24.00 — 60.00

223 10 YUAN
1937. Blue and green. SYS at l., vessel at r. Back blue-green;
Confucius, men w/2 horse-drawn carts.
a. Issued note. — 8.00 — 25.00 — 75.00
b. W/o sign. — 5.00 — 15.00 — 45.00

		VG	VF	UNC
218	10 YUAN			
(217)				

218 10 YUAN
(217) 1936. Dk. blue and black on m/c unpt. SYS at l. and as wmk. Back
blue-green; Palace of China in Peking at r.
a. Sign. 5. — .10 — .30 — 1.00
b. Sign. 6. — .10 — .30 — 1.00
c. Sign. 7. — .25 — 1.00 — 3.00
d. Sign. 8 (heavier or lighter print). — .10 — .30 — 1.00
e. Sign. 9. — .25 — 1.00 — 2.00
f. Ovpt: Tibetan characters on face and back. Sign. 5; 7. — 20.00 — 50.00 — —

219 50 YUAN
1936. Dk. blue and brown on m/c unpt. SYS at l. and as wmk. Back
red; Palace of China in Peking at ctr. Printer: W&S.
a. Issued note. Sign. 11 in red. — .50 — 2.00 — 5.00
b. Ovpt: *Chungking* in Chinese at l. and r. and in English at upper ctr. on back. Sign. 10 in black. — 25.00 — —

1939 ISSUES

		VG	VF	UNC
224	1 FEN = 1 CENT			

224 1 FEN = 1 CENT
1939. Red. Pagoda at l. Back red; coin at r.
a. Printer: Union Publishers & Printers. — .20 — .65 — 2.00
b. Printer: Union Printing Co. — .50 — 1.50 — 4.50

225 5 FEN = 5 CENTS

	VG	VF	UNC
1939. Green. Pagoda at l. Back green; coin in ctr.			
a. Printer: Union Publishers & Printers.	.20	.65	2.00
b. Printer: Union Printing Co.	1.00	3.25	10.00

225A 5 FEN = 5 CENTS

	VG	VF	UNC
1939. Green. Face like #225 but back w/date 1936 and Chinese text (pass for the Nanking Military Government).	—	140.00	350.00

1940 ISSUE

#226-229 printer: CHB.

228 10 YUAN

	VG	VF	UNC
1940. Blue-gray. Portr. SYS at r. Back gray-green.	.20	.50	1.50

229 50 YUAN

	VG	VF	UNC
1940. Orange. Portr. SYS at r. Back blue. *CHUNG-KING.*			
a. Sign. 5.	1.65	5.00	15.00
b. Sign. 8.	1.00	3.00	9.00

226 1 CHIAO = 10 CENTS

	VG	VF	UNC
1940. Green. Portr. SYS at r.	.10	.25	.75

227 2 CHIAO = 20 CENTS

	VG	VF	UNC
1940. Blue. Portr. SYS at r. Like #226.			
a. Issued note.	.15	.35	1.00
r. Remainder w/o sign.	—	—	—

1941 ISSUES

#239-240 printer: SBNC.
#241 *Deleted.*

230 2 YUAN

	VG	VF	UNC
1941. Purple on lt. orange and blue unpt. SYS at r. Back blue. Printer: CHB.	.40	1.00	3.00

231 2 YUAN

	VG	VF	UNC
1941. Blue and m/c. SYS at l. Back blue; temple behind trees at ctr. 3 serial # varieties. Printer: TDLR.	1.00	2.50	8.50

232 2 YUAN

	VG	VF	UNC
1941. Blue and m/c. SYS at l. Back blue; pagoda near mountain slope (Wang He Lou). Printer: TDLR.	8.00	25.00	75.00

233 5 YUAN

	VG	VF	UNC
1941. Green. SYS at l. Back olive. Similar to #237. Printer: W&S.	5.50	16.50	50.00

234 5 YUAN

	VG	VF	UNC
1941. Green on m/c unpt. Portr. SYS at lower r. Back green. 2 serial # varieties. Printer: CHB.			
a. Issued note.	.25	.75	2.00
b. Ovpt: *Chungking* in Chinese at l. and r. on face. *CHUNGKING* in English on back.	1.00	3.00	12.50

235 5 YUAN

	VG	VF	UNC
1941. Lilac-brown. SYS at l. Back lilac-brown; pagoda near mountain slope (Wang He Lou). 2 serial # varieties. Printer: TDLR.	.40	1.00	4.00

236 5 YUAN

	VG	VF	UNC
1941. Dk. brown. SYS at l. Back dk. brown; temple behind trees at ctr. 3 serial # varieties. Printer: TDLR.	1.00	3.00	10.00

237 10 YUAN

	VG	VF	UNC
1941. Dk. blue. SYS at l. Back green-blue. Printer: W&S.			
a. Sign. 5.	.75	3.00	8.00
b. Sign. 6.	.30	1.00	4.00
c. Sign. 7.	.30	1.00	4.00
d. Sign. 8.	.75	3.00	8.00
e. Sign. 9.	.30	1.00	4.00

238 10 YUAN

1941. Blue. P'ai-Lou Gate at l. Back dk. green. 2 serial # varieties. Chinese printer.

	VG	VF	UNC
a. Sign. 7.	3.00	10.00	25.00
b. Sign. 9.	2.25	8.00	20.00

239 10 YUAN

1941. Blue. SYS at l. Back green.

	VG	VF	UNC
a. Sign. 7 in black.	.30	1.50	4.00
b. Sign. 12 in green as part of plate.	1.50	5.50	17.50

240 20 YUAN

1941. Red and m/c. Portr. SYS at l. Back brown.

	VG	VF	UNC
a. Sign. 7 in black. Blue serial # and sign. seals.	1.00	5.00	25.00
b. As a but w/red serial # and sign. seals.	.75	4.00	20.00
c. Sign. 12 in brown as part of plate.	.30	1.00	5.00

242 50 YUAN

1941. Green. P'ai-Lou Gate at r. Back brown. 2 serial # varieties.

	VG	VF	UNC
a. Chinese printer 8 characters.	4.00	10.00	30.00
b. Chinese printer 7 characters.	8.50	20.00	60.00
c. Chinese printer 6 characters.	8.50	20.00	60.00

243 100 YUAN

1941. Greenish gray on m/c unpt. Portr. SYS at l. Back purple. Printer: SBNC.

	VG	VF	UNC
a. Issued note.	.10	.25	1.00
b. W/o serial #.	3.00	10.00	25.00

1942 ISSUES

#244 and 245 printer: TDLR.

#251-253 printer: TDLR.

244 5 YUAN

1942. Green. SYS at l. Airplane on back.

	VG	VF	UNC
a. Sign. 6.	1.00	3.50	10.00
b. Sign. 7.	1.00	3.50	10.00

245 10 YUAN

1942. Blue. Portr. SYS at l. Military trumpeter near Great Wall on back.

	VG	VF	UNC
a. Sign. 5.	1.00	3.50	10.00
b. Sign. 6.	.50	1.50	6.00
c. Sign. 7.	.50	1.50	6.00
d. Ovpt. *Chungking.* Sign. 7.	5.00	15.00	40.00

246 10 YUAN

1942. Blue. SYS at l. Back w/o vignette. Printer: Dah Tung Book Company.

	VG	VF	UNC
	2.50	7.50	30.00

247 10 YUAN

1942. Brown. P'ai-lou Gate at r. Back yellow-brown. 2 serial # and 2 paper varieties. Chinese printer.

	VG	VF	UNC
	2.50	7.50	30.00

248 20 YUAN

1942. Brown. P'ai-lou Gate at r. Back red. Chinese printer.

	VG	VF	UNC
	3.25	10.00	40.00

249 100 YUAN

1942. Red. Victory Gate at ctr. Back blue.

	VG	VF	UNC
a. Chinese printer 8 characters. Sign. 7.	3.00	9.00	35.00
b. As a. Sign. 9.	2.00	5.00	17.50
c. Chinese printer 7 characters. Sign. 7.	3.00	10.00	40.00

250 100 YUAN

1942. Red. SYS at r. Back green. Chinese printer.

	VG	VF	UNC
	2.00	8.00	30.00

251 500 YUAN

1942. Red on gold unpt. SYS at l. Back red; ship at ctr.

	VG	VF	UNC
	.40	2.00	8.00

252 1000 YUAN

1942. Lilac on lt. green unpt. SYS at l. Great Wall at ctr. on back.

	VG	VF	UNC
	.40	2.00	8.00

253 2000 YUAN

1942. Red on lt. green unpt. SYS at l. Back red; pagoda at shoreline.

	VG	VF	UNC
	1.00	3.00	9.00

1943 ISSUE

254 100 YUAN

1943. Green-black. Victory Gate at l. Chinese printer.

	VG	VF	UNC
	1.50	5.00	20.00

1944 ISSUES

#255-256 printer: TDLR.

NOTE: Also see special issues for Manchuria #375-379.

			VG	VF	UNC
255	**50 YUAN**				
	1944. Deep purple on m/c unpt. SYS at l. and as wmk.		1.00	4.00	12.50
256	**100 YUAN**				
	1944. Dk. brown on m/c unpt. SYS at l. and as wmk.		.75	3.00	10.00

			VG	VF	UNC
257	**100 YUAN**				
	1944. Green on red unpt. SYS at l. Back brown; SYS memorial at r. Printer: W&S.		30.00	125.00	300.00

			VG	VF	UNC
258	**100 YUAN**				
	1944. Gray on lt. blue and pale orange unpt. P'ai-lou gateway at ctr. 150 x 64mm. Chinese printer.		3.00	10.00	30.00
259	**100 YUAN**				
	1944. Blue. P'ai-lou gateway at l. 151 x 77mm. Chinese printer.		3.00	10.00	30.00
260	**100 YUAN**				
	1944. Black on lt. gray and pale violet unpt. P'ai-lou gateway at l. 165 x 65mm. Chinese printer.		3.00	10.00	30.00
260A	**100 YUAN**				
	1944. Dk. gray on pale green unpt. Portr. SYS at r. Chinese printer 6 characters.		2.00	7.50	20.00

			VG	VF	UNC
261	**100 YUAN**				
	1944. Dk. brown. P'ai-lou gateway at ctr. 165 x 63mm. Chinese printer 8 characters.		2.00	7.50	25.00
262	**200 YUAN**				
	1944. Dk. green. Portr. SYS at lower l. Back brown. Chinese printer 6 characters.		2.00	7.50	25.00

			VG	VF	UNC
263	**400 YUAN**				
	1944. Green. Portr. SYS at lower l. Back brown. Chinese printer 6 characters.		2.00	7.50	30.00

			VG	VF	UNC
264	**500 YUAN**				
	1944. Red. SYS at l. and as wmk. Printer: TDLR.		.50	2.00	8.00

			VG	VF	UNC
265	**500 YUAN**				
	1944. Red-brown. on pale orange and lt. yellow-green unpt. SYS at l. and as wmk. Printer: W&S.		1.00	4.00	16.00
266	**500 YUAN**				
	1944. Black on yellow-green and tan unpt. Portr. SYS at r. 179 x 76mm. Chinese printer 8 characters.		4.50	12.50	50.00

			VG	VF	UNC
267	**500 YUAN**				
	1944. Dk. brown on pale orange and lt. olive-green unpt. Portr. SYS at l. Back blue. 2 serial # varieties. Printer: BABNC.		.30	1.00	5.00
268	**1000 YUAN**				
	1944. Dp. purple on m/c unpt. Portr. SYS at l. P'ai-lou gateway at r. Chinese printer 8 characters.				
	a. Issued note.		1.00	4.00	12.50
	b. W/2 red Chinese handstamps: "Army Command Northeast" and *Tung Pei* on face.		15.00	40.00	120.00
269	**1000 YUAN**				
	1944. Blue-gray. Portr. SYS at lower r. Chinese printer 6 characters.		12.00	35.00	80.00

1945 ISSUES

NOTE: #273 w/5 character ovpt. for Vietnam is believed to be a modern fabrication.

#291A *Deleted.* See #290.

#291B *Deleted.* See #294.

269A 5 YUAN
1945. Green on red unpt. Portr. SYS at lower l. Back green. Vietnam.
(S/M #C300-).

	VG	VF	UNC
	—	—	—

269B 5 YUAN
1945. Blue. SYS at l. Back green. Taiwan. (S/M #C300-219).

	VG	VF	UNC
	—	—	—

270 10 YUAN
1945. Green on pale green unpt. Portr. SYS at lower l. Chinese printer.

	VG	VF	UNC
	.30	1.00	4.50

271 10 YUAN
1945. Orange. SYS at l. Naval battle on back. Taiwan. (Not issued).

	VG	VF	UNC
	—	—	—

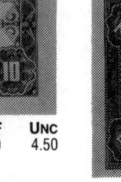

272 10 YUAN
1945. Burgundy. Portr. SYS at lower l. Vietnam.

	VG	VF	UNC
	—	—	—

273 50 YUAN
1945. Red on pale red unpt. Portr. SYS at l. Chinese printer.

	VG	VF	UNC
	.25	1.00	4.50

274 50 YUAN
1945. Olive. SYS at l. Printer: CPF. Sinkiang.

	VG	VF	UNC
	25.00	75.00	200.00

275 50 YUAN
1945. Red. SYS at l. Back blue; mirror printing of naval battle. Taiwan.
(Not issued).

	VG	VF	UNC
	—	—	—

276 50 YUAN
1945. Blue. Portr. SYS at lower l. Vietnam.

	VG	VF	UNC
	—	Rare	—

277 50 YUAN
1945. Green. Victory Gate.

	VG	VF	UNC
	10.00	30.00	90.00

277A 100 YUAN
1945. Blue-gray. Portr. SYS at lower l. Sinkiang. Printer: CPF.

	VG	VF	UNC
	60.00	150.00	325.00

277B 100 YUAN
1945. Taiwan.

	VG	VF	UNC
	—	—	—

278 100 YUAN
1945. Blue on pale blue unpt. Portr. SYS at lower l. lower l. Chinese
printer.

	VG	VF	UNC
	1.50	5.00	17.50

279 200 YUAN
1945. Gray-blue. SYS at l. Chinese printer.

	VG	VF	UNC
	3.00	10.00	25.00

280 400 YUAN
1945. Lilac. Portr. SYS at lower l. Chinese printer.

	VG	VF	UNC
	2.50	7.50	25.00

281 400 YUAN
1945. Dk. blue-black on lt. blue-green and pink unpt. SYS at l. in unpt.
Back: blue.

	VG	VF	UNC
	8.00	25.00	75.00

282 500 YUAN
1945. Greenish black on lt. blue unpt. Portr. SYS at lower l. Chinese
printer 8 characters.

	VG	VF	UNC
	2.50	7.50	22.50

283 500 YUAN
1945. Black w/lt. blue national sunbursts in unpt. at l. and r. Portr.
SYS at ctr. Back lt. olive-green. Chinese printer 8 characters.

	VG	VF	UNC
a. Issued note.	1.00	2.50	10.00
b. 2 Chinese handstamps: "Army Command Northeast" and *Tung Pei* on face.	21.50	65.00	200.00

284 500 YUAN
1945. Green. SYS at l. Chinese printer 5 characters.
1.25 5.00 15.00

285 500 YUAN
1945. Brown on lilac unpt. P'ai-lou Gate at r. Chinese printer 7
characters.

VG	VF	UNC
3.75	15.00	45.00

286 500 YUAN
1945. Red. Chinese printer 8 characters.
8.00 25.00 60.00

287 1000 YUAN
1945. Red-orange on lilac unpt. Portr. SYS at lower l. Chinese printer
8 characters.

VG	VF	UNC
2.50	7.50	25.00

288 1000 YUAN
1945. Brown-violet on pink unpt. Portr. SYS at lower l. Chinese printer
8 characters.

VG	VF	UNC
1.75	7.50	22.50

289 1000 YUAN
1945. Brown. Portr. SYS at ctr. Chinese printer 8 characters.

VG	VF	UNC
1.00	4.00	12.00

290 1000 YUAN
1945. Purple. SYS at ctr. National sunburst at l. and r. on back.
Printer: SBNC.
.25 1.00 3.00

291 1000 YUAN
1945. Black. SYS at r. Gray paper. Chinese printer 7 characters.
1.50 6.50 20.00

292 1000 YUAN
1945. Brown on lilac unpt. SYS at l. Chinese printer 5 characters.
1.50 6.50 20.00

293 1000 YUAN
1945. Blue-gray on pale blue and lilac unpt. SYS at l. Chinese printer 5
characters.
1.50 6.50 20.00

294 1000 YUAN
1945. Brown on red-brown unpt. SYS at l. Chinese printer 10
characters.
.75 3.00 9.00

295 1000 YUAN
1945. Dk. blue on pale blue and lilac unpt. Chinese printer 5
characters.
1.50 6.50 20.00

296 1000 YUAN
1945. Red on pink unpt. P'ai-lou Gate at ctr. Back blue. Chinese
printer 7 characters.
3.75 15.00 45.00

297 1000 YUAN
1945. Green. SYS at l. Back dk. blue. Chinese printer 6 characters.

VG	VF	UNC
2.50	10.00	30.00

298 1000 YUAN
1945. Blue. Portr. SYS at lower l. Chinese sign. in thick or thin
characters. Chinese printer 6 characters. White to gray paper.

VG	VF	UNC
1.50	6.50	20.00

299 2000 YUAN
1945. Green. Great Wall at r. Back brown. Chinese printer 7
characters.

VG	VF	UNC
5.00	20.00	60.00

300 2000 YUAN
1945. Brown-violet. SYS at r. Chinese printer 5 characters.
1.75 7.50 22.50

301 2000 YUAN
1945. Violet. SYS at l. Chinese printer 5 character.

	VG	VF	UNC
a. Issued note.	1.75	7.50	22.50
b. W/2 Chinese handstamps: "Army Command Northeast" and *Tung Pei* on face.	15.00	40.00	125.00

302 2000 YUAN
1945. Green. SYS at l. Back: black. Chinese printer 6 characters.
1.50 6.50 20.00

303 2500 YUAN
1945. Blue-lt. blue. Portr. SYS at l. Back dk. olive-green. 3 serial #
varieties. Chinese printer 7 characters.

VG	VF	UNC
2.50	10.00	30.00

304 2500 YUAN
1945. Blue on green unpt. SYS at l. Back blue. Chinese printer 6
characters.

VG	VF	UNC
3.75	15.00	45.00

305 5000 YUAN
1945. Blue-black on m/c unpt. Portr. SYS at l. P'ai-lou Gate at r.
Chinese printer 5 characters.

VG	VF	UNC
2.50	10.00	30.00

306 5000 YUAN
1945. Brown. SYS at l. 2 Chinese sign. varieties. 2 serial # varieties.
Chinese printer 6 characters.
2.00 8.00 25.00

1946 ISSUE

307 2000 YUAN
1946. Purple on gold unpt. SYS at l. Back dull red; SYS Mausoleum at
ctr. r. Printer: W&S.

VG	VF	UNC
1.25	5.00	15.00

1947 Issues

#316 *Deleted*. See 320c.

			VG	VF	UNC
308	**2000 YUAN**		3.00	12.50	37.50
	1947. Green on pale green and pink unpt. Portr. SYS at lower l. P'ailou Gate at r. Back black. Chinese printer 8 characters.				
309	**5000 YUAN**		1.50	6.50	20.00
	1947. Dk. blue on lt. green unpt. SYS at l. Back green. Chinese printer 8 characters.				
310	**5000 YUAN**		1.25	5.00	15.00
	1947. Purple. SYS at l. Printer: TDLR.				
311	**5000 YUAN**		1.00	4.00	12.50
	1947. Dk. lilac on gold unpt. SYS at l. Back lilac; SYS Mausoleum at ctr.				

			VG	VF	UNC
312	**5000 YUAN**		1.50	5.00	15.00
	1947. Blue on green unpt. Portr. SYS at lower l. Like #309. Back green. Chinese printer 5 characters.				
313	**5000 YUAN**		1.50	5.00	15.00
	1947. Green on lt. violet unpt. at ctr. Back green. Chinese printer 6 characters.				
314	**10,000 YUAN**		.75	2.50	7.50
	1947. Brown. SYS at l., mountains and river at r. Back blue. Chinese printer 8 characters.				

			VG	VF	UNC
315	**10,000 YUAN**		1.75	7.50	22.50
	1947. Olive on m/c unpt. Portr. SYS at l., mountains and river at r. Back olive-green. 159 x 75mm. Chinese printer 8 characters.				

			VG	VF	UNC
317	**10,000 YUAN**		1.50	6.00	18.00
	1947. Red on pale blue and lt. green unpt. Portr. SYS at ctr. Back dull red. Printer: TDLR.				
318	**10,000 YUAN**		1.75	7.50	22.50
	1947. Gray-blue. SYS at l. 164 x 74mm. Chinese printer 8 characters.				
319	**10,000 YUAN**		.75	2.50	7.50
	1947. Red-brown. SYS at ctr. Back gray-black. Printer: SBNC.				

			VG	VF	UNC
320	**10,000 YUAN**				
	1947. Blue-violet. Portr. SYS at lower l. Back blue-violet.				
	a. Chinese printer 5 characters. 2 paper and serial # varieties.		1.00	4.00	12.50
	b. Chinese printer 6 characters.		1.00	4.00	12.50
	c. Chinese printer 8 characters.		1.00	4.00	12.50
321	**10,000 YUAN**		1.75	7.50	22.50
	1947. Dk. brown on m/c unpt. SYS at l. Back dk. lilac. Chinese printer 6 characters.				

			VG	VF	UNC
322	**10,000 YUAN**		1.75	7.50	22.50
	1947. Lilac. Portr. SYS at lower l. Back brown. 162 x 74mm. Chinese printer 8 characters.				
322A	**50,000 YUAN**		—	—	—
	1947. Brown on green unpt. SYS at r. Small house at ctr. on back. Printer: HBNC. (Not issued).				

1930 SHANGHAI CUSTOMS GOLD UNITS ISSUES

#323-374 portr. SYS at top ctr. Bank bldg. at l. ctr. on back. Vertical format except for #333 and #334 which are horizontal.

NOTE: This issue was primarily intended to facilitate customs payments, but during and after World War II they were used for general circulation. The 1930 issue was printed into the 1940's.

#323-331 w/m/c guilloche. Sign. varieties. Printer: ABNC.

			VG	VF	UNC
325	**1 CUSTOMS GOLD UNIT**				
	1930. Brown.				
	a. Sign. 4.		2.50	10.00	40.00
	b. Sign. 5.		2.00	8.00	22.50
	c. Sign. 7 in black. Sign. title: *ASSISTANT MANAGER* at r. Serial # on face and back.		2.00	10.00	40.00
	d. Sign. 7 in brown as part of plate. Sign. title: *ASST. GENERAL MANAGER* at r. Serial # on back only.		.25	1.00	4.50
326	**5 CUSTOMS GOLD UNITS**				
	1930. Black.				
	a. Sign. 4.		2.50	10.00	40.00
	b. Sign. 5.		2.00	8.00	25.00
	c. Sign. 7. Sign title: *ASSISTANT MANAGER* at r. Serial # on face and on back.		2.00	8.00	25.00
	d. Sign. 7 in plate. Sign. title: *ASST. GENERAL MANAGER* at r. Serial # on back only.		.25	.60	1.50
327	**10 CUSTOMS GOLD UNITS**				
	1930. Olive-gray.				
	a. Sign. 4.		2.50	10.00	40.00
	b. Sign. 5.		1.00	4.00	12.00
	c. Sign. 7 in black. Sign. title: *ASSISTANT MANAGER* at r. Serial # on face and on back.		1.00	4.00	12.00
	d. Sign. 7 in plate. Sign. title: *ASST. GENERAL MANAGER* at r. Serial # on back only.		.20	.40	1.25
328	**20 CUSTOMS GOLD UNITS**				
	1930. Dk. green.		.15	.40	1.00

			VG	VF	UNC
329	**50 CUSTOMS GOLD UNITS**		.25	.75	2.00
	1930. Purple.				

330	100 CUSTOMS GOLD UNITS	VG	VF	UNC
	1930. Red.	.35	1.00	4.00
	a. Issued note.			
	b. W/2 red Chinese handstamps: "Army Command Northeast" and *Tung Pei.*	—	—	—
331	250 CUSTOMS GOLD UNITS			
	1930. Brown.	1.25	3.75	15.00

323	10 CENTS	VG	VF	UNC
	1930. Purple.			
	a. Sign. 4.	1.50	5.00	25.00
	b. Sign. 5.	1.00	3.50	15.00
324	20 CENTS			
	1930. Green.			
	a. Sign. 4.	2.50	7.50	30.00
	b. Sign. 5.	1.50	5.00	25.00

1930 (1947) CUSTOMS GOLD UNITS ISSUES

332	500 CUSTOMS GOLD UNITS	VG	VF	UNC
	1930 (1947). Blue.	.50	1.50	5.00

1947 CUSTOMS GOLD UNITS ISSUE

#332-334 horizontal format w/m/c guilloche. Printer: W&S.
#335-374 vertical format w/m/c guilloche.
#337 *Deleted.* See #339c.
#341A *Deleted.* See #342c.
#345 *Deleted.* See #364A.

333	100 CUSTOMS GOLD UNITS			
	1947. Violet. Back blue. Specimen.	—	—	90.00

334	500 CUSTOMS GOLD UNITS	VG	VF	UNC
	1947. Blue on m/c unpt. Back brown.	4.00	20.00	50.00

335	500 CUSTOMS GOLD UNITS	VG	VF	UNC
	1947. Blue. *SHANGHAI.* Printer: ABNC.	.75	3.50	9.00
336	500 CUSTOMS GOLD UNITS			
	1947. Lt. green. Printer: SBNC.	.80	4.00	10.00

338	1000 CUSTOMS GOLD UNITS	VG	VF	UNC
	1947. Olive. Olive guilloche. Printer: CHB.	.50	2.00	6.00
339	1000 CUSTOMS GOLD UNITS			
	1947. Gray. Brown and lilac guilloche.			
	a. Chinese printer 8 characters. Serial # 2mm tall.	.50	2.00	6.00
	b. Chinese printer 6 characters. Serial # 3mm tall.	.35	2.00	6.00
	c. Chinese printer 5 characters. 2 serial # varieties.	.75	3.00	9.00

340	**2000 CUSTOMS GOLD UNITS**	**VG**	**VF**	**UNC**
	1947. Orange. Printer: ABNC.	.50	2.00	6.00
341	**2000 CUSTOMS GOLD UNITS**			
	1947. Lt. olive-brown. Printer: SBNC.	.50	2.00	6.00

342	**2000 CUSTOMS GOLD UNITS**	**VG**	**VF**	**UNC**
	1947. Green.			
	a. Chinese printer 5 characters.	.60	2.50	7.50
	b. Chinese printer 6 characters.	.60	2.50	7.50
	c. Chinese printer 9 characters.	.60	2.50	7.50

343	**2000 CUSTOMS GOLD UNITS**	**VG**	**VF**	**UNC**
	1947. Dk. brown. Printer: CHB.	.50	2.00	6.00
344	**2000 CUSTOMS GOLD UNITS**			
	1947. Blue-violet. Printer: TDLR.	.50	2.00	6.00

345	**2500 CUSTOMS GOLD UNITS**	**VG**	**VF**	**UNC**
	1947. Olive. Printer: CHB.	1.00	4.00	12.00
346	**2500 CUSTOMS GOLD UNITS**			
	1947. Violet. Chinese printer 5 characters.		Reported Not Confirmed	
347	**5000 CUSTOMS GOLD UNITS**			
	1947. Brown. Printer: TDLR.	.50	2.00	6.00
348	**5000 CUSTOMS GOLD UNITS**			
	1947. Green. Printer: TDLR.		Reported Not Confirmed	
349	**5000 CUSTOMS GOLD UNITS**			
	1947. Blue. Printer: SBNC.	.50	2.00	6.00

350	**5000 CUSTOMS GOLD UNITS**	**VG**	**VF**	**UNC**
	1947. Green. Chinese printer 5 characters.	.75	3.00	9.00
351	**5000 CUSTOMS GOLD UNITS**			
	1947. Red. Chinese printer 5 characters.			
	a. Issued note.	.50	2.00	6.00
	p. Proof.	—	—	150.00

352	**5000 CUSTOMS GOLD UNITS**	**VG**	**VF**	**UNC**
	1947. Brown on gold unpt. Back black. Chinese printer 5 characters.	.75	3.00	9.00
	Lg. or sm. serial #.			

353	5000 CUSTOMS GOLD UNITS	VG	VF	UNC
	1947. Brown. Back slate blue. Printer: CHB.	.50	2.00	6.00
354	10,000 CUSTOMS GOLD UNITS			
	1947. Blue. Printer: TDLR.	.50	2.00	6.00
355	10,000 CUSTOMS GOLD UNITS			
	1947. Printer: SBNC.		Reported Not Confirmed	

1948 CUSTOMS GOLD UNITS ISSUES

357	2000 CUSTOMS GOLD UNITS	VG	VF	UNC
	1948. Orange. Chinese printer 5 characters.	.50	2.00	6.00
358	2500 CUSTOMS GOLD UNITS			
	1948. Lilac-brown. Chinese printer 5 characters. Large or small serial #.	1.00	4.00	12.00

359	5000 CUSTOMS GOLD UNITS	VG	VF	UNC
	1948. Purple. Printer: ABNC.	.50	2.00	6.00
360	5000 CUSTOMS GOLD UNITS			
	1948. Blue. Printer: SBNC.	.50	2.00	6.00

361	5000 CUSTOMS GOLD UNITS	VG	VF	UNC
	1948. Purple. Chinese printer 5 characters. Large or small serial # and 2 paper varieties.	.50	2.00	6.00
362	5000 CUSTOMS GOLD UNITS			
	1948. Blue. Printer: CHB.	.50	2.00	6.00
363	10,000 CUSTOMS GOLD UNITS			
	1948. Blue. Printer: SBNC.	.75	5.00	9.00
364	10,000 CUSTOMS GOLD UNITS			
	1948. Blue. Chinese printer 5 characters. 2 serial # varieties.	.50	2.00	6.00
364A	10,000 CUSTOMS GOLD UNITS			
	1948. Printer: W&S.	—	—	—
365	25,000 CUSTOMS GOLD UNITS			
	1948. Brown. Printer: ABNC.	3.50	14.00	42.00

366	25,000 CUSTOMS GOLD UNITS	VG	VF	UNC
	1948. Green. Chinese printer 5 characters. Large or small serial #.	1.25	5.00	15.00
367	25,000 CUSTOMS GOLD UNITS			
	1948. Lilac-brown. Printer: CHB.	1.75	7.50	22.50
368	50,000 CUSTOMS GOLD UNITS			
	1948. Red. Printer: CHB.			
	a. Issued note.	—	—	—
	s. Specimen.	—	Unc	100.00
369	50,000 CUSTOMS GOLD UNITS			
	1948. Pink. Similar to #368 but different guilloche. Specimen. Printer: CHB.	—	Unc	100.00
369A	50,000 CUSTOMS GOLD UNITS			
	1948. Purple. Printer: SBNC. (Not issued).	—	—	—
370	50,000 CUSTOMS GOLD UNITS			
	1948. Red. Chinese printer 5 characters. 2 serial # varieties. 64 x 154mm.	1.50	6.00	18.00
371	50,000 CUSTOMS GOLD UNITS			
	1948. Orange. Chinese printer 5 characters. 70 x 162mm.			
	a. Issued note.	2.25	9.00	27.50
	p. Proof.	—	—	150.00
372	50,000 CUSTOMS GOLD UNITS			
	1948. Deep purple on lt. blue unpt. Chinese printer 5 characters.	2.25	9.00	27.50

373	50,000 CUSTOMS GOLD UNITS	VG	VF	UNC
	1948. Brown-violet. Chinese printer 5 characters.	3.00	12.00	48.00
374	250,000 CUSTOMS GOLD UNITS			
	1948. Red and m/c.	15.00	60.00	200.00

1945-48 "9 NORTHEASTERN PROVINCES" BRANCH ISSUES

Issued at a rate of 20 to 1 current yuan.

#375-386 city gate at l. Under the bank title are 7 Chinese characters which translates "note for circulation in the northeast 9 provinces."

#380A *Deleted.* See #380b.

#381-386 Great Wall on back.

東北九省流通券
Tung Pei Chiu Sheng Liu T'ung Ch'üan

		VG	VF	UNC
375	**1 YUAN**			
	1945. Brown on pink unpt. (S/M #C303-1).	5.00	12.50	30.00
376	**5 YUAN**			
	1945. Orange. (S/M #C303-2).	2.50	7.50	20.00
376A	**5 YUAN**			
	1945. Red. Peking printer. (SM #C303-2.5).	—	600.00	1000.
377	**10 YUAN**			
	1945. Blue on purple unpt. Back blue. (S/M #C303-3).	1.00	4.00	17.50
378	**50 YUAN**			
	1945. Purple on green unpt. (S/M #C303-4).	1.00	4.00	17.50
379	**100 YUAN**			
	1945. Olive-green on lt. tan unpt. Back dk. olive-green. 2 serial # varieties. (S/M #C303-5).	.25	1.00	3.00

		VG	VF	UNC
380	**500 YUAN**			
	1946; 1947. Dk. green on lilac unpt. Back dk. green.			
	a. Shanghai printer. (S/M #C303-10). (1946).	.25	1.00	3.00
	b. Peking printer. (S/M #C303-21). (1947).	1.00	3.00	15.00
381	**500 YUAN**			
	1947. Dk. brown on orange unpt. (S/M #C303-20).	.25	1.00	3.00
382	**1000 YUAN**			
	1947. Blue-black on pink unpt.			
	a. Chinese printer 5 characters. (S/M #C303-22).	1.00	3.00	10.00
	b. Chinese printer 8 characters. (S/M #C303-23).	.25	1.00	3.00
383	**2000 YUAN**			
	1947. Brown. (S/M #C303-24).	1.00	3.00	10.00
384	**2000 YUAN**			
	1948. Brown-violet on m/c unpt. (S/M #C303-30).	.25	1.00	3.00

		VG	VF	UNC
385	**5000 YUAN**			
	1948. Dk. blue-black on red and tan guilloche. 2 serial # varieties. (S/M #C303-31a).	.25	1.00	3.00
385A	**5000 YUAN**			
	1948. Greenish blue-black on brown and olive-green guilloche. (S/M #C303-31b).	.50	2.00	6.00
386	**10,000 YUAN**			
	1948. Brown on m/c unpt. Back: brown. (S/M #C303-32).	.25	1.00	2.50

1948 (1945 DATED) GOLD *CHIN YUAN* ISSUE

This system was introduced in August 1948, to replace the previous currency at an exchange rate of GY$1 for $3,000,000 in the old currency.

#387-394 *Fa Pi* currency withheld because of high inflation and later issued as gold yuan. Printer: ABNC.

		VG	VF	UNC
387	**1 YUAN**			
	1945. (1948). Blue on m/c unpt. CKS at ctr. (S/M #C302-1).	.15	.75	3.50

		VG	VF	UNC
388	**5 YUAN**			
	1945 (1948). Olive-green on m/c unpt. Lin Sun at l. 3 sign. varieties. (S/M #C302-2).	.25	1.00	4.00
389	**5 YUAN**			
	1945 (1948). Blue on m/c unpt. SYS at ctr. National sunbursts at l. and r. Junks at ctr. on back. Printer: SBNC. Specimen. (S/M #C302-3).	7.50	30.00	120.00
389A	**5 YUAN**			
	1945. Like #389 but black. Green back. Wide margin. Specimen.	—	—	—

		VG	VF	UNC
390	**10 YUAN**			
	1945 (1948). Brown on m/c unpt. CKS at r. Bridge at l. on back. 3 sign. varieties. (S/M #C302-4).	.35	1.50	6.00

		VG	VF	UNC
391	**20 YUAN**			
	1945 (1948). Green. Lin Sun at ctr.	.35	1.50	6.00
392	**50 YUAN**			
	1945 (1948). Black on m/c unpt. SYS at ctr. 2 sign. varieties. (S/M #C302-6).	.35	1.50	6.00

		VG	VF	UNC
393	**50 YUAN**			
	1945 (1948). Black on m/c unpt. CKS at ctr. 3 sign. varieties. (S/M #C302-7).	.35	1.50	6.00
394	**100 YUAN**			
	1945 (1948). Red on m/c unpt. Lin Sun at l. CKS at r. 2 sign. varieties. (S/M #C302-8).	1.00	4.00	16.00

1948 (1946 DATED) GOLD *CHIN YUAN* ISSUE
Portr. CKS at r. Printer: TDLR.

			VG	VF	UNC
395	**10 CENTS**				
	1946. Brown. Shoreline village, pagoda at ctr. on back. (S/M #C302-10).		.25	1.00	3.00
395A	**20 CENTS**				
	1946. Black. Back green; sampans at anchor. Specimen.		—	Unc	40.00
396	**20 CENTS**				
	1946. Orange. Sampans at anchor on back. (S/M #C302-11).		.40	1.25	4.00

1948 GOLD *CHIN YUAN* ISSUE

			VG	VF	UNC
399	**10 YUAN**				
	1948. Green on m/c unpt. CKS at r. Printer: CPF. (S/M #C302-30).		.25	1.00	4.00
400	**20 YUAN**				
	1948. Brown on m/c unpt. CKS at r. Printer: CHB. (S/M #C302-32).		.25	1.00	4.00
401	**20 YUAN**				
	1948. Red on m/c unpt. CKS at r. Printer: CPF. (S/M #C302-31).		.50	1.50	5.00

			VG	VF	UNC
402	**50 YUAN**				
	1948. Deep red on gold and lt. blue unpt. CKS at ctr. Printer: CHB. (S/M #C302-41).		1.00	3.00	10.00
403	**50 YUAN**				
	1948. Violet on m/c unpt. CKS at r. Printer: CPF. (S/M #C302-40).		.50	1.50	5.00

			VG	VF	UNC
404	**50 YUAN**				
	1948. Black on m/c unpt. CKS at ctr. Yangtze Ganges at ctr. on back. Printer: TDLR. (S/M #C302-42).		35.00	100.00	300.00
405	**50 YUAN**				
	1948. Red. CKS at r. Printer: SBNC. (S/M #C302-43).		10.00	30.00	90.00
406	**100 YUAN**				
	1948. Green. CKS at ctr. Printer: CHB. (S/M #C302-45).		1.00	3.00	9.00

			VG	VF	UNC
407	**100 YUAN**				
	1948. Dk. blue on m/c unpt. CKS at r. Printer: CPF. (S/M #C302-44).		1.00	3.00	9.00
396A	**10 CENTS**				
	1948. CKS at ctr. Printer: CPF. (Not issued).		—	—	—

			VG	VF	UNC
397	**50 CENTS**				
	1948. Brown. CKS at r. Printer: CPF. (S/M #C302-20).		.50	1.50	5.00
398	**50 CENTS**				
	1948. Violet. CKS at r. Printer: SBNC. (S/M #C302-21).		5.00	15.00	45.00

1949 GOLD *CHIN YUAN* ISSUES

			VG	VF	UNC
408	**100 YUAN**				
	1949. Orange on m/c unpt. CKS at r. Printer: CPF. (S/M #C302-50).		1.00	3.00	9.00

			VG	VF	UNC
409	**500 YUAN**				
	1949. Dk. green on m/c unpt. CKS at r. Printer: CPF. (S/M #C302-51).		.75	2.00	7.00
410	**500 YUAN**				
	1949. Violet on m/c unpt. CKS at r. Printer: CHB. (S/M #C302-52).		.35	1.00	4.00
411	**1000 YUAN**				
	1949. Brown. CKS at r. Back red; temple at r. Printer: CHB. (S/M #C302-55).		.40	1.25	5.00

			VG	VF	UNC
412	**1000 YUAN**				
	1949. Blue-gray on m/c unpt. CKS at r.				
	a. Printer: CPF. (S/M #C302-54a).		.50	1.50	5.00
	b. Printer: CPF1. (S/M #C302-54b).		1.00	3.00	10.00
	c. Printer: CPF2. (S/M #C302-54c).		1.00	3.00	10.00
	d. Printer: CPF3. (S/M #C302-54d).		1.00	3.00	10.00
	e. Printer: CPF4. (S/M #C302-54e).		1.00	3.00	10.00
413	**1000 YUAN**				
	1949. Brown. CKS at r. Printer: CPF. (S/M #C302-55).		.50	1.50	5.00
414	**5000 YUAN**				
	1949. Red. CKS at r. Back red; w/bridge. Printer: CHB. (S/M #C302-57).		.50	1.50	5.00

			VG	VF	UNC
415	**5000 YUAN**				
	1949. Red on m/c unpt. CKS at r. Back red; w/bank at l.				
	a. Printer: CPF. (S/M #C302-56a).		.35	1.00	5.00
	b. Printer: CPF3. (S/M #C302-56b).		1.00	3.00	10.00
416	**10,000 YUAN**				
	1949. Blue on m/c unpt. CKS at r. Back blue; w/bridge. Printer: CHB. (S/M #C302-61).		.50	1.50	5.00

			VG	VF	UNC
417	**10,000 YUAN**				
	1949. Blue on m/c unpt. CKS at r. Back blue; bank at l.				
	a. Printer: CPF. (S/M #C302-60a).		.75	3.00	9.00
	b. Printer: CPF1. (S/M #C302-60b).		1.50	6.00	20.00
	c. Printer: CPF2. (S/M #C302-60c).		1.50	6.00	20.00
418	**50,000 YUAN**				
	1949. Red-orange on m/c unpt. CKS at r. Printer: CPF. (S/M #C302-62).		1.00	3.00	10.00

419 50,000 YUAN
1949. Brown and m/c. CKS at r. Similar to $418 but w/different guilloche.

		VG	VF	UNC
a.	Printer: CPF. (S/M #C302-63a).	.75	2.00	7.50
b.	Printer: CPF1. (S/M #C302-63b).	1.00	5.00	15.00
c.	Printer: CPF2. (S/M #C302-63c).	1.00	4.00	12.50
p.	Proof.	—	—	50.00

420 50,000 YUAN
1949. Red. CKS at ctr. Printer: TDLR. (S/M #C302-64).   10.00 30.00 100.00

421 100,000 YUAN
1949. Lilac. CKS at r. Printer: CHB. (S/M #C302-71).   .65 1.75 7.50

422 100,000 YUAN
1949. Grayish green. CKS at r.

		VG	VF	UNC
a.	Printer: CPF. (S/M # #C302-72a).	.60	1.75	7.00
b.	Printer: CPF1. (S/M #C302-72b).	1.50	6.00	20.00
c.	Printer: CPF2. (S/M #C302-72c).	1.50	6.00	20.00
d.	Printer: CPF3. (S/M #C302-72d).	1.50	6.00	20.00
e.	Printer: CPF4. (S/M #C302-72e).	1.50	6.00	20.00
f.	Printer: CPF-Taipei. (S/M #C302-72f).	10.00	35.00	125.00

423 500,000 YUAN
1949. Greenish black on m/c unpt. Temple at ctr. on back. Printer: CHB. (S/M #C302-73).   1.00 2.50 8.00

424 500,000 YUAN
1949. Lilac-brown on m/c unpt. Back lilac; bank at ctr.

		VG	VF	UNC
a.	Printer: CPF. (S/M #C302-72a).	1.25	4.00	12.50
b.	Printer: CPF1. (S/M #C302-72b).	2.00	7.00	25.00
c.	Printer: CPF2. (S/M #C302-72c).	2.00	7.00	25.00
d.	Printer: CPF3. (S/M #C302-72d).	2.00	7.00	25.00
e.	Printer: CPF4. (S/M # #C302-72e).	2.00	7.00	25.00
f.	Printer: CPF-Taipei. (S/M #C302-72f).	12.00	35.00	175.00

425 500,000 YUAN
1949. Green. CKS at r. Printer: SBNC. (S/M #C302-74).   10.00 30.00 100.00

426 1,000,000 YUAN
1949. Brown and blue. CKS at r. Back brown. Printer: CHB. (S/M #C302-75).   6.00 18.00 60.00

427 5,000,000 YUAN   VG   VF   UNC
1949. Red and blue. CKS at r. Back red. Printer: CHB. (S/M #C302-77).   25.00 75.00 200.00

1949 SILVER *YIN YUAN* ISSUE

#439-448 printer: CHB.
#439-447 Silver 'junk' 1-Yuan coin at ctr. on back.

428 1 CENT   VG   VF   UNC
1949. Green. CKS at ctr. Vertical format. Printer: CPF-Chungking. (S/M #C304-1).   3.00 15.00 50.00

429 5 CENTS
1949. Red. CKS at ctr. Vertical format. Printer: CPF-Chungking. (S/M #C304-2).   3.00 15.00 50.00

430 5 CENTS
1949. Green. SYS at r. Temple of Heaven on back. Printer: CPF-Taipei. (S/M #C304-3).   10.00 30.00 90.00

431 5 CENTS   VG   VF   UNC
1949. Red-violet. Pier at ctr. *Tsingtao.* (S/M #C304-4).   11.00 32.50 100.00

432 10 CENTS
1949. Blue on red unpt. CKS at ctr. Vertical format. Printer: CPF-Chungking. I(S/M #C304-5).   5.00 20.00 60.00

433 10 CENTS   VG   VF   UNC
1949. Purple. SYS at r. Printer: CHB. (S/M #C304-6).   .25 .75 3.00

434 10 CENTS
1949. Gray-green. Pier at ctr. *Tsingtao.* (S/M #C304-7).   11.00 32.50 100.00

435 20 CENTS
1949. Orange. CKS at ctr. Vertical format. Printer: CPF-Chungking. (S/M #C304-10).   10.00 32.50 100.00

436 20 CENTS
1949. Green. SYS at r. Printer: CHB. (S/M #C304-11).   .50 1.25 5.00

437 50 CENTS   VG   VF   UNC
1949. Lilac. CKS at ctr. Vertical format. Printer: CPF-Chungking. (S/M #C304-12).   12.00 35.00 110.00

438 50 CENTS
1949. Brown. SYS at r. Printer: CPF-Taipei. *(S/M #C304-13).*   3.00   12.00   65.00

438A 50 CENTS
1949. Yellow-green. *Tsingtao. (S/M #C304-14).*   Reported Not Confirmed

439 1 DOLLAR   VG   VF   UNC
1949. Blue on m/c unpt. Portr. SYS at r. Printer: CHB. *(S/M #C304-*   .25   .75   3.00
20).

440 1 DOLLAR   VG   VF   UNC
1949. Lilac-brown. SYS at r. *CHUNGKING.* Printer: CHB. *(S/M #C304-*   .25   1.00   4.00
22).

441 1 DOLLAR   VG   VF   UNC
1949. Black-blue. SYS at r. *CANTON.* Printer: CHB. *(S/M #C304-21).*   .25   1.00   4.00

442 5 DOLLARS
1949. SYS at r. Printer: CHB. *(S/M #C304-23).*   2.50   7.50   22.50

443 5 DOLLARS
1949. Dk. brown on m/c unpt. SYS at r. *CHUNGKING.* Printer: CHB.   .50   2.00   6.00
(S/M #C304-25).

444 5 DOLLARS
1949. Brown and red. SYS at r. *CANTON.* Printer: CHB. *(S/M #C304-*
24).
   a. Issued note.   .50   2.00   6.00
   b. Sign. on back.   15.00   45.00   —

445 10 DOLLARS   VG   VF   UNC
1949. Red. SYS at r. Printer: CHB. *(S/M #C304-30).*   2.50   7.50   22.50

446 10 DOLLARS
1949. Pink. SYS at r. *CHUNGKING.* Printer: CHB. *(S/M #C304-32).*   3.00   10.00   30.00

447 10 DOLLARS
1949. Black on m/c unpt. SYS at r. *CHUNGKING.* Printer: CHB. *(S/M*   .50   1.50   6.00
#C304-31).

448 100 DOLLARS
1949. Green. SYS at r. *CHUNGKING.* Printer: CHB. Specimen. *(S/M*   —   —   90.00
#C304-33).

CENTRAL BANK OF CHINA
(BRANCHES - NATIONAL RESUMED)
GENERAL ISSUE - SHANGHAI BRANCH 上港

1949 GENERAL GOLD *CHIN YUAN* ISSUE
Circulating Bearer Cashier's Checks.

		GOOD	FINE	XF
449	**50,000 YUAN**			
	1949. Green on blue unpt. *(S/M #C302-).*	6.50	20.00	80.00
449A	**100,000 YUAN**			
	1949. Red on pink unpt. *(S/M #C302-).*	6.50	20.00	80.00
449B	**300,000 YUAN**			
	1949. Green. *(S/M #C302-).*	6.50	20.00	80.00
449C	**500,000 YUAN**			
	28.4.1949. Blue on pink unpt. *(S/M #C302-).*	6.50	20.00	80.00
449D	**1,000,000 YUAN**			
	1949. Violet on green unpt. *(S/M #C302-).*	6.50	20.00	80.00
449E	**5,000,000 YUAN**			
	7.5.1949. Brown on yellow unpt. *(S/M #C302-93).*	6.50	20.00	80.00
		VG	VF	UNC
449F	**10,000,000 YUAN**			
	1949. (Not issued). *(S/M #C302-).*	—	—	—

CHANGCHUNG BRANCH 長春

1948 FIRST ISSUE

		GOOD	FINE	XF
449G	**100,000 YUAN**			
	1948. Green on violet unpt. *(S/M #C302-).*	6.50	20.00	80.00
449GE	**200,000 YUAN**			
	1948. *(S/M #C302-).*	6.50	20.00	80.00
449GF	**500,000 YUAN**			
	1948. *(S/M #C302-).*	6.50	20.00	80.00
449GG	**1,000,000 YUAN**			
	1948. *(S/M #C302-).*	6.50	20.00	80.00
449GH	**2,000,000 YUAN**			
	1948. *(S/M #C302-).*	6.50	20.00	80.00
449H	**10,000,000 YUAN**			
	1948. *(S/M #C302-).*	6.50	20.00	80.00
449HH	**15,000,000 YUAN**			
	1948. *(S/M #C302-).*	6.50	20.00	80.00
449I	**30,000,000 YUAN**			
	1948. Gray on blue unpt. *(S/M #C302-).*	6.50	20.00	80.00
449J	**50,000,000 YUAN**			
	1948. Gray on blue unpt. *(S/M #C302-).*	6.50	20.00	80.00

     #449K   #449M

		GOOD	FINE	XF
449K	**60,000,000 YUAN**			
	1948. Purple on lilac unpt. *(S/M #C302-95).*	6.50	20.00	80.00
449L	**120,000,000 YUAN**			
	1948. Blue on gray unpt. *(S/M #C302-).*			
449M	**180,000,000 YUAN**			
	1948. Purple on brown unpt. *(S/M #C302-).*	6.50	20.00	80.00

1948 SECOND ISSUE

		GOOD	FINE	XF
449N	**5,000,000 YUAN**			
	24.8.1948. *(S/M #C302-).*	6.50	20.00	80.00
449O	**50,000,000 YUAN**			
	1948. *(S/M #C302-).*	6.50	20.00	80.00

1948 PROVISIONAL ISSUE

449P	**4,500,000 YUAN**			
	1948. Ovpt. on #449N. *(S/M #C302-).*	6.50	20.00	80.00
449Q	**30,000,000 YUAN**			
	1948. Ovpt. on #449O. *(S/M #C302-).*	6.50	20.00	80.00

CHENGTU BRANCH 成都

1949 GOLD *CHIN YUAN* FIRST ISSUE

449Z 5000 YUAN
7.4.1949-18.4.1949. Brown on yellow unpt., black text. *(S/M #C302-).*
a. Issued note. — 7.50 22.50 90.00
b. Remainder w/counterfoil. — 5.00 15.00 60.00

1949 GOLD *CHIN YUAN* SECOND ISSUE

	#449Y		**#449Z**	
		GOOD	FINE	XF

449Y 2000 YUAN
30.3.1949-13.4.1949. Violet-brown on lt. blue unpt., black text. *(S/M #C302-).* — 7.50 22.50 90.00

449AA 10,000 YUAN
25.4.1949-28.4.1949. Red-violet on lt. green unpt. *(S/M #C302-).* — 7.50 22.50 90.00

449R 10,000,000 YUAN
1949. *(S/M #C302-).* — 8.00 25.00 100.00

CHUNGKING BRANCH 重慶

1949 GOLD *CHIN YUAN* ISSUE

	#499U		**#449V**	
		GOOD	FINE	XF

449S 50,000 YUAN
1949. Brown. *(S/M #C302-).* — 6.50 20.00 80.00

449T 500,000 YUAN
1949. Red. *(S/M #C302-).* — 6.50 20.00 80.00

449U 1,000,000 YUAN
14.6.1949. Red on yellow unpt. *(S/M #C302-91).* — 6.50 20.00 80.00

449V 5,000,000 YUAN
1.6.1949. Green. *(S/M #C302-92).* — 6.50 20.00 80.00

449W 5,000,000 YUAN
1949. Purple on yellow unpt. *(S/M #C302-94).* — 6.50 20.00 80.00

	GOOD	FINE	XF

449X 10,000,000 YUAN
14.6.1949. Red on lt. blue unpt. *(S/M #C302-).* — 6.50 20.00 80.00

FOOCHOW BRANCH 福州

1949 GOLD *CHIN YUAN* FIRST ISSUE

449AF 50,000 YUAN
1.9.1949. Bank title in seal script w/flower bud outline in all 4 corners. *(S/M #C302-).* — 6.50 20.00 80.00

1949 GOLD *CHIN YUAN* SECOND ISSUE

#450A *Deleted.*

450B 20,000 YUAN
April 1949. Red-brown. *(S/M #C302-).* — 6.50 20.00 80.00

450BB 50,000 YUAN
April 1949. *(S/M #C302-).* — 6.50 20.00 80.00

	#450		**#450B**	
		GOOD	FINE	XF

450
April 1949. Purple. *(S/M #C302-80).* — 6.50 20.00 80.00

1949 NATIONAL *KUO PI YUAN* ISSUE

#450C-450G printer: CPF.

450C 20,000 YUAN
ND (1949). Red. (Not issued). *(S/M #C302-).* — — — —

450D 30,000 YUAN
ND (1949). Green. (Not issued). *(S/M #C302-).* — — — —

450E 40,000 YUAN
ND (1949). Lt. blue. (Not issued). *(S/M #C302-).* — — — —

450F 50,000 YUAN
ND (1949). Dk. blue. (Not issued). *(S/M #C302-).* — — —

450G	100,000 YUAN	GOOD	FINE	XF
	ND (1949). Brown on yellow unpt. (Not issued). *(S/M #C302-).*	—	—	—

1949 GOLD *CHIN YUAN* PROVISIONAL ISSUE

#450H   #450J

450H	20,000 YUAN	GOOD	FINE	XF
	25.4.1949. Ovpt. on #450C. *(S/M #C302-81).*	5.00	15.00	60.00
450I	30,000 YUAN			
	25.4.1949. Ovpt. on #450D. *(S/M #C302-82).*	5.00	15.00	60.00
450J	40,000 YUAN			
	25.4.1949. Ovpt. on #450E. *(S/M #C302-83).*	5.00	15.00	60.00
450K	50,000 YUAN			
	25.4.1949. Ovpt. on #450F. *(S/M #C302-84).*	5.00	15.00	60.00
450L	100,000 YUAN			
	25.4.1949. Ovpt. on #450G. *(S/M #C302-85).*	5.00	15.00	60.00

1949 GOLD *CHIN YUAN* FOURTH ISSUE
#450M, 450N SYS at upper ctr.

#450M   #450N

450M	100,000 YUAN	GOOD	FINE	XF
	April 1949. Brown on lt. blue unpt. *(S/M #C302-).*	6.50	20.00	80.00
450N	500,000 YUAN			
	April 1949. Blue on yellow unpt. *(S/M #C302-90).*	6.50	20.00	80.00

KUNMING BRANCH 明昆

1945-47 ISSUE

450O	100,000 YUAN			
	1945. Violet on yellow unpt. *(S/M #C302-).*	7.50	22.50	90.00
450P	300,000 YUAN			
	1947. Green on brown unpt. *(S/M #C302-).*	7.50	22.50	90.00

MUKDEN, MANCHURIA BRANCH 京盛

1948 NORTHWEST *YUAN* ISSUE

450Q	100,000 YUAN	GOOD	FINE	XF
	1948. Dk. brown on lt. gray unpt., black text. *(S/M #C303-).*	8.00	25.00	100.00
450R	500,000 YUAN			
	1948. Blue on yellow-orange unpt. black text. *(S/M #C303-).*	8.00	25.00	100.00
450S	5,000,000 YUAN			
	2.4.1948. *(S/M #C30-).*	8.00	25.00	100.00

YIBIN BRANCH

1944 NATIONAL *KUO PI YUAN* ISSUE

450T	5000 YUAN	GOOD	FINE	XF
	12.9.1944. Brown-violet on lt. blue unpt., black text. *(S/M #C302-).*	10.00	30.00	120.00

FARMERS BANK OF CHINA   行銀民農國中
Chung Kuo Nung Min Yin Hang

1934 ISSUE
#451-456 Chinese printer: TYPC. Sign. varieties.

453	1 YUAN	GOOD	FINE	XF
	1934. Red on lt. green and lilac unpt. 3 farm laborers at l. Back green; farmer plowing w/ox.			
	a. CHENGCHOW. (S/M #C290-10c).	5.00	15.00	60.00
	b. FOOCHOW. (S/M #C290-10a).	5.00	15.00	60.00
	c. LANCHOW. (S/M #C290-10d).	5.00	15.00	60.00
	d. W/o place name. (S/M #C290-10b).	5.00	15.00	60.00
	e. CHANGSHA. (S/M #C290-10e).	5.00	15.00	60.00
	f. HANKOW. (S/M #C290-10f).	5.00	15.00	60.00
	g. KWEIYANG. (S/M #C290-10g).	5.00	15.00	60.00
	h. SIAN. (S/M #C290-10h).	5.00	15.00	60.00
453A	1 YUAN			
	1934. Similar to #453 but face dk. blue. Back brown. Chinese ovpt: *Shanghai* on face. (S/M #C290-).	10.00	25.00	85.00

451	1 CHIAO = 10 CENTS	GOOD	FINE	XF
	ND. (1934) Red. Farm laborer at ctr. Back green. Vertical format. (S/M #C290-1).	3.00	10.00	40.00
452	2 CHIAO = 20 CENTS			
	ND. (1934) Red. (S/M #C290-2).	5.00	15.00	60.00

1935 FIRST ISSUE

454	20 CENTS = 2 CHIAO	VG	VF	UNC
	Feb. 1935. Red. Farmer plowing w/ox at top. Back green. 2 sign. varieties. (S/M #C290-20).	2.50	7.50	30.00

1935 SECOND ISSUE
#457-460 printer: TDLR.

457	1 YUAN	VG	VF	UNC
	1.4.1935. Red and m/c. Farming scenes at l. and r. Back red; house at ctr., sheep at r. 2 sign. varieties. (S/M #C290-30).	1.00	4.50	13.50
458	5 YUAN			
	1935. Green and m/c. Agricultural occupations at l. and r. Back green, temple at ctr., ox at r. 2 sign. varieties. (S/M #C290-31).			
	a. Issued note.	1.25	5.00	15.00
	b. W/various numerical ovpt.	2.25	9.00	27.50

459	10 YUAN	VG	VF	UNC
	1935. Purple and m/c. Agricultural occupations at l. and r. Pagoda at ctr., horse at r. on back. 3 sign. varieties. (S/M #C290-32).			
	a. Issued note.	1.00	4.00	12.00
	b. W/various numerical ovpt.	2.25	9.00	27.50

455	10 CENTS = 1 CHIAO	VG	VF	UNC
	1.3.1935. Red. Farmer in irrigation system at top. Back green. 2 sign. varieties. (S/M #C290-21).	2.25	9.00	27.50
456	20 CENTS = 2 CHIAO			
	1.4.1935. Black and red. Farmer plowing w/ox at top. Back orange. 2 sign. varieties. (S/M #C290-22).	2.25	9.00	27.50

1936 ISSUE

460	50 CENTS	VG	VF	UNC
	1936. Blue. Agricultural occupations at l. and r. Hillside pagoda at ctr., goat head at r. on back. (S/M #C290-40).	1.00	4.50	13.50

1937 ISSUE
#461-465 Chinese printer: TYPC.

461	10 CENTS	VG	VF	UNC
	1937. Blue. Landscape. Back brown, green and purple. 2 serial # varieties. (S/M #C290-50).	.25	1.00	3.00
461A	10 CENTS			
	1937. Blue. Face like #461 but back w/Chinese text (pass for the Nanking Military Government).	60.00	180.00	—

462 20 Cents
1937. Green. Agricultural scene. Back green, brown and blue. 2 serial # varieties. *(S/M #C290-51)*.

	VG	VF	UNC
	.25	1.00	3.00

1940 Regular Issue

463 1 Yuan
1940. Red. Workers at lower r. Back brown, blue and green. *(S/M #C290-60)*.

	VG	VF	UNC
	.25	1.00	3.00

464 10 Yuan
1940. Red. Farmer working in irrigation system. Back blue, lilac and brown. 2 serial # varieties. *(S/M #C290-65)*.

	VG	VF	UNC
	1.75	7.50	22.50

465 20 Yuan
1940. Blue. Worker by houses along river. 2 serial # varieties. *(S/M #C290-70)*.

	VG	VF	UNC
	1.00	4.50	13.50

1940 First Provisional Issue

#466-468 new issuer name ovpt. on notes of the Hupeh Provincial Bank.

466 1 Yuan
ND (1940 - old date 1929). Purple and m/c. Ovpt. on #S2104. *(S/M #C290-62)*.

	GOOD	FINE	XF
	15.00	60.00	180.00

467 5 Yuan
ND (1940 - old date 1929). Green and m/c. Ovpt. on #S2105.

	GOOD	FINE	XF
a. HANKOW. *(S/M #C290-63b)*.	16.50	50.00	150.00
b. HUPEH. *(S/M #C290-63c)*.	16.50	50.00	150.00
c. SHANTUNG. *(S/M #C290-63d)*.	16.50	50.00	150.00

		GOOD	FINE	XF
d. W/o place name. *(S/M #C290-63a)*.		16.50	50.00	150.00

468 10 Yuan
ND (1940 - old date 1929). Red and m/c. Ovpt. on #S2106. *(S/M #C290-66)*.

	GOOD	FINE	XF
	16.50	50.00	150.00

1940 Second Provisional Issue

#469, new issuer name ovpt. on notes of the Provincial Bank of Kwangtung Province. It is considered spurious by some authorities.

469 1 Yuan
ND (1940 - old date 1.1.1918). Blue and m/c. Ovpt. on #S2401b. *(S/M #C290-61)*.

	GOOD	FINE	XF
	—	—	—

1940 Third Provisional Issue

#470 and 471 new issuer name ovpt. on notes of the Szechuan Provincial Bank.

470	5 YUAN	GOOD	FINE	XF
	ND (1940 - old date 1.7.1937). Green and m/c. Ovpt. on #S2823. *(S/M #C290-64).*	5.00	20.00	80.00
471	10 YUAN			
	ND (1940 - old date 1.7.1937). Purple and m/c. Ovpt. on #S2824. *(S/M #C290-67).*	5.00	20.00	80.00

1940 FOURTH PROVISIONAL "RECONSTRUCTION" ISSUE
#472 and 473 new issuer m/c name ovpt. on notes of the Szechuan Provincial Government.

472	50 YUAN	GOOD	FINE	XF
	ND (1940 - old date 1937). Blue and green. Ovpt. on #S2816. Chungking. *(S/M #C290-71).*	8.50	35.00	—

473	100 YUAN	GOOD	FINE	XF
	ND (1940 - old date 1937). Orange and yellow. Ovpt. on #S2817. Chungking. *(S/M #C290-72).*	8.50	35.00	—

1941 ISSUE
#474 and 475 printer: TDLR.

#476-478 boats near bridge at ctr. Bridge at ctr. on back. Printer: ABNC.

474	1 YUAN	VG	VF	UNC
	1941. Brown on m/c unpt. SYS at l. House at ctr., sheep at r. on back. 3 serial # varieties. *(S/M #C290-80).*	.25	1.00	5.00

475	5 YUAN	VG	VF	UNC
	1941. Blue on m/c unpt. SYS at l. Temple at ctr., ox at r. on back. 3 serial # varieties. *(S/M #C290-81).*	.50	2.50	10.00

476	50 YUAN	VG	VF	UNC
	1941. Brown on green and m/c unpt. *(S/M #C290-82b).*			
	a. Issued note.	Reported Not Confirmed		
	b. Ovpt: *Chungking (S/M #C290-82a).*	1.00	3.00	12.00
477	100 YUAN			
	1941. Purple on green and m/c unpt. *(S/M #C290-83b).*			
	a. Serial # on face only.	.75	2.50	10.00
	b. Ovpt: *Chungking.* Serial # on face and back. *(S/M #C290-83a).*	.75	2.25	9.00

478	500 YUAN	VG	VF	UNC
	1941. Green on brown and m/c unpt. Similar to #476. *(S/M #C290-84b).*			
	a. Issued note.	3.00	10.00	40.00
	b. Black ovpt. *Chungking.* Specimen *(S/M #C290-84a).*	—	—	75.00

1942 ISSUE

479	50 YUAN	VG	VF	UNC
	1942. Brown. Steam passenger train at l. Chinese printer: TTBC. *(S/M #C290-90).*	1.50	6.00	24.00

484	1000 YUAN	GOOD	FINE	XF
	1945. Purple. Chinese printer: YAWY. *Shang Jao. (S/M #C290-111)*.	5.50	22.50	90.00

GREAT NORTHWESTERN BANK

行銀藏蒙
Men Tsang Yin Hang

Its Chinese name means "Mongolian-Tibetan Bank" but its issues had limited circulation.

1924 ISSUE

485	10 CENTS	GOOD	FINE	XF
	1924. Red. *TIENTSIN. (S/M #M14-1)*.	6.00	25.00	100.00

486	20 CENTS	GOOD	FINE	XF
	1924. Dk. brown. *TIENTSIN. (S/M #M14-2)*.	9.00	35.00	140.00
487	50 CENTS			
	1924. *TIENTSIN. (S/M #M14-3)*.		Reported Not Confirmed	
488	1 DOLLAR			
	1924. *(S/M #M14-10)*.		Reported Not Confirmed	
489	5 DOLLARS			
	1924. *(S/M #M14-11)*.		Reported Not Confirmed	
490	10 DOLLARS			
	1924. *(S/M #M14-12)*.		Reported Not Confirmed	

480	100 YUAN	VG	VF	UNC
	1942. Green. Landscape and agricultural scene at r. Chinese printer: TYPC. *(S/M #C290-91)*.	2.00	8.00	32.50

1943 ISSUE

#480A-482 agricultural scenes at l. and r. Ovpt: 7 characters below bank title. Printer: CTPA.

480A	5 YUAN	GOOD	FINE	XF
	1.10.1943. *(S/M #C290-97)*.	—	—	—
480B	10 YUAN			
	1.10.1943. Purple. Uniface. *(S/M #C290-98)*.	—	—	—

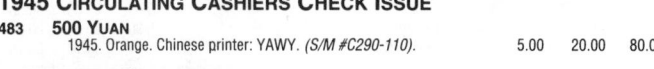

481	50 YUAN	GOOD	FINE	XF
	1.10.1943. Red. Like #480A. Back blue. *(S/M #C290-100)*.	—	30.00	120.00
482	100 YUAN			
	1.10.1943. Brown. Like #480A. *(S/M, #C290-101)*.	—	35.00	140.00

1945 CIRCULATING CASHIERS CHECK ISSUE

483	500 YUAN			
	1945. Orange. Chinese printer: YAWY. *(S/M #C290-110)*.	5.00	20.00	80.00

INDUSTRIAL DEVELOPMENT BANK OF CHINA

行銀業勸
Ch'uan Yeh Yin Hang

1921 ISSUES

491	1 YUAN	GOOD	FINE	XF
	1.2.1921. Red and m/c. Village gateway, bldg. at ctr. Printer: ABNC.			
	a. *PEKING. (S/M #C245-1a)*.	3.75	15.00	60.00
	b. *CHENGCHOW. (S/M #C245-1b)*.	3.75	15.00	60.00
	r. Remainder w/o place name. *(S/M #C245-1c)*.	—	Unc	75.00
	p. Proof.	—	Unc	110.00
	s. Specimen.	—	Unc	65.00
492	1 YUAN			
	1921. Green and black. Bldg. at ctr. Printer: BEPP.			
	a. *PEKING. (S/M #C245-2a)*.	3.75	15.00	60.00
	b. Remainder w/o place name. *(S/M #C245-2b)*.	—	Unc	60.00

1927 ISSUE

#497 and 498 w/ovpt: *King Ching Tung Chun* at top on back. Printer: BEPP.

		GOOD	FINE	XF
497	**10 CENTS**			
	1927. Dk. green. Waterfront palace at top ctr.			
	a. *TIENTSIN.* (S/M #C245-10a).	3.00	12.50	50.00
	r. Remainder, w/o place name. (S/M #C245-10b).	—	Unc	40.00
498	**20 CENTS**			
	1927. Orange. Hillside pagoda at top ctr.			
	a. *TIENTSIN/PEKING.* (S/M #C245-11a).	3.75	15.00	60.00
	r. Remainder, w/o place name. (SM #C245-11b).	—	Unc	48.00

		GOOD	FINE	XF
493	**5 YUAN**			
	1.2.1921. Dk. blue and m/v. Village gateway, bldg. at ctr. Also w/various control letter ovpts. Printer: ABNC.			
	a. *PEKING.* (S/M #C245-3a).	10.00	30.00	120.00
	b. *CHENGCHOW.* (S/M #C245-3b).	10.00	30.00	120.00
	p. Proof.	—	Unc	120.00
	s. Specimen.	—	Unc	65.00
494	**5 YUAN**			
	1.5.1921. Black and m/c. Back: brown. Printer: BEPP.			
	a. *PEKING.* (S/M #C245-4a).	8.00	25.00	100.00
	b. *NANKING.* (S/M #C245-4b).	8.00	25.00	100.00
	c. *TIENTSIN.* (S/M #C245-4c).	8.00	25.00	100.00

1928 ISSUE

#499-500 fortress city at l. Temple of Heaven at ctr. on back. Printer: BEPP.

		GOOD	FINE	XF
499	**10 CENTS**			
	1.9.1928. Red. *PEIPING.* (S/M #C245-20a).			
	a. Issued note.	3.00	12.50	50.00
	r. Remainder, w/o place name.	—	Unc	40.00
499A	**10 CENTS**			
	1.9.1928. Brown. *TIENTSIN.* (S/M #C245-20b).			
	a. Issued note.	3.00	12.50	50.00
	r. Remainder, w/o place name.	—	Unc	40.00

		GOOD	FINE	XF
495	**10 YUAN**			
	1.2.1921. Dk. green and m/c. Village gateway, bldg. at ctr. Printer: ABNC.			
	a. *PEKING.* (S/M #C245-5b).	7.00	20.00	80.00
	r. Remainder w/o place name. (S/M #C245-5b).	—	Unc	55.00
	p. Proof.	—	Unc	110.00
	s. Specimen.	—	Unc	65.00

		GOOD	FINE	XF
500	**20 CENTS**			
	1.9.1928. Purple.			
	a. *PEIPING.* (S/M #C245-21a).	5.00	20.00	80.00
	b. *TIENTSIN.* (S/M #C245-21b).	5.00	20.00	80.00
	r. Remainder, w/o place name. (S/M #C245-21c).	—	Unc	50.00

LAND BANK OF CHINA, LIMITED

中國墾業銀行

Chung Kuo K'en Yeh Yin Hang

1926 ISSUE

#501-506 cliffs at l., shoreline temple at ctr. r. Shoreline at l. on back. Also w/various numerical, letter and Chinese character control ovpt. Printer: W&S.

		GOOD	FINE	XF
496	**10 YUAN**			
	1.7.1921. Green and m/c. Back: brown. Printer: BEPP. *PEKING.* (S/M #C245-6).	8.00	25.00	100.00
496A	**50 YUAN**			
	1.2.1921. Orange on red and green unpt. Village gateway at ctr. Back: orange. (S/M #C245-7).			
	p. Proof w/o office of issue.	—	Unc	440.00
	s. Specimen w/o office of issue.	—	Unc	330.00
496B	**100 YUAN**			
	1.2.1921. Lt. blue on orange and olive-green unpt. Village gateway at ctr. Back: blue. *PEKING.* (S/M #C245-8).			
	a. Issued note.	Reported Not Confirmed		
	p. Proof w/o office of issue.	—	Unc	725.00
	s. Specimen w/o office of issue.	—	Unc	550.00

		GOOD	FINE	XF
501	**1 DOLLAR**			
	1.6.1926. Brown and m/c.			
	a. *SHANGHAI.* (S/M #C285-1a).	7.50	30.00	120.00
	b. *TIENTSIN.* (S/M #C285-1b).	7.50	30.00	120.00

		Good	Fine	XF
502	**5 DOLLARS**			
	1.6.1926. Purple and green.			
	a. *SHANGHAI. (S/M #C285-2a).*	11.00	45.00	180.00
	b. *TIENTSIN. (S/M #C285-2b).*	11.00	45.00	180.00
503	**10 DOLLARS**			
	1.6.1926. Green and m/c.			
	a. *SHANGHAI. (S/M #C285-3a).*	12.50	50.00	200.00
	b. *TIENTSIN. (S/M #C285-3b).*	12.50	50.00	200.00

1931 ISSUE

		Good	Fine	XF
504	**1 DOLLAR**			
	1.6.1931. Red and green. *SHANGHAI. (S/M #C285-10).*	6.00	25.00	100.00
505	**5 DOLLARS**			
	1.6.1931. Green and red. *SHANGHAI. (S/M #C285-11).*	6.00	25.00	100.00
506	**10 DOLLARS**			
	1.6.1931. Yellow. *SHANGHAI. (S/M #C285-12).*	11.00	45.00	180.00

NATIONAL BANK OF CHINA - NANKING

中華家國銀行

Chung Hua Kuo Chia Yin Hang

Established 1930 by Marshal Yen Hsi-shan at Peking in opposition to the Kuomintang in Nanking.

1930 ISSUE

#507-510 Temple of Heaven at ctr. PEKING. Printer: BEPP.

507	**20 CENTS**			
	1930. Specimen. *(S/M #C260-1).*	—	Unc	90.00

		Good	Fine	XF
508	**1 DOLLAR**			
	1930. Brown. Specimen. *(S/M #C260-10).*	—	Unc	110.00

		Good	Fine	XF
509	**5 DOLLARS**			
	1930. Deep olive-green. Specimen. *(S/M #C260-11).*	—	Unc	120.00
510	**10 DOLLARS**			
	1930. Orange. Specimen. *(S/M #C260-12).*	—	Unc	135.00

NATIONAL BANK OF CHINA - CANTON

Established by Kuomintang Party in 1920-21 at Canton. Merged into Central Bank of China about 1923. It had no affiliation w/the previous bank, which has a similar English name.

1921 ISSUE

#511-516 SYS at ctr. w/palm trees at l. and r. 3 men and a farmer w/an ox at ctr. on back.

511	**10 CENTS**			
	1921. Blue and black on pink unpt. Back brown. *(S/M #C261-1).*	10.00	40.00	160.00
512	**20 CENTS**			
	1921. *(S/M #C261-2).*		Reported Not Confirmed	
513	**50 CENTS**			
	1921. *(S/M #C261-3).*		Reported Not Confirmed	
514	**1 DOLLAR**			
	1921. Blue and black on pink unpt. Back brown. *(S/M #C261-10).*	12.50	50.00	200.00
515	**5 DOLLARS**			
	1921. Green and black on pink unpt. Back brown on blue unpt. *(S/M #C261-11).*	22.50	90.00	360.00

		Good	Fine	XF
516	**10 DOLLARS**			
	1921. Red and black on yellow unpt. Back blue on yellow unpt. *(S/M #C261-12).*	30.00	125.00	500.00

THE NATIONAL COMMERCIAL BANK, LIMITED

中華民國銀行

Che Chiang Hsing Yeh Yin Hang

Established 1908.

LAW 4.7.1907

		Good	Fine	XF
516A	**1 DOLLAR**			
	ND. Mandarin at l. Rooster at r. on back.			
	a. *HUPEH. (S/M #C22-).*	15.00	60.00	240.00
	b. *SHANGHAI. (S/M #C22-).*	15.00	60.00	240.00

		Good	Fine	XF
516B	**5 DOLLARS**			
	ND. Orange. Mandarin at r. *(S/M #C22-).*			
	a. *HUPEH. (S/M #C22-).*	18.50	75.00	300.00
	b. *SHANGHAI. (S/M #C22-).*	18.50	75.00	300.00

516C   10 DOLLARS
ND. Brown. Mandarin at l. Rooster at r. on back. *SHANGHAI.*
Specimen. *(S/M #C22-).*

	GOOD	FINE	XF
	—	Unc	400.00

1923 ISSUE
#517-519 printer: ABNC.

517   1 DOLLAR
1.10.1923. Black and m/c. Mandarin at r. Rooster on back. Also
w/various control letter ovpts.

	GOOD	FINE	XF
a. *SHANGHAI. (S/M #C22-1a).*	5.00	20.00	80.00
b. *TIENTSIN. (S/M #C22-1b).*	5.00	20.00	80.00
c. *HUPEH. (S/M #C22-1c).*	9.00	36.50	145.00

518   5 DOLLARS
1.10.1923. Red and m/c. Mandarin at ctr. Rooster at r. on back. Also
w/various control letter and Chinese character ovpts.

	GOOD	FINE	XF
a. *SHANGHAI. W/o sign. on face (S/M #C22-2a).*	9.00	36.50	145.00
b. *SHANGHAI. Sign. on face. (S/M #C22-2b).*	9.00	36.50	145.00
c. *TIENTSIN. (S/M #C22-2c).*	9.00	36.50	145.00
d. *NANKING. (S/M #C22-2d).*	12.50	50.00	200.00
e. *HUPEH. (S/M #C22-2e).*	12.50	50.00	200.00

519   10 DOLLARS
1.10.1923. Green and m/c. Old man at ctr. Rooster at l. on back.

	GOOD	FINE	XF
a. *HUPEH. (S/M #C22-3c).*	17.50	75.00	300.00
b. *SHANGHAI. (S/M #C22-3a).*	12.50	50.00	200.00
c. *TIENTSIN. (S/M #C22-3b).*	12.50	50.00	200.00

519C   10 DOLLARS
1.10.1929. Fortress at l. *SHANGHAI.* Specimen. *(S/M #C22-).*

	GOOD	FINE	XF
	—	Unc	145.00

NATIONAL INDUSTRIAL BANK OF CHINA
中國實業銀行
Chung Kuo Shih Yeh Yin Hang

1922 ISSUE
#520-524 landscape at l. Landscape at ctr. on back. Printer: BEPP.

520   1 YUAN
1.6.1922.

	VG	VF	UNC
a. *HANKOW. (S/M #C291-).*	30.00	120.00	—
b. *PEKING. Specimen. (S/M #C291-).*	—	Unc	72.50
c. *SHANGHAI. Specimen. (S/M #C291-).*	—	Unc	72.50
d. *TIENTSIN. (S/M #C291-).*	30.00	120.00	—

521   5 YUAN
1.6.1922.

	VG	VF	UNC
a. *HANKOW. Specimen. (S/M #C291-).*	—	Unc	110.00
b. *PEKING. (S/M #C291-).*	—	Unc	110.00

522   10 YUAN
1.6.1922.

	VG	VF	UNC
a. *PEKING. Specimen. (S/M #C291-1).*	—	Unc	140.00
s. *W/o place name. Specimen. (S/M #C291-).*	—	Unc	110.00

523   50 YUAN
1.6.1922.

	VG	VF	UNC
a. *PEKING. Specimen. (S/M #C291-).*	—	Unc	165.00
s. *W/o place name. Specimen. (S/M #C291-).*	—	Unc	140.00

524   100 YUAN
1.6.1922.

	VG	VF	UNC
a. *PEKING. Specimen. (S/M #C291-).*	—	Unc	165.00
s. *W/o place name. Specimen. (S/M #C291-).*	—	Unc	140.00

1924 ISSUES
#525-530 Great Wall at ctr. on back. Sign. varieties. Also w/various numerical, letter and Chinese character ovpt. Printer: ABNC.

525   1 YUAN

1924. Violet on m/c unpt. Running horse at upper l.

		GOOD	FINE	XF
a.	SHANGHAI. (S/M #C291-1c).	2.50	10.00	40.00
b.	TSINGTAO. (S/M #C291-1a).	2.75	11.00	45.00
c.	WEIHAIWEI. (S/M #C291-1b).	5.50	22.50	90.00
d.	PEKING. (S/M #C291-1e).	2.50	11.00	45.00
e.	TIENTSIN (S/M #C291-1d).	2.50	11.00	45.00
f.	SHANTUNG. (S/M #C291-1f).	2.50	11.00	45.00

526   5 YUAN

1924. Red and m/c. Running horse at ctr.

		GOOD	FINE	XF
a.	HANKOW. (S/M #C291-2b).	10.00	40.00	160.00
b.	SHANGHAI. (S/M #C291-2a).	5.50	22.50	90.00
c.	TIENTSIN. (S/M #C291-2c).	5.50	22.50	90.00
d.	TSINGTAO. (S/M #C291-2d).	11.00	45.00	180.00
e.	PEKING. (S/M #C291-2e).	9.00	37.50	150.00
f.	WEIHAIWEI. (S/M #C291-2f).	11.00	45.00	180.00

527   10 YUAN

1924. Green and m/c. Running horse at ctr.

		GOOD	FINE	XF
a.	SHANGHAI. (S/M #C291-3a).	4.50	18.50	75.00
b.	TIENTSIN. (S/M #C291-3b).	10.00	40.00	85.00
c.	PEKING. (S/M #C291-3c).	10.00	40.00	85.00
d.	SHANTUNG. (S/M #C291-3d).	18.50	75.00	300.00

528   50 YUAN

1924. Orange. Running horse at ctr.

		GOOD	FINE	XF
a.	PEKING. (S/M #C291-4a).	25.00	100.00	400.00
b.	SHANTUNG. (S/M #C291-4b).	25.00	100.00	400.00
s.	Specimen. (S/M #C291-4).	—	Unc	350.00

529   100 YUAN

1924. Blue and m/c. Running horse at ctr.

		GOOD	FINE	XF
a.	PEKING. (S/M #C291-5b).	25.00	100.00	400.00
b.	SHANGHAI. (S/M #C291-5a).	30.00	125.00	500.00
s.	Specimen. (S/M #C291-5).	—	Unc	350.00

530   100 YUAN

1924. Red. Specimen. (S/M #C291-6). — Unc 300.00

1931 ISSUE

#531-533 Running horse at ctr. Bank bldg. at ctr. on back. Sign. varieties. Also w/various numerical, letter and Chinese characters ovtp. Printer: ABNC.

531   1 YUAN

1931. Purple and m/c. 2 sign. varieties.

		GOOD	FINE	XF
a.	FUKIEN. (S/M #C291-).	10.00	30.00	120.00
b.	Shanghai on face; SHANGHAI on back. (S/M #C291-10a).	5.00	15.00	60.00
c.	Shanghai on face only. (S/M #C291-10b).	5.00	15.00	60.00
d.	SHANTUNG. (S/M #C291-10c).	10.00	30.00	120.00
e.	TSINGTAO. (S/M #C291-10d).	10.00	30.00	120.00
r.	Remainder, w/o place name. (S/M #C291-10).	—	Unc	90.00

532	5 YUAN	GOOD	FINE	XF
	1931. Red and m/c.			
	a. *SHANGHAI.* 2 sign. varieties. *(S/M #C291-11a).*	5.00	15.00	60.00
	b. *TIENTSIN. (S/M #C291-11b).*	5.00	15.00	60.00
	c. *FUKIEN. (S/M #C291-11c).*	7.50	20.00	80.00
	d. *FOOCHOW/FUKIEN. (S/M #C291-11d).*	7.50	20.00	80.00
	r. Remainder, w/o place name. *(S/M #C291-11).*	—	Unc	75.00
533	10 YUAN			
	1931. Green and m/c. *SHANGHAI. (S/M #C291-12).*	10.00	30.00	120.00

1935 ISSUE

534	1 YUAN			
	1935. Red. Printer: W&S. *Shanghai. (S/M #C291-20).*	20.00	50.00	140.00

NINGPO COMMERCIAL AND SAVINGS BANK LIMITED

NINGPO COMMERCIAL BANK LIMITED

NINGPO COMMERCIAL BANK

行銀明四

Szu Ming Yin Hang

NOTE: For earlier issues see #A61A-A61D. Shanghai office.

1920 ISSUES

**#540-544 also w/various Chinese character ovpt. Printer: ABNC.
ovpt. see #170.**

539	1 DOLLAR			
	1920. Blue and m/c. *Shanghai. (S/M #S107-10).*			
	a. Issued note.	6.50	20.00	80.00
	b. Ovpt: *SH.*	6.50	20.00	80.00
540	1 DOLLAR			
	1.9.1920. Blue. Back orange. *Shanghai. (S/M #S107-11).*			
	a. Issued note.	6.50	20.00	80.00
	b. Ovpt: *SH.*	6.50	20.00	80.00

541	5 DOLLARS	GOOD	FINE	XF
	1.9.1920. Red and m/c. Bank at ctr. Floral pot at ctr on back. *SHANGHAI. (S/M #S107-12).*			
	a. Issued note.	2.50	10.00	40.00
	b. Ovpt: *NP.*	3.00	12.50	50.00
	c. Ovpt: *SH.*	3.00	12.50	50.00
	d. Ovpt: *Y.*	3.00	12.50	50.00
542	10 DOLLARS			
	1.9.1920. Green. *SHANGHAI. (S/M #S107-13).*	5.00	20.00	80.00
543	50 DOLLARS			
	1.9.1920. Red and m/c. *SHANGHAI. (S/M #S107-14).*	18.50	75.00	300.00
544	100 DOLLARS			
	1.9.1920. Blue and m/c. *SHANGHAI. (S/M #S107-15).*	22.50	90.00	360.00

1921 ISSUE

545	1 DOLLAR	GOOD	FINE	XF
	1.11.1921. Red. Bank at ctr. Printer: BEPP. *SHANGHAI. (S/M #S107-20).*	3.75	15.00	60.00

1925 ISSUES

#546-548B printer: G&D.

546	1 DOLLAR	GOOD	FINE	XF
	1.9.1925. Brown. Mountain landscape at ctr. *SHANGHAI (S/M #S107-30).*	10.00	25.00	75.00

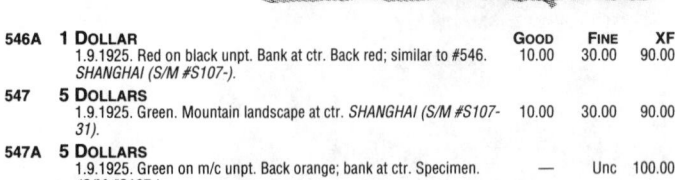

546A	1 DOLLAR	GOOD	FINE	XF
	1.9.1925. Red on black unpt. Bank at ctr. Back red; similar to #546. *SHANGHAI (S/M #S107-).*	10.00	30.00	90.00
547	5 DOLLARS			
	1.9.1925. Green. Mountain landscape at ctr. *SHANGHAI (S/M #S107-31).*	10.00	30.00	90.00
547A	5 DOLLARS			
	1.9.1925. Green on m/c unpt. Back orange; bank at ctr. Specimen. *(S/M #S107-).*	—	Unc	100.00

548	10 DOLLARS	GOOD	FINE	XF
	1.9.1925. Black and red. Mountain landscape at ctr. *SHANGHAI. (S/M #S107-32).*	15.00	45.00	125.00
548A	10 DOLLARS			
	1.9.1925. Black and red. Bank at ctr. *(S/M #S107-33).*	55.00	140.00	350.00

548B 100 DOLLARS

		GOOD	FINE	XF
1.9.1925. Violet and m/c. Mountain landscape. Back similar to #541. *SHANGHAI (S/M #S107-35).*		18.50	75.00	300.00

1932-34 ISSUE

#549 and 550 printer: W&S.

NOTE: Mismatched dates on face and back.

549 1 DOLLAR

Jan. yr. 21(1932) 11.1.1933. Red-brown. Mountain landscape at l. Back green. *SHANGHAI.*

		GOOD	FINE	XF
a.	Green serial #. *(S/M #S107-40a).*	1.75	7.50	30.00
b.	Blue serial #. *(S/M #S107-40b).*	1.75	7.50	30.00
c.	W/o serial # on face. *(S/M #S107-40c).*	1.75	7.50	30.00

550 10 DOLLARS

	GOOD	FINE	XF
January 1934. Red. Mountain landscape at l. *SHANGHAI. (S/M #S107-50).*	3.75	15.00	60.00

TAH CHUNG BANK

行銀中大

Ta Chung Yin Hang

1921 FIRST ISSUE

#551-556 landscape at l., Great Wall at r. Printer: BEPP.

554 1 YUAN

15.7.1921. Green and black.

		GOOD	FINE	XF
a.	*HANKOW.* Specimen. *(S/M #T12-10a).*	—	Unc	70.00
b.	*TSINGTAU.* Specimen. *(S/M #T12-10b).*	—	Unc	70.00
c.	*TIENTSIN. (S/M #T12-10c).*	6.00	25.00	100.00

555 5 YUAN

15.7.1921. Orange and black.

		GOOD	FINE	XF
a.	*HANKOW.* Specimen. *(S/M #T12-11a).*	—	Unc	80.00
b.	*TSINGTAU.* Specimen. *(S/M #T12-11b).*	—	Unc	80.00

556 10 YUAN

15.7.1921. Purple and black.

		GOOD	FINE	XF
a.	*HANKOW.* Specimen. *(S/M #T12-12a).*	—	Unc	90.00
b.	*TSINGTAU.* Specimen. *(S/M #T12-12b).*	—	Unc	90.00
c.	*TIENTSIN. (S/M #T12-).*	7.50	30.00	120.00
d.	*CHUNGKING. (S/M #T12-).*	7.50	30.00	120.00

551 10 CENTS

1921. Green.

		GOOD	FINE	XF
a.	*HANKOW.* Specimen. *(S/M #T12-1b).*	—	Unc	85.00
b.	*TIENTSIN. (S/M #T12-1a).*	6.00	25.00	100.00
c.	*TSINGTAU.* Specimen. *(S/M #T12-1c).*	—	Unc	85.00

552 20 CENTS

1921. Orange.

		GOOD	FINE	XF
a.	*HANKOW.* Specimen. *(S/M #T12-2b).*	—	Unc	85.00
b.	*TIENTSIN. (S/M #T12-2a).*	6.00	25.00	100.00
c.	*TSINGTAU.* Specimen. *(S/M #T12-2c).*	—	Unc	85.00

553 50 CENTS

1921. Purple.

		GOOD	FINE	XF
a.	*HANKOW.* Specimen. *(S/M #T12-3b).*	—	Unc	85.00
b.	*TIENTSIN.* Specimen. *(S/M #T12-3a).*	—	Unc	85.00
c.	*TSINGTAU.* Specimen. *(S/M #T12-3c).*	—	Unc	85.00

1921 SECOND ISSUE

#557 and 557A printer: BEPP.

557 1 DOLLAR

	GOOD	FINE	XF
1.1.1921. Brown. Landscape at ctr. *CHUNGKING.* Specimen. *(S/M #T12-).*	—	Unc	80.00

557A 10 DOLLARS

1.1.1921. Green and m/c. Landscape at ctr.

		GOOD	FINE	XF
a.	*PEKING.* Specimen. *(S/M #T12-13a).*	—	Unc	100.00
b.	*CHUNGKING. (S/M #T12-13b).*	—	—	—

1932 ISSUE

561 1 YUAN

	VG	VF	UNC
1.9.1932. Green. Back black; dollar coin at ctr. *SHANGHAI.* Specimen. *(S/M #T12-30).*	—	—	100.00

		VG	VF	Unc
562	**5 YUAN**	—	VF	**Unc**
	1.9.1932. Black on m/c unpt. Bell at ctr. Back black; five 1-Yuan coins. *SHANGHAI*. Specimen. (S/M #T12-31).		—	90.00
563	**10 YUAN**			
	1.9.1932. *SHANGHAI*. (S/M #T12-32).	—	—	100.00

		VG	VF	Unc
558	**10 CENTS**	**VG**	**VF**	**Unc**
	1932. Brown. Bell at ctr. *Tientsin*. (S/M #T12-20).	6.00	25.00	100.00

		VG	VF	Unc
559	**20 CENTS**	**VG**	**VF**	**Unc**
	1932. Green. Bell at ctr. *Tientsin*. (S/M #T12-21).	7.50	30.00	120.00
560	**50 CENTS**			
	1932. (S/M #T12-22).	9.00	37.50	150.00

1938 ISSUE
#564-565 *PEKING*. Printer: BEPP.

		VG	VF	Unc
564	**1 YUAN**	**VG**	**VF**	**Unc**
	15.1.1938. Green and black. Landscape at l., Great Wall at r. (S/M #T12-40).	1.00	3.00	10.00
565	**5 YUAN**			
	15.1.1938. Orange and black. (S/M #T12-41).	1.25	4.00	14.00

BANK OF TERRITORIAL DEVELOPMENT
ТЕРРИТОРІАЛЦНО ПРОМЫШЛЕННЫЙ БАНКЪ КИТАЪ

行銀邊殖

Chih Pien Yin Hang

This institution collapsed in 1917, leaving behind quantities of unpaid notes and shares. Its branches, however, enjoyed considerable autonomy and not all were immediately affected. The Yunnan office was still in operation and probably issuing notes in the mid-1920s although none of the latter has been seen.

1914 ISSUE
#566-572 printer: BEPP. Changchun issues w/ovpt: *N.B. Payable in subsidiary (silver) coins at par... on back.*

		GOOD	FINE	XF
566	**1 DOLLAR**	**GOOD**	**FINE**	**XF**
	1.12.1914. Green and black. Workers and camels along road at ctr.			
a.	*CHANGCHUN*. W/ovpt: *N.B. Payable by Ten Coins to The Dollar*, on back. (S/M #C165-1a).	3.75	15.00	60.00
b.	*CHANGCHUN/CHEKIANG*. (S/M #C165-2a).	3.75	15.00	60.00
c.	*CHANGCHUN/DOLONOR*. (S/M #C165-2b).	7.50	22.50	90.00
d.	*CHANGCHUN/HANKOW*. (S/M #C165-2c).	3.75	15.00	60.00
e.	*CHANGCHUN/KIANGSU*. (S/M #C165- 2d).	3.75	15.00	60.00
f.	*CHANGCHUN/SHANGHAI*. (S/M #C165-2e).	1.50	6.00	25.00
g.	*CHANGCHUN/TIENTSIN*. (S/M #C165-2f).	1.50	6.00	25.00
h.	*CHEKIANG*. (S/M #C165-1b).	3.75	15.00	60.00
i.	*HARBIN*. (S/M #C165-1c).	3.75	15.00	60.00
j.	*KIANGSU*. (S/M #C165-1d).	3.75	15.00	60.00
k.	*KIRIN*. (S/M #C165-1e).	3.75	15.00	60.00
l.	*Fengtien//MOUKDEN*. (S/M #C165-1f).	3.75	15.00	60.00
m.	*Fengtien// MOUKDEN/CHANGCHUN*. (S/M #C165-3a).	3.75	15.00	60.00
n.	*Fengtien//MOUKDEN/YUNNAN*. (S/M #C165-3b).	3.75	15.00	60.00
o.	*SHANGHAI*. (S/M #C165-1g).	1.50	6.00	25.00
p.	*TIENTSIN*. (S/M #C165-1h).	1.50	6.00	25.00
q.	*CHANGCHUN/MUKDEN*. (S/M #C165-).	3.75	15.00	60.00
r.	Remainder, w/o place name or sign. (S/M #C165-1i).	.75	3.00	12.00

		GOOD	FINE	XF
567	**5 DOLLARS**	**GOOD**	**FINE**	**XF**
	1.12.1914. Purple on yellow unpt. Hut along shoreline, ships at ctr.			
a.	*CHANGCHUN*. (S/M #C165-4a).	2.75	11.00	45.00
b.	*CHANGCHUN/CHEKIANG*. (S/M #C165-5a).	2.75	11.00	45.00
c.	*CHANGCHUN/HANKOW*. (S/M #C165-5b).	2.75	11.00	45.00
d.	*CHANGCHUN/HARBIN*. (S/M #C165-5c).	2.75	11.00	45.00
e.	*CHANGCHUN/KIANGSU*. (S/M #C165-5d).	2.75	11.00	45.00
f.	*CHANGCHUN/SHANGHAI*. (S/M #C165-5e).	2.75	11.00	45.00
g.	*DOLONOR*. (S/M #C165-4b).	11.00	45.00	180.00
h.	*HARBIN*. (S/M #C165-4c).	2.75	11.00	45.00
i.	*MANCHURIA*. w/N.B. payable in silver... and *To be converted into silver dollars... on back*. (S/M #C165-4d).	2.75	11.00	45.00
k.	*Fengtien-MOUKDEN*. (S/M #C165-4e).	2.75	11.00	45.00

l.	*Fengtien-MOUKDEN/SHANGHAI*. (S/M #C165-6a).	2.75	11.00	45.00
m.	*Fengtien-MOUKDEN/YUNNAN*. (S/M #C165-6b).	2.75	11.00	45.00
n.	*SHANGHAI*. (S/M #C165-4f).	2.75	11.00	45.00
o.	*TIENTSIN*. (S/M #C165-4g).	2.75	11.00	45.00

		Good	Fine	XF
p.	CHEKIANG. (S/M #C165-).	2.75	11.00	45.00
q.	KIANGSI. (S/M #C165-).	2.75	11.00	45.00
r.	KIANGSU. (S/M #C165-).	2.75	11.00	45.00
s.	YUNNAN. (S/M #C165-).	2.75	11.00	45.00
t.	Remainder, w/o place or sign. (S/M #C165-).	1.85	7.50	30.00

568 10 DOLLARS
1.12.1914. Yellow and red. Roadbuilding at ctr.

		Good	Fine	XF
a.	CHANGCHUN. (S/M #C165-7a).	5.00	20.00	80.00
b.	CHANGCHUN/HANKOW. (S/M #C165-8a).	5.00	20.00	80.00
c.	CHANGCHUN/KIANGSU. (S/M #C165-8b).	5.00	20.00	80.00
d.	DOLONOR. (S/M #C165-7b).	10.00	40.00	160.00
e.	KIANGSU. (S/M #C165-7c).	5.00	20.00	80.00
f.	KIRIN. (S/M #C165-7d).	5.00	20.00	80.00
g.	MANCHURIA. (S/M #C165-7e).	5.00	20.00	80.00
h.	SHANGHAI. (S/M #C165-7f).	5.00	20.00	80.00
i.	TIENTSIN. (S/M #C165-7g).	5.00	20.00	80.00
j.	CHANGCHUN/KALGAN. (S/M #C165-).	5.00	20.00	80.00
k.	CHANGCHUN/Fengtien//MOUKDEN. (S/M #C165-).	5.00	20.00	80.00
l.	CHANGCHUN/SHANGHAI. (S/M #C165-).	5.00	20.00	80.00
m.	CHANGCHUN/TIENTSIN. (S/M #C165-).	5.00	20.00	80.00
r.	Remainder, w/o place name or sign. (S/M #C165-7h).	2.50	10.00	40.00

1915 ISSUE
#573-575 Russian text on back. Printer: CMN.

569 5 CENTS
1915. Red. (S/M #C165-10). 5.00 15.00 45.00

570 10 CENTS
1915. Purple. (S/M #C165-11). 5.00 15.00 45.00

571 20 CENTS

	Good	Fine	XF
1.11.1915. Green. Farm workers at l. MANCHURIA. (S/M #C165-12).	3.75	15.00	60.00

572 50 CENTS

	Good	Fine	XF
1.11.1915. Black. Landscape at l. MANCHURIA. (S/M #C165-13).	5.00	20.00	80.00

573 1 DOLLAR
1915. Green. (S/M #C165-20). Reported Not Confirmed

574 5 DOLLARS
1915. Brown and black on pink unpt. Similar to #575. Urga. Remainder w/o sign. (S/M #C165-21). Good — Unc 125.00

575 10 DOLLARS
1915. Blue. Urga. Remainder w/o sign. (S/M #C165-22). Good — Unc 200.00

1916 ISSUE
#576 and 577 w/# fields.
#582-585 printer: ABNC.

576 100 COPPERS
1916. Red and yellow. Remainder w/o place name, serial # or sign. (S/M #C165-30). Good — Unc 40.00

577 200 COPPERS
1916. Dk. green. Remainder w/o place name, serial # or sign. (S/M #C165-31). Good — Unc 60.00

578 10 CENTS
1.11.1916. Purple. Cows at l.

		VG	VF	UNC
a.	CHANGCHUN. (S/M #C165-40b).	1.85	7.50	30.00
b.	MANCHURIA. (S/M #C165-40a).	2.25	9.00	35.00
r.	Remainder w/o serial #. (S/M #C165-40).	—	Unc	25.00

579 20 CENTS
1916. (S/M #C165-41). Reported Not Confirmed

		VG	**VF**	**UNC**
580	**40 CENTS**	6.50	25.00	100.00
	1.11.1916. Black and red. Houses along shoreline at l. Back brown. CHANGCHUN. (S/M #C165-42).			
581	**50 CENTS**	6.50	25.00	100.00
	1916. Black. MANCHURIA. Printer: BEPP. (S/M #C165-43).			

		VG	**VF**	**UNC**
584	**10 DOLLARS**			
	ND. (1916) Black on m/c unpt. Bldg. at l.			
	a. SHANGHAI. (S/M #C165-52b).	3.00	12.50	50.00
	b. TIENTSIN. (S/M #C165-52a).	3.00	12.50	50.00
	r. Remainder w/o place name. (S/M #C165-52).	—	Unc	40.00

		VG	**VF**	**UNC**
585	**50 DOLLARS**	—	Unc	150.00
	ND. (1916) Black on m/c unpt. Bldg. r. Remainder w/o place name. (S/M #C165-53).			

		VG	**VF**	**UNC**
582	**1 DOLLAR**			
	ND. (1916) Black on m/c unpt. City gate at l.			
	a. KALGAN. (S/M #C165-50a).	5.00	10.00	40.00
	b. CHANGCHUN. W/ovpt: N.B. payable in sudsidiary (silver) coins... on back. (S/M #C165-50c).	2.50	10.00	40.00
	c. TIENTSIN. (S/M #C165-50d).	5.00	10.00	40.00
	r. Remainder, w/o place name. (S/M #C165-50b).	—	Unc	20.00

1918 ISSUE

		VG	**VF**	**UNC**
585A	**1 DOLLAR**	15.00	45.00	180.00
	1918. Green and black. Temple at l., rural bldgs. at r. Back green; rural bldgs. at ctr. KIRIN. (S/M #C165-61).			

		VG	**VF**	**UNC**
583	**5 DOLLARS**			
	ND. (1916) Black on m/c unpt. Bldg. at shoreline at r.			
	a. KALGAN. (S/M #C165-51b).	3.00	12.50	50.00
	b. TIENTSIN. (S/M #C165-51a).	3.00	12.50	50.00
	c. ANHWEI. (S/M #C165-51c).	3.00	12.50	50.00
	d. CHANGCHUN. W/ovpt: N.B. payable in subsidiary (silver) coins... on back. (S/M #C165-51).	3.00	12.50	50.00
	r. Remainder, w/o place name. (S/M #C165-51).	—	Unc	40.00

585B 5 DOLLARS
1918. Lilac and green. Temple at l. *Kirin. (S/M #C165-).*

VG	VF	UNC
18.50	75.00	300.00

MINISTRY OF COMMUNICATIONS - PEKING-HANKOW RAILWAY

券付支路鐵漢京部通交

Chiao T'ung Pu Ching Han T'ieh Lu Chih Fu Ch'üan

#585C-594 similar except for denomination and period in months in Chinese below bank name.
Printer: BEPP.

16 MONTH SERIES 期六十第

585C 10 DOLLARS
Feb. 1922. Blue and red. *(S/M #C125-2c).*

VG	VF	UNC
.75	2.00	8.00

24 MONTH SERIES 期四十二第

586 5 DOLLARS
Feb. 1922. Purple and red. *(S/M #C125-1a).*

	.75	2.00	8.00

587 10 DOLLARS
Feb. 1922. Blue and red. *(S/M #C125-2a).*

	.75	2.00	8.00

588 50 DOLLARS
Feb. 1922. Green and red. *(S/M #C125-3a).*

	4.00	12.00	45.00

25 MONTH SERIES 期五十二第

588B 10 DOLLARS
Feb. 1921. Blue and red. *(S/M #C125-2d).*

	.75	2.00	8.00

32 MONTH SERIES 期二十三第

589 5 DOLLARS
Feb. 1922. Purple and red. *(S/M #C125-1b).*

VG	VF	UNC
.75	2.00	8.00

590 10 DOLLARS
Feb. 1922. Blue and red. *(S/M #C125-2b).*

	.75	2.00	8.00

591 50 DOLLARS
Feb. 1922. Green and red. *(S/M #C125-3b).*

	4.00	12.00	45.00

36 MONTH SERIES 期六十三第

592 5 DOLLARS
Feb. 1922. Purple and red. *(S/M #C125-1e).*

	.75	2.00	8.00

593 10 DOLLARS
Feb. 1922. Blue and red. *(S/M #C125-2e).*

	.75	2.00	8.00

594 50 DOLLARS
Feb. 1922. Green and red. *(S/M #C125-3e).*

	4.00	12.00	45.00

MILITARY EXCHANGE BUREAU

局兌滙需軍部政財

Ts'ai Cheng Pu Chün Hsü Hui Tui Chü

1927 ISSUE

595 1 YUAN
1927. Black and m/c. Junks at upper l., ships at upper r. Back green; Great Wall at ctr. *(S/M #T181-1).*

VG	VF	UNC
12.50	50.00	200.00

MARKET STABILIZATION CURRENCY BUREAU

局錢官市平部政財

Ts'ai Cheng Pu P'ing Shih Kuan Ch'ien Chü

1910's (ND) ISSUE

#597 and 598 Temple of Heaven at ctr.

597 20 COPPERS
ND. Brown. Back: green. *Peking. (S/M #T183-).*

—	—	—

598 50 COPPERS
ND. (1910) Brown and blue. Back blue. *Honan.* Printer: BEPP. *(S/M #T183-).*

VG	VF	UNC
50.00	200.00	—

1915 ISSUE

#599-603 have hillside pagoda at l.; Temple of Heaven at r.

599 10 COPPERS
1915. Black, blue and yellow.

		VG	VF	UNC
a.	*Ching Chao* (Peking). *(S/M #T183-1a).*	2.00	6.00	22.50
b.	*Ching Chao/Three Eastern Provinces. (S/M #T183-1c).*	2.50	7.50	27.50
c.	*Tientsin/Chihli. (S/M #T183-1b).*	2.50	7.50	27.50
d.	*Kiangsi. (S/M #T183-1d).*	2.50	7.50	27.50

600	**20 COPPERS**	**VG**	**VF**	**UNC**
	1915. Black, purple and blue.			
	a. *Ching Chao. (S/M #T183-2a).*	2.00	6.00	22.50
	b. *Ching Chao/Chihli. (S/M #T183-2d).*	2.50	7.50	25.00
	c. *Ching Chao/Honan. (S/M #T183-2f).*	2.50	7.50	27.50
	d. *Ching Chao/Kiangsi. (S/M #T183-2c).*	2.50	7.50	27.50
	e. *Ching Chao/Shantung. (S/M #T183-2e).*	2.50	7.50	27.50
	f. *Ching Chao/Three Eastern Provinces. (S/M #T183-2g).*	2.50	7.50	27.50
	g. *Tientsin/Chihli. (S/M #T183-2b).*	2.50	7.50	27.50
601	**40 COPPERS**			
	1915. Black, brown and green.			
	a. *Chihli. (S/M #T183-3b).*	2.50	7.50	27.50
	b. *Ching Chao. (S/M #T183-3a).*	2.00	6.00	22.50
	c. *Ching Chao/Anhwei. (S/M #T183-3d).*	2.50	7.50	27.50
	d. *Ching Chao/Chihli. (S/M #T183-3e).*	2.50	7.50	27.50
	e. *Ching Chao/Honan. (S/M #T183-3f).*	2.50	7.50	27.50
	f. *Ching Chao/Kiangsi. (S/M #T183-3g).*	2.50	7.50	27.50
	g. *Ching Chao/Shantung. (S/M #T183-3h).*	2.50	7.50	27.50
	h. *Kiangsu. (S/M #T183-3c).*	2.50	7.50	27.50
	i. *Ching Chao/Peking. (S/M #T183-3i).*	2.50	7.50	27.50
	j. *Shantung. (S/M #T183-3).*	2.50	7.50	27.50

602	**50 COPPERS**	**VG**	**VF**	**UNC**
	1915. Black, red and green.			
	a. *Chihli. (S/M #T183-4b).*	2.00	6.00	22.50
	b. *Ching Chao. (S/M #T183-4a).*	1.00	3.00	11.00
	c. *Ching Chao/Heilungkiang. (S/M #T183-4f).*	2.00	6.00	22.50
	d. *Ching Chao/Honan. (S/M #T183-4g).*	2.00	6.00	22.50
	e. *Ching Chao/Kiangsi. (S/M #T183-4h).*	2.00	6.00	22.50
	f. *Ching Chao/Kiangsu. (S/M #T183-4i).*	2.00	6.00	22.50
	g. *Honan. (S/M #T183-4c).*	2.00	6.00	22.50
	h. *Kiangsu. (S/M #T183-4d).*	2.00	6.00	22.50
	i. *Kiangsu/Heilungkiang. (S/M #T183-4j).*	2.00	6.00	22.50
	j. *Shantung. (S/M #T183-4e).*	2.00	6.00	22.50
	k. *Peking. (S/M #T183-4k).*	2.00	6.00	22.50
	l. *KIANGSI/HONAN. (S/M #T183-4l).*	2.00	6.00	20.00
	r. Remainder, w/o place name. *(S/M T183-4).*	2.00	6.00	22.50

603	**100 COPPERS**	**VG**	**VF**	**UNC**
	1915. Black, green and orange.			
	a. *Anhwei. (S/M #T183-5b).*	2.00	6.00	27.50
	b. *Chihli. (S/M #T183-5c).*	2.00	6.00	27.50
	c. *Ching Chao. (S/M #T183-5a).*	2.00	6.00	27.50
	d. *Ching Chao/Heilungkiang. (S/M #T183-5h).*	2.00	6.00	27.50
	e. *Honan. (S/M #T183-5d).*	2.00	6.00	27.50
	f. *Kiangsi. (S/M #T183-5d).*	2.00	6.00	27.50
	g. *Shansi. (S/M #T183-5f).*	2.00	6.00	27.50
	h. *Shantung. (S/M #T183-5g).*	2.00	6.00	27.50
	i. *Peking. (S/M #T183-5i).*	2.00	6.00	27.50

1919 FIRST ISSUE

603A	**10 COPPERS**			
	Jan. 1919. Blue on green unpt. *Ching Chao. (S/M #T183-).*	7.50	15.00	45.00
603B	**20 COPPERS**			
	Jan. 1919. Blue-green on orange unpt. *Tientsin. (S/M #T183-).*	5.00	15.00	50.00

1919 SECOND ISSUES

604	**10 COPPERS**	**VG**	**VF**	**UNC**
	1919. Black and dk. blue-violet on lt. orange unpt. Back ochre and gray. Printer: BEPP.			
	a. *Ching Chao. (S/M #T183-10a).*	5.00	15.00	55.00
	b. *Ching Chao/Yen T'ai. (S/M #T183-10b).*	6.00	20.00	65.00
	c. *Ching Chao/Peking. (S/M #T183-10c).*	6.00	20.00	65.00
	d. *ChiNan. (S/M #T183-10d).*	6.00	20.00	65.00

1919 THIRD ISSUES

604A	**10 COPPERS**	**VG**	**VF**	**UNC**
	1919. Like #604 but back red-brown and lt. green.			
	a. *Chefoo, Shantung. (S/M #T183-).*	5.00	15.00	55.00
	b. *Peking/? (S/M #T183-).*	5.00	15.00	55.00
605	**20 COPPERS**			
	1919. Black, purple and blue. Printer: BEPP.			
	a. *Ching Chao. (S/M #T183-11a).*	5.00	15.00	50.00
	b. *Ching Chao/Yen T'ai. (S/M #T183-11b).*	6.00	17.50	65.00
	c. *Ching Chao/Peking. (S/M #T183-11c).*	6.00	17.50	65.00
	d. *ChiNan. (S/M #T183-11d).*	6.00	17.50	65.00

1920 ISSUE

606	**20 COPPERS**	**VG**	**VF**	**UNC**
	1920. Black, blue and m/c. Printer: ABNC.			
	a. *Chihli. (S/M #T183-20b).*	6.00	17.50	65.00
	b. *Ching Chao. (S/M #T183-20a).*	6.00	17.50	65.00

1921 FIRST ISSUES

607	**10 COPPERS**			
	1921. Black, blue and orange. Back w/o English.			
	a. *Chihli. (S/M #T183-30b).*	2.00	6.00	20.00
	b. *Ching Chao. (S/M #T183-30a).*	2.00	6.00	20.00
	c. *Peking. (S/M #T183-30c).*	2.00	6.00	20.00
607A	**10 COPPERS**			
	1921. Similar to #607, but w/10 COPPER COINS on back. *Ching Chao. (S/M #T183-).*	2.50	7.50	25.00
608	**20 COPPERS**			
	1921. Black, purple and blue.			
	a. *Ching Chao. (S/M #T183-31a).*	2.50	7.50	25.00
	b. *Ching Chao/Chihli. (S/M #T183-31b).*	2.50	7.50	25.00

1922 ISSUES

609	**10 COPPERS**			
	1922. Black, blue and yellow. Printer: BEPP. *Ching Chao. (S/M #T183-40).*	2.50	7.50	27.50

610	**20 COPPERS**	**VG**	**VF**	**UNC**
	1922. Black, purple and blue. Printer: BEPP. 120 x 72mm.			
	a. *Ching Chao. (S/M #T183-41a).*	2.00	6.00	22.50
	b. *Ching Chao/Kiangsu. (S/M #T183-41b).*	2.00	6.00	22.50
	c. *Shantung. (S/M #T183-41c).*	2.00	6.00	22.50

611	**20 COPPERS**	**VG**	**VF**	**UNC**
	1922. Black, purple and blue. 139 x 82mm. *Ching Chao. (S/M #T183-42).*	2.50	7.50	27.50

1923 ISSUE

612	**10 COPPERS**			
	1923. Black, blue and yellow. 112 x 60mm.			
	a. *Ching Chao. (S/M #T183-50a).*	.50	1.50	4.50
	b. *Shantung. (S/M #T183-50b).*	1.50	4.50	14.00
	c. *Tientsin. (S/M #T183-50c).*	1.50	4.50	14.00
613	**10 COPPERS**			
	1923. Black, blue and yellow. 110 x 55mm. *Ching Chao. (S/M #T183-51).*	2.00	5.00	15.00

614	**20 COPPERS**	**VG**	**VF**	**UNC**
	1923. Black, purple and blue.			
	a. *Ching Chao. (S/M #T183-52a).*	2.00	5.00	14.00
	b. *SHANTUNG. (S/M #T183-52b).*	2.50	7.50	27.50
615	**40 COPPERS**			
	1923. Black, brown and green. *Ching Chao. (S/M #T183-53).*	2.50	7.50	27.50

1923 SECOND ISSUES
#616-622 printer: BEPP.

619	**1 YUAN**			
	ND. (1923) Brown. Shrine at ctr. Remainder, w/o place name. *(S/M #T183-70).*	—	Unc	65.00
620	**5 YUAN**			
	ND. (1923) Purple. *(S/M #T183-71).*	7.50	22.50	82.50
621	**10 YUAN**			
	ND. (1923) *(S/M #T183-72).*		Reported Not Confirmed	
622	**100 YUAN**			
	ND. (1923). *(S/M #T183-73).*		Reported Not Confirmed	

616	**10 CENTS**	**VG**	**VF**	**UNC**
	1.6.1923. Blue. Palace at ctr. Back maroon.			
	a. *Peking. (S/M #T183-60b).*	.75	2.50	8.50
	r. *Remainder, w/o place name. (S/M #T183-60a).*	.50	1.50	5.50
617	**20 CENTS**			
	1.6.1923. Purple. Similar to #531. Back orange.			
	a. *Peking. (S/M #T183-61b).*	.75	2.50	8.50
	r. *Remainder, w/o place name. (S/M #T183-61a).*	.50	1.50	5.50
618	**50 CENTS**			
	1.6.1923. Green. Similar to #531. Back dk. brown.			
	a. *Kalgan. (S/M #T183-62c).*	2.50	7.50	27.50
	b. *Peking. (S/M #T183-62b).*	2.50	7.50	27.50
	r. *Remainder, w/o place name. (S/M #T183-62a).*	1.00	3.00	11.00

SPECIAL CIRCULATING NOTES

券通流別特部政財

Ts'ai Cheng Pu T'e Pieh Liu T'ung Ch'üan

#623-625 various dates 1923-24 w/an elongated purple hand stamped seal diagonally. This indicates that they were once presented for payment and then affixed to a separate document providing for redemption on a monthly installment basis through 1926. The full sheet has 39 stamp-sized coupons for the holder to clip and turn in. Peking: Printer: BEPP.

1923 ISSUE

623	**1 YUAN**	**VG**	**VF**	**UNC**
	1923. Blue. Arched bridge over stream at ctr. *(S/M #T184-1).*	1.00	3.00	10.00
624	**5 YUAN**			
	1923. Brown. Arched bridge over stream at ctr. *(S/M #T184-2).*	1.50	4.50	15.00
625	**10 YUAN**			
	1923. Red. Temple at ctr. *(S/M #T184-3).*	2.00	6.00	20.00

FIXED TERM, INTEREST-BEARING TREASURY NOTES

券庫國利有期定部政財

Ts'ai Cheng Pu Ting Ch'i Yu Li Kuo K'u Chüan

1919-20 ISSUE

#626-628 original date October 1919, vertically at lower r. and reissue date vertically at lower l.
Printer: BEPP.

626	**1/2 YUAN**	**VG**	**VF**	**UNC**
	1919-20. Blue.			
	a. *Aug., Oct., Dec. 1919. (S/M #T185-1a).*	.50	1.25	10.00
	b. *April 1920. (S/M #T185-1b).*	.50	1.25	10.00
	c. *June 1920. (S/M #T185-1c).*	.50	1.25	10.00
	r. *Remainder, w/o date. (S/M #T185-1d).*	—	Unc	7.50

627	**1 YUAN**	**VG**	**VF**	**UNC**
	1919-20. Orange.			
	a. *Aug. 1919. (S/M #T185-10a).*	.50	1.25	10.00
	b. *April 1920. (S/M #T185-10b).*	.50	1.25	10.00
	c. *June 1920. (S/M #T185-10c).*	.50	1.25	10.00
	r. *Remainder, w/o date. (S/M #T185-10d).*	—	Unc	7.50
628	**5 YUAN**			
	1919-20. Green.			
	a. *Aug., Oct., Dec. 1919. (S/M #T185-11a).*	.50	1.25	12.50
	b. *Feb., April, June, July 1920. (S/M #T185-11b).*	.50	1.25	12.50
	c. *Aug., Oct. 1920. (S/M #T185-11c).*	.50	1.25	12.50
	r. *Remainder, w/o date. (S/M #T185-11d).*	—	Unc	10.00

1922 ISSUE

#629-631 Peking. Printer: BEPP.

			VG	VF	UNC
629	**1 YUAN**		1.25	4.00	13.50
	1922. Brown. Back red. (S/M #T185-20).				
630	**5 YUAN**		1.75	6.00	20.00
	1922. Purple. Back red. (S/M #T185-21).				
631	**10 YUAN**		2.50	8.00	26.50
	1922. Green. Back red. (S/M #T185-22).				

1923 ISSUES

#632-637 Peking. Printer: BEPP.

			VG	VF	UNC
632	**1 YUAN**		1.25	4.00	13.50
	Feb. 1923. Red. Back blue. (S/M #T185-30).				
633	**1 YUAN**		1.25	4.00	13.50
	June 1923. Blue. Back green. (S/M #T185-31).				
634	**5 YUAN**		1.75	6.00	20.00
	Feb. 1923. Blue. (S/M #T185-32).				
635	**5 YUAN**		1.75	6.00	20.00
	June 1923. Brown. Back green. (S/M #T185-33).				
636	**10 YUAN**		2.50	8.00	26.50
	Feb. 1923. Purple. Back blue. (S/M #T185-34).				
637	**10 YUAN**		2.50	8.00	26.50
	June 1923. Red. Back green. (S/M #T185-35).				

SHORT TERM, INTEREST-BEARING EXCHANGE NOTES

券換兌利有期短部政財

Ts'ai Cheng Pu Tuan Ch'i Yu Li Tui Huan Ch'üan

#638-640 Peking. Printer: BEPP.

1922 ISSUE

			VG	VF	UNC
638	**1 YUAN**		1.00	3.00	10.00
	1922. Brown. Temple at ctr. (S/M #T186-1).				

			VG	VF	UNC
639	**5 YUAN**		1.50	4.50	15.00
	1922. Purple. (S/M #T186-2).				
640	**10 YUAN**		2.50	7.50	25.00
	1922. Green. (S/M #T186-3).				

INTEREST-BEARING, CIRCULATING NOTES

券通流利有部政財

Ts'ai Cheng Pu Yu Li Liu T'ung Ch'üan

#641-643 Peking. Printer: BEPP.

1923 ISSUE

			VG	VF	UNC
641	**1 YUAN**				
	1.2.1923. Red. Pagoda on hill shoreline at ctr. (S/M #T187-1).				
	a. Issued note.		.60	2.00	6.50
	b. Ovpt: 2 vertical columns 20 Chinese characters at l. on back.		1.00	3.00	10.00
	c. Punched hole cancelled.		—	Unc	3.25

			VG	VF	UNC
642	**5 YUAN**		.85	3.00	10.00
	1.2.1923. Blue. Arched bridge over stream at ctr. (S/M #T187-2).				

			VG	VF	UNC
643	**10 YUAN**		1.25	4.00	13.50
	1.2.1923. Purple. House, bridge at ctr. (S/M #T187-3).				

PEOPLES REPUBLIC OF CHINA

The Peoples Republic of China, located in eastern Asia, has an area of 3,696,100 sq. mi. (9,572,900 sq. km.), including Manchuria and Tibet, and a population of 1.14 billion. Capital: Beijing (Peking). The economy is based on agriculture, mining and manufacturing. Textiles, clothing, metal ores, tea and rice are exported.

In the fall of 1911, the middle business class of China and Chinese students educated in Western universities started a general uprising against the Manchu dynasty which forced the abdication on Feb. 12, 1912, of the boy emperor Hsuan T'ung (Pu-yi), thus bringing to an end the Manchu dynasty that had ruled China since 1644. Five days later, China formally became a republic with physician and revolutionist Sun Yat-sen as first provisional president.

Dr. Sun and his supporters founded a new party called the Kuomintang, and planned a Chinese republic based upon the Three Principles of Nationalism, Democracy and People's Livelihood. They failed, however, to win control of all China, and Dr. Sun resigned the presidency in favor of Yuan Shih Kai, the most powerful of the Chinese generals. Yuan ignored the constitution of the republic and tried to make himself emperor.

After the death of Yuan in 1917, Sun Yat-sen and the Kuomintang established a republic in Canton. It also failed to achieve the unification of China, and in 1923 Dr. Sun entered into an agreement with the Soviet Union known as the Canton-Moscow Entente. The Kuomintang agreed to admit Chinese communists to the party. The Soviet Union agreed to furnish military advisers to train the army of the Canton Republic. Dr. Sun died in 1925 and was succeeded by one of his supporters, General Chiang Kai-shek.

Chiang Kai-shek launched a vigorous campaign to educate the Chinese and modernize their industries and agriculture. Under his command, the armies of the Kuomintang captured Nanking (1927) and Peking (1928). In 1928, Chiang was made president of the Chinese Republic. His government was recognized by most of the great powers, but he soon began to exercise dictatorial powers. Prodded by the conservative members of the Kuomintang, he initiated a break between the members and the Chinese Communists which, once again, prevented the unification of China.

Persuaded that China would fare better under the leadership of its businessmen in alliance with the capitalist countries than under the guidance of the Chinese Communists and in alliance with the Soviet Union, Chiang expelled all Communists from the Kuomintang, sent the Russian advisers home, and hired German generals to train his army.

The Communists responded by setting up a government and raising an army that during the period of 1930-34 acquired control over large parts of Kiangsi, Fukien, Hunan, Hupeh and other provinces. These early Communist centers issued currency in the form of copper and silver coins and many varieties of notes printed on paper and cloth. A lack of minting facilities limited the issue of coins. Low mintage and the demonetization of silver in China in 1935 have elevated the surviving coinage specimens to the status of highly valued numismatic rarities. The issues of notes, the majority of which bore revolutionary slogans and often cartoon-like vignetts have also suffered a high attrition rate and certain issues command appreciable premiums in today's market.

When his army was sufficiently trained and equipped, Chiang Kai-shek led several military expeditions against the Communist Chinese which, while unable to subdue them, dislodged them south of the Yangtze, forcing them to undertake in 1935 a celebrated "Long March" of 6,000 miles (9,654 km.) from Hunan northwest to a refuge in Shensi province just south of Inner Mongolia from which Chiang was unable to displace them.

The Japanese menace had now assumed warlike proportions. Chiang rejected a Japanese offer of cooperation against the Communists, but agreed to suppress the movement himself. His generals, however, persuaded him to negotiate a truce with the Communists to permit united action against the greater menace of Japanese aggression. Under the terms of the truce, Communists were again admitted to the Kuomintang. They, in turn, promised to dissolve the Soviet Republic of China and to cease issuing their own currency.

The war with Japan all but extinguished the appeal of the Kuomintang, appreciably increased the power of the Communists, and divided China into three parts. The east coast and its principal cities - Peking, Tientsin, Nanking, Shanghai and Canton - were in Japanese-controlled, puppet-ruled states. The Communists controlled the countryside in the north where they were the de facto rulers of 100 million peasants. Chiang and the Kuomintang were driven toward the west, from where they returned with their prestige seriously damaged by their wartime performance.

At the end of World War II, the United States tried to bring the Chinese factions together in a coalition government. American mediation failed, and within weeks the civil war resumed.

By the fall of 1947, most of northeast China was under Communist control. During the following year, the war turned wholly in favor of the Communists. The Kuomintang armies in the northeast surrendered, two provincial capitals in the north were captured, a large Kuomintang army in the Huai river basin surrendered. Four Communist armies converged upon the demoralized Kuomintang forces. The Communists crossed the Yangtse in April 1949. Nanking, the Nationalist capital, fell. The civil war on the mainland was virtually over.

Chiang Kai-shek relinquished the presidency to Li Tsung-jen, his deputy, and after moving to Canton, to Chungking and Chengtu, retreated from the mainland to Taiwan (Formosa) where he resumed the presidency.

The Communist Peoples Republic of China was proclaimed on September 2, 1949. Thereafter relations between the Peoples Republic and the Soviet Union steadily deteriorated. China emerged as independent center of Communist power in 1958.

During and following World War II, the Chinese Communists again established banks at the various Communist centers to issue local currency. Prominent among Communist regional banks were the Bank of Central China, Bank of Peihai, and Bank of Shansi, Chahar and Hopeh.

The complexity of regional banks with their widely varying exchange rates were replaced in December 1948 by the Peoples Bank of China. Beneficial effects of the centralization were not immediately apparent. The pace of inflation was unslowed and regional note-issuing agencies continued to operate in remote areas for more than a year. Upon the defeat of the Kuomintang and the establishment of the Peoples Republic of China, the Communist government issued a new form of currency, the "Peoples Currency," as a replacement for all other notes in an effort to inject a stabilizing influence into the disorganized economy. Peoples Currency, Foreign Exchange Certificates and certain local or emergency issues are the only forms of paper money permitted to circulate by the Communist government.

TITLES:
Issuer's name reads from r. to l. until 1951 and from then on it reads from l. to r.

DATING:
The new Peoples Republic carried on w/the years of the old Republic into 1949. Then they converted to western dating reading r. to l. in Chinese into 1951 when it was then reversed to be read from l. to r.

MONETARY SYSTEM:
1 Yuan = 10 Chiao
1 Chiao = 10 Fen

PEOPLES BANK OF CHINA 中國人民銀行

Chung Kuo Jen Min Yin Hang Zhong Guo RenMin Yin Hang

1948 ISSUES
#809 *Deleted.*

			GOOD	FINE	XF
800	**1 YUAN** 1948. Blue and red. 2 workers at l. Back brown. *(S/M #C282-1).*		.90	3.75	15.00

			GOOD	FINE	XF
801	**5 YUAN** 1948. Dk. blue. Junks at l. Back green. *(S/M #C282-3).*		1.00	4.50	18.00

			GOOD	FINE	XF
802	**5 YUAN** 1948. Green. Sheep at l. *(S/M #C282-2).*		.90	3.75	15.00

			GOOD	FINE	XF
803	**10 YUAN** 1948. Blue-green on lt. green unpt. Farm laborers at l., coal mine at r. *(S/M #C282-4).*		1.00	4.50	18.00

			GOOD	FINE	XF
804	**20 YUAN** 1948. Brown. Chinese w/donkeys at l., steam passenger trains at r. *(S/M #C282-5).*		1.00	4.50	18.00

805	50 YUAN	GOOD	FINE	XF
	1948. Red-brown and black on lt. green unpt. Donkey operated well at l., coal mine at r. Back tan on ochre unpt. (S/M #C282-6).	2.50	7.50	22.50

806	100 YUAN	GOOD	FINE	XF
	1948. Dk. green. Hillside pagoda, shoreline at r. Steam passenger train at ctr. on back. (S/M #C282-11).	3.00	9.00	27.50

807	100 YUAN	GOOD	FINE	XF
	1948. Brown-violet. Factory at l., steam passenger trains at r. (S/M #C282-10).			
	a. Green unpt. on face.	3.00	9.00	27.50
	b. W/o unpt. on face.	3.00	9.00	27.50

808	100 YUAN	GOOD	FINE	XF
	Black and orange-brown. Farm couple plowing w/ox at l., factory at r. (S/M #C282-9).	1.75	7.00	28.00

810	1000 YUAN	GOOD	FINE	XF
	1948. Gray-violet. Farmer plowing w/horses at l. Back brown-violet; Temple of Heaven at ctr. 2 serial # varieties. (S/M #C282-14).	1.75	7.00	28.00

1949 ND PROVISIONAL ISSUE

811 (836A)	150 YUAN	GOOD	FINE	XF
	ND (-old date 1949). Ovpt: 150 Yuan on #821.	11.00	32.50	130.00

1949 ISSUES
#854A Deleted.

812	1 YUAN	GOOD	FINE	XF
	1949. Violet. Factory at l. (S/M #C282-20).	.75	3.00	12.00

813	5 YUAN	GOOD	FINE	XF
	1949. Brown. 2 women weaving at l. (S/M #C282-21).	.75	3.00	12.00

813A	5 YUAN	GOOD	FINE	XF
	1949. Red. Vertical format. *Kiangsi.* (S/M #C282-22).	7.50	30.00	120.00

814	5 YUAN	GOOD	FINE	XF
	1949. Lt. blue. Plow at l., man w/donkey cart at ctr., steer at r. Back purple. (S/M #C282-).	22.50	67.50	200.00

814A	5 YUAN	GOOD	FINE	XF
	1949. Blue. Factory at l. Back: brown w/hydro-electric plant at ctr. Specimen. (S/M #C282-).	—	Unc	150.00

814B	5 YUAN	GOOD	FINE	XF
	1949. Purple. Sawing wood, planting rice, steam passenger train at l. W/o serial #. (S/M #C282-).	—	—	—

815	10 YUAN	GOOD	FINE	XF
	1949. Red. Workers at l., farmer plowing w/ox at r. 2 serial # varieties. (S/M #C282-25).	.75	3.00	12.00

		GOOD	FINE	XF
823	**20 YUAN**			
	1949. Blue on lt. blue unpt. Agricultural occupations. *(S/M #C282-)*.	1.35	5.50	22.50

		GOOD	FINE	XF
816	**10 YUAN**			
	1949. Gray-blue on green unpt. Farmer and worker at l. *(S/M #C282-23)*.	1.00	4.50	18.00

		GOOD	FINE	XF
824	**20 YUAN**			
	1949. Blue. 2 workers pushing ore car at ctr. *(S/M #C282-33)*.	.75	3.00	12.00

		GOOD	FINE	XF
817	**10 YUAN**			
	1949. Brown on yellow and olive-green unpt. Steam passenger train in front of factory at l. Back olive-green. *(S/M #C282-24)*.			
	a. Issued note.	1.00	4.50	18.00
	s. Specimen.	—	—	—
818	**10 YUAN**			
	1949. Vertical format. *Kiangsi. (S/M #C282-26)*.	11.50	32.50	130.00
818A	**10 YUAN**			
	1949. Purple and yellow. Truck by factory at l., ox drawn irrigation system at r. W/o serial #. *(S/M #C282-)*.	—	—	—
818B	**10 YUAN**			
	1949. Blue and brown. Like #818A. W/o serial #. *(S/M #C282-)*.	—	—	—

		GOOD	FINE	XF
825	**20 YUAN**			
	1949. Blue. Vertical format. *Kiangsi. (S/M #C282-34)*.	11.50	32.50	130.00
825A	**20 YUAN**			
	1949. Blue and orange. Steam passenger train passing under viaduct, factories at ctr. r. W/o serial #. *(S/M #C282-)*.	—	—	—
825B	**20 YUAN**			
	1949. Blue, yellow and green. Like #825A. *(S/M #C282-)*.	11.50	32.50	130.00

		GOOD	FINE	XF
819	**20 YUAN**			
	1949. Lilac-brown. Pagoda at shoreline in foreground at l. *(S/M #C282-31)*.	1.00	4.50	18.00
820	**20 YUAN**			
	1949. Blue. Similar to #819. *(S/M #C282-30)*.	1.00	4.50	18.00

		GOOD	FINE	XF
826	**50 YUAN**			
	1949. Blue. Steam passenger train at l., bridge at r. Back red. *(S/M #C282-41)*.	4.00	12.00	36.00
827	**50 YUAN**			
	1949. Red. Similar to #826. Back blue. *(S/M #C282-41)*.	4.00	12.00	36.00

		GOOD	FINE	XF
821	**20 YUAN**			
	1949. Green. Factory, bridge and steam passenger train at l. *(S/M #C282-32)*.	1.00	4.50	18.00

		GOOD	FINE	XF
828	**50 YUAN**			
	1949. Gray-olive. Steam roller at r. *(S/M #C282-37)*.	6.00	18.00	55.00

		GOOD	FINE	XF
822	**20 YUAN**			
	1949. Violet on lt. ochre unpt. Junks at l., coal mine at r. Back tan. *(S/M #C282-27)*.	3.50	10.00	30.00

		GOOD	FINE	XF
829	**50 YUAN**			
	1949. Blue and black. Steam passenger train at ctr. 2 serial # varieties. *(S/M #C282-35)*.	4.00	12.00	36.00

		GOOD	**FINE**	**XF**
830	**50 YUAN**	3.00	9.00	27.00

1949. Brown. Farmer and laborer at ctr. 2 serial # varieties. *(S/M #C282-36)*.

		GOOD	**FINE**	**XF**
831	**100 YUAN**	.75	3.00	12.00

1949. Red on orange and black. Ship dockside at r. *(S/M #C282-43)*.

		GOOD	**FINE**	**XF**
832	**100 YUAN**	1.00	4.50	18.00

1949. Dk. brown and black on blue unpt. Bridge and Peking pagoda at l., shrine at r. 3 serial # varieties. *(S/M #C282-44)*.

		GOOD	**FINE**	**XF**
833	**100 YUAN**			

1949. Brown and black on orange unpt. Similar to #832. *(S/M #C282-45)*.

		GOOD	**FINE**	**XF**
a.	Red sign. seals 20mm apart.	1.35	5.50	22.50
b.	Red sign. seals 42mm apart.	1.35	5.50	22.50

		GOOD	**FINE**	**XF**
834	**100 YUAN**	1.35	5.50	22.50

1949. Red. Factories at l. and r. *(S/M #C282-42)*.

		GOOD	**FINE**	**XF**
835	**100 YUAN**	10.00	30.00	90.00

1949. Brown on green unpt. Sampans at l. *(S/M #C282-)*.

		GOOD	**FINE**	**XF**
836	**100 YUAN**	.75	3.00	12.00

1949. Brown and black. Donkey train w/factories behind at l. ctr., peasants hoeing at r. *(S/M #C282-46)*.

		GOOD	**FINE**	**XF**
837	**200 YUAN**	1.00	4.50	18.00

1949. Lilac-brown. Pagoda near shoreline at r. 2 serial # varieties. *(S/M #C282-51)*.

		GOOD	**FINE**	**XF**
838	**200 YUAN**	3.00	9.00	27.50

1949. Violet and green. Great Wall at r. Back violet. *(S/M #C282-47)*.

		GOOD	**FINE**	**XF**
838A	**200 YUAN**	2.00	6.00	18.50

1949. Like #838 but blue-gray on yellow-green unpt. Back brown-violet. *(S/M #C282-47.5)*.

		GOOD	**FINE**	**XF**
839	**200 YUAN**	5.00	15.00	45.00

1949. Blue-green. Harvesting at l. *(S/M #C282-52)*.

		GOOD	**FINE**	**XF**
840	**200 YUAN**	2.00	6.00	15.00

1949. Brown. Steel plant at l. White or tan paper. *(S/M #C282-53)*.

841 **200 YUAN**
1949. Blue. House at l. behind bronze cow, bridge at r. (S/M #C282-50).

	GOOD	FINE	XF
	2.00	6.00	18.50

842 **500 YUAN**
1949. Brown. Peasant walking at l., small bridge at r. (S/M #C282-56).

	GOOD	FINE	XF
	6.00	18.00	55.00

843 **500 YUAN**
1949. Brown and black. Steam shovel at r. (S/M #C282-55).

	GOOD	FINE	XF
	4.00	12.00	36.00

844 **500 YUAN**
1949. Gray and blue. City gate at ctr. (S/M #C282-57).

	GOOD	FINE	XF
	4.00	12.00	36.00

845 **500 YUAN**
1949. Violet and black on brown and lt. blue unpt. Farmer plowing w/mule at ctr. Back brown. (S/M #C282-).

	GOOD	FINE	XF
	4.00	12.00	36.00

846 **500 YUAN**
1949. Green. Tractor plowing at l. (S/M #C282-54).

	GOOD	FINE	XF
	3.00	9.00	27.50

847 **1000 YUAN**
1949. Gray-green. Town view at r. (S/M #C282-61).

	GOOD	FINE	XF
	2.50	7.50	22.50

848 **1000 YUAN**
1949. Black. Tractors at l. and at r. Farmer at ctr. on back. (S/M #C282-63).

	GOOD	FINE	XF
	2.50	7.50	22.50

849 **1000 YUAN**
1949. Green. Harvesting scene w/donkey cart at r. (S/M #C282-60).

	GOOD	FINE	XF
	2.50	7.50	22.50

850 **1000 YUAN**
1949. Lilac-brown on gray and brown unpt. Factory at l. w/man pushing ore hopper in foreground, farmer plowing w/2 donkeys at r. Back lilac-brown; ship dockside at ctr. (S/M #C282-62).

	GOOD	FINE	XF
	2.50	7.50	22.50

		GOOD	FINE	XF
851	**5000 YUAN**	4.00	12.00	36.00
	1949. Dk. gray-green. Tractor tilling at ctr. (S/M #C282-65).			

		GOOD	FINE	XF
852	**5000 YUAN**	4.00	12.00	36.00
	1949. Dk. green. 3 tractors at l., factory at r. (S/M #C282-64).			

		GOOD	FINE	XF
853	**10,000 YUAN**	3.00	9.00	27.50
	1949. Dk. brown and yellow. Farmers plowing w/horses at ctr. (S/M #C282-67).			

		GOOD	FINE	XF
854	**10,000 YUAN**	2.50	7.50	22.50
	1949. Green on m/c unpt. Warship at ctr. (S/M #C282-66).			

1950 ISSUE

		GOOD	FINE	XF
855	**50,000 YUAN**	16.50	50.00	150.00
	1950. Dk. green. Combine harvester at l. Back dk. brown-violet; foundry workers at ctr. (S/M #C282-).			

		GOOD	FINE	XF
856	**50,000 YUAN**	16.50	50.00	150.00
	1950. Blue on lt. green unpt. Bldg. at r. (S/M #C282-).			

1951 ISSUE

NOTE: Specimen books of #857-859 were "liberated" from the Peoples Bank. They usually have glue stains on back at l. and r. edges.

		GOOD	FINE	XF
857	**500 YUAN**			
	1951. Violet. City gate, Arabic legends w/*Sinkiang* on back. (S/M #C282-70).			
	a. Issued note.	16.50	50.00	150.00
	s. Specimen.	—	Unc	100.00

		GOOD	FINE	XF
857A	**1000 YUAN**			
	1951. Horses grazing by tents. Arabic legends w/*Singkiang* on back. (S/M #C282-).			
	a. Issued note.	32.50	100.00	300.00
	s. Specimen.	—	Unc	100.00

857B	5000 YUAN	GOOD	FINE	XF
	1951. Blue-green and black. Tents and camel at r. Back dk. blue. *(S/M #C282-).*			
	a. Issued note.	57.50	175.00	525.00
	b. Specimen.	—	Unc	125.00

857C	5000 YUAN	GOOD	FINE	XF
	1951. Purple and black on yellow unpt. Sheep grazing at r. Back green; Arabic legends w/*Sinkiang* at ctr. (S/M #C282-).			
	a. Issued note.	50.00	150.00	450.00
	s. Specimen.	—	Unc	125.00

858	10,000 YUAN	GOOD	FINE	XF
	1951. Red-brown on purple. Camel caravan. Arabic legends w/*Sinkiang* on back. (S/M #C282-).			
	a. Issued note.	40.00	120.00	360.00
	s. Specimen.	—	Unc	110.00

858A	10,000 YUAN	GOOD	FINE	XF
	1951. Brown-violet on black unpt. Herdsman w/horses at l. ctr. Back brown. (S/M #C282-).			
	a. Issued note.	50.00	150.00	450.00
	s. Specimen.	—	Unc	125.00

1953 FIRST ISSUE

859	5000 YUAN	GOOD	FINE	XF
	1953. Brown-violet on m/c unpt. Steam passenger train crossing bridge at l. ctr. Back brown, green and blue. (S/M #C282-).			
	a. Issued note.	26.50	80.00	240.00
	s. Specimen.	—	Unc	60.00

1953 SECOND ISSUE

860	1 FEN	VG	VF	UNC
	1953. Brown on yellow-orange unpt. Produce truck at r.			
	a. Roman control numerals and serial #. (S/M #C282-1a).	.25	.75	2.50
	b. Roman control numerals only. (S/M #C283-1b).	FV	.10	.25

861	2 FEN	VG	VF	UNC
	1953. Dk. blue on lt. blue unpt. Airplane at r.			
	a. Roman control numerals and serial #. (S/M #C283-2a).	.25	.75	2.50
	b. Roman control numerals only. (S/M #C283-2b).	FV	.10	.25

862	5 FEN	VG	VF	UNC
	Dk. green on green unpt. Cargo ship at r.			
	a. Roman control numerals and serial #. (S/M #C283-3a).	.35	1.00	3.00
	b. Roman control numerals only. (S/M #C283-3b).		.10	.30

863	1 JIAO	VG	VF	UNC
	1953. Brown-violet. Farm tractor at l. (S/M #C283-4).	.55	1.75	4.50

864	2 JIAO	VG	VF	UNC
	1953. Dk. green. Steam passenger train at l. (S/M #C283-5).	1.25	6.00	18.00

865	5 JIAO	VG	VF	UNC
	1953. Violet on lilac and lt. blue unpt. Dam at l. (S/M #C283-6).	.25	.85	2.25

			VG	VF	UNC
866	**1 YUAN**		1.10	3.50	9.00
	1953. Red. Great Hall at ctr. *(S/M #C283-10)*.				

			VG	VF	UNC
867	**2 YUAN**		2.35	6.00	25.00
	1953. Blue. Pagoda near rock at ctr. *(S/M #C283-10)*.				

			VG	VF	UNC
868	**3 YUAN**		16.00	48.00	120.00
	1953. Green. Old bridge at ctr. *(S/M #C283-12)*.				

			VG	VF	UNC
869	**5 YUAN**		10.00	30.00	75.00
	1953. Lilac-brown. Demonstrators at ctr. *(S/M #C283-13)*.				

			VG	VF	UNC
870	**10 YUAN**		25.00	75.00	300.00
	1953. Gray-black. Farm couple at ctr. *(S/M #C283-14)*.				

1956 ISSUE

			VG	VF	UNC
871	**1 YUAN**		.80	2.50	8.00
	1956. Black. Similar to #866. *(S/M #C283-40)*.				
872	**5 YUAN**		1.65	5.00	15.00
	1956. Dk. brown and m/c. Similar to #869. *(S/M #C283-43)*.				

1960 ISSUE
#873-876 arms at r. on back.

			VG	VF	UNC
873	**1 JIAO**		.80	2.50	8.00
	1960. Red-brown. Workers at ctr. *(S/M #C284-1)*.				

			VG	VF	UNC
874	**1 YUAN**		.25	.75	2.25
	1960. Red-brown and red-violet on m/c unpt. Woman driving tractor at ctr. *(S/M #C284-)*.				

		VG	VF	UNC
875	**2 YUAN**			
	1960. Black and green on m/c unpt. Machinist working at lathe at ctr.			
	a. Wmk: Lg. star and 4 small stars. *(S/M #C284-10a)*.	.35	1.00	3.00
	b. Wmk: Lt. stars and dark spades. *(S/M #C284-106)*.	.25	.75	2.25

			VG	VF	UNC
876	**5 YUAN**		.60	1.85	5.50
	1960. Brown and black on m/c unpt. Foundry worker at ctr. Wmk: Lg. star and 4 small stars. *(S/M #C284-11)*.				

REPUBLIC OF CHINA - TAIWAN

The Republic of China, comprising Taiwan (an island located 90 miles (145 km.) off the southeastern coast of mainland China), the offshore islands of Quemoy and Matsu and nearby islets of the Pescadores chain, has an area of 14,000 sq. mi. (35,981 sq. km.) and a population of 20.2 million. Capital: Taipei. During the past decade, manufacturing has replaced agriculture in importance. Fruits, vegetables, plywood, textile yarns and fabrics and clothing are exported.

Chinese migration to Taiwan began as early as the sixth century. The Dutch established a base on the island in 1624 and held it until 1661, when they were driven out by supporters of the Ming dynasty who used it as a base for their unsuccessful attempt to displace the ruling of Manchu dynasty of mainland China. After being occupied by Manchu forces in 1683, Taiwan remained under the suzerainty of China until its cession to Japan in 1895. It was returned to China following World War II. On December 8, 1949, Taiwan became the last remnant of Sun Yatsen's Republic of China when Chiang Kai-shek moved his army and government from mainland China to the island following his defeat by the Communist forces of Mao Tse-tung.

RULERS:
Japanese, 1895-1945

MONETARY SYSTEM:
Chinese:
1 Chiao = 10 Fen (Cents)
1 Yuan (Dollar) = 10 Chiao
Japanese:
1 Yen = 100 Sen

NOTE: S/M # in reference to *CHINESE BANKNOTES* by Ward D. Smith and Brian Matravers.

T'AI-NAN KUAN YIN P'IAO

T'AI-NAN OFFICIAL SILVER NOTES

票銀官南臺
Tai Nan Kuan Yin P'iao

忠堂正府南臺理護
Hu Li T'ai Nan Fu Cheng Tang Chung

1895 FIRST ISSUE

#900-902 are dated in the 21st year of the reign of Kuang Hsu and are in the Chinese lunar calendar. Add approximately 7 weeks for western dates. Uniface with occasion endorsements on back.

900	1 DOLLAR	GOOD	FINE	XF
	June Yr. 21 (1895). Blue. Red seal. (S/M #T63-1).			
	a. Issued note.	50.00	150.00	375.00
	b. Reissue w/2 additional smaller vertical chinese character ovpt. (S/M #T63-1-).	40.00	120.00	300.00

Reissue ovpt.:

901	5 DOLLARS	GOOD	FINE	XF
	June Yr. 21 (1895). Blue. Red seal. (S/M #T63-2).			
	a. Issued note.	50.00	150.00	375.00
	b. Reissue w/2 additional smaller vertical Chinese character ovpt. (S/M #T63-2-).	40.00	120.00	300.00

Reissue ovpt.:

902	10 DOLLARS	GOOD	FINE	XF
	June Yr. 21 (1895). Blue. Red seal. (S/M #T63-3).			
	a. Issued note.	75.00	225.00	550.00
	b. Reissue w/2 additional smaller vertical Chinese character ovpt. (S/M #T63-3-).	60.00	175.00	450.00

1895 SECOND ISSUE

#903-906 dated June or August in the 21st year of the reign of Kuang Hsu and are in the Chinese lunar calendar. Add approximately 7 weeks for western dates. Uniface except for occasional endorsements on back.

Reissue ovpt.:

903	500 CASH	GOOD	FINE	XF
	Aug. Yr. 21 (1895). Green. Red seals.			
	a. 131 x 237mm. (S/M #T63-10).	75.00	225.00	550.00
	b. 128 x 246mm. (S/M #T63-11).	70.00	210.00	525.00
	c. Reissue w/2 additional smaller vertical Chinese character ovpt. (S/M #T63-).	65.00	185.00	450.00

官銀錢票總局

Reissue ovpt.:

904   1 DOLLAR

		GOOD	FINE	XF
	June/July Yr. 21 (1895). Blue. Red handstamped seals.			
a.	Thick paper. (S/M #T63-20b).	45.00	135.00	335.00
b.	Thin paper. (S/M #T63-20a).	40.00	125.00	300.00
c.	Reissue w/2 additional smaller vertical Chinese character ovpt. (S/M #T63-20-).	35.00	105.00	275.00

905   5 DOLLARS

		GOOD	FINE	XF
	June/July Yr. 21 (1895). Blue. Red handstamped seals.			
a.	Thick paper. (S/M #T63-21b).	50.00	150.00	375.00
b.	Thin paper. (S/M #T63-21a).	50.00	150.00	375.00
c.	Reissue w/2 additional smaller vertical Chinese character ovpt. (S/M #T63-21-).	40.00	120.00	300.00

906   10 DOLLARS

		GOOD	FINE	XF
	June/July Yr. 21 (1895.) Blue. 2 red handstamped seals.			
a.	Thick paper. (S/M #T63-22b).	60.00	180.00	400.00
b.	Thin paper. (S/M #T63-22a).	60.00	180.00	400.00
c.	Reissue w/2 additional smaller vertical Chinese character ovpt. (S/M #T63-22-).	40.00	120.00	300.00

JAPANESE INFLUENCE

BANK OF TAIWAN

行銀灣臺
T'ai Wan Yin Hang

1899-1901 ND SILVER NOTE ISSUE

#907-910 vertical format w/2 facing Onagadori cockerels at upper ctr. 2 facing dragons below. W/text: *THE BANK OF TAIWAN Promises to pay the bearer on demand... Yen in Silver* on back.

907   1 YEN

		GOOD	FINE	XF
907	ND (1899). Black on lt. green unpt. Back ochre. (S/M #T70-1).	1000.	1500.	3500.
908	**5 YEN** ND (1899). Black on brown-orange unpt. Back gray-violet. (S/M #T70-2).	2500.	5000.	—
909	**10 YEN** ND (1901). Black on gray-violet unpt. Back green. (S/M #T70-3).	—	—	—
910	**50 YEN** ND (1900). Black on lt. orange unpt. Back blue-gray. Specimen. (S/M #T70-4).	—	—	—

1904-1906 ND GOLD NOTE ISSUE

#911-913 vertical format w/2 Onagadori cockerels at upper ctr. 2 facing dragons below. W/text: *THE BANK OF TAIWAN Promises to pay the bearer on demand ... Yen in Gold* on back.

911   1 YEN

		GOOD	FINE	XF
911	ND (1904). Black on yellow-orange unpt. Back purple. (S/M #70-10).	12.00	30.00	80.00
912	**5 YEN** ND (1904). Black on blue unpt. Back ochre. (S/M #T70-11).	100.00	250.00	600.00

913	**10 YEN**		GOOD	FINE	XF
	ND (1906). Black on pale gray unpt. Back green. (S/M #T70-12).		200.00	325.00	800.00

TAIWAN GOVERNMENT GENERAL

1917 EMERGENCY POSTAGE STAMP SUBSIDIARY COINAGE
Japanese postage stamps (Type Tazawa) pasted on special forms called *Tokubetsu Yubin Kitte Daishi* (Special Postage Stamp Cards).

#914-917 black text and circle on back.

#918-920 only black circle on back.

914	**5 SEN**	GOOD	FINE	XF
	ND (1917). Purple adhesive stamp on blue form. (S/M #T70-).	300.00	500.00	700.00

915	**10 SEN**	GOOD	FINE	XF
	ND (1917). Blue adhesive stamp on pink form. (S/M #T70-).	300.00	500.00	700.00
916	**20 SEN**			
	ND (1917). Purple adhesive stamp on green form. (S/M #T70-).	300.00	500.00	700.00

917	**50 SEN**	GOOD	FINE	XF
	ND (1917). Two *20 Sen* plus one *10 Sen* adhesive stamps on orange form. (S/M #T70-).	500.00	700.00	900.00

1918 EMERGENCY POSTAGE STAMP SUBSIDIARY COINAGE ISSUE

918	**1 SEN**	GOOD	FINE	XF
	ND (1918). Orange adhesive stamp on orange form. (S/M #T70-1).	300.00	500.00	700.00

919	**3 SEN**	GOOD	FINE	XF
	ND (1918). Red adhesive stamp on purple form. (S/M #T70-).	300.00	500.00	700.00
920	**5 SEN**			
	ND (1918). Purple adhesive stamp on red form. (S/M #T70-).	300.00	500.00	700.00

BANK OF TAIWAN LIMITED - TAIWAN BANK

券行銀灣臺

Tai Wan Yin Hang Ch'uan

1914-16 ND ISSUE
#921-932 various seascapes of a lighthouse point on back.

#921-28, 930, 931 and 933 engraved.

921	**1 YEN**	VG	VF	UNC
	ND (1915). Blue on lilac and lt. green unpt. Temple and stairs at r. Back dk. green on ochre unpt. (S/M #T70-20).	10.00	30.00	100.00
922	**5 YEN**			
	ND (1914). Gray on ochre and pink unpt. Temple and stairs at r. Back lt. violet-brown on lt. green unpt. (S/M #T70-21).	75.00	200.00	500.00

923	**10 YEN**	VG	VF	UNC
	ND (1916). Black on tan unpt. Temple and stairs at r. Back dk. purple and pale green. (S/M #T70-22).	75.00	200.00	500.00

1921 ISSUE

924 **50 YEN**
1921. Black on ochre and lt. brown unpt. Temple and stairs at r. Back VG 400.00 VF 1000. UNC 2500.
black and pale violet. (S/M #T70-23).

1932-37 ND ISSUE

925 **1 YEN**
(926) ND (1933; 1944). Black on gray, ochre and olive-green unpt. Temple
and stairs at l. Back dull greenish black on ochre unpt.

		VG	VF	UNC
a.	Serial # and block # (1933). (S/M #T70-30).	1.00	4.00	12.00
b.	Block # only (1944). (S/M #T70-40).	1.25	5.50	16.00
s1.	As a. Specimen.	—	—	150.00
s2.	As b. Specimen.	—	—	400.00

926 **5 YEN**
(927) ND (1934). Black on pink and green unpt. Pillared portico at l. Shrine
and stairs in background. Back dk. brown, olive-green and violet;
Japanese characters 5 YEN at r. (S/M #T70-31).

		VG	VF	UNC
a.	Issued note.	8.00	25.00	100.00
s1.	Specimen.	—	—	400.00
s2.	Specimen w/normal serial #.	—	—	150.00

927 **10 YEN**
(925) ND (1932). Black on dk. green, gray and ochre unpt. Lanterns on road
to Taiwan Jinja. Back dk. blue-gray on ochre unpt.; 10 YEN at lower
ctr.(S/M #T70-32).

		VG	VF	UNC
a.	Issued note.	5.00	22.50	90.00
s1.	Specimen.	—	—	400.00
s2.	Specimen w/normal serial #.	—	—	150.00

928 **100 YEN**
ND (1937). Black on lt. green, ochre and purple unpt. Temple and
stairs at l. Back lt. green and dk. brown; 100's in border. Black serial #.
(S/M #T70-33)..

		VG	VF	UNC
a.	Issued note.	12.50	40.00	160.00
s1.	Specimen.	—	—	400.00
s2.	Specimen w/normal serial #.	—	—	150.00

1944 ND ISSUE

929 **5 YEN**
(930) ND (1944). Like #927 but green, purple and brown unpt. Back lt.
brown on green unpt.; golden kite over 5 at r. (S/M #T70-42).

		VG	VF	UNC
a.	Issued note.	10.00	30.00	100.00
s1.	Specimen.	—	—	400.00
s2.	Specimen w/normal serial #.	—	—	150.00

930 **10 YEN**
(931) ND (1944-45). Face like #925 but lt. green and lilac unpt. Back dk.
blue-gray on lt. lilac unpt.; golden kite at r., palm trees at ctr. r., 10's in
border.

		VG	VF	UNC
a.	Black serial # and block # (1944). (S/M #T70-).	10.00	30.00	120.00
b.	Red block # only (1945). (S/M #T70-43).	10.00	30.00	120.00
s1.	Specimen. Wmk: Bank of Taiwan logos. (S/M #T70-).	—	—	175.00
s2.	As a. Specimen.	—	—	400.00
s3.	As a. Specimen w/normal serial #.	—	—	150.00
s4.	As b. Specimen.	—	—	150.00

1945 ND ISSUE

931 **10 YEN**
(932) ND (1945). Face like #931 but olive unpt. w/green at ctr. (color shade
varieties). Crude paper. Back dk. blue-green w/o lilac unpt. Red block
only. (S/M #T70-45).

		VG	VF	UNC
a.	Issued note.	8.00	35.00	125.00
s.	Specimen.	—	—	175.00

932 **100 YEN**
(929) ND (1945). Face like #928 but black on lt. blue and blue-violet to gray
unpt. Back purple to grayish purple w/golden kite at lower l., 100 at
bottom ctr. Crude paper.

		VG	VF	UNC
a.	W/o wmk. Block #1-2. (S/M #T70-46b).	15.00	50.00	185.00
b.	Wmk.: Bank of Taiwan logos. Block #2-7. (S/M #T70-46b).	8.00	35.00	125.00
s1.	As a. Specimen	—	—	150.00
s2.	As b. Specimen.	—	—	150.00

937	**10 YUAN**	**VG**	**VF**	**UNC**
	1946. Gray. *(S/M #T72-3).*	.75	3.00	8.00
938	**50 YUAN**			
	1946. Brown. *(S/M #T72-4).*	7.00	35.00	140.00

933	**1000 YEN**	**VG**	**VF**	**UNC**
	ND (1945). Ovpt. on Japan #45. Red seal of the Bank of Taiwan and vertical characters; *Tai Wan Yin Hang* at ctr. on back. *(S/M #T70-).*			
	a. Issued note.	1250.	2350.	4250.
	s. Specimen.	—	—	2500.

939	**100 YUAN**	**VG**	**VF**	**UNC**
	1946. Green. *(S/M #T72-5).*	1.00	3.00	9.00
940	**500 YUAN**			
	1946. Red. 2 serial # varieties. *(S/M #T72-6).*	1.00	5.00	20.00

1947-49 ISSUES

934	**1000 YEN**	**VG**	**VF**	**UNC**
	ND (1945). Black on yellow-green and gray unpt. Shrine at r. Back black on tan unpt., mountain range. Specimen. *(S/M #T70-47)*	—	Rare	—

TAIWAN - CHINESE ADMINISTRATION

BANK OF TAIWAN

行銀灣台

T'ai Wan Yin Hang

PRINTERS, 1946-

CPF:
   (Central Printing Factory)

CPFT:
   (Central Printing Factory, Taipei)

FPFT:
   (First Printing Factory)

PFBT:
   (Printing Factory of Taiwan Bank)

1946 ISSUE
#935-944 bank bldg. at l., portr. SYS at ctr. Naval battle scene at ctr. on back.
#935-940 printer: CPF.

935	**1 YUAN**	**VG**	**VF**	**UNC**
	1946. Blue. *(S/M #T72-1).*	.75	2.00	6.00
936	**5 YUAN**			
	1946. Red. *(S/M #T72-2).*	.75	2.00	7.00

941	**100 YUAN**	**VG**	**VF**	**UNC**
	1947. Green. Like #939 but bank bldg. w/o car, w/flag at top of front of bldg. Naval battle scene in circular ornament on back. Chinese printer: FPFT. *(S/M #T72-10).*	1.00	2.00	10.00
942	**1000 YUAN**			
	1948. Blue. Like #939 w/car in front of bldg., flag over l. side of bldg. Naval battle scene in oval ornament on back. Printer: CPF. *(S/M #T72-20).*	1.00	5.00	20.00
943	**1000 YUAN**			
	1948. Blue. Like #942 but bank bldg. w/o car at l., w/flag on top of front of bldg. Naval battle scene in circular ornament on back. Chinese printer: FPFT. *(S/M #T72-21).*	2.00	10.00	40.00

944	**10,000 YUAN**	**VG**	**VF**	**UNC**
	1948. Dk. green. Chinese Printer: FPFT. *(S/M #T72-23).*	5.00	20.00	100.00

945	**10,000 YUAN**	**VG**	**VF**	**UNC**
	1949. Red and green. Portr. SYS at l. Bank bldg. on back. Printer: CPF. (S/M #T72-30).	2.00	6.00	14.00
945A	**100,000 YUAN**	—	—	—
	1949. SYS at ctr. Printer: FPFT. (S/M #T72-). (Not issued.)			

1949 ISSUES

#946 and 947 bank bldg. at upper ctr. Taiwan outlined on back. Printer: CPF.
#948-957 portr. SYS at upper ctr. Bank at upper ctr. on back.
#952-954 Chinese printer: FPFT.
#955-0957 printer: CPF.

#950

#951

950	**1 YUAN**	**VG**	**VF**	**UNC**
	1949. Brown-violet. Bank in circular frame at top on back. Chinese printer: FPFT. 2 serial # varieties. (S/M #T73-11).	2.00	10.00	40.00
951	**1 YUAN**			
	1949. Red. Printer: CPF. (S/M #T73-10).	15.00	60.00	240.00

#952

#953

952	**5 YUAN**	**VG**	**VF**	**UNC**
	1949. Green. Back lt. orange; *1949* above lower frame. (S/M #T73-13).	—	Rare	—
953	**5 YUAN**			
	1949. Red w/red and purple guilloche. *1949* within lower frame on back. (S/M #T73-12).	5.00	20.00	80.00

#954

#955

954	**10 YUAN**	**VG**	**VF**	**UNC**
	1949. Blue on lt. blue unpt. Back brown; *1949* above lower frame. (S/M #T73-15).	30.00	125.00	500.00
955	**10 YUAN**			
	1949. Blue-black on lt. green and pink unpt. Portr. SYS in simple oval frame at top. Back blue-black; *1949* in lower ornamental frame. (S/M #T73-14).	2.00	8.00	20.00

#956

#957

956	**100 YUAN**	**VG**	**VF**	**UNC**
	1949. Brown-violet w/blue and pink guilloche. (S/M #T73-17).	50.00	200.00	800.00
957	**100 YUAN**			
	1949. Brown-violet w/brown-violet guilloche. (S/M #T73-16).	35.00	175.00	700.00

#946

#947

946	**1 CENT**	**VG**	**VF**	**UNC**
	1949. Blue. (S/M #T73-1).	1.00	2.00	6.00
947	**5 CENTS**			
	1949. Brown. (S/M #T73-2).	1.00	3.00	7.00

#948

#949

948	**10 CENTS**	**VG**	**VF**	**UNC**
	1949. Green. Printer: CPF. (S/M #T73-3).	2.00	10.00	45.00
949	**50 CENTS**			
	1949. Orange. Printer: CPF. (S/M #T73-4).			
	a. Serial # w/2 letter prefix.	.50	1.00	4.00
	b. Serial # w/1 letter prefix and suffix.	.10	.50	2.00

1948-49 CIRCULATING BANK CASHIER'S CHECK ISSUE

#958-961 uniface w/occasional Chinese endorsements on back, vertical format w/bank at upper ctr. Chinese printer: FPFT.

5000 Yuan	10,000 Yuan	100,000 Yuan

			GOOD	FINE	XF
958	**5000 YUAN**		10.00	40.00	100.00
	(1948). Orange. *(S/M #T72-22).*				
959	**10,000 YUAN**		10.00	40.00	100.00
	(1948). Blue. *(S/M #T72-24).*				
960	**100,000 YUAN**		12.00	35.00	90.00
	(1949). Red. *(S/M #T72-31).*				
961	**1,000,000 YUAN**		20.00	50.00	125.00
	(1949). Brown. *(S/M #T72-32).*				

1950 ISSUE

		VG	VF	UNC
962	**10 YUAN**	—	—	100.00
	1950. M/c. Similar to #R105. Specimen. *(S/M #T73-).*			

1954 ISSUE

#964-969 Chinese printer: PFBT.

964	**1 YUAN**	1.00	3.00	9.00
	1954. Blue. *(S/M #T73-31).*			

#965   #967

		VG	VF	UNC
965	**1 YUAN**	1.00	2.00	6.00
	1954. Deep green on lt. blue-green unpt. *(S/M #T73-30).*			
966	**1 YUAN**	1.00	2.00	6.00
	1954. Deep green on lt. green unpt. Back dull olive-green on lt. green unpt. (litho). *(S/M #T73-31).*			
967	**10 YUAN**	1.00	4.00	11.00
	1954. Blue. *(S/M #T73-32).*			
963	**1 CENT**	.50	2.00	5.00
	1954. Blue. Bank. Printer: CPF. *(S/M #T73-20).*			

1955 ISSUE

968	**5 YUAN**	1.00	3.00	12.00
	1955. Red w/red and blue guilloche. *(S/M #T73-40).*			

1960 ISSUE

969	**10 YUAN**	1.00	2.00	4.00
	1960. Blue on m/c unpt. SYS at l., bridge at r. *(S/M#T73-50).*			

		VG	VF	UNC
970	**10 YUAN**	1.00	2.00	4.00
	1960. Red on yellow and lt. green unpt. Like #969 but w/o printer. *(S/M #T73-51).*			

OFF-SHORE ISLAND CURRENCY

BANK OF TAIWAN

行銀灣臺
Tai Wan Yin Hang

Notes of the Bank of Taiwan and later notes of the Republic of China/Bank of Taiwan w/ovpt: #R101-R109 portr. SYS at upper ctr. Vertical format.

KINMEN (QUEMOY) BRANCH

Notes of the Bank of Taiwan and later notes of the Republic of China/Bank of Taiwan w/ovpt:

1949 ISSUES

#R101-R109 portr. SYS at upper ctr. Vertical format.

		VG	VF	UNC
R102	**1 YUAN**	5.00	20.00	80.00
(R1002)	1949 (1952). Green. Printer: FPFT. *(S/M #T74-2).*			

#R1002B

		VG	VF	UNC
R102A	**1 YUAN**	150.00	400.00	800.00
(R1002A)	1949. Reddish brown on lt. orange unpt. Back blue; lg. red outlined character ovpt: *Chin Men.* Buff paper. *(S/M #T74-3)*			

R102B 5 YUAN
(R1002B) 1949. Dk. green on lt. blue and m/c unpt. Back dk. green on lt. green unpt.; lg. red outlined character ovpt: *Chin Men. (S/M #T74-4).*

	VG	VF	UNC
	250.00	650.00	1200.

1950-51 ISSUES

R105 10 YUAN
(R1005) 1950 (1952). Blue on m/c unpt. Printer: FPFT. *(S/M #T74-21).*

	VG	VF	UNC
	5.00	15.00	45.00

R106 10 YUAN
(R1006) 1950 (1963). Blue. Printer: CPF. *(S/M #T74-20).*

	.50	1.50	7.50

R107 50 YUAN
(R1007) 1951 (1967). Green. Printer: FPFT. *(S/M #T74-30).*

	VG	VF	UNC
	3.00	10.00	55.00

R103 10 CENTS
(R1003) 1950 (1952). Blue.

		VG	VF	UNC
a.	Ovpt. at bottom of face. *(S/M #T74-10a).*	5.00	20.00	70.00
b.	Ovpt. at middle and bottom of face. *(S/M #T74-10b).*	4.00	15.00	45.00

R104 50 CENTS
(R1004) 1950 (1952). Brown. Ovpt: *Chin Men* at lower l. and r. on face. Printer: CPF. *(S/M #T74-11).*

		VG	VF	UNC
a.	Ovpt: *Chin* at r., *Men* at l. on back.	10.00	30.00	95.00
b.	Ovpt: *Chin Men* at l. and r. on back.	10.00	30.00	95.00

1955-72 ISSUES

R108 5 YUAN
(R1008) 1955 (1956). Violet. Printer: PFBT. *(S/M #T74-40).*

	VG	VF	UNC
	2.00	10.00	45.00

MATSU BRANCH

Notes of the Bank of Taiwan and later notes of the Republic of China/Bank of Taiwan w/ovpt.

1950-51 ISSUES

#R113-R115 horizontal format.
#R116, R119-R121 portr. SYS at upper ctr. Vertical format.

R115 1 YUAN
(R1015) 1950. Red.

		VG	VF	UNC
a.	W/ imprint. Specimen. *(S/M #T75-).*	—	Unc	110.00
b.	W/o imprint. Specimen. *(S/M #T75-).*	—	Unc	110.00

 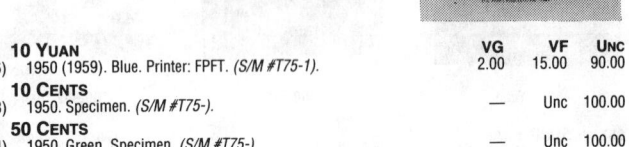

R116 10 YUAN
(R1016) 1950 (1959). Blue. Printer: FPFT. *(S/M #T75-1).*

	VG	VF	UNC
	2.00	15.00	90.00

R113 10 CENTS
(R1013) 1950. Specimen. *(S/M #T75-).*

	—	Unc	100.00

R114 50 CENTS
(R1014) 1950. Green. Specimen. *(S/M #T75-).*

	—	Unc	100.00

1954-72 ISSUES

R119 1 YUAN
(R1019) 1954 (1959). Brown. Printer: PFBT. *(S/M #T75-20).*

	VG	VF	UNC
	.25	.75	3.50

R120 1 YUAN
(R1020) 1954. Brown. Printer: CPF. *(S/M #T75-).*

	.25	.75	3.00

R121 5 YUAN
(R1021) 1955 (1959). Dk. green. Printer: PFBT. *(S/M #T75-30).*

	VG	VF	UNC
	.50	1.00	5.00

TACHEN BRANCH

Notes of the Bank of Taiwan w/ovpt: 陳大

1949 ISSUES
#R140-R143 vertical format w/SYS at upper ctr.

R140	1 YUAN		VG	VF	UNC
(R1040)	1949 (1953). Green. Printer: FPFT. (S/M #T76-1).		50.00	150.00	475.00

1950 ISSUE

R143	10 YUAN		VG	VF	UNC
(R1043)	1950 (1953). Blue. Printer: FPFT. (S/M #T76-20).		90.00	300.00	1200.

#R1041 #R1042

R141	10 CENTS		VG	VF	UNC
(R1041)	1950 (1953). Red. Printer: CPF. (S/M #T76-10).		90.00	300.00	650.00
R142	50 CENTS				
(R1042)	1950 (1953). Green. Printer: CPF. (S/M #T76-11).		50.00	175.00	700.00

JAPANESE PUPPET BANKS

Japan's attempt to assert political and economic control over East Asia, an expansionist program called "Asia for the Asiatics," and later the "Co-Prosperity Sphere for East Asia," was motivated by economic conditions and the military tradition of the Japanese people. Living space, food, and raw materials were urgently needed. To secure them and also markets for their manufactured goods, the Japanese thought they had to establish control over the markets and resources of East Asia. They planned: (1) to add nearby islands to the islands of Japan, (2) to obtain possession of Korea, (3) to absorb the Malay Peninsula, Indo-China, Thailand, the Philippines, and the numerous Southwest Pacific islands into the Empire of Japan, and (4) to assert at least economic control over China.

By the eve of World War I, the Japanese had succeeded in occupying the Bonin Islands (1874), annexing Formosa and the Pescadores Islands (1895), annexing the Liaotung peninsula and the southern half of Sakhalin island (Russo-Japanese War), and annexing Korea (1910).

During World War I, Japan managed to gain economic control over Manchuria and Inner Mongolia, and to take the Shantung Peninsula from Germany. Further territorial expansion was achieved by the Paris Peace Settlement (1919) which mandated to Japan all of the Caroline, Marshall, and Mariana islands except Guam. The Japanese were, however, forced to give the Shantung Peninsula back to China.

Japan's military thrust against mainland China began in earnest on Sept. 18, 1931, when with a contrived incident for an excuse, the Japanese army seized the strategic centers in Manchuria and set up (1932) the puppet nation of Manchukuo with Henry Pu-Yi, ex-emperor of China, as emperor under the protection and control of the Japanese army. Not content with the seizure of Manchuria, the Japanese army then invaded the Chinese province of Jehol and annexed it to Manchukuo (1933). In 1934, Japan proclaimed Manchukuo an independent nation and the Japanese army penetrated into Inner Mongolia and some of China's northern provinces, and established a garrison near Peiping. Although determined to resist the invasion of their country, the Chinese were able to do little more than initiate a boycott of Japanese goods.

War between the two powers quickened in July 1937, when Japanese and Chinese troops clashed at the Marco Polo Bridge near Peiping, an incident Japanese leaders used as an excuse to launch a full-fledged invasion of China without a declaration of war. Peiping and Tientsin were taken in a month. Shanghai fell in Nov. 1937. Nanking fell in Dec. 1937 and was established as a puppet state under a Chinese president. Canton fell in 1938.

Though badly mauled and weakened by repeated Japanese blows, the Chinese continued to fight, and to meet defeat, while Japanese armies overran large sections of Eastern China and occupied the essential seaports. Trading space for time, Chiang Kai-shek kept his army intact and moved his capital from Nanking to Chungking behind the mountains in western China. Factory machinery, schools and colleges were moved to the west. With the aid of the Flying Tigers, a volunteer force of American aviators commanded by General Claire Chennault, and military supplies from the United States and Great Britain moved slowly over the dangerous Burma Road, the Chinese continued to resist the hated invader. The war came to a stalemate. The Japanese made no attempt to take Chungking. The Chinese could not drive the Japanese armies from the provinces they had conquered.

The defeat of Japan was brought about by the decision of the Japanese government to execute their plan to drive the United States, France, Great Britain, and the Netherlands out of the East, a plan initiated by an air attack on U.S. military installations at Pearl Harbor, Hawaii. Japan's dream of dominance in East Asia began to fade with the defeat of a powerful Japanese fleet at the Battle of Midway (June 3, 1942), and flickered out at Hiroshima and Nagasaki in Aug. 1945 in the wake of "a rain of ruin from the air, the like of which had never been seen on this earth." Upon the defeat of Japan by the Allies, control of the China-Japanese puppet states reverted to Chinese factions.

During the existence of the China-Japanese puppet states, Japanese occupation authorities issued currency through Japanese puppet banks, the most important of which were the Central Reserve Bank of China, Federal Reserve Bank of China, Hua-Hsing Commercial Bank, and Chi Tung Bank.

Operations of the Central Reserve Bank of China, the state bank of the puppet Republic of China government at Nanking, began sometime in 1940, although the official inauguration date is Jan. 1, 1941. To encourage public acceptance, the notes of this puppet bank carried, where size permitted, the portrait of Sun Yat-sen, Chinese nationalist revolutionary leader and founder of the Chinese republic, on the face, and his mausoleum on the back. The number of notes issued by the Central Reserve Bank of China exceeds the total number issued by all other Japanese puppet banks in China.

An interesting feature of the issues of the Central Reserve Bank of China is the presence of clandestine propaganda messages engraved on some of the plates by patriotic Chinese engravers. The 50-cent notes of 1940 carry a concealed propaganda message in Chinese. The initials "U S A C" and the date 1945 ("U.S. Army Coming, 1945") appear on the 1944 200-yuan note. Two varieties of the 1940 10-yuan note include in the face border design devices resembling bisected turtles, an animal held in low esteem in China.

A small number of notes issued by the Central Reserve Bank of China carry overprints, the exact purpose of which is unclear, with the exception of those which indicate a circulation area. Others are thought to be codes referring to branch offices or Japanese military units.

The Federal Reserve Bank of China, located in Peiping, was the puppet financial agency of the Japanese in northeast China. This puppet bank issued both coins and currency, but in modest amounts. The first series of notes has a curious precedent. The original plates were prepared by two American engravers who journeyed to China in 1909 to advise officials of the Bureau of Engraving and Printing, Peking (BEPP) on engraving techniques of the Western World. The Chinese gentleman appearing on the 1-yuan notes of 1938 is said to be making an obscene gesture to indicate Chinese displeasure with the presence of the Japanese.

The Hua Hsing Commercial Bank was a financial agency created and established by the government of Japan and its puppet authorities in Nanking. Notes and coins were issued until sometime in 1941, with the quantities restricted by Chinese aversion to accepting them.

The Chi Tung Bank was the banking institution of the "East Hopei Autonomous Government" established by the Japanese in 1938 to undermine the political position of China in the northwest provinces. It issued both coins and notes between 1937 and 1939 with a restraint uncharacteristic of the puppet banks of the China-Japanese puppet states. The issues were replaced in 1940 by those of the Federal Reserve Bank of China.

* * * This section has been renumbered in part. * * *

CENTRAL RESERVE BANK OF CHINA
行銀備儲央中
Chung Yang Ch'u Pei Yin Hang

1940 ISSUE
#J9A Deleted.
#J13 Deleted. See #J12.
NOTE: Many are of the opinion that ovpt: *Wuhan* and *Kwangtung* on #J12 are fantasies.

J1 1 FEN = 1 CENT

	VG	VF	UNC
1940. Red on lt. brown unpt.			
a. Imprint and serial #.	1.00	4.00	16.00
b. W/o imprint, w/block letters and #.	.25	1.00	4.00
s1. As a. Specimen w/blue ovpt: *Yang Pen. Specimen* on back. Uniface pair.	—	—	60.00
s2. As b. Specimen w/ovpt: *Yang Pen. Specimen* on back.	—	—	60.00

J2 5 FEN = 5 CENTS

	VG	VF	UNC
1940. Green on pale green unpt.			
a. Imprint and serial #.	.25	1.00	4.00
b. W/o imprint, w/block letters and #.	.25	1.00	4.00
s1. As a. Specimen w/red ovpt: *Yang Pen. Specimen* on back. Uniface pair.	—	—	60.00
s2. As b. Specimen w/red ovpt: *Yang Pen. Specimen* on back.	—	—	60.00

J8 1 YUAN

	VG	VF	UNC
1940. Green on yellow unpt. Portr. SYS at l., mausoleum of SYS at ctr. Back green w/black sign. 150 x 78mm.			
a. Issued note.	.60	2.50	10.00
b. Red ovpt: *HSING* twice on face and back.	3.25	8.00	20.00
c. Control ovpt: *I (Yi)* twice on face and back.	16.00	40.00	—
s. Specimen w/red ovpt: *Yang Pen. Specimen* on back.	—	—	125.00

J9 1 YUAN

	VG	VF	UNC
1940. Violet on lt. blue unpt. Like #J8. Back violet on pink and yellow-green unpt.			
a. Black sign. on back 151 x 79mm. (1.5.1942).	1.65	5.00	15.00
b. Violet sign. Serial # format: LL123456L. 151 x 79mm.	.90	2.75	8.00
c. Violet sign. Serial # format: L/L 123456L. 146 x 78mm.	.90	2.75	8.00
s1. As a. Specimen w/red ovpt: *Yang Pen. Specimen* on back.	—	—	125.00
s2. As b. Specimen w/red ovpt: *Yang Pen. Specimen* on back.	—	—	125.00

J10 5 YUAN

	VG	VF	UNC
1940. Red. Portr. SYS at ctr. Back red; mausoleum at ctr.			
a. Face w/ yellow and blue-green unpt. Serial # on face and back. Black sign. (6.1.1941).	5.00	15.00	45.00
b. As a. Black control ovpt. on face and back.	11.00	35.00	100.00
c. Face w/pink and blue unpt. Serial # on face only. Black sign. (19.12.1941).	1.00	3.00	9.00
d. As c. Black control ovpt. on face and back.	3.00	10.00	30.00
e. As c. Red sign.	.25	.75	2.25
f. As e. Red ovpt: *Wuhan* over seals on face.	3.25	10.00	30.00
g. As e. Black ovpt: *Kwangtung* horizontally on lower corners of face.	3.25	10.00	30.00
s1. As a. Specimen.	—	—	125.00
s2. As c. Specimen w/blue ovpt: *Yang Pen. Specimen* on back.	—	—	125.00
s3. As c. Specimen w/red ovpt: *Mi-hon.*	—	—	125.00

J11 5 YUAN

	VG	VF	UNC
1940. Red w/repeated gold Chinese 4 character unpt. Proof.	—	—	100.00

J12 10 YUAN

	VG	VF	UNC
1940. Blue on blue-green and lt. brown unpt. Similar to #J10. Back blue.			
a. Bright blue face and back. Serial # on face and back. Black sign. (6.1.1941).	12.50	37.50	150.00
b. As a. Red control ovpt. on face and back.	37.50	150.00	—
c. Dk. blue face and back. Serial # on face only, black sign.	.75	2.25	8.00
d. As c. Red control ovpt. on face and back.	6.50	20.00	60.00

	VG	VF	UNC
e. As c. Black ovpt: *Kwangtung* vertically at l. and r.	2.50	7.50	25.00
f. As e. Smaller blue ovpt: *Kwangtung.*	2.50	7.50	25.00

	VG	VF	UNC
g. As c. Lt. blue ovpt: *Wuhan* over red seals on face.	2.50	7.50	25.00
h. Color similar to c. Serial # on face only, blue sign. (19.12.1941).	.25	.75	2.50
i. As h. Ovpt: *Wuhan* over sign. seals at lower l. and r. (as g).	2.50	7.50	25.00
j. As h. Ovpt: *Wuhan* vertically at sides on face.	2.50	7.50	25.00
k. As h. Black ovpt: *Kwangtung* at l. and r. (as e).	2.50	7.50	25.00
l. As h. Blue ovpt: *Kwangtun* at l. and r. in different style of type.	2.50	7.50	25.00
s1. As a. Specimen w/red ovpt: *Yang Pen. Specimen* on back.	—	—	150.00
s2. As c. Specimen w/red ovpt: *Yang Pen. Specimen* on back.	—	—	125.00
s3. As c. Specimen w/red ovpt: *Mi-hon.* Regular serial #.	—	—	100.00
s4. As h. Specimen w/red ovpt: *Yang Pen. Specimen* on back.	—	—	125.00
s5. As h. Specimen w/red ovpt: *Mi-hon.* Regular serial #.	—	—	100.00

J3 10 CENTS = 1 CHIAO

	VG	VF	UNC
1940. Green. Back m/c.			
a. Issued note.	.25	1.00	4.00
s1. Specimen w/red ovpt: *Yang Pen. Specimen* on back. Uniface pair.	—	—	60.00
s2. Specimen w/red ovpt: *Yang Pen. Specimen* on back.	—	—	60.00

1943 ISSUES

#J21-J28 portr. SYS at ctr. SYS Mausoleum at ctr. on back.
#J22 *Deleted.* See #J21.

J4	20 CENTS = 2 CHIAO	VG	VF	UNC
	1940. Blue. Back m/c.			
	a. Issued note.	.30	1.25	5.00
	s1. Specimen w/red ovpt: *Yang Pen. Specimen* on back. Uniface pair.	—	—	60.00
	s2. Specimen w/red ovpt: *Yang Pen. Specimen* on back.	—	—	60.00
J5	50 CENTS = 5 CHIAO			
	1940. (1941). Red-brown. Back m/c.			
	a. Issued note.	.60	2.50	10.00
	s. Specimen w/blue ovpt: *Yang Pen.* Red *Specimen* on back.	—	—	60.00
J6	50 CENTS = 5 CHIAO			
	1940. Orange. Back m/c.	1.00	4.00	12.00

J7	50 CENTS = 5 CHIAO	VG	VF	UNC
	1940. Violet. Back m/c.			
	a. Issued note.	.50	2.00	8.00
	s1. Specimen w/red ovpt: *Yang Pen. Specimen* on back. Uniface pair.	—	—	60.00
	s2. Specimen w/red ovpt: *Yang Pen. Specimen* on back.	—	—	50.00

1942 ISSUE

J14	100 YUAN	VG	VF	UNC
	1942. Dk. green on m/c unpt. Portr. SYS at ctr. SYS Mausoleum at ctr. on back.			
	a. Blue sign.	.75	2.25	8.00
	b. Black sign. (17.6.1942).	11.00	33.00	100.00
	s. As b. Specimen w/red ovpt: *Yang Pen. Specimen* on back.	—	—	150.00

J19	1 YUAN	VG	VF	UNC
	1943. Green on lt. blue unpt. Portr. SYS at ctr. SYS Mausoleum at ctr. on back.			
	a. Issued note.	.50	1.50	4.50
	s. Specimen w/red ovpt: *Yang Pen.*	—	—	125.00

J20	10 YUAN	VG	VF	UNC
	1943. Brown on m/c unpt. Portr. SYS at l. SYS Mausoleum at ctr. on back.			
	a. Issued note.	1.00	3.00	10.00
	b. Ovpt: *Kwangtung.* vertically at l. and r.	3.00	10.00	30.00
	s. As a. Specimen w/red ovpt: *Yang Pen.*	—	—	125.00

J21	100 YUAN	VG	VF	UNC
	1943. Dk. olive-green on m/c unpt. Back lt. green-dk. green. W/serial #.			
	a. Issued note.	.50	1.50	4.50
	b. Red ovpt: *Wuhan.*	3.00	10.00	30.00
J23	100 YUAN			
	1943 (1944). Blue on m/c unpt. Back green; w/block letters.			
	a. Wmk: Clouds.	.50	1.50	5.00
	b. W/o wmk.	.50	1.50	5.00
	s. Specimen w/ovpt: *Yang Pen.*	—	—	125.00

Wuhan ovpt.

J15	500 YUAN	VG	VF	UNC
	1942. Brown on m/c unpt. Portr. SYS at l. SYS Mausoleum at r. on back. *Kwangtung* at lower l. and r.			
	a. Wmk: *500 Yuan.*	3.25	10.00	30.00
	b. W/o wmk.	3.25	10.00	30.00
	s. Specimen w/red ovpt: *Yang Pen. Specimen* on back. W/o *Kwangtung.*	—	—	150.00

J24 500 YUAN

	VG	VF	UNC
1943 (1944). Brown on m/c unpt. 180 x 96mm. Block letters.			
a. Wmk: *500* in Chinese characters.	3.25	10.00	30.00
b. W/o wmk.	1.35	4.00	12.00
c. Red ovpt: *Kwangtung.*	2.50	7.50	25.00
d. Red ovpt: *Wuhan* vertically at l. and r.	2.50	7.50	25.00
s1. Specimen w/red ovpt. *Yang Pen. Specimen* on back.	—	—	125.00
s2. Specimen w/red ovpt: *Mi-hon.*	—	—	125.00
s3. As d. Specimen w/red ovpt: *Yang Pen. Specimen* on back.	—	—	125.00

J24A 500 YUAN

	VG	VF	UNC
1943 (1944). Dk. brown on m/c unpt. Back dk. brown. Serial #. 187 x 95mm.			
a. Issued note.	5.50	16.50	50.00
s. Specimen w/red ovpt: *Yang Pen. Specimen* on back.	—	—	125.00

J25 500 YUAN

	VG	VF	UNC
1943 (1944). Deep purple-brownish purple on m/c unpt. 187 x 95mm. Serial #. Guilloche in the unpt. Back violet, lithographed.			
a. Wmk: *500* in Chinese characters.	3.00	10.00	30.00
b. Wmk: Cloud forms.	2.25	7.00	20.00
c. W/o wmk.	1.00	4.00	12.00
s1. Specimen w/red ovpt: *Yang Pen. Specimen* on back.	—	—	125.00
s2. Specimen w/red ovpt: *Mi-hon.*	—	—	125.00

J26 500 YUAN

	VG	VF	UNC
1943 (1944). Pale purple on pink unpt. Like #J25 but w/o guilloche in the unpt. Back w/plate varieties. Wmk: cloud form.			
a. Issued note.	1.00	4.00	12.00
s. Specimen w/red ovpt: *Yang Pen. Specimen* on back.	—	—	125.00

J27 500 YUAN

	VG	VF	UNC
1943 (1945). Brown on lt. brown unpt. Brown guilloche. Block letters. 169 x 84mm.			
a. Issued note.	2.00	6.00	15.00
s. Specimen w/red ovpt: *Yang Pen. Specimen* on back.	—	—	125.00

J28 500 YUAN

	VG	VF	UNC
1943. Brown on lilac. M/c guilloche. Block letters. 169 x 84mm.			
a. Wmk: Cloud forms.	2.00	6.00	15.00
b. W/o wmk.	1.00	3.00	10.00
s. Specimen w/red ovpt: *Yang Pen. Specimen* on back.	—	—	125.00

J16 10 CENTS = 1 CHIAO

	VG	VF	UNC
1943. Green. SYS Mausoleum at ctr. W/o imprint, w/block #.			
a. Issued note.	.40	1.25	4.00
s. Specimen w/red ovpt: *Yang Pen.* Uniface pair.	—	—	60.00

J17 20 CENTS = 2 CHIAO

	VG	VF	UNC
1943. Blue. SYS Mausoleum at ctr. W/o imprint, w/block #.			
a. Issued note.	.55	1.65	5.00
s. Specimen w/red ovpt: *Yang Pen.* Uniface pair.	—	—	60.00

J18 50 CENTS = 5 CHIAO

	VG	VF	UNC
1943. Red-brown. SYS Mausoleum at ctr.			
a. W/o imprint, w/block #.	.65	2.00	6.00
b. W/o imprint, w/block letter and #.	1.25	4.00	12.00
s. As a. Specimen w/blue ovpt: *Yang Pen.* Uniface pair.	—	—	60.00

1944 ISSUES

#J29-J39 portr. SYS at ctr. SYS Mausoleum at ctr. on back. Wmk: Cloud forms may be vertical or horizontal.

J29 100 YUAN

	VG	VF	UNC
1944 (1945). Blue on pale green unpt. Back blue. Wmk: Cloud forms.			
a. Issued note.	2.75	11.50	35.00
s. Specimen w/red ovpt: *Yang Pen. Specimen* on back.	—	—	125.00

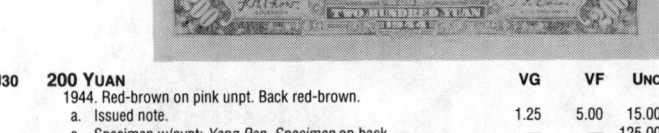

J30 200 YUAN

	VG	VF	UNC
1944. Red-brown on pink unpt. Back red-brown.			
a. Issued note.	1.25	5.00	15.00
s. Specimen w/ovpt: *Yang Pen. Specimen* on back.	—	—	125.00

J31 1000 YUAN

	VG	VF	UNC
1944 (1945). Dk. blue on m/c unpt. Back deep blue-gray on m/c unpt. Serial #. 185 x 94mm.			
a. Issued note.	2.75	11.50	35.00
s. Specimen w/red ovpt: *Yang Pen. Specimen* on back.	—	—	125.00

J32 **1000 Yuan**
1944 (1945). Deep gray-blue on m/c unpt. Block letters. 185 x 94mm.

		VG	VF	UNC
a.	Wmk: Cloud forms.	.90	2.75	8.00
b.	W/o wmk.	.65	2.00	6.00
c.	Red ovpt: *Wuhan.*	3.00	10.00	30.00
s.	Specimen w/red ovpt: *Yang Pen. Specimen* on back.			

J33 **1000 Yuan**
1944 (1945). Deep gray-blue on ochre unpt. Block letters. 169 x 84mm.

		VG	VF	UNC
a.	Issued note.	1.25	4.00	12.00
s.	Specimen w/red ovpt: *Yang Pen. Specimen* on back.	—	—	125.00

J34 **1000 Yuan**
1944 (1945). Gray. Block letters. 163 x 65mm.

a.	Issued note.	6.50	20.00	60.00
s.	Specimen w/red ovpt: *Yang Pen. Specimen* on back.	—	—	125.00

J35 **1000 Yuan**
1944 (1945). Green on lt. blue unpt. Back green. Block #. 149 x 79mm.

		VG	VF	UNC
a.	Issued note.	5.00	20.00	60.00
s1.	Specimen w/red ovpt: *Yang Pen. Specimen* on back.	—	—	125.00
s2.	As s1. W/o *Specimen* on back.	—	—	100.00
s3.	Specimen w/red ovpt: *Mi-hon.*	—	—	100.00

J36 **10,000 Yuan**
1944 (1945). Dk. brown on pink unpt. Serial #. 184 x 94mm.

a.	Wmk: Cloud forms.	8.00	25.00	75.00
s.	Specimen w/red ovpt: *Yang Pen. Specimen* on back.	—	—	125.00

J37 **10,000 Yuan**
1944 (1945). Dk. green on tan or pale yellow-brown unpt. Serial #. 184 x 94mm. Backs w/vignette varieties.

		VG	VF	UNC
a.	Back w/pink sky in ctr.	2.50	10.00	30.00
b.	Back w/green sky in ctr.	4.50	13.50	40.00
s1.	Specimen w/red ovpt: *Yang Pen. Specimen* on back.	—	—	125.00
s2.	Specimen w/red ovpt: *Mi-hon.*	—	—	150.00

J38 **10,000 Yuan**
1944 (1945). Green on pale yellow-brown unpt. Block letters. 170 x 83mm.

a.	Issued note.	2.50	10.00	30.00
s.	Specimen w/red ovpt: *Yang Pen. Specimen* on back.	—	—	125.00

J39 **10,000 Yuan**
1944 (1945). Green on pale yellow-brown unpt. Block letters. 166 x 65mm.

		VG	VF	UNC
a.	Issued note.	4.00	12.00	36.00
s.	Specimen w/red ovpt: *Yang Pen. Specimen* on back.	—	—	125.00

1945 Issues

#J40-J44 portr. SYS at ctr. SYS Mausoleum at ctr. on back.

J40 **5000 Yuan**
1945. Gray-green on pale green unpt. Back gray-green. Serial #. 166 x 90mm.

a.	Printer: CRBCPW.	2.50	10.00	30.00
b.	W/o imprint.	5.50	16.50	50.00
s.	As a. Specimen w/red ovpt: *Yang Pen. Specimen* on back.	—	—	125.00

J41 **5000 Yuan**
1945. Dk. gray-green on pale green unpt. Like #J40. Block letters. 170 x 84mm.

		VG	VF	UNC
a.	Issued note.	2.50	8.00	25.00
s.	Specimen w/red ovpt: *Yang Pen. Specimen* on back.	—	—	125.00

J42 **5000 Yuan**
1945. Black. Back dk. gray. Block letters. 166 x 65mm.

		VG	VF	UNC
a.	Issued note.	5.50	16.50	50.00
s.	Specimen w/red ovpt: *Yang Pen. Specimen* on back.	—	—	125.00

J43 **100,000 Yuan**
1945. Red-violet on pale green unpt. Serial #. 185 x 95mm.

a.	Issued note.	45.00	140.00	425.00
s.	Specimen w/ovpt: *Mi-hon.*	—	—	300.00

J44 **100,000 Yuan**
1945. Purple on yellow-brown unpt. 168 x 64mm.

		VG	VF	UNC
a.	Block letters.	90.00	275.00	825.00
r.	Remainder w/o block letters or sign. seals. Back purple to red-violet.	50.00	150.00	450.00

FEDERAL RESERVE BANK OF CHINA

行銀備準合聯國中
Chung Kuo Lien Ho Chun Pei Yin Hang

1938 First Issue

#J45-J47 17 arch bridge at summer palace at ctr.
#J51-J54 printer: BEPP.

J45 **1/2 Fen**
1938. Lt. blue on yellow unpt. *(S/M #C286-1).*

		VG	VF	UNC
a.	Issued note.	2.75	8.00	25.00
s.	Specimen w/ovpt: *Yang Pen. Specimen* on back. Uniface pair.	—	—	60.00

J46 **1 Fen**
1938. Lt. brown on pale green unpt. *(S/M #C286-2).*

		VG	VF	UNC
a.	Issued note.	1.65	5.00	15.00
s.	Specimen w/ovpt: *Yang Pen. Specimen* on back. Uniface pair.	—	—	60.00

J47 5 FEN

1938. Red on pink unpt.

		VG	VF	UNC
a.	1938. (S/M #C286-3).	.85	2.50	8.00
b.	1939. (S/M #C286-30).	.40	1.25	4.00
s.	As a. Specimen w/red ovpt: *Yang Pen* on face. Blue ovpt. on back. Uniface pair.	—	—	60.00

J48 10 FEN = 1 CHIAO

1938; 1940. Red-brown on pink unpt. Tower of summer palace at r.

		VG	VF	UNC
a.	1938. (S/M #C286-4).	.40	1.20	4.00
b.	1940. (S/M #C286-31).	.65	2.00	6.00
s.	As a. Specimen w/red ovpt: *Yang Pen* on face and back. Uniface pair.	—	—	60.00

J49 20 FEN = 2 CHIAO
(J50)

1938; 1940. Blue on pale blue unpt. Temple of Heaven at r.

		VG	VF	UNC
a.	1938. (S/M #C286-5).	.85	2.50	8.00
b.	1940. (S/M #C286-32).	1.00	3.25	10.00
s.	As a. Specimen w/red ovpt: *Yang Pen* on face and back. Uniface pair.	—	—	60.00

J50 50 FEN = 5 CHIAO
(J70)

ND (1938). Orange on pale green unpt. Marco Polo bridge at ctr. *(S/M #C286-60)*.

		VG	VF	UNC
a.	Issued note.	2.50	8.00	25.00
s.	Specimen w/ovpt: *Yang Pen. Specimen* on back.	—	—	100.00

1938 SECOND ISSUE

J59 100 YUAN
(J64)

1938 (1944). Brown. Face like #J63. Plain pattern on back. Outer frame of back has color varieties. *(S/M #C286-22)*.

	VG	VF	UNC
	2.50	10.00	30.00

J51 10 CENTS = 1 CHIAO

1938. Brown-violet. Dragon at r. *(S/M #C286-5)*.

		VG	VF	UNC
a.	Issued note.	10.00	30.00	100.00
s.	Specimen w/red ovpt: *Yang Pen. Specimen* on back. Uniface pair.	—	—	100.00

J52 20 CENTS = 2 CHIAO

1938. Green. Dragon at r. *(S/M #C286-7)*.

		VG	VF	UNC
a.	Issued note.	12.50	40.00	125.00
s.	Specimen w/ovpt: *Yang Pen. Specimen* on back. Uniface pair.	—	—	110.00

J53 50 CENTS = 5 CHIAO

1938. Orange. Dragon at r. *(S/M #C286-8)*.

		VG	VF	UNC
a.	Issued note.	15.00	50.00	150.00
s.	Specimen w/ovpt: *Yang Pen. Specimen* on back. Uniface pair.	—	—	100.00

J54 1 DOLLAR

1938. Green. Portr. Confucius at l., junks at lower ctr. r., dragon above. 183 x 93mm. *(S/M #C286-10)*.

		VG	VF	UNC
a.	Issued note.	7.50	30.00	90.00
s.	Specimen w/ovpt: *Yang Pen. Specimen* on back.	—	—	125.00

J55 1 DOLLAR

1938. Green. Like #J54 but poor printing. *(S/M #C286-11)*.

	VG	VF	UNC
	15.00	60.00	180.00

J56 5 DOLLARS
(J57)

1938. Orange. Portr. Yüeh Fei at l., horseback patrol at lower r., dragon above. 184 x 97mm. *(S/M #C286-13)*.

		VG	VF	UNC
a.	Issued note.	75.00	225.00	600.00
s.	Specimen w/ovpt: *Yang Pen. Specimen* on back.	—	—	250.00

J57 **10 DOLLARS**   VG   VF   UNC
(J59)
1938. Blue. Portr. Kuan-yü at l., Great Wall at lower r., dragon above.
190 x 102mm. *(S/M #C286-15)*.
  a.   Issued note.   75.00 225.00 600.00
  s.   Specimen w/ovpt: *Yang Pen. Specimen* on back.   —   —   250.00

J58 **100 DOLLARS**   VG   VF   UNC
(J62)
1938. Purple. Portr. Huang Ti at l., farm laborer at lower r., dragon
above. 190 x 107mm. *(S/M #C286-20)*.
  a.   Issued note.   200.00 600.00 1800.
  s.   Specimen w/ovpt: *Yang Pen. Specimen* on back.   —   —   600.00

1938 (1939) ISSUE

#J60 *Deleted.*
#J65 *Deleted.* See #J47.
#J66 *Deleted.* See #J48.
#J67 *Deleted.* See #J49.

J61 **1 YUAN**
(J56)
1938 (1939). Yellow-green. Boats at ctr., dragon above, portr.
Confucius at r. 148 x 72mm. *(S/M #C286-12)*.
  a.   Issued note.   2.50   10.00   30.00
  s.   Specimen w/red ovpt: *Yang Pen. Specimen* on back. Uniface   —   —   125.00
    pair.

J62 **5 YUAN**
(J58)
1938 (1939). Orange. Horseback patrol at ctr., dragon above, portr.
Yüeh Fei at r. 155 x 76mm. *(S/M #C286-14)*.
  a.   Issued note.   3.75   15.00   45.00
  s.   Specimen w/red ovpt: *Yang Pen. Specimen* on back. Uniface   —   —   125.00
    pair.

J63 **10 YUAN**
(J61)
1938 (1939). Blue. Great Wall at ctr., dragon above, portr. Kuan-yü at
r. Paper w/many or few fibers. 164 x 83mm. *(S/M #C286-16)*.
  a.   Issued note.   6.50   25.00   75.00
  s.   Specimen w/red ovpt: *Yang Pen. Specimen* on back. Uniface   —   —   125.00
    pair.

J64 **100 YUAN**
(J63)
1938 (1939). Violet. Ships along shoreline at l., farm laborers at r. ctr.,
w/dragon above, portr. Huang Ti at r. Pagoda at ctr. on back. 178 x
95mm. *(S/M #C286-21)*.
  a.   Issued note.   22.50   70.00 210.00
  s.   Specimen w/red ovpt: *Yang Pen. Specimen* on back. Uniface pair.   —   —   150.00

1944 ISSUE

J68 **50 FEN = 5 CHIAO**   VG   VF   UNC
1944. Violet on ochre and violet unpt. Temple of the clouds at l. *(S/M
#C286-40)*.
  a.   Issued note.   1.00   3.00   10.00
  s.   Specimen perforated: *Yang Pen*. Uniface pair.   —   —   75.00

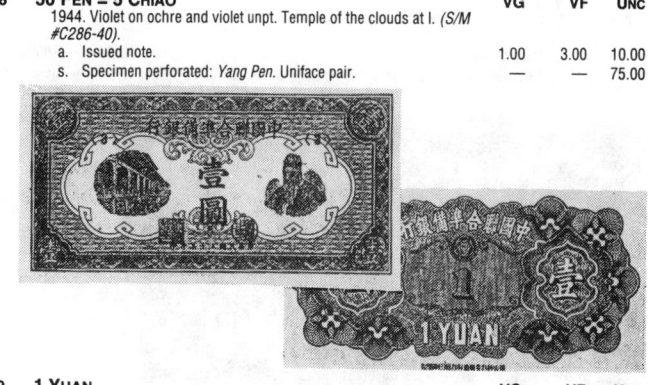

J69 **1 YUAN**   VG   VF   UNC
1944. Dk. gray on dk. olive-green or olive-brown (shades) unpt.
Partial view of temple, Confucius at r. 125 x 65mm. *(S/M #C286-50)*.
  a.   Issued note.   1.25   4.00   12.00
  s.   Specimen perforated: *Yang Pen*. Uniface pair.   —   —   75.00

1941 ND ISSUE

#J70 *Deleted.* See #J50.
#J71 *Deleted.* See #J73.

J72 **1 YUAN**   VG   VF   UNC
ND (1941). Gray-green on green and pink ovpt. Partial view of temple
at l., Confucius at r. 146 x 70mm. *(S/M #C286-70)*.
  a.   Issued note.   .85   2.50   7.50
  s.   Specimen w/red ovpt. and perforated: *Yang Pen. Specimen* on   —   —   100.00
    back.

J73 **5 YUAN**   VG   VF   UNC
(J74)
ND (1941). Orange on m/c unpt. Temple at l., Yüeh Fei at r. *(S/M
#C286-71)*.
  a.   Issued note.   2.50   8.00   25.00
  s.   Specimen w/ovpt. and perforated: *Yang Pen. Specimen* on back.   —   —   100.00
    Uniface pair.

J74
(J81)

10 YUAN

ND (1941). Blue on m/c unpt. Wu Ying Hall at l., man w/cap at r. *(S/M #C286-74).*

	VG	VF	UNC
a. Issued note.	2.65	8.00	25.00
s. Specimen w/red ovpt. and perforated: *Yang Pen. Specimen* on back.	—	—	100.00

J75
(J86)

100 YUAN

ND (1941). Brown on green and purple unpt. House w/stairs at l., Huang Ti at r. 174 x 93mm. Chinese printer. *(S/M #C286-84).*

	VG	VF	UNC
a. Issued note.	8.00	25.00	75.00
s. Specimen w/red ovpt. and perforated: *Yang Pen. Specimen* on back.	—	—	150.00

1943 ND ISSUE

J76

10 YUAN

ND (1943). Dk. blue-gray on green and brown unpt. Kuan Yü at l. Jade Peak Pagoda at r. 160 x 85mm. *S/M #C286-73.*

	VG	VF	UNC
a. Issued note.	4.00	12.00	36.00
s. Specimen perforated: *Yang Pen.* Uniface pair.	—	—	125.00

J77
(J83)

100 YUAN

ND (1943). Brown on m/c unpt. Huang Ti at l. temple near mountainside at r. 176 x 95mm *(S/M #C286-83).*

	VG	VF	UNC
a. Issued note.	4.00	12.00	36.00
s. Specimen w/ovpt. and perforated *Yang Pen. Yang Pen* on back. Uniface pair.	—	—	125.00

J78
(J90)

500 YUAN

ND (1943). Brownish black on pale green and olive unpt. Temple of Heaven at l. Confucius at r. Onagadori cocks unpt. at l. and at r. of vertical denomination at ctr. *500* once on back. Block letters and serial #. 179 x 98mm. *(S/M #C286-90).*

	VG	VF	UNC
a. Back frame brown. Imprint 26mm.	8.00	25.00	75.00
b. Back frame brown. Imprint 29mm.	5.50	16.50	50.00
s. Back frame red-brown. Imprint 24mm. Specimen perforated: *Yang Pen.* Uniface pair.	—	—	125.00

1944 ND ISSUE

J79
(J75)

5 YUAN

ND (1944). Brown on yellow unpt. Small house at l., Yüeh Fei w/book at r. *(S/M #C286-72).*

	VG	VF	UNC
a. Black on yellow unpt. Seal 8mm high at l. Wmk: Clouds and *FRB* logo.	1.65	5.00	15.00
b. Wmk: *FRB* logo.	1.65	5.00	15.00
c. Dk. brown on lt. brown unpt. Seal 7mm high at l. W/o wmk.	2.50	7.50	22.50
s. Specimen perforated: *Yang Pen.* Uniface pair.	—	—	125.00

J80
(J77)

10 YUAN

ND (1944). Blue on lt. brown unpt. Kuan-yü at l., wall of house w/tree and rock at r. w/*10 YUAN* at bottom ctr. on back. 158 x 78mm. *(S/M #C286-75).*

	VG	VF	UNC
a. Issued note.	1.65	5.00	15.00
s1. Specimen w/red ovpt: *Yang Pen. Yang Pen* on back. Uniface pair.	—	—	125.00
s2. Specimen perforated: *Yang Pen.* Uniface pair.	—	—	125.00

J81
(J79) **10 YUAN**
ND (1944). Purple on m/c unpt. Man w/mustache at r. *(S/M #C286-80).*

	VG	VF	UNC
a. Issued note.	2.50	8.00	25.00
s. Specimen w/red ovpt. and perforated: *Yang Pen.*	—	—	125.00

J82
(J80) **10 YUAN**
ND (1944). Blue on m/c unpt. Similar to #J79. *(S/M #C286-81).*

	VG	VF	UNC
a. Issued note.	4.00	12.50	40.00
s1. Specimen w/red ovpt. and perforated: *Yang Pen.*	—	—	125.00
s2. Specimen w/red ovpt. *Mi-hon.*	—	—	100.00

J83
(J85) **100 YUAN**
ND (1944). Dk. brown on green-blue and violet. House w/stairs at l., Huang Ti at r. Back brown and violet. 178 x 95mm. W/o imprint. *(S/M #C286-85).*

	VG	VF	UNC
a. Issued note.	5.50	16.50	50.00
b. Horizontal quadrille paper.	5.50	16.50	50.00
s1. Specimen w/red ovpt. and perforated: *Yang Pen.*	—	—	150.00
s2. Specimen w/red ovpt: *Mi-hon.*	—	—	150.00

J84
(J89) **500 YUAN**
ND (1944). Dk. green on tan and purple unpt. Temple of Heaven at l., Confucius at r. Unpt. w/Onagadori cock above guilloche at ctr. Back brown on yellow-brown unpt; *500* five times. 181 x 99mm. *(S/M #C286-91).*

	VG	VF	UNC
a. Horizontal quadrille paper.	15.00	45.00	135.00
b. Non-quadrille paper.	15.00	45.00	135.00
s1. Specimen w/red ovpt. and perforated: *Yang Pen.* Uniface pair.	—	—	125.00
s2. Specimen w/red ovpt: *Mi-hon.*	—	—	150.00

J84A
(J89A) **500 YUAN**
ND (1944). Like #J89 but litho. Back brown on yellow unpt. Block #1. Specimen w/red ovpt: *Mi-hon.*

	VG	VF	UNC
	—	—	150.00

1945 ND ISSUE

J85
(J73) **1 YUAN**
ND (1945). Dk. brown on lt. orange-brown unpt. Bridge and pavilion at l., numeral at r. 123 x 63mm. (Not issued). *(S/M #C286-65).*

	VG	VF	UNC
a. Block #.	—	200.00	500.00
s. Specimen perforated: *Yang Pen.* Uniface pair.	—	—	500.00

J86
(J78) **10 YUAN**
ND (1945). Violet on lt. brown unpt. Kuan-yü at l., wall of house w/tree and rock at r. W/o *10 YUAN* on back. 143 x 72mm.

	VG	VF	UNC
a. Chinese printer (11 characters). *(S/M #C286-77).*	1.65	5.00	15.00
b. Chinese printer (14 characters). *(S/M #C286-76).*	1.65	5.00	15.00
s. As b. Specimen perforated: *Yang Pen.*	—	—	125.00

J87
(J82) **50 YUAN**
ND (1945). Violet-brown. Man w/beard at l. *(S/M #C286-82).*

	VG	VF	UNC
a. Wmk. *FRB* logo and clouds. Block #1.	5.50	16.50	50.00
b. W/o wmk. Block #2.	8.00	25.00	75.00
s. As a. Specimen perforated: *Yang Pen.* Uniface pair.	—	—	150.00

J88
(J84) **100 YUAN**
ND (1945). Brown to red-brown. Imperial Resting Quarters near mountainside at at l., Huang Ti at r. Back red-brown. 170 x 90mm. *S/M #C286-86).*

	VG	VF	UNC
a. Issued note.	.65	2.00	6.00
s. Specimen perforated: *Yang Pen.* Uniface pair.	—	—	125.00

J88A
(J84A) **100 YUAN**
ND (1945). Gray and red-brown. Like #J84. Back brown. Block #16. | 2.65 | 8.00 | 25.00 |

J89
(J87) **500 YUAN**
ND (1945). Blue on lt. blue-green and yellow-brown unpt. Temple of Heaven at l. Wmk: *FRB* logo and clouds. 185 x 83mm. *(S/M #C286-92).*

	VG	VF	UNC
a. Issued note.	2.65	8.00	25.00
s. Specimen perforated: *Yang Pen.* Uniface pair.	—	—	150.00

J90
(J88) **500 YUAN**
ND (1945). Blue-gray on orange-yellow to salmon unpt. Like #J87 but reduced size 168 x 78mm. *(S/M #C286-93).*

	VG	VF	UNC
	2.50	7.50	22.50

		VG	VF	UNC
J98	**5 YUAN** 1938. Dk. green and black on ochre and gray. House, arch, bridge, and pagoda at ctr. *(S/M #H184-12).*			
	a. Black ovpt. Sign of bank president Ch'en Chin Tao on back.	—	—	350.00
	s. Specimen w/ovpt: *Yang Pen* on face and back.	—	—	300.00
J99	**10 YUAN** ND (1938). Black on m/c unpt. Ta Ch'eng Tien bldg. at l. Confucius at r. *(S/M #H184-13).*			
	a. Issued note. (Sea salvaged).	400.00	—	—
	s. Specimen w/ovpt: *Yang Pen* on face and back.	—	—	1250.

		VG	VF	UNC
J91	**1000 YUAN** ND (1945). Dk. green. Great Wall at ctr. r. Ch'ien Men fortress at ctr. on back. *(S/M #C286-94).*			
	a. Engraved, w/serial # and block #1-3. Wmk: *1* in oval, ovals horizontal.	3.00	10.00	30.00
	b. Engraved, w/serial # and block #1-3. Wmk: *1* in oval, ovals vertical.	3.00	10.00	30.00
	c. Wmk: *FRB* logo repeated.	5.50	16.50	50.00
	s. As b. Specimen perforated: *Yang Pen.* Uniface pair.	—	—	150.00
	r. Remainder, w/o serial #, block #, or sign. seals.	—	—	35.00

		VG	VF	UNC
J100	**10 YUAN** 1938. Brown-orange and black on ochre and lt. green unpt. Temple at ctr. *(S/M #H184-14).*			
	a. Issued note.	175.00	175.00	350.00
	s. Specimen w/ovpt: *Yang Pen* on face and back.	—	—	300.00
	r. Remainder w/o sign.	—	—	300.00

		VG	VF	UNC
J92	**5000 YUAN** ND (1945). Brown. State stone barge at l. (Empress Dowager's summer palace, *I Ho Yuan*). Wmk: *FRB* logo. *(S/M #C286-95).*			
	a. Issued note.	60.00	240.00	600.00
	r. Remainder w/o serial # or block #.	—	100.00	250.00

HUA-HSING COMMERCIAL BANK

行銀業商興華

Hua Hsing Shang Yeh Yin Hang

1938 ISSUES
#J95 Deleted.

		VG	VF	UNC
J96	**1 YUAN** 1938. Green on yellow and gray unpt. Trees along roadway at l. ctr. *(S/M #H184-10).*			
	a. Issued note.	100.00	300.00	800.00
	s. Specimen w/ovpt: *Yang Pen. Specimen* on back.	—	—	500.00
J97	**5 YUAN** ND (1938). Blue on m/c unpt. Liu Ho Pagoda at l., Yüeh Fei at r. *(S/M #184H-11).*			
	a. Issued note.	—	Rare	
	s. Specimen w/ovpt: *Yang Pen. Specimen* on back.	—	—	1250.

		VG	VF	UNC
J93	**10 CENTS = 1 CHIAO** 1938. Green on pink and lt. blue unpt. Junks at l. *S/M #H184-1).*			
	a. Issued note.	55.00	165.00	400.00
	s. Specimen w/ovpt: *Yang Pen. Specimen* on back.	—	—	400.00

		VG	VF	UNC
J94	**20 CENTS = 2 CHIAO** 1938. Brown. Pagoda at ctr. Back lt. blue. *(S/M #H184.2).*			
	a. Issued note.	55.00	165.00	400.00
	s. Specimen w/ovpt: *Yang Pen. Specimen* on back.	—	—	400.00

MENGCHIANG BANK

行銀疆蒙
Meng Chiang Yin Hang

1938-45 ND ISSUES

J101	**5 FEN**	**VG**	**VF**	**UNC**
	ND (1940). Gray. Herd of sheep at ctr. Back brown-orange. *(S/M #M11-1)*.			
	a. Issued note.	1.50	5.00	15.00
	s. Specimen w/ovpt: *Yang Pen.* on face and back.	—	—	60.00

J105	**1 YUAN**	**VG**	**VF**	**UNC**
	ND (1938). Dk. green and black on ochre and m/c unpt. Herd of sheep at ctr. Back blue-gray. *(S/M #M11-11)*.			
	a. Issued note.	4.00	12.00	50.00
	s. Specimen w/red ovpt: *Yang Pen* on face and back. Toppan Printing Co. imprint. Uniface pair.	—	—	150.00

J101A	**1 CHIAO**	**VG**	**VF**	**UNC**
	ND (1940). Brown and black on lt. blue unpt. Herd of camels at ctr. Back blue-gray. *(S/M #M11-2)*.			
	a. Issued note.	1.50	5.00	15.00
	s. Specimen w/red ovpt: *Yang Pen* on face and back.	—	—	60.00

J106	**5 YUAN**	**VG**	**VF**	**UNC**
	ND (1938). Orange-brown and black w/violet guilloche. Pagoda at l., fortress at r. Back tan; rural bldg. at ctr. *(S/M #M11-12)*.			
	a. Issued note.	2.65	8.00	25.00
	s. Specimen w/red ovpt: *Yang Pen* on face and back. Toppan Printing Co. imprint. Uniface pair.	—	—	150.00

J102	**5 CHIAO**	**VG**	**VF**	**UNC**
	ND (1944). Black on yellow-brown unpt. Temple courtyard. Back green. *(S/M #M11-4)*.			
	a. Issued note.	40.00	120.00	360.00
	s. Specimen w/red-orange ovpt: *Mi-hon.*	—	—	200.00

J107	**5 YUAN**	**VG**	**VF**	**UNC**
	ND (1944). Purple on pale purple and orange unpt. Lama monastery at l. ctr. Back dk. blue. Specimen. *(S/M #M11-13)*.	—	Rare	—

J103	**5 CHIAO = 50 FEN**	**VG**	**VF**	**UNC**
	ND (1940). Dk. purple and black on green and pale blue unpt. Herd of camels at ctr. Back blue-gray. *(S/M #M11-3)*.			
	a. Issued note.	3.00	12.00	40.00
	s. Specimen w/red ovpt: *Yang Pen* on face and back.	—	—	60.00

J104	**1 YUAN**	**VG**	**VF**	**UNC**
	ND. Dk. green on ochre unpt. Great Wall at l. ctr. Back blue. *(S/M #M11-10)*.	1.00	5.00	15.00

J108	**10 YUAN**	**VG**	**VF**	**UNC**
	ND (1944). Dk. blue-gray on yellow unpt. Camel at l., men on horseback, w/oxen and horses at ctr. Back lt. blue w/Buddhas at ctr.			
	a. Wmk: Bank logo. Serial # and block #. *(S/M #M11-15)*.	15.00	50.00	150.00
	b. W/o wmk. Serial # and block #. *(S/M #M11-)*.	5.00	15.00	50.00
	c. Block # only. *(S/M #M11-)*.	8.00	25.00	75.00

J108A 10 YUAN
ND (1944). Brown and black on ochre unpt. Like #J108. Back dk. red. (S/M #M11-).

	VG	VF	UNC
r. Remainder. Block # only.	8.00	25.00	75.00
s. Specimen w/red-orange ovpt:	—	—	125.00

J109 10 YUAN
ND (1938). Dk. brown. Sheep at ctr. Back blue. (S/M #M11-14).

	VG	VF	UNC
a. Issued note.	5.00	25.00	75.00
s. Specimen w/red ovpt: Yang Pen on face and back. Toppan Printing Co. imprint. Uniface pair.	—	—	150.00

J110 100 YUAN
ND (1945). Dk. green on lt. brown unpt. Herdsman w/goats. (S/M #M11-22).

	VG	VF	UNC
a. Issued note.	3.00	10.00	30.00
s. Specimen w/red-orange ovpt: Mi-hon.	—	—	125.00

J111 100 YUAN
ND (1945). Black on yellow-green unpt. Lama monastary. (S/M #M11-21).

	VG	VF	UNC
	5.00	15.00	40.00

J112 100 YUAN
ND (1938). Purple and black on olive-geen and m/c unpt. Pavilion at l., camel at r. (S/M #M11-21).

	VG	VF	UNC
a. Issued note.	3.00	10.00	40.00
s. Specimen w/red ovpt: Yang Pen on face and back. Toppan Printing Co. imprint. Uniface pair.	—	—	150.00

CHI TUNG BANK

行銀東冀
Chi Tung Yin Hang

1937 ISSUE

J113 5 CHIAO = 50 FEN
ND (1937). Dk. green on lt. blue and pink unpt. Gateway at l. ctr. Back pale green. (S/M #C84-1).

	VG	VF	UNC
a. Issued note.	275.00	700.00	1750.
s1. Specimen w/ovpt: Yang Pen. and SPECIMEN.	—	—	750.00
s2. As a. Specimen w/ovpt: Yang Pen and Specimen on face and back, perforated serial #.	—	—	700.00

J114 1 YUAN
ND (1937). Orange on lt. green and ochre unpt. Great Wall at r. Back tan. (S/M #C284-2).

	VG	VF	UNC
a. Issued note.	275.00	700.00	1750.
s1. Specimen (English).	—	—	750.00
s2. As a. Specimen w/ovpt: Yang Pen and Specimen on face and back, perforated serial #.	—	—	700.00

J115 5 YUAN
ND (1937). Purple on m/c unpt. Tower at Tunghsien at r. (S/M #C84-3).

	VG	VF	UNC
s1. Specimen (English).	—	—	1500.
s2. Specimen w/ovpt: Yang Pen and Specimen on face and back, perforated serial #.	—	—	1400.

J116 10 YUAN
ND (1937). Black on m/c unpt. Temple at r. Back ochre. (S/M #C84-4).

	VG	VF	UNC
s1. Specimen (English).	—	—	2500.
s2. Specimen w/ovpt: Yang Pen and Specimen on face and back. Perforated serial #.	—	—	2400.

J117 100 YUAN
ND (1937). Dk. blue on m/c unpt. Bldg. at r. Back blue. *(S/M #C84-5).*

	VG	VF	UNC
s1. Specimen (English).	—	—	4000.
s2. Specimen w/ovpt: *Yang Pen* and *Specimen* on face and back. Perforated serial #.	—	—	4000.

CHANAN BANK

行銀南察

Ch'a Nan Yin Hang

PROVISIONAL ISSUE

#J118-J119 ovpt. on notes of the Central Bank of Manchukuo. This is the second ovpt. w/*Ch'a Nan Yin Hang* in Chinese vertically at l. and r. on face. First ovpt. is for Central Bank of Manchukuo. Chanan Bank notes have the face ovpt. for CBM line out, but w/o any new ovpt. on back leaving the CBM ovpt.

J118 1 YUAN
ND (1937- old date 1929). Black and m/c. Ovpt. on #J120. *(S/M #C4-1).*

	VG	VF	UNC
a. Double line through red ovpt. below pavilion.	300.00	600.00	2000.
b. Single line through red ovpt. below pavilion.	300.00	600.00	2000.
s. Specimen w/red handstamp: *Yang Pen.* Punched hole cancelled.	—	—	600.00

J119 10 YUAN
ND (1937- old date 1929). Green and m/c. Ovpt. on #J122. *(S/M #C4-3).*

	VG	VF	UNC
a. Issued note.	1500.	2500.	—
s. Specimen w/red handstamp: *Yang Pen.* Punched hole cancelled.	—	—	2500.

MANCHUKUO

Under the lax central government of the Republic of China, Manchuria attained a relatively large measure of independence. This occurred in 1917, under the leadership of Marshal Chang Tso-lin and his son, Chang Hsueh-Liang. Following the Japanese occupation, the State of Manchukuo was established on February 18, 1932, with the annexation of the Chinese Province of Jehol. Under japanese auspices, Manchukuo was ruled by Pu Yi, the last emperor of the Manchu (Ching) Dynasty. In 1934, Manchukuo was declared an empire; and Pu Yi proclaimed emperor. The empire was dissolved when Soviet troops occupied the territory in August, 1945. Following the Soviet evacuation, Manchukuo was re-incorporated into China. Capital: Hsinking.

RULERS:
Ta Tung, Years 1-3, 1932-1934
Kang Teh, Years 1-12, 1934-1945

MONETARY SYSTEM:
1 Yuan = 10 Chiao = 100 Fen

CENTRAL BANK OF MANCHUKUO

行銀央中洲滿

Man Chou Chung Yang Yin Hang

Formed in 1932 by a merger of the following banks: Provincial Bank of the Three Eastern Provinces, Frontier Bank, Heilungkiang Provincial Bank and Kirin Provincial Bank.

PROVISIONAL ISSUE

#J120-J122 ovpt. new bank name on notes of the Provincial Bank of the Three Eastern Provinces. Dated first year of Ta Tung (1932).

NOTE: For #J120 and J122 w/additional vertical Chinese ovpt: *Cha Nan Yin Hang*, see Chanan Bank #J118 and #J119.

#J123 *Deleted.*

J120 1 YUAN
1932 (-old date Nov. 1929). Black and m/c. ovpt. on #S2962a. *(S/M #M2-1).*

	VG	VF	UNC
a. Issued note.	400.00	1000.	3000.
s1. Specimen w/ovpt: *Yang Pen* and *Specimen. Specimen* on back. Uniface pair.	—	—	1000.
s2. As a. Specimen w/ovpt: *Yang Pen* and *Specimen.* Punched hole cancelled.	—	—	800.00

J121 5 YUAN
1932 (- old date Nov. 1929). Brown and m/c. ovpt. on #S2963a. Specimen w/ovpt: *Yang Pen* and *Specimen* on back. Uniface pair. *(S/M #M2-).*

	VG	VF	UNC
	—	—	1200.

J122 10 YUAN
1932 (- old date Nov. 1929). Green and m/c. ovpt. on #S2964a. *(S/M #M2-2).*

	VG	VF	UNC
a. Issued note.	1200.	3000.	—
s1. Specimen w/ovpt: *Yang Pen* and *Specimen. Specimen* on back. Uniface pair.	—	—	1000.
s2. As a. Specimen w/ovpt: *Yang Pen.* Punched hole cancelled.	—	—	800.00

1932 ISSUE

J124 5 CHIAO = 50 FEN
ND (1932). Dk. blue on ochre unpt. Back pale green. *(S/M #M2-10).*

	VG	VF	UNC
a. Issued note.	50.00	200.00	450.00
s. Specimen w/ovpt: *Yang Pen* and *Specimen* on face and back. Uniface pair.	—	—	200.00

1932-33 ND ISSUE

#J125-J128 m/c flag at l., bldg. at r.

J125 1 YUAN
ND (1932). Blue on yellow yellow unpt. *(S/M #M2-20).*

	VG	VF	UNC
a. Issued note.	16.50	50.00	150.00
s. Specimen w/ovpt: *Yang Pen* and *Specimen* on face and back. Uniface pair.	—	—	100.00

		VG	VF	UNC
J131	**5 YUAN** ND (1938). Black on brown unpt. at ctr. Man w/beard wearing feather crown at r. Back brown. *(S/M #M2-41)*.			
	a. 6-digit serial #.	15.00	50.00	150.00
	b. 7-digit serial #.	8.00	25.00	75.00
	s. Specimen w/ovpt: *Yang Pen* and *Specimen* on face and back. Punched hole cancelled. Uniface pair.	—	—	60.00

		VG	VF	UNC
J126	**5 YUAN** ND (1933). Dk. brown on tan unpt. *(S/M #M2-21)*.			
	a. Issued note.	50.00	150.00	450.00
	s. Specimen w/ovpt: *Yang Pen* and *Specimen* on face and back. Punched hole cancelled. Uniface pair.	—	—	100.00
J127	**10 YUAN** ND (1932). Blue on orange unpt. *(S/M #M2-22)*.			
	a. Issued note.	55.00	165.00	500.00
	s. Specimen w/ovpt: *Yang Pen* and *Specimen* on face and back. Uniface pair.	—	—	175.00

		VG	VF	UNC
J128	**100 YUAN** ND (1933). Blue on yellow-orange unpt. *(S/M #M2-23)*.			
	a. Issued note.	65.00	200.00	600.00
	s. Specimen w/ovpt: *Yang Pen* and *Specimen* on face and back. Uniface pair.	—	—	285.00

1935-38 ND ISSUE

		VG	VF	UNC
J132	**10 YUAN** ND (1937). Black on brown unpt. at ctr. Emperor Ch'ien Lung at r. Back purple. *(S/M #M2-42)*.			
	a. 6-digit serial #.	5.50	16.50	50.00
	b. 7-digit serial #.	2.75	8.00	25.00
	s. Specimen w/ovpt: *Yang Pen* and *Specimen* on face and back. Uniface pair.	—	—	60.00
J133	**100 YUAN** ND (1938). Black on green unpt. at ctr. Confucius at r., Ta Ch'eng Tien bldg. at l. Back blue; w/sheep. *(S/M #M2-43)*.			
	a. 6-digit serial #.	30.00	90.00	200.00
	b. 7-digit serial #.	3.00	8.00	25.00
	s. Specimen w/ovpt: *Yang Pen* and *Specimen* on face and back. Uniface pair.	—	—	60.00

1944 ND ISSUE
#J135-J138 w/block # and serial #. New back designs.

		VG	VF	UNC
J129	**5 CHIAO = 50 FEN** ND (1935). Brown on green and lilac unpt. Ch'ien Lung at r. Back brown and olive. *(S/M #M2-30)*.			
	a. Issued note.	2.00	5.00	15.00
	s. Specimen w/ovpt: *Yang Pen* and *Specimen* on face and back. Uniface pair.	—	—	60.00

		VG	VF	UNC
J134	**5 CHIAO = 50 FEN** ND (1944). Blue-green on pale blue unpt. Ta Ch'eng Tien bldg. at l. ctr. Back brown. *(S/M #M2-50)*.	10.00	35.00	100.00
J135 (J142)	**1 YUAN** ND (1944). Face like #J130 but violet unpt. at ctr. Back violet.			
	a. Block # and serial #. *(S/M #M2-60)*.	.50	1.50	7.50
	b. Block # only. *(S/M #M2-80)*.	1.00	3.00	15.00
	s1. As a. Specimen w/ovpt: *Yang Pen*. *Specimen* on back. Uniface pair.	—	—	60.00
	s2. As b. Specimen w/ovpt: *Yang Pen*.	—	—	75.00

		VG	VF	UNC
J130	**1 YUAN** ND (1937). Black on green and yellow unpt. at ctr. T'ien Ming at r. Back green. *(S/M #M2-40)*.			
	a. 6-digit serial #.	3.00	10.00	30.00
	b. 7-digit serial #.	.50	1.75	7.50
	s. Specimen w/ovpt: *Yang Pen* and *Specimen* on face and back. Uniface pair.	—	—	60.00

J136 5 YUAN
(J143) ND (1944). Face like #J131 but orange unpt. at ctr. Back green.

	VG	VF	UNC
a. Block # and serial #. (S/M #M2-61).	1.00	4.00	12.00
s. Block # only. Specimen w/ovpt: *Yang Pen*. (S/M #M2-81).	—	—	175.00

J137 10 YUAN
(J144) ND (1944). Face like #J132 but green unpt. at ctr. Back blue.

	VG	VF	UNC
a. Block # and serial #. Wmk: *MANCHU CENTRAL BANK*. (S/M #M2-62).	1.00	3.00	10.00
b. Revalidation *10 Yuan* adhesive stamp on face. See #M35.	—	—	—
c. Block # only. Wmk. as a. (S/M #M2-82).	1.00	4.00	12.00
d. Revalidation *10 Yuan* adhesive stamp on face. See #M35.	—	—	—
e. Block # only. Wmk: Chinese character: *Man* in clouds repeated.	2.00	6.50	20.00
s1. As a. Specimen w/ovpt: *Yang Pen*. Specimen on back. Uniface pair.	—	—	60.00
s2. As e. Specimen w/ovpt: *Yang Pen*.	—	—	60.00

J138 100 YUAN
ND (1944). Face like #J133 but w/blue unpt. at ctr. Back brown w/men and donkey carts by storage silos at ctr. (S/M #M2-63).

	VG	VF	UNC
a. Wmk: *MANCHU CENTRAL BANK*.	1.00	4.00	12.00
b. Wmk: Chinese character: *Man* in clouds repeated.	2.00	6.50	20.00
s1. As a. Specimen w/ovpt: *Yang Pen*. Specimen on back. Block #1. Uniface pair.	—	—	60.00
s2. As b. Specimen w/ovpt: *Yang Pen*.	—	—	75.00

1941-45 ISSUE
#J139-J141; J145-J146 w/o serial #, only block letters.
#J142-J144 *Deleted*. See #J135b, J136s, J137c.

J139 5 FEN
ND (1945). Blue-green. Back orange; tower at ctr. (S/M #M2-70).

	16.50	50.00	150.00

J140 10 FEN = 1 CHIAO
ND (1944). Yellow-orange unpt. Back green; house at ctr. on back. (S/M #M2-71).

	VG	VF	UNC
	1.00	3.00	10.00

J141 5 CHIAO = 50 FEN
ND (1941). Green on pink and orange unpt. Ch'ien Lung at r. Back blue. (S/M #M2-72).

	VG	VF	UNC
a. Issued note.	.50	1.50	7.50
s. Specimen w/ovpt: *Yang Pen* and *Specimen*. Uniface pair.	—	—	60.00

J145 100 YUAN
ND (1945). Like #J138 but w/only 1 serial #. Local printer. (S/M #M2-83).

	VG	VF	UNC
	350.00	1000.	—

J146 1000 YUAN
ND (1944). Dk. brown and violet. Confucius at r., Ta Ch'eng Tien bldg. at l. Back green and brown; bank bldg. at ctr. (S/M #M2-84).

	VG	VF	UNC
	150.00	400.00	1000.

JAPANESE MILITARY - WWII
NOTE: See also Japan #M7-M12.

JAPANESE IMPERIAL GOVERNMENT
大日本帝國政府
Ta Jih Pen Ti Kuo Cheng Fu

1937 ISSUE
#M1-M5 2 facing Onagadori cockerels at upper ctr., 2 facing dragons below. Showa yr. 12.

#M1 #M3

M1 10 SEN
Yr. 12 (1937). Black on blue unpt. (S/M #T27-20).

	VG	VF	UNC
a. Issued note.	20.00	65.00	150.00
s. Specimen w/red ovpt: *Mi-hon*. Specimen on back.	—	—	200.00

M2 50 SEN
Yr. 12 (1937). Black on yellow unpt. (S/M #T27-22).

	VG	VF	UNC
a. Issued note.	35.00	100.00	250.00
s. Specimen w/red ovpt: *Mi-hon*. Specimen on back.	—	—	250.00

			VG	VF	UNC
M3	**1 YEN**				
	Yr. 12 (1937). Black on lt. lilac unpt. (S/M #T27-30).				
	a. Issued note.		35.00	100.00	300.00
	s. Specimen w/red ovpt: Mi-hon. Specimen on back.		—	—	350.00
M4	**5 YEN**				
	Yr. 12 (1937). Black on pink unpt. (S/M #T27-31).				
	a. Issued note.		400.00	750.00	2250.
	s. Specimen w/red ovpt: Mi-hon. Specimen on back.		—	—	2000.
M5	**10 YEN**				
	Yr. 12 (1937). Black on lt. green unpt. (S/M #T27-32).				
	a. Issued note.		800.00	2000.	3500.
	s. Specimen w/red ovpt: Mi-hon. Specimen on back.		—	—	2500.

1939-40 ND ISSUES

Line A: 府政國帝本日大

TITLES:
A: Ta Jih Pen Ti Kuo Cheng Fu.
B: Ta Jih Pen Ti Kuo Cheng Fu Chung Yung Shou Piao.

Line B: 票手用軍 府政國帝本日大

NOTE: Forgeries exist of #M10. Forgeries exist on #M21 on plain white paper.
NOTE: For similar notes in different color printings see French Indochina #M1-M7.

			VG	VF	UNC
M6	**2 1/2 RIN**				
	ND (1940). Black on brown unpt. Vertical note. Title A. (S/M #T30-1).		180.00	450.00	900.00

			VG	VF	UNC
M7	**1 SEN**				
	ND (1939). Brown on blue-gray unpt. Dragon at r. Title A. (S/M #T30-2).				
	a. Issued note.		.30	1.00	3.00
	s. Specimen w/ovpt: Mi-hon.		—	—	100.00
M8	**1 SEN**				
	ND (1939). Brown on blue-gray unpt. Dragon at r. Title B. (S/M #T31-1).		.55	1.65	5.00
M9	**5 SEN**				
	ND (1940). Blue and brown on pink unpt. Dragon at r. Title A. (S/M #T30-3).				
	a. Issued note.		.30	1.00	3.00
	s. Specimen w/ovpt: Mi-hon.		—	—	100.00
M10	**5 SEN**				
	ND (1939). Blue and brown on pink ovpt. Dragon at r. Title B. (S/M #T31-2).		2.50	8.00	25.00

			VG	VF	UNC
M11	**10 SEN**				
	ND (1940). Black on yellow-orange and violet unpt. Dragon at r. Title A. (S/M #T30-4).				
	a. Issued note.		.55	1.65	5.00
	s. Specimen w/ovpt: Mi-hon.		—	—	100.00
M12	**10 SEN**				
	ND (1938). Black on yellow-orange and violet unpt. Dragon at r. Title B. (S/M #T31-3).		4.50	13.50	40.00
M13	**50 SEN**				
	ND (1940). Black on green and pink unpt. Dragon at l. Title A. (S/M #T30-5).		.30	1.00	3.00

			VG	VF	UNC
M14	**50 SEN**				
	ND (1938). Black on green and pink unpt. Dragon at l. Title B. (S/M #T31-4).		.45	1.35	4.00

			VG	VF	UNC
M15	**1 YEN**				
	ND (1940). Black on pink and yellow unpt. Onagadori cock at l. Title A. (S/M #T30-10).				
	a. Issued note.		1.00	3.25	10.00
	s. Specimen w/ovpt: Mi-hon.		—	—	100.00
M16	**1 YEN**				
	ND (1939). Black on pink and yellow unpt. Onagadori cock at l. Title B. (S/M #T31-10).		10.00	40.00	200.00

			VG	VF	UNC
M17	**5 YEN**				
	ND (1940). Black on blue and yellow unpt. Onagadori cock at l. and r. Title A. (S/M #T30-11).				
	a. Issued note.		.65	2.00	6.00
	r. Remainder w/o serial #, block # or seal.		—	13.50	40.00
	s. Specimen w/ovpt: Mi-hon.		—	—	100.00
M18	**5 YEN**				
	ND (1939). Black on blue and yellow unpt. Onagadori cock at l. and r. Title B. (S?M #T31-11).				
	a. Issued note.		2.00	6.50	20.00
	r. Remainder w/o seal.		—	13.50	40.00

			VG	VF	UNC
M19	**10 YEN**				
	ND (1940). Black on pale blue-green and lilac unpt. Dragon. Title A. (S/M #T30-13).				
	a. Issued note.		.65	2.00	6.00
	r. Remainder w/o serial #, block # or seal.		—	13.50	40.00
	s. Specimen w/ovpt: Mi-hon.		—	—	100.00
M20	**10 YEN**				
	ND (1939). Black on pale blue-green and lilac unpt. Dragon. Title B. (S/M #T31-12).				
	a. Issued note.		4.50	13.50	40.00
	r. Remainder w/o serial # or block #.		—	13.50	40.00

1945 ND ISSUE

M21	**100 YEN**	VG	VF	UNC
	ND (1945). Black on yellow-green unpt. Onagadori cock at l. and r. Title A. Back green. *(S/M #T30-14)*.			
	a. Issued note.	1.00	5.00	15.00
	s. Specimen w/ovpt: *Mi-hon.*	—	—	100.00

MILITARY NOTE

票手用軍
Chun Yung Shou P'iao

Although issued for all of occupied China, these notes were later replaced by Federal Reserve and Central Reserve Bank of China issues. They did remain in circulation in Hong Kong and Hainan Island through the occupation.

HANDSTAMP VARIETIES:

Type I: Hiragana (rare)   Type II: Hentaigana (common)

The CANTON ovpt. is Japanese Hiragana or Hentaigana characters in a 10-11mm circle. It exists in red, green, black and purple and was applied in March, 1939. Most of Type II - Hentaigana encountered in today's market in high grade are considered to be forgeries. Most notes are w/o either handstamp.

1938 ND ISSUES

M22	**1 YEN**	VG	VF	UNC
	ND (1938). Lt. brown. Ovpt: 4 Japanese characters across ctr., 11 characters below, 8 characters (Bank of Japan) blocked out at top. Ovpt: red. *(S/M #J11-1)*.			
	a. Issued note.	7.50	21.50	75.00
	b. W/handstamp: Type II.	10.00	35.00	—

M23	**1 YEN**	VG	VF	UNC
	ND (1938). Lt. brown. Ovpt: 4 Japanese characters across ctr. *(S/M #T32-1)*.			
	a. Issued note.	2.50	7.50	25.00
	b. W/handstamp: Type II.	4.00	10.00	—

M24	**5 YEN**	VG	VF	UNC
	ND (1938). Green and brown unpt. Hooded man at r. Ovpt: 4 Japanese characters across ctr., 11 characters below, 7 characters (Bank of Japan Convertible Note) blocked out at top. *(S/M #J11-2)*.			
	a. Issued note.	7.50	21.50	75.00
	b. W/handstamp: Type II.	10.00	35.00	—

M25	**5 YEN**	VG	VF	UNC
	ND (1938; 1944). Green and brown unpt. Ovpt: 4 Japanese characters across ctr.			
	a. Wmk: Plum flowers (1938). *(S/M #T32-2)*.	.50	1.50	15.00
	b. Wmk: 2 birds (1944). *(S/M #32-3)*.	.50	1.50	15.00

M26	**10 YEN**	VG	VF	UNC
	ND (1938). Green unpt. Ovpt: 4 Japanese characters across ctr., 11 characters below, 7 characters (Bank of Japan Convertible Note) blocked out at top. *(S/M #J11-3)*.			
	a. Issued note.	7.50	21.50	75.00
	b. W/handstamp: Type II.	10.00	35.00	—

M27	**10 YEN**	VG	VF	UNC
	ND (1938). Green unpt. Ovpt: 4 Japanese characters across ctr. *(S/M #T32-4)*.			
	a. Issued note.	1.00	4.00	12.00
	b. W/handstamp: Type II.	2.00	6.00	—
	s. Specimen w/red ovpt: *Mi-hon.*	—	—	100.00

1945 ND HONG KONG ISSUES

M28	**100 YEN**	VG	VF	UNC
	ND (1945). Black on lt. blue and brown unpt. Ovpt: 4 Japanese characters across ctr., 7 characters below, 5 characters at top and 4 vertical characters at l. blocked out. *(S/M #J11-4)*.	.50	2.00	10.00
M29	**100 YEN**			
	ND (1945). Black on green and violet unpt. Like #M28. Ovpt: 4 Japanese characters across ctr. and seal at l. *(S/M #T32-5)*.	.25	1.00	5.00
M30	**100 YEN**			
	ND (1945). Red-brown on green unpt. Similar to #M29. Ovpt: 4 Japanese characters at ctr. *(S/M #T32-6)*.	.10	.30	2.50

SOUTH CHINA EXPEDITIONARY ARMY

1944 ISSUE

			VG	VF	UNC
M30A	**1000 YEN**		300.00	800.00	—
	Yr. 33 (1944). Red, blue and black on yellow-green unpt. Back purple				
	on yellow unpt. *(S/M #T32-7)*.				

RUSSIAN MILITARY - WWII

SOVIET RED ARMY HEADQUARTERS

蘇聯紅軍司令部
Su Lien Hung Chun Szu Ling Pu

Issued for general circulation in the Russian occupied territory of Manchuria (the disolved puppet state of Manchukuo).

1945 ISSUE

		VG	VF	UNC
M31	**1 YUAN**	5.50	17.50	45.00
	1945. Blue on green unpt. *(S/M #S82-1a)*.			
M32	**5 YUAN**	5.50	17.50	45.00
	1945. Brown on green unpt. *(S/M #S82-2a)*.			

		VG	VF	UNC
M33	**10 YUAN**	2.00	5.00	20.00
	1945. Red on lilac unpt. *(S/M #S82-3a)*.			
M34	**100 YUAN**	3.00	7.50	30.00
	1945. Blue on pink unpt. *(S/M #S82-4a)*.			

1945 ND REVALIDATED ISSUE

NOTE: The 10 Yuan adhesive stamp is also known affixed to Manchukuo 10 Yuan notes. Refer to Manchukuo listings.

		VG	VF	UNC
M35	**10 YUAN**	3.00	7.50	30.00
	ND (1946 - old date 1945). Brown revalidation *10 Yuan* adhesive			
	stamp on #M33. *(S/M #S82-3b)*.			

		VG	VF	UNC
M36	**100 YUAN**	3.00	7.50	30.00
	ND (1946 - old date 1945). Green revalidation *100 Yuan* adhesive			
	stamp on #M34. *(S/M #S82-4b)*.			

The Republic of Colombia, located in the northwestern corner of South America, has an area of 439,737 sq. mi. (1,138,914 sq. km.) and a population of 33.4 million. Capital: Bogota. The economy is primarily agricultural with a mild, rich coffee the chief crop. Colombia has the world's largest platinum deposits and important reserves of coal, iron ore, petroleum and limestone; precious metals and emeralds are also mined. Coffee, crude oil, bananas, sugar, coal and flowers are exported.

The northern coast of present Colombia was one of the first parts of the American continent to be visited by Spanish navigators, and the site, at Darien in Panama, of the first permanent European settlement on the American mainland in 1510. New Granada, as Colombia was known until 1861, stemmed from the settlement of Santa Maria in 1525. New Granada was established as a Spanish Colony in 1549. Independence was declared in 1813, and secured in 1824. In 1819, Simon Bolivar united Colombia, Venezuela, Panama and Ecuador as the Republic of Greater Colombia. Venezuela withdrew from the Republic in 1829; Ecuador in 1830; and Panama in 1903.

MONETARY SYSTEM:
   1 Peso = 100 Centavos

NOTE: Certain listings encompassing issues circulated by various bank and regional authorities are contained in Vol. 1.

NEW GRANADA

REPÚBLICA DE COLOMBIA

#1-4 uniface. Printer: Peter Maverick, New York, U.S.A.

1819 ISSUE

		GOOD	FINE	XF
1	**6 1/4 CENTAVOS = MEDIO REAL**	40.00	100.00	250.00
	ND (ca.1819). Black. Pineapple at upper ctr.			
2	**12 1/2 CENTAVOS = 1 REAL**	40.00	100.00	250.00
	ND (ca.1819). Black. Similar to #1.			

		GOOD	FINE	XF
3	**25 CENTAVOS = 2 REALES**	40.00	100.00	250.00
	ND (ca.1819). Black. Loaded burro at upper ctr.			
4	**50 CENTAVOS = 4 REALS**	30.00	75.00	
	ND (ca.1819). Black. Similar to #3.			

1820s ISSUE

#5-8 *BOLIVAR* above arms at ctr. Uniface. Printer: Peter Maverick, New York, U.S.A. (From cut up 4-subject sheets of unissued remainders.)

		GOOD	FINE	XF
5	**1 PESO**	—	Unc	175.00
	182x. Black.			
6	**2 PESOS**	—	Unc	175.00
	182x. Black.			
7	**3 PESOS**	—	Unc	175.00
	182x. Black.			

8	5 PESOS	GOOD	FINE	XF
	182x. Black.	—	Unc	175.00

TESORERIA JENERAL DE LOS ESTADOS UNIDOS DE NUEVA GRANADA

1860s ISSUE

#9-58, 60 *Deleted.*

59	20 CENTAVOS = 2 REALES			
	(ca.1860)	40.00	100.00	250.00
61	1 PESO = 10 REALES			
	186x. Pink unpt. Steamship at upper r. and at upper l.	60.00	150.00	360.00

62	2 PESOS = 20 REALES	GOOD	FINE	XF
	Dec. 1862. Yellow unpt. Steamship at upper r. and at upper l.	75.00	180.00	450.00

63	3 PESOS = 30 REALES	GOOD	FINE	XF
	186x. Implements.	80.00	200.00	500.00
64	10 PESOS = 100 REALES			
	186x. Implements.	90.00	225.00	550.00
65	20 PESOS = 200 REALES			
	186x. Implements.	110.00	260.00	650.00
66	100 PESOS = 1000 REALES			
	1.3.1861. Blue unpt. Implements.	—	Rare	—

ESTADOS UNIDOS DE COLOMBIA

ESTADOS UNIDOS DE COLOMBIA

1863 TREASURY ISSUE

#74-78 printer: ABNC.

71	5 CENTAVOS			
	ND. Blue. Tools.	80.00	200.00	500.00
72	10 CENTAVOS			
	ND. Blue. Horse.	80.00	200.00	500.00
73	20 CENTAVOS			
	ND. Black. Seated woman w/shield at ctr. Printer sign. on back.	80.00	200.00	500.00

74	1 PESO	GOOD	FINE	XF
	2.1.1863. Black on brown unpt. Man at lower l., bldg. at upper l. ctr., arms at lower r.	65.00	160.00	400.00

75	2 PESOS	GOOD	FINE	XF
	2.1.1863. Black on red unpt. Arms at lower l., horse and rider at top ctr., Bolívar at lower r. Series A-C.	90.00	225.00	550.00

76	5 PESOS	GOOD	FINE	XF
	2.1.1863. Black on green unpt. Man at lower l., standing woman at ctr., arms at r.	100.00	250.00	600.00
77	10 PESOS			
	2.1.1863. Black on green unpt. Arms at l., steamboat at r. ctr., man at lower r.	125.00	300.00	750.00
78	20 PESOS			
	2.1.1863. Black on yellow unpt. Arms at l., man w/mule cart at ctr., Caldas at r.	—	Rare	—

1869 ISSUE

80	3 PESOS			
	28.8.1869.	—	Rare	—

1876 ISSUE

#82-100 held in reserve.

#101-112 *Deleted.* See Vol. I.

81	5 CENTAVOS			
	24.11.1876. Black. Tobacco, beehive, plow and shovel at ctr. Printed sign. and dk. red oval stamping on back. Printer: Ayala i Medrano.	80.00	200.00	500.00

BANCO NACIONAL DE LOS ESTADOS UNIDOS DE COLOMBIA

ND ISSUE

122	20 CENTAVOS	GOOD	FINE	XF
	ND. Black on blue unpt. R. Nuñez at upper ctr. Back red-brown. Series Y. Printer: Chaix.	30.00	75.00	185.00
123	20 CENTAVOS			
	ND. Black on blue unpt. Like #122. Printer: Litografia de Villaveces, Bogotá.	—	—	—

1881 FIRST ISSUE

#134, 135, and 138 Liberty seated at l., arms at top ctr. r. Printer: Lit D. Paredes, Bogotá. **Partially printed date.**

134	**1 Peso**	GOOD	FINE	XF
	1.3.1881. Blue. Series A.	100.00	250.00	600.00
135	**5 Pesos**			
	1.3.1881. Black and red, stamping and handwritten sign. on plain back.	100.00	250.00	600.00
138	**20 Pesos**			
	1.3.1881. Date partially handwritten.	—	Rare	—

1881 SECOND ISSUE
#141-146 printer: ABNC.
#147-152 held in reserve.

141	**1 Peso**	GOOD	FINE	XF
	1.3.1881. Black on brown unpt. Portr. helmeted Athena at lower l., portr. S. Bolívar at upper ctr., arms at lower r. Back brown. Series A.	100.00	250.00	600.00
142	**5 Pesos**			
	1.3.1881. Black on green unpt. Woman at l., man in uniform at ctr., arms at r. Back green.	100.00	250.00	600.00

143	**10 Pesos**	GOOD	FINE	XF
	1.3.1881. Black on orange unpt. Arms at lower l., steam locomotive at ctr., portr. Caldas at r. Back red.	125.00	300.00	750.00

144	**20 Pesos**	GOOD	FINE	XF
	1.3.1881. Black on blue unpt. Arms at l., unloading bales at ctr., Nariño at r. Back blue.	150.00	360.00	900.00
145	**50 Pesos**			
	1.3.1881. Black on brown unpt. Arms at l., globe w/ship and train at ctr., Torres at r. Back brown.	300.00	750.00	—
146	**100 Pesos**			
	1.3.1881. Black on brown-orange unpt. Miners at lower l., Allegorical woman flanking shield at ctr., Santander at lower r. Back brown-orange. Specimen.	375.00	950.00	—

1882 ISSUE

153	**50 Centavos**	GOOD	FINE	XF
	1.3.1882. Orange and black. Arms at ctr. Purple stamping on back.	35.00	90.00	225.00

1885 ISSUE
#161-165 printer: Lit. D. Paredes.
#172-174, 176-181 held in reserve.
#175 *Deleted*. See #135.

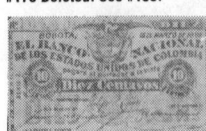

161	**10 Centavos**	GOOD	FINE	XF
	1885. Black on orange-gold unpt. Arms at upper ctr. Printed sign. and stamping on back. Series Z.			
	a. 15.3.1885.	6.00	18.00	55.00
	b. 5.8.1885.	6.50	20.00	60.00

162	**20 Centavos**	GOOD	FINE	XF
	15.3.1885. Black on aqua unpt. Similar to #161. Printed sign. and stamping on back. Series Y.	6.00	18.00	55.00
164	**1 Peso**			
	6.10.1885. Black on green unpt. Arms at upper ctr. Sign. and stamping on back. Series A.	6.50	20.00	60.00
165	**1 Peso**			
	6.10.1885. Black on pink unpt. Like #164.	6.50	20.00	60.00
170	**50 Pesos**			
	22.7.1885. Condor.	—	—	—
171	**100 Pesos**			
	3.3.1885. Black on orange unpt. Woman.	—	—	—

BANCO NACIONAL DE COLOMBIA

1885 ISSUE

181	**1 Real**	GOOD	FINE	XF
	5.8.1885. Black on green unpt. Arms at l. Back green; printed sign. across. Red seal at ctr. Series C-I; K; M. Printer: HLBNC.	2.50	10.00	25.00
182	**10 Centavos = 1 Real**			
	5.8.1885. Like #181, but blue seal on face and back. Series F; K; O; Q; T; Printer: CABB (ABNC).	2.50	10.00	25.00

1886 ISSUE

186	**20 Centavos**	GOOD	FINE	XF
	ND. (1886). Black on orange unpt. Man at l. Back blue; stamped date in oval *21.11.1886*. Printer: Villaveces, Bogotá.	8.00	25.00	50.00

1887 ISSUE

189	**2 Reales**	GOOD	FINE	XF
	1.1.1887. Black on gold unpt. Portr. man at lower l., arms at lower r. Back brown. Series D; E; H; I; K; M; N. Printer: HLBNC.	5.00	20.00	50.00
190	**50 Centavos**			
	1.5.1887. Printer: Villaveces, Bogotá.	—	—	—

BANCO NACIONAL DE LA REPÚBLICA DE COLOMBIA

1886 ISSUE
#191-195 printer: HLBNC.

191	**50 Centavos**	GOOD	FINE	XF
	1.9.1886. Green. Justice at upper l., shield at lower r. Series 1.	7.50	30.00	90.00

192	**1 Peso**	GOOD	FINE	XF
	1.9.1886. Green. Helmeted woman at upper l., arms at upper r. Back green. Series 2A.	6.00	25.00	75.00
193	**1 Peso**			
	1.9.1886. Like #192. Back blue.	7.00	27.50	85.00

194 5 PESOS

	Good	Fine	XF
1.9.1886. Green on orange unpt. Shield at lower l., helmeted Minerva	27.50	110.00	335.00

195 10 PESOS

	Good	Fine	XF
1.9.1886. Brown. Reclining allegorical seated figures w/arms at ctr. Back blue. Series 2A.	35.00	140.00	425.00

1888 ISSUE

#211-218 circular red bank seal on back. Printer: ABNC.
#219 and 220 held in reserve.

211 10 CENTAVOS = 1 REAL

	Good	Fine	XF
1.3.1888. Black on yellow unpt. Arms at lower l. Back green; printed sign. At least 11 Greek and English series letters.	3.00	12.00	36.00

214 1 PESO

	Good	Fine	XF
1.3.1888. Black on orange and yellow unpt. Arms at l., portr. S. Bolívar at r. Back brown. At least 15 Greek and English series letters.	4.50	18.00	55.00

215 5 PESOS

	Good	Fine	XF
1.3.1888. Black on orange and yellow unpt. Arms at l., allegorical woman w/bale seated at l. ctr., portr. S. Bolívar at r. Back brown. Series A.	8.00	32.50	100.00

216 10 PESOS

	Good	Fine	XF
1.3.1888. Black on brown and yellow unpt. Standing allegorical woman and pedestal of Liberty at l., S. Bolívar at ctr., arms at r. Back brown. Series A.	12.50	50.00	150.00

217 50 PESOS

	Good	Fine	XF
1.3.1888. Black on blue and yellow unpt. S. Bolívar at l., arms at ctr., seated allegorical woman at lower r. Back blue. Series A.	22.00	87.50	265.00

218 100 PESOS

	Good	Fine	XF
1.3.1888. Black on green and yellow unpt. Arms at l., cherub at upper ctr., portr. S. Bolívar at r. Back orange. Series A.	37.50	150.00	450.00

1893 ISSUE

#221, 224, 227-228 printer: ABNC.
#222, 223, 225, 226, 229-233 held in reserve.

221 10 CENTAVOS = 1 REAL

	Good	Fine	XF
2.1.1893. Like #211. At least 16 Greek and English series letters.	1.00	4.00	12.00

224 1 PESO

	Good	Fine	XF
2.1.1893. Like #214. At least 13 Greek and English series letters.	2.50	10.00	30.00

227 50 PESOS

2.1.1893. Like #217. Series A.	17.50	70.00	210.00

228 100 PESOS

2.1.1893. Like #218.	30.00	125.00	375.00

1895 ISSUE

#234-236, 238-239 printer: ABNC.
#242-250 held in reserve.

234 1 PESO

	Good	Fine	XF
4.3.1895. Like #214. At least 21 Greek and English series letters.	1.50	6.00	24.00

235 5 PESOS

	Good	Fine	XF
4.3.1895. Like #215. Series A.	5.50	22.50	90.00

236	**10 PESOS**	GOOD	FINE	XF
	4.3.1895. Like #216. Series A.	7.50	30.00	120.00

237	**25 PESOS**	GOOD	FINE	XF
	4.3.1895. Black on orange and green unpt. Dog at l., Liberty at lower r. Back brown. Series 1. Printer: FLBN.	32.50	135.00	400.00

238	**50 PESOS**	GOOD	FINE	XF
	4.3.1895. Like #217. Series A.	16.00	65.00	200.00
239	**100 PESOS**			
	4.3.1895. Like #218. Series A.	32.50	135.00	400.00

241	**1000 PESOS**	GOOD	FINE	XF
	4.3.1895. Black on pink and blue unpt. Woman at l. Woman w/h ead covered on red back. Printer: FLBN.	—	725.00	1800.

REPUBLIC

BANCO NACIONAL DE LA REPÚBLICA DE COLOMBIA

Notes of 1899 and 1900 show great variance in printing quality, color shades, types of paper used. There was also a considerable amount of forgery of these notes.

1899 CIVIL WAR ISSUES
#257-259, 261 held in reserve.

251	**2 PESOS**			
	28.10.1899. Black on pink unpt. Liberty facing l. at l. Back blue. Series A-C; G; K; M; N.	2.00	8.00	35.00
	a. Issued note.	2.50	10.00	42.00
	b. Punch cancelled.	1.00	4.50	18.00

252	**2 PESOS**	GOOD	FINE	XF
	28.10.1899. Black on pink unpt. Liberty facing r. at l. *SEGUNDA EDICION* at lower l. Back blue. Series A-L. Printer: LN.	2.50	12.00	48.00
253	**5 PESOS**			
	29.10.1899. Black on blue unpt. Arms and allegorical seated figures at ctr. Back slate green. Series B; D; E; F. Imprint: Otto Schroeder.	5.00	25.00	72.00
254	**5 PESOS**			
	29.10.1899. Face like #253 w/Schroeder imprint. *SEGUNDA EDICION* at lower r. on back, along with LN imprint. Series A; D.	4.00	20.00	60.00

255	**5 PESOS**	GOOD	FINE	XF
	29.10.1899. Like #253, but *2A EMISION* at lower ctr. and LN imprint at lower r. on face. Back green. Series A; B; E.	4.00	20.00	60.00
256	**5 PESOS**			
	29.10.1899. Like #255, but *3A EMISION* at lower ctr. on face. Series A-C; E; F.	4.50	22.00	66.00

260	**100 PESOS**	GOOD	FINE	XF
	29.10.1899. Black on orange-tan unpt. S. Bolívar at l., Spaniards landing at ctr., arms at r. Back brown; arms at ctr. Series A. Imprint: Otto Schroeder.	40.00	125.00	375.00

1900 CIVIL WAR ISSUES
#272, 277, 283-300 held in reserve.

 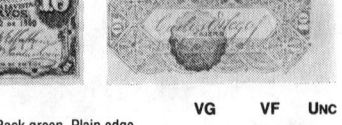

262	**10 CENTAVOS**	VG	VF	UNC
	2.1.1900. Black on green unpt. Arms at l. Back green. Plain edge. Series A. Imprint: Villaveces, Bogotá.			
	a. Serial # across lower ctr.	1.00	4.50	18.00
	b. W/o serial #.	1.00	4.50	18.00
	c. Numeral 2 for day in date miss ing. Perforated edge.	—	—	—
	d. W/o serial #. Perforated edge.	—	—	—

263	**10 CENTAVOS**	VG	VF	UNC
	30.9.1900. Blue on orange unpt. Arms at upper l. Back orange. At least 10 series letters. Printer: LN.	1.00	5.00	18.00

264 **20 Centavos**

	VG	VF	UNC
25.3.1900. Black on lt. blue-gray unpt. Arms at l. Back blue to deep blue. At least 13 series letters.	1.00	4.50	18.00

265 **20 Centavos**

	VG	VF	UNC
30.9.1900. Black on wine or lilac unpt. Arms at lower l. Back shades of purple or violet, arms at ctr. At least 17 series letters. Printer: LN.	.75	3.00	12.00

266 **50 Centavos**

	Good	Fine	XF
20.7.1900. Black on blue unpt. Arms at r. Back brown (shades); inverted position. Series B; E. Imprint: Otto Schroeder (both sides of note).	2.25	9.00	36.00

267 **50 Centavos**

20.7.1900. Similar to #266 but *2A EMISION* at lower l. and no Schroeder imprint at lower r. Back has Schroeder imprint at bottom and is not inverted. Series F.	2.25	9.00	36.00

268 **50 Centavos**

20.7.1900. Blue or green unpt. Like #267. Back has *2A EMISION* at bottom margin, and no Schroeder imprint. Series B; C; E; G; I; J; V.	1.85	7.50	30.00

269 **1 Peso**

	Good	Fine	XF
25.4.1900. Black on lt. red unpt. Arms at ctr. Back black. Series B; E; I; O; P. Printer: Lit. D. Paredes.	3.00	12.00	48.00

270 **1 Peso**

	Good	Fine	XF
30.9.1900. Black on lt. red unpt. Man at l. Back blue; arms at ctr. At least 12 series letters. Printer: LN.	1.85	7.50	30.00

271 **5 Pesos**

	Good	Fine	XF
30.9.1900. Black on red-orange unpt. Man and woman watering horses at l., blue bank seal at r. ctr. *2A EMISION* at lower l. margin. Back brown or violet; *2A EMISION* at lower ctr. in margin. Series A; h; I; K; n. Printer: LN.	3.00	12.00	48.00

273 **5 Pesos**

30.9.1900. *2A EMISION.*		Reported Not Confirmed	

274 **10 Pesos**

30.9.1900. Black on orange-brown unpt. Miners at l., arms at ctr. Printer: LN.			
a. No imprint at lower r. Back purple. Series A; B; I.	7.50	30.00	90.00
b. Like a., but back blue. Series A; B.	8.00	32.00	100.00
c. Imprint at lower r. Back purple. Series H; M.	6.50	26.50	80.00
d. Like a.; back inverted and blue. Series M.	6.50	26.50	80.00

275 **10 Pesos**

	Good	Fine	XF
30.9.1900. Like #274 but *2A EMISION* at lower ctr. Back blue; name *LEHNER* at l., LN imprint at bottom r. Series A; N; O.	6.50	26.50	80.00

276 **20 Pesos**

30.9.1900. Black. Arms at ctr., farmer at r. Back brown; mules and boys on mountain trail at ctr. Printer: LN.	Good	Fine	XF
a. Blue unpt. Series B.	7.50	30.00	90.00
b. Green unpt. Series A; C; F; M; O; P; Q.	6.50	26.50	80.00

278 **50 Pesos**

15.2.1900. Black on green unpt. Arms at upper l., sailing ship and steam passenger train at upper ctr. Portr. man at upper r. Back red; arms at ctr. Series A; C. Imprint: Otto Schroeder.	Good	Fine	XF
a. Series A; C.	17.50	70.00	210.00
b. Perforated *B de B (Banco de Bogotá)* at ctr. Series B.	17.50	70.00	210.00

279 **50 Pesos**

	Good	Fine	XF
30.9.1900. Black on dull orange unpt. Woman and trough at lower l., arms at upper ctr., S. Bolívar at lower r. Back pinkish orange; woman at ctr. Series A; C; D. Printer: LN.	17.50	70.00	210.00

280 **50 Pesos**

30.9.1900. Blue on dull orange unpt. Like #279. Back orange. Series A-D. Printer: LN.	17.50	70.00	210.00

		GOOD	FINE	XF
281	**100 PESOS**	25.00	100.00	300.00
	30.9.1900. Black on orange unpt. Man at lower l., condor at upper ctr., arms at lower r. *SEGUNDA EDICION* at lower ctr. Back blue and pinkish violet; funeral of Atahualpa scene at ctr. Series A; C; F. Printer: LN.			
282	**500 PESOS**	800.00	1250.	2000.
	28.2.1900. Brown. Arms at upper l. Back black text, large blue eagle at ctr., 4 hand sign. below. Series A.			

TREASURY

Treasury and Junta de Conversion issues leading to the establishment of the Banco de la Répública in 1923.

1904 ISSUE

#301-307 printer: W&S.

#310 *Deleted.* #309 and 310 held in reserve.

		GOOD	FINE	XF
301	**1 PESO**	2.25	9.00	36.00
	April 1904. Black on gold unpt. Arms at l., Cordoba at ctr. Back purple; plantation scene.			

		GOOD	FINE	XF
302	**2 PESOS**	2.50	10.00	42.00
	April 1904. Black on blue unpt. Arms at l., sheep at ctr. Back brown; portr. Rigaurte at ctr.			

		GOOD	FINE	XF
303	**5 PESOS**	5.00	20.00	60.00
	April 1904. Black on green unpt. Arms at upper l., church at ctr. Back dk. red; portr. Torres at ctr.			

		GOOD	FINE	XF
304	**10 PESOS**	7.50	30.00	90.00
	April 1904. Black on red unpt. Gen. A. Nariño at l., arms at r. Back brown; standing helmeted woman at l., riverboats at ctr.			
305	**25 PESOS**	10.00	40.00	120.00
	April 1904. Black on orange unpt. Portr. Caldas at l., arms at r. Back green; observatory at ctr.			

		GOOD	FINE	XF
306	**50 PESOS**	22.50	90.00	270.00
	April 1904. Black on green unpt. Gen. Santander at l., arms and cherubs at ctr., plantation scene at r. Back red-brown; standing Liberty and eagle at l., bridge scene at ctr.			

		GOOD	FINE	XF
307	**100 PESOS**	17.50	70.00	210.00
	April 1904. Black on red unpt. Standing S. Bolívar at l., arms at ctr. Back orange; Plaza de Bolívar at ctr.			

1908 ISSUE

#312-315 held in reserve.

		GOOD	FINE	XF
311	**1000 PESOS**	—	Rare	—
	March 1908. Black on green unpt. Portr. S. Bolívar at ctr. between seated allegorical woman at l., Mercury at r. Printer: W&S.			

REPÚBLICA DE COLOMBIA

This issuing body was established in 1909.

1910 *JUNTA DE CONVERSION* ISSUE

#316 and 317 printer: ABNC.

#318-320 held in reserve.

		GOOD	FINE	XF
316	**50 PESOS**	8.00	40.00	120.00
	Aug. 1910. Black on olive unpt. Arms at l., portr. S. Bolívar at r. Back olive; printed sign. across ctr. Series A; B; C; D..			
317	**100 PESOS**	20.00	100.00	300.00
	Aug. 1910. Black on orange and yellow unpt. Arms at l., portr. S. Bolívar at ctr. r. Back brown; like #316. Series A.			

1915 JUNTA DE CONVERSION ISSUE
#321-327 printer: ABNC.

#323 Series F and #324 Series D were actually issued by the Banco de la República.

#328-330 held in reserve.

322	2 PESOS	GOOD	FINE	XF
	20.7.1915. Black on blue and m/c unpt. Portr. Gen. A. Nariño at ctr. Back blue; arms at ctr. Series A-E.	17.00	85.00	300.00

323	5 PESOS	GOOD	FINE	XF
	20.7.1915. Black on orange and m/c unpt. Portr. Córdoba at l. ctr., condor at r. Back orange; arms at ctr. Series A-F.	10.00	50.00	250.00

324	10 PESOS	GOOD	FINE	XF
	20.7.1915. Black on green, purple and orange unpt. Gen. Santander at l., large dollar sign. at ctr., arms at r. Back lt. orange; national capitol, 3 printed sign. beneath. Series A-D.	18.00	90.00	325.00

1922 BONO DEL TOSERO (TREASURY BOND) PROVISIONAL ISSUE
#331 and 332 are a Junta de Conversion issue authorized by Law 6 and Decree #166 of 1922, and Public Notive #206 of 8.2.1922.

#333-335 held in reserve.

331	1 PESO	VG	VF	UNC
	1922 (-old date 20.7.1915). Red ovpt. *BONO DEL TESORO* across face. Red ovpt. Lg. heading at top w/10-line text in square at ctr. on back of #321. Series J.	50.00	175.00	—
332	5 PESOS			
	1922 (-old date 20.7.1915). Ovpt. on face and back of #323 as above.	100.00	300.00	—

1938 TREASURY ISSUE
#336 and 337 printer: ABNC.

#342-350 held in reserve.

NOTE: Since the Banco de la República could not issue notes without gold backing after 1923, the Treasury issued the 5 and 10 Pesos dated 1938 and the 1/2 Pesos of 1948 and 1953 (#336, 337 and 341). These notes were signed by the Minister of Finance, the Treasurer and the Comptroller, and were designed to contravene the law. In reality these notes are emergency issues that eventually became legal tender within system.

336	5 PESOS	VG	VF	UNC
	22.3.1938. Black on m/c unpt. Córdoba at ctr. Back red; arms at ctr. Series A.	7.50	25.00	70.00

337	10 PESOS	VG	VF	UNC
	22.3.1938. Black on m/c unpt. Gen. Santander at l., bust S. Bolívar at r. Back lt. orange; arms at ctr. Series B.	10.00	40.00	125.00

1948 TREASURY ISSUE
#342-350 held in reserve.

341	1/2 PESO	VG	VF	UNC
	1948; 1953. Brown on m/c unpt. Portr. Gen. A. Nariño at ctr. Back brown; arms at ctr. Printer: ABNC.			
	a. Series A; B. 16.1.1948.	1.00	3.50	25.00
	b. Series C. 18.2.1953.	1.00	3.50	25.00

BANCO DE LA REPÚBLICA

1923 CERTIFICADOS SOBRE CONSIGNACIÓN DE ORO (GOLD CERTIFICATES) PROVISIONAL ISSUE
#351-354 Gold Certificates. New bank name ovpt: *BANCO DE LA REPÚBLICA / BILLETE PROVISIONAL* on Casa de Moneda de Medellin #S1026-S1029 (See Vol. 1). Printer: ABNC.

#355-360 held in reserve.

351	2 1/2 PESOS	GOOD	FINE	XF
	ND (- old date 1.5.1920). Black on green and m/c unpt. Black green. Blue ovpt. on #S1026.	50.00	200.00	500.00
352	5 PESOS			
	ND (- old date 15.9.1919). Black on brown and m/c unpt. Back brown. Ovpt. on #S1027.	—	Rare	—
353	10 PESOS			
	ND. Black on orange and m/c unpt. Back orange. Ovpt. on #S1028.	—	Rare	—
354	20 PESOS			
	ND. Black on blue and m/c unpt. Back blue. Ovpt. on #S1029.	—	Rare	—

1923 ISSUE

#361-367 bank name below upper frame in Gothic lettering. Backs w/Liberty head at ctr., printed sign. below. Printer: ABNC.

#368-370 held in reserve.

		VG	VF	UNC
361	**1 PESO** 20.7.1923. Blue on m/c unpt. Portr. Caldas at ctr. Back red-brown. Series A.	20.00	95.00	450.00

		VG	VF	UNC
362	**2 PESOS** 20.7.1923. Green on m/c unpt. Portr. C. Torres at ctr. Back dk. brown. Series B.	45.00	150.00	750.00
363	**5 PESOS** 20.7.1923. Brown on m/c unpt. Portr. Córdoba at l. Back green. Series C.	45.00	150.00	750.00
364	**10 PESOS** 20.7.1923. Black on m/c unpt. Portr. Gen. A. Nariño at r. Back red. Series D.	42.50	140.00	700.00
365	**50 PESOS** 20.7.1923. Dk. brown on m/c unpt. Portr. A. J. de Sucre at l. Back orange. Series E.	150.00	600.00	—
366	**100 PESOS** 20.7.1923. Purple on m/c unpt. Portr. Gen. Santander at ctr. Back red-brown. Series F.	125.00	500.00	—
367	**500 PESOS** 20.7.1923. Olive green on m/c unpt. Portr. S. Bolívar at r. Back orange. Series G.	—	Rare	—

1926-28 ISSUE

#371-375A w/bank name as part of upper frame in standard lettering. Back design and sign. like #361-367. Printer: ABNC.

		VG	VF	UNC
371	**1 PESO** 1.1.1926. Orange on m/c unpt. Portr. S. Bolívar at ctr. Back blue. Series H.	9.00	37.50	150.00
372	**2 PESOS** 1.1.1926. Olive on m/c unpt. Portr. C. Torres at ctr. Series I. Back purple.	30.00	125.00	600.00

		VG	VF	UNC
373	**5 PESOS** 1926; 1928. Blue on m/c unpt. Portr. Córdoba at l. Back brown.			
	a. Series J. 1.1.1926.	25.00	100.00	500.00
	b. Series M. 1.1.1928.	3.50	17.50	95.00
374	**10 PESOS** 1926; 1928. Purple on m/c unpt. Portr. Gen. A. Nariño at r. Back green.			
	a. Series K. 1.1.1926.	30.00	100.00	575.00
	b. Series N. 1.1.1928.	10.00	35.00	200.00
375	**50 PESOS** 1926; 1928. Green on m/c unpt. Portr. A.J. de Sucre at l. Back blue-black.			
	a. Series L. 1.1.1926.	50.00	200.00	700.00
	b. Series P. 20.7.1928.	30.00	110.00	475.00

		VG	VF	UNC
375A	**100 PESOS** 20.7.1928. Brown on m/c unpt. Portr. Gen. Santander at ctr. Back red. Series Q.	50.00	300.00	850.00

1927 ISSUE

#376-378 wmk. area at r. Backs w/various branches of the Banco de la República and printed sign. below. Printer: TDLR.

#379 *Deleted.* See #375A.

		VG	VF	UNC
376	**5 PESOS** 20.7.1927. Green on m/c unpt. Portr. Córdoba and seated allegorical woman at l. Older bank at Bogotá on back. Series M.	10.00	50.00	225.00
377	**10 PESOS** 20.7.1927. Blue on m/c unpt. Portr. Gen. A. Nariño and Mercury at l. Bank at Medellin on back. Series N.	20.00	125.00	475.00

		VG	VF	UNC
378	**20 PESOS** 20.7.1927. Violet on m/c unpt. Portr. Caldas and allegorical woman at l. Older bank at Barranquilla on back. Series O.	25.00	125.00	475.00

1929 ISSUE

		VG	VF	UNC
380	**1 PESO** 1929-54. Blue on m/c unpt. Portr. Gen. Santander and standing allegorical woman at l., bust of S. Bolívar at r. Back blue; Liberty at ctr. Printer: ABNC.			
	a. Series R in red. 20.7.1929.	.75	3.50	25.00
	b. Sign. and series like a. 20.7.1940.	.30	2.00	20.00
	c. Series R in red. 20.7.1942; 20.7.1943.	.25	1.50	15.00
	d. Series R in blue. 20.7.1944; 1.1.1945; 20.7.1946.	.40	2.00	18.00
	e. Series R in blue. 20.7.1946; 7.8.1947 (prefixes A-F).	.40	2.00	18.00
	f. Series HH. 1.1.1950.	.25	.75	7.00
	g. Series HH. 1.1.1954.	.25	.75	7.00

1931 *CERTIFICADOS DE PLATA* (SILVER CERTIFICATES) PROVISIONAL ISSUE

		VG	VF	UNC
381	**5 PESOS** ND (1931- old date 20.7.1915). Black ovpt: *CERTIFICADO DE PLATA* on back of #323.	75.00	200.00	650.00

1932 REGULAR ISSUE

#382-383 Printer: ABNC.

		VG	VF	UNC
382	**1 PESO** 1.1.1932. Green on m/c unpt. Portr. Gen. Santander at ctr. Liberty at ctr. on back. Prefix A.	6.50	40.00	185.00

383 5 Pesos

	VG	VF	UNC
1.1.1932. Blue on m/c unpt. Portr. Gen. A. Nariño at ctr. Back red; like #382. Prefix B.	25.00	200.00	550.00

1935 Issue

384 1/2 Peso

	VG	VF	UNC
20.7.1935. Brown on m/c unpt. Bust of Caldas at l. ctr., bust of S. Bolívar at r. Liberty at ctr. on back. Series S. Printer: ABNC.	20.00	125.00	425.00

1938 Commemorative Issue

#385, 400th Anniversary Founding of Bogota 1538-1938.

385 1 Peso

	VG	VF	UNC
6.8.1938. Blue on m/c unpt. Portr. G. Ximenez de Quesada in medallion supported w/2 allegorical angels at ctr. Back brown; scene of founding of Bogotá at ctr. Series T. Printer: ABNC.	15.00	50.00	225.00

1940 Issue

386 5 Pesos

	VG	VF	UNC
1940-50. Like #373, but w/o title: *CAJERO* and sign. on back.			
a. Series M in red. 20.7.1940.	1.00	6.00	40.00
b. Series M in red. 20.7.1942; 20.7.1943.	.50	3.00	35.00
c. Series M in blue. 20.7.1944; 1.1.1945; 20.7.1946; 7.8.1947.	.50	3.00	35.00
d. Series M. 12.10.1949.	.25	1.50	22.50
e. Series FF. 1.1.1950.	.25	1.50	22.50

1941 Certificados de Plata (Silver Certificates) Issue

387 1 Peso

	VG	VF	UNC
1.1.1941. Green on m/c unpt. Portr. Gen. Santander at l. Liberty at ctr. on back. Prefix B.	7.00	25.00	150.00

388 5 Pesos

	VG	VF	UNC
1.1.1941. Black on m/c unpt. Portr. Gen. A. Nariño at l. Back blue; like #387. Prefix C.	4.00	15.00	80.00

1941 *Certificados de Oro* (Gold Certificates) Issue

389 10 Pesos

	VG	VF	UNC
1941-63. Portr. Gen. A. Nariño at lower r. w/o title: *CAJERO* and sign. on back.			
a. Series N in red. 20.7.1941; 20.7.1943.	1.00	6.00	35.00
b. Series N in violet. 20.7.1944; 1.1.1945; 7.8.1947.	.50	4.00	30.00
d. Series N. 12.10.1949.	.25	2.00	25.00
e. Series EE. 1.1.1950.	.25	2.00	22.50
f. Series EE. 2.1.1963.	.20	1.50	20.00

1942 Issue

#390-391 printer: ABNC.

390 2 Pesos

	VG	VF	UNC
1942-55. Like #372, but w/o title: *CAJERO* and sign. on back.			
a. Series I in red. 20.7.1942; 20.7.1943.	.50	4.00	35.00
b. Series I in olive. 20.7.1944; 1.1.1945; 7.8.1947.	.50	3.00	30.00
c. Series GG. 1.1.1950.	.50	2.50	25.00
d. Series GG. 1.1.1955.	.25	1.00	8.00

391 500 Pesos

	VG	VF	UNC
1942-53. Like #367, but w/o title: *CAJERO* and sign. on back.			
a. Series G in red. 10.7.1942.	50.00	225.00	850.00
b. Series G in olive. 1.1.1944; 1.1.1945; 7.8.1947 (prefix A).	40.00	100.00	385.00
c. Series AA. 1.1.1950.	15.00	60.00	325.00
d. Series AA. 1.1.1951; 1.1.1953.	10.00	30.00	90.00

1943 Issue

#392-394 printer: ABNC.

#392-397 *Deleted.* See #392-394.

392			VG	VF	UNC
(395)	**20 PESOS** 1943-63. Purple and m/c. Bust of Caldas at l., bust of S. Bolívar at r. Liberty at ctr. on back.				
	a. Series U in red. 20.7.1943.		12.50	50.00	200.00
	b. Series U in purple. 20.7.1944; 1.1.1945.		10.00	40.00	150.00
	c. Series U. Prefix A. 7.8.1947.		1.00	4.00	40.00
	d. Series DD. 1.1.1950; 1.1.1951.		1.00	3.00	30.00
	e. Series DD. 2.1.1963.		.50	2.00	20.00

393			VG	VF	UNC
(396)	**50 PESOS** 1944-58. Like #375, but w/o title: *CAJERO* and sign. on back.				
	a. Series P. 20.7.1944; 1.1.1945.		6.00	20.00	95.00
	b. Series P. Prefix A. 7.8.1947.		1.00	5.00	50.00
	c. Series CC. 1.1.1950; 1.1.1951.		1.00	4.00	30.00
	d. Series CC. 1.1.1953.		1.00	4.00	30.00
	e. Series CC. 1.1.1958.		1.00	3.00	25.00

394			VG	VF	UNC
(397)	**100 PESOS** 1944-57. Like #375A, but w/o *CAJERO* title and sign. on back.				
	a. Series Q. 20.7.1944; 1.1.1945; 7.8.1947. Prefix A.		6.00	40.00	135.00
	b. Series BB. 1.1.1950.		5.00	25.00	125.00
	c. Series BB. 1.1.1951.		2.00	12.50	60.00
	d. Series BB. 1.1.1953; 20.7.1957.		1.50	6.00	32.50

1946 PROVISIONAL ISSUE

Because of a scarcity of coins in circulation the Banco de la República took certain quantities of *R* series 1 Peso notes dated 1942 and 1943, and sliced them in halves and ovpt. each half as a Half Peso. The 1942 dated notes are Serial #70,000,001-70,250,000 while the 1943 dated notes are Serial #57,000,001-58,000,000.

397			VG	VF	UNC
(393)	**1/2 PESO** ND (1946-old dates 20.7.1942 and 20.7.1943). Halves of *R* series of #380c ovpt. in black squares as Half Peso on face, words *MEDIO PESO* w/oi square on back.				
	a. Printer's name: *LITOGRAFIA COLOMBIA, S.A. - BOGOTA* as part of black ovpt. on face (old date 20.7.1942).		40.00	150.00	400.00
	b. W/o local printer's name as part of black ovpt. on face (old dates 20.7.1942; 20.7.1943).		25.00	75.00	225.00

1953 ISSUE
#399-401 printer: TDLR.

398			VG	VF	UNC
	1 PESO 7.8.1953. Blue on m/c unpt. Standing S. Bólivar statue at l., bridge of Boyaca at ctr., Gen. Santander at r. Liberty at ctr. on back. Series A. Printer: W&S.		.25	.75	4.50

399			VG	VF	UNC
	5 PESOS 1.1.1953. Green on m/c unpt. Similar to #376, but numeral in guilloche instead of wmk. at r. Newer bank at Bogota on back. Series M.		.25	1.50	12.50

400			VG	VF	UNC
	10 PESOS 1953-61. Blue on m/c unpt. Portr. Gen. A. Nariño at l., palm trees at r. Bank w/Mercury alongside at Cali on back. Series N.				
	a. 1.1.1953.		.25	2.00	25.00
	b. 1.1.1958; 1.1.1960.		.25	1.25	20.00
	c. 2.1.1961.		.25	1.00	17.50

401			VG	VF	UNC
	20 PESOS 1953-65. Red-brown on m/c unpt. Portr. Caldas and allegory at l. Liberty in frame at r. Newer bank at Barranquilla on back. Series O.				
	a. 1.1.1953.		.25	3.00	25.00
	b. 1.1.1960.		.25	3.00	20.00
	c. 2.1.1961; 2.1.1965.		.20	1.00	17.50

1958 ISSUE
#402-403 printer: ABNC.

402			VG	VF	UNC
	50 PESOS 1958-67. Lt. brown on m/c unpt. Portr. A.J. de Sucre at lower l. Back olive-green; Liberty at ctr. Series Z.				
	a. 20.7.1958; 7.8.1960.		.50	3.50	22.50
	b. 1.1.1964; 12.10.1967.		.25	2.50	20.00

403	100 Pesos	VG	VF	UNC
	1958-67. Gray on m/c unpt. Portr. Gen. Santander at r. Back green; Like #402. Series Y.			
a.	7.8.1958.	.50	3.00	22.50
b.	1.1.1960; 1.1.1964; 20.7.1965; 20.7.1967.	.50	1.25	10.00

1959-60 ISSUE

404	1 Peso	VG	VF	UNC
	1959-77. Blue on m/c unpt. Portr. S. Bolívar at l., portr. Gen. Santander at r. Liberty head and condor w/waterfall and mountain at ctr. on back.			
a.	Security thread. 12.10.1959.	.10	1.00	4.00
b.	Security thread. 2.1.1961; 7.8.1962; 2.1.1963; 12.10.1963; 2.1.1964; 12.10.1964.	.10	.50	2.00
c.	W/o security thread. 20.7.1966; 20.7.1967; 1.2.1968; 2.1.1969.	.10	.25	1.00
d.	W/o security thread. 1.5.1970; 12.10.1970; 7.8.1971; 20.7.1972; 7.8.1973; 7.8.1974.	.10	.25	1.00
e.	As d. 1.1.1977.	.50	1.50	10.00
405	5 Pesos			
	20.7.1960. Green on m/c unpt. Portr. Córdoba and seated allegory at l. New bank bldg. at Bogotá on back. Series M. Printer: TDLR.	.25	1.50	8.50

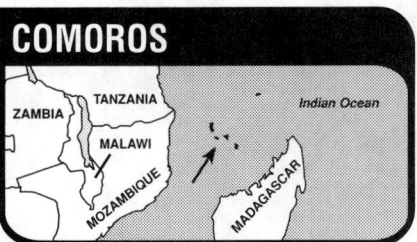

The Federal Islamic Republic of the Comoros, a volcanic archipelago located in the Mozambique Channel of the Indian Ocean 300 miles (483 km.) northwest of Madagascar, has an area of 838 sq. mi. (1,797 sq. km.) and a population of 570,000. Capital: Moroni. The economy of the islands is based on agriculture. There are practically no mineral resources. Vanilla, essence for perfumes, copra and sisal are exported.

Ancient Phoenician traders were probably the first visitors to the Comoros Islands, but the first detailed knowledge of the area was gathered by Arab sailors. Arab dominion and culture were firmly established when the Portuguese, Dutch and French arrived in the 16th century. In 1843 a Malagasy ruler ceded the island of Mayotte to France; the other three principal islands of the archipelago - Anjouan, Moheli and Grand Comore - came under French protection in 1886. The islands were joined administratively with Madagascar in 1912. The Comoros became partially autonomous, with the status of a French overseas territory in 1946 and achieved complete internal autonomy in 1961. On Dec. 31, 1975, after 133 years of French association, the Comoros Islands became the independent Republic of the Comoros.

Mayotte retained the option of determining its future ties and in 1976 voted to remain French. Its present status is that of a French Territorial Collectivity. French coinage and currency also circulates there.

RULERS:
French to 1975

MONETARY SYSTEM:
1 Franc = 100 Centimes

FRENCH INFLUENCE

GOVERNMENT OF THE COMOROS

1920 ND EMERGENCY POSTAGE STAMP ISSUE

#A1-1C small adhesive postage stamps of Madagascar depicting Navigation and Commerce, Scott #32, 43, 44, and 46; Moheli, Scott #12 affixed to rectangular pressboard w/animals printed on the back (similar to the Madagascar stamps, Scott #A7)

#1   #1A

A1	0.05 Franc			
	ND (1920). Green adhesive stamp. Blue legend at bottom *MADAGASCAR ET DEPENDANCES*. Dog on back.		Reported Not Confirmed	
		GOOD	FINE	XF
1	0.50 Franc			
	ND (1920). Pink adhesive Stamp. Blue legend at bottom *MADAGASCAR ET DEPENDANCES*. Dog on back.	350.00	600.00	—
1A	0.50 Franc			
	ND (1920). Brown adhesive stamp. Red legend at bottom *MOHELI*. Dog on back.	350.00	600.00	—
1B	0.50 Franc			
	ND (1920). Dk. pink adhesive stamp. Blue legend at bottom *MADAGASCAR ET DEPENDANCES*. Zebu on back.	—	—	—
1C	1 Franc			
	ND (1920). Green adhesive stamp. Red legend at bottom *MADAGASCAR ET DEPENDANCES*. Dog on back.	—	—	—

REPUBLIC

BANQUE DE MADAGASCAR ET DES COMORES

1960 ND PROVISIONAL ISSUE

#2-6 additional red ovpt: *COMORES*.

#4-6 dated through 1952 have titles 'A', those dated 1955 or ND have titles 'B'.

2	50 Francs	VG	VF	UNC
	ND (1960-63). Brown and m/c. Woman w/hat at r. Man on back. Ovpt. on Madagascar #45.			
a.	Sign. titles: *LE CONTROLEUR GAL.* and *LE DIRECTEUR GAL.* ND (1960).	5.00	20.00	70.00
b.	Sign. titles: *LE DIRECTEUR GAL. ADJOINT* and *LE PRESIDENT DIRECTEUR GAL.* ND (1963). 2 sign varieties.	1.00	5.00	20.00

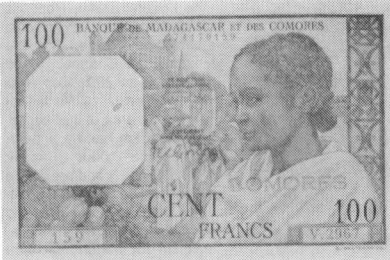

3 **100 FRANCS**
ND (1960-63). M/c. Woman at r., palace of the Qn. of Tananariva in background. Woman, boats and animals on back. Ovpt. on Madagascar #46.

		VG	VF	UNC
	a. Sign. titles: *LE CONTROLEUR GAL.* and *LE DIRECTEUR GAL.* ND (1960).	6.00	25.00	80.00
	b. Sign. titles: *LE DIRECTEUR GAL. ADJOINT* and *LE PRESIDENT DIRECTEUR GAL.* ND (1963).	1.00	5.00	18.50

4 **500 FRANCS**
ND (1960-63). M/c. Man w/fruit at ctr. Ovpt on Madagascar #47.

		VG	VF	UNC
	a. Sign. titles: *LE CONTROLEUR GAL* and *LE DIRECTEUR GAL.* - old date 30.6.1950; 9.10.1952 (1960).	30.00	100.00	325.00
	b. Sign. titles: *LE DIRECTEUR GAL. ADJOINT* and *LE PRESIDENT DIRECTEUR GAL.* ND (1963).	15.00	75.00	250.00

5 **1000 FRANCS**
ND (1960-63). M/c. Woman and man at l. ctr. Ox-cart on Back. Ovpt. on Madagascar #48.

		VG	VF	UNC
	a. Sign. titles: *LE CONTROLEUR GAL.* and *LE DIRECTEUR GAL.* - old date 1950-52; 9.10.1952 (1960).	45.00	125.00	425.00
	b. Sign. titles: *LE DIRECTEUR GAL. ADJOINT* and *LE PRESIDENT DIRECTEUR GAL.* ND (1963).	25.00	90.00	350.00

6 **5000 FRANCS**
ND (1960-63). M/c. Portr. Gallieni at upper l., young woman at r. Huts at l., woman w/baby at r. on back. Ovpt. on Madagascar #49.

		VG	VF	UNC
	a. Sign. titles: *LE CONTROLEUR GAL.* and *LE DIRECTEUR GAL.* - old date 30.6.1950 (1960).	175.00	425.00	875.00
	b. Sign. titles: *LE DIRECTEUR GAL. ADJOINT* and *LE PRESIDENT DIRECTEUR GAL.* ND (1963).	125.00	325.00	750.00

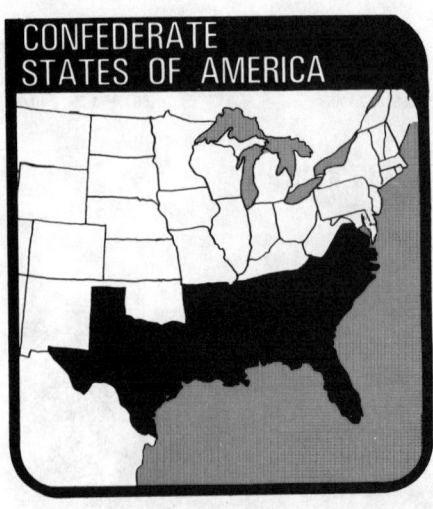

CONFEDERATE STATES OF AMERICA

The Confederate States of America (1861-1865) was a federal republic constituted by the 11 Southern states which seceded from the United States after the election of Abraham Lincoln as President. In the order of their secession, the 11 members of the Confederate States of America were South Carolina, Mississippi, Florida, Alabama, Georgia, Louisiana, Texas, Arkansas, North Carolina, Virginia and Tennessee.

The seceded states had left the Union separately and were in effect separate nations, each too small to withstand economic pressures or attack by the Union Army. On Feb. 4, 1861, delegations from South Carolina, Mississippi, Florida, Alabama, Georgia, and Louisiana - Texas arrived later - met in Montgomery, Alabama to organize a Southern nation dedicated to states' rights and the protection of slavery. A provisional government was formed and Jefferson Davis was elected President. The secession crisis precipitated the Civil War - officially known as the War of the Rebellion and, in the South, as the War Between the States - which ended in Union victory and the collapse of the Confederate States of America. The secession states were eventually readmitted to the Union.

To finance the war, both the Confederacy and its constituent states issued paper currency, the redemption of which is specifically forbidden by Section 4 of the 14th Amendment to the U.S. Constitution. WATERMARKS "NY" "TEN" "FIVE" "CSA" in Block letters "CSA" in Script letters "J. WHATMAN 1862" "HODGKINSON & CO. WOOKEY HOLE MILL" "CSA" in block letters with wavy borderline.

MONETARY SYSTEM
1 Dollar = 100 Cents

NOTE: *SL#* in the listings refer to *Confederate States Paper Money, 8th Edition* by Arlie R. Slabaugh.

CONFEDERATE STATES

CONFEDERATE STATES OF AMERICA

MONTGOMERY, ALABAMA BRANCH

1861 ISSUE
#1-4 Handwritten dates of May-June, 1861. Interest Bearing Notes. Printer: NBNC.

1 **50 DOLLARS**

	VG	VF	UNC
5.6.1861. Green and black. Blacks hoeing cotton at ctr. Plate letter A. 1,606 issued. *(SL #1)*.	2000.	5000.	8500.

2 **100 DOLLARS**

	VG	VF	UNC
5.6.1861. Green and black. Columbia at l., steam train depot scene at ctr. Plate letter A. 1,606 issued. *(SL #1)*.	2000.	5000.	8750.

3 **500 DOLLARS**

	VG	VF	UNC
5.6.1861. Green and black. Steam passenger train crossing vladuct, cattle below. Plate letter A. 607 issued. *(SL #3)*.	3500.	7500.	—

4	**1000 DOLLARS**	**VG**	**VF**	**UNC**
	5.6.1861. Green and black. Calhoun at lower l., Jackson at lower r. Plate letter A. 607 issued. *(SL #4).*	4000.	8000.	—

RICHMOND, VIRGINIA BRANCH

1861 (FIRST) ISSUE, AUG.-SEPT.

#5-6 usually have handwritten dates of Aug.-Sept. 1861. Interest Bearing Notes.

5	**50 DOLLARS**	**VG**	**VF**	**UNC**
	8.9.1861. Green and black. Justice at l., Pallas and Ceres seated on cotton bale at ctr., Washington at r. Plate letter B. Printer: Southern BNC. *(SL #5).* 5,798 issued.	225.00	450.00	900.00

6	**100 DOLLARS**	**VG**	**VF**	**UNC**
	8.9.1861. Green and black. Justice at lower l., steam passenger train at ctr., Minerva at r. Plate letter B. Printer: Southern BNC. *(SL #6).* 5,798 issued.	250.00	500.00	1000.

1861 (SECOND) ISSUE, JULY

7	**5 DOLLARS**	**VG**	**VF**	**UNC**
	25.7.1861. *FIVE* at l. and *Confederate States of America* in blue. Plate letters F-I. Back blue. Printer: J. Manouvrier. *(SL #7)*	350.00	1750.	5000.

8	**5 DOLLARS**	**VG**	**VF**	**UNC**
	25.7.1861. Sailor at lower l., Liberty seated above *5* w/eagle at ctr. Plate letters B; Bb. Printer: H & L. *(SL #8).*	500.00	2500.	—

9	**10 DOLLARS**	**VG**	**VF**	**UNC**
	25.7.1861. Woman at lower l., Liberty seated above shield w/flag and eagle at ctr. Plate letters A; B; C. Printer: H & L. *(SL #9).*	65.00	350.00	—

10	**20 DOLLARS**	**VG**	**VF**	**UNC**
	25.7.1861. Sailing ship at ctr. Plate letters B, C; Cc; Ccc; D. Printer: H & L. *(SL #10).*	28.50	75.00	150.00

11	**50 DOLLARS**	**VG**	**VF**	**UNC**
	25.7.1861. Tellus at l., Washington at ctr. Plate letters B; Bb; C. Printer: H & L. *(SL #11).*	35.00	85.00	175.00

12	**100 DOLLARS**	**VG**	**VF**	**UNC**
	25.7.1861. Washington at l., Ceres and Proserpine in flight at ctr. Plate letters B; C. Printer: H & L. *(SL #12).*	175.00	350.00	650.00

1861 (THIRD) ISSUE, SEPT.

NOTE: #13 was incorrectly dated for an 1862 issue.

13	**2 DOLLARS**	**VG**	**VF**	**UNC**
	2.9.1861. Benjamin at upper l., personification of the South striking down the Union w/a sword at top ctr. Series 1-10. Printer: B. Duncan (S.C.). *(SC #26).*	250.00	1750.	—

14 5 DOLLARS
2.9.1861. Black and red on red fibre paper. Minerva at l., Commerce, Agriculture, Justice, Liberty and Industry at upper ctr., Washington statue at r. Plate letters A; B; C. Printer: Southern BNC. *(SL #22).*

	VG	VF	UNC
	140.00	300.00	750.00

15 5 DOLLARS
2.9.1861. Black and orange. boy at lower l., blacksmith w/hammer, steam passenger train at lower r. Plate letters A; AA. Printer: Leggett, Keatinge & Ball. *(SL #31).*

	VG	VF	UNC
	225.00	600.00	—

16 5 DOLLARS
2.9.1861. Black w/blue-green or yellow-green ornamentation. C. G. Memminger at ctr., Minerva at r. above Roman numeral V. *(SL #32).*

	VG	VF	UNC
a. Printer: Leggett, Keatinge & Ball.	65.00	225.00	500.00
b. Printer: K & B(V.).	65.00	225.00	500.00

17 5 DOLLARS
2.9.1861. Black. C. G. Memminger at ctr., Minerva at r. *(SL #33).*

	VG	VF	UNC
a. Printer: K & B (V.).	35.00	100.00	250.00
b. W/o imprint.	35.00	100.00	250.00

18 5 DOLLARS
1.9.1861. Loading cotton at dockside at lower l., Indian Princess at r. Printer H & L. *(SL #14).*

	VG	VF	UNC
	3000.	8000.	

19 5 DOLLARS
2.9.1861. Sailor at lower l., Ceres seated on a bale of cotton at top ctr. Serial #9A-16A. W/o series, also *SECOND* and *THIRD SERIES*. *(SL #19).*

	VG	VF	UNC
a. Printer: H & L.	12.50	25.00	75.00
b. Printer: J. T. Paterson.	10.00	20.00	60.00
c. Printer: J. T. Paterson & C.	10.00	20.00	60.00

20 5 DOLLARS
2.9.1861. C. G. Memminger at lower l., sailor reclining by cotton bales at upper ctr., Justice standing w/Ceres kneeling at r. *(SL #27).*

	VG	VF	UNC
a. Plate letters A-H. Printer: B. Duncan (V.).	22.50	85.00	275.00
b. *SECOND SERIES,* serial #1-8. Printer: B. Duncan (S.C.)	20.00	60.00	300.00

21 10 DOLLARS
2.9.1861. Black and red. Thetis at upper l., Indian family at top ctr., Indian maiden at upper r. Plate letters A; B; C. Printer: Southern BNC. *(SL #23).*

	VG	VF	UNC
	85.00	215.00	550.00

22 10 DOLLARS
2.9.1861. Black and orange-red. J.E. Ward at lower l., horse cart loaded w/cotton at ctr., man carrying sugar cane at lower r. Plate letters, A, A1. Printer: Leggett, Keatinge & Ball. *(SL #34).*

	VG	VF	UNC
	225.00	575.00	—

23 10 DOLLARS
2.9.1861. Black and orange-red. R. M. T. Hunter at lower l., child at lower r. Plate letters: H-K. *(SL #35).*

	VG	VF	UNC
a. Printer: Leggett, Keatinge & Ball.	45.00	125.00	350.00
b. Printer: K & B.	45.00	125.00	350.00

24 10 DOLLARS
2.9.1861. R. M. T. Hunter at lower l., Hope w/anchor at lower ctr., C. G. Memminger at lower r. Plate letters W-Z. Printer: K & B. *(SL #36).*

	VG	VF	UNC
	35.00	90.00	325.00

25 10 DOLLARS
2.9.1861. Red or orange protector in unpt. R. M. T. *X - X* protector in unpt. R. M. T. Hunter at lower l., Hope w/anchor at lower ctr., C. G. Memminger at lower r. Plate letters W-Z. Printer: K & B. *(SL #37).*

	VG	VF	UNC
	30.00	75.00	250.00

26	**10 DOLLARS**	VG	VF	UNC
	2.9.1861. Liberty seated by shield and eagle at upper l., train at r. Printer: H & L (litho). *(SL #15).*			
	a. Plate letter Ab.	2250.	6500.	—
	b. Plate letters A9-A16.	—	Rare	—

27	**10 DOLLARS**	VG	VF	UNC
	2.9.1861. Ceres and Commerce seated by an urn at upper l., train at r. Plate letters A9-A16. *(SL #20).*			
	a. Printer: J. T. Paterson.	25.00	50.00	235.00
	b. Printer: H & L.	27.50	55.00	250.00

28	**10 DOLLARS**	VG	VF	UNC
	2.9.1861. Black picking cotton at top ctr. Plate letters A-H. Printer: B. Duncan (V.). *(SL #28).*	80.00	250.00	800.00

29	**10 DOLLARS**	VG	VF	UNC
	2.9.1861. R. M. T. Hunter at l., Gen. F. Marion's "Sweet Potato Dinner" scene at ctr., Minerva standing at r. *FIRST - FOURTH SERIES.* *(SL #29).*			
	a. Printer: B. Duncan (S.C.).	20.00	50.00	125.00
	b. W/o imprint.	20.00	50.00	125.00

30	**20 DOLLARS**	VG	VF	UNC
	2.9.1861. Black w/green ornamentation. Liberty at l., Ceres seated between Commerce and Navigation at upper r. ctr. Serial letter A. Printer: H & L. *(SL #16).*	75.00	175.00	350.00

31	**20 DOLLARS**	VG	VF	UNC
	2.9.1861. Sailor leaning on capstan at lower l., sailing ship at upper ctr. *(SL #21).*			
	a. Printer: H & L.	25.00	50.00	140.00
	b. Printer: J. T. Paterson.	15.00	30.00	60.00

32	**20 DOLLARS**	VG	VF	UNC
	2.9.1861. Minerva reclining w/shield at lower l., Navigation kneeling at top ctr., blacksmith by anvil at lower r. Plate letter A. Printer: Southern BNC. *(SL #24).*	425.00	1000.	2750.

33	**20 DOLLARS**	VG	VF	UNC
	2.9.1861. V. Pres. A. H. Stevens at l., Industry seated between Cupid and beehive at ctr., Navigation at r. Plate #1-10. *FIRST-THIRD SERIES.* Printer: B. Duncan (V or SC). *(SL #30).*	15.00	30.00	85.00

34	**20 DOLLARS**	VG	VF	UNC
	2.9.1861. A. H. Stephens at ctr. between industrial and agricultural goods. Plate letters W-Z. Printer: K & B (S.C.) *(SL #38).*	60.00	175.00	350.00

35	**50 DOLLARS**	VG	VF	UNC
	2.9.1861. 2 sailors at lower lower l., Moneta seated with chest at upper ctr. Various serial letters and #'s. Printer: H & L. *(SL #17).*	20.00	35.00	60.00

36	**50 DOLLARS**	VG	VF	UNC
	2.9.1861. Hope w/anchor at lower l., steam passenger train at top ctr., Justice at r. Plate letter A. Printer: Southern BNC. *(SL #25)*	800.00	2000.	—

37	**50 DOLLARS**	VG	VF	UNC
	2.9.1861. Black and green. Pres. J. Davis at ctr. W/o series, also *SECOND SERIES.* Plate letters WA-ZA. Printer: K & B (V.). *(SL #39).*	40.00	150.00	250.00

38 **100 DOLLARS**

	VG	VF	UNC
2.9.1861. Sailor w/anchor at lower l., slaves loading cotton on wagon at upper ctr. Various serial letters and #'s. Printer: H & L. *(SL #18).*	25.00	40.00	75.00

1862 (FOURTH) ISSUE, JUNE

NOTE: #46-48 incorrectly dated for an 1861 Issue.

#47-48 printer: K. & B. (S.C.) (Not regularly issued.)

39 **1 DOLLAR**

	VG	VF	UNC
2.6.1862. Liberty standing at l., steam powered sailing ships at top ctr. r., L. H. Pickens at lower r., *FIRST-THIRD SERIES.* Printer: B. Duncan (S.C.). *(SL #43).*	20.00	60.00	120.00

40 **1 DOLLAR**

	VG	VF	UNC
2.6.1862. Green *1* and *ONE* protector unpt. Liberty standing at l., steam powered sailing ships at top ctr. r., L. H. Pickens at lower r. *FIRST, SECOND SERIES.* Printer: B. DUNCAN (S.C.). *(SL #44).*	35.00	175.00	400.00

41 **2 DOLLARS**

	VG	VF	UNC
2.6.1862. Benjamin at upper l., personification of the South striking down the Union w/a sword at top ctr. *FIRST-THIRD SERIES.* Printer: B. Duncan (S.C.). *(SL #45).*	20.00	45.00	125.00

42 **2 DOLLARS**

	VG	VF	UNC
2.6.1862. Green *2* and *TWO* protector unpt. Benjamin at upper l., personification of the South striking down the Union w/a sword at top ctr. *SECOND SERIES.* Printer: B. Duncan. (S.C.). *(SL #46).*	35.00	175.00	950.00

46 **10 DOLLARS**

	VG	VF	UNC
2.9.1862. Ceres reclining on cotton bales at top ctr. w/sailing ship in background, R. M. T. Hunger at lower r. Printer: H. & L. (w/o imprint). *(SL #47).*			
a. Terms of redemption read: *Six Months after...*	22.00	40.00	150.00
b. Error: terms of redemption read: *Six Months after...*	22.00	40.00	150.00

47 **10 DOLLARS**

	VG	VF	UNC
2.9.1862. Ceres holding sheaf of wheat at top ctr., R. M. T. Hunter at lower r. *(SL #48).*	2000.	3500.	—

48 **20 DOLLARS**

	VG	VF	UNC
2.9.1862. Liberty seated w/shield on bale of cotton top ctr., R. M. T. Hunter at lower r. *(SL #49).*	1800.	3000.	—

43 **100 DOLLARS**

	VG	VF	UNC
1862. Milkmaid at lower l., steam passenger train at top ctr. w/straight steam blowing out of locomotive boiler. W/ or w/o various interest paid markings on back. *(SL #40).*			
a. Plate letters A, Ab-Ah. Printer: H & L. 5.5.1862-5.9.1862.	30.00	55.00	100.00
b. Plate letters Aa-Ah. Printer: J. T. Paterson. 8.4.1862; May, 1862.	18.50	32.50	60.00

44 **100 DOLLARS**

	VG	VF	UNC
1862-63. Milkmaid at lower l., steam passenger train at top ctr. w/diffused steam blowing out of locomotive boiler. Plate letters Aa-Ah. W/ or w/o various interest paid markings on back. Printer: J. T. Patterson & C. *(SL #41).*	18.50	32.50	60.00

45 **100 DOLLARS**

	VG	VF	UNC
26.8.1862. Red-orange *HUNDRED* ovpt. Calhoun at lower l., blacks hoeing cotton at top ctr., Columbia at r. W/ or w/o various interest paid markings on back. Printer: K & B (S.C.). H. *(SL #42).*	18.50	32.50	60.00

1862 (FIFTH) ISSUE, DEC.

49 1 DOLLAR
2.12.1862. C. C. Clay at top ctr. *(SL #50).*

	VG	VF	UNC
a. *FIRST* or *SECOND* SERIES Printer: K & B. (S.C.).	30.00	65.00	135.00
b. W/o Series. Printer: B. Duncan.	30.00	65.00	135.00

50 2 DOLLARS
2.12.1862. J.P. Benjamin at r. *(SL #51).*

	VG	VF	UNC
a. *FIRST* or *SECOND SERIES.* Printer: K & B (S.C.).	25.00	60.00	120.00
b. W/o series. Printer: J. T. Paterson & C.	25.00	60.00	120.00

51 5 DOLLARS
2.12.1862. Capital at Richmond, Va. at top ctr., C. G. Memminger at lower r. Ornate blue back. *(SL #52).*

	VG	VF	UNC
a. *FIRST* or *SECOND SERIES*, w/o imprint.	15.00	30.00	60.00
b. *FIRST* or *SECOND SERIES.* Printer: J. T. Paterson & C.	40.00	90.00	300.00
c. *FIRST-THIRD SERIES*, lithog'd by J. T. Paterson & C.	15.00	30.00	60.00
d. *SECOND SERIES.* Printer: E & C.	15.00	30.00	60.00
e. *SECOND SERIES*, Printer: E & C. Lithog'd by J. T. Paterson & C.	17.50	35.00	85.00
f. *SECOND SERIES*, Printers: E & C. and J. T. Paterson & C.	17.50	35.00	75.00

52 10 DOLLARS
2.12.1862. Capital at Columbia, S.C., at top ctr., R. M. T. Hunter at lower r. Ornate blue back. *(SL #53).*

	VG	VF	UNC
a. W/o series. Printer: B. Duncan, K & B (S.C.).	35.00	75.00	175.00
b. *SECOND, THIRD* or *FOURTH SERIES*, Printer: B. Duncan.	15.00	30.00	60.00
c. W/o series, also *THIRD SERIES* Printer: E & C.	15.00	30.00	60.00
d. *THIRD* or *FOURTH SERIES.* Printer: E & C, B. Duncan.	15.00	30.00	60.00

53 20 DOLLARS
2.12.1862. Capital at Nashville, Tenn. at top ctr., A. H. Stephens at lower r. Ornate blue back. *(SL #54).*

	VG	VF	UNC
a. *FIRST SERIES.* Printer: J. T. Paterson & C.	25.00	60.00	150.00
b. *FIRST SERIES.* Printer: J. T. Paterson & C.	25.00	60.00	150.00
c. *FIRST SERIES.* w/o imprint.	25.00	30.00	150.00
d. *FIRST SERIES.* Printer: B. Duncan.	27.50	65.00	160.00
e. *FIRST SERIES.* Printer: B. Duncan.	30.00	70.00	185.00

54 50 DOLLARS
2.12.1862. Pres. J. Davis at ctr. Ornate green back. Engravers' names above or below *FUNDABLE...* at l. *(SL #55).*

	VG	VF	UNC
a. Printer: K & B (V).	35.00	100.00	225.00
b. Printer: K & B (S.C.).	35.00	100.00	225.00

55 100 DOLLARS
2.12.1862. 2 soldiers at lower l., L. H. Pickens at ctr., G. W. Randolph at lower r. W/o series; also *SECOND SERIES*. Printer: K & B (S.C.). *(SL #56).*

	VG	VF	UNC
	45.00	75.00	175.00

1863 (SIXTH) ISSUE, APRIL

56 50 CENTS
6.4.1863. Pink paper. Pres. J. Davis at top ctr. Printed sign. *FIRST* or *SECOND SERIES*. Printer: Archer & Daly. *(SL #57).*

	VG	VF	UNC
	7.50	12.00	30.00

57 1 DOLLAR
6.4.1863. C. C. Clay at top ctr. *(SL #58).*

	VG	VF	UNC
a. *FIRST* or *SECOND SERIES.* Printer: K & B. (S.C.)	20.00	40.00	80.00
b. W/o series, also *SECOND SERIES.* Printer: E & C. (litho)	22.00	45.00	90.00

58 2 DOLLARS
6.4.1863. Pink paper. J. P. Benjamin at r. *(SL #59).*

	VG	VF	UNC
a. *FIRST* or *SECOND SERIES.* Printer: K & B. (S.C.).	25.00	75.00	190.00
b. W/o series, also *SECOND SERIES.* Printer: E & C (litho) and K & B. (S.C.)	27.00	82.00	210.00

59 **5 DOLLARS**
6.4.1863. Capital at Richmond, Va. at top ctr., C. G. Memminger at lower r. Date ovpt. from April, 1863 - Feb. 1864. Ornate blue back. *(SL #60).*

		VG	VF	UNC
a.	*SECOND-THIRD SERIES.* Printer: K & B. (S.C.)	20.00	40.00	75.00
b.	*FIRST-THIRD SERIES.* Printer: K & B and J. T. Paterson & C.	11.50	22.50	50.00
c.	W/o series, *THIRD SERIES.* Printer: K & B, E & C.	11.50	22.50	50.00
d.	W/o series, *FIRST SERIES.* Printer: K & B, J. T. Paterson & C., E & C.	40.00	90.00	175.00

60 **10 DOLLARS**
6.4.1863. Capital at Columbia, S.C. at top ctr., R. M. T. Hunter at lower r. Date ovpt. from April, 1863 - Feb. 1864. Ornate blue back. *(SL #61).*

		VG	VF	UNC
a.	W/o series, *FIRST* and *FIFTH SERIES.* Printer: K & B (S.C.), E & C.	10.00	20.00	50.00
b.	*FIRST, SECOND, FIFTH SERIES.* Printer: K & B, B. Duncan.	30.00	60.00	100.00
c.	*SECOND SERIES.* Printer: K & B, J. T. Paterson & C.	40.00	75.00	150.00

61 **20 DOLLARS**
6.4.1863. Capital at Nashville, Tenn. at top ctr., A. H. Stephens at lower r. Date ovpt. from April - Oct. 1863. Ornate blue back. *((SL #62).*

		VG	VF	UNC
a.	*FIRST SERIES.* Printer: K & B. (S.C.)	15.00	30.00	60.00
b.	W/o series, *FIRST-THIRD SERIES.* Printer: K & B, E & C.	15.00	30.00	60.00
c.	*FIRST SERIES.* Printer: K & B, J. T. Paterson & C.	30.00	60.00	120.00

62 **50 DOLLARS**
6.4.1863. Pres. J. Davis at ctr. Date ovpt. from April, 1863 - Feb., 1864. Ornate green back. Plate letters WA-ZA. W/o series, also *FIRST SERIES.* Imprint above or below *FUNDABLE...* at l.

		VG	VF	UNC
a.	Printer: K & B (Va.).	35.00	85.00	140.00
b.	Printer: K & B (S.C.).	35.00	85.00	140.00

63 **100 DOLLARS**
6.4.1863. 2 soldiers at l. L. H. Pickens at ctr., G. W. Randolph at lower r. Date ovpt. from May, 1863 - Jan., 1864. W/o series, also *FIRST SERIES.* Printer: K & B (S.C.).

VG	VF	UNC
25.00	75.00	175.00

1864 (SEVENTH) ISSUE, FEB.

64 **50 CENTS**
17.2.1864. Pink paper. President J. Davis at top ctr. Printed sign. Printer: Archer & Halpin. *(SL #65).*

		VG	VF	UNC
a.	*FIRST SERIES.*	4.00	10.00	27.50
b.	*SECOND SERIES.*	5.00	12.50	27.50

65 **1 DOLLAR**
17.2.1864. Red unpt. C. C. Clay at top ctr. *(SL #66).*

		VG	VF	UNC
a.	*ENGRAVED BY* K & B. (S.C.)	22.00	40.00	125.00
b.	*ENGRAVED & PRINTED BY* K & B. (S.C.)	22.00	40.00	125.00
c.	*ENGRAVED BY* K & B. (S.C.) & *LITHOG'D BY* E & C.	22.00	40.00	125.00

66 **2 DOLLARS**
17.2.1864. Red unpt. Pink J. P. Benjamin at r. *(SL #67).*

		VG	VF	UNC
a.	*ENGRAVED BY* K & B. (S.C.)	12.00	32.50	95.00
b.	*ENGRAVED & PRINTED BY* K & B. (S.C.).	18.00	40.00	110.00
c.	*ENGRAVED BY* K & B. (S.C.) *LITHOG'D BY* E & C.	18.00	40.00	110.00

67 **5 DOLLARS**
17.2.1864. Red unpt. Capital at Richmond, Va. at top ctr., C. G. Memminger at lower r. Date ovpt. from April 1863 - Feb., 1864. Blue *FIVE* on back. W/o series, also *SERIES 1-7.* Printer: K & B. (S.C.) *(SL #68).*

VG	VF	UNC
11.50	22.50	30.00

68 **10 DOLLARS**
17.2.1864. Red unpt. Artillery horseman pulling cannon at upper ctr. R. M. T. Hunter at lower r. Blue *TEN* on back. W/o series, also *FIRST-TENTH SERIES.* Printer: K & B. (S.C.) *(SL #69).*

VG	VF	UNC
10.00	20.00	28.00

69	**20 DOLLARS**	**VG**	**VF**	**UNC**
	17.2.1864. Red unpt. Capital at Nashville, Tenn. at top ctr., A. H. Stephens at lower r. Date ovpt. from April - Oct., 1863. Blue *TWENTY* on back. W/o series, also *SERIES 1-5,*also *VI-XI.* Printer: K & B. (S.C.) (*SL #70*).	11.50	22.50	30.00

70	**50 DOLLARS**			
	17.2.1864. Red unpt. Pres. J. Davis at ctr. Date ovpt. from Apr., 1863 - Feb., 1864. Blue *FIFTY* on back. W/o series, also *FIRST - FOURTH SERIES.* (*SL #71*).	20.00	35.00	65.00

71	**100 DOLLARS**	**VG**	**VF**	**UNC**
	17.2.1864. Red unpt. 2 soldiers at l. L. H. Pickens at ctr., G. W. Randolph at lower r. Date ovpt. from May, 1863 - Jan., 1864. Blue *HUNDRED* on back. W/o series, also *SERIES I, II.* (*SL #72*).	20.00	35.00	80.00

72	**100 DOLLARS**			
	17.2.1864. Reduced size. 2 soldiers at l. L. H. Pickens at ctr., G. W. Randolph at lower r. Plate letter D. "Havana counterfeit". (*SL #-*).	18.00	30.00	60.00

73	**500 DOLLARS**	**VG**	**VF**	**UNC**
	17.2.1864. Red unpt. Confederate seal w/equestrian statue of G. Washington below Confederate flag at l., Gen. T. J. "Stonewall" Jackson at lower r. (*SL #73*).	150.00	275.00	450.00

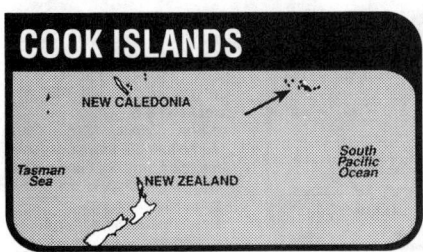

COOK ISLANDS

Cook Islands, a political dependency of New Zealand consisting of 15 islands located in the South Pacific Ocean about 2,000 miles (3,218 km.) northeast of New Zealand, has an area of 93 sq. mi. (234 sq. km.) and a population of 16,900. Capital: Avarua. The United States claims the islands of Danger, Manahiki, Penrhyn and Rakahanga atolls. Citrus and canned fruits and juices, copra, clothing, jewelry and mother- of-pearl shell are exported.

The islands were first sighted by Spanish navigator Alvaro de Mendada in 1595. Portuguese navigator Pedro Fernandes de Quieros landed on Rakahanga in 1606. English navigator Capt. James Cook sailed to the islands on three occasions: 1773, 1774 and 1777. He named them Hervey Islands, in honor of Augustus John Hervey, a lord of the Admiralty. The islands were declared a British protectorate in 1888, and were annexed to New Zealand in 1901. They were granted internal self-government in 1965. New Zealand provides an annual subsidy and retains responsibility for defense and foreign affairs.

As a territory of New Zealand, the Cook Islands are considered to be within the Commonwealth of Nations.

RULERS:
New Zealand, 1901-

MONETARY SYSTEM:
1 Shilling = 12 Pence
1 Pound = 20 Shillings, to 1967
1 Dollar = 100 Cents, 1967-

NOTE: In June 1995 the Government of the Cook Islands began redeeming all 10, 20 and 50 dollar notes in exchange for New Zealand currency while all coinage and their 3 dollar notes will remain in circulation.

NEW ZEALAND INFLUENCE

GOVERNMENT OF THE COOK ISLANDS

1894 ISSUE
#1-2 crossed flags of Cook Islands at top ctr.

1	**2 SHILLINGS**	**GOOD**	**FINE**	**XF**
	7.8.1894. Blue on pink unpt. (Not issued).	—	—	2750.

2	**4 SHILLINGS**	**GOOD**	**FINE**	**XF**
	7.8.1894. Blue on green and orange unpt. (Not issued).	—	—	2750.

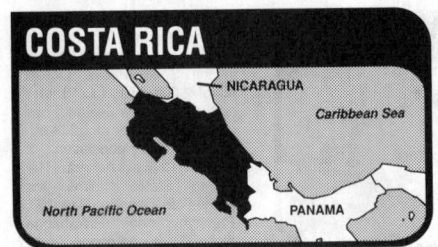

The Republic of Costa Rica, located in southern Central America between Nicaragua and Panama, has an area of 19,575 sq. mi. (50,700 sq. km.) and a population of 3.03 million. Capital: San Jose. Agriculture predominates; coffee, bananas, beef and sugar contribute heavily to the country's export earnings.

Costa Rica was discovered by Christopher Columbus in 1502, during his last voyage to the new world, and was a colony of Spain from 1522 until independence in 1821. Columbus named the territory Nueva Cartago; the name Costa Rica wasn't generally employed until 1540. Bartholomew Columbus attempted to found the first settlement but was driven off by Indian attacks and the country wasn't pacified until 1530. Costa Rica was absorbed for two years (1821-23) into the Mexican Empire of Agustin de Iturbide. From 1823 to 1848 it was a constituent state of the Central American Republic (q.v.). It was established as a republic in 1848. Today, Costa Rica remains a model of orderly democracy in Latin America.

MONETARY SYSTEM:
1 Peso = 100 Centavos to 1896
1 Colon = 100 Centavos, 1896-

NOTE: Certain listings encompassing issues circulated by various bank and regional authorities are contained in Volume 1.

REPUBLIC

REPUBLICA DE COSTA RICA

1865-71 ISSUE

#101-105 uniface. Printer: BWC. NOTE: A number of issues earlier than 1865 are reported but not confirmed.

		GOOD	FINE	XF
101	**1 PESO**			
	2.1.1865. Black on green unpt. Arms at l., Mercury w/bales at r.			
	a. W/o circular stampings on back.	100.00	350.00	700.00
	b. Circular stampings on back: *EMISION DE GUERRA* w/arms arms at ctr. em-bossed at l. *SECRETARIA DE HACIENDA Y COMERCIO.* stamped w/arms at ctr. r.	100.00	350.00	—

		GOOD	FINE	XF
102	**2 PESOS**			
	27.3.1871. Black on brown unpt. Arms at l., portr. young woman at r. W/stampings as #101b above on back.	150.00	400.00	—

		GOOD	FINE	XF
103	**5 PESOS**			
	2.1.1865. Black on reddish tan unpt. Arms at l., sailing boat at r. W/o stampings on back.	200.00	500.00	—
104	**10 PESOS**			
	2.1.1865. Black on green unpt. Arms at l., vignette at r.	—	—	—
105	**25 PESOS**			
	2.1.1865. Black on blue unpt. Arms at l., oxen and cart at r.	—	—	—
106	**50 PESOS**			
	2.1.1865. Black on orange unpt. Arms at l., standing woman w/fruit basket at r.	—	—	—
107	**50 PESOS**			
	2.1.1865. Black on olive unpt. Arms at l., bldg. at r.	—	—	—

1877 ISSUE

		GOOD	FINE	XF
111	**1 PESO**			
	4.4.1877. Black and red. Arms at lower ctr. Uniface.	—	Rare	—

1880's ISSUE

#120-124 printer: ABNC.

		GOOD	FINE	XF
120	**5 PESOS**			
	ND. Black on red-orange unpt. Standing woman at l., arms at lower ctr., Raphael's Angel at r. Back: red-orange. Specimen.	—	Unc	350.00

		GOOD	FINE	XF
121	**10 PESOS**			
	ND (c.1887-89). Black on green unpt. Seated woman w/globe at l., arms at ctr., seated woman w/plants at r.			
	a. Circular black stamp: *JEFATURA DE SECCION DEL SELLO NACIONAL 26 DIC 89*, and hand sign. Back: green; flowers.	—	Rare	—
	p. W/o circular black stamp or handsign.	—	Unc	350.00

		GOOD	FINE	XF
122	**25 PESOS**			
	ND. Black on orange unpt. arms at l., Prospect Pt., Niagara Falls and Canadian Horseshoe Falls at ctr., military bust at r. Back: brown.			
	a. Issued note, text like #121a.	—	Rare	—
	p1. Brown unpt. Uniface proof.	—	Unc	350.00
	p2. Blue unpt. Uniface proof.	—	Unc	350.00

		GOOD	FINE	XF
123	**50 PESOS**			
	ND (ca.1887-89). Black on green unpt. Bldg. at l., military bust at ctr., arms at lower r.			
	a. Circular black hand stamp and hand sign. on face like #121. Back: olive.	—	Rare	—
	p. W/o stamping. Proof.	—	Unc	350.00
124	**100 PESOS**			
	14.11.1888. Black on lt. orang e unpt. Bldg. at l., head at c tr., arms at r. Back orange-br own. Specimen.	—	—	450.00

1897 GOLD CERTIFICATE ISSUE
#131-135 arms at ctr. on back. Printer: ABNC.

131	5 COLONES	GOOD	FINE	XF
	1.1.1897. Black on yellow and green unpt. Portr. C. Columbus at ctr. Back: blue-green. Series A. Proof.	—	—	—
132	10 COLONES			
	1.1.1897. Black on green and yellow unpt. Portr. C. Columbus at ctr. Back: green. Series B. Proof.	—	—	—
133	25 COLONES			
	1.1.1897. Black on blue and yellow unpt. Portr. C. Columbus at ctr. Back: blue. Series C. Proof.	—	—	—
134	50 COLONES			
	1.1.1897. Black on orange and yellow unpt. Portr. C. Columbus at l., seated Agriculture at ctr. Back: orange. Series D. Proof.	—	—	—
135	100 COLONES			
	yellow unpt. Portr. C. 1.1.1897. Black on brown and yellow unpt. Portr. C. Columbus at l., allegorical woman w/globe and lute at ctr. Back: brown. Sereis E. Proof.	—	—	—

1902-10 SILVER CERTIFICATE ISSUE
A. Payable in 25 and 50 Centimos coins. Printer: ABNC.

141	1 COLON	GOOD	FINE	XF
	5.4.1902 (filled in by hand). Black on green and yellow unpt., uniface. Portr. C. Columbus at l., arms w/flags at r. Black circular stamping of arms at ctr. on back.	75.00	350.00	—

142	1 COLON	GOOD	FINE	XF
	1.10.1905; 1.7.1906. Like #141. Back dk. green w/black circular stamping of arms at l.	15.00	50.00	175.00

143	1 COLON	GOOD	FINE	XF
	23.5.1910-1.10.1914. Like #142 but arms w/o flags. Black stamping of arms w/o circle at r. on back.	6.00	40.00	125.00
144	2 COLONES			
	190(2). Black on yellow and and orange unpt. Face like #141. Black circular stamping of arms on back. Uniface.	100.00	350.00	—
145	2 COLONES			
	1.10.1905; 1.7.1906. Black on yellow and orange unpt. Like #142. Back red-orange.	25.00	75.00	250.00
146	2 COLONES			
	1.11.1910; 1.12.1912; 1.10.1914. Like #143.	12.50	45.00	125.00

1917 SILVER CERTIFICATE ISSUE
B. Notes backed by coined silver. Printer: ABNC.

147	50 CENTIMOS	GOOD	FINE	XF
	11.10.1917-21.11.1921. Black on olive unpt. Portr. C. Columbus at ctr. Back: olive-brown, w/arms. Black stamped arms at r.	3.00	15.00	40.00

148	1 COLON	GOOD	FINE	XF
	1.10.1917; 24.10.1917; 5.6.1918; 3.7.1918. Similar to #143 but w/diff. text below heading and diff. sign. titles.	6.00	25.00	75.00

149	2 COLONES	GOOD	FINE	XF
	2.2.1917; 22.9.1917; 5.11.1917. Similar to #146 but w/changes as #148.	50.00	200.00	—

150	50 COLONES	GOOD	FINE	XF
	ND (1917). Black on brown and m/c unpt. Portr. C. Columbus at ctr. Back: brown; arms at ctr. Proof.			
150A	100 COLONES			
	ND (1917). Black on blue and m/c unpt. Similar to #150. Back: blue; arms at ctr. Specimen			

1918-20 PROVISIONAL ISSUES

151	2 COLONES			
	17.8.1918; 1.10.1918. Red ovpt: *LEY NO. 3 BILLETE DE PLATA 23 JUNIO 1917* on face of #146. Red sign. and date.	15.00	50.00	125.00

152	2 COLONES	GOOD	FINE	XF
	11.8.1920. Black ovpt: Aunque la leyenda...... *1917* on back of #146 in 5 lines. Black sign. and date.	15.00	50.00	125.00

BANCO INTERNACIONAL DE COSTA RICA

SERIES A
#162 the illustration is of a counterfeit note.

		Good	Fine	XF
156	**25 CENTIMOS**			
	9.10.1918-25.7.1919. Dk. green. Portr. Liberty at l.	2.50	15.00	50.00

		Good	Fine	XF
157	**50 CENTIMOS**			
	18.1.1918-24.10.1921. Black on brown unpt. Portr. woman at ctr. Back: brown.	4.00	20.00	65.00

		Good	Fine	XF
158	**1 COLON**			
	1918-35. Black on m/c unpt. Seated woman at ctr. Back: blue; Liberty head.			
	a. 18.1.1918; 9.10.1918; 21.10.1918.	5.00	25.00	65.00
	b. 17.11.1922; 18.4.1923.	4.00	20.00	55.00
	c. 27.9.1929; 12.4.1935-9.10.1935.	3.00	17.50	50.00

		Good	Fine	XF
159	**2 COLONES**			
	1918-31. Black on m/c unpt. Reclining Liberty w/lion and book at ctr. Back: olive; Liberty head.			
	a. 18.1.1918; 28.6.1919.	25.00	75.00	200.00
	b. 24.5.1923-8.7.1931.	20.00	60.00	175.00

		Good	Fine	XF
160	**5 COLONES**			
	1.11.1914. Black. Indian girl w/pineapple basket at l., banana tree at r. Back: orange; lg. V5.	35.00	115.00	375.00

		Good	Fine	XF
161	**10 COLONES**			
	1.11.1914. Black. 5 coffee bean pickers at ctr. Back: brown.	45.00	225.00	475.00

		Good	Fine	XF
162	**20 COLONES**			
	1.11.1914. Black. Draped woman w/ship's wheel at r. Back: olive-green.	—	Rare	—
163	**50 COLONES**			
	1.11.1914. Black. Woman playing mandolin at ctr. Back: blue-black.	—	Rare	—

		Good	Fine	XF
164	**100 COLONES**			
	1.11.1914. Black. Seated feamale artist at l. Back: green.	75.00	200.00	450.00

SERIES B - PROVISIONAL ISSUE (1918)

		Good	Fine	XF
165	**50 CENTIMOS**			
	12.4.1935. Like #147. Red ovpt: *BANCO INTERNACIONAL DE COSTA RICA/AUNQUE LA LEYENDA 1935* on back in 7 lines. 2 red sign. below. Sign. titles: *EL SECRETARIO DE HACIENDA* and *EL DIRECTOR DEL BANCO* ovpt. on face.	4.00	25.00	70.00

1916-35 ISSUES
#168-170 printer: ABNC.

		Good	Fine	XF
166	**1 COLON**			
	9.10.1935. Green on m/c unpt. Like #158. Back brown. Printer: ABNC.	5.00	30.00	85.00

		Good	Fine	XF
167	**2 COLONES**			
	20.1.1932-6.10.1936. Brown on red, blue and green unpt. Portr. Mona Lisa at ctr. Back: black; ox-cart. Printer W&S.	12.50	60.00	225.00

		Good	Fine	XF
168	**5 COLONES**			
	1.12.1916. Black on m/c unpt. Portr. Pres. A. Gonzalez Flores at ctr. Back: blue-gray.	35.00	150.00	—

			GOOD	FINE	XF
169	**10 COLONES**				
	1.12.1916; 9.10.1918. Black on m/c unpt. Portr. W. J. Field Spencer first director of the Banco, at ctr. Back: orange.		50.00	185.00	—

			GOOD	FINE	XF
169A	**20 COLONES**				
	1.12.1916. Deep blue on m/c unpt. Liberty seated w/sword and shield at ctr. French Marianne at ctr. on back. Series B. Printer: ABNC.				
	a. Issued note w/date.		—	—	—
	s. Black on blue unpt. Back: green. ND. Specimen.		—	—	—
170A	**50 COLONES**				
	1.3.1916. Black. Seated woman at ctr.		Reported Not Confirmed		
170B	**100 COLONES**				
	ND. Like #164. (Not issued).		Reported Not Confirmed		

1918-19 PROVISIONAL ISSUE

#171 and 172 black ovpt: *Acuerdo No. 225/de 9 de Octubre de 1918.*

			GOOD	FINE	XF
171	**5 COLONES**				
	9.10.1918 (-old date 1.12.1916). Ovpt. at ctr. on back of #168.		45.00	150.00	400.00
172	**10 COLONES**				
	9.10.1918 (-old date 1.12.1916). Ovpt. at ctr. on back of #169.		35.00	125.00	325.00

SERIES C

#173-178 printer: ABNC.

			GOOD	FINE	XF
173	**50 CENTIMOS**				
	21.6.1935; 21.7.1935; 1.8.19.5. Blue on tan unpt. Portr. woman at ctr. Back: green. Like #157.		5.00	17.50	60.00

			GOOD	FINE	XF
174	**5 COLONES**				
	1919-30. Dk. blue on m/c unpt. Indian girl w/pineapple basket at l., banana tree at r. Like #160. Back: dk. brown.				
	a. 4.1.1919; 28.6.1919.		15.00	65.00	225.00
	b. 2.11.1926-22.12.1930.		10.00	50.00	200.00

			GOOD	FINE	XF
175	**10 COLONES**				
	1919-32. Blue on m/c unpt. Like #161. Back olive-brown.				
	a. Date at lower r. 4.1.1919.		25.00	85.00	250.00
	b. Date at lower ctr. 13.9.1927 -20.1.1932		17.50	60.00	200.00

			GOOD	FINE	XF
176	**20 COLONES**				
	1919-36. Dk. blue on m/c unpt. People cutting sugar cane at ctr. Back: orange.				
	a. 4.1.1919.		25.00	100.00	325.00
	b. Sign. title: *EL SUBDIRECTOR* ovpt. at r. 31.7.1933.		22.50	85.00	250.00
	c. W/o sign. title changes. 10.6.1936; 3.7.1936.		20.00	70.00	200.00
177	**50 COLONES**				
	1919-32. Dk. blue on m/c unpt. Woman playing mandolin at ctr. Like #163. Back: green.				
	a. 4.1.1919.		35.00	150.00	425.00
	b. 23.6.1927-11.2.1932.		25.00	100.00	350.00

			GOOD	FINE	XF
178	**100 COLONES**				
	1919-32. Dk. blue on m/c ovpt. Seated female artist at l. Like #164. Back: blue-black.				
	a. 4.1.1919-24.5.1923.		30.00	100.00	325.00
	b. 22.4.1930-11.2.1932.		25.00	85.00	225.00
	x. Error date: 14.12.2931.		50.00	150.00	—

SERIES D

179   10 COLONES

	Good	Fine	XF
7.11.1931. Olive and blue on pink unpt. 3 workers on horseback at ctr. Red ovpt: *CERTICADO DE PLATA . . . 1931* in 3 lines. Red date and sign. Back: brown; Columbus at ctr. Lg. red ovpt: *CERTIFICADO DE PLATA* across ctr. on back. Printer TDLR.	90.00	250.00	600.00

1931-33 ISSUE

180   5 COLONES

	Good	Fine	XF
1931-36. Red-orange and blue on tan unpt. 3 coffee bean workers at r. Back: tan; monument. Printer: TDLR.			
a. 8.7.1931-31.10.1936.	5.00	50.00	160.00
b. Sign. title: *EL SUBDIRECTOR* ovpt. at r. 27.8.1936.	5.00	50.00	160.00

181   10 COLONES

	Good	Fine	XF
20.1.1932; 21.12.1935-17.12.1936. Like #179 but w/o ovpt. Black date and sign.	15.00	75.00	225.00

182   100 COLONES

	Good	Fine	XF
1933-35. Blue on m/c unpt. woman standing w/basket of vegetable at l. Back: red-brown; lg. bldg. Printer: W&S.			
a. Sign. title: *EL SUBDIRECTOR* ovpt. at r. 2.6.1933-4.9.1933.	12.50	75.00	200.00
b. W/o sign. title changes. 30.10.1934; 26.3.1935.	12.50	75.00	200.00

1933 SERIES E

183   50 COLONES

	Good	Fine	XF
1933. Dk. green on m/c unpt. woman standing at l. Back: Dk. blue; monument at ctr. Printer: W&S.			
a. Sign. title: *EL SUBDIRECTOR* ovpt. at r. 31.7.1933.	15.00	90.00	225.00
b. W/o sign. title changes. 24.11.1933.	15.00	90.00	225.00

1924-25 ISSUE

#184-189 series A. Printer: ABNC. NOTE: The 2, 5 and 10 Colones of Series B were used w/provisional ovpts. of the Banco Nacional, as were some of #184 and #187.

184   2 COLONES

	Good	Fine	XF
24.12.1924-5.2.1929. Dk. blue on m/c unpt. Allegorical woman standing w/model airplane by woman seated at r. Back: brown.	7.50	60.00	150.00

185   5 COLONES

	Good	Fine	XF
4.11.1925-11.5.1928. Dk. blue on m/c unpt. Woman seated at r. Back: purple.	17.50	100.00	—

186   10 COLONES

	Good	Fine	XF
15.7.1924; 6.1.1925; 29.11.1927. Dk. Blue on m/c unpt. woman holding steam locomotive and woman seated at l. Back: orange.	35.00	175.00	

187	**20 COLONES**	GOOD	FINE	XF
	15.7.1924-29.11.1927. Dk. blue m/c unpt. Seated woman holding book and wreath at r. Back: lt. brown.	60.00	225.00	—

188	**50 COLONES**	GOOD	FINE	XF
	24.12.1924. Dk. blue on m/c unpt. Helmeted woman seated holding sword and palm branch at l. Back: black.	—	Rare	—

189	**100 COLONES**	GOOD	FINE	XF
	24.12.1924-24.1.1927. Dk. blue on m/c unpt. Seated woman holding branch at r. Back: green.	—	Rare	—

BANCO NACIONAL DE COSTA RICA

1937-43 PROVISIONAL ISSUE, OVPT. TYPE A, W/O LEY

#190-194 ovpt: *BANCO NACIONAL DE COSTA RICA/DEPARTAMENTO EMISOR* on face of Banco Internacional notes w/sign titles changed.

190	**1 COLON**	GOOD	FINE	XF
	23.6.1943. Red ovpt. on #166. Series C/B. Red date and sign.	3.50	10.00	50.00

191	**10 COLONES**	GOOD	FINE	XF
	10.3.1937. Black ovpt on #181.	12.50	60.00	175.00
192	**20 COLONES**			
	1937-38. Black ovpt. on #176.			
	a. Sign. titles: *PRESIDENTE* and *GERENTE* 10.3.1937; 7.7.1937;2.3.1938.	17.50	75.00	225.00
	b. Sign title: *VICEPRESIDENTE* at l. 22.6.1938.	17.50	75.00	225.00

193	**50 COLONES**	GOOD	FINE	XF
	8.4.1941; 4.2.1942. Red ovpt. on #183. Red date and sign.	22.50	100.00	300.00

194	**100 COLONES**	GOOD	FINE	XF
	1937-42. Red ovpt. on #182. Red date and sign.			
	a. Sign title: *GERENTE* at r. 3.11.1937; 29.3.1939; 30.10.1940; 4.2.1942.	12.50	75.00	200.00
	b. Sign title: *SUB-GERENTE* at r. 9.7.1941.	12.50	75.00	200.00

1937-38 PROVISIONAL ISSUE, OVPT. TYPE B, LEY No. 16 DE 5 DE NOVIEMBRE DE 1936

#195 black ovpt: *BANCO NACIONAL DE COSTA RICA/DEPARTAMENTO EMISOR* over text on back of Banco Internacional - Caja de Conversion Series B notes.

195	**2 COLONES**	GOOD	FINE	XF
	1937-38. Red-orange and purple on gold unpt. Columbus Back: blue; plantation plantation workers. Series C/B. Printer: TDLR.			
	a. 4 lines of ovpt. added. Sign. titles: *PRESIDENTE* and GERENTE 4.1.1937-3.11.1937.	3.50	12.50	50.00
	b. Sign. titles: *VICE PRESIDENTE* at 22.6.1938.	3.50	12.50	50.00
	c. 5 lines of ovpt. added. Sign. title: *PRESIDENTE* at l. 2.3.1938.	3.50	12.50	50.00

1939-40 PROVISIONAL ISSUE, OVPT. TYPE C, LEY No. 16 DE 5 DE NOVIEMBRE DE 1936

#196 and 197 ovpt: *BANCO NACIONAL DE COSTA RICO/DEPARTAMENTO EMISOR* over text on face only of Banco Internacional - Caja de Conversion notes.

196	**2 COLONES**	GOOD	FINE	XF
	15.2.1939. Black ovpt. on #195. Issue date at end of ovpt text. Series C/B.	4.00	15.00	60.00

197	2 COLONES	GOOD	FINE	XF
	1940. Red ovpt. on #184. Series D/A.			
	a. 7.2.1940.	7.50	30.00	85.00
	b. 9.5.1940.	2.00	7.50	35.00

1937-39 PROVISIONAL ISSUE, OVPT. TYPE D, LEY NO. 16 DE 5 DE NOVIEMBRE DE 1936

#198-200 ovpt: *BANCO NACIONAL DE COSTA RICA/DEPARTAMENTO EMISOR* on face and back, back w/extra extra text on Banco Internacional - Caja de Conversion notes.

198	5 COLONES	GOOD	FINE	XF
	1937-38. Purple. Workers loading train w/bananas at l., mountain view at r. Arms on back. Black ovpt: Series E/B. Printer: TDLR.			
	a. Sign. title: *PRESIDENTE* at l. 10.3.1937-2.3.1938.	15.00	75.00	225.00
	b. Sign. title: *VICE PRESIDENTE* at l. 22.6.1938.	15.00	75.00	225.00

199	10 COLONES	GOOD	FINE	XF
	3.11.1937; 2.3.1938. Orange on yellow unpt. Workers field drying coffee beans at l. ctr. Back: orange; lg. bldg. Black ovpt: Series E/B. Printer: TDLR.	25.00	100.00	325.00

200	20 COLONES	GOOD	FINE	XF
	1.2.1939. Red ovpt. on #187. Red date and sign. Series D/A.	30.00	125.00	375.00

1941 SERIES E
#201-202 printer: W&S.

201	2 COLONES	VG	VF	UNC
	1941-45. Brown on m/c unpt. Portr. Juan V. de Coronado at ctr. Back: brown; rescue scene w/Coronado at ctr.			
	a. W/o sign. title changes. 5.2.1941; 4.2.1942; 20.1.1943-16.2.1944.	1.50	6.00	27.00
	b. Sign. title: *SUB-GERENTE* ovpt at r. 18.6.1941; 12.11.1941; 15.7.1942.	1.50	6.00	27.00
	c. Sign. title: *VIE-PRESIDENTE* at l. 10.12.1942; 18.11.1942.	1.50	6.00	27.00
	d. Both sign. titles ovpt. 28.2.1945.	1.50	6.00	27.00

202	20 COLONES	VG	VF	UNC
	1941-44. Red on m/c unpt. Portr Juan de Cavallon at ctr. Back: red; church at Orosi.			
	a. Sign. title: *SUB-GERENTE* ovpt. at r. 10.9.1941; 21.7.1943.	20.00	150.00	375.00
	b. Sign. title: *VICE-PRESIDENTE* ovpt. at l. 12.11.1942.	20.00	150.00	375.00
	c. W/o sign. title changes: 17.3.1942; 12.1.1944.	20.00	150.00	375.00

1939-46 SERIES F

203	2 COLONES	VG	VF	UNC
	1946-49. Red on m/c unpt. Portr. Joaquin B. Calvo at ctr. Back: dk. brown; plaza in San Jose. Printer ABNC.			
	a. Both sign. titles ovpt. 18.9.1946; 13.11.1946; 14.12.1949.	1.00	4.00	15.00
	b. Sign. title: *SUB-GERENTE* ovpt at r. 23.4.1947-13.8.1947; 7.12.1949.	1.00	4.00	15.00
	c. Sign. title: *VICE-PRESIDENTE* ovpt at l. 28.1.1948.	1.00	4.00	15.00

204	5 COLONES	VG	VF	UNC
	5.7.1939-28.10.1942. Green on m/c unpt. Portr. Juan Mora Fernandez at ctr. Back: green; ruins in Cartago. Printer: W&S.	3.00	20.00	85.00

205 **10 COLONES**

	VG	VF	UNC
1939-41. Blue on m/c unpt. Florencio del Castillo at ctr. Back: blue; Cacique Indian. Printer: W&S.			
a. W/o sign. title changes. 8.9.1939-20.3.1941.	10.00	60.00	275.00
b. Sign. title: *SUB-GERENTE* ovpt. at r. 10.9.1941.	10.00	60.00	275.00

206 **20 COLONES**

	VG	VF	UNC
1945-48. Olive on m/c unpt. Portr. Gregorio J. Ramirez at r. Back: orange; view of Poas Volcano. Printer: ABNC.			
a. Both sign. titles ovpt. 28.2.1945.	15.00	100.00	475.00
b. Sign. title: *SUB-GERENTE* ovpt. at r. 23.4.1947.	15.00	100.00	475.00
c. W/o sign. title changes. 3.3.1948.	15.00	100.00	475.00

207 **50 COLONES**

	VG	VF	UNC
1942. Black on green and gold unpt. Portr. C. Columbus at ctr. Back: black; scene of Columbus at cariari in 1502. Printer: W&S.			
a. W/o sign. title changes. 9.9.1942.	15.00	100.00	350.00
b. Sign. title: *VICE-PRESIDENTE* at l. 1.12.1942.	15.00	100.00	350.00

208 **100 COLONES**

	VG	VF	UNC
3.6.1942; 19.8.1942; 26.8.1942. Olive on m/c unpt. Vaso Policromo artifact at ctr. Back: olive; ceremonial altar. Printer: W&S.	25.00	125.00	425.00

1942-44 SERIES G
#209-212 Printer: ABNC.

209 **5 COLONES**

	VG	VF	UNC
1943-49. Brown on m/c unpt. Portr. B. Carillio at r. Back: green; bridge.			
a. W/o sign. title changes. 3.3.1943; 28.1.1948; 3.3.1948.	1.50	6.00	30.00
b. Both sign. titles ovpt. 28.2.1945; 14.12.1949.	1.50	6.00	30.00
c. Sign. title: *SUB-GERENTE* ovpt. at r. 16.10.1946; 13.8.1947; 31.8.1949; 30.11.1949.	1.50	6.00	30.00

210 **10 COLONES**

	VG	VF	UNC
1942-48. Lt. orange on m/c unpt. Portr. Manuel J. Carazo at l. Back: blue; large sailing ship at ctr.			
a. W/o sign. title changes. 28.10.1942-12.1.1944; 28.1.1948-3.3.1948.	3.00	15.00	150.00
b. Sign. title: *SUB-GERENTE* ovpt. at r. 16.10.1946; 13.8.1947-18.12.1947.	3.00	15.00	150.00

211 **50 COLONES**

	VG	VF	UNC
1944-47. Grayish green on m/c unpt. Portr. Manuel G. Escalante at l. Back: black; church in Heredia.			
a. Both sign. titles ovpt. 24.5.1944; 7.6.1944.	10.00	60.00	250.00
b. Sign. title: *VICE-PRESIDENTE* ovpt. at l. 4.6.1947.	10.00	60.00	250.00

212	**100 COLONES**	VG	VF	UNC
	1943-49. Green on m/c unpt. Portr. Dr. Jose M. Castro Madriz at l. Back: olive; old University of Santo Tomas.			
	a. Sign. title: *SUB-GERENTE* ovpt at r. 21.7.1943; 21.12.1949.	15.00	100.00	325.00
	b. W/o sign. title changes. 10.10.1943; 20.10.1943; 16.2.1944; 22.10.1947; 3.3.1948.	15.00	100.00	325.00

BANCO CENTRAL DE COSTA RICA

1950-67 PROVISIONAL ISSUE

Ovpt: *BANCO CENTRAL DE COSTA RICA/SERIE PROVISIONAL* on Banco Nacional notes.

216	**5 COLONES**			
	1950 Blue ovpt on #210. Series G.			
	a. W/o sign. title changes. 3.4.1950.	1.00	5.00	25.00
	b. *SUB-GERENTE* sign. ovpt at r. 20.0.1950.	1.00	5.00	25.00
	c. Sign. Title: *VICE-PRESIDENTE* ovpt at l. 5.9.1951.	1.00	5.00	25.00
215	**10 COLONES**			
	1950-51. Blue ovpt.on #209. Series G.			
	a. W/o sign. title changes. 20.7.1950; 5.10.1950; 6.12.1950.	3.00	10.00	125.00
	b. POR (for) added to l. of sign. title at l. 8.8.1951.	3.00	10.00	125.00
217	**20 COLONES**			
	8.11.1950; 7.3.1951. Blue ovpt on #206. Series F.	6.00	25.00	225.00
218	**50 COLONES**			
	1950-53. Blue ovpt. on #211. Series G.			
	a. W/o sign. title changes. 3.4.1950; 4.7.1951; 5.3.1952.	8.00	40.00	275.00
	b. POR (for) added to left of sign. title on l. 10.10.1951; 5.12.1951; 25.3.1953.	8.00	40.00	275.00
219	**100 COLONES**			
	1952-55. Blue ovpt on #212. Series G.			
	a. W/o sign. title changes. 23.4.1952; 28.10.1953; 16.6.1954.	15.00	65.00	300.00
	b. Sign. title: *SUB-GERENTE* ovpt at r. 2.3.1955.	15.00	65.00	300.00

1951-73 SERIES A ISSUE

#221-224 printer: W&S.

#225-226 printer: ABNC.

220	**5 COLONES**			
	1951-58. Green on m/c unpt. B. Carillo at r. Back green; coffee worker. Printer: ABNC.			
	a. POR (for) added to l. of sign. title at r. 20.11.1952.	1.00	6.00	25.00
	b. W/o sign. title changes. 8.7.1953; 6.8.1953; 3.12.1953; 21.7.1954-19.10.1955; 12.9.1956-6.8.1958.	1.00	5.00	20.00
	c. Sign. title: *SUB-GERENTE* ovpt at r. 11.7.1956.	1.00	5.00	20.00
	d. POR added to l. of sign. title at l. 12.9.1951; 26.5.1954.	1.00	5.00	20.00

221	**10 COLONES**	VG	VF	UNC
	1951-62. Blue on m/c unpt. Portr. A. Echeverria at ctr. Back: blue; ox-cart at ctr.			
	a. W/POR added to l. of sign. title at l. 8.11.1951; 29.10.1952.	3.00	8.00	50.00
	b. W/o sign. title changes. 7.9.1955-27.6.1962.	2.00	6.00	40.00
	c. W/POR added to both sign. titles. 28.11.1951	3.00	8.00	50.00

222	**20 COLONES**	VG	VF	UNC
	1952-64. Red on m/c unpt. Portr. C. Picado at ctr. at ctr. Back: red, university bldg. at ctr.			
	a. Date at l. ctr., w/o sign. title changes. 11.6.1952; 10.12.1952; 11.8.1954; 14.10.1955; 13.2.1957.	3.00	15.00	75.00
	b. Sign. title: *SUB-GERENTE* ovpt at r. 20.4.1955.	2.25	11.00	65.00
	c. Date at lower l. 7.11.1957-9.9.1964.	2.00	10.00	60.00
	d. *POR* added at l. of sign. title at l. 25.3.1953; 25.2.1954.	3.00	15.00	75.00

223	**50 COLONES**	VG	VF	UNC
	31.1.1957-27.11.1963. Olive on m/c unpt. Portr. R. F. Guardia at ctr. Back: olive; National Library at ctr.	5.00	25.00	115.00

224	**100 COLONES**	VG	VF	UNC
	1955-60. Black on m/c unpt. Portr. J. R. Mora at ctr. Back: black; statue of J. Santamaria at ctr.			
	a. W/o sign. title changes. 19.10.1955; 6.10.1959; 25.11.1959; 29.4.1960.	7.50	27.50	175.00
	b. Sign. title: *SUB-GERENTE* ovpt at r. 27.3.1957.	7.50	27.50	175.00

226	**1000 COLONES**	VG	VF	UNC
	26.3.1958; 2.4.1973; 18.10.1973; 12.6.1974. Red on m/c unpt. Portr. J. Pena at l. Back: red; Central and National Bank at ctr.	50.00	165.00	450.00

1959-80 SERIES B ISSUE

#228-232 printer: TDLR.

227	**5 COLONES**	VG	VF	UNC
	20.5.1959-3.11.1962. Green on m/c unpt. Portr. B. Carrillo at ctr. Back: green; coffee worker at ctr. Printer: W&S.	1.00	4.00	25.00

CROATIA

Croatia (Hrvatska), formerly a federal republic of the Socialist Federal Republic of Yugoslavia, has an area of 21,829 sq. mi. (56,538 sq. km.) and a population of about 5 million. Capital: Zagreb.

The country was attached to the Kingdom of Hungary until Dec. 1, 1918, when it joined with Serbia, Slovenia, Bosnia-Herzegovina, Macedonia and Montenegro to form the Kingdom of the Serbs, Croats and Slovenes, which changed its name to the Kingdom of Yugoslavia on Oct. 3, 1929. On April 6, 1941, Hitler, angered by the coup d'etat that overthrew the pro-Nazi regime of regent Prince Paul, sent Nazi forces into Yugoslavia Within a week the army of the Balkan Kingdom was broken. Yugoslavia was dismembered to reward Hitler's Balkan allies. Croatia, reconstituted as a nominal kingdom, was given to the administration of an Italian princeling, who wisely decided to remain in Italy. At the conclusion of World War II, Croatia was one of the 6 Socialist Rebuplics which formed Yugoslavia.

Croatia proclaimed its independence from Yugoslavia on Oct. 8, 1991. Serbian forces had developed a military stronghold in the area around Knin, located in southern Croatia. In August 1995 Croat forces overan this political-military enclave.

RULERS:
Austrian, 1527-1918

MONETARY SYSTEM:
1 Dinar = 100 Para 1918-1941, 1945-
1 Kuna = 100 Banica 1941-1944
1 Kuna = 100 Lipa, 1994-

NOTE: The word "kuna", derived from the Russian "cunica" which means marten, reflects the use of furs for money in medieval eastern Europe.
NOTE: Certain listings encompassing issues circulated by various bank and regional authorities are contained in Volume 1.

REVOLUTION OF 1848
CROATIA-SLAVONIA-DALMATIA
1848 ASSIGNAT ISSUE
#A1-A3 have arms at upper ctr. Hand sign. of Count Jelacic, governor of the triple kingdom.
NOTE: In 1850 all but apparently 8 pieces were burned. 240 x 170mm. (Not issued.)

A1	**25 FORINT** 5.5.1848. Grayish blue.	—	Rare	—
A2	**100 FORINT** 5.5.1848.		Reported Not Confirmed	
A3	**1000 FORINT** 5.5.1848. Olive green.	—	Rare	—

KINGDOM, WWII AXIS INFLUENCE
NEZAVISNA DRZAVA HRVATSKA
INDEPENDENT STATE OF CROATIA
GOVERNMENT NOTES
1941 ISSUE
#1-5 printer: G&D.

		VG	VF	UNC
1	**50 KUNA** 26.5.1941. Red-brown. Arms at upper l.			
	a. Issued note.	1.50	5.00	20.00
	b. Specimen.	—	—	—

		VG	VF	UNC
2	**100 KUNA** 26.5.1941. Blue-gray. Arms at l.			
	a. Issued note.	.90	3.00	12.50
	b. Specimen.	—	—	—
3	**500 KUNA** 26.5.1941. Green. Corn sheaves at r. ctr. Arms in unpt. at l. on face, and at l. on back.			
	a. Issued note.	3.75	12.50	50.00
	b. Specimen.	—	—	—

		VG	VF	UNC
4	**1000 KUNA** 26.5.1941. Brown. Croatian farmer's wife at l. Arms in unpt. at ctr. Low mountain range across ctr. on back.			
	a. Issued note.	1.25	3.75	15.00
	b. Specimen.	—	—	—

1942 FIRST ISSUE

		VG	VF	UNC
5	**10 KUNA** 30.8.1941. Olive and brown. Arms at lower r.			
	a. Issued note.	.75	2.50	10.00
	b. Specimen.	—	—	—

1942 SECOND ISSUE

6 50 BANICA
25.9.1942. Blue and lt. brown. Vertical format. Arms at upper ctr. on back.

	VG	VF	UNC
a. Issued note.	.75	2.50	12.50
b. Specimen.	—	—	—

7 1 KUNA
25.9.1942. Dk. blue and brown. Arms at r.

	VG	VF	UNC
a. Issued note.	.60	2.00	10.00
b. Specimen.	—	—	—

8 2 KUNA
25.9.1942. Dk. brown and red-brown. Arms at r.

	VG	VF	UNC
a. Issued note.	.60	2.00	10.00
b. Specimen.	—	—	—

1944 ISSUE

9 20 KUNA
15.1.1944. Brown on tan unpt. Arms at r. (Not issued).

	VG	VF	UNC
	—	13.50	45.00

10 50 KUNA
15.1.1944. Black on green and lt. orange unpt. Arms at r. (Not issued).

	VG	VF	UNC
a. W/o serial #.	—	52.50	175.00
b. W/normal serial #.	—	—	500.00

HRVATSKA DRZAVNA BANKA

CROATIAN STATE BANK

1943 ISSUE
#11-13 printer: G&D.

11 100 KUNA
1.9.1943. Dk. blue and brown. Round design of birds and flowers at r. Mother and child in Croatian dress at ctr. on back.

	VG	VF	UNC
a. Issued note.	2.25	7.50	25.00
b. Specimen.	—	—	—

11A 500 KUNA
1.9.1943. Lilac and violet. (Not issued).

	VG	VF	UNC
a. Normal serial #.	—	150.00	450.00
b. Specimen.	—	—	600.00

12 1000 KUNA
1.9.1943. Dk. brown on yellow and green unpt. Frieze at ctr. Two Croatian women on back.

	VG	VF	UNC
	.50	1.50	5.00

13 5000 KUNA
1.9.1943. Red-brown, blue and brown. Hexagonal receptacle at r. Croatian couple on back.

	VG	VF	UNC
	.65	2.25	7.50

14 5000 KUNA
15.7.1943. Brown on violet and green unpt. Woman in national costume at l. Back blue on lilac, brown and lt. green unpt.

	VG	VF	UNC
a. Issued note.	2.00	6.50	22.50
b. Specimen.	—	—	—

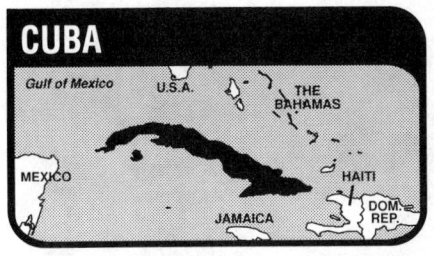

CUBA

The Republic of Cuba, situated at the northern edge of the Caribbean Sea about 90 miles (145 km.) south of Florida, has an area of 44,218 sq. mi. (114,524 sq. km.) and a population of 10.7 million. Capital: Havana. The Cuban economy is based on the cultivation and refining of sugar, which provides 80 percent of export earnings.

Discovered by Columbus in 1492 and settled by Diego Velasquez in the early 1500s, Cuba remained a Spanish possession until 1898, except for a brief British occupancy in 1762-63. Cuban attempts to gain freedom were crushed, even while Spain was granting independence to its other American possessions. Ten years of warfare, 1868-78, between Spanish troops and Cuban rebels exacted guarantees of right which were never implemented. The final revolt, begun in 1895, evoked American sympathy, and with the aid of U.S. troops independence was proclaimed on May 20, 1902. Fulgencio Batista seized the government in 1952 and established a dictatorship. Opposition to Batista, led by Fidel Castro, drove him into exile on Jan. 1, 1959. A communist-type, 25-member collective leadership headed by Castro was inaugurated in March 1962.

RULERS:
Spanish to 1898

MONETARY SYSTEMS:
1 Peso = 100 Centavos
1 Peso Convertibles = 1 U.S.A. Dollar, 1995-

SPANISH INFLUENCE

EL BANCO ESPAÑOL DE LA HABANA

HABANA BRANCH

1857 ISSUE

#A1-4 allegorical female seated w/Indian, lion and symols of commerce at top ctr. Various date and sign. combinations.

		GOOD	FINE	XF
A1	**50 PESOS** 18xx.	—	Rare	—
1	**100 PESOS** 1857-59. Black on blue paper.	—	Rare	—
2	**300 PESOS** 1857-59. Black.	—	Rare	—

3	**500 PESOS** 1.2.1857-59. Black on pink pink paper.	GOOD —	FINE Rare	XF —
4	**1000 PESOS** 1857-59. Black.	—	Rare	—

1867 ISSUE

#5-9 allegorical female seated w/Indian, lion and symbols of commerce at top ctr. Various date and sign. combinations.

5	**25 PESOS** 1867-68. Black on green unpt.	GOOD 1250.	FINE 3150.	XF —
6	**50 PESOS** 1867-68. Black on tan unpt. Green paper.	1500.	3750.	—
7	**100 PESOS** 1867-68. Black on green unpt. Yellow paper.	1650.	4350.	—

8	**300 PESOS** 13.7.1867-69. Black on tan unpt. Lt. purple paper.	GOOD 2250.	FINE 5600.	XF —
9	**500 PESOS** 1867-68. Black on green unpt. Red paper.	—	Rare	—

10	**1000 PESOS** 26.8.1867-68. Black on green unpt. Allegorical female standing w/indian, lion and symbol of commerce at top ctr. White paper.	GOOD —	FINE Rare	XF —

1869 ISSUE

#11-18 seated allegorical figure at upper ctr. Various date and sign. combinations. Printer: NBNC.

11	**5 PESOS** 1869-79. Rust and black.	GOOD —	FINE Rare	XF —
12	**10 PESOS** 1869-79. Rust and black.	—	Rare	—

		GOOD	FINE	XF
13	**25 PESOS** 1869-79. Blue and black.	—	Rare	—
14	**50 PESOS** 1869-79. Yellow and black.	—	Rare	—
15	**100 PESOS** 1869-79. Red and black.	—	Rare	—
16	**300 PESOS** 1869-79. Brown and black.	—	Rare	—
17	**500 PESOS** 1869-79. Tan and black.	—	Rare	—

		GOOD	FINE	XF
18	**1000 PESOS** 1869-79. Green and black.	—	Rare	—

1872 FIRST ISSUE
#19-22 various date and sign. combinations. Printer: BWC (w/o imprint).

		GOOD	FINE	XF
19	**5 PESOS** 1872-87. Black on pink and green unpt. Woman at top ctr.	450.00	1500.	3750.

		GOOD	FINE	XF
20	**10 PESOS** 1872-92. Woman by a beehive at top ctr.	675.00	2250.	—
21	**25 PESOS** 1872-91. Mercury holding a caduceus at top ctr.	900.00	3000.	—
22	**50 PESOS** 1872-90. Youth carrying a bundle of sugar cane at top ctr.	1100.	3750.	—
23	**100 PESOS** 1872-87.			
24	**300 PESOS** 1872-87.		Reported Not Confirmed	
25	**500 PESOS** 1872-87.		Reported Not Confirmed	
26	**1000 PESOS** 1872-87. Woman at ctr.	—	Rare	—

1872 SECOND ISSUE
#27 and 28 various date and sign. varieties. Printer: CNBB.

27 **1 PESO**
1872-83. Black. Vignette like #11-18. Back black and green. Columbus in sight of land at ctr.

		GOOD	FINE	XF
a.	15.6.1872.	30.00	75.00	260.00
b.	11.7.1872.	30.00	75.00	260.00
c.	15.5.1876.	30.00	75.00	260.00
d.	31.5.1879.	30.00	75.00	260.00
e.	16.8.1883.	30.00	75.00	260.00

28 **3 PESOS**
1872-83. Black. Vignette like #11-18. Back black and deep orange; Columbus in sight of land at ctr.

		GOOD	FINE	XF
a.	15.6.1872.	60.00	150.00	525.00
b.	1.7.1872.	60.00	150.00	525.00
c.	1.12.1877.	60.00	150.00	525.00
d.	7.3.1879.	Reported Not Confirmed		
e.	31.5.1879.	60.00	150.00	525.00
f.	6.8.1883.	60.00	150.00	525.00

1872 THIRD ISSUE
#29-31 crowned shields at l. Allegorical figure seated on back. Pritner: NBNC.

29 **5 CENTAVOS**
1872-83. Black on lt. tan or yellow paper. Back green.

		GOOD	FINE	XF
a.	1.7.1872.	2.50	7.50	25.00
b.	ABNC monogram. 15.5.1876.	1.75	5.50	18.50
c.	W/o imprint. 15.5.1876.	Reported Not Confirmed		
d.	6.8.1883.	1.75	5.50	18.50

30 **10 CENTAVOS**
1872-83. Black on lt. tan paper. Back brown.

		GOOD	FINE	XF
a.	1.7.1872.	3.00	9.00	30.00
b.	Imprint. 15.5.1876.	2.50	7.50	25.00
c.	W/o imprint. 15.5.1876.	2.50	7.50	25.00
d.	6.8.1883.	2.50	7.50	25.00

31 **25 CENTAVOS**
1872-76. Black. Back orange.

		GOOD	FINE	XF
a.	1.7.1872.	6.00	18.50	62.50
b.	15.5.1876.	Reported Not Confirmed		

32 **50 CENTAVOS**
1872-76. Black. Crowned shield at ctr. Back orange. Printer: NBNC.

		GOOD	FINE	XF
a.	1.7.1872.	8.00	24.00	80.00
b.	15.5.1876.	6.00	18.00	60.00

33 **50 CENTAVOS**
28.10.1889. Black on tan paper. Spaniard and Indian at r. Back orange; monument at ctr. Printer: ABNC.

		GOOD	FINE	XF
a.	W/counterfoil.	32.50	80.00	200.00
b.	W/o counterfoil.	9.00	27.50	95.00

CARDENAS BRANCH

1860's ISSUE

		GOOD	FINE	XF
33A	**10 PESOS** 186x.	—	Rare	—
33B	**25 PESOS** 186x.	—	Rare	—
33C	**50 PESOS** 186x.	—	Rare	—
33D	**100 PESOS** 186x.	—	Rare	—
33E	**300 PESOS** 186x.	—	Rare	—
33F	**500 PESOS** 186x.	—	Rare	—
33G	**1000 PESOS** 186x.	—	Rare	—

MATANZAS BRANCH

1860's ISSUE
#34-38 similar to #11-15. Printer: NBNC.

34 **5 PESOS**
186x.   Reported Not Confirmed

		GOOD	FINE	XF
35	**10 PESOS** 186x. Lt. blue.	—	Rare	—
36	**25 PESOS** 186x.	Reported Not Confirmed		

		GOOD	FINE	XF
37	**50 PESOS** 186x.	—	Rare	—
38	**100 PESOS** 186x.	Reported Not Confirmed		

SAGUA LA GRANDE BRANCH

1860's ISSUE
#38A-38G similar to #12-17. Printer: NBNC.

38A	**10 PESOS** 186x.	—	Rare	—
38B	**25 PESOS** 186x.	—	Rare	—
38C	**50 PESOS** 186x.	—	Rare	—

38D	**100 PESOS** 186x. Red and black.	—	Rare	—
38E	**300 PESOS** 186x.	—	Rare	—
38F	**500 PESOS** 186x. Brown and black.	—	Rare	—
38G	**1000 PESOS** 186x.	—	Rare	—

EL TESORO DE LA ISLA DE CUBA

1891 TREASURY NOTE ISSUE
#39-44 almost always found w/o sign. Values for such notes. Printer: BWC.

		Good	Fine	XF
39	**5 PESOS** 12.8.1891. Black on blue and orange unpt. Winged woman w/trumpet by woman w/book at l.	35.00	90.00	225.00

		Good	Fine	XF
40	**10 PESOS** 12.8.1891. Black on blue-green unpt. Mercury w/shield at r.	50.00	125.00	300.00

		Good	Fine	XF
41	**20 PESOS** 12.8.1891. Black on violet and green unpt. Woman seated w/shield at l.	52.50	135.00	335.00

		Good	Fine	XF
42	**50 PESOS** 12.8.1891. Black on purple and orange unpt. Mercury and youth seated at l.	70.00	175.00	425.00

		Good	Fine	XF
43	**100 PESOS** 12.8.1891. Black on purple and orange unpt. Young boy seated w/lamb at l., young girl seated at r.	80.00	200.00	485.00

		Good	Fine	XF
44	**200 PESOS** 12.8.1891. Black on brown and red unpt. Justice standing at l., young farm couple at r.	120.00	300.00	750.00

BANCO ESPAÑOL DE LA ISLA DE CUBA

1896 ISSUE
#45-49, 51-51B printer: ABNC.

		VG	VF	UNC
45	**5 CENTAVOS** 15.5.1896. Black. Arms at l. Back green; plant at ctr.			
	a. Issued note w/o ovpt.	.30	1.25	4.50
	b. Red ovpt: PLATA across face on a.	2.00	9.50	32.50

		VG	VF	UNC
46	**50 CENTAVOS** 15.5.1896. Black. Arms at r. Back deep orange; plant at ctr. Series H.			
	a. Issued note w/o ovpt.	.70	2.75	9.00
	b. Red ovpt: PLATA on a.	2.75	11.50	37.50

		VG	VF	UNC
47	**1 PESO** 15.5.1896. Black. Arms at ctr. Back blue; Qn. Isabel II at ctr. Series G.			
	a. Issued note w/o ovpt.	1.00	4.50	15.00
	b. Red ovpt: PLATA on a.	2.75	11.50	37.50

48   5 PESOS
1896-97. Black on orange and gold unpt. Woman seated w/bales at
ctr. Back brown; arms at ctr.

		VG	VF	UNC
a.	Issued note w/o ovpt. 15.5.1896.	.90	3.50	11.50
b.	Ovpt: PLATA on a. 15.5.1896.	.85	3.75	12.50
c.	W/o ovpt. 15.2.1897.	.90	3.50	11.50

49   10 PESOS
15.5.1896. Black on green unpt. Ox cart at top ctr. Back green; arms at
ctr.

		VG	VF	UNC
a.	Handwritten or hand stamped partially printed date, w/o ovpt.	1.25	5.00	16.50
b.	Handwritten date and month, handstamped sign.	75.00	200.00	—
c.	Printed date, w/o ovpt.	.90	3.50	11.50
d.	Printed date, ovpt: PLATA on c.	1.00	4.50	15.00

50   50 PESOS
15.5.1896. Black on red and green unpt. Allegorical woman at r.
Printer: BWC.

		VG	VF	UNC
a.	Issued note w/o ovpt.	27.50	65.00	160.00
b.	Ovpt: PLATA on a.	20.00	50.00	110.00

51   100 PESOS
15.5.1896. Black on orange and green unpt. Woman and cow at l.
Back orange and green.

VG	VF	UNC
75.00	185.00	625.00

51A   500 PESOS
15.5.1896. Black on orange and blue unpt. Winged woman and spear
at l. Columbus at ctr. on back.

VG	VF	UNC
725.00	1850.	—

51B   1000 PESOS
15.5.1896. Black on brown and gray unpt. Justice w/scales at l. Back
blue and brown.

VG	VF	UNC
—	Rare	—

1897 ISSUE

#52-53 printer: ABNC.

NOTE: For 5 Pesos dated 1897, see #48c.

52   10 CENTAVOS
15.2.1897. Black. Arms at r. Back brown; ships at ctr. Series K.

VG	VF	UNC
.50	1.50	7.50

53   20 CENTAVOS
15.2.1897. Black. Arms at ctr. Back gray; harvesting sugar cane at ctr.
Series I.

VG	VF	UNC
.50	1.50	7.50

1868-76 REVOLUTION

LA REPUBLICA DE CUBA

1869 ISSUE

#55-60 day and month handwritten on some notes.

54   50 CENTAVOS
1869. Black on gray unpt. Uniface. Flag at ctr.

GOOD	FINE	XF
6.00	15.00	35.00

55   1 PESO
1869. Black. Uniface. Arms at upper l. W/o sign.

		GOOD	FINE	XF
a.	Red seal.	8.00	25.00	62.50
b.	W/o red seal.	11.00	32.50	82.50
c.	Signed note, sign. stamped.	35.00	105.00	265.00

56   5 PESOS
1869. Black. Uniface. Draped shield at l.

		GOOD	FINE	XF
a.	W/o sign.	12.50	37.50	92.50
b.	Hand sign.	24.00	72.00	187.50

57   10 PESOS
1869. Black. Uniface. Draped shield at l.

		GOOD	FINE	XF
a.	W/o sign.	45.00	125.00	320.00
b.	Hand sign. of Cespedes.	100.00	300.00	750.00

58	50 PESOS	GOOD	FINE	XF
	1869. Black. Uniface. Draped shield at l.	—	Rare	

59	500 PESOS	GOOD	FINE	XF
	8.9.1869. Black. Angel at l., 3 women seated at r., eagle at lower ctr.	500.00	1500.	—

60	1000 PESOS	GOOD	FINE	XF
	6.9.1869. Red and brown. Angel at l., 3 women seated at r., eagle at lower ctr.	250.00	750.00	1650.

JUNTA CENTRAL REPUBLICANA DE CUBA Y PUERTO RICO

1869 ISSUE

#61-64 issued by a military revolutionist group located in New York City.

61	1 PESO	GOOD	FINE	XF
	17.8.1869. Black. Uniface.	10.00	40.00	100.00

62	5 PESOS	GOOD	FINE	XF
	17.8.1869. Blue. Like #61.	35.00	140.00	365.00
63	10 PESOS			
	17.8.1869. Green.	165.00	500.00	—
64	20 PESOS			
	17.8.1869. Red.	—	Rare	

REPUBLIC

BANCO NACIONAL DE CUBA
NATIONAL BANK OF CUBA

1905 FIRST ISSUE

#65-68 back green; fortress at ctr. (Not issued). Printer: ABNC.

#67-68 text on face: *EN ORO DEL CUÑO ESPAÑOL PAGARA AL PORTADOR A LA PRESENTACION.*

65	1 PESO	GOOD	FINE	XF
	ND (1905). Black. Portr. D. Capote at ctr.	—	Rare	

66	2 PESOS	GOOD	FINE	XF
	ND (1905). Black. Portr. M. Gomez at r.	—	Rare	

67	5 PESOS	GOOD	FINE	XF
	ND (1905). Black. Portr. J. Montes at l.	—	Rare	

68	10 PESOS	GOOD	FINE	XF
	ND (1905). Black. Portr. T. Palma at ctr.	—	Rare	

1905 SECOND ISSUE

#68A-68B text on face: *ORO, O SU EQUIVALENTE EN MONEDA DE LOS E.U. DE AMERICA, PAGARA AL PORTADOR A LA VISTA.* Printer: ABNC.

68A	5 DOLLARS			
	ND (ca.1905). Black. Similar to #67. Proof.	—	—	—
68B	10 DOLLARS			
	ND (ca.1905). Black. Similar to #68. Proof.	—	—	—

REPÚBLICA DE CUBA

CERTIFICADOS DE PLATA (SILVER CERTIFICATES)

69	**1 PESO**	GOOD	FINE	XF
	1934-49. Black on blue unpt. J. Martí at ctr. Back blue.			
a.	1934.	6.00	20.00	67.50
b.	1936.	9.00	32.50	110.00
c.	1936A.	7.50	25.00	82.50
d.	1938.	5.50	18.00	60.00
e.	1943.	5.50	18.00	60.00
f.	1945.	5.50	18.00	60.00
g.	1948.	5.50	18.00	60.00
h.	1949.	6.50	22.50	75.00

70	**5 PESOS**	GOOD	FINE	XF
	1934-49. Black on orange Unpt. J. Martí at ctr. Back blue.			
a.	1934.	18.50	45.00	150.00
b.	1936.	18.50	45.00	150.00
c.	1936A.	18.50	45.00	150.00
d.	1938.	16.00	40.00	135.00
e.	1943.	18.50	45.00	150.00
f.	1945.	16.00	40.00	135.00
g.	1948.	16.00	40.00	135.00
h.	1949.	18.50	45.00	150.00

71	**10 PESOS**	GOOD	FINE	XF
	1934-48. Black on brown unpt. C. Manuel de Céspedes at ctr. Back brown.			
a.	1934.	33.50	82.50	275.00
b.	1936.	33.50	82.50	275.00
c.	1936A.	33.50	82.50	275.00
d.	1938.	32.50	80.00	265.00
e.	1943.	33.50	82.50	275.00
f.	1945.	32.50	80.00	265.00
g.	1948.	32.50	80.00	265.00

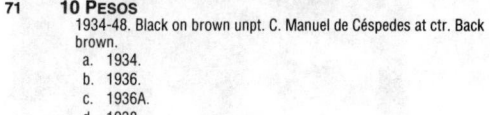

72	**20 PESOS**	GOOD	FINE	XF
	1934-48. Black on olive unpt. A. Maceo at ctr. Back olive.			
a.	1934.	52.50	135.00	450.00
b.	1936.	52.50	135.00	450.00
c.	1936A.	52.50	135.00	450.00
d.	1938.	50.00	125.00	425.00
e.	1943.	52.50	135.00	450.00
f.	1945.	50.00	125.00	425.00
g.	1948.	50.00	125.00	425.00

73	**50 PESOS**	GOOD	FINE	XF
	1934-48. Black on lt. orange unpt. G. Iniguez at ctr. Back lt. orange.			
a.	1934.	100.00	250.00	825.00
b.	1936.	100.00	250.00	825.00
c.	1936A.	100.00	250.00	825.00
d.	1938.	100.00	250.00	825.00
e.	1943.	100.00	250.00	825.00
f.	1948.	100.00	250.00	825.00

74	**100 PESOS**	GOOD	FINE	XF
	1936-48. Black on purple unpt. F. Aguilera at ctr. Back purple; capitol at l., cathedral at r.			
a.	1936.	125.00	325.00	1100.
b.	1938.	125.00	325.00	1100.
c.	1943.	125.00	325.00	1100.
d.	1945.	125.00	325.00	1100.
e.	1948.	125.00	325.00	1100.
75	**500 PESOS**			
	1944. Black on red and violet unpt. S. Betancourt at ctr. Back red. Printer: ABNC. Specimen.	—	Unc	1000.
75A	**500 PESOS**			
	1947. Similar to #75, but w/*LEY NO. 5 DE 2 DE MAYO DE 1942* beneath l. sign. title. Printer: ABNC.			
a.	Issued note.	—	Rare	—
s.	Specimen.	—	Unc	1000.
76	**1000 PESOS**			
	1944; 1945. Black on dk. green unpt. T. Palma at ctr. Back green. Printer: ABNC.			
a.	1944.	1650.	3350.	—
b.	1945.	750.00	1500.	3750.
76A	**1000 PESOS**			
	1947. Similar to #76, but w/*LEY NO. 5 DE 2 DE MAYO DE 1942* beneath l. sign. title.			
a.	Issued note.	1250.	2500.	6000.
s.	Specimen.	—	—	—

BANCO NACIONAL DE CUBA (RESUMED)

1949-50 ISSUE
#77-85 head at ctr. Arms. at ctr. on back. Printer: ABNC.

77	**1 PESO**	VG	VF	UNC
	1949; 1960. Black on blue unpt. J. Martí at ctr. Back blue.			
a.	Red serial #. 1949.	1.50	6.00	30.00
b.	Black serial #. 1960.	1.10	4.50	22.50
s1.	As a. Specimen ovpt: *MUESTRA*.	—	—	125.00
s2.	As b. Specimen ovpt: *MUESTRA*.	—	—	100.00

78	**5 PESOS**	VG	VF	UNC
	1949-50. Black on orange unpt. Portr. M. Gómez at ctr. Back orange.			
a.	1949.	2.85	11.50	57.50
b.	1950.	3.00	12.00	60.00
s1.	As a. Specimen ovpt: *MUESTRA*.	—	—	125.00
s2.	As b. Specimen ovpt: *MUESTRA*.	—	—	100.00

79	**10 PESOS**	VG	VF	UNC
	1949; 1960. Black on brown unpt. Portr. C. de Céspedes at ctr. Back brown.			
a.	Red serial #. 1949.	1.85	7.50	37.50
b.	Black serial #. 1960.	1.10	4.50	22.50
s1.	As a. Specimen ovpt: *MUESTRA*.	—	—	125.00
s2.	As b. Specimen ovpt: *MUESTRA*.	—	—	100.00

80 20 PESOS
1949-60. Black on olive unpt. Portr. A. Maceo at ctr. Back olive.

	VG	VF	UNC
a. Red serial #. 1949.	1.10	4.50	22.50
b. Red serial #. 1958.	.75	3.00	15.00
c. Black serial #. 1960.	.75	3.00	15.00
s1. As a. Specimen ovpt: *MUESTRA*.	—	—	125.00
s2. As b. Specimen ovpt: *MUESTRA*.	—	—	125.00
s3. As c. Specimen ovpt: *MUESTRA*.	—	—	100.00

81 50 PESOS
1950-60. Black on yellow unpt. Portr. C. Iniguez at ctr. Back yellow-orange.

	VG	VF	UNC
a. Red serial #. 1950.	1.50	6.00	30.00
b. Red serial #. 1958.	1.35	5.50	27.50
c. Black serial #. 1960.	2.50	10.00	52.50
s1. As a. Specimen ovpt: *MUESTRA*.	—	—	125.00
s2. As b. Specimen ovpt: *MUESTRA*.	—	—	125.00
s3. As c. Specimen ovpt: *MUESTRA*.	—	—	100.00

82 100 PESOS
1950-58. Black on purple unpt. Portr. F. Aguilera at ctr. Red serial #. Back purple.

	VG	VF	UNC
a. 1950.	2.25	9.00	45.00
b. 1954.	1.60	6.50	32.50
c. 1958.	2.50	10.00	52.50
s1. As a. Specimen ovpt: *MUESTRA*.	—	—	125.00
s2. As b. Specimen ovpt: *MUESTRA*.	—	—	125.00
s3. As c. Specimen ovpt: *MUESTRA*.	—	—	100.00

83 500 PESOS

	VG	VF	UNC
1950. Black on red unpt. Portr. S. Betancourt at ctr. Back red.	30.00	75.00	300.00

84 1000 PESOS

	VG	VF	UNC
1950. Black on dk. green unpt. Portr. T. Palma at ctr. Back green.	11.00	27.50	110.00

85 10,000 PESOS
1950. Black on olive unpt. Portr. I. Agramonte at ctr. Back olive.

	VG	VF	UNC
a. Issued note (2 known).	—	Rare	—
p. Proofs, face and back.	—	—	650.00
s. Specimen.	—	—	3000.

1953 COMMEMORATIVE ISSUE
#86, José Marté's birth centennial.

86 1 PESO

	VG	VF	UNC
1953. Black on blue unpt. Portr. J. Martí at lower l. *MANIFESTO DE MONTECRISTI 1895* at ctr. Back blue; map of Cuba over arms at ctr., commemorative dates at l. Printer: ABNC.	11.50	45.00	140.00

1956 ISSUE
Replacement notes #87 and 88: Small crosslet design in place of prefix letter.

87 1 PESO
1956-58. Black on blue unpt. Monument at ctr. J. Martí at r. Back blue; farm scene at l., arms at ctr., factory at r. Printer: TDLR

	VG	VF	UNC
a. 1956	1.65	5.00	20.00
b. 1957	1.35	4.00	16.50
c. 1958	1.35	4.00	16.50
s1. As a. Specimen perforated: *SPECIMEN*.	—	—	125.00
s2. As b. Specimen perforated: *SPECIMEN*.	—	—	125.00

88 10 PESOS
1956-60. Black on brown unpt. Wheels at ctr., portr. C. de Céspedes at r. Back brown; cows at l., arms at ctr., milk bottling factory at r. Printer: TDLR.

	VG	VF	UNC
a. 1956.	2.00	6.25	25.00
b. 1958.	1.50	4.50	18.50
c. 1960.	1.00	3.00	12.50
s1. As a. Specimen perforated: *SPECIMEN*.	—	—	125.00
s2. As b. Specimen perforated: *SPECIMEN*.	—	—	125.00
s3. As c. Specimen perforated: *SPECIMEN*.	—	—	125.00

1958-60 ISSUES
Replacement notes #90-93: Small crosslet design in place of prefix letter.

Note: Several examples of #92b in "issued" form (w/serial #) are verified.

90	**1 PESO**	VG	VF	UNC
(91)	1959. Black on blue unpt. J. Martí addressing assembly at ctr., portr. J. Martí at r. Back blue; farm scene at l., arms at ctr., factory at r. Printer: TDLR.			
	a. Issued note.	1.00	3.25	10.00
	s. Specimen perforated: SPECIMEN.	—	—	125.00
91	**5 PESOS**			
(90)	1958-60. Black on green unpt. Riders on horseback at ctr., Portr. M. Gómez at r. Back green; plantation at l., arms at ctr., cigar factory at r. Printer: TDLR.			
	a. 1958.	1.50	4.50	18.50
	b. 1959. (Not issued).	—	—	—
	c. 1960.	1.50	4.50	18.50
	s1. As a. Specimen perforated: SPECIMEN.	—	—	125.00
	s2. As c. Specimen perforated: SPECIMEN.	—	—	100.00
92	**5 PESOS**			
(93)	1960. Black on green unpt. Portr. M. Gómez at ctr. Arms at ctr. on green back. Printer: ABNC.			
	a. Issued note.	1.25	3.75	15.00
	s. Specimen perforated: SPECIMEN.	—	—	100.00

93	**100 PESOS**	VG	VF	UNC
(92)	1959-60. Black on orange unpt. Portr. F. Aguilera at ctr. Black serial #. Arms at ctr. on orange back. Printer: ABNC.			
	a. 1959.	1.00	3.00	12.50
	s1. As a. Specimen perforated: SPECIMEN.	—	—	125.00
	s2. Specimen perforated: SPECIMEN.	—	—	225.00

CURACAO

The island of Curacao, the largest of the Netherlands Antilles, which is an autonomous part of the Kingdom of the Netherlands located in the Caribbean Sea 40 miles off the coast of Venezuela, has an area of 173 sq. mi. (472 sq. km.) and a population of 150,000. Capital: Willemstad. The chief industries are the refining of crude oil imported from Venezuela and Colombia and tourism. Petroleum products, salt, phosphates and cattle are exported.

Curacao was discovered by Spanish navigator Alonso de Ojeda in 1499 and was settled by Spain in 1527. The Dutch West India Company took the island from Spain in 1634 and administered it until 1787, when it was surrendered to the crown. The Dutch held it thereafter except for two periods during the Napoleonic Wars, 1800-1803 and 1807-1816, when it was occupied by the British. During World War II, Curacao refined 60 percent of the oil used by the Allies; the refineries were protected by U.S. forces after Germany invaded the Netherlands in 1940.

RULERS:
Dutch

MONETARY SYSTEM:
1 Gulden = 100 Cents

NOTE: For later issues see Netherland Antilles.

DUTCH INFLUENCE

CURACAOSCHE BANK

1892 ISSUE
#A1-A4 Uniface. Handsigned on back. Printer: HBNC.

A1	**25 CENTEN**	GOOD	FINE	XF
	1892. Black on green unpt.	750.00	1250.	—
A2	**50 CENTEN**			
	1892. Black on blue unpt.	850.00	1500.	—

A3	**1 GULDEN**	GOOD	FINE	XF
	1892. Black on yellow unpt.	—	Rare	—

A4	**2 1/2 GULDEN**	GOOD	FINE	XF
	1892. Black on red unpt.	—	Rare	—

1900s ISSUE
1	**5 GULDEN** Ca. 1900.	—	Rare	—
2	**10 GULDEN** Ca. 1900.	—	Rare	—
3	**25 GULDEN** Ca. 1900.	—	Rare	—
4	**50 GULDEN** Ca. 1900.	—	Rare	—
5	**100 GULDEN** Ca. 1900.	—	Rare	—

		GOOD	FINE	XF
6	**250 GULDEN** Ca. 1900.	—	Rare	—
7	**500 GULDEN** Ca. 1900.	—	Rare	—

1918-20 ISSUE

		GOOD	FINE	XF
7A	**1 GULDEN** ND; 1918. Black on yellow unpt.	75.00	275.00	—

		GOOD	FINE	XF
7G	**1 GULDEN** 1920. Black on yellow unpt. Larger size.	200.00	550.00	—

		GOOD	FINE	XF
7B	**2 1/2 GULDEN** ND (c.1918). Black on red unpt.	150.00	450.00	—

		GOOD	FINE	XF
7C	**2 1/2 GULDEN** 1.7.1918; 1920. Red and yellow. a. Issued note. r. Unsigned remainder.	 125.00 —	 375.00 125.00	 — 250.00

		GOOD	FINE	XF
7E	**5 GULDEN** 1918; 1920.	—	Rare	—
7F	**10 GULDEN** 1920. Like #7E.	—	Rare	—

1925 ISSUE

		GOOD	FINE	XF
8	**5 GULDEN** 1925. Purple. City view at lower ctr.	150.00	500.00	—
9	**10 GULDEN** 1925. Like #8.	—	Rare	—
11	**50 GULDEN** 1925.	—	Rare	—
12	**100 GULDEN** 1925.	—	Rare	—
13	**250 GULDEN** 1925.	—	Rare	—
14	**500 GULDEN** 1925.	—	Rare	—

1930 ISSUE
#15-21 woman seated w/scroll and flag at l. Arms on back. Printer: JEZ.

		GOOD	FINE	XF
15	**5 GULDEN** 1930. Green on red and green unpt. Back blue on red and blue unpt.	20.00	60.00	175.00
16	**10 GULDEN** 1930.	40.00	225.00	—
17	**25 GULDEN** 1930.	—	—	—
18	**50 GULDEN** 1930.	—	—	—
19	**100 GULDEN** 1930.	—	—	—
20	**250 GULDEN** 1930.	—	—	—
21	**500 GULDEN** 1930.	—	—	—

1939 ISSUE
#22-24 printer: JEZ.

		GOOD	FINE	XF
22	**5 GULDEN** 1939. Green. Coastline city at ctr. Back blue.	5.00	30.00	150.00

		GOOD	FINE	XF
23	**10 GULDEN** 1939. Green. Ships dockside at ctr.	10.00	50.00	250.00
24	**25 GULDEN** 1939.	35.00	125.00	350.00

1943 ISSUE
#25-27 similar to #22-24 but w/printing in wmk. area at lower ctr. Printer: ABNC.

		VG	VF	Unc
25	**5 GULDEN** 1943. Green. Coastline city at ctr. Back blue and m/c.	10.00	60.00	250.00
26	**10 GULDEN** 1943. Green. Ships dockside at ctr. Back green and m/c.	15.00	80.00	375.00
27	**25 GULDEN** 1943. Green. View of city at ctr. Back black and m/c.	35.00	150.00	500.00
28	*DELETED.*			

1948 ISSUE
#29-32 printer: JEZ.

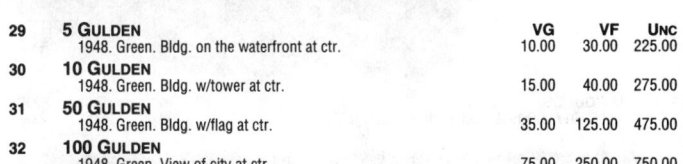

		VG	VF	Unc
29	**5 GULDEN** 1948. Green. Bldg. on the waterfront at ctr.	10.00	30.00	225.00
30	**10 GULDEN** 1948. Green. Bldg. w/tower at ctr.	15.00	40.00	275.00
31	**50 GULDEN** 1948. Green. Bldg. w/flag at ctr.	35.00	125.00	475.00
32	**100 GULDEN** 1948. Green. View of city at ctr.	75.00	250.00	750.00

1954 ISSUE
woman seated with scroll and flag at l. Title: *NEDERLANDSE ANTILLEN* over crowned supported arms at ctr. on back. Printer: JEZ.

		VG	VF	Unc
38	**5 GULDEN** 25.11.1954. Blue. View of Curacao at ctr.	7.00	20.00	125.00
39	**10 GULDEN** 25.11.1954. Green. Beach in Aruba at ctr.	10.00	30.00	85.00
40	**25 GULDEN** 25.11.1954. Black-gray. View of Bonaire at ctr.	15.00	85.00	275.00
41	**50 GULDEN** 25.11.1954. Red-brown. Coastline city of St. Maarten at ctr.	50.00	175.00	450.00
42	**100 GULDEN** 25.11.1954. Violet. Monument in St. Eustatius at ctr.	75.00	200.00	550.00

		VG	VF	Unc
43	**250 GULDEN** 25.11.1954. Olive. Boats on the beach in Saba at ctr.	150.00	350.00	—
44	**500 GULDEN** 25.11.1954. Red. Oil refinery in Curacao at ctr.	300.00	550.00	—

1958 ISSUE

		VG	VF	Unc
45	**5 GULDEN** 1958. Blue. Like #38.	8.00	25.00	110.00
46	**10 GULDEN** 1958. Green. Like #39.	10.00	40.00	140.00

		VG	VF	Unc
47	**25 GULDEN** 1958. Black-gray. Like #40.	17.50	70.00	250.00
48	**50 GULDEN** 1958. Brown. Like #41.	35.00	125.00	325.00
49	**100 GULDEN** 1958. Violet. Like #42.	70.00	225.00	500.00
50	**250 GULDEN** 1958. Olive. Like #43.	150.00	350.00	—

1960 ISSUE

		VG	VF	Unc
51	**5 GULDEN** 1960. Blue. Like #38.	7.00	20.00	100.00
52	**10 GULDEN** 1960. Green. Like #39.	10.00	25.00	120.00
53	**25 GULDEN** 1960. Black-gray. Like #40.	15.00	60.00	225.00
54	**50 GULDEN** 1960. Brown. Like #41.	35.00	110.00	300.00

		VG	VF	Unc
55	**100 GULDEN** 1960. Violet. Like #42.	70.00	200.00	450.00

CURACAO MUNTBILJETTEN
CURRENCY NOTES

1942 ISSUE
#35-36 printer: ABNC.

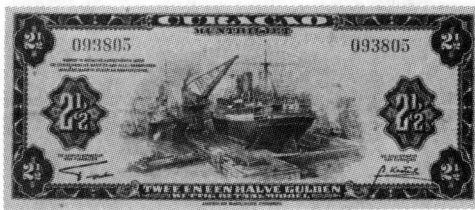

		VG	VF	Unc
35	**1 GULDEN** 1942; 1947. Red. Mercury seated between ships at ctr. Arms at ctr. on back.			
	a. 1942. 2 sign. var.	3.00	20.00	100.00
	b. 1947.	3.00	25.00	135.00

		VG	VF	Unc
36	**2 1/2 GULDEN** 1942. Blue. Ship at dockside at ctr. Back like #35.	7.50	30.00	185.00

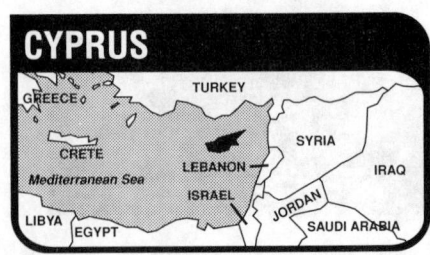

The Republic of Cyprus, a member of the European Commonwealth and Council, lies in the eastern Mediterranean Sea 44 miles (71 km.) south of Turkey and 60 miles (97 km.) west of Syria. It is the third largest island in the Mediterranean Sea, having an area if 3,572 sq. mi. (9,251 sq. km.) and a population of 710,200. Capital: Nicosia. Agriculture and mining are the chief industries. Asbestos, copper, citrus fruit, iron pyrites and potatoes are exported.

The importance of Cyprus dates from the Bronze Age when it was desired as a principal souce of copper (from which the island derived its name) and as a strategic trading center. Its role as an international marketplace made it a prime disseminator of the then prevalent cultures, a role that still influences the civilization of Western man. Because of its fortuitous position and influential role, Cyprus was conquered by a succession of empires; the Assyrian, Egyptian, Persian, Macedonian, Ptolemaic, Roman and Byzantine. It was taken from Isaac Comnenus by Richard the Lion-Hearted in 1191, sold to the Knights Templars, conquered by Venice and Turkey, and made a crown colony of Britain in 1925. Finally on Aug. 16, 1960, it became an independent republic.

In 1964, the ethnic Turks, who favor partition of Cyprus into separate Greek and Turkish states, withdrew from active participation in the government. Turkish forces invaded Cyprus in 1974 and gained control of 40 percent of the island. In 1975, Turkish Cypriots proclaimed their own Federated state in northern Cyprus. The UN held numerous discussions from 1985-92, without any results towards unification.

The president is Chief of State and Head of Government.

RULERS:
British to 1960

MONETARY SYSTEM:
1 Shilling = 9 Piastres
1 Pound = 20 Shillings to 1963
1 Shilling = 50 Mils
1 Pound = 1000 Mils, 1963-83
1 Pound = 100 Cents, 1983-

BRITISH INFLUENCE

GOVERNMENT OF CYPRUS

1914 FIRST ISSUE

		GOOD	FINE	XF
1	**1 POUND**			
	10.9.1914. Black. Coat of arms at ctr.			

		GOOD	FINE	XF
2	**5 POUNDS**	—	Rare	—
	10.9.1914. Red. Coat of arms at upper ctr.			

1914 SECOND ISSUE

		GOOD	FINE	XF
3	**5 SHILLINGS**	—	Rare	—
	30.10.1914; 6.11.1914. Blue. Portr. Kg. George V at l.			
4	**10 SHILLINGS**	—	Rare	—
	30.10.1914; 6.11.1914. Green. Portr. Kg. George V at l. Uniface.			
5	**1 POUND**	—	Rare	—
	30.10.1914; 6.11.1914. Black. Portr. Kg. George V at ctr.			
6	**5 POUNDS**	—	Rare	—
	30.10.1914; 6.11.1914; 1.9.1916. Red-brown. Portr. Kg. George V at ctr.			

1917 ISSUE

		GOOD	FINE	XF
7 (9)	**5 SHILLINGS**	250.00	750.00	1850.
	1.12.1917; 1.3.1918. Brown on blue and gray unpt. Portr. Kg. George V at ctr.			

		GOOD	FINE	XF
8 (10)	**10 SHILLINGS**	300.00	850.00	2000.
	30.6.1917; 1.3.1918; 1.4.1922. Blue. Portr. Kg. George at top ctr. Uniface.			

		GOOD	FINE	XF
9 (11)	**1 POUND**			
	1917-28. Purple on blue and green unpt. Portr. Kg. George V at r. Uniface.			
	a. Date at l. 30.6.1917-1.7.1925.	250.00	750.00	1850.
	b. Date at ctr. 1.4.1926; 1.5.192 6; 1.7.1927; 1.10.1928.	250.00	750.00	1850.

		GOOD	FINE	XF
10 (13)	**10 POUNDS**	750.00	2000.	
	30.6.1917; 1.9.1919. Red. Portr. Kg. George V at r.			

		VG	FINE	UNC
11 (6A)	**100 POUNDS**			
	1.11.1917. Coat of arms in upper frame at ctr. (Not issued).			

1919 EMERGENCY ISSUE

		GOOD	FINE	XF
12 (6C)	**1 SHILLING**			
	1919.			
	a. Green. Printed on 1/3 cut piece of #9 (-old date 1918). 12.11.1919.	—	Rare	—
	p. Proof. 38 x 64mm. 1.11.1919.	—	Rare	—
13 (6D)	**2 SHILLINGS**	—	Rare	—
	1.11.1919. Printer's proof. 42 x 78mm.			

1920; 1926 ISSUE

		GOOD	FINE	XF
14 (7)	**1 SHILLING**	175.00	650.00	1350.
	1.3.1920. Dk. green. Portr. Kg. George V at r. Back blue.			

15   **2 SHILLINGS**
(8)   1.3.1920. Dk. red on blue unpt., green border. Portr. Kg. George V at ctr. Back green.

	GOOD	FINE	XF
	225.00	700.00	1500.

16   **5 POUNDS**
(12)   1.8.1926; 1.11.1927. Green. Portr. Kg. George V at r. Uniface.

	GOOD	FINE	XF
	500.00	1250.	—

1930; 1933 ISSUE
#17-19 w/text: *GOVERNMENT OF CYPRUS* and arms on back.

17   **10 SHILLINGS**
(14)   1.8.1933; 1.9.1934; 2.1.1936. Gray and violet. Portr. Kg. George V at top ctr. Back violet.

	150.00	475.00	1200.

18   **1 POUND**
(15)   2.1.1930; 1.9.1934; 3.9.1935; 2.1.1936. Gray-violet and brown. Portr. Kg. George V at upper r.

	GOOD	FINE	XF
	125.00	450.00	950.00

19   **5 POUNDS**
(16)   2.1.1930; 2.1.1936. Green. Portr. Kg. George V at r.

	350.00	950.00	2000.

1937; 1939 ISSUE
#20-25 various date and sign. varieties.
#23-25 printer: TDLR.

20   **1 SHILLING**
(17)   3.1.1939-25.8.1947. Brown and green. Kg. George VI at ctr. Back red, green and blue.

	VG	VF	UNC
	5.00	35.00	150.00

21   **2 SHILLINGS**
(18)   3.1.1939-25.8.1947. Green and violet. Portr. Kg. George VI at ctr. Similar to #20. Back purple and violet.

	VG	VF	UNC
	8.00	45.00	185.00

22   **5 SHILLINGS**
(19)   3.1.1939-1.11.1950. Brown-violet and blue. Portr. Kg. George VI at ctr. Values in Greek and Arabic characters. Back red and purple.

	15.00	50.00	300.00

23   **10 SHILLINGS**
(20)   12.5.1937-1.11.1950. Maroon on pink and olive unpt. Portr. Kg. George VI at top ctr. Values in Greek and Arabic characters.

	VG	VF	UNC
	35.00	125.00	575.00

24   **1 POUND**
(21)   12.5.1937-30.9.1951. Brown on green unpt. Portr. Kg. George VI at upper r. Back brown.

	VG	VF	UNC
	25.00	100.00	375.00

25   **5 POUNDS**
(22)   1.9.1938-30.9.1951. Green. Portr. Kg. George VI at upper r. Values in Greek and Arabic characters.

	100.00	450.00	1200.

1943 PROVISIONAL ISSUE
NOTE: Previously listed #23b, back w/ovpt: *3* at lower l. and upper r. corners only; also lg. *3* at ctr., is now believed to be an altered #26.

26   **3 PIASTRES ON 1 SHILLING**
(23)   ND (1943-old date 30.8.1941). Brown and green. Ovpt: *THREE PIASTRES* and in Greek on #17.

	VG	VF	UNC
a. Ovpt: *3* in all four corners; also lg. *3* at ctr. on back.	50.00	125.00	250.00

27   **3 PIASTRES**
(24)   1.3.1943. Brown on green. Ovpt: *THREE PIASTRES* and in Greek on 2/5 cut of #17.

	VG	VF	UNC
	75.00	175.00	450.00

1943 REGULAR ISSUE

28	3 PIASTRES	VG	VF	UNC
(25)	1943-44. Blue. Portr. Kg. George VI at ctr.			
	a. 18.6.1943; 6.4.1944.	2.00	5.00	22.50
	b. 15.9.1944; 25.9.1944. (Not issued).	—	—	—

1952-53 ISSUES

29	5 SHILLINGS	VG	VF	UNC
(19A)	1.2.1952. Brown-violet and blue. Portr. Kg. George VI at ctr. Similar to #22 but values in Greek and modern Turkish characters.	20.00	85.00	375.00

30	5 SHILLINGS	VG	VF	UNC
(25A)	1.9.1952. Brown-violet and blue. Portr. Qn. Elizabeth II at ctr.	15.00	75.00	450.00

31	10 SHILLINGS	VG	VF	UNC
(20A)	1.9.1953; 31.7.1954. Maroon on pink and olive unpt. Portr. Kg. George VI at top ctr. Similar to #23 but values in Greek and modern Turkish characters.	45.00	150.00	625.00
32	5 POUNDS			
(22A)	1.11.1953. Green. Portr. Kg. George VI at upper r. Similar to #25 but values in Greek and modern Turkish characters.	125.00	600.00	1500.

1955 ISSUE

#33-36 portr. Qn. Elizabeth II at r., map at lower r. Various date and sign. varieties. Arms at r. on back.

33	250 MILS	VG	VF	UNC
(26)	1.6.1955; 1.2.1956; 1.3.1957; 1.3.1960. Blue on m/c unpt.	5.00	30.00	200.00

34	500 MILS	VG	VF	UNC
(27)	1.6.1955; 1.2.1956; 1.3.1957. Green on m/c unpt.	17.50	100.00	550.00

35	1 POUND	VG	VF	UNC
(28)	1.6.1955; 1.2.1956; 1.3.1957. Brown on m/c unpt.	8.00	35.00	250.00

36	5 POUNDS	VG	VF	UNC
(29)	1.6.1955; 1.2.1956; 1.3.1957; 15.3.1958; 1.3.1960. Green on m/c unpt.	20.00	85.00	475.00

The Republic of Czechoslovakia (Ceskoslovenská), located in central Europe, had an area of 49,365 sq. mi. (127,859 sq. km.) and a population of 15.7 million. Capital: Prague. Machinery was the chief export of the highly industrialized economy.

Czechoslovakia proclaimed itself a republic on Oct. 28, 1918. with T. G. Masaryk as president. Hitler provoked Czechoslovakia's German minority in the Sudentenland to agitate for autonomy. At Munich in Sept. of 1938, France and Britain, forced the cession of the Sudentenland to Germany. In March 1939, Germany invaded Czechoslovakia and established the Protectorate of Bohemia and Moravia. Slovakia, a province in southeastern Czechoslovakia, was constituted as a republic under Nazi influence. After the World War II defeat of the Axis powers re-established the physical integrity and independence of Czechoslovakia, while bringing it within the Russian sphere of influence. On Feb. 23-25, 1948, the Communists seized control of the government in a coup d'etat, and adopted a constitution making the country a "people's republic." A new constitution adopted June 11, 1960, converted the country into a "socialist republic" which lasted until 1989. On Nov. 11, 1989, public demonstrations against the communist government began and in Dec. of that same year, communism was overthrown and the Czech and Slovak Federal Republic was formed. On January 1, 1993 this was split to form the Czech Republic and the Republic of Slovakia.

MONETARY SYSTEM:
1 Koruna = 100 Haleru

SPECIMEN NOTES

Large quantities of specimens were formerly made available to collectors. Most notes issued after 1945 are distinguished by a perforation consisting of a few small holes or letter S. Since the difference in price between original and specimen notes is frequently very great, both types of notes are valued. The earlier issues were recalled from circulation and then perforated: *SPECIMEN* or *NEPLATNE* for collectors. Caution should be exercised while examining notes as we have been notified of examples of perforated specimen notes having the holes filled back in.

* * * This section has been partially renumbered. * * *

REPUBLIC

REPUBLIKA CESKOSLOVENSKÁ

1919 PROVISIONAL ISSUE

		Good	Fine	XF
1	**10 KORUN**			
	1919 (-old date 2.1.1915). Blue imperforate 10 Haleru adhesive stamp on Austria #19.	3.00	8.00	10.00

		Good	Fine	XF
2	**20 KORUN**			
	1919 (-old date 2.1.1913). Red perforated 20 Haleru adhesive stamp on Austria #13.	2.00	6.00	12.00
2A	**20 KORUN**			
	1919 (-old date 2.1.1913). Red 20 Haleru adhesive stamp on Austria #14.	2.00	6.00	12.00

		Good	Fine	XF
3	**50 KORUN**			
	1919 (-old date 2.1.1914). Brown perforated 50 Haleru adhesive stamp on Austria #15.	3.00	6.00	12.00

		Good	Fine	XF
4	**100 KORUN**			
	1919 (-old date 2.1.1912). Orange-brown imperforate 1 Koruna adhesive stamp on Austria #12 (II Auflage).			
	a. Stamp w/straight edge.	3.00	6.00	12.00
	b. Stamp w/perforations.	3.00	7.00	15.00
5	**1000 KORUN**			
	1919 (-old date 2.1.1902). Reddish black 10K(orun) stamplike printed ovpt. on Austria #8.	4.00	10.00	20.00

1919 ISSUE

		Good	Fine	XF
6	**1 KORUNA**			
	15.4.1919. Blue. Arms at ctr. on red back.			
	a. Issued note.	.25	.75	4.00
	x. Error date: 5.4.1919 (Series 014).	—	—	100.00
	s. Specimen.	—	2.50	7.50

		Good	Fine	XF
7	**5 KORUN**			
	15.4.1919. Red and black. woman at l. and r. Back blue on brown unpt. Red text.			
	a. Issued note.	2.00	8.00	35.00
	s. Specimen.	2.00	4.00	8.00

		Good	Fine	XF
8	**10 KORUN**			
	15.4.1919. Purple on brown unpt. Helmeted man at lower l. and lower r. Back purple and tan; girl at l. and r.			
	a. Issued note.	4.00	15.00	40.00
	s. Specimen.	2.00	6.00	17.50

340 CZECHOSLOVAKIA

9   20 KORUN

	GOOD	FINE	XF
15.4.1919. Blue and brown. 4 women's heads. Back red w/green text; head at l. and r.			
a. Issued note.	10.00	40.00	150.00
x. Error: back w/o green printed legend.	—	—	—
s. Specimen.	1.00	4.00	12.50

10   50 KORUN

	GOOD	FINE	XF
15.4.1919. Brown and dk. red on lt. brown and green unpt. Woman at l. and r. Arms at ctr. on back.			
a. Issued note.	20.00	60.00	225.00
s. Specimen.	2.00	6.00	17.50

11   100 KORUN

	GOOD	FINE	XF
15.4.1919. Blue and violet. 4 arms across lower ctr. Woman at l. and r. of eagle on back.			
a. Issued note.	20.00	95.00	275.00
s. Specimen.	4.50	15.00	45.00

12   500 KORUN

	GOOD	FINE	XF
15.4.1919. Red and brown. Seated figures at ctr. Arms at upper l. and woman at upper r. above eagles on back.			
a. Issued note.	—	Rare	—
x. Counterfeit.	60.00	150.00	300.00
s. Specimen.	300.00	500.00	1000.

13   1000 KORUN

	GOOD	FINE	XF
15.4.1919. Blue on m/c unpt. Allegorical figure w/globe at r. Standing women at l. on back. Printer: ABNC.			
a. Issued note. Series D.	80.00	200.00	450.00
s1. Perforated: SPECIMEN.	40.00	100.00	225.00
s2. Brown. Special uniface print by ABNC of "archive series" for collectors.	—	—	15.00

14   5000 KORUN

	GOOD	FINE	XF
15.4.1919. Red. Woman at r. Like Austria #8.			
a. Issued note.	—	Rare	—
s. Perforated: NEPLATNÉ (invalid).	—	350.00	750.00

1920-23 ISSUE

15 (17)   5 KORUN

	GOOD	FINE	XF
28.9. 1921. Blue and red-brown. J. A. Komensky at l. Arms at ctr. on back.	2.50	10.00	35.00

16 (18)   50 KORUN

	GOOD	FINE	XF
12.7.1922. Brown, red and blue. Arms at upper l., woman's head at lower r. Farmer w/castle in background on purple back.	35.00	100.00	350.00

17 (15)   100 KORUN

	GOOD	FINE	XF
14.1.1920. Green. Pagan priestess at r. Printer: ABNC.			
a. Issued note.	15.00	35.00	125.00
s. Perforated: SPECIMEN.	—	25.00	45.00

18 (19)   500 KORUN

	GOOD	FINE	XF
6.10.1923. Brown. Arms at l., legionnaire at r. Lion, Liberty head and child on back. Printer: ABNC.			
a. Issued note.	100.00	350.00	775.00
s. Perforated: SPECIMEN.	—	175.00	375.00

19 (16)	**5000 KORUN**	GOOD	FINE	XF
	6.7.1920. Brown-violet on m/c unpt. River Elbe w/Rip mountain at l. ctr., girl in national costume at r. Back purple on green unpt. Standing allegorical woman at ctr. Printer: ABNC.			
	a. Issued note.	30.00	75.00	160.00
	s. Perforated: *SPECIMEN.* Series B.	—	8.00	25.00

NARODNI (A) BANKA CESKOSLOVENSKÁ

CZECHOSLOVAK NATIONAL BANK

1926-34 ISSUES

20 (21)	**10 KORUN**	VG	VF	UNC
	2.1.1927. Dk. purple on lilac unpt. Helmeted man at lower l. and lower r.			
	a. Issued note.	1.00	3.00	20.00
	s. Perforated: *SPECIMEN* or *NEPLATNÉ.*	—	1.50	10.00

21 (20)	**20 KORUN**			
	1.10.1926. Blue-violet, brown and red. Gen. Stefanik at l., arms at r. Back dk. blue on brown unpt. Pres. Masaryk at r.			
	a. Issued note.	.75	2.00	10.00
	s. Perforated: *SPECIMEN.*	—	1.25	5.00

22 (23)	**50 KORUN**	VG	VF	UNC
	1.10.1929. Red-violet on brown unpt. Girl at upper l., ornate arms at ctr. Farmer, wife and tools on back.			
	a. Issued note.	2.00	6.00	25.00
	s. Perforated: *SPECIMEN.*	—	2.50	10.00

23 (24)	**100 KORUN**	VG	VF	UNC
	10.1.1931. Dk. green on m/c unpt. Boy w/falcon at l., arms at ctr., woman at r. Allegorical figures at l., Pres. Masaryk at r. on back.			
	a. Issued note.	2.00	6.00	30.00
	p. Black proofs. Uniface pair.	—	—	85.00
	s. Perforated: *SPECIMEN.*	—	3.50	15.00

24 (22)	**500 KORUN**	VG	VF	UNC
	2.5.1929. Red on m/c unpt. Arms at l., legionnaire at r.			
	a. Issued note.	7.00	20.00	100.00
	s. Perforated: *SPECIMEN.* Series D; G.	—	3.00	18.50

25	**1000 KORUN**	VG	VF	UNC
	8.4.1932. Allegorical figure w/globe at r.			
	a. Issued note. Series A.	12.00	40.00	150.00
	s. Perforated: *SPECIMEN.*	—	6.00	20.00

	26 **1000 KORUN**	**VG**	**VF**	**UNC**
	25.5.1934. Blue on lt. blue and green unpt. Woman w/book and 2 children at l. Back dk. brown and m/c; F. Palacky at r.			
	a. Issued note.	5.00	15.00	60.00
	s. Perforated: *SPECIMEN.*	—	3.50	20.00

REPUBLIKA ČESKOSLOVENSKÁ(RESUMED)

REPUBLIC OF CZECHOSLOVAKIA

1938 ISSUE

#27 and 28 were prepared for use by the mobilized Czech army in 1938, but were not released. After the Nazis occupied Czechoslovakia, these notes were ovpt. for the new Bohemia dn Moravia Protectorate (Refer to those listings #1 and 2).

#29-43 Deleted. See Bohemia and Moravia #3-17.

	27 **1 KORUNA**	**VG**	**VF**	**UNC**
	ND (1938). Blue. Lettering in unpt. in l. circle, Liberty wearing cap at r. circle. Arms at l., *RADA* (series) in white rectangle and 5 lines of text on back. (Not issued).	8.00	20.00	40.00

	28 **5 KORUN**	**VG**	**VF**	**UNC**
	ND (1938). Lilac and purple. J. Jungmann at r. Woman's head at l. on back. (Not issued).	20.00	50.00	100.00

1944-45 ISSUE

#45-50 Russian printing.

	45 **1 KORUNA**	**VG**	**VF**	**UNC**
	1944. Red-brown on brown unpt.			
	a. Issued note.	.50	1.50	3.00
	s. Perforated: *SPECIMEN.*	—	1.00	2.00

	46 **5 KORUN**	**VG**	**VF**	**UNC**
	1944. Dk. blue on lt. blue unpt.			
	a. Unpt. horizontal wavy lines.	.50	2.00	5.00
	b. Unpt. vertical wavy lines.	.50	2.00	5.00
	s. Perforated: *SPECIMEN* (a or b).	—	1.00	3.00

	47 **20 KORUN**	**VG**	**VF**	**UNC**
	1944. Black on tan unpt. 2 serial # varieties.			
	a. Issued note.	2.00	4.00	8.00
	s. Perforated: *SPECIMEN* or *NEPLATNÉ.*	—	1.50	3.00
	48 **100 KORUN**			
	1944. Green on lt. green unpt. 2 serial # varieties.			
	a. Issued note.	2.00	5.00	10.00
	s. Perforated: *SPECIMEN.*	—	2.00	5.00

	49 **500 KORUN**	**VG**	**VF**	**UNC**
	1944. Red on lt. brown unpt.			
	a. Issued note.	3.00	9.00	30.00
	s. Perforated: *SPECIMEN* or *NEPLATNÉ.*	—	2.00	5.00
	50 **1000 KORUN**			
	1944. Dk. blue on green unpt.			
	a. Issued note.	4.00	10.00	50.00
	s. Perforated: *SPECIMEN.*	—	3.00	6.00

	50A **2000 KORUN**	**VG**	**VF**	**UNC**
(44)	1945. Blue and black on green unpt. Arms w/produce at r. Back brown on lt. green and lt. orange unpt.			
	a. Issued note.	75.00	150.00	450.00
	s. Perforated: *SPECIMEN.*	—	1.50	6.00

1945 (ND) PROVISIONAL ISSUES

#51-57 issues of Slovakia and Republic w/Czechoslovak revalidation adhesive stamps portraying Pres. T. G. Masaryk (w/or w/o cap) affixed.

NOTE: These special adhesive stamps are still available in the philatelic market place.

	51 **100 KORUN**	**VG**	**VF**	**UNC**
	ND (1945 - old date 7.10.1940). Yellow *K* adhesive stamp on Slovakia #9.			
	a. Issued note.	1.00	4.00	15.00
	s. Perforated: *SPECIMEN.*	—	1.00	3.00

52 100 KORUN
ND (1945 - old date 7.10.1940). Yellow *K* adhesive stamp on Slovakia #10. *II. Emisia* at l. margin on back.

		VG	VF	UNC
a.	Issued note.	1.00	4.00	20.00
s.	Perforated: *SPECIMEN*.	—	1.00	3.00

53 100 KORUN
(55) ND (1945 - old date 1944). Blue *E* adhesive stamp w/black ovpt: *100* on #48.

		VG	VF	UNC
a.	Issued note.	.50	2.00	7.50
s.	Perforated: *SPECIMEN*.	—	1.50	4.00

54 500 KORUN
(53) ND (1945 - old date 12.7.1941). Orange *B* adhesive stamp on Slovakia #13.

		VG	VF	UNC
a.	Issued note.	2.00	7.00	35.00
s.	Perforated: *SPECIMEN*.	—	2.00	6.00

55 500 KORUN
(56) ND (1945 - old date 1944). Blue *E* adhesive stamp w/red ovpt: *500* on #49.

		VG	VF	UNC
a.	Issued note.	1.00	5.00	20.00
s.	Perforated: *SPECIMEN*.	—	1.50	4.00

56 1000 KORUN
(54) ND (1945 - old date 25.11.1940). Red *Y* adhesive stamp on Slovakia #12.

		VG	VF	UNC
a.	Issued note.	3.00	10.00	40.00
s.	Perforated: *SPECIMEN*.	—	3.00	8.00

57 1000 KORUN
ND (1945 - old date 1944). Blue *E* adhesive stamp w/red ovpt: *1000* on #50.

		VG	VF	UNC
a.	Issued note.	2.00	7.00	30.00
s.	Perforated: *SPECIMEN*.	—	1.50	4.00

1945-46 (ND) ISSUE

58 1 KORUNA
ND (1946). Blue. Similar to #27 but w/o unpt. in l. circle on face. Different unpt. design, w/o *RADA* (series), and 4 lines of text on back. (Not issued.)

		VG	VF	UNC
a.	W/o perforation holes.	—	—	6.00
s.	Perforated w/3 holes.	—	—	3.00

59 5 KORUN
ND (1945). Red on yellow unpt. Arms at ctr. on back. Printer: TDLR.

		VG	VF	UNC
a.	Issued note.	.25	.50	3.00
s.	Perforated w/3 holes, *S*, or *SPECIMEN*.	—	1.00	2.00

60 10 KORUN
ND (1945). Green on pink and green unpt. Printer: TDLR.

		VG	VF	UNC
a.	Issued note.	.25	1.00	3.00
s.	Perforated w/3 holes, *S*, or *SPECIMEN*.	—	1.00	2.00

61 20 KORUN
ND (1945). Blue on yellow and green unpt. K. Havlicek at l. Arms at lower ctr. on back.

		VG	VF	UNC
a.	Issued note.	.25	1.00	4.00
s.	Perforated w/3 holes, *S*, or *SPECIMEN*.	—	.50	1.50

62 50 KORUN
ND (1945). Purple on lt. green unpt. Gen. M. Stefanik at l. Ornate arms at ctr. on back.

		VG	VF	UNC
a.	Issued note.	.25	1.50	5.00
s.	Perforated w/3 holes, *S*, or *SPECIMEN*.	—	.75	2.00

63 **100 KORUN**

	VG	VF	UNC
ND (1945). Black-green on orange and green unpt. Pres. Masaryk at l. Prague Castle at ctr. on back.			
a. Issued note.	.50	2.00	10.00
s. Perforated w/3 holes, *S*, or *SPECIMEN*.	—	1.50	4.00

64 **500 KORUN**

	VG	VF	UNC
ND (1945). Brown on orange and m/c unpt. J. Kollar at l. w/black serial # and *MINISTER FINANCI* sign. and title. Lake and mountains on back.			
a. Issued note.	3.00	12.00	45.00
s. Perforated w/3 holes, *S*, or *SPECIMEN*.	—	1.75	10.00

65 **1000 KORUN**

	VG	VF	UNC
ND (1945). Black on m/c unpt. Kg. J. Z. Podebrad at l. Castle at ctr. on back.			
a. Issued note.	.50	3.00	15.00
s. Perforated w/3 holes, *S*, or *SPECIMEN*.	—	1.75	6.00

1945-48 DATED ISSUE

66
(67) **50 KORUN**

	VG	VF	UNC
3.7.1948. Deep blue. Gen. Stefanik at r. 3 serial # varieties. Scene of Banska Bystricka on back.			
a. Issued note.	.50	2.00	8.00
s. Perforated w/3 holes, *S*, or *SPECIMEN*.	—	1.00	3.00

67
(66) **100 KORUN**

	VG	VF	UNC
16.5.1945. Gray-brown on blue and peach unpt. Liberty wearing cap at r. 3 serial # varieties. Back blue on red and blue unpt.			
a. Issued note.	.30	1.00	6.00
s. Perforated w/3 holes, *S*, or *SPECIMEN*.	—	.75	2.00

1949-50 ISSUE

68 **5 KORUN**

	VG	VF	UNC
25.1.1949. Red on lt. brown unpt. Similar to #59.			
a. Issued note.	.25	1.50	4.00
s. Perforated w/3 holes or *SPECIMEN*.	—	.75	2.00

69
(70) **10 KORUN**

	VG	VF	UNC
4.4.1950. Green. Similar to #60.			
a. Issued note.	.25	1.00	3.00
s. Perforated w/3 holes, *S*, or *SPECIMEN*.	—	.75	1.50

70
(69) **20 KORUN**

	VG	VF	UNC
1.5.1949. Orange-brown and m/c. Girl w/floral wreath at r. Farm woman and vase of flowers on back.			
a. Margin w/fibers at l., bluish paper. Series A.	.50	2.00	9.00
b. Margin w/o fibers at l., yellowish paper. Series B.	.50	1.50	8.00
s. Perforated w/3 holes, *S*, or *SPECIMEN* (a or b).	—	1.00	2.00

71	**50 KORUN**	VG	VF	UNC
	29.8.1950. Dk. brown on tan unpt. Miner at r. Back green.			
	a. Margin w/fibers at l., bluish paper. Series A.	.50	3.00	9.00
	b. Margin w/o fibers at l., yellowish paper. Series B.	.50	2.00	8.00
	s. Perforated w/3 holes, *S,* or *SPECIMEN* (a or b).	—	1.50	3.00

1953 ISSUE

72A	**20 KORUN**	VG	VF	UNC
	25.2.1953. Blue. (Not issued).	—	—	550.00

NARODNI (A) BANKA CESKOSLOVENSKÁ (RESUMED)
1945-46 ISSUE

73	**500 KORUN**	VG	VF	UNC
(75)	12.3.1946. Brown on orange and m/c unpt. Similar to #64, but w/orange serial # and 3 sign. w/o title.			
	a. Issued note.	1.00	2.50	10.00
	s. Perforated w/3 holes, *S,* or *SPECIMEN.*	—	1.75	5.00

74	**1000 KORUN**	VG	VF	UNC
(73)	16.5.1945. Dk. grayish brown on gray unpt. Girl at r. Back blue, red-orange and m/c; arms at ctr. r.			
	a. Wmk: Outlined repeated "X" design. Yellowish, dense paper.	1.00	4.00	15.00
	b. Wmk: Outlined repeated "X" design. Bluish, transparent paper.	1.00	4.00	15.00
	c. Wmk: Small circles added between outlined repeated "X" design. Yellowish, dense paper.	1.00	4.00	15.00
	d. Wmk: Small circles added between outlined repeated "X" design. Bluish, transparent paper.	1.00	4.00	15.00
	s. Perforated: w/3 holes, *S, S-S,* or *SPECIMEN.* (a, b, c, or d).	—	2.50	7.50

75	**5000 KORUN**	VG	VF	UNC
(74)	1.11.1945. Black on brownish gray unpt. B. Smetana at r. Back green; National Theater in Prague at ctr., wreath at r.			
	a. Issued note.	1.50	4.00	15.00
	s. Perforated w/3 holes, *S,* or *SPECIMEN.*	—	2.50	7.00

STÁTNÍ BANKA CESOSLOVENSKÁ
CZECHOSLOVAK STATE BANK
1951 ISSUE

76	**100 KORUN**	VG	VF	UNC
(77)	24.10.1951. Brown. Woman at r. Coat of arms w/lion on m/c back. (Not issued).	—	—	300.00
77	**1000 KORUN**			
(76)	9.5.1951. Brown. Like #73. (Not issued).	—	—	800.00

PEOPLES REPUBLIC
STÁTNÍ REPUBLICY CESKOSLOVENSKÁ
STATE OF THE CZECHOSLOVAK REPUBLIC

1953 ISSUE
#78-82 w/o pictorial design on face, arms at ctr. on back.

 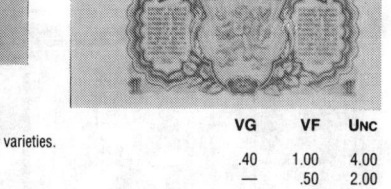

78	**1 KORUNA**	VG	VF	UNC
	1953. Brown on tan unpt. 2 serial # varieties.			
	a. Issued note.	.40	1.00	4.00
	s. Perforated: *SPECIMEN.*	—	.50	2.00
79	**3 KORUN**			
	1953. Blue on lt. blue unpt. 2 serial # varieties.			
	a. Issued note.	.50	2.00	8.00
	s. Perforated w/1 hole or *SPECIMEN.*	—	.50	2.00

80	**5 KORUN**	VG	VF	UNC
	1953. Olive on lt. green unpt. 2 serial # varieties.			
	a. Issued note.	1.00	3.50	12.50
	s. Perforated: *SPECIMEN.*	—	.50	2.00

SOCIALIST REPUBLIC

STÁTNÍ BANKY CESKOSLOVENSKE

CZECHOSLOVAK STATE BANK

		VG	VF	UNC
83	**10 KORUN**			
	1953. Brown on lt. green and orange unpt. Arms at l. on back. 2 serial # varieties.			
	a. Issued note.	.50	2.00	8.00
	s. Perforated w/3 holes.	—	—	2.00

		VG	VF	UNC
86	**100 KORUN**			
	1953. Brown on tan and pink unpt. Worker and farmer at l. 2 serial # varieties. Scene of Prague on back.			
	a. Issued note.	1.00	5.00	20.00
	s. Perforated w/3 holes.	—	—	5.00

1953 ISSUE
#83-86 wmk: Star in circle repeated.

1958 ISSUE

		VG	VF	UNC
84	**25 KORUN**			
	1953. Blue on lt. blue unpt. Equestrian statue of J. Zizka at l. 2 serial # varieties. Scene of Tabor on back.			
	a. Issued note.	1.50	7.50	25.00
	s. Perforated w/3 holes.	—	—	6.00

		VG	VF	UNC
87	**25 KORUN**			
	1958. Blue. Arms at l. ctr., J. Zizka at r. Town and church on back.			
	a. Issued note.	2.00	8.00	20.00
	s. Perforated w/1 hole or *SPECIMEN*.	—	—	6.00

1960-64 ISSUE
#88-98 printer: STC-Prague.

		VG	VF	UNC
85	**50 KORUN**			
	1953. Green on lt. green unpt. Statue of partisan w/Russian soldier at l. 2 serial # varieties. Back blue and olive; scene of Banska Bystricka at ctr.			
	a. Issued note.	1.00	6.00	22.50
	s. Perforated w/3 holes.	—	—	5.00

		VG	VF	UNC
88	**10 KORUN**			
	1960. Brown on m/c unpt. 2 girls w/flowers at r. Orava Dam on back.	.10	.50	4.00

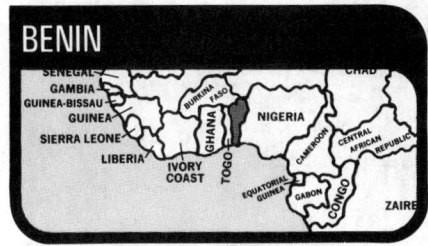

BENIN

The Peoples Republic of Benin (former French colony that became the Republic of Dahomey), located on the south side of the West African bulge between Togo and Nigeria, has an area of 43,484 sq. mi. (112,622 sq. km.) and and a population of 3.6 million. Capital: Porto-Novo. The principal industry of Benin, one of the poorest countries of West Africa, is the processing of palm oil products. Palm kernel oil, peanuts, cotton and coffee are exported.

Porto-Novo, on the Bight of Benin, was founded as a trading post by the Portuguese in the 17th century. At that time, Benin was composed of an aggregation of mutually suspicious tribes, the majority of which were tributary to the powerful northern Kingdom of Abomey. In 1863, the King of Porto-Novo petitioned France for protection from Abomey. The French subjugated other militant tribes as well, and in 1892 organized the area as a protectorate of France; in 1904 it was incorporated into French West Africa as the Territory of Dahomey. After the establishment of the Fifth French Republic, the Territory of Dahomey became an autonomous state within the French community. On Aug. 1, 1960, it became the fully independent Republic of Dahomey. In 1974, the republic began a transition to a socialist society with Marxism-Leninism as its revolutionary philosophy. On Nov. 30, 1975, the name of the Republic of Dahomey was changed to the Peoples Republic of Benin.

Benin is a member of the "Union Monetaire Ouest-Africaine" with other west African states.

Also see French West Africa, West African States.

RULERS:
French to 1960

MONETARY SYSTEM:
1 Franc = 100 Centimes

FRENCH INFLUENCE

GOUVERNEMENT GÉNÉRAL DE L'A.O.F. (AFRIQUE OCCIDENTALE FRANCAISE)

COLONIE DU DAHOMEY

1917 EMERGENCY ISSUE
#1-2 Décret du 11.2.1917. French coin design at l. and r.

		GOOD	FINE	XF
1	**0.50 FRANC**			
	D.1917. Orange and black. Back: Black text.			
	a. Wmk: Bees.	27.50	60.00	150.00
	b. Wmk: Laurel leaves.	27.50	60.00	150.00

		GOOD	FINE	XF
2	**1 FRANC**			
	D.1917. Orange and yellow unpt.			
	a. Wmk: Bees.	27.50	60.00	150.00
	b. Wmk: Laurel leaves.	30.00	65.00	175.00

DANISH WEST INDIES

The Danish West Indies (now the organized unincorporated territory of the Virgin Islands of the United States) consists of the islands of St. Thomas, St. John, St. Croix, and 62 islets located in the Caribbean Sea 40 miles (64 km.) east of Puerto Rico. The islands have a combined area of 133 sq. mi (344 sq. km.) and a population of 110,000. Capital: Charlotte Amalie. Tourism is the principal industry. Watch movements, costume jewelry, pharmaceuticals and rum are exported.

The Virgin Islands were discovered by Columbus in 1493, during his second voyage to America. During the 17th century the islands, actually the peaks of a submerged mountain range, were held at various times by Spain, Holland, England, France and Denmark, and during the same period were favorite resorts of the buccaneers operating in the Caribbean and the coastal waters of eastern North America. Control of the 100-island chain finally passed to Denmark and England. The Danish islands were purchased by the United States in 1917 for $25 million, mainly because they command the Anegada Passage into the Caribbean Sea, a strategic point on the defense perimeter of the Panama Canal.

Currency of the United States of America is now in circulation.

RULERS:
Danish to 1917

MONETARY SYSTEM:
25 West Indies Rigsdaler Courant = 20 Danish Rigsdaler Courant
1 Franc = 20 Cents
1 Daler = 5 Francs
1 Dollar = 100 Cents

DANISH INFLUENCE

TREASURY

ST. CROIX BRANCH

1784-85 PROVISIONAL ISSUE
#A1 reissue of 1775 Danish State notes.

NOTE: For similar revalued Danish notes refer to Faeroe Islands and Iceland listings.

		GOOD	FINE	XF
A1	**6 1/4 RIGSDALER**	—	—	—
	4.9.1784; 2.3.1785 (-old date 1775). Black on white paper. Printed on back of Denmark 5 Rigsdaler #A29a.			

1788 ISSUE
#A2-A74 Various hand sign. across bottom.

		GOOD	FINE	XF
A2	**20 RIGSDALER**			
	1788. Black. Uniface.	—	Rare	—
A3	**50 RIGSDALER**			
	1788. Black. Uniface.	—	Rare	—
A4	**100 RIGSDALER**			
	1788. Black. Uniface.	—	Rare	—

1799 Issue

			Good	Fine	XF
A11	**20 Rigsdaler**	1799. Black. Uniface.	—	Rare	
A12	**50 Rigsdaler**	1799. Black. Uniface.	—	Rare	
A13	**100 Rigsdaler**	1799. Black. Uniface.	—	Rare	

1806 Issue

A21	**5 Rigsdaler**	1806. Black. Uniface.	—	Rare	—
A22	**10 Rigsdaler**	1806. Black. Uniface.	—	Rare	—
A23	**50 Rigsdaler**	1806. Black. Uniface.	—	Rare	—
A24	**100 Rigsdaler**	1806. Black. Uniface.	—	Rare	—

1814-15 Issue

A31	**5 Rigsdaler**	1814-15. Black. Uniface.	—	Rare	—
A32	**10 Rigsdaler**	1814-15. Black. Uniface.	—	Rare	—
A33	**50 Rigsdaler**	1814-15. Black. Uniface.	—	Rare	—
A34	**100 Rigsdaler**	1814-15. Black. Uniface.	—	Rare	—

1822 Issue

A41	**5 Rigsdaler**	1822. Black. Uniface.	—	Rare	—
A42	**10 Rigsdaler**	1822. Black. Uniface.	—	Rare	—
A43	**50 Rigsdaler**	1822. Black. Uniface.	—	Rare	—
A44	**100 Rigsdaler**	1822. Black. Uniface.	—	Rare	—

1829 Issue

A51	**5 Rigsdaler**	1829. Black. Uniface.	—	Rare	—
A52	**10 Rigsdaler**	1829. Black. Uniface.	—	Rare	—
A53	**50 Rigsdaler**	1829. Black. Uniface.	—	Rare	—
A54	**100 Rigsdaler**	1829. Black. Uniface.	—	Rare	—

1836 Issue

A61	**5 Rigsdaler**	1836. Black. Uniface.	—	Rare	—
A62	**10 Rigsdaler**	1836. Black. Uniface.	—	Rare	—
A63	**50 Rigsdaler**	1836. Black. Uniface.	—	Rare	—
A64	**100 Rigsdaler**	1836. Black. Uniface.	—	Rare	—

1842 Issue

#A71-A74 w/text in Gothic lettering. Denomination line across top.

A71	**5 Rigsdaler**	1842. Black. Uniface.	—	Rare	—
A72	**10 Rigsdaler**	1842. Black. Uniface.	—	Rare	—
A73	**50 Rigsdaler**	1842. Black. Uniface.	—	Rare	—
A74	**100 Rigsdaler**	1842. Black. Uniface.	—	Rare	—

STATE TREASURY

LAW OF 4.4.1849

#1-6 various dates and sign. varieties w/denominations in *BESTINDISKE DALERE* (West Indies dollars).

NOTE: Issued examples required 7 sign.

			Good	Fine	XF
1	**2 Dalere**	L. 1849. Pink paper. Portr. Mercury in frame at l., portr. Zeus at r., arms at lower ctr.	125.00	250.00	475.00
2	**3 Dalere**	L. 1849. Pink paper. Like #1.	250.00	500.00	850.00
3	**5 Dalere**	L. 1849. Lt. violet paper. Like #1.	300.00	550.00	800.00
4	**10 Dalere**	L. 1849 (1900). Lt. green paper. Like #1.	350.00	650.00	1100.

			Good	Fine	XF
5	**50 Dalere**	L. 1849. Lt. blue paper. Like #1.	—	Rare	—
6	**100 Dalere**	L. 1849. Like #1.	—	Rare	—

LAWS OF 4.4.1849 AND 1860

7	**2 Dalere**	L. 1860. Like #1.	200.00	450.00	750.00

LAWS OF 4.4.1849 AND 1898

			Good	Fine	XF
8	**2 Dalere**	L. 1898. Brown paper. Like #1.			
	a.	Issued note w/7 sign. 1.8.1899.	125.00	250.00	700.00
	r.	Remainder w/3 sign.	20.00	45.00	100.00

BANK OF ST. THOMAS

1837 Issue

#9-12 printer: New England Bank Note Co., Boston.

9	**5 Dollars**	1837. Harbor scene at ctr., allegorical figures at l. and r.	—	Rare	—
10	**10 Dollars**	1837. Similar to #9.	—	Rare	—
11	**100 Dollars**	1837. Columbus and steamship at l., landing of Columbus at ctr., allegorical figures at r.	—	Rare	—
12	**500 Dollars**	1837. 4 women seated on globe, allegorical figures at l. and r.	—	Rare	—

1860 Issue

13	**5 Dollars**	1860. Blue. Bank arms at top ctr. Denomination: *$5* on back. Printer: ABNC.	—	Rare	—

			Good	Fine	XF
14	**10 Dollars**	1860. Black. Uniface.	—	Rare	—
14A	**10 Dollars**	1860. Orange. Uniface.	—	Rare	—
14B	**100 Dollars**	1860. Brown. Bank arms at upper ctr. Uniface.	—	Rare	—

1889 ISSUE
#15-16 have bank arms at l. Uniface.

15	1 DOLLAR		GOOD	FINE	XF
	1.7.1889. Lt. green.				
	a.	Issued note.	—	Rare	—
	r.	Unsigned remainder. 188x.	—	Rare	—
16	2 DOLLARS				
	1889.				
	a.	Issued note.	—	Rare	—
	r.	Unsigned remainder. 188x.	—	Rare	—

DANSK-VESTINDISKE NATIONALBANK

NATIONAL BANK OF THE DANISH WEST INDIES

1905 ISSUE
#17-20 printer: BWC.

17	5 FRANCS	GOOD	FINE	XF
	1905. Green and gray. Portr. Kg. Christian IX at lower l., palm tree at r. Village on back.	125.00	325.00	850.00

18	10 FRANCS		GOOD	FINE	XF
	1905. Black and red. Palm tree at l., portr. Kg. Christian IX at top ctr., village scene at r. Plants on back.				
	a.	Issued note.	550.00	1250.	2750.
	b.	Cut and handstamped: *CANCELLED.*	150.00	350.00	650.00

19	20 FRANCS		GOOD	FINE	XF
	1905. Red and lt. green. Palm tree at l., portr. Kg. Christian IX at top ctr., harbor scene at r. Several local scenes at l. and ctr. on back.				
	a.	Issued note.	—	Rare	—
	b.	Cut and handstamped: *CANCELLED.*	250.00	550.00	1000.

20	100 FRANCS		GOOD	FINE	XF
	1905. Gray and black. Portr. Kg. Christian IX at l., street scene at upper ctr., palm tree at r. Town scene at ctr. on back.				
	a.	Issued note.	—	Rare	—
	b.	Cut and handstamped: *CANCELLED.*	—	Rare	—

Danzig (Gdansk), the capital of Gdansk province, north-central Poland, is situated at the mouth of the Vistula River on the Baltic Sea.

Danzig was first mentioned in 997 as belonging to Poland. It began its development as a trade center in 1260, upon the attainment of municipal autonomy. In 1308, the city was seized by the Teutonic Knights who held it until it was regained by Poland in 1466. It reached its peak during the Renaissance, becoming the most prosperous port on the Baltic.

Danzig's decline began during the Swedish wars of the 17th century. In 1772 it was seized by Prussia and in 1793 was incorporated as part of Prussia. Napoleon granted it the status of a free city in 1807, which it didn't want because it had a German majority, and later was relegated to the province of West Prussia.

From 1919 to 1939, Danzig again had the status of a free city. It was given to Poland in March 1945, following the defeat of the Axis powers. Polish currency is now in circulation.

MONETARY SYSTEM:
1 Mark = 100 Pfennige
1 MO (Million) = 1,000,000
1 MD (Milliarde) = 1,000,000,000 to 1923
1 Gulden = 100 Pfennig, 1923-1937

NOTE: Certain listings encompassing issues circulated by various bank and regional authorities are contained in Volume 1 under German States.

DANZIG - FREE CITY

CITY COUNCIL

1914 EMERGENCY ISSUE

NOTE: #1-12 were issued by the city before its free city status began in 1919.

		VG	VF	UNC
1	**50 PFENNIG**			
	10.8.1914. Violet.			
	a. Wmk: Scales.	25.00	75.00	300.00
	b. Wmk: Wavy lines.	18.00	65.00	300.00
	c. Wmk: Spades.	18.00	65.00	300.00

		VG	VF	UNC
2	**1 MARK**			
	10.8.1914. Brown.			
	a. Wmk: Wavy lines.	25.00	90.00	325.00
	b. Wmk: Spades.	18.00	80.00	325.00
3	**2 MARK**			
	10.8.1914. Pink.	25.00	90.00	350.00
4	**3 MARK**			
	10.8.1914. Green.			
	a. Wmk: Spades.	25.00	100.00	400.00
	b. Wmk: Crosses in squares.	37.50	125.00	425.00

1916 ISSUE

		VG	VF	UNC
5	**10 PFENNIG**			
	9.12.1916. Black on blue unpt.	2.00	7.00	25.00

		VG	VF	UNC
6	**50 PFENNIG**			
	9.12.1916. Black on orange unpt.	2.00	7.00	25.00

1918 FIRST ISSUE

		VG	VF	UNC
7	**5 MARK**			
	12.10.1918. Black on green unpt.			
	a. Wmk: Drops.	25.00	60.00	165.00
	b. W/o wmk.	18.00	45.00	150.00
8	**20 MARK**			
	12.10.1918. Black on brown unpt.			
	a. Wmk: Drops.	30.00	70.00	200.00
	b. Wmk: Spades.	25.00	50.00	175.00
	c. W/o wmk.	18.00	45.00	160.00

1918 SECOND ISSUE

		VG	VF	UNC
9	**50 PFENNIG**			
	1.11.1918. Brown. City Hall. 2 stylized lions and arms on back.	3.50	10.00	35.00

		VG	VF	UNC
10	**20 MARK**			
	15.11.1918. Black on lilac-brown unpt. Hanseatic galleon at l. Town view, 2 stylized lions and arms on back.	15.00	50.00	185.00

1919 ISSUE

		VG	VF	UNC
11	**50 PFENNIG**			
	15.4.1919. Brown and violet. Town view on back.	1.50	5.00	12.00
12	**50 PFENNIG**			
	15.4.1919. Dk. green and olive-green. Like #11.	1.50	6.00	17.50

SENATE OF THE MUNICIPALITY

1922 ISSUE

13   100 MARK
    31.10.1922. Green on gray unpt. St. Mary's Church. Bldg. at l. and r.
    on back.

	VG	VF	UNC
	10.00	25.00	85.00

14   500 MARK
    31.10.1922. Blue. Arms at l., tall church at r. Krantor on back.

	VG	VF	UNC
	12.00	40.00	185.00

15   1000 MARK
    31.10.1922. Olive-green and dk. brown. Arms at l., Hanseatic galleon
    at r. Town view on back.

	VG	VF	UNC
	10.00	35.00	165.00

1923 FIRST ISSUE

16   1000 MARK
    15.3.1923. Dk. green. Similar to #15.

	VG	VF	UNC
	12.00	50.00	200.00

17   10,000 MARK
    20.3.1923. Dk. blue on lt. brown unpt. Town views at l. and r. Large
    bldg. on back.

	VG	VF	UNC
	10.00	35.00	165.00

18   10,000 MARK
(20)   26.6.1923. Dk. brown and blue. Portr. Danzig merchant at l. (painting
    by Hans Holbein the younger), ship at r. City view at l. and r. on back.

	VG	VF	UNC
	7.50	25.00	90.00

19   50,000 MARK
(19018) 20.3.1923. Lt. green on pale yellow unpt. St. Mary's Church at l. Arms
    at l., bldgs. at ctr. on back.

	VG	VF	UNC
	10.00	35.00	165.00

20   50,000 MARK
(19)   20.3.1923. Dk. brown. Like #18.

	VG	VF	UNC
	10.00	35.00	170.00

1923 PROVISIONAL ISSUE

21   1 MILLIONEN ON 50,000 MARK
    8.8.1923 (-old date 20.3.1923). Red ovpt. on #19.

	12.00	40.00	175.00

22   1 MILLIONEN ON 50,000 MARK
    8.8.1923 (-old date 20.3.1923). Dk. blue ovpt. on #19.

	VG	VF	UNC
	10.00	35.00	180.00

23   5 MILLIONEN ON 50,000 MARK
(24)   15.10.1923 (-old date 20.3.1923). Green ovpt. on #19.

	VG	VF	UNC
	10.00	37.50	180.00

1923 INFLATION ISSUES

24   1 MILLIONEN MARK
(23)   8.8.1923. Lilac and green. Arms at l., Chodowiecki at r. Ornate
    gateway on back.

	VG	VF	UNC
	8.00	25.00	100.00

25 10 MILLIONEN MARK
31.8.1923. Green. Portr. J. Hevelius at upper l., arms at r. Margin printing upright. City view across back.

	VG	VF	UNC
a. Lg. *A* at lower r. corner.	8.00	25.00	95.00
b. W/o *A* at lower r. corner.	10.00	30.00	110.00

26 10 MILLIONEN MARK
31.8.1923. Green. Like #25, but margin printing inverted.

	VG	VF	UNC
	9.00	25.00	135.00

27 100 MILLIONEN MARK
22.9.1923. Black on lt. orange unpt. Uniface.

	VG	VF	UNC
a. Wmk: Triangles.	10.00	30.00	180.00
b. Wmk: Tear drops.	10.00	30.00	180.00

28 500 MILLIONEN MARK
26.9.1923. Dk. brown on violet unpt. Portr. Schopenhauer at top ctr. City view on back.

	VG	VF	UNC
a. Upright lt. blue margin inscription.	10.00	30.00	180.00
b. Upright lt. yellow margin inscription.	10.00	30.00	180.00

29 500 MILLIONEN MARK
26.9.1923. Dk. brown on violet unpt. Like #28.

	VG	VF	UNC
a. Inverted lt. blue margin inscription.	10.00	30.00	175.00
b. Inverted lt. yellow margin inscription.	10.00	30.00	185.00

30 5 MILLIARDEN MARK
11.10.1923. Black on blue unpt., uniface.

	VG	VF	UNC
	12.00	40.00	185.00

31 10 MILLIARDEN MARK
11.10.1923. Black on brown unpt.

	VG	VF	UNC
a. Wmk: Interlaced lines.	10.00	37.50	185.00
b. Wmk: Tear drops.	10.00	40.00	190.00

DANZIGER ZENTRALKASSE

DANZIG CENTRAL FINANCE DEPARTMENT

1923 FIRST GULDEN ISSUE, OCT.
#32-37 uniface.

32 1 PFENNIG
22.10.1923. Dk. blue on lt. brown unpt.

	VG	VF	UNC
	6.00	15.00	57.50

33 2 PFENNIG
22.10.1923. Dk. green on orange unpt.

	VG	VF	UNC
	7.50	20.00	65.00

34 5 PFENNIGE
22.10.1923. Black on green unpt. Like #35.

	VG	VF	UNC
a. Wmk: Interlaced lines.	10.00	25.00	90.00
b. Wmk: Octagons.	15.00	40.00	100.00

35 10 PFENNIGE
22.10.1923. Dk. red on blue unpt.

	VG	VF	UNC
a. Wmk: Interlaced lines.	10.00	30.00	100.00
b. Wmk: Hanseatic galleon.	12.00	45.00	150.00

36 25 PFENNIGE
22.10.1923. Black on lilac-brown unpt.

	VG	VF	UNC
	12.00	45.00	175.00

37 50 PFENNIGE
22.10.1923. Black on gray unpt. 2 serial # varieties.

	VG	VF	UNC
	20.00	50.00	195.00

38 1 GULDEN
22.10.1923. Black on green unpt.

	VG	VF	UNC
a. Wmk: Interlaced lines.	25.00	65.00	250.00
b. Wmk: Hanseatic galleon.	45.00	90.00	300.00

39 2 GULDEN
22.10.1923. Lilac-brown. Hanseatic galleon at ctr. 2 serial # varieties.

	VG	VF	UNC
	60.00	125.00	375.00

40 5 GULDEN
22.10.1923. Black on lt. brown and gray-green unpt. Hanseatic galleon at ctr.

	VG	VF	UNC
a. Wmk: Interlaced lines.	80.00	200.00	600.00
b. Wmk: Hanseatic galleon.	100.00	250.00	700.00

41 10 GULDEN
22.10.1923. Black on reddish brown unpt. Hanseatic galleon at l.

	VG	VF	UNC
	100.00	300.00	1000.

42 25 GULDEN
22.10.1923. Black on olive unpt. Hanseatic galleon at l.

	VG	VF	UNC
	200.00	500.00	1500.

1923 SECOND GULDEN ISSUE, NOV.
#43-47 like #32-37. Uniface.

43 1 PFENNIG
1.11.1923. Dk. blue on lt. brown unpt.

	VG	VF	UNC
	35.00	70.00	200.00

43A 2 PFENNIG
1.11.1923. Dk. green on orange unpt.

	VG	VF	UNC
	100.00	175.00	500.00

44 5 PFENNIG
1.11.1923. Black on green unpt.

	VG	VF	UNC
	45.00	110.00	350.00

45 10 PFENNIGE
1.11.1923. Dk. red on blue unpt.

	VG	VF	UNC
	60.00	120.00	375.00

46 25 PFENNIGE
1.11.1923. Black on lilac-brown unpt.

	VG	VF	UNC
	70.00	140.00	400.00

47 50 PFENNIGE
1.11.1923. Black on gray unpt.

	VG	VF	UNC
	70.00	140.00	400.00

48	**1 GULDEN**	VG	VF	UNC
	1.11.1923. Black on green unpt.	100.00	170.00	500.00
49	**2 GULDEN**			
	1.11.1923. Lilac-brown. Hanseatic galleon at ctr.	120.00	250.00	600.00
50	**5 GULDEN**			
	1.11.1923. Black on lt. brown & gray-green unpt. Hanseatic galleon at ctr.	200.00	350.00	900.00
51	**50 GULDEN**			
	1.11.1923. Black on reddish brown unpt. Hanseatic galleon at l.	300.00	500.00	—
52	**100 GULDEN**			
	1.11.1923. Black on olive unpt. Hanseatic galleon at l.	300.00	600.00	—

BANK VON DANZIG

BANK OF DANZIG

1924 ISSUE

53	**10 GULDEN**			
	10.2.1924. Brown. Artushof (Artus' courtyard) at ctr.	150.00	350.00	900.00
54	**25 GULDEN**			
	10.2.1924. St. Mary's Church at ctr.	200.00	500.00	1750.00
55	**100 GULDEN**			
	10.2.1924. Blue. River Mottlau dock scene at ctr.	210.00	550.00	1800.

56	**500 GULDEN**	VG	VF	UNC
	10.2.1924. Green. Zeughaus (the arsenal) at ctr.	50.00	120.00	550.00

57	**1000 GULDEN**	VG	VF	UNC
	10.2.1924. Red-orange. City Hall at ctr.	50.00	175.00	600.00

1928-30 ISSUE

58 (59)	**10 GULDEN**			
	1.7.1930. Brown, Artushof (Artus' courtyard) at ctr.	35.00	85.00	550.00
59 (58)	**25 GULDEN**			
	1.10.1928. Dk. green. St. Mary's Church at ctr.	90.00	350.00	1000.

1931-32 ISSUE

60 (62)	**20 GULDEN**			
	2.1.1932. Lilac-brown. Stockturm (local tower) at ctr. 2 serial # varieties. Neptune at r. on back.	20.00	50.00	250.00
61 (60)	**25 GULDEN**			
	2.1.1931. Dk. green. St. Mary's Church at ctr.	40.00	100.00	600.00

62 (61)	**100 GULDEN**	VG	VF	UNC
	1.8.1931. Blue. River Mottlau dock scene at ctr. Allegorical man at r. on back.	30.00	90.00	300.00

1937-38 ISSUE

63 (64)	**20 GULDEN**	VG	VF	UNC
	1.11.1937. Dk. green. Artushof (Artus' courtyard) at ctr. 2 serial # varieties. Back like #62.	15.00	45.00	250.00
64 (65)	**20 GULDEN**			
	2.1.1938. Like #64. Blue-green and orange face, lilac-rose and green back. Specimen.	—	Rare	—
65 (63)	**50 GULDEN**			
	5.2.1937. Brown. The "Vorlaubenhaus" (building) at ctr. Allegorical man at r. on back.	20.00	70.00	275.00

The Kingdom of Denmark, a constitutional monarchy located at the mouth of the Baltic Sea, has an area of 16,633 sq. mi. (43,069 sq. km.) and a population of 5.16 million. Capital: Copenhagen. Most of the country is arable. Agriculture, which employs the majority of the people, is conducted by small farmers served by cooperatives. The largest industries are food processing, iron and metal, and fishing. Machinery, meats (chiefly bacon), dairy products and chemicals are exported.

Denmark, a great power during the Viking period of the 9th-11th centuries, conducted raids on western Europe and England, and in the 11th century united England, Denmark and Norway under the rule of King Canute. Despite a struggle between the crown and the nobility (13th-14th centuries) which forced the King to grant a written constitution, Queen Margaret (1353-1412) succeeded in uniting Denmark, Norway, Sweden, Finland and Greenland under the Danish crown, placing all of Scandinavia under the rule of Denmark. An unwise alliance with Napoleon contributed to the dismembering of the empire and fostered a liberal movement which succeeded in making Denmark a constitutional monarchy in 1849.

RULERS:

Frederik IV, 1690-1730
Christian VI, 1730-1746
Frederik V, 1746-1766
Christian VII, 1766-1808
Frederik VI, 1808-1839
Christian VIII, 1839-1848
Frederik VII, 1848-1863
Christian IX, 1863-1906
Frederik VIII, 1906-1912
Christian X, 1912-1947
Frederik IX, 1947-1972

MONETARY SYSTEM:

1 Rigsdaler dansk Courant = 96 Skilling Courant = 6 Mark; at the same time, 1 Rigsdaler Species = 120 Skilling Courant, 1713-1813
1 Rigsbankdaler = 96 Rigsbankskilling (= 1/2 Rigsdaler Species), 1813-54
1 Rigsbankdaler Rigsmont = 96 Skilling Rigsmont (= 1 Rigsbankdaler), 1854-74
1 Krone = 100 Ore (= 1/2 Rigsdaler), 1874-

KINGDOM

TREASURY

DECREE OF 8.4.1713 - "AUTHORIZED NOTES"

#A1-A6 have crowned double monogram F4 printed at top l., handwritten denomination, 6 hand sign.

		GOOD	FINE	XF
A1	1 RIGSDALER 1713.	—	—	—
A2	5 RIGSDALER 1713.	—	—	—
A3	10 RIGSDALER 1713.	—	—	—
A4	25 RIGSDALER 1713.	—	—	—
A5	50 RIGSDALER 1713.	—	—	—
A6	100 RIGSDALER 1713.	—	—	—

DECREE OF 8.4.1713 - 2ND GROUP

#A7-A9 printed denominations, 6 hand sign.

		GOOD	FINE	XF
A7	1 RIGSDALER 1713.	400.00	1000.	
A8	5 RIGSDALER 1713.			
A9	10 RIGSDALER 1713.			

DECREE OF 8.4.1713 - 3RD GROUP

#A10-A13 crowned double monogram F4 printed at top l. 5 hand sign.

		GOOD	FINE	XF
A10	1 (EEN) MARK 1713.	750.00	1500.	
A11	2 (TOE) MARK 1713.	850.00	1700.	
A12	3 MARK 1713. a. Value expressed as: Tree Mark. b. Value expressed as: Tre Mark.	900.00	1800.	

		GOOD	FINE	XF
A13	1 (EEN) RIGSDALER 1713.	800.00	1600.	

DECREE OF 8.4.1713 - 4TH GROUP

#A14-A17 w/o monogram; impressed stamp w/imperial arms, 3 hand sign.

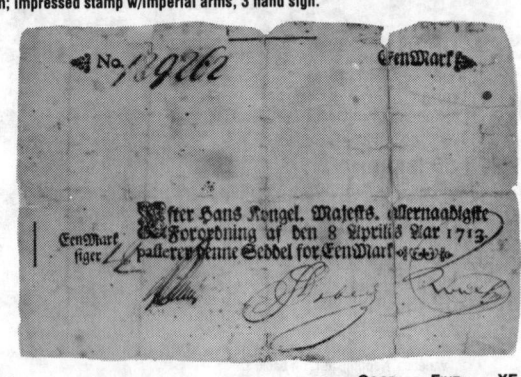

		GOOD	FINE	XF
A14	1 (EEN) MARK 1713.	600.00	1200.	—
A15	2 (TOE) MARK 1713.	700.00	1400.	—
A16	3 (TREE) MARK 1713.	800.00	1600.	—

A17	1 (EEN) RIGSDALER	GOOD	FINE	XF
	1713.	400.00	800.00	—

KIÖBENHAVNSKE ASSIGNATION-, VEXEL- OG LAANE-BANQUE

COPENHAGEN NOTES, EXCHANGE AND MORTGAGE BANK

COPENHAGEN BRANCH

1737 ISSUE
#A18-A23 have ornate column at l., handwritten denomination.

A18	10 RIGSDALER			
	1737.	—	—	—
A19	20 RIGSDALER			
	1737.	—	—	—
A20	30 RIGSDALER			
	1737.	—	—	—
A21	40 RIGSDALER			
	1737; 1740.	—	—	—
A22	50 RIGSDALER			
	1737; 1740.	—	—	—
A23	100 RIGSDALER			
	1737; 1739; 1740.	—	—	—

1748-1762 ISSUE
#A24-A27 have printed denomination, design at l. in 3 styles. #A24-A25 have 3 hand sign.; #A26-A27 have 5 hand sign.

A24	1 RIGSDALER COURANT	GOOD	FINE	XF
	(1762-92).			
	a. 1762-63 (only 1762 and 1763 known). No wmk.	—	—	—
	b. 1766-67 (only 1766 known). Wmk.: crowned monogram *F5* w/letters A-F, *C7* w/impressed stamp.	—	—	—
	c. 1769-92. Wmk: crowned monogram w/impressed stamp *C7*.	—	—	—

A25	10 RIGSDALER COURANT	GOOD	FINE	XF
	(1748-88).			
	a. 1748-63. Wmk: crowned monogram *F5* w/impressed stamp *F5*. No examples known.	—	—	—
	b. 1768-80. Wmk: crowned monogram *F5* w/impressed stamp *C7*.	45.00	225.00	—
	c. 1772-88. Wmk: crowned monogram *C7* and impressed stamp *C7*.	325.00	800.00	—
A26	50 RIGSDALER COURANT			
	(1748-87).			
	a. 1748-61. Wmk. and impressed stamp w/*F5*. No examples known.	—	—	—
	b. 1770-87. Wmk. and impressed stamp w/*C7*. No examples known.	—	—	—
A27	100 RIGSDALER COURANT			
	(1748-88).			
	a. 1748-61. Wmk. and impressed stamp w/*F5*. No examples known.	—	—	—
	b. 1768. Wmk.: *F5*, impressed stamp *C7*. No examples known.	—	—	—
	c. 1772-88 (only 1782 known). Wmk. and impressed stamp w/*C7*.	—	—	—

1775-88 ISSUE
#A28-32 similar to previous issue. Anti-counterfeiting text added vertically at r. White paper (#A29a) or blue paper (#A28, A29b, A30-32).

A28	1 RIGSDALER COURANT	GOOD	FINE	XF
	1788-1804. Issued until 1813.	40.00	100.00	200.00

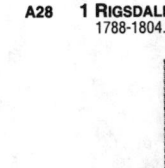

A29	5 RIGSDALER COURANT	GOOD	FINE	XF
	1775-1800.			
	a. White paper. 1775-91. Issued until 1793.	60.00	150.00	275.00
	b. Blue paper. 1786-1800. Issued until 1813.	50.00	125.00	225.00

A30	10 RIGSDALER COURANT	GOOD	FINE	XF
	1778-98. Issued until 1813.	70.00	175.00	—
A31	50 RIGSDALER COURANT			
	1785-94. Issued until 1812.	200.00	500.00	—

A32	100 RIGSDALER COURANT	GOOD	FINE	XF
	1785-98. Issued until 1813.	160.00	400.00	—

DANSKE OG NORSKE SPECIES BANKE I KIÖBENHAVN

DANISH-NORWEGIAN SPECIE BANK IN COPENHAGEN

1791-98 ISSUE
#A33-A37 in demoninations of *Rigsdaler Specie*.

		Good	Fine	XF
A33	**8 RIGSDALER SPECIE** 1791; 1797.	—	—	—
A34	**20 RIGSDALER SPECIE** 1791.	—	—	—
A35	**40 RIGSDALER SPECIE** 1792-96. No examples known.	—	—	—
A36	**80 RIGSDALER SPECIE** 1791-97. Only a *formular* of 1791 is known.	—	—	—
A37	**4 RIGSDALER SPECIE** 1798-1800. Only 1798 is known.	—	—	—

DRAFTS ON THE REVENUE OF THE TREASURY - COMPENSATION FUND

DECREE OF 8.4.1808

		Good	Fine	XF
A38	**2 RIGSDALER D.C.** D.1808.	48.00	180.00	—

		Good	Fine	XF
A39	**20 RIGSDALER D.C.** D.1808.	40.00	150.00	—

DECREES OF 28.8.1809 AND 6.6.1810.
#A40-A42 small change notes.

		Good	Fine	XF
A40	**8 SKILLING** D.1809.	20.00	75.00	—

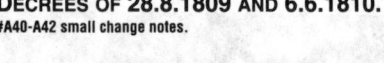

		Good	Fine	XF
A41	**12 SKILLING** D.1809.	25.00	85.00	—

		Good	Fine	XF
A42	**24 SKILLING** D.1810.	30.00	90.00	—

ROYAL BANK

1813 DRAFTS

A43	**100 RIGSBANKDALER** 6.2.1813. No examples known.	—	—	—
A44	**250 RIGSBANKDALER** 6.2.1813.	—	—	—
A45	**500 RIGSBANKDALER** 6.2.1813. No examples known.	—	—	—

DANISH STATE

DRAFTS - ROYAL DECREE OF 30.9.1813

A46	**100 RIGSBANKDALER** 1813. No examples known.	—	—	—
A47	**200 RIGSBANKDALER** 1813. No examples known.	—	—	—

RIGSBANKEN I KIOBENHAVN

RIGSBANK IN COPENHAGEN

1813 ISSUE
#A48-A52 uniface.

		Good	Fine	XF
A48	**1 RIGSBANKDALER** 1813-15.	65.00	165.00	—
A49	**5 RIGSBANKDALER** 1813-14.	100.00	250.00	—
A50	**10 RIGSBANKDALER** 1813-14.	120.00	300.00	—

		Good	Fine	XF
A51	**50 RIGSBANKDALER** 1813.	200.00	500.00	—

A52	100 RIGSBANKDALER			
	1813.	350.00	850.00	—

NATIONALBANKEN I KIOBENHAVN

NATIONAL BANK IN COPENHAGEN

1819 ISSUE
#A53-A57 uniface.

A53	1 RIGSBANKDALER	GOOD	FINE	XF
	1819.	35.00	90.00	—
A54	5 RIGSBANKDALER			
	1819.	70.00	175.00	—
A55	10 RIGSBANKDALER			
	1819.	100.00	250.00	—
A56	50 RIGSBANKDALER			
	1819.	—	—	—

A57	100 RIGSBANKDALER	GOOD	FINE	XF
	1819.	250.00	600.00	—

1834-51 ISSUE

A58	5 RIGSBANKDALER	GOOD	FINE	XF
	1835.	100.00	250.00	—
A59	20 RIGSBANKDALER			
	1851.			
	a. Hand serial #, impressed stamps, back w/3 hand sign.	—	—	—
	b. Printed serial #, no impressed stamps, no sign. on back (issued 1872).	175.00	400.00	—
A60	50 RIGSBANKDALER			
	1834.			
	a. Plain back, impressed stamps, 5 hand sign.	—	—	—
	b. Brown back, impressed stamps, 5 hand sign. (issued 1850).	—	—	—
	c. Like b. but no impressed stamp, 2 hand sign. (issued 1870, no examples known).	—	—	—
A61	100 RIGSBANKDALER			
	1845.	—	—	—

1860-74 ISSUE

A62	5 RIGSDALER			
	1863-74.			
	a. Wmk. w/o wavy lines, impressed stamp, hand serial #. 1863.	120.00	300.00	—
	b. Wmk. has wavy lines, no impressed stamp, printed serial #. 1872-74.	100.00	250.00	—
A63	10 RIGSDALER			
	1860-74.			
	a. Impressed stamp, hand serial #, back w/3 hand sign. 1860.	—	—	—
	b. No impressed stamp, printed serial #, no sign. 1872-74.	—	—	—
A64	50 RIGSDALER			
	1873-74.	—	—	—
A65	100 RIGSDALER			
	1870-74.	—	—	—

INTEREST-BEARING CREDIT NOTES 1848-70
Various Decrees and Laws

A66	5 RIGSBANKDALER			
	D.1848.	—	—	—
A67	5 RIGSBANKDALER			
	L.1850.	—	—	—

LAW OF 27.1.1851

A68	5 RIGSBANKDALER			
	L.1851.	—	—	—
A69	50 RIGSBANKDALER			
	L.1851. No examples known.	—	—	—
A70	100 RIGSBANKDALER			
	L.1851. No examples known.	—	—	—

LAW OF 26.8.1864

A71	20 RIGSDALER			
	L.1864.	—	—	—
A72	50 RIGSDALER			
	L.1864.	—	—	—
A73	100 RIGSDALER			
	L.1864.	—	—	—

LAW OF 27.3.1866

A74	20 RIGSDALER			
	L.1866.	—	—	—
A75	50 RIGSDALER			
	L.1866.	—	—	—
A76	100 RIGSDALER			
	L.1866.	—	—	—
A77	500 RIGSDALER			
	L.1866.	—	—	—

LAW OF 1.8.1870

A78	50 RIGSDALER			
	L.1870.	—	—	—
A79	100 RIGSDALER			
	L.1870.	—	—	—
A80	500 RIGSDALER	GOOD	FINE	XF
	L.1870.	—	—	—

1875-1903 ISSUE

A81	10 KRONER	GOOD	FINE	XF
	1875-90. Arms at upper ctr.	100.00	300.00	—
A82	50 KRONER			
	1875-81. Ornate panels at side s.	—	—	—

A83	100 KRONER	GOOD	FINE	XF
	1875-87. Head at l. and r., or nate oval design between.	—	—	—
A84	500 KRONER			
	1875; 1903. Heads of Mercury a t l. and Ceres at r., arms at bottom ctr.			
	a. Issued note.	—	—	—
	b. Handstamped: *MAKULATOR* (waste paper) w/2 punched holes.	350.00	1100.	—

1898-1904 ISSUE

1	5 KRONER	GOOD	FINE	XF
	1898-1904. Blue. Ornamental design of *5s* and *FEM KRONER*. Serial # at bottom l. and r.	60.00	150.00	350.00
2	10 KRONER			
	1891-1904. Black on brown unpt. Shield at l. ten 1 krone coins along bottom on back.	70.00	160.00	400.00
3	50 KRONER			
	1883-1904. Brown. Woman seated at l.	300.00	700.00	1200.
4	100 KRONER			
	1888-1904. Green. Woman standing w/scrolls at ctr.	300.00	800.00	1300.

1904-11 ISSUE

6	5 KRONER	GOOD	FINE	XF
	1904-11. Blue. Similar to #1 but different wmk. of wavy lines. Serial # at top l. and r.	50.00	135.00	300.00

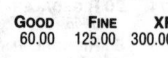

7	10 KRONER	GOOD	FINE	XF
	1904-11. Black on brown unpt. Like #2 but different wmk. of wavy lines.	60.00	125.00	300.00

8	50 KRONER	GOOD	FINE	XF
	1904-10. Brown. Like #3 but different wmk. of wavy lines.	275.00	650.00	1100.

9	100 KRONER	GOOD	FINE	XF
	1904. Green. Like #4 but different wmk. of wavy lines.	275.00	650.00	1100.

1914-16 ISSUES
#10-15 w/o pictorial design. Arms on back.

10	1 KRONE	VG	VF	UNC
	1914. Black on red paper. Arms in shield w/fish at lower l. for Iceland on back.	3.00	20.00	65.00

11	1 KRONE	VG	VF	UNC
	1914. Black on red paper. Arms in shield w/falcon at lower l. for Iceland on back.	2.00	15.00	50.00

12	1 KRONE	VG	VF	UNC
	1916; 1918; 1920; 1921. Blue o n blue-green unpt.	.85	3.00	12.00

STATSBEVIS

STATE TREASURY NOTES

1914 ISSUE
5% interest bearing notes that passed as legal tender.

16	10 KRONER	GOOD	FINE	XF
	1.10.1914.	50.00	100.00	200.00
17	50 KRONER			
	1.10.1914.	100.00	200.00	400.00
18	100 KRONER			
	1.10.1914.	—	—	—
19	500 KRONER			
	1.10.1914.	—	—	—

NATIONALBANKEN I KJOBENHAVN

NATIONAL BANK, COPENHAGEN

1910-31 ISSUE

#20-24 first sign. always V. Lange. Second sign. changes.

Text commences: *VEXLES MED GULDMONT* or *VEXLES PAA ANFORDRING MED GULDMONT.* Wmk: Dk. numerals of the notes' denominations.

		VG	VF	UNC
20	**5 KRONER** 1912-31. Blue-green. Coastline at ctr. Arms on back.	12.00	30.00	80.00
21	**10 KRONER** 1913-30. Brown. Mercury on back.			
	a. Lt. brown. 1913-15.	25.00	55.00	125.00
	b. Brown. 1917-30.	12.00	30.00	75.00
22	**50 KRONER** 1911-30. Blue-green. Fishermen in boat pulling in a net. Vines surrounding arms on back.	60.00	150.00	300.00
23	**100 KRONER** 1910-30. Brown. Sea-god w/shell-trumpet to l. and r. of arms on back.	30.00	75.00	175.00
24	**500 KRONER** 1910-31. Gray-blue. Farmer plowing w/horses at ctr. Vines surrounding arms on back.	125.00	300.00	600.00

1930-31 ISSUE

#25-29 first sign. V. Lange ot 31.3.1935. Svendsen from 1.4.1935. Second sign. changes.

Text commences: *NATIONALBANKENS SEDLER.* Wmk: Lt. numerals of value.

25	**5 KRONER** 1931-36. Blue-green. Like #20.	3.00	15.00	40.00
26	**10 KRONER** 1930-36. Brown. Like #21.	3.00	15.00	40.00
27	**50 KRONER** 1930-36. Blue-green. Like #22.	30.00	75.00	175.00
28	**100 KRONER** 1930-36. Brown. Like #23.	22.50	60.00	135.00
29	**500 KRONER** 1931-39. Gray-blue. Like #24.	100.00	225.00	450.00

DANMARKS NATIONALBANK

1937-38 ISSUE

#30-34 like #20-29 but w/new bank name; first sign. Svendsen. Second sign. changes (17 different.)

		VG	VF	UNC
30	**5 KRONER** 1937-43. Blue-green. Like #20 and #25.	.75	4.00	18.00
31	**10 KRONER** 1937-43. Brown. Like #21 and #26.	1.00	5.00	20.00

		VG	VF	UNC
32	**50 KRONER** 1938-42. Blue-green. Like #22 and #27.	7.00	25.00	70.00

		VG	VF	UNC
33	**100 KRONER** 1938-43. Brown. Like #23 and #28.	10.00	35.00	70.00
34	**500 KRONER** 1938-41. Gray-blue. Like #24 and #29.	75.00	160.00	325.00

1944-46 ISSUE

#35-41 first sign. Svendsen for #35, 36, 37a, 38, 39 - 1944-45. Halberg for #35, 37a, 37b, 38, 40 1945-49. Riim for #35, 37b, 38, 40, 41 - 1948-62.

		VG	VF	UNC
35	**5 KRONER** 1944-50. Blue. *KRO 5 NER.* Arms on back.	1.50	7.50	40.00

		VG	VF	UNC
36	**10 KRONER** 1944-45. Brown. *10 TI KRONER 10.* Arms on back.	1.50	7.50	40.00

		VG	VF	UNC
37	**10 KRONER** 1945-50. Dk. green. Face like #31. Arms on back.			
	a. Hand-made paper, wmk: Floral ornaments at l. and r.	4.00	20.00	50.00
	b. Wmk: Wavy lines (later issue).	1.50	7.50	35.00

		VG	VF	UNC
38	**50 KRONER** 1944-55. Violet. Fishermen in boat pulling in net. Face like #32. Arms at ctr. on back.	20.00	50.00	85.00
39	**100 KRONER** 1944-45. Green. Face like #33. Arms only on back.	50.00	90.00	165.00
40	**100 KRONER** 1946-60. Lt. green. Like #39.	30.00	55.00	80.00

41	500 KRONER	VG	VF	UNC
	1944-62. Orange. Face like #34. Arms only on back.	110.00	160.00	225.00

1950-63 ISSUE

Law of 7.4.1936

#42-47 first sign. changes. Second sign. Riim, 1952-67 for #42a, 42b, 43, 44, 45a, 45b, 46a, 46b, 47; Valeur from 1970- for #44, 45b, 46b.

42	5 KRONER	VG	VF	UNC
	(19)50-60. Blue-green. Portr. Thorvaldsen at l., 3 Graces at r. Kalundborg city view on back. Wmk: 5 repeated.			
a.	5 in the wmk. 10.55mm high. W/o dot after 7 in law date. (19)52. Series A0; A1; A2.	2.75	13.50	45.00
b.	As a but w/dot after 7 in law date. (19)52.	1.85	9.00	30.00
c.	5 in the wmk. 13mm high. (19)55-60.	1.50	7.50	25.00
r.	Replacement note. (19)50 (sic).	1.50	7.50	25.00

43	10 KRONER	VG	VF	UNC
	(19)50-52. Black and olive-brown. Portr. Andersen at l., birds in nest at r. Green landscape on back. Wmk: 5 repeated.			
a.	Issued note. (19)51-52.	4.00	20.00	65.00
r.	Replacement note. (19)50 (sic).	5.00	25.00	85.00

44	10 KRONER	VG	VF	UNC
	(19)50-74. Black and brown. Portr. Andersen at l. Black landscape on back.			
a.	Top and bottom line in frame commences w/10.	7.50	37.50	125.00
b.	As a but w/10's in wmk. 14mm high. (19)54-57.	5.50	27.50	90.00
c.	1957-74. Top and bottom line in frame commences with TI. (19)57-59.	2.00	9.00	30.00
d.	As c. (19)60-69.	2.00	6.00	20.00
e.	As c. (19)70-74.	FV	2.75	5.50
r.	Replacement note. (19)50 (sic).	2.50	4.50	10.00

45	50 KRONER	VG	VF	UNC
	(19)50-70. Blue on green unpt. Portr. O. Romer at l., tower at r. Rock formation on blue back.			
a.	Hand-made paper. Wmk: Crowns and 50 (19)56-61.	15.00	35.00	150.00
b.	Wmk: Rhombuses and 50. (19)62-70.	10.00	15.00	35.00
r.	Replacement note. (19)50 (sic).	12.50	22.50	75.00

MILITARY

KGL. DANSKA FÄLT-COMMISARIATET, 1809

ROYAL DANISH COMMISSION

1809 ISSUE

#M1A-M4A printed w/Danish and Swedish values, printed for planned occupation of south Sweden. (Not issued).

NOTE: Trial printings exist for 12 Skillingar; 1, 6, 20 and 24 Riksdaler Riksgald.

M1A	8 SKILLINGAR RIKSGALDS-MYNT			
	1809.	—	—	—
M2A	16 SKILLINGAR RIKSGALDS-MYNT			
	1809.	—	—	—
M3A	2 RIXDALER BANCO SPECIE			
	1809.	—	—	—
M4A	20 RIXDALER BANCO SPECIE			
	1809.	—	—	—

ALLIEREDE OVERKOMMANDO TIL BRUG I DANMARK

ALLIED COMMAND IN DENMARK, WWII

1945 ISSUE

M1	25 ORE			
	ND (1945). Brown and lilac.	10.00	20.00	45.00
M2	1 KRONE			
	ND (1945). Blue and lilac.	8.50	17.50	40.00
M3	5 KRONER			
	ND (1945). Green.	20.00	50.00	150.00
M4	10 KRONER			
	ND (1945). Dk. brown and blue.	25.00	60.00	175.00
M5	50 KRONER			
	ND (1945). Violet.	60.00	160.00	350.00
M6	100 KRONER			
	ND (1945). Green-blue. Specime ns only.	—	Unc	500.00

DANSKE KRIGSMINISTERIUM, DEN DANSKE BRIGADE

ROYAL DANISH MINISTRY OF WAR,

POST LIBERATION WWII.

1947-58 ISSUE

#M7-M12 issued for the troops first stationed in Germany, and later in other parts of the world.

M7	5 ORE			
	ND (1947-58). Blue. Arms at l.	6.50	13.00	30.00
M8	10 ORE			
	ND (1947-58). Brown. Like #M7.	6.50	13.00	30.00
M9	25 ORE			
	ND (1947-58). Blue. Like #M7.	10.00	20.00	40.00
M10	1 KRONE			
	ND (1947-58). Brown. Like #M12 .	15.00	30.00	50.00
M11	5 KRONER			
	ND (1947-58). Blue. Like #M12.	30.00	100.00	250.00
M12	10 KRONER			
	ND (1947-58). Brown.	50.00	150.00	350.00

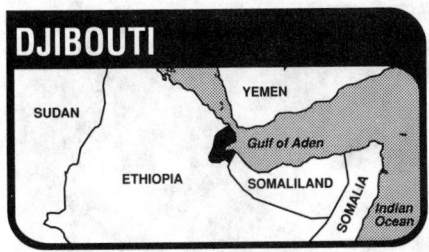

DJIBOUTI

The Republic of Djibouti (formerly French Somaliland or the French Overseas Territory of Afars and Issas), located in northeast Africa at the Bab el Mandeb Strait connecting the Suez Canal and the Red Sea with the Gulf of Aden and the Indian Ocean, has an area of 8,494 sq. mi. (22,000 sq. km.) and a population of 542,000. Capital: Djibouti. The tiny nation has less than one sq. mi. of arable land, and no natural resources except salt, sand and camels.

The commercial activities of the trans-shipment port of Djibouti and the Addis Ababa-Djibouti railroad are the basis of the economy. Salt, fish and hides are exported.

French interest in former French Somaliland began in 1839 with concessions obtained by a French naval lieutenant from the provincial sultans. French Somaliland was made a protectorate in 1884 and its boundaries were delimited by the Franco-British and Ethiopian accords of 1887 and 1897. It became a colony in 1896 and a territory within the French Union in 1946. In 1958, it voted to join the new French Community as an overseas territory, and reaffirmed that choice by a referendum in March 1967. Its name was changed from French Somaliland to the French Territory of Afars and Issas on July 5, 1967.

The French Tricolor, which had flown over the strategically important territory for 115 years, was lowered for the last time on June 27, 1977, when French Afars and Issas became Africa's 49th independent state, under the name of the Republic of Djibouti.

Djibouti, a seaport and capital city of the Republic of Djibouti (and formerly of French Somaliland and French Afars and Issas) is located on the east coast of Africa and the southernmost entrance to the Red Sea. The capital was moved from Obok to Djibouti in 1892 and established as the transshipment point for Ethiopia's foreign trade via the Franco-Ethiopian railway linking Djibouti and Addis Ababa.

RULERS:
French to 1977

MONETARY SYSTEM:
1 Franc = 100 Centimes

FRENCH SOMALILAND

BANQUE DE L'INDO-CHINE

DJIBOUTI BRANCH

DECRETS DES 21.1.1875, 20.2.1888, 16.5.1900 ET 3.4.1901
#1-3 Various dates (until 1921) and sign. varieties.

	5 FRANCS	**GOOD**	**FINE**	**XF**
1	1913; 1919. Blue. Oriental woman seated below FRANCE seated holding caduceus at l.			
	a. Issued note. 14.3.1913; 26.8.1919.	250.00	850.00	—
	b. Cancelled note handstamped: *ANNULÉ.* 26.8.1919.	100.00	400.00	—

	20 FRANCS	**GOOD**	**FINE**	**XF**
2	4.5.1910. Blue. Neptune reclining holding trident at lower left.			
	a. Issued note.	375.00	1650.	—
	b. Cancelled note handstamped: *ANNULÉ.*	125.00	700.00	—

	100 FRANCS	**GOOD**	**FINE**	**XF**
3	19.6.1915. Elephant columns at l. and r., 2 women reclining with ox and tiger at bottom.			
	a. Issued note.	375.00	1800.	—
	b. Cancelled note handstamped: *ANNULÉ.*	125.00	650.00	—

1920 PROVISIONAL ISSUE

	100 FRANCS	**GOOD**	**FINE**	**XF**
4	2.1.1920 (-old date 10.3.1914). Like #5. Red ovpt. on Tahiti #3.			
	a. Issued note.	50.00	125.00	285.00
	b. Cancelled note handstamped: *ANNULÉ.*	20.00	65.00	135.00

1920-23 REGULAR ISSUE
#4A-5 w/o decrets.

	5 FRANCS	**GOOD**	**FINE**	**XF**
4A	1.8.1923. Like #1.			
	a. Issued note.	200.00	800.00	—
	s. Perforated: *SPECIMEN.*	—	Unc	100.00
4B	**20 FRANCS**			
	3.1.1921. Like #2.	325.00	1250.	—

	100 FRANCS	**GOOD**	**FINE**	**XF**
5	2.1.1920. Brown. Like #3.	35.00	85.00	175.00

1928-38 ISSUES
#6-10 issued ca. 1926-38.

	5 FRANCS	**GOOD**	**FINE**	**XF**
6	ND. Blue and red on lt. gold unpt. Woman wearing helmet at l.			
	a. Sign. titles: *UN ADMINISTRATEUR* and *LE DIRECTEUR.*	2.00	7.00	37.50
	b. Sign. titles: *LE PRÉSIDENT* and *LE DIRECTEUR GÉNÉRAL.*	2.00	7.00	37.50

10	1000 FRANCS	GOOD	FINE	XF
	ND (1938). M/c. Market scene at l. and in background, woman sitting at r. Sign. titles: *LE PRÉSIDENT and LE DIRECTEUR GÉNÉRAL*.	20.00	50.00	225.00
10A	1000 FRANCS			
	ND (1938). Like #10 but bank title and denomination *1000* w/red background on face and back. Sign. titles: *LE PRÉSIDENT* and *LE DIRECTEUR GÉNÉRAL ADJOINT*. Perforated: *SPECIMEN*.	—	Rare	—

1943 PROVISIONAL ISSUES

11	5 FRANCS	GOOD	FINE	XF
	1.1.1943. Ovpt: Double cross of Lorraine and head of antelope on #6.	40.00	150.00	350.00
12	20 FRANCS			
	1.1.1943. Ovpt: Double cross of Lorraine and head of antelope on #7A.	—	Rare	—

7	20 FRANCS	GOOD	FINE	XF
	ND. Lilac-brown and dk. lilac on lt. green unpt. Dk. blue text. Woman at r. Peacock at l. ctr. on back.			
	a. Run # through 18.	3.00	12.50	55.00
	b. Similar coloring but much much lighter lilac and more visible lt. green unpt. Run #19-20 only.	4.00	15.00	75.00
7A	20 FRANCS			
	ND. Blue and lt. lilac on lt. gold unpt. Like #7. Heavier green on back. Run #21-23.	4.00	15.00	75.00
7B	20 FRANCS			
	ND. Like #7 but legend in black, and circle at bottom ctr. is red w/white numeral. numeral Red *20 Fr* on back. Different from #7 or 7A. Specimen.	—	Unc	750.00

8	100 FRANCS	GOOD	FINE	XF
	ND. M/c. Woman w/head in laurel wreath holding small figure of Athena at ctr.	8.00	20.00	90.00

12A	20 FRANCS	GOOD	FINE	XF
	ND. Blue and red. Ovpt: *COTE FRANCAISE DES SOMALIS. B.I.C. DJIBOUTI* in rectangle on #7.	75.00	150.00	450.00
13	100 FRANCS			
	1.1.1943. Ovpt: Double cross of Lorraine and head of antelope on #8.	100.00	250.00	550.00
13A	100 FRANCS			
	ND. Ovpt: *COTE FRANCAISE...* on #8.	100.00	250.00	550.00
13B	500 FRANCS			
	1.1.1943. Ovpt: Double cross of Lorraine and head of antelope on #9.	—	—	—
13C	500 FRANCS			
	ND. Ovpt: *COTE FRANCAISE...* on #9.	—	—	—
13D	1000 FRANCS			
	1.1.1943. Ovpt: Double cross of Lorraine and head of antelope on #10.	—	—	—
13E	1000 FRANCS			
	ND. Ovpt: *COTE FRANCAISE...* on #10.	—	—	—

1945 ISSUE

#14-18 printer: Government Printer Palestine.

9	500 FRANCS	GOOD	FINE	XF
	1927; 1938. Woman w/coat of arms and branch at l., ships in background.			
	a. Sign. titles: *UN ADMINISTRATEUR* and *LE DIRECTEUR*. 20.7.1927.	17.50	55.00	185.00
	b. Sign. titles: *LE PRÉSIDENT* and *LE DIRECTEUR GÉNÉRAL*. 8.3.1938.	15.00	50.00	175.00

14	**5 FRANCS** ND (1945). Lt. brown. Boat at ctr. on back.	GOOD 15.00	FINE 50.00	XF 200.00

24	**1 FRANC** 30.11.1919. Brown. 3 sign. varieties.	GOOD 30.00	FINE 60.00	XF 180.00

15	**20 FRANCS** ND (1945). Red on yellow unpt. Bldg. on back.	GOOD 25.00	FINE 85.00	XF 275.00
16	**100 FRANCS** ND (1945). Green. Palms on back.	60.00	225.00	—
17	**500 FRANCS** ND (1945). Purple. Swords and spears on back.	175.00	600.00	—

TRÉSOR PUBLIC, CÔTE FRANÇAISE DES SOMALIS

1952 ISSUE

25	**50 FRANCS** ND (1952). Lt. brown and m/c. Boat anchored at r. Camels on back.	VG 1.00	VF 8.00	UNC 30.00

18	**1000 FRANCS** ND (1945). Green, yellow and blue. Fish at ctr. on back.	GOOD 300.00	FINE 1000.	XF —

26	**100 FRANCS** ND (1952). M/c. Stylized corals. Trunk of palm tree on back.	VG 2.00	VF 25.00	UNC 80.00
27	**500 FRANCS** ND (1952). Ochre and m/c. Ships at l. ctr. Jumping gazelle on back.	10.00	80.00	325.00

1946 ISSUE

19	**10 FRANCS** ND (1946). M/c. Youth at l. Camel caravan on back.	15.00	50.00	200.00

19A	**100 FRANCS** ND (1946). M/c. Woman at l., farmer plowing w/oxen at r.	GOOD 20.00	FINE 90.00	XF 275.00
20	**1000 FRANCS** ND (1946). M/c. Woman holding jug at l. ctr. on front and back.	40.00	160.00	500.00

CHAMBRE DE COMMERCE, DJIBOUTI

1919 EMERGENCY ISSUE

21	**5 CENTIMES** ND (1919). Green cardboard; w/ or w/o perforations at l.	20.00	35.00	125.00
22	**10 CENTIMES** ND (1919). Lt. brown cardboard; w/ or w/o perforations at l.	20.00	35.00	125.00
23	**50 CENTIMES** 30.11.1919. Violet. 3 sign. varieties.	25.00	50.00	165.00

		VG	VF	UNC
28	**1000 FRANCS** ND (1952). M/c. Like #20.	25.00	120.00	400.00

		VG	VF	UNC
29	**5000 FRANCS** ND (1952). M/c. Aerial view of harbor at Djibouti at ctr.	75.00	275.00	700.00

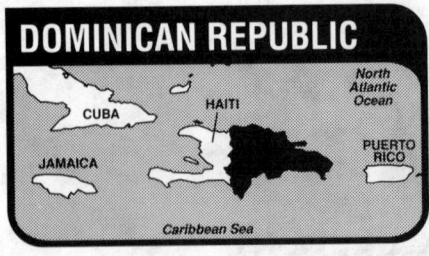

The Dominican Republic, which occupies the eastern two-thirds of the island of Hispaniola, has an area of 18,816 sq. mi. (48,734 sq. km.) and a population of 7.3 million. Capital: Santo Domingo. The agricultural economy produces sugar, coffee, tobacco and cocoa.

Columbus discovered Hispaniola in 1492, and named it *La Isla Espanola* - "the Spanish Island." Santo Domingo, the oldest white settlement in the Western Hemisphere, was the base from which Spain conducted its exploration of the New World. Later, French buccaneers settled the western third of Hispaniola, which in 1697 was ceded to France by Spain, and in 1804 became the Republic of Haiti - "mountainous country." At this time, the Spanish called their part of Hispaniola Santo Domingo, and the French called their part Saint-Domingue. In 1822, the Haitians conquered the entire island and held it until 1844, when Juan Pablo Duarte, the national hero of the Dominican Republic, drove them out of eastern Hispaniola and established an independent Dominican Republic. The republic returned voluntarily to Spanish dominion - after being rejected by France, Britain and the United States - from 1861 to 1865, when independence was restored.

MONETARY SYSTEM:
1 Peso = 100 Centavos

NOTE: This section has been renumbered from the old 7th Edition of General Issues.

ST. DOMINGUE

FRENCH ADMINISTRATION

1810's ISSUE
#2-5 held in reserve.

		GOOD	FINE	XF
1	**4 ESCALINS** ND (1810). Arms at ctr. Uniface.	—	—	—

SPANISH INFLUENCE

REPÚBLICA DOMINICANA

1848 PROVISIONAL ISSUE
#A1 and A2 ovpt:...*del decreto Congreso Nacional de 19 de Mayo de 1853...* on blank back. Printer: Durand, Baldwin & Co. N.Y.

NOTE: #A1 and A2 are seen most often with punched cancellation. Uncancelled notes are worth 30% more.

#8 held in reserve.

		GOOD	FINE	XF
6 (A1)	**20 PESOS ON 1 PESO = 40 CENTAV** 1848. Black. Like #A2.	75.00	175.00	—

7	40 PESOS ON 2 PESOS = 80 CENTA	GOOD	FINE	XF
(A2)	1848. Brown. Farm boy raking at l., arms at top ctr.	100.00	225.00	—

DECRETO 23.7.1849
#12 and 13 held in reserve.

9	1 PESO	GOOD	FINE	XF
(A3)	D.1849. Black.	150.00	300.00	450.00
10	2 PESOS			
(A4)	D.1849. Black.	150.00	300.00	450.00
11	5 PESOS			
(A4A)	D.1849. Black.	175.00	325.00	500.00

DECRETO 19.5.1853
#16 and 17 held in reserve.

14	1 PESO
(A4B)	D.1853. Arms at upper ctr.

15	2 PESOS	GOOD	FINE	XF
(A5A)	D.1853. Black. Arms at upper ctr.	150.00	300.00	450.00

DECRETO 16.8.1858
#20 held in reserve.

18	10 PESOS	GOOD	FINE	XF
(A5C)	D.1858	—	—	—
19	50 PESOS			
(A5E)	D.1858. Black.	—	—	—

1864 ISSUE
#23 held in reserve.

21	10 PESOS
(A5G)	20.9.1864. Black on brown paper. Issued at Santiago de los Caballeros.
22	20 PESOS
(A5H)	1864. Black on white paper.

COMISION DE HACIENDA

DECRETO 12 JULIO 1865
#25 and 27 held in reserve.

24	50 PESOS
(A5J)	D.1865.

26	200 PESOS	GOOD	FINE	XF
(A5L)	D.1865. 2 circular handstamps on face. Series J.	—	—	—

JUNTA DE CREDITO

DECRETO 23 OCTOBRE 1865
#30 held in reserve.

28	10 CENTAVOS FUERTES	GOOD	FINE	XF
(A5N)	D.1865. Arms in rectangular frame at upper ctr., oval handstamp below. Series C.	—	—	—
29	20 CENTAVOS FUERTES			
(A5P)	D.1865. Black. Small allegorical figure in oval at l., arms at upper ctr. Uniface.	—	—	—

DECRETO 12 MARZO 1866
#32 held in reserve.

31	40 CENTAVOS	GOOD	FINE	XF
(A5R)	D.1866. Design in vertical guilloche at l., lg. arms at upper ctr. r., oval handstamp below. Uniface. Series B.			

DECRETO 29 JULIO 1866
#37 held in reserve.

33	5 CENTAVOS			
(A5U)	ND. Arms at top ctr. Uniface.	85.00	200.00	350.00

			GOOD	FINE	XF
34 (A5V)	**10 CENTAVOS** *D.1866.* Black. Arms at top ctr., circular handstamp below. Uniface. Series D; E.		—	—	—
35 (A6)	**10 CENTAVOS** 29.7.1866. Black. Arms at top ctr. Uniface.		50.00	125.00	250.00

			GOOD	FINE	XF
36 (A7)	**20 CENTAVOS** ND. Lg. arms at ctr. r., circular handstamp below to r. Series B. Uniface.		75.00	175.00	350.00

DECRETO 26 MARZO 1867
#44 held in reserve.

			GOOD	FINE	XF
38 (A8)	**40 CENTAVOS** *D.1867.* Sm. arms at top ctr., handstamp below to r. Uniface. Series A; B.		75.00	175.00	—
39 (A9)	**1 PESO** ND.		75.00	175.00	—
40 (A10)	**2 PESOS** 1867.		75.00	175.00	—
42 (A11)	**5 PESOS** 1867.		75.00	175.00	—
43 (A12)	**10 PESOS** *D.1867.*		75.00	175.00	—

DECRETO 30.9.1867
#46 held in reserve.

45 (A13)	**20 CENTAVOS** *D.1867.* Black.		—	—	—

INTENDENCIA DE SANTO DOMINGO

1860's ISSUE
#47-51 w/red handstamped oval seal: *MINISTERIO LA GUERRA Y...* around crowned Spanish arms. Issued during the period Spain considered Santo Domingo as a Spanish territory, March 3, 1861 to July 11, 1865.

			GOOD	FINE	XF
47 (A41)	**1/2 PESO** 1.5.1862. Blue. Series A.		300.00	500.00	750.00

			GOOD	FINE	XF
48 (A42)	**2 PESOS** 1.5.1862. Green. Series B.		300.00	500.00	750.00
49 (A43)	**5 PESOS** ca.1862. Series C.		350.00	600.00	900.00
50 (A44)	**15 PESOS** ca.1862. Series D.		400.00	700.00	1000.
51 (A45)	**25 PESOS** ca.1862. Series E.		600.00	900.00	1250.

TREASURY

RESTORATION OF 16.8.1863
#56-58 held in reserve.

			GOOD	FINE	XF
55 (A51)	**1 PESO** 1870. Red. Allegorical figure of the Republic at l., arms at upper ctr. Uniface.		350.00	750.00	—

REPUBLICA DOMINICANA

BANCO CENTRAL DE LA REPÚBLICA DOMINICANA

1947 ISSUE
#59-67 face black w/orange seal w/text over seal: *CIUDAD TRUJILLO/DISTRITO DE SANTO DOMINGO/REPUBLICA DOMINICANA.* Unless otherwise stated, all notes have Indian (Liberty) head and national arms on back. Sign. and title varieties. Printer: ABNC.

			VG	VF	UNC
60 (18)	**1 PESO** ND (1947-55). Portr. Duarte at ctr. Back green.				
	a. Sign. title: *Secretario de Estado del Tesoro y Credito Publico* at r.		2.00	8.00	35.00
	b. Sign. title: *Secretario de Estado de Finanzas* at r.		2.00	8.00	35.00
61 (19)	**5 PESOS** ND (1947-50). Portr. Sanchez at ctr. Back brown.		7.00	20.00	80.00

| 62 | 10 PESOS | | VG | VF | UNC |
| (20) | ND (1947-50). Portr. Mella at ctr. Back orange. | | 15.00 | 35.00 | 150.00 |

63	20 PESOS		VG	VF	UNC
(21)	ND (1947-50). Gate (Puerta del Conde) at ctr. Back blue.		30.00	100.00	375.00
64	50 PESOS				
(22)	ND (1947-50). Tomb of Columbus at ctr. Back green.		60.00	200.00	450.00
65	100 PESOS				
(23)	ND (1947-50). Woman w/coffeepot and cup at ctr. Back green.		120.00	275.00	650.00
66	500 PESOS				
(24)	ND (1947-50). Obelisco de Ciudad Trujillo at ctr. Back green.		—	—	—

| 67 | 1000 PESOS | | VG | VF | UNC |
| (25) | ND (1947-50). Basilica Menor de Santa Maria at ctr. Back green. | | — | — | — |

1952 ISSUE

#68-70 printer: TDLR.

| 68 | 5 PESOS | | | | |
| (19A) | ND (1952). Similar to #61. | | 8.00 | 30.00 | 100.00 |

| 69 | 10 PESOS | | VG | VF | UNC |
| (20A) | ND (1952). Similar to #62 but many major differences. | | 20.00 | 50.00 | 185.00 |

| 70 | 20 PESOS | | VG | VF | UNC |
| (21A) | ND (1952). Portr. Trujillo at ctr. Trujillo's Peace Monument at ctr. between Indian head and arms on turquoise back. | | 50.00 | 160.00 | 425.00 |

1956 ISSUE

| 71 | 1 PESO | | VG | VF | UNC |
| (26) | ND (1957-61). Like #60. Printer: ABNC. | | 1.50 | 6.00 | 27.50 |

72	5 PESOS		VG	VF	UNC
(27)	ND (1956-58). Similar to #61. Printer: ABNC.		3.50	15.00	55.00
73	10 PESOS				
(28)	ND (1956-58). Similar to #62. Printer: ABNC.		8.00	25.00	95.00
74	20 PESOS				
(29)	ND (1956-58). Similar to #63. Printer: ABNC.		20.00	50.00	155.00
75	50 PESOS				
(31)	ND (1956-58). Like #64. Printer: ABNC.		60.00	140.00	275.00
76	100 PESOS				
(32)	ND (1956-58). Like #65. Printer: ABNC.		40.00	100.00	250.00
77	500 PESOS				
(33)	ND (1956-58). Like #66. Printer: ABNC.		—	—	—
78	1000 PESOS				
(34)	ND (1956-58). Like #67. Printer: ABNC.		—	—	—

1956 COMMEMORATIVE ISSUE

| 79 | 20 PESOS | | VG | VF | UNC |
| (30) | ND (1956). Black. Trujillo at ctr., red ovpt: *AÑO DEL BENEFACTOR DE LA PATRIA* at upper l. Printer: ABNC. | | — | — | — |

1958 ISSUE

80	1 PESO		VG	VF	UNC
(26A)	ND (1958-59). Similar to #71. Printer: W&S.		2.00	8.00	35.00
81	5 PESOS				
(27A)	ND (1959). Similar to #72. Printer: W&S.		5.00	25.00	85.00
82	10 PESOS				
(28A)	ND (1959). Similar to #73. Printer: W&S.		10.00	32.50	110.00
83	20 PESOS				
(30A)	ND (ca.1958). Like #79 but w/o commemorative text on face.		—	—	—

| 84 | 100 PESOS | | VG | VF | UNC |
| (32A) | ND (1959). Like #76. Printer: W&S. | | 25.00 | 90.00 | 200.00 |

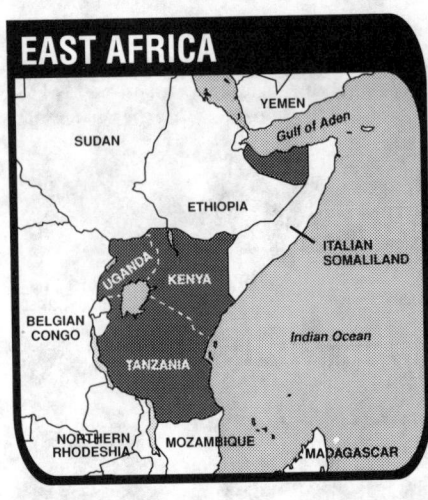

EAST AFRICA

East Africa was an administrative grouping of five separate British territories: Kenya, Tanganyika (now part of Tanzania), the Sultanate of Zanzibar and Pemba (now part of Tanzania), Uganda and British Somaliland (now part of Somalia). See individual entries for specific statistics and history.

The common interest of Kenya, Tanzania and Uganda invited cooperation in economic matters and consideration of political union. The territorial governors, organized as the East Africa High Commission, met periodically to administer such common activities as taxation, industrial development and education. The authority of the Commission did not infringe upon the constitution and internal autonomy of the individual colonies. A common coinage and banknotes, which were also legal tender in Aden, was provided for use of the member colonies by the East Africa Currency Board.

Also see British Somaliland, Zanzibar, Kenya, Uganda and Tanzania.

RULERS:
British

MONETARY SYSTEM:
1 Rupee = 100 Cents to 1920
1 Florin = 100 Cents, 1920-1921
1 Shilling = 100 Cents, 1921-

BRITISH INFLUENCE

GOVERNMENT OF THE EAST AFRICA PROTECTORATE

MOMBASA BRANCH

1905 ISSUE

			GOOD	FINE	XF
1A	**5 RUPEES**		450.00	1000.	—
	1.9.1905. Green unpt.				
2A	**10 RUPEES**		550.00	2000.	—
	1.9.1905. Yellow unpt.				
3A	**20 RUPEES**		1250.	3000.	—
	1.9.1905. Red unpt.				

			GOOD	FINE	XF
4A	**50 RUPEES**		—	Rare	
	1.9.1905. Purple unpt.				
5A	**100 RUPEES**		—	Rare	
	1.9.1905. Reddish brown unpt.				

		GOOD	FINE	XF
				Rare
6A	**500 RUPEES**			
	1.9.1905.			

1912-16 ISSUE

		GOOD	FINE	XF
1	**5 RUPEES**	275.00	650.00	1500.
	1.5.1916; 1.12.1918.			
2	**10 RUPEES**	350.00	1200.	2250.
	1.7.1912; 15.1.1914; 1.5.1916; 1.12.1918.			
3	**20 RUPEES**	800.00	1750.	3500.
	1.7.1912; 1.5.1916; 1.12.1918.			
4	**50 RUPEES**	1000.	2250.	4500.
	1.7.1912.			
5	**100 RUPEES**	—	Rare	—
	1.7.1912.			
6	**500 RUPEES**	—	Rare	—
	1.7.1912; 1.5.1916.			

EAST AFRICAN CURRENCY BOARD

MOMBASA BRANCH

1920 FIRST ISSUE

		GOOD	FINE	XF
7	**1 RUPEE**	60.00	250.00	750.00
	7.4.1920. Olive-brown and red. Portr. Kg. George V at r. Back blue; hippo at ctr. Printer: TDLR.			

1920 SECOND ISSUE

#10-12B Portr. Kg. George V at top ctr. Printer: BWC.

		GOOD	FINE	XF
8	**1 FLORIN**	35.00	125.00	400.00
	1.5.1920. Olive-brown and red. Portr. Kg. George V at r. Back blue; hippo at ctr. on back.			
9	**5 FLORINS**	250.00	650.00	1400.
	1.5.1920. Blue and green. Portr. Kg. George V at r. Hippo at ctr. on back.			

		GOOD	FINE	XF
10	**10 FLORINS = 1 POUND**	—	Rare	
	1.5.1920. Blue and orange.			
11	**20 FLORINS = 2 POUNDS**	—	Rare	
	1.5.1920.			

12	50 FLORINS = 5 POUNDS	GOOD	FINE	XF
	1.5.1920.	—	Rare	—
12A	100 FLORINS = 10 POUNDS			
	1.5.1920.	—	Rare	—
12B	500 FLORINS = 50 POUNDS			
	1.5.1920.	—	Rare	—

1921 ISSUE
#13-19 portr. Kg. George V at upper or lower r. Lion at ctr. on back. Printer: TDLR.

13	5 SHILLINGS	GOOD	FINE	XF
	15.12.1921. Blue-black on brown and orange unpt.	50.00	150.00	425.00
14	10 SHILLINGS			
	15.12.1921. Blue-black on green and pink unpt.	70.00	225.00	650.00
15	20 SHILLINGS = 1 POUND			
	15.12.1921. Blue-black on yellow and orange unpt.	140.00	450.00	1000.
16	100 SHILLINGS = 5 POUNDS			
	15.12.1921. Blue-black on lilac unpt.	250.00	750.00	2000.
17	200 SHILLINGS = 10 POUNDS			
	15.12.1921. Blue-black on gray-blue unpt.	700.00	1500.	3250.
18	1000 SHILLINGS = 50 POUNDS			
	15.12.1921. Blue-black on lt. brown unpt.	—	Rare	—
19	10,000 SHILLINGS = 500 POUNDS			
	15.12.1921. Blue-black on blue unpt.	—	Rare	—

NAIROBI BRANCH

1933 ISSUE
#20-26 portr. Kg. George V at upper or lower r. Printer: TDLR.

20	5 SHILLINGS	GOOD	FINE	XF
	1.1.1933. Blue-black on brown and orange unpt. Back orange-brown; lion at ctr.	30.00	85.00	300.00

21	10 SHILLINGS	GOOD	FINE	XF
	1.1.1933. Blue-black on green and pink unpt. Back green; lion at ctr.	40.00	135.00	450.00

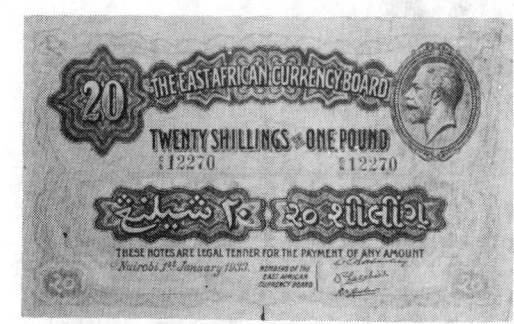

22	20 SHILLINGS = 1 POUND	GOOD	FINE	XF
	1.1.1933. Blue-black on yellow and orange unpt. Back brown; lion at ctr.	75.00	225.00	650.00
23	100 SHILLINGS = 5 POUNDS			
	1.1.1933. Blue-black on green and lilac unpt. Back red-brown, lion at ctr.	175.00	400.00	1400.
24	200 SHILLINGS = 10 POUNDS			
	1.1.1933. Blue-black on gray-blue unpt.	—	Rare	—
25	1000 SHILLINGS = 50 POUNDS			
	1.1.1933. Blue-black on lt. brown unpt.	—	Rare	—
26	10,000 SHILLINGS = 500 POUNDS			
	1.1.1933. Blue-black on blue unpt.	—	Rare	—

1938-52 ISSUE
#27-32 portr. Kg. George VI at upper or lower l. Various date, sign. and serial # varieties.

27	1 SHILLING	VG	VF	UNC
	1.1.1943. Blue-black on purple unpt. Back purple; lion at ctr.	2.00	7.00	50.00

28	5 SHILLINGS	VG	VF	UNC
	1938-52. Blue-black on brown unpt. Printer: TDLR.			
	a. 3 sign. 1.1.1938-42.	6.00	25.00	185.00
	b. 4 sign. 1943-1.1.1952.	5.00	20.00	150.00
28A	5 SHILLINGS			
	1.8.1942. Like #28 but w/India style serial #. W/o imprint	15.00	60.00	350.00

29	10 SHILLINGS	VG	VF	UNC
	1938-52. Dk. blue on green and pink unpt. Printer: TDLR.			
	a. 3 sign. 1.1.1938-42.	8.00	30.00	200.00
	b. 4 sign. 1943-1.1.1952.	7.00	25.00	185.00

29A 10 SHILLINGS
1.8.1942. Like #29 but w/India style serial #. W/o imprint.

	VG	VF	UNC
	30.00	125.00	550.00

30 20 SHILLINGS = 1 POUND
1938-52. Blue-black on yellow and orange unpt. Printer: TDLR.

	VG	VF	UNC
a. 3 sign. 1.1.1938-42.	10.00	40.00	350.00
b. 4 sign. 1943-1.1.1952.	8.00	35.00	275.00

30A 20 SHILLINGS = 1 POUND
1.8.1942. Like #30 but w/India style serial #. W/o imprint.

	VG	VF	UNC
	37.50	150.00	650.00

31 100 SHILLINGS = 5 POUNDS
1938-51. Blue-black on green and lilac unpt. Printer: TDLR.

	VG	VF	UNC
a. 3 sign. 1.1.1938-42.	80.00	275.00	800.00
b. 4 sign. 1943-1.8.1951.	75.00	260.00	700.00

32 10,000 SHILLINGS = 500 POUNDS
1.1.1947; 1.8.1951. Blue-black on blue unpt. Printer: TDLR.

	—	Rare	—

1953 ISSUE

#33-36 portr. Qn. Elizabeth II at upper or lower r. Various date and sign. varieties. Printer: TDLR.

33 5 SHILLINGS
31.3.1953-1.10.1957. Blue-black on lt. brown unpt.

	VG	VF	UNC
	3.00	15.00	125.00

34 10 SHILLINGS
31.3.1953-1.10.1957. Blue-black on green and pink unpt.

	VG	VF	UNC
	7.00	30.00	300.00

35 20 SHILLINGS = 1 POUND
31.3.1953-1.2.1956. Blue-black on yellow and orange unpt.

	VG	VF	UNC
	6.00	25.00	180.00

36 100 SHILLINGS = 5 POUNDS
31.3.1953-1.2.1956. Blue-black on green and lilac unpt.

	VG	VF	UNC
	50.00	175.00	700.00

W/O OFFICE OF ISSUE

37 5 SHILLINGS
ND (1958-60). Brown on m/c unpt.

	VG	VF	UNC
	2.50	10.50	135.00

38 10 SHILLINGS
ND (1958-60). Green on m/c unpt.

	VG	VF	UNC
	2.50	12.50	180.00

39 20 SHILLINGS
ND (1958-60). Blue on m/c unpt.

	VG	VF	UNC
	3.00	15.00	225.00

40 100 SHILLINGS
ND (1958-60). Red on m/c unpt.

	VG	VF	UNC
	20.00	100.00	750.00

ECUADOR

The Republic of Ecuador, located astride the equator on the Pacific coast of South America, has an area of 109,484 sq. mi. (283,561 sq. km.) and a population of 9.65 million. Capital: Quito. Agriculture is the mainstay of the economy but there are appreciable deposits of minerals and petroleum. It is the world's largest exporter of bananas and balsa wood. Coffee, cacao and shrimp are also valuable exports.

Ecuador was first sighted, 1526, by Bartolome Ruiz. Conquest was undertaken by Sebastian de Benalcazar who founded Quito in 1534. Ecuador was part of the province, later Vice-royalty, of Peru until 1739 when it became part of the Vice-royalty of New Granada. After two failed attempts to attain independence in 1810 and 1812, it successfully declared its independence in October 1820, and won final victory over Spanish forces May 24, 1822. Incorporated into the Gran Colombia confederacy, it loosened its ties in 1830 and regained full independence in 1835.

MONETARY SYSTEM:
1 Peso = 100 Centavos
1 Sucre = 10 Decimos = 100 Centavos
1 Condor = 25 Sucres

REPUBLIC

BANCO CENTRAL DEL ECUADOR

1928 ISSUE
#84-88 black on m/c unpt., w/text: *CAPITAL AUTORIZADO 10,000,000 SUCRES.* 2 sign.; sign. title ovpt: *TESORERO/GERENTE* at r. on #84b and 85b. Arms on back. Printer: ABNC.

#89 and 90 *Deleted*.

		Good	Fine	XF
84	**5 SUCRES**			
	1928-38. Woman seated w/wreath, sickle and fruit at ctr. Back red.			
	a. 14.1.1928; 6.11.1928; 9.11.1932; 21.12.1933; 7.11.1935; 5.10.1937.	5.50	17.50	55.00
	b. Sign. title ovpt: *Delegado de la Superintendencia de Bancos* across ctr. 27.10.1938.	8.00	25.00	75.00

		Good	Fine	XF
85	**10 SUCRES**			
	1928-38. Woman w/basket at ctr. Steam locomotive at l., ox carts at r. in background. Back blue.			
	a. 20.5.1928; 30.5.1928; 6.11.1928; 9.11.1933; 21.12.1933; 7.11.1935; 5.10.1937.	5.50	17.50	55.00
	b. Sign. title ovpt: *Delegado de la Superintendencia de Bancos* across ctr. 27.10.1938.	6.50	20.00	65.00
86	**20 SUCRES**	20.00	50.00	125.00
	30.5.1928; 6.11.1928; 9.11.1932; 21.12.1933; 7.11.1935; 12.2.1937. Woman seated at ctr. Back brown.			

		Good	Fine	XF
87	**50 SUCRES**	30.00	80.00	200.00
	30.5.1928; 6.11.1928; 9.11.1932; 21.12.1933; 8.8.1934; 1.10.1936. Ship at l., woman seated w/globe and anvil at ctr., train at r. Back green.			

		Good	Fine	XF
88	**100 SUCRES**	50.00	150.00	300.00
	30.5.1928; 6.11.1928; 9.11.1932; 8.8.1934; 1.10.1936. Woman seated w/globe at ctr. Back purple.			

1939-44 ISSUE
#91-97 slight modifications from previous issue, w/text: *CAPITAL AUTORIZADO 20,000,000 SUCRES.* 3 sign.; various sign. title ovpts. Printer: ABNC.

		VG	VF	UNC
91	**5 SUCRES**			
	1940-49. Similar to #84.			
	a. Printed sign. title: *TESORERO DE RESERVA* at r. 12.3.1940-28.11.1941.	2.50	10.00	50.00
	b. Sign. title ovpt: *GERENTE GENERAL* at r. 3.2.1945-21.10.1947.	2.25	9.00	45.00
	c. Like b., but sign. title printed. 21.10.1947-21.6.1949.	2.00	8.00	37.50

		VG	VF	UNC
92	**10 SUCRES**			
	1939-49. Similar to #85.			
	a. Sign. title ovpt: *PRESIDENTE* at l. Date at r. 17.10.1939-6.6.1944.	3.75	15.00	75.00
	b. Printed sign. titles. 6.2.1942; 3.12.1947; 19.2.1948; 22.11.1948; 21.6.1949.	3.50	14.00	70.00
	c. Sign. title ovpt: *PRESIDENTE* at l., *GERENTE GENERAL* at r. Date at l. 5.10.1944; 19.12.1944; 23.1.1945.	3.00	12.00	60.00
	d. Sign title ovpt: *GERENTE GENERAL* at r. 22.8.1945; 7.11.1945; 8.2.1946; 25.7.1946; 22.11.1948; 21.6.1949.	2.75	11.00	55.00

		VG	VF	UNC
93	**20 SUCRES**			
	1939-49. Similar to #86.			
	a. Sign. title ovpt: *PRESIDENTE* at l. Date at lower r. 17.10.1939-27.3.1944.	6.00	24.00	120.00
	b. Printed sign. titles. Date at lower r. 5.6.1940-27.3.1944.	5.50	22.50	110.00
	c. Sign. title ovpt: *PRESIDENTE* at l., *GERENTE GENERAL* at r. 25.10.1944.	5.00	20.00	100.00
	d. Sign title ovpt: *GERENTE GENERAL* at r. Date at upper r. 21.9.1945; 26.12.1945; 12.6.1947; 22.11.1948; 17.3.1949.	4.50	18.00	90.00
	e. As b. but date at upper r. 27.4.1948; 17.3.1949.	4.00	16.00	80.00
	f. Printed sign. titles w/*GERENTE GENERAL* at r.	4.25	17.00	85.00

		VG	VF	UNC
94	**50 SUCRES**			
	1939-1949. Similar to #87.			
	a. 17.10.1939-3.12.1943.	16.00	90.00	225.00
	b. Sign. title ovpt: *GERENTE GENERAL* at r. 16.10.1946; 12.7.1947; 22.11.1948; 27.1.1949.	15.00	75.00	175.00

		VG	VF	UNC
95	**100 SUCRES**			
	1939-49. Similar to #88.			
	a. 17.10.1939-16.10.1946.	40.00	125.00	300.00
	b. 12.7.1947.	20.00	60.00	150.00
	c. 27.1.1949.	25.00	75.00	225.00

96	500 SUCRES	VG	VF	UNC
	1944-1966. Mercury seated at ctr. Back deep orange.			
	a. Sign. title ovpt. *PRESIDENTE* at l. 12.5.1944; 27.6.1944.	175.00	325.00	—
	b. Sign. title ovpt. *GERENTE GENERAL* at l., *VOCAL* at r. 31.7.1944; 7.9.1944.	150.00	300.00	—
	c. Sign. title ovpt. *GERENTE GENERAL* at r. 12.1.1945-12.7.1947.	125.00	250.00	—
	d. As c. 21.4.1961-17.11.1966	100.00	200.00	550.00
	s. Specimen.	—	—	400.00

97	1000 SUCRES	VG	VF	UNC
	1944-67. Woman reclining w/globe and telephone at ctr. Back gray.			
	a. Sign. title ovpt. *PRESIDENTE* at l. 12.5.1944; 7.6.1944.	275.00	—	—
	b. Sign. title ovpt. *GERENTE GENERAL* at l., *VOCAL* at r. 31.7.1944; 7.9.1944.	250.00	—	—
	c. Sign. title ovpt. *PRESIDENTE* at l., *GERENTE GENERAL* at r. 12.1.1945.	225.00	—	—
	d. Sign. title ovpt. *GERENTE GENERAL* at r. 16.10.1945; 12.7.1947.	200.00	—	—
	e. As d. 21.4.1961; 27.2.1962; 4.3.1964; 23.7.1964; 17.11.1966; 6.4.1967.	100.00	—	—
	s. Specimen.	—	—	400.00

1950 ISSUE

Various dates found w/ or w/o dot after *1* in year.

#98 and 101 sign. title varieties.

#98-101 black on m/c unpt. Many date varieties. Arms at ctr. on back, 31mm wide w/o flagpole stems below. Printer: ABNC.

98	5 SUCRES	VG	VF	UNC
	11.5.1950-28.11.1955. Black on green unpt. Portr. A. J. de Sucre at ctr. Date at l. or r. Back red. Printer: W&S.			
	a. 11.5.1950-26.3.1953.	2.25	11.00	55.00
	b. Sign. title ovpt. *SUBGERENTE GENERAL* at l. 21.9.1953.	2.00	10.00	50.00
	c. 31.5.1954-28.11.1955.	1.75	8.50	42.50

99	10 SUCRES	VG	VF	UNC
(101)	1950-74. Portr. S. de Benalcazar at ctr. Back blue.			
	a. Plain background. 14.1.1950-28.11.1955.	1.50	5.00	20.00
	b. Ornate background, different background guilloches. 15.6.19566-27.4.1966.	.50	2.00	8.50
	c. 24.5.1968-2.1.1974.	.25	1.00	4.00

100	20 SUCRES	VG	VF	UNC
(102)	28.2.1950-28.7.1960. Church facade at ctr. Back brown.	1.00	4.50	20.00
101	50 SUCRES			
(99)	11.5.1950-8.4.1959. Black on green unpt. National monument at ctr. w/ bldgs. in background. Back green. Printer: W&S.			
	a. 11.5.1950; 26.7.1950; 13.10.1950; 3.4.1951; 26.9.1951.	5.00	25.00	100.00
	b. Sign. title ovpt. *SUBGERENTE GENERAL* at l. 3.9.1952; 8.10.1953.	4.50	22.50	90.00
	c. 10.12.1953; 19.6.1956; 8.4.1959.	4.00	20.00	80.00

1952 ISSUE

A105	100 SUCRES	VG	VF	UNC
	3.9.1952-2.4.1957. Black on m/c unpt. Portr. S. Bolívar at ctr. Different guilloches. Back purple.	15.00	75.00	200.00

1956 ISSUE

102	5 SUCRES	VG	VF	UNC
(100)	1956-73. Portr. A. J. de Sucre at ctr. Back red-violet.			
	a. 19.6.1956; 29.8.1956; 2.4.1957; 2.1.1958.	.50	2.50	10.00
	b. Sign. title: *SUBGERENTE GENERAL*. 24.9.1957.	.25	1.25	5.00
	c. 1.1.1966.	.20	.55	3.50
	d. 27.2.1970; 3.9.1973. Serial # varieties.	.15	.50	2.00

1957-58 ISSUE

#113 and 116 black on m/c unpt. Several sign. title ovpt. varieties. Security thread used intermittently through 1969. Printer: TDLR.

113	5 SUCRES	VG	VF	UNC
	1958-88. Portr. A.J. de Sucre at ctr. Back red-violet; arms at ctr.			
	a. 2.1.1958-7.11.1962.	.60	2.00	7.50
	b. 23.5.1963-27.2.1970.	.25	.50	3.00
	c. 25.7.1979-24.5.1980.	FV	FV	1.00
	d. 22.11.1988.	FV	FV	.50
	s. Specimen. ND; 24.5.1968.	—	—	27.50

116 **50 SUCRES**
1957-82. National Monument w/bldgs. in background at ctr. Back green; arms at ctr.

	VG	VF	UNC
a. 2.4.1957; 7.7.1959; 7.4.1960; 7.11.1962; 29.10.1963; 29.1.1965; 6.8.1965.	2.00	8.00	25.00
b. 1.1.1966; 27.4.1966; 17.11.1966; 4.10.1967; 30.5.1969; 17.7.1974.	.50	2.00	6.00
c. 24.5.1980; 20.8.1982.	FV	FV	1.50
s. Specimen. ND; 1.1.1966.	—	—	30.00

116A **100 SUCRES**
(105) 1957-80. Like #A105 but w/different guilloches.

	VG	VF	UNC
a. Sign. title: *SUBGERENTE GENERAL.* 24.9.1957.	10.00	50.00	125.00
b. 6.6.1958; 8.4.1959; 21.4.1961.	4.00	20.00	60.00
c. 1.1.1966-7.7.1970.	2.00	4.00	15.00
d. 1.2.1980.	1.00	2.00	5.00

The Arab Republic of Egypt, located on the northeastern corner of Africa, has an area of 386,650 sq. mi. (1,000,000 sq. km.) and a population of 56 million. Capital: Cairo. Although Egypt is an almost rainless expanse of desert, its economy is predominantly agricultural. Cotton, rice and petroleum are exported.

Egyptian history dates back to about 4000 B.C. when the empire was established by uniting the upper and lower kingdoms. Following its 'Golden Age' (16th to 13th centuries B.C.), Egypt was conquered by Persia (525 B.C.) and Alexander the Great (332 B.C.) The Ptolemies ruled until the suicide of Cleopatra (30 B.C.) when Egypt became a Roman colony. Arab caliphs ruled Egypt from 641 to 1517, when the Turks took it for their Ottoman Empire. Turkish rule, interrupted by the occupation of Napoleon (1798-1801), became increasingly casual, permitting Great Britain to inject its influence by purchasing shares in the Suez Canal. British troops occupied Egypt in 1882, becoming the de facto rulers. On Dec. 14, 1914, Egypt was made a protectorate of Britain. British occupation ended on Feb. 28, 1922, when Egypt became a sovereign, independent kingdom. The monarchy was abolished and a republic proclaimed on June 18, 1952.

On Feb. 1, 1958, Egypt and Syria formed the United Arab Republic. Yemen joined on March 8 in an association known as the United Arab States. Syria withdrew from the United Arab Republic on Sept. 29, 1961, and on Dec. 26 Egypt dissolved its ties with Yemen in the United Arab States. On Sept. 2, 1971, Egypt shed the name United Arab Republic in favor of the Arab Republic of Egypt.

RULERS:
Abdul Hamid II, AH1293-1327, 1876-1909AD
Muhammad V, AH1327-1332, 1909-1914AD
Hussein Kamil, 1915-1917AD
Fuad I (Sultan), 1917-1922AD
Fuad I (King), 1922-1936AD
Farouk I, 1936-1952AD

MONETARY SYSTEM:
1 Piastre = 10 Ochr-El-Guerches
1 Pound = 100 Piastres to 1916
1 Piastre (Guerche) = 10 Milliemes
1 Pound (Junayh) = 100 Piastres, 1916-

* * * This section has been renumbered. * * *

KINGDOM

NATIONAL BANK OF EGYPT

Bank notes issued since 1899. Many sign., serial # and date varieties. Valuations are for the most common dates; earlier dates usually deserve higher prices.

#A1 *Deleted.*

DECREE OF 25.6.1898

1 **50 PIASTRES**
(3) 1.1.1899. Black on green and pink unpt. Sphinx at ctr. Back green.

	VG	VF	UNC
a. Sign. Palmer.	600.00	1500.	3500.
b. Sign. Rowlatt.	600.00	1500.	3500.

2 **1 POUND**
(7) 5.1.1899. Black on red and orange unpt. 2 camels at ctr. Back orange. Printer: BWC.

	VG	VF	UNC
a. Sign. Palmer.	1250.	3000.	5000.
b. Sign. Rowlatt.	850.00	2500.	5000.
s. Specimen.	—	—	—

11	50 PIASTRES	VG	VF	UNC
(4)	1.8.1914-12.12.1920. Brown. Sphinx at l.	125.00	385.00	1000.

3	5 POUNDS	VG	VF	UNC
(14)	10.1.1899. Yellow, green and rose. Pyramids and palms at l. Specimen.	—	Rare	—

4	10 POUNDS	VG	VF	UNC
(19)	13.1.1899. Rose and lt. blue. Philae Temple w/2 sailboats at l. Specimen.	—	Rare	—

5	50 POUNDS			
(23)	15.1.1899. Blue, yellow and rose. Philae Temple at l. Specimen.	—	Rare	—

12	1 POUND	VG	VF	UNC
(8)	21.9.1914-20.1.1924. Blue on pink and lt. green unpt. Ruins at l. Back green.			
	a. Sign. Rowlatt. 1914-20.	70.00	250.00	600.00
	b. Sign. Hornsby. 1923-24.	75.00	275.00	650.00

6	100 POUNDS			
(27)	15.1.1899. Olive. Philae Temple at l. Specimen.	—	Rare	—

1912 ISSUE

8	10 POUNDS			
(19A)	1.1.1912. Like #4, but rose and dk. blue.	—	Rare	—

13	5 POUNDS	VG	VF	UNC
(15)	1.9.1913-11.11.1919. Pink and black. Small sailing ship at l.	225.00	600.00	2000.

1913-17 ISSUE

10	25 PIASTRES	VG	VF	UNC
(1)	1917-51. Brown-olive. Banks of the Nile at ctr.			
	a. Sign. Rowlatt. 5.8.1917-18.6.1918.	25.00	95.00	375.00
	b. Sign. Cook. 6.6.1940; 7.6.1940.	7.50	15.00	85.00
	c. Sign. Nixon. 18.12.1940-1946	1.50	8.50	45.00
	d. Sign. Leith-Ross. 1948-7.7.1950.	1.50	8.50	50.00
	e. Sign. Saad (Arabic). 15.5.1951-21.5.1951.	2.00	8.50	50.00
	f. As e. But w/Arabic serial #. 22.5.1951-23.5.1951.	2.00	8.50	50.00

14	10 POUNDS	VG	VF	UNC
(20)	2.9.1913-30.5.1920. Brown and m/c. Mosque of Sultan Qala'un and street in Cairo. Printer: BWC.	150.00	500.00	1850.

		VG	VF	UNC
15 (24)	**50 POUNDS** 1913-45. Purple and m/c. Mameluke tombs w/caravan in front.			
	a. Sign. Rowlatt. 4.9.1913.	400.00	1500.	—
	b. Sign. Rowlatt 14.11.1918-21.1.1920.	200.00	650.00	—
	c. Sign. Nixon. 6.2.1942-2.5.1945.	75.00	225.00	750.00

		VG	VF	UNC
16 (27A)	**100 POUNDS** 5.9.1913; 7.10.1919. Blue and green. Citadel and mosque of Mohammed Ali at ctr.	7500.	—	—

1921 ISSUE

		VG	VF	UNC
17 (28)	**100 POUNDS** 1921-45. Brown, red and green. Citadel of Cairo at l. Mosque at r. Small sailing boat and island of Philae on back.			
	a. Sign. Rowlatt (?). 1.3.1921.	—	—	—
	b. Sign. Hornsby. 1.9.1921.	700.00	2000.	—
	c. Sign. Cook. 4.6.1936.	75.00	400.00	—
	d. Sign. Nixon. 1942-45.	50.00	225.00	700.00

1924 ISSUE

		VG	VF	UNC
18 (9)	**1 POUND** 1.6.1924-20.9.1924. Red and blue. Camel at ctr.	85.00	285.00	700.00

		VG	VF	UNC
19 (16)	**5 POUNDS** 1924-45. Green and violet. Bank at ctr. Back blue and red on green and orange unpt; palms and bldg. at ctr.			
	a. Sign. Hornsby. 1.8.1924-13.1.1929.	35.00	125.00	500.00
	b. Sign. Cook. 1930-40.	15.00	45.00	165.00
	c. Sign. Nixon. 1940-45.	12.50	35.00	125.00

1926 ISSUE

		VG	VF	UNC
20 (10)	**1 POUND** 1.7.1926-10.1.1930. Green and dk. blue. Fellah at r. Back purple.	35.00	125.00	475.00

1930-35 ISSUE

21 (5)	**50 PIASTRES**	**VG**	**VF**	**UNC**
	7.5.1935-18.5.1951. Green and m/c. Tutankhamen at l. Back blue; crescent and stars at l. Wmk: Scarab.			
	a. Sign. Cook. 1935-40.	2.50	12.50	47.50
	b. Lg. sign. Nixon. 1940-41.	2.00	10.00	40.00
	c. Sm. sign. Nixon. 1945-47.	2.00	10.00	40.00
	d. Sign. Leith-Ross. 1948-50.	2.00	10.00	40.00
	e. Sign. Saad (Arabic). 1951.	2.00	12.50	50.00

22 (11)	**1 POUND**	**VG**	**VF**	**UNC**
	1930-48. Blue and brown. circle over wmk. at l. unprinted, portr. Tutankhamen in brown at r. Back green; mosque at ctr. Wmk: Sphinx.			
	a. Sign. Hornsby. 23.4.1930; 24.4.1930; 25.4.1930.	20.00	65.00	170.00
	b. Sign. Cook. 5.12.1931-10.6.1940.	5.00	15.00	55.00
	c. Sign. Nixon. 25.11.1940-31.1.1945.	1.50	7.50	30.00
	d. Sign. Leith-Ross. 26.5.1948-10.6.1948.	2.00	8.50	40.00

23 (21)	**10 POUNDS**	**VG**	**VF**	**UNC**
	3.3.1931-24.5.1951. Brown, yellow-green and m/c. Mosque of Sultan Qala'un and street in Cairo at r. Back blue; farm scene and trees. Printer: BWC.			
	a. Sign. Cook. 3.3.1931-1940.	25.00	65.00	250.00
	b. Sign. Nixon. 1940-47.	15.00	50.00	150.00
	c. Sign. Leith-Ross. 1948-50.	15.00	50.00	150.00
	d. Sign. Saad (Arabic). 1951.	15.00	55.00	165.00

1946-50 ISSUE

24 (12)	**1 POUND**	**VG**	**VF**	**UNC**
	1.7.1950-10.5.1952. Blue and lilac. Portr. Kg. Farouk at r.			
	a. European and Arabic serial #. 1.7.1950-13.7.1950.	3.50	22.50	90.00
	b. Arabic serial #. 15.5.1951-22.5.1951.	3.50	22.50	90.00
	c. Like b. w/o imprint. 8.5.1952-10.5.1952.	3.50	22.50	90.00

25 (17)	**5 POUNDS**	**VG**	**VF**	**UNC**
	1.5.1946-6.6.1951. Blue-green, violet and brown. Citadel of Cairo at l., Farouk at r.			
	a. Sign. Leith-Ross. 1.5.1946-1950.	10.00	45.00	135.00
	b. Sign. Saad (Arabic). 1951.	12.00	50.00	150.00

26 (25)	**50 POUNDS**	**VG**	**VF**	**UNC**
	1.11.1949-16.5.1951. Green and brown. Portr. Kg. Farouk at r. City scene on back.			
	a. Sign. Leith-Ross. 1.11.1949-1950.	25.00	125.00	600.00
	b. Sign. Saad (Arabic). 1951.	25.00	125.00	600.00

27 (29)	**100 POUNDS**	**VG**	**VF**	**UNC**
	1.7.1948-16.5.1951. Lt. violet and green. Minaret at l., Portr. Kg. Farouk at r. Mosque on back.			
	a. Sign. Leith-Ross. 1.7.1948-50.	35.00	200.00	750.00
	b. Sign. Saad (Arabic). 1951.	30.00	175.00	700.00

1952 ISSUE

28 (2)	**25 PIASTRES**	**VG**	**VF**	**UNC**
	8.5.1952-14.12.1957. Green. Tutankhamen's mask at r. Mosque on back.	1.00	5.00	15.00
29 (6)	**50 PIASTRES**			
	8.5.1952-3.8.1960. Brown on m/c unpt. Tutankhamen at r. Ruins on back. Wmk: Sphinx.	1.00	3.00	15.00
30 (13)	**1 POUND**			
	12.5.1952-23.8.1960. Blue and lilac. Circle over wmk. at l. w/unpt., Tutankhamen in lilac at r. Back blue; ruins. Wmk: Sphinx.	1.00	5.00	15.00

31	**5 POUNDS**		VG	VF	UNC
(18)	8.5.1952-11.8.1960. Dk. green, gray-blue and brown. Mosque at l., Tutankhamen at r. Back green; allegorical figures. Wmk: Flower.		5.00	12.00	25.00

32	**10 POUNDS**		VG	VF	UNC
(22)	1.11.1952-31.5.1960. Red and lilac. Tutankhamen's mask at r. Ruins on back. Wmk: Sphinx.		7.50	20.00	40.00
33	**50 POUNDS**				
(26)	29.10.1952; 30.10.1952. Green and brown. Tutankhamen's mask at r. Back like #26.		20.00	100.00	500.00

34	**100 POUNDS**		VG	VF	UNC
(30)	29.10.1952; 30.10.1952. Violet and green. Minaret at l. Tutankhamen's mask at r. Back like #27.		15.00	100.00	550.00

EGYPTIAN GOVERNMENT

1916-17 ISSUE

158	**5 PIASTRES**		VG	VF	UNC
(58)	27.5.1917. Blue on green and tan unpt. Back olive-green; ruins at ctr. (Not issued).		—	—	250.00
159	**10 PIASTRES**				
(59)	ND (ca. 1917). Green and black. Specimen.		—	—	—

160	**10 PIASTRES**		VG	VF	UNC
(60)	1916-17. Green on tan and lt. green unpt. Back blue; Colossi of Memnon on at ctr. Printer: TDLR.				
	a. 17.7.1916.		25.00	75.00	300.00
	b. 27.5.1917.		10.00	35.00	125.00

1918 ISSUE

161	**5 PIASTRES**		VG	VF	UNC
(61)	1.5.1918-10.6.1918. Purple on green and orange unpt. Back green; ruins at ctr. Printer: Survey of Egypt.		15.00	40.00	250.00

162	**5 PIASTRES**		VG	VF	UNC
(62)	1.6.1918. Lilac-brown on green unpt. Caravan at lower ctr. Back blue. Printer: BWC.		8.50	30.00	100.00

LAW 50/1940 ND ISSUES

163	**5 PIASTRES**		VG	VF	UNC
(63)	ND. Green on brown unpt. Aswan Dam on lilac back.		1.00	5.00	30.00
164	**5 PIASTRES**				
(64)	ND. Brown on yellow unpt. Mosque of Emir Khairbak at l. Back gray.		1.00	4.50	25.00

165	**5 PIASTRES**		VG	VF	UNC
(65)	ND. Brown on yellow unpt. Portr. Kg. Farouk at l. Back gray-blue; like #164.				
	a. Sign. title: *MINISTER OF FINANCE* on back.		1.00	3.00	20.00
	b. Sign. title: *MINISTER OF FINANCE AND ECONOMY* on back.		1.00	4.00	30.00

166	**10 PIASTRES**		VG	VF	UNC
(66)	ND. Brown on lilac unpt. Nile scene w/Citadel on blue back.				
	a. W/o wmk. Arabic serial #.		4.00	15.00	120.00
	b. Wmk: Geometric shape. Arabic serial #.		3.00	12.50	75.00
	c. Wmk: Geometric shape Western serial #.		4.00	15.00	100.00

167 **10 PIASTRES**
(67)   ND. Blue on green unpt. Temple of Philae at ctr. Color shading
       varieties. Back green on lt. orange unpt.

	VG	VF	UNC
	1.00	4.00	30.00

168 **10 PIASTRES**
(68)   ND. Blue on green unpt. Portr. Kg. Farouk at r. Back green on lt.
       orange unpt.

	VG	VF	UNC
a. Sign. title: *MINISTER OF FINANCE* on back.	1.00	4.00	30.00
b. Sign. title: *MINISTER OF FINANCE AND ECONOMY* on back.	2.00	5.00	40.00

EGYPTIAN ROYAL GOVERNMENT

Face A1: *EGYPTIAN ROYAL GOVERNMENT* in Arabic. (Regency of Farouk's son, Ahmed Fuad II).
Back 1A: as following issue.

1952 REVOLUTIONARY PROVISIONAL ISSUE

169 **5 PIASTRES**
(69)   ND. (1952). Similar to #170 but different heading at top.

	VG	VF	UNC
	—	—	—

169A **10 PIASTRES**
(69A)   ND. (1952). Similar to #171 but different heading at top.

	VG	VF	UNC
	—	—	—

EGYPTIAN STATE

Face 1: *EGYPTIAN STATE CURRENCY NOTE* in Arabic.
Back 1A: *EGYPTIAN CURRENCY NOTE* in English. Sign. title: *MINISTER OF FINANCE AND ECONOMY.* Imprint: Survey of Egypt.

1952 ND ISSUE

170 **5 PIASTRES**
(70)   ND. (1952). Lilac on gray-olive unpt. Portr. Qn. Nefertiti at r. Ovpt.
       pattern on Kg. Farouk wmk. at l. Back brown.

	VG	VF	UNC
	25.00	75.00	150.00

171 **10 PIASTRES**
(71)   ND (1952). Gray-blue on brown unpt. Group of people and flag w/3
       stars and crescent at r. Ovpt. pattern on Farouk wmk. at l. Back black
       and red.

	VG	VF	UNC
	45.00	125.00	300.00

EGYPTIAN REPUBLIC

Face 2: *EGYPTIAN REPUBLIC CURRENCY NOTE* in Arabic.
Back 1A: Like previous issue *(EGYPTIAN CURRENCY NOTE)* and sign. as above).

1952 PROVISIONAL ISSUE

172 **5 PIASTRES**
(72)   ND (1952). Similar to #170 w/ovpt. pattern on Farouk wmk. at l.

	VG	VF	UNC
	25.00	85.00	165.00

1952 REGULAR ISSUE

174 **5 PIASTRES**
(74)   ND (1952-58). Lilac. Like #172 but w/o pattern ovpt. on wmk. area.

	VG	VF	UNC
a. Wmk: Pyramids. 3 sign. varieties.	1.00	5.00	17.50
b. Wmk: Crown and letters (paper from #165 and #168).	1.00	5.00	22.50

175 **10 PIASTRES**
(75)   ND (1952-58). Gray-blue to black. Similar to #171 but w/o ovpt.
       pattern on wmk. area.

	VG	VF	UNC
a. Wmk: Pyramids. 3 sign. varieties.	1.00	5.00	35.00
b. Wmk: Crown and letters (paper as on #174b).	1.00	6.00	35.00

UNITED ARAB REPUBLIC

ARAB REPUBLIC OF EGYPT

Face 3: *UNITED ARAB REPUBLIC-EGYPTIAN REGION* in Arabic (main heading plus small lines of Arabic text underneath).
Back 1B: *EGYPTIAN CURRENCY NOTE* in English. Sign. title changed to : *MINISTER OF TREASURY.* Imprint: Survey of Egypt.
Face r: Main heading unchanged from Face 3 but *EGYPTIAN REGION* (small line of Arabic text) is deleted.
Back 2: *UNITED ARAB REPUBLIC* in English. Various sign. Imprint: Survey Dept.

1958 FIRST ND ISSUE

		VG	VF	UNC
176 (76)	**5 PIASTRES** ND. Red-lilac to violet. Similar to #174.			
	a. Wmk: Pyramids.	1.50	5.00	20.00
	b. Wmk: Eagles. 2 sign. varieties.	1.50	5.00	20.00
	c. Wmk: *U A R* letters in Arabic and English. Lilac or dk. purple.	.25	2.00	10.00

		VG	VF	UNC
177 (77)	**10 PIASTRES** ND. Blue-black to black. Similar to #175 but flag w/2 stars and w/o crescent.			
	a. Wmk: Pyramids. 2 sign. varieties.	1.50	5.00	20.00
	b. Wmk: Eagles.	1.50	5.00	20.00
	c. Wmk: *U A R* letters in Arabic and English.	.25	1.50	12.50
178 (77A)	**10 PIASTRES** ND. "Mule" note combining Face 3. W/back 1A.	15.00	75.00	300.00

ITALIAN OCCUPATION - WWII

Italian issue prepared for the occupation of Egypt during WWII. Specimens only, except for #M2 and M3. "Issued" notes would mean only that they were saved during the destruction of the entire printing. They were not released to general circulation.

CASSA MEDITERRANEA DI CREDITO PER L'EGITTO

1942 ND ISSUE

NOTE: Only one complete specimen set is known. For similar notes w/*PER IL SVDAN* refer to Sudan #M1-M8; for similar notes w/*CASSA MEDITERRANEA...LA GRECIA* refer to Greece #M1-M9.

		VG	VF	UNC
M1	**5 PIASTRES** ND (1942). Purple on blue. Bust of Apollo at r. Stylized grain at l. on back.			
	a. Issued note.	—	Rare	—
	s. Specimen.	—	—	2500.
M2	**10 PIASTRES** ND (1942). Red-orange. Bust of Apollo at r. Stylized ancient galley prows at l. on back.			
	a. Issued note.	—	Rare	—
	s. Specimen.	—	—	2500.

		VG	VF	UNC
M3	**50 PIASTRES** ND (1942). Red-orange. Portr. Emperor Octavian at l.			
	a. Issued note.	—	Rare	—
	s. Specimen.	—	—	2500.
M4	**1 LIRA** ND (1942). Dull purple and dk. brown on ochre unpt. Portr. Emperor Octavian at l.			
	a. Issued note.	—	Rare	—
	s. Specimen.	—	—	2500.

		VG	VF	UNC
M5	**5 LIRE** ND (1942). Dk. brown and purple on ochre unpt. Portr. Emperor Octavian at l.			
	a. Issued note.	—	Rare	—
	s. Specimen.	—	—	2500.
M6	**10 LIRE** ND (1942). Violet and purple. Specimen.	—	—	2500.

		VG	VF	UNC
M7	**50 LIRE** ND (1942). Dk. gray on lt. gray unpt. Portr. David (by Michelangelo) at l.			
	a. Issued note.	—	Rare	—
	s. Specimen.	—	—	2500.
M8	**100 LIRE** ND (1942). Portr. David (by Michelangelo) at l.			
	a. Issued note.	—	Rare	—
	s. Specimen.	—	—	2500.

EL SALVADOR

GUATEMALA
HONDURAS
NICARAGUA
North Pacific Ocean

The Republic of El Salvador, a Central American country bordered by Guatemala, Honduras and the Pacific Ocean, has an area of 8,260 sq. mi. (21,041 sq. km.) and a population of 5.05 million. Capital: San Salvador. This most intensely cultivated country of Latin America produces coffee (the major crop), cotton, sugar and balsam for export. Gold, silver and other metals are largely unexploited.

The first Spanish attempt to subjugate the area was undertaken in 1523 by Pedro de Alvarado, Cortes' lieutenant. He was forced to retreat by superior Indian forces, but returned in 1525 and succeeded in bringing the region under control of the captain generalcy of Guatemala, where it remained until 1821. In 1821, El Salvador and the other Central American provinces declared their independence from Spain. In 1823, the Federal Republic of Central America was formed by the five Central American States. When this federation was dissolved in 1829, El Salvador became an independent republic.

MONETARY SYSTEM:
1 Peso = 100 Centavos to 1919
1 Colon = 100 Centavos 1919-

NOTE: This section has been reorganized by date issues from printing firms. The catalog numbers have been changed and are referenced to the old 7th Edition of General Issues.

REPUBLIC
GOBIERNO DEL SALVADOR
GOVERNMENT OF EL SALVADOR

1877 ISSUE
#1-8 have arms at upper ctr. on face, arms at ctr. on back. 180x82mm. Printer: NBNC.

		VG	VF	UNC
1	**1 PESO**			
	1.4.1877. Blue and black. Back brown. (11)			
	a. Issued note.	—	—	—
	s. Specimen.	—	—	300.00
2	**2 PESOS**			
	1.4.1877. Brown and black. Back blue. Specimen.	—	—	300.00
3	**5 PESOS**			
	1.4.1877. Green and black. Back orange. Specimen.	—	—	300.00
4	**10 PESOS**			
	1.4.1877. Orange and black. Back green. Specimen.	—	—	300.00
5	**25 PESOS**			
	1.4.1877. Orange-brown and black. Back blue. Specimen.	—	—	400.00
6	**50 PESOS**			
	1.4.1877. Red-orange and black. Back brown. Specimen.	—	—	400.00
7	**100 PESOS**			
	1.4.1877. Blue and black. Back red-orange. Specimen.	—	—	500.00
8	**500 PESOS**			
	1.4.1877. Gold and black. Back orange-brown. Specimen.	—	—	500.00

DEUDA INTERIOR DEL PAIS
Circulating Interior Debit Notes.
#9-15 similar in color and design to #1-8.
#9-18 larger size, 215 x 127mm. Printer: NBNC.

		VG	VF	UNC
9	**1 PESO**			
	1.4.1877.			
	a. Issued note.	—	—	—
	s. Specimen.	—	—	300.00
10	**2 PESOS**			
	1.4.1877. Specimen.	—	—	300.00
11	**5 PESOS**			
	1.4.1877. Specimen.	—	—	300.00
12	**10 PESOS**			
	1.4.1877. Specimen.	—	—	300.00
13	**25 PESOS**			
	1.4.1877. Specimen.	—	—	
14	**50 PESOS**			
	1.4.1877.			
	a. Issued note.	—	—	—
	s. Specimen.	—	—	
15	**100 PESOS**			
	1.4.1877. Specimen.	—	—	
16	**200 PESOS**			
	1.4.1877. Black on brown unpt. Back deep red. Specimen.	—	—	
17	**500 PESOS**			
	1.4.1877. Gold and black. Back orange-brown. Specimen.	—	—	
18	**1000 PESOS**			
	1.4.1877. Black on deep red unpt. Back yellow. Specimen.	—	—	

DEUDA PUBLICA DEL SALVADOR
Circulating Public Debit Notes. Ca. 1880.

		VG	VF	UNC
35	**25 PESOS**			
	18xx. Brown and black. Mercury l., arms at upper ctr. Printer: BWC. Specimen.	—	—	—

BANCO CENTRAL DE RESERVA DE EL SALVADOR
VALIDATION OVERPRINTS

The Government decreed that after 1907 all issued banknotes should have a validation stamp with the text: *TOMADO RAZON* accompanied by the official seal and sign. Varieties of sign. and numerous dates may exist for some issues. Later issues have only the seal, sign. and date after San Salvador. The dates listed throughout are only those found on the face of the note.

TRIBUNAL DE CUENTAS

Sergio Castellanos	1907–1910

TRIBUNAL SUPERIOR DE CUENTAS

Sergio Castellanos	1910–1916	Alb. Galindo	1924–1927
Jose E. Suay	1917–1918	D. Rosales Sol	1928–1929
Luis Valle M.	1919	C.V. Martinez	1939

JUNTA DE VIGILANCIA DE BANCOS Y S.A.

V.C. Barriere	1935–1944	B. Glower V.	1952
C. Valmore M.	1940	M. Ant. Ramirez	1954–1958
V.M. Valdes	1946–1948	Antonio Serrano L.	1956–1958
M.E. Hinds	1949	Pedro A. Delgado	1959
Jorge Sol	1950–1953	R. Rubio	1961

CORTE DE CUENTAS

M.E. Hinds	1940–1943

SUPERINTENDENCIA DE BANCOS Y OTRAS INSTITUCIONES FINANCIERAS

Juan S. Quinteros	1962–1975	Marco T. Guandique	1977–Feb. 1981
Jose A. Mendoza	1968–1975	Rafael T. Carbonell	1981–
Jorge A. Dowson	1975–1977	Raul Nolasco	1981–

NOTE: Certain listings encompassing issues circulated by various bank and regional authorities are contained in Volume 1.

1934 ISSUE
#75-80 portr. C. Columbus at ctr. on back. Printer: ABNC.

75 **1 COLON**
(69) 31.8.1934; 4.9.1941; 14.1.1943. Black on pale blue and m/c unpt.
Allegorical woman Allegorical woman reclining w/fruits and branch at
ctr. Back orange.

	VG	VF	UNC
	6.00	15.00	60.00

76 **2 COLONES**
(73) 31.8.1934-14.5.1952. Black on m/c unpt. Allegorical woman reclining
w/fruits and branch at ctr. Back red-brown.

	VG	VF	UNC
	10.00	35.00	110.00

77 **5 COLONES**
(74) 31.8.1934. Black on m/c unpt. Allegorical woman reclining w/fruits
and branch at ctr. Back green.

	VG	VF	UNC
	12.00	40.00	120.00

78 **10 COLONES**
(77) 31.8.1934. Black on m/c unpt. Allegorical woman reclining w/fruits
and branch at ctr. Back dk. brown.

	VG	VF	UNC
	25.00	75.00	195.00

79 **25 COLONES**
31.8.1934; 14.2.1951; 17.3.1954. Allegorical woman reclining w/fruits
and branch at ctr. Back deep blue.

	VG	VF	UNC
	25.00	65.00	175.00

80 **100 COLONES**
31.8.1934; 9.2.1937. Brown and green unpt. Allegorical woman
reclining w/fruits and branch at ctr. Back dull olive-green.

	VG	VF	UNC
	30.00	85.00	225.00

1938 ISSUE
#81 and 82 portr. C. Columbus at ctr. on back. Printer: W&S.

81 **1 COLON**
(70) 10.5.1938. Black on m/c unpt. Woman w/basket of fruit on her head at
l. Back orange.

	VG	VF	UNC
	6.00	15.00	60.00

			VG	VF	Unc
82	**5 Colones**		10.00	27.50	95.00
(75)	10.5.1938-17.3.1954. Black on m/c unpt. Woman w/basket of fruit on her head at l. Back green.				

1942-44 Issue
#83-86 portr. C. Columbus at ctr. on back. Printer: W&S.

			VG	VF	Unc
83	**1 Colon**		4.00	12.50	55.00
(71)	26.9.1944-14.5.1952. Black on pale blue and m/c unpt. Farmer plowing w/oxen at ctr. Back orange.				

			VG	VF	Unc
84	**5 Colones**		7.50	20.00	85.00
(76)	11.8.1942-14.5.1952. Black on m/c unpt. Delgado addressing crowd at ctr. Back green.				

			VG	VF	Unc
85	**10 Colones**		10.00	45.00	125.00
(78)	14.3.1943-14.5.1952. Black on m/c unpt. Portr. M.J. Arce at l. Back brown.				

			VG	VF	Unc
86	**100 Colones**		25.00	75.00	225.00
(81)	11.8.1942-31.1.1951. Brown and green unpt. Independence monument at ctr. Back olive-green.				

1950; 1954 Issue

			VG	VF	Unc
87	**1 Colon**		3.00	10.00	40.00
(72)	10.1.1950; 6.11.1952; 17.3.1954. Coffee bush at l., Lake Coatepeque at r. Back orange. Printer: W&S.				

			VG	VF	Unc
88	**10 Colones**		10.00	40.00	100.00
(99)	17.3.1954. Black on dull purple and m/c unpt. M.J. Arce at upper ctr. Back dk. brown. Series ZA.				
89	**100 Colones**		25.00	75.00	225.00
	17.3.1954. Black on green unpt. Independence monument at ctr. Back olive-green. Printer: ABNC.				

1955 Issue
#90-92 portr. C. Columbus at ctr. on back. Printer: W&S.

			VG	VF	Unc
90	**1 Colon**				
(82)	1955-60. Black on m/c unpt. Coffee bush at lower l., bank at r. Back orange.				
	a. Paper w/o metal thread. 13.4.1955.		2.50	5.00	18.00
	b. Paper w/metal thread. 15.2.1956-17.8.1960.		1.00	2.50	12.50

			VG	VF	Unc
91	**2 Colones**				
(88)	1955-58. Black on m/c unpt. Coffee bush at l. w/field workers in background. Back red-brown.				
	a. Plain paper w/o security thread. 13/4/1955.		4.00	12.00	40.00
	b. Paper w/metal thread. Wmk: *BANCO CENTRAL*. 27.8.1958.		3.00	10.00	35.00

			VG	VF	Unc
92	**5 Colones**				
	1955-59. Black on m/c unpt. Woman w/basket of fruit on her head. Back green.				
	a. Plain paper w/o security thread. 13.4.1955.		4.00	15.00	50.00
	b. Paper w/metal thread. Wmk: *BANCO CENTRAL*. 23.1.1957-25.11.1959.		4.00	15.00	50.00

1957-58 Issue
#93-98 portr. C. Columbus at ctr. on back. Printer: ABNC.

93	**1 COLON**	**VG**	**VF**	**UNC**
(83)	4.9.1957. Black on pink and pale green unpt. *SAN SALVADOR* at lower l., farmer plowing w/oxen at ctr. Red serial # and series letters. Back orange.	2.00	8.00	22.50

94	**2 COLONES**	**VG**	**VF**	**UNC**
(89)	9.11.1960. Black on m/c unpt. Allegorical woman reclining w/fruits and branch at ctr. Reduced size.	3.00	12.50	40.00

95	**5 COLONES**	**VG**	**VF**	**UNC**
(93)	15.2.1956; 9.11.1960. Black on m/c unpt. *SAN SALVADOR* at lower l., Delgado addressing crowd at ctr. Red serial # at upper l. and r. Back green.	3.00	8.00	30.00

96	**10 COLONES**	**VG**	**VF**	**UNC**
(100)	4.9.1957. Black on m/c unpt. Portr. M.J. Arce at l. Back brown.	8.00	30.00	85.00

97	**25 COLONES**	**VG**	**VF**	**UNC**
(104)	29.12.1958; 9.11.1960. Black on m/c unpt. Reservoir in frame at ctr. Back blue.	7.50	30.00	85.00

98	**100 COLONES**	**VG**	**VF**	**UNC**
(109)	29.12.1958; 9.11.1960. Black on m/c unpt. *SAN SALVADOR* at lower l., Independence monument at ctr. Serial # at upper l. and upper r. Back olive.	25.00	75.00	250.00

1959 ISSUE

99	**10 COLONES**	**VG**	**VF**	**UNC**
(101)	25.11.1959. Black on pale green and m/c unpt. Portr. M.J. Arce at upper ctr. Reduced size, 67 x 156mm. Back slate gray; portr. C. Columbus at ctr. Printer: W&S.	4.00	15.00	55.00

ESTONIA

The Republic of Estonia (formerly the Estonian Soviet Socialist Republic of the U.S.S.R.) is the northernmost of the three Baltic states in eastern Europe. It has an area of 17,413 sq. mi. (45,100 sq. km.) and a population of 1.6 million. Capital: Tallinn. Agriculture and dairy farming are the principal industries. Butter, eggs, bacon, timber and petroleum are exported.

This small and ancient Baltic state has enjoyed but two decades of independence since the 13th century. After having been conquered by the Danes, the Livonian Knights, the Teutonic Knights of Germany (who reduced the people to serfdom), the Swedes, the Poles and Russia, Estonia declared itself an independent republic on Nov. 15, 1917, but was not freed until Feb. 1919. The peace treaty was signed Feb. 2, 1920. Shortly after the start of World War II, it was again occupied by Russia and incorporated as the 16th state of the U.S.S.R. Germany occupied the tiny state from 1941 to 1944, after which it was retaken by Russia. Some of the nations of the world, including the United States and Great Britain, did not recognize Estonia's incorporation as an S.S.R. into the Soviet Union.

On August 20, 1991, the Parliament of the Estonian S.S.R. voted to reassert the republic's independence.

MONETARY SYSTEM
1 Mark = 100 Penni to 1928
1 Kroon = 100 Senti, 1928-1941
In 1919 the notes of the Russian Northwest Army (Gen. Yudenich) were also circulating in Estonia and in some areas also the notes of the Special Corps of the North Army under Gen. Rodzianko.
The U.S.S.R. ruble circulated in the early days of WW II and again from 1944 until 1991 while the German reichsmark circulated between 1941 to 1944.

REPUBLIC

EESTI WABARIIGI 5% WÕLAKOHUSTUS

REPUBLIC DEBT OBLIGATORS OF 5% INTEREST

#1-38 bonds w/o pictorial design that were declared legal tender on 20.1.1919. Dates given are redemption dates.

1919 SERIES A ISSUES

		GOOD	**FINE**	**XF**
1	**50 MARKA** 1.5.1919. Gray.	10.00	30.00	—
2	**100 MARKA** 1.5.1919. Gray.	12.00	32.50	—
3	**200 MARKA** 1.5.1919. Gray.	15.00	37.50	—
4	**500 MARKA** 1.5.1919. Gray. Printed on both sides.	18.00	45.00	—
5	**500 MARKA** 1.5.1919. Uniface.	18.00	45.00	—
6	**1000 MARKA** 1.5.1919. Gray. Uniface.			

1919 SERIES B ISSUES

7	**50 MARKA** 1.6.1919. Yellow-brown. Printed on both sides.	12.00	35.00	—
8	**50 MARKA** 1.6.1919. Yellow-brown. Uniface.	12.00	35.00	—
9	**100 MARKA** 1.6.1919. Yellow-brown.	10.00	30.00	—

		GOOD	**FINE**	**XF**
10	**200 MARKA** 1.6.1919. Yellow-brown. Printed on both sides.	—	—	—
11	**200 MARKA** 1.6.1919. Yellow. Uniface.	—	—	—
12	**500 MARKA** 1.6.1919. Yellow-brown.	—	—	—
		GOOD	**FINE**	**XF**
13	**1000 MARKA** 1.6.1919. Yellow-brown.	—	—	—

1919 SERIES D ISSUES

			GOOD	FINE	XF
14	**50 MARKA**				
	1.7.1919. Green.		12.00	37.50	—
15	**100 MARKA**				
	1.7.1919. Green.		15.00	42.50	—
16	**200 MARKA**				
	1.7.1919. Green. Printed on both sides.		—	—	—
17	**200 MARKA**				
	1.7.1919. Green. Uniface.		—	—	—
18	**500 MARKA**				
	1.7.1919. Green. Printed on both sides.		—	—	—
19	**500 MARKA**				
	1.7.1919. Green, uniface.		—	—	—
20	**1000 MARKA**				
	1.7.1919. Green.		—	—	—

1919 W/O SERIES FIRST ISSUE

			GOOD	FINE	XF
21	**50 MARKA**				
	1.11.1919. Gray.		12.00	37.50	—
22	**100 MARKA**				
	1.11.1919. Yellow-brown.		15.00	42.50	—
23	**200 MARKA**				
	1.11.1919. Orange.		—	—	—
24	**500 MARKA**				
	1.11.1919. Green.		—	—	—

1919 W/O SERIES SECOND ISSUE

			GOOD	FINE	XF
25	**50 MARKA**				
	1.12.1919. Gray.		12.00	37.50	—
26	**100 MARKA**				
	1.12.1919. Yellow-brown.		15.00	42.50	—
27	**200 MARKA**				
	1.12.1919. Orange.		—	—	—
28	**500 MARKA**				
	1.12.1919. Green.		—	—	—

1920 FIRST ISSUE

			GOOD	FINE	XF
29	**50 MARKA**				
	1.1.1920. Gray.		12.00	32.50	—
30	**50 MARKA**				
	1.1.1920. Green.		12.00	35.00	—
31	**100 MARKA**				
	1.1.1920. Gray.		12.00	32.50	—
32	**100 MARKA**				
	1.1.1920. Yellow-brown.		12.00	35.00	—
33	**200 MARKA**				
	1.1.1920. Orange.		—	—	—
34	**500 MARKA**				
	1.1.1920. Gray.		—	—	—
35	**500 MARKA**				
	1.1.1920. Green.		—	—	—
36	**1000 MARKA**				
	1.1.1920. Green.		—	—	—

1920 SECOND ISSUE

			GOOD	FINE	XF
37	**100 MARKA**				
	1.5.1920. Gray.		12.00	32.50	—
38	**200 MARKA**				
	1.5.1920. Gray.		—	—	—

EESTI VABARIIGI KASSATÄHT

REPUBLIC OF ESTONIA TREASURY

1919-1920 ISSUE

NOTE: #42 and 43 also exist w/ovpt: *POHJAN POJAT RYKMENTIN*.... See #M1 and M3.

			VG	VF	UNC
39	**5 PENNI**				
	ND (1919). Green. Owl in tree at ctr.		1.00	2.00	5.00

			VG	VF	UNC
40	**10 PENNI**				
	ND (1919). Brown. Ship at ctr.		1.00	2.00	5.00

			VG	VF	UNC
41	**20 PENNI**				
	ND (1919). Yellow. Windmill at ctr.		1.00	2.50	6.50

			VG	VF	UNC
42	**50 PENNI**				
	1919. Blue. Ornamental design at ctr.		1.50	4.00	12.50

			VG	VF	UNC
43	**1 MARK**				
	1919. Brown on gold unpt. Sheaves of wheat and sickles at ctr.		1.50	4.00	12.50

			VG	VF	UNC
44	**3 MARKA**				
	1919. Green on olive unpt. Agricultural symbols at ctr.		2.50	6.00	18.00

			VG	VF	UNC
45	**5 MARKA**				
	1919. Blue and lt. brown. Farmer plowing at ctr. Field scene on back.		2.50	7.50	25.00

			VG	VF	UNC
46	**10 MARKA**				
	1919. Brown. Shepherd blowing a horn while standing between a cow and some sheep. Man w/horse between cornucopiae on back.				
	a. *KÜMME MARKA* in black border on back.		3.00	10.00	30.00
	b. *KÜMME MARKA* w/o border.		3.00	10.00	30.00

47	**25 MARKA**	VG	VF	UNC
	1919. Blackish purple and brown. Tree at l. and r., harvesting potatoes at ctr. Fishermen w/boats and nets on back.			
	a. Wmk: Horizontal wavy lines.	5.00	20.00	45.00
	b. Wmk: Vertical lines.	5.00	20.00	45.00

48	**100 MARKA**	VG	VF	UNC
	1919. Brown on tan unpt. Woman at spinning wheel at ctr. Man at l., woman at r.			
	a. Wmk: Horizontal wavy lines.	10.00	30.00	85.00
	b. *SEERIA II.*	10.00	30.00	85.00
	c. *SEERIA III.*	10.00	30.00	85.00
	d. Wmk: Vertical lines.	10.00	30.00	85.00
49	**500 MARKA**			
	ND (1920-21). Lilac. Back black on olive unpt. Lt. green eagle and shield at ctr.			
	a. Wmk: *500.* (1920).	20.00	65.00	175.00
	b. *SEERIA II.* (1920).	20.00	65.00	175.00
	c. *SEERIA II.* (1920).	17.50	55.00	150.00
	d. *SEERIA A.* Wmk: *EV.* (1920)	15.00	50.00	135.00
	e. *SEERIA B.* (1920).	12.50	45.00	110.00
	f. *SEERIA D.* (1921).	12.50	45.00	110.00

50	**1000 MARKA**	VG	VF	UNC
	ND (1920-21). Green and brown. Birth of Liberty on back.			
	a. W/o series. ND (1920).	100.00	350.00	—
	b. *SEERIA A.* Wmk: *EV.* (1921).	100.00	350.00	—
	c. *SEERIA B.* Wmk: *EV.* (1921).	100.00	350.00	—

1923 ISSUE

51	**100 MARKA**	VG	VF	UNC
	1923. Green and brown. Bank at ctr.			
	a. W/o series.	10.00	40.00	120.00
	b. *SEERIA* (series) *A.* (1927).	10.00	40.00	120.00

52	**500 MARKA**	VG	VF	UNC
	1923. Brown on blue and lt. tan unpt. Toompea Castle at ctr.	60.00	175.00	425.00

EESTI VABARIIGI VAHETUSTÄHT

REPUBLIC OF ESTONIA EXCHANGE NOTE

1922 ISSUE

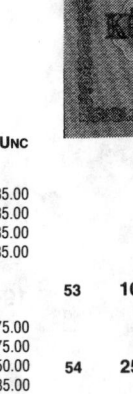

53	**10 MARKA**	VG	VF	UNC
	1922. Blackish green on red-brown unpt. Back red-brown and brown.			
	a. W/o serial # prefix letters. Wmk: *EV.*	2.00	6.00	25.00
	b. Series A. Wmk: Squares. (1924).	3.00	8.00	30.00
54	**25 MARKA**			
	1922. Brown on olive and lilac unpt. Back lilac on gray unpt.			
	a. W/o serial # prefix letters. Wmk: Horizontal wavy lines.	10.00	25.00	75.00
	b. Series A. Different sign. (1926).	8.00	20.00	60.00
	c. Series A. Wmk: Vertical wavy lines. (1926).	8.00	20.00	60.00

EESTI PANGATÄHT

ESTONIA BANKNOTE

1919-1921 ISSUE

55	**50 MARKA**	VG	VF	UNC
	1919. Brown on olive unpt. Globe at ctr. on back.	15.00	35.00	85.00

56	**100 MARKA**	VG	VF	UNC
	1921. Brown. 2 blacksmiths at ctr. Monogram at ctr. on back.	20.00	65.00	125.00

57	500 MARKA			
	1921. Lt. green and gray. Ornamental design.	125.00	275.00	—

1922-1923 ISSUE

58	100 MARKA			
	1922. Black on lilac, brown and green unpt. Galleon on back.	35.00	100.00	225.00

59	1000 MARKA	VG	VF	UNC
	ND (1922). Black on lilac and green unpt. Port view of the city of Tallinn (Reval) on back.			
	a. Issued note.	100.00	250.00	475.00
	p. Face proof.	—		

60	5000 MARKA	VG	VF	UNC
	1923. Blue, brown and green. Arms at ctr. r. Bank at l. ctr. on back.	—	Rare	—

EESTI VABARIIGI KASSATÄHT (RESUMED)

1928 PROVISIONAL ISSUE

61	1 KROON ON 100 MARKA	VG	VF	UNC
	ND. (1928-old date 1923). Red ovpt. on #51.	10.00	30.00	100.00

EESTI PANK

BANK OF ESTONIA

1928-35 ISSUE

#62-65 arms at upper l. on back.

62 (63)	5 KROONI			
	1929. Red-brown. Fisherman holding oar at l. Back red-brown and m/c.	3.00	8.50	25.00

63 (62)	10 KROONI	VG	VF	UNC
	1928. Blue. Woman in national costume carrying sheaf of wheat and sickle at l. 2 sign. Back blue and m/c.	2.00	6.00	17.50

64 (65)	20 KROONI			
	1932. Green. Shepherd blowing horn at l. Back m/c on gray-green unpt.	2.00	5.00	14.00

65 (64)	50 KROONI			
	1929. Brown. Coastline of Rannamoisa at l.	3.00	6.00	17.50

66	100 KROONI	VG	VF	UNC
	1935. Blue. Blacksmith working at an anvil at l.	8.00	20.00	60.00

1937 ISSUE

67	10 KROONI	VG	VF	UNC
	1937. Blue. Woman in national costume carrying sheaf of wheat and sickle at l. 3 sign. Back blue and m/c.	2.00	5.00	15.00

1940 ISSUE

68	10 KROONI			
	1940. Blue. Like #67. Wide or narrow margins. (Not issued).	—	150.00	300.00

MILITARY - WWI

FINNISH REGIMENT - SONS OF THE NORTH

Finnish and Estonian notes w/circular violet ovpt. of Paymaster of the Regiment, Sons of the North that were circulating in 1919 in Southern Estonia and Northern Latvia. Possibly a spurious issue.

1919 ND ISSUES

#M1-M3 ovpt: *Pohjan Pojat Rykmentin Rahaston hoitaja.*

M1 (M2)	50 PENNI			
	ND (1919-old date 1919). Ovpt. on #42.	—	—	—
M2 (M1)	1 MARKKA			
	ND (1919-old date 1916). Ovpt. on Finland #19.	—	—	—
M3	1 MARKA			
	ND (1919-old date 1919). Ovpt. on #43.	—	—	—

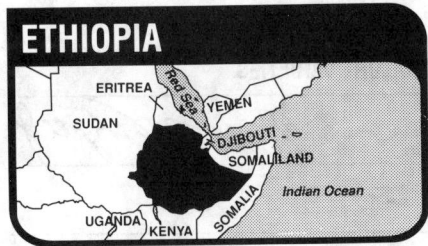

ETHIOPIA

The Peoples Democratic Republic of Ethiopia, faces on the Red Sea in east-central Africa. The country has an area of 424,214 sq. mi. (1.099,900 sq. km.) and a population of 55 million people who are divided among 40 tribes and speak 270 languages and dialects. Capital: Addis Ababa. The economy is predominantly agricultural and pastoral. Gold and platinum are mined and petroleum fields are being developed.

Coffee, oilseeds, hides and cereals are exported.

Legend claims that Menelik I, the son born to Solomon, King of Israel, by the Queen of Sheba, settled in Axum in Northern Ethiopia to establish the dynasty which then reigned - with only brief interruptions - until 1974. Modern Ethiopian history began with the reign of Emperor Menelik II (1889-1913) under whose guidance the country emerged from medieval isolation. Ethiopia was invaded by Mussolini in 1935, and together with Italian Somaliland and Eritrea became part of Italian East Africa until liberated by British and Ethiopian troops in 1941. Haile Selassie I, 225th consecutive Solomonic ruler, was deposed by a military committee on Sept. 12, 1974. In July 1976, Ethiopia's military provisional government referred to the country as Socialist Ethiopia.

Eritrea, a former Ethiopian province fronting on the Red Sea, was an Italian colony from 1890 until its incorporation into Italian East Africa in 1936. It was under British military administration from 1941 to Sept. 15, 1952, when the United Nations designated it an autonomous unit within the federation of Ethiopia and Eritrea. On Nov. 14, 1962, it was fully integrated with Ethiopia. On May 24, 1993, Eritrea became an independent nation.

RULERS:
Menelik II, 1889-1913
Lij Yasu, 1913-1916
Zauditu, Empress, 1916-1930
Haile Selassie I, 1930-1936, 1941-1974

MONETARY SYSTEM:
1 Thaler = 16 Gersh (Piastres) to 1936
1 Birr (Dollar) = 100 Canteems (Cents), 1941-

KINGDOM

BANK OF ABYSSINIA

The bank was closely associated with the National Bank of Egypt and was also administered by Cairo. Notes issued from 1915 until liquidated by decree of Aug. 29, 1931. Hand stamped or handwritten dates for all notes prior to June 1, 1929; the June 1, 1929 date is printed.

1915 ISSUE

1   5 THALERS
1915-1.6.1929. Gazelle at ctr.
a. Issued note. — Rare —
s. Specimen. — Unc 1000.

2   10 THALERS
1915-1.6.1929. Leopard at ctr.
a. Issued note. — Rare —
s. Specimen. — Unc 1350.

3   50 THALERS
1915-1.6.1929. Lion at ctr.
a. Issued note. — Rare —
s. Specimen. — Unc 1850.

4   100 THALERS
1915-1.6.1929. Elephant at r.
a. Issued note. — Rare —
s. Specimen. — Unc 2650.

5   500 THALERS
1915-1.6.1929. Warrior standing at l.
a. Issued note. — Rare —
s. Specimen. — Unc 3250.

BANK OF ETHIOPIA

1932-33 ISSUE

#6-11 printer: BWC.

NOTE: Recalled by Italian authorities in 1936.

		GOOD	FINE	XF
6	**2 THALERS** 1.6.1933. Dk. blue on green and m/c unpt. Jugate busts of Emperor Haile Selassie and Empress at ctr.	15.00	60.00	185.00

		GOOD	FINE	XF
7	**5 THALERS** 1.5.1932; 29.4.1933. Purple on m/c unpt. Head of gazelle at ctr., bank bldg. at l., arms at r.	20.00	100.00	300.00

8	10 THALERS	GOOD	FINE	XF
	1.5.1932; 29.4.1933; 31.5.1935. Blue-green on m/c unpt. Leopard at ctr., arms at l., bank bldg. at r.	20.00	100.00	325.00

9	50 THALERS	GOOD	FINE	XF
	1.5.1932; 29.4.1933. Blue-green on m/c unpt. Lion at ctr., bank bldg. at upper l., arms at upper l. ctr.	40.00	125.00	350.00

10	100 THALERS	GOOD	FINE	XF
	1.5.1932; 29.4.1933. Blue on m/c unpt. Elephant at r., bank bldg. at l., arms at upper l. ctr.	50.00	175.00	550.00

11	500 THALERS	GOOD	FINE	XF
	1.5.1932; 29.4.1933. Purple on m/c unpt. Warrior standing at l., arms at top ctr., bank bldg. at r.	250.00	500.00	1500.

STATE BANK OF ETHIOPIA

SIGNATURE VARIETIES			
1	*[signature]*	3	*[signature]*
2	*[signature]*		

1945 ISSUE
#12-17 Emperor Haile Selassie at l. Arms at ctr. on back. Printer: SBNC.

12	1 DOLLAR	VG	VF	UNC
	ND (1945). Black on orange unpt. Farmer plowing w/oxen at ctr. Back green.			
	a. Sign. 1.	8.00	30.00	120.00
	b. Sign. 2.	5.00	20.00	80.00
	c. Sign. 3.	4.00	15.00	55.00

13	5 DOLLARS	VG	VF	UNC
	ND (1945). Black and lilac on orange unpt. Tree with beehive at ctr. r. Back orange.			
	a. Sign. 1.	15.00	80.00	320.00
	b. Sign. 2.	10.00	55.00	210.00
	c. Sign. 3.	7.50	40.00	150.00

14	10 DOLLARS	VG	VF	UNC
	ND (1945). Black on orange and blue unpt. Equestrian monument to Menelik II w/domed bldg. in background at ctr. Back red.			
	a. Sign. 1.	40.00	150.00	475.00
	b. Sign. 2.	28.00	110.00	325.00
	c. Sign. 3.	20.00	75.00	225.00

15	50 DOLLARS	VG	VF	UNC
	ND (1945). Black on green and yellow unpt. Parliament at ctr.			
	a. Sign. 1.	75.00	300.00	950.00
	b. Sign. 2.	55.00	215.00	650.00
	c. Sign. 3.	37.50	150.00	450.00

16 | **100 Dollars**
ND (1945). Black on green unpt. Palace of Haile Selassie I (now a university) at ctr.

	VG	VF	UNC
a. Sign. 1.	120.00	450.00	1150.
b. Sign. 2.	90.00	340.00	850.00
c. Sign. 3.	60.00	225.00	550.00

17 | **500 Dollars**
ND (1945). Black on yellow and olive unpt. Trinity Church in Addis Ababa at ctr.

	VG	VF	UNC
a. Sign. 1.	500.00	900.00	1650.
b. Sign. 2.	375.00	675.00	1200.
c. Sign. 3.	250.00	450.00	800.00

The Faeroe Islands, a self-governing community within the kingdom of Denmark, are situated in the North Atlantic between Iceland and the Shetland Islands. The 17 inhabited islets and reefs have an area of 540 sq. mi. (1,399 sq. km.) and a population of 48,000. Capital: Thorshavn. The principal industries are fishing and grazing. Fish and fish products are exported.

While it is thought that Irish hermits lived on the islands in the 7th and 8th centuries, the present inhabitants are descended from the 6th century Norse settlers. The Faeroe Islands became a Norwegian fief in 1035 and became Danish in 1380 when Norway and Denmark were united. They have ever since remained in Danish possession and were granted self-government (except for an appointed governor-general) with their own legislature, executive and flag in 1948.

The islands were occupied by British troops during World War II, after the German occupation of Denmark.

RULERS:
Danish

MONETARY SYSTEM:
1 Króne = 100 Øre

NOTE: This section has been reorganized by date

DANISH INFLUENCE

GOVERNMENT

1809-12 EMERGENCY ISSUE
#A3-A9 handwritten on card stock or paper. Uniface. Thorshavn.
A1, A2 and A10 Held in reserve.

		GOOD	FINE	XF
A3	**3 SKILLING** 1809.	—	—	—
A4	**4 SKILLING** 1809.	—	—	—
A5	**5 SKILLING** 1812.	—	—	—
A6	**6 SKILLING** 1809.	—	—	—
A9	**5 MARK** 1810.	—	—	—

1815 PROVISIONAL ISSUE
#A11 reissue of Danish Rigsbanken i Kiøbenhavn notes dated 1814.

| A11 | **1 RIGSBANKDALER** 15.4.1815 (-old date 1814). Printed on back of Denmark #A48. | — | — | — |

FAERØ AMT

1940 WWII PROVISIONAL ISSUE
#1-6 red ovpt: *KUN GYLDIG PAA FAERØERNE, FAERØ AMT, JUNI 1940* w/sign. of Hilbert on Danish notes.

| 1 | **5 KRONER** June 1940. Blue-green. Printed sign. | 50.00 | 160.00 | 400.00 |

| 2 | **10 KRONER** June 1940. Brown. Handwritten sign. and ovpt. on Denmark #31. Serial #M9627001-9627500. | GOOD 30.00 | FINE 90.00 | XF 225.00 |

| 3 | **10 KRONER** June 1940. Brown. Printed sign. | GOOD 35.00 | FINE 110.00 | XF 275.00 |
| 4 | **50 KRONER** June 1940. Blue. Printed sign. | 200.00 | 600.00 | — |

		GOOD	FINE	XF
5	**100 KRONER** June 1940. Brown. Printed sign.	175.00	525.00	—
6	**500 KRONER** June 1940. Gray-blue. Printed sign.	850.00	1850.	—

FAERØERNE

1940 FIRST EMERGENCY ISSUE

		GOOD	FINE	XF
7	**10 KRONER** 1.10.1940.			
	a. Brown.	75.00	225.00	625.00
	b. Olive.	95.00	285.00	750.00
8	**100 KRONER** 1.10.1940. Red-brown. Ram's head at upper r.	385.00	1000.	2250.

1940 SECOND EMERGENCY ISSUE

		VG	VF	UNC
9	**1 KRONE** Nov. 1940. Blue on lilac and lt. red unpt. Like #10.	3.75	15.00	50.00

		VG	VF	UNC
10	**5 KRONER** Nov. 1940. Green and blue-green.	18.50	75.00	250.00
11	**10 KRONER** Nov. 1940. Brown on lilac and green unpt. Like #10.	18.50	75.00	225.00

		VG	VF	XF
12	**100 KRONER** Nov. 1940. Green and brown. Like #10.	150.00	500.00	1250.

FØROYAR

1951-54 ISSUE
Law of 12.4.1949

		VG	VF	UNC
13	**5 KRÓNER** L.1949 (1951-60). black on green unpt. Coin w/ram at l. Fishermen w/boat on green back.			
	a. Sign. C. A. Vagn-Hansen and Kr. Djurhuus.	5.00	30.00	100.00
	b. Sign. N. Elkaer-Hansen and Kr. Ojurhuus.	5.00	30.00	100.00

		VG	VF	UNC
14	**10 KRÓNER** L.1949 (1954). Black on orange unpt. Shield w/ram at l. Rural scene on orange back.			
	a. Sign. C. A. Vagn-Hansen and Kr. Djurhuus. Wmk: 10. 10.5mm.	3.00	5.00	25.00
	b. Sign. M. Wahl and P. M. Dam. Wmk: 10. 13mm.	2.50	4.00	12.50
	c. Sign. M. Wahl and A. P. Dam.	2.00	3.50	8.00

		VG	VF	UNC
15	**100 KRÓNER** L.1949 (1952-63). Blue-green. Porpoises on back. Irregular margins at l. and r. (straight margins are trimmed).			
	a. Sign. C. A. Vagn-Hansen and Kr. Djurhuus.	25.00	65.00	200.00
	b. Sign. N. Elkaer-Hansen and Kr. Djurhuus.	25.00	65.00	200.00
	c. Sign. M. Wahl and P. M. Dam.	25.00	65.00	200.00

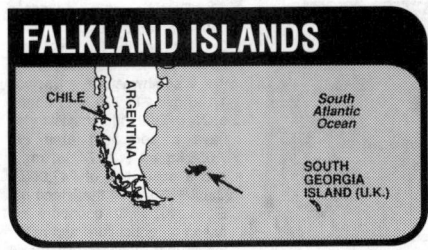

FALKLAND ISLANDS

The Colony of the Falkland Islands and Dependencies, a British colony located in the South Atlantic about 500 miles northeast of Cape Horn, has an area of 4,700 sq. mi. (12,173 sq. km.) and a population of 2,100. East Falkland, West Falkland, South Georgia, and South Sandwich are the largest of the 200 islands. Capital: Stanley. Sheep grazing is the main industry. Wool, whale oil, and seal oil are exported.

The Falklands were discovered by British navigator John Davis (Davys) in 1592, and named by Capt. John Strong - for Viscount Falkland, treasurer of the British navy - in 1690. French navigator Louis De Bougainville established the first settlement, at Port Louis, in 1764. The following year Capt. John Byron claimed the islands for Britain and left a small party at Saunders Island. Spain later forced the French and British to abandon their settlements but did not implement its claim to the islands. In 1829 the Republic of Buenos Aires, which claimed to have inherited the Spanish rights, sent Louis Vernet to develop a colony on the islands. In 1831 he seized three American sailing vessels, whereupon the men of the corvette, *U.S.S. Lexington*, destroyed his settlement and proclaimed the Falklands to be "free of all governance." Britain, which had never renounced its claim, then re-established its settlement in 1833.

RULERS:
British

MONETARY SYSTEM:
1 Shilling = 12 Pence
1 Pound = 20 Shillings to 1966
1 Pound = 100 Pence, 1966-

BRITISH INFLUENCE

GOVERNMENT OF THE FALKLAND ISLANDS

1899-1905 ISSUE
#A1-A4 uniface. Printer: TDLR.

		GOOD	FINE	XF
A1	**5 SHILLINGS** 12.1.1901; 15.1.1901. Green on pink unpt.	—	—	—
A1A	**5 SHILLINGS** 1.2.1905; 1908; 27.11.1916. Brown on pink unpt. Like #A1.	1000.	2000.	—
A2	**10 SHILLINGS** Like #A1.	Reported Not Confirmed		

		GOOD	FINE	XF
A3	**1 POUND** 16.10.1899; 28.8.1915. Blue on pink unpt.	1750.	3500.	—
A4	**5 POUNDS** Like #A3.	Reported Not Confirmed		

1921 ISSUE
#1-3 portr. Kg. George V. at r. Printer TDLR.

1	**10 SHILLINGS**		GOOD	FINE	XF
	1921-32. Brown-gray unpt.				
	a. 2 sign. 1.2.1921; 10.1.1927.		550.00	2000.	3500.
	b. 1 sign. 10.2.1932.		400.00	1500.	2500.

2	**1 POUND**		GOOD	FINE	XF
	1921-32. Blue on green unpt.				
	a. 2 sign. 1.2.1921; 10.1.1927.		800.00	2500.	5000.
	b. 1 sign. 10.2.1932.		600.00	1500.	3250.
3	**5 POUNDS** 1.2.1921; 10.2.1932. Red on green unpt.		—	Rare	—

1938-51 ISSUE
#4-6 portr. Kg. George VI at r. Printer: TDLR.

4	**10 SHILLINGS**	VG	VF	UNC
	19.5.1938. Brown on gray unpt.	12.50	55.00	175.00

5	**1 POUND**	VG	VF	UNC
	19.5.1938. Blue on green and lilac unpt.	15.00	65.00	375.00

6	**5 POUNDS**	VG	VF	UNC
	20.2.1951. Red on green, blue and lt. tan unpt.	65.00	250.00	900.00

THE GOVERNMENT OF THE FALKLAND ISLANDS

1960-67 ISSUE

			VG	VF	UNC
7	**10 SHILLINGS**				
	10.4.1960. Brown on gray unpt.		5.00	20.00	90.00

			VG	VF	UNC
9	**5 POUNDS**				
	1960; 1975. Red on green unpt.				
	a. Sign: L. Gleadell: 10.4.1960.		9.00	20.00	95.00
	b. Sign: H. T. Rowlands: 30.1.1975.		7.50	15.00	75.00

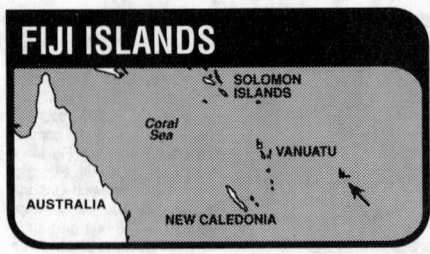

FIJI ISLANDS

The Dominion of Fiji, an independent member of the British Commonwealth, consists of about 320 islands located in the southwestern Pacific 1,100 miles (1,770 km.) north of New Zealand. The islands have a combined area of 7,056 sq. mi. (18,274 sq. km.) and a population of 747,000. Capital: Suva on the island of Biti Levu. Fiji's economy is based on agriculture and mining. Sugar, coconut products, manganese and gold are exported.

The Fiji Islands were discovered by Dutch navigator Abel Tasman in 1643 and visited by British naval captain James Cook in 1774. The first complete survey of the island was conducted by the United States in 1840. Settlement by missionaries from Tonga and traders attracted by the sandalwood trade began in 1835. Following a lengthy period of intertribal warfare, the islands were unconditionally and voluntarily ceded to Great Britain in 1874 by King Thakombau. The trading center was Levuka on the island of Ovalau which was also the capital under the British from 1874-82. Fiji became a sovereign and independent nation on Oct 10, 1970, the 96th anniversary of the cession of the islands to Queen Victoria. It is a member of the Commonwealth of Nations. The Queen of England is Chief of State.

RULERS:
Thakombau, until 1874
British, 1874-

MONETARY SYSTEM:
1 Shilling = 12 Pence
1 Pound = 20 Shillings to 1969
1 Dollar = 100 Cents, 1969-

KINGDOM

C.R. - CAKOBAU REX

1867 TREASURY NOTE ISSUE

#1 held in reserve.

			GOOD	FINE	XF
2	**1 DOLLAR**				
(A1)	1867. Black on buff paper.		—	—	—

1871-73 ISSUES

#4 and 9 held in reserve.

			GOOD	FINE	XF
3	**12 1/2 CENTS**				
(A1A)	1873. Blue. Single chain border.				
	a. Issued Note. 1.9.1873.		85.00	180.00	360.00
	b. Pen cancelled. 13.10.1873.		70.00	150.00	300.00

			GOOD	FINE	XF
5	**25 CENTS**				
(2)	1.9.1873. Red. Double chain border.		60.00	125.00	275.00
6	**50 CENTS**				
(1A)	5.1.1872. Black. Single chain border.		120.00	225.00	425.00

			GOOD	FINE	XF
7	**50 CENTS**				
(3)	1.9.1873. Green. Double chain border.		60.00	125.00	275.00

8 (1B)	**100 CENTS**	GOOD	FINE	XF
	1.4.1872. Brown. Like #1.	70.00	150.00	300.00

LEVUKA, OVALAU, FIJI
1871 TREASURY NOTE ISSUE
#10 and 11, printer: Gazette Office, Levuka, Ovalau (Island).

10 (5C)	**5 DOLLARS**	GOOD	FINE	XF
	16.11.1871. Lt. brown.			
	a. Issued note.	—	—	—
	r. Remainder.	—	—	—
11	**10 DOLLARS**			
	ca.1871.	—	—	—

1872 TREASURY NOTE ISSUE
#12-16 arms at top ctr. Handwritten various dates, partially printed date: *187.* Printer: S. T. Leigh & Co., Sydney.

12 (5B)	**1 DOLLAR**	GOOD	FINE	XF
	10.2.1872; 11.11.1872; 11.1.1873; 11.2.1873; 1.9.1873. Black.			
	a. Handstamped: *CANCELLED.*	90.00	225.00	425.00

13 (6)	**5 DOLLARS**	GOOD	FINE	XF
	20.2.1872; 4.4.1872; 12.6.1873; 16.11.1873. Pale purple.			
	a. Handstamped: *CANCELLED.*	100.00	250.00	450.00

14 (7)	**10 DOLLARS**	GOOD	FINE	XF
	1.3.1872-1.6.1872; 17.3.1873. Brown.			
	a. Handstamped: *CANCELLED.*	90.00	225.00	425.00
15 (8)	**25 DOLLARS**			
	23.3.1872; 5.4.1872; 15.7.1872; 11.11.1872; 12.6.1873. Blue.			
	a. Pen cancelled through sign., w/ or w/o handstamps: *CANCELLED.*	120.00	300.00	550.00

16 (9)	**50 DOLLARS**	GOOD	FINE	XF
	1.4.1872; 15.7.1872; 11.3.1873; 12.6.1873. Red.			
	a. Pen cancelled through sign., w/ or w/o handstamps: *CANCELLED.*	90.00	225.00	425.00
	r. Remainder w/sign.	90.00	225.00	425.00

BRITISH INFLUENCE
GOVERNMENT OF FIJI
1917-26 ISSUE
#17-22 printer: TDLR.

17 (10)	**5 SHILLINGS**	GOOD	FINE	XF
	1.9.1920-8.12.1933. Brown and green. Arms at upper ctr. Uniface.	150.00	550.00	1750.

18 (11)	**10 SHILLINGS**	GOOD	FINE	XF
	1918-32. Blue and green. Arms at l. Uniface.			
	a. 29.10.1918.	600.00	250.00	—
	b. 1.1.1920-23.9.1932.	375.00	1000.	3500.

19 (12)	**1 POUND**	GOOD	FINE	XF
	1.3.1917; 5.12.1925; 21.1.1930. Green on pink unpt. Uniface.	350.00	950.00	3250.
20 (13)	**5 POUNDS**			
	20.8.1926. Black, dk. red and orange.	—	—	—

21	10 POUNDS	GOOD	FINE	XF
(14)	5.12.1925. Blue on gray unpt.	—	—	—
22	20 POUNDS			
(15)	1914-33.	Reported Not Confirmed		

1934 ISSUE
#23-28 portr. Kg. George V at r. Printer: BWC.

23	5 SHILLINGS			
(15A)	1.1.1934; 1.6.1934; 1.3.1935. Dk. blue and brown.	90.00	200.00	1100.
24	10 SHILLINGS			
(15B)	1.1.1934; 1.6.1934; 1.3.1935. Dk. brown and blue.	250.00	850.00	2500.
25	1 POUND			
(16)	1.1.1934; 1.6.1934; 1.3.1935. Green and red.	125.00	485.00	1500.
26	5 POUNDS			
(17)	13.9.1934; 1.3.1935. Pink, red and green.	350.00	1000.	2250.
27	10 POUNDS			
(17A)	1.1.1934; 12.7.1934; 1.3.1935. Blue.	575.00	1500.	3750.

28	20 POUNDS	GOOD	FINE	XF
(17B)	12.7.1934; 2.9.1934. Purple and black.	850.00	2200.	5500.

1937-42 ISSUE
#29-35 portr. Kg. George VI at r. Various date and sign. varieties. Printer: BWC.

29	5 SHILLINGS	VG	VF	UNC
(24)	1937-51. Dk. blue and brown. Portr. Kg. George VI facing l. at r.			
	a. 1.3.1937; 1.3.1938.	12.50	50.00	450.00
	b. 1.7.1940-1.7.1943; 1.1.1946.	8.50	35.00	325.00
	c. 1.9.1948-1.6.1951.	7.50	20.00	225.00
30	10 SHILLINGS			
(25)	1937-51. Dk. brown and blue. Portr. Kg. George VI facing l. at r.			
	a. 1.3.1937-1.7.1943.	15.00	65.00	500.00
	b. 1.1.1946; 1.9.1948.	12.50	55.00	450.00
	c. 1.8.1949; 1.7.1950; 1.6.1951.	10.00	45.00	375.00
31	1 POUND			
(26)	1937-40. Green and red. Portr. Kg. George VI facing l. at r.			
	a. 1.3.1937; 1.3.1938.	30.00	125.00	700.00
	b. 1.7.1940; 1.10.1940.	20.00	100.00	600.00

32	1 POUND	VG	VF	UNC
(26A)	1941-51. Green and red. Portr. Kg. George VI facing l. at r.			
	a. 1.1.1941; 1.6.1941; 1.1.1942; 1.7.1943; 1.1.1946.	20.00	75.00	550.00
	b. 1.9.1948; 1.8.1949; 1.7.1950; 1.6.1951.	15.00	55.00	425.00
33	5 POUNDS			
(27)	1941-51. Pink, red and green. Portr. Kg. George VI facing l. at r.			
	a. 1.1.1941; 1.7.1943.	150.00	650.00	1500.
	b. 1.1.1946; 1.8.1949; 1.6.1951.	100.00	400.00	1250.

34	10 POUNDS	VG	VF	UNC
(28)	1942-51. Blue and black.			
	a. 1.1.1942; 1.7.1943; 1.1.1946.	275.00	950.00	2600.
	b. 1.9.1948; 1.8.1949; 1.6.1951.	200.00	750.00	2000.
35	20 POUNDS			
(29)	1937-51. Black and purple.			
	a. 1.3.1937; 1.3.1938.	850.00	2250.	—
	b. 1.9.1948; 1.6.1951.	550.00	1750.	—

1940s PROVISIONAL ISSUE
#36-38 ovpt: *GOVERNMENT OF FIJI...* on local reprints of Reserve Bank of New Zealand notes. W/o imprint.

36	10 SHILLINGS			
(21A)	ND (1940 - old date 1.8.1934). Ovpt. on local reprint of New Zealand #154.	—	Rare	—

37	1 POUND	VG	VF	UNC
(22)	ND (1940 - old date 1.8.1934). Ovpt. on Australian reprint of New Zealand #155.			
	a. W/o wmk., 1D prefix serial #.	85.00	275.00	850.00
	b. W/o wmk., difference in width of ovpt. and position. 6D prefix serial #.	50.00	150.00	550.00
	c. Wmk. (postal stamp) Crown/A repeated. F1/0 prefix serial #.	55.00	175.00	650.00
38	5 POUNDS			
(23)	ND (1940 - old date 1.8.1934). Ovpt on local reprint of New Zealand #156.	1000.	2000.	—

1942 EMERGENCY ISSUES

39	1 PENNY	VG	VF	UNC
(20)	1.7.1942. Black on green unpt. Arms in unpt. at l., penny coin at lower r. Back green; penny coin at lower l.			
	a. Issued note.	.50	2.00	7.00
	s. Specimen.	—	—	90.00

40
(18)
1 SHILLING
1.1.1942. Black on gray paper. Arms at top ctr. Uniface.

	VG	VF	UNC
a. Issued note.	3.00	15.00	65.00
r. Remainder, w/o serial #.	—	—	100.00
s. Specimen.	—	—	125.00

41
(21)
1 SHILLING
1.9.1942. Black on yellow unpt. words, yellow paper. Arms at top ctr.

	VG	VF	UNC
a. Issued note. Block letters A, B.	3.00	17.50	55.00
s. Specimen.	—	—	125.00

42
(19)
2 SHILLINGS
1.1.1942. Black on red unpt. words. Like #31.

	VG	VF	UNC
a. Issued note.	4.00	22.50	75.00
r. Remainder, w/o serial #.	—	—	125.00
s. Specimen.	—	—	125.00

1953-57 ISSUE
#43-49 arms at upper ctr., portr. Qn. Elizabeth II at r. Printer: BWC.

43
(30)
5 SHILLINGS
1957-65. Green and blue on lilac and green unpt.

	VG	VF	UNC
a. 1.6.1957; 28.4.1961; 1.12.1962.	2.00	7.50	65.00
b. 1.9.1964; 1.12.1964; 1.10.1965.	1.50	6.00	50.00

44
(31)
10 SHILLINGS
1957-65. Brown on lilac and green unpt.

	VG	VF	UNC
a. 1.6.1957; 28.4.1961; 1.12.1962.	3.00	22.50	275.00
b. 1.9.1964; 1.10.1965.	2.50	15.00	250.00

45
(32)
1 POUND
1954-67. Green on yellow and blue unpt.

	VG	VF	UNC
a. 1.7.1954; 1.6.1957; 1.9.1959.	8.00	25.00	300.00
b. 1.12.1961-1.1.1967.	3.00	20.00	250.00

46
(33)
5 POUNDS
1954-67. Purple on lt. orange and green unpt.

	VG	VF	UNC
a. 1.7.1954; 1.9.1959; 1.10.1960.	40.00	225.00	1000.
b. 1.12.1962; 20.1.1964; 1.12.1964; 1.1.1967.	30.00	200.00	750.00

47
(34)
10 POUNDS
1954-64. Blue.

	VG	VF	UNC
a. 1.7.1954.	75.00	375.00	1500.
b. 1.9.1959; 1.10.1960; 20.1.1964; 11.6.1964.	50.00	285.00	700.00

48
(35)
20 POUNDS
1.1.1953. Black and violet. Title: *GOVERNMENT OF FIJI* at top on back.

	VG	VF	UNC
	350.00	1500.	3750.

49
(36)
20 POUNDS
1.1.1953; 1.7.1954; 1.11.1958. Red. Titles: *GOVERNMENT OF FIJI* at top on back.

	VG	VF	UNC
	350.00	1500.	4000.

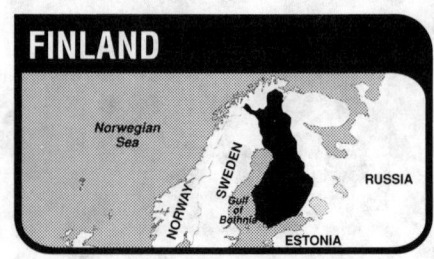

FINLAND

The Republic of Finland, the second most northerly state of the European continent, has an area of 130,120 sq. mi. (337,009 sq. km.) and a population of 5 million. Capital: Helsinki. Lumbering, shipbuilding, metal and woodworking are the leading industries. Paper, timber, woodpulp, plywood and metal products are exported.

The Finns, who probably originated in the Volga region of Russia, took Finland from the Lapps late in the 7th century. They were conquered in the 12th century by Eric IX of Sweden, and brought into contact with Western Christendom. In 1809, Sweden was conquered by Alexander I of Russia, and the peace terms gave Finland to Russia which became a grand duchy within the Russian Empire until Dec. 6, 1917, when, shortly after the Bolshevik revolution, it declared its independence. After a brief but bitter civil war between the Russian sympathizers and Finnish nationalists in which the Whites (nationalists) were victorious, a new constitution was adopted, and on Dec. 6, 1917 Finland was established as a republic. In 1939 Soviet troops invaded Finland over disputed territorial concessions which were later granted in the peace treaty of 1940. When the Germans invaded Russia, Finland also became involved and in the Armistice of 1944 lost the Petsamo area also to the Soviets.

RULERS:
Gustaf III, 1771-1792, of Sweden
Gustaf IV Adolph, 1792-1809
Alexander I, 1809-1825, of Russia
Nicholas I, 1825-1855
Alexander II, 1855-1881
Alexander III, 1881-1894
Nicholas II, 1894-1917

MONETARY SYSTEM:
(With Sweden to 1809)
1 Riksdaler Specie = 48 Skilling Specie
(With Russia 1809-1917)
1 Ruble = 100 Kopeks
1 Markka = 100 Pennia 1860-1963
1 New Markka = 100 Old Markkaa 1963-

SWEDISH INFLUENCE

KONGL. GENERAL KRIGS COMMISSARIATET

KING'S GENERAL WAR COMMISSARIAT

1790 ISSUE
#A1-A12 w/o pictorial design. Various handwritten dates w/ printed 1790. Embossed seal w/legend: K. FINSKA G: KRIGS COMMISARIATET around crowned arms at top ctr. Printed sign. of Fahnehjeim with an additional handwritten sign. Uniface. Minor varieties exist.

		GOOD	FINE	XF
A1	**8 SKILLING SPECIE** 1790.	300.00	1200.	—
A2	**12 SKILLING SPECIE** 1790.	300.00	1200.	—
A3	**16 SKILLING SPECIE** 1790.	300.00	1200.	—
A4	**24 SKILLING SPECIE** 1790.	300.00	1200.	—
A5	**32 SKILLING SPECIE** 1790.	—	—	—
A6	**1 RIKSDALER SPECIE** 1790.	—	—	—
A7	**1 RIKSDALER 8 SKILLING SPECIE** 1790.	—	—	—
A8	**1 RIKSDALER 16 SKILLING SPECIE** 1790.	—	—	—
A9	**1 RIKSDALER 24 SKILLING SPECIE** 1790.	—	—	—
A10	**1 RIKSDALER 32 SKILLING SPECIE** 1790.	—	—	—
A11	**1 RIKSDALER 40 SKILLING SPECIE** 1790.	—	—	—
A12	**2 RIKSDALER SPECIE** 1790.	—	—	—

RUSSIAN INFLUENCE

WAXEL-LANE-OCH DEPOSITIONS-CONTOR

ABO BRANCH

1812 ISSUE
#A13-15 Denominations in oval, w/o pictorial design. Various sign. and handwritten dates w/printed 18, w/ or w/o various wmks.

		GOOD	FINE	XF
A13	**20 KOPEKS** 1812-18.	250.00	1200.	3500.
A14	**50 KOPEKS** 1812-19.	235.00	1100.	3250.
A15	**75 KOPEKS** 1812-21.	200.00	1000.	3000.

WAXEL-DEPOSITIONS-OCH LANE BANK

ABO BRANCH

1819-22 ISSUE

A16	**20 KOPEKS** 1818-19.	400.00	1500.	4000.
A17	**50 KOPEKS** 1819-20.	—	Rare	—
A18	**75 KOPEKS** 1821.	—	Rare	—

HELSINGSFORS BRANCH

1819-22 ISSUE

A19	**20 KOPEKS** 1820-22. W/ or w/o wmk.	—	Rare	—
A20	**50 KOPEKS** 1822.	—	Rare	—
A21	**1 RUBLE** 1819-20.	—	Rare	—
A22	**2 RUBLES** 1819-20.	—	Rare	—
A23	**4 RUBLES** 1819-20.	—	Rare	—

WAXEL DEPOSITIONS-OCH LANE BANK

1819-22 ISSUE
#A24-A28 w/double headed eagle at top ctr. Various printed dates (on A27a and 28a handwritten). Uniface.

		GOOD	FINE	XF
A24	**20 KOPEKS** 1824-26; 1829-38; 1840.	60.00	150.00	300.00
A25	**50 KOPEKS** 1824-26; 1830; 1835-40.	60.00	175.00	350.00

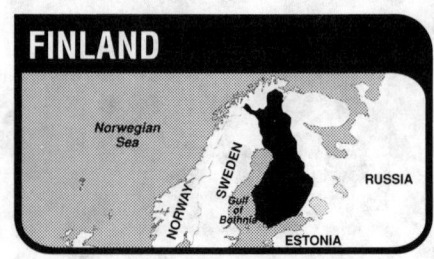

		GOOD	FINE	XF
A26	**75 KOPEKS** 1824-26; 1831; 1836; 1839-40.	100.00	300.00	700.00
A27	**1 RUBLE** 1822-29.			
	a. Handwritten serial #. 1822-24.	200.00	500.00	1000.
	b. Printed serial #. 1826-29.	140.00	450.00	700.00
A28	**2 RUBLES** 1823-28.			
	a. Handwritten serial #. 1823-24.	400.00	750.00	1200.
	b. Printed serial #. 1826-28.	300.00	650.00	1000.

FINSKA BANKEN

BANK OF FINLAND

1840-41 RUBLE ISSUE
#A29-A32 w/double headed eagle at top ctr. Various date and sign. varieties. Russian and Swedish text on face and Finnish text on back.

A29	**3 RUBLES** 1840-43; 1845-48; 1852-53; 1855-57; 1859-62. Green.	400.00	800.00	1500.
A30	**5 RUBLES** 1840-43; 1847-48; 1851-53; 1855-57; 1860-62. Blue.	1000.	2000.	3000.
A31	**10 RUBLES** 1841-42; 1847; 1849; 1852-53; 1855-57; 1862. Red.	4000.	8000.	—
A32	**25 RUBLES** 1841-44; 1846-47; 1851-52; 1855-57; 1862 (Not issued). Olive.	1200.	3000.	—

FINLANDS BANK

SUOMEN PANKKI

1860-62 MARKKA ISSUE
Various date and sign. varieties.

A33	**1 MARKKA** 1860-61; 1864; 1866. Lilac on lt. blue. Embossed eagle on top.	300.00	550.00	850.00
A34	**3 MARKKAA** 1860-66. Green on yellow. Embossed eagle on top.	300.00	600.00	1000.

A35 12 MARKKAA
1862. Green. Man w/stick and cap at l., young woman w/scarf at r.

	GOOD	FINE	XF
a. W/o series.	120.00	200.00	400.00
b. Series B.	200.00	500.00	1000.
c. Series C.	150.00	300.00	750.00

A36 20 MARKKAA
1862. Red. Crowned mantled arms consisting of crowned double headed eagle between man and woman at l.

	GOOD	FINE	XF
a. W/o series.	175.00	300.00	700.00
b. Series B.	250.00	500.00	—
c. Series C.	200.00	450.00	900.00

A37 40 MARKKAA
1862. Yellow. Crowned mantled arms consisting of crowned double headed eagle at l., seated woman w/anchor and caduceus at r.
2150. 4500. 6000.

A38 100 MARKKAA
1862. M/c. Young man w/stick and cap at l., young woman at r.

	GOOD	FINE	XF
a. W/o series.	250.00	500.00	800.00
b. Series B.	400.00	1000.	2000.
c. Series C.	350.00	750.00	1200.

1866-75 ISSUE

A39 1 MARKKA
1866-67. Like #A33. Eagle on top in black.

a. 1866.	300.00	600.00	1000.
b. 1867.	50.00	125.00	300.00

A40 3 MARKKAA
1866-75. Like #A34. Pink unpt. Eagle on top in black.

a. 1866.	70.00	200.00	400.00
	1500.	2000.	4000.
b. 1867; 1869-70; 1872-75.	70.00	200.00	400.00

A41 5 MARKKAA
1875. Bluish-gray. Arms at l. *I SILFVER* below *FEM MARK*.
125.00 350.00 750.00

A42 10 MARKKAA
1875. Red and gray. Arms at l. *I SILFVER* below *TIO MARK*.
400.00 1000. 2000.

1878 ISSUE

A43 5 MARKKAA
1878. Bluish-gray. Like #A41, but *FINSKT MYNT* below *FEM MARK*.
50.00 100.00 250.00

A44 10 MARKKAA
1878. Red and gray. Like #A42, but *I GULD* below *TIO MARK*.
200.00 500.00 1000.

A45 500 MARKKAA
1878. Yellow and gray. Arms w/2 cherubs.

a. Printed in Copenhagen. Serial #000001-079000.	500.00	1200.	3500.
b. Printed in Helsinki. Serial #079001-.	300.00	600.00	1750.

1882-84 ISSUE

A46 10 MARKKAA
1882. Black and yellow. Like #A44, but slightly altered design.

a. W/lines under sign.	50.00	125.00	350.00
b. W/o lines under sign.	50.00	125.00	350.00

A47 20 MARKKAA
1882; 1883. Black and brown. Arms at l.

a. 1882.	300.00	650.00	1200.
b. 1883.	50.00	100.00	250.00

A49 50 MARKKAA
1884. Black and blue. Arms at ctr.
125.00 250.00 500.00

A48 100 MARKKAA
1882. Black and red. Arms at ctr.

a. Printed in Copenhagen. 3mm serial #000001-481300.	150.00	400.00	750.00
b. Printed in Helsinki. 3.8mm serial #481301-683000.	125.00	300.00	750.00

1886-94 ISSUE

A50 5 MARKKAA
1886. Black and blue. Arms at ctr.

	GOOD	FINE	XF
a. Wmk. at ctr. r.	25.00	65.00	200.00
b. Wmk. at ctr.	15.00	40.00	125.00

A51 10 MARKKAA
1889. Dk. brown and red. Arms at ctr.
20.00 50.00 125.00

A52 20 MARKKAA
1894. Black and dk. brown. Arms at ctr. Wmk. at l. and r.

a. Dk. red. Serial # up to 0096584.	40.00	100.00	225.00
b. Red-brown. Serial #123023-324770.	30.00	85.00	200.00
c. Brown. Serial #403209 onward.	20.00	60.00	150.00

1897-98 ISSUE

1 5 MARKKAA
1897. Blue on brown unpt. Arms at l., woman at ctr., head at r. Round shield on back. Vertical format.

GOOD	FINE	XF
15.00	45.00	175.00

2 5 MARKKAA
1897. Like #1, but shield w/point at ctr. on back.

GOOD	FINE	XF
7.50	20.00	75.00

398 FINLAND

3	10 MARKKAA	GOOD	FINE	XF
	1898. Purple on brown unpt. Woman standing at l. Back purple-brown.	10.00	25.00	75.00

5	20 MARKKAA	GOOD	FINE	XF
	1898. Woman w/youth and globe.			
	a. Back green.	15.00	50.00	250.00
	b. Back red. (Not issued).	—	—	—
6	50 MARKKAA			
	1898. Blue. Woman w/tablet at l.			
	a. Handwritten sign. to #1000.	40.00	100.00	300.00
	b. Lines under sign. Serial #1001-342000.	40.00	100.00	300.00
	c. W/o lines under sign. Serial #342001 & up.	40.00	100.00	300.00
7	100 MARKKAA			
	1898. Young farming couple at l.			
	a. Back purple.	50.00	150.00	300.00
	b. Back red. (Not issued).	—	—	—

8	500 MARKKAA	GOOD	FINE	XF
	1898. Blue. Woman w/lion at l.	200.00	500.00	1000.

1909 FIRST ISSUE

Begining w #9, isses are affected by WWI and many re-issues of earlier dates.

#9-32 have Czarist eagle at upper ctr.

NOTE: The wmk. is only found on about half of the printings of #9a. Notes with prefex letters A, B & C are believed to be special printings.

9	5 MARKKAA	VG	VF	UNC
	1909. Blue. Rowboat in river in black on back.			
	a. Wmk: SPFB.	3.00	10.00	30.00
	b. W/o wmk.	5.00	15.00	45.00
	c. Serial # prefix A; B or C.	200.00	350.00	750.00
10	10 MARKKAA			
	1909. Lilac. Stylized tree at ctr. House/w 2 cows in black on back. Serial # and series varieties.	3.00	15.00	40.00

11	20 MARKKAA	VG	VF	UNC
	1909. Orange on gray unpt. Caduceus at ctr. Stylized tree on back. Serial # varieties.			
	a. Wmk: SPFB.	5.00	15.00	50.00
	b. W/o wmk.	7.00	20.00	70.00
12	50 MARKKAA			
	1909. Blue. Lighthouse on back.	20.00	50.00	175.00
13	100 MARKKAA			
	1909. Violet. Farmer plowing at l. and r. Serial # varieties.	40.00	100.00	250.00
14	500 MARKKAA			
	1909. Orange and brown. 2 blacksmiths at anvil at ctr. Serial # varieties.	300.00	600.00	1000.
15	1000 MARKKAA			
	1909. Yellow and brown. 2 men holding a caduceus at ctr.	500.00	1000.	2000.

1915 ISSUE

16	1 MARKKA	VG	VF	UNC
	1915. Red. Uniface. Serial # varieties.			
	a. W/o series.	1.00	5.00	15.00
	b. Series A.	1.00	2.00	5.00

1916 ISSUE

17	25 PENNIÄ			
	1916. Yellow-brown. (Not issued).	500.00	750.00	1000.
18	50 PENNIÄ			
	1916. Gray-blue. (Not issued).	500.00	750.00	1000.

19	1 MARKKA	VG	VF	UNC
	1916. Dk. brown on lt. brown unpt. Serial # varieties.	.50	1.00	3.00

1916 PEOPLES COMMISSARIAT ISSUE

19A	1 MARKKA			
	1916. Like #19 but serial #20232001-20880000.	10.00	30.00	60.00

1918 ISSUE OF 1909 DATED NOTES
Issued in 1918 w/old date 1909. Notes have high serial #.

20	5 MARKKAA	VG	VF	UNC
	1909 (1918). Blue. Like #9, but serial #19397001-20789000.	1.00	3.00	10.00
21	20 MARKKAA			
	1909 (1918). Orange-brown. Like #11, but serial #9874001-10019000.	2.00	10.00	50.00
22	100 MARKKAA			
	1909 (1918). Violet. Like #13, but serial #2775001-2983000.	5.00	15.00	40.00

23	**500 MARKKAA**	**VG**	**VF**	**UNC**
	1909 (1918). Orange and brown. Like #14, but serial #170001-262000.	7.50	20.00	60.00

REPUBLIC OF FINLAND

FINLANDS BANK

1909 DATED ISSUE (1918), LITT. A

24	**5 MARKKAA**			
	1909 (1918). Blue. Like #9.			
	a. Wmk.	7.50	20.00	50.00
	b. W/o wmk.	5.00	15.00	60.00
25	**10 MARKKAA**			
	1909 (1918). Lilac. Like #10.	5.00	15.00	50.00
26	**20 MARKKAA**			
	1909 (1918). Orange-brown. Like #11.	200.00	500.00	1000.
27	**50 MARKKAA**			
	1909 (1918). Blue. Like #12.	25.00	50.00	200.00
28	**100 MARKKAA**			
	1909 (1918). Violet. Like #13.	350.00	750.00	1250.
29	**500 MARKKAA**			
	1909 (1918). Orange and brown. Like #14.	—	Rare	—

1909 DATED ISSUE (1918), *SARJA II* (SERIES II)

30	**5 MARKKAA**	**VG**	**VF**	**UNC**
	1909 (1918). Green. Like #9.	2.00	10.00	25.00
31	**100 MARKKAA**			
	1909 (1918). Orange and gray. Like #13.	20.00	50.00	100.00
32	**500 MARKKAA**			
	1909 (1918). Gray and yellow. Like #14.	100.00	300.00	750.00

1918 ISSUE

#33-41 w/o Czarist eagle at upper ctr.

33	**25 PENNIÄ**	**VG**	**VF**	**UNC**
	1918. Dk. brown on lt. brown unpt.	.50	1.50	3.00

34	**50 PENNIÄ**	**VG**	**VF**	**UNC**
	1918. Dk. brown on blue unpt.	.50	1.50	4.00

35	**1 MARKKA**	**VG**	**VF**	**UNC**
	1918. Dk. brown on lt. brown unpt. Similar to #19.	.50	1.50	5.00
36	**5 MARKKAA**			
	1918. Green. Similar to #9.	2.00	10.00	20.00
37	**10 MARKKAA**			
	1918. Lilac. Similar to #10.	3.00	10.00	25.00

38	**20 MARKKAA**	**VG**	**VF**	**UNC**
	1918. Blue. Similar to #11.	5.00	15.00	40.00

39	**50 MARKKAA**	**VG**	**VF**	**UNC**
	1918. Blue. Similar to #12.	15.00	50.00	125.00
40	**100 MARKKAA**			
	1918. Lt. brown on gray unpt. Similar to #13.	15.00	50.00	150.00
41	**1000 MARKKAA**			
	1918. Similar to #15.	300.00	600.00	1500.

1922 DATED ISSUE

#42-74 arms on back.

42	**5 MARKKAA**	**VG**	**VF**	**UNC**
	1922. Green. Fir tree at ctr.	1.00	5.00	25.00
43	**10 MARKKAA**			
	1922. Brown. Pine tree at ctr.	1.00	5.00	25.00
44	**20 MARKKAA**			
	1922 (1926). Red. Pine tree at ctr.	10.00	25.00	75.00
45	**50 MARKKAA**			
	1922 (1926). Dk. blue. Allegorical group of 6 people.	25.00	100.00	225.00

46	**100 MARKKAA**	**VG**	**VF**	**UNC**
	1922. Dk. brown. Allegorical group of 6 people.	50.00	125.00	250.00
47	**500 MARKKAA**			
	1922 (1924). Brown on green unpt. Allegorical group of 11 people.	75.00	200.00	350.00
48	**1000 MARKKAA**			
	1922 (1923). Brown. Allegorical group of 13 people.	60.00	150.00	300.00

1922 DATED ISSUE, LITT. A

		VG	VF	UNC
49	**5 MARKKAA** 1922 (1926). Green. Like #42.	1.00	5.00	25.00
50	**10 MARKKAA** 1922 (1926). Brown. Like #43.	1.00	5.00	25.00
51	**20 MARKKAA** 1922 (1927). Violet. Like #44.	30.00	100.00	200.00
52	**50 MARKKAA** 1922 (1925). Dk. blue. Like #45.	25.00	100.00	250.00
53	**100 MARKKAA** 1922 (1923). Dk. brown. Like #46.	20.00	70.00	150.00
		VG	VF	UNC
54	**500 MARKKAA** 1922 (1930). Brown on green unpt. Like #47.	100.00	350.00	750.00
55	**1000 MARKKAA** 1922 (1929). Brown. Like #48.	150.00	400.00	1000.

1922 DATED ISSUE, LITT. B

		VG	VF	UNC
56	**5 MARKKAA** 1922 (1929). Green. Like #42.	5.00	20.00	50.00
57	**10 MARKKAA** 1922 (1929). Brown. Like #43.	5.00	10.00	30.00
58	**20 MARKKAA** 1922 (1929). Violet. Like #44.	50.00	125.00	300.00
59	**50 MARKKAA** 1922 (1929). Dk. blue. Like #45.	100.00	400.00	700.00
60	**100 MARKKAA** 1922 (1929). Dk. brown. Like #46.	50.00	120.00	300.00

1922 DATED ISSUE, LITT. C

		VG	VF	UNC

61	**5 MARKKAA**
	1922 (1930). Green. Like #42.
	  a. Issued note.
	  s. Specimen.
		1.00
		—
			5.00
			—
				15.00
				100.00

62	**10 MARKKAA**
	1922 (1930). Brown. Like #43.
	  a. Issued note.
	  s. Specimen.
		1.00
		—
			5.00
			—
				15.00
				100.00

63	**20 MARKKAA**
	1922 (1931). Red. Like #44.
	  a. Issued note.
	  s. Specimen.
		1.00
		—
			5.00
			—
				15.00
				100.00

		VG	VF	UNC

64	**50 MARKKAA**
	1922 (1931). Dk. blue. Like #45.
	  a. Issued note.
	  s. Specimen.
		5.00
		—
			20.00
			—
				50.00
				175.00

		VG	VF	UNC

65	**100 MARKKAA**
	1922 (1932-45). Dk. brown. Like #46.
	  a. Issued note.
	  s. Specimen.
		5.00
		—
			20.00
			—
				50.00
				175.00

		VG	VF	UNC

66	**500 MARKKAA**
	1922 (1931-42). Brown on green unpt. Like #47.
	  a. Issued note.
	  s. Specimen.
		12.00
		—
			25.00
			—
				100.00
				200.00

		VG	VF	UNC

67	**1000 MARKKAA**
	1922 (1931-45). Brown. Like #48.
	  a. Issued note.
	  s. Specimen.
		10.00
		—
			25.00
			—
				75.00
				200.00

1922 DATED ISSUE, LITT. D

67A	**1000 MARKKAA** 1922 (1939). Green. *Litt. D.* Like #48.	100.00	200.00	500.00

1939 PROVISIONAL ISSUE

68	**5000 MARKKAA** 1922 (1939). Brown. *Litt. A.* Blue ovpt. on #47.	3000.	4500.	6000.

1939-41 DATED ISSUE

69	**5 MARKKAA**
	1939 (1942-45). Green. Like #42.
	  a. Issued note.
	  s. Specimen.
		1.00
		—
			4.00
			—
				12.00
				100.00

70	**10 MARKKAA**	VG	VF	UNC
	1939 (1939-45). Brown. Like #43.			
	a. Issued note.	.50	3.00	7.50
	s. Specimen.	—	—	100.00

71	**20 MARKKAA**	VG	VF	UNC
	1939 (1939-45). Purple. Like #44.			
	a. Issued note.	1.00	4.00	12.00
	s. Specimen.	—	—	100.00

77	**10 MARKKAA**	VG	VF	UNC
	1945. Red. Pine at ctr.			
	a. Issued note.	1.00	4.00	15.00
	s. Specimen.	—	—	100.00

78	**20 MARKKAA**	VG	VF	UNC
	1945. Blue. Pine at ctr.			
	a. Issued note.	1.00	4.00	15.00
	s. Specimen.	—	—	100.00

79	**50 MARKKAA**			
	1945. Brown. Young farm couple on back.			
	a. Printed area on face 93 x 96mm . (A serial #).	5.00	15.00	50.00
	b. Printed area on face 88 x 92mm .	3.00	10.00	30.00
	s. Specimen.	—	—	125.00

80	**100 MARKKAA**			
	1945. Blue-green. Woman w/lion on back.			
	a. Issued note.	3.00	10.00	30.00
	s. Specimen.	—	—	125.00

81	**500 MARKKAA**	VG	VF	UNC
	1945. Blue. Similar to #47.			
	a. Issued note.	20.00	50.00	160.00
	s. Specimen.	—	—	200.00

72	**50 MARKKAA**	VG	VF	UNC
	1939 (1939-45). Dk. blue. Like #45.			
	a. Issued note.	6.00	15.00	50.00
	s. Specimen.	—	—	150.00

73	**100 MARKKAA**			
	1939 (1940-45). Dk. brown. Like #46.			
	a. Issued note.	5.00	12.50	50.00
	s. Specimen.	—	—	150.00

74	**1000 MARKKAA**			
	1941 (1944-45). Brown. *Litt. E.* Like #48.	500.00	1000.	1500.

82	**1000 MARKKAA**	VG	VF	UNC
	1945. Blue-violet. Similar to #48.			
	a. Issued note.	15.00	50.00	135.00
	s. Specimen.	—	—	200.00

75	**5000 MARKKAA**	VG	VF	UNC
	1939 (1940). Dk. blue and violet. Snellman at l.			
	a. Denomination at ctr. and at r. w/o reddish unpt. (1940-1943) .	150.00	300.00	600.00
	b. Denomination at ctr. and at r. w/reddish unpt. (1945).	250.00	500.00	1000.
	s. Specimen.	—	—	1000.

1945 DATED ISSUE, LITT. A

76	**5 MARKKAA**			
	1945 (1946). Yellow. Fir at ctr.			
	a. Issued note.	1.00	4.00	15.00
	s. Specimen.	—	—	100.00

		VG	VF	UNC
83	**5000 MARKKAA**			
	1945. Dk. brown. Like #75.			
	a. Issued note.	75.00	150.00	300.00
	s. Specimen.	—	—	500.00

1945 DATED ISSUE, LITT. B

		VG	VF	UNC
84	**5 MARKKAA**			
	1945 (1948). Yellow. Like #76.	1.50	5.00	15.00
85	**10 MARKKAA**			
	1945 (1948). Red. Like #77.	.50	2.00	6.50

		VG	VF	UNC
86	**20 MARKKAA**			
	1945 (1948). Blue. Like #78.	1.00	2.50	8.50

		VG	VF	UNC
87	**50 MARKKAA**			
	1945 (1948). Brown. Like #79.	2.00	6.00	20.00

		VG	VF	UNC
88	**100 MARKKAA**			
	1945 (1948). Blue-green. Like #80.	2.00	5.00	20.00
89	**500 MARKKAA**			
	1945 (1948). Blue. Like #81.	12.00	40.00	95.00

		VG	VF	UNC
90	**1000 MARKKAA**			
	1945 (1948). Violet. Like #82.	10.00	30.00	85.00

1955 ISSUE

		VG	VF	UNC
91	**100 MARKKAA**			
	1955. Brown on olive unpt. Ears of wheat at ctr.			
	a. Issued note.	1.00	3.50	12.00
	s. Specimen.	—	—	150.00
92	**500 MARKKAA**			
	1955. Brown on blue unpt. Conifer branch at ctr. 2 sign. varieties.			
	a. Issued note.	20.00	40.00	80.00
	s. Specimen.	—	—	200.00
93	**1000 MARKKAA**			
	1955. Dk. green. Paasikivi at l.			
	a. Issued note.	5.00	20.00	45.00
	s. Specimen.	—	—	200.00

		VG	VF	UNC
94	**5000 MARKKAA**			
	1955. Brown and lilac. K. J. Stahlberg at l.			
	a. Issued note.	15.00	40.00	75.00
	s. Specimen.	—	—	250.00

		VG	VF	UNC
95	**10,000 MARKKAA**			
	1955. Lilac. J. V. Snellman at l. ctr.			
	a. Issued note.	25.00	60.00	120.00
	s. Specimen.	—	—	300.00

1956 ISSUE

		VG	VF	UNC
96	**500 MARKKAA**			
	1956. Blue. Conifer branch.			
	a. Issued note.	5.00	20.00	50.00
	s. Specimen.	—	—	125.00

1957 ISSUE

		VG	VF	UNC
97	**100 MARKKAA**			
	1957. Dk. red on lt. brown unpt. Ears of wheat.			
	a. Issued note.	.50	2.00	6.00
	s. Specimen.	—	—	125.00

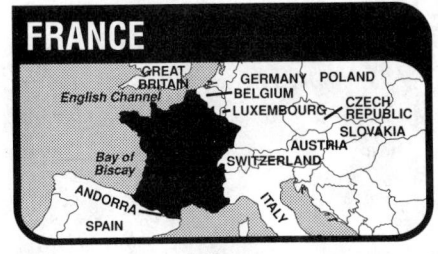

FRANCE

The French Republic, largest of the West European nations, has an area of 220,668 sq. mi. (547,026 sq. km.) and a population of 57.5 million. Capital: Paris. Agriculture, mining and manufacturing are the most important elements of France's diversified economy. Textiles and clothing, iron and steel products, machinery and transportation equipment, agricultural products and wine are exported.

France, the Gaul of ancient times, emerged from the Renaissance as a modern centralized national state which reached its zenith during the reign of Louis XIV (1643-1715) when it became an absolute monarchy and the foremost power in Europe. Although his reign marks the golden age of French culture, the domestic abuses and extravagance of Louis XIV plunged France into a series of costly wars. This, along with a system of special privileges granted the nobility and other favored groups, weakened the monarchy, brought France to bankruptcy - and laid the way for the French Revolution of 1789-94 that shook Europe and affected the whole world.

The monarchy was abolished and the First Republic formed in 1793. The new government fell in 1799 to a coup led by Napoleon Bonaparte who, after declaring himself First Consul for life, had himself proclaimed emperor of France and king of Italy. Napoleon's military victories made him master of much of Europe, but his disastrous Russian campaign of 1812 initiated a series of defeats that led to his abdication in 1814 and exile to the island of Elba. The monarchy was briefly restored under Louis XVIII. Napoleon returned to France in March 1815, but his efforts to regain power were totally crushed at the Battle of Waterloo. He was exiled to the island of St. Helena where he died in 1821.

The monarchy under Louis XVIII was again restored in 1815, but the ultrareactionary regime of Charles X (1824-30) was overthrown by a liberal revolution and Louis Philippe of Orleans replaced him as monarch. The monarchy was ousted by the Revolution of 1848 and the Second Republic proclaimed. Louis Napoleon Bonaparte (nephew of Napoleon I) was elected president of the Second Republic. He was proclaimed emperor in 1852. As Napoleon III, he gave France two decades of prosperity under a stable, autocratic regime, but led it to defeat in the Franco-Prussian War of 1870, after which the Third Republic was established.

The Third Republic endured until 1940 and ended by the capitulation of France to the swiftly maneuvering German forces. Marshal Henri Petain formed a puppet government that sued for peace and ruled unoccupied France from Vichy. Meanwhile, General Charles de Gaulle escaped to London where he formed a wartime government in exile and the Free French army. De Gaulle's provisional exile government was officially recognized by the Allies after the liberation of Paris in 1944, and De Gaulle, who had been serving as head of the provisional government, was formally elected to that position. In October 1945, the people overwhelmingly rejected a return to the prewar government, thus paving the way for the formation of the Fourth Republic.

De Gaulle was unanimously elected president of the Fourth Republic, but resigned in January 1946 when leftists withdrew their support. In actual operation, the Fourth Republic was remarkably like the Third, with the National Assembly the focus of power. The later years of the Fourth Republic were marked by a burst of industrial expansion unmatched in modern French history. The growth rate, however, was marred by a nagging inflationary trend that weakened the franc and undermined the competitive posture of France's export trade. This and the Algerian conflict led to the recall of De Gaulle to power, the adoption of a new constitution vesting strong powers in the executive, and establishment in 1958 of the current Fifth Republic.

* * * This section has been reorganized by issue, and beginning w/Bank of France, renumbered. * * *

RULERS:
Louis XIV, 1643-1715
Louis XV, 1715-74
Louis XVI, 1774-93
First Republic, 1793-94, L'An 2
Directory, 1795-99, L'An 4-7
Consulate, 1799-1803, L'An 8-11
Napoleon as Consul, 1799-1804
Napoleon I as Emperor, 1804-14
(First Restoration)
Louis XVIII, 1814-15
Napoleon I, 1815
(Second Restoration)
Louis XVIII, 1815-24
Charles X, 1824-30
Louis Philippe, 1830-48
Second Republic, 1848-52
Napoleon III, 1852-70

MONETARY SYSTEM
1 Livre = 20 Sols (Sous)
1 Ecu = 6 Livres
1 Louis D'or = 4 Ecus to 1794
1 Franc = 10 Decimes = 100 Centimes, 1794-
1 Nouveaux Franc = 100 "old" Francs, 1960-

FRENCH DENOMINATIONS
1 Un	13 Treize	125 Cent Vingt-Cinq
2 Deux	14 Quatorze	200 Deux Cents
3 Trois	15 Quinze	250 Deux Cent Cinquante
4 Quatre	16 Seize	300 Trois Cents
5 Cinq	20 Vingt	400 Quatre Cents
6 Six	25 Vingt-Cinq	500 Cinq Cents
7 Sept	30 Trente	750 Sept Cent Cinquante
8 Huit	40 Quarante	1000 Mille
9 Neuf	10 Cinquante	2000 Deux Mille
10 Dix	80 Quatre-Vingts	5000 Cinq Mille
11 Onze	90 Quatre-Vingt-Dix	10,000 Quatre-Vingt-Dix
12 Douze	100 Cent	

KINGDOM

BILLETS DE MONOYE

1701-1710 ISSUE

A1	25-10,000 LIVRES	GOOD	FINE	XF
	1701-1710.			

a. Crowned double *L* monogram. 1701-07.	1500.	3500.	5500.

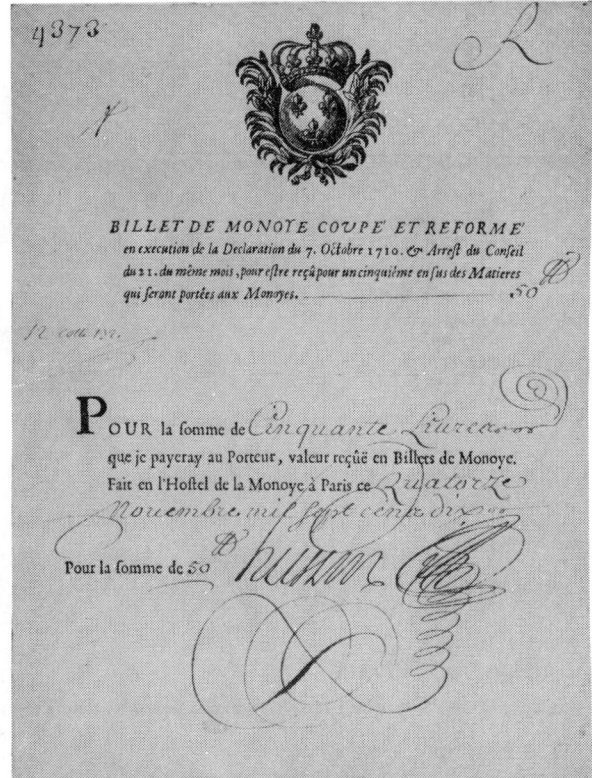

b. Crowned fleur-de-lis. 1709-10.	1500.	3500.	5500.

BILLETS DE L'ESTAT

1716 ISSUE

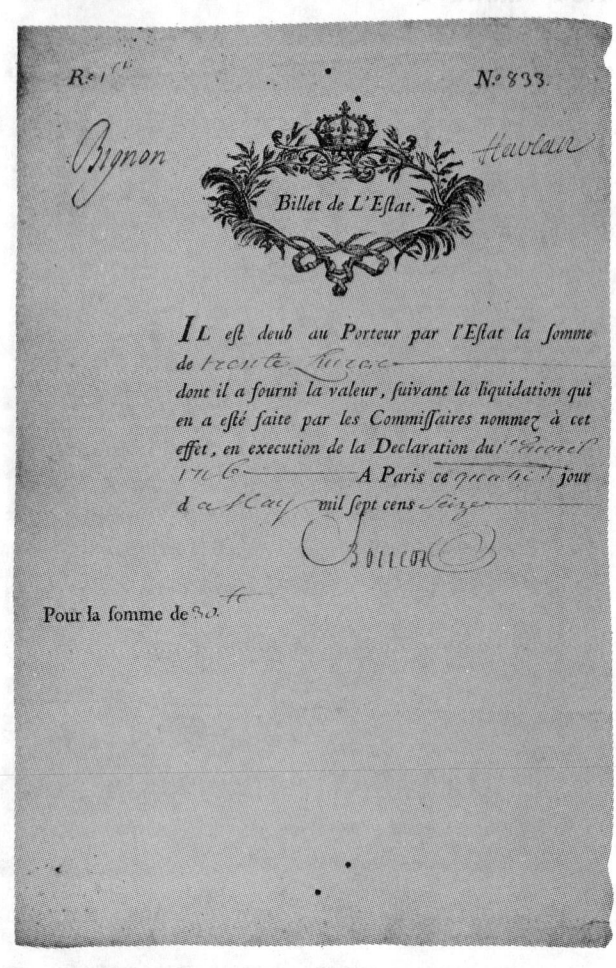

A2	30-1000 LIVRES 1716.	GOOD 1500.	FINE 3500.	XF 5500.

LA BANQUE GÉNÉRALE

Issued by John Law in Louisiana. In 1720 a 50% devaluation occurred causing a great panic.

1716 ISSUE

A3	10 ECUS 16.6.1716-9.11.1717.	—	—	—
A4	40 ECUS 13.10.1716-9.11.1717	—	—	—
A5	100 ECUS 16.6.1716-8.3.1718.	—	—	—
A6	400 ECUS 13.10.1716-8.3.1718.	—	—	—
A7	1000 ECUS 16.6.1716-8.3.1718.	—	—	—

1718 ISSUE

A8	10 ECUS 8.6.1718; 30.8.1718.	—	—	—
A9	50 ECUS 8.6.1718; 30.8.1718; 18.10.1718.	—	—	—
A10	500 ECUS 8.6.1718; 30.8.1718; 18.10.1718.	—	—	—

LA BANQUE ROYALE

Issued by John Law in Louisiana. In 1720 a 50% depreciation occurred and caused a great panic.

1719-20 ISSUE

#A12-A15 engraved ornamented monogram at l. edge.

A12	10 LIVRES 1.4.1719; 25.7.1719.	300.00	700.00	1200.

A13	100 LIVRES 10.1.1719-1.1.1720.	GOOD 500.00	FINE 1250.	XF 2250.
A14	1000 LIVRES 10.1.1719-1.1.1720.	500.00	1250.	2250.
A15	10,000 LIVRES 1.1.1720.	—	—	—

1720 FIRST ISSUE

#A16-A23 lettered l. edge.

A16	10 LIVRES 1.1.1720.	GOOD	FINE	XF
	a. W/o text: ...en Especes d'Argent.	250.00	600.00	1000.
	b. W/text: ...en Especes d'Argent.	60.00	150.00	300.00
A17	100 LIVRES 1.1.1720.			
	a. W/o text: ...en Especes d'Argent.	300.00	700.00	1200.
	b. W/text: ...en Especes d'Argent.	60.00	150.00	300.00

A18	1000 LIVRES 1.1.1720.	GOOD	FINE	XF
	a. W/o text: ...en Especes d'Argent.	—	—	—
	b. W/text: ...en Especes d'Argent.	200.00	500.00	900.00
A19	10,000 LIVRES 1.1.1720.			

1720 SECOND ISSUE

A20	10 LIVRES 1.7.1720.			
	a. W/text: ...payer au Porteur a vue Dix livres Tournois.	65.00	175.00	275.00
	b. W/text: ...payer au Porteur Dix livres a vue Tournois.	250.00	600.00	1000.
	c. W/text: ...especes (instead of Especes).			
A21	100 LIVRES 1.7.1720.	200.00	500.00	900.00

1720 THIRD ISSUE

A22	10 LIVRES 2.9.1720.	200.00	500.00	900.00

A23	50 LIVRES	GOOD	FINE	XF
	2.9.1720.	150.00	350.00	650.00

CAISSE D'ESCOMPTE

1776 ISSUE

#A24-A27 w/o text: *Promesse d'Assignat.*

A24	200 LIVRES	GOOD	FINE	XF
	1776-90. Green paper.	700.00	1750.	2750.
A25	300 LIVRES			
	1776-90. Blue paper.	800.00	2000.	3500.
A26	600 LIVRES			
	1776-90.	—	—	—

A27	1000 LIVRES	GOOD	FINE	XF
	1776-90.	250.00	600.00	1000.

1790 ISSUE

#A24A-A27A w/text: *Promesse d'Assignat.*

A24A	200 LIVRES			
	1790-93.	—	—	—
A25A	300 LIVRES			
	1790-93.	—	—	—
A26A	600 LIVRES			
	1790-93.	—	—	—
A27A	1000 LIVRES			
	1790-93.	—	—	—

ASSIGNATS

DOMAINES NATIONAUX

1789 ISSUE

#A28-A30 bust Kg. Louis XVI at upper ctr.

A28	200 LIVRES	GOOD	FINE	XF
	19&21.12.1789 and 16&17.4.1790.			
	a. Issued note complete w/3 coupons.	—	—	—
	b. Issued note w/o coupons.	350.00	1250.	1750.
	c. Cancelled w/ovpt: *ANNULE.*			
A29	300 LIVRES	GOOD	FINE	XF
	19&21.12.1789 and 16&17.4.1790. Pink paper.			
	a. Issued note complete w/3 coupons.	—	—	—
	b. Issued note w/o coupons.	450.00	1500.	2000.

A30	1000 LIVRES	GOOD	FINE	XF
	19&20.12.1789 and 16&17.4.1790. Red. Kg. Louis XVI at top l.			
	a. Issued note complete w/3 coupons.	—	—	—
	b. Issued note w/o coupons.	1200.	2200.	4000.

1790 INTEREST COUPONS

A32	9 LIVRES			
	16/17.4.1790. Coupon of #A29.			
	a. Single coupon.	—	Rare	—
	b. Sheet of 3 coupons.	—	Rare	—
A33	30 LIVRES			
	16/17.1790. Coupon of #A30.			
	a. Single coupon.	—	Rare	—
	b. Sheet of 3 coupons.	—	Rare	—

1790 ISSUE

A34	50 LIVRES	GOOD	FINE	XF
	29.9.1790. Kg. Louis XVI at top ctr.	30.00	100.00	150.00
A35	60 LIVRES			
	29.9.1790. Kg. Louis XVI at top ctr.	40.00	120.00	175.00
A36	70 LIVRES			
	29.9.1790. Kg. Louis XVI at top ctr.	40.00	120.00	175.00
A37	80 LIVRES			
	29.9.1790. Kg. Louis XVI at top ctr.	40.00	120.00	175.00

			GOOD	FINE	XF
A38	**90 LIVRES**		45.00	125.00	175.00
	29.9.1790. Kg. Louis XVI at top ctr.				
A39	**100 LIVRES**		50.00	135.00	200.00
	29.9.1790. Kg. Louis XVI at top ctr.				

			GOOD	FINE	XF
A48	**300 LIVRES**		45.00	160.00	250.00
	19.6/12.9.1791. Kg. Louis XVI at top ctr.				

1791 THIRD ISSUE

			GOOD	FINE	XF
A49	**5 LIVRES**		3.00	6.00	15.00
	28.9.1791.				
A50	**5 LIVRES**		3.00	6.00	15.00
	1.11.1791.				

			GOOD	FINE	XF
A40	**500 LIVRES**		70.00	225.00	350.00
	29.9.1790. Kg. Louis XVI at top l.				
A41	**2000 LIVRES**		1200.	2200.	4000.
	29.9.1790. Red. Kg. Louis XVI at top l.				

1791 FIRST ISSUE

			GOOD	FINE	XF
A42	**5 LIVRES**		3.00	7.00	15.00
	6.5.1791.				
A43	**50 LIVRES**		30.00	100.00	150.00
	19.6.1791. Kg. Louis XVI at top ctr.				
A44	**60 LIVRES**		40.00	120.00	175.00
	19.6.1791. Kg. Louis XVI at top ctr.				

			GOOD	FINE	XF
A51	**10 LIVRES**		1.50	4.00	12.00
	16.12.1791.				

			GOOD	FINE	XF
A52	**25 LIVRES**		12.00	25.00	60.00
	16.12.1791. Kg. Louis XVI at top r.				

1792 FIRST ISSUE

			VG	VF	UNC
A53	**10 SOUS**		1.00	2.00	3.00
	4.1.1792.				
A54	**15 SOLS**		1.00	2.00	3.00
	4.1.1792.				
A55	**25 SOLS**		1.50	3.00	4.00
	4.1.1792.				

			GOOD	FINE	XF
A44A	**100 LIVRES**		30.00	100.00	150.00
(A45)	19.6.1791. Kg. Louis XVI at top. ctr.				
A46	**500 LIVRES**		150.00	450.00	600.00
	19.6.1791. Kg. Louis XVI at top ctr.				

1791 SECOND ISSUE

			GOOD	FINE	XF
A47	**200 LIVRES**		40.00	120.00	175.00
	19.6/12.9.1791. Kg. Louis XVI at top ctr.				

			VG	VF	UNC
A56	**50 SOLS**		1.00	2.00	3.00
	4.1.1792.				
A57	**5 LIVRES**		5.00	8.00	15.00
	30.4.1792.				
A58	**50 LIVRES**		35.00	70.00	100.00
	30.4.1792. Kg. Louis XVI at top ctr.				
A59	**200 LIVRES**		45.00	85.00	120.00
	30.4.1792. Kg. Louis XVI at top ctr.				

1792 SECOND ISSUE

		VG	VF	UNC
A60	**5 LIVRES** 27.6.1792.	2.00	6.00	12.00
A61	**5 LIVRES** 31.7.1792.	2.00	6.00	12.00
A62	**50 LIVRES** 31.8.1792. Kg. Louis XVI at top ctr.	40.00	80.00	110.00
A63	**200 LIVRES** 31.8.1792. Kg. Louis XVI at top ctr.	45.00	90.00	120.00

1792 THIRD ISSUE

		VG	VF	UNC
A64	**10 SOUS** 24.10.1792.			
	a. Issued note.	1.50	3.00	4.50
	b. Error note w/text: *La loi punit...* at lower l., repeated at lower r.	50.00	200.00	400.00
A65	**15 SOLS** 24.10.1792.	1.50	3.00	4.50
A66	**10 LIVRES** 24.10.1792.			
	a. Wmk. Fleur-de-lis.	5.00	12.00	25.00
	b. Wmk. *RP-FR* top left. *X*.	1.50	3.00	4.50
A67	**25 LIVRES** 24.10.1792. Kg. Louis XVI at top r.	8.00	20.00	40.00

1793 ISSUE

		VG	VF	UNC
A68 (A70)	**10 SOUS** 23.5.1793.			
	a. Wmk. *LA NATION...* Series 1/16.	3.00	7.50	15.00
	b. Wmk. *RF/Xs*.	1.50	3.00	4.50
	c. Error note w/text: *La loi puni...*at lower l., repeated at lower r.	50.00	200.00	400.00

		VG	VF	UNC
A69 (A71)	**15 SOLS** 23.5.1793.			
	a. Wmk: *LA NATION...* Series 1/42.	3.00	7.50	15.00
	b. Wmk. *RF/15s*.	1.50	3.00	4.50
	c. Error note w/text: *LA NATION...*at lower r., repeated at lower l.	50.00	200.00	400.00
A70 (A72)	**50 SOLS** 23.5.1793.			
	a. Wmk. *LA NATION...* Series 1/36.	3.00	7.50	15.00
	b. Wmk. *RF/50s*.	1.50	3.00	4.50

		VG	VF	UNC
A71 (A73)	**25 LIVRES** 6.6.1793.	1.50	4.00	8.00

RÉPUBLIQUE FRANÇAISE

1792 ISSUE

		VG	VF	UNC
A72 (A69)	**50 LIVRES** 14.12.1792.	6.00	15.00	30.00

		VG	VF	UNC
A73 (A68)	**400 LIVRES** 21.11.1792.	10.00	20.00	40.00

1793 FIRST ISSUE

		VG	VF	UNC
A74	**125 LIVRES** 7 Vendemiaire An II (28.9.1793).	4.00	8.00	15.00

		VG	VF	UNC
A75	**250 LIVRES** 7 Vendemiaire An II (28.9.1793).	5.00	10.00	20.00

1793 SECOND ISSUE

A76	5 LIVRES	VG	VF	UNC
	10 Brumaire An II (31.10.1793).	2.00	4.00	6.50

1794 ISSUE

A77	500 LIVRES	VG	VF	UNC
	20 Pluviose An II (8.2.1794).	5.00	10.00	20.00

1795 FRANC ISSUE

A78	100 FRANCS	GOOD	FINE	XF
	18 Nivose An III (7.1.1795).	3.00	6.00	15.00

A79	750 FRANCS	GOOD	FINE	XF
	18 Nivose An III (7.1.1795).	400.00	1100.	1600.

A80	1000 FRANCS	GOOD	FINE	XF
	18 Nivose An III (7.1.1795). Red.	15.00	40.00	75.00

A81	2000 FRANCS	GOOD	FINE	XF
	18 Nivose An III (7.1.1795).	25.00	60.00	150.00

A82	10,000 FRANCS	GOOD	FINE	XF
	18 Nivose An III (7.1.1795).	60.00	150.00	250.00

PROMESSES DE MANDATS TERRITORIAUX

1796 ISSUE
Sign. varieties.

A83	25 FRANCS	GOOD	FINE	XF
	28 Ventose An IV (18.3.1796). Black and olive.			
	a. W/o *Serie*.	15.00	30.00	60.00
	b. W/*Serie*.	6.00	15.00	25.00

A84	**100 FRANCS**	GOOD	FINE	XF
	28 Ventose An IV (18.3.1796). Red and blue-gray.			
	a. W/o *Serie*.	30.00	70.00	125.00
	b. W/*Serie*.	8.00	25.00	50.00
A85	**250 FRANCS**			
	28 Ventose An IV (18.3.1796). Olive and black.			
	a. W/o *Serie*.	25.00	70.00	125.00
	b. W/*Serie*.	12.00	35.00	75.00

A86	**500 FRANCS**	GOOD	FINE	XF
	28 Ventose An IV (18.3.1796). Gray-blue and red.			
	a. W/o *Serie*.	30.00	70.00	125.00
	b. W/*Serie*.	15.00	30.00	65.00

MANDATS TERRITORIAL
1796 ISSUE

A87	**5 FRANCS**	GOOD	FINE	XF
	28 Ventose An IV (18.3.1796).			
	a. W/o handstamp.	400.00	800.00	1300.
	b. Black handstamp: *Rep. Fra*.	50.00	100.00	200.00
	c. Red handstamp: *Rep. Fra*.	50.00	100.00	200.00

RESCRIPTIONS DE L'EMPRUNT FORCÉ
1796 ISSUE

A88	**25 FRANCS**			
	21 Nivose An IV (11.1.1796).	175.00	400.00	650.00
A89	**50 FRANCS**			
	21 Nivose An IV (11.1.1796).	300.00	700.00	1100.

(Rescription document image)

A90	**100 FRANCS**	GOOD	FINE	XF
	21 Nivose An IV (11.1.1796).	175.00	400.00	650.00
A91	**250 FRANCS**			
	21 Nivose An IV (11.1.1796).	350.00	750.00	1200.
A92	**500 FRANCS**			
	21 Nivose An IV (11.1.1796).	500.00	1200.	2000.
A93	**1000 FRANCS**			
	21 Nivose An IV (11.1.1796).	650.00	1500.	2500.

ARMÉE CATHOLIQUE ET ROYALE
1793 ISSUE

A94				
	2.8.1793. Assignats w/handwritten notice: *Au nom du Roi bon pour...*	—	—	—
	(In the name of the king good for...)			

1793-94 BONS DE MANLEVRIER

A94A	**10 SOUS**	GOOD	FINE	XF
	ND (1794).	35.00	100.00	250.00
A94B	**15 SOUS**			
	ND (1794).	35.00	100.00	250.00

#A95   #A96

A95	**5 LIVRES**	GOOD	FINE	XF
	ND (Nov. 1793).	35.00	100.00	250.00
A96	**10 LIVRES**			
	ND (Nov. 1793).	50.00	150.00	400.00
A97	**25 LIVRES**			
	ND (Nov. 1793).	65.00	200.00	500.00
A98	**50 LIVRES**			
	ND (Nov. 1793).	75.00	225.00	550.00
A99	**100 LIVRES**			
	ND (Nov. 1793).	85.00	250.00	600.00

1794 BONS DE PASSAGE

A100	**LIVRES-VARIOUS HANDWRITTEN AMT**	GOOD	FINE	XF
	ND (1794). Deep red. Louis XVII at top ctr. Uniface.			
	a. Issued note.	750.00	1500.	—
	r. Remainder w/o sign. or value filled in.	500.00	1000.	—
	x. Printed *500 Livre* (counterfeit).	25.00	50.00	100.00

CONSULATE THRU SECOND REPUBLIC
BANQUE DE FRANCE
1800 PROVISIONAL ISSUE

1 (A112)	**500 FRANCS** 1800. Blue and red. Ovpt: *Payable a la Banque de France* on Caisse de Comptes Courants notes.	—	—	—
2 (A120)	**1000 FRANCS** 1800. Black and red. Ovpt: *Payable a La Banque de France* on Caisse de Compte Courants notes.	—	—	—

1800 REGULAR ISSUE

5 (A113)	**500 FRANCS** 21.6.1800-27.10.1802. Blue and red. Name as *Banque de France*.	—	—	—
10 (A121)	**1000 FRANCS** 21.6.1800-28.4.1802. Black and red. Name as *Banque de France*.	—	—	—

1803-06 ISSUE

15 (A114)	**500 FRANCS** 19.2.1806-29.8.1806. Allegorical figures at l. and r.	—	—	—
16 (A122)	**1000 FRANCS** 14.4.1803-16.4.1812. Allegorical figures at l. and r. 4 sign. varieties.	—	—	—

1810-14 ISSUE

20 (A110)	**250 FRANCS** 27.9.1810-2.1.1812. Green paper. W/text: *Comptair de Lille...*	—	—	—
21 (A123)	**1000 FRANCS** 25.4.1814-4.4.1816. Printed seal at upper l. and r.	—	—	—

1817-18 ISSUE

25 (A115)	**500 FRANCS** 2.1.1818-3.7.1828. Women at top ctr. and at l., Mercury at r.			

		GOOD	FINE	XF
	a. Wmk: *Cinq Cents 500 Fr.* Date handwritten. 6 sign. varieties. Up to 8.8.1822.	—	—	—
	b. Wmk: *Cinq Cents Fr. Banque de France BF.* Date handwritten. 8.4.1824-22.5.1825.	—	—	—
	c. Date printed. 19.4.1827-3.7.1828.	—	—	—

26 **1000 FRANCS**
(A124) 1817-29. Woman in chariot drawn by lions at top ctr., seated allegorical figures at l. and r.
a. Wmk: *Mille Francs 1000 Fr.* Rose field. 3 sign. varieties. 17.4.1817-8.4.1824.
b. Wmk: Like "a", but rusty-brown field. 6 sign. varieties. 27.11.1817-13.3.1823.
c. Wmk: *Mille Francs - Banque de France.* 20.1.1825-14.5.1829.

1829 ISSUE

30 **500 FRANCS**
(A116) 5.3.1829-15.9.1831. Women at top ctr. and l. Mercury at r. Top l. and r. text in circle.
a. Sign. title: *LE DIRECTEUR.* 2 sign. varieties. Up to 22.4.1830.
b. Sign. title: *LE SECRÉTAIRE DU GOUVERNEMENT DELA BANQUE.* 2 sign. varieties. 15.9.1831.

31 **1000 FRANCS**
(A125) 26.11.1829-3.2.1831. Women in chariot drawn by lions at top ctr. Seated allegorical figures at l. and r. *Banque de France* stamped.
a. Sign. title: *LE DIRECTEUR.* 3 sign. varieties. 25.3.1830.
b. Sign. title: *LE SECRÉTAIRE DU GOUVERNEMENT DE LA BANQUE.*

1831-37 ISSUE

35 **250 FRANCS**
(A111) 9.6.1836-13.8.1846. Green paper. Women at top ctr. and at l., Mercury at r., 2 reclining women at bottom ctr.
a. Sign. title: *Secrétaire du Gouvernement de la Banque.* Up to 14.10.1841.
b. Sign. title: *Secrétaire Général* 14.12.1843.

36 **500 FRANCS**
(A117) 1831-43. Women at top ctr. and l. Mercury at r. Top l. and r. text in circle. Back reversed.
a. Sign. title: *LE SECRÉTAIRE DU GOUVERNEMENT DE LA BANQUE.* 3 sign. varieties. 15.9.1831-25.11.1841.
b. Sign. title: *LE SECRÉTAIRE GÉNÉRAL.* 25.6.1842-13.7.1843.

37 **1000 FRANCS**
(A126) 15.9.1831-25.11.1841. Women in chariot drawn by lions at top ctr., seated allegorical figures at l. and r. *Bank de France* stamped. Back reversed. 3 sign. varieties

38 **1000 FRANCS**
(A127) 28.2.1837-17.2.1848. Women in chariot drawn by lions at top ctr., seated allegorical figures at l. and r. *Comptoir de ...* (name of place) stamped.

1842-46 ISSUE

40 **500 FRANCS**
(A118) 1844-63. Woman at l., man at r., woman seated at bottom ctr. w/2 cherubs.

		GOOD	FINE	XF
	a. Wmk: *Cinq Cents Fr. Banque de France.* 22.2.1844.	—	—	—
	b. wmk: *Cinq Cents Fr. Banque de France BF.* 5.9.1844-21.10.1847.	—	—	—
	c. Wmk: *500 F. Cinq Cents Fr. Banque de France.* 6 sign. varieties. 21.4.1848-15.1.1863.	—	—	—

41 **1000 FRANCS**
(A128) 25.6.1842-13.11.1862. 2 female allegorical figures at l., r., top ctr. and at bottom ctr.
a. Wmk: *Mille Francs - Banque de France.* 25.6.1842-24.10.1844.
b. Wmk: *1000 Fr. Mille Francs - Banque de France.* 7 sign. varieties. From 24.10.1844.
c. Name of branch bank below *Banque de France.* 12.10.1848-27.9.1849.
d. Name of branch bank on counterfoil at r. 28.1.1850-23.8.1860.

42 **5000 FRANCS**
(A130) 28.5.1846. Red. Women in chariot drawn by lions at top ctr. Seated allegorical figure at l. and r. 2 sign. varieties.

1848 PROVISIONAL ISSUE

44 **100 FRANCS**
(A105) 1848. Black on Green unpt.

		GOOD	FINE	XF
	a. Sign. in script. 16.3.1848.	—	Rare	—
	b. Printed sign. Serial # at l. and r. 4.5.1848.	—	Rare	—
	c. Printed sign. Serial # at r., series letter at l. 15.7.1848.	—	Rare	—

1848 REGULAR ISSUES

45 **100 FRANCS**
(A106) 1848-63. Woman at top ctr., woman at l., 2 recumbent women at bottom.
a. Sign. black. 14.9.1848-24.1.1856.
b. Sign. blue. 2 sign. Varieties. 25.1.1856-8.1.1863.

46 **200 FRANCS**
(A108) 10.6.1847-27.10.1864. Women at l., Mercury at r., 2 recumbent women at bottom ctr. Oval frame. Various succursales (branches).
a. W/o name of branch bank below *BANQUE DE FRANCE* and w/3 sign. varieties.
b. Name of branch bank below *BANQUE DE FRANCE* and w/4 sign.
c. Name of branch bank in blue printing on counterfoil at r.

47 **200 FRANCS**
(A109) 9.3.1848-30.3.1848. Yellowish paper. Woman in chariot drawn by lions at top ctr. Square frame.

1862-68 ISSUE

50 **50 FRANCS**
(A103) 1864-66. Blue. 2 cherubs, coat of arms at bottom ctr.
a. Wmk: *B-F.* 2.3.1864-6.6.1864.
b. Wmk: Head of Mercury. 7.6.1864-8.6.1866.

		GOOD	FINE	XF
51 **50 FRANCS**				
(A104)	26.11.1868-16.11.1883. Blue and black. 2 cherubs, coat of arms at bottom ctr.			
	a. Printed serial # at upper l. and lower r. 4 sign. varieties. Paris printing.	1150.	2250.	4250.
	b. Handwritten serial # at upper l. and lower r., star at l., r., and above denomination. Clermont-Ferrand printing. 15.9.1870-27.10.1870.	—	—	—

52 **100 FRANCS**
(A107) 1863-82. Blue. Allegorical figures of 4 women and numerous cherubs.
a. Blue serial #, date on back. 8.1.1863-19.6.1866.
b. Black serial #, date on face, 4 sign. varieties. 23.8.1866-13.4.1882.

53 **500 FRANCS**
(A119) 1863-87. Woman at l., man at r., woman seated at bottom ctr. w/2 cherubs. Back and face w/same imprint.
a. Blue serial #. 5.11.1863-2.4.1868.
b. Black serial #. Sign. title: *LE CONTROLEUR.* 5 sign. varieties. 25.6.1868-19.6.1882.
c. Sign. title: *LE CONTROLEUR GÉNÉRAL.* 3 sign. varieties. 20.6.1882-20.8.1887.

54 **1000 FRANCS**
(A129) 4.12.1862-28.6.1889. Blue. 2 female allegorical figures at l., r., top and bottom ctr.
a. Blue serial #. 4.12.1862-2.11. 1866.
b. Like "a", but name of branch bank below *Banque de France.*
c. Black serial #. Sign. title: *LE CONTROLEUR.* 20.6.1867-16.8.1882.
d. Like "c", but sign. title: *LE CONTROLEUR GÉNÉRAL* 4 sign. varieties. 17.8.1822-28.6.1889.
e. Name of branch bank below *BANQUE DE FRANCE* and in red on counterfoil at r.

1870 ISSUE

		GOOD	FINE	XF
55 **20 FRANCS**				
(A101)	23.12.1870-29.5.1873. Blue. Seated woman.	150.00	450.00	1250.

			Good	Fine	XF
56 (A102)	**25 Francs** 1870-73. Blue. Seated woman.				
	a.	Printed serial # at upper l. and lower r. Paris printing. 16.8.1870-17.11.1870; 10.3.1873.	1000.	2000.	4000.
	b.	Handwritten serial # at upper l. and lower r., star at l., r. and above denomination (in letters). Clermont-Ferrand printing. 18.11.1870-15.9.1870.	350.00	750.00	2000.

THIRD REPUBLIC - WWII

BANQUE DE FRANCE

1871-74 ISSUE

Consecutive dates of the day of printing, thus many varieties of dates and also of sign. quoted were the first and last date of printing (not the date of issue). Listings are given by sign. combination for each note, w/values according to relative scarcity. The signs of the zodiac are used in place of the date on some notes.

Zodiac Signs

≈	AQUARIUS: January
♓	PISCES: February
♈	ARIES: March
♉	TAURUS: April
♊	GEMINI: May
♋	CANCER: June
♌	LEO: July
♍	VIRGO: August
♎	LIBRA: September
♏	SCORPIO: October
♐	SAGITTARIUS: November
♑	CAPRICORN: December

		VG	VF	UNC
60 (1)	**5 FRANCS** 1.12.1871-19.1.1874. Blue. man standing at l., woman standing w/staff at r. 3 allegorical figures on back.	25.00	125.00	525.00

		VG	VF	UNC
61 (9)	**20 FRANCS** 1874-1905. Blue on ochre unpt., denomination in black. Mercury seated at l., woman seated at r. Woman's head at l. and r. on back.			
	a. A. Mignot and Marsaud. 1.7.1874-7.8.1875.	45.00	225.00	900.00
	b. V. d'Anfreville and Giraud. 1.6.1904.	40.00	200.00	725.00
	c. Sign. as b. 11.1.1905.	45.00	225.00	975.00

1882-84 ISSUE

		VG	VF	UNC
62 (14)	**50 FRANCS** 1884-89. Blue. Women at l. and r., 2 small angels above, caduceus at each corner. Allegorical figures on back.			
	a. Sign. A. Mignot and F. Carre. 1.8.1884-23.10.1885.	—	—	—
	b. Sign. E. Bertin and F. Carre. 2.1.1886-15.2.1886.	—	—	—
	c. Sign. E. Bertin and Billotte. 18.10.1888-4.3.1889.	—	—	—
63 (21)	**100 FRANCS** 1882-88. Blue. 2 women seated.			
	a. Sign. A. Mignot and de Jancigny. 2.1.1882-10.1.1882.	—	—	—
	b. Sign. A. Mignot and F. Carre. 11.1.1882-31.12.1885.	—	—	—
	c. Sign. C. Bertin and F. Carre. 2.1.1886-13.1.1888.	—	—	—
	d. Sign. C. Bertin and Billotte. 16.7.1888-11.9.1888.	—	—	—

1888-89 ISSUE

		VG	VF	UNC
64 (15)	**50 FRANCS** 1889-1927. Blue on lilac unpt. Women l. and r., 2 small angels above, caduceus at each corner. 5 women in medallion at ctr. Allegorical figures on back.			
	a. Sign. E. Bertin and Billotte. 1.5.1889-3.8.1889.	250.00	1000.	—
	b. Sign. V. d'Anfreville and Billotte. 27.2.1890-26.5.1900.	100.00	400.00	—
	c. Sign. V. d'Anfreville and Giraud. 2.1.1901-30.12.1905.	105.00	425.00	—
	d. Sign. V. d'Anfreville and E. Picard. 2.1.1906-13.7.1907.	125.00	500.00	—
	e. Sign. J. Laferriere and E. Picard. 16.7.1907-8.11.1919.	12.00	60.00	225.00
	f. Sign. J. Laferriere and A. Aupetit. 15.11.1920-6.6.1921.	55.00	275.00	—
	g. Sign. L. Platet and A. Aupetit. 1.5.1922-20.4.1925.	11.00	55.00	200.00
	h. Sign. L. Platet and P. Strohl. 1.7.1926-25.3.1927.	18.00	90.00	240.00

		VG	VF	UNC
65 (22)	**100 FRANCS** 1888-1909. Blue on pink unpt. Like #63 but 4 women at ctr.			
	a. Sign. C. Bertin and Billotte. 12.9.1888-31.12.1889.	100.00	325.00	1000.
	b. Sign. V. d'Anfreville and Billotte. 2.1.1890-5.7.1900.	45.00	140.00	600.00
	c. Sign. V. d'Anfreville and Giraud. 18.7.1900-30.12.1905.	42.50	135.00	525.00
	d. Sign. V. d'Anfreville and E. Picard. 2.1.1906-12.3.1907.	55.00	165.00	650.00
	e. Sign. J. Laferriere and E. Picard. 1.8.1907-29.1.1909.	55.00	165.00	650.00

70 (2)	**5 FRANCS**	**VG**	**VF**	**UNC**
	2.1.1912-2.2.1917. Blue. Man standing at l. woman standing w/staff at r. Ornaments on back.	10.00	55.00	225.00
71 (24)	**100 FRANCS**			
	1909-23. M/c. Like #69 but bale w/o *L O M 02* at r.			
	a. Sign. J. Laferriere and E. Picard. 11.5.1909-12.4.1920.	5.00	15.00	60.00
	b. Sign. J. Leferriere and A. Aupetit. 15.11.1920-21.9.1921.	15.00	45.00	175.00
	c. Sign. L. Platet and A. Aupetit. 1.5.1922-29.11.1923.	4.50	12.50	52.50

66 (30)	**500 FRANCS**	**VG**	**VF**	**UNC**
	1888-1937. Blue on lilac unpt. Woman at l., Mercury at r. Ornate oval border w/cherubs, animals and 3 figures at bottom. Allegorical figures on back. Sign. title: *LE CAISSIER PRINCIPAL* added.			
	a. Sign. A. Delmotte, C. Bertin and Billote. 2.11.1888-8.7.1889.	450.00	1500.	—
	b. Sign. A. Delmotte, V. d'Anfreville and Billotte. 9.1.1890-24.4.1897.	300.00	950.00	—
	c. Sign. Bouchet, V. d'Anfreville and Billotte. 23.3.1899-30.6.1900.	300.00	1050.	—
	d. Sign. Panhard, V. d'Anfreville and Giraud. 7.2.1901-17.4.1902.	300.00	900.00	—
	e. Sign. Frachon, V. d'Anfreville and Giraud. 27.8.1903-26.12.1904.	300.00	900.00	—
	f. Sign. Frachon, V. d'Anfreville and E. Picard. 22.2.1906-10.9.1906.	300.00	900.00	—
	g. Sign. Frachon, J. Laferriere and E. Picard. 24.10.1907-4.10.1917.	50.00	150.00	350.00
	h. Sign. A. Aupetit, J. Laferriere and E. Picard. 1.4.1920-21.6.1920.	75.00	225.00	—
	i. Sign. J. Emmery, J. Laferriere and A. Aupetit. 3.1.1921-9.2.1921.	90.00	275.00	—
	j. Sign. J. Emmery, L. Platet and A. Aupetit. 1.5.1922-11.9.1924.	30.00	125.00	450.00
	k. Sign. J. Emmery, L. Platet and P. Strohl. 1.7.1926-26.10.1929.	15.00	65.00	285.00
	l. Sign. Roulleau, L. Platet and P. Strohl. 1.4.1930-29.12.1932.	13.50	55.00	275.00
	m. Sign. Roulleau, J. Boyer and P. Strohl. 12.1.1933-10.6.1937.	13.00	52.50	275.00

72 (3)	**5 FRANCS**	**VG**	**VF**	**UNC**
	1917-33. Lilac. Female wearing helmet at l. Dock worker and sailing ship on back. Sign. titles: *LE CAISSIER PRINCIPAL* and *LE SECRÉTAIRE GÉNÉRAL*.			
	a. Sign. J. Laferriere and E. Picard. 1.12.1917-23.1.1919.	3.00	15.00	75.00
	b. Sign. J. Laferriere and A. Aupetit. 15.11.1920-11.6.1921.	5.00	25.00	125.00
	c. Sign. L. Platet and A. Aupetit. 1.5.1922-21.7.1925.	2.50	12.50	60.00
	d. Sign. L. Platet and P. Strohl. 1.7.1926-29.12.1932.	.90	4.50	22.50
	e. Sign. J. Boyer and P. Strohl. 5.1.1933-14.9.1933.	1.25	6.00	30.00

67 (33)	**1000 FRANCS**	**VG**	**VF**	**UNC**
	1889-1926. Blue on lilac unpt. Mercury at l., woman in medallion at r., many allegorical figures in border Allegorical figures on back.			
	a. Sign. A. Delmotte, C. Bertin and Billotte. 7.11.1889-29.11.1889.	600.00	1800.	—
	b. Sign. A. Delmotte, V. d'Anfreville and Billotte. 23.1.1890-14.3.1898.	365.00	1100.	—
	c. Sign. Bouchet, V. d'Anfreville and Billotte. 27.10.1898-21.6.1900.	365.00	1100.	—
	d. Sign. Panhard, V. d'Anfreville and Giraud. 9.4.1901-10.2.1902.	365.00	1100.	—
	e. Sign. Frachon, V. d'Anfreville and Giraud. 23.10.1902-30.12.1905.	300.00	900.00	—
	f. Sign. Frachon, V. d'Anfreville and E. Picard. 2.1.1906-23.5.1907.	275.00	825.00	—
	g. Sign. Frachon, J. Laferriere and E. Picard. 7.5.1908-24.1.1919.	22.50	67.50	325.00
	h. Sign. A. Aupetit, J. Laferriere and E. Picard. 15.5.1919-27.2.1920.	22.50	67.50	325.00
	i. Sign. J Emmery, J. Laferriere and A. Aupetit. 15.11.1920-29.4.1921.	22.50	67.50	375.00
	j. Sign. J. Emmery, L. Platet and A. Aupetit. 1.5.1922-26.6.1926.	12.50	37.50	275.00
	k. Sign. J. Emmery, L. Platet and P. Strohl. 1.7.1926-16.9.1926.	12.50	37.50	285.00

73 (6)	**10 FRANCS**	**VG**	**VF**	**UNC**
	1916-37. Blue. Minerva at l. Sitting farm woman on back. Sign. titles: *LE CAISSIER PRINCIPAL* and *LE SECRÉTAIRE GÉNÉRAL*.			
	a. Sign. J. Laferriere and E. Picard. 3.1.1916-15.11.1918.	2.50	12.50	100.00
	b. Sign. J. Laferriere and A. Aupetit. 15.11.1920-6.6.1921.	3.50	17.50	120.00
	c. Sign. L. Platet and A. Aupetit. 1.5.1922-26.6.1926.	1.00	5.00	67.50
	d. Sign. L. Platet and P. Strohl. 1.7.1926-8.9.1932.	.50	2.50	22.50
	e. Sign. J. Boyer and P. Strohl. 17.12.1936-25.2.1937.	10.00	50.00	140.00

1906-08 ISSUE

68 (10)	**20 FRANCS**	**VG**	**VF**	**UNC**
	1906-13. Blue on ochre unpt., denomination in blue. Mercury seated at l. woman seated at r. Woman's head at l. and r. on back			
	a. Sign. V. d'Anfreville and E. Picard. 2.1.1906-25.10.1906.	50.00	250.00	600.00
	b. Sign. J. Laferriere and E. Picard. 2.1.1912-12.2.1913.	45.00	225.00	525.00
	c. Sign. as b. 12.2.1913.	50.00	250.00	600.00

69 (23)	**100 FRANCS**			
	2.1.1908-10.5.1909. M/c. Woman w/child at l. and r. Bale marked *L O M 02* at r. Blacksmith at l., woman and child at r. on back.	30.00	90.00	325.00

		VG	VF	UNC
74 (11)	**20 FRANCS** 1.7.1916-21.2.1919. Blue. Bayard at l. Farmer w/scythe on back.	15.00	75.00	250.00

		VG	VF	UNC
75 (23A)	**100 FRANCS** ND (1917). Black on m/c unpt. Standing woman at ctr. Printer : ABNC. Face proof.	—	—	2500.

		GOOD	FINE	XF
76 (38)	**5000 FRANCS** 2.1.1918-29.1.1918 (1938). M/c. Worker seated w/Mercury at upper l., angelic child figure w/symbols of agriculture and painting at upper r. Paris on back.	125.00	375.00	2000.

1923-27 ISSUE

		VG	VF	UNC
77 (16)	**50 FRANCS** 11.2.1927-17.7.1930. Brown, blue and m/c. 2 angels above, Mercury below. Woman and man in 2 wreaths on back. Artist's name *Luc Olivier - Merson* below frame on face and back.			
	a. 11.2.1927-13.12.1929.	13.00	65.00	250.00
	b. 10.7.1930-24.7.1930.	18.00	90.00	300.00

		VG	VF	UNC
78 (25)	**100 FRANCS** 1923-37. M/c. Like #24, but recess in the frame for serial number expanded from 20 to 23 mm. Sign. title: *LE CAISSIER PRINCIPAL.*			
	a. Sign. L. Platet and A. Aupetit. 30.11.1923-26.6.1926.	2.00	10.00	50.00
	b. Sign. L. Platet and P. Strohl. 1.7.1926-29.12.1932.	1.50	7.50	40.00
	c. Sign. J. Boyer and P. Strohl. 12.1.1933-30.6.1937.	1.25	6.50	37.50

		VG	VF	UNC
79 (34)	**1000 FRANCS** 1927-37. Lt. brown, blue and m/c. Ceres at l., Mercury at r., 2 small angels below. 4 different craftsmen on back. Sign. title: *LE CAISSIER PRINCIPAL.*			
	a. Sign. J. Emmery, L. Platet and P. Strohl. 11.2.1927-2.1.1930.	2.50	7.50	67.50
	e. Sign. Roulleau, L. Platet and P. Strohl. 1.4.1930-29.12.1932.	2.00	6.00	60.00
	f. Sign. Roulleau, J. Boyer and P. Strohl. 12.1.1933-30.6.1937.	2.00	6.00	60.00

1930 ISSUE

		VG	VF	UNC
80 (17)	**50 FRANCS** 1930-34. Brown, blue and m/c. 2 angels above, Mercury below. Woman and man in 2 wreaths on back. W/o artist's name below frame.			
	a. Sign. L. Platet and P. Strohl. 24.7.1930-29.12.1932.	9.00	45.00	165.00
	b. Sign. J. Boyer and P. Strohl. 12.1.1933-16.8.1934.	9.00	45.00	165.00

1934 ISSUE

		VG	VF	UNC
81 (18)	**50 FRANCS** 15.11.1934-30.6.1937. Brown and m/c. Ceres and Park of Versailles at l., reclining figure at r. Mercury at r. w/caduceus on back. Sign. title: *LE CAISSIER PRINCIPAL.*	4.50	22.50	75.00

		VG	VF	UNC
82 (39)	**5000 FRANCS** 1934. Purple and m/c. Woman w/Victory statuette and olive branch at ctr. Statuette in rotogravure on back. Sign. title: *LE CAISSIER PRINCIPAL.*			
	a. 8.11.1934.	40.00	200.00	600.00
	b. 16.5.1935; 11.5.1935.	32.50	165.00	525.00

1937-39 ISSUE

		VG	VF	UNC
83 (4)	**5 FRANCS** 13.7.1939-9.1.1941. Lilac. Like #72, but w/sign. titles: *LE CAISSIER GÉNÉRAL.*	.50	2.50	12.50

		VG	VF	UNC
84 (7)	**10 FRANCS** 2.2.1939-5.3.1942. Blue. Like #73, but w/sign. title: *LE CAISSIER GÉNÉRAL.*	.90	4.50	18.00

		VG	VF	UNC
85 (19)	**50 FRANCS** 1937-40. Like #81 but w/sign. title: *LE CAISSIER GÉNÉRAL.*			
	a. Sign. J. Boyer and R. Favre-Gilly. 5.8.1937-9.9.1937.	10.00	50.00	175.00
	b. Sign. P. Rousseau and R. Favre-Gilly. 4.11.1937-4.4.1940.	3.00	15.00	60.00

		VG	VF	UNC
86 (26)	**100 FRANCS** 1937-39. M/c. Like #78 but w/sign. title: *LE CAISSIER GÉNÉRAL.* Thin or thicker paper.			
	a. Sign. J. Boyer and R. Favre-Gilly. 9.9.1937-2.12.1937.	9.00	45.00	125.00
	b. Sign. P. Rousseau and R. Favre-Gilly. 9.12.1937-14.9.1939.	.50	2.25	30.00

		VG	VF	UNC
87 (29)	**300 FRANCS** ND (1938). Brown and m/c. Ceres at l. Mercury at r. on back.	50.00	150.00	550.00
88 (31)	**500 FRANCS** 1937-40. Blue on pink unpt. Like #66, but w/sign. title: *LE CAISSIER GÉNÉRAL.*			
	a. Sign. P. Strohl, J. Boyer and R. Favre-Gilly. 5.8.1937-9.9.1937.	30.00	120.00	475.00
	b. Sign. P. Strohl, P. Rousseau and R. Favre-Gilly. 2.12.1937-9.12.1937.	30.00	85.00	300.00
	c. Sign. H. de Bletterie, P. Rousseau and R. Favre-Gilly. 24.3.1938-18.1.1940.	10.00	40.00	175.00
89 (32B)	**500 FRANCS** ND. Ovpt. on 300 Francs, Like #87. Proof	—	—	—

		VG	VF	UNC
90 (35)	**1000 FRANCS** 1937-40. Ochre, blue and m/c. Like #79 but w/sign. title: *LE CAISSIER GÉNÉRAL.* Thin or thicker paper.			
	a. Sign. P. Strohl, J. Boyer and R. Favre-Gilly. 8.7.1937-26.8.1937.	17.00	52.50	165.00
	b. Sign. P. Strohl, P. Rousseau and R. Favre-Gilly. 4.11.1937-23.12.1937.	11.50	45.00	135.00
	c. Sign. H. de Bletterie, P. Rousseau and R. Favre-Gilly. 24.3.1938-25.7.1940.	2.25	7.00	45.00
91 (40)	**5000 FRANCS** 13.10.1938. Like #39, but w/sign. title: *LE CAISSIER GÉNÉRAL.*	65.00	250.00	675.00

1939-40 ISSUE

		VG	VF	UNC
92 (12)	**20 FRANCS** 1939. Blue on m/c. unpt. Allegories of Science and Labor at r. Scientist and city view w/bridge at l. on back.			
	a. 7.12.1939-3.10.1940.	3.50	18.00	75.00
	b. 17.10.1940-4.12.1941.	3.00	15.00	65.00
	c. 8.1.1942.	4.50	22.50	90.00

		VG	VF	UNC
93 (20)	**50 FRANCS** 13.6.1940-15.5.1942. Brown, green and m/c. Jacques Coeur at l. Scene in Bourges, woman at r. on back.	.50	3.50	20.00

94 (27)	**100 FRANCS**	VG	VF	UNC
	19.5.1939-23.4.1942. Brown and m/c. Woman and child w/background of Paris. Man in ruffled collar looking over field scene w/farm, castle, rivers on back.	.50	2.00	10.00

95 (32)	**500 FRANCS**	VG	VF	UNC
	1940-45. Green, lilac and m/c. Pax w/wreath at l. Man and woman at r. on back.			
	a. Sign. H. de Bletterie, P. Rousseau and R. Favre-Gilly. 4.1.1940-16.1.1941.	5.50	27.50	52.50
	b. Sign. as a.16.5.1940.	2.50	12.50	30.00
	c. Sign. J. Belin, P. Rousseau and R. Favre-Gilly. 4.1.194-5.11.1942.	1.50	7.50	27.50

96 (36)	**1000 FRANCS**	VG	VF	UNC
	1940-44. M/c. Woman at l. and r. Blacksmith and Mercury back.			
	a. Sign. H. de Bletterie, P. Rousseau and R. Favre-Gilly. 24.10.1940-19.12.1940.	5.50	27.50	67.50
	b. Sign. J. Belin, P. Rousseau and R. Favre-Gilly. 6.2.1941-29.6..1944.	6.00	30.00	82.50
	c. Sign. as b. 6.4.1944; 17.5.1944; 6.7.1944-20.7.1944.	4.50	22.50	67.50
	d. Sign. as b. 1.6.1944; 22.6.1944.	7.50	37.50	105.00

97 (41)	**5000 FRANCS**			
	1938-44. Like #91 but w/o statuette in rotogravure on back (not copied exactly from engraving on face).			
	a. Sign. H. de Bletterie, P. Rosseau and R. Favre-Gilly. 8.12.1938-26.12.1940.	15.00	75.00	225.00
	b. Sign. as a. 19.1.1939.	6.50	20.00	60.00
	c. Sign. J. Belin, P. Rosseau, and R. Favre-Gilly. 10.4.1941-10.12.1942.	5.00	15.00	50.00
	d. Sign. as c. 7.1.1943-18.3.1943.	9.00	27.50	75.00
	e. Sign. as c. 23.3.1944-27.4.1944.	12.50	37.50	105.00

1941-43 ISSUE

98 (5)	**5 FRANCS**	VG	VF	UNC
	1943-47. Blue, green and m/c. Pyrenean shepherd at r. Woman and flowers on back.			
	a. Sign. P. Rousseau and R. Favre-Gilly. 2.6.1943-5.4.1947.	.25	1.00	5.00
	b. Sign. P. Rousseau and P. Gargam. 30.10.1947.	.50	2.25	11.00

99 (8)	**10 FRANCS**	VG	VF	UNC
	1941-49. Brown and m/c. Miners at l., another at r. Cows at l., farm woman and child at r. on back.			
	a. Sign. P. Rousseau and R. Favre-Gilly. 11.9.1941.	3.00	15.00	60.00
	b. Sign as a. 9.10.1941; 19.11.1942; 19.4.1945.	1.25	6.00	22.50
	c. Sign. as a. 11.6.1942; 20.1.1944.	.40	2.25	12.00
	d. Sign. as a. 15.10.1942; 9.9.1943.	.40	2.00	9.00
	e. Sign. as a. 26.11.1942; 25.3.1943; 13.1.1944; 22.6.1944-9.1.1947.	.15	.75	5.50
	f. Sign. P. Rousseau and P. Gargam. 30.10.1947-30.6.1949.	.30	1.50	9.00

100 (13)	**20 FRANCS**	VG	VF	UNC
	1942-50. Red and m/c. Breton fisherman at r. 2 women and child at l. and ctr., statuary at r. on back.			
	a. Sign. P. Rousseau and R. Favre-Gilly. 12.2.1942-17.5.1944.	.40	2.00	7.50
	b. Sign. as a. 5.7.1945; 9.1.1947.	.40	2.25	12.00
	c. Sign. P. Rousseau and P. Gargam. 28.1.1948-3.11.1949.	.40	2.00	9.00
	d. Sign. as c. 9.2.1950.	3.00	15.00	50.00

101 (28)	**100 FRANCS**	VG	VF	UNC
	15.5.1942-14.12.1944. M/c. Descartes at r. Angel on back.	4.00	22.50	55.00

| 102 | 1000 FRANCS | VG | VF | UNC |
| (37) | 1942. Brown and m/c. Ceres seated w/Hermes at r. Mercury on back. | 4.00 | 10.00 | 22.50 |

103	5000 FRANCS	VG	VF	UNC
(42)	1942-47. Brown, red and m/c. Female (France) w/3 men (French colonies) at ctr. Same Female on back alone, but w/scenes from colonies.			
	a. Sign. J. Belin, P. Rousseau and R. Favre-Gilly. 5.3.1942-12.11.1942.	10.00	52.50	135.00
	b. Sign. as a. 27.4.1944; 5.10.1944.	15.00	75.00	200.00
	c. Sign. as a. 18.1.1945-9.1.1947.	6.50	18.50	82.50
	e. Sign. J. Belin, P. Rousseau and P. Gargam. 20.3.1947-25.9.1947.	7.50	22.50	90.00

1943 ND PROVISIONAL ISSUE

| 104 | 3000 FRANCS | | | |
| (37A) | ND. Provisional printing Proof. | — | — | — |

WW II

TRESOR CENTRAL

GOVERNMENT NOTES

#105, 111-113 were issued in Corsica.

#105-108 English printing.

105	100 FRANCS	VG	VF	UNC
(43)	2.10.1943. Blue on green and violet unpt. Portr. Marianne at ctr. Anchor, barrel, bale ctr. other implements on back.			
	a. Issued notes.	15.00	60.00	180.00
	s. Specimen.	—	—	400.00

| 106 | 500 FRANCS | VG | VF | UNC |
| (44) | ND (1944). Brown. Portr. Marianne at l. 2 serial # varieties. Printer: TDLR (w/o imprint). | 5.00 | 25.00 | 75.00 |

| 107 | 1000 FRANCS | VG | VF | UNC |
| (45) | ND (1944). Green. Portr. Marianne at ctr. 2 serial # varieties. | 5.00 | 25.00 | 75.00 |

108	1000 FRANCS	VG	VF	UNC
(A45)	2.10.1943. Green. Phoenix rising. at ctr. Similar to Fr. Equatorial Africa #14. Printer: BWC (w/o imprint).			
	a. (Not issued)	—	Rare	—
	s. Specimen.	—	—	6500.00

109	5000 FRANCS	VG	VF	UNC
(45A)	ND. Blue. Portr. Marianne at r. Printer: TDLR (w/o imprint).			
	a. Issued note.	—	Rare	—
	s. Specimen.	—	Rare	—

| 110 | 5000 FRANCS | | | |
| (45B) | ND. Marianne w/flag and torch. Specimen. | — | Rare | — |

1945 PROVISIONAL ISSUE

French printing.

			VG	VF	UNC
111 (46)	**500 FRANCS** ND (1945). Blue on green unpt. ovpt: *TRESOR* on Algeria #24		85.00	250.00	750.00

			VG	VF	UNC
112 (47)	**1000 FRANCS** ND (1945). M/c. ovpt: *TRESOR* on Algeria #30.				
	a. Ovpt. on #30a. Wmk: Head. (-old date 2.7.1942).		75.00	225.00	70.00
	b. Ovpt. on #30b. Wmk: Lettering. (-old dates 14.8.1942; 17.8.1942; 2.11.1942).		90.00	265.00	800.00
113 (48)	**5000 FRANCS** 1945. Brown-violet on pink unpt. ovpt. *TRESOR* on Algeria #32. All notes were destroyed. No examples known.		—	—	—

ALLIED MILITARY CURRENCY

1944 FIRST ISSUE - SUPPLEMENTAL FRENCH FRANC CURRENCY

#114-121 w/text: *EMIS EN FRANCE.* Tricolor in blue, white and red on back. Printer: Forbes Lithograph Manufacturing Co., Boston (Massachusetts, U.S.A.). Replacement notes w/*X* near serial #.

		VG	VF	UNC
114 (49)	**2 FRANCS** 1944. Green w/black border. Torch at l. and r. in green unpt. Back blue on red unpt.	.15	.50	2.50
	a. Issued note.	.25	.80	4.00
	b. Block #2.	.20	.80	4.00
	s. Specimen.	—	—	125.00

		VG	VF	UNC
115 (50)	**5 FRANCS** 1944. Blue and black on green unpt. Like #114.	.15	.40	4.50
	a. Issued note.	.20	.80	4.00
	b. Block #2.	.20	.80	4.00
	s. Specimen.	—	—	125.00

		VG		UNC
116 (51)	**10 FRANCS** 1944. Lilac and black on green unpt. Like #114.			
	a. Issued note.	1.00		.25	5.50
	s. Specimen.	—		—	125.00

		VG	VF	UNC
117 (52)	**50 FRANCS** 1944. Lilac and black on green and blue unpt. Back blue on blue and red unpt.			
	a. Issued note.	1.00	5.00	35.00
	s. Specimen.	—	—	200.00
118 (53)	**100 FRANCS** 1944. Dk. blue and black on green and blue unpt. Like #117.			
	a. Issued note.	1.00	5.00	30.00
	b. Block #2.	—	5.00	40.00
	s. Specimen.	—	—	200.00

		VG	VF	UNC
119 (54)	**500 FRANCS** 1944. Brown and black on green and blue unpt. Like #117.			
	a. Issued note.	30.00	105.00	450.00
	s. Specimen.	—	—	350.00

		VG	VF	UNC
120 (55)	**1000 FRANCS** 1944. Red and black on green and blue unpt. Like #117.			
	a. Issue note.	150.00	600.00	2400.
	s. Specimen.	—	—	1800.

		VG	VF	UNC
121 (55A)	**5000 FRANCS** 1944. Green and black on green and blue unpt. Like #117. Specimen.	—	—	2000.

1944 SECOND ISSUE - PROVISIONAL FRENCH FRANC CURRENCY

NOTE: Authorized by French Committee of National Liberation.

#122-126 replacement notes w/*X* near serial #.

		VG	VF	UNC
122 (56)	**50 FRANCS** 1944. Similar to #117.			
	a. Issue note.	1.00	5.00	25.00
	b. Block #2.	1.35	7.00	35.00
	c. Block #3. Specimen w/*W.*	1.50	8.00	40.00

		VG	VF	UNC
123 (57)	**100 FRANCS** 1944. Similar to #118.			
	a. Issued note.	1.00	5.00	20.00
	b. Block #2. Numbered at USA-BEP; position of small #2 at l. is at l. ctr.	1.00	5.00	25.00
	c. Blocks #3-8. Numbered at Forbes; position of larger run # at l. is near l. corner.	1.00	5.00	25.00
	d. Block #9.	10.00	50.00	250.00
	e. Block #10.	3.00	15.00	75.00
	s. Specimen.	—	—	350.00
124 (57A)	**500 FRANCS** 1944. Similar to #119.			
	a. Not officially issued.	1750.	—	—
	s. Specimen perforated: *SPECIMEN.*	—	—	1250.

125	**1000 FRANCS**	VG	VF	UNC
(58)	1944. Similar to #120.			
	a. Issued note.	75.00	225.00	550.00
	b. Block #2.	75.00	225.00	550.00
	c. Block #3.	80.00	240.00	600.00
	s. Specimen w/X.	—	—	1000.
126	**5000 FRANCS**			
(58A)	1944. Similar to #121. Specimen perforated: SPECIMEN.	—	—	1250.

REPUBLIC - POST WWII

BANQUE DE FRANCE

1945-49 ISSUE

For notes dated after 1945 in the old Franc currency see #98, 99, 100 and 103.

127	**50 FRANCS**	VG	VF	UNC
(59)	1946-51. Red, blue and m/c. Leverrier at r. Neptune and date 1846 on back.			
	a. Sign. P. Rousseau and R. Favre-Gilly. 14.3.1946-3.10.1946.	1.00	4.00	20.00
	b. Sign. P. Rousseau and P. Gargam. 20.3.1947-2.3.1950.	.50	3.50	17.50
	c. Sign. J. Cormier and P. Gargam. 29.6.1950-1.2.1951.	1.50	9.00	40.00
	d. Sign. G. Gouin d'Ambrieres and P. Gargam. 7.6.1951.	4.00	45.00	125.00

128	**100 FRANCS**	VG	VF	UNC
(60)	1945-54. Brown, red and m/c. Farmer w/2 oxen. Wmk: Woman w/hair parted on her l. Man, woman and children at dockside on back.			
	a. Sign. P. Rousseau and R. Favre-Gilly. 7.11.1945-9.1.1947.	.50	3.00	12.50
	b. Sign. P. Rousseau and P. Gargam. 3.4.1947-19.5.1949.	.50	3.00	12.50
	c. Sign. J. Cormier and P. Gargam. 29.6.1950-16.11.1950.	1.50	9.00	30.00
	d. Sign. G. Gouin d'Ambrieres and P. Gargam. 6.9.1951-1.4.1954.	.50	3.00	13.50
	e. Wmk: Reversed, hair parted on her r. 2.10.1952; 6.8.1953; 1.10.1953; 4.3.1954.	8.00	50.00	135.00

129	**500 FRANCS**	VG	VF	UNC
(61)	1945-53. Purple and m/c. Chateaubriand at ctr. w/musical instrument. Allegorical figures on back.			
	a. Sign. J. Belin, P. Rousseau and R. Favre-Gilly. 19.7.1945-9.1.1947.	3.00	22.50	85.00
	b. Sign. J. Belin, P. Rousseau and P. Gargam. 13.5.1948.	10.00	55.00	150.00
	c. Sign. J. Belin, G. Gouin d'Ambrieres and P. Gargam. 3.7.1952-2.7.1953.	3.00	22.50	85.00

130	**1000 FRANCS**	VG	VF	UNC
(63)	1945-50. Blue and m/c. Minerva and Hercules at ctr. Woman at ctr. on back.			
	a. Sign. J. Belin, P. Rousseau and R. Favre-Gilly. 12.4.1945-9.1.1947.	2.50	12.00	40.00
	b. Sign. J. Belin, P. Rousseau and P. Gargam. 11.3.1948-20.4.1950.	2.50	12.00	40.00
	c. Sign. J. Belin, J. Cormier and P. Gargam. 29.6.1950.	7.00	20.00	100.00

131	**5000 FRANCS**	VG	VF	UNC
(65)	1949-57. M/c. 2 allegorical figures (Sea and Countryside) at ctr. Mercury and allegorical woman on back.			
	a. Sign. J. Belin, P. Rousseau and P. Gargam. 10.3.1949-3.11.1949.	25.00	60.00	150.00
	b. Sign. J. Belin, J. Cormier and P. Gargam. 1.2.1951-5.4.1951.	25.00	60.00	150.00
	c. Sign. J. Belin, G. Gouin d'Ambrieres and P. Gargam. 16.8.1951-6.12.1956.	17.50	40.00	115.00
	d. Sign. G. Gouin d'Ambrieres, R. Favre-Gilly and P. Gargam. 7.3.1957-7.11.1957.	25.00	60.00	150.00

132 (67)	**10,000 FRANCS**	VG	VF	UNC
	1945-56. M/c. Young girl w/book and globe.			
	a. Sign. J. Belin, P. Rousseau and R. Favre-Gilly. 27.12.1945-9.1.1947.	40.00	125.00	275.00
	b. Sign. J. Belin, P. Rousseau and P. Gargam. 3.11.1949-16.2.1950.	40.00	125.00	275.00
	c. Sign. J. Belin, J. Cormier and P. Gargam. 8.6.1950-5.4.1951.	40.00	115.00	250.00
	d. Sign. J. Belin, G. Gouin d'Ambrieres and P. Gargam. 4.5.1951-7.6.1956.	30.00	85.00	210.00

1953-57 ISSUE

133 (62)	**500 FRANCS**	VG	VF	UNC
	1954-58. Blue, orange and m/c. Bldg. at l., V. Hugo at r. Hugo at l., Pantheon in Paris on back.			
	a. Sign. J. Belin, G. Gouin d'Ambrieres and P. Gargam. 7.1.1954-4.8.1955.	1.00	15.00	65.00
	b. Sign. G. Gouin d'Ambrieres, R. Favre-Gilly and P. Gargam. 7.2.1957-30.10.1958.	1.00	15.00	65.00

134 (64)	**1000 FRANCS**	VG	VF	UNC
	1953-57. M/c. Village across, Richelieu at r. Similar scene on back w/Richelieu at l.			
	a. Sign. J. Belin, G. Gouin d'Ambrieres and P. Gargam. 2.4.1953-6.12.1956.	3.00	12.50	55.00
	b. Sign. G. Gouin d'Ambrieres, R. Favre-Gilly and P. Gargam. 7.3.1957-5.9.1957.	3.00	20.00	85.00
135 (66)	**5000 FRANCS**			
	1957-58. M/c. Henry IV at ctr., bridge in background. Henry IV at ctr., castle at r. on back.			
	a. Sign. G. Gouin d'Ambrieres, R. Favre-Gilly, and P. Gargam. 7.2.1957-30.10.1958.	20.00	45.00	135.00
136 (68)	**10,000 FRANCS**			
	1955-58. M/c. Arch at l., Napoleon Bonaparte at r. Napoleon at l., capital bldg. at r. on back.			
	a. Sign. J. Belin, G. Gouin d'Ambrieres and P. Gargam. 1.12.1955-6.12.1956.	30.00	60.00	145.00
	b. Sign. G. Gouin d'Ambrieres, R. Favre-Gilly, P. Gargam. 4.4.1957-30.10.1958.	30.00	60.00	145.00

1958 PROVISIONAL ISSUE
#137-140 Ovpt: *Nouveaux Francs* (NF).

137 (69)	**5 NOUVEAUX FRANCS ON 500 FRANCS**	VG	VF	UNC
	ND (1960-old dates 1958-59) Ovpt. on #133.			
	a. 30.10.1958.	45.00	175.00	600.00
	b. 12.2.1959.	30.00	125.00	400.00

138 (70)	**10 NOUVEAUX FRANCS ON 1000 FRANCS**	VG	VF	UNC
	ND (-old date 7.3.1957). Ovpt. on #134.	25.00	120.00	350.00

139 (71)	**50 NOUVEAUX FRANCS ON 5000 FRANCS**	VG	VF	UNC
	ND (-old dates 1958-59). Ovpt. on #135.			
	a. Sign. G. Gouin d'Ambrieres, R. Favre-Gilly and P. Gargam. 30.10.1958.	20.00	100.00	250.00
	b. Sign. G. Gouin d'Ambrieres, R. Tondu and P. Gargam. 5.3.1959.	25.00	120.00	300.00

140 (72)	**100 NOUVEAUX FRANCS ON 10,000 FRANCS**	VG	VF	UNC
	ND (-old date 30.10.1958). Ovpt. on #136.	35.00	100.00	350.00

1959 ISSUE
#141-145 denomination: *NOVEAUX FRANCS* (NF).

141 (73)	**5 NOUVEAUX FRANCS**	VG	VF	UNC
	5.3.1959-5.11.1965. Blue, orange and m/c. Bldg. at l. Village at l. Pantheon in Paris on back.	1.50	9.00	30.00
142 (74)	**10 NOUVEAUX FRANCS**			
	5.3.1959-4.1.1963. M/c. Skyline across, Richelieu at r. Similar scene on back, Richelieu at l.	2.50	10.00	35.00
143 (75)	**50 NOUVEAUX FRANCS**			
	5.3.1959-5.4.1962. M/c. Henry IV at ctr., castly and bridge in background. Similar scene on back.	12.50	37.50	125.00
144 (76)	**100 NOUVEAUX FRANCS**			
	5.3.1959-6.5.1964. M/c. Arch at l. Bonaparte at r. Capital bldg. at r. Bonaparte at l. on back.	20.00	33.50	110.00

145 (77)	500 NOUVEAUX FRANCS 1959-66. M/c. Moliere at ctr.	VF	VF	UNC
	a. Sign. G. Gouin d'Ambrieres, R. Tondu and P. Gargam. 2.7.1959-8.1.1965.	FV	200.00	300.00
	b. Sign. H. Morant, R. Tondu and P. Gargam. 6.1.1966-1.9.1966.	200.00	250.00	350.00

REGIONAL

RÉGIE DES CHEMINS DE FER DES TERRITOIRES OCCUPÉS

FRANCO-BELGIAN RAILWAYS ADMINISTRATION IN OCCUPIED GERMAN TERRITORY

1923 ISSUE

#R1-10 steam locomotive at top ctr. Rhine landscape in unpt. at ctr. Neptune at r. on back.

R1	.05 FRANC ND (1923). Dk. blue on orange unpt., red border.	VG .20	VF 1.50	UNC 6.00
R2	.10 FRANC ND (1923). Dk. brown on lt. blue unpt., green border.	.50	1.50	6.00
R3	.25 FRANC ND (1923). Violet on lilac unpt., gold border.	.75	2.00	7.50

R4	.50 FRANC ND (1923). Dk. green on olive unpt., gold border.	VG 1.00	VF 2.50	UNC 8.00
R5	1 FRANC ND (1923). Dk. blue on gray-green unpt., gold border.	1.25	3.00	10.00

R6	5 FRANCS ND (1923). Dk. blue on gray unpt., red border.	VG 2.00	VF 4.50	UNC 12.50
R7	10 FRANCS ND (1923). Gray-green unpt.	4.50	15.00	35.00
R8	20 FRANCS ND (1923). Violet unpt.	VG 8.00	VF 25.00	UNC 65.00
R9	50 FRANCS ND (1923). Pink unpt.	35.00	100.00	250.00
R10	100 FRANCS ND (1923). Black on pink unpt., gold border.	50.00	150.00	275.00

MILITARY - WWI

TRESAR ARMIEE

1917 ISSUE

#M1-M5 woman w/child at l., soldier w/dog at r. RF monogram in shield at ctr. on back.

#M1-M3 French text on back: 'up to the end of the second year after the armistice.'

M1	50 CENTIMES ND (1917). Blue.	.50	1.00	4.00
M4	50 CENTIMES ND (1919). Blue. Like #M1.	1.00	2.50	8.00
M2	1 FRANC ND (1917). Brown.	.75	1.50	6.00
M5	1 FRANC ND (1919). Brown. Like #M2.	1.50	3.50	10.00
M3	2 FRANCS ND (1917). Purple.	1.50	4.00	20.00

MILITARY - POST WWII

TRESOR FRANÇAIS

Post-Liberation issues for occupied Germany and Austria after 1945.

1947 ISSUE

#M6-M10 TRESOR FRANÇAIS.

#M8-M10 Mercury at ctr. Reclining woman on back.

M6	5 FRANCS ND (1947). Brown, red and m/c. Woman at ctr. Wheat harvesting on back.	2.50	6.00	30.00
M7	10 FRANCS ND (1947). Lt. blue and m/c. Like #M6.	2.50	7.00	35.00

M8	50 FRANCS ND (1947). Blue and m/c.	VG 7.50	VF 17.50	UNC 65.00
M9	100 FRANCS ND (1947). Brown and m/c.	7.50	17.50	65.00
M10	1000 FRANCS ND (1947). Blue-green and m/c.	100.00	225.00	500.00

1955 ISSUE

#M11-M15 TRESOR PUBLIC.

M11	100 FRANCS ND (1955). Like #M9.	8.50	20.00	75.00
M12	1000 FRANCS ND (1955). M/c. Mercury at l. ctr.	100.00	325.00	650.00
M13	5000 FRANCS ND (1955). M/c. Young farm couple at ctr.			
	a. Issued note.	275.00	650.00	1500.
	s. Specimen.	—	—	1000.

1960 ISSUE

M14	5 NOUVEAUX FRANCS ON 500 FRANCS ND (1960). M/c. Mercury facing. (Not issued w/o ovpt.).	100.00	250.00	550.00
M14A	10 NOUVEAUX FRANCS ON 1000 FRANCS ND (1960). M/c. Mercury at l. ctr. Ovpt. on #M12.	175.00	375.00	750.00
M15	50 NOUVEAUX FRANCS ON 5000 FRANCS ND (1960). M/c. Ovpt. on #M13.	500.00	1000.	2500.

SUEZ CRISIS, 1956

FORCES FRANÇAISES EN MEDITERRANEE ORIENTALE

1956 ISSUE

#M16-M18 ovpt: FORCES FRANÇAISES EN MEDITERRANEE ORIENTALE.

M16	50 FRANCS ND (1956). M/c. Ovpt. on #M8.	200.00	350.00	600.00
M17	100 FRANCS ND (1956). Ovpt. on #M9.	200.00	350.00	600.00
M18	1000 FRANCS ND (1956). Ovpt. on #M10.	600.00	1100.	1750.

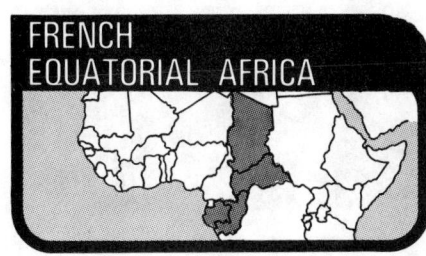

FRENCH EQUATORIAL AFRICA

French Equatorial Africa, an area consisting of four self governing dependencies (Middle Congo, Ubangi-Shari, Chad and Gabon) in west-central Africa, has an area of 969,111 sq. mi. (2,509,987 sq. km.) and a population of 3.5 million. Capital: Brazzaville. The area, rich in natural resources, exported cotton, timber, coffee, cacao, diamonds and gold.

Little is known of the history of these parts of Africa prior to French occupation - which began with no thought of territorial acquisition. France's initial intent was simply to establish a few supply stations along the west coast of Africa to service the warships assigned to combat the slave trade in the early part of the 19th century. French settlement began in 1839. Gabon (then Gabun) and the Middle Congo were secured between 1885 and 1891; Chad and the Ubangi- Shari between 1894 and 1897. The four colonies were joined to form French Equatorial Africa in 1910. The dependencies were changed from colonies to territories within the French Union in 1946, and all the inhabitants were made French citizens. In 1958, they voted to become autonomous republics within the new French Community, and attained full independence in 1960.

RULERS:
French to 1960

MONETARY SYSTEM:
1 Franc = 100 Centimes

FRENCH INFLUENCE
GOUVERNEMENT GÉNÉRAL
DE L'AFRIQUE EQUATORIALE FRANÇAISE
1917 ND EMERGENCY ISSUE

1	**50 CENTIMES**	VG	VF	UNC
	ND (1917). Green on blue unpt.			
	a. W/o wmk. 3 sign. varieties.	20.00	80.00	150.00
	b. Wmk: Laurel leaves.	20.00	80.00	150.00

2	**1 FRANC**	VG	VF	UNC
	ND (1917). Red on blue unpt.			
	a. W/o wmk. 3 sign. varieties.	25.00	90.00	180.00
	b. Wmk: Laurel leaves.	25.00	90.00	180.00

3	**2 FRANCS**	VG	VF	UNC
	ND (1917). Blue on yellow unpt. Like #2. 2 sign. varieties.	40.00	125.00	300.00

1925 PROVISIONAL ISSUE

3A	**25 FRANCS**	VG	VF	UNC
	9.7.1925. Ovpt: *AFRIQUE EQUATORIALE FRANÇAISE* on French West Africa #7B.	—	Rare	—

BONS DE CAISSE
1940 EMERGENCY WWII ISSUE

4	**1000 FRANCS**	VG	VF	UNC
	25.10.1940; 20.12.1940. Green on yellow paper. Man rowing boat at ctr.	—	Rare	—

4A	**1000 FRANCS**	VG	VF	UNC
	ND (1940). Man at ctr. Specimen.	—	Rare	—

		VG	VF	UNC
5	**5000 FRANCS** 25.10.1940. Red. Dancer at ctr. Specimen.	—	Rare	—

AFRIQUE FRANÇAISE LIBRE

1941 ISSUE
#6-9 flag in upper r. corner.

		VG	VF	UNC
6	**5 FRANCS** ND (1941). Green, brown and m/c. Man at ctr. Man weaving on back.	5.00	20.00	60.00
7	**25 FRANCS** ND (1941). Red, blue and m/c. Man wearing turban w/horse. Lion on back.			
	a. Issued note.	17.50	75.00	225.00
	s. Specimen.	—	—	175.00

		VG	VF	UNC
8	**100 FRANCS** ND (1941). Dk. brown, lilac and m/c. 2 women at ctr. Woman w/basket on back.	62.50	250.00	—
9	**1000 FRANCS** ND (1941). Brown, yellow and green. French woman w/African woman and child. Printer: BWC.			
	a. Issued note.	1000.	2250.	—
	s. Specimen.	—	—	2500.

CAISSE CENTRALE DE LA FRANCE LIBRE

ORDONNANCE DU 2 DEC. 1941
#10-14A printed in England. Printer: BWC (w/o imprint).

		VG	VF	UNC
10	**5 FRANCS** L.1941. Red on orange and lilac unpt. Marianne at ctr.			
	a. Issued note.	20.00	80.00	240.00
	s. Specimen, punched hole cancelled.	—	—	175.00
11	**10 FRANCS** L.1941. Purple on lt. brown and lt. blue unpt. Like #10.			
	a. Issued note.	22.50	110.00	—
	s. Specimen, punched hole cancelled.	—	—	200.00
12	**20 FRANCS** L.1941. Green on lilac and olive unpt. Like #10.			
	a. Issued note.	30.00	120.00	—
	s. Specimen, punched hole cancelled.	—	—	225.00
13	**100 FRANCS** L.1941. Blue-green on gold and orange unpt. Face similar to #10. Anchor, barrel, bale and other implements on back. Like France #43.			
	a. Issued note.	42.50	185.00	550.00
	s. Specimen, punched hole cancelled.	—	—	300.00

		VG	VF	UNC
14	**1000 FRANCS** L.1941. Dk. blue. Phoenix rising from flames. Like #19.			
	a. Issued note.	300.00	1200.	—
	p. Red. Proof.	—	—	750.00
	s1. Specimen, punched hole cancelled.	—	—	950.00
	s2. As a. Specimen w/ovpt. and perforated: *SPÉCMEN*.	—	—	950.00

		VG	VF	UNC
14A	**5000 FRANCS** L.1941. Violet. Marianne w/torch in l. hand and flag in r. hand. Proof.	—	Rare	—

CAISSE CENTRALE DE LA FRANCE D'OUTRE-MER

ORDONNANCE DU 2 FEB. 1944
#15-19 w/o imprinted name of colony. For notes w/imprinted name see Guadeloupe, French Guiana or Martinique. Printer: BWC (w/o imprint).

NOTE: #18, 19 issues for Reunion w/special serial # ranges, see Reunion.

NOTE: #15, 16, 17, 19 issues for St. Pierre w/special serial # ranges, see St. Pierre.

		VG	VF	UNC
15	**5 FRANCS** L.1944. Red. Marianne at ctr. Similar to #10.			
	a. Sign. A. Duval. Blue serial #.	5.00	25.00	100.00
	b. Sign. A. Postel-Vinay. Blue serial #.	4.00	20.00	80.00
	c. Sign. A. Postel-Vinay. W/o serial #.	6.00	30.00	120.00
	d. Black serial # w/prefix A (in plate).	7.00	35.00	140.00
	e. Black serial # w/prefix B (in plate).	6.00	30.00	120.00
	f. Black serial # w/prefix C (in plate).	6.00	30.00	120.00
	g. Black serial # w/prefix D (in plate).	6.00	30.00	120.00
16	**10 FRANCS** L.1944. Purple. Like #15.			
	a. Sign. A. Duval. Red serial #.	7.50	35.00	110.00
	b. Sign. A. Postel-Vinay. Red serial #.	7.50	35.00	110.00
	c. Sign. A. Postel-Vinay. Black serial #.	10.00	45.00	125.00
	d. Black serial # w/prefix A (in plate).	10.00	50.00	200.00
	e. Black serial # w/prefix B (in plate).	11.00	55.00	220.00

17	**20 FRANCS**	**VG**	**VF**	**UNC**
	L.1944. Green. Like #15.			
	a. Sign. A. Duval. Red serial #.	14.00	70.00	280.00
	b. Sign. A. Postel-Vinay. Red serial #.	13.00	65.00	260.00
	c. Sign. A. Postel-Vinay. Black serial #.	13.00	65.00	260.00
	d. Black serial # w/prefix A (in plate).	13.00	65.00	260.00
18	**100 FRANCS**			
	L.1944. Green. Like #13.	40.00	125.00	500.00

22	**20 FRANCS**	**VG**	**VF**	**UNC**
	ND (1947). Brown and m/c. E. Gentil at r., villagers at l. ctr. Man at l. and r. on back.	4.00	17.50	75.00

23	**50 FRANCS**	**VG**	**VF**	**UNC**
	ND (1947). M/c. Belain d'Esnambuc at l., sailing ship at r. Woman at l. on back.	7.50	25.00	115.00

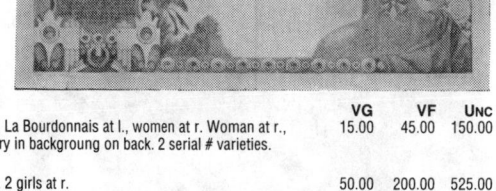

19	**1000 FRANCS**	**VG**	**VF**	**UNC**
	L.1944. Dk. blue Phoenix rising from flames. War-town landscape at l., peaceful landscape at r., on back.			
	a. Black serial #.	450.00	1000.	—
	s1. As a. Specimen ovpt: *SPÉCIMEN.*	—	—	1200.
	s2. Specimen ovpt. and perforated SPÉCIMEN. Red serial #.	—	—	1350.

24	**100 FRANCS**	**VG**	**VF**	**UNC**
	ND (1947). M/c. La Bourdonnais at l., women at r. Woman at r., mountain scenery in backgroung on back. 2 serial # varieties.	15.00	45.00	150.00
25	**500 FRANCS**			
	ND (1949). M/c. 2 girls at r.	50.00	200.00	525.00
26	**1000 FRANCS**			
	ND (1947). M/c. 2 women (symbol of the "Union Francaise") at r. 2 serial # varieties.	45.00	165.00	425.00

1947-52 ISSUE

#20B-27 w/o imprinted name of colony. For notes w/imprinted name see French Antilles, French Guiana, Guadeloupe, Martinique, Reunion or Saint Pierre et Miquelon. Printed in France.

20B	**5 FRANCS**			
	ND (1947). Blue and m/c. Ship at l., Bougainville at r. Woman w/fruits on back.	2.50	12.00	45.00

21	**10 FRANCS**	**VG**	**VF**	**UNC**
	ND (1947). Blue and m/c. Colbert at l. River scene on back.	3.00	15.00	55.00

27	**5000 FRANCS**	**VG**	**VF**	**UNC**
	ND (1952). Brown. Gen. Schoelcher at ctr r.	95.00	350.00	850.00

INSTITUT D'EMISSION DE L'AFRIQUE EQUATORIALE FRANÇAISE ET DU CAMEROUN

1957 ISSUE

28	**5 FRANCS** ND. M/c. Like #20B.	15.00	45.00	140.00
29	**10 FRANCS** ND. M/c. Like #21.	20.00	55.00	150.00
30	**20 FRANCS** ND. Olive-brown. Like #22.	25.00	75.00	185.00

		VG	**VF**	**UNC**
31	**50 FRANCS** ND (1957). Green and m/c. Woman picking coffee beans at l. Men logging in river on back.	6.00	17.50	75.00
32	**100 FRANCS** ND (1957). Blue and m/c. Gov. Gen. Felix Eboue at ctr. Cargo ships, man on back.	8.50	22.50	90.00

		VG	**VF**	**UNC**
33	**500 FRANCS** ND (1957). Brown and m/c. Woman in front of huts. Freight train crossing bridge at ctr. on back.	35.00	125.00	360.00

		VG	**VF**	**UNC**
34	**1000 FRANCS** ND (1957). M/c. Woman w/harvest of cocoa. Man picking cotton on back.	45.00	135.00	385.00

FRENCH GUIANA

The French Overseas Department of French Guiana, located on the northeast coast of South America, bordered by Surinam and Brazil, has an area of 32,252 sq. mi. (91,000 sq. km.) and a population of 114,800. Capital: Cayenne. Placer gold mining and shrimp processing are the chief industries. Shrimp, lumber, gold, cocoa and bananas are exported.

The coast of Guiana was sighted by Columbus in 1498 and explored by Amerigo Vespucci in 1499. The French established the first successful trading stations and settlements, and placed the area under direct control of the French Crown in 1674. Portuguese and British forces occupied French Guiana for five years during the Napoleonic Wars. Devil's Island, the notorious penal colony in French Guiana where Capt. Alfred Dreyfus was imprisoned, was established in 1852 - and finally closed in 1947. When France adopted a new constitution in 1946, French Guiana voted to remain within the French Union as an overseas department.

RULERS:
French

MONETARY SYSTEM:
1 Franc = 10 Decimes = 100 Centimes
1 Nouveaux Franc = 100 "old" Francs

FRENCH INFLUENCE

TREASURY

1795 EMERGENCY ISSUE

		GOOD	**FINE**	**XF**
A5	**40 LIVRES** 13.12.1795. Black. Uniface.	200.00	350.00	—

BANQUE DE LA GUYANE

1888-1922 ISSUES
Sign. varieties.

		GOOD	**FINE**	**XF**
1	**5 FRANCS** L.1901 (1922-47). Blue man at l., woman at r.			
	a. Sign. title: *Directeur* H. Poulet. (1922).	20.00	50.00	170.00
	b. Sign. title: *Directeur* P. L. Lamer. (1933).	18.00	45.00	150.00
	c. Sign. titles: *Directeur* C. Halleguen and Caissier E. Brais. (1939).	15.00	35.00	125.00
	d. Sign. titles: *Directeur* C. Halleguen, and Caissier? (1942).	9.00	22.50	110.00
	e. Sign. title: *Directeur* M. Buy. (1947).	9.00	22.50	100.00
2	**25 FRANCS** ND (1910). Black and green. Back pink.	200.00	725.00	—

3	100 FRANCS	GOOD	FINE	XF
	ND. Red and blue. Back green.	—	Rare	—
4	500 FRANCS			
	ND (1888-89). Red.	—	Rare	—

1916 EMERGENCY ISSUE

5	1 FRANC			
	16.12.1916 (1917-19). Blue and gray. 2 sign. varieties.	15.00	45.00	150.00
6	2 FRANCS			
	16.12.1916 (1917-19). Red and blue. 2 sign. varieties.	20.00	65.00	175.00

1933-1938 ISSUE
#10 *Deleted.*

7	25 FRANCS	GOOD	FINE	XF
	ND (1933-45). Purple and m/c. Woman w/wreath at ctr. Trees l. and r., ship in water at ctr. on back. 5 sign. varieties.	35.00	125.00	375.00

8	100 FRANCS	GOOD	FINE	XF
	ND (1933-42). M/c. Woman holding staff at l. 4 sign. varieties.	110.00	325.00	650.00
9	500 FRANCS			
	ND (1938-40). M/c. Like #8. 2 sign. varieties.	250.00	750.00	—

1942; 1945 WWII EMERGENCY ISSUE
#11-11A Bank name 40mm long. Border w/design element at upper and lower ctr. Bank name stamped in oval on back. Hand stamped sign. 2 sign. varieties. Local printing.

11A	2 FRANCS	VG	VF	UNC
	ND (1942). Blue-green.	70.00	150.00	300.00

	#11		#11C	
		VG	VF	UNC
11	1 FRANC			
	ND (1942). Red.	60.00	135.00	250.00
11B	1 FRANC			
	ND (1945). Red.	70.00	150.00	300.00
11C	2 FRANCS			
	ND (1945). Blue-green.			
	a. Hand sign.	75.00	175.00	350.00
	b. Stamped sign.	70.00	150.00	300.00

1942 ISSUE

12	5 FRANCS			
	ND (1942). Black on green unpt. . Justice at l.			
	r. Remainder, w/o sign.	—	—	2000.
	s. Specimen.	—	—	1500.

13	100 FRANCS	VG	VF	UNC
	ND (1942). Black on red unpt. Map of Guiana at l. Back dk. green on brown unpt. 2 sign. varieties.			
	a. Sign. Halleguen as *LE DIRECTEUR*.	200.00	650.00	1350.
	b. Sign. Buy as *LE DIRECTEUR*.	240.00	775.00	1600.

14	500 FRANCS	VG	VF	UNC
	ND (1942). Black on yellow unpt. "Flying boat" at ctr. Back dk. red on blue unpt.; caravelle Santa Maria at ctr. 2 sign. varieties.			
	a. Sign. Collat as *LE CENSEUR*.	1250.	2750.	—
	b. Sign. St.-Clair as *LE CENSEUR*.	1250.	2750.	—
	s. Specimen.	—	—	1150.
15	1000 FRANCS			
	ND (1942). Green. Seated woman at l. and r. Back brown; Liberty at ctr. 3 sign varieties.	1750.	3500.	—

CAISSE CENTRALE DE LA FRANCE LIBRE

ORDONNANCE DU 2 DEC. 1941
#16 and 16A English printing.

16	100 FRANCS	VG	VF	UNC
	L.1941. Green on orange unpt. Marianne at ctr. Anchor, barrel, bale and other implements on back. Ovpt: *GUYANE*.			
	a. Issued note.	110.00	275.00	700.00
	s. Specimen.	—	—	450.00

16A	**1000 F**RANCS	**VG**	**VF**	**UNC**
	L.1941. Blue. Phoenix rising from flames. Black handstamp: *GUYANE FRANÇAISE* twice. Handstamp: *ANNULE* (cancelled).	—	850.00	2250.

C<small>AISSE</small> C<small>ENTRALE DE LA</small> F<small>RANCE D</small>'O<small>UTRE</small>-M<small>ER</small>

O<small>RDONNANCE DU</small> 2 F<small>EB.</small> 1944

#17 and 18 ovpt. or handstamped: *GUYANE.* **English printing.**

17	**100 F**RANCS	**VG**	**VF**	**UNC**
	L.1944. Green on orange unpt. Like #16.			
	a. Issued note.	45.00	175.00	525.00
	s. Specimen.	—	—	400.00
18	**1000 F**RANCS			
	L.1944. Blue. Phoenix rising from flames. Like #16A.			
	a. Dk. blue serial #.	750.00	1650.	—
	b. Red serial #. Ovpt: *GUYANE.* W/o wmk.	750.00	1650.	—
	c. Red serial #. Hand-stamped: *GUYANE FRANÇAISE.* Wmk. paper.	850.00	1750.	—
	d. As c. Cancelled w/black stamp *ANNULÉ.*	—	—	—
	s. As a. Specimen.	—	—	1250.

1947 I<small>SSUE</small>

#19-26 ovpt: GUYANE French printing. Standard designs.

19	**5 F**RANCS	**VG**	**VF**	**UNC**
	ND (1947-49). M/c. Bougainville at r.			
	a. Issued note.	3.00	12.50	50.00
	s. Specimen.	—	—	37.50
20	**10 F**RANCS			
	ND (1947-49). M/c. Colbert at l.			
	a. Issued note.	4.00	17.50	55.00
	s. Specimen.	—	—	40.00
21	**20 F**RANCS			
	ND (1947-49). M/c. E. Gentil at r.			
	a. Issued note.	5.00	22.50	75.00
	s. Specimen.	—	—	50.00

22	**50 F**RANCS	**VG**	**VF**	**UNC**
	ND (1947-49). M/c. B. d'Esnambuc at l., sailing ship at r.			
	a. Issued note.	9.00	35.00	150.00
	s. Specimen.	—	—	100.00
23	**100 F**RANCS			
	ND (1947-49). M/c. La Bourdonnais at l., women at r.			
	a. Issued note.	12.50	45.00	165.00
	s. Specimen.	—	—	110.00
24	**500 F**RANCS			
	ND (1947-49). M/c. 2 women at r.			
	a. Issued note.	17.50	150.00	525.00
	s. Specimen.	—	—	250.00
25	**1000 F**RANCS			
	ND (1947-49). M/c. 2 women at r.			
	a. Issued note.	37.50	175.00	575.00
	s. Specimen.	—	—	275.00

26	**5000 F**RANCS	**VG**	**VF**	**UNC**
	ND (1947-49). M/c. Gen. Schoeicher at ctr. r.			
	a. Issued note.	75.00	300.00	825.00
	s. Specimen.	—	—	325.00

1960 I<small>SSUE</small>

27	**1000 F**RANCS	**VG**	**VF**	**UNC**
	ND (1960). M/c. Fishermen. Specimen.	—	—	850.00
28	**5000 F**RANCS			
	ND (1960). M/c. Woman w/fruit bowl.			
	a. Issued note.	325.00	650.00	1500.
	s. Specimen.	—	—	500.00

FRENCH INDIA

French India consisted of five settlements in India that formerly constituted a territory of France: Pondicherry (Pondichery), Chandernagpr. Karikal and Yanam on the east coast, and Mahe on the west coast. The combined settlements had an area of 197 sq. mi. (500 sq. km). Capital: Pondicherry. French interest in the East was evident as early as the opening of the 16th century, but initial individual efforts were checked by the Portuguese.

After a number of false starts, the acquired Pondicherry, 85 miles (137 Km.) south of Madras, in 1654. Chandernagor, 16 iles (26 km.) north of Calcutta was acquired in 1690-92. Mahe was acquired in 1725 and Karikai in 1739. Yanam was founded in 1750. The French enclaves were captured (by the Dutch and British) and restored several times before French possession was established, by treaties, 1914-17.

Chandernagor voted in 1949 to join India and became part of the Republic of India in 1950. Pondicherry, Karikal, Yanam and Mahe formed the Pondicherry Union Territory and joined the Republic of India in 1954.

RULERS
French to 1954

MONTETARY SYSTEM
1 Roupie = 8 fanons = 16 Annas

FRENCH INFLUENCE

BANQUE DE l'INDOCHINE, PONDICHERY
NOTE: Emergency *Bons de Caisse* are reported to have been issued during 1918-19.

DÉCRET DU 21.1.1875
#A1 and A2 various date and sign. varieties.

		GOOD	FINE	XF
A1	**10 ROUPIES** 3.4.1901; 24.5.1909. Blue. Neptune reclining holding trident at lower l. Multiple language texts on back.	—	Rare	—
A2	**50 ROUPIES** (1877-). Blue-gray and red-brown. Elephant columns l. and r., 2 reclining women w/ox l., tiger r. at lower border. Decree in ribbon in border at top ctr.	—	Rare	—

DÉCRETS DES 21.1.1875 ET 20.2.1888

		GOOD	FINE	XF
A3	**50 ROUPIES** 10.9.1898. Like #A2 but printed date.	—	Rare	—

DÉCRETS DES 21.1.1875, 20.2.1888 ET 16.5.1900

		GOOD	FINE	XF
1	**50 ROUPIES** (1902-). Like #A3, but printed decree. W/counterfeiting clause replacing decrees in ribbon in border at top ctr.	—	Rare	—

DÉCRETS DES 21.1.1875, 20.2.1888, 16.5.1900 ET 3.4.1901

		GOOD	FINE	XF
2	**10 ROUPIES** 3.11.1919. Like #A1 but printed date. a. Issued note. b. Cancelled w/handstamp: *ANNULÉ.*	— —	Rare —	— 2500.
3	**50 ROUPIES** 17.6.1915. Like #a. a. Issued note. b. Cancelled w/handstamp: *ANNULÉ.*	— —	Rare Rare	— —

W/O DÉCRETS

		GOOD	FINE	XF
4	**1 ROUPIE** 1919-45. Blue and brown on lt. orange unpt. Helmeted woman at l. Back orange-brown. a. Sign titles: *L'ADMININSTRATEUR-DIRECTEUR* and *UN ADMINISTRATEUR.* 12.11.1919. b. Sign titles: *L'ADMINISTRATEUR* and *LE DIRECTEUR.* 2 sign varieties. 1.8.1923; 1.1.1928. c. Sign. titles: *UN ADMININSTRATEUR* and *LE DIRECTEUR GÉNÉRAL.* 5.4.1932. d. Sign. titles: *LE PRÉSIDENT* and *LE DIRECTEUR GÉNÉRAL.* 2 sign. varieties. 13.2.1936; 8.3.1938; 8.9.1945. e. As d. Punched hole cancelled w/handstamp: *ANNULÉ.* 8.9.1945.	85.00 75.00 70.00 25.00 15.00	225.00 175.00 150.00 75.00 45.00	450.00 350.00 300.00 175.00 —
4A	**1 ROUPIE** 8.9.1945. Face like #4. Back guilloche w/3 cross-shapes instead of 2.	60.00	200.00	—

1936-37 ND ISSUE

		GOOD	FINE	XF
5	**5 ROUPIES** ND (1937). M/c. Brown and orange on m/c unpt. Women wearing helmet holding lance at l., denomination numeral *5* over wreath at upper r. Woman w/headress at l., ancient statues at r. on back. a. Sign. titles: *LE PRÉSIDENT* and *LE DIRECTEUR GÉNÉRAL.* (1937). b. Sign titles: *LE PRÉSIDENT and LE DIRECTEUR GAL. ADJOINT.* (1946). c. As b. Punched hole cancelled w/handstamp: *ANNULÉ.* s. As b. Specimen perforated *SPECIMEN.*	85.00 75.00 45.00	185.00 150.00 90.00	350.00 300.00 —

7 50 ROUPIES
ND (1936). M/c. Ornamental stove at I. Dupleix on back.

		GOOD	FINE	XF
a.	Sign. Thion de la Chaume as *LE PRÉSIDENT* and Baudouin as *LE DIRECTEUR GÉNÉRAL* (1936).	—	Rare	—
b.	Sign. Borduge-Baudouin. (1947-40).	600.00	1500.	—
c.	Sign. Minost-Laurent. (1945).	700.00	1800.	—
d.	Punched hole cancelled w/handstamp: *ANNULÉ*.	350.00	900.00	—
s.	Specimen perforated: *SPECIMEN*.	—	—	—

FRENCH INDO-CHINA

French Indo-China (l'Indo-Chine) was located on the Indo-Chinese peninsula of Southeast Asia. It was a French colonial possession from the later 19th century until 1954. A French Governor-General headed a federal-type central government and colonial administration, but reported directly to France which retained exclusive authority over foreign affairs, defense, customs, finance and public works.

The colony covered 286,194 sq. mi. (741,242 sq. km.) and had a population of 24 million. It consisted of 5 protectorates: Tonkin (northern Vietnam), Annam (central Vietnam), Cochin-China (southern Vietnam), Laos and Cambodia. Principal cities were: Saigon, Hanoi, Haiphong, Pnom-Penh and Vientiane. From 1875 to 1951, the exclusive right to issue banknotes within the colony was held by the Bank of Indochina (Banque de l'Indochine). On December 31, 1951 this privilege was transferred to the Issuing Authority of the States of Cambodia, Laos and Vietnam (Institut d'Emission des Etats du Cambodge, du Laos et du Vietnam).

From the moment of their conquest, the Indochinese people resisted French rule. The degree of resistance varied, being strongest in central and northern Vietnam, but was evident throughout Indochina. There were unsuccessful attempts by Vietnamese nationals, headed by Nguyen Ai Quoc (later known as Ho Chi Minh), to gain recognition/independence at the Versailles Peace Conference following World War I.

Japan occupied French Indochina at the start of World War II, but allowed the local French (Vichy) government to remain in power until March 1945. Meanwhile, many nationalists (communist and non-communist alike) followed Ho Chi Minh's leadership in the formation of the League for Independence of Vietnam (Viet-Minh) which took an active anti-Japanese part during the war. France reoccupied the area after the Japanese surrender, and established the Associated States of Indochina, with each of the five political subdivisions having limited independence within the French Union. Disagreement over the degree of independence and the reunification of the three Vietnamese subdivisions led to armed conflict with the Viet-Minh and a protracted war (The First Indochina War). In 1949/1950, in an attempt to retain her holdings, France recognized Laos, Cambodia and Vietnam as semi-independent self governing States within the French Union, but retained financial and economic control. Fighting continued and culminated with the French military disaster at Dien Bien Phu in May 1954. The subsequent Geneva Agreement brought full independence to Laos, Cambodia and Vietnam ("temporarily" divided at the 17th parallel of latitude), and with it, an end to French rule in Indochina.

See also Vietnam, South Vietnam, Laos and Cambodia.

* * * This section has been partially renumbered. * * *

RULERS:
French to 1954

MONETARY SYSTEM:
1 Piastre = 1 (Mexican Silver) Dollar = 100 Cents,1875-1903
1 Piastre = 100 Cents, 1903-1951
1 Piastre = 100 Cents = 1 Riel (Cambodia), 1951-1954
1 Piastre = 100 Cents = 1 Kip (Laos)
1 Piastre = 100 Cents = 1 Dong (Vietnam)

SIGNATURE VARIETIES/TITLE COMBINATIONS BANQUE DE L'INDOCHINE, 1875–1951		
1	Edwuoard Delessert Un Administrateur a Paris NOTE: Also handsigned by Le Cassier and Le Directeur de la Succursale.	
2	Aduoard Delessert Un Administrateur	Stanislas Simon Le Directeur
3	Ernest Denormandie Un Administrateur	Stanislas Simon Le Directeur
4	Baron Hely D'Oissel Un Administrateur	Stanislas Simon Le Directeur
5	Baron Hely D'Oissel Un Administrateur	Stanislas Simon Le Administrateur-Directeur
6	Albert de Monplanet Un Administrateur	René Thion de la Chaume Le Directeur
7	Stanislas Simon Un Administrateur	René Thion de la Chaume Le Directeur
8	René Thion de la Chaume Le President	Paul Baudouin Le Directeur-General
9	Macel Borduge Le President	Paul Baudouin Le Directeur-General
10	Paul Gannay L'Inspecteur-General	Edmond Bruno Le Directeur de la Succursale de Salgon
11	Emile Minost Le President	Jean Laurent Le Directeur-General Adjoin

FRENCH INFLUENCE

BANQUE DE L'INDO-CHINE

HAIPHONG BRANCH

DÉCRET DU 21.1.1875

1 (1B)	**5 DOLLARS = 5 PIASTRES** 17.10.1896. Ovpt: *HAIPHONG* on #21.		—	Rare	—

DÉCRETS DES 21.1.1875 ET 20.2.1888

#2-4 handstamped city name. Date printed.
#2 w/text: *Emission autorisée 3 Aôut 1891.*

		GOOD	FINE	XF
2 (4B)	**1 DOLLAR = 1 PIASTRE** ND (1892-98). Like #24.	225.00	575.00	—
3 (7B)	**20 DOLLARS = 20 PIASTRES** 25.4.1893; 28.4.1893. Like #25.	—	—	—
4 (8B)	**100 DOLLARS = 100 PIASTRES** 5.5.1893. Like #26.	—	—	—

1897-99 ISSUE

#5 w/text: *Emission autorisée 3 Aôut 1891.*
#6 w/printed city and date.

		GOOD	FINE	XF
5 (5B)	**1 DOLLAR = 1 PIASTRE** ND (1899-1903). Like #27.	175.00	525.00	—
6 (9B)	**5 DOLLARS = 5 PIASTRES** 4.2.1897; 6.2.1897. Like #28.	—	—	—
7 (10B)	**20 DOLLARS = 20 PIASTRES** Like #22. Specimens only.	—	—	—

1899-1900 ISSUE

		GOOD	FINE	XF
8 (15)	**5 DOLLARS = 5 PIASTRES** 19.9.1900. Red. Like #29.	—	—	—
9 (16)	**20 DOLLARS = 20 PIASTRES** 12.9.1898; 15.9.1898. Red. Like #30.	—	—	—
10 (17)	**100 DOLLARS = 100 PIASTRES** 17.2.1899. Red. Like #31.	—	—	—

DÉCRETS DES 21.1.1875, 20.2.1888 ET 16.5.1900

11 (21)	**100 DOLLARS = 100 PIASTRES** (1903). Red. Like #10.		Reported Not Confirmed

		GOOD	FINE	XF
12 (25)	**100 PIASTRES** 3.7.1903-22.3.1907. Red. Like #11. Sign. 4.	850.00	1750.	

DÉCRETS DES 21.1.1875, 20.2.1888, 16.5.1900 ET 3.4.1901

#13 w/text: *Emission autorisée 3 Aôut 1891.*

		GOOD	FINE	XF
13 (29)	**1 PIASTRE** ND (1903-21). Like #34. City of issue handstamped.			
	a. Sign. 4 w/titles: *Un Administrateur* and *Le Directeur.* (1903-09).	Reported Not Confirmed		
	b. Sign. 5 w/titles: *Un Administrateur* and *L'Administrateur - Directeur.*(1909-21).	15.00	50.00	150.00

		GOOD	FINE	XF
14 (30)	**5 PIASTRES** 9.6.1905; 10.6.1905; 2.3.1907. Red. Like #35. Sign. 4	—	—	—
15 (31)	**20 PIASTRES** 10.6.1905; 11.3.1907. Red. Like #36. Sign. 4.			
	a. Issued note.	150.00	450.00	—
	s. Specimen. 30.2.1905.			

1909-11 ISSUE

16 (35)	**5 PIASTRES** 1.9.1910-29.11.1915. Green. Like #37.			
	a. Sign. 4 w/titles: *Un Administrateur* and *Le Directeur.* (1909).	Reported Not Confirmed		
	b. Sign. 5 w/titles: *Un Administrateur* and *L'Administrateur - Directeur.* (1910-15).	40.00	150.00	425.00

		GOOD	FINE	XF
17 (36)	**20 PIASTRES** 12.1.1909-6.4.1917. Green.			
	a. Sign. 4 w/titles: *Un Administrateur* and *Le Directeur.* (1909).	85.00	200.00	—
	b. Sign. 5 w/titles: *Un Administrateur* and *L'Administrateur - Directeur.* (1917).	50.00	175.00	500.00

18	**100 PIASTRES**	GOOD	FINE	XF
(37)	6.5.1911-11.4.1919. Green and brown. Like #39. Sign. 5 w/titles: *Un Administrateur* and *L'Administrateur - Directeur*.	150.00	450.00	1000.

1920; 1925 ISSUE

#19 and 20 w/o décrets or autograph sign., w/sign. titles: *Le Caissier...*

19	**5 PIASTRES**	GOOD	FINE	XF
(41)	27.5.1920. (1926-27). Green. Like #37. Sign. 5.	35.00	125.00	—

20	**100 PIASTRES**	GOOD	FINE	XF
(42)	1.9.1925. Green and brown. Sign. 6.	125.00	425.00	950.00

SAIGON BRANCH

DÉCRET DU 21.1.1875

#21-23 city of issue printed. Dates handwritten or handstamped.

21	**5 DOLLARS = 5 PIASTRES**	GOOD	FINE	XF
(1A)	19.7.1893; 30.1.1896. Blue. Neptune reclining holding trident at lower l. Sign. I.	—	Rare	—

22	**20 DOLLARS = 20 PIASTRES**	GOOD	FINE	XF
(2A)	(1876-92). Blue. Elephant columns l. and r. 2 reclining women w/ox l., tiger r. at lower border. Sign I.	—	Rare	—

23	**100 DOLLARS = 100 PIASTRES**	GOOD	FINE	XF
(3A)	(1879-92). Blue. Vasco da Gama at l., sailing ships at lower ctr., Polynesian man w/paddle by dragon boat at r. Sign I.	—	Rare	—

DÉCRETS DES 21.1.1875 ET 20.2.1888

#24-26 handstamped city name. Dates printed.

#24 w/text: *Emission autorisée 3 Aôut 1891.*

24	**1 DOLLAR = 1 PIASTRE**			
(4A)	ND (1892-98). Blue. Oriental woman seated below France seated holding cadeuces at l. Sign 2.	150.00	425.00	
25	**20 DOLLARS = 20 PIASTRES**			
(7A)	25.4.1893. Like #22. Issue date printed. Sign. 2.	—	—	—
26	**100 DOLLARS = 100 PIASTRES**			
(8A)	2.5.1893; 5.5.1893; 9.5.1893; 12.5.1893. Like #23. Issue date printed. Sign. 2.			
	a. Issued note.	—	—	—
	b. 9.5.1893. Cancelled w/handstamp: *ANNULÉ.* 2.5.1893;	—	—	—

1897-1900 ISSUE

#27 w/text: *Emission autorisée 3 Aôut 1891.*

#28 printed city name and date.

27	**1 DOLLAR = 1 PIASTRE**			
(5A)	ND (1899-1903). Red-brown. Like #24. Sign. 3.	90.00	250.00	700.00

28	**5 DOLLARS = 5 PIASTRES**	GOOD	FINE	XF
(9A)	9.1.1897; 23.1.1897. Like #21. Sign. 2.			
	a. Issued note.	—	—	—
	s. Specimen. 30.2.1899.	—	—	—

1900 ISSUE

29	**5 DOLLARS = 5 PIASTRES**			
(12)	26.9.1900; 27.9.1900; 1.10.1900; 4.10.1900. Blue. Like #28. Sign. 3.	—	—	—
30	**20 DOLLARS = 20 PIASTRES**			
(13)	3.9.1898; 5.9.1898. Blue. Like #22. Sign. 3.	350.00	650.00	—
31	**100 DOLLARS = 100 PIASTRES**			
(14)	16.2.1899. Blue. Like #23. Sign. 3.	—	—	—

DÉCRETS DES 21.1.1875, 20.2.1888 ET 16.5.1900

32	**100 DOLLARS = 100 PIASTRES**			
(19)	9.3.1903. Blue. Like #31. Sign. 4.	400.00	850.00	—

1903 "PIASTRES" ISSUE

33	**100 PIASTRES**			
(23)	4.7.1903-20.3.1907. Blue w/black text. Like #32. Sign 4.	300.00	850.00	—

DÉCRETS DES 21.1.1875, 20.2.1888, 16.5.1900 ET 3.4.1901

#34 w/text: *Emission autorisée 3 Aôut 1891.*

34	**1 PIASTRE**	GOOD	FINE	XF
(26)	ND (1903-21). Red-brown. Like #27. City of issue handstamped.			
	a. Sign. 4 w/titles: *Un Adminisatrateur* and *Le Directeur.* (1903-09).	25.00	100.00	350.00
	b. Sign. 5 w/titles: *Un Administrateur* and *L'Administrateur - Directeur.* (1909-21).	8.00	25.00	85.00
35	**5 PIASTRES**			
(27)	5.6.1905; 6.6.1905; 8.6.1905; 4.3.1907; 6.3.1907. Like #29. Sign. 4.	175.00	450.00	950.00

36	**20 PIASTRES**	GOOD	FINE	XF
(28)	5.6.1905; 6.6.1905; 14.3.1907; 15.3.1907; 16.3.1907. Blue. Like #22. Sign. 4.	125.00	350.00	850.00

1911-15 ISSUE

37	**5 PIASTRES**	GOOD	FINE	XF
(32)	2.1.1909-15.11.1911. Purple. Ships in background at l., flowers at ctr. Dragon on back.			
	a. Sign. 4 w/titles: *Un Administrateur* and *Le Directeur.* (1909).	50.00	150.00	450.00
	b. Sign. 5 w/titles: *Un Administrateur* and *L'Administrateur - Directeur.* (1910-16).	25.00	100.00	275.00
38	**20 PIASTRES**			
(33)	23.5.1917. (1909). Purple. Seated woman w/sword at l., couple at r. 2 dragons on back. Like #17.			
	a. Sign. 4 w/titles: *Un Administrateur* and *Le Directeur.* (1909).		Reported Not Confirmed	
	b. Sign. 5 w/titles: *Un Administrateur* and *L'Administrateur - Directeur.* (1913-17).	25.00	100.00	275.00

39	**100 PIASTRES**	GOOD	FINE	XF
(34)	3.5.1911-14.4.1919. Purple. Woman w/branch and wreath at r., mandarin in front. Dragon design on back. Sign 5.	40.00	150.00	500.00

1920 ISSUE

#40-42 w/o décrets or autograph sign., w/titles: *Le Caissier…*

40	**5 PIASTRES**			
(38)	5.1.1920-13.3.1920. Purple. Like #37. Sign. 5.	12.50	60.00	225.00

41 (39)	**20 PIASTRES** 1.8.1920. Purple. Sign. 6.	**GOOD** 20.00	**FINE** 100.00	**XF** 275.00

42 (40)	**100 PIASTRES** 5.1.1920-27.1.1920. Purple. Like #39. Sign. 5.	**GOOD** 35.00	**FINE** 150.00	**XF** 500.00

BANQUE DE L'INDO-CHINE (1920S)

1920 FRACTIONAL ISSUE

Décret of 3.4.1901 and authorization date 6.10.1919 (on back).

#43-47 printer: Chaix.

43	**10 CENTS** L.1919 (1920-23). Blue. Black serial #. Sign. 5.	**GOOD** 7.50	**FINE** 25.00	**XF** 85.00

44	**10 CENTS** L.1919 (1920-23). Blue like #43 but red serial #. Red Chinese and Vietnamese denomination ovpt. on back. Sign. 6.	**GOOD** 9.00	**FINE** 30.00	**XF** 150.00

45	**20 CENTS** L.1919 (1920-23) Purple on gold unpt. Black serial #. Sign. 5.	**GOOD**	**FINE**	**XF**
	a. Printer's name at lower r. on back.	7.50	25.00	85.00
	b. W/o imprint.	7.50	50.00	150.00

46	**50 CENTS** L.1919 (1920-23). Red. Black serial #. Sign. 5.	**GOOD** 12.00	**FINE** 60.00	**XF** 200.00

47	**50 CENTS** L.1919 (1920). Red. Like #46. Blue Chinese and Vietnamese denomination ovpt. Black serial #.	**GOOD**	**FINE**	**XF**
	a. Issued note.	200.00	350.00	—
	s. Specimen perforated: *SPECIMEN / IMPRIMERIE CHAIX.*	—	—	—

1921-28 ND ISSUE

48	**1 PIASTRE** ND (1921-31). Brown and blue on lt. tan unpt. Helmeted woman at l. Large *$1* on back.	**VG**	**VF**	**UNC**
	a. Sign. 6. (1921-26).	5.00	25.00	100.00
	b. Sign. 7. (1927-31).	1.00	5.00	25.00

49	**5 PIASTRES** ND (1926-31). M/c. Woman w/wreath at r. Peacock on back.	**VG**	**VF**	**UNC**
	a. Sign. 6. (1926).	12.50	45.00	125.00
	b. Sign. 7. (1927-31).	8.50	35.00	85.00

50   20 PIASTRES
ND (1928-31). M/c. Woman w/wreath holding branch and golden sphere at ctr. Ancient statue on back. Sign. 7.

	VG	VF	UNC
	15.00	65.00	200.00

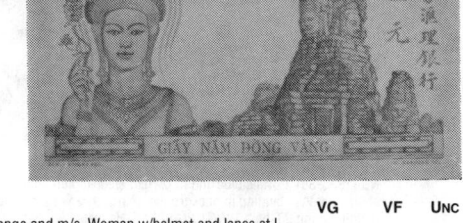

53   5 PIASTRES
ND. (1932) Brown, orange and m/c. Woman w/helmet and lance at l., denomination numeral 5 over wreath at upper r. Women w/headdress at l., ancient statues at r. on back. Sign. 8.

	VG	VF	UNC
a. Issued note.	60.00	175.00	350.00
x. Contemporary counterfeit on genuine wmk. paper.	—	Unc	10.00

51   100 PIASTRES
ND (1925-39). M/c. Golden vessel w/dog on top at l. Duplex at ctr., head at r. on back.

	VG	VF	UNC
a. Sign. 6. (1925-26).	10.00	40.00	165.00
b. Sign. 7. (1927-31).	8.00	35.00	135.00
c. Sign. 8. (1932-35).	7.50	30.00	110.00
d. Sign. 9. (1936-39).	3.50	15.00	75.00

1932-39 ND ISSUE

#54-55 Lao text added on back.

NOTE: For note of similar design but different heading see #92.

NOTE: For 100 Piastres of this series, see #51c and #51d.

BANQUE DE L'INDO-CHINE (1930S)

Issues starting in 1932 when the Piastre was removed from silver standard and defined in terms of gold w/defacto exchange rate of 1 Piastre = 10 French Francs.

1932 ND ISSUE

#52-53 w/o Lao text on back.

1 Piastre
Type I - Old Lao text

1 Piastre
Type II - New Lao text

54   1 PIASTRE
ND. (1932-39) Like #52 but red denomination I.

	VG	VF	UNC
a. Lao text Type I (Old Lao). Sign. 8. (1932).	1.50	12.00	50.00
b. Lao text Type I. Sign. 9. (1936).	.25	1.00	3.50
c. Lao text Type I, Sign. 11. (1946).	.75	3.00	15.00
d. Lao text Type II (New Lao). W/dot under O in MOT on back. Sign. 11. (1949).			
e. As d but w/o dot under O in MOT on back.	1.50	5.00	25.00

5 Piastres
Type I - Old Lao text

5 Piastres
Type II - New Lao text

52   1 PIASTRE
ND. (1932) Brown, red amd m/c. Woman at r., bldg. at ctr., blue denomination numeral 1. Man w/baskets on back. Sign. 8.

	VG	VF	UNC
	7.50	40.00	120.00

55   5 PIASTRES
ND. (1932-39) Like #53, but larger 5 at upper r. on white background.

	VG	VF	UNC
a. Lao text Type I (Old Lao). Sign. 8.. (1932).	3.00	12.50	65.00
b. Lao text Type I. Sign.9. (1936).	1.00	5.00	20.00
c. Lao text Type I. Sign. 11. (1946).	1.00	7.50	35.00
d. Lao text Type II (New Lao). Sign. 11. (1949).	1.00	5.00	17.50

56 20 PIASTRES
ND (1936-39). Purple, blue and m/c. Helmeted woman holding wreath
at ctr., Athens standing in background, maroon bank name and
denomination 20, blue *VINGT PIASTRES*. Helmeted woman holding
wreath at ctr r. on back.

		VG	VF	UNC
a.	Sign. 8. (1936). Specimen only.	—	—	—
b.	Sign. 9. (1936-39).	6.50	25.00	85.00

57 500 PIASTRES
ND (from 1939). M/c. Woman and child examining globe; blue bank
name and denomination numerals. 2 elephants behind woman and
child on back. Sign. 9.

VG	VF	UNC
3.00	15.00	60.00

1942-45 ND ISSUES

#58-73 printed in French Indochina by the Imprimerie de l'Extreme Orient (I.D.E.O.) in Hanoi. Sign. 10.

#65-69 autograph sign. w/titles: *LE CAISSIER DE LA SUCCURSALE*.

58 1 PIASTRE
ND. (1942-45) Dk. blue-black on orange unpt. Junks at l. Figure
w/hands together on back.

		VG	VF	UNC
a.	7-digit serial #, 2.4mm tall.	1.00	6.50	22.50
b.	7-digit serial #, 2.0mm tall.	1.00	7.50	25.00
c.	Letter and 6 digits in serial #, w/o serifs.	1.00	7.50	25.00

59 1 PIASTRE
ND. (1942-45) Black on blue unpt. Like #58.

		VG	VF	UNC
a.	7-digit serial #.	1.00	6.50	22.50
b.	Letter and 6 digits in serial #, w/o serifs.	1.00	7.50	25.00

60 1 PIASTRE
ND. (1942-45) Dk. brown on purple unpt. (color shades). Like #58. 7-
digit serial #.

VG	VF	UNC
.40	1.50	4.50

61 5 PIASTRES
ND (1942-45). Dk. green on red and m/c unpt. Back dk. brown on
green unpt. Pavillion at water's edge.

VG	VF	UNC
3.00	22.50	55.00

62 5 PIASTRES
ND (1942-45). Like #61. Back gray and black.

		VG	VF	UNC
a.	Serial # 4mm tall, w/serifs.	12.50	65.00	—
b.	Serial # 4.5mm tall, w/o serifs.	12.50	65.00	

63 5 PIASTRES
ND (1942-45). Dk. brown on pinkish brown and m/c unpt. Like #61.

VG	VF	UNC
2.00	15.00	35.00

64 5 PIASTRES
ND (1942-45). Violet, bright pink and m/c unpt. Like #61.

VG	VF	UNC
7.50	45.00	110.00

65 20 PIASTRES
ND (1942-45). Blue on gray unpt. Like #71. Walled fortress at r.
Seated figure on back. Letters: A-F.

VG	VF	UNC
6.00	27.50	95.00

66 100 PIASTRES
ND (1942-45). Lilac and orange frame and vignette. Market scenes at
l. and r. Back orange and red; w/pagoda. Letters: A-G.

VG	VF	UNC
3.50	17.50	55.00

67 100 PIASTRES
ND (1942-45). Violet frame, green and violet vignette. Like #66. Back
violet. Letters: A-G.

VG	VF	UNC
3.00	15.00	50.00

68 500 PIASTRES
ND (1944-45). Blue on yellow unpt. Red value at ctr. r., 6 men on
irrigation work. Back blue and m/c; dragon.

VG	VF	UNC
3.00	17.50	60.00

69 500 PIASTRES
ND (1945). Dk. green and gray. Like #68.

	3.00	15.00	50.00

1942-45 ND SECOND ISSUES

#70-73 printed sign. w/titles: *LE CAISSIER*…

70 20 PIASTRES
ND (1942-45). Green and yellow. Like #71. Letters: A-E.

VG	VF	UNC
4.00	27.50	75.00

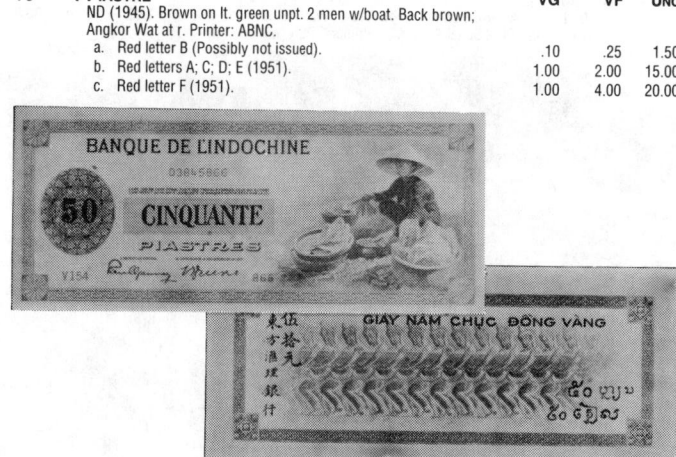

76	1 PIASTRE	VG	VF	UNC
	ND (1945). Brown on lt. green unpt. 2 men w/boat. Back brown; Angkor Wat at r. Printer: ABNC.			
	a. Red letter B (Possibly not issued).	.10	.25	1.50
	b. Red letters A; C; D; E (1951).	1.00	2.00	15.00
	c. Red letter F (1951).	1.00	4.00	20.00

71	20 PIASTRES	VG	VF	UNC
	ND (1942-45). Black and gray on brown unpt. Letters: A-L.	1.00	4.00	15.00
72	20 PIASTRES			
	ND (1942-45). Pink and black Like #65. Letters: A-E.	35.00	125.00	425.00
73	100 PIASTRES			
	ND (1942-45). Black-green frame, orange, brown and yellow vignette. Back dk. brown. Like #66. Letters: A-Q.	2.00	12.50	30.00

1949; 1951 ND Issue
#74-75 printed in Japan in 1944 for issue in Indochina.

77	50 PIASTRES	VG	VF	UNC
	ND (1945). Green. Man w/straw hat and baskets at r. Frieze from Angkor Wat on back. Printer: ABNC (w/o imprint).	15.00	75.00	350.00

74	1 PIASTRE	VG	VF	UNC
	ND (1949). Green, orange and m/c. 2 farmers w/ox. 2 women w/branches on back. Sign. 10.	2.50	10.00	30.00

78	100 PIASTRES	VG	VF	UNC
	ND (1945). Blue. Statues at Angkor Wat at l. 5 workers carrying baskets on back. Printer: ABNC (w/o imprint).	2.00	10.00	100.00

1946 ND Issue

75	5 PIASTRES	VG	VF	UNC
	ND. (1951) Green and m/c. Farmers working in rice fields. Temple w/Buddhists on back. Sign. 10.			
	a. Issued note w/regular serial #.	225.00	450.00	—
	b. Unfinished, w/o signs. or serial #.	—	Unc	275.00
	s. Finished specimen w/2 signs. and serial # all zeros.	—	Unc	350.00

79	100 PIASTRES	VG	VF	UNC
	ND (1946). Blue on m/c unpt. BIC bank bldg. at ctr. Back blue; 2 junks. Printer: TDLR (w/o imprint).			
	a. Issued note.	15.00	50.00	300.00
	x. Contemporary counterfeit, brown paper.	1.00	5.00	20.00

1945 ND Issue
#76-79 printed in the U.S. and England for issue in Indochina after WW II. All with Sign. 10.

1947-51 ND Issue
NOTE: 3 known of #84s1, and only 1 of #84s2. For issued note of similar design, see #98d and 109.

		VG	VF	UNC
80	**10 PIASTRES** ND (1947). Dk. purple on m/c unpt. Angkor Wat at l. Back red; field worker. Sign. 11. 2 Serial # varieties. Printer: TDLR (w/o imprint).	1.00	6.00	30.00

		VG	VF	UNC
81	**20 PIASTRES** ND (1949). M/c. Like #56, but white bank name and value 20 on red background, red *VINGT PIASTRES*. Sign. 11.	3.00	15.00	45.00

		VG	VF	UNC
82	**100 PIASTRES** ND (1947-54). M/c. Mercury at l. Man w/2 elephants at l., man at r. on back. Sign 11.			
	a. Type I Lao text on back. (1947 -49).	2.50	20.00	60.00

		VG	VF	UNC
83	**500 PIASTRES** ND (1951). M/c. Like #57, but white bank name and value numerals on red background. Sign. 11.	45.00	200.00	700.00

		VG	VF	UNC
84	**1000 PIASTRES** ND (printed 1951). Gray, orange and m/c. Elephant at l., water buffaloes at r. Bayon head (Angkor) at l., tree at r. on back. Wmk. Woman in Cambodian dancer's headdress. Sign. E. Minost and J. Laurent w/title: *Le Directeur General*.			
	s1. Specimen (serial # all O's).	—	—	2500.
	s2. Note w/regular serial # perforated: *SPECIMEN*.	—	Rare	—

GOUVERNEMENT GENERAL DE L'INDOCHINE

#85-91 issued during WW II by French Indochina colonial administration. Printed by the Imprimerie de l'Extreme Orient (I.D.E.O.) in Hanoi.

SIGNATURE VARIETIES/TITLE COMBINATIONS BANQUE DE L'INDOCHINE ISSUES, 1939–43			
12	Emile Henry *Le Tresorier Payeur General*	Yves Cazaux *Le Directeur des Finances*	
13	Louis Mayet *Le Tresorier General*	Yves Cazaux *Le Directeur des Finances*	
14	Louis Mayet *Le Tresorier General*	Jean Cousin *Le Directeur des Finances*	

1939 ND ISSUE

		VG	VF	UNC
85	**10 CENTS** ND. (1939) Red-brown. Sculptures at l., dancer at r. Market scene w/elephants on back.			
	a. *Le Tresorier Payeur General* in 2 lines at lower l. Denominations in Chinese, Cambodian and Vietnamese on back. Sign. 12.	6.50	25.00	75.00
	b. Like #85a, but denomination in Lao added on back. Sign. 12.	8.00	37.50	100.00
	c. *Le Tresorier General* 1 line at lower l. Sign. 13.	1.00	5.00	20.00
	d. Like #85c, serial # format 123456LL. Sign. 14.	.25	1.00	6.00
	e. Like #85d, but serial # format LL 123.456. Color is dk. brown.	.25	1.00	6.00

		VG	VF	UNC
86	**20 CENTS** ND. (1939) Brown and green. Women w/conical hat at l., boat at ctr. on back.			
	a. Like #85a. Sign. 12.	7.00	27.50	85.00
	b. *Deleted.*			
	c. Like #85c. Sign. 13.	2.50	10.00	30.00
	d. Like #85d. Sign. 14.	1.50	6.00	15.00

		VG	VF	UNC
87	**50 CENTS** ND. (1939) Red-brown and purple. Woman w/pole on back.			
	a. Like #85a. Sign. 12.	8.00	32.50	100.00
	b. *Deleted.*			
	c. Like #85c. Sign. 13.	2.00	10.00	30.00
	d. Like #85d. Sign. 14.	2.00	10.00	30.00
	e. Like #87d, but coffee-brown and black.	3.75	15.00	45.00

1942 ND ISSUE

#89-91, (from 1942-43) Pham-Ngoc-Khue, designer. Color shades vary. Sign. 14.

		VG	VF	UNC
88	**5 CENTS** ND. (1942) Green on pale blue unpt.			
	a. Signs., titles and penalty clause in black. Serial # format: 123456L.	.25	2.00	6.00
	b. Green unpt. Sign., titles and penalty clause in green. Serial # format: LL123456.	.25	1.00	4.00

89 10 CENTS
ND (1942) Brown on tan unpt.
a. Serial # format: LL123.456. | | .25 | 1.00 | 3.00
b. Serial # format: 1LL234.567. | | 1.25 | 5.00 | 15.00

| | VG | VF | UNC |

90 20 CENTS
ND (1942) Red-violet on pinkish unpt. Dragons and flames at ctr. .40 1.65 5.00

91 50 CENTS
ND (1942) Green on lt. green unpt. Dragon w/rice underneath on back.
a. Serial # format: LL123.456. .50 2.00 6.00
b. Serial # format: 1LL234.567. 1.25 5.00 15.00

INSTITUT D'EMISSION DES ETATS DU CAMBODGE,
DU LAOS ET DU VIETNAM

On 3I.12.1951 the exclusive privilege of banknote issue was withdrawn from the Banque de l'Indochine and transferred to the "Issuing Authority of the (Associated) States of Cambodia, Laos and Vietnam." Institut d'Emission notes, with but one exception, distinct for each state, were legal tender in all three until 1955. They were exchangeable at par with Banque de l'Indochine notes which not only remained in circulation but continued to be issued until existing stocks, transferred to the Institut d'Emission, were exhausted. The Piastre-French Franc exchange rate, reset at 1:17 in 1946, continued unchanged until May 1953 when France unilaterally adjusted it to 1:10.

SIGNATURE VARIETIES/TITLE COMBINATIONS ON INSTITUT D'EMISSION NOTES

15	Gaston Cusin — Le President	M. Lacoutre — Le Caissier Central	ALL THREE STATES
16		Le Caissier General (unidentified)	
17		Chhean Vam	CAMBODIA
18		Son Sann	
19		Khun One Voravong — Un Administrateur	LAOS
20		Le Ky Huong	
21		Nghiem Van Tri — Un Administrateur	VIET-NAM

CAMBODIA, LAOS AND VIETNAM BRANCH
1953 ND Issue

92 1 PIASTRE
ND (1953). Brown, red and m/c. Woman at r. Similar to #54, but modified legends in red. Sign. 15.
VG .50 VF 3.00 UNC 10.00

CAMBODIA BRANCH
1953-54 ND ISSUES
#93-98 wmk: Elephant head. Cambodian title on back:
NOTE: For later issues see Cambodia.

93 1 PIASTRE = 1 RIEL
ND (1953). Green and blue on yellow and m/c unpt. Young Kg. Sihanouk at ctr. Back red on yellow unpt. Sign. 16.
VG 17.50 VF 75.00 UNC 175.00

94 1 PIASTRE = 1 RIEL
ND (1954). Blue and green. Face like #100 and 105 w/trees. Back blue and brown; Royal houseboat at l. Sign. 18.
VG 2.00 VF 10.00 UNC 55.00

95 5 PIASTRES = 5 RIELS
ND (1953). Green on pink and green unpt. Face like #101 and 106 w/banana trees at l., palms at r. Naga (mythical snake) head at l. on back. Sign. 18.
VG 4.00 VF 25.00 UNC 80.00

96 10 PIASTRES = 10 RIELS
ND (1953). Red on blue and gold unpt. Face like #102 and 107 w/stylized sunburst at ctr. 2 dancers at l. on back.
a. Sign. 17. 5.00 30.00 175.00
b. Sign. 18. 8.00 40.00 250.00

97   100 Pɪᴀsᴛʀᴇs = 100 Rɪᴇʟs
ND (1954). Orange and m/c. Face like #103 and 108 w/3 women at l.
Back brown and m/c; Temple of Angkor. Sign. 18.

	VG	VF	UNC
	6.00	40.00	200.00

98   200 Pɪᴀsᴛʀᴇs = 200 Rɪᴇʟs
ND (1953). Green, brown w/elephant at l., 2 water buffaloes at r.
Bayon head (Angkor) at l., tree at r. on back. Sign. 17.

	VG	VF	UNC
	30.00	100.00	300.00

Lᴀᴏs BʀᴀɴᴄH

1953-54 ND Issues

#99-103 wmk: Elephant head. Laotian title on back:

NOTE: For later issues see Laos.

---

99   1 Pɪᴀsᴛʀᴇ = 1 Kɪᴘ
ND (1953). Green and blue on yellow and m/c unpt. Kg. Sisavang
Vong at ctr. Back deep red on yellow unpt. Sign. 16.

	VG	VF	UNC
	1.50	6.00	50.00

100   1 Pɪᴀsᴛʀᴇ = 1 Kɪᴘ
ND (1954). Blue and green. Face like #94 and 105. Back brown and
blue; horse w/3 roofs at l. Sign. 19.

	VG	VF	UNC
	.50	2.50	15.00

101   5 Pɪᴀsᴛʀᴇs = 5 Kɪᴘ
ND (1953). Green on pink and green unpt. Face like #96 and 106.
Temple of That Luang at l. on back. Sign. 19.

	VG	VF	UNC
	3.00	20.00	60.00

102   10 Pɪᴀsᴛʀᴇs = 10 Kɪᴘ
ND (1953). Red on blue and gold unpt. Face like #96 and 107. Woman
at l. on back. Sign. 19.

	VG	VF	UNC
	3.00	25.00	90.00

103   100 Pɪᴀsᴛʀᴇs = 100 Kɪᴘ
ND (1954). M/c. Face like #97 and 108. Bldg at ctr., woman w/bowl of
roses at r. on back. Sign. 20.

	VG	VF	UNC
	3.00	22.50	85.00

Vɪᴇᴛɴᴀᴍ BʀᴀɴᴄH

1953-54 ND Issues

#104-109 wmk: Tiger head. Vietnamese title on back: VIÊN PHÁT-HÀNH.

NOTE: For later issues see Vietnam.

104   1 Pɪᴀsᴛʀᴇ = 1 Dᴏɴɢ
ND (1953). Green and blue on yellow and m/c unpt. Bao Dai at ctr.
Back red on yellow unpt. Sign. 16.

	.50	3.00	17.50

105   1 Pɪᴀsᴛʀᴇ = 1 Dᴏɴɢ
ND (1954). Blue and green. Face like #94 and 100. Back brown and
blue; lion at l. Sign. 21. Thin white or white/tan paper.

	.25	.50	5.00

109   200 PIASTRES = 200 DONG
ND (1953). Green, brown and pink. Face like #98. Bao Dai at l., pagoda at ctr. on back. Sign. 21.

	VG	VF	UNC
	6.00	35.00	90.00

106   5 PIASTRES = 5 DONG
ND (1953). Green on pink and green unpt. Face like #95 and 101. Bao Dai at l. on back. Sign. 21.

	VG	VF	UNC
	.25	2.00	10.00

JAPANESE OCCUPATION, WW II

JAPANESE IMPERIAL GOVERNMENT

府政國帝本日大
Ta Jih Pen Ti Kuo Cheng Fu

Like the Japanese Imperial Government issues for China #M13, M15, M17, M19 and M21 except for changes in colors and back inscriptions and having an additional Japanese character *Ro* which appears similar to a flat topped "3" prefix to the block # on #M1-M4.

NOTE: For 100 Yen of same design but diff. color printing, see China #M21.

1938-40 ND ISSUE
NOTE: for 100 Yen of same design but diff. color printing, see China #M21.

107   10 PIASTRES = 10 DONG
ND (1953). Red on blue and gold unpt. Face like #96 and 102. Rock in water at l. on back. Sign. 21.

	VG	VF	UNC
	.50	2.50	12.50

			VG	VF	UNC
M1	50 SEN	ND (1940). Blue on yellow-green and lt. purple unpt. Dragon at l. Back blue.	50.00	125.00	250.00
M2	1 YEN	ND (1940). Purple on yellow-green and brown unpt. Onagadori cockerel at l. Back purple.	150.00	250.00	500.00
M3	5 YEN	ND (1940). Gray-green on gray-blue and lt. purple unpt. Onagadori cockerel at l. and r. Back dk. green.	600.00	1250.	2500.
M4	10 YEN	ND (1940). Brown on lt. blue and pink unpt. Onagadori cockerel at l. and r. Block # and serial #. Back brown.	750.00	1500.	3000.
M5 (M7)	100 YEN	ND (1938). Blue-green on lt. lilac unpt. Onagadori cockerel at l. and r. Specimen.	—	—	500.00

1942 ND ISSUE

			VG	VF	UNC
M6 (M5)	1 YEN	ND (ca.1942). Dk. brown and green lithograph. Like #M2 but only 2 block #. W/o *Ro* prefix. Back dk. brown. Specimen.	—	Rare	—

108   100 PIASTRES = 100 DONG
ND (1954). M/c. Face like #97 and 103. Small bldg. at ctr., Bao Dai at r. on back. Sign. 21.

	VG	VF	UNC
	2.00	12.50	60.00

			VG	VF	UNC
M7 (M6)	10 YEN	ND (ca.1942) Brown and blue lithograph. Like #M4 but only 2 block #. W/o *Ro* prefix. Back brown. Specimen.	.35	1.00	4.00

The colony of French Oceania (now the Territory of French Polynesia), comprising 130 basalt and coral islands scattered among five archipelagoes in the South Pacific, had an area of 1,544 sq. mi. (3,999 sq. km.) and a population of about 185,000, mostly Polynesians. Capital: Papeete. The colony produced phosphates, copra and vanilla. Tahiti of the Society Islands, the hub of French Oceania, was visited by Capt. Cook in 1769 and by Capt. Bligh in the Bounty 1788-89. The Society Islands were claimed by France in 1768, and in 1903 grouped with the Marquesas Islands, the Tuamotu Archipelago, the Gambier Islands and the Austral Islands under a single administrative head located at Papeete, Tahiti, to form the colony of French Oceania.

RULERS:
French

MONETARY SYSTEM:
1 Franc = 100 Centimes

FRENCH INFLUENCE

CHAMBRE DE COMMERCE DES ETABLISSEMENTS FRANÇAIS DE L'OCÉANIE

1919 FIRST EMERGENCY ISSUE
Arrêté du 29 Decembre 1919
#1-4 woman leaning on arch at l. and r. Helmeted head at l. and r. on back. Printer: Halpin Lithograph Co., San Francisco.

		GOOD	FINE	XF
1	**25 CENTIMES** *L.1919.* Brown.	50.00	100.00	225.00

		GOOD	FINE	XF
2	**50 CENTIMES** *L.1919.* Green.	50.00	100.00	225.00

		GOOD	FINE	XF
3	**1 FRANC** *L.1919.* Orange. Black or red serial #.	50.00	100.00	300.00

		GOOD	FINE	XF
4	**2 FRANCS** *L.1919.* Purple.	50.00	100.00	300.00

1919 SECOND ISSUE
#1A-2A, 5-6 w/o design, but same date as previous issue. Local printer.

		GOOD	FINE	XF
1A	**25 CENTIMES** *L.1919.* Brown.	60.00	150.00	350.00

		GOOD	FINE	XF
2A	**50 CENTIMES** *L.1919.* Blue.	60.00	150.00	350.00

		GOOD	FINE	XF
5	**1 FRANC** *L.1919.* Black. Dk. brown paper.	60.00	150.00	350.00

6	2 FRANCS *L.1919*. Black. Tan paper.	GOOD 60.00	FINE 150.00	XF 350.00

BONS DE CAISSE DES ETABLISSEMENTS FRANÇAIS LIBRES DE L'OCÉANIE

1941 EMERGENCY WWII ISSUE
Décret du 18 Août 1941

#6A and 6B small rectangular cardboards.

6A	1 FRANC *D.1941*. Black. Soccer player at ctr. on back.	—	Rare	—
6B	2 FRANCS *D.1941*.	—	Rare	—

1942 ISSUE
Arrêté No. 300 A.G.F. du 7 Avril 1942

#7-9 Upright hand holding torch of freedom behind shield of Lorraine at ctr.

7	50 CENTIMES *L.1942*. Orange and green. 2 sign. varieties.	VG 100.00	VF 325.00	UNC 475.00
8	1 FRANC *L.1942*. Green and red. 2 sign. varieties.	105.00	350.00	500.00

9	2 FRANCS *L.1942*. Blue and black. 2 sign. varieties.	VG 125.00	VF 425.00	UNC 575.00

BONS DE CAISSE DES ETABLISSEMENTS FRANÇAIS DE L'OCÉANIE

1943 EMEREGENCY WWII ISSUE
Arrêté No. 698 S.G. du 25 Septembre 1943.

10	50 CENTIMES *L.1943*. Orange and black. Map outline on back w/text inside.	VG	VF	UNC
	a. Circular violet handstamp.	37.50	125.00	275.00
	b. Wreath in circular violet handstamp.	40.00	135.00	325.00
	c. Embossed seal.	37.50	125.00	275.00
11	1 FRANC *L.1943*. Green and purple. like #10.			
	a. Circular violet handstamp.	37.50	125.00	275.00
	b. Wreath in circular violet handstamp.	40.00	135.00	325.00
	c. Embossed seal.	37.50	125.00	275.00

13	2.50 FRANCS *L.1943*. Black and red. Like #10.	VG	VF	UNC
	a. Circular violet handstamp.	50.00	165.00	350.00
	b. Wreath in circular violet handstamp.	52.50	175.00	400.00
	c. Embossed seal.	50.00	165.00	350.00

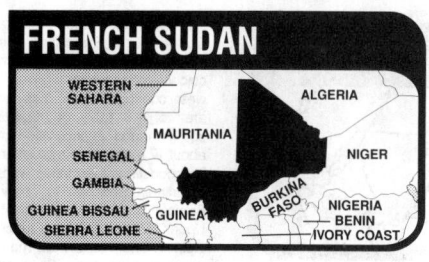

FRENCH SUDAN

The French Sudan, a land-locked country in the interior of West Africa southwest of Algeria, has an area of 478,764 sq. mi. (1,240,000 sq. km.). Capital: Bamako. Livestock, fish, cotton and peanuts are exported.

French Sudanese are descendants of the ancient Malinke Kingdom of Mali that controlled the middle Niger from the 11th to the 17th centuries. The French penetrated the Sudan (now Mali) about 1880, and established their rule in 1898 after subduing fierce native resistance. In 1904 the area became the colony of Upper Senegal-Niger (changed to French Sudan in 1920), and became part of the French Union in 1946. In 1958 French Sudan became the Sudanese Republic with complete internal autonomy. Senegal joined with the Sudanese Republic in 1959 to form the Mali Federation which, in 1960, became a fully independent member of the French Community. Upon Senegal's subsequent withdrawal from the Federation, the Sudanese, on Sept. 22, 1960, proclaimed their nation the fully independent Republic of Mali and severed all ties with France.

Note: For later issues see Mali, Vol. 3.

RULERS:
French to 1960

MONETARY SYSTEM:
1 Franc = 100 Centimes

FRENCH INFLUENCE

GOUVERNEMENT GÉNÉRAL DE L'AFRIQUE

OCCIDENTALE FRANÇAISE

COLONIE DU SOUDAN FRANÇAISE

1917 EMERGENCY WWI ISSUE
Décret du Soudan Française

NOTE: Denominations of 1 Franc and 2 Francs probably exist.

A1	0.50 FRANC *L.1917*.	VG	VF	UNC
	a. Wmk: Bees.	65.00	185.00	350.00
	b. Wmk: Laurel leaves.	65.00	185.00	350.00

FRENCH W. AFRICA

French West Africa (Afrique Occidentale Francaise), a former federation of French colonial territories on the northwest coast of Africa, has an area of 1,831,079 (4,742,495 sq. km.) and a population of about 17 million. Capital: Dakar. The constituent territories were Mauritania, Senegal, Dahomey, French Sudan, Ivory Coast, Upper Volta, Niger, French Guinea, and later on the mandated area of Togo. Peanuts, palm kernels, cacao, coffee and bananas were exported.

Prior to the mid-19th century, France, as the other European states, maintained establishments on the west coast of Africa for the purpose of trading in slaves and gum, but made no serious attempt at colonization. From 1854 onward, the coastal settlements were gradually extended into the interior until, by the opening of the 20th century, acquisition ended and organization and development began. French West Africa was formed in 1895 by grouping the several colonies under one administration (at Dakar) while retaining a large measure of autonomy to each of the constituent territories. The inhabitants of French West Africa were made French citizens in 1946. With the exception of French Guinea, all of the colonies voted in 1958 to become autonomous members of the new French Community. French Guinea voted to become the fully independent Republic of Guinea. The present-day independent states are members of the "Union Monetaire Ouest-Africaine."

Also see West African States.

MONETARY SYSTEM:
1 Franc = 100 Centimes
1 Unit = 5 Francs

FRENCH INFLUENCE

BANQUE DE L'AFRIQUE OCCIDENTALE

SIGNATURE TITLES:

a, c, f, h, j, l: *Un Administrateur, Le Directeur*
b, e: *Un Administrateur, Le Directeur, Le Caissier*
d, g, i, k: *Le Président, L'Administrateur- Directeur*
m: *Le Président, Le Directeur General*

CITIES OF ISSUE:
In addition to city of issue designation, the back color is the same for all denominations within a city.
A - Conakri, Conakry (French Guinea) Back: green.
B - Dakar (Sengal) Back: red (5 Francs green)
C - Duala (Cameroon) Ovpt. on Conakry or Dakar notes.
D - Grand-Bassam (Ivory Coast) Back: blue.
E - Porto Novo (Dahomey) Back: dk. brown or red.
F - St. Louis (Sengal) Back: red.
NOTE: The first issue of the bank also circulated in Equatorial Africa, Togo and Cameroon. Dakar is most frequenty encountered. Notes with Lome (Togo) imprint allegedly exist but no examples have been reported.

CONAKRY BRANCH

1903-24 ISSUE

		GOOD	FINE	XF
5A	**5 FRANCS**			
	8.2.1904. Blue and yellow. Lio n at l.; bowl, drum and other objects at r.			
	a. *CONAKRI.*Sign. titles: a. 8.2.1904.	85.00	225.00	500.00
	b. *CONAKRY*. Sign. titles: c. 10.7.1919.	75.00	200.00	450.00
9A	**50 FRANCS**			
	1920-24. Blue and yellow. Elephant head and tree and l. at r. *CONAKRY*. Sign. titles: h.			
	a. Sgn. titles: e. 12.2.1920.	—	—	—
	b. Sign. titles: h. 12.6.1924.	100.00	350.00	650.00
10A	**100 FRANCS**			
	1903-24. Red and green. Like #9A. *CONAKRY*.			
	a. Sign. titles: a. 3.11.1903.	140.00	500.00	—
	b. Sign. titles: e. 12.2.1920.	100.00	350.00	650.00
	c. Sign. titles: i. 13.11.1924.	110.00	375.00	700.00
13A	**500 FRANCS**			
	1912-24. Blue and yellow. Like #9A. *CONAKRY*.			
	a. Sign. titles: b. 12.9.1912.	350.00	850.00	—
	b. Sign. titles: g.10.11.1921.	300.00	750.00	—
	c. Sign. titles: i. 10.4.1924.	300.00	750.00	—

		GOOD	FINE	XF
15A	**1000 FRANCS**			
	10.4.1924. Red and green. Like #9A. *CONAKRY*. Sign. titles: i.	375.00	1000.	—

DAKAR BRANCH

1892(ND)PROVISIONAL ISSUE

		GOOD	FINE	XF
3	**100 FRANCS**			
(20)	ND (old dates 26;30.11.1892). Blue on pink unpt. Ovpt. new heading at top and *DAKAR* at lower ctr. on unissued 1892 France 100 Francs.	—	Rare	—

1916-24 ISSUE

		GOOD	FINE	XF
5B	**5 FRANCS**			
	1916-32. Blue and yellow. Like #5A.			
	a. Sign. titles: c. 8.6.1916; 28.5.1918; 10.7.1919.	17.50	55.00	135.00
	b. Sign. titles: h. 14.12.1922.	15.00	40.00	125.00
	c. Sign. titles: i. 10.4.1924; 9.7.1925.	20.00	65.00	150.00
	d. Sign. titles: j. 1.8.1925; 17.2.1926.	12.00	35.00	120.00
	e. Sign. titles: k. 10.6.1926.	12.00	35.00	120.00
	6. Sign. titles: l. 21.10.1926; 13.1.1928.	12.00	35.00	120.00
	g. Sign. titles: m. 16.5.1929; 1.9.1932.	17.50	55.00	135.00

		GOOD	FINE	XF
7B	**25 FRANCS**			
	1925-26. Gray-brown and green. Like #9A.			
	a. Sign. titles: i. 9.7.1925.	30.00	125.00	300.00
	b. Sign. titles: k. 10.6.1926.	30.00	125.00	300.00
9B	**50 FRANCS**			
	1919; 1926; 1929. Blue and yellow. Like #9A.			
	a. Sign. titles: b. 11.9.1919.	50.00	150.00	425.00
	b. Sign. titles: b. 11.9.1919.	40.00	125.00	375.00
	c. Sign. titles: j. 17.2.1926.	35.00	115.00	300.00
	d. Sign. titles: m. 14.3.1929.	50.00	150.00	425.00

PORTO NOVO BRANCH

1916-24 ISSUE

5E	**5 FRANCS** 8.6.1916; 28.5.1918; 10.7.1919. Like #5A. Sign. titles: c.	85.00	225.00	500.00
7E	**25 FRANCS** 1920; 1923. Like #7B.			
	a. Sign. titles: e. 12.2.1920.	180.00	500.00	950.00
	b. Sign. titles: i. 12.7.1923.	180.00	500.00	950.00
10E	**50 FRANCS** 1920; 1924. Like #9A.			
	a. Sign. titles: e. 12.2.1920.	300.00	675.00	—
	b. Sign. titles: i. 12.6.1924.	300.00	675.00	—
11E	**100 FRANCS** 1920; 1924. Like #11B. Sign. titles: f.			
	a. Sign. titles: f. 15.4.1920.	325.00	750.00	—
	b. Sign. titles: i. 13.11.1924.	325.00	750.00	—
12E	**100 FRANCS** 9.3.1916. Like #12D. Ovpt: *PORTO NOVO* on GRAND BASSAM. Ovpt: *DAHOMEY* in lg. lettering across back. Sign. titles: b.	325.00	750.00	—
13E	**500 FRANCS** 15.4.1924. Like #13A. Sign. titles: f.	450.00	1100.	
14E	**1000 FRANCS** 11.9.1919. Red and green. Ovpt: *PORTO-NOVO* on DAKAR. Ovpt: *DAHOMEY* in lg. lettering across red back. Sign. titles: d.	600.00	1500.	
15E	**1000 FRANCS** 10.4.1924. Like #9A. Sign. titles: i.	600.00	1500.	

SAINT LOUIS BRANCH

1904-17 ISSUES

5F	**5 FRANCS** 1904; 1916. Like #5A.			
	a. Sign. titles: a. 1.2.1904.	200.00	550.00	—
	b. Sign. titles: c. 8.6.1916; 15.8.1918.	140.00	400.00	650.00
7F	**25 FRANCS** 9.11.1917. Sign. titles: b.	250.00	600.00	
13F	**500 FRANCS** 12.2.1912; 11.9.1913. Like #13A. Sign. titles: b.	500.00	1150.	
14F	**1000 FRANCS** 14.10.1905. Sign. titles: a.	600.00	1500.	

W/O BRANCH

1919 ISSUE

5G	**5 FRANCS** 10.7.1919. Like #5A. Sign. titles: c.	100.00	275.00	575.00

1934-37 ISSUE

#21-27 w/o city of issue. Printed by the Banque de France (w/o imprints). Various dates and sign. varieties.

NOTE: For issues similar to #21-27 but w/heading *Afrique Française Libre*, see French Equatorial Africa #6-9. For #21-27 w/*RF-FEZZAN* ovpt. see Libya.

		VG	VF	UNC
21	**5 FRANCS** 17.7.1934-6.3.1941. Brown, green and m/c. Man at ctr. Man weaving on back. Value in dk. blue.	1.50	7.50	27.50
22 (24)	**25 FRANCS** 1.5.1936-9.3.1939. M/c. Young man wearing turban w/horse at l. ctr. Value in blue. Lion at r. on back.	5.00	17.50	55.00

1941-42 ISSUES

25 (22)	**5 FRANCS** 6.3.1941-1.10.1942. M/c. Like #21 but va-lue in lt. blue.	1.50	8.50	30.00
26 (23)	**5 FRANCS** 2.3.1943. M/c. Like #22 but value, date and sign. in red.	6.00	20.00	57.50
27 (25)	**25 FRANCS** 9.1.1942; 24.2.1942; 22.4.1942; 1.10.1942. M/c. Like #24 but value in red.	7.00	27.50	65.00

		GOOD	FINE	XF
10B	**100 FRANCS** 15.4.1920. Red and green. Like #9A. Ovpt: *DAKAR* on CONAKRY. Ovpt: *SENEGAL* in large lettering across green back. Sign. titles: f.	100.00	250.00	550.00
11B	**100 FRANCS** 1924; 1926. Normally printed city of issue, otherwise face like #10B.			
	a. Sign. titles: i. 13.11.1924.	50.00	150.00	425.00
	b. Sign. titles: k. 24.9.1926.	50.00	150.00	425.00
12B	**500 FRANCS** 10.11.1921. Blue and yellow. Ovpt: *DAKAR* on CONAKRY. Ovpt: *Senegal* in lg. lettering across green back. Sign. titles: g.	300.00	650.00	—
13B	**500 FRANCS** 1919-24. Blue and yellow. Like #13A.			
	a. Sign. titles: d. 11.9.1919.	350.00	850.00	—
	b. Sign. titles: g. 10.11.1921.	300.00	750.00	—
	c. Sign. titles: i. 10.4.1924.	275.00	675.00	—
15B	**1000 FRANCS** 10.4.1924. Red and green. Like #9A. Sign. i.	325.00	900.00	—

DUALA BRANCH

1919-21 ISSUE

6C	**25 FRANCS** 15.4.1920. Ovpt: *DUALA* on CONAKRY. Sign. titles: f.	250.00	550.00	—
13C	**500 FRANCS** 10.11.1921. Blue and yellow. Ovpt: *DUALA* on DAKAR. *DUALA* in lg. lettering across green back. Sign. titles: g	500.00	1500.	
14C	**1000 FRANCS** 11.9.1919. Ovpt: *DUALA* similar to #13C. Sign. d.	600.00	1750.	

GRAND BASSAM BRANCH

1904-24 ISSUES

5D	**5 FRANCS** 1904-19. Like #5A.			
	a. Sign. titles: a. 26.2.1904; 1.3.1904.	90.00	250.00	600.00
	b. Sign. titles: c. 8.6.1916; 18.5.1918; 28.5.1918; 10.7.1919.	85.00	235.00	475.00
6D	**25 FRANCS** 12.7.1923. Gray-brown. Like #9A. Ovpt: *GRAND-BASSAM* on CONAKRI. Ovpt: *COTE de IVOIRE* in lg. lettering across green back. Sign. titles: h.	265.00	550.00	—
7D	**25 FRANCS** 1920; 1923. Normally printed city of issue, otherwise like #6D.			
	a. Sign. titles: f. 12.2.1920.	180.00	500.00	1000.
	b. Sign. titles: i. 12.7.1923.	180.00	500.00	1000.
9D	**50 FRANCS** 1920; 1924. Like #9A.			
	a. Sign. titles: f. 12.2.1920.	275.00	675.00	—
	b. Sign. titles: i. 12.6.1924.	275.00	675.00	—
11D	**100 FRANCS** 1910-24. Like #11B.			
	a. Sign. titles: b. 18.8.1910; 9.3.1916.	325.00	750.00	—
	b. Sign. titles: e. 12.2.1920.	325.00	750.00	—
	c. Sign. titles: f. 15.4.1920.	325.00	750.00	—
	d. Sign. titles: i. 13.11.1924.	325.00	750.00	—
12D	**100 FRANCS** 15.4.1920. Ovpt: *GRAND-BASSAM* similar to #6D. sign. titles: f.	375.00	750.00	—
13D	**500 FRANCS** 15.4.1924. Like #13A. Sign. titles: f.	450.00	950.00	—
14D	**1000 FRANCS** 15.4.1924. Like #9A. Sign. titles: f.	600.00	1500.	

1942-43 EMERGENCY WWII ISSUE
#28-30 Printer: E.A. Wright. Phila. sign. varieties.

28	5 FRANCS	VG	VF	UNC
	14.12.1942. Black on gold unpt. Woman at ctr. Back red-violet on blue unpt.			
	a. Serial #. 2 sign. style varieties.	3.25	10.00	25.00
	b. W/o serial #.	10.00	30.00	75.00
	s1. As a. Specimen.	—	—	100.00
	s2. As b. Specimen.	—	—	85.00

29 (32)	10 FRANCS	VG	VF	UNC
	2.1.1943. Violet on gold unpt. Woman at r. Algerian printing.	25.00	75.00	225.00

30 (29)	25 FRANCS	VG	VF	UNC
	14.12.1942. Black on green unpt. Woman at l. Back blue on brown unpt; plane and palms at ctr.			
	a. Serial # at ctr., block letter at upper l. and r.	4.50	13.50	50.00
	b. Block letter and # at upper l. and lower r., # at lower l. and upper r., serial # at ctr.	7.00	22.50	85.00
	c. W/o serial #.	18.50	57.50	175.00
	s. Specimen.	—	—	150.00

31 (30)	100 FRANCS	VG	VF	UNC
	14.12.1942. Black on pink unpt. Tree at ctr. Back green on gold unpt; huts and palms at ctr.			
	a. Serial #.	15.00	45.00	150.00
	b. W/o serial #.	30.00	90.00	200.00
	s. Specimen	—	—	175.00

32 (31)	1000 FRANCS			
	14.12.1942. Purple on lt. green and pinkish unpt. Ships and train at ctr. BAO in wreath on back. Printer: ABNC.	225.00	675.00	1200.

AFRIQUE OCCIDENTALE FRANÇAISE

1944 (ND) ISSUE

33	0.50 FRANC	VG	VF	UNC
	ND (1944). Orange. Fortress at ctr. W/ or w/o security strip.	2.00	6.00	20.00

34	1 FRANC	VG	VF	UNC
	ND (1944). Dk. brown. Fisherman in boat at l., woman at r.			
	a. Lt. blue paper.	2.00	6.00	20.00
	b. Lt. brown on yellow paper.	2.00	6.00	20.00

35	2 FRANCS	VG	VF	UNC
	ND (1944). Blue. Beach w/palm tree at l.	20.00	60.00	225.00

BANQUE DE L'AFRIQUE OCCIDENTALE (RESUMED)

1943-48 ISSUE

36	5 FRANCS	VG	VF	UNC
	17.8.1943(1945)-28.10.1954. M/c. 2 woamn, 1 w/finery, w/jug. Men poling in long boats at l. ctr. on back.	1.25	3.75	15.00

37	10 FRANCS	VG	VF	UNC
	18.1.1946-28.10.1954. M/c. 2 bow hunters at ctr. Man carring deer on back.	2.00	7.00	27.50

38	25 FRANCS	VG	VF	UNC
	17.8.1943(1945)-28.10.1954. M.c. Woman at ctr. Man w/bull at ctr. back.	4.00	17.50	75.00

39   50 FRANCS
27.9.1944(1945)-28.10.1954. M/c. Women at ctr., old man wearing
fez at r. Man w/stalk of bananas at ctr. on back

	VG	VF	UNC
	5.00	25.00	100.00

40   100 FRANCS
10.5.1945-5.10.1955. M/c. woman w/fruit bowl at ctr. Family on back.

	VG	VF	UNC
	7.50	27.50	110.00

41   500 FRANCS
6.2.1946-21.11.1953. M/c. Woman w/flag at ctr. Colonial soldiers on
back.

	VG	VF	UNC
	35.00	175.00	650.00

42   1000 FRANCS
16.4.1948-28.10.1954. M/c. Woman w/2 jugs at ctr. Woman w/high
headdress at ctr. on back.

	VG	VF	UNC
	60.00	185.00	750.00

43   5000 FRANCS
15.11.1948; 22.12.1950. M/c. France w/2 native women at ctr

	VG	VF	UNC
	300.00	700.00	—

INSTITUT D'EMISSION DE L'A.O.F. ET DU TOGO

1955-56 ISSUE

44   50 FRANCS
5.10.1955. M/c. Like #39.

	VG	VF	UNC
	30.00	100.00	350.00

45   50 FRANCS
ND (1956). Black and m/c. 3 women at ctr. Woman w/headdress, city
in background at ctr.

	VG	VF	UNC
	3.50	15.00	75.00

46   100 FRANCS
23.10.1956; 20.5.1957. M/c. mask at l., woman w/braids at r. Woman
at l. on back.

	VG	VF	UNC
	6.00	25.00	100.00

47   500 FRANCS
23.10.1956. M/c. People at field work at l., mask at r.

	VG	VF	UNC
	30.00	100.00	350.00

48   1000 FRANCS
5.10.1955. M/c. Like #42.

	VG	VF	UNC
	125.00	225.00	550.00

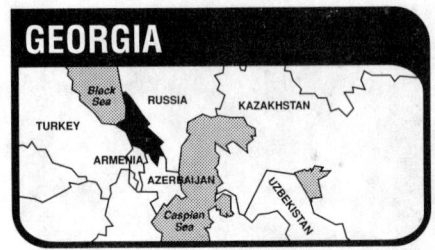

GEORGIA

Georgia (formerly the Georgian Social Democratic Republic under the U.S.S.R.), is bounded by the Black Sea to the west and by Turkey, Armenia and Azerbaijan. It occupies the western part of Transcaucasia covering an area of 26,900 sq. mi. (69,700 sq. km.) Capital: Tbilisi. Hydro-electricity, minerals, forestry and agriculture are the chief industries.

The Georgian dynasty first emerged after the Macedonian victory over the Achaemenid Persian empire in the 4th century B.C. Roman "friendship" was imposed in 65 B.C. after Pompey's victory over Mithradates. The Georgians embraced Christianity in the 4th century A.D. During the next three centuries Georgia was involved in the ongoing conflicts between the Byzantine and Persian empires. The latter developed control until Georgia regained its independence in 450-503 A.D. but then it reverted to a Persian province in 533 A.D., Then restored as a kingdom by the Byzantines in 562 A.D. It was established as an Arab emirate in the 8th century. The Seljuk Turks invaded but the crusades thwarted their interests. Over the following centuries Turkish and Persian rivalries along with civil strife divided the area under the two influences.

Czarist Russian interests increased and a treaty of alliance was signed on July 24, 1773 whereby Russia guaranteed Georgian independence and it acknowledged Russian suzerainty. Persia invaded again in 1795 leaving Tiflis in ruins. Russia slowly took over annexing piece by piece and soon developed total domination. After the Russian Revolution the Georgians, Armenians and Azerbaijanis formed the short- lived Transcaucasian Federal Republic on Sept. 20, 1917 which broke up into three independent republics on May 26, 1918. A Germano-Georgian treaty was signed on May 28, 1918, followed by a Turko- Georgian peace treaty on June 4. The end of WW I and the collapse of the central powers allowed free elections.

On May 20, 1920, Soviet Russia concluded a peace treaty, recognizing its independence, but later invaded on Feb. 11, 1921 and a soviet republic was proclaimed. On March 12, 1922 Stalin included Georgia in a newly formed Transcaucasian Soviet Federated Socialist Republic. On Dec. 5, 1936 the T.S.F.S.R. was dissolved and Georgia became a direct member of the U.S.S.R. The collapse of the U.S.S.R. allowed full transition to independence and on April 9, 1991 a unanimous vote declared the republic an independent state based on its original treaty of independence of May 1918.

ГРУЗИНСКОИ РЕСПУБЛИКИ

Georgia, Autonomous Republic

TREASURY

1919 ОБЯЗАТЕЛЬСТВО КАЗНАЧЕИСТВА DEBENTURE BONDS

			VG	VF	UNC
1	**25 RUBLES** 15.1.1919.		2.50	10.00	30.00

			VG	VF	UNC
2	**100 RUBLES** 15.1.1919.		3.00	12.00	36.00
3	**500 RUBLES** 15.1.1919.		4.00	16.00	48.00
4	**1000 RUBLES** 15.1.1919.		3.50	15.00	45.00
5	**5000 RUBLES** 15.1.1919.		6.00	25.00	75.00

1919-21 STATE NOTES
#6-15, St. George on horseback on back.
#16-22 held in reserve.

				VG	VF	UNC
6	**50 KOPEKS** ND (1919). Blue on lt. brown unpt.			.35	1.50	4.50

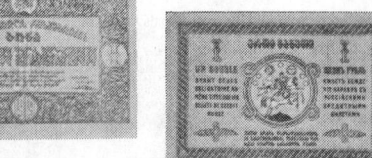

			VG	VF	UNC
7	**1 RUBLE** 1919. Brown on pink unpt.		.50	2.25	6.75
8	**3 RUBLES** 1919. Black on green unpt.		.75	3.00	9.00

			VG	VF	UNC
9	**5 RUBLES** 1919. Black on orange unpt.		.75	3.00	9.00
10	**10 RUBLES** 1919. Brown on red-brown unpt.		.75	3.00	9.00
11	**50 RUBLES** 1919. Violet on brown unpt. green also in unpt. on back.		1.00	4.00	12.00

			VG	VF	UNC
12	**100 RUBLES** 1919. Green. Lilac in unpt. on back.		1.25	5.00	15.00

			VG	VF	UNC
13	**500 RUBLES** 1919. Black-green on red-brown unpt. Woman seated w/shield and lance at ctr.				
	a. Wmk: plaited lines.		2.50	10.00	30.00
	b. Thick or thin paper w/o wmk.		1.00	4.00	12.00
14	**1000 RUBLES** 1920. Brown on blue and tan unpt.				
	a. Wmk: Plaited lines.		3.00	12.00	36.00
	b. W/o wmk.		1.50	6.00	18.00

			VG	VF	UNC
15	**5000 RUBLES** 1921. Lilac to brown. Bldg. w/flags at ctr. Margin circles around corner numerals are ringed once at each side.				
	a. Wmk: Monograms.		2.25	9.00	27.00
	b. W/o wmk.		1.25	5.00	15.00
	c. Ruled on back.		3.00	12.00	36.00

GERMAN EAST AFRICA

German East Africa (Tanganyika), located on the coast of east-central Africa between British East Africa (now Kenya) and Portuguese East Africa (now Mozambique), has an area of 362,284 sq. mi. (938,216 sq. km.) and a population of about 6 million. Capital: Dar es Salam. Chief products prior to German control were ivory and slaves; after German control, sisal, coffee and rubber.

The East African coast first felt the impact of foreign influence in the eighth century, when Arab traders arrived. By the 12th century, traders and immigrants from the Near East and India had built highly developed city/trading states along the coast. By 1506, Portugal claimed control along the entire coast, but made no attempt to establish a colony or to explore the interior.

Germany acquired control of the area by treaties in 1884, and established it as a protectorate administered by the German East Africa Company. In 1891, the German Government assumed direct administration of the area, which was proclaimed the Colony of German East Africa in 1897.

German colonial domination of Tanganyika ended with World War I. Control of most of the territory passed to Great Britain, under a League of Nations mandate. British control was continued after World War II, under a United Nations trusteeship. Thereafter, Tanganyika moved gradually toward self-government. It became autonomous in May 1961. Full independence was achieved on Dec. 9 of the same year.

RULERS:
   German, 1884-1918
   British, 1918-1961

MONETARY SYSTEM:
   1 Rupie = 100 Heller

GERMAN INFLUENCE

DEUTSCH-OSTAFRIKANISCHE BANK

1905-12 ISSUE
#1-5 printer: G&D.

		GOOD	FINE	XF
1	**5 RUPIEN**			
	15.6.1905. Blue on brown and m/c unpt. 2 lions at bottom ctr.	8.50	25.00	150.00

		GOOD	FINE	XF
2	**10 RUPIEN**			
	15.6.1905. Black on red unpt. Daressalam Harbor at lower ctr.	12.00	45.00	190.00

		GOOD	FINE	XF
3	**50 RUPIEN**			
	15.6.1905. Black on blue unpt. Portr. Kaiser Wilhelm II in cavalry uniform at l.			
	a. 2 serial # on face.	50.00	110.00	350.00
	b. 2 serial # each on face and back.	25.00	85.00	250.00

		GOOD	FINE	XF
4	**100 RUPIEN**			
	15.6.1905. Black on green unpt. Portr. Kaiser Wilhelm II in cavalry uniform at ctr.	35.00	100.00	300.00

		GOOD	FINE	XF
5	**500 RUPIEN**			
	2.9.1912. Black on purple unpt. Portr. Kaiser Wilhelm II in admiral's uniform at l.	500.00	1000.	1800.

1915-17 EMERGENCY WWI ISSUES
Many varieties of sign., serial #, wmk., eagle types and letters.
#23-28 w/ovpt: *W, X* or *Z* dateline or letterhead notes.
#38-49 serial # and sign. varieties.
#26B Deleted. See #24A. #26C Deleted. See #25A.

		VG	VF	UNC
6	**1 RUPIE**			
	1.9.1915. Blue-gray paper. Letter A.	4.00	8.00	16.00
7	**1 RUPIE**			
	1.11.1915. Blue-gray paper. Letter A on back. W/text: *Gebucht von* below date at l.			
	a. W/bank handstamp.	5.00	10.00	25.00
	b. W/o bank handstamp.	2.00	5.00	10.00

		VG	VF	UNC
8	**1 RUPIE**			
	1.11.1915. Lt. green paper. Letter B W/o text: *Gebucht von.*	2.00	8.00	15.00

9 **1 RUPIE**
1.11.1915. W/text: *Kraft besonderer Ermächtigung* below date at l.
Both sign. handwritten.

		VG	VF	UNC
a.	Lt. green paper. Letter B.	.50	2.00	5.00
b.	Gray-brown paper. Letters B; C.	1.00	3.00	7.00
c.	Gray-brown paper. Letter P, E2, F2.	10.00	25.00	60.00

9A **1 RUPIE**
1.11.1915. W/text:*Kraft besonderer Ermächtigung* below date at l.
Stamped sign. at r.

		VG	VF	UNC
a.	Gray-brown paper. Letter B, C.	5.00	10.00	25.00
b.	Gray-white paper. Letters P, Q (2 diff. types), R, S, T, U, V, Y, A2, B2, C2, D2, E2, F2.	.50	1.50	4.00

10 **1 RUPIE**
1.11.1915. w/text: *Kraft besonderer Ermächtigung* below sign. at l.
Stamped sign. at r.

		VG	VF	UNC
a.	Gray-brown paper. Letter C.	.50	2.00	5.00
b.	Thick olive-brown paper. Letter D.	.50	2.00	6.00
c.	Thick gray paper. Letter D.	.50	1.50	4.00

11 **1 RUPIE**
1.11.1915. *Gez.: A Frühling* printed at r.

		VG	VF	UNC
a.	Thick gray paper. Letter E.	.50	1.50	4.00
b.	Thin gray-white paper. Letters E; F; G.	.50	1.00	3.00

12 **1 RUPIE**
1.11.1915. *A. Frühling (w/o gez.)* printed at r.

		VG	VF	UNC
a.	W/o wmk. Letter H.	.50	1.00	3.00
b.	W/wmk. Letter H.	.50	1.00	3.00
c.	Wmk: Meander stripe. Letters H; P.	2.00	5.00	10.00

13 **1 RUPIE**
1.12.1915. W/text: *Gebucht von* below date at l. Letter H.   1.00   3.00   7.00

14 **1 RUPIE**
1.12.1915. W/o text: *Gebucht von.* Letters H; J.   2.50   6.00   12.00

15 **1 RUPIE**
1.12.1915. W/text: *Kraft besonderer Ermächtigung* below date at l.,
gez. A. Frühling printed at r.

		VG	VF	UNC
a.	Red-brown paper. Letter J.	.50	2.00	5.00
b.	Gray-brown paper. Letters J; K (3 different positions).	.50	2.00	5.00

16 **1 RUPIE**
1.12.1915. W/text: *Kraft besonderer Ermächtigung* below date at l. *A. Frühling (w/o gez.)* printed at r.

		VG	VF	UNC
a.	Gray-brown paper. Letter K (3 different positions).	.50	2.00	5.00
b.	Dk. brown wrapping paper. Letters K; L.	.50	2.00	5.00

17 **1 RUPIE**
1.12.1915. W/text: *Kraft besonderer Ermächtigung* below date at l.,
stamped sign. at r. Letter L.   VG 1.00   VF 3.00   UNC 7.00

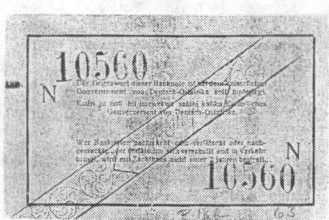

18 **1 RUPIE**
1.2.1916. W/o text: *Gebucht von* at l., eagle on face 20mm high.

		VG	VF	UNC
a.	Brown transparent oil paper. Letters L; M; N.	.50	2.00	5.00
ax.	Error, w/o sign. Letter L.	4.00	10.00	30.00
b.	Thick gray-brown paper. Letter N.	5.00	15.00	50.00

19 **1 RUPIE**
1.2.1916. W/text: *Gebucht von* at l., eagle on face 15mm high; frame
at upper l. has 7 stars and at upper r. 14 stars. Black printing. Letters
F2; G2; H2; J2; K2; L2; M2; N2; O2; P2; Q2; R2; S2; T2; U2; V2; W2;
X2; Y2; Z2; A3; B3; C3; D3; E3; F3; G3.   VG .30   VF .80   UNC 1.50

20 **1 RUPIE**
1.2.1916. W/text: *Gebucht von* at l., eagle on face 15mm high; frame
at upper l. has 6 stars and at upper r. 13 stars. Black printing.

		VG	VF	UNC
a.	Letters G3; H3; J3; K3; L3; M3; N3; O3; P3; Q3 (4 different types); R3; S3; T3; U3; V3.	.30	.80	1.50
b.	Square lined paper. Letter Q3 (4 different types).	1.00	3.00	7.00
x.	Error: 3 instead of N3.	4.00	8.00	—
y.	Error w/o sign. (V).	3.00	6.00	—
z.	Error w/word on back: *Kaiserl chen* w/letter "i" dropped out.	4.00	8.00	—

21 **1 RUPIE**
1.2.1916. Like #19 but blue and blue-green printing. Letter A4.   .50   1.00   2.00

22 **1 RUPIE**
1.7.1917. Printed w/rubber type (so-called "bush notes"). Eagle stamp
on back in different sizes.

		VG	VF	UNC
a.	Eagle on back 15mm high. Letters EP.	2.00	5.00	10.00
b.	Eagle on back 23mm high. Letters EP.	.50	1.50	4.00
c.	Letters ER.	1.00	3.00	7.00
cx.	Error w/letters EP on face, ER on back.	—	Rare	—
d.	Eagle on back 15mm high. Letters FP.	4.00	8.00	20.00
dx.	Error w/back inverted.	4.00	8.00	20.00
e.	Eagle on back 19mm high. Letters FP.	4.00	8.00	20.00
ex.	Error w/back inverted.	4.00	8.00	20.00
f.	Letters IP.	5.00	10.00	35.00

23 **1 RUPIE**
ND. #15b (J) and #18a (N) on back w/lg. violet stamp: *W* over original
letter.   10.00   25.00   50.00

24 **1 RUPIE**
ND. #10f (Q, V, Y) on back w/violet stamp: *X* over original letter, 1
serial # crossed out and 2 new serial # added.   7.50   15.00   30.00

24A
(26B) **1 RUPIE**
ND. Violet. Handstamp: *Z* on back over original letter, 1 serial #
crossed out and 2 new serial # added. The following notes are known
with stamp: 10 (P, Q, R, S, T, U, V); 18 (N); 19 (N2, O2, P2, Q2, R2,
A3).   5.00   10.00   35.00

25 1 RUPIE
ND. Stamp: *X* as on #24 but 2 serial # crossed out and 2 new serial # added. The following notes are known: 7b (A); 8 (B); 10f (T, V, Y, A2, B2, C2, D2); 11a (E); 18a (M); 19 (X2, B3, C3).

VG	VF	UNC
2.50	5.00	10.00

25A 1 RUPIE
(26C)
ND. Violet. Handstamp: *Z* 2 serial #'s crossed out and 2 serial # added. The following notes are known with stamp: 10 (P, Q, R, T, U,V); 18 (L, M, N); 19 (F2, N2, O2, P2, R2, S2, T2, X2, Z2, A3).

VG	VF	UNC
2.00	4.00	10.00

26 1 RUPIE
ND. Stamp: *X* as on #24 but w/o change of serial #. The following notes are known: 8 (B); 10d (P, Q. R. T, U, Y, B2, C2, E2, F2); 11b (F, G); 12a (H); 14 (J); 16b (K, L); 17 (L); 18a (M, N); 19 (H2, L2, O2, Q2, S2, V2, W2, Y2, A3, B3, C3, D3, E3, F3, G3); 20 (G3, H3, J3, K3, L3, M3, N3, O3, P3, Q3, R3, S3, T3, U3, V3); 21 (A4).

VG	VF	UNC
15.00	30.00	60.00

26A 1 RUPIE
ND. Violet. Handstamp *Z* over original letter w/o change of serial #. The following notes are known with stamp: 10 (C, S, U); 11 (E, F, G); 12 (H); 14 (H); 15 (J); 16 (K); 17 (L); 18 (M, N); 19 (J2, M2, N2, R2, S2, U2).

VG	VF	UNC
2.00	4.00	10.00

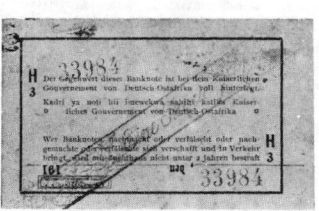

27 1 RUPIE
ND. Date (from stationery used as printing paper); 5 different dateline types exist.

	VG	VF	UNC
a. Dateline on back of the following notes: 19 (F3, G3); 20 (H3, J3, K3, L3, M3, N3, O3, P3, Q3, R3, S3, T3, U3, V3).	4.00	8.00	20.00
b. Dateline on back of the following notes: 22a (EP); 22b (EP); 22c (ER); 22e (FP); 22f (IP); 26 (M3, V3).	4.00	8.00	20.00
c. Dateline on front of the following notes: 22b (EP); 22c (ER).	10.00	25.00	50.00

28 1 RUPIE
ND. Letterhead on back (from stationery used as printing paper), so-called "letterhead notes". 14 different types of letterheads exist on the following notes: 22a (EP); 22b (EP); 22c (ER); 22d (FP); 22e (FP); 22f (IP).

VG	VF	UNC
50.00	80.00	160.00

29 5 RUPIEN
15.8.1915. Value in letters only, both sign. handwritten. W/o series letter.

VG	VF	UNC
3.00	6.00	15.00

30 5 RUPIEN
15.8.1915. Like #29 but sign. at r. facsimile stamped. W/o series letter.

VG	VF	UNC
12.50	25.00	50.00

31 5 RUPIEN
15.8.1915. Value in letters and #, both sign. handwritten. Series letters B (2 varieties); C.

VG	VF	UNC
3.00	6.00	15.00

32 5 RUPIEN
15.8.1915. Like #31 but sign. at r. facsimile stamped. Letter C.

3.00	6.00	15.00

33 5 RUPIEN
1.11.1915. *Daressalam/Tabora* in 2 lines. Letter D.

3.00	6.00	15.00

34 5 RUPIEN
1.11.1915. *Daressalam/Tabora* in 1 line, w/text: *Kraft besonderer Ermächtigung* at lower I. Sign. at l. handwritten.

	VG	VF	UNC
a. Gray-green cardboard w/blue fibres. Letters D; E.	3.00	6.00	15.00
b. Gray-green cardboard w/blue fibres (darker than #34a) and impressed jute texture. Letters D; E.	3.00	6.00	15.00
c. Gray-green cardboard w/o blue fibres. Letter E.	3.00	6.00	15.00
d. Dk. green cardboard w/o impressed jute texture. Letters E; F.	3.00	6.00	15.00

35 5 RUPIEN
1.11.1915. Like #34 but both sign. facsimile stamped. Letters E; F.

	VG	VF	UNC
	3.00	6.00	15.00

36 5 RUPIEN
1.2.1916. *Gebucht von* below date at I.

	VG	VF	UNC
a. Stiff gray-blue cardboard. Letter F.	3.00	6.00	15.00
b. Soft dk. blue cardboard. Letters F; G.	3.00	6.00	15.00
c. Stiff dk. gray cardboard. Letter F.	3.50	7.00	17.50
d. Green cardboard. Letters G; F.	3.50	7.00	20.00
e. Green paper. Letters G; H.	3.50	7.00	20.00
f. Letter X/F, new serial #. Dk. blue.	—	Rare	—

37 5 RUPIEN
1.7.1917. Printed w/rubber type, (so-called "bush notes").

	VG	VF	UNC
a. Value 5 3.5mm high.	15.00	30.00	60.00
b. Value 5 5mm high.	12.00	22.50	45.00

38 10 RUPIEN
1.10.1915. Dk. brown cardboard.

	VG	VF	UNC
a. W/o serial letter.	5.00	10.00	20.00
b. Handwritten B.	10.00	20.00	40.00

39 10 RUPIEN
1.10.1915. Like #38 but w/violet stamp: *Z* on back.

VG	VF	UNC
10.00	20.00	40.00

40 10 RUPIEN
1.2.1916. Dk. brown cardborad W/o letter or w/B. *DOAB* in ornamental letters on top r. and bottom l.

10.00	20.00	40.00

	47	**50 RUPIEN**	VG	VF	UNC
		1.10.1917. Printed w/rubber type, (so-called "bush notes").			
		a. W/sign., back printed.	125.00	250.00	450.00
		b. W/o sign. Back black. (Not issued).	75.00	150.00	300.00
	48	**200 RUPIEN**			
		15.4.1915. W/o wmk.	65.00	150.00	300.00

	41	**10 RUPIEN**	VG	VF	UNC
		1.6.1916. Yellow-brown paper. Letter B.	7.50	12.50	25.00
	42	**10 RUPIEN**			
		1.6.1916. Like #41 but violet stamp: X over B on back.	10.00	20.00	40.00
	43	**10 RUPIEN**			
		1.7.1917. Printed w/rubber type, (so-called "bush notes").			
		a. Value 3mm high and 4mm wide.	9.00	17.50	35.00
		b. Value 5mm high and 4-5mm wide.	9.00	17.50	35.00
		c. Value 5mm high and 7mm wide.	9.00	17.50	35.00
	44	**20 RUPIEN**			
		15.3.1915. White cardboard.			
		a. Both sign. handwritten. Serial # on face handwritten.	12.50	25.00	50.00
		b. British forgery on thick cardboard. Serial # on face and back mis-matched.	100.00	200.00	400.00

	49	**200 RUPIEN**	VG	VF	UNC
		15.6.1915. Wmk: Wavy lines.	60.00	135.00	285.00

	45	**20 RUPIEN**	VG	VF	UNC
		15.3.1915. Lilac cardboard. Both sign. handwritten. Serial # on back only.	12.50	17.50	35.00

	46	**50 RUPIEN**	VG	VF	UNC
		1.10.1915.			
		a. Soft gray cardboard.	15.00	25.00	70.00
		b. Stiff brown cardboard.	20.00	40.00	80.00

German New Guinea (also known as Neu Guinea or Kaiser Wilhelmsland, and now part of Papua New Guinea) includes the northeast corner of the island of New Guinea, the islands of the Bismarck Archipelago, Bougainville and Buka Islands, and about 600 small offshore islands. Bounded on the west coast by West Irian, to the north and east by the Pacific Ocean and to the south by Papua, it has an area of 92,159 sq. mi. (238,692 sq. km.) and, under German administration, had a population of about 250,000. Capital: Herbertshohe, later moved to Rabaul. Copra was the chief export.

Germany took formal possession of German New Guinea in 1884. It was administered by the German New Guinea Company until 1899, when control was assumed by the German imperial government. On the outbreak of World War I in 1914, Australia occupied the territory and it remained under military control until 1921, when it became an Australian mandate of the League of Nations. During World War II, between 1942 and 1945, the territory was occupied by Japan. Following the Japanese surrender, it was administered by Australia under the United Nations trusteeship system. In 1949, Papua and New Guinea were combined as one administrative unit known as Papua New Guinea, which attained internal autonomy on Dec. 1, 1973. Papua New Guinea achieved full independence on Sept. 16, 1975.

German Reichsbanknoten and Reichskassenscheine circulated until 1914.

RULERS:
German, 1884-1914
Australian, 1914-1942, 1945-1975
Japanese, 1942-1945

MONETARY SYSTEM:
1 Mark = 100 Pfennig

AUSTRALIAN OCCUPATION - WWI

TREASURY NOTES

1914-15 ISSUE
#1-5 w/o pictorial design, w/text: *Payable in coin at the Treasury, Rabaul.*

1	5 MARKS	VG	VF	UNC
	1914-15.			
	a. 14.10.1914.	—	Rare	—
	b. Pen *cancelled* 1.1.1915.	—	Rare	—

2	10 MARKS			
	1914-15.			
	a. 14.10.1914.	—	Rare	—
	b. Pen *cancelled* 1.1.1915.	—	Rare	—
3	20 MARKS			
	1914.			
	a. 1914.	—	Rare	—
	b. Pen *cancelled* 1.1.1915.	—	Rare	—

4	50 MARKS	VG	VF	UNC
	1914.			
	a. 16.10.1914.	3500.	7500.	—
	b. Pen *cancelled* 1.1.1915.	—	Rare	—

5	100 MARKS	VG	VF	UNC
	5.11.1914.	—	Rare	—

German South West Africa (Deutsch-Sudwestafrika) is a former German territory situated on the Atlantic coast of southern Africa. The colony had an area of 318,261 sq. mi. (824,293 sq. km.). Capital: Windhoek.

The first Europeans to land on the shores of the area were 15th-century Portuguese navigators. The interior, however, was not explored until the middle of the 18th century. Great Britain annexed the Walvis Bay area in 1878; it was incorporated into the Cape of Good Hope in 1884. The rest of the coastal area was annexed by Germany in 1885. South African forces occupied German South West Africa during World War I. South Africa received it as a League of Nations mandate on Dec. 17, 1920.

South Africa's mandate was terminated by the United Nations on Oct. 27, 1966. In June 1968 the UN General Assembly voted to rename the country Namibia. South Africa found both actions unacceptable, and the status of the territory remains in dispute.

German Reichsbanknoten and Reichskassenscheine circulated until 1914.

RULERS:
German to 1914

MONETARY SYSTEM:
1 Mark = 100 Pfennig

GERMAN INFLUENCE

KAISERLICHE GOUVERNEMENT KASSENSCHEINE

1914 ISSUE

NOTE: So-called "Seitz notes", named after the governor whose sign. is printed on some of the notes.

		GOOD	FINE	XF
1	**5 MARK**			
	8.8.1914. Green.			
	a. Issued note.	65.00	200.00	500.00
	b. Cancelled.	50.00	150.00	300.00

		GOOD	FINE	XF
2	**10 MARK**			
	8.8.1914. Red-brown.			
	a. Issued note.	65.00	200.00	500.00
	b. Cancelled.	50.00	150.00	300.00
3	**20 MARK**			
	8.8.1914. Brown-violet.			
	a. Issued note.	65.00	200.00	525.00
	b. Cancelled.	50.00	150.00	350.00
4	**50 MARK**			
	8.8.1914. Red.			
	a. Issued note.	90.00	275.00	575.00
	b. Cancelled.	65.00	200.00	400.00

		GOOD	FINE	XF
5	**100 MARK**			
	8.8.1914. Blue.			
	a. Issued note.	125.00	400.00	950.00
	b. Cancelled.	100.00	300.00	700.00

SWAKOPMUNDER BUCHHANDLUNG

These notes were issued by order of the Windhoek Chamber of Commerce and used for payment by the authorities and public institutions (police, post office, railroad, etc.) These notes circulated all over the colony.

1915-18 ISSUE

		GOOD	FINE	XF
6	**10 PFENNIG**			
	ND (1916-18). Green linen. Value: *Zehn Pfg.*; w/o *NUMMER* at upper r.			
	a. 1 sign.	16.50	50.00	135.00
	b. 2 sign.	11.50	35.00	100.00

		GOOD	FINE	XF
7	**10 PFENNIG**			
	ND (1916-18). Green linen. Value: *10 Pfennig; NUMMER* at upper r. W/ or w/o letter *B*.	11.50	35.00	100.00

		GOOD	FINE	XF
8	**25 PFENNIG**			
	ND (1916-18). Pale blue or white paper (cloth fabric between paper layers). Red-brown text, green value (diagonal). W/o *NUMMER* at upper r.			
	a. Rounded corners. 2 handwritten sign.	11.50	35.00	100.00
	b. Square corners. 1 facsimile sign.	13.00	40.00	100.00
9	**25 PFENNIG**			
	ND (1916-18). Pale blue paper (cloth fabric between paper layers). Red-brown text, black value on green unpt. *NUMMER* at upper r.	35.00	100.00	250.00
10	**50 PFENNIG**			
	ND (1916-18). Blue on lt. blue linen. Value: *Funfzig Pfg;* w/o *NUMMER* at upper r.			
	a. Rounded corners. 2 handwritten sign.	18.50	57.50	170.00
	b. Square corners. 1 facsimile sign.	21.00	63.50	190.00

		GOOD	FINE	XF
11	**50 PFENNIG**			
	ND (1916-18). Blue-green on white linen. Value: *0,50 Mark; NUMMER* at upper r. (2 varieties of *M* in Mark; w/ or w/o period after Mark).	13.00	40.00	125.00
12	**1 MARK**			
	ND (1916-18). Yellowish cardboard. Black text on green unpt. W/o *NUMMER* at upper r. 2 sign. varieties.	13.00	40.00	125.00
13	**1 MARK**			
	ND (1916-18). Lt. green cardboard. Black and red-brown on dk. green unpt. *NUMMER* at upper l.	13.00	40.00	125.00

		GOOD	FINE	XF
14	**1 MARK**			
	ND (1916-18). Rose linen. Red-brown unpt. extending over entire note. *Ausgabe B* at upper r.	11.50	35.00	100.00
15	**2 MARK**			
	ND (1916-18). Black and salmon text. Value: *Zwei;* w/o *NUMMER* at r. 1 or 2 sign.			
	a. Rose colored cardboard w/impressed linen texture.	35.00	90.00	225.00
	b. Yellowish cardboard w/impressed linen texture.	35.00	90.00	225.00
16	**2 MARK**			
	ND (1916-18). Brown. Value: *2; NUMMER* at upper r. (2 varieties of *M* in *Mark*).			
	a. Lt. gray cardboard w/impressed linen texture.	21.00	63.50	190.00
	b. Lt. brown cardboard w/impressed linen texture.	30.00	90.00	225.00

		GOOD	FINE	XF
17	**3 MARK**			
	ND (1916-18). Green unpt. Lt. green cardboard w/linen texture. W/o *NUMMER* at upper r.	32.50	100.00	275.00
18	**3 MARK**			
	ND (1916-18). Brown unpt. Lt. brown cardboard. *NUMMER* at upper r. (2 varieties of *M* in *Mark*).	36.50	110.00	300.00

GERMANY

Germany, a nation of north-central Europe which from 1871 to 1945 was, successively, an empire, a republic and a totalitarian state, attained its territorial peak as an empire when it comprised a 208,780 sq. mi. (540,740 sq. km.) homeland and an overseas colonial empire.

As the power of the Roman Empire waned, several warlike tribes residing in northern Germany moved south and west, invading France, Belgium, England, Italy and Spain. In 800 AD the Frankish King Charlemagne, who ruled most of France and Germany, was crowned Emperor of the Holy Roman Empire, a loose federation of an estimated 1,800 German States that lasted until 1806. Modern Germany was formed from the eastern part of Charlemagne's empire.

After 1812, the German States were reduced to a federation of 32, of which Prussia was the strongest. In 1871, Prussian Chancellor Otto Von Bismarck united the German States into an empire ruled by Wilhelm I, the Prussian king. The empire initiated a colonial endeavor and became one of the world's greatest powers. Germany disintegrated as a result of World War I, and was reestablished as the Weimar Republic. The humiliation of defeat, economic depression, poverty and discontent gave rise to Adolf Hitler, 1933, who reconstituted Germany as the Third Reich and after initial diplomatic and military triumphs, led it to disaster in World War II. East Germany and West Germany were established in 1949.

For subsequent history, see German Federal Republic and German Democratic Republic.

RULERS:
Wilhelm I, 1871-1888
Friedrich III, 1888
Wilhelm II, 1888-1918

MONETARY SYSTEM:
1 Mark = 100 Pfennig to 1923
1000 Milliarden Mark = 1 Rentenmark = 100 Rentenpfennig, 1923-1924
1 Rentenmark = 1 Reichsmark = 100 Reichspfennig, 1924-1948
1 AMC Mark = 100 AMC Pfennig, 1945-1948
1 Million = 1,000,000
10 Millionen = 10,000,000
1 Milliarde = 1,000,000,000 (English 1 Billion)
10 Milliarden = 10,000,000,000
1 Billion = 1,000,000,000,000 (English 1 Trillion)
10 Billionen = 10,000,000,000,000

WATERMARK VARIETIES

A. Wavy lines Diagonally - Congruent

B. Pattern of triangles with concave sides within circles

C. 6-pointed stars within rounded triangle pattern

D. Small crucifera blossoms

E. G, D within 6-pointed stars and Z's

F. Greek pattern

G. Lattice

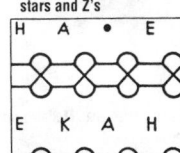

H. Knotted rope and EKAHA

I. Thorns

J. Horizontally opposed wavy lines

K. Diamonds in maze

L. Small circles

M. S in 6-pointed stars within clouds

N. Diamond pattern

O. Tuning fork H's pattern

P. HUDS-in circular pattern

Q. RSV-Linear pattern

R. Contoured chain pattern

S. Straight chain pattern

NOTE: The above wmks. are from "Papiergeld-Spezialkatalog Deutschland. 1874–1980" by Pick/Rixen (published by Battenburg Verlag. Munich).

EMPIRE
REICHSKASSENSCHEINE
IMPERIAL TREASURY NOTES

1874 ISSUE

		GOOD	FINE	XF
1	**5 MARK** 11.7.1874. Dk. blue and gray-blue. 2 children seated at lower ctr. w/arms between them.	350.00	700.00	2500.

		GOOD	FINE	XF
2	**20 MARK** 11.7.1874. Green and yellow. Allegorical man wearing shirt w/arms and holding a staff w/arms at l. ctr.	1350.	3500.	7500.
3	**50 MARK** 11.7.1874. Dk. violet, brown and dk. green. 2 allegorical figures at ctr., arms at each corner.	1200.	2500.	6000.

1882 ISSUE

	5 MARK	GOOD	FINE	XF
4	10.1.1882. Dk. blue. Knight in armor w/shield of arms at r.	40.00	350.00	550.00

	20 MARK	GOOD	FINE	XF
5	10.1.1882. Green. 2 small boys w/fruit at l. and r.	600.00	1500.	5000.
6	**50 MARK**			
	10.1.1882. Dk. brown. Allegorical winged figure at r.	1500.	2700.	5500.

1899 ISSUE

	50 MARK	GOOD	FINE	XF
7	5.1.1899. Dk. green and brown-olive. Germania seated at l.	1500.	2500.	4200.

1904-06 ISSUE

	5 MARK	GOOD	FINE	XF
8	31.10.1904. Blue and blue-green. Germania w/child and dove at l. Dragon on back.			
	a. 6 digit serial #.	.50	3.50	14.00
	b. 7 digit serial #.	.50	2.00	12.00

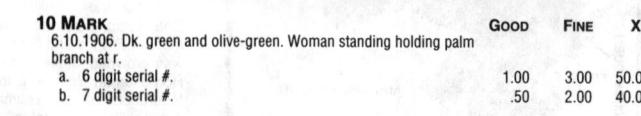

	10 MARK	GOOD	FINE	XF
9	6.10.1906. Dk. green and olive-green. Woman standing holding palm branch at r.			
	a. 6 digit serial #.	1.00	3.00	50.00
	b. 7 digit serial #.	.50	2.00	40.00

REICHSBANKNOTEN

IMPERIAL BANK NOTES

1876 ISSUE

	100 MARK	GOOD	FINE	XF
10	1.1.1876. Dk. blue and gray-blue. Arms at l., Minerva in wreath at r.	3000.	5500.	12,000.

	1000 MARK	GOOD	FINE	XF
11	1.1.1876. Brown. Arms at l. Woman w/small angels on back. Specimen. (Not issued).	—	—	15,000.

1883-84 ISSUE

	100 MARK	GOOD	FINE	XF
12	3.9.1883. Dk. blue on lt. blue unpt. 1 red seal. Medallic woman's head supported by 2 women on back.	500.00	850.00	1600.
13	**1000 MARK**			
	2.1.1884. Brown. 1 red seal. Allegorical figures of 2 women (Navigation and Agriculture) on back.	900.00	1500.	3000.

1891 FIRST ISSUE

	1000 MARK			
14	1.1.1891. Brown. Like #13. 1 red seal.	600.00	900.00	1700.

1891 SECOND ISSUE

	100 MARK			
15	1.5.1891. Blue. Like #12. 1 red seal.	300.00	600.00	1250.

1895 ISSUE

			GOOD	FINE	XF
16	**100 MARK**				
	1.3.1895. Blue. Like #12.				
	a. Issued note. 2 red seals.		300.00	600.00	1200.
	s. Specimen. 1 red seal.		—	—	—
17	**1000 MARK**				
	1.3.1895. Brown. Like #13. 2 red seals.		1100.	1800.	3500.

1896 ISSUE

18	**100 MARK**				
	10.4.1896. Blue. Like #12. 2 red seals.		100.00	225.00	450.00

			GOOD	FINE	XF
19	**1000 MARK**				
	10.4.1896. Brown. Like #17. 2 red seals.		225.00	425.00	850.00

1898 ISSUE

20	**100 MARK**				
	1.7.1898. Blue. Like #16. 2 seals.				
	a. Issued note.		1.50	5.00	60.00
	b. W/ovpt: *Im Ausland ungiltig, nur zahlbar bei der Staatsbenk Munchen.*				
21	**1000 MARK**				
	1.7.1898. Brown. Like #17. 2 seals.		5.00	25.00	175.00

1903 ISSUE

			VG	VF	UNC
22	**100 MARK**				
	17.4.1903. Blue. Like #16. 2 seals.		.75	9.50	60.00
23	**1000 MARK**				
	10.10.1903. Brown. Like #17. 2 seals.		3.00	15.00	120.00

1905 ISSUE

24	**100 MARK**				
	18.12.1905. Blue. Like #16. 2 seals.				
	a. 24mm serial #.		.50	1.50	35.00
	b. 29mm serial #.		.50	1.50	35.00

1906 ISSUE

			VG	VF	UNC
25	**20 MARK**				
	10.3.1906. Blue. Eagle at upper r. Back red and blue.				
	a. 6 digit serial #.		.25	10.00	35.00
	b. 7 digit serial #.		.25	10.00	35.00

			VG	VF	UNC
26	**50 MARK**				
	10.3.1906. Green on pink unpt. Germania at upper l. and r.				
	a. 6 digit serial #.		.25	8.00	25.00
	b. 7 digit serial #.		.25	8.00	25.00
27	**1000 MARK**		VG	VF	UNC
	26.7.1906. Brown. Like #17.		5.00	45.00	100.00

1907 ISSUE

28	**20 MARK**				
	8.6.1907. Blue. Like #25.		.25	3.00	30.00
29	**50 MARK**				
	8.6.1907. Green. Like #26b.		40.00	125.00	400.00
30	**100 MARK**				
	8.6.1907. Blue. Like #16.		1.00	7.00	50.00

1908 ISSUE

31	**20 MARK**				
	7.2.1908. Blue. Like #25b.		.25	4.00	45.00
32	**50 MARK**				
	7.2.1908. Green. Like #26b.		.25	1.50	35.00

			VG	VF	UNC
33	**100 MARK**				
	7.2.1908. Dk. blue on lt. blue unpt. Like #16.				
	a. Red serial # and seal, serial # 29mm long.		.25	.50	4.00
	b. Serial # 24mm long.		.50	12.00	150.00

34	**100 MARK**				
	7.2.1908. Dk. blue on lt. blue unpt. Like #16 but green serial # and seal (reprint 1918-22).		.25	.50	6.00
35	**100 MARK**				
	7.2.1908. Blue. Mercury at l., Ceres at r. Germania seated w/shield and sword on back. Wmk: Wilhelm I and *100*. 207 x 102mm.		.50	3.00	60.00
36	**1000 MARK**				
	7.2.1908. Brown. Like #17.		3.00	15.00	100.00

1909 ISSUE

37	**20 MARK**				
	10.9.1909. Blue. Like #25b.		.25	1.50	30.00

			VG	VF	UNC
38	**100 MARK**		.50	3.00	60.00
	10.9.1909. Blue. Like #35.				
39	**1000 MARK**		2.00	8.00	120.00
	10.9.1909. Brown. Like #17.				

1910 ISSUE

			VG	VF	UNC
40	**20 MARK**				
	a. W/o wmk. 6 digit serial #.		.50	1.50	12.50
	b. W/o wmk. 7 digit serial #.		.25	1.00	10.00
	c. Wmk: *20 Mark*.		1.00	6.00	50.00

			VG	VF	UNC
41	**50 MARK**		.25	1.50	20.00
	21.4.1910. Green. Like #26b.				

			VG	VF	UNC
42	**100 MARK**		.25	1.00	8.50
	21.4.1910. Dk. blue on lt. blue-gray unpt. Like #35 but red serial # and seal.				
43	**100 MARK**		.25	1.00	10.00
	21.4.1910. Dk. blue on lt. blue unpt. Like #35 but green serial # and seal.				
44	**100 MARK**				
	21.4.1910. Brown. Like #17 but red serial # and seal.				
	a. 6 digit serial # (until 1916).		.25	3.00	50.00
	b. 7 digit serial #.		.25	.50	1.00

			VG	VF	UNC
45	**1000 MARK**				
	21.4.1910. Dk. brown on tan unpt. Like #17 but green serial # and seal.				
	a. 6 digit serial #.		1.00	5.00	40.00
	b. 7 digit serial #.		.25	.50	2.00

1914 ISSUE

			VG	VF	UNC
46	**20 MARK**				
	19.2.1914. Like #25.				
	a. 6 digit serial #.		.50	2.00	50.00
	b. 7 digit serial #.		.25	.50	7.00

DARLEHENSKASSENSCHEINE

STATE LOAN CURRENCY NOTES

1914 FIRST ISSUE

			VG	VF	UNC
47	**5 MARK**				
	5.8.1914. Black on gray-violet unpt. Germania at l. and r. on blue back.				
	a. 6 digit serial #.		1.00	5.00	150.00
	b. 7 digit serial #.		.25	.50	35.00
	c. 8 digit serial #.		.25	.50	35.00

48	**20 MARK**	VG	VF	UNC
	5.8.1914. Dk. brown on brown and lilac unpt. Minerva at l., Mercury at r. on brown back.			
	a. 6 digit serial #.	.25	5.00	175.00
	b. 7 digit serial #.	.25	3.00	150.00

49	**50 MARK**	VG	VF	UNC
	5.8.1914. Black and lilac-red on gray unpt. Germania at l. and r. on green back.			
	a. 6 digit serial #.	.25	3.00	175.00
	b. 7 digit serial #.	.25	3.00	25.00

1914 SECOND ISSUE

50	**1 MARK**	VG	VF	UNC
	12.8.1914. Black on lt. green and lilac unpt. Red serial # and seal. White paper. Back green w/o unpt.	.20	.50	2.50

51	**1 MARK**	VG	VF	UNC
	12.8.1914. Black on lt. green and lilac unpt. LIke #50 but lt. brown pattern over entire note. Back w/green unpt.	.20	.50	2.50
52	**1 MARK**			
	12.8.1914. Like #51 but blue serial # and seal.	.20	.50	2.50

53	**2 MARK**	VG	VF	UNC
	12.8.1914. Black on red unpt. Red serial # and seal. White paper. Back red w/o unpt.	.25	.50	2.50
54	**2 MARK**			
	12.8.1914. Black on red unpt. Like #53 but lt. red pattern over entire note. Back w/lt. red unpt.	.25	.50	2.50
55	**2 MARK**			
	12.8.1914. Like #54 but blue serial # and seal.	.25	.50	2.50

1917-18 ISSUE

NOTE: Spelling of heading changed to *Darlehnskassenschein* from 1917 onwards.

56	**5 MARK**	VG	VF	UNC
	1.8.1917. Black and purplish blue. Girl at upper r. Back black on green and blue unpt.			
	a. 7 digit serial #.	.20	1.50	6.50
	b. 8 digit serial #.	.20	1.50	5.00

57	**20 MARK**	VG	VF	UNC
	20.2.1918. Dk. brown on carmine unpt. Minerva at l., Mercury at r. Back brown. Man in armor at l., allegorical woman at r.	.25	2.00	13.00

1920 ISSUES

58	**1 MARK**	VG	VF	UNC
	1.3.1920. Dk. brown on green and olive unpt. Back dk. green.	.10	.25	1.00

59	**2 MARK**	VG	VF	UNC
	1.3.1920. Red on lt. brown unpt. Brown serial # and seal. Back red-brown.	.10	.25	1.00
60	**2 MARK**			
	1.3.1920. Dk. brown on blue and lt. brown unpt. Red serial # and seal. Back darker red-brown.	.10	.25	1.00

1922 ISSUE

61	**1 MARK**	VG	VF	UNC
	15.9.1922. Dk. green on lt. green unpt.			
	a. Lt. green paper.	.10	.25	1.00
	b. Gray paper.	5.00	12.00	40.00
62	**2 MARK**	VG	VF	UNC
	15.9.1922. Brown on pink unpt.	.10	.25	1.00

REICHSBANKNOTEN (RESUMED)

IMPERIAL BANK NOTES

NOTE ON VARIETIES: There are many differences in serial #, sheet mark letters and paper among the inflation period notes in addition to the wmk. varieties quoted.

1915-19 ISSUE

		VG	VF	UNC
63	**20 MARK**	.25	2.00	7.50
	4.11.1915. Dk. blue on lt. blue unpt. 2 men w/cornucopias filled w/money at upper ctr. Man and woman on back.			

		VG	VF	UNC
64	**50 MARK**			
	20.10.1918. Dk. brown on gray-violet unpt. Green guilloche at l. Dk. line margin (known as the "Mourning Note").			
	a. Wmk: J.	30.00	75.00	225.00
	b. Wmk: A.	27.50	60.00	200.00
	c. Wmk: B.	25.00	55.00	170.00

		VG	VF	UNC
65	**50 MARK**	1.50	9.00	30.00
	30.11.1918. Olive-brown on gray unpt. Broad margin, w/egg-shaped white area on back (known as the "Egg Note").			

		VG	VF	UNC
66	**50 MARK**	.25	2.00	12.00
	24.6.1919. Green on lt. brown unpt. Woman at upper r. Reihe 1-4. Back blue.			

WEIMAR REPUBLIC

REICHSBANKNOTEN

REPUBLIC TREASURY NOTES

1920 ISSUE

		VG	VF	UNC
67	**10 MARK**			
	6.2.1920. Dk. green and black on olive unpt.			
	a. Unpt. letters.	.10	.25	3.00
	b. W/o unpt. letters.	50.00	100.00	250.00

		VG	VF	UNC
68	**50 MARK**	.25	.50	12.00
	23.7.1920. Dk. green and green. Woman w/flowers and fruit at r. Farmer and worker on back.			

69   100 MARK
   1.11.1920. Dk. brown w/black text on blue and red unpt. "Bamberg
   Horseman" (in Bamberg Cathedral) at upper l. and r.

		VG	VF	UNC
a.	7 digit serial #.	.15	.25	6.00
b.	8 digit serial #.	.15	.25	4.00

1922 FIRST ISSUE

70   10,000 MARK
   19.1.1922. Blue-green on olive-green unpt. Male portr. at r. by A.
   Durer, like #71. Eagle in rectangular ornament on back.

VG	VF	UNC
.25	.50	6.00

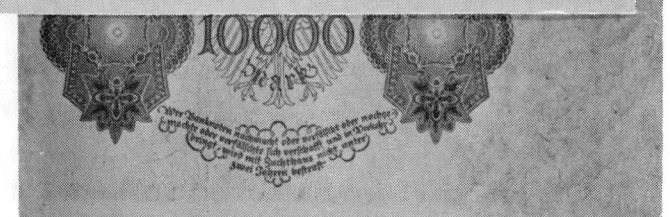

71   10,000 MARK
   19.1.1922. Blue-green on olive-green unpt. Face like #70 but
   monochrome below eagle on back. 210 x 124mm.

VG	VF	UNC
.25	.75	6.00

72   10,000 MARK
   19.1.1922. Blue-green on olive-brown unpt. Like #71, but 180 x
   100mm.

VG	VF	UNC
.20	.40	6.00

1922 SECOND ISSUE

73   500 MARK
   27.3.1922. Dk. blue and olive-green. Portr. J. Mayer at upper r.

VG	VF	UNC
.50	5.00	30.00

74   500 MARK
   7.7.1922. Black. R. margin tinted. Uniface.

		VG	VF	UNC
a.	Red serial # (valid until 1.1.1923).	.50	2.50	150.00
b.	Green 7 digit serial # (valid until 1.4.1923).	.20	.50	4.50
c.	Green 8 digit serial # (valid until 1.4.1923).	—	—	—

1922 THIRD ISSUE

75   100 MARK
   4.8.1922. Black-blue. L. and r. margins tinted.

VG	VF	UNC
.25	2.00	6.00

76	**1000 MARK**	VG	VF	UNC
	15.9.1922. Dk. green on green and lilac unpt.			
	a. Wmk: E. White paper.	.10	.25	1.00
	b. Wmk: L. Yellow paper.	.10	.25	1.00
	c. Wmk: F. White paper.	.10	.25	1.00
	d. Wmk: D. White paper.	.10	.25	1.00
	e. Wmk: G. White paper.	.10	.25	1.00
	f. Wmk: H. White paper.	.10	.25	1.00
	g. Wmk: J. Pale green paper.	.10	.25	1.00
	h. Wmk: K. Pale green paper.	.10	.25	1.00

77	**5000 MARK**	VG	VF	UNC
	16.9.1922. Blue and brown on gray and green unpt. Portr. mintmaster Spinelli at r.	2.00	16.00	100.00
78	**5000 MARK**			
	19.11.1922. Dk. brown on brown unpt. Chamberlain H. Urmiller at l.	1.25	4.00	38.00

79	**50,000 MARK**	VG	VF	UNC
	19.11.1922. Black on white w/green tint at r. Portr. Burgermaster Brauweiler at upper l. by B. Bruyn, w/o unpt.	.50	1.50	8.00
80	**50,000 MARK**			
	19.11.1922. Dk. brown on pink and green. Like #79 but w/unpt.	.50	1.50	8.00

1922 FOURTH ISSUE

81	**5000 MARK**	VG	VF	UNC
	2.12.1922. Brown on green and lt. brown unpt. Portr. merchant Imhof at r. by A. Durer.			
	a. Wmk: G/D in stars, E.	.10	.25	1.50
	b. Wmk: Lattice, G.	.10	.25	1.50
	c. Wmk: Thorns, I.	.10	.25	1.50
	d. Wmk: Greek pattern, F.	.10	.25	1.50
	e. Wmk: Wavy lines, J.	.25	1.00	3.00

1922 FIFTH ISSUE

NOTE: For #82 w/ovpt: *1 MILLARDE*, see #113.

82	**1000 MARK**	VG	VF	UNC
	15.12.1922. Black on dk. brown unpt. Portr. mintmaster J. Herz at upper l. by G. Penz. (Not issued).			
	a. Various styles of serial #, w/o prefix letter A.	—	1.00	8.00
	b. Lg. serial # w/prefix letter A.	—	150.00	400.00

1923 FIRST ISSUE

83	**100,000 MARK**	VG	VF	UNC
	1.2.1923. Dk. brown on lilac w/lilac tint at r. Portr. merchant Gisze at l. by H. Holbein.			
	a. W/o *T* at l. of portr.	2.00	3.50	10.00
	b. *T* at l. of portr.	2.00	3.50	10.00

1923 SECOND ISSUE

84	**10,000 MARK**	VG	VF	UNC
	3.2.1923. Dk. blue on green and red unpt. (Not issued).			
	r. Remainder.	—	250.00	450.00
	s. Specimen ovpt: *MUSTER*.	—	—	250.00

85   20,000 MARK

	VG	VF	UNC
20.2.1923. Blue-black on pink and green unpt.			
a. Wmk: Small circles, L. 2 serial # varieties.	.15	.30	3.00
b. Wmk: *G/D* in stars, E.	.15	.30	3.00
c. Wmk: Lattice, G.	.25	.50	3.00
d. Wmk: Thorns, I.	.25	.75	5.00
e. Wmk: Greek pattern, F.	.25	.75	5.00
f. Wmk: Wavy lines, J.	.25	.75	5.00

86   1 MILLION MARK

	VG	VF	UNC
20.2.1923. Dk. brown on lt. brown and dk. green unpt. Uniface.			
a. Series letters and serial # at l. and r.	.20	1.50	15.00
b. Series leters and serial # at upper l. and upper r.	.20	1.50	15.00

1923 THIRD ISSUE

NOTE: #87 w/ovpt: *500 MILLIARDEN*, see #124.

87   5000 MARK

	VG	VF	UNC
15.3.1923. Dk. brown on olive-brown. Chamberlain H. Urmiller. (Not issued).	—	200.00	400.00

88   500,000 MARK

	VG	VF	UNC
1.5.1923. Dk. green on lilac and green unpt. Portr. man wearing Jacobite cap at l. and r.			
a. Serial # on face and back.	4.00	10.00	48.00
b. Serial # on face only.	4.00	10.00	48.00

89
(90)   2 MILLIONEN MARK

	VG	VF	UNC
23.7.1923. Dk. brown on pink and green unpt. Merchant Gisze at l. and r. by H. Holbein.			
a. Issued note.	4.00	9.00	25.00
b. Error: *MULIONEN*.	25.00	75.00	160.00

90
(89)   5 MILLIONEN MARK

	VG	VF	UNC
1.6.1923. Brown on lilac and green w/yellow tint at r. Portr. woman (Constitutional Medallion) at upper l. ctr.	7.00	20.00	75.00

1923 FOURTH ISSUES

91   100,000 MARK

	VG	VF	UNC
25.7.1923. Black on green unpt. Uniface.			
a. Wmk: *G/D* in stars, E, green paper.	.15	.50	1.25
b. Wmk: Wavy lines, J, white paper.	.15	.50	1.25

92   500,000 MARK

	VG	VF	UNC
25.7.1923. Carmine w/violet tint at r. Uniface.	.25	1.20	5.00

		VG	VF	UNC
93	**1 MILLION MARK** 25.7.1923. Dk. blue on lilac and lt. brown unpt. Denomination field like #85 w/new denomination ovpt. at l. on face. Printed back.	2.00	5.00	30.00

		VG	VF	UNC
94	**1 MILLION MARK** 25.7.1923. Black on white w/yellow tint at r., uniface.	.20	.50	4.50
95	**5 MILLIONEN MARK** 25.7.1923. Black on white w/blue-green tint at l.	.20	1.00	6.00

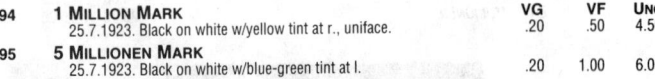

		VG	VF	UNC
96	**10 MILLIONEN MARK** 25.7.1923. Black and dk. green w/yellow tint at r.	.20	.50	3.00

		VG	VF	UNC
97	**20 MILLIONEN MARK** 25.7.1923. Black and lt. blue w/lilac tint at r.			
	a. 7 digit serial #.	.20	.50	3.00
	b. 8 digit serial #.	.20	.50	3.00

		VG	VF	UNC
98	**50 MILLIONEN MARK** 25.7.1923. Black and lilac-brown w/lilac tint at r. Uniface.			
	a. 7 digit serial #.	.20	.50	3.00
	b. 8 digit serial #.	.20	.50	3.00

1923 FIFTH ISSUES

NOTE: There are also notes w/wmk. meander ribbon (good forgery).

		VG	VF	UNC
99	**50,000 MARK** 9.8.1923. Black on lt. brown unpt. Uniface.	.50	1.00	5.00

		VG	VF	UNC
100	**200,000 MARK** 9.8.1923. Black on gray unpt. Uniface.	.20	1.00	5.00

		VG	VF	UNC
101	**1 MILLION MARK** 9.8.1923. Black. White paper, w/green tint at r. Serial # at bottom. Wmk: Oak leaves. Uniface.	.20	.50	2.00

		VG	VF	UNC
102	**1 MILLION MARK** 9.8.1923. Black. Green unpt. panel at r. W/o serial #. Uniface.			
	a. Wmk: *G/D* in stars, E.	.10	.50	2.00
	b. Wmk: Small circles, L.	.15	.50	2.00
	c. Wmk: Lattice, G.	.15	.50	2.00
	d. Wmk: Wavy lines, J.	.20	.75	2.50

		VG	VF	UNC
103	**2 MILLIONEN MARK** 9.8.1923. Black. White paper, w/lilac tint at r. Serial # at bottom. Wmk: Oak leaves. Uniface.	.20	.50	2.00

		VG	VF	UNC
104	**2 MILLIONEN MARK** 9.8.1923. Black. Lilac guilloche at r. W/o serial #. Uniface.			
	a. Wmk: *G/D* in stars, E.	.20	.50	1.50
	b. Wmk: Small circles, L.	.20	.50	1.50
	c. Wmk: Lattice w/*8*, G.	.20	.50	1.50
	d. Wmk: Wavy lines, J.	.20	1.00	3.00

105	**5 MILLIONEN MARK**	VG	VF	UNC
	20.8.1923. Black on gray-green unpt. Pink paper. Uniface.	.50	1.50	5.00

106	**10 MILLIONEN MARK**	VG	VF	UNC
	22.8.1923. Black on pale olive-green and blue-gray unpt. Uniface.			
	a. Wmk: *G/D* in stars, E.	.15	.45	3.00
	b. Wmk: Small circles, L.	.15	.45	3.00
	c. Wmk: Lattice w/*8*, G.	.15	.45	3.00
	d. Wmk: Wavy lines, J.	.15	.45	3.00

107	**100 MILLIONEN MARK**	VG	VF	UNC
	22.8.1923. Black on blue-green and olive-brown unpt. Uniface.			
	a. Wmk: Oak leaves, gray tint at r.	.25	1.00	4.00
	b. Wmk: Small crucifera blossoms, D. W/embedded fibre strips in paper on back.	.25	1.00	4.00
	c. Wmk: Small crucifera blossoms, D. W/o embedded fibre strips in paper on back.	.25	1.00	4.00
	d. Wmk: *G/D* in stars, E.	.25	1.00	4.00
	e. Wmk: Small circles, L.	.25	1.00	4.00
	f. Wmk: *S* in stars, M.	.25	1.00	4.00
	g. Wmk: Lozenges, N.	.25	1.00	4.00

1923 SIXTH ISSUE

108	**20 MILLIONEN MARK**	VG	VF	UNC
	1.9.1923. Black on olive-brown and dk. green unpt. Uniface.			
	a. Wmk: Small circles. L.	.15	.50	3.00
	b. Wmk: Lozenges, N.	.25	1.00	4.00
	c. Wmk: *G/D* in stars, E.	.15	.50	3.00
	d. Wmk: Wavy lines, J.	.25	.50	1.00
	e. Wmk: Lattice, G.	.25	.50	1.00
	f. Wmk: *S* in stars, M.	2.00	10.00	30.00

109	**50 MILLIONEN MARK**	VG	VF	UNC
	1.9.1923. Black on gray and lilac unpt. Uniface.			
	a. Wmk: Small crucifera blossoms, gray paper. D.	.20	.50	3.00
	b. Wmk: *G/D* in stars, E. White paper.	.20	.50	3.00
	c. Wmk: Small circles, L. White paper.	.25	.50	3.00
	d. Wmk: Lozenges, N. White paper.	.25	.50	3.00
	e. Wmk: *S* in stars, M. White paper.	.25	.50	3.00
	f. Wmk: Lattice, G. White paper.	.25	.50	3.00

110	**500 MILLIONEN MARK**	VG	VF	UNC
	1.9.1923. Dk. brown on lt. brown and lilac unpt. *500* facing inwardly at r. margin. Uniface.			
	a. Wmk: Thistle leaves, lilac tint at r.	—	1.00	5.00
	b. Like C: but *500* facing inwardly at r. margin.	.25	1.00	5.00
	c. Wmk: Small crucifera blossoms. *500* facing outwardly at r. margin, D.	50.00	150.00	250.00
	d. Wmk: *G/D* in stars, E.	.25	1.00	5.00
	e. Wmk: Small circles, L.	.25	1.00	5.00
	f. Wmk: *S* in stars. M.	.40	1.00	5.00
	g. Wmk: Lozenges. N.	6.00	20.00	35.00
	h. Wmk: Lattice. G.	.50	2.00	5.00

111	**500 MILLIARDEN MARK**			
	1.9.1923. Blue, lilac and green. Vienna printing. Allegorical head at upper r. Specimens only.	—	Unc	2000.

112	**1 BILLION MARK**	VG	VF	UNC
	1.9.1923 Violet and lilac. Allegorical head at r. Vienna printing. Specimens only.	—	Unc	2000.

1923 SEVENTH ISSUES

113 **1 MILLIARDE MARK ON 1000 MARK**

	VG	VF	UNC
ND (Sept. 1923 - old date 15.12.1922). Black on dk. brown. Red new denomination ovpt. on #82.			
a. Wmk: *1000*, brown tint at r. White paper.	2.00	4.50	10.00
b. Wmk: Small crucifera blossoms, D. Brown paper.	2.00	4.50	10.00
c. Wmk: Small crucifera blossoms, D. White paper.	2.00	4.50	10.00
d. Ovpt. inverted.	—	100.00	—
e. Ovpt. on back only.	—	120.00	—
f. Ovpt. on face only.	—	120.00	—

114 **1 MILLIARDE MARK**

	VG	VF	UNC
5.9.1923. Black on dk. green, lilac and blue. Blue-green tint at r. Uniface.	.50	1.50	10.00

115 **5 MILLIARDEN MARK**

	VG	VF	UNC
10.9.1923. Black on olive-brown unpt. Uniface.			
a. Wmk: Oak leaves, lilac tint at r.	2.00	5.00	15.00
b. Wmk: Small crucifera blossoms, D.	2.00	5.00	15.00

116 **10 MILLIARDEN MARK**

	VG	VF	UNC
15.9.1923. Black on gray-lilac and blue-green unpt. Format similar to #114. Uniface.			
a. Wmk: Thistle leaves, yellow tint at r.	2.00	6.00	20.00
b. Wmk: Small crucifera blossoms, D.	2.00	9.00	25.00

117 **10 MILLIARDEN MARK**

	VG	VF	UNC
1.10.1923. Black-green (shades) on lilac and green unpt. Uniface. 160 x 105mm.			
a. Wmk: *G/D* in stars, E.	2.00	7.00	30.00
b. Wmk: Small circles, L.	2.00	7.00	30.00
c. Wmk: *S* in stars, M.	2.00	7.00	30.00
d. Wmk: Lozenges, N.	10.00	25.00	45.00
e. Wmk: Lattice, G.	2.00	7.00	30.00

118 **20 MILLIARDEN MARK**

	VG	VF	UNC
1.10.1923. Dk. green on blue and orange unpt. 140x93 (90)mm. Uniface.			
a. Wmk: *G/D* in stars. 5 or 6 digit serial #. E.	4.00	10.00	25.00
b. Wmk: *G/D* in stars, E. Error w/*20 MILLIARDEN* on l. edge. Format 175x85mm.	40.00	90.00	175.00
c. Wmk: Small circles. L.	3.00	7.00	25.00
d. Wmk: Small circles, L. W/error *20 MILLIARDEN* on l. edge.	40.00	90.00	175.00
e. Wmk: Lozenges, N.	3.00	7.00	25.00
f. Wmk: Lattice, G.	3.00	7.00	25.00
g. Wmk: *S* in stars, M.	3.00	7.00	25.00

119 **50 MILLIARDEN MARK**

	VG	VF	UNC
10.10.1923. Black on orange and blue unpt. Uniface.			
a. Wmk: Oak leaves, green tint at r.	3.50	9.00	30.00
b. Wmk: Small crucifera blossoms, D. White paper.	3.50	9.00	30.00
c. Wmk: Small crucifera blossoms, D. White paper. W/o serial #.	3.00	7.00	30.00
d. Wmk: Small crucifera blossoms, D. Gray paper. W/o srial #.	3.00	7.00	30.00

120 **50 MILLIARDEN MARK**

	VG	VF	UNC
10.10.1923. Black on orange, blue and green. Like #119b but green rectangular unpt. at r. Uniface.			
a. Wmk: *G/D* in stars, E.	3.00	7.00	35.00
b. Wmk: Small circles, L.	3.50	10.00	40.00
c. Wmk: *S* in stars, M.	1.00	10.00	40.00

121 **200 MILLIARDEN MARK**

	VG	VF	UNC
15.10.1923. Black on violet and green unpt. Uniface.			
a. Wmk: *G/D* in stars, E.	1.50	7.00	30.00
b. Wmk: Small circles, L.	3.00	8.00	30.00
c. Wmk: *S* in stars,M.	4.50	10.00	30.00
d. Wmk: Lattice, G.	15.00	40.00	100.00

1923 EIGHTH ISSUE

122 **1 MILLIARDE MARK**

	VG	VF	UNC
20.10.1923. Black on blue-green unpt. Uniface.	.25	.75	6.50

123 **5 MILLIARDEN MARK**

	VG	VF	UNC
20.10.1923. Black on violet-brown unpt. Uniface.			
a. With serial #.	.40	1.00	9.00
b. W/o serial #.	.40	1.00	9.00

124 **500 MILLIARDEN MARK ON 5000 MARK**

	VG	VF	UNC
ND (Oct. 1923 - old date 15.3.1923). Dk. brown on olive-brown unpt. New denomination ovpt. on #87.			
a. Ovpt. on face and back.	12.50	30.00	150.00
b. Ovpt. on back only (error).	30.00	70.00	500.00
c. Ovpt. on face only (error).	30.00	70.00	500.00

1923 NINTH ISSUE

125 **50 MILLIARDEN MARK**

	VG	VF	UNC
26.10.1923. Black on blue-green unpt. Uniface.			
a. Gray paper.	1.50	14.00	25.00
b. Green paper.	1.50	14.00	25.00

126 **100 MILLIARDEN MARK**
26.10.1923. Dk. blue on white, blue tint at r. Uniface.

	VG	VF	UNC
	1.25	10.00	26.00

127 **500 MILLIARDEN MARK**
26.10.1923. Dk. brown on white. Uniface.

	VG	VF	UNC
a. Wmk: Oak leaves, green tint at r.	5.00	15.00	55.00
b. Wmk: *500M,* blue or violet tint at r.	5.00	15.00	55.00

128 **100 BILLIONEN MARK**
26.10.1923. Black on lilac and gray, brown tint at r. Uniface.

	VG	VF	UNC
	250.00	800.00	1500.

1923 TENTH ISSUE

129 **1 BILLION MARK**
1.11.1923. Brown-violet, lilac tint at r. Uniface.

	VG	VF	UNC
	12.00	35.00	120.00

130 **5 BILLIONEN MARK**
1.11.1923. Black and pink unpt. Uniface.

	VG	VF	UNC
a. Wmk: Thistles, yellow tint at r.	35.00	100.00	250.00
b. Wmk: Small crucifera blossoms. D.	50.00	125.00	400.00

131 **10 BILLIONEN MARK**
1.11.1923. Black on green and lt. brown unpt. Uniface.

	VG	VF	UNC
a. Wmk: Thistles, blue-green tint at r.	45.00	135.00	300.00
b. Wmk: Small crucifera blossoms. D.	65.00	150.00	400.00

132 **10 BILLIONEN MARK**
1.11.1923. Black on brown and blue-green unpt. Uniface.

	VG	VF	UNC
a. Wmk: *G/D* in stars. E.	40.00	180.00	450.00
b. Wmk: Small circles. L.	55.00	200.00	550.00

1923 ELEVENTH ISSUE

133 **100 MILLIARDEN MARK**
5.11.1923. Red-brown on olive and blue-green unpt. Uniface.

	VG	VF	UNC
	1.00	12.00	25.00

134 **1 BILLION MARK**
5.11.1923. Black on violet and brown unpt. Uniface.

	VG	VF	UNC
	10.00	60.00	125.00

135 **2 BILLIONEN MARK**
5.11.1923. Black on green and pink unpt. Uniface.

	VG	VF	UNC
a. Wmk: *G/D* in stars, E.	15.00	35.00	150.00
b. Wmk: Small circles, L.	15.00	35.00	150.00
c. Wmk: *S* in stars, M.	20.00	50.00	150.00

136 **5 BILLIONEN MARK**
7.11.1923. Black on blue and pink unpt. Uniface.

	VG	VF	UNC
a. Wmk: Thistles. Yellow tint at r.	35.00	120.00	500.00
b. Wmk: Small crucifera blossoms, D.	70.00	200.00	500.00
c. Wmk: *G/D* in stars, E.	35.00	120.00	500.00
d. Wmk: Small circles, L.	35.00	120.00	500.00

1924 FIRST ISSUE

137 **10 BILLIONEN MARK**
1.2.1924. Brown on green, lilac tint at r. Uniface.

	VG	VF	UNC
	30.00	120.00	300.00

138	20 B<small>ILLIONEN</small> M<small>ARK</small>	**VG**	**VF**	**UNC**
	5.2.1924. Blue-green and violet, lt. violet tint at r. Portr. woman at upper r. by A. Durer.	150.00	350.00	700.00

139	50 B<small>ILLIONEN</small> M<small>ARK</small>	**VG**	**VF**	**UNC**
	10.2.1924. Brown and olive, green tint at r. Portr. Councillor J. Muffel at ctr. r. by A. Durer.	300.00	750.00	1200.

140	100 B<small>ILLIONEN</small> M<small>ARK</small>	**VG**	**VF**	**UNC**
	15.2.1924. Red-brown and blue, lt. blue tint at r. Portr. W. Pirkheimer at r. by A. Durer.	700.00	1600.	3000.

1924 S<small>ECOND</small> I<small>SSUE</small>

141	5 B<small>ILLIONEN</small> M<small>ARK</small>	**VG**	**VF**	**UNC**
	15.3.1924. Dk. brown on green and lilac unpt. Back green.	30.00	90.00	265.00

R<small>EICHSSCHULDENVERWALTUNG</small>

I<small>MPERIAL</small> D<small>EBT</small> A<small>DMINISTRATION</small>

1915 E<small>MERGENCY</small> I<small>NTEREST</small> C<small>OUPON</small>I<small>SSUE</small>

In October 1918 all interest coupons of war loans, due on 2.1.1919 (letter q), were temporarily declared legal tender.

142	2.50 M<small>ARK</small>	**VG**	**VF**	**UNC**
	Year of loan: 1915; 1916; 1917; 1918.	3.00	8.00	25.00

143	5.00 M<small>ARK</small>	**VG**	**VF**	**UNC**
	Year of loan: 1915; 1916; 1917; 1918.	4.00	12.50	35.00

144	12.50 M<small>ARK</small>	**VG**	**VF**	**UNC**
	Year of loan: 1915; 1916; 1917; 1918.	5.00	15.00	45.00

145	25.00 M<small>ARK</small>	**VG**	**VF**	**UNC**
	Year of loan: 1915; 1916; 1917; 1918.	8.00	25.00	60.00
146	50.00 M<small>ARK</small>			
	Year of loan: 1915; 1916; 1917; 1918.	12.00	30.00	85.00
147	125.00 M<small>ARK</small>			
	Year of loan: 1915; 1916; 1917; 1918.	20.00	35.00	110.00

Z<small>WISCHENSCHEINE</small> - S<small>CHATZANWEISUNGEN</small>

I<small>MPERIAL</small> T<small>REASURY</small>

1923 I<small>NTERIM</small> N<small>OTE</small> I<small>SSUE</small>

In October 1923, interim notes of the Reich's Bank for Treasury certificates, partial bonds of the treasury certificates of the German Reich were declared legal tender.

148	0.42 G<small>OLDMARK</small> = 1/10 D<small>OLLAR</small> (U.S.A.)	**VG**	**VF**	**UNC**
	23.10.1923. Wmk: O.	4.00	40.00	85.00
149	1.05 G<small>OLDMARK</small> = 1/4 D<small>OLLAR</small> (U.S.A.)			
	23.10.1923. Wmk: 5. Uniface.	10.00	60.00	100.00
150	1.05 G<small>OLDMARK</small> = 1/4 D<small>OLLAR</small> (U.S.A.)			
	23.10.1923. Wmk: 50. Capital letters on back.	8.00	60.00	100.00

151	2.10 G<small>OLDMARK</small> = 1/2 D<small>OLLAR</small> (U.S.A.)	**VG**	**VF**	**UNC**
	23.10.1923. Wmk: 20 MARK.	10.00	200.00	350.00

1923 P<small>ARTIAL</small> B<small>OND OF</small> T<small>REASURY</small> C<small>ERTIFICATES</small> I<small>SSUES</small>

152	0.42 G<small>OLDMARK</small> = 1/10 D<small>OLLAR</small> (U.S.A.)			
	26.10.1923. Wmk: Oak and thistles.	4.00	35.00	75.00
153	1.05 G<small>OLDMARK</small> = 1/4 D<small>OLLAR</small> (U.S.A.)			
	26.10.1923. Wmk: 5.	12.00	40.00	110.00

154	1.05 G<small>OLDMARK</small> = 1/4 D<small>OLLAR</small> (U.S.A.)	**VG**	**VF**	**UNC**
	26.10.1923. Wmk: 10.	10.00	40.00	125.00
155	1.05 G<small>OLDMARK</small> = 1/4 D<small>OLLAR</small> (U.S.A.)			
	26.10.1923. Wmk: 50.	7.50	40.00	120.00
156	2.10 G<small>OLDMARK</small> = 1/2 D<small>OLLAR</small> (U.S.A.)			
	26.10.1923. Wmk: 5.	18.00	65.00	200.00

		VG	VF	UNC
157	2.10 GOLDMARK = 1/2 DOLLAR (U.S.A.)	10.00	45.00	150.00
	26.10.1923. Wmk: 20.			

1923 WHOLE TREASURY CERTIFICATES ISSUES

3 different issues each:
1. Wmk: Ornaments.
2. *Ausgefertigt*, at lower r. Wmk: Lines and *RSV*.
3. Like #2 but w/o *Ausgefertigt* at lower r.

		VG	VF	UNC
158	4.20 GOLDMARK = 1 DOLLAR (U.S.A.)			
	25.8.1923.			
	a. Wmk: P.	30.00	150.00	275.00
	b. Wmk: Q.	30.00	150.00	275.00
159	8.40 GOLDMARK = 2 DOLLARS (U.S.A.)			
	25.8.1923.			
	a. Wmk: P.	100.00	650.00	1000.
	b. Wmk: Q.	100.00	650.00	1000.

		VG	VF	UNC
160	21.00 GOLDMARK = 5 DOLLARS (U.S.A.)			
	25.8.1923.			
	a. Wmk: P.	150.00	1200.	2500.
	b. Wmk: Q.	150.00	1200.	2500.

RENTENBANK - STABILIZATION BANK
Introduced the Rentenmarkscheine w/1 Rentenmark equal to 1,000 Milliarden Reichsmark.

1923 RENTENMARKSCHEINE ISSUE

		VG	VF	UNC
161	1 RENTENMARK	2.00	20.00	80.00
	1.11.1923. Olive.			
162	2 RENTENMARK	7.00	45.00	250.00
	1.11.1923. Red and green.			
163	5 RENTENMARK	20.00	80.00	275.00
	1.11.1923. Blue-green and violet.			

		VG	VF	UNC
164	10 RENTENMARK	50.00	280.00	900.00
	1.11.1923. Lilac and green.			

		VG	VF	UNC
165	50 RENTENMARK	250.00	800.00	3000.
	1.11.1923. Brown and violet.			
166	100 RENTENMARK	120.00	350.00	2000.
	1.11.1923. Brown and blue-green.			
167	500 RENTENMARK			
	1.11.1923. Blue-gray and green.			
	a. Issued note.	1750.	3500.	5500.
	s. Specimen ovpt: *MUSTER*.	—	Unc	4000.

		VG	VF	UNC
168	1000 RENTENMARK			
	1.11.1923. Brown and lt. green.			
	a. Issued note.	1800.	3600.	7000.
	s. Specimen ovpt: *MUSTER*.	—	Unc	4000.

1925-26 ISSUE

		VG	VF	UNC
169 (171)	5 RENTENMARK	1.00	8.50	55.00
	2.1.1926. Dk. green and olive. Portr. farm girl at upper ctr. r.			

		VG	VF	UNC
170	**10 RENTENMARK** 3.7.1925. Green and brown. Portr. farm woman at l.	60.00	225.00	1200.

		VG	VF	UNC
171 (169)	**50 RENTENMARK** 20.3.1925. Brown, green and lilac. Farmer at r.	60.00	250.00	750.00

1934 ISSUE

		VG	VF	UNC
172	**50 RENTENMARK** 6.7.1934. Dk. brown on olive. Freiherr vom Stein at r.	20.00	100.00	600.00

1937 ISSUE

#173 and 174 blind embossed seal at lower r.

		VG	VF	UNC
173	**1 RENTENMARK** 30.1.1937. Olive. Yellow stripe at right. Lg. or sm. size numerals in serial #.			
	a. 7 digit serial #.	2.00	15.00	40.00
	b. 8 digit serial #.	.10	.25	4.00

		VG	VF	UNC
174	**2 RENTENMARK** 30.1.1937. Brown. Yellow strip at right. Lg. or sm. size numerals in serial #.			
	a. 7 digit serial #.	2.00	15.00	50.00
	b. 8 digit serial #.	.10	.25	7.00

DEUTSCHE GOLDDISKONTBANK

GERMAN GOLD DISCOUNT BANK

This bank did not exercise its right of issuing banknotes. The notes that were printed in anticipation of release were destroyed but for only 3 specimens of each.

1924 ISSUE

		VG	VF	UNC
174A	**5 POUNDS** 20.4.1924. Brown. Youth. Specimen.	—	Unc	4000.

		VG	VF	UNC
174B	**10 POUNDS** 20.4.1924. Gray-green. Portr. youth w/wreath at upper ctr. r. Specimen.	—	Unc	4000.

REICHSBANKNOTES

Issued Reichsmarks on par w/the Rentenmarks.

1924 ISSUE

		VG	VF	UNC
175	**10 REICHSMARK** 11.10.1924. Dk. green and red-lilac. Portr. merchant Dietrich Born at upper ctr. r. by H. Holbein at r. ctr.	20.00	95.00	650.00

		VG	VF	UNC
176	**20 REICHSMARK** 11.10.1924. Brown and red-lilac. Portr. woman at upper ctr. r. by H. Holbein.	40.00	100.00	700.00

		VG	VF	UNC
177	**50 REICHSMARK** 11.10.1924. Brown and dk. green. Portr. man at upper ctr r. by H. Holbein.	8.00	25.00	120.00
178	**100 REICHSMARK** 11.10.1924. Brown and blue-green. Portr. English Lady at upper ctr. r. by H. Holbein.	8.00	25.00	120.00

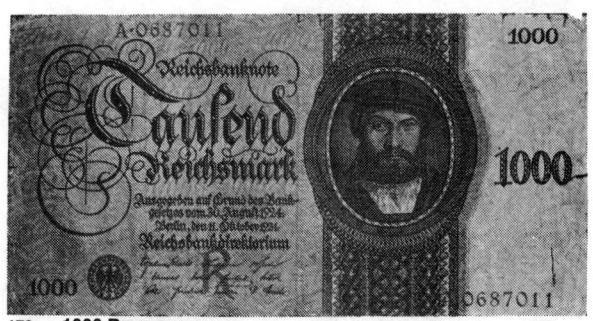

179 1000 REICHSMARK
11.10.1924. Brown and blue. Portr. Patrician Wedigh at upper ctr. r. by H. Holbein.

	VG	VF	UNC
	30.00	85.00	225.00

1929-36; (1945) ISSUE

#180-183 serial # on face and back for first variety; serial # on face only for second variety.

180 10 REICHSMARK
22.1.1929. Dk. green and black on tan and gray unpt. Portr. A. D. Thaer at r.

	VG	VF	UNC
a. Wmk: Head of Thaer at l. W/unpt. letters.	.20	1.50	6.50
b. Wmk: Ornament at l. W/o unpt. letters (1945).	.30	4.00	16.00

181 20 REICHSMARK
22.1.1929. Dk. brown on m/c unpt. Portr. W. von Siemens at r.

	VG	VF	UNC
a. Wmk: W. von Siemens at l. W/unpt. letters.	.25	1.50	6.50
b. Wmk: Ornament at l. W/o unpt. letters (1945).	1.00	4.00	16.00

182 50 REICHSMARK
30.3.1933. Green and black on m/c unpt. Portr. Hansemann at r.

	VG	VF	UNC
a. Wmk: D. Hansemann at l. W/unpt. letters.	.30	2.00	6.50
b. Wmk: Ornament at l. W/o unpt. letters (1945)	1.00	4.00	12.00

183 100 REICHSMARK
24.6.1935. Blue. Portr. J. von Liebig at r., swastika in unpt. at ctr.

	VG	VF	UNC
a. Wmk: J. von Liebig at l., w/unpt. letters.	2.00	4.50	8.00
b. Wmk: Ornament at l., w/o unpt. letters (1945).	4.00	9.00	17.50

184 1000 REICHSMARK
22.2.1936. Brown and olive. Portr. K. F. Schinkel at r., swastika unpt. at ctr.

	VG	VF	UNC
	22.50	70.00	120.00

1939 ISSUE

185 20 REICHSMARK
16.6.1939. Brown. Portr. woman holding edelweiss at r. (Similar to Austria #101).

	VG	VF	UNC
	.50	5.00	18.00

1942 ISSUE

186 5 REICHSMARK
1.8.1942. Red-brown. Portr. young soldier at r. Wmk: *5* straight up at l., either frontwards or backwards.

	VG	VF	UNC
a. Issued note.	.75	2.00	8.00
b. Wmk: *5* upside down at l.	10.00	25.00	60.00

LOCAL

EUPEN-MALMEDY

In the territory of Eupen-Malmedy, before the entry of the Allied troops in 1944, the locally valid German banknotes, occasionally also Reich's Credit Treasury Notes, were handstamped by various municipalities, previously Belgian. The handstamped notes were legal tender until exchanged for Belgian notes. Almost all handstamped notes of this type are very scarce.

SUDETENLAND AND LOWER SILESIA (REICHENBERG)

1945 KASSENSCHEINE EMERGENCY ISSUE

187 20 REICHSMARK
28.4.1945. Red-brown on tan unpt. Back brown.

VG	VF	UNC
.50	1.00	3.00

REICHSBANK OFFICES IN GRAZ, LINZ AND SALZBURG

1945 EMERGENCY REISSUE

Photo-mechanically produced notes, following the pattern of the notes already in circulation. All notes of a particular denomination have identical serial #.

187A 5 REICHSMARK
ND (1945-old date 1/8/1942). Red-brown. Portr. young soldier at r. Reported Not Confirmed
Serial #G.13663932.

188 10 REICHSMARK
ND (1945-old date 22.1.1929). Blue-green. Portr. A. D. Thaer at r., blurred printing. Serial #D.02776733.

	VG	VF	UNC
a. W/o holes.	30.00	250.00	500.00
b. W/holes.	12.00	100.00	250.00

189 50 REICHSMARK
ND (1945-old date 30.3.1933). Green. D. Hansemann at r., blurred printing. Serial #E.06647727.

	VG	VF	UNC
a. W/o holes.	20.00	120.00	200.00
b. W/holes.	8.00	50.00	85.00

190 100 REICHSMARK
ND (1945-old date 24.6.1935). Blue J. von Liebig at r., blurred printing. Serial #T.7396475.

	VG	VF	UNC
a. W/o holes.	20.00	40.00	130.00
b. W/holes.	8.00	15.00	78.00

ALLIED OCCUPATION - WW II

ALLIED MILITARY CURRENCY

The notes issued by the Western Allies carry a secret sign. of Forbes the printers: *F*, whereas those printed by the Russians (they were given the glass positives by the USA) are w/o this initial. The notes were in circulation w/the Reichsmark and Rentenmark notes, and were also used by the population.

1944 ISSUE

191 1/2 MARK
1944. Green on lt. blue unpt.

	VG	VF	UNC
a. 9 digit serial # w/*F.*	.15	.65	2.00
b. 8 digit serial # w/dash, w/*F.*	15.00	35.00	85.00
c. 8 digit serial # w/dash, w/o *F.*	3.00	10.00	120.00

192 1 MARK
1944. Blue on lt. blue unpt.

	VG	VF	UNC
a. 9 digit serial # w/*F.*	.25	.75	3.00
b. 9 digit serial # w/o *F.*	.50	2.00	6.00
c. 8 digit serial # w/dash, w/*F.*	15.00	100.00	150.00
d. 8 digit serial # w/dash, w/o *F.*	.75	3.00	10.00

193 5 MARK
1944. Lilac on lt. blue unpt.

	VG	VF	UNC
a. 9 digit serial # w/*F.*	.25	1.50	5.00
b. 9 digit serial # w/o *F.*	8.00	12.00	30.00
c. 8 digit serial # w/dash, w/*F.*	20.00	100.00	250.00
d. 8 digit serial # w/dash, w/o *F.*	1.00	3.00	20.00

194 10 MARK
1944. Blue on lt. blue unpt.

	VG	VF	UNC
a. 9 digit serial # w/*F.*	1.50	15.00	30.00
b. 9 digit serial # w/o *F.*	11.00	22.00	40.00
c. 8 digit serial # w/dash, w/*F.*	25.00	185.00	400.00
d. 8 digit serial # w/dash, w/o *F.*	1.00	10.00	25.00

195 20 MARK
1944. Red on lt. blue unpt.

	VG	VF	UNC
a. 9 digit serial # w/*F.*	1.00	4.00	35.00
b. 9 digit serial # w/o *F.*	2.00	5.00	40.00
c. 8 digit serial # w/dash, w/*F.*	40.00	260.00	450.00
d. 8 digit serial # w/dash, w/o *F.*	1.00	5.00	15.00

196 50 MARK
1944. Blue on lt. blue unpt.

	VG	VF	UNC
a. 9 digit serial # w/*F.*	1.50	5.00	40.00
b. 9 digit serial # w/o *F.*	4.00	8.00	25.00
c. 8 digit serial # w/dash, w/*F.*	60.00	150.00	600.00
d. 8 digit serial # w dash, w/o *F.*	1.50	5.00	20.00

197	**100 MARK**	VG	VF	UNC
	1944. Lilac on lt. blue unpt.			
	a. 9 digit serial # w/F.	1.50	5.00	40.00
	b. 9 digit serial # w/o F.	4.00	8.00	25.00
	c. 8 digit serial # w/dash, w/F.	100.00	250.00	1000.
	d. 8 digit serial # w/dash, w/o F.	1.00	4.00	25.00
198	**1000 MARK**			
	1944. Green on lt. blue unpt.			
	a. 9 digit serial # w/F.	75.00	165.00	275.00
	b. 8 digit serial # w/dash, w/o F.	30.00	60.00	120.00

THIRD REICH

KONVERSIONSKASSE FÜR DEUTSCHE

AUSLANDSSCHULDEN

CONVERSION FUND FOR GERMAN FOREIGN DEBTS

Promissory notes issued to refugees from Germany during 1933-35 in place of regular German currency not permitted out of the country. At the times when Jewish refugees were paid for their confiscated properties it was with these notes. They were not legal tender nor transferable. It was sometimes possible to convert them at half their face value by selling them to the German Golddiskontbank. Eventually the owner found them to be worthless.

1933 ISSUE

199	**5 REICHSMARK**			
	28.8.1933. Black, green and brown.	10.00	20.00	35.00

200	**10 REICHSMARK**	VG	VF	UNC
	28.8.1933. Black and lilac.	12.50	25.00	50.00
201	**30 REICHSMARK**			
	28.8.1933. Black, red and brown.	30.00	60.00	200.00
202	**40 REICHSMARK**			
	28.8.1933. Black, blue and brown.	50.00	100.00	250.00
203	**50 REICHSMARK**			
	28.8.1933. Black, brown and blue.	30.00	60.00	200.00
204	**100 REICHSMARK**			
	28.8.1933. Black, brown and green.	12.50	25.00	150.00
205	**500 REICHSMARK**			
	28.8.1933.	—	—	—
206	**1000 REICHSMARK**			
	28.8.1933.	—	—	—

1934 ISSUE

#207-214 ovpt. 2 red guilloches at l., the lower one containing the date 1934.

207	**5 REICHSMARK**			
	1934. Ovpt. on #199.	10.00	20.00	40.00
208	**10 REICHSMARK**			
	1934. Ovpt. on #200.	15.00	30.00	50.00
209	**30 REICHSMARK**			
	1934. Ovpt. on #201.	27.50	55.00	150.00
210	**40 REICHSMARK**			
	1934. Ovpt. on #202.	30.00	60.00	200.00

211	**50 REICHSMARK**	VG	VF	UNC
	1934. Ovpt. on #203.	20.00	35.00	150.00
212	**100 REICHSMARK**			
	1934. Ovpt. on #204.	12.50	25.00	150.00
213	**500 REICHSMARK**			
	1934. Ovpt. on #205.	—	—	—
214	**1000 REICHSMARK**			
	1934. Ovpt. on #206.	—	—	—

REGIONAL - OCCUPATION OF LITHUANIA - WWI

OSTBANK FÜR HANDEL UND GEWERBE,

DARLEHNSKASSENSCHEINE

STATE LOAN BANK CURRENCY NOTES, EASTERN BANK OF COMMERCE AND INDUSTRY, POSEN (POZNAN)

1916 ISSUE

#R120-R126 circulated in Lithuania until 1922.

R120	**20 KOPEKEN**			
	17.4.1916. Blue-green.	1.50	4.00	15.00

R121	**50 KOPEKEN**	VG	VF	UNC
	17.4.1916. Black on red-brown and blue-green unpt.			
	a. *ASTUN GADEEM* last 2 words at bottom r. on back. Capital letters of bottom text 1.8mm tall. *AISDEWU KASES SIME* at r. w/*S* in form of *f*.	1.50	4.00	30.00
	b. As above but capital letters only. 1.2-1.4mm tall.	3.50	10.00	85.00
	c. *ASTONI GADEEM* last 2 words at bottom r. on back. Capital letter of bottom text 1.8mm tall. *AISDEWU KASES SIHME* at r.	1.50	4.00	25.00
	d. As above but capital letters only 1.2-1.4mm tall. Text poorly printed.	1.50	4.00	25.00

R122	**1 RUBEL**	VG	VF	UNC
	17.4.1916. Black on blue and brown unpt.			
	a. Like #R121a.	1.50	4.00	30.00
	b. Like #R121b.	3.00	15.00	85.00
	c. Like #R121c.	1.50	4.00	25.00
	d. Like #R121d.	1.50	4.00	25.00
R123	**3 RUBEL**			
	17.4.1916. Dk. brown on green and lilac unpt.			
	a. *AIFDEWU* w/crossed *F* (Gothic *F*).	7.00	14.00	200.00
	b. *AIFDEWU* w/uncrossed *F* (Gothic *S*).	3.00	7.00	50.00
R124	**10 RUBEL**			
	17.4.1916. Red-brown on red and green unpt.	7.00	14.00	60.00

R125	**25 RUBEL**	VG	VF	UNC
	17.4.1916. Dk. blue on lilac unpt.	12.00	35.00	150.00

R126 100 RUBEL

	VG	VF	UNC
17.4.1916. Blue. Woman at l., man wearing helmet at r.	12.00	60.00	150.00

DARLEHNSKASSE OST
STATE LOAN BANK EAST
KOWNO (KAUNAS) BRANCH
1918 ISSUE
#R127-R134 circulated in Lithuania until 1922.

R127 1/2 MARK

	VG	VF	UNC
4.4.1918. Black on lilac and lt. brown unpt.	1.50	4.00	12.50

R128 1 MARK

	VG	VF	UNC
4.4.1918. Dk. brown on green unpt.	1.50	4.00	15.00

R129 2 MARK

	VG	VF	UNC
4.4.1918. Red-brown on lilac unpt.	1.50	6.00	50.00

R130 5 MARK

	VG	VF	UNC
4.4.1918. Brown and blue.	2.00	5.00	25.00

R131 20 MARK

	VG	VF	UNC
4.4.1918. Red-brown on green and pink unpt.	4.00	10.00	50.00

R132 50 MARK

	VG	VF	UNC
4.4.1918. Dk. blue on gray-violet unpt.	5.00	10.00	40.00

R133 100 MARK

	VG	VF	UNC
4.4.1918. Brown. Woman at l., man wearing helmet at r. Similar to #R126.	7.00	17.50	45.00

R134 1000 MARK

	VG	VF	UNC
4.4.1918. Green. Mercury and youth in armor at r.			
a. 6 digit serial #, black sign.	12.00	27.50	125.00
b. 7 digit serial #, green sign.	7.00	20.00	100.00

GERMAN OCCUPIED TERRITORIES - WWII
REICHSKREDITKASSEN
REICH'S CREDIT TREASURY NOTES
NOTE: Immediately after the end of the war, Reich's Credit Treasury Notes were authorized in the British zone of occupation in the denominations of 5, 20 and 50 Reichsmark, provided they had been given a stamp of a Reichsbank office located in the British zone of occupation. All notes which exist with different stamps are scarce.

1939 ISSUE
#R135-R140 legal tender alongside the currency of the country in numerous occupied countries and territories during WW II.

R135 50 REICHSPFENNIG

	VG	VF	UNC
ND (1939-45). Green on tan unpt.	.50	1.50	5.00

 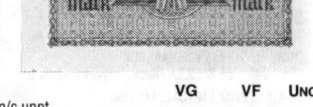

R136 1 REICHSMARK

	VG	VF	UNC
ND (1939-45). Greenish black on brown and m/c unpt.			
a. Embossed stamp. Series 1-480.	.25	1.00	2.50
b. W/o embossed stamp. Series 481-702.	.50	1.00	15.00

R137 2 REICHSMARK

	VG	VF	UNC
ND (1939-45). Grayish brown on green and tan unpt.			
a. Embossed stamp. 7 digit serial #.	.25	1.00	2.50
b. W/o embossed stamp. 8 digit serial #.	.50	1.50	10.00

R138 5 REICHSMARK

	VG	VF	UNC
ND (1939-45). Blue-black on brown and gray unpt. Portr. farmer at l., factory worker at r. Berlin War Memorial at ctr. on back.			
a. Embossed stamp. 7 digit serial #.	.50	1.25	4.00
b. W/o embossed stamp. 8 digit serial #.	.50	1.50	5.00

R139 20 REICHSMARK

	VG	VF	UNC
ND (1939-45). Dk. brown on red-brown and pale olive unpt. "The Architect" by A. Dürer at r. Brandenburg Gate at ctr. on back.	.75	2.00	15.00

R140 50 REICHSMARK
ND (1939-45). Blue-black on dull violet unpt. Portr. woman at upper r.
Marienburg castle at ctr. on back.

	VG	VF	UNC
	1.00	3.00	20.00

MILITARY PAYMENT CERTIFICATES

ETAPPEN - INSPEKTION

BASE INSPECTORATE I, 1ST ARMY

1915 ISSUE
#M1-M4 issued in the occupied French territory. All w/different dates in script, only "1915" in print.

			VG	VF	UNC
M1	**50 CENTIMES**				
	1915.		40.00	70.00	120.00
M2	**1 FRANC**				
	1915.		40.00	70.00	120.00

			VG	VF	UNC
M3	**2 FRANCS**		30.00	50.00	100.00
	1915.				
M4	**5 FRANCS**		GOOD	FINE	XF
	1915.		30.00	50.00	100.00

ETAPPEN - KOMMANDANTUR

BASE LOCAL HEADQUARTERS

1915 ISSUE
#M5-M8 like #M1-M4. Issued in occupied French territory.

			VG	VF	UNC
M5	**50 CENTIMES**		40.00	70.00	120.00
	1915.				
M6	**1 FRANC**		30.00	50.00	100.00
	1915.				
M7	**2 FRANCS**		30.00	50.00	100.00
	1915.				

			VG	VF	UNC
M8	**5 FRANCS**		30.00	50.00	100.00
	1915.				

ETAPPEN - INSPEKTION

BASE INSPECTORATE, 2ND ARMY

1914-15 ISSUE
#M9-M13 issued in occupied French territory, so-called "Deichmann-Bons", w/different handstamps of various French municipalities.

			VG	VF	UNC
M9	**5 FRANCS**				
	1914-15.		40.00	100.00	175.00
M10	**10 FRANCS**				
	1914-15.		40.00	100.00	175.00
M11	**20 FRANCS**				
	1914-15.		40.00	100.00	175.00

			VG	VF	UNC
M12	**50 FRANCS**				
	1914-15.		40.00	100.00	175.00
M13	**100 FRANCS**				
	1914-15.		40.00	100.00	175.00

ETAPPEN - KOMMANDANTUR (RESUMED)

BASE LOCAL HEADQUARTERS

1914-15 ISSUE
#M14-18 issued in occupied French territory "Deichmann-Bons," Like #M9-M13.

			VG	VF	UNC
M14	**5 FRANCS**				
	1914-15.		40.00	100.00	175.00
M15	**10 FRANCS**				
	1914-15.		40.00	100.00	175.00

			VG	VF	UNC
M16	**20 FRANCS**				
	1914-15.		40.00	100.00	175.00
M17	**50 FRANCS**				
	1914-15.		40.00	100.00	175.00
M18	**100 FRANCS**				
	1914-15.		40.00	100.00	175.00

ETAPPEN - INSPEKTION (RESUMED)

BASE INSPECTORATE, 3RD ARMY

1915 ISSUE
#M19-M26 issued in occupied French territory.

			VG	VF	UNC
M19	**1 FRANC**				
	1915.		40.00	100.00	175.00

		VG	VF	UNC
M20	**2 FRANCS** 1915.	40.00	100.00	175.00
M21	**3 FRANCS** 1915.	40.00	100.00	175.00
M22	**5 FRANCS** 1915.	40.00	100.00	175.00
M23	**10 FRANCS** 1915.	40.00	100.00	175.00
M24	**25 FRANCS** 1915.	40.00	100.00	175.00
M25	**100 FRANCS** 1915.	40.00	100.00	175.00
M26	**100 FRANCS** 1915.	40.00	100.00	175.00

REICHSMARINE DES OSTSEEBEREICHES

REICH'S NAVY OF THE BALTIC SEA ZONE

KIEL BRANCH

1923 ISSUE

M27	**1 MILLIARDE MARK** 27.10.1923.	10.00	20.00	35.00

		VG	VF	UNC
M28	**5 MILLIARDEN MARK**	7.00	15.00	30.00
M29	**20 MILLIARDEN MARK**	3.00	6.00	12.00
M30	**50 MILLIARDEN MARK**	3.00	6.00	12.00

BEHELFSZAHLUNGSMITTEL FÜR DIE DEUTSCHE

WEHRMACHT

AUXILIARY PAYMENT CERTIFICATES, GERMAN ARMED FORCES

1940 ND ISSUE

Intended as legal tender within the services during World War II. Worth 10 times the face value if spent in military channels.

NOTE: Also see Greece #M19-M22.

		VG	VF	UNC
M31	**1 REICHSPFENNIG** ND (1940). Lilac-brown. Swastika at ctr. in unpt.	25.00	65.00	400.00

1942 ND ISSUE

#M32-M37 have unpt. eagle w/small swastika in unpt. at ctr.

M32	**1 REICHSPFENNIG** ND (1942). Blue.	2.00	4.00	8.00
M33	**5 REICHSPFENNIG** ND (1942). Red.	2.00	4.00	10.00

		VG	VF	UNC
M34	**10 REICHSPFENNIG** ND (1942). Green.	1.00	3.00	12.00
M35	**50 REICHSPFENNIG** ND (1942). Red-orange.	2.00	6.00	20.00
M36	**1 REICHSMARK** ND (1942). Brown on orange unpt.	5.00	15.00	60.00

		VG	VF	UNC
M37	**2 REICHSMARK** ND (1942). Dk. blue on lilac unpt.	15.00	40.00	120.00

VERRECHNUNGSSCHEINE FÜR DIE DEUTSCHE

WEHRMACHT

CLEARING NOTES FOR GERMAN ARMED FORCES

Superseded the Auxiliary Payment Certificates in 1944; face value corresponded to the actual value as legal tender.

1944 ISSUE

		VG	VF	UNC
M38	**1 REICHSMARK** 15.9.1944. Green.	.50	1.00	4.50
M39	**5 REICHSMARK** 15.9.1944. Blue.	.75	1.50	8.00

		VG	VF	UNC
M40	**10 REICHSMARK** 15.9.1944. Red.	.50	1.00	5.00
M41	**50 REICHSMARK** 15.9.1944. Lilac-brown.	5.00	10.00	35.00

GERMAN FED. REP.

The Federal Republic of Germany (formerly West Germany), located in north-central Europe, since 1990 with the unification of East Germany, has an area of 137.82 sq. mi. (356,854 sq. km.) and a population of 81.30 million. Capital: Bonn. The economy centers about one of the world's foremost industrial establishments. Machinery, motor vehicles, iron, steel, yarns and fabrics are exported.

During the post-Normandy phase of World War II, Allied troops occupied the western German provinces of Schleswig-Holstein, Hamburg, Lower Saxony, Bremen, North Rhine-Westphalia, Hesse, Rhineland- Palatinate, Baden-Wurttemberg, Bavaria and Saarland. The conquered provinces were divided into American, British and French occupation zones. Five eastern German provinces were occupied and administered by the forces of the Soviet Union.

The western occupation forces restored the civil status of their zones on Sept. 21, 1949, and resumed diplomatic relations with the provinces on July 2, 1951. On May 5, 1955, nine of the ten western provinces, organized as the Federal Republic of Germany, became fully independent. The tenth province, Saarland, was restored to the republic on Jan. 1, 1957.

The post-WW II division of Germany ended on Oct. 3, 1990, when the German Democratic Republic (East Germany) ceased to exist and its five constituent provinces were formally admitted to the Federal Republic of Germany. An election Dec. 2, 1990, chose representatives to the united federal parliament (Bundestag), which then conducted its opening session in Berlin in the old Reichstag building. Although Berlin technically is the capital of the reunited Germany, the actual seat of government remains for the time being in Bonn.

MONETARY SYSTEM:
1 Deutsche Mark (DM) = 100 Pfennig

ALLIED OCCUPATION - POST WWII

U.S. ARMY COMMAND

1948 FIRST ISSUE

#1 and 2 printer: Forbes Litho (w/o imprint).

#1-10 were known as "Special Army Currency" and were issued under military authority and w/o name of country.

#1-10, also #13-17 may come w/stamped: *B* in circle, perforated: *B* or w/both varieties on the same note. These markings were made as a temporary check on currency circulating in West Berlin.

#5-8 printer: ABNC (w/o imprint).

#3, 4, 9 and 10 printer: Tudor Press, Boston, Mass. U.S.A. (W/o imprint).

NOTE: #10 was in circulation for only a very few days.

1 1/2 DEUTSCHE MARK
	VG	VF	UNC
1948. Green on lt. green and lt. brown unpt. Back brown and blue.			
a. Issued note.	2.50	17.50	100.00
b. Stamped: *B* in circle.	2.50	17.50	150.00
c. Perforated: *B*.	2.50	17.50	225.00
d. Stamped and perforated: *B* on the same note.	3.00	60.00	250.00
s1. As a. perforated: *SPECIMEN*.	—	—	150.00
s2. Specimen w/red ovpt: *MUSTER*.	—	—	150.00

2 1 DEUTSCHE MARK
	VG	VF	UNC
1948. Blue on blue-green and lilac unpt. Back brown on lilac unpt.			
a. Issued note.	2.00	20.00	80.00
b. Stamped: *B* in circle.	2.00	20.00	150.00
c. Perforated: *B*.	2.00	30.00	225.00
d. Stamped and perforated: *B* on the same note.	2.50	60.00	250.00
s1. As a. perforated: *SPECIMEN*.	—	—	125.00
s2. Specimen w/red ovpt: *MUSTER*.	—	—	125.00

3 2 DEUTSCHE MARK
	VG	VF	UNC
1948. Lilac on blue-green unpt. Allegorical woman seated at l. holding tablet. Back green on red unpt.			
a. Issued note.	7.50	60.00	400.00
b. Stamped: *B* in circle.	7.50	100.00	600.00
c. Perforated: *B*.	7.50	120.00	1000.
d. Stamped and perforated: *B* on the same note.	9.00	400.00	1200.
s1. As a. perforated: *SPECIMEN*.	—	—	250.00
s2. Specimen w/red ovpt: *MUSTER*.	—	—	200.00

4 5 DEUTSCHE MARK
	VG	VF	UNC
1948. Brown on green and gold unpt. Man seated at r. Back lilac and blue.			
a. Issued note.	6.00	45.00	150.00
b. Stamped: *B* in circle.	7.50	50.00	250.00
c. Perforated: *B*.	7.50	50.00	500.00
d. Stamped and perforated: *B* on the same note.	7.50	50.00	700.00
s1. As a. perforated: *SPECIMEN*	—	—	175.00
s2. Specimen w/44mm red ovpt: *MUSTER*.	—	—	175.00
s3. Specimen w/54mm red ovpt: *MUSTER*.	—	—	175.00

1948 SECOND ISSUE

5 10 DEUTSCHE MARK
	VG	VF	UNC
1948. Blue on m/c unpt. Allegorical figures of 2 women and a man at ctr.			
a. Issued note.	8.00	25.00	200.00
b. Handstamped: *B* in circle.	9.00	30.00	225.00
c. Perforated: *B*.	9.00	30.00	300.00
d. Handstamped and perforated: *B* on the same note.	9.00	30.00	500.00
s1. As a. perforated: *SPECIMEN*.	—	—	200.00
s2. Specimen w/red ovpt: *MUSTER*.	—	—	200.00
s3. As s2. perforated *SPECIMEN*.	—	—	200.00

6 20 DEUTSCHE MARK
	VG	VF	UNC
1948. Green on m/c unpt. 2 allegorical figures at l.			
a. Issued note.	17.50	55.00	200.00
b. Handstamped: *B* in circle.	17.50	55.00	225.00
c. Perforated: *B*.	17.50	55.00	300.00
d. Handstamped and perforated: *B* on the same note.	17.50	55.00	500.00
s1. As a. perforated *SPECIMEN*.	—	—	200.00
s2. Speciman w/red ovpt: *MUSTER*.	—	—	200.00

7 50 DEUTSCHE MARK
	VG	VF	UNC
1948. Purple on m/c unpt. Allegorical woman at ctr.			
a. Issued note.	50.00	120.00	600.00
b. Handstamped: *B* in circle.	50.00	120.00	800.00
c. Perforated: *B*.	100.00	250.00	—
d. Handstamped and perforated: *B* on the same note.	50.00	120.00	1000.
s1. Specimen w/red ovpt: *MUSTER*.	—	—	200.00

8 100 DEUTSCHE MARK
	VG	VF	UNC
1948. Red on m/c unpt. Allegorical woman w/globe at ctr.			
a. Issued note.	85.00	225.00	1500.
b. Handstamped: *B* in circle.	85.00	225.00	2000.
c. Perforated: *B*.		Rare	—
d. Handstamped and perforated: *B* on the same note.	85.00	225.00	3000.
s1. As d. perforated *SPECIMEN*.	—	—	250.00
s2. Specimen w/red ovpt: *MUSTER* perforated *SPECIMEN*.	—	—	250.00

1948 ND THIRD ISSUE

9	20 DEUTSCHE MARK	VG	VF	UNC
	ND (1948). Blue on blue-green and orange unpt. Medallic woman's head at l. Back red on green unpt.			
	a. Issued note.	150.00	300.00	550.00
	b. Handstamped: *B* in circle.	150.00	300.00	800.00
	c. Perforated: *B*.	150.00	300.00	1200.
	d. Handstamped and perforated: *B* on the same note.	150.00	300.00	1600.
	s1. As a. perforated *SPECIMEN*.	—	—	200.00
	s2. Specimen w/red ovpt: *MUSTER*.	—	—	200.00
	s3. As s2. perforated: *SPECIMEN*.	—	—	200.00

10	50 DEUTSCHE MARK	VG	VF	UNC
	ND (1948). Green-blue. Allegorical woman at ctr.			
	a. Issued note.	1000.	1500.	3000.
	b. Handstamped: *B* in circle.	1000.	1500.	—
	s1. Specimen.	—	—	1000.
	s2. Specimen w/red ovpt: *MUSTER*.	—	—	1000.
	s3. Specimen perforated: *B*.	—	—	—

BANK DEUTSCHER LÄNDER

1948 ISSUE

#16-17 printer: ABNC (w/o imprint).
#14-15 portr. as wmk. Printer: Banque de France.

11	5 PFENNIG	VG	VF	UNC
	ND (1948). Green on lilac unpt. Back lilac.			
	a. Issued note.	.60	3.00	12.00
	s. Specimen w/red ovpt: *MUSTER*.	—	—	60.00
12	10 PFENNIG			
	ND (1948). Blue on brown unpt. Back brown.			
	a. Issued note.	.60	3.00	12.00
	s. Specimen w/red ovpt: *MUSTER*.	—	—	60.00

13	5 DEUTSCHE MARK	VG	VF	UNC
	9.12.1948. Black on green and yellow unpt. Woman (Europa) on the bull at r. Wmk: Woman's head.			
	a. Series letter A-6A. Printer: TDLR (w/o imprint).	6.00	30.00	90.00
	b. As a. handstamped *B* in circle.	18.00	60.00	125.00
	c. As a. perforated *B*.	20.00	65.00	150.00
	d. As a. handstamped and perforated *B* on same note.	22.50	75.00	175.00
	e. Number w/series letter 1A-6A.	4.00	10.00	30.00
	f. As e. handstamped *B* in circle.	10.00	20.00	50.00
	g. As e. perforated *B*.	10.00	20.00	50.00
	h. As e. handstamped and perforated *B* on same note.	15.00	30.00	75.00
	i. Number w/series letter 7A-(?). Printer: BDK (w/o imprint).	4.00	7.50	20.00
	s1. Series letter A w/red ovpt: *SPECIMEN* perforated *SPECIMEN*.	—	—	150.00
	s2. Series letter 7A w/red ovpt: *MUSTER* on face and back.	—	—	150.00
14	50 DEUTSCHE MARK			
	9.12.1948. Brown and black on yellow-green unpt. Merchant Imhof by A. Durer at l. Imhof at l., men w/ship at r. on back.			
	a. Issued note.	32.50	45.00	80.00
	b. Handstamped: *B* in circle.	32.50	75.00	350.00
	s. Specimen w/red ovpt: *MUSTER*.	—	—	200.00

15	100 DEUTSCHE MARK	VG	VF	UNC
	9.12.1948. Black and brown on blue unpt. Councillor J. Muffel by A. Durer at r. Muffel at l., old city view at ctr. on back.			
	a. Issued note.	62.50	75.00	125.00
	b. Stamped: *B* in circle.	62.50	250.00	500.00
	s1. Specimen w/89mm red ovpt: *MUSTER*.	—	—	200.00
	s2. Specimen w/99mm red ovpt: *MUSTER*.	—	—	200.00

1949 ISSUE

16	10 DEUTSCHE MARK	VG	VF	UNC
	22.8.1949. Blue. Similar to #5 but w/bank name.			
	a. Issued note.	6.50	10.00	35.00
	b. Stamped: *B* in circle.	6.50	10.00	250.00
	s1. As a. w/red ovpt: *MUSTER*.	—	—	100.00
	s2. As s1. perforated *SPECIMEN*.	—	—	100.00

17	20 DEUTSCHE MARK	VG	VF	UNC
	22.8.1949. Green. Similar to #6 but w/bank name.			
	a. Issued note.	12.50	25.00	200.00
	b. Handstamped: *B* in circle.	12.50	125.00	400.00
	s1. As a. perforated: *SPECIMEN*.	—	—	100.00
	s2. As s1. w/red ovpt: *MUSTER*.	—	—	100.00

FEDERAL REPUBLIC

DEUTSCHE BUNDESBANK

1960 ISSUE

#18-43 portr. as wmk.
#19-21 and 23 w/ or w/o ultraviolet senstive features.

18	5 DEUTSCHE MARK	VG	VF	UNC
	2.1.1960. Green on m/c unpt. Young Venetian woman by A. Durer at r. Sprig on back.	FV	5.00	13.00
19	10 DEUTSCHE MARK			
	2.1.1960. Blue on m/c unpt. Young man at r. Sailing ship *Gorch Fock* on back.	FV	20.00	45.00
20	20 DEUTSCHE MARK			
	2.1.1960. Black and green on m/c unpt. E. Tucher by A. Durer ar r. Violin, bow and clarinet on back.	FV	35.00	80.00
21	50 DEUTSCHE MARK	VG	VF	UNC
	2.1.1960. Brown and olive-green on m/c unpt. Chamberlain H. Urmiller at r. Lubecker Holsten-Tor gate on back.	FV	45.00	95.00

22	**100 DEUTSCHE MARK**	**VG**	**VF**	**UNC**
	2.1.1960. Blue on m/c unpt. Master Seb. Munster at r. Eagle on back.	FV	80.00	175.00
23	**500 DEUTSCHE MARK**	**VG**	**VF**	**UNC**
	2.1.1960. Brown-lilac on m/c unpt. Male portrait by Hans Maler zu Schwaz. Castle Felz on back.	FV	FV	650.00

24	**1000 DEUTSCHE MARK**			
	2.1.1960. Dk. brown on m/c unpt. Astronomer Schoner (by Lucas Cranach the Elder) at r. and as wmk. Cathedral of Limburg on the Lahn on back.	FV	FV	1500.

The German Democratic Republic (East Germany), located on the great north European plain ceased to exist in 1990. During the closing days of World War II in Europe, Soviet troops advancing into Germany from the east occupied the German provinces of Mecklenburg, Brandenburg, Saxony-Anhalt, Saxony and Thuringia. These five provinces comprised the occupation zone administered by the Soviet Union after the cessation of hostilities. The other three zones were administered by the U.S., Great Britain and France. Under the Potsdam agreement, questions affecting Germany as a whole were to be settled by the commanders in chief of the occupation zones acting jointly and by unanimous decision. When Soviet intransigence rendered the quadripartite commission inoperable, the three western zones were united to form the Federal Republic of Germany, May 23, 1949. Thereupon the Soviet Union dissolved its occupation zone and established it as the Democratic Republic of Germany, Oct. 7, 1949. East and West Germany became reunited as one country on July 1, 1990.

MONETARY SYSTEM:
   1 Mark = 100 Pfennig

SOVIET OCCUPATION - POST WWII

TREASURY

1948 PROVISIONAL ISSUE
Introduction of the Deutsche Mark-Ost (East).
#1-7 adhesive validation stamps on old Rentenmark and Reichsbank notes.
NOTE: Germany #171, 172, 177 and 178 are also encountered with these adhesive stamps although they were not officially issued as such.

1	**1 DEUTSCHE MARK**	**VG**	**VF**	**UNC**
	1948 (-old date 30.1.1937). Blue adhesive stamp on Germany 1 Rentenmark #173.	1.00	3.50	10.00
2	**2 DEUTSCHE MARK**			
	1948 (-old date 30.1.1937). Green adhesive stamp on Germany 2 Rentenmark #174.	1.50	4.50	15.00

3	**5 DEUTSCHE MARK**	**VG**	**VF**	**UNC**
	1948 (-old date 1.8.1942). Brown adhesive stamp on Germany 5 Reichsmark #186.	1.75	5.00	15.00

4	**10 DEUTSCHE MARK**	**VG**	**VF**	**UNC**
	1948 (-old date 22.1.1929). Lilac adhesive stamp.			
	a. On Germany 10 Reichsmark #180a.	1.50	4.50	17.50
	b. On Germany 10 Reichsmark #180b.	1.50	4.50	17.50

5	**20 DEUTSCHE MARK**	**VG**	**VF**	**UNC**
	1948 (-old dates 1929; 1939). Brown adhesive stamp.			
	a. On Germany 20 Reichsmark #181a. (-old date 22.1.1929).	2.50	7.50	30.00
	b. On Germany 20 Reichsmark #181b. (-old date 22.1.1929).	2.50	7.50	30.00
	c. On Germany 20 Reichsmark #185. (-old date 16.6.1939).	3.00	8.50	40.00

6   50 DEUTSCHE MARK

		VG	VF	UNC
	1948 (-old date 30.3.1933). Blue-gray adhesive stamp.			
a.	On Germany 50 Reichsmark #182a.	2.50	7.50	30.00
b.	On Germany 50 Reichsmark #182b.	2.50	7.50	30.00

7   100 DEUTSCHE MARK

		VG	VF	UNC
	1948 (-old date 24.6.1935). Blue-green adhesive stamp.			
a.	On Germany 100 Reichsmark #183a.	4.00	10.00	45.00
b.	On Germany 100 Reichsmark #183b.	4.00	10.00	45.00

DEMOCRATIC REPUBLIC

DEUTSCHE NOTENBANK

1948 ISSUE
#8-16 w/o pictorial design.
#8a-13a printer: Goznak, USSR.
#8b-13b printer: East Germany.

8   50 DEUTSCHE PFENNIG

		VG	VF	UNC
	1948. Blue on brown unpt.			
a.	6 digit serial #.	2.50	7.50	35.00
b.	7 digit serial #.	.50	1.65	6.50

9   1 DEUTSCHE MARK

	1948. Olive-brown on olive and brown unpt.			
a.	6 digit serial #.	2.00	6.00	27.50
b.	7 digit serial #.	.35	1.00	4.00

10   2 DEUTSCHE MARK

		VG	VF	UNC
	1948. Brown on lt. brown and green unpt.			
a.	6 digit serial #.	2.00	6.00	27.50
b.	7 digit serial #.	.45	1.35	5.50

11   5 DEUTSCHE MARK

	1948. Dk. brown on green and lt. brown unpt.			
a.	6 digit serial 3, w/o plate #.	1.75	5.00	25.00
b.	7 digit serial #, w/plate #.	.35	1.00	4.00

12   10 DEUTSCHE MARK

	1948. Black on green and lt. brown unpt.			
a.	6 digit serial #, w/o plate #.	2.50	7.50	30.00
b.	7 digit serial #, w/plate #.	.50	1.65	6.50

13   20 DEUTSCHE MARK

		VG	VF	UNC
	1948. Dk. brown on red-brown and green unpt.			
a.	6 digit serial #, w/o plate #.	2.00	6.00	27.50
b.	7 digit serial #, w/plate #.	.65	2.00	8.00

14   50 DEUTSCHE MARK

	1948. Green on brown unpt.			
a.	W/o plate #. Single letter prefix.	1.50	4.50	20.00
b.	W/plate #. Double letter prefix.	.50	1.65	6.50

15   100 DEUTSCHE MARK
1948. Blue on green and lt. brown unpt.   1.00   3.00   12.00

16   1000 DEUTSCHE MARK

	VG	VF	UNC
1948. Brown on green and lt. brown unpt.	7.50	22.50	90.00

1955 ISSUE

17   5 DEUTSCHE MARK
1955. Gray and black on brown and red-brown unpt.   1.25   3.50   7.00

18   10 DEUTSCHE MARK

	1955. Lt. purple on olive and dk. orange unpt.			
a.	Issued note.	2.00	6.00	17.00
s.	Specimen ovpt: *MUSTER*.	—	—	75.00

19   20 DEUTSCHE MARK

	VG	VF	UNC
1955. Dk. blue on lt. tan and red-brown unpt.	2.00	6.00	23.00

20   50 DEUTSCHE MARK
1955. Dk. red on orange and lt. green unpt.   3.00   8.50   35.00

21   100 DEUTSCHE MARK
1955. Brown on lt. blue, green and pink unpt.   6.00   20.00   65.00

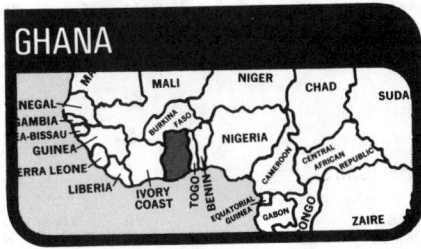

GHANA

The Republic of Ghana, a member of the British Commonwealth situated on the West Coast of Africa between the Ivory Coast and Togo, has an area of 92,098 sq. mi. (238,537 sq. km.) and a population of 15.6 million, almost entirely African. Capital: Accra. Cocoa (the major crop), coconuts, palm kernels and coffee are exported. Mining, second in importance to agriculture, is concentrated on gold, manganese and industrial diamonds.

Ghana was first visited by Portuguese traders in 1470, and through the 17th century was used by various European powers - England, Denmark, Holland, Germany - as a center for their slave trade. Britain achieved control of the Gold Coast in 1821, and established the colony of Gold Coast in 1874. In 1901, Britain annexed the neighboring Ashanti Kingdom; the same year a northern region known as the Northern Territories became a British protectorate. Part of the former German colony of Togoland was mandated to Britain by the League of Nations and administered as part of the Gold Coast. The state of Ghana, comprising the Gold Coast and British Togoland, obtained independence on March 6, 1957, becoming the first black African colony to do so. On July 1, 1960, Ghana adopted a republican constitution, changing from a ministerial to a presidential form of government. The government was overthrown, the constitution suspended and the National Assembly dissolved by the Ghanaian Army and police on Feb. 24, 1966. The government was returned to civilian authority in Oct. 1969, but was again seized by military officers in a bloodless coup on Jan. 13, 1972. Ghana remains a member of the Commonwealth of Nations, with executive authority vested in the Supreme Military Council.

Ghana's monetary denomination of "cedi" is derived from the word "sedie" meaning cowrie, a shell money commonly employed by coastal tribes.

MONETARY SYSTEM:
1 Shilling = 12 Pence
1 Pound = 20 Shillings to 1965
1 Cedi = 100 Pesewas, 1965-

REPUBLIC

BANK OF GHANA

1958-63 ISSUE
#1-3 various date and sign. varieties. Wmk: *GHANA* in star.

1	10 SHILLINGS	VG	VF	UNC
	1958-63. Green and brown. Bank bldg. in Accra at ctr r. Star on back.			
	a. 2 sign. Printer: TDLR. 1.7.1958.	2.00	5.00	20.00
	b. W/o imprint. 1.7.1961; 1.7.1962.	1.00	3.00	12.00
	c. 1 sign. 1.7.1963.	.75	2.50	10.00

2	1 POUND	VG	VF	UNC
	1958-62. Red-brown and blue. Bank bldg. in Accra at ctr. Coconuts in 2 piles on back.			
	a. Printer: TDLR. 1.7.1958. 1.4.1959.	1.00	3.00	12.00
	b. W/o imprint. 1.7.1961; 1.7.1962.	1.00	2.50	10.00

3	5 POUNDS	VG	VF	UNC
	1.7.1958-1.7.1962. Purple and orange. Bank bldg. in Accra at ctr. Cargo ships, logs in water on back.	5.00	15.00	45.00

4	1000 POUNDS	VG	VF	UNC
	1.7.1958. Black-brown. Bank in Accra at lower r. Used in inter-bank transactions.	—	100.00	300.00

The British Colony of Gibraltar, located at the southernmost point of the Iberian Peninsula, has an area of 2.25 sq. mi. (5.8 sq. km.) and a population of 29,048 Capital (and only town): Gibraltar. Aside from its strategic importance as guardian of the western entrance to the Mediterranean Sea, Gibraltar is also a free port, British naval base, and coaling station.

Gibraltar, rooted in Greek mythology as one of the Pillars of Hercules, has long been a coveted stronghold. Moslems took it from Spain and fortified it in 711. Spain retook it in 1309, lost it again to the Moors in 1333, and retook it in 1462. After Barbarossa sacked Gibraltar in 1540, Spain strengthened its defenses and held it until the War of the Spanish Succession when it was captured by a combined British and Dutch force, 1704. Britain held it against the Franco-Spanish attacks of 1704-05 and through the historic "Great Siege" of 1779-83. Recently Spain has attempted to discourage British occupancy by harassment and economic devices. In 1967, Gibraltar's inhabitants voted 12,138 to 44 to remain under British rule.

RULERS:
British

MONETARY SYSTEM:
1 Shilling = 12 Pence
1 Pound = 20 Shillings to 1971
1 Pound = 100 New Pence, 1971-

BRITISH INFLUENCE

GOVERNMENT OF GIBRALTAR

1914 EMERGENCY WWI SERIES A
#1-5 embossed stamp of the Anglo-Egyptian B.

		GOOD	FINE	XF
1	**2 SHILLINGS = 2 CHELINES** 6.8.1914. Red.	425.00	1000.	—
2	**10 SHILLINGS = 10 CHELINES** 6.8.1914. Blue.	850.00	2000.	—
3	**1 POUND = 1 LIBRA** 6.8.1914. Black. Yellow paper.	1250.	500.00	—
4	**5 POUNDS = 5 LIBRAS** 6.8.1914. Black. Blue paper.	—	Rare	—
5	**50 POUNDS = 50 LIBRAS** 6.8.1914. Black. Blue paper.	—	Rare	—

1914 SERIES B

		GOOD	FINE	XF
6	**2 SHILLINGS = 2 CHELINES** 6.8.1914. Green on pink. Arms at top ctr.	100.00	250.00	500.00

		GOOD	FINE	XF
7	**10 SHILLINGS = 10 CHELINES** 6.8.1914. Lilac on pink.	200.00	500.00	—
8	**1 POUND = 1 LIBRA** 6.8.1914. Blue on green.	275.00	750.00	—
9	**5 POUNDS = 5 LIBRAS** 6.8.1914. Brown on green.	—	Rare	—
10	**50 POUNDS = 50 LIBRAS** 6.8.1914. Pink on green.	—	Rare	—

1927 ORDINANCE, REGULAR ISSUE
#11-13 printer: W&S.

		VG	VF	UNC
11	**10 SHILLINGS = 10 CHELINES** 1.10.1927. Blue on yellow-brown unpt. Rock of Gibraltar at upper l.	30.00	100.00	400.00
12	**1 POUND** 1.10.1927. Green on yellow-brown unpt. Rock of Gilbraltar at bottom ctr.	37.50	125.00	500.00
13	**5 POUNDS** 1.10.1927. Brown. Rock of Gilbraltar at bottom ctr.	75.00	250.00	1000.

1934 ORDINANCE, 1938-42 ISSUE
#14-16 printer: W&S.

		VG	VF	UNC
14	**10 SHILLINGS** 1937-58. Blue on yellow-brown unpt. Rock of Gibraltar at upper l. 2 serial # varieties and 4 sign. varieties.			
	a. Sign. title: *TREASURER*. 1.2.1937.	15.00	65.00	275.00
	b. Sign. title: *FINANCIAL SECRETARY*. 1.6.1942; 1.7.1954; 3.10.1958.	5.00	17.50	75.00

		VG	VF	UNC
15	**1 POUND** 1938-58. Green on yellow-brown unpt. Rock of Gibraltar at bottom ctr. 2 serial varieties and 5 sign. varieties.			
	a. Sign. title: *TREASURER*. 1.6.1938.	25.00	90.00	350.00
	b. Sign. title: *FINANCIAL SECRETARY*. 1.6.1942; 1.12.1949.	5.00	20.00	85.00
	c. As b. 1.7.1954; 3.10.1958.	3.00	15.00	70.00
16	**5 POUNDS** 1942-58. Brown. Rock of Gilbraltar at bottom ctr. 2 serial # varieties and 4 sign. varieties.			
	a. 1.6.1942.	20.00	90.00	300.00
	b. 1.12.1949.	15.00	45.00	185.00
	c. 1.7.1954; 3.10.1958.	12.50	35.00	135.00

1958 ISSUE
#17-19 printer: TDLR.

		VG	VF	UNC
17	**10 SHILLINGS** 3.10.1958; 1.5.1965. Blue on yellow-brown unpt. Rock of Gibraltar at l.	2.50	15.00	95.00

18 1 POUND
1958-75. Green on yellow-brown unpt. Rock of Gibraltar at bottom ctr.

		VG	VF	UNC
a.	Sign. title: *FINANCIAL SECRETARY*. 3.10.1958; 1.5.1965.	2.50	8.50	37.50
b.	Sign. title: *FINANCIAL AND DEVELOPMENT SECRETARY*. 20.11.1971.	2.00	5.00	17.00
c.	20.11.1975.	3.00	15.00	85.00

19 5 POUNDS
1958-75. Brown. Rock of Gibraltar at bottom ctr.

		VG	VF	UNC
a.	Sign. title: *FINANCIAL SECRETARY*. 3.10.1958; 1.5.1965.	12.50	35.00	165.00
b.	Sign. title: *FINANCIAL AND DEVELOPMENT SECRETARY*. 1.5.1965; 20.11.1971; 20.11.1975.	10.00	27.50	125.00

The Gilbert and Ellice Islands comprised a British colony made up of 40 atolls and islands in the western Pacific Ocean. The colony consisted of the Gilbert Islands, the Ellice Islands, Ocean Island, Fanning, Washington and Christmas Island in the Line Islands, and the Phoenix Islands. The principal industries were copra production and phosphate mining.

Early inhabitants were Melanesian but the Ellice Islands were occupied in the 16th century by the Samoans, who established the Polynesian race there. The first Europeans to land in the islands came in 1764. James Cook was there in 1777. Britain declared a protectorate over the islands in 1892 and made it a colony in 1915. In World War II the Gilberts were occupied by the Japanese from Dec. 1941 to Nov. 1943. The colony adopted a new constitution and became self-governing in 1971. The Ellice Islands became Tuvalu in 1976 with independence in 1978. The balance of the colony became Kiribati in 1979.

Australian currency is currently used in circulation.

RULERS:
British until 1978-79

MONETARY SYSTEM:
1 Pound = 20 Shillings
1 Shilling = 12 Pence

BRITISH INFLUENCE

GILBERT AND ELLICE ISLANDS COLONY

1942 EMERGENCY WWII ISSUE
#1-5 made by mimeograph process. Embossed seal: *COURT OF H.R.H. HIGH COMMISSIONER FOR WESTERN PACIFIC* at l. Uniface

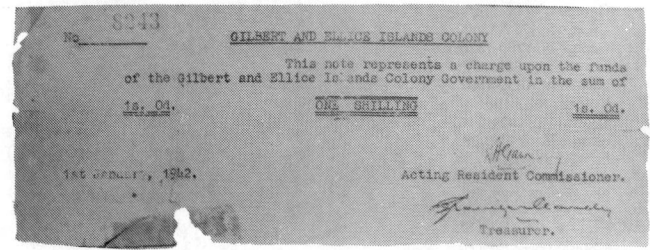

1 1 SHILLING
1.1.1942. White paper. — Rare —

2 2 SHILLINGS
1.1.1942. Reported Not Confirmed

3 5 SHILLINGS
1.1.1942. Reported Not Confirmed

4 10 SHILLINGS
1.1.1942. Reported Not Confirmed

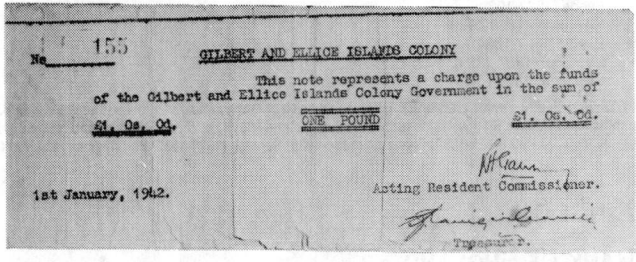

5 1 POUND
1.1.1942. Pink paper. — Rare —

The United Kingdom of Great Britain and Northern Ireland, located off the northwest coast of the European continent, has an area of 94,227 sq. mi. (244,046 sq. km.) and a population of 57.7 million. Capital: London. The economy is based on industrial activity and trading. Machinery, motor vehicles, chemicals, and textile yarns and fabrics are exported.

After the departure of the Romans, who brought Britain into an active relationship with Europe, Britain fell prey to invaders from Scandinavia and the Low Countries who drove the original Britons into Scotland and Wales, and established a profusion of kingdoms that finally united in the 11th century under the Danish King Canute. Norman rule, following the conquest of 1066, stimulated the development of those institutions which have since distinguished British life. Henry VIII (1509-47) turned Britain from continental adventuring and faced it to the sea - a decision that made Britain a world power during the reign of Elizabeth I (1558-1603). Strengthened by the Industrial Revolution and the defeat of Napoleon, 19th century Britain turned to the remote parts of the world and established a colonial empire of such extent and prosperity that the world has never seen its like. World Wars I and II sealed the fate of the Empire and relegated Britain to a lesser role in world affairs by draining her resources and inaugurating a worldwide movement toward national self-determination in her former colonies.

By the mid-20th century, most of the territories formerly comprising the British Empire had gained independence, and the empire had evolved into the Commonwealth of Nations, an association of equal and autonomous states which enjoy special trade interests. The Commonwealth is presently (1983) composed of 49 member nations, including the United Kingdom. All recognize the British monarch as head of the Commonwealth. Fourteen continue to recognize the British monarch as Chief of State. They are: United Kingdom, Australia, New Zealand, Bahamas, Barbados, Canada, Fiji, Jamaica, Mauritius, Papua New Guinea, Solomon Islands, St. Lucia, Kiribati and Tuvalu.

* * * This section has been renumbered. * * *

RULERS:
William III, 1694-1702
Anne, 1702-1714
George I, 1714-1727
George II, 1727-1760
George III, 1760-1820
George IV, 1820-1830
William IV, 1830-1837
Victoria, 1837-1901
Edward VII, 1901-1910
George V, 1910-1936
Edward VIII, 1936
George VI, 1936-1952
Elizabeth II, 1952-

MONETARY SYSTEM:
1 Shilling = 12 Pence
1 Pound = 20 Shillings to 1971
1 Pound = 100 New Pence, 1971-
1 Guinea = 21 Shillings

BRANCH OFFICES:
Branch office notes were introduced beginning w/Henry Hase in 1826.
Birmingham (1826-1939)
Gloucester (1826-1939)
Manchester (1826-1939)
Bristol (1827-1939)
Leeds (1827-1939)
Newcastle (1828-1939)
Exeter (1827-1834)
Liverpool (1827-1939)
Swansea (1826-)

NOTE: Branch office notes are worth from twice as much or more compared with the more common "London" issues. Thomas Rippon, 1829-1835 Market value from $2000. in VF. Additional branch offices of this series includes Hull (1829-1939) Plymouth (1834-1939) Norwich (1829-1852) Portsmouth (1834-1914).

KINGDOM

BANK OF ENGLAND

Founded in 1694, the Bank of England is the greatest banking institution formed. Although torn by crisis in its infancy, today it enjoys the public's confidence in the expression "As safe as the Bank of England".

The earliest recorded notes were all handwritten promissory notes and certificates of deposit of 1694. The first partially printed notes were introduced ca. 1696 with handwritten amounts. By 1745 all notes were printed with partial denominations of round figures in denominations of 20 Pounds through 1000 Pounds, allowing handwritten denominations of shillings to be added on.

In 1759 the word *POUNDS* was also printed on the notes.

From 1752 the Chief Cashier's handwritten name as payee is usually found and from 1782 it was used exclusively. From 1798 until 1855 it was actually printed on the notes. In 1855 notes were produced made simply payable to *bearer*. Notes were issued in denominations of 1 Pound through 1000 Pounds.

For specialized listings of early Bank of England notes refer to *English Paper Money*, by Vincent Duggleby.

1694-95 ISSUE

#25-29 signed by Thomas Speed. Handwritten.

		GOOD	FINE	XF
25	**5 POUNDS** 1695-99. Black			
	a. 1695-97. W/o wmk in paper.	—	Rare	—
	b. 1697-99. W/wmk. in paper.	—	Rare	—
26	**10 POUNDS** 1694-99. Black.			

		GOOD	FINE	XF
27	**20 POUNDS** 1694-99. Black.	—	Rare	—
28	**50 POUNDS** 1694-99. Black.	—	Rare	—
29	**100 POUNDS** 1694-99. Black	—	Rare	—

1699 ISSUE

#35-39 medallion of Britannia w/spear and olive branch. Handwritten denominations. Signed by Thomas Madocks.

35	**5 POUNDS** 1699-1707. Black.	—	Rare	—
36	**10 POUNDS** 1699-1707. Black.	—	Rare	—
37	**20 POUNDS** 1699-1707. Black.	—	Rare	—
38	**50 POUNDS** 1699-1707. Black.	—	Rare	—
39	**100 POUNDS** 1699-1707. Black.	—	Rare	—

1707 ISSUE

#40-44 medallion of Britannia within foliate border. Signed by Thomas Madocks.

40	**5 POUNDS** 1707-25. Black.		Rare	—
41	**10 POUNDS** 1707-25. Black.		Rare	—
42	**20 POUNDS** 1707-25. Black.		Rare	—
43	**50 POUNDS** 1707-25. Black.		Rare	—
44	**100 POUNDS** 1707-25. Black.		Rare	—

1725 ISSUE

50	**20 POUNDS** 1725-39. Black.	—	Rare	
51	**30 POUNDS** 1725-39. Black.	—	Rare	
52	**40 POUNDS** 1725-39. Black.	—	Rare	
53	**50 POUNDS** 1725-39. Black.	—	Rare	
54	**60 POUNDS** 1725-39. Black.	—	Rare	
55	**70 POUNDS** 1725-39. Black.	—	Rare	
56	**80 POUNDS** 1725-39. Black.	—	Rare	
57	**90 POUNDS** 1725-39. Black.	—	Rare	
58	**100 POUNDS** 1725-39. Black.	—	Rare	
59	**200 POUNDS** 1725-39. Black.	—	Rare	
60	**300 POUNDS** 1725-39. Black.	—	Rare	
61	**400 POUNDS** 1725-39. Black.	—	Rare	
62	**500 POUNDS** 1725-39. Black.	—	Rare	
63	**1000 POUNDS** 1725-39. Black.	—	Rare	

1739 ISSUE

#66-78 signed by James Collier and Daniel Race.

65	**20 POUNDS** 1739-51. Black.	—	Rare	—
66	**30 POUNDS** 1739-51. Black.	—	Rare	—
67	**40 POUNDS** 1739-51. Black.	—	Rare	—
68	**50 POUNDS** 1739-51. Black.	—	Rare	—
69	**60 POUNDS** 1739-51. Black.	—	Rare	—
70	**70 POUNDS** 1739-51. Black.	—	Rare	—
71	**80 POUNDS** 1739-51. Black.	—	Rare	—
72	**90 POUNDS** 1739-51. Black.	—	Rare	—
73	**100 POUNDS** 1739-51. Black.	—	Rare	—
74	**200 POUNDS** 1739-51. Black.	—	Rare	—
75	**300 POUNDS** 1739-51. Black.	—	Rare	—
76	**400 POUNDS** 1739-51. Black.	—	Rare	—
77	**500 POUNDS** 1739-51. Black.	—	Rare	—
78	**1000 POUNDS** 1739-51. Black.	—	Rare	—

1751; 1759 Issue
#80-95 signed by Daniel Race and Elias Simes

		GOOD	FINE	XF
80	**10 POUNDS** 1759. Black.	—	Rare	—
81	**15 POUNDS** 1759. Black.	—	Rare	—
82	**20 POUNDS** 1751-59. Black.	—	Rare	—
83	**30 POUNDS** 1751-59. Black.	—	Rare	—
84	**40 POUNDS** 1751-59. Black.	—	Rare	—
85	**50 POUNDS** 1751-59. Black.	—	Rare	—
86	**60 POUNDS** 1751-59. Black.	—	Rare	—
87	**70 POUNDS** 1751-59. Black.	—	Rare	—
88	**80 POUNDS** 1751-59. Black.	—	Rare	—
89	**90 POUNDS** 1751-59. Black.	—	Rare	—
90	**100 POUNDS** 1751-59. Black.	—	Rare	—
91	**200 POUNDS** 1751-59. Black.	—	Rare	—
92	**300 POUNDS** 1751-59. Black.	—	Rare	—
93	**400 POUNDS** 1751-59. Black.	—	Rare	—
94	**500 POUNDS** 1751-59. Black.	—	Rare	—
95	**1000 POUNDS** 1751-59. Black.	—	Rare	—

1759; 1765 Issue
#100-115 signed by Danie Race.

		GOOD	FINE	XF
100	**10 POUNDS** 1759-75. Black.	—	Rare	—
101	**15 POUNDS** 1759-75. Black.	—	Rare	—
102	**20 POUNDS** 1759-75. Black.	—	Rare	—
103	**25 POUNDS** 1765-75. Black.	—	Rare	—
104	**30 POUNDS** 1759-75. Black.	—	Rare	—
105	**40 POUNDS** 1759-75. Black.	—	Rare	—
106	**50 POUNDS** 1759-75. Black.	—	Rare	—
107	**60 POUNDS** 1759-75. Black.	—	Rare	—
108	**70 POUNDS** 1759-75. Black.	—	Rare	—
109	**80 POUNDS** 1759-75. Black.	—	Rare	—
110	**90 POUNDS** 1759-75. Black.	—	Rare	—
111	**100 POUNDS** 1759-75. Black.	—	Rare	—
116	**100 POUNDS** 1759-75. Black.	—	Rare	—
112	**200 POUNDS** 1759-75. Balck.	—	Rare	—
113	**300 POUNDS** 1759-75. Black.	—	Rare	—
114	**400 POUNDS** 1759-75. Black.	—	Rare	—
115	**500 POUNDS** 1759-75. Black.	—	Rare	—

1775 Issue
#130-146 signed by Charles Jewson.

		GOOD	FINE	XF
130	**10 POUNDS** 1775-78. Black.	—	Rare	—
131	**15 POUNDS** 1775-78. Black.	—	Rare	—
132	**20 POUNDS** 1775-78. Black.	—	Rare	—
133	**25 POUNDS** 1775-78. Black.	—	Rare	—
134	**30 POUNDS** 1775-78. Black.	—	Rare	—
135	**40 POUNDS** 1775-78. Black.	—	Rare	—
136	**50 POUNDS** 1775-78. Black.	—	Rare	—
137	**60 POUNDS** 1775-78. Black.	—	Rare	—
138	**70 POUNDS** 1775-78. Black.	—	Rare	—
139	**80 POUNDS** 1775-78. Black.	—	Rare	—
140	**90 POUNDS** 1775-78. Black.	—	Rare	—

		GOOD	FINE	XF
141	**100 POUNDS** 1775-78. Black.	—	Rare	—
142	**200 POUNDS** 1775-78. Black.	—	Rare	—
143	**300 POUNDS** 1775-78. Black.	—	Rare	—
144	**400 POUNDS** 1775-78. Black.	—	Rare	—
145	**500 POUNDS** 1775-78. Black.	—	Rare	—
146	**1000 POUNDS** 1775-78. Black.	—	Rare	—

1778 Issue
#150-166 signed by Abraham Newland.

		GOOD	FINE	XF
150	**10 POUNDS** 1778-97. Black.	—	Rare	—
151	**15 POUNDS** 1778-1807. Black.	—	Rare	—
152	**20 POUNDS** 1778-1807. Black.	—	Rare	—
153	**25 POUNDS** 1778-1807. Black.	—	Rare	—
154	**30 POUNDS** 1778-1807. Black.	—	Rare	—
155	**40 POUNDS** 1778-1807. Black.	—	Rare	—
156	**50 POUNDS** 1778-1807. Black.	—	Rare	—
157	**60 POUNDS** 1778-1807. Black.	—	Rare	—
158	**70 POUNDS** 1778-1807. Black.	—	Rare	—
159	**80 POUNDS** 1778-1807. Black.	—	Rare	—
160	**90 POUNDS** 1778-1807. Black.	—	Rare	—
161	**100 POUNDS** 1778-1807. Black.	—	Rare	—
162	**200 POUNDS** 1778-1807. Black.	—	Rare	—
163	**300 POUNDS** 1778-1807. Black.	—	Rare	—
164	**400 POUNDS** 1778-1807. Balck.	—	Rare	—
165	**500 POUNDS** 1778-1807. Black.	—	Rare	—
166	**1000 POUNDS** 1778-1807. Black.	—	Rare	—

1793 Issue

		GOOD	FINE	XF
168	**5 POUNDS** 1793-1807. Black.	—	Rare	—

1797 Issue
#170-172 handwritten date, serial # and Cashier's name.

		GOOD	FINE	XF
170	**1 POUND** 1797. Black.	—	Rare	—
171	**2 POUNDS** 1797. Black.	—	Rare	—
172	**10 POUNDS** 1797. Black.	—	Rare	—

1798 Issue
#175-177 printed Cashier's name. Smaller size.

		GOOD	FINE	XF
175	**1 POUND** 1798-1801. Black.	—	Rare	—
176	**2 POUNDS** 1798-1801. Black.	—	Rare	—
177	**10 POUNDS** 1798-1805. Black.	—	Rare	—

1801 I<small>SSUE</small>

#180-181 new Watermark, standard size.

		G<small>OOD</small>	F<small>INE</small>	XF
180	**1 P<small>OUND</small>**			
	1801-03. Black.	—	Rare	—
181	**2 P<small>OUNDS</small>**			
	1801-03. Balck.	—	Rare	—

1803 I<small>SSUE</small>

#184-185 denomination in watermark.

184	**1 P<small>OUND</small>**			
	1803-07. Black.	—	Rare	—
185	**2 P<small>OUNDS</small>**			
	1803-05. Black.	—	Rare	—

1805 I<small>SSUE</small>

#187-188 bank of England head.

187	**2 P<small>OUNDS</small>**			
	1805-07. Black.	—	Rare	—
188	**10 P<small>OUNDS</small>**			
	1805-07. Black.	—	Rare	—

1807 I<small>SSUE</small>

#190-204 Henry Hase as Chief Cashier. Branch as London. Additional branches opened: 1826 - Gloucester, Manchester, Swansea; 1827 - Birmingham, Bristol, Exter, Leeds, Liverpool; 1828 - Newcastle.

190 **1 P<small>OUND</small>**

1807-29. Black.

	a. Handwritten date, w/countersignature.	—	Rare	—
	b. Handwritten date, w/o countersignature.	—	Rare	—
	c. Printed date and serial #.	—	Rare	—

191	**2 P<small>OUNDS</small>**			
	1807-29. Black.			
	a. Handwritten date, w/countersignature.	—	Rare	—
	b. Handwritten date, w/o countersignature.	—	Rare	—
	c. Printed date and serial #.	—	Rare	—
192	**5 P<small>OUNDS</small>**			
	1807-29. Black.			
	a. Handwritten date.	—	Rare	—
	b. Printed date and serial #.	—	Rare	—
193	**10 P<small>OUNDS</small>**			
	1807-29. Black.	—	Rare	—
194	**15 P<small>OUNDS</small>**			
	1807-22. Balck.	—	Rare	—
195	**20 P<small>OUNDS</small>**			
	1807-29. Black.	—	Rare	—
196	**25 P<small>OUNDS</small>**			
	1807-22. Black.	—	Rare	—
197	**30 P<small>OUNDS</small>**			
	1807-29. Black.	—	Rare	—
198	**40 P<small>OUNDS</small>**	F		
	1807-29. Black.	—	Rare	—

		G<small>OOD</small>	F<small>INE</small>	XF
199	**50 P<small>OUNDS</small>**			
	1807-29. Black.	—	Rare	—
200	**100 P<small>OUNDS</small>**			
	1807-29. Black.	—	Rare	—
201	**200 P<small>OUNDS</small>**			
	1807-29. Black.	—	Rare	—
202	**300 P<small>OUNDS</small>**			
	1807-29. Black.	—	Rare	—
203	**500 P<small>OUNDS</small>**			
	1807-29. Black.	—	Rare	—
204	**1000 P<small>OUNDS</small>**			
	1807-29. Black.	—	Rare	—

1829 I<small>SSUE</small>

#210-220 Thomas Rippon as Chief Cashier. Branch as London. Additional Branches were opened at Hull and Norwich (1829); Portsmouth (1834). Exeter closed in 1834.

210	**5 P<small>OUNDS</small>**			
	1829-35. Black.	—	Rare	—
211	**10 P<small>OUNDS</small>**			
	1829-35. Black.	—	Rare	—
212	**20 P<small>OUNDS</small>**			
	1829-35. Black.	—	Rare	—
213	**30 P<small>OUNDS</small>**			
	1829-35. Black.	—	Rare	—
214	**40 P<small>OUNDS</small>**			
	1829-35. Black.	—	Rare	—
215	**50 P<small>OUNDS</small>**			
	1829-35. Black.	—	Rare	—
216	**100 P<small>OUNDS</small>**			
	1829-35. Black.	—	Rare	—
217	**200 P<small>OUNDS</small>**			
	1829-35. Black.	—	Rare	—
218	**300 P<small>OUNDS</small>**			
	1829-35. Black.	—	Rare	—
219	**500 P<small>OUNDS</small>**			
	1829-35. Black.	—	Rare	—
220	**1000 P<small>OUNDS</small>**			
	1829-35. Black.	—	Rare	—

1835 I<small>SSUE</small>

#221-231 payable to Matthew Marshall as Chief Cashier.

221	**5 P<small>OUNDS</small>**			
	1835-53. Black.	—	Rare	—
222	**10 P<small>OUNDS</small>**			
	1835-53. Black.	—	Rare	—
223	**20 P<small>OUNDS</small>**			
	1835-53. Black.	—	Rare	—
224	**30 P<small>OUNDS</small>**			
	1835-52. Black.	—	Rare	—
225	**40 P<small>OUNDS</small>**			
	1835-51. Black.	—	Rare	—
226	**50 P<small>OUNDS</small>**			
	1835-53. Black.	—	Rare	—
227	**100 P<small>OUNDS</small>**			
	1835-53. Black.	—	Rare	—
228	**200 P<small>OUNDS</small>**			
	1835-53. Black.	—	Rare	—
229	**300 P<small>OUNDS</small>**			
	1835-53. Black.	—	Rare	—
230	**500 P<small>OUNDS</small>**			
	1835-53. Black.	—	Rare	—
231	**1000 P<small>OUNDS</small>**			
	1835-53. Black.	—	Rare	—

1853 I<small>SSUE</small>

#232-240 payable to Matthew Marshall as Chief Cashier. Printed signatures of Bank Officals: J. Vautin, H. Bock, J. Ferraby, J. Williams and J. Luson.

232	**5 P<small>OUNDS</small>**			
	1853-55. Black.	—	Rare	—
233	**10 P<small>OUNDS</small>**			
	1853-55. Black.	—	Rare	—
234	**20 P<small>OUNDS</small>**			
	1853-55. Black.	—	Rare	—
235	**50 P<small>OUNDS</small>**			
	1853-55. Black.	—	Rare	—
236	**100 P<small>OUNDS</small>**			
	1853-55. Black.	—	Rare	—
237	**200 P<small>OUNDS</small>**			
	1853-55. Black.	—	Rare	—
238	**300 P<small>OUNDS</small>**			
	1853-55. Black.	—	Rare	—
239	**500 P<small>OUNDS</small>**			
	1853-55. Black.	—	Rare	—
240	**1000 P<small>OUNDS</small>**			
	1853-55. Black.	—	Rare	—

1855 I<small>SSUE</small>

#241-249 "Pay to the bearer" notes, London. Modified Britannia vignette. The wmk. of Matthew Marshall's sign. was added to that of the value and bank name.

241	**5 P<small>OUNDS</small>**			
(1)	1855. London.			
	a. Sign. J. Vautin.	—	—	XF
	b. Sign. H. Bock.	—	—	—
	c. Sign. J. Ferraby.	—	—	—

		GOOD	FINE	XF
242 (2)	**10 POUNDS** 1855. London.	—	—	—
	a. Sign. J. Vautin.	—	—	—
	b. Sign. H. Bock.	—	—	—
	c. Sign. J. Ferraby.	—	—	—
243 (3)	**20 POUNDS** 1855. Sign. J. Williams. Londo n.	—	—	—
244 (4)	**50 POUNDS** 1855. Sign. J. Williams. Londo n.	—	—	—
245 (5)	**100 POUNDS** 1855. Sign. J. Williams. Londo n.	—	—	—
246 (6)	**200 POUNDS** 1855. Sign. J. Luson. London.	—	Rare	—
247 (7)	**300 POUNDS** 1855. Sign. J. Luson. London.	—	Rare	—
248 (8)	**500 POUNDS** 1855. Sign. J. Luson. London.	—	Rare	—
249 (9)	**1000 POUNDS** 1855. Sign. J. Luson. London.	—	Rare	—

1860 ISSUE

#250-258 additional branch office of this series is: Leicester (1843-1872).

250 (10)	**5 POUNDS** 1860. Sign. W. P. Gattie. London.	—	—	—
251 (11)	**10 POUNDS** 1860. Sign. W. P. Gattie. London.	—	—	—
252 (12)	**20 POUNDS** 1860. Sign. T. Kent. London.	—	—	—
253 (13)	**50 POUNDS** 1860. Sign. T. Kent. London.	—	—	—
254 (14)	**100 POUNDS** 1860. Sign. T. Kent. London.	—	—	—
255 (15)	**200 POUNDS** 1860. Sign. C. T. Whitmell. London.	—	Rare	—
256 (16)	**300 POUNDS** 1860. Sign. C. T. Whitmell. London.	—	Rare	—
257 (17)	**500 POUNDS** 1860. Sign. C. T. Whitmell. London.	—	Rare	—
258 (18)	**1000 POUNDS** 1860. Sign. C. T. Whitmell. London.	—	Rare	—

1864 ISSUE

#259-267 William Miller as Chief Cashier.

259 (19)	**5 POUNDS** 1864-66. Sign. W. P. Gattie. London.	—	—	—
260 (20)	**10 POUNDS** 1864-66. Sign. W. P. Gattie. London.	—	—	—
261 (21)	**20 POUNDS** 1864-66. Sign. T. Kent. London .	—	—	—
262 (22)	**50 POUNDS** 1864-66. Sign. T. Kent. London .	—	—	—
263 (23)	**100 POUNDS** 1864-66. Sign. T. Kent. London .	—	—	—
264 (24)	**200 POUNDS** 1864-66. Sign. C. T. Whitmell. London.	—	Rare	—
265 (25)	**300 POUNDS** 1864-66. Sign. C. T. Whitmell. London.	—	Rare	—
266 (26)	**500 POUNDS** 1864-66. Sign. C. T. Whitmell. London.	—	Rare	—
267 (27)	**1000 POUNDS** 1864-66. Sign. C. T. Whitmell. London.	—	Rare	—

1866 ISSUE

#268-276 signature of George Forbes in wmk.

268 (28)	**5 POUNDS** 1866-70. Sign. Hy Dixon. London.	—	—	—
269 (29)	**10 POUNDS** 1866-70. Sign. Hy Dixon. London.	—	—	—
270 (30)	**20 POUNDS** 1866-70. Sign. T. Puzey. London.	—	—	—
271 (31)	**50 POUNDS** 1866-70. Sign. T. Puzey. London.	—	—	—
272 (32)	**100 POUNDS** 1866-70. Sign. T. Puzey. London.	—	—	—
273 (33)	**200 POUNDS** 1866-70. Sign. W. O. Wheeler. London.	—	Rare	—
274 (34)	**300 POUNDS** 1866-70. Sign. W. O. Wheeler. London.	—	Rare	—
275 (35)	**500 POUNDS** 1866-70. Sign. W. O. Wheeler. London.	—	Rare	—
276 (36)	**1000 POUNDS** 1866-70. Sign. W. O. Wheeler. London.	—	Rare	—

1870 ISSUE

#277-285 the printed sign. of the chief cashier appears on all the notes from 1870 onward w/title: *Chief Cashier* printed under his name.

277 (37)	**5 POUNDS** 1870-73. London.	—	—	—
278 (38)	**10 POUNDS** 1870-73. London.	—	—	—
279 (39)	**20 POUNDS** 1870-73. London.	—	—	—

		GOOD	FINE	XF
280 (40)	**50 POUNDS** 1870-73. London.	—	—	—
281 (41)	**100 POUNDS** 1870-73. London.	—	—	—
282 (42)	**200 POUNDS** 1870-73. London.	—	Rare	—
283 (43)	**300 POUNDS** 1870-73. London.	—	Rare	—
284 (44)	**500 POUNDS** 1870-73. London.	—	Rare	—
285 (45)	**1000 POUNDS** 1870-73. London.	—	Rare	—

1873 ISSUE

#286-294 Frank May as Chief Cashier.

286 (46)	**5 POUNDS** 1873-93. London.	—	—	—
287 (47)	**10 POUNDS** 1873-93. London.	—	—	—
288 (48)	**20 POUNDS** 1873-93. London.	—	—	—
289 (49)	**50 POUNDS** 1873-93. London.	—	—	—
290 (50)	**100 POUNDS** 1873-93. London.	—	—	—
291 (51)	**200 POUNDS** 1873-93. London.	—	Rare	—
292 (52)	**300 POUNDS** 1873-93. London.	—	Rare	—
293 (53)	**500 POUNDS** 1873-93. London.	—	Rare	—
294 (54)	**1000 POUNDS** 1873-93. London.	—	Rare	—

1893 ISSUE

Horace G. Bowen as Chief Cashier.

295 (55)	**5 POUNDS** 1893-1902. London.	—	—	—
296 (56)	**10 POUNDS** 1893-1902. London.	—	—	—
297 (57)	**20 POUNDS** 1893-1902. London.	—	—	—
298 (58)	**50 POUNDS** 1893-1902. London.	—	—	—
299 (59)	**100 POUNDS** 1893-1902. London.	—	—	—
300 (60)	**200 POUNDS** 1893-1902. London.	—	Rare	—
301 (61)	**500 POUNDS** 1893-1902. London.	—	Rare	—
302 (62)	**1000 POUNDS** 1893-1902. London.	—	Rare	—

1902 ISSUE

#303-311 John G. Narine as Chief Cashier.

		GOOD	FINE	XF
303 (62A)	**1 POUND** ND. London. (Not issued). Specimen only.	—	3000.	4000.
304 (63)	**5 POUNDS** 1902-18. London.	120.00	250.00	475.00
305 (64)	**10 POUNDS** 1902-18. London.	250.00	500.00	1000.
306 (65)	**20 POUNDS** 1902-18. London.	—	—	—
307 (66)	**50 POUNDS** 1902-18. London.	—	—	—
308 (67)	**100 POUNDS** 1902-18. London.	—	—	—
309 (68)	**200 POUNDS** 1902-18. London.	—	Rare	—

310	**500 POUNDS**		GOOD	FINE	XF
(69)	1902-18. London.		—	Rare	
311	**1000 POUNDS**				
(70)	1902-18. London.		—	Rare	—

1918 ISSUE

#312-319 Ernest M. Harvey as Chief Cashier.

312	**5 POUNDS**	GOOD	FINE	XF
(71)	1918-25.			
	a. London.	30.00	85.00	185.00
	b. Birmingham.	50.00	125.00	325.00
	c. Leeds.	85.00	175.00	350.00
	d. Liverpool.	85.00	175.00	350.00
	e. Manchester.	85.00	175.00	350.00
313	**10 POUNDS**			
(72)	1918-25. London.	70.00	150.00	350.00
314	**20 POUNDS**			
(73)	1918-25. London.	85.00	350.00	750.00
315	**50 POUNDS**			
(74)	1918-25. London.	250.00	750.00	1500.

316	**100 POUNDS**	GOOD	FINE	XF
(75)	1918-25. London.	300.00	900.00	2250.
317	**200 POUNDS**			
(76)	1918-25. London.		Rare	
318	**500 POUNDS**			
(77)	1918-25. London.	—	Rare	—
319	**1000 POUNDS**			
(78)	1918-25. London.	—	Rare	—

1925 ISSUE

#320-327 Cyril P. Mahon as Chief Cashier.

320	**5 POUNDS**			
(79)	1925-29. London.	60.00	130.00	275.00
321	**10 POUNDS**			
(80)	1925-29. London.	50.00	120.00	250.00
322	**20 POUNDS**			
(81)	1925-29. London.	75.00	175.00	600.00
323	**50 POUNDS**			
(82)	1925-29. London.	200.00	325.00	900.00
324	**100 POUNDS**			
(83)	1925-29. London.	400.00	600.00	1500.
325	**200 POUNDS**			
(84)	1925-29. London.	—	Rare	—
326	**500 POUNDS**			
(85)	1925-29. London.	—	Rare	—

327	**1000 POUNDS**		GOOD	FINE	XF
(86)	1925-29. London.		—	Rare	—

1929 ISSUE

#328-334 Basil G. Catterns as Chief Cashier.

328	**5 POUNDS**	100.00	150.00	300.00
(87)	1929-34. London.			
329	**10 POUNDS**	150.00	300.00	450.00
(88)	1929-34. London.			
330	**20 POUNDS**	250.00	450.00	900.00
(89)	1929-34. London.			

331	**50 POUNDS**	GOOD	FINE	XF
(90)	1929-34. London.	250.00	450.00	900.00
332	**100 POUNDS**			
(91)	1929-34. London.	300.00	650.00	1500.
333	**500 POUNDS**			
(92)	1929-34. London.	—	—	7500.
334	**1000 POUNDS**			
(93)	1929-34. London.	—	Rare	

1934 ISSUE

#335-341 Kenneth O. Peppiatt as Chief Cashier.

OPERATION BERNHARD FORGERIES

During World War II "almost perfect" forgeries of Bank of England Pound notes were produced by prisoners in a German concentration camp. The enterprise was code named "Operation Bernhard". The following occur: 5, 10, 20 and 50 Pound notes with different dates and also include branch office issues such as Leeds and Bristol. There are a number of very small but discernible differences between the Operation Bernhard counterfeits and genuine notes. For example, most counterfeits have a dull look in Britiannia's eyes and less clarity on the cross at top of her crown. Average market value in XF condition $45.00-90.00. For further information and details, see *Nazi Counterfeiting of British & Currency During World Ware II* by Bryan Burke.

335	5 POUNDS	GOOD	FINE	XF
(94)	Aug. 1934-Aug. 1943. London.	45.00	80.00	180.00

336	10 POUNDS	GOOD	FINE	XF
(95)	Aug. 1934-Aug. 1943. London.	65.00	150.00	300.00
337	20 POUNDS			
(96)	Aug. 1934-Aug. 1943.			
	a. London.	150.00	300.00	650.00
	b. Liverpool	200.00	400.00	750.00
338	50 POUNDS			
(97)	Aug. 1934-Aug. 1943.			
	a. London.	200.00	450.00	900.00
	b. Liverpool	200.00	500.00	1000.
339	100 POUNDS			
(98)	Aug. 1934-Aug. 1943. London.	300.00	900.00	1500.
340	500 POUNDS			
(99)	Aug. 1934-Aug. 1943. London.	1500.	4000.	6000.

341	1000 POUNDS	GOOD	FINE	XF
(100)	April 1934-Aug. 1943. London.	—	Rare	—

1944-47 ISSUE

#342 and 343 metal thread introduced in paper.

342	5 POUNDS	GOOD	FINE	XF
(101)	1944-47. Thick paper. London.	45.00	60.00	135.00
343	5 POUNDS			
(102)	1947. Thin paper. London.	40.00	60.00	135.00

1949 ISSUE

#344, Percival S. Beale as Chief Cashier.

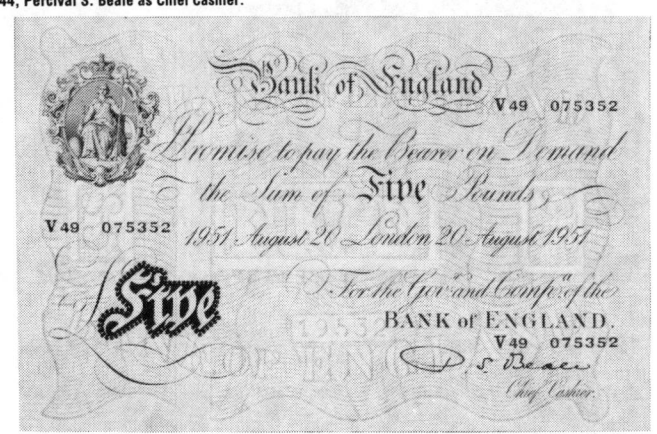

344	5 POUNDS	GOOD	FINE	XF
(103)	1949-55. London.	40.00	60.00	135.00

1955 ISSUE

#345, Leslie O'Brien as Chief Cashier.

345	5 POUNDS			
(104)	16.6.1955; 20.9.1956. London.	25.00	60.00	135.00

TREASURY NOTES

1914 ND ISSUE

#346-347 Portr. Kg. George V at l. Sign. John Bradbury. Uniface.

#346-359 w/title: *UNITED KINGDOM OF GREAT BRITAIN AND IRELAND.*

346	10 SHILLINGS	GOOD	FINE	XF
(105)	ND (Aug. 1914). Red. 3 serial # varieties.	75.00	200.00	500.00
347	1 POUND			
(106)	ND (Aug. 1914). Black. 7 serial # varieties.	200.00	400.00	800.00

1914-15 ISSUE

#348-349 portr. Kg. George V at upper l., St. George at upper r. Uniface.

NOTE: For examples of #348 and 349 w/Turkish ovpt. see Turkey #M1 and M2.

348	10 SHILLINGS			
(107)	ND (Jan. 1915). Red. 5 serial # varieties.	80.00	150.00	350.00

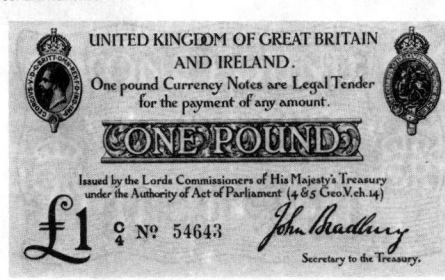

349	1 POUND	GOOD	FINE	XF
(108)	ND (23.10.1914). Black. 2 serial # varieties.	75.00	200.00	450.00

1917-18 ND ISSUE

350	10 SHILLINGS			
(109)	ND (1918). Green. Britannia at at l., portr. Kg. George V at r.			
	a. Black serial #. (Nov.)	100.00	200.00	450.00
	b. Red serial #. (Dec.)	100.00	200.00	450.00

		GOOD	FINE	XF
351	**1 POUND**			
(110)	ND (Feb. 1917). Brown and green. St. George slaying dragon at l., portr. Kg. George V at r.	45.00	100.00	250.00

1919 ND FIRST ISSUE

		GOOD	FINE	XF
352	**5 SHILLINGS**			
(111)	ND (1919). Red-violet and green. Kg. George V at ctr. Back gray.	1000.	2000.	—

1919 ND SECOND ISSUE

#353-361 sign. N. F. Warren Fisher.

#353-359 w/*GREAT BRITAIN AND IRELAND* text in heading.

NOTE: #352-355 were never officially released, but a few apparently found their way into circulation.

		GOOD	FINE	XF
353	**1 SHILLING**			
(111A)	ND (1919). Green and brown. Portr. Kg. George V at ctr. Coin on back. Not issued.	—	Rare	—

		GOOD	FINE	XF
354	**2 SHILLINGS - 6 PENCE**			
(112)	ND (1919). Olive-green and deep brown. Similar to #351A.	—	Rare	—
355	**5 SHILLINGS**			
(112A)	ND (1919). Deep violet and green. Like #351.	—	Rare	—

1919 ND THIRD ISSUE

		GOOD	FINE	XF
356	**10 SHILLINGS**			
(113)	ND (Oct. 1919). Green. Like #349. Serial # w/No.	20.00	60.00	150.00
357	**1 POUND**			
(114)	ND (Oct. 1919). Brown and green. Like #350. Wmk: *ONE POUND* at ctr. in 1 line.	10.00	40.00	90.00

1922 ND ISSUE

		GOOD	FINE	XF
358	**10 SHILLINGS**			
(115)	ND (1922-23). Green. Like #353 but serial # w/o *No*.	10.00	35.00	90.00
359	**1 POUND**			
(116)	ND (1922-23). Brown. Like #354 but wmk: *ONE POUND* at ctr.	7.00	20.00	80.00

1928 ND ISSUE

#360 and 361 w/title: *UNITED KINGDOM OF GREAT BRITAIN AND NORTHERN IRELAND.*

		GOOD	FINE	XF
360	**10 SHILLINGS**			
(117)	ND (1928). Green. Britannia at l., portr. Kg. George V at r.	20.00	70.00	185.00
361	**1 POUND**			
(118)	ND (1928). Brown. St. George slaying dragon at l., portr. Kg. George V at r.	10.00	60.00	130.00

BANK OF ENGLAND (CONTINUED)

1928-48 ND ISSUE

		VG	VF	UNC
362	**10 SHILLINGS**			
(119)	ND (1928-48). Brown. Seated Britannia at l. Paper w/o security thread.			
	a. Sign. C. P. Mahon (1928-29).	35.00	85.00	175.00
	b. Sign. B. G. Catterns (1929-34).	15.00	40.00	95.00
	c. Sign. K. O. Peppiatt. (1934-39).	20.00	45.00	100.00
	d. Sign. like C. Series w/L (1948).	25.00	65.00	150.00
363	**1 POUND**			
(120)	ND (1928-48). Green. Seated Britannia at upper l. Paper w/o security thread.			
	a. Sign. C. P. Mahon (1928-29).	18.00	50.00	130.00
	b. Sign. B. G. Catterns (1929-34).	10.00	25.00	60.00
	c. Sign. K. O. Peppiatt (1934-39).	10.00	30.00	70.00
	d. Sign. like c. Series letters R-A; S-A (1948).	10.00	25.00	50.00
	e. Ovpt: *Withdrawn from circulation September 18th, 1941* on c.	100.00	300.00	—
	f. Ovpt. on b.	100.00	300.00	—
	g. Ovpt: *Withdrawn from circulation November 10th, 1941.* on c.	100.00	250.00	400.00

1940-41 EMERGENCY ISSUE

		VG	VF	UNC
364	**2 SHILLINGS - 6 PENCE**			
(121)	ND (1941). Black on lt. blue unpt. Sign. K. O. Peppiatt. (Not issued).	—	3000.	

		VG	VF	UNC
365	**5 SHILLINGS**			
(122)	ND (1941). Olive on pink unpt. Sign. K. O. Peppiatt. (Not issued).	—	3000.	—

		VG	VF	UNC
366	**10 SHILLINGS**			
(123)	ND (1940-48). Mauve. Seated Britannia at l. Paper w/security thread. Sign. K. O. Peppiatt.	6.00	20.00	50.00
367	**1 POUND**			
(124)	ND (1940-48). Lt. or dk. blue and pink. Seated Britannia at upper l. Paper w/security thread. Sign. K. O. Peppiatt.			
	a. Issued note.	6.00	12.00	20.00
	b. Ovpt: *Withdrawn from circulation September 18th, 1941.*	250.00	450.00	—

1948 ISSUE

368 **10 SHILLINGS**
(126) ND (1948-60). Brown-violet and brown on gray and pink unpt. Like #119 but paper w/security thread. Wmk: Head of Minerva.

		VG	VF	UNC
a.	Sign. K. O. Peppiatt. (1948-49).	8.00	20.00	40.00
b.	Sign. P. S. Beale. (1949-55).	5.00	12.00	30.00
c.	Sign. L. K. O'Brien. (1955-60).	5.00	12.00	30.00

369 **1 POUND**
(127) ND (1948-60). Green. Like #120 but paper w/security thread.

		VG	VF	UNC
a.	Sign. K. O. Peppiatt. (1948-49).	5.00	10.00	24.00
b.	Sign. P. S. Beale. (1949-55).	5.00	8.00	15.00
c.	Sign. L. K. O'Brien. (1955-60).	5.00	8.00	15.00

1957 ISSUE

370 **5 POUNDS**
(128) ND (1957-61). Blue and m/c. Portr. helmeted head of Britannia at upper l. St. George slaying dragon at lower ctr., denomination £5 in blue print on back. Sign. L.K. O'Brien.

VG	VF	UNC
10.00	30.00	50.00

1960 ISSUE

#373 and 374 portr. Qn. Elizabeth II at r.

371 **10 SHILLINGS**
(130) ND (1960-70). Brown on m/c unpt.

		VG	VF	UNC
a.	Sign. L. K. O'Brien. (1960-61).	2.00	4.00	12.00
b.	Sign. J. Q. Hollom. (1962-66).	1.50	3.00	10.00
c.	Sign. J. S. Fforde. (1966-70).	1.50	2.50	7.00

372 **1 POUND**
(131) ND (1960-77). Deep green on m/c unpt.

		VG	VF	UNC
a.	Sign. L. K. O'Brien. (1960-61).	2.00	4.00	12.00
b.	Sign. J. Q. Hollom. (1962-66).	2.00	4.00	9.00
c.	Sign. J. S. Fforde. (1966-70).	2.00	4.00	8.00
d.	Sign. J. B. Page. (1970-77).	2.00	4.00	7.00

MILITARY

BRITISH MILITARY AUTHORITY

1943 ND ISSUE

Originally issued in 1943 for use by British troops in North Africa. One Pound notes w/ovpt: *BULGARIA*, *FRANCE* and *GREECE* were prepared but not issued. The remaining stock was later sent to Cyprus in 1956.

#M1-M6 have lion on crown device.

M1 **6 PENCE**
ND (1943). Red-brown on green and peach unpt. Back red, green, blue and purple.

VG	VF	UNC
6.00	20.00	60.00

M2 **1 SHILLING**
ND (1943). Black on gray and violet unpt. Back purple on brown, green and blue unpt.

VG	VF	UNC
3.00	12.00	35.00

M3 **2 SHILLINGS - 6 PENCE**
ND (1943). Green on pink unpt. Back olive green and brown on lilac and olive unpt.

VG	VF	UNC
4.00	17.50	40.00

M4 **5 SHILLINGS**
ND (1943). Brown on blue and green unpt. Back violet on green and blue unpt.

VG	VF	UNC
5.00	20.00	45.00

M5	**10 SHILLINGS**	**VG**	**VF**	**UNC**
	ND (1943). Blue on olive and lilac unpt. Back olive brown on gray and brown unpt.	8.00	35.00	80.00

M6	**1 POUND**	**VG**	**VF**	**UNC**
	ND (1943-45). Violet on orange and green unpt. Back orange, green and black.	15.00	45.00	100.00
	a. Issued note w/o ovpt.	15.00	45.00	100.00
	b. Ovpt: *BULGARIA*. 25 prepared.	—	—	1500.
	c. Ovpt: *FRANCE*. 50 prepared.	—	—	1000.
	d. Ovpt: *GREECE*. 25 prepared.	—	—	1500.

BRITISH ARMED FORCES

1946 ND TOKEN ISSUE

#M7-M8 text printed on paper, then laminated for issue. Printer: TDLR (w/o imprint).

M7	**1/2 PENNY**	**VG**	**VF**	**UNC**
	ND (1946). Black on dk. brown. Round printed disk of laminated paper.	4.00	10.00	25.00

M8	**1 PENNY**	**VG**	**VF**	**UNC**
	ND (1946). Black on dk. brown. Round printed disk of laminated paper.	4.00	10.00	25.00

BRITISH ARMED FORCES, SPECIAL VOUCHERS

NOTE: The Ministry of Defense sold large quantities of remainders #M20c, M26a, M27a, M28a, M32 and M35 2-hole punch cancelled w/normal serial # a few years ago. Original specimens of #M20c, M27a, M28 and M35 have one punched hole and special serial # 123456 and larger denominations sometimes have an additional serial # 789012.

1946 ND FIRST SERIES

Originally issued on Aug. 1, 1946 for use by British forces in occupied Germany and Austria. They were later released to British Forces in occupied Japan on May 6, 1947. Some notes are found w/ovpt: *IS-SUED IN H.M. SHIPS AFLOAT FOR USE IN NAAFI CANTEENS ONLY*, which were used by Force T marines also assigned to Japan. They were part of the B.C.O.F.

#M9-M15 printer: TDLR.

M9	**3 PENCE**	**VG**	**VF**	**UNC**
	ND (1946). Lilac on orange and green unpt.			
	a. Issued note.	3.00	35.00	80.00
	b. Ovpt: ....*NAAFI CANTEENS ONLY.*	40.00	150.00	300.00
M10	**6 PENCE**			
	ND (1946). Brown on lilac and blue unpt.			
	a. Issued note.	3.00	20.00	60.00
	b. Ovpt:....*NAAFI CANTEENS ONLY.*	40.00	150.00	300.00

M11	**1 SHILLING**	**VG**	**VF**	**UNC**
	ND (1946). Gray-blue on olive green and orange unpt.			
	a. Issued note.	6.00	35.00	90.00
	b. Ovpt:....*NAAFI CANTEENS ONLY.*	40.00	150.00	300.00

M12	**2 SHILLINGS - 6 PENCE**	**VG**	**VF**	**UNC**
	ND (1946). Pale red on green and violet unpt. Back pale red and violet.			
	a. Issued note.	10.00	45.00	120.00
	b. Ovpt:....*NAAFI CANTEENS ONLY.*	40.00	150.00	300.00
M13	**5 SHILLINGS**			
	ND (1946). Green on violet and orange unpt. Back green and pale red.			
	a. Issued note.	15.00	50.00	130.00
	b. Ovpt:....*NAAFI CANTEENS ONLY.*	40.00	150.00	300.00
M14	**10 SHILLINGS**			
	ND (1946). Purple on orange and red-brown unpt.			
	a. Issued note.	12.00	50.00	130.00
	b. Ovpt:....*NAAFI CANTEENS ONLY.*	40.00	150.00	300.00

M15	**1 POUND**	**VG**	**VF**	**UNC**
	ND (1946). Blue on red and green unpt.			
	a. Issued note.	20.00	55.00	150.00
	b. Ovpt:....*NAAFI CANTEENS ONLY.*	100.00	250.00	—

1948 ND SECOND SERIES

#M16-M23 printer: TDLR.

NOTE: This series was retired in 1971.

M16	**3 PENCE**	**VG**	**VF**	**UNC**
	ND (1948). Brown on lt. red and green unpt.			
	a. Paper w/metal strip. (1948).	1.00	4.00	16.00
	b. Wmk. paper. (1961).	.50	2.50	10.00

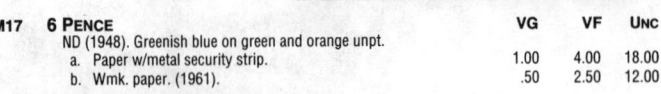

M17	**6 PENCE**	**VG**	**VF**	**UNC**
	ND (1948). Greenish blue on green and orange unpt.			
	a. Paper w/metal security strip.	1.00	4.00	18.00
	b. Wmk. paper. (1961).	.50	2.50	12.00

M18	**1 SHILLING**	**VG**	**VF**	**UNC**
	ND (1948). Red-orange on purple and green unpt.			
	a. Paper w/metal security strip. (1948).	1.00	4.50	30.00
	b. Wmk. paper. (1961).	.50	2.50	15.00
M19	**2 SHILLINGS - 6 PENCE**			
	ND (1948). Lilac on lt. green and ornage unpt.			
	a.. Paper w/metal security strip.	1.25	4.50	20.00
	b.. Wmk. paper. (1961).	1.00	3.00	15.00

M20	**5 SHILLINGS**	VG	VF	UNC
	ND (1948). Blue on orange and lt. red unpt.			
	a. Paper w/metal security strip. (1948).	6.00	15.00	30.00
	b. Wmk. paper. Black serial #. (1961).	4.00	10.00	25.00
	c. Wmk. paper, red serial #. 4.10.30.	4.00	10.00	25.00
	d. Cancelled remainder w/normal serial # and 2 punched holes.	—	—	4.00
M21	**10 SHILLINGS**			
	ND (1948). Green.			
	a. Paper w/metal security strip. (1948).	2.00	5.00	25.00
	b. Wmk. paper. (1961).	2.00	5.00	25.00

M22	**1 POUND**	VG	VF	UNC
	ND (1948). Lilac on red and blue unpt.			
	a. Paper w/metal strip. (1948).	.50	1.50	3.00
	b. Wmk. paper.	.75	2.00	5.00

M23	**5 POUNDS**	VG	VF	UNC
	ND (1958). Dk. blue on olive and brown unpt. Wmk. paper r.	.75	2.00	5.00

1956 ND THIRD SERIES

Printed in 1948, they were not issued until 1956 for use during the Suez Canal crisis which was a very limited issue lasting only 2 months.

#M24-M29 Imprint: TDLR; printer: J. Waddington Ltd.

M24	**3 PENCE**	VG	VF	UNC
	ND (1956). Green, orange and pink. Back green.	60.00	150.00	250.00
M25	**6 PENCE**			
	ND (1956). Lilac and green.	20.00	60.00	120.00
M26	**1 SHILLING**			
	ND (1956). Blue and pink.			
	a. W/o punch cancel holes.	10.00	35.00	100.00
	b. Cancelled remainder w/2 punched holes.	—	—	5.00
	s. Specimen w/1 punched hole.	—	—	35.00

M26A	**2 SHILLINGS - 6 PENCE**	VG	VF	UNC
	ND. Specimen.	—	—	300.00
M27	**5 SHILLINGS**			
	ND (1956). Orange and green.	60.00	150.00	250.00

M28	**10 SHILLINGS**	VG	VF	UNC
	ND (1956). Red, green and orange.			
	a. W/o punch cancel holes.	4.00	20.00	80.00
	b. Cancelled remainder w/normal serial # and 2 punched holes.	—	—	5.00

M29	**1 POUND**	VG	VF	UNC
	ND (1956). Brown, pink and purple.	—	—	3.00

GREECE

The Hellenic Republic of Greece is situated in south-eastern Europe on the southern tip of the Balkan Peninsula. The republic includes many islands, the most important of which are Crete and the Ionian Islands. Greece (including islands) has an area of 51,146 sq. mi. (131,944 sq. km.) and a population of 10.3 million. Capital: Athens. Greece is still largely agricultural. Tobacco, cotton, fruit and wool are exported.

Greece, the Mother of Western civilization, attained the peak of its culture in the 5th century BC, when it contributed more to government, drama, art and architecture than any other people to this time. Greece fell under Roman domination in the 2nd and 1st centuries BC, becoming part of the Byzantine Empire until Constantinople fell to the Crusaders in 1202. With the fall of Constantinople to the Turks in 1453, Greece became part of the Ottoman Empire. Independence from Turkey was won with the revolution of 1821-27. In 1833, Greece was established as a monarchy, with sovereignty guaranteed by Britain, France and Russia. After a lengthy power struggle between the monarchist forces and democratic factions, Greece was proclaimed a republic in 1925. The monarchy was restored in 1935 and reconfirmed by a plebiscite in 1946. The Italians invaded Greece via Albania on Oct. 28,1940 but were driven back well within the Albanian border. Germany began its invasion on April 6, 1941 and quickly overran the entire country, driving off a British Expeditionary force by the end of April. King George II and his new government went into exile. The German - Italian occupation of Greece lasted until Oct. 1944. On April 21, 1967, a military junta took control of the government and suspended the constitution. King Constantine II made an unsuccessful attempt against the junta in the fall of 1968 and consequently fled to Italy. The monarchy was formally abolished by plebiscite, Dec. 8, 1974, and Greece established as the "Hellenic Republic," the third republic in Greek history.

The island of Crete (Kreti), located 60 miles southeast of the Peloponnesus, was the center of a brilliant civilization that flourished before the advent of Greek culture. After being conquered by the Romans, Byzantines, Moslems and Venetians, Crete became part of the Turkish Empire in 1669. As a consequence of the Greek Revolution of the 1820s, it was ceded to Egypt. Egypt returned the island to the Turks in 1840, and they ceded it to Greece in 1913, after the Second Balkan War.

The Ionian Islands, situated in the Ionian Sea to the west of Greece, is the collective name for the islands of Corfu, Cephalonia, Zante, Santa Maura, Ithaca, Cthera and Paxo, with their minor dependencies. Before Britain acquired the islands, 1809-1814, they were at various times subject to the authority of Venice, France, Russia and Turkey. They remained under British control until their cession to Greece on March 29, 1864.

RULERS:

John Capodistrias, 1827-1831
Othon (Otto of Bavaria) 1832-1962
George I, 1863-1913
Constantine I, 1913-1923
George II, 1922-1923, 1935-1947
Paul I, 1947-1964
Constantine II, 1964-1973

MONETARY SYSTEM:

1 Phoenix = 100 Lepta, 1828-31
1 Drachma = 100 Lepta, 1831-

DENOMINATIONS

1 - ΜΙΑ
2 - ΔΥΟ
5 - ΠΕΝΤΕ
10 - ΔΕΚΑ
20 - ΕΙΚΟΣΙ
25 - ΕΙΚΟΣΙΠΕΝΤΕ
50 - ΠΕΝΤΗΚΟΝΤΑ
100 - ΕΚΑΤΟΝ
200 - ΔΙΑΚΟΣΙΑ
250 - ΔΙΑΚΟΣΙΑ ΠΕΝΤΗΚΟΝΤΑ
500 - ΠΕΝΤΑΚΟΣΙΑΙ
750 - ΕΠΤΑΚΟΣΙΑ ΠΕΝΤΗΚΟΝΤΑ
1000 - ΧΙΛΙΑΙ
2000 - ΔΥΟ ΧΙΛΙΑΔΕΣ
5000 - ΠΕΝΤΕ ΧΙΛΙΑΔΕΣ
10,000 - ΔΕΚΑ ΧΙΛΙΑΔΕΣ
20,000 - ΕΙΚΟΣΙ ΧΙΛΙΑΔΕΣ
25,000 - ΕΙΚΟΣΙ ΠΕΝΤΕ ΧΙΛΙΑΔΕΣ
50,000 - ΠΕΝΤΗΚΟΝΤΑ ΧΙΛΙΑΔΕΣ
100,000 - ΕΚΑΤΟΝ ΧΙΛΙΑΔΕΣ
500,000 - ΠΕΝΤΑΚΟΣΙΑΙ ΧΙΛΙΑΔΕΣ
1,000,000 - ΕΝ ΕΚΑΤΟΜΜΥΡΙΟΝ
5,000,000 - ΠΕΝΤΕ ΕΚΑΤΟΜΜΥΡΙΑ
10,000,000 - ΔΕΚΑ ΕΚΑΤΟΜΜΥΡΙΑ
25,000,000 - ΕΙΚΟΣΙ ΠΕΝΤΕ ΕΚΑΤΟΜΜΥΡΙΑ
50,000,000 - ΠΕΝΤΗΚΟΝΤΑ ΕΚΑΤΟΜΜΥΡΙΑ
100,000,000 - ΕΚΑΤΟΝ ΕΚΑΤΟΜΜΥΡΙΑ
200,000,000 - ΔΙΑΚΟΣΙΑ ΕΚΑΤΟΜΜΥΡΙΑ
500,000,000 - ΠΕΝΤΗΑΚΟΝΤΑ ΕΚΟΤΟΜΜΥΡΙΑ
2,000,000,000 - ΔΥΟ ΧΙΛΙΑΔΕΣ ΕΚΑΤΟΜΜΥΡΙΑ
10,000,000,000 - ΔΕΚΑ ΔΙΣΕΚΑΤΟΜΜΥΡΙΑ
100,000,000,000 - ΕΚΑΤΟΝ ΔΙΣΕΚΑΤΟΜΜΥΡΙΑ

EKDOSIS ISSUES

Many notes can be differentiated by the designation of the Ekdosis (EK.) on the back of the notes. The issue numbers quoted here are found on the note in Greek letters in each case following " " i.e.

1	ΠΡΩΤΗ	**6**	ΕΚΤΗ	**11**	ΕΝΔΕΚΑΤΗ
2	ΔΕΥΤΕΡΑ	**7**	ΕΒΔΟΜΗ	**12**	ΔΩΔΕΚΑΤΗ
3	ΤΡΙΤΗ	**8**	ΟΓΔΟΗ	**13**	ΔΕΚΑΤΗ ΤΡΙΤΗ
4	ΤΕΤΑΡΤΗ	**9**	ΕΝΑΤΗ (ΕΝΝΑΤΗ)	**14**	ΔΕΚΑΤΗ ΤΕΤΑΡΤΗ
5	ΠΕΜΠΤΗ	**10**	ΔΕΚΑΤΗ		

GREEK ALPHABET

Α	α	Alpha	(ä)	Ι	ι	Iota	(ē)	Ρ	ρ	Rho	(r)		
Β	β	Beta	(b)	Κ	κ	Kappa	(k)	Σ	σ	Sigma	(s)6		
Γ	γ	Gamma	(g)	Λ	λ	Lambda	(l)	Τ	τ	Tau	(t)		
Δ	δ	Delta	(d)	Μ	μ	Mu	(m)	Υ	υ	Upsilon	(ōō)		
Ε	ε	Epsilon	(e)	Ν	ν	Nu	(n)	Φ	φ	Phi	(f)		
Ζ	ζ	Zeta	(z)	Ξ	ξ	Xi	(ks)	Χ	χ	Chi	(H)		
Η	η	Eta	(ā)	Ο	ο	Omicron	(o)	Ψ	ψ	Psi	(ps)		
Θ	θ	Theta	(th)	Π	π	Pi	(p)	Ω	ω	Omega	(ō)		

NOTE: Certain listings encompassing issues encompassing issues circulated by various bank and regional authorities are contained in Volume 1.

INDEPENDENT GREECE
ΠΡΟΣΩΡΙΝΗ ΔΙΟΙΚΗΣΙΣ ΤΗΣ ΕΛΛΑΔΟΣ
PROVISIONAL ADMINISTRATION OF GREECE

1822 ISSUE

#1-5 bonds which circulated as currency. Issued in Corinth and Nauplion. Denominations in Gr. (Grossi = Piastres).

		GOOD	FINE	XF
1	**100 GROSSI**			
	1822.	100.00	300.00	700.00
2	**250 GROSSI**			
	1822.	100.00	300.00	700.00
3	**500 GROSSI**			
	1822.	100.00	300.00	700.00
4	**750 GROSSI**			
	1822.	200.00	500.00	1200.

5	**1000 GROSSI**	**GOOD**	**FINE**	**XF**
	1822.	200.00	500.00	1200.

NATIONAL FINANCE BANK

1831 ISSUE

6	**5 PHOENIX**			
	30.6.1831. Red.	300.00	750.00	1250.
7	**10 PHOENIX**			
	30.6.1831. Red.	600.00	1500.	2500.
8	**50 PHOENIX**			
	30.6.1831. Lt. blue.	—	Rare	—
9	**100 PHOENIX**			
	30.6.1831. Lt. blue.	—	Rare	—

KINGDOM (PRE 1935)

ΕΛΛΗΝΙΚΗ ΤΡΑΠΕΖΑ

BANK OF GREECE
A bank of issue from 1841-48.

1841 ISSUE
#10-13 uniface.

10	**25 DRACHMAI**	**GOOD**	**FINE**	**XF**
	30.3.1841. Black on green paper. Arms of Kg. Othon at upper ctr.	—	Rare	—
11	**50 DRACHMAI**			
	30.3.1841. Like #10.	—	Rare	—

12	**100 DRACHMAI**	**GOOD**	**FINE**	**XF**
	30.3.1841. Black on lt. brown paper. Like #10 but oval at ctr.	—	Rare	—
13	**500 DRACHMAI**			
	30.3.1841. Like #10.	—	Rare	—

ΕΘΝΙΚΗ ΤΡΑΠΕΖΑ ΤΗΣ ΕΛΛΑΔΟΣ

NATIONAL BANK OF GREECE

LAW OF 30.2.1841
#14-18 statue at l. and r. Embossed seat at r.

14	**10 DRACHMAI**	**GOOD**	**FINE**	**XF**
	L.1841. Blue.	—	Rare	—
15	**25 DRACHMAI**			
	L.1841.	—	Rare	—
16	**50 DRACHMAI**			
	L.1841.	—	Rare	—
17	**100 DRACHMAI**			
	L.1841.	—	Rare	—
18	**500 DRACHMAI**			
	L.1841. Black.	—	Rare	—

1852 ISSUE
#19-21 uniface.

#22 *Deleted.*

19	**10 DRACHMAI**	**GOOD**	**FINE**	**XF**
	1852. Arms of Kg. Othon at top ctr.	—	Rare	—
20	**25 DRACHMAI**			
	1852. Arms of Kg. Othon.	—	Rare	—

21	**100 DRACHMAI**	**GOOD**	**FINE**	**XF**
	1852. Green denomination guilloches. Arms of Kg. Othon at upper l.	—	Rare	—

1863-67 ISSUE
#23-25 G. Stavros, first governor of the National Bank of Greece. Uniface. Printer: ABNC.

#26 *Deleted.*

23	**10 DRACHMAI**			
	15.7.1863; 10.3.1867. Black on red and green unpt. Arms of Kg. Othon at l., G. Stavros at top ctr., Nereid at lower r.	1000.	2500.	4500.

24	**25 DRACHMAI**	**GOOD**	**FINE**	**XF**
	Black on red and green unpt. G. Stavros at upper l., 2 women at upper ctr., arms of Kg. Othon at lower r. Specimen.	—	—	5000.
25	**100 DRACHMAI**			
	Black on red and green unpt. Woman reclining w/shield at upper ctr., arms of Kg. Othon at bottom r. Specimen.	—	—	5000.

1867-69 ISSUE
#27-29 G. Stavros, arms of Kg. George I. Uniface. Printer: ABNC.

27	**10 DRACHMAI**			
	ca. 1867. Like #23 but arms of Kg. George I.		Reported Not Confirmed	

28	25 DRACHMAI	GOOD	FINE	XF
	3.7.1867; 8.3.1868; 28.6.1868. Black, red and green. Like #24 but arms of Kg. George I.	1000.	1600.	3000.

29	100 DRACHMAI	GOOD	FINE	XF
	4.8.1867; 25.8.1869. Black, red and green. Like #25 but arms of Kg. George I.	—	Rare	—
29A	500 DRACHMAI			
	Similar to #33.		Reported Not Confirmed	

1870-78 ISSUE
#30-33 G. Stavros. 2 lg. *N*'s on face (for New Drachmai of Latin Monetary Union). Printer: ABNC.

30	10 DRACHMAI	GOOD	FINE	XF
	18.8.1878-3.8.1883. Black, blue and red. Like #23 but arms of Kg. George I. Back red.	600.00	1000.	2000.
31	25 DRACHMAI			
	30.12.1871; 20.5.1882-12.8.1886. Black on blue and green unpt. Like #28. Back green.	300.00	600.00	1200.

32	100 DRACHMAI	GOOD	FINE	XF
	1870-20.5.1882. Black, red and green. Like #29.	—	Rare	—
33	500 DRACHMAI			
	1872-5.8.1886. Green and brown. Arms of Kg. George I at upper l., women at lower r. Back brown.	—	Rare	—

LAW OF 21.12.1885
#34 and 35 printer: BWC.

34	1 DRACHMA	GOOD	FINE	XF
	L.1885. Black on blue yellow unpt. Portr. Hermes at lower l. Back blue; arms of Kg. George I at ctr.	20.00	65.00	160.00

35	2 DRACHMAI	GOOD	FINE	XF
	L.1885. Black on blue and yellow unpt. Portr. Hermes at l., Athena at r. Back like #34.	25.00	80.00	175.00

1885 ND PROVISIONAL ISSUE
NOTE: Excessive demand for the 5 Drachmai denomination was satisfied by cutting 10 Drachmai notes in half. This practice continued apparently beyond 1910 despite the issuance of 5 Drachmai notes in 1897.

36	5 DRACHMAI	GOOD	FINE	XF
	ND (-old dates 1878-1900). L. or r. half of 10 Drachmai #30, 37, 43 and 46.	50.00	100.00	300.00

1886-97 ISSUE
#37-39 G. Stavros at l. Printer: ABNC.

37	10 DRACHMAI	GOOD	FINE	XF
	18.9.1889-5.8.1893. Orange and blue. Arms of Kg. George I at ctr., Hermes at r. Back red; woman and sheep.	300.00	700.00	1200.
38	25 DRACHMAI			
	30.5.1888-12.6.1897. Black on red and green unpt. Reclining woman at ctr., arms of Kg. George I at r. Back brown; woman at ctr.	500.00	900.00	1600.
39	100 DRACHMAI			
	25.2.1886; 6.3.1886; 18.9.1887. Like #32, but red denomination in unpt.	—	Rare	—

1897 ND ISSUE
Law of 21.12.1885
#40-42 printer: BWC.
NOTE: For #40 and 41 w/red ovpt: *1917* see #301 and 302.

40	1 DRACHMA	GOOD	FINE	XF
	L.1885. (1897). Black on blue and orange unpt. Athena at l. Back similar to #34.	10.00	40.00	90.00
41	2 DRACHMAI			
	L.1885. (1897). Black on blue and orange unpt. Hermes at r. Back similar to #34.	12.00	45.00	100.00

1897 ISSUE

42	5 DRACHMAI	GOOD	FINE	XF
	2.10.1897; 10.11.1897; 12.12.1897. Black on orange and purple unpt. Arms of Kg. George I at l., portr. G. Stavros at top ctr. Back blue; Athena at ctr.	75.00	175.00	450.00

1892; 1897 ISSUE

43 10 DRACHMAI
14.9.1892-June 1900. Purple on tan unpt. Mercury at l., arms of Kg. George I at ctr. Printed in Vienna.

	GOOD	FINE	XF
	650.00	1400.	—

44 25 DRACHMAI
12.8.1897-31.8.1900. Black on orange and blue unpt. Athena at l., male portr. at ctr. r., arms of Kg. George I at r. Back blue; Hermes at ctr. Printer: W&S.

	GOOD	FINE	XF
	600.00	1150.	—

45 100 DRACHMAI
12.2.1892-12.4.1893; 20.5.1899. Purple. Athena reclining on lion chair at l., arms of Kg. George I at top ctr., male portr. at r. Printed in Vienna.

	GOOD	FINE	XF
	800.00	1800.	—

1900; 1903 ISSUE
#46-48 portr. G. Stavros at l., arms of Kg. George I at r.

46 10 DRACHMAI
1.6.1900; 20.6.1900; 15.7.1900. Green. Hermes at ctr. on back. Printer: BWC.

	GOOD	FINE	XF
	150.00	400.00	950.00

47 25 DRACHMAI
1.5.1903-2.9.1903. EK. 8. Black on red and blue unpt. 2 women at ctr. Child and fish at ctr. on back. Printer: ABNC.

	GOOD	FINE	XF
	125.00	275.00	600.00

48 100 DRACHMAI
10.6.1900; 1.7.1900; 15.7.1900. Black on purple and orange unpt. Back green; Athena at ctr. Printer: BWC.

	GOOD	FINE	XF
	250.00	650.00	1250.

1901 ISSUE
#49 and 50 portr. G. Stavros at l., arms of Kg. George I at r. Printer: ABNC.

49 500 DRACHMAI
2.1.1901. EK. 6. Brown and green. Portr. Athena at ctr. Woman and sheep on back.
  a. Issued note.
  s. Specimen.

	GOOD	FINE	XF
a.	300.00	850.00	—
s.	—	—	—

50 1000 DRACHMAI
30.3.1901; 30.5.1901. Black on m/c unpt. Hermes at ctr. Woman at ctr. on back.
  a. Issued note.
  s. Specimen.

	GOOD	FINE	XF
a.	400.00	1250.	—
s.	—	—	—

1905-10 ISSUE
#51-53 portr. G. Stavros at l., arms of Kg. George I at r. Sign. varieties. Printer: ABNC.

51 10 DRACHMAI
12.3.1910-24.3.1917. Black on purple and green unpt. Hermes at ctr. on back.

	GOOD	FINE	XF
	25.00	75.00	225.00

52 25 DRACHMAI
2.1.1909-14.2.1918. EK. 9. Similar to #47 but different guilloches.

	GOOD	FINE	XF
	8.00	40.00	125.00

53 100 DRACHMAI
1.10.1905-12.11.1917. EK. 9. Black on purple and green unpt. Woman holding child at ctr. on back.

	GOOD	FINE	XF
	12.50	60.00	200.00

1905-17 ISSUE
#54-57 portr. G. Stavros at l., arms of Kg. George I at r. Printer: ABNC.
NOTE: Illustration of 57 is mismatched halves patched back together.

54	5 DRACHMAI	GOOD	FINE	XF
	1.10.1905-15.3.1918. EK. 2. Black on purple and green unpt. Hermes at ctr. on back.	3.00	10.00	40.00

55	100 DRACHMAI	GOOD	FINE	XF
	10.12.1917-Sept.1918. EK. 10. Similar to #53 but different guilloches. Temple at ctr. on back.	50.00	225.00	—

56	500 DRACHMAI	GOOD	FINE	XF
	5.5.1914-20.12.1918. EK. 7. Black on m/c unpt. Similar to #49 but different guilloches. Back black, violet and m/c.	125.00	425.00	—

57	1000 DRACHMAI	GOOD	FINE	XF
	15.4.1917-16.12.1918. Black on m/c unpt. Similar to #50.	300.00	750.00	—

1922 EMERGENCY ISSUE
Law of 25.3.1922
NOTE: Many National Bank notes in circulation were cut in half. The l. half remained legal tender until 1927 at half face value. The r. half was considered a compulsory loan, equally valued at half face value.

58	5 DRACHMI = 2 1/2 DRACHMAI	GOOD	FINE	XF
	L.1922. EK. 2 (#54).	4.00	12.00	25.00
59	10 DRACHMAI = 5 DRACHMAI			
	L.1922. EK. 8, 9 (#46, 51).	5.00	15.00	35.00

60	25 DRAHCAMI = 12 1/2 DRACHMAI	GOOD	FINE	XF
	L.1922. EK. 7, 8, 9 (#44, 47, 52).	7.50	20.00	40.00
61	100 DRACHMAI = 50 DRACHAMI			
	L.1922. EK. 8, 9, 10 (#48, 53, 55).	7.50	20.00	45.00
62	500 DRACHMAI = 250 DRACHAMI			
	L.1922. EK. 5, 6, 7 (#33, 49, 56).	30.00	90.00	150.00
63	1000 DRACHAMI = 500 DRACHAMI			
	L.1922. EK. 1 (#50, 57).	50.00	125.00	300.00

1918-22 NEON ISSUE
#64-69 portr. G.Stavros at l., ovpt: NEON over arms of Kg. George I at r.
#64-66, 68 and 69 printer: ABNC.

64	5 DRACHMAI	GOOD	FINE	XF
	31.5.1918-8.1.1919. Black on red and m/c unpt. Black ovpt: NEON. Athena at ctr. on back.	3.00	12.00	40.00

65   25 DRACHMAI

	GOOD	FINE	XF
2.5.1918-25.11.1919. Black on blue unpt. Seated figure at ctr. Red ovpt: *NEON*. 2 allegorical women on back.	8.00	30.00	75.00

66   50 DRACHMAI

	GOOD	FINE	XF
16.9.1921-24.2.1922. Brown on green unpt. Relief from Sarcophagus at ctr. Red ovpt: *NEON*. Back blue; Alexander at ctr.	20.00	85.00	250.00

67   100 DRACHMAI

	GOOD	FINE	XF
1.1922; 8.2.1922; 17.2.1922. Blue on lt. green and red-orange unpt. 2 women reclining at ctr. Red ovpt: *NEON*. Back brown on lt. green and ornage unpt. Temple at ctr. Printer: BWC.	15.00	65.00	200.00

68   500 DRACHMAI

	GOOD	FINE	XF
13.10.1921; 25.1.1922. Black on brown and green unpt. Woman at ctr. Red ovpt: *NEON*. Statue at l. and r., temple at ctr. on back.	60.00	150.00	275.00

69   1000 DRACHMAI

	GOOD	FINE	XF
15.6.1921-25.1.1922. Blue on m/c unpt. Woman at ctr. Red ovpt: *NEON*. Back black on red and m/c unpt. Urn at l. and r., temple at ctr.	125.00	250.00	600.00

1923 FIRST ISSUE

#70-72 portr. G. Stavros at l. Printer: ABNC.

70   5 DRACHMAI

	GOOD	FINE	XF
24.3.1923. Green on orange unpt. Back red-brown; Alexander at ctr.	5.00	17.50	45.00

71   25 DRACHMAI

	GOOD	FINE	XF
5.3.1923. Brown. Back blue; temple at ctr.	7.50	30.00	85.00

72   1000 DRACHMAI

	GOOD	FINE	XF
5.1.1923. Blue on brown unpt. Parthenon at ctr. on back.	—	Rare	—

1923 SECOND ISSUE

#73-77 and 79 printer: ABNC.

73   5 DRACHMAI

	GOOD	FINE	XF
28.4.1923. Black on orange and green unpt. Back green and m/c; Athena at ctr.	4.00	15.00	45.00

		Good	Fine	XF
74	**25 DRACHMAI** 15.4.1923. Black on green and m/c unpt. Ancient coin at l. and r. on brown and purple back.	12.00	45.00	125.00
75	**50 DRACHMAI** 12.3.1923. Black on m/c unpt. Back brown on blue unpt; Hermes at ctr.	100.00	250.00	550.00

		Good	Fine	XF
76	**100 DRACHMAI** 1.3.1923. Black and m/c. Back blue and m/c; relief of Elusis at ctr.	100.00	250.00	600.00
77	**500 DRACHMAI** 8.1.1923. Black on yellow and green unpt. Church at ctr. on back.	—	Rare	—
78	**500 DRACHMAI** 8.1.1923. Similar to #77. Ruins at ctr. on back. Printer: Gebr. Parcus, Munich (w/o imprint). Specimen.	—	—	800.00
79	**1000 DRACHMAI** 4.4.1923; 14.7.1923. Black on m/c unpt. Statue at l. and r. 4 columns and view of ruins at ctr. on back.	—	Rare	—

REPUBLIC

ΕΘΝΙΚΗ ΤΡΑΠΕΖΑ ΤΗΣ ΕΛΛΑΔΟΣ

NATIONAL BANK OF GREECE (CONTINUED)

1926 EMERGENCY ISSUE
Law of 23.1.1926

Older National Bank 50-1000 Drachmai notes were cut w/the left-hand portion 3/4 of the width leaving the right-hand portion 1/4 in width. Later on, the large left-hand pieces were exchanged at 3/4 of original face value and at 1/4 of the 3/4 face value for debentures of compulsory loan. The smaller 1/4 right-hand pieces were also exchanged for debentures.

		Good	Fine	XF
80	**50 DRACHMAI** L.1926. EK. 3, 4 (#66, 75).	7.50	20.00	45.00

		Good	Fine	XF
81	**100 DRACHMAI** L.1926. EK. 11, 12 (#67, 76).	7.50	20.00	45.00
82	**500 DRACHMAI** L.1926. EK. 8, 9 (#68, 77).	20.00	75.00	150.00

		Good	Fine	XF
83	**1000 DRACHMAI** L.1926. EK. 2, 3, 4 (#69, 72, 79).	40.00	100.00	250.00

1926 *NEON* ISSUE
#84-86 w/red ovpt: *NEON* in circle. Printer: BWC.

		Good	Fine	XF
84	**50 DRACHMAI** ND(1926-old date 6.5.1923). Purple on green and orange unpt. Portr. G. Stavros at l. Back purple; statue at ctr.	6.00	25.00	85.00

		Good	Fine	XF
85	**100 DRACHMAI** ND(1926-old date 20.4.1923). Green. Portr. G. Stavros at ctr. Back olive; church at ctr.			
	a. Black sign. of Royal Commissioner.	12.00	45.00	160.00
	b. Red sign. of Royal Commissioner.	6.00	30.00	100.00

		Good	Fine	XF
86	**500 DRACHMAI** ND(1926-old date 12.4.1923). Brown. Portr. G. Stavros at ctr. Back brown; city at ctr.	12.00	50.00	150.00

1926 THIRD ISSUE
#88 and 89 portr. G. Stavros at ctr. Printer: ABNC.

NOTE: #87 was issued as a provisional note of the Bank of Greece. See #94.

87	**5 DRACHMAI** 17.12.1926. Brown on green unpt. Back brown; ancient coin at l. and r.		Reported Not Confirmed

		Good	Fine	XF
88	**10 DRACHMAI** 15.7.1926; 5.8.1926. Blue on yellow and orange unpt. Ancient coin at l. and r. on back.	6.00	30.00	85.00

		Good	Fine	XF
89	**500 DRACHMAI** 21.11.1926. Purple on m/c unpt. Back purple; church at ctr., mythical animal at l. and r.			
	a. Black sign. of Commissioner.	12.50	50.00	150.00
	b. Red sign. of Commissioner.	8.00	35.00	130.00

1927 ISSUE
#90 and 91 printer: ABNC.

NOTE: #90 and 91 were only issued as provisional notes of the Bank of Greece. See #97 and 98.

		GOOD	FINE	XF
90	**50 DRACHMAI**			
	30.4.1927; 13.5.1927; 24.5.1927. Brown on orange and green unpt. Columns at l. and r., portr. G. Stavros at ctr. Ancient coin at l. and r. on back. (Not issued).	20.00	45.00	125.00

		GOOD	FINE	XF
91	**100 DRACHMAI**			
	25.5.1927; 6.6.1927; 14.6.1927. Green on orange and brown unpt. Portr. G. Stavros at l., ancient coin at r. Coin w/Apollo at ctr. on back. (Not issued).	20.00	45.00	125.00

ΤΡΑΠΕΖΑ ΤΗΣ ΕΛΛΑΔΟΣ

BANK OF GREECE

CA. 1928 FIRST PROVISIONAL ISSUE
#92 and 93 ovpt: new bank name on notes of the National Bank of Greece.

		GOOD	FINE	XF
92	**50 DRACHMAI**			
	ND (-old date 6.5.1923). Ovpt. on #84.	5.00	35.00	85.00

		GOOD	FINE	XF
93	**100 DRACHMAI**			
	ND (-old date 20.4.1923). Ovpt. on #85.	4.50	30.00	80.00

CA. 1928 SECOND PROVISIONAL ISSUE
#94-101 ovpt: new bank name on notes of the National Bank of Greece.

		GOOD	FINE	XF
94	**5 DRACHMAI**			
	ND (-old date 17.11.1926). Black ovpt. on lower r. on #87.	3.00	17.50	45.00

CA. 1928 THIRD PROVISIONAL ISSUE

		GOOD	FINE	XF
95	**20 DRACHMAI**			
	ND (-old dates 19.10.1926; 5.11.1926. Brown on m/c unpt. G. Stavros at l. Back brown; woman at ctr.	20.00	65.00	175.00
96	**25 DRACHMAI**			
	ND (-old date 15.4.1923). Ovpt. on #74.	30.00	150.00	300.00
97	**50 DRACHMAI**			
	ND (-old date 30.4.1927). Ovpt. on #90.	2.00	6.00	15.00
98	**100 DRACHMAI**			
	ND (-old date 6.6.1927). Ovpt. on #91.	1.50	5.00	12.50
99	**500 DRACHMAI**			
	ND (-old date 21.11.1926). Ovpt. on #89.	20.00	80.00	200.00

		GOOD	FINE	XF
100	**1000 DRACHMAI**			
	ND (-old date 1926). Black on green and m/c unpt. Portr. G. Stavrosk w/blue at ctr. Back w/blue and pink unpt. Stone carving at ctr.			
	a. W/o sign. under red bar at lower r. Old date 15.10.1926.	1.00	3.00	7.50
	b. W/o sign. under red bar at lower r. Old date 4.11.1926.	1.00	2.00	5.00
	c. Red bar ovpt. over sign. at lower r.	20.00	75.00	

		GOOD	FINE	XF
101	**5000 DRACHMAI**			
	ND (-old date 5.10.1926).. Brown on green unpt. Frieze at top, portr. G. Stavros at ctr. Back brown; stone carving at ctr.	60.00	200.00	450.00

1932 ISSUE
#102 and 103 printer: ABNC.

		VG	VF	UNC
102	**500 DRACHMAI**			
	1.10.1932. M/c. Portr. Athena at ctr. Stone carving at ctr. on back.	1.00	3.00	8.50

103	5000 DRACHMAI		VG	VF	UNC
	1.9.1932. Brown. Portr. Athena at ctr. Back green; mythical bird at ctr.		1.25	3.50	12.00

KINGDOM 1935-41

ΤΡΑΠΕΖΑ ΤΗΣ ΕΛΛΑΔΟΣ

BANK OF GREECE (CONTINUED)

1935 ISSUE

#104-106 printed in France.

104	50 DRACHMAI		VG	VF	UNC
	1.9.1935. M/c. Girl w/sheaf of wheat at I. Relief of Elusis at ctr., woman at r. on back.		1.50	4.50	15.00

105	100 DRACHMAI		VG	VF	UNC
	1.9.1935. M/c. Hermes at ctr. Woman holding basket at ctr. on back.		2.00	6.00	20.00

106	1000 DRACHMAI		VG	VF	UNC
	1.5.1935. M/c. Girl in national costume at ctr. Workman at l. and r., girl in national costume at ctr. on back.		2.00	7.50	25.00

1939 ISSUE

NOTE: For similar #107 but red-brown see #168.

107	50 DRACHMAI			
	1.1.1939. Green. Hesiod at I. Frieze at ctr. on back. Printer: TDLR (w/o imprint).	.50	1.50	3.00

108	100 DRACHMAI		VG	VF	UNC
	1.1.1939. Green and yellow. 2 peasant women at lower I. Stone carving in country scene on back. Printer: W&S (w/o imprint). (Not issued).		1.00	4.50	12.50

109	500 DRACHMAI		VG	VF	UNC
	1.1.1939. Purple and lilac. Portr. woman in national costume at I. Back blue-green; view of city and woman in oval. Printer: BWC (w/o imprint).				
	a. ΕΠΙ in line below Greek denomination.		.50	1.50	5.00
	b. Error: ΕΝΙ instead of ΕΠΙ		1.00	3.50	10.00
110	1000 DRACHMAI				
	1.1.1939. Green. Woman in national costume at r. Back blue-green; Athena at I. and view of Parthenon ruins at ctr. Printer: BWC (w/o imprint).		.75	1.50	4.00

1939 PROVISIONAL ISSUE

111	1000 DRACHMAI ON 100 DRACHMAI		VG	VF	UNC
	1939. Ovpt. on #108.		1.00	3.00	8.00

GERMAN / ITALIAN OCCUPATION -WW II

BANK OF GREECE

1941 EMERGENCY REISSUE

Because of a shortage of notes caused by the German-Italian occupation, Greek authorities on April 25, 1941 reissued cancelled notes readied for destruction. These were in use for about a year, and were redeemed on 1.4.1942 by exchanging them for new notes. Some are hole- cancelled (probably issued in Athens), while others also bear local stamps of branches of the Bank of Greece. Clear stamps are worth considerably more. The condition of all these notes is usually very low.

		GOOD	FINE	XF
112	**50 DRACHMAI** (1941). Reissue of #97, 104.	6.00	—	—

		GOOD	FINE	XF
113	**100 DRACHMAI** (1941). Reissue of #98, 105.	5.00	—	—
114	**500 DRACHMAI** (1941). Reissue of #102.	4.00	—	—
115	**1000 DRACHMAI** (1941). Reissue of #100a, 100b, 106.	3.00	—	—
115A	**5000 DRACHMAI** (1941). Reissue of #103.	—	—	—

1941 INFLATION ISSUE

Serial # varieties including positioning.

		VG	VF	UNC
116	**100 DRACHMAI** 10.7.1941. Brown. Bird frieze at l. and r. Back brown and green; Kapnikarea Church at ctr.	.25	.50	2.50

		VG	VF	UNC
117	**1000 DRACHMAI** 1.10.1941. Blue and brown. Coin of Alexander at l. Back green and yellow.			
	a. Title of picture on illustration.	.25	1.00	4.00
	b. Title of picture on white background.	.25	1.00	4.00

1942 INFLATION ISSUE

		VG	VF	UNC
118	**1000 DRACHMAI** 21.8.1942. Black on blue-gray and pale orange unpt. Bust of young girl from Thasos at ctr. Statue of Lion of Amphipolis at ctr. on back.	.25	.50	2.50

		VG	VF	UNC
119	**5000 DRACHMAI** 20.6.1942. Black on pale red, blue and m/c unpt. Factories and ships at lower l., statue of Nike of Samothrace between male workers at l., fisherman and shoreline at lower r. Back dk. brown on lt. blue and yellow-orange unpt.; farmers sowing and plowing w/horses at ctr.			
	a. Paper w/o wmk.	.25	.75	3.00
	b. Wmk. paper (same paper used for Agricultural Bonds #136-144).	1.00	4.00	12.00
120	**10,000 DRACHMAI** 29.12.1942. Brown. Young farm couple from Delphi at l. Treasure of the Athenians on back.			
	a. Title of picture on illustration.	.25	.60	3.00
	b. Title of picture in lt. background.	.25	.60	4.00

1943 INFLATION ISSUE

		VG	VF	UNC
121	**50 DRACHMAI** 1.2.1943. Brown on blue unpt. Woman from Paramithia at l. Back brown; ancient coin at l. and r.	.25	.50	2.00

		VG	VF	UNC
122	**5000 DRACHMAI** 19.7.1943. Green and brown. Frieze at l. and r., Athena at ctr. Back brown; relief at ctr.	.25	.50	2.50
123	**25,000 DRACHMAI** 12.8.1943. Black on brown and lt. blue-green unpt. Bust of Nymph Deidamia at l. Back black on olive green; ruins of Olympian Temple of Zeus at ctr.	.25	.50	2.50

1944 FIRST INFLATION ISSUE

		VG	VF	UNC
124	**50,000 DRACHMAI** 14.1.1944. Blue. Athlete at ctr. Back dk. brown.	.75	3.00	12.50

125 100,000 DRACHMAI
21.1.1944. Black on brown and lt. blue-green unpt. Ancient silver tetradrachm coin of Athens at l. and r. Ruins of the Temple of Aphaea Athena in Aegina at ctr. on back.

		VG	VF	UNC
a.	Serial number w/prefix letters.	.25	1.00	6.00
b.	Serial number w/suffix letters.	.25	1.00	6.00

126 500,000 DRACHMAI
20.3.1944. Black on dull violet-brown unpt. Head of Zeus at l. Back black on blue-green and pale olive green unpt; ears of wheat at ctr. — .25 .50 2.00

127 1,000,000 DRACHMAI
29.6.1944. Black on blue-green and pale orange unpt. Bust of youth from Antikythera at ctr. Back black on blue and pink unpt; ruins of Temple of Poseidon in Sounion at ctr.

		VG	VF	UNC
a.	Serial numbers w/prefix letters.	.25	.50	2.50
b.	Serial numbers w/suffix letters.	.25	.50	2.50

128 5,000,000 DRACHMAI
20.7.1944. Brown. Arethusa on dekadrachm of Syracuse at l. Back dk. brown and gray. .25 .50 2.00

129 10,000,000 DRACHMAI
29.7.1944. Brown. Dk. brown fringe around denomination guilloche and sign. .25 .50 1.25

130 25,000,000 DRACHMAI
10.8.1944. Green. Ancient Greek coin at l. and r. .25 .50 1.25

131 200,000,000 DRACHMAI
9.9.1944. Brown and red-brown. Parthenon frieze at ctr. Back brown.

		VG	VF	UNC
a.	Unpt. in tightly woven pattern w/o circles.	.25	.50	1.25
b.	Unpt. interconnecting circles w/dots.	3.00	7.00	25.00

132 500,000,000 DRACHMAI
1.10.1944. Blue-green. Apollo at l. Relief at ctr. on back. .25 .50 2.00

133 2,000,000,000 DRACHMAI
11.10.1944. Black on pale lt. green unpt. Like #131. Back aqua. .25 .50 1.25

134 10,000,000,000 DRACHMAI
20.10.1944. Black and blue-black on tan unpt. Face like #128. Back dull dk. blue. .25 .50 2.00

135 100,000,000,000 DRACHMAI
3.11.1944. Red-brown. Nymph Deidamia at l. Ancient coin at l. and r. on back. .50 1.00 4.00

ΤΑΜΕΙΑΚΟΝ ΓΡΑΜΜΑΤΙΟΝ
AGRICULTURAL TREASURY BONDS
NOTE: There is some question as to whether or not this series of Agricultural Treasury Bonds circulated as banknotes.

1942 ISSUE
136 25,000 DRACHMAI
26.11.1942. Lt. orange. Back brown. Series 1. 25.00 50.00 75.00

137 100,000 DRACHMAI
27.11.1942. Dk. green. Back blue-green. Series 1. — — 95.00

138 500,000 DRACHMAI
27.11.1942. Brown and green Series 1. — — 350.00

1943 FIRST ISSUE
139 25,000 DRACHMAI
5.3.1943. Blue and gray. Series 2. — — 75.00

140 100,000 DRACHMAI
5.3.1943. Blue and red. Series 2. — — 95.00

141 500,000 DRACHMAI
5.3.1943. Lt. orange. Series 2. — — 150.00

1943 SECOND ISSUE
142 25,000 DRACHMAI
15.5.1943. Gray, blue and green. Series 3. (Not issued). — — 250.00

143 100,000 DRACHMAI
15.5.1943. Green. Series 3. (Not issued). — — 250.00

144 500,000 DRACHMAI
15.5.1943. Green and brown. Series 3. (Not issued). — — 250.00

REGIONAL - WW II

BANK OF GREECE

ΑΓΡΙΝΙΟΥ - AGRINION BRANCH

1944 TREASURY NOTES
#145-150 bank name in capital or small letters. Uniface.

145	**100,000,000 DRACHMAI** Oct. 1944.	20.00	60.00	150.00
146	**200,000,000 DRACHMAI** Oct. 1944.	25.00	75.00	200.00
147	**300,000,000, DRACHMAI** Oct. 1944.	25.00	75.00	200.00

		VG	VF	UNC
148	**500,000,000 DRACHMAI** 9.10.1944. Blue text.	25.00	75.00	200.00
149	**1,000,000,000 DRACHMAI** Oct. 1944.	25.00	75.00	200.00
150	**2,000,000,000 DRACHMAI** 2.10.1944.			
	a. Bank name w/capital letters.	25.00	75.00	200.00
	b. Bank name w/small letters.	25.00	75.00	200.00
150A	**VARIOUS AMOUNTS** Sept.-Oct. 1944. Regular checks of the Agrinion branch made payable to *Ourselves* by bank manager. Amounts in millions of drachmai.	100.00	175.00	300.00

ΚΕΦΑΛΛΗΝΙΑ – ΙΘΑΚΑ CEPHALONIA - ITHAKA BRANCH

1944 TREASURY NOTES

		VG	VF	UNC
151	**50,000,000 DRACHMAI** 6.10.1944. Yellowish paper.	30.00	90.00	250.00

		VG	VF	UNC
152	**100,000,000 DRACHMAI** 6.10.1944. Bluish paper.	20.00	60.00	175.00

ΚΕΡΚΨΡΑ - CORFU BRANCH

1944 PROVISIONAL ISSUE
Red ovpt. on Ionian Islands notes #M14, M15 and M16 for use in Corfu.

153	**20 DRACHMAI ON 50 DRACHMAI** 18.12.1944.	—	Rare	—

		VG	VF	UNC
154	**100 DRACHMAI ON 100 DRACHMAI** 18.12.1944.	—	Rare	—
155	**500 DRACHMAI ON 1000 DRACHMAI** 18.12.1944.	—	Rare	—

1944 TREASURY NOTE W/KERKYRA NAME

		VG	VF	UNC
156	**100,000,000 DRACHMAI** 17.10.1944. Green on yellow.	8.00	20.00	50.00

ΚΑΛΑΜΑΤΑ - KALAMATA BRANCH

1944 FIRST ISSUE TREASURY NOTES
#157-160 uniface. Flag at l. and r.

157	**25,000,000 DRACHMAI** 20.9.1944. Brown.	25.00	65.00	150.00

		VG	VF	UNC
158	**50,000,000 DRACHMAI** 20.9.1944. Violet.	15.00	40.00	100.00
159	**100,000,000 DRACHMAI** 20.9.1944. Lt. blue.	12.00	30.00	75.00
160	**500,000,000 DRACHMAI** 20.9.1944. Green.	25.00	65.00	150.00

1944 SECOND ISSUE

		VG	VF	UNC
161	**200,000,000 DRACHMAI** 5.10.1944. Orange. Back brown.			
	a. Greek handstamp on back.	12.00	30.00	75.00
	b. French handstamp on back.	15.00	40.00	100.00
	c. Stamp for *TRIPOLIS* branch on back.	100.00	200.00	300.00

ΝΑΥΠΛΙΟΥ - NAUPLIA BRANCH

1944 PROVISIONAL TREASURY NOTES

#162-163 ovpt. on Bank of Greece notes.

			VG	VF	UNC
162	**100,000,000 DRACHMAI** 19.9.1944. Red ovpt. on back of #128.		30.00	80.00	200.00

			VG	VF	UNC
163	**500,000,000 DRACHMAI** 19.9.1944. Black ovpt. on back of #119.		—	Rare	—

ΥΠΟΚΑΤΑΣΤΗΜΑ ΠΑΤΡΩΝ - PATRAS BRANCH

1944 TREASURY NOTES

#164-165 uniface.

			VG	VF	UNC
164	**100,000,000 DRACHMAI** 7.10.1944. Brown. Ancient Greek coin at l.		6.00	15.00	40.00

			VG	VF	UNC
165	**500,000,000 DRACHMAI** 7.10.1944. Blue-gray. Ancient Greek coin at ctr.		6.00	15.00	40.00

ΤΡΙΚΑΛΩΝ - TRIKALA BRANCH

1944 PROVISIONAL TREASURY NOTES

#166-167 ovpt. on Bank of Greece notes.

NOTE: A 500 Million Drachmai issue from the Zakinthos Branch dated Oct. 1944 is reported.

166	**10,000,000 DRACHMAI** 29.9.1944. Black ovpt. on back of #118.		—	—	—

			VG	VF	UNC
167	**200,000,000 DRACHMAI** 29.9.1944. Black ovpt. and red German stamping on back of #122.		100.00	300.00	—

KINGDOM - POST WW II

ΤΡΑΠΕΖΑ ΤΗΣ ΕΛΛΑΔΟΣ

BANK OF GREECE

1941-44 ISSUE

NOTE: For similar #168 but green dated 1939 see #107.

			VG	VF	UNC
168	**50 DRACHMAI** 1.1.1941 (2.1.1945). Red-brown on lilac unpt. Like #107. Wmk: Young male head. Printer: TDLR (w/o imprint).		.50	1.25	3.50

			VG	VF	UNC
169	**50 DRACHMAI** 9.11.1944. Brown on blue and gold unpt. Statue of Nike of Samothrake at l. Phoenix at ctr. on back.		1.50	4.50	20.00

1944-46 ISSUE

#171-176 printer: BWC (w/o imprint).

#170-176 issued 1944-46.

			VG	VF	UNC
170	**100 DRACHMAI** ND (1944). Blue on gold unpt. Canaris (maritime hero) at r. Goddess at ctr. on back. Printer: W&S (w/o imprint).		.75	2.50	12.00

			VG	VF	UNC
171	**500 DRACHMAI** ND (1945). Green. Portr. Capodistrias (statesman) at l. University of Athens at bottom ctr. on back.		1.00	4.00	17.50
172	**1000 DRACHMAI** ND (1944). Brown. Portr. Kolokotronis (hero of freedom) at l. Soldier at ctr. on back. 161 x 80mm.		1.50	4.50	27.50
173	**5000 DRACHMAI** ND (1945). Red. Portr. woman w/children at ctr. 2 women w/mythical horse at ctr. on back. 170 x 84mm.		10.00	50.00	145.00
174	**10,000 DRACHMAI** ND (1945). Orange. Aristotle at l., ancient coins around border. Back brown; chariot driven Polyzalos (found in Delphi) at ctr. 180 x 90mm.		10.00	50.00	145.00

175	**10,000 DRACHMAI**	**VG**	**VF**	**UNC**
	ND (1946). Blue. Like #174. 180 x 90mm.	10.00	50.00	145.00
176	**20,000 DRACHMAI**			
	ND (1946). Dk. green. Athena at l., ancient coin at bottom. Medusa at upper ctr., chicken at lower ctr. on back. 180 x 90mm.	10.00	50.00	145.00

1947 ND ISSUE
#177-179 reduced size, issued 1947.

177	**5000 DRACHMAI**	**VG**	**VF**	**UNC**
	ND (1947). Purple on orange unpt. Like #173 but 153 x 80mm.	7.00	20.00	70.00
178	**10,000 DRACHMAI**			
	ND (1947). Orange. Like #174 but 153 x 80mm.	8.00	35.00	95.00
179	**20,000 DRACHMAI**			
	ND (1947). Dk. green. Like #176 but 153 x 80mm.			
	a. W/o security strip.	7.00	25.00	95.00
	b. W/security strip.	7.00	30.00	110.00

1947; 1949 ISSUE

180	**1000 DRACHMAI**	**VG**	**VF**	**UNC**
	1947. Brown. Like #172 but 145 x 75mm.			
	a. 9.1.1947. Wmk: Ancient warrior w/helmet.	1.50	6.00	22.50
	b. 14.11.1947. W/o wmk.	1.00	5.00	20.00
181	**5000 DRACHMAI**			
	9.6.1947. Brown. Like #173 but 153 x 80mm.	2.00	15.00	57.50

182	**10,000 DRACHMAI**	**VG**	**VF**	**UNC**
	29.12.1947. Orange. Like #174 but 150 x 79mm.			
	a. W/o printer's name at bottom on back. (Printer: BWC).	1.00	15.00	57.50
	b. Greek printer's name at bottom on back. Same numeral style as a.	4.00	35.00	110.00
	c. Printer like b., but series letters small and in front of serial #.	2.00	30.00	80.00

183	**20,000 DRACHMAI**	**VG**	**VF**	**UNC**
	29.12.1949. Blue on m/c unpt. Like #176 but 147 x 78mm.	2.00	15.00	62.50

1950 ISSUE

184	**5000 DRACHMAI**	**VG**	**VF**	**UNC**
	28.10.1950. Brown. Portr. Solomos at l. Battle of Mesolonghi on back.	2.00	15.00	62.50

185	**50,000 DRACHMAI**	**VG**	**VF**	**UNC**
	1.12.1950. Olive and gray. Portr. woman at l. Ruins at ctr. on back.	2.00	9.00	50.00

1953 ND ISSUE
#185A-185C printer: W&S (w/o imprint).

185A	**1 NEW DRACHMA**			
	ND (1953). Dull blue on m/c unpt. Portr. Athena at r. Specimen.	—	—	—
185B	**5 NEW DRACHMAI**			
	ND (1953). Dk. olive-brown on m/c unpt. Portr. Homer at lower r. Specimen.	—	—	—
185C	**10 NEW DRACHMAI**			
	ND (1953). Green on m/c unpt. Portr. archaic woman at lower r. Specimen.	—	—	—

1954 ISSUE
#186-188 NEA EKΔOΣIΣ (New Issue) at r.

186	**10 DRACHMAI**			
	15.1.1954. Orange. Like #182.	12.00	60.00	150.00

		VG	VF	UNC
187	**20 DRACHMAI**	8.00	40.00	120.00
	15.1.1954. Blue. Like #183.			
188	**50 DRACHMAI**	5.00	25.00	75.00
	15.1.1954. Green and gray. Like #185.			

1954-56 ISSUE

		VG	VF	UNC
189	**10 DRACHMAI**			
	1954-55. Orange. Kg. George I at l. Church at ctr. on back.			
	a. 15.5.1954.	3.00	12.00	50.00
	b. 1.3.1955.	2.00	6.00	30.00

		VG	VF	UNC
190	**20 DRACHMAI**	4.00	15.00	60.00
	1.3.1955. Blue. Demokritos at l. Mythical scene on back.			

		VG	VF	UNC
191	**50 DRACHMAI**	1.50	5.00	20.00
	1.3.1955. Dk. green. Pericles at ctr. Pericles speaking on back.			

		VG	VF	UNC
192	**100 DRACHMAI**			
	1954-55. Red on m/c unpt. Themistocles at l., galley at bottom r. Sailing ships on back.			
	a. 31.3.1954.	4.00	15.00	50.00
	b. 1.7.1955.	1.50	5.00	20.00

		VG	VF	UNC
193	**500 DRACHMAI**	4.00	15.00	50.00
	8.8.1955. Green on m/c unpt. Socrates at ctr. Apostle Paul speaking to assembly on back.			

		VG	VF	UNC
194	**1000 DRACHMAI**	8.00	25.00	60.00
	16.4.1956. Brown. Alexander at l., frieze at bottom. Alexander in battle on back.			

MINISTRY OF FINANCE

GREEK STATE

1917 PROVISIONAL ISSUE
#301 and 302 red ovpt: *NOMOE/991/1917.* Printer: BWC.

		VG	VF	UNC
301	**1 DRACHMA**	15.00	45.00	100.00
	1917 (-old date 21.12.1885). Ovpt. on #40.			

		VG	VF	UNC
302	**2 DRACHMAI**	15.00	50.00	130.00
	1917 (-old date 21.12.1885). Ovpt. on #41.			

ΒΑΣΙΛΕΙΟΝ ΤΗΣ ΕΛΛΑΔΟΣ

KINGDOM OF GREECE

1917-20 ND ISSUE
#303-307 arms of Kg. George I. Printer: Aspiotis Freres.

		VG	VF	UNC
303	**50 LEPTA**			
	ND (1920). Blue. Standing Athena at ctr. Back blue; ancient coins at l. and r.			
	a. Square perforations.	1.50	5.00	10.00
	b. Zig-zag perforations.	3.00	15.00	30.00

304	**1 DRACHMA** 27.10.1917. Brown. Hermes seated at ctr. Back blue.	VG	VF	UNC
	a. Brown on gold unpt. W/o inner line in diamond surrounding Hermes, diamond dk. brown.	2.50	8.50	20.00
	b. Darker brown w/o unpt. Inner line in diamond surrounding Hermes, diamond brown.	1.00	3.00	10.00

305	**1 DRACHMA** ND (1918). Brown. Pericles at r. Back green; medal at ctr.	VG 3.00	VF 10.00	UNC 30.00
306	**2 DRACHMAI** 27.10.1917. Blue and brown. Like #304. Back brown.	3.00	10.00	30.00
307	**2 DRACHMAI** ND (1918). Black on gold unpt. Pericles at l. Back brown; ancient coin at middle l. and r.	12.00	50.00	120.00

1917 (1918) ISSUE

#308-312 printer: BWC.

NOTE: All issues w/1917 date were released in 1918.

308	**1 DRACHMA** 27.10.1917 (1918). Black on lt. green and pink unpt. Homer at ctr. Back green and lt. brown.	VG 2.00	VF 7.50	UNC 35.00

309	**1 DRACHMA** 27.10.1917 (1918). Purple on lilac and m/c unpt. Hermes seated at r. Back green and brown.	VG 1.00	VF 4.00	UNC 20.00

310	**2 DRACHMAI** 27.10.1917 (1918). Blue on brown and orange unpt. Zeus at l. Back green.	VG 2.00	VF 7.50	UNC 35.00

311	**2 DRACHMAI** 27.10.1917 (1918). Red-brown on m/c unpt. Orpheus w/lyre at ctr. Back blue and lilac.	VG 3.00	VF 9.00	UNC 45.00

1918 ISSUE

312	**5 DRACHMAI** 14.6.1918. Green and m/c. Athena at l. Back purple and red. (Not issued).	VG 100.00	VF 250.00	UNC 500.00

ΕΛΛΑΣ
1922 ND POSTAGE STAMP CURRENCY ISSUE

313	**10 LEPTA** ND (1922). Brown. Hermes. Same design in reverse on back. Postage stamp of the 1911-21 issue (Michel #162, Scott #202).	VG	VF	UNC
	a. Square perforations.	2.00	7.50	20.00
	b. Zig-zag perforations.	2.00	6.00	15.00

ΒΑΣΙΛΕΙΟΝ ΤΗΣ ΕΛΛΑΔΟΕ (continued)
1940 ISSUE

314	**10 DRACHMAI** 6.4.1940. Blue on green and lt. brown unpt. Ancient coin w/Demeter at l. Back blue and brown; university at ctr.	VG .10	VF .25	UNC .75

315	**20 DRACHMAI** 6.4.1940. Green on lt. lilac and orange unpt. Ancient coin w/Poseidon at l. Back purple and green; Parthenon at ctr.	VG .10	VF .25	UNC .75

ΕΛΛΗΝΙΚΗ ΠΟΛΙΤΕΙΑ
GREEK STATE (RESUMED)
1941 ISSUE

#316-319 printer: Aspiotis - ELKA.

316	**50 LEPTA** 18.6.1941. Red and black on lt. brown unpt. Nike of Samothrake at l. Church on back.	VG .25	VF .50	UNC 1.50

317	**1 DRACHMA** 18.6.1941. Red and blue on gray unpt. Aristotle at l. Back blue and brown; ancient coin at ctr.	VG .25	VF .40	UNC 1.00

318	**2 DRACHMAI** 18.6.1941. Purple and black on lt. brown unpt. Ancient coin of Alexander at l. Back blue and gray; ancient coin at ctr.	VG .25	VF .40	UNC 1.00

319 5 DRACHMAI
18.6.1941. Black and red on pale yellow unpt. 3 women of Knossos at ctr. Back yellow and brown; column at ctr.

	VG	VF	UNC
	.25	.50	1.25

ΒΑΣΙΛΕΙΟΝ ΤΗΣ ΕΛΛΑΔΟΣ
KINGDOM OF GREECE (RESUMED)
1944; 1945 ISSUE

320 1 DRACHMA
9.11.1944. Blue on green unpt. Back blue; Phoenix at ctr.

	VG	VF	UNC
	.25	.50	1.25

321 5 DRACHMAI
15.1.1945. Brown and yellow-orange.

	VG	VF	UNC
	.25	.50	1.25

322 10 DRACHMAI
9.11.1944. Brown on green and orange unpt. Laborer at l. and r. Church at ctr. on back.

	VG	VF	UNC
	.25	.50	1.25

323 20 DRACHMAI
9.11.1944. Blue on orange unpt. Zeus on ancient coin at ctr. Angel at ctr. on back.

	VG	VF	UNC
	.25	.50	1.25

1950 ISSUE

324 100 DRACHMAI
1950-53. Blue on orange unpt. Constantine at ctr. Church at ctr. on back.

	VG	VF	UNC
a. 10.7.1950.	.25	1.00	3.00
b. 1.11.1953.	.50	2.00	4.50

325 500 DRACHMAI
1950-53. Green on brown unpt. Byzantine coin at l. Church at ctr. on back.

	VG	VF	UNC
a. 10.7.1950.	.25	1.00	4.00
b. 1.11.1953.	.75	2.50	7.50

326 1000 DRACHMAI
1950-53. Brown on orange and green unpt. Ancient coin at l. and r. Back brown and pink; stone carving of a lion at ctr.

	VG	VF	UNC
a. 10.7.1950.	.25	1.50	4.50
b. 1.11.1953.	.75	2.50	7.50

ITALIAN OCCUPATION - WW II
CASSA MEDITERRANEA DI CREDITO PER LA GRECIA
1941 ISSUE

#M1-M4 Hermes at r. on back. Circulated 1941-44.

#M5-M10 David (sculpture by Michaelangelo) at l.

		VG	VF	UNC
M1	**5 DRACHMAI** ND (1941). Green. Wheat at l.	1.00	5.00	25.00
M2	**10 DRACHMAI** ND (1941). Red-orange. Prows of ancient ships at l.	1.00	5.00	25.00
M3	**50 DRACHMAI** ND (1941). Blue. Wheat at l.	1.25	6.00	30.00
M4	**100 DRACHMAI** ND (1941). Brown on orange unpt. Prow of ship at l.	1.25	6.00	30.00

		VG	VF	UNC
M5	**500 DRACHMAI** ND (1941). Dk. green.	5.00	20.00	100.00
M6	**1000 DRACHMAI** ND (1941). Lt. brown.	3.00	10.00	50.00
M7	**5000 DRACHMAI** ND (1941). Lilac.	8.00	35.00	160.00
M8	**10,000 DRACHMAI** ND (1941). Gray.	6.00	20.00	200.00
M9	**20,000 DRACHMAI** ND (1941). Blue.	8.00	35.00	160.00

IONIAN ISLANDS
BIGLIETTO A CORSO LEGALE PER LE ISOLE JONIE
1941 ND ISSUE
#M11-M18 issued for the Ionian Islands.

		VG	VF	UNC
M11	**1 DRACHMA** ND (1941). Dk. green. Back w/tan unpt.	.75	3.50	20.00

		VG	VF	UNC
M12	**5 DRACHMAI** ND (1941). Red. Alexander at l. Alexander at l. Ancient picture at ctr. on back.	.75	3.50	20.00
M13	**10 DRACHMAI** ND (1941). Green. Like #M12.	.75	3.75	22.50
M14	**50 DRACHMAI** ND (1941). Brown. Old man at l.	.75	4.00	25.00

		VG	VF	UNC
M15	**100 DRACHMAI** ND (1941). Blue. Like #M14.	.75	3.75	22.50
M16	**500 DRACHMAI** ND (1941). Lilac on blue unpt. Caesar from coin at l. Ancient picture on back.			
	a. Issued note.	2.00	8.00	45.00
	b. Blue Imperial handstamp w/sign. at l.	—	Rare	—
M17	**1000 DRACHMAI** ND (1941). Brown. Like #M18.			
	a. Issued note.	2.00	8.50	48.00
	b. Blue Imperial handstamp w/sign. at l.	—	Rare	—

		VG	VF	UNC
M18	**5000 DRACHMAI** ND (1941). Blue on gray unpt. Like #M16. Ionian emblems and landscape at ctr. on back.			
	a. Issued note.	7.50	30.00	100.00
	b. Blue Imperial handstamp w/sign. at l.	—	Rare	—

GERMAN OCCUPATION - WW II
GERMAN ARMED FORCES
AUXILIARY PAYMENT CERTIFICATES
#M19-M22 issued for the German Armed Forces.
German Nazi (3 varieties), Salonika-Aegean and Greek handstamps on back of Germany #M32-M35.

		VG	VF	UNC
M19	**1 PFENNIG** ND. Blue. Stamped on Germany #M32.	2.50	10.00	30.00

		VG	VF	UNC
M20	**5 PFENNIG** ND. Red. Stamped on Germany #M33.	2.50	10.00	30.00
M21	**10 PFENNIG** ND. Green. Stamped on Germany #M34.	2.50	10.00	30.00
M22	**50 PFENNIG** ND. Orange. Stamped on Germany #M35.	27.00	75.00	250.00

GREENLAND

Greenland, an integral part of the Danish realm, is a huge island situated between the North Atlantic Ocean and the Polar Sea, almost entirely within the Artic Circle. It has an area of 840,000 sq. mi. (2,175,600 sq. km.) and a population of 54,000. Capital: Godthab. Greenland is the world's only source of natural cryolite, a fluoride of sodium and aluminum important in making aluminum. Fish products and minerals are exported.

Eric the Red discovered Greenland in 982 and established the first settlement in 986. Greenland was a republic until 1261, when the sovereignty of Norway was extended to the island. The original colony was abandoned about 1400 when increasing cold interfered with the breeding of cattle. Successful recolonization was undertaken by Denmark in 1721. In 1921 Denmark extended its claim to include the entire island, and made it a colony of the crown in 1924. The island's colonial status was abolished by amendment to the Danish constitution on June 5, 1953, and Greenland became an integral part of the Kingdom of Denmark. It has been an autonomous state since May 1, 1979.

RULERS:
Danish

MONETARY SYSTEM:
1 Rigsbankdaler = 96 Skilling to 1874
1 Krone = 48 Skilling
1 Krone = 100 Ore, 1874-

DANISH INFLUENCE
KONGEL. GRØNLANDSKE HANDEL
1803 ISSUE
#A1-A4 value text at upper r. Julianehaab District.

		GOOD	FINE	XF
A1	**12 SKILLING** 1803.	400.00	—	—

		GOOD	FINE	XF
A2	**24 SKILLING** 1803.	425.00	650.00	—
A3	**1/2 RIGSDALER** 1803.	500.00	800.00	—
A4	**1 RIGSDALER** 1803.	400.00	—	—

HANDELSSTEDERNE I GRØNLAND
1804 ISSUE

		GOOD	FINE	XF
A5	**6 SKILLING** 1804. Text in diamond at ctr.	250.00	750.00	—
A6	**12 SKILLING** 1804. Similar to #A5.	400.00	1000.	—

		GOOD	FINE	XF
A7	**1/4 RIGSDALER** 1804.	350.00	700.00	—
A8	**1/2 RIGSDALER** 1804. Text in triangle at ctr.	400.00	700.00	—
A9	**1 RIGSDALER** 1804.	400.00	950.00	—

		GOOD	FINE	XF
A10	**5 RIGSDALER** 1804.	600.00	1200.	—

1819 ISSUE

A11	**6 SKILLING** 1819.	—	—	—
A12	**12 SKILLING** 1819.	—	—	—
A13	**24 SKILLING** 1819.	—	—	—
A14	**1 RIGSBANKDALER** 1819.	—	—	—

1837 ISSUE

A15	**6 SKILLING** 1837.	—	—	—
A16	**12 SKILLING** 1837.	—	—	—
A17	**24 SKILLING** 1837.	—	—	—
A18	**1 RIGSBANKDALER** 1837.	—	—	—

1841 ISSUE

A19	**6 SKILLING** 1841.	—	—	—
A20	**12 SKILLING** 1841.	—	—	—
A21	**24 SKILLING** 1841.	—	—	—
A22	**1 RIGSBANKDALER** 1841.	—	—	—

1844 ISSUE

A23	**6 SKILLING** 1844.	—	—	—
A24	**12 SKILLING** 1844.	—	—	—
A25	**24 SKILLING** 1844.	—	—	—
A26	**1 RIGSBANKDALER** 1844.	—	—	—

1848 ISSUE

A27	**6 SKILLING** 1848.	—	—	—
A28	**12 SKILLING** 1848.	—	—	—
A29	**24 SKILLING** 1848.	—	—	—
A30	**1 RIGSBANKDALER** 1848.	—	—	—

1853 ISSUE

		GOOD	FINE	XF
A31	**6 SKILLING** 1853.	—	—	—
A32	**1 RIGSBANKDALER** 1853.	—	—	—

1856 ISSUE

		GOOD	FINE	XF
A33	**6 SKILLING R.M.** 1856. Red on blue paper. a. Issued note. b. Unsigned remainder.	 150.00 —	 550.00 Unc	 850.00 500.00

		GOOD	FINE	XF
A34	**12 SKILLING R.M.** 1856. a. Issued note. b. Unsigned remainder.	 175.00 —	 650.00 Unc	 — 500.00
A35	**24 SKILLING R.M.** 1856.	200.00	750.00	—
A36	**1 RIGSBANKDALER** 1856. Blue and red on blue paper.	250.00	1000.	—

1874 ISSUE
#A37-A39 monogram at l., crowned small polar bear at r.

		GOOD	FINE	XF
A37	**50 ØRE** 1874. Gray. a. Issued note. r. Unsigned remainder.	 175.00 —	 550.00 Unc	 900.00 350.00

		GOOD	FINE	XF
A38	**1 KRONE** 1874. Blue. a. Issued note. r. Unsigned remainder.	 200.00 —	 675.00 Unc	 1050. 450.00

1875 ISSUE

		GOOD	FINE	XF
A39	**25 ØRE** 1875. Lt. brown. a. Issued note. r. Unsigned remainder.	 100.00 —	 300.00 Unc	 700.00 400.00

1883; 1887 ISSUE

A40 1 KRONE
1883. Blue. Crowned polar bears at l. and r.   150.00   575.00   950.00

A40A 1 KRONE
1887. Like #A40.   175.00   600.00   1000.

A41	5 KRONEN	GOOD	FINE	XF
	1887. Green. Polar bear at l. facing l.			
	a. Serial # handwritten.	175.00	600.00	1000.
	b. Serial # printed.	140.00	550.00	925.00
	r. Unsigned remainder.	—	Unc	550.00

1888 ISSUE
#1-21 have all been demonetized.

1	50 ØRE	GOOD	FINE	XF
	1888. Brown. Greenland seal on ice slab at ctr. Polar bear in l. shield facing r.			
	a. Serial # handwritten.	125.00	350.00	700.00
	b. Serial # printed.	125.00	350.00	700.00

1892 ISSUE

2	25 ØRE			
	1892. Black. Polar bear in l. shield facing r.			
	a. Serial # handwritten.	100.00	300.00	650.00
	b. Serial # printed.	100.00	300.00	650.00

1897 ISSUE

5	1 KRONE			
	1897; 1905. Blue. Polar bear in l. shield facing l.			
	a. 1897.	100.00	275.00	650.00
	b. 1905.	75.00	225.00	575.00

1905 ISSUE

4	25 ØRE	GOOD	FINE	XF
	1905. Red. Polar bear in l. shield facing l.	30.00	50.00	100.00

DEN KONGELIGE GRØNLANDSKE HANDEL

1911 PROVISIONAL ISSUE

6	1 KRONE	GOOD	FINE	XF
	1911 (-old date 1905). Blue.			
	a. Ovpt.: *Den kgl. grønlandske Handel 1911* across lower ctr. on #5.	250.00	500.00	1050.
	b. W/additional ovpt.: *kolonien Holstensborg* at top.	250.00	850.00	1700.

1911 ISSUE
#7, 8, 10: 2 wmk. varieties.

7	25 ØRE			
	1911. Red. Eider duck on rock in water at ctr.	100.00	500.00	750.00
8	50 ØRE			
	1911. Brown. Greenland seal on ice at ctr.	125.00	350.00	800.00

9	1 KRONE	GOOD	FINE	XF
	1911. Blue. Reindeer in mountains at ctr.	125.00	400.00	925.00
10	5 KRONER			
	1911. Green. Polar bear on ice at ctr. Outer edges perforated.			
	a. W/o ovpt.	150.00	500.00	1050.
	b. W/ovpt.: *Kolonien Holstensborg* at top.	350.00	1250.	—

STYRELSEN AF KOLONIERNE I GRØNLAND
STATE NOTES
1913 ISSUE

11	25 ØRE	VG	VF	UNC
	ND (1913). Red. Eider duck on rock in water at ctr.	15.00	50.00	100.00

12	50 ØRE	VG	VF	UNC
	ND (1913). Brown. Sea lion on ice at ctr.	15.00	85.00	275.00

13	1 KRONE	VG	VF	UNC
	ND (1913). Blue. Reindeer in mountains at ctr.	25.00	95.00	275.00
14	5 KRONER			
	ND (1913). Green. Polar bear on ice at ctr.	20.00	65.00	225.00

GRØNLANDS STYRELSE
STATE NOTES
1926-52 ISSUE
#15-17 w/text: *GRØNLANDS STYRELSE* on all sides of face and around map at ctr. on back.

15	5 KRONER			
	ND (1926-52). Green. Polar bear on ice at ctr.			
	a. Green unpt. of diagonal lines; white border. W/o wmk.	25.00	85.00	275.00
	b. Green unpt. fine screening through border. W/o wmk.	25.00	85.00	275.00
	c. Wmk: Wavy lines. (1945-52).	15.00	45.00	200.00

16	**10 KRONER**	**VG**	**VF**	**UNC**
	ND (1926-52). Brown. Hump-back whale at ctr.			
	a. W/o wmk. (1926-44).	40.00	120.00	350.00
	b. Wmk: Wavy lines. (1945-52).	25.00	80.00	300.00
17	**50 KRONER**	**GOOD**	**FINE**	**XF**
	ND (1926-52). Lilac. Clipper ship at ctr.			
	a. W/o wmk. (1926-44).	—	—	—
	b. Wmk: Wavy lines. (1945-52).	300.00	700.00	1700.

DEN KONGELIGE GRØNLANDSKE HANDEL (RESUMED)

1953 ISSUE

18	**5 KRONER**	**VG**	**VF**	**UNC**
	ND (1953-67). Green. Similar to #15.	10.00	40.00	125.00

19	**10 KRONER**	**VG**	**VF**	**UNC**
	ND (1953-67). Brown. Similar to #16.	12.00	65.00	200.00

20	**50 KRONER**	**VG**	**VF**	**UNC**
	ND (1953-67). Lilac. Similar to #17.	75.00	375.00	825.00

KREDITSEDDEL
CREDIT NOTES

1953 ISSUE

21	**100 KRONER**	**VG**	**VF**	**UNC**
	16.1.1953. Black, orange and blue-green. K. Rasmussen at at l., dog sled, lake and hill at lower r. Back red; crown at l. ctr., map at r.			
	a. Issued note.	125.00	525.00	1250.
	s. Specimen.	—	—	550.00

MILITARY

GRØNLANDS ADMINISTRATION

1940'S TRADE CERTIFICATES

#M1-M4 are perforated, narrow cardboard tokens w/denomination and *Grl. Adm.* Issued for American troops stationed in Greenland during World War II.

M1	**1 ØRE**	**VG**	**VF**	**UNC**
	ND. Brown cardboard.	10.00	20.00	45.00
M2	**2 ØRE**			
	ND. Yellow cardboard.	10.00	20.00	45.00
M3	**5 ØRE**			
	ND. Violet cardboard.	10.00	20.00	50.00
M4	**10 ØRE**			
	ND. White cardboard.	15.00	25.00	60.00

1941 TRADE CERTIFICATES

#M5-M7 embossed circular seal w/crown over *GRØNLANDS ADMINISTRATION* at l.

M5	**1 SKILLING**			
	ND (1941). Red. Like #M6.	100.00	250.00	500.00

M6	**5 SKILLING**	**VG**	**VF**	**UNC**
	ND (1941). Blue.	100.00	350.00	550.00
M7	**20 SKILLING**			
	ND (1941). Green. Like #M6.	125.00	275.00	600.00

1942 TRADE CERTIFICATES

#M8-M10 black handstamp: *GRØNLANDS ADMINISTRATION* around crown at l.

M8	**1 SKILLING**			
	ND (1942). Red. Like #M10.	—	8.00	25.00
M9	**5 SKILLING**			
	ND (1942). Blue. Like #M10.	—	8.00	25.00

M10	**20 SKILLING**	**VG**	**VF**	**UNC**
	ND (1942). Green.	—	8.00	25.00

GRENADA

Grenada, located in the Windward islands of the Caribbean Sea 90 miles (145 km.) north of Trinidad, has (with Carriacou and Petit Martinique) an area of 133 sq. mi. (344 sq. km.). Capital: St. George's. Grenada is the smallest independent nation in the Western Hemisphere. Columbus discovered Grenada in 1498 during his third voyage to the Americas. Spain failed to colonize the island, and in 1627 granted it to the British who sold it to the French who colonized it in 1650. Grenada was captured by the British in 1763, retaken by the French in 1779, and finally ceded to the British in 1783. In 1958 Grenada joined the Federation of the West Indies, which was dissolved in 1962. In 1967, it became an internally self-governing British associated state. Full independence was attained on Feb. 4, 1974. Grenada is a member of the Commonwealth of Nations. The prime minister is the Head of Government.

NOTE: For earlier commerical bank issues, see Volume I. For later issues see East Caribbean States and Volume III.

RULERS:
British

MONETARY SYSTEM:
1 Shilling = 12 Pence
1 Pound = 20 Shillings to 1970
1 Dollar = 100 cents

BRITISH INFLUENCE

GOVERNMENT OF GRENADA

1920 ISSUE
#1-3 portr. of Kg. George V at r. on face. Sailing ship at ctr. on back. Printer: TDLR.

1	2 SHILLINGS 6 PENCE			
	1.7.1920. Red and olive-gray. Back olive.	—	Rare	—

2	5 SHILLINGS			
	1.7.1920. Blue and green. Back brown.	—	Rare	—

3	10 SHILLINGS			
	1.7.1920. Blue-gray and green. Back blue.	—	Rare	—

GUADELOUPE

The French Overseas Department of Guadeloupe, located in the Leeward Islands of the West Indies about 300 miles (493 km.) southeast of Puerto Rico, has an area of 687 sq. mi. (1,779 sq. km.) and a population of 335,000. Actually it is two islands separated by a narrow salt water stream: volcanic Basse-Terre to the west and the flatter limestone formation of Grande-Terre to the east. Capital: Basse-Terre, on the island of that name. The principal industries are agriculture, the distillation of liquors, and tourism. Sugar, bananas and rum are exported.

Guadeloupe was discovered by Columbus in 1493 and settled in 1635 by two Frenchmen, L'Olive and Dupiessis, who took possession in the name of the French Company of the Islands of America. When repeated efforts by private companies to colonize the island failed, it was relinquished to the French crown in 1674, and established as a dependency of Martinique. The British occupied the island on two occasions, 1759-1763 and 1810-1816, before it passed permanently to France. A colony until 1946, Guadeloupe was then made an overseas territory of the French Union. In 1958 it voted to become an Overseas Department within the new French Community.

Grande-Terre, as noted in the first paragraph, is the eastern member of two-island Guadeloupe. Isle Desirade (La Desirade), located east of Grande-Terre, and Les Saintes (Iles des Saintes), located south of Basse-Terre, are dependencies of Guadeloupe.

RULERS
French

MONETARY SYSTEM
1 Franc = 100 Centimes
1 Nouveaux Franc = 100 "old" Francs, 1960-

FRENCH INFLUENCE

BANQUE DE PRET

1848 ISSUE

A1	5 FRANCS			
	1848.	—	Rare	—
A2	10 FRANCS			
	1848.	—	Rare	—
A3	50 FRANCS			
	1848.	—	Rare	—
A4	100 FRANCS			
	1848.	—	Rare	—
A5	500 FRANCS			
	1848.	—	Rare	—
A6	1000 FRANCS			
	1848.	—	Rare	—

1851 ISSUE

A7	5 FRANCS			
	13.5.1851.	—	Rare	—
A8	10 FRANCS			
	13.5.1851.	—	Rare	—

GUADELOUPE TRÉSOR COLONIAL

BONS DE CAISSE

DÉCRET DU 25.5.1854

A12	1 FRANC			
	1.6.1854. Black on lt. green paper. Uniface.	—	Rare	—

DÉCRETS DES 23.4.1855 ET 3.3.1858

A12A	1 FRANC			
	6.11.1863. Red.		Rare	

DÉCRETS DES 23.4.1855, 3.3.1858 ET 2.6.1863
#A13-15 various date and sign. varieties. Sailing ship at lower l. Border of trees, barrels, arms etc. Uniface.

A13	1 FRANC			
	6.3.1863; 13.11.1863; 15.11.1863. Red.	—	Rare	—
A14	2 FRANCS			
	9.12.1864. Red.	—	Rare	—
A15	5 FRANCS			
	ND. (Not issued).	—	Rare	—

GUADELOUPE ET DEPENDANCES, TRÉSOR COLONIAL

DÉCRET DU 18.8.1884

1	50 CENTIMES	GOOD	FINE	XF
	D.1884. Brown.			
	a. Issued note.	—	—	—
	r. Unsigned remainder.	100.00	350.00	750.00
1A	1 FRANC			
	D.1884. Black on gray unpt. Format as #1.	—	—	—

2	1 FRANC	GOOD	FINE	XF
	D.1884. Different format.			
	a. Issued note.	—	—	—
	r. Unsigned remainder.	150.00	425.00	—
3	2 FRANCS			
	D.1884. Brown unpt. Uniface.			
	a. Issued note.	—	—	—
	r. Unsigned remainder.	175.00	500.00	—

3A	2 FRANCS	GOOD	FINE	XF
	D.1884. Black on purple paper. Uniface.	—	Rare	—

4	5 FRANCS	GOOD	FINE	XF
	D.1884. Blue on green unpt. Uniface. Format as #1.			
	a. Issued note.	—	—	—
	r. Unsigned remainder.	250.00	650.00	—
5	10 FRANCS			
	D.1884. Black on cream paper.	—	Rare	—

BANQUE DE LA GUADELOUPE

LAW OF 1901, FIRST ISSUE

7	5 FRANCS	GOOD	FINE	XF
	L.1901 (1928-45). Red. Man at l., woman at r. Law date on back.			
	a. Sign. title: Le Directeur C. Damoiseau. (1928).	30.00	70.00	175.00
	b. Sign. title: Le Directeur H. Marconnet. (1934, 1943).	15.00	40.00	130.00
	c. Sign. title: Le Directeur G. Devineau. (1944).	20.00	55.00	150.00
	d. Sign. title: Le Directeur A. Boudin. (1945).	10.00	30.00	120.00

8	25 FRANCS	GOOD	FINE	XF
	ND (1920-44). Red. Scales and cornucopias at ctr. of lower frame. 6 sign. varieties.	150.00	450.00	—

9	100 FRANCS	GOOD	FINE	XF
	ND (1920-21; 1925). Red and blue. Like #8. 2 sign. varieties.	225.00	725.00	—
10	500 FRANCS			
	ND (1887-1929). Red. Standing figures at l. and r. 5 sign. varieties.	—	Rare	—

LAW OF 1901, SECOND ISSUE

11	50 CENTIMES	GOOD	FINE	XF
	1920. Blue on purple unpt.	35.00	125.00	300.00

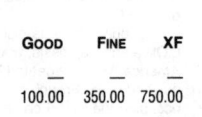

12	**1 FRANC**	**GOOD**	**FINE**	**XF**
	1920. Brown on aqua unpt.	45.00	135.00	325.00

13	**2 FRANCS**	**GOOD**	**FINE**	**XF**
	1920. Green on orange unpt.	65.00	200.00	450.00

14	**25 FRANCS**	**GOOD**	**FINE**	**XF**
	ND (1934; 1944). M/c. Woman w/wreath at ctr., flowers on top, fruit on bottom. 2 sign. varieties.	40.00	145.00	475.00

1920 (ND) PROVISIONAL ISSUE
Ovpt: *BANQUE DE LA GUADELOUPE* on unissued Banque de France notes (old dates of 1892-93).

15	**100 FRANCS**		**FINE**	
	ND (1920-old dates 1892-93). Violet, blue and brown. Woman seated at l. and r. Ovpt. on France #22b.	—	Rare	—

1934 ND ISSUE
#18 *Deleted.*
#19 *Deleted.* See #15.

16	**100 FRANCS**	**GOOD**	**FINE**	**XF**
	ND (1934; 1944). M/c. Woman w/staff at l., ship in background at lower ctr. r. 2 sign. varieties.	150.00	350.00	950.00

17	**500 FRANCS**	**GOOD**	**FINE**	**XF**
	ND (1934). M/c. Like #16.	250.00	650.00	—

EMERGENCY BANK CHECK ISSUES
#20A-20E early bank checks w/partially printed date and value.

20A	**50 CENTIMES**			
	ca. 1870-1900. Printed partial dates 187x, 189x, 190x. Blue-green.	—	Rare	—
20B	**50 CENTIMES**			
	ca. 1890-1900. Printed partial dates 189x, 190x. Orange-brown.	—	Rare	—

20C	**1 FRANC**	**GOOD**	**FINE**	**XF**
	ca. 1870-1900. Printed partial dates 187x, 190x. (1902 reported). Blue.	—	Rare	—
20D	**2 FRANCS**			
	189x. Red.	—	Rare	—
20E	**5 FRANCS**			
	187x. Red.	—	Rare	—

1940 EMERGENCY WWII BANK CHECK ISSUE

20F	**1000 FRANCS**	**GOOD**	**FINE**	**XF**
	24.6.1940; 27.1.1942. Purple. View of island w/2 sailing ships sideways at l. Printer: Fortin, Paris.	700.00	1800.	—

1942 ISSUE
#21-26A various sign. varieties. Printer E.A. Wright, Philadelphia, PA, U.S.A.

21	**5 FRANCS**	**VG**	**VF**	**UNC**
	ND (1942). Black on yellow unpt. Columbus at ctr. Back red-brown.			
	a. Sign. G. Devineau w/title: *LE DIRECTEUR.*	30.00	150.00	425.00
	b. Sign. A. Boudin w/title: *LE DIRECTEUR.*	27.50	135.00	375.00
	s. Specimen.	—	—	185.00

22 **25 FRANCS**
ND (1942). Black on green unpt. Map of Guadeloupe at l. Back blue; woman at ctr.

	VG	VF	UNC
a. Sign. G. Devineau w/title: *LE DIRECTEUR*.	40.00	165.00	450.00
b. Sign. A. Boudin w/title: *LE DIRECTEUR*.	36.00	150.00	400.00
s. Specimen.	—	—	235.00

23 **100 FRANCS**
ND (1942). Black on red-orange unpt. Oxcart at ctr. Back green; small sailing boat at ctr.

	VG	VF	UNC
a. Sign. G. Devineau w/title: *LE DIRECTEUR*.	125.00	375.00	950.00
b. Sign. A. Boudin w/title: *LE DIRECTEUR*.	110.00	335.00	850.00
s. Specimen.	—	—	475.00

24 **500 FRANCS**
ND (1942). Black on red unpt. Sailing ship "Santa Maria" at l. Flying boat on back. 161 x 115mm.

	VG	VF	UNC
a. Sign. H. Marconnet w/title: *LE DIRECTEUR*.	750.00	1750.	—
b. Sign. G. Devineau w/title: *LE DIRECTEUR*.	675.00	1500.	—
s. Specimen.	—	—	2000.

25 **500 FRANCS**
ND (1942). Face similar to #24. 150 x 85mm.

	VG	VF	UNC
a. Issued note.	850.00	2000.	—
s. Specimen.	—	—	1500.

26 **1000 FRANCS**
ND (1942). Black on blue unpt. Bust of Karukera at ctr. Back orange on lt. red unpt. 178 x 117mm.

	VG	VF	UNC
a. Sign. H. Marconnet w/title: *LE DIRECTEUR*.	750.00	1500.	2850.
b. Sign. G. Devineau w/title: *LE DIRECTEUR*.	675.00	1350.	2500.
s. Specimen.	—	—	1250.

26A **1000 FRANCS**
ND (1942). Similar to #26 but reduced size.

	VG	VF	UNC
a. Issued note.	1100.	2850.	—
s. Specimen.	—	—	1750.

CAISSE CENTRALE DE LA FRANCE D'OUTRE-MER

GUADELOUPE BRANCH

1944 ISSUE
#27-30 ovpt: *GUADELOUPE*. English printing.

27 **10 FRANCS**
2.2.1944. Violet. Marianne at ctr.

	VG	VF	UNC
a. Issued note.	15.00	40.00	145.00
s. Specimen.	—	—	225.00

28 **20 FRANCS**
2.2.1944. Green. Marianne at ctr.

	VG	VF	UNC
a. Issued note.	20.00	50.00	160.00
s. Specimen.	—	—	225.00

29 **100 FRANCS**
2.2.1944. Green. Marianne at ctr.

	VG	VF	UNC
a. Issued note.	50.00	175.00	575.00
s. Specimen.	—	—	450.00

30	**1000 FRANCS**	**VG**	**VF**	**UNC**
	2.2.1944. Blue. Phoenix rising from flames. War/peace scenes on back.			
a.	W/o wmk.	400.00	1200.	—
b.	Wmk: Marianne.	400.00	1200.	—
s.	As a. Specimen.	—	—	1200.

1947-52 ISSUE
#31-40 ovpt: *GUADELOUPE*. French printing w/standard designs.

31	**5 FRANCS**			
	ND (1947-49). M/c. Bougainville at r.	2.50	8.50	45.00

32	**10 FRANCS**	**VG**	**VF**	**UNC**
	ND (1947-49). M/c. Colbert at l., sailing ships at ctr. r.	2.50	10.00	55.00
33	**20 FRANCS**			
	ND (1947-49). M/c. E. Gentil at r., natives at l. ctr.	3.00	12.50	65.00
34	**50 FRANCS**			
	ND (1947-49). M/c. B. d'Esnambuc at l., sailing ship at r.	4.00	15.00	110.00

35	**100 FRANCS**	**VG**	**VF**	**UNC**
	ND (1947-49). M/c. La Bourdonnais at l., 2 women at r.	6.00	20.00	135.00

36	**500 FRANCS**	**VG**	**VF**	**UNC**
	ND (1947-49). M/c. 2 women at r., sailboat at l.	25.00	140.00	425.00

37	**1000 FRANCS**	**VG**	**VF**	**UNC**
	ND (1947-49). M/c. 2 women at r.			
a.	Issued note.	40.00	160.00	500.00
s.	Specimen.	—	—	350.00
38	**5000 FRANCS**			
	ND (1952). M/c. Gen. Schoelcher.			
a.	Issued note.	250.00	650.00	—
s.	Specimen.	—	—	325.00

1960 ISSUE

39	**1000 FRANCS**			
	ND (1960). M/c. Fishermen from the Antilles.			
a.	Issued note.	100.00	260.00	575.00
s.	Specimen.	—	—	325.00

40	**5000 FRANCS**	**VG**	**VF**	**UNC**
	ND (1960). M/c. Woman w/fruit bowl at ctr. r., palm trees at l.	150.00	600.00	—

1960 PROVISIONAL ISSUE
#41-44 ovpt: *GUADELOUPE* and new denomination.

41	**1 NOVEAUX FRANCS ON 100 FRANCS**			
	ND (1960). Ovpt. on #35.	10.00	55.00	195.00
42	**5 NOVEAUX FRANCS ON 500 FRANCS**			
	ND (1960). Ovpt. on #36.	30.00	150.00	475.00

43	**10 NOVEAUX FRANCS ON 1000 FRANCS**	**VG**	**VF**	**UNC**
	ND (1960). Ovpt. on #39.	100.00	280.00	675.00
44	**50 NOVEAUX FRANCS ON 5000 FRANCS**			
	ND (1960). Ovpt. on #40.	150.00	775.00	—

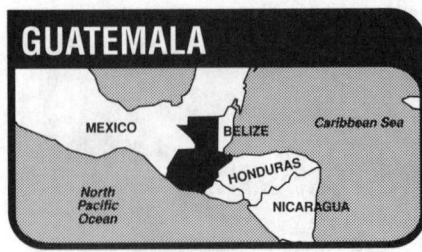

The Republic of Guatemala, the northernmost of the five Central American republics, has an area of 42,042 sq. mi. (108,889 sq. km.) and a population of 9.4 million. Capital: Guatemala City. The economy of Guatemala is heavily dependent on resources which are being developed. Coffee, cotton and bananas are exported. Guatemala, once the site of the ancient Mayan civilization, was conquered by Pedro de Alvarado, the lieutenant of Cortes who undertook the conquest from Mexico. Skilled in strategy and cruelty, he progressed rapidly along the Pacific coastal lowlands to the highland plain of Quezaltenango where the decisive battle for Guatemala was fought. After routing the Mayan forces, he established the first capital of Guatemala in 1524.

Guatemala of the colonial period included all of Central America but Panama. Guatemala declared its independence of Spain in 1821 and was absorbed into the short-lived Mexican empire of Augustin Iturbide, 1822-23. From 1823 to 1839 Guatemala was a constituent state of the Central American Republic. Upon dissolution of the federation, Guatemala became an independent republic.

* * * This section has been renumbered * * *

MONETARY SYSTEM:
   1 Peso = 100 Centavos to 1924
   1 Quetzal = 100 Centavos, 1924-

NOTE: Certain listings encompassing issues circulated by various bank and regional authorities are contained in Volume 1.

REPUBLIC

TESORERIA NACIONAL DE GUATEMALA
Issuer from 1881 until closed in 1885.

1881 ND PROVISIONAL ISSUE

		Good	Fine	XF
1	**1 PESO**			
(S201)	ND (ca.1881). Black on red unpt. Seated allegorical woman "Abundance" w/steam passenger train in background at lower l., male portr. at l. ctr., arms at r. ctr., Liberty w/staff at lower r. Back green. Printer: CCBB.			
	a. Ovpt. *PAGADERO EN LA ADMINISTRACION DE COBAN* and circular Treasury Seal on back.	—	—	—
	b. Ovpt.*PAGADERO EN LA ADMINISTRACION DE QUEZALT-ENANGO* and circular Treasury Seal on back.	—	—	—

1882 ND REGULAR ISSUE
#2-5 printer: ABNC.

		Good	Fine	XF
2	**1 PESO**			
(S202)	ND (ca.1882). Black on orange and olive unpt. Reclining woman w/book at l., arms at ctr., woman w/scales and cornucopia filled w/coins at lower r. Back green.			
	a. Black sign. W/o series, series A; B; C; E; Plate A.	10.00	35.00	125.00
	b. Red sign. Plate A.	15.00	40.00	130.00

		Good	Fine	XF
3	**5 PESOS**			
(S203)	ND (ca.1882). Black on orange and blue unpt. Steam locomotive at l., arms at r. Black sign. Back blue. Series A; B; E.	40.00	125.00	300.00

		Good	Fine	XF
4	**10 PESOS**			
(S204)	ND (ca.1882). Black on green and red unpt. 2 cherubs at lower l., young woman at upper ctr., arms at lower r. Back brown.			
	a. Red sign. Plate C.	75.00	175.00	450.00
	b. Black sign. Series B; C; D; Plate E.	75.00	175.00	450.00

		Good	Fine	XF
5	**25 PESOS**			
(S205)	ND (ca. 1882). Black on orange and yellow unpt. Arms at l., house in forest scene beneath, allegorical woman reclining holding wheat sheaves and sickle at ctr. r. Back orange.			
	a. Issued note.	—	Rare	—
	p. Proof.	—	—	—

BANCO CENTRAL DE GUATEMALA

LAW 7 DE JULIO DE 1926
#6-10 printer: TDLR.

		Good	Fine	XF
6	**1 QUETZAL**			
(70)	21.4.1927-31.10.1928. Green on orange unpt. Gen. J. María Orellana at l., workers loading bales w/steam crane in background. Monolith of Quirigua at ctr. on back.	7.50	30.00	100.00

		Good	Fine	XF
7	**2 QUETZALES**			
(73)	13.4.1928. Orange on lt. green and lilac unpt. Portr. Gen. J. María Orellana, palm trees at l., mountains at ctr. Back orange; seascape and mountains at ctr.			
	a. W/law date.	17.50	80.00	300.00
	b. W/*Acuerdo de* and issue date, w/o law date.	15.00	75.00	275.00
	c. W/o *Acurdo de.*	15.00	75.00	275.00

8 (76)	**5 QUETZALES**	**GOOD**	**FINE**	**XF**
	21.11.1927; 13.4.1928; 7.4.1934. Purple on lt. green and blue unpt. Workers by Gen. J. María Orellana at l. Town and mountains on back.	15.00	55.00	190.00

9 (82)	**20 QUETZALES**	**GOOD**	**FINE**	**XF**
	1927-45. Blue on yellow and green unpt. Portr. Gen. J. María Orellana at lower l., w/Mercury reclining at upper r. Palace of the Captains General on back.			
	a. W/o *Acuerdo de.* Sign. title *GERENTE* at r. 25.7.1927; 13.4.1928.	60.00	175.00	425.00
	b. *Acuerdo de.* Sign. title: *SUB-GERENTE* at r. 1.2.1945.	50.00	150.00	375.00

10 (84A)	**100 QUETZALES**	**GOOD**	**FINE**	**XF**
	L.1926. Dk. green on orange and yellow unpt. Portr. Gen. J. María Orellana at l. Printer: TDLR. Specimen.	—	—	—

1928 ISSUE

#11 and 12 printer: W&S.

11 (71)	**1 QUETZAL**	**GOOD**	**FINE**	**XF**
	13.4.1928; 31.10.1928; 17.3.1934. Green. Like #6.			
	a. Issued note.	6.00	25.00	90.00
	s. Speciman.	—	Unc	100.00

12 (80)	**10 QUETZALES**	**GOOD**	**FINE**	**XF**
	24.12.1929; 11.5.1931; 21.4.1934; 21.5.1935. Red on yellow and green unpt. Portr. Gen. J. María Orellana at l. Back red; ornate bridge.			
	a. Issued note.	27.50	85.00	375.00
	s. Specimen.	—	Unc	400.00

1933-36 ISSUE

#13-18 printer: W&S.

13 (69)	**1/2 QUETZAL**	**GOOD**	**FINE**	**XF**
	1933-42. Brown on blue unpt. Banana plantation at r. Lake and mountain on back.			
	a. Sign. title: *GERENTE* at r. 26.1.1933; 2.12.1938; 19.2.1941; 21.10.1942.	1.25	6.00	25.00
	b. Sign. title: *SUB-GERENTE* at r. 21.10.1942.	1.50	8.00	30.00

14 (72)	**1 QUETZAL**	**GOOD**	**FINE**	**XF**
	1934-45. Deep green on lilac and ochre unpt. Farm bldgs. and truck at l. ctr. Back like #6.			
	a. Sign. title: *GERENTE* at r. 17.3.1934-19.9.1942.	2.00	9.00	35.00
	b. Sign. title: *SUB-GERENTE* at r. 19.9.1942; 31.10.1945.	2.00	8.00	30.00

15 (75)	**2 QUETZALES**	**GOOD**	**FINE**	**XF**
	1936-42. Orange on green and violet unpt. Mountains and lake at l. Back like #7.			
	a. Sign. title: *GERENTE* at r. 25.1.1936; 4.2.1942.	7.50	25.00	125.00
	b. Sign. title: *SUB-GERENTE* at r. 4.2.1942.	8.00	35.00	135.00

16 (78)	**5 QUETZALES**	**GOOD**	**FINE**	**XF**
	1934-45. Purple on orange and green unpt. Ship at dockside at l. Quetzal on back.			
	a. Sign. title: *GERENTE* at r. 7.4.1934-8.1.1943.	10.00	30.00	150.00
	b. Sign. title: *SUB-GERENTE* at r. 29.1.1945.	12.50	35.00	175.00

17 (81)	**10 QUETZALES**	**GOOD**	**FINE**	**XF**
	1935-45. Dk. red on green unpt. Mountains and lake at l. Back like #12.			
	a. Sign. title: *GERENTE* at r. 21.5.1935-12.6.1943.	15.00	35.00	120.00
	b. Sign. title: *SUB-GERENTE* at r. 1.2.1945; 22.5.1945.	22.50	50.00	155.00

18 (84)	**20 QUETZALES**	**GOOD**	**FINE**	**XF**
	1936-44. Blue on green and m/c unpt. Dock workers at l. Back like #9. Sign. title: *GERENTE* at r.			
	a. 2.5.1936.	40.00	120.00	250.00
	b. 14.1.1937/2.5.1936.	65.00	200.00	—
	c. 4.2.1942; 3.9.1943; 3.2.1944; 9.8.1944.	40.00	120.00	250.00

1936 ISSUE

		GOOD	FINE	XF
18A (74)	**2 QUETZALES** 25.1.1936. Orange on lt. green and lilac unpt. Mountains and lake at l. Printer: TDLR.			
	a. Issued note.	20.00	125.00	400.00
	s. Specimen.	—	Unc	350.00

BANCO DE GUATEMALA

1946 PROVISIONAL ISSUE

#19-22 ovpt: *BANCO DE GUATEMALA* on Banco Central de Guatemala notes. Sign. title ovpt: *PRESIDENTE TRIBUNAL DE CUENTAS* at l., *PRESIDENTE DEL BANCO* at r.

		VG	VF	UNC
19 (85)	**1/2 QUETZAL** 1946; 1948. Ovpt. on #13.			
	a. 12.8.1946.	2.00	6.00	27.50
	b. 10.3.1948.	15.00	50.00	125.00

		VG	VF	UNC
20 (86)	**1 QUETZAL** 12.8.1946. Ovpt. on #14.	4.50	12.50	45.00

		VG	VF	UNC
21 (88)	**5 QUETZALES** 12.8.1946. Ovpt. on #8.	17.50	65.00	175.00

		VG	VF	UNC
22 (90)	**20 QUETZALES** 12.8.1946; 28.3.1947. Ovpt. on #18.	40.00	175.00	375.00

1948 ISSUE

#23-28 sign. title: *PRESIDENTE DEL...* at r. Sign. varieties. Printer: ABNC.

		VG	VF	UNC
23 (91)	**1/2 QUETZAL** 15.9.1948-5.1.1954. Brown. Hermitage of Cerro del Carmen at l. 2 Guatemalans on back.	1.00	6.00	40.00

		VG	VF	UNC
24 (92)	**1 QUETZAL** 1948-55. Green. Palace of the Captains General at l. Lake Atitlan on back.			
	a. W/o *Acuerdo de.* 15.9.1948-5.1.1954.	1.50	7.50	45.00
	b. W/*Autorizacion de.* 5.1.1955.	2.00	10.00	60.00
25 (93)	**5 QUETZALES** 15.9.1948-5.1.1954. Purple. Vase (Vasija de Uaxactun) at l. Mayan-Spanish conflict on back.	17.50	50.00	130.00
26 (94)	**10 QUETZALES** 1948-55. Red. Round stone carving (Ara de Tikal) at l. Founding of old Guatemala on back.			
	a. Date alone at r. 15.9.1948-5.1.1954.	25.00	60.00	175.00
	b. W/*Autorizacion de.* 5.1.1955.	25.00	60.00	175.00
27 (95)	**20 QUETZALES** 15.9.1948; 18.2.1949; 3.5.1950; 5.1.1954. Blue. R. Landivar at l. Meeting of Independence on back.	30.00	100.00	265.00
28 (96)	**100 QUETZALES** 15.9.1948; 3.8.1949; 21.5.1952. Black on m/c unpt. Indio de Nahuala at l. Valley and mountain on back.			
	a. 15.9.1948.	65.00	175.00	400.00
	b. 3.8.1949.	100.00	200.00	500.00

1955-56 ISSUE

#30-34 sign. varieties. Printer: W&S.

		VG	VF	UNC
29 (97)	**1/2 QUETZAL** 5.1.1955; 22.2.1956; 16.1.1957. Brown. Similar to #23 but bldg. at r.	1.00	8.00	40.00

		VG	VF	UNC
30 (98)	**1 QUETZAL** 5.1.1955; 22.2.1956; 16.1.1957. Green. Similar to #24 but bldg. at ctr. r.	1.00	8.00	40.00

		VG	VF	UNC
31 (99)	**5 QUETZALES** 5.1.1955; 22.2.1956; 16.1.1957. Purple. Similar to #25 but vase at r.	5.00	30.00	80.00
32 (100)	**10 QUETZALES** 22.2.1956; 16.1.1957; 22.1.1958. Red. Similar to #26 but round stone at r.	12.00	50.00	180.00
33 (101)	**20 QUETZALES** 5.1.1955-18.2.1959. Blue. Similar to #27 but R. Landivar at ctr.	25.00	100.00	265.00
34 (102)	**100 QUETZALES** 5.1.1955; 16.1.1957; 22.1.1958. Dk. blue. Similar to #28 but Indio de Nahuala at ctr.	100.00	250.00	525.00

1957-58 ISSUE

#35-50 sign. title: *JEFE DE...* at r.
#35-39 printer: ABNC.

			VG	VF	UNC
35 (91A)	1/2 QUETZAL	22.1.1958. Brown. Hermitage of Cerro del Carmen at l. 2 Guatemalans on back.	2.00	7.50	40.00
36 (92A)	1 QUETZAL	16.1.1957; 22.1.1958. Green. Palace of the Captains General at l. Lake Atitlan on back.	2.00	6.00	32.50

			VG	VF	UNC
37 (93A)	5 QUETZALES	22.1.1958. Purple vase (Vasija de Uaxactum)at l. Mayan-Spanish battle scene on back.	8.00	30.00	100.00
38 (94A)	10 QUETZALES	22.1.1958; 12.1.1962; 9.1.1963; 8.1.1964. Like #26.	10.00	50.00	145.00
39 (95A)	20 QUETZALES	1958(?); 9.1.1963; 8.1.1964; 15.1.1965. Like #27.	20.00	75.00	235.00

1959-60 ISSUES

#A97A-102A sign. varieties. Printer: W&S.

			VG	VF	UNC
40 (A97A)	1/2 QUETZAL	18.2.1959. Like #29. Lighter brown shadings around value guilloche at l. Printed area 2mm smaller than #41. 6-digit serial #.	2.00	7.00	40.00
41 (97A)	1/2 QUETZAL	18.2.1959; 13.1.1960; 18.1.1961. Similar to #40 but darker brown shadings around value guilloche at l. 7-digit serial #.	.75	2.50	20.00
42 (A98A)	1 QUETZAL	18.2.1959. Green palace. Like #30. Dull green back. 6-digit serial #.	2.00	6.00	45.00
43 (98A)	1 QUETZAL	18.2.1959-8.1.1964. Black and green. Like #42, but black palace. Back bright green. 7-digit serial #.	1.00	3.50	20.00
44 (99A)	5 QUETZALES	18.2.1959. Like #31. Vase in purple.	8.00	25.00	90.00
45 (99B)	5 QUETZALES	18.2.1959-8.1.1964. Similar to #44 but redesigned guilloche. Vase in brown.	5.00	20.00	80.00
46 (100A)	10 QUETZALES	18.2.1959. Like #32. Stone in red.	15.00	40.00	135.00

			VG	VF	UNC
47 (100B)	10 QUETZALES	18.2.1959; 13.1.1960; 18.1.1961. Similar to #46 but redesigned guilloche. Stone in brown.	12.50	30.00	110.00
48 (101A)	20 QUETZALES	13.1.1960-15.1.1965. Blue. Similar to #33, but portr. R. Landivar at r.	20.00	65.00	180.00
49 (101B)	100 QUETZALES	18.2.1959. Dk. blue. Like #34, w/Indio de Nahuala in blue at ctr.	115.00	250.00	500.00
50 (102A)	100 QUETZALES	13.1.1960-15.1.1965. Dk. blue. Indio de Nahuala in brown at r.	115.00	250.00	450.00

GUERNSEY

The Bailiwick of Guernsey, a British crown dependency located in the English Channel 30 miles (48 km.) west of Normandy, France, has an area of 30 sq. mi. (78 sq. km.), including the Isles of Alderney, Jethou, Herm, Brechou and Sark, and a population of 53,794. Capital: St. Peter Port. Agriculture and cattle breeding are the main occupations.

Militant monks from the Duchy of Normandy established the first permanent settlements on Guernsey prior to the Norman invasion of England, but the prevalence of prehistoric monuments suggests an earlier occupancy. The island, the only part of the Duchy of Normandy belonging to the British crown, has been a possession of Britain since the Norman Conquest of 1066. During the Anglo-French Wars, the harbors of Guernsey were employed in the building and outfitting of ships for the English privateers preying on French shipping. Guernsey is administered by its own laws and customs. Acts passed by the British Parliament are not applicable to Guernsey unless the island is specifically mentioned. During World War II, German troops occupied the island from June 30, 1940 to June 6, 1944.

RULERS:

British to 1940, 1944-
German Occupation, June 1940-June 1944

MONETARY SYSTEM:

1 Penny = 8 Doubles
1 Shilling = 12 Pence
5 Shillings = 6 Francs
1 Pound = 20 Shillings to 1971
1 Pound = 100 New Pence 1971-

BRITISH INFLUENCE

STATES OF GUERNSEY

1825; 1857 GOVERNMENT NOTES

A1	1 POUND	1827-36. Britannia standing w/shield and lion at upper l., allegorical woman standing at upper r. Lg. *ONE* in guilloche at lower l.			
		a. 21.11.1827; 15.4.1828.	—	Rare	—
		b. 10.7.1829; 1.12.1829; 1.10.1836.	—	Rare	—

A2	1 POUND	28.3.1857-22.5.1894. Similar to #A1, but lg. *One Pound* in guilloche at lower l.	—	Rare	—

1895; 1903 GOVERNMENT NOTES

1	**1 POUND**			
	15.7.1895. Sailing ships anchored along coastline across upper ctr. (St. Sampson's Harbor). Back green; arms medallion at ctr. in ornate pattern. Printer: PBC.	—	Rare	—
1A	**1 POUND**			
	23.3.1903.	—	Rare	—
2	**5 POUNDS**			
			Reported Not Confirmed	

1914 EMERGENCY WWI ISSUE
#3 and 4 denominated in British sterling and French francs. Arms at ctr. in unpt.

3	**5 SHILLINGS = 6 FRANCS**			
	5.8.1914. Printer: The Star, Guernsey.	—	Rare	—
4	**10 SHILLINGS = 12 FRANCS**			
	7.8.1914. Printer: The Evening Press, Guernsey.	—	Rare	—

1914 ISSUE
#5 and 6 denomiated in British sterling and French francs. Arms medallion at ctr. In guilloche on back. Printer: PBC.

5	**5 SHILLINGS = 6 FRANCS**			
	1.9.1914. Black on red unpt. Back red.	—	Rare	—
6	**10 SHILLINGS = 12 FRANCS**			
	1.9.1914; 19.7.1919. Similar to #5.	—	Rare	—
7	**1 POUND**			
	3.4.1914; 1.9.1916; 1.8.1919. Like #1.	—	Rare	—

1921 PROVISIONAL ISSUE
#8-9A ovpt: *BRITISH*.

8	**5 SHILLINGS = 6 FRANCS**			
	ND (Apr. 1921-old date 1.9.1914). Red ovpt: *BRITISH* on #5.	—	Rare	—
9	**10 SHILLINGS = 12 FRANCS**			
	ND (Apr. 1921-old date 1.9.1914). Red ovpt: *BRITISH* on #6.	—	Rare	—

9A	**1 POUND**			
	ND (Apr. 1921-old date 1.8.1919). Red ovpt: *BRITISH* on #7.	—	Rare	—

1921-24 ISSUE
#10 and 11 St. Sampson's Harbor scene across upper ctr.

		GOOD	FINE	XF
10	**10 SHILLINGS**			
	17.5.1924. Black and gray. w/o denomination in numerals at ctr.	150.00	450.00	1000.
11	**1 POUND**			
	1.3.1921; 9.2.1924; 17.5.1924. Black and gray on orange unpt. W/o denomination in numerals at ctr. Like #10.	—	Rare	—

1927 ISSUE

		GOOD	FINE	XF
12	**1 POUND**			
	6.12.1927; 12.4.1928. Black and gray on red unpt. Like #10. Denomination *1* in unpt. at ctr.	150.00	450.00	1000.

1933 ISSUE
NOTE: Other dates for #10-13 may exist and need confirmation. *All* dates for #14 need confirmation.

		GOOD	FINE	XF
13	**10 SHILLINGS**			
	18.11.1933. Lt. blue and brown. Like #10. Denomination *10* unpt. at ctr., only 1 sign. English wording on back.	100.00	400.00	900.00
14	**1 POUND**			
	3.1.1933-18.11.1933. Gray on red unpt. Like #12 but w/o *ENTD* at lower l., only 1 sign. English wording on back.	100.00	400.00	950.00

1934 ISSUE

		GOOD	FINE	XF
15	**10 SHILLINGS**			
	29.3.1934; 5.6.1937; 1.7.1939; 9.3.1940. Lt. blue and orange Like #13. Back red; *S'BALLIVIE INSULE DEGERNEREYE* (Seal of the Island of Guernsey).	100.00	400.00	950.00

		GOOD	FINE	XF
16	**1 POUND**			
	1934-40. Gray. Like #14. Back blue. *S'BALLIVIE INSULE DEGERNEREYE* (Seal of the Island of Guernsey).			
	a. 29.3.1934-1.7.1939.	185.00	500.00	1100.
	b. 9.3.1940.	75.00	250.00	550.00

GERMAN OCCUPATION - WW II

GOVERNMENT OF GUERNSEY

1941 FIRST ISSUE

		GOOD	FINE	XF
18	**2 SHILLINGS 6 PENCE**			
	25.3.1941. Blue on orange unpt unpt. Back dk. blue.	45.00	90.00	200.00

		GOOD	FINE	XF
19	**5 SHILLINGS**			
	25.3.1941. Black on red unpt. Back red.	50.00	120.00	300.00

1941 SECOND ISSUE

		GOOD	FINE	XF
20	**2 SHILLINGS 6 PENCE** Like #18.			
	17.5.1941.	50.00	110.00	250.00
21	**5 SHILLINGS**			
	17.5.1941. Like #19.	60.00	150.00	400.00

1941 THIRD ISSUE

		GOOD	FINE	XF
22	**6 PENCE**			
	16.10.1941. Black on lt. blue and orange unpt. Back purple.	35.00	75.00	175.00

		GOOD	FINE	XF
23	**1 SHILLING 3 PENCE**			
	16.10.1941. Black on yellow and brown unpt. Back brown.	55.00	160.00	350.00

1942 FIRST ISSUE

		GOOD	FINE	XF
24	**6 PENCE**			
	1.1.1942. Like #22. Blue paper.	50.00	130.00	300.00
25	**1 SHILLING ON 1/3D**			
	1.1.1942. Orange ovpt. of new denomination. Blue paper.	20.00	80.00	165.00

		GOOD	FINE	XF
25A	**2 SHILLINGS 6 PENCE**			
	1.1.1942. Like #18. Blue paper.	20.00	80.00	165.00
25B	**5 SHILLINGS**			
	1.1.1942.	25.00	95.00	200.00

1942 SECOND ISSUE

		GOOD	FINE	XF
27	**1 SHILLING ON 1/3D**			
	18.7.1942. Orange ovpt. on #26.	30.00	100.00	250.00
26	**1 SHILLING 3 PENCE**			
	18.7.1942. Black on yellow unpt. Blue paper. Back gray.	20.00	85.00	200.00

1943 ISSUE

		GOOD	FINE	XF
28 (27A)	**6 PENCE**			
	1.1.1943. Like #22. White paper.	30.00	95.00	200.00
29	**1 SHILLING ON 1/3D**			
	1.1.1943. Orange ovpt. on #26.	35.00	110.00	250.00
30	**2 SHILLINGS 6 PENCE**			
	1.1.1943. Blue.	30.00	100.00	250.00

		GOOD	FINE	XF
31	**5 SHILLINGS**			
	1.1.1943. Black on red denomination. Back red.	35.00	160.00	400.00

		GOOD	FINE	XF
32	**10 SHILLINGS**			
	1.1.1943. Blue on red denomination. Back red.	85.00	250.00	600.00

		GOOD	FINE	XF
33	**1 POUND**			
	1.1.1943. Black on red unpt. Sailing ships and coastline across upper ctr. (St. Sampson's Harbor). Back blue.	80.00	200.00	600.00

BRITISH INFLUENCE - POST WW II

STATES OF GUERNSEY

1945 FIRST ISSUE

NOTE: #33B was withdrawn shortly after its release.

		GOOD	FINE	XF
33A	**1 POUND**			
	1.1.1945. Like #33. Blue paper.	80.00	200.00	600.00
33B	**5 POUNDS**			
	1.1.1945. Green on green paper. Arms at upper l.	—	Rare	—

1945 SECOND ISSUE

#34-37 w/text...backed by Guernsey Notes. Printed on blue French paper.

		GOOD	FINE	XF
34	**5 SHILLINGS**			
	1.1.1945.	—	Rare	—

			GOOD	FINE	XF
35	**10 SHILLINGS** 1.1.1945.		—	Rare	—
36	**1 POUND** 1.1.1945. Like #33.		—	Rare	—
37	**5 POUNDS** 1.1.1945.		—	Rare	—

1945 THIRD ISSUE

#38-41 w/text...*backed by British Notes.*

38	**5 SHILLINGS** 1.1.1945.		—	Rare	—
39	**10 SHILLINGS** 1.1.1945.		—	Rare	—
40	**1 POUND** 1.1.1945.		—	Rare	—
41	**5 POUNDS** 1.1.1945.		—	Rare	—

1945; 1956 ISSUE

			VG	VF	UNC
42	**10 SHILLINGS** 1945-66. Lilac on lt. green un pt. Back purple.				
	a. 1.8.1945-1.9.1957.		18.00	65.00	250.00
	b. 1.7.1958-1.3.1965.		5.00	45.00	90.00
	c. 1.7.1966.		8.00	20.00	60.00

			VG	VF	UNC
43	**1 POUND** 1945-66. Purple on green unpt. Harbor entrance across ctr. Back: green.				
	a. 1.8.1945-1.3.1957.		7.50	50.00	180.00
	b. 1.9.1957-1.3.1962; 1.6.1963; 1 ; 1.3.1965.		5.00	20.00	65.00
	c. 1.7.1966.		3.50	15.00	65.00

			VG	VF	UNC
44	**5 POUNDS** 1.12.1956; 1.3.1965; 1.7.1966. Green and blue. Flowers at l.		60.00	200.00	500.00

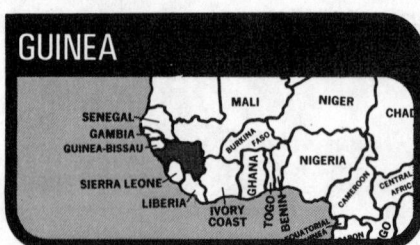

GUINEA

The Republic of Guinea (formerly French Guinea), situated on the Atlantic coast of Africa between Sierra Leone and Guinea-Bissau, has an area of 94,964 sq. mi. (245,957 sq. km.) and a population of 6.1 million. Capital: Conakry. Although Guinea contains one-third of the world's reserves of bauxite and significant deposits of iron ore, gold and diamonds, the economy is still dependent on agriculture. Aluminum, bananas, copra and coffee are exported.

The coast of Guinea was known to Portuguese navigators of the 15th century but was seldom visited by European traders of the 16th-18th centuries because of its dangerous coastal waters. French penetration of the area began in the mid-19th century with the entering into of protectorate treaties with several of the coastal chiefs. After a long struggle with Guinea's native leader Samory Toure, France secured the area and until 1890 administered it as a part of Senegal. In 1895 the colony (Guinee Francaise) became an autonomous part of the federation of French West Africa. The inhabitants were extended French citizenship in 1946 when the colony became an overseas territory of the French Union. Guinea became an independent republic on Oct. 2, 1958, when it declined to enter the new French Community.

RULERS:
French to 1958

MONETARY SYSTEM:
1 Franc = 100 Centimes to 1971
1 Syli = 10 Francs, 1971-1980
Franc System 1985-

FRENCH INFLUENCE

GOUVERNEMENT GÉNÉRAL DE L'AFRIQUE

OCCIDENTALE FRANÇAISE

COLONIE DE LA GUINÉE FRANÇAISE

DÉCRET DU 11.2.1917

#1   #2

			VG	VF	UNC
1	**0.50 FRANC** *D.1917.* Dk. brown on lt. brown unpt. Reverse and obverse of 50 Centimes coin on face. Back black text.				
	a. Wmk: Bees. Imprint on back 23mm long.		30.00	85.00	225.00
	b. Wmk: Bees. Imprint on back 26mm long.		37.50	100.00	260.00
	c. Wmk: Laurel leaves.		37.50	110.00	275.00
	d. W/o wmk.		30.00	85.00	225.00
2	**1 FRANC** *D.1917.* Blue on green unpt. Reverse and obverse of 1 Franc coin on face.				
	a. Wmk: Bees.		40.00	125.00	275.00
	b. Wmk: Laurel leaves.		45.00	135.00	325.00
	c. W/o wmk.		32.50	110.00	265.00

1920 EMERGENCY POSTAGE STAMP ISSUE

#3-5 adhesive postage stamps (Michel #66, 67 and 70; or Scott #54, 56 and 61) affixed to colored cardboard w/ovpt: *VALEUR D'ECHANGE* in two lines on face. Value in ornate frame at ctr. on back.

			VG	VF	UNC
3	**5 CENTIMES** ND (1920). Green. Orange cardboard.		75.00	175.00	300.00
4	**10 CENTIMES** ND (1920). Rose. Green cardboard.		75.00	175.00	300.00
5	**25 CENTIMES** ND (1920). Blue. Red cardboard.		85.00	200.00	325.00

REPUBLIC

BANQUE DE LA RÉPUBLIQUE DE GUINÉE

1958 ISSUE

#6-11 Pres. Sekou Toure at l.

10	5000 FRANCS	VG	VF	UNC
	2.10.1958. Green. Banana harvesting on back.	85.00	350.00	—

6	50 FRANCS	VG	VF	UNC
	2.10.1958. Brown. Mask at ctr. on back.	10.00	50.00	225.00

7	100 FRANCS,	VG	VF	UNC
	2.10.1958. Lilac. Woman and child w/village on back.	20.00	50.00	250.00
8	500 FRANCS			
	2.10.1958. Red-orange. Pineapple field on back.	40.00	150.00	500.00

11	10,000 FRANCS	VG	VF	UNC
	2.10.1958. Dk. brown. Mining on back.	125.00	475.00	—

BANQUE CENTRALE DE LA RÉPUBLIQUE DE GUINÉE

1960 ISSUE

9	1000 FRANCS	VG	VF	UNC
	2.10.1958. Blue. Small boats at shore, man at ctr. r. on back.	25.00	110.00	450.00

12	50 FRANCS	VG	VF	UNC
	1.3.1960. Brown and m/c. Heavy machinery on back.	1.00	3.00	12.50

13	100 FRANCS	VG	VF	UNC
	1.3.1960. Brown-violet and m/c. Pineapple harvesting on back.	1.00	3.00	15.00
14	500 FRANCS			
	1.3.1960. Blue and m/c. Men pulling long boats ashore on back.	3.00	10.00	65.00

			VG	VF	UNC
15	**1000 FRANCS** 1.3.1960. Green and m/c. Banana harvesting on back.		2.50	8.00	40.00

HAITI

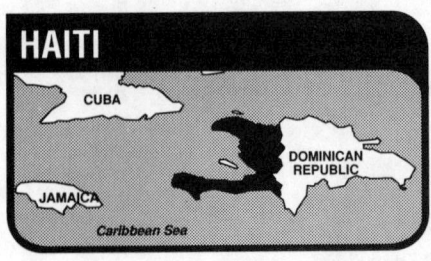

The Republic of Haiti, which occupies the western one third of the island of Hispañola in the Caribbean Sea between Puerto Rico and Cuba, has an area of 10,714 sq. mi. (27,750 sq. km.) and a population of 6.2 million. Capital: Port-au-Prince. The economy is based on agriculture, light manufacturing and tourism which is becoming increasingly important. Coffee, bauxite, sugar, essential oils and handicrafts are exported.

Columbus discovered Hispañola in 1492. Spain colonized the island, making Santo Domingo the base for exploration of the Western Hemisphere. Later French buccaneers settled the western third of Hispañola which was ceded to France by Spain in 1697. Slaves brought over from Africa to work the coffee and sugar cane plantations made it one of the richest colonies of the French Empire. The Republic of Haiti was established in 1804 by the slave revolt of the 1790's, making it the oldest black republic in the world and the second oldest republic (after the United States) in the Western Hemisphere.

MONETARY SYSTEM:
- 1 Gourde = 100 Centimes
- 1 Piastre = 300 Gourdes, 1873
- 5 Gourdes = 1 U.S. Dollar, 1919-89

FRENCH INFLUENCE

DEPARTMENT OF PORT-DU-PAIX

1790's ND ISSUE

A1	**4 ESCALINS** ND. Arms at ctr. Uniface.	—	Rare	—

REPUBLIC (FIRST)

RÉPUBLIQUE D'HAITI

LOI DU 16 AVRIL 1827 - FIRST ISSUE

#1-10 lg. format w/arms at upper ctr.

			GOOD	FINE	XF
1	**1 GOURDE** L.1827. Black or gray on large, thin white or off-white paper. Very wide margins (often trimmed). Print frame ca. 204 x 112mm.		25.00	60.00	150.00
2	**2 GOURDES** L.1827.				
	a. Thin paper w/o wmk.		15.00	35.00	100.00
	b. Thick paper w/o wmk.		15.00	35.00	100.00
	c. Thin yellow paper. Wmk: *REPUBLIQUE D'HAITI*.		15.00	35.00	100.00

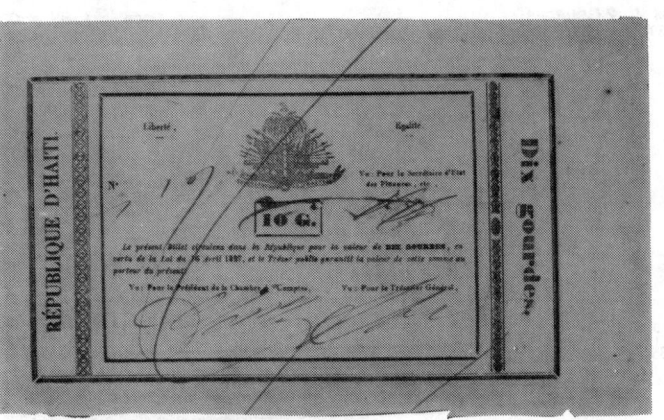

	10 GOURDES	GOOD	FINE	XF
4	*L.1827*. Value *10 G.* in ctr. frame. W/o wmk.			
	a. Thin paper.	10.00	25.00	95.00
	b. Thick paper.	10.00	25.00	95.00

	10 GOURDES	GOOD	FINE	XF
5	*L.1827*. Value *$10* in ctr. frame.			
	a. Thin paper. Wmk: *REPUBLIQUE D'HAITI*.	15.00	35.00	100.00
	b. Thick paper w/o wmk.	15.00	35.00	100.00

	10 GOURDES	GOOD	FINE	XF
6	*L.1827*. Thin yellow paper. Large lozenge around ctr. Wmk. in 2 lines.	20.00	50.00	125.00
7	**25 GOURDES**			
	L.1827. Thin white paper. Numeral *2* has straight bottom.	15.00	40.00	110.00

	25 GOURDES	GOOD	FINE	XF
8	*L.1827*. Thick brown paper. Numeral *2* has curved bottom.	15.00	40.00	110.00

	100 GOURDES	GOOD	FINE	XF
10	*L.1827*. Heavy paper. Similar to #6. Wmk: Lg. oval.	25.00	75.00	225.00

EMPIRE D'HAITI

TREASURY

LOI DU 16 AVRIL 1851

	2 GOURDES	GOOD	FINE	XF
15	*L.1851*. Black. Arms at upper ctr. Very wide margins (often trimmed). Frame 200 x 112mm.			
	a. Yellow paper. Lg. 2-line wmk: *EMPIRE D'HAYTI* (sometimes w/crown in wmk.)	25.00	60.00	150.00
	b. Wmk: *REPUBLIQUE D'HAYTI*.	25.00	60.00	150.00
	c. Pale blue-green paper w/o wmk.	30.00	75.00	175.00

RÉPUBLIQUE D'HAITI

TREASURY (1827)

LOI DU 16 AVRIL 1827 - SECOND ISSUE

#18-21 'Simple format' style. Arms at upper ctr.

	2 GOURDES	GOOD	FINE	XF
18	*L.1827*. Thin white paper w/o wmk. Frame about 134 x 75mm.	25.00	60.00	150.00
20	**10 GOURDES**			
	L.1827. W/ or w/o printed *Serie A* and *No.1*.	25.00	60.00	150.00

21	20 GOURDES	GOOD	FINE	XF
	L.1827. Like #20.	25.00	60.00	150.00

LOI DU 16 AVRIL 1827 - THIRD ISSUE
#25 'Long format' style.

25	20 GOURDES	GOOD	FINE	XF
	L.1827. Arms at upper ctr. Printed Serie A and No 1. Frame about 174 x 74mm.	30.00	75.00	175.00

LOI DU 16 AVRIL 1827 - FOURTH ISSUE
#28-30 'Diamond frame format' style. w/o Arms.

27	4 GOURDES			
	L.1827. Value *400* in box at upper ctr. W/o arms. *Le Membre Signataire* in italics.	40.00	85.00	—

28	8 GOURDES	GOOD	FINE	XF
	L.1827. Frame about 120 x 84mm.			
	a. *HUIT GOURDES* at l. reads bottom to top.	25.00	60.00	150.00
	b. *HUIT GOURDES* at l. reads top to bottom.	25.00	60.00	150.00
30	16 GOURDES			
	L.1827.			
	a. "Le Membre Signataire" in standard type.	25.00	60.00	150.00
	b. *Le Membre Signataire* in italics.	25.00	60.00	150.00

LOI DU 16 AVRIL 1827 - FIFTH ISSUES
#33-36 ornate format w/oval arms at top ctr. Printer: CS&E.

33	2 GOURDES	GOOD	FINE	XF
	L.1827. Black on yellow paper w/wmk. Frame ca.94 x 61mm. Series A-D.	4.00	15.00	50.00

34	2 GOURDES	GOOD	FINE	XF
	L.1827. Black on white paper. Similar to #33. Series A-D.	10.00	30.00	75.00

35	2 GOURDES	GOOD	FINE	XF
(39)	*L.1827.* Black on white paper w/wmk. Series D11-K12. Printer: W&S.	7.50	17.50	45.00

36	10 GOURDES	GOOD	FINE	XF
(35)	*L.1827.* Black on blue paper w/wmk. Printed back. Series A-F.	8.00	20.00	50.00

37	25 GOURDES	GOOD	FINE	XF
(36)	*L.1827.* Black on green paper w/wmk. Series G.	10.00	25.00	65.00

LOI DU 16 AVRIL 1827 - SIXTH ISSUE
#41 and 42 'Fancy format' style. Pres. Fabre-Nicolas Geffrard (1859-67). Printer: W&S.

41	1 GOURDE	GOOD	FINE	XF
	L.1827. Black on pink or rose paper w/fancy wmk. (rarely w/o). Portr. Pres. Geffrard at upper l. Frame about 94 x 62mm. Wide margins (sometimes trimmed).	5.00	20.00	50.00

42	2 GOURDES	GOOD	FINE	XF
	L.1827. Black on white paper w/wmk. Portr. Pres. Geffrard at upper l and r. Series A1-U10.	5.00	20.00	50.00

GOUVERNEMENT DU SUD D'HAITI
GOVERNMENT OF SOUTH HAITI

EN DATE DU 13 OCTOBRE 1868
#51-58 black print. Arms at upper ctr.

51	2 GOURDES			
	L.1868. Series A-D.	35.00	95.00	225.00
52	4 GOURDES			
	L.1868. Series A; C; F; L; N; O; P.			
	a. White or off-white paper.	35.00	95.00	225.00
	b. Blue paper.	35.00	95.00	225.00

	54	**12 GOURDES**	**GOOD**	**FINE**	**XF**
		L.1868. Paper color varieties: orange, yellow, blue, pink, green, violet etc. W/o Series, or Series E-V.	40.00	100.00	275.00
	55	**24 GOURDES**			
		L.1868. Series B.	50.00	110.00	—

	56	**25 GOURDES**	**GOOD**	**FINE**	**XF**
		L.1868. Series D.	50.00	110.00	—

	57	**48 GOURDES**	**GOOD**	**FINE**	**XF**
		L.1868. W/o Series.	—	60.00	150.00
	58	**100 GOURDES**			
		L.1868. Frame ca.196 x 72mm.	65.00	175.00	—

LOI DU 28 OCTOBRE 1869

	60	**10 PIASTRES FORTES**			
		L.1869. Thin white paper. Frame 170 x 75mm.	125.00	275.00	—

LOI DU 22 JUILLET 1871

	64	**10 GOURDES**	**GOOD**	**FINE**	**XF**
		L.1871. Green or blue-green paper. Series E-X4.	15.00	60.00	150.00
	65	**20 GOURDES**			
		L.1871. White or off-white paper. Series A-Q5.	15.00	60.00	150.00

LA BANQUE NATIONALE D'HAITI

SEPTRE. 1875
#68-72 Pres. Michel Domingue. Issued w/o signs. (but some have had fraudulent signs. added later). Printer: ABNC.

	68	**25 CENTIMES**	**GOOD**	**FINE**	**XF**
		Sept.1875. Black on pink unpt. Portr. Pres. Domingue at l., arms at r. Frame 112 x 56mm. Back red.	4.00	12.50	50.00

	70	**1 PIASTRE**	**GOOD**	**FINE**	**XF**
		Sept. 1875. Black on blue and orange unpt. Portr. Pres. Domingue at l., arms at ctr., allegorical woman (Agriculture) at r. Frame 155 x 77mm. Back blue.	5.00	25.00	75.00

	72	**5 PIASTRES**	**GOOD**	**FINE**	**XF**
		Sept. 1875. Black on lt. green and pink unpt. Alllegorical woman at l., arms at ctr., portr. Pres. Domingue at r. Back orange.	7.50	30.00	85.00

TREASURY (1883-89)

LOI DU 28 AOUT 1883
#75,76 *Salomon Jeune* first issue. Printer: ABNC.

	75	**1 GOURDE**	**GOOD**	**FINE**	**XF**
		L.1883. Black on blue unpt. Arms at upper ctr., Portr. Qn. Isabella at r. Frame 177 x 77mm. Back blue. Series through A48.	110.00	475.00	—

	76	**2 GOURDES**	**GOOD**	**FINE**	**XF**
		L.1883. Black on pink unpt. Dog at upper l., arms at upper r. Back salmon-pink. Series through B14.	125.00	500.00	—

LOI DU 6 OCTOBRE 1884
#77,78 *Salomon Jeune* second issue. Printer: ABNC.

			Good	Fine	XF
77	**1 GOURDE**		125.00	475.00	—
	L.1884. Black on orange and blue unpt. Ceres reclining at l., arms at r. Frame 170 x 74mm. Back orange. Series through C54.				
78	**2 GOURDES**		125.00	475.00	—
	L.1884. Black on green and orange unpt. Ceres seated at l. Back green. Series through D32.				

LOI DU 3 NOVEMBRE 1887
#79,80 *Salomon Jeune* third issue. Printer: CS&E.

			Good	Fine	XF
79	**1 GOURDE**		125.00	475.00	—
	L.1887. Black on orange and blue unpt. Arms at upper l., Ceres reclining at r. Back red. Series through E100.				

			Good	Fine	XF
80	**2 GOURDES**		125.00	475.00	—
	L.1887. Black on green and orange unpt. Farmers and horse at l., portr. girl at upper r., arms at lower r. Back green. Series through F50.				

DECRET DU 28 JUIN 1889
#83-85 issued in Port-au-Prince by Pres. Francois Denis Légitime.

			Good	Fine	XF
83	**10 CENTIMES**				
	ND. Black on heavy gray wmk. paper. Frame 118 x 61mm.				
	a. Black print.		60.00	150.00	325.00
	b. Blue print.		60.00	150.00	325.00
84	**20 CENTIMES**		65.00	175.00	350.00
	ND. Green on heavy gray wmk. paper. Frame 118 x 61mm.				

			Good	Fine	XF
85	**1 GOURDE**		85.00	250.00	550.00
	D.1889. Green on heavy white wmk. paper. Frame 166 x 61mm.				

RÉPUBLIQUE SEPTENTRIONALE D'HAITI

1888 ND ISSUE
Govt. of Gen. Floraville Hippolyte 1888-89 in North Haiti.
#88-95 printer: HLBNC.

			Good	Fine	XF
88	**10 CENTIMES**		75.00	225.00	450.00
	ND (1888). Black on gray unpt. Arms at upper l. Back green. Series A. 82 x 42mm.				

			Good	Fine	XF
89	**25 CENTIMES**		75.00	225.00	450.00
	ND (1888). Black on lt. blue unpt. Arms at r. Back blue. Series A. 110 x 62mm.				

			Good	Fine	XF
90	**50 CENTIMES**		60.00	200.00	400.00
	ND (1888). Black on pale orange unpt. Arms at l. Back violet-brown. Series A. 110 x 64mm.				

			Good	Fine	XF
91	**1 GOURDE**		75.00	250.00	500.00
	ND (1888). Black on pink and green unpt. Justice and Youth at upper l., arms at r. Back. Green. Series A. 154 x 100mm.				

| 92 | 2 GOURDES
ND (1888). Black on orange and blue unpt. Arms at l., woman seated
w/globe at r. Back red. Series A. 154 x 100mm. | **GOOD**
100.00 | **FINE**
400.00 | **XF**
950.00 |

1889 ND ISSUE

| 95 | 1 GOURDE
ND (1889). Woman at l. Serial # and 2 of 3 signs. in red. Back blue.
Series T. 165 x 74mm. | **GOOD**
100.00 | **FINE**
350.00 | **XF**
800.00 |

TREASURY (1892)

LOI DU 29 SEPTEMBRE 1892
#101 and 102 J. J. Dessalines at l., arms at r. Printer: ABNC.

| 101 | 1 GOURDE
L.1892. Black on yellow and blue unpt. Back red. Series B-V. 182 x
80mm. | **GOOD**
20.00 | **FINE**
85.00 | **XF**
285.00 |

| 102 | 2 GOURDES
L.1892. Black on yellow and pink unpt. Back blue. Series BC-OP. | **GOOD**
25.00 | **FINE**
125.00 | **XF**
375.00 |

BANQUE NATIONALE D'HAITI

1890's ISSUE

| 107 | 5 GOURDES
ND. Blue and buff. Justice at l., arms in orange at r. Back pale blue.
136 x 79mm. Printer: Imp. Filigranique G. Richard et Cie., Paris. | **GOOD**
150.00 | **FINE**
450.00 | **XF**
1000. |

TREASURY (1903-08)

LOI DU 10 AOUT 1903 - COMMEMORATIVE
#110 and 111, Centennial of Haitian Independence, 1804-1904.

#110 and 111 J. J. Dessalines and date 1804 at l., arms at ctr. Nord Alexis and date 1904 at r. Printer: ABNC.

| 110 | 1 GOURDE
L.1903. Black on blue-gray unpt. Back green, w/o vignette, 176 x
80mm. Series A-G. | **GOOD**
7.50 | **FINE**
50.00 | **XF**
175.00 |

| 111 | 2 GOURDES
L.1903. Black on green-gray unpt. Back red, w/o vignette. Series AA-
JJ. | **GOOD**
7.50 | **FINE**
55.00 | **XF**
185.00 |

LOI DU 27 FEVRIER 1904 - COMMEMORATIVE
#120 and 121, Centennial of Haitian Independence, 1804-1904.

#120 and 121 like #110 and 111.

| 120 | 1 GOURDE
L.1904. Series A-R. | **GOOD**
6.00 | **FINE**
30.00 | **XF**
150.00 |

| 121 | 2 GOURDES
L.1904. Series BB-OO. | **GOOD**
7.00 | **FINE**
25.00 | **XF**
175.00 |

LOI DU 14 MAI 1908

| 125 | 5 GOURDES
L.1908. Black on pink Nord Alexis at both l. and r. Back red. Series
C3-19. 169 x 73mm. Printer: ABNC. | **GOOD**
150.00 | **FINE**
485.00 | **XF**
— |

BON DU TRESOR

TREASURY

L'ARRETE DU 22 JANVIER 1915
#127-129 local print.

127	**1 Gourde**	Good	Fine	XF
	L.1915. Black. Arms at ctr. Back dk. blue. Heavy manila paper. Series A; B.	4.00	25.00	85.00
128	**2 Gourdes**			
	L.1915. Like #127. Back pale red. Series AA.	15.00	50.00	150.00
129	**5 Gourdes**			
	L.1915. Like #127. Back red-brown. Series AAA.			
	a. Red serial #.	7.50	35.00	100.00
	b. Black serial #.	4.00	25.00	85.00

Loi du 22 Decembre 1914 (Issued Feb. 1915)
#131 and 132 printer: ABNC.

131	**1 Gourde**	Good	Fine	XF
	L.1914. Face similar to #110 W/o ovpt. Farming scene at ctr. on back. Series A.	8.00	50.00	150.00

132	**2 Gourdes**	Good	Fine	XF
	L.1914. Face similar to #110. W/o ovpt. Mining scene at ctr. on back. Series AA-FF.	10.00	50.00	165.00

1916 ND Issue
#135-136 local printing.

135	**1 Gourde**	Good	Fine	XF
	ND (1916). Blue and black w/red title and text. Back blue. 184 x 82mm. Series D; E; J.	125.00	250.00	550.00
136	**2 Gourdes**			
	ND (1916). Red and black w/blue title and text. Like #135. Back red. Series K-O.	150.00	275.00	600.00

Banque Nationale de la République d'Haiti

1916 Provisional Issue
#137-141 w/vertical red ovpt. lines on unsigned notes of the Eighteenth Issue of Republique (1914). Red dates either 1916 and 1913, or 1919 and 1913. The distinguishing 1916 or 1919 date is vertical in red near the top ctr. of the note.

137	**1 Gourde**	Good	Fine	XF
	L.1916. 1916 ovpt. on #131. Series A-D.	7.50	35.00	135.00
138	**2 Gourdes**			
	IL.1916. 1916 ovpt. on #132. Series AA-II.	20.00	95.00	—

1919 Provisional Issue

140	**1 Gourde**	Good	Fine	XF
	L.1919. 1919 ovpt. on #131. Series D-M.	3.00	15.00	100.00

141	**2 Gourdes**	Good	Fine	XF
	L.1919. 1919 ovpt. on #132. Series HH-RR.	7.00	25.00	110.00

Convention du 2 Mai 1919 - First Issue (ca.1920-24)
#150-153 banana plant on face, coffee plant on back. Size: 163 x 87mm. Printer: ABNC.

150	**1 Gourde**	Good	Fine	XF
	L.1919. Black on green and brown unpt. Plant at l. Back dk. brown. Prefix letters. A-L. 2 sign. varieties.	5.00	35.00	175.00

151	**2 Gourdes**	Good	Fine	XF
	L.1919. Black on green and brown unpt. Plant at r. Back blue. Prefix letters A-J. 2 sign. varieties.	15.00	85.00	350.00

152	**5 Gourdes**	Good	Fine	XF
	L.1919. Black on red, blue and green unpt. Plant at r. ctr. Back orange. Prefix Letters A and B. 2 sign. varieties.	35.00	170.00	525.00
153	**10 Gourdes**			
	L.1919. Black on green and brown unpt. Like #152. Back green. Prefix letter A.	65.00	275.00	—
154	**20 Gourdes**			
	L.1919. Black on blue and m/c unpt. Similar to #152. Back orange. (Not issued). Archive example.	—	—	—

CONVENTION DU 12 AVRIL 1919 - SECOND ISSUE (1925-32)
#160-166 third sign. title: *Pour Controle…* Arms on back. Printer: ABNC.

		VG	VF	UNC
160	**1 GOURDE**			
	L.1919. Dk. brown and m/c. Distant aerial view of Citadel le Ferriere at ctr. Black sign. 121 x 61mm. Prefix letters M-AC (but w/o W). 5 sign. varieties.	1.50	10.00	30.00
161	**2 GOURDES**			
	L.1919. Deep blue and m/c. Like #160. Prefix letters K-M; P-R. 5 sign. varieties.	2.00	15.00	40.00

		VG	VF	UNC
162	**5 GOURDES**			
	L.1919. Orange on lt. green and m/c. unpt. Women harvesting coffee at l. Black sign. 162 x 70mm. Prefix letters C; D. 3 sign. varieties.	1.50	10.00	30.00
163	**10 GOURDES**			
	L.1919. Green and m/c. Coffee plant at ctr. Prefix letter B. 2 sign. varieties.	5.00	25.00	75.00

		VG	VF	UNC
164	**20 GOURDES**			
	L.1919. Red-brown and m/c. Palm tree at r. Prefix letter A.	150.00	350.00	—
165	**50 GOURDES**			
	L.1919. Dk. olive and m/c. Cotton bolls at ctr. Prefix letter A.	20.00	75.00	200.00
166	**100 GOURDES**			
	L.1919. Purple and m/c. Field workers at l. Prefix letter A.	25.00	85.00	225.00

CONVENTION DU 12 AVRIL 1919 - THIRD ISSUE
#167 and 168 portr. Pres. Stenio Vincent at ctr. Printer ABNC.

		VG	VF	UNC
167	**1 GOURDE**			
	L.1919. Dk. brown and m/c. Prefix letter W.	30.00	125.00	275.00
168	**2 GOURDES**			
	L.1919. Blue and m/c. Like #167. Prefix letter N.	30.00	150.00	325.00

CONVENTION DU 12 AVRIL 1919 - FOURTH ISSUE
#170-173 first and third sign. title each: *Un Administrateur.* Printer: ABNC.

		VG	VF	UNC
170	**1 GOURDE**			
	L.1919. Like #160, but brown sign. Prefix letters AD-AR. 4 sign. varieties.	1.00	4.00	15.00

		VG	VF	UNC
171	**2 GOURDES**			
	L.1919. Like #161, but blue sign. Prefix letters S-Y. 4 sign. varieties.	1.00	5.00	25.00
172	**5 GOURDES**			
	L.1919. Like #162. Prefix letters D; E. 3 sign. varieties.			
	a. Orange sign. Prefix letter D.	2.00	12.50	35.00
	b. Black sign. Prefix letter E.	1.50	8.00	17.50
173	**10 GOURDES**			
	L.1919. Like #163. Prefix letter B.	5.00	25.00	55.00

CONVENTION DU 12 AVRIL 1919 - FIFTH ISSUE
#174-177 printer: W&S.

		VG	VF	UNC
174	**1 GOURDE**			
	L.1919. Dk. brown and m/c. Citadel Rampart at ctr. Back dk. brown. Prefix letters WA-WD. 2 sign. varieties.	20.00	60.00	175.00
175	**2 GOURDES**			
	L.1919. Blue and m/c. Like #174. Back blue. Prefix letters WA and WB. 2 sign.. varieties.	40.00	120.00	325.00

		VG		UNC
176	**50 GOURDES**			
	L.1919. Dk. olive and m/c. Like #165. Back olive.			
	a. Issued note.	—		—
	s. Specimen, punched hole cancelled.	—		200.00
177	**100 GOURDES**	VG	VF	UNC
	L.1919. Brown. Like #166. Uniface specimen pair.	—	—	250.00

REPUBLIC (SECOND)
BANQUE NATIONALE DE LA RÉPUBLIQUE D'HAITI
COVENTION DU 12 AVRIL 1919 - SIXTH ISSUE (CA.1951-64)
#178-181, 183 and 184 arms at ctr. on back. First sign. title: *Le President.* Printer: ABNC.

		VG	VF	UNC
178	**1 GOURDE**			
	L.1919. Dk. brown on lt. blue and m/c. unpt. Citadel rampart at ctr. Prefix letters AS-BM. 5 sign. varieties.	.75	2.00	10.00
179	**2 GOURDES**			
	L.1919. Blue and m/c. lt. green in unpt. Like #178. Prefix letters Z-AF. 6 sign. varieties.	1.00	3.00	15.00
180	**5 GOURDES**			
	L.1919. Orange on green unpt. Woman harvesting coffee beans at l. Prefix letters G-M. 3 sign. varieties.	1.50	4.50	12.50

		VG	VF	UNC
181	**10 GOURDES**			
	L.1919. Green on m/c unpt. Coffee plant at ctr. Prefix letters B-D. 2 sign. varieties.	3.00	10.00	30.00
183	**50 GOURDES**			
	L.1919. Olive-green on m/c unpt. Cotton bolls at ctr. Specimen.	—	—	160.00
184	**100 GOURDES**	VG	VF	UNC
	L.1919. Purple on m/c unpt. Field workers at l. Back purple. Prefix letter A.			
	a. Issued note.	20.00	50.00	200.00
	s. Specimen, punched hole cancelled.	—	—	175.00

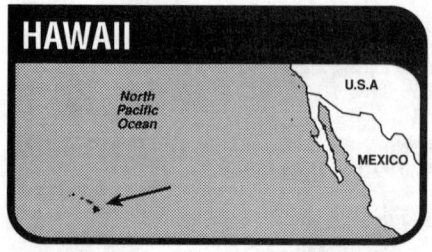

The State of Hawaii, 50th state of the United States, consists of eight main islands and numerous smaller islands of coral and volcanic origin situated in the central Pacific Ocean 2,400 miles (3,862 km.) from San Francisco. The archipelago has an area of 6,471 sq. mi. (16,641 sq. km.) and a population of 1.1 million. Capital: Honolulu. The principal industries are tourism and agriculture. Cane sugar and pineapples are exported.

The islands, originally populated by Polynesians who traveled from the Society Islands, were discovered by British navigator Capt. James Cook in 1778. He named them the Sandwich Islands. King Kamehameha the Great united the islands under one kingdom (1795-1810) which endured until 1893 when Queen Liliuokalani, the gifted composer of 'Aloha Oe' and other songs, was deposed and a provisional government established. This was followed by a republic which governed Hawaii until 1898 when it ceded itself to the United States. Hawaii was organized as a territory in 1900 and attained statehood on Aug. 21, 1959.

RULERS
King Kalakaua, 1874-1891
Queen Liliuokalani, 1891-1893
Provisional Govt., 1893-1894
Republic, 1894-1898
Annexed to U.S., 1898-1900
Territory, 1900-1959

MONETARY SYSTEM
1 Dollar = 100 Cents

KINGDOM

DEPARTMENT OF FINANCE

1879 (1880) SILVER CERTIFICATE OF DEPOSIT
#1-5 arms at ctr. on back. Printer: ABNC.

		VG	VF	UNC
1	**10 DOLLARS**			
	ND (1880). Black on orange unpt. Sailing ship at l. cowboy roping steers at ctr., steam locomotive at r. Back orange.			
	a. Issued note.	—	10000.	
	b. Punched or cut cancelled.	Unknown In Private Hands		
	p. Proof pair, face and back.	—	—	3000.

		VG	VF	UNC
2	**20 DOLLARS**			
	ND (1879). Black on brown unpt. Portr. girl w/dog at lower l., Portr. woman between steam paddlewheel ship and steam passenger train at lower r. Back brown.			
	a. Issued note.	Reported Not Confirmed		
	b. Punched or cut cancelled.	2500.	—	—
	p. Proof pair, face and back	—	—	3500.

		VG	VF	UNC
3	**50 DOLLARS**			
	ND (1879). Black on green unpt. Ram at l., allegorical woman at ctr., girl at r. Back green.			
	a. Issued note.	5000.	—	—
	b. Punched or cut cancelled.	Unknown In Private Hands		
	p. Proof pair, face and back.	—	—	4000.

		VG	VF	UNC
4	**100 DOLLARS**			
	ND (1879). Black on blue unpt. Galloping horse at lower l., globe between steam passenger train and sailing ship at ctr., cow at lower r. Back blue.			
	a. Issued note.	—	—	15000.
	b. Punched or cut cancelled.	2500.	—	7500.
	p. Proof pair, face and back.	—	—	5000.

		VG	VF	UNC
5	**500 DOLLARS**			
	ND (1879). Black on orange unpt. Kg. Kalakaua I at l., steam locomotive between sailing ships at ctr., farmer carrying produce at r. Back orange. Proof pair, face and back.	—	—	25000.

REPUBLIC OF HAWAII

DEPARTMENT OF FINANCE

1895 (1899) GOLD CERTIFICATE OF DEPOSIT ISSUE
#6-10 black on gold unpt. Back gold; arms in circle at ctr. Printer: ABNC.

		VG	VF	UNC
6	**5 DOLLARS**			
	1895 (1899). Woman at l., bldg. and trees at ctr., steer at r.			
	a. Issued note.	—	15000.	
	b. Cancelled.	—	—	6000.
	p. Proof pair, face and back.	—	—	5500.

		VG	VF	UNC
7	**10 DOLLARS**			
	1895 (1899). Steamship at l., sugar cane harvest at ctr., woman at r.			
	a. Issued note	Reported Not Confirmed		
	b. Cancelled.	—	—	7000.
	p. Proof pair, face and back.	—	—	6000.

		VG	VF	Unc
8	**20 DOLLARS** 1895 (1899). Woman standing at l., sugar cane harvest at ctr., horse's head at r.			
	a. Issued note.	5000.	—	—
	b. Cancelled.	—	—	8000.
	p. Proof pair, face and back.	—	—	7000.

		VG	VF	Unc
9	**50 DOLLARS** 1895 (1899). Woman at l., longhorns w/cowboy on horseback at ctr., tree at r.			
	a. Issued note.	Reported Not Confirmed		
	b. Cancelled. Unknown in private hands.	—	—	—
	p. Proof pair, face and back.	—	—	8000.
10	**100 DOLLARS** 1895 (1899). 2 allegorical women at l., cowboys and steam passenger train at ctr., horse at r.			
	a. Issued note.	Reported Not Confirmed		
	b. Cancelled.	—	—	10000.
	p. Proof pair, face and back.	—	—	9000.

1895 (1897) SILVER CERTIFICATE OF DEPOSIT ISSUE
#11-15 Black on blue unpt. Back blue; arms at ctr. Printer: ABNC.

		VG	VF	Unc
11	**5 DOLLARS** 1895 (1897). Palm tree at l., Iolani Palace at ctr., kneeling man at r.			
	a. Issued note.	4500.	8000.	—
	b. Cancelled.	Reported Not Confirmed		
	p. Proof pair, face and back.	—	—	5000.
12	**10 DOLLARS** 1895 (1897). Similar to #1.			
	a. Issued note.	10000.	—	—
	b. Cancelled.	3500.	—	—
	p. Proof pair, face and back.	—	—	5500.
13	**20 DOLLARS** 1895 (1897). Similar to #2.			
	a. Issued note.	Reported Not Confirmed		
	b. Cancelled.	Unknown In Private Hands		
	p. Proof pair, face and back.	—	—	6000.
14	**50 DOLLARS** 1895 (1897). Similar to #3.			
	a. Issued note.	Reported Not Confirmed		
	b. Cancelled. Unknown in private hands.	—	—	—
	p. Proof pair, face and back.	—	—	7500.
15	**100 DOLLARS** 1895 (1897). Similar to #4.			
	a. Issued note.	Reported Not Confirmed		
	b. Cancelled. Unknown in private hands.	—	—	—
	p. Proof pair, face and back.	—	—	8500.

UNITED STATES OF AMERICA - TERRITORIAL
Issued in 1942 after the Japanese attack on Pearl Harbor. Used as a financial precaution to a possible invasion of the islands and capture of U.S. currency.

TREASURY

1935A (1942) EMERGENCY SILVER CERTIFICATE ISSUE
#36, ovpt: *HAWAII* of face and back of 1935A series.

		VG	VF	Unc
36	**1 DOLLAR** 1935A (1942). Portr. G. Washington at ctr. Brown serial # and seal at r. Back green.	6.00	10.00	35.00

FEDERAL RESERVE

1934 (1942) EMERGENCY ISSUE
#37-41 w/brown serial # and seal at r. Ovpt: *HAWAII* on face and back of San Francisco 1934 and 1934A Series 'L' notes.

		VG	VF	Unc
37	**5 DOLLARS** 1934 (1942). Portr. A. Lincoln at ctr. Back green; Lincoln Memorial at ctr.	20.00	32.50	100.00

		VG	VF	Unc
38	**5 DOLLARS** 1934A (1942). Like #37.	20.00	30.00	90.00

		VG	VF	Unc
39	**10 DOLLARS** 1934A (1942). Black. Portr. A. Hamilton at ctr. Back green; Treasury bldg. at ctr.	20.00	30.00	200.00
40	**20 DOLLARS** 1934 (1942). Black. Portr. A. Jackson at ctr. Back green; White House at ctr.	28.50	40.00	300.00
41	**20 DOLLARS** 1934A (1942). Like #40.	30.00	50.00	400.00

Hejaz, a province of Saudi Arabia and a former vilayet of the Ottoman Empire, occupies an 800-mile-long (1,287 km.) coastal strip between Nejd and the Red Sea. Population: 1.4 million. Hejaz contains the holy cities of Mecca and Medina. The economy is based on pilgrimage spending, light industries, limited agriculture production and the wealth generated by the oil deposits of Saudi Arabia.

The province was a Turkish dependency until freed in World War I. Husain Ibn Ali, Amir of Mecca, opposed the Turkish control and, with the aid of Lawrence of Arabia, wrested much of Hejaz from the Turks and in 1916 assumed the title of King of Hejaz. Ibn Sa'ud of Nejd conquered Hejaz in 1925, and in 1932 combined it with Nejd and other provinces under his control to form the Kingdom of Saudi Arabia.

RULERS
Husain Ibn Ali, AH1334-1373 (AD 1916-1924)
Abd Al-Aziz Ibn Sa'ud, AH1342-1373 (AD 1924-1953)

MONETARY SYSTEM
1 Pound (Riyal) = 20 Ghirsh (Piastres)

HEJAZ
ARABIAN NATIONAL BANK OF HEDJAZ
DECREE OF 23 SHAWAL AH1343 (1924)

1	**1/2 POUND**			
	D. AH1343 (1924). Red. Kaaba (or Ka'bah-Moslem shrine in Mecca). Indian coin on back.	—	Rare	—
2	**1 POUND**			
	D. AH1343 (1924).	—	Rare	—

3	**10 POUNDS**			
	D. AH1343 (1924). Temple at ctr., columns at l. and r.	—	Rare	—

4	**50 POUNDS**			
	D. AH1343 (1924). Tree at l., ruins at r.	—	Rare	—

5	**100 POUNDS**			
	D. AH1343 (1924). Oasis at ctr., facing ancient winged statues at l. and r. of archway.	—	Rare	—

The Republic of Honduras, situated in Central America between Nicaragua and Guatemala, has an area of 43,277 sq. mi. (112,088 sq. km.) and a population of 5.1 million. Capital: Tegucigalpa. Agriculture, mining (gold and silver), and logging are the chief industries. Bananas, timber and coffee are exported.

Honduras, a site of the ancient Mayan Empire, was claimed for Spain by Columbus in 1502, during his last voyage to the Americas. The first settlement was made by Cristobal de Olid under orders of Hernan Cortes, then in Mexico. The area, regarded as one of the most promising sources of gold and silver in the new world, was a part of the Captaincy General of Guatemala throughout the colonial period. After declaring its independence from Spain, in 1821, Honduras fell briefly to the Mexican empire of Agustin de Iturbide, and then joined the Central American Federation (1823-39). Upon dissolution of the federation, Honduras became an independent republic.

* * * This section has been partially renumbered. * * *

MONETARY SYSTEM:
l Peso = 100 Centavos, 1871-1926
1 Lempira = 100 Centavos, 1926-

NOTE: Certain listings encompassing issues circulated by provincial, state and commercial banking authorities are contained in Volume 1.

RÉPUBLICA DE HONDURAS
VALE AL PORTADOR
1889 ISSUE

#9-13 receipts issued by the Bogran government w/circular handstamp: *REPUBLICA DE HONDURAS* at l., embossed circular seal:...*PUBLICO*...at ctr. and w/ or w/o oval handstamp: *OFICINA GENERAL* at r.

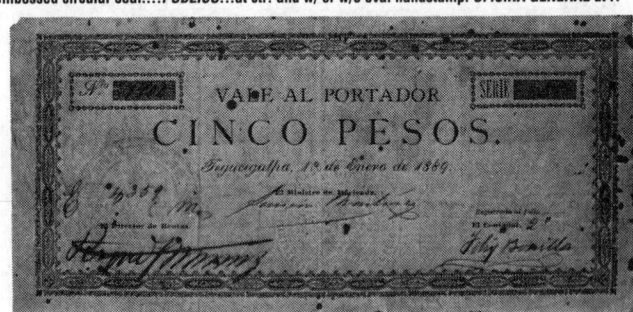

		GOOD	FINE	XF
9 (A9)	**5 PESOS** 1.1.1889.	—	—	—
10 (A10)	**10 PESOS** 1.1.1889.	—	—	—
11 (A11)	**20 PESOS** 1.1.1889.	—	—	—
12 (A12)	**50 PESOS** 1.1.1889. Gray w/maroon denomination at l. and r. w/2 red handstamps.	750.00	1500.	2250.

		GOOD	FINE	XF
13 (A13)	**100 PESOS** 1.1.1889. Orange-brown w/2 handstamps.			

BILLETE PRIVILEGIADO
1891 ISSUE

14 **2 Pesos**   GOOD   FINE   XF
(A14)   15.7.1891. Brown. Arms at ctr. Back black.   —   —

15 **25 Pesos**   GOOD   FINE   XF
(A15)   15.7.1891. Gray-green. Like #A14. Back black.   —   —

BILLETES DEL TESORO

TREASURY NOTES

1889 ISSUE

16 **5 Pesos**
(A16)   1889.   —   —   —
17 **10 Pesos**
(A17)   1889.   —   —   —
18 **20 Pesos**
(A18)   1889.   —   —   —
19 **50 Pesos**
(A19)   1889.   —   —   —
20 **100 Pesos**
(A20)   1889.   —   —   —

BANCO DE HONDURAS

1889 ISSUE
Various dates including authorization dates on backs and sign. varieties.
#24-27 printer: ABNC.

22 **5 Pesos**   GOOD   FINE   XF
(30)   1.10.1889. Black on orange and yellow unpt. Steer's head at l., arms   —   Rare   —
      at r. Back red.

23 **50 Pesos**   GOOD   FINE   XF
(32A)   1.10.1889. Black on brown and yellow unpt. Allegorical woman w/3   —   —   —
      children and globe at l., arms at lower l. Indian w/bow at r. Back
      brown. Archive copy.

24 **100 Pesos**   GOOD   FINE   XF
(33)   1.10.1889. Black on orange and yellow unpt. Seated woman at l.,   —   Rare   —
      steer's head at ctr., arms at r. Back orange.

1913 ISSUE

25 **10 Pesos**   FINE
(31)   1.10.1913. Black on m/c unpt. Steer's head at l. Back red; arms at ctr.   —   Rare   —
      Series A.

26 **20 Pesos**   GOOD   FINE   XF
(32)   1.10.1913. Black on m/c unpt. Steer's head at r. Back olive-green;   —   Rare   —
      arms at ctr.

27 **50 Pesos**   GOOD   FINE   XF
(32B)   1.10.1913. Black on m/c unpt. Steer's head at ctr. Back green; arms at   —   —   —
      ctr. Proof.

1922 ISSUE

28 **50 Centavos**   GOOD   FINE   XF
      27.5.1922. M/c. Steer's head at l., church at ctr. Arms on back.   —   Unc   300.00
      Printer: W&S. Specimen, punched hole cancelled.

29	1 PESO	GOOD	FINE	XF
	27.5.1922. Black on purple and m/c unpt. Steer's head at r. Back dk. blue; arms at ctr. New authorization date of 13.7.1925 and text ovpt. in upper margin on back.			
	a.. Authorization ovpt. in black.	75.00	250.00	—
	b.. Authorization ovpt. in red.	95.00	300.00	—

1932 ISSUE
#34-41 bank at ctr. on back. Printer: W&S.
#34-37 Lempira at l., arms at r.

34	1 LEMPIRA	GOOD	FINE	XF
	11.2.1932. Blue on m/c unpt. Series A.	15.00	65.00	200.00

35	2 LEMPIRAS	GOOD	FINE	XF
	11.2.1932. Green on m/c unpt. Series A.	50.00	300.00	—
36	5 LEMPIRAS			
	11.2.1932. Brown on m/c unpt. Series A.	75.00	450.00	—

37	10 LEMPIRAS	GOOD	FINE	XF
	11.2.1932. Black on lt. green and m/c unpt. Series A.	90.00	550.00	—
38	20 LEMPIRAS			
	11.2.1932. Series A.		Reported Not Confirmed	
39	25 LEMPIRAS			
	11.2.1932. Series A.		Reported Not Confirmed	
40	50 LEMPIRAS			
	11.2.1932. Series A.		Reported Not Confirmed	
41	100 LEMPIRAS			
	11.2.1932. Series A.		Reported Not Confirmed	

1941 ISSUE
#42-44 printer: ABNC.

42	5 LEMPIRAS	GOOD	FINE	XF
	5.3.1941. Brown on red unpt. Portr. Morazan at l. Steer's head on brown back. Series B.	25.00	100.00	275.00

43	10 LEMPIRAS	GOOD	FINE	XF
	5.3.1941. Green on brown unpt. Portr. S. Soto at r. Back green; like #42. Series B.			
	a. W/o red ovpt. on back.	65.00	225.00	—
	b. Red ovpt: *Autorizada su circulacion...25.5.1948* in 3 lines of text and sign. on back.	65.00	225.00	—

44	20 LEMPIRAS	GOOD	FINE	XF
	5.3.1941. Black on olive unpt. l. Portr. Agurcia at l. Steer's head at ctr. on black back. Series A.			
	a. W/o red ovpt. on back.	75.00	325.00	—
	b. Red ovpt: *Autorizada su circulacion...25.5.1948* in 3 lines of text and sign. on back.	75.00	325.00	—

BANCO CENTRAL DE HONDURAS
Established 1950 by merger of Banco Atlantida and Banco de Honduras. Various date and sign. varieties.
1950-51 ISSUE

45	1 LEMPIRA	VG	VF	UNC
	1951. Red on lt. tan unpt. Lempira at l., arms at r. Monolith on back. Red serial #. Printer: W&S.			
	a. 16.3.1951; 4.5.1951.	2.00	6.00	32.50
	b. 28.12.1951.	1.50	4.50	25.00
	s. Specimen, punched hole cancelled.	—	—	40.00
46	5 LEMPIRAS			
	1950-51. Dk. blue-gray on m/c unpt. Portr. Morazan at l. Arms at ctr. on back. Printer: ABNC.			
	a. 1.7.1950; 11.7.1950; 22.9.1950; 22.12.1950.	12.50	65.00	—
	b. 16.2.1951.	8.50	50.00	—
	s. Specimen, punched hole cancelled.	—	—	100.00

47	10 LEMPIRAS	VG	VF	UNC
	25.5.1951-26.3.1954. Brown on m/c unpt. Portr. Cabanas at l. Plantation work on back. Printer: W&S.			
	a. Issued note.	25.00	85.00	—
	s. Specimen, punched hole cancelled.	—	—	135.00

48 20 LEMPIRAS
25.5.1951-4.6.1954. Purple on m/c unpt. D. Herrera at l. Castle on back. Printer: W&S.

	VG	VF	UNC
a. Issued note.	20.00	85.00	200.00
s. Specimen, punched hole cancelled.	—	—	175.00

49 100 LEMPIRAS
1951-72. Yellow on m/c unpt. Valle at l., arms at r. Village and bridge on back.

	VG	VF	UNC
a. W/o security thread, lilac-pink unpt. Printer: W&S. 16.3.1951; 8.3.1957.	85.00	225.00	—
b. W/o security thread, w/fibers at r. ctr., lt. green and lt. orange unpt. Printer: W&S. 10.12.1969.	65.00	150.00	—
c. W/security thread, yellow unpt. 13.10.1972.	55.00	125.00	225.00
s. Specimen, punched hole cancelled.	—	—	200.00

1953-56 ISSUE

51 5 LEMPIRAS
1953-67. Gray on m/c unpt. Morazan at l., arms at r. Serial # at upper l. and upper r. Battle of Trinidad on back. Printer: ABNC.

	VG	VF	UNC
a. Date horizontal. 17.3.1953; 19.2.1960; 25.10.1963; 12.3.1965; 7.1.1966.	4.00	20.00	75.00
b. Date vertical. 15.4.1966; 29.9.1967.	3.50	17.50	60.00

52 10 LEMPIRAS
1954-70. Brown on m/c unpt. Cabanas at l., arms at r. Old bank on back. Date and sign. Style varieties. Printer: TDLR.

	VG	VF	UNC
a. R. sign. title: *MINISTRO DE HACIENDA*... 19.11.1954.	15.00	60.00	125.00
b. R. sign. title: *MINISTRO DE ECONOMIA*... 19.2.1960-15.1.1970.	10.00	25.00	75.00

53 20 LEMPIRAS
4.6.1954; 8.5.1959-18.2.1972. Green. D. Herrera at l., arms at r. Waterfalls on back. Printer: TDLR.

VG	VF	UNC
15.00	37.50	125.00

54 50 LEMPIRAS
20.1.1956. Deep blue on m/c unpt. Dr. J. Trinidad Reyes at l., arms at r. University of Honduras on back. Printer: TDLR.

	VG	VF	UNC
a. Issued note.	35.00	100.00	350.00
s. Specimen, punched hole cancelled.	—	—	275.00

HONG KONG

Hong Kong, a British colony situated at the mouth of the Canton or Pearl River 90 miles (145 km.) southeast of Canton, has an area of 409 sq. mi. (1,045 sq. km.) and a population of 5.6 million. Capital: Victoria. The free port of Hong Kong, the commercial center of the Far East, is a transshipment point for goods destined for China and the countries of the Western Pacific. Light manufacturing and tourism are important components of the economy.

Long a haven for fishermen-pirates and opium smugglers, the island of Hong Kong was ceded to Britain at the conclusion of the first Opium War (1839-1842). At the time, the acquisition of "a barren rock" was ridiculed by both London and English merchants operating in the Far East. The Kowloon Peninsula and Stonecutter's Island were ceded in 1860 and the so-called New Territories, comprising most of the mainland of the colony, were leased to Britain for 99 years in 1898. They will return to mainland China's rule on Dec. 20, 1999.

When the Japanese opened hostilities in World War II, on Dec. 7, 1941, they immediately attacked Hong Kong which fell, after some bitter fighting, on Christmas day. The colony was liberated by British troops on Aug. 30, 1945, when it was found that the population was no more than 600,000, of whom 80 percent were suffering from malnutrition. Hong Kong's economic life was dead. A brief period of military administration was followed by the formal re-establishment of civil government in May 1946. Hong Kong made a dramatic recovery and at the close of 1947 the population had reached 1,800,000. With the disintegration of the Nationalist Chinese forces and the establishment of the Central Peoples government, from 1948 to April 1950, an unprecedented influx of refugees took place, raising the population to about 2,360,000.

RULERS:
British (1845-1999)

MONETARY SYSTEM:
1 Dollar = 100 Cents

COMMERCIAL BANKS:
Agra & United Service Bank, Limited - #5-8
Asiatic Banking Corporation - #13-14
Bank of Hindustan, China & Japan - #20
Chartered Bank of India, Australia & China - #21-59
Chartered Bank - #62-67
Chartered Mercantile Bank of India, London & China - #82-91
Hong Kong & Shanghai Banking Company, Limited - #96-101
Hong Kong & Shanghai Banking Corporation - #111-183
Mercantile Bank of India, Limited - #235-241
Mercantile Bank Limited - #242-243
National Bank of China Limited - #247-251
Oriental Bank Corporation - #260-270

NOTE ON VALUATIONS: Most valuations are for issued notes. At times specimen or proof notes are listed w/valuations, but these are only cases where a regularly issued example is not known to exist.

BRITISH INFLUENCE

AGRA & UNITED SERVICE BANK, LIMITED

行銀理匯剌加呵
A Jai La Hui Li Yin Hang

Later became Agra & Masterman's Bank, Limited.

1862 ISSUE
#5-8 Royal arms at top ctr. Printer: John Biden, London.

		GOOD	FINE	XF
5	**100 DOLLARS** ca.1862. Proof.	—	Rare	—
6	**200 DOLLARS** ca.1862. Proof.	—	Rare	—
7	**300 DOLLARS** ca.1862. Proof.	—	Rare	—
8	**500 DOLLARS** ca.1862. Proof.	—	Rare	—

ASIATIC BANKING CORPORATION

行銀理匯特鴉西亞

Ya Hsi Ya De Hui Li Yin Hang

1800's ISSUE

#13, 14 arms at upper ctr.

			GOOD	FINE	XF
13	**50 DOLLARS**		—	Rare	—
	18xx.				

			GOOD	FINE	XF
14	**100 DOLLARS**		—	Rare	—
	18xx. Specimen.				

BANK OF HINDUSTAN CHINA & JAPAN

行銀理匯本日國中丹士度慳

Keng Tu Shi Dan Chung Kuo Jih Ben Hui Li Yin Hang

Founded 1863; closed 1865.

HONG KONG BRANCH

1863 ISSUE

			GOOD	FINE	XF
20	**1000 DOLLARS**		—	Rare	—
	18xx. Arms at upper ctr. Printer: Batho, Sprague & Co., London. Remainder.				

CHARTERED BANK OF INDIA, AUSTRALIA & CHINA

行銀理滙國中山金新度印

Yin Tu Hsin Chin Shan Chung Kuo Hui Li Yin Hang

行銀利加麥國中山金新度印

Yin Tu Hsin Chin Shan Chung Kuo Ta Cha Yin Hang

In the 1950's became the Chartered Bank. These listings are for notes w/*HONG KONG* as branch office of issue. Similar notes w/other branch offices of issue such as *HANKOW, PEKING, SHANGHAI* and *TIEN-TSIN* were Chinese branch office issues while those of *PENANG* and *SINGAPORE* were issued in the Straits Settlements, *BANGKOK* issues were for Thailand. Refer to Volume 1.

HONG KONG BRANCH

1865 ISSUE

#21-26 arms at upper or top ctr. Printer: Batho, Sprague & Co.

			GOOD	FINE	XF
21	**5 DOLLARS**				
	1865-79. Gray frame. 2 hand-written sign.				
	a. 2.1.1865.		2000.	6500.	16,000.
	b. 1.1.1874; 1.1.1879.		—	Rare	—

			GOOD	FINE	XF
22	**10 DOLLARS**		—	Rare	—
	18xx. Gray frame. Back red-orange. Proof.				

			GOOD	FINE	XF
23	**25 DOLLARS**		—	Rare	—
	18xx. Blue. Back red-orange. Proof.				
24	**50 DOLLARS**		—	Rare	—
	18xx. Lt. blue frame. Back orange. Proof.				

			GOOD	FINE	XF
25	**100 DOLLARS**		—	Rare	—
	18xx. Red-orange. Proof.				
26	**500 DOLLARS**		—	Rare	—
	18xx. Gray frame. Gray *500* below arms. Back red-orange; lg. *500* in guilloche. Proof.				

1879 ISSUE

#27-32 arms at upper ctr. Printer: WWS.

				FINE	XF
27	**5 DOLLARS**		—	Unc	17,500.
	1.1.1879. Blue-gray frame. Back green. Proof.				
28	**10 DOLLARS**		—	Unc	17,500.
	1.1.1879. Brown frame. Back green. Proof.				
29	**25 DOLLARS**		—	Unc	25,000.
	1.1.1879. Green on red unpt. Back green. Proof.				
30	**50 DOLLARS**		—	Unc	21,000.
	1.1.1879. Orange on red unpt. Back dk. green. Proof.				
31	**100 DOLLARS**		—	Unc	21,000.
	1.1.1879. Black on red unpt. Back dk. green. proof.				

32	500 DOLLARS	GOOD	FINE	XF
	1.1.1879. Black. Back red; dragon at ctr. Proof.	—	Unc	25,000.

1897-1910 ISSUES
#37-40 printer: WWS.

33	5 DOLLARS	GOOD	FINE	XF
	1.11.1897; 15.11.1897. Gray frame. Like #21. Sign. at r. printed. Printer: Batho, Sprague & Co.	1200.	4500.	—

34	5 DOLLARS	GOOD	FINE	XF
	1.10.1903; 1.1.1905; 19.1.1910; 1.7.1911; 1.10.1912. Blue-green frame on brown-orange unpt. Last 2 digits of year stamped on printed 190x. Printer: WWS.	600.00	1250.	3500.
35	10 DOLLARS			
	19.1.1910. 190x. Brown frame on brown-orange unpt. w/purple TEN at lower ctr. Back gray. Printer: WWS.	3000.	6500.	—
36	25 DOLLARS			
	1.1.1897. Green. Arms at upper ctr. Back green. Printer: Batho, Sprague & Co.	—	Rare	—

37	25 DOLLARS	GOOD	FINE	XF
	189x.; 1903. Green on purple and red unpt. Like #36.	—	Rare	—
38	50 DOLLARS			
	6.10.1910; 8.9.1910. Yellow-orange on purple and yellow unpt. Back green.	—	Rare	—
39	100 DOLLARS			
	8.9.1910. Gray on purple and pink unpt. Back green.	3000.	8000.	17,500.

40	500 DOLLARS	GOOD	FINE	XF
	8.9.1910; 6.10.1910; 20.10.1910; 1.7.1911. Red on olive-green and pink unpt. Arms at top ctr., lg. 500 below. Back greenish black.	—	Rare	—

1911-23 ISSUES
#41-46 printer: W&S.

41	5 DOLLARS	GOOD	FINE	XF
	1.11.1911-1.7.1922. Blue and black. Workmen at l., arms at upper ctr., river scene at r. Large blue 5 in unpt. at bottom ctr. Bldg. at ctr. on back.	375.00	1200.	3500.

42	10 DOLLARS	GOOD	FINE	XF
	1.12.1911-1.7.1922. Black and red-violet on m/c unpt. Boats and pagoda at l., boats in cove at r. Bldg. at ctr. on back.	500.00	1350.	4250.

43	**50 DOLLARS**	**GOOD**	**FINE**	**XF**
	1.1.1912. Black and orange-brown. *50* at upper l. and at each side of vignette. Back yellow-green; old bank bldg. at ctr.	1850.	5000.	12,000.

44	**50 DOLLARS**	**GOOD**	**FINE**	**XF**
	1.11.1923; 1.5.1924; 1.11.1929. Black and orange-brown on m/c unpt. Red *FIFTY* at each side of central vignette. Back olive-green and brown-violet; old back bldg. at ctr.	1000.	3000.	6300.

45	**100 DOLLARS**	**GOOD**	**FINE**	**XF**
	1.2.1912; 1.5.1924; 1.2.1926. Black and green on m/c unpt. Bridge at upper l., pavilion at upper r. Back black and red; old bank bldg. at ctr.	1400.	3500.	14,000.
46	**500 DOLLARS**			
	1912-26. Pale red and blue-black on m/c unpt. Boat, coastline at ctr. Back blue and black; old bank bldg. at ctr.			
	a. 1.3.1912; 1.7.1912;	2000.	5500.	18,000.
	b. 1.2.1921; 1.7.1922; 1.10.1926.	1750.	4500.	16,000.

1923-29 ISSUES
#47-52 printer: W&S.

47	**5 DOLLARS**	**GOOD**	**FINE**	**XF**
	1.9.1923; 1.11.1923. Blue and black. Like #41 but w/red *FIVE* at lower ctr. Back red.	350.00	900.00	3250.
48	**5 DOLLARS**			
	1.5.1924; 1.9.1927. Blue. Like #47 but Chinese character *Wu* in red at either side of arms. Back brown.	300.00	850.00	3000.
49	**10 DOLLARS**			
	1.3.1923-1.11.1923. Black and violet unpt. Like #42 but w/red *TEN* at lower ctr.	450.00	1200.	3750.

50	**10 DOLLARS**	**GOOD**	**FINE**	**XF**
	1.5.1924; 1.9.1927; 1.8.1929. Like #49 but w/red *TEN* between red Chinese characters *Shih* (ten) at lower ctr.	400.00	1000.	3500.
51	**50 DOLLARS**			
	1.5.1923. Black and orange-brown on m/c unpt. *50* at upper r. Back olive-green and violet.	1350.	3500.	8500.
52	**100 DOLLARS**			
	2.12.1929; 2.6.1930. Black and dk. blue on m/c unpt. Britannia at l. Junk and sampan at ctr. on back.	650.00	1750.	3850.

1930-34 ISSUES
#53-59 printer: W&S.

53	**5 DOLLARS**	**GOOD**	**FINE**	**XF**
	18.8.1930; 1.9.1931. Green. Short red 30mm *5* in unpt. at ctr. Helmeted warrior's head at l.	200.00	450.00	1450.

54	**5 DOLLARS**	**GOOD**	**FINE**	**XF**
	1934-56. Like #53 but tall red 50mm *5* in unpt. at ctr.			
	a. Sign. at r. printed. 2.4.1934-20.9.1940.	100.00	350.00	900.00
	b. 2 sign. printed. 28.10.1941-26.2.1948.	55.00	140.00	425.00

55	**10 DOLLARS**	GOOD	FINE	XF
	1931-56. Black and red on green unpt. Helmeted warrior's head at l., arms at ctr. Woman harvesting rice at ctr. on back.			
	a. Sign. at r. printed. 1.7.1931.	90.00	275.00	1000.
	b. 2.4.1934-20.9.1940.	80.00	250.00	850.00
	c. 2 sign. printed. 18.11.1941-1.9.1956.	25.00	75.00	250.00
56	**50 DOLLARS**			
	1.7.1931; 2.4.1934; 1.11.1934. Black and brown on m/c unpt. Helmeted warrior's head at l. Woman harvesting rice at r. on back.	350.00	1000.	3500.

57	**100 DOLLARS**	GOOD	FINE	XF
	1934-56. Dk. green and dk. brown on m/c unpt. Britannia seated holding trident w/shield and lion at ctr., arms at upper r. Statue Square, Supreme Court bldg. at ctr. r. on back.			
	a. Sign. at r. printed. 1.5.1934; 12.7.1934.	400.00	1000.	2800.
	b. 28.3.1936-1.11.1939.	325.00	850.00	2000.
	c. 2 sign. printed. 8.12.1941-1.9.1956.	150.00	475.00	1250.

59	**500 DOLLARS**	GOOD	FINE	XF
	1934-52. Black and dk. brown on m/c unpt. Man at l. Boat, harbor view at ctr. r. on back.			
	a. 1.6.1934.	375.00	1000.	2500.
	b. 14.9.1936.	275.00	800.00	2000.
	c. 1.11.1939.	225.00	750.00	1950.
	d. 6.8.1947.	175.00	700.00	1900.
	e. 1.8.1951; 1.11.1952.	125.00	650.00	1850.

CHARTERED BANK

行銀打渣[1]

Cha Ta Yin Hang

Prior to the 1950's was known as The Chartered Bank of India, Australia & China. In the 1980's it became the Standard Bank. Later became the Standard Chartered Bank.

1956-59 ISSUE

#62-67 wmk: Helmeted warrior's head. Printer: W&S.

62	**5 DOLLARS**	VG	VF	UNC
	9.4.1959. Black and dk. green on m/c unpt. Arms at lower l. Chinese junk and sampan at ctr. on back.	20.00	55.00	135.00
63	**10 DOLLARS**			
	6.12.1956. Black and red. Helmeted warrior's head at l. Woman harvesting rice at ctr. on back.	50.00	150.00	550.00

58	**500 DOLLARS**	GOOD	FINE	XF
	1.8.1930. Dk. blue on m/c unpt. Helmeted warrior's head at lower ctr. Sampan at r. on back.	—	Rare	—

64	**10 DOLLARS**	VG	VF	UNC
	9.4.1959. Black and red-violet on red unpt. Arms at l. Bank bldg. at ctr. on back.	15.00	35.00	120.00
65	**100 DOLLARS**			
	6.12.1956. Dk. green and brown on m/c unpt. Britannia seated holding trident w/shield and lion at ctr., arms at upper r. Statue Sqaure, Supreme Court bldg. at ctr. r. on back.	400.00	950.00	2750.
66	**100 DOLLARS**			
	9.4.1959. Dk. green and brown on m/c unpt. Arms at ctr. Harbor view on back.	42.50	125.00	725.00

			VG	VF	UNC
67	**500 DOLLARS**		275.00	750.00	2250.

1.9.1957; 14.12.1959. Black and dk. brown on m/c unpt. Man at l. Boat, harbor view at ctr. r. on back.

CHARTERED MERCANTILE BANK OF INDIA, LONDON & CHINA

印度倫頓中國處匯理銀行

Yin Tu Lun Dun Chung Kuo San Zhu Hui Li Yin Hang

In 1912 this bank became The Mercantile Bank of India.

HONG KONG BRANCH

1858 ISSUE

#82-86 black. Britannia seated w/crowned shield at upper ctr. Uniface. Printer: Batho & Co.

			GOOD	FINE	XF
82 (89)	**5 DOLLARS**	18xx. Lg. blue *FIVE* in unpt. Proof.	—	—	—
83 (90)	**10 DOLLARS**	18xx. Lg. gray *TEN* in Proof.	—	—	—

			GOOD	FINE	XF
84 (91)	**25 DOLLARS**	18xx. Lg. red-orange *TWENTY FIVE* in unpt. Proof.	—	—	—

			GOOD	FINE	XF
85 (92)	**50 DOLLARS**	18xx. Lg. green *FIFTY* in unpt. Proof.	—	—	—

			GOOD	FINE	XF
86 (93)	**100 DOLLARS**	18xx. Lg. red-orange *ONE HUNDRED* in unpt. Proof.	—	—	—

1873-90 ISSUE

#87-91 arms at upper ctr. Printer: PBC.

			GOOD	FINE	XF
87 (82)	**5 DOLLARS**	1873-90. Red *FIVE* in unpt.			
		a. Perforated: *CANCELLED.* 8.1.1873; 1.9.1880; 1.5.1882.	—	Rare	—
		b. 1.12.1888; 1.9.1889; 1.1.1890.	—	Rare	—
88 (83)	**10 DOLLARS**	16.7.1883; 16.12.1887; 16.5.1889.	—	Rare	—
89 (84)	**25 DOLLARS**	1.1.1880; 1.9.1880; 1.1.1890. Proof.	—	Unc	25,000.

			GOOD	FINE	XF
90 (85)	**50 DOLLARS**	1.9.1888; 1.1.1890. Proof.	—	Unc	14,000.
91 (86)	**100 DOLLARS**	18xx; 1.9.1880; 1.9.1880; 1.9.1888. Proof.	—	Unc	14,000.

HONG KONG & SHANGHAI BANKING COMPANY, LIMITED

英商香港上海匯豐銀行

Ying Shang Hsiang K'ang Shang Hai Hui Feng Yin Hang

In the early 1870's, this bank became The Hong Kong and Shanghai Banking Corporation.

1865 ISSUE

			GOOD	FINE	XF
96	**5 DOLLARS**	18xx. Proof.	—	Unc	10,000.
97	**10 DOLLARS**	18xx. Proof.	—	Unc	10,000.

			GOOD	FINE	XF
98	**25 DOLLARS**	18xx. Black. Back orange. Proof.	—	Rare	

99	**50 DOLLARS**	GOOD	FINE	XF
	16.4.1865.	—	Rare	
100	**100 DOLLARS**			
	18xx. Proof.	—	Unc	15,000.
101	**500 DOLLARS**			
	18xx. Proof.	—	Unc	19,500.

HONG KONG & SHANGHAI BANKING CORPORATION

行銀理滙海上港香

Hsiang K'ang Shang Hai Hui Li Yin Hang

Formerly The Hong Kong and Shanghai Banking Company, Limited. These listings are for notes w/*HONG KONG* as city of issue. Similar notes with branch offices in cities of issue such as *AMOY, CHEFOO, FOOCHOW, HANKOW, PEKING, SHANGHAI* and *TIENTSIN* were Chinese branch office issues while *PENANG* and *SINGAPORE* were issued in the Straits Settlements, *BANGKOK* issues were of Thailand and *HIOGO* and *YOKOHAMA* were of Japan. Various early handwritten, partially printed and later fully printed dates and sign. varieties exist.

HONG KONG BRANCH

1867-89 ISSUE
#111-135 arms at upper ctr. Bank arms at ctr. on back. Printer: Ashby & Co.

111	**1 DOLLAR**	GOOD	FINE	XF
	1.10.1872-30.11.1872. Gray frame w/red-orange *$1-* Chinese character-*1$* in unpt. Back lilac.	700.00	1800.	4000.
112	**1 DOLLAR**			
	1.4.1873-1.6.1874. Like #111 but w/lilac unpt.	700.00	1800.	4000.
113	**1 DOLLAR**			
	30.6.1879-1.9.1879. Like #112 but w/red unpt. Back red-orange.	700.00	1800.	4000.

114	**1 DOLLAR**	GOOD	FINE	XF
	1.6.1884-20.9.1888. Face like #113. Back red-orange.	500.00	1500.	3250.
115	**5 DOLLARS**			
	1.1.1867. Lt. green unpt. Back lt. brown.	—	Rare	—
116	**5 DOLLARS**			
	16.7.1877. Green unpt. 198 x 117mm.	—	Rare	—

117	**5 DOLLARS**	GOOD	FINE	XF
	3.1.1882; 1.2.1883; 6.2.1883. Gray frame on green unpt. w/dk. blue *$5 - 5$* at l. and r. Back dk. green.	—	Rare	—
119	**10 DOLLARS**			
	16.7.1877. Blue and black. Back red-orange. Proof.	—	Unc	8000.

121	**25 DOLLARS**	GOOD	FINE	XF
	18xx; 1880; 1884. Black w/blue-black *$25-25$* at l. and r. Arms at upper ctr. Back lt. orange. 201 x 105mm.			
	a. 1.11.1880; 1.12.1884.	—	Rare	
	r. Remainder w/oval handstamp: *CANCELLED-JUL 16 1877.* 18xx.	—	Rare	
	p. Proof. 18xx.			
122	**25 DOLLARS**			
	1.11.1889. Brown w/red *$25 - 25$* at l. and r. Arms at upper ctr. Back red-orange.	—	Rare	—
125	**50 DOLLARS**			
	16.7.1877. Blue and black. Arms at top ctr. Back dk. gray, 203 x 120mm. Remainder w/oval handstamp: *CANCELLED-SEP 4 1877.*	—	Unc	16,000.
127	**50 DOLLARS**			
	1.1.1884. Lt. brown. Like #125.	—	Rare	—
129	**100 DOLLARS**			
	16.7.1877. Blue and black. Arms at top ctr. Back orange. Proof.	—	Unc	17,500.
131	**100 DOLLARS**			
	6.2.1885; 10.2.1888. Red. 196 x 125mm.	—	Rare	—
132	**100 DOLLARS**			
	31.12.1888; 2.1.1890; 1.9.1893. Red w/lg. outlined *100* in blue oval frame in unpt. Back red-orange.	—	Rare	—
134	**500 DOLLARS**			
	18xx. Black w/dk. blue *$500-500$* at l. and r. Back black. Printer: Ashby & Co. Proof.	—	Unc	20,000.
135	**500 DOLLARS**			
	16.7.1877. Blue and black. Back blue. Proof.	—	Rare	—

1884-96 ISSUES
#136-149 printer: BFL.

136	**1 DOLLAR**	GOOD	FINE	XF
	1889-99. Black frame on lt. blue and brown unpt. Back red-orange.			
	a. Handwritten date. 1.11.1889.	250.00	700.00	2000.
	b. 2.1.1890.	200.00	700.00	1600.
	c. Printed dates. 18.11.1895; 2.1.1899.	150.00	400.00	1250.
137	**5 DOLLARS**			
	1.5.1884-1.12.1889. Gray frame on green unpt. w/red-orange *$5-5$* at l. and r. Back red-orange.	—	Rare	—
138	**5 DOLLARS**			
	2.1.1890-1.9.1893. Gray frame on lt. green unpt. Back red.	1500.	3500.	7500.

		GOOD	FINE	XF
139	**5 DOLLARS**			
	1.3.1897; 1.9.1897; 1.3.1898. Gray frame on yellow unpt. Back red-orange.	1250.	2750.	6500.
141	**10 DOLLARS**			
	26.4.1888. Lt. blue. Back orange.	—	Rare	—
142	**10 DOLLARS**			
	1.3.1890, 15.12.1890. Lt. green. Back lt. brown.	—	Rare	—

		GOOD	FINE	XF
143	**10 DOLLARS**			
	1.4.1893-1.3.1898. Blue-gray on pink unpt. Back brown-orange.	2000.	4500.	7500.

		GOOD	FINE	XF
145	**50 DOLLARS**			
	2.1.1890; 1.3.1897; 1.3.1898. Violet on red unpt. Back red-orange.	—	Rare	—

		GOOD	FINE	XF
146	**100 DOLLARS**			
(108)	18xx. Black on brown unpt. Qn. Victoria at l., colony arms at r. Specimen.	—	Rare	—

		GOOD	FINE	XF
147	**100 DOLLARS**			
	1895-96. Red on blue unpt. arms at top ctr.			
	a. 1.1.1895.	—	Rare	—
	b. 1.3.1897.	1500.	4500.	15,000.

		GOOD	FINE	XF
149	**500 DOLLARS**			
	1896-97. Red-orange on lt. green unpt. Back red-orange w/colony arms at ctr.			
	a. Issued note. 1.3.1896.	—	Rare	—
	r. Remainder, perforated: *CANCELLED.* 1897.	—	Unc	19,000.

1900-01 ISSUE
#150-154 printer: BWC.

150   5 DOLLARS
1.12.1900; 1.1.1901. Olive-green on yellow unpt. Lg. curved *FIVE* in
unpt. below arms at upper ctr.

	GOOD	FINE	XF
	750.00	1750.	5500.

151   10 DOLLARS
1.12.1900; 1.1.1901; 1.7.1902. Dk. blue on red unpt. Lg. *TEN* in unpt.
below arms at upper ctr. Back red.

	GOOD	FINE	XF
	700.00	2500.	6000.

152   50 DOLLARS
1.1.1901. Violet on tan unpt. Lg. *FIFTY* below arms at upper ctr. Arms
at upper ctr. under arched bank name. Back red-orange; allegorical
woman reclining at ctr. Specimen.

	GOOD	FINE	XF
	—	Unc 10,000.	

153   100 DOLLARS
1.1.1901. Red on green. Lg. curved *ONE HUNDRED* in unpt. below arms
at upper ctr. Allegorical woman artist seated at ctr. on back. Specimen.

	GOOD	FINE	XF
	—	Unc 12,500.	

154   500 DOLLARS
1.1.1901. Brown on blue unpt. Lg. curved *FIVE HUNDRED* in upt.
under arms at upper ctr. Back red; seated allegorical woman w/3
cherubs at ctr.

	GOOD	FINE	XF
	—	Unc 15,000.	

1904-05 ISSUE
#155-160 printer: BWC.

155 1 DOLLAR

	Good	Fine	XF

1904-06; 1913. Black on blue and yellow unpt. Helmeted woman at l., port scene and arms at lower r. Bank name in cureved line. Back

		Good	Fine	XF
a.	1 printed sign. 1.1.1904; 1.5.1906.	150.00	450.00	1000.
b.	2 printed sign. 1.7.1913.	50.00	150.00	425.00

156 5 DOLLARS

	Good	Fine	XF

1.5.1904; 1.6.1905. Olive on yellow unpt. Arms at upper ctr. Back red-orange.

Good	Fine	XF
650.00	1750.	5250.

157 10 DOLLARS

1.5.1904; 1.1.1905; 1.6.1905. Dk. blue on tan unpt. Similar to #151 but different unpt. design.

Good	Fine	XF
500.00	2000.	6000.

158 50 DOLLARS

1905; 1909. Black, purple and dk. green on lt. green unpt. Bank shield at l., head of Greek male statue at ctr., Great Wall of China vignette at r. Back red-orange and black; old bank bldg. at ctr.

		Good	Fine	XF
a.	1.1.1905.	1000.	4500.	9000.
b.	1.1.1909.	850.00	4000.	8000.

159 100 DOLLARS

	Good	Fine	XF

1.5.1904; 1.1.1906. Red on m/c unpt. Arms at upper ctr. Back brown. 198 x 127mm.

Good	Fine	XF
1500.	5000.	12,500.

160 500 DOLLARS

	Good	Fine	XF

1.5.1904; 1.1.1905; 1.6.1907. Brown on m/c unpt. Arms at upper ctr. Back dk. red like #154.

Good	Fine	XF
2250.	7000.	17,500.

1905-15 ISSUE
#161-165 printer: W&S.

161 5 DOLLARS

	Good	Fine	XF

1.1.1906; 1.1.1909. Olive and brown on orange unpt. Water carrier and sedan bearers at l., ship at r. Back red and black.

Good	Fine	XF
500.00	1500.	4000.

162 10 DOLLARS

1.1.1909. Black and dk. blue on lt. blue and pink unpt. Back lt. red-brown and black. Waterfront at l., horseman and walkers at r., ships and houses in background. Old bank bldg. at ctr. on back.

Good	Fine	XF
500.00	1500.	4000.

163 100 DOLLARS

	Good	Fine	XF

1906; 1909. Orange and black on lt. blue unpt. Bank shield at upper l., Chinese laborers w/baskets at l. and r. Back red-brown and black; old bank bldg. at ctr.

		Good	Fine	XF
a.	Issued note. 1.1.1909.	1250.	4500.	10,000.
s.	Specimen. 1.1.1906.	—	Unc	13,500.

164 500 DOLLARS

	GOOD	FINE	XF
1909; 1912. Black and brown on lt. blue unpt. Farmer w/ox at l., arms at ctr., Botanic Garden at r. Old bank bldg. at ctr. on back.			
a. 1.1.1909.	2500.	6000.	14,500.
b. 1.1.1912.	2500.	6000.	14,500.

165 500 DOLLARS

1.1.1915. Deep brown and black on lt. blue unpt. Like #164. Back red-violet and black.	2500.	6000.	14,500.

1912-21 ISSUE
#166-170 printer: W&S.

166 5 DOLLARS

	GOOD	FINE	XF
1.7.1916; 1.1.1921; 1.1.1923; 1.5.1923. Like #161 but olive and brown back.	550.00	1400.	4000.

167 10 DOLLARS

	GOOD	FINE	XF
1.7.1913; 1.1.1921; 1.1.1923. Blue on red unpt. Like #162 but back olive-green and dk. brown.	275.00	900.00	2500.

168 50 DOLLARS

	GOOD	FINE	XF
1.1.1921; 1.1.1923. Like #158 but back green and black.	2000.	3500.	8000.

169 100 DOLLARS

	GOOD	FINE	XF
1912-23. Orange and black on lt. blue unpt. Like #163 but back olive and brown.			
a. 1.1.1912.	1250.	5000.	12,000.
b. 1.1.1921; 1.1.1923.	1000.	4500.	10,000.

170 500 DOLLARS

1.1.1921; 1.7.1925. Like #165, but back olive-green and olive-brown.	2000.	6000.	12,500.

1923 ISSUE
#171-188 printer: BWC.

171 1 DOLLAR

	VG	VF	UNC
1.1.1923; 1.1.1925. Black on blue and yellow unpt. Similar to #155 but bank name in straight line. Maroon and brown back.	45.00	150.00	550.00

1926-27 ISSUE
#173-177 old bank bldg. below angel playing trumpet at ctr. on back.

172 1 DOLLAR

	VG	VF	UNC
1926-35. Blue on yellow and lt. green unpt. Helmeted woman at l. Back purple.			
a. 1.1.1926.	60.00	200.00	700.00
b. 1.1.1929.	35.00	110.00	300.00
c. 1.6.1935.	20.00	50.00	225.00

173 **5 DOLLARS**
1927-46. Dk. brown on m/c unpt. Woman seated at r. *HONGKONG* at date not divided. W/4 serial # on back.

		VG	VF	UNC
a.	1 printed sign. 1.10.1927; 1.1.1929; 1.9.1930.	70.00	225.00	875.00
b.	1.1.1930-1.1.1938.	40.00	125.00	650.00
c.	2 printed sign. w/additional vertical serial # on face and back. 1.4.1940; 1.4.1941.	32.50	125.00	300.00
d.	W/o serial # on back. 1.4.1941.	7.00	20.00	100.00
e.	30.3.1946.	5.00	15.00	70.00

174 **10 DOLLARS**
1927-30. Dk. blue on m/c unpt. Woman holding sheaf of grain at l., *HONGKONG* at date not divided. W/4 serial # on back.

a.	1.10.1927.	100.00	250.00	1250.
b.	1.1.1929; 1.1.1930.	65.00	200.00	850.00
c.	1.9.1930.	100.00	275.00	1400.

175 **50 DOLLARS**
1927-1937. Dk. green on m/c unpt. Woman standing on winged wheel w/vines and fruit at l., arms at top ctr.

		VG	VF	UNC
a.	1.10.1927.	300.00	850.00	3500.
b.	1.10.1930.	250.00	700.00	2600.
c.	1.1.1934.	200.00	500.00	2250.
d.	"Duress" note issued during Japanese occupation w/serial #B350,001 to B550,000. 1934-37.	250.00	700.00	2600.

176 **100 DOLLARS**
1927-59. Red. Woman seated w/book at l., arms at upper ctr.

a.	1 printed sign. 1.10.1927; 1.9.1930; 2.1.1933.	175.00	650.00	2250.
b.	2.1.1934; 1.1.1936.	135.00	400.00	1900.
c.	1.7.1937.	120.00	350.00	1700.
d.	"Duress" note issued during Japanese occupation w/serial #B485,001 to B650,000. 1934-37.	135.00	400.00	1900.
e.	1.4.1941-1.3.1955.	100.00	300.00	950.00
f.	5.9.1956; 25.2.1958; 24.9.1958.	90.00	275.00	850.00
g.	4.2.1959.	110.00	350.00	1050.

177 **500 DOLLARS**
1927; 1930. Dk. brown on purple and m/c unpt. Woman seated holding tablet at r. Back purple and yellow-brown.

		VG	VF	UNC
a.	1.10.1927.	800.00	2500.	8500.
b.	1.7.1930.	650.00	2000.	6500.
c.	"Duress" note issued during Japanese occupation w/serial #C126,001 to C300,000. 1.7.1930.	650.00	2000.	6500.

1932-35 ISSUE

178 **10 DOLLARS**
1932-48. Dk. green on m/c unpt. Like #174.

		VG	VF	UNC
a.	1 printed sign. W/4 serial # on back. 1.1.1932-1.1.1938.	8.50	100.00	500.00
b.	W/ additional small serial # printed vertically on face and back. 1.4.1941.	35.00	125.00	—
c.	2 printed sign. W/o serial # on back. 1.4.1941.	6.00	25.00	100.00
d.	30.3.1946; 31.3.1947; 1.4.1941.	5.00	20.00	90.00

179 **500 DOLLARS**
1935-69. Brown and blue. Arms at top ctr., Sir T. Jackson at r. Back blue; allegorical female head at l., bank bldg. at ctr.

		VG	VF	UNC
a.	Handsigned. 1.6.1935-1.7.1937.	250.00	700.00	2850.
b.	Printed sign. 1.4.1941-1.8.1952.	170.00	275.00	850.00
c.	11.7.1960-1.8.1966.	FV	250.00	750.00
d.	31.7.1967.	FV	225.00	650.00
e.	11.2.1968; 27.3.1969.	FV	135.00	350.00

1949 ISSUE

179A **10 DOLLARS**
(181A) 1949-59. Dk. green on m/c unpt. Like #178 but w/*HONG KONG* at date divided.

a.	1.7.1949; 31.12.1953.	10.00	25.00	90.00
b.	1.7.1954-14.1.1958.	6.00	15.00	75.00
c.	26.3.1958.	15.00	60.00	200.00
d.	14.9.1958; 24.9.1958.	6.00	15.00	75.00
e.	4.2.1959.	10.00	25.00	85.00

1954 ISSUE

180	5 DOLLARS	VG	VF	UNC
	1954-59. Brown. Like #173 but w/*HONG KONG* at date divided.			
	a. 1.7.1954-7.8.1958.	3.00	12.00	65.00
	b. 4.2.1959.	8.00	20.00	85.00

1959 ISSUE

181 (C21)	5 DOLLARS			
	1959-75. Brown. Similar to #173 and 180 but smaller size. New bank bldg. at ctr. on back.			
	a. Sign. titles: *CHIEF ACCOUNTANT* and *CHIEF MANAGER*. 2.5.1959-29.6.1960.	1.75	5.00	14.00
	b. 1.5.1963.	5.50	14.00	140.00
	c. 1.5.1964-27.3.1969.	1.50	4.00	10.00
	d. Sign. titles: *CHIEF ACCOUNTANT* and *GENERAL MANAGER*. 1.4.1970-18.3.1971.	.60	1.35	6.00
	e. 13.3.1972; 31.10.1972.	.50	1.25	3.50
	f. Sm. serial #. 31.10.1973; 31.3.1975.	FV	1.00	2.00

182	10 DOLLARS			
	1959-83. Dk. green on m/c unpt. Woman w/sheaf of grain at upper l., arms below. Back similar to #184.			
	a. Sign. titles: *CHIEF ACCOUNTANT* and *CHIEF MANAGER*. 21.5.1959-1.9.1962.			
	b. 1.5.1963; 1.9.1963.	1.85	5.50	35.00
	c. 1.5.1964; 1.9.1964.	FV	2.75	14.00
	d. 1.10.1964.	4.00	10.00	100.00
	e. 1.2.1965; 1.8.1966; 31.7.1967.	FV	2.50	12.50
	f. 20.3.1968; 23.11.1968; 27.3.1969; 18.3.1971.	FV	2.00	7.00
	g. Sign. titles: *CHIEF ACCOUNTANT* and *GENERAL MANAGER*. 1.4.1970-31.3.1977.	FV	1.75	6.00
	h. Sign. titles: *CHIEF ACCOUNTANT* and *EXECUTIVE DIRECTOR*. 31.3.1978; 31.3.1979.	FV	FV	5.00
	i. Sign. titles: *CHIEF ACCOUNTANT* and *GENERAL MANAGER*. 31.3.1980; 31.3.1981.	FV	FV	3.50
	j. Sign. titles: *MANAGER* and *GENERAL MANAGER*. 31.3.1982; 31.3.1983.	FV	FV	3.00

183	100 DOLLARS			
	1959-72. Red on m/c unpt. Woman seated at l. w/open book, arms at upper ctr. Wmk: Helmeted warrior's head and denomination.			
	a. Sign. titles: *CHIEF ACCOUNTANT* and *CHIEF MANAGER*. 21.8.1959-1.10.1964.	18.00	40.00	125.00
	b. 1.2.1965-27.3.1969.	14.00	30.00	90.00
	c. Sign. titles: *CHIEF ACCOUNTANT* and *GENERAL MANAGER*. 1.4.1970; 18.3.1971; 13.3.1972.	14.00	30.00	90.00

MERCANTILE BANK OF INDIA, LIMITED

行銀利有港香

Hsiang K'ang Yu Li Yin Hang

Formerly The Chartered Mercantile Bank of India, London and China. In 1959 it became The Mercantile Bank Limited. Various date and sign. varieties. These listings are for notes w/*HONG KONG* as city of issue. Similar notes w/*SHANGHAI* were Chinese branch office issue.

HONG KONG BRANCH

1912 ISSUE

#235-241 printer: W&S.

#235-239 Mercury at ctr. on back.

235	5 DOLLARS	GOOD	FINE	XF
	1912-41. Olive on tan unpt. Boats at ctr. w/houses and towers in background. Back dk. red and black.			
	a. W/2 serial # on back. 1.3.1912.	1000.	2000.	4750.
	b. As a. 1.5.1924; 1.1.1930.	750.00	1600.	4250.
	c. W/4 serial # on back. 1.7.1936; 1.12.1937.	675.00	1450.	2850.
	d. 2 serial # on back. 29.11.1941.	600.00	1300.	3500.

236	10 DOLLARS	GOOD	FINE	XF
	1912-41. Red-brown on lt. yellow-green unpt. Houses and mountains near water, bridge at ctr. Back green and black.			
	a. W/2 serial # on back. 1.3.1912.	800.00	2000.	5000.
	b. As a. 1.1.1930.	500.00	1200.	4000.
	c. W/4 serial # on back. 1.7.1936.	550.00	1200.	4000.
	d. As c. 1.12.1937.	750.00	1350.	4700.
	e. 2 serial # on back. 29.11.1941.	275.00	650.00	2000.

237	25 DOLLARS	GOOD	FINE	XF
	1.3.1912. Blue on yellow unpt. River view w/boats and houses at l.	3000.	8000.	22,000.

238	50 DOLLARS	GOOD	FINE	XF
	1.3.1912; 1.5.1924; 1.1.1930. Brown and black. Ships at ctr., mountains in background.	1800.	3750.	6250.

239	100 DOLLARS	GOOD	FINE	XF
	1912-56. Red-violet on orange and lt. blue unpt. Houses below mountains at water's edge at ctr.			
	a. 1.3.1912.	1500.	4000.	10,000.
	b. 1.5.1924; 1.1.1930.	1200.	3000.	8000.
	c. W/4 serial # on back. 1.7.1936.	1200.	3000.	8000.
	d. W/2 serial # on back. 24.8.1948; 28.3.1950; 10.3.1953; 26.10.1954; 4.10.1955; 2.1.1956.	375.00	950.00	2850.

1935 ISSUE

240	50 DOLLARS	GOOD	FINE	XF
	1935-41. Dk. brown on m/c unpt. Male bust at l. and as wmk. Chinese mansion on back.			
	a. W/2 serial # on back. 1.7.1935.	450.00	1300.	3750.
	b. W/4 serial # on back. 1.12.1937.	750.00	2200.	7000.
	c. W/2 serial # on back. 29.11.1941.	600.00	1700.	5000.

1948 ISSUE

241	500 DOLLARS	GOOD	FINE	XF
	24.8.1948. Dk. blue on yellow and lt. blue unpt. Mercury at r. Gateway on back. Handsigned. Wmk: 500.	—	Rare	—

MERCANTILE BANK LIMITED

行銀利有港香

Hsiang K'ang Yu Li Yin Hang

Formerly The Mercantile Bank of India Limited. In 1978 this bank was absorbed by the Hong Kong & Shanghai Banking Corp. and its note issuing right ended.

1958-60 ISSUE
#242-243 printer: W&S.

242	100 DOLLARS	VG	VF	UNC
	1958-60. Brown-violet on orange and lt. blue unpt. Similar to #239 but w/new bank name.			
	a. 3.1.1958; 12.8.1958; 26.5.1959.	375.00	1250.	3500.
	b. 20.9.1960; 6.12.1960.	325.00	1150.	3000.

243	500 DOLLARS	VG	VF	UNC
	26.5.1959. Blue on yellow and lt. blue unpt. Similar to #241 w/new bank name. Printed sign. Wmk: 500.	—	Rare	—

NATIONAL BANK OF CHINA LIMITED

行銀理滙華中港香

Hsiang K'ang Chung Hua Hui Li Yin Hang

A British bank based in Hong Kong also having a branch in Shanghai.

HONG KONG BRANCH

1892 ISSUE
#247-251 black text. Arms at upper ctr. Junks over harbor view at ctr. on back. Various dates between 1892-1911. Printer: W&S.

247	5 DOLLARS	GOOD	FINE	XF
	1894. Deep red on yellow and orange unpt. Back red-orange.			
	a. Issued note w/printed date. 2.5.1894.	3000.	9000.	—
	b. Partially printed date, 2 handwritten sign. 189x.	—	Rare	—
	r1. Remainder w/partially printed date, printed sign. at r., punched holed and perforated: CANCELLED. 189x.	—	Rare	—
	r2. Remainder w/o sign. 189x.	—	Rare	—
	s. Salesman's sample punched hole cancelled, w/W&S printer's seal, ovpt: SPECIMEN.	—	Rare	—

248	10 DOLLARS			
	2.5.1894. Green on lt. green and yellow unpt. Remainder.	3500.	11,000.	—

249	50 DOLLARS	GOOD	FINE	XF
	189x. Red on yellow unpt. Back brown. Unsigned remainder punch holed and perforated: CANCELLED.	—	Unc	22,000.
250	100 DOLLARS			
	189x. Purple on lilac and yellow unpt. Unsigned remainder punched holed and perforated: CANCELLED.	—	Unc	17,000.
251	500 DOLLARS			
	189x. Brown on gold and yellow unpt. Back brown. Unsigned remainder punched holed and perforated: CANCELLED.	—	Unc	19,500.

ORIENTAL BANK CORPORATION

行銀理滙藩東
Tung Fan Hui Li Yin Hang

Founded about 1845, it later became The Oriental Banking Corporation and was a moderately important
bank in the 1870's and 1880's. All notes have arms at top ctr.

VICTORIA, HONG KONG BRANCH

1860'S ISSUE
#260, 263 and 264 royal crowned shield between lion and unicorn at upper ctr. Printer: PBC.

260 5 DOLLARS
18xx. Black. Proof handstamped: *SPECIMEN.* — — —

		GOOD	FINE	XF
263	**50 DOLLARS**			
	18xx. Black. Proof handstamped: *SPECIMEN.*	—	—	—

		GOOD	FINE	XF
264	**100 DOLLARS**			
	18xx. Black. Proof handstamped: *SPECIMEN.*	—	—	—

HONG KONG BRANCH

1866 ISSUE
#267-270 crowned shield between lion and unicorn at upper ctr. Printer: PBC.

		GOOD	FINE	XF
267	**5 DOLLARS**			
	1866-82.			
	a. Issued note. 7.3.1866.	8000.	20,000.	—
	b. Issued note. 7.3.1879.	—	Rare	—
	s. Specimen. 4.9.1866; 1.9.1882.	—	Rare	—

		GOOD	FINE	XF
268	**25 DOLLARS**			
	7.5.1866; 7.5.1879/1866. Orange on yellow unpt.	—	Rare	—
269	**50 DOLLARS**			
	7.3.1866; 1.5.1883. Black. Pro of.	—	Rare	—

		GOOD	FINE	XF
270	**100 DOLLARS**			
	7.3.1866; 1.5.1883. Proof.	—	Rare	—

GOVERNMENT OF HONG KONG

1935 ISSUE
#311-312 printer: BWC.

府政港香
Hsiang K'ang Cheng Fu

		VG	VF	UNC
311	**1 DOLLAR**			
	ND (1935). Purple on m/c unpt. Portr. Kg. George V at r.	25.00	300.00	1000.

1936 ISSUE

		VG	VF	UNC
312	**1 DOLLAR**			
	ND (1936). Purple on m/c unpt. Portr. Kg. George VI at r.	7.00	20.00	125.00

1940-41 ISSUES

		VG	VF	UNC
313	**1 CENT**			
	ND (1941). Brown on ochre unpt. Back red.			
	a. W/o serial # prefix.	.25	1.50	5.00
	b. Prefix A.	.25	1.00	3.00
	c. Prefix B.	.25	.50	2.00

		VG	VF	UNC
314	**5 CENTS**			
	ND (1941). Green on pale orange unpt. Back violet.	3.00	20.00	50.00
315	**10 CENTS**			
	ND (1941). Red on yellow unpt. Back blue.			
	a. W/o serial # prefix.	.50	3.00	18.00
	b. Prefix A.	.35	2.50	15.00
316	**1 DOLLAR**			
	ND (1940-41). Dk. blue on m/c unpt. Portr. Kg. George VI at r. Printer: BWC.	8.00	20.00	75.00

1941 EMERGENCY ISSUE

		VG	VF	UNC
317	**1 DOLLAR ON 5 YUAN**			
	ND (Dec. 1941 - old date 1941). Dk. blue on m/c unpt. Red ovpt. on Bank of China #93.	35.00	100.00	275.00

1945 EMERGENCY ISSUE

#318-320 prepared by the British Military Administration to replace the "duress" notes of the Hong Kong and Shanghai Banking Corporation in circulation immediately following the Japanese surrender. (Not issued).

		VG	VF	UNC
318	**1 DOLLAR ON 1000 YEN**			
	ND. Red. W/ or w/o yellow unpt. Temple at l., man at r. Plate includes all legends and lineout bar.	70.00	250.00	500.00

		VG	VF	UNC
319	**5 DOLLARS ON 1000 YUAN**			
	ND (1945 - old date 1944). blue. Ovpt. on Central Reserve Bank of China #J32.	150.00	400.00	900.00

		VG	VF	UNC
320	**10 DOLLARS ON 5000 YUAN**			
	ND (1945 - old date 1945). gray. Ovpt. on Central Reserve Bank of China #J42.	150.00	450.00	1000.

1945-49 ISSUE

#321-324 Portr. Kg. George VI at r.
#321-323 uniface.

		VG	VF	UNC
321	**1 CENT**			
	ND (1945). Brown on lt. blue unpt.	.15	.30	1.00
322	**5 CENTS**			
	ND (1945). Green on lilac unpt.	.35	3.00	25.00

		VG	VF	UNC
323	**10 CENTS**			
	ND (1945). Red on grayish unpt.	.25	1.00	12.50

		VG	VF	UNC
324	**1 DOLLAR**			
	1949; 1952. Dk. green on m/c unpt. Printer: BWC.			
	a. Sign. C.G. Follows. 9.4.1949.	8.00	20.00	65.00
	b. Sign. A.G. Clark. 1.1.1952.	9.00	22.50	80.00

1952 ISSUE

328	1 DOLLAR		VG	VF	UNC
	1952-59. Dk. green on m/c unpt. Portr. Qn. Elizabeth II at r. Printer: BWC.				
	a. 1.7.1952; 1.7.1954; 1.7.1955.		.75	3.00	18.50
	b. 1.6.1956-1.7.1959.		.35	2.00	15.00

The Hungarian Republic, located in central Europe, has an area of 35,919 sq. mi. (93,030 sq. km.) and a population of 10.6 million. Capital: Budapest. The economy is based on agriculture, bauxite and a rapidly expanding industrial sector. Machinery, chemicals, iron and steel, and fruits and vegetables are exported.

The ancient kingdom of Hungary, founded by the Magyars in the 9th century, achieved its greatest extension in the mid-14th century when its dominions touched the Baltic, Black and Mediterranean Seas. After suffering repeated Turkish invasions, Hungary accepted Habsburg rule to escape Turkish occupation, regaining independence in 1867 with the Emperor of Austria as king of a dual Austro- Hungarian Empire. Sharing the defeat of the Central Powers in World War I, Hungary lost the greater part of its territory and population and underwent a period of drastic political revision. The short-lived republic of 1918 was followed by a chaotic interval of communist rule, 1919, and the restoration of the monarchy in 1920 with Admiral Horthy as regent of a kingdom without a king. Although a German ally in World War II, Hungary was occupied by German troops who imposed a pro-Nazi dictatorship, 1944. Soviet armies drove out the Germans in 1945 and assisted the communist minority in seizing power. A revised constitution published on Aug. 20, 1949, had established Hungary as a "People's Republic" of the Soviet type, but it is once again a republic as of Oct. 23, 1989.

RULERS:
Austrian to 1918

MONETARY SYSTEM:
1 Korona = 100 Fillér to 1926
1 Pengö = 100 Fillér to 1946
1 Milpengö = 1 Million Pengö
1 B(illió) Pengö = 1 Billion Pengö
1 Adopengö = 1 Tax Pengö
1 Forint = 100 Fillér 1946-
1 Forint (florin) = 60 Krajczar

DENOMINATIONS

Egy = 1	Ötven = 50
Két = 2	Száz = 100
Öt = 5	Ezer = 1000
Tiz = 10	Millió = Million
Húsz = 20	Milliárd = 1,000 Million
Huszonöt = 25	

These words used separately or in combination give denomination.

AUSTRO-HUNGARIAN EMPIRE

MAGYAR KIRÁLY KÖLCSÖNPÉNZTÁR-JEGY

ROYAL HUNGARIAN WAR LOAN BANK

1914 ISSUE

1	250 KORONA	VG	VF	UNC
	27.9.1914. Specimen perforated: *MINTA*.	—	—	750.00

556 HUNGARY

2	**2000 KORONA**	VG	VF	UNC
	27.9.1914. Portr. Empress Zita at r. Specimen perforated: *MINTA*.	—	—	750.00

3	**10,000 KORONA**	VG	VF	UNC
	27.9.1914. Specimen perforated: *MINTA*.	—	—	750.00

AZ OSZTRÁK-MAGYAR BANK PÉNZTÁRJEGYE

AUSTRO-HUNGARIAN BANK

#4-9, non-interest bearing Treasury notes of Hungarian branches. Text in Hungarian, various dates (ca.1918) and place names handstamped.

KOLOZSVAR BRANCH

1918 ISSUE

4	**1000 KORONA** 1918.	500.00	1000.	2000.
5	**5000 KORONA** 1918.	500.00	1000.	2000.
6	**10,000 KORONA** 1918.	500.00	1000.	2000.

SZATMÁR-NEMETI BRANCH

1918 ISSUE

7	**1000 KORONA** 29.11.1918.	550.00	1100.	2200.
8	**5000 KORONA** 29.11.1918.	550.00	1100.	2200.
9	**10,000 KORONA** 29.11.1918.	550.00	1100.	2200.

1919 ISSUE
#10-16, notes printed in Budapest in 1919 w/variations from the regular notes printed in Austria. Bilingual text.

10	**1 KORONA**	VG	VF	UNC
	1.12.1916. (1919). Red. Helmeted warrior's head at ctr. Woman's head at upper l. and r. on back. Like Austria #20. Series # above 7000. (Communist regime in Budapest).	2.50	5.00	12.50
11	**2 KORONA** 1.3.1917 (1919). Red. Like Austria #21 but series # above 7000.			
	a. Issued note.	1.50	4.00	10.00
	x. Error: w/*Genenalsekretar*.	5.00	15.00	35.00

12	**25 KORONA**	VG	VF	UNC
	27.10.1918 (1919). Blue on lt. brown unpt., uniface. Like Austria #23 but series # above 3000. 2 serial # varieties. (Soviet Republic of Bela Kun. 21.3.1919-4.8.1919).	3.00	7.50	17.50
13	**25 KORONA**	VG	VF	UNC
	27.10.1918 (1919). Blue on lt. brown unpt. Like #12 but wavy lines on back. Series #1001-1999. 3 serial # varieties.	3.50	9.00	20.00

14	**200 KORONA**			
	27.10.1918 (1919). Green on red-brown unpt. Like Austria #24 but series A up to 2000. (People's Republic, 16.11.1918-21.3.1919).	4.00	10.00	22.50

15	200 KORONA	VG	VF	UNC
	27.10.1918 (1919). Green on red-brown unpt., uniface. Like #14 but series A above 2000. (Soviet Republic of Bela Kun 21.3.1919-4.8.1919).	3.00	7.50	17.50
16	200 KORONA			
	27.10.1918 (1919). Green on red-brown unpt. Like #15 but wavy lines on back. Series B1001-B1999.	3.00	7.50	17.50

AZ OSZTRÁK-MAGYAR BANK - BUDAPESTI FÖINTÉZETE
TREASURY NOTE OF THE BUDAPEST HEAD OFFICE
1918 ISSUE

17	200 KORONA	VG	VF	UNC
	3.11.1918. Hungarian legends on face. Specimens only.	—	350.00	750.00

1920 PROVISIONAL ISSUE

#18-32 ovpt: *MAGYARORSZAG* and Hungarian coat of arms. Issued as state notes w/seal upright or turned to l. Only the 1000 and 10,000 Korona w/seal turned to r. are rare.

NOTE: #18-32 are also found with additional South Slavonian or Romanian handstamps. Notes with forged MAGYARORSZAG ovpt. were given a black, thick-ruled cross (18#-23, 25,27-32) w/handstamp: *Stempel wurde von ...als unecht befunden.*

NOTE: The numerous local or military ovpt. and cancellations are beyond the scope of this catalog.

18	10 KORONA			
	ND (1920 - old date 2.1.1904). Ovpt. on Austria #9.	5.00	12.00	30.00

19	10 KORONA	VG	VF	UNC
	ND (1920 - old date 2.1.1915). Ovpt. on Austria #19.	1.00	2.00	5.00

20	20 KORONA	VG	VF	UNC
	ND (1920 - old date 2.1.1913). Ovpt. on Austria #13.	1.00	2.00	5.00

21	20 KORONA	VG	VF	UNC
	ND (1920 - old date 2.1.1913). Ovpt. on Austria #14. W/II. Auflage. (2nd issue).	1.00	—	5.00
22	25 KORONA			
	ND (1920 - old date 27.10.1918). Ovpt. on Austria #23. Series up to 3000.	5.00	15.00	40.00

23	25 KORONA	VG	VF	UNC
	ND (1920 - old date 27.10.1918). Series above 3000.	6.00	20.00	50.00
24	50 KORONA			
	ND (1920 - old date 2.1.1902). Ovpt. on Austria #6.	45.00	120.00	300.00
25	50 KORONA			
	ND (1920 - old date 2.1.1914). Ovpt. on Austria #15.	1.00	2.00	5.00

26	100 KORONA	VG	VF	UNC
	ND (1920 - old date 2.1.1910). Ovpt. on Austria #11.	75.00	225.00	600.00
27	100 KORONA			
	ND (1920 - old date 2.1.1912). Ovpt. on Austria #12.	1.00	2.00	4.00

28	200 KORONA	VG	VF	UNC
	ND (1920 - old date 27.10.1918). Ovpt. on Austria #24. Series A.			
	a. Wavy lines on back.	30.00	75.00	175.00
	b. W/o wavy lines on back.	30.00	75.00	175.00
29	200 KORONA			
	ND (1920 - old date 27.10.1918). Ovpt. on Austria #24. Series B.	40.00	100.00	250.00
30	200 KORONA			
	ND (1920 - old date 27.10.1918). 6 digit serial #.	40.00	100.00	250.00
31	1000 KORONA			
	ND (1920 - old date 2.1.1902). Ovpt. on Austria #8.	1.50	4.00	10.00
32	10,000 KORONA			
	ND (1920 - old date 2.11.1918). Ovpt. on Austria #25.	5.00	15.00	40.00

REGENCY

MAGYAR POSTATAKARÉKPÉNZTÁR

HUNGARIAN POST OFFICE SAVINGS BANK

1919 FIRST ISSUE
#38-39, color trials also exist.

			VG	VF	UNC
33	5 KORONA				
	1.5.1919. Specimen. (1 known).		—	—	—
34	5 KORONA				
	15.5.1919. Blue on green unpt. Man sowing at r. *AZ OSZTRAK-MAGYAR BANK BANKJEGYEIRE* on face.		1.00	2.50	7.50

			VG	VF	UNC
35	5 KORONA				
	15.5.1919. Blue on green unpt. Like #34. *MAS TORVENYES PENZNEMEKRE* on face.		1.00	2.50	7.50
36	10 KORONA				
	15.5.1919. Specimens.				

			VG	VF	UNC
37	10 KORONA				
	15.7.1919. Blue on green-blue unpt. Woman wearing Phrygian cap at l.		1.50	8.00	30.00

			VG	VF	UNC
38	20 KORONA				
	15.7.1919. Dk. blue. Woman w/2 small children at ctr. 2 serial # varieties.				
	a. Olive unpt.		2.00	10.00	35.00
	b. Yellow unpt.		2.00	10.00	35.00

			VG	VF	UNC
39	100 KORONA				
	15.7.1919. Blue and olive. Man seated w/sword at ctr. (Not issued.) (2 known.)		—	—	—

			VG	VF	UNC
39A	1000 KORONA				
	15.7.1919. Specimen.		—	—	—

1919 SECOND ISSUE

40	5 KORONA				
	9.8.1919. Specimen. (1 known.)		—	—	—

			VG	VF	UNC
41	10 KORONA				
	9.8.1919. Gray-blue on brown unpt. Similar to #37, but woman w/o cap. 3 serial # varieties.		3.00	12.50	60.00

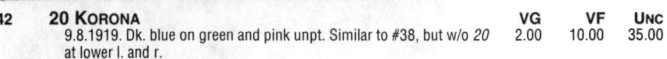

42	**20 KORONA** 9.8.1919. Dk. blue on green and pink unpt. Similar to #38, but w/o *20* at lower l. and r.	**VG** 2.00	**VF** 10.00	**UNC** 35.00

1919 THIRD ISSUE

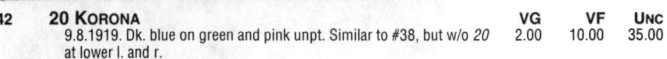

43	**20 FILLÉR** 2.10.1920. Brown. Arms at upper ctr. Back gray.	**VG** .25	**VF** 1.00	**UNC** 3.00
44	**50 FILLÉR** 2.10.1920. Blue. Arms at l. Back purple.	.25	1.00	3.00

1920 ISSUE

45	**10 MILLION KORONA** 1.5.1921. Specimen.	—	—	—

MAGYAR NEMZETI BANK

1919 FIRST ISSUE

46	**50 KORONA** 15.3.1919.	—	—	—
47	**1000 KORONA** 15.3.1919.	—	—	—

1919 SECOND ISSUE

48	**25 KORONA** 2.5.1919. (1 known.)	—	—	—

1919 THIRD ISSUE

49	**2 KORONA** 2.6.1919.	—	—	—
50	**20 KORONA** 2.6.1919.	—	—	—

1919 FOURTH ISSUE

51	**10 KORONA** 1.8.1919.	—	—	—
52	**100 KORONA** 15.8.1919. (2 known.)	—	—	—
53	**1000 KORONA** 15.8.1919.	—	—	—

PÉNZÜGYMINISZTÉRIUM

STATE NOTES OF THE MINISTRY OF FINANCE

1920 FIRST ISSUE
#54-56 specimens only.

54	**50 FILLÉR** 1920. Circular, 30mm.	—	—	—
55	**1 KORONA** 1920. Circular, 35mm.	—	—	—
56	**2 KORONA** 1920. Circular, 40mm.	—	—	—

1920 SECOND ISSUE
#62-63, 65-68 printer: OFZ.

57	**1 KORONA** 1.1.1920. Blue. Woman at r. Serial # red or dk. red. Arms at r. on back.	**VG** .20	**VF** .50	**UNC** 2.50

58	**2 KORONA** 1.1.1920. Red on lt. brown unpt. Arms at l., reaping farmer at r. 2 serial # varieties.	**VG** .20	**VF** .50	**UNC** 2.50
59	**5 KORONA** 1.1.1920. Specimen. Circular, 44mm.	—	—	—

60	**10 KORONA** 1.1.1920. Brown on blue-green unpt. Chain bridge, Budapest at upper ctr. Serial # varieties.	**VG** .20	**VF** .50	**UNC** 2.50

61	**20 KORONA** 1.1.1920. Black on green and pale orange unpt. Mátyás Church (Budapest) at r. 2 serial # varieties.	**VG** .20	**VF** .50	**UNC** 2.50

62	**50 KORONA** 1.1.1920. Dk. brown on brown and tan unpt. Prince F. Rákóczi at r.	**VG** .25	**VF** 1.00	**UNC** 5.00

63	**100 KORONA** 1.1.1920. Brown on lt. brown unpt. Kg. Mátyas at r. 155 x 100mm.	**VG** .25	**VF** 1.00	**UNC** 5.00
64	**100 KORONA** 1.1.1920. 119 x 70mm. Specimen perforated: *MINTA.*	—	—	—
65	**500 KORONA** 1.1.1920. Dk. green on brown-olive unpt. Prince Arpad wearing helmet.	.50	2.00	9.50

66 1000 KORONA
1.1.1920. Dk. brown on brown unpt. St. Stephan at r.

	VG	VF	UNC
a. Issued note.	1.00	3.00	12.00
s. Specimen perforated: *MINTA*.	—	—	50.00

67 5000 KORONA
1.1.1920. Dk. brown on green and gray unpt. "Patrona Hungariae" at r.

VG	VF	UNC
1.50	5.00	25.00

68 10,000 KORONA
1.1.1920. Dk. green and violet. "Patrona Hungariae" at r.

VG	VF	UNC
2.00	8.00	30.00

1922 ISSUE

69 25,000 KORONA
15.8.1922. Violet. "Patrona Hungariae" at r.

	VG	VF	UNC
a. Paper w/o silk thread.	7.00	17.50	60.00
b. Paper w/silk thread.	15.00	50.00	110.00
s. As a. perforated: *MINTA*.	—	—	100.00

70 50,000 KORONA
15.8.1922. Proof.

	VG	VF	UNC
	—	—	—

1923 FIRST ISSUE

71 50,000 KORONA
1.5.1923. Red. Young man at r.

	VG	VF	UNC
a. Imprint: Orell Füssli.	6.00	20.00	60.00
b. W/o imprint.	8.00	25.00	75.00

72 100,000 KORONA
1.5.1923. Dk. blue. Young man at r.

	VG	VF	UNC
a. Imprint: Orell Füssli.	20.00	50.00	150.00
b. Imprint: Magyar Pénzjegynyomda Rt.	25.00	65.00	175.00
s. As a. perforated: *MINTA*.	—	—	125.00

1923 SECOND ISSUE

NOTE: Treasury certificates of the State Note Issuing Office (5, 10, 50 and 100 million Korona w/date 14.7.1923) are also reputed to have been printed, but up to now none of these notes have been confirmed.

73 100 KORONA
1.7.1923. Brown. Kg. Mátyas wearing a wreath at r.

	VG	VF	UNC
a. Imprint: Magyar Pénzjegynyomda Rt.	.25	1.00	3.00
b. W/o imprint.	.25	1.00	3.00

74 500 KORONA
1.7.1923. Green on lt. brown unpt. Prince Árpád wearing helmet at r.

	VG	VF	UNC
a. Imprint: Magyar Pénzjegynyomda Rt.	.50	1.00	3.00
b. W/o imprint.	.25	.75	2.00

75 1000 KORONA
1.7.1923. Black on brown unpt. St. Stephan at r.

	VG	VF	UNC
a. Imprint: Magyar Pénzjegynyomda Rt.	.50	1.00	3.00
b. W/o imprint.	.50	1.00	4.00

76 5000 KORONA
1.7.1923. Dk. brown on tan and lt. blue unpt. Woman wearing crown at r.

	VG	VF	UNC
a. Imprint: Magyar Pénzjegynyomda Rt.	.75	1.75	5.00
b. W/o imprint.	1.00	2.50	6.00

77 **10,000 KORONA**
1.7.1923. Dk. green on tan and lilac unpt. "Patrona Hungariae" at r.

	VG	VF	UNC
a. Imprint: Magyar Pénzjegynyomda Rt.	1.00	2.00	7.00
b. W/o imprint.	1.25	2.50	9.00
c. Imprint: Orell Füssli, Zürich.	1.25	2.50	9.00

78 **25,000 KORONA**
1.7.1923. Violet. Kg. Ladislaus wearing crown at at r. Printer: Orell Füssli, Zürich.

	VG	VF	UNC
	10.00	30.00	100.00

79 **500,000 KORONA**
1.7.1923. Violet and brown. Woman wearing a wreath at r.

	VG	VF	UNC
a. Imprint: Magyar Pénzjegynyomda Rt.	40.00	130.00	300.00
b. Imprint: Orell Füssli.	60.00	170.00	350.00

80 **1,000,000 KORONA**
4.9.1923. Blue on green unpt. Like #79.

	VG	VF	UNC
a. Imprint: Magyar Pénzjegynyomda. Rt.	150.00	350.00	650.00
b. W/o imprint.	150.00	350.00	650.00
c. W/o portr. and w/o serial #. (Half-finished printing).	—	—	500.00

1925 PROVISIONAL ISSUE
#81-88 new denominations ovpt. on old notes.

81 **8 FILLÉR ON 1000 KORONA**
ND (1925 - old date 1.7.1923). Red ovpt. on #75.

	VG	VF	UNC
a. Imprint: Magyar Pénzjegynyomda Rt.	5.00	12.00	40.00
b. W/o imprint.	4.00	10.00	35.00

82 **40 FILLÉR ON 5000 KORONA**
ND (1925 - old date 1.7.1923). Green ovpt. on #76.

	VG	VF	UNC
a. Imprint: Magyar Pénzjegynyomda Rt.	7.00	15.00	50.00
b. W/o imprint.	6.00	12.50	45.00

83 **80 FILLÉR ON 10,000 KORONA**
ND (1925 - old date 1.7.1923). Red ovpt. on #77.

	VG	VF	UNC
a. Imprint: Magyar Pénzjegynyomda Rt.	10.00	25.00	75.00
b. W/o imprint.	10.00	25.00	75.00
c. Imprint: Orell Füssli.	12.00	30.00	85.00

84 **2 PENGÖ ON 25,000 KORONA**
ND (1925 - old date 1.7.1923). Red ovpt. on #78.

	VG	VF	UNC
	20.00	60.00	150.00

85 **4 PENGÖ ON 50,000 KORONA**
ND (1925 - old date 1.5.1923). Green ovpt. on #71.

	VG	VF	UNC
a. Imprint: Orell Füssli.	35.00	100.00	250.00
b. W/o imprint.	35.00	100.00	250.00

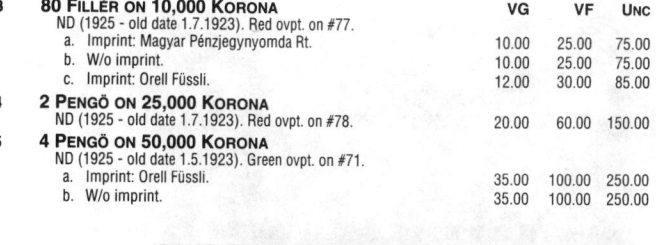

86 **8 PENGÖ ON 100,000 KORONA**
ND (1925 - old date 1.5.1923). Red ovpt. on #72.

	VG	VF	UNC
a. Imprint: Orell Füssli.	75.00	175.00	400.00
b. Imprint: Magyar Pénzjegynyomda Rt.	75.00	175.00	400.00

87 **40 PENGÖ ON 500,000 KORONA**
ND (1925 - old date 1.7.1923). Red ovpt. on #79.

	VG	VF	UNC
a. Imprint: Magyar Pénzjegynyomda Rt.	—	—	—
b. W/o imprint.	—	—	—

88 **80 PENGÖ ON 1,000,000 KORONA**
ND (1925 - old date 4.9.1923). Red ovpt. on #80.

	VG	VF	UNC
a. Imprint: Magyar Pénzjegynyomda Rt.	—	—	—
b. W/o imprint.	—	—	—

MAGYAR NEMZETI BANK (RESUMED)
HUNGARIAN NATIONAL BANK
1926-27 ISSUE

89 **5 PENGÖ**
1.3.1926. Brown. Portr. Count I. Széchenyi at r. Bridge on back.

	VG	VF	UNC
a. Issued note.	10.00	30.00	140.00
s. Specimen perforated: *MINTA*.	—	—	85.00

90 **10 PENGÖ**
1.3.1926. Green on lt. tan unpt. Portr. F. Deák at r. Parliament House on back.

	VG	VF	UNC
a. Issued note.	50.00	200.00	600.00
s. Specimen perforated: *MINTA*.	—	—	350.00

91   20 PENGÖ

		VG	VF	UNC
	1.3.1926. Brown on green unpt. Portr. L. Kossuth at r.			
a.	Issued note.	100.00	425.00	1050.
s.	Specimen perforated: *MINTA.*	—	—	475.00

92   50 PENGÖ

		VG	VF	UNC
	1.3.1926. Blue. Portr. Prince F. Rákóczi at r.			
a.	Issued note.	200.00	675.00	1700.
s.	Specimen perforated: *MINTA.*	—	—	750.00

93   100 PENGÖ

		VG	VF	UNC
	1.3.1926. Brown-lilac. Portr. Kg. Mátyas at r.			
a.	Issued note.	200.00	675.00	1700.
s.	Specimen perforated: *MINTA.*	—	—	750.00

94   1000 PENGÖ

		VG	VF	UNC
	1.7.1927. Blue, green and red. Portr. "Hungaria" at upper r.			
a.	Issued note.	400.00	1000.	2700.
s.	Specimen perforated: *MINTA.*	—	—	850.00

1928-30 ISSUE

95   5 PENGÖ

	VG	VF	UNC
1.8.1928. Blue. Count I. Szóchenyi at r. Bridge on back.	8.00	22.50	75.00

96   10 PENGÖ

	VG	VF	UNC
1.2.1929. Green. F. Déak at r. Parliament House on back.	3.00	10.00	40.00

97   20 PENGÖ

	VG	VF	UNC
2.1.1930. Dk. blue. L. Kossuth at r. Hungarian National Bank bldg. on back.	.25	2.00	12.50

98   100 PENGÖ

	VG	VF	UNC
1.7.1930. Lilac. Kg. Mátyas at r. Series # w/o asterisk. Royal Palace at Budapest on back.	.25	.75	3.00

1932 ISSUE

99   50 PENGÖ

	VG	VF	UNC
1.10.1932. Red-brown on green and blue unpt. S. Petófi at r. Rider on horseback on back.	.25	.75	3.00

1936 ISSUE

100   10 PENGÖ

	VG	VF	UNC
22.12.1936. Green on orange and green unpt. "Patrona Hungariae" at l., girl at r. Series # w/o asterisk. Equestrian statue of St. Stephan on back.	.25	.50	2.00

1938 ISSUE

101	50 FILLÉR	VG	VF	UNC
	15.1.1938. Proof.	—	—	—

102	1 PENGŐ	VG	VF	UNC
	15.1.1938. Blue on brown unpt. Girl at r. Series # w/o asterisk.	1.00	2.50	8.50
103	2 PENGŐ			
	15.1.1938. Specimen.	—	—	65.00

104	5 PENGŐ	VG	VF	UNC
	15.1.1938. Brown on green unpt. Girl at r.	10.00	30.00	80.00
105	20 PENGŐ ON 50 FILLÉR			
	15.1.1938. Proof.	—	—	—

1939 ISSUE

106	5 PENGŐ	VG	VF	UNC
	25.10.1939. Brown. Girl at r. Man w/balalaika on back.	1.00	4.00	9.00
107	100 PENGŐ ON 5 PENGŐ			
	25.10.1939. Proof.	—	—	—

1940-45 ISSUE

108	2 PENGŐ	VG	VF	UNC
	15.7.1940. Green. Girl at r. Woman and child on back. White or yellow paper.	1.00	3.00	10.00

109	20 PENGŐ	VG	VF	UNC
	15.1.1941. Blue on tan and lt. green unpt. Shepherd and sheep at lower ctr., woman wearing national costume at and young woman on back.	.25	.50	2.00

110	50 PENGŐ	VG	VF	UNC
	5.4.1945. Brown on green unpt. Prince F. Rákóczi at r. Horses in field w/dk. clouds above on back.	.30	1.00	4.00

111	100 PENGŐ	VG	VF	UNC
	5.4.1945. Purple on lt. blue and lilac unpt. Kg. Mátyas at r. Royal Palace at Budapest on back.			
	a. W/wmk.	.30	1.00	4.00
	b. W/o wmk.	.30	1.00	4.00

SZALASI GOVERNMENT IN VESZPREM, 1944-1945

MAGYAR NEMZETI BANK

1930 ISSUE

112	100 PENGŐ	VG	VF	UNC
	1.7.1930. Violet. Like #98, but series # w/asterisk.	1.00	2.00	6.00

1936 ISSUE

113	10 PENGŐ			
	22.12.1936. Green. Like #100, but series # w/asterisk.	2.50	7.50	20.00

1938 ISSUE

114	1 PENGŐ	VG	VF	UNC
	15.1.1938. Blue on brown unpt. Like #102 but series # w/asterisk.	3.00	10.00	30.00

1943 ISSUE

115   100 PENGÖ

		VG	VF	UNC
24.2.1943. Lilac-brown on lt. brown. Young man w/fruits and doves at l., girl at r. Allegorical figures to l. and r. of arms at ctr. on back.				
a.	Printed on both sides.	10.00	27.50	70.00
b.	Printed on back only.	3.00	10.00	30.00
c.	Printed on face only.	—	—	—

116   1000 PENGÖ

	VG	VF	UNC
24.2.1943. Violet-brown. Portr. "Hungaria" at r.	.50	2.00	5.00

POST WW II INFLATIONARY ERA

MAGYAR NEMZETI BANK

HUNGARIAN NATIONAL BANK

1945-46 PENGÖ ISSUE
#118, 119 and 121 adhesive stamps have 2 types of letter B in MNB.

117   500 PENGÖ

		VG	VF	UNC
15.5.1945. Blue. Portr. woman wearing wreath at r. First Russian word at upper l. on back correctly spelled ПЯТЬСОТ.				
a.	Issued note.	.25	.75	2.00
x.	Error w/ word incorrectly spelled НЯТЬСОТ.	.50	3.00	15.00

118   1000 PENGÖ

		VG	VF	UNC
15.7.1945. Dk. green on red-brown unpt. Woman wearing flowers at r. 2 serial # varieties.				
a.	W/o adhesive stamp.	.25	.75	2.00
b.	Red adhesive stamp.	.25	.75	2.50

119   10,000 PENGÖ

		VG	VF	UNC
15.7.1945. Lilac-brown on green unpt. Portr. woman at r.				
a.	W/o adhesive stamp.	.25	.50	2.00
b.	Brown on lt. green adhesive stamp.	.25	.75	2.00

120   100,000 PENGÖ

	VG	VF	UNC
23.10.1945. Brown on green-blue unpt. Portr. woman wearing national costume at r. Arms at ctr. on back.	.25	.50	2.00

121   100,000 PENGÖ

		VG	VF	UNC
23.10.1945. Blue. Like #120.				
a.	W/o adhesive stamp.	25.00	60.00	150.00
b.	Green adhesive stamp.	35.00	75.00	200.00

122   1,000,000 PENGÖ

	VG	VF	UNC
16.11.1945. Blue on brown and green unpt. Portr. L. Kossuth at r. Painting "At the shore of Lake Balaton" (by M. Geza) on back.	.25	.75	2.00

123   10,000,000 PENGÖ

	VG	VF	UNC
16.11.1945. Dk. green on m/c unpt. Portr. L. Kossuth at r. Dove w/olive branch on back.	.25	.75	2.50

124   100,000,000 PENGÖ

	VG	VF	UNC
18.3.1946. Brown on green unpt. Portr. woman wearing headscarf at r. Parliament House on back.	.25	.75	2.50

125	1 MILLIARD PENGÖ	VG	VF	UNC
	18.3.1946. Violet on lt. orange unpt. Woman at r. Like #137.	.25	.75	2.50

1946 MILPENGÖ ISSUES

126	10,000 MILPENGÖ	VG	VF	UNC
	29.4.1946. Dk. blue and red. Like #119.	.25	.75	2.50

127	100,000 MILPENGÖ	VG	VF	UNC
	29.4.1946. Dk. green. Like #120.	.25	.75	2.50

128	1 MILLION MILPENGÖ	VG	VF	UNC
	24.5.1946. Brown on yellow unpt. Like #122.	.25	.75	2.50

129	10 MILLION MILPENGÖ	VG	VF	UNC
	24.5.1946. Brown on blue unpt. Like #123.	.25	.75	2.50
130	100 MILLION MILPENGÖ			
	3.6.1946. Green. Like #124.	.25	.75	2.50

131	1 MILLIARD MILPENGÖ	VG	VF	UNC
	3.6.1946. Blue. Woman at r. Like #125.	.25	.75	2.50

1946 "B.-PENGÖ" ISSUES
#132-137 w/o serial #.

132	10,000 B.-PENGÖ	VG	VF	UNC
	3.6.1946. Brown on violet unpt. Like #126.	.25	.75	2.50
133	100,000 B.-PENGÖ			
	3.6.1946. Red-brown. Like #127.	.25	.75	3.00
134	1,000,000 B.-PENGÖ			
	3.6.1946. Dk. brown. Like #128.	.25	.75	3.00
135	10,000,000 B.-PENGÖ			
	3.6.1946. Violet. Like #129.	.25	.75	5.00

136	100,000,000 B.-Pengö	VG	VF	UNC
	3.6.1946. Blue. Like #130.	.50	1.50	10.00

137	1 MILLIARD B.-Pengö	VG	VF	UNC
	3.6.1946. Green. Like #131. (Not issued.)	10.00	45.00	185.00

MINISTRY OF FINANCE

1946 ADÓPENGÖ (TAX PENGÖ) SYSTEM FIRST ISSUE

NOTE: In accordance w/an ordinance by the Ministry of Finance, numerous tax-accounting letters of credit, law courts, fee and deed stamps were declared legal tender.

138	50,000 (ÖTVENEZER) ADÓPENGÖ	VG	VF	UNC
	25.5.1946. Green.			
	a. Gray paper w/wmk. and serial #.	.60	2.00	5.00
	b. Gray paper w/wmk., w/o serial #.	.60	2.00	5.00
	c. White paper w/o wmk.,w/o serial #.	.60	2.00	5.00

139	500,000 (OTSZAZEZER) ADOPENGO	VG	VF	UNC
	25.5.1946. Dk. blue.			
	a. Gray paper w/wmk. and serial #.	.60	2.00	6.00
	b. White paper w/o wmk., w/o serial #.	.60	2.00	5.00
140	1,000,000 (EGYMILLIÓ) ADÓPENGÖ			
	25.5.1946. Red on gray unpt.			
	a. Gray paper w/wmk. and serial #.	.60	2.00	5.00
	b. Like a, but arms in unpt. on back at l. and r. reversed (cross at l.).	.75	3.00	7.00
	c. White paper w/o wmk. w/o serial #.	.60	2.00	5.00
141	10,000,000 (TIZMILLIÓ) ADÓPENGÖ			
	25.5.1946. Blue on yellow unpt.			
	a. White paper w/o wmk., w/o serial #.	.60	2.00	6.00
	b. Like a, but arms in unpt. on back at l. and r. reversed (cross at l.).	2.50	7.50	20.00
	c. Gray paper w/wmk., w/o serial # but arms in unpt. on back at l. and r. reversed (cross at l.).	2.50	7.50	20.00

142	10,000,000 (TIZMILLIÓ) ADÓPENGÖ	VG	VF	UNC
	25.5.1946. Gray-blue on pink unpt.			
	a. White paper w/o wmk., w/o serial #.	1.25	5.00	15.00
	b. Like a, but arms in unpt. on back at l. and r. reversed (cross at l.).	4.50	15.00	40.00
	c. Gray paper, w/o serial #.	2.00	6.00	20.00

1946 ADÓPENGÖ (TAX PENGÖ) SYSTEM SECOND ISSUE

142A	1 MD. (EGYMILLIÁRD) ADÓPENGÖ			
	25.5.1946. Lilac on lt. blue unpt. (Not issued).	—	Rare	—
143	10,000 (TIZEZER) ADÓPENGÖ	VG	VF	UNC
	28.5.1946. Brown.			
	a. Gray paper w/wmk. and serial #. 5.970/1946, M.E. on back.	.60	2.00	5.00
	b. Gray paper w/wmk., w/o serial #.	.60	2.00	5.00
	c. White paper w/o wmk., w/o serial #. 5.600/1946 M.E. on back.	4.50	12.00	40.00

144	100,000 (EGYSZÁZEZER) ADÓPENGÖ	VG	VF	UNC
	28.5.1946. Brown-lilac on pink unpt.			
	a. Gray paper w/wmk. and serial #. 5.970/1946. M.E. on back.	.60	2.00	5.00
	b. Gray paper w/wmk., w/o serial #. 5.970/1946. M.E. on back.	.60	2.00	5.00
	c. Like b, but arms in unpt. on back at l. and r. reversed (cross at l.).	4.50	15.00	45.00
	d. Gray paper w/wmk. and serial #. 5.600/1946. M.E. on back.	4.50	15.00	45.00
	e. White paper w/o wmk., w/o serial #. 5.600/1946. M.E. on back.	1.00	5.00	15.00

MAGYAR POSTATAKARÉKPÉNZTÁR

HUNGARIAN POSTAL SAVINGS BANK

RESZBETETJEGY

1946 FIRST ISSUE

#145-148, regulations on back. Issued 29.6.1946.

145	10,000 (TIZEZER) ADÓPENGÖ			
	22.4.1946. Black. *Kir.*	8.00	20.00	50.00
146 (147)	10,000 (TIZEZER) ADÓPENGÖ			
	22.4.1946. Black. W/o *Kir.*	5.00	15.00	45.00
147 (146)	100,000 (SZÁZEZER) ADÓPENGÖ			
	22.4.1946. Red. *Kir.*	8.00	20.00	50.00
148	100,000 (SZÁZEZER) ADÓPENGÖ			
	22.4.1946. Red. W/o *Kir.*	8.00	20.00	50.00

1946 SECOND ISSUE

#149-152, dated 1946 within the postal handstamp. Face w/*MASRA AT NEM RUHAZHATO* at bottom, text on back.

NOTE: #149-158 exist w/postal handstamp on lower l. or w/o handstamp. Unfinished partially printed notes exist for #157 and 158.

149	10,000 (TIZEZER) ADÓPENGÖ	VG	VF	UNC
	1946. Black on gray unpt.	2.00	5.00	15.00

		VG	VF	UNC
150	**100,000 (SZÁZEZER) ADÓPENGÖ** 1946. Red on lt. red unpt.	2.00	5.00	15.00
151	**1,000,000 (EGYMILLIÓ) ADÓPENGÖ** 1946. Dk. blue on lt. blue unpt.	2.00	5.00	15.00
152	**10,000,000 (TIZMILLIÓ) ADÓPENGÖ** 1946. Dk. green on lt. green unpt.	2.00	5.00	15.00

1946 THIRD ISSUE
#153 and 154 like #148 - but uniface, w/o text on back.

		VG	VF	UNC
153	**100,000 (SZÁZEZER) ADÓPENGÖ** 1946.			
	a. W/serial #.	—	—	—
	b. W/o serial #.	3.00	10.00	30.00
154	**1,000,000 (EGYMILLIÓ) ADÓPENGÖ** 1946.			
	a. W/serial #.	—	—	—
	b. W/o serial #.	3.00	10.00	30.00

1946 FOURTH ISSUE
#155 and 156 like #149 - but w/o Masra at Nem Ruhazhato on face. Text on back.

		VG	VF	UNC
155	**10,000 (TIZEZER) ADÓPENGÖ** 1946.			
	a. W/serial #.	—	—	—
	b. W/o serial #.	3.00	10.00	30.00
156	**1,000,000 (EGYMILLIÓ) ADÓPENGÖ** 1946.			
	a. W/serial #.	—	—	—
	b. W/o serial #.	3.00	10.00	30.00

1946 FIFTH ISSUE
#157 and 158 like #149 - but uniface, w/o text on back.

		VG	VF	UNC
157	**10,000 (TIZEZER) ADÓPENGÖ** 1946.	2.00	8.00	20.00
158	**10,000,000 (TIZMILLIÓ) ADÓPENGÖ** 1946.	2.00	8.00	20.00

MAGYAR NEMZETI BANK (RESUMED)

HUNGARIAN NATIONAL BANK

1946 FORINT ISSUE

		VG	VF	UNC
159	**10 FORINT** 3.6.1946. Green on lt. tan unpt. Blue denomination guilloche at r. Portr. young man w/hammer at l. Arms on back.			
	a. Issued note.	5.00	15.00	60.00
	s. Specimen perforated: *MINTA*.	—	—	50.00

			VF	UNC
160	**100 FORINT** 3.6.1946. Blue on green unpt. Red denomination guilloche at r. Portr. young woman w/sickle and ear of corn at at l. Hands grasping hammer and wheat on back.			
	a. Issued note.		5.00 15.00	60.00
	s. Specimen perforated: *MINTA*.		—	50.00

1947 ISSUE

		VG	VF	UNC
161	**10 FORINT** 27.2.1947. Green. Portr. S. Petófi at r. Painting "Birth of the Song" (by J. Jankó) on back.	10.00	30.00	70.00
162	**20 FORINT** 27.2.1947. Blue. Gy. Dózsa at r. Man w/hammer and wheat on back.	10.00	35.00	80.00

		VG	VF	UNC
163	**100 FORINT** 27.2.1947. Red-brown. Arms at upper ctr., portr. L. Kossurth at r. Horses pulling wagon on back.	10.00	35.00	80.00

1949 ISSUE

		VG	VF	UNC
164	**10 FORINT** 24.10.1949. Green. Like #161 but arms w/star.	1.00	5.00	20.00

		VG	VF	UNC
165	**20 FORINT** 24.10.1949. Blue. Like #162 but arms w/star.	1.50	7.00	25.00
166	**100 FORINT** 24.10.1949. Red-brown. Like #157 but arms w/star.	1.50	7.00	25.00

1951 ISSUE

		VG	VF	UNC
167	**50 FORINT** 1.9.1951. Brown. Prince F. Rákóczi at r. Men fighting on horseback on back.	1.00	4.00	15.00

REPUBLIC

MAGYAR NEMZETI BANK

HUNGARIAN NATIONAL BANK

1957 ISSUE
#168-173 arms of 3-bar shield w/star and wreath.

		VG	VF	UNC
168	**10 FORINT** 1957-75. Deep olive-green and blue-black on m/c unpt. Value at l., portr. S. Petófi at r. Trees and river at ctr. on back.			
	a. 23.5.1957.	.75	3.00	7.50
	b. 24.8.1960.	.50	2.00	7.00
	c. 12.10.1962.	.50	1.50	5.00
	d. 30.6.1969.	.25	1.00	3.00
	e. 28.10.1975.	.10	.35	2.00
	s. As d. Specimen w/red ovpt. and perforated: *MINTA*.	—	—	25.00

169 20 FORINT
1957-80. Deep blue on m/c unpt. Value at l., portr. G. Dózsa at r. Nude male with hammer and wheat at ctr. on back.

		VG	VF	UNC
a.	23.5.1957.	.75	3.00	10.00
b.	24.8.1960.	2.00	5.00	25.00
c.	12.10.1962.	.75	2.00	7.50
d.	3.9.1965.	.50	1.00	6.00
e.	30.6.1969.	.20	.65	5.00
f.	28.10.1975. Serial # varieties.	.50	1.00	4.50
g.	30.9.1980.	.25	.50	2.00
s.	As e. Specimen w/red ovpt. and perforated: *MINTA*.	—	—	25.00

171 100 FORINT
1957-89. Violet and deep brown on m/c unpt. Value at l., portr. L. Kossath at r. Horse drawn wagon at ctr. on back.

		VG	VF	UNC
a.	23.5.1957.	4.00	8.00	25.00
b.	24.8.1960.	4.00	8.00	25.00
c.	12.10.1962.	2.00	4.00	12.00
d.	24.10.1968.	FV	3.00	10.00
e.	28.10.1975. Serial # varieties.	FV	2.00	8.50
f.	30.9.1980.	FV	FV	6.50
g.	30.10.1984.	FV	FV	5.50
h.	10.1.1989.	FV	FV	2.25
s.	As b. Specimen w/red ovpt. and perforted: *MINTA*.	—	—	25.00

RUSSIAN ARMY OCCUPATION - WW I

A VÖRÖSHADSEREG PARANCSOKSÁGA

1944 ISSUE

M1 1 PENGŐ
1944. Blue on brown unpt. Printing size on date side 106 x 49mm.

		VG	VF	UNC
a.	Unpt. horizontal wavy lines.	.50	1.50	6.00
b.	Unpt. vertical wavy lines.	.50	1.50	6.00

M2 1 PENGŐ
1944. Blue on brown unpt. Printing size on date side 118 x 54mm.

		VG	VF	UNC
a.	W/o serial #, w/horizontal wavy lines.	.25	.75	3.00
b.	W/o serial #, w/vertical wavy lines.	.25	.75	3.00
c.	W/serial #.	8.00	20.00	50.00

M3 2 PENGŐ

	VG	VF	UNC
1944. Blue on green unpt.	.25	.75	3.00

M4 5 PENGŐ

	VG	VF	UNC
1944. Lilac on lt. blue unpt.	.25	.50	3.00

M5 10 PENGŐ

	VG	VF	UNC
1944. Dk. green on lilac unpt.	.50	2.00	8.00

M6 20 PENGŐ
1944. Gray on dull olive unpt.

		VG	VF	UNC
a.	W/o serial #.	10.00	25.00	60.00
b.	W/serial #. 2 serial # varieties.	.50	2.00	8.00

M7 50 PENGŐ

	VG	VF	UNC
1944. Olive. 2 serial # varieties.	.50	1.50	10.00

M8 100 PENGŐ

	VG	VF	UNC
1944. Dk. brown. 2 serial # varieties.	.50	1.50	10.00

M9	1000 Pengö		VG	VF	UNC
	1944. Red.		3.50	8.00	30.00

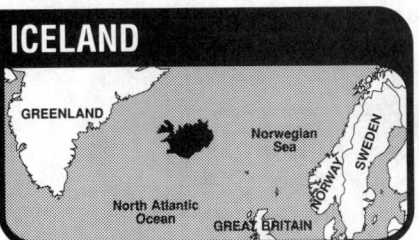

The Republic of Iceland, an island of recent volcanic origin in the North Atlantic east of Greenland and immediately south of the Arctic Circle, has an area of 39,768 sq. mi. (103,000 sq. km.) and a population of 262,193. Capital: Reykjavík. Fishing is the chief industry and accounts for more than 70 percent of the exports.

Iceland was settled by Norwegians in the 9th century and established as an independent republic in 930. The Icelandic assembly called the "Althing," also established in 930, is the oldest parliament in the world. Iceland came under Norwegian sovereignty in 1262, and passed to Denmark when Norway and Denmark were united under the Danish crown in 1384. In 1918, it was established as a virtually independent kingdom in union with Denmark. On June 17, 1944, while Denmark was still under occupation by troops of the Third Reich, Iceland was established by plebiscite as an independent republic.

RULERS:
Christian IX, 1863-1906
Frederik VIII, 1906-1912
Christian X, 1912-1944

MONETARY SYSTEM:
Danish until 1873
1 Krona = 100 Aurar, 1874-

DANISH INFLUENCE

COURANT BANK

1777-78 PROVISIONAL ISSUE
#A1, A2, A5, A6 and A11 reissue of early Danish State notes.

		GOOD	FINE	XF
A1	1 RIGSDALER	—	—	—
	1777-80; 1783-84; 1788-92. black. Printed on the back of Denmark #A24c.			
A2	5 RIGSDALER	—	—	—
	1778-79. Black. Printed on the back of Denmark #A29a.			

1792-1800 ISSUE

A5	1 RIGSDALER	GOOD	FINE	XF
	1792-94; 1801. Black. Printed on the back of Denmark #A28.			
	a. Issued note.	—	—	—
	b. Handstamped: "A" in circle. 1792-94.	—	—	—
	c. Handstamped: "B" in circle. 1794.	—	—	—
	d. Handstamped: "C" in circle. 1801.	—	—	—
	e. Handstamped: "D" in circle. 1801.	—	—	—
A6	5 RIGSDALER			
	1800-01. Black on blue paper. Printed on the back of Denmark #A29b. Handstamped: "C" in circle.	—	—	—

RIGSBANK

1815 PROVISIONAL ISSUE

A11	RIGSBANKDALER	VG	VF	UNC
	20.3.1815 (-old date 1814). printed on the back of Rigsbanken i Kiøbenhavn notes.	—	—	—

LANDSSJOD ÍSLANDS

LAW OF 18.9.1885
#1-3 Kg. Christian IX at l. in profile.

1	5 KRÓNUR	GOOD	FINE	XF
	L.1885. Gray-brown and black.			
	a. Issued note.	300.00	550.00	1000.
	b. Unissued remainder.	—	Unc	1000.
2	10 KRÓNUR			
	L.1885. Blue.			
	a. Issued note.	350.00	600.00	1150.
	b. Unissued remainder.	—	Unc	1250.
3	50 KRÓNUR			
	L.1885. Gray-green and lt. brown. Allegorical figure at ctr. on back.			
	a. Issued note.	—	Rare	
	b. Unissued remainder.	—	Unc	1500.

LAWS OF 18.9.1885 AND 12.1.1900 FIRST ISSUE
#4 and 5 portr. Kg. Christian IX at l. facing.
#6 Kg. Frederik VIII at l.

4	5 KRÓNUR	GOOD	FINE	XF
	L.1885 and 1900 (1900-06). Brown and gray. Bird at ctr. on back.	150.00	300.00	650.00
	a. Issued note.	150.00	300.00	650.00
	b. Punched hole cancelled.	—	200.00	
5	10 KRÓNUR			
	L.1885 and 1900 (1900-06), blue and brown. Allegorical figure at ctr. on back.			
	a. Issued note.	200.00	400.00	850.00
	b. Punched hole cancelled.	—	250.00	
6	50 KRÓNUR			
	L.1885 and 1900 (1906-12). Gray-green and brown. Back like #5.			
	a. Issued note.	—	Rare	
	b. Punched hole cancelled.	—	350.00	—

LAWS OF 18.9.1885 AND 12.1.1900 SECOND ISSUE
#7-9 Kg. Christian X at l.

7	5 KRÓNUR			
	L.1885 and 1900 (1912). Brown and green-gray.			
	a. Issued note.	200.00	400.00	800.00
	b. Punched hole cancelled.	—	200.00	
8	10 KRÓNUR			
	L.1885 and 1900 (1912). Blue and brown.			
	a. Issued note.	200.00	400.00	800.00
	b. Punched hole cancellation.	—	275.00	
9	50 KRÓNUR			
	L.1885 and 1900 (1912). Gray-green and lt. brown.			
	a. Issued note.	—	Rare	
	b. Punched hole cancelled.	—	400.00	

ÍSLANDS BANKI

1904 ISSUE
#10-13 printer: G&D.
#10-14 portr. Kg. Christian IX at l.

10	5 KRÓNUR	GOOD	FINE	XF
	1904. Gray and violet. Bird at l. on back.	60.00	150.00	375.00

11	10 KRÓNUR	GOOD	FINE	XF
	1904. Dk. blue. Bird at r. on back.	75.00	200.00	475.00
12	50 KRÓNUR			
	1904. Blue and gray. Volcano and river at r. Back similar to #11.	—	Rare	—

13	100 KRÓNUR	GOOD	FINE	XF
	1904. Dk. blue. Geyser at r. Bird at ctr. on back.	—	Rare	

1919 PROVISIONAL ISSUE

14	100 KRÓNUR	GOOD	FINE	XF
	1919. Blue and gray. Ovpt. on back of #1.			
	a. Issued note.	—	Rare	—
	b. Unissued remainder.	—	Unc	1500.

1920 ISSUE
#15-16 printer: G&D.

15	5 KRÓNUR	GOOD	FINE	XF
	1920. Black on red and blue unpt. Geyser at l. Back red and blue.			
	a. Issued note.	150.00	300.00	650.00
	b. Remainder (1 signature).	—	Unc	350.00

16	10 KRÓNUR	GOOD	FINE	XF
	1920. Dk. blue. Volcano and river at l. Back blue and brown.	150.00	300.00	650.00

RIKISSJOD ÍSLANDS

LAWS OF 18.9.1885 AND 12.1.1900 (1921)
#17 and 18 printer: R. Gutenberg, Reykjavik.
#19-21 portr. Kg. Christian X at l.

17	1 KRÓNA	GOOD	FINE	XF
	L.1885 and 1900. Dk. blue. Unpt. of double-line circles. Arms on back.			
	a. Blue serial # at bottom ctr. (1921).	17.50	65.00	150.00
	b. Dk. blue serial # at upper l. (1922).	17.50	65.00	150.00
	c. Black serial # at upper l. (1922).	17.50	65.00	150.00

18	1 KRÓNA	GOOD	FINE	XF
	L.1885 and 1900. Dk. blue. Unpt. of simple circles. Arms on back.			
	a. Black serial #. (1921).	15.00	55.00	125.00
	b. Series A, red serial #. (1924-25).	15.00	55.00	125.00
	c. Series B, red serial #. (1925).	15.00	55.00	125.00
19	5 KRÓNUR			
	ND. Brown and green. Like #7 but w/Fyrir Rikissjod Íslands.	80.00	175.00	375.00
20	10 KRÓNUR			
	ND. Dk. green on green unpt. Like #8 but w/Fyrir Rikissjod Íslands.	100.00	200.00	425.00
21	50 KRÓNUR			
	ND. Gray-green and lt. brown. Like #9 but w/Fyrir Rikiossjod Íslands.	225.00	600.00	1250.

1941 EMERGENCY WW II ISSUE

22	1 KRÓNA	VG	VF	UNC
	1941 (1941-47). All on very thin paper. Arms on back. Printer: R. Gutenberg, Reykjavik.			
	a. Green on lt. green paper (1941-42).	2.50	15.00	75.00
	b. Brown on lt. brown paper (1942).	2.50	10.00	50.00
	c. Brown on white paper (1942-43).	2.50	10.00	50.00
	d. Blue-green on white paper (1944-47).	2.00	8.00	40.00
	e. Dk. blue on white paper (1944-45).	2.50	10.00	45.00
	f. Dk. blue on yellow paper (1945).	2.50	12.50	50.00
	g. Lt. blue on white paper (1947).	2.50	10.00	45.00

LANDSBANKI ÍSLANDS

LAWS OF 31.5.1927 AND 15.4.1928
#23-26 portr. Kg. Christian X at l. Varieties in r. h. sign.
#23-25 mention 1928 law date; #26 shows the 1927 date.

23	5 KRÓNUR	GOOD	FINE	XF
	L.1928 (1929). Brown on green unpt. Like #19 but w/Landsbanki Íslands.	60.00	150.00	350.00
24	10 KRÓNUR			
	L.1928 (1929). Dk. blue on lt. blue unpt. Like #2Q but w/Landsbanki Íslands.	75.00	175.00	400.00
25	50 KRÓNUR			
	L.1928 (1929). Gray-green on lt. brown unpt. Like #21 but w/Landsbanki Íslands.	150.00	500.00	1150.
26	100 KRÓNUR			
	31.5.1927. Gray-blue on gray unpt. Back like #24.	225.00	700.00	1300.

LAW OF 15.4.1928

SIGNATURE VARIETIES		
1	*Jón Árnason*	*Magnús Sigurthsson*
	Jón Árnason – Magnús Sigurthsson, 1917-1945	
2		*Kaaber*
	Jón Árnason – Lúthvik Kaaber, 1918–1940	
3		*Georg Ólafsson*
	Jón Árnason – Georg Ólafsson, 1921–1941	
4		*Vilhjalmur Þór*
	Jón Árnason – Vilhjálmur Thor, 1940–1945	
5		*Petur Magnússon*
	Jón Árnason – Pétur Magnússon, 1941–1944	

#27-31 notes issued 1934-47. Sign. of Bank Director at l., sign. of Bank Governor at r. Printer: BWC.

		VG	VF	UNC
27	**5 KRÓNUR**			
	L.1928. Blue and violet. J. Eriksson at l. Sign. 1-4. Bldg. at r. on back.			
	a. Issued note.	3.00	10.00	45.00
	s. Specimen.	—	Unc	150.00

		VG	VF	UNC
28	**10 KRÓNUR**			
	L.1928. Blue. J. Sigurdsson at l. Sign. 1-5. Waterfalls at r. on back.			
	a. Issued note.	3.00	10.00	45.00
	s. Specimen.	—	Unc	175.00
29	**50 KRÓNUR**			
	L.1928. Violet. Like #27. Sign. 1-5. Men w/fishing boats and freighter on back.			
	a. Issued note.	15.00	50.00	150.00
	s. Specimen.	—	Unc	225.00

		VG	VF	UNC
30	**100 KRÓNUR**			
	L.1928. Red. Like #28. Sign. 1-5. Flock of sheep on back.			
	a. Issued note.	15.00	40.00	135.00
	s. Specimen.	—	Unc	250.00
31	**500 KRÓNUR**			
	L.1928. Green. Like #28. Sign. 1, 4-5. River, rocks and mountains on back.			
	a. Issued note.	50.00	165.00	450.00
	s. Specimen.	—	Unc	400.00

REPUBLIC

LANDSBANKI ÍSLANDS

LAW OF 15.4.1928

	SIGNATURE VARIETIES	
6	Magnús Jónsson – Magnús Sigurthsson, 1946-1947	
7	Magnús Jónsson – Vilhjálmur Thor, 1955–1957	
8	Magnús Jónsson – Jón Árnason, 1946–1954	
9	Magnús Jónsson – Jón G. Maríasson, 1943-1957	

10	Magnús Jónsson – Gunnar Vithar, 1948–1955	
11	Magnús Jónsson – Pétur Benediktsson, 1956–1957	

#32-36 notes issued 1948-56. Sign. of Bank Director at l., sign. of Bank Governor at r. Printer: BWC.

		VG	VF	UNC
32	**5 KRÓNUR**			
	L.1928. Green. Like #27. Sign. 6-11.			
	a. Issued note.	1.00	4.00	17.50
	s. Specimen.	—	—	100.00

		VG	VF	UNC
33	**10 KRÓNUR**			
	L.1928. Red. Like #28. Sign. 6, 8-10.			
	a. Issued note.	1.00	5.00	20.00
	s. Specimen.	—	—	125.00

		VG	VF	UNC
34	**50 KRÓNUR**			
	L.1928. Green. Like #29. Sign. 6, 8-10.			
	a. Issued note.	8.00	25.00	80.00
	s. Specimen.	—	—	150.00

		VG	VF	UNC
35	**100 KRÓNUR**			
	L.1928. Blue. Like #30. Sign. 6-11.			
	a. Issued note.	10.00	30.00	120.00
	s. Specimen.	—	—	175.00

36 500 KRÓNUR

	VG	VF	UNC
L.1928. Brown. Like #31. Sign. 6, 8-10.			
a. Issued note.	20.00	60.00	185.00
s. Specimen.	—	—	250.00

LANDSBANKI ÍSLANDS-SEDLABANKINN

LAW OF 21.6.1957
#37-41 printer: BWC (w/o imprint).

37 5 KRÓNUR

	VG	VF	UNC
L.1957. Red-brown on m/c unpt. Viking I. Arnarson at l. Farm bldgs. on gray back.			
a. Buff paper (first printing).	.75	2.00	5.00
b. White paper (second printing).	.60	1.50	4.00
s1. As a. Specimen.	—	—	125.00
s2. As b. Specimen.	—	—	150.00

38 10 KRÓNUR

	VG	VF	UNC
L.1957. Violet-brown green and orange unpt. J. Eiriksson at l. Dock scene on on green back.			
a. Letter *O* in *REYKJAVIKURHOFN* on back w/o umlaut (error).	2.00	6.00	15.00
b. Letter *Ö* w/umlauts on top. (corrected).	1.00	3.00	10.00
s1. As a. Specimen.	—	—	125.00
s2. As b. Specimen.	—	—	150.00

39 25 KRÓNUR

	VG	VF	UNC
L.1957. Purple on m/c unpt. M. Stephensen Logmadur at l., fjord at ctr. Fishing boats near large rock formation in water on back.			
a. Issued note.	1.00	5.00	20.00
s. Specimen.	—	—	150.00

40 100 KRÓNUR

	VG	VF	UNC
L.1957. Blue-green. T. Gunnarsson at l. Back green; herd of sheep and mountain at ctr.			
a. Issued note.	1.00	2.50	7.00
s. Specimen.	—	—	150.00

41 1000 KRÓNUR

	VG	VF	UNC
L.1957. Blue and green. Bldg at lower ctr., J. Sigurdsson at r. Rock formations on back.			
a. Issued note.	10.00	35.00	95.00
s. Specimen.	—	—	175.00

INDIA

The Republic of India, a subcontinent jutting southward from the mainland of Asia, has an area of since about 2500 BC, when an urban culture based 1,266,595 sq. mi. (3,287,590 sq. km.) and a population of 833.4 million, second only to that of the Peoples Republic of China. Capital: New Delhi. India's economy is based on agriculture and industrial activity. Engineering goods, cotton apparel and fabrics, handicrafts, tea, iron and steel are exported.

The people of India have had a continuous civilization on commerce and trade, and to a lesser extent, agriculture, was developed by the inhabitants of the Indus River Valley. The origins of this civilization are uncertain, but it declined about 1500 B.C., when the region was conquered by the Aryans. Over the following 2,000 years, the Aryans developed a Brahmanic civilization and introduced the caste system. Several successive empires flourished in India over the following centuries, notably those of the Mauryans, Guptas and Mughals. In the 7th and 8th centuries AD, the Arabs expanded into western India, bringing with them the Islamic faith. A Muslim dynasty (the Mughal Empire) controlled virtually the entire subcontinent during the period preceding the arrival of the Europeans; an Indo-Islamic style of art and architecture evolved, of which the Taj Mahal is a splendid example.

The Portuguese were the first to arrive, off Calicut in May 1498. It wasn't until 1612, after Portuguese and Spanish power began to wane, that the English East India Company established its initial settlement at Surat. By the end of the century, English traders were firmly established in Bombay, Madras and Calcutta, as well as in some parts of the interior, and Britain was implementing a policy to create the civil and military institutions that would insure British dominion over the country. By 1757, following the successful conclusion of a war of colonial rivalry with France, the British were firmly established in India as not only traders, but as conquerors. During the next 60 years, the English East India Company acquired dominion over most of India by bribery and force, and ruled directly, or through puppet princelings.

The Indian Mutiny (also called Sepoy Mutiny) of 1857-59, begun by Indian troops in the service of the British East India Company, revealed the intensity of the growing resentment against British domination. The widespread rebellion against British rule was unsuccessful, but resulted in the transfer of government from the company to the British crown, and was a source of inspiration to later Indian nationalists. Agitation for representation in the government continued.

Following World War I, in which India sent six million troops to fight at the side of the Allies, Indian nationalism intensified under the banner of the Indian National Congress and the leadership of Mohandas Karamchand Gandhi, who called the non-violent revolt against British authority. The Government of India Act of 1935 proposed a federal status linking the British India provinces with the many princely states; in addition, provincial legislatures were to be created. The federal status was never implemented, but the legislatures were created after the election of 1937, with the National Congress winning majorities in most of the provinces.

When Britain declared war on Germany in Sept., 1939, the viceroy declared India also to be at war with a common enemy. The Congress, however, demanded independence as a condition for cooperation. Britain refused. But as the Japanese advanced into Asia, Britain offered to transfer to Indians power over all but military affairs during the war, and set forth a plan for postwar independence. Congress was willing to accept the wartime transfer of power, but both Congress and the Muslim League rejected Britain's plan for independence; Congress because it did not sufficiently safeguard Indian unity, the Muslims (who wanted a separate Muslim state) because of fears of what would happen to Muslims within a united India.

Early in 1947, Prime Minister Clement Attlee announced that Britain would leave India "by a date not later than June 1948," even though the Hindus and Muslims could not agree among themselves on a plan for self-government. The National Congress, aware that the Muslim League would revolt rather than accept an all-India government, reluctantly agreed to the formation of a separate Muslim state. The Muslim-populated provinces of the northwest frontier, Sindh and West Punjab in the west, and East Bengal in the east were separated from India to form the Muslim state of Pakistan, which became independent on August 14, 1947. India became independent on the following day. Initially, Pakistan consisted of East and West Pakistan, two areas separated by 1,000 miles of Indian territory. East Pakistan seceded from Pakistan on March 26, 1971, and with the support of India established itself as the independent Peoples Republic of Bangladesh.

The Republic of India is a member of the Commonwealth of Nations. The president is the Chief of State. The prime minister is the Head of Government.

RULERS:
British to 1947

MONETARY SYSTEM:
1 Rupee = 16 Annas to 1957
1 Rupee = 100 Naye Paise, 1957-1964
1 Rupee = 100 Paise, 1964-

STAPLE HOLES AND CONDITION

Perfect uncirculated notes are rarely encountered without having at least two tiny holes made by staples, stick pins or stitching having been done during age old accounting practices before and after a note is released to circulation.

NOTE: Certain listings encompassing issues circulated by various bank and regional authorities are contained in Volume 1.

COLONIAL OFFICES

	Allahabad	K	Karachi
B	Bombay	L	Lahore
C	Calcutta	M	Madras
	Calicut	R	Rangoon, refer to Myanmar listings
A	Cawnpore		

DENOMINATION LANGUAGE PANELS

Bengali		Marathi	
Burmese		Tamil	
Gujarati		Telugu	
Gujarati (var.)		Persian (Farsi)	
Hindi		Urdu	
Kannada			

SIGNATURE VARIETIES

Dates appearing on notes are not when the notes were printed. Dates of manufacture may be deduced from a wmk. code, i.e. A 41 06 means Vat A, week 41, year 1906. This date is sometimes one or two years later than the printed date. Signatures are left off until the notes are actually issued, sometimes many years after the notes were printed. Therefore, the dates below do not correspond exactly with the years the signers held office.

A.V.V. Alyar, 1919		Stephen Jacob, 1886–1896	
J.A. Ballard, 1861–1863		E. Jay, 1884	
O.T. Barrow, 1899–1906		C.E. Jones, 1941	
C.W.C. Cassog, 1913–1915		J.W. Kelly, 1935	
A.F. Cox, 1891–1905		A. Kingstocke, 1913	
H. Denning, 1920–1925		R. Logan, 1887–1899	
C.D. Deshmukh, 1943–1947		A.C. McWatters, 1916–1922	
R.W. Gillan, 1907–1913		W.H. Michael, 1906	
M.M.S. Gubbay, 1913–1919		Hugh Sandeman, 1872	
E.F. Harrison, 1873		I.L. Sundtrayton (?), 1872	
F.C. Harrison, 1904–1905		J.B. Taylor, 1925	
D. Hastings, 1901		A.C. Merell Tupps, 1872–1886	
H.F. Howard, 1912–1916		J. Westland, 1882	

BRITISH INFLUENCE

GOVERNMENT OF INDIA

1861-65 ISSUE

#A1-A1A Qn. Victoria in sprays at upper l. Two language panels. Uniface. Sign. J. A. Ballard w/title: COM-MISSIONER.

		A1	**10 RUPEES**			
A1	10 RUPEES					
	6.8.1861; 9.5.1862; 7.6.1862; 8.6.1863; 14.6.1864; 6.6.1865.		—	Rare	—
A1A	20 RUPEES					
	10.6.1864. Second sign. of S. K. Lambert (?).		—	Rare	—

1872-1927 ISSUE

#A2-A20 uniface Colonial types w/o portrait. Issued 1872-1927.

			GOOD	FINE	XF
A2	**5 RUPEES**				
	1872-1901. Green unpt. 4 language panels, 2 serial #.				
	a.	ALLAHABAD or CALCUTTA. Sign. Edw. A. Harrison. 19.1.1872.	150.00	250.00	900.00
	b.	BOMBAY. Sign. A. C. Merell Tupps. 27.5.1872; 11.11.1886.	150.00	250.00	900.00
	c.	BOMBAY. Sign. A. F. Cox. 7.5.1891; 5.2.1899-8.6.1899.	100.00	200.00	800.00
	d.	BOMBAY. Sign. O. T. Barrow. 1.11.1894-9.1.1901.	100.00	200.00	800.00
	e.	CALCUTTA. Sign. E. Jay. 10.5.1884.	150.00	250.00	850.00
	f.	CALCUTTA. Sign. Stephen Jacob. 1.10.1886; 1.6.1888.	150.00	250.00	850.00

			GOOD	FINE	XF
A3	**5 RUPEES**				
	1901-03. Green unpt. 6 language panels, 4 serial #.				
	a.	BOMBAY. Sign. A. F. Cox. 3.3.1902-1.8.1903.	70.00	150.00	350.00
	b.	BOMBAY. Sign. O. T. Barrow. 9.1.1901; 1.3.1902.	70.00	150.00	350.00
	c.	CALCUTTA. Sign. A. F. Cox. 4.2.1901.	70.00	150.00	350.00

			GOOD	FINE	XF
A4	**5 RUPEES**				
	1903. Black and pink. 8 language panels and 4 serial #. at any Office of Issue Not Situated in Burma added to text. L (Lahore).				
	a.	Letter L. Sign. A. F. Cox.	Reported Not Confirmed		
	b.	Letter B. Sign. O. T. Barrow. 12.7.1905; 6.4.1907; 8.4.1907.	100.00	200.00	400.00

			GOOD	FINE	XF
A5	**5 RUPEES**				
	1907-15. Red-pink unpt. 8 lanuage panels, 4 serial #. at any Office of Issue added to text. Letter for city of issue.				
	a.	B (Bombay). Sign. H. F. Howard. 9.11.1907; 7.2.1912; 31.10.1913; 14.10.1913; 31.10.1913.	25.00	50.00	125.00
	b.	B (Bombay). Sign. M. M.S. Gubbay. 7.1.1914; 18.5.1914; 19.5.1914; 8.4.1915.	25.00	50.00	125.00
	c.	B (Bombay). Sign. R. W. Gillan. 8.2.1909; 2.10.1909.	25.00	50.00	125.00
	d.	C (Calcutta). Sign. R. W. Gillan. 20.5.1907; 12.10.1907.	25.00	50.00	125.00
	e.	C (Calcutta). Sign. M. M. S. Gubbay. 4.3.1914.	25.00	50.00	125.00
	f.	C (Calcutta). Sign. H. F. Howard. 23.9.1912; 25.10.1912; 30.10.1912; 31.7.1913.	25.00	50.00	125.00
	g.	A (Cawnpore). Sign. H. F. Howard. 2.10.1912.	25.00	50.00	125.00
	h.	M (Madras). Sign. M. M. S. Gubbay. 22.7.1914.	25.00	50.00	125.00

			GOOD	FINE	XF
A6	**5 RUPEES**				
	1914-24. Black on pink unpt. 3 serial #.				
	a.	B (Bombay). Sign. M. M. S. Gubbay. 8.4.1915-8.8.1916.	20.00	40.00	100.00
	b.	C (Calcutta). Sign. M. M. S. Gubbay. 9.1.1915-21.7.1916.	25.00	50.00	125.00
	c.	C (Calcutta). Sign. H. F. Howard. 4.5.1916; 13.7.1916.	25.00	50.00	125.00
	d.	A (Cawnpore). Sign. M. M. S. Gubbay. 2.2.1915; 28.12.1915.	20.00	40.00	100.00
	e.	L (Lahore). Sign. M. M. S. Gubbay. 31.7.1916.	30.00	60.00	135.00
	f.	M (Madras). Sign. M. M. S. Gubbay. 12.8.1914-23.10.1918.	20.00	40.00	100.00
	g.	W/o letter. Sign. M. M. S. Gubbay. 26.10.1918-23.1.1920.	15.00	30.00	85.00
	h.	W/o letter. Sign. A. C. McWatters. 12.1.1922-8.2.1924.	15.00	30.00	85.00
	i.	W/o letter. Sign. H. Denning. 24.1.1924; 25.1.1924; 8.2.1924; 11.2.1924.	15.00	30.00	85.00

			GOOD	FINE	XF
A7	**10 RUPEES**				
	1872-1906. Green unpt. 4 languages on 2 panels, 2 serial #.				
	a.	ALLAHABAD or CALCUTTA. Sign. E. Jay. 24.3.1884.	100.00	250.00	900.00

		GOOD	FINE	XF
b.	BOMBAY. Sign. R. Logan. 10.3.1887; 16.6.1899.	100.00	200.00	800.00
c.	BOMBAY. Sign. O. T. Barrow. 1.7.1899; 2.2.1900.	100.00	200.00	800.00
d.	BOMBAY. Sign. I. L. Sundtrayton. 7.5.1872.	—	Rare	—
e.	CALCUTTA. Sign. H. Sandeman. 1872.	100.00	200.00	800.00
f.	CALCUTTA. Sign. J. Westland. 15.4.1882; 10.12.1883.	100.00	200.00	800.00
g.	CALCUTTA. Sign. Stephen Jacob. 6.1.1893; 10.2.1893.	100.00	200.00	800.00
h.	CALCUTTA. Sign. A. F. Cox. 17.1.1898-14.10.1901.	100.00	200.00	800.00
i.	LAHORE or CALCUTTA. Sign. Stephen Jacob. 25.11.1896.	—	Rare	—
j.	MADRAS/Rangoon. 1896.	Reported Not Confirmed		
k.	MADRAS /L. 1896.	—	Rare	—

A8 **10 RUPEES**
1903-06. Green unpt. 4 language panels, 4 serial #. BOMBAY.

		GOOD	FINE	XF
a.	Sign. O. T. Barrow. 14.8.1903; 19.8.1903; 1.9.1905.	60.00	125.00	375.00
b.	Sign. F. C. Harrison. 2.9.1905; 6.9.1905; 3.10.1905; 12.10.1905.	60.00	125.00	375.00
c.	Sign. W.H. Michael. 3.1.1906.	60.00	125.00	375.00

A9 **10 RUPEES**
1903-06. Green unpt. 4 languages on 2 panels, 4 serial #. CALCUTTA.

		GOOD	FINE	XF
a.	Sign. A. F. Cox. 10.6.1903; 5.8.1904; 20.12.1904.	60.00	125.00	375.00
b.	Sign. O. T. Barrow. 1.11.1904-3.12.1906.	60.00	125.00	375.00
c.	CAWNPORE or CALCUTTA. Sign. R. W. Gillan. 29.8.1906.	60.00	125.00	375.00

A14 **20 RUPEES**
1902-05. Green unpt. 4 languages on 2 panels, 4 serial #.

		GOOD	FINE	XF
a.	CALCUTTA. Sign. A. F. Cox. 3.2.1902.	200.00	575.00	—
b.	CALCUTTA. Sign. O. T. Barrow. 10.3.1905.	200.00	575.00	—
c.	LAHORE or CALCUTTA. Sign. A. A. Cox. 27.3.1902.	200.00	575.00	—
d.	LAHORE or CALCUTTA. Sign. O. T. Barrow. 30.8.1905.	200.00	575.00	—

A10 **10 RUPEES**
1910-20. Red unpt. 8 language panels, 4 serial #. *at any Office of Issue* added to text. Letter for city of issue.

		GOOD	FINE	XF
a.	B (Bombay). Sign. R. W. Gillan. 24.8.1910; 26.8.1910; 16.11.1911.	17.50	45.00	140.00
b.	B (Bombay). Sign. H. F. Howard. 1914-26.4.1916; 29.5.1916.	17.50	45.00	140.00
c.	B (Bombay). Sign. M. M. S. Gubbay. 1916-17.2.1919.	17.50	45.00	140.00
d.	C (Calcutta). Sign. R. W. Gillan. 21.2.1910; 31.5.1912.	17.50	45.00	140.00
e.	C (Calcutta). Sign. H. F. Howard. 31.5.1912; 6.4.1916.	17.50	45.00	140.00
f.	C (Calcutta). Sign. M. M. S. Gubbay. 1916-19.	17.50	45.00	140.00
g.	A (Cawnpore). Sign. M. M. S. Gubbay. 23.12.1915-1919.	20.00	50.00	140.00
h.	K (Karachi). Sign. M. M. S. Gubbay. 27.2.1918.	20.00	50.00	140.00
i.	L (Lahore). Sign. M. M. S. Gubbay. 10.10.1917.	20.00	50.00	140.00
j.	M (Madras). Sign. M. M. S. Gubbay. 1914-19.	20.00	50.00	140.00
k.	W/o letter. Sign. M. M. S. Gubbay. 27.2.1919-16.8.1920.	15.00	40.00	125.00
l.	W/o letter. Sign. A. C. McWatters. 10.2.1920.	15.00	40.00	125.00

A11 **20 RUPEES**
5.7.1899; 1.1.1901. Green unpt. 4 language panels, 2 serial #. BOMBAY. Sign. O. T. Barrow.

	GOOD	FINE	XF
	250.00	800.00	—

A12 **20 RUPEES**
1904-06. Green unpt. 4 language panels, 4 serial #. BOMBAY.

		GOOD	FINE	XF
a.	Sign. F. C. Harrison. 11.1.1904; 12.1.1904; 17.10.1905.	200.00	650.00	—
b.	Sign. W. H. Michael. 18.10.1905; 16.1.1906.	200.00	650.00	—

A13 **20 RUPEES**
1894-1901. Green unpt. 4 languages on 2 panels, 2 serial #.

		GOOD	FINE	XF
a.	ALLAHABAD or CALCUTTA. Sign. A. F. Cox. 26.6.1894; 26.2.1901.	300.00	875.00	—
b.	LAHORE or CALCUTTA. Sign. A. F. Cox. 28.8.1900.	300.00	875.00	—

A14A **50 RUPEES**

	GOOD	FINE	XF
19.9.1905. Green unpt. 4 language panels, 4 serial #. BOMBAY. Sign. F.C. Harrison.	350.00	825.00	—

A15 **50 RUPEES**
1913-22. Red unpt. 8 language panels, 4 serial #. Letter for city of issue.

		GOOD	FINE	XF
a.	B (Bombay). Sign. H. F. Howard. 11.6.1913; 17.6.1913; 10.6.1920.	300.00	725.00	—
b.	B (Bombay). Sign. A. C. McWatters. 8.2.1916.	300.00	725.00	—
c.	B (Bombay). Sign. H. Denning. 8.6.1920.	300.00	725.00	—
d.	C (Calcutta). Sign. H. Denning. 15.1.1918; 9.3.1920; 10.3.1920; 28.10.1922.	300.00	725.00	—
e.	A (Cawnpore). Sign. A. C. McWatters. 29.4.1919.	300.00	725.00	—
f.	K (Karachi). Sign. M. M. S. Gubbay. 1.12.1913.	300.00	725.00	—
g.	L (Lahore). 21.3.1918.	—	Rare	—
h.	M (Madras). Sign. H. F. Howard. 23.6.1913.	—	Rare	—
i.	C (Calcutta). Sign. A. C. McWa McWatters. 11.1.1918.	—	Rare	—

A16	100 RUPEES	GOOD	FINE	XF
	1.7.1900; 15.10.1900. Green unpt. 4 language panels, 2 serial #. BOMBAY. Sign. O. T. Barrow.	150.00	400.00	700.00
A17	100 RUPEES			
	1904-27. Green unpt. 4 language panels, 4 serial #.			
	a. BOMBAY. Sign. H. F. Howard. 26.2.1913.	100.00	200.00	425.00
	b. Bombay. Sign. M. M. S. Gubbay 1.7.1914; 26.41916; 16.7.1916.	100.00	200.00	425.00
	c. BOMBAY. Sign. A.C. McWatters. 10.6.1918-10.7.1918.	100.00	200.00	425.00
	d. BOMBAY. Sign. H. Denning. 3.7.1920; 17.7.1920; 26.7.1920; 4.1.1923; 24.1.1925.	100.00	200.00	425.00
	e. CALCUTTA. Sign. A. F. Cox. 22.9.1904; 23.3 1905.	100.00	200.00	425.00
	f. CALCUTTA. Sign. A. C. McWatters. 31.1.1918-22.11.1925.	100.00	200.00	425.00
	g. CALCUTTA. Sign. O. T. Burrow. 23.3.1905.	100.00	200.00	425.00
	h. CALCUTTA. Sign. H. Denning. 27.3.1920; 30.10.1922; 31.10.1922.	100.00	200.00	425.00
	i. CAWNPORE. Sign. H. Denning. 11.3.1918; 6.6.1919; 14.6.1919; 15.4.1920.	100.00	200.00	425.00
	j. KARACHI. 30.12.1915.	125.00	280.00	525.00
	k. 6.9.1913-24.5.1920	100.00	200.00	425.00
	l. LAHORE. 1901-27.(25.41918).	100.00	200.00	425.00
	m. MADRAS. Sign. H. Denning. 3.9.1920-13.21925.	100.00	200.00	425.00

A18	500 RUPEES	GOOD	FINE	XF
	1907-19. Green unpt. 4 language panels at top, 4 serial #.			
	a. BOMBAY. Sign. A Kingstocke. 8.5.1913.	500.00	1250.	—
	b. BOMBAY. Sign. C. W. Cassog. 9.5.1913.	500.00	1250.	—
	c. BOMBAY. Sign. H. Denning. 10.5.1913.	500.00	1250.	—
	d. CALCUTTA. Sign. A. V. V. Aiyar. 22.4.1919.	—	Rare	
	e. CALCUTTA. Sign. H. Denning. 2.5.1922; 29.5.1922.	—	Rare	

	f. CAWNPORE or CALCUTTA. Sign. J. W. Kelly. 26.6.1907; 27.6.1907.	—	Rare	—

A19	1000 RUPEES	GOOD	FINE	XF
	1909-27. Lt. green unpt. 4 language panels at top, 4 serial #.			
	a. BOMBAY. Sign. A. Kingstocke. 1909; 2.6.1913.	250.00	750.00	—
	b. BOMBAY. Sign. C. W. C. Cassog. 20.9.1915.	250.00	750.00	—
	c. BOMBAY. Sign. H. Denning. 20.9.1915; 9.8.1918; 10.8.1918; 12.8.1925; 14.8.1925; 7.7.1926.	250.00	750.00	—
	d. BOMBAY. Sign. A. V. V. Aiyar. 22.9.1919; 12.8.1925-7.7.1926.	250.00	750.00	—
	e. CALCUTTA. Sign. H. Denning. 6.4.1920; 19.8.1927; 22.8.1927.	250.00	750.00	—
A20	10,000 RUPEES			
	22.4.1899. Green unpt. 4 languages on 1 panel, 4 serial #. CALCUTTA.	—	Rare	

1917-30 ISSUE
#1-16 Kg. George V.
#9 and 10 w/*RAGOON* ovpt. are listed in Burma.
#10 with *T* prefix may have been officially used to denote thin paper, as all such notes are on thinner stock.

1	1 RUPEE	VG	VF	UNC
	1917. Black on red unpt. Coin w/Kg. George V at upper l. W/ or w/o perforation on l. border. Also isssued in booklets of 25 pcs.			
	a. Wmk: Rayed star in plain field at r. Sign. M. M. S. Gubbay.	2.00	5.00	20.00
	b. Wmk: Rayed star in plain field at r. Sign. A. C. McWatters.	2.00	5.00	20.00
	c. Wmk: Rayed star in plain field at r. Sign. H. Denning.	3.00	7.00	27.50
	d. Wmk: Rayed star in square at r. Smaller letters in last line (Gujarati) on back. Sign. H. Denning.	2.00	5.00	20.00
	e. Wmk: Rayed star in square at r. Larger letters in last line on back. Sign. A. C. McWatters.	1.50	3.00	15.00
	f. Wmk: Rayed star in square at r. Larger letters in last line on back. Sign. H. Denning.	1.50	3.00	15.00
	g. Wmk: Rayed star in square. Sign. M. M. S. Gubbay.	1.50	3.00	15.00

2	2 RUPEES 8 ANNAS	VG	VF	UNC
	ND (1917). Black on green and red-brown unpt. Kg. George V in octagon at upper l. Sign. M. M. S. Gubbay.	40.00	100.00	300.00

3   **5 RUPEES**
ND. Green on brown unpt. Oval portr. of Kg. George V at upper r.
Inverted 5 at lower l. on back. Trial pieces. Sign. M. M. S. Gubbay.

	VG	VF	UNC
	—	—	650.00

4   **5 RUPEES**
ND. Brown-violet, green and lt. brown. Kg. George V at upper r.

	VG	VF	UNC
a. Sign. H. Denning.	5.00	15.00	65.00
b. Sign. J. B. Taylor.	5.00	15.00	65.00

5   **10 RUPEES**
ND. Blue and brown. Kg. George V at upper r. Serial # at upper l. and lower r.

	VG	VF	UNC
a. Sign. A. C. McWatters.	10.00	27.50	90.00
b. Sign. H. Denning.	10.00	27.50	90.00

6   **10 RUPEES**
ND. Green and brown. Similar to #5 but serial # at lower l. and upper r.
Sign. H. Denning.

	7.00	20.00	80.00

7   **10 RUPEES**
ND. Dk. blue on gray and purple unpt. Kg. George V at r.

	VG	VF	UNC
a. Sign. H. Denning.	5.00	15.00	55.00
b. Sign. J. B. Taylor.	5.00	15.00	55.00

8   **50 RUPEES**
ND. Coin w/Kg. George V at upper r. CAWNPORE. W/o sign. Uniface.
Perforated: *SPECIMEN.*

	VG	VF	UNC
a. Blue, green and brown.	—	Unc	900.00
b. Brown, red and yellow.	—	Unc	900.00

9   **50 RUPEES**
ND (1930). Lilac and brown. Kg. George V in oval at r.

a. BOMBAY. Sign. H. Denning.	100.00	225.00	650.00
b. BOMBAY. Sign. J. B. Taylor.	100.00	225.00	650.00
c. CALCUTTA. Sign. H. Denning.	100.00	225.00	650.00
d. CALCUTTA. Sign. J. B. Taylor.	100.00	225.00	650.00
e. CAWNPORE. Sign. J. B. Taylor.	110.00	250.00	700.00
f. KARACHI. Sign. J. B. Taylor.	110.00	250.00	700.00
g. MADRAS. Sign. J. B. Taylor.	110.00	250.00	700.00

10   **100 RUPEES**
ND. Violet and green. Oval portr. of Kg. George V at upper r.

	VG	VF	UNC
a. Sm. BOMBAY in black. Sign. H. Denning.	30.00	80.00	275.00
b. Lg. (13mm) BOMBAY in green. Sign. J. B. Taylor.	30.00	80.00	275.00
c. Lg. BOMBAY in green, prefix letter: T. Sign. J. W. Kelly.	30.00	80.00	275.00
d. Sm. CALCUTTA in black. Sign. H. Denning.	30.00	80.00	275.00
e. Lg. or sm. CALCUTTA in green. Sign. H. Denning.	30.00	80.00	275.00
f. Lg. CALCUTTA in green. Sign. J. B. Taylor.	30.00	80.00	275.00
g. Lg. CALCUTTA in green, prefix letter: T. Sign. J. B. Taylor.	30.00	80.00	200.00
h. Lg. CALCUTTA in green, prefix letter: T. Sign. J. W. Kelly.	30.00	80.00	275.00
i. Sm. CAWNPORE in green. Sign. H. Denning.	30.00	80.00	275.00
j. Lg. CAWNPORE in green. Sign. J. B. Taylor.	30.00	80.00	275.00
k. Lg. CAWNPORE in green, prefix letter: T. Sign. J. W. Kelly.	30.00	80.00	275.00
l. Lg. or sm. KARACHI in green. Sign. H. Denning.	30.00	80.00	275.00
m. Lg. LAHORE in green. Sign. H. Denning.	30.00	80.00	275.00
n. Lg. LAHORE in green. Sign. J. B. Taylor.	30.00	80.00	275.00
o. Lg. LAHORE in green, prefix letter: T. Sign. J. W. Kelly.	30.00	80.00	275.00
p. Sm. MADRAS in green. Sign. H. Denning.	30.00	80.00	275.00
q. Lg. MADRAS in green. Sign. J. B. Taylor.	30.00	80.00	275.00
r. Lg. MADRAS in green, prefix letter: T. Sign. J. W. Kelly.	30.00	80.00	275.00

11   **500 RUPEES**
ND (1928).

	—	Rare	—

12   **1000 RUPEES**
ND (1928). Violet and green. oval portr. of Kg. George V in sprays at r.
Farmer plowing w/oxen at ctr. on back.

	VG	VF	UNC
a. BOMBAY. Sign. J. B. Taylor.	150.00	450.00	—
b. CALCUTTA. Sign. J. B. Taylor.	150.00	450.00	—
c. CALCUTTA. Sign. J. W. Kelly.	150.00	450.00	—
d. LAHORE. Sign. J. B. Taylor.	150.00	450.00	—

13 **10,000 RUPEES**
ND (1928). Green and brown. oval portr. of Kg. George V at ctr., wmk. at l. at r. Back blue.

		VG	VF	UNC
a.	BOMBAY. Sign. J. B. Taylor.	—	Rare	—
b.	CALCUTTA. Sign. J. B. Taylor.	—	Rare	—
c.	KARACHI. Sign. J. W. Kelly.	—	Rare	—

1928-35 ISSUE

14 **1 RUPEE**
1935. Green-blue. Coin w/Kg. George V at r. Reverse of coin w/date on back. W/ or w/o perforation on l. border. Those perforated were issued in booklets of 25 notes.

		VG	VF	UNC
a.	Wm: Portr. Sign. J. W. Kelly.	1.00	3.00	10.00
b.	Wmk: W/o Portr. Sign. J. W. Kelly.	2.00	5.00	15.00

15 **5 RUPEES**
ND.(1928-1935) Brown-violet and lt. brown. Oval portr. Kg. George V at r.

		VG	VF	UNC
a.	Sign. J.B. Taylor.	1.00	4.50	20.00
b.	Sign. J.W. Kelly.	1.00	4.50	20.00

16 **10 RUPEES**
ND. Blue or dk. blue. Palm tree, lake and mountains at ctr. Elephants on back.

		VG	VF	UNC
a.	Sign. J. B. Taylor.	2.00	7.50	30.00
b.	Sign. J. W. Kelly.	2.00	7.50	30.00

RESERVE BANK OF INDIA

1937 ISSUE
#17-24 Kg. George VI at r.
#17-19 w/o place names.
#20-22 w/place names.

17 **2 RUPEES**
ND. Lilac and m/c.

		VG	VF	UNC
a.	Black serial #. Sign. J. B. Taylor (1937).	.50	2.00	5.00
b.	Black serial #. Sign. C. D. Deshmukh (1943).	.50	2.50	5.00
c.	Red serial #. Sign. C. D. Deshmukh (1943).	1.00	4.50	15.00

18 **5 RUPEES**
ND. Brown and green. Similar to #15.

		VG	VF	UNC
a.	Sign. J. B. Taylor (1937).	.50	1.50	6.00
b.	Sign. C. D. Deshmukh (1943).	.50	1.50	6.00

19 **10 RUPEES**
ND. Blue-violet and olive. Back blue w/elephants.

		VG	VF	UNC
a.	Sign. J. B. Taylor (1937).	1.00	4.00	12.50
b.	Sign. C. D. Deshmukh (1943).	1.00	4.00	12.50

20 **100 RUPEES**
ND. Dk. green and lilac. Back dk. green w/tiger. Wmk: Kg. George VI.

		VG	VF	UNC
a.	BOMBAY. Wmk: Profile. Sign. J. B. Taylor (1937).	15.00	30.00	75.00
b.	BOMBAY. Wmk: Profile. Sign. C. D. Deshmukh (1943).	15.00	30.00	75.00
c.	BOMBAY. Wmk: Facing portr. Sign. C. D. Deshmukh (1943).	16.00	35.00	85.00
d.	CALCUTTA. Wmk: Profile. Sign. J. B. Taylor (1937).	15.00	30.00	75.00
e.	CALCUTTA. Wmk: Profile. Sign. C. D. Deshmukh (1943).	15.00	30.00	75.00
f.	CALCUTTA. Wmk: Facing portr. Sign. C. D. Deshmukh (1943).	16.00	35.00	85.00
g.	CAWNPORE. Wmk: Profile. Sign. J. B. Taylor (1937).	15.00	30.00	75.00
h.	CAWNPORE. Wmk: Profile. Sign. C. D. Deshmukh (1943).	15.00	30.00	75.00
i.	KANPUR (Cawnpore). Wmk: facing portr. Sign. C. D. Deshmukh (1943).	25.00	60.00	—
j.	DELHI. Wmk: Profile. Sign. C. D. Deshmukh (1943).	17.00	37.50	95.00
k.	KARACHI. Wmk: Profile. Sign. C. D. Deshmukh (1943).	15.00	30.00	75.00
l.	LAHORE. Wmk: Profile. Sign. J. B. Taylor (1937).	15.00	30.00	75.00
m.	LAHORE. Wmk: Profile. Sign. C. D. Deshmukh (1943).	15.00	30.00	75.00
n.	MADRAS. Wmk: Profile. Sign. J. B. Taylor (1937).	15.00	30.00	70.00
o.	MADRAS. Wmk: Profile. Sign. C. D. Deshmukh (1943).	15.00	30.00	75.00
p.	MADRAS. Wmk: Facing. Sign. C. D. Deshmukh (1943).	16.00	35.00	85.00
q.	KARACHI. Wmk: Profile. Sign. J. B. Taylor.	15.00	30.00	75.00

21	1000 RUPEES		VG	VF	UNC
	ND (1937). Lilac, violet and green. Mountain scene on back. Sign. J. B. Taylor.				
	a.	BOMBAY.	50.00	110.00	325.00
	b.	CALCUTTA.	50.00	110.00	325.00
	c.	CAWNPORE.	50.00	110.00	325.00
	d.	KARACHI.	50.00	110.00	325.00
	e.	LAHORE.	50.00	110.00	325.00
	f.	MADRAS.	50.00	110.00	325.00
22	10,000 RUPEES		—	Rare	—
	ND (1938).				

1943 ISSUE
#23-24 Kg. George VI facing at r.

23	5 RUPEES				
	ND (1943). Green and m/c. antelope on back. Sign. C. D. Deshmukh.				
	a.	Black serial #.	1.00	3.00	12.00
	b.	Red serial #.	4.00	15.00	40.00

24	10 RUPEES	VG	VF	UNC
	ND (1943). Violet and m/c. Dhow on back. Sign. C. D. Deshmukh.	1.00	3.00	10.00

GOVERNMENT OF INDIA (RESUMED)

1940 ISSUE

25	1 RUPEE	VG	VF	UNC
	1940. Blue-gray and m/c. Coin w/Kg. George VI at r. Coin w/date on back. Sign. C. E. Jones.			
	a. Black serial #.	.20	.75	2.00
	b. Red serial #.	1.00	6.00	30.00
	c. Black serial #, letter A.	2.00	6.00	30.00
	d. Green serial #, letter A.	.20	.75	1.50

REPUBLIC OF INDIA

SIGNATURE VARIETIES	
Governors, Reserve Bank of India (all except 1 Rupee notes)	
C.D. Deshmukh February 1943–June 1949	*C.D. Deshmukh*
B. Rama Rau July 1949–January 1957	*B Rama Rau*
K.G. Ambegaokar January 1957–February 1957	*K.G.Ambegaokar*
H.V.R. Iengar March 1957–February 1962	*H.V.R.Iengar*

RESERVE BANK OF INDIA

FIRST SERIES
#27-47 Asoka column at r. Lg. letters in unpt. beneath serial #. Wmk: Asoka column.

Error singular Hindi = RUPAYA   Corrected plural Hindi = RUPAYE

VARIETIES: #27-28, 33, 38, 42, 46, 48 and 50 have large headings in Hindi expressing value incorrectly in the singular form Rupaya.

NOTE: For similar notes but in different colors, please see Haj Pilgrim and Persian Gulf listings at the end of this country listing.

27	2 RUPEES	VG	VF	UNC
	ND. Red-brown on violet and green unpt. Tiger head at l. on back. Value in English and error Hindi on face and back. Gujarati numberal 2 at upper r. 8 value text lines on back. Sign. B. Rama Rau. Rau.	.50	2.50	8.00

28	2 RUPEES	.50	2.50	8.00
	ND. Similar to #27 but English 2 at upper l. and r. Redesigned panels on face. 7 value text lines on back; third 18mm long. Sign B. Rama Rau.			

29	2 RUPEES	VG	VF	UNC
	ND. Red-brown on violet and green unpt. Tiger head at l. on back. Value in English and corrected Hindi on both sides. Third value text line on back 24mm long. Tiger's head to l.			
	a. Sign. 2.	.75	3.00	12.00
	b. Sign. 4.	.50	2.00	10.00

32 **5 RUPEES**
ND. Green on brown unpt. English value only on face, serial # at ctr.
Rs. 5 and antelope on back. Sign 2.

	VG	VF	UNC
	1.00	4.00	15.00

33 **5 RUPEES**
ND. Like #32 but value in English and error Hindi on face, serial # at r.
8 value lines on back, fourth line 21mm long. Sign. 2.

VG	VF	UNC
.75	2.00	9.00

34 **5 RUPEES**
ND. Fourth value text line on back 26mm long. Sign. 2.

VG	VF	UNC
.75	3.00	9.00

35 **5 RUPEES**
ND. Green on brown unpt. Value in English and correct Hinki. *Rs. S*
and antelope on back, but redesigned panels at l. and r.
a. W/o letter. Sign. 4.   .75 2.00 9.00
b. Letter A. Sign. 4.   .50 2.00 6.00

37 **10 RUPEES**

	VG	VF	UNC
a. Sign. C. D. Deshmukh.	6.00	12.50	30.00
b. Sign. B. Rama Rau.	1.50	5.00	15.00

38 **10 RUPEES**
ND. Like #37 but value in English and error Hindi on face and back. 2
serial #. Third value text line on back. 24mm long. Sign. B. Rama Rau.   .75 3.00 15.00

39 **10 RUPEES**
ND. Violet on m/c unpt. English and correct Hindi value. Dhow at ctr.
on back. Third value text line on back 29mm long.

	VG	VF	UNC
a. W/o letter. Sign. 2.	1.50	4.00	12.50
b. W/o letter. Sign. 4.	.75	3.00	9.00
c. Letter A. Sign. 4.	.75	3.00	9.00

41 **100 RUPEES**

	VG	VF	UNC
a. Dk. blue. Sign. B. Rama Rau.	30.00	60.00	135.00
b. Lt. blue. Sign. B. Rama Rau.	25.00	55.00	110.00

42 **100 RUPEES**

	VG	VF	UNC
a. Black serial #. Sign. B. Rama Rau.	15.00	40.00	85.00
b. Red serial #. Sign. B. Rama Rau.	15.00	40.00	85.00

43   100 RUPEES
ND. Purplish blue on m/c unpt. Value in English and correct Hindi.
Bank emblem at l. on back. Third value text line 40mm long.

		VG	VF	UNC
a.	W/o letter, thin paper. Sign. 2.	15.00	40.00	85.00
b.	W/o letter, thin paper. Sign. 4.	15.00	40.00	85.00
c.	Letter A, thick paper. Sign. 4.	15.00	40.00	85.00

44   100 RUPEES
ND. Violet and m/c. Heading in rectangle at top, serial # at upper l. and
lower r. title: *GOVERNOR* at ctr. r. Dam at ctr. w/13 value text lines at l.
on back. Sign. 4.

VG	VF	UNC
12.50	25.00	65.00

46   1000 RUPEES
ND. Brown on green and blue unpt. Value in English and in error Hindi
on face and back. Tanjore Temple at ctr. w/7 value text lines at l. on
back.

		VG	VF	UNC
a.	BOMBAY. Sign. B. Rama Rau.	50.00	125.00	—
b.	CALCUTTA. Sign. B. Rama Rau.	50.00	125.00	—
c.	DELHI. Sign. B. Rama Rau.	50.00	125.00	—
d.	MADRAS. Sign. B. Rama Rau.	50.00	125.00	—

48   5000 RUPEES
ND. Green, violet and brown. Asoka column at l. Value in English and
in error Hindi on face and back. Gateway of India on back. Sign. 2.

		VG	VF	UNC
a.	BOMBAY.	—	Rare	—
b.	CALCUTTA.	—	Rare	—
c.	DELHI.	—	Rare	—

49   5000 RUPEES
ND. Green, violet and brown. Asoka column at l. Value in English and
correct Hindi. Gateway of India on back. BOMBAY. Sign. 4.

VG	VF	UNC
—	Rare	—

50   10,000 RUPEES
ND. Blue, violet and brown. Asoka column at ctr. Value in English and
in error Hindi on face and back.

		VG	VF	UNC
a.	BOMBAY. Sign. 2.	—	Rare	—
b.	CALCUTTA. Sign. 2.	—	Rare	—
c.	MADRAS. Sign. 4.	—	Rare	—

50A   10,000 RUPEES
ND. Like #50 but Hindi corrected. BOMBAY. Sign. 4.

VG	VF	UNC
—	Rare	—

GOVERNMENT OF INDIA

SIGNATURE VARIETIES	
SECRETARIES, MINISTRY OF FINANCE (1 Rupee notes only)	
K.R.K. Menon **K.R.K. Menon, 1949**	*A.K. Roy* **A.K. Roy, 1957**
K.G. Ambegaokar **K.G. Ambegaokar, 1949–1951**	*L.K. Jha* **L.K. Jha, 1957–1963**
H.M. Patel **H.M. Patel, 1951–1957**	

NOTE: The sign. H. M. Patel is often misread as "Mehta." There was never any such individual serving as
Secretary. Do not confuse H. M. Patel with I. G. Patel who served later.

1949-51 ISSUE

71   1 RUPEE
ND (1949-50). Green-gray and m/c. Asoka column at r. W/o coin
design on face or back.

		VG	VF	UNC
a.	Sign. 31. (1949).	.40	1.50	6.00
b.	Sign. 32. (1949-50).	.40	1.50	6.00

22	**1000 LIVRES**	**GOOD**	**FINE**	**XF**
	L.1790. Wavy bar under title.			
	a. Off-white paper.	400.00	800.00	1600.
	b. Bluish paper.		Rare	
	x. Error: inverted *D* in *DE BOURBON*.		Rare	
23	**1000 LIVRES**			
	L.1790. Straight bar under title.	400.00	800.00	1600.

24	**10,000 LIVRES**	**GOOD**	**FINE**	**XF**
	L.1790	—	Rare	—

1795-96 ISSUE
#26 and 28 w/text: *Bon pour...*

26	**2 LIVRES 10 SOLS**	**GOOD**	**FINE**	**XF**
	1795. Black. Uniface.	—	—	—

28	**10 LIVRES**	**GOOD**	**FINE**	**XF**
	1795-96. Black. Uniface.	—	—	—

ISLE OF MAN

IRELAND
UNITED KINGDOM

The Isle of Man, a dependency of the British Crown located in the Irish Sea equidistant from Ireland, Scotland and England, has an area of 227 sq. mi. (588 sq. km.) and a population of 61,000. Capital: Douglas. Agriculture, dairy farming, fishing and tourism are the chief industries.

The prevalence of prehistoric artifacts and monuments on the island give evidence that its mild, almost sub-tropical climate was enjoyed by mankind before the dawn of history. Vikings came to the Isle of Man during the 9th century and remained until ejected by Scotland in 1266. The island came under the protection of the British Crown in 1288, and in 1406 was granted, in perpetuity, to the Earls of Derby, from whom it was inherited, 1736, by the Duke of Atholl. Rights and title were purchased from the Duke of Atholl in 1765 by the British Crown; the remaining privileges of the Atholl family were transferred to the crown in 1829. The Isle of Man is ruled by its own legislative council and the House of Keys, one of the oldest legislative assemblies in the world. Acts of Parliament passed in London do not affect the island unless it is specifically mentioned.

RULERS:
  British

MONETARY SYSTEM:
  1 Pound = 20 Shillings to 1971

NOTE: Certain private or commercial bank listings have been deleted and will appear together with other early bank issues in Vol. I.

BRITISH INFLUENCE

BARCLAYS BANK LIMITED

1924 ISSUE

A1A, 1A-1E *Deleted.*

1	**1 POUND**	**GOOD**	**FINE**	**XF**
	1924-60. Brown and green. Triskele in unpt. at ctr. Douglas harbor on back. Printer: W&S.			
	a. 7.6.1924-7.4.1937.	375.00	750.00	1500.
	b. 17.12.1937-4.12.1953.	100.00	300.00	600.00
	c. 10.4.1954-10.3.1959.	80.00	150.00	400.00
	d. 30.3.1960.	100.00	200.00	450.00

ISLE OF MAN BANKING CO. LIMITED

In 1926 became Isle of Man Bank Limited.

1865 ISSUE

#2-3, Douglas harbor at upper ctr. Triskele at ctr. on back. Printer: W. & A. K. Johnston Ltd., Edinburgh. Various date and sign. varieties.

2	**1 POUND**	**GOOD**	**FINE**	**XF**
	1865-1915. Black and brown. Vertical blue lines and border on back.	500.00	1000.	—

3	5 POUNDS	GOOD	FINE	XF
	1894-1920. Black and blue. Seal of arms at l.			
	a. 1.11.1894; 1.1.1900; 4.12.1911; 7.8.1914; 1.3.1920.	2500.	5000.	10000.
	r. Unsigned remainder. ND.	—	—	—

1914 ISSUE

3A (2A)	1 POUND			
	1914-26. Black and brown. Like #2 but w/o vertical blue lines or border on back.			
	a. 1.8.1914.	250.00	500.00	1200.
	b. 8.1.1916-1.3.1926.	150.00	400.00	800.00

ISLE OF MAN BANK LIMITED
Formerly the Isle of Man Banking Co. Limited.

1926-27 ISSUE
#4 and 5, Douglas harbor above bank title. Triskele at ctr. on back. Various date and sign. varieties.

4	1 POUND			
	1.12.1926-4.9.1933. Black and pink. Printer: W. & A. K. Johnston Ltd., Edinburgh.	200.00	400.00	800.00

5	5 POUNDS	GOOD	FINE	XF
	1.11.1927. Blue, green and pink. 2 sign. varieties. Printer: W&S.	37.50	150.00	300.00

1934-36 ISSUE
#6 and 6A Douglas harbor above bank title. Triskele at ctr. on back. Various date and sign. varieties.

6	1 POUND	GOOD	FINE	XF
	1934-60. Blue, brown and green. Printer: W&S.			
	a. 1.10.1934-5.5.1937.	40.00	95.00	250.00
	b. 4.2.1938-18.10.1952.	20.00	60.00	120.00
	c. 1.12.1953; 29.11.1954. 2 sign. varieties.	40.00	90.00	175.00
	d. 5.1.1956-24.10.1960.	20.00	60.00	125.00

6A (5A)	5 POUNDS			
	1936-60. Brown, pink and green. Like #5.			
	a. 1.12.1936.	50.00	150.00	300.00
	b. 3.1.1945; 7.4.1960.	150.00	300.00	600.00

LANCASHIRE & YORKSHIRE BANK LIMITED
Taken over in 1928 by Martins Bank Limited.

MANX BANK BRANCH

1904 ISSUE
#7-8, various date and sign. varieties.

7	1 POUND	GOOD	FINE	XF
	10.11.1904-30.10.1920. Slate gray. Tower of Refuge at ctr. Title: *MANX BANK / BRANCH OF THE / LANCASHIRE & YORKSHIRE BANK LIMITED.* Bank arms on back. Douglas.	275.00	550.00	1100.

1920 W/O BRANCH NAME ISSUE

8	1 POUND	GOOD	FINE	XF
	13.12.1920-28.12.1927. Slate gray. Bank arms at l., Tower of Refuge at r. Title: *LANCASHIRE & YORKSHIRE BANK LIMITED.* Castle Rushen at l., Triskele at ctr., Laxey wheel at r. on back.	375.00	750.00	1500.

LLOYDS BANK LIMITED

1919-29 ISSUES
#9-13 various date and sign. varieties.

9	1 POUND			
	23.4.1919-10.12.1920. Black and green.	375.00	750.00	1500.
10	1 POUND			
	23.3.1921-21.1.1927. Like #9 but pink unpt. *ONE POUND.*	375.00	750.00	1500.
11	1 POUND			
	1.8.1929-14.2.1934. Black and green on pink unpt. Text: *INCORPORATED IN ENGLAND* in 1 line.	300.00	600.00	1200.

1935 ISSUE

12	1 POUND			
	1935-54. Like #11 but w/text: *INCORPORATED IN ENGLAND* divided. Letters of bank name w/shading on back.			
	a. 28.1.1935-27.4.1949.	200.00	350.00	700.00
	b. 27.2.1951-26.2.1954.	100.00	250.00	500.00

1955 ISSUE

13	1 POUND	GOOD	FINE	XF
	21.1.1955-14.3.1961. Black on green unpt. Bank arms at upper ctr.			
	a. Issue note.	75.00	150.00	300.00
	r. Unsigned remainder. ND.	—	—	100.00

LONDON COUNTY WESTMINSTER AND PARR'S BANK LIMITED

In 1923 the name was changed to "Westminster Bank". See also #22-23.

1918 PROVISIONAL ISSUE

#14, various date and sign. varieties.

14	**1 POUND**				
	28.3.1918-22.11.1918. Ovpt: *LONDON COUNTY WESTMINSTER* on #21.	500.00	1000.	2000.	

1919 REGULAR ISSUE

#15, various date and sign. varieties.

15	**1 POUND**				
	11.10.1919; 11.1.1921; 25.11.1921. Like #14 but newly printed bank name. Printer: W&S.	500.00	1000.	2000.	

MANX BANK LIMITED

Taken over in 1901 by the Mercantile Bank of Lancashire Limited.

1882 ISSUE

#16, various date and sign. varieties.

16	**1 POUND**				
	11.11.1882-30.5.1900. Black. Tower of Refuge at ctr. Printer: W&S.	500.00	1000.	2000.	

MARTINS BANK LIMITED

Absorbed the Lancashire & Yorkshire Bank Limited in 1928.

1928 PROVISIONAL ISSUE

17	**1 POUND**				
	9.10.1928; 3.11.1928. Ovpt: *MARTINS BANK LIMITED* on #8.	500.00	1000.	2000.	

1928 ISSUE

18	**1 POUND**				
	1929-38. Black. Tower of Refuge at r. Castle Rushen at l. Bird on dk. hatched field in bank shield at l. Albert Tower at r. on back.				
	a. Red serial #. 2.4.1929; 1.12.1931; 31.12.1932.	150.00	300.00	600.00	
	b. Black serial #. 1.8.1934; 1.10.1938.	100.00	200.00	400.00	

1946 ISSUE

		GOOD	FINE	XF
19	**1 POUND**			
	1946-57. Black. Like #18 but bird on lightly stippled field in bank shield at l.			
	a. 1.3.1946.	50.00	130.00	300.00
	b. 1.6.1950; 1.5.1953; 1.2.1957.	20.00	75.00	200.00

MERCANTILE BANK OF LANCASHIRE LIMITED

Absorbed Manx Bank Limited in 1901. Taken over in 1904 by the Lancashire and Yorkshire Bank.

1901 ISSUE

#20, various date and sign. varieties.

20	**1 POUND**				
	13.6.1901-6.9.1902. Black. Tower of Refuge at ctr. Like #16. Printer: W&S.	500.00	1000.	2000.	

PARR'S BANK LIMITED

Amalgamated in 1918 with the London County and Westminster Bank.

1900 ISSUE

#21, various date and sign. varieties.

21	**1 POUND**				
	1900-16. Gray. Crowned Triskele supported by lion l., unicorn r.				
	a. Handwritten dates. 20.8.1900; 23.1.1901; 1.6.1906.	500.00	1000.	2000.	
	b. Printed dates. 2.4.1909-10.11.1916.	500.00	1000.	2000.	

WESTMINSTER BANK LIMITED

Formerly the London County Westminster and Parr's Bank Limited.

1923 PROVISIONAL ISSUE

#22, various date and sign. varieties.

22	**1 POUND**				
	1923-27. Ovpt: *WESTMINSTER BANK LIMITED* on #15.				
	a. 4.7.1923; 17.12.1923; 5.2.1924.	500.00	1000.	2000.	
	b. 20.10.1924-4.4.1927.	500.00	1000.	2000.	

1929 REGULAR ISSUE

#23 various date and sign. varieties.

23	**1 POUND**				
	1929-55. Black on lt. yellow unpt. Crowned Triskele supported by lion l., unicorn r., at upper ctr. Printer: W&S.				
	a. 9.1.1929; 24.10.1929; 14.11.1933.	150.00	300.00	600.00	
	b. 22.1.1935-4.2.1943.	110.00	225.00	450.00	
	c. 11.2.1944-18.3.1949.	80.00	160.00	325.00	
	d. 7.11.1950-30.3.1955.	60.00	125.00	250.00	

1955 ISSUE

#23A, various date and sign. varieties.

		GOOD	FINE	XF
23A	**1 POUND**			
	1955-61. Black on lt. yellow unpt. Crowned Triskele supported by lion and unicorn at upper ctr. W/text: *INCORPORATED IN ENGLAND* added below bank name. Printer: W&S.			
	a. 23.11.1955.	125.00	250.00	500.00
	b. 4.4.1956-10.3.1961.	50.00	120.00	250.00

ISRAEL

The State of Israel, at the eastern end of the Mediterranean Sea, bounded by Lebanon on the north, Syria on the northeast, Jordan on the east, and Egypt on the southwest, has an area of 7,847 sq. mi. (23,309 sq. km.) and a population of 4.5 million. Capital: Jerusalem. Diamonds, chemicals, citrus, textiles, and minerals are exported.

Palestine, which corresponds to Canaan of the Bible, was settled by the Philistines about the 12th century B.C. and shortly thereafter was invaded by the Jews who established the kingdoms of Israel and Judah. Because of its position as part of the land bridge connecting Asia and Africa, Palestine was invaded and conquered by nearly all of the historic empires of ancient Europe and Asia. In the 16th century it became a Turkish satrap. After falling to the British in World War I, it, together with Transjordan, was mandated to Great Britain by the League of Nations, 1922.

For more than half a century prior to the termination of the British mandate over Palestine, 1948, Zionist leaders had sought to create a Jewish homeland for Jews dispersed throughout the world. For almost as long, Jews fleeing persecution had immigrated to Palestine. The Nazi persecutions of the 1930s and 1940s increased the Jewish movement to Palestine and generated international support for the creation of a Jewish state, first promulgated by the Balfour Declaration of 1917 which asserted British support for the endeavor. The dream of a Jewish homeland was realized on May 14, 1948 when Palestine was proclaimed the State of Israel.

MONETARY SYSTEM:
1 Palestine Pound = 1000 Mils to 1948
1 Lira = 1000 Prutot, 1948-1960   1 Sheqel = 10 "old" Lirot, 1980-85
1 Lira = 100 Agorot, 1960-1980   1 New Sheqel = 1000 "old" Sheqalim, 1985-
1 Sheqel = 100 New Agorot, 1980-1985
1 New Sheqel = 100 Agorot, 1985-

STATE OF ISRAEL

ANGLO-PALESTINE BANK LIMITED

1948 PROVISIONAL ISSUE
Printed in the event that notes ordered might not be ready on time; destroyed in October, only a few sets preserved.
#1-4 uniface.

		VG	VF	UNC
1	**500 MILS** 16.5.1948. Purple.	—	—	1500.
2	**1 PALESTINE POUND** 16.5.1948. Green.	—	—	1500.
3	**5 PALESTINE POUNDS** 16.5.1948. Brown.	—	—	1200.
4	**10 PALESTINE POUNDS** 16.5.1948. Blue.	—	—	1200.

ISRAEL GOVERNMENT

SIGNATURE VARIETIES

SIGNATURE VARIETIES			
Zagaggi	*(signature)*	E. Kaplan	*(signature)*
Zagaggi	*(signature)*	L. Eshkol	*(signature)*
A. Neeman	*(signature)*	L. Eshkol	*(signature)*

1952-53 FRACTIONAL NOTE ISSUES
NOTE: Paper Thickness varies.

NOTE: *Adeph, Bet* and *Gimel* series refer to the first 3 letters of the Hebrew alphabet. The series suffix letter follows the serial #. On some series, a very faint gold-colored Menorah appears on face at upper l. or upper r. when exposed to ultra-violet lighting.

#5 Deleted.
#10A Deleted. See #10a.

#6

6	**50 MILS** ND (printed 1948, issued 1952). Dk. red and orange. Vertical format.	VG 25.00	VF 50.00	UNC 250.00

#7

		VG	VF	UNC
7	**100 MILS** ND (printed 1948, issued 1952). Green. Vertical format.	25.00	50.00	250.00
8	**50 PRUTA** ND (1952). Blue-black. Horizontal format. Sign. 1.	15.00	40.00	175.00

		VG	VF	UNC
9	**50 PRUTA** ND (1952). Red on pink unpt. Back gray. Sign. 1.	10.00	25.00	85.00
10	**50 PRUTA** ND (1952). Red on red or orange unpt. Back red or orange.			
	a. Sign. 1.	10.00	25.00	85.00
	b. Sign. 2.	10.00	25.00	85.00
	c. Sign. 3.	1.00	3.00	7.50

		VG	VF	UNC
11	**100 PRUTA** ND (1952). Green on lt. green unpt. Back gray. Sign. 1.	12.00	25.00	100.00
12	**100 PRUTA** ND (1952). Blue on green unpt. Back green.			
	a. Sign. 1.	12.00	25.00	100.00
	b. Sign. 2.	12.00	25.00	100.00
	c. Sign. 3.	1.00	3.00	7.50
	d. Sign. 3 w/A. Neeman inverted (error).	500.00	1200.00	3000.

SERIAL NUMBER SUFFIXES

01005א	*Aleph*
01004ב	*Bet*
01011ג	*Gimel*

13 **250 Pruta**
ND (1953). Dk. brown on green unpt. Back dk. green on orange unpt; Sea of Galilee w/Arbel mountain at ctr. r.

	VG	VF	UNC
a. Aleph series w/menorah.	4.00	15.00	65.00
b. Aleph series w/o menorah.	4.00	15.00	35.00
c. Bet series w/o menorah.	3.00	10.00	25.00
d. Gimel series w/menorah at l.	4.00	15.00	65.00
e. Gimel series w/menorah at r.	4.00	15.00	75.00
f. Aleph series w/*250* under guilloche on face.	—	—	—

ANGLO-PALESTINE BANK LIMITED

1948-51 ISSUE
#14-18 printer: ABNC (w/o imprint). Serial # varieties.

14 **500 MILS**
ND (1948-51). Gray.

	VG	VF	UNC
a. Issued note.	30.00	75.00	750.00
s. Specimen.	—	—	300.00

15 **1 POUND**
ND (1948-51). Blue. Similar to #14.

	VG	VF	UNC
a. Issued note.	7.00	30.00	125.00
s. Specimen.	—	—	300.00

16 **5 POUNDS**
ND (1948-51). Brown. Similar to #14.

	VG	VF	UNC
a. Issued note.	10.00	25.00	150.00
s. Specimen.	—	—	300.00

17 **10 POUNDS**
ND (1948-51). Red. Similar to #14.

	VG	VF	UNC
a. Issued note.	15.00	45.00	250.00
s. Specimen.	—	—	300.00

18 **50 POUNDS**
ND (1948-51). Lilac. Similar to #14.

	VG	VF	UNC
a. Issued note.	2000.	3250.	—
s. Specimen.	—	—	400.00

BANK LEUMI LE-ISRAEL B.M.

1952 ISSUE
#19-23 printer: ABNC (w/o imprint).

19 **500 PRUTAH**
ND (9.6.1952). Gray-green on lt. blue unpt.

	VG	VF	UNC
a. Issued note.	8.00	75.00	550.00
s. Specimen.	—	—	300.00

20 **1 POUND**
ND (9.6.1952). Olive on pink unpt.

	VG	VF	UNC
a. Issued note.	4.00	15.00	55.00
s. Specimen.	—	—	300.00

21 **5 POUNDS**
ND (9.6.1952). Brown on yellow unpt.

	VG	VF	UNC
a. Issued note.	12.00	40.00	185.00
s. Specimen.	—	—	300.00

22	**10 POUNDS**	VG	VF	UNC
	ND (9.6.1952). Gray on orange unpt.			
	a. Issued note.	15.00	45.00	300.00
	s. Specimen.	—	—	300.00

23	**50 POUNDS**	VG	VF	UNC
	ND (9.6.1952). Dk. brown on lt. blue unpt.			
	a. Issued note.	200.00	475.00	1350.
	s. Specimen.	—	—	400.00

BANK OF ISRAEL

1955 / 5715 ISSUE
#24-28 wmk: Menorah. Printer: TDLR (w/o imprint).

24	**500 PRUTA**	VG	VF	UNC
	1955/5715. Red on green unpt. Ruin of an ancient synagogue near Bir'am at l., flowers at upper r. Modernistic design on back.			
	a. Issued note.	3.00	8.00	35.00
	s. Specimen.	—	—	150.00

25	**1 LIRA**	VG	VF	UNC
	1955/5715. Blue on m/c unpt. Landscape in Upper Galilee across bottom, flowers at upper r.			
	a. Issued note.	3.00	10.00	45.00
	s. Specimen.	—	—	150.00

26	**5 LIROT**	VG	VF	UNC
	1955/5715. Brown on lt. blue unpt. Negev landscape across ctr., flowers at upper r.			
	a. Issued note.	3.00	12.50	60.00
	s. Specimen.	—	—	150.00

27	**10 LIROT**	VG	VF	UNC
	1955/5715. Dk. green on m/c unpt. Landscape in the Plain of Jezreel across ctr., flowers at upper r.			
	a. Red serial #.	5.00	15.00	40.00
	b. Black serial #.	4.00	10.00	30.00
	s. Specimen.	—	—	150.00

28	**50 LIROT**	VG	VF	UNC
	1955/5715. Dk. blue and m/c. Jerusalem Road between mountains, flowers at upper r. on face.			
	a. Black serial #.	10.00	40.00	100.00
	b. Red serial #.	20.00	60.00	160.00
	s. Specimen.	—	—	200.00

1958-60 / 5718-20 ISSUE
#29 and 30 printer: JEZ (w/o imprint).
#31 and 32 printer: TDLR (w/o imprint).

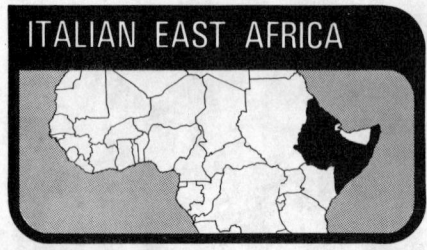

ITALIAN EAST AFRICA

Italian East Africa was a former Italian possession made up of Eritrea (Italian colony since 1890), Ethiopia (invaded by Italy from Eritrea in 1935 and annexed in 1936) and Italian Somaliland (under Italian influence since 1889). Founded in 1936, it lasted until British-led colonial forces came into each of the areas in 1941.

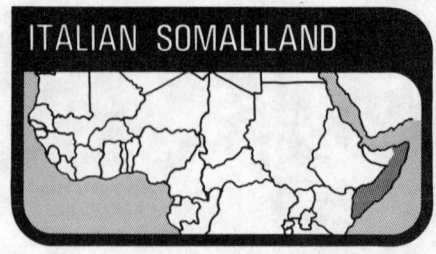

ITALIAN SOMALILAND

Italian Somaliland, a former Italian colony in East Africa, extended south from Ras Asir to Kenya. Area: 178,218 sq. mil. (461,585 sq. km.). Captial: Mogadisho.

In 1885, Italy obtained commercial concessions in the area from the sultan of Zanzibar,and in 1905 purchased the coast from Warshek to Brava. The Italians then extended their occupation inward. Cession of Jubaland Province by Britain in 1924, and seizure of the sultanates of Obbia and Mijertein in 1925-27 brought direct Italian administration over the whole territory. Italian dominance continued until World War II.

British troops occupied Italian Somaliland in 1941. Britain administered the colony until 1950, when it became a UN trust territory administered by Italy. On July 1, 1960, Italian Somaliland united with British Somaliland to form the independent Somali Democratic Republic.

RULERS:
Italian, 1892-1941, 1950-1960
British, 1941-1950

MONETARY SYSTEM:
1 Rupia = 100 Bese to 1925
1 Somali = 1 Lira = 100 Centesimi, 1925-1960
1 Shilling = 100 Cents, WW II British occupation

ITALIAN OCCUPATION - WW II

BANCA D'ITALIA

AFRICA ORIENTALE ITALIANA BRANCH

1938-39 ISSUE
NOTE: This issue circulated in all the Italian occupied ares and colonies in Africa.
#1-4 ovpt: *SERIE SPECIALE AFRICA ORIENTALE ITALIANA.*

		VG	VF	UNC
1	**50 LIRE**			
	1938-39. Green on lt. green unpt. Head of Italia seal at r. Back blue-green; statue of She-wolf w/Romulus and Remus at ctr.			
	a. 14.6.-12.9.1938.	10.00	50.00	120.00
	b. 14.1.1939.	12.00	60.00	150.00
2	**100 LIRE**			
	1938-39. Blue-green on orange unpt. Reclining Roma w/shield and spear holding Victory, statue of She-wolf w/Romulus and Remus at botton ctr. Back blue-green and brown; eagle.			
	a. 14.6.-12.9.1938.	12.00	60.00	150.00
	b. 14.1.1939.	15.00	80.00	200.00

		VG	VF	UNC
3	**500 LIRE**			
	1938-39. Blue and green. Peasant woman w/sheaf of grain and sickle at r. Back green and red-brown; crowned arms at l., Roma seated between allegorical male figures at ctr., fasces seal below.			
	a. 14.6.-12.9.1938.	80.00	250.00	550.00
	b. 14.1.1939.	100.00	300.00	700.00

		VG	VF	UNC
4	**1000 LIRE**			
	1938-39. Violet, brown and blue. 2 women (Venezia and Genova) reclining at bottom ctr. Back violet and green; allegorical woman seated between reclining male and Mercury at ctr. on back, fasces seal above.			
	a. 14.6.-12.9.1938.	80.00	250.00	550.00
	b. 14.1.1939.	110.00	325.00	750.00

ITALIAN INFLUENCE

BANCA D'ITALIA

SOMALIA ITALIANA BRANCH

1920 BUONI DE CASSA ISSUE

		GOOD	FINE	XF
2	**1 RUPIA**			
	13.5.1920. Black and red. Back brown.	150.00	400.00	900.00

		GOOD	FINE	XF
3	**5 RUPIAS**			
	13.5.1920. Pink and brown. Back brown.	325.00	950.00	—

4	10 RUPIAS		GOOD	FINE	XF
	13.5.1920. Yellowish brown and m/c. Back blue-green.		450.00	1150.	
5	20 RUPIAS		—	—	—
	13.5.1920. (Not issued).				
6	50 RUPIAS		—	—	—
	13.5.1920. (Not issued).				

CASSA PER LA CIRCOLAZIONE MONETARIA DELLA SOMALIA

1950 ISSUE

11	1 SOMALI		VG	VF	UNC
	1950. Brown and yellow. Leopard at ctr.				
	a. Issued note.		45.00	250.00	750.00
	s. Specimen.		—	—	575.00
12	5 SOMALI				
	1950. Blue.				
	a. Issued note.		35.00	200.00	675.00
	s. Specimen.		—	—	500.00
13	10 SOMALI				
	1950. Green. 3 sign. varieties.				
	a. Issued note.		10.00	55.00	260.00
	s. Specimen.		—	—	200.00

14	20 SOMALI		VG	VF	UNC
	1950. Brown. 3 sign. varieties.				
	a. Issued note.		10.00	70.00	285.00
	s. Specimen.		—	—	210.00

15	100 SOMALI		VG	VF	UNC
	1950. Violet and lt. brown. Lion at l. 3 sign. varieties.				
	a. Issued note.		125.00	450.00	1000.
	s. Specimen.		—	—	750.00

1951 ISSUE

16	5 SOMALI				
	1951. Brown-violet and lt. Blue. Leopard at ctr. Like #11.		12.50	50.00	200.00

The Italian Republic, a 700-mile-long peninsula extending into the heart of the Mediterranean Sea, has an area of 116,304 sq. mi. (301,255 sq. km.) and a population of 57.4 million. Capital: Rome. The economy centers about agriculture, manufacturing, forestry and fishing. Machinery, textiles, clothing and motor vehicles are exported.

From the fall of Rome until modern times, "Italy" was little more than a geographical expression. Although nominally included in the Empire of Charlemagne and the Holy Roman Empire, it was in reality divided into a number of independent states and kingdoms presided over by wealthy families, soldiers of fortune or hereditary rulers. The 19th century unification movement fostered by Mazzini, Garibaldi and Cavor attained fruition in 1860-1870 with the creation of the Kingdom of Italy and the installation of Victor Emanuele, King of Italy. Benito Mussolini came to power during the post-World War I period of economic and political unrest, installed a Fascist dictatorship with a figurehead king as titular Head of State.

Mussolini entered Italy into the German-Japanese anti-Comintern pact (Tri-Partite Pact) and withdrew from the League of Nations. The war did not go well for Italy and Germany was forced to assist Italy in its failed invasion of Greece. The Allied invasion of Sicily on July 10, 1943 and bombing of Rome brought the Fascist council to a no vote of confidence on July 24, 1943. Mussolini was arrested but soon escaped and set up a government in Saló. Rome fell to the Allied forces in June 1944 and the country was allowed the status of co-belligerent against Germany. The Germans held northern Italy for another year. Mussolini was eventually captured and executed by partisans. Following the defeat of the Axis powers the Italian monarchy was dissolved by plebiscite, and the Italian Republic proclaimed on June 10, 1946.

* * * This section has been renumbered. * * *

RULERS:

Umberto I, 1878-1900
Vittorio Emanuele III, 1900-1946

MONETARY SYSTEM:

1 Lira = 100 Centesimi

DECREES:

There are many different dates found on the following notes of the Banca d'Italia. These include ART. DELLA LEGGE (law date) and the more important DECRETO MINISTERIALE (D. M. date). The earliest D.M. date is usually found on the back of the note while later D.M. dates are found grouped together. The actual latest date (of issue) is referred to in the following listings.

PRINTERS:

Further differentiations are made in respect to the printers w/the place name Roma or L'Aquila (1942-44).

NOTE: Certain listings encompassing issues circulated by various bank and regional authorities are contained in Volume 1.

FACE SEAL VARIETIES

Type A
Italia facing l.

Type B
Facing head of Medusa

Type C
Winged lion of St. Mark of Venice above 3 shields of Genoa, Pisa and Amalfi

BACK SEAL VARIETIES

Type D
"Decreto Ministeriale De 30 Luglio 1896"
(17.7.1896-17.1.1930)

Type E
"Otto-Bre 1922"
w/fasces
(19.5.1926-6.8.1943)

Type F
Banco d'Italia monogram
(7.8.1943-21.3.1947)

KINGDOM

FEDERAL BIGLIETTI CONSORZIALE

A unified bank note issue imposed by the governmet to reduce the amount of coinage in circulation. These were released by the following banks: Banca Nazionale nel Regno d'Italia, Banco Nazionale Toscana, Banca Romana, Banca Toscana di Credito, Banco di Napoli and Banco di Sicilia.

LAW OF 30.4.1874

NOTE: All notes mention this law date, but Regal Decrees from 2.7.1875 to 3.11.1877 were the authorizing determinants.

			GOOD	FINE	XF
1 (S491)	40 CENTESIMI	*L. 1874/* Black and blue on brown unpt. Back blue; Italia at l.	3.00	10.00	30.00

			GOOD	FINE	XF
2 (S492)	1 LIRA	*L. 1874.* Black and brown on green unpt. Back brown; Italia at l.	2.00	8.00	25.00

			GOOD	FINE	XF
3 (S493)	2 LIRE	*L. 1874.* Green and black on peach unpt. Italia at l. Back dk. green.	2.00	8.00	25.00

			GOOD	FINE	XF
4 (S494)	5 LIRE	*L. 1874.* Brown, tan and black on lt. orange unpt. Back brown; Italia at l. and r.	2.00	8.00	25.00

			GOOD	FINE	XF
5 (S495)	10 LIRE	*L. 1874.* Blue and black on brown unpt. Back blue; Italia at l. and r.	3.00	10.00	30.00
6 (S496)	20 LIRE	*L. 1874.* Black text, blue on orange unpt. Arms at upper ctr., cherubs at lower ctr., ornamental border. Back black; crowned Italia at ctr.	50.00	150.00	450.00

			GOOD	FINE	XF
7 (S497)	100 LIRE	*L. 1874.* Black text, blue on gold unpt. Crowned supported arms at top ctr., allegorical figures around border. Back dk. brown; crowned Italia at ctr.	40.00	125.00	375.00
8 (S498)	250 LIRE	*L. 1874.* Black on brown unpt. Allegorical figures at bottom and around border. Back black on green unpt; crowned Italia at ctr.	100.00	300.00	—

			GOOD	FINE	XF
9 (S499)	1000 LIRE	*L. 1874.* Black on lt. green unpt. Crowned supported arms at top ctr., allegorical women and cherubs at sides and bottom. Back black on lt. blue unpt; crowned Italia at ctr.	150.00	450.00	—

FEDERAL BIGLIETTI GIÀ CONSORZIALE

LAW OF 25.12.1881

NOTE: All notes mention this law date but Regal Decrees of 1881 and 1882 actually governed their issuance. Like previous issue, but different colors.

			GOOD	FINE	XF
10 (S501)	1 LIRA	*L. 1881.* Black text, red on lt. tan unpt. Back red. Like #2.	3.00	10.00	30.00

			GOOD	FINE	XF
11 (S502)	2 LIRE	*L. 1881.* Black text, blue on blue-gray unpt. Back blue. Like #3.	3.00	10.00	30.00
12 (S503)	5 LIRE	*L. 1881.* Black text, lt. blue on gold unpt. Back lt. blue. Like #4.	8.00	35.00	100.00
13 (S504)	10 LIRE	*L. 1881.* Black text, orange on green unpt. Back orange. Like #5.	10.00	40.00	125.00
14 (S505)	20 LIRE	*L. 1881.* Gray on blue unpt. Back Gray. Like #6.	50.00	150.00	450.00
15 (S506)	100 LIRE	*L. 1881.* Black and green on lt. blue unpt. Back blue and green. Like #7.	65.00	250.00	850.00
16 (S507)	250 LIRE	*L. 1881.* Blue and green. Like #8.	175.00	450.00	—
17 (S508)	1000 LIRE	*L. 1881.* Black and green. Like #9.	250.00	650.00	—

TREASURY BIGLIETTI DI STATO

1882-95 ISSUES

			VG	VF	UNC
18 (47)	5 LIRE	*D.1882-92.* Blue. Kg. Umberto I at l.			
		a. Sign. Dell'Ara and Crodara. 17.12.1882.	15.00	40.00	350.00
		b. Sign. Dell'Ara and Pia. 6.8.1889.	15.00	35.00	220.00
		c. Sign. Dell'Ara and Righetti. 25.10.1892.	10.00	20.00	150.00
19 (48)	10 LIRE	*D.11.3.1883.* Blue. Kg. Umberto I at l. on face and on back. Sign. Dell'Ara and Crodara.	120.00	400.00	1600.

			VG	VF	UNC
20 (49)	10 LIRE	*1888-1925.* Blue on pink unpt. Portr. Kg. Umberto I at l. Only denomination in oval at l. on back.			
		a. Sign. Dell'Ara and Crodara. 5.2.1888.	100.00	200.00	800.00
		b. Sign. Dell'Ara and Pia. 6.8.1889.	20.00	50.00	250.00
		c. Sign. Dell'Ara and Righetti. 25.10.1892.	5.00	10.00	70.00
		d. Sign. Dell'Ara and Altamura. 22.1.1911.	5.00	10.00	80.00
		e. Sign. Dell'Ara (or Giu. Dell'Ara) and Righetti. 23.4.1914-11.10.1915.	5.00	10.00	80.00
		f. Sign. Dell'Ara (or Giu. Dell'ara) and Porena. 29.7.1918.	5.00	10.00	80.00
		g. Sign. Maltese and Rossolini. 10.9.1923.	5.00	10.00	80.00
		h. Sign. Maltese and Rosi Bernardini. 20.12.1925.	5.00	10.00	80.00

			VG	VF	UNC
21 (50)	**25 LIRE** 21.7.1895. Blue on pink unpt. "Italia" at l. Back green.		225.00	500.00	1800.

1902 ISSUE

			VG	VF	UNC
22 (51)	**25 LIRE** 23.3.1902. Blue on orange unpt. Kg. V. Emanuele III at l. Heraldic eagle at r. on back.		1800.	2250.	—

1904 ISSUE

			VG	VF	UNC
23 (52)	**5 LIRE** 1904-25. Blue and black on pink unpt. Portr. Kg. V. Emanuele III at r.				
	a.	Sign. Dell'Ara and Righetti. 19.10.1904.	2.00	6.00	60.00
	b.	Sign. Dell'Ara and Altamura. 21.1.1911.	4.00	10.00	80.00
	c.	Sign. Dell'Ara (or Giu. Dell'Ara) and Righetti. 29.3.1914; 17.6.1915.	2.00	6.00	60.00
	d.	Sign. G. Dell'Ara and Porena. 29.7.1918.	2.00	7.00	65.00
	e.	Sign. Maltese and Rossolini. 10.9.1923.	2.00	6.00	60.00
	f.	Sign. Maltese and Rosi Bernardini. 20.12.1925.	2.00	6.00	60.00

REGNO D'ITALIA BIGLIETTO DI STATO

1923 ISSUE

NOTE: For similar type but headed *Banca d'Italia* and dated 1918-19, see #42.

			VG	VF	UNC
24 (53)	**25 LIRE** 20.8.1923. Brown. Similar to #42. Seals: Type A/E.				
	a.	Sign. Maltese and Rossolini. Series 001-116.	120.00	300.00	1600.
	b.	Sign. Maltese and Rosi Bernardini. Series 117-120.	400.00	800.00	

1935 ISSUE

			VG	VF	UNC
25 (54)	**10 LIRE** 1935; 1938-XVII; 1939-XVIII; 1944-XXII. Blue. Portr. Kg. V. Emanuele III at l. Portr. Italia at r. on back. Date at bottom ctr. edge.				
	a.	Sign. Grassi, Rosi Bernardini and Collari. 18.6.1935.	1.00	2.00	20.00
	b.	Sign. Grassi, Cossu and Collari. 1938.	1.00	3.00	25.00
	c.	Sign. Grassi, Porena and Cossu. 1939; 1944.	1.00	2.00	15.00

1939; 1940 ISSUE

			VG	VF	UNC
26 (56)	**1 LIRA** 14.11.1939. Dk. brown on lt. brown unpt. Caesar Augustus at ctr. on back.		.10	.30	3.00
27 (57)	**2 LIRE** 14.11.1939. Blue-violet. Julius Caesar on back.		.10	.30	4.00

			VG	VF	UNC
28 (55)	**5 LIRE** 1940; 1944. Violet on brown unpt. Portr. Kg. V. Emanuele III at l. Date at bottom ctr. edge. Eagle w/sword at ctr. on back.		1.00	2.00	15.00

ITALIA - BIGLIETTO DI STATO

1944 ISSUE

			VG	VF	UNC
29 (58)	**1 LIRA** 23.11.1944. Brown on pink unpt. "Italia" at l. Back green.				
	a.	Sign. Ventura, Simoneschi and Giovinco.	.10	.25	3.00
	b.	Sign. Bolaffi, Cavallaro and Giovinco.	.10	.25	3.00
	c.	Sign. DiCristina, Cavallaro and Zaini.	.10	.25	5.00

			VG	VF	UNC
30 (59)	**2 LIRE** 23.11.1944. Green on lt. orange unpt. "Italia" at l. Back orange or gold.				
	a.	Sign. Ventura, Simoneschi and Giovinco.	.10	.25	5.00
	b.	Sign. Bolaffi, Cavallaro and Giovinco.	.10	.25	6.00

			VG	VF	UNC
31 (60)	**5 LIRE** 23.11.1944. Violet-brown. Archaic helmeted female head at l.				
	a.	Sign. Ventura, Simoneschi and Giovinco.	.10	.35	5.00
	b.	Sign. Bolaffi, Simoneschi and Giovinco.	.10	.25	3.00
	c.	Sign. Bolaffi, Cavallaro and Giovinco.	.10	.25	3.00

32 (61)	**10 LIRE**	**VG**	**VF**	**UNC**
	23.11.1944. Blue. Jupiter at l. Engraved or lithographed. (The lithographed note has a blue line design in wmk. area at ctr.)			
a.	Sign. Ventura, Simoneschi and Giovinco.	.10	.25	7.00
b.	Sign. Bolaffi, Simoneschi and Giovinco.	.10	.30	5.00
c.	Sign. Bolaffi, Cavallaro and Giovinco.	.10	.25	5.00

TREASURY BUONI DI CASSA

R. DECRETO 4.8.1893/DECRETO MINISTERIALE 22.2.1894

33 (65)	**1 LIRA**			
	D.1893 (1893-94). Red-brown w/black text on green unpt. Kg. Umberto I at l. Back blue. Series 001-032.	20.00	40.00	300.00

1894 ISSUE

34 (67)	**1 LIRA**			
	L.1894 (1894-98). Like #33. Series 033-112. Sign. Dell'Ara and Righetti.	20.00	40.00	300.00

35 (66)	**2 LIRE**	**VG**	**VF**	**UNC**
	D.1894 (1894-98). Dk. blue w/black text on grayish brown unpt. Kg. Umberto I at l. Back red-brown. Series 001-069.	60.00	120.00	750.00

1914 ISSUE

36 (68)	**1 LIRA**			
	D.1914 (1914-21). Dk. olive-brown on lt. blue unpt. Kg. V. Emanuele III at l. Back red.			
a.	Sign. Dell'Ara and Righetti. Series 001-157 (1914-17).	2.00	5.00	30.00
b.	Sign. Giu. Dell'Ara and Righetti. Series 158-216.	2.00	5.00	30.00
c.	Sign. Giu. Dell'Ara and Porena. Series 217-266 (1921).	25.00	50.00	200.00

37 (69)	**2 LIRE**	**VG**	**VF**	**UNC**
	D.1914 (1914-22). Brown-violet on lt. red-brown unpt. Kg. V. Emanuele III at l. Back brown.			
a.	Sign. Dell'Ara and Righetti. Series 001-082 (1914-17).	2.00	5.00	50.00
b.	Sign. Giu. Dell'Ara and Righetti. Series 083-107.	2.00	5.00	50.00
c.	Sign. Giu. Dell'Ara and Porena. Series 108-165 (1920-22).	2.00	5.00	50.00

BANCA D'ITALIA

BANK OF ITALY

DECRETO MINISTERIALE 30.7.1896 AND 12.9.1896

38 (2)	**50 LIRE**			
	1896-1926. Blue on green unpt. W/counterfoil, large letter L and woman w/3 children at l. Woman on back. Seals: Type A/D.			
a.	Sign. Marchiori and Nazari. 17.7.1896; 9.12.1899.	80.00	150.00	600.00
b.	Sign. Stringher and Accame. 1.2.1906-9.6.1910.	40.00	80.00	350.00
c.	Sign. Stringher and Sacchi. 2.1.1912-4.10.1918.	30.00	60.00	300.00
d.	Sign. Canavai and Sacchi. 22.1.1919; 12.5.1919.	50.00	100.00	350.00
e.	Sign. Stringher and Sacchi. 15.8.1919-29.6.1926.	25.00	50.00	250.00

39 (11)	**100 LIRE**	**VG**	**VF**	**UNC**
	1896-1926. Brown and pink. w/counterfoil, lg. B and woman seated w/small angels at l. Seals: Type A/D. Wmk: Head of Mercury.			
a.	Sign. Marchiori and Nazari. 17.7.1896.	100.00	180.00	700.00
b.	Sign. Marchiori and Accame. 9.12.1899.	100.00	180.00	700.00
c.	Sign. Stringher and Accame. 9.12.1899-9.6.1910.	40.00	80.00	350.00
d.	Sign. Stringher and Sacchi. 10.9.1911-4.10.1918.	30.00	80.00	350.00
e.	Sign. Canovai and Sacchi. 22.1.1919; 12.5.1919.	50.00	100.00	500.00
f.	Sign. Stringher and Sacchi. 15.8.1919-8.9.1926.	30.00	80.00	350.00

40 (21)	**500 LIRE**			
	1898-1921. Dk. blue on pink-brown unpt. W/counterfoil, oval ornament w/allegorical figures. Seals: Type A/D. Wmk: Head of Roma.			
a.	Sign. Marchiori and Nazari. 25.10.1898.	450.00	900.00	2000.
b.	Sign. Marchiori and Accame. 25.10.1898.	450.00	900.00	2000.
c.	Sign. Stringher and Accame. 9.12.1899-9.6.1910.	375.00	750.00	1800.
d.	Sign. Stringher and Sacchi. 15.6.1912; 15.12.1918.	350.00	700.00	1500.
e.	Sign. Canovai and Sacchi. 12.5.1919.	400.00	850.00	1700.
f.	Sign. Stringher and Sacchi. 15.8.1919; 12.2.1921.	350.00	700.00	1500.

41 (30)	**1000 LIRE**			
	1897-1920. Violet-brown and brown. W/counterfoil, lg. M at l. Seals: Type A/D. Wmk: Head of "Italia" at r. and 1000 at l.			
a.	Sign. Marchiori and Nazari. 16.12.1897.	500.00	1000.	2200.
b.	Sign. Stringher and Accame. 9.12.1899; 21.10.1906; 15.10.1908; 9.6.1910.	400.00	800.00	1600.
c.	Sign. Stringher and Sacchi. 13.11.1911-1.7.1918.	350.00	700.00	1500.
d.	Sign. Canavai and Sacchi. 22.1.1919.	400.00	900.00	1800.
e.	Sign. Stringher and Sacchi. 15.8.1919-17.8.1920.	350.00	700.00	1400.

1915-21 ISSUES

42 (1)	**25 LIRE**	**VG**	**VF**	**UNC**
	1918-19. Deep brown on brown unpt. Medallic head of "Italia" at r., eagle w/flag above. Back blue-black on blue-gray w/head of Minerva in oval at l. and as wmk. Seals: Type A/D.			
a.	Sign. Stringher and Sacchi. 24.1.1918; 1.7.1918.	100.00	250.00	1000.
b.	Sign. Canavai and Sacchi. 22.1.1919; 12.5.1919.	100.00	250.00	1000.

43 (6)	**50 LIRE**	**VG**	**VF**	**UNC**
	15.6.1915-4.10.1918. Black on orange unpt. Seated "Italia" at r. Farmer w/oxen on back. Seals: Type A/D. Wmk: Dante. Sign. Stringher and Sacchi.	120.00	300.00	1500.

44 (6A)	**50 LIRE**			
	1919-20. Like #43. Seals: Type A/D.			
a.	Sign. Canovai and Sacchi. 22.1.1919; 12.5.1919.	120.00	300.00	1500.
b.	Sign. Stringher and Sacchi. 15.8.1919; 13.11.1919; 7.6.1920.	110.00	280.00	1400.

	500 LIRE	VG	VF	UNC
45 (25)	16.7.1919-13.4.1926. olive-brown on violet and m/c unpt. Peasant woman w/sickle and sheaf at r. Crowned arms at l. Roma seated between allegorical male figures at ctr. Seals: Type A/D. Wmk: L. da Vinci.	30.00	80.00	500.00
46 (31)	19.8.1921-8.8.1926. voilet-brown and brown. W/o counterfoil. Seals: Type A/D. Wmk: Banca d'Italia at l., head of "Italia" at r.	80.00	180.00	600.00

1926 ISSUE

	50 LIRE	VG	VF	UNC
47 (3)	1926-36. Blue on green unpt. Like #38 w/counterfoil at l. Seals: Type A/D.			
	a. Sign. Stringher and Sacchi. 8.9.1926-17.12.1928.	25.00	50.00	250.00
	b. Sign. Stringher and Cima. 15.1.1929-17.11.1930.	25.00	50.00	250.00
	c. Sign. Azzolini and Cima. 2.3.1931-17.3.1936.	25.00	50.00	250.00
48 (12)	1926-30. Brown and pink. W/counterfoil. Seals: Type A/E/			
	a. Sign. Stringher and Sacchi. 8.9.1926-2.6.1928.	35.00	90.00	375.00
	b. Sign. Stringher and Cima. 15.1.1929-17.11.1930.	35.00	90.00	375.00
49 (13)	**100 LIRE** 2.2.1926; 8.8.1926. Blue. W/o counterfoil. Seals: Type A/D. Wmk: Head of "Italia".	60.00	120.00	600.00
50 (14)	**100 LIRE** 1926-34. Blue. Seals: Type A/E.			
	a. Sign. Stringher and Sacchi. 18.11.1926; 12.2.1927; 9.4.1928.	30.00	80.00	350.00
	b. Sign. Stringher and Cima. 12.4.1929-22.4.1930.	30.00	80.00	350.00
	c. Sign. Azzolini and Cima. 2.3.1931-17.10.1934.	30.00	80.00	350.00

	500 LIRE			
51 (26)	1926-42. Violet and olive-brown. Seals: Type A/E. *ROMA* at end of imprint.			
	a. Sign. Stringher and Sacchi. 6.12.1926-21.6.1928.	20.00	60.00	325.00
	b. Sign. Stringher and Cima. 6.6.1929; 21.3.1930.	20.00	60.00	300.00
	c. Sign. Azzolini and Cima. 18.2.1932-16.10.1935.	15.00	50.00	260.00
	d. Sign. Azzolini and Urbini. 22.12.1937-23.3.1942.	15.00	50.00	250.00
52 (32)	**1000 LIRE** 1926-32. Violet-brown and brown. W/o counterfoil. Seals: Type A/E.			
	a. Sign. Stringher and Sacchi. 8.8.1926-21.6.1928.	40.00	80.00	350.00
	b. Sign. Stringher and Cima. 12.4.1929; 5.12.1929; 20.10.1930.	40.00	80.00	350.00
	c. Sign. Azzolini and Cima. 2.1.1932.	50.00	100.00	400.00

1930-33 ISSUE

	50 LIRE	VG	VF	UNC
54 (7)	1933-40. Blue-violet and yellow brown on orange and yellow unpt. She/wolf w/Romulus and Remus on back. Seals: Type A/E. Wmk: Julius Caesar. *Roma* at end of imprint on back. 128 x 75mm.			
	a. Sign. Azzolini and Cima. 11.10.1933-30.4.1937.	3.00	12.00	120.00
	b. Sign. Azzolini and Urbini. 27.8.1937-23.10.1940.	3.00	12.00	100.00

	100 LIRE	VG	VF	UNC
55 (17)	1931-42. Olive and brown. Roma reclining w/spear and shield holding Victory, wolf w/twins at bottom ctr. Seals: Type A/E. Wmk: "Italia" and Dante. *ROMA* at end of imprint.			
	a. Sign. Azzolini and Cima. 5.10.1931-16.12.1936.	5.00	10.00	110.00
	b. Sign. Azzolini and Urbini. 13.3.1937-11.6.1942.	4.00	8.00	90.00
56 (35)	**1000 LIRE** 1930-41. Blue and brown. 2 women reclining at bottom ctr. (Venezia and Genova). Seals: Type A/D. Wmk: "Italia" at l., Columbus at r. *ROMA* at end of imprint.			
	a. Sign. Stringher and Cima. 7.7.1930.	30.00	80.00	400.00
	b. Sign. Azzolini and Cima. 28.6.1930-17.3.1936.	15.00	50.00	300.00
	c. Sign. Azzolini and Urbini. 21.10.1938-13.11.1941.	15.00	50.00	300.00

1941-42 ISSUE

	50 LIRE			
57 (7A)	19.8.1941; 24.1.1942; 18.7.1942. Design like #54 but slightly reduced size. 120 x 70mm.	3.00	12.00	100.00

58 (8)	**50 LIRE** 28.8.1942-6.8.1943. blue-violet and yellow-brown on orange and yellow unpt. Like #54 but w/*L'AQUILA* at end of imprint. Seals: Type A/E.	**VG** 5.00	**VF** 15.00	**UNC** 120.00

59 (15)	**100 LIRE** 9.12.1942; 15.3.1943. Brown on yellow unpt. Seals: Type A/E.	**VG** 5.00	**VF** 15.00	**UNC** 120.00
60 (18)	**100 LIRE** 28.8.1942-17.5.1943. olive-green and brown. Seals: Type A/E. *L'AQUILA* at end of imprint.	8.00	20.00	130.00

61 (27)	**500 LIRE** 21.10.1942; 18.1.1943; 17.5.1943. Olive-brown on violet and m/c unpt. Seals: Type A/E. *L'AQUILA* at end of imprint.	**VG** 50.00	**VF** 100.00	**UNC** 550.00
62 (32A)	**1000 LIRE** 12.12.1942; 6.2.1943. Like #52. Seals: Type A/E. Sign. Azzolini and Urbini.	25.00	60.00	450.00

63 (36)	**1000 LIRE** 28.8.1942-6.8.1943. Blue and brown. *L'A-QUILA* at end of imprint.	**VG** 40.00	**VF** 80.00	**UNC** 350.00

1943 ISSUES

64 (4)	**50 LIRE** 31.3.1943. Blue on green unpt. Like #47 but w/o counterfoil. Woman's head at r. on back. Seals: Type A/E. Sign. Azzolini and Urbini.	**VG** 8.00	**VF** 20.00	**UNC** 120.00
65 (5)	**50 LIRE** 11.8.1943; 8.10.1943; 11.11.44. Blue on green unpt. Like #64 but w/seals: Type A/F.	8.00	20.00	120.00

66 (9)	**50 LIRE** 23.8.1943; 8.10.1943; 1.2.1944. Blue-violet and yellow-brown. Like #58. Seals: Type A/F.	**VG** 10.00	**VF** 20.00	**UNC** 150.00
67 (16)	**100 LIRE** 1943-44. Brown on yellow unpt. Seals: Type A/F.			
	a. Sign. Azzolini and Urbini. 23.8.1943-11.11.1944.	5.00	15.00	120.00
	b. Sign. Introna and Urbini. 20.12.1944.	35.00	70.00	300.00
68 (19)	**100 LIRE** 23.8.1943; 8.10.1943. olive-green and brown. Seals: Type A/F.	8.00	25.00	160.00
69 (22)	**500 LIRE** 31.3.1943. Dk. red on pink unpt. W/o counterfoil. Seals: Type A/E.	15.00	80.00	500.00

70 (23)	**500 LIRE** 1943-47. Dk. red on pink unpt. Seals: Type A/F.	**VG**	**VF**	**UNC**
	a. Sign. Azzolini and Urbini. 23.8.1943-17.8.1944.	20.00	60.00	300.00
	b. Sign. introna and Urbini. 7.10.1944.	25.00	70.00	350.00
	c. Sign. Azzolini and Urbini. 10.10.1944; 13.2.1945; 8.6.1945.	20.00	60.00	300.00
	d. Sign. Einaudi and Urbini. 9.6.1945-19.2.1947.	20.00	60.00	300.00
71 (28)	**500 LIRE** 23.8.1943. Colors as #61. Seals: Type A/F.	70.00	150.00	650.00

72 (33)	**1000 LIRE**	VG	VF	UNC
	1943-47. Violet-brown and brown. Seals: Type A/F.			
	a. Sign. Azzolini and Urbini. 11.8.1943-1.8.1944; 11.11.1944.	10.00	30.00	250.00
	b. Sign. Introna and Urbini. 7.10.1944; 30.11.1944.	15.00	50.00	280.00
	c. Sign. Einaudi and Urbini. 8.3.1945-12.7.1947.	12.00	40.00	260.00
73 (37)	**1000 LIRE**			
	23.8.1943; 8.10.1943. Blue and brown. Seals: Type A/F.	40.00	80.00	500.00

INTERIM GOVERNMENT
BANCA D'ITALIA
1944 ISSUE

74 (10)	**50 LIRE**	VG	VF	UNC
	10.12.1944. Green on orange unpt. Medallic head of "Italia" in oval at l. Seal: Type A. Wmk: *50*.	1.00	5.00	50.00

75 (20)	**100 LIRE**	VG	VF	UNC
	10.12.1944. Red on blue unpt. Medallic head of "Italia" at l. Seal: Type A. Wmk: *100*.	1.00	5.00	50.00
76 (28A)	**500 LIRE**			
	10.12.1944. Dk. red on yellow unpt. Medallic head of "Italia" at l. (Not issued).	—	Rare	—
77 (37A)	**1000 LIRE**			
	10.12.1944. Blue on blue-green unpt. Medallic head of "Italia" at l. (Not issued).	—	Rare	—

REPUBLIC
BANCA D'ITALIA
BANK OF ITALY
1945 PROVISIONAL ISSUE

78 (40)	**5000 LIRE**	VG	VF	UNC
	4.8.1945-12.7.1947. Blue w/text: *Titolo provvisorio...* at l. and r. in head of "Italia" unpt. Seal: Type A. Wmk: Head of "Italia".			
	a. 4.8.1945.	30.00	100.00	600.00
	b. 4.1.1947-12.7.1947.	30.00	80.00	500.00
79 (44)	**10,000 LIRE**			
	4.8.1945; 4.1.1947; 12.7.1947. Red-brown w/text: *Titolo provvisorio...* in head of "Italia" unpt. at l. and r. Seal: Type A. Wmk: Head of "Italia". Sign. Einaudi and Urbini.	40.00	100.00	500.00

1947 ISSUES

80 (29)	**500 LIRE**	VG	VF	UNC
	1947-61. Purple on lt. brown unpt. "Italia" at l. Back purple on gray unpt. Seal: Type B. Wmk: Head of "Italia".			
	a. Sign. Einaudi and Urbini. 20.3.1947; 10.2.1948.	3.00	15.00	120.00
	b. Sign. Carli and Ripa. 23.3.1961.	3.00	17.50	130.00

81 (34)	**1000 LIRE**	VG	VF	UNC
	1947-50. Violet-brown and brown. Seals: Type B/F.			
	a. Sign. Einaudi and Urbini. 22.11.1947; 14.4.1948.	40.00	100.00	600.00
	b. Sign. Menichella and Urbini. 14.11.1950.	120.00	200.00	1000.

82 (38)	**1000 LIRE**	VG	VF	UNC
	L.1947. Purple and brown. "Italia" at l. Seal: Type A. Wmk: Head of "Italia". Back blue on gray unpt. Sign. Einaudi and Urbini.	3.00	15.00	180.00
83 (38A)	**1000 LIRE**			
	20.3.1947. Like #82. Seal: Type B. Sign. Einaudi and Urbini.	3.00	8.00	100.00
84 (41A)	**5000 LIRE**			
	17.1.1947. Green and brown. 2 women seated at lower ctr. (Venezia and Genova). Seal: Type A. Sign. Einaudi and Urbini.	75.00	250.00	750.00
85 (42)	**5000 LIRE**			
	1947-63. Green and brown. 2 women seated at ctr. (Venezia and Genova). Seals: Type A/F. Wmk: Dante at l., "Italia" at r.			
	a. Sign. Einaudi and Urbini. 7.1.1947; 27.10.1947; 23.4.1948.	200.00	500.00	1600.
	b. Sign. Menichella and Urbini. 10.2.1949; 5.5.1952; 7.2.1953.	40.00	100.00	500.00
	c. Sign. Menichella and Boggione. 23.3.1961; 7.1.1963.	40.00	100.00	500.00
	d. Sign. Carli and Ripa. 23.3.1961; 7.1.1963.	40.00	100.00	500.00

1947 PROVISONAL ISSUE

86 (41)	**5000 LIRE**	VG	VF	UNC
	1947-49. Blue. Like #76. Seal: Type B.			
	a. Sign. Einaudi and Urbini. 8.9.1947; 18.11.1947; 17.12.1947; 28.1.1948.	30.00	75.00	450.00
	b. Sign. Menichella and Urbini. 22.11.1949.	30.00	75.00	450.00
87 (45)	**10,000 LIRE**			
	1947-50. Red-brown. Like #79 but w/seal: Type B.			
	a. Sign. Einaudi and Urbini. 8.9.1947; 18.11.1947; 17.12.1947; 28.1.1948.	20.00	50.00	275.00
	b. Sign. Menichella and Urbini. 6.9.1949; 12.6.1950.	20.00	50.00	275.00

1948 ISSUE

88 (39)	**1000 LIRE**	VG	VF	UNC
	1948-61. Purple and brown. Portr. "Italia" at l. and as wmk. Back blue on gray unpt. Seal: Type B.			
	a. Sign. Einaudi and Urbini. 10.2.1948.	2.00	10.00	140.00
	b. Sign. Menichella and Urbini. 11.2.1949.	2.00	10.00	140.00
	c. Blue-gray. Sign. Menichella and Boggione. 15.9.1959.	3.00	20.00	200.00
	d. Color like *c*. Sign. Carli and Ripa. 25.9.1961.	2.00	10.00	140.00

89 (46)	**10,000 LIRE**	VG	VF	UNC
	1948-62. Brown, orange and m/c. 2 women seated at ctr. (Venezia and Genova). Seal: Type B. Wmk: Verdi at l., Galilei at r.			
	a. Sign. Einaudi and Urbini. 8.5.1948.	25.00	50.00	300.00
	b. Sign. Menichella and Urbini. 10.2.1949-7.2.1953.	20.00	45.00	280.00
	c. Sign. Menichella and Boggione. 27.10.1953-12.5.1960.	20.00	45.00	280.00
	d. Sign. Carli and Ripa. 23.3.1961-24.3.1962.	20.00	40.00	250.00

1950 ISSUE

90 (24)	**500 LIRE**	VG	VF	UNC
	14.11.1950. Dk. red on pink unpt. Seals: Type B/F.	400.00	1800.	

REPUBBLICA ITALIANA - BIGLIETTO DI STATO

1951 ISSUE

91 (62)	50 LIRE 31.12.1951. Green. "Italia" at l.	VG	VF	UNC
	a. Sign. Bolaffi, Cavallaro and Giovinco.	1.00	2.00	25.00
	b. Sign. DiCristina, Cavallaro and Parisi.	1.00	3.00	30.00

92 (63)	100 LIRE 31.12.1951. Violet-brown. "Italia" at l.	VG	VF	UNC
	a. Sign. Bolaffi, Cavallaro and Giovinco.	1.00	2.00	25.00
	b. Sign. DiCristina, Cavallaro and Parisi.	1.00	3.00	30.00

MILITARY

CASSA VENETA DEI PRESTITI

CURRENCY NOTES

AUSTRIAN OCCUPATION OF VENEZIA, 1918

BUONI DI CASSA

#M4-M9 archaic helmeted female head at l.

M1	5 CENTESIMI 2.1.1918. Black on blue unpt. Serial # w/ or w/o *No*.	VG	VF	UNC
		.50	1.00	3.00

M2	10 CENTESIMI 2.1.1918. Black on lt. brown unpt.	VG	VF	UNC
		.50	1.00	3.00
M3	50 CENTESIMI 2.1.1918. Black on red unpt.			
		.50	1.00	3.00

M4	1 LIRA 2.1.1918. Lilac. 2 serial # varieties.	VG	VF	UNC
		1.00	2.00	4.00
M5	2 LIRE 2.1.1918. Green. 3 serial # varieties.			
		1.00	2.50	5.00

M6	10 LIRE 2.1.1918. Blue. 2 serial # varieties.	VG	VF	UNC
		1.50	4.00	9.00
M7	20 LIRE 2.1.1918. Red-violet. 2 serial # varieties.			
		3.00	7.50	15.00
M8	100 LIRE 2.1.1918. Brown and green.			
		12.00	35.00	70.00
M9	1000 LIRE 2.1.1918. Brown.			
		60.00	150.00	500.00

ALLIED MILITARY CURRENCY

ALLIED OCCUPATION - WW II Printers: US Bureau of Engraving - w/o indication; Forbes Litho., Boston - w/F.

SERIES 1943

M10	1 LIRA 1943. Blue and brown.	VG	VF	UNC
	a. *F.*	.10	.30	3.00
	b. W/o *F.*	.10	.30	3.00
M11	2 LIRE 1943. Violet and brown.			
	a. *F.*	.10	.30	4.00
	b. W/o *F.*	.10	.30	4.00
M12	5 LIRE 1943. Green and brown.			
	a. *F.*	.10	.30	8.00
	b. W/o *F.*	.10	.30	10.00

M13	10 LIRE 1943. Black and brown.	VG	VF	UNC
	a. *F.*	1.00	3.00	25.00
	b. W/o *F.*	1.00	3.00	30.00
M14	50 LIRE 1943. Blue.			
	a. *F.*	.50	3.00	25.00
	b. W/o *F.*	.50	4.00	50.00
M15	100 LIRE 1943. Violet and blue.			
	a. *F.*	1.00	4.00	40.00
	b. W/o *F.*	1.00	4.00	50.00
M16	500 LIRE 1943. Green and blue.			
	a. *F.*	40.00	70.00	485.00
	b. W/o *F.*	35.00	60.00	400.00

M17	1000 LIRE 1943. Black and blue.	VG	VF	UNC
	a. *F.*	60.00	100.00	500.00
	b. W/o *F.*	50.00	90.00	400.00

SERIES OF 1943 A

Printer: Forbes.

M18	5 LIRE 1943. A. Green and brown.	VG	VF	UNC
	a. Serial # prefix/suffix A-A.	.20	1.00	6.00
	b. b. Serial # prefix/suffix A-B.	.20	1.00	6.00
	s. Specimen perforated: *SPECIMEN*.	—	—	125.00
M19	10 LIRE 1943 A. Black and brown.			
	a. Serial # prefix/suffix A-A.	.50	2.00	12.00
	b. Serial # prefix/suffix A-B.	.50	2.25	12.00
	s. Specimen perforated: *SPECIMEN*.	—	—	125.00
M20	50 LIRE 1943 A. Blue.			
	a. Serial # prefix/suffix A-A.	1.00	3.00	30.00
	b. Serial # prefix/suffix A-B.	1.00	3.00	30.00
	s. Specimen perforated: *SPECIMEN*.	—	—	150.00

			VG	VF	UNC
M21	**100 LIRE**				
	1943 A. Violet and blue.				
	a. Serial # prefix/suffix A-A.	1.00	3.00	30.00
	b. Serial # prefix/suffix A-B.	1.00	3.00	30.00
	c. Serial # prefix/suffix A-C.	1.00	3.00	30.00
	s. Specimen perforated: *SPECIMEN*.	—	—	125.00
M22	**500 LIRE**				
	1943 A. Green and blue.				
	a. Issued note.	15.00	35.00	350.00
	s. Specimen perforated: *SPECIMEN*.	—	—	700.00
M23	**1000 LIRE**				
	1943 A. Black and blue.				
	a. Issued note.	12.50	30.00	300.00
	s. Specimen perforated: *SPECIMEN*.	—	—	700.00

GOVERNO DELLE ISOLE ITALIANE DELL'EGEO

DODECANESE

GOVERNMENT OF ITALIAN ISLANDS IN THE AEGEAN

ITALIAN OCCUPATION - WW II

NOTE: During 1943-45 different notes were issued by various groups of partisans such as the Brigata Garibaldi, Brigata Osoppo and Comitato Liberazone Ligure. All these notes are practically unobtainable in the trade and all are considered rare.

1944 ISSUE

			Good	Fine	XF
M24	**50 LIRE**		250.00	450.00	800.00
	15.4.1944-21.4.1944. Green, yellow and brown. Wolf w/Romulus and Remus at ctr., island fortress in background.				

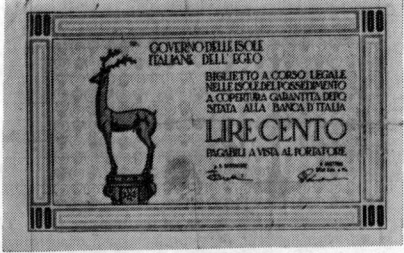

			Good	Fine	XF
M25	**100 LIRE**		225.00	400.00	750.00
	15.4.1944-21.4.1944. Blue, yellow and brown. Stag at l.				

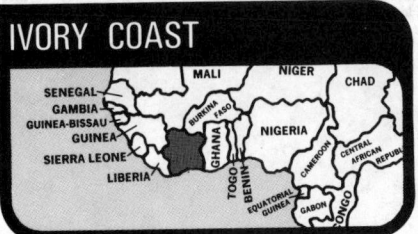

IVORY COAST 635

The Republic of Cote d'Ivoire (Ivory Coast), a former French overseas territory located on the south side of the African bulge between Nigeria and Ghana, has an area of 124,504 sq. mi. (322,463 sq. km.) and a population of 11.8 million. Capital: Abidjan. The predominantly agricultural economy is one of Africa's most prosperous. Coffee, tropical woods, cocoa, and bananas are exported.

The Ivory Coast was first visited by French and Portuguese navigators in the 15th century. French traders set up establishments in the 19th century, and gradually extended their influence along the coast and inland. The area was organized as a territory in 1893, and from 1904 to 1958 was a constituent unit of the Federation of French West Africa - as a Colony under the Third Republic and an Overseas Territory under the Fourth. In 1958 the Ivory Coast became an autonomous republic within the French Community. Independence was attained on Aug. 7, 1960.

Together with other West African states, the Cote d'Ivoire is a member of the "Union Monetaire Ouest-Africaine."

Also see French West Africa and West African Monetary Union.

RULERS:
French to 1960

MONETARY SYSTEM:
1 Franc = 100 Centimes

FRENCH INFLUENCE

GOUVERNEMENT GÉNÉRAL DE L'AFRIQUE

OCCIDENTALE FRANÇAISE (A.O.F.)

COLONIE DE LA COTE D'IVOIRE BRANCH

DÉCRET DU 11.2.1917
#1-3 obverse and reverse of French coin at l. and r.

		VG	VF	UNC
1	**.50 FRANC**			
	D.1917. Black and orange on yellow unpt. Back black text.			
	a. Wmk: Bees.	15.00	50.00	125.00
	b. Wmk: Laurel leaves.	20.00	60.00	140.00
	c. W/o wmk.	10.00	45.00	120.00

		VG	VF	UNC
2	**1 FRANC**			
	D.1917. Black and green on yellow unpt. Obverse and reverse of 1 Franc French coin.			
	a. Wmk: Bees.	15.00	50.00	145.00
	b. Wmk: Laurel leaves.	20.00	60.00	155.00
3	**2 FRANCS**			
	D.1917.			
	a. Wmk: Bees.	20.00	60.00	190.00
	b. Wmk: Laurel leaves.	20.00	60.00	190.00

1920 POSTAGE STAMP ISSUE
#4-6 postage stamps of the Ivory Coast (Michel #44, 45, and 48, or Scott #45, 47 and 52 w/natives in boat) pasted on cardboard and w/ovpt: *Valeur d'echange* **and value.**

			VG	VF	UNC
4	**.05 FRANC ON 5 CENTIMES** ND (1920). Yellow-green and blue-green.		15.00	25.00	60.00

			VG	VF	UNC
5	**10 CENTIMES** ND (1920). Red-orange and rose.		15.00	25.00	60.00

			VG	VF	UNC
6	**.25 FRANC ON 25 CENTIMES** ND (1920). Ultramarine and blue.		15.00	25.00	60.00

COTE D'IVOIRE

1943 EMERGENCY WW II ISSUE
#A7-8 elephant head in unpt. at ctr.

			VG	VF	UNC
A7	**50 CENTIMES** ND. Dk. blue and yellow.		—	Rare	—

			VG	VF	UNC
7	**1 FRANC** ND. Blue on yellow unpt.		—	Rare	—

			VG	VF	UNC
8	**2 FRANCS** ND. Blue on yellow unpt.		—	Rare	—

JAMAICA

Jamaica, a member of the British Commonwealth situated in the Caribbean Sea 90 miles south of Cuba, has an area of 4,232 sq. mi. (10,991 sq. km.) and a population of 2.4 million. Capital: Kingston. The economy is founded chiefly on mining, tourism and agriculture. Alumina, bauxite, sugar, rum and molasses are exported.

Jamaica was discovered by Columbus on May 3, 1494, and settled by Spain in 1509. The island was captured in 1655 by a British naval force under the command of Admiral William Penn, and ceded to Britain by the Treaty of Madrid, 1670. For more than 150 years, the Jamaican economy of sugar, slaves and piracy was one of the most prosperous in the new world. Dissension between the property-oriented island legislature and the home government prompted parliament to establish a crown colony government for Jamaica in 1866. From 1958 to 1961 Jamaica was a member of the West Indies Federation, withdrawing when Jamaican voters rejected the association. The colony attained independence on Aug. 6, 1962. Jamaica is a member of the Commonwealth of Nations. The Queen of England is Chief of State.

A decimal standard currency system was adopted on Sept. 8, 1969.

RULERS:
British

MONETARY SYSTEM:
1 Shilling = 12 Pence
1 Pound = 20 Shillings to 1969
1 Dollar = 100 Cents, 1969-

NOTE: Certain listings encompassing issues circulated by various bank and regional authorities are contained in Volume 1.

BRITISH INFLUENCE

TREASURY
Currency Note Issue

LAW 27/1904 AND 17/1918
#27-30 printer: TDLR.
#29 *Deleted.*

			GOOD	FINE	XF
27	**2 SHILLINGS 6 PENCE** L.1904/18. Green. Portr. Kg. George V at r. Back orange; woman w/hat at ctr.		500.00	1250.	2500.

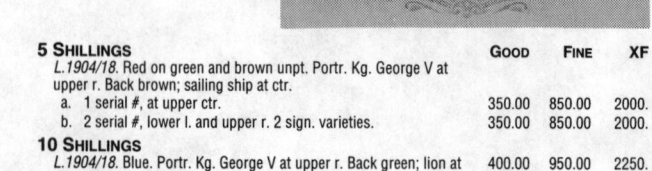

			GOOD	FINE	XF
28	**5 SHILLINGS** L.1904/18. Red on green and brown unpt. Portr. Kg. George V at upper r. Back brown; sailing ship at ctr.				
	a. 1 serial #, at upper ctr.		350.00	850.00	2000.
	b. 2 serial #, lower l. and upper r. 2 sign. varieties.		350.00	850.00	2000.
30	**10 SHILLINGS** L.1904/18. Blue. Portr. Kg. George V at upper r. Back green; lion at ctr. 2 sign. varieties.		400.00	950.00	2250.

GOVERNMENT OF JAMAICA

LAW 27/1904 AND 17/1918
#32 and 33 arms at upper l., waterfalls at ctr., Portr. Kg. George V at upper r. Printer: W&S.
#31, 34-36 *Deleted.*

39	**10 SHILLINGS**		**VG**	**VF**	**UNC**
	15.6.1950-17.3.1960. Purple. Back like #38.		5.00	25.00	125.00
40	**1 POUND**				
	1.11.1940. Blue. Back m/c.				
	a. Red serial #.		40.00	150.00	500.00
	b. Black serial #.		40.00	125.00	450.00
41	**1 POUND**				
	1942-60. Green. Back like #40, w/*ONE POUND* in 2 lines.				
	a. 30.11.1942; 2.1.1948.		15.00	75.00	375.00
	b. 15.6.1950-17.3.1960.		7.50	45.00	250.00
42	**5 POUNDS**				
	30.11.1942. Maroon.		250.00	800.00	—

32	**5 SHILLINGS**	**GOOD**	**FINE**	**XF**
	L.1904/18. Brown. River and bridge at ctr. on back.			
	a. 2 serial #. 2 sign varieties.	125.00	400.00	950.00
	b. 1 serial #.	250.00	750.00	1500.

33	**10 SHILLINGS**	**GOOD**	**FINE**	**XF**
	L.1904/18. Green.			
	a. 2 serial #. 2 sign. varieties.	250.00	750.00	1750.
	b. 1 serial #.	250.00	750.00	1750.

43	**5 POUNDS**	**VG**	**VF**	**UNC**
	1.8.1952; 7.4.1955; 15.8.1957; 1.9.1957. Brown. Like #42.	150.00	550.00	1400.

1939-52 ISSUES

#37-43 Portr. Kg. George V at l. Printer: TDLR.

1960 ISSUE

#45-47 Portr. Kg. George VI at l. New back design. Printer: TDLR.

45	**5 SHILLINGS**			
	17.3.1960; 4.7.1960. Orange. *FIVE SHILLINGS* in 1 line on back.	7.50	35.00	160.00

37	**5 SHILLINGS**	**VG**	**VF**	**UNC**
	1939-58. Orange. Back m/c; w/*FIVE SHILLINGS* in 2 lines.			
	a. 2.1.1939-15.6.1950.	7.50	40.00	150.00
	b. 1.3.1953-15.8.1958.	5.00	27.50	120.00
38	**10 SHILLINGS**			
	2.1.1939; 1.11.1940; 2.1.1948. Blue. Back m/c; w/*TEN SHILLINGS* in 2 lines.	10.00	40.00	100.00
	a. 2.1.1939.	12.50	75.00	200.00
	b. 1.11.1940.	10.00	40.00	140.00
	c. 2.1.1948.	12.50	75.00	200.00

46	**10 SHILLINGS**	**VG**	**VF**	**UNC**
	4.7.1960. Purple. *TEN SHILLINGS* in 1 line on back.	9.00	45.00	200.00
47	**1 POUND**			
	19.5.1960. Green. *ONE POUND* in 1 line on back.	12.00	65.00	250.00

48	**5 POUNDS**	**VG**	**VF**	**UNC**
	17.3.1960; 4.7.1960. Blue and m/c. Qn. Elizabeth II at l. Factory and banana tree on back.	75.00	375.00	1000.

BANK OF JAMAICA

SIGNATURE VARIETIES

1	Stanley W. Payton, 1960–64	3	Richard T. P. Hall **Governor** – 1966–67
2	Richard T. P. Hall, **Acting Governor** – 1964–66	4	G. Arthur Brown, 1967–77

LAW 1960

FIRST ND ISSUE

Pound System

Law 1960

#49-51 Qn. Elizabeth II at l. Latin motto below arms. Sign. S. W. Payton. Printer: TDLR.

49	**5 SHILLINGS**				
	L.1960. Red on m/c unpt. River rapids on back.		3.00	12.50	60.00
50	**10 SHILLINGS**				
	L.1960. Purple on m/c unpt. Men w/bananas on back.		5.00	17.50	170.00

		VG	**VF**	**UNC**
51	**1 POUND**			
	L.1960. Green on m/c unpt. Harvesting on back.	5.00	20.00	170.00

SECOND ND ISSUE

#49A-51A like previous issue, but English motto below arms. Printer: TDLR.

		VG	**VF**	**UNC**
49A	**5 SHILLINGS**			
	L.1960. Red on m/c unpt.			
	a. Sign. 1. 2 serial # varieties.	2.00	7.00	55.00
	b. Sign. 2.	2.50	8.00	75.00
	c. Sign. 4.	1.50	5.00	50.00
50A	**10 SHILLINGS**			
	L.1960. Purple on m/c unpt.			
	a. Sign. 1. 2 serial # varieties.	3.00	7.50	110.00
	b. Sign. 2.	3.00	8.50	125.00
	c. Sign. 3.	3.50	12.50	150.00
	d. Sign. 4.	2.00	6.00	100.00
51A	**1 POUND**			
	L.1960. Green on m/c unpt.			
	a. Sign. 1. 2 serial # varieties, Gothic and Roman.	5.00	17.50	150.00
	b. Sign. 2.	5.00	17.50	165.00
	c. Sign. 3.	7.50	25.00	200.00
	d. Sign. 4.	4.00	15.00	140.00

		VG	**VF**	**UNC**
52	**5 POUNDS**			
	L.1960. Blue on m/c unpt. Storage plant at ctr., woman w/fruit basket at r. on back.			
	a. Sign. 1. 2 serial # varieties, Gothic and Roman.	30.00	150.00	600.00
	b. Sign. 3.	27.50	135.00	550.00
	c. Sign. 4.	25.00	125.00	500.00

JAPAN

Japan, a constitutional monarchy situated off the east coast of Asia, has an area of 145,856 sq. mi. (377,644 sq. km.) and a population of 123.2 million. Capital: Tokyo. Japan, one of the three major industrial nations of the free world, exports machinery, motor vehicles, textiles and chemicals.

Japan, founded (so legend holds) in 660 BC by a direct descendant of the Sun Goddess, was first brought into contact with the west by a storm-blown Portuguese ship in 1542. European traders and missionaries proceeded to enlarge the contact until the Shogunate, sensing a military threat in the foreign presence, expelled all foreigners and severed relations with the outside world in the 17th century. After contact was reestablished by Commodore Perry of the U.S. Navy in 1854, Japan rapidly industrialized, abolished the Shogunate and established a parliamentary form of government, and by the end of the 19th century achieved the status of a modern economic and military power. A series of wars with China and Russia, and participation with the Allies in World War I, enlarged Japan territorially but brought its interests into conflict with the Far Eastern interests of the United States and Britain, causing it to align with the Axis powers for the pursuit of World War II. After its defeat in World War II, Japan renounced military aggression as a political instrument, established democratic self-government, and quickly reasserted its position as an economic world power.

See also Burma, China (Japanese military issues, Central Reserve Bank, Federal Reserve Bank, Hua Hsing Commercial Bank, Mengchiang Bank, Chanan Bank and Chi Tung Bank and Manchukuo), Hong Kong, Indochina, Malaya, Netherlands East Indies, Oceania, the Philippines, Korea and Taiwan.

* * * This section has been partially renumbered. * * *

RULERS:

Mutsuhito (Meiji), 1867-1912	明治
Yoshihito (Taisho), 1912-1926	大正
Hirohito (Showa), 1926-1989	昭和
Akihito (Heisei), 1989-	平成

MONETARY SYSTEM:

1 Sen = 10 Rin
1 Yen = 100 Sen

NOTE: Certain listings encompassing issues circulated by various bank and regional authorities are contained in Volume 1.

MONETARY UNITS

厘 Rin;   錢 Sen;   圓 or 圓 or ¥ or 円 Yen

PORTRAIT VARIETIES

#1 Takeuchi Sukune

#2 Sugawara Michizane

#3 Wakeno Kiyomaro

#4 Fujiwara Kamatari

#5 Wakeno Kiyomaro

#6 Shotoku-taishi

#7 Yamato Takeru No Mikoto

CONSTITUTIONAL MONARCHY

GREAT JAPANESE GOVERNMENT - MINISTRY OF FINANCE

省蔵大府政本日大

Dai Nip-pon Sei-fu O-kura-sho

1872 ISSUE
#1-9 Meiji Tsuho-Satsu w/facing Onagadori cockerels at top and 2 facing dragons at bottom. Printer: Dondorf and Naumann,

		10 SEN		20 SEN		1/2 YEN

			GOOD	FINE	XF
1	**10 SEN**				
	ND (1872). Black on pink unpt. Back green.		15.00	35.00	70.00
2	**20 SEN**				
	ND (1872). Black on brown unpt. Back blue.		40.00	80.00	150.00
3	**1/2 YEN**				
	ND (1872). Black on green unpt. Back brown.		60.00	125.00	250.00

		GOOD	FINE	XF
4	**1 YEN**			
	ND (1872). Black on brown unpt. Back blue.	55.00	120.00	200.00
5	**2 YEN**			
	ND (1872). Black on blue unpt. Back brown.	350.00	650.00	1000.

		GOOD	FINE	XF
6	**5 YEN**			
	ND (1872). Black on brown unpt. Back blue.	1000.	2000.	3500.
7	**10 YEN**			
	ND (1872). Black on blue unpt. Back lilac.	600.00	1250.	2500.
8	**50 YEN**			
	ND (1872). Black on lilac unpt. Back blue.	—	Rare	—
9	**100 YEN**			
	ND (1872). Black on blue unpt. Back red.	—	Rare	—

GREAT IMPERIAL JAPANESE GOVERNMENT

幣紙用通國帝本日大

Dai Nip-pon Tei-koku Tus-yo Shi-hei

1873 "PAPER CURRENCY" ISSUE
#10-14 black w/number of issuing national bank and location at lower ctr. All have black face, green and black back showing equivalent gold coin. Printer: CONB.

		GOOD	FINE	XF
10	**1 YEN**	1250.	3000.	5000.
	ND (1873). Prow of a ship at l. Warrior w/bow and arrows at r. Gold 1 yen coin at l. and r., ancient Japanese warrior scene at ctr. on back.			

		GOOD	FINE	XF
11	**2 YEN**	2500.	5500.	—
	ND (1873). Warrior in armor at l. and r. Castle gateway on back.			

		GOOD	FINE	XF
12	**5 YEN**	5000.	9000.	—
	ND (1873). Field work at l. and r. Arch bridge on back.			

13	**10 YEN**		GOOD	FINE	XF
	ND (1873). Musicians at l. and r. Horseman arriving on beach on back.		—	Rare	—

14	**20 YEN**		GOOD	FINE	XF
	ND (1873). Dragon at l., kneeling man at r. Warriors at beach on back.		—	Rare	—

GREAT IMPERIAL JAPANESE GOVERNMENT

大日本帝國政府紙幣

Dai Nip-pon Tei-koku Sei-fu Shi-hei

1881-83 "PAPER MONEY" ISSUE
#17-19 brown unpt. Empress Jingu at r. Ornate denomination w/red seal on back.

15	**20 SEN**	GOOD	FINE	XF
	1881 (1882) Brown unpt. w/brown seal at r.	40.00	90.00	200.00
16	**50 SEN**			
	1881 (1882) Brown unpt. w/brown seal at r.	175.00	450.00	1000.

17	**1 YEN**	GOOD	FINE	XF
	1878 (1881).	200.00	450.00	850.00
18	**5 YEN**			
	1880 (1882).	1500.	3000.	5500.

19	**10 YEN**	GOOD	FINE	XF
	1881 (1883).	2500.	5000.	9500.

GREAT IMPERIAL JAPANESE NATIONAL BANK

大日本帝國國立銀行

Dai Nip-pon Tei-koku Koku-ritsu Gin-ko

1877-78 ISSUE
#20 and 21 have the various issuing bank number on face; issue location and bank number on back.

20	**1 YEN**	GOOD	FINE	XF
	ND (1877). Black on yellow-brown unpt. 2 sailors at r. Back dk. green w/Ebisu, god of household thrift and industry.	350.00	850.00	1750.
21	**5 YEN**			
	ND (1878). Black on green unpt. 3 blacksmiths at r. Back black and green w/Ebisu.	800.00	2250.	3750.

BANK OF JAPAN

日本銀行兌換銀券

Nip-pon Gin-ko Da Kan Gin Ken

1885-86 CONVERTIBLE SILVER NOTE ISSUE
#22-25 Daikoku (God of Fortune) sitting on rice bales.
#22, 23 and 25 w/text: *Nippon Ginko Promises to Pay the Bearer on Demand...Yen in Silver* on face.

22	**1 YEN**	GOOD	FINE	XF
	ND (1885). Blue. Daikoku at r.	175.00	400.00	950.00
23	**5 YEN**			
	ND (1886). Blue. Daikoku on back.	2000.	3500.	6500.
24	**10 YEN**			
	ND (1885). Blue. Daikoku at r.	3500.	7500.	—
25	**100 YEN**			
	ND (1885). Blue. Daikoku at r.	—	Rare	—

1889-91 CONVERTIBLE SILVER NOTE ISSUE
#26-29 serial # in Japanese numerals.

		Good	Fine	XF
26 (27)	**1 YEN** ND (1889). Black on lt. orange unpt. Portr. #1 at r. Japanese serial #. 1 yen coin at ctr. and l. on back.	45.00	135.00	375.00
27 (26)	**5 YEN** ND (1888). Black on green unpt. Portr. #2 at r.	1500.	3500.	7000.
28	**10 YEN** ND (1890). Black on lt. brown unpt. Portr. #3 at r. Back lt. brown.	2000.	4500.	8500.
29	**100 YEN** ND (1891). Black on lt. brown unpt. Portr. #4 at r. Back lt. blue.	—	Rare	—

1916 CONVERTIBLE SILVER NOTE ISSUE
Issuer's name reads l. to r. or r. to l.

		Good	Fine	XF
30	**1 YEN** ND (1916). Like #27 but Western serial #.			
	a. Block # below 200.	20.00	50.00	100.00
	b. Block #200-299.	2.50	7.50	15.00
	c. Block #300 and higher.	1.00	3.00	7.00
	s. As c. Vermilion ovpt: *Mi-hon.* Regular serial #.	—	Unc	300.00

BANK OF JAPAN (RESUMED)

日本銀行兌換券
Nip-pon Gin-ko Da Kan Ken

1899-1900 CONVERTIBLE GOLD NOTE ISSUE
#31-37 w/text: *NIPPON GINGKO promises to pay the bearer on demand...yen in gold* on back.
#31-33 dated from Meiji year 32 (1899) to Taisho year 2 (1913) on back.

		Good	Fine	XF
31	**5 YEN** 1899-1910. Black on pale green unpt. Portr. #1 at ctr. Back orange.			
	a. Japanese block character.	250.00	700.00	1300.
	b. Western block #.	350.00	1000.	2000.

		Good	Fine	XF
32	**10 YEN** 1899-1913. Black on lt. brown unpt. Goo Shrine at l., portr. #3 at r. Back green; boar at ctr.			
	a. Japanese block character.	350.00	1000.	2000.
	b. Western block #.	450.00	1200.	2500.

		Good	Fine	XF
33	**100 YEN** 1900-13. Black on lt. brown unpt. Park w/Danzan Shrine at l., portr. #4 at r. Back purple; Bank of Japan.			
	a. Japanese block character.	3000.	7000.	—
	b. Western block #.	2000.	5000.	—

1910 CONVERTIBLE GOLD NOTE ISSUE

		Good	Fine	XF
34	**5 YEN** ND (1910). Green on purple unpt. Portr. #2 at r. Back purple. Wmk: Daikoku.	300.00	600.00	1250.

1915-17 CONVERTIBLE GOLD NOTE ISSUE

		Good	Fine	XF
35	**5 YEN** ND (1916). Black on lt. green unpt. Ube Shrine w/stairs at l., portr. #1 at r. Back brown.	75.00	150.00	350.00

		Good	Fine	XF
36	**10 YEN** ND (1915). Gray. Portr. #5 at l., Goo Shrine at r. Back green and brown.	75.00	150.00	300.00
37	**20 YEN** ND (1917). Black on m/c unpt. Portr. #2 at r. Back purple; Kitano Shrine.	500.00	1250.	3250.

1927 EMERGENCY ISSUE

37A **50 YEN**
ND (1927). Guilloche at l. and r. of ctr. Uniface. Specimen.

	GOOD	FINE	XF
	—	Rare	—

37B **200 YEN**
ND (1927). Greenish black w/black text. Guilloche at ctr. w/o portr. Uniface.

	GOOD	FINE	XF
	—	Rare	—

1927 ND ISSUE

NOTE: For similar note but w/pale blue unpt., see #43A.

	GOOD	FINE	XF
z. Face as a. Propaganda message in Japanese text on back. (4 varieties).	12.50	35.00	—

38 **200 YEN**
ND (1927). Black on green unpt. Portr. #1 at r. Back red. Specimen.

	GOOD	FINE	XF
	—	Rare	—

1930-31 ND ISSUE

#39-45 Japanese text w/denomination in English on back.

NOTE: 4 different propaganda notes w/face of #40 and different messages on back in Japanese are frequently encountered. Values range from $25.-$60. in Fine.

39 **5 YEN**
ND (1930). Black on green and orange unpt. Kitano Shrine at l., green guilloche at ctr., Portr. #2 at r. Back brown and olive.

	VG	VF	UNC
a. Issued note.	4.00	20.00	150.00
s1. Specimen w/ovpt. and perforated *Mi-hon.*	—	—	700.00
s2. Specimen w/sm. vermilion ovpt: *Mi-hon.* Regular serial #.	—	—	200.00

41
(42) **20 YEN**
ND (1931). Black on green unpt. Danzon Shrine at l., portr. #4 at r. Back blue and brown; another view of same shrine.

	VG	VF	UNC
a. Issued note.	50.00	200.00	600.00
s1. Specimen w/ovpt. and perforated: *Mi-hon.*	—	—	3000.
s2. Specimen w/sm. vermilon ovpt: *Mi-hon. SPECIMEN* on back. Regular serial #.	—	—	800.00
s3. Specimen w/blue ovpt: *SPECIMEN* on face and back. Regular serial #.	—	—	750.00

40 **10 YEN**
ND (1930). Black on green and brown unpt. Portr. #3 at r. Back green and brown.

	VG	VF	UNC
a. Issued note.	3.00	8.00	35.00
s1. Specimen w/ovpt. and perforated: *Mi-hon.*	—	—	900.00
s2. Specimen w/sm. vermilion ovpt: *Mi-hon.* Regular serial #.	—	—	200.00

42
(41) **100 YEN**
ND (1930). Black on blue and brown unpt. Yumedono Pavilion at l., portr. #6 at r. Back green and brown; Horyuji Temple at ctr.

	VG	VF	UNC
a. Issued note.	15.00	50.00	150.00
s. Specimen w/sm. vermilion ovpt: *Mi-hon.* Regular serial #.	—	—	700.00

1942 ND ISSUE

43 5 YEN
ND (1942). Similar to #39 but w/o ctr. guilloche. Back red-brown and lilac.

	VG	VF	UNC
a. Issued note.	3.00	10.00	45.00
s1. Specimen w/ovpt. and perforated: *Mi-hon.*	—	—	900.00
s2. Specimen w/sm. vermilion ovpt: *Mi-hon.* Regular serial #.	—	—	250.00
s3. Specimen w/red ovpt: *SPECIMEN* on face and back. Regular serial #.	—	—	175.00

1945 ND PROVISIONAL ISSUE

43A 200 YEN
(38) ND (1945). Black on pale blue unpt. Portr. #1 at r. Back red; English denomination. (Originally printed in 1927).

	GOOD	FINE	XF
a. Issued note.	550.00	1000.	2250.
s1. Specimen w/ovpt. and perforated *Mi-hon.*	—	Unc	9000.
s2. Specimen w/vermilion ovpt: *Mi-hon. Specimen* on back. Regular serial #.	—	Unc	2500.
s3. Specimen w/sm. vermilion ovpt: *Mi-hon.* Regular serial #,	—	Unc	2000.

1945 ND ISSUES

44 200 YEN

	VG	VF	UNC
a. Issued note.	80.00	250.00	550.00
s1. Specimen w/ovpt. and perforated: *Mi-hon.*	—	—	3250.
s2. Specimen w/vermilion ovpt: *Mi-hon. SPECIMEN* on back. Regular serial #.	—	—	1000.
s3. Specimen w/sm. vermilion ovpt: *Mi-hon.* Regular serial #.	—	—	750.00
s4. Specimen w/blue ovpt: *SPECIMEN* on face and back. Regular serial #.	—	—	700.00

45 1000 YEN
ND (1945). Black on brown, green and yellow unpt. Takebe Shrine at l., portr. #7 at r. Back brown and orange.

	VG	VF	UNC
a. Issued note.	1000.	2500.	4000.
s1. Specimen w/ovpt. and perforated: *Mi-hon.*	—	—	12,000.
s2. Specimen w/vermilion ovpt: *Mi-hon. SPECIMEN* on back. Regular serial #.	—	—	4000.
s3. Specimen w/sm. vermilion ovpt: *Mi-hon.* Regular serial #.	—	—	3000.
s4. Specimen w/blue ovpt: *SPECIMEN.* Regular serial #.	—	—	3000.

GREAT IMPERIAL JAPANESE GOVERNMENT (RESUMED)

1917 "PAPER MONEY" ISSUE

大日本帝國政府紙幣
Dai Nip-pon Tei-koku Sei-fu Shi-hei

46 10 SEN
1917-21. Black on orange unpt. Red seal at l., denomination numeral at r.

	VG	VF	UNC
a. Taisho yr. 6.	3.00	10.00	30.00
b. Taisho yrs. 7; 8.	2.00	6.00	20.00
c. Taisho yrs. 9; 10.	2.00	6.00	15.00

47 20 SEN
1917-19. Black on green unpt. Like #48.

	VG	VF	UNC
a. Taisho yr. 6.	20.00	50.00	175.00
b. Taisho yrs. 7; 8.	10.00	30.00	125.00

48 50 SEN
1917-22. Black on pink unpt. Red seal at l., denomination numeral at r.

	VG	VF	UNC
a. Taisho yr. 6.	7.00	20.00	75.00
b. Taisho yrs. 7; 8.	5.00	15.00	60.00
c. Taisho yrs. 9; 10; 11.	4.00	10.00	40.00

BANK OF JAPAN (RESUMED)

日本銀行券
Nip-pon Gin-ko Ken

1943 ND ISSUE
#49-51, Japanese text only.

		VG	VF	UNC
49 (51)	**1 YEN** ND (1943). Black on lt. blue unpt. Portr. #1 at ctr., serial # and block #1-34. Ube Shrine at ctr. on back.			
	a. Issued note.	1.00	4.00	17.50
	s1. Specimen w/ovpt. and perforated: *Mi-hon.*	—	—	1200.
	s2. Specimen w/red ovpt. *SPECIMEN* on face and back.	—	—	800.00
	s3. Specimen w/sm. ovpt. *Mi-hon.*	—	—	250.00
	s4. Specimen w/blue ovpt: *SPECIMEN.*	—	—	225.00
50 (53)	**5 YEN** ND (1943). Black on lt. green and purple unpt. Kitano Shrine at l., portr. #2 at r. Black serial # and block #. Back green and lt. brown.			
	a. Issued note.	2.00	8.00	50.00
	s. Specimen w/ovpt. and perforated: *Mi-hon.*	—	—	1400.

		VG	VF	UNC
55 (54)	**5 YEN** ND (1944). Like #53 but only red block #.			
	a. Issued note.	75.00	250.00	450.00
	s1. Specimen w/ovpt. and perforated: *Mi-hon.*	—	—	1900.
	s2. Specimen w/sm. ovpt: *Mi-hon.* Regular block #.	—	—	500.00

		VG	VF	UNC
51 (55)	**10 YEN** ND (1943-44). Black on brown and lt. blue unpt. Portr. #3 at r. Black serial # and block #. Back blue; Goo Shrine at ctr.			
	a. Wmk: *10 Yen* in Japanese characters at top ctr. (1943).	2.00	6.00	20.00
	b. Wmk: Repeating characters *NIHON* and *JU. (10). (1944).*	2.50	7.00	25.00
	s1. As a. Specimen w/ovpt. and perforated: *Mi-hon.*	—	—	1000.
	s2. As a. Specimen w/blue ovpt: *SPECIMEN.* Regular serial #.	—	—	250.00

		VG	VF	UNC
56	**10 YEN** ND (1944-45). Like #55 but w/only red block #.			
	a. Wmk: Repeating characters *NIHON* and *JU.* (10) (1944).	3.00	10.00	35.00
	b. Wmk: Repeating Bank of Japan logos (circles) (1945).	4.00	12.00	40.00
	c. Wmk: Outline of Kiri leaf (1945).	5.00	15.00	50.00
	s1. As a. Specimen w/ovpt. and perforated: *Mi-hon.*	—	—	1000.
	s2. As b. Specimen w/ovpt: *Mi-hon.* Regular block #.	—	—	500.00

1944 ND ISSUE
#52-57, Japanese text only.

		VG	VF	UNC
52 (49)	**5 SEN** ND (1944). Black on yellow unpt. Equestrian statue at l.			
	a. Issued note.	.10	.50	2.50
	s1. Specimen ovpt: *Mi-hon.* Block #1.	—	—	550.00
	s2. Specimen w/sm. ovpt: *Mi-hon.* Regular block #.	—	—	150.00

		VG	VF	UNC
57	**100 YEN** ND (1944). Black on brown unpt. of leaves. Yumedono Pavilion at l., portr. #6 at r. Back lilac; temple.			
	a. Wmk: Arabesque phoenix design at l.	8.00	25.00	95.00
	b. Wmk: Kiri leaves.	15.00	45.00	125.00
	s1. As a. Specimen w/ovpt. and perforated: *Mi-hon.*	—	—	2250.
	s2. As a. Specimen w/sm. ovpt: *Mi-hon.* Regular block #.	—	—	600.00

GREAT IMPERIAL JAPANESE GOVERNMENT (CONT.)

1938 "PAPER MONEY" ISSUE

		VG	VF	UNC
53 (50)	**10 SEN** ND (1944). Black on purple unpt. Tower monument at l.			
	a. Issued note.	.10	.50	4.00
	s1. Specimen w/ovpt: *Mi-hon.* Block #1.	—	—	550.00
	s2. Specimen w/sm. ovpt: *Mi-hon.* Regular block #.	—	—	150.00
54 (52)	**1 YEN** ND (1944-45). Like #51. Block # only.			
	a. Wmk: Fancy floral design. Block #35-47 (1944).	1.50	5.00	20.00
	b. Wmk: Outline of kiri leaf. Block #48-49 (1945).	3.50	10.00	35.00
	s1. As a. Specimen w/ovpt. and perforated: *Mi-hon.*	—	—	950.00
	s2. As a. Speciman w/red ovpt: *SPECIMEN.*	—	—	600.00

		VG	VF	UNC
58	**50 SEN** 1938. Black on yellow and blue unpt. Fuji and cherry blossoms. (Showa yr. 13 at l.) Back lt. green.			
	a. Issued note.	.50	1.25	9.00
	s1. Specimen w/sm. ovpt: *Mi-hon.* Regular block #.	—	—	250.00

1942 "PAPER MONEY" ISSUE

		VG	VF	UNC
65	**50 SEN** ND (1945). B in unpt.	1.00	2.50	7.00
66	**1 YEN** ND (1946). A in unpt.	5.00	12.50	40.00

		VG	VF	UNC
59	**50 SEN** 1942-44. Black on green and brown unpt. Yasukuni Shrine. Back green; mountain at ctr.			
	a. Showa yr. 17.	.50	2.50	17.50
	b. Showa yr. 18.	.20	.75	5.00
	c. Showa yr. 19.	.30	1.00	7.00
	s1. As c. Specimen w/sm. ovpt: *Mi-hon*. Regular block #.	—	—	250.00
	s2. As c. Specimen w/red ovpt: *SPECIMEN*. Regular block.	—	—	200.00

IMPERIAL JAPANESE GOVERNMENT

幣紙府政國帝本日

Nip-pon Tei-koku Sei-fu Shi-hei

1945 "PAPER MONEY" ISSUE

		VG	VF	UNC
60	**50 SEN** 1945. Lilac unpt. Like #59. Showa yr. 20.			
	a. Issued note.	.25	.75	4.00
	s1. Specimen w/ovpt: *MI-hon*. Blcok #1.	—	—	550.00
	s2. Specimen w/red ovpt: *SPECIMEN*. Block #22.	—	—	550.00

		VG	VF	UNC
67	**1 YEN** ND. B in unpt.			
	a. Serial # prefix - suffix A-A. (1945).	1.00	2.50	7.00
	b. Serial # prefix - suffix B-B. (1955).	4.50	12.00	30.00
	c. Serial # prefix - suffix C-C. (1956).	3.50	10.00	25.00
	d. Serial # prefix - suffix D-D. (1957).	3.50	10.00	25.00
68	**5 YEN** ND (1946). A in unpt.	30.00	70.00	200.00

JAPANESE GOVERNMENT

日本政府紙幣

Nip-pon Sei-fu Shi-hei

1948 "PAPER MONEY" ISSUE

#61, issuer's name reads l. to r.

		VG	VF	UNC
69	**5 YEN** ND (1945). B in unpt.			
	a. Serial # prefix - suffix A-A.	1.50	4.00	12.00
	b. Serial # prefix - suffix B-B.	5.00	15.00	40.00
70	**10 YEN** ND (1946). A in unpt.	35.00	100.00	250.00
71	**10 YEN** ND (1945). B in unpt.	1.50	4.00	12.00

		VG	VF	UNC
61	**50 SEN** 1948. Black on lilac unpt. Portr. Itagaki Taisuke at r. Back green; Diet Bldg. at ctr.	.30	.75	3.50

ALLIED MILITARY CURRENCY - WWII

Initially printed in the U.S.A., subsequently printed in Japan having different serial # style.

Notes w/*A* unpt. circulated only a few weeks in Japan in 1946 and were never legal tender for Japanese citizens. *A* notes were also legal tender in Korea from Sept., 1945 - June, 1946. Notes w/*B* unpt. were legal tender for Japanese citizens from Sept. 1945 - July 1948. *B* yen were used in Okinawa until 1958.

1945-51 ND ISSUE

#62-76 black on lt. blue unpt. Back brown.

		VG	VF	UNC
62	**10 SEN** ND (1946). A in unpt.	4.00	10.00	35.00

		VG	VF	UNC
72	**20 YEN** ND (1946). A in unpt.	100.00	200.00	525.00
73	**20 YEN** ND (1945). B in unpt.	3.50	12.00	40.00

		VG	VF	UNC
63	**10 SEN** ND (1945). B in unpt.	1.00	2.50	7.00
64	**50 SEN** ND (1946). A in unpt.	4.00	10.00	35.00

		VG	VF	UNC
74	**100 YEN** ND (1946). A in unpt.	150.00	325.00	750.00

			VG	VF	UNC
75	**100 YEN** ND (1945). B in unpt.		3.50	12.00	40.00

			VG	VF	UNC
76	**1000 YEN** ND (1951). B in unpt.				
	a. Block letters A; B; C.		450.00	900.00	1750.
	b. Block letters D; E.		300.00	700.00	1250.

BANK OF JAPAN (RESUMED)

券行銀本日
Nip-pon Gin-ko Ken

1945 ND ISSUE
Issuer's name reads l. to r. or r. to l.

			VG	VF	UNC
77	**10 YEN** ND (1945). Black. Portr. #3 at ctr. Back brown.				
	a. Green and gray unpt. Wmk: Quatrefoil. Blocks #1-69.		25.00	60.00	200.00
	b. Lilac unpt. W/o wmk. Blocks #70-165.		35.00	100.00	300.00
	s1. As a. Specimen w/ovpt. and perforated: *Mi-hon*.		—	—	1400.
	s2. As a. Specimen w/sm. ovpt: *Mi-hon*. Regular block #.		—	—	350.00
78 (78A)	**10 YEN** ND (1945). Black, green and lilac. Portr. #3 at r. Back green. Specimen.		—	—	—
78A (78)	**100 YEN** ND (1945). Black on green unpt. Portr. #6 at ctr. Back dk. green.				
	a. Wmk: Quatrefoil. Shaded gray to dull gray-green to gray unpt. Block#1-43.		35.00	100.00	275.00
	b. Wmk: Kiri leaves. Dull gray-green unpt. Block #44-190.		25.00	75.00	250.00
	s1. As a. Specimen w/ovpt. and perforated: *Mi-hon*.		—	—	1900.
	s2. As b. Specimen w/sm. ovpt. *Mi-hon*. Regular block #.		—	—	500.00
78B	**500 YEN** ND (1945). Black on orange unpt. Portr. #1 at ctr. Back brown. Specimen.		—	—	—
78C	**1000 YEN** ND (1945). Black and blue. Similar to #45 but lithographed. Back lt. blue. Specimen.		—	—	—

1946 PROVISIONAL ISSUE
#79-82 March 1946 Currency Reform. Old notes from 10 to 1000 Yen were revalidated w/validation adhesive stamps (Shoshi) of corresponding values.

			VG	VF	UNC
79	**10 YEN** ND (1946). Validation adhesive stamp.				
	a. Affixed to 10 Yen #40.		8.00	17.50	35.00
	b. Affixed to 10 Yen #55.		8.00	17.50	35.00
	c. Affixed to 10 Yen #56.		8.00	17.50	35.00
	d. Affixed to 10 Yen #77.		15.00	30.00	95.00

			VG	VF	UNC
80	**100 YEN** ND (1946). Validation adhesive stamp.				
	a. Affixed to 100 Yen #41.		18.00	35.00	95.00
	b. Affixed to 100 Yen #57.		15.00	27.50	65.00
	c. Affixed to 100 Yen #78.		20.00	40.00	110.00
81	**200 YEN** ND (1946). Validation adhesive stamp.				
	a. Affixed to 200 Yen #38.		—	—	—
	b. Affixed to 200 Yen #44.		—	—	—
82	**1000 YEN** ND (1946). Validation adhesive stamp affixed to 1000 Yen #45.		—	—	—

1946-51 ND ISSUE

			VG	VF	UNC
83	**5 SEN** ND (1948). Black on yellow unpt. Plum blossoms at r. Back lt. brown.		.50	1.50	6.00

			VG	VF	UNC
84	**10 SEN** ND (1947). Black on blue unpt. Doves at r. Back lt. red-brown; Diet Bldg. at l.		.20	.50	2.50

		VG	VF	UNC
85	**1 YEN**			
	ND (1946). Black on lt. brown unpt. Cockerel at lower ctr., portr. Ninomiya Sontoku at r. Back blue.			
	a. Issued note.	.10	.30	2.00
	s. Specimen w/ovpt: *Mi-hon. SPECIMEN* on back.	—	—	750.00
86	**5 YEN**			
	ND (1946). Dk. brown on green unpt. W/o vignette. Back blue.			
	a. Issued note.	.50	2.00	10.00
	s. Specimen w/ovpt: *Mi-hon. SPECIMEN* on back.	—	—	750.00

		VG	VF	UNC
87	**10 YEN**			
	ND (1946). Black on gray-blue unpt. Diet Bldg. at l. Back green.			
	a. Issued note.	.50	1.75	8.00
	s1. Specimen w/ovpt: *SPECIMEN.*	—	—	750.00
	s2. Specimen w/sm. ovpt: *Mi-hon.* Regular block #.	—	—	200.00

		VG	VF	UNC
88	**50 YEN**			
	ND (1951). Black on orange and olive unpt. Portr. Takahashi Korekiyo at r. Back brown; Bank of Japan at bldg. at l.	4.00	12.50	45.00

		VG	VF	UNC
89	**100 YEN**			
	ND (1946). Like #57 but lilac unpt. of leaves. Back blue. Black control and serial #. Horyuji Temple on back.			
	a. Wmk: Kiri leaves.	3.50	10.00	25.00
	b. Wmk: Arabesque - phoenix design.	5.00	15.00	50.00
	s1. As a. Specimen w/ovpt: *SPECIMEN.*	—	—	1000.
	s2. As a. Specimen w/sm. ovpt: *Mi-hon.* Regular block #.	—	—	250.00
89A	**1000 YEN**			
	ND. Black on rose unpt. Similar to #45. Back green and lt. blue. Specimen.	—	Rare	

1950-58 ND ISSUE

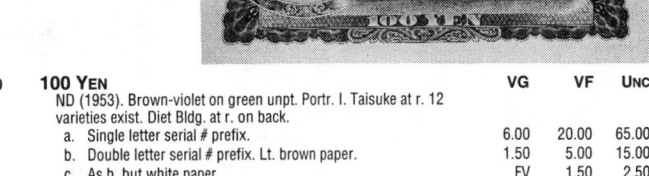

		VG	VF	UNC
90	**100 YEN**			
	ND (1953). Brown-violet on green unpt. Portr. I. Taisuke at r. 12 varieties exist. Diet Bldg. at r. on back.			
	a. Single letter serial # prefix.	6.00	20.00	65.00
	b. Double letter serial # prefix. Lt. brown paper.	1.50	5.00	15.00
	c. As b, but white paper.	FV	1.50	2.50
	s. As a. Specimen w/red ovpt. and perforated: *Mi-hon.*	—	—	1000.

		VG	VF	UNC
91	**500 YEN**			
	ND (1951). Blue. Portr. I. Tomomi at r. Back gray and pale green; Mt. Fuji at r.			
	a. Single letter serial # prefix.	8.00	25.00	80.00
	b. Double letter serial # prefix. Cream paper.	5.50	7.00	30.00
	c. As b, but white paper.	FV	5.50	11.50
	s. As a. Specimen w/red ovpt. and perforated: *Mi-hon.*	—	—	1000.

		VG	VF	UNC
92	**1000 YEN**			
	ND (1950). Black on green unpt. Portr. Shotoku-Taishi at r. Back brown and blue; Yumedono Pavilion at l.			
	a. Single letter serial # prefix.	15.00	40.00	125.00
	b. Double letter serial # prefix.	FV	15.00	50.00

		VG	VF	UNC
93	**5000 YEN**			
	ND (1957). Green and m/c. Portr. Shotoku-Taishi at ctr. and as wmk. Back green; Bank of Japan at ctr.			
	a. Single letter serial # prefix.	FV	65.00	125.00
	b. Double letter serial # prefix.	FV	FV	70.00

94	**10,000 Yen**	**VG**	**VF**	**Unc**
	ND (1958). Dk. brown and dk. green. Portr. Shotohu-Taishi at r. Back brown; phoenix at l. and r. in unpt. within ornate frame. Wmk: Yumedono Pavilion.			
	a. Single letter serial # prefix.	FV	125.00	200.00
	b. Double letter serial # prefix.	FV	FV	130.00

JAPANESE MILITARY CURRENCY

See also China, Hong Kong and occupation issues for Burma, French Indochina, Malaya, Netherlands Indies, Oceania and the Philippines.

GREAT IMPERIAL JAPANESE GOVERNMENT - MINISTRY OF FINANCE

省蔵大府政本日大

Dai Nip-pon Sei-fu O-kura-sho

1895 SINO-JAPANESE WAR ISSUE

Issued in North China.

#MA1-M18 2 Onagadori cockerels at top and 2 dragons at bottom. Meiji yr. 28.

MA1 (AM1)	**2 MACE 5 CANDAREENS** 1895. Black on ochre unpt. Back brown.	—	Rare	—
MA2 (AM2)	**5 MACE** 1895. Black on gray-violet unpt. Back black.	—	Rare	—

MA3 (AM3)	**1 TAEL** 1895. Black on lt. blue unpt. Back dk. blue.	**VG** —	**VF** Rare	**Unc** —

MA4 (AM4)	**5 TAELS** 1895. Black on green unpt. Back green.	**VG** —	**VF** Rare	**Unc** —
MA5 (AM5)	**10 TAELS** 1895. Black on ochre unpt. Back brown-orange.	—	Rare	—

1904 RUSSO-JAPANESE WAR ISSUE

Issued in Korea, North China and Sakhalin in Eastern Siberia. Meiji yr. 37.

NOTE: For issues like #M1-M3 but w/10-pointed star above cockerels' heads, see Korea #7-9.

	10 SEN		**50 SEN**	
			GOOD	**FINE**	**XF**
M1	**10 SEN** 1904. Black on lt. red-brown unpt. Back red-brown.				
	a. W/serial # at top on back.		25.00	70.00	150.00
	b. W/o serial # on back.		15.00	35.00	75.00
M2	**20 SEN** 1904. Black on green unpt. Back green.				
	a. W/serial # at top on back.		90.00	225.00	450.00
	b. W/o serial # on back.		60.00	150.00	300.00
M3	**50 SEN** 1904. Black on lt. gray-violet unpt. Back lt. gray-violet.				
	a. W/ serial # at top on back.		150.00	350.00	700.00
	b. W/o serial # on back.		75.00	200.00	350.00

		GOOD	**FINE**	**XF**
M4	**1 YEN** 1904. Black on ochre unpt. Back yellow-brown.			
	a. W/serial # at top on back.	300.00	700.00	1400.
	b. W/o serial # on back.	150.00	400.00	700.00
M5	**5 YEN** 1904. Black on lt. blue-gray unpt. Back blue-gray.			
	a. W/serial # at top of rack.	1000.	2000.	4000.
	b. W/o serial # on back.	750.00	1500.	3500.
M6	**10 YEN** 1904. Black on lt. brown-violet unpt. Back brown-violet.			
	a. W/serial # at top on back.	1500.	3000.	—
	b. W/o serial # on back.	1250.	2500.	—

1914 OCCUPATION OF TSINGTAO ISSUE

#M7-M12 English legends - in silver at l., and r. and at top on back. Taisho yr. 3.

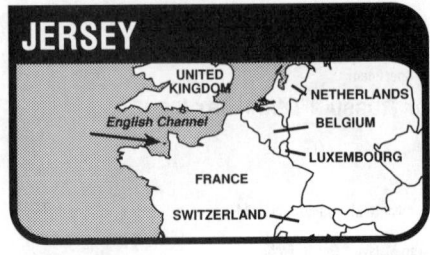

The Bailiwick of Jersey, a British Crown dependency located in the English Channel 12 miles (19 km.) west of Normandy, France, has an area of 45 sq. mi. (117 sq. km.) and a population of 72,691. Capital: St. Helier. The economy is based on agriculture and cattle breeding - the importation of cattle is prohibited to protect the purity of the island's world-famous strain of milk cows.

Jersey was occupied by Neanderthal man 100,000 years B.C., and by Iberians of 2000 B.C. who left their chamber tombs in the island's granite cliffs. Roman legions almost certainly visited the island although they left no evidence of settlement. The country folk of Jersey still speak an archaic form of Norman- French, lingering evidence of the Norman annexation of the island in 933 B.C. Jersey was annexed to England in 1206, 140 years after the Norman Conquest. The dependency is administered by its own laws and customs; laws enacted by the British Parliament do not apply to Jersey unless it is specifically mentioned. During World War II, German troops occupied the island from July 1, 1940 until June 6, 1944.

RULERS:
British

MONETARY SYSTEM:
1 Shilling = 12 Pence
1 Pound = 20 Shillings, 1877-1971

NOTE: Certain listings encompassing issues circulated by various bank and regional authorities are contained in Vol. 1.

BRITISH INFLUENCE

STATES OF THE ISLAND OF JERSEY

1840 INTEREST BEARING NOTES

A1   5 POUNDS
1.9.1840. Black. Arms at upper ctr. *JERSEY STATES BOND FOR FIVE POUNDS BRITISH.* on back. Printer: W. Adams.

		Rare	
a. Issued note.	—	Rare	—
b. Pen cancelled.	20.00	40.00	80.00
r. Remainder. 18xx.	20.00	40.00	80.00

GERMAN OCCUPATION - WWII

STATES OF JERSEY

1941 ND ISSUES
#1-6 arms at upper l.

			VG	VF	UNC
1	**6 PENCE**				
	ND (1941-42). Black on orange unpt. Back orange. Wmk: Thick or thin chain.				
	a. Issued note.		10.00	25.00	65.00
	b. Cancelled.		6.00	15.00	45.00
	r. Remainder. W/o serial #.		—	—	—

			VG	VF	UNC
2	**1 SHILLING**				
	ND (1941-42). Dk. brown on blue unpt. 2 men in unpt. Same 2 men in brown on back. Wmk: Thick chain.				
	a. Issued note.		10.00	25.00	65.00
	b. Cancelled.		6.00	15.00	45.00
	r. Remainder. W/o serial #.		—	—	—

			VG	VF	UNC
3	**2 SHILLINGS**				
	ND (1941-42). Blue on lt. brown unpt. Horse-drawn cart in unpt. Same cart in blue on back. Wmk: Thick chain.				
	a. Issued Note.		10.00	25.00	70.00
	b. Cancelled.		6.00	15.00	45.00
	r. Remainder. W/o serial #.		—	—	—

			VG	VF	UNC
4	**2 SHILLINGS**				
	ND (1941-42). Dk. blue-violet and pale orange unpt. W/o cart scene on back. Wmk: Thick chain.				
	a. Issued note.		20.00	60.00	125.00
	b. Cancelled.		12.00	35.00	75.00

			VG	VF	UNC
5	**10 SHILLINGS**				
	ND (1941-42). Green. Girl w/cows on back. Wmk: Thick or thin chain.				
	a. Issued note.		45.00	95.00	200.00
	b. Cancelled.		25.00	55.00	125.00

			VG	VF	UNC
6	**1 POUND**				
	ND (1941-42). Purple on green unpt. Face similar to #5. Back purple; men w/horse and cart gathering seaweed. Wmk: Thick chain.				
	a. Issued note.		60.00	120.00	300.00
	b. Cancelled.		36.00	72.00	180.00

JORDAN

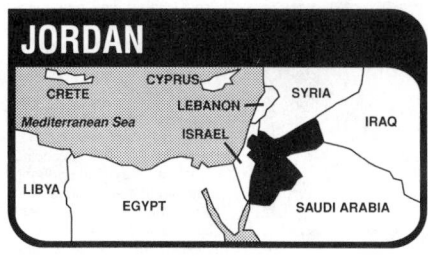

The Hashemite Kingdom of Jordan, a constitutional monarchy in southwest Asia, has an area of 37,738 sq. mi. (97,740 sq. km.) and a population of 3 million. Capital: Amman. Agriculture and tourism comprise Jordan's economic base. Chief exports are phosphates, tomatoes and oranges.

Jordan is the Edom and Moab of the time of Moses. It became part of the Roman province of Arabia in 106 AD, was conquered by the Arabs in 633-36, and was part of the Ottoman Empire from the 16th century until World War I. At that time, the regions presently known as Jordan and Israel were mandated to Great Britain by the League of Nations as Transjordan and Palestine. In 1922 Transjordan was established as the semi-autonomous Emirate of Transjordan, ruled by the Hashemite Prince Abdullah but still nominally a part of the British mandate. The mandate over Transjordan was terminated in 1946, the country becoming the independent Hashemite Kingdom of Transjordan. The kingdom was renamed the Hashemite Kingdom of The Jordan in 1950.

RULERS:
 Abdullah Ibu al-Hussein, 1946-51
 Hussein I, 1952-

MONETARY SYSTEM:
 1 Dirham = 100 Fils
 1 Dinar = 10 Dirhams, until 1993
 1 Dinar = 10 Piastres, 1993-

SIGNATURE VARIETIES					
1	رضا		6		
2			6A		
3			7		
4			8		
5			9		

KINGDOM

HASHEMITE KINGDOM OF THE JORDAN

LAW 1949 FIRST ISSUE

#1-5 wmk. Kg. Abdullah. Printer: TDLR.
#2-5 Kg. Abdullah at r.

	500 FILS	VG	VF	UNC
1	L.1949. Lilac. Landscape w/irrigation system. Cows in hayfield on back. Sign. 1; 2.			
	a. Issued note.	15.00	50.00	200.00
	s. Specimen perforated: Cancelled. Sign. 1.	—	—	150.00

	5 DINARS	VG	VF	UNC
3	L.1949. Red. El Hazne, Treasury of Pharaoh at Petra at ctr. on back. Sign 1; 2.			
	a. Issued note.	35.00	135.00	285.00
	s. Specimen perforated: CANCELLED. Sign. 1.	—	—	210.00

	10 DINARS	VG	VF	UNC
4	L.1949. Blue. Sign. 1; 2.			
	a. Issued note.	40.00	165.00	400.00
	s. Specimen perforated: CANCELLED. Sign. 1.	—	—	300.00

HASHEMITE KINGDOM OF JORDAN

LAW 1949

#A6-8 backs like #1-5. Wmk: Toung Kg. Hussein w/o head covering. Printer: TDLR.
#6-8 Kg. Hussein at r.

	500 FILS	VG	VF	UNC
A6	L.1949. (1952) Lilac. Like #1. Sign. 3-6; 7; 9.	5.00	30.00	125.00
6	**1 DINAR**			
	L.1949. (1952). Green and black. Back like #2. Sign. 3-6; 6A; 7; 9.	5.00	25.00	120.00

7	**5 DINARS**	VG	VF	UNC
	L.1949. (1952). Red and black. Back like #3. Sign. 3-6; 7; 9.	20.00	80.00	225.00

8	**10 DINARS**	VG	VF	UNC
	L.1949. (1952). Blue and black. Back like #4. Sign. 3-6; 7; 9.	40.00	150.00	375.00

KIAU CHAU

Kiau Chau (Kiao Chau, Kiao-chow, Kiautscho), a former German trading enclave, including the port of Tsingtao, was located on the Shantung Peninsula of eastern China. Following the murder of two missionaries in Shantung in 1897, Germany occupied Kiaochow Bay, and during subsequent negotiations with the Chinese government obtained a 99-year lease on 177 sq. mi. of land. The enclave was established as a free port in 1899, and a customs house set up to collect tariffs on goods moving to and from the Chinese interior. The Japanese took siege to the port on Aug. 27, 1914 as their first action in World War I to deprive German sea marauders of their east Asian supply and refitting base. Aided by British forces the siege ended on Nov. 7. Japan retained possession until 1922, when it was restored to China by the Washington Conference on China and naval armaments. It fell again to Japan in 1938, but not until the Chinese had destroyed its manufacturing facilities. Since 1949 it has been a part of the Peoples Republic of China.

RULERS:
German, 1897-1914
Japanese, 1914-1922, 1938-1945

MONETARY SYSTEM:
1 Dollar = 10C Cents

NOTE: *S/M #* refer to *Chinese Banknotes* by Ward D. Smith and Brian Matravers.

GERMAN INFLUENCE

DEUTSCH-ASIATISCHE BANK

行銀華德
Te Hua Yin Hang

For notes of the Deutsch-Asiatische Bank issued by branches *HANKOW, PEKING* or *SHANGHAI* other than *TSINGTAO,* refer to Foreign Banks in China listings, Volume 1.

TSINGTAO BRANCH

1907; 1914 ISSUE
#1-7 printer: G&D.
NOTE: Denominations of 1, 50, 100 and 200 Dollars dated 1.7.1914 are reported.

		GOOD	FINE	XF
1	**1 DOLLAR**			
	1.3.1907. Blue and rose. "Germania" standing at r. w/spear. *(S/M #T101-40).*			
	a. Wmk: 8 cornered crossflower.	750.00	1750.	—
	b. Wmk: *GD.*	750.00	1750.	—
2	**5 DOLLARS**			
	1907; 1914. Dk. green and violet. Like #1. *(S/M #T101-41).*			
	a. Wmk: 8 cornered crossflower. 1.3.1907.	350.00	850.00	—
	b. Wmk: *GD.* 1.3.1907.	350.00	850.00	—
	c. Wmk: *GD.* 1.7.1914. (Not issued).	—	Rare	—

		GOOD	FINE	XF
3	**10 DOLLARS**			
	1907; 1914. Brown and blue. Like #1. *(S/M #T101-42).*			
	a. Wmk: 8 cornered crossflower.	450.00	950.00	—
	b. Wmk: *GD.* 1.3.1907.	Reported Not Confirmed		
	c. Wmk: *GD.* 1.7.1914. (Not issued).	—	Rare	—
4	**25 DOLLARS**			
	1.3.1907. Green and rose. Like #1. *(S/M #T101-43).*			
	a. Wmk: 8 cornered crossflower.	—	Rare	—
	b. Wmk: *GD.*	—	—	—
5	**50 DOLLARS**			
	1.3.1907. Violet and gray. Like #1. *(S/M #T101-44).*			
	a. Wmk: 8 cornered crossflower.	—	Rare	—
	b. Wmk: *GD.*	Reported Not Confirmed		
6	**200 DOLLARS**			
	1.7.1914. Like #1. Wmk: *GD. (S/M #T101-45).*	—	—	—
7	**500 DOLLARS**			
	1.7.1914. Like #1. Wmk: *GD. (S/M #T101-46).*	—	Rare	—

1914 TAEL ISSUE
#8-10 printer: G&D.

NOTE: Denominations of 1, 5, 10 and 20 Taels dated 1914 have been reported.

8 50 TAELS
1.7.1914. Like #1. Wmk: GD. (S/M #T101-51). — — —

9 100 TAELS
1.7.1914. Like #1. Wmk: GD. (S/M #T101-52). — — —

10 500 TAELS
1.7.1914. Like #1. (S/M #T101-53). — — —

Korea, "Land of the Morning Calm," occupies a mountainous peninsula in northeast Asia bounded by Manchuria, the Yellow Sea and the Sea of Japan. According to legend, the first Korean dynasty, that of the House of Tangun, ruled from 2333 BC to 1122 BC. It was followed by the dynasty of Kija, a Chinese scholar, which continued until 193 BC and brought a high civilization to Korea. The first recorded period in the history of Korea, the Period of the Three Kingdoms, lasted from 57 BC to 935 AD and achieved the first political unification on the peninsula. The Kingdom of Koryo, from which Korea derived its name, was founded in 935 and continued until 1392, when it was superseded by the Yi dynasty of King Yi, Sung Kye which was to last until the Japanese annexation in 1910.

At the end of the 16th century Korea was invaded and occupied for 7 years by Japan, and from 1627 until the late 19th century it was a semi-independent tributary of China. Japan replaced China as the predominant foreign influence at the end of the Sino-Japanese War (1894-95), only to find its position threatened by Russian influence from 1896 to 1904. The Russian threat was eliminated by the Russo-Japanese War (1904-05) and in 1905 Japan established a direct protectorate over Korea. On Aug. 22, 1910, the last Korean ruler signed the treaty that annexed Korea to Japan as a government general in the Japanese Empire. Japanese suzerainty was maintained until the end of World War II. The Potsdam conference in 1945 set the 38th parallel as the line dividing the occupation forces of the United States in the South and Russia in the north.

A contingent of the United States Army landed at Inchon to begin the acceptance of the Surrender of Japanese forces in the South on Sept. 8, 1945. Unissued Japanese printed stock was released during the U.S. Army's administration for circulation in the southern sector.

NOTE: For later issues see Korea/North and Korea/South.

* * * This section has been partially renumbered. * * *

RULERS
Kojong, 1864-1897
Kwang Mu, 1897-1907
Yung Hi, 1907-1910
Japanese, 1910-1945

MONETARY SYSTEM:
1 Yen = 100 Sen
1 Yang = 100 Fun
1 Whan = 5 Yang to 1902
1 Won = 100 Chon 1902-

MONETARY UNITS:
Fun 分
Mun 文
Yang, Niang 兩
Chon 錢
Won 圜
Hwan 圜

KINGDOM OF KOREA
TREASURY DEPARTMENT
HOJO

1893 CONVERTIBLE NOTES
#1-3 dragons around text in circle at ctr. Printed in 1893 (30th year of King Kojong). Issuing Agency: Tai Whan Shou (Conversion Office). (Not issued).

1	**5 YANG**			
	Yr. 30 (1893).	—	Rare	—
2	**10 YANG**			
	Yr. 30 (1893).	—	Rare	—
2A	**20 YANG**			
	Yr. 30 (1893).	—	Rare	—

3	**50 YANG**			
	Yr. 30 (1893).	—	Rare	—

JAPANESE PROTECTORATE

DAI ICHI GINKO

FIRST NATIONAL BANK OF JAPAN

1902 ISSUE

#4-12 w/10 pronged star at top ctr.

#4-6 S. Eiichi at r.

NOTE: For issues similar to #7-9 but w/chrysanthemum crest above cockerels' heads see Japan-Military Issues #M1-M3.

4	**1 YEN**	GOOD	FINE	XF
	1902; 1904. Black on blue-green unpt. Back dk. blue.			
	a. Stars in corners on face. 1902. (Meiji yr. 35).	200.00	500.00	1000.
	b. Numerals in corners on face. 1904. (Meiji yr. 37).	175.00	450.00	900.00

5	**5 YEN**	GOOD	FINE	XF
	1902; 1904. Black on ochre unpt. Like #4. Back grayish blue-green.			
	a. Stars in corners on face. 1902. (Meiji yr. 35).	350.00	800.00	2500.
	b. Numerals in corners on face. 1904. (Meiji yr. 37).	300.00	750.00	2250.
6	**10 YEN**			
	1902; 1904. Black on lt. blue unpt. Like #4. Back dark red-brown.			
	a. Stars in corners on face. 1902. (Meiji yr. 35).	—	Rare	—
	b. Numerals in corners on face. 1904. (Meiji yr. 37).	—	Rare	—

1904 ISSUE

7	**10 SEN**	GOOD	FINE	XF
	1904. Red. 2 Onagadori cockerels at top w/2 dragons below (Meiji yr. 37).	60.00	125.00	—
8	**20 SEN**			
	1904. Blue. Like #7. (Meiji yr. 37).	150.00	275.00	700.00
9	**50 SEN**			
	1904. Yellow. Like #7. Back purple. (Meiji yr. 37).	200.00	400.00	1200.

1907 ISSUE

9A	**5 YEN**	GOOD	FINE	XF
	1907. Black. Peacock at l., temple at ctr. Back purple on ochre unpt. (Meiji yr. 39). Specimen ovpt: *Mi-hon.*	—	Rare	—

1908-09 ISSUE

10	**1 YEN**	GOOD	FINE	XF
	1908. Blue on pink unpt. Bridge shelter at l. Back red on lt. blue unpt. (Meiji yr. 40).	125.00	300.00	500.00

11   5 YEN
1909. Black on lt. orange-brown unpt. Shrine at r. Back purple w/black text on lt. green unpt. (Meiji yr. 41).

	GOOD	FINE	XF
	—	Rare	—

12   10 YEN
1909. Green. Back brown-violet; house at r. (Meiji yr. 41).

	GOOD	FINE	XF
	—	Rare	—

BANK OF KOREA

1909 ISSUE

#13-15 plum blossom at top ctr. Dated Yung Hi yr. 3.

		GOOD	FINE	XF
13	**1 YEN** 1909 (1910). Similar to #10. Back: brown-orange.	75.00	200.00	500.00
14	**5 YEN** 1909 (1911). Black on lt. violet-brown unpt. Like #11. Back: blue-black on lt. green unpt.	350.00	750.00	2500.
15	**10 YEN** 1909 (1911). Dk. gray-green on lilac unpt. Like #12. Back: brown.	300.00	500.00	2000.

BANK OF CHOSEN

1911 (1914) FIRST ISSUE

		GOOD	FINE	XF
16	**100 YEN** 1911 (1914). Purple on lilac and ochre unpt. God of Fortune sitting on rice bales w/sack over shoulder. Stylized serial # (Korean).	50.00	150.00	700.00
16A	**100 YEN** 1911 (1914). Like #16 but blue. Regular style serial # (Japanese).	40.00	125.00	600.00

1911 (1915) SECOND ISSUE

#16-19 2 printers, distinguished by serial # style. Dated Meiji yr. 44 (1911).

Stylized serial # (Korean). Regular style serial # (Japanese).

		VG	VF	UNC
17	**1 YEN** 1911 (1915). Black on lt. red unpt. Man w/beard. *ONE YEN* at l.			
	a. Stylized serial # (Koren).	10.00	40.00	125.00
	b. Regular style serial # (Japanese).	5.00	30.00	100.00
18	**5 YEN** 1911 (1915). Brown. Man w/beard at r.			
	a. Stylized serial # (Koren).	50.00	275.00	1000.
	b. Regular style serial # Japanese).	40.00	225.00	800.00

		VG	VF	UNC
19	**10 YEN** 1911 (1915). Green. *TEN YEN* at l., man w/beard at at r.			
	a. Stylized serial # (Koren).	40.00	225.00	800.00
	b. Regular style serial # (Japanese).	30.00	200.00	700.00

1916 ISSUE

#20-22 dated Taisho yr. 5.

20	**10 SEN** 1916. Blue on pink unpt. W/o Western numerals for denomination on face.	25.00	75.00	200.00
21	**20 SEN** 1916. Blue on orange unpt. W/o Western numerals for denomination on face.	100.00	350.00	1000.

		VG	VF	UNC
22	**50 SEN** 1916. Blue on lt. green unpt. W/o Western numerals for denomination on face.	100.00	350.00	1000.

1919 ISSUE

#23-25 Russian, Japanese and English text: *payable in Japanese currency at any of its Manchurian offices.* Dated Taisho yr. 8.

23	**10 SEN** 20.10.1919. Green on pink unpt. Western numerals for denomination at r. on face. Russian and English wording on pink back.			
	a. 7 character imprint (Korean).	10.00	35.00	100.00
	b. 14 character imprint (Japanese).	15.00	45.00	110.00

		VG	VF	UNC
24	**20 SEN** 20.10.1919. Black on yellow unpt. Western numerals for denomination at r. on face. Russian legends on back.	35.00	85.00	200.00
25	**50 SEN** 20.10.1919. Black on green unpt. Western numerals for denomination at r. on face. Russian legends on back.			
	a. 7 character imprint (Korean). Blocks 1-6.	15.00	60.00	200.00
	b. 14 character imprint (Japanese). Blocks 6-7.	20.00	65.00	225.00

1917 PROVISIONAL POSTAL STAMP ISSUE

			VG	VF	UNC
26 (28)	**5 SEN** 1917. Japanese 5 Sen postal adhesive stamp (type Tazawa) affixed to a special form.		—	Unc	700.00

1932-38 ND AND DATED ISSUE

#29-32 w/o bank name in English on back.

			VG	VF	UNC
27 (26)	**10 SEN** 1937. Like #23 but w/o Russian wording on back. (Showa yr. 12).		8.00	25.00	150.00
28 (27)	**50 SEN** 1937. Like #25 but w/o Russian legends on back. (Showa yr. 12).				
	a. Issued note.		10.00	30.00	150.00
	s. Specimen w/red ovpt: *Mi-hon*.		—	—	200.00

			VG	VF	UNC
29	**1 YEN** ND (1932). Black on lt. brown unpt. Brown guilloche at l., green guilloche at ctr., man w/beard at r. Serial # and block #. 14 character imprint.				
	a. Issued note.		.25	2.00	6.00
	s1. Specimen w/red ovpt. and perforated: *Mi-hon*.		—	—	200.00
	s2. Specimen w/vermilion ovpt: *Mi-hon*.		—	—	150.00
	s3. Specimen w/red ovpt: *Mi-hon*, punched hole cancelled.		—	—	100.00
30	**5 YEN** ND (1935). Black on lt. brown, green and lilac unpt. Man w/beard at r. Back green; *5 YEN* at bottom. 7 character imprint.				
	a. Issued note.		50.00	20.00	175.00
	s1. Specimen w/red ovpt. and perforated: *Mi-hon*.		—	—	200.00
	s2. Specimen w/red ovpt: *Mi-hon*, punched hole cancelled.		—	—	100.00
31	**10 YEN** ND (1932). Black. Green and olive guilloche at ctr., man w/beard at r. Back green and brown; bldg. at ctr., *10 YEN* at bottom. 14 character imprint.				
	a. Issued note.		2.00	5.00	15.00
	s. Specimen w/red ovpt. and perforated: *Mi-hon*.		—	—	200.00

			VG	VF	UNC
32	**100 YEN** ND (1938). Black on pink, green and violet unpt. Man w/beard at r. *100 YEN* at bottom on back. Wmk: Plum branches. 12 character imprint.				
	a. Issued note.		6.00	20.00	75.00
	s. Specimen w/red ovpt: *Mi-hon*, punched hole cancelled.		—	—	200.00

1944 ND ISSUES

			VG	VF	UNC
33 (35)	**1 YEN** ND (1944). Like #29 but block # only.				
	a. Issued note.		1.00	4.00	12.00
	s1. Specimen w/red ovpt: *Mi-hon*.		—	—	200.00
	s2. Specimen w/vermilion ovpt: *Mi-hon* on face and back.		—	—	150.00
34	**5 YEN** ND (1944). Like #30 but w/o 5 YEN at bottom on back. Serial # and block #. 10 character imprint.				
	a. Issued note.		4.00	25.00	125.00
	s1. Specimen w/red ovpt. and perforated: *Mi-hon*.		—	—	200.00
	s2. Specimen w/vermilion ovpt: *Mi-hon* on face and back.		—	—	250.00
	s3. Specimen w/vermilion ovpt: *Mi-yo* in frame. *Specimen* on back.		—	—	100.00
35 (33)	**10 YEN** ND (1944). Black on blue unpt. Brown and green guilloche at ctr., man w/beard at r. W/o *10 YEN* at bottom on dull green back. Serial # and block #. 7 character imprint.				
	a. Issued note.		3.00	10.00	75.00
	s. Specimen w/red ovpt. and perforated: *Mi-hon*.		—	—	200.00

			VG	VF	UNC
36 (40)	**10 YEN** ND (1944-45). Like #33 but block # only. 7 character imprint.				
	a. Wmk: *CHOSEN GINKO* (4 characters) at bottom, ornaments at ctr. (1944).		3.75	15.00	50.00
	b. Wmk: *CHO* character and cherry blossoms repeated. (1945).		3.00	12.00	40.00
	s1. As a. Specimen w/vermilion ovpt: *Mi-hon* on face and back.		—	—	150.00
	s2. As a. Specimen w/vermilion ovpt: *Mi-hon*.		—	—	100.00
	s3. As a. Specimen w/purple ovpt: *Mi-yo* in frame. *Specimen* on back.		—	—	100.00
	s4. As b. Specimen w/vermilion ovpt: *Mi-hon* on face and back.		—	—	150.00
37 (36)	**100 YEN** ND (1944). Black on green, blue and violet unpt. Guilloche at ctr., man w/beard at r. W/o *100 YEN* at bottom on back. Serial and block #. W/ or w/o wmk. 10 character imprint.				
	a. Issued note.		3.50	12.50	40.00
	s1. Specimen w/red ovpt: *Mi-hon*.		—	—	200.00
	s2. Specimen w/vermilion ovpt: *Mi-hon* on face and back.		—	—	150.00
	s3. Specimen w/vermilion ovpt: *Mi-hon*.		—	—	100.00

1945 ND ISSUE

			VG	VF	UNC
38	**1 YEN** ND (1945). Black on pale green and brown unpt. Guilloche brown at l. W/o guilloche at ctr. Man w/beard at r. Block # only. Back green. Lithographed.				
	a. Issued note.		.25	2.00	6.00
	s1. Specimen w/red ovpt: *Mi-hon*. Special serial# on back.		—	—	150.00
	s2. Specimen w/red ovpt: *Mi-hon* in frame.		—	—	100.00
	s3. Specimen w/vermilion ovpt: *Mi-hon* in frame on face and back.		—	—	100.00
	s4. Specimen w/vermilion ovpt: *Mi-yo* in frame. *Specimen* on back.		—	—	100.00
39	**5 YEN** ND (1945). Like #34 but block # only.				
	a. Issued note.		3.00	10.00	60.00
	s. Specimen w/vermilion ovpt: *Mi-yo* in frame. *Specimen* on back.		—	—	100.00

			VG	VF	UNC
40 (42)	**10 YEN** ND (1945-46). Black on purple unpt., gray guilloche at ctr. Man w/beard at r., paulownia crest at top ctr. Block# only. Back gray to grayish purple. 7 character imprint.				
	a. Block # 1; 2 (1945).		10.00	40.00	300.00
	b. Block # 3; 4 (1946).		11.00	45.00	350.00
	s1. As a. Specimen w/red ovpt: *Mi-hon.* Special serial# on back.		—	—	150.00
	s2. As a. Specimen w/vermilion ovpt: *Mi-yo* in frame. *Specimen* on back.		—	—	100.00
	s3. As b. Specimen w/vermilion ovpt: *Mi-yo* in frame.		—	—	100.00

			VG	VF	UNC
46	**100 YEN = 100 WON** ND (1947). Like #45. Face guilloche orange to yellow (varies). Back green w/violet guilloche. Wmk. varieties.				
	a. a. Gray paper, w/wmk.		.50	2.00	10.00
	b. b. White paper, w/o wmk.		.25	1.00	3.00

			VG	VF	UNC
41	**100 YEN** ND (1945). Black. Face like #32 and #36 but litho. Lt. blue unpt. and guilloche at l. Paulownia crest above portr. Blocks 1 and 2 only. Back dull gray-brown; design like #36.		300.00	800.00	2500.
42 (37)	**1000 YEN** ND (1945). Lt. purple. Man w/beard at r. Back gray.				
	a. Block #1. (Not issued).		—	2000.	3000.
	s. Specimen w/red ovpt: *Mi-hon.*		—	2000.	3000.

1945 ND PROVISIONAL ISSUE

				VF	UNC
42A (37A)	**1000 YEN** ND (1945). 5 character red ovpt: *Chosen Ginko Ken* (Bank of Chosen Note) on Japan #45. (Not issued).		—	3000.	4000.

U.S. ARMY ADMINISTRATION
Issued for circulation in the southern sector.

BANK OF CHOSEN

1946-47 ISSUE

			VG	VF	UNC
43	**10 YEN = 10 WON** ND (1946). Black on pale green unpt, blue-green guilloche at ctr. Man w/beard at r. 5 petaled white hibiscus flower at upper ctr. Block # only. Back: gray. 12 character imprint.		.75	4.00	20.00
44	**100 YEN = 100 WON** ND (1946). Black. Olive guilloche at l.Mman w/beard at r., paulownia crest at r. Block # only.		15.00	50.00	250.00

			VG	VF	UNC
45	**100 YEN = 100 WON** ND (1946). Blue. Orange guilloche at ctr. 5 petaled white hibiscus flower above portr. Back brown w/orange guilloche. Color variations.		2.50	15.00	40.00

658 NORTH KOREA

The Democratic Peoples Republic of Korea, situated in northeastern Asia on the northern half of the Korean peninsula between the Peoples Republic of China and the Republic of Korea, has an area of 46,540 sq. mi. (120,538 sq. km.) and a population of 22.4 million. Capital: Pyongyang. The economy is based on heavy industry and agriculture. Metals, minerals and farm produce are exported.

Japan replaced China as the predominant foreign influence in Korea in 1895 and annexed the peninsular country in 1910. Defeat in World War II brought an end to Japanese rule. U.S. troops entered Korea from the south and Soviet forces entered from the north. The Cairo conference (1943) had established that Korea should be "free and independent." The Potsdam conference (1945) set the 38th parallel as the line dividing the occupation forces of the United States and Russia. When Russia refused to permit a U.N. commission designated to supervise reunification elections to enter North Korea, an election was held in South Korea which established the Republic of Korea on Aug. 15, 1948. North Korea held an unsupervised election on Aug. 25, 1948, and on the following day proclaimed the establishment of the Democratic Peoples Republic of Korea.

MONETARY SYSTEM:
1 Won = 100 Chon

SOVIET MILITARY OCCUPATION

RUSSIAN ARMY HEADQUARTERS

1945 ISSUE
#1-4 design w/o vignettes.

		VG	VF	UNC
1	**1 WON** 1945. Green on lt. brown unpt.	10.00	40.00	100.00
2	**5 WON** 1945. Brown on blue unpt.	12.50	50.00	120.00
3	**10 WON** 1945. Violet on lt. green unpt.	13.50	55.00	140.00

		VG	VF	UNC
4	**100 WON** 1945. Red on gray unpt. a. Wmk., serial # 17mm long. b. W/o wmk., serial # 15 mm long.	 22.50 22.50	 67.50 67.50	 170.00 170.00

NORTH KOREA CENTRAL BANK

1947 ISSUES
#8-11 worker and farmer at l. ctr. Mountain on back.

		VG	VF	UNC
5	**15 CHON** 1947. Brown a. W/wmk. b. W/o wmk.	 .30 —	 1.00 —	 3.00 .75
6	**20 CHON** 1947. Green. a. W/wmk. b. W/o wmk.	 .30 —	 1.00 —	 3.00 .75

		VG	VF	UNC
7	**50 CHON** 1947. Blue on lt. olive unpt. a. W/wmk. b. W/o wmk.	 .20 —	 .50 —	 2.00 .75

		VG	VF	UNC
8	**1 WON** 1947. Black on orange and green unpt. a. W/wmk. b. W/o wmk.	 .30 —	 1.00 —	 50.00 1.00
9	**5 WON** 1947. Black on blue and red unpt. 4 lines between second and third character at bottom; segmented Korean numeral at lower r. Back blue.	.25	.75	3.00

		VG	VF	UNC
10	**5 WON** 1947. Like #9 but 8 lines between second and third character at bottom; more connected Koren numeral at lower r. a. W/wmk. b. W/o wmk.	 .25 —	 .50 —	 3.00 1.00
10A	**10 WON** 1947. Black on red and green unpt. a. W/wmk. b. W/o wmk.	 1.00 —	 3.00 —	 10.00 1.50
11	**100 WON** 1947. Black on red, orange and lilac unpt. a. W/wmk. b. W/o wmk.	 1.50 —	 7.50 —	 25.00 2.00

DEMOCRATIC PEOPLES REPUBLIC

KOREAN CENTRAL BANK

1959 ISSUE

12	**50 CHON**	VG	VF	UNC
	1959. Blue. Arms at upper l.	.15	.50	2.00

17	**100 WON**	VG	VF	UNC
	1959. Green and m/c. Arms at l., steam freight train in factory area at ctr. River w/cliffs on back.	.25	.75	3.00

13	**1 WON**	VG	VF	UNC
	1959. Red-brown. Fishing boat at ctr.	.15	.50	2.00

14	**5 WON**	VG	VF	UNC
	1959. Green and m/c. Lg. bldg. at ctr.	.15	.40	2.00

15	**10 WON**	VG	VF	UNC
	1959. Red and m/c. Pagoda at ctr. r. Woman picking fruit on back.	.20	.50	2.00

16	**50 WON**	VG	VF	UNC
	1959. Purple and m/c. Arms at l., bridge and city at ctr. Woman w/wheat on back.	.20	.50	2.00

SOUTH KOREA

The Republic of Korea, situated in northeastern Asia on the southern half of the Korean peninsula between North Korea and the Korean Strait, has an area of 38,025 sq. mi. (98,484 sq. km.) and a population of 43.27 million. Capital: Seoul. The economy is based on agriculture and textiles. Clothing, plywood and textile products are exported. Japan replaced China as the predominant foreign influence in Korea in 1895 and annexed the peninsular country in 1910. Defeat in World War II brought an end to Japanese rule. U.S. troops entered Korea from the south and Soviet forces entered from the north. The Cairo Conference (1943) had established that Korea should be "free and independent." The Potsdam Conference (1954) set the 38th parallel as the line dividing the occupation forces of the United States and Russia. When Russia refused to permit a U.N. commission designated to supervise reunification elections to enter North Korea, an election was held in South Korea on May 10, 1948. By its determination, the Republic of Korea was inaugurated on Aug. 15, 1948.

NOTE: For Bank of Chosen notes issued in South Korea under the Allied Occupation during the post WWII period 1945 to 1948 refer to Korea listings.

MONETARY SYSTEM:
1 Won (Hwan) = 100 Chon
1 new Won = 10 old Hwan, 1962-

DATING:
The modern notes of Korea are dated according to the founding of the first Korean dynasty, that of the house of Tangun, in 2333 BC.

REPUBLIC

BANK OF CHOSEN

1949 ND ISSUE
NOTE: #3 was issued unofficially by the North Korean Army in 1950 during the Korean conflict.

			VG	VF	UNC
1	**5 WON**		1.50	3.50	37.50
	ND (1949). Black on orange unpt.. Archway at r. Back red-brown; bldg. at ctr.				

			VG	VF	UNC
2	**10 WON**		1.00	2.50	25.00
	ND (1949). Black on lilac unpt. Like #1. Back black.				

			VG	VF	UNC
3	**1000 WON**		.50	1.50	12.50
	ND (1950). Lilac. Man w/beard at l. Back lt. blue.				

BANK OF KOREA

1949 ISSUE

		VG	VF	UNC
4	**5 CHON**	1.50	4.00	45.00
	1949. Red. Like #6.			
5	**10 CHON**	2.00	5.00	55.00
	1949. Brown. Like #6.			

		VG	VF	UNC
6	**50 CHON**	2.00	5.00	65.00
	1949. Blue. 5-petaled blossom within circle at ctr.			

1950 ISSUE

		VG	VF	UNC
7	**100 WON**	.50	1.00	7.50
	ND (1950). Brown. City gate at l. Color varieties.			

		VG	VF	UNC
8	**1000 WON**	.50	1.50	12.50
	ND (1950). Green. Portr. Syngman Rhee at l. Color varieties.			

1952 ISSUE

		VG	VF	UNC
9	**500 WON**	2.50	30.00	170.00
	4285 (1952). Blue. Portr. Syngman Rhee at l. Back brown; pagoda at ctr.			

		VG	VF	UNC
10	**1000 WON**			
	4285 (1952); 4286 (1953). Black-green. Portr. Syngman Rhee at l. Back like #9.			
	a. Lg. date. 4285	.50	2.00	12.00
	b. Sm. date. 4286.	.50	2.00	12.00

1953 ND ISSUE
#11-12 printed in Korea from glass positives furnished by the U.S.A. BEP.

#13-15 medieval tortoise warship at r. Printed by Tudor Press, Boston, U.S.A. through the BEP.

		VG	VF	UNC
11	**1 WON**			
	ND (1953). Lilac. Wreath of guilloches at l. ctr.			
	a. Thin wmk. paper.	.40	1.00	5.50
	b. Thick paper, w/o wmk.	.40	1.00	5.50

| 12 | **5 WON**
ND (1953). Red. Wreath of guilloches at l. ctr. | VG
1.00 | VF
5.00 | UNC
45.00 |

13	**10 WON** ND (1953). Blue.	VG 2.00	VF 12.00	UNC 85.00
14	**100 WON** ND (1953). Green	4.00	25.00	150.00
15	**1000 WON** ND (1953). Brown.	25.00	100.00	350.00

1953-56 ISSUES

| 16 | **10 HWAN**
4286 (1953). Green-black on lt. blue unpt. on gray paper. Pagoda portal at r. Rock formations in water on purple back. | VG
2.00 | VF
7.50 | UNC
65.00 |

| 17 | **10 HWAN**
4286 (1953)-4291 (1958). Gray-blue on white paper. Like #16. Back purple. | VG
.50 | VF
1.50 | UNC
17.50 |
| 18 | **100 HWAN**
4286 (1953). Dk. green on yellowish paper. Portr. Syngman Rhee at l. Archway on back. | 30.00 | 275.00 | 950.00 |

| 19 | **100 HWAN**
4287 (1954); 4288 (1955); 4289 (1956). Dk. green on white paper. Like #18. | VG
1.00 | VF
2.50 | UNC
35.00 |

| 20 | **500 HWAN**
4289 (1956); 4290 (1957). Gray-blue on green unpt. Portr. Syngman Rhee at ctr. Back brown. | VG
5.00 | VF
45.00 | UNC
250.00 |

1957 ISSUE

| 21 | **100 HWAN**
4290 (1957). Gray on olive-green and brown unpt. Portr. Syngman Rhee at r. Back green. | VG
3.50 | VF
20.00 | UNC
120.00 |

| 22 | **1000 HWAN**
4290 (1957)-4293 (1960). Purple on brown and green unpt. Portr. Syngman Rhee at r. Back black on green unpt; date at ctr. | VG
3.00 | VF
30.00 | UNC
145.00 |

1958-60 ISSUE

| 23 | **50 HWAN**
4291 (1958). Green-blue on olive-green unpt. Archway at l. Back green; statue at ctr. medieval tortoise warship at r. | VG
25.00 | VF
85.00 | UNC
400.00 |

| 24 | **500 HWAN**
4291 (1958); 4292 (1959). Dk. green. Portr. Syngman Rhee at r. Back brownish purple. | VG
5.00 | VF
35.00 | UNC
250.00 |

| 25 | **1000 HWAN**
4293 (1960); 4294 (1961); 1962. Black on olive unpt. Kg. Sejong the Great at r. Back blue-green and lt. brown; flaming torch at ctr. | VG
1.50 | VF
10.00 | UNC
75.00 |

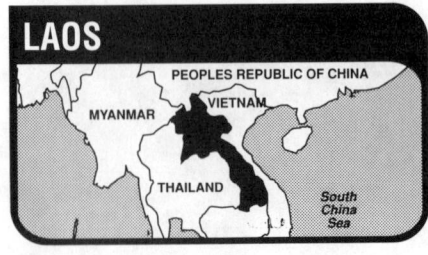

LAOS

The Lao People's Democratic Republic, located on the Indo-Chinese Peninsula between the Socialist Republic of Vietnam and the Kingdom of Thailand, has an area of 91,429 sq. mi. (236,800 sq. km.) and a population of 4.2 million. Captial: Vientiane. Agriculture employs 95 percent of the people. Tin, lumber and coffee are exported.

The first United Kingdom of Laos was established in the mid-14th century by King Fa Ngum who ruled an area including present Laos, northeastern Thailand, and the southern part of China's Yunnan province from his capital at Luang Prabang. Thailand and Vietnam obtained control over much of the present Lao territory in the 18th century and remained dominant until France established a protectorate over the area in 1893 and incorporated it into the Union of Indo-China. The Independence of Laos was proclaimed in March of 1945, during the last days of the Japanese occupation of World War II. France reoccupied Laos in 1946, and established it as a constitutional monarchy within the French Union in 1949. In 1953, war erupted between the government and the Pathet Lao, a Communist movement supported by the Vietnamese Communist forces. Peace was declared in 1954 with Laos becoming fully independent in 1955 and the Pathet Lao being permitted to occupy two northern provinces. Civil war broke out again in 1960 with the United States supporting the government of the Kingdom of Laos and the North Vietnamese helping the Communist Pathet Lao, and continued, with intervals of truce and political compromise, until the formation of the Lao People's Democratic Republic on Dec. 2, 1975.

RULERS:
Sisavang Vong, 1949-1959
Savang Vatthana, 1959-1975

MONETARY SYSTEM:
1 Piastre = 100 Cents to 1955
1 Kip = 100 At, 1955-1978

FREE LAO GOVERNMENT

Government of 1945-46 established in Vientiane after the Japanese surrender.

LAO ISSARA

FREE LAO GOVERNMENT

1945-46 ISSUE

#A3, some minor varieties exist in rendition of characters also.

A1	10 AT	GOOD	FINE	XF
	ND. Kneeling Buddhist monk w/parasol at ctr.	40.00	100.00	175.00

A2	20 AT	GOOD	FINE	XF
	ND. Lao temple at ctr.	40.00	100.00	175.00

A3	50 AT	GOOD	FINE	XF
	ND. Symbol of constitution at ctr.			
	a. W/o *50* on back. Plain paper. Series 1.	2.00	10.00	35.00
	b. Sm. *50* 4mm high on back, top of 5 curved. Plain paper. Series 2-7.	1.00	5.00	25.00

ກ
ຫ

Word for c. and d.

c.	Sm. *50* 4mm high on back, top of 5 straight, first character on fifth line is as illustration. Vertical lined paper. Series 2; 6.	2.00	10.00	30.00
d.	Like #A3c but character as illustrated is last on fourth line. Vertical lined paper. Series 10.	2.00	10.00	30.00
e.	Lg. *50* 5.5mm high on back, text on front similar to #A3d. Vertical lined paper. Series 10; 13.	2.00	10.00	30.00
f.	Lg. *50* 5.5mm high on back, but w/o printer's identification line on front. Vertical lined paper. Series 9.	2.00	10.00	30.00
g.	Like #A3e but w/designer name Phong on front on a vertical line inside the lower l. Letters VS in lower corner.	—	—	—
h.	Series # on front (Lao numeral) different from the # (in words) on back.	—	Rare	—
i.	As b. but bottom line missing on back. Series 4.	—	—	—
j.	As b. Vertical lined paper. Series 2-7.	1.00	5.00	25.00
k.	As d. Horizontal lined paper. Series 10.	—	—	—
l.	As f. Horizontal lined paper. Series 9.	—	—	—

A4	10 KIP	GOOD	FINE	XF
	ND. Purple. W/or w/o pink unpt. Garuda bird at top ctr. Temple on back.			
	a. Serial # in Western numerals Sign. Khammao Vilay.	40.00	100.00	250.00
	b. Serial # in Lao and European characters. Sign. Katay Don Sasorith.	20.00	70.00	200.00

KINGDOM

BANQUE NATIONALE DU LAOS

SIGNATURE VARIETIES		
	LE GOUVERNEUR	UN CENSEUR
1	*Phou Panya*	*H. Mouradr*
2	*Phou Panya*	*Bently*
3	*Aly Gibnya*	*Saven*

1957 ND ISSUE

#1-6 sign. 1.

#1-3, and 5 were also printed by the Pathet Lao during the Civil War. These counterfeits were printed in Bulgaria on paper w/o planchettes (security dots). Serial # style is also different from genuine notes.

1	1 KIP	VG	VF	UNC
	ND (1957). Green. That de Ing Hang at l. Farmer w/water buffalo on back.			
	a. Security dots. Printer: SBNC.	.25	1.00	15.00
	b. W/o security dots (counterfeit).	.10	.25	1.00
	s. As a. Specimen.	—	—	—

2	5 KIP	VG	VF	UNC
	ND (1957). Brown. That de Tion-Si at r. Ox cart on back.			
	a. Security dots. Printer: SBNC.	1.00	10.00	50.00
	b. W/o security dots (counterfeit).	.10	.25	1.00
	s. As a. Specimen.	—	—	—

3 **10 KIP**
ND (1957). Blue. Pagoda Vat Ong Tu at r. Workers in rice field on back.

	VG	VF	UNC
a. Security dots. Printer: SBNC.	.50	3.00	30.00
b. W/o security dots (counterfeit).	.25	.50	2.00
s. As a. Specimen.	—	—	—

4 **20 KIP**
ND (1957). Purple. Govt. palace. Woman weaving on back. Printer: SBNC.

	VG	VF	UNC
a. Issued note.	2.00	15.00	75.00
s. Specimen.	—	—	—

5 **50 KIP**
ND (1957). Red. Government bldg. Back orange; logger on elephant.

	VG	VF	UNC
a. Security dots. Printer: SBNC.	7.50	35.00	200.00
b. W/o security dots (counterfeit).	.50	1.00	4.00
s. As a. Specimen.	—	—	—

6 **100 KIP**
ND (1957). Brown and m/c. S. Vong at l., vessels at ctr., dragons at r. Woman w/bowl of roses at r., bldg. at ctr. on back (like Fr. Indochina #103). Printer: Bank of France (w/o imprint).

	VG	VF	UNC
	.20	.60	8.00

1957 COMMEMORATIVE ISSUE
#7, 2500th Year of Buddhist Era

7 **500 KIP**
Yr. 2500 (1957). Red and m/c. S. Vong at l., bldg. at ctr. Back purple on blue unpt; bldgs. Sign. 3.

	VG	VF	UNC
	2.00	20.00	85.00

The Republic of Latvia, the central Baltic state in east Europe, has an area of 24,595 sq. mi. (43,601 sq. km.) and a population of *2.6 million. Capital: Riga. Livestock raising and manufacturing are the chief industries. Butter, bacon, fertilizers and telephone equipment are exported.

The Latvians, of Aryan descent, were nomadic tribesmen who settled along the Baltic prior to the 13th century. Lacking a central government, they were easily conquered by the German Teutonic knights, Russia, Sweden and Poland. Following the third partition of Poland by Austria, Prussia and Russia in 1795, Latvia came under Russian domination and did not experience autonomy until the Russian Revolution of 1917 provided an opportunity for freedom. The Latvian republic was established on Nov. 18, 1918. It was occupied by Soviet troops in 1939 and annexed to the Soviet Union in 1940. Following the German occupation of 1941-44, it was retaken by Russia and reestablished as a member S.S. Republic of the Soviet Union. Western countries, including the United States, did not recognize Latvia's incorporation into the Soviet Union. Latvia declared its independence from the former U.S.S.R. on Aug. 22, 1991.

MONETARY SYSTEM:
- 1 Rublis = 100 Kapeikas, 1919-22
- 1 Lat = 100 Santimu, 1923-40
- 1 Lat = 200 Rublu, 1993
- 1 Rublis = 1 Russian Ruble, 1992

REPUBLIC

LATWIJAS WALSTS KASES SIHMES

(LATVIAN GOVERNMENT CURRENCY NOTES)

1919-20 ISSUE

NOTE: Many serial # varieties exist.

NOTE: Excellent Russian forgeries exist of #6 and #8.

		VG	VF	UNC
1	**1 RUBLIS** 1919. Blue and brown. Flaming ball with L and 3 stars above legend. Wmk: Wavy lines.	4.00	20.00	55.00

		VG	VF	UNC
2	**1 RUBLIS** 1919. Lt. and dk. green.			
	a. Wmk: Wavy lines.	1.00	3.00	20.00
	b. Wmk: Lt. lines.	1.00	3.00	15.00

		VG	VF	UNC
3	**5 RUBLI** ND (1919). Lt. and dk. blue. Fennhe head facing l.			
	a. Wmk: Wavy lines.	3.00	15.00	45.00
	b. Wmk: Lt. lines. 3 legend varieties.	2.50	10.00	35.00

		VG	VF	UNC
4	**10 RUBLI** 1919. Red-brown and green. Sailing ship at ctr.			
	a. Wmk: Wavy lines.	5.00	17.50	50.00
	b. Wmk: Lt. lines. 3 legend varieties.	3.00	12.50	35.00

		VG	VF	UNC
5	**25 RUBLI** 1919. Brown. 3 stylized ears of corn on back.			
	a. Blue serial #. Wmk: Bunches wavy lines.	30.00	90.00	250.00
	b. Red serial #. Wmk. as a.	30.00	90.00	250.00
	c. Green serial #. Wmk: Stars and hexagons.	15.00	35.00	125.00
	d. 1 serial # at r., *Serija* at l. Wmk: Lt. lines.	15.00	30.00	110.00
	e. Wmk. like d. 2 serial #.	8.00	30.00	100.00

		VG	VF	UNC
6	**50 RUBLI** 1919. Green and gray.	45.00	125.00	300.00

		VG	VF	UNC
7	**100 RUBLI** 1919. Brown and dk. brown. Oak tree on back. 3 legend varieties.	10.00	25.00	90.00

		VG	VF	UNC
8	**500 RUBLI** 1920. Lt. and dk. green. Symbols of agriculture, industry and navigation on back.			
	a. Wmk: Lt. lines. 2 legend varieties.	50.00	125.00	325.00
	b. Wmk: Bunches of wavy lines.	45.00	110.00	300.00

LATWIJAS MAINAS SIHMES

LATVIAN SMALL EXCHANGE NOTES

1920 ISSUE

#9-12 face like back.

		VG	VF	UNC
9	**5 KAPEIKAS** ND (1920). Red.	1.00	2.00	5.00

		VG	VF	UNC
10	**10 KAPEIKAS** ND (1920). Blue.	1.00	2.00	5.00
11	**25 KAPEIKAS** ND (1920). Brown.	1.25	2.50	6.00
12	**50 KAPEIKAS** ND (1920). Purple.	1.25	2.50	6.00
	a. Back upright.	1.25	2.50	6.00
	b. Back inverted.	20.00	60.00	150.00

LATVIJAS BANKAS

BANK OF LATVIA

PROVISIONAL ISSUE

		VG	VF	UNC
13	**10 LATU ON 500 RUBLI** ND (-old date 1920). Red ovpt. on #8b.	35.00	225.00	450.00

1923 ISSUE

		VG	VF	UNC
14	**100 LATU** 1923. Blue. 2 seated women in national costume on back. 2 legend varieties.	60.00	135.00	375.00

1924 ISSUE

		VG	VF	UNC
15	**20 LATU** 1924. Black on orange unpt. Lt. tan paper. Farmer sowing. Back red; arms at ctr. (Issued only briefly.)	—	Rare	—

		VG	VF	UNC
16	**50 LATU** 1924. Brown on green unpt. River Dvina (Daugava) w/view of Riga. Arms at l. on back.			
	a. Issued note.	175.00	450.00	—
	s. Specimen.	—	—	—

1925 ISSUE

		VG	VF	UNC
17	**20 LATU** 1925. Black on yellow and green unpt. Portr. Pres. J. Cakste at top ctr. Arms on back. Printer: W&S.	40.00	90.00	275.00

1928-29 ISSUE

		VG	VF	UNC
18	**25 LATU** 1928. Black on yellow unpt. K. Valdemars at top ctr., ships l. and r. Back blue; arms at ctr. Printer: W&S.	8.00	35.00	110.00

		VG	VF	UNC
19	**500 LATU** 1929. Blue and brown. Girl in national costume at r. Cows and sheaves on back. Printer: BWC.	30.00	125.00	400.00

666 LATVIA

1934 ISSUE

20	50 LATU	VG	VF	UNC
	1934. Blue. Prime Minister K. Ulmanis at r. Printer: TDLR.	5.00	15.00	40.00

1938-39 ISSUE

21	25 LATU	VG	VF	UNC
	1938. Green. National hero Lacpiesis (the slayer of bears) at r. River barge on back. Printer: BWC.	3.50	8.00	25.00

22	100 LATU	VG	VF	UNC
	1939. Red. Farm couple w/daughter. Cargo ship dockside on back.	5.00	12.50	37.50

LATVIJAS VALSTS KASES ZIME

LATVIAN GOVERNMENT CURRENCY NOTES

1925-26 ISSUE

23 (24)	5 LATI			
	1926. Brown. Symbols of commerce and navigation on back.	75.00	275.00	—

24 (23)	10 LATU	VG	VF	UNC
	1925. Red-brown. Oak tree and cornfield on back. 5 sign. varieties.	25.00	85.00	230.00

1933 ISSUE

25	10 LATU	VG	VF	UNC
	1933-34. Blue-green. Seated woman in national costume on back.			
	a. 1933.	5.00	17.50	45.00
	b. 1934.	7.00	25.00	65.00

1935 ISSUE

26	10 LATU	—	—	—
	1935. Deep brown and deep violet on m/c unpt. Bondage (?) monument at l. Back blue-black on lt. blue w/arms at ctr. r. Specimen perforated: *PARAUGS*.			

27 (26A)	20 LATU	VG	VF	UNC
	1935. Deep brown on gray unpt. Lacpiesis w/bear at l., arms at upper ctr. on back. Specimen perforated: *PARAUGS*.	—	—	—

1935-37 ISSUE

29	10 LATU	VG	VF	UNC
	1937-40. Dk. brown and m/c. Fishermen and net at ctr. Back blue-black; man sowing at ctr.			
	a. 1937.	2.50	5.00	22.50
	b. 1938.	2.50	5.00	22.50
	c. 1939.	3.00	6.00	25.00
	d. 1940.	3.00	6.00	25.00

30 (27)	20 LATU	VG	VF	UNC
	1935-36. Brown. Castle of Riga. Farmer at l., woman in national costume at r. on back.			
	a. 1935.	6.00	22.50	55.00
	b. 1936.	4.00	17.50	50.00

1940 ISSUE

33	20 LATU	VG	VF	UNC
	1940. Blue. Academy of Agriculture in Jelgava.	125.00	250.00	500.00

LATVIJAS VALSTS KASES MAINAS ZIME
LATVIAN GOVERNMENT CURRENCY VOUCHERS

1940 ISSUE
NOTE: The 5 Lait 1940 (#34), 10 Latu 1937 (#29), 20 Latu 1935 (#30), 100 Latu 1939 (#22), 500 Latu 1929 (#19), also exist w/the probably unofficial ovpt. *Latuja 1941, 1. Juljs.*

		VG	VF	UNC
34	**5 LATI**			
	1940. Blue, gray and brown. Bridge across the River Guaja. Back brown; arms at ctr.			
	a. Sign. title at l: *Finansu Ministrs.*	10.00	35.00	85.00
	b. Sign. title at l: *Finansu Tautas Komisars.*	15.00	40.00	120.00

REGIONAL
RIGAS STRADNEEKU DEPUTATU PADOMES
RIGA'S WORKERS DEPUTIES' SOVIET

1919 ISSUE
#R1-R4 star, w/hammer and sickle. Wmk. paper. Circulated in all parts of Latvia.

NOTE: #R1-R4 also exist as unfinished notes. Unfinished sheets of #R3 and R4 w/printing on only 1 side were used in producing some Latvian postage stamps.

		VG	VF	UNC
R1	**1 RUBLIS**	.50	1.00	2.50
	1919. Red and brown.			

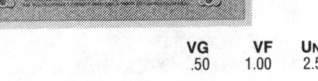

		VG	VF	UNC
R2	**3 RUBLI**	.50	1.00	2.50
	1919. Red, olive green and black.			

		VG	VF	UNC
R3	**5 RUBLI**			
	1919. Red and blue.			
	a. Issued note.	.50	1.00	3.00
	x. Back inverted.	7.00	30.00	65.00

		VG	VF	UNC
R4	**10 RUBLI**	.50	1.50	3.00
	1919. Red, green and lilac.			

The Republic of Lebanon, situated on the eastern shore of the Mediterranean Sea between Syria and Israel, has an area of 4,015 sq. mi. (10,400 sq. km.) and a population of 2.8 million. Capital: Beirut. The economy is based on agriculture, trade and tourism. Fruit, other foodstuffs and textiles are exported.

Almost at the beginning of recorded history, Lebanon appeared as the well-wooded hinterland of the Phoenicians who exploited its famous forests of cedar. The mountains were a Christian refuge and a Crusader stronghold. Lebanon, the history of which is essentially the same as that of Syria, came under control of the Ottoman Turks early in the 16th century. Following the collapse of the Ottoman Empire after World War I, Lebanon, along with Syria, became a French mandate. The French drew a border around the predominantly Christian Lebanon Sanjak or administrative subdivision and on Sept. 1, 1920 proclaimed the area the State of Grand Lebanon (Etat du Grand Liban), a republic under French control. France announced the independence of Lebanon during WWII after Vichy control was deposed on Nov. 26, 1941. It became fully independent on Jan. 1, 1944, but the last British and French troops did not leave until the end of Aug. 1946.

* * * This section has been partially renumbered. * * *

RULERS
French to 1943

MONETARY SYSTEM
1 Livre (Pound) = 100 Piastres

OVERPRINT VARIETIES

OVERPRINT VARIETIES				
/	//	V	W	◇
Type A	Type B	Type C	Type D	Type E

FRENCH INFLUENCE
BANQUE DE SYRIE ET DU GRAND-LIBAN

1925 ISSUE
#1-8 *GRAND-LIBAN* heading on notes similar to some Syrian issues.

		GOOD	FINE	XF
1	**25 PIASTRES**	30.00	150.00	425.00
	15.4.1925. M/c. Similar to Syria #21. Water mill on back.			
2	**50 PIASTRES**	60.00	275.00	750.00
	15.4.1925. M/c. Similar to Syria #22.			
3	**1 LIVRE**	100.00	425.00	—
	15.4.1925. M/c.			
4	**5 LIVRES**	125.00	550.00	—
	15.4.1925. Blue, orange and m/c.			
5	**10 LIVRES**	150.00	650.00	—
	15.4.1925. M/c.			
6	**25 LIVRES**	—	—	—
	15.4.1925. M/c.			

		GOOD	FINE	XF
7	**50 LIVRES**	—	—	—
	15.4.1925. M/c. Bldgs. across ctr. on back.			
8	**100 LIVRES**	—	—	—
	15.4.1925. M/c.			

1930 ISSUE
#8A-11 *GRAND-LIBAN* heading on notes similar to some Syrian issues.

8A	**1 LIVRE**	—	—	—
	1.11.1930. M/c. Similar to Syria #29A.			

		GOOD	FINE	XF
9	**5 LIVRES**	125.00	550.00	—
	1.11.1930. M/c. Similar to Syria #30. Hillside fortress on back.			
10	**10 LIVRES**	175.00	750.00	—
	1.11.1930. M/c. Similar to Syria #31. Ornate ruins at l. ctr. on back.			
11	**25 LIVRES**	—	—	—
	1.11.1930. M/c. Similar to Syria #32.			

1935 ISSUE

12	**1 LIVRE**	15.00	75.00	225.00
	1.2.1935. M/c. Similar to Syria #34. Harbor and mountain landscape across l. and ctr. panels on back.			

		GOOD	FINE	XF
12A	**5 LIVRES**	60.00	250.00	—
	1.2.1935. M/c. Similar to Syria #36. Bldg. across ctr., *LIBAN* at upper ctr. on back.			
12F	**100 LIVRES**			
	1.2.1935. Violet ovpt. Type A. Printer: BWC.			

1939 PROVISIONAL ISSUE
A13-14 ovpt: *LIBAN 1939* on various earlier Lebanese and Syrian notes.

A13	**1 LIVRE**			
	1939 (- old date 1935). Ovpt. on face of #12.			
	a. Ovpt. at upper ctr.	12.00	65.00	225.00
	b. Ovpt. at lower ctr.	12.00	65.00	225.00
13	**5 LIVRES**	40.00	175.00	—
	1939 (- old date 1935). Ovpt. across upper ctr. on face of Syria #36. *SYRIE* at upper ctr. on back.			

		GOOD	FINE	XF
13A	**5 LIVRES**	50.00	200.00	—
	1939 (- old date 1935). Ovpt. across lower ctr. of Lebanon #12A.			
13B	**10 LIVRES**	150.00	650.00	—
	1939 (- old date 1930). Ovpt. at upper ctr. on Lebanon #10.			

		GOOD	FINE	XF
13C	**25 LIVRES**	225.00	850.00	—
	1939 (- old date 1.2.1935). M/c. Ovpt. at upper ctr. Ornamented flower pattern at l. and r. on back, bridge and bldgs. at ctr.			
13D	**50 LIVRES**	—	—	—
	1939 (- old date 1938). Ovpt. at upper ctr. on Syria #39.			
14	**100 LIVRES**			
	1939 (- old date 1935). Ovpt. on Lebanon #12F.			
	a. Green ovpt. Type A.	—	—	—
	b. Orange ovpt. Type B.	—	—	—
	c. Lilac ovpt. Type C.	—	—	—

BANQUE DE SYRIE ET DU LIBAN

1939 FIRST ISSUE

15	1 LIVRE	GOOD	FINE	XF
	1.9.1939. M/c. View of Cyprus on back. Like #48.	5.00	40.00	175.00
16	5 LIVRES			
(17)	1.9.1939. Type C1. Serveau. City views on back. Like #49.	25.00	150.00	650.00
17	10 LIVRES			
(19)	1.9.1939. Type C1. Serveau w/*Livres*, bldg. on back.	75.00	375.00	—
18	25 LIVRES			
(21)	1.9.1939. Type Seb. Laurent w/*Livres*, columns on face.	—	—	—
19	50 LIVRES			
(23)	1.9.1939. Type Seb. Laurent w/*Livres*. City scene at ctr.	—	—	—
21	250 LIVRES			
(25)	1.9.1939. M/c. Well w/dome on face.	—	—	—

1939 SECOND ISSUE

#22-24 like #17-19 but w/*Livres Libanaises*.

25 *Deleted.* See #21.

22	10 LIVRES			
(20)	1.9.1939. Like #17 but w/*Livres Libanaises*.	100.00	450.00	—
23	25 LIVRES			
(22)	1.9.1939. Like #18 but w/*Livres Libanaises*.	—	—	—
24	50 LIVRES			
	1.9.1939. Like #19 but w/*Livres Libanaises*.	—	—	—

1939 PROVISIONAL ISSUE

In 1947, new Syrian notes were introduced and all former issues of Syria were cancelled, whereas Lebanese notes remained valid (and were redeemable for many years afterwards); therefore, some attempts were made to 'change' Syrian notes into Lebanese issues. This series, however, is different for the two countries and allow easy identification.

NOTE: Notes w/*BETROUTH* ovpt. on *DAMAS* are forgeries.

26	1 LIVRE	GOOD	FINE	XF
	1.9.1939. Green. Columns of Baalbek at l. Ovpt: *LIBAN* Printer: BWC.			
	a. Blue ovpt. Type A.	4.00	15.00	80.00
	b. Lilac ovpt. Type B.	4.00	15.00	80.00
	c. Olive ovpt. Type C.	4.00	15.00	80.00
	d. Pink ovpt. Type D.	4.00	15.00	80.00
	e. Blue ovpt. Type E.	4.00	15.00	80.00

27	5 LIVRES	GOOD	FINE	XF
	1.9.1939. Brown. Cedar tree at r. Ovpt: *LIBAN*. Printer: BWC.			
	a. Violet ovpt. Type A.	15.00	50.00	175.00
	b. Pink ovpt. Type B.	15.00	50.00	175.00
	c. Green ovpt. Type C.	15.00	50.00	175.00
	d. Blue ovpt. Type E.	15.00	50.00	175.00
28	10 LIVRES			
	1.9.1939. Brown-violet. Clock tower at l. Like Syria #42. Ovpt: *LIBAN*.			
	a. Pink ovpt. Type A.	30.00	150.00	425.00
	b. Green ovpt. Type B.	30.00	150.00	425.00
	c. Blue ovpt. Type C.	30.00	150.00	425.00
29	25 LIVRES			
	1.9.1939. Violet. Caravan at lower ctr. Like Syria #43. Ovpt: *LIBAN*.			
	a. Blue-gray ovpt. Type A.	50.00	250.00	650.00
	b. Orange ovpt. Type C.	50.00	250.00	650.00

30	50 LIVRES	GOOD	FINE	XF
	1.9.1939. Brown and m/c. Like Syria #44. Ovpt: *LIBAN*.			
	a. Brown ovpt. Type A.	125.00	550.00	—
	b. Olive ovpt. Type E.	125.00	550.00	—

1942 ISSUE

31	5 LIVRES			
	1.8.1942. Dk. brown. Ovpt: *BEYROUTH* on Syria #46.	60.00	225.00	650.00
32	50 LIVRES			
	1.8.1942. Dk. brown. Ovpt: *BEYROUTH* on Syria #47.	—	—	—
33	100 LIVRES			
	1.8.1942. Blue. Ovpt: *BEYROUTH* on Syria #48.	—	—	—

RÉPUBLIQUE LIBANAISE

GOVERNMENT BANKNOTES

1942 ISSUE

34	5 PIASTRES	VG	VF	UNC
	15.7.1942. Purple and green. Cedar tree at l. Back dk. blue.	1.00	4.00	20.00
35	10 PIASTRES			
	31.7.1942. Dk. blue on lt. green. 3 Arabs sitting near coastline on back.	1.00	4.50	30.00

36	25 PIASTRES	VG	VF	UNC
	1.8.1942. Lilac and tan. Omayyad Mosque in Damascus at ctr. Printer: BWC.	3.00	8.00	60.00

37   50 PIASTRES
1.8.1942. Green. Trees at top ctr., mosque w/2 minarets at r. Printer: BWC.

	VG	VF	UNC
	5.00	15.00	75.00

1944 ISSUE

38   5 PIASTRES
15.2.1944. Purple and green. Like #34.

	VG	VF	UNC
	1.00	3.50	13.50

39   10 PIASTRES
15.2.1944. Dk. blue on lt. green unpt. Like #35. Back brown.

	VG	VF	UNC
	1.00	4.50	20.00

1948 ISSUE

40   5 PIASTRES
12.1.1948. Blue and yellow. Like #38. Back green.

	VG	VF	UNC
	1.00	2.50	12.00

41   10 PIASTRES
12.1.1948. Lilac-brown on lt. blue unpt. Like #39. Back blue.

	VG	VF	UNC
	1.00	4.50	18.50

42   25 PIASTRES
12.1.1948; 6.11.1950. Violet on green and orange unpt. Cedar tree at r. Lion at ctr. on back.

	VG	VF	UNC
	1.50	6.00	35.00

43   50 PIASTRES
12.1.1948; 6.11.1950. Green and m/c. Columns of Baalbek at ctr. Ruins on back.

	VG	VF	UNC
	2.00	8.50	55.00

1950 ISSUE

46   5 PIASTRES
21.11.1950. Brown. Fortress on back.

	VG	VF	UNC
	1.50	5.00	20.00

47   10 PIASTRES
21.11.1950. Lilac and violet. Back blue, w/courtyard of a mosque.

	VG	VF	UNC
	1.00	3.50	17.00

BANQUE DE SYRIE ET DU LIBAN

1945 ISSUE

48   1 LIVRE
1.12.1945; 1.8.1950. M/c. Like #15.

	GOOD	FINE	XF
	7.50	35.00	150.00

49   5 LIVRES
1.12.1945; 1.8.1950. Blue, orange and m/c. Like #17.

	GOOD	FINE	XF
	25.00	100.00	450.00

50   10 LIVRES
1.12.1945; 1.8.1950. M/c. Like #20.

	GOOD	FINE	XF
	35.00	150.00	550.00

51	25 LIVRES	GOOD	FINE	XF
	1.12.1945; 1.8.1950. M/c. Like #22.	50.00	200.00	600.00

56	5 LIVRES	VG	VF	UNC
	1.1.1952-64. Blue and m/c. Courtyard of the Palais de Beit-Eddine. Snowy mountains w/trees on back. W/ or w/o security strip.	2.00	20.00	85.00

52	50 LIVRES	GOOD	FINE	XF
	1.12.1945; 1.8.1950. M/c. Like #24.	60.00	225.00	650.00

57	10 LIVRES	VG	VF	UNC
	1.1.1956; 1.1.1961; 1.1.1963. Green and m/c. Ruins of pillared temple. Shorelilne w/city on hills on back.	5.00	35.00	150.00

53	100 LIVRES	GOOD	FINE	XF
	1.12.1945; 1.8.1950. M/c. Cedar tree and mountain on back.	75.00	275.00	—

58	25 LIVRES	VG	VF	UNC
	1.1.1952; 1.1.1953. Blue-gray on m/c unpt. Harbor town. stone arch bridge at ctr. r. on back. Wmk: Lion's head.	25.00	90.00	400.00

1952; 1956 ISSUE
#55-60 all dated 1 January. Sign. varieties. Printer: TDLR.

55	1 LIVRE	VG	VF	UNC
	1.1.1952-64. Brown and m/c. Boats at dockside (Saida) at l. Columns of Baalbek on back. W/ or w/o security strip.	.50	5.00	25.00

59	**50 LIVRES**	**VG**	**VF**	**UNC**
	1.1.1952; 1.1.1953; 1.1.1964. Deep brown on m/c unpt. Coast landscape. Lg. rock formations in water on back. Wmk: Lion's head.	35.00	125.00	500.00

60	**100 LIVRES**	**VG**	**VF**	**UNC**
	1.1.1952; 1.1.1953; 1.1.1958; 1.1.1963. Blue. View of Beyrouth. Cedar tree at ctr. on back and as wmk.	10.00	45.00	135.00

LEEWARD ISLANDS

Leeward Islands is a geographical name, always distinguished from the Windward Islands. In English terminology, the term "Leeward Islands" applies to the northernmost Lesser Antilles, from the Virgin Islands to Guadeloupe, sometimes including Dominica.

From 1871 to 1956, the British colonies of Antigua (with Barbuda and Redonda), St. Kitts-Nevis-Anguilla, Montserrat, and the British Virgin Islands were collectively administered as the Leeward Islands.

See separate listings for the individual colonies; also see British Caribbean Territories.

RULERS:
British

MONETARY SYSTEM:
1 Shilling = 12 Pence
1 Pound = 20 Shillings

BRITISH INFLUENCE

GOVERNMENT OF THE LEEWARD ISLANDS

1921 ISSUE
#1 and 2 Portr. Kg. George V at top ctr. Arms at ctr. on back. Printer: TDLR.

Note: A 2 Shillings 6 Pence (2/6d) note possibly exists.

1	**5 SHILLINGS**			
	1.1.1921. Red on gray unpt. Back green.	—	Rare	—

2	**10 SHILLINGS**			
	1.1.1921. Green on blue unpt. Like #1. Back lt. brown.	—	Rare	—

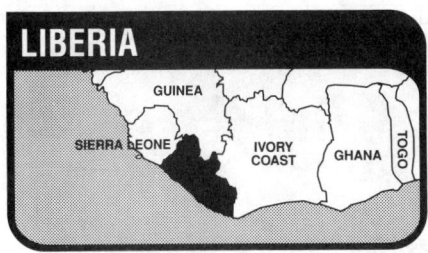

LIBERIA

GUINEA

SIERRA LEONE

IVORY COAST

GHANA

TOGO

The Republic of Liberia, located on the southern side of the west African bulge between Sierra Leone and the Ivory Coast, has an area of 38,250 sq. mi. (111,369 sq. km.) and a population of 2.5 million. Capital: Monrovia. The major industries are agriculture, mining and lumbering. Iron ore, diamonds, rubber, coffee and cocoa are exported.

The Liberian coast was explored and chartered by Portuguese navigator Pedro de Cintra in 1461. For the following three centuries Portuguese traders visited the area regularly to trade for gold, slaves and pepper. The modern country of Liberia, Africa's first republic, was settled in 1822 by the American Colonization Society as a homeland for American freed slaves, with the U.S. government furnishing funds and assisting in negotiations for procurement of land from the native chiefs. The various settlements united in 1839 to form the Commonwealth of Liberia, and in 1847 established the country as a republic with a constitution modeled after that of the United States.

Notes were issued from 1857 through 1880; thereafter the introduction of dollar notes of the United States took place. U.S. money was declared legal tender in Liberia in 1943, replacing British West African currencies. Not until 1989 was a distinctive Liberian currency again issued.

MONETARY SYSTEM:
1 Dollar = 100 Cents

NOTE: Certain listings encompassing issues circulated by various bank and regional authorities are contained in Volume 1.

REPUBLIC

TREASURY DEPARTMENT

1857-63 ISSUE
#6-9 various partly handwritten dates. Black printing; notes w/ctr. design shore w/plow and palm tree w/sailing ship in background.
TYPE I: W/text: *Pay to bearer in Gold or Silver coin;* handsigned by Secretary of the Treasury and President.

		GOOD	FINE	XF
6	**50 CENTS** 1858-64.			
	a. 26.2.1858.	300.00	750.00	—
	b. 6.2.1862; 26.2.1862; 24.8.1863; 26.8.1863; 28.12.1863; 18.2.1864.	160.00	400.00	—

		GOOD	FINE	XF
7	**1 DOLLAR** 25.4.1857; 21.8.1862-18.2.1864.	175.00	425.00	—

		GOOD	FINE	XF
8	**3 DOLLARS** 26.7.1862; 28.12.1863; 18.2.1864.	185.00	475.00	—
9	**5 DOLLARS** 26.8.1858; 24.8.1863; 28.12.1863.	225.00	525.00	—

1876-80 ISSUE
TYPE II: W/o specie payment clause. Handsigned by Treasurer and Secretary of the Treasury.

			GOOD	FINE	XF
10	**10 CENTS** 26.8.1880.		225.00	525.00	—

		GOOD	FINE	XF
11	**50 CENTS** 24.1.1876.	250.00	625.00	—
12	**1 DOLLAR** 24.1.1876; 26.8.1880.	250.00	625.00	—
13	**2 DOLLARS** 24.1.1876; 26.8.1880.	275.00	650.00	—

		GOOD	FINE	XF
14	**3 DOLLARS** 26.8.1880.	300.00	750.00	—
15	**5 DOLLARS** 24.1.1876; 1.3.1880; 26.8.1880.	275.00	650.00	—

		GOOD	FINE	XF
16	**10 DOLLARS** 26.8.1880.	325.00	850.00	—

TREASURY DEPARTMENT PAYMENT CERTIFICATES

MONROVIA BRANCH

1880'S ISSUE

17	**VAR. HANDWRITTEN DENOMINATIONS** Various handwritten dates.	50.00	100.00	200.00

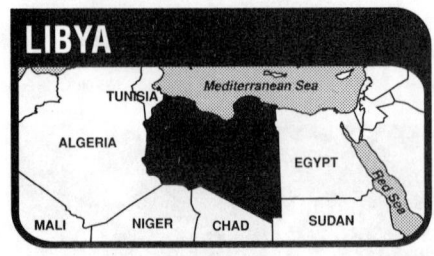

The Socialist People's Libyan Arab Jamahiriya, located on the north central coast of Africa between Tunisia and Egypt, has an area of 679,359 sq. mi. (1,759,540 sq. km.) and a population of 4 million. Capital: Tripoli. Crude oil, which accounts for 90 per cent of the export earnings, is the mainstay of the economy.

Libya has been subjected to foreign rule throughout most of its history, various parts of it having been ruled by the Phoenicians. Carthaginians, Vandals, Byzantines, Greeks, Romans, Egyptians, and in the following centuries the Arab's language, culture and religion were adopted by the indigenous population. Libya was conquered by the Ottoman Turks in 1553, and remained under Turkish domination, becoming a Turkish vilayet in 1835, until it was conquered by Italy and made into a colony in 1911. The name "Libya", the ancient Greek name for North Africa exclusive of Egypt, was given to the colony by Italy in 1934. Libya came under Allied administration after the fall of Tripoli on Jan. 23, 1943 and was divided into zones of British and French control. On Dec. 24, 1951, in accordance with a United Nations resolution, Libya proclaimed its independence as a constitutional monarchy, thereby becoming the first country to achieve independence through the United Nations. The monarchy was overthrown by a coup d'etat on Sept. 1, 1969, and Libya was established as a republic.

RULERS:
Idris I, 1951-1969

MONETARY SYSTEM:
1 Piastre = 10 Milliemes
1 Pound = 100 Piastres = 1000 Milliemes, 1951-1971
1 Dinar = 1000 Dirhams, 1971-

UNITED KINGDOM
NOTE: Previously listed #1-4 are now shown as Italian East Africa.

TREASURY

LAW OF 24.10.1951
#8-11 arms at l. denomination in lg. # at r. over wmk. area.

			VG	VF	UNC
5	**5 PIASTRES**		1.50	5.00	17.50
	L.1951. Red on lt. yellow unpt. Colonnade at l., palm tree at r.				

			VG	VF	UNC
6	**10 PIASTRES**		2.00	7.00	25.00
	L.1951. Green on lt. orange unpt. Ruins of gate at l., palm tree at r.				

			VG	VF	UNC
7	**1/4 POUND**		7.50	25.00	160.00
	L.1951. Blue on lt. orange unpt. Ruins of Columns at l., palm tree at r.				
			GOOD	FINE	XF
8	**1/2 POUND**		12.50	50.00	150.00
	L.1951. Purple on m/c unpt.				

			GOOD	FINE	XF
9	**1 POUND**		10.00	50.00	150.00
	L.1951. Blue on m/c unpt.				
10	**5 POUNDS**		45.00	150.00	—
	L.1951. Green on m/c unpt.				
11	**10 POUNDS**		55.00	225.00	—
	L.1951. Brown on m/c unpt.				

KINGDOM

TREASURY

1952 ISSUE
#12-14 Kg. Idris I at l., palm tree at r.
#15-18 Kg. Idris I at l., bush at lower ctr.

			VG	VF	UNC
12	**5 PIASTRES**		2.00	8.50	30.00
	1.1.1952. Red on lt. yellow unpt.				

			VG	VF	UNC
13	**10 PIASTRES**		4.00	15.00	60.00
	1.1.1952. Green.				

			VG	VF	UNC
14	**1/4 POUND**		10.00	35.00	160.00
	1.1.1952. Orange.				

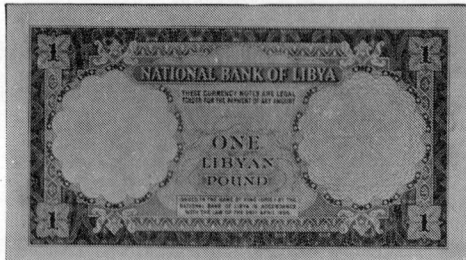

15	1/2 POUND	VG	VF	UNC
	1.1.1952. Purple.	12.50	40.00	150.00
16	1 POUND	GOOD	FINE	XF
	1.1.1952. Blue.	15.00	65.00	200.00
17	5 POUNDS			
	1.1.1952. Green.	50.00	225.00	—
18	10 POUNDS			
	1.1.1952. Brown.	100.00	425.00	—

NATIONAL BANK OF LIBYA

LAW OF 26.4.1955; 1958-59 ISSUE
#19-22 arms at l. 2 sign. varieties.

19	1/2 POUND	GOOD	FINE	XF
	L.1955 (1959). Purple. similar to #8.			
	a. Black serial #	8.50	25.00	100.00
	b. Red serial #.	8.50	25.00	100.00

20	1 POUND	GOOD	FINE	XF
	L.1955 (1959). Blue. Similar to #9.	8.50	30.00	125.00

21	5 POUNDS	GOOD	FINE	XF
	L.1955 (1958). Green. Similar to #10	25.00	125.00	—
22	10 POUNDS			
	L.1955 (1958). Brown. Similar to #11.	40.00	150.00	—

BRITISH OCCUPATION - WW II
MILITARY AUTHORITY IN TRIPOLITANIA

1943 ND ISSUE
#M1-M8, Lion on crown at ctr. or at r.

M1	1 LIRA	VG	VF	UNC
	ND (1943). Green.			
	a. Issued note.	1.00	8.00	35.00
	s. Specimen.	—	—	135.00
M2	2 LIRE			
	ND (1943). Blue on green unpt.			
	a. Issued note.	4.50	22.50	90.00
	s. Specimen.	—	—	150.00
M3	5 LIRE			
	ND (1943). Green on red-brown unpt.			
	a. Issued note.	1.00	7.50	35.00
	s. Specimen.	—	—	150.00
M4	10 LIRE			
	ND (1943). Lilac on green unpt.			
	a. Issued note.	4.00	12.50	50.00
	s. Specimen.	—	—	175.00

M5	50 LIRE	VG	VF	UNC
	ND (1943). Brown.			
	a. Issued note.	10.00	40.00	120.00
	s. Specimen.	—	—	200.00
M6	100 LIRE			
	ND (1943). Red-orange on blue unpt.			
	a. Issued note.	15.00	57.50	160.00
	s. Specimen.	—	—	200.00

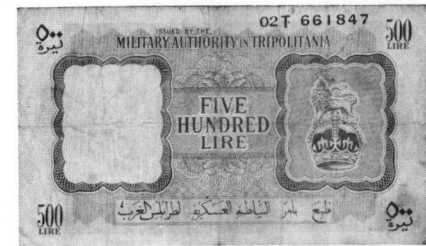

M7	500 LIRE	VG	VF	UNC
	ND (1943). Green on blue unpt.			
	a. Issued note.	80.00	400.00	1000.
	s. Specimen.	—	—	600.00
M8	1000 LIRE			
	ND (1943). Blue on brown unpt.			
	a. Issued note.	125.00	550.00	1350.
	s. Specimen.	—	—	800.00

FRENCH OCCUPATION OF THE FEZZAN - WW II

REPUBLIQUE FRANCAISE

1936-38 ND ISSUE
#M9-M11, black handstamp: *R-F/FEZZAN*; (in rectangle) letters in stamp 12 and 14mm high on Banque de l'Afrique Occidentale notes. Forgeries, created for collectors, exist (w/letters in stamp taller and different dates after 1940).
NOTE: There is a possibility that all Fezzan ovpt. notes except some of #M9 are spurious.

		VG	VF	UNC
M9	**5 FRANCS** ND (-old date 10.3.1938). M/c. Ovpt. on French West Africa #21.	150.00	275.00	—

		VG	VF	UNC
M10	**25 FRANCS** ND (-old date 10.3.1938). Ovpt. on French West Africa #24.	—	—	—

		VG	VF	UNC
M11	**100 FRANCS** ND (-old date 17.11.1936). Ovpt. on French West Africa #26.	—	—	—

LIECHTENSTEIN

The Principality of Liechtenstein, located in central Europe on the east bank of the Rhine between Austria and Switzerland, has an area of 62 sq. mi. (157 sq. km.) and a population of 30,000. Capital: Vaduz. The ecomomy is based on agriculture and light manufacturing. Canned goods, textiles, ceramics and precision instruments are exported. Liechtenstein assumed its present form in 1719 when the lordships of Schellenburg and Vaduz were merged into a principality. It was a member of the Rhine Confederation from 1806 to 1815, and of the German Confederation from 1815 to 1866 when it became independent. Liechtenstein's long and close association with Austria was terminated by World War I. In 1921 it adopted the coinage of Switzerland, and two years later entered into a customs union with the Swiss, who also operate its postal and telegraph systems and represent it in international affairs. The tiny principality abolished its army in 1868 and has avoided involvement in all European wars since that time.

RULERS:
Prince John II, 1858-1929
Prince Franz I, 1929-1938
Prince Franze Josef II, 1938-1989
Prince Hans Adam II, 1989-

MONETARY SYSTEM:
1 Krone = 100 Heller to 1924
1 Frank = 100 Rappen, 1924-

PRINCIPALITY

FURSTENTUM LIECHTENSTEIN GUTSCHEINE

DUCHY OF LEICHTENSTEIN CREDIT NOTES

1920 ISSUE

		VG	VF	UNC
1	**10 HELLER** ND (1920). Red and blue. Arms at l. Villa on back.	.50	1.00	5.00

		VG	VF	UNC
2	**20 HELLER** ND (1920). Red and blue. Arms at l. Castle at Vaduz on back.	.50	1.00	5.00

		VG	VF	UNC
3	**50 HELLER** ND (1920). Red and blue w/arms in unpt. at ctr. Landscape on back.	.50	1.00	5.00

LITHUANIA

The Republic of Lithuania (formally the Lithuanian Soviet Federated Socialist Republic), southernmost of the Baltic states in east Europe, has an area of 26,173 sq. mi. (65,201 sq. km.) and a population of 3.72 million. Capital: Vilnius. The economy is based on livestock raising and manufacturing. Hogs, cattle, hides and electric motors are exported. Lithuania emerged as a grand duchy joined to Poland through the Lublin Union in 1569. In the 15th century it

was a major power of central Europe, stretching from the Baltic to the Black Sea. Following the third partition of Poland by Austria, Prussia and Russia, 1795, Lithuania came under Russian domination and did not regain its independence until shortly before the end of World War I when it declared itself a sovereign republic. The republic was occupied by Soviet troops in June of 1940 and annexed to the U.S.S.R. Following the German occupation of 1940-44, it was retaken by Russia and reestablished as a member republic of the Soviet Union. Western countries, including the United States, did not recognize Lithuania's incorporation into the Soviet Union.

Lithuania declared its independence March 11, 1990, and it was recognized by the United States on Sept. 2, 1991, followed by the Soviet government in Moscow on Sept. 6. They were seated in the UN General Assembly on Sept. 17, 1991.

MONETARY SYSTEM:
1 Litas = 100 Centu

NOTE: For notes issued by the Darlehnskasse Ost at Kaunas in 1918 w/Lithuanian language, see Germany, Occupied Territories WW I.

REPUBLIC

LIETUVOS UKIO BANKAS

1919 ISSUE

		VG	VF	UNC
A1	50 OST. MARKIU ND (1919-20).	50.00	200.00	300.00
A2	100 OST. MARKIU ND (1919-20). Black and gold.	75.00	300.00	500.00
A3	500 OST. MARKIU ND (191-20). Black.	100.00	350.00	550.00

		VG	VF	UNC
A4 (A1)	1000 OST. MARKIU ND (1919-20). Green. Back m/c.	150.00	450.00	600.00

LIETUVOS BANKAS

BANK OF LITHUANIA

1922 SEPTEMBER ISSUE

#1-6 knight on horseback at ctr. on back. Printer: Otto Elsner, Berlin.

		VG	VF	UNC
1	1 CENTAS 10.9.1922. Blue. a. Issued note. s1. Specimen perforated: PAVYZDYS. s2. Specimen ovpt: VALEUR NON VALABLE! ECHANTILLON!	8.00 — —	25.00 — —	50.00 70.00 —

		VG	VF	UNC
2	5 CENTAI 10.9.1922. Green. a. Issued note. s1. Specimen perforated: PAVYZDYS. s2. Specimen ovpt: VALEUR NON VALABLE! ECHANTILLON!	8.00 — —	25.00 — —	50.00 70.00 70.00
3	20 CENTU 10.9.1922. Red-brown. a. Issued note. s1. Specimen perforated: PAVYZDYS. s2. Specimen ovpt: VALEUR NON VALABLE! ECHANTILLON!	12.50 — —	45.00 — —	90.00 125.00 125.00
4	50 CENTU 10.9.1922. Purple. a. Issued note. s1. Specimen perforated: PAVYZDYS. s2. Specimen ovpt: VALEUR NON VALABLE! ECHANTILLON!	17.50 — —	60.00 — —	100.00 135.00 135.00

		VG	VF	UNC
5	1 LITAS 10.9.1922. Gray. a. Wmk: Strands. b. Wmk: Loop. s1. Specimen perforated: PAVYZDYS. s2. Specimen ovpt: VALEUR NON VALABLE! ECHANTILLON!	50.00 50.00 — —	100.00 100.00 — —	250.00 250.00 265.00 265.00

		VG	VF	UNC
6	5 LITAI 10.9.1922. Dk. brown. a. Issued note. s1. Specimen perforated: PAVYZDYS. s2. Specimen ovpt: VALEUR NON VALABLE! ECHANTILLON!	70.00 — —	165.00 — —	325.00 375.00 375.00

1922 NOVEMBER ISSUE

#7-B21 printer: Andreas Haase, Prague.

		VG	VF	UNC
7	1 CENTAS 16.11.1922. Blue and burgundy-red. Back green and dk. red. a. Issued note. s1. Specimen perforated: PAVYZDYS. s2. Specimen ovpt: VALEUR NON VALABLE! ECHANTILLON!	8.00 — —	25.00 — —	50.00 70.00 70.00

		VG	VF	UNC
8	2 CENTU 16.11.1922. Dk. green on gray-violet. Back lt. and dk. brown. a. Issued note. s1. Specimen perforated: PAVYZDYS. s2. Specimen ovpt: VALEUR NON VALABLE! ECHANTILLON!	9.00 — —	25.00 — —	60.00 80.00 80.00

9   5 CENTAI

	VG	VF	UNC
16.11.1922. Blue on green. Back brown and purple.			
a. Issued note.	10.00	30.00	60.00
s1. Specimen perforated: PAVYZDYS.	—	—	80.00
s2. Specimen ovpt: VALEUR NON VALABLE! ECHANTILLON!	—	—	80.00

10   10 CENTU

	VG	VF	UNC
16.11.1922. Red-brown on gray-violet. Back red on brown.			
a. Issued note.	12.00	35.00	65.00
s1. Specimen perforated: PAVYZDYS.	—	—	90.00
s2. Specimen ovpt: VALEUR NON VALABLE! ECHANTILLON!	—	—	90.00

11   20 CENTU

	VG	VF	UNC
16.11.1922. Dk. blue on gray. Back dk. and lt. brown.			
a. Issued note.	15.00	40.00	90.00
s1. Specimen perforated: PAVYZDYS.	—	—	110.00
s2. Specimen ovpt: VALEUR NON VALABLE! ECHANTILLON!	—	—	110.00

12   50 CENTU

	VG	VF	UNC
16.11.1922. Purple and green. Back dk. green and brown.			
a. Issued note.	20.00	55.00	125.00
s1. Specimen perforated: PAVYZDYS.	—	—	175.00
s2. Specimen ovpt: VALEUR NON VALABLE! ECHANTILLON!	—	—	175.00

13   1 LITAS

	VG	VF	UNC
16.11.1922. Red-brown on gray. Back red and purple on tan.			
a. Issued note.	30.00	100.00	250.00
s1. Specimen perforated: PAVYZDYS.	—	—	225.00
s2. Specimen ovpt: VALEUR NON VALABLE! ECHANTILLON!	—	—	225.00

14   2 LITU

	VG	VF	UNC
16.11.1922. Blue on gray. Back dk. blue and purple.			
a. Issued note.	50.00	150.00	275.00
s1. Specimen perforated: PAVYZDYS.	—	—	250.00
s2. Specimen ovpt: VALEUR NON VALABLE! ECHANTILLON!	—	—	250.00

15   5 LITAI

	VG	VF	UNC
16.11.1922. Purple and blue. Farmer sowing at ctr. Black Serial # at lower ctr. Back green and brown; woman at r.			
a. Issued note.	50.00	175.00	375.00
s1. Specimen perforated: PAVYZDYS.	—	—	400.00
s2. Specimen ovpt: VALEUR NON VALABLE! ECHANTILLON!	—	—	400.00

16   5 LITAI

	VG	VF	UNC
16.11.1922. Olive-green, blue and black. Similar to #15 but ornamentation on face slightly changed. Red serial # at upper r.			
a. Issued note.	40.00	125.00	300.00
s1. Specimen perforated: PAVYZDYS.	—	—	325.00
s2. Specimen ovpt: VALEUR NON VALABLE! ECHANTILLON!	—	—	325.00

17   5 LITAI

	VG	VF	UNC
16.11.1922. Red-brown and dk. gray. Face like #16. Ornamentation on back is changed. Green serial #.			
a. Issued note.	45.00	175.00	325.00
s1. Specimen perforated: PAVYZDYS.	—	—	450.00
s2. Specimen ovpt: VALEUR NON VALABLE! ECHANTILLON!	—	—	450.00

18	10 LITU		VG	VF	UNC
	16.11.1922. Blue, purple and brown. Raftsman at r. Woman at l. and r. on back.				
	a. Issued note.		75.00	225.00	400.00
	s1. Specimen perforated: *PAVYZDYS*.		—	—	520.00
	s2. Specimen ovpt: *VALEUR NON VALABLE! ECHANTILLON!*		—	—	520.00

19	50 LITU		VG	VF	UNC
	16.11.1922. Dk. green and brown. Lithuanian Grand Duke Gediminas at r. Bldg. behind ornamented gate on back.				
	a. Issued note.		200.00	475.00	900.00
	s1. Specimen perforated: *PAVYZDYS*.		—	—	1000.
	s2. Specimen ovpt: *VALEUR NON VALABLE! ECHANTILLON!*		—	—	1000.

20	100 LITU		VG	VF	UNC
	16.11.1922. Blue and purple. Arms at l; Vytautas the Great at r.				
	a. Issued note.		200.00	500.00	950.00
	s1. Specimen perforated: *PAVYZDYS*.		—	—	1000.
	s2. Specimen ovpt: *VALEUR NON VALABLE! ECHANTILLON!*		—	—	1000.

20A	500 LITU	VG	VF	UNC
(A21)	10.8.1924. Back brown; Lithuanian emblem. (Not issued).	—	Rare	—

20B	1000 LITU	VG	VF	UNC
(B21)	10.8.1924. Blue and orange. Face similar to #A21. Map at l., snakes in limbs on back. (Not issued).	—	Rare	—

1924 NOVEMBER-DECEMBER ISSUE
#21-25 printer: BWC.

21	500 LITU		VG	VF	UNC
	11.12.1924. Dk. brown. Back blue.				
	a. Issued note.		150.00	300.00	575.00
	s1. Specimen perforated: *PAVYZDYS*.		—	—	650.00
	s2. Specimen ovpt: *VALEUR NON VALABLE! ECHANTILLON!*		—	—	650.00

22	1000 LITU		VG	VF	UNC
	11.12.1924. Green. Arms at ctr. Girl in Lithuanian national costume at l., seated youth at r. on back.				
	a. Issued note.		200.00	475.00	900.00
	s1. Specimen perforated: *PAVYZDYS*.		—	—	1000.
	s2. Specimen ovpt: *VALEUR NON VALABLE! ECHANTILLON!*		—	—	1000.

1927-28 ISSUE

23	10 LITU		VG	VF	UNC
	24.11.1927. Green. Farmers tilling the fields on back.				
	a. Issued note.		12.50	25.00	60.00
	s1. Specimen perforated: *PAVYZDYS*.		—	—	100.00
	s2. Specimen ovpt: *VALEUR NON VALABLE! ECHANTILLON!*		—	—	100.00

24	50 LITU		VG	VF	UNC
	31.3.1928. Dk. blue. Dr. J. Basanavicius at l. Ornate bldg. on back.				
	a. Issued note.		10.00	35.00	75.00
	s1. Specimen perforated: *PAVYZDYS*.		—	—	100.00
	s2. Specimen ovpt: *VALEUR NON VALABLE! ECHANTILLON!*		—	—	100.00

27	20 LITU		VG	VF	UNC
	5.7.1930. Brown on green and blue unpt. Grand Duke Vytautas the Great at l. Vytautas Church at ctr. Cargo ship and statue on back.				
	a. Issued note.		15.00	40.00	95.00
	s1. Specimen perforated: *PAVYZDYS*.		—	—	125.00
	s2. Specimen ovpt: *VALEUR NON VALABLE! ECHANTILLON!*		—	—	125.00

1938 COMMEMORATIVE ISSUE
#28, 20th Anniversary of Independence.

28	10 LITU		VG	VF	UNC
	16.2.1938. Green and orange. Pres. A. Smetona at l. Council of Lithuania on back. Specimen. Printer: BWC.				
	a. Issued note.		—	—	1500.
	s1. Specimen ovpt: *PAVYZDYS*.		—	—	—
	s2. Specimen ovpt: *VALEUR NON VALABLE! ECHANTILLON!*		—	—	2000.

25	100 LITU		VG	VF	UNC
	31.3.1928. Dk. purple. Seated woman at l., boy w/staff of Mercury at r. Bldg. on back.				
	a. Issued note.		15.00	40.00	85.00
	s1. Specimen perforated: *PAVYZDYS*.		—	—	125.00
	s2. Specimen ovpt: *VALEUR NON VALABLE! ECHANTILLON!*		—	—	125.00

1929-30 COMMEMORATIVE ISSUE
#26 and 27, 500th Anniversary Vytautas the Great. Printer: BWC.

26	5 LITAI		VG	VF	UNC
	24.6.1929. Brown. Grand Duke Vytautas the Great at l. Medieval warriors on horseback on back.				
	a. Issued note.		12.00	45.00	90.00
	s1. Specimen perforated: *PAVYZDYS*.		—	—	125.00
	s2. Specimen ovpt: *VALEUR NON VALABLE! ECHANTILLON!*		—	—	125.00

LUXEMBOURG

The Grand Duchy of Luxembourg is located in western Europe between Belgium, Germany and France, has an area of 998 sq. mi. (2,586 sq. km.) and a population of 390,000. Capital: Luxembourg. The economy is based on steel - Luxembourg's per capita production of 16 tons is the highest in the world.

Founded about 963, Luxembourg was a prominent country of the Holy Roman Empire; one of its sovereigns became Holy Roman Emperor as Henry VII, 1308. After being made a duchy by Emperor Charles IV, 1534, Luxembourg passed under the domination of Burgundy, Spain, Austria and France in 1443-1815. It regained autonomy under the Treaty of Vienna, 1815, as a grand duchy in union with the Netherlands, though ostensibly a member of the German Confederation. When Belgium seceded from the Kingdom of the Netherlands, in 1830, Luxembourg was forced to cede its greater western section to Belgium. The tiny duchy left the German Confederation in 1867 when the Treaty of London recognized it as an independent state and guaranteed its perpetual neutrality. Luxembourg was occupied by Germany and liberated by American troops in both World Wars.

RULERS:
William III (Netherlands), 1849-1890 (represented by brother Henry)
Adolphe, 1890-1905
William IV, 1905-12
Marie Adelaide, 1912-1919
Charlotte, 1919-1964
Jean, 1964-

MONETARY SYSTEM:
1 Thaler = 30 Groschen
1 Mark = 100 Pfennig = 1 Franc (Franken) 25 Centimes
1 Franc = 100 Centimes

GRAND DUCHY

DIE INTERNATIONALE BANK IN LUXEMBURG

INTERNATIONAL BANK IN LUXEMBOURG

1856 GULDEN ISSUE

		GOOD	FINE	XF
A1	**5 GULDEN** 1.9.1856. Proof.	—	—	—
A2	**10 GULDEN** 1.9.1856. Proof.	—	—	—
A3	**25 GULDEN** 1.9.1856. Proof.	—	—	—

1856 THALER ISSUE

1	**10 THALER** 1.9.1856; 30.9.1885; 15.9.1894. Black on yellow unpt. Back blue; seated woman and 3 cherubs.	—	Rare	—

1856 FRANC/MARK ISSUE

2	**25 FRANCS = 20 MARK** 1.9.1856; 30.9.1886; 15.4.1894. Brown on yellow unpt. Back like #1.	—	Rare	—
3	**100 FRANCS = 80 MARK** 1.9.1856; 30.9.1886; 15.9.1894. Brown on yellow unpt. Back like #1.	—	—	—

1900 ISSUE
#4 and 5 printer: G&D.

		GOOD	FINE	XF
4	**20 MARK** 1.7.1900. Blue and brown on m/c unpt. Foundry worker w/factory in background at l.	500.00	1200.	2750.

		GOOD	FINE	XF
5	**50 MARK** 1.7.1900. Green and red-brown. Miner at l., farmer at r.	650.00	1750.	—

1914 WW I EMERGENCY ISSUE
#6-8 circular arms at l. on back.

		GOOD	FINE	XF
6	**1 MARK** 5.8.1914. Blue. Like #7.	37.50	100.00	275.00

		GOOD	FINE	XF
7	**2 MARK** 5.8.1914. Brown.	50.00	150.00	375.00
8	**5 MARK** 5.8.1914. Blue text (w/o vignette). Black text on back.	100.00	300.00	500.00

1923 ISSUE

9	**100 FRANCS** 10.2.1923; 1.4.1930. Yellow and blue. City of Luxembourg on face. Back red and blue; Vianden Castle at r.	120.00	250.00	575.00
10	**100 FRANCS** 18.12.1930. Yellow and blue. Like #9.	100.00	225.00	525.00

1936 ISSUE

		GOOD	FINE	XF
11	**100 FRANCS** 1.8.1936; 18.12.1940. Yellow and blue. Like #9.	120.00	275.00	600.00

1947 ISSUE

		VG	VF	UNC
12	**100 FRANCS** 15.5.1947. Brown and blue. Farm wife at l., Grand Duchess Charlotte at ctr. facing l., farmer at r. 3 steelworkers on back.	12.00	65.00	400.00

1956 ISSUE

		VG	VF	UNC
13	**100 FRANCS** 21.4.1956. Dk. green. Farm wife at l., Grand Duchess Charlotte at ctr. facing r., farmer at r. Back similar to #12.			
	a. Issued note.	6.00	25.00	225.00
	s. Specimen w/red ovpt. *SPECIMEN.*	—	—	165.00

GROSSHERZOGLICH LUXEMBURGISCHE NATIONAL BANK
GRAND DUKAL LUXEMBOURG NATIONAL BANK

1873 THALER ISSUE

		VG	VF	UNC
15	**5 THALER**			
	1.7.1873. Brown. Arms at l. and r.			
	a. Issued note.	—	Rare	—
	s. Specimen.	—	—	1250.
16	**10 THALER**			
	1.7.1873. Gray.			
	a. Issued note.	—	Rare	—
	s. Specimen.	—	—	1250.

		VG	VF	UNC
17	**20 THALER**			
	1.7.1873. Lt. brown. Arms at l., allegorical figures at r.			
	a. Issued note.	—	Rare	—
	s. Specimen.	—	—	1250.

1873 FRANC ISSUE

		VG	VF	UNC
17A	**20 FRANCS**			
	1.7.1873. Blue on pink unpt.	—	Rare	
17B	**100 FRANCS**			
	1.7.1873.	—	Rare	

1876 MARK ISSUE

		VG	VF	UNC
18	**5 MARK**			
	25.3.1876. Blue on violet unpt. Arms at l., bust at r.			
	a. Issued note.	—	Rare	—
	s. Specimen.	—	—	1250.
19	**10 MARK**			
	25.3.1876. Brown.			
	a. Issued note.	—	Rare	—
	s. Specimen.	—	—	1250.
20	**20 MARK**			
	25.3.1876. Gray-green.			
	a. Issued note.	—	Rare	—
	s. Specimen.	—	—	1250.

ÉTAT DU GRAND-DUCHÉ DE LUXEMBOURG
GROSSHERZOGLICH LUXEMBURGISCHER STAAT

KASSENSCHEINE
State Treasury Notes · Bons de Caisse

LAW OF 28.11.1914
#21-25 sign. varieties. Printer: G&D.

		GOOD	FINE	XF
21	**1 FRANK = 80 PFENNIG**			
	L. 1914. Black on blue unpt.	10.00	25.00	125.00

		GOOD	FINE	XF
22	**2 FRANKEN = 1 MARK**			
	L.1914. Dk. brown on orange and green unpt.	15.00	35.00	175.00

		GOOD	FINE	XF
23	**5 FRANKEN = 4 MARK**			
	L.1914. Brownish purple on lilac and green unpt. Sign. title: _Le Directeur...Finances._	22.50	75.00	235.00
23A	**5 FRANKEN = 4 MARK**			
	L.1914. Like #23 but sign. title:_Le Ministre d'État, President du Gouvernment._	30.00	100.00	—
24	**25 FRANKEN = 20 MARK**			
	L.1914. Violet and green.	65.00	150.00	450.00
25	**125 FRANKEN = 100 MARK**			
	L.1914. Lilac and green.			
	a. Issued note.	125.00	300.00	—
	r. Remainder.	—	Unc	300.00

LAW OF 28.11.1914 AND 11.12.1918
#26-33 have Law dates 28.11.1914-11.12.1918 but were issued in 1919.
#26-31 printer: G&D.

		GOOD	FINE	XF
26	**50 CENTIMES**			
	L.1914-1918 (1919). Dk. brown on lilac unpt. Sign. varieties.	5.00	20.00	75.00
27	**1 FRANC**			
	L.1914-1918 (1919). Black on blue unpt.	7.00	25.00	100.00
28	**2 FRANCS**			
	L.1914-1918 (1919). Dk. brown on orange and green unpt.	9.00	30.00	150.00

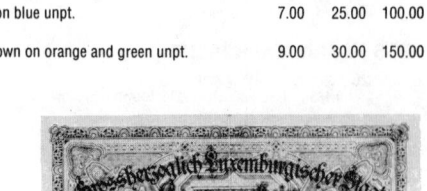

		GOOD	FINE	XF
29	**5 FRANCS**			
	L.1914-1918 (1919). Brownish purple on lilac and green unpt.			
	a. Red seal.	10.00	50.00	185.00
	b. Dk. brown seal.	10.00	50.00	185.00
	c. Black seal.	10.00	50.00	185.00

		GOOD	FINE	XF
30 (33)	**10 FRANCS** L.1914-1918 (1919). Blue on blue-gray. Allegorical woman at l. and r.	325.00	700.00	—

		GOOD	FINE	XF
31 (30)	**25 FRANCS** L.1914-1918 (1919). Blue-green on lt. green unpt.			
	a. W/o serial # (unfinished).	—	Unc	40.00
	b. W/serial #, blue and green.	45.00	135.00	275.00
32 (31)	**125 FRANCS** L.1914-1918 (1919). Lilac and green.	100.00	325.00	—

		GOOD	FINE	XF
33 (32)	**500 FRANCS** L.1914-1918 (1919).			
	a. W/o seal or serial # on back (unfinished).	—	Unc	50.00
	b. w/serial #, Pink unpt.	150.00	400.00	—

1923-27 ISSUE
#35-36 printer: G&D.

		GOOD	FINE	XF
34	**10 FRANCS** ND (1923). Blue. Farmer's wife at l., worker at r. Grand Duchess Charlotte at l. on back.	65.00	225.00	575.00

		GOOD	FINE	XF
35	**20 FRANCS** L.1914-1918 (1926). Violet and green. Arms at ctr. Duchess Charlotte and bldgs. on back.	55.00	200.00	500.00
36	**100 FRANCS** ND (1927). Brown and green. Grand Duchess Charlotte at l. 12 coats of arms on back.	75.00	250.00	575.00

GRAND DUCHÉ DE LUXEMBOURG

1929-39 ISSUE

		GOOD	FINE	XF
37	**20 FRANCS** 1.10.1929. Blue. Grape harvest. Farmer plowing on back. Printer: JEZ.			
	a. Issued note.	25.00	75.00	200.00
	s. Specimen w/red ovpt: SPECIMEN.	—	Unc	135.00

		GOOD	FINE	XF
38	**50 FRANCS** 1.10.1932. Green-blue on tan unpt. Grand Duchess Charlotte at upper r. Palace in Luxembourg on back. Printer: JEZ.			
	a. Issued note.	20.00	65.00	150.00
	s1. As a. Specimen w/red ovpt: SPECIMEN.	—	Unc	110.00
	s2. Lilac. Specimen.	—	Unc	250.00
39	**100 FRANCS** ND (1934). Black on green, brown and m/c unpt. Grand Duchess Charlotte at l., arms at ctr. Back green; seated woman w/globe and anvil at ctr., Adolphe Bridge and city of Luxembourg behind. Printer: ABNC.			
	a. Issued note.	17.50	55.00	125.00
	s. Specimen.	—	Unc	85.00

40   1000 FRANCS

		GOOD	FINE	XF
1.9.1939. (Issued 1940). Dk. brown and green. Arms in unpt. Printer: G&D.				
a.	Issued note.	250.00	775.00	—
s.	Specimen.	—	Unc	1000.

GERMAN OCCUPATION - WW II

LETZBURG

1940 ISSUE

41   10 (ZENG) FRANG

20.4.1940. Brown w/pink unpt. P. Eyschen at l. Arms on back. Printer: G&D. (Not issued).	—	Rare	—

41A   20 FRANG

ND (ca. 1939-40). Blue and brown. Harvesting at l. and r. (Not issued).	—	Rare	—

ALLIED OCCUPATION - WW II

GRAND DUCHÉ DE LUXEMBOURG

LETZBURG

1943 ISSUE

42   20 FRANG

		VG	VF	UNC
1943. Brown. Grand Duchess Charlotte at r. Back purple; Farmer w/sickle and corn. Printer: W&S.				
a.	Issued note.	1.50	6.00	65.00
s.	Specimen w/red ovpt: *SPECIMEN*, punched hole cancelled.	—	—	140.00

1944 ND ISSUE

43   5 FRANCS

		VG	VF	UNC
ND (1944). Olive-green. Grand Duchess Charlotte at ctr. Back red. Printer: ABNC.				
a.	Issued note.	.75	5.00	40.00
p.	Proof. Uniface pair.	—	—	175.00
s.	Specimen w/red ovpt: *SPECIMEN*.	—	—	125.00

44   10 FRANCS

		VG	VF	UNC
ND (1944). Purple. Like #43. Back olive. Printer: ABNC.				
a.	Issued note.	.75	5.00	40.00
p.	Proof. Uniface pair.	—	—	175.00
s.	Specimen w/red ovpt: *SPECIMEN*.	—	—	150.00

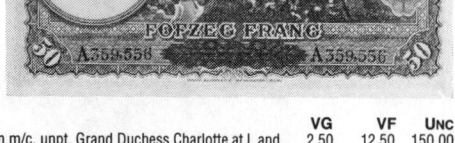

45   50 FRANCS

	VG	VF	UNC
ND (1944). Dk. green on m/c unpt. Grand Duchess Charlotte at l. and as wmk. Vianden Castle at lower ctr., guilloche ovpt. covering German wording below on back. Serial # prefix A. Printer: BWC.	2.50	12.50	150.00

46   50 FRANCS

		VG	VF	UNC
ND (1944). Dk. green on m/c unpt. Like #45 but back w/o wording at bottom and also w/o guilloche. Serial # prefix B-D. Printer: BWC.				
a.	Issued note.	2.00	7.50	135.00
s.	Specimen w/red ovpt: *SPECIMEN*, punched hole cancelled.	—	—	225.00

47	100 FRANCS	VG	VF	UNC
	ND (1944). Blue on m/c unpt. Back red-brown. Like #39. Printer: ABNC.			
	a. Issued note.	12.50	40.00	200.00
	p. Proof. Uniface pair.	—	—	225.00
	s. Specimen w/red ovpt: *SPECIMEN*, punched hole cancelled.	—	—	175.00

1954-56 ISSUE
#48-50 wmk: Grand Duchess Charlotte.

48	10 FRANCS	VG	VF	UNC
	ND (1954). Green. Grand Duchess Charlotte at r. Vianden Castle on back. Sign. varieties.			
	a. Issued note.	1.50	4.50	15.00
	s. Specimen w/red ovpt: *SPECIMEN*, punched hole cancelled.	—	—	18.50

49	20 FRANCS	VG	VF	UNC
	ND (1955). Blue. Grand Duchess Charlotte at r. Moselle River w/village of Ehnen on back.			
	a. Issued note.	1.00	4.00	12.00
	s. Specimen w/red ovpt: *SPECIMEN*, punched hole cancelled.	—	—	15.00

50	100 FRANCS	VG	VF	UNC
	15.6.1956. Red-brown on blue unpt. Grand Duchess Charlotte at r. Differdange steelworks on back.			
	a. Issued note.	5.00	10.00	30.00
	s. Specimen w/red ovpt: *SPECIMEN*, punched hole cancelled.	—	—	55.00

MACAO

The Province of Macao, a Portuguese overseas province located in the South China Sea 35 miles southwest of Hong Kong, consists of the peninsula and the islands of Taipa and Coloane. It has an area of 6 sq. mi. (16. sq. km.) and a population of 433,000. Capital: Macao. Macao's economy is based on light industry, commerce, tourism, fishing and gold trading - Macao is one of the few entirely free markets for gold in the world. Cement, textiles, firecrackers, vegetable oils and metal products are exported.

Established by the Portuguese in 1557, Macao is the oldest European settlement in the Far East. The Chinese, while agreeing to Portuguese settlement, did not recognize Portuguese sovereign rights and the Portuguese remained largely under control of the Chinese until 1849, when the Portuguese abolished the Chinese custom house and declared the independence of the port. The Manchu government formally recognized the Portuguese right to "perpetual occupation" of Macao in 1887, but its boundaries are still not delimited. In Mar. 1940 the Japanese army demanded recognition of the nearby "puppet" government at Changshan. in Sept. 1943 they demanded installation of their "advisors" in lieu of a military occupation.

Macao is scheduled to become a special administrative area under The Peoples Republic of China in 1999.

* * * This section has been partially renumbered. * * *

RULERS:
Portuguese

MONETARY SYSTEM:
1 Pataca = 100 Avos

PRIVATE BANKS
During the 1920's and early 1930's the private banks of Macao issued various circulating checks in dollars to facilitate trade with Chinese firms. These apparently circulated freely along with the Pataca issues of the Banco Nacional Ultramarino which quite obviously were in short supply. Most examples known have appropriate colonial revenue adhesive stamps affixed as found on bills of exchange and private checks. The additional large brush strokes or marks obliterating the denomination indicates the sum has been paid. A similar circulating check was issued in 1944 by the Tai Fong Cambista.

PORTUGUESE INFLUENCE

BANCO NACIONAL ULTRAMARINO

行銀理滙外海國洋西大
Ta Hsi Yang Kuo Hai Wai Hui Li Yin Hang

1905-07 ISSUE
#1-6 printer: BFL.

1	1 PATACA	GOOD	FINE	XF
	4.9.1905. Brown on blue unpt. Imprint: *Lisboa... 19...*, date partially handwritten. Crowned arms at ctr. on back.	50.00	175.00	900.00
2	5 PATACAS			
	4.9.1905; 4.10.1910; 4.12.1910. Blue on orange unpt. Sailing ship at upper ctr.	450.00	2250.	—

3 **10 PATACAS**
(5)   2.1.1907; 31.3.1924; 4.12.1924; 18.6.1936; 23.12.1941. Lt. red on
        green unpt. Crowned arms at upper l., sailing ship at upper ctr.
        Serrated l. edge.

	GOOD	FINE	XF
	300.00	1250.	3000.

6 **100 PATACAS**
(4)   1.1.1906. Dk. green on green, lt. brown and yellow unpt. Crowned
        arms at upper l., sailing ship at upper l. ctr., lg. *100* in unpt. at ctr.

	GOOD	FINE	XF
	—	—	—

1912-24 ISSUE

4 **25 PATACAS**
(6)   2.1.1907; 22.1.1907. Black on rose unpt. Like #5.

	GOOD	FINE	XF
	—	Rare	—

7 **1 PATACA**
1.1.1912. Brown on blue unpt. Like #1 but place and date printed.
Arms w/o crown at ctr. on back. Printer: BWC.

	GOOD	FINE	XF
	15.00	75.00	550.00

8 **5 PATACAS**
(9)   1.1.1924. Green on yellow unpt. Steamship at l., junks at r. Printer:
        TDLR.

	GOOD	FINE	XF
	50.00	175.00	1200.

5 **50 PATACAS**
(3)   1.1.1906. Blue on rose unpt. Sailing ship at upper ctr., lg. red *50* in
        unpt. at lower ctr.

	GOOD	FINE	XF
a. Issued note.	600.00	2000.	—
s. Specimen.	—	—	—

9 (8)	100 PATACAS	GOOD	FINE	XF
	22.7.1919. Brown on m/c unpt. Arms at upper l., steamship at upper l. ctr., steamship seal at lower r.	—	Rare	—

1920 ND SUBSIDIARY NOTE ISSUE
#10-12 printer: HKP.

10	5 AVOS	VG	VF	UNC
	ND (1920). Brown on green unpt. Arms at upper l.	1.50	6.00	45.00

11	10 AVOS	VG	VF	UNC
	ND (1920). Green on yellow unpt. Arms at upper l.	2.50	10.00	45.00
12	50 AVOS			
	ND (1920). Black on green unpt. Arms at top ctr. Handwritten sign. Back orange.	3.00	12.50	100.00

1942 ND SUBSIDIARY NOTE ISSUE
#13-17 printer: HKP.

NOTE: Also see #19 and 21.

13	1 AVO	VG	VF	UNC
	ND (1942). Grayish brown. Arms at upper l.	2.00	5.00	12.50
14	5 AVOS			
	ND (1942). Brown on green unpt. Like #10.	3.00	10.00	50.00

15	10 AVOS	VG	VF	UNC
	ND (1942). Blue on yellow unpt. Arms at upper l.	3.50	12.00	70.00
16	20 AVOS			
	ND (1942). Brown on green unpt.	4.50	15.00	40.00
17	50 AVOS			
	ND (1942). Purple on green unpt. Arms at top ctr.	5.00	17.50	90.00

JAPANESE INFLUENCE - WW II
BANCO NACIONAL ULTRAMARINO
1944 ND SUBSIDIARY NOTE ISSUE

18	5 AVOS	VG	VF	UNC
	ND (1944). Red on green unpt. Arms at upper l.	1.00	4.00	45.00

19	10 AVOS	VG	VF	UNC
	ND (1944). Blue on yellow unpt. Like #15 but 100 x 55mm.	1.00	4.00	35.00
20	20 AVOS			
	ND (1944). Red on lt. olive unpt. Back lt. orange.	2.00	6.00	25.00

21	50 AVOS	VG	VF	UNC
	ND (1944). Purple on lt. green unpt. Like #17 but w/letters A-J at l. and r. Also on thin paper. Back orange.	1.00	4.00	12.00

1944 EMERGENCY CERTIFICATE ISSUE
Decreto No. 33:517

#22-27 arms at l., steamship seal at r., vertical backs. Sign. varieties. Printer: Sin Chun and Company.

22	5 PATACAS	VG	VF	UNC
	D.5.2.1944. Black-blue w/maroon guilloche. Back green.	10.00	35.00	125.00

23	10 PATACAS	VG	VF	UNC
	D.5.2.1944. Brown w/maroon guilloche. Back brown.	22.50	75.00	200.00
24	25 PATACAS			
	D.5.2.1944. Brown.	62.50	210.00	550.00

25	50 PATACAS	VG	VF	UNC
	D.5.2.1944. Olive w/maroon guilloche. Back brown.	60.00	200.00	500.00

			VG	VF	UNC
26	**100 PATACAS**				
	D.5.2.1944. Red-violet w/lt. blue guilloche. Back red.		185.00	600.00	—
27	**500 PATACAS**				
	D.5.2.1944. Brown on m/c unpt.		—	—	—

PORTUGUESE INFLUENCE - POST WW II

BANCO NACIONAL ULTRAMARINO

1945 REGULAR ISSUE
#28-34 temple at r. Steamship seal at ctr. on back. Sign. varieties. Printer: W&S.

			VG	VF	UNC
28	**1 PATACA**				
	16.11.1945. Blue on red and green unpt.		.75	2.25	11.50

			VG	VF	UNC
29	**5 PATACAS**				
	16.11.1945. Green on green and red unpt.		2.50	7.50	60.00
30	**10 PATACAS**				
	16.11.1945. Brown.		7.50	22.50	110.00
31	**25 PATACAS**				
	16.11.1945. Red-orange on lt. green unpt.		50.00	120.00	600.00
32	**50 PATACAS**				
	16.11.1945. Blue-gray.		27.50	85.00	375.00

			VG	VF	UNC
33	**100 PATACAS**				
	16.11.1945. Violet.		170.00	500.00	—
34	**500 PATACAS**				
	16.11.1945. Brown.		400.00	1350.	—

1946-50 ISSUE
#35-38 printer: HKP.

			VG	VF	UNC
35	**5 AVOS**				
	6.8.1946. Dk. brown on green u npt. Back green.				
	a. Issued note.		1.50	5.00	40.00
	r. Remainder w/o serial #.		—	—	9.00

			VG	VF	UNC
36	**10 AVOS**				
	6.8.1946. Red on blue unpt. Ship and light tower at ctr. Back gray.				
	a. Issued note.		2.50	7.50	40.00
	r. Remainder w/o serial #.		—	—	12.00

			VG	VF	UNC
37	**20 AVOS**				
	6.8.1946. Violet on gray unpt. Ruins of S. Paulo at l. Back red-brown.				
	a. Issued note.		2.50	7.50	50.00
	r. Remainder w/o serial #.		—	—	12.00

			VG	VF	UNC
38	**50 AVOS**				
	6.8.1946. Blue on tan unpt. Junks at l., steamship seal at r. Back violet.				
	a. Issued note.		2.50	6.00	20.00
	r. Remainder w/o serial #.		—	—	7.50
39	**25 PATACAS**				
	20.4.1948. Brown. L. de Camoes at r. MACAU below.		35.00	100.00	250.00

			VG	VF	UNC
39A	**100 PATACAS**				
	27.11.1950. Brown on m/c unpt. Portr. Colonel J. M. Ferreira da Amabal at r. Printer: W&S. Specimen.		—	—	—

1952 FIRST ISSUE
#42a was not officially released. A quantity of approximately 5000 notes mysteriously found its way into today's market.

			VG	VF	UNC
40	**2 AVOS**				
	19.1.1952. Purple. Like #42. Specimen.		—	—	180.00

41	**5 AVOS**	VG	VF	UNC
	19.1.1952. Brown. Like #42. Specimen.	—	—	180.00

42	**10 AVOS**	VG	VF	UNC
	19.1.1952. Green on lt. brown and blue unpt.			
	r. Remainder.	—	4.00	18.50
	s. Specimen.	—	—	150.00

43	**20 AVOS**	VG	VF	UNC
	19.1.1952. Olive. Like #42. Specimen.	—	—	180.00

DECRETO NO. 17154

44	**100 PATACAS**			
	19.5.1952. Brown on lt. green unpt. Portr. M. de Arriaga Brum da Silveira at r. Archway w/flag at ctr. on back. Sign. varieties. Printer: W&S.			
	a. Issued note.	15.00	45.00	240.00
	s. Specimen.	—	—	180.00

1958 ISSUE

Decreto - Lei No. 39.221

#45-48 portr. L. de Camoes at r. and as wmk. Printer: BWC.

45	**10 PATACAS**	VG	VF	UNC
	20.11.1958. Blue on m/c unpt. Sign. varieties.			
	a. Issued note.	3.00	6.00	40.00
	s. Specimen.	—	—	30.00

46	**25 PATACAS**			
	20.11.1958. Brown on m/c unpt. *MACAU* at upper ctr.			
	a. Issued note.	5.00	10.00	100.00
	s. Specimen.	—	—	75.00

47	**50 PATACAS**			
	20.11.1958. Dk. green on m/c unpt.			
	a. Issued note.	12.00	25.00	150.00
	s. Specimen.	—	—	110.00

48	**500 PATACAS**	VG	VF	UNC
	20.11.1958. Olive-brown on m/c unpt.			
	a. Issued note.	135.00	165.00	450.00
	s. Specimen.	—	—	335.00

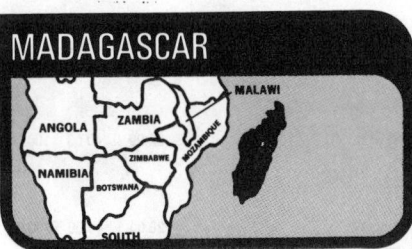

The Democratic Republic of Madagascar, an independent member of the French Community located in the Indian Ocean 250 miles (402 km.) off the southeast coast of Africa, has an area of 226,658 sq. mi. (587,041 sq. km.) and a population of 12.4 million. Capital: Antananarivo. The economy is primarily agricultural; large bauxite deposits are presently being developed. Coffee, vanilla, graphite and rice are exported.

Diago Diaz, a Portuguese navigator, sighted the island of Madagascar on Aug. 10, 1500, when his ship became separated from an India-bound fleet. Attempts at settlement by the British during the reign of Charles I and by the French during the 17th and 18th centuries were of no avail, and the island became a refuge and supply base for Indian Ocean pirates. Despite considerable influence on the island, the British accepted the imposition of a French protectorate in 1886 in return for French recognition of Britain's sphere of influence in Zanzibar. Madagascar was made a French colony in 1896 after absolute control had been established by military force. Britain occupied the island after the fall of France in 1942, to prevent its seizure by the Japanese, and gave it to the Free French in 1943. On Oct. 14, 1958, following a decade of intermittent but bitter warfare, Madagascar, as the Malagasy Republic, became an autonomous state within the French Community. On June 27, 1960, it became a sovereign independent nation, though remaining nominally within the French Community. The Malagasy Republic was renamed the Democratic Republic of Madagascar in 1976.

MONETARY SYSTEM:
1 French Franc = 100 Centimes to 1945
1 CFA Franc = 1.70 French Francs, 1945-1948
1 CFA Franc = 2 French Francs, 1948-1959
1 CFA Franc = 0.02 French Franc, 1959-1961
5 Malagasy Francs (F.M.G.) = 1 Ariary, 1961-

REPUBLIC

GOUVERNEUR GÉNÉRAL

TANANARIVE

DÉCRET DU 17.9.1914

1	**5 FRANCS**	VG	VF	UNC
	D.1914.	—	—	—
2	**10 FRANCS**			
	29.3.1917.	—	—	—
3	**20 FRANCS**			
	29.3.1917.	—	—	—

POSTAGE STAMPS

Postage stamps of type "Filanzane" (Michel #77, 78, 81, 86, 88, 89, or Scott #82, 84, 91, 102, 109, 113, transportation by sedan chair) pasted on rectangular cardboard.

Type I	Type II	Type III

Type I: Gray cardboard. Dog on back; value on stamps only.

Type II: Gray cardboard. Dog on back; value in numerals at r. on back.

Type III: Gray cardboard. Dog on back; value on back in numerals at r. and in words at l., imprinted separately.

Type IV: Gray cardboard. Dog on back; value on back in numerals at r. and in words at l., printed simultaneously w/picture.

Type V: Like Type IV but cardboard of varnished stock.

Type VI: Gray cardboard. Zebu on back.

Type VII: Brown cardboard. Zebu on back.

Type VIII: Like Type VII but cardboard of varnished stock.

NOTE: For smaller stamps w/*MADAGASCAR ET DEPENDANCES* or *MOHELI* pasted on square cardboard w/dog on back, see Comoros.

1916 ISSUE TYPE I

4	**0.25 FRANC**	VG	VF	UNC
	ND (1916). Blue. Type I.	20.00	40.00	100.00
5	**0.50 FRANC**			
	ND (1916). Violet. Type I.	20.00	40.00	100.00
5A	**1 FRANC**			
	ND (1916). Brown and green. Type I.			Reported Not Confirmed
6	**2 FRANCS**			
	ND (1916). Blue and olive. Type I.	20.00	40.00	100.00

1916 ISSUE TYPE II

		VG	VF	UNC
7	**0.10 FRANC** ND (1916). Red and brown. Type II.	20.00	40.00	100.00

1916 ISSUE TYPE III

8	**0.05 FRANC** ND (1916). Blue-green and olive. Type III.	20.00	40.00	100.00

1916 ISSUE TYPE IV

9	**0.05 FRANC** ND (1916). Blue-green and olive. Type IV.	20.00	40.00	100.00
10	**0.10 FRANC** ND (1916). Red and brown. Type IV.	20.00	40.00	100.00
11	**0.25 FRANC** ND (1916). Blue. Type IV.	20.00	40.00	100.00
11A	**0.50 FRANC** ND (1916). Type IV.	20.00	40.00	100.00
11B	**1 FRANC** ND (1916). Type IV.	20.00	40.00	100.00
11C	**2 FRANCS** ND (1916). Type IV.	20.00	40.00	100.00

1916 ISSUE TYPE V

12	**0.05 FRANC** ND (1916). Green. Type V.	20.00	40.00	100.00
13	**0.50 FRANC** ND (1916). Violet. Type V.	20.00	40.00	100.00
14	**1 FRANC** ND (1916). Brown and green. Type V.	20.00	40.00	100.00
15	**2 FRANCS** ND (1916). Blue and green. Type V.	20.00	40.00	100.00

1916 ISSUE TYPE VI

		VG	VF	UNC
16	**0.05 FRANC** ND (1916). Blue-green and olive. Type VI.	20.00	40.00	100.00
17	**0.10 FRANC** ND (1916). Red and brown. Type VI.	20.00	40.00	100.00
18	**0.25 FRANC** ND (1916). Blue. Type VI.	20.00	40.00	100.00
19	**0.50 FRANC** ND (1916). Violet. Type VI.	20.00	40.00	100.00
20	**1 FRANC** ND (1916). Brown and green. Type VI.	20.00	40.00	100.00
21	**2 FRANCS** ND (1916). Blue and green. Type VI.	20.00	40.00	100.00

1916 ISSUE TYPE VII

22	**0.05 FRANC** ND (1916). Blue-green and olive. Type VII.		Reported Not Confirmed	
23	**0.10 FRANC** ND (1916). Red and brown. Type VII.	20.00	40.00	100.00
24	**0.25 FRANC** ND (1916). Blue. Type VII.	20.00	40.00	100.00
25	**0.50 FRANC** ND (1916). Violet. Type VII.	20.00	40.00	100.00
26	**1 FRANC** ND (1916). Brown and green. Type VII.	20.00	40.00	100.00
27	**2 FRANCS** ND (1916). Blue and green. Type VII.		Reported Not Confirmed	

1916 ISSUE TYPE VIII

28	**0.05 FRANC** ND (1916). Blue-green and olive. Type VIII.	20.00	40.00	100.00
29	**0.10 FRANC** ND (1916). Red and green. Type VIII.	20.00	40.00	100.00
30	**0.25 FRANC** ND (1916). Blue. Type VIII.	20.00	40.00	100.00

		VG	VF	UNC
31	**0.50 FRANC** ND (1916). Violet. Type VIII.	20.00	40.00	100.00
32	**1 FRANC** ND (1916). Brown and green. Type VIII.	20.00	40.00	100.00
33	**2 FRANCS** ND (1916). Blue and green. Type VIII.	20.00	40.00	100.00

BANQUE DE MADAGASCAR

1926 ISSUE

		GOOD	FINE	XF
34	**100 FRANCS** ND (1926 - old dates 3.12.1892-13.2.1893). Ovpt: *BANQUE DE MADAGASCAR.* on unissued notes of the Banque de France (#22b).	150.00	450.00	—

1930's ISSUE

		VG	VF	UNC
35	**5 FRANCS** ND (ca.1937). Red-brown on blue and green unpt. Goddess Juno at l. 2 sign. varieties.	4.00	17.50	50.00

		VG	VF	UNC
36	**10 FRANCS** ND (ca. 1937-47). Green and blue. Woman w/fruit at r. Farmer plowing on back. 3 sign. varieties.	7.00	25.00	70.00

		VG	VF	UNC
37	**20 FRANCS** ND (ca. 1937-47). Yellow-brown. France and African woman w/child at r. Man at l. on back. 3 sign. varieties.	10.00	35.00	100.00

38	**50 FRANCS**	**GOOD**	**FINE**	**XF**
	ND (ca. 1937-47). Lt. green and m/c Minerva at l., female allegory of science at r. 3 sign. varieties.	30.00	95.00	325.00
39	**100 FRANCS**			
	ND (ca. 1937-47). Female allegory of wisdom at l., Fortuna and symbols of agriculture and industry at r.	Reported Not Confirmed		
40	**100 FRANCS**			
(41)	ND (ca.1937). Violet, brown and yellow. Man w/woman and child. 2 sign. varieties.	25.00	95.00	260.00

41	**1000 FRANCS**	**GOOD**	**FINE**	**XF**
(42)	11.7.1933; 19.5.1945; 28.12.1948. M/c. Female allegory of the French Republic at l., African woman at r. 3 sign. varieties.	100.00	375.00	900.00

42	**1000 FRANCS**	**GOOD**	**FINE**	**XF**
(40)	ND (ca. 1937). Blue and m/c. Female allegory of industry at l., female allegory of agriculture at r.	150.00	450.00	1150.

1941 EMERGENCY ISSUE

43	**1000 FRANCS**	**GOOD**	**FINE**	**XF**
	1941; 1946. Blue and brown. Sailing ships at l., coastal scenery.			
	a. Sign. handwritten. 15.12.1941.	1650.	—	—
	b. Sign. handwritten or stamped. 15.3.1946.	1650.	—	—

1942 BONS DE CAISSE

44	**5000 FRANCS**	**GOOD**	**FINE**	**XF**
	30.4.1942. Green. 2 oxen. Animals, woman w/fruit, and workers on back.			
	a. Issued note.	—	Rare	—
	s. Specimen.	—	Unc	3000.

BANQUE DE MADAGASCAR ET DES COMORES

1950-51 ISSUE

#45-49 wmk: Woman's head.

NOTE: For #48 dated 9.10.1952 w/provisional ovpt., see #54.

45	**50 FRANCS**	**VG**	**VF**	**UNC**
	ND. Brown and m/c. Woman w/hat at r. Man on back. 2 sign. varieties.			
	a. Sign. title: *LE CONTROLEUR GÉNÉRAL.*	3.00	17.50	60.00
	b. Sign. title: *LE DIRECTOR GÉNÉRAL ADJOINT.*	3.00	17.50	60.00
46	**100 FRANCS**			
	ND. M/c. Woman at r., w/palace of the qn. of Tananarive in background. Woman, boats, and animals on back.			
	a. Sign. title: *LE CONTROLEUR GÉNÉRAL.*	4.00	20.00	75.00
	b. Sign. title: *LE DIRECTEUR GÉNÉRAL ADJOINT.*	4.00	20.00	75.00
47	**500 FRANCS**			
	30.6.1950; 18.6.1951; 9.10.1952. M/c. Man w/fruit at ctr.			
	a. Sign. title: *LE CONTROLEUR GÉNÉRAL.*	15.00	75.00	300.00
	b. Sign. title: *LE DIRECTOR GÉNÉRAL ADJOINT.*	15.00	75.00	300.00

48	**1000 FRANCS**	**VG**	**VF**	**UNC**
	1.2.1951. M/c. Woman and man at l. ctr. Ox cart on back. 158 x 104mm.			
	a. Sign. title: *LE CONTROLEUR GÉNÉRAL.*	30.00	150.00	475.00
	b. Sign. title: *LE DIRECTOR GÉNÉRAL ADJOINT.*	30.00	150.00	475.00

49	**5000 FRANCS**	**VG**	**VF**	**UNC**
	30.6.1950; 23.11.1955. M/c. Portr. Gallieni at upper l., portr. young woman at r. Huts at l., woman w/baby at r. on back.			
	a. Sign. title: *LE CONTROLEUR GÉNÉRAL.*	175.00	425.00	950.00
	b. Sign. title: *LE DIRECTOR GÉNÉRAL ADJOINT.*	175.00	425.00	950.00

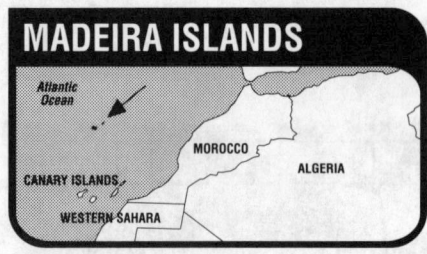

The Madeira Islands, which belong to Portugal, are located 360 miles (492 km.) off the northwest coast of Africa. They have an area of 307 sq. mi. (795 sq. km.) and a population of 267,000. The group consists of two inhabited islands named Madeira and Porto Santo and two groups of uninhabited rocks named Desertas and Selvagens. Capital: Funchal. The three staple products are wine, flowers and sugar.

Although the evidence is insufficient, it is thought that the Phoenicians visited Madeira at an early period. The Portuguese navigator Goncalvez Zarco first sighted Porto Santo in 1418, having been driven there by a storm while he was exploring the coast of West Africa. Madeira itself was discovered in 1420. The islands were uninhabited when visited by Zarco, but their colonization was immediately begun by Prince Henry the Navigator, aided by the knights of the Order of Christ. British troops occupied the islands in 1801, and again in 1807-14. Since 1976 Madeira is politically and administratively an autonomous region with a regional government and a parliament.

RULERS:
Portuguese

PORTUGUESE INFLUENCE

BANCO DE PORTUGAL

AGENCIA NO FUNCHAL BRANCH

1875 ISSUE

1	**20,000 REIS** 2.3.1875-4.3.1876. Blue. Seated figure at l. and r., arms at ctr. Oval ovpt. vertically at l. and r. Uniface.	—	Rare	—

1878 ISSUE

2	**10,000 REIS** 5.11.1878. Brown on blue-green unpt. Arms w/2 women in oval at ctr. Back green.	—	Rare	—

1879 PROVISIONAL ISSUE

3	**10,000 REIS** ND (1879 -old date 5.11.1878). Ovpt: *MOEDA FORTE* across bottom and at upper l. and r. on #2.	—	Rare	—

1891 PROVISIONAL ISSUE

#5-11 oval ovpt. at r.
#4 *Deleted.* See #9.

5	**500 REIS** 18.7.1891.	Reported Not Confirmed	
6	**1000 REIS** 18.7.1891.	Reported Not Confirmed	
7	**2500 REIS** 18.7.1891.	Reported Not Confirmed	
8	**5000 REIS** 18.7.1891.	Reported Not Confirmed	

9 (4)	**10,000 REIS** 18.7.1891. Blue oval ovpt: *DOMICILIADA NA AGENCIA DO FUNCHAL....BANCO DE PORTUGAL* at r. on #3. Punched hole cancelled: *SEM VALOR.*	—	Rare	—
10	**20,000 REIS** 18.7.1891.	Reported Not Confirmed		
11	**50,000 REIS** 18.7.1891.	—	Rare	—

1892 PROVISIONAL ISSUE

			GOOD	FINE	XF
12	**100 REIS** 3.2.1892. (- old date 6.8.1891). W/3 line diagonal ovpt: *Domiciliada para circular no districto do Funchal em virtude do Decreto de 3 de Fevereiro de 1892* on Portugal #35.		300.00	700.00	

MALAYA

Malaya, a former member of the British Commonwealth located in the southern part of the Malay Peninsula, consisted of 11 states: the unfederated Malay states of Johore, Kedah, Kelantan, Perlis and Trengganu; the federated Malay states of Negri Sembilan, Pahang, Perak and Selangor; and former members of the Straits Settlements, Malacca and Penang. The federation had an area of about 60,000 sq. mi. (155,400 sq. km.). Capital: Kuala Lumpur. It was occupied by Japan from 1941-1945. Malaya was organized February 1, 1948, was granted full independence on August 31, 1957, and became part of the Federation of Malaysia on September 16, 1963.

See also Straits Settlements and Malaysia.

RULERS:
British

MONETARY SYSTEM:
1 Dollar = 100 Cents

BRITISH INFLUENCE

BOARD OF COMMISSIONERS OF CURRENCY

1940 FIRST ISSUE
NOTE: A shipload of 1 and 5 Dollar bills dated 1940 was captured by the Germans. The bills were not issued. Later ovpt. in 1945 by the British Military Government. See #9 and 10.

			VG	VF	UNC
1	**10 DOLLARS**		40.00	150.00	500.00
	1.1.1940. Violet and m/c. Portr. Kg. George VI at r. Arms of the 11 states on back. Printer: W&S.				

1940 SECOND ISSUE
#2 and 3 designed and printed by Survey Dept. F. M. S.

			VG	VF	UNC
2	**10 CENTS**		5.00	20.00	50.00
	15.8.1940. Dk. blue on lilac and brown unpt. Portr. Kg. George VI at l.				
3	**25 CENTS**		17.50	60.00	200.00
	1.9.1940. Aqua on blue, orange and lilac unpt. Portr. Kg. George VI at r. Arms of the 11 states on back.				

1940 (1945) ISSUE
#4 and 5 States' arms on back. Printer: W&S.

			VG	VF	UNC
4 (9)	**1 DOLLAR**				
	1.1.1940 (Aug. 1945). Green and m/c. Portr. Kg. George VI. Ovpt: *Not Legal Tender. Specimens only. No value by the British Government.*				
	a. w/o Ovpt.		250.00	700.00	2000.
	b. W/o ovpt.		250.00	700.00	2000.
5 (10)	**5 DOLLARS**		500.00	1500.	4000.
	1.1.1940 (Aug. 1945). Blue and m/c. Portr. Kg. George VI. Ovpt: *Not Legal...*				

1941-42 (1945) ISSUE
#6-8 printer: TDLR.

#6-10 portr. Kg. George VI at l.

#9 and 10 printer: W&S.

#11-15 portr. Kg. George VI at r. States' arms on back.

#11-13 printer: W&S.

#14-16 wmk: Lion's head. Printer: BWC.

17 *Deleted*.

PORTRAIT VARIETIES

TYPE 1 TYPE 2 TYPE 3

			VG	VF	UNC
6 (4)	**1 CENT**		.25	.50	2.00
	1.7.1941 (1945). Violet on orange unpt. Uniface.				

			VG	VF	UNC
7 (5)	**5 CENTS**				
	2.7.1941 (1945). Red on green unpt. Uniface.				
	a. Jawi script at lower l.: ليم سين		.50	1.00	3.00
	b. Jawi script at lower l.: ليما سين		.50	1.00	3.00

			VG	VF	UNC
8 (6)	**10 CENTS**		.50	1.00	3.00
	1.7.1941 (1945). Blue on pink unpt. Uniface. 3 varieties of portr.				

			VG	VF	UNC
9 (7)	**20 CENTS**				
	1.7.1941 (1945). Brown on orange and green unpt. States' arms on back.				
	a. Jawi script at lower l.: سين		1.25	3.00	15.00
	b. Jawi script at lower l.: سن		1.25	3.00	15.00

			VG	VF	UNC
10 (8)	**50 CENTS**				
	1.7.1941 (1945). Violet on orange and blue unpt. Similar to #7. Portr. varieties.				
	a. Jawi script at lower l.: ليما فوله		1.50	3.00	15.00
	b. Jawi script at lower l.: ليم ڤوله		1.50	3.00	15.00

			VG	VF	UNC
11	**1 DOLLAR**		1.50	4.50	17.50
	1.7.1941 (1945). Blue and m/c.				
12	**5 DOLLARS**		6.00	15.00	65.00
	1.7.1941 (1945). Green and m/c.				

			VG	VF	UNC
13	**10 DOLLARS**		8.50	30.00	140.00
	1.7.1941 (1945). Red and m/c.				

			VG	VF	UNC
14	**50 DOLLARS**		100.00	250.00	650.00
	1.1.1942 (1945). Blue.				

			VG	VF	UNC
15	**100 DOLLARS**		120.00	275.00	750.00
	1.1.1942 (1945). Red and green. Like #14.				
16	**1000 DOLLARS**		2000.	4000.	—
	1.1.1942 (1945). Violet.				

JAPANESE OCCUPATION - WW II

JAPANESE GOVERNMENT

1942-45 ISSUE

#M1-M10 block letters commencing w/M.

NOTE: Many modern *'replicas'* from paste-up plates in strange colors have entered the market from sources in Southeast Asia.

		VG	VF	UNC
M1	**1 CENT**			
	ND (1942). Dk. blue on lt. green unpt.			
	a. 2 block letters, format: MA.	.25	.75	2.25
	b. Fractional block letters, format: M/AA.	.5	.10	.40
	s. As a. Specimen w/red ovpt: *Mi-hon. SPECIMEN* on back.	—	—	100.00

		VG	VF	UNC
M2	**5 CENTS**			
	ND (1942). Brown-violet and gray.			
	a. 2 block letters.	.25	.75	2.25
	b. Fractional block letters.	.10	.20	.50
	s. As a. Specimen w/red ovpt: *Mi-hon. SPECIMEN* on back.	—	—	100.00

		VG	VF	UNC
M3	**10 CENTS**			
	ND (1942). Green and lt. blue.			
	a. 2 block letters.	.25	.75	2.25
	b. Fractional block letters.	.10	.20	.50
	s. As a. Specimen w/red ovpt: *Mi-hon. SPECIMEN* on back.	—	—	100.00

M4	50 CENTS		VG	VF	UNC

ND (1942). Brown. Fan-like tree at r.

		VG	VF	UNC
a.	W/o wmk. Block letters: MA; MB.	.25	1.50	6.00
b.	W/wmk. Block letters: MC-MT.	.10	.20	.50
s.	As a. Specimen w/red ovpt: *Mi-hon. SPECIMEN* on back.	—	—	100.00

M5	1 DOLLAR		VG	VF	UNC

ND (1942). Dk. blue on pink unpt. Breadfruit tree at l., coconut palm at r.

		VG	VF	UNC
a.	W/o wmk. Block letters: MA w/serial #.	8.00	30.00	100.00
b.	W/wmk. Block letters: MB-MH; MJ-MN; MR.	.35	1.00	4.00
c.	W/wmk. Block letters: MI; MO; MS.	.10	.25	.75
s.	Block letters: MB. Specimen w/red ovpt: *Mi-hon. SPECIMEN* on back.	—		

M6	5 DOLLARS		VG	VF	UNC

ND (1942). Lilac on orange unpt. Coconut palm at l., paw-paw tree at r.

		VG	VF	UNC
a.	Block letters: MB w/serial #.	3.00	10.00	40.00
b.	Block letters MB-MJ; MO; MP.	1.00	3.00	9.00
c.	Block letters MK; MR.	.10	.25	.85
d.	Woven paper.	.25	1.00	3.00
s.	As b. Specimen w/red ovpt: *Mi-hon. SPECIMEN* on back.	—	—	100.00

M7	10 DOLLARS		VG	VF	UNC

ND (1942-44). Blue-green on lt. yellow unpt. Trees and fruits. Back green to bluish green or lt. blue; ship on horizon.

		VG	VF	UNC
a.	Block letters w/serial #.	3.00	15.00	45.00
b.	Block letters: MB-MP. M w/vertical upstroke and downstroke. W/wmk.	.25	.50	1.50
c.	Block letters w/o serial #. *M* w/sloping upstroke and downstroke. Paper w/silk threads, w/o wmk. MP. (1944).	.10	.25	.85
s.	As b. Specimen w/red ovpt: *Mi-hon. SPECIMEN* on back.	—	—	100.00
x.	As b. Ship w/o smoke. W/o wmk. (counterfeit).	2.50	5.00	10.00

M8	100 DOLLARS		VG	VF	UNC

ND (1944). Brown. Hut and trees on the water. Man w/buffalos in river on back.

		VG	VF	UNC
a.	M w/vertical upstroke and downstroke. Wmk. paper.	.25	1.00	4.50
b.	*M* w/sloping upstroke and downstroke. Paper w/silk threads, w/o wmk.	.15	.50	3.00
c.	Block letters only. Wmk. woven paper.	.50	2.00	5.00
s.	As a. Specimen w/red ovpt: *Mi-hon. SPECIMEN* on back.	—	—	100.00
x.	Purple face (probable error). Block letters MT.	1.50	6.00	17.50

M9	100 DOLLARS		VG	VF	UNC
	ND (1945). Brown. Workers on a rubber estate at r. Back green; houses and seashore at ctr.		.75	3.00	10.00

M10	1000 DOLLARS		VG	VF	UNC

ND (1945). Greenish black on green unpt. Ox cart at ctr. back green; design like #M8.

		VG	VF	UNC
a.	Black block letters. M w/vertical upstroke and downstroke. W/wmk.	20.00	50.00	175.00
b.	Red block letters. *M* w/sloping upstroke and dowstroke. Paper w/silk threads, w/o wmk.	1.75	6.50	20.00
s.	As a. Specimen w/red ovpt: *Mi-hon.*	—	—	200.00
x.	Red block letters, vertical up/down strokes, crude paper (counterfeit).	.25	1.00	2.00

MALAYA & BRITISH BORNEO

Malaya and British Borneo, a Currency Commission named the Board of Commissioners of Currency, Malaya and British North Borneo, was initiated on Jan. 1, 1952, for the purpose of providing a common currency for use in Johore, Kelantan, Kedah, Perlis, Trengganu, Negri Sembilan, Pahang, Perak, Salangor, Penang, Malacca, Singapore, North Borneo, Sarawak and Brunei.

For later issues see Brunei, Malaysia and Singapore.

RULERS:
British

MONETARY SYSTEM:
1 Dollar = 100 Cents

BRITISH INFLUENCE

BOARD OF COMMISSIONERS OF CURRENCY

1953 ISSUE

#1-7 Qn. Elizabeth II at r.
#1-3 arms of the 16 states on back. Wmk: Tiger's head. Printer: W&S.
#4-7 printer: BWC.

			VG	VF	UNC
1	**1 DOLLAR**				
	21.3.1953. Blue on m/c unpt.		3.00	8.00	35.00

			VG	VF	UNC
2	**5 DOLLARS**				
	21.3.1953. Green on m/c unpt.		10.00	32.00	200.00

			VG	VF	UNC
3	**10 DOLLARS**				
	21.3.1953. Red on m/c unpt.		12.00	32.00	210.00

			VG	VF	UNC
4	**50 DOLLARS**				
	21.3.1953. Blue and green.		80.00	210.00	400.00

			VG	VF	UNC
5	**100 DOLLARS**				
	21.3.1953. Violet and brown.		200.00	480.00	1600.
6	**1000 DOLLARS**				
	21.3.1953. Violet on m/c unpt.		—	Rare	—
7	**10,000 DOLLARS**				
	21.3.1953. Green on m/c unpt.		—	Rare	—

1959 ISSUE

			VG	VF	UNC
8	**1 DOLLAR**				
	1.3.1959. Blue on m/c unpt. Sailing boat at l. Men w/boat and arms of 5 states on back. Wmk: Tiger's head.				
	a. Printer: W&S.		6.00	16.00	60.00
	b. Printer: TDLR.		3.00	8.00	30.00

The Republic of Maldives, an archipelago of 2,000 coral islets in the northern Indian Ocean 417 miles (671 km.) southwest of Ceylon, has an area of 115 sq. mi. (298 sq. km.) and a population of 213,200. Capital: Malâ. Fishing employs 95 percent of the work force. Dried fish, copra and coir yarn are exported.

The Maldive Islands were visited by Arab traders and converted to Islam in 1153. After being harassed in the 16th and 17th centuries by Mopla pirates of the Malabar coast and Portuguese raiders, the Maldivians voluntarily placed themselves under the suzerainty of Ceylon. In 1887, the islands became an internally self-governing British protectorate and a nominal dependency of Ceylon. Traditionally a sultanate, the Maldives became a republic in 1953 but restored the sultanate in 1954. The Sultanate of the Maldive Islands attained complete internal and external autonomy on July 26, 1965, and on Nov. 11, 1968 again became a republic.

RULERS:
British to 1965

MONETARY SYSTEM:
1 Rupee = 100 Lari

REPUBLIC

MALDIVIAN STATE, GOVERNMENT TREASURER

1947; 1960 ISSUE
#2-7 palm tree and dhow at l., dhow at r.

		VG	VF	UNC
1	**1/2 RUPEE**			
	14.11.1947/AH1367. Orange and m/c. Palm tree and dhow at ctr. Uniface.	3.50	20.00	100.00

		VG	VF	UNC
2	**1 RUPEE**			
	1947; 1960. Blue and green on m/c unpt. Bldgs. at r. on back.			
	a. 14.11.1947/AH1367.	2.00	6.00	15.00
	b. 4.6.1960/AH1379.	.50	1.00	2.50

		VG	VF	UNC
3	**2 RUPEES**			
	1947; 1960. Brown and blue on m/c unpt. Pavilion at ctr. r. on back.			
	a. 14.11.1947/AH1367.	2.50	7.50	17.50
	b. 4.6.1960/AH1379.	.75	1.50	3.00

		VG	VF	UNC
4	**5 RUPEES**			
	1947; 1960. Violet and orange on m/c unpt. Bldg. at ctr. on back.			
	a. 14.11.1947/AH1367.	2.00	6.00	15.00
	b. 4.6.1960/AH1379.	1.00	2.50	7.50

		VG	VF	UNC
5	**10 RUPEES**			
	1947; 1960. Brown on m/c unpt. Bldg. at ctr. on back.			
	a. 14.11.1947/AH1367.	2.50	5.00	20.00
	b. 4.6.1960/AH1379.	3.00	7.00	25.00

1951; 1960 ISSUE

		VG	VF	UNC
6	**100 RUPEES**			
(7)	1951; 1960. Green on m/c unpt. Back brown, violet and m/c; park and bldg. complex at ctr.			
	a. 1951/AH1371.	45.00	125.00	375.00
	b. 4.6.1960/AH1379.	7.50	20.00	45.00

1951-80 ISSUE

7 (6)	**50 RUPEES**	VG	VF	UNC
	1951-80. Blue on m/c unpt. Waterfront bldg. at ctr. on back.			
	a. 1951/AH1371.	35.00	90.00	250.00
	b. 4.6.1960/AH1379.	5.00	15.00	35.00
	c. Litho. 1.8.1980/AH17.7.1400. .	6.00	17.50	40.00

MALTA

The Republic of Malta, an independent parliamentary democracy within the British Commonwealth, is situated in the Mediterranean Sea between Sicily and North Africa. With the islands of Gozo and Comino, Malta has an area of 122 sq. mi. (316 sq. km.) and a population of 359,900. Capital: Valletta. Malta has no proven mineral resources, an agriculture insufficient to its needs and a small but expanding, manufacturing facility. Clothing, textile yarns and fabrics, and knitted wear are exported.

For more than 3,500 years Malta was ruled, in succession, by Phoenicians, Carthaginians, Romans, Arabs, Normans, the Knights of Malta, France and Britain. Napoleon seized Malta by treachery in 1798. The French were ousted by a Maltese insurrection assisted by Britain, and in 1814 Malta, of its own free will, became part of the British Empire. Malta obtained full independence in Sept., 1964; electing to remain within the Commonwealth with the British monarch as the nominal head of state.

Malta became a republic on Dec. 13, 1974, but remained a member of the Commonwealth of Nations. The president is Chief of State, while the prime minister is the Head of Government.

* * * This section has been partially renumbered. * * *

RULERS:
British to 1974

MONETARY SYSTEM:
1 Shilling = 12 Pence
1 Pound = 20 Shillings to 1971
1 Cent = 10 Mils
1 Lira (Pound) = 100 Cents, 1971-

BRITISH INFLUENCE

THE GOVERNMENT OF MALTA

1914 FIRST ISSUE
#2 and 3, arms at upper ctr.

2 (4)	**5 SHILLINGS**	GOOD	FINE	XF
	13.8.1914. Black on blue unpt. Like #3.	100.00	350.00	750.00

3	**10 SHILLINGS**	GOOD	FINE	XF
	12.8.1914. Black on red unpt. Back pink.	125.00	400.00	850.00

4 (7)	**1 POUND**	GOOD	FINE	XF
	20.8.1914. Black.	125.00	450.00	850.00

5	5 POUNDS	GOOD	FINE	XF
	14.8.1914. Black on ornate green unpt.	185.00	700.00	1500.

6	10 POUNDS	GOOD	FINE	XF
	14.8.1914. Black on yellow unpt.	—	Rare	—

1914 SECOND ISSUE

7 (8)	5 SHILLINGS			
	4.9.1914. Black on blue unpt. Like #3.	75.00	350.00	650.00
8 (9)	1 POUND			
	14.9.1914. Black on pink unpt. Like #4.	95.00	425.00	750.00

1918 ISSUE

9 (10)	2 SHILLINGS			
	20.11.1918. Green on lt. blue unpt. Portr. Kg. George V at r. Back blue. Printer: TDLR. (Not issued, see #15).	—	Rare	—
10 (10A)	5 SHILLINGS			
	20.11.1918. Red on blue unpt. Like #10. Back green; Grand Harbour. Printer: TDLR.	—	Rare	—

1939 ISSUE
#11-14 portr. Kg. George VI at r. Date in written style under sign. at bottom. Uniface. Printer: BWC (w/o imprint).

11 (12)	2 SHILLINGS 6 PENCE	VG	VF	UNC
	13.9.1939. Violet, blue and green.	12.00	50.00	180.00

12 (13)	5 SHILLINGS	VG	VF	UNC
	13.9.1939. Green and red.	10.00	37.50	165.00
13 (14)	10 SHILLINGS			
	13.9.1939. Blue, violet and olive.	10.00	40.00	140.00
14 (15)	1 POUND			
	13.9.1939. Brown and purple.	12.50	45.00	175.00

1940 PROVISIONAL ISSUE

15 (11)	1 SHILLING ON 2 SHILLINGS	VG	VF	UNC
	ND (1940 - old date 20.11.1918). Green and lt. blue. Red ovpt. on #10.	6.00	20.00	70.00

1940-43 ISSUE
#16-20 w/o date. Uniface. Printer: BWC (w/o imprint).

#17-20 portr. Kg. George VI at r.

16	1 SHILLING	VG	VF	UNC
	ND (1943). Violet and lilac. Portr. Kg. George VI at ctr.	2.00	8.00	27.50
17	2 SHILLINGS			
	ND (1942). Brown and green.			
	a. Sign. J. Pace. No wmk.	4.00	22.50	80.00
	b. Sign. E. Cuschieri. No wmk.	3.50	20.00	80.00
	c. Sign. like b. Heavier paper w/wmk: Map of Malaya.	5.00	25.00	100.00

18	2 SHILLINGS 6 PENCE	VG	VF	UNC
	ND (1940). Violet and blue.	7.00	25.00	145.00
19	10 SHILLINGS			
	ND (1940). Blue, violet and olive.	4.00	12.50	40.00

20	1 POUND	VG	VF	UNC
	ND (1940). Brown and purple.			
	a. Sign. J. Pace.	8.00	20.00	65.00
	b. Sign. E. Cuschieri w/title: *Treasurer* below sign. in script.	7.50	15.00	37.50
	c. Sign. E. Cuschieri w/title: *Treasurer* below sign. in small block letters.	8.00	20.00	55.00

ORDINANCE 1949 (1951 ISSUE)
#21-22 English George Cross at l., portr. Kg. George VI at r. Printer: TDLR.

21	10 SHILLINGS	VG	VF	UNC
	L.1949 (1951). Green.	5.00	25.00	110.00

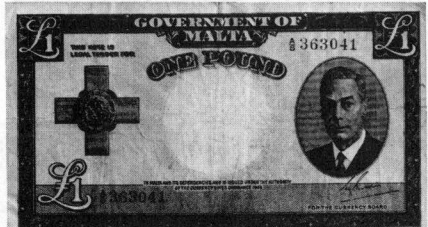

22   1 POUND
   L.1949 (1951). Brown.

	VG	VF	UNC
	3.00	10.00	35.00

ORDINANCE 1949 (1954 ISSUE)
#23-24 English George Cross at l., portr. Qn. Elizabeth II at r. Printer: TDLR.

23   10 SHILLINGS
   L.1949 (1954). Green.

		VG	VF	UNC
	a. Sign. E. Cuschieri (1954).	10.00	35.00	150.00
	b. Sign. D. A. Shepherd.	15.00	40.00	185.00

24   1 POUND
   L.1949 (1954). Brown. Like #23.

		VG	VF	UNC
	a. Sign. E. Cuschieri (1954).	5.00	20.00	125.00
	b. Sign. D. A. Shepherd.	3.00	12.50	80.00

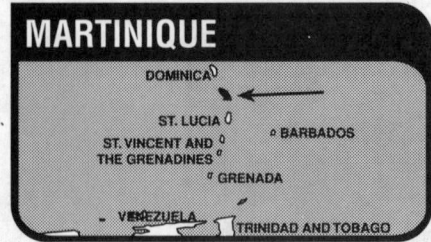

MARTINIQUE

The French Overseas Department of Martinique, located in the Lesser Antilles of the West Indies between Dominica and Saint Lucia, has an area of 425 sq. mi. (1,101 sq. km.) and a population of 329,000. Capital: Fort-de-France. Agriculture and tourism are the major sources of income. Bananas, sugar and rum are exported. Christopher Columbus discovered Martinique, probably on June 15, 1502. France took possession on June 25, 1635, and has maintained possession since that time except for three short periods of British occupation during the Napoleonic Wars. A French department since 1946, Martinique voted a reaffirmation of that status in 1958, remaining within the new French Community. Martinique was the birthplace of Napoleon's Empress Josephine, and the site of the eruption of Mt. Pelee in 1902 that claimed over 40,000 lives.

RULERS:
   French

MONETARY SYSTEM:
   1 Franc = 100 Centimes

FRENCH INFLUENCE
NOTE: For later issues see French Antilles.

TRÉSOR COLONIAL

FORT DE FRANCE OFFICE

DÉCRET DU 23.4.1855
#A1 and 1 breadfruit tree, snake, shrubbery at upper l., old sailing ship at lower l., crowned arms at top ctr, palm tree, snake and shrubbery at r., various cargo along bottom border. Uniface.

A1   1 FRANC
   D.1855. W/text: Remboursalbe le 31 Mai 1858.

	a. Issued note. 27.2.1856.	—	Rare	—
	r. Unsigned remainder.	—	Rare	—

1   5 FRANCS
   D.1855.

	—	Rare	—

DÉCRETS DES 23.4.1855 ET DU 3.3.1858

A2   1 FRANC
   D.1855 & 1858. Black. W/text: *Remboursable le 31 Mai 1863*. Uniface.

	a. Issued note. 6.2.1869.	—	Rare	—
	r. Unsigned remainder w/counterfoil, ND.	—	Rare	—

A3   5 FRANCS
   D.1855 & 1858. Similar to #A2.

	—	Rare	—

DÉCRET DU 18.8.1884
#3A-5 w/o border of trees and plants. Uniface.

			Good	Fine	XF
2	**1 FRANC** *D.1884.* Red. Border of trees and plants. 2 sign. varieties. Uniface.		600.00	1000.	—
3A	**1 FRANC** *D.1884.* Red. Similar to #4.		—	Rare	—
3	**2 FRANCS** *D.1884.* Green. Similar to #2.		—	Rare	—

			Good	Fine	XF
4	**5 FRANCS** *D.1884.* Black. Thin border design, and space for serial # at ctr.		—	Rare	—
4A	**5 FRANCS** *D.1884.* Black on yellow-green paper. Similar to #4 but thicker border design, w/o space for serial # at ctr.		—	Rare	—
4B	**5 FRANCS** *D.1884.* Similar to #4A, but gray paper.		—	Rare	—
5	**10 FRANCS** *D.1884.* Orange paper. Similar to #4A.		—	Rare	—

BANQUE DE LA MARTINIQUE

1870's PROVISIONAL ISSUE
#5A and 5B chéques (checks) w/printed value.

			Good	Fine	XF
5A	**1 FRANC** 187x. Violet w/lt. blue text. Uniface.		15.00	50.00	115.00
5B	**5 FRANCS** 3.11.1878. Blue w/red value. W/ or w/o sign. Like #5A.		—	Rare	—

LAW OF 1874
5C	**5 FRANCS** *L.1874.* Blue. Similar to #6.		—	—	—

LAW OF 1901

			Good	Fine	XF
6	**5 FRANCS** *L.1901* (1934-45). Purple. Man at l., woman at r. Law date on blue-green back. 3 sign. varieties.		15.00	45.00	150.00
6A	**5 FRANCS** *L.1901* (1903-34). Red. Like #6. Back blue-green. 5 sign. varieties.		20.00	75.00	200.00

			Good	Fine	XF
7	**25 FRANCS** ND (1922-30). Brown and blue. Back blue. 2 sign. varieties.		300.00	950.00	—
8	**100 FRANCS** ND (1905-32). Black and green. Similar to #7. Back brown. 3 sign. varieties.		450.00	1350.	—

			Good	Fine	XF
9	**500 FRANCS** ND (1905-22). Brown and gray. Allegorical figures on borders. Back reverse image. 4 sign varieties.		—	Rare	—

1915 ISSUE
#10 and 11, 2 sign. varieties.

			Good	Fine	XF
10	**1 FRANC** 1915. Red on blue unpt. Date in unpt. Arms at ctr. on back.		15.00	50.00	175.00
11	**2 FRANCS** 1915. Blue. Woman's head at ctr. on back.		17.50	60.00	200.00

1930-32 ISSUE
#15 *Deleted.*

12   25 FRANCS
ND (1930-45). M/c. Woman w/wreath at ctr., floral drapery behind
fruit at bottom. 3 sign. varieties.

	GOOD	FINE	XF
	25.00	140.00	425.00

13   100 FRANCS
ND (1932-45). M/c. Woman w/screptre at l., ship in background at ctr.
4 sign. varieties.

	GOOD	FINE	XF
	100.00	400.00	950.00

14   500 FRANCS
ND (1932-45). M/c. Like #13. 4 sign. varieties.

	GOOD	FINE	XF
	250.00	850.00	—

1942 EMERGENCY ISSUES
#16, 17 and 20 printer: EAW.

16   5 FRANCS
ND (1942). Black on dull red unpt. Allegorical female figure at l. Back
blue; women at ctr.

	GOOD	FINE	XF
a. Red serial #.	30.00	85.00	225.00
b. Blue serial #.	20.00	50.00	160.00

16A   5 FRANCS
ND (1942). Blue. Column at l., lg. *5* at r. Back like #18. Local printing.

	GOOD	FINE	XF
	350.00	800.00	—

17   25 FRANCS
ND (1943-45). Black on yellow unpt. Woman seated w/fruit at r. Back
green; ship and tree at ctr. 3 sign. varieties.

	GOOD	FINE	XF
	22.50	50.00	250.00

18   25 FRANCS
ND (1942). Violet w/black text on rose paper. Column at l. Bank
monogram at ctr. on back. Local printing.

	GOOD	FINE	XF
	400.00	900.00	—

1942 ISSUE
#19 and 21 printer: ABNC.

19   100 FRANCS
ND (1942). Green on m/c unpt. Allegorical woman seated w/fruit at l.
Seated allegorical woman w/child on back. 2 sign. varieties.

	GOOD	FINE	XF
	100.00	300.00	900.00

		Good	Fine	XF
20	**1000 Francs** ND (1942). Blue. Women seated at l. and r. Back orange; woman at ctr.	650.00	1500.	3250.
21	**1000 Francs** ND (1942). Red-brown on lt. green and m/c unpt. Allegorical man, woman and child at r. 3 sign. varieties. Allegorical figures on back.	650.00	1500.	3250.

CAISSE CENTRALE DE LA FRANCE LIBRE

1941 ISSUE
#22 ovpt: *MARTINIQUE.* English printing.

22	**1000 Francs** *L. 2.12.1941* (1944-47). Blue. Phoenix rising from flames. War/peace scenes on back.			
	a. Ovpt. below *Caisse Centrale.*	400.00	1000.	2500.
	b. Ovpt. like a., cancelled w/stamp *ANNULE.*	—	—	1750.
	c. Ovpt. at top and diagonally from lower l. to upper r.	400.00	1000.	2500.
	s. Specimen.	—	—	1750.

CAISSE CENTRALE DE LA FRANCE D'OUTRE-MER

LAW OF 2.2.1944
#23-25 Marianne at ctr., red ovpt: *MARTINIQUE* at l. and r. English printing.

		VG	VF	UNC
23	**10 Francs** *L. 2.2.1944.* Violet on red unpt.	7.50	30.00	135.00
24	**20 Francs** *L. 2.2.1944.* Green on red unpt.	15.00	35.00	160.00

		VG	VF	UNC
25	**100 Francs** *L. 2.2.1944.* Green on orange unpt. Anchor, barrel, bale and other implements on back.	45.00	135.00	475.00
26	**1000 Francs** *L. 2.2.1944.* Blue. Like #22.			
	a. Issued note.	350.00	850.00	2500.
	s. Specimen.	—	—	1500.

1947 ND ISSUE
#27-36 ovpt: *MARTINIQUE.* French printing, w/usual designs.

27	**5 Francs** ND (1947-49). M/c. Bougainville at r. 2 wmk. varieties.	3.00	7.00	40.00

		VG	VF	UNC
28	**10 Francs** ND (1947-49). M/c. Colbert at l. Boat at ctr. r. on back.	4.00	15.00	60.00
29	**20 Francs** ND (1947-49). M/c. E. Gentil at r.	5.00	17.50	75.00
30	**50 Francs** ND (1947-49). M/c. Belain d'Esnambuc at l.	10.00	30.00	110.00

		VG	VF	UNC
31	**100 Francs** ND (1947-49). M/c. La Bourdonnais at l.	15.00	45.00	150.00

		VG	VF	UNC
32	**500 Francs** ND (1947-49). M/c. 2 women at r. Ox-carts on back.	30.00	125.00	475.00

33	**1000 FRANCS**	**VG**	**VF**	**UNC**
	ND (1947-49). M/c. 2 women at r.	90.00	210.00	550.00

1952 ND ISSUE

34	**5000 FRANCS**			
	ND (1952). M/c. Gen. Schoelcher.			
	a. Issued note.	200.00	500.00	1000.
	s. Specimen.	—	—	325.00

1960 ND ISSUE

35	**1000 FRANCS**			
	ND (1960). M/c. Fishermen from Antilles.	75.00	150.00	475.00

36	**5000 FRANCS**	**VG**	**VF**	**UNC**
	ND (1960). M/c. Woman holding fruit bowl.			
	a. Issued note.	300.00	750.00	—
	s. Specimen w/ovpt. and perforated: *SPECIMEN.*	—	—	600.00

MAURITIUS

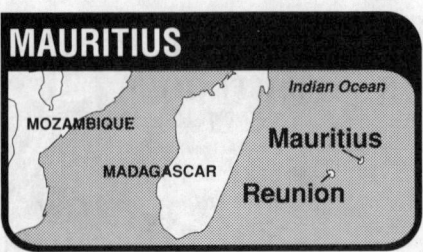

The island of Mauritius, a member nation of the British Commonwealth located in the Indian Ocean 500 miles (805 km.) east of Madagascar, has an area of 790 sq. mi. (2,045 sq. km.) and a population of 1.01 million. Capital: Port Louis. Sugar provides 90 percent of the export revenue. Cartographic evidence indicates that Arabs and Malays arrived at Mauritius during the Middle Ages. Domingo Fernandez, a Portuguese navigator, visited the island in the early 16th century, but Portugal made no attempt at settlement. The Dutch took possession, and named the island, in 1598. Their colony failed to prosper and was abandoned in 1710. France claimed Mauritius in 1715 and developed a strong and prosperous colony that endured until the island was captured by the British in 1810, during the Napoleonic Wars. British possession was confirmed by the Treaty of Paris, 1814. Mauritius became independent on March 12, 1968. It is a member of the Commonwealth of Nations. The Queen of England is Chief of State.

RULERS:
British

MONETARY SYSTEM:
1 Shilling = 12 Pence
1 Pound = 20 Shillings
1 Pound = 5 Dollars to 1848
1 Rupee = 100 Cents, 1848-
1 Crown = 10 Mauritius Livres

BRITISH INFLUENCE

SPECIAL FINANCE COMMITTEE

1842 EMERGENCY ISSUE
NOTE: #1F is printed on back of cut up and cancelled Mauritius Commercial Bank issues.

1F	**1 DOLLAR**	**GOOD**	**FINE**	**XF**
	1.9.1842. Port Louis. 5 sign. varieties.	85.00	225.00	375.00

CURRENCY COMMISSIONERS OF MAURITIUS

1848 ISSUE
#8-9 arms at upper ctr. Sign. varieties.

8	**5 RUPEES**	**GOOD**	**FINE**	**XF**
	5.6.1848; 1849. Currency Commissioners' seal at top ctr. Port Louis.	—	Rare	—
9	**10 RUPEES**			
	1848-49.	—	Rare	—

GOVERNMENT OF MAURITIUS

1860-66 ISSUE
#10-11 arms at upper ctr. Various dates and sign. Counterfoil at l.

10	**5 SHILLINGS**			
	1866.	—	Rare	—

11	**10 SHILLINGS**	**GOOD**	**FINE**	**XF**
	22.8.1860; 1866; 1.11.1867. Black and green on cream paper. Arms at top ctr.	—	Rare	—
12	**1 POUND**			
	1866.	—	Rare	—

12A	**5 POUNDS/25 DOLLARS**	**GOOD**	**FINE**	**XF**
	186x. Arms at upper ctr. Specimen w/counterfoil.	—	Rare	—

1876; 1877 ISSUE
#13-15 arms at top ctr. Various dates and sign. Counterfoil at l.

NOTE: Spink Mauritius collection 10-96, #15 in fine $10,600., one of 2 known.

13	**5 RUPEES**	**GOOD**	**FINE**	**XF**
	1876; 1878; 1902.			
	a. 1876; 23.10.1878.	—	Rare	—
	b. 5.10.1896; 13.11.1900; 17.11.1902.	500.00	1000.	—
14	**10 RUPEES**			
	1.10.1877.	700.00	1400.	—

15	**50 RUPEES**	**GOOD**	**FINE**	**XF**
	1.12.1876. Black. Arms at top ctr.	—	Rare	—

1907-14 ISSUE
#16-18 arms at top ctr. Sign. title varieities.

16	**5 RUPEES**	**GOOD**	**FINE**	**XF**
(17)	19.10.1907-1.10.1930. Greenish brown paper.	225.00	450.00	950.00
17	**10 RUPEES**			
(18)	1.10.1914-1.10.1930. Lilac paper.	300.00	700.00	1500.
18	**50 RUPEES**			
(19)	19.10.1907; 1.1.1920.	—	Rare	—

1919 ISSUE

19	**1 RUPEE**	**GOOD**	**FINE**	**XF**
(16)	1.7.1919; 1.7.1928. Brown on green unpt. Sailing ship and mountains at r. Printer: TDLR.	100.00	350.00	750.00

1930 ISSUE
#20 and 21 arms at l., portr. Kg. George V at r. Wmk: Stylized sailing ship. Printer: W&S.

20	**5 RUPEES**	**GOOD**	**FINE**	**XF**
	ND (1930). Blue.	30.00	125.00	600.00

21	**10 RUPEES**	**GOOD**	**FINE**	**XF**
	ND (1930). Brown.	65.00	275.00	1200.

1937 ISSUE
#22 and 23 portr. Kg. George VI at r. Printer: W&S.

22	**5 RUPEES**			
	ND (1937). Blue on m/c unpt.	17.50	50.00	185.00

23 10 RUPEES
ND (1937). Brown on m/c unpt.

	GOOD	FINE	XF
	40.00	125.00	550.00

1940 ISSUE
#24-26 portr. Kg. George at r. W/o imprint.

#24   #25

24 25 CENTS
ND (1940). Blue. Uniface.

		VG	VF	UNC
a.	Serial # at ctr. Prefix A.	25.00	85.00	375.00
b.	Serial # at lower l. Prefix A.	35.00	120.00	475.00
c.	Serial # position like b. Prefix B.	25.00	85.00	350.00
d.	Like b. Prefix C.	25.00	85.00	350.00

25 50 CENTS
ND (1940). Lilac. Uniface.

		VG	VF	UNC
a.	Serial # at ctr. Prefix A.	35.00	110.00	450.00
b.	Serial # at lower l. Prefix A.	50.00	150.00	525.00
c.	Serial # position like b. Prefix B.	25.00	100.00	425.00

26 1 RUPEE
ND (1940). Green on lilac unpt. Sign. varieties.

	VG	VF	UNC
	15.00	50.00	425.00

1942 EMERGENCY ISSUE

26A 1 RUPEE
27.3.1942 (-old date 1.7.1924; 1.10.1930). Printed on partial backs of 10 Rupees notes #18.

	VG	VF	UNC
	500.00	1000.	—

1954 ISSUE
#27-29A portr. Qn. Elizabeth II at r. Sign. varieties. Wmk: Stylized sailing ship. Printer: BWC.

27 5 RUPEES
ND (1954). Blue on m/c unpt. Mountain scene at lower l. Arms on back.

	VG	VF	UNC
	7.00	30.00	200.00

28 10 RUPEES
ND (1954). Red on m/c unpt. Mountain scene at lower ctr.

	VG	VF	UNC
	20.00	100.00	450.00

29 25 RUPEES
ND (1954). Green on m/c unpt. Bldg. at lower ctr.

	VG	VF	UNC
	70.00	500.00	1200.

29A 1000 RUPEES
ND (1954). Mauve on m/c unpt. Bldg. like #29 at lower ctr.

	VG	VF	UNC
	—	Rare	—

MEMEL

Memel is the German name for Klaipeda, a town and port of Lithuania on the Baltic Sea at the mouth of Nemunas River. It is the base of a large fishing fleet, and has major shipbuilding and repair yards. Founded as a fort in the early 13th century, Klaipeda was seized and destroyed in 1252 by the Teutonic Knights, who built a new fortress called Memelburg. The town, later called Memel, and adjacent territory was held by the Swedes through most of the 17th century. After the Swedish occupation, the area became part of East Prussia though briefly occupied by the Russians in 1757 and 1813. During WW I, Memel was captured by the Russians again and after 1919 was administered by France under a League of Nations mandate. On Jan. 15, 1923, it was seized by the Lithuanians as their only good port and made a part of the autonomous Klaipeda territory. It was taken by Soviet forces in Jan. 1945 and made a part of the Lithuanian Soviet Socialist Republic until Lithuanian independence was achieved later in 1991.

MONETARY SYSTEM:
1 Mark = 100 Pfennig

FRENCH ADMINISTRATION - POST WW I
HANDELSKAMMER DES MEMELGEBIETS
CHAMBER OF COMMERCE, TERRITORY OF MEMEL

1922 ISSUE
#1-9 authorized by the Interallied Commission.

1	1/2 MARK	VG	VF	UNC
	22.2.1922. Blue. Bay on back.	1.25	2.50	7.50

2	1 MARK	VG	VF	UNC
	22.2.1922. Brown. Spit of land on back.	1.50	3.50	8.00

3	2 MARK	VG	VF	UNC
	22.2.1922. Blue and olive-brown. Memel in 1630 on back.			
	a. Wmk: Sculptured chain.	1.75	4.50	12.00
	b. Wmk: Contoured chain.	1.50	4.00	12.00

4	5 MARK	VG	VF	UNC
	22.2.1922. Blue and yellow. Stock exchange on back.			
	a. Wmk: Sculptured chain.	2.50	5.00	15.00
	b. Wmk: Contoured chain.	2.25	4.50	15.00

5	10 MARK	VG	VF	UNC
	22.2.1922. Yellow-brown and blue. Couple, lighthouse and man on back.			
	a. Wmk: Sculptured chain.	3.00	6.00	20.00
	b. Wmk: Contoured chain.	2.50	5.00	18.00

6	20 MARK	VG	VF	UNC
	22.2.1922. Lilac and violet. Cow, farmhouse and horse on back.			
	a. Wmk: Sculptured chain.	4.00	8.00	35.00
	b. Wmk: Contoured chain.	3.50	7.50	30.00

7	50 MARK	VG	VF	UNC
	22.2.1922. Brown on green and violet. Manu-facturing, logging and shipbuilding on back.			
	a. Wmk: Sculptured chain.	6.00	17.50	65.00
	b. Wmk: Contoured chain.	6.00	17.50	65.00

		VG	VF	UNC
8	**75 MARK** 22.2.1922. Brown on blue and pink unpt. New and old sawmills on back.	8.00	20.00	65.00

		VG	VF	UNC
9	**100 MARK** 22.2.1922. Blue and lt. brown. General view of Memel on back.	9.00	30.00	85.00

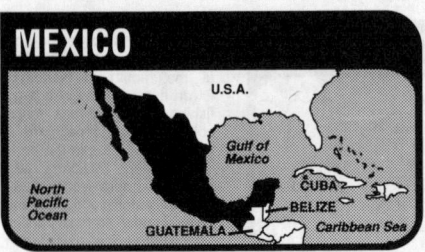

MEXICO

The United Mexican States located immediately south of the United States has an area of 759,529 sq. mi. (1,967,183 sq. km.) and a population of 84.4 million. Capital: Mexico City. The economy is based on agriculture, manufacturing and mining. Cotton, sugar, coffee and shrimp are exported.

Mexico was the site of highly advanced Indian civilizations 1,500 years before conquistador Hernando Cortes conquered the wealthy Aztec empire of Montezuma. 1519-1521, and founded a Spanish colony which lasted for nearly 300 years. During the Spanish period, Mexico, then called New Spain, stretched from Guatemala to the present states of Wyoming and California, its present northern boundary having been established by the secession of Texas during (1836) and the war of 1846-1848 with the United States.

Independence from Spain was declared by Father Miguel Hidalgo on Sept. 16, 1810, (Mexican Independence Day) and was achieved by General Augustin de Iturbide in 1821. Iturbide became emperor in 1822 but was deposed when a republic was established a year later. For more than half a century following the birth of the republic, the political scene of Mexico was characterized by turmoil which saw two emperors (including the unfortunate Maximilian), several dictators and an average of one new government every nine months passing swiftly from obscurity to oblivion. The land, social, economic and labor reforms promulgated by the Reform Constitution of Feb. 5, 1917 established the basis for a sustained economic development and participative democracy that have made Mexico one of the most politically stable countries of modern Latin America.

* * * This section has been renumbered. * * *

MONETARY SYSTEM:
- 1 Peso = 100 Centavos
- 1 Nuevo Peso = 1000 old Pesos, 1992-

NOTE: Catalog numbers in ( ) are cross references to *The Complete Encyclopedia of Mexican Paper Money* by Duane Douglas, Claudio Verrey & Alberto Hidalgo, 1982, Krause Publications.

EMPIRE OF ITURBIDE

EL IMPERIO MEXICANO, DISTRITO FEDERAL

1823 ISSUE
#1-3 issued by Emperor Agustin de Iturbide in 1823. All have arms in oval at upper ctr. Black on thin white paper, uniface. Most were cancelled with a 2-inch cut at bottom.

		GOOD	FINE	XF
1	**1 PESO** 1.1.1823. *(PR-DF-1)*.			
	a. Issued note.	20.00	40.00	65.00
	b. Cut cancelled. *PR-DF-5)*.	15.00	25.00	55.00
	c. Handwritten cancellation: *Ynutilizado, Oaxaca 16.5.1825. (PR-DF-3)*.	20.00	40.00	60.00
	d. Ovpt: *LEON* on face in red.	30.00	70.00	125.00
2	**2 PESOS** 1.1.1823. *(PR-DF-6)*.			
	a. Issued note.	30.00	60.00	100.00
	b. Cut cancelled. *PR-DF-6)*.	20.00	40.00	60.00
	c. Handwritten cancellation like #1c. *(PR-DF-7)*.	20.00	45.00	75.00
3	**10 PESOS** 1.1.1823. *(PR-DF-11)*.			
	a. Issued note.	200.00	300.00	400.00
	b. Cut cancelled. *PR-DF-12)*.	35.00	75.00	125.00

REPUBLIC

LAS TESORERÍAS DE LA NACIÓN

THE TREASURY OF THE NATION

DECREE OF APRIL 11, 1823
#4-6 designs similar to Empire issue. Many are cut cancelled. Printed on backs of Papal Bulls (Lent authorizations) dated 1818 and 1819. There is great controversy concerning possible counterfeits of these notes.

4	**1 PESO** 5.5.1823. *(PR-DF-13)*.			
	a. Issued note.	40.00	100.00	200.00
	b. Cut cancelled. *(PR-DF-13)*.	20.00	50.00	100.00

5	**2 PESOS** 5.5.1823. *(PR-DF-17).*	GOOD	FINE	XF
	a. Issued note.	40.00	100.00	200.00
	b. Cut cancelled. *(PR-DF-19).*	25.00	75.00	150.00

6	**10 PESOS** 5.5.1823. *(PR-DF-21).*	GOOD	FINE	XF
		100.00	150.00	275.00

EMPIRE OF MAXIMILIAN

BANCO DE MÉXICO
#7, prepared for Emperor Maximilian (1864-67).

1866 ISSUE

7	**10 PESOS** 1866. Blue. Allegorical man and woman seated at lower ctr.	GOOD —	FINE Rare	XF —

ESTADOS UNIDAS DE MEXICO

UNITED STATES OF MEXICO

BANCO DE LA REPÚBLICA MEXICANA

In 1917, Venustiano Carranza decreed the creation of a new bank issue to replace all other banks of issue in order to do away with the multiple issues of paper money and help bring about financial peace. This bank never came into being as such, but it was of vital historical importance because it served as a basis for the founding of the Bank of Mexico in 1925.

1918 SERIES A
#11-15 Aztec calendar at ctr. on back. Printer: ABNC.

11	**5 PESOS** 1918. Black. Minerva seated w/globe at ctr. Back deep blue.	VG	VF	UNC
	p1. Face proof.	—	—	200.00
	p2. Back proof.	—	—	50.00
	s. Specimen, punched hole cancelled.	—	—	200.00

12	**10 PESOS** 1918. Black. Ceres reclining w/lion at ctr. Back deep green.	VG	VF	UNC
	p1. Face proof.	—	—	200.00
	p2. Back proof.	—	—	50.00
	s. Specimen, punched hole cancelled.	—	—	200.00

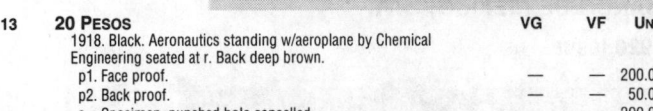

13	**20 PESOS** 1918. Black. Aeronautics standing w/aeroplane by Chemical Engineering seated at r. Back deep brown.	VG	VF	UNC
	p1. Face proof.	—	—	200.00
	p2. Back proof.	—	—	50.00
	s. Specimen, punched hole cancelled.	—	—	200.00

14	**50 PESOS** 1918. Black. Agriculture seated w/sheaf and scythe at l., Maritime Commerce seated w/ship and rudder at r. Back olive-brown.	VG	VF	UNC
	p1. Face proof.	—	—	200.00
	p2. Back proof.	—	—	50.00
	s. Specimen, punched hole cancelled.	—	—	200.00

15	100 PESOS	VG	VF	UNC

15 100 PESOS
1918. Black. Cherub standing between reclining Truth and Wisdom at ctr. Back deep red.

		VG	VF	UNC
p1.	Face proof.	—	—	200.00
p2.	Back proof.	—	—	50.00
s.	Specimen, punched hole cancelled.	—	—	200.00

COMISION MONETARIA

1920 ISSUE

#16 and 17 printer: Oficina Imp. de Hacienda.

16 50 CENTAVOS
(408) 10.1.1920. Black on gray. Minerva at l. Back green; allegorical figures at ctr.

	VG	VF	UNC
	8.00	15.00	45.00

17 1 PESO
(409) 10.1.1920. Brown. Goddess of Plenty w/2 cherubs at ctr. Back blue; like #16.

	GOOD	FINE	XF
	12.00	25.00	55.00

BANCO DE MÉXICO, S.A.

1920 ISSUE

19 2 PESOS
(698) ND (1920). Woman standing before Aztec calendar stone. Face proof. Printer: Talleresde Impresion de Estampillasy Valores. (Not issued).

	GOOD	FINE	XF
	—	Unc	350.00

1925; 1931 ISSUE

#21-27 lg. size notes (180 x 83mm). Sign. varieties. Statue of Victory in Mexico City at ctr. on back. Printer: ABNC.

21 5 PESOS
(699) 1925-34; ND. Black on m/c unpt. Portr. G. Faure at ctr. Back black.

		GOOD	FINE	XF
a.	1.9.1925. Series: A.	125.00	225.00	450.00
b.	1.8.1931. Series: C.	7.00	20.00	50.00
c.	30.4.1932. Series D.	7.00	20.00	50.00
d.	22.6.1932. Series E.	5.00	12.00	50.00
e.	18.1.1933. Series: F.	5.00	12.00	50.00
f.	9.8.1933. Series G.	4.00	10.00	40.00
g.	7.3.1934. Series: H.	3.00	8.00	35.00
h.	ND. Series: I.	3.00	8.00	35.00

22 10 PESOS
(700) 1925-34; ND. Black on m/c unpt. 2 winged women supporting book "The Law". Back brown.

		GOOD	FINE	XF
a.	1.9.1925. Series: A.	300.00	550.00	—
b.	1.8.1931. Series: C.	5.00	25.00	85.00
c.	30.4.1932. Series: D.	4.00	20.00	65.00
d.	22.6.1932. Series: E.	4.00	17.00	55.00
e.	18.1.1933. Series: F.	4.00	17.00	55.00
f.	9.8.1933. Series: G.	7.00	35.00	—
g.	7.3.1934. Series: H.	2.50	8.00	35.00
h.	ND. Series: I.	2.50	8.00	35.00

23 20 PESOS
(701) 1925-34; ND. Black on m/c unpt. Dock scene w/ship and steam locomotive. Back red.

		GOOD	FINE	XF
a.	1.9.1925. Series: A.	350.00	750.00	—
b.	1.8.1931. Series: C.	15.00	40.00	250.00
c.	30.4.1932. Series: D.	12.00	30.00	195.00
d.	22.6.1932. Series: E.	12.00	30.00	195.00
e.	18.1.1933. Series: F.	12.00	30.00	195.00
f.	9.8.1933. Series: G.	10.00	25.00	175.00
g.	7.3.1934. Series: H.	10.00	25.00	165.00
h.	ND. Series: I.	10.00	25.00	165.00

24 50 PESOS
(702) 1925-34. Black on m/c unpt. "Navigation" at l. Back olive-green.

		GOOD	FINE	XF
a.	1.9.1925. Series: A.	600.00	1150.	—
b.	1.8.1931. Series: C.	40.00	80.00	300.00
c.	30.4.1932. Series: D.	35.00	70.00	250.00
d.	22.6.1932. Series: E.	35.00	70.00	250.00
e.	18.1.1933. Series: F.	35.00	70.00	250.00
f.	9.8.1933. Series: G.	30.00	60.00	215.00
g.	7.3.1934. Series: H.	30.00	60.00	215.00

25	**100 PESOS**	GOOD	FINE	XF
(703)	1925-34. Black on m/c unpt. "Maritime Commerce" seated w/youth at ctr. Back dk. green.			
	a. 1.9.1925. Series: A.	800.00	1500.	—
	b. 1.8.1931. Series: C.	50.00	150.00	—
	c. 30.4.1932. Series: D.	45.00	125.00	—
	d. 22.6.1932. Series: E.	45.00	125.00	—
	e. 18.1.1933. Series: F.	45.00	125.00	350.00
	f. 9.8.1933. Series: G.	35.00	100.00	300.00
	g. 7.3.1934. Series: H.	35.00	100.00	300.00

26	**500 PESOS**	GOOD	FINE	XF
(704)	1931-34. Black on m/c unpt. "Electrical Energy" seated at ctr. Back blue.			
	a. 1.8.1931. Series: C.	225.00	550.00	1400.
	b. 18.1.1933. Series: F.	225.00	550.00	1400.
	c. 9.8.1933. Series: G.	200.00	400.00	1200.
	d. 7.3.1934. Series: H.	200.00	450.00	1250.

27	**1000 PESOS**	GOOD	FINE	XF
(705)	1931-34. Black on m/c unpt. "Wisdom" seated w/globe. Back orange.			
	a. 1.8.1931. Series: C.	650.00	1500.	—
	b. 9.8.1933. Series: G.	650.00	1500.	—
	c. 7.3.1934. Series: H.	650.00	1350.	2250.

1936 ISSUE
#28-33 small size notes (157 x 67mm). Sign. varieties. Printer: ABNC.

28	**1 PESO**	GOOD	FINE	XF
(709)	ND (1936); 1943. Black on m/c unpt. Aztec calendar stone at ctr. *UN* in background under sign. at l. and r. Back red; Statue of Victory at ctr.			
	a. ND. Series: A.	10.00	40.00	115.00
	b. ND. Series: B.	12.00	50.00	150.00
	c. ND. Series: C.	4.00	12.00	70.00
	d. ND. Series: D-F.	2.00	7.00	20.00
	e. 14.4.1943. Series: G-K.	.75	3.00	7.00

29	**5 PESOS**	GOOD	FINE	XF
(705A)	1.4.1936. Black on m/c unpt. Like #21 but smaller, w/text: *PAGARA CINCO PESOS EN EFECTIVO* below portr., w/curved *SERIE* at l. and r. Large BdM seal on back. Series: J.	15.00	50.00	125.00

30	**10 PESOS**	GOOD	FINE	XF
(706)	1.4.1936. Black on m/c unpt. Like #22 but smaller. Statue of Victory at ctr. on back. Series: J.	7.00	15.00	65.00

31	**100 PESOS**	GOOD	FINE	XF
(708)	1.9.1936. Black on m/c unpt. Portr. I. Madero at r. Bank of Mexico at ctr., lg. seal on back. Series: K			
	a. Issued note.	75.00	225.00	400.00
	s. Specimen, punched hole cancelled.	—	Unc	225.00

32	**500 PESOS**	GOOD	FINE	XF
(708A)	9.1.1936. Black on m/c unpt. Portr. J. M. Morelos y Pavon at r., w/text: *PAGARAEN EFECTIVO* below *500* at ctr. Middle sign. title: *INTERVENTOR DEL GOBIERNO*. Printed date. Back green; miners' palace. Printed date. Series: K.	150.00	400.00	800.00

33	**1000 PESOS**	GOOD	FINE	XF
(708B)	9.1.1936. Black on m/c upt. Portr. Cuauhtemoc at r. w.text: *PAGAR...EN EFECTIVO* beneath *1000* at ctr. Middle sign. title: *INTERVENTOR DEL GOBIERNO*. Back dk. brown; El Bastillo Chichen-Itza, w/lg. seal. Printed date. Series: K.	200.00	450.00	900.00

1937 ISSUE
#34-37 sign. varieties. Printer: ABNC.

34 (713)	5 PESOS 1937-50. Black on m/c unpt. Like #29 but w/text: *PAGARA .... AL PORTADOR* below portr., w/*EL* and *S.A.* added to face. Back gray; *S.A.* added to *BANCO DE MEXICO* w/small BdeM seal.	VG	VF	UNC
	a. 22.9.1937. Series: M.	4.00	7.50	30.00
	b. 26.6.1940. Series: N.	1.50	5.00	18.00
	c. 12.11.1941. Series: O.	1.50	5.00	18.00
	d. 25.11.1942. Series: P.	1.00	3.50	10.00
	e. 7.4.1943. Series: Q.	1.00	3.00	7.50
	f. 1.9.1943. Series: R.	1.00	3.50	10.00
	g. 17.1.1945. Series: S-Z.	1.00	3.50	10.00
	h. 14.8.1946. Series: AA-AK.	1.00	3.00	8.00
	i. 3.9.1947. Series: AL-AZ.	1.00	3.00	7.00
	j. 22.12.1948. Series: BA-BT.	1.00	3.00	7.00
	k. 23.11.1949. Series: BU-BV.	.75	2.00	6.00
	l. 26.7.1950. Series: BY-CB.	.75	2.00	5.00
	s. Specimen, punched hole cancelled.	—	—	175.00

35 (715)	10 PESOS 1937-42. Black on m/c unpt. Portr. E. Ruiz de Velazquez at r. Middle sign. title: *INTERVENTOR DEL GOBIERNO*. Road to Guanajuato at ctr. on back. Printed date.	VG	VF	UNC
	a. 22.9.1937. Series: M.	4.00	8.00	30.00
	b. 26.6.1940. Series: N.	2.50	6.00	18.00
	c. 12.11.1941. Series: O.	1.50	5.00	15.00
	d. 25.11.1942. Series: P.	1.50	5.00	15.00
	s. Specimen, punched hole cancelled.	—	—	175.00

36 (717)	20 PESOS 21.4.1937. Black on m/c unpt. Portr. J. Ortiz de Dominguez at l. Middle sign. title: *INTERVENTOR DEL GOBIERNO*. Back olive-green; Federal palace courtyard at ctr., lg. seal. Printed date. Series: L.	VG 8.00	VF 25.00	UNC 70.00

37 (707)	50 PESOS 1937; 1940. Purple, green, brown and m/c. Portr. I. Zaragoza at r. View of Ixtaccihuatl-Popocatepetl and volcanoes on back.	GOOD	FINE	XF
	a. 21.4.1937. Series: L.	40.00	125.00	250.00
	b. 26.6.1940. Series: N.	45.00	135.00	—

1940-43 ISSUE
#38-45 sign. varieties. Printer: ABNC.

38 (710)	1 PESO 1943-48. Like #28 but w/o "No" above serial #. *UNO* in background under sign. at l. and r.			
	a. 7.7.1943. Series: L-Q.	.50	3.00	6.00
	b. 1.9.1943. Series: R.	3.00	10.00	45.00
	8. 17.1.1945. Series: S-Z.	.50	4.00	9.00
	d. 12.5.1948. Series: AA-AJ.	.50	3.00	6.00

39 (715A)	10 PESOS 1943-45. Black on m/c unpt. Like #35 but *MEXICO D.F.* and printed dates higher.	VG	VF	UNC
	a. 7.4.1943. Series: Q.	1.50	3.50	10.00
	b. 1.9.1943. Series: R.	1.75	4.50	15.00
	c. 17.1.1945. Series: S-Z.	1.50	3.50	12.00

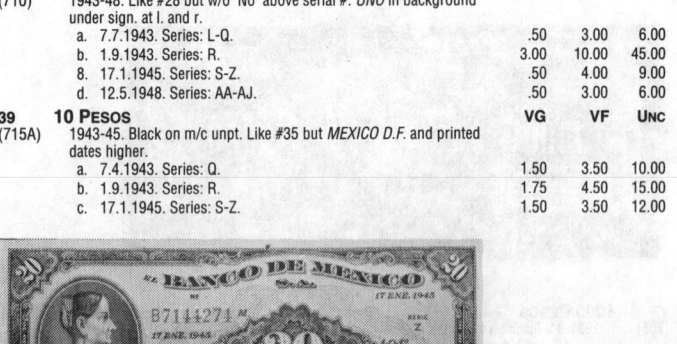

40 (717A)	20 PESOS 1940-45. Black on m/c unpt. Like #36 but small seal on back. Printed date.	VG	VF	UNC
	a. 26.6.1940. Series: N.	5.00	9.00	30.00
	b. 11.11.1941. Series: O.	2.50	6.00	20.00
	c. 11.11.1491 at l., 11.11.1941 at r. (error). Series: O.	125.00	275.00	—
	d. 11.11.1941. Series: O.	2.50	7.00	25.00
	e. 25.11.1942. Series: P.	2.25	4.50	15.00
	f. 7.4.1943. Series: Q.	2.25	4.50	15.00
	g. 1.9.1943. Series: R.	2.25	4.50	15.00
	h. 17.1.1945. Series: S-Z.	2.25	4.50	15.00
	s. Specimen, punched hole cancelled.	—	—	175.00

41 (718)	**50 PESOS**	VG	VF	UNC
	1941-45. Dp. blue on m/c unpt. Portr. I. de Allende at l. Middle sign. title: *INTERVENTOR DEL GOBIERNO.* Back blue; Statue of Victory at ctr. on back. Printed date.			
	a. 12.11.1941. Series: O-Q.	4.00	10.00	25.00
	b. 25.10.1944. Series: R.	3.00	6.00	15.00
	c. 17.1.1945. Series: S-W.	2.00	5.00	12.00
	s. Specimen, punched hole cancelled.	—	—	175.00

42 (718B)	**100 PESOS**	VG	VF	UNC
	1940-42. Black on m/c unpt. Portr. F. I. Madero at r. Back purple; Bank of Mexico bldg. at ctr. on back.			
	a. See #31.			
	b. 26.6.1940. Series: N.	20.00	35.00	100.00
	c. 12.11.1941. Series: O.	12.00	20.00	70.00
	d. 25.11.1942. Series: P.	20.00	35.00	100.00

43 (720A)	**500 PESOS**	VG	VF	UNC
	1940-43. Black on m/c unpt. Like #32 but w/text: *PAGARA...AL PORTADOR* beneath *500* at ctr. Printed dates. Back green; Miner's palace and small seal on back.			
	a. 26.6.1940. Series: N.	15.00	45.00	165.00
	b. 11.11.1941. Series: O.	15.00	45.00	165.00
	c. 25.11.1942. Series: P.	15.00	40.00	150.00
	d. 7.4.1943. Series: Q.	15.00	40.00	150.00
	e. 1.9.1943. Series: R.	15.00	40.00	125.00
	s. Specimen, punched hole cancelled.	—	—	225.00

44 (721A)	**1000 PESOS**	VG	VF	UNC
	1941-45. Black on m/c unpt. Cuauhtemoc at l. w/text: *PAGARA.... AL PORTADOR* beneath *1000* at ctr. Back dk. brown; El Bastillo Chichenitza at ctr. on back. Printed dates.			
	a. 11.11.1941. Series: O.	35.00	60.00	150.00
	b. 25.11.1942. Series: P.	35.00	60.00	150.00
	c. 7.4.1943. Series: Q.	30.00	50.00	125.00
	d. 11.20.1945. Series: R.	15.00	40.00	100.00
	s. Specimen, punched hole cancelled.	—	—	175.00

45 (722)	**10,000 PESOS**	VG	VF	UNC
	1943-53. Purple on m/c unpt. Portr. M. Romero at l. Government palace on back.			
	a. 1.9.1943. Series: R.	100.00	400.00	—
	b. 27.12.1950. Series: CS.	100.00	400.00	—
	c. 19.1.1953. Series: DK.	75.00	300.00	1000.
	s. Specimen, punched hole cancelled.	—	—	850.00

1945-48 ISSUE
#46-52 sign. varieties. Printer: ABNC.

46 (711)	**1 PESO**	GOOD	FINE	XF
	1948; 1950. Like #38 but *EL* and *S.A.* added to *BANCO DE MEXICO* on face. *S.A.* added on back.			
	a. 22.12.1948. Series: BA-BJ.	.25	1.00	5.00
	b. 26.7.1950. Series: BY-CR.	.25	1.00	4.00

47 (715B)	**10 PESOS**	VG	VF	UNC
	1946-50. Black on m/c unpt. Like #39 but middle sign. title: *INTERVENTOR DE LA COM. NAC. BANCARIA.* Engraved dates.			
	a. 14.8.1946. Series: AA-AJ.	1.00	3.50	9.00
	b. 3.9.1947. Series: AK-AZ.	1.00	3.50	9.00
	c. 22.12.1948. Series: BA-BJ.	1.00	2.80	8.00
	d. 23.11.1949. Series: BU.	.30	2.00	6.50
	e. 26.7.1950. Series: BY, BZ.	.30	2.00	6.50

48 (717B)	**20 PESOS**	VG	VF	UNC
	22.12.1948. Black on m/c unpt. Like #40 but middle sign. title: *INTERVENTOR DE LA COM. NAC. BANCARIA.* Engraved date. Series: BA-BE.	1.25	2.50	10.00

49 (718A)	**50 PESOS**	VG	VF	UNC
	1948-72. Deep blue on m/c unpt. Portr. I. de Allende at l. Middle sign. title: *INTERVENTOR DE LA COM. NAC. BONCARIA.* Engraved dates. Back blue; Independence Monument at ctr.			
	a. 22.12.1948. Black series letters. Series: BM-BD.	3.00	6.00	15.00
	b. 23.11.1949. Series: BU-BX.	3.00	6.00	15.00
	c. 26.7.1950. Series: BY-CF.	3.00	5.00	12.50
	d. 27.12.1950. Series: CS-DH.	3.00	5.00	12.50
	e. 19.1.1953. Series: DK-DV.	2.00	4.00	11.00
	f. 10.2.1954. Series: DW-EH.	2.00	4.00	10.00
	g. 8.9.1954. Series: EI-FF.	2.00	4.00	10.00
	h. 11.1.1956. Series: FK-FV.	2.00	4.00	10.00
	i. 19.6.1957. Series: FW-GP.	2.00	4.00	10.00
	j. 20.8.1958. Series: HC-HR.	2.00	4.00	10.00
	k. 18.3.1959. Red series letters. Series: HS-IP.	2.00	4.00	10.00
	l. 20.5.1959. Series: IQ-JN.	2.00	4.00	10.00
	m. 25.1.1961. Series: JO-LB.	1.50	3.00	8.00
	n. 8.11.1961. Series: LC-AID.	1.50	3.00	8.00
	o. 24.4.1963. Series: AIE-BAP.	1.50	3.00	8.00
	p. 17.2.1965. Series: BAQ-BCD.	1.00	2.50	5.50
	q. 10.5.1967. Series: BCY-BEG.	1.00	2.50	5.00
	r. 19.11.1969 Series: BGK-BIC.	1.00	2.50	4.50
	s. 22.7.1970. Series: BIG-BKN.	1.00	2.50	4.50
	t. 27.6.1972. Series: BLI-BMG.	1.00	2.50	4.50
	u. 29.12.1972. Series: BNG-BRB.	1.00	2.00	4.00
	v. Specimen, punched hole cancelled.	—	—	125.00

50 (719)	**100 PESOS**	VG	VF	UNC
	17.1.1945. Brown on m/c unpt. Portr. M. Hidalgo at l., series letters above serial #. Middle sign. title: *INTERVENTOR DEL GOBIERNO.* Printed date. Back olive-green. Coin w/national coat-of-arms at ctr. Series: S-Z.			
	a. Issued note.	12.00	20.00	50.00
	s. Specimen, punched hole cancelled.	—	—	200.00

51 (720B)	500 PESOS	VG	VF	UNC
	1948-78. Black on m/c unpt. Portr. J. M. Morelos y Pavon at r. W/o "No" above serial #. Middle sign. title: *INTERVENTOR DE LA COM. NAC. BANCARIO.* Back green; Palace of Mining at ctr.			
a.	22.12.1948. Series: BA.	15.00	40.00	150.00
b.	27.12.1950. Series: CS-CT.	15.00	40.00	150.00
c.	3.12.1951. Series: DI-DJ.	15.00	40.00	150.00
d.	19.1.1953. Series: DK-DN.	12.00	25.00	60.00
e.	31.8.1955. Series: FG-FJ.	12.00	20.00	50.00
f.	11.1.1956. Series: FK-FL.	12.00	20.00	50.00
g.	19.6.1957. Series: FW-GB.	12.00	20.00	50.00
h.	20.8.1958. Series: HC-HH.	10.00	20.00	40.00
i.	18.3.1959. Series: HS-HX.	10.00	20.00	40.00
j.	20.5.1959. Series: IQ-IV.	10.00	20.00	40.00
k.	25.1.1961. Series: JO-JT.	10.00	20.00	40.00
l.	8.11.1961. Series: LC-MP.	10.00	20.00	40.00
m.	17.2.1965. Series: BAQ-BCN.	6.00	12.00	25.00
n.	24.3.1971. Series: BKD-BKT.	2.50	5.00	12.50
o.	27.6.1972. Series: BLI-BLM.	2.50	5.00	12.50
p.	29.12.1972. Series: BNG-BNP.	2.50	5.00	12.50
q.	18.7.1973. Series: BUY-BWB.	1.75	5.00	12.50
r.	2.8.1974. Series: BXV-BZI.	1.75	3.50	8.00
s.	18.2.1977. Series: BZJ-CCK.	1.00	3.50	7.50
t.	18.1.1978. Series: CCL-CDY.	1.00	3.50	7.50

52 (721B)	1000 PESOS	VG	VF	UNC
	1948-77. Black on m/c unpt. Cuauhtemoc at r. Middle sign. title: *INTERVENTOR DE LA COM. NAC. BANCARIO.* Back brown; Chichen Itzfl pyramid at ctr.			
a.	22.12.1948. Series: BA.	25.00	45.00	150.00
b.	23.11.1949. Series: BU.	25.00	45.00	150.00
c.	27.12.1950. Series: CS.	25.00	45.00	125.00
d.	3.12.1951. Series: DI-DJ.	25.00	45.00	125.00
e.	19.1.1953. Series: DK-DL.	25.00	45.00	125.00
f.	31.8.1955. Series: FG-FH.	20.00	40.00	75.00
g.	11.1.1956. Series: FK-FL.	20.00	40.00	75.00
h.	19.6.1957. Series: FW-FZ.	20.00	35.00	60.00
i.	20.8.1958. Series: HC-HE.	20.00	35.00	60.00
j.	18.3.1959. Series: HS-HU.	18.00	30.00	50.00
k.	20.5.1959. Series: IQ-IS.	18.00	30.00	50.00
l.	25.1.1961. Series: JO-JQ.	18.00	30.00	45.00
m.	8.11.1961. Series: LC-LV.	18.00	30.00	45.00
n.	17.2.1965. Series: BAQ-BCN.	7.00	15.00	30.00
o.	24.3.1971. Series: BKO-BKT.	2.00	4.00	10.00
p.	27.6.1972. Series: BLI-BLM.	2.00	4.50	12.00
q.	29.12.1972. Series: BNG-BNK.	2.00	4.50	12.00
r.	18.7.1973. Series: BUY-BWB.	2.00	4.50	12.00
s.	2.8.1974. Series: BXV-BYY.	2.00	4.50	12.00
t.	18.2.1977. Series: BZL-CBQ.	2.00	4.00	10.00

1950; 1951 ISSUE

#53-55 sign. varieties. Printer: ABNC.

53 (715C)	10 PESOS	VG	VF	UNC
	1951; 1953. Black on m/c unpt. Like #715B but w/o "No" above serial #.			
a.	3.12.1951. Series: DI, DJ.	.30	2.00	6.50
b.	19.1.1953. Series: DK-DM.	.30	2.00	6.50

54 (717C)	20 PESOS	VG	VF	UNC
	1950-70. Black on m/c unpt. Portr. J. Ortiz de Dominguez at l. W/o "No" above serial #. Back olive-green; Federal Palace courtyard at ctr.			
a.	27.12.1950. Black series letters. Series: CS-CT.	1.10	3.00	9.00
b.	19.1.1953. Series: DK.	1.10	3.00	9.00
c.	10.2.1954. Red series letters. Series: DW.	1.10	2.50	8.50
d.	11.1.1956. Series: FK.	1.10	2.50	8.50
e.	19.6.1957. Series: FW.	1.10	2.50	8.00
f.	20.8.1958. Series: HC, HD.	1.10	2.50	8.00
g.	18.3.1959. Series: HS, HT.	1.10	2.00	7.00

		VG	VF	UNC
h.	20.5.1959. Series: IQ, IR.	1.10	2.00	7.00
i.	25.1.1961. Series: JO, JP.	.75	1.50	6.00
j.	8.11.1961. Series: LC-LG.	.75	1.50	6.00
k.	24.4.1963. Series: AIE-AIH.	.50	1.25	5.00
l.	17.2.1965. Series: BAQ-BAV.	.50	1.25	5.00
m.	10.5.1967. Series: BCY-BDB.	.50	1.25	5.00
n.	27.8.1969. Series: BGA-BGB.	.50	1.25	5.00
o.	18.3.1970. Series: BID-BIF.	.50	1.25	5.00
p.	22.7.1970. Series: BIG-BIK.	.50	1.25	5.00
s.	Specimen, punched hole cancelled.	—	—	125.00

55 (719A)	100 PESOS	VG	VF	UNC
	1950-61. Brown on m/c unpt. Portr. M. Hidalgo at l. Middle sign. title: *INTERVENTOR DE LA COM. NAC. BANCARIA.* Engraved dates. Back olive-green; coin w/national seal at ctr.			
a.	27.12.1950. Black series letters. Series: CS-CZ.	6.00	10.00	25.00
b.	19.1.1953. Series: DK-DP.	3.50	7.00	15.00
c.	10.2.1954. Series: DN-DZ.	3.50	7.00	15.00
d.	8.9.1954. Series: EI-ET.	3.50	7.00	15.00
e.	11.1.1956. Series: FK-FV.	3.50	7.00	12.00
f.	19.6.1957. Series: FW-GH.	3.50	7.00	12.00
g.	20.8.1958. Series: HC-HR.	3.50	7.00	12.00
h.	18.3.1959. Series: HS-IH.	3.50	7.00	12.00
i.	20.5.1959. Series: IQ-JF.	3.50	7.00	12.00
j.	25.1.1961. Series: JO-KL.	3.50	7.00	12.00

1953; 1954 ISSUE

#56-58 sign. varieties. Printer: ABNC.

56 (711A)	1 PESO	GOOD	FINE	XF
	1954. Like #46 but series letters in red at lower l. and r.			
a.	10.2.1954. Series: DW-EF.	.25	1.00	4.00
b.	8.9.1954. Series: EI-FB.	.25	1.00	4.00

57 (714)	5 PESOS	VG	VF	UNC
	1953-54. Black on m/c unpt. Like #34 but w/o *No* above serial #, w/series letters lower.			
a.	19.1.1953. Series: DK-DN.	.75	2.00	5.00
b.	10.2.1954. Series: DW-DZ.	.20	1.00	4.00
c.	8.9.1954. Series: EI-EP.	.20	1.00	4.00

58 (716)	10 PESOS	VG	VF	UNC
	1954-67. Black on m/c unpt. Portr. E. Ruiz de Valezquez at r. Text: *MEXICO D.F.* above series letters. Back brown; road to Guanajuato at ctr.			
a.	10.2.1954. Series: DW, DX.	.50	1.00	7.00
b.	8.9.1954. Series: EI-EN.	.25	1.00	4.00
c.	19.6.1957. Series: FW, FX.	.60	2.50	8.00
d.	24.7.1957. Series: GQ.	.60	2.50	8.00
e.	20.8.1958. Series: HC-HF.	.25	1.50	5.00
f.	18.3.1959. Series: HS-HU.	.25	1.50	5.00
g.	20.5.1959. Series: IQ-IS.	.25	1.50	5.00
h.	25.1.1961. Series: JO-JT.	.25	1.00	4.00
i.	8.11.1961. Series: LC-LV.	.25	1.00	4.00
j.	24.4.1963. Series: AIE-AIT.	.25	1.00	4.00
k.	17.2.1965. Series: BAQ-BAX.	.25	1.00	4.00
l.	10.5.1967. Series: BCY-BDA.	.25	1.00	3.00
s.	Specimen, punched hole cancelled.	—	—	150.00

1957 ISSUE

#59 and 60 sign. varieties. Printer: ABNC.

59	**1 Peso**			VG	VF	Unc
(712)	1957-70. Black on m/c unpt. Aztec calendar stone at ctr. Text: *MEXICO D.F.* added above date at lower l. Back red. Independence monument at ctr.					
	a.	19.6.1957. Series: FW-GF.		.10	1.00	3.00
	b.	24.7.1957. Series: GH-GR.		.10	.75	3.00
	c.	4.12.1957. Series: GS-HB.		.10	.75	2.50
	d.	20.8.1958. Series: HC-HL.		.10	.75	2.50
	e.	18.3.1959. Series: HS-IB.		.10	.50	2.00
	f.	20.5.1959. Series: IQ-IZ.		.10	.50	2.00
	g.	25.1.1961. Series: JO-KC.		.10	.25	1.50
	h.	8.11.1961. Series: LC-LD.		.10	.25	1.50
	i.	9.6.1965. Series: BCO-BCX.		.10	.20	1.00
	j.	10.5.1967. Series: BCY-BEB.		.10	.25	1.00
	k.	27.8.1969. Series: BGA-BGJ.		.10	.25	1.00
	l.	22.7.1970. Series: BIG-BIP.		.10	.20	.75

60	**5 Pesos**			VG	VF	Unc
(714A)	1957-70. Black on m/c unpt. Portr. G. Faure at ctr. Text: *MEXICO D.F.* before date. Back gray; Independence Monument at ctr.					
	a.	19.6.1957. Series: FW, FX.		.40	2.00	6.00
	b.	24.7.1957. Series: GQ, GR.		.40	2.00	6.00
	c.	20.8.1958. Series: HC-HJ.		.25	1.50	5.00
	d.	18.3.1959. Series: HS-HV.		.25	1.50	5.00
	e.	20.5.1959. Series: IQ-IT.		.25	1.50	5.00
	f.	25.1.1961. Series: JO-JV.		.15	.75	3.00
	g.	8.11.1961. Series: LC-MP.		.15	.75	3.00
	h.	24.4.1963. Series: AIE-AJJ.		.15	.50	2.00
	i.	19.11.1969. Series: BGK-BGT.		.15	.50	2.00
	j.	22.7.1970. Series: BIG-BII.		.15	.50	2.00

Romanian, until 1940 The Republic of Moldova (formerly the Moldavian S.S.R.) is bordered in the east and south by the Ukraine and on the west by Romania. It has an area of 13,000 sq. mi. (33,700 sq. km.) and a population of 4.4 million. (This includes the area and people of Transdniestria, an area in dispute.) Fish, agricultural products including canned goods, steel, concrete and dairy products are leading industries.

The Moldavian A.S.S.R. was created on Oct. 12, 1924, as part of the Ukrainian S.S.R., a Soviet protest against the recovery of Bessarabia by Romania. In 1940 Romania yielded to a Soviet ultimatum and ceded Bessarabia to the U.S.S.R. and the Soviet government formed a Moldavian S.S.R. comprised of the major part of Bessarabia. In June 1941, the Romanians allied with Germany reincorporated the whole of Bessarabia into Romania. Soviet armies reconquered it late in 1944 restoring the Moldavian S.S.R. A new constitution was adopted in April 1978. A declaration of republican sovereignty was adopted in June 1990 and the area was renamed Moldova, an independent republic, declared in Aug. 1991. In Dec. 1991 Moldova became a member of the Commonwealth of Independent States. Separatists and government forces clashed in 1992. A joint declaration by Russian and Moldavian presidents on July 3, 1992 envisaged a demarcation line held by neutral forces and withdrawal of the Russian army from Transdniestria, which had developed into a self-styled republic.

MONETARY SYSTEM:
3 Ducati = 100 Lei

REPUBLIC

BANCA NATIONALA A MOLDAVEI

1857 ISSUE

A1	**3 Ducats = 100 Lei**			
	1.9.1857. Arms at top ctr. Printer: G&D.	—	Rare	—

CEMITETUL NATIONAL REVOLUTIONAR ROMAN

1853 REVOLUTIONARY ISSUE

A2	**10 Ducati**			
	1853. Eagle at top ctr.	—	Rare	—

716 MONACO

The Principality of Monaco, located on the Mediterranean coast nine miles off Nice, has an area of 0.6 sq. mi. (1.49 sq. km.) and a population of 29,000. Capital: Monaco-Ville. The economy is based on tourism and the manufacture of perfumes and liqueurs. Monaco derives most of its revenue from a tobacco monopoly, the sale of postage stamps for philatelic purpose, and the gambling tables of Monte Carlo Casino.

Monaco derived its name from "Monoikos", the Greek surname for Hercules, the mythological strong man in whose honor the Greeks erected a temple on the Monacan headland. Probably founded by the Phoenicians, Monaco has been ruled by the Genoa Grimaldi family since 1297 - Prince Rainier III, the present and 30th monarch of Monaco, is still of that line - except for a period during the French Revolution and the First Republic when it was annexed to France. Since 1865, Monaco has maintained a customs union with France which guarantees its privileged position as long as the royal male line remains intact. Under the new constitution proclaimed on December 17, 1962, the Prince shares his power with an 18-member unicameral National Council.

RULERS:
Albert I, 1889-1922
Louis II, 1922-1949
Rainier III, 1949-

MONETARY SYSTEM:
1 Franc = 100 Centimes

PRINCIPALITY

PRINCIPAUTÉ DE MONACO

1920 EMERGENCY ISSUES

		VG	VF	UNC
1	**25 CENTIMES**			
	16.3.(20.3) 1920. (Dated 1920.) Brown. First issue.			
	a. W/o embossed arms.	10.00	20.00	65.00
	b. Embossed arms in 17mm stamp.	15.00	35.00	95.00
	c. Embossed arms in 22mm stamp.	10.00	20.00	65.00
2	**25 CENTIMES**			
	16.3.(20.3) 1920. (Dated 1921.) Blue-violet.			
	a. W/o embossed arms.	10.00	17.00	55.00
	b. Embossed arms in 17mm stamp.	10.00	20.00	65.00
	c. Embossed arms in 22mm stamp.	12.00	25.00	70.00

		VG	VF	UNC
3	**50 CENTIMES**			
	16.3.(20.3) 1920. (Issued 28.4.1920.) Blue-gray. Series A-H.			
	a. Issued note.	10.00	20.00	75.00
	r. Remainder w/o serial #. Series E.	—	—	50.00

		VG	VF	UNC
4	**1 FRANC**			
	16.3.(20.3) 1920. (Issued 28.4.1920.) Brown. First issue. Lettered cartouche.			
	a. Series A.	10.00	30.00	100.00
	b. Series B; C.	75.00	160.00	—

		VG	VF	UNC
5	**1 FRANC**			
	16.3.(20.3) 1920. (Issued 28.4.1920.) Blue-gray and brown. Second issue. Plain cartouche. Series A-E.	10.00	20.00	65.00

The State of Mongolia (formerly the Mongolian Peoples Republic), a landlocked country in central Asia between the Soviet Union and the Peoples Republic of China, has an area of 604,247 sq. mi. (1,565,000 060 km.) and a population of 2.26 million. Capital: Ulan Bator. Animal herds and flocks are the chief economic asset. Wool, cattle, butter, meat and hides are exported.

Mongolia (often referred to as Outer Mongolia), one of the world's oldest countries, attained its greatest power in the 13th century when Genghis Khan and his successors conquered all of China and extended their influence westward as far as Hungary and Poland. The empire dissolved in later centuries and in 1691 was brought under suzerainty of the Manchus, who had conquered China in 1644. After the Chinese republican movement led by Sun Yat-sen overthrew the Manchus and set up the Chinese Republic in 1911. Mongolia, with the support of Russia, proclaimed its independence from China, on March 13, 1921, when the Provisional Peoples Government was established. Later, on Nov. 26, 1924, the government proclaimed the Mongolian Peoples Republic. Opposition to the communist party developed in late 1989 and after demonstrations and hunger strikes the Politburo resigned on Mar. 12, 1990 and the new State of Mongolia was organized.

RULERS:
   Chinese to 1921

MONETARY SYSTEM:
   1 Tugrik (Tukhrik) = 100 Mongo

PROVISIONAL PEOPLE'S GOVERNMENT

MONGOLIAN GOVERNMENT'S TREASURE

1921 ISSUE
#A1-A4 payable on or after November 20, 1921.

		GOOD	FINE	XF
A1	**10 DOLLARS** 20.11.1921. Lt. blue w/red-brown text. White, blue, pink and yellow arms at upper ctr. Emblem at top ctr., ram at bottom ctr. on back.	350.00	850.00	—
A2	**25 DOLLARS** 21.11.1921. Red and blue. Cow at bottom ctr. on back.	350.00	950.00	—

		GOOD	FINE	XF
A3	**50 DOLLARS** 20.11.1921. Gold and red frame, red text. White, blue, pink and yellow arms at upper ctr. Back dk. blue frame w/red text; emblem at top ctr., horse at bottom ctr.	450.00	1100.	—
A4	**100 DOLLARS** 20.11.1921. Yellow and red. Camel at bottom ctr. on back.	550.00	1400.	—

1924 ISSUE
#1-6 m/c. Ornamental. (Not issued).

		VG	VF	UNC
1	**50 CENTS** 1924. Yellow and m/c.			
	r. Remainder.	—	—	185.00
	s. Specimen perforated: ОБРАЗЕЦЪ.	—	—	450.00

		VG	VF	UNC
2	**1 DOLLAR** 1924. Blue and m/c.			
	r. Remainder.	—	—	200.00
	s. Specimen perforated: ОБРАЗЕЦЪ.	—	—	500.00
3	**3 DOLLARS** 1924. Brown and m/c.			
	r. Remainder.	—	—	225.00
	s. Specimen perforated: ОБРАЗЕЦЪ.	—	—	550.00
4	**5 DOLLARS** 1924. Green and m/c.			
	r. Remainder.	—	—	250.00
	s. Specimen perforated: ОБРАЗЕЦЪ.	—	—	600.00

		VG	VF	UNC
5	**10 DOLLARS** 1924. Lilac and m/c.			
	r. Remainder.	—	—	275.00
	s. Specimen perforated: ОБРАЗЕЦЪ.	—	—	650.00
6	**25 DOLLARS** 1924. Blue and m/c.			
	r. Remainder.	—	—	325.00
	s. Specimen perforated: ОБРАЗЕЦЪ.	—	—	750.00

COMMERCIAL AND INDUSTRIAL BANK

1925 FIRST ISSUE
#A7-A10 "Soembo" arms at ctr., perforated: 1.12.1925 vertically at l. Serial # prefix A.

		GOOD	FINE	XF
A7	**1 TUGRIK** 1.12.1925. Yellow-brown.	15.00	40.00	100.00
A8	**2 TUGRIK** 1.12.1925. Green.	20.00	55.00	150.00
A9	**5 TUGRIK** 1.12.1925. blue and m/c. Back red.	20.00	65.00	175.00
A10	**10 TUGRIK** 1.12.1925. Red and m/c. Back green and brown.	30.00	80.00	225.00

1925 SECOND ISSUE
#7-10 w/o perforated date.

7	**1 TUGRIK** 1925. Yellow-brown.	7.50	30.00	80.00

		GOOD	FINE	XF
8	**2 TUGRIK** 1925. Green.	12.00	45.00	120.00
9	**5 TUGRIK** 1925. Blue and m/c. Back red-brown.	15.00	50.00	140.00

		GOOD	FINE	XF
10	**10 TUGRIK** 1925. Red and m/c. Back green and brown.	25.00	55.00	185.00
11	**25 TUGRIK** 1925. Brown and m/c. Back green.	30.00	80.00	275.00
12	**50 TUGRIK** 1925. Green and m/c. Back brown.	35.00	125.00	450.00
13	**100 TUGRIK** 1925. Blue and red.	75.00	225.00	650.00

MONGOLIAN PEOPLES REPUBLIC

COMMERCIAL AND INDUSTRIAL BANK

1939 ISSUE
#14-20 portr. Sukhe-Bataar at r., "Soembo" arms at l. Mongolian text.

		GOOD	FINE	XF
14	**1 TUGRIK** 1939. Brown.	3.50	12.50	45.00
15	**3 TUGRIK** 1939. Green.	5.00	18.00	75.00

		GOOD	FINE	XF
16	**5 TUGRIK** 1939. Blue.	7.50	20.00	85.00
17	**10 TUGRIK** 1939. Red.	15.00	30.00	95.00
18	**25 TUGRIK** 1939. Gray-brown.	15.00	55.00	150.00
19	**50 TUGRIK** 1939. Green-brown.	35.00	75.00	200.00
20	**100 TUGRIK** 1939. Lt. blue.	75.00	135.00	275.00

1941 ISSUE
#21-27 portr. Sukhe-Bataar at r., Socialist arms at l. Mongolian and Russian text.

		GOOD	FINE	XF
21	**1 TUGRIK** 1941. Brown.	3.00	8.00	45.00
22	**3 TUGRIK** 1941. Green.	5.00	12.00	60.00
23	**5 TUGRIK** 1941. Blue.	7.00	15.00	80.00

		GOOD	FINE	XF
24	**10 TUGRIK** 1941. Red.	12.00	25.00	110.00
25	**25 TUGRIK** 1941. Gray-brown.	20.00	40.00	135.00

		GOOD	FINE	XF
26	**50 TUGRIK** 1941. Green-brown.	40.00	65.00	175.00
27	**100 TUGRIK** 1941. Lt. blue.	60.00	85.00	200.00

УЛСЫН БАНК - State Bank

1955 ISSUE
#28-34 portr. Sukhe-Bataar at r., Socialist arms at l. Mongolian and Russian text. Wmk: Symbol repeated.

		GOOD	FINE	XF
28	**1 TUGRIK** 1955. Black on pale brown-orange and m/c unpt. Back dk. brown text on pale brown-orange unpt.	.15	.50	1.50
29	**3 TUGRIK** 1955. Black on lt. green and m/c unpt. Back dk. green text on lt. green and m/c unpt.	.20	.60	1.75

30	**5 TUGRIK**	**GOOD**	**FINE**	**XF**
	1955. Black on lt. blue and m/c unpt. Back blue-black text on lt. blue and m/c unpt.	.25	.80	2.50
31	**10 TUGRIK**			
	1955. Dp. red and red on pink and m/c unpt. Back dk. brown text on pale orange and m/c unpt.	.40	1.20	3.50

32	**25 TUGRIK**	**GOOD**	**FINE**	**XF**
	1955. Black on lt. blue and m/c unpt. Back dk. brown text on tan and m/c unpt.	.50	1.50	4.50
33	**50 TUGRIK**			
	1955. Black on lt. green and m/c unpt. Back dk. green text on lt. green and m/c unpt.	.60	1.75	5.50

34	**100 TUGRIK**	**GOOD**	**FINE**	**XF**
	1955. Black on lt. blue and m/c unpt. Back dk. blue-green text on lt. blue and m/c unpt.	.80	2.50	7.50

The former independent kingdom of Montenegro, now one of the nominally autonomous federated units of Yugoslavia, was located in southeastern Europe north of Albania. As a kingdom, it had an area of 5,333 sq. mi. (13,812 sq. km.) and a population of about 250,000. Capital: Titograd. The predominantly pastoral kingdom had few industries.

Montenegro became an independent state in 1355 following the breakup of the Serb empire. During the Turkish invasion of Albania and Herzegovina in the 15th century, the Montenegrins moved their capital to the remote mountain village of Cetinje where they maintained their independence through two centuries of intermittent attack, emerging as the only one of the Balkan states not subjugated by the Turks. When World War I began, Montenegro joined with Serbia and was subsequently invaded and occupied by the Austrians. Austria withdrew upon the defeat of the Central Powers, permitting the Serbians to move in and maintain the occupation. Montenegro then joined the kingdom of the Serbs, Croats and Slovenes, which later became Yugoslavia.

RULERS:

Nicholas I, 1910-1918

MONETARY SYSTEM:

1 Perper = 100 Para = 1 Austrian Crown

NOTE: During World War II Italian ovpt. notes of Yugoslavia with *Verificato* were circulated in Montenegro. There was also an issue of "Socialniki Dinara" in 1945 (stamp money). For details see Yugoslavia, Volume I.

KINGDOM

TREASURY

1912 ISSUE

#1-6 arms at ctr.

1	**1 PERPER**	**GOOD**	**FINE**	**XF**
	1.10.1912. Dk. blue on green paper. Arms at ctr.			
	a. Issued note.	4.00	20.00	50.00
	b. Handstamped: *CETINJE*.	15.00	50.00	—
	c. Punched hole cancelled.	2.00	7.50	20.00

2	**2 PERPERA**	**GOOD**	**FINE**	**XF**
	1.10.1912. Lilac on reddish paper.			
	a. Issued note.	5.00	25.00	60.00
	b. Punched hole cancelled.	3.00	10.00	25.00
3	**5 PERPERA**			
	1.10.1912. Dk. green on olive-green paper.			
	a. Issued note.	7.50	35.00	85.00
	b. Punched hole cancelled.	4.00	15.00	35.00

4	**10 PERPERA**	GOOD	FINE	XF
	1.10.1912. Red-brown on yellowish paper.			
	a. Issued note	30.00	100.00	200.00
	b. Punched hole cancelled.	15.00	45.00	90.00

5	**50 PERPERA**	GOOD	FINE	XF
	1.10.1912. Blue on brown unpt. Reddish paper.			
	a. Issued note.	200.00	600.00	1200.
	b. Punched hole cancelled.	100.00	300.00	750.00
6	**100 PERPERA**			
	1.10.1912. Brown paper.			
	a. Issued note.	300.00	800.00	1600.
	b. Punched hole cancelled.	200.00	500.00	1000.

ROYAL GOVERNMENT

1914 FIRST ISSUE

7	**1 PERPER**	GOOD	FINE	XF
	25.7.1914 (-old date 1.10.1912). Red ovpt. on #1.			
	a. Issued note.	7.00	25.00	65.00
	b. W/handstamp: *CETINJE.*	10.00	35.00	—
8	**2 PERPERA**			
	25.7.1914 (-old date 1.10.1912). Red ovpt. on #2.	15.00	45.00	90.00

1914 SECOND ISSUE

#9-14 arms at ctr. on both sides. All notes are 155 x 107mm. Valuations are for notes w/o additional hand-stamps. Cancelled notes are worth 30% less.

9	**5 PERPERA**	GOOD	FINE	XF
	25.7.1914. Blue.			
	a. Issued note.	2.00	10.00	35.00
	b. Punched hole cancelled.	1.00	4.00	12.00
10	**10 PERPERA**			
	25.7.1914. Red.	2.00	12.00	40.00
11	**20 PERPERA**			
	25.7.1914. Brown.	4.00	20.00	60.00

12	**50 PERPERA**	GOOD	FINE	XF
	25.7.1914. Olive.	4.00	30.00	70.00
13	**100 PERPERA**			
	25.7.1914. Lt. brown.	12.00	60.00	150.00
14	**100 PERPERA**			
	11.8.1914. Lt. brown. (Probably a trial note only).	—	—	1000.

1914 THIRD ISSUE

#15-21 arms at ctr. on back. Valuations are for notes w/o additional handstamps. Cancelled notes are worth 30% less.

15	**1 PERPER**	GOOD	FINE	XF
	25.7.1914. Blue on gray paper. Ornamental anchor at top.	1.00	3.00	12.00
16	**2 PERPERA**			
	25.7.1914. Brown. Like #15.	1.50	4.50	17.50

17	**5 PERPERA**	GOOD	FINE	XF
	25.7.1914. Red. Like #15.	2.00	5.00	20.00

18	**10 PERPERA**	GOOD	FINE	XF
	25.7.1914. Blue. Arms at upper l.	2.00	5.00	20.00
19	**20 PERPERA**			
	25.7.1914. Brown. Like #18.	4.00	10.00	35.00
20	**50 PERPERA**			
	25.7.1914. Red. Like #21.	8.00	30.00	85.00

		Good	Fine	XF
21	**100 Perpera** — 25.7.1914. Blue. Angels at top ctr., women seated holding cornucopias at bottom ctr.	12.50	45.00	110.00

Austrian Occupation - WW I

K.u.K. Militar Generalgouvernement

Kreiskommando, 1916-18

Military Government District Command

#9-13 and #15-21 all dated 25.7.1914. Ovpt: *K.u.K. MILITAR GENERALGOUVERNEMENT IN MONTENEGRO KREISKOMMANDO* (and place name) handstamped on both sides in black, red or violet.

Cetinje Branch

1916 ND First Provisional Issue

#M1-M5 width of *CETINJE* in ovpt. 11mm.

		Good	Fine	XF
M1	**5 Perpera** — ND(1916-old date 25.7.1914). Ovpt. on #9.	2.00	8.00	20.00

		Good	Fine	XF
M2	**10 Perpera** — ND(1916-old date 25.7.1914). Ovpt. on #10.	3.00	10.00	25.00
M3	**20 Perpera** — ND(1916-old date 25.7.1914). Ovpt. on #11.	3.00	10.00	25.00
M4	**50 Perpera** — ND(1916-old date 25.7.1914). Ovpt. on #12.	3.00	10.00	25.00
M5	**100 Perpera** — ND(1916-old date 25.7.1914). Ovpt. on #13.	6.00	20.00	50.00

1916 ND Second Provisional Issue

#M6-M12 width of *CETINJE* in ovpt. 11mm.

		Good	Fine	XF
M6	**1 Perper** — ND(1916-old date 25.7.1914). Ovpt. on #15.	2.00	5.00	10.00

		Good	Fine	XF
M7	**2 Perpera** — ND(1916-old date 25.7.1914). Ovpt. on #16.	2.00	5.00	10.00
M8	**5 Perpera** — ND(1916-old date 25.7.1914). Ovpt. on #17.	2.00	5.00	10.00
M9	**10 Perpera** — ND(1916-old date 25.7.1914). Ovpt. on #18.	3.00	9.00	18.00

		Good	Fine	XF
M10	**20 Perpera** — ND(1916-old date 25.7.1914). Ovpt. on #19.	3.50	10.00	20.00
M11	**50 Perpera** — ND(1916-old date 25.7.1914). Ovpt. on #20.	5.00	15.00	30.00
M12	**100 Perpera** — ND(1916-old date 25.7.1914). Ovpt. on #21.	7.00	20.00	40.00

1916 ND Third Provisional Issue

#M13-M17 width of *CETINJE* in ovpt. 16mm.

		Good	Fine	XF
M13	**5 Perpera** — ND(1916-old date 25.7.1914). Ovpt. on #9.	3.50	10.00	20.00

		Good	Fine	XF
M14	**10 Perpera** — ND(1916-old date 25.7.1914). Ovpt. on #10.	3.50	10.00	20.00
M15	**20 Perpera** — ND(1916-old date 25.7.1914). Ovpt. on #11.	4.00	12.00	25.00

		GOOD	FINE	XF
M16	**50 PERPERA** ND(1916-old date 25.7.1914). Ovpt. on #12.	5.00	15.00	30.00
M17	**100 PERPERA** ND(1916-old date 25.7.1914). Ovpt. on #13.	7.00	20.00	40.00

1916 ND FOURTH PROVISIONAL ISSUE
#M18-M24 width of *CETINJE* in ovpt. 16mm.

		GOOD	FINE	XF
M18	**1 PERPER** ND(1916-old date 25.7.1914). Ovpt. on #15.	2.00	5.00	10.00
M19	**2 PERPERA** ND(1916-old date 25.7.1914). Ovpt. on #16.	2.00	6.00	12.00
M20	**5 PERPERA** ND(1916-old date 25.7.1914). Ovpt. on #17.	3.00	9.00	18.00
M21	**10 PERPERA** ND(1916-old date 25.7.1914) Ovpt. on #18.	3.50	10.00	20.00
M22	**20 PERPERA** ND(1916-old date 25.7.1914). Ovpt. on #19.	4.00	12.00	25.00
M23	**50 PERPERA** ND(1916-old date 25.7.1914). Ovpt. on #20.	5.00	15.00	30.00
M24	**100 PERPERA** ND(1916-old date 25.7.1914). Ovpt. on #21.	7.00	20.00	40.00

IPEK BRANCH

1916 ND FIRST PROVISIONAL ISSUE

		GOOD	FINE	XF
M25	**5 PERPERA** ND(1916-old date 25.7.1914). Ovpt. on #9.	3.50	10.00	20.00
M26	**10 PERPERA** ND(1916-old date 25.7.1914). Ovpt. on #10.	5.00	15.00	30.00

		GOOD	FINE	XF
M27	**20 PERPERA** ND(1916-old date 25.7.1914). Ovpt. on #11.	7.00	20.00	40.00
M28	**50 PERPERA** ND(1916-old date 25.7.1914). Ovpt. on #12.	10.00	30.00	60.00
M29	**100 PERPERA** ND(1916-old date 25.7.1914). Ovpt. on #13.	12.00	35.00	70.00

1916 ND SECOND PROVISIONAL ISSUE

		GOOD	FINE	XF
M30	**1 PERPER** ND(1916-old date 25.7.1914). Ovpt. on #15.	2.00	6.00	12.00
M31	**2 PERPERA** ND(1916-old date 25.7.1914). Ovpt. on #16.	3.50	10.00	20.00
M32	**5 PERPERA** ND(1916-old date 25.7.1914). Ovpt. on #17.	5.00	15.00	30.00
M33	**10 PERPERA** ND(1916-old date 25.7.1914). Ovpt. on #18.	7.00	20.00	40.00
M34	**20 PERPERA** ND(1916-old date 25.7.1914). Ovpt. on #19.	10.00	25.00	50.00

		GOOD	FINE	XF
M35	**50 PERPERA** ND(1916-old date 25.7.1914). Ovpt. on #20.	12.00	30.00	60.00
M36	**100 PERPERA** ND(1916-old date 25.7.1914). Ovpt. on #21.	12.50	35.00	70.00

KOLASIN BRANCH

1916 ND FIRST PROVISIONAL ISSUE

		GOOD	FINE	XF
M37	**5 PERPERA** ND(1916-old date 25.7.1914). Ovpt. on #9.	4.00	12.00	25.00
M38	**10 PERPERA** ND(1916-old date 25.7.1914). Ovpt. on #10.	5.00	15.00	30.00
M39	**20 PERPERA** ND(1916-old date 25.7.1914). Ovpt. on #11.	10.00	25.00	50.00
M40	**50 PERPERA** ND(1916-old date 25.7.1914). Ovpt. on #12.	12.00	30.00	60.00

		GOOD	FINE	XF
M41	**100 PERPERA** ND(1916-old date 25.7.1914). Ovpt. on #13.	25.00	75.00	150.00

1916 ND SECOND PROVISIONAL ISSUE

		GOOD	FINE	XF
M42	**1 PERPER** ND(1916-old date 25.7.1914). Ovpt. on #15.	2.50	7.50	15.00
M43	**2 PERPERA** ND(1916-old date 25.7.1914). Ovpt. on #16.	4.00	12.00	25.00
M44	**5 PERPERA** ND(1916-old date 25.7.1914). Ovpt. on #17.	5.00	15.00	30.00
M45	**10 PERPERA** ND(1916-old date 25.7.1914). Ovpt. on #18.	6.00	17.50	35.00
M46	**20 PERPERA** ND(1916-old date 25.7.1914). Ovpt. on #19.	8.00	25.00	50.00
M47	**50 PERPERA** ND(1916-old date 25.7.1914). Ovpt. on #20.	12.00	35.00	70.00
M48	**100 PERPERA** ND(1916-old date 25.7.1914). Ovpt. on #21.	20.00	60.00	120.00

NIKSIC BRANCH

1916 ND FIRST PROVISIONAL ISSUE
#M49-M53 width of *NIKSIC* in ovpt. 11mm.

		GOOD	FINE	XF
M49	**5 PERPERA** ND(1916-old date 25.7.1914). Ovpt. on #9.	6.00	17.50	35.00
M50	**10 PERPERA** ND(1916-old date 25.7.1914). Ovpt. on #10.	12.00	35.00	70.00
M51	**20 PERPERA** ND(1916-old date 25.7.1914). Ovpt. on #11.	15.00	50.00	100.00
M52	**50 PERPERA** ND(1916-old date 25.7.1914). Ovpt. on #12.	20.00	60.00	120.00
M53	**100 PERPERA** ND(1916-old date 25.7.1914). Ovpt. on #13.	35.00	100.00	200.00

1916 ND SECOND PROVISIONAL ISSUE
#M54-M60 width of *NIKSIC* in ovpt. 11mm.

		GOOD	FINE	XF
M54	**1 PERPER** ND(1916-old date 25.7.1914). Ovpt. on #15.	3.50	10.00	20.00
M55	**2 PERPERA** ND(1916-old date 25.7.1914). Ovpt. on #16.	6.00	17.50	35.00

M56	**5 PERPERA** ND(1916-old date 25.7.1914). Ovpt. on #17.	6.00	17.50	35.00
M57	**10 PERPERA** ND(1916-old date 25.7.1914). Ovpt. on #18.	7.50	22.50	45.00
M58	**20 PERPERA** ND(1916-old date 25.7.1914. Ovpt. on #19.	10.00	30.00	60.00

M59	**50 PERPERA** ND(1916-old date 25.7.1914). Ovpt. on #20.	**GOOD** 12.50	**FINE** 37.50	**XF** 75.00

M60	**100 PERPERA** ND(1916-old date 25.7.1914). Ovpt. on #21.	**GOOD** 25.00	**FINE** 75.00	**XF** 150.00

1916 ND THIRD PROVISIONAL ISSUE
#M61-M65 width of *NIKSIC* in ovpt. 14mm.

M61	**5 PERPERA** ND(1916-old date 25.7.1914). Ovpt. on #9.	5.00	15.00	30.00
M62	**10 PERPERA** ND(1916-old date 25.7.1914). Ovpt. on #10.	7.50	22.50	45.00
M63	**20 PERPERA** ND(1916-old date 25.7.1914). Ovpt. on #11.	10.00	30.00	60.00
M64	**50 PERPERA** ND(1916-old date 25.7.1914). Ovpt. on #12.	12.50	37.50	75.00

M65	**100 PERPERA** ND(1916-old date 25.7.1914). Ovpt. on #13.	**GOOD** 25.00	**FINE** 75.00	**XF** 150.00

1916 ND FOURTH PROVISIONAL ISSUE
#M66-M72 width of *NIKSIC* in ovpt. 14mm.

M66	**1 PERPER** ND(1916-old date 25.7.1914). Ovpt. on #15.	4.00	12.00	25.00
M67	**2 PERPERA** ND(1916-old date 25.7.1914). Ovpt. on #16.	5.00	16.00	32.00
M68	**5 PERPERA** ND(1916-old date 25.7.1914). Ovpt. on #17.	5.00	16.00	32.00
M69	**10 PERPERA** ND(1916-old date 25.7.1914). Ovpt. on #18.	7.00	20.00	40.00

M70	**20 PERPERA** ND(1916-old date 25.7.1914). Ovpt. on #19.	8.00	22.50	45.00
M71	**50 PERPERA** ND(1916-old date 25.7.1914). Ovpt. on #20.	10.00	30.00	60.00
M72	**100 PERPERA** ND(1916-old date 25.7.1914). Ovpt. on #21.	15.00	50.00	100.00

PLEVLIE BRANCH

1916 ND FIRST PROVISIONAL ISSUE

M73	**5 PERPERA** ND(1916-old date 25.7.1914). Ovpt. on #9.	5.00	16.00	32.00
M74	**10 PERPERA** ND(1916-old date 25.7.1914). Ovpt. on #10.	7.50	22.50	45.00

M75	**20 PERPERA** ND(1916-old date 25.7.1914). Ovpt. on #11.	**GOOD** 10.00	**FINE** 30.00	**XF** 60.00

M76	**50 PERPERA** ND(1916-old date 25.7.1914). Ovpt. on #12.	**GOOD** 12.50	**FINE** 37.50	**XF** 75.00
M77	**100 PERPERA** ND(1916-old date 25.7.1914). Ovpt. on #13.	30.00	100.00	200.00

1916 ND SECOND PROVISIONAL ISSUE

M78	**1 PERPER** ND(1916-old date 25.7.1914). Ovpt. on #15.	5.00	15.00	30.00
M79	**2 PERPERA** ND(1916-old date 25.7.1914). Ovpt. on #16.	5.00	15.00	30.00
M80	**5 PERPERA** ND(1916-old date 25.7.1914). Ovpt. on #17.	5.00	15.00	30.00
M81	**10 PERPERA** ND(1916-old date 25.7.1914). Ovpt. on #18.	6.00	17.50	35.00
M82	**20 PERPERA** ND(1916-old date 25.7.1914). Ovpt. on #19.	7.50	22.50	45.00
M83	**50 PERPERA** ND(1916-old date 25.7.1914). Ovpt. on #20.	9.00	27.50	55.00

M84	**100 PERPERA** ND(1916-old date 25.7.1914). Ovpt. on #21.	**GOOD** 12.50	**FINE** 37.50	**XF** 75.00

PODGORICA BRANCH

1916 ND FIRST PROVISIONAL ISSUE
#M85-M89 width of *Podgorica* in ovpt 13mm.

			Good	Fine	XF
M85	**5 PERPERA** ND(1916-old date 25.7.1914). Ovpt. on #9.		7.50	22.50	45.00
M86	**10 PERPERA** ND(1916-old date 25.7.1914). Ovpt. on #10.		10.00	30.00	60.00
M87	**20 PERPERA** ND(1916-old date 25.7.1914). Ovpt. on #11.		12.50	37.50	75.00
M88	**50 PERPERA** ND(1916-old date 25.7.1914). Ovpt. on #12.		15.00	50.00	100.00
M89	**100 PERPERA** ND(1916-old date 25.7.1914). Ovpt. on #13.		30.00	100.00	200.00

1916 ND SECOND PROVISIONAL ISSUE
#M90-M96 width of *Podgorica* in ovpt. 13mm.

			Good	Fine	XF
M90	**1 PERPER** ND(1916-old date 25.7.1914). Ovpt. on #15.		4.00	12.50	25.00
M91	**2 PERPER** ND(1916-old date 25.7.1914). Ovpt. on #16.		5.00	15.00	30.00
M92	**5 PERPERA** ND(1916-old date 25.7.1914). Ovpt. on #17.		7.50	22.50	45.00
M93	**10 PERPERA** ND(1916-old date 25.7.1914). Ovpt. on #18.		7.50	22.50	45.00
M94	**20 PERPERA** ND(1916-old date 25.7.1914). Ovpt. on #19.		10.00	30.00	60.00
M95	**50 PERPERA** ND(1916-old date 25.7.1914). Ovpt. on #20.		12.50	37.50	75.00
M96	**100 PERPERA** ND(1916-old date 25.7.1914). Ovpt. on #21.		15.00	50.00	100.00

1916 ND THIRD PROVISIONAL ISSUE
#M97-M101 width of *PODGORICA* in ovpt. 13mm.

			Good	Fine	XF
M97	**5 PERPERA** ND(1916-old date 25.7.1914). Ovpt. on #9.		7.50	22.50	45.00
M98	**10 PERPERA** ND(1916-old date 25.7.1914). Ovpt. on #10.		7.50	22.50	45.00
M99	**20 PERPERA** ND(1916-old date 25.7.1914). Ovpt. on #11.		12.50	37.50	75.00
M100	**50 PERPERA** ND(1916-old date 25.7.1914). Ovpt. on #12.		15.00	50.00	100.00
M101	**100 PERPERA** ND(1916-old date 25.7.1914). Ovpt. on #13.		30.00	100.00	200.00

1916 ND FOURTH PROVISIONAL ISSUE
#M102-M108 width of *PODGORICA* in ovpt. 13mm.

M102	**1 PERPER** ND(1916-old date 25.7.1914). Ovpt. on #15.		7.50	22.50	45.00
M103	**2 PERPER** ND(1916-old date 25.7.1914). Ovpt. on #16.		9.00	27.50	55.00

			Good	Fine	XF
M104	**5 PERPERA** ND(1916-old date 25.7.1914). Ovpt. on #17.		12.50	37.50	75.00
M105	**10 PERPERA** ND(1916-old date 25.7.1914). Ovpt. on #18.		15.00	50.00	100.00
M106	**20 PERPERA** ND(1916-old date 25.7.1914). Ovpt. on #19.		25.00	75.00	150.00
M107	**50 PERPERA** ND(1916-old date 25.7.1914). Ovpt. on #20.		30.00	100.00	200.00
M108	**100 PERPERA** ND(1916-old date 25.7.1914). Ovpt. on #21.		35.00	125.00	250.00

1916 ND FIFTH PROVISIONAL ISSUE
#M109-M113 width of *PODGORICA* in ovpt. 17mm.

			Good	Fine	XF
M109	**5 PERPERA** ND(1916-old date 25.7.1914). Ovpt. on #9.		6.00	17.50	35.00
M110	**10 PERPERA** ND(1916-old date 25.7.1914). Ovpt. on #10.		7.50	22.50	45.00
M111	**20 PERPERA** ND(1916-old date 25.7.1914). Ovpt. on #11.		10.00	30.00	60.00
M112	**50 PERPERA** ND(1916-old date 25.7.1914). Ovpt. on #12.		7.50	22.50	45.00
M113	**100 PERPERA** ND(1916-old date 25.7.1914). Ovpt. on #13.	Good	Fine	XF
			12.50	37.50	75.00

1916 ND SIXTH PROVISIONAL ISSUE
#M114-M120 width of *PODGORICA* in ovpt. 17mm.

M114	**1 PERPER** ND(1916-old date 25.7.1914). Ovpt. on #15.		7.50	22.50	45.00
M115	**2 PERPER** ND(1916-old date 25.7.1914). Ovpt. on #16.		7.50	22.50	45.00
M116	**5 PERPERA** ND(1916-old date 25.7.1914). Ovpt. on #17.		7.50	22.50	45.00
M117	**10 PERPERA** ND(1916-old date 25.7.1914). Ovpt. on #18.		12.50	37.50	75.00
M118	**20 PERPERA** ND(1916-old date 25.7.1914). Ovpt. on #19.		15.00	50.00	100.00
M119	**50 PERPERA** ND(1916-old date 25.7.1914). Ovpt. on #20.		20.00	60.00	125.00
M120	**100 PERPERA** ND(1916-old date 25.7.1914). Ovpt. on #21.		25.00	75.00	150.00

STARI BAR BRANCH

1916 ND FIRST PROVISIONAL ISSUE
#M121-125 width of *STARI BAR* in ovpt 11mm.

M121	**5 PERPERA** ND(1916-old date 25.7.1914). Ovpt. on #9.		12.50	37.50	80.00
M122	**10 PERPERA** ND(1916-old date 25.7.1914). Ovpt. on #10.		20.00	60.00	130.00
M123	**20 PERPERA** ND(1916-old date 25.7.1914). Ovpt. on #11.		20.00	60.00	130.00
M124	**50 PERPERA** ND(1916-old date 25.7.1914). Ovpt. on #12.		25.00	75.00	175.00
M125	**100 PERPERA** ND(1916-old date 25.7.1914). Ovpt. on #13.		30.00	100.00	200.00

1916 ND SECOND PROVISIONAL ISSUE
#M126-M132 width of *STARI BAR* in ovpt. 11mm.

M126	**1 PERPER** ND(1916-old date 25.7.1914). Ovpt. on #15.		15.00	50.00	120.00
M127	**2 PERPER** ND(1916-old date 25.7.1914). Ovpt. on #16.		20.00	50.00	140.00
M128	**5 PERPERA** ND(1916-old date 25.7.1914). Ovpt. on #17.		25.00	75.00	160.00
M129	**10 PERPERA** ND(1916-old date 25.7.1914). Ovpt. on #18.		30.00	100.00	200.00
M130	**20 PERPERA** ND(1916-old date 25.7.1914). Ovpt. on #19.		30.00	100.00	200.00
M131	**50 PERPERA** ND(1916-old date 25.7.1914). Ovpt. on #20.		40.00	125.00	275.00
M132	**100 PERPERA** ND(1916-old date 25.7.1914). Ovpt. on #21.		50.00	150.00	350.00

1916 ND THIRD PROVISIONAL ISSUE
#M133-M137 width of *STARI BAR* in ovpt. 16mm.

M133	**5 PERPERA** ND(1916-old date 25.7.1914). Ovpt. on #9.		12.50	37.50	85.00
M134	**10 PERPERA** ND(1916-old date 25.7.1914). Ovpt. on #10.		25.00	75.00	170.00
M135	**20 PERPERA** ND(1916-old date 25.7.1914). Ovpt. on #11.		25.00	75.00	170.00
M136	**50 PERPERA** ND(1916-old date 25.7.1914). Ovpt. on #12.		40.00	125.00	250.00

		GOOD	**FINE**	**XF**
M137	**100 PERPERA** ND(1916-old date 25.7.1914). Ovpt. on #13.	50.00	150.00	350.00

1916 ND FOURTH PROVISIONAL ISSUE
#M138-M144 width of *STARI BAR* in ovpt. 16mm.

		GOOD	**FINE**	**XF**
M138	**1 PERPER** ND(1916-old date 25.7.1914). Ovpt. on #15.	7.50	22.50	50.00
M139	**2 PERPERA** ND(1916-old date 25.7.1914). Ovpt. on #16.	7.50	22.50	50.00
M140	**5 PERPERA** ND(1916-old date 25.7.1914). Ovpt. on #17.	7.50	22.50	50.00
M141	**10 PERPERA** ND(1916-old date 25.7.1914). Ovpt. on #18.	12.50	37.50	80.00
M142	**20 PERPERA** ND(1916-old date 25.7.1914). Ovpt. on #19.	15.00	50.00	120.00
M143	**50 PERPERA** ND(1916-old date 25.7.1914). Ovpt. on #20.	20.00	60.00	125.00
M144	**100 PERPERA** ND(1916-old date 25.7.1914). Ovpt. on #21.	25.00	75.00	150.00

BELGRAD BRANCH

1916 ND PROVISIONAL ISSUE

M145	**1 PERPER** ND(1916-old date 25.7.1914). Ovpt. on #15.	150.00	450.00	1000.
M146	**10 PERPERA** ND(1916-old date 25.7.1914). Ovpt. on #18.	150.00	450.00	1000.

STEUER-U. ZOLLAMT KOLASIN BRANCH

1916 ND PROVISIONAL ISSUE

		GOOD	**FINE**	**XF**
M147	**1 PERPER** ND(1916-old date 25.7.1914). Ovpt. on #1.	150.00	450.00	1000.

K.u.K. KREISKOMMANDO UNTERABTEILUNG

DISTRICT COMMAND SUBDIVISION

1916 ND PROVISIONAL ISSUE

M147A	**1 PERPER** ND(1916-old date 25.7.1914). Ovpt. w/o place name on #15.	150.00	450.00	1000.

K.u.K. MILITARVERWALTUNG

ARMY ADMINISTRATION, 1917-18

1917 CONVERTABLE VOUCHER ISSUE

		VG	**VF**	**UNC**
M148 (M149)	**1 PERPER = 50 MUNZPERPER = 5 HELLER** 5.7.1917. Blue-green on orange unpt.	7.00	20.00	55.00
M149 (M150)	**2 PERPERA = 1 MUNZPERPER = 1 KRONE** 5.7.1917. Violet on green unpt.	7.00	25.00	60.00

		VG	**VF**	**UNC**
M150 (M151)	**5 PERPERA = 2 MUNZPERPER 50 PARA =** **2 KRONEN 50 HELLER** 5.7.1917. Lilac on green unpt.	10.00	30.00	70.00

		VG	**VF**	**UNC**
M151 (M148)	**10 PERPERA = 5 MUNZPERPER = 5 KRONEN** 1.6.1917. Blue on brown unpt.	7.00	25.00	60.00

		VG	**VF**	**UNC**
M152	**20 PERPERA = 10 MUNZPERPER = 10 KRONEN** 20.11.1917. Red-brown on green unpt.	15.00	40.00	90.00

		VG	**VF**	**UNC**
M153	**50 PERPERA = 25 MUNZPERPER = 25 KRONEN** 20.11.1917. Lilac on green unpt.	25.00	50.00	135.00
M154	**100 PERPERA = 50 MUNZPERPER = 50 KRONEN** 20.11.1917. Blue on olive unpt.	30.00	60.00	160.00

726 MOROCCO

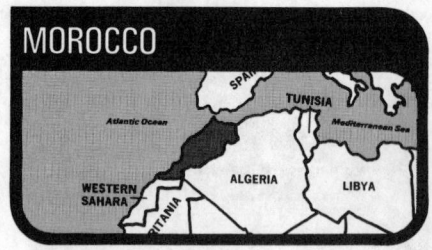

The Kingdom of Morocco situated on the northwest corner of Africa south of Spain, has an area of 172,413 sq. mi. (712,550 sq. km.) and a population of 25.7 million. Capital: Rabat. The economy is essentially agricultural. Phosphates, fresh and preserved vegetables, canned fish, and raw material are exported.

Morocco's strategic position at the gateway to western Europe has been the principal determinant of its violent, frequently unfortunate history.

Time and again the fertile plain between the rugged Atlas Mountains and the sea has echoed the battle's trumpet as Phoenicians, Romans, Vandals, Visigoths, Byzantine Greeks and Islamic Arabs successively conquered and occupied the land. Modern Morocco is a remnant of an early empire formed by the Arabs at the close of the 7th century which encompassed all of northwest Africa and most of the Iberian Peninsula. During the 17th and 18th centuries, while under the control of native dynasties, it was the headquarters of the famous Sale pirates. Morocco's strategic position involved it in the competition of 19th century European powers for political influence in Africa, and resulted in the division of Morocco into French and Spanish spheres of interest which were established as protectorates in 1912. Morocco became independent on March 2, 1956, after France agreed to end its protectorate. Spain signed similar agreements on April 7 of the same year.

* * * This section has been partially renumbered. * * *

RULERS:
Abd Al-Aziz, AH1311-1325/1894-1908AD
Hafiz, AH1325-1330/1908-1912AD
Yusuf, AH1330-1346/1912-1927AD
Muhammad V, AH1346-1380/1927-1961AD
Hassan II, AH1380- /1961- AD

MONETARY SYSTEM:
1 Dirham = 50 Mazunas
1 Rial = 10 Dirhams to 1921
1 Franc = 100 Centimes
1 Dirham = 100 Francs, 1921-1974
1 Dirham = 100 Santimat, 1974-
1 Riffan = 1 French Gold Franc = 10 British Pence

KINGDOM

BANQUE D'ETAT DU MAROC
Established April 7, 1906.

1910; 1917 ISSUE
#1 and 2 w/text: *PAYABLES A VUE AU PORTEUR.*

NOTE: Other denominations and issues may exist like Bons de Caisse (issue of 1919).

			GOOD	FINE	XF
1 (2)	**4 RIALS = 40 FRANCS** 2.7.1917; 6.7.1917; 9.7.1917. Salmon, ochre and blue. Tower at ctr.		200.00	500.00	1250.
2 (1)	**20 RIALS = 100 FRANCS** 31.2.1910; 15.7.1910; 18.7.1910. Violet, yellow and blue. Palm tree at ctr.		225.00	600.00	1500.

PROTECTORAT DE LA FRANCE AU MAROC

1919 EMERGENCY ISSUE

			GOOD	FINE	XF
4	**25 CENTIMES** Oct. 1919. Rose cardboard. Octagonal ovpt: *MAROC 25c.*				
	a. *Octobre* in date. W/or w/o series letters.		20.00	50.00	125.00
	b. OCTOBRE in date.		20.00	50.00	125.00
	c. *OCTOBRE* in date.		20.00	50.00	125.00
5	**50 CENTIMES** Oct. 1919. Orange cardboard. Octagonal ovpt: *MAROC 50c.*				
	a. *Octobre* in date. W/or w/o series letters.		20.00	50.00	125.00
	b. OCTOBRE in date.		20.00	50.00	125.00
	c. *OCTOBRE* in date.		20.00	50.00	125.00

			GOOD	FINE	XF
6	**1 FRANC** Oct. 1919. Yellow cardboard. Octagonal ovpt: *MAROC 1F.*				
	a. *Octobre* in date. W/or w/o series letters.		20.00	50.00	125.00
	b. OCTOBRE in date.		20.00	50.00	125.00
	c. *OCTOBRE* in date.		20.00	50.00	125.00

			GOOD	FINE	XF
7	**2 FRANCS** Oct. 1919. Green cardboard. Octagonal ovpt: *MAROC 2F.*				
	a. *Octobre* in date. Series A.		20.00	50.00	140.00
	b. OCTOBRE in date.		20.00	50.00	140.00
	c. *OCTOBRE* in date.		20.00	50.00	140.00

BANQUE D'ETAT DU MAROC (RESUMED)

STATE BANK OF MOROCCO
Established April 7, 1906

1920-24 ISSUE
#8 and 9 w/o text: *PAYABLES A VUE* on face. Sign. varieties.
#10 *Deleted.* See 23A.
#11-15 various dates and sign. varieties.
#12-14 w/text: *PAYABLES A VUE..*

			VG	VF	UNC
8	**5 FRANCS** ND (1921). Blue and green. W/title: *BANQUE D'ETAT DU MAROC* in 1 line on back. Serial # at bottom only. 2 sign. varieties. Printer: Chaix, Paris.		15.00	50.00	225.00

			VG	VF	UNC
9	**5 FRANCS** ND (1924). Blue and green. Similar to #8 but w/title: *BANQUE D'ETAT DU MAROC* in 2 lines on back. Serial # at top and bottom. 4 sign. varieties.		10.00	35.00	135.00

			VG	VF	UNC
11	**10 FRANCS** 1920-28. Blue and sepia.				
	a. Serial # only at bottom. 2 Sign. varieties. 4.5.1920-1.12.1923.		20.00	80.00	250.00
	b. Serial # at top printed over and below ornamentation. 3 sign. varieties. 15.5.1924-1.7.1928.		15.00	70.00	200.00
12	**20 FRANCS** 7.1.1920-17.4.1926. Gray, blue and sepia. Tower at ctr. Serial # at top in white fields (l. and r.) and bottom l. and r. in special blank fields. 3 sign. varieties		25.00	100.00	250.00
13	**50 FRANCS** 13.9.1920-8.8.1928. Blue-green and lt. brown. Design style similar to #11. Serial # at l. and r. at top printed over ornamentation, and bottom l. and r. 4 sign. varieties. 170 x 98mm.		50.00	130.00	375.00

14	**100 FRANCS**	VG	VF	UNC
	15.12.1919-1.9.1926. Red. Palm tree at ctr. 3 sign. varieties. Back red w/blue text.	100.00	350.00	750.00

18	**20 FRANCS**	VG	VF	UNC
	1929-45. Gray-blue and sepia. Tower at ctr. Like #12 but serial # at top in special blank field.			
	a. W/text: *PAYABLES A VUE AU PORTEUR.* 2 sign. varieties. 12.6.1929; 2.12.1931.	20.00	50.00	185.00
	b. W/o text: *PAYABLES A VUE.. ..* 3 sign. varieties. 6.3.1941; 14.11.1941; 9.11.1942; 1.3.1945.	3.00	12.50	70.00

19	**50 FRANCS**	VG	VF	UNC
	12.6.1929; 2.12.1931; 17.11.1932. Blue-green and lt. brown. Like #13 but serial # at top and bottom in blank field. 2 sign. varieties.	30.00	85.00	250.00

15	**500 FRANCS**	VG	VF	UNC
	1923-48. Brown, red and m/c. View of city of Fez.			
	a. W/text: *PAYABLES A VUE AU PORTEUR.* 5 sign. varieties. 1.10.1923-29.6.1937.	150.00	350.00	900.00
	b. W/o text: *PAYABLES A VUE.. ..* 3.5.1946-10.11.1948.	15.00	45.00	85.00
16 (22)	**1000 FRANCS** 1921-50. Green, blue and ochre. View of city. 5 sign. varieties.			
	a. 1.2.1921.	75.00	175.00	550.00
	b. 12.6.1929-27.9.1934.	45.00	140.00	485.00
	c. 13.1.1937-9.2.1950.	25.00	100.00	350.00

20	**100 FRANCS**	VG	VF	UNC
	1.7.1928-28.10.1947. M/c. Fortress (Kasbah) at ctr. 4 sign. varieties.	3.00	20.00	90.00

1936; 1938 ISSUE
#22 *Deleted.* See #16.

1928-29 ISSUES

21	**50 FRANCS**	VG	VF	UNC
	23.9.1936-2.12.1949. Green, blue and sepia. 4 sign. varieties.	3.00	20.00	90.00

17	**10 FRANCS**	VG	VF	UNC
	1929-42. Blue and sepia. Like #11 but serial # on top in blank field.			
	a. W/text: *PAYABLES A VUE AU PORTER.* 2 sign. varieties. 12.6.1929; 20.5.1931.	12.00	40.00	125.00
	b. W/o text: *PAYABLES A VUE.. ..* 6.3.1941; 25.9.1942.	1.50	7.50	45.00

23   5000 FRANCS

	VG	VF	UNC
1938-51. Brown and blue. Moroccan city overlooking the sea Wmk: Lion. 3 sign. varieties.			
a. 28.9.1938; 14.11.1941.	90.00	275.00	650.00
b. 9.11.1942.	80.00	250.00	600.00
c. 21.12.1945-19.4.1951.	70.00	225.00	550.00

1941 ISSUE

23A   5 FRANCS
(10)

	VG	VF	UNC
1922-41. Red, blue and sepia.			
a. W/text: *PAYABLES A VUE AU PORTEUR.* 1.8.1922 (issued 1941).	3.00	17.50	75.00
b. W/o text: *PAYABLES A VUE...* 24.7.1941; 27.7.1941; 14.11.1941.	1.00	3.50	30.00

1943 FIRST ISSUE

Notes printed in Morocco or the United States during World War II.

#29 and 31 *Deleted.*

24   5 FRANCS
(27)

	VG	VF	UNC
1.8.1943; 1.3.1944. Blue on yellow unpt. Printer: EAW.	.75	2.50	7.00

25   10 FRANCS
(24)

	VG	VF	UNC
1.5.1943; 1.8.1943; 1.3.1944. Black on green unpt. 5 pointed star. Back blue on red unpt. Printer: EAW.	1.00	4.50	17.50

26   50 FRANCS
(29)

	VG	VF	UNC
1.8.1943; 1.3.1944. Black and lt. brown. Fortress at l., sailing ship at r. Back green on yellow unpt. Printer: EAW.	3.00	15.00	75.00

27   100 FRANCS
(25)

	VG	VF	UNC
1.5.1943; 1.8.1943; 1.3.1944. M/c. Gate in city wall. Printer: EAW.	6.00	20.00	80.00

28   1000 FRANCS
(26)

	VG	VF	UNC
1.5.1943; 1.8.1943; 1.3.1944. Brown. Printer: ABNC.	75.00	200.00	600.00

32   5000 FRANCS

	VG	VF	UNC
1.8.1943. Green. Printer: ABNC.	500.00	1250.	—

1943 SECOND ISSUE

#33, 39 and 40 printer: Imp. Réunies, Casablanca.

#34-38 deleted.

33   5 FRANCS

	VG	VF	UNC
14.9.1943. Yellow and blue.	.75	2.00	7.00

39	**20 FRANCS** ND (1943). Red-brown and blue. Bldgs. on hillside.	**VG** 2.00	**VF** 15.00	**UNC** 85.00
40	**50 FRANCS** ND (1943). Green on orange unpt. Similar to #26. 170 x 106mm.	3.00	17.50	90.00

EMPIRE CHERIFIEN, PROTECTORAT DE LA RÉPUBLIQUE FRANÇAISE

1944 EMERGENCY ISSUE

41	**50 CENTIMES** 6.4.1944. Red. Fortress on back.	**VG** .75	**VF** 2.00	**UNC** 12.00

42	**1 FRANC** 6.4.1944. Green. City of Fes on back.	**VG** .75	**VF** 2.50	**UNC** 14.00

43	**2 FRANCS** 6.4.1944. Violet-brown. House on the shore (La Menara) on back.	**VG** 1.00	**VF** 3.50	**UNC** 16.00

BANQUE D'ETAT DU MAROC - POST WW II

1948-51 ISSUES

44	**50 FRANCS** 2.12.1949. Green, blue and sepia. Like #21 but reduced size.	**VG** 1.00	**VF** 5.00	**UNC** 20.00

45	**100 FRANCS** 10.11.1948-22.12.1952. M/c. Like #20 but reduced size.	**VG** 1.50	**VF** 6.00	**UNC** 30.00

45A	**500 FRANCS** 29.5.1951. Brown on m/c unpt. Monument in front of State Bank bldg. at ctr. r. City view on back. Wmk: Male lion's head. Printer: TDLR (w/o imprint). Specimen.	**VG** —	**VF** —	**UNC** 850.00

45B	**500 FRANCS** 29.5.1951. City view at ctr. r. Printer: TDLR (w/o imprint). Specimen.	**VG** —	**VF** —	**UNC** 850.00

46	**500 FRANCS** 18.7.1949-14.2.1958. M/c. Doorway of house w/Moroccan city in background. 2 sign. varieties.	**VG** 2.50	**VF** 17.50	**UNC** 100.00

46A	**1000 FRANCS** 29.1.1951. Green. Bldg. at ctr. Printer: TDLR (w/o imprint). Specimen.	**VG** —	**VF** —	**UNC** 900.00

47	**1000 FRANCS** 19.4.1951-7.8.1958. M/c. Mosque, city and hills in background. 2 sign. varieties.	**VG** 5.00	**VF** 35.00	**UNC** 180.00

48	5000 FRANCS	VG	VF	UNC
	ND. Red-brown. Bldg. at ctr. Printer: TDLR (w/o imprint). Specimen.	—	—	1000.

52	100 DIRHAMS ON 10,000 FRANCS	VG	VF	UNC
	ND (-old dates 2.8.1954; 28.4.1955). Ovpt. on #50.	20.00	80.00	325.00

REGIONAL

STATE BANK OF THE RIFF

1923 ISSUE
Issued during the Berber uprising under Abd el-Krim, 1921-26. #R3 *Deleted*.

R1	1 RIFFAN		VF	UNC
	10.10.1923. Red. Horsemen at l. and r. Uniface.	—	60.00	90.00
R2	5 RIFFANS			
	10.10.1923. Lt. green. Like #R1.	—	75.00	120.00

49	5000 FRANCS	VG	VF	UNC
	2.4.1953; 23.7.1953; 7.8.1958. M/c. Mosque w/hills in background.	25.00	140.00	425.00
50	10,000 FRANCS			
	13.8.1953-28.4.1955. M/c. Aerial view of Casablanca.	30.00	165.00	485.00

1959 PROVISIONAL DIRHAM ISSUE

51	50 DIRHAMS ON 5000 FRANCS	VG	VF	UNC
	ND (-old date 23.7.1953). Ovpt. on #49.	25.00	90.00	385.00

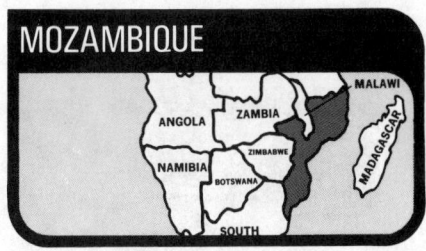

MOZAMBIQUE

The People's Republic of Mozambique, a former overseas province of Portugal stretching for 1,430 miles (2,301 km.) along the southeast coast of Africa, has an area of 309,494 sq. mi. (783,030 sq. km.) and a population of 16.1 million, 99 percent of whom are native Africans of the Bantu tribes. Capital: Maputo. Agriculture is the chief industry. Cashew nuts, cotton, sugar, copra and tea are exported.

Vasco da Gama explored all the coast of Mozambique in 1498 and found Arab trading posts already along the coast. Portuguese settlement dates from the establishment of the trading post of Mozambique in 1505. Within five years Portugal absorbed all the former Arab sultanates along the east African coast. The area was organized as a colony in 1907 and became an overseas province in 1952. In Sept. of 1974, after more than a decade of guerrilla warfare with the forces of the Mozambique Liberation Front, Portugal agreed to the independence of Mozambique, effective June 25, 1975.

* * * This section has been partially renumbered. * * *

RULERS:
Portuguese to 1975

MONETARY SYSTEM:
Pound Sterling = Libra Esterlina (pound sterling)
1 Mil Reis = 1000 Reis to 1907
1 Escudo = 100 Centavos, 1907-1975

STEAMSHIP SEAL VARIETIES:

Type I LORENÇO / Type II MARQUES LISBOA / Type III C, C, A.

C, C, A = Colonias, Commercio, Agricultura.

3 types of BANCO NACIONAL ULTRAMARINO seals are found on bank notes issued for Lourenço Marques.

PORTUGUESE INFLUENCE

BANCO NACIONAL ULTRAMARINO

1877 ISSUE
#1-8 Lourenço Marques.

		GOOD	FINE	XF
1	**5000 REIS** 2.4.1877. Note of Loanda w/ovpt. for Mozambique.	—	Rare	—
2	**20,000 REIS** 2.4.1877. Note of Loanda w/ovpt. for Mozambique.	—	Rare	—

1878 ISSUE

		GOOD	FINE	XF
3	**1000 REIS** 29.1.1878.	—	—	—
4	**2000 REIS** 29.1.1878. Green. Steamship at ctr.	—	—	—
5	**2500 REIS** 29.1.1878.	—	—	—
6	**5000 REIS** 29.1.1878.	—	—	—
7	**10,000 REIS** 29.1.1878.	—	—	—

		GOOD	FINE	XF
8	**20,000 REIS** 29.1.1878.	—	—	—

1884; 1897 ISSUES
#9-15 w/text...Succursal em Mozambique...

9	**1000 REIS** 28.1.1884; 2.1.1897. Green.	—	—	—
10	**2000 REIS** 2.1.1897.	—	—	—
11	**2500 REIS** 2.1.1897.	—	—	—
12	**5000 REIS** 2.1.1897.	—	—	—
13	**10,000 REIS** 2.1.1897.	—	—	—
14	**20,000 REIS** 2.1.1897.	—	—	—
15	**50,000 REIS** 2.1.1897.	—	—	—

1897 SECOND ISSUE
#16-29 W/text: ...em Lourenço Marques...

16	**1000 REIS** 2.1.1897. Standing Indian at l., ship at ctr.	—	—	—
17	**2000 REIS** 2.1.1897.	—	—	—

		GOOD	FINE	XF
18	**2500 REIS** 2.1.1897. Steamship at l., field at ctr., woman standing at ctr. r.	—	—	—
19	**5000 REIS** 2.1.1897.	—	—	—
20	**10,000 REIS** 2.1.1897.	—	—	—
21	**20,000 REIS** 2.1.1897.	—	—	—
22	**50,000 REIS** 2.1.1897.	—	—	—

1906 ISSUE

23	**1000 REIS** 20.2.1906. Lt. brown. Standing Indian at l., ship at ctr. Uniface.	—	—	—
24	**2000 REIS** 20.2.1906.	—	—	—
25	**2500 REIS** 20.2.1906.	—	—	—
26	**5000 REIS** 20.2.1906. Green.	—	—	—
27	**10,000 REIS** 20.2.1906.	—	—	—
28	**20,000 REIS** 20.2.1906.	—	—	—
29	**50,000 REIS** 20.2.1906. Brown.	—	—	—

1907 ISSUE

52	**10 CENTAVOS** 1.1.1907. Red-brown. Sailing ship.	—	—	—

1908 ISSUE
#30-31 portr. Vasco da Gama at l., sailing ships in passage Cape of Boa Esperanca in 1498 at r. W/ovpt: *LOURENÇO MARQUES*. Printer: BWC.

30	**2500 REIS** 2.1.1908. Black on green and m/c unpt. Red Steamship Seal Type I.	—	—	—

31	**5000 REIS**	GOOD	FINE	XF
	2.1.1908. Black on green and m/c unpt. Red Steamship Seal Type I.	—	—	—

1909 ISSUE

#34-43 portr. Vasco da Gama at I., sailing ships in passage Cape of Boa Esperanca in 1498. Printer: BWC.
#40-43 embarkation of Vasco da Gama in 1497 at r.

32	**1000 REIS**			
	1.3.1909. Black on green and yellow unpt. Red Steamship Seal Type I. Printer: BWC.	50.00	150.00	400.00

33	**1000 REIS**	GOOD	FINE	XF
	1.3.1900. Black on green and yellow unpt. Red Steamship Seal Type III. Printer: BWC.	35.00	125.00	300.00
34	**2500 REIS**			
	1.3.1909. Black on blue and yellow unpt. Red Steamship Seal Type I.	100.00	200.00	400.00

35	**2500 REIS**	GOOD	FINE	XF
	1.3.1909. Black on blue and yellow unpt. Red Steamship Seal Type III.	100.00	200.00	400.00
36	**5000 REIS**			
	1.3.1909. Black on m/c unpt. Red Steamship Seal Type I.	125.00	250.00	500.00
37	**5000 REIS**			
	1.3.1909. Black on m/c unpt. Red Steamship Seal Type III.	125.00	250.00	500.00
38	**10,000 REIS**			
	1.3.1909. Black on blue and yellow unpt. Red Steamship Seal Type I.	175.00	350.00	700.00
39	**10,000 REIS**			
	1.3.1909. Black on blue and yellow unpt. Red Steamship Seal Type III.	175.00	350.00	700.00
40	**20,000 REIS**			
	1.3.1909. Black on tan and pale blue unpt. Red Steamship Seal Type III.	350.00	750.00	1500.
41	**20,000 REIS**			
	1.3.1909. Black on tan and pale blue unpt. Red Steamship Seal Type III.	350.00	750.00	1500.
42	**50,000 REIS**			
	1.3.1909. Black on brown, tan and pale blue unpt. Red Steamship Seal Type I.	500.00	1000.	2000.
43	**50,000 REIS**			
	1.3.1909. Black on brown, tan and pale blue unpt. Red Steamship Seal Type III.	500.00	1000.	2000.

1909 LIBRA ESTERLINA ISSUE

#44-49 printer: BWC.

44	**1 LIBRA**			
	1.3.1909. Black on orange and green unpt. Back brown. Red Steamship Seal Type I.	75.00	—	—
45	**1 LIBRA**			
	1.3.1909. Black on orange and green unpt. Back brown. Red Steamship Seal Type III.	50.00	—	—
46	**5 LIBRAS**			
	1.3.1909. Black on pink, blue and yellow unpt. Red Steamship Seal Type I.	100.00	—	—
47	**10 LIBRAS**			
	1.3.1909. Black on pale green, pale blue and red unpt. Red Steamship Seal Type I.	125.00	—	—
48	**20 LIBRAS**			
	1.3.1909. Brown on m/c unpt. Red Steamship Seal Type I.	150.00	—	—
49	**20 LIBRAS**			
	1.3.1909. Brown on m/c unpt. Red Steamship Seal Type III.	150.00	—	—

1914 FIRST ISSUE

#53-55 woman seated, sailing ships in background at ctr. on back. Printer: BWC.

53	**10 CENTAVOS**	GOOD	FINE	XF
	5.11.1914. Purple on m/c unpt. Counterfoil at I. Dk. green Steamship Seal Type II. Back deep blue.	2.50	10.00	25.00
54 (56)	**20 CENTAVOS**			
	5.11.1914. Blue on m/c unpt. Counterfoil at I. Red Steamship Seal Type II. Back purple.	4.50	15.00	40.00

55 (59)	**50 CENTAVOS**	GOOD	FINE	XF
	5.11.1914. Green on m/c unpt. Counterfoil at I. Purple Steamship Seal Type II. Back brown.	5.00	15.00	40.00

1914 SECOND ISSUE

#56-58 woman seated, sailing ships in background at ctr. on back. Printer: BWC.

56 (54)	**10 CENTAVOS**	GOOD	FINE	XF
	5.11.1914. Purple on m/c unpt. Counterfoil at I. Dk. green Steamship Seal Type III. Back deep blue.	2.00	8.00	25.00
57	**20 CENTAVOS**			
	5.11.1914. Blue on m/c unpt. Counterfoil at I. Red Steamship Seal Type III. Back purple.	3.00	10.00	40.00
58 (60)	**50 CENTAVOS**			
	5.11.1914. Green on m/c unpt. Counterfoil at I. Purple Steamship Seal Type III. Back brown.	4.00	12.00	40.00

1914 THIRD ISSUE

#59-61 woman seated, sailing ships in background at ctr. on back. Printer: BWC.

59 (55)	**10 CENTAVOS**			
	5.11.1914. Purple on m/c unpt. W/o counterfoil at I. Steamship Seal Type III. Back deep blue.	1.50	6.00	20.00
60 (58)	**20 CENTAVOS**			
	5.11.1914. Blue on m/c unpt. W/o counterfoil at I. Red Steamship Seal Type III. Back purple.	2.00	8.00	25.00
61	**50 CENTAVOS**			
	5.11.1914. Green on m/c unpt. W/o counterfoil at I. Purple Steamship Seal Type III. Back brown.	3.50	10.00	40.00

1920 EMERGENCY ISSUE

#62-65 offset printed on low-grade yellowish paper in Oporto.

62	**10 CENTAVOS**	**GOOD**	**FINE**	**XF**
	1.1.1920. Red. Back violet. Sailing ships at l. and r.	100.00	180.00	250.00
63	**20 CENTAVOS**			
	1.1.1920. Green. Allegorical figures at l. and r. Back blue.	60.00	100.00	200.00
64	**50 CENTAVOS**			
	1.1.1920. Blue. Allegorical figures at l. and r.	80.00	150.00	250.00
65	**50 ESCUDOS**			
	1.1.1920. Dk. blue on pale green unpt. Arms at upper ctr. Back brown	500.00	1000.	2000.
	on pale yellow-orange; palm trees at ctr.			

1921 ISSUE

#66-73 Provincia de Mozambique. F. de Oliveira Chamico at l. Seated allegorical woman and ships on back. Sign. varieties.

#66, 68-72 printer: BWC.

66	**1 ESCUDO**			
	1.1.1921. Green on m/c unpt.			
	a. *Decreto.*	5.00	20.00	80.00
	b. W/o *Decreto.*	5.00	20.00	80.00
67	**2 1/2 ESCUDOS**			
	1.1.1921. Blue on m/c unpt. Printer: TDLR.			
	a. *Decreto.*	10.00	30.00	100.00
	b. W/o *Decreto.*	10.00	30.00	100.00

68	**5 ESCUDOS**	**GOOD**	**FINE**	**XF**
	1.1.1921. Brown on m/c unpt.			
	a. *Decreto.*	15.00	50.00	135.00
	b. W/o *Decreto.*	15.00	50.00	135.00
69	**10 ESCUDOS**			
	1.1.1921. Brown-violet on m/c unpt.			
	a. *Decreto.*	20.00	75.00	200.00
	b. W/o *Decreto.*	20.00	75.00	200.00
70	**20 ESCUDOS**			
	1.1.1921. Blue-green on m/c unpt.			
	a. *Decreto.*	50.00	150.00	450.00
	b. W/o *Decreto.*	50.00	150.00	450.00
71	**50 ESCUDOS**			
	1.1.1921. Red-brown on m/c unpt.			
	a. *Decreto.*	125.00	325.00	750.00
	b. W/o *Decreto.*	125.00	325.00	750.00
72	**100 ESCUDOS**			
	1.1.1921. Blue-green on m/c unpt.			
	a. *Decreto.*	180.00	450.00	1000.
	b. W/o *Decreto.*	180.00	450.00	1000.

1929 PROVISIONAL ISSUE

Decreto No. 17,154 de 26 de Julho de 1929

72A	**100 ESCUDOS ON 1 LIBRA**	**GOOD**	**FINE**	**XF**
(50)	ND (1929-old date 1.3.1909). Black ovpt. on #45	100.00	450.00	—

72B	**1000 ESCUDOS ON 20 LIBRAS**	**GOOD**	**FINE**	**XF**
(51)	ND (1929-old date 1.3.1909). Black ovpt. on #49.	250.00	600.00	

1932 ISSUE

73	**500 ESCUDOS**			
	25.8.1932. Black on m/c unpt. Unique.	—	Rare	—

1937; 1938 ISSUE

#74-79 A. Ennes at l.

74	**20 ESCUDOS**	**GOOD**	**FINE**	**XF**
	6.4.1937. Blue. Printer: BWC.	7.50	30.00	125.00
75	**50 ESCUDOS**			
	11.1.1938. Gray-olive. Printer: BWC.	12.00	40.00	200.00
76	**100 ESCUDOS**			
	11.1.1938. Purple.	20.00	75.00	260.00

1941 FIRST ISSUE

77	**100 ESCUDOS**			
	27.3.1941. Purple.	20.00	70.00	230.00
78	**500 ESCUDOS**			
	27.3.1941. Lilac.	35.00	125.00	425.00
79	**1000 ESCUDOS**			
	27.3.1941. Brown.	120.00	300.00	850.00

1941 EMERGENCY SECOND ISSUE

80	**50 CENTAVOS**	**VG**	**VF**	**UNC**
	1.9.1941. Green on cream paper. Arms at l. Back purple; arms at ctr.	4.00	15.00	45.00
	Printer: Imprensa Nac. de Moçambique.			

1941 THIRD ISSUE

#81-84 portr. F. de Oliveira Chamico at l., steamship seal at r. Like #66-69 but diff. sign. titles. Sign. varieties.

81	**1 ESCUDO**	**VG**	**VF**	**UNC**
	1.9.1941. Green. Printer: BWC.	3.00	12.00	45.00

82	2 1/2 ESCUDOS	VG	VF	UNC
	1.9.1941. Blue. Printer: TDLR.	6.00	25.00	90.00

83	5 ESCUDOS	VG	VF	UNC
	1.9.1941. Dk. brown. Printer: BWC.			
a.	Issued note.	10.00	50.00	125.00
s.	Specimen, punched hole cancelled. W/o serial #.	—	—	175.00

84	10 ESCUDOS	VG	VF	UNC
	1.9.1941. Lt. brown. Printer: BWC.	12.00	60.00	150.00

1941 FOURTH ISSUE
#85-88 A. Ennes at l., steamship seal at r.

85	20 ESCUDOS			
	1.11.1941. Black on blue and m/c unpt. Printer: BWC.	7.50	25.00	95.00

86	50 ESCUDOS	VG	VF	UNC
	1.11.1941. Black on brown and m/c unpt. Printer: BWC.	10.00	35.00	150.00
87	500 ESCUDOS			
	1.11.1941. Black on lilac and m/c unpt.	40.00	125.00	425.00
88	1000 ESCUDOS			
	1.11.1941. Black on brown and m/c unpt.	125.00	250.00	825.00

1943 ISSUE
#89-91 A. Ennes at l., steamship seal at r.
#89 and 90 printer: BWC.

89	5 ESCUDOS			
(90)	15.4.1943. Black on green and m/c unpt.	3.50	12.50	55.00
90	10 ESCUDOS			
(91)	15.4.1943. Black on brown-violet and m/c unpt.	7.50	20.00	75.00

91	100 ESCUDOS	VG	VF	UNC
(89)	27.1.1943. Black on orange and m/c unpt.	15.00	50.00	170.00

1944; 1945 ISSUE
#92-99 portr. A. Ennes at l., Steamship Ship Seal at r.

92	1 ESCUDO	VG	VF	UNC
	23.5.1944. Black on olive and m/c unpt.	1.00	5.00	22.50

93	2 1/2 ESCUDOS	VG	VF	UNC
	23.5.1944. Blue.	2.00	8.00	45.00
94	5 ESCUDOS			
	29.11.1945. Green on m/c unpt.	3.00	10.00	45.00
95	10 ESCUDOS			
	29.11.1945. Brown on m/c unpt.	7.00	15.00	80.00
96	20 ESCUDOS			
	29.11.1945. Blue on m/c unpt.	10.00	25.00	100.00

96A	50 ESCUDOS			
	29.11.1945. Brown on m/c unpt. Printer: BWC.	10.00	35.00	145.00
97	100 ESCUDOS	VG	VF	UNC
	29.11.1945. Orange on m/c unpt.	15.00	45.00	175.00
98	500 ESCUDOS			
	29.11.1945. Lilac on m/c unpt.	35.00	85.00	300.00

99 **1000 ESCUDOS**

		VG	VF	UNC
	1945; 1947. Blue on m/c unpt.			
	a. 29.11.1945.	90.00	200.00	600.00
	b. 27.3.1947.	50.00	100.00	425.00

1947 ISSUE
#100 and 101 portr. A. Ennes at l., steamship seal at r.

100 **100 ESCUDOS**

		VG	VF	UNC
	27.3.1947. Orange on m/c unpt.	15.00	35.00	125.00

101 **500 ESCUDOS**

		VG	VF	UNC
	27.3.1947. Lilac on m/c unpt.	30.00	75.00	265.00

1950; 1953 ISSUE
#102 and 103 ornate church doorway at ctr. on back. Wmk: Arms. Printer: TDLR.
#104 and 105 printer: BWC.

102 **50 ESCUDOS**

		VG	VF	UNC
	16.2.1950. Black on m/c unpt. E. Costa at r., w/text: *COLONIA PORTUGUESA* belwo bank name.	7.50	15.00	50.00

103 **100 ESCUDOS**

		VG	VF	UNC
	16.2.1950. Orange on m/c unpt. A. de Ornelas Evasconcelos at r., w/text: *COLONIA PORTUGUESA* below bank name.	10.00	25.00	80.00

104 **500 ESCUDOS**

		VG	VF	UNC
	31.7.1953. Brown-violet on m/c unpt. C. Xavier at r.			
	a. Issued note.	17.50	30.00	85.00
	s. Specimen, punched hole cancelled.	—	—	75.00

105 **1000 ESCUDOS**

		VG	VF	UNC
	31.7.1953. Blue on m/c unpt. Mousinho de Albuquerque at r.			
	a. Issued note.	15.00	40.00	125.00
	s. Specimen, punched hole cancelled.	—	—	100.00

1958 ISSUE
#106 and 107 wmk: Arms. Printer: TDLR.

106 **50 ESCUDOS**

		VG	VF	UNC
	24.7.1958. Black on m/c. E. Costa at r. Like # 102 but w/o text: *COLONIA PORTUGUESA* below bank name; w/o printing over wmk. at l. Back green.	1.00	2.50	8.00

107 **100 ESCUDOS**

		VG	VF	UNC
	24.7.1958. Like #103 but w/o text: *COLONIA PORTUGUESA* below bank name; w/o printing over wmk. at l.	2.50	7.50	25.00

108 **500 ESCUDOS**

		VG	VF	UNC
	24.7.1958. Brown-violet. C. Xavier at r.	15.00	35.00	85.00

REGIONAL

BANCO DA BEIRA

1919 LIBRA ISSUES
#R1-R33 values are primarily for cancelled notes. Most of those except for #R2-R4 w/o cancellations are worth at least double the valuations shown. Cancellations: *CANCELADO* in lg. letters or *PAGO 30.*(or other day) 11.1942 in small letters and #.
#R1-R9 printer: BWC.

R1 **10 CENTAVOS**

		GOOD	FINE	XF
	15.9.1919. Green and yellow.	2.00	6.00	15.00

R2 **20 CENTAVOS**

		GOOD	FINE	XF
	15.9.1919. Green.			
	a. Issued note.	2.00	6.00	15.00
	b. Cancelled.	2.00	6.00	15.00

R3 **50 CENTAVOS**

		GOOD	FINE	XF
	15.9.1919. Black on orange-brown and m/c unpt. Back blue.			
	a. Lg. hand sign. at l.	3.00	8.00	17.50
	b. Sm. printed sign. at l.	2.00	6.00	15.00
	c. Cancelled.	3.00	8.00	17.50

R4 **50 CENTAVOS**

		GOOD	FINE	XF
	15.9.1919. Brown. *PRATA* deep blue in frame at top ctr.			
	a. Issued note.	2.00	6.00	15.00
	b. Cancelled.	2.00	6.00	15.00

R5 **1/2 LIBRA**

		GOOD	FINE	XF
	15.9.1919. Red on m/c unpt.	2.00	6.00	15.00

R6	1 LIBRA	GOOD	FINE	XF
	15.9.1919. Blue on m/c unpt.			
	a. Lg. hand sign. at l.	2.00	6.00	15.00
	b. Sm. printed sign. at l.	2.00	6.00	15.00

R7	1 LIBRA	GOOD	FINE	XF
	15.9.1919. Blue o m/c unpt. *OURO* in frame at bottom ctr.	2.00	6.00	15.00

R8	5 LIBRAS	GOOD	FINE	XF
	15.9.1919. Blue on m/c unpt.			
	a. Lg. hand sign. at l.	4.00	12.00	30.00
	b. Sm. printed sign. at l.	4.00	12.00	30.00
R9	5 LIBRAS			
	15.9.1919. Blue. *OURO* in frame at bottom ctr.	5.00	12.00	30.00
R10	10 LIBRAS			
	15.9.1919.	15.00	50.00	150.00
R11	20 LIBRAS			
	15.9.1919.	25.00	75.00	200.00

1919 ESCUDO ISSUE

R11A	1 ESCUDO	GOOD	FINE	XF
	15.9.1919. Brown. Printer: BWC.	5.00	12.00	30.00

1921 ISSUE

R12	10 LIBRAS			
	1.2.1921.	25.00	100.00	200.00
R13	20 LIBRAS			
	1.2.1921.	25.00	100.00	200.00

COMPANHIA DE MOÇAMBIQUE, BEIRA

ND PROVISIONAL LIBRA ISSUE

#R14-R23 ovpt. new issuer name in rectanglar frame.

R14	10 CENTAVOS			
	ND (-old date 15.9.1919). Ovpt. on #R1.	2.00	6.00	20.00
R15	20 CENTAVOS			
	ND (-old date 15.9.1919). Ovpt. on #R2.	2.00	6.00	20.00
R16	50 CENTAVOS			
	ND (-old date 15.9.1919). Ovpt. on #R3.	2.00	6.00	20.00

R17	50 CENTAVOS	GOOD	FINE	XF
	ND (-old date 15.9.1919). Ovpt. on #R4.	2.00	6.00	20.00
R18	1/2 LIBRA			
	ND (-old date 15.9.1919). Ovpt. on #R5.	2.00	6.00	20.00
R19	1 LIBRA			
	ND (-old date 15.9.1919). Ovpt. on #R6.			
	a. Lg. hand sign. at l.	2.00	6.00	20.00
	b. Sm. printed sign. at l.	2.00	6.00	20.00

R20	1 LIBRA	GOOD	FINE	XF
	ND (-old date 15.9.1919). Ovpt. on #R7.	3.00	8.00	20.00
R21	5 LIBRAS			
	ND (-old date 15.9.1919). Ovpt. on #R8.	4.00	15.00	40.00
R21A	5 LIBRAS			
	ND (-old date 15.9.1919). Ovpt. on #R9.	4.00	15.00	40.00
R22	10 LIBRAS			
	ND (-old date 1.2.1921). Ovpt. on #R12.	25.00	100.00	200.00
R23	20 LIBRAS			
	ND (-old date 1.2.1921). Ovpt. on #R13.	25.00	100.00	200.00

ND PROVISIONAL ESCUDO ISSUE

R23A (R21B)	1 ESCUDO			
	ND (-old date 15.9.1919). Ovpt. on #R11A.	4.00	15.00	40.00

1930 REGULAR ISSUE

R24	1 LIBRA	GOOD	FINE	XF
	1.11.1930. Blue on m/c unpt. Printr: BWC.	2.00	6.00	15.00

1931 ISSUE

R25 (R26)	10 CENTAVOS			
	1.10.1931. Green.	2.00	6.00	15.00

			GOOD	FINE	XF
R26 (R27)	**50 CENTAVOS** 1.10.1931. Sepia. Printer: BWC.		2.00	6.00	15.00
R27 (R25)	**1/2 LIBRA** 1.9.1931.		2.00	6.00	15.00

1933 ISSUE
#R28 and R29 printer: BWC.

			GOOD	FINE	XF
R28	**10 CENTAVOS** 20.10.1933. Green.		2.00	6.00	15.00

			GOOD	FINE	XF
R29	**20 CENTAVOS** 25.11.1933. Blue.		2.00	6.00	12.00

1934 ISSUE

			GOOD	FINE	XF
R30 (R31)	**1/2 LIBRA** 15.3.1934. Red.		2.00	6.00	15.00

			GOOD	FINE	XF
R31 (R32)	**1 LIBRA** 15.3.1934. Blue.		2.00	6.00	15.00
R32 (R30)	**5 LIBRAS** 15.1.1934. Blue.		3.00	15.00	30.00

1937 ISSUE

			GOOD	FINE	XF
R33	**1 ESCUDO** 12.5.1937. Violet.		2.00	6.00	15.00

NEPAL 737

The Kingdom of Nepal, the world's only Hindu kingdom, is a landlocked country located in central Asia along the southern slopes of the Himalayan Mountains. It has an area of 56,136 sq. mi. (140,797 sq. km.) and a population of 19.4 million. Capital: Kathmandu. Nepal has substantial deposits of coal, copper, iron and cobalt but they are largely unexploited. Agriculture is the principal economic activity. Livestock, rice, timber and jute are exported.

Prithvi Narayan Shah, ruler of the principality of Gurkha, formed Nepal from a number of independent mountain states in the latter half of the 18th century. After his death a period of political instability ensued which lasted until the 1840's when the Rana family reduced the monarch to a figurehead and established itself as hereditary Prime Ministers. A popular revolution (1950-51) toppled the Rana family and reconstituted the power in the throne. In 1959 King Mahendra declared Nepal a constitutional monarchy. A new constitution promulgated in 1962 instituted a system of panchayat (village council) democracy from the village to the national levels.

RULERS:
Tribhuvana Vira Vikrama Shahi Deva, 1911-1950; 1951-1955
Jnanendra Vira Vikrama Shahi Deva, 1950-1951
Mahendra Vira Vikrama Shahi Deva, 1955-1972
Birendra Bir Bikram Shahi Deva, 1972-

MONETARY SYSTEM:
1 Rupee = 100 Paisa

HEADING VARIETIES

Type I: नेपाल सर्कार   Type II: नेपाल मरकार

NOTE: Issues in the Mohru System have reference to Rupees in English on the notes. The difference is in the Nepalese designation of the value.

For those notes in Mohru the first character at the left appears thus: म

When the Nepalese designation changes to Rupees, this character appears thus: रू

Lines where either of these appear are in the lower center on the face, or on the back. Both will never appear on the same note. All notes from the second issue of Mahendra to the present are in rupees.

SIGNATURE VARIETIES

1	Janaph Raja	जनफ राज	5	Laxminath Gautam	
2	Bharana Raja	भरतराज	6	Besh Bahadur Thapa	
3	Narendra Raja	नरेन्द्रराज	7	Prhadimhalal Rajbhandari	
4	Himalaya Shamsher		8	Yadavnath Panta	

KINGDOM

GOVERNMENT OF NEPAL

1951 ND FIRST ISSUE
#2-4 portr. Kg. Tribhuvana Vira Vikrama w/plumed crown at r. Type I heading.

		VG	VF	UNC
1	**1 MOHRU** ND (1951). Blue and brown. Coin at r. w/date VS2008 (1951). Back w/coin at l., mountains at ctr. Sign. 2; 3.	1.00	2.00	6.00

		VG	VF	UNC
2	**5 MOHRU** ND (1951). Purple and m/c. Tiger on back. Sign. 1; 2.	3.00	10.00	30.00

3	10 MOHRU	VG	VF	UNC
	ND (1951). Purple and m/c. Arms on back. Sign. 2.	6.00	18.50	55.00

10	10 MOHRU	VG	VF	UNC
	ND (1956). Dk. brown and red. Temple at ctr. Back brown and gold; arms at ctr. Sign. 4; 5.	2.00	6.50	20.00

4	100 MOHRU	VG	VF	UNC
	ND (1951). Dk. green and m/c. Rhinoceros on back.			
	a. Sign. 1.	30.00	75.00	225.00
	b. Sign. 2.	28.00	57.50	175.00

1951 ND SECOND ISSUE
#5-7 Type II heading.

5	5 MOHRU			
	ND (1951). Purple and m/c. Like #2. Sign. 3.	2.00	6.00	18.00
6	10 MOHRU			
	ND (1951). Purple and m/c. Like #3. Sign. 3.	2.75	8.00	25.00
7	100 MOHRU			
	ND (1951). Dk. green and m/c. Like #4. Sign. 3.	13.50	40.00	120.00

STATE BANK OF NEPAL

1956 ND MOHRU ISSUE
#9-11 portr. Kg. Mahendra Vira Vikrama in civilian clothes at l.

11	100 MOHRU	VG	VF	UNC
	ND (1956). Green and brown. Temple at Lalitpur at ctr. Back green on brown unpt.; rhinoceros. Sign. 4; 5.	7.50	22.50	65.00

1956 ND RUPEE ISSUE
#12-15 like previous issue. Denominations in Nepalese language changed from "Mohru" to "Rupees" on both face and back.

8	1 MOHRU	VG	VF	UNC
	ND (1956). Violet and olive. Coin at l. w/date VS2013 (1956). Back lilac and green. Sign 4.	.75	1.50	2.50

12	1 RUPEE	VG	VF	UNC
	ND (1956). Violet and olive. Coin at l., temple at ctr. Sign. 8.	.20	.85	3.50

9	5 MOHRU	VG	VF	UNC
	ND (1956). Violet and aqua. Stupa at ctr. Back violet; Himalayas. Sign. 4; 5.	1.50	5.00	12.00

13	5 RUPEES	VG	VF	UNC
	ND (1956). Violet and aqua. Stupa at ctr. Himalayas on back. Sign. 5; 6; 7; 8.	.40	1.65	5.00

14   10 RUPEES
ND (1956). Dk. brown and red. Temple at ctr. Arms at ctr. on back.
Sign. 5; 6; 7; 8.

	VG	VF	UNC
	.65	2.75	8.00

15   100 RUPEES
ND (1956). Green and brown. Temple at Lalitpor at ctr. Rhinoceros on back. Sign. 5; 6; 7; 8.

	VG	VF	UNC
	2.75	10.00	35.00

NETHERLANDS

The Kingdom of the Netherlands, a country of western Europe fronting on the North Sea and bordered by Belgium and Germany, has an area of 15,770 sq. mi. (40,844 sq. km.) and a population of 15.1 million. Capital: Amsterdam, but the seat of government is at The Hague. The economy is based on dairy farming and a variety of industrial activities. Chemicals, yarns and fabrics, and meat products are exported.

After being a part of Charlemagne's empire in the 8th and 9th centuries, the Netherlands came under the control of Burgundy and the Austrian Hapsburgs, and finally was subjected to Spanish domination in the 16th century. Lead by William of Orange, the Dutch revolted against Spain in 1568 the seven northern provinces formed the Union of Utrecht and declared their independence in 1581, becoming the Republic of the United Netherlands. In the following century, the 'Golden Age' of Dutch history, the Netherlands became a great sea and colonial power, a patron of the arts and a refuge for the persecuted. In 1814, all the provinces of Holland and Belgium were merged into the Kingdom of the United Netherlands under William I. The Belgians withdrew in 1830 to form their own Kingdom, the last substantial change in the configuration of European Netherlands. German forces invaded in 1940 and the royal family soon fled with cargos of wealth to England where a government in exile was formed. German High Commissioner, Arthur Seyss-Inquart, was placed in command until 1945 and the arrival of Allied military forces.

* * * This section has been partially renumbered. * * *

RULERS:
William I, 1815-1840
William II, 1840-1849
William III, 1849-1890
Wilhelmina I, 1890-1948
Juliana I, 1948-1981
Beatrix, 1981-

MONETARY SYSTEM:
1 Gulden = 100 Cents
1 Rijksdaalder = 2 1/2 Gulden

KONINKRIJK - KINGDOM

DE NEDERLANDSCHE BANK

NETHERLANDS BANK

1814 ISSUE

		GOOD	FINE	XF
A2	**25 GULDEN** 1814-38. Rose.	—	Rare	—
A3	**40 GULDEN** 1814-38. Rose.	—	Rare	—
A4	**60 GULDEN** 1814-38. Rose.	—	Rare	—
A5	**80 GULDEN** 1814-25. Rose.	—	Rare	—
A6	**100 GULDEN** 1814-38. Rose.	—	Rare	—
A7	**200 GULDEN** 1814-38. Rose.	—	Rare	—
A8	**300 GULDEN** 1814-38. Rose.	—	Rare	—
A9	**500 GULDEN** 1814-38. Rose.	—	Rare	—
A10	**1000 GULDEN** 1814-38. Rose. Earlier notes w/value written, later notes w/value printed.	—	Rare	—

KONINKRIJK DER NEDERLANDEN

MUNTBILJETTEN - STATE NOTES

LAW OF 18.12.1845
#A11-A15 wmk: *RIJKS MUNT*. Uniface.

A11	**5 GULDEN** 1.1.1846. Red.	—	Rare	—
A12	**10 GULDEN** 1.1.1846. Brown.	—	Rare	—

A13	**20 GULDEN**	GOOD	FINE	XF
	1.1.1846. Green.	—	Rare	—

A14	**100 GULDEN**	GOOD	FINE	XF
	1.1.1846. Blue.	—	Rare	—
A15	**500 GULDEN**			
	1.1.1846. Yellow.	—	Rare	—

LAW OF 17.9.1849
#A16-A18 various printed or handwritten dates in 1849. #A20 - 3 various date and sign. varieties.

A16	**10 GULDEN**	GOOD	FINE	XF
	15.10.1849. Blue.	—	Rare	—
A17	**100 GULDEN**			
	1849. Red on gray unpt.	—	Rare	—
A18	**500 GULDEN**			
	1849. Brown on blue unpt.	—	Rare	—
A19	**1000 GULDEN**			
	1849. Green on red unpt.	—	Rare	—

1852 ISSUE
#A20, various date and sign. varieties.

A20	**10 GULDEN**	GOOD	FINE	XF
	1852-78. Lt. blue. allegorical figures on borders, arms at upper ctr.	—	Rare	—

1878 ISSUE
#1, various date and sign. varieties.

1	**10 GULDEN**	GOOD	FINE	XF
	1878-94. Lt. brown. Arms at upper ctr., ornate border.	—	Rare	—

1884-94 ISSUE
#2 and 3, various date and sign. varieties.

2	**10 GULDEN**	GOOD	FINE	XF
	1894-98. Brown. Standing woman and lion at l., portr. Qn. Wilhelmina as child at r.	—	Rare	—
3	**50 GULDEN**			
	1884-1914. Blue. Standing women and lion at l. similar to #2. Portr. Kg. William III at r.	—	Rare	—

1898 ISSUE
#3A, various date and sign. varieties.

3A (2A)	**10 GULDEN**	GOOD	FINE	XF
	1898-1914. Similar to #2 but older portr. Qn. Wilhelmina at r.	—	Rare	—

ZILVERBONNEN - SILVER NOTES

1914 ISSUE

4	**1 GULDEN**	GOOD	FINE	XF
	7.8.1914. Brown. Value *1* at ctr.			
	a. Issued note.	15.00	60.00	150.00
	p. Proof.	—	Unc	30.00

5	**2 1/2 GULDEN**	GOOD	FINE	XF
	7.8.1914. Blue on green unpt. Value *2.50* at ctr. thick and thin paper.			
	a. Issued note.	50.00	150.00	350.00
	p. Proof.	—	Unc	50.00

6	**5 GULDEN**	GOOD	FINE	XF
	7.8.1914. Green.			
	a. Issued note.	70.00	225.00	500.00
	p. Proof.	—	Unc	75.00

1915 ISSUE

		GOOD	FINE	XF
7	**2 1/2 GULDEN** 30.3.1915. Blue. Value *2.50* at ctr. and at the 4 corners.	30.00	100.00	300.00

1916 ISSUE

		GOOD	FINE	XF
8 (9)	**1 GULDEN** 1.5.1916. Brown. Value *1* at ctr. and at the 4 corners.	12.00	50.00	125.00
9 (8)	**2 1/2 GULDEN** 31.3.1916. Blue. Like #7.	30.00	100.00	300.00

1917 ISSUE

10 (11)	**1 GULDEN** 1.11.1917. Brown. Like #8.	12.00	50.00	125.00
11 (10)	**2 1/2 GULDEN** 1.8.1917. Blue. Like #7.	20.00	80.00	250.00

1918 FIRST ISSUE

		GOOD	FINE	XF
12	**2 1/2 GULDEN** 1.7.1918. Blue on gray and yellow unpt. Value *2.50* at l., at ctr. and upper and lower r.	10.00	40.00	125.00

1918 SECOND ISSUE

13	**1 GULDEN** 1.10.1918. Brown. Like #8.	12.00	50.00	125.00
14	**2 1/2 GULDEN** 1.10.1918. Like #12.	10.00	40.00	125.00

1920 ISSUE

		GOOD	FINE	XF
15	**1 GULDEN** 1.2.1920. Brown on lt. green unpt. Qn. Wilhelmina at l.	5.00	25.00	100.00
16	**2 1/2 GULDEN** 1.10.1920. Like #12.	6.00	30.00	125.00

1922 ISSUES

17	**2 1/2 GULDEN** 1.5.1922. Like #12.			
	a. Issued note.	6.00	30.00	125.00
	x. Counterfeit w/date: 1.10.1922.	6.00	30.00	125.00

		GOOD	FINE	XF
18	**2 1/2 GULDEN** 1.12.1922. Like #12.	6.00	30.00	125.00

1923 ISSUE

		GOOD	FINE	XF
19	**2 1/2 GULDEN** 1.10.1923. Face like #12. Back w/o unpt. in inner rectangle.			
	a. Issued note.	6.00	30.00	125.00
	p. Proof.	20.00		

1927 ISSUE

20	**2 1/2 GULDEN** 1.10.1927. Like #19.	6.00	25.00	100.00

DE NEDERLANDSCHE BANK

NETHERLANDS BANK

1904-11 "OLD STYLE" ISSUE

#21-27 various date and sign. varieties.
#21-23 arms w/caduceus and lion at top ctr.
#24-27 portr. Minerva at top ctr.

		GOOD	FINE	XF
21	**25 GULDEN** 27.9.1904-7.12.1921. Black on orange unpt. 7 sign. varieties. Uniface.	150.00	450.00	750.00

		GOOD	FINE	XF
22	**40 GULDEN** 6.6.1910; 11.7.1921; 13.9.1921; 11.12.1922. Black on green unpt. 6 sign. varieties.	300.00	800.00	1500.

23   60 GULDEN
11.8.1910-1.9.1924. Black on lilac-brown unpt. 6 sign. varieties.

GOOD	FINE	XF
300.00	800.00	1500.

24   100 GULDEN
1.3.1911; 17.2.1919; 2.1.1920; 13.10.1921. Black. Back blue. 4 sign. varieties.

GOOD	FINE	XF
300.00	750.00	1750.

25   200 GULDEN
18.10.1910; 2.7.1921. Black. Back lt. brown. 3 sign. varieties.

500.00	1250.	2250.

26   300 GULDEN
15.2.1909; 3.1.1921. Black Back lt. brown. 3 sign. varieties.

500.00	1250.	2250.

27   1000 GULDEN
3.10.1910; 22.5.1916. Black and blue. Back red. 4 sign. varieties.

—	Rare	—

1914 "OLD STYLE" ISSUE
#32-33 portr. Minerva at top ctr.

28   10 GULDEN
1.8.1914. Red on green unpt. W/o vignette. Back blue.

GOOD	FINE	XF
—	Rare	—

29   25 GULDEN
1.8.1914. Red on green unpt. Like #28.

GOOD	FINE	XF
—	Rare	—

30   40 GULDEN
1.8.1914. Green on lt. green unpt. Like #28.

GOOD	FINE	XF
—	Rare	—

31   60 GULDEN
1.8.1914. Brown on green unpt. Like #28.

GOOD	FINE	XF
—	Rare	—

32   100 GULDEN
1.8.1914. Black on rose unpt.

GOOD	FINE	XF
—	Rare	—

32A   200 GULDEN
1.8.1914. Black on orange unpt.

GOOD	FINE	XF
—	Rare	—

32B   300 GULDEN
1.8.1914. Black on green unpt.

GOOD	FINE	XF
—	Rare	—

33	1000 GULDEN	GOOD	FINE	XF
	1.8.1914. Black on blue unpt.	—	Rare	—

1906 "NEW STYLE" ISSUE

34	10 GULDEN			
	18.6.1906; 24.9.1913; 18.3.1914; 29.6.1916; 20.10.1920-30.11.1920. Blue. Allegorical figures of Labor at l., and Welfare at r. *AMSTERDAM* and serial # on face. 4 sign varieties. Back brown and green.	200.00	500.00	800.00

1919-23 "NEW STYLE" ISSUE
#39-42 woman seated at l.

35	10 GULDEN	GOOD	FINE	XF
	7.7.1921-16.5.1923. Like #34 but *AMSTERDAM* and serial # on back.	12.00	40.00	100.00
36	25 GULDEN			
	1921. Red-orange. Mercury seated at l., portr. William of Orange at top ctr., galleon at r. Bank on back. Sign. handwritten. Thick or thin paper.			
	a. *AMSTERDAM* in date 17mm wide; serial # prefix letters extra bold. 26.9.1921; 30.9.1921.	75.00	175.00	450.00
	b. *AMSTERDAM* in date 19mm wide; serial # prefix letters in 1 or 2 lines. 9.8.1921; 15.8.1921.	50.00	125.00	350.00

37 (39)	40 GULDEN	GOOD	FINE	XF
	1.2.1923; 12.2.1923; 15.2.1923. Green. Mercury seated at l., Prince Maurits at top ctr., galleon at r.	350.00	750.00	1750.

38 (40)	60 GULDEN	GOOD	FINE	XF
	9.4.1923. Brown-violet. Mercury seated at l., Prince Frederik Hendrik at top ctr., galleon at r.	300.00	650.00	1250.

39 (41)	100 GULDEN	GOOD	FINE	XF
	1922-28. Blue.			
	a. Prefix letter and serial # 4mm. W/o serial # on back. 23.1.1922; 4.2.1922.	30.00	120.00	350.00
	b. Prefix letter and serial # 4mm. Serial # and text on back. *Hij die biljetten...* 10.9.1924; 15.9.1924.	25.00	100.00	300.00
	c. Prefix letter and serial # 4mm. Serial # and text on back: *Het Namaken...* 12.3.1926.	20.00	75.00	200.00
	d. Prefix letter and serial # 3mm. Serial # and text on back: *Het Namaken...* 11.2.1927; 4.12.1928; 7.12.1928; 8.12.1928.	20.00	75.00	200.00

40 (42)	200 GULDEN	GOOD	FINE	XF
	1.12.1922; 3.1.1925; 8.4.1926. Red-brown.	300.00	850.00	1750.

41 (43)	300 GULDEN	GOOD	FINE	XF
	2.12.1922; 9.4.1926; 19.2.1927. Green.	300.00	850.00	.1750.
42 (44)	1000 GULDEN			
	23.6.1919-5.3.1921. Sepia.	225.00	500.00	1000.

1924-29 ISSUES

43 (46)	10 GULDEN	GOOD	FINE	XF
	1924-32. Dk. blue. Zeeland farmer's wife at lower ctr. Back purple and brown.			
	a. Black sign. w/text: *Het in vooraad...* on back. 29.3.1924; 10.7.1924.	5.00	15.00	50.00
	b. Black sign. w/text: *Het namaken...* Prefix letter before serial # on back. (2 types). 1.3.1924 - 8.4.1930.	4.00	12.00	45.00
	c. Blue sign. w/text: *Het namaken...* Prefix letter before serial # at lower l. and at upper r. on back. 2 sign. varieties. Vissering/Delprat or Trip/Delprat. 20.4.1930; 11.9.1930; 2.1.1931; 7.4.1931; 1.8.1931; 8.4.1932.	4.00	12.00	45.00
	d. Blue sign. w/text: *Wetboek van Strafrecht...* on back. 21.3.1932; 6.5.1932.	4.00	12.00	45.00

48	**1000 GULDEN**	GOOD	FINE	XF
(45)	1.10.1926-19.9.1938. Dk. green and violet. Like #39. Serial # over serial letter prefix unpt. on back. 3 sign. varieties (Delprat/Vissering; Delprat/Trip; Westermann/Trip).	20.00	60.00	200.00

1930-33 ISSUE

44	**20 GULDEN**	GOOD	FINE	XF
(47)	2.1.1926-25.11.1936. Black on olive unpt. Sailor at the helm at bottom ctr. r. 2 sign. varieties. (Delprat/Vissering or Westermann/Trip).	10.00	30.00	125.00

49	**10 GULDEN**	GOOD	FINE	XF
(52)	1.6.1933-18.9.1939. Dk. blue. Portr. old man wearing a cap at r. by Rembrandt. Back green, brown and m/c.	1.50	6.00	22.50

45	**25 GULDEN**	GOOD	FINE	XF
(37)	15.7.1929-28.6.1930. Red. Like #36 but w/o picture on back. Sign. printed.	12.00	40.00	100.00
46	**25 GULDEN**			
(38)	27.7.1927-3.8.1928. Blue. Like #45. Sign. handwritten.	20.00	50.00	125.00

50	**25 GULDEN**	GOOD	FINE	XF
(51)	1.6.1931-19.3.1941. Red and m/c. Bank president W.C. Mees at lower r. 2 sign. varieties.	2.00	8.00	40.00

47	**50 GULDEN**	GOOD	FINE	XF
(48)	18.4.1929-18.5.1931. Gray-blue. Helmeted Minerva at r. (Wisdom), black or blue sign.	8.00	25.00	100.00

51	**100 GULDEN**	GOOD	FINE	XF
(49)	1930-44. Brown and m/c. Portr. women at top l. ctr. and upper r. (reflected issues).			
	a. Date at ctr. on back. 4 sign. varieties (Delprat/Vissering; Delprat/Trip; Westermann/Trip; Robertson/Rost van Tonningen) 1.10.1930; 9.3.1931; 28.11.1936; 1.12.1936.	5.00	20.00	80.00
	b. As a. 13.3.1939-28.5.1941.	3.75	12.00	60.00
	c. Date at upper l. and at lower r. on back. 12.1.1942-7.3.1944.	2.50	8.00	40.00

52	**500 GULDEN**	GOOD	FINE	XF
(50)	1.12.1930; 2.12.1930; 4.12.1930. Gray-blue and m/c. Portr. Stadhouder, Kg. William III at top ctr. r. Galleon in unpt.	100.00	350.00	950.00

1939-41 ISSUES

53	**10 GULDEN**	GOOD	FINE	XF
(56)	1.6.1940-2.1.1941. Brown and dk. green. Qn. Emma at r.	4.00	15.00	45.00

54	**20 GULDEN**	GOOD	FINE	XF
(53)	20.7.1939-19.3.1941. Violet and olive. Qn. Emma at r. "Men-O-War" of the 17th century at l. Schreiers Tower l. and St. Nicolaas Church r. on back. Both in Amsterdam.	4.00	12.00	50.00

55	**20 GULDEN**	GOOD	FINE	XF
(54)	19.3.1941. Ovpt: *AMSTERDAM* new date w/bar obliterating old date on #54.	40.00	100.00	225.00

1940; 1941 ISSUE

56	**10 GULDEN**		GOOD	FINE	XF
(55)	1940-42. Blue and green. Young girl at r. by P.J. Moreelsen..				
	a. Wmk: Head of an old man. 19.7. 1940-18.3.1941.		1.25	4.00	17.50
	b. Wmk: Grapes. 10.4.1941-19.9.1942.		1.00	3.00	12.50

57	**25 GULDEN**	GOOD	FINE	XF
	20.5.1940. Olive-brown. Young girl at r. by P.J. Moreelsen. Wide margin unprinted at l. Geometric designs on back.	5.00	20.00	65.00

58	**50 GULDEN**	GOOD	FINE	XF
(59)	7.1.1941-6.2.1943. Dk. brown and m/c. Woman at l. and at r. by J. Steen. "Winter Landscape" by I. van Ostade on back.	6.00	20.00	50.00

1943 ISSUE

59 (60)	**10 GULDEN** 4.1.1943-21.4.1944. Blue, violet-blue and m/c. Man w/hat painting by Rembrandt.	**GOOD** 1.00	**FINE** 3.00	**XF** 10.00

60 (58)	**25 GULDEN** 4.10.1943-13.4.1944. Red-brown. Like #57 but *DNB* in frame in l. margin.	**GOOD** 2.00	**FINE** 7.00	**XF** 25.00

KONINKRIJK DER NEDERLANDEN

ZILVERBONNEN - SILVER NOTES

1938 ISSUE

61	**1 GULDEN** 1.10.1938. Brown. Similar to #15.	**VG** .25	**VF** .50	**UNC** 5.00

62	**2 1/2 GULDEN** 1.10.1938. Blue. Similar to #12.	**VG** .30	**VF** .75	**UNC** 7.00

1944 ISSUE

63	**5 GULDEN** 16.10.1944. Green. Large *5's* at l. and r. 3 serial # varieties.	3.00	8.00	40.00

MUNTBILJETTEN - STATE NOTES

1943 ISSUE

#64-69 portr. Qn. Wilhelmina at ctr. Back orange; arms at ctr. Printer: ABNC.

64	**1 GULDEN** 4.2.1943. Red.	.75	4.00	15.00

65	**2 1/2 GULDEN** 4.2.1943. Green.	**VG** 2.00	**VF** 7.00	**UNC** 30.00
66	**10 GULDEN** 4.2.1943. Blue.	7.00	40.00	80.00

67	**25 GULDEN** 4.2.1943. Olive.	**VG** 100.00	**VF** 275.00	**UNC** 550.00

68	**50 GULDEN** 4.2.1943. Brown.	**VG** 150.00	**VF** 375.00	**UNC** 750.00

69	**100 GULDEN** 4.2.1943. Black.	**VG** 95.00	**VF** 200.00	**UNC** 350.00

1945 ISSUE
#70-71 printer: TDLR.

70	**1 GULDEN** 18.5.1945. Brown on lt. green unpt. Portr. Qn. Wilhelmina at ctr. 2 serial # varieties.	**VG** .50	**VF** 3.00	**UNC** 15.00
71	**2 1/2 GULDEN** 18.5.1945. Blue and violet. Like #70. 3 serial # varieties.	.50	4.00	20.00

1949 ISSUE
#72-73 printer: JEZ.

72	**1 GULDEN** 8.8.1949. Brown on lt. blue unpt. Qn. Juliana at l.	**VG** .25	**VF** 1.00	**UNC** 8.00
73	**2 1/2 GULDEN** 8.8.1949. Blue. Like #72.	.25	1.50	10.00

DE NEDERLANDSCHE BANK

1945 ISSUE
#75-76 printer: TDLR.

74   10 GULDEN

	VG	VF	UNC
7.5.1945. Blue and brown-violet. Stylized arms w/lion at bottom ctr. 2 serial # varieties.	6.00	30.00	85.00

75   10 GULDEN

	VG	VF	UNC
7.5.1945. Blue. Kg. William I at r. Back red and olive; colliery. 2 serial # varieties.			
a. Date at r. 1788-1843 (incorrect).	12.00	30.00	85.00
b. Date at r. 1772-1843.	10.00	20.00	60.00

76   20 GULDEN

	VG	VF	UNC
7.5.1945. Brown. Stadhouder/Kg. William III at r. Back green; Moerdyk bridge. 2 serial # varieties.	15.00	35.00	80.00

77   25 GULDEN

	VG	VF	UNC
7.5.1945. Maroon and tan. Young girl at r. 2 serial # varieties.	15.00	55.00	110.00

78   50 GULDEN

	VG	VF	UNC
7.5.1945. Brown. Prince William II as a youth at r.	25.00	65.00	135.00

79   100 GULDEN

	VG	VF	UNC
7.5.1945. Brown. W/o vignette.	70.00	150.00	300.00

80   1000 GULDEN

	VG	VF	UNC
7.5.1945. Blue-black on orange and green unpt. William the Silent at r. Back blue and gray; dike at ctr. Printer: W&S.	200.00	500.00	1000.

1947 ISSUE

81   25 GULDEN

	VG	VF	UNC
19.3.1947. Red and green. young girl wearing flowers in her hair at r.	20.00	50.00	135.00

82   100 GULDEN

	VG	VF	UNC
9.7.1947. Brown. Woman at r. Back m/c.	30.00	70.00	150.00

1949 ISSUE

#84-100 printer: JEZ.

83	10 GULDEN	VG	VF	UNC
	4.3.1949. Blue. Face like #75b. Landscape w/windmill (after a painting by J. I. Ruisdael) on back. Printer: TDLR.	7.00	15.00	55.00

84	25 GULDEN	VG	VF	UNC
	1.7.1949. Brownish orange. Kg. Solomon at r.	8.00	20.00	70.00

1953; 1956 ISSUE

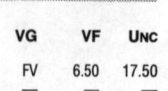

85	10 GULDEN	VG	VF	UNC
(86)	23.3.1953. Blue, brown and green. H. de Groot. at r.			
	a. Issued note.	FV	6.50	17.50
	s. Specimen.	—	—	—

86	20 GULDEN	VG	VF	UNC
(88)	8.11.1955. Green and lilac. Boerhaave at r. Serpent at l. on back.			
	a. Issued note.	5.00	17.50	60.00
	s. Specimen.	—	—	—
87	25 GULDEN			
	10.4.1955. Red, orange and brown. C. Huygens at r.			
	a. Issued note.	FV	15.00	35.00
	s. Specimen.	—	—	—

88	100 GULDEN	VG	VF	UNC
(85)	2.2.1953. Dk. brown. Erasmus at r. Back red-brown; stylized bird at l.			
	a. Issued note.	FV	75.00	175.00
	s. Specimen.	—	—	—

89	1000 GULDEN	VG	VF	UNC
	15.7.1956. Brown and green. Rembrandt at r. Hand w/brush and palette on back.			
	a. Issued note.	FV	700.00	850.00
	s. Specimen.	—	—	—

OCCUPATION OF GERMANY, POST -WW II

MINISTERIE VAN OORLOG

#M1-M3, issued for the Royal Dutch Army stationed in occupied Germany. Printer: JEZ.

ND ISSUES

M1	1 GULDEN			
	ND. Brown. Like #M3.	75.00	150.00	275.00
M2	5 GULDEN	VG	VF	UNC
	ND. Green. Like #M3.	100.00	200.00	350.00

[Ministerie van Oorlog 25 Gulden note image]

M3	25 GULDEN	VG	VF	UNC
	ND. Violet.	125.00	250.00	425.00

NETHERLANDS ANTILLES

The Netherlands Antilles, part of the Netherlands realm, comprise two groups of islands in the West Indies: Bonaire and Curacao near the Venezuelan coast; and St. Eustatius, Saba and the southern part of St. Martin (St. Maarten) southeast of Puerto Rico. The island group has an area of 385 sq. mi. (961 sq. km.) and a population of 191,000. Capital: Willemstad. Chief industries are the refining of crude oil, and tourism Petroleum products and phosphates are exported.

On Dec. 15, 1954, the Netherlands Antilles were given complete domestic autonomy and granted equality within the Kingdom with Surinam and the Netherlands.

The island of Aruba gained independence in 1986.

RULERS:
Dutch

MONETARY SYSTEM:
1 Gulden = 100 Cents

DUTCH INFLUENCE

WEST-INDISCHE BANK

1800's ISSUE

		GOOD	FINE	XF
A5	50 GULDEN	—	—	—
	ND. (1800's) Uniface. Remainder w/o sign.			

BANK VAN DE NEDERLANDSE ANTILLEN

1955 ISSUE
MUNTBILJETTEN - Currency Notes

		VG	VF	UNC
14	2 1/2 GULDEN			
	1955; 1964. Blue. Ship in dry dock at ctr. Crowned supported arms at ctr. on back. Printer: ABNC.			
	a. 1955.	5.00	22.00	100.00
	b. 1964.	5.00	25.00	120.00

NETHERLANDS INDIES

Netherlands Indies (now Indonesia) comprised Sumatra and adjacent islands, Java with Madura, Borneo (except for Sabah, Sarawak and Brunei), Celebes with Sanger and Talaud Islands, and the Moluccas and Lesser Sunda Islands east of Java (excepting the Portuguese half of Timor and the Portuguese enclave of Oe-Cusse). Netherlands New Guinea (now Irian Jaya) was ceded to Indonesia in 1962. The Dutch colonial holdings formed an archipelago of more than 13,000 islands spread across 3,000 miles (4,824 km.) in southeast Asia. The area is rich in oil, rubber, timber and tin.

Portuguese traders established posts in the East Indies in the 16th century, but they were soon outnumbered by the Dutch VOC (United East India Company) who arrived in 1602 and gradually established themselves as the dominant colonial power. Dutch dominance, interrupted by British incursions during the Napoleonic Wars, established the Netherlands Indies as one of the richest colonial possessions in the world.

One day after the Japanese attack on Pearl Harbor the Netherlands declared war against Japan and therefore a state of war existed between Japan and the Dutch East Indies. The main islands of the archipelago were taken by the Japanese during the first three months of 1942; on March 8, 1942 the Royal Netherlands Indies Army surrendered in Kalidjati (between Jakarta and Bandung on Java island). The Japanese placed Sumatra and former British Malaya (including Singapore) under the administration of the 25th army, Java and Madura under the 16th army and the rest of Indonesia, including Borneo and Sulawesi (Celebes), under the administration of the Japanese navy. The 1942 series was placed in circulation immediately after the conquest of Borneo. Initially the notes were printed in Japan, later they were printed locally.

From September 1944 the 1942 series was replaced by a set in the Indonesian (and Japanese) language instead of Dutch as the Japanese wanted to support the growing nationalist movement in Indonesia in this way as well.

The 100 and 1000 rupiah which are similar to Malayan notes issued in 1942 (M 8/9 and 10) are believed to have been issued in Sumatra only; the 1000 rupiah never reached normal circulation at all (see #126 and 127).

The Japanese surrendered on August 15, 1945 (effective for Java and Sumatra on September 12) and the Republic of Indonesia was proclaimed on August 17, 1945. During 1946-1949 (the first Dutch troops returned to Java March 6, 1946) the struggle for independence by the Indonesian nationalists against the Dutch caused monetary chaos (see also the Indonesia section in Volume One of this catalog) and the Japanese invasion money remained valid in both the Dutch and Indonesian nationalist-controlled areas as late as 1948 and 1949 at different rates to the Netherlands Indies gulden and the Indonesian rupiah.

RULERS:
United East India Company, 1602-1799
Batavian Republic, 1799-1806
Louis Napoleon, King of Holland, 1806-1811
British Administration, 1811-1816
Kingdom Of The Netherlands, 1816-1942
Dutch to 1949

MONETARY SYSTEM:
1 Gulden = 100 Cent
1 Roepiah (1943-45) = 100 Sen
Dutch:
1 Rijksdaalder = 48 Stuivers = 0.60 Ducatoon
1 Gulden = 120 Duits = 100 Cents 1854-
British:
1 Spanish Dollar = 66 Stuivers
1 Java Rupee = 30 Stuivers

NOTE: Various issues of notes from about #53-85 are known w/oval ovpt: *REPUBLIK MALUKU-SELATAN*, etc. on back. For details see Volume I at end of Indonesia listing.

DUTCH INFLUENCE

GOVERNMENT - STATE NOTES

1815 CREATIE ISSUE
#1-9 issued after the Dutch regained control over their possessions in the East Indies. All have handwritten signatures and serial #'s; Stamped crowned 'W' (King Willem I). Border w/musical notation and 'Netherlandsch Oostindien / India 'Olland' (Both meaning Netherlands East Indies.) Dated in Arabic numerals. Uniface. Wmk: Waves. Printer: JEZ.

		GOOD	FINE	XF
1	1 GULDEN			
	1815. Black.			
	a. Issued note.	—	—	—
	r. Unsigned remainder, w/o stamp or serial #.	50.00	75.00	100.00

2	5 GULDEN	GOOD	FINE	XF
	1815. Brown.			
	a. Issued note.	—	—	—
	r. Unsigned remainder, w/o stamp or serial #.	50.00	75.00	100.00
3	10 GULDEN			
	1815. Blue.			
	a. Issued note.	—	—	—
	r. Unsigned remainder, w/o stamp or serial #.	50.00	75.00	100.00
4	25 GULDEN			
	1815. Black.			
	a. Issued note.	—	—	—
	r. Unsigned remainder, w/o stamp or serial #.	50.00	75.00	100.00
5	50 GULDEN			
	1815. Red.			
	a. Issued note.	—	—	—
	r. Unsigned remainder, w/o stamp or serial #.	75.00	150.00	200.00
6	100 GULDEN			
	1815. Blue.			
	a. Issued note.	—	—	—
	r. Unsigned remainder, w/o stamp or serial #.	75.00	150.00	200.00
7	300 GULDEN			
	1815. Black.			
	a. Issued note.	—	—	—
	r. Unsigned remainder, w/o stamp or serial #.	100.00	200.00	400.00
8	600 GULDEN			
	1815. Brown.			
	a. Issued note.	—	—	—
	r. Unsigned remainder, w/o stamp or serial #.	100.00	200.00	400.00

9	1000 GULDEN	GOOD	FINE	XF
	1815. Blue.			
	a. Issued note.	—	—	Rare
	r. Unsigned remainder, w/o stamp or serial #.	100.00	200.00	400.00

DE JAVASCHE BANK

1828 GOED VOOR ISSUE

#10-16 three handwritten sign., serial #. Value ovpt. Border w/musical notation and 'Oost-Indien' (East Indies). Wmk: *JAVASCHE BANK*. Uniface. Printer: JEZ. Authorized 30.1.1827. Issued 11.3.1828.

10	25 GULDEN	—	—	—
	1827. Black.			
11	50 GULDEN	—	—	—
	1827. Black.			
12	100 GULDEN	—	—	—
	1827. Black.			
13	200 GULDEN	—	—	—
	1827. Black.			
14	300 GULDEN	—	—	—
	1827. Black.			
15	500 GULDEN	—	—	—
	1827. Black.			
16	1000 GULDEN	—	—	—
	1827. Black.			

1832 KOPERGELD ISSUE

#17-24 two handwritten sign., serial # and value. Value also printed. Border w/musical notation and 'Kopergeld' (Copper money) These notes were only redeemable in copper coin. Wmk: *JAVASCHE BANK*. Uniface. Printer: JEZ. Authorized 23.8.1832. Issued Oct. 1832.

NOTE: All *Kopergeld* notes (#17-24, #33-38) were withdrawn in Oct. 1858.

17	1 GULDEN	—	—	—
	ND. Green. W/o series letter.			
18	5 GULDEN	—	—	—
	ND. Black. Series A.			
19	10 GULDEN	—	—	—
	ND. Black. Series B.			
20	25 GULDEN	—	—	—
	ND. Black. Series C.			
21	50 GULDEN	—	—	—
	ND. Black. Series D.			
22	100 GULDEN	—	—	—
	ND. Blue. Series E.			

23	500 GULDEN	GOOD	FINE	XF
	ND. Red. Series F.			
24	1000 GULDEN			
	ND. Red. Series G.			

1853 GOED VOOR ISSUE

#25-32 similar to #10-16, date, three handwritten sign. and serial #. Value printed. Border w/musical notation and 'Neerlands-Indie' (Netherlands Indies). Wmk: *JAVASCHE BANK*. Uniface. Printer: JEZ. Issued from 1.4.1853.

25	10 GULDEN	—	—	—
	Handwritten dates from 1.4.1858. Dk. green and black, value in red.			
26	25 GULDEN	—	—	—
	Handwritten dates from 1.4.1858. Blue, value in black.			
27	50 GULDEN	—	—	—
	Handwritten dates from 1.4.1858. Blue, value in black.			
28	100 GULDEN	—	—	—
	Handwritten dates from 1.4.1858. Red, value in black.			
29	200 GULDEN	—	—	—
	Handwritten dates from 1.4.1858. Red, value . in black.			
30	300 GULDEN	—	—	—
	Handwritten dates from 1.4.1858. Red, value in black.			
31	500 GULDEN	—	—	—
	Handwritten dates from 1.4.1858. Red, value, in black.			
32	1000 GULDEN	—	—	—
	Handwritten dates from 1.4.1858. Red, value in black.			

1840s ND KOPERGELD ISSUE

#33-38 similar to #18-28 (Second series). Authorized 14.10.1842.

#33-38 Series N.

33	5 GULDEN			
	ND.			

34	10 GULDEN	GOOD	FINE	XF
	ND.			
35	25 GULDEN			
	ND.			
36	50 GULDEN			
	ND.			
37	100 GULDEN			
	ND.			
38	500 GULDEN			
	ND.			

GOVERNMENT (RESUMED)

1846 RECEPIS ISSUE

#39-44 handwritten sign., date and serial #. Border w/musical notation. Wmk: Waves. 'Recepis' (Script, certificate.) Uniface. Printer: JEZ. Authorized 4.2.1846. Issued from 1.4.1846.

NOTE: All Recepis notes withdrawn 30.6.1861.

39	1 GULDEN	GOOD	FINE	XF
	Various handwritten dates from 1.4.1846. Black.			
	a. Issued note.	60.00	90.00	190.00
	r. Unsigned remainder, w/o serial #.	25.00	50.00	100.00
40	5 GULDEN			
	Various handwritten dates from 1.4.1846. Red.			
	a. Issued note.	—	—	—
	r. Unsigned remainder, w/o serial #.	25.00	50.00	100.00
41	10 GULDEN			
	Various handwritten dates from 1.4.1846. Green.			
	a. Issued note.	—	—	—
	r. Unsigned remainder, w/o serial #.	25.00	50.00	100.00

42	25 GULDEN	GOOD	FINE	XF
	Various handwritten dates from 1.4.1846. Brown.			
	a. Issued note.	—	—	—
	r. Unsigned remainder, w/o serial #.	60.00	90.00	190.00
43	100 GULDEN			
	Various handwritten dates from 1.4.1846. Blue.			
	a. Issued note.	—	—	—
	r. Unsigned remainder, w/o serial #.	60.00	90.00	190.00
44	500 GULDEN			
	Various handwritten dates from 1.4.1846. Orange.			
	a. Issued note.	—	—	—
	r. Unsigned remainder, w/o serial #.	60.00	90.00	190.00

DE JAVASCHE BANK (RESUMED)

1864-95 ISSUE

#45-51 printer: JEZ.

#49 and 51 portr. J. Pieterzoon Coen at top ctr. 2 sign. varieties.

#45-52 legal text in 4 languages: Dutch, Javanese, Chinese, and Arabic on back.

NOTE: #48 withdrawn from circulation due to counterfeiting.

45	5 GULDEN	GOOD	FINE	XF
	1866-1895. Black and brown. Dutch arms at top. 3 sign. varieties.			
	a. 1.10.1866.	230.00	625.00	—
	b. 5.4.1895.	250.00	685.00	—
	s. Ovpt: SPECIMEN.	15.00	210.00	375.00

46	10 GULDEN	GOOD	FINE	XF
	1864-1895. Black. Batavian arms w/lion at lower ctr. Back green and black. 4 sign. varieties.			
	a. 1.2.1864; 1.3.1879.	350.00	1050.	—
	b. 1.2.1888; 1.2.1890.	—	—	—
	s. Ovpt: SPECIMEN.	115.00	210.00	375.00
47	25 GULDEN			
	1864-1895. Black. Like #46. Back blue and red. 3 sign varieties.			
	a. 1.8.1864; 1.3.1879.	—	Rare	—
	b. -1888; -1890.	—	—	—
	s. Ovpt: SPECIMEN.	115.00	210.00	375.00

48	50 GULDEN	GOOD	FINE	XF
	1864-1873. Violet. Like #46. Back blue. 1 sign. variety.			
	a. 1.9.1864.	—	Rare	—
	s. Ovpt: SPECIMEN.	115.00	210.00	375.00
49	100 GULDEN			
	1864-1895. Black. Back green and brown.			
	a. 1.3.1864; 1.3.1879.	—	Rare	—
	b. -1888; -1890.	—	—	—
	s. Ovpt: SPECIMEN.	115.00	210.00	375.00
49A	200 GULDEN			
	1864-1895.			
	a. 1.1.1864.	—	—	—
	b. -1876.	—	—	—
	s. Ovpt: SPECIMEN.	—	—	—
49B	300 GULDEN			
	1864-1895.			
	a. 2.5.1864.	—	—	—
	b. -1876.	—	—	—
	s. Ovpt: SPECIMEN.	—	—	—
50	500 GULDEN			
	1864-1895. Black. Back orange and brown.			
	a. 1.6.1864.	—	Rare	—
	b. -1872.	—	—	—
	s. Ovpt: SPECIMEN.	115.00	210.00	375.00

51	1000 GULDEN	GOOD	FINE	XF
	1864-1895. Black. J. Pieterszoon Coen at upper ctr. Back violet and black. Legal text in 4 languages: Dutch, Indonesian, Chinese and Arabic. Printer: JEZ. 2 sign. varieties.			
	a. 1.7.1864.	—	Rare	—
	b. 1.7.1873.	—	—	—
	s. Ovpt: SPECIMEN.	115.00	210.00	375.00

ND 1875 ISSUE

52 2 1/2 GULDEN

	GOOD	FINE	XF

ND (1875) Blue on brown unpt. Landscape at l. and r., Dutch arms at bottom ctr. Shield at ctr., varieties in law text on back. Printer: Albrecht & Co. (Not issued).

| | — | — | — |

1895-1924 ISSUE

#53-60 varieties in law text on back. Printer: JEZ

#56-60 Mercury at l., 3 crowned arms in wreaths at upper ctr., J. P. Coen w/ruffled collar at r.

53 10 GULDEN

	GOOD	FINE	XF

11.11.1899-26.7.1924. Blue-green. Arms at top. Back green. 8 sign. varieties.

| a. Issued note. | 60.00 | 200.00 | 565.00 |
| s. Ovpt: SPECIMEN. | 55.00 | 85.00 | 160.00 |

54 25 GULDEN

8.6.1897-4.2.1921. Brown. Back purple. 6 sign. varieties.

| a. Issued note. | 85.00 | 300.00 | — |
| s. Ovpt: SPECIMEN | 55.00 | 85.00 | 160.00 |

55 50 GULDEN

1876-1922. Brown. 3 sign. varieties.

a. 15.2.1876; 15.2.1879.	—	Rare	—
b. 1895-30.8.1922.	230.00	750.00	—
s. Ovpt: SPECIMEN.	55.00	85.00	160.00

56 100 GULDEN

	GOOD	FINE	XF

1.6.1897-15.6.1921. Blue-gray and deep blue-green. Back blue-gray and brown. 6 sign. varieties.

| a. Issued note. | 230.00 | 575.00 | 1700. |
| s. Ovpt: SPECIMEN. | 55.00 | 85.00 | 160.00 |

57 200 GULDEN

1.3.1897-19.8.1922. Brown. Back brown and violet. 4 sign. varieties.

| a. Issued note. | 400.00 | 1050. | — |
| s. Ovpt: SPECIMEN. | 55.00 | 85.00 | 160.00 |

58 300 GULDEN

1.6.1897-30.4.1901. Green. Back green and brown. 2 sign. varieties.

| a. Issued note. | 400.00 | 1050. | — |
| s. Ovpt: SPECIMEN. | 85.00 | 145.00 | 250.00 |

59 500 GULDEN

2.6.1897-5.7.1919. Gray and brown. Back purple and brown. 3 sign. varieties.

| a. Issued note. | 400.00 | 1050. | — |
| s. Ovpt: SPECIMEN. | 55.00 | 85.00 | 160.00 |

60 1000 GULDEN

23.8.1898-5.7.1919. Brown. Back yellow, brown and green. 3 sign. varieties.

| a. Issued note. | 575.00 | 1800. | — |
| s. As a. w/ovpt: SPECIMEN 3.1.1919. | 55.00 | 85.00 | 160.00 |

1901 ISSUE

#62 held in reserve.

61 5 GULDEN

	GOOD	FINE	XF

1901-24. Blue. Portr. J. P. Coen at r. Black or red serial #. Back brown on blue unpt. Printer: JEZ. 7 sign. varieties.

a. 3.10.1901-22.2.1911.	65.00	220.00	—
b. -1912-11.10.1924.	35.00	140.00	310.00
s. As b. w/ovpt: SPECIMEN. 21.1.1923.	28.00	55.00	110.00

1904 ISSUE

#64 held in reserve.

63 200 GULDEN

May 1904. Similar to #57 but serial # panels and lg. *200* replace 3 crowned arms in wreath at upper ctr. (Not issued).

| | — | — | — |

65 1000 GULDEN

	GOOD	FINE	XF

May 1904. Similar to #60 but serial # panels and lg. *1000* replace 3 crowned arms in wreath at upper ctr. (Not issued).

| | — | — | — |

1919-21 ISSUE

#66-68 Javasche Bank in Batavia at ctr. Printer: ABNC.

NOTE: #66 was withdrawn from circulation due to counterfeiting.

NOTE: Two varieties of word Batavia on #68.

66 20 GULDEN

12.8.1919-8.1.1921. Orange. Back orange, green and blue. 2 sign. varieties.

| a. Issued note. | 150.00 | 550.00 | 1200. |
| s. As a. w/ovpt: SPECIMEN. | 65.00 | 140.00 | 310.00 |

67 30 GULDEN

	GOOD	FINE	XF

8.9.1919-18.1.1921. Blue. Back blue, green and brown. 2 sign. varieties.

| a. Issued note. | 120.00 | 525.00 | 1250. |
| s. As a. w/ovpt: SPECIMEN. | 65.00 | 140.00 | 310.00 |

68 40 GULDEN

22.8.1919-21.1.1921. Green. Back green, brown and blue. 2 sign. varieties.

| a. Issued note. | 120.00 | 525.00 | 1250. |
| s. As a. w/ovpt: SPECIMEN. | 65.00 | 140.00 | 310.00 |

1925-31 ISSUE
#69-77 printer: JEZ.
#70-77 portr. J. P. Coen at upper r.

		Good	Fine	XF
69	**5 GULDEN**	2.50	9.50	45.00
	8.1.1926-1.4.1931. Violet. W/o vignette. Back violet and brown. 3 sign. varieties.			
70	**10 GULDEN**	3.50	11.50	55.00
	2.1.1926-20.4.1931. Green. Back green and red. 3 sign. varieties.			

		Good	Fine	XF
71	**25 GULDEN**	4.50	14.00	70.00
	1.12.1925-2.4.1931. Brown. Back brown and purple. 3 sign. varieties.			

		Good	Fine	XF
72	**50 GULDEN**	4.50	16.50	75.00
	5.11.1925-30.10.1930. Orange. Back brown and orange. 4 sign. varieties.			

		Good	Fine	XF
73	**100 GULDEN**	3.50	14.00	70.00
	2.11.1925-28.10.1930. Black. Back blue-gray. 3 sign. varieties.			
74	**200 GULDEN**	65.00	220.00	565.00
	2.11.1925-20.10.1930. Red. Back red and brown. 3 sign. varieties.			

		Good	Fine	XF
75	**300 GULDEN**	110.00	330.00	810.00
	2.1.1926-11.1.1926. Violet. Back violet and green. 1 sign. variety.			
76	**500 GULDEN**	45.00	140.00	410.00
	2.1.1926-19.8.1930. Blue. Back brown and blue. 2 sign. varieties.			

		Good	Fine	XF
77	**1000 GULDEN**	55.00	165.00	410.00
	1.4.1926-8.5.1930. Red. Back brown and red. 2 sign. varieties.			

1933-38 ISSUE
#78-85 printer: JEZ.
#81-85 wmk: Head.

		VG	VF	UNC
78	**5 GULDEN**	3.00	9.00	32.50
	23.4.1934-17.8.1939. Brown on lt. brown and pale green unpt. Javanese dancer at l. Back m/c. 3 sign. varieties.			

1942 ISSUE

			VG	VF	UNC
79	**10 GULDEN**		4.00	10.00	37.50

2.10.1933-31.8.1939. Dk. blue on lt. blue and pink unpt. Javanese dancer at l. and at r. Back green, red and blue. 3 sign. varieties.

			VG	VF	UNC
86	**5 GULDEN**		—	—	125.00

15.1.1942. Black on lt. blue and gray unpt. Floral design at r. Back m/c; ornate tree at ctr. Printer: G. Kolff & Co., Batavia. (Not issued).

1946 ISSUE

#87-96 printer: JEZ.

#87-90 wmk: Floral design.

#91-96 wmk: Diamond design.

NOTE: Also encountered perforated: *INGETROKKEN 2.4.47* (withdrawn).

NOTE: The Javasche Bank notes cut in half (from 5 Gulden) and those of the Republic of Indonesia originate from the currency reform of March 1950. The left half of a note was valid for exchange against new notes (see Indonesia #37/37) at 50% of face value; the right half was also accepted at half its face value for a 3% government bond issue until 1st May 1950.

			VG	VF	UNC
80	**25 GULDEN**		5.00	15.00	60.00
	14.12.1934-4.7.1939. Purple on m/c unpt. Javanese dancer at l. and r. Back brown on red and blue unpt. 2 sign. varieties.				
81	**50 GULDEN**		17.50	50.00	135.00
	19.4.1938; 25.4.1938; 14.4.1939. Black on red, green and blue unpt. Javanese dancer at l. and at r. Back brown and violet.				
82	**100 GULDEN**		30.00	75.00	225.00
	7.2.1938-22.4.1939. Violet and orange. Javanese dancers at l. and at r. Back m/c.				
83	**200 GULDEN**		200.00	550.00	1150.
	23.5.1938-24.4.1939. Green and brown. Javanese dancer at l. and at r. Back m/c.				

			VG	VF	UNC
87	**5 GULDEN**		3.50	14.00	50.00
	1946. Violet and red. Lotus at l.				
88	**5 GULDEN**		3.50	14.00	50.00
	1946. Green and orange. Like #87.				
89	**10 GULDEN**		3.50	14.00	50.00
	1946. Green. Mangosteen at l.				
90	**10 GULDEN**		4.00	16.50	55.00
	1946. Purple. Like #89.				

			VG	VF	UNC
91	**25 GULDEN**		5.50	14.00	50.00
	1946. Green. Beach w/palms at l.				
92	**25 GULDEN**		6.00	22.00	65.00
	1946. Red-orange. Like #91.				

			VG	VF	UNC
84	**500 GULDEN**		175.00	500.00	1000.
	2.6.1938-27.4.1939; Green and brown. Javanese dancer at l. and at r. Back m/c.				

			VG	VF	UNC
93	**50 GULDEN**		10.00	35.00	100.00
	1946. Dk. blue. Sailboat at l.				
94	**100 GULDEN**		9.00	22.00	95.00
	1946. Brown. Rice fields w/mountain in background at l.				
95	**500 GULDEN**		45.00	90.00	625.00
	1946. Red. Like #94.				

			VG	VF	UNC
85	**1000 GULDEN**				
	30.5.1938-29.4.1939. Green. Javanese dancers at l. and at r. Back m/c.				
	a. Issued note.		250.00	750.00	1350.
	p. Proof perforated: 32.9.(19)36.		—	—	1000.
	s. Specimen w/ovpt. *SPECIMEN* perforated: 34.5.(19)68(sic).		—	—	1000.

96	1000 GULDEN	VG	VF	UNC
	1946. Gray. Like #94.	275.00	550.00	1250.

1948 ISSUE
#97-99 printer: TDLR.

97	1/2 GULDEN			
	1948. Lilac. Moon orchids at l., 2 serial # varieties.	1.25	4.00	13.50
98	1 GULDEN			
	1948. Blue. Palms at l., 2 serial # varieties.	1.25	4.00	13.50
99	1 GULDEN			
	1948. Red. Blossoms at l., 2 serial # varieties.	2.75	7.00	23.50

GOVERNMENT (20TH CENTURY)

1919 MUNTBILJETTEN ISSUE
#100 and 101 portr. Qn. Wilhelmina at ctr. Arms at ctr. on back. Printer: ABNC.

NOTE: Earlier dates of #100-101 w/sign. title ovpt. at l. Later dates have same sign. title printed.

100	1 GULDEN	GOOD	FINE	XF
	1.8.1919-11.10.1920. Black. Back blue.	14.00	50.00	150.00
101	2 1/2 GULDEN			
	4.8.1919-28.2.1920. Dk. green. Back brown.	16.00	70.00	185.00

1920 MUNTBILJETTEN ISSUE
#103 and 104 printer: De Bussy (Amsterdam).

102	1/2 GULDEN	GOOD	FINE	XF
	14.1.1920. Black on green unpt. Crowned supported arms at ctr. Back gray-green. Plain or textured paper. Printer: Topografische Inrichting Batavia.	10.00	35.00	135.00
103	1 GULDEN			
	1.1.1920. Green and blue. W/o vignette. Back blue.	10.00	35.00	135.00

104	2 1/2 GULDEN	GOOD	FINE	XF
	1.5.1920. Green, brown and violet. Similar to #103. Back brown.	20.00	50.00	170.00

1939 MUNTBILJETTEN ISSUE
#105-107 coin at ctr. r. Printer: G. Kolff & Co., Batavia.

105	1 GULDEN	VG	VF	UNC
	1.11.1939. Brown and green. Back blue. Proof.	—	—	340.00
106	1 GULDEN			
	1.11.1939. Brown and lilac. Back brown. Proof.	—	—	340.00
107	1 GULDEN			
	1.11.1939. Blue, green and orange. Back brown. Proof.	—	—	340.00

1940 MUNTBILJETTEN ISSUE
#108 and 109 printer: G. Kolf & Co., Batavia.

NOTE: #108 and 109 issued 24.4.1941 due to a shortage of coins normally minted in U.S.A.

108	1 GULDEN	VG	VF	UNC
	15.6.1940. Brown, blue and m/c. Coin at ctr. r. Back brown, w/Borubudur Temple at ctr.			
	a. Serial # and letters.	2.00	5.50	20.00
	b. Letters only.	2.00	5.50	20.00

109	2 1/2 GULDEN	VG	VF	UNC
	15.6.1940. Gray-brown. J. P. Coen at ctr. Back brown and violet; arms.	4.00	9.50	27.00

1943 MUNTBILJETTEN ISSUE
#110-118 portr. Qn. Wilhelmina at r. , crowned supported arms at l. Back green. Printer: ABNC.

#113-118 plane, soldier and warship on back.

110	50 CENTS			
	2.3.1943. Orange.			
	a. Issued note.	1.00	3.00	10.00
	p. Proof.	—	—	200.00
	s. Specimen.	—	—	125.00

111	1 GULDEN	VG	VF	UNC
	2.3.1943. Black.			
	a. Issued note.	.50	2.00	10.00
	p. Proof.	—	—	200.00
	s. Specimen.	—	—	125.00

112	2 1/2 GULDEN	VG	VF	UNC
	2.3.1943. Violet.			
	a. Issued note.	1.25	5.00	12.50
	p. Proof.	—	—	225.00
	s. Specimen.	—	—	150.00
113	5 GULDEN			
	2.3.1943. Blue.			
	a. Issued note.	1.25	4.00	10.00
	p. Proof.	—	—	225.00
	s. Specimen.	—	—	150.00
114	10 GULDEN			
	2.3.1943. Red.			
	a. Issued note.	2.50	6.00	15.00
	p. Proof.	—	—	225.00
	s. Specimen.	—	—	150.00

115	25 GULDEN	VG	VF	UNC
	2.3.1943. Brown.			
	a. Issued note.	4.00	11.50	45.00
	p. Proof.	—	—	275.00
	s. Specimen.	—	—	200.00
116	50 GULDEN			
	2.3.1943. Green.			
	a. Issued note.	4.00	11.50	50.00
	p. Proof.	—	—	275.00
	s. Specimen.	—	—	225.00

117	100 GULDEN	VG	VF	UNC
	2.3.1943. Dk. brown.			
	a. Issued note.	6.00	18.50	70.00
	p. Proof.	—	—	325.00
	s. Specimen.	—	—	275.00
118	500 GULDEN			
	2.3.1943. Gray-blue.			
	a. Issued note.	200.00	500.00	1200.
	p. Proof.	—	—	600.00
	s. Specimen.	—	—	550.00

JAPANESE OCCUPATION - WW II

DE JAPANSCHE REGEERING

THE JAPANESE GOVERNMENT

1942 ISSUE

#119-133 plate letter *S* prefix (from Japanese *Shonan*, (the great eastern territories), the Japanese name for Indonesia).

#119-133 w/2 lg. Japanese characters *Mi-hon* in red and w/ or w/o *Specimen* on the back are all various types of specimens.

#122-125 w/Dutch text: *DE JAPANSCHE REGEERING BETAALT AAN TOONDER* (The Japanese Government pays to bearer).

#122-125 all have the repeated kiri-flower wmk., but the wmk. is sometimes not discernible. (Exceptions: #122a, block SA, and #123a.)

#123-125 w/ovpt: *Republik Islam Indonesia* see Volume 1, Indonesia #S511-S529. Other ovpts. exist, but are believed to be recent fantasies for collectors. These include black bar ovpt: *Republik Maluku Selatan R.M.S.* and *Persatuan Islam Borneo* with sign.

119	1 CENT	VG	VF	UNC
	ND (1942). Green and pink. Back green.			
	a. 2 block letters, format SA.	.25	.50	1.25
	b. Fractional block letters, form at S/AA.	.10	.30	.90
	s. As a. Specimen w/red ovpt: *Mi-hon. SPECIMEN* on back.	—	—	100.00
120	5 CENTS			
	ND (1942). Blue and lt. brown. Back blue.			
	a. Letter *S* followed by a one or two digit number, format S1 to S31.	.50	1.50	5.00
	b. 2 block letters.	.35	1.00	2.00
	c. Fractional block letters.	.20	.40	1.00
	s. As a. Specimen w/red ovpt: *Mi-hon. SPECIMEN* on back.	—	—	100.00
121	10 CENTS			
	ND (1942). Purple and yellow. Back purple.			
	a. Letter *S* followed by number, S1 to S31.	.50	1.50	5.00
	b. 2 block letters.	7.00	20.00	75.00
	c. Fractional block letters.	.25	.50	1.00
	s. As a. Specimen w/red ovpt: *Mi-hon. SPECIMEN* on back.	—	—	100.00

122	1/2 GULDEN	VG	VF	UNC
	ND (1942). Blue, gray and yellow. Fan palm at r. Back blue.			
	a. Block letters SA-SK, SM.	.50	1.50	4.00
	b. Block letters SL.	.25	.75	2.00
	s. As a. Specimen w/ovpt: *Mi-hon. SPECIMEN* on back.	—	—	100.00

123	1 GULDEN	VG	VF	UNC
	ND (1942). Brown and green. Breadfruit tree at l., coconut palm at r. Back brown.			
	a. Block letters SA; SB, serial #, w/o wmk.	25.00	60.00	125.00
	b. Block letters SB-SH; SL.	.50	1.50	4.00
	c. Block letters SI; SN.	.25	.50	1.00
	s. As a. Specimen w/ovpt: *Mi-hon. SPECIMEN* on back.	—	—	100.00

124 5 GULDEN
ND (1942). Green and yellow. Coconut palm at l., papaw at r. Back green.

		VG	VF	UNC
a.	Block letters SA; SB serial #.	25.00	60.00	125.00
b.	Block letters SB-SF.	1.00	2.50	6.00
c.	Block letters SG.	.25	1.00	2.50
s.	As a. Specimen w/ovpt: *Mi-hon. SPECIMEN* on back.	—	—	100.00

125 10 GULDEN
ND (1942). Purple and lt. green. Banana tree at ctr., coconut palm at r. Back purple; ship at ctr.

		VG	VF	UNC
a.	Block letters SA only, serial #.	25.00	60.00	130.00
b.	Block letters SB-SH; SK.	1.00	2.50	6.00
c.	Block letters SI; SL.	.25	1.00	3.00
s.	As a. Specimen w/ovpt: *Mi-hon. SPECIMEN* on back.	—	—	100.00

PEMERINTAH DAI NIPPON

THE JAPANESE GOVERNMENT

1944-45 ISSUE
#126 and 127 w/Indonesian text: *Pemerintah Dai Nippon* (The Japanese Government)

126 100 ROEPIAH
ND (1944-45). Brown-violet and dk. green. Hut under trees on a shore at ctr. Back red-brown. Framer in stream w/2 water buffalo at ctr.

		VG	VF	UNC
a.	Engraved face. Standard kiri-flowers wmk.	10.00	25.00	75.00
b.	Lithographed face, paper w/o silk threads, block letters SO sans serif, 4mm. high. W/o wmk.	5.00	10.00	25.00
c.	Lithographed face, paper w/silk threads, block I letters SO not sans serif, 4mm. high. W/o wmk.	5.00	10.00	25.00
r.	Remainder, w/o block letters SO.	2.00	6.00	15.00
s.	As a. Specimen w/ovpt: *Mi-hon. SPECIMEN* on back.	—	—	100.00

127 1000 ROEPIAH
ND (1945). Blue-green and purple. Pair of oxen pulling cart at ctr. Back same as #126, dk. green. Lithographed face. Standard kiri-flowers wmk.

		VG	VF	UNC
a.	Issued note.	75.00	200.00	650.00
s.	Specimen w/ovpt: *Mi-hon.*	—	Unc	400.00

DAI NIPPON TEIKOKU SEIHU

IMPERIAL JAPANESE GOVERNMENT

1944 ISSUE
#128-133 w/Japanese text: *Dai Nippon Teikoku Seihu* (Imperial Japanese Government).

128 1/2 ROEPIAH
ND (1944). Gray-black on lt. Brown. Stylized dragon. Back gray-black.

		VG	VF	UNC
a.	Issued note.	1.00	2.00	5.00
s.	Specimen w/red ovpt: *Mi-hon.*	—	—	100.00

129 1 ROEPIAH
ND (1944). Black-green and green. Field work (rice growing). Back brown; Banyan tree and temples of Dieng Plateau.

		VG	VF	UNC
a.	Issued note.			
s.	Specimen w/red ovpt: *Mi-hon.*	—	—	100.00

130 5 ROEPIAH
ND (1944). Olive-green and green. Batak house at l. Back green; Batak woman (Sumatera).

		VG	VF	UNC
a.	Issued note.	1.00	2.00	6.00
s.	Specimen w/red ovpt: *Mi-hon.*	—	—	100.00

131 10 ROEPIAH
ND (1944). Black-brown and brown. Javanese dancer at l. Back purple; stupas and statues of Buddha from Borobudur Temple.

		VG	VF	UNC
a.	Issued note.	1.00	2.00	6.00
p.	Proof w/pale blue unpt.	—	Rare	—
s.	Specimen w/red ovpt: *Mi-hon.*	—	—	100.00

Dutch New Guinea (Irian Jaya, Irian Barat, West Irian, West New Guinea), a province of Indonesia consisting of the western half of the island of New Guinea and adjacent islands, has an area of 159,376 sq. mi. (412,781 sq. km.) and a population of 930,000. Capital: Jayapura. Many regions are but partially explored. Rubber, copra and tea are produced.

Northwest New Guinea was first visited by Dutch navigators in the 17th century. Dutch sovereignty was established and extended throughout the 18th century. In 1828, Dutch New Guinea was declared a dependency of Tidore (an island of the Moluccas conquered by the Dutch in 1654). The boundary was established by treaties with Great Britain (1884) and Germany (1885). Japanese forces occupied only the northern coastal area in 1942; they were driven out by the Allies in 1944.

The Netherlands retained sovereignty over Dutch New Guinea when independence was granted to Indonesia in 1949. It was placed under United Nations administration in 1962, and was transferred to Indonesia in 1963 with provision for the holding of a plebiscite by 1969 to decide the country's future. As a result, it became a province of Indonesia.

RULERS:
Dutch to 1963

MONETARY SYSTEM:
1 Gulden = 100 Cents to 1963

NOTE: Refer to Netherlands Indies for issues before and during WWII. For later issues see Irian Barat (Indonesia).

		VG	**VF**	**UNC**
132	**100 ROEPIAH** ND (1944). Black-brown on pale green and violet unpt. Lion statue at l., statue of Vishnu on Garuda at r. and Saruda at l. Back dk. green; Wayang puppet at ctr.			
	a. Issued note.	2.50	10.00	45.00
	s. Specimen w/red ovpt: *Mi-hon.*	—	—	100.00
133	**100 ROEPIAH** ND (1943). Violet on yellow unpt. *DAI NIPPON* on face 59mm, *SERATOES ROEPIAH* on back 75mm. Proof.	—	Rare	—

NOTES: #119-132 known w/o block letters, and for most of the notes proofs also in modified designs are known. Unfinished notes, especially of the 1944 series #128-132, some of them uniface, are printers' leftovers which became available after the Japanese surrendered in 1945. Of #131 two different types of falsifications exist.

There is controversy about the legitimacy of #120, 121, 125, 128-130 and possibly others of this series w/o block letters. Very deceptive counterfeits of some notes from #128-132 have recently been seen.

DUTCH INFLUENCE
NOTE: #1-3 *Deleted.*

NIEUW-GUINEA

1950 ISSUE
#4-10 Portr. Qn. Juliana at l. Printer: JEZ.
#6-10 Portr. Qn. Juliana at l., birds of paradise at r.

		GOOD	**FINE**	**XF**
4	**1 GULDEN** 2.1.1950. Green and orange. Back green and brown.			
	a. Issued note.	15.00	50.00	175.00
	s. Specimen.	—	Unc	110.00
5	**2 1/2 GULDEN** 2.1.1950. Red-brown on blue unpt. Back red-brown and blue.			
	a. Issued note.	17.50	90.00	300.00
	b. Specimen.	—	Unc	180.00
6	**5 GULDEN** 2.1.1950. Blue on tan unpt.			
	a. Issued note.	35.00	150.00	375.00
	s. Specimen.	—	Unc	225.00

		GOOD	**FINE**	**XF**
7	**10 GULDEN** 2.1.1950. Brown on gray unpt.			
	a. Issued note.	50.00	200.00	500.00
	s. Specimen.	—	Unc	300.00
8	**25 GULDEN** 2.1.1950. Green on brown unpt.			
	a. Issued note.	125.00	500.00	—
	s. Specimen.	—	Unc	550.00
9	**100 GULDEN** 2.1.1950. Lilac on green unpt.			
	a. Issued note.	175.00	700.00	—
	s. Specimen.	—	Unc	750.00
10	**500 GULDEN** 2.1.1950. Lt. brown on gray unpt.	**GOOD**	**FINE**	**XF**
	a. Issued note.	—	—	—
	s. Specimen.	—	Unc	1000.

NEDERLANDS NIEUW-GUINEA

1954 ISSUE
#11-17 Portr. Qn. Juliana at r., different types of birds at l.

NOTE: Several notes of Netherlands Indies #29-33, 35 and Javasche Bank 5 Gulden are known w/lg. circular handstamp: FINANCIEN NIEUW GUINEA GVT. and other local ovpt. Further documentation is needed.

		GOOD	FINE	XF
11	**1 GULDEN**			
	8.12.1954. Green and brown. Back green and red.			
	a. Issued note.	7.50	25.00	100.00
	s. Specimen.	—	Unc	100.00

		GOOD	FINE	XF
12	**2 1/2 GULDEN**			
	8.12.1954. Blue and brown. Back blue and green.			
	a. Issued note.	10.00	45.00	150.00
	s. Specimen.	—	Unc	150.00

		GOOD	FINE	XF
13	**5 GULDEN**			
	8.12.1954. Lilac and brown.			
	a. Issued note.	15.00	60.00	185.00
	s. Specimen.	—	Unc	185.00

		GOOD	FINE	XF
14	**10 GULDEN**			
	8.12.1954. Purple and green. Back purple and brown; stylized bird of paradise at ctr. r.			
	a. Issued note.	40.00	125.00	375.00
	s. Specimen.	—	Unc	250.00
15	**25 GULDEN**			
	8.12.1954. Brown and violet. Owl on back.			
	a. Issued note.	85.00	250.00	650.00
	s. Specimen.	—	Unc	275.00
16	**100 GULDEN**			
	8.12.1954. Lt. and dk. olive-brown and dk. blue. Back like #15.			
	a. Issued note.	150.00	450.00	—
	s. Specimen.	—	Unc	325.00
17	**500 GULDEN**			
	8.12.1954. Lilac, brown and m/c. Back like # 15			
	a. Issued note.	225.00	800.00	—
	s. Specimen	—	Unc	400.00

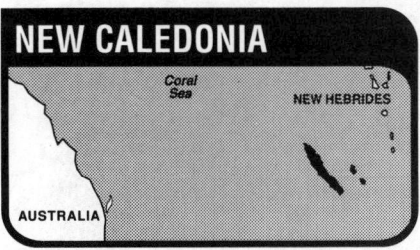

The French Overseas Territory of New Caledonia, a group of about 25 islands in the South Pacific, is situated about 750 miles (1,207 km.) east of Australia. The territory, which includes the dependencies of Ile des Pins, Loyalty Islands, Ile Huon, Isles Belep, Isles Chesterfield, and Ile Walpole, has a total land area of 6,530 sq. mi. (19,058 sq. km.) and a population of 152,000. Capital: Noumea. The islands are rich in minerals; New Caledonia has the world's largest known deposit of nickel. Nickel, nickel castings, coffee and copra are exported.

British navigator Capt. James Cook discovered New Caledonia in 1774. The French took possession in 1853, and established a penal colony on the island in 1854. The European population of the colony remained disproportionately convict until 1894. New Caledonia became an overseas territory within the French Community in 1946, and in 1958 and 1972 chose to remain affiliated with France.

* * * This section has been renumbered. * * *

RULERS:
French

MONETARY SYSTEM:
1 Franc = 100 Centimes

FRENCH INFLUENCE

COMPAGNIE DE LA NOUVELLE CALÉDONIE

1873 SUCCURSALE DE NOUMÉA ISSUE
#1-3 seal at upper l. Back reversed image. Various dates.

		GOOD	FINE	XF
1 (A1A)	**5 FRANCS** 1.7.1873. Black.	Reported Not Confirmed		
2 (A1)	**5 FRANCS** 1.7.1874. Yellow-brown.	400.00	1000.	—
3 (A2)	**20 FRANCS** Sept. 1874. Black on green unpt.	450.00	1150.	—

BANQUE DE LA NOUVELLE CALÉDONIE

1874 ISSUE
#4 farmer w/implements and cow at l., islander w/produce and implements at r.

		GOOD	FINE	XF
4	**100 FRANCS** 187x. Blue. Remainder cancelled w/ovpt: ANNULÉ.	—	Rare	—

1875 ETABLISSEMENT DE NOUMÉA ISSUE
Décret du 14 Juillet 1874
#6-9 seal at upper l. Back reversed image. Various dates.

		GOOD	FINE	XF
6 (A3)	**5 FRANCS** 1875. Yellow-brown.	450.00	1200.	—
7 (A4)	**20 FRANCS** 10.4.1875. Black on green unpt.	500.00	1350.	—
8 (A5)	**100 FRANCS** 10.7.1875. Pale blue.	—	Rare	—
9 (A6)	**500 FRANCS** 25.1.1875. Blue.			
	a. Issued note.	—	Rare	—
	r. Remainder cancelled w/ovpt: ANNULÉ 187x.	—	Rare	—

DÉCRETS DES 21.2.1875/20.2.1888

		GOOD	FINE	XF
10 (1)	**5 FRANCS**	Reported Not Confirmed		
11 (2)	**20 FRANCS** (ca.1890). Handwritten or handstamped dates. Blue. Neptune reclining holding trident at lower l. 3 sign.	—	—	—

16	**20 FRANCS**	GOOD	FINE	XF
(4B)	1905; 25.9.1913. Blue. Like #11 and 14.			
	a. Issued note. 25.9.1913.	—	—	—
	b. Cancelled w/ovpt: *Annulé*	—	—	—
	s. Specimen 3.7.1905; 25.9.1913.	—	—	—

12	**100 FRANCS**	GOOD	FINE	XF
(3)	1895; 1898. Blue and red. Elephant columns at l. and r., 2 reclining women w/ox l., tiger r. at lower border. Back blue.			
	a. Issued note 15.1.1895; 26.10.1898.	—	—	—
	p. Proof w/o serial #, ovpt: *ANNULÉ*. 1.7.1898.	—	—	—

17	**100 FRANCS**	GOOD	FINE	XF
(5)	3.3.1914; 10.3.1914; 11.3.1914. Blue and red. Like #12. 3 sign.	175.00	350.00	850.00

1916-25 ISSUE (W/O DÉCRETS)

18	**5 FRANCS**	GOOD	FINE	XF
(6)	6.6.1916; 19.6.1916. Lt. green. 2 sign.	75.00	200.00	550.00

19	**5 FRANCS**	GOOD	FINE	XF
(7)	2.6.1924. Blue.	75.00	200.00	475.00

13	**500 FRANCS**	GOOD	FINE	XF
(4)	1.7.1898. Blue and red. Vasco da Gama at l., sailing ships at lower ctr., Polynesian man holding paddle on "sea-dragon" boat at r.			
	a. Issued note.	—	—	—
	p. Proof w/o block or serial #, ovpt: *Annulé*.	—	—	—

BANQUE DE L'INDO-CHINE

NOUMÉA BRANCH

DÉCRETS DES 21.2.1875/20.2.1888/16.5.1900

14	**20 FRANCS**	GOOD	FINE	XF
	3.3.1902. Like #11. Series X.6.			

DÉCRETS DES 21.2.1875/20.2.1888/16.5.1900/3.4.1901

20	**20 FRANCS**	GOOD	FINE	XF
(8)	3.1.1921; 2.6.1924; 2.6.1925. Blue and red. Like #11. 2 sign.	150.00	350.00	700.00

21	**100 FRANCS**	GOOD	FINE	XF
(9)	2.6.1925. Blue and red. Like #12.	200.00	500.00	900.00

15	**5 FRANCS**	GOOD	FINE	XF
(4A)	15.6.1916; 17.6.1916. Blue and red. Oriental woman seated below Liberty seated holding caduceus at l. Back blue.			
	a. Issued note.	250.00	650.00	—
	b. Cancelled w/ovpt: *Annulé*.	150.00	350.00	—

22	500 FRANCS	GOOD	FINE	XF
(10)	3.1.1921. Blue and red. Like #13.	500.00	1250.	—

1914 EMERGENCY POSTAGE STAMP CARD ISSUES

#23-27 adhesive postal stamps affixed to cardboard w/handstamp: *TRESORIER PAYEUR DE LA NOUVELLE CÁLEDONIE* and *SECRETARIAT GENERAL* on back.

23	25 CENTIMES	VG	VF	UNC
(11)	ND (1914-23). Kanaka village on stamp. Hand stampings on back. 52 x 39mm. to 61 x 40mm.	160.00	300.00	550.00

24	50 CENTIMES (35 AND 15)	VG	VF	UNC
(12)	ND (1914-23). Kanaka village and Kagu bird on stamps.	250.00	400.00	650.00
25	50 CENTIMES			
(13)	ND (1914-23). Kanaka village on stamp.	200.00	350.00	600.00
26	1 FRANC			
(14)	ND (1914-23).	200.00	350.00	600.00
27	2 FRANCS			
(15)	ND (1914-23).	250.00	400.00	650.00

1922 ENCAPSULATED POSTAGE STAMP

28	25 CENTIMES	VG	VF	UNC
(15A)	ND (1922). Stamp encapsuled in aluminum w/embossing: *BANQUE DE L'INDOCHINE, NOUMÉA.*	15.00	25.00	85.00
29	50 CENTIMES			
(15B)	ND (1922). Like #28 but different stamp.	30.00	50.00	125.00

TRÉSORERIE DE NOUMÉA

1918 FIRST ISSUE

30	0.50 FRANC	GOOD	FINE	XF
(16)	14.11.1918-13.1.1919. *L'Article 139 du Code penal* in 3 lines on back.	35.00	110.00	275.00
31	1 FRANC			
(17)	14.11.1918-13.1.1919. Like #30.	40.00	125.00	300.00
32	2 FRANCS			
(18)	14.11.1918-13.1.1919. Like #30.	60.00	150.00	375.00

1918 SECOND ISSUE

#33-35 similar to #30-32 except for arrangement of text as indicated.

33	0.50 FRANC	GOOD	FINE	XF
(19)	14.11.1918-13.1.1919. Blue. *L'Article 139 du Code penal* in 4 lines on back.			
	a. Sm. numerals on back.	15.00	50.00	175.00
	b. Lg. numerals on back.	15.00	50.00	175.00
34	1 FRANC			
(20)	14.11.1918-13.1.1919. Brown. Like #33.			
	a. Sm. numerals on back.	20.00	65.00	200.00
	b. Lg. numerals on back.	20.00	65.00	200.00

35	2 FRANCS			
(21)	14.11.1918-13.1.1919. Blue-green. Like #33.			
	a. Sm. numerals on back.	25.00	75.00	225.00
	b. Lg. numerals on back.	25.00	75.00	225.00

BANQUE DE L'INDOCHINE, NOUMÉA

1926-29 ISSUE

36	5 FRANCS	VG	VF	UNC
(22)	ND (ca. 1926). Brown on lt. green unpt. Woman w/helmet at lower l. Imprint: Ch. Walhain and E. Deloche.			
	a. Sign. titles: *UN ADMINISTRATEUR* and *LE DIRECTEUR.*	3.00	20.00	75.00
	b. Sign. titles: *LE PRÉSIDENT* and *LE DIRECTEUR GÉNÉRAL.*	1.50	5.00	25.00

37	20 FRANCS	VG	VF	UNC
(24)	ND (ca.1929). Lilac-brown. Woman at r. Peacock on back. Imprint: Cl. Serveau and E. Deloche.			
	a. Sign. titles: *UN ADMINISTRATEUR* and *LE DIRECTEUR.*	8.00	30.00	125.00
	b. Sign. titles: *LE PRÉSIDENT* and *LE DIRECTEUR GÉNÉRAL.*	7.00	25.00	100.00

38	500 FRANCS	VG	VF	UNC
(31)	27.12.1927; 8.3.1938. Lilac-brown and olive. Woman standing at l., ships at top ctr.	100.00	250.00	600.00

1939 ND PROVISIONAL ISSUE

		VG	VF	UNC
39 (28)	**100 FRANCS ON 20 PIASTRES** ND (1939). M/c. Ovpt. on French Indochina #56b.	50.00	200.00	600.00

		VG	VF	UNC
40 (28A)	**1000 FRANCS ON 100 PIASTRES** ND (1939-old date 1920). Ovpt. on French Indochina #40.	—	Rare	—

1939 EMERGENCY BEARER CHECK ISSUE

		VG	VF	UNC
41 (34A)	**5000 FRANCS** 16.9.1939-16.7.1943. Black, check format.	—	Rare	—

1937; 1940 ND ISSUE

		VG	VF	UNC
42 (27)	**100 FRANCS** ND (1937-67). M/c. Woman w/wreath and sm. figure of Athena at ctr. Statue of Angkor at ctr. on back. Imprint: Seb. Laurent and Rita. 205 x 120mm.			

a.	Sign. titles: *UN ADMINISTRATEUR* and *LE DIRECTEUR GEN-ERAL.* (1937).	5.00	15.00	75.00
b.	Sign. titles: *LE PRESIDENT* Borduge and *LE DIRECTEUR GEN-ERAL* Baudouin (1937).	4.00	12.00	70.00
c.	Sign. titles: *LE PRESIDENT* and *L'ADMINISTRATEUR DIRECTOR GENERAL* (1953).	4.00	12.00	60.00
d.	Sign. titles: *LE PRESIDENT* and *LE VICE-PRESIDENT DIRECT-EUR-GENERAL* (1957).	4.00	12.00	55.00
e.	Sign. titles: *LE PRESIDENT* de Flers and *LE DIRECTEUR GEN-ERAL* Robert (1963).	3.00	10.00	50.00

		VG	VF	UNC
43 (32)	**1000 FRANCS** ND (1940-65). M/c. Market scene in background and at l., woman sitting at r. Imprint: L. Jonas and G. Beltrand.			
a.	Sign. M. Borduge w/title *LE PRÉSIDENT* and P. Baudouin w/title: *LE DIRECTEUR GÉNÉRAL* (1940).	40.00	125.00	375.00
b.	Sign. titles: *LE PRÉSIDENT* and *LE L'ADMINISTRATEUR DIREC-TEUR GÉNÉRAL*.	55.00	160.00	480.00
c.	Sign. titles: *LE PRÉSIDENT* and *LE VICE-PRÉSIDENT DIRECT-EUR GÉNÉRAL*.	30.00	90.00	275.00
d.	Sign. F. de la Motte Angode Flers w/title: *LE PRÉSIDENT* and M. Robert w/title: *LE DIRECTEUR GÉNÉRAL*. (1963).	32.50	100.00	300.00

1942; 1943 ND ISSUE

		VG	VF	UNC
44 (29)	**100 FRANCS** ND (1942). Brown. Woman wearing wreath and holding sm. figure of Athena at ctr. Statue of Angkor on back. 160 x 102mm. Australian printing.	30.00	100.00	350.00

45   **1000 FRANCS**
(33)   ND (1943). Blue. Statues of Angkor at l. W/o *EMISSION* and date ovpt.   150.00   250.00   650.00
     Printer: ABNC (w/o imprint).

1943 ISSUE

46   **100 FRANCS**   VG   VF   UNC
(30)   1943; 1944. Brown. Like #44.
     a. Ovpt: *EMISSION 1943.*   50.00   145.00   475.00
     b. Ovpt: *EMISSION 1944.*   65.00   175.00   550.00

47   **1000 FRANCS**   VG   VF   UNC
(34)   1943; 1944. Blue. Like #45.   Reported Not Confirmed
     a. Ovpt: *EMISSION 1943.*
     b. Ovpt: *EMISSION 1944.*   150.00   275.00   700.00

1944 ND ISSUE

48   **5 FRANCS**   VG   VF   UNC
(23)   ND (1944). Dk. blue. Woman wearing wreath and holding sm. figure   15.00   55.00   160.00
     of Athena at ctr. Statue of Angkor at ctr. on back. Australian printing.

49   **20 FRANCS**   VG   VF   UNC
(25)   ND (1944). Green. Woman at l., boat at ctr.; fisherman at r. Mask on   8.00   18.00   70.00
     back. Australian printing.

1951 ND ISSUE

50   **20 FRANCS**   VG   VF   UNC
(26)   ND. (1951-63). M/c. Youth at l., flute player at r. Fruit bowl at l.,
     woman at r. ctr. on back.
     a. Sign. titles: *LE PRESIDENT* and *LE DIRECTEUR GAL.* (1951).   3.00   8.00   30.00
     b. Sign. titles: *LE PRESIDENT* and *LE VICE-PRESIDENT DIRECT-*   1.50   4.50   20.00
       EUR GENERAL. (1954; 1958).
     c. Sign. titles: *LE PRESIDENT* and *LE DIRECTOR GENERAL.* (1963).   1.25   4.00   19.50

NOUVELLE CALÉDONIE

TRÉSORERIE DE NOUMÉA, BON DE CAISSE

#51-58 ship near crane at l., factory at r. Black text w/cross of Lorraine and stag head on back. Sign. varieties. Some notes on wmk. paper.

ARRÊTÉ DU 9.7.1942

51   **50 CENTIMES**   VG   VF   UNC
(35)   15.7.1942. Dk. green.   1.50   5.00   22.50

52   **1 FRANC**
(36)   15.7.1942. Purple.   1.50   5.00   22.50

53   **2 FRANCS**   VG   VF   UNC
(37)   15.7.1942. Brown.   2.50   7.00   25.00

ARRÊTÉ DU 29.1.1943

			VG	VF	UNC
54 (38)	**50 CENTIMES** 29.3.1943. Green.		1.50	5.00	22.50
55 (39)	**1 FRANC** 29.3.1943. Blue.				
	a.	Thin numerals *1* at upper l. and r.	1.50	5.00	22.50
	b.	Thick numerals *1* at upper l. and r.	1.50	5.00	22.50

			VG	VF	UNC
56 (40)	**2 FRANCS** 29.3.1943. Brown.				
	a.	Thin numerals *2* at upper l. and r.	3.00	8.00	27.50
	b.	Thick numerals *2* at upper l. and r.	3.00	8.00	27.50

			VG	VF	UNC
57 (41)	**20 FRANCS** 30.4.1943; 1943. Red.				
	a.	W/o *Deuxieme Emission* at bottom ctr. on back. 30.4.1943.	10.00	40.00	140.00
	b.	*Deuxieme Emission.* 1943.	10.00	40.00	140.00

ARRÊTÉ DU 11.6.1943

		VG	VF	UNC
58 (42)	**5 FRANCS** 15.6.1943. Pale green w/lt. brown text.	1.50	6.50	35.00

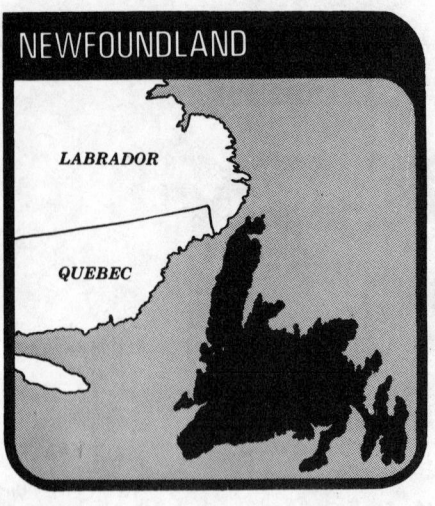

John Cabot, who visited Newfoundland in 1497, is given the title of discoverer although it is likely that Vikings visited its shore on their various trips to the west. Early settlement efforts were made by the British involving such men as Sir Humphrey Gilbert, John Guy and Sir George Calvert. There was much dispute between the French and the British for the island and its fishing rights. Awarded to England by the Treaty of Utrecht of 1713. Granted first governor in 1728. Adequate local government did not develop until the mid 1800s. Made a British colony in 1934 and became a province of Canada (along with Labrador) in 1949.

RULERS:
British

MONETARY SYSTEM:
1 Pound = 20 Shillings
1 Dollar = 100 Cents

NEWFOUNDLAND

ISLAND OF NEWFOUNDLAND

1850 TREASURY NOTE

			GOOD	FINE	XF
A3A	**1 POUND** 16.10.1850. Sailing ship at top ctr.				
	a.	2 sign.	125.00	275.00	—
	b.	3 sign.	—	Rare	—
	r.	Unsigned remainder.	35.00	85.00	135.00

NEWFOUNDLAND GOVERNMENT

DEPARTMENT OF PUBLIC WORKS BRANCH

1901 CASH NOTE ISSUE
#A4-A8 consecutive year dates from 1901 to 1908. Printer: ABNC.

		GOOD	FINE	XF
A4	**40 CENTS** 1901-08.	60.00	185.00	450.00
A5	**50 CENTS** 1901-08. Like #A4.	60.00	185.00	450.00
A6	**80 CENTS** 1901-08. Like #A4.	75.00	225.00	550.00

		GOOD	FINE	XF
A7	**1 DOLLAR** 1901-08.	100.00	375.00	750.00

A8	5 DOLLARS	GOOD	FINE	XF
	1901-08. Like #A7.	150.00	500.00	1000.

1910 ISSUE
#A9-A13 view of waterfall at upper ctr. Consecutive "double" year dates 1910-11; 1911-12; 1912-13; 1913-14. Printer: Whitehead, Morris & Co., Engravers, London.

A9	25 CENTS	GOOD	FINE	XF
	1910-11-1913-14. Black on maroon unpt. Back brown and gray.	17.50	55.00	200.00
A10	50 CENTS			
	1910-11-1913-14. Red unpt.	20.00	65.00	225.00
A11	1 DOLLAR			
	1910-11-1913-14. Green and pink.	35.00	125.00	425.00
A12	2 DOLLARS			
	1910-11-1913-14. Yellow-brown.	90.00	350.00	—
A13	5 DOLLARS			
	1910-11-1913-14. Blue.	150.00	750.00	—

GOVERNMENT OF NEWFOUNDLAND

1920 TREASURY NOTE ISSUE
#A14-A15 caribou head at r., sailing ship at l., ornate seal at ctr., anchor against rocks at r. on back. Printer: ABNC.

A14	1 DOLLAR	VG	VF	UNC
	2.1.1920. Black on blue unpt. Portr. Kg. George V at l. Back blue.			
	a. Sign. Bursell and Brownrigg.	100.00	250.00	1000.
	b. Sign. Hickey and Brownrigg.	50.00	140.00	725.00
	c. Sign. Keating and Brownrigg.	50.00	140.00	725.00
	d. Sign. Renouf and Brownrigg.	50.00	140.00	725.00

A15	2 DOLLARS	VG	VF	UNC
	2.1.1920. Black on yellow brown and blue unpt. Mine workers at ctr. Back brown.			
	a. Sign. Bursell and Brownrigg.	125.00	325.00	1350.
	b. Sign. Hickey and Brownrigg.	110.00	300.00	1200.
	c. Sign. Keating and Brownrigg.	120.00	320.00	1250.
	d. Sign. Renouf and Brownrigg.	110.00	300.00	1200.

NEW HEBRIDES

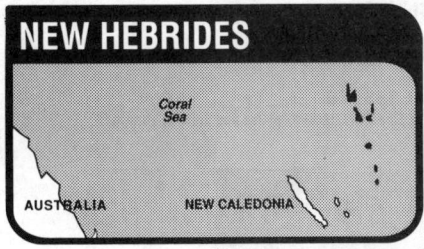

New Hebrides Condominium, a group of islands located in the South Pacific 500 miles (800 km.) west of Fiji, were under the joint sovereignty of Great Britain and France. The islands have an area of 5,700 sq. mi. (14,763 sq. km.) and a population of mainly Melanesians of mixed blood. Capital: Port-Vila. The volcanic and coral islands, while material and subject to frequent earthquakes, are extremely fertile, and produce copra, coffee, tropical fruits and timber for export.

The New Hebrides were discovered by Portuguese navigator Pedro de Quiros in 1606, visited by French explorer Bougainville in 1768, and named by British navigator Capt. James Cook in 1774. Ships of all nations converged on the islands to trade for sandalwood, prompting France and Britain to relinquish their individual claims and declare the islands a neutral zone in 1878. The New Hebrides were placed under the control of a mixed Anglo-French commission of naval officers during the native uprisings of 1887, and established as a condominium under the joint sovereignty of France and Great Britain in 1906.

RULERS:
British and French to 1980

MONETARY SYSTEM:
1 Franc = 100 Centimes

BRITISH AND FRENCH INFLUENCE

COMPTOIRS FRANCAIS DES NOUVELLES-HÉBRIDES

1921 ISSUE

A1	25 FRANCS	GOOD	FINE	XF
	22.8.1921. Red and blue. Thatched house at lower l., bridge at ctr., trees at l. and r. Back; red; pottery at l. and r.	300.00	600.00	—

SERVICES NATIONAUX FRANÇAIS DES NOUVELLES HÉBRIDES

1943 EMERGENCY WW II ISSUE
#1-3B black on green and pink unpt. Cross of Lorraine at top ctr. above 2 palm branches.

1	5 FRANCS	GOOD	FINE	XF
	ND (1943). 2 sign. varieties.	30.00	80.00	200.00
2	20 FRANCS			
	ND (1943). 2 sign. varieties.	50.00	125.00	350.00
3	100 FRANCS			
	ND (1943).	250.00	650.00	—
3A	500 FRANCS			
	ND (1943). Orange value and Serial #.	—	Rare	—
3B	1000 FRANCS			
	ND (1943).	—	Rare	—

B<small>ANQUE DE L</small>'I<small>NDOCHINE</small>

N<small>OUVELLES</small> H<small>ÉBRIDES</small> B<small>RANCH</small>

1941-45 ND P<small>ROVISIONAL</small> I<small>SSUES</small>

Ovpt. A: Red oval w/*NOUVELLES HÉBRIDES FRANCE LIBRE,* palms and Cross of Lorraine.
Ovpt. B: Red *NOUVELLES HÉBRIDES.*

	4	**5 F<small>RANCS</small>**	G<small>OOD</small>	F<small>INE</small>	XF
		ND (1941). Brown and green. Ovpt. A on New Caledonia #22.			
		a. Sign. de la Chaume and Baudouin.	12.50	50.00	175.00
		b. Sign. Borduge and Baudouin.	10.00	35.00	150.00

5	**5 F<small>RANCS</small>**	G<small>OOD</small>	F<small>INE</small>	XF
	ND (1945). Blue. Ovpt. A on New Caledonia #23.	20.00	75.00	200.00

6	**20 F<small>RANCS</small>**	G<small>OOD</small>	F<small>INE</small>	XF
	ND (1941). Lilac-brown. Ovpt. A on New Caledonia #24.	25.00	85.00	225.00

7	**20 F<small>RANCS</small>**	G<small>OOD</small>	F<small>INE</small>	XF
	ND (1945). Green. Ovpt. A on New Caledonia #25.	30.00	100.00	275.00

8	**20 F<small>RANCS</small>**	VG	VF	U<small>NC</small>
	ND. (1941-45) M/c. Ovpt. B on New Caledonia #26.			
	a. Sign. titles: *LE PRÉSIDENT* and *VICE-PRÉSIDENT DIRECTEUR GÉNÉRAL.*	3.00	6.00	30.00
	b. Sign. titles: *LE PRÉSIDENT* and *LE DIRECTEUR GÉNÉRAL.*	2.00	4.00	25.00

9	**100 F<small>RANCS</small>**	G<small>OOD</small>	F<small>INE</small>	XF
	ND. (1941-45) M/c. Ovpt. A at ctr.			
	a. Ovpt. on New Caledonia #27a.	125.00	275.00	700.00
	b. Ovpt. on New Caledonia #27b.	150.00	325.00	750.00

10	**100 F<small>RANCS</small>**	G<small>OOD</small>	F<small>INE</small>	XF
	ND. (1941-45)M/c. Like #9, but ovpt. B across lower ctr.			
	a. Sign. titles: *PRÉSIDENT* and *DIRECTEUR,* length of ovpt. 89mm.	7.50	50.00	125.00
	b. Sign. titles: *PRÉSIDENT* and *ADMINISTRATEUR,* length of ovpt. 68mm.	9.00	60.00	150.00
	c. Sign. titles: *PRÉSIDENT* and *VICE-PRÉSIDENT,* length of ovpt. 68mm.	7.50	50.00	125.00
10A	**100 F<small>RANCS</small>**			
	ND (1945). Brown. Ovpt. A on New Caledonia #29.	135.00	300.00	550.00

			GOOD	FINE	XF
11	**100 FRANCS** ND (1946-old date 1943). Brown. Ovpt. A on New Caledonia #30a.		125.00	275.00	500.00
12	**100 FRANCS** ND (1947-old date 1944). Brown. Ovpt. A on New Caledonia #30b.		125.00	275.00	500.00

			GOOD	FINE	XF
12A	**500 FRANCS** ND (-old date 8.3.1938). Lilac-brown. Ovpt. A at ctr. on New Caledonia #31.		—	Rare	—

			GOOD	FINE	XF
13	**1000 FRANCS** ND (1945-47 - old date 1944). Blue. Ovpt. A on New Caledonia #34b.		150.00	300.00	600.00
14	**1000 FRANCS** 1944. Blue. Like #13, but ovpt. B.		125.00	250.00	500.00

			GOOD	FINE	XF
14A	**1000 FRANCS** ND (1941). M/c. Ovpt. A on New Caledonia #32.		—	Rare	—

			GOOD	FINE	XF
15	**1000 FRANCS** ND. (1941-45) M/c. Like #A15 but ovpt. B across bottom ctr.		35.00	75.00	235.00

NEW ZEALAND

New Zealand, a parliamentary state located in the southwestern Pacific 1,250 miles (2,011 km.) east of Australia, has an area of 103,736 sq. mi. (269,056 sq. km.) and a population of 3.46 million. Capital: Wellington. Wool, meat, dairy products and some manufactured items are exported.

New Zealand was discovered and named by Dutch navigator Abel Tasman in 1642, and explored by British navigator Capt. James Cook who surveyed it in 1769 and annexed the land to Great Britain. The British government disavowed the annexation and for the next 70 years the only white settlers to arrive were adventurers attracted by the prospects of lumbering, sealing and whaling. Great Britain annexed the land in 1840 by treaty with the native chiefs and made it a dependency of New South Wales. The colony was granted self-government in 1852, a ministerial form of government in 1856, and full dominion status on Sept. 26, 1907. Full internal and external autonomy, which New Zealand had in effect possessed for many years, was formally extended in 1947. New Zealand is a member of the Commonwealth of Nations. The Queen of England is Chief of State.

RULERS:
British

MONETARY SYSTEM:
1 Pound = 20 Shillings (also 2 Dollars) to 1967
1 Dollar = 100 Cents, 1967-
1 Shilling = 12 Pence

BRITISH INFLUENCE

RESERVE BANK OF NEW ZEALAND

1934 ISSUE
Pound System
#154-157 kiwi at l. arms at upper ctr., portr. Maori chief at r. Lake, mountains at ctr. on back. Printer: TDLR.

154	**10 SHILLINGS**	VG	VF	UNC
	1.8.1934. Red on m/c unpt.	25.00	140.00	650.00

155	**1 POUND**	VG	VF	UNC
	1.8.1934. Purple on m/c unpt.	15.00	55.00	275.00

156	**5 POUNDS**	VG	VF	UNC
	1.8.1934. Blue on m/c unpt.	25.00	100.00	450.00
157	**50 POUNDS**			
	1.8.1934. Red on m/c unpt.	650.00	2000.	3500.

1940 ND ISSUE
#158-162 portr. Capt. J. Cook at lower r. Sign. title: *CHIEF CASHIER*. Wmk: Maori chief. Printer: TDLR.

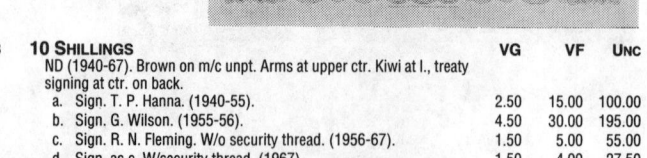

158	**10 SHILLINGS**	VG	VF	UNC
	ND (1940-67). Brown on m/c unpt. Arms at upper ctr. Kiwi at l., treaty signing at ctr. on back.			
	a. Sign. T. P. Hanna. (1940-55).	2.50	15.00	100.00
	b. Sign. G. Wilson. (1955-56).	4.50	30.00	195.00
	c. Sign. R. N. Fleming. W/o security thread. (1956-67).	1.50	5.00	55.00
	d. Sign. as c. W/security thread. (1967).	1.50	4.00	27.50

---

159 1 POUND

		VG	VF	UNC
	ND (1940-67). Purple on m/c unpt. Arms at upper ctr. Sailing ship on sea at l. on back.			
a.	Sign. T. P. Hanna. (1940-55).	3.00	9.00	110.00
b.	Sign. G. Wilson. (1955-56).	4.00	15.00	120.00
c.	Sign. R. N. Fleming. W/o security thread. (1956-67).	3.00	7.00	70.00
d.	Sign. as c. W/security thread. (1967).	2.00	5.00	35.00

160 5 POUNDS

		VG	VF	UNC
	ND (1940-67). Blue on m/c unpt. Crowned arms at upper ctr. Island, water and mountains on back.			
a.	Sign. T. P. Hanna. (1940-55).	9.00	20.00	135.00
b.	Sign. G. Wilson. (1955-56).	9.00	25.00	175.00
c.	Sign. R. N. Fleming. W/o security thread. (1956-67).	9.00	17.50	120.00
d.	Sign. as c. W/security thread. (1967).	6.50	10.00	50.00

161 10 POUNDS

		VG	VF	UNC
	ND (1940-67). Green on m/c unpt. Crowned arms, sailing ship at l. Herd of animals on back.			
a.	Sign. T. P. Hanna. (1940-55).	30.00	55.00	360.00
b.	Sign. G. Wilson. (1955-56).	35.00	70.00	400.00
c.	Sign. R. N. Fleming. (1956-67).	17.50	30.00	90.00
d.	Sign. as c. W/security thread. (1967).	10.00	18.50	70.00

162 50 POUNDS

		VG	VF	UNC
	ND (1940-67). Red on m/c unpt. Crowned arms, sailing ship at l. Dairy farm and mountain on back.			
a.	Sign. T. P. Hanna. (1940-55).	220.00	450.00	1750.
b.	Sign. G. Wilson. (1955-56).	220.00	450.00	2000.
c.	Sign. R. N. Fleming. (1956-67).	125.00	400.00	850.00

NICARAGUA

The Republic of Nicaragua, situated in Central America between Honduras and Costa Rica, has an area of 50,193 sq. mi (130,000 sq. km.) and a population of 3.87 million. Capital: Managua. Agriculture, mining (gold and silver) and hardwood logging are the principal industries. Cotton, meat, coffee and sugar are exported.

Columbus sighted the coast of Nicaragua in 1502 during the course of his last voyage of discovery. It was first visited in 1522 by conquistadors from Panama, under command of Gonzalez Davola. After the first settlements were established in 1524 at Granada and Leon, Nicaragua was incorporated, for administrative purpose, in the Captaincy General of Guatemala, which included every Central American state but Panama. The Captaincy General declared its independence from Spain on Sept. 15, 1821. The next year Nicaragua united with the Mexican Empire of Agustin de Iturbide, then in 1823 with the Central American Republic. When the federation was dissolved, Nicaragua declared itself an independent republic in 1838.

MONETARY SYSTEM:
  1 Peso = 100 Centavos to 1912
  1 Cordoba = 100 Centavos, 1912-1987

NOTE: Certain listings encompassing issues circulated by various bank and regional authorities are contained in Volume 1.

REPUBLIC

#173-177 sign. varieties.

TESORERÍA GENERAL

1896 PROVISIONAL ISSUE

DECRETO 30.3.1896

Ovpt: *TESORERÍA GENERAL* on face and back of issues of Banco Agricola-Mercantil. Issued by revolutionary forces in Leon.

A13 50 CENTAVOS

		GOOD	FINE	XF
	D.1896. Dk. blue ovpt. on l. half of #S107. Treasury registration stamp diagonally at ctr. on back.	—	—	—

A14 1 PESO

		GOOD	FINE	XF
	1.4.1896 (-old date 6.11.1888). Dk. green ovpt. on #S107.			
a.	Circular handstamp: *TESORERÍA GENERAL NICARAGUA* on back.	20.00	65.00	160.00
b.	Handstamp: Tesorería General *LEON NIC* on back.	30.00	85.00	175.00
c.	W/o circular handstamp on back.	25.00	75.00	160.00

A15 5 PESOS

		GOOD	FINE	XF
	1.4.1896 (-old date 6.11.1888). Orange ovpt. on #S108.			
a.	Ovpt: Text w/circular handstamp on back.	20.00	65.00	160.00
b.	Ovpt: Text w/o circular handstamp on back.	15.00	55.00	140.00
c.	W/o ovpt. text or circular handstamp on back.	45.00	125.00	225.00

BILLETES DEL TESORO NACIONAL

These notes were redeemable in silver and gold. They were recognized as legal tender in 1885.

DECRETO 15.9.1880

		VG	VF	UNC
A22	**1 PESO** *D.1880.* Series I. Black on lt. blue unpt. Seated Liberty w/shield of national arms and staff at lower l. Two dry seals. Wmk. paper. Uniface.	—	—	—

DECRETO 24.9.1881

#1-5 printer: HLBNC.

		GOOD	FINE	XF
1	**1 PESO** *D.1881.* Liberty bust at bottom ctr., arms at upper l. Series I.	250.00	400.00	—
2	**5 PESOS** *D.1881.* Series II. Like #1. Remainder w/stub.	—	—	—
3	**25 PESOS** *D.1881.* Series III.	—	—	—
4	**50 PESOS** *D.1881.* Series IV.	—	—	—
5	**100 PESOS** *D.1881.* Series V.	—	—	—

DECRETO 30.6.1883

		GOOD	FINE	XF
6	**25 PESOS** *D.1883.* Series III.	—	—	—
7	**50 PESOS** *D.1883.* Series IV.	—	—	—
8	**100 PESOS** *D.1883.* Series V.	—	—	—

DECRETO 20.3.1885

#9-10 printer: HLBNC.

		GOOD	FINE	XF

9	**20 CENTAVOS**
	D.1885. Black. Arms at r. Round purple handstamp on back. Uniface. Series VII.
	  a. Issued note.
	  r. Remainder w/stub.
		—
		—
			—
			—
				—
				—

		GOOD	FINE	XF

10	**50 CENTAVOS**
	D.1885. Black on pink paper. Arms at ctr. Purple handstamps on face and back. Uniface. Series VI.
	  a. Issued note.
	  r. Remainder w/stub.
		—
		—
			—
			—
				—
				—

DECRETO 10.11.1885

		GOOD	FINE	XF
11	**10 CENTAVOS** *D.1885.* Red. Purple handstamps on face and back. Local printing. Uniface.	—	—	—

12	**10 CENTAVOS**
	D.1885. Black. Arms at upper l. Purple handstamps of *Secretaria de Hacienda*, facsimile sign. of *EL TESORERO* on back. Uniface. Series VIII. Printer: HLBNC.
	  a. Issued note.
	  r. Remainder w/stub.
		—
		—
			—
			—
				—
				—

DECRETO 20.3.1886

		GOOD	FINE	XF
13	**20 CENTAVOS** *D.1886.* Series VII.	—	—	—
14	**50 CENTAVOS** *D.1886.* Series VI.	—	—	—
15	**1 PESO** *D.1886.* Series I.	—	—	—

DECRETO 12.10.1894

#17-19 printer: Paydt, Upham & Co. S.F.

		GOOD	FINE	XF
16	**5 CENTAVOS** ND (1894). Black on blue-green unpt. W/o decreto. Back dk. green. Local printing. Series 9.	25.00	60.00	140.00

		GOOD	FINE	XF

17	**10 CENTAVOS**
	D.1894. Dk. brown on orange and green unpt. Arms at upper l. Back brown. Series XI.
	  a. Red sign.
	  b. Black sign.
		
		25.00
		17.50
			
			65.00
			55.00
				
				150.00
				125.00

		GOOD	FINE	UNC

18	**20 CENTAVOS**
	D.1894. Dk. brown on brown and green unpt. Arms at upper l. Back green. Series X.
	  a. 2 sign. varieties.
	  b. W/o sign.
		
		25.00
		—
			
			75.00
			—
				
				165.00
				—

19	**50 CENTAVOS**	GOOD	FINE	XF
	D.1894. Dk. brown on green and tan unpt. Arms at upper l. Back blue. Series I; 6; IX.			
	a. *Series I* at top, blue serial #. 2 sign. varieties.	35.00	90.00	190.00
	b. *Series 6* at top, red serial #. 3 sign. varieties.	35.00	90.00	190.00
	c. *Series IX* at top, red serial #. 2 sign. varieties.	35.00	100.00	200.00
	d. Like c., but w/o sign.	20.00	60.00	110.00

1894 COMMEMORATIVE ISSUE
#20-23, 402nd Anniversary of the Discovery of America. Local printing.

23	**5 PESOS**	GOOD	FINE	XF
	D. 1894. Black and red. Seated Liberty (Ms. Herrera) w/arms at l., Chief Nicarao at r. on back.	—	Rare	—
23A	**10 PESOS**			
	D. 1894. Black and orange. Arms on back.	—	—	—

1894 ISSUE

20	**20 CENTAVOS**	GOOD	FINE	XF
	D.1894. Blue. Back black on brown unpt. w/seated Liberty at l. looking at 5 mountains and sunrise at r. Series 1.	—	Rare	—
21	**50 CENTAVOS**			
	D.1894. Black on lt. tan unpt. Similar to #20. Back black on green unpt.	—	Rare	—

24	**1 PESO**	GOOD	FINE	XF
	D.1894. Black. Portr. S. Bolívar at ctr., arms in blue at lower r. Back dk. green; arms at ctr.			
	a. *Series No. VII.* Imprint: Paydt Upham & Co. S.F.	300.00	500.00	800.00
	b. *Series No. VIII.* Imprint: Paydt Upham & Co. S.F. 2 sign. varieties.	300.00	450.00	750.00
	r. Remainder w/o sign.	175.00	425.00	—

25	**5 PESOS**	GOOD	FINE	XF
	D.1894. Black on pink and lt. blue unpt. Portr. Herrera at upper l., arms at lower r. Back green; arms at ctr. Series III.	275.00	450.00	—

22	**1 PESO**	GOOD	FINE	XF
	D.1894. Black. Arms at upper ctr. Seated Liberty (Ms. Rafaela Herrera) w/arms and bales at l., seated Indian w/huts at r. on back.			
	a. Sign. title: *El Ministro General* at l. All titles in sm. lettering.	400.00	750.00	1300.
	b. Sign. title: *El Ministro de Hacienda* at l. All titles in lg. lettering.	400.00	750.00	—

26	**10 PESOS**	GOOD	FINE	XF
	D.1894. Black. Red arms at ctr. Portr. Jerez at r. Back blue and inverted; arms at ctr. Imprint: Lith. Paydt, Upham & Co. S.F. Series IV.			
	a. Sign. titles: *El Ministro General* and *El Tesorero.*	—	1000.	—
	b. Ovpt. sign. titles: *El Ministro de Hacienda* and *El Tesorero General.*	—	1000.	—

27 **50 Pesos**
D.1894. Black on green unpt. Morazán at l. Back lt. brown; arms at ctr. Series V.
   a. Issued note.
   r. Unsigned remainder.

	GOOD	FINE	XF
a.	—	—	—
r.	—	—	—

1900 ISSUE
#28-33 printer: W&S.

#		GOOD	FINE	XF
28	**50 CENTAVOS** 15.9.1900. Black on blue and red unpt. Woman seated at ctr. Back blue.	25.00	65.00	200.00

#		GOOD	FINE	XF
29	**1 PESO** 15.9.1900. Black on green and gold unpt. Jerez at l., cattle at r. Back brown.			
	a. Issued note.	25.00	100.00	250.00
	s. Specimen. Yellow and orange, back green.	—	—	—

#		GOOD	FINE	XF
30	**5 PESOS** 15.9.1900. Black on red unpt. Portr. Zelaya at l., steam passenger train at ctr. Back brown.	100.00	300.00	—
31	**10 PESOS** 15.9.1900. Black and purple on gold unpt. Herrera at top ctr., farmer plowing w/oxen below. Back dull purple; arms.			
	a. Issued note.	150.00	400.00	—
	s. Specimen. Punch cancelled w/large holes.	—	—	—
32	**25 PESOS** 15.9.1900. Black on blue-green unpt. Portr. D. F. Morazán at l., Liberty in winged chariot drawn by lions at ctr. Back pale green; arms at ctr.			
	a. Issued note.	—	—	—
	s. Specimen. Punch cancelled w/small holes.	—	—	—

#		GOOD	FINE	XF
33	**50 PESOS** 15.9.1900. Black on yellow and orange unpt. Liberty and portr. S. Bolívar at l. Back brown. Specimen.	—	—	—

1906-08 ISSUE
#34-39 printer: Waterlow Bros. & Layton, Ltd., London.

#		GOOD	FINE	XF
34	**50 CENTAVOS** 1.1.1906. Black on red and green unpt. Allegorical woman seated w/sword and trumpet at l. Back blue; arms at ctr.			
	a. Issued note.	12.50	40.00	100.00
	s. Specimen.	—	—	—

#		GOOD	FINE	XF
35	**1 PESO** 1.1.1906. Black on red and orange unpt. 2 women and child gathering fruit at upper l., portr. woman at r. Back brown; arms at ctr.			
	a. Issued note.	15.00	65.00	135.00
	s. Specimen, punched hole cancelled.	—	—	—

#		GOOD	FINE	XF
36	**5 PESOS** 1.1.1908. Black on tan and purple unpt. Steam locomotive at l., protr. Zelaya at ctr. r. Back orange; arms at r.	200.00	500.00	—
37	**10 PESOS** 1.1.1908. Red and brown. Portr. Gen. D. M. Jerez at l. Back purple; arms at r.	300.00	600.00	—

38   50 PESOS   GOOD   FINE   XF
      1.1.1908. Black on yellow and green unpt. Portr. S. Bolívar at l.,man   —   —   —
      w/ox-cart at ctr. Back brown; arms at r.

39   100 PESOS   GOOD   FINE   XF
      1.1.1908. Black on green and tan unpt. Seated woman at l., equestrian   —   —   —
      statue of Nicarao at r. Back green.

1909 ISSUE

40   50 PESOS   GOOD   FINE   XF
      D.24.11.1909. Black on red unpt., blue border. J.S. Zelaya at l. Arms   —   Rare   —
      at ctr. on back. Local printing.

1910 PROVISIONAL ISSUE

41   5 PESOS   GOOD   FINE   XF
      D.3.2.1910. Dr. J. Madriz at l. Local printing.   185.00 475.00   —

42   5 PESOS   GOOD   FINE   XF
      D.3.3.1910. Black on blue and lt. red unpt. Arms at ctr. on back. Local 175.00 400.00   —
      printing.

1911 ISSUE (DATED 1910)
#43-49 Columbus on face. Sign. varieties. Printer: ABNC.

43   50 CENTAVOS   GOOD   FINE   XF
      1.1.1910. Black on green and m/c unpt. C. Columbus at r. Back dk.
      green. Series A.
      a. Ctr. sign. Pres. *José Madriz.*   15.00   30.00   100.00
      b. Ctr. sign. Pres. *Juan J. Estrada.*   15.00   30.00   100.00

44   1 PESO   GOOD   FINE   XF
      1.1.1910. Black on orange-brown unpt. Portr. C. Columbus at l. Back
      orange. Series B.
      a. Ctr. sign. Pres. *José Madriz.*   15.00   30.00   100.00
      b. Ctr. sign. Pres. *Juan J. Estrada.*   15.00   30.00   100.00

45   5 PESOS   GOOD   FINE   XF
      1.1.1910. Black on blue and m/c unpt. Seated woman at l., portr. C.
      Columbus at ctr. r. Back dk. blue. Series C.
      a. Ctr. sign. Pres. *José Madriz.*   45.00   110.00 275.00
      b. Ctr. sign. Pres. *Juan J. Estrada.*   50.00   150.00 375.00

46   10 PESOS
   1.1.1910. Black on red and m/c unpt. Woman and child at l., portr. C.
   Columbus at r. Back red-brown. Series D.

   a.   Ctr. sign. Pres. *José Madriz.*   65.00   225.00   —
   b.   Ctr. sign. Pres. *Juan J. Estrada.*   75.00   250.00

52   10 CENTAVOS   GOOD   FINE   XF
   L.1912. Black on green unpt. Portr. Liberty at l. Back green.
   a.   W/o prefix. Pres. sign. *Adolfo Diaz* (Oct. 1914).   8.00   22.50   50.00
   b.   Prefix A. Pres. sign. as a.   8.00   22.50   50.00
   c.   Prefix B. Pres. sign. *E. Chamorro* (Oct. 1918).   8.00   22.50   50.00
   d.   Prefix C. Pres. sign. *Diego M. Chamorro.* (July 1922). 12.00   30.00   75.00
   e.   Prefix D. Pres. sign. as d.   6.00   15.00   40.00
   f.   Prefix E. Pres. sign. *Emiliano Chamorro* (Sept. 1926).   6.00   15.00   40.00
   s.   Specimen.

47   25 PESOS   GOOD   FINE   XF
   1.1.1910. Black on m/c unpt. Portr. C. Columbus at l., arms at ctr.
   Back olive; monument at ctr. Series E.
   a.   Ctr. sign. Pres. *José Madriz.*   100.00   325.00   —
   b.   Ctr. sign. Pres. *Juan J. Estrada.*   125.00   350.00

48   50 PESOS
   1.1.1910. Black on purple m/c unpt. Arms at ctr., portr. C. Columbus
   at r. Back purple; lg. bldg. at ctr. Series F.
   a.   Ctr. sign. Pres. *José Madriz.*   —   Rare
   b.   Ctr. sign. Pres. *Juan J. Estrada.*   Reported Not Confirmed

49   100 PESOS
   1.1.1910. Black on orange and m/c unpt. Portr. C. Columbus at l. ctr.,
   arms at r. Back red; gateway to govt. bldg. at ctr. Series G. Sign. of
   Pres. *José Madriz.*
   a.   Ctr. sign. Pres. *José Madriz.*   —   Rare   —
   b.   Ctr. sign. Pres *Juan J. Estrada.*   —   Rare   —

1912 PROVISIONAL ISSUE
Ovpt: *ESTE BILLETE VALE … CENTAVOS DE CÓRDOBA* vertically in red on face.

53   25 CENTAVOS   GOOD   FINE   XF
   L. 1912. Black on orange unpt. Portr. Liberty at r. Back orange.
   a.   W/o prefix. Pres. sign. *Adolfo Diaz* (Oct. 1914). Red serial #.   10.00   25.00   55.00
   b.   Prefix A. Pres. sign. *E. Chamorro* (Oct. 1918). Blue serial #.   10.00   27.50   60.00
   s.   Specimen.

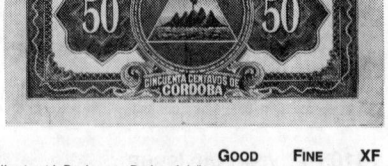

50   4 (CUATRO) CENTAVOS ON 50 CENTAVO   GOOD   FINE   XF
   ND (-old date 1.1.1910). Black on green and m/c unpt. Ovpt. on #43b.   35.00   85.00   165.00

54   50 CENTAVOS   GOOD   FINE   XF
   L. 1912. Black on blue unpt. Portr. Liberty at l. Back gray. Red serial #.
   a.   W/o prefix. Pres. sign. *Adolfo Diaz* (Oct. 1914).   12.50   30.00   65.00
   b.   Prefix A. Pres. sign. *E. Chamorro* (Oct. 1918).   15.00   35.00   75.00
   s.   Specimen.   —   —

51   8 (OCHO) CENTAVOS ON 1 PESO   GOOD   FINE   XF
   ND (-old date 1.1.1910). Black on orange-brown unpt. Ovpt. on #44b.   40.00   100.00   200.00

BANCO NACIONAL DE NICARAGUA

LEY DE 20 DE MARZO DE 1912

#52-54 fractional notes w/o date. Arms at ctr. on back. Printer: ABNC.

#55-60, portr. Córdoba at l.

#55-61 larger notes. Printer: HBNC.

NOTE: For similar issues but w/later dates see #85-89.

55   1 CORDOBA   GOOD   FINE   XF
   L. 1912. Black on green unpt. Portr. Nicarao at lower r. Back green;
   arms at ctr.
   a.   W/o prefix. Pres. sign. *Adolfo Diaz* (Oct. 1914). Red serial #.   70.00   175.00   —
   b.   Prefix A. Pres. sign. *E. Chamorro* (Oct. 1918). Blue serial #.   70.00   175.00   —
   c.   Prefix B. Pres. Sign. *Carlos José Solórzano.*   140.00   350.00   —
   s.   Specimen. Pres. sign. *Carlos José Solórzano.*   —   —

56	2 CORDOBAS	GOOD	FINE	XF
	L. 1912. Black on brown unpt. Portr. De la Cerda at r. Back maroon; arms at ctr.			
	a. W/o prefix. Pres. sign. Adolfo Diaz (Oct. 1914).	—	—	—
	b. Prefix A. Pres. sign. E. Chamorro (Oct. 1918).	—	—	—
	s. Specimen.	—	—	—

57	5 CORDOBAS	GOOD	FINE	XF
	L. 1912. Portr. Larreynaga at r.			
	a. Issued note.	—	—	—
	s. Specimen.	—	—	—

58	10 CORDOBAS	GOOD	FINE	XF
	L. 1912. Black on orange unpt. Portr. Chamerra at r. Back orange.			
	a. Issued note.	—	—	—
	s. Specimen.	—	—	—
59	20 CORDOBAS			
	L. 1912. Martinez at r.			
	a. Issued note.	—	—	—
	s. Specimen.	—	—	—
60	50 CORDOBAS			
	L. 1912. Estrada at r.			
	a. Issued note.	—	—	—
	s. Specimen.	—	—	—

61	100 CORDOBAS	GOOD	FINE	XF
	L. 1912. Palm trees, Lake Managua and volcano at ctr.			
	a. Issued note.	—	—	—
	s. Specimen.	—	—	—

1927-39 ISSUE

#62-69, bank name in English in upper frame above Spanish name. National arms on back. Printer: ABNC.

62	1 CORDOBA	GOOD	FINE	XF
	1927; 1930. Green on m/c unpt. Woman at ctr. Back dk. brown.			
	a. Minister Guzman. 1927 (Mar. 1927).	60.00	180.00	350.00
	b. Minister Lopez. 1927 (July, 1928).	60.00	180.00	350.00
	c. 1930 (Dec. 1929).	—	—	—
	s. Specimen.	—	—	—

63	1 CORDOBA	GOOD	FINE	XF
	1932-39. Blue on m/c unpt. Like #62. Back dk. olive brown.			
	a. 1932.	20.00	60.00	150.00
	b. 1937; 1938; 1939.	8.00	25.00	65.00
	s. Specimen.	—	—	—

64	2 CORDOBAS	GOOD	FINE	XF
	1939. Green on m/c unpt. Ox-cart in front of sugar cane mill at l. Back red-orange.			
	a. Issued note.	10.00	35.00	100.00
	s. Specimen.	—	—	—

65	5 CORDOBAS	GOOD	FINE	XF
	1927-39. Gray on m/c unpt. Cattle at ctr. Back brown.			
	a. 1927.	—	—	—
	b. 1938; 1939.	8.50	30.00	75.00
	s. Specimen.	—	—	—
66	10 CORDOBAS			
	1929-39. Brown on m/c unpt. Portr. Liberty at r. Like #94. Back carmine.			
	a. 1929.	—	—	—
	b. 1938; 1939.	22.50	65.00	175.00
	s. Specimen.	—	—	—

67	20 CORDOBAS	GOOD	FINE	XF
	1929-39. Orange on m/c unpt. Bay and port of Corinto. Back blue.			
	a. 1929.	—	—	—
	b. 1937; 1939.	60.00	175.00	—
	s. Specimen, punched hole cancelled.			
68	50 CORDOBAS			
	1929; 1937; 1939. Purple on m/c unpt. 2 women w/wheat laureates at l. Back orange.			
	a. Issued note.	—	—	—
	s. Specimen, punched hole cancelled.	—	—	—

69	100 CORDOBAS	GOOD	FINE	XF
	1939. Red on m/c unpt. Woman w/fruits before altar at r. Back dk. olive brown.	—	—	—

1934 REVALIDATION

The Decree of January 2, 1934, ordered all circulating notes to be exchanged against new notes w/red ovpt: *REVALIDADO.* The ovpt. was printed on notes in stock in the vaults of the B.N.N.

NOTE: The old notes w/o ovpt. became worthless on June 1, 1934. Later dates (1937-39) of the 2nd issue were put into circulation w/o ovpt. No. 2 Cordobas notes or fractional currency notes were issued w/ovpt.

70	1 CORDOBA	GOOD	FINE	XF
	ND (D.1934). Ovpt. on #62.	25.00	85.00	225.00

71	1 CORDOBA	GOOD	FINE	XF
	ND (D.1934). Ovpt. on #63a.	20.00	65.00	175.00
72	5 CORDOBAS			
	ND (D.1934). Ovpt. on #65a.	30.00	100.00	—

73	10 CORDOBAS	GOOD	FINE	XF
	ND (D.1934). Ovpt. on #58.	100.00	300.00	—
74	10 CORDOBAS			
	ND (D.1934). Ovpt. on #66a.	75.00	175.00	—
75	20 CORDOBAS			
	ND (D.1934). Ovpt. on #59.	—	—	—
76	20 CORDOBAS			
	ND (D.1934). Ovpt. on #67a.	—	—	—

77	50 CORDOBAS	GOOD	FINE	XF
	ND (D.1934). Ovpt. on #68.	—	—	—
78	100 CORDOBAS			
	ND (D.1934). Ovpt. on #61.	—	—	—

1935-38 ISSUE
#79-84 arms at ctr. on back. Printer: HBNC.

79	10 CENTAVOS	GOOD	FINE	XF
	1938. Black on green unpt. Portr. Liberty at l. Back green.	4.50	20.00	65.00

80	25 CENTAVOS	GOOD	FINE	XF
	1938. Black on orange unpt. Portr. Liberty at r. Back orange.	6.00	25.00	75.00

81	50 CENTAVOS	GOOD	FINE	XF
	1938. Black on dk. blue unpt. Portr. Liberty at l. Back blue.	9.00	45.00	125.00

82	1 CORDOBA	GOOD	FINE	XF
	1935; 1938. Blue on peach unpt. 2 allegories people on cliff above sea at ctr. Back green.	12.50	60.00	150.00
83	5 CORDOBAS			
	1935. Black on lt. green and red unpt. Woman's head at ctr. Back brown.	20.00	80.00	250.00

84 **10 CORDOBAS**

	GOOD	FINE	XF
1935. Brown on purple and green unpt. Palm trees, lake and volcano at ctr. Back carmine.	30.00	150.00	—

1937 ND ISSUE

#85 and 86 portr. Liberty. Arms at ctr. on back. Similar to #87 and 88. Printer: ABNC.

85 **10 CENTAVOS**

	GOOD	FINE	XF
ND (1937). Similar to #87 but w/o the 6 lines of text on face referring to Law of 1912.			
a. Sign. title: *DIRECTOR GERENTE* at bottom.	4.00	15.00	45.00
b. Sign. title: *GERENTE GENERAL* at bottom.	5.00	17.50	55.00

86 **25 CENTAVOS**

ND (1937). Similar to #88 but w/o text on face referring to Law of 1912.			
a. Sign. title: *DIRECTOR GERENTE* at bottom.	5.00	17.50	60.00
b. Sign. title: *GERENTE GENERAL* at bottom.	10.00	20.00	60.00

1938 ISSUE

#87-89 similar to previous issue. Printer: ABNC.

87 **10 CENTAVOS**

	VG	VF	UNC
1938. Black on green unpt. Like #52.	3.50	12.50	35.00

88 **25 CENTAVOS**

	VG	VF	UNC
1938. Black on orange unpt. Like #53.	4.50	17.50	55.00

89 **50 CENTAVOS**

	VG	VF	UNC
1938. Black on blue unpt. Like #54.	6.50	22.50	75.00

1941-45 ISSUE

The English bank name in upper frame has been removed. Face and back designs and colors similar to second issue notes except for #90 and 91. Printer: ABNC.

90 **1 CORDOBA**

	VG	VF	UNC
1941-45. Blue on m/c unpt. Portr. Indian girl wearing feather at ctr. Back dk. olive-brown. *SERIE DE* (date) engraved and printed in blue.			
a. 1941.	1.00	3.50	12.50
b. 1942; 1945.	2.00	7.00	35.00

91 **1 CORDOBA**

1949; 1951. Like #90 but *SERIE DE* (date) typographed and printed in red.			
a. 1949.	2.00	8.00	45.00
b. 1951.	1.50	5.00	25.00

92 **2 CORDOBAS**

	VG	VF	UNC
1941; 1945. Green on m/c unpt. Similar to #64.			
a. 1941.	3.50	15.00	60.00
b. 1945.	3.25	13.50	55.00

93 **5 CORDOBAS**

	VG	VF	UNC
1942; 1945; 1951. Gray on m/c unpt. Similar to #65.			
a. 1942.	5.00	20.00	80.00
b. 1945.	4.50	18.50	75.00
c. 1951.	4.00	17.50	70.00

94 **10 CORDOBAS**

	VG	VF	UNC
1942; 1945; 1951. Brown on m/c unpt. Similar to #66.			
a. 1942.	10.00	40.00	160.00
b. 1945.	9.00	37.50	150.00
c. 1951.	8.00	32.50	130.00

95 **20 CORDOBAS**

1942; 1945; 1951. Orange on m/c unpt. Similar to #67.			
a. 1942.	25.00	100.00	300.00
b. 1945.	22.50	90.00	275.00
c. 1951.	20.00	82.50	250.00

96 **50 CORDOBAS**

1942; 1945. Purple on m/c unpt. Similar to #68.			
a. 1942.	50.00	125.00	—
b. 1945. 2 sign. varieties for r. h. sign.	35.00	65.00	150.00

97	**100 CORDOBAS**	VG	VF	UNC
	1941; 1942; 1945. Red on m/c unpt. Similar to #69.			
	a. 1941; 1942.	110.00	225.00	—
	b. 1945. 2 sign. varieties for r. h. sign.	100.00	200.00	—

98	**500 CORDOBAS**	VG	VF	UNC
	1945. Black on m/c unpt. Portr. R. Dario at ctr. Back green. 2 sign. varieties for r. h. sign.	200.00	300.00	—

1953-54 ISSUE

#99-106, all notes except #105 and 106 come in two date varieties:
a. *SERIE DE* (date) engraved, printed in note color. 1953-58.
b. *SERIE DE* (date) typographed, printed in black. 1959-60. Printer: TDLR.

99	**1 CORDOBA**	VG	VF	UNC
	1953-60. Dk. blue on m/c unpt. Portr. indian girl wearing feather at ctr. Bank on back.			
	a. Engraved date. 1953; 1954; 1957; 1958.	2.00	6.00	20.00
	b. Typographed date. 1959; 1960.	1.50	4.50	17.50
	s. Specimen.	—	—	—

100	**5 CORDOBAS**	VG	VF	UNC
	1953-60. Dk. green on m/c unpt. C. Nicarao at ctr. Carved statue on back at ctr., arms at r.			
	a. Engraved date. 1953.			
	b. Engraved date. 1954; 1957; 1958.	3.00	12.50	85.00
	c. Typographed date. 1959; 1960.	2.00	10.00	75.00
	s. Specimen.			

101	**10 CORDOBAS**	VG	VF	UNC
	1953-60. Red on m/c unpt. Arms at l., portr. M. de Larreynaga at r. Independence meeting on back.			
	a. Engraved date. 1953; 1954; 1957; 1958.	6.00	45.00	175.00
	b. Typographed date. 1959; 1960.	4.00	35.00	150.00
	s. Specimen.	—	—	—

102	**20 CORDOBAS**	VG	VF	UNC
	1953-60. Orange-brown on m/c unpt. Scene w/R. Herrera at ctr. Map on back.			
	a. Engraved date. 1953; 1954; 1957; 1958.	10.00	60.00	325.00
	b. Typographed date. 1959; 1960.	7.50	50.00	275.00
	c. Specimen.			

103	**50 CORDOBAS**	VG	VF	UNC
	1953-60. Dk. blue on m/c unpt. Portr. M. Jerez at l., Gen. T. Martinez at r. Flag on back.			
	a. Engraved date. 1953; 1954; 1957; 1958.	20.00	90.00	500.00
	b. Typographed date. 1959; 1960.	17.50	75.00	425.00
	s. Specimen.	—	—	—

104	**100 CORDOBAS**	VG	VF	UNC
	1953-60. Purple on m/c unpt. Portr. J. Dolores Estrada at r. National Palace on back.			
	a. Engraved date. 1953; 1954; 1957; 1958.	12.00	55.00	400.00
	b. Typographed date. 1959; 1960.	10.00	45.00	250.00
	s. Specimen.	—	—	—

105 500 CORDOBAS
    1953-54. Black on m/c unpt. Portr. R. Dario at ctr. Monument in Dario
    Park at ctr. on back.

	VG	VF	UNC
a. Engraved date. 1953; 1954.	125.00	450.00	—
b. Typographed date. 1959; 1960.	100.00	350.00	—
s. Specimen.	—	—	—

106 1000 CORDOBAS
    1953-54. Brown on m/c unpt. Portr. Pres. Gen. A. Somoza at lower l.,
    arms at r. Stadium on back.

	VG	VF	UNC
a. Engraved date. 1953; 1954.	150.00	500.00	—
b. Typographed date. 1959; 1960.	125.00	400.00	—
s. Specimen.	—	—	—

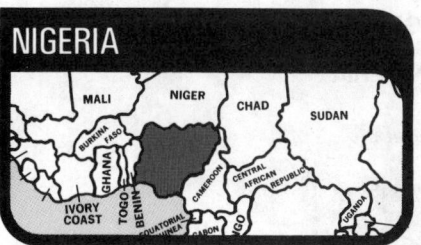

The Federal Republic of Nigeria, situated on the Atlantic coast of Africa between Benin and Cameroon, has an area of 356,667 sq. mi. (923,768 sq. km.) and a population of 88.5 million. Capital: Lagos. The economy is based on petroleum and agriculture. Crude oil, cocoa, tobacco and tin are exported. Following the Napoleonic Wars, the British expanded their trade with the interior of Nigeria. British claims to a sphere of influence in that area were recognized by the Berlin Conference of 1885, and in the following year the Royal Niger Company was chartered. Direct British control of the territory was initiated in 1900, and in 1914 the amalgamation of northern and southern Nigeria into the Colony and Protectorate of Nigeria was effected. In 1960, following a number of territorial and constitutional changes, Nigeria was granted independence within the British Commonwealth as a federation of the northern, western and eastern regions. Nigeria altered its political relationship with Great Britain on Oct. 1, 1963, by proclaiming itself a republic. It did, however, elect to remain a member of the Commonwealth of Nations. The Supreme Commander of Armed Forces is the Head of the Federal Military Government.

On May 30, 1967, the Eastern Region of the republic - an area occupied principally by the proud and resourceful Ibo tribe - seceded from Nigeria and proclaimed itself the independent Republic of Biafra. Civil war erupted and raged for 31 months. Casualties, including civilian, were about two million, the majority succumbing to malnutrition and disease. Biafra surrendered to the federal government on January 15, 1970. After military coups in 1983 and 1985 the government was assumed by an Armed Forces Ruling Council. A transitional civilian council was formed in 1993.

RULERS:
    British to 1963

MONETARY SYSTEM:
    1 Shilling = 12 Pence
    1 Pound = 20 Shillings to 1973
    1 Naira (10 Shillings) = 100 Kobo, 1973-

BRITISH INFLUENCE

GOVERNMENT OF NIGERIA

1918 WW I EMERGENCY ISSUE

		GOOD	FINE	XF
1	**1 SHILLING** Dec. 1918. Green.	400.00	1200.	2500.
1A	**10 SHILLINGS** Dec. 1918. Red.	—	Rare	—

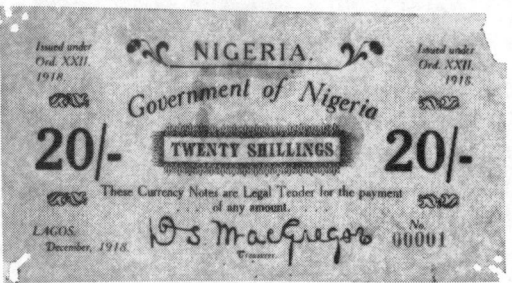

		GOOD	FINE	XF
1B	**20 SHILLINGS** Dec. 1918. Black.	—	Rare	—

FEDERATION OF NIGERIA

CENTRAL BANK OF NIGERIA

1958 ISSUE
#2-5 river scene and palm trees. Printer: W&S.

		VG	VF	UNC
2	**5 SHILLINGS** 15.9.1958. Lilac and blue-green. Back lilac; palms.	5.00	20.00	60.00
3	**10 SHILLINGS** 15.9.1958. Green and brown. Back green; crop sowing and man w/produce.	10.00	50.00	150.00
4	**1 POUND** 15.9.1958. Red and dk. brown. Back red; harvesting coconuts.	2.00	8.00	25.00

		VG	VF	UNC
5	**5 POUNDS** 15.9.1958. Dk. green on green and purple unpt. Back purple; fruit farming at r.	15.00	50.00	175.00

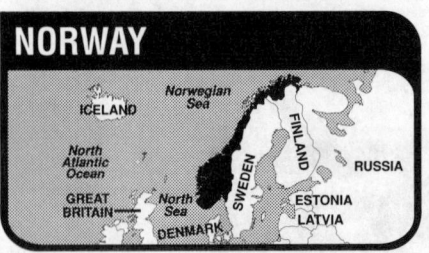

NORWAY

The Kingdom of Norway, a constitutional monarchy located in northwestern Europe, has an area of 150,000 sq. mi. (388,500 sq. km.) including the island territories of Spitzbergen (Svalbard) and Jan Mayen, and a population of 4.27 million. Capital: Oslo (Christiania until 1924). The diversified economic base of Norway includes shipping, fishing, forestry, agriculture, and manufacturing. Nonferrous metals, paper and paperboard, paper pulp, iron, steel and oil are exported.

A United Norwegian kingdom was established in the 9th century, the era of the indomitable Norse Vikings who ranged far and wide, visiting the coasts of northwestern Europe, the Mediterranean, Greenland and North America. In the 13th century, the Norse kingdom was united briefly with Sweden, then passed, through the Union of Kalmar, 1397, to the rule of Denmark which was maintained until 1814. In 1814, Norway fell again under the rule of Sweden. The union lasted until 1905 when the Norwegian Parliament arranged a peaceful separation and invited a Danish prince (King Haakon VII) to occupy the throne of an independent Kingdom of Norway.

RULERS:
Christian V, 1670-1699
Frederik IV, 1699-1730
Christian VI, 1730-1746
Frederik V, 1746-1766
Christian VII, 1766-1808
Frederik VI, 1808-1814
Carl XIII, 1814-1818
Carl XIV Johan, 1818-1844
Oscar I, 1844-1859
Carl XV, 1859-1872
Oscar II, 1872-1905
Haakon VII, 1905-1957
Olav V, 1957-1991
Harald V, 1991-

MONETARY SYSTEM:
1 Speciedaler = 96 Skilling to 1816
1 Speciedaler = 120 Skilling, 1816-1873
1 Krone = 100 Øre, 1873-

KINGDOM

THOR MØHLEN NOTES

1695 ISSUE
#A1-A5 black w/red wax seals. Uniface.

NOTE: All valuations for notes w/o tallon (counterfoil). Tallon may bring 30-50% of actual note valuations.

		GOOD	FINE	XF
A1	**10 RIXDALER CRONER** 1695.	1000.	2000.	3500.
A2	**20 RIXDALER CRONER** 1695.	1000.	2000.	3500.

		GOOD	FINE	XF
A3	**25 RIXDALER CRONER** 1695.	1000.	2000.	3500.
A4	**50 RIXDALER CRONER** 1695.	1200.	2500.	4500.
A5	**100 RIXDALER CRONER** 1695.	1200.	2500.	4500.

REGERINGS KOMMISSION

CHRISTIANIA BRANCH

1807-10 ISSUES

		GOOD	FINE	XF
A12 (A17)	**1 RIGSBANKDALER** 1813-14.	100.00	200.00	600.00
A13 (A18)	**5 RIGSBANKDALER** 1813-14.	125.00	300.00	700.00
A15 (A20)	**50 RIGSBANKDALER** 1813-14.	—	Rare	—
A16 (A21)	**100 RIGSBANKDALER** 1813-14.	—	Rare	—

		GOOD	FINE	XF
A6	**1 RIGSDALER** 1.10.1807.	100.00	250.00	600.00
A7	**5 RIGSDALER** 1.10.1807.	100.00	250.00	600.00

STATTHOLDERBEVIS (PRINSEDLER)

CHRISTIANIA BRANCH

1815 ISSUE

		GOOD	FINE	XF
A8	**10 RIGSDALER** 1.10.1807.	125.00	275.00	700.00
A10	**100 RIGSDALER** 1.10.1807.	150.00	300.00	750.00

		GOOD	FINE	XF
A17 (A22)	**1 RIGSBANKDALER** 1815.	200.00	400.00	1000.
A18 (A23)	**5 RIGSBANKDALER** 1815.	—	Rare	—
A19 (A24)	**15 RIGSBANKDALER** 1815.	—	Rare	—
A20 (A25)	**25 RIGSBANKDALER** 1815.	—	Rare	—

		GOOD	FINE	XF
A21 (A26)	**50 RIGSBANKDALER** 1815.	—	Rare	—

		GOOD	FINE	XF
A11	**12 SKILLING** 1810.	40.00	90.00	200.00

NORGES MIDLERTIDIGE RIGSBANK

RIGSBANKENS NORSKE AVDELING

CHRISTIANIA BRANCH

CHRISTIANIA BRANCH

1813 ISSUE

1814 FRACTIONAL NOTE ISSUE

		GOOD	FINE	XF
A22 (A12)	**3 RIGSBANK-SKILLING** 1814.	60.00	150.00	300.00

		GOOD	FINE	XF
A23 (A13)	**6 RIGSBANK-SKILLING** 1814.	60.00	150.00	300.00
A24 (A14)	**8 RIGSBANK-SKILLING** 1814.	60.00	150.00	300.00
A25 (A15)	**16 RIGSBANK-SKILLING** 1814.	60.00	150.00	300.00

		GOOD	FINE	XF
A30	**1 SPECIEDALER** 1817-24.	500.00	1300.	2000.
A31	**5 SPECIEDALER** 1817-18. Blue paper.	—	Rare	—
A32	**10 SPECIEDALER** 1818-34. Yellow paper.	—	Rare	—
A33	**50 SPECIEDALER** 1818-47. Green paper.	—	Rare	—
A34	**100 SPECIEDALER** 1818-46. Red paper. Ornate arms at l.	—	Rare	—

1825-34 ISSUE
#A35-A38 w/handwritten serial #.

		GOOD	FINE	XF
A35	**24 SKILLING SPECIES** 1834-42.	200.00	400.00	700.00
A36	**1/2 SPECIEDALER** 1834-39.	300.00	500.00	900.00
A37	**1 SPECIEDALER** 1825-43.	500.00	1200.	2000.

		GOOD	FINE	XF
A26 (A16)	**1/2 RIGSBANKDALER-48 SKILLING** 1814.	75.00	200.00	400.00

NORGES BANK

TRONDHJEM BRANCH

1817-22 ISSUES
#A28-A34 w/handwritten serial #.

		GOOD	FINE	XF
A38	**5 SPECIEDALER** 1826-28. Blue paper.	500.00	1200.	2000.

1841-47 ISSUE
#A39 and A40 w/handwritten serial #.

		GOOD	FINE	XF
A39	**1 SPECIEDALER** 1845-49. Gray.	500.00	1200.	2000.
A40 (A42)	**5 SPECIEDALER** 1841-54. Blue-black. Crowned arms at upper ctr.	—	Rare	—

1847-54 ISSUES

		GOOD	FINE	XF
A41 (A40)	**1 SPECIEDALER** 1849-53. Black. Crowned arms at upper ctr.	450.00	1000.	2000.

		GOOD	FINE	XF
A28	**24 SKILLING SPECIES** 1822-26.	200.00	400.00	700.00

		GOOD	FINE	XF
A42 (A41)	**1 SPECIEDALER** 1854-66. Blue. Crowned arms at upper ctr.	450.00	800.00	1500.
A43	**5 SPECIEDALER** 1853-66. Black-blue on blue paper. Ornate crowned arms at upper ctr.	—	Rare	—
A44	**10 SPECIEDALER** 1847-64. Black-yellow on yellow paper.	—	Rare	—

		GOOD	FINE	XF
A29	**1/2 SPECIEDALER** 1822-30.	200.00	400.00	700.00

A45 50 SPECIEDALER
1849-66. Black-green on green paper. Orante crowned arms at upper ctr. — Rare —

A46 100 SPECIEDALER
1847-65. Black and red on red paper. — Rare —

1865-68 ISSUE
#A47-A52 black, red and green on different colors of paper. 4 allegorical figures supporting crowned arms at upper ctr. Crowned arms at ctr. on back. Printer: Saunders, London.

		GOOD	FINE	XF
A47	**1 SPECIEDALER** 1865-77. White paper.	250.00	500.00	1000.
A48	**5 SPECIEDALER** 1866-77. Blue paper.	—	Rare	—
A49	**10 SPECIEDALER** 1866-77. Yellow paper.	—	Rare	—
A50	**50 SPECIEDALER** 1866-77. Green paper.	—	Rare	—
A51	**100 SPECIEDALER** 1866-69. Red paper.	—	Rare	—
A52	**100 SPECIEDALER** 1868-77. Red paper.	—	Rare	—

1877 ISSUE
#1-6 portr. Kg. Oscar II at l. or at top ctr.

		GOOD	FINE	XF
1	**5 KRONER** 1877-99. Black on blue unpt.	135.00	400.00	750.00

		GOOD	FINE	XF
2	**10 KRONER** 1877-99. Black on yellow unpt.	250.00	500.00	950.00

		GOOD	FINE	XF
3	**50 KRONER** 1877-99. Black on green unpt.	—	Rare	—
4	**100 KRONER** 1877-98. Black on pink unpt.	—	Rare	—
5	**500 KRONER** 1877-96. Black on brown unpt.	—	Rare	—

		GOOD	FINE	XF
6	**1000 KRONER** 1877-98. Black on orange-brown unpt.	—	Rare	—

1901 ISSUE
#7-12 portr. Pres. Christie at l. Arms at r. on back.

NOTE: 150 sets of remainders ovpt. *SPECIMEN*, w/4 punch hole cancellations, were distributed by the Norges Bank in 1945, after the series was replaced.

		GOOD	FINE	XF
7	**5 KRONER** 1901-44. Dk. green. Back blue.			
	a. Sign. H. V. Hansen. 1901-16.	50.00	125.00	325.00
	b. Sign. S. Cederholm. 1916-34.	10.00	30.00	75.00
	c. Sign. G. Meldahl Nielsen. 1935-44.	4.00	10.00	30.00
	r. As c. Remainder ovpt. *SPECIMEN*. 1944.	—	Unc	90.00
8	**10 KRONER** 1901-44. Violet. Portr. Adm. Tordenskjold at r. Back tan.			
	a. Sign. H. V. Hansen. 1901-16.	30.00	100.00	200.00
	b. Sign. S. Cederholm. 1917-34.	7.00	20.00	50.00
	c. Sign. G. Meldahl Nielsen. 1935-44.	1.50	5.00	15.00
	r. As c. Remainder ovpt. *SPECIMEN*. 1944.	—	Unc	75.00

9	**50 KRONER**	GOOD	FINE	XF
	1901-45. Green. Bldg. at ctr. on back. Square format.			
	a. Sign. H. V. Hansen. 1901-15.	250.00	500.00	—
	b. Sign. S. Cederholm. 1917-34.	15.00	60.00	100.00
	c. Sign. G. Meldahl Nielsen. 1935-45.	8.00	20.00	60.00
	r. As c. Remainder ovpt: *SPECIMEN.* 1945.	—	Unc	150.00

10	**100 KRONER**	GOOD	FINE	XF
	1901-45. Violet. Portr. Adm. Tordenskjold at r. Bldg. at ctr. on back. Square format.			
	a. Sign. H. V. Hansen. 1901-16.	200.00	400.00	—
	b. Sign. S. Cederholm. 1917-34.	12.00	55.00	110.00
	c. Sign. G. Meldahl Nielsen. 1935-45.	8.00	25.00	60.00
	r. As c. Remainder ovpt: *SPECIMEN.* 1945.	—	Unc	150.00

11	**500 KRONER**	GOOD	FINE	XF
	1901-44. Blue-gray. Bldg. at ctr. on back.			
	a. Sign. H. V. Hansen. 1901-16.	—	Rare	—
	b. Sign. S. Cederholm. 1918-32.	350.00	1000.	—
	c. Sign. G. Meldahl Nielsen. 1936-44.	250.00	500.00	1000.
	r. As c. Remainder ovpt: *SPECIMEN.* 1944.	—	Unc	400.00

12	**1000 KRONER**	GOOD	FINE	XF
	1901-43. Violet. Portr. Adm. Tordenskjold at r. Church at ctr. on back.			
	a. Sign. H. V. Hansen. 1901-16.	—	Rare	—
	b. Sign. S. Cederholm. 1917-32.	150.00	300.00	650.00
	c. Sign. G. Meldahl Nielsen. 1936-43.	100.00	250.00	500.00
	r. As c. Remainder ovpt: *SPECIMEN.* 1943.	—	Unc	300.00

1917-18 SKILLEMYNTSEDLENE ISSUE
Small change notes.

13	**1 KRONE**	VG	VF	UNC
	1917. Black on green unpt. Back green; crowned arms at ctr.	8.00	25.00	70.00
14	**2 KRONER**			
	1918; 1922. Black on pink unpt. Like #13. Back red.	15.00	40.00	100.00

1940 SKILLEMYNTSEDLENE ISSUE

15	**1 KRONE**	VG	VF	UNC
	1940-50. Brown on green unpt. Back green.			
	a. Sign. G. Meldahl Nielsen. 1940-45.	12.00	40.00	90.00
	b. Sign. E. Thorp. 1946-50.	9.00	30.00	75.00
16	**2 KRONER**			
	1940-50. Brown on pink unpt. Like #15. Back red.			
	a. Sign. G. Meldahl Nielsen. 1940-45.	7.00	20.00	50.00
	b. Sign. E. Thorp. 1946-50.	6.00	16.00	40.00

1942 ISSUE
WW II Government in Exile
#17-24 printer: W&S.
#19b-24b w/*KRIGSSEDDEL.*

17	**1 KRONE**	VG	VF	UNC
	1942. Dk. brown on green unpt. Back green.			
	a. Issued note.	20.00	75.00	150.00
	r. As a. Remainder w/ovpt: *SPECIMEN*, punched hole cancelled.	—	—	55.00
	s. Specimen w/red ovpt: *SPECIMEN.*	—	—	110.00
18	**2 KRONER**			
	1942. Dk. brown on pink unpt. Back red.			
	a. Issued note.	25.00	85.00	175.00
	r. As a. Remainder w/ovpt: *SPECIMEN*, punched hole cancelled.	—	—	55.00
	s. Specimen w/red ovpt: *SPECIMEN.*	—	—	110.00

NORGES BANK - POST WW II

1945 ISSUE

			VG	VF	UNC
19	**5 KRONER**				
	1942; 1944. Purple on green, red and brown unpt. Arms at l. Back brown.				
	a. 1942. (Not officially issued).		—	—	1500.
	b. 1944.		50.00	150.00	400.00
	r1. As a. Remainder w/ovpt: *SPECIMEN*, punched hole cancelled.		—	—	200.00
	r2. As b. Remainder w/ovpt: *SPECIMEN*, punched hole cancelled.		—	—	175.00
	s1. As a. Specimen w/red ovpt: *SPECIMEN*.		—	—	350.00
	s2. As b. Specimen w/red ovpt: *SPECIMEN*.		—	—	200.00

			VG	VF	UNC
25	**5 KRONER**				
	1945-54. Blue. Arms at l.				
	a. Sign. G. Meldahl Nielsen. 1945.		6.00	15.00	60.00
	b. Sign. E. Thorp. 1946-54.		8.00	20.00	90.00
26	**10 KRONER**				
	1945-53. Yellow-brown. Arms at l.				
	a. Sign. G. Meldahl Nielsen. 1945-46.		4.00	10.00	55.00
	b. Sign. E. Thorp. 1946-53.		5.00	14.00	65.00

			VG	VF	UNC
20	**10 KRONER**				
	1942; 1944. Red on blue-green and green unpt. Arms at top ctr. Back green.				
	a. 1942. (Not officially issued).		—	—	1500.
	b. 1944.		40.00	100.00	300.00
	r1. As a. Remainder w/ovpt: *SPECIMEN*, punched hole cancelled.		—	—	300.00
	r2. As b. Remainder w/ovpt: *SPECIMEN*, punched hole cancelled.		—	—	100.00
	s1. As a. Specimen w/red ovpt: *SPECIMEN*.		—	—	500.00
	s2. As b. Specimen w/red ovpt: *SPECIMEN*.		—	—	150.00
21	**50 KRONER**				
	1942; 1944. Brown and m/c. Arms at top l. ctr. Back blue.				
	a. 1942. (Not officially issued).		—	—	1500.
	b. 1944.		300.00	700.00	—
	r1. As a. Remainder w/ovpt: *SPECIMEN*, punched hole cancelled.		—	—	300.00
	r2. As b. Remainder w/ovpt: *SPECIMEN*, punched hole cancelled.		—	—	300.00
	s1. As a. Specimen w/red ovpt: *SPECIMEN*.		—	—	600.00
	s2. As b. Specimen w/red ovpt: *SPECIMEN*.		—	—	550.00

			VG	VF	UNC
27	**50 KRONER**				
	1945-50. Green. Arms at l.				
	a. Sign. G. Meldahl Nielsen. 1945.		22.00	50.00	200.00
	b. Sign. E. Thorp. 1947-50.		75.00	200.00	500.00
	s. Specimen, punched hole cancelled.		—	—	—
28	**100 KRONER**				
	1945-49. Red. Arms at l.				
	a. Sign. G. Meldahl Nielsen. 1945-46.		22.00	50.00	200.00
	b. Sign. E. Thorp. 1947-49.		25.00	80.00	250.00
29	**1000 KRONER**				
	1945-47. Lt. brown. Similar to #12, but *GULD* (gold) blocked out at ctr.				
	a. Sign. G. Meldahl Nielsen. 1945-46.		350.00	600.00	1000.
	b. Sign. E. Thorp. 1947.		600.00	900.00	—

1948-55 ISSUE

			VG	VF	UNC
22	**100 KRONER**				
	1942; 1944. Blue and m/c. Arms at top l. ctr. Back orange.				
	a. 1942. (Not officially issued).		—	—	1500.
	b. 1944.		400.00	900.00	1800.
	r1. As a. Remainder w/ovpt: *SPECIMEN*, punched hole cancelled.		—	—	300.00
	r2. As b. Remainder w/ovpt: *SPECIMEN*, punched hole cancelled.		—	—	500.00
	s1. As a. Specimen w/red ovpt: *SPECIMEN*.		—	—	500.00
	s2. As b. Specimen w/red ovpt: *SPECIMEN*.		—	—	550.00
23	**500 KRONER**				
	1942. Green and m/c.				
	a. Not officially issued.		—	—	1750.
	r. Remainder w/ovpt: *SPECIMEN*, punched hole cancelled.		—	—	400.00
	s. Specimen w/red ovpt: *SPECIMEN*.		—	—	650.00
24	**1000 KRONER**				
	1942. Brown and m/c.				
	a. Not officially issued.		—	—	2000.
	r. Remainder w/red ovpt: *SPECIMEN*, punched hole cancelled.		—	—	500.00
	s. Specimen w/red ovpt: *SPECIMEN*.		—	—	750.00

			VG	VF	UNC
30	**5 KRONER**				
	1955-63. Blue. Portr. F. Nansen at l. Fishing scene on back.				
	a. Sign. Brofoss - Thorp. 1955-57.		5.00	20.00	50.00
	b. Sign. Brofoss - Ottesen. 1959-63.		3.00	10.00	40.00

31   10 KRONER

1954-73. Yellow-brown. Portr. C. Michelsen at l. Mercury w/ships on back.

		VG	VF	UNC
a.	Sign. Jahn - Thorp. 1954. Series A-D.	3.00	8.00	40.00
b.	Sign. Brofoss - Thorp. 1954 Series D-1958 Series N.	3.00	8.00	30.00
c.	Sign. Brofoss - Ottesen. 1959-1965 Series A.	FV	3.00	20.00
d.	Sign. Brofoss - Petersen. 1965 Series F-1969.	FV	2.50	12.00
e.	Sign. Brofoss - Odegaard. 1970.	FV	2.50	11.00
f.	Sign. Wold - Odegaard. 1971-73.	FV	FV	8.00

34   500 KRONER

1948-76. Dk. green. Portr. N. Henrik Abel at upper l. and as wmk., crowned supported arms at upper ctr. Factory workers on back.

		VG	VF	UNC
a.	Sign. Jahn - Thorp. 1948; 1951.	115.00	225.00	—
b.	Sign. Brofoss and Thorp. 1954; 1956; 1958.	90.00	200.00	—
c.	Sign. Brofoss - Ottesen. 1960-64.	FV	165.00	—
d.	Sign. Brofoss - Petersen. 1966-69.	FV	140.00	—
e.	Sign. Brofoss - Odegaard. 1970.	FV	125.00	—
f.	Sign. Wold - Odegaard. 1971-76.	FV	115.00	200.00
s.	Specimen.	—	—	—

32   50 KRONER

1950-65. Dk. green. Portr. B. Bjornson at upper l. and as wmk., crowned arms at upper ctr. Harvesting on back.

		VG	VF	UNC
a.	Sign. Jahn - Thorp. 1950-54 Series A; B.	15.00	50.00	200.00
b.	Sign. Brofoss - Thorp. 1954 Series B-1958.	13.50	30.00	125.00
c.	Sign. Brofoss - Ottesen. 1959-65.	10.00	28.50	100.00

33   100 KRONER

1949-62. Red. Portr. H. Wergel at upper l. and as wmk., crowned arms at upper ctr. Logging on back.

		VG	VF	UNC
a.	Sign. Jahn - Thorp. 1949-54 Series C.	22.50	50.00	200.00
b.	Sign. Brofoss - Thorp. 1954-58.	20.00	30.00	125.00
c.	Sign. Brofoss - Ottesen. 1959-62.	20.00	30.00	100.00

35	**1000 KRONER**	**VG**	**VF**	**UNC**
	1949-74. Red-brown. Portr. H. Ibsen at l. and as wmk., crowned supported arms at upper ctr. Old man and child on back.			
	a. Sign. Jahn - Thorp. 1949; 1951; 1953.	175.00	250.00	—
	b. Sign. Brofoss - Thorp. 1955; 1958.	175.00	250.00	—
	c. Sign. Brofoss - Ottesen. 1961; 1962.	170.00	225.00	—
	d. Sign. Brofoss - Petersen. 1965-70.	FV	200.00	—
	e. Sign. Brofoss - Odegaard. 1971-74.	FV	175.00	300.00

MILITARY - WW II

IHENDEHAVARGJELDSBREV

ARMY HIGH COMMAND

1940 ISSUE

#M1-M3 ornamental border at l. Uniface.

NOTE: Issued by Maj. Gen. W. Steffens in Voss w/approval of the branch of the Norges Bank.

M1	**5 KRONER**	**VG**	**VF**	**XF**
	14.4.1940. Black.	60.00	175.00	350.00

M2	**10 KRONER**	**VG**	**VF**	**XF**
	14.4.1940. Black.	65.00	200.00	400.00
M3	**100 KRONER**	**VG**	**VF**	**UNC**
	14.4.1940. Black.	100.00	300.00	600.00

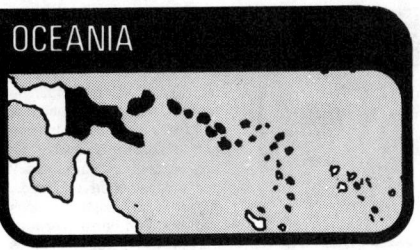

In general usage, Oceania is the collective name for the islands scattered throughout most of the Pacific Ocean. It has traditionally been divided into four parts: Australasia (Australia and New Zealand), Melenesia, Micronesia and Polynesia.

Numismatically, Oceania is the name applied to the Gilbert and Solomon Islands, New Britain, and Papua New Guinea, hence the British denominations.

See also French Oceania.

MONETARY SYSTEM:
1 Pound = 20 Shillings

JAPANESE OCCUPATION - WW II

JAPANESE GOVERNMENT

1942 ND ISSUE

NOTE: Spurious 1/4 Shilling notes exist.

NOTE: Block letters OC may be 42mm or 53mm apart.

1	**1/2 SHILLING**	**VG**	**VF**	**UNC**
	ND (1942). Violet on yellow-brown unpt. Palm trees along the beach at r. Block letters OA-OC.			
	a. Block letters spaced 42mm apart.	1.00	4.00	10.00
	b. Block letters spaced 50-53mm apart.	1.00	2.50	6.00
	c. Block letters: OC spaced 50-53mm apart.	.25	.75	2.50
	s. Specimen w/red ovpt: *Mi-hon. Specimen* on back.	—	—	100.00
2	**1 SHILLING**			
	ND (1942). Blue on green unpt. Breadfruit tree at l., palm trees along the beach at r. Block letters: OA-OC.			
	s1. Specimen w/red ovpt: *Mi-hon. Specimen* on back.	—	—	100.00
	s2. Specimen w/lg. red ovpt: *Mi-hon.*	—	—	100.00
3	**10 SHILLINGS**			
	ND (1942). Brown. Palm trees along the beach at r. Block letters : OA.			
	a. Issued note.	3.00	12.50	50.00
	s. Specimen w/red ovpt: *Mi-hon. Specimen* on back.	—	—	100.00

4	**1 POUND**	**VG**	**VF**	**UNC**
	ND (1942). Green on lt. blue unpt. Palm trees along beach at r. Block letters : OA.			
	a. Issued note.	.65	2.50	10.00
	s. Specimen w/red ovpt: *Mi-hon. Specimen* on back.	—	—	100.00

AUSTRALIAN "REPLICAS"

1943 ISSUE

NOTE: Reprints of #1, 2 and 4 were made in Australia in 1943 (Poor printing paper w/weak wmk.), mostly w/ovpt: *REPLICA* on back. Modern copies are also reported.

R1	**1/2 SHILLING**			
	ND (1943). Violet on yellow-brown unpt. Like #1 w/red ovpt: *REPLICA.* Block letters : OC.	12.00	30.00	75.00
R2	**1 SHILLING**			
	ND (1943). Bright blue. on green unpt. Like #1 w/red ovpt: *REPLICA.* Block letters: OC.	12.00	30.00	75.00
R3	**1 SHILLING**			
	ND (1943). Dk. blue-gray w/o guilloche or ovpt: *REPLICA.* Block letters : OC.	12.00	30.00	—
R4	**1 POUND**			
	ND (1943). Green w/modified blue guilloche. Red ovpt: *REPLICA* on back. Block letters : OA.	16.50	40.00	100.00
R5	**1 POUND**			
	ND (1943). W/o ovpt: *REPLICA* on back.			
	a. Green w/modified pale blue guilloche.	12.00	30.00	75.00
	b. Dk. olive-green.	16.50	40.00	—
	c. Bright Green.	16.50	40.00	—

The Islamic Republic of Pakistan, located on the Indian subcontinent between India and Afghanistan, has an area of 310,404 sq. mi. (803,943 sq. m.) and a population of 114 million. Capital: Islamabad. Pakistan is mainly an agricultural land. Yarn, cotton, rice and leather are exported.

Afghan and Turkish intrusions into norhtern India between the 11th and 18th centuries resulted in large numbers of indians being converted to Islam. The idea of a separate Moslem state indepenent of Hindu India developed in the 1930's and was agreed to by Britain in 1946. The Islamic majority areas of india, consisting of the separate geographic entities known as East and West Pakistan, achieved self-government as Pakistan, with dominion status in the British Commonwealth, when the British withdrew from India on Aug. 14, 1947. Pakistan became a republic in 1956. When a basic constitutional crisis initiated by the election of Dec. 1, 1970 - the first direct general election in Pakistani history - could not be resolved by the leaders of East and West Pakistan, the East Pakistanis seceded from the Islamic Republic of Pakistan (March 26, 1971) and formed the independent People's Republic of Bangladesh.

MONETARY SYSTEM:
1 Rupee = 16 Annas to 1961
1 Rupee = 100 Paisa (Pice), 1961-

REPUBLIC

GOVERNMENT OF PAKISTAN

1947 ND PROVISIONAL ISSUE
#1-3A ovpt: *GOVERNMENT OF PAKISTAN* in English and Urdu on Government and Reserve Bank of India notes.

1	1 RUPEE	GOOD	FINE	XF
	ND (1947-48). Gray-green. Ovpt. on India #25c.	5.00	20.00	45.00

1A	2 RUPEES	GOOD	FINE	XF
	ND (1947-48). Lilac.			
	a. Ovpt. on India #17b.	10.00	40.00	85.00
	b. Ovpt. on India #17c.	7.00	30.00	65.00

2	5 RUPEES	GOOD	FINE	XF
	ND (1947-48). Green. Ovpt. on India #23a.	15.00	50.00	100.00

3	10 RUPEES	GOOD	FINE	XF
	ND (1947-48). Violet. Ovpt. on India #24.	15.00	60.00	100.00
3A	100 RUPEES			
	ND (1947-48). Dk. green and lilac. Ovpt. on India #20k.	35.00	150.00	250.00

1949 ND ISSUE
#4-10 arms at r.

4	1 RUPEE	VG	VF	UNC
	ND (1949). Green on m/c unpt. Archway on back. Wmk: Arms.	2.00	10.00	25.00

5	5 RUPEES	VG	VF	UNC
	ND (1949). Blue on tan unpt.	5.00	20.00	60.00

6	10 RUPEES	VG	VF	UNC
	ND (1949). Orange on green unpt.	8.00	30.00	85.00

7	100 RUPEES	VG	VF	UNC
	ND (1949). Green on tan unpt.	5.00	110.00	375.00

1952 ISSUE

		VG	VF	UNC
8	**1 RUPEE** ND (1952). Blue on m/c unpt. Similar to #4. Back blue. Sign. varieties.	.25	1.75	4.00

STATE BANK OF PAKISTAN

CITY OVERPRINT VARIETIES

Dacca   Karachi   Lahore

Some notes exist w/Arabic and some w/Sanskrit ovpt. denoting city of issue, Dacca, Karachi or Lahore. These are much scarcer than the regular issues. Sign. varieties.

1953 ND ISSUE
#11-14 wmk: Arms. Printer: TDLR (w/o imprint).

		VG	VF	UNC
11	**2 RUPEES** ND (1953). Brown on pink and lt. green unpt. Tower at r. Mosque at l. ctr. on back.	10.00	30.00	75.00

		VG	VF	UNC
12	**5 RUPEES** ND (1953). Purple on lt. green unpt. Boat w/cargo at ctr. Mountain scene on back. 3. sign. varieties.	.75	5.00	12.50

		VG	VF	UNC
13	**10 RUPEES** ND (1953). Brown on lt. yellow unpt. Park scene. Mosque on back. 2 serial # varieties. 4 sign. varieties.	2.00	10.00	35.00
14	**100 RUPEES** ND (1953). Red-brown. Similar to #7. Wmk. area at r. on face. 2 sign. varieties.	20.00	75.00	175.00

1957 ISSUE
#15-18 portr. of M. Ali Jinnah and as wmk.

		VG	VF	UNC
15	**5 RUPEES** ND (1957). Purple on lt. blue and maroon unpt. Jinnah at ctr. Terraces on back. 3 sign. varieties	.50	2.00	7.50

		VG	VF	UNC
16	**10 RUPEES** ND (1957). Brown and m/c. Jinnah at l. Park scene on back. 2 sign. varieties w/sign. in Urdu or Latin letters.	.50	3.00	10.00
17	**50 RUPEES** ND (1957). Blue-green on peach unpt. Jinnah at ctr. Back green; sailing ships. 3 sign. varieties.			
	a. 1. sign.	2.50	5.00	35.00
	b. 2. sign.	2.50	6.00	40.00

790 PAKISTAN

18	**100 RUPEES**			
		VG	**VF**	**UNC**
	ND (1957). Green on violet and peach unpt. Jinnah at ctr. Mosque on back. 3 sign. varieties.			
	a. Issued note.	2.00	6.00	35.00
	b. Ovpt: *Dacca.*	3.00	10.00	55.00
	c. Ovpt: *Karachi.*	3.00	8.00	50.00
	d. Ovpt: *Lahore.*	3.00	10.00	55.00

REGIONAL

GOVERNMENT OF PAKISTAN

CA. 1950'S ND ISSUE
#R1 ovpt: *FOR PILGRIMS FROM PAKISTAN/FOR USE IN SAUDI ARABIA AND IRAQ.*

R1	**100 RUPEES**	**VG**	**VF**	**UNC**
	ND. (ca. 1950's) Red.	450.00	1150.	—

STATE BANK OF PAKISTAN

CA. 1950'S ND ISSUE
#R2 ovpt: *FOR HAJ PILGRIMS FROM PAKISTAN/FOR USE IN SAUDI ARABIA ONLY.*

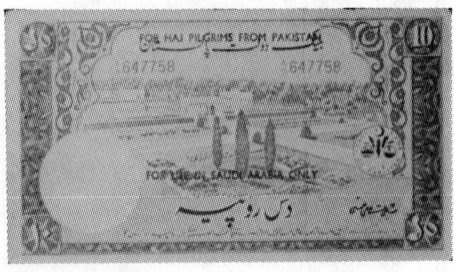

R2	**10 RUPEES**	**VG**	**VF**	**UNC**
	ND (ca.1950's). Green. 2 sign. varieties.	20.00	55.00	165.00

Palestine, a former British mandate in southwest Asia at the eastern end of the Mediterranean Sea, had an area of 10,160 sq. mi. (26,315 sq. km.). It included Israel and that part of Jordan lying west of the Jordan River. Ancient Palestine (the territory occupied in biblical times by the kingdoms of Israel and Judah) was somewhat larger, including lands east of the Jordan River.

Because of its position as part of the land bridge connecting Asia and Africa, Palestine was invaded and conquered by virtually all the historic powers of Europe and the Near East. From 1516 to 1917, it was held by the Ottoman Empire. In 1917, it was conquered by the British under Allenby and assigned as a British mandate, effective 1922. The British ruled Palestine until 1948, and succeeded in satisfying neither the Arab majority nor the growing Jewish population. The United Nations recommended the establishment of separate Jewish and Arab states in Palestine.

The British left Palestine on May 14, 1948, and the State of Israel was proclaimed. In 1950, the Kingdom of Jordan annexed the west bank of the Jordan River. This was seized by Israel in 1967, bringing the entire former mandate under Israeli administration.

RULERS:
British, 1917-1948

MONETARY SYSTEM:
1 Pound = 1000 Mils

NOTE: For issues of the Anglo-Palestine Bank Ltd., refer to Israel.

BRITISH INFLUENCE

PALESTINE CURRENCY BOARD

1927 ISSUE
#6-11 Citadel of Jerusalem (commonly called the Tower of David) at ctr. on back. Printer: TDLR.

NOTE: According to Bank of England records, only 6 pcs. of #11 are outstanding. Four are known.

6	**500 MILS**	**GOOD**	**FINE**	**XF**
	1927-45. Purple on green unpt. Rachel's tomb near Bethlehem at lower l.			
	a. 1.9.1927.	80.00	180.00	300.00
	b. 30.9.1929.	70.00	110.00	250.00
	c. 20.4.1939.	60.00	100.00	200.00
	d. 15.8.1945.	70.00	110.00	250.00

7	**1 POUND**	**GOOD**	**FINE**	**XF**
	1927-44. Green and black. Dome on the Rock at l.			
	a. 1.9.1927.	85.00	200.00	550.00
	b. 30.9.1929.	50.00	125.00	350.00

PANAMA

The Republic of Panama, a Central American country situated between Costa Rica and Colombia, has an area of 29,206 sq. mi. (77,083 sq. km.) and a population of 2.4 million. Capital: Panama City. The Panama Canal is the country's biggest asset; servicing world related transit trade and international commerce. Bananas, refined petroleum, sugar and shrimp are exported.

Panama was visited by Christopher Columbus in 1502 during his fourth voyage to the Americas. It was explored by Vasco de Balboa in 1513. Panama City, founded in 1519, was a primary trans-shipment center for treasure and supplies both to and from Spain and the Colonies. Panama declared its independence in 1821 and joined the Confederation of Greater Colombia. In 1903, after Colombia rejected a treaty enabling the United States to build the Canal across the Isthmus, Panama, with the support of the United States, proclaimed its independence from Colombia and became a sovereign republic.

Notes of the United States have normally circulated throughout Panama.

MONETARY SYSTEM:
  1 Balboa = 100 Centesimos

NOTE: Certain listings encompassing issues circulated by various bank and regional authorities are contained in Volume 1 under Colombia.

c. 20.4.1939.		45.00	100.00	300.00
d. 1.1.1944.		50.00	125.00	350.00

REPUBLIC OF PANAMA
The Sosa Project was conceived by Don Martin Sosa, Comptroller General of Panama in 1933.

REPÚBLICA DE PANAMA

1933 "SOSA" ISSUE

		GOOD	FINE	XF
21	**1 BALBOA** 5.8.1933. Arms at l., Balboa standing w/sword and flag at r. (Not issued).	—	—	—
21A	**10 BALBOAS** 1933.		Reported Not Confirmed	

BANCO CENTRAL DE EMISIÓN
Issued under the Government of President Arnulfo Arias.

1941 "ARIAS" ISSUE
#22-25 arms at ctr. on back. Printer: HBNC.

NOTE: After a very short circulation period #22-25 were recalled and almost all were destroyed.

		GOOD	FINE	XF
8	**5 POUNDS** 1927-44. Red and black. Crusader's Tower at Ramleh at l.			
	a. 1.9.1927.	—	Rare	—
	b. 30.9.1929.	110.00	275.00	500.00
	c. 20.4.1939.	100.00	275.00	400.00
	d. 1.1.1944.	110.00	225.00	500.00

		VG	VF	UNC
22	**1 BALBOA** 1941. Black on green and red unpt. Balboa at ctr. Back green.			
	a. Issued note.	275.00	650.00	1250.
	s. Specimen.	—	—	700.00

		VG	VF	UNC
23	**5 BALBOAS** 1941. Black on blue, violet and orange unpt. Urraca at l. Back blue.			
	a. Issued note.	750.00	1500.	2750.
	s. Specimen.	—	—	1250.

		GOOD	FINE	XF
9	**10 POUNDS** 1927-44. Blue and black. Like #8.			
	a. 1.9.1927.	—	Rare	—
	b. 30.9.1929.	125.00	400.00	900.00
	c. 7.9.1939.	100.00	300.00	650.00
	d. 1.1.1944.	100.00	350.00	750.00
10	**50 POUNDS** 1927-39. Purple and black. Like #8.			
	a. 1.9.1927.	—	Rare	—
	b. 30.9.1929.	—	Rare	—
	c. 7.9.1939.	—	Rare	—
11	**100 POUNDS** 1927-42. Green and black. Like #8.			
	a. 1.9.1927.	—	Rare	—
	b. 30.9.1929.	—	Rare	—
	c. 10.9.1942.	Reported Not Confirmed		

24	**10 BALBOAS**	**VG**	**VF**	**UNC**
	1941. Black on violet, orange and green unpt. Old fortress at ctr. Back brown.			
	a. Issued note.	950.00	2000.	4000.
	s. Specimen.	—	—	1800.

25	**20 BALBOAS**	**VG**	**VF**	**UNC**
	1941. Black on orange, red and violet. Ox cart at ctr. Back orange.			
	a. Issued note.	1250.	3000.	6000.
	s. Specimen.	—	—	3000.

The Republic of Paraguay, a landlocked country in the heart of South America surrounded by Argentina, Bolivia and Brazil, has an area of 157,048 sq. mi. (406,752 sq. km.) and a population of 4.4 million, 95 percent of whom are of mixed Spanish and Indian descent. Capital: Asuncion. The country is predominantly agrarian, with no important mineral deposits or oil reserves. Meat, timber, oilseeds, tobacco and cotton account for 70 percent of Paraguay's export revenue.

Paraguay was first visited by Alejo Garcia, a shipwrecked Spaniard, in 1520. The interior was explored by Sebastian Cabot in 1526 and 1529, when he sailed up the Parana and Paraguay Rivers. Asuncion, which would become the center of a province embracing much of southern South America, was established by the Spanish explorer Juan de Salazar on Aug. 15, 1537. For a century and a half the history of Paraguay was largely the history of the agricultural colonies established by the Jesuits in the south and east to Christianize the Indians. In 1811, following the outbreak of the South American wars of independence, Paraguayan patriots overthrew the local Spanish authorities and proclaimed their country's independence.

MONETARY SYSTEM:
- 1 Peso = 100 Centesimos to 1870
- 1 Peso = 100 Centavos (Centesimos) to 1944
- 1 Guarani = 100 Centimos, 1944-

REPÚBLICA DEL PARAGUAY

EL TESORO NACIONAL

NATIONAL TREASURY
#1-30 lithographed notes. Uniface.
#1-17 w/monogram of Carlos Antonio Lopez, President of the Republic.

DECRETO DE 13 DE FEBRERO DE 1856
#1-4 black seal at ctr.

1	**1/2 REAL**	**GOOD**	**FINE**	**XF**
	ND (1856). Black. Flowers at l. 175 x 120mm.	25.00	80.00	200.00

2	**4 REALES**	**GOOD**	**FINE**	**XF**
	ND (1856). Black. Burro at upper l. 155 x 105mm.	30.00	100.00	225.00
3	**1 PESO**			
	ND (1856). Black. Leopard at upper l. 165 x 120mm.	20.00	50.00	125.00
4	**2 PESOS**			
	ND (1856). Black. Goat looking l. at upper l. 160 x 120mm.	20.00	50.00	125.00

DECRETO DE 29 DE ABRIL DE 1859

5	**1 REAL**	**GOOD**	**FINE**	**XF**
	ND (1859). Black. Bottle at upper l., black seal at ctr. 170 x 110mm.	45.00	75.00	175.00

DECRETO DE 17 DE MAYO DE 1859

6	**1 PESO**	**GOOD**	**FINE**	**XF**
	ND (1859). Black. Leopard at upper ctr. 160 x 115mm.			

DECRETO DE 10 DE JUNIO DE 1860

		Good	Fine	XF
7	**1/2 REAL**			
	ND (1860). Black. Flowers at upper l., arms at upper ctr. 105 x 65mm.	25.00	80.00	200.00

		Good	Fine	XF
8	**1 REAL**			
	ND (1860). Black. Bottle at l., arms at upper ctr. 120 x 75mm.	20.00	50.00	125.00
9	**2 REALES**			
	ND (1860). Black. Man w/horse at upper l., arms at upper ctr. and r. 2 sign. varieties. 125 x 80mm.	7.50	17.50	50.00

		Good	Fine	XF
10	**4 REALES**			
	ND (1860). Black. Burro at upper l., arms at upper ctr. 2 sign. varieties. 140 x 100mm.	10.00	30.00	80.00

		Good	Fine	XF
11	**1 PESO**			
	ND (1860). Black. Leopard at upper l., arms at upper ctr. 3 sign. varieties. 150 x 105mm.	10.00	30.00	80.00

		Good	Fine	XF
12	**2 PESOS**			
	ND (1860). Black and pink. Goat looking r. at upper l., arms at upper ctr. 165 x 105mm.	6.00	15.00	50.00

		Good	Fine	XF
13	**3 PESOS**			
	ND (1860). Black and lt. green. Woman, harvest and ship at upper l., arms at upper ctr. 185 x 115mm.	7.50	17.50	50.00

DECRETO DE 21 DE SETIEMBRE DE 1861

		Good	Fine	XF
14	**5 PESOS**			
	ND (1861). Black. Steam passenger train at upper l., arms at upper ctr. 175 x 115mm.	7.50	20.00	60.00

DECRETO DE 14 DE NOVIEMBRE DE 1861

		Good	Fine	XF
15	**4 PESOS**			
	ND (1861). Blue. Blindfolded Justice seated at upper l., oval arms at upper ctr. 180 x 115mm.	10.00	30.00	80.00

DECRETO DE 31 DE MARZO DE 1862
#16-17 oval arms at ctr.

	20	4 REALES		GOOD	FINE	XF
		ND (1865). Black. Ram at upper l. 145 x 95mm.		3.50	17.50	40.00

16	4 PESOS		GOOD	FINE	XF
	ND (1862). Black. Oxen w/plow at l. 190 x 125mm.		3.00	10.00	35.00

	21	1 PESO		GOOD	FINE	XF
		ND (1865). Blue. Ox at upper l. 155 x 105mm.		3.50	17.50	40.00

	22	2 PESOS		GOOD	FINE	XF
		ND (1865). Blue. Man w/horse-drawn cart at upper l. 165 x 95mm.		3.50	17.50	40.00

17	5 PESOS		GOOD	FINE	XF
	ND (1862). Black. Man riding w/2 burros at upper l. 180 x 120mm.		7.50	20.00	55.00

DECRETO DE 25 DE MARZO DE 1865
Issues of Mariscal Lopez, the son of Carlos Antonio Lopez who took the presidency of the Republic in 1862.
#18-30 black seal at upper ctr.

18	1 REAL		GOOD	FINE	XF
	ND (1865). Black. Man walking w/sack on stick at upper l. 140 x 90mm.		10.00	40.00	100.00

	23	3 PESOS		GOOD	FINE	XF
		ND (1865). Blue. Ship at upper l. 160 x 110mm.		3.50	17.50	40.00

19	2 REALES		GOOD	FINE	XF
	ND (1865). Black. Floral design at l. 140 x 95mm.		3.50	17.50	40.00

24	**4 PESOS**	GOOD	FINE	XF
	ND (1865). Blue. Oxen w/plow at l. 190 x 115mm.	3.50	17.50	40.00

25	**5 PESOS**	GOOD	FINE	XF
	ND (1865). Blue. Similar to #17, but w/o monogram at r. Slightly reduced size, 170 x 115mm.	3.00	15.00	35.00

26	**10 PESOS**	GOOD	FINE	XF
	ND (1865). Blue. Woman carrying sack at l., arms at l. and r. 190 x 125mm.	3.50	17.50	40.00

1865-70 ISSUE

#27-30, reduced size notes.

27	**3 PESOS**	GOOD	FINE	XF
	ND (1865-70). Black. Ship at upper l. 160 x 90mm.	7.50	25.00	75.00
28	**4 PESOS**	GOOD	FINE	XF
	ND (1865-70). Black. Oxen w/plow at l. 175 x 95mm.	7.50	25.00	75.00
29	**5 PESOS**			
	ND (1865-70). Black. Similar to #25. 155 x 95mm.	15.00	40.00	100.00
30	**10 PESOS**			
	ND (1865-70). Black. Similar to #26, but w/o arms at l. and r. 200 x 95mm.	3.50	17.50	40.00

WAR OF THE TRIPLE ALLIANCE, 1864-70

NOTE: Apparently, during one stage of the war, these notes of the reduced size (#27-29) were ovpt. w/red circle inscribed: *TERCERA SERIE.*

1868 ISSUE

31	**3 PESOS**	GOOD	FINE	XF
	ND (1868). Red ovpt. on #27.	3.50	12.50	35.00

32	**4 PESOS**	GOOD	FINE	XF
	ND (1868). Red ovpt. on #28.	3.50	12.50	35.00
33	**5 PESOS**			
	ND (1868). Red ovpt. on #29.	3.50	12.50	35.00

1870 ISSUE

#37-39 issued w/o or w/2 oval handstamps on back of *MINISTERIO DE HACIENDA* **and the** *TESORERIA GENERAL-ASUNCION* **around arms.**

#40 *Deleted.*

34	**1 REAL**	GOOD	FINE	XF
	29.12.1870. Black and green. Arms at l.			
35	**2 REALES**			
	29.12.1870.			
36	**4 REALES**			
	29.12.1870. Black and green. Dog at l., arms at upper ctr.			

37	**50 CENTESIMOS**	GOOD	FINE	XF
	29.12.1870. Black. W/ w/o 2 oval handstamps on back. Uniface.			
	a. W/o 2 oval handstamps on back.	—	Rare	—
	b. W/2 oval handstamps on back.	—	Rare	—

38	**1 PESO**	GOOD	FINE	XF
	29.12.1870. Black. Bull at ctr. W/ w/o 2 oval handstamps on back.			
	a. W/o 2 oval handstamps on back.	—	Rare	—
	b. W/2 oval handstamps on back.	—	Rare	—

39	**5 PESOS**	GOOD	FINE	XF
	29.12.1870. Black. Arms at ctr. W/ w/o 2 oval handstamps on back.			
	a. W/o 2 oval handstamps on back.	—	Rare	—
	b. W/2 oval handstamps on back.			

1871 ISSUE

		GOOD	FINE	XF
41	**1/2 REAL** 1871. Black. Arms at upper l., rooster at ctr.			
	a. Issued note.	—	—	—
	r. Signed remainder.	—	—	—

		GOOD	FINE	XF
42	**1 REAL** 15.7.1871. Black. Arms at l. 2 sign. varieties.			
43	**2 REALES** 15.7.1871.	—	—	—

		GOOD	FINE	XF
44	**4 REALES** 15.7.1871. Black. Dog at l., arms at upper ctr. 2 sign. varieties.	—	—	—
45	**1 PESO** 15.7.1871.	—	—	—
46	**5 PESOS** 15.7.1871.	—	—	—
47	**10 PESOS** 15.7.1871.	—	—	—

CAJA DE CONVERSION

LAW OF 9.1.1874; DECREE OF 4.3.1874

#48-52 printer: Ludovico Sartori y Cia. Uniface.

NOTE: Some examples of #48 appear w/2 oval overstamps on back.

		GOOD	FINE	XF
48	**10 CENTAVOS** 15.3.1874. Black. 2 sign. varieties.	—	Rare	—
49	**20 CENTAVOS** 15.3.1874. Brown. 2 sign varieties.	—	Rare	—
50	**50 CENTAVOS** 15.3.1874. Black. Sheep at ctr. 2 sign. varieties.	—	Rare	—
51	**1 PESO** 15.3.1874. Orange and black. 4 sign. varieties.			
	a. Issued note.	—	Rare	—
	b. W/2 oval handstamps on back (like #37b-39b).	—	Rare	—
52	**5 PESOS** 1874. 2 sign. varieties.	—	Rare	—

TESORO NACIONAL

NATIONAL TREASURY

LEY DE 22.4.1875

#60, 61, 66 and 67 printer: Lit. San Martin-Argentina.

#62-65 Held in reserve.

#68-86 held in reserve.

NOTE: Apparently #60 and 61 are part of a later series because of their signatures.

		GOOD	FINE	XF
60	**5 CENTAVOS** L.1875. Green. Ram at upper ctr. 2 sign. varieties.	—	Rare	—
61	**20 CENTAVOS** L.1875.	—	—	—
66	**10 PESOS** L.1875. Orange and black. woman's head at l. and r., mountain scene at ctr.			
67	**20 PESOS** L.1875. M/c. Boy standing at l., paddle steamer at upper ctr.			

REPÚBLICA DEL PARAGUAY

Government Notes

LEY DE 24 DE SETIEMBRE DE 1894

#87-94 printer: G&D.

		GOOD	FINE	XF
87	**50 CENTAVOS** L.1894. Orange and black. Arms at ctr. 4 sign. varieties.	8.00	25.00	80.00
88	**1 PESO** L.1894. Black, dk. red and blue. Arms at l. Back dk. red. 3 sign. varieties.	8.00	25.00	80.00
89	**5 PESOS** L.1894. Blue and orange. Arms at r. 3 sign. varieties.	15.00	50.00	125.00
90	**10 PESOS** L.1894.	Reported Not Confirmed		
91	**20 PESOS** L.1894. Arms at l.	—	Rare	—
92	**50 PESOS** L.1894.	Reported Not Confirmed		
93	**100 PESOS** L.1894. Black and orange. Woman w/torch at l., arms at ctr. 2 sign. varieties.	—	Rare	—

		GOOD	FINE	XF
94	**200 PESOS** L.1894. Lt. blue and orange unpt. Arms at l., portr. Gen. Egusquiza at top ctr. 2 sign. varieties.	150.00	550.00	—

LEY DE 18 DE NOVIEMBRE DE 1899

#95-157 have identical designs for each denomination (some with minor variations).

#95-104 arms on back. Printer: ABNC.

		GOOD	FINE	XF
95	**50 CENTAVOS** L.1899. Black on orange unpt. Minerva wearing helmet at l. Back orange.	2.50	6.50	20.00
96	**1 PESO** L.1899. Black on green unpt. Woman wearing straw hat at ctr. Back green. 2 sign. varieties.	3.50	10.00	25.00
97	**2 PESOS** L.1899. Black on lt. brown unpt. Government palace at ctr. Back brown. 2 sign. varieties.	4.50	15.00	40.00

98	**5 PESOS**			
	L.1899. Black on lilac, peach and blue unpt. View of city of Asuncion from river. Back dk. blue.	6.00	25.00	60.00
99	**10 PESOS**			
	L.1899. Black on green unpt. Cathedral at r. ctr. Back gray-green.	10.00	35.00	80.00
100	**20 PESOS**			
	L.1899. Black on blue and yellow unpt. Congressional palace at ctr. Back dk. blue. 2 sign. varieties.	15.00	40.00	100.00
101	**50 PESOS**			
	L.1899. Black on yellow and brown unpt. Municipal theater at r. Back dk. brown; man's head at ctr.	20.00	60.00	150.00
102	**100 PESOS**			
	L.1899. Black on red and yellow unpt. Guaira waterfall at ctr. Back red; woman's head at ctr.	22.50	75.00	175.00
103	**200 PESOS**			
	L.1899. Black on yellow and orange unpt. Mountain and farm at ctr. r. Back orange; woman's head at l.	40.00	125.00	300.00

		GOOD	FINE	XF
104	**500 PESOS**			
	L.1899. Black on lilac and yellow unpt. Woman w/child at l., ruins at Humaita at r. Back blue-gray.	50.00	200.00	500.00

LEY DE 14 DE JULIO DE 1903

#105-114 date of the law in 1 or 2 lines, arms on back. Printer: ABNC.

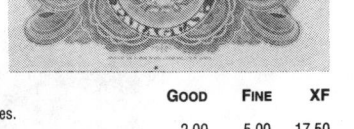

		GOOD	FINE	XF
105	**50 CENTAVOS**			
	L.1903. Like #95. Back green. 4 sign. varieties.			
	a. Date in 2 lines.	2.00	5.00	17.50
	b. Date in 1 line.	2.00	5.00	17.50

		GOOD	FINE	XF
106	**1 PESO**			
	L.1903. Like #96. Date in 1 line. Back brown. 4 sign. varieties.			
	a. Serial # at upper r.	3.00	8.00	25.00
	b. Serial # at bottom ctr.	2.50	7.50	22.50

		GOOD	FINE	XF
107	**2 PESOS**			
	L.1903. Like #97. Date in 1 line. Back brown. 2 sign. varieties.			
	a. Serial # at upper r.	4.00	12.50	27.50
	b. Serial # at bottom ctr.	3.00	10.00	25.00

		GOOD	FINE	XF
108	**5 PESOS**			
	L.1903. Like #98. Back brown. 5 sign. varieties.			
	a. Date in 2 lines.	5.00	17.50	50.00
	b. Date in 1 line.	4.00	15.00	40.00
109	**10 PESOS**			
	L.1903. Like #99. Date in 1 line. Back olive. 5 sign. varieties.			
	a. Serial # at bottom l. and r.	8.00	25.00	75.00
	b. Serial # at bottom ctr.	7.00	22.50	60.00
110	**20 PESOS**			
	L.1903. Like #100. 2 sign. varieties.			
	a. Date in 2 lines.	10.00	35.00	90.00
	b. Date in 1 line.	12.50	37.50	100.00
111	**50 PESOS**			
	L.1903. Like #101. Date in 2 lines. Back brown. 5 sign. varieties.			
	a. Serial # at bottom l. and r.	17.50	50.00	115.00
	b. Serial # at bottom ctr.	15.00	45.00	100.00
112	**100 PESOS**			
	L.1903. Like #102. Date in 1 line. Back red. 3 sign. varieties.			
	a. Serial # at upper l. and r.	20.00	65.00	150.00
	b. Serial # at bottom ctr.	17.50	55.00	125.00
113	**200 PESOS**			
	L.1903. Like #103. Date in 1 line. Back orange. 6 sign varieties.			
	a. Serial # at lower l. and upper r.	35.00	100.00	260.00
	b. Serial # at bottom ctr.	30.00	90.00	225.00
114	**500 PESOS**			
	L.1903. Like #104. Date in 2 lines. Back blue. 5 sign. varieties.			
	a. Serial # at upper l. and lower r.	35.00	160.00	375.00
	b. Serial # at bottom ctr.	40.00	165.00	350.00

LEY DE 26 DE DICIEMBRE DE 1907

#115-124 arms on back. Printer: ABNC.

#115-120 sign. Evaristo Acosta and Juan Y. Ugarte.

		VG	VF	UNC
115	**50 CENTAVOS**			
	L.1907. Black on green unpt. Like #95. Back green.	2.00	4.00	10.00
116	**1 PESO**			
	L.1907. Black on orange unpt. Like #96. Back orange.	2.50	6.00	20.00

		VG	VF	UNC
117	**2 PESOS**			
	L.1907. Black on blue unpt. Like #97. Back blue.	3.00	8.50	25.00

118	**5 PESOS**	**VG**	**VF**	**UNC**
	L.1907. Black on yellow and orange unpt. Like #98.	4.00	12.50	35.00
119	**10 PESOS**			
	L.1907. Black on yellow and green unpt. Like #99.	6.00	15.00	45.00
120	**20 PESOS**			
	L.1907. Black on yellow unpt. Like #100.	10.00	25.00	75.00

132	**50 PESOS**	**GOOD**	**FINE**	**XF**
	L.1912. Ovpt. on #158.	25.00	55.00	160.00
133	**100 PESOS**			
	L.1912. Ovpt. on #111.	35.00	75.00	200.00
134	**100 PESOS**			
	L.1912. Ovpt. on #159.	30.00	65.00	180.00
135	**200 PESOS**			
	L.1912. Ovpt. on #112.	30.00	65.00	180.00
136	**500 PESOS**			
	L.1912. Ovpt. on #114.	30.00	65.00	180.00

LEY DE 28 DE ENERO DE 1916
#137-142 w/text: *LA OFICINA DE CAMBIOS* below serial #. Arms on back. Printer: ABNC.

121	**50 PESOS**	**VG**	**VF**	**UNC**
	L.1907. Black on rose and yellow unpt. Like #101. 2 sign. varieties.	10.00	25.00	75.00
122	**100 PESOS**	**GOOD**	**FINE**	**XF**
	L.1907. Black on yellow and tan unpt. Like #102. 3 sign. varieties.	12.50	30.00	90.00
123	**200 PESOS**			
	L.1907. Back lilac. Like #103. 6 sign. varieties.	30.00	80.00	200.00

137	**50 CENTAVOS**	**VG**	**VF**	**UNC**
	L.1916. Like #115. Back green. 4 sign. varieties.	1.50	3.50	10.00

124	**500 PESOS**	**GOOD**	**FINE**	**XF**
	L.1907. Back orange. Like #104. 7 sign. varieties.	30.00	80.00	200.00

1912 PROVISIONAL ISSUE
#125-136 arms on back. Printer: ABNC.

#125-133 w/black oval ovpt: *EMISION DEL ESTADO LEY 11 DE ENERO DE 1912.*

#127, 129, 132 and 134 w/ *PESOS ORO SELLADO* barred out.

#126, 128 and 130 *Deleted.*

125	**2 PESOS**	**GOOD**	**FINE**	**XF**
	L.1912. Ovpt. on #107.	15.00	35.00	95.00
127	**5 PESOS**			
	L.1912. Ovpt. on #156.	15.00	35.00	95.00

138	**1 PESO**	**VG**	**VF**	**UNC**
	L.1916. Like #116. Back orange. 4 sign. varieties.	2.00	5.00	17.50
139	**2 PESOS**			
	L.1916. Like #117. Back blue. 5 sign. varieties.	2.50	7.50	25.00
140	**5 PESOS**			
	L.1916. Like #118. Back brown. 3 sign. varieties.	3.00	10.00	35.00
141	**10 PESOS**			
	L.1916. Like #119. Back gray. 3 sign. varieties.	10.00	40.00	100.00

142	**20 PESOS**	**VG**	**VF**	**UNC**
	L.1916. Like #120. Back: olive. 2 sign. varieties.	20.00	60.00	175.00

LEY NO. 463 DE 30 DE DICIEMBRE DE 1920
#143-148 arms on back. Printer: ABNC.

129	**10 PESOS**	**GOOD**	**FINE**	**XF**
	L.1912. Ovpt. on #157.	15.00	35.00	95.00
131	**50 PESOS**			
	L.1912. Ovpt. on #110.	30.00	60.00	175.00

143	5 PESOS	VG	VF	UNC
	L.1920. Like #140. 2 sign. varieties.	1.50	3.50	12.50
144	10 PESOS			
	L.1920. Like #141. 2 sign. varieties.	3.00	6.50	17.50

145	50 PESOS	VG	VF	UNC
	L.1920. Like #121. Back brown. 2 sign. varieties.	6.00	20.00	60.00

146	100 PESOS	VG	VF	UNC
	L.1920. Like #122. Back blue. 2 sign. varieties.	10.00	30.00	85.00

147	200 PESOS			
	L.1920. Back orange. Like #123..	Reported Not Confirmed		

148	500 PESOS	VG	VF	UNC
	L.1920. Back lilac. Like #124.	30.00	90.00	200.00

LEYS 1920 & 1923
#149-155 sign. varieties, arms on back. Printer: ABNC.

149	5 PESOS	VG	VF	UNC
	L.1920 & 1923. Like #143. 3 sign. varieties.	1.50	6.00	15.00

150	10 PESOS	VG	VF	UNC
	L.1920 & 1923. Like #144. 3 sign. varieties.	2.50	8.00	20.00
151	50 PESOS			
	L.1920 & 1923. Like #145. Back brown. 4 sign. varieties.	5.00	15.00	35.00

152	100 PESOS	VG	VF	UNC
	L.1920 & 1923. Like #146. Back blue. 5 sign. varieties.	8.50	25.00	65.00

153	200 PESOS	VG	VF	UNC
	L.1920 & 1923. Back orange. Like #123. 5 sign. varieties.	17.50	65.00	150.00
154	500 PESOS			
	L.1920 & 1923. Back lilac, Like #148. 7 sign. varieties.	20.00	80.00	175.00

155	1000 PESOS	VG	VF	UNC
	L.1920 & 1923. Black on m/c unpt. Woman holding fasces at l. Back black; arms at ctr. 8 sign. varieties.	30.00	100.00	250.00

BANCO DE LA REPÚBLICA

LEY DE 26 DE DICIEMBRE DE 1907
#156-159 arms at ctr. on back. Printer: W&S.

156	5 PESOS M.N. = 1/2 PESO ORO	VG	VF	UNC
	L.1907. Black on blue unpt. Woman wearing Liberty cap at ctr. Back brown. 2 sign. varieties.	.25	1.00	5.00

			VG	VF	UNC
157	**10 PESOS M.N. = 1 PESO ORO**		4.00	10.00	35.00
	L.1907. Black on red unpt. Railroad station at ctr. Back: green. 2 sign. varieties.				
158	**50 PESOS M.N. = 5 PESOS ORO**		30.00	85.00	200.00
	L.1907. Black on green unpt. National Congress at ctr.				

			VG	VF	UNC
159	**100 PESOS M.N. = 10 PESOS ORO**		1.00	4.00	11.50
	L.1907. Black on yelow unpt. Bldg. at ctr. 2 sign. varieties. Back: blue. 4 sign. varieties.				
160	**1000 PESOS M.N. = 100 PESOS ORO**		35.00	110.00	250.00
	L.1907. Woman w/children. Printer: P. Bouchard-Buenos Aires.				

LEY 8.9.1920

			VG	VF	UNC
161	**1000 PESOS**		—	—	—
	L.1920. Rectangular ovpt: *EL BANCO DE LA REPÚBLICA, LEY No. 432, 8 de Setiembre de 1920* on #160.				

LEY 469, DEC. 31, 1920

			VG	VF	UNC
162	**1000 PESOS**		—	—	—
	L.1920. Rectangular ovpt. on #160.				

LEY 30.12.1920/25.10.1923

#163-164 printer: ABNC.

			VG	VF	UNC
163	**5 PESOS**		3.50	12.50	35.00
	L.1920, 1923. Like #149 but w/text: *POR EL BANCO DE LA REPÚBLICA DEL PARAGUAY* at bottom. 4 sign. varieties.				
164	**10 PESOS**		4.50	15.00	40.00
	L.1920, 1923. Like #150 w/text: *POR EL BANCO DE LA REPÚBLICA DEL PARAGUAY* at bottom. 2 sign. varieties.				

LEY No. 550 DE 25 DE OCTUBRE DE 1923

#165-168 printer: ABNC.

			VG	VF	UNC
165	**50 PESOS**		40.00	100.00	250.00
	L.1923. Blue on m/c unpt. Bldg. at ctr. Back red; star at ctr.				

			VG	VF	UNC
166	**50 PESOS**		2.00	10.00	35.00
	L.1923. Blue on m/c unpt. Bldg. at ctr. Back red; shield w/lion at ctr.				

			VG	VF	UNC
167	**100 PESOS**		45.00	125.00	275.00
	L.1923. Blue on m/c unpt. Face like #168. Back brown; star at ctr.				

			VG	VF	UNC
168	**100 PESOS**		2.00	10.00	35.00
	L.1923. Olive-green on brown and m/c unpt. Bldg. at ctr. Back brown; shield w/lion at ctr.				

			VG	VF	UNC
169	**500 PESOS**		15.00	40.00	90.00
	L.1923. Gray-green. Portr. C. A. Lopez at upper l. ctr., cow at lower r. Printer: W&S.				
170	**1000 PESOS**		30.00	85.00	250.00
	L.1923. Like #155. Printer: ABNC.				

1943 PROVISIONAL ISSUE

			VG	VF	UNC
171	**50 CENTIMOS ON 50 PESOS FUERTES**			Reported Not Confirmed	
	ND (1943). Red ovpt. on #165.				

			VG	VF	UNC
172	**50 CENTIMOS ON 50 PESOS FUERTES**				
	ND (1943).				
	a. Red ovpt. on #166.		10.00	40.00	100.00
	b. Black ovpt. on #166.			Reported Not Confirmed	
173	**1 GUARANI ON 100 PESOS FUERTES**				
	ND (1943).				
	a. Red ovpt. on #168.		10.00	40.00	100.00
	b. Black ovpt. on #168.			Reported Not Confirmed	

			VG	VF	UNC
174	**5 GUARANIES ON 500 PESOS FUERTES**		25.00	75.00	175.00
	ND (1943). Red ovpt. on #169.				
175	**5 GUARANIES ON 500 PESOS FUERTES**		40.00	100.00	175.00
	ND (1943). Ovpt. on #154.				

176	10 GUARANIES ON 1000 PESOS FUERTES	VG	VF	UNC
	ND (1943). Ovpt. on #155.	45.00	110.00	275.00

BANCO DEL PARAGUAY

LEY NO. 11, 22.2.1936

177   1 GUARANI
L.1936. (Not issued).   Reported Not Confirmed

DECRETO LEY 655 DEL 5 DE OCTUBRE DE 1943

#178-184 arms at upper r. Series A. Printer: TDLR, Sign. varieties.
NOTE: For later issues of similar design see Banco Central. #185-191.

178	1 GUARANI	VG	VF	UNC
	L.1943. Green. Soldier at ctr. Back brown; bldg. at ctr. 4 sign. varieties.	.75	2.50	9.00

179	5 GUARANIES	VG	VF	UNC
	L.1943. Blue. Gen. J. E. Diaz at ctr. Back dk. red; bldg. 2 sign. varieties.	2.00	6.00	15.00

180	10 GUARANIES	VG	VF	UNC
	L.1943. Red. D. Carlos Antonio Lopez at ctr. Back purple; bldg. 3 sign. varieties.	3.00	8.00	20.00
181	50 GUARANIES			
	L.1943. Brown. Dr. J. Gaspar Rodriguez de Francia at ctr. Back gray-brown; bldg. 3 sign. varieties.	5.00	15.00	40.00

182	100 GUARANIES	VG	VF	UNC
	L.1943. Green. M. Jose F. Estigarribia at ctr. Back blue; lg. bldg. facing r. 2 sign. varieties.	8.00	25.00	60.00
183	500 GUARANIES			
	L.1943. Blue. M. Francisco Solano Lopez at ctr. Back red; lg. bldg. 3 sign. varieties.	25.00	60.00	125.00
184	1000 GUARANIES	VG	VF	UNC
	L.1943. Red-violet. Declaration of Independence on 14.4.1811 at ctr. Back orange; Presidential palace. 2 sign. varieties.	35.00	90.00	200.00

BANCO CENTRAL DEL PARAGUAY

DECRETO LEY NO. 18 DEL 25 DE MARZO DE 1952

#185-191 have black security thread in l. half of notes. Later issues have m/c fibers in r. half of notes. Arms at r. Sign. title: *Gerente* at l., lg. or sm. size signs. Sign varieties. Printer: TDLR.

185	1 GUARANI	VG	VF	UNC
	L.1952. Green. Like #178.			
	a. 1 red serial #. Lg. or sm. sign. Series A.	.75	1.50	6.00
	b. 1 red serial #. Fibers at r. Series B.	.50	1.25	3.50
	c. 2 black serial #. Fibers at r. Serial # prefix B.	.25	.50	1.50

186	5 GUARANIES	VG	VF	UNC
	L.1952. Blue. Like #179.			
	a. 1 red serial #. Lg. or sm. sign. Series A.	.75	1.50	5.00
	b. 1 red serial #. Fibers at r. Series A.	.50	1.25	3.50
	c. 2 black serial #. Fibers at r. Serial # prefix A.	.25	.60	2.00

187	10 GUARANIES	VG	VF	UNC
	L.1952. Red. Like #180.			
	a. 1 black serial #. Lg. or sm. sign. Series A.	1.00	2.50	9.00
	b. 1 black serial #. Fibers at r. Series A.	.75	1.50	4.00
	c. 2 black serial #. Fibers at r. Serial # prefix B.	.50	1.25	3.50

188	50 GUARANIES	VG	VF	UNC
	L.1952. Brown. Like #181.			
	a. W/o fibers at r. Lg. or sm. sign.	1.00	4.00	15.00
	b. Fibers at r.	1.00	4.00	10.00
189	100 GUARANIES			
	L.1952. Green. Face like #182. Back blue; bldg. facing l. Lg. or sm. sign.			
	a. W/o fibers at r.	2.00	8.00	20.00
	b. Fibers at r.	1.50	6.00	15.00

190 500 GUARANIES
L.1952. Blue. Face I like #183. Back red; domed bldg. at ctr.

	VG	VF	UNC
a. W/o fibers at r.	30.00	75.00	150.00
b. Fibers at r.	25.00	60.00	125.00

191 1000 GUARANIES
L.1952. Lilac. Face like #184. Back orange; bldg. w/courtyard.

	VG	VF	UNC
a. W/o fibers at r.	40.00	90.00	200.00
b. Fibers at r.	35.00	75.00	150.00

The Republic of Peru, located on the Pacific coast of South America, has an area of 496,222 sq. mi. (1,285,216 sq. km.) and a population of 21.6 million. Capital: Lima. The diversified economy includes mining, fishing and agriculture. Fish meal, copper, sugar, zinc and iron ore are exported.

Once part of a great Inca Empire that reached from northern Ecuador to Central Chile, Peru was conquered in 1531-33 by Francisco Pizarro. Desirable as the richest of the Spanish viceroyalties, it was torn by warfare between avaricious Spaniards until the arrival in 1569 of Francisco de Toledo, who initiated 2 1/2 centuries of efficient colonial rule which made Lima the most aristocratic colonial capital and the stronghold of Spain's American possessions. Jose de San Martin of Argentina proclaimed Peru's independence on July 28, 1821; Simon Bolivar of Venezuela secured it in Dec. of 1824 when he defeated the last Spanish army in South America. After several futile attempts to re-establish its South American empire, Spain recognized Peru's independence in 1879.

MONETARY SYSTEM:
- 1 Sol = 100 Centavos (10 Dineros) to 1985
- 1 Libra = 10 Soles
- 1 Inti = 1000 Soles de Oro, 1986-1991
- 1 Nuevo Sol = 1 Million 1 Units, 1991-

REPÚBLICA DEL PERU

JUNTA ADMINISTRADORA

1879 ISSUE
#1-10 sign. varieties. Printer: ABNC.

1 1 SOL
30.6.1879. Black on yellow-brown and blue unpt. Cupids at l. and r., woman w/fruit at ctr. Back brown; sailing ship at ctr.

GOOD	FINE	XF
1.50	8.00	40.00

2 2 SOLES
30.6.1879. Black on green and brown unpt. Steam passenger trains at lower l. and r., woman at fountain at lower ctr. Back: red-orange. 3 serial # varieties.

GOOD	FINE	XF
1.50	8.00	45.00

3 5 SOLES
30.6.1879. Black on green and red unpt. Woman and child at l., woman w/2 children at r. Red numeral *V's* at upper l. and r. in unpt. Upper line of lg. green *5* at ctr. measures 16mm across. Back brown.

GOOD	FINE	XF
2.50	10.00	50.00

4	**5 SOLES**	GOOD	FINE	XF
	30.6.1879. Black on green and red unpt. Like #3 but w/o red *V's* in unpt. Lg. green numeral *5* at ctr. measures 20.5mm across at top.	2.00	10.00	50.00

5	**10 SOLES**	GOOD	FINE	XF
	30.6.1879. Black on brown and lt. blue unpt. Woman sitting w/staff and scales at l., woman w/wreath at ctr., arms at r. Back green; woman sitting w/llama at ctr.	3.00	30.00	90.00

6	**20 SOLES**	GOOD	FINE	XF
	30.6.1879. Black on brown unpt. Woman w/book and pen at ctr. W/o green *20* in unpt. Back blue.	2.00	10.00	50.00

7	**20 SOLES**	GOOD	FINE	XF
	30.6.1879. Black on yellow and lt. green unpt. Like #6 but w/lg. green *20's* at lower l. and r. in unpt. Back blue.			
	a. Issued note.	2.00	10.00	50.00
	b. Cut cancelled, w/circular ovpt: *DIRECCION DEL TESORO* (arms) *LIMA JULIO 30 DE 1899* at r.	5.00	20.00	75.00

8	**50 SOLES**	GOOD	FINE	XF
	30.6.1879. Black on blue-green unpt. Woman w/2 shields at l., woman and child at lower r. Back brown; allegorical woman and 2 children at ctr.	15.00	75.00	175.00

9	**100 SOLES**	GOOD	FINE	XF
	30.6.1879. Black on red and green unpt. Young sailor at l., arms flanked by women on each side at ctr., filleted woman at r. Back red and black; horse and girl.	20.00	90.00	200.00

10	**500 SOLES**	GOOD	FINE	XF
	30.6.1879. Black on yellow and gold unpt. Heraldic shield and 4 angels at ctr. Back green and black; funeral of Atahualpa.	60.00	175.00	400.00

1881 AREQUIPA PROVISIONAL ISSUE

1A	**1 SOL**	GOOD	FINE	XF
	1881 (- old date 30.6.1879). Black circular ovpt: *COMISION DE SUBSIDIOS AREQUIPA 1881* at r. on #1. (For circulation in Arequipa).	40.00	100.00	—
2A	**2 SOLES**			
	1881 (- old date 30.6.1879). Black circular ovpt: *COMISION DE SUBSIDIOS AREQUIPA 1881* at ctr. on #2.	45.00	110.00	—
3A	**5 SOLES**			
	1881 (- old date 30.6.1879). Black circular ovpt: *COMISION DE SUBSIDIOS AREQUIPA 1881* at r. on #3.	45.00	110.00	—
7A	**20 SOLES**			
	1881 (- old date 30.6.1879). Black circular ovpt: *COMISION DE SUBSIDIOS AREQUIPA 1881* at r. on #7.	50.00	125.00	—

1881 PROVISIONAL ISSUE

#11-13 *BILLETE PROVISIONAL* w/new denomination and new date ovpt. on face and/or back of 1873 notes of the Banca de la Compania General del Peru. Printers: NBNC for face, ABNC for back.

NOTE: #11-13 sometimes have an additional sign. guaranteeing the authenticity of the note. This sign. was an official endorsement.

11   1 REAL DE INCA ON 1 SOL
   1.9.1881 (- old date 1873). Ovpt. on #S131. W/ or w/o sign.

	GOOD	FINE	XF
	5.00	20.00	50.00

12   5 REALES DE INCA ON 5 SOLES
   1.9.1881 (- old date 1873). Ovpt. on #S132. W/ or w/o sign.

	GOOD	FINE	XF
	7.50	25.00	65.00

13   100 CENT. DE INCA ON 100 SOLES
   1.9.1881 (- old date 1873). Ovpt. on #S134. W/ or w/o sign.

	GOOD	FINE	XF
	15.00	60.00	130.00

1881 INCA ISSUE
#14-17 sign. titles: *SECRETARIO DE HACIENDA Y COMERCIO* and *JUNTA FISCAL* on new notes.

14   1 INCA
   1.9.1881. Blue.

	GOOD	FINE	XF
	25.00	85.00	200.00

15   5 INCAS
   1.9.1881. Blue. Cherub at upper l. and r., arms at top ctr. W/o ovpt.

	GOOD	FINE	XF
	12.50	30.00	75.00

16   5 INCAS
   1.9.1881. Blue. Ovpt: *LEGITIMO* on #15.

	GOOD	FINE	XF
	9.00	20.00	60.00

17   100 INCAS
   1.9.1881. Blue. Seated Mercury at l., seated allegorical woman at r. W/o ovpt.

	GOOD	FINE	XF
	40.00	120.00	250.00

1881 SOLES PROVISIONAL ISSUE
#18-20 ovpt. for Soles on Incas notes.

18   50 SOLES
   1.9.1881. Blue. Oval ovpt: *VALE POR / CINCUENTA SOLES / 1881 / EMISION FISCAL* on #15.

	GOOD	FINE	XF
	9.00	20.00	60.00

19   50 SOLES
   1.9.1881. Blue. Oval ovpt: *VALE POR....* on #16.

	GOOD	FINE	XF
	9.00	20.00	60.00

20   1000 SOLES
   1.9.1881. Blue. Oval ovpt: *VALE POR / MIL SOLES / 1881 / EMISION FISCAL* on #17.

	GOOD	FINE	XF
	30.00	80.00	200.00

JUNTA DE VIGILANCIA

1914 CHEQUES CIRCULARES FIRST ISSUE
Circulating drafts issued on the following banks: Banco del Peru y Londres, Banco Italiano, Banco Internacional del Peru, Banco Popular del Peru, Banco Aleman Transatlantico, Caja de Ahorros de Lima.

#21-24 printer: T. Scheuch, Lima.

30	50 Centavos		Good	Fine	XF
(31)	17.8.1917. Dk. blue on green unpt. Liberty seated w/shield and staff at ctr. Back brown; arms at ctr. Printer: Scheuch.		2.50	15.00	50.00

21	1/2 Libra		Good	Fine	XF
	3.10.1914. Black on green unpt. Worker at ctr. Back green.		25.00	80.00	200.00
22	1 Libra				
	8.9.1914. Woman seated w/caduceus at l.		50.00	150.00	350.00
23	5 Libras				
	8.9.1914. Black on blue unpt. Justice seated at l.		35.00	100.00	225.00

24	10 Libras		Good	Fine	XF
	8.9.1914. Black on green unpt. Woman w/flag at l.		—	—	—

31	1 Sol		Good	Fine	XF
(29)	10.8.1917. Dk. blue. Similar to #40. Back brown. Printer: ABNC.		4.00	17.50	40.00

1914 Cheques Circulares Second Issue
#25-28 have issuing banks listed in 3 lines of text under top heading. Printer: ABNC.

1918 Cheques Circulares First Issue
#32-35 printer: Fabbri.

25	1/2 Libra		Good	Fine	XF
	3.10.1914. Black on green unpt. Liberty at ctr. Back green.		20.00	75.00	160.00
26	1 Libra				
	3.10.1914. Black on red-orange unpt. Woman seated at l. Back red-orange; drill worker at ctr.		20.00	70.00	150.00
27	5 Libras				
	3.10.1914. Black on blue unpt. Child and lamb at r. Back blue; 2 allegorical women at ctr.		40.00	110.00	250.00

32	1/2 Libra		Good	Fine	XF
	13.6.1918.		Reported Not Confirmed		
33	1 Libra				
	13.6.1918. Winged woman at l. and r.		—	—	—

34	5 Libras		Good	Fine	XF
	13.6.1918. Black. Liberty at l., globe at r.		—	—	—
35	10 Libras				
	13.6.1918.		Reported Not Confirmed		

1918 Cheques Circulares Second Issue
#36-39 have issuing banks listed in 2 lines of text under top heading. Printer: ABNC.

28	10 Libras		Good	Fine	XF
	3.10.1914. Black on m/c unpt. Rubber tree worker at l. Back orange; steam train at ctr.		50.00	150.00	—

36	1/2 Libra		Good	Fine	XF
	14.9.1918. Similar to #25.		40.00	110.00	250.00
37	1 Libra				
	14.9.1918. Similar to #26.		40.00	110.00	250.00

1917 Certificado De Deposito De Oro Issue

29	5 Centavos		Good	Fine	XF
(30)	17.8.1917. Black on blue unpt. Back dk. orange; sun face at ctr. Printer: Scheuch, Lima.		2.00	12.50	35.00

38	5 Libras		Good	Fine	XF
	14.9.1918. Similar to #27.		45.00	120.00	265.00
39	10 Libras				
	14.9.1918. Similar to #28. Uniface proof.		—	—	—

1918 SOL ISSUE

40	1 SOL	GOOD	FINE	XF
	14.9.1918. Dk. blue. Liberty seated w/shield and staff at ctr. Back brown; arms at ctr. Printer: ABNC.	4.00	12.50	35.00

BANCO DE RESERVA DEL PERU

1922 ISSUE
#48-51 dated 1922. Printer: ABNC.

48	1/2 LIBRA	GOOD	FINE	XF
	12.4.1922. Similar to #36.	10.00	35.00	90.00

49	1 LIBRA	GOOD	FINE	XF
	12.4.1922. Similar to #37.	15.00	40.00	100.00

50	5 LIBRAS	GOOD	FINE	XF
	12.4.1922. Similar to #38.	25.00	70.00	150.00

51	10 LIBRAS	GOOD	FINE	XF
	12.4.1922. Black on yellow unpt. Similar to #39.	35.00	90.00	180.00

1926 ISSUE
#52-55 like #48-51 but dated 1926. Printer: ABNC.

52	1/2 LIBRA	GOOD	FINE	XF
	11.8.1926. Black on green unpt. (Not issued).	—	—	—
53	1 LIBRA	GOOD	FINE	UNC
	11.8.1926. Black on red unpt. (Not issued).	—	—	—
54	5 LIBRAS	GOOD	FINE	XF
	11.8.1926. Black on blue unpt. (Not issued).	—	—	—
55	10 LIBRAS	GOOD	FINE	UNC
	11.8.1926. Black on yellow unpt. (Not issued).	—	Rare	—

BANCO CENTRAL DE RESERVA DEL PERU

1935 PROVISIONAL ISSUE (1922 DATED NOTES)
#56-59 ovpt. new bank name and new denomination ovpt. on backs of notes of the Banco de Reserva del Peru dated 1922.

56	5 SOLES ON 1/2 LIBRA	GOOD	FINE	XF
	ND (- old date 12.4.1922). Ovpt. on #48.	20.00	60.00	150.00
57	10 SOLES ON 1 LIBRA			
	ND (- old date 12.4.1922). Ovpt. on #49.	25.00	75.00	175.00

58	50 SOLES ON 5 LIBRAS	GOOD	FINE	XF
	ND (- old date 12.4.1922). Ovpt. on #50.	40.00	120.00	250.00
59	100 SOLES ON 10 LIBRAS			
	ND (- old date 12.4.1922). Ovpt. on #51.	50.00	150.00	—

1935 PROVISIONAL ISSUE (1926 DATED NOTES)
#60-63 ovpt. on notes dated 1926.

60	5 SOLES ON 1/2 LIBRA	GOOD	FINE	XF
	ND (- old date 11.8.1926). Ovpt. on #52.	20.00	60.00	150.00

61	10 SOLES ON 1 LIBRA	GOOD	FINE	XF
	ND (- old date 11.8.1926). Ovpt. on #53.	25.00	75.00	175.00
62	50 SOLES ON 5 LIBRAS			
	ND (- old date 11.8.1926). Ovpt. on #54.	40.00	120.00	250.00
63	100 SOLES ON 10 LIBRAS			
	ND (- old date 11.8.1926). Ovpt. on #55.	50.00	150.00	—

1935 ISSUES

64 (65)	50 CENTAVOS	VG	VF	UNC
	3.5.1935. Blue. Similar to #64. Back lt. brown. Printer: Fabbri, Lima. Series A-D.	4.00	10.00	40.00

65 (64)	1 SOL	VG	VF	UNC
	26.4.1935. Blue. Liberty seated w/shield and staff at ctr. Back brown; arms at ctr. Printer: ABNC. Series A-E.	2.00	6.00	20.00

1933 ISSUE (LEY 7137)
#66-69 printer: ABNC. Sign. title varieties; title above ctr. sign:

a. *PRESIDENTE DEL DIRECTORIO* (to 1941)

b. *VICE-PRESIDENTE* (1944-45)

c. *PRESIDENTE* (1946-47)

		VG	**VF**	**UNC**
66	**5 SOLES** 31.3.1933-8.9.1939. Black on m/c unpt. Portr. Liberty at ctr. Back green; mine workers at ctr. 135 x 67mm.	3.00	8.00	20.00

		VG	**VF**	**UNC**
67	**10 SOLES** 31.3.1933-8.9.1939. Black on m/c unpt. Seated woman holding basket w/flowers at l. Back orange; mine driller at ctr. 144 x 76mm.	3.00	10.00	25.00

		VG	**VF**	**UNC**
68	**50 SOLES** 31.3.1933-8.9.1939. Black on m/c unpt. Girl w/lamb and sheep at r. Back blue; two allegorical women at ctr. 158 x 77mm.	6.00	25.00	65.00
69	**100 SOLES** 31.1.1933-8.9.1939. Black on m/c unpt. Similar to #28. Back orange; steam train at ctr. 172 x 79mm.	25.00	60.00	140.00

1941 ISSUE

		VG	**VF**	**UNC**
66A	**5 SOLES** 26.9.1941-17.10.1947. Like #66. 141 x 68mm.	2.00	5.00	17.50

		VG	**VF**	**UNC**
67A	**10 SOLES** 26.9.1941-17.10.1947. Black on m/c unpt. Like #67. 152 x 77mm.	2.00	6.00	17.50
68A	**50 SOLES** 26.9.1941-28.9.1950. Black. Like #68. 165 x 78mm.	5.00	15.00	60.00

		VG	**VF**	**UNC**
69A	**100 SOLES** 26.9.1941-28.9.1950. Black. Like #69. 177 x 80mm.	12.00	50.00	110.00

1946-51 ISSUE
#70-74 portr. seated Liberty holding shield and staff at ctr. Arms at ctr. on back. Sign. varieties.

		VG	**VF**	**UNC**
70	**5 SOLES** 20.3.1952; 16.9.1954. Green on plain lt. blue unpt. Serial # at upper l. and r. Printer: TDLR.	1.00	3.00	7.00
71 (72)	**10 SOLES** 12.7.1951-17.2.1955. Black on m/c unpt. Back orange. Printer: TDLR.	1.00	4.00	8.00
72 (77)	**50 SOLES** 31.3.1949; 12.7.1951; 16.9.1954. Black on m/c unpt. Back blue. Printer: TDLR.	2.00	5.00	20.00
73 (79)	**100 SOLES** 31.3.1949-16.9.1954. Black on m/c unpt. Back orange. Printer: TDLR.	4.00	10.00	30.00

		VG	**VF**	**UNC**
74 (81)	**500 SOLES** 4.10.1946; 10.7.1952. Brown on m/c unpt. Back deep red. Printer: W&S.	12.00	30.00	90.00

1955 ISSUE

		VG	**VF**	**UNC**
75 (73)	**10 SOLES** 17.2.1955. Black, green-black and brown. Like #71. Printer: G&D. Proof.	—	—	100.00

1956 ISSUE
#76-80 portr. seated Liberty holding shield and staff at ctr. Arms at ctr. on back. Sign. varieties.

		VG	**VF**	**UNC**
76 (70A)	**5 SOLES** 22.3.1956; 18.3.1960. Green on patterned lt. blue unpt. Like #70.	.50	1.50	5.00

		VG	**VF**	**UNC**
77 (74)	**10 SOLES** 9.7.1956. Orange on m/c unpt. Similar to #71. Printer: G&D.	2.00	6.00	20.00

			VG	VF	UNC
78	**50 SOLES**		1.50	4.50	17.50
	22.3.1956; 24.10.1957; 13.5.1959. Dk. blue on lilac unpt. Like #72. Serial # at upper l. and r. Printer: TDLR.				
79 (80)	**100 SOLES**				
	1956-61. Black on lt. blue unpt. Like #73 but different guilloche. Back black.				
	a.	*LIMA* at lower l. 22.3.1956; 24.10.1957.	4.00	12.00	30.00
	b.	*LIMA* at lower r. w/date. 13.5.1959.	4.00	12.00	30.00
	c.	As b. Series and serial # at lower l. and upper r. 1.2.1961.	4.00	12.00	30.00
80 (82)	**500 SOLES**				
	1956-61. Brown on lt. brown and lilac unpt. Similar to #74. Back brown.				
	a.	Series and serial # at upper corners. 22.3.1956; 24.10.1957.	8.00	25.00	75.00
	b.	Series and serial # at lower l. and upper r. 10.12.1959; 16.6.1961.	8.00	25.00	75.00

1958 ISSUE

			VG	VF	UNC
81 (71)	**5 SOLES**		1.00	4.00	6.00
	21.8.1958. Green. Like #70 but different guilloche on back. Printer: W&S.				

		VG	VF	UNC
82 (75)	**10 SOLES**	1.00	4.00	15.00
	21.8.1958. Orange on m/c unpt. Similar to #71. Printer: W&S.			

1960 ISSUE

		VG	VF	UNC
82A (76)	**10 SOLES**	.75	1.50	5.00
	8.7.1960; 1.2.1961. Orange on lt. green unpt. Similar to #82 but different guilloche. Serial # and series at lower l. and upper r. Printer: TDLR.			

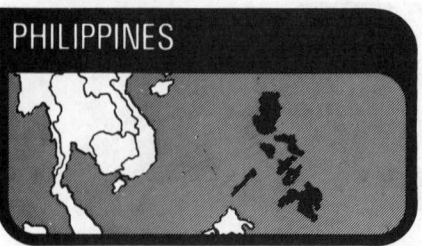

PHILIPPINES

The Republic of the Philippines, an archipelago in the western Pacific 500 miles (805 km.) from the southeast coast of Asia, has an area of 115,830 sq. mi. (300,000 sq. km.) and a population of 60.9 million. Capital: Manila. The economy of the 7,000-island group is based on agriculture, forestry and fishing. Timber, coconut products, sugar and hemp are exported.

Migration to the Philippines began about 30,000 years ago when land bridges connected the islands with Borneo and Sumatra. Ferdinand Magellan claimed the islands for Spain in 1521. The first permanent settlement was established by Miguel de Legazpi at Cebu in April of 1565; Manila was established in 1572. A British expedition captured Manila and occupied the Spanish colony in Oct. of 1762, but it was returned to Spain by the treaty of Paris, 1763. Spain held the Philippines amid a growing movement of Filipino nationalism until 1898 when they were ceded to the United States of the end of the Spanish-American War. The Filipinos then fought unsuccessfully against the United States to maintain their independent Republic proclaimed by Emilio Aguinaldo. The country became a self-governing commonwealth of the United States in 1935, and attained independence as the Republic of the Philippines on July 4, 1946. During World War II the Japanese had set up a puppet republic, but this quasi-government failed to achieve worldwide recognition. The occupation lasted from late 1941 to 1945. Ferdinand Marcos lost to Corazón Aquino in elections of 1986. Marcos then fled the country. In 1992 Fidel Ranos was elected President.

RULERS:
Spanish to 1898
United States, 1898-1946

MONETARY SYSTEM:
1 Peso = 100 Centavos to 1967
1 Piso = 100 Sentimos, 1967-

SPANISH INFLUENCE

BANCO ESPAÑOL FILIPINO DE ISABEL 2A

1852 ISSUE
#A1-A3 crowned portr. Qn. Isabel II at top ctr. Printer: BWC.

A1	**10 PESOS**			
	1.5.1852; 1.1.1865. Black on brown or white paper.	—	Rare	—
A2	**25 PESOS**			
	1.5.1852; 1.1.1865. Green paper.	—	Rare	—

A3	**50 PESOS**			
	1.5.1852; 1.1.1865. Brown paper.	—	Rare	—

BANCO ESPAÑOL FILIPINO

1883 ISSUE
#A4-A6 bank arms at top ctr. Uniface.

		VG	VF	UNC
A4	**10 PESOS** 1.1.1883. Brown paper.	—	—	—
A5	**25 PESOS** 1.1.1883. Green paper.	—	—	—

		VG	VF	UNC
A6	**50 PESOS** 1.1.1883. Brown paper.	—	—	—

1896 ISSUE
#A7-A10 bank arms at upper ctr. Printed on both sides. Printer: BFL.

		GOOD	FINE	XF
A7	**5 PESOS** 1.6.1896. Black on brown paper. a. Issued note. b. Cancelled w/handstamp: *PAGADO*.	 1250. —	 2500. —	 — —

		GOOD	FINE	XF
A8	**10 PESOS** 1.6.1896. Black on yellow paper. a. Issued note. b. Cancelled w/handstamp: *PAGADO*.	 — —	 — —	 — —

A9	**25 PESOS** 1.6.1896. Black on blue paper.	—	—	—
A10	**50 PESOS** 1.6.1896. Black on pink paper.	—	—	—

BILLETE DEL TESORO

TREASURY NOTE

1877 ISSUE
#A11-A15 uniface.

		GOOD	FINE	XF
A11	**1 PESO** 26.4.1877. Black. Arms at upper ctr.	—	Rare	—
A13	**4 PESOS** 26.4.1877. Black on orange paper. Arms at l.	—	Rare	—

		GOOD	FINE	XF
A15	**25 PESOS** 26.4.1877. Black on blue paper. Arms at upper ctr.	—	Rare	—

REPUBLIC (19C)

REPÚBLICA FILIPINA

LEY 26 NOVIEMBRE 1898

		VG	VF	UNC
A25	**5 PESOS** *L.1898.* Black on red unpt. W/serial #, w/o sign. Back black.	200.00	500.00	1200.

LEY 30.11.1898 AND 24.4.1899
Most notes are w/o sign. and w/o serial #.

		VG	VF	UNC
A26	**1 PESO** *L. 1898-99.* Black. a. Issued note w/sign. and serial #. r. Remainder w/o sign. or serial #.	 — 40.00	 Rare 150.00	 — 350.00

A27	**5 PESOS**	**VG**	**VF**	**UNC**
	L.1898-99. Black. Similar to #A25.			
a.	Issued note w/sign. and serial #.	—	Rare	—
r.	Remainder w/o sign. or serial #.	50.00	175.00	450.00

LEY 24.4.1899

NOTE: 2, 10, 20, 25, 50 and 100 Peso notes were authorized but no examples are known to exist.

A28	**1 PESO**	**VG**	**VF**	**UNC**
	L.1899. Black. Similar to #A26. Remainder w/o sign. or serial #.	40.00	150.00	350.00

UNITED STATES ADMINISTRATION

BANCO ESPAÑOL FILIPINO

1904 ISSUE

#A31-A36 bank arms at upper ctr. Denominations w/o *FUERTES*. Printer: BFL.

A31	**5 PESOS**	**VG**	**VF**	**UNC**
	1.1.1904. Black on pink paper.	—	Rare	—
A32	**10 PESOS**			
	1.1.1904. Black on green paper.	—	Rare	—

A33	**25 PESOS**	**VG**	**VF**	**UNC**
	1.1.1904. Black on lt. purple paper.	—	Rare	—
A34	**50 PESOS**			
	1.1.1904. Black on green paper.	—	Rare	—

A35	**100 PESOS**	**VG**	**VF**	**UNC**
	1.1.1904. Black on yellowish brown paper.	—	Rare	—

A36	**200 PESOS**	**VG**	**VF**	**UNC**
	1.1.1904. Black on yellowish brown paper. Back m/c.	—	Rare	—

1908 ISSUE

#1-6 printer: USBEP (w/o imprint).

#1 and 2 w/1 stamped sign. (at l.) and 2 printed sign.

#4-6 w/only 2 printed sign.

1	**5 PESOS**	**GOOD**	**FINE**	**XF**
	1.1.1908. Black on red unpt. Woman seated at l. Back red. Sign. J. Serrano at l.	25.00	100.00	275.00

2	**10 PESOS**	**GOOD**	**FINE**	**XF**
	1.1.1908. Black on brown unpt. Woman w/flowers at ctr. Back brown.			
a.	Sign. Julian Serrano at l.	—	Rare	
b.	Sign. J. Serrano at l.	60.00	200.00	
3	**20 PESOS**			
	1.1.1908. Black on lilac unpt. Woman at l. Back tan.			
a.	Sign. Julian Serrano at l.	—	Rare	
b.	Sign. J. Serrano at l.	200.00	500.00	

4	**50 PESOS**	**GOOD**	**FINE**	**XF**
	1.1.1908. Black on blue unpt. Woman standing w/flower at l. Back red.	200.00	500.00	
5	**100 PESOS**			
	1.1.1908. Black on green unpt. Woman seated w/scroll and globe at l. Back olive.	250.00	600.00	
6	**200 PESOS**			
	1.1.1908. Black on tan unpt. Justice w/scales and shield at ctr. Back orange.	—	—	—

BANK OF THE PHILIPPINE ISLANDS

A name change to English for the Banco Espanol Filipino.

1912 ISSUE

#7-12 designs like previous issue. Printer: USBEP (w/o imprint). Replacement notes of b. varieties: Star prefix.

1920 ISSUE

#13-15 like #7b-9b except for date and serial # prefix-suffix. Sign. D. Garcia and E. Sendres. Printer: US-BEP (w/o imprint). Replacement notes: Star prefix.

			Good	Fine	XF
7	**5 PESOS**				
	1.1.1912. Black on red unpt. Similar to #1.				
	a. Sign. D. Garcia and Jno. S. Hord. Back red.		2.00	8.00	45.00
	b. Sign. D. Garcia and E. Sendres. Back orange.		2.00	8.00	45.00
8	**10 PESOS**				
	1.1.1912. Black on brown unpt. Similar to #2.				
	a. Sign. D. Garcia and Jno. S. Hord.		3.00	10.00	50.00
	b. Sign. D. Garcia and E. Sendres.		3.00	10.00	50.00

		Good	Fine	XF
13	**5 PESOS**			
	1.1.1920. Black on red unpt. Like #7b.	2.00	9.00	40.00

		Good	Fine	XF
14	**10 PESOS**			
	1.1.1920. Black on brown unpt. Like #8b.	3.00	10.00	50.00

			Good	Fine	XF
9	**20 PESOS**				
	1.1.1912. Black on lilac unpt. Similar to #3.				
	a. Sign. D. Garcia and Jno. S. Hord.		4.00	20.00	75.00
	b. Sign. D. Garcia and E. Sendres.		4.00	20.00	75.00

		Good	Fine	XF
15	**20 PESOS**			
	1.1.1920. Black on lilac unpt. Like #9b.	4.00	20.00	80.00

1928 ISSUE

#16-21 designs like #7-12 but w/o unpt. Sign. D. Garcia and Fulg. Borromeo. Printer: USBEP (w/o imprint). Replacement notes: Star prefix.

		Good	Fine	XF
16	**5 PESOS**			
	1.1.1928. Black Like #7.	2.00	8.00	35.00
17	**10 PESOS**			
	1.1.1928. Black. Like #8.	3.00	9.00	40.00
18	**20 PESOS**			
	1.1.1928. Black. Like #9.	4.00	17.50	65.00

			Good	Fine	XF
10	**50 PESOS**				
	1.1.1912. Black on blue unpt. Similar to #4.				
	a. Sign. D. Garcia and Jno. S. Hord.		15.00	75.00	250.00
	b. Sign. D. Garcia and E. Sendres.		12.50	65.00	225.00

		Good	Fine	XF
19	**50 PESOS**			
	1.1.1928. Black. Like #10.	10.00	40.00	150.00

			Good	Fine	XF
11	**100 PESOS**				
	1.1.1912. Black on green unpt. Similar to #5.				
	a. Sign. D. Garcia and Jno. S. Hord.		50.00	150.00	400.00
	b. Sign. D. Garcia and E. Sendres.		50.00	150.00	400.00

		Good	Fine	XF
20	**100 PESOS**			
	1.1.1928. Black. Like #11.	50.00	125.00	350.00

		Good	Fine	XF
12	**200 PESOS**			
	1.1.1912. Black on tan unpt. Similar to #6. Sign. D. Garcia and Jno. S. Hord.	150.00	500.00	—

		Good	Fine	XF
21	**200 PESOS**			
	1.1.1928. Black. Like #12.	85.00	200.00	450.00

1933 ISSUE

#22-24 like #16-18 except for date and serial # prefix-suffix. Sign. D. Garcia and P.J. Campos. Printer: US-BEP (w/o imprint). Replacement notes: Star prefix.

		GOOD	FINE	XF
22	**5 PESOS**			
	1.1.1933. Black. Like #16.	2.00	8.00	35.00
23	**10 PESOS**			
	1.1.1933. Black. Like #17.	2.50	9.00	40.00
24	**20 PESOS**			
	1.1.1933. Black. Like #18.	3.50	17.50	65.00

PHILIPPINE ISLANDS

Silver Certificates

1903 ISSUE

#25-38 printer: USBEP (w/o imprint).

NOTE: The chief executive's title before 1905 was: *Civil Governor.*

		GOOD	FINE	XF
25	**2 PESOS**			
	1903. Black on blue unpt. Portr. J. Rizal at upper l. Back blue.			
	a. Sign. Wm. H. Taft and F. A. Branagan.	90.00	250.00	600.00
	b. Sign. L. E. Wright and F. A. Branagan.	100.00	300.00	800.00

		GOOD	FINE	XF
26	**5 PESOS**			
	1903. Black on red unpt. Portr. Pres. W. McKinley at l. Back red.			
	a. Sign. Wm. H. Taft and F. A. Branagan.	100.00	300.00	850.00
	b. Sign. L. E. Wright and F. A. Branagan.	125.00	400.00	1000.
27	**10 PESOS**			
	1903. Black on brown unpt. Portr. G. Washington at lower ctr. Back brown.			
	a. Sign. Wm. H. Taft and F. A. Branagan.	150.00	500.00	1100.
	b. Sign. L. E. Wright and F. A. Branagan.	200.00	600.00	—

		GOOD	FINE	XF
27A	**10 PESOS**	—	—	—
	1903. Like #27 but black vertical text ovpt: *Subject to the provisions of the/Act of Congress approved/ June 23, 1906* on face. Sign. H. C. Ide w/title: *Governor General* and F. A. Branagan.			

1905 ISSUE

#28-31 issued w/ovpt. like #27A. Sign. L. E. Wright w/title: *Governor General* and F. A. Branagan.

		GOOD	FINE	XF
28	**20 PESOS**			
	1905. Black on yellow unpt. Mt. Mayon at ctr. Back tan.	—	Rare	—
29	**50 PESOS**			
	1905. Black on red unpt. Gen. H. W. Lawton at l. Back red.	—	Rare	—
30	**100 PESOS**			
	1905. Black on green unpt. F. Magellan at ctr. Back olive.	—	Rare	—
31	**500 PESOS**			
	1905. Black. M. Lopez de Legazpi at ctr. Back purple.	—	Rare	—

1906 ISSUE

		GOOD	FINE	XF
32	**2 PESOS**			
	1906. Black on blue unpt. Similar to #25 but new authorization date, and payable in silver or gold.			
	a. Sign. J. F. Smith and F. A. Branagan.	40.00	100.00	250.00
	b. Sign. W. C. Forbes and J. L. Barrett.	60.00	200.00	—
	c. Sign. W. C. Forbes and J. L. Manning.	60.00	200.00	—
	d. Sign. F. B. Harrison and J. L. Manning.	50.00	150.00	350.00
	e. Sign. like d., but w/o blue unpt. (error).	40.00	175.00	—
	f. Sign. F. B. Harrison and A. P. Fitzsimmons.	17.50	40.00	135.00
33	**500 PESOS**			
	1906. Black. Similar to #31.	—	Rare	—

1908 ISSUE

		GOOD	FINE	XF
34	**20 PESOS**			
	1908. Black on yellow unpt. Similar to #28.			
	a. Sign. J. F. Smith and F. A. Branagan.	75.00	250.00	300.00
	b. Sign. W. C. Forbes and J. L. Barrett.	100.00	300.00	—
	c. Sign. W. C. Forbes and J. L. Manning.	125.00	400.00	—
	d. Sign. F. B. Harrison and J. L. Manning.	100.00	300.00	—
	e. Sign. F. B. Harrison and A. P. Fitzsimmons.	65.00	225.00	—

1910 ISSUE

		GOOD	FINE	XF
35	**5 PESOS**			
	1910. Black on red unpt. Similar to #26.			
	a. Sign. W. C. Forbes and J. L. Barrett.	50.00	150.00	—
	b. Sign. W. C. Forbes and J. L. Manning.	45.00	125.00	—
	c. Sign. F. B. Harrison and J. L. Manning.	60.00	175.00	—
	d. Sign. F. B. Harrison and A. P. Fitzsimmons.	40.00	100.00	250.00

1912 ISSUE

1912. Black on brown unpt. Similar to #27.

		GOOD	FINE	XF
36	**10 PESOS**			
	a. Sign. W. C. Forbes and J. L. Barrett.	75.00	250.00	—
	b. Sign. W. C. Forbes and J. L. Manning.	75.00	250.00	—
	c. Sign. F. B. Harrison and J. L. Manning.	75.00	250.00	—
	d. Sign. F. B. Harrison and A. P. Fitzsimmons.	40.00	150.00	350.00

1916 ISSUE

		GOOD	FINE	XF
37	**50 PESOS**			
	1916. Black on red unpt. Similar to #29.	—	Rare	—
38	**100 PESOS**			
	1916. Black on green unpt. Similar to #30.	—	Rare	—

PHILIPPINE NATIONAL BANK

1917 EMERGENCY WW I ISSUE

#39-42 American bald eagle on back. Local printing.

#43-45 new bank name, seal, sign. ovpt on Bank of the Philippine Islands notes.

			VG	VF	UNC
39	**10 CENTAVOS** 20.11.1917. Gold on yellow unpt. Back yellow.		5.00	15.00	50.00

			VG	VF	UNC
40	**20 CENTAVOS** 20.11.1917. Blue on yellow unpt. Back blue.		5.00	15.00	50.00

			VG	VF	UNC
41	**50 CENTAVOS** 22.9.1917. Black on green unpt. Back green.		4.00	10.00	35.00
42	**1 PESO** 22.9.1917. Black on red unpt. Back red.		6.00	25.00	60.00

			GOOD	FINE	XF
43	**5 PESOS** ND (1917 - old date 1912). Ovpt. on #7.		—	—	—

			GOOD	FINE	XF
43A	**10 PESOS** ND (1917 - old date 1912). Ovpt. on #8.		—	—	—
43B	**20 PESOS** ND (1917 - old date 1912). Ovpt. on #9.		—	Rare	—

1916-20 ISSUE

#44-50 printer: USBEP (w/o imprint). Replacement notes: Star prefix.

NOTE: #49 was never officially issued. 10,000 pieces were captured and issued during WW II by the Japanese (serial #90001-100000). The others were looted by Moros in the province of Mindanao who sold them at one-tenth of their face value. This accounts for their relative availability.

			GOOD	FINE	XF
44 (47)	**1 PESO** 1918. Black on orange unpt. C. A. Conant at l. Back green.		45.00	150.00	450.00

			VG	VF	UNC
45 (44)	**2 PESOS** 1916. Black on blue unpt. J. Rizal at l. (similar to Silver and Treasury Certificates). Back blue.		65.00	250.00	—
46 (45)	**5 PESOS** 1916. Black on red unpt. Pres. Wm. McKinley at l. (similar to Silver and Treasury Certificates). Back red-orange.				
	a. Sign. S. Ferguson and H. P. Willis.		100.00	350.00	—
	b. Sign. S. Mercado and V. Concepcion.		1.50	4.00	15.00

			GOOD	FINE	XF
47 (46)	**10 PESOS** 1916. Black on brown unpt. Washington at ctr. (similar to Silver and Treasury Certificates). Back brown.				
	a. Sign. S. Ferguson and H. P. Willis.		100.00	350.00	—
	b. Sign. S. Mercado and V. Concepcion.		4.00	20.00	65.00

			GOOD	FINE	XF
48	**20 PESOS** 1919. Black on yellow unpt. Portr. Congressman W. A. Jones at lower ctr. Back tan.		75.00	300.00	—

			GOOD	FINE	XF
49	**50 PESOS** 1920. Black on green unpt. Portr. Gen. Lawton at l. Back red.		6.00	25.00	75.00

			GOOD	FINE	XF
50	**100 PESOS** 1920. Green on red unpt. F. Magellan at ctr. Back olive.		—	Rare	—

1921 ISSUE

#51-55 designs like previous issue but notes w/o unpt. Printer: USBEP (w/o imprint). Replacemnet notes: Star prefix.

			GOOD	FINE	XF
51	**1 PESO** 1921. Like #44.		25.00	85.00	225.00
52	**2 PESOS** 1921. Like #45.		30.00	100.00	300.00

			GOOD	FINE	XF
53	**5 PESOS** 1921. Like #46.		1.50	4.00	10.00

			GOOD	FINE	XF
54	**10 PESOS** 1921. Like #47.		3.00	15.00	45.00

			GOOD	FINE	XF
55	**20 PESOS** 1921. Like #48.		7.50	40.00	110.00

1924 ISSUE

#56, replacement notes: Star prefix.

			GOOD	FINE	XF
56	**1 PESO** 1924. Like #51.		10.00	50.00	125.00

1937 ISSUE

#57-59 printer: USBEP w/imprint on back. Title reads: *PHILIPPINES* instead of *PHILIPPINE ISLANDS*. Replacement notes: Star prefix.

			VG	VF	UNC
57	**5 PESOS** 1937. Similar to #53.		5.00	20.00	50.00

			VG	VF	UNC
58	**10 PESOS** 1937. Similar to #54.		10.00	25.00	75.00
59	**20 PESOS** 1937. Similar to #55.		15.00	60.00	175.00

PHILIPPINE ISLANDS (RESUMED)

Treasury Certificates

1918 ISSUE

#60-67 printer: USBEP (w/o imprint). Replacement notes: Star suffix.

		GOOD	FINE	XF
60	**1 PESO** 1918. Black on green unpt. A. Mabini at l. Back green.			
	a. Sign. F. B. Harrison and A. P. Fitzsimmons.	7.50	45.00	150.00
	b. Sign. F.B. Harrison and V. Carmona.	10.00	60.00	200.00
61	**2 PESOS** 1918. Black on blue unpt. J. Rizal at l. Back blue.	25.00	125.00	350.00
62	**5 PESOS** 1918. Black on lt. red unpt. Wm. McKinley at l. Back red-orange.	40.00	175.00	—
63	**10 PESOS** 1918. Black on brown unpt. G. Washington at ctr. Back brown.	150.00	650.00	—

		GOOD	FINE	XF
63A	**20 PESOS** 1918. Black on yellow unpt. Mayon volcano at ctr. Ornate blue XX at upper l. Back tan. Sign. F.B. Harrison and A. P. Fitzsimmons	40.00	175.00	450.00

		GOOD	FINE	XF
64	**20 PESOS** 1918. Like #63A but w/o ornate XX at l. Sign. F. B. Harrison and V. Carmona.	50.00	200.00	500.00
65	**50 PESOS** 1918. Black on green unpt. Gen. Lawton at l. Back red.			
	a. Sign. F. B. Harrison and A. P. Fitzsimmons.	100.00	400.00	—
	b. Sign. F. B. Harrison and V. Carmona.	100.00	400.00	—

		GOOD	FINE	XF
66	**100 PESOS** 1918. Black on green unpt. Magellan at ctr. Back olive.			
	a. Sign. F. B. Harrison and A. P. Fitzsimmons.	—	Rare	—
	b. Sign. F. B. Harrison and V. Carmona.	—	Rare	—
67	**500 PESOS** 1918. Black on orange unpt. Legazpi at ctr. Back purple.	—	Rare	—

1924 ISSUE

#68-72 w/o unpt., otherwise designs like previous issue. Printer: USBEP (w/o imprint). Replacement notes: Star suffix.

NOTE: Though official records indicate that the backs of #72 were printed in purple, two examples are known with green backs. Further reports are requested.

		GOOD	FINE	XF
68	**1 PESO**			
	1924. Like #60.			
	a. Sign. L. Wood and Salv. Lagdameo w/title: *Acting Treasurer*.	7.50	35.00	100.00
	b. Sign. L. Wood and Salv. Lagdameo w/title: *Treasurer*.	10.00	40.00	125.00
	c. Sign. H. L. Stimson and Salv. Lagdameo.	7.50	35.00	100.00
69	**2 PESOS**			
	1924. Like #61, but lg. denomination numeral added in red at lower l. ctr.			
	a. Sign. Leonard Wood and Salv. Lagdameo w/title: *Acting Treasurer*.	12.50	75.00	200.00
	b. Sign. Leonard Wood and Salv. Lagdameo w/title: *Treasurer*.	10.00	60.00	150.00
	c. Sign. Henry L. Stimson and Salv. Lagdameo.	8.00	50.00	140.00

		GOOD	FINE	XF
70	**5 PESOS**			
	1924. Black. Like #62.	20.00	100.00	250.00

		GOOD	FINE	XF
71	**10 PESOS**			
	1924. Black. Like #63.	8.00	45.00	200.00

		GOOD	FINE	XF
72	**500 PESOS**			
	1924. Like #67. Blue unpt. and numeral.	750.00	1750.	—
	a. Back purple.	750.00	2000.	—
	b. Back green.	—	—	—

1929 ISSUE

#73-80 printer: USBEP (w/o imprint). Replacement notes: Star suffix.

Many changes were effected on US-Philippine currency with the 1929 Issue, as the United States changed from the large to small size formats. Significant design alterations were introduced as well as some color changes.

		GOOD	FINE	XF
73	**1 PESO**			
	1929. Black on orange unpt. A. Mabini at l. Similar to #60 but several minor alterations in plate. Back orange.			
	a. Sign. D. F. Davis and Salv. Lagdameo.	5.00	25.00	75.00
	b. Sign. T. Roosevelt and Salv. Lagdameo.	6.00	45.00	150.00
	c. Sign. F. Murphy and Salv. Lagdameo.	3.00	15.00	65.00
74	**2 PESOS**			
	1929. Black on blue unpt. J. Rizal at l. Similar to #61 but several minor alterations in plate. Back blue.			
	a. Sign. Theodore Roosevelt and Salv. Lagdameo.	6.00	45.00	125.00
	b. Sign. Frank Murphy and Salv. Lagdameo.	3.00	15.00	65.00

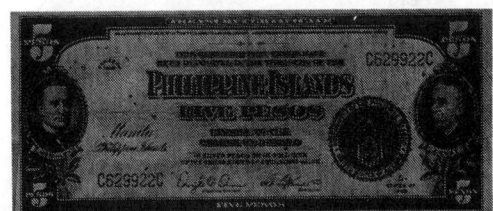

		GOOD	FINE	XF
75	**5 PESOS**			
	1929. Black on yellow unpt. Portr. Wm. McKinley at l., portr. Adm. Dewey at r. Back yellow.	7.50	40.00	175.00

		GOOD	FINE	XF
76	**10 PESOS**			
	1929. Black on brown unpt. Portr. G. Washington at l. Back brown.	12.50	50.00	225.00

		GOOD	FINE	XF
77	**20 PESOS**			
	1929. Black on yellow unpt. Mayon volcano at ctr. Similar to #64 but several minor alterations in plate. Back tan.	25.00	75.00	300.00
78	**50 PESOS**			
	1929. Black on pink unpt. Gen. Lawton at l. Back dk. red.	65.00	250.00	—

		GOOD	FINE	XF
79	**100 PESOS**			
	1929. Black on green unpt. Magellan at l. Back green.	—	Rare	—

		GOOD	FINE	XF
80	**500 PESOS**			
	1929. Black on orange unpt. Legazpi at l. Back purple.	—	Rare	—

COMMONWEALTH

PHILIPPINES

TREASURY CERTIFICATES

1936 ISSUE

#81-88 new red Commonwealth seal. Sign. Manuel Quezon and Antonio Ramos. Title reads: *PHILIPPINES* instead of *PHILIPPINE ISLANDS*. Printer: USBEP (w/o imprint). Replacement notes: Star suffix.

81	1 PESO 1936. Similar to #73.	VG 2.00	VF 5.00	UNC 12.00

82	2 PESOS 1936. Similar to #74.	VG 3.00	VF 7.00	UNC 25.00
83	5 PESOS 1936. Similar to #75.			
	a. Regular issue. Serial # D1D to D3 244 000D.	2.50	6.00	17.50
	b. U.S.A. War Dept. issue (1944). D3 244 001D to D3 544000D.	30.00	100.00	250.00

84	10 PESOS 1936. Similar to #76.	VG	VF	UNC
	a. Regular issue. Serial # D1D to D2 024 000D.	4.00	15.00	55.00
	b. U.S.A. War Dept. issue (1944). D2 024 001D to D2 174 000D.	50.00	160.00	350.00
85	20 PESOS 1936. Similar to #77.			
	a. Regular issue. D1D to D1 664 000D.	10.00	75.00	300.00
	b. U.S.A. War Dept. issue (1944). D1 664 001D to D1 739 000D.	50.00	150.00	350.00
86	50 PESOS 1936. Similar to #78.	75.00	225.00	—
87	100 PESOS 1936. Similar to #79.			
	a. Regular issue. Serial # D1D to D41 000D.	150.00	350.00	—
	b. U.S.A. War Dept. issue (1944). D41 001D to D56 000D.	—	Rare	—
88	500 PESOS 1936. Similar to #80.	—	Rare	—

1941 ISSUE

#89-93 like previous issue. Sign. Manuel Quezon and A.S. de Leon. Printer: USBEP (w/o imprint). Replacement notes: Star suffix.

NOTE: 50, 100 and 500 Pesos notes Series of 1941 were printed but never shipped because of the outbreak of WW II. All were destroyed in 1949, leaving extant only proof impressions and specimen sheets.

89	1 PESO 1941. Like #81.	VG	VF	UNC
	a. Regular issue. Serial # E1E to E6 000 000E.	1.50	4.00	9.00
	b. Processed to simulate used currency (condition - fine, $175.00) at Bureau of Standards (1943). #E6 008 001E to E6 056 000E; E6 064 0001E to E6 072 000E; E6 080 001E to E6 324 000E. Total 300,000 notes.	—	—	—
	c. Naval Aviators' Emergency Money Packet notes (1944). E6 324 001E to E6 524 000E.	5.00	15.00	50.00
90	2 PESOS 1941. Like #82.	3.50	15.00	60.00

91	5 PESOS 1941. Like #83.	VG	VF	UNC
	a. Regular issue. Serial #E1E to E1 188 000E.	5.00	20.00	65.00
	b. Processed like #89b (1943). (Condition - Fine, $300.00). #E1 208 001E to E1 328 000E.	—	—	—
	c. Packet notes like #89c #E1 328 001E to E1 348 000E.	15.00	50.00	200.00

92	10 PESOS 1941. Like #84.	VG	VF	UNC
	a. Regular issue. Serial #E1E to E800 000E.	5.00	20.00	65.00
	b. Processed like #89b (1943). (Condition - Fine, $350.00). E810 0011E to E870 000E.	—	—	—
	c. Packet notes like #89c (1944). #E870 001E to E890 000E.	20.00	70.00	200.00
93	20 PESOS 1941. Like #85.	60.00	250.00	—

1944 ND VICTORY ISSUE

#94-101 w/text: VICTORY Series No. 66 twice on face instead of date, blue seal. Black ovpt: VICTORY in lg. letters on back. Printer: USBEP (w/o imprint). Replacement notes: Star suffix.

94	1 PESO ND (1944). Like #89. Sign. Osemena and Hernandez.	VG .75	VF 1.50	UNC 6.00

95	2 PESOS ND (1944). Like #90.	VG	VF	UNC
	a. Sign. S. Osmena and J. Hernandez w/title: Auditor General.	1.00	2.00	12.50
	b. Sign. M. Roxas and M. Guevara w/title: Treasurer.	3.00	12.00	50.00
96	5 PESOS ND (1944). Like #91. Sign. S. Osmena and J. Hernandez.	2.50	7.50	40.00
97	10 PESOS ND (1944). Like #92. Sign. Osmena and Hernandez.	3.00	12.50	75.00

98	20 PESOS ND (1944). Like #93.	VG	VF	UNC
	a. Sign. S. Osmena and J. Hernandez w/title: Auditor General.	5.00	25.00	100.00
	b. Sign. M. Roxas and M. Guevara w/title: Treasurer.	12.50	50.00	250.00

99	50 PESOS ND (1944). Like #86.	VG	VF	UNC
	a. Sign. S. Osmena and J. Hernandez w/title: Auditor General.	30.00	100.00	300.00
	b. Sign. M. Roxas and M. Guevara w/title: Treasurer.	40.00	150.00	—
100	100 PESOS ND (1944). Like #87.			
	a. 1944. S. Osmena and J. Hernandez w/title: Auditor General.	60.00	20.00	—
	b. Sign. S. Osmena and M. Guevara w/title: Treasurer.	75.00	275.00	—
	c. Sign. M. Roxas and M. Guevara.	60.00	200.00	—

101	**500 Pesos**	VG	VF	UNC
	ND (1944). Like #88.			
	a. Sign. S. Osmena and J. Hernandez w/title: *Auditor General.*	300.00	—	—
	b. Sign. S. Osmena and M. Guevara w/title: *Treasurer.*	300.00	—	—
	c. Sign. M. Roxas and M. Guevara.	300.00	—	—

JAPANESE OCCUPATION - WW II

JAPANESE GOVERNMENT

1942 ND ISSUE

Notes w/block letter *P* preceding other letter(s).

102	**1 CENTAVO**	VG	VF	UNC
	ND (1942). Black on green unpt. Back green.			
	a. 2 block letters.	.10	.20	.50
	b. Fractional block letters.	.10	1.00	1.00
	s. As a. Specimen w/red ovpt: *Mi-hon. SPECIMEN* on back.	—	—	100.00

103	**5 CENTAVOS**	VG	VF	UNC
	ND (1942). Black on blue unpt. Back blue.			
	a. 2 block letters.	.10	.20	.50
	b. Fractional block letters.	.20	.50	1.50
	s. As a. Specimen w/red ovpt: *Mi-hon. SPECIMEN* on back.	—	—	100.00

104	**10 CENTAVOS**	VG	VF	UNC
	ND (1942). Black on lt. brown unpt. Back brown.			
	a. 2 block letters.	.10	.20	.50
	b. Fractional block letters.	.10	.20	.60
	s. As a. Specimen w/red ovpt: *Mi-hon. SPECIMEN* on back.	—	—	100.00

105	**50 CENTAVOS**	VG	VF	UNC
	ND (1942). Black on lt. purple unpt. Plantation at r. Back purple.			
	a. Buff colored paper.	.20	.50	1.00
	b. White paper.	.10	.20	.60
	s. Specimen w/red ovpt: *Mi-hon. SPECIMEN* on back.	—	—	100.00

106	**1 Peso**	VG	VF	UNC
	ND (1942). Black on lt. green unpt. Plantation at l. Back green.			
	a. Buff to lt. brown paper.	.50	1.25	3.00
	b. White paper.	.25	.75	2.00
	s. Specimen w/red ovpt: *Mi-hon. SPECIMEN* on back.	—	—	100.00

107	**5 Pesos**	VG	VF	UNC
	ND (1942). Black on lt. blue unpt. Plantation at ctr. Back orange.			
	a. Buff to lt. brown paper.	.50	1.25	3.00
	b. White paper.	.25	.75	2.00
	s. Specimen w/red ovpt: *Mi-hon. SPECIMEN* on back.	—	—	100.00
107A	**5 Pesos**			
	ND (1942). Black on lt. orange unpt. Like #107b. Back gold-yellow.	.50	1.25	5.00

108	**10 Pesos**	VG	VF	UNC
	ND (1942). Black on blue unpt. Plantation at r. Back brown.			
	a. Buff paper.	.25	.50	1.25
	b. White paper.	.20	.30	.75
	s. Specimen w/red ovpt: *Mi-hon. SPECIMEN* on back.	—	—	100.00

1943 ND ISSUE

#109-112 engraved face plates w/Rizal Monument at l. or r. Wmk: Banana tree.

109	**1 Peso**	VG	VF	UNC
	ND (1943). Black on lt. green and pink unpt. Monument at l. Back blue on pink unpt.			
	a. Serial # and block #. (#1-80).	.20	.50	1.00
	b. Block # only (81-87).	1.50	5.00	15.00
	s. As a. Specimen w/red ovpt: *Mi-hon. SPECIMEN* on back.	—	—	150.00

110	**5 Pesos**	VG	VF	UNC
	ND (1943). Black on green and yellow unpt. Monument at l. Back brown on gray unpt.			
	a. Issued note.	.25	.75	2.00
	s. Specimen w/ovpt: *Mi-hon.*	—	—	150.00

111	10 PESOS	VG	VF	UNC
	ND (1943). Black on green unpt. Monument at l. Back green on yellow unpt.			
	a. Issued note.	.25	.75	2.00
	s. Specimen w/red ovpt: *Mi-hon.*	—	—	150.00

112	100 PESOS	VG	VF	UNC
	ND (1944). Black on lt. blue and tan unpt. Monument at r. Back purple on green unpt.			
	a. Issued note.	.25	.75	2.50
	s. Specimen w/red ovpt: *Mi-hon.*	—	—	150.00

1944-45 ND INFLATION ISSUE

113	100 PESOS	VG	VF	UNC
	ND (1945). Black on brown on lt. green unpt. Back yellow-brown. W/o wmk. Similar to #115. Block letters PV.	—	Rare	—

114	500 PESOS	VG	VF	UNC
	ND (1944). Black on purple unpt. Rizal Monument at r. Back brown. Lithographed.			
	a. Wmk: Banana tree. Buff paper. Block letters PF.	.75	2.00	10.00
	b. Wmk: Quatrefoil kiri flower. Most on white paper. Block letters PG.	.50	1.50	4.00
	s1. Specimen w/red ovpt: *Mi-hon. SPECIMEN* on back.	—	—	150.00
	s2. Specimen w/ovpt: *Mi-hon.*	—	—	150.00

115	1000 PESOS	VG	VF	UNC
	ND (1945). Blue-purple. Like #113. Back olive. Block letter PU.			
	a. Purple on lilac unpt. (shades). Back dk. olive-green w/o offset.	1.50	3.00	10.00
	b. As a., but back lt. olive-green w/o offset.	1.50	3.00	10.00
	c. As a., but back w/offset from face plate.	.20	.50	3.00
	d. As b., but back w/offset from face plate.	.20	.50	3.00

OVERPRINT VARIETIES:

A. The Filipino organization called JAPWANCAP, Inc., (Japanese War Notes Claimants Association of the Philippines) made a very serious attempt in 1967 to obtain funds from the United States for redemption of millions of pesos in Japanese occupation currency. Notes being held by that group were marked with a number of different stampings. Most are seen on higher denomination notes, but occasionally lower values are found thus marked as well. Such marked notes have no particular value above the unmarked pieces.

B. Various Japanese occupation notes exist with propaganda ovpt: *THE CO-PROSPERITY SPHERE: WHAT IS IT WORTH?* Also, many copies of the ovpt. have been applied to the otherwise common occupation notes. It is extremely difficult to ascertain genuine ovpt. at this time.

BANGKO SENTRAL NG PILIPINAS

1944 ISSUE

115A	10 PISO	VG	VF	UNC
	L.29.2.1944. Brown on brown unpt. J. Rizal at l. (A few made in 1944 as essays; not approved for circulation).	—	Rare	—

116	100 PISO	VG	VF	UNC
	L.29.2.1944. Black on pink unpt. J. Rizal at l. Back red and orange. (Printed 1944; not issued).			
	s1. Specimen w/red ovpt: *MI-HON.* W/block # and serial #.	—	—	900.00
	s2. As s1. Specimen w/red ovpt: *Specimen* w/serial # all zeros.	—	—	—
	s3. Specimen w/o block and serial #.	200.00	325.00	550.00

REPUBLIC

CENTRAL BANK OF THE PHILIPPINES

1949 PROVISIONAL ISSUE

#117-124 Treasury Certificates of Victory Series w/red ovpt: *CENTRAL BANK/OF THE PHILIPPINES* on back.

117	1 PESO	VG	VF	UNC
	ND (1949). Ovpt. on #94.			
	a. Thick lettering in ovpt.	1.00	3.00	12.50
	b. Medium-thick lettering in ovpt.	1.50	4.00	15.00
	c. Thin lettering in ovpt.	1.00	3.00	10.00
118	2 PESOS			
	ND (1949). Ovpt. on #95. Thick lettering in ovpt.			
	a. Sign. S. Osmeña and J. Hernandez.	—	Rare	—
	b. Sign. M. Roxas and M. Guevara.	4.00	10.00	45.00
119	5 PESOS			
	ND (1949). Ovpt. on #96.			
	a. Thick lettering in ovpt.	3.00	12.00	55.00
	b. Thin lettering in ovpt.	2.00	10.00	50.00

120	10 PESOS	VG	VF	UNC
	ND (1949). Ovpt. on #97. Thick lettering in ovpt.	5.00	20.00	75.00
121	20 PESOS			
	ND (1949). Ovpt. on #98. Thick lettering in ovpt.			
	a. Sign. S. Osmeña and J. Hernandez.	7.50	30.00	110.00
	b. Sign. M. Roxas and M. Guevara.	7.50	30.00	110.00
122	50 PESOS			
	ND (1949). Ovpt. on #99. Thin lettering in ovpt.			
	a. Sign. S. Osmeña and J. Hernandez.	25.00	80.00	200.00
	b. Sign. M. Roxas and M. Guevara.	25.00	80.00	200.00

123 100 PESOS
ND (1949). Ovpt. on #100. Thick lettering in ovpt.

	VG	VF	UNC
a. Sign. S. Osmeña and J. Hernandez.	40.00	120.00	250.00
b. Sign. S. Osmeña and M. Guevara.	40.00	120.00	250.00
c. Sign. M. Roxas and M. Guevara.	35.00	100.00	225.00

124 500 PESOS
ND (1949). Ovpt. on #101. Thick lettering in ovpt.

	VG	VF	UNC
a. Sign. S. Osmeña and J. Hernandez.	25.00	550.00	1250.
b. Sign. S. Osmeña and M. Guevara.	250.00	550.00	1250.
c. Sign. M. Roxas and M. Guevara.	225.00	500.00	1000.

1949 ND "ENGLISH" ISSUES

#125, 127, and 129 sign. E. Quirino and M. Cuaderno. Printer: SBNC.

#130-141 printer: TDLR.

#133-141 bank seal at lower r.

125 5 CENTAVOS
ND. Red on tan unpt. Back red.

	VG	VF	UNC
	.10	.30	1.25

126 5 CENTAVOS
(128) ND. Llke #125. Sign. R. Magsaysay and M. Cuaderno. Printer: W&S.

	VG	VF	UNC
	.10	.25	1.00

127 10 CENTAVOS
(126) ND. Brownish purple on tan unpt. Back brownish purple.

	VG	VF	UNC
a. Issued note.	.25	.50	2.50
r. Remainder w/o serial #.	—	100.00	250.00

128 10 CENTAVOS
(129) ND. Llke #126. Sign. R. Magsaysay and M. Cuaderno. Printer: W&S.

	VG	VF	UNC
	.10	.25	1.00

129 20 CENTAVOS
(127) ND. Green on lt. green unpt. Back green.

	VG	VF	UNC
a. Issued note.	.30	.60	3.50
r. Remainder w/o serial # (error).	—	100.00	250.00

130 20 CENTAVOS
ND. Green on lt. green unpt. Back green.

	VG	VF	UNC
a. Sign. R. Magsaysay and M. Cuaderno.	.20	.50	2.00
b. Sign. C. Garcia and M. Cuaderno.	.10	.25	1.00

131 50 CENTAVOS
ND. Blue on lt. blue unpt. Back blue. Sign. R. Magsaysay and M. Cuaderno.

	VG	VF	UNC
	.20	.50	2.25

132 1/2 PESO
ND. Green on yellow and blue unpt. Ox-cart w/Mt. Mayon in background at ctr. Back green. Sign. C. Garcia and M. Cuaderno.

	VG	VF	UNC
	.20	.50	2.25

133 1 PESO
ND. Black on lt. gold and blue unpt. A. Mabini at l. Back Black; Barasoain Church at ctr.

	VG	VF	UNC
a. Sign. E. Quirino and M. Cuaderno. *GENUINE* in very lt. tan letters just beneath top heading on face.	7.00	22.00	85.00
b. Sign. E. Quirino and M. Cuaderno w/o *GENUINE* on face.	.50	1.50	5.00
c. Sign. R. Magsaysay and M. Cuaderno.	.25	.75	3.00
d. Sign. C. Garcia and M. Cuaderno.	.25	.75	2.00
e. Sign. C. Garcia and A. Castillo w/title: *Acting Governor*.	.50	1.00	3.50
f. Sign. D. Macapagal and A. Castillo w/title: *Governor*.			
g. Sign. F. Marcos and A. Castillo.	.25	.75	2.00
h. Sign. F. Marcos and A. Calalang.	.10	.30	1.00
s. Sign. as f. Specimen.	—	—	55.00

134 2 PESOS
ND. Black on blue and gold unpt. Portr. J. Rizal at l. Back blue; landing of Magellan in the Philippines.

	VG	VF	UNC
a. Sign. E. Quirino and M. Cuaderno.	1.00	4.00	15.00
b. Sign. R. Magsaysay and M. Cuaderno.	.75	2.00	5.00
c. Sign. C. Garcia and A. Castillo w/title: *Acting Governor*.	.75	1.50	4.00
d. Sign. D. Macapagal and A. Castillo w/title: *GOVERNOR*.	.15	.50	1.50
s. Sign. as b. Specimen.	—	—	60.00
s. Sign. as d. Specimen.	—	—	60.00

135 **5 PESOS**
ND. Black on yellow and gold unpt. Portr. M. H. del Pilar at l., Lopez
Jaena at r. Back gold; newspaper "La Solidaridad".

	VG	VF	UNC
a. Sign. E. Quirino and M. Cuaderno.	2.00	7.50	25.00
b. Sign. R. Magsaysay and M. Cuaderno.	1.00	3.50	10.00
c. Sign. C. Garcia and M. Cuaderno.	1.50	4.00	15.00
d. Sign. C. Garcia and A. Castillo w/title: *Acting Governor*.	1.25	3.00	12.00
e. Sign. D. Macapagal and A. Castillo w/title: *Governor*.	.20	.40	1.25
f. Sign. F. Marcos and G. Licaros.	.20	.40	1.25
s. Sign. as e. Specimen.	—	—	65.00

136 **10 PESOS**
ND. Black on tan and lt. red unpt. Fathers Burgos, Gomez and Zamora
at l. Back brown; monument.

	VG	VF	UNC
6. Sign. E. Quirino and M. Cuaderno.	8.00	25.00	75.00
b. Sign. R. Magsaysay and M. Cuaderno.	2.50	7.00	20.00
c. Sign. C. Garcia and M. Cuaderno.	3.00	7.50	22.50
d. Sign. C. Garcia and A. Castillo w/title: *Acting Governor*.	2.50	7.00	17.50
e. Sign. D. Macapagal and A. Castillo w/title: *Governor*.	.25	.75	2.25
f. Sign. F. Marcos and G. Licaros.	1.00	2.50	7.50
s. Sign. as b. Specimen.	—	—	70.00
s. Sign. as d. Specimen.	—	—	70.00

137 **20 PESOS**
ND. Black on yellow unpt. Portr. A. Bonifacio at l., E. Jacinto at r. Back
brownish orange; flag and monument.

	VG	VF	UNC
a. Sign. E. Quirino and M. Cuaderno.	10.00	30.00	85.00
b. Sign. R. Magsaysay and M. Cuaderno.	2.75	8.00	25.00
c. Sign. C. Garcia and A. Castillo w/title: *Acting Governor*.	2.25	7.00	20.00
d. Sign. D. Macapagal and A. Castillo w/title: *Governor*.	.50	1.50	4.50
e. Sign. F. Marcos and G. Licaros.	.35	1.00	3.00
s. Sign. as a. Specimen.	—	—	100.00
s. Sign. as d. Specimen.	—	—	75.00

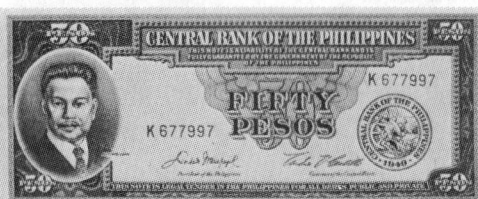

138 **50 PESOS**
ND. Black on pink and lt. tan unpt. Portr. A. Luna at l. Back red; scene
of blood compact of Sikatuna and Legaspi.

	VG	VF	UNC
a. Sign. E. Quirino and M. Cuaderno.	50.00	170.00	—
b. Sign. R. Magsaysay and M. Cuaderno.	20.00	45.00	90.00
c. Sign. C. Garcia and M. Cuaderno.	8.00	20.00	40.00
d. Sign. D. Macapagal and A. Castillo.	.65	2.00	6.00
s. Sign. as d. Specimen.	—	—	85.00

139 **100 PESOS**
ND. Black on gold unpt. T. Sora at l. Back yellow; regimental flags.
Sign. E. Quirino and M. Cuaderno.

VG	VF	UNC
1.65	5.00	15.00

140 **200 PESOS**
ND. Green on pink and lt. blue unpt. Pres. Manuel Quezon at l. Back
green; Legislative bld g. Sign. E. Quirino and M. Cuaderno.

VG	VF	UNC
2.75	8.00	25.00

141 **500 PESOS**
ND. Black on purple and lt. tan unpt. Pres. Manuel Roxas at l. Back
purple; Central Bank. Sign. E. Quirino and M. Cuaderno.

VG	VF	UNC
7.00	20.00	65.00

POLAND

The Republic of Poland, formerly the Polish Peoples Republic, located in central Europe, has an area of 120,725 sq. mi. (312,677 sq. km.) and a population of 38 million. Capital: Warsaw. The economy is essentially agricultural, but industrial activity provides the products for foreign trade. Machinery, coal, coke, iron, steel and transport equipment are exported.

Poland, which began as a Slavic duchy in the 10th century and reached its peak of power between the 14th and 16th centuries, has had a turbulent history of invasion, occupation or partition by Mongols, Turkey, Hungary, Sweden, Austria, Prussia and Russia.

The first partition took place in 1772. Prussia took Polish Pomerania. Russia took part of the eastern provinces. Austria took Galicia, in which lay the fortress city of Krakow (Cracow). The second partition occurred in 1793 when Russia took another slice of the eastern provinces and Prussia took what remained of western Poland. The third partition, 1795, literally removed Poland from the map. Russia took what was left of the eastern provinces. Prussia seized most of central Poland, including Warsaw. Austria took what was left of the south. Napoleon restored to Poland much of the territory lost to Prussia and Austria, but after his defeat another partition returned the Duchy of Warsaw to Prussia, made Kracow into a tiny republic, and declared what remained to be the Kingdom of Poland under the czar and in permanent union with Russia.

Poland re-emerged as an independent state recognized by the Treaty of Versailles on June 28, 1919, and maintained its independence until 1939 when it was invaded by, and partitioned between Germany and Russia. Poland's present boundaries were determined by the U.S.-British-Russian agreement of Aug. 16, 1945. The Government of National Unity was replaced when the Polish Communist-Socialist faction won a decisive victory at the polls in 1947 and established a "People's Democratic Republic" of the Soviet type. In Dec. 1989, Poland became a republic once again.

RULERS:
Stanislaw Augustus, 1764-1795
Fryderyk August I, King of Saxony, as Grand Duke, 1807-1814
Alexander I, Czar of Russia, as King, 1815-1825
Nikolaj (Mikolay) I, Czar of Russia, as King, 1825-1855

MONETARY SYSTEM:
1 Marka = 100 Fenigow to 1919
1 Zloty = 100 Groszy 1919

KINGDOM

BILET SKARBOWY

TREASURY NOTE

1794 TREASURY NOTE
#A1-A11 issued by General Kosciuszko.

A2

A3

		GOOD	FINE	XF
A2	**10 ZLOTYCH** 8.6.1794.	12.00	25.00	55.00
A3	**25 ZLOTYCH** 8.6.1794. White paper.	12.00	30.00	65.00
A4	**50 ZLOTYCH** 8.6.1794. Dk. brown paper.	25.00	50.00	100.00
A5	**100 ZLOTYCH** 8.6.1794. Red paper.	25.00	55.00	120.00
A6	**500 ZLOTYCH** 8.6.1794.	250.00	500.00	1000.
A7	**1000 ZLOTYCH** 8.6.1794.	—	Rare	—

1794 TREASURY NOTE SECOND ISSUE
#A8-A11 uniface w/name: *F. MALINOWSKI* on back (as illustrated) are modern reproductions.

		GOOD	FINE	XF
A8	**5 GROSZY** 13.8.1794.	6.00	15.00	35.00

		GOOD	FINE	XF
A9	**10 GROSZY** 13.8.1794.			
A10	**1 ZLOTY** 13.8.1794.	75.00	150.00	300.00

		GOOD	FINE	XF
A1	**5 ZLOTYCH** 8.6.1794.	7.50	20.00	50.00
A11	**4 ZLOTE** 4.9.1794.	5.00	10.00	25.00

DUCHY OF WARSAW

KASSOWY-BILLET XIESTWA WARSZAWSKIEGO

1810 STATE TREASURY NOTE
#A12-A14 have 9 different sign. Also exist as "Formulare" w/red stamps but w/o the printed seal. Market value: $500.00.

		GOOD	FINE	XF
A12	**1 TALAR** 1.12.1810. Black.	40.00	100.00	275.00
A13	**2 TALARY** 1.12.1810. Black.	50.00	125.00	325.00
A14	**5 TALAROW** 1.12.1810. Black.	75.00	175.00	450.00

BILLET KASSOWY KROLESTWA POLSKIEGO

1824 ISSUE

		GOOD	FINE	XF
A15	**5 ZLOTYCH** 1824.	75.00	175.00	350.00

		GOOD	FINE	XF
A16	**10 ZLOTYCH** 1824.	150.00	300.00	550.00
A17	**50 ZLOTYCH** 1824.			
A18	**100 ZLOTYCH** 1824.			

INSURRECTION OF 1831

ASSYGNACYA SKARBOWA

1831 ISSUE

		GOOD	FINE	XF
A18A	**200 ZLOTYCH** 1831.	—	—	500.00

		GOOD	FINE	XF
A18B	**500 ZLOTYCH** 1831. Black and blue. Ornate border w/tridents. Black text on back.	—	—	350.00

RUSSIAN INFLUENCE

BANK POLSKI

1830 ISSUE

		GOOD	FINE	XF
A19	**5 ZLOTYCH** 1.5.1830.	70.00	150.00	350.00
A20	**50 ZLOTYCH** 1.5.1830.	200.00	400.00	850.00

		GOOD	FINE	XF
A21	**100 ZLOTYCH** 1.5.1830.	150.00	325.00	550.00

1831 ISSUE

		GOOD	FINE	XF
A22	**1 ZLOTY** 1831.	60.00	125.00	275.00

1841 ISSUE

		GOOD	FINE	XF
A23	**3 RUBEL** 1841.	80.00	175.00	375.00

1842 ISSUE

		GOOD	FINE	XF
A24	**3 RUBEL** 1842.	80.00	175.00	375.00

1843 ISSUE

		GOOD	FINE	XF
A25	**3 RUBEL** 1843.	80.00	175.00	375.00
A25A	**10 RUBEL** 1843.	80.00	175.00	375.00

1844 ISSUE

		GOOD	FINE	XF
A26	**10 RUBEL** 1844.	200.00	400.00	850.00
A27	**25 RUBEL** 1844.	275.00	550.00	1200.

1846 ISSUE

		GOOD	FINE	XF
A28	**3 RUBEL** 1846.	80.00	175.00	375.00

1847 ISSUE

		GOOD	FINE	XF
A29	**1 RUBEL** 1847.	70.00	150.00	350.00

		GOOD	FINE	XF
A30	**10 RUBEL** 1847. Crowned imperial eagle at top ctr.	200.00	400.00	850.00

1848 ISSUE

		GOOD	FINE	XF
A31	**25 RUBEL** 1848.	275.00	550.00	1200.

1849 ISSUE

		GOOD	FINE	XF
A32	**1 RUBEL** 1849.	70.00	150.00	350.00

1850 ISSUE

		GOOD	FINE	XF
A33	**3 RUBEL** 1850.	80.00	175.00	375.00

1851 ISSUE

		GOOD	FINE	XF
A34	**1 RUBEL** 1851.	70.00	150.00	350.00
A35	**3 RUBEL** 1851.	80.00	175.00	375.00

1852 ISSUE

		GOOD	FINE	XF
A36	**1 RUBEL** 1852.	70.00	150.00	350.00
A37	**3 RUBEL** 1852.	80.00	175.00	375.00

1853 ISSUE

		GOOD	FINE	XF
A38	**1 RUBEL** 1853.	70.00	150.00	350.00
A39	**3 RUBEL** 1853.	80.00	175.00	375.00

1854 ISSUE

		GOOD	FINE	XF
A40	**1 RUBEL** 1854.	70.00	150.00	350.00
A41	**3 RUBEL** 1854.	80.00	175.00	375.00

1855 ISSUE

		GOOD	FINE	XF
A42	**1 RUBEL** 1855.	70.00	150.00	350.00

1856 ISSUE

		GOOD	FINE	XF
A43	**1 RUBEL** 1856.	70.00	150.00	350.00

1857 ISSUE

		GOOD	FINE	XF
A44	**1 RUBEL** 1857.	100.00	200.00	450.00

1858 ISSUE

		GOOD	FINE	XF
A45	**1 RUBEL** 1858.	70.00	150.00	350.00
A46	**3 RUBEL** 1858.	80.00	175.00	375.00

1864 ISSUE

		GOOD	FINE	XF
A47	**1 RUBEL** 1864. Crowned imperial eagle at ctr.	70.00	150.00	350.00

1865 ISSUE

		GOOD	FINE	XF
A48	**3 RUBEL** 1865.	80.00	175.00	375.00
A49	**25 RUBEL** 1865.	275.00	550.00	1200.

1866 FIRST ISSUE

		GOOD	FINE	XF
A50	**1 RUBEL** 1866.	70.00	150.00	350.00
A51	**3 RUBEL** 1866.	80.00	175.00	375.00
A52	**10 RUBEL** 1866.	200.00	400.00	850.00

		GOOD	FINE	XF
A53	**25 RUBEL** 1866. Crowned imperial eagle at upper ctr.	275.00	550.00	1200.

1866 SECOND ISSUE

		GOOD	FINE	XF
A54	**1 RUBEL** ND.(1866).	—	—	—

GERMAN OCCUPATION, WW I

POLSKA KRAJOWA KASA POZYCZKOWA

POLISH STATE LOAN BANK

1916-17 FIRST ISSUE

#1-6 face red and black w/text: *Zarzad jeneral-gubernatorstwa*.

		VG	VF	UNC
1	**1/2 MARKI** 1917. Crowned eagle at l. Back blue and olive.	.75	3.00	20.00

				VG	VF	UNC
2	**1 MARKA**			1.50	5.00	25.00
	1917. Crowned eagle at l. Back blue and red.					

				VG	VF	UNC
3	**2 MARKI**			1.50	6.00	22.50
	1917. Crowned eagle at l. Back orange and green.					
3A	**5 MAREK**			—	—	—
	1917. Back gray-blue and yellow (Not issued). Proof.					
3B	**10 MAREK**			—	—	—
	1917. Back violet-brown and green (Not issued). Proof.					

				GOOD	FINE	XF
4	**20 MAREK**			6.00	20.00	60.00
	1917. Crowned eagle at ctr. Back violet and lt. brown.					

				GOOD	FINE	XF
5	**50 MAREK**			5.00	15.00	40.00
	1917. Crowned eagle at ctr. Back green and pink.					
6	**100 MAREK**					
	9.12.1916. Crowned eagle at l. Back dk. blue and orange.					
	a. 6-digit serial #.			6.00	20.00	60.00
	b. 7-digit serial #.			6.00	20.00	55.00

1916-17 SECOND ISSUE

#7-16 w/text: *Zarzad General-Gubernatorstwa*.

				VG	VF	UNC
7	**1/2 MARKI**			1.00	3.00	15.00
	1917. Like #1. Back blue and olive.					
8	**1 MARKA**			1.00	3.00	20.00
	1917. Like #2. Back blue and red.					

				GOOD	FINE	XF
9	**2 MARKI**			1.00	5.00	22.50
	1917. Like #3. Back orange and green.					
10	**5 MAREK**			2.00	8.00	30.00
	1917. Red and black. Text at l.: ...*Biletiej Polskiej Krajowej...* Back gray-blue and yellow.					
11	**5 MAREK**			2.00	8.50	35.00
	1917. Like #10 but text l.: ...*Biletow Kasy Pozyczkowej...* Back gray-blue and yellow.					
12	**10 MAREK**			2.00	8.50	35.00
	1917. Red and black. Crowned eagle at ctr. Text at l.: ...*Biletow Polskiej Krajowej...* Back violet-brown and green.					
13	**10 MAREK**			15.00	45.00	120.00
	1917. Like #12 but text at l.: ...*Biletow Kasy Pozyczkowej...* Back violet-brown and green.					

				GOOD	FINE	XF
14	**20 MAREK**			8.00	20.00	60.00
	1917. Like # 4. Back violet and lt. brown.					

15	100 MAREK		GOOD	FINE	XF
	9.12.1916. Like #6. Blue and red.		3.00	12.50	30.00

16	1000 MAREK	GOOD	FINE	XF
	1917. Brown and red. Crowned eagle at l. Back dk. blue, green and lt. tan.	10.00	40.00	100.00

REPUBLIC

POLSKA KRAJOWA KASA POZYCZKOWA

POLISH STATE LOAN BANK

1919 FIRST ISSUE

21	20 MAREK	VG	VF	UNC
	17.5.1919. Brown. Crowned eagle at ctr. Back brown and green; Kosciuszko at ctr. 3 serial # varieties.	2.00	7.00	25.00

17	100 MAREK		VG	VF	UNC
(18)	15.2.1919. Green and gray-violet. Portr. T. Kosciuszko at l.				
	a.	Wmk: Honeycombs. Brownish paper w/engraver's name at lower l. and r.	1.00	3.00	9.00
	b.	Wmk: Honeycombs. Brownish paper w/o engraver's name.	1.50	5.00	15.00
	c.	Indistinct wmk: (Polish eagle). White paper.	2.00	7.00	17.50
18	500 MAREK				
(17)	15.1.1919. Green and red. Crowned eagle at l. Back dk. and lt. green.		12.50	50.00	145.00

22	1000 MAREK		VG	VF	UNC
	17.5.1919. Green and brown. Kosciuszko at l.				
	a.	Wmk: Honeycombs. Brownish paper w/engraver's name at lower l. and r. on back. 2 serial # varieties.	1.00	3.00	10.00
	b.	Wmk: Honeycombs. Brownish paper w/o engraver's name.	2.00	5.00	15.00
	c.	Indistinct wmk: (crowned eagle). White paper w/engraver's name at lower l. and r. on back.	1.00	3.00	10.00
	d.	Indistinct wmk: (crowned eagle). White paper w/o engraver's name. 2 serial # varieties.	1.00	3.00	10.00

1919 THIRD ISSUE

1919 SECOND ISSUE

19	1 MARKA	VG	VF	UNC
	17.5.1919. Gray-violet and violet. Eagle at ctr. on back. 3 serial # varieties.	.50	3.00	10.00

23	1 MARKA	VG	VF	UNC
	23.8.1919. Red on brown unpt. Arms at l., woman at r. 2 serial # varieties.	.25	.60	2.50

20	5 MAREK		VG	VF	UNC
	17.5.1919. Black. Small eagle at upper ctr. Back green; B. Glowacki (Pres.) at r.				
	a.	Engraver's name at lower l. and r. on back.	.75	3.00	12.50
	b.	W/o engraver's name. 2 serial # varieties.	.75	3.00	12.50

24	5 MAREK	VG	VF	UNC
	23.8.1919. Green on brown unpt. Arms at l., portr. T. Kosciuszko at r. 2 serial # varieties.	.25	.50	2.50
25	10 MAREK			
	23.8.1919. Blue-green on brown unpt. Similar to #24. 2 serial # varieties.	.25	.75	3.50

			VG	VF	UNC
26	**20 MAREK** 23.8.1919. Red on brown unpt. Portr. woman at r. 2 serial # varieties.		.50	1.00	3.50

			VG	VF	UNC
27	**100 MAREK** 23.8.1919. Blue on brown unpt. Portr. T. Kosciuszko at r. 2 serial # varieties.		.75	1.50	4.50
28	**500 MAREK** 23.8.1919. Green on brown unpt. Portr. woman at r. 3 serial # varieties.		.75	3.00	9.00

			VG	VF	UNC
29	**1000 MAREK** 23.8.1919. Violet on brown unpt. Portr. T. Kosciuszko at r. 6 serial # varieties.		.25	.60	3.00

1920 ISSUE

			VG	VF	UNC
30	**1/2 MARKI** 7.2.1920. Green on brown unpt. Portr. T. Kosciuszko at r.		.25	1.00	3.00
31	**5000 MAREK** 7.2.1920. Blue on brown unpt. Portr. woman at l., man at r. 4 serial # varieties.		.75	3.00	10.00

1922-23 INFLATION ISSUES
NOTE: For #34 there exists 2 error dates: 25.4.1922 and 25.4.1923.

			GOOD	FINE	XF
32	**10,000 MAREK** 11.3.1922. Greenish black on lt. tan unpt. Woman's head at l. and r. Eagle at ctr. on back.		2.00	7.50	25.00

			GOOD	FINE	XF
33	**50,000 MAREK** 10.10.1922. Brown on lt. tan and blue unpt. Eagle at l. on back.		1.50	5.00	17.50
34 (35)	**100,000 MAREK** 30.8.1923. Brown. Back blue-gray; eagle at ctr.		4.00	12.50	45.00

			GOOD	FINE	XF
35 (34)	**250,000 MAREK** 25.4.1923. Gray-brown on lt. bluish unpt. Eagle at ctr. on back. 2 serial # varieties.		3.00	10.00	40.00

36 500,000 MAREK — GOOD 3.00 FINE 10.00 XF 40.00
30.8.1923. Gray on lt. green unpt. Eagle at ctr. on back. 5 serial # varieties.

37 1,000,000 MAREK — 5.00 15.00 60.00
30.8.1923. Olive-brown on lt. blue unpt. Town view at l. Back green; eagle at ctr. 2 serial # varieties.

38 5,000,000 MAREK — 10.00 40.00 100.00
20.11.1923. Brown on pink and blue unpt. Eagle at upper ctr. Back blue-gray; eagle at l.

39 10,000,000 MAREK — GOOD 20.00 FINE 75.00 XF 175.00
20.11.1923. Green and blue on lt. tan and green unpt. Town view w/2 towers at l., crowned eagle at r. Back brown; eagle at upper l. 2 serial # varieties.

40 50,000,000 MAREK — 50.00 200.00 450.00
20.11.1923. Blue unpt.

41 100,000,000 MAREK — GOOD 75.00 FINE 225.00 XF 500.00
20.11.1923. Pink unpt.

MINISTERSTWO SKARBU
MINISTRY OF FINANCE
1924 PROVISIONAL BILET ZDAWKOWY ISSUE

42 1 GROSZ — VG / VF / UNC
28.4.1924. Red ovpt. w/new denomination and coin on bisected note #36.
a. L. half. — 3.00 10.00 30.00
b. R. half. — 3.00 10.00 30.00

43 5 GROSZY — VG / VF / UNC
28.4.1924. Red ovpt. w/new denomination and coin on bisected note #39.
a. L. half. — 5.00 17.50 50.00
b. R. half. — 5.00 17.50 50.00

1924-25 BILET ZDAWKOWY ISSUE

44 10 GROSZY — VG 1.50 VF 7.00 UNC 27.50
28.4.1924. Blue. Bldg. w/column at ctr., coin at l. and r.

45 20 GROSZY — VG 2.00 VF 8.00 UNC 35.00
28.4.1924. Brown. Copernicus monument at ctr., coin at l. and r.

46 50 GROSZY — VG 3.00 VF 15.00 UNC 50.00
28.4.1924. Red. Equestrian statue of J. Poniatowski at ctr., coin at lower l. and r.

47 2 ZLOTE
1.5.1925. Gray-violet on gray-green. Obverse and reverse of 2 Zlote coin.
a. Back right side up. — 30.00 60.00 140.00
b. Misprint: back inverted. — — —

48 5 ZLOTYCH — VG 40.00 VF 130.00 UNC 300.00
1.5.1925. Green and brown. Obv. of coin at l.

1926 BILET PANSTWOWY ISSUE

		VG	VF	UNC
49	**5 ZLOTYCH** 25.10.1926. Dk. olive and brown. Woman at ctr. Worker on back.	30.00	70.00	150.00

1938 BILET PANSTWOWY ISSUE

		VG	VF	UNC
50	**1 ZLOTY** 1.10.1938. Gray on yellow-brown unpt. Portr. man w/crown at r.	10.00	32.50	70.00

BANK POLSKI

1919 DATED ISSUE
#51-56 2 sign. w/o titles.
#57-59 printer: W&S.

		GOOD	FINE	XF
51	**1 ZLOTY** 28.2.1919 (1924). Purple on lilac unpt. Portr. T. Kosciuszko at l. Eagle at r. on back.	5.00	15.00	50.00
52	**2 ZLOTE** 28.2.1919 (1924). Lt. and dk. blue on lt. brown unpt. Portr. T. Kosciuszko at l.	17.50	45.00	110.00

		GOOD	FINE	XF
53	**5 ZLOTYCH** 28.2.1919 (1924). Brown. Portr. Prince J. Poniatowski at r. Eagle at l. on back.	25.00	60.00	165.00

		GOOD	FINE	XF
54	**10 ZLOTYCH** 28.2.1919 (1924). Purple and brown. Portr. T. Kosciuszko at upper l. and as wmk.	35.00	80.00	175.00
55	**20 ZLOTYCH** 28.2.1919 (1924). M/c. Portr. Kosciuszko at l.	50.00	120.00	250.00
56	**50 ZLOTYCH** 28.2.1919 (1924). Violet-brown and violet. Kosciuszko at l. Eagle at ctr. r. on back.	150.00	350.00	—
57	**100 ZLOTYCH** 28.2.1919 (1924). Blue and brown. Kosciuszko at l.	12.00	30.00	70.00

		GOOD	FINE	XF
58	**500 ZLOTYCH** 28.2.1919 (1924). Purple and green. Kosciuszko at l.	2.50	7.50	20.00

		GOOD	FINE	XF
59	**1000 ZLOTYCH** 28.2.1919 (1924). Brown. Kosciuszko at l.			
	a. Issued note.	175.00	325.00	—
	s. Specimen.	—	—	225.00

60	**5000 Zlotych**			**XF**
	28.2.1919 (1924). Green. Portr. T. Kosciuszko at lower l. Specimen.			300.00

1924 Issue
#61-63 designs like previous issue, but 3 sign. w/titles.

		Good	**Fine**	**XF**
61	**5 Zlotych**			
	15.7.1924. Brown. Like #53.	20.00	65.00	140.00
62	**10 Zlotych**			
	15.7.1924. Purple. Like #54.			
	a. White paper.	35.00	85.00	165.00
	b. Gray paper.	35.00	85.00	165.00

		Good	**Fine**	**XF**
63	**20 Zlotych**			
	15.7.1924. M/c. Like #55.			
	a. White paper.	55.00	175.00	400.00
	b. Gray paper.	55.00	175.00	400.00
64	**50 Zlotych**			
	28.8.1925. Green, brown and blue. Farmer's wife at l. Mercury at r. 2 bldgs. on back.	20.00	60.00	135.00

1926 Issue

		Good	**Fine**	**XF**
65 (66)	**10 Zlotych**			
	20.7.1926. Brown, olive and blue. Allegorical female at l. and r. Three standing figures on back.			
	a. Wmk: Kg. w/numbers.	25.00	65.00	165.00
	b. Wmk: Kg. w/values.	15.00	30.00	75.00
66 (65)	**20 Zlotych**			
	1.3.1926. Blue and olive. Like #64.	50.00	130.00	300.00

1928 Issue
#67-68 printer: Orell Fussli, Zurich (w/o imprint).

67	**10 Zlotych**	**VG**	**VF**	**UNC**
	2.1.1928. Dk. blue. Portr. youth at upper r.	—	500.00	800.00

68	**20 Zlotych**	**VG**	**VF**	**UNC**
	2.1.1928. Dk. purple. Woman at r. Specimen only.	—	450.00	650.00

1929 Issue

		VG	**VF**	**UNC**
69	**10 Zlotych**			
	20.7.1929. Brown-olive and blue. Like #65. Wmk: Kg., 10Z1.	1.00	2.50	7.50
70	**20 Zlotych**			
	1.9.1929. Blue and olive. Like #66.	40.00	90.00	200.00

		VG	VF	UNC
71	**50 ZLOTYCH** 1.9.1929. Green, brown and blue. Like #64. Wmk: Man's head.	.50	2.00	5.00

1930-32 ISSUE

		VG	VF	UNC
72	**5 ZLOTYCH** 2.1.1930. Blue on gray unpt. Woman at r. Wmk: Head.	.50	2.00	5.00

		VG	VF	UNC
73	**20 ZLOTYCH** 20.6.1931. Blue on brown and tan unpt. Portr. E. Plater at upper r. Back brown and blue; farm woman and 2 children at l. ctr. Wmk: Kg.	.50	2.00	5.00

		VG	VF	UNC
74	**100 ZLOTYCH** 2.6.1932. Brown on gold unpt. Portr. Prince J. Poniatowski at r. Back brown, orange and m/c. Allegorical figures at l. and r., lg. tree at ctr.			
	a. Wmk: Qn. Jadwigi/100 Zt.	1.00	2.50	6.00
	b. Wmk: Qn. Jadwigi/100Zt. +x+.	1.00	2.50	6.00

1934 ISSUE

		VG	VF	UNC
75	**100 ZLOTYCH** 9.11.1934. Brown. Like #74. Wmk. like #74a or b.	1.00	2.50	6.00

1936 ISSUE

		VG	VF	UNC
76	**2 ZLOTE** 26.2.1936. Grayish brown on yellow and lt. blue unpt. Portr. girl in Dabrowki national costume at r. Eagle at ctr. on back.			
	a. Issued note.	.50	2.00	6.00
	r. Remainder w/o serial #.	—	3.00	10.00

		VG	VF	UNC
77	**20 ZLOTYCH** 11.11.1936. Blue on lt. peach unpt. Statue of woman w/2 children at l., E. Plater at upper r. Standing figures at l. and r., church at ctr. on back. Wmk: Girl's head.	.50	2.00	5.00
78	**50 ZLOTYCH** Man at r. (Not issued).			
	a. Face and back.	—	—	500.00
	b. Back only.	—	—	125.00

GOVERNMENT IN EXILE, WW II

BANK POLSKI

1939 FIRST ISSUE

#79-81 printer: BWC.

#79-88 printed in England and the United States.

#82-86 printer: TDLR.

		VG	VF	UNC
79	**1 ZLOTY** 15.8.1939. Purple. (Not issued).			
	r. Remainder.	—	—	275.00
	s. Specimen.	—	—	150.00

		VG	VF	UNC
80	**2 ZLOTE** 15.8.1939. Green. (Not issued).			
	r. Remainder.	—	—	275.00
	s. Specimen.	—	—	150.00

		VG	VF	UNC
81	**5 ZLOTYCH** 15.8.1939. Blue. Portr. girl wearing national costume at r. (Not issued).			
	r. Remainder.	—	—	300.00
	s. Specimen.	—	—	150.00

		VG	VF	UNC
85	**100 ZLOTYCH** 15.8.1939. Brown. Man w/mustache at r. (Not issued).			
	r. Remainder.	—	—	275.00
	s. Specimen.	—	—	150.00

		VG	VF	UNC
82	**10 ZLOTYCH** 15.8.1939. Red-orange. Young woman wearing head scarf at r. (Not issued).			
	r. Remainder.	—	—	275.00
	s. Specimen.	—	—	150.00

		VG	VF	UNC
83	**20 ZLOTYCH** 15.8.1939. Blue. Old woman wearing head scarf at r. (Not issued).			
	r. Remainder.	—	—	275.00
	s. Specimen.	—	—	150.00

		VG	VF	UNC
86	**500 ZLOTYCH** 15.8.1939. Purple. Sailor w/pipe at r. (Not issued).			
	r. Remainder.	—	—	275.00
	s. Specimen.	—	—	150.00

1939 SECOND ISSUE
#87 and 88 printer: ABNC.

		VG	VF	UNC
84	**50 ZLOTYCH** 15.8.1939. Green. Man wearing national costume at r. (Not issued).			
	r. Remainder.	—	—	275.00
	s. Specimen.	—	—	150.00

		VG	VF	UNC
87	**20 ZLOTYCH** 20.8.1939. Blue. Young woman in national costume at r. Church on back. (Not issued).			
	r. Remainder.	—	—	275.00
	s. Specimen.	—	—	150.00

88	50 ZLOTYCH	VG	VF	UNC
	20.8.1939. Green. Young farmer's wife at r. River and mountains on back. (Not issued).			
	r. Remainder.	—	—	275.00
	s. Specimen w/ovpt: WZOR, punched hole cancelled.	—	—	150.00

GERMAN OCCUPATION, WW II

GENERALGOUVERNEMENT

1939 PROVISIONAL ISSUE

#89 and 90 ovpt: *Generalgouvernement für die besetzten polnischen Gebiete.*
NOTE: #89 and #90 are frequently found with forged ovpt.

89	100 ZLOTYCH	VG	VF	UNC
	ND (1939 - old date 2.6.1932). Red ovpt. on #74.	6.00	15.00	60.00
90	100 ZLOTYCH			
	ND (1939 - old date 9.9.1934). Red ovpt. on #75.	5.00	12.50	55.00

BANK EMISYJNY W POLSCE

EMISSION BANK OF POLAND

1940 ISSUE

91	1 ZLOTY	VG	VF	UNC
	1.3.1940. Gray-blue on lt. tan unpt.	.25	1.00	5.00

92	2 ZLOTE	VG	VF	UNC
	1.3.1940. Brown on blue and brown unpt. Portr. woman wearing head scarf at upper r.	.25	1.00	6.00
93	5 ZLOTYCH			
	1.3.1940. Green-blue on tan and blue unpt. Man in cap at l.; girl at r. Similar to #72.	7.50	25.00	50.00

94	10 ZLOTYCH	VG	VF	UNC
	1.3.1940. Brown on tan and blue unpt. Girl in headdress on wmk. area at l., allegorical female at l. and r. Sculpture on back.	.25	.75	3.00

95	20 ZLOTYCH	VG	VF	UNC
	1.3.1940. Gray-blue on blue and red unpt. Man in cap on wmk. area at l., female statue w/2 children at l. ctr. E. Plater at r. Similar to #77.	.50	1.00	3.00
96	50 ZLOTYCH			
	1.3.1940. Blue-green on brown unpt. Man in cap at l., woman's statue at l. ctr., young man at r. Ornate bldg. on back.	3.00	8.00	40.00

97	100 ZLOTYCH	VG	VF	UNC
	1.3.1940. Brown on lt. green and orange unpt. Patrician of old Warsaw at l. Bldg. at l. on back.	.75	1.50	5.00

98	500 ZLOTYCH	VG	VF	UNC
	1.3.1940. Gray-blue on olive unpt. Portr. Gorale at upper r. and as wmk. River in mountains on back.	2.50	5.00	15.00

1941 ISSUE

NOTE: Various notes of #91-103 also exist w/handstamps of the Warsaw Resistance Fighters of 1944, *A. K. Regula; Pierwszy zold powstancy, Sierpien 1944; Okreg Warszawski-Dowodztwo zgrup. IV or Braterstwo Broni Anglii Ameryki Polski Niech Zyje* (long live the Anglo-American-Polish brotherhood in arms).

99	1 ZLOTY	VG	VF	UNC
	1.8.1941. Gray-blue. Like #91.	.25	.50	2.00

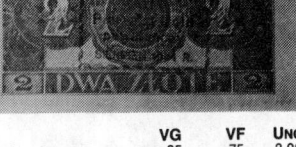

100	2 ZLOTE	VG	VF	UNC
	1.8.1941. Brown. Like #92.	.25	.75	3.00

101	5 ZLOTYCH	VG	VF	UNC
	1.8.1941. Green-blue. Like #93.	.25	.50	2.50
102	50 ZLOTYCH			
	1.8.1941. Dk. green and blue. Similar to #96. Wmk: Man in cap.	.25	.75	3.00

103	100 ZLOTYCH	VG	VF	UNC
	1.8.1941. Brown and blue on lt. brown and gold unpt. Allegorical figure at upper ctr. Six church spires at ctr. on back. Wmk: Man w/beard.	.50	1.25	4.00

103A	1000 ZLOTYCH	VG	VF	UNC
	1.8.1941. Man at r. Bldg. and Russian text on back. (Not issued).	—	—	—

RUSSIAN INFLUENCE - POST WW II COMMITTEE OF NATIONAL LIBERATION

NARODOWY BANK POLSKI

POLISH NATIONAL BANK

1944 ISSUE

#104, 105, 107, 109, 111, 113, 115, 117 and 119 were reprinted w/inscription: *EMISJA PAMIATKOWA ODBITA W 1974 r.Z ORYGINALNYCH KLISZ* imprint across top border of face. Arms on face. Russian printing.

104	50 GROSZY	VG	VF	UNC
	1944. Reddish maroon.			
	a. 1944.	1.00	3.00	15.00
	b. 1974 (-old date 1944). Reprint w/leg: EMISJA...	—	—	2.00
105	1 ZLOTY			
	1944. Dk. green on orange unpt.			
	a. 1944.	1.00	3.50	9.00
	b. 1974 (-old date 1944). Reprint Reprint w/leg: EMISJA... Serial #764560.	—	—	2.00

106	2 ZLOTE	VG	VF	UNC
	1944. Brown on lt. blue unpt. *OBOWIAZKOWYM* at bottom. 3 serial # varieties.	1.00	3.00	8.50
107	2 ZLOTE			
	1944. Brown on lt. blue unpt. *OBOWIAZKOWE* at bottom.			
	a. 1944.	1.50	5.00	15.00
	b. 1974 (-old date 1944). Reprint w/leg: *EMISJA...* Serial # 11111.	—	—	2.00
108	5 ZLOTYCH			
	1944. Violet-brown on green unpt. *OBOWIAZKOWYM* at bottom.	1.00	3.50	9.00

109	5 ZLOTYCH	VG	VF	UNC
	1944. Violet-brown on green unpt. *OBOWIAZKOWE* at bottom.			
	a. 1944.	1.00	3.50	10.00
	b. 1974 (-old date 1944). Reprint Reprint w/leg: *EMISJA...* Serial #518823.	—	—	2.00
110	10 ZLOTYCH			
	1944. Blue on lt. green unpt. *OBOWIAZKOWYM* at bottom.	1.00	4.00	12.50
111	10 ZLOTYCH			
	1944. Blue on lt. green unpt. *OBOWIAZKOWE* at bottom.			
	a. 1944.	1.00	3.50	10.00
	b. 1974 (-old date 1944). Reprint w/leg: *EMISJA...* Serial #823518.	—	—	2.00

112	20 ZLOTYCH	VG	VF	UNC
	1944. Blue-black on lilac unpt. *OBOWIAZKOWYM* at bottom.	1.00	3.50	10.00

113	20 ZLOTYCH	VG	VF	UNC
	1944. Blue-black on lilac unpt. *OBOWIAZKOWE* at bottom. 2 Serial # varieties.			
	a. 1944.	1.50	5.00	15.00
	b. 1974 (-old date 1944). Reprint w/leg: *EMISJA...* Serial #671154.	—	—	2.00
114	50 ZLOTYCH			
	1944. Blue on lilac unpt. *OBOWIAZKOWYM* at bottom.	3.00	7.50	25.00

115	50 ZLOTYCH	VG	VF	UNC
	1944. Deep blue-violet on lilac unpt. *OBOWIAZKOWE* at bottom. 2 serial # varieties.			
	a. 1944.	3.00	7.50	20.00
	b. 1974 (-old date 1944). Reprint w/leg: *EMISJA...* Serial #889147.	—	—	2.00
116	100 ZLOTYCH			
	1944. Red on blue unpt. *OBOWIAZKOWYM* at bottom.	5.00	15.00	35.00

117	100 ZLOTYCH	VG	VF	UNC
	1944. Red on blue unpt. *OBOWIAZKOWE* at bottom. 3 serial # varieties.			
	a. 1944.	4.00	12.50	30.00
	b. 1974 (-old date 1944). Reprint Reprint w/leg: *EMISJA...* Serial #778093.	—	—	2.00
	s. Specimen w/ovpt: *WZOR*, regular serial #.	—	—	20.00

118	500 ZLOTYCH	VG	VF	UNC
	1944. Black on orange unpt. *OBOWIAZKOWYM* at bottom.	7.50	20.00	50.00
119	500 ZLOTYCH			
	1944. Black on orange unpt. *OBOWIAZKOWE* at bottom. 2 serial # varieties.			
	a. 1944.	5.00	15.00	35.00
	b. 1974 (-old date 1944). Reprint Reprint w/leg: *EMISJA...* Serial #780347.	—	—	2.00
	s. Specimen w/ovpt: *WZOR*, regular serial #.	—	—	25.00

GOVERNMENT OF NATIONAL UNITY - POST WW II

NARODOWY BANK POLSKI

POLISH NATIONAL BANK

1945 ISSUE

120	1000 ZLOTYCH	VG	VF	UNC
	1945. Brown on tan unpt. Eagle in unpt. at ctr. 2 serial # varieties.	20.00	45.00	100.00

1946 First Issue

121	**500 Zlotych**	**VG**	**VF**	**Unc**
	15.1.1946. Dk. blue and green. Man holding boat at l., fisherman at r. View of old town on back.	17.50	40.00	85.00
122	**1000 Zlotych**			
	15.1.1946. Brown. Miner at l., worker at r. 4 serial # varieties.	15.00	35.00	70.00

1946 Second Issue

123	**1 Zloty**	**VG**	**VF**	**Unc**
	15.5.1946. Deep lilac.	.50	1.25	2.50

124	**2 Zlote**	**VG**	**VF**	**Unc**
	15.5.1946. Green on buff paper. Wmk: Stars.	.75	1.75	3.50

125	**5 Zlotych**	**VG**	**VF**	**Unc**
	15.5.1946. Gray-blue.	1.25	2.50	5.00
126	**10 Zlotych**			
	15.5.1946. Red-brown on green and gold unpt. Eagle at upper ctr.	1.25	2.50	5.00
127	**20 Zlotych**			
	15.5.1946. Green and brown. Eagle at upper ctr. 2 airplanes at ctr. on back.	5.00	10.00	30.00

128	**50 Zlotych**	**VG**	**VF**	**Unc**
	15.5.1946. Brown and purple on gold unpt. Sailing ship at l., ocean freighter at r., eagle at upper ctr. Ships and sailboat on back.	7.50	15.00	40.00
129	**100 Zlotych**			
	15.5.1946. Red on orange unpt. Farmer's wife at l., farmer at r. Farmer w/tractor on back.	6.00	12.50	35.00

Peoples Democratic Republic

Narodowy Bank Polski

Polish National Bank

1947 Issue

130	**20 Zlotych**	**VG**	**VF**	**Unc**
	15.7.1947. Green on olive unpt. Eagle at lower ctr. Tools, globe and book on back.	6.00	12.50	35.00

131	**100 Zlotych**	**VG**	**VF**	**Unc**
	1947; 1948. Red on lilac unpt. Farmer's wife at ctr. Horses on back.			
	a. Issued note. 15.7.1947.	8.00	17.50	42.50
	p. Proof. 1.7.1948.	—	—	—

132	**500 Zlotych**	**VG**	**VF**	**Unc**
	15.7.1947. Blue on tan and olive unpt. Eagle at l. ctr., woman w/oar and anchor at ctr. Ships and loading dock on back.	10.00	20.00	45.00

133	**1000 Zlotych**	**VG**	**VF**	**Unc**
	15.7.1947. Brown and olive. Worker at ctr.	12.00	25.00	65.00

1948 ISSUE
#134-140 arms on face.

134	2 ZLOTE	VG	VF	UNC
	1.7.1948. Dk. olive green on lt. olive and lt. orange unpt. Bldg. on back. 2 serial # varieties.	.15	.65	2.50

135	5 ZLOTYCH	VG	VF	UNC
	1.7.1948. Red-brown on brown and red-brown unpt. Farmer plowing on back. 2 serial # varieties. Wmk: Woman.	.50	1.25	5.00

136	10 ZLOTYCH	VG	VF	UNC
	1.7.1948. Brown on lt. brown and lt. red unpt. Portr. man at r. Stacking hay on back. 2 serial # varieties. Wmk: Woman.	.40	1.25	5.00

137	20 ZLOTYCH	VG	VF	UNC
	1.7.1948. Dk. blue on pale blue and lt. red unpt. Portr. woman wearing a head scarf at r. Ornate bldg. on back. 4 serial # varieties.			
a.	Issued note.	.30	1.00	4.00
s.	Specimen w/ovpt: WZOR, normal serial #.	—	—	7.50

138	50 ZLOTYCH	VG	VF	UNC
	1.7.1948. Green on lt. green and olive unpt. Portr. sailor at r. Ships at dockside on back. 4 serial # varieties. Wmk: Woman.			
a.	Issued note.	.40	1.25	5.00
s.	Specimen w/ovpt: WZOR, normal serial #.	—	—	8.50

139	100 ZLOTYCH	VG	VF	UNC
	1.7.1948. Red on lt. red and m/c unpt. Man at r. Factory on back. 3 serial # varieties. Wmk: Woman.			
a.	100 in ctr. guilloche w/fine line around edge. Buff or white paper.	.75	2.25	6.50
b.	100 in ctr. guilloche w/o fine line around edge. Series GF.	3.00	10.00	30.00
s.	As a. Specimen w/ovpt: WZOR, normal serial #.	—	—	10.00

140	500 ZLOTYCH	VG	VF	UNC
	1.7.1948. Dk. brown on lt. brown and m/c unpt. Portr. coal miner at r. Coal miners on back. 2 serial # varieties. Wmk: Woman.			
a.	Issued note.	.50	2.00	8.00
s.	Specimen w/ovpt: WZOR, normal serial #.	—	—	12.50

RZECZPOSPOLITA POLSKA

NARODOWY BANK PLOSKI

PLISH NATIONAL BANK

COLLECTOR SERIES

CS1	1948; 1965 20-1000 ZLOTYCH	VG	VF	UNC
	#137, 138, 139a, 140 & 141a w/deep red ovpt: WZOR on face; normal serial #.	—Issue Price		—

PORTUGAL

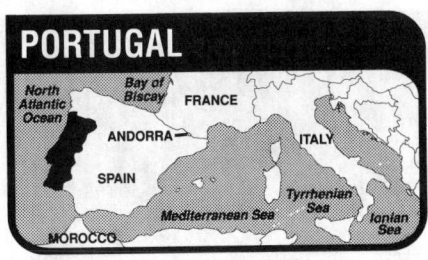

The Portuguese Republic, located in the western part of the Iberian Peninsula in southwestern Europe, has an area of 35,553 sq. mi. (92,080 sq. km.) and a population of 9.86 million. Capital: Lisbon. Portugal's economy is based on agriculture and a small but expanding industrial sector. Textiles, machinery, chemicals, wine and cork are exported.

After centuries of domination by Romans, Visigoths and Moors, Portugal emerged in the 12th century as an independent kingdom financially and philosophically prepared for the great period of exploration that would follow. Attuned to the inspiration of Prince Henry the Navigator (1394-1460), Portugal's daring explorers of the 14th and 15th centuries roamed the world's oceans from Brazil to Japan in an unprecedented burst of energy and endeavor that culminated in 1494 with Portugal laying claim to half the transoceanic world. Unfortunately for the fortunes of the tiny kingdom, the Portuguese proved to be inept colonizers. Less than a century after Portugal laid claim to half the world, English, French and Dutch trading companies had seized the lion's share of the world's colonies and commerce, and Portugal's place as an imperial power was lost forever. The monarchy was overthrown in 1910 and a republic established.

On April 25, 1974, the government of Portugal was seized by a military junta which reached agreements providing for independence for the Portuguese overseas provinces of Portuguese Guinea (Guinea-Bissau), Mozambique, Cape Verde Islands, Angola, and St. Thomas and Prince Islands (Sao Tome Principe).

* * * This section has been reordered and renumbered. * * *

RULERS:
Spanish, 1493-1898
Luiz I, 1861-1889
Carlos I, 1889-1908
Manuel II, 1908-1910
Republic, 1910-

MONETARY SYSTEM:
1 Mil Reis = 1000 Reis to 1910
1 Escudo = 100 Centavos, 1910-

NOTE: Prata = Silver, Ouro = Gold.

COLONIAL ISSUE OVERPRINTS
AÇÔRES, see Azores and Madeira
BOLAMA, see Portuguese Guinea
CABO VERDE, see Cape Verde
GUINÉ, see Portuguese Guinea
LOANDA, see Angola

LOURENÇO MARQUES, see Mozambique
MOEDA INSULANA, see Azores and Madeira
NOVA GOA, see Portuguese India
S. TIAGO or S. THIAGO, see Cape Verde
S. TOMÉ, see St. Thomas and Prince

KINGDOM

Notes were first issued in Portugal in 1797 because of poor economic conditions brought about by the war between Spain and France. Many of these notes were officially repaired and handstamped on the back (and sometimes on the face) with various dates and endorsements as they continued to circulate. Most are found in very worn condition. Variations on the notes include partially or fully printed year dates both in numerals and in words, also printed date altered to a later date by hand.

1797 ISSUE
#1 and 2 brown. Impressed royal arms at top ctr. Uniface.

		GOOD	FINE	XF
1 (S101)	**5000 REIS** 1797. 4 allegorical vignettes in ovals across top.	—	—	—
2 (S102)	**10,000 REIS** 1797. Vignettes of barrels, animal, soldiers, spinning across top in octagons.	—	—	—

1798 ISSUES
#3-7 brown. Impressed royal arms at top ctr. Various handwritten dates. Uniface.

3 (S103)	**2400 REIS** 1798. Bldg. in ornate rectangle at upper l. and r.	—	—	—
4 (S104)	**2400 REIS** 1798-99. Walled cities at upper l. and r., 2 cherubs w/garlands at top ctr.	—	—	—
5 (S105)	**10,000 REIS** 1798. Winged cherub approaching stylized beehive at upper l., pastoral scene w/barn behind, cherub w/dog at upper r.	—	—	—
6 (S106)	**20,000 REIS** 1798-99. Cherubs at upper l. and r.	—	—	—
7 (S107)	**20,000 REIS** 1798. 4 allegorical vignettes in ornate squarish frames across top.	—	—	—

1799 ISSUES
#8-15 brown. Impressed royal arms at top ctr. Various handwritten dates. Uniface.

8 (S108)	**1200 REIS** 24.4.1799. Ornate vines at l. and r. across top.	—	—	—
9 (S109)	**2400 REIS** 1799. Vignettes in 2 oval frames at l. and r.	—	—	—
10 (S110)	**5000 REIS** 1799. Young couples w/the males playing musical instruments at upper l. and r.	—	—	—

		GOOD	FINE	XF
11 (S111)	**5000 REIS** 1799. Vignettes of animals (goats, birds, chickens, lions) across upper l. and r.	—	—	—
12 (S112)	**6400 REIS** 1799. 2 facing dogs (under the sun and under the moon) in oval frames at top ctr.	—	—	—

		GOOD	FINE	XF
13 (S113)	**10,000 REIS** 1799. 6 vignettes in oval frames across top.	—	—	—
	a. Date w/handwritten last numeral *9*.	—	—	—
	b. Entire date printed.	—	—	—
14 (S114)	**12,800 REIS** 1799. 2 long-necked birds, oyster and pearl in ornate frames at top ctr.	—	—	—
15 (S115)	**20,000 REIS** 1799. 8 vignettes in oval frames across top.	—	—	—

1805 ISSUE
Law of 2.4.1805

#16 and 17 brown. Various handwritten dates. Uniface.

16 (S116)	**1200 REIS** 28.6.1805. 2 children watering a flower at top ctr.	15.00	—	—
17 (S117)	**2400 REIS** 5.10.1805. Youthful helmeted warrior w/lion in frame at top ctr.	20.00	—	—

1807 ISSUE
Decree of 31.10.1807

#18 and 19 brown. Uniface.

18 (S118)	**1200 REIS** 28.11.1807. Like #16.	—	—	—
19 (S119)	**2400 REIS** 5.12.1807. Like #17.	—	—	—

WAR OF THE BROTHERS

IMPERIAL TREASURY

The later struggle for the Portuguese throne necessitated a reissue of the old imperial issues dated 1798, 1799, 1805, and 1807 w/red revalidation ovpt. of each of the warring brothers.

1826 REVALIDATION ISSUES
#20-28 red crowned ovpt: *D./PEDRO IV/1826* in starburst.

		GOOD	FINE	XF
20 (S120)	**1200 REIS** 1826 (- old date 1807). Ovpt. on #18.	15.00	—	—

		GOOD	FINE	XF
21 (S121)	**2400 REIS** 1826 (- old date 1805). Ovpt. on #17.	12.00	—	—

			GOOD	FINE	XF
24	**5000 REIS**		**12.00**	—	—
(S123)	1826 (- old date 1799). Ovpt. on #10.				

			GOOD	FINE	XF
25	**5000 REIS**		**12.00**	—	—
(S124)	1826 (- old date 1799). Ovpt. on #11.				

			GOOD	FINE	XF
27	**6400 REIS**		**15.00**	—	—
(S125)	1826 (- old date 1799). Ovpt. on #12.				

			GOOD	FINE	XF
28	**10,000 REIS**		**15.00**	—	—
(S126)	1826 (- old date 1798). Ovpt. on #5.				

			GOOD	FINE	XF
31	**20,000 REIS**				
(S128)	1826 (- old date 1799).				
	a. Ovpt. on #13a.		20.00	—	—
	b. Ovpt. on #13b.		20.00	—	—

1828 REVALIDATION ISSUES

#33-46 red ovpt: Crowned *D./MIGUEL I/1828* in starburst.

			GOOD	FINE	XF
33	**1200 REIS**		**15.00**	—	—
(S130)	1828 (- old date 1805). Ovpt. on #16.				

			GOOD	FINE	XF
34	**2400 REIS**		**12.00**	—	—
(S131)	1828 (- old date 1799). Ovpt. on #4.				

			GOOD	FINE	XF
35	**2400 REIS**		**12.00**	—	—
(S132)	1828 (- old date 1805). Ovpt. on #17.				

			GOOD	FINE	XF
38	**2400 REIS**		12.00	—	—
(S133)	1828 (- old date 1807). Ovpt. on #19.				
40	**10,000 REIS**		20.00	—	—
(S135)	1798. Ovpt. on #5.				

BANCO DE PORTUGAL

1847 ISSUE

			GOOD	FINE	XF
49	**10 MIL REIS**		—	—	—
(19)	30.6.1847-16.6.1873 (handwritten dates). Brown. Allegorical figure in each corner. Back blue.				
50	**20 MIL REIS**		—	—	—
(22BA)	1.5.1847-1.5.1850. Red. Allegorical figure in each corner. Back blue.				

1854 ISSUE

51	**18 MIL REIS**		—	—	—
(22B)	20.6.1854-12.4.1867 (handwritten dates). Black. Seated allegorical figure at either side of arms at upper ctr. Back blue.				

1867 ISSUE

52	**20 MIL REIS**		—	—	—
(22C)	29.10.1867; 20.12.1867. Black on yellow unpt. Ctr. design similar to #51. Figure in yellow at l. and r. Uniface.				

1869 ISSUE

53	**20 MIL REIS**		—	—	—
(22CA)	4.3.1869; 25.1.1870; 22.2.1870 22.2.1870. Black on green unpt. Design like #52. Figures at l. and r. in red.				

1871 ISSUE

			GOOD	FINE	XF
41	**10,000 REIS**				
(S136)	1828 (- old date 1799).				
	a. Ovpt. on #13a.		20.00	—	—
	b. Ovpt. on #13b.		20.00	—	—

			GOOD	FINE	XF
54	**20 MIL REIS**		—	—	—
(22CB)	4.11.1871-17.8.1875. Blue. Design like #52. Figures at l. and r. in black.				

1876 ISSUE

55	**10 MIL REIS**		—	—	—
(20)	15.5.1876-28.12.1877. Violet. Design like #49.				
56	**20 MIL REIS**		—	—	—
(22CC)	15.5.1876. Blue. D. Luis I at ctr. Back red.				

			GOOD	FINE	XF
44	**12,800 REIS**		25.00	—	—
(S137)	1828 (- old date 1799). Ovpt. on #14.				

1877 ISSUE

57	**20 MIL REIS**		—	—	—
(22DC)	6.7.1877-17.12.1886. Blue-black. 3 allegorical figures w/arms at l. Back brown, arms at ctr.				

1878 ISSUE

58	**10 MIL REIS**		—	—	—
(20A)	28.1.1878-21.3.1882. Brown on pink unpt. Ctr. design like #83. Back red.				

1879 ISSUE

59	**10 MIL REIS**		—	—	—
(20B)	24.10.1879-18.10.1881. Black. Seated figure at either side of arms at ctr. Back lilac.				

			GOOD	FINE	XF
45	**20,000 REIS**		25.00	—	—
(S138)	1828 (- old date 1799). Ovpt. on #7.				

1883-86 ISSUE

60	**5 MIL REIS**		—	—	—
(12)	2.1.1883-17.4.1889 (handwritten dates). Brown on yellow unpt. Standing figure at l. and r. Arms at ctr. on back.				
61	**20 MIL REIS**		—	—	—
(22CE)	4.1.1884-20.8.1889. Brown. Seated woman w/arms at upper ctr. Back blue.				
62	**50 MIL REIS**		—	—	—
(26A)	25.6.1886-26.2.1892 (handwritten dates). Black on lt. red unpt. Allegorical figure at l. and r., arms at lower ctr. Back brown.				

			GOOD	FINE	XF
46	**20,000 REIS**		25.00	—	—
(S139)	1828 (- old date 1799). Ovpt. on #15.				
47	**20,000 REIS**		25.00	—	—
(S140)	1828 (-old date 1799/8). Ovpt. on #6.				

1890-91 ISSUE

63	**200 REIS**				
(A1)	1.8.1891. Blue on gray unpt. Arms at l. Arms at ctr. r. on back.				

	64 500 REIS	GOOD	FINE	XF
(1)	12.5.1891. Black. (Not issued.)	—	—	—
65 (1A)	500 REIS 1.7.1891. Lilac on tan unpt. Arms at ctr. on face and back.	30.00	80.00	200.00
66 (5)	1 MIL REIS 1.7.1891. Brown on pink unpt. Arms at upper ctr. and at ctr. on back.	—	—	—
67 (8)	2 1/2 MIL REIS 1.6.1891. Red on green unpt. Arms at l. Arms at ctr. on back.	—	Rare	—
68 (13)	5 MIL REIS 26.5.1890. Blue. Woman at l., arms at upper ctr.	—	—	—

	69 5 MIL REIS	GOOD	FINE	XF
(14)	8.11.1890. Blue. Allegorical seated figures w/arms at upper ctr. Back pale brown.	—	Rare	—
70 (14A)	5 MIL REIS 3.3.1891-15.6.1892. Blue. Mercury head at upper ctr. Back brown.	—	—	—
71 (22D)	20 MIL REIS 8.11.1890-23.6.1898. Blue. Allegorical figures at l. and r., arms at upper ctr. Back gray on lilac unpt. Wmk: Bank name and date *29.7.87.*	—	—	—

1893-99 ISSUE

	72 500 REIS	GOOD	FINE	XF
(2)	22.7.1899; 25.5.1900. Brown. Woman and shield at l. Back red and blue unpt; arms at ctr.	30.00	80.00	200.00

	73 1 MIL REIS	GOOD	FINE	XF
(6)	24.3.1896; 31.12.1897; 31.10.1899; 30.11.1900. Blue on pink unpt. Arms at upper l. woman w/winged cap and staff at r. Back brown; arms at ctr.	30.00	100.00	225.00

	74 2 1/2 MIL REIS	GOOD	FINE	XF
(9)	16.2.1893-25.5.1900. Black on violet and brown unpt. Standing woman at l. and r., arms at upper ctr. Back blue-gray; arms at ctr.	—	—	—
75 (15)	5 MIL REIS 16.4.1894. Pink-violet. Peace at l., arms at upper ctr. r. Vertical design at l. and r., arms at ctr. on back.	—	—	—
76 (20C)	10 MIL REIS 1.12.1894. Aqua. Seated allegorical figure at l. and r., arms at upper ctr. Standing allegorical figure at l. and r. Medallion of Lusitania at top ctr. on back.	—	—	—
77 (27)	50 MIL REIS 18.10.1898; 31.10.1898; 3.11.1898; 30.10.1900. Brown. Seated woman at either side of arms at lower ctr., vertical design at l. and r. Arms at ctr. on back. Wmk: Allegorical heads.	—	—	—

	78 100 MIL REIS	GOOD	FINE	XF
(30)	1.12.1894-10.3.1909. Blue. Allegorical figures at l. and r., arms at lower ctr. Back blue and gray; allegorical figure on tall pedestal at l. and r. Wmk: Allegorical heads.	350.00	950.00	—

1901-03 ISSUE, W/O CHAPA; CHAPA 3

Listed in accordance w/the nominal denomination and plate numbers (Ch. = Chapa = plate), which describes the different types of notes. Various date and sign. varieties.

	79 2 1/2 MIL REIS	GOOD	FINE	XF
(10)	29.9.1903; 11.3.1904; 30.8.1904; 25.8.1905. Ch. 3. Brown. Helmeted woman seated w/arms at l. Arms at r. on back.	45.00	125.00	300.00
80 (16)	5 MIL REIS 20.9.1901. W/o Chapa. Blue on yellow unpt. Angel at l., 6 busts across upper border, old boats at bottom ctr. r. Back green; arms at r.	—	—	—

	81 10 MIL REIS	GOOD	FINE	XF
(21)	29.11.1902; 26.6.1903; 30.8.1904; 22.5.1908; 30.12.1909. Ch. 3. Brown on yellow unpt. Luis de Camões at l., 2 figures and globe at lower ctr., ships at r. Infante D. Henrique at upper l. on back. Wmk: A. de Albuquerque.	175.00	425.00	900.00
82 (23)	20 MIL REIS 26.2.1901. W/o *Chapa.* Blue on tan unpt. Standing figure at l. and r., arms at lower ctr. Back orange and blue.	—	—	—

1903-06 ISSUE, CHAPA 3, 6 AND 8

	83 5 MIL REIS	GOOD	FINE	XF
(17)	31.7.1903-25.8.1905; 9.7.1907. Ch. 6. Blue on brown unpt. 3 figures w/arms at ctr. Arms at ctr. on back.	60.00	150.00	—
84 (24)	20 MIL REIS 12.10.1906. Ch. 8. Blue on gold unpt. Face similar to #82. D. Affonso Henriques at ctr., helmeted figure at l. and r. on back.	175.00	550.00	—

		Good	Fine	XF
85 (28)	**50 Mil Reis** 29.1.1904-30.9.1910. Ch. 3. Blue-gray. Statues of Principe Perfetto and B. Dias at l. and r., heads of Pero de Alenquer and Diogo Cao at lower l. and r., w/anchor and ships, allegorical woman at ctr.r. Back brown; arms at l. Wmk: L. de Camoes.	250.00	750.00	—

CASA DA MOEDA

1891 REIS ISSUES
NOTE: #89 w/3-line diagonal ovpt. Funchal district, see Madeira #12.

		VG	VF	UNC
86 (32)	**50 Reis** 6.8.1891. Green on lilac unpt. Arms at l. and r.	7.00	17.50	40.00

		VG	VF	UNC
87 (33)	**50 Reis** 6.8.1891. Blue. Arms at upper ctr.	7.00	17.50	40.00
88 (34)	**100 Reis** 6.8.1891. Brown on lt. brown unpt. Arms at l. and r. Back pale gray.	7.00	17.50	40.00

		VG	VF	UNC
89 (35)	**100 Reis** 6.8.1891. Dk. brown on lt. green unpt. Back green; arms in circle at ctr.	7.00	17.50	40.00
90 (36)	**100 Reis** D.6.8.1891. Brown. Curtain, man sitting on anvil at l., figures of cherubs at r. Arms at ctr. on back. Similar to #93.	7.00	17.50	40.00
	a.. Many proof prints in different colors each.	—	—	30.00

REPUBLIC

CASA DA MOEDA

STATE NOTES OF THE MINT

1917 PROVISIONAL ISSUES
#91 and 92 old date 6.8.1891 blocked out.

91 (37)	**5 Centavos** ND (-old date 6.8.1891). Bronze and blue-green. Probably only proof print.	—	—	—
92 (38)	**5 Centavos** ND (-old date 6.8.1891). Bronze and blue. Probably only proof print.	—	—	—

DECRETO DE 15 DE AGOSTO DE 1917

		VG	VF	UNC
93 (39)	**10 Centavos** D.1917. Bronze and dk. brown. Curtain, man sitting on anvil. Back green; arms at ctr.			
	a. Issued note.	1.50	3.50	12.50
	p. Proof prints (10 different colors) each.	—	—	20.00

		VG	VF	UNC
94 (40)	**10 Centavos** D.1917. Dk. blue on lt. tan unpt. Columns at l. and r., arms at upper ctr. Paper gray and thin or yellowish and thicker. Back blue-green.			
	a. Issued note.	1.00	3.00	10.00
	p. Proof print in different colors.	—	—	20.00

		VG	VF	UNC
95 (41)	**10 Centavos** D.1917. Blue on green unpt. Seated woman at l. and r., arms at lower ctr. Back blue; seated figures at ctr., arms above.			
	a. Wmk: Ovals.	1.50	4.00	15.00
	b. Wmk: Casa da Moeda.	1.00	2.50	7.50
	c. W/o wmk.	1.00	2.50	7.50

		VG	VF	UNC
96 (42)	**10 Centavos** D.1917. Red-brown on lt. brownish gray unpt. Seated man at l. Chimney stacks, ships, bridge in background. Arms at upper r. Back lt. brown; coin at ctr. White, gray, yellow-brown or brown paper.	1.00	2.50	8.00

1918-22 ISSUES

		VG	VF	UNC
97 (43)	**5 Centavos** 5.4.1918. Blue-green on gray-violet unpt. Arms at upper ctr. Back brown. Gray and thin or yellowish and thicker paper.	1.00	2.50	8.00

		VG	VF	UNC
98 (44)	**5 Centavos** D.5.4.1918. Red on pale orange unpt. Small child at l., bust at r., coin at ctr. below. Back aqua; arms at ctr.	1.00	2.50	8.00

99 **5 CENTAVOS**
(47)

	VG	VF	UNC
D.5.4.1918. Dk. brown on yellow-brown unpt. Arms at upper ctr. White and yellowish paper.	1.00	2.50	7.50

100 **20 CENTAVOS**
(49)

	VG	VF	UNC
D.4.8.1922. Dk. brown on blue unpt. Seated man at l., woman at r., arms at upper ctr. Back purplish black; allegorical figures and ship.	1.00	3.00	10.00

1925 FIRST ISSUE - DECRETOS DE 15.8.1917 AND 11.4.1925

101 **10 CENTAVOS**
(50)

	VG	VF	UNC
D.1917 and 1925. Red-brown on gray unpt. Arms at l. woman w/torch at r. Back brown; Comercio Square in Lisbon at ctr. Printer: W&S.	1.00	2.50	7.50

1925 SECOND ISSUE - DECRETOS DE 4.8.1922 AND 1.4.1925

102 **20 CENTAVOS**
(51)

	VG	VF	UNC
D.1922 and 1925. Brown on gray unpt. Woman at l., arms above. Back gray; Casa da Moeda at ctr. Printer: W&S.	2.00	5.00	15.00

BANCO DE PORTUGAL

1911 INTERIM ISSUE

104 **5 MIL REIS**
(18)

	GOOD	FINE	XF
14.11.1906; 30.12.1909; 30.3.1910 (1911). Ch. 7. Black on blue and m/c unpt. Marquez de Pombal at l. Arms at ctr., woman seated at r. on back. Wmk: Minerva. Printer: BWC.	60.00	150.00	—

1912-17 ND PROVISIONAL ISSUE

105 **500 REIS**
(3)

	GOOD	FINE	XF
ND (1917 - old dates 27.12.1904; 30.9.1910). Ch. 3. Black on green unpt. *Republica* over crowned arms at top ctr. Back brown; woman's head at l. Wmk: Mercury.			
a. Black ovpt: *REPUBLICA*.	3.50	10.00	50.00
b. Engraved *REPUBLICA*.	1.50	6.00	40.00

106 **1 MIL REIS**
(7)

	GOOD	FINE	XF
ND (1917 - old date 30.9.1910). Ch. 3. Blue. Arms at lower l. ctr., seated woman at r. W/*REPUBLICA* over crowned arms at bottom. Back red; seated woman at l.	20.00	65.00	150.00

107 **2 1/2 MIL REIS**
(11)

	GOOD	FINE	XF
ND (1916 - old dates 20.6.1909; 30.6.1909; 30.9.1910; 27.6.1919). Ch. 4. Black and green on orange unpt. A. de Albuquerque at r. Mercury at l. on back. Black ovpt: *REPUBLICA* over crowned arms at ctr. on back.	20.00	60.00	150.00

108 **10 MIL REIS**
(22)

	GOOD	FINE	XF
ND (1917 - old dates 22.5.1908; 30.9.1910). Ch. 4. Black on tan unpt. 5 men representing sculpture, painting, reading, music and writing. Back green and pink; allegorical woman at l., helmeted woman at r. Wmk: Woman's head. Printer: BWC.			
a. Ovpt: *Republica* over crowned arms on back. 30.9.1910.	150.00	375.00	850.00
b. Engraved *Republica* over crowned arms on back.	150.00	375.00	850.00

109 **20 MIL REIS**
(26)

	GOOD	FINE	XF
ND (1912 - old dates 30.12.1909; 30.3.1912). Ch. 9. Blue on tan unpt. Portr. Vasco da Gama in pillar at l., Luis de Camoes in pillar at r., arms at lower ctr. Back blue-green ovpt: *REPUBLICA* on crowned arms at l. Wmk: D. Joao II.	150.00	475.00	—

110 **50 MIL REIS**
(29)

	GOOD	FINE	XF
ND (1917 - old date 30.9.1910). Ch. 4. Blue. Middle East kg. on throne at l., voyagers at r. Ovpt: *REPUBLICA.* on crowned arms at lower ctr., medallion of Luisitania at r. on back. Wmk: Man w/turban.	200.00	600.00	—

111
(31)
100 MIL REIS

ND (1916 - old dates 22.5.1908; 10.3.1909; 30.9.1910). Green on yellow unpt. Scene of arrival of P. A. Cabral at Lisbon 8.3.1500. Back red-brown and tan; arms at upper ctr. Black ovpt: *REPUBLICA* on crowned arms at top ctr. on back.

	GOOD	FINE	XF
	300.00	850.00	—

1913-18 REGULAR ISSUE

112
(52)
50 CENTAVOS

1918; 1920. Ch. 1. Purple and m/c. Woman w/ship in her hand at l. Back purple and green; woman w/staff and scale at ctr. Wmk: Minerva head.

	GOOD	FINE	XF
a. Serial #. 5.7.1918.	3.50	7.50	35.00
b. Block # and letters in 2 lines. 5.7.1918; 25.6.1920.	2.00	5.00	30.00

113
(53)
1 ESCUDO

1917-20. Ch. 1. Red, violet and m/c. Woman seated holding book at l. Back brown; woman w/lyre at r. Wmk: Allegorical head.

	GOOD	FINE	XF
a. 7.9.1917; 25.6.1920.	3.50	10.00	45.00
b. 29.11.1918.	—	Rare	—

114
(56)
5 ESCUDOS

29.7.1913-1.2.1923. Ch. 1. Purple on lt. blue unpt. Woman seated at l. offering wreath, portr. A. Herculano at top ctr. Back brown; fortress at ctr. Wmk: Minerva head.

	GOOD	FINE	XF
	40.00	100.00	175.00

115
(63)
20 ESCUDOS

5.1.1915-26.3.1918. Ch. 1. Brown-lilac and green. Woman at l. and r., portr. A. Garrett at ctr. Back blue on lt. green unpt; arms at ctr.

	GOOD	FINE	XF
a. Issued note. 5.1.1915-26.3.1918.	75.00	250.00	500.00
b. Kingdom of the North ovpt: *REINO DE PORTUGAL / 19 de Janeiro de 1919* (-old date 14.4.1915).	—	Rare	—

116
(81)
100 ESCUDOS

13.8.1918; 5.2.1920. Ch. 1. Deep blue on m/c unpt. Indians, ships (discovery of Brazil) and medallic portr. of P. Alvares Cabral at ctr. r. Back brown and m/c; 2 heads and Cabral's arrival in 1500 (similar to #111) at ctr. Wmk: Man's head.

	GOOD	FINE
	600.00	1250.

1919 ISSUE, CHAPA 1 AND 2

117
(60)
10 ESCUDOS

21.10.1919; 7.7.1920. Ch. 1. Blue on yellow and brown unpt. Portr. A. de Albuquerque at l., explorer scene at bottom ctr. Back brown on yellow unpt; allegorical figures at bottom ctr., head at r. Wmk: Allegorical head.

	GOOD	FINE	XF
	100.00	200.00	500.00

118
(64)
20 ESCUDOS

12.8.1919-7.7.1920. Ch. 2. Blue on brown and green unpt. J. DeCastro at l. Back maroon and m/c; bldg. at ctr. arms at r. Wmk: Allegorical head.

	GOOD	FINE	XF
	75.00	200.00	500.00

1920 ISSUES, CHAPA A, 1, 2 AND 3

119 **2 ESCUDOS 50 CENTAVOS**
(54)   10.7.1920; 3.2.1922. Ch. 1. Green and m/c. Portr. D. Nuno Álvarez Pereira at r. Back blue-green and red; woman w/globe at l.

Good	Fine	XF
30.00	80.00	150.00

120 **5 ESCUDOS**
(57)   10.7.1920-13.1.1925. Ch. 2. Violet-brown and green. Portr. J. das Regras at l. Back blue; convent at r. Wmk: Allegorical head.

Good	Fine	XF
30.00	60.00	150.00

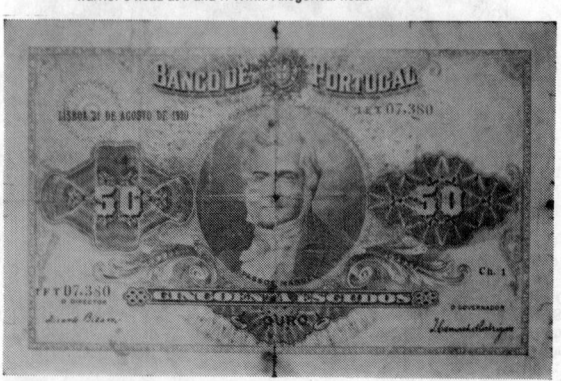

121 **10 ESCUDOS**
(61)   9.8.1920; 31.8.1926; 2.11.1927; 28.1.1928. Ch. 2. Brown on yellow-green unpt. Portr. M. de Sa da Bandeira at ctr. Back blue; arms at upper ctr.

Good	Fine	XF
50.00	175.00	475.00

122 **20 ESCUDOS**
(65)   9.8.1920-3.2.1927. Ch. 3. Brown, green and m/c. J. Estevao Coelho de Magalhaes at l., woman seated w/arms and globe at r. Back brown; warrior's head at l. and r. Wmk: Allegorical head.

100.00	300.00	300.00

123 **50 ESCUDOS**
(71)   31.8.1920; 3.2.1927. Ch. 1. Red-brown and m/c. Portr. Passos Manoel at ctr. Statue and ornate archway on back. Wmk: Allegorical head. Printer: BWC.

Good	Fine	XF
175.00	450.00	950.00

124 **100 ESCUDOS**
(82)   31.8.1920; 27.4.1922; 13.4.1926; 15.8.1927; 28.1.1928. Ch. 2. Brown. Portr. D. do Couto at l. Back maroon and brown; castle at ctr., allegorical figures at r. Wmk: Man's head.

Good	Fine	XF
600.00	1200.	—

125 **1000 ESCUDOS**
(99)   10.7.1920. Ch. A. Blue on m/c unpt. Portr. Duque da Terceira at upper l., arms at upper r. Back brown on yellow unpt; vertical design at l. and r. Wmk: Bank name.

—	Rare	—

126 **1000 ESCUDOS**
(100)   28.7.1920. Ch. 1. Slate blue on m/c unpt. Portr. L. de Camões at r. Allegorical women at l. and r. on back. Printer: BWC (w/o imprint).

—	Rare	—

1922 ISSUES, CHAPA 1 AND 2

127 **2 ESCUDOS 50 CENTAVOS**
(55)   17.11.1922; 18.11.1925; 18.11.1926. Ch. 2. Blue on orange and yellow unpt. Portr. M. da Silveira at ctr. Back orange on yellow unpt., arms at ctr. Wmk: Bank name repeated. Printer: W&S.

Good	Fine	XF
15.00	45.00	90.00

128 **50 ESCUDOS**
(72)   6.2.1922; 18.11.1925. Ch. 2. Blue on m/c unpt. Angel of Peace at l., cherubs at r. corners. Back brown and m/c; radiant sun at ctr., woman and lions at r. Wmk: Head.

350.00	700.00	1500.

129 **500 ESCUDOS**
(89)   4.5.1922; 8.12.1925. Ch. 1. Brown on m/c unpt. João de Deus at l., arms at upper r. Back brown and green; allegorical child w/flute at r. Wmk: Head representing the Republic.

700.00	1500.	—

130 **500 ESCUDOS**
(90)   17.11.1922. Ch. 2. Purple and black on tan unpt. Vasco da Gama at l., sailing ships at r. Back purple ; arms at ctr. Wmk: Bank name repeated. Printer: W&S.

300.00	800.00	1500.

131 **1000 ESCUDOS**
(101)   27.4.1922; 13.4.1926. Ch. 2. Dk. blue and purple. A. F. Castilho at ctr., arms at r. Back purple and lilac; 2 allegorical women w/lyre and torch at ctr. Printer: BWC (w/o imprint).

—	Rare	—

1924-25 ISSUES, CHAPA 3 AND 4

132 **5 ESCUDOS**
(58)   10.11.1924. Ch. 3. Black on orange and blue unpt. Allegorical woman and child at l., Agriculture at r. Back blue; Palacio da Bolsa in Porto at ctr. Wmk: Allegorical head. Printer: BWC.

—	—	—

133 **5 ESCUDOS**
(59)   13.1.1925. Ch. 4. Gray on yellow-brown and lt. blue unpt. Portr. D. Alvaro Vaz d'Almada at lower ctr. Back blue; arms at ctr. Wmk: Bank name repeated. Printer: W&S.

Good	Fine	XF
25.00	60.00	125.00

134
(62)
10 ESCUDOS
13.1.1925. Ch. 3. Black on pink unpt. Monastery in Lisbon at l., portr. E. de Queiroz at r. Back brown; arms at l. Wmk: Bank name repeated. Printer: W&S.

GOOD	FINE	XF
40.00	100.00	250.00

135
(66)
20 ESCUDOS
13.1.1925. Ch. 4. Red on yellow unpt. Portr. M. de Pombal at top ctr. Comercio Square below. Back red; arms at ctr. Wmk: Bank name repeated. Printer: W&S.

GOOD	FINE	XF
75.00	200.00	550.00

136
(73)
50 ESCUDOS
13.1.1925. Ch. 3. Blue on lt. pink and green unpt. Portr. Vasco da Gama at l., Monastery of Mafra at ctr r. Arms at ctr. on back. Wmk: Bank name repeated. Printer: W&S.

GOOD	FINE	XF
150.00	400.00	750.00

137
(83)
100 ESCUDOS
13.1.1925. Ch. 3. Black on salmon unpt. Mareshal Duque de Saldanha at l., monument w/city scene at ctr. r. Arms at ctr. on back. Wmk: Bank name repeated. Printer: W&S (Not issued).

—	—	—

138
(91)
500 ESCUDOS
13.1.1925. Ch. 3. Brown on lt. green unpt. Camillo Branco at l., city scene w/river at r. Arms at ctr. on back. Wmk: Bank name repeated. Printer: W&S (Not issued).

—	—	—

139
(101A)
1000 ESCUDOS
13.1.1925. Ch. 3. Tan and black. Visconde de Seabra at l., cathedral at r. Arms at ctr. on back. Printer: W&S. Specimen.

1927-28 ISSUE, CHAPA 3 AND 4

140
(84)
100 ESCUDOS
4.4.1928; 12.8.1930. Ch. 4. Blue on green and red unpt. G. Freire at l., allegorical figures w/arms at upper ctr., pillars at lower ctr. Back red-brown; horsecart and town at ctr., bank arms at r. Wmk: Head symbolizing the Republic.

GOOD	FINE	XF
75.00	200.00	350.00

141
(92)
500 ESCUDOS
4.4.1928; 19.4.1929. Ch. 4. Red-violet on m/c unpt. Castle at l., portr. D. de Palmella at r. and as wmk. Back green; bank arms at l., horse-drawn carts at lower ctr. Printer: BWC (w/o imprint).

GOOD	FINE	XF
500.00	1000.	—

142
(102)
1000 ESCUDOS
25.11.1927. Ch. 3. Blue on lt. tan unpt. Convent at ctr., O. Martins at r. and as wmk. Back red-brown; bank arms at ctr. Printer: BWC (w/o imprint).

GOOD	FINE	XF
—	—	—

1929 ISSUE, CHAPA 4 AND 5

143
(67)
20 ESCUDOS
17.9.1929-27.2.1940. Ch 5. Red-violet and m/c. Portr. M. d' Albuquerque at l., and as wmk., ornate bldg. at r. Back violet; Guimaraes Castle at l.

GOOD	FINE	XF
35.00	75.00	150.00

144
(74)
50 ESCUDOS
17.9.1929; 7.3.1933. Ch. 4. Violet and m/c. Portr. B. Carneiro at l. ctr. Back blue and m/c; Coimbra University at ctr., warrior head at r. Wmk: Allegorical head of Justice.

GOOD	FINE	XF
80.00	200.00	300.00

145
(103)
1000 ESCUDOS
17.9.1929. Ch. 4. Green, violet and m/c. Bridge at ctr., Gen. M. de Sa da Bandeira at r. Bank arms, woman's head and field workers on back. Wmk: Allegorical head. Printer: BWC (w/o imprint).

GOOD	FINE	XF
700.00	1500.	—

1932 ISSUE, CHAPA 5

146 **50 ESCUDOS**
(75) 18.11.1932. Ch. 5. Violet and m/c. D. de Saldanha at l., monument at ctr. Back blue; farmer and oxen plowing at ctr., bank arms at r. Wmk: Head.

	Good	Fine	XF
	75.00	200.00	350.00

147 **500 ESCUDOS**
(93) 18.11.1932; 31.8.1934. Ch. 5. Brown-violet and blue on m/c unpt. J. da Silva Carvalho at l., palace at ctr. Back green; river and wall at ctr., Liberty at r. Wmk: Homer. Printer: BWC (w/o imprint).

	Good	Fine	XF
	200.00	500.00	—

148 **1000 ESCUDOS**
(104) 18.11.1932. Ch. 5. Dk. green and purple on m/c unpt. C. de Castelo-Melhor at l., National Palace at ctr., bank arms at lower r. Back brown; island castle at ctr. Wmk: Allegorical head. Printer: BWC (w/o imprint).

	Good	Fine	XF
	500.00	1000.	—

1935; 1938 ISSUE, CHAPA 5 AND 6

149 **50 ESCUDOS**
(76) 3.3.1938. Ch. 6. Brown-violet and dk. blue on m/c unpt. Arms at ctr., R. Ortigao at r. Back blue-green; head at l., monastery at ctr. Wmk: Woman's head.

	Good	Fine	XF
	40.00	80.00	150.00

150 **100 ESCUDOS**
(85) 21.2.1935; 13.3.1941. Ch. 5. Blue-green and brown. J. Pinto Ribeiro at l., arms at upper ctr. Back dk. red,. monument for 1.12.1640 (restoration of independence) at ctr., bank arms at r. Wmk: Head of Victory from monument.

	Good	Fine	XF
	40.00	80.00	200.00

151 **500 ESCUDOS**
(94) 26.4.1938. Ch. 6. Brown on green and gold unpt. Arms at lower l., Infante Don Henriques in black at r. Back green; tomb at l. ctr. Wmk: Allegorical head. Printer: W&S (w/o imprint).

	Good	Fine	XF
	75.00	200.00	350.00

152 **1000 ESCUDOS**
(105) 17.6.1938. Ch. 6. Green on tan and blue unpt. Arms at lower l., portr. M. de Aviz in black at r. ctr., spires at r. Back brown; monastery at ctr. Wmk: Woman's head. Printer: W&S (w/o imprint).

	Good	Fine	XF
	60.00	100.00	200.00

1941 ISSUE, CHAPA 6 AND 6A

153 **20 ESCUDOS**
(68) 1941-59. Ch. 6. Green and violet on m/c unpt. Portr. D. Antonio Luiz de Menezes at r. Back green on m/c unpt; bank arms at ctr. Wmk: Man's head.

	Good	Fine	XF
a. Sign. title at l.: *O VICE-GOVERNADOR*. 28.1.1941-25.5.1954.	8.00	15.00	30.00
b. Sign. title at l.: *O GOVERNADOR*. 27.1.1959.	8.00	15.00	30.00

154 **50 ESCUDOS**
(77) 25.11.1941-28.6.1949. Ch. 6A. Similar to #149. Back brown-violet and green.

	Good	Fine	XF
	15.00	30.00	80.00

1942 ISSUE, CHAPA 1 AND 7

155 **500 ESCUDOS**
(95) 29.9.1942. Ch. 7. Brown-violet and green on m/c unpt. Cherubs at ctr., D. de Goes at r. Back blue; ornate pulpit at ctr. Wmk: Bank name repeated. Printer: W&S (w/o imprint).

	Good	Fine	XF
	35.00	100.00	150.00

1953 ISSUE, CHAPA 7

		Good	FINE	XF
156 (106)	**1000 ESCUDOS** 29.9.1942. Ch. 7. Dk. green and blue on m/c unpt. Knight and Arab on horseback at l., portr. D. Afonso Henriques at r. and as wmk. Back brown; head at l., ornate tomb at ctr. Printer: BWC (w/o imprint).	12.00	40.00	100.00
157 (111B)	**5000 ESCUDOS** 29.9.1942. Ch. 1. Purple and m/c. Allegorical children at lower l., Qn. D. Leonor at r. Allegorical figures on back. Printer: BWC (w/o imprint). Specimen.	—	—	—

1944 ISSUE, CHAPA 8

		VG	VF	UNC
158 (96)	**500 ESCUDOS** 28.11.1944; 11.3.1952. Ch. 8. Dk. red and black on m/c unpt. Arms at upper ctr., D. Joao IV at r. Kg. and crowd on back. Wmk: Allegorical head. Printer: BWC (w/o imprint).	20.00	40.00	100.00

		VG	VF	UNC
160 (78)	**50 ESCUDOS** 28.4.1953; 24.6.1955. Ch. 7. Blue on m/c unpt. Arms at top ctr., F. Pereira de Mellow at r. and in profile as wmk. Back olive and green; bank arms at l., statue "The Thinker" at ctr.	8.00	15.00	25.00

1956 ISSUE, CHAPA 8

161 (107)	**1000 ESCUDOS** 31.1.1956. Ch. 8. Greenish gray and violet on m/c unpt. Castle at l., arms at lower ctr., D. Filipa de Lencastre at r. Back green; Qn. in oval at l., Qn. and 2 men at ctr. Wmk: Man's head. Printer: BWC (w/o imprint).	10.00	40.00	100.00

1958 ISSUE, CHAPA 9

162 (97)	**500 ESCUDOS** 27.5.1958. Ch. 9. Olive-brown on m/c unpt. D. Francisco d' Almeida at r. and as wmk. Back brown; 3 medieval men at l. Printer: BWC (w/o imprint).	35.00	100.00	150.00

1960 ISSUE, CHAPA 6A AND 7A

163 (69)	**20 ESCUDOS** 26.7.1960. Ch. 6A. Dk. green and purple. Portr. of D. Antonio Luiz de Menezes at r. and as wmk. Back purple and m/c; bank arms at l.	2.50	7.50	30.00
164 (79)	**50 ESCUDOS** 24.6.1960. Ch. 7A. Blue on m/c unpt. Arms at upper ctr. F. Pereira de Mello at r. and as wmk. Back dk. green and m/c; statue "The Thinker" at l.	4.00	8.00	15.00

1947 ISSUE, CHAPA 6

		VG	VF	UNC
159 (86)	**100 ESCUDOS** 28.10.1947; 24.10.1950; 22.6.1954; 25.6.1957. Ch. 6. Dk. green and lilac on m/c unpt. Arms at upper ctr., P. Nunes at r. and as wmk. Back brown; fountain in arches at ctr.	6.00	12.50	28.00

PORTUGUESE GUINEA

Portuguese Guinea (now Guinea-Bissau), a former Portuguese province of the west coast of Africa bounded on the north by Senegal and on the east and southeast by Guinea, had an area of 13,948 sq. mi. (36,125 sq. km.). Capital: Bissau. The province exported peanuts, timber and beeswax. Portuguese Guinea was discovered by Portuguese navigator Nuno Tristao in 1446. Trading rights in the area were granted to Cape Verde islanders but few prominent posts were established before 1851, and they were principally coastal installations. The chief export of this colony's early period was slaves for South America, a practice that adversely affected trade with the native people and retarded subjection of the interior. Territorial disputes with France delayed final demarcation of the colony's frontiers until 1905.

The African Party for the Independence of Guinea-Bissau was founded in 1956, and several years later began a guerrilla warfare that grew in effectiveness until 1974, when the rebels controlled most of the colony. Portugal's costly overseas wars in her African territories resulted in a military coup in Portugal in April 1974, that appreciably brightened the prospects for freedom for Guinea-Bissau. In August, 1974, the Lisbon government signed an agreement granting independence to Portuguese Guinea effective Sept. 10, 1974. The new republic took the name of Guinea-Bissau.

RULERS:
Portuguese to 1974

MONETARY SYSTEM:
1 Mil Reis = 1000 Reis to 1910
1 Escudo = 100 Centavos 1910-1975

NOTE: Three types of *BANCO NACIONAL ULTRAMARINO* seals are found on the bank notes originally issued for Bolama.

PORTUGUESE INFLUENCE

BANCO NACIONAL ULTRAMARINO, GUINÉ

1909 FIRST ISSUE
#1-11 ovpt: *BOLAMA*. Printer: BWC.

			GOOD	FINE	XF
1	**1 MIL REIS**	1.3.1909. Steamship Seal Type I at r.	100.00	200.00	450.00
2	**2.5 MIL REIS**	1.3.1909. Steamship Seal Type I at r.	120.00	300.00	650.00
3	**5 MIL REIS**	1.3.1909. Steamship Seal Type I at r.	150.00	400.00	800.00
4	**10 MIL REIS**	1.3.1909. Steamship Seal Type I at r.	200.00	500.00	1000.
5	**20 MIL REIS**	1.3.1909. Steamship Seal Type I at r.	250.00	600.00	1200.
5B	**50 MIL REIS**	1.3.1909.	800.00	1500.	—

1909 SECOND ISSUE

			GOOD	FINE	XF
1A	**1 MIL REIS**	1.3.1909. Steamship Seal Type III at r.	100.00	200.00	450.00
2A	**2.5 MIL REIS**	1.3.1909. Steamship Seal Type III at r.	120.00	300.00	650.00
3A	**5 MIL REIS**	1.3.1909. Steamship Seal Type III at r.	150.00	400.00	800.00
4A	**10 MIL REIS**	1.3.1909. Steamship Seal Type III at r.	200.00	500.00	1000.
5A	**20 MIL REIS**	1.3.1909. Steamship Seal Type III at r.	250.00	600.00	1200.

1909 PROVISIONAL ISSUE

			GOOD	FINE	XF
5F	**5 MIL REIS**	1.3.1909. Rectangular ovpt: *PAVEL... ces agencies de Guiné* on Cape Verde #6b.	—	—	—

1914 FIRST FRACTIONAL ISSUE

			GOOD	FINE	XF
6	**10 CENTAVOS**	5.11.1914. Purple on m/c unpt. Steamship Seal Type II at bottom ctr.	25.00	75.00	150.00

			GOOD	FINE	XF
7 (8)	**20 CENTAVOS**	5.11.1914. Blue on m/c unpt. Steamship Seal Type II.	25.00	75.00	150.00
8 (10)	**50 CENTAVOS**	5.11.1914. Green on m/c unpt. Steamship Seal Type II.	25.00	75.00	150.00

1914 SECOND FRACTIONAL ISSUE

			GOOD	FINE	XF
9 (7)	**10 CENTAVOS**	5.11.1914. Purple on m/c unpt. Like #6 but Steamship Seal Type III.	20.00	40.00	120.00
10 (9)	**20 CENTAVOS**	5.11.1914. Blue on m/c unpt. Like #7 but Steamship Seal Type III.	20.00	40.00	120.00
11	**50 CENTAVOS**	5.11.1914. Green on m/c unpt. Like #8 but Steamship Seal Type III.	20.00	50.00	120.00

1921 ISSUE

#12-18 portr. Oliveira Chamico at l. Ovpt: *GUINÉ*.
#12, 14-18 printer: BWC.

			GOOD	FINE	XF
12	**1 ESCUDO**	1.1.1921. Green.	20.00	40.00	125.00
13	**2 1/2 ESCUDOS**	1.1.1921. Dk. blue on yellow and red-violet unpt. Printer: TDLR.	20.00	70.00	200.00
14	**5 ESCUDOS**	1.1.1921. Black.	20.00	80.00	250.00
15	**10 ESCUDOS**	1.1.1921. Brown.	40.00	120.00	350.00
16	**20 ESCUDOS**	1.1.1921. Dk. blue.	100.00	200.00	500.00
17	**50 ESCUDOS**	1.1.1921. Blue.	150.00	400.00	750.00
18	**100 ESCUDOS**	1.1.1921. Brown.	180.00	500.00	1000.

1937 ISSUE

#21-24 J. Texeira Pinto at l. Ovpt: *GUINÉ*. Printer: BWC.

			GOOD	FINE	XF
21	**10 ESCUDOS**	14.9.1937. Red-brown on m/c. unpt.	25.00	85.00	175.00
22	**20 ESCUDOS**	14.9.1937. Blue on m/c unpt.	60.00	150.00	350.00
23	**50 ESCUDOS**	14.9.1937. Red on m/c unpt.	100.00	250.00	650.00
24	**100 ESCUDOS**	14.9.1937. Purple on m/c unpt.	125.00	300.00	750.00

1944 ISSUE

25	**5 ESCUDOS**	**VG**	**VF**	**UNC**
	2.11.1944. Olive and m/c. J. Texeira Pinta at l., steamship seal at r. Ovpt: *GUINÉ*. Printer: BWC.	20.00	50.00	100.00

1945 ISSUE

#26-32 portr. J. Texeira Pinto at l., steamship at r. Ovpt: *GUINÉ*. Printer: BWC.

26	**2 1/2 ESCUDOS**	**VG**	**VF**	**UNC**
	2.1.1945. Purple and m/c.	10.00	35.00	100.00
27	**5 ESCUDOS**			
	16.11.1945. Green.	12.50	45.00	150.00
28	**10 ESCUDOS**			
	16.11.1945. Brown.	15.00	60.00	200.00
29	**20 ESCUDOS**			
	16.11.1945. Blue.	15.00	65.00	220.00
30	**50 ESCUDOS**			
	16.11.1945. Yellow and green.	22.50	75.00	285.00
31	**100 ESCUDOS**			
	16.11.1945. Red.	30.00	100.00	350.00
32	**500 ESCUDOS**			
	16.11.1945. Green.	50.00	150.00	500.00

1947 ISSUE

#33-42 J. Texeira Pinto at l., steamship seal at r. Ovpt: *GUINÉ*. Printer: BWC.

33	**20 ESCUDOS**	**VG**	**VF**	**UNC**
	27.3.1947. Blue.	15.00	65.00	200.00
34	**50 ESCUDOS**			
	27.3.1947. Red.	20.00	85.00	275.00
35	**100 ESCUDOS**			
	27.3.1947. Purple.	25.00	100.00	325.00
36	**500 ESCUDOS**			
	27.3.1947. Green.	40.00	150.00	450.00

1958 ISSUE

#37-39 J. Texeira Pinto at l., steamship seal at r. Ovpt: *GUINÉ*. Serial # prefix B.
Printer: BWC.

37	**50 ESCUDOS**	**VG**	**VF**	**UNC**
	20.11.1958. Red, green and m/c.			
	a. Issued note.	10.00	40.00	150.00
	s. Specimen, punched hole cancelled.	—	—	120.00
38	**100 ESCUDOS**			
	20.11.1958. Purple and m/c.			
	a. Issued note.	12.50	60.00	250.00
	s. Specimen, punched hole cancelled.	—	—	200.00

39	**500 ESCUDOS**	**VG**	**VF**	**UNC**
	20.11.1958. Green and m/c.			
	a. Issued note.	50.00	100.00	350.00
	s. Specimen, punched hole cancelled.	—	—	275.00

PORTUGUESE INDIA

The former Portuguese possessions of Goa, Daman and Diu (now a union territory of west-central India), occupied an area of 1,441 sq. mi. (3,733 sq. km.) and had a population of about 200,000. Capital: Panaji. It is the site of a fine natural harbor and of iron and manganese deposits.

Vasco da Gama, the Portuguese explorer, first visited the west coast of India in 1498. Shortly thereafter the Portuguese arrived in strength and captured Goa (1510), Diu (1535), Daman (1559), and a number of other coastal enclaves and small islands, and for more then a century enjoyed a virtual monopoly on trade. With the arrival of powerful Dutch and English fleets in the first half of the 17th century, Portuguese power in the area declined, until virtually all that remained under Portuguese control were the enclaves of Goa (south of Bombay), Daman (due north of Bombay) and Diu (northwest of Bombay). They were invaded by India in 1961 and annexed to India in 1962.

RULERS:
Portuguese to 1961

MONETARY SYSTEM:
1 Rupia = 16 Tanga = 960 Reis to 1958
1 Escudo = 100 Centavos, 1958-1962

STEAMSHIP SEALS VARIETIES

Type I	Type II	Type III
LISBOA/C,C,A	LISBOA	C, C, A

C,C,A = Colonias, Commercio, Agricultura

NOTE: Three types of *BANCO NACIONAL ULTRAMARINO* seals are found on the bank notes issued for Bolama.

PORTUGUESE INFLUENCE

JUNTA DA FAZENDA PUBLICA

1882 ISSUE

		VG	VF	XF
A2	**10 RUPIAS** 2.11.1882. Portr. Kg. Carlos I at upper ctr.	—	—	—
A3	**20 RUPIAS** 2.11.1882; 3.11.1882. Portr. Kg. Carlos I at upper ctr.	—	—	—

GOVERNO GERAL DO ESTADO DA INDIA

1883 ISSUE

		GOOD	FINE	XF
1	**5 RUPIAS** 1883.	—	—	—
2	**10 RUPIAS** 1883.	—	—	—
3	**20 RUPIAS** 1883.	—	—	—
4	**50 RUPIAS** 1883.	—	—	—
5	**100 RUPIAS** 1883.	—	—	—
6	**500 RUPIAS** 1883.	—	—	—

1896 ISSUE

		GOOD	FINE	XF
7	**5 RUPIAS** 1.12.1896. Green and black. Portr. Kg. Carlos I at upper ctr.	—	—	—
8	**10 RUPIAS** 1.12.1896.	—	—	—
9	**20 RUPIAS** 1.12.1896.	—	—	—
10	**50 RUPIAS** 1.12.1896.	—	—	—

1899 ISSUE

		GOOD	FINE	XF
11	**5 RUPIAS** 15.11.1899. Brown and black. Kg. Carlos I and lg. *CINCO.* at ctr.	—	—	—
12	**10 RUPIAS** 15.11.1899.	—	—	—
13	**20 RUPIAS** 15.11.1899.	—	—	—
14	**50 RUPIAS** 15.11.1899.	—	—	—

BANCO NACIONAL ULTRAMARINO

NOVA GOA BRANCH

1906 ISSUE

#15-18A printer: BWC.

#16-18A allegorical woman w/trident at ctr.

		GOOD	FINE	XF
15	**5 RUPIAS** 1.1.1906. Blue and m/c. Allegorical woman w/trident at l. Back blue and maroon.			
	a. Steamship seal Type I (1906-18).	350.00	650.00	—
	b. Steamship seal Type III (1918-21).	300.00	600.00	—

		GOOD	FINE	XF
16	**10 RUPIAS** 1.1.1906. Black and m/c. Back green and maroon.			
	a. Steamship seal Type I (1906-18).	350.00	650.00	—
	b. Steamship seal Type III (1918-21).	300.00	600.00	—
17	**20 RUPIAS** 1.1.1906. Black on lt. green unpt. Back lt. brown. Steamship seal Type I (1906-18).	—	Rare	—
17A	**20 RUPIAS** 1.1.1906. Dk. blue and m/c. Back purple and brown. Steamship seal Type III (1918-21).	—	Rare	—
18	**50 RUPIAS** 1.1.1906. Black and m/c. Back maroon and green. Steamship seal Type I (1906-18).	—	Rare	—

			GOOD	FINE	XF
18A	**50 RUPIAS**	1.1.1906. Blue on m/c. Steamship seal Type III (1918-21).	—	Rare	—

1917 ISSUE
#19-22A printer: BWC.
#19-21A allegorical woman seated, anchor, sailing ship, sailboat in harbor at ctr.

			GOOD	FINE	XF
24	**2 1/2 RUPIAS**	1.1.1924. Blue and purple. Like #23. Back purple.	150.00	375.00	750.00

			GOOD	FINE	XF
19	**4 TANGAS**	1.10.1917. Red-brown and green. Back olive and maroon w/woman at ctr. Deep green steamship seal Type II.	30.00	75.00	250.00
19A	**4 TANGAS**	1.10.1917. Violet and m/c. Like #19. Back blue and maroon. Blue steamship seal Type II.			

			GOOD	FINE	XF
25	**5 RUPIAS**	1.1.1924. Green. Palace at ctr. Tiger on back.	100.00	350.00	650.00
26	**10 RUPIAS**	1.1.1924. Violet and blue. Similar to #25. Back violet.	150.00	375.00	750.00
27	**20 RUPIAS**	1.1.1924. Violet and pink. Similar to #25. Back brownish violet.	175.00	425.00	—
28	**50 RUPIAS**	1.1.1924. Purple and maroon. Elephant at ctr. Back purple; sailing ship.	—	Rare	—

			GOOD	FINE	XF
20	**8 TANGAS**	1.10.1917. Green and red. Back green.	40.00	100.00	300.00
20A	**8 TANGAS**	1.10.1917. Blue and m/c. Like #20. Back blue and maroon.			
21	**1 RUPIA**	1.10.1917. Brown. Back red.			
	a.	Blue steamship seal Type I.	75.00	200.00	550.00
	b.	Blue steamship seal Type II.	50.00	175.00	425.00
21A	**1 RUPIA**	1.10.1917. Blue. Like #21. Back Maroon; woman w/caduceus seated by globe, cornucopia w/produce and anchor at ctr. on back. Brown steamship seal Type III.	50.00	175.00	425.00
22	**2 1/2 RUPIAS**	1.10.1917. Maroon and m/c. Like 22A. Back brown. Dull red steamship seal Type II.	125.00	300.00	700.00

			GOOD	FINE	XF
22A	**2 1/2 RUPIAS**	1.10.1917. Red and m/c. Back green. Violet steamship seal Type III.	75.00	225.00	550.00

W/O DECRETO

			GOOD	FINE	XF
23	**1 RUPIA**	1.1.1924. Blue and gold. Tiger head at ctr. Local bldg. on back.	25.00	70.00	200.00

			GOOD	FINE	XF
29	**100 RUPIAS**	1.1.1924. Purple and brown. Similar to #28. Back purple.	—	Rare	—
30	**500 RUPIAS**	1.1.1924. Blue and maroon. Similar to #28. Back grayish purple.	—	Rare	—

DECRETO NO. 17 154 (1929)
#23-30 printer: TDLR.

		GOOD	FINE	XF
23A	**1 RUPIA** 1.1.1924 (1929). Like #23.	20.00	50.00	150.00

		GOOD	FINE	XF
25A	**5 RUPIAS** 1.1.1924 (1929). Green. Like #25.	100.00	350.00	650.00
26A	**10 RUPIAS** 1.1.1924 (1929). Like #26.			
	a. Sign. titles: *VICE GOVERNADOR* and *GOVERNADOR*.	100.00	350.00	650.00
	b. Sign. titles: *ADMINISTRADOR* and *PRESIDENTE DO CONSELHO* *ADMINISTRATIVO*.	150.00	385.00	750.00

1938 ISSUE

		GOOD	FINE	XF
31	**5 RUPIAS** 11.1.1938. Green on lilac unpt. Like #25 but date at upper l.	50.00	100.00	225.00

		GOOD	FINE	XF
32	**10 RUPIAS** 11.1.1938. Red-violet on blue unpt. Like #26 but date at upper l.	50.00	100.00	225.00
33	**20 RUPIAS** 11.1.1938. Olive-brown on peach unpt. Like #27 but date at upper l.	70.00	120.00	250.00

		GOOD	FINE	XF
34	**50 RUPIAS** 11.1.1938. Blue on brown unpt. Like #28.	—	Rare	—

INDIA PORTUGUESA BRANCH

1945 ISSUE
#35-40 steamship seal at upper l., portr. A. de Albuquerque at r. Woman, sailing ships at ctr., arms at upper r. on back. Printer: BWC.

		GOOD	FINE	XF
35	**5 RUPIAS** 29.11.1945. Green on blue and brown unpt.	6.00	20.00	45.00

1959 ISSUE

#41-46 portr. A. de Albuquerque at r. Steamship seal at upper l. Early explorer, sailing ships at ctr. on back. Sign. varieties. Printer: TDLR.

			VG	VF	UNC
41	**30 ESCUDOS**		3.00	12.00	45.00
	2.1.1959. Dk. red and m/c.				

			VG	VF	UNC
42	**60 ESCUDOS**		5.00	20.00	70.00
	2.1.1959. Black and m/c.				

			GOOD	FINE	XF
36	**10 RUPIAS**		7.50	22.50	55.00
	29.11.1945. Brown and m/c.				

			GOOD	FINE	XF
37	**20 RUPIAS**		10.00	35.00	100.00
	29.11.1945. Blue and m/c.				
38	**50 RUPIAS**		20.00	65.00	175.00
	29.11.1945. Dk. red and m/c.				

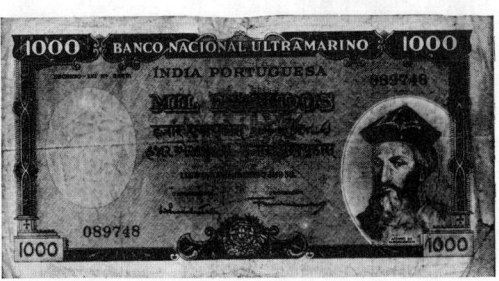

			VG	VF	UNC
43	**100 ESCUDOS**		7.50	37.50	125.00
	2.1.1959. Blue and m/c.				
44	**300 ESCUDOS**		20.00	60.00	200.00
	2.1.1959. Violet and m/c.				
45	**600 ESCUDOS**		35.00	95.00	325.00
	2.1.1959. Green and m/c.				

			GOOD	FINE	XF
39	**100 RUPIAS**		40.00	120.00	350.00
	29.11.1945. Violet and m/c.				

			VG	VF	UNC
46	**1000 ESCUDOS**		65.00	135.00	450.00
	2.1.1959. Brown and m/c.				

			GOOD	FINE
40	**500 RUPIAS**		375.00	850.00
	29.11.1945. Green and m/c.			

The Commonwealth of Puerto Rico, the easternmost island of the Greater Antilles in the West Indies, has an area of 3,435 sq. mi. (9,104 sq. km.) and a population of 3.3 million. Capital: San Juan. The commonwealth has its own constitution and elects its own governor. Its people are citizens of the United States, liable to the draft - but not to federal taxation. The chief industries of Puerto Rico are manufacturing, agriculture, and tourism. Manufactured goods, cement, dairy and livestock products, sugar, rum, and coffee are exported, mainly to the United States.

Puerto Rico ("Rich Port") was discovered by Columbus who landed on the island and took possession for Spain on Oct. 19, 1493 - the only time Columbus set foot on the soil of what is now a possession of the United States. The first settlement, Caparra, was established by Ponce de Leon in 1508. The early years of the colony were not promising. Considerable gold was found, but the supply was soon exhausted. Efforts to enslave the Indians caused violent reprisals. Hurricanes destroyed crops and homes. French, Dutch, and English freebooters burned the towns. Puerto Rico remained a Spanish possession until 1898, when it was ceded to the United States following the Spanish-American War. Puerto Ricans were granted a measure of self-government and U.S. citizenship in 1917. Effective July 25, 1952, a Congressional resolution elevated Puerto Rico to the status of a free commonwealth associated with the United States.

Vieque (or Crab Island), located to the east of Puerto Rico, is the largest of the Commonwealth's major offshore islands. The others are Culebra, a naval station to the east, and Mona to the west.

RULERS:
Spanish, 1493-1898

MONETARY SYSTEM:
1 Peso = 100 Centavos to 1898
1 Dollar = 100 Cents, 1898-

Note: Certain listings encompassing issues circulated by various bank and regional authorities are included in Volume 1.

SPANISH INFLUENCE

TESORERÍA NACIONAL

1812 ISSUE

			GOOD	FINE	XF
1	**8 REALES** 1812. Black. Arms in circle of dots at ctr.		—	Rare	—

1813 ISSUE

			GOOD	FINE	XF
2	**8 REALES** 1813. Black. Paschal lamb at ctr.				
	a. White paper.		1500.	—	—
	b. Blue paper.		—	Rare	—

DECREES OF 3.9.1811 AND 29.6.1813
Issued in 1814.

			GOOD	FINE	XF
3	**3 PESOS** 1814 (Roman Numerals). Black. Uniface, vertical format.		—	Rare	—

			GOOD	FINE	XF
4	**5 PESOS** 1814 (Roman Numerals). Black. Uniface, horizontal format.		—	Rare	—

1815-19 ISSUE
#5-6 uniface. Printer: Murray Draper Fairman.

			GOOD	FINE	XF
5	**3 PESOS** July 1815; 4.8.1815. Black. Crowned Spanish arms at upper ctr.		1500.	2500.	4000.

			GOOD	FINE	XF
6	**5 PESOS** 25.7.1819; 31.7.1819. Black. Portr. Kg. Ferdinand VII at top ctr.		1500.	2500.	4000.

MINISTERIO DE ULTRAMAR

1895 BILLETE DE CANJE
Circulating Bill

			GOOD	FINE	XF
7	**1 PESO** 17.8.1895. Black on yellow unpt. Portr. man at l. Back blue; crowned arms of Spain at ctr.				
	a. W/counterfoil.		20.00	45.00	90.00
	b. W/o counterfoil.		15.00	35.00	75.00

SERIES A
#8-11 Paschal lamb at l. Printer: ABNC.
#9-13 crowned Spanish arms at ctr. on back.
#12-13 Paschal lamb at r.

			GOOD	FINE	XF
8	**5 PESOS** ND (ca.1889). Black on green and yellow unpt. Seated child painting at r. Back green; crowned Spanish arms at l. Speciman or proof.		—	—	—

27	**10 PESOS**	GOOD	FINE	XF
	1894-97. Black on blue and yellow unpt. Similar to #9. Back orange.	850.00	2500.	5000.
28	**20 PESOS**			
	1894-97. Black on blue and yellow unpt. Similar to #10. Back blue. Specimen or proof.	—	—	—

9	**10 PESOS**	GOOD	FINE	XF
	ND (ca.1889). Black on yellow and brown unpt. 2 coastwatchers at r. Back brown.			
	a. Issued note.	—	Rare	—
	p. Proof.	—	—	—
10	**20 PESOS**			
	ND (ca.1889). Black on orange and yellow unpt. 3 men lifting crate at upper ctr. Back orange. Specimen or proof.	—	—	—
11	**50 PESOS**			
	ND (ca.1889). Black on blue and yellow unpt. Columbus sighting land at ctr. r. Back blue. Proof.	—	—	—
12	**100 PESOS**			
	ND (ca.1889). Black on yellow and brown unpt. Man w/globe and map at l., 2 allegorical women at ctr. Back brown. Proof.	—	—	—
13	**200 PESOS**			
	ND (ca.1889). Black on orange and yellow unpt. Justice at l., seated woman w/globe at ctr. Back orange. Archive copy.	—	—	—

SERIES B

#14-19 designs like previous issue. Printer: ABNC.

14	**5 PESOS**	GOOD	FINE	XF
	ND. Black on brown and yellow unpt. Like #8. Back brown. Archive copy.	—	—	—
15	**10 PESOS**			
	ND. Black on yellow and blue unpt. Like #9. Back tan. Archive copy.	—	—	—
16	**20 PESOS**			
	ND. Black on orange and blue unpt. Like #10. Back blue. Archive copy.	—	—	—
17	**50 PESOS**			
	ND. Black on brown and yellow unpt. Like #11. Back blue. Specimen.	—	—	—
18	**100 PESOS**			
	ND. Black on yellow and red unpt. Like #12. Back red. Archive copy.	—	—	—
19	**200 PESOS**			
	ND. Black on green and yellow unpt. Like #13. Back green. Archive copy.	—	—	—

SERIES C

#20-25 designs like previous issue. Printer: ABNC.

20	**5 PESOS**	GOOD	FINE	XF
	ND. Black on red and yellow unpt. Like #8. Back tan. Archive copy.	—	—	—
21	**10 PESOS**			
	ND. Black on green and red unpt. Like #9. Back blue. Archive copy.	—	—	—
22	**20 PESOS**			
	ND. Black on orange and brown unpt. Like #10. Back brown. Archive copy.	—	—	—
23	**50 PESOS**			
	ND. Black on red and yellow unpt. Like #11. Back red. Specimen or proof.	—	—	—
24	**100 PESOS**			
	ND. Black on yellow and green unpt. Like #12. Back green. Specimen or proof.	—	—	—
25	**200 PESOS**			
	ND. Black on brown and yellow unpt. Like #13. Back brown. Specimen.	—	—	—

29	**50 PESOS**	GOOD	FINE	XF
	1894-97. Black on brown and yellow unpt. Similar to #11. Back brown. Specimen or proof.	—	—	—
30	**100 PESOS**			
	1894-97. Black on orange and yellow unpt. Similar to #12. Back orange. Specimen or proof.	—	—	—
31	**200 PESOS**			
	1895-97. Black on green and yellow unpt. Similar to #13. Back green. Specimen.	—	—	—

UNITED STATES ADMINISTRATION

BANCO ESPAÑOL DE PUERTO RICO

1900 ISSUE

1894 SERIES D

#26-29 portr. Qn. mother and regent of Spain's Maria Chistina. Printer: ABNC.

#30-34 portr. regent at r.

26	**5 PESOS**	GOOD	FINE	XF
	1.12.1894; 2.3.1896; 3.11.1896; 1.7.1897. Black on brown and yellow unpt. Similar to #8. Back brown.			
	a. Issued note.	800.00	2000.	—
	b. Ovpt: *MAYAGUEZ.* 1.12.1894.	1000.	2800.	—

		Good	Fine	XF
32	**5 PESOS**			
	1.5.1900. Ovpt: *MONEDA AMERICANA* on #20. Series C.	850.00	2500.	—

FIRST NATIONAL BANK OF PORTO RICO AT SAN JUAN
Charter #6484.

This bank was in operation from 1902 until its placement in voluntary liquidation Sept. 8, 1911. Thirteen notes known.

1902 THIRD CHARTER PERIOD
#33-36 red seal at lower r.

		Good	Fine	XF
33 (S121)	**10 DOLLARS** 1902. Black. Portr. McKinley at l. Back deep green.	8500.	14,000.	—
34 (S122)	**20 DOLLARS** 1902. Black. Portr. McCulloch at l. Back deep green.	10,000.	16,000.	—
35 (S123)	**50 DOLLARS** 1902. Black. Portr. Sherman at l. Back deep green.	—	Unique	—
36 (S124)	**100 DOLLARS** 27.10.1902. Black. Portr. Knox at l. Back green.	—	Unique	—

1908 ISSUE
#37-40 blue seal at lower r. Dates *1902, 1908* on back. Designs like #33-36.

37 (S125)	**10 DOLLARS** 27.10.1902. Black. Back green.	—	Unique	—
38 (S126)	**20 DOLLARS** c.1908.	Unknown In Private Hands		
39 (S127)	**50 DOLLARS** c.1908.	Unknown In Private Hands		
40 (S128)	**100 DOLLARS** c.1908.	Unknown In Private Hands		

BANCO DE PUERTO RICO

1901-04 SERIES E
#41-46 have "U.S. Cy." (U.S. Currency) on face, Paschal lamb at ctr. on back. Printer: ABNC.

		Good	Fine	XF
41	**5 PESOS = 5 DOLLARS** 1.7.1904. Black on orange unpt. Seated woman holding scale by cornucopia w/money and chest at ctr. Back orange.	800.00	2000.	4250.
42	**10 PESOS = 10 DOLLARS** ND (ca.1901-04). Black on brown and yellow unpt. Seated allegorical woman w/marine implements at ctr. Back brown. Proof.	—	—	—
43	**20 PESOS = 20 DOLLARS** ND (ca.1901-04). Black on blue and yellow unpt. Seated allegorical woman w/harvest at ctr. Back blue. Proof.	—	—	—
44	**50 PESOS = 50 DOLLARS** ND (ca.1901-04). Black on olive and yellow unpt. Train, allegorical women w/industrial implements, and sailing ships at ctr. r. Back olive. Archive copy.	—	—	—
45	**100 PESOS = 100 DOLLARS** ND (ca.1901-04). Black on olive and red unpt. Allegorical woman w/sacks and barrels at ctr. Back red. Proof.	—	—	—
46	**200 PESOS = 200 DOLLARS** ND (ca.1901-04). Black on yellow and purple unpt. Cherub at upper l. and r., allegorical woman w/plants and bird at ctr. Back purple. Proof.	—	—	—

1909 SERIES F
NOTE: Uniface trial designs similar to #47 and #48 but dated 1.7.1907 were in ABNC archives.

		Good	Fine	XF
47	**5 DOLLARS** 1.7.1909. Black. Columbus at l., red Paschal lamb seal at r. Back green; seated woman w/lamb at ctr.			
	a. Issued note.	450.00	950.00	2250.
	b. Cancelled w/ovpt: *CANCELADO* w/or w/o punched holes.	175.00	350.00	850.00

		Good	Fine	XF
48	**10 DOLLARS** 1.7.1909. Black. Ponce de Leon at l., red Paschal lamb seal at r. Back brown; Liberty at ctr.			
	a. Issued note.	700.00	1750.	4750.
	b. Cancelled w/punched holes.	225.00	450.00	1000.

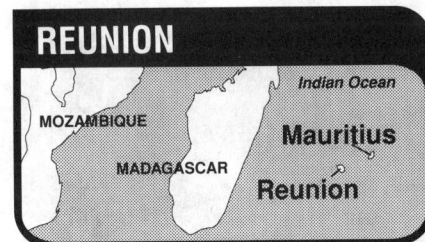

REUNION

Indian Ocean

MOZAMBIQUE

Mauritius

MADAGASCAR

Reunion

The Department of Reunion, an overseas department of France located in the Indian Ocean 400 miles (640 km.) east of Madagascar, has an area of 969 sq. mi. (2,510 sq. km.) and a population of 556,000. Capital: Saint-Denis. The island's volcanic soil is extremely fertile. Sugar, vanilla, coffee and rum are exported.

Although first visited by Portuguese navigators in the 16th century, Reunion was uninhabited when claimed for France by Capt. Goubert in 1638. It was first colonized as Isle de Bourbon by the French in 1662 as a layover station for ships rounding the Cape of Good Hope to India. It was renamed Reunion in 1793. The island remained in French possession except for the period of 1810-15, when it was occupied by the British. Reunion became an overseas department of France in 1946, and in 1958 voted to continue that status within the new French Union. Bauque du France notes were introduced 1.1.1973.

RULERS:
French, 1638-1810, 1815
British, 1810-1815

MONETARY SYSTEM:
1 Franc = 100 Centimes
1 Nouveau Franc = 100 Old Francs, 1960

NOTE: For earlier issues see Isles of France and of Bourbon.

FRENCH INFLUENCE

ILE DE LA RÉUNION - TRÉSOR COLONIAL

DECRET DU 2.5.1879 (1884 FIRST ISSUE)

#1-4 uniface.
NOTE: Denominations of 30, 50 and 100 Francs are reported.

		GOOD	FINE	XF
1	**50 CENTIMES** 8.7.1884. Black.	150.00	450.00	—
2	**1 FRANC** 8.7.1884. Black. Like #1. 2 plate varieties.	165.00	500.00	—
3	**2 FRANCS** 8.7.1884. Black on yellow paper.	200.00	600.00	—

		GOOD	FINE	XF
4	**3 FRANCS** 4.6.1884. Black on green paper.	—	Rare	—

DECRET DU 2.5.1879 (1884 SECOND ISSUE)

#5-7 w/different appearance of text and border (similar to Guadeloupe #1).

		GOOD	FINE	XF
5	**50 CENTIMES** 4.6 1884. Black on cream paper.	450.00	—	—
6	**1 FRANC** 4.6 1884 Black on dark blue paper.	500.00	—	—
7	**2 FRANCS** 4.6. 1884. Black on gray paper.	550.00	—	—

1886 ISSUE

#8-10 cherub w/pillar and cornucopia at l. and r., allegories of Agriculture and Commerce at ctr. on face. Head at l. and r., value over anchor at ctr. on back.

		GOOD	FINE	XF
8	**50 CENTIMES** 21.6.1886. Black on lt. gray paper.	150.00	450.00	—
9	**1 FRANC** 10.5.1886. Black on pale blue or lt. green paper.	185.00	550.00	—

		GOOD	FINE	XF
10	**2 FRANCS** 1886. Black.	225.00	675.00	—

BANQUE DE LA RÉUNION

VICHY FRENCH GOVERNMENT - WW II FREE FRENCH GOVERNMENT - WW II

LAW OF 12.9.1873

		GOOD	FINE	XF
11	**5 FRANCS** L. 1873. Border of trees and cornucopia. Brown paper. Uniface.	—	Rare	—
12	**10 FRANCS** L.1873. Border of flowers and 3 cherubs. White paper. Uniface.	—	Rare	—

LAW OF 1874

		GOOD	FINE	XF
13	**5 FRANCS** L.1874 (1890-1912). Blue. Medallic heads at l. and r. 10 sign. varieties.	200.00	—	—

LAW OF 1901

		GOOD	FINE	XF
14	**5 FRANCS** L1901 (1912-44). Red. Like #13. Back: gray. 6 sign. varieties.	20.00	60.00	150.00

1874; 1875 ISSUE

		GOOD	FINE	XF
15	**25 FRANCS** ND (1876-1908). Blue. Flowers and fruit w/landscape in background on brown back. 3 sign. varieties.	250.00	550.00	1250.

16	**100 FRANCS**	GOOD	FINE	XF
(17)	ND (1874-1917). Red. Like #15. 6 sign. varieties.	—	Rare	—
17	**500 FRANCS**			
(19)	ND (1875-1929). Black on cream unpt. Like #17. 5 sign. varieties.	—	Rare	—

1912; 1914 ISSUE

18	**25 FRANCS**	GOOD	FINE	XF
(16)	ND (1912-30). Blue w/black text. Like #15. Back maroon. 5 sign. varieties.	175.00	450.00	950.00
19	**100 FRANCS**			
(18)	ND (1914-29). Maroon. Like #17 Back blue. 4 sign. varieties.	—	Rare	—

1917 EMERGENCY FRACTIONAL ISSUE

#22 *Deleted.*

20	**5 CENTIMES**	VG	VF	UNC
	ND (1917). Black on red cardboard w/embossed seal. Uniface.	15.00	45.00	135.00

21	**10 CENTIMES**	VG	VF	UNC
	ND (1917). Black on brown cardboard w/embossed seal. Uniface.	32.50	100.00	300.00

1923-30 ISSUE

23	**25 FRANCS**	GOOD	FINE	XF
	ND (1930-44). Purple and m/c. Woman wearing wreath at ctr., flowers and fruit in background. 4 sign. varieties.	40.00	100.00	425.00

24	**100 FRANCS**	GOOD	FINE	XF
	ND (1926-44). M/c. Woman w/staff at l. 5 sign. varieties.	150.00	350.00	900.00
25	**500 FRANCS**			
	ND (1923-44). M/c. Like #24. 5 sign. varieties.	225.00	600.00	—

1937-40 EMERGENCY CIRCULATING BEARER CHECK ISSUE

26	**100 FRANCS**	GOOD	FINE	XF
	29.11.1937; 8.10.1940; 5.11.1940. Apricot paper.	—	Rare	—
27	**500 FRANCS**			
	29.11.1937; 8.10.1940; 5.11.1940; 25.11.1940.	—	Rare	—
28	**1000 FRANCS**			
	29.11.1937; 8.10.1940; 5.11.1940.	—	Rare	—
29	**5000 FRANCS**			
	8.10.1940; 5.11.1940.	—	Rare	—

VICHY FRENCH GOVERNMENT

BANQUE DE LA RÉUNION

ARRETÉ LOCAL DU 8.10.1942

#30-32 Francisque (Vichy axe) at upper l. and r.

30	**50 CENTIMES**	GOOD	FINE	XF
	L. 1942. Lt. purple unpt.	175.00	400.00	900.00
31	**1 FRANC**			
	L. 1942. Lt. blue unpt.	175.00	400.00	900.00

32	**2 FRANCS**	GOOD	FINE	XF
	L. 1942. Orange unpt.	175.00	400.00	900.00

FREE FRENCH GOVERNMENT

BANQUE DE LA RÉUNION

1942 ISSUE

32A	**2 FRANCS**	GOOD	FINE	XF
	ND (-old date 8.10.1942). Like #35 but w/black ovpt. line on *Décret du 8 October 1942.* Both Crosses of Lorraine in black.	—	Rare	—

ARRETÉ LOCAL DU 12.8.1943

#33-35 Cross of Lorraine in red at upper l. and r.

33	**50 CENTIMES**	GOOD	FINE	XF
	L. 1943. Lt. purple unpt.	160.00	325.00	725.00
34	**1 FRANC**			
	L. 1943. Lt. blue unpt.	160.00	325.00	725.00
35	**2 FRANCS**			
	L. 1943. Orange unpt.	160.00	325.00	725.00

CAISSE CENTRALE DE LA FRANCE LIBRE

1943 ND PROVISIONAL ISSUE

#36-38 types of French Equatorial Africa w/special serial # ranges. Reunion not mentioned. Printer: BWC (w/o imprint).

NOTE: See also St. Pierre & Miquelon #10-14.

		GOOD	FINE	XF
36	**5 FRANCS**			
	L.1941 (ca. 1943). Type of FEA #10. Serial # AN 100 001-AN 260 000.	20.00	60.00	—
37	**100 FRANCS**			
	L.1941 (1944-45). Tyype of FEA #13.			
	a. Serial # range PA 270 001-PA 470000. July 1944).	50.00	150.00	—
	b. Serial # range PB 700 001-000. PA 900000. (Jan. 1945).	70.00	150.00	
	c. Serial # range PE 590 001-PF 090000. (31.12.1945).	70.00	150.00	
38	**1000 FRANCS**			
	L.1941 (ca. 1943). Type of FEA #14. Serial TA 030 001-TA 060 000; TA 215 001-TA 235 000; TA 255 001-TA 275 000.	400.00	1000.	1600.

CAISSE CENTRALE DE LA FRANCE D'OUTRE-MER

1944 ND PROVISIONAL ISSUE

#39-40 types of French Equatorial Africa w/special serial # ranges. Reunion not mentioned. Printer: BWC 9 w/o imprint).

NOTE: See also St. Pierre & Miquelon #15-18.

		GOOD	FINE	XF
39	**100 FRANCS**			
	L.1944. Similar to FEA #18.			
	a. Serial # PQ 200 001-PQ 700 000.	50.00	150.00	—
	b. Serial # PS 700 001-PS 800 000.	50.00	150.00	
40	**1000 FRANCS**			
	L.1944. Similar to FEA #19. Serial # TD 125 001-TD 135 000; TD 185 001-TD 235 000.	600.00	1200.	—

1947 ND PROVISIONAL ISSUE

#41-48 ovpt: *LA RÉUNION* on French Equatorial Africa Issues.

		VG	VF	UNC
41	**5 FRANCS**			
	ND (1947). M/c. Ovpt. on F.E.A. #10.			
	a. Issued note.	3.00	15.00	100.00
	s. Specimen.	—	—	90.00
42	**10 FRANCS**			
	ND (1947). M/c. Ovpt. on F.E.A. #21.			
	a. Issued note.	3.50	20.00	125.00
	s. Specimen.	—	—	100.00
43	**20 FRANCS**			
	ND (1947). Olive-brown. Ovpt. on F.E.A. #22.			
	a. Issued note.	5.00	25.00	140.00
	s. Specimen.	—	—	110.00

		VG	VF	UNC
44	**50 FRANCS**			
	ND (1947). M/c. Ovpt. on F.E.A. #23.			
	a. Issued note.	7.50	30.00	175.00
	s. Specimen.	—	—	150.00
45	**100 FRANCS**			
	ND (1947). M/c. Ovpt. on F.E.A. #24.			
	a. Issued note.	9.00	37.50	225.00
	s. Specimen.	—	—	175.00
46	**500 FRANCS**			
	ND (1947). M/c. Ovpt. on F.E.A. #25.			
	a. Issued note.	25.00	75.00	350.00
	s. Specimen.	—	—	225.00

		VG	VF	UNC
47	**1000 FRANCS**			
	ND (1947). M/c. Ovpt. on F.E.A. #26.			
	a. Issued note.	30.00	95.00	450.00
	s. Specimen.	—	—	250.00
48	**5000 FRANCS**			
	ND (1947). Brown and m/c ovpt. on F.E.A. #27.			
	a. Issued note.	60.00	175.00	675.00
	s. Specimen.	—	—	375.00

INSTITUT D'EMISSION DES DÉPARTEMENTS D'OUTRE-MER

1960 ND PROVISIONAL ISSUE

#49 and 50 ovpt: *LA RÉUNION*.

		VG	VF	UNC
49	**100 FRANCS**			
	ND (1960). M/c. Like #45.			
	a. Issued note.	10.00	50.00	260.00
	s. Specimen.	—	—	200.00

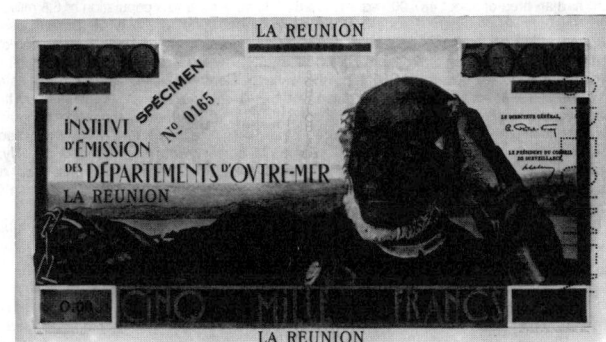

		VG	VF	UNC
50	**5000 FRANCS**			
	ND (1960). Brown and m/c. Like #48.			
	a. Issued note.	35.00	145.00	600.00
	s. Specimen.	—	—	450.00

Rhodesia and Nyasaland (now the Republic of Zimbabwe) located in the east-central part of southern Africa, has an area of 150,804 sq. mi. (390,580 sq. km.) and a population of 6.9 million. Capital: Salisbury. The economy is based on agriculture and mining. Tobacco, sugar, asbestos, copper and chrome ore and coal are exported.

The Rhodesian area, the habitat of paleolithic man, contains extensive evidence of earlier civilizations, notably the world-famous ruins of Zimbabwe, a gold-trading center that flourished about the 14th or 15th century AD. The Portuguese of the 16th century were the first Europeans to attempt to develop south-central Africa, but it remained for Cecil Rhodes and the British South Africa Co. to open the hinterlands. Rhodes obtained a concession for mineral rights from local chiefs in 1888 and administered his African empire (named Southern Rhodesia in 1895) through the British South Africa Co. until 1923, when the British government annexed the area after the white settlers voted for existence as a separate entity, rather than for incorporation into the Union of South Africa. From Sept. of 1953 through 1963 Southern Rhodesia was joined with the British protectorates of Northern Rhodesia and Nyasaland into a multiracial federation. When the federation was dissolved at the end of 1963, Northern Rhodesia and Nyasaland became the independent states of Zambia and Malawi.

Britain was prepared to grant independence to Southern Rhodesia but declined to do so when the politically dominant white Rhodesians refused to give assurances of representative government. On May 11, 1965, following two years of unsuccessful negotiation with the British government, Prime Minister Ian Smith issued an unilateral declaration of independence. Britain responded with economic sanctions supported by the United Nations. After further futile attempts to effect an accommodation, the Rhodesian Parliament severed all ties with Britain, and on March 2, 1970, established the Republic of Rhodesia.

On March 3, 1978, Prime Minister Ian Smith and three moderate black nationalist leaders signed an agreement providing for black majority rule. The name of the country was changed to Zimbabwe Rhodesia.

After the election of March 3, 1980, the country again changed its name to the Republic of Zimbabwe. The Federation of Rhodesia and Nyasaland (or the Central African Federation), comprising the British protectorates of Northern Rhodesia and Nyasaland and the self-governing colony of Southern Rhodesia, was located in the east-central part of southern Africa. The multiracial federation had an area of about 487,000 sq. mi. (1,261,330 sq. km.) and a population of 6.8 million. Capital: Salsbury, in Southern Rhodesia. The geographical unity of the three British possessions suggested the desirability of political and economic union as early as 1924. Despite objections by the African constituency of Northern Rhodesia and Nyasaland, who by the dominant influence of prosperious and self governing Southern Rhodesia, the Central African Federation was established in Sept. of 1953. As feared, the Federation was effectively and profitably dominated by the European consituency of Southern Rhodesia despite the fact that the three component countries largely retained their prefederation political structure. It was dissolved at the end of 1963, largely because of the effective opposition of the Nyasaland African Congress. Northern Rhodesia and Nyasaland became independent states of Zambia and Malawi in 1964. Southern Rhodesia unilaterally decalred its independence as Rhodesia the following year which was not recognized by the British Government.

For earlier issues refer to Southern Rhodesia. For later issues refer to Malawi, Zambia, Rhodesia and Zimbabwe.

RULERS:
British to 1970

MONETARY SYSTEM:
1 Shilling = 12 Pence
1 Pound = 20 Shillings to 1970

BRITISH INFLUENCE

BANK OF RHODESIA AND NYASALAND

1956 ISSUE
#20-23 portr. Qn. Elizabeth II at r. Various date and sign. varieties. Wmk: C. Rhodes. Printer: BWC.

20	10 SHILLINGS	VG	VF	UNC
	1956-61. Reddish brown on m/c unpt. River scene on back.			
	a. Sign. Graffery-Smith. 3.4.1956-6.5.1960.	10.00	50.00	250.00
	b. Sign. H. J. Richards. 30.12.1960-30.1.1961.	8.00	40.00	200.00

21	1 POUND	VG	VF	UNC
	1956-61. Green on m/c unpt. Zimbabwe ruins at ctr. on back.			
	a. Sign. Graffery-Smith. 22.5.1956-17.6.1960.	7.50	50.00	350.00
	b. Sign. H. J. Richards. 23.11.1960-23.1.1961.	6.00	47.50	325.00
22	5 POUNDS			
	1956-61. Blue on m/c unpt. Victoria Falls on back.			
	a. Sign. Graffery-Smith. 3.4.1956-19.6.1959.	15.00	90.00	450.00
	b. Sign. H. J. Richards. 30.1.1961; 1.2.1961.	13.50	85.00	400.00
23	10 POUNDS			
	1956-61. Brown on m/c unpt. Back gray-green; elephants at ctr.			
	a. Sign. Graffery-Smith. 3.4.1956; 15.4.1957; 3.7.1959; 3.6.1960.	150.00	500.00	1750.
	b. Sign. H. J. Richards. 1.2.1961.	125.00	450.00	1500.

ROMANIA

The Republic of Romania (formerly the Socialist Republic of Romania), a Balkan country in southeast Europe, has an area of 91,699 sq. mi. (237,500 sq. km.) and a population of 23.2 million. Capital: Bucharest. The economy is predominantly agricultural; heavy industry and oil have become increasingly important since 1959. Machinery, foodstuffs, raw minerals and petroleum products are exported.

Romania, the ancient Roman province of Dacia, endured wave after wave of barbarian conquest, until the late 13th century. The Vlach tribes of south of the Danube river moved north, mixing in with the Slavs and Tatars developing the two principalities of Walachia and Moldavia.

The early years of the principality of Walachia were involved in struggles with Hungary. Soon afterwards they found themselves at war with the Turks. Final capitulation to Turkey came in 1417.

Moldavia first appeared as an independent state in 1349. Polish overlordship came about at the end of the 14th century. Stephen the Great (1457-1504) was a champion of Christendom against the Turks. When Peter Rares (1527-38 and 1541-46) came to the throne, he allied himself with the Turks as he made war on the imperial forces in Transylvania and Poland. Later he allied himself with the emperor against Poland and the sultan, but was defeated and deposed in 1538. In 1541 he returned to the throne with Turkish help.

The treaty of Kuchuk Kainarji, which ended the Russo-Turkish war in 1774, resulted in Moldavia losing its northern tip, Bukovina, to Austria. As a result of Russia's continuing interests in the area and the peace of Bucharest in 1812, southeastern Moldavia, known as Bessarabia, ceded.

Peasant uprisings in 1848 were put down by the Turks and a Russo-Turkish military intervention returned things back to normal. Russian troops did not evacuate the principalities until 1851 and during the Crimean War were occupied in turn by Russia and Austria. The treaty of Paris (1856) placed the principalities with their existing privileges, ending the Russian protectorate.

Union of the principalities was voted for unanimously in 1848 and the two assemblies elected a single Prince in the person of Alexander Cuza on Jan. 17, 1859, accomplishing the *defacto* union of Romania. The prince through lack of agrarian reform was compelled to abdicate in Feb. 1866, and was succeeded by Prince Carol I who later became king in 1881. Later, in 1888 it changed to a constitutional monarchy with a bicameral legislation in 1888.

The First Balkan War in 1912 gave birth to the claim for Silistra, awarded in May 1917. The intervention and deployment of Romanian troops into Bulgaria in the Second Balkan War of 1913 resulted in the acquisition of southern Dobruja.

Crossing into Transylvania, Romania declared war on Austro-Hungary on Aug. 22, 1916. They were soon expelled and the Central Powers occupied Bucharest by Dec. 6, 1916. The Treaty of Bucharest was signed on May 7, 1918, and the Central Powers disorganized the finance of the Kingdom, ensuring financial ruin. On Nov. 9, 1918, when the defeat of the Central Powers was eminent, war was declared again. The king re-entered Bucharest on Nov. 30, 1918, after the German troops had evacuated Romania under the terms of the Armistice. Bessarabia was incorporated along with Transylvania and the old frontier borders were recognized by the treaties of St. Germain and Trianon.

The government was reorganized along Fascist lines in 1940, and in the following year Romania joined Germany's attack on the Soviet Union. The country was subsequently occupied by the Russian Army which actively supported the program and goals of the Romanian Communists. On Nov. 19, 1946, a Communist-dominated government was installed and prompted the abdication of King Michael. Romania became a "People's Republic" on Dec. 30, 1947. With the accession of N. Ceausescu to power in 1965, a repressive and impoverished domestic scene worsened. A popular protest to the eviction of a protestant pastor in 1989 escalated into a massive demonstration against the government which spread rapidly to other areas. An official rally in Bucharest turned also against the government. A state of emergency was declared but armed forces supported the uprising. Later the Ceausescus were captured and executed on Dec. 25, 1989. A provisional government was set up and after protests and riots, it fell, being replaced by an interim government.

* * * This section has been reordered and renumbered. * * *

RULERS:
Carol I (as Prince), 1866-81 (as King) 1881-1914
Ferdinand I, 1914-1927
Mihai I, 1927-1930
Carol II, 1930-1940
Mihai I, 1940-1947

MONETARY SYSTEM:
1 Leu = 100 Bani

DATING
as found on certain issues

19	- VII	- 31	- 34
Century	Month	Day	Year

KINGDOM
BILET HYPOTHECAR
STATE NOTES OF THE PRINCIPALITY
1877 ISSUE
#1-4 Wmk: Trajan.
#5 and 6 wmk: Minerva and Trajan.

			Good	Fine	XF
1	**5 Lei** 12.6.1877. Blue. 2 allegorical women at lower ctr., children at l. and r. Arms at lower ctr. on back.				
	a. Issued note.		100.00	250.00	600.00
	s. Specimen.		—	Rare	

			Good	Fine	XF
2	**10 Lei** 12.6.1877. Blue. Similar to #1. Eagle w/outstretched wings at top ctr.				
	a. Issued note.		150.00	350.00	850.00
	s. Specimen.		—	Rare	
3	**20 Lei** 12.6.1877. Blue. 2 men and a woman at l., river and bridge scene at lower ctr., arms at r. 2 farm wives w/poles at r. on back.				
	a. Issued note.		175.00	500.00	—
	s. Specimen.		—	Rare	—

			Good	Fine	XF
4	**50 Lei** 12.6.1877. Blue. Similar to #3. Eagle added as on #2.				
	a. Issued note.		250.00	800.00	—
	s. Specimen.		—	Rare	—

			Good	Fine	XF
5	**100 Lei** 12.6.1877. Blue. Woman w/children at lower ctr. Allegorical figures, arms and eagle at ctr. on back.				
	a. Issued note.		300.00	1000.	—
	s. Specimen.		—	Rare	—

6	500 LEI	GOOD	FINE	XF
	12.6.1877. Blue. 2 women and girl at l., arms at lower ctr., 3 women w/boy at r. Standing figure at l. and r., bust at ctr. on back.			
	a. Issued note.	400.00	1250.	—
	s. Specimen.	—	Rare	—

BANCA NATIONALA A ROMANIEI

1880 PROVISIONAL ISSUE
#6A-6F ovpt. of new bank name on Bilet Hypothecar notes dates 12.8.1877.

7 (6A)	5 LEI	GOOD	FINE	XF
	9.9.1880 (-old date 12.6.1867). Ovpt. on #1. (Not Issued).	—	—	—
8 (6B)	10 LEI			
	9.9.1880 (-old date 12.6.1867). Ovpt. on #2.			

9 (6C)	20 LEI	GOOD	FINE	XF
	9.9.1880 (-old date 12.6.1867). Ovpt. on #3.	—	—	—
10 (6D)	50 LEI			
	9.9.1880 (-old date 12.6.1867). Ovpt. on #4.			
	a. Issued note.	—	—	—
	b. Cancelled note hand-stamped and perforated: ANULAT.	—	—	—
11 (6E)	100 LEI			
	9.9.1880 (-old date 12.6.1867). Ovpt. on #5.			
	a. Issued note.	—	—	—
	b. Cancelled note hand-stamped and perforated: ANULAT.	—	—	—
12 (6F)	500 LEI			
	9.9.1880 (-old date 12.6.1867). Ovpt. on #6.	—	—	—

1881 ISSUE

13 (29)	20 LEI	VG	VF	UNC
	19.1.1881-31.8.1895. Blue. 2 boys at ctr., boy at r. w/staff of mercury. 7 sign. varieties.	100.00	300.00	—

14 (33)	100 LEI	VG	VF	UNC
	28.2.1881-11.11.1907. Blue. 2 little children on upper l. and r.; eagle at top ctr. 9 sign. varieties.	20.00	90.00	200.00
15 (46)	1000 LEI			
	1881-1906. Blue. Woman w/sickle at l., woman w/oar at r. Round medallion w/bust of Trajan at upper ctr. on back. Sign. varieties.			
	a. 28.2.1881-1.6.1895.	—	Rare	
	b. 19.9.1902-23.3.1906.	140.00	325.00	—

1896 ISSUE

16 (30)	20 LEI	VG	VF	UNC
	14.3.1896-28.8.1908. Blue. Woman w/6 children at ctr. 3 sign. varieties.	40.00	100.00	300.00

1909-16 ISSUE

17 (21)	1 LEU	VG	VF	UNC
	12.3.1915; 27.3.1916. Violet-blue on pale pink unpt. (Unpt. usually barely visible; notes thus appear to be blue). Columns at l., woman at r. 3 signs. Wolf w/Romulus and Remus on back.	.50	2.00	7.50

18 (24)	2 LEI	VG	VF	UNC
	12.3.1915. Violet-blue on pink unpt. (see #21). Woman at l., Eagle w/cross in its mouth at r. Soldier w/sword at l., soldier w/bugle at r. on back. 3 sign., 2 sign. varieties.	1.00	3.00	10.00

19 (27)	5 LEI	VG	VF	UNC
	31.7.1914-22.11.1928. Violet. Farmer's wife w/distaff at l., arms at r. Woman and child picking apples at ctr. on back. Value numerals in violet. Wmk: Heads of Trajan and Minerva. 3 sign., w/6 sign. varieties.			
	a. Issued note.	1.00	3.00	12.50
	s. Specimen. 25.3.1920.	—	—	30.00

20 **20 Lei**
(31) 26.2.1909-31.1.1929. Bue-violet. Girl w/fruit at l., boy w/oar at r. Flying eagle w/cross and arms flying over river on back. Wmk: Minerva and Trajan. 12 sign. varieties.

	VG	VF	UNC
	2.00	6.00	30.00

21 **100 Lei**
(34) 14.1.1910-31.1.1929. Violet-blue. Woman seated wearing national costume at l. Wmk: head of Trajan and Minerva. 9 sign. varieties.

	VG	VF	UNC
	5.00	17.50	45.00

22 **500 Lei**
(40) 11.2.1916-12.2.1920. Violet-blue. Woman w/boy at l., seated farmer's wife at r. 2 farm wives on back. 9 sign. varieties.

	VG	VF	UNC
a. Issued note.	10.00	30.00	100.00
s. As a. specimen.	—	—	200.00

23 **1000 Lei**
(46A) 20.5.1910-22.10.1931. Woman w/sickle at l., woman w/oar at r. Round medallion blank on back.

a. Issued note.	100.00	200.00	400.00
s. Specimen. 31.1.1929.	—		

1917 ISSUE

24 **5 Lei**
(28) 16.2.1917. Violet-brown. Like #19. Numerals of value on back in yellow. Wmk: Lt. and dk. half-spheres.

	VG	VF	UNC
a. 133 x 79mm.	2.00	6.00	25.00
b. 139 x 87mm.	2.00	6.00	25.00

25 **100 Lei**
(35) 16.2.1917. Violet. Like #21. Wmk: Lt. and dk. half-spheres.

a. Issued note.	10.00	30.00	100.00
b. Specimen w/o date, sign. or serial #.	—	—	35.00

1920 ISSUE

26 **1 Leu**
(22) 17.7.1920. Violet-blue on lt. pink unpt. Columns at l., woman at r. Wolf w/Romulus and Remus and lg. date on back.

	VG	VF	UNC
a. Issued note.	.75	3.00	10.00
s. Specimen w/o sign., series or serial #.	—	—	25.00

27 **2 Lei**
(25) 17.7.1920. Blue-black on pale pink. Woman at l. Eagle w/cross in its mouth at r. Soldier w/sword at l., soldier w/bugle at r. on back. Large date on gray back.

	VG	VF	UNC
a. Issued note.	.75	2.50	8.50
s. As a. w/red ovpt: *SPECIMEN.*	—		30.00

1924 ISSUE

28 **500 Lei**
(41) 12.6.1924. M/c. Farmer's wife w/distaff at l., woman w/infant at r. 3 sign. varaieties.

	VG	VF	UNC
	10.00	30.00	100.00

1925-29 ISSUE

29 **5 Lei**
(27A) 19.9.1929. Farmer's wife w/distaff at l., arms at r. Woman and child picking apples at ctr. on back. Wmk: Heads of Trajan and Minerva. 2. sign.

	VG	VF	UNC
	1.00	3.50	15.00

30 **20 Lei**
(32) 19.9.1929. Blue-violet. Girl w/fruit at l., boy w/oar at r. Flying eagle w/cross and arms flying over river on back. Wmk: Heads of Minerva and Trajan. 2 sign.

	2.00	6.00	30.00

31 **100 Lei**
(36) 19.9.1929. Violet. Woman seated wearing national costume at l. Wmk: Heads of Trajan and Minerva. 2 sign.

	VG	VF	UNC
	6.00	25.00	65.00

32 **500 Lei**
(42) 1.10.1925-27.1.1938. M/c. Farmer's wife w/distaff at l. woman w/infant at r. 2 sign. 6 sign. varieities.

	VG	VF	UNC
	5.00	15.00	35.00

1930-33 ISSUE

33 **100 LEI**
(37)   13.5.1930-13.5.1932. Olive-brown. Woman seated wearing national costume at l. Wmk: Heads of Trajan and Minerva. 3 sign. varieties.

	VG	VF	UNC
	5.00	20.00	45.00

34 **1000 LEI**
(47)   15.6.1933. Blue and m/c. Woman at lower l. and man at lower r. Mercury at l. and r. on back.

	VG	VF	UNC
a. Issued note.	100.00	200.00	400.00
s. Specimen.	—	—	—

35 **5000 LEI**
(55A)   31.3.1931. Dk. blue. Corwned *M1* in cross design on upper l. wmk. area., Danube view below, arms at ctr. Portr. Kg. Carol II at r. Medieval scene on back. Printer: BWC. Specimen only.

	VG	VF	UNC
	—	—	500.00

1934 ISSUE

36 **500 LEI**
(43)   31.7.1934. Dk. green on m/c unpt. Portr. Kg. Carol II at l. Villa w/trees on back. Printer: BWC.

	VG	VF	UNC
a. Issued note.	6.00	17.50	45.00
s. Specimen w/o sign., series or serial #.	—	—	60.00

37 **1000 LEI**
(48)   15.3.1934. Brown and m/c. Portr. Kg. Carol II at l. Complex design w/2 women and child at r. on back.

	VG	VF	UNC
a. Issued note.	50.00	100.00	200.00
s. Specimen.	—	—	200.00

1936-39 ISSUES

38 **1 LEU**
(23)   28.10.1937; 21.12.1938. Lilac-brown. Columns at l. woman at r. Date on face. 2 sign., 2 sign. varieties.

	VG	VF	UNC
a. Issued note.	1.00	5.00	20.00
s. Specimen w/o sign., series or serial #. 28.10.1937.	—	—	30.00

39 **2 LEI**
(26)   1937-40. Lilac-brown. Woman at l. Eagle w/cross in its mouth at r. Soldier w/sword at l., soldier w/bugle at r. on back. 2 sign., 2 sign. varieties.

	VG	VF	UNC
a. Lilac-brown. 28.10.1937; 21.12.1938.	1.00	5.00	20.00
b. Deep purple on red unpt. 1.11.1940.	—	—	—
s. As a. w/red ovpt: *SPECIMEN*. 21.12.1938.	—	—	40.00

40 **5 LEI**
(28A)   21.12.1938. Farmer's wife w/distaff at l., arms at r. Woman and child picking apples at ctr. on back. Wmk: *BNR*. Specimen.

	VG	VF	UNC
	—	—	225.00

41 **20 LEI**
(32A)   28.4.1939. Green. Girl w/fruit at l., boy w/oar at r. Flying eagle w/cross and arms over river on back. Denomination stated *DOUA ZECI LEI*. Wmk: *BNR*. Specimen.

	VG	VF	UNC
	—	—	275.00

42 **500 LEI**
(44)   30.4.1936; 26.5.1939; 1.11.1940. Gray-blue on m/c unpt. Similar to #36.

	VG	VF	UNC
a. Issued note.	2.50	6.00	25.00
s. Specimen. 30.4.1936.	—	—	60.00

43 **500 LEI**
(44A) 30.1.1936; 30.4.1936; 26.5.1939; 1.9.1940. Gray. Like #42, but vignette ovpt. of 2 farm wives at l. on back.

	VG	VF	UNC
	5.00	12.50	35.00

44 **1000 LEI**
(49) 25.6.1936. Brown and green. 2 farm wives w/3 children each at l. and r. 2 farm wives at l. and r. on back. Wmk: Kg. Carol II w/wreath.

	VG	VF	UNC
a. Issued note.	2.50	6.00	20.00
s. Specimen.	—	—	50.00

45 **1000 LEI**
(50) 25.6.1936. Brown and green. Like #44, but w/vignette ovpt: 2 farm wives.

	VG	VF	UNC
	25.00	50.00	100.00

46 **1000 LEI**
(51) 19.12.1938-1.11.1940. Brown and green. Like #44, but wmk: Kg. Carol II w/o wreath.

	VG	VF	UNC
	1.00	3.00	10.00

47 **1000 LEI**
(52) 21.12.1938; 28.4.1939; 1.11.1940. Brown and green. Like #46, but w/vignette ovpt: 2 farm wives

	VG	VF	UNC
	25.00	50.00	100.00

1940 COMMEMORATIVE ISSUE

48 **5000 LEI**
(56) 6.9.1940 (-old date 31.1.1931). Dk. blue. Crowned *MI* monogram in cross design on wmk. area at upper l., Danube landscape below, arms at ctr. Portr. Kg. Carol II at r. *6 SEPTEMVRIE 1940* text in plate over Kg. Carol. Medieval scene on back. Printer: BWC.

	VG	VF	UNC
	25.00	50.00	100.00

1940 ISSUE

49 **100 LEI**
(38) 19.2.1940. Dk. brown. Like #31. Wmk: Heads of Trajan and Minerva.

	VG	VF	UNC
	5.00	20.00	45.00

50 **100 LEI**
(39) 19.2.1940; 1.11.1940. Dk. brown. Like #49. Wmk: *BNR*. 2 sign. varieties.

	VG	VF	UNC
a. Issued note.	5.00	17.50	45.00
s. Specimen.	—	—	100.00

51 **500 LEI**
(45) 1.11.1940-26.1.1943. Brown on m/c unpt. 2 farm wives at l. Villa w/trees on back. Wmk: *BNR* horizontal or vertical. 2 sign. varieties.

	VG	VF	UNC
a. Issued note.	.75	2.00	6.00
s. Specimen. 20.4.1942.	—	—	50.00

1941 ISSUE

52 **1000 LEI**
(53) 10.9.1941-20.3.1945. Blue and green on pink unpt. Similar to #44, but wmk: Head of Trajan. Value *UNA MIE LEI* at lower ctr. 3 sign. varieties.

	VG	VF	UNC
	.40	1.00	5.00

53
(54)
2000 LEI
18.11.1941; 10.10.1944. Brown, violet and yellow. Farm wife w/distaff at l., woman w/infant at r. 2 farm wives at l., oil refinery at r. on back. Wmk: Head of Trajan. 2 sign. varieties.

	VG	VF	UNC
	.75	3.00	15.00

1943 ISSUE

54
(55)
2000 LEI
23.3.1943-20.3.1945. Brown, violet and yellow. Like #53. Wmk: *BNR* in shield. 2 sign. varieties.

	VG	VF	UNC
a. Issued note.	.50	2.50	10.00
s. Specimen. 23.3.1943.	—	—	40.00

55
(57)
5000 LEI
28.9.1943; 2.5.1944; 22.8.1944. Lt. blue on m/c unpt. 2 male heads of Trajan and Decebal at upper l., arms at ctr. Wmk: Portr. of Trajan. Man and oxen looking towards city on back. 2 sign. varieties.

	VG	VF	UNC
	.50	1.50	5.00

1944 ISSUE

56
(58)
5000 LEI
10.10.1944-20.12.1945. Lt. blue. Like #55. Wmk: *BNR* horizontal or vertical. 2 sign. varieties.

	VG	VF	UNC
a. Issued note.	.50	1.50	5.00
s. Specimen. 10.10.1944.	—	—	40.00

1945 ISSUE

57
(59)
10,000 LEI
18.5.1945; 20.12.1945; 28.5.1946. Brown and red. Similar to #44. 2 sign. varieties.

	VG	VF	UNC
a. Issued note.	.75	2.00	8.00
s. Specimen. 18.5.1945.	—	—	50.00

58
(60)
100,000 LEI
7.8.1945-8.5.1947. Green and gray. Woman w/boy at l., farm wife at r. 2 farm wives on back. Wmk: *BNR*.

	VG	VF	UNC
a. Issued note.	.50	1.50	5.00
s. Specimen. 7.8.1945.	—	—	30.00

1947 ISSUE

59
(61)
100,000 LEI
25.1.1947. Lilac, brown and m/c. Trajan and Decebal at ctr. 2 farmers at l., arms at ctr. 2 women and child at r. on back.

	VG	VF	UNC
a. Issued note.	.75	3.00	12.00
s. Specimen.	—	—	80.00

60
(62)
1,000,000 LEI
16.4.1947. Blue-green and gray-brown on lt. tan and blue unpt. Like #61.

	VG	VF	UNC
a. Issued note.	2.00	5.00	15.00
s. Specimen.	—	—	80.00

61
(63)
5,000,000 LEI
25.6.1947. Olive and brown on m/c unpt. Women and children at l. and r., wolf w/Romulus and Remus at ctr. 2 farm wives at l. and r. on back.

	VG	VF	UNC
a. White wmk. paper.	10.00	25.00	50.00
b. Ruled paper.	5.00	15.00	40.00
s. Specimen.	—	—	100.00

1947 FIRST ISSUE
#62-64 issued after 1947 currency reform.

			VG	VF	UNC
62 (73)	**100 LEI** 25.6.1947. Dk. brown on lt. brown unpt. 3 men w/torch, ears of corn and hammer at r.		2.00	6.00	15.00

			VG	VF	UNC
63 (74)	**500 LEI** 25.6.1947. Brown. Woman at cttr. Farmer and wheat on back.				
	a. Issued note.		8.00	17.50	40.00
	s. Specimen.		—	—	50.00
64 (75)	**1000 LEI** 25.6.1947. Blue on m/c unpt. T. Vladimirescu at ctr. Arms at ctr. on back.				
	a. Issued note.		10.00	20.00	50.00
	s. Specimen.		—	—	150.00

1947 SECOND ISSUE

			VG	VF	UNC
65 (76)	**100 LEI** 27.8.1947. Brown. Like #73.		.75	2.50	10.00
66 (77)	**1000 LEI** 30.9.1947. Blue. Like #75.		8.00	25.00	60.00

1947 THIRD ISSUE

			VG	VF	UNC
67 (78)	**100 LEI** 5.12.1947. Brown. Like #73.				
	a. Issued note.		1.00	5.00	15.00
	s. Specimen.		—	—	30.00
68 (79)	**1000 LEI** 5.12.1947. Blue. Like #75.		7.00	22.50	50.00

MINISTERUL FINANTELOR
MINISTRY OF FINANCE

1917 EMERGENCY WW I ISSUE
#69-71 Kg. Ferdinand I at ctr. Crowned supported arms on back. Small rectangular notes.

#69 (#7)   #70 (#8)   #71 (#9)

			VG	VF	UNC
69 (7)	**10 BANI** 1917. Dk. green on olive ovpt.		.75	2.50	5.00
70 (8)	**25 BANI** 1917. Dk. brown on ochre ovpt.		1.00	3.00	8.00
71 (9)	**50 BANI** 1917. Dk. blue on lt. brown on peach unpt.		1.00	4.00	12.00

1918 ND ISSUE
#72-75 portr. Kg. Ferdinand I over crowned supported arms at ctr. *MF* monograms at l. and r. Printer ABNC. (Not issued.)

			VG	VF	UNC
72 (9A)	**10 LEI** ND (ca.1918). Black. Proof, punched hole cancelled.		—	—	250.00
73 (9B)	**50 LEI** ND (ca.1918). Proof.				

			VG	VF	UNC
74 (9C)	**200 LEI** ND (ca.1920). Proof, punched hole cancelled.		—	—	—

			VG	VF	UNC
75 (9D)	**2000 LEI** ND (ca.1920). Proof, punched hole cancelled. *MF* monograms at l. and r.		—	—	—

1945; 1947 ND ISSUE
1 New Leu = 20,000 Old Lei

			VG	VF	UNC
76 (64)	**20 LEI** 1945. Brown on lt. brown unpt. Portr. Kg. Michael at ctr.		.25	.75	2.50
77 (66)	**20 LEI** ND (1947). Dk. brown on green unpt. Trajan and Decebal at at upper l. Woman sitting on woodpile on back. Wmk: *M. F.* Sign. title: *DIRECTORUL GENERAL AL BUGETULUI.* 2 sign. varieties.		.75	3.00	12.50

			VG	VF	UNC
78 (65)	**100 LEI** 1945. Blue on lt. blue unpt. Like #64.		.25	.50	1.50

PEOPLES REPUBLIC

MINISTERUL FINANTELOR

MINISTRY OF FINANCE

1948 ND ISSUE

			VG	VF	UNC
79 (67)	**20 LEI** ND (1948). Brown and green. Like #78. Wmk: *RPR*.		.75	3.00	12.50

			VG	VF	UNC
80 (68)	**20 LEI** ND (1948). Dk. brown on green unpt. Like #72. Lower sign. title: *DIRECTORUL BUGETULUI*.		1.00	4.00	15.00

1952 ISSUE

			VG	VF	UNC
81 (70)	**1 LEU** 1952. Brown on lt. orange unpt. Arms at ctr. on back.				
	a.	Red series and serial #.	.50	1.50	5.00
	b.	Blue series and serial #.	.25	.75	2.00
	s.	As b. Specimen.	—	—	15.00

			VG	VF	UNC
82 (71)	**3 LEI** 1952. Violet-brown on greenish gray unpt. Arms at ctr. on back.				
	a.	Red series and serial #.	.75	2.00	8.00
	b.	Blue series and serial #.	.50	1.25	3.00
	s.	As b. Specimen.	—	—	15.00

			VG	VF	UNC
83 (72)	**5 LEI** 1952. Blue on lt. brown and lt. orange unpt. Girl at l., arms at upper r. Dam construction on back.				
	a.	Red series and serial #.	.75	3.00	10.00
	b.	Blue series and serial #.	.50	1.50	3.50
	s.	As b. Specimen.	—	—	15.00

			VG	VF	UNC
84 (69)	**20 LEI** 15.6.1950. Dk. green on gray unpt. Girl's head at r. Arms at ctr. on back.				
	a.	Issued note.	.50	1.50	4.00
	s.	Specimen.	—	—	30.00

BANCA NATIONALA A ROMANIEI

ROMANIAN NATIONAL BANK

1948 ISSUE

			VG	VF	UNC
85 (80)	**1000 LEI** 18.6.1948. Blue. Like #75.				
	a.	Issued note.	2.00	5.00	17.50
	s.	Specimen.	—	—	150.00

BANCA REPUBLICII POPULARE ROMANE - BANCA DE STAT

1949-52 ISSUE

			VG	VF	UNC
86 (81)	**500 LEI** 15.10.1949. Brown. 3 men at l. ctr.				
	a.	Issued note.	4.00	12.00	35.00
	s.	Specimen.	—	—	50.00

87 (82)	1000 LEI 20.9.1950. Blue and m/c. Balcescu at l. River and mountains on back.	VG 3.00	VF 8.00	UNC 27.50

1952 ISSUE
1 New Leu = 20 Old Lei

88 (83)	10 LEI 1952. Brown on m/c unpt. Worker at l., arms at ctr. r. Rock loaded onto train on back.	VG	VF	UNC
	a. Red serial #.	1.50	4.00	12.00
	b. Blue serial #.	.50	1.50	4.00
	s. As b. Specimen.	—	—	15.00

89 (84)	25 LEI 1952. Brown on violet unpt. T. Vladimirescu at l. Wheat harvesting on back.	VG	VF	UNC
	a. Red serial #.	1.50	5.00	17.00
	b. Blue serial #.	.50	1.50	4.00
	s. As b. Specimen.	—	—	20.00

90 (85)	100 LEI 1952. Blue on lt. blue unpt. N. Balcescu at l., arms at ctr. r. Lg. bldgs. on back.	VG	VF	UNC
	a. Red serial #.	3.00	10.00	25.00
	b. Blue serial #.	1.50	4.00	12.50
	s. As b. Specimen.	—	—	25.00

GERMAN OCCUPATION - WW I
BANCA GENERALA ROMANA

1917 ISSUE
#M1-M8 often found w/numerous different handstamps of military units and Romanian authorities. Such
notes are generally well worn.

M1	25 BANI ND (1917). Olive-brown. Mercury at r.	VG .50	VF 2.00	UNC 7.50

M2	50 BANI ND (1917). Pale blue-gray. Woman at upper l.	VG .75	VF 2.50	UNC 10.00

M3	1 LEU ND (1917). Black text on green unpt. Mercury at l., laureate woman's head at r.	VG 1.00	VF 3.00	UNC 12.00
M4	2 LEI ND (1917). Black text on pale red unpt. Woman at l., Mercury at r.	1.00	4.00	15.00

M5	5 LEI ND (1917). Black text on lilac unpt. Woman at l. and at r. Back blue- gray.	VG 1.50	VF 5.00	UNC 17.50
M6	20 LEI ND (1917). Black text on brown unpt. Woman at l., Mercury at r. on back.	2.00	8.00	30.00
M7	100 LEI ND (1917). Black text on olive and blue unpt. Mercury at l., woman at r. on back.	6.00	15.00	60.00

M8	**1000 Lei**		VG	VF	UNC
	ND (1917). Brown and m/c. Back like #M7.		12.00	30.00	80.00

RUSSIAN OCCUPATION - WW II

COMANDAMENTUL ARMATEI ROSSII

NOTE: For previously listed #M17-M22 see Transdniestra.

1944 ISSUE

#M9 Deleted.

M10	**5 Lei**		VG	VF	UNC
	1944. Blue.		15.00	30.00	70.00

M11	**10 Lei**		VG	VF	UNC
	1944. Brown.		15.00	35.00	80.00
M12	**20 Lei**				
	1944. Blue.		25.00	50.00	100.00
M13	**100 Lei**				
	1944. Brown-olive.		50.00	100.00	200.00

M14	**500 Lei**		VG	VF	UNC
	1944. Brown on blue unpt.		60.00	120.00	240.00
M15	**1000 Lei**				
	1944.		75.00	150.00	300.00

M16	**5000 Lei**		VG	VF	UNC
	1944.		—	Rare	—

REGIONAL

TREASURY

1919 FIRST PROVISIONAL ISSUE

Romania Timbru Special handstamp on the Austrian (for Bukovina) or Hungarian (for Siebenbérgen and Banat) side of Austro-Hungarian bank notes. All issued in 1919.

#R1-R11 handstamp on Austrian side (Bukovina). Also frequently encountered w/additional Hungarian or Yugoslav handstamps (usually of military units).

R1	**10 KRONEN**		GOOD	FINE	XF
(10)	ND (1919 - old date 2.1.1904). Handstamp on Austria #9.		6.00	15.00	30.00

R2	**10 KRONEN**		GOOD	FINE	XF
(11)	ND (1919 - old date 2.1.1915). Handstamp on Austria #19.		4.00	10.00	20.00
R3	**20 KRONEN**				
(12)	ND (1919 - old date 2.1.1907). Handstamp on Austria #10.		60.00	150.00	300.00
R4	**20 KRONEN**				
(13)	ND (1919 - old date 2.1.1913). Handstamp on Austria #13.		6.00	15.00	30.00
R5	**20 KRONEN**				
(14)	ND (1919 - old date 2.1.1913). Handstamp on Austria #14.		2.00	5.00	10.00
R6	**50 KRONEN**				
(15)	ND (1919 - old date 2.1.1902). Handstamp on Austria #6.		60.00	150.00	300.00

R7	**50 KRONEN**		GOOD	FINE	XF
(16)	ND (1919 - old date 2.1.1914). Handstamp on Austria #15.		4.00	10.00	20.00
R8	**100 KRONEN**				
(17)	ND (1919 - old date 2.1.1910). Handstamp on Austria #11.		60.00	150.00	300.00
R9	**100 KRONEN**		GOOD	FINE	XF
(18)	ND (1919 - old date 2.1.1912). Handstamp on Austria #12.		2.00	5.00	10.00
R10	**1000 KRONEN**				
(19)	ND (1919 - old date 2.1.1902). Handstamp on Austria #8.		4.00	10.00	20.00
R11	**10,000 KRONEN**				
(20)	ND (1919 - old date 2.11.1918). Handstamp on Austria #25.		10.00	25.00	50.00

1919 SECOND PROVISIONAL ISSUE

#R12-R22 handstamp on Hungarian side (Siebenbérgen and Banat). Also frequently encountered w/additional Hungarian or Yugoslav handstamps (usually of military units).

R12	**10 KORONA**		GOOD	FINE	XF
(10A)	ND (1919 - old date 2.1.1904). Handstamp on Austria #9.		6.00	15.00	30.00
R13	**10 KORONA**				
(11A)	ND (1919 - old date 2.1.1915). Handstamp on Austria #19.		4.00	10.00	20.00
R14	**20 KORONA**				
(12A)	ND (1919 - old date 2.1.1907). Handstamp on Austria #10.		60.00	150.00	300.00
R15	**20 KORONA**		GOOD	FINE	XF
(13A)	ND (1919 - old date 2.1.1913). Handstamp on Austria #13.		6.00	15.00	30.00
R16	**20 KORONA**				
(14A)	ND (1919 - old date 2.1.1913). Handstamp on Austria #14.		2.00	5.00	10.00

R17	**50 KORONA**		GOOD	FINE	XF
(15A)	ND (1919 - old date 2.1.1902). Handstamp on Austria #6.		60.00	150.00	300.00
R18	**50 KORONA**				
(16A)	ND (1919 - old date 2.1.1914). Handstamp on Austria #15.		4.00	10.00	20.00
R19	**100 KORONA**				
(17A)	ND (1919 - old date 2.1.1910). Handstamp on Austria #11.		60.00	150.00	300.00
R20	**100 KORONA**				
(18A)	ND (1919 - old date 2.1.1912). Handstamp on Austria #12.		2.00	5.00	10.00
R21	**1000 KORONA**				
(19A)	ND (1919 - old date 2.1.1902). Handstamp on Austria #8.		4.00	10.00	20.00
R22	**10,000 KORONA**				
(20A)	ND (1919 - old date 2.11.1918). Handstamp on Austria #25.		10.00	25.00	50.00

RUSSIA (U.S.S.R.)

Russia, (formerly the central power of the Union of Soviet Socialist Republics and now of the Commonwealth of Independent States) which occupies the northern part of Asia and the far eastern part of Europe, in 1991 had an area of 8,649,538 sq. mi. (22,402,200 sq. km.) and a population of *288.7 million. Capital: Moscow. Exports include machinery, iron and steel, crude oil, timber and nonferrous metals.

The first Russian dynasty was founded in Novgorod by the Viking Rurik in 862 AD. Under Yaroslav the Wise (1019-54) the subsequent Kievan state became one of the great commercial and cultural centers of Europe before falling to the Mongols of the Batu Khan, 13th century, who ruled Russia until late in the 15th century when Ivan III threw off the Mongol yoke. The Russian Empire was enlarged, solidified and Westernized during the reigns of Ivan the Terrible, Peter the Great and Catherine the Great, and by 1881 extended to the Pacific and into Central Asia.

Assignats, the first government paper money of the Russian Empire, were introduced in 1769, and gave way to State Credit Notes in 1843. Russia was put on the gold standard in 1897 through the efforts of Finance Minister Count Sergei Witte, and Russia reformed her currency at that time.

All pre-1898 notes were destroyed as they were turned in to the Treasury, accounting for their uniform scarcity today.

The last Russian Czar, Nicholas II (1894-1917), was deposed by the provisional government under Prince Lvov and later Alexander Kerensky during the military defeat in World War I. This government rapidly lost ground to the Bolshevik wing of the Socialist Democratic Labor Party which attained power following the Bolshevik Revolution. During the Russian Civil War (1917-1922) many regional governments, national states and armies in the field were formed which issued their own paper money.

After the victory of the Red armies, these areas became federal republics of the Russian Socialist Federal Soviet Republic (RSFSR), or autonomous soviet republics which united on Dec. 30, 1922, to form the Union of Soviet Socialist Republics (USSR) under the premiership of Lenin.

Beginning with the downfall of the communist government in Poland, other European countries occupied since WW II began democratic elections which spread into Russia itself, leaving the remaining states united in a newly founded Commonwealth of Independent States (C.I.S.) developed after Mikhail Gorbachev resigned on Dec. 25, 1991. The USSR Supreme Soviet voted a formal end to the treaty of union signed in 1992 and dissolved itself.

RULERS:
Catherine II (the Great), 1762-1796
Paul I, 1796-1801
Alexander I, 1801-1825
Nicholas I, 1825-1855
Alexander II, 1855-1881
Alexander III, 1881-1894
Nicholas II, 1894-1917

MONETARY SYSTEM:
1 Ruble = 100 Kopeks
1 Chervonetz = 10 Gold Rubles

NOTE: Certain listings encompassing issues circulated by various bank and regional authorities are contained in Volume 1.

MONETARY UNITS

KOPEK	КОПЕЙКА
KOPEKS	КОПЕЙКИ, КОПЕЕКЪ
RUBLE	РУБЛЬ
RUBLES	РУБЛЯ or РУБЛЕЙ
CHERVONETZ	ЧЕРВОНЕЦ
CHERVONTSA	ЧЕРВОНЦА
CHERVONTSEV	ЧЕРВОНЦЕВ

DENOMINATIONS

1	ОДИН, ОДИНЪ or ОДНА
2	ДВА or ДВЕ
3	ТРИ
5	ПЯТЬ
10	ДЕСЯТЬ
20	ДВАДЦАТЬ
25	ДВАДЦАТЬ ПЯТЬ
30	ТРИДЦАТЬ
40	СОРОК or СОрОКЪ
50	ПЯТЬДЕСЯТ or ПЯТЬДЕСЯТЬ
60	ШЕСТЬДЕСЯТ or ЩЕСТЬДЕСЯТЬ
100	СТО
250	ДВЬСТИ ПЯТЬДЕСЯТЬ or ДВЕСТИ ПЯТЬДЕСЯТ
500	ПЯТЬСОТ or ПЯТЬСОТЪ
1,000	ТЫСЯЧА
5,000	ПЯТЬ ТЫСЯЧ or ТЫСЯЧЪ
10,000	ДЕСЯТЬ ТЫСЯЧ or ТЫСЯЧЪ
15,000	ПЯТНАДЦАТЬ ТЫСЯЧ or ТЫСЯЧЪ
25,000	ДВАДЦАТЬ ПЯТЬ ТЫСЯЧ
50,000	ПЯТЬ ДЕСЯТ ТЫСЯЧ or ПЯТЬДЕСЯТ ТЫСЯЧЪ
100,000	СТО ТЫСЯЧ or ТЫСЯЧЪ
250,000	ДВЬСТИ ПЯТЬДЕСЯТ ТЫСЯЧ
500,000	ПЯТЬ СОТЪ ТЫСЯЧ
1,000,000	ОДИН MILLION or МИЛЛИОНЪ
5,000,000	ПЯТЬ МИЛЛИОНОВ

ISSUE IDENTIFICATION CHART

CZARIST EMPIRE, 1769-1917

DATE	ISSUER	CAT.#
1769-1843	ГОСУДАРСТВЕННОЙ АССИГНАЦИИ	A1-A24
1840	ГОСУДАРСТВЕННЫЙ КОММЕРЧЕСКІЙ БАНКЪ	A25-A30
1841	КРЕДИТНЫЙ БИЛЕТЪ СОХРАН НЫХЪ КАЗЕНЪ И ГОСУДАРСТВЕННАГО БАНКА	A31-32
1843-1895	ГОСУДАРСТВЕННЫЙ КРЕДИТНЫЙ БИЛЕТЪ	A33-A64
1895	ГОСУДАРСТВЕННЫЙ БАНКЪ: ДЕПОЗИТНАЯ МЕТАЛЛИЧЕСКАЯ КВИТАНЦІЯ	A65-83
1898-1915	ГОСУДАРСТВЕННЫЙ КРЕДИТНЫЙ БИЛЕТЪ	1-15
1915-1917	КАЗНАЧЕЙСКІЙ РАЗМѢННЫЙ ЗНАКЪ	24-31

PROVISIONAL GOVERNMENT, 1917-1918

1918	ГОСУДАРСТВЕННЫЙ КРЕДИТНЫЙ БИЛЕТЪ	35-37
	КАЗНАЧЕЙСКІЙ ЗНАКЪ	38-39
1918	ГОСУДАРСТВЕННЫЙ КРЕДИТНЫЙ БИЛЕТЪ	40-42C
	АКЦИОНЕРНОЕ (ОБЩЕСТВО) КОММЕРЧЕСКИХ БАНКОВЪ	43-47

RUSSIAN SOCIALIST FEDERATED SOVIET REPUBLIC, 1918-1924

1918	БИЛЕТЬ ГОСУДАРСТВЕННАГО КАЗНА ЧЕЙСТВА	48-60
	5% КРАТКОСРОЧНОЕ ОБЯЗАТЕЛЬСТВО ГСУДАР. (СТВЕННАГО) КАЗНАЧЕЙСТВА	61-76
	5% ОБЛИГАЦІЯ ЗАЕМЪ СВОБОДЫ	77-80E
	РАСЧЕТНЫЙ ЗНАК	81-85
	ГОСУДАРСТВЕННЫЙ КРЕДИТНЫЙ БИЛЕТЪ	86-97
1919-1921	РАСЧЕТНЫЙ ЗНАК	98-119
1921	КРАТКОСРОЧНОЕ ОБЯЗАТЕЛЬСТВО	120-125
1922	ГОСУДАРСТВЕННЫЙ ДЕНЕЖНЫЙ ЗНАК	126-138
	БАНКОВЫЙ БИЛЕТ	139-145
1922-1923	ГОСУДАРСТВЕННЫЙ ДЕНЕЖНЫЙ ЗНАК	146-171
	ПЛАТЕЖНОЕ ОБЯЗАТЕЛЬСТВО НКФ Р. С.Ф.С.Р.	172-175
1924	ТРАНСПОРТНЫЙ СЕРТИФИКАТ	176-180

UNION OF SOVIET SOCIALIST REPUBLICS, 1924-91

1924-1925	ГОСУДАРСТВЕННЫЙ ДЕНЕЖНЫЙ ЗНАК	181-183, 186-190
1924-1929	ПЛАТЕЖНОЕ ОБЯЗАТЕЛЬСТВО НКФ С.С.С.Р. НАРОДНОГО КОМИССАРІАТА ФИНАНСОВ СОЮЗА С.С.Р.	184-185A 185B-185E
1924-1961	БИЛЕТ ГОСУДАРСТВЕННОТО БАНКА С.С.С.Р.	197-205, 225-236
1928-1961	ГОСУДАРСТВЕННЫЙ КАЗНАЧЕЙСКИЙ БИЛЕТЪ	206-224

EMERGENCY ISSUE

1915-17	Postage Stamp Currency	16-23, 32-34

FRACTIONAL ISSUE

1924	Small Change Notes	191-196

CYRILLIC ALPHABET

А	а	*А*	*а*	**A**	С	с	*Ст*	*ст*	**S**
Б	б	*Б*	*б*	**B**	Т	т	*Т*	*т*	**T**
В	в	*В*	*в*	**V**	У	у	*У*	*у*	**U**
Г	г	*Г*	*г*	**G**	Ф	ф	*Ф*	*ф*	**F**
Д	д	*Д*	*д,g*	**D**	Х	х	*Х*	*х*	**Kh**
Е	е	*Е*	*е*	**ye**	Ц	ц	*Ц*	*ц*	**C**
Ё	ё	*Ё*	*і*	**yo**	Ч	ч	*Ч*	*ч*	**ch**
Ж	ж	*Ж*	*ж*	**zh**	Ш	ш	*Ш*	*ш*	**sh**
З	з	*З*	*з*	**Z**	Щ	щ	*Щ*	*щ*	**shch**
И	и	*И*	*и*	**I**	Ъ *)| ъ *)	–	*ъ*	**'**
Й	й	*И*	*й*	**J**	Ы	ы	–	*ы*	**'**
К	к	*К*	*к.к*	**K**	Ь **)| ь **)	–	*ь*	**'**
Л	л	*Л*	*л*	**L**	Э	э	*Э*	*э*	**E**
М	м	*М*	*м*	**M**	Ю	ю	*Ю*	*ю*	**yu**
Н	н	*Н*	*н*	**N**	Я	я	*Я*	*я*	**ya**
О	о	*О*	*о*	**O**	I	I	*У*	*і*	**I**
П	п	*П*	*п*	**P**	Ѣ	ѣ	*Ж*	*ѣ*	**ye**
Р	р	*Р*	*р*	**R**					

*) "hard", and **) "soft" signs; both soundless. I and Ѣ were dropped in 1918.

NOTE: Some other areas whose notes are listed in this volume had local currencies.

IMPERIAL RUSSIA

ГОСУДАРСТВЕННОЙ АССИГНАЦИ

STATE ASSIGNATS

Large size notes, printed in black on white paper w/text in frame, different year dates. 4 handwritten sign. (many varieties).

1774 ISSUE

#A5, 25 RUBLES, 1777

TYPES

a. In text: САНКТ ПЕТЕРБУОЙ ЪАНКЪ — САНКТ ПЕТЕРБУРГЪ
Saint Petersburg Bank — Saint Petersburg

b. In text: САНКТ ПЕТЕРБУРГОЙ БАНКЪ — МОСКВА
Saint Petersburg Bank — Moscow

c. In text: МОСКОВСКОЙ БАНКЪ — САНКТ ПЕТЕРБУРГЪ
Moscow Bank — Saint Petersburg

c. In text: МОСКОВСКОЙ БАНКЪ — МОСКВА
Moscow Bank — Moscow

1769 ISSUE

			GOOD	FINE	XF
A1	**25 RUBLES** 1769-73. 1 serial # at ctr. above *ASSIGNAT*.		1000.	1800.	—
A2	**50 RUBLES** 1769-73. 1 serial # at ctr. above *ASSIGNAT*.		1400.	2000.	—
A3	**75 RUBLES** 1769-71. 1 serial # at ctr. above *ASSIGNAT*.		2800.	4000.	—
A4	**100 RUBLES** 1769-73. 1 serial # at ctr above *ASSIGNAT*.		2600.	3800.	—
			GOOD	FINE	XF
A5	**25 RUBLES** 1774-84. 3 serial #: at ctr., at lower l. and lower r.		900.00	1600.	—
A6	**50 RUBLES** 1774-84. 3 serial #: at ctr., at lower l. and lower r.		1000.	2000.	—
A7	**100 RUBLES** 1774-84. 3 serial #: at ctr., at lower l. and lower r.		2200.	3400.	—

1785-87 ISSUE

#A8-A12 are smaller size than #A1-A7; text w/o frame, various year dates, 2 handwritten sign. on face and 1 handwritten sign. on back. Many sign. varieties. Also Napoleonic forgeries w/2 or 3 printed sign. exist and some of these have printing errors in 1 or 2 words.

Correct:

ГОСУДАРСТВЕННОЙ ХОДЯЧЕЮ

Error:

ГОСУДАРСТВЕННОЙ ХОЛЯЧЕЮ

NOTE: Some forged notes have Cyrillic Л (L) instead of Д (D) in text.

VALUATIONS: Napoleonic forgeries are generally worth as much as their genuine counterparts.

		GOOD	FINE	XF
A8	**5 RUBLES** 1787-1818. Gray to bluish paper.			
	a. 1787-1801.	400.00	850.00	—
	b. 1803-1818.	250.00	500.00	—

A9	10 RUBLES		GOOD	FINE	XF
	1787-1817. Pink paper.				
	a. 1787-1801.		550.00	950.00	—
	b. 1803-1817.		300.00	550.00	—

A10	25 RUBLES		GOOD	FINE	XF
	1785-1818. White paper. Issued w/clipped corners.				
	a. 1785-1801.		—	Rare	—
	b. 1803-1818.		300.00	650.00	—
A11	50 RUBLES				
	1785-1818. White paper.				
	a. a. 1785-1801.		—	Rare	—
	b. b. 1803-1818.		600.00	1000.	—
A12	100 RUBLES				
	1785-1817. White paper.				
	a. 1785-1801.		—	Rare	—
	b. 1803-1817.		—	Rare	—

1802 ISSUE
#A13-A16 black on white paper.

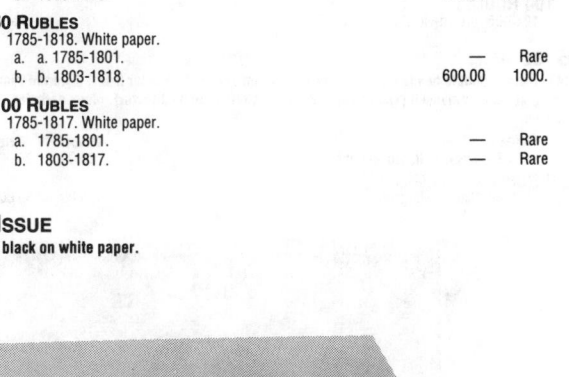

A13	5 RUBLES		GOOD	FINE	XF
	1802. Specimen.		—	—	—
A14	10 RUBLES				
	1802-03. Specimen.		—	—	—
A15	25 RUBLES				
	1802. Specimen.		—	—	—
A16	100 RUBLES				
	1802. Specimen.		—	—	—

1818-22 ISSUES
#A17-A24 crowned double headed eagle w/shield; different year dates; first sign. (director) Hovanskii (printed), second sign. (cashier, handwritten). Many varieties.

A17	5 RUBLES		GOOD	FINE	XF
	1819-43. Blue paper.		200.00	550.00	—
A18	10 RUBLES				
	1819-43. Pink paper.		300.00	650.00	—
A19	20 RUBLES				
	1822. Green paper. Specimen.		—	—	—
A20	20 RUBLES				
	1822. Reddish paper. Specimen.		—	—	—

A21	25 RUBLES		GOOD	FINE	XF
	1818-43. White paper.		450.00	900.00	—
A22	50 RUBLES				
	1818-43. Yellowish paper.		1000.	2000.	—
A23	100 RUBLES				
	1819-43. White paper.		—	Rare	—
A24	200 RUBLES				
	1819-43. Gray paper.		—	Rare	—

ГОСУДАРСТВЕННЫЙ КОММЕРЧЕСКІЙ БАНКЪ

STATE COMMERCIAL BANK

1840-41 ISSUE
#A25-A30 first sign. printed, second and third sign. handwritten. Many sign. varieties.

A25	3 RUBLES		GOOD	FINE	XF
	1840. Green.		700.00	1500.	—
A26	5 RUBLES				
	1840. Blue.		1000.	2000.	—
A27	10 RUBLES				
	1840. Pink.		—	Rare	—
A28	25 RUBLES				
	1840. Black.		—	Rare	—
A29	50 RUBLES				
	1840. Brown.		—	Rare	—
A30	100 RUBLES				
	1841. M/c.		—	Rare	—

КРЕДИТНЫЙ БИЛЕТЪ СОХРАННЫХЪ КАЗЕНЪ И ГОСУДАРСТВЕННЫХЪ ЗАЕМНАГО БАНКА

CUSTODY TREASURY AND STATE LOAN BANK CREDIT NOTES

1841 ISSUE

		Good	Fine	XF
A31	**50 RUBLES** 1841. Black-olive. Yellowish paper.	—	—	—
A32	**50 RUBLES** 1841. Black, red and orange. White paper.	—	—	—

ГОСУДАРСТВЕННЫЙ КРЕДИТНЫЙ БИЛЕТЪ

STATE CREDIT NOTES

1843-56 ISSUE

#A33-A40 crowned double headed eagle in shield within sprays or ornate frame at top ctr. Different year dates on face. First sign. printed (until 1851 Halchinskii); handwritten (1854 Jurev, 1855-1860 Rostov-chev, 1861-1865 Lamanskii), second and third sign. handwritten varieties. From 1851 all sign. were printed.

NOTE: State Credit Notes dated 1843 or 1847 are worth about 30% more than market values indicated.

		Good	Fine	XF
A33	**1 RUBLE** 1843-65. Brown on yellow.	90.00	175.00	450.00

		Good	Fine	XF
A34	**3 RUBLES** 1843-65. Green on lt. green.	150.00	300.00	—
A35	**5 RUBLES** 1843-65. Blue on lt. blue.	200.00	400.00	—
A36	**10 RUBLES** 1843-65. Red on pink unpt.	350.00	850.00	—
A37	**15 RUBLES** 1856. M/c. Specimen.	—	—	—

		Good	Fine	XF
A38	**25 RUBLES** 1843-65. Violet on lilac unpt.	500.00	950.00	—
A39	**50 RUBLES** 1843-65. Black on gray unpt.	—	Rare	—
A40	**100 RUBLES** 1843-65. Brown-violet on brown.	—	Rare	—

1866 ISSUE

#A41-A47 crowned double headed eagle above monogram of Czar Alexander II at l. Different year dates on back; first sign: Lamanskii (1866 as vice-director, 1870-1880 as director). Many varieties of the second sign.

		Good	Fine	XF
A41	**1 RUBLE** 1866-80. Black on lt. brown unpt.	60.00	125.00	250.00
A42	**3 RUBLES** 1866-80. Black on lt. green unpt.	125.00	250.00	—

		Good	Fine	XF
A43	**5 RUBLES** 1866-80. Black on lt. blue unpt. Portr. D. Ivanovich Donskoi at ctr. on back.	175.00	350.00	—
A44	**10 RUBLES** 1866-80. Black on red unpt. M. Feodorovich at ctr. on back.	350.00	650.00	—
A45	**25 RUBLES** 1866-76. Black on lilac unpt. A. Mikhailovich at ctr. on back.	600.00	1250.	—

		GOOD	FINE	XF
A46	**50 RUBLES** 1866. Black on gray unpt. Portr. Peter the Great at ctr. on back.	—	Rare	—
A47	**100 RUBLES** 1866-80. Black on yellow unpt. Catherine the Great at ctr. on back.	—	Rare	—

1882-86 ISSUE

#A48-A53 design like #A41-A47 but w/monogram of Czar Alexander III. Different year dates on back. First sign. Cimsen (until 1886), Zhukovskii (1889-1892), Pleske (1894-1896); second sign. varieties.

		GOOD	FINE	XF
A48	**1 RUBLE** 1882; 1884; 1886. Black on lt. brown unpt.	50.00	100.00	250.00
A49	**3 RUBLES** 1882; 1884; 1886. Black on lt. green unpt.	100.00	225.00	450.00

		GOOD	FINE	XF
A50	**5 RUBLES** 1882; 1884; 1886. Black on lt. blue unpt.	175.00	350.00	—
A51	**10 RUBLES** 1882; 1884; 1886. Black on red unpt.	350.00	650.00	—
A52	**25 RUBLES** 1886. Black on gray-blue and violet unpt.	550.00	950.00	—
A53	**100 RUBLES** 1882-94. Black on yellow unpt.	—	Rare	—

1887-94 ISSUE

#A54-A60 new type of notes w/monogram of Czar Alexander III. Different year dates; first sign. Cimsen (1887), Zhukovskii (1889-1892), E. Pleske (1894). Many varieties of second sign.

NOTE: Only 1 example of #A59 is known uncancelled.

		GOOD	FINE	XF
A54	**1 RUBLE** 1887-94. Crowned arms at l., monogram at r. Back brown.	35.00	100.00	225.00
A55	**3 RUBLES** 1887-94. Crowned arms at l. Back green.	125.00	250.00	475.00
A56	**5 RUBLES** 1887-94. Back blue.	125.00	300.00	650.00
A57	**10 RUBLES** 1887-92. Back red.	225.00	500.00	—

		GOOD	FINE	XF
A58	**10 RUBLES** 1894. Red on m/c unpt. Vertical format.	175.00	350.00	—
A59	**25 RUBLES** 1887. Back violet.	500.00	950.00	—
A60	**25 RUBLES** 1892. Lilac. Like #7.	500.00	950.00	—

1895 ISSUE

#A61-A64 monogram of Nicholas II at l. Sign. E. Pleske. Second sign. varies.

		GOOD	FINE	XF
A61	**1 RUBLE** 1895. Like #A54.	40.00	100.00	250.00
A62	**3 RUBLES** 1895. Similar to #A55.	100.00	200.00	425.00
A63	**5 RUBLES** 1895. Blue and m/c. Like #3.	150.00	350.00	—
A64	**100 RUBLES** 1895, 1896. Like #A53.	—	Rare	—

ГОСУДАРСТВЕННЫЙ БАНКЪ ДЕПОЗИТНАЯ МЕТАЛІЧЕСКАЯ КВИТАНЦІЯ

STATE BANK METAL DEPOSIT RECEIPTS

1876 ISSUE

		VG	VF	UNC
A65	**50 RUBLES = 10 HALF IMPERIALS** 1876. Specimen, perforated: ОБРАЗЕЦЪ.	—	—	—
A66	**100 RUBLES = 10 IMPERIALS** 1876. Specimen.	—	—	—

1886 ISSUE

		VG	VF	UNC
A67	**50 RUBLES** 1886. Specimen, perforated: ОБРАЗЕЦЪ.	—	—	—
A68	**100 RUBLES** 1886. Specimen.	—	—	—
A69	**500 RUBLES** 1886. Specimen.	—	—	—
A70	**1000 RUBLES** 1886. Specimen.	—	—	—

1895 ISSUE

		VG	VF	UNC
A71	**5 RUBLES** 1895. Specimen, perforated: ОБРАЗЕЦЪ.	—	—	700.00
A72	**10 RUBLES** 1895. Specimen.	—	—	700.00
A73	**25 RUBLES** 1895. Specimen.	—	—	700.00
A74	**50 RUBLES** 1895. Specimen.	—	—	700.00
A75	**100 RUBLES** 1895. Specimen.	—	—	700.00
A76	**500 RUBLES** 1895. Specimen.	—	—	700.00

A77	**1000 RUBLES**	**VG**	**VF**	**UNC**
	1895. Specimen.	—	—	700.00

1896 ISSUE

		VG	**VF**	**UNC**
A78	**5 RUBLES**			
	1896. Specimen, perforated:	—	—	—
A79	**10 RUBLES**			
	1896. Specimen.	—	—	—
A80	**30 RUBLES**			
	1896. Specimen.	—	—	—
A81	**100 RUBLES**			
	1896. Specimen.	—	—	—
A82	**500 RUBLES**			
	1896. Specimen.	—	—	—
A83	**1000 RUBLES**			
	1896. Specimen.	—	—	—

ГОСУДАРСТВЕННЫЙ КРЕДИТНЫЙ БИЛЕТЪ (resumed)

STATE CREDIT NOTES

1898 ISSUE

These notes can be dated according to the sign. of the State Bank Director: E. Pleske (1898-1903); S. Timashev (1903-09); A. Konshin (1909-12); I. Shipov (1912-17).

SIGNATURE VARIETIES	
E. Pleske, to 1903	S. Timashev, 1903–1909
A. Konshin, 1909–1912	I. Shipov, 1912–1917

1	**1 RUBLE**	**GOOD**	**FINE**	**XF**
	1898. Blue on red-brown unpt. Russian eagle at l., monogram at r. Full serial #. Back red-brown.			
	a. Sign. Pleske.	2.00	4.00	15.00
	b. Sign. Timashev.	2.00	4.00	15.00
	c. Sign. Konshin.	3.00	7.00	20.00
	d. Sign. Shipov.	.25	.75	4.00

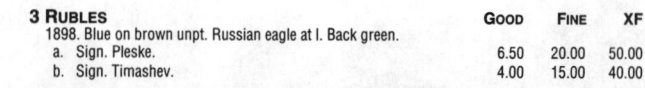

2	**3 RUBLES**	**GOOD**	**FINE**	**XF**
	1898. Blue on brown unpt. Russian eagle at l. Back green.			
	a. Sign. Pleske.	6.50	20.00	50.00
	b. Sign. Timashev.	4.00	15.00	40.00

3	**5 RUBLES**	**GOOD**	**FINE**	**XF**
	1898. Blue on m/c. Allegorical figure of seated woman holding shield and sword.			
	a. Sign. Pleske.	10.00	35.00	100.00
	b. Sign. Timashev.	8.00	25.00	70.00
4	**10 RUBLES**			
	1898. Red on m/c. Allegorical figure of seated woman holding shield and laurel branch.			
	a. Sign. Pleske.	10.00	40.00	140.00
	b. Sign. Timashev.	12.50	55.00	175.00

5	**100 RUBLES**	**GOOD**	**FINE**	**XF**
	1898. Black on tan unpt. Portr. Catherine II at l. Back blue on green and lilac unpt.			
	a. Sign. Pleske.	15.00	60.00	185.00
	b. Sign. Timashev.	15.00	60.00	185.00
	c. Sign. Konshin.	10.00	35.00	100.00
6	**500 RUBLES**			
	1898. Black. Peter I at l.			
	a. Sign. Pleske.	40.00	95.00	325.00
	b. Sign. Timashev.	20.00	50.00	175.00
	c. Sign. Konshin.	15.00	40.00	150.00

1899 ISSUE

7	25 RUBLES	GOOD	FINE	XF
	1899. Lilac. Allegorical figures of Russia standing w/shield, 2 seated children at l. Back blue and maroon; 6 heads at r.			
	a. Sign. Pleske.	20.00	65.00	200.00
	b. Sign. Timashev.	15.00	60.00	175.00

8	50 RUBLES	GOOD	FINE	XF
	1899. Black. Portr. Nicholas I at l. Back green and m/c.			
	a. Sign. Pleske.	20.00	60.00	175.00
	b. Sign. Timashev.	20.00	60.00	175.00
	c. Sign. Konshin.	2.00	6.00	15.00
	d. Sign. Shipov.	1.00	3.00	8.00

1905-12 ISSUE

For #10 w/series # of 2 letters and 3 numerals, rather than a serial # see #35.

NOTE: Some of the Shipov notes were later printed by the Provisional Government and still later by the Soviet Government. Those notes are of lighter colors than the original Imperial printing.

9	3 RUBLES	VG	VF	UNC
	1905. Black on green and m/c.			
	a. Sign. Timashev.	1.00	2.50	6.00
	b. Sign. Konshin.	.25	.50	2.50
	c. Sign. Shipov.	.25	.50	1.00
10	5 RUBLES			
	1909. Blue-black on m/c unpt. Eagle at top ctr. Vertical format. Back dk. gray on m/c unpt. Full serial #.			
	a. Sign. Konshin.	.20	.40	2.25
	b. Sign. Shipov.	.20	.40	1.00

11	10 RUBLES	VG	VF	UNC
	1909. Deep olive-green on green and red unpt. Imperial eagle at top ctr., produce at l. and r. Vertical format.			
	a. Sign. Timashev.	1.00	4.00	12.50
	b. Sign. Konshin.	.20	.40	2.00
	c. Sign. Shipov.	.20	.40	1.00

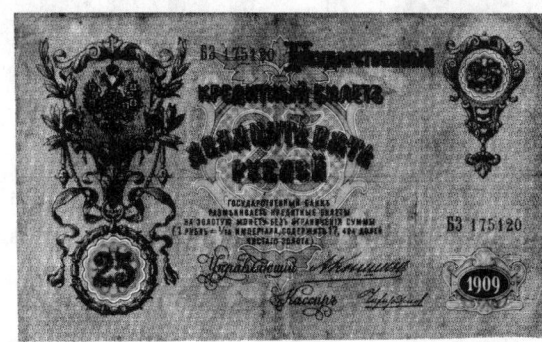

12	25 RUBLES	VG	VF	UNC
	1909. Red and blue. Alexander III at r. on back.			
	a. Sign. Konshin.	.50	1.50	6.00
	b. Sign. Shipov.	.50	1.00	2.00
13	100 RUBLES			
	1910. Lt. brown. Allegorical man w/sword, Catherine II at l. on back. 258 x 121mm.			
	a. Sign. Konshin.	1.00	3.00	7.50
	b. Sign. Shipov.	.50	1.50	3.50
14	500 RUBLES			
	1912. Green and m/c. Peter I at l. on back. 272 x 126mm.			
	a. Sign. Konshin.	2.00	5.00	10.00
	b. Sign. Shipov.	1.00	2.50	6.00

1915 ISSUE

15	1 RUBLE	VG	VF	UNC
	ND(1915 -old date 1898). Blue on brown unpt. Like #1 but control # instead of serial #. 13 sign. varieties. Top sign. Shipov.	.25	.50	1.25

СВЕРНАЯ РОССІЯ

POSTAGE STAMP CURRENCY ISSUE

1915-16 ISSUE

Romanov Tercentenary stamps of 1913 printed on thin card stock; legend and eagle on back. The 1 and 2 Kopek pieces also carry a denomination ovpt. Portraits: #16-17 Peter I, #18-19 Alexander II, #20 Alexander III, #21 Nicholas II, #22 Nicholas I, #23 Alexander I.

NOTE: For postage stamp cuurency issue w/o eagle on back, see #32-34.

16	1 KOPEK	VG	VF	UNC
	ND (1916-17). Brown-orange. Ovpt: 1 on face. (Scott #112).	.75	1.50	3.50
17	1 KOPEK			
	ND (1916-17). Brown-orange. #16 w/o 1 ovpt. (Scott #114).	5.00	17.50	35.00
18	2 KOPEKS			
	ND (1916-17). Yellow-green. Ovpt: 2 on face. (Scott #113).	.75	1.50	3.50
19	2 KOPEKS			
	ND (1916-17). Yellow-green. #18 w/o 2 ovpt., (Scott #115).	10.00	20.00	50.00

20	3 KOPEKS	VG	VF	UNC
	ND (1916-17). Red. (Scott #116).	.50	1.00	2.75

		VG	VF	UNC
21	**10 KOPEKS** ND (1915). Blue. (Scott #105).	.25	.75	2.00
22	**15 KOPEKS** ND (1915). Brown. (Scott #106).	.25	.75	2.00
23	**20 KOPEKS** ND (1915). Green. (Scott #107).	.25	.75	2.00

КАЗНАЧЕЙСКІЙ РАЗМѢННЫЙ ЗНАКЪ
TREASURY SMALL CHANGE NOTES
1915 ISSUE
#24-31 arms at upper ctr. on face; at ctr. on back.

		VG	VF	UNC
24	**1 KOPEK** ND (1915-17). Lt. brown on dull red unpt.	.20	.50	2.00
25	**2 KOPEKS** ND (1915-17). Gray-brown on lt. brown unpt.	.20	.50	2.00
26	**3 KOPEKS** ND (1915-17). Green on lt. green unpt.	.20	.50	2.00
27	**5 KOPEKS** ND (1915-17). Black on lt. blue unpt.	.20	.50	2.00
28	**10 KOPEKS** ND (1915-17). Blue on red-orange unpt. (Not issued).	—	60.00	175.00
29	**15 KOPEKS** ND (1915-17). Red-brown on yellow unpt. (Not issued).	—	60.00	175.00
30	**20 KOPEKS** ND (1915-17). Green on lilac unpt. (Not issued).	—	60.00	175.00

		VG	VF	UNC
31	**50 KOPEKS** ND (1915-17). Blue on yellow unpt.	.20	.50	2.00

PROVISIONAL GOVERNMENT
POSTAGE STAMP CURRENCY
1917 ISSUE

		VG	VF	UNC
32	**1 KOPEK** ND (1917). Brown-orange. Like #16-17 but w/o eagle on back. (Scott #139).	.75	1.50	4.00
33	**2 KOPEKS** ND (1917). Green. Like #18-19 but w/o eagle on back. (Scott #140).	.75	1.50	4.00

		VG	VF	UNC
34	**3 KOPEKS** ND (1917). Red. Like #20 but w/o eagle on back. (Scott #141).	.75	1.50	4.00

ГОСУДАРСТВЕННЫЙ КРЕДИТНЫЙ БИЛЕТЪ
GOVERNMENT CREDIT NOTES
1917 ISSUE

		VG	VF	UNC
35	**5 RUBLES**			
	a. Issued note.	.25	.50	1.50
	x. Error. Series letters "AY" above and "YA" below.	15.00	40.00	100.00

		VG	VF	UNC
36	**250 RUBLES** (4.9.) 1917. Black on lilac unpt. Swastika in unpt. on back. 13 sign. varieties.	.50	1.50	5.00
37	**1000 RUBLES** (9.5.) 1917. Dk. brown on green unpt. Swastika in unpt. on face. Back blue; Duma bldg. at ctr. 5 sign. varieties.	1.00	3.00	7.00

1918; 1919 ISSUE
Notes printed in the United States; most never issued by the Provisional Government.

#38-40C printer: ABNC (w/o imprint).

NOTE: For #38 and 40 issued by other authorities during the Civil War, see Volume 1, #S1196-S1197, S1213-S1214 and S1248-S1249.

		VG	VF	UNC
38 (40)	**25 RUBLES** 1918. Black on blue and m/c unpt. Commerce seated at ctr. Double-headed eagle on back.			
	a. Sign.	2.50	5.00	15.00
	b. W/o sign.	2.00	4.50	10.00
39 (41)	**50 RUBLES** 1919. Proof.	—	Rare	—
40 (42)	**100 RUBLES** 1918. Agriculture seated at ctr. Back brown; like #40.			
	a. Sign.	3.50	7.50	18.50
	b. W/o sign.	2.50	6.00	12.50

40A	250 RUBLES			
(42A)	1919. Proof.	—	Rare	—
40B	500 RUBLES			
(42B)	1919. Proof.	—	Rare	—
40C	1000 RUBLES			
(42C)	1919. Proof.	—	Rare	—

КАЗНАЧЕЙСКІЙ ЗНАКЪ

TREASURY NOTES

1917 ND ISSUE

#41 and 42 so-called "Kerenki," they are frequently also called "Kerensky rubles." They were printed on plates adapted from consular revenue stamps. Eagle at upper ctr.

NOTE: #41 and 42 may also appear in sheets up to 100 subjects.

		VG	VF	UNC
41	**20 RUBLES**			
(38)	ND (4.9.1917). Brown on red-brown unpt.	.20	.40	1.00
42	**40 RUBLES**			
(39)	ND (4.9.1917). Red on green unpt.	.20	.40	1.00

АКЦИОНЕРНОЕ (ОБЩЕСТВО) КОММЕРЧЕСКИХ БАНКОВЪ

UNION OF RUSSIAN STOCK COMMERCE BANKS

1917 (ND) ISSUE

		VG	VF	UNC
43	**25 RUBLES**			
	ND (1917). Green.	75.00	150.00	250.00

		VG	VF	UNC
44	**50 RUBLES**			
	ND (1917). Brown.	100.00	200.00	350.00
45	**100 RUBLES**			
	ND (1917).	100.00	200.00	350.00
46	**100 RUBLES**			
	ND (1917). Govt. check.	175.00	350.00	700.00
47	**500 RUBLES**			
	ND (1917). Govt. check.	175.00	350.00	700.00

Р.С.Ф.С.Р.

РОССИЙСКИЙ СОЦИАЛИСТИЧЕСКИХ ФЕДЕРАТИВНОЙ

СОВЕТСКИХ РЕСПУБЛИК

R.S.F.S.R.-RUSSIAN SOCIALIST FEDERATED SOVIET REPUBLIC

БИЛЕТЪ ГОСУДАРСТВЕННАГО КАЗНАЧЕЙСТВА

STATE TREASURY NOTES

1908-1916 (1918) ISSUES

		VG	VF	UNC
48	**25 RUBLES**			
	1915 (1918). Green on violet unpt.	1.00	2.00	5.00
49	**50 RUBLES**			
	1908 (1918). Brown on green unpt.	4.00	8.00	17.50
50	**50 RUBLES**			
	1912 (1918). Brown on green unpt.	2.50	5.00	10.00
51	**50 RUBLES**			
	1913 (1918). Brown on green unpt.	2.50	5.00	10.00

		VG	VF	UNC
52	**50 RUBLES**			
	1914 (1918). Brown on green unpt.	1.50	3.00	6.00
53	**50 RUBLES**			
	1915 (1918). Brown on green unpt.	2.00	5.00	10.00
54	**100 RUBLES**			
	1908 (1918). Black on pink unpt.	6.00	12.00	25.00
55	**100 RUBLES**			
	1912 (1918). Black on pink unpt.	3.50	7.50	15.00
56	**100 RUBLES**			
	1913 (1918). Black on pink unpt.	3.00	6.00	12.00
57	**100 RUBLES**			
	1914 (1918). Black on pink unpt.	2.00	5.00	10.00
58	**100 RUBLES**			
	1915 (1918). Black on pink unpt.	2.00	4.00	8.00
59	**500 RUBLES**			
	1915 (1918). Black on blue unpt.	1.75	3.50	7.00
60	**500 RUBLES**			
	1916 (1918). Black on lt. blue unpt.	2.00	5.00	10.00

5% КРАТКОСРОЧНОЕ ОБЯЗАТЕЛЪСТВО ГОСУДАР СТВЕННАГОКАЗНАЧЕЙСТВА

STATE TREASURY 5% SHORT-TERM OBLIGATIONS

1916-17 (1918) ISSUE

NOTE: For similar issue w/crownless eagle, see Volume 1-Siberia #S831-S870.

		VG	VF	UNC
61	**1000 RUBLES**			
	1916 (1918). Lilac-brown. (12 month).	4.00	8.00	20.00
62	**1000 RUBLES**			
	1917 (1918). Lilac-brown. (9 month).	4.00	8.00	20.00

		VG	VF	UNC
63	**1000 RUBLES**			
	1917 (1918). Red-violet on brown and orange unpt. (12 month).	2.50	5.00	15.00
64				
	1916-17 (1918). Orange. (12 month).	4.00	8.00	20.00

65	**10,000 RUBLES** 1916 (1918). Red. (12 month).	7.50	15.00	35.00
66	**10,000 RUBLES** 1916 (1918). Red. (9 month).	10.00	20.00	45.00
67	**10,000 RUBLES** 1917 (1918). Red. (12 month).	7.50	15.00	35.00
68	**25,000 RUBLES** 1916 (1918). (12 month).	12.00	25.00	70.00
69	**25,000 RUBLES** 1917-18 (1918). (9 month).	15.00	30.00	75.00
70	**25,000 RUBLES** 1917 (1918). (12 month).	10.00	20.00	60.00
71	**50,000 RUBLES** 1916-17 (1918). (12 month).	15.00	30.00	80.00
72	**50,000 RUBLES** 1917 (1918). (9 month).	20.00	40.00	90.00
73	**100,000 RUBLES** 1916-17 (1918). (12 month).	25.00	50.00	130.00
74	**500,000 RUBLES** 1916-17 (1918). (12 month).	40.00	80.00	200.00
75	**500,000 RUBLES** 1917 (1918). (9 month).	50.00	100.00	225.00
76	**1,000,000 RUBLES** 1916-17 (1918). (12 month).	60.00	125.00	250.00

5% ОБЛИГАЦІЯ ЗАЕМЪ СВОБОДЫ

5% FREEDOM LOANS DEBENTURE BONDS

1917 (1918) ISSUE

#77-80E issue of interest coupons (payment term from 1.1.1908); 1917-20 in the territories of Generals Denikin, Wrangel, Yudenich and Admiral Kolchak; 1917-19 in the Ukrainian Peoples Republic.

		VG	VF	UNC
77	**20 RUBLES** 1917 (1918). Black on yellow unpt.			
	a. W/o ovpt. of value.	1.75	3.50	7.00
	b. W/ovpt. of value.	3.50	7.00	15.00
78	**40 RUBLES** 1917 (1918). Black.			
	a. W/o ovpt. of value.	1.75	3.50	7.00
	b. W/ovpt. of value.	3.50	7.00	15.00
79	**50 RUBLES** 1917 (1918). Black on green unpt.			
	a. W/o ovpt. of value.	1.50	3.00	6.00
	b. W/ovpt. of value.	3.00	6.00	12.00
80	**100 RUBLES** 1917 (1918). Black on brown unpt.			
	a. W/o ovpt. of value.	4.00	8.00	16.00
	b. W/ovpt. of value.	10.00	20.00	40.00
80A	**500 RUBLES** 1917 (1918). Black on blue.			
	a. W/o ovpt. of value.	4.00	8.00	16.00
	b. W/ovpt. of value.	10.00	20.00	40.00
80B	**1000 RUBLES** 1917 (1918). Black on rose. 200 x 155mm.			
	a. W/o ovpt. of value.	7.00	15.00	30.00
	b. W/ovpt. of value.	12.00	25.00	50.00
80C	**5000 RUBLES** 1917 (1918). Black.			
	a. W/o ovpt. of value.	7.00	15.00	30.00
	b. W/ovpt. of value.	15.00	30.00	60.00
80D	**10,000 RUBLES** 1917 (1918). Black.			
	a. W/o ovpt. of value.	—	—	—
	b. W/ovpt. of value.	—	—	—
80E	**25,000 RUBLES** 1917 (1918). Black.			
	a. W/o ovpt. of value.	—	—	—
	b. W/ovpt. of value.	—	—	—

РАСЧЕТНЫЙ ЗНАК

CURRENCY NOTES

1919 ND ISSUE

		VG	VF	UNC
81	**1 RUBLE** ND (1919). Brown. Back m/c.	.25	.50	1.00
82	**2 RUBLES** ND (1919). Dk. brown. Back m/c.	.25	.50	1.00
83	**3 RUBLES** ND (1919). Green. Back m/c. Wmk: Lozenges.	.25	.50	1.00

1921 ND ISSUE

		VG	VF	UNC
84	**3 RUBLES** ND (1921). Green.			
	a. Wmk: Spades.	.50	1.00	2.00
	b. Wmk: Stars.	.25	.50	1.00
85	**5 RUBLES** ND (1921). Dk. blue.			
	a. Wmk: Lozenges.	.35	.75	1.50
	b. Wmk: Spades.	1.75	3.50	7.00
	c. Wmk: Stars.	2.00	4.00	8.00
	d. W/o wmk.	.50	1.00	2.00

ГОСУДАРСТВЕННЫЙ КРЕДИТНЫЙ БИЛЕТЪ

STATE TREASURY NOTES

1918 ISSUE

		VG	VF	UNC
86	**1 RUBLE** 1918. Brown on tan unpt.	.50	1.00	2.50
87	**3 RUBLES** 1918. Green on lt. green unpt.	.50	1.00	2.50
88	**5 RUBLES** 1918. Blue-black on lt. blue unpt.	.50	1.00	2.50
89	**10 RUBLES** 1918. Red-brown on lt. red unpt. Back dk. brown on red-brown unpt.	.50	1.00	2.50
90	**25 RUBLES** 1918. Red-brown on lt. brown unpt. Back dull purple on brown unpt.	.50	1.00	3.00
91	**50 RUBLES** 1918. Dk. brown on lt. brown unpt.	.50	1.00	3.00

		VG	VF	UNC
92	**100 RUBLES** 1918. Brown on lt. red unpt.	.75	1.25	3.50
93	**250 RUBLES** 1918. Green on lt. green unpt.	.75	1.50	4.00
94	**500 RUBLES** 1918. Dull black on pale olive-green. Back dull black on brown and pale olive-green unpt.	1.00	2.00	5.00
95	**1000 RUBLES** 1918. Brown on tan unpt.			
	a. Issued note.	1.75	3.50	8.50
	x. Error. Back top to top w/back inverted.	7.50	20.00	50.00
96	**5000 RUBLES** 1918. Black on blue unpt. Swastika in unpt. Back brown on blue unpt.	1.00	3.00	8.00
97	**10,000 RUBLES** 1918. Dk. brown on brown and red unpt. Swastika in unpt.	1.50	4.00	10.00

РАСЧЕТНЫЙ ЗНАК

CURRENCY NOTES

1919-20 (ND) ISSUE

Because of the multi-language text, these notes are sometimes called "Babylonians".
#101-106 w/10 sign. varieties. Text, in 7 languages, says "Workers of the World, Unite!"

		VG	VF	UNC
98	**15 RUBLES**	.50	1.00	2.50
	ND (1919). Brown on lt. brown unpt. Back m/c; arms at ctr. 8 sign. varieties.			
99	**30 RUBLES**			
	ND (1919). Brown on green unpt. Arms at ctr. on back.			
	a. Issued note.	.50	1.00	3.00
	x. Error. Back top to top w/back inverted.	5.00	15.00	35.00
100	**60 RUBLES**	.50	1.00	3.50
	ND (1919). Blue on gray unpt. Arms at ctr. on back.			

		VG	VF	UNC
101	**100 RUBLES**	.25	.50	2.00
	1919 (1920). Dk. brown or black on lt. brown unpt. Arms at upper l. on back.			
102	**250 RUBLES**			
	1919 (1920). Black on red-brown unpt. Back like #101.			
	a. Wmk: 250.	.25	.50	2.00
	b. Wmk: Stars.	.50	1.50	4.00
103	**500 RUBLES**			
	1919 (1920). Black on olive unpt. Back like #101.			
	a. Wmk: 500.	.50	1.00	3.50
	b. Wmk: Stars.	1.00	2.00	5.00

		VG	VF	UNC
104	**1000 RUBLES**			
	1919 (1920). Black on green unpt.			
	a. Wmk: 1000.	.50	1.25	3.00
	b. Wmk: Sm. stars.	.50	1.50	4.00
	c. Wmk: Lg. stars.	.50	1.50	4.00
	d. Wmk: Lozenges.	.50	1.50	4.00

		VG	VF	UNC
105	**5000 RUBLES**			
	1919 (1920). Blue on yellow and m/c unpt. Arms at ctr. on back.			
	a. Wmk: Broad waves.	.75	2.00	6.00
	b. Wmk: Narrow waves.	.75	2.00	6.00
	c. Wmk: Stars.	1.00	2.50	8.00
106	**10,000 RUBLES**			
	1919 (1920). Red on purple and m/c unpt. Back like #105.			
	a. Wmk: Broad waves.	1.00	2.50	8.00
	b. Wmk: Narrow waves.	1.50	3.00	10.00
	c. Wmk: Stars.	1.50	3.00	10.00

1921 ISSUE

NOTE: #107-112 may be found in various uncut forms, i.e. block of 4, vertical or horizontal pair, etc.
#113-117 w/10 sign. varieties.

		VG	VF	UNC
107	**50 RUBLES**			
	ND (1921). Brown. Arms at ctr.			
	a. Wmk: Lozenges.	.50	1.00	2.00
	b. Wmk: Lg. stars.	.25	.75	1.50
	c. Wmk: Sm. stars.	.50	1.00	2.00
108	**100 RUBLES**	.75	1.25	3.00
	1921. Yellow. Arms at r.			
109	**100 RUBLES**	.50	1.00	2.50
	1921. Orange. Arms at r.			
110	**250 RUBLES**			
	1921. Green. Arms at l.			
	a. Wmk: 250.	.50	1.00	2.50
	b. Wmk: Stars.	1.00	2.00	4.00

		VG	VF	UNC
111	**500 RUBLES**			
	1921. Blue-black. Arms at ctr.			
	a. Wmk: 500.	.50	1.00	3.00
	b. Wmk: Stars.	.50	1.00	3.00
	c. Wmk: Lozenges.	.50	1.00	3.50
112	**1000 RUBLES**			
	1921. Red. Arms at l.			
	a. Wmk: 1000.	.50	1.00	3.00
	b. Wmk: Sm. stars.	.50	1.00	3.00
	c. Wmk: Lg. stars.	.75	1.50	4.00
	d. Wmk: Lozenges.	.50	1.00	3.00

		VG	VF	UNC
113	**5000 RUBLES**			
	1921. Blue on brown unpt. Arms at upper ctr. on back.			
	a. Issued note.	.50	1.50	5.00
	x. Error. Misprint: PROLETAPIER instead of PROLETARIER at upper l. on back.	1.00	3.00	7.00
114	**10,000 RUBLES**			
	1921. Dk. red on lt. red unpt. Arms at ctr. on back.	1.00	4.00	9.00

115   25,000 RUBLES
1921. Red brown.

	VG	VF	UNC
a. Wmk: Lg. stars.	.75	2.00	5.00
b. Wmk: Sm. stars.	1.00	3.00	7.00

116   50,000 RUBLES
1921. Blue-green. Arms at lower ctr.

	VG	VF	UNC
a. Wmk: Lg. stars.	.50	1.25	4.00
b. Wmk: Sm. stars.	1.00	3.00	8.00
c. Wmk: Crosses.	2.00	5.00	12.00

117   100,000 RUBLES
1921. Red. Arms at l. ctr. Wmk: lg. stars.

VG	VF	UNC
.50	1.00	3.00

1921 WAR LOAN CURRENCY NOTE

118   50,000 RUBLES
1921. War loan type.

VG	VF	UNC
6.00	12.00	22.50

119   100,000 RUBLES
1921. War loan type.

VG	VF	UNC
7.00	15.00	27.50

ОБЯЗАТЕЛЬСТВО РОССИЙСКОЙ СОЦИАЛИСТИЧЕСКОЙ ФЕДЕРАТИВНОЙ СОВЕТСКОЙ РЕСПУБЛИКИ

TREASURY SHORT-TERM CERTIFICATES

1921 ISSUE
1 New Ruble = 10,000 Old Rubles.

120   1,000,000 RUBLES
1921. Black on yellowish paper.

VG	VF	UNC
5.00	15.00	60.00

121   5,000,000 RUBLES
1921. Black on bluish paper.

7.50	20.00	80.00

122   10,000,000 RUBLES
1921. Black on bluish paper.

8.50	25.00	100.00

1922 ISSUE

123   5000 RUBLES
1922.

VG	VF	UNC
5.00	12.00	50.00

124   10,000 RUBLES
1922. Black on gray-blue paper.

7.00	17.50	70.00

125   25,000 RUBLES
1922. Specimen.

VG	VF	UNC
20.00	50.00	200.00

ГОСУДАРСТВЕННЫЙ ДЕНЕЖНЫЙ ЗНАК

STATE CURRENCY NOTES

1922 ISSUE
#127-130 arms at upper l.
#128-138 each have 10 sign. varieties.

126   50 KOPEKS
1922. Proof.

VG	VF	UNC
—	—	—

127   1 RUBLE
1922. Brownish orange. 9 sign. varieties.

VG	VF	UNC
.50	1.50	4.50

128   3 RUBLES
1922. Green.

.50	1.50	4.50

129   5 RUBLES
1922. Blue.

.50	1.50	4.50

130   10 RUBLES
1922. Red.

.50	1.50	4.50

131   25 RUBLES
1922. Brown-lilac on yellow and blue unpt.

VG	VF	UNC
.50	2.00	5.00

132   50 RUBLES
1922. Blue on pink unpt.

.50	2.00	5.00

133   100 RUBLES
1922. Red on blue unpt.

1.00	3.00	7.00

134   250 RUBLES
1922. Dk. green on blue and orange unpt.

1.50	4.00	9.00

135   500 RUBLES
1922. Dk. blue on lt. brown unpt.

2.00	5.00	12.00

136   1000 RUBLES
1922. Brown on red, blue and green unpt.

5.00	12.00	30.00

137   5000 RUBLES
1922. Black. Back green and pink.

8.00	22.00	60.00

138   10,000 RUBLES
1922. Red. Back red and green.

12.00	35.00	100.00

БАНКОВЫЙ БИЛЕТ

STATE BANK NOTES

1922 ISSUE
#139-145 have m/c guilloche at l.

NOTE: Trial pieces and proofs of later notes include 1 Chervonetz 1924 (2 diff. designs), and 5 Chervontsev 1924.

139   1 CHERVONETZ
1922. 2 sign. varieties.

VG	VF	UNC
20.00	40.00	120.00

140   2 CHERVONTSA
1922. Specimen.

—	—	600.00

141   3 CHERVONTSA
1922.

35.00	75.00	300.00

142   5 CHERVONTSEV
1922.

35.00	75.00	225.00

1923 FIRST ISSUE
1 "New" Ruble = 1,000,000 "Old" Rubles.
#156-162 text on back in 7 lines.
#157-162 w/10 sign. varieties.

			VG	VF	UNC
143	**10 CHERVONTSEV**		60.00	120.00	250.00
	1922.				
144	**25 CHERVONTSEV**		75.00	150.00	500.00
	1922.				
145	**50 CHERVONTSEV**		—	Rare	—
	1922. Proof.				

1923 ISSUE

			VG	VF	UNC
145A	**1/2 CHERVONETZ**		—	—	—
	1923. Specimen. Brown text.				

ГОСУДАРСТВЕННІЙ ДЕНЕЖНЫЙ ЗНАК (resumed)

STATE CURRENCY NOTES

1922 ISSUE
#146-151 "Promissory note" type. Arms at upper ctr.

			VG	VF	UNC
146	**1 RUBLE**		.75	2.00	5.00
	1922. Brown on gold unpt.				

			VG	VF	UNC
147	**3 RUBLES**		.75	2.00	5.00
	1922. Green.				
148	**5 RUBLES**		1.00	3.00	7.00
	1922. Blue.				
149	**10 RUBLES**		1.00	3.00	7.00
	1922. Red.				
150	**25 RUBLES**		1.50	3.50	8.50
	1922. Purple.				
151	**50 RUBLES**		1.50	3.50	8.50
	1922. Brown on green unpt.				

1923 ISSUE
#152-155 "coin notes" w/o promissory designation. Image of coin shown.

			VG	VF	UNC
152	**10 KOPEKS**		—	—	—
	1923.				
153	**15 KOPEKS**		—	—	—
	1923.				
154	**20 KOPEKS**		—	—	—
	1923.				

			VG	VF	UNC
156	**1 RUBLE**		.50	1.00	3.00
	1923. Brown. 3 sign. varieties.				
157	**5 RUBLES**		.50	1.00	3.00
	1923. Green.				
158	**10 RUBLES**		.50	1.00	3.00
	1923. Dk. purple. Back brown.				
159	**25 RUBLES**		.50	1.00	3.00
	1923. Blue.				
160	**50 RUBLES**		.50	1.00	3.00
	1923. Olive.				
161	**100 RUBLES**		.75	2.00	5.00
	1923. Purple and m/c.				
162	**250 RUBLES**		1.00	3.00	7.50
	1923. Dk. blue.				

1923 SECOND ISSUE
#163-171 text on back in 8 lines.
#164-171 w/10 sign. varieties.
#168-171 arms at ctr. in unpt.

			VG	VF	UNC
163	**1 RUBLE**		.50	1.00	3.00
	1923. Brown. 3 sign. varieties.				
164	**5 RUBLES**		.50	1.00	3.00
	1923. Green.				
165	**10 RUBLES**				
	1923. Black on gray unpt. Back brown.				
	a. Wmk: Lozenges.		.50	1.00	3.00
	b. Wmk: Stars.		1.00	2.00	5.00
166	**25 RUBLES**				
	1923. Blue.				
	a. Wmk: Lozenges.		.50	1.00	3.00
	b. Wmk: Stars.		1.00	2.00	5.00
167	**50 RUBLES**				
	1923. Brown.				
	a. Wmk: Lozenges.		.50	1.25	3.50
	b. Wmk: Stars.		1.00	2.50	5.50

			VG	VF	UNC
155	**50 KOPEKS**		1.50	4.00	10.00
	1923. Blue.				

168	100 RUBLES	VG	VF	UNC
	1923. Purple on m/c unpt.			
	a. Wmk: Lozenges.	1.00	2.50	6.00
	b. Wmk: Stars.	1.00	2.00	5.00
169	500 RUBLES			
	1923. Dk. brown on m/c unpt.	3.00	7.00	20.00
170	1000 RUBLES			
	1923. Red on m/c unpt.	4.00	10.00	25.00
171	5000 RUBLES			
	1923. Green on m/c unpt.	6.00	15.00	35.00

С.С.С.Р.

СОЮЗ СОВЕТСКИХ СОЦИАЛИСТИЧЕСКИХ

РЕСПУБЛИК

U.S.S.R.-UNION OF SOVIET SOCIALIST REPUBLIC

ГОСУДАРСТВЕННЫЙ ДЕНЕЖНЫЙ ЗНАК

STATE CURRENCY NOTES

1923 (1924) ISSUE
#181-183 w/10 sign. varieties. Arms at upper l.

181	10,000 RUBLES	VG	VF	UNC
	1923 (1924). Lilac on green un pt. View of Kremlin.	10.00	35.00	100.00

182	15,000 RUBLES	VG	VF	UNC
	1923 (1924). Brown. Man at ctr .	12.00	45.00	115.00

171A	10,000 RUBLES	VG	VF	UNC
	1923. Red on lt. brown paper. 6-pointed star at upper ctr. Wmk: Lozenges. (Not issued).	—	Rare	—

ПЛАТЕЖНОЕ ОБЯЗАТЕЛЬСТВОН.К.Ф.Р.С.Ф.С.Р.

N.K.F. PAYMENT OBLIGATIONS OF THE R.S.F.S.R.

1 Gold Ruble = 5000 Rubles

1923 (1924) ISSUE

172	100 GOLD RUBLES	VG	VF	UNC
	1923 (1924). Specimen, perforated: ОБРАЗЕЦ.	—	—	225.00
173	250 GOLD RUBLES			
	1923 (1924). Specimen.	—	Rare	—
174	500 GOLD RUBLES			
	1923 (1924). Specimen.	—	Rare	—
175	1000 GOLD RUBLES			
	1923 (1924). Specimen.			225.00

ТРАНСПОРТНЫЙ СЕРТИФИКАТ

TRANSPORT CERTIFICATES

1924 ISSUE

183	25,000 RUBLES	VG	VF	UNC
	1923 (1924). Dk. blue and gree n on lilac unpt. Soldier at ct r.	15.00	50.00	135.00

ПЛАТЕЖНОЕ ОБЯЗАТЕЛЬСТВО Н.К.Ф. С.С.С.Р.

N.K.F. PAYMENT OBLIGATIONS OF THE U.S.S.R.

1923 ISSUE

184	100 GOLD RUBLES	VG	VF	UNC
	(1923-29). Specimen, perforated: ОБРАЗЕЦ.	—	—	300.00
184A	250 GOLD RUBLES			
	(1923-29). Specimen.	—	—	300.00
185	500 GOLD RUBLES			
	(1923-29). Specimen.	—	—	300.00

176	3 GOLD RUBLES	VG	VF	UNC
	1.3.1924. Front view steam locomotive at ctr., axe and anchor at upper r.	50.00	150.00	350.00
177	5 GOLD RUBLES			
	1.3.1924. Series 1-5.	25.00	50.00	150.00
178	5 GOLD RUBLES			
	1.5.1924. Series 6-10.	25.00	50.00	150.00
179	5 GOLD RUBLES			
	1.5.1924. Series 11-15. Like #178 but change in text on back.	25.00	50.00	150.00
180	5 GOLD RUBLES			
	1.5.1924. Series 16-24. Like #179 but repeated change in text on back.	25.00	50.00	150.00

		VG	VF	UNC
185A	1000 GOLD RUBLES (1923-29). Specimen.	—	—	300.00

НАРОДНОГО КОМИССАРІАТА ФИНАНСОВ

СОЮЗА С.С.Р. КРАТКОСРОЧНОЕ ПЛАТЕЖНОЕ ОБЯЗАТЕЛЬСТВО

N.F.K. SHORT-TERM PAYMENT OBLIGATIONS OF THE U.S.S.R.

1928 ISSUE

		VG	VF	UNC
185B	100 GOLD RUBLES 1928-29.	—	—	—
185C	250 GOLD RUBLES 1928-29.	—	—	—
185D	500 GOLD RUBLES 1928-29.	—	—	—
185E	1000 GOLD RUBLES 1928-29.	—	—	—

ГОСУДАРСТВЕННЫЙ ДЕНЕЖНЫЙ ЗНАК (resumed)

STATE CURRENCY NOTES

1924 ISSUE
#186-188 w/5 sign. varieties.

		VG	VF	UNC
186	1 GOLD RUBLE 1924. Blue on lt. brown and m/c unpt. Arms at upper ctr. Vertical size, w/and w/o series СЕРИЯ.	4.00	15.00	65.00
187	3 GOLD RUBLES 1924. Green. 2 reclining men a t lower ctr.	50.00	150.00	500.00
188	5 GOLD RUBLES 1924. Blue. Tractor plowing at lower ctr.	60.00	200.00	600.00

1925 ISSUE
#189-190 w/10 sign. varieties. Arms at upper ctr.

		VG	VF	UNC
189	3 RUBLES 1925. Dk. green.	1.50	5.00	17.50

		VG	VF	UNC
190	5 RUBLES 1925. Dk. blue. Worker at l.	1.50	4.00	15.00

SMALL CHANGE NOTES

1924 ISSUE
#191-195 arms at upper ctr.

		VG	VF	UNC
191	1 КОРЕК 1924. Lt. brown.	1.50	5.00	15.00

		VG	VF	UNC
192	2 КОРЕКS 1924. Brown.	1.50	5.00	17.50
193	3 КОРЕКS 1924. Green.	1.50	5.00	17.50
194	5 КОРЕКS 1924. Blue.	1.50	5.00	17.50
195	20 КОРЕКS 1924. Brown on rose unpt. Specimen.	20.00	75.00	200.00

		VG	VF	UNC
196	50 КОРЕКS 1924. Blue on brown unpt. Arms at upper l.	2.50	8.00	45.00

БИЛЕТ ГОСТДАРСТВЕННОГО БАНКА С.С.Р.

1924 ISSUE

		VG	VF	UNC
197	3 CHERVONTSA 1924 (date in wmk.). Black. uniface. Farmer sowing at l., arms at upper ctr. 2 sign. varieties.	30.00	85.00	200.00

1926; 1928 ISSUE

198	1 CHERVONETZ	VG	VF	UNC
	1926. Dk. blue. Arms at upper l. 4 sign. varieties.	10.00	27.50	65.00

199	2 CHERVONTSA	VG	VF	UNC
	1928. Green. Arms at upper ctr. 4 sign. varieties.			
	a. Green sign.	10.00	27.50	65.00
	b. Black sign.	8.00	25.00	50.00

200	5 CHERVONTSEV	VG	VF	UNC
	1928. Dk. blue. Uniface. Arms at upper l. 4 sign. varieties.	30.00	85.00	200.00

1932 ISSUE

201	3 CHERVONTSA	VG	VF	UNC
	1932. Green. Arms at upper ctr.	5.00	15.00	45.00

1937 ISSUE
#202-205 portr. V. Lenin at r.

202	1 CHERVONETZ	VG	VF	UNC
	1937. Gray.	.50	1.50	6.00
203	3 CHERVONTSA			
	1937. Red-brown.	.50	1.50	6.00
204	5 CHERVONTSEV			
	1937. Dk. olive-green.	.75	2.00	7.00
205	10 CHERVONTSEV			
	1937. Slate gray.	1.00	3.00	8.50

ГОСУДАРСТВЕННЫЙ КАЗНАЧЕЙСКИЙ БИЛЕТ
STATE TREASURY NOTES

1928 ISSUE

206	1 GOLD RUBLE	VG	VF	UNC
	1928. Blue on lt. brown and m/c unpt. Like #186. 5 sign. varieties. W/ and w/o series СЕРИЯ.	2.50	8.00	22.50

1934 ISSUE
#207-212 arms at upper ctr.

207	1 GOLD RUBLE	VG	VF	UNC
	1934. Dk. blue. Back brown on m/c unpt. W/sign.	1.50	4.00	12.00

208	1 GOLD RUBLE	VG	VF	UNC
	1934. Dk. blue. Like #207. W/o sign.	.50	1.50	5.00
209	3 GOLD RUBLES			
	1934. Green. W/sign.	2.00	4.00	12.00

210	3 GOLD RUBLES	VG	VF	UNC
	1934. Green. Like #209. W/o sign.	.75	2.00	6.00
211	5 GOLD RUBLES			
	1934. Gray-blue on lt. blue. W/sign.	2.50	6.00	20.00
212	5 GOLD RUBLES			
	1934. Gray-blue on lt. blue. Like #211. W/o sign.	1.00	3.00	7.00

1938 ISSUE
#213-215 arms at upper l.

		VG	VF	UNC
213	**1 RUBLE** 1938. Brown on gold unpt. Miner at r.	.50	1.00	3.50

		VG	VF	UNC
214	**3 RUBLES** 1938. Dk. green. Soldiers at l.	.50	1.00	4.50

		VG	VF	UNC
215	**5 RUBLES** 1938. Dk. blue. Aviator at r.	.50	1.50	4.50

1947 ISSUE
Type I: 16 scrolls of denominations on wreath around arms (8 at l., 7 at r., 1 at ctr.).
Type II: 15 scrolls of denominations on wreath around arms (7 at l., 7 at r., 1 at ctr.).

		VG	VF	UNC
216	**1 RUBLE** 1947. Blue-black on pale orange unpt. Back m/c. Type I.	.25	1.00	3.00
217	**1 RUBLE** 1947 (1957). Type II.	.25	1.00	3.00
218	**3 RUBLES** 1947. Dk. green on lt. green and lilac unpt. Type I.	.50	1.50	4.00
219	**3 RUBLES** 1947 (1957). Type II.	.50	1.50	4.00

		VG	VF	UNC
220	**5 RUBLES** 1947. Black on blue and lt. orange unpt. Back blue and m/c. Type I.	.75	2.00	5.00
221	**5 RUBLES** 1947 (1957). Type II.	.50	1.50	4.00

БИЛЕТ ГОСУДАРСТВЕННОГО БАНКА С.С.С.Р.
STATE BANK NOTE U.S.S.R.

1947 ISSUE

		VG	VF	UNC
225	**10 RUBLES** 1947. Black on blue and m/c unpt. Type I. V. Lenin at l. on back.	1.00	3.00	10.00
226	**10 RUBLES** 1947 (1957). Type II.	.75	2.50	9.00

		VG	VF	UNC
227	**25 RUBLES** 1947. Blue on green and m/c unpt. V. Lenin at l. Type I. Back black on blue and green unpt. Similar to #225.	1.25	3.50	12.50
228	**25 RUBLES** 1947 (1957). Type II.	1.00	3.00	10.00
229	**50 RUBLES** 1947. Blue-black on yellow-green and pink m/c unpt. V. Lenin at l. Type I. Back blue-black on m/c unpt. Similar to #225.	1.50	5.00	15.00
231	**100 RUBLES** 1947. Black on m/c unpt. Type I. V. Lenin at l. Back black on ochre and lilac unpt.; view of Kremlin.	2.00	6.00	20.00
232	**100 RUBLES** 1947 (1957). Type II.	2.00	6.00	20.00

888 SAAR

Saar (Sarre, Saarland), the smallest of the ten states of West Germany, is bounded by France to the south and by Luxembourg to the west. It has an area of 991 sq. mi. (2,568 sq. km.) and a population of 1.2 million. Capital: Saarbrucken. Principal products are iron and steel, chemicals, glass and coal.

The area of the Saar became part of France in 1766, but was divided between Prussia and Bavaria by the Treaty of Paris, 1815. The Treaty of Versailles, 1919, made the Saar an autonomous territory of the League of Nations, while assigning the coal mines to France. It was returned to Germany, by plebiscite, in 1935. France reoccupied the Saar in 1945. In 1946 it was assigned to the French occupation zone, and was united economically to France in 1947. Following a plebiscite, the Saar became a state of West Germany in 1957.

The Saar mark had no actual fractional divisions produced.

MONETARY SYSTEM:
1 Franc = 100 Centimes to 1930
1 Mark = 100 Pfennig, 1930-1957

AUTONOMOUS TERRITORY

MINES DOMANIALES DE LA SARRE, ETAT FRANCÇAIS

1919 ISSUE
#1 and 2 circulated from 1919 until 1.1.1930.

			VG	VF	UNC
1	**50 CENTIMES** ND (1919). Blue-gray w/brown text. Portr. woman at l.		12.50	22.50	60.00

			VG	VF	UNC
2	**1 FRANC** ND (1919). Red-brown on gold unpt. Portr. woman at r. Obverse and reverse of 1-franc coin dated 1919 at l. ctr. on back.		15.00	30.00	75.00

SARRE

TREASURY

1947 ISSUE
#6-8 wmk: Head at l. and r.

			VG	VF	UNC
3	**1 MARK** 1947. Blue and brown. Bearded classic man at ctr. Woman w/fruit on back.		10.00	20.00	65.00
4	**2 MARK** 1947. Lilac and brown on yellow unpt. Like #3.		70.00	150.00	300.00
5	**5 MARK** 1947. Pink and violet on lt. blue and orange unpt. Like #3.		20.00	50.00	185.00

			VG	VF	UNC
6	**10 MARK** 1947. Green, red and m/c. woman at ctr. Man and horse on back.		40.00	120.00	275.00
7	**50 MARK** 1947. Green, yellow and m/c. Like #6.		300.00	650.00	—
8	**100 MARK** 1947. Yellow-brown, blue-green and m/c. Like #6.		—	Rare	—

The Colony of St. Helena, a British colony located about 1,150 miles (1,850 km.) from the west coast of Africa, has an area of 47 sq. mi. (122 sq. km.) and a population of 5,700. Capital: Jamestown. Flax, lace and rope are produced for export. Ascension and Tristan da Cunha are dependencies of St. Helena.

The island was discovered and named by the Portuguese navigator Joao de Nova Castella in 1502. The Portuguese imported livestock, fruit trees and vegetables but established no permanent settlement. The Dutch occupied the island temporarily, 1645-1651. The original European settlement was founded by representatives of the British East India Company sent to annex the island after the departure of the Dutch. The Dutch returned and captured St. Helena from the British on New Year's Day, 1673, but were in turn ejected by a British force under Sir Richard Munden. Thereafter St. Helena was the undisputed possession of Great Britian. The island served as the place of exile for Napoleon, several Zulu chiefs, and an ex-sultan of Zanzibar.

RULERS:
British

MONETARY SYSTEM:
1 Pound = 20 Shillings to 1971
1 Pound = 100 New Pence, 1971

BRITISH INFLUENCE

GOVERNOR AND COUNCIL OF THE ISLAND OF ST. HELENA

1722 ISSUE
NOTE: #1 brought over $8500 at auction in Oct. 1989 (Phillips London, Lot #315).

1	**2 SHILLINGS 6 PENCE** 17.4.1722. Black. Uniface.	—	Rare	—

ST. HELENA CURRENCY BOARD

1917 ISSUE
2	**5 SHILLINGS** ca. 1917.	—	Rare	—
3	**20 SHILLINGS** ca. 1917.	—	Rare	—
4	**40 SHILLINGS** ca. 1917.	—	Rare	—

Saint Lucia, an independent island nation located in the Windward Islands of the West Indies between St. Vincent and Martinique, has an area of 238 sq. mi. (616 sq. km). Capital: Castries.

St. Lucia was discovered by Columbus in 1502. The first attempts at settlements undertaken by the British in 1605 and 1638 were frustrated by sickness and the determined hostility of the fierce Carib inhabitants. The French settled it in 1650 and made a treaty with the natives. Until 1814, when the island became a definite British possession, it was the scene of a continuous conflict between the British and French which saw the island change loyalty on at least 14 occasions.

RULERS:
British

MONETARY SYSTEM:
1 Pound = 20 Shillings until 1948
1 Dollar = 100 Cents, 1949-

NOTE: For later issues refer to East Caribbean States/British East Caribbean Territories.

BRITISH INFLUENCE

GOVERNMENT

1920 ISSUE
#1 and 2 printer: TDLR.

1	**5 SHILLINGS** 1.10.1920. Green and violet. Portr. Kg. George V at ctr. Back pale blue; local arms at ctr.	—	Rare	—
2	**10 SHILLINGS** 1.10.1920.		Reported Not Confirmed	

The Territorial Collectivity of St. Pierre and Miquelon, a French overseas territory located 10 miles (16 km.) off the south coast of Newfoundland, has an area of 93 sq. mi. (242 sq. km.) and a population of *6,000. Capital: St. Pierre. The economy of the barren archipelago is based on cod fishing and fur farming. Fish and fish products, and mink and silver fox pelts are exported.

The islands, occupied by the French in 1604, were captured by the British in 1702 and held until 1763 when they were returned to the possession of France and employed as a fishing station. They passed between France and England on six more occasions between 1778 and 1814 when they were awarded permanently to France by the Treaty of Paris. The rugged, soil-poor granite islands, which will support only evergreen shrubs, are all that remain to France of her extensive colonies in North America. In 1958 St. Pierre and Miquelon voted in favor of the new constitution of the Fifth Republic of France, thereby choosing to remain within the French Community.

Notes of the Banque de France circulated 1937-1942; afterwards notes of the Caisse Centrale de la France Libre and the Caisse Centrale de la France d'Outre-Mer.

RULERS:
French

MONETARY SYSTEM:
1 Franc = 100 Centimes
5 Francs 40 Centimes = 1 Canada Dollar
1 Nouveaux Franc = 100 'old', 1960-

FRENCH INFLUENCE

BANQUE DES ISLES SAINT-PIERRE ET MIQUELON

SAINT-PIERRE BRANCH

1890 ISSUE

1	**27 FRANCS**			
	1890. Blue. Sailing ship at l., woman seated at upper ctr., fish at r. Hand cancelled.	—	Rare	—

SAINT-PIERRE-MIQUELON BRANCH

1890-95 ISSUE

2	**27 FRANCS**			
	1895. Blue. Woman seated, sailing ship at l., fish, woman seated at r. on back. 2 sign. varieties. Hand cancelled, handstamped: *ANNULÉ*.	—	Rare	—

3	**54 FRANCS**			
	1890-95. Blue. Like #2. Hand cancelled, handstamped: *ANNULÉ*.	—	Rare	—

CHAMBRE DE COMMERCE

1920 ISSUE

		GOOD	FINE	XF
4	**0.05 FRANC**			
	15.5.1920.	—	—	—
5	**0.10 FRANC**			
	15.5. 1920.	—	—	—
6	**0.25 FRANC**			
	15.5.1920. (1st and 2nd issue).	—	—	—
7	**0.50 FRANC**			
	15.5.1920.	—	—	—
8	**1 FRANC**			
	15.5.1920.	—	—	—
9	**2 FRANCS**			
	15.5.1920.	—	—	—

CAISSE CENTRALE DE LA FRANCE LIBRE
PROVISIONAL WW II ISSUES W/O ST. PIERRE NAME

ORDONNANCE DU 2.12.1941
#10-14 types of French Equatorial Africa w/special serial # ranges. Printer: BWC (w/o imprint).
NOTE: See also Reunion #36-38.

		GOOD	FINE	XF
10	**5 FRANCS**			
	L.1941 (1943). Type of F.E.A. #10. Serial # AA 000 002-AA 030 000 (20.1.1943).	20.00	60.00	—
11	**10 FRANCS**			
	L.1941 (1943). Type of F.E.A. #11.			
	a. Serial # FA 000 001-FA 015 000 (20.1.1943).	25.00	75.00	—
	b. Serial # 2 520 001-2 533 120.	25.00	75.00	—
12	**20 FRANCS**			
	L.1941 (ca. 1943). Type of F.E.A. #12. Serial # LA 000 001-LA 030 000.	30.00	95.00	—
13	**100 FRANCS**			
	L.1941. (1943).Type of F.E.A. #13. Serial # PA 000 001-PA 070 000 (July 1943).	70.00	150.00	—
14	**1000 FRANCS**			
	1941. (1943). Type of F.E.A. #14.			
	a. Serial # TA 000 001-TA 030 000 (July 1943).	400.00	1000.	—
	b. Serial # TA 275 001-TA 295 000 (Oct. 1944).	400.00	1000.	—

CAISSE CENTRALE DE LA FRANCE D'OUTRE-MER

SAINT PIERRE ET MIQUELON

ORDONNANCE DU 2.2.1944
#15-18 types of French Equatorial Africa w/special serial # ranges. Printer: BWC (w/o imprint).
NOTE: See also Reunion #39-40.

		GOOD	FINE	XF
15	**5 FRANCS**			
	L.1944 (1945). Type of F.E.A. #15. Serial # AM 000 001-AM 020 000 (3.10.1945).	20.00	60.00	—
16	**10 FRANCS**			
	L.1944 (1946). Type of F.E.A. #16. Serial # 2520 001-2533 120 (4.2.1946).	25.00	75.00	—
17	**20 FRANCS**			
	L.1944 (1945-46). Type of F.E.A. #17.			
	a. Serial # 2 509 001-2 509 279 (22.1.1945).	30.00	95.00	—
	b. Serial # 2 510 001-2 531 200 (4.2.1946).	30.00	95.00	—

18	1000 FRANCS	GOOD	FINE	XF
	L.1944 (1945-46). Type of F.E.A. #19.			
	a. Serial # TD 021 001-TD 046 000 (5.9.1945).	400.00	1000.	—
	b. Serial # TD 235 001-TD 255 000 (17.6.1946).	400.00	1000.	—

1947 ND ISSUE
#19-21 types of French Equatorial Africa post WW II Issue.

19	10 FRANCS	GOOD	FINE	XF
	ND (1947). Type of FEA #21, also St. Pierre #23.			
	a. Serial # 2 520 001-2 550 00 Printer: Desfosses, Paris.	5.00	15.00	45.00
	b. Serial # 19 100 001-19 200 000. Printer: Banque de France.	5.00	15.00	45.00

20	20 FRANCS	GOOD	FINE	XF
	ND (1947). Type of FEA #22, also St. Pierre #24. Serial # 2 509 001-2 509 279; 2 510 001-2 531 200.	7.50	25.00	65.00
21	50 FRANCS			
	ND (1947). Type of FEA #23, also St. Pierre # 25. Serial # 8 600 001-8 700 000.	9.00	35.00	95.00

1950 ND ISSUE
#22-29 ovpt: *SAINT-PIERRE-ET-MIQUELON.*

22	5 FRANCS	VG	VF	UNC
	ND (1950-60). Blue and m/c. Ship at l., Bougainville at r. Woman w/fruit and house on back.	.25	1.00	6.00

23	10 FRANCS	VG	VF	UNC
	ND (1950-60). Blue and m/c. Colbert at l., ships at r. River scene and plants on back.	.50	1.50	9.00

24	20 FRANCS	VG	VF	UNC
	ND (1950-60). Brown and m/c. 4 people w/huts at l., E. Gentil at r. 2 men on back.	1.00	2.00	12.50

25	50 FRANCS	VG	VF	UNC
	ND (1950-60). M/c. B. d'Esnambuc at l., ship at r. Woman on back.	10.00	35.00	135.00
26	100 FRANCS			
	ND (1950-60). M/c. La Bourdonnais at l., 2 women at r. Woman looking at mountains on back.	12.00	40.00	185.00
27	500 FRANCS			
	ND (1950-60). M/c. Bldgs. and sailboat at l., 2 women at r. Ox-carts w/wood and plants on back.	30.00	150.00	425.00

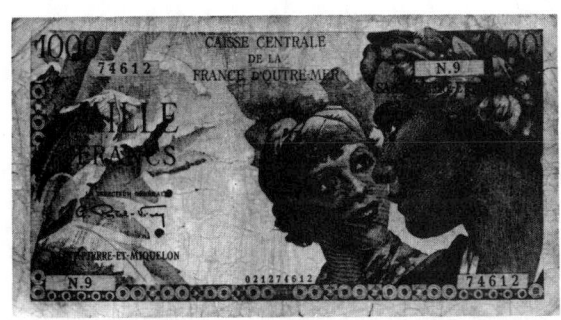

28	1000 FRANCS	VG	VF	UNC
	ND (1950-60). M/c. 2 women at r. Woman at r, 2 men in small boat on back.	50.00	200.00	675.00
29	5000 FRANCS			
	ND (1950-60). M/c. Gen. Schoelcher at r. ctr. Family on back.	120.00	350.00	—

1960 ND PROVISIONAL ISSUE
#30, 31 and 35 ovpt: *SAINT-PIERRE-ET-MIQUELON* and new denomination.

30	1 NOUVEAUX FRANC ON 50 FRANCS	VG	VF	UNC
	ND (1960). M/c. Ovpt. on Reunion #25.	3.00	8.00	32.50
31	1 NOUVEAUX FRANC ON 50 FRANCS	VG	VF	UNC
	ND (1960). M/c. B. d'Esnambuc at l., ship at r. Woman on back.	35.00	150.00	350.00

			Good	Fine	XF
54 (A65)	**1 Pound** 1.5.1902.		55.00	125.00	350.00
55 (A66)	**5 Pounds** 1902.				
		a. 1.3.1902.	40.00	100.00	225.00
		b. 1.4.1902.	50.00	120.00	350.00
		c. 1.5.1902.	37.50	90.00	220.00
56 (A67)	**10 Pounds** 1902.				
		a. 1.3.1902.	135.00	225.00	650.00
		b. 1.4.1902.	85.00	185.00	450.00
		c. 1.5.1902.	55.00	125.00	310.00

UNION OF SOUTH AFRICA

After the Union came into being (1910), only six note issuing banks remained. The South African Reserve Bank was established in 1921 and received the exclusive note issuing privilege.

TREASURY

PRETORIA BRANCH

1920 Currency and Banking Act

1920 GOLD CERTIFICATE ISSUE

Issued in 1920 and circulated for only a short period. All notes have one side in English and the other in Afrikaans.

#69-73 arms at upper ctr. Wmk: *UNION/OF/SOUTH AFRICA* in wavy frame. Market values are for punched hole cancelled notes.

		VG	VF	UNC
69	**1 Pound** L. 1920. Black.	60.00	150.00	350.00
70	**5 Pounds** L. 1920. Black.	65.00	170.00	400.00

		VG	VF	UNC
71	**100 Pounds** L. 1920. Black.	90.00	225.00	600.00
72	**1000 Pounds** L. 1920. Black.	165.00	475.00	1200.

		VG	VF	UNC
73	**10,000 Pounds** L. 1920. Black.	250.00	650.00	1650.

SOUTH AFRICAN RESERVE BANK

1921 ISSUE

			VG	VF	UNC
74	**10 Shillings** 30.11.1921-1922. Blue. Wmk: Sailing ship and portr. J. van Riebeeck. Sign. W. H. Clegg.		120.00	400.00	1000.
75 (79)	**1 Pound** 1921-22. Black on red unpt. Sailing ship on face and back. Sign. W. H. Clegg.		40.00	180.00	525.00
76 (85)	**5 Pounds** 1921-22. Green and brown. Sailing ship at l. Sign. W. H. Clegg.		75.00	285.00	825.00
77 (96)	**20 Pounds** 29.9.1921. Blue. Sailing ship at l. Sign. W. H. Clegg.		165.00	650.00	2300.
78 (98)	**100 Pounds** 30.9.1921. Red-brown. Sailing ship at l. Sign. W. H. Clegg.		800.00	2500.	5100.

1925-28 ISSUES

			VG	VF	UNC
79 (75)	**10 Shillings** 20.9.1926. Dk. brown on pink and pale green unpt. Wmk: Sailing ship and portr. J. van Riebeeck.		70.00	200.00	575.00

			VG	VF	UNC
80 (76)	**10 Shillings** 1928-47. Like #79 but English and Afrikaans text. Wmk: Sailing ship and portr. J. van Riebeeck.				
		a. Sign. W. H. Clegg. 1.9.1928-1931.	60.00	160.00	450.00
		b. Sign. W. H. Clegg. Date ovpt: 17.11.1931/2.4.1932.	120.00	325.00	850.00
		c. Sign. J. Postmus. 12.9.1932-1945.	8.00	32.00	100.00
		d. Sign. Dr. M. H. de Kock. 5.9.1945-1947.	8.00	22.00	75.00
81 (80)	**1 Pound** 1925-28. Dk. brown. Sailing ship at l.		60.00	225.00	650.00
82 (86)	**5 Pounds** 7.4.1926. Dk. green and brown. New type.		100.00	360.00	975.00

1928; 1929 ISSUES

			VG	VF	UNC
83 (81)	**1 Pound** 1.9.1928. Dk. brown. Like #81 but altered design on back. English and Dutch text.		40.00	180.00	550.00

			VG	VF	UNC
84 (82)	**1 Pound** 1928-47. Dk. brown. Like #83 but English and Afrikaans text.				
		a. Sign. W. M. Clegg. 3.12.1928-1931.	50.00	145.00	450.00
		b. Sign. J. Postmus. 5.9.1932-1944.	5.50	18.00	80.00
		c. Sign. J. Postmus. Paper w/metal thread (only series A78). 19.9.1938.	48.00	170.00	625.00
		d. Sign. Dr. M. H. de Kock. 13.9.1945-1947.	4.00	18.00	75.00
85 (87)	**5 Pounds** 2.4.1928. Like #82 but altered design on back. English and Dutch text.		75.00	225.00	700.00
86 (88)	**5 Pounds** 1929-47. Like #85 but English and Afrikaans text.				
		a. Sign. W. H. Clegg. 2.9.1929-1931.	52.00	175.00	485.00
		b. Sign. J. Postmus. 1.9.1933-1944.	16.00	55.00	150.00
		c. Sign. Dr. M. H. de Kock. 6.4.1946-1947.	10.00	35.00	100.00

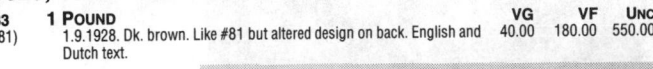

87
(97) **20 POUNDS**
1928; 1933. Blue. New type.

	VG	VF	UNC
a. Sign. W. H. Clegg. 3.9.1928.	165.00	585.00	2100.
b. Sign. J. Postmus. 4.9.1933.	125.00	525.00	1650.

88
(99) **100 POUNDS**
1928; 1933. Brown. New type.

a. Sign. W. H. Clegg. 4.9.1928.	700.00	2250.	4600.
b. Sign. J. Postmus. 8.9.1933.	425.00	1900.	3400.

1943 ISSUE

89
(93) **10 POUNDS**
14.4.1943; 19.4.1943. Brown. Sailing ship at l. Sign. J. Postmus.

	VG	VF	UNC
	25.00	60.00	185.00

1948 ISSUES

90
(77) **10 SHILLINGS**
1948-59. Brown. Portr. Jan van Riebeeck at l., first lines of bank name and value in English. Sign. Dr. M. H. de Kock.

	VG	VF	UNC
a. Date w/name of month. 12.4.1948-1951.	6.50	22.00	75.00
b. Date w/month by #. 1.12.1951-1959.	5.50	18.00	65.00

91
(78) **10 SHILLINGS**
1948-59. Like #90 but first line of bank name and value in Afrikaans. Sign. Dr. M. H. de Kock.

a. Date w/name of month. 10.4.1948-1951.	6.50	22.00	75.00
b. Date w/month by #. 1.12.1951-1959.	5.50	18.00	65.00

92
(83) **1 POUND**
1948-59. Blue. Portr. Jan van Riebeeck at l.; first line of bank name and value in English. Sign. Dr. M. H. de Kock.

	VG	VF	UNC
a. Date w/name of month. 1.9.1948-1951.	3.25	13.50	50.00
b. Date w/month by #. 1.12.1951-1959.	2.50	9.00	40.00

93
(84) **1 POUND**
1948-59. Like #92 but first line of bank name and value in Afrikaans. Sign. Dr. M. H. de Kock.

a. Date w/name of month. 3.9.1948-1951.	3.25	11.00	50.00
b. Like #84a but thicker paper (only series B28). 12.4.1949.	8.00	40.00	110.00
c. Date w/month by #. 1.12.1951-1959.	2.50	9.00	40.00

94
(89) **5 POUNDS**
1.11.1948-1949. Green. Portr. Jan van Riebeeck at l., first line of bank name and value in English. Sign. Dr. M. H. de Kock.

	12.00	36.00	115.00

95
(90) **5 POUNDS**
1.11.1948-1949. Green. Like #94 but first line of bank name and value in Afrikaans. Sign. Dr. M. H. de Kock.

	12.00	36.00	115.00

1950 ISSUES

96
(91) **5 POUNDS**
1950-59. Dk. green. Like #94; first line of bank name and value in English. Sign. Dr. M. H. de Kock.

	VG	VF	UNC
a. Date w/name of month. 1950-52.	7.50	22.00	75.00
b. Date w/month by #. 2.1.1953-1959.	5.00	18.00	65.00

97
(92) **5 POUNDS**
1950-59. Like #96 but first line of bank name and value in Afrikaans. Sign. Dr. M. H. de Kock.

a. Date w/name of month. 1950-52.	7.50	22.00	75.00
b. Date w/month by #. 2.1.1953-1959.	5.00	18.00	65.00

1952 ISSUES

98
(94) **10 POUNDS**
18.12.1952-1959. Brown-violet. Portr. Jan van Riebeeck at l. First line of bank name and value in English. Sign. Dr. M. H. de Kock.

	VG	VF	UNC
	15.00	50.00	175.00

99
(95) **10 POUNDS**
18.12.1952-1959. Brown-violet. Like #98 but first line of bank name and value in Afrikaans. Sign. Dr. M. H. de Kock.

	15.00	50.00	175.00

100 **100 POUNDS**
29.1.1952. Blue and m/c. Portr. Jan van Riebeeck at l. First line of bank name and value in English. Sign. Dr. M. H. de Kock.

	VG	VF	UNC
a. Issued note.	160.00	775.00	2000.
b. Perforated: *CANCELLED.*	150.00	550.00	1900.

101 **100 POUNDS**
29.1.1952. Blue and m/c. Like #100 but first line of bank name and value in Afrikaans. Sign. Dr. M. H. de Kock.

a. Issued note.	160.00	775.00	2000.
b. Perforated: *CANCELLED.*	150.00	550.00	1900.

Southern Rhodesia (now Zimbabwe), located in the east-central part of southern Africa, has an area of 150,804 sq. mi. (390,580 sq. km.) and a population of *10.1 million. Capital: Salisbury. The economy is based on agriculture and mining. Tobacco, sugar, asbestos, copper and chrome ore and coal are exported.

The Rhodesian area, the habitat of paleolithic man, contains extensive evidence of earlier civilizations, notably the world-famous ruins of Zimbabwe, a gold-trading center that flourished about the 14th or 15th century AD. The Portuguese of the 16th century were the first Europeans to attempt to develop south-central Africa, but it remained for Cecil Rhodes and the British South Africa Co. to open the hinterlands. Rhodes obtained a concession for mineral rights from local chiefs in 1888 and administered his African empire (named Southern Rhodesia in 1895) through the British South Africa Co. until 1923, when the British government annexed the area after the white settlers voted for existence as a separate entity, rather than for incorporation into the Union of South Africa. From September of 1953 through 1963 Southern Rhodesia was joined with the British protectorates of Northern Rhodesia and Nyasaland into a multiracial federation. When the federation was dissolved at the end of 1963, Northern Rhodesia and Nyasaland became the independent states of Zambia and Malawi.

Britain was prepared to grant independence to Southern Rhodesia but declined to do so when the politically dominant white Rhodesians refused to give assurances of representative government. On May 11, 1965, following two years of unsuccessful negotiation with the British government, Prime Minister Ian Smith issued a unilateral declaration of independence. Britain responded with economic sanctions supported by the United Nations. After further futile attempts to effect an accommodation, the Rhodesian Parliament severed all ties with Britain, and on March 2, 1970, established the Republic of Rhodesia.

On March 3, 1978, Prime Minister Ian Smith and three moderate black nationalist leaders signed an agreement providing for black majority rule. The name of the country was changed to Zimbabwe Rhodesia.

After the election of March 3, 1980, the country changed its name again and became the Republic of Zimbabwe.

Also see Rhodesia and Nyasaland.

RULERS:
British to 1970

MONETARY SYSTEM:
1 Shilling = 12 Pence
1 Pound = 20 Shillings to 1970

BRITISH INFLUENCE

SOUTHERN RHODESIA CURRENCY BOARD

1939-45 ISSUES
#8-11 portr. Kg. George VI at r. Various date and sign. varieties. Printer: BWC.

		VG	VF	UNC
8	**5 SHILLINGS** 1.1.1943. Purple. 89 x 57mm.	35.00	125.00	500.00

		VG	VF	UNC
8A	**5 SHILLINGS** 1945; 1948. Purple. Like #8, but 114 x 70mm.			
	a. 1.2.1945; 1.10.1945.	30.00	125.00	400.00
	b. 1.1.1948.	30.00	100.00	350.00

		VG	VF	UNC
9	**10 SHILLINGS** 15.12.1939-1.9.1951. Brown and m/c. Antelope at l., Victoria Falls at ctr. on back.	35.00	200.00	550.00
10	**1 POUND** 15.12.1939-1.9.1951. Green and m/c. Antelope at l., Zimbabwe ruins at ctr. on back.	30.00	175.00	500.00

		VG	VF	UNC
11	**5 POUNDS** 1939-52. Blue, brown and m/c. Factory at lower ctr. Antelope at l., Victoria Falls at ctr. on back.			
	a. W/o white *5* in unpt. on face. 15.12.1939.	175.00	550.00	—
	b. White *5* in unpt. on face. 1.3.1944-1.9.1951.	70.00	275.00	800.00
	c. Sign. title: *CHAIRMAN* above *MEMBER.* 15.1.1952.	70.00	300.00	900.00

1952-53 ISSUE
#12-15 Qn. Elizabeth II at r. *SOUTHERN RHODESIA CURRENCY BOARD* in text. Various date and sign. varieties. Printer: BWC.

		VG	VF	UNC
12	**10 SHILLINGS** 1.12.1952; 3.1.1953. Brown and m/c. Antelope at l., Victoria Falls at ctr. on back.	35.00	250.00	575.00

		VG	VF	UNC
13	**1 POUND** 1.12.1952; 3.1.1953; 10.3.1954. Green and m/c. Antelope at l., Zimbabwe ruins at ctr. on back.	25.00	150.00	525.00
14	**5 POUNDS** 3.1.1953. Blue and m/c. Antelope at l., Victoria Falls at ctr. on back.	120.00	450.00	—
15	**10 POUNDS** 15.4.1953; 10.3.1954. Brown and m/c.	600.00	1800.	—

CENTRAL AFRICA CURRENCY BOARD

1955 ISSUE

#16-19 Qn. Elizabeth II at r. *CENTRAL AFRICA CURRENCY BOARD* in text. Various sign. varieties. Printer: BWC.

		VG	VF	UNC
16	**10 SHILLINGS** 10.9.1955. Brown and m/c. Like #12.	35.00	225.00	550.00
17	**1 POUND** 10.9.1955. Green and m/c. Like #13.	25.00	175.00	525.00
18	**5 POUNDS** 10.9.1955. Blue and m/c. Like #14.	85.00	550.00	1250.
19	**10 POUNDS** 10.9.1955. Brown and m/c. Like #15.	Reported Not Confirmed		

The Spanish State, forming the greater part of the Iberian Peninsula of southwest Europe, has an area of 195,988 sq. mi. (504,714 sq. km.) and a population of *39.4 million including the Balearic and the Canary Islands. Capital: Madrid. The economy is based on agriculture, industry and tourism. Machinery, fruit, vegtables and chemicals are exported.

It is not known when man first came to the Iberian peninsula - the Altamira caves off the Cantabrian coast approximately 50 miles west of Santander were fashioned in Paleolithic times. Spain was a battleground for centuries before it became a united nation, fought for by Phoenicians, Carthaginians, Greeks, Celts, Romans, Vandals, Visigoths and Moors. Ferdinand and Isabella destroyed the last Moorish stronghold in 1492, freeing the national energy and resources for the era of discovery and colonization that would make Spain the most powerful country in Europe during the 16th century. After the destruction of the Spanish Armada, 1588, Spain never again played a major role in European politics. Napoleonic France ruled Spain between 1808 and 1814. The monarchy was restored in 1814 and continued, interrupted by the short-lived republic of 1873-74, until the exile of Alfonso XIII in 1931, when the Second Republic was established.

The monarchy was reconstituted in 1947 under the regency of General Francisco Franco, the king designate to be crowned after Franco's death. Franco died on Nov. 30, 1975. Two days after his passing, Juan Carlos de Borbon, the grandson of Alfonso XIII, was proclaimed King of Spain.

* * * **This section has been partially renumbered.** * * *

RULERS:
Ferdinand VII, 1808-1833
Isabella II, 1833-1868
Amadeo I, 1871-1873
Regency, 1874
Alfonso XII, 1875-1885
Alfonso XIII, 1886-1931
2nd Republic and Civil War, 1932-1936
Francisco Franco, 1937-1975
Juan Carlos I, 1975-

MONETARY SYSTEM:
1 Peseta = 100 Centimos 1874-

FIRST REPUBLIC, 1873-74

BANCO DE ESPAÑA

Some early issues had branch city names stamped on face or back. In some issues serial # may or may not have a prefix letter.

1874 ISSUE

		GOOD	FINE	XF
1	**25 PESETAS** 1.7.1874. Gray and cream. Bearers at l. and r. of ctr.	750.00	1500.	—
2	**50 PESETAS** 1.7.1874. Black and chestnut. D. Martinez at l.	1200.	2000.	—
3	**100 PESETAS** 1.7.1874. Ochre and black. J. de Herrera at l., fortified monastery at ctr.	1000.	2000.	—
4	**500 PESETAS** 1.7.1874. Black and cream. Woman seated at l., Goya at r.	1250.	2500.	—
5	**1000 PESETAS** 1.7.1874. Black and cream. Minerva at l., A. Cano at r.	2000.	4000.	—

KINGDOM

BANCO DE ESPAÑA

1875 ISSUE

#6-10 printer: BWC. (W/o imprint).

		GOOD	FINE	XF
6	**25 PESETAS** 1.1.1875. Black on lilac unpt. Woman at l.	850.00	1750.	—

	500 PESETAS	**GOOD**	**FINE**	**XF**
9	1.1.1875. Gray and blue. Women at l. and r.	1250.	2500.	—

	50 PESETAS	**GOOD**	**FINE**	**XF**
7	1.1.1875. Gray, green and salmon. Women leaning against coat of arms at top ctr., woman at bottom ctr., children at upper l. and r., lions at lower l. and r.	1350.	2000.	—

	100 PESETAS	**GOOD**	**FINE**	**XF**
8	1.1.1875. Gray, green and orange. Woman by castle at l., woman at r.	1000.	2000.	—

	1000 PESETAS	**GOOD**	**FINE**	**XF**
10	1.1.1875. Gray and brown. Woman w/shield and spear at at l., woman at r.	1600.	3250.	—

1876 ISSUE
#11-13 Lope de Vega at l. Printer: ABNC.

	100 PESETAS	**GOOD**	**FINE**	**XF**
11	1.7.1876. Black on m/c unpt. Woman w/children at ctr., woman seated at r. Back dk. brown; ship at l. and r., allegorical woman at ctr.			
	a. Issued note.	500.00	1200.	—
	s. Specimen.	—	—	—
12	**500 PESETAS**			
	1.7.1876. Black on m/c unpt. Woman reclining w/children at top ctr., woman at lower r. Back red-brown; steam train at ctr.			
	a. Issued note.	1000.	2500.	—
	s. Specimen.	—	—	—

		GOOD	FINE	XF
13	**1000 PESETAS** 1.7.1876. Black on m/c unpt. Spaniard w/indian maiden at ctr., Liberty at lower r. Back brown; allegorical women at l. and r., two allegorical women at ctr.			
	a. Issued note.	500.00	1200.	—
	s. Specimen.	—	—	—

1878 ISSUE
#16 Deleted.

		GOOD	FINE	XF
14	**50 PESETAS** 1.1.1878. Gray and black. P. Calderon de la Barca at r.	750.00	1500.	—
15	**100 PESETAS** 1.1.1878. Ochre and gray. G. de la Vega at l., woman w/laureate at r.	750.00	1500.	—
17	**250 PESETAS** 1.1.1878. Orange and gray. F. de Herrera at l.	600.00	1200.	—
18	**500 PESETAS** 1.1.1878. Cream and gray-black. P. de Cespedes at l., woman w/helmet at r.	1250.	2500.	—
19	**1000 PESETAS** 1.1.1878. Green and black. M. de Cervantes at l., rider on donkey at ctr.	2000.	4000.	—

1880 ISSUE

		GOOD	FINE	XF
20	**50 PESETAS** 1.4.1880. Rose and gray-green. Count de Campomanes at l.	1000.	1500.	—
21	**100 PESETAS** 1.4.1880. Green and orange. F. de Quevedo at l., woman w/laureate at r.	1000.	2000.	—
22	**500 PESETAS** 1.4.1880. Chestnut and ochre. C. Coello at l.	1250.	2500.	—
23	**1000 PESETAS** 1.4.1880. Green and black. B. Murillo at l.	2000.	4000.	—

1884 FIRST ISSUE
#24-28 printer: ABNC.

#25-27 portr. Juan Alvarez de Mendizábal at r.

		GOOD	FINE	XF
24	**25 PESETAS** 1.1.1884. Red and black. Woman w/2 children at ctr. Back orange; arms at ctr.	400.00	1000.	—

		GOOD	FINE	XF
25	**50 PESETAS** 1.1.1884. Black on green unpt. Woman seated by globe at l. Back green; woman and eagle at ctr.	500.00	1200.	—

		GOOD	FINE	XF
26	**100 PESETAS** 1.1.1884. Black on orange unpt. Cherubs at ctr. Back orange.	250.00	800.00	—
27	**500 PESETAS** 1.1.1884. Black on ochre unpt. Woman w/sword at l., cherub at ctr. Back ochre; arms at ctr.	650.00	1500.	—

		GOOD	FINE	UNC
28	**1000 PESETAS** 1.1.1884. Black on orange unpt. Woman bearer at l., Mendizábal at ctr., woman standing at r. Back brown; dog and safe at ctr.			
	a. Issued note.	1250.	2500.	—
	p. Proof.	—	—	—

1884 SECOND ISSUE

		GOOD	FINE	XF
29	**25 PESETAS** 1.7.1884. Ochre and black. R. de Santillan at ctr.	600.00	1200.	—
30	**50 PESETAS** 1.7.1884. Black on tan unpt. B. Murillo at ctr. Back blue.	400.00	850.00	—

		GOOD	FINE	XF
31	**100 PESETAS** 1.7.1884. Black on lt. tan unpt. Portr. A. Mon at top ctr. Back green; old locomotive at ctr.	200.00	550.00	—
32	**500 PESETAS** 1.7.1884. Black, chestnut and green. Girl w/dog at l., portr. Count de Floridablanca at r.	1250.	2500.	—
33	**1000 PESETAS** 1.7.1884. Green and black. Marquis de la Ensenada at l., women at r., one holding sheaf and sickle.	1600.	3250.	—

1886 ISSUE

		GOOD	FINE	XF
34	**25 PESETAS** 1.10.1886. Black on pale gold unpt. Goya at ctr. Back red.	175.00	450.00	750.00
35	**50 PESETAS** 1.10.1886. Chestnut. Woman w/child at l., Goya at r.	420.00	950.00	1750.
36	**100 PESETAS** 1.10.1886. Chestnut. Man standing at l., Goya at r.	300.00	650.00	1350.
37	**500 PESETAS** 1.10.1886. Ochre and black. Goya at l., woman seated at r.	1000.	2500.	4500.
38	**1000 PESETAS** 1.10.1886. Yellow and black. Woman seated w/harp at l. Goya seated behind table at r.	1250.	2500.	5000.

1889 ISSUE

#39-41 back designs different from previous issue.

		GOOD	FINE	XF
39	**25 PESETAS** 1.6.1889. Black on gold unpt. Similar to #34. Back brown; Creso at ctr.	150.00	350.00	650.00
40	**50 PESETAS** 1.6.1889. Black on yellow unpt. Similar to #35. Back green; 2 cherubs.	350.00	650.00	900.00

		GOOD	FINE	XF
41	**100 PESETAS** 1.6.1889. Black on yellow unpt. Similar to #36. Back brown; woman and cherub at ctr.	95.00	175.00	375.00

1893 ISSUE

#42-44 portr. Jovellanos at l.

		GOOD	FINE	XF
42	**25 PESETAS** 24.7.1893. Blue and yellow. Medallion at ctr., standing figure at r. on back.	120.00	250.00	550.00
43	**50 PESETAS** 24.7.1893. Black on yellow unpt. Seated woman at r. w/sword across lap. Back green; cherubs and winged head at ctr.	220.00	400.00	575.00

		GOOD	FINE	XF
44	**100 PESETAS** 24.7.1893. Blue on pale yellow unpt. Back brown; heads at l. and r.	95.00	175.00	375.00

1895 ISSUE

		GOOD	FINE	XF
45	**1000 PESETAS** 1.5.1895. Black on lt. tan unpt. El Conde de Cabarrus at l. w/child leaning on frame. Back brown; Kg. Carlos III and lion.	150.00	350.00	600.00

1898 ISSUE

		GOOD	FINE	XF
46	**5 PESETAS** 1898. Qn. Isabel la Católica at l. (Not issued).			

		GOOD	FINE	XF
47	**50 PESETAS** 2.1.1898. Black and yellow. Jovellanos at l., helmeted woman at r.	160.00	300.00	550.00
48	**100 PESETAS** 24.6.1898. Blue and yellow. Jovellanos at l.	80.00	150.00	350.00

1899 ISSUE

		GOOD	FINE	XF
49	**25 PESETAS** 17.5.1899. Blue on pale green unpt. Quevedo at l. Back brown; head at ctr., Mercury at r.	90.00	185.00	400.00
50	**50 PESETAS** 25.11.1899. Black on pale green unpt. Quevedo at l., statue of man at r. Back green; woman reclining at l., man at r.	130.00	275.00	475.00

1900 ISSUE

		GOOD	FINE	XF
51	**100 PESETAS** 1.5.1900. Blue on lt. green unpt. Quevedo at l., medallic portr. at r. Back brown; cherubs and Athena.	130.00	275.00	475.00

1902-03 ISSUE

		GOOD	FINE	XF
52	**50 PESETAS** 30.11.1902. Black and yellow. Velázquez at l.	150.00	350.00	650.00

		GOOD	FINE	XF
53	**100 PESETAS** 1.7.1903. Gray. Man standing w/spade in hand at l., small child on knees w/arm uplifting palm branch at r.			
	a. Issued note.	600.00	1500.	—
	r. Remainder.	—	—	—

54 **500 PESETAS**
 1.10.1903. Grayish-blue. Man and arms spread as if in flight at top ctr.

		Good	Fine	XF
a.	Issued note.	1500.	3000.	—
b.	Half finished print w/o unpt. Punched hole cancelled.	—	Unc	250.00

1904-05 ISSUE

Certain issues following have a round embossed validation applied by the Republic in 1931. This validation consists of crowned Spanish arms with 2 laurel branches at ctr., legend around: *GOBIERNO PROVISIONAL DE LA REPÚBLICA 14 ABRIL 1931*. Notes of 25, 50 and 100 Pesetas had it applied to the upper l. corner, and those of 500 and 1000 Pesetas to the upper r. corner. The embossing is not easily discernible.

			Good	Fine	XF
55	**25 PESETAS**	1.1.1904. Blue-green. Standing figures at l. and r.	15.00	35.00	85.00
56	**50 PESETAS**	19.3.1905. Ochre, green and gray. Echegaray at l.	150.00	350.00	700.00

1906 ISSUE
#57-59 printer: BWC.

57 **25 PESETAS**
 24.9.1906. Black and blue. Woman seated at l.

		Good	Fine	XF
a.	Issued note.	12.50	40.00	70.00
b.	Round embossed Republic validation at upper l. corner (1931).	25.00	50.00	100.00

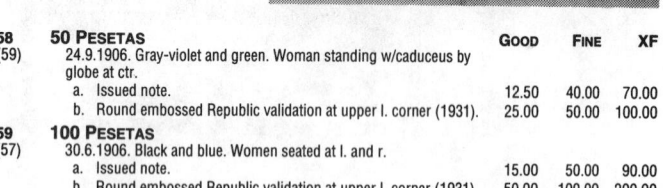

58
(59) **50 PESETAS**
 24.9.1906. Gray-violet and green. Woman standing w/caduceus by globe at ctr.

		Good	Fine	XF
a.	Issued note.	12.50	40.00	70.00
b.	Round embossed Republic validation at upper l. corner (1931).	25.00	50.00	100.00

59
(57) **100 PESETAS**
 30.6.1906. Black and blue. Women seated at l. and r.

a.	Issued note.	15.00	50.00	90.00
b.	Round embossed Republic validation at upper l. corner (1931).	50.00	100.00	200.00

1907 FIRST ISSUE
#60 printer: BWC.

60 **500 PESETAS**
 28.1.1907. Black on green and violet unpt. Women reclining at l. and r. leaning against medallic portr. of king at ctr. Back green; arms at ctr.

	Good	Fine	XF
	150.00	350.00	750.00

61 **1000 PESETAS**
 10.5.1907. Black on blue unpt. Mercury w/globe on shoulder at l., shield w/castle at lower l., shield w/rampant lion at lower r. Back brown; woman w/sword and lion at ctr.

		Good	Fine	XF
a.	Issued note.	200.00	450.00	850.00
b.	Round embossed Republic validation at upper r. corner (1931).	200.00	450.00	850.00

1907 SECOND ISSUE
#62-66 printer: BWC.

62 **25 PESETAS**
 15.7.1907. Black on dk. pink and green unpt. Woman reclining at ctr. Alhambra de Granada on back.

		Good	Fine	XF
a.	Issued note.	12.50	40.00	100.00
b.	Round embossed Republic validation at upper l. corner (1931).	25.00	50.00	125.00

63 **50 PESETAS**
 15.7.1907. Black on yellow, red and blue unpt. Woman standing at l. and r. Cathedral of Burgos on back.

		Good	Fine	XF
a.	Issued note.	12.50	45.00	75.00
b.	Round embossed Republic validation at upper l. corner (1931).	25.00	50.00	125.00

64 **100 PESETAS**
 15.7.1907. Green, red, yellow and black. Woman seated at l., medallic male portr. at ctr. Cathedral of Seville on back.

		Good	Fine	XF
a.	Issued note.	12.50	30.00	50.00
b.	Round embossed Republic validation at upper l. corner (1931).	25.00	50.00	125.00

65 **500 PESETAS**
 15.7.1907. Red, green and black. Woman standing at l., cherubs at lower r. Alcázar de Segovia on back.

		Good	Fine	XF
a.	Issued note.	85.00	200.00	400.00
b.	Round embossed Republic validation at upper r. corner (1931).	65.00	150.00	300.00

	1000 PESETAS	GOOD	FINE	XF
66	15.7.1907. Black on ochre and red unpt. Woman seated on throne by medallic female portr. at ctr. Palacio Real de Madrid on back.			
	a. Issued note.	100.00	250.00	500.00
	b. Round embossed Republic validation at upper r. corner (1931).	100.00	225.00	450.00

1908 ISSUE

	25 PESETAS	VG	VF	UNC
67	1.12.1908. Quintana at l. Back half finished printing, proofs in different colors.	—	—	100.00
68	100 PESETAS	—	—	—
	1.12.1908. Blue. Conjoined portraits of Kg. Fernando and Qn. Isabel at l. (Not issued).			

1914; 1915 ISSUE

	5 PESETAS	VG	VF	UNC
68A	1914. Fernando VI at l. (Not issued).	—	—	—
68B	1000 PESETAS	—	—	—
	23.5.1915. Conjoined portraits of Alfonso XIII and Victoria Eugenia at l. (Not issued).			

1925 ISSUE

NOTE: 5 million Series G notes #69 were printed but never released.

	100 PESETAS	VG	VF	UNC
69	1.7.1925. Dk. blue and green on m/c unpt. Felipe II at l. and as wmk. Monastery of El Escorial at lower ctr. Retreat of Felipe II on blue and orange back. Printer: BWC.			
	a. Serial # w/o series letter, Series A-C, and Series D to 2,000,000.	5.00	20.00	—
	b. Round embossed Republic validation at upper l. corner (1931).	5.00	20.00	—
	c. Serial # D2,000,001 through Series F, Republic issue (1936).	.75	2.00	4.00
69A (68C)	500 PESETAS	—	—	—
	23.1.1925. Cardinal Cisneros at l. (Not issued).			

	1000 PESETAS	VG	VF	UNC
70	1.7.1925. Chestnut, red and violet. Kg. Carlos I at r., gorgon head at top ctr. Alcázar de Toledo on back. Printer: BWC.			
	a. Serial # to 3,646,000.	7.50	25.00	—
	b. Round embossed Republic validation at upper r. corner (1931).	7.50	30.00	—
	c. Serial # 3,646,001 to 5,000,000, Republic issue (1936).	2.50	7.50	20.00

1926; 1927 ISSUE
#71-73 printer: BWC.

	25 PESETAS	VG	VF	UNC
71	12.10.1926. Blue and violet on m/c unpt. St. Xavier at l. St. Xavier baptizing Indians on red-brown back. Wmk: Qn.			
	a. Issued note.	2.00	6.00	15.00
	b. Round embossed Republic validation at upper l. corner (1931).	5.00	20.00	—

72   50 PESETAS
17.5.1927. Purple and violet on orange and yellow unpt. Kg. Alfonso
XIII at l., fortified city at lower ctr. Founding of Buenos Aires on blue
back. Wmk: Qn.

		VG	VF	UNC
a.	Issued note.	6.00	17.50	45.00
b.	Round embossed Republic validation at upper l. corner (1931).	10.00	45.00	—

73   500 PESETAS
24.7.1927. Blue and brown on orange and green unpt. Lions Court at
Alhambra at ctr., Isabella Cátolica at r. Arms on red and purple back.

		VG	VF	UNC
a.	Serial # to 1,602,000.	15.00	40.00	—
b.	Round embossed Republic validation at upper r. corner (1931).	15.00	40.00	—
c.	Serial # 1,602,001 to 2,00,000, Republic issue (1936).	4.00	10.00	25.00

75   50 PESETAS
15.8.1928. Violet and black on pale blue and dull orange unpt. Prado
Museum in Madrid at lower l. and ctr., Velázquez at r. Painting "La
rendición de Breda" by Velázquez on back. Wmk: Woman.

		VG	VF	UNC
a.	Serial # w/o series letter, also Series A through 8,640,000.	3.00	8.00	—
b.	Serial # A8,640,001 through Series E, Republic issue.	.50	1.00	2.00

1928 ISSUE

Circulation of 1928-dated notes: part of the issue of 25 and 50 Pesetas was released before July 18, 1936,
the date at which recognition by the Nationalist government of further issues was cut off. None of the
100, 500 or 1000 Pesetas were released before that date; therefore, they are all considered as issues
of the Republic only.

#74-78 printer: BWC.

76   100 PESETAS
15.8.1928. Purple and black on m/c unpt. Cervantes at l. and as wmk.,
monument at ctr. Painting of D. Quijote by Pidal on back.

VG	VF	UNC
.30	2.00	6.00

77   500 PESETAS
15.8.1928. Purple and green on m/c unpt. Cathedral of Toledo at
lower l., Cardinal Cisneros above. Picture by Casanova showing
liberation of captives on back.

VG	VF	UNC
2.50	15.00	35.00

74   25 PESETAS
15.8.1928. Blue and brown on m/c unpt. Monument at ctr., Cáderon
de la Barca at r. Religious comedy scene on lilac back. Wmk: Woman.

		VG	VF	UNC
a.	Serial # w/o series letter, also Series A through 7,780,000.	3.50	10.00	—
b.	Serial # A7,780,001 through Series E, Republic issue.	.50	1.25	2.25

78   1000 Pesetas
15.8.1928. Blue and purple on m/c unpt. Cathedral of Seville at lower l., San Fernando at r. Painting of King receiving communion (by A. Ferrant) on red-brown back.

	VG	VF	UNC
	4.00	8.00	25.00

REPUBLIC

BANCO DE ESPAÑA

1931 PROVISIONAL ISSUE

Aside from the embossed notes (see #56b, 58b, 59b, 61b, 62b, 63b, 64b, 65b, 66b, 69b, 70b, 71b, 72b, 73b), the Provisional Government had at first authorized the overstamping of the 50 Pesetas (#72, with portr. of Alfonso XIII) with a purple oval handstamp consisting of arms at ctr. and legend *REPÚBLICA ESPAÑOLA* around. An earlier 50 Pesetas issue (#59) is also reported with this handstamp.

80   50 Pesetas
ND (1931 -old date 17.5.1927) . Republican handstamp over portr. at l. on #72.

	VG	VF	UNC
	7.50	17.50	45.00

1931 ISSUE
#81-85 printer: BWC.

81   25 Pesetas
25.4.1931. Green and brown on m/c unpt. V. López at r. Back brown; López's "Music". Wmk: Woman in Phrygian cap.

	VG	VF	UNC
	.50	2.00	5.00

82   50 Pesetas
25.4.1931. Blue, lilac and violet. E. Rosales at l. Rosales' "The Death of Lucretia" on back. Wmk: Woman.

	VG	VF	UNC
	.75	2.50	5.00

83   100 Pesetas
25.4.1931. Purple and black on blue, tan and m/c unpt. G. F. de Córdoba at l. Back green; painting by Casado del Alisal. Wmk: Helmeted man.

	VG	VF	UNC
	.50	2.00	4.00

84   500 Pesetas
25.4.1931. Chestnut and blue on m/c unpt. Juan S. de Elcano at l. Elias Salaverria's "Disembarkation" on back. Wmk: Kg.

	VG	VF	UNC
	1.50	10.00	30.00

84A   1000 Pesetas
25.4.1931. Green. J. Zorrilla at upper l. Zorrilla reading his poems at gathering on back. (Not issued).

	VG	VF	UNC
	—	Unc	200.00

1935 (1936) SILVER CERTIFICATE
#85 and 86 printer: BWC.

		VG	VF	UNC
85	**5 PESETAS**	.25	1.00	2.50
	1935 (1936). Green and violet. Woman at l.			

		VG	VF	UNC
86	**10 PESETAS**	.25	1.00	2.50
	1935 (1936). Red-brown and b blue. Woman at r.			

1935; 1936 (1938) REGULAR ISSUE

		VG	VF	UNC
87 (89)	**25 PESETAS**	20.00	50.00	125.00
	31.8.1936 (1938). Blue, chestnut and purple. J. Sorolla at l., church steeple at r. ctr. Back purple; picture by Sorolla. Printer: TDLR.			

		VG	VF	UNC
88	**50 PESETAS**	1.00	6.00	15.00
	22.7.1935. Purple and black on m/c unpt. S. Ramón y Cajal at r. and as wmk., woman on column supports at l. and r. Monument on blue back. Printer: TDLR.			

		VG	VF	UNC
89 (87)	**500 PESETAS**	35.00	75.00	190.00
	7.1.1935. Chestnut, green and blue. H. Cortez at l., his palace in Mexico at lower r. ctr. Back red and purple; painting of Cortez burning his ships. Printer: TDLR.			

1938 ISSUES
#90-92 not issued.

		VG	VF	UNC
90	**100 PESETAS**	—	—	—
	11.3.1938. Barcelona. Carving of Dame of Elche at l., boat at ctr. Roadway w/palms on on back. Printer: TDLR.			

		VG	VF	UNC
91 (92)	**100 PESETAS**	—	—	—
	15.8.1938. Gray. Barcelona. W/o vignettes. Spanish printing.			
92 (91)	**5000 PESETAS**	—	—	—
	11.6.1938. Barcelona. M. Fortuny at r. Fortuny's picture "La Vicaria" on back. Printer: BWC.			

MINISTERIO DE HACIENDA

MINISTRY OF FINANCE

1937-38 ISSUE

		VG	VF	UNC
93	**50 CENTIMOS**	.25	1.00	2.50
	1937. Blue on pink unpt. Woman at ctr. Back green.			

		VG	VF	UNC
94	**1 PESETA**	.40	1.50	3.00
	1937. Brown and green. Nike of Samothrace at l. Back purple and gold, w/La Cibeles Fountain in Madrid.			

		VG	VF	UNC
95	**2 PESETAS**	.40	1.50	3.00
	1938. Blue, brown and green. Woman at ctr. Back gray and purple, w/Toledo Bridge in Madrid.			

POSTAGE STAMP/DISK

Brown cardboard disks, Spanish coat of arms with *PLUS ULTRA* printed on face, back affixed w/postage stamps or revenue stamps. Initially issued only by the Ministry of Finance, later also by the banks as small change.

The decree of 24.2.1938 authorized the use of 5 and 25 centimos postage stamps (correos), and 10 and 15 centimos revenue stamps (especial movil), to be affixed to cardboard disks. A later decree, of 22.10.1938, authorized the 10 centimos postage stamp as well because of color confusion with the revenue stamps of that denomination. Specific design types are not mentioned in the decrees; thus, only the denominations themselves under their respective categories can be listed. Many other types and denominations were affixed to the disks and circulated; however, all of these must be considered unofficial. The following listing includes commonly encountered official and unofficial types.

1938 CORREOS "NUMERAL" SERIES
#96-96E postage stamps w/large numerals; w/o portr.
#96F-96N postage stamps w/portr.
#96-96N arms on face.

		VG	VF	UNC
96	**5 CENTIMOS**	1.00	3.00	5.00
	ND (1938). Brown.			
96A	**10 CENTIMOS**	1.00	3.50	6.00
	ND (1938). Green.			
96B	**15 CENTIMOS**	1.00	3.50	6.00
	ND (1938). Gray.			
96C	**20 CENTIMOS**	1.00	4.50	7.00
	ND (1938). Violet.			

			VG	VF	UNC
96D	**25 CENTIMOS**		1.00	3.00	5.00
	ND (1938). Brown-violet.				
96E	**30 CENTIMOS**		1.00	4.50	8.00
	ND (1938). Rose.				

1938 CORREOS "PORTRAIT" SERIES

			VG	VF	UNC
96F	**5 CENTIMOS**		1.00	3.00	5.00
	ND (1938). Dk. brown.				
96G	**10 CENTIMOS**		1.00	3.50	6.00
	ND (1938).				
96H	**15 CENTIMOS**		1.00	3.50	6.00
	ND (1938).				
96I	**25 CENTIMOS**		1.00	3.00	5.00
	ND (1938). Red-violet.				
96J	**30 CENTIMOS**		1.00	3.50	6.00
	ND (1938).				
96K	**40 CENTIMOS**		1.00	3.50	6.00
	ND (1938).				
96L	**45 CENTIMOS**		1.00	3.50	6.00
	ND (1938). Red.				
96M	**50 CENTIMOS**		1.00	3.50	6.00
	ND (1938).				
96N	**60 CENTIMOS**		1.00	3.50	6.00
	ND (1938).				

1938 ESPECIAL MOVIL (REVENUE) SERIES
#96O-96T revenue stamps w/o portraits; w/large crowned arms between pillars (Type I) or sprays (Type II).

			VG	VF	UNC
96O	**5 CENTIMOS**		1.00	3.50	6.00
	ND (1938). Blue. Type I.				
96P	**10 CENTIMOS**		1.00	3.50	6.00
	ND (1938). Brown. Type I.				
96Q	**15 CENTIMOS**		1.00	3.50	6.00
	ND (1938). Gray-green. Type I.				
96R	**15 CENTIMOS**		1.00	3.50	6.00
	ND (1938). Red. Type II.				
96S	**30 CENTIMOS**		1.00	3.50	6.00
	ND (1938).				
96T	**50 CENTIMOS**		1.00	3.50	6.00
	ND (1938). Red. Type I.				

REGENCY

BANCO DE ESPAÑA

1936 ISSUE
#99-103 printer: G&D (w/o imprint).

			VG	VF	UNC
97	**5 PESETAS**		37.50	75.00	175.00
	21.11.1936. Brown on blue-green unpt. Arms at r.				
98	**10 PESETAS**		37.50	75.00	175.00
	21.11.1936. Blue and orange. Arms at r.				

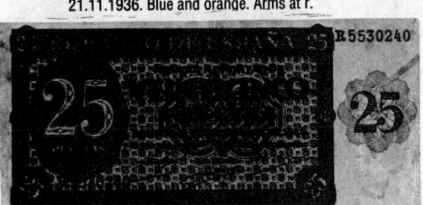

			VG	VF	UNC
99	**25 PESETAS**		2.50	6.00	27.50
	21.11.1936. Blue on olive unpt. Head on back.				

			VG	VF	UNC
100	**50 PESETAS**		3.00	8.00	35.00
	21.11.1936. Brown on green unpt. Head at l. and r. on back.				

			VG	VF	UNC
101	**100 PESETAS**		5.00	12.00	45.00
	21.11.1936. Green on lt. green and orange unpt. Catherdral of Burgos on back.				

			VG	VF	UNC
102	**500 PESETAS**		37.50	80.00	250.00
	21.11.1936. Dk. blue. Bldg. and viaduct on back.				
103	**1000 PESETAS**		60.00	125.00	300.00
	21.11.1936. Green. Old bridge and bldg. on back.				

1937 ISSUE
#104 and 105 printer: Coen, Milano.

#106A-106C printed by an Italian firm. (Not issued).

			VG	VF	UNC
104 (105)	**1 PESETA**		1.00	6.00	15.00
	12.10.1937. Lilac on blue unpt. Arms at l. Back purple on brown unpt.				
105 (106)	**2 PESETAS**		1.00	6.00	15.00
	12.10.1937. Dk. green on lt. orange and lt. lilac unpt. Gothic church at l. Back bluish black.				

			VG	VF	UNC
106 (104)	**5 PESETAS**	18.7.1937. Brown on tan unpt. Woman holding caduceus at r. Series A-C. Back orange; arms at ctr. Imprint: Litl M. Portabella Zaragoza.	10.00	35.00	95.00
106A (104A)	**25 PESETAS**	18.7.1937. Columbus at l. Columbus at the "New World" on back.	—	—	—
106B (104B)	**100 PESETAS**	18.7.1937. Gen. Castanos at r. Battle of Bailén on back.	—	—	—
106C (104C)	**1000 PESETAS**	18.7.1937. Carlos V at ctr. Battle scene on back.	—	—	—

			VG	VF	UNC
113 (112)	**100 PESETAS**	20.5.1938. Lilac-brown and orange. House of Cordon on back.	4.00	12.00	35.00
114 (113)	**500 PESETAS**	20.5.1938. Yellow-green and lilac. Cathedral on back.	20.00	60.00	135.00

1938 ISSUE
#107-109 printer: Coen, Milano.
#110-115 arms unpt. Printer: G&D.

			VG	VF	UNC
107	**1 PESETA**	28.2.1938. Brown on green unpt. Arms at l. Back purple.	3.00	8.00	27.50

			VG	VF	UNC
108	**1 PESETA**	30.4.1938. Brown on green unpt. Like #107.	1.25	4.50	17.50

			VG	VF	UNC
115 (114)	**1000 PESETAS**	20.5.1938. Blue and red. Historic picture on back.	35.00	80.00	185.00

1940 FIRST ISSUE
#116-120 printer: Calcografia & Cartevalori, Milano, Italia.

			VG	VF	UNC
109	**2 PESETAS**	30.4.1938. Dk. green on orange and lilac unpt. Like #105.	1.50	10.00	30.00

			VG	VF	UNC
116	**25 PESETAS**	9.1.1940 (1943). Gray-blue on lt. brown unpt. J. de Herrera at l., Patio de Evangelistas at r. Arms at l. on back.	3.00	18.00	50.00
117	**50 PESETAS**	9.1.1940 (1943). Green on blue and orange unpt. M. Pelayo at l. Back lt. blue-gray; arms at ctr.	3.00	12.00	30.00

			VG	VF	UNC
110 (115)	**5 PESETAS**	10.8.1938. Green and red on lt. brown unpt.	1.50	5.00	25.00
111 (110)	**25 PESETAS**	20.5.1938. Green and pink. Church in Seville on back.	2.00	6.00	22.50

			VG	VF	UNC
112 (111)	**50 PESETAS**	20.5.1938. Red-brown and green. Castle at Olite on back.	4.00	12.00	37.50

			VG	VF	UNC
118	**100 PESETAS**	9.1.1940 (1943). Lilac-brown on green unpt. Columbus at ctr., allegorical woman at either side. Arms at ctr. on back	6.00	22.50	60.00
119	**500 PESETAS**	9.1.1940 (1945). Dk. green. John of Austria at r. Battle of Lepanto w/old ships on back.	40.00	95.00	225.00

120   1000 Pesetas
9.1.1940. Issue of 12.11.1943. Gray and brown. B. Murillo at ctr. Back maroon and brown; Murillo painting "Children Counting Money."

VG	VF	UNC
50.00	110.00	250.00

1940 Second Issue

121   1 Peseta
1.6.1940. Blue and orange. Cortez on horseback at r. Back brown. Imprint: Graficas Reunidas S. A., Madrid.

VG	VF	UNC
3.00	8.00	30.00

122   1 Peseta
4.9.1940. Black on gold and blue unpt. Sailing ship Santa Maria at ctr. Back dk. green on purple unpt. Imprint: Rieusset S.A. Barcelona.

VG	VF	UNC
1.00	8.00	20.00

123   5 Pesetas
4.9.1940. Dk. brown and blue-green on orange and green unpt. Arms at l., palace of Segovia at r. Back blue and green. Printer: G&D.

VG	VF	UNC
3.00	10.00	35.00

124   500 Pesetas
21.10.1940. Issue of Feb. 1947. Black on lt. green, gold and pink unpt. Conde Orgas (Death Scene) by El Greco at r. Back gray on gold unpt.; view of Toledo at ctr.

VG	VF	UNC
25.00	75.00	185.00

125   1000 Pesetas
21.10.1940. Lilac and violet. Portr. helmeted Kg. Carlos I at l. Arms of Kg. Carlos I on back.

VG	VF	UNC
35.00	95.00	225.00

1943 Issue
#126 and 127 printer: FNMT.

126   1 Peseta
(127)
21.5.1943. Dk. brown on m/c unpt. Kg. Ferdinand the Catholic at l. Columbus landing on back.

VG	VF	UNC
.50	3.00	10.00

127   5 Pesetas
(126)
13.2.1943. Black on m/c unpt. Qn. Isabel la Católica at l. Columbus w/his men at ctr. on back.

VG	VF	UNC
1.00	8.00	25.00

1945 Issue
#128 and 129 printer: FNMT.

128   1 Peseta
15.6.1945. Brown on m/c unpt. Qn. Isabel la Católica at l. Man w/old map on back.

VG	VF	UNC
.25	3.00	6.00

129   5 Pesetas
15.6.1945. Black and green on m/c unpt. Qn. Isabel la Católica and Columbus at l. Medieval battle on back. W/o series, and Series A-M.

VG	VF	UNC
.75	5.00	15.00

1946 Issue
#130-133 printer: FNMT.

		VG	VF	UNC
130	**25 PESETAS** 19.2.1946 (1948). Purple and black on m/c unpt. F. Estrada at l. View of Pola de Somiedo on back. Wmk: Greek man's head.	.50	4.00	10.00

		VG	VF	UNC
131	**100 PESETAS** 19.2.1946 (1949). Brown on lilac unpt. Goya at r. and as wmk. "The Sun Shade" by Goya on back. Series A-B.	1.50	10.00	25.00

		VG	VF	UNC
132	**500 PESETAS** 19.2.1946 (1949). Blue on m/c unpt. F. de Vitoria at r. and as wmk. University of Salamanca on back.	15.00	45.00	120.00
133	**1000 PESETAS** 19.2.1946 (1948). Green and brown. J. L. Vives at r. and as wmk. Cloister at college in Valencia on back.	25.00	65.00	165.00

1947 Issue

		VG	VF	UNC
134	**5 PESETAS** 12.4.1947. Brown-lilac on lt. green and lt. orange unpt. Seneca at r. Back blue-black. Printre: FNMT.	.50	5.00	12.00

1948 Issue
#135-137 printer: FNMT.

		VG	VF	UNC
135 (137)	**1 PESETA** 19.6.1948. Brown on m/c unpt. Lady from Elche at r. Orange plant on back.	.25	3.00	8.00

		VG	VF	UNC
136 (135)	**5 PESETAS** 5.3.1948. Dk. green on lilac unpt. J.S. Elcano at l. Wmk: Man's head.	.25	3.00	10.00

		VG	VF	UNC
137 (136)	**100 PESETAS** 2.5.1948 (1950). Brown. F. Bayeu at l. Goya's "El Cacharrero" on back. Wmk: Goya.	1.00	6.00	20.00

1949 (1951) Issue

		VG	VF	UNC
138	**1000 PESETAS** 4.11.1949 (1951). Black and green. R. de Santillan at r. Goya's "El bebedor" on back. Wmk: Goya. Printer: FNMT.	25.00	55.00	135.00

1951 Issue
139-143 printer: FNMT.

		VG	VF	UNC
139 (141)	**1 PESETA** 19.11.1951. Brown on m/c unpt. D. Quijote at r. Shields and lance on back.	.15	3.00	6.00

			VG	VF	UNC
140 (139)	**5 PESETAS** 16.8.1951. Dk. green and black on olive and orange unpt. Balmes at l. and as wmk. Old bldg. on back.		.25	3.00	8.00

			VG	VF	UNC
141 (142)	**50 PESETAS** 31.12.1951 (1956). Lilac-red on m/c unpt. S. Rusiñol at r. and as wmk. Rusiñol's "Jardines de Aranjuez" on back.		.50	5.00	10.00

			VG	VF	UNC
142 (140)	**500 PESETAS** 15.11.1951 (1952). Dk. blue. M. Benlliure at l. Sculpture by Benlliure on back.		15.00	40.00	85.00
143	**1000 PESETAS** 31.12.1951 (1953). Green. J. Sorolla at ctr. Sorolla's "La fiesta del naranjo" on back.		12.00	35.00	85.00

1953 ISSUE
#144 and 145 printer: FNMT.

			VG	VF	UNC
144 (145)	**1 PESETA** 22.7.1953. Brown and black on m/c unpt. M. de Santa Cruz at r. Old sailing ship on back.		.15	3.00	6.00

			VG	VF	UNC
145 (144)	**100 PESETAS** 7.4.1953 (1955). Brown on m/c unpt. J. Romero de Torres at ctr. Painting by Torres on back. Wmk: Woman's head.		FV	2.50	9.00

1954 ISSUE
#146-148 printer: FNMT.

			VG	VF	UNC
146	**5 PESETAS** 22.7.1954. Green on lt. lilac unpt. Kg. Alfonso X at r. and as wmk. Library and museum bldg. in Madrid on back.		.15	3.00	6.00
147	**25 PESETAS** 22.7.1954. Purple on orange and m/c unpt. I. Albeniz at l. and as wmk. Patio scene of the Lion's Court of Alhambra on back.		.35	4.00	10.00

			VG	VF	UNC
148	**500 PESETAS** 22.7.1954 (1958). Blue on m/c unpt. I. Zuloaga at ctr. and as wmk. Zuloaga's "Vista de Toledo" on back.		FV	10.00	30.00

1957 (1958) ISSUE

			VG	VF	UNC
149	**1000 PESETAS** 29.11.1957 (1958). Green. "Reyes Católicos" at ctr. Arms on back. Printer: FNMT.		FV	20.00	50.00

Straits Settlements is a former British crown colony on the south and west coast of Malay Peninsula consisting of Malacca, Penang, Singapore, Labuan (Borneo), Cocos Island and Christmas Island. Cocos Island, Christmas Island and Labuan were placed under control of the Governor of Straits Settlements in 1886.

The colony was united under one government as a presidency of India in 1826, was incorporated under Bengal in 1830, and was removed from control of the Indian government and placed under direct British control in 1867. Japanese forces occupied the colony in 1941-45.

Cocos Island and Christmas Island were ceded to Australia in 1955 and 1958 respectively. Penang and Malacca were made states of independent Federation of Malaya in 1957, and became states of Malaysia in 1963. Labuan was incorporated as part of Singapore in 1907, was constituted as a separate settlement in 1912, was made part of North Borneo in 1946, and became part of Malaysia in 1963. Singapore was made a separate colony in 1946, was part of Malaysia in 1963-65, and became an independent republic in 1965.

RULERS:
British

MONETARY SYSTEM:
1 Dollar = 100 Cents

NOTE: Certain listings encompassing issues circulated by various commercial bank and regional authorities are contained in Volume 1.

BRITISH INFLUENCE

GOVERNMENT OF THE STRAITS SETTLEMENTS

1898-1906 ISSUE
#1-4B arms at upper ctr. Various dates and sign. varieties. Printer: TDLR.

NOTE: At Singapore, in the Spink-Taisei Sale of February, 1989, #4A, $50 dated 1901 brought $7,150 in Fine condition; #4B, $100 dated 1901 brought $17,600 in VG-F condition.

		GOOD	FINE	XF
1	**1 DOLLAR**			
	1906-24. Black. Tiger at ctr. on back.			
	a. Lt. pink paper. 2 sign. varieties. 1.9.1906.	100.00	500.00	780.00
	b. Dk. red paper. Unpt. like #A1. 4 sign. varieties. 8.6.1909; 17.3.1911.	90.00	400.00	780.00
	c. Paper and unpt. like b. 2.1.1914-5.9.1924	35.00	75.00	175.00

		GOOD	FINE	XF
1A	**1 DOLLAR**			
	1.9.1906. Like #1a but unpt. Shows numeral 1 at l. and ctr. r.	100.00	500.00	780.00
2	**5 DOLLARS**			
	1.9.1898; 1.3.1900. Black on lt. purple unpt. Tiger at ctr. on back. 195 x 120mm.	700.00	1600.	3800.

		GOOD	FINE	XF
3	**5 DOLLARS**			
	1.2.1901-5.9.1924. Black and purple on lt. yellow paper. Similar to #2 but changes in frame ornaments on face and back. 119 x 75mm. 6 sign. varieties.	300.00	1000.	2400.

		GOOD	FINE	XF
4	**10 DOLLARS**			
	1898-1924. Blue on lt. purple unpt. Tiger on back. 7 sign. varieties.			
	a. 1.9.1898; 1.2.1901; 8.6.1909; 17.3.1911.	—	Rare	—
	b. 2.1.1914-5.9.1924.	600.00	1500.	—

		GOOD	FINE	XF
4A	**50 DOLLARS**			
	1.2.1901. Green on lt. purple unpt.	—	Rare	—

4B	**100 DOLLARS**	**GOOD**	**FINE**	**XF**
	1.2.1901. Red on lt. purple unpt.	—	Rare	—
4C	**100 DOLLARS**			
	1.2.1901. Red on dk. olive unpt. *HUNDRED* on back.	—	Rare	—

1916 ISSUE

#A5 and 5 portr. Kg. George V above tiger at ctr. Uniface. Printer: TDLR.

NOTE: The authenticity of #A5 dated 1.6.1920 has not been determined.

A5	**50 DOLLARS**	**GOOD**	**FINE**	**XF**
	7.3.1916. Dk. blue on gray-violet unpt.	400.00	1000.	—

5	**100 DOLLARS**	**GOOD**	**FINE**	**XF**
	7.3.1916; 1.6.1920. Dk. red on olive unpt.	600.00	1650.	—

1917 ISSUE

6	**10 CENTS**	**GOOD**	**FINE**	**XF**
	1917-20. Green on yellow unpt. Arms at upper ctr. 2 sign. varieties. Date in red seal on back, day at l. of crown, month at r., year at bottom. Printer: Survey Dept. F.M.S.			
	a. Sign. H. Marriot, w/title: *Ag. Treasurer.* W/*No.* before serial #. 1.7.1917-1.10.1917.	15.00	50.00	135.00
	b. As a. but w/o *No.* before serial #. 1.11.1917-1.9.1918.	12.50	45.00	125.00
	c. Sign. A.M. Pountney w/title: *Treasurer.* 2.1.1919-10.6.1920.	8.00	25.00	85.00

7	**25 CENTS**	**GOOD**	**FINE**	**XF**
	ND (1917). Black on yellow-orange unpt. Arms at top ctr. Tiger at ctr. on back. Printer: Survey Dept. F.M.S.	100.00	250.00	450.00

1919 ISSUE

8	**10 CENTS**	**GOOD**	**FINE**	**XF**
	14.10.1919. Red and green on gray-brown unpt. Arms at top ctr. Back green; dragon at ctr. Printer: TDLR.			
	a. Sign. title: *Ag. Treasurer.*	10.00	40.00	100.00
	b. Sign. title: *Treasurer.*	6.00	15.00	40.00

1925; 1930 ISSUE

#9-15 printer: TDLR.

NOTE: #15 was used only in interbank transactions.

9	**1 DOLLAR**	**GOOD**	**FINE**	**XF**
	1925-30. Red on gray-violet unpt. Palm trees at l., palm trees and huts at r. Beach w/palms at ctr. on back. 4 sign. varieties (red or black).			
	a. Red date in plate. 1.1.1925; 1.9.1927; 1.1.1929.	15.00	70.00	165.00
	b. Black ovpt. date. 1.1.1930.	12.00	60.00	135.00

10	**5 DOLLARS**	**GOOD**	**FINE**	**XF**
	1925-30. Green. Farmer w/water buffalo ridden by child at r. Tiger in ornate cartouche at upper ctr. on back. 4 sign. varieties (red or black).			
	a. Green date in plate. 1.1.1925; 1.9.1927; 1.1.1929.	60.00	225.00	400.00
	b. Black ovpt. date 1.1.1930.	60.00	225.00	400.00

11 10 DOLLARS

	GOOD	FINE	XF
1925-30. Purple. Palm trees and huts w/fishing boats at ctr. Animal cart in ornate cartouche on back. 4 sign. varieties (red or black).			
a. Purple date in plate. 1.1.1925; 1.9.1927; 1.1.1929.	90.00	300.00	650.00
b. Black ovpt. date 1.1.1930.	90.00	300.00	650.00

12 50 DOLLARS

	GOOD	FINE	XF
1925; 1927. Like #A5.			
a. 24.9.1925.	1200.	2600.	—
b. 1.11.1927.	—	Rare	—

13 100 DOLLARS

	GOOD	FINE	XF
24.9.1925; 1.11.1927. Like #5. 2 sign. varieties.	900.00	2200.	—

14 1000 DOLLARS

	GOOD	FINE	XF
1.10.1930. Like #5.	—	Rare	—

15 10,000 DOLLARS

	GOOD	FINE	XF
(ca. 1925). Like #5.	—	Rare	—

1931 ISSUE

#16-18 portr. Kg. George V at r. Tiger at ctr., woman's head at l. on back. Printer: BWC.

16 1 DOLLAR

	GOOD	FINE	XF
1931-35. Dk. blue. 2 sign. varieties.			
a. 1.1.1931-1.1.1934.	20.00	90.00	340.00
b. 1.1.1935.	5.00	15.00	30.00

17 5 DOLLARS

	GOOD	FINE	XF
1931-35. Violet. 2 sign. varieties.			
a. 1.1.1931-1.1.1934.	50.00	160.00	500.00
b. 1.1.1935.	20.00	60.00	240.00

18 10 DOLLARS

	GOOD	FINE	XF
1931-35. Green. 2 sign. varieties.			
a. 1.1.1931-1.1.1934.	50.00	160.00	500.00
b. 1.1.1935.	20.00	60.00	240.00

SUDAN

The Democratic Republic of the Sudan, located in north-east Africa on the Red Sea between Egypt and Ethiopia, has an area of 967,500 sq. mi. (2,505,810 sq. km.) and a population of 29.97 million. Capital: Khartoum. Agriculture and livestock raising are the chief occupations. Cotton, gum arabic and peanuts are exported.

The Sudan, site of the powerful Nubian kingdom of Roman times, was a collection of small independent states from the 14th century until 1820-22 when it was conquered and united by Mohammed Ali, Pasha of Egypt. Egyptain forces were driven from the area during the Mahdist revolt, 1881-98, but the Sudan was retaken by Anglo-Egyptian expeditions, 1896-98, and established as an Anglo-Egyptian condominium in 1899. Britain supplied the administrative apparatus and personnel, but the appearance of joint Anglo-Egyptian administration was continued until Jan. 9, 1954, when the first Sudanese self-government parliament was inaugurated. The Sudan achieved independence on Jan. 1, 1956 with the consent of the British and Egyptian governments. On June 30, 1989 Gen. Omar Hassan Ahmad al-Bashir overthrew the civilian government in a military coup. The rebel guerrilla PLA forces are active in the south. Notes of Egypt were in use before 1956.

RULERS:
British, 1899-1954
Italian, 1940

MONETARY SYSTEM:
1 Ghirsh (Piastre) = 10 Millim (Milliemes)
1 Sudanese Pound = 100 Piastres to 1992
1 Dinar = 10 Old Sudanese Pounds, 1992

REPUBLIC

SUDAN GOVERNMENT - TREASURY

1955 ISSUE

#A1-A5 arms (desert camel soldier) at ctr. r. on back. Printer: W&S. (Not issued.)

		VG	VF	UNC
A1	**25 PIASTRES** 6.7.1955. Red on pale green and pale orange unpt. Soldiers in formation at l. Specimen, punched hole cancelled.	—	—	—

A2	**50 PIASTRES** 6.7.1955. Green on ochre and dull violet unpt. Elephants at l. Specimen, punched hole cancelled.	—	—	—

A3	**1 POUND** ND (1955). Blue on yellow and m/c unpt. Dam at l. Specimen, punched hole cancelled.	—	—	—

A4	**5 POUNDS** 6.7.1955. Dk. brown on m/c unpt. Dhow at l. Specimen, punched hole cancelled.	—	—	—
A5	**10 POUNDS** ND (1955). Black on m/c unpt. Bldg. at l. Specimen, punched hole cancelled.	—	—	—

SUDAN CURRENCY BOARD

1956 ISSUE

#1A-5 Arabic dates at lower r. Arms (desert camel soldier) at ctr. r. on back.

		VG	VF	UNC
1A	**25 PIASTRES** 15.9.1956. Red on pale green and pale orange unpt. Soldiers in formation at l. 3rd line of text 31mm long.	7.50	25.00	125.00

		VG	VF	UNC
1B	**25 PIASTRES** 15.9.1956. Red on pale green and pale orange unpt. Like #1A but 3rd line of text 45mm long.	5.00	20.00	140.00
2A	**50 PIASTRES** 15.9.1956. Green on ochre and dull violet unpt. Elephants at l. 3rd line of text 31mm long.	20.00	70.00	450.00

		VG	VF	UNC
2B	**50 PIASTRES** 15.9.1956. Green on ochre and dull violet unpt. Like #2A but 3rd line of text 45mm long.	15.00	50.00	425.00

		VG	VF	UNC
3	**1 POUND** 15.9.1956. Blue on yellow and m/c unpt. Dam at l.	15.00	45.00	250.00
4	**5 POUNDS** 15.9.1956. Dk. brown on m/c unpt. Dhow at l.	25.00	75.00	700.00

5	**10 POUNDS** 15.9.1956. Black on m/c unpt. Bldg. at l.	**VG** 35.00	**VF** 150.00	**UNC** 950.00

ITALIAN OCCUPATION - WW II

CASSA MEDITERRANEA DI CREDITO PER IL SUDAN

1940 ISSUE

#M1-M8 prepared for the Italian occupation of Sudan during World War II. Specimen.

		VG	**VF**	**UNC**
M1	**5 PIASTRES** ND (1940). Blue. Like #M2.	—	Rare	
M2	**10 PIASTRES** ND (1940). Orange. Man at r.	—	Rare	
M3	**50 PIASTRES** ND (1940). Blue-green.	—	Rare	
M4	**1 LIRA** ND (1940). Green. Roman warrior at l.	—	Rare	
M5	**5 LIRE** ND (1940). Like #M4.	—	Rare	

		VG	**VF**	**UNC**
M6	**10 LIRE** ND (1940). Like #M4.	—	Rare	
M7	**50 LIRE** ND.	—	Rare	

		VG	**VF**	**UNC**
M8	**100 LIRE** ND (1940). Blue. Man at l.	—	Rare	

The Republic of Surinam, formerly known as Dutch Guiana, located on the north central coast of South America between Guyana and French Guiana, has an area of 63,037 sq. mi. (163,270 sq. km.) and a population of 404,300. Capital: Paramaribo. The country is rich in minerals and forests, and self-sufficient in rice, the staple food crop. The mining, processing and exporting of bauxite is the principal economic activity.

Lieutenants of Amerigo Vespucci sighted the Guiana coast in 1499. Spanish explorers of the 16th century, disappointed at finding no gold, departed leaving the area to be settled by the British in 1652. The colony prospered and the Netherlands acquired it in 1667 in exchange for the Dutch rights in Nieuw Nederland (state of New York). During the European wars of the 18th and 19th centuries, which were fought in part in the New World, Surinam was occupied by the British from 1799-1814. Surinam became an autonomous part of the Kingdom of the Netherlands on Dec. 15, 1954. Full independence was achieved on Nov. 25, 1975.

RULERS:
Dutch to 1975

MONETARY SYSTEM:
1 Gulden = 1 Florin = 100 Cents

DUTCH INFLUENCE

ALGEMENE NEDERLANDSCHE MAATSCHAPPIJ

GENERAL NETHERLANDS COMPANY

1826 ISSUE

A11	**1/2 GULDEN** 1.10.1826. Black. Uniface.	**GOOD** —	**FINE** Rare	**XF** —

SOCIÉTÉ GÉNÉRALE POUR FAVORISER L'INDUSTRIE NATIONALE

1826 ISSUE

A15	**3 GULDEN** 1.10.1826. Black. Uniface.	**GOOD** —	**FINE** Rare	**XF** —

WEST-INDISCHE BANK

1829 ISSUE
#A21-A32 uniface. Printer: JEZ.

		GOOD	FINE	XF
A21	**1/2 GULDEN** 1829. Black.	—	Rare	—
A22	**1 GULDEN** 1829.	—	—	—
A23	**2 GULDEN** 1829.	—	—	—
A24	**3 GULDEN** 1829.	—	—	—
A25	**5 GULDEN** 1829.	—	—	—
A26	**10 GULDEN** 1829.	—	—	—
A28	**50 GULDEN** 1829. Uniface. Unsigned remainder.	—	—	—

1837 ISSUE

		GOOD	FINE	XF
A31	**10 CENTEN** 1837. Black.	—	Rare	—
A32	**15 CENTEN** 1837. Red.	—	Rare	—
A33	**25 CENTEN** 1837. Hexagonal.	—	—	—
A40	**25 GULDEN** 1837.	—	—	—
A41	**50 GULDEN** 1837.	—	—	—

1865 ISSUE

		GOOD	FINE	XF
A45	**10 GULDEN** 1.7.1865. Supported arms at top ctr.	—	—	—
A46	**25 GULDEN** 1.7.1865.	—	—	—
A47	**50 GULDEN** 1.7.1865.	—	—	—
A48	**100 GULDEN** 1.7.1865.	—	—	—
A49	**200 GULDEN** 1.7.1865.	—	—	—
A50	**300 GULDEN** 1.7.1865.	—	—	—

DE SURINAAMSCHE BANK

1901 ISSUE
Various date and sign. varieties.

		GOOD	FINE	XF
A55	**50 GULDEN** 1.7.1901.			

1915-48 ISSUE
#1A-5 printer: JEZ.
#2A-5 w/4 oval vignettes in corners depicting various aspects of local economy.

		GOOD	FINE	XF
1A	**5 GULDEN** 1.10.1935; 3.6.1940. Blue on lt. green unpt. Arms at l., woman at r.	75.00	250.00	550.00
2A	**10 GULDEN** 1.8.1915; 15.6.1932; 15.6.1933. Red.	250.00	1500.	750.00

		GOOD	FINE	XF
3A	**25 GULDEN** 1.9.1941. Green on tan unpt.	300.00	2000.	—
1	**50 GULDEN** 15.4.1926; 28.11.1938. Blue.	400.00	2700.	—
2	**100 GULDEN** 1.9.1927. Brown.	—	Rare	—
3	**200 GULDEN** 1.7.1925; 1.9.1941. Brown.	—	Rare	—

		GOOD	FINE	XF
4	**300 GULDEN** 1.12.1948. Violet.	—	Rare	—
5	**1000 GULDEN** 9.11.1943. Brown-violet.	—	Rare	—

1940 ND PROVISIONAL ISSUE

		GOOD	FINE	XF
5A	**2 1/2 GULDEN** ND (-old date 1940). Red ovpt. on face and back of r. half of #1A.	—	Rare	—

1940-42 ISSUE
#6-10 printer: ABNC.
#7-10 bldg. w/flag at ctr.

		GOOD	FINE	XF
6	**2 1/2 GULDEN** 1940-42. Lilac-red on brown unpt. Woman reclining w/branch at ctr. Arms at top ctr. on back.			
	a. Date on face. 1.10.1940; 7.4.1941; 1.9.1941.	30.00	65.00	225.00
	b. Date on back. 1.1.1942.	15.00	45.00	165.00
	p. Proof.	—	Unc	250.00
	s. Specimen.	—	Unc	225.00

		GOOD	FINE	XF
7	**5 GULDEN** 1.9.1942. Blue on m/c unpt. Arms at lower ctr. on back.			
	a. Issued note.	60.00	175.00	450.00
	p. Proof.	—	Unc	350.00
	s. Specimen.	—	Unc	325.00

		GOOD	FINE	XF
8	**10 GULDEN** 1.6.1942. Orange on m/c unpt.			
	a. Issued note.	100.00	600.00	1250.00
	p. Proof.	—	Unc	650.00
	s. Specimen.	—	Unc	600.00

		GOOD	FINE	XF
9	**25 GULDEN** 1.2.1942; 1.12.1948. Green on m/c unpt.			
	a. 1.2.1942.	150.00	750.00	1600.
	b. 1.12.1948.	120.00	600.00	1250.
	p. Proof.	—	Unc	750.00
	s. Specimen.	—	Unc	700.00

		GOOD	FINE	XF
10	**100 GULDEN** 1.9.1941; 1.4.1943; 1.4.1948. Purple on m/c unpt.			
	a. Issued note.	350.00	1250.	
	p. Proof.	—	Unc	850.00
	s. Specimen.	—	Unc	800.00

1951 ISSUE
#11-13 printer: De Bussy, Amsterdam.

		GOOD	FINE	XF
11	**10 GULDEN** 1.8.1951. Green. Hut and trees at r. Cancelled.	100.00	400.00	850.00

		GOOD	FINE	XF
12	**25 GULDEN** 1.8.1951. Bldg. w/flag at lower r. Cancelled.	125.00	475.00	950.00

		GOOD	FINE	XF
13	**100 GULDEN** 1.8.1951. Violet and lilac. Arms w/Indian as shield supporter (Justitia, Pietas, Fides) at r. Cancelled.	175.00	550.00	1250.

ZILVERBONNEN

1918 ISSUE
#13A-13C various date and sign. varieties.

		GOOD	FINE	XF
13A	**HALF GULDEN**	300.00	650.00	—
	12.4.1918; 2.2.1920. Brown. Uniface.			

		GOOD	FINE	XF
13B	**1 GULDEN**	300.00	650.00	—
	12.4.1918. Brown. Like #13A.			
13C	**2 1/2 GULDEN**	—	500.00	900.00
	12.4.1918. Red-brown on lt. brown unpt. Like #13A. Unissued remainder.			

1920 FIRST ISSUE

		GOOD	FINE	XF
13D	**1 GULDEN**	300.00	650.00	—
	2.2.1920. Like #13B, but sign. title at r. changed.			

1920 SECOND ISSUE

		GOOD	FINE	XF
14	**50 CENT**	75.00	200.00	525.00
	1.8.1920. Blue, olive and m/c. Similar to #16.			
15	**1 GULDEN**	85.00	235.00	575.00
	1.8.1920. Green, orange and m/c. Similar to #16.			

		GOOD	FINE	XF
16	**2 1/2 GULDEN**	100.00	325.00	650.00
	1.8.1920. Brown on green unpt. Back green.			

1940 ISSUE
#17 and 18 printer: ABNC.

		GOOD	FINE	XF
17	**50 CENT**			
	1940-42. Orange. Helmeted woman at l.			
	a. 1 serial #. 27.9.1940; 5.10.1940; 30.10.1940.	5.00	35.00	140.00
	b. As a. 1.7.1941.	4.50	32.50	130.00
	c. 2 serial #. 30.4.1942.	4.00	25.00	100.00
	p. Proof.	—	Unc	160.00
	s. Specimen.	—	Unc	135.00

		GOOD	FINE	XF
18	**1 GULDEN**			
	1940-47. Gray-blue. Like #17.			
	a. 1 serial #. 26.6.1940; 5.7.1940; 19.9.1940; 30.10.1940.	8.50	35.00	150.00
	b. As a. 1.7.1941.	7.50	32.50	140.00
	c. 2 serial #. 30.4.1942.	7.50	30.00	110.00
	d. 1.7.1947.	12.50	50.00	200.00
	p. Proof.	—	Unc	200.00
	s. Specimen.	—	Unc	175.00

1949-55 ISSUES
#19-22 helmeted woman at l. Printer: JEZ.

		VG	VF	UNC
19	**1 GULDEN**	5.00	30.00	125.00
	1.7.1949. Green, dk. brown and blue. Back brown and violet.			
19A	**1 GULDEN**	5.00	30.00	110.00
	1.3.1951. Like #19, but back brown and green.			

		VG	VF	UNC
20	**1 GULDEN**			
	1954-60. Blue and brown.			
	a. Sign. title: *De Landsminister van Financien* at l. 1.7.1954.	4.00	25.00	95.00
	b. Sign. title: *De Minister van Financien* at l. 1.5.1956; 1.4.1960.	3.75	15.00	85.00
21	**2 1/2 GULDEN**	6.00	50.00	200.00
	1.7.1950. Red-brown on yellow-green unpt. 3 lines of text at lower ctr.			
	r. Back red-violet and purple.			

22	**2 1/2 GULDEN**	VG	VF	UNC
	1.7.1955. Red-brown. 4 lines of text at lower ctr. r. Back red and brown.	5.00	40.00	165.00

CENTRALE BANK VAN SURINAME

1957 ISSUE
#25-29 arms on back. Wmk: Toucan's head. Printer: JEZ.

25	**5 GULDEN**	VG	VF	UNC
	2.1.1957. Blue on m/c unpt. Woman w/fruit basket at r.	3.00	7.50	35.00
26	**10 GULDEN**			
	2.1.1957. Orange on m/c unpt. Like #25.	5.00	12.50	60.00
27	**25 GULDEN**			
	2.1.1957. Green on m/c unpt. Girl and fruit at r.	10.00	25.00	100.00
28	**100 GULDEN**			
	2.1.1957. Purple on m/c unpt. Like #27.	35.00	75.00	275.00
29	**1000 GULDEN**			
	2.1.1957. Olive green on m/c unpt. Like #27.	200.00	450.00	850.00

SWEDEN

The Kingdom of Sweden, a limited constitutional monarchy located in northern Europe between Norway and Finland, has an area of 173,732 sq. mi. (449,960 sq. km.) and a population of 8.6 million. Capital: Stockholm. Mining, lumbering and a specialized machine industry dominate the economy. Machinery, paper, iron and steel, motor vehicles and wood pulp are exported.

Sweden was founded as a Christian stronghold by Olaf Skottkonung late in the 10th century. After conquering Finland late in the 13th century, Sweden, together with Norway, came under the rule of Denmark, 1397-1523, in an association known as the Union of Kalmar. Modern Sweden had its beginning in 1523 when Gustavus Vasa drove the Danes out of Sweden and was himself chosen king. Under Gustavus Adolphus II and Charles XII, Sweden was one of the great powers of the 17th century Europe - until Charles invaded Russia, 1708, and was defeated at the Battle of Pultowa in June 1709. Early in the 18th century, a coalition of Russia, Poland and Denmark took away Sweden's Baltic empire and in 1809 Sweden was forced to cede Finland to Russia. Norway was ceded to Sweden by the Treaty of Kiel in January 1814. The Norwegians resisted for a time but later signed the Act of Union at the Convention of Moss in August 1814. The Union was dissolved in 1905 and Norway became independent. A new constitution which took effect on Jan. 1, 1975, restricts the function of the king to a ceremonial role.

* * * This section has been renumbered. * * *

RULERS:
Carl XI, 1660-1697
Carl XII, 1697-1718
Ulrica Eleonora, 1719-1720
Fredric I, 1720-1751
Adolf Fredric, 1751-1771
Gustav III, 1771-1792
Gustaf IV Adolf, 1792-1809
Carl XIII, 1809-1818
Carl XIV John, 1818-1844
Oscar I, 1844-1859
Carl XV, 1859-1872
Oscar II, 1872-1907
Gustaf V, 1907-1950
Gustaf VI, 1950-1973
Carl XVI Gustaf, 1973-

MONETARY SYSTEM:
1 Daler Smt. = 32 Öre Smt. (= 3 Daler Kmt.), 1665
1 Riksdaler = 48 Skilling (= 18 Daler Kmt.), 1777
1 Riksdaler = 1 1/2 Riksdaler Riksgäld, 1803
1 Riksdaler Specie - 2 2/3 Riksdaler Banco = 4 Risdaler Riksgäld, 1834
1 Riksdaler Riksmynt = 100 Öre (= 1/4 Riksdaler Specie = 1 Riksdaler Riksgäld), 1855
1 Korona = 100 Öre (= 1 Riksdaler Riksmynt), 1873

MONETARY ABBREVIATIONS
DALER SMT. = Daler Silvermynt
DALER KMT. = Daler Kopparmynt
RKD. = Riksdaler
RKD. SP. = Riksdaler Specie
RKD. BC. = Riksdaler Banco
RKD. RGD. = Riksdaler Riksgäld
SK. = Schillingar
SK. Kop. = Kopparschillingar
SK. SP = Skillingar Specie
SK. BC. = Skillingar Banco
Kr. = Krona (Kronor)

NOTE ON VALUES: Indicated values apply only to uncancelled examples. Notes with cancellations are worth up to 50% less. Swedish printers referred to in the following listings:
C.A. Broling CAB
AB Jacob Bagges JB
Per Axel Nyman PAN
Carl Axel Nyman CAN

KINGDOM

STOCKHOLMS BANCO
#A1-A45 are unknown in private hands.

1661 DUCAT ISSUE

A1	**VARIOUS HANDWRITTEN VALUES**	GOOD	FINE	XF
	1661.	—	—	—

1661 RIKSDALER SPECIE ISSUE
#A2-A45 handwritten denominations.

A2	**50 RIKSDALER SPECIE**	GOOD	FINE	XF
	1661-62.	—	—	—
A3	**100 RIKSDALER SPECIE**			
	1661-62.	—	—	—
A4	**200 RIKSDALER SPECIE**			
	1661-62.	—	—	—
A5	**300 RIKSDALER SPECIE**			
	1661-62.	—	—	—

A60	100 DALER SILVERMYNT	GOOD	FINE	XF
	1666.	3000.	7000.	20,000.

1667 TRANSPORT (TRANSFER) ISSUE

A61	100 DALER SILVERMYNT	GOOD	FINE	XF
	1667. Copper money. (Only negotiable w/endorsement.)	—	—	—

CONTRIBUTION OFFICE AND PURCHASING COMMISSION

1716 DALER SILVERMYNT ISSUE

A62	25 DALER SILVERMYNT	GOOD	FINE	XF
	1716. Completely handwritten.	40.00	120.00	320.00

1717 ISSUE

A63	5 DALER SILVERMYNT	GOOD	FINE	XF
	1717.			
	a. 3 sign.	20.00	60.00	160.00
	r. Unsigned remainder.	10.00	30.00	80.00

A64	10 DALER SILVERMYNT	GOOD	FINE	XF
	1717.			
	a. W/3 sign.	20.00	60.00	160.00
	r. Unsigned remainder.	10.00	30.00	80.00

ASURANCE NOTES

1719 ISSUE

A65	2 ÖRE	GOOD	FINE	XF
	1719-29. Handwritten dates. Exchangeable for emergency coins.	—	—	—
A66	2 ÖRE			
	1719-29. Handwritten dates. Exchangeable for paper money.	—	—	—
A67	14 ÖRE			
	1719-29. Handwritten dates. Exchangeable for emergency coins and notes.	—	—	—
A68	14 ÖRE			
	1719-29. Printed dates. Redeemable for taxes.	—	—	—
A69	14 ÖRE			
	1719-29. Printed dates.	—	—	—

KONGL. MAY: TZ STÄNDERS WEXEL-BANCO

1701-19 ISSUE

A70	VARIOUS HANDWRITTEN VALUES	GOOD	FINE	XF
(A71)	1702-19.	—	Rare	
A71	200 DALER SILVERMYNT			
(A70)	1701. Handwritten. 1 known.	—	Rare	

RIKSENS STÄNDERS WEXEL-BANCO

1719 ISSUE

A72	VARIOUS HANDWRITTEN VALUES	GOOD	FINE	XF
	1719-28. 1 known.	—	Rare	

1729 ISSUE

A73	VARIOUS HANDWRITTEN VALUES	GOOD	FINE	XF
	1729-31. 1 known.	—	Rare	

1732 ISSUE

A74	VARIOUS HANDWRITTEN VALUES	GOOD	FINE	XF
	1732-47. Comprised of 4 pages.	—	Rare	

1743-45 ISSUE

A75	6 DALER KOPPARMYNT	GOOD	FINE	XF
	1745-47. Banco Sigill seal at upper I. Exchanged in 1749 for #A81.	—	Rare	
A76	9 DALER KOPPARMYNT			
	1745-47. Like #A75. Exchanged in 1749 for #A82.	—	Rare	
A77	12 DALER KOPPARMYNT			
	1745-47. Like #A75.	—	Rare	
A78	24 DALER KOPPARMYNT			
	1743-47. Comprised of 4 pages.	—	Rare	
A79	36 DALER KOPPARMYNT			
	1743-47. Comprised of 4 pages.	—	Rare	

1748 ISSUE

A80	VARIOUS HANDWRITTEN VALUES	GOOD	FINE	XF
	1748-60. Comprised of 4 pages.	—	Rare	
A81	6 DALER KOPPARMYNT			
	1748-61. *BANCO TRANSPORT SEDEL* in uneven line.	—	Rare	—

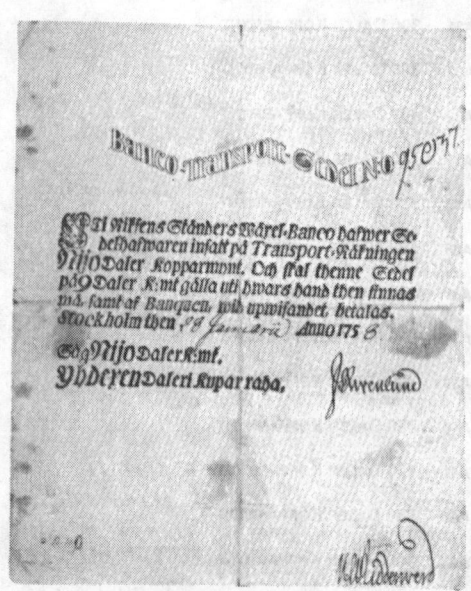

A82	9 DALER KOPPARMYNT	GOOD	FINE	XF
	1748-61. Like #A81.	—	Rare	—

A83	12 DALER KOPPARMYNT	GOOD	FINE	XF
	1748-54. Like #A81.	—	Rare	—
A84	24 DALER KOPPARMYNT			
	1748-58. Like #A81. Comprised of 4 pages.	—	Rare	—
A85	36 DALER KOPPARMYNT			
	1748-58. Like #A81. Comprised of 4 pages.	—	Rare	—

1759-60 ISSUE

A86	VARIOUS HANDWRITTEN VALUES	GOOD	FINE	XF
	1759-76. Comprised of 4 pages.	—	—	—

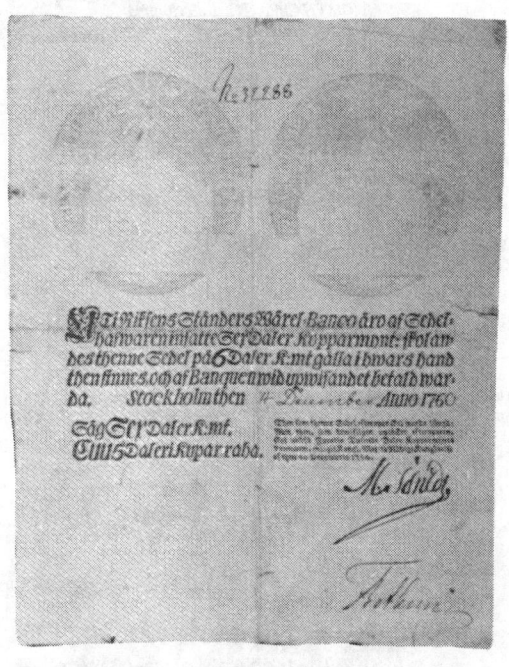

A87	6 DALER KOPPARMYNT	GOOD	FINE	XF
	1759-76. Embossed seals at top. Withdrawn in 1777, devalued in 1840.	60.00	180.00	700.00
A88	9 DALER KOPPARMYNT			
	1759-76. Like #A87.	70.00	200.00	800.00

A89	12 DALER KOPPARMYNT	GOOD	FINE	XF
	1760-76. Like #A87.	100.00	300.00	1200.

1777 TRANSPORT (TRANSFER) ISSUE

A90	VARIOUS HANDWRITTEN VALUES	GOOD	FINE	XF
	1777-1836. Comprised of 4 pages.	—	—	—

A91	2 RIKSDALER SPECIE	GOOD	FINE	XF
	1777-1812. Comprised of 4 pages.			
	a. 1777-86.	—	Rare	—
	b. 1787-1806; 1812.	—	Rare	—
	c. Printed value above obligation. 1807-1811.	125.00	350.00	1400.

A92 (A93)	3 RIKSDALER SPECIE	GOOD	FINE	XF
	1777-1812. Like #A91. Comprised of 4 pages.			
	a. 1777-86.	—	Rare	—
	b. 1787-1805.	—	Rare	—
	c. 1806-12.	100.00	300.00	1200.

1802 ISSUE

A93 (A95)	8 SCHILLINGAR SPECIE	GOOD	FINE	XF
	1802-34. Like #A91. Comprised of 4 pages.			
	a. 1802-18.	30.00	80.00	325.00
	b. Change in punishment clause. 1819-30.	30.00	80.00	325.00
	c. Printed value above obligation. Punishment clause in frame. 1831-34.	20.00	65.00	275.00

A94 (A97)	12 SCHILLINGAR SPECIE			
	1802-34. Like #A93.			

		GOOD	FINE	XF
a.	1802-18.	40.00	120.00	475.00
b.	Change in punishment clause. 1819-34.	30.00	100.00	400.00

A95 **16 SCHILLINGAR SPECIE**
(A99)   1802-34. Like #A91.

		GOOD	FINE	XF
a.	1802; 1806; 1808-09; 1811-12; 1815-18.	50.00	125.00	525.00
b.	1803-05; 1807; 1810; 1813-14.	—	Rare	—
c.	Change in punishment clause. 1819; 1823; 1825.	—	Rare	—
d.	Change in punishment clause. 1820-22; 1824; 1826-30.	40.00	125.00	475.00
e.	Horizontal format. 1831-34.	50.00	125.00	500.00

1803 ISSUE

A96 **10 KOPPAR SCHILLINGAR**
(A101)   1803-04. Embossed seal at top ctr.

	GOOD	FINE	XF
	20.00	50.00	175.00

A97 **14 KOPPAR SCHILLINGAR**
(A102)   1803-04. Like #A96.

	GOOD	FINE	XF
	20.00	50.00	175.00

1812 ISSUE

A98 **2 RIKSDALER SPECIE**
(A92)   1812-34. Like #A91. (Withdrawn in 1848, devalued in 1949.)
Comprised of 2 pages.

		GOOD	FINE	XF
a.	1812-13; 1815.	70.00	200.00	800.00
b.	1814; 1816-18.	—	Rare	—
c.	Change in punishment clause. 1819-22; 1828; 1831; 1834.	—	Rare	—
d.	Change in punishment clause. 1823-27; 1829-30; 1832-33.	80.00	250.00	1000.

A99 **3 RIKSDALER SPECIE**
(A94)   1812-36. Like #A93. Horizontal format. Comprised of 2 pages.

		GOOD	FINE	XF
a.	1812-18.	—	Rare	—
b.	Change in punishment clause. 1819-23; 1825-30; 1832; 1835-36.	—	Rare	—
c.	Change in punishment clause. 1824; 1831; 1833-34.	70.00	200.00	800.00

1834 ISSUE

#A103 *Deleted.* See #A94.

A100 **8 SCHILLINGAR BANCO**
(A96)   1834-49. Like #A93.

		GOOD	FINE	XF
a.	Contoured letters in wmk. 1834-36.	20.00	45.00	175.00
b.	Different wmk. 1836-49.	10.00	25.00	100.00

A101 **12 SCHILLINGAR BANCO**
(A98)   1834-49. Like #A100.

		GOOD	FINE	XF
a.	Contoured letters in wmk. 1834-36.	25.00	70.00	200.00
b.	Different wmk. 1836-49.	20.00	40.00	125.00

A102 (A100)	**16 SCHILLINGAR BANCO** 1834-49. Like #A99c. Horizontal format.	GOOD	FINE	XF
	a. Contoured letters in wmk. 1834-36.	25.00	75.00	300.00
	b. Different wmk. 1836-49.	20.00	50.00	200.00
A104	**2 RIKSDALER BANCO** 1834-36.	75.00	225.00	900.00
A105	**3 RIKSDALER BANCO** 1834-36.	75.00	225.00	900.00

RIKSENS STÄNDERS RIKSGALDS CONTOIR

1790 ISSUE

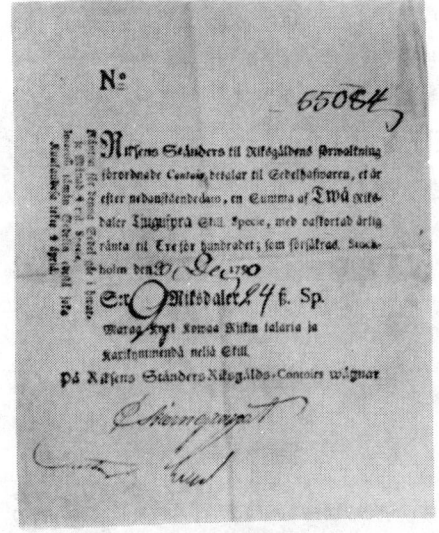

A106	**VARIOUS HANDWRITTEN VALUES** 1790-92. Comprised of 4 pages.	GOOD —	FINE —	XF —

1791 ISSUE

A107	**12 SCHILLINGAR** 1791-92.	GOOD 70.00	FINE 200.00	XF 800.00

A108	**16 SCHILLINGAR** 1791-92.	GOOD 80.00	FINE 225.00	XF 900.00
A109	**24 SCHILLINGAR** 1791-92.	90.00	250.00	1000.
A110	**1 RIKSDALER SPECIE** 1791-92.	—	—	—
A111	**2 RIKSDALER SPECIE** 1791-92.	—	—	—
A112	**5 RIKSDALER SPECIE** 1791-92.	—	—	—

1792; 1793 ISSUE

A113	**VARIOUS HANDWRITTEN VALUES** 1793-1816. Comprised of 4 pages.	GOOD —	FINE —	XF —

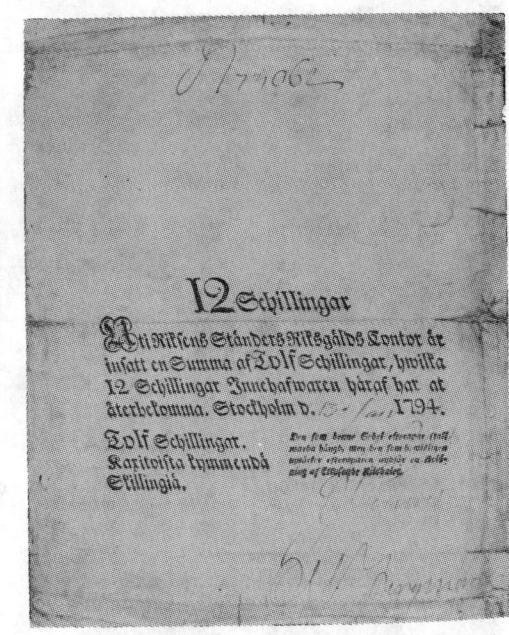

A114	**12 SCHILLINGAR** 1792-1805.	GOOD	FINE	XF
	a. 1792-94. Uniface.	25.00	80.00	325.00
	b. 1795-1805. Value on back.	20.00	60.00	250.00
A115	**16 SCHILLINGAR** 1792-1834.			
	a. 1792-94. Uniface.	50.00	150.00	625.00
	b. 1795-1818. Value on back.	35.00	120.00	425.00
	c. 1819-34. Punishment clause change.	30.00	100.00	400.00
A116	**24 SCHILLINGAR** 1792-1804.			
	a. 1792-94. Uniface.	60.00	175.00	675.00
	b. 1795-1804. Value on back.	50.00	150.00	575.00

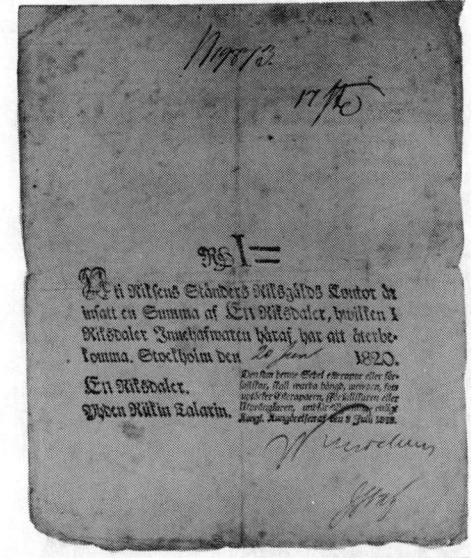

A117	**1 RIKSDALER** 1792-1834.	GOOD	FINE	XF
	a. 1792-94. Uniface.	50.00	175.00	650.00
	b. 1795-1818. Value on back.	30.00	90.00	350.00
	c. 1819-34. Punishment clause change.	30.00	90.00	350.00
A118	**2 RIKSDALER** 1792-1818.			
	a. 1792-94.	50.00	150.00	650.00
	b. 1795-1818. Value on back.	40.00	125.00	500.00
	c. 1819-34. Horizontal format. Punishment clause change.	30.00	100.00	400.00

1816 ISSUE

#A122 *Deleted.* See #A118c.

A119	**10 RIKSDALER** 1816-34.	GOOD —	FINE —	XF —
A120	**50 RIKSDALER** 1816-34.	—	—	—
A121	**100 RIKSDALER** 1816-34.	—	—	—

SVERIGES RIKES STÄNDERS BANK
1835-36 ISSUE

A123 32 SCHILLINGAR BANCO
1836-58. Black on yellow paper. Lion lying in front of of crowned arms at top ctr.

	Good	Fine	XF
a. Handwritten serial #. 1836.	30.00	110.00	450.00
b. Handwritten serial #. 1839.	—	Rare	—
c. Printed serial #. 1840-58.	10.00	30.00	150.00

A124 2 RIKSDALER SCHILLINGAR
1836-57. Black on lt. blue paper. Like #A123.

	Good	Fine	XF
a. Handwritten serial #. 1836.	80.00	250.00	1000.
b. Printed serial #. 1840; 1845; 1849; 1851; 1853; 1855; 1857.	15.00	50.00	200.00
c. Printed serial #. 1848.	30.00	100.00	400.00

A125 6 2/3 RIKSDALER BANCO
1835-56. Black on green paper. Like #A123.

	Good	Fine	XF
a. Handwritten serial #. 1835.	200.00	600.00	2400.
b. Printed serial #. 1841; 1850; 1852; 1854; 1856.	70.00	200.00	800.00
c. Printed serial #. 1848-49.	—	Rare	—

A126 10 RIKSDALER BANCO
1836-57. Black on yellow paper. Like #A125.

	Good	Fine	XF
a. Handwritten serial #. 28.1.1836.	300.00	750.00	3000.
b. Printed serial #. 1841; 1852; 1854-55; 1857.	100.00	300.00	1200.
c. Printed serial #. 1848; 1850.	—	Rare	—

A127 16 2/3 RIKSDALER BANCO
1836-55. Black on lt. red paper. Like #A125.

	Good	Fine	XF
a. Handwritten serial #. 28.1.1836.	—	Rare	—
b. Printed serial #. 1844; 1852; 1855.	400.00	1200.	4000.
c. Printed serial #. 1847; 1850.	—	Rare	—

A128 33 1/3 RIKSDALER BANCO
1836-57. Black on lt. blue paper. Like #A125.

	Good	Fine	XF
a. Handwritten serial #. 28.1.1836.	—	Rare	—
b. Printed serial #. 1840-52; 1857.	—	Rare	—
c. Printed serial #. 1854; 1856.	600.00	2000.	5000.

A129 100 RIKSDALER BANCO
1836-54. Black on lt. yellow paper. Seva seated below radiant crown at top ctr.

	Good	Fine	XF
a. Handwritten serial #. 1836.	—	Rare	—
b. Printed serial #. 1843-54.	—	Rare	—

A130 500 RIKSDALER BANCO
1836-54. Blue on lt. blue paper. Like #A129.

	Good	Fine	XF
a. Handwritten serial #. 1836.	—	Rare	—
b. Printed serial #. 1840-54.	—	Rare	—

1859 ISSUE

A131 1 RIKSDALER
1859-65. Green. Like #A138 but *EN* in ctr. rectangle.

	Good	Fine	XF
	15.00	40.00	150.00

A132 5 RIKSDALER
(A133)
1858-67. Red. Like #A131.

	Good	Fine	XF
a. 1858; 1863.	100.00	300.00	1100.
b. Frame patterned. 1863; 1867.	70.00	250.00	1000.

A133 10 RIKSDALER
(A134)
1859; 1866. Green. Like #A131, but handwritten sign.

	Good	Fine	XF
	100.00	300.00	1200.

A134 50 RIKSDALER
(A135)
1859; 1861; 1865. Red. Like #A131, but handwritten sign.

	Good	Fine	XF
	—	Rare	—

A135 100 RIKSDALER
(A136)
1859; 1864. Green. Like #A131, but handwritten sign.

	Good	Fine	XF
	—	Rare	—

A136 500 RIKSDALER
(A137)
3.1.1859. Red. Like #A131, but handwritten sign.

	Good	Fine	XF
	—	Rare	—

A137 1000 RIKSDALER
(A138)
3.1.1859. Yellow. Like #A131.

	Good	Fine	XF
	—	Rare	—

1865 ISSUE

A138 1 RIKSDALER
(A132)
1865-69. Green on green unpt. Like #A131 but *EN* in oval at ctr.

	Good	Fine	XF
	10.00	30.00	125.00

SW(V)ERIGES RIKSBANK
1869-70 ISSUE

A139 1 RIKSDALER
1869-73. Black on green unpt. Like #A138, but w/different wmk.

	Good	Fine	XF
a. 2 handwritten sign. 1869-72.	10.00	30.00	125.00
b. L. sign. printed. 1872-73.	8.00	25.00	100.00
c. 2 sign. printed. 1873.	6.00	20.00	80.00

A140 5 RIKSDALER
1870-73. Black on red unpt. Like #A132.

	Good	Fine	XF
a. 2 serial #. 1870-72.	75.00	225.00	900.00
b. L. sign. printed. 1872-73.	60.00	175.00	700.00

A141 10 RIKSDALER
1870-73. Black on green unpt. Like #A133.

	Good	Fine	XF
a. 2 serial #. 1870-73.	75.00	250.00	1000.
b. L. sign. printed. 1873.	75.00	250.00	1000.

A142 50 RIKSDALER
3.1.1870. Black on red unpt. Like #A134.

	Good	Fine	XF
	—	Rare	—

A143 100 RIKSDALER
1870; 1872. Black on green unpt. Like #A135.

	Good	Fine	XF
	—	Rare	—

A144 500 RIKSDALER
1870. Black on red unpt. Like #A136.

	Good	Fine	XF
	—	Rare	—

A145 1000 RIKSDALER
1870. Black on yellow. Like #A137.

	Good	Fine	XF
	—	Rare	—

1874 ISSUE
#1-6 consecutive year dates. Sign. varieties.

1 1 KRONA
1874-75. Black on green unpt. Crowned and supported arms at top ctr. 134 x 76mm.

	Good	Fine	XF
a. 1874.	7.00	20.00	90.00
b. 1875.	5.00	15.00	60.00

2 5 KRONOR
(3)
1874-78. Red and black. Like #1. 135 x 75mm.

	Good	Fine	XF
a. 1874.	60.00	180.00	700.00
b. 1875.	70.00	200.00	800.00
c. 1876.	60.00	180.00	700.00
d. 1877.	60.00	180.00	700.00
e. 1878.	70.00	200.00	800.00

3 (15)	**10 KRONOR** 1874-79. Green and black. Crowned and supported arms at top ctr. ca. 150 x 135mm.	**GOOD**	**FINE**	**XF**
		60.00	160.00	700.00
	a. 1874.	70.00	200.00	900.00
	b. 1875.	60.00	180.00	800.00
	c. 1876.	70.00	200.00	900.00
	d. 1877.	60.00	160.00	700.00
	e. 1878.	60.00	160.00	700.00
	f. 1879.	—	Rare	—
4 (25)	**50 KRONOR** 1874; 1876-79. Red and black. Crowned and supported arms over value. ca. 150 x 135mm.	—	Rare	—
5 (35)	**100 KRONOR** 1874-79. Green and black. Crowned and supported arms over value. ca. 220 x 135mm.	—	Rare	—
6 (45)	**1000 KRONOR** 1874-93. Yellow and black. Like #35. ca. 220 x 135mm.	—	Rare	—

1879-81 ISSUES

7 (4)	**5 KRONOR** 1879. Like #5. Back blue. 120 x 70mm. Sign. at r. handwritten.	**GOOD** 120.00	**FINE** 350.00	**XF** 1400.

8 (5)	**5 KRONOR** 1879-88. Black on brown design. Arms at upper ctr. back green; crowned shield at top ctr. Sign at r. handwritten.	**GOOD**	**FINE**	**XF**
	a. 1879.	70.00	200.00	800.00
	b. 1880.	40.00	120.00	500.00
	c. 1881.	40.00	120.00	500.00
	d. 1882.	40.00	120.00	500.00
	e. 1883.	40.00	120.00	500.00
	f. 1884.	40.00	120.00	500.00
	g. 1885.	40.00	120.00	500.00
	h. 1886.	40.00	120.00	500.00
	i. 1887.	40.00	120.00	500.00
	j. 1888.	40.00	120.00	500.00

9 (16)	**10 KRONOR** 1879-91. Black and blue. Crowned arms in upper corners, value at ctr. ca. 120x 70mm.	**GOOD**	**FINE**	**XF**
		—	Rare	—
	a. 1879.	100.00	300.00	1200.
	b. 1881.	100.00	300.00	1200.
	c. 1882.	100.00	300.00	1200.
	d. 1883.	100.00	300.00	1200.
	e. 1884.	100.00	300.00	1200.
	f. 1885.	100.00	300.00	1200.
	g. 1886.	80.00	250.00	1000.
	h. 1887.	80.00	250.00	1000.
	i. 1888.	80.00	250.00	1000.
	j. 1889.	70.00	200.00	800.00
	k. 1890.	70.00	200.00	800.00
	l. 1891.	70.00	200.00	800.00
10 (26)	**50 KRONOR** 1880-84; 1886; 1888-96. Maroon and black. Crowned arms over value. C. 140 x 120mm.	—	Rare	—
11 (36)	**100 KRONOR** 1880-96. Blue and black. Crowned arms in upper corners. Handwritten sign. ca. 140 x 120mm.	—	Rare	—
12 (46)	**1000 KRONOR** 1881. Blue and black. Crowned arms at top ctr. 210 x 120mm.	—	Rare	—

1888-96 ISSUE

13 (6)	**5 KRONOR** 1888-90. Like #8. Back green. 2 sign. printed.	**GOOD**	**FINE**	**XF**
	a. 1888.	30.00	100.00	400.00
	b. 1889.	25.00	75.00	300.00
	c. 1890.	20.00	60.00	250.00

14 (7)	**5 KRONOR** 1890-98. Black on beige paper. Red and green guilloche. Svea seated at r. Gustav Vasa on back.	**GOOD** 40.00	**FINE** 120.00	**XF** 500.00

15 (17)	**10 KRONOR** 1892-97. Black on gray paper. Red and blue guilloche. Svea seated at r. Portr. G. Vasa on back.	**GOOD**	**FINE**	**XF**
	a. 1892-93.	50.00	150.00	600.00
	b. 1894.	50.00	150.00	600.00
	c. 1895.	50.00	150.00	600.00
	d. 1896.	50.00	150.00	600.00
	e. 1897.	50.00	150.00	600.00
16 (27)	**50 KRONOR** 1896-97. Black. Red and green guilloche. Svea seated at lower r. G. Vasa on back.	150.00	400.00	1600.
17 (37)	**100 KRONOR** 1896-98. Like #11. L. sign. printed.	—	Rare	—
18 (47)	**1000 KRONOR** 1894; 1895; 1897. Bluish paper w/red imbedded fibers. Svea seated. G. Vasa on back.	—	Rare	—

1898; 1899 ISSUE

19 (8)	**5 KRONOR** 1899-1905. Like #14 but letter at lower l. and r. on back.	**GOOD** 30.00	**FINE** 90.00	**XF** 350.00
20 (18)	**10 KRONOR** 1898-1905. Like #15 but letter at l. and r. on back.			
	a. 1898-1900.	50.00	150.00	600.00
	b. 1901-05.	30.00	120.00	500.00
21 (28)	**50 KRONOR** 1898-1903. Like #16 but letter at lower l. and r. on back.			
	a. 1898.	140.00	400.00	1600.
	b. 1899-1900.	140.00	400.00	1600.
	c. 1901-02.	120.00	350.00	1400.
	d. 1903.	120.00	350.00	1400.
22 (38)	**100 KRONOR** 1898-1903. Red and blue. Svea seated at lower r. G. Vasa on back.			
	a. 1898.	125.00	400.00	1600.
	b. 1900-01.	125.00	400.00	1600.
	c. 1902-03.	120.00	350.00	1400.
23 (48)	**1000 KRONOR** 1898-1905. Like #18. 1 letter at lower l. and r. on back.	—	Rare	—

1903 ISSUE

24 (29)	**50 KRONOR** 1903-06. Like #21 but printed sign.	**GOOD**	**FINE**	**XF**
	a. 1903.	100.00	300.00	1200.
	b. 1904-06.	80.00	250.00	1000.
25 (39)	**100 KRONOR** 1903-06. Like #22. Both sign. printed.			
	a. 1903-05.	80.00	250.00	1000.
	b. 1906.	80.00	250.00	1000.

1906-1909 ISSUE

26 (9)	**5 KRONOR** 1907-17. Like #19 but green guilloche.	**GOOD**	**FINE**	**XF**
	a. 1907-13.	20.00	60.00	250.00
	b. 1914.	15.00	45.00	200.00
	c. 1915.	80.00	250.00	1000.
	d. 1916-17.	15.00	45.00	200.00

27 (19)	10 KRONOR 1906-17. Like #20 but green guilloche.	GOOD	FINE	XF
	a. 1906.	25.00	80.00	400.00
	b. 1907.	25.00	75.00	300.00
	c. 1908-11.	25.00	75.00	275.00
	d. 1912.	20.00	60.00	240.00
	e. 1913.	25.00	75.00	300.00
	f. 1914.	20.00	60.00	240.00
	g. 1915-16.	15.00	50.00	200.00
	h. 1917.	10.00	35.00	150.00

28 (30)	50 KRONOR 1907-17. Like #24 but yellow unpt. added.			
	a. 1907-15.	55.00	175.00	675.00
	b. 1916.	50.00	150.00	600.00
	c. 1917.	40.00	125.00	525.00

29 (40)	100 KRONOR 1907-17. Like #25. Yellow added to unpt.			
	a. 1907-09.	125.00	225.00	550.00
	b. 1910-11.	110.00	200.00	500.00
	c. 1912.	95.00	170.00	375.00
	d. 1913-14.	110.00	190.00	450.00
	e. 1915-17.	80.00	150.00	325.00

30 (49)	1000 KRONOR 1907. Maroon added to unpt. Like #23.	—	Rare	—

31 (50)	1000 KRONOR 1909-17. Paper color changes to reddish w/blue imbedded fibers. Like #30.	—	Rare	—

1914; 1918 ISSUE

32 (2)	1 KRONA 1914-39. Black on green unpt. Like #1. 120 x 70mm.	GOOD	FINE	XF
	a. 1914.	3.00	10.00	30.00
	b. 1915-17.	5.00	15.00	50.00
	c. 1918-21.	3.00	10.00	30.00
	d. 1924; 1938; 1939.	—	—	900.00
	s. Specimen. 1939.	—	Rare	—
	x. Error: legend missing, *lagen om rikets mynt av de.* 1920.	200.00	500.00	1000.

33 (10)	5 KRONOR 1918-52. Like #26 but numeral of value in red. Wmk: Mercury head.	GOOD	FINE	XF
	a. 1918-19.	15.00	40.00	160.00
	b. 1920.	30.00	90.00	350.00
	c. 1921-22.	12.00	35.00	150.00
	d. 1923.	10.00	30.00	130.00
	e. 1924.	12.00	40.00	150.00
	f. 1925.	10.00	30.00	120.00
	g. 1926-28.	8.00	22.50	90.00
	h. 1929-32.	7.00	20.00	75.00
	i. 1933-35.	2.00	9.00	35.00
	j. 1936.	1.50	5.00	20.00
	k. 1937.	1.50	5.00	20.00
	l. 1938-39.	1.00	4.00	16.00
	m. 1940-46.	.50	2.00	9.00
	n. 1947-49.	.50	1.00	4.00
	o. 1950.	1.00	3.00	12.00
	p. 1951.	.50	1.00	4.00
	q. 1952.	.50	1.00	2.00

34 (20)	10 KRONOR 1918-40. Like #27 but numeral of value in red. Wmk: Mercury head.			
	a. 1918.	16.00	50.00	200.00
	b. 1919-21.	12.00	40.00	160.00
	c. 1922-24.	10.00	30.00	125.00
	d. 1925.	8.00	25.00	110.00
	e. 1926-28.	5.00	17.50	70.00
	f. 1929.	4.00	12.00	50.00
	g. 1930-31.	3.00	9.00	35.00

		GOOD	FINE	XF
	h. 1932-34.	2.00	6.00	25.00
	i. 1935-36.	2.00	6.00	25.00
	j. 1937-40.	1.00	4.00	15.00

35 (31)	50 KRONOR 1918-54. Like #28. Safety letter after 5 digit serial #.			
	a. 1918.	30.00	90.00	350.00
	b. 1919.	30.00	90.00	350.00
	c. 1920.	25.00	70.00	275.00
	d. 1921.	20.00	60.00	240.00
	e. 1922.	20.00	60.00	240.00
	f. 1923-26.	20.00	60.00	240.00
	g. 1927-30.	14.00	40.00	160.00
	h. 1931-36.	10.00	25.00	100.00
	i. 1937-38.	9.00	20.00	80.00
	j. 1939-54.	8.00	17.50	70.00

36 (41)	100 KRONOR 1918-46. Like #29. 5 digit serial # ends w/safety letter.			
	a. 1918-19.	35.00	100.00	400.00
	b. 1920-21.	35.00	100.00	400.00
	c. 1922.	25.00	75.00	275.00
	d. 1923.	25.00	75.00	275.00
	e. 1924.	25.00	75.00	275.00
	f. 1925-26.	12.50	50.00	200.00
	g. 1927.	12.50	50.00	200.00
	h. 1928-29.	12.50	50.00	200.00
	i. 1930.	10.00	40.00	160.00
	j. 1931-33.	10.00	30.00	120.00
	k. 1934-35.	8.00	25.00	100.00
	l. 1936-38.	8.00	25.00	100.00
	m. 1939-41.	8.00	20.00	80.00
	n. 1942.	8.00	20.00	80.00
	o. 1943.	8.00	20.00	80.00
	p. 1945.	8.00	20.00	80.00
	q. 1946.	8.00	20.00	80.00

37 (51)	1000 KRONOR 1918-30. Like #31. Numeral of value in red.			
	a. 1918.	150.00	450.00	1800.
	b. 1919.	150.00	450.00	1800.
	c. 1920-21.	125.00	400.00	1600.
	d. 1922.	125.00	400.00	1600.
	e. 1926.	125.00	350.00	1400.
	f. 1929.	125.00	350.00	1400.
	g. 1930.	125.00	300.00	1200.

1932 ISSUE

38 (52)	1000 KRONOR 1932-50. Like #37. 2 printed sign.	VG	VF	UNC
	a. 1932.	300.00	600.00	1200.
	b. 1936.	200.00	450.00	900.00
	c. 1938.	200.00	400.00	800.00
	d. 1939.	200.00	350.00	700.00
	e. 1950.	200.00	350.00	700.00

1939 ISSUE

39 (55)	**10,000 KRONOR** 1939. Black and blue. Coat of arms at ctr. Uniface. Wmk: Mercury head and wavy lines.	VG —	VF Rare	UNC —

1940 ISSUE

40 (21)	**10 KRONOR** 1940-52. Gray-blue on m/c unpt. G. Vasa at l. and as wmk., red dates and serial #. Arms on back.	VG	VF	UNC
	a. 1940.	50.00	200.00	800.00
	b. 1941.	3.00	10.00	40.00
	c. 1942-43.	3.00	8.00	30.00
	d. 1944-45.	1.75	4.00	16.00
	e. 1946.	2.00	7.00	30.00
	f. 1947.	1.75	3.00	12.00
	g. 1948-52. Engraved back.	1.75	3.00	10.00
	h. 1952. Offset back.	1.75	3.00	10.00

1948 COMMEMORATIVE ISSUE

#41, 90th Birthday of Kg. Gustaf V.

NOTE: #41 was sold at twice normal face value in special packaging.

41 (11)	**5 KRONOR** 1948. Olive on m/c unpt. Portr. Kg. Gustaf V at l., monogram at r. Back brown; arms.	VG	VF	UNC
	a. W/o package.	3.00	8.00	30.00
	b. W/original package.	3.00	16.00	60.00

1952-55 ISSUE

42 (12)	**5 KRONOR** 1954-61. Dk. brown on red and blue unpt. Beige paper. Portr. Kg. Gustaf VI Adolf at r. ctr. and as wmk. Svea standing w/shield on back.	VG	VF	UNC
	a. W/safety letter. 1954-56.	1.00	3.00	6.00
	b. W/o safety letter. 1959-61.	1.00	3.00	6.00
	c. W/star. 1956; 1959-61.	10.00	40.00	150.00

43 (22)	**10 KRONOR** 1953-62. Gray-blue. Portr. G. Vasa at l. and as wmk. Blue date and serial #.	VG	VF	UNC
	a. 1953-54.	1.65	2.25	6.00
	b. 1955-56.	1.65	2.25	6.00
	c. 1957-59.	1.65	2.25	6.00
	d. 1960.	2.00	4.00	10.00
	e. 1962.	1.65	2.25	6.00
	f. W/star. 1956-60; 1962.	15.00	40.00	160.00

44 (32)	**50 KRONOR** 1955-58. Like #35. No safety letter after 6 digit serial #.	VG	VF	UNC
	a. 1947-54. Single lg. letter at lower l. and r. on back.	15.00	30.00	100.00
	b. 1955-58. Two sm. letters at lower l. and r. on back.	10.00	25.00	80.00
	c. w/star. 1956-58.	60.00	150.00	300.00

45 (42)	**100 KRONOR** 1955-59. Like #11. 6 digit serial # w/o safety letter.	VG	VF	UNC
	a. 1947-54. Single lg. letter at lower l. and r. on back.	25.00	50.00	100.00
	b. 1955-59. Two sm. letters at lower l. and r. on back.	20.00	40.00	80.00
	c. W/star. 1956-58.	60.00	100.00	200.00

46 (53)	**1000 KRONOR** 1952-73. Brown and m/c. Svea standing (modelled by Greta Hoffstrom). Kg. on back and as wmk.	VG	VF	UNC
	a. Blue and red safety fibers. 1952.	165.00	250.00	500.00
	b. 1957.	165.00	250.00	500.00
	c. 1962.	165.00	250.00	450.00
	d. 1965.	165.00	250.00	450.00
	e. One vertical filament. 1971.	165.00	200.00	400.00
	f. 1973.	165.00	200.00	400.00

1958; 1959 ISSUE

47 (33)	**50 KRONOR** 1959-62. Like #44. Second sign. at l. Sm. serial #.	VG	VF	UNC
	a. 1959-62.	10.00	20.00	60.00
	b. W/star. 1959-62.	20.00	50.00	120.00

48 (43)	**100 KRONOR** 1959-63. Like #45. Second sign. at l. Sm. date and serial #.			
	a. 1959-63.	17.50	30.00	60.00
	b. W/star. 1959-63.	20.00	60.00	120.00

49 (56)	**10,000 KRONOR** 1958. Green and m/c. King Gustav VI Adolf at r. and as wmk. Seva standing w/shield at crt. on back.	**VG** 1600.	**VF** 2000.	**UNC** 3000.

SWITZERLAND

The Swiss Confederation, located in central Europe north of Italy and south of Germany, has an area of 15,941 sq. mi. (41,290 sq. km.) and a population of 6.9 million. Capital: Bern. The economy centers about a well developed manufacturing industry. Machinery, chemicals, watches and clocks, and textiles are exported.

Switzerland, the habitat of lake dwellers in prehistoric times, was peopled by the Celtic Helvetians when Julius Caesar made it a part of the Roman Empire in 58 BC. After the decline of Rome, Switzerland was invaded by Teutonic tribes, who established small temporal holdings which, in the Middle Ages, became a federation of fiefs of the Holy Roman Empire. As a nation, Switzerland originated in 1291 when the districts of Nidwalden, Schwyz and Uri united to defeat Austria and attain independence as the Swiss Confederation. After acquiring new cantons in the 14th century, Switzerland was made independent from the Holy Roman Empire by the 1648 Treaty of Westphalia. The revolutionary armies of Napoleonic France occupied Switzerland and set up the Helvetian Republic, 1798-1803. After the fall of Napoleon, the Congress of Vienna, 1815, recognized the independence of Switzerland and guaranteed its neutrality. The Swiss Constitutions of 1848 and 1874 established a union modeled upon that of the United States.

MONETARY SYSTEM:
1 Franc (Franken) = 10 Batzen = 100 Centimes (Rappen)

The banknotes of the SNB bore three signatures until the 5th Series (1956/57 to 1980):

(1) President of the Bank Council (Präsident des Bankrates, Président du Conseil)

2) A member of the Board of Directors (Mitglid des Direktoriums, membre de la direction générale)

(3) Chief Cashier (Hauptkassier)

In the Board of Directors of the Swiss National Bank there are three members: The president of the National Bank and Chairman of Department I, the Vice-president and chairman of Department II and the Chairman of Department III. So, there are always three possible signature combinations with a single date

The Presidents of the Bank Council Der Präsident des Bankrates Le Président du Conseil		The Chief Cashiers Der Hauptkassier Le caissier principal	
Johann-Daniel Hirter 1906-23		A. Chevallier 1907-13	
Dr. Paul Usteri 1923-27		K. Bornhauser 1913-36	
Dr. h. c. Alfred Sarasin 1927-35		Erich Blumer 1936-54	
Dr. Gustav Schaller 1935-39 (Schaller[1])		Otto Kunz 1954-66	
(Schaller[2])		Rudolf Aebersold 1966-1981	
Prof. Dr. Gottlieb Bachmann 1939-47			
Dr. Alfred Müller 1947-59			
Dr. Brenno Galli 1959-78			

The Members of the Board of Directors Ein Mitglied des Direktoriums Un membre de la direction générale	
Heinrich Kundert 1907-15	
Rodolphe de Haller 1907-20	
August Burckhardt 1907-24	
Dr. Adolf Jöhr 1915-18	
Prof. Dr. Gottlieb Bachmann 1918-39	
Charles Schnyder von Wartensee 1920-37 (Schnyder[1])	
(Schnyder[2])	

Ernst Weber 1925-47	
Dr. h. c. Paul Rossy 1937-55	
Fritz Schnorf 1939-42	
Dr. h. c. Alfred Hirs 1942-54	
Prof. Dr. Paul Keller 1947-56	
Dr. Walter Schwegler 1954-66	
Dr. Riccardo Motta 1955-66	
Dr. Max Iklé 1956-68	

CONFEDERATION

SCHWEIZERISCHE NATIONALBANK
Established in 1905.

1907 ISSUE
#142-145 standing allegorical woman at l., cherub at lower r.

NOTE: Similar to previous issue of Concordat note issues but w/new issuer name and a white cross in red guilloche in unpt. at upper r. For Concordat issues see Vol. 1.

		GOOD	FINE	XF
142	**50 FRANKEN**			
	1.2.1907. Yellow-green.	500.00	1000.	1800.

		GOOD	FINE	XF
143	**100 FRANKEN**			
	1.2.1907. Blue.	800.00	1600.	2400.
144	**500 FRANKEN**			
	1.2.1907. Green.	2250.	—	—

		GOOD	FINE	XF
145	**1000 FRANKEN**			
	1.2.1907. Violet.	3250.	—	—

GESETZ VOM 6 OKT. 1905 (LAW OF OCT. 6. 1905)
Printer: W&S.

		GOOD	FINE	XF
146	**50 FRANKEN**			
	1910-20. Green. Portr. woman at lower l. F. Hodler's *Woodcutter* on back.			
	a. 1.1.1910.	75.00	150.00	400.00
	b. 1.1.1914; 1.1.1917; 1.8.1920. (w/sign. 7 add 20%).	50.00	100.00	300.00

		GOOD	FINE	XF
147	**100 FRANKEN**			
	1910-20. Dk. blue. Portr. woman at l. F. Hodler's *Scyther* on back.			
	a. 1.1.1910.	100.00	200.00	550.00
	b. 1.1.1914; 1.8.1920.	50.00	100.00	300.00
	c. 1.1.1917. (w/sign. 7 add 20%).	60.00	125.00	350.00
148	**500 FRANKEN**			
	1.1.1910; 1.1.1914; 1.1.1917. Dark red and lilac. Woman from Appenzell at I. E. Burnand's *Embroidering Appenzell Women* on back. Printer: W&S.			
	a. 1.1.1910.	500.00	800.00	1200.
	b. 1.1.1914; 1.1.1917.	300.00	500.00	900.00

151A 40 FRANKEN

		Good	Fine	XF
	1.9.1914. Violet on lt. green. Winkelried at l.	—	—	—

1918 ISSUES
#152 and 153 printer: OFZ.

149 1000 FRANKEN

		Good	Fine	XF
	1910-17. Violet and orange. Portr. woman at lower l. E. Burnand's *Foundry* on back.			
a.	1.1.1910.	500.00	1100.	1500.
b.	1.1.1914.	450.00	1000.	1350.
c.	1.1.1917.	400.00	800.00	1250.
s.	Specimen, punched hole cancelled.	—	—	—

152 100 FRANKEN

		Good	Fine	XF
	1.1.1918. Blue and brown. Wm. Tell at l., Tell's Chapel at Lake Vierwaldstätten at r. Letters *T.W.* at lower l., *R.K.* at lower r. Mount Jungfrau on back. Printer: OFZ. Offset.			
a.	Issued note.	300.00	600.00	1100.
s.	Specimen, punched hole cancelled.	—	—	—

1911-14 ISSUE

150
(151) **5 FRANKEN**

		Good	Fine	XF
	1913-52. Black and brown on green and orange unpt. William Tell monument in Altdorf at l. Rutli Mountain in l. background. Shade variations in brown tones. Back olive.			
a.	Lt. brown. 1.8.1913.	60.00	125.00	200.00
b.	Lt. brown. 1.8.1914; 1.1.1916.	30.00	50.00	100.00
c.	Green. 1.8.1914.	50.00	100.00	150.00
d.	Dk. brown. 1.1.1919.	30.00	60.00	100.00
e.	1.1.1921.	10.00	25.00	40.00
f.	1.7.1922.	30.00	60.00	100.00
g.	2.12.1926-28.3.1952.	10.00	25.00	40.00
h.	15.1.1953; 22.10.1953 (not issued).	8.00	17.50	30.00

151
(150) **20 FRANKEN**

		Good	Fine	XF
	1911-22. Blue, green and brown. Woman's head "Vreneli" at l.			
a.	1.12.1911.	175.00	300.00	575.00
b.	1.9.1915; 1.1.1916; 1.1.1918. (w/sign. 7 add 20%).	100.00	200.00	450.00
c.	1.1.1920; 1.9.1920; 1.1.1922.	85.00	175.00	425.00

153 100 FRANKEN

		Good	Fine	XF
	1.1.1918. Blue and brown. Similar to #152 but modified portr. of Wm. Tell. Letters *Ekn.* R. K. in the l. medallion at lower r. Partly engraved. Specimen, punched hole cancelled.	—	Rare	—

EIDGENÖSSISCHE STAATSKASSE

LA CAISSE LA CASSA FÉDÉRALE

1914 ISSUES
#154-162 arms at top ctr.
NOTE: Same design issued in either German, Italian or French.

		GOOD	FINE	XF
154	**5 FRANKEN** 10.8.1914. Blue. Portr. Libertas at l., Winkelreid at r. German text.	275.00	500.00	950.00

		GOOD	FINE	XF
155	**5 FRANKEN** 10.8.1914. Blue. Like #154 but French text.	375.00	600.00	1200.

		GOOD	FINE	XF
156	**5 FRANKEN** 10.8.1914. Blue. Like #154 but Italian text.	900.00	1250.	3000.

		GOOD	FINE	XF
157	**10 FRANKEN** 10.8.1914. Blue. Portr. Libertas at l., William Tell at r. German text.	400.00	750.00	1500.
158	**10 FRANKEN** 10.8.1914. Blue. Like #157 but French text.	600.00	1100.	2000.
159	**10 FRANKEN** 10.8.1914. Blue. Like #157 but Italian text.	1250.	2000.	3750.
160	**20 FRANKEN** 10.8.1914. Blue. Portr. Libertas at l., Winkelreid at r. German text.	1000.	1650.	3000.

		GOOD	FINE	XF
161	**20 FRANKEN** 10.8.1914. Blue. Like #160 but French text.	1500.	2250.	3250.
162	**20 FRANKEN** 10.8.1914. Blue. Like #160 but Italian text.	2000.	3000.	4250.

DARLEHENSKASSE DER SCHWEIZERISCHEN

EIDGENOSSENSCHAFT

STATE LOAN BANK OF THE SWISS FEDERATION

1914 ISSUE
NOTE: Currency notes for 1 and 2 Franken dated 27.4.1915 and 100 Franken dated 9.9.1914 were printed, but not issued.

		GOOD	FINE	XF
163	**25 FRANKEN** 9.9.1914. Dk. green and yellow-brown. 2 serial # varieties. Printer: OFZ.	500.00	750.00	1700.

SCHWEIZERISCHE NATIONALBANK (RESUMED)

SWISS NATIONAL BANK

GESETZ VOM 7.4.1921 (LAW OF 7.4.1921)

1922; 1923 ISSUE

		VG	VF	UNC
164	**20 FRANKEN** 1.7.1922. Blue, green and brown. Like #150.	100.00	210.00	450.00

		VG	VF	UNC
164A	**20 FRANKEN** 16.5.1923. Dk. blue. Portr. woman in national costume at l. Printer: OFZ. (Not issued).	—	—	—

165	100 FRANKEN	VG	VF	UNC
	1.1.1923. Blue. Like #147.	80.00	175.00	500.00
166	500 FRANKEN			
	1.1.1923. Red. Like #148.	400.00	650.00	1250.
167	1000 FRANKEN			
	1.1.1923. Violet. Like #149.	650.00	1000.	2100.

1921-28 ISSUE

#168-172 *GESETZGEBUNG ÜBER DIE SCHWEIZERISCHE NATIONALBANK* (Legislation governing the Swiss National Bank). Sign. varieties.

169	50 FRANKEN	VG	VF	UNC
	1924-55. Green. Like #146.			
	a. 1.4.1924; 30.9.1926.	65.00	200.00	325.00
	b. 23.11.1927.	55.00	150.00	290.00
	c. 25.9.1929; 16.9.1930; 21.7.1931.	55.00	125.00	300.00
	d. 27.8.1937; 31.8.1938; 17.3.1939; 3.8.1939; 15.2.1940; 12.12.1941; 1.10.1942; 7.5.1943; 16.10.1947; 20.1.1949. (w/sign. 27 add 20%).	40.00	100.00	250.00
	e. 29.10.1955.	40.00	125.00	325.00

168	10 FRANKEN	VG	VF	UNC
(168A)	1.4.1921. Brown on yellow unpt. Portr. woman in national costume at lower l. Printer: W&S. Specimen.	—	—	—

170	100 FRANKEN	VG	VF	UNC
	1924-49. Dk. blue. Like #147.			
	a. 1.4.1924.	60.00	150.00	250.00
	b. 16.9.1926; 30.3.1927; 23.11.1927.	35.00	75.00	225.00
	c. 4.10.1928; 16.9.1930; 21.7.1931.	35.00	70.00	200.00
	d. 19.7.1934; 27.8.1937; 31.8.1938; 17.3.1939; 3.8.1939.	25.00	60.00	180.00
	e. 15.2.1940-20.1.1949. (w/sign. 27 add 10%).	25.00	55.00	165.00

168A	20 FRANKEN	VG	VF	UNC
(168)	1.5.1923-18.4.1929. Blue, green and brown. Like #150.	75.00	175.00	400.00

171 500 FRANKEN
1928-49. Dk. red and lilac. Like #148.

	VG	VF	UNC
a. 4.10.1928.	300.00	750.00	1400.
b. 16.6.1931; 7.9.1939.	275.00	650.00	1300.
c. 4.12.1942; 31.8.1946; 16.10.1947.	250.00	600.00	1250.
d. 20.1.1949 (not issued and destroyed).			

172 1000 FRANKEN
1927-55. Violet and orange. Like #149.

	VG	VF	UNC
a. 23.11.1927; 16.9.1930.	325.00	750.00	1850.
b. 16.6.1931; 10.12.1931; 7.9.1939; 4.12.1942; 11.11.1943; 16.10.1947; 29.4.1955.	275.00	600.00	1650.

1929-50 ISSUE

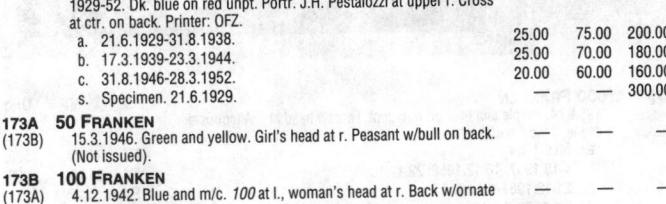

173 20 FRANKEN
1929-52. Dk. blue on red unpt. Portr. J.H. Pestalozzi at upper r. Cross at ctr. on back. Printer: OFZ.

	VG	VF	UNC
a. 21.6.1929-31.8.1938.	25.00	75.00	200.00
b. 17.3.1939-23.3.1944.	25.00	70.00	180.00
c. 31.8.1946-28.3.1952.	20.00	60.00	160.00
s. Specimen. 21.6.1929.	—	—	300.00

173A 50 FRANKEN
(173B) 15.3.1946. Green and yellow. Girl's head at r. Peasant w/bull on back. (Not issued).

	—	—	—

173B 100 FRANKEN
(173A) 4.12.1942. Blue and m/c. *100* at l., woman's head at r. Back w/ornate designs. (Not issued).

	—	—	—

173C 1000 FRANKEN
1.1.1950. Black, blue and violet on m/c unpt. Girl's head at r. Turbine and mountains on back. (Not issued).

	VG	VF	UNC
	—	—	—

1954-57 ISSUE
#174-175 printer: OFZ.

174 10 FRANKEN
1955-77. Red-brown and purple. Gottfried Keller at r. Carnation flower across back.

	VG	VF	UNC
a. 25.8.1955; 20.10.1955.	10.00	18.00	35.00
b. 29.11.1956; 18.12.1958; 23.12.1959.	FV	FV	25.00
c. 22.12.1960-15.1.1969.	FV	FV	17.50
d. 5.1.1970-6.1.1977.	FV	FV	12.50

175 20 FRANKEN
1954-76. Blue and m/c. Gen. G.H. Dufour at r. Thistle at l. ctr. on back.

	VG	VF	UNC
a. 1.7.1954.	15.00	32.50	85.00
b. 7.7.1955; 20.10.1955; 5.7.1956; 4.10.1957	FV	25.00	60.00
c. 18.12.1958; 23.12.1959.	FV	17.50	32.50
d. 22.12.1960-15.1.1969.	FV	FV	30.00
e. 5.1.1970-9.4.1976	FV	FV	27.50

176　50 FRANKEN
7.7.1955; 4.10.1957; 18.12.1958. Green and red on m/c unpt. Girl at r.
Apple harvesting scene on back (symbolizing fertility). Printer: W&S.

		VG	VF	UNC
a.	7.7.1955.	FV	60.00	125.00
b.	4.10.1957; 18.12.1958.	FV	50.00	85.00

177　100 FRANKEN
1956-73. Blue and brown on m/c unpt. Boy's head at r. St. Martin
sharing his cape on back. Printer: TDLR.

		VG	VF	UNC
a.	25.10.1956.	FV	90.00	200.00
b.	1.10.1957; 18.12.1958.	FV	80.00	165.00
c.	21.12.1961-15.1.1969.	FV	FV	150.00
d.	5.1.1970-7.3.1973.	FV	FV	125.00

179　1000 FRANKEN
1954-74. Purple and blue on m/c unpt. Female head at r. Allegorical
scene "dance macabre" on back.

		VG	VF	UNC
a.	30.9.1954.	FV	900.00	1500.
b.	4.10.1957; 18.12.1958; 22.12.1960.	FV	850.00	1250.
c.	21.12.1961-1.1.1967.	FV	FV	1175.
d.	5.1.1970-7.2.1974.	FV	FV	1100.

178　500 FRANKEN
31.1.1957; 4.10.1957; 18.12.1958. Brown-orange and olive m/c unpt.
Woman looking in mirror at r. Elders w/4 girls bathing at ctr. r. on
back (Fountain of Youth). Printer: W&S.

	VG	VF	UNC
	FV	450.00	750.00

The Syrian Arab Republic, located in the Near East at the eastern end of the Mediterranean Sea, has an area of 71,498 sq. mi. (185,180 sq. km.) and a population of 12.6 million. Capital: Greater Damascus. Agriculture and animal breeding are the chief industries. Cotton, crude oil and livestock are exported.

Ancient Syria, a land bridge connecting Europe, Africa and Asia, has spent much of its history in thrall to the conqueror's whim. Its subjection by Egypt about 1500 BC was followed by successive conquests by the Hebrews, Phoenicians, Babylonians, Assyrians, Persians, Macedonians, Romans, Byzantines and finally, in 636 AD, by the Moslems. The Arabs made Damascus, one of the oldest continuously inhabited cities of the world, the trade center and capital of an empire stretching from India to Spain. In 1517, following the total destruction of Damascus by the Mongols of Tamerlane, Syria fell to the Ottoman Turks and remained a Turkish province until World War I. The League of Nations gave France a mandate to the Levant states of Syria and Lebanon in 1920. In 1930, following a series of uprisings, France recognized Syria as an independent republic, but still subject to the mandate. Lebanon became fully independent on Nov. 22, 1943, and Syria on Jan. 1, 1944.

On Feb. 1, 1958, Egypt and Syria formed the United Arab Republic. Yemen joined on March 8 in an association known as the United Arab States. Syria withdrew from the United Arab Republic on Sept. 29, 1961, and on Dec. 26 Egypt dissolved its ties with Yemen in the United Arab States.

RULERS:
French, 1920-1944

MONETARY SYSTEM:
1 Pound (Livre) = 100 Piastres

OVERPRINT VARIETIES

| Type A | Type B | Type C | Type D | Type E |

FRENCH INFLUENCE

BANQUE DE SYRIE

1919 ISSUE
#1-19 printer: BWC.

		Good	Fine	XF
1	**5 PIASTRES** 1.8.1919. Dk. green on m/c unpt. Ruins of Baalbek at lower ctr. Back blue and lilac w/lion's head at ctr.			
	a. Sign. title: *LE SECRETAIRE GENERAL.*	5.00	27.50	75.00
	b. Sign title: *LE ADMINISTRATEUR DELEGUE.*	5.50	30.00	85.00

		Good	Fine	XF
2	**25 PIASTRES** 1.8.1919. Dk. blue and m/c. Omayyad Mosque in Damascus at ctr.	12.50	45.00	150.00

		Good	Fine	XF
3	**50 PIASTRES** 1.8.1919. Purple and m/c. Damascus at upper ctr.	22.50	85.00	250.00

		Good	Fine	XF
4	**100 PIASTRES** 1.8.1919. Brown and m/c. Pillars of Baalbek at l.	40.00	125.00	450.00
5	**500 PIASTRES** 1.8.1919. Dk. purple and m/c. Cedar tree at r. City view at ctr. on back.			
	a. Issued note.	40.00	250.00	600.00
	s. Specimen.	—	—	—

1920 FIRST ISSUE

		VG	VF	UNC
6	**1 PIASTRE** 1.1.1920. Blue on lt. green and lt. orange unpt. Back brown and red-brown; ruins of Baalbek at ctr.	2.50	8.00	25.00
7	**10 LIVRES** 1.1.1920. Lt. brown. Tower of Great Serai of Beyrouth at l.			
	a. Issued note.	—	—	—
	s. Specimen.	—	—	250.00
8	**25 LIVRES** 1.1.1920. Green. Arab cemetery at l., caravan by city gate at r.			
	a. Issued note.	—	—	—
	s. Specimen.	—	—	325.00
9	**50 LIVRES** 1.1.1920. Blue. Road at l.			
	a. Issued note.	—	—	—
	s. Specimen.	—	—	400.00

		VG	VF	UNC
10	**100 LIVRES** 1.1.1920. Gray.			
	a. Issued note.	—	—	—
	s. Specimen.	—	—	550.00

1920 SECOND ISSUE

		Good	Fine	XF
11	**5 PIASTRES** 1.7.1920. Dk. green and m/c. Like #1.	5.00	25.00	75.00

12   10 PIASTRES

	Good	Fine	XF
1.7.1920. Dk. blue and m/c. Shepherds gathered around a campfire, goats in background.	7.50	40.00	135.00

13   25 PIASTRES

	Good	Fine	XF
1.7.1920. Dk. blue. Bldg. w/clock tower at lower ctr.	12.50	45.00	150.00

14   50 PIASTRES

1.7.1920. Purple.	22.50	100.00	300.00

15   100 PIASTRES

1.7.1920. Brown. Pillars of Baalbek.	65.00	225.00	500.00

16   500 PIASTRES

	Good	Fine	XF
1.7.1920. Dk. purple. Like #5. Back blue.	—	Rare	—

17   10 LIVRES

1.7.1920. Lt. brown. Tower of the Great Serai of Beyrouth.	—	—	—

18   25 LIVRES

1.7.1920. Green. Arab cemetery at l., caravan near city gate at r.	—	—	—

19   100 LIVRES

1.7.1920. Green. Bank of Beyrouth at upper ctr.	—	—	—

BANQUE DE SYRIE ET DU GRAND-LIBAN

1925 FIRST ISSUE

21   25 PIASTRES

	Good	Fine	XF
15.4.1925. Mill on back.	25.00	75.00	200.00

22   50 PIASTRES

15.4.1925. Type Cl. Serveau. W/o ovpt: *SYRIE.*	30.00	100.00	275.00

23   50 PIASTRES

15.4.1925. Like #22, w/ovpt: *SYRIE.*	—	—	—

24   100 PIASTRES

15.4.1925.	—	—	—

1925 SECOND ISSUE

25   5 LIVRES

	Good	Fine	XF
15.4.1925.	—	—	—

26   10 LIVRES

15.4.1925.	—	—	—

27   25 LIVRES

15.4.1925.	—	—	—

28   50 LIVRES

15.4.1925.	—	—	—

29   100 LIVRES

15.4.1925.	—	—	—

1930 ISSUE

29A   1 LIVRE

	Good	Fine	XF
1.11.1930. M/c. Harbor and mountainous landscape on back.	30.00	90.00	225.00

30   5 LIVRES

1.11.1930. M/c.	35.00	110.00	400.00

31   10 LIVRES

1.11.1930. M/c. Ornate ruins on back.	40.00	175.00	600.00

32   25 LIVRES

1.11.1930. M/c.	—	—	—

33   100 LIVRES

1.11.1930. M/c.	—	—	—

1935 ISSUE
#35 *Deleted.*

34   1 LIVRE

	VG	VF	UNC
1.2.1935. Brown and m/c. Like #29A. Harbor and mountain landscape on back.	7.50	30.00	190.00

36   5 LIVRES

	VG	VF	UNC
1.2.1935. M/c. Azam Palace at ctr. on back.	25.00	100.00	400.00

38	100 Livres	VG	VF	UNC
	1.2.1935. Similar to #19. Ovpt: *SYRIE*. Printer: BWC.			
	a. W/o line ovpt.	—	—	—
	b. Orange ovpt. Type B.	—	—	—
	c. Lilac ovpt. Type C.	—	—	—
	d. Green ovpt. Type A.	—	—	—

1938 Issue

39	50 Livres	VG	VF	UNC
	1.1.1938. Type CI. Serveau.	125.00	450.00	1000.

1939 Provisional Issues

#39A-39F ovpt: *SYRIE 1939*.

39A	1 Livre	Good	Fine	XF
	1939 (-old date 1.2.1935). Ovpt. on #34.	8.00	30.00	135.00

39B	5 Livres	Good	Fine	XF
	1939 (-old date 1.2.1935). Ovpt. on #36.			
	a. W/ovpt: *SYRIE 1939* below central Arabic text.	20.00	80.00	275.00
	b. W/ovpt: *SYRIE 1939* above central Arabic text.	20.00	80.00	275.00

39C	10 Livres	Good	Fine	XF
	1939 (-old date 1.11.1930). Ovpt. on #31.	200.00	700.00	—
39D	100 Livres			
	1939 (-old date 1.11.1930). Ovpt. on #33.	150.00	600.00	1100.

39E	100 Livres	Good	Fine	XF
	1939 (-old date 1.2.1935).			
	a. Ovpt. on #38a.	120.00	350.00	—
	b. Ovpt. on #38b.	120.00	350.00	—
	c. Ovpt. on #38c.	120.00	350.00	—
	d. Ovpt. on #38d.	120.00	350.00	—

39F	100 Livres	Good	Fine	XF
	1939 (-old date 1.2.1935).			
	a. Ovpt. on Lebanon #14a.	120.00	350.00	—
	c. Ovpt. on Lebanon #14c.	175.00	500.00	

BANQUE DE SYRIE ET DU LIBAN

BON DE CAISSE BRANCH

1939 ISSUE
#47 and #48 printer: Government Printer, Palestine.

40	**1 LIVRE**	VG	VF	UNC
	1.9.1939. Green and m/c. Pillars of Baalbek at l. Back red on m/c unpt.; city view at ctr.			
	a. W/o line ovpt.	4.50	30.00	90.00
	b. Violet Type A ovpt.	4.50	30.00	90.00
	c. Lilac-colored Type B ovpt.	4.50	30.00	90.00
	d. Green Type C ovpt.	4.50	30.00	90.00
	e. Red Type D ovpt.	4.50	30.00	90.00
	f. Blue Type E ovpt.	4.50	30.00	90.00

41	**5 LIVRES**	VG	VF	UNC
	1.9.1939. Brown and m/c. Cedar at r. Landscape w/bldgs. oval at ctr. on back.			
	a. W/o line ovpt.	9.00	40.00	150.00
	b. Violet Type A ovpt.	9.00	40.00	150.00
	c. Pink or green Type B ovpt.	9.00	40.00	150.00
	d. Green Type C ovpt.	9.00	40.00	150.00
	e. Blue Type E ovpt.	9.00	40.00	150.00

43	**25 LIVRES**	GOOD	FINE	XF
	1.9.1939. Brown-lilac and m/c. Caravan at ctr. Back olive and m/c; ruins at ctr.			
	a. Lilac Type A ovpt.	10.00	60.00	250.00
	b. Red Type C ovpt.	10.00	60.00	250.00
	c. Green Type D ovpt.	10.00	60.00	250.00
	d. W/o ovpt.	10.00	60.00	250.00

44	**50 LIVRES**	GOOD	FINE	XF
	1.9.1939. Brown, blue and m/c. Street scene at l. Ovpt: *SYRIE* and green Type E.	30.00	125.00	475.00

45	**100 LIVRES**	GOOD	FINE	XF
	1939. Green and yellow. W/o *SYRIE* ovpt.			
	a. Green type A ovpt.	30.00	95.00	350.00
	b. Orange type B ovpt.	30.00	95.00	350.00
	c. Pink type C ovpt.	30.00	95.00	350.00

1942 ISSUE

42	**10 LIVRES**	GOOD	FINE	XF
	1.9.1939. Brown-violet and m/c. Clock tower at l.			
	a. W/o ovpt.	8.50	35.00	125.00
	b. Green Type A ovpt.	8.50	35.00	125.00
	c. Green Type B ovpt.	8.50	35.00	125.00
	d. Blue Type C ovpt.	8.50	35.00	125.00

46	**5 LIVRES**	GOOD	FINE	XF
	1.8.1942. Dk. green on yellow paper. Back blue. Imprint: R. Soriano I.C. Beyrouth.	65.00	200.00	450.00

54	50 PIASTRES	VG	VF	UNC
	31.8.1942. Blue on green unpt. Pillars. Back brown.	7.50	27.50	100.00

1944 ISSUE

#55 and 56 printer: Moharrem Press; Alexandrie.

55	5 PIASTRES	VG	VF	UNC
	15.2.1944. Green on lt. green unpt. Similar to #49. Back blue.	1.25	4.50	20.00

CA.1945 ND PROVISIONAL ISSUE

56A	2 1/2 PIASTRES	VG	VF	UNC
	ND. Tax adhesive stamp affixed to cardboard w/red text on back.	15.00	35.00	100.00

56	10 PIASTRES	VG	VF	UNC
	15.2.1944. Brown on gold unpt. Similar to #50. Back maroon.	2.00	8.50	50.00

BANQUE DE SYRIE ET DU LIBAN

1947 ISSUE

#59-61 w/green ovpt: State arms and *Ministry of Finance* in Arabic.

57	1 LIVRE	VG	VF	UNC
	1.4.1947. Brown and m/c. Similar to #34.	5.00	25.00	100.00
58	10 LIVRES	25.00	85.00	375.00
	1.4.1947. M/c. Roman temple ruins. Type CI. Serveau.			

47	50 LIVRES	GOOD	FINE	XF
	1.8.1942. Green.	100.00	300.00	850.00
48	100 LIVRES	200.00	500.00	1500.
	1.8.1942. Blue on green and yellow unpt. Back green.			

REPUBLIC

REPUBLIQUE SYRIENNE

1942 FIRST ISSUE

#49-50 printer: Survey of Egypt.

#51-52 printer: BWC.

49	5 PIASTRES	VG	VF	UNC
	15.7.1942. Green on lt. lilac unpt. Back purple; Citadel of Aleppo at ctr.	1.25	5.00	25.00
50	10 PIASTRES	2.00	10.00	50.00
	31.7.1942. Brown on yellow unpt. Mosque w/2 minarets. Back red-brown.			

51	25 PIASTRES	VG	VF	UNC
	1.8.1942. Red and m/c. Similar to #2.	5.00	17.50	75.00
52	50 PIASTRES	7.50	27.50	100.00
	1.8.1942. Blue and m/c. Similar to #3.			

1942 SECOND ISSUE

#53-54 printer; Survey of Egypt.

#55-56 printer: Moharrem Press, Alexandrie.

53	25 PIASTRES	VG	VF	UNC
	31.8.1942. Dk. brown on gold unpt. Mosque of Si Kabib of Homs. Back maroon.	5.00	17.50	80.00

59	**25 LIVRES**	**VG**	**VF**	**UNC**
	1.4.1947. M/c. Citadel on back. Type Cl. Serveau.	35.00	175.00	500.00

61	**100 LIVRES**	**VG**	**VF**	**UNC**
	1.4.1947. M/c. View of Damascu s. Type Laurent.	100.00	400.00	1000.

1948 ISSUE

62	**5 LIVRES**	**VG**	**VF**	**UNC**
	15.12.1948. M/c. Similar to #36.	8.50	35.00	300.00

1949 ISSUE

#65-67 w/green ovpt: State arms and Ministry of Finance in Arabic.

63	**1 LIVRE**	**VG**	**VF**	**UNC**
	1.7.1949. M/c. Like #57.	5.00	25.00	100.00

60	**50 LIVRES**	**VG**	**VF**	**UNC**
	1.4.1947. M/c. Oriental house on back. Type Cl. Serveau.	60.00	275.00	700.00

64	**10 LIVRES**	**VG**	**VF**	**UNC**
	1.7.1949. M/c. Like #58.	25.00	85.00	375.00
65	**25 LIVRES**			
	1.7.1949. M/c.	25.00	125.00	500.00

			VG	VF	UNC
66	**50 LIVRES**		85.00	300.00	700.00
	1.7.1949. M/c. Like #60, but w /ovpt. like #65.				

			VG	VF	UNC
67	**100 LIVRES**		65.00	250.00	900.00
	1.7.1949. M/c. Like #61, but w/ovpt. like #65.				

1949 BONS DE CAISSE PROVISIONAL ISSUE

			VG	VF	UNC
68	**250 LIVRES**		—	—	—
	1.7.1949. Form filled out in handwriting.				
69	**500 LIVRES**		—	—	—
	1.7.1949. Form filled out in handwriting.				

1950 REGULAR ISSUE

			VG	VF	UNC
70	**25 LIVRES**		20.00	75.00	450.00
	15.8.1950. M/c. Like #65.				
71	**50 LIVRES**		40.00	150.00	600.00
	15.8.1950. M/c. Like #66.				
72	**100 LIVRES**		85.00	285.00	800.00
	15.8.1950. M/c. Like #67.				

INSTITUT D'EMISSION DE SYRIE

1950'S FIRST ISSUE
#73-78 arms at r., *Premiere Emission*. Wmk: Horse's head.

			VG	VF	UNC
73	**1 LIVRE**		5.00	17.50	60.00
	ND. Dk. brown on m/c unpt. Bldg. w/minaret on back.				

			VG	VF	UNC
74	**5 LIVRES**		10.00	37.50	150.00
	ND. Orange-brown on m/c unpt. Citadel of Aleppo on back.				

			VG	VF	UNC
75	**10 LIVRES**		20.00	65.00	225.00
	ND. Blue-green on m/c unpt. City view on back.				

			VG	VF	UNC
76	**25 LIVRES**		35.00	125.00	400.00
	ND. Red on m/c unpt. Ornate doorway on back.				
77	**50 LIVRES**		40.00	200.00	575.00
	ND. Green on m/c ovpt. Arches on back.				

			VG	VF	UNC
78	**100 LIVRES**		55.00	300.00	775.00
	ND. Blue on m/c unpt.				

1955 ISSUE
#75A and 76A arms at r. *Deuxieme Emission*.

			VG	VF	UNC
75A	**10 LIVRES**		15.00	60.00	225.00
	1955. Blue green on m/c unpt. Like #75.				

76A	25 LIVRES	VG	VF	UNC
	1955. Red on m/c unpt. Like #76.	40.00	150.00	500.00

BANQUE CENTRALE DE SYRIE
CENTRAL BANK OF SYRIA

1957-58 ISSUE

#79-85 bank name is French on back.
#81 *Deleted.*

79	1 LIVRE	VG	VF	UNC
	1957. Brown on m/c unpt. Similar to #73.	7.50	25.00	75.00

80	5 LIVRES	VG	VF	UNC
	1957. Brown on m/c unpt. Similar to #74.	12.00	45.00	200.00
82	10 LIVRES			
	1957. Blue-green on m/c unpt. Similar to #75.	22.50	75.00	300.00
83	25 LIVRES			
	1957. Red on m/c unpt. Similar to #76.	37.50	150.00	400.00

84	50 LIVRES	VG	VF	UNC
	1957; 1958. Green on m/c unpt. Similar to #77.	50.00	160.00	485.00
85	100 LIVRES			
	1958. Blue on m/c unpt. Similar to #78.	55.00	200.00	675.00

1958 ISSUE

#86-92 bank name in English on back.
#86-88 wmk: Arabian horse's head. Printer: The Pakistan Security Printing Corporation, Ltd., Karachi (w/o imprint).
#89-92 wmk: Arabian horse's head. Printer: JEZ.

86	1 POUND	VG	VF	UNC
	1958. Brown on m/c unpt. Worker at r. Water wheel of Hama on back.			
	a. Issued note.	1.50	5.00	20.00
	s. Specimen.	—	—	25.00
87	5 POUNDS			
	1958. Green on m/c unpt. Like #86. Citadel of Aleppo on back.			
	a. Issued note.	3.00	15.00	65.00
	s. Specimen.	—	—	45.00
88	10 POUNDS			
	1958. Purple on m/c unpt. Like #86. Courtyard of Omayad Mosque on back.			
	a. Issued note.	5.00	25.00	100.00
	s. Specimen.	—	—	90.00
89	25 POUNDS	VG	VF	UNC
	1958. Blue on m/c unpt. Girl w/ basket at r. Interior view of El-Azm Palace in Damascus on back.			
	a. Issued note.	12.50	65.00	200.00
	s. Specimen.	—	—	165.00
90	50 POUNDS			
	1958. Red and brown on m/c unpt. Like #89. Mosque of Sultan Selim on back.			
	a. Issued note.	17.50	75.00	225.00
	s. Specimen.	—	—	200.00
91	100 POUNDS			
	1958;1962 Olive on m/c unpt. Like #89. Old ruins of Palmyra on back.			
	a. Issued note.	25.00	125.00	350.00
	s. Specimen.	—	—	225.00
92	500 POUNDS			
	1958. Brown and purple on m/c unpt. Motifs from ruins of Kingdom of Ugarit, head at r. Ancient religious wheel and cuneiform clay tablet on back.			
	a. Issued note.	100.00	400.00	—
	s. Specimen.	—	—	500.00

TAHITI

Tahiti, the largest island of the central South Pacific French overseas territory of French Polynesia, has an area of 402 sq. mi. (1,042 sq. km.) and a population of 79,500. Papeete on the northwest coast is the capital and administrative center of French Polynesia. Copra, sugar cane, vanilla and coffee are exported. Tourism is an important industry.

Capt. Samuel Wallis of the British Navy discovered Tahiti in 1768 and named it King George III Island. Louis-Antoine de Bougainville arrived in the following year and claimed it for France. Subsequent English visits were by James Cook in 1769 and William Bligh in the HMS "Bounty" in 1788.

Members of the Protestant London Missionary Society established the first European settlement in 1797, and with the aid of the local Pomare family gained control of the entire island and established a "missionary kingdom" with a scriptural code of law. Nevertheless, Tahiti was subsequently declared a French protectorate (1842) and a colony (1880), and since 1958 is part of the overseas territory of French Polynesia.

* * * This section has been partially renumbered. * * *

RULERS:
French

MONETARY SYSTEM:
1 Franc = 100 Centimes

FRENCH INFLUENCE

BANQUE DE L'INDOCHINE

PAPEETE BRANCH

DÉCRETS DES 21.1.1875 - 20.2.1888 - 16.5.1900 - 3.4.1901

	5 FRANCS	GOOD	FINE	XF
1	14.3.1914. Red. Seated oriental woman below seated Liberty holding caduceus at l. 2 sign.			
	a. Ovpt: *PAPEETE (TAHITI)* in red below decrees at ctr. r. 14.3.1914.	125.00	400.00	900.00
	b. Ovpt: *PAPEETE (TAHITI)* in black. 14.3.1914.	125.00	400.00	900.00

	20 FRANCS	GOOD	FINE	XF
2	20.3.1914. Blue-green w/black text. Neptune reclining holding trident at lower l. 3 sign.	150.00	575.00	—

	100 FRANCS			
3	10.3.1914; 12.3.1914. Elephant columns l. and r., 2 reclining women w/ox l., tiger r., at lower border. 3 sign.	—	Rare	—

1920 ISSUE (W/O DECRETS)

	5 FRANCS	GOOD	FINE	XF
4	2.1.1920; 1.8.1923. Red. Like #1, but 3 sign.	100.00	285.00	700.00
5	20 FRANCS 1.5.1920. Green w/black text. Like #2.	150.00	525.00	—

	100 FRANCS	GOOD	FINE	XF
6	2.1.1920. Brown. Like #3 but 2 sign.			
	a. Hand sign.	75.00	250.00	—
	b. Printed sign.	50.00	175.00	375.00

BANQUE ANDRÉ KRAJEWSKI

PAPEETE BRANCH

1920 ND ISSUE

#7-10 seated woman holding branch and frame around denomination at lower l. Printer: A. Carlisle and Co., S.F.

		GOOD	FINE	XF
7	25 CENTIMES ND (1920). Brown.	75.00	300.00	650.00
8	50 CENTIMES ND (1920). Green.	100.00	325.00	725.00

		GOOD	FINE	XF
9	1 FRANC ND (1920). Red.	120.00	425.00	850.00
10	2 FRANCS ND (1920). Orange and red.	120.00	425.00	850.00

BANQUE DE L'INDOCHINE (RESUMED)

PAPEETE BRANCH

1923-28 ISSUE
#11-13 sign. varieties.

		GOOD	FINE	XF
11	**5 FRANCS** ND (1927). Brown. Helmeted woman at lower l.			
	a. Sign. titles: *Un Administrateur* and *Le Directeur*.	8.00	25.00	90.00
	b. Sign. R. Thion de la Chaume and P. Baudouin w/titles: *Le Président* and *Le Directeur Général*.	5.00	12.50	55.00
	c. Sign. M. Borduge and P. Baudouin w/titles as b.	3.00	7.50	35.00

		GOOD	FINE	XF
12 (13)	**20 FRANCS** ND (1928). Brown, lilac and red. Woman at r. Peacock on back.			
	a. Sign. titles: *Le Directeur* and *Le Administrateur*.	20.00	65.00	175.00
	b. Sign. R. Thion de la Chaume and P. Baudouin w/titles: *Le Président* and *Le Directeur Général*.	15.00	45.00	95.00
	c. Sign. M. Borduge and P. Baudouin w/titles as b.	7.50	25.00	65.00
	d. Sign. titles like b., but w/ovpt: *BANQUE DE L'INDOCHINE/SUCCURSALE DE PAPEETE*.	15.00	45.00	95.00

		GOOD	FINE	XF
13 (19)	**500 FRANCS** 1923; 1938. Dk. violet. Standing woman at l., ships at top ctr.			
	a. Sign. titles: *LE DIRECTEUR* and *UN ADMINISTRATEUR*. 1.4.1923.	120.00	350.00	750.00
	b. Sign. titles: *LE PRÉSIDENT* and *LE DIRECTEUR GÉNÉRAL*. 8.3.1938.	120.00	350.00	750.00

1939-40 ND ISSUE

		GOOD	FINE	XF
14 (16)	**100 FRANCS** ND (1939-65). Brown and m/c. woman wearing wreath and holding sm. figure of Athena at ctr. Angkor statue on back.			
	a. Sign. M. Borduge and P. Baudouin w/titles: *LE PRÉSIDENT* and *LE ADMINISTRATEUR DIRECTEUR GÉNÉRAL*.	6.00	20.00	60.00
	b. Sign. titles: *LE PRÉSIDENT* and *LE ADMINISTRATEUR DIRECTEUR GÉNÉRAL*.	5.00	17.50	50.00
	c. Sign. titles: *LE PRÉSIDENT* and *LE VICE-PRÉSIDENT DIRECTEUR GÉNÉRAL*.	4.00	15.00	35.00
	d. Sign. titles: *LE PRÉSIDENT* and *LE DIRECTEUR GÉNÉRAL*.	3.00	12.50	27.50
15 (20)	**1000 FRANCS** ND (1940-57). M/c. Market scene at l. and in background, seated woman at r.			
	a. Sign. M. Borduge and P. Baudouin w/titles: *LE PRÉSIDENT* and *LE VICE-PRÉSIDENT DIRECTEUR GÉNÉRAL*.	30.00	100.00	275.00
	b. Sign. titles: *LE PRÉSIDENT* and *LE VICE-PRÉSIDENT DIRECTEUR GÉNÉRAL*.	25.00	85.00	250.00
	c. Sign. F.M.A. de Flers and M. Robert w/titles like a.	15.00	45.00	200.00

1940 ND PROVISIONAL ISSUE

		GOOD	FINE	XF
16 (16A)	**100 FRANCS ON 20 FRANCS** ND (ca.1940). Black ovpt: *CENT FRANCS* and 2 sign. vertically at l. ctr., also ovpt: *CENT* across upper ctr. and *100* at lower ctr. on #12c.			
	a. Issued note.	—	Rare	—
	b. Punch cancelled handstamped: *ANNULÉ*.	—	Rare	—

1943 ND PROVISIONAL ISSUE

		GOOD	FINE	XF
17 (18)	**100 FRANCS ON 50 PIASTRES** Piastres ND(1943). Green. Man w/straw hat and baskets at r. Ovpt. on unfinished 50 Piastres, French Indo-China #77. Printed sign. Printer: ABNC (w/o imprint).			
	a. Text: *DE SAIGON* in r. sign. title not lined out.	50.00	110.00	350.00
	b. Text: *DE SAIGON* in r. sign. title lined out.	35.00	85.00	325.00
	s. Specimen, handstamped: *ANNULÉ*.	—	Unc	275.00

		GOOD	FINE	XF
18 (21)	**1000 FRANCS ON 100 PIASTRES** ND (1943). Blue. Angkor statues at l. Ovpt. on unfinished 100 Piastres French Indo-China #78. Printer: ABNC (w/o imprint).			
	a. Handwritten sign. at r.	125.00	350.00	725.00
	b. Both sign. printed.	120.00	310.00	700.00

1944 ND ISSUE

		GOOD	FINE	XF
19 (12)	**5 FRANCS** ND (1944). Blue. Woman wearing wreath and holding sm. figure of Athena at ctr. Angkor statue on back. Australian printing. 2 sign. varieties.			
	a. Issued note.	25.00	85.00	225.00
	s. Specimen.	—	Unc	200.00

		GOOD	FINE	XF
20 (14)	**20 FRANCS** ND (1944). Brown. Woman at l., sailboat at ctr., fisherman at r. Stylized mask on back. Australian printing.			
	a. Issued note.	30.00	110.00	250.00
	s. Specimen.	—	Unc	250.00

1951 ND ISSUE

		VG	VF	UNC
21 (15)	**20 FRANCS** ND (1951-63). M/c. Youth at l., flute player at r. Fruit at l., woman at r. on back. Wmk: Man w/hat.			
	a. Sign. titles: *LE PRÉSIDENT* and *LE DIRECTEUR GAL.* (1951).	3.50	9.00	35.00
	b. Sign. titles: *LE PRÉSIDENT* and *LE VICE-PRÉSIDENT DIRECT- EUR GÉNÉRAL* (1954-1958).	1.50	6.00	20.00
	c. Sign. titles: *LE PRÉSIDENT* and *LE DIRECTEUR GÉNÉRAL.* (1963).	1.25	5.00	15.00

1954 PROVSIONAL ISSUE

		GOOD	FINE	XF
22	**1000 FRANCS ON 100 PIASTRES** 1954. Blue. Similar to #21. Ovpt. elements on back as well as on face.	110.00	300.00	675.00

TANGIER

Tangier (Tangiers) is a port and city of the province of the same name in northern Morocco, at the west end of the Strait of Gibraltar, 17 miles (27 km.) from the southern tip of Spain. Tangier province has an area of 141 sq. mi. (365 sq. km.) and a population of 240,000. The town has a population of 190,000. Fishing and a textile industry supplement Tangier's role as a tourist center.

Tangier began as a 15th century BC Phoenician trading post, later becoming a Carthaginian and then a Roman settlement called Tingis. After five centuries of Roman rule, it was captured successively by the Vandals, Byzantines and Arabs. It was occupied by Islamic dynasties from about 682 to 1471, and by the Portuguese and Spanish until 1662, when sovereignty was transferred to the English crown. It was returned to Morocco in 1684 and was the diplomatic capital of Morocco during the 19th century. In 1923 it became an international zone governed by representatives from Great Britain, France, Spain, Portugal, Italy, Belgium, The Netherlands, Sweden, and later, the United States. It remained an international zone except for a period of Spanish occupation during World War II and then again until 1956, when it became a part of the Kingdom of Morocco.

RULERS:
French, 1912-1923
International Zone, 1923-1940, 1945-1956
Spanish, 1940-1945
Morocco, 1956-

SPANISH OCCUPATION - WWII

SERVICIOS MUNICIPALES

1941 EMERGENCY ISSUE

		GOOD	FINE	XF
1	**0.25 FRANCOS** Aug. 1941; March 1942; Oct. 1942. Blue.	225.00	600.00	—
2	**0.50 FRANCOS** Aug. 1941; March 1942; Oct. 1942. Brown.	225.00	600.00	—

		GOOD	FINE	XF
3	**1 FRANCO** Aug. 1941; March 1942; Oct. 1942. Violet.	200.00	500.00	—
4	**2 FRANCOS** (ca. 1941-42.) Orange.	300.00	700.00	—

TANNU TUVA

The Tannu-Tuva Peoples Republic (Tuva), an autonomous part of the former Union of Soviet Socialist Republics located in central Asia on the northwest border of Outer Mongolia, has an area of 64,000 sq. mi. (165,760 sq. km.) and a population of about 175,000. Capital: Kyzyl. The economy is based on herding, forestry and mining. As Urianghi, Tuva was part of Outer Mongolia of the Chinese Empire when Czarist Russia, after fomenting a separatist movement, extended its protection to the mountainous country in 1914. Tuva declared its independence as the Tannu-Tuva People's Republic in 1921 under the auspices of the Tuva People's Revolutionary Party. In 1926, following Russia's successful mediation of the resultant Tuvinian-Mongolian territorial dispute, Tannu-Tuva and Outer Mongolia formally recognized each other's independence. The Tannu-Tuva People's Republic became an autonomous region of the U.S.S.R. on Oct. 13, 1944.

Russian notes circulated between 1925-1933.

MONETARY SYSTEM:
1 Lan = 1 Aksha (Ruble) = 100 Kopejek (Kopeks)

PEOPLE'S REPUBLIC

TREASURY

1924 ND PROVISIONAL ISSUE
#1-4 ovpt. lines of script and a square stamp w/script on Russian Imperial notes. Most of these are spurious.

		VG	VF	UNC
1	**1 LAN ON 1 RUBLE** ND (1924 - old date 1898). Blue on brown unpt. Ovpt. on Russia #1.	4.00	7.50	12.50

2 3 LAN ON 3 RUBLES
ND (1924 - old date 1905). Green and pink. Ovpt. on Russia #9.

	VG	VF	UNC
	4.00	7.50	12.50

3 5 LAN ON 5 RUBLES
ND (1924 - old date 1909). Blue. Ovpt. on Russia #10.

	VG	VF	UNC
	4.00	7.50	12.50

4 10 LAN ON 10 RUBLES
ND (1925 - old date 1909). Red and green. Ovpt. on Russia #11.

	VG	VF	UNC
	4.00	7.50	12.50

1933 ND PROVISIONAL ISSUE
#5-9 vignette ovpt. on Union of Soviet Socialist Republics notes.

		VG	VF	UNC
5	3 RUBLES ND (1933 - old date 1925). Ovpt. on Russia #189.	—	—	—
6	5 RUBLES ND (1933 - old date 1925). Ovpt. on Russia #190.	—	—	—
7	1 CHERVONETZ ND (1933 - old date 1926). Ovpt. on Russia #198.	—	—	—
8	2 CHERVONETZA ND (1933 - old date 1926). Ovpt. on Russia #199.	—	—	—
9	1 GOLD RUBLE ND (1933 - old date 1928). Ovpt. on Russia - U.S.S.R. #206.	—	—	—

TANNU TUVA REPUBLIC

1935 ISSUE
#10-14 arms at upper ctr.

		GOOD	FINE	XF
10	1 AKSHA 1935. Green and m/c.	250.00	600.00	1250.
11	3 AKSHA 1935. M/c.	250.00	600.00	1250.
12	5 AKSHA 1935. Red and m/c.	250.00	600.00	1250.

		GOOD	FINE	XF
13	10 AKSHA 1935. Red and m/c.	—	Rare	—
14	25 AKSHA 1935. Brown and m/c.	—	Rare	—

1940 ISSUE
#15-19 farmer plowing w/2 horses at ctr.

		GOOD	FINE	XF
15	1 AKSHA 1940. Brown on orange and green unpt.	175.00	375.00	750.00
16	3 AKSHA 1940. Green.	175.00	375.00	750.00
17	5 AKSHA 1940. Blue.	175.00	375.00	750.00
18	10 AKSHA 1940. Red.	200.00	450.00	875.00
19	25 AKSHA 1940. Brown-violet.	200.00	450.00	875.00

The Kingdom of Thailand (formerly Siam), a constitutional monarchy located in the center of mainland southeast Asia between Burma and Laos, has an area of 198,457 sq. mi. (514,000 sq. km.) and a population of 57.6 million. Capital: Bangkok. The economy is based on agriculture and mining. Rubber, rice, teakwood, tin and tungsten are exported.

The history of Thailand, the only country in south and southeast Asia that was never colonized by an European power, dates from the 6th century AD when tribes of the Thai stock migrated into the area from the Asiatic continent, a process that accelerated with the Mongol invasion of China in the 13th century. After 400 years of sporadic warfare with the neighboring Burmese, King Taksin won the last battle in 1767. He founded a new capital, Dhonburi, on the west bank of Chao Praya River. King Rama I moved the capital to Bangkok in 1782.

The Thai were introduced to the Western world by the Portuguese, who were followed by the Dutch, British and French. Rama III of the present ruling dynasty negotiated a treaty of friendship and commerce with Britain in 1826, and in 1896 the independence of the kingdom was guaranteed by an Anglo-French accord. The absolute monarchy was changed into a constitutional monarchy in 1932.

In 1909 Siam ceded to Great Britain its suzerain rights over the dependencies of Kedah, Kelantan, Trengganu and Perlis, Malay states situated in southern Siam just north of British Malaya. This eliminated any British jurisdiction in Siam proper.

On Dec. 8, 1941, after five hours of fighting, Thailand agreed to permit Japanese troops passage through the country to invade northern British Malaya. This eventually led to increased Japanese intervention and finally occupation of the country. On Jan. 25, 1942, Thailand declared war on Great Britain and the United States. A free Thai guerrilla movement was soon organized to counteract the Japanese. In July 1943, Japan transferred the four northern Malay States back to Thailand. These were returned to Great Britain after peace treaties were signed in 1946.

* * * This section has been partially renumbered. * * *

RULERS:
Rama IV (Phra Chom Klao Mongkut), 1851-1868
Rama V (Phra Maha Chulalongkorn), 1868-1910
Rama VI (Vajiravudh), 1910-1925
Rama VII (Prajadhipok), 1925-1935
Rama VIII (Ananda Mahidol), 1935-1946
Rama IX (Bhumiphol Adulyadej), 1946-

MONETARY SYSTEM:
1 Baht (Tical) = 100 Satang
1 Tamlung = 4 Baht, 1853

KINGDOM OF SIAM

GRAND TREASURY

PHRA MAHA CHULALONGKORN

1853 ISSUE
#A1-A4 represent the first paper currency issued in Siam. Size: 140 x 102mm.

		Good	Fine	XF
A1	3 TAMLUNGS = 12 TICALS 1853.	Reported Not Confirmed		
A2	4 TAMLUNGS = 16 TICALS 1853.	Reported Not Confirmed		
A3	6 TAMLUNGS = 24 TICALS 1853.	Reported Not Confirmed		
A4	10 TAMLUNGS = 40 TICALS 1853.	—	Rare	—

1850's SECOND ISSUE
Bluish paper. Size: 87 x 62mm.

A5

A6

		Good	Fine	XF
A5	20 TICALS ND.	—	Rare	—
A6	80 TICALS ND.	—	Rare	—

1850's THIRD ISSUE
Bluish paper. Size: 87 x 50mm.

		Good	Fine	XF
A7	1/8 TICAL ND (1851-68).	700.00	1100.	2250.

		Good	Fine	XF
A8	1/4 TICAL ND (1851-68).	600.00	1000.	2000.
A9	3/8 TICAL ND (1851-68).	1500.	2500.	4500.
A10	1/2 TICAL ND (1851-68).	Reported Not Confirmed		
A11	1 TICAL ND (1851-68).	Reported Not Confirmed		

1850's FOURTH ISSUE
Thick cream unwmk. paper. Size: 108 x 85mm.

		Good	Fine	XF
A12	3 TAMLUNGS = 12 TICALS ND.	Reported Not Confirmed		
A13	4 TAMLINGS ND.	Reported Not Confirmed		
A14	5 TAMLUNGS = 20 TICALS ND.	Reported Not Confirmed		
A15	7 TAMLUNGS ND.	Reported Not Confirmed		
A16	8 TAMLUNGS ND.	Reported Not Confirmed		
A17	10 TAMLUNGS = 40 TICALS ND.	Reported Not Confirmed		
A18	12 TAMLUNGS ND.	Reported Not Confirmed		
A19	15 TAMLUNGS ND.	Reported Not Confirmed		
A20	1 CHANG = 80 TICALS ND.	Reported Not Confirmed		
A21	1 CHANG = 5 TAMLUNGS = 100 TICALS ND.	Reported Not Confirmed		

		Good	Fine	XF
A22	1 CHANG = 10 TAMLUNGS = 120 TICALS ND.	—	Rare	—

ROYAL SIAMESE TREASURY

1874 ISSUE

		Good	Fine	XF
A23	1 ATT = 1/64 TICAL 1874. Black. Blind embossed w/lg. circular seal and smaller rectangle seal. Size: 147 x 93mm.	350.00	700.00	—

1892 ISSUE
#1-8 Royal arms at upper ctr. Printer: G&D. (Not issued).

GOVERNMENT OF SIAM

ANANDA MAHIDOL

1902 ISSUE, SERIES 1

	1 TICAL	GOOD	FINE	XF
1	ND (1892). Green on blue and lt. red unpt. Back gray-blue.	375.00	950.00	—
2	**5 TICALS** ND (1892). Pink on green unpt. Back brown.	—	—	—
3	**10 TICALS** ND (1892). Maroon and m/c.	—	—	—
4	**40 TICALS** ND (1892). Red-orange and m/c.	GOOD —	FINE —	XF —

	80 TICALS	GOOD	FINE	XF
5	ND (1892). Blue-green and m/c.	—	—	—
6	**100 TICALS** ND (1892). Blue, tan and m/c.	—	—	—
7	**400 TICALS** ND (1892). a. Purple, green and m/c. b. Green on m/c unpt. Back green-gray, arms at ctr. c. Orange on m/c unpt. Back orange on blue and m/c unpt. arms at ctr.	GOOD — — —	FINE — — —	XF — — —
8	**800 TICALS** ND (1892). Brown, blue-green and m/c. Arms in ctr. on BACK.	—	—	—

SIGNATURE VARIETIES

	CHIEF OF THE BANKNOTE DEPARTMENT เจ้าพนักงาน		MINISTER OF FINANCE เสนาบดีกระทรวงพระคลัง
1	*(signature)*		*(signature)*
2	*(signature)*		*(signature)*
3	*(signature)*		*(signature)*
4	*(signature)*		*(signature)*
5	*(signature)*		*(signature)*
6	*(signature)*		*(signature)*
7			*(signature)*
8	*(signature)*		*(signature)*
9	*(signature)*		*(signature)*
	MINISTER OF FINANCE (to 1928) เสนาบดีกระทรวงพระคลง		
10	*(signature)*		
11	*(signature)*		
	MINISTER OF FINANCE (from 1928) รัฐมนตรีว่าการกระทรวงการคลัง		
12	*(signature)* *		
13	*(signature)* *		
14	*(signature)* *		
15	*(signature)* *		
16	*(signature)* *		

	5 TICALS	GOOD	FINE	XF
9	1902-25. Gray on green unpt.			
	a. Serial # at top only, green unpt. (1902-05). Sign. 1; 2; 3.	300.00	700.00	1750.
	b. Serial # at top only, purple-gray on tan unpt. (1905-11). Sign. 3; 5.	200.00	650.00	1600.
	c. Serial # at top and bottom, purple-gray on tan unpt. (1911-25). Sign. 5; 6; 8; 9.	225.00	600.00	1500.

	10 TICALS	GOOD	FINE	XF
10	1902-24. Brown on yellow unpt.			
	a. Serial # at top only, tan unpt. (1902-06). Sign. 1; 2.	250.00	750.00	1750.
	b. Serial # at top only, green unpt. (1906-13). Sign. 3; 4; 5.	200.00	700.00	1600.
	c. Serial # at top and bottom, green unpt. (1913-24). Sign. 5; 6; 8; 9.	225.00	600.00	1500.
	p. Brown. Proof. 1.1.1903.	—	—	—

11	**20 TICALS**	GOOD	FINE	XF
	1902-25. Green on pale pink unpt.			
	a. Serial # at top only, yellow unpt. (1902-06). Sign. 1; 2.	300.00	1000.	—
	b. Serial # at top only, lt. green unpt. (1906-10). Sign. 5.	300.00	1000.	—
	c. Serial # at top and bottom, lt. green unpt. (1910-25). Sign. 6; 8; 9.	300.00	950.00	—
	p. Green. Proof. 1.4.1902.	—	—	—

12	**100 TICALS**	GOOD	FINE	XF
	1902-25. Purple on pale brown unpt.			
	a. Serial # at top only, brown on yellow unpt. (1902-08). Sign. 1; 2. 3.	450.00	1100.	2700.
	b. Serial # at top only, violet on brown unpt. (1908-10). Sign. 3; 4; 5.	400.00	1000.	2500.
	c. Serial # at top and bottom, violet on brown unpt. (1910-25). Sign. 5; 6; 8; 9.	350.00	450.00	2350.
	p. Purple. Proof. 1.4.1902.	—	—	—

13	**1000 TICALS**	GOOD	FINE	XF
	1.4.1902-25. Red on pale red unpt.			
	a. Serial # at top only, lt. brown unpt. (1902-09). Sign. 1; 2.	—	Rare	—
	b. Serial # at top only, brown unpt. (1909-12). Sign. 5.	—	Rare	—
	c. Serial # at top and bottom, brown unpt. (1912-25). Sign. 5; 6; 8; 9.	—	Rare	—
	p. Proof. 1.4.1902.	—	—	—

16	**1 BAHT**	GOOD	FINE	XF
	1925-33. Blue on yellow unpt.			
	a. Type I text. 1.4.1925-20.4.1928. Sign. 10.	2.00	10.00	35.00
	b. Type II text. 8 8.9.1928-11.6.1933. Sign. 10; 11; 12; 13.	2.00	10.00	20.00

1918 ISSUE

14	**1 TICAL**	GOOD	FINE	XF
	1918-25. Black on gray or gray-brown unpt. Sign. 6; 8; 9.	150.00	250.00	650.00

17	**5 BAHT**	GOOD	FINE	XF
	1925-32. Purple on green unpt.			
	a. Type I text. 1.4.1925-15.2.1928. Sign. 10.	20.00	85.00	250.00
	b. Type II text. 29.6.1929-1.2.1932. Sign. 10; 11.	15.00	65.00	175.00

18	**10 BAHT**	GOOD	FINE	XF
	1925-34. Red-brown on pink unpt.			
	a. Type I text. 29.6.1925-15.11.1926. Sign. 10.	15.00	75.00	250.00
	b. Type II text. 15.5.1929-21.3.1934. Sign. 10; 11; 12; 13.	12.00	50.00	225.00

1918 ND PROVISIONAL ISSUE

15	**50 TICALS**	GOOD	FINE	XF
	ND (1918). Ovpt. on #14. Sign. 7.			
	a. W/o embossed stamp.	—	Rare	—
	b. Embossed stamp of 3-headed elephant on back.	—	Rare	—

1925 ISSUE, SERIES 2

Dates and single sign. of Finance Minister on bottom ctr., mythological winged Garuda bird at upper l., 3-headed elephant at lower r. Common vignette at ctr. shows ceremonial parade of first plowing on back. Officially described as "Series Two."

TEXT VARIETIES (in second line on face):

Type I สัญฌาจะชายสินให้แก่ผู้นำ ฯบัตรน้มาชินเปนสินๅกรสยาม

"Contract to pay in Siamese Currency to anyone who presents this note".

Type II ธนบัตร์เป็นเงินที่ชำระหนี้ได้ตวบกฎหมาย

"Banknote is legal tender for any debt".

#16-21 ceremonial procession on back. Printer: TDLR.

19	**20 BAHT**	GOOD	FINE	XF
	1925-33. Green on gray unpt.			
	a. Type I text. 15.4.1925; 29.7.1925; 15.8.1925; 15.11.1926; 15.7.1927. Sign. 10.	25.00	100.00	275.00
	b. Type II text. 29.5.1928-1.1.1933. Sign. 10; 11; 13.	20.00	90.00	225.00

			GOOD	FINE	XF
20	**100 BAHT**				
	1925-38. Blue on green unpt.				
	a. Type I text. 1.4.1925-1.11.1927. Sign. 10; 11.		20.00	100.00	295.00
	b. Type II text. 11.9.1928-16.9.1938. Sign. 14; 15; 16.		15.00	80.00	275.00
21	**1000 BAHT**				
	1925-38. Red-brown on yellow unpt.				
	a. Type I text. 1.4.1925-1.11.1927. Sign. 10; 11.		100.00	325.00	800.00
	b. Type II text. 1.10.1930-11.9.1938. Sign. 11; 15.		90.00	300.00	750.00

1934-35 ISSUE, SERIES 3

Single sign. of Finance Minister at bottom ctr. Winged mythological figure (Garuda) at top ctr. and 3-headed elephant at lower r. corner. Temple and pagoda on an island on back. Officially described as "Series Three".

#22-25 Rama VII facing at l. Printer: TDLR.

NOTE: #22-25 come with 2 variations in the Finance Minister title line at bottom center of face.

			VG	VF	UNC
22	**1 BAHT**		1.50	6.00	35.00
	1.4.1934-25.2.1935. Dk. blue on lt. yellow-green and pale orange unpt. Royal barge at ctr. Sign. 13; 14.				

			VG	VF	UNC
23	**5 BAHT**		5.00	45.00	175.00
	29.5.1934-18.2.1935. Purple on yellow and orange unpt. Emerald Buddha Temple complex at ctr. Sign. 13; 14.				
24	**10 BAHT**		5.00	20.00	150.00
	1.2.1934-1.3.1935. Brown on pink unpt. River and mountains at ctr. Sign. 13; 14.				

			VG	VF	UNC
25	**20 BAHT**		10.00	25.00	125.00
	15.1.1935; 25.1.1935; 8.2.1935; 13.2.1935; 25.2.1935. Green on pale blue and tan unpt. River, village and pagoda at ctr. Sign. 14.				

1935-36 ISSUE

#26-29 King Rama VIII as a boy 3/4 face at l. Back design like previous issue.

			VG	VF	UNC
26	**1 BAHT**		2.00	8.00	35.00
	18.4.1935-11.9.1938. Blue. Similar to #22. Sign. 14; 15.				
27	**5 BAHT**		6.00	35.00	150.00
	29.4.1935-15.5.1937. Purple. Similar to #23. Sign. 14; 15.				

			VG	VF	UNC
28	**10 BAHT**		5.00	25.00	140.00
	29.5.1935-1.10.1936. Brown. Similar to #24. Sign. 14; 15.				
29	**20 BAHT**		7.00	35.00	160.00
	1.4.1936-1.7.1936. Green. Similar to #25. Sign. 15.				

1939 ND ISSUE, SERIES 4A

Officially described as "Series Four (Thomas)" (notes printed in England by Thomas De La Rue) to differentiate from similar, but cruder, notes printed later by the Thai Map Department. W/o dates. Kg. Rama VIII as a boy 3/4 face at l. and 3-headed elephant at lower r. M/c guilloche unpt. at ctr. Single sign. of Finance Minister at bottom ctr. Royal Throne Hall on back.

NOTE: In 1939 the name *SIAM* was changed to *THAILAND*. By decree of 7.3.1939 this change was made in the main heading at top on faces of all notes, as shown below:

HEADING VARIETIES

รัฐบาล สยาม	รัฐบาล ไทย
TYPE I:	TYPE II:
GOVERNMENT OF SIAM	GOVERNMENT OF THAILAND

			VG	VF	UNC
30	**1 BAHT**		2.00	10.00	50.00
	ND (from 1938). Blue. Phra Samut Chedi Temple and pagoda at ctr. Type I heading. Sign. 15, 16.				

		VG	VF	UNC
31	**1 BAHT** ND (from 1939). Blue. Like #30. Type II heading.			
	a. Serial # at l. w/European characters, Thai at r. Sign. 16.	2.00	10.00	30.00
	b. Both serial # w/European characters Sign. 23 (from 1946).	1.00	8.00	27.50
32	**5 BAHT** ND (from 1939). Purple. Entrance to Phra Pathom Chedi at ctr. Type I heading. Sign. 16.	5.00	25.00	115.00
33	**5 BAHT** ND (from 1939). Purple. Like #32 but Type II heading. Sign. 16.	5.00	20.00	110.00

		VG	VF	UNC
34	**10 BAHT** ND (from 1939). Brown. Mahagal Fortress at ctr. Type I heading. Sign. 16.	5.00	30.00	140.00
35	**10 BAHT** ND (from 1939). Brown. Like #34 but Type II heading.			
	a. Sign. 16 (from 1939).	5.00	25.00	125.00
	b. Sign. 23 (from 1946).	5.00	22.00	110.00
36	**20 BAHT** ND (from 1939). Green. Throne Halls at ctr. Type I heading. Sign. 16.	3.00	15.00	45.00
37	**1000 BAHT** ND (from 1939). Red-brown. Temple of the Dawn at ctr. Type I heading. Sign. 16.	100.00	325.00	—
38	**1000 BAHT** ND (from 1939). Red-brown. Like #37 but w/Type II heading. Sign. 16.	100.00	325.00	—

JAPANESE INTERVENTION - WW II
GOVERNMENT OF THAILAND

1942-44 ND ISSUE, SERIES 4B
Officially described as "Series Four (Map)". Printed by Royal Thai Army Map Department, w/imprint in the bottom margin face and back. Similar to their counterparts in Series Four (Thomas), but of inferior quality. Single sign. of Minister of Finance at bottom ctr. Top legend is changed from: รัฐบาล ไทย

To: รัฐบาลไทย

SIGNATURE VARIETIES		
	CHIEF OF THE BANKNOTE DEPARTMENT	**MINISTER OF FINANCE**
17		
	DIRECTOR GENERAL OF THE TREASURY DEPARTMENT อธิบดีกรมคลัง	**MINISTER OF FINANCE** รัฐมนตรีว่าการกระทรวงการคลัง
18		
	MINISTER OF FINANCE รัฐมนตรีว่าการกระทรวงการคลัง	
19		
20		
21		
22		
23		
24		

		VG	VF	UNC
39	**1 BAHT** ND (from 1942). Blue. Similar to #31. Wmk: Constitution on tray on pedestal.			
	a. R. serial # in Thai. Sign. 17.	2.00	15.00	45.00
	b. Both serial # in European numbers. Sign. 17; 19; 20.	2.00	12.00	40.00
40	**10 BAHT** ND (from 1943). Brown. Similar to #35.			
	a. Wmk: Constitution. Sign. 17.	8.00	25.00	140.00
	b. Wmk: Constitution. Sign. 20.	8.00	20.00	130.00
	c. Sign. 21 (probably conterfeit; # and sign. fraudulently applied to genuine note; not issued).	—	—	—
	d. Wmk: Wavy lines w/constitution printed in window. Sign. 21 (from 1945).	8.00	25.00	130.00
	e. Wmk: Like d. Sign. 24.	8.00	50.00	160.00
	f. Sign. 20 (like c, probably counterfeit; not issued).	—	—	—

		VG	VF	UNC
41	**20 BAHT** ND (from 1943). Green. Like #36. Unpt. orange and green on face. Wmk: Constitution. Sign. 17; 19; 20.	2.00	25.00	140.00
42	**100 BAHT** ND (1944). Blue. Temple, w/walkway flanked by 2 mythological statues, at ctr. Pink and green unpt. design on face. Wmk: Constitution. Silk threads. Sign. 19; 20.	10.00	75.00	175.00

1942-45 ND ISSUES, SERIES 5
Printed in Japan by Mitsui Trading Company. Officially described as "Series Five". Kg. Rama VIII full face at r. Single sign. of Finance Minister at bottom ctr. Walled temple and pagoda complex on river bank (Royal Palace) on back.

#44-53 wmk: Constitution on tray on pedestal.

		VG	VF	UNC
43	**50 SATANG** ND (1942). Green on pink unpt. design. Wmk. paper. 17; 20.			
	a. Issued note.	1.00	5.00	14.00
	r. Remainder w/o sign. or block #.	—	—	125.00
	s1. Specimen w/ovpt: *Mi-hon*.	—	—	—
	s2. Specimen w/ovpt: *Specimen*.	—	—	—

		VG	VF	UNC
44	**1 BAHT** ND (1942; 1944). Brown on pink unpt. at ctr. Entrance to Wat Phumintr, flanked by mythological snakes at l.			
	a. 3 serial #, lower l. in Thai. Sign. 17.	7.00	20.00	50.00
	b. 3 serial # all w/European numerals. Sign. 17.	2.00	10.00	30.00
	c. 2 serial # (lower l. deleted). Sign. 17; 19; 20.	2.00	10.00	30.00
	r. Remainder w/o sign. or serial #.	—	—	125.00
	s1. Specimen w/ovpt: *Mi-hon*.	—	—	—
	s2. Specimen w/ovpt: *Specimen*.	—	—	—
45	**5 BAHT** ND (1942; 1944). Green on green unpt. Marble Temple at l.			
	a. 3 serial #, lower l. in Thai. Sign. 17.	10.00	40.00	175.00
	b. 3 serial #, all w/European numbers. Sign. 17.	10.00	40.00	175.00
	c. 2 serial # (lower l. deleted). Sign. 17; 19; 20.	10.00	35.00	160.00
	d. W/o sign.	—	—	150.00
	s. Specimen w/ovpt: *Specimen*.	—	—	—

46 **5 BAHT**
ND (1945). Green. Like #45. 2 serial #. Back purple, w/constitution printed in purple on window.

	VG	VF	UNC
a. Sign. 20.	5.00	30.00	140.00
b. W/o sign.	5.00	30.00	130.00

47 **10 BAHT**
ND (from 1942). Purple on pink and lt. blue unpt. Part of wall and gateway to Wat Chetupon at l. Back purple.

	VG	VF	UNC
a. 3 serial #, lower l. in Thai. Sign. 17.	10.00	40.00	160.00
b. 3 serial #, all w/European numbers. Sign. 17.	10.00	35.00	150.00
c. 2 serial # (lower l. deleted). Sign. 17; 20.	10.00	35.00	140.00
s. Specimen w/ovpt: *Specimen*.	—	—	—

48 **10 BAHT**
ND (1945). Purple. Like #47c, but back lt. green. Sign. 20.

	VG	VF	UNC
	12.00	60.00	180.00

49 **20 BAHT**
ND (from 1942). Blue on brown unpt. Throne Hall at l. Back blue.

	VG	VF	UNC
a. 3 serial #. Upper r. and l. w/European letters and numerals, lower l. in Thai. Sign. 17.	5.00	40.00	150.00
b. 3 serial #, all w/European numbers. Upper l. and r. have Western letter in control prefix, lower has Thai letter prefix. Sign. 17.	5.00	40.00	150.00
c. 3 serial #, all w/European numbers. Upper r. and lower have Thai letter in control prefix (P/31-P/33 only). Sign. 17.	10.00	50.00	175.00
d. 2 serial # (lower l. deleted). Western control letter in upper l., Thai control letter in upper r. Sign. 17; 19; 20.	5.00	40.00	140.00
s. Specimen w/ovpt: *Specimen*.	—	—	—

50 **20 BAHT**
ND (1945). Like #49d, but back lt. brown.

	VG	VF	UNC
a. Sign. 20.	5.00	35.00	140.00
b. W/o sign.	5.00	35.00	140.00

51 **100 BAHT**
ND (1943). Red on blue and olive unpt. Temple of the Dawn at l. Back red. Sign. 17.

	VG	VF	UNC
a. Issued note.	35.00	125.00	350.00
s1. Specimen w/ovpt: *Mi-hon*.	—	—	—
s2. Specimen w/ovpt: *Specimen*.	—	—	—

52 **100 BAHT**
ND (1945). Red. Like #51 but back blue.

	VG	VF	UNC
a. Sign. 20.	25.00	125.00	300.00
b. W/o sign.	25.00	125.00	275.00
s1. Specimen w/ovpt: *Mi-hon*.	—	—	—
s2. Specimen w/ovpt: *Specimen*.	—	—	—

53 **1000 BAHT**
ND (1944). Olive on pink and blue unpt. The Chakri and Dusit Maha Prasad Throne Halls at l. Back olive. Silk threads. Sign. 17.

	VG	VF	UNC
a. Issued note.	275.00	650.00	—
s1. Specimen w/ovpt: *Mi-hon*.	—	—	—
s2. Specimen w/ovpt: *Specimen*.	—	—	—

1945 ND FIRST ISSUE, SERIES 6

Kg. Rama VIII as a boy at l., single sign. of Finance Minister at bottom ctr. Royal Throne Hall on back. Officially described as "Series Six". Printed by Army Map Department (w/imprint) and Navy Hydrological Department (w/o imprint).

53A **20 BAHT**
ND (1945). Green. Like #41 but unpt. design pink. W/imprint. Sign. 20.

	VG	VF	UNC
a. Wmk: Constitution on tray on pedestal, silk threads.	15.00	50.00	150.00
b. Wmk: Wavy lines. Silk threads throughout; tan constitution ovpt. in circle. W/imprint. Sign. 20; 21.	15.00	60.00	160.00
c. Wmk: Like b. W/o imprint. Sign. 21.	15.00	60.00	160.00

53B **100 BAHT**
ND (1945). Blue. Like #42 but unpt. design mostly purple.

	VG	VF	UNC
a. Wmk: Constitution. Silk threads throughout. W/imprint.	Reported Not Confirmed		
b. Wmk: Like a. W/o imprint. Sign. 20.	15.00	60.00	160.00
c. Wmk: Wavy lines. Silk threads, purple constitution ovpt. in circle. W/imprint. Sign. 20; 21.	20.00	80.00	190.00
d. Wmk: Like c. W/o imprint. Sign. 20; 21.	15.00	55.00	150.00

1945 ND SECOND ISSUE, SERIES 7

Kg. Rama VIII full face at l., single sign. of Finance Minister at bottom ctr. Royal Throne Hall on back. Officially described as "Series Seven". Crudely printed by private printers contracted by the Bank of Thailand.

54 **1 BAHT**
ND (1945). Blue on lt. pink unpt. Similar to #30.

	VG	VF	UNC
a. Wmk: Multiple wavy lines. Sign. 20; 21.	1.00	6.00	18.00
b. W/o wmk. Sign. 21.	2.00	8.00	25.00

55 **5 BAHT**
ND (1945). Purple and lt. green. Similar to #32. Lt. green constitution ovpt. in circle. Wmk: Wavy lines. Red serial #. 135 x 76mm. Sign. 20; 21.

VG	VF	UNC
10.00	50.00	150.00

55A **5 BAHT**
ND (1945). Like #55 but black serial #. 115 x 65mm. Sign. 20; 21.

VG	VF	UNC
10.00	50.00	150.00

56 **10 BAHT**
ND (1945). Dk. brown. Similar to #34.

	VG	VF	UNC
a. Wmk: Constitution. Sign. 20.	5.00	30.00	140.00
b. Wmk: Multiple wavy lines. brown constitution ovpt. in circle. Sign. 20.	5.00	30.00	140.00

57 **50 BAHT**
ND (1945). Pale red on green unpt. Marble Temple at ctr.

	VG	VF	UNC
a. W/o wmk. Sign. 20.	10.00	60.00	190.00
b. Wmk: Multiple wavy lines. Sign. 20; 21.	10.00	60.00	190.00

KINGDOM
GOVERNMENT OF THAILAND

SIGNATURE VARIETIES		
	MINISTER OF FINANCE รัฐมนตรีว่าการกระทรวงการคลัง	GOVERNOR OF THE BANK OF THAILAND ผู้ว่าการธนาคารแห่งประเทศไทย
25	*(signature)*	*(signature)*
26	*(signature)*	*(signature)*
	MINISTER OF FINANCE รัฐมนตรีว่าการกระทรวงการคลัง	
27	*(signature)*	
	MINISTER OF FINANCE	GOVERNOR OF THE BANK OF THAILAND
28	*(signature)*	*(signature)*
29	*(signature)*	*(signature)*
30	*(signature)*	*(signature)*
31	*(signature)*	*(signature)*
32	*(signature)*	*(signature)*
33	*(signature)*	*(signature)*
34	*(signature)*	*(signature)*
35	*(signature)*	*(signature)*
36	*(signature)*	*(signature)*
37	*(signature)*	*(signature)*
38	*(signature)*	*(signature)*
39	*(signature)*	*(signature)*
40	*(signature)*	*(signature)*
41	*(signature)*	*(signature)*
42	*(signature)*	*(signature)*
43	*(signature)* **	*(signature)*

**signed as Undersecretary/Deputy Finance Minister

44	*(signature)*	*(signature)*

1942-44 ND ISSUE

58 (59)	**1 BAHT** ND (1942). Blue on red unpt. Portr. Kg. Rama VIII 3/4 face at l. Constitution on tray on pedestal embossed in oval at r. Sign. 18. Wmk.: Vertical white stripe 8mm. wide at l. ctr.	VG	VF	UNC
	a. Red to orange flower in unpt. at ctr.	30.00	100.00	300.00
	b. Yellow flower in unpt. at ctr. (Counterfeit?).	30.00	90.00	265.00

59 (58A)	**10 BAHT** ND. Like #62 but w/o ovpt. or sign. (Not issued).	VG 5.00	VF 20.00	UNC 40.00

60 (62)	**1000 BAHT** ND (1943). Deep red and yellow. Kg. Rama VIII tilted to r. of vertical at r. Phrang Sam Yod (3 ornate towers) at l. Wmk: Constitution. Sign. 18.	VG 150.00	VF 500.00	UNC 1200.
61 (62A)	**1000 BAHT** ND (1944). Like #62A, but deep brown and yellow. Sign. 18.	150.00	500.00	1200.

1945; 1946 ND PROVISIONAL ISSUE

Different types of wartime notes, some of which were issued after the war but before supplies of new notes could be obtained for normal use. A "hodgepodge" having no common characteristics, this series, officially described as "Series Special", was printed in part in Thailand, in part in other countries.

62 (58)	**50 SATANG ON 10 BAHT** ND (1946). Dk. purple on gray unpt. Portal at l., Kg. Rama VIII full face at r. Royal palace on river bank on back. New value ovpt. in 3 corners on face, twice on back on #58. Sign. 22.	VG 5.00	VF 10.00	UNC 25.00

62A (60)	**1 BAHT** ND (1946). Blue on pale olive unpt. ONE BAHT at ctr. 3-line black ovpt on face. English printing. Sign. 23.	VG	VF	UNC
	a. 2nd line of ovpt. complete (29 characters).	5.00	8.00	17.50
	b. 12th character of 2nd line missing.	2.00	10.00	22.50

62B (61)	**50 BAHT ON 1 DOLLAR** ND (1945). Purple and greenish yellow. Ovpt. on #R1.	VG	VF	UNC

a. Red 50 in white circle on face and back. Sign. 17; 20.	60.00	150.00	425.00
b. Red 50 in white circle on face only. Sign. 20.	60.00	150.00	425.00

c. W/o red 50 or obliterative ovpts. on face or back. Black denomination in words ovpt. on face. Sign. 17; 19; 20.	60.00	150.00	425.00

1948 ND FIRST ISSUE, SERIES 8

Printed in the U.S. by Tudor Press, Boston. This is a regular (not "Liberation") issue, officially described as "Series Eight". Kg. Rama VIII full face at l. Unpt. road w/monuments and pagoda. All have brown back, w/constitution on ceremonial vessel at ctr. Replacement notes identified by absence of letter at end of serial #. Wmk: *MILITARY AUTHORITY* repeated.

		VG	VF	UNC
63	**1 BAHT** ND (1948). Green and blue. Sign. 22.	.25	1.00	5.00

		VG	VF	UNC
64	**5 BAHT** ND (1948). Dk. and lt. blue. Sign. 22.	1.00	6.00	25.00

		VG	VF	UNC
65	**10 BAHT** ND (1948). Brown on blue.			
	a. Black sign. ovpt. at r. Sign. 25.	2.00	15.00	50.00
	b. 2 black sign. ovpt. Sign. 26.	2.00	15.00	50.00

		VG	VF	UNC
66	**20 BAHT** ND (1948). Dk. and lt. blue.			
	a. Black sign. ovpt. at r. Sign. 25.	10.00	50.00	135.00
	b. 2 black sign. ovpt. Sign. 26.	10.00	50.00	135.00

		VG	VF	UNC
67	**100 BAHT** ND (1948). Brown on lt. blue. Black sign. 25 (unconfirmed); 26; 28 ovpt.	25.00	100.00	250.00

1948 ND SECOND ISSUE, SERIES 9

W/o dates. Printed in England by TDLR and officially described as "Series Nine". With exception of #68, all have Kg. Rama IX full face at l., sign. of Finance Minister at l. and Governor of the Bank of Thailand at r., wmk. in circular window at r. Royal Throne Hall on back.

#69-73 Kg. in uniform w/o collar insignia. Wmk: Constitution on tray on pedestal. Blue and red security threads. Printer: TDLR.

		VG	VF	UNC
68	**50 SATANG** ND (1948). Green on pink unpt. Constitution on tray on pedestal in unpt. Phra Samut Chedi on back. Sign. 27.	1.00	2.00	4.00
69	**1 BAHT** ND (1948). Blue on m/c unpt. Similar to #30.			
	a. Red serial #. Sign. 28; 30; 31; 32; 33; 34.	1.00	3.00	10.00
	b. Black serial #. Sign. 28; 31; 32.	1.00	3.00	10.00
70	**5 BAHT** ND (1948). Purple on m/c unpt. Similar to #32.			
	a. Red serial #. Sign. 28; 32.	2.00	5.00	25.00
	b. Black serial #. Sign. 28; 30; 31.	1.00	3.00	20.00
71	**10 BAHT** ND (1948). Brown on m/c. unpt. Similar to #34.			
	a. Red serial #. Sign. 28; 29; 32.	1.00	4.00	20.00
	b. Black serial #. Sign. 28; 30; 31; 32.	1.00	3.00	18.00

		VG	VF	UNC
72	**20 BAHT** ND (1948). Green on m/c unpt. Similar to #36.			
	a. Red serial #. Sign. 28; 29; 30; 31; 32.	2.00	6.00	25.00
	b. Black serial #. Sign. 28; 30; 31; 32.	2.00	5.00	22.00

73	100 BAHT	VG	VF	UNC
	ND (1948). Red on m/c. unpt. Similar to #37. Black serial # only. Sign. 28; 31; 32; 33; 34.	5.00	15.00	45.00

1953-56 ND ISSUE

#74-78 slightly modified Kg. in Field Marshall's uniform w/collar insignia and 3 decorations. Black serial #. Printer: TDLR.

Small letters in 2-line text on back.

Large letters in 2-line text on back.

74	1 BAHT	VG	VF	UNC
	ND (1955). Blue on m/c unpt. Like #69.			
a.	Wmk: Constitution. Red and blue security threads. Sign. 34.	.25	1.00	6.00
b.	Wmk: Constitution. Metal security strip. Sign. 34; 35 (lg. size).	.25	1.00	5.00
c.	Wmk: Kg. profile. Sm. letters in 2-line text on back. Sign. 35.	.25	1.00	5.00
d.	Wmk: Kg. profile. Larger letters in 2-line text on back. Sign. 36; 37; 38; 39; 40; 4l.	.20	.60	4.00

75	5 BAHT	VG	VF	UNC
	ND (1956). Purple on m/c unpt. Like #70.			
a.	Wmk: Constitution. Red and blue security threads. Sign. 34.	.50	2.00	4.00
b.	Wmk: Constitution. Metal security strip. Sign. 34; 35 (lg. size).	.50	1.50	3.50
c.	Wmk: Kg. profile. Sm. letters in 2-line text on back. Sign. 35; 36.	.50	1.50	3.50
d.	Wmk: Kg. profile. Larger letters in 2-line text on back. Sign. 38; 39; 40; 41.	.25	1.00	2.00

76	10 BAHT	VG	VF	UNC
	ND (1953). Brown on m/c unpt. Like #71.			
a.	Wmk: Constitution. Red and blue security threads. Sign. 34.	.50	2.00	6.00
b.	Wmk: Constitution. Metal security strip. Sign. 34; 35 (lg. size).	.50	2.00	4.50
c.	Wmk: Kg. profile. Sm. letters in 2-line text on back. Sign. 35; 36; 37; 38.	.50	1.00	2.50
d.	Wmk: Kg. profile. Larger letters in 2-line text on back. Sign. 39; 40; 41; 42; 44.	.50	1.00	2.25

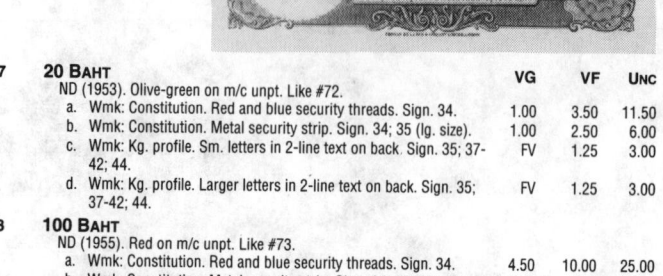

77	20 BAHT	VG	VF	UNC
	ND (1953). Olive-green on m/c unpt. Like #72.			
a.	Wmk: Constitution. Red and blue security threads. Sign. 34.	1.00	3.50	11.50
b.	Wmk: Constitution. Metal security strip. Sign. 34; 35 (lg. size).	1.00	2.50	6.00
c.	Wmk: Kg. profile. Sm. letters in 2-line text on back. Sign. 35; 37-42; 44.	FV	1.25	3.00
d.	Wmk: Kg. profile. Larger letters in 2-line text on back. Sign. 35; 37-42; 44.	FV	1.25	3.00
78	100 BAHT			
	ND (1955). Red on m/c unpt. Like #73.			
a.	Wmk: Constitution. Red and blue security threads. Sign. 34.	4.50	10.00	25.00
b.	Wmk: Constitution. Metal security strip. Sign. 34; 35; 37; 38.	4.25	8.50	20.00
c.	Wmk: Kg. profile. Sm. letters in 2-line text on back. Sign. 38-41.	FV	6.00	15.00
d.	Wmk: Kg. profile. Larger letters in 2-line text on back. Sign. 38-41.	FV	6.00	15.00

REGIONAL - WW II

#R1 was issued in the northern Malay States of Kedah, Kelantan, Perlis and Trengganu which were ceded to Thailand by Japan during WW II. They were later ovpt: 50 Baht and issued for general circulation; see #62B.

TREASURY

1943 PROVISIONAL ISSUE

R1	1 DOLLAR	VG	VF	UNC
	ND (1943). Purple and green. Vertical line of Chinese inscription at l., Malay at r. Throne Hall on back.			
a.	Issued note.	—	—	—
r.	Unsigned remainder.	—	100.00	300.00

Tibet, an autonomous region of China located in central Asia between the Himalayan and Kunlun Mountains, has an area of 471,660 sq. mi. (1,221,599 sq. km.) and a population of 1.3 million. Capital: Lhasa. The economy is based on agriculture and livestock raising. Wool, livestock, salt and hides are exported. Lamaism, a form of Buddhism, developed in Tibet in the 8th century. From that time until the 1900s, the country remained isolated from the outside world, ruled from the 17th century by the Dalai Lama. The British in India achieved some influence in the early 20th century, and encouraged Tibet to declare its independence from China in 1913. The communist revolution in China marked a new era in Tibetan history. Chinese Communist troops invaded Tibet in Oct., 1950. After a token resistance, Tibet signed an agreement with China in which China recognized the spiritual and temporal leadership of the Dalai Lama, and Tibet recognized the suzerainty of China. In 1959, a nationwide revolt triggered by Communist-initiated land reform broke out. The revolt was ruthlessly crushed. The Dalai Lama fled to India, and on Sept. 1, 1965, the Chinese made Tibet an autonomous region of China.

NOTE: Chinese notes in Tibetan script or w/Tibetan ovpt. were not intended for circulation in Tibet, but for use in bordering Chinese Provinces having a Tibetan speaking population. Refer to China #209b, 214b, 217b, 219d and 220c in this volume. Also #S1739 and S1740 (Sikang Provincial Bank) in Volume 1.

MONETARY SYSTEM:
7.5 Srang = 50 Tam (Tangka)

DENOMINATONS   VALUES

Tam (Tangka):   Five: Twenty-five:

Srang: Ten: Twenty-five:

                   Fifteen: Fifty:

                   100:             Hundred:

DATING
Tibetan notes simply give the number of solar years which have elapsed since the legendary founding of the government in 255 AD, which is year 1 on this reckoning. Thus, Tibetan era dates are converted to AD dates merely by adding 254 to the former. Some of the later Tibetan notes give only the 'rab byung' cycle (without the year) in which issued. Thus a note of the 16th cycle would imply issuance any time during the 60-year period 1927-86AD.

TYPES I & II

1st Line:

2nd Line:

Decades: 165X   (Units
           166X   see below)
           167X
           168X
           169X

Units (to be   1.   4.   7.
added to above):   2.   5.   8.
                   3.   6.   9.

3rd Line:

4th Line:

                   15th:
                   16th:

TYPE III

1st Line:

2nd Line:

TYPE IV
Same as Type III, but 2nd line ends:

25 Srang:

100 Srang:

AUTONOMOUS
GOVERNMENT OF TIBET
1658-59 (1912-13) ISSUE
#1-7A many varieties in size, printing and color.

			GOOD	FINE	XF
1	**5 TAM**		100.00	300.00	—
	1658 (1912). Green. Lion and flowers. 4 lines of text. Back lt. green. 180 x 100mm.				
1A	**5 TAM**		100.00	300.00	—
	1658 (1912). Blue. Like #1. Back blue.				

			GOOD	FINE	XF
2	**10 TAM**		150.00	500.00	—
	1658-59 (1912-13). Red. Lion at ctr. 4 lines of text. 175 x 95mm.				

			GOOD	FINE	XF
3	**15 TAM**		125.00	400.00	—
	1659 (1913). Purple. Lion w/platter of fruit at ctr. 4 lines of text. 185 x 100mm.				
4	**25 TAM**		125.00	400.00	—
	1659 (1913). Yellow. Lion. 4 lines of text. Mountains and elephant on back. 180 x 95mm.				

		GOOD	**FINE**	**XF**
5	**50 TAM**	125.00	400.00	—
	1659 (1913). Blue. 2 lions at ctr. 4 lines of text. Seated figure on back. 185 x 100mm.			
6	**50 TAM**	100.00	300.00	—
	1659 (1913). Purple. Like #5 except for color.			

1672-77 (1926-31) ISSUE

		GOOD	**FINE**	**XF**
7	**50 TAM**			
	1672-87 (1926-41). Blue and red on yellow unpt. 2 lions at ctr. Back red and blue; lion, dragon, tiger and stylized creature. 201 x 118mm.			
	a. Short serial # frame. 1672 (Cycle 15); 1673-77 (Cycle 16).	25.00	75.00	250.00
	b. Long serial # frame. 1673-87 (Cycle 16).	25.00	75.00	250.00
7A	**50 TAM**			
	1677 (1931). Like #7, but additional red circular seal over the serial # at upper r.	35.00	100.00	280.00

1685-90 (1939-43) ISSUE

#8-12 many varieties in size, printing and color. These notes were made by pasting together 3 sheets, the middle one having a 2-line security legend printed on it.

		GOOD	**FINE**	**XF**
8	**5 SRANG**	12.50	25.00	65.00
	ND (1942-46). Blue and red on yellow unpt. Lion at ctr. 2 lines of text. Back red and lt. blue; fountain between dragons. 121 x 73mm.			

		GOOD	**FINE**	**XF**
9	**10 SRANG**	5.00	12.00	40.00
	1687-94 (1941-48). Blue on pink unpt. 2 lions at ctr. 4 lines of text. Dragons and lions on back. 180 x 112mm.			

		GOOD	**FINE**	**XF**
10	**25 SRANG**			
	ND (1941-48). Orange on yellow unpt. 2 lions at ctr. 2 lines of text. Back orange and blue; people, bldgs., elephant and rider. 183 x 110mm.			
	a. Lg. text 83mm long (1941-47).	5.00	12.00	35.00
	b. Sm. text 75mm long (1948).	5.00	12.00	35.00

		GOOD	**FINE**	**XF**
11	**100 SRANG**			
	ND (1942-59). Orange on yellow unpt. 2 lions w/fruit bowl at ctr. 2 lines of text. Round seal at l. Back orange, green red and black; seated figure. 215 x 138mm.			
	a. Lg. text 93-94mm long.	1.50	4.00	15.00
	b. Sm. text 85-87mm long.	1.50	4.00	15.00
	c. Center sheet w/security legend inverted.			
	d. Inverted seal.	20.00	40.00	80.00
12	**100 TAM SRANG**			
	ND (1939-40). Like #11, but w/octagonal seal at l.	25.00	50.00	120.00

TIMOR

Timor, an island of Indonesia between the Savu and Timor Seas, has an area, including the former colony of Portuguese Timor, of 11,883 sq. mi. (30,775 sq. km.) and a population of 1.5 million. Western Timor is administered as part of Nusa Tenggara Timur (East Nusa Tenggara) province. Capital: Kupang. The eastern half of the island, the former Portuguese colony, forms a single province, Timor Timur (East Timor). Capital: Dili.

Timor exports sandalwood, coffee, tea, hides, rubber and copra.

Portuguese traders reached Timor about 1520, and moved to the north and east when the Dutch established themselves in Kupang, a sheltered bay at the southwestern tip, in 1613. Treaties effective in 1860 and 1914 established the boundaries between the two colonies. Japan occupied the entire island during World War II. The former Dutch colony in the western part of the island became part of Indonesia in 1950.

At the end of Nov., 1975, the Portuguese Province of Timor attained independence as the People's Democratic Republic of East Timur. In Dec., 1975 or early in 1976 the government of the People's Democratic Republic was seized by a guerrilla faction sympathetic to the Indonesian territorial claim to East Timur which ousted the constitutional government and replaced it with the Provisional Government of East Timur. On July 17, 1976, the Provisional Government enacted a law which dissolved the free republic and made East Timur the 24th province of Indonesia.

NOTE: For later issues see Indonesia listing.

MONETARY SYSTEM:
1 Pataca = 100 Avos to 1958
1 Escudo = 100 Centavos, 1958-1975

NOTE: In March 1912, before any notes were made especially for Timor, certain issues from Macao were declared legal tender there. The following list shows exact details:

1 PATACA 1905.	Serial #	83,751 to 84,000	87,251 to 90,750
		84,251 to 84,500	91,001 to 92,000
		84,571 to 85,750	93,001 to 93,500
		86,001 to 86,500	94,001 to 97,000
10 PATACAS 1907.	Serial #	87,001 to 93,000	93,001 to 95,500
25 PATACAS 1907.	Serial #	47,501 to 50,000	

PORTUGUESE INFLUENCE

BANCO NACIONAL ULTRAMARINO

1910 ISSUE
#1-4 arms on back. Sign. varieties. Printer: BWC.

		GOOD	FINE	XF
1	**1 PATACA** 1.1.1910. Purple and lt. green.	90.00	220.00	500.00
2	**5 PATACAS** 1.1.1910. Brown and yellow.	250.00	500.00	1000.
3	**10 PATACAS** 1.1.1910. Dk. blue and green.	300.00	600.00	1600.
4	**20 PATACAS** 1.1.1910. Green and gray.	400.00	850.00	2000.

1920 PROVISIONAL ISSUE

		GOOD	FINE	XF
5	**25 PATACAS** 2.1.1920. Ovpt: *PAGAVEL EM DILLY TIMOR* at bottom border on Macao #6.	—	Rare	—

1933 ND PROVISIONAL ISSUE

		GOOD	FINE	XF
6	**5 PATACAS** ND (1933 - old date 1.1.1924). Green on yellow unpt. Ovpt. *Pagaveis em TIMOR* at r. on Macao #9.	200.00	475.00	950.00

1940; 1943 ND PROVISIONAL WW II ISSUE

		GOOD	FINE	XF
7	**5 AVOS** ND (1940). Brown. Ovpt: *PAGAVEL EM TIMOR* on Macao #10.	50.00	150.00	425.00

		GOOD	FINE	XF
8	**10 AVOS** ND (1940). Green. Ovpt: *PAGAVEL EM TIMOR* on Macao #11.	150.00	350.00	850.00

		GOOD	FINE	XF
9	**50 AVOS** ND (1943). Purple. Ovpt: *PAGAVEL EM TIMOR* on Macao #17.	100.00	300.00	700.00

1945 ND PROVISIONAL ISSUE
#10-11B Ovpt: *PAGAVEL EM TIMOR* on older Macao notes.

			Good	Fine	XF
10	**5 PATACAS** ND (1945 - old date 1.1.1924). Green on yellow unpt. Ovpt. on Macao #9.		300.00	700.00	—

			Good	Fine	XF
11	**25 PATACAS** ND (1945 - old date 1.1.1907). Black on rose unpt. Ovpt. on Macao #6.		—	Rare	—
11A	**100 PATACAS** ND (1945 - old date 1.1.1906). Green on yellow unpt. Ovpt. on Macao #4.		—	Rare	—
11B	**100 PATACAS** ND (1945 - old date 22.7.1919). Brown on m/c unpt. Ovpt. on Macao #8.		—	Rare	—

1940 ISSUE
#12-14 printer: BWC.

		VG	VF	UNC
12	**5 AVOS** 19.7.1940. Red on m/c unpt. Steamship seal at upper l.	10.00	25.00	95.00

		VG	VF	UNC
13	**10 AVOS** 19.7.1940. Green on m/c unpt. Like #12.	10.00	30.00	125.00
14	**50 AVOS** 19.7.1940. Purple. Steamship seal at ctr.	15.00	60.00	240.00

1945 FIRST ISSUE

		VG	VF	UNC
15	**1 PATACA** 8.3.1945. Black on pink unpt. Steamship seal at l. Back brown; arms at ctr. Printer: Litografia Nacional.	30.00	70.00	240.00

1945 SECOND ISSUE
#16-20 native huts at l., arms at r. Printer: W&S.

		VG	VF	UNC
16	**1 PATACA** 16.11.1945. Green.	12.50	30.00	85.00

		VG	VF	UNC
17	**5 PATACAS** 16.11.1945. Brown.	15.00	35.00	100.00
18	**10 PATACAS** 16.11.1945. Red.	20.00	60.00	190.00
19	**20 PATACAS** 16.11.1945. Blue.	25.00	85.00	275.00
20	**25 PATACAS** 16.11.1945. Lilac.	30.00	110.00	450.00

1948 ISSUE

		VG	VF	UNC
21	**20 AVOS**	10.00	85.00	—

17.7.1948. Olive-brown on m/c unpt. Arms at upper ctr. Back olive and red-brown; steamship seal at ctr. Printer: BWC.

1959 ISSUE

#22-25 portr. J. Celestino da Silva at. r. Bank seal and crowned arms on back. Printer: BWC.

		VG	VF	UNC
22	**30 ESCUDOS**			
	2.1.1959. Blue on m/c unpt.			
	a. Issued note.	5.00	20.00	125.00
	s. Specimen.	—	—	100.00
23	**60 ESCUDOS**			
	2.1.1959. Red on m/c unpt.			
	a. Issued note.	5.00	25.00	170.00
	s. Specimen.	—	—	135.00
24	**100 ESCUDOS**			
	2.1.1959. Brown on m/c unpt.			
	a. Issued note.	7.50	37.50	225.00
	s. Specimen.	—	—	175.00
25	**500 ESCUDOS**			
	2.1.1959. Dk. brown and black on m/c unpt.			
	a. Issued note.	40.00	170.00	475.00
	s. Specimen.	—	—	375.00

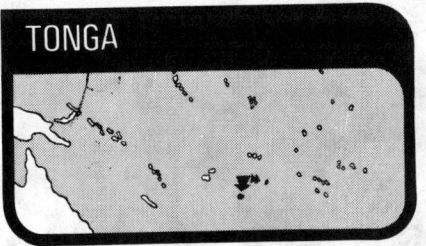

TONGA

The Kingdom of Tonga (or Friendly Islands), a member of the British Commonwealth, is an archipelago situated in the southern Pacific Ocean south of Western Samoa and east of Fiji comprising 150 islands. Tonga has an area of 270 sq. mi. (748 sq. km.) and a population of 103,000. Capital: Nuku'alofa. Primarily agricultural, the kingdom exports bananas and copra.

Dutch navigators Willem Schouten and Jacob Lemaire were the first Europeans to visit Tonga in 1616. They were followed by the noted Dutch explorer Abel Tasman who visited the Tongatapu group in 1643. No further European contact was made until 1773 when British navigator Capt. James Cook arrived and, impressed by the peaceful deportment of the natives, named the islands the Friendly Islands. Within a few years of Cook's visit, Tonga was embroiled in a civil war that lasted until the great chief Taufa'ahau, who reigned as George Tubou I (1845-93), was converted to Christianity and brought unity and peace to the islands. Tonga became a self-governing protectorate of Great Britain in 1900 and a fully independent state on June 4, 1970. The monarchy is a member of the Commonwealth of Nations. The monarch is Chief of State and Head of Government.

RULERS:
Queen Salote, 1918-1965
King Taufa'ahau, 1965-

MONETARY SYSTEM:
1 Shilling = 12 Pence
1 Pound = 20 Shillings to 1967
1 Pa'anga = 100 Seniti, 1967-

KINGDOM

GOVERNMENT OF TONGA

1921-33 TREASURY NOTE ISSUE

#1-4 palms at l. and r., arms at ctr., *STERLING* at r. Various date and sign. varieties. Printer: TDLR.

1	**4 SHILLINGS**		
	26.6.1933.	—	Rare	—
2	**10 SHILLINGS**		
	28.6.1933.	—	Rare	—
3	**1 POUND**		
	28.6.1933.	—	Rare	—
4	**5 POUNDS**		
	1.1.1921.	—	Rare	—

1936-39 ISSUE

#5-8 palms at l. and r., arms at ctr., ovpt. of several lines or solid block over *STERLING* at r. Various date and sign. varieties. Printer: TDLR.

		GOOD	FINE	XF
5	**4 SHILLINGS**			
	16.12.1936-1.12.1941. Brown. *FOUR SHILLINGS* at l.	40.00	125.00	350.00
6	**10 SHILLINGS**			
	21.4.1937; 4.5.1937; 24.1.1938; 19.5.1939. Green. *TEN* at l.	65.00	200.00	500.00

		GOOD	FINE	XF
7	**1 POUND**	125.00	350.00	850.00
	10.12.1936; 22.1.1937; 21.4.1937; 4.5.1937; 19.5.1939. Red. *ONE POUND* at l.			
8	**5 POUNDS**	—	Rare	
	19.5.1939. Dk. blue. *FIVE POUNDS* at l.			

1940-42 ISSUE
#9-12 w/denomination spelled out on both sides of arms at ctr. Printer: TDLR.

9	**4 SHILLINGS**	GOOD	FINE	XF
	1941-66. Brown on m/c unpt. *FOUR SHILLINGS* at l. and r.			
	a. 1.12.1941-22.10.1946. 3 sign.	20.00	75.00	225.00
	b. 7.2.1949; 15.2.1951; 20.7.1951; 6.9.1954.	15.00	60.00	150.00
	c. 19.9.1955-30.11.1959.	5.00	25.00	65.00
	d. 24.10.1960-27.9.1966.	3.00	7.50	25.00
	e. 3.11.1966. 2 sign.	1.50	4.00	16.50
10	**10 SHILLINGS**			
	1941-66. Green on m/c unpt. *TEN SHILLINGS* at l. and r.			
	a. 19.5.1939; 17.10.1941-28.11.1944. 3 sign.	30.00	100.00	325.00
	b. 6.6.1950-1955.	25.00	70.00	150.00
	c. 2.5.1956; 22.7.1957; 10.12.1958.	6.00	15.00	70.00
	d. 24.10.1960; 28.11.1962; 29.7.1964; 22.6.1965.	3.00	8.50	30.00
	e. 3.11.1966. 2 sign.	2.00	5.00	20.00

11	**1 POUND**	GOOD	FINE	XF
	1940-66. Red on m/c unpt. *ONE POUND* at l. and r.			
	a. 3.5.1940-7.11.1944. 3 sign.	35.00	110.00	325.00
	b. 15.6.1951; 11.9.1951; 19.9.1955.	30.00	85.00	175.00
	c. 2.5.1956; 10.12.1958; 30.11.1959; 12.12.1961.	10.00	22.50	50.00
	d. 28.11.1962; 30.10.1964; 2.11.1965; 3.11.1966.	5.00	12.00	35.00
	e. 2.12.1966. 2 sign.	2.00	6.00	25.00

12	**5 POUNDS**	GOOD	FINE	XF
	1942-66. Dk. blue on m/c unpt. *FIVE POUNDS* at l. and r.			
	a. 11.3.1942-1945. 3 sign.	500.00	750.00	1000.
	b. 15.6.1951; 5.7.1955; 11.9.1956; 26.6.1958.	200.00	385.00	700.00
	c. 30.11.1959; 2.11.1965.	100.00	250.00	500.00
	d. 2.12.1966. 2 sign.	10.00	25.00	45.00

The Transdniester Moldavian Republic was formed in 1990, even before the separation of Moldavia from Russia. It has an area of 11,544 sq. mi. (29,900 sq. km). and a population of 742,000. Capital: Tiraspol. Once the Moldavian SSR declared independence in August 1991, the natural independence route for Transdniestria was pushed to a head when Russian occupation forces quelled demonstrations by force in Bendery and Doubossary.

Transdniestria has a president, parliament, army and police forces, but as yet it is lacking international recognition.

The area was conquered from the Turks in the last 18th Century, and in 1792 the capital city of Tiraspol was founded. After 1812, the area called Bessarabia (present Moldova and part of the Ukraine) became part of the Russian Empire. During the Russian Revolution, in 1918, the area was taken by Romanian troops, and in 1924 the Moldavian Autonomous SSR was formed. On 22 June 1941, Romania declared war on the U.S.S.R. and Romanian troops fought alongside the Germans up to Stalingrad. A Romanian occupation area between the Dniester and Bug Rivers called *Transdniestria* was established in October 1941, and was used mainly as a dumping ground for Jews deported by Romania. Its center was the port of Odessa. A special issue of notes for use in Transdniestria was made by the Romanian government. In 1944 the Russians recaptured Transdniestria, advancing into Romania itself and occupying Bucharest in August of that year.

See also Romania #M10-16.

ROMANIAN OCCUPATION (OF U.S.S.R.) - WW II

INSTITUTUL DE FINANTARE EXTERNA (INFINEX)

1941 ND BON DE CREDIT ISSUE
NOTE: This issue bears unusual denominations because of the exchange rate set by Germany, as follows:

6 Lei = 10 Reichspfennig or 1 Ruble/Karbowanez (Ukrainian German Issue).

1200 Lei = 20 Reichsmark or 200 Rubles/Karbowanez.

		GOOD	FINE	XF
M1 (M17)	**1 LEU** ND (1941-44). Gray.	100.00	300.00	600.00
M2 (M18)	**6 LEI** ND (1941-44). Gray-blue.	100.00	300.00	600.00

M3 (M19)	**24 LEI** ND (1941-44). Brown.	GOOD 100.00	FINE 300.00	XF 600.00

		GOOD	FINE	XF
M4 (M20)	**120 LEI** ND (1941-44). Blue. Sunflower at r.	125.00	375.00	750.00
M5 (M21)	**600 LEI** ND (1941-44). Gray on brown-violet unpt. Cross at ctr.	125.00	375.00	750.00
M6 (M22)	**1200 LEI** ND (1941-44). Gray on tan unpt. Grapes at ctr. Boat on river at ctr. on back.	225.00	675.00	1350.

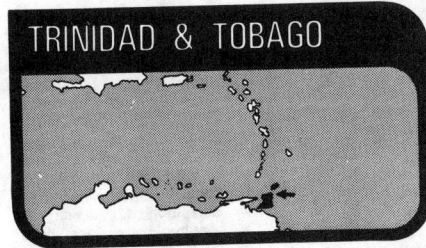

The Republic of Trinidad and Tobago, a member of the British Commonwealth, situated 7 miles (11 km.) off the coast of Venezuela, has an area of 1,981 sq. mi. (5,130 sq. km.) and a population of 1.25 million. Capital: Port-of-Spain. The Island of Trinidad contains the world's largest natural asphalt bog. Birds of Paradise live on little Tobago, the only place outside of their native New Guinea where they can be found in a wild state. Petroleum and petroleum products are the mainstay of the economy. Petroleum products, crude oil and sugar are exported.

Trinidad and Tobago were discovered by Columbus in 1498. Trinidad remained under Spanish rule from the time of its settlement in 1592 until its capture by the British in 1797. It was ceded to the British in 1802. Tobago was occupied at various times by the French, Dutch and English before being ceded to Britain in 1814. Trinidad and Tobago were merged into a single colony in 1888. The colony was part of the Federation of the West Indies until Aug. 31, 1962, when it became an independent member of the Commonwealth of Nations. A new constitution establishing a republican form of government was adopted on Aug. 1, 1976. Trinidad and Tobago is a member of the Commonwealth of Nations. The president is Chief of State. The prime minister is Head of Government.

Notes of the British Caribbean Territories circulated between 1950-1964.

* * * This section has been renumbered. * * *

RULERS:
British to 1976

MONETARY SYSTEM:
1 Dollar = 100 Cents
5 Dollars = 1 Pound 10 Pence

BRITISH INFLUENCE

GOVERNMENT OF TRINIDAD AND TOBAGO

1905 ISSUE
#1-2A mountain w/sailing ship on back. Various date and sign. varieties. Printer: TDLR.

		GOOD	FINE	XF
1	**1 DOLLAR**			
	1905-26. Blue. Landing of Columbus at l., arms at top ctr.			
	a. Black vignette at l. 1.4.1905.	200.00	400.00	1000.
	b. Blue vignette. 1.4.1905.	125.00	300.00	800.00
	c. 1.1.1924; 1.3.1926.	75.00	250.00	700.00

		GOOD	FINE	XF
2	**2 DOLLARS**			
	1.4.1905. Sailing ship in harbor at l., palm tree w/sailing ship in background at r., vignettes in circles.			
	a. Red.	250.00	650.00	1750.
	b. Green and red.	—	Rare	—

1929 ISSUE

		GOOD	FINE	XF
3 (1A)	**1 DOLLAR** 1.1.1929; 1.1.1932. Blue. Landing of Columbus at l., tree at r.	75.00	250.00	600.00

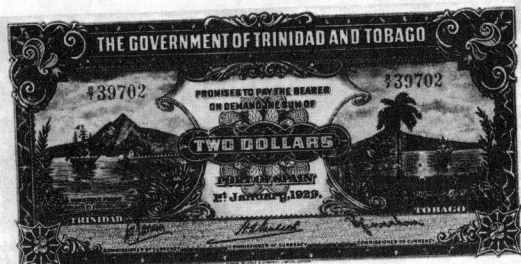

		GOOD	FINE	XF
4 (2A)	**2 DOLLARS** 1.1.1929. Red. Sailing ship in harbor at l., palm tree w/sailing ship in background at r. 178 x 89mm.	150.00	325.00	850.00

1934; 1935 ISSUE
#3-7 like #2A but reduced size. Various date and sign. varieties. Printer: TDLR.

		GOOD	FINE	XF
5 (3)	**1 DOLLAR** 1935-49. Dk. blue on m/c unpt. 150 x 82mm.			
	a. 1.9.1935.	10.00	25.00	100.00
	b. 2.1.1939.	1.00	5.00	35.00
	c. 1.5.1942; 1.1.1943.	1.00	5.00	35.00
	d. 1.7.1948.	1.50	6.00	50.00
	e. 1.7.1949.	1.50	6.00	65.00

		GOOD	FINE	XF
6 (4)	**2 DOLLARS** 1934-39. Bright red on blue and m/c unpt. 150 x 82mm.			
	a. 1.5.1934; 1.9.1935.	25.00	75.00	350.00
	b. 2.1.1939.	7.50	35.00	185.00

		GOOD	FINE	XF
7 (5)	**5 DOLLARS** 1935-42. Purple on m/c unpt.			
	a. 1.9.1935.	50.00	175.00	475.00
	b. 2.1.1939; 1.5.1942.	15.00	65.00	225.00

1939-42 ISSUE

		GOOD	FINE	XF
8 (4A)	**2 DOLLARS** 1.5.1942; 1.1.1943; 1.7.1949. Dk. red on green and m/c. unpt. Like #4.	7.50	40.00	225.00
9 (6)	**10 DOLLARS** 1939; 1942. Red-brown on m/c unpt.			
	a. 2.1.1939.	100.00	350.00	—
	b. 1.5.1942.	75.00	275.00	650.00
10 (6A)	**20 DOLLARS** 1.5.1942; 1.1.1943. Green on m/c unpt.	450.00	1000.	—

1943 ISSUE

		GOOD	FINE	XF
11 (7)	**20 DOLLARS** 1.1.1943. Purple on m/c unpt.	500.00	1250.	—

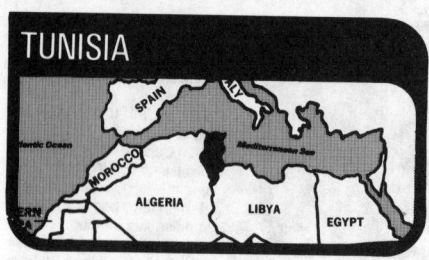

TUNISIA

The Republic of Tunisia, located on the northern coast of Africa between Algeria and Libya, has an area of 63,170 sq. mi. (163,610 sq. km.) and a population of *7.9 million. Capital: Tunis. Agriculture is the backbone of the economy. Crude oil, phosphates, olive oil, and wine are exported. Tunisia, settled by the Phoenicians in the 12th century BC, was the center of the seafaring Carthaginian empire. After the total destruction of Carthage, Tunisia became part of Rome's African province. It remained a part of of the Roman Empire (except for the 439-533 interval Vandal conquest) until taken by the Arabs, 648, who administered it until the Turkish invasion of 1570. Under Turkish control, the public revenue was heavily dependent upon the piracy of Mediterranean shipping, an endeavor that wasn't abandoned until 1819 when a coalition of powers threatened appropriate reprisal. Deprived of its major source of income, Tunisia underwent a financial regression that ended in bankruptcy, enabling France to establish a protectorate over the country in 1881. National agitation and guerrilla fighting forced France to grant Tunisia internal autonomy in 1955 and to recognize Tunisian independence on March 20, 1956. Tunisia abolished the monarchy and established a republic on July 25, 1957.

* * * The first part of this section has been reordered and renumbered * * *

RULERS:
    French, 1881-1956

MONETARY SYSTEM:
    1 Franc = 100 Centimes to 1960
    1 Dinar = 1000 Millim, 1960-

OTTOMAN INFLUENCE

DAR EL-MAL

STATE BANK

1846 ISSUE

A2	**50 RIYALS** AH1263/1846. Ornate knotted border. W/o wmk. (Discounted at 4%).	—	Rare	—

FRENCH INFLUENCE

BANQUE DE L'ALGÉRIE

1903-1908 ISSUE
#1-5 black ovpt: *TUNISIE.*

		GOOD	FINE	XF
1	**5 FRANCS** 1903-14.5.1925. Blue. Mercury at l., peasant at r. Ovpt. on Algeria #2.	15.00	40.00	175.00

		GOOD	FINE	XF
2 (5)	**20 FRANCS** 1908-42. Blue. Mercury at l., Hercules at r. Ovpt. on Algeria #8.			
	a. 15.4.1908; 29.4.1908.	32.50	125.00	300.00
	b. 22.2.1939-28.9.1942.	12.00	45.00	135.00
3 (10)	**50 FRANCS** 2.3.1908. Blue. Cherubs at l. and r., woman at lower ctr. Ovpt. on Algeria #14.	65.00	150.00	350.00

1921-26 ISSUE

#8-11 black ovpt: *TUNISIE*.

			GOOD	FINE	XF
8 (2)	**5 FRANCS** 1925-41. Red-brown and violet. Girl wearing kerchief at r. 128 x 88mm. Ovpt. on Algeria #77.				
	a.	14.9.1925-28.2.1933.	2.50	7.50	40.00
	b.	2.3.1939-31.5.1941. Serial # varieties.	1.50	4.50	25.00
	c.	1941. W/o serial #.	—	—	—
9 (11)	**50 FRANCS** 18.1.1924-2.4.1937. Green. Mosque w/tower at r., city of Algiers at ctr. background. Ovpt. on Algeria #80.		10.00	42.50	90.00

			GOOD	FINE	XF
10 (15)	**100 FRANCS** 1921-39. Blue and violet. 2 boys at l., Arab w/camel at r. Ovpt. on Algeria #81.				
	a.	11.3.1921; 25.7.1921; 17.4.1928.	15.00	50.00	150.00
	b.	16.1.1933; 21.8.1933.	10.00	35.00	100.00
	c.	14.3.1936-1939.	7.50	25.00	75.00
11 (24)	**1000 FRANCS** 1926-39. Brown-violet. Woman w/sword and child at l., Algerian woman w/child at r. Ovpt. on Algeria #83.				
	a.	Ovpt. at l. 19.7.1926.	50.00	250.00	600.00
	b.	Ovpt. at r. 14.2.1938; 19.4.1938; 3.8.1939; 23.9.1939.	40.00	220.00	500.00

1938-39 ISSUE

#12-14 black ovpt: *TUNISIE*.

			GOOD	FINE	XF
12	**50 FRANCS** 1939-45. M/c. Veiled woman w/man wearing red fez at r. Ovpt. on Algeria #84.				
	a.	Wmk: Head. 3.1.1939-28.5.1942; 1.5.1945.	4.00	12.50	55.00
	b.	Wmk: Lettering. 6.7.1942; 27.8.1942; 1.3.1945.	2.00	10.00	35.00

			GOOD	FINE	XF
4 (14)	**100 FRANCS** 6.2.1908; 11.2.1908; 8.11.1911. Blue. Boy standing w/oar and hammer at l., boy standing w/shovel and sickle at r. Ovpt. on Algeria #74.		70.00	175.00	450.00

			GOOD	FINE	XF
5 (18)	**500 FRANCS** 1904; 1909; 1924. Blue. Fortuna at l., Mercury at r., 2 boys sitting at bottom. Ovpt. on Algeria #75.				
	a.	9.5.1904; 4.1.1909.	—	Rare	—
	b.	3.1.1924-16.4.1924	60.00	135.00	400.00

1914; 1918 ISSUE

#6 and 7 black ovpt: *TUNISIE*.

			GOOD	FINE	XF
6	**20 FRANCS** 1914-41. Purple on lt. blue unpt. Girl at r. 165 x 105mm. Ovpt. on Algeria #9.				
	a.	3.8.1914.	3.00	15.00	70.00
	b.	26.2.1929-2.12.1941.	2.00	7.50	35.00

			GOOD	FINE	XF
7 (23)	**1000 FRANCS** 1918-24. Blue. Woman sitting w/oar at l., blacksmith at r., 2 boys sitting w/lion at bottom. Ovpt. on Algeria #76.				
	a.	5.11.1918.	165.00	375.00	850.00
	b.	5.3.1923; 18.1.1924; 16.4.1924; 25.4.1924.	150.00	325.00	700.00

	17 (7)	**20 FRANCS** 9.1.1943-10.2.1944. Similar to #6, but 122 x 90mm. Sign titles: *L'INSPECTEUR GÉNÉRAL* and *CAISSIER PRINCIPAL*. Ovpt. on Algeria #94.	**GOOD** 1.50	**FINE** 5.00	**XF** 20.00
	18 (8)	**20 FRANCS** 2.2.1945; 3.4.1945; 7.5.1945. Purple. Like #17 but sign. titles: *CAISSIER PRINCIPAL* and *LE'SECRETAIRE GÉNÉRAL*.	2.00	7.00	25.00
	19 (20)	**500 FRANCS** 15.3.1943; 18.5.1943; 20.5.1943; 16.7.1943; 3.2.1944. Blue and green. 2 boys at l., Arab w/camel at r. Ovpt. on Algeria #93.	30.00	140.00	300.00

	13 (16)	**100 FRANCS** 1939-42. M/c. Algerian w/turban at l. Ovpt. on Algeria #85.	**GOOD**	**FINE**	**XF**
		a. Wmk: Head. 26.9.1939-5.1.1942.	2.50	8.50	47.50
		b. Wmk: Lettering. 27.4.1942; 6.6.1942; 26.9.1942; 2.11.1942.	3.00	12.50	55.00

	20 (25)	**1000 FRANCS** 1941-42. M/c. Horses at ctr., French farm family at r. French text on back. Ovpt. on Algeria #86.	**GOOD**	**FINE**	**XF**
		a. Wmk: Woman's head. 24.6.1941; 4.9.1941; 2.1.1942.	30.00	65.00	185.00
		b. Wmk: Lettering. 2.11.1942.	37.50	85.00	250.00
	21 (28)	**5000 FRANCS** 1942. Red-orange. Young Algerian woman at l., woman w/torch and shield at r. Ovpt. on Algeria #90.	65.00	225.00	500.00

	14 (19)	**500 FRANCS** 30.9.1938; 26.7.1939; 3.1.1942-13.1.1942. Blue-violet and m/c. Girl at l., woman w/torch and youth at r. Ovpt. on Algeria #82.	**GOOD** 30.00	**FINE** 85.00	**XF** 350.00

1946-49 ISSUE

1941-45 ISSUES

#15-28 black ovpt: *TUNISIE.*

	15 (3)	**5 FRANCS** 8.2.1944; 8.3.1944. Red-brown and violet. Similar to #8 but 97 x 59mm. Sign. titles: *L' Inspecteur Gal.* and *Caissier Pal.* Ovpt. on Algeria #92.	**GOOD** 1.00	**FINE** 3.50	**XF** 12.50
	16 (4)	**5 FRANCS** 2.10.1944. Red-brown and violet. Like #15 but sign. titles: *Le Secreteur Gal.* and *Caissier Pal.*	2.00	5.00	22.50

	22 (9)	**20 FRANCS** 4.6.1948; 7.6.1948. Green and brown. Ornamental design. Like Algeria #103 w/title: *BANQUE DE L'ALGÉRIE/ TUNISIE.*	**GOOD** 3.00	**FINE** 15.00	**XF** 40.00

	23 (13)	**50 FRANCS** 3.2.1949. Blue and rose. Ornamental design w/title: *BANQUE DE L'ALGÉRIE & DE LA TUNISIE.*	**GOOD** 12.00	**FINE** 50.00	**XF** 150.00

	24	**100 FRANCS**	**GOOD**	**FINE**	**XF**
(17)		5.11.1946-18.2.1948. Blue, yellow and brown. Hermes at r., Roman gate in background. Ancient mosiac w/boat and 3 people on back. Title: *BANQUE DE L'ALGÉRIE/ TUNISIE* at top. Wmk: Woman's head.	12.00	50.00	175.00
25		**500 FRANCS**			
(21)		30.1.1947; 16.5.1947. Green and yellow. Winged Victory w/Roman ruins in background. W/titles: *BANQUE DE L'ALGÉRIE/TUNISIE.*	15.00	75.00	200.00
26		**1000 FRANCS**			
		4.9.1946; 5.9.1946. M/c. Similar to #20 but w/title: *BANQUE DE L'ALGÉRIE / TUNISIE* on face. Arabic text on back.	35.00	140.00	275.00

	27	**5000 FRANCS**	**GOOD**	**FINE**	**XF**
(29)		1946. M/c. P. Apollo at l. Like Algeria #109 but w/*TUNISIE* in front of engraver's name at lower r. Arabic text on back different from #21.	40.00	125.00	325.00

1950 ISSUE

	28	**500 FRANCS**	**GOOD**	**FINE**	**XF**
(22)		31.1.-17.3.1950; 11.2.-30.7.1952; 1.12.1954. Green and yellow. Similar to #25 but w/title: *BANQUE DE L'ALGÉRIE ET DE LA TUNISIE.*	15.00	75.00	200.00

	29	**1000 FRANCS**	**GOOD**	**FINE**	**XF**
(27)		1950-57. Dk. brown and blue. Ruins of Roman temples at l. W/title: *BANQUE DE L'ALGÉRIE ET DE LA TUNISIE.* Neptune w/trident, horses and allegorical figures at ctr. on back. Wmk: Woman's head.			
		a. 17.2.1950-26.12.1950.	20.00	65.00	140.00
		b. 20.3.1957.	20.00	65.00	140.00

	30	**5000 FRANCS**	**GOOD**	**FINE**	**XF**
		9.1.1950-7.5.1952. Violet. Roman ruins at l. Roman Emperor Vespasian at r., w/title: *BANQUE DE L'ALGÉRIE ET DE LA TUNISIE.*	25.00	95.00	300.00

GERMAN OCCUPATION - WW II

BANQUE DE L'ALGÉRIE

1942 PROVISIONAL ISSUE

Ovpt: *BANQUE DE L'ALGÉRIE* and new denomination on unissued 100 Francs note of the Banque de France (old dates May to August 1892). Issued during the German occupation between Dec. 1942-May 1943.

	31	**1000 FRANCS ON 100 FRANCS**	**GOOD**	**FINE**	**XF**
		ND. Violet, blue and brown. Woman seated at l. and r.	8.00	20.00	80.00

REGENCE DE TUNIS

DIRECTION GÉNÉRALE DES FINANCES - TREASURY

1918 FIRST ISSUE

NOTE: #32-53 exchangeable w/notes of the Banque de l'Algérie. Several different heading and frame styles used. All w/o black stamping: *Regence de Tunis*. Arms at ctr. on back.

		VG	VF	UNC
32	**50 CENTIMES**			
	16.2.1918. Green.			
	a. Monogram at ctr. on back. Engraver and printer on both sides.	6.00	15.00	50.00
	b. Monogram at ctr. on back. Engraver and printer on face only.	6.00	15.00	50.00
	c. W/o monogram on back. Engraver and printer on face only.	6.00	15.00	50.00
33	**1 FRANC**			
	16.2.1918. Red.			
	a. Wmk: *1896*.	7.00	20.00	60.00
	b. Wmk: *1910*.	7.00	20.00	60.00
34	**2 FRANCS**			
	16.2.1918. Brown.	8.00	27.50	70.00

1918 SECOND ISSUE

		VG	VF	UNC
35	**50 CENTIMES**			
	27.4.1918. Green.	4.00	17.50	60.00

		VG	VF	UNC
36	**1 FRANC**			
	27.4.1918. Red.			
	a. Wmk: *1912*.	4.00	17.50	60.00
	b. Wmk: *1913*.	4.00	17.50	60.00
	c. Wmk: *1916*.	4.00	17.50	60.00
	d. Wmk: *1917*.	4.00	17.50	60.00
	e. Wmk: *1918*.	4.00	17.50	60.00
37	**2 FRANCS**			
	27.4.1918. Brown.			
	a. Wmk: *1896*. Printer: PICARD.	8.00	30.00	70.00
	b. Wmk: *1910*. Printer: PICARD.	8.00	30.00	70.00
	c. Printer: YVORRA-BARLIER-CLAVE.	4.00	17.50	70.00
38	**2 FRANCS**			
	14.8.1918. Brown.	8.00	25.00	65.00

1918 THIRD ISSUE

		VG	VF	UNC
39	**50 CENTIMES**			
	30.9.1918. Green.	7.00	20.00	65.00
40	**1 FRANC**			
	30.9.1918. Red.	7.00	20.00	65.00
41	**2 FRANCS**			
	30.9.1918. Brown.	7.00	20.00	65.00

1918 FOURTH ISSUE

		VG	VF	UNC
42	**50 CENTIMES**			
	4.11.1918. Green.	7.00	20.00	65.00

		VG	VF	UNC
43	**1 FRANC**			
	4.11.1918. Red.	7.00	20.00	65.00
44	**2 FRANCS**			
	4.11.1918. Brown.	7.00	20.00	65.00

1919 ISSUE

		VG	VF	UNC
45	**50 CENTIMES**			
	17.3.1919. Green.			
	a. Printer: YVORRA-BARLIER-CLAVE.	4.00	16.00	50.00
	b. Printer: YVORRA-BARLIER.	4.00	16.00	50.00
46	**1 FRANC**			
	17.3.1919. Red.			
	a. Printer: YVORRA-BARLIER-CLAVE.	4.00	16.00	50.00
	b. Printer: YVORRA-BARLIER.	4.00	16.00	50.00

		VG	VF	UNC
47	**2 FRANCS**			
	17.3.1919. Brown.			
	a. Printer: YVORRA-BARLIER-CLAVE.	7.00	20.00	60.00
	b. Printer: YVORRA-BARLIER.	7.00	20.00	60.00

1920 ISSUE

		VG	VF	UNC
48	**50 CENTIMES**			
	3.3.1920. Green. 3 sign. varieties.	4.00	16.00	50.00

		VG	VF	UNC
49	**1 FRANC**			
	3.3.1920. Red. 3 sign. varieties.	4.00	16.00	50.00

		VG	VF	UNC
50	**2 FRANCS**			
	3.3.1920. Brown. 3 sign. varieties.	7.00	20.00	65.00

1921 ISSUE

		VG	VF	UNC
51	**50 CENTIMES**			
	25.1.1921. Green.	7.00	20.00	60.00

			VG	VF	UNC
52	**1 FRANC**		7.00	20.00	60.00
	25.1.1921. Red				
53	**2 FRANCS**		8.00	25.00	65.00
	25.1.1921. Brown.				

DIRECTION DES FINANCES - TREASURY

1943 ISSUE
NOTE: #54-56 veiled woman carrying a water jug at l., mountain at ctr., palm tree at r. Archway on back.

			VG	VF	UNC
54	**50 CENTIMES**		1.50	4.00	15.00
	15.7.1943. Brown-violet.				
55	**1 FRANC**		2.00	5.00	15.00
	15.7.1943. Green and brown.				
56	**2 FRANCS**		2.00	6.00	20.00
	15.7.1943. Brown-violet and blue.				

REPUBLIC

BANQUE CENTRALE DE TUNISIE

1960 ISSUE

			VG	VF	UNC
60	**5 DINARS**		7.50	25.00	120.00
	1.11.1960. Brown. H. Bourguiba at r., bridge at l. Western numerals value *5* and serial *#*.				

TURKEY

The Republic of Turkey, a parliamentary democracy of the Near East located partially in Europe and partially in Asia between the Black and the Mediterranean seas, has an area of 301,382 sq. mi. (780,580 sq. km.) and a population of 59.9 million. Capital: Ankara. Turkey exports cotton, hazelnuts, and tobacco, and enjoys a virtual monopoly in meerschaum.

The Ottoman Turks, a tribe from Central Asia, first appeared in the early 13th century, and by the 17th century had established the Ottoman Empire which stretched from the Persian Gulf to the southern frontier of Poland, and from the Caspian Sea to the Algerian plateau. The defeat of the Turkish navy by the Holy League in 1571, and of the Turkish forces besieging Vienna in 1683, began the steady decline of the Ottoman Empire which, accelerated by the rise of nationalism, contracted its European border, and by the end of World War I deprived it of its Arab lands. The present Turkish boundaries were largely fixed by the Treaty of Lausanne in 1923. The sultanate and caliphate, the political and spiritual ruling institutions of the old empire, were separated and the sultanate abolished in 1922 by Mustafa Kemal Atatürk. On Oct. 29, 1923, Turkey formally became a republic and Atatürk was selected as the first president.

* * * This section has been renumbered * * *

RULERS:
Abdul Mejid, AH1255-1277/1839-1861AD
Abdul Aziz, AH1277-1293/1861-1876AD
Murad V, AH1293/1876AD
Abdul Hamid II, AH1293-1327/1876-1909AD
Muhammad V, AH1327-1336/1909-1918AD
Muhammad VI, AH1336-1341/1918-1923AD
Republic, AH1341-/1923-AD

MONETARY SYSTEM:
1 Kurush (Gurush, Piastre) = 40 Para
1 Lira (Livre, Pound) = 100 Piastres

FINANCE MINISTER SEAL VARIETIES, 1858-1878

SAFVETI
ND(AH1274)

AHMED MUHTAR
ND(AH1276)

TASCI TEVFIK
ND(AH1277)

GALIP
AH(1)293

YUSEF
AH1294

MEHMED KANI
AH1295

OTTOMAN EMPIRE

NOTE: Early notes circulated in Constantinople, Western Anatolia and Cyprus.

TREASURY

Embossed tughra w/flower at r. of Abdul Mejid

1840 FIRST "KAIME" ISSUE, SERIES 1
Handwritten 12 1/2% Interest Bearing Notes

		GOOD	FINE	XF
1 (A1)	**500 KURUSH** AH1256 (1840).	—	Rare	

1840 SECOND "KAIME" ISSUE, SERIES 2
#2-6 reduced size. Seal of Saib Pasha on back.

2 (A2)	**50 KURUSH** AH1256 (1840).	—	Rare	—
3 (A3)	**100 KURUSH** AH1256 (1840).	—	Rare	—
4 (A4)	**250 KURUSH** AH1256 (1840).	—	Rare	—

1840 THIRD "KAIME" ISSUE, SERIES 3

5 (A5)	**500 KURUSH** AH1256 (1840).	—	Rare	—
6 (A6)	**1000 KURUSH** AH1256 (1840).	—	Rare	—
7	**2000 KURUSH** AH1256 (1840).	—	Rare	—

1842 "KAIME" ISSUE
Printed 12 1/2% Interest Bearing Notes w/handwritten serial # and values w/seal of Safveti.

NOTE: The year dates indicated are determined by the term of office of the Finance Minister's seal.

8	**50 KURUSH** AH1257 (1841). Black. Yellow paper. 104 x 160mm.	—	Rare	—
9 (A7)	**100 KURUSH** AH1257 (1841). Black. Blue paper. 105 x 165mm.	—	Rare	—

1843 FIRST "KAIME" ISSUE
10% Interest Bearing Notes

		GOOD	FINE	XF
10 (A8)	**250 KURUSH** AH1259 (1843). Black. Cream paper. 104 x160mm.	—	Rare	—

1843 SECOND "KAIME" ISSUE, SERIES A
6% Interest Bearing Notes w/handwritten serial # w/seal of Hüsnü.

		GOOD	FINE	XF
11	**50 KURUSH** AH1259 (1843). 98 x 152mm.	—	Rare	—
12	**100 KURUSH** AH1259 (1843). 132 x 195mm.	—	Rare	—

1843 THIRD "KAIME" ISSUE, SERIES B
6% Interest Bearing Notes w/seal of Safveti.

13 (A14)	**50 KURUSH** AH1259-62 (1843-46).	—	Rare	—
14 (A15)	**100 KURUSH** AH1259-62 (1843-46).	—	Rare	—

1848 "KAIME" ISSUE, SERIES C
6% Interest Bearing Notes w/seal of Safveti.

15	**500 KURUSH** AH1264-65 (1848-49). 185 x 110mm.	—	Rare	—
16	**1000 KURUSH** AH1264-65 (1848-49). Blue. Cream paper.	—	Rare	—

1852 "KAIME" ISSUE
6% Interest Bearing Notes w/seal of Halid.

17 (A16)	**250 KURUSH** AH(1)268 (1852). 178 x 117mm.	—	Rare	—
18	**500 KURUSH** AH1268 (1852). 185 x 125mm.	—	Rare	—

19	1000 KURUSH	GOOD	FINE	XF
(A18)	AH(1)268 (1852). Brown. Yellow paper. 185 x 125mm.	—	Rare	—
20	5000 KURUSH			
(A20)	AH(1)268 (1852).	—	Rare	—

1851-52 ND "KAIME" ISSUE

#21 and 22 w/octagonal control seal and seal of Nafiz, A. Muhtar or Safveti.

21	10 KURUSH	GOOD	FINE	XF
(A23)	ND (1852).	100.00	250.00	550.00

22	20 KURUSH	GOOD	FINE	XF
(A27)	ND (1852). 94 x 151mm.	100.00	250.00	550.00

1853; 1854 ND "KAIME" ISSUE

#23 and 24 w/seal of Safveti, A. Muhtar or Tevfik.

23	10 KURUSH	GOOD	FINE	XF
(A23)	ND (1853-54). Black on yellow and lt. green unpt. 68 x 105mm.	70.00	165.00	400.00

24	20 KURUSH	GOOD	FINE	XF
(A24)	ND (1854). Black on yellow and lt. green unpt. 89 x 130mm.	70.00	175.00	350.00

1855-57 ND "KAIME" ISSUE

#25 and 26 issued for the Ordu Kaimesi (Army Corps) w/seals of Savfeti, Sefik or A. Muhtar, and "Orduyu Humayun".

25	10 KURUSH	GOOD	FINE	XF
(A27)	ND (1854). Black on lt. green unpt.	—	Rare	—

26	20 KURUSH	GOOD	FINE	XF
(A26)	ND (1855-57). Black on lt. green unpt.	70.00	175.00	350.00

1858 ISSUE, SERIES E

Engraved plates exist for notes #27-31 w/the date AH1273, but no notes have been seen w/seal of Hasib (hexagonal shaped).

27	100 KURUSH	GOOD	FINE	XF
	AH1274 (1858). 170 x 102mm.	—	—	—
28	250 KURUSH			
	AH1274 (1858). 173 x 103mm.	—	—	—
29	500 KURUSH			
	AH1274 (1858). 179 x 107mm.	—	—	—

30	1000 KURUSH	GOOD	FINE	XF
	AH1274 (1858). 184 x 110mm on yellow paper, blue unpt.	—	—	—
31	5000 KURUSH			
	AH1274 (1858). 185 x 110mm.	—	—	—

1858-61 ISSUE

32	20 KURUSH	GOOD	FINE	XF
	AH1273 (1858-61). Brown. 176 x 126mm. 6 lines of text above AH1273 and seal of Savfeti on back.	—	Rare	—

1861 FIRST "KAIME" ISSUE

#33-35A w/6 lines of text above AH1277 and seal of Tevfik on back.

NOTE: Most notes of AH1277 are w/o handwritten serial # at l. and r. bottom in oval gaps on face.

33	10 KURUSH	GOOD	FINE	XF
(A28)	AH1277 (1861). Blue unpt. 122 x 173mm.	90.00	225.00	450.00
34	20 KURUSH			
(A29)	AH1277 (1861). Yellow unpt. 126 x 176mm.	90.00	225.00	450.00
35	50 KURUSH			
(A30)	AH1277 (1861). Red-brown on rose unpt. 133 x 184mm.	125.00	250.00	500.00

35A	**100 KURUSH**		GOOD	FINE	XF
	AH1277 (1861). Blue unpt.		—	—	—

1861 SECOND "KAIME" ISSUE
#36-38 like #33-35 but w/5 lines of text above AH1277 within wreath, and seal of Tevfik on back.

36	**20 KURUSH**		GOOD	FINE	XF
(A31)	AH1277. Black on gold unpt.		6.00	15.00	45.00

37	**50 KURUSH**		GOOD	FINE	XF
(A32)	AH1277. Red-brown.		8.00	20.00	50.00
38	**100 KURUSH**				
(A33)	AH1277. Yellow unpt. 133 x 185mm.		12.00	32.00	70.00

1861 THIRD "KAIME" ISSUE

#39 w/tughra of Abdul Aziz w/o flower at r. 6 lines of of text over AH date 1277 within wreath and w/seal of Tevfik on back.

39	**50 KURUSH**		GOOD	FINE	XF
(A36)	AH1277. Red-brown w/rose unpt.		75.00	175.00	450.00

1861 FOURTH "KAIME" ISSUE
#40 and 41 w/tughra of Abdul Aziz w/o flower at r.. 5 lines of new text above AH date 1277 on back.

40	**50 KURUSH**		GOOD	FINE	XF
(A38)	AH1277. Red-brown.		50.00	125.00	300.00

41	**100 KURUSH**		GOOD	FINE	XF
(A39)	AH1277. Gray unpt. 185 x 133mm.		20.00	60.00	150.00

BANQUE IMPERIALE OTTOMANE
1876 FIRST "KAIME" ISSUE

#42-45 w/tughra of Murad V.

NOTE: #42-45 usually occur on paper w/o wmk. Occasionally they are found on wmk. or handmade (laid) paper. Seal of Galip on back.

42	**10 KURUSH**		GOOD	FINE	XF
(A47)	AH1293 (1876). Lilac on lt. green unpt. W/round AH1293 handstamp. Oblong 1876 handstamp on back.		12.00	25.00	75.00
43	**20 KURUSH**				
(A48)	AH1293 (1876). Brown-lilac on yellow unpt. W/round AH1293 handstamp. Oblong 1876 handstamp on back.		12.00	25.00	75.00
44	**50 KURUSH**				
(A49)	AH1293 (1876). Brown-lilac on yellow unpt. Vertical format. W/round AH1293 handstamp. Oval 1876 handstamp on back.		16.00	32.50	100.00
45	**100 KURUSH**				
(A50)	AH1293 (1876). Brown-lilac on gray unpt. W/round AH1293 handstamp. Oblong 1876 hand-stamp on back.		12.00	25.00	75.00

1876 SECOND "KAIME" ISSUE

#46-51 w/tughra of Abdul Hamid II. Seal of Galip on back.

NOTE: Prior to WW I and until 1933, the Banque Imperiale Ottomane issued notes which were not legal tender in the real sense of the word, since they were traded like stocks and shares at a rate in excess of the nominal value of I, 5, 50 and 100 Pounds.

46	**1 KURUSH**		GOOD	FINE	XF
(1)	AH1293-95 (1876-78). Gray to gray-blue. Perforated edges.				
	a. W/round AH1293 handstamp, box 1876 handstamp on back.		15.00	30.00	80.00
	b. W/round AH1293 handstamp, box 1877 handstamp on back.		3.50	10.00	40.00
	c. W/15mm round AH1294 handstamp, straight line 1877 hands-tamp on back.		2.00	6.00	20.00
	d. W/18mm round AH1295 handstamp, straight line 1877 hands-tamp on back.		3.00	8.00	30.00

#47   #49

47	**5 KURUSH**		GOOD	FINE	XF
(2)	AH1293-95 (1876-78). Red-brown.				
	a. W/round AH1293 handstamp, box 1876 handstamp on back.		10.00	25.00	75.00
	b. W/round AH1293 handstamp, box 1877 handstamp on back. W/o wmk.		6.00	15.00	50.00
	c. W/round AH1294 handstamp, box 1877 handstamp on back.		6.00	15.00	50.00
	d. W/round AH1295 handstamp, box 1877 handstamp on back.		7.50	25.00	70.00

48 (3)	**10 KURUSH**	GOOD	FINE	XF
	AH1293-95 (1876-78). Lilac on lt. green.			
	a. W/round AH1293 handstamp, box 1876 or 1877 handstamp on back.	6.00	20.00	60.00
	b. W/round AH1294 handstamp, box 1877 handstamp on back.	6.00	15.00	50.00
	c. W/round AH1295 handstamp, box 1877 handstamp on back.	7.50	25.00	75.00
49 (4)	**20 KURUSH**			
	AH1293-95 (1876-78). Brown-lilac and yellow.			
	a. W/round AH1293 handstamp, box 1876 or 1877 handstamp on back.	7.50	25.00	75.00
	b. W/round AH1294 handstamp, box 1877 handstamp on back.	6.00	15.00	50.00
	c. W/round AH1295 handstamp, box 1877 handstamp on back.	7.50	25.00	75.00
50 (5)	**50 KURUSH**			
	AH1293-95 (1876-78). Brown-lilac on yellow unpt. Vertical format.	7.50	25.00	75.00
	a. W/round AH1293 handstamp, box 1876 or 1877 handstamp on back.			
	b. W/round AH1294 handstamp, box 1877 handstamp on back.	6.00	15.00	50.00
	c. W/round AH1295 handstamp, box 1877 handstamp on back.	7.50	25.00	75.00
51 (6)	**100 KURUSH**			
	AH1293-95 (1876-78). Brown-lilac on gray unpt. Vertical format.	6.00	20.00	60.00
	a. W/round AH1293 handstamp, oval 1877 handstamp on back.	6.00	15.00	50.00
	b. W/round AH1294 handstamp, oval 1877 handstamp on back.			
	c. W/round AH1295 handstamp, oval 1877 handstamp on back.	15.00	40.00	125.00

1877 "KAIME" ISSUE

52 (7)	**50 KURUSH**	GOOD	FINE	XF
	AH1294-95 (1877-78). Black on lt. blue unpt. Horizontal format.			
	a. W/round AH1294 handstamp, box 1877 handstamp on back.	25.00	50.00	160.00
	b. W/round AH1295 handstamp, box 1877 handstamp on bacl.	20.00	40.00	125.00

53 (8)	**100 KURUSH**	GOOD	FINE	XF
	AH1294-95 (1877-78). Black on orange-brown unpt. Horizontal format.			
	a. W/round AH1294 handstamp, box 1877 handstamp on back.	10.00	30.00	75.00
	b. W/round AH1295 handstamp, box 1877 handstamp on back.	12.00	35.00	85.00

LAW OF 15 DECEMBER AH1279 (1863)

54 (A40)	**200 PIASTRES**	GOOD	FINE	XF
	L.1279. Black, brown and green. Reimbursable in Constantinople.	350.00	750.00	—
55 (A41)	**200 PIASTRES**			
	L.1279. Reimbursable in Smyrna. 4 sign. and 2 seals.	200.00	550.00	—

56 (A42)	**200 PIASTRES**	GOOD	FINE	XF
	L.1279. Similar to #42 but w/text: *Remboursable seulement en 10 Medjidies d'Argent* (payable only in 10 Medjidies in silver) at upper l.	—	Rare	
57 (A43)	**2 MEDJIDIES D'OR**			
	L.1279. Green and brown on blue-gray unpt.			
	a. Issued note.	300.00	650.00	—
	b. Handstamped *ANNULÉ.*	—	—	—
	c. Pin hole cancelled *PAYE.*	—	—	—

58 (A44)	**5 MEDJIDIES D'OR**	GOOD	FINE	XF
	L.1279. Black and blue.			
	a. Issued note.	—	Rare	—
	b. Handstamped *ANNULÉ.*	—	—	—
	c. Pin hole cancelled *PAYE.*	—	—	—

LAW OF 20 DECEMBER AH1290 (1874)

59 (A45)	**1 LIVRE**	GOOD	FINE	XF
	L.1290 (1873). Denomination in 4 languages. Tan on brown and blue unpt. 2 sign. varieties.			
	a. Issued note.	—	Rare	—
	b. Handstamped *ANNULÉ.*	—	—	—

LAW OF DECEMBER AH1299 (1882)

60 (A46)	**5 LIVRES**	GOOD	FINE	XF
	L.1299 (1882). Black and blue on orange and green unpt. Tughra of Abdul Hamid at top ctr.			
	a. Issue note.	350.00	750.00	—
	s. Specimen.	—	Unc	300.00

1909 ND ISSUE

61	**100 LIVRES**	GOOD	FINE	XF
	ND (AH1327/1909). Green.	—	—	—

1908 ISSUE

#62 and 63 w/tughra of Abdul Hamid II. Printer: W&S.

62 (8A)	**5 LIVRES**	GOOD	FINE	XF
	AH1326 (1908). Blue. Back brown. Specimen.	—	Unc	150.00
63 (8B)	**100 LIVRES**			
	AH1326 (1908). Green. Specimen.	—	Unc	300.00

LAW OF 1 JANUARY AH1326 (1909)

#64-66 w/tughra of Muhammad V. Printer: W&S.

64 (8D)	**5 LIVRES**	GOOD	FINE	XF
	AH1326 (1909). Gray blue on lt. green, brown and lt. red unpt. Back brown. 2 sign. varieties.			
	a. Issued note.	50.00	200.00	400.00
	s. Specimen.	—	Unc	300.00
65 (8E)	**50 LIVRES**			
	AH1326 (1909). Brown on red, orange and yellow unpt.			
	a. Issued note.	—	Rare	—
	s. Specimen.	—	Unc	600.00
66 (8F)	**100 LIVRES**			
	AH1326 (1909). Green.			
	a. Issued note.	—	Rare	—
	s. Specimen.	—	Unc	450.00

LAW OF JULY AH1332 (1914)

67	**1 LIVRE**	GOOD	FINE	XF
	July AH1332 (1914). Blue. Specimen.	—	—	—

LAW OF AUGUST AH1332 (1914)

68 (8C)	1 LIVRE Aug. AH1332 (1914). Brown on lt. green and lt. red unpt. Back gray-green.	GOOD	FINE	XF
	a. Issued note.	10.00	25.00	85.00
	b. Remainder.	—	Unc	45.00

DETTE PUBLIQUE OTTOMANE

STATE NOTES OF THE MINISTRY OF FINANCE

Arabic sign. of Talat, Cahit and Cavid; English sign. of Janko, Taufing and Pritsch. Legend and numerals in Arabic, "Mali" year dates.

LAW OF 30 MARCH AH1331 (1915-16)

#69 and 70 printer: G&D.

69 (9)	1 LIVRE L.1331. Black on blue frame. Pink, green and brown unpt.	VG 5.00	VF 20.00	UNC 75.00
70 (10)	5 LIVRES L.1331. Red-brown and m/c., black text.	30.00	100.00	250.00

LAW OF 18 OCTOBER AH1331 (1915-16)

71 (11)	1/4 LIVRE L.1331. Dk. brown on green unpt., brown text.	VG 5.00	VF 20.00	UNC 75.00
72 (12)	1/2 LIVRE L.1331. Black on pink unpt., black text.	8.00	30.00	85.00
73 (13)	1 LIVRE L.1331. Black on brown and m/c unpt.	7.00	25.00	75.00

74 (14)	5 LIVRES L.1331. Black on blue frame. Pink, blue and brown unpt. Printer: G&D.	VG 25.00	VF 90.00	UNC 225.00

LAW OF 16 DECEMBER AH1331 (1915-16)

#75-78 new denomination ovpt. on halved notes of earlier issue.

75 (15)	1/2 LIVRE L.1331. Ovpt. on l. or r. half of #73.	VG —	VF Rare	UNC —
76 (16)	1/2 LIVRE L.1331. Ovpt. on l. or r. half of #73.	—	Rare	—
77 (17)	2 1/2 LIVRES L.1331. Ovpt. on l. or r. half of #70. (Not issued).	VG —	VF Rare	UNC —
78 (18)	2 1/2 LIVRES L.1331. Ovpt. on l. or r. half of #74. (Not issued).	—	Rare	—

LAW OF 22 DECEMBER AH1331 (1912)

79 (19)	5 PIASTRES L.1331. Black on brown unpt.	VG 2.00	VF 5.00	UNC 15.00
80 (20)	20 PIASTRES L.1331. Black on purple unpt.	2.50	7.50	25.00
81 (21)	1/4 LIVRE L.1331. Dk. brown on green unpt.	4.00	15.00	50.00

82 (22)	1/2 LIVRE L.1331. Black on pink unpt.	VG 5.00	VF 17.50	UNC 55.00
83 (23)	1 LIVRE L.1331. Black, brown frame on blue, green and pink unpt.	3.00	10.00	35.00
84 (24)	1 LIVRE L.1331. Black, brown frame on pale green and pink unpt.	3.00	10.00	35.00

LAW OF 23 MAY AH1332 (1916-17)

85 (25)	1 PIASTRE L.1332. Green w/black text. River w/palms and caravan.	VG 1.00	VF 2.00	UNC 6.00

86 (26)	2 1/2 PIASTRES L.1332. Pink w/black text. The Dardanelles.	VG 1.00	VF 2.00	UNC 6.00

LAW OF 6 AUGUST AH1332 (1916-17)

NOTE: #95 was deposit note made w/the Imperial Ottoman Bank to cover the issue of #85 and #86.

87 (32)	5 PIASTRES L.1332. Black text on olive unpt. White paper. Uniface. Wmk. varieties.	VG 1.00	VF 4.00	UNC 12.00

		VG	VF	UNC
88 (33)	**20 PIASTRES** L.1332. Black text on red unpt. Purple paper. Uniface.	2.00	6.00	20.00
89 (34)	**1/2 LIVRE** L.1332. Pink unpt., black text. Brownish paper.	5.00	12.50	37.50
90 (35)	**1 LIVRE** L.1332. Black. Green frame on blue-green and pink unpt.			
	a. Wmk: Hook pattern.	3.00	8.00	35.00
	b. Wmk: Sm. crucifereae.	4.00	12.00	45.00
91 (36)	**5 LIVRES** L.1332. Blue frame on m/c unpt.	30.00	75.00	210.00
92 (37)	**10 LIVRES** L.1332. Black text on lt. blue unpt. Brown frame.	40.00	125.00	350.00

		GOOD	FINE	UNC
93 (38)	**50 LIVRES** L.1332. Lt. blue and yellow-brown.			
	a. Wmk: Hook pattern.	150.00	500.00	—
	b. Wmk: Squared stars.	150.00	500.00	—
94 (41)	**500 LIVRES** L.1332.	—	Rare	
95 (42)	**50,000 LIVRES** L.1332. Blue on pink unpt.			
	a. Issued note.	—	Rare	
	s. Specimen.	—	—	10,000.

LAW OF 4 FEBRUARY AH1332 (1916-17)

		VG	VF	UNC
96 (43)	**5 PIASTRES** L.1332. Green unpt., black text. Bluish paper. Uniface.	1.00	4.00	12.50
97 (44)	**20 PIASTRES** L.1332. Brown unpt., black text. Brownish paper. Uniface.	2.00	6.00	17.50
98 (45)	**1/2 LIVRE** L.1332. Red unpt., black text. Violet paper. Uniface.	3.00	10.00	40.00
99 (46)	**1 LIVRE** L.1332. Black on brown frame. Violet, pink and green unpt.			
	a. Wmk: Fork pattern.	3.00	8.00	35.00
	b. Wmk: Sm. cruciferae.	3.00	8.00	35.00

		GOOD	FINE	XF
100 (47)	**2 1/2 LIVRES** L.1332. Orange and green.	25.00	80.00	250.00
101 (48)	**10 LIVRES** L.1332. Gray-brown on lt. gray unpt.	40.00	200.00	425.00
102 (49)	**25 LIVRES** L.1332. Maroon and gray on lt. blue unpt. Back brown.	75.00	300.00	600.00

		GOOD	FINE	XF
103 (50)	**100 LIVRES** L.1332. Brown on lt. blue unpt.	175.00	450.00	—

LAW OF 28 MARCH AH1333 (1917)

		GOOD	FINE	XF
104 (53)	**5 LIVRES** L.1333. Red-blue frame. Green and m/c unpt.	25.00	60.00	180.00
105 (54)	**25 LIVRES** L.1333. Red. Brown frame. Lt. blue unpt.	60.00	220.00	550.00
106 (55)	**100 LIVRES** L.1333. Brown and red on lt. blue unpt. Back brown; black text.	175.00	450.00	1100.
107 (56)	**1000 LIVRES** L.1333.	—	Rare	

LAW OF 28 MARCH AH1334 (1918) FIRST ISSUE
#107A and 107B w/tughra of Muhammad V.

		GOOD	FINE	XF
107A (A56A)	**100 LIVRES** L.1334.	—	Rare	
107B (A56B)	**500 LIVRES** L.1334.	—	Rare	

LAW OF 28 MARCH AH1334 (1918) SECOND ISSUE
#108-115 tughra of Muhammad VI.

		GOOD	FINE	XF
108 (56A)	**2 1/2 LIVRES** L.1334. Orange and blue-green, w/black text. Similar to #110.			
	a. Stamp: 2 eme emission.	40.00	125.00	300.00
	b. Stamp: 3 eme emission.	25.00	75.00	200.00
	c. Stamp: 5 eme emission.	12.00	50.00	125.00
109 (56B)	**5 LIVRES** L.1334. Brown frame. Similar to #110.			
	a. Stamp: 2 eme emission.	40.00	125.00	300.00
	b. Stamp: 6 eme emission.	20.00	40.00	125.00

		GOOD	FINE	XF
110 (56C)	**10 LIVRES** L.1334. Brown frame, black text. Lt. blue unpt.			
	a. 1st emission (no stamping)	40.00	125.00	350.00
	b. 2 eme emission stamping.	50.00	150.00	500.00
	c. 3 eme emission stamping.	60.00	150.00	450.00
	d. 4 eme emission stamping.	30.00	100.00	300.00
	e. 5 eme emission stamping.	30.00	100.00	300.00
	x. 2 eme emission. Thought to be a British military counterfeit paper w/o wmk. Small "10s" in denomination in l. border on back facing out instead of in. (illustrated).			

			Good	Fine	XF
111 (56D)	**25 Livres** *L.1334.*		60.00	220.00	550.00
112 (56E)	**50 Livres** *L.1334.* Lt. gray on blue unpt. Back yellow		150.00	375.00	800.00
113 (56F)	**100 Livres** *L.1334.* Dk. brown on yellow unpt. Back blue.		200.00	500.00	
114 (56G)	**500 Livres** *L.1334.* Blue on lt. blue.		—	Rare	—
115 (56H)	**1000 Livres** *L.1334.* Brown and dk. blue.		—	Rare	—

POSTAGE STAMP MONEY

1917 ISSUE

#116-118 non-issued adhesive postage stamps (#116 and #117) and adhesive revenue stamp (#118) affixed to colored cardboard.

#116 **#117** **#118**

			VG	VF	UNC
116 (57)	**5 PARA** ND (1917). Carmine on yellow or pink cardboard. Gun emplacement.		1.00	3.00	9.00
117 (58)	**10 PARA** ND (1917). Green on blue, green, yellow or pink cardboard. Hagia Sophia Mosque.		1.00	3.00	9.00
118 (59)	**10 PARA** ND (1917). Green and pink on blue, yellow or pink cardboard. Camel. Arabic ovpt: *10 Para.*		2.00	6.00	15.00

REPUBLIC

STATE NOTES OF THE MINISTRY OF FINANCE

1926 ISSUE

#119-125 Arabic legend and *Law #701 of 30 KANUNUEVVEL (AH)1341* (January 12, 1926) at ctr. Wmk: Ataturk. Printer: TDLR.

#122-125 Kemal Ataturk at r.

			VG	VF	UNC
119 (60)	**1 Livre** *L.1341* (1926). Green. Farmer w/2 oxen. Bldg. on back.				
	a. Issued note.		10.00	33.00	110.00
	s. Specimen.		—	—	100.00
120 (61)	**5 Livres** *L.1341* (1926). Blue. Bounding wolf at ctr., bldgs. at r. Bridge and city view on back.				
	a. Issued note.		30.00	125.00	550.00
	s. Specimen.		—	—	400.00

			VG	VF	UNC
121 (62)	**10 Livres** *L.1341* (1926). Purple. Bounding wolf at r. Rock mountain w/bridge on back.				
	a. Issued note.		—	65.00	200.00
	s. Specimen.		—	—	500.00

			VG	VF	UNC
122 (63)	**50 Livres** *L.1341* (1926). Brown. Town view w/mountains on back.				
	a. Issued note.		175.00	575.00	—
	s. Specimen.		—	—	1000.
123 (64)	**100 Livres** *L.1341* (1926). Green. Ankara new town on back.				
	a. Issued note.		—	Rare	—
	s. Specimen.		—	—	1250.

			VG	VF	UNC
124 (65)	**500 Livres** *L.1341* (1926). Red-brown on blue and gold unpt. Mosque at l. Town view on back.				
	a. Issued note.		—	Rare	—
	s. Specimen.		—	—	1500.

			VG	VF	UNC
125 (66)	**1000 Livres** *L.1341* (1926). Dk. blue. Railroad through mountain pass on back.				
	a. Issued note.		—	Rare	—
	s. Specimen.		—	—	1750.

TÜRKIYE CÜMHURIYET MERKEZ BANKASI
CENTRAL BANK OF TURKEY

CENTRAL BANK LAW OF 11 HAZIRAN 1930; SECOND ISSUE (1937-39)

#126-132 portr. Pres K. Ataturk at r. and as wmk. Printer: TDLR.

126 (67)	2 1/2 LIRA	VG	VF	UNC
	L.1930 (25.4.1939). Green. Monument of the Square of the Nation on back.	6.00	20.00	70.00

127 (68)	5 LIRA	VG	VF	UNC
	L.1930 (15.10.1937). Dk. blue. Back green, Monument of Secuity in Ankara.	12.00	40.00	130.00

128 (69)	10 LIRA	VG	VF	UNC
	L.1930 (16.5.1938). Red-brown. Citadel of Ankara on back.	20.00	70.00	175.00
129 (70)	50 LIRA			
	L.1930 (1.4.1938). Purple. Angora sheep and farmhouse on back.	25.00	80.00	275.00
130 (71)	100 LIRA			
	L.1930 (1.3.1938). Dk. brown. The Dardanelles on back.	67.50	225.00	—
131 (72)	500 LIRA			
	L.1930 (15.6.1939). Olive. Rumeli-Hissar Palace on back.	—	Rare	—
132 (73)	1000 LIRA			
	L.1930 (15.6.1939). Dk. blue. Monument of Security in Ankara on back.	—	Rare	—

CENTRAL BANK LAW OF 11 HAZIRAN 1930; INTERIM ISSUE (1942-44)

#133, 135-139 pres. I. Inonu at r. and as wmk.

#136-139 printer: TDLR.

133 (74)	50 KURUS	VG	VF	UNC
	L.1930. Dk. brown on lilac. Bank on back. Printer: BWC. (Not issued).	1.50	4.50	15.00

134 (75)	50 KURUS	VG	VF	UNC
	L.1930 (26.6.1944). brown and green. Portr. Pres. Inonu at ctr. Bank on back. No wmk. Printer: Reichsdruckerei.	10.00	33.00	110.00

135 (76)	1 LIRA	VG	VF	UNC
	L.1930 (25.4.1942). Lilac. The Bosporus Strait on back. Printer: BWC.	5.00	16.50	55.00
136 (76A)	50 LIRA			
	L.1930. Purple. Back like #129 (Not issued).	—	—	—

137 (77)	100 LIRA	VG	VF	UNC
	L.1930. Brown. The Dardanelles on back.	500.00	1250.	—
138 (78)	500 LIRA			
	L.1930 (18.11.1940). Dk. green. Rumeli-Hissar Palace on back.	250.00	850.00	—
139 (79)	1000 LIRA			
	L.1930 (18.11.1940). Blue. Monument of Security on back.	375.00	1150.	—

CENTRAL BANK LAW OF 11 HAZIRAN 1930; THIRD ISSUE (1942-47)

#141-146 w/o wmk.

#142, 143, 145 and 146 printer: ABNC.

140 (80)	2 1/2 LIRA	VG	VF	UNC
	L.1930 (27.3.1947). Dk. brown on lilac unpt. Portr. Pres. Inonu at r. and as wmk. Bank on back. Printer: BWC.	4.00	28.00	70.00

141 (81)	10 LIRA	VG	VF	UNC
	L.1930 (15.1.1942). Brown and red-brown. Portr. Pres. Inonu at l. 3 peasant women on back. Printer: Reichsdruckerei.	8.00	55.00	140.00

142 (82)	50 LIRA	VG	VF	UNC
	L.1930 (25.4.1942). Purple on m/c unpt. Portr. Pres. Inonu w/long tie at r. Goats on back.	50.00	150.00	375.00
143 (83)	50 LIRA			
	L.1930 (17.2.1947). Slate blue on m/c unpt. Like #142, Pres. Inonu w/white bowtie at r.	50.00	150.00	375.00

	153	2 1/2 LIRA	VG	VF	UNC
	(93)	L.1930 (15.2.1960). Lilac, Like #150 but back lt. green.	1.50	5.50	40.00

	144	100 LIRA	VG	VF	UNC
	(84)	L.1930 (15.8.1942). Dk. and lt. brown. Portr. Pres. Inonu at l. Girl w/grapes on back. Printer: Reichsdruckerei.			
		a. Imprint: REICHSDRUCKEREI at bottom margin on face.	16.50	50.00	150.00
		b. W/o imprint at bottom.	17.50	55.00	165.00
		c. Semi-finished note w/imprint.	16.50	50.00	150.00
	145	500 LIRA			
	(85)	L.1930 (24.4.1946). Dk. olive on m/c unpt. Pres. Inonu at ctr. Factory workers at machines on back.	125.00	375.00	775.00
	146	1000 LIRA			
	(86)	L.1930 (24.4.1946). Blue on m/c unpt. Pres. Inonu at r. Military buglers on back.	—	—	—

CENTRAL BANK LAW 11 HAZIRAN 1930; FOURTH ISSUE (1947-48)

#147-149 printer: ABNC.

	154	5 LIRA	VG	VF	UNC
	(94)	L.1930 (10.11.1952). Blue on m/c unpt. Back blue; 3 peasant women w/baskets of hazelnuts at ctr. Series A-D. Printer: BWC.	1.50	5.50	40.00
	155	5 LIRA			
	(94A)	L.1930 (8.6.1959). Like #154, but back green. Series E.	1.75	6.50	45.00
	156	10 LIRA			
	(96A)	L.1930. Green face and back. River and bridge on back. Series A-J. Printer: TDLR.	2.50	10.00	65.00

	147	10 LIRA	VG	VF	UNC
	(87)	L.1930 (7.2.1947). Red on m/c unpt. Portr. Pres. Inonu w/tie at r. Fountain of Ahmed III on back.	22.50	90.00	225.00
	148	10 LIRA			
	(88)	L.1930 (15.9.1948). Brown on m/c unpt. Pres. Inonu w/bow tie at r. Similar to #147.	20.00	80.00	200.00

	157	10 LIRA	VG	VF	UNC
	(97)	L.1930 (2.6.1952). Green. Like #156. Back brownish-red. Series K-U. Printe: TDLR.	1.50	6.00	42.50
	158	10 LIRA			
	(98)	L.1930 (24.3.1958). Green face. Like #159 but lt. blue and red on face. Brownish red back. Series V; Y. Printer: TDLR.	1.50	5.00	32.50
	159	10 LIRA			
	(98A)	L.1930. Green face and back. Similar to #157 but different guilloche on face. Series Z1-Z36. W/o imprint.	1.50	5.00	32.50
	160	10 LIRA			
	(99)	L.1930 (26.10.1953). Green. Like #159 but back red. Series Z37-.	2.50	10.00	65.00
	161	10 LIRA			
	(100)	L.1930 (25.4.1960). Green. Like #160 but back green. Different sign. Series A; B. W/o imprint.	1.50	5.00	32.50

	149	100 LIRA	VG	VF	UNC
	(89)	L.1930 (18.7.1947). Green on m/c unpt. Portr. Pres. Inonu at ctr. Rumeli-Hissar Fortress on back.	45.00	135.00	400.00

CENTRAL BANK LAW 11 HAZIRAN 1930; FIFTH ISSUE (1951-60)

#150-172 portr.Pres. K. Ataturk at r. similar to First Issue. Earlier issues printed by TDLR and BWC. Later issues by Devlet Banknot Matbasi, Ankara (w/o imprint). Sign. varieties.

All notes have Ataturk wmk. from #150 on.

#150-153 printer: TDLR.

#162-165, #167,168 and #170-172 printer: BWC.

	150	2 1/2 LIRA	VG	VF	UNC
	(90)	L.1930 (15.7.1952). Lilac on m/c unpt. Central bank on back.	2.00	9.00	65.00
	151	2 1/2 LIRA			
	(91)	L.1930 (3.1.1955). Lilac, Like #90 but back brown.	1.75	6.50	45.00
	152	2 1/2 LIRA			
	(92)	L.1930 (1.7.1957). Lilac. Like #90 but back red.	1.50	5.50	40.00

	162	50 LIRA	VG	VF	UNC
	(101)	L.1930 (1.12.1951). Brown on m/c unpt. Back brown; statue of soldier holding rifle at l. ctr.	3.00	11.50	45.00
	163	50 LIRA			
	(102)	L.1930 (2.2.1953). Brown on m/c unpt. Like #162 but back orange.	4.00	15.00	57.50

		VG	VF	UNC
164 (103)	**50 LIRA** L.1930 (15.10.1956). Brown on m/c unpt. Like #162 but back red.	4.00	15.00	57.50
165 (104)	**50 LIRA** L.1930 (1.10.1957). Brown on unpt. Like #162 but back blue-gray.	3.00	10.00	42.50
166 (105)	**50 LIRA** L.1930 (15.2.1960). Purple on m/c unpt. Similar to #162 but different style of numbers. Reddish guilloche at ctr. W/o imprint.	3.00	13.00	52.50
167 (107)	**100 LIRA** L.1930 (10.10.1952). Olive on m/c unpt. Park w/bridge in Ankara on back, Ankara fortress behind.	5.00	22.50	90.00

		VG	VF	UNC
168 (108)	**100 LIRA** L.1930 (2.7.1956). Like #167 but back lt. blue. SERI H, I and J.	5.00	22.50	90.00
169 (108A)	**100 LIRA** L.1930. Olive on m/c unpt. Similar to #167 but w/o imprint, and w/o SERI in front of number Different sign. Series K-P.	3.00	13.00	52.50
170 (109)	**500 LIRA** L.1930 (15.4.1953). Red-brown and m/c. Byzantine hippodrom w/mosque in Istanbul on back.	30.00	125.00	500.00
171 (110)	**500 LIRA** L.1930 (16.2.1959). Brown and m/c. Like #170, but w/o SERI in front of number. Different sign.	22.50	90.00	350.00

		VG	VF	UNC
172 (111)	**1000 LIRA** L.1930 (15.4.1953). Violet. Bosporus and fortress on back.	30.00	115.00	450.00

GALLIPOLI CAMPAIGN - WW I

BRITISH TREASURY

PROVISIONAL ISSUE

#M1-M2 issued for circulation in British occupied Gallipoli, Palestine and Iraq w/Arabic text ovpt. in 2 lines.

		GOOD	FINE	XF
M1 (M1)	**60 PIASTRES ON 10 SHILLINGS** ND (1915-16). Red. Ovpt. on Great Britain #348.	125.00	350.00	750.00
M2 (M2)	**120 PIASTRES ON 1 POUND** ND (1915-16). Black. Ovpt. on Great Britain #349.	850.00	2000.	—

The Colony of the Turks and Caicos Islands, a British colony situated in the West Indies at the eastern end of the Bahama Islands, has an area of 166 sq. mi. (430 sq. km.) and a population of *10,000. Capital: Cockburn Town, on Grand Turk. The principal industry of the colony is the production of salt, which is gathered by raking. Salt, crayfish and conch shells are exported.

The Turks and Caicos Islands were discovered by Juan Ponce de Leon in 1512, but were not settled until 1678 when Bermudians arrived to rake salt from the salt ponds. The British settlers were driven from the island by the Spanish in 1710, during the long War of the Spanish Succession. They returned and throughout the remaining years of the war repulsed repeated attacks by France and Spain. In 1799 the islands were granted representation in the Bahamian assembly, but in 1848, on petition of the inhabitants, they were made a separate colony under Jamaica. They were annexed by Jamaica in 1873 and remained a dependency until 1959 when they became a unit territory of the Federation of the West Indies. When the Federation was dissolved in 1962, the Turks and Caicos Islands became a separate Crown Colony with its economy based on the USA dollar currently in circulation.

RULERS:
British

MONETARY SYSTEM:
1 Shilling = 12 Pence
1 Pound = 20 Shillings to 1971
1 Dollar (USA) = 100 Cents

BRITISH INFLUENCE

GOVERNMENT OF THE TURKS AND CAICOS ISLANDS

1903-28 ISSUE

#1-4 arms at top ctr. Various date and sign. varieties. Printer: TDLR.

		GOOD	FINE	XF
1	**5 SHILLINGS** 10.1.1928. Black and blue on yellow unpt. Back blue; arms at ctr.	1250.	4000.	—

		GOOD	FINE	XF
2	**10 SHILLINGS** 1.6.1924. Dk. brown.			
	a. Issued note.	1750.	4500.	—
	s. Specimen.	—	—	—

		GOOD	FINE	XF
3	**1 POUND** Red on blue-green unpt.			
	a. 2.12.1903. Handdated and handsigned.	2500.	5750.	—
	b. 12.11.1918.	2000.	4750.	—
4	**1 POUND** 12.11.1928. Red and pink on yellow unpt. Uniface.	—	Rare	

UKRAINE

The Ukraine (formerly the Ukrainian Soviet Socialist Republic) is bordered by Russia to the east, Russia and Belarus to the north, Poland, Slovakia and Hungary to the west, Romania and Moldova to the south-west and in the south by the Black Sea and the Sea of Azov. It has an area of 233,088 sq. mi. (603,700 sq. km.) and a population of 51.9 million. Capital: Kyiv (Kiev). Ukraine was the site of the Chernobyl nuclear power station disaster in 1986. Coal, grain, vegetables and heavy industrial machinery are major exports.

The territory of Ukraine has been inhabited for over 30,000 years. As the result of its location, Ukraine has served as the gateway to Europe for millennia and its early history has been recorded by Arabic, Greek, Roman, as well as Ukrainian historians.

Ukraine, which was known as Rus' until the sixteenth century (and from which the name Russia was derived in the 17th century), became the major political and cultural center of Eastern Europe in the 9th century. The Rus' Kingdom, under a dynasty of Varangian origin, due to its position on the intersection of the north-south Scandinavia to Byzantium and the east-west Orient to Europe trade routes, became a focal point of world trade. At its apex Rus' stretched from the Baltic to the Black Sea and from the upper Volga River in the east, almost to the Vistula River in the west. It has family ties to many European dynasties. In 988 knyaz (king) Volodymyr adopted Christianity from Byzantium. With it came church books written in the Cyrillic alphabet, which originated in Bulgaria. The Mongol invasion in 1240 brought an end to the might of the Rus' Kingdom.

In the seventeenth century, after almost four hundred years of Mongol, Lithuanian, Polish, and Turkish domination, the Cossack State under Hetman Bohdan Khmelnytsky regained Ukrainian independence. The Hetman State lasted until the mid-eighteenth century and was followed by a period of foreign rule: Eastern Ukraine was controlled by Russia, which enforced russification through introduction of the Russian language and prohibiting the use of the Ukrainian language in schools, books and public life. Western Ukraine came under relatively benign Austro-Hungarian rule.

With the disintegration of the Russian and Austro-Hungarian Empires in 1917 and 1918, Eastern Ukraine declared its full independence on January 22, 1918 and Western Ukraine followed suit on November 1 of that year. On January 22, 1919 both parts united into one state that had to defend itself on three fronts: from the "Red" Bolsheviks and their puppet Ukrainian Soviet Republic formed in Kharkiv, from the "White" czarist Russian forces, and from Poland. Ukraine lost the war. In 1920 Eastern Ukraine was occupied by the Bolsheviks and in 1922 was incorporated into the Soviet Union. There followed a brief resurgence of Ukrainian language and culture until Stalin suppressed it in 1928. The artificial famine-genocide of 1932-33 killed 7-10 million Ukrainians, and Stalinist purges in the mid-1930s took a heavy toll. Western Ukraine was partitioned between Poland, Romania, Hungary and Czechoslovakia.

During the period of independence 1917-1920, Ukraine issued its own currency in Karbovanets denominations under the Central Rada of social-democrats (#1-11) and in Hryvnia denominations during the monarchy of Hetman Pavlo Skoropadsky (#12-19 and #29-34). During WW II German occupation forces issued Karbowanez currency.

On August 24, 1991 Ukraine once again declared its independence. On December 1, 1991 over 90% of Ukraine's electorate approved full independence from the Soviet Union. On December 5, 1991 the Ukrainian Parliament abrogated the 1922 treaty which incorporated Ukraine into the Soviet Union. Later, Leonid Kravchuk was elected president by a 65% majority.

During the changeover from the Ruble currency of the Soviet Union to the Karbovanets of Ukraine, as a transition measure and to restrict unlicensed export of scarce goods, coupon cards (202 x 82mm), similar to ration cards, were issued in various denominations (#80). They were valid for one month and were given to employees in amounts equal to their pay. Each card contained multiples of 1, 3, 5, and sometimes 10 Karbovanets valued coupons, to be cut apart. They were supposed to be used for purchases together with ruble notes. In January 1992 Ukraine began issuing individual coupons in Karbovanets denominations (printed in France and dated 1991), which are presently functioning as sole currency (#81-).

Ukraine is a charter member of the United Nations and has inherited the third largest nuclear arsenal in the world, which by recent agreement with the USA will be dismantled within the next decade. Ukrainians in the homeland and the diaspora make up 1% of the world's population.

RULERS:

Polish, 1569-1666
Polish and Russian, 1667-1671
Polish and Ottoman, 1672-1684
Polish, 1685-1792
Russian, 1793-1917

MONETARY SYSTEM:

1 Karbovanets (Karbovantsiv) КАРБОВАНЕЦЬ, КАРБОВАНЦІВ = 2 Hryven ГРИВЕНЬ
1917-1920 = 200 Shahiv ШАГІВ

AUTONOMOUS REPUBLIC

УКРАЇНСЬКА НАРОДНЯ РЕСПУБЛІКА

UKRAINIAN NATIONAL REPUBLIC

CENTRAL RADA BRANCH

1917 ISSUE

1	**100 KARBOVANTSIV**			
	1917. Brown, orange and yellow. Inscription on back in Polish, Russian and Yiddish.			
	a. Printing same way up on both sides.	—	Rare	—
	b. Back inverted.	20.00	60.00	150.00

ЗНАК ДЕРЖАВНОЇ СКАРБНИЦІ

STATE TREASURY NOTES

1918 (ND) ISSUE

		VG	VF	UNC
2	**25 KARBOVANTSIV**			
	ND (1918). Green. Man standing w/spade at l., woman w/sheafs at r. W/o serial # prefix letters (issued in Kiev).			
	a. W/text: КРЕДИТОВИМ.	6.00	15.00	40.00
	b. W/text: КРЕДИТОВИМ.	20.00	50.00	100.00

		VG	VF	UNC
3	**25 KARBOVANTSIV**			
	ND (1918). Green. Like #2 but serial # prefix letters: *AO* (issued in Odessa).	2.00	5.00	12.00
4	**50 KARBOVANTSIV**			
	ND (1918). Green. Type of #2 (issued in Kiev).			
	a. W/text: КРЕДИТОВИМ.	5.00	10.00	20.00
	b. W/text: КРЕДИТОВИМИ.	2.00	5.00	12.00
5	**50 KARBOVANTSIV**			
	ND (1918). Green. Like #4 but serial # prefix letters: *AKI* or *AKII* (issued in Kiev).			
	a. Issued note.	1.50	4.00	7.00
	b. Error, w/back only in red. (AKII).	10.00	20.00	35.00

6	**50 KARBOVANTSIV**	**VG**	**VF**	**UNC**
	ND (1918). Green. Like #4 but w/serial # prefix letters: *AO* (issued in Odessa).			
	a. Serial # to 209.	1.00	3.00	5.00
	b. Serial # from 210 (issued by Gen. Denikin and labeled as false by the Ukrainian Government).	1.00	3.00	5.00

POSTAGE STAMP CURRENCY

1918; 1919 EMERGENCY ISSUE

#7-11 postage stamp designs, Michel catalogue #1-5 or Scott #67-71, printed on ungummed cardboard w/trident arms over black text within single line or double line border.

	#7	#8	#9	Common back

		VG	**VF**	**UNC**
7	**10 SHAHIV**			
	ND (1918). Yellow-brown. Arms.	1.00	2.50	6.00
8	**20 SHAHIV**			
	ND (1918). Dk. brown. Peasant.	1.00	2.50	6.00
9	**30 SHAHIV**			
	ND (1918). Head of Ceres.			
	a. Ultramarine.	1.50	3.00	7.00
	b. Gray-violet.	2.00	4.00	10.00

	#10		#11	

		VG	**VF**	**UNC**
10	**40 SHAHIV**			
	ND (1918). Green. Trident arms.			
	a. Perforated.	1.00	2.50	6.00
	b. Imperforate.	17.50	30.00	50.00
11	**50 SHAHIV**			
	ND (1918). Red. Wreath around value *50*.			
	a. Perforated.	1.00	2.50	5.00
	b. Imperforate.	17.50	30.00	50.00
10A	**5 KARBOWANEZ**			
	ND (1919). Ovpt.: Soviet arms in wreath on back of #10.	—	—	—

3.6% БІЛЕТ ДЕРЖАВНОЇ СКАРБНИЦІ

BOND CERTIFICATES, 3.6%

1918 ISSUE

#12-15 bond certificates w/interest coupons.

12	**50 HRYVEN**	**GOOD**	**FINE**	**XF**
	1918. Green and brown.	3.00	8.00	15.00

13	**100 HRYVEN**	**GOOD**	**FINE**	**XF**
	1918. Brown on green and red.	2.00	6.00	14.00
14	**200 HRYVEN**			
	1918. Blue.	3.00	8.00	15.00

15	**1000 HRYVEN**	**GOOD**	**FINE**	**XF**
	1918. Brown on yellow-brown.	3.00	8.00	15.00

INTEREST COUPONS

1918 ISSUE

16	**90 SHAHIV**	**GOOD**	**FINE**	**XF**
	1918. Black on pale green unpt. Back red on pale green unpt.	.50	1.00	2.00
17	**1 HRYVEN 80 SHAHIV**			
	1918. Red-brown.	.50	1.00	2.00

18	**3 HRYVEN 60 SHAHIV**	**GOOD**	**FINE**	**XF**
	1918. Black on lt. blue and gray unpt. Back pale red on lt. blue unpt.	.50	1.00	2.00
19	**18 HRYVEN**			
	1918. Yellow-brown.	.50	1.00	2.00

ДЕРЛАВНИЙ КРЕДИТОВИЙ БІЛЕТ

STATE CREDIT NOTES

1918 ISSUE

20	**2 HRYVEN**	**VG**	**VF**	**UNC**
	1918. Green.			
	a. Yellowish background. Serial # prefix letter: *A*.	1.50	3.00	8.00
	b. Brown background. Serial # prefix letter: *B*.	2.00	5.00	12.00

21	**10 HRYVEN**	**VG**	**VF**	**UNC**
	1918. Red-brown.	1.00	2.50	6.50

22	**100 HRYVEN**	VG	VF	UNC
	1918. Blue-violet. Farmer's wife at l., worker at r.			
	a. Blue background. Serial # prefix letter: *A*.	4.00	10.00	20.00
	b. Gray-violet unpt. Serial # prefix letter: *B*. (Not issued).	—	150.00	300.00

23	**500 HRYVEN**	VG	VF	UNC
	1918. Green and orange. Ceres head at upper ctr.	4.00	10.00	20.00
24	**1000 HRYVEN**			
	1918. Blue on orange and yellow unpt.	4.00	12.00	25.00
25	**2000 HRYVEN**			
	1918. Red on blue unpt.	8.00	25.00	50.00

1920 ISSUE

#26-28 Austrian printing.

NOTE: It is reported that only 2 sets of these proofs exist.

26 (39)	**50 HRYVEN**	VG	VF	UNC
	1920. Black and blue. Allegorical figures at l. and r., arms at upper ctr. Portr. of Petro Loroshenko in cartouche at l., arms above. Proof.	—	Rare	—
27 (40)	**50 HRYVEN**			
	1920. Brown. Proof.	—	Rare	—
28 (41)	**1000 HRYVEN**			
	1920. Gray and orange. Proof.	—	Rare	—

5% КР. ОБЯЗАТ. ГОСУД. КАЗНАЧ.

RUSSIAN STATE DEBENTURE BONDS, 5%

1918 ISSUE

#29-34 exist w/different stamps on the State Bank branches. Validated Oct.-Dec. 1918.

29 (26)	**1000 RUBLES**	GOOD	FINE	XF
	ND (1918). Red-brown on gray.	3.00	8.00	15.00
30 (27)	**5000 RUBLES**			
	ND (1918).	4.00	10.00	18.00
31 (28)	**10,000 RUBLES**			
	ND (1918).	6.00	12.00	30.00
32 (29)	**25,000 RUBLES**			
	ND (1918).	8.00	15.00	40.00
33 (30)	**50,000 RUBLES**			
	ND (1918).	10.00	25.00	60.00
34 (31)	**500,000 RUBLES**			
	ND (1918).	—	—	—

ЗНАК ДЕРЖАВНОЇ СКАРБНИЦІ

STATE TREASURY NOTES

1918 ISSUE

35 (32)	**1000 KARBOVANTSIV**	VG	VF	UNC
	ND (1918). Deep brown and m/c on tan unpt. Black sign. Back brown; trident arms at top ctr. between 2 standing allegorical women supporting frame w/value.			
	a. Wmk: Wavy lines.	2.00	10.00	20.00
	b. Zigzag lines of varnish printed on paper.	3.00	12.00	25.00

SEMEN PETLYURA DIRECTORATE

1918-19 ISSUE

NOTE: #S293 was issued under the Ukrainian Socialist Soviet Republic and is not considered to be a truly independent issue. It is similar to #36 but is w/o serial #, only a block #.

36	**10 KARBOVANTSIV**	VG	VF	UNC
	ND (1919). Brown or red-brown on gray paper. Wmk: Spades. 3 serial # varieties. See also #S293 (Russia-Vol. I).	4.00	15.00	40.00
37	**25 KARBOVANTSIV**			
	1919. Violet-brown w/ and w/o serial #.	4.00	8.00	30.00
38 (34)	**100 KARBOVANTSIV**			
	1918. Brown and gray-green.			
	a. Wmk: Stars. 2 serial # varieties.	3.00	6.00	15.00
	b. Wmk: Spades. 2 serial # varieties.	5.00	10.00	30.00

39 (35)	**250 KARBOVANTSIV**	VG	VF	UNC
	1918. Brown and gray on olive unpt.			
	a. Lg. letters; serial # prefix: АА, АБ, АГ.	3.00	8.00	30.00
	b. Sm. letters; serial # prefix: АБ, АВ, АГ.	3.00	8.00	30.00

40 (33)	**1000 KARBOVANTSIV**	VG	VF	UNC
	ND (1918). Brown-violet and m/c on tan unpt. Brown-violet sign. Like #35. Back brown-violet.			
	a. Wmk: Wavy lines.	4.00	12.00	25.00
	b. Wmk: Stars.	3.00	10.00	20.00

РОЗМІННИЙ ЗНАК ДЕРЖАВНОЇ СКАРБНИЦІ

STATE UNCERTAINS

1920 ISSUE

41	5 HRYVEN	VG	VF	UNC
(38)	ND (1920). Gray. Trident at l.			
	a. Issued note.	3.00	8.00	20.00
	x. Error: ГИБЕИЬ. (w/o Р).	35.00	100.00	175.00

GERMAN OCCUPATION - WW II

ЗМИССИОННЫЙ БАНК

STATE BANK

KIEV BRANCH

1941 ISSUE

#42-48 were printed by the German government for use in occupied areas during WW II, but the Germans rejected the idea of Russian language on occupation notes and instead issued the Ukrainian occupation notes of the Zentralnotenbank type. Proofs perforated: *DRUCKPROBE.*

NOTE: Technically #42-48 were not intended as occupation notes for Ukraine. Instead, they were for possible issue in an area the Germans call "Ostland" which was to be administered from Kiev.

42	1 RUBLE	VG	VF	UNC
	1941. Brown. Lt. brown and green unpt. Proof.	—	—	800.00
43	3 RUBLES			
	1941. Violet and green unpt. Proof.	—	—	800.00
44	5 RUBLES			
	1941. Violet and green unpt. Proof.	—	—	800.00
45	1 CHERVONETS			
	1941. Blue, lt. blue and green unpt. Proof.	—	—	800.00

46	3 CHERVONTSA	VG	VF	UNC
	1941. Green and violet unpt. Proof.	—	—	800.00
47	5 CHERVONTSIV			
	1941. Brown. Green and violet unpt. Proof.			
	a. Regular serial #.	—	—	3000.
	p. Proof.	—	—	800.00
48	10 CHERVONTSIV			
	1941. Brown. Green and brown unpt. Proof.	—	—	800.00

ZENTRALNOTENBANK UKRAINE

UKRAINIAN CENTRAL BANK

1942 ISSUE

49	1 KARBOWANEZ	VG	VF	UNC
	10.3.1942. Olive.	1.50	5.00	15.00

50	2 KARBOWANEZ	VG	VF	UNC
	10.3.1942. Young boy wearing fur cap at r. (Not issued).	—	175.00	500.00

51	5 KARBOWANEZ	VG	VF	UNC
	10.3.1942. Brown-violet. Portr. young girl at r.	1.00	4.00	15.00
52	10 KARBOWANEZ			
	10.3.1942. Red-brown. Farmer's wife at r.	1.00	4.50	20.00
53	20 KARBOWANEZ			
	10.3.1942. Gray-brown. Industrial worker at r.	1.50	6.00	32.50
54	50 KARBOWANEZ			
	10.3.1942. Green. Miner at r.	3.00	12.50	55.00

55	100 KARBOWANEZ	VG	VF	UNC
	10.3.1942. Blue. Portr. seaman at r.	7.00	20.00	85.00
56	200 KARBOWANEZ			
	10.3.1942. Olive. Peasant woman at r.	10.00	35.00	110.00

57	500 KARBOWANEZ	VG	VF	UNC
	10.3.1942. Violet. Portr. chemist at r.	20.00	60.00	140.00

The United States of America as politically organized under the Articles of Confederation consisted of the 13 former British-American colonies - New Hampshire, Massachusetts, Rhode Island, Connecticut, New York, New Jersey, Pennsylvania, Delaware, Maryland, Virginia, North Carolina, South Carolina and Georgia - clustered along the eastern seaboard of North America between the forests of Maine (then part of Massachusetts) and the marshes of Georgia. The United States had no national capital; Philadelphia, where the Continental Congress met, was the "seat of the government." The population during this formative phase of America's history (1777-1789) was about 3 million, most of whom lived on self-sufficient family farms. Fishing, lumbering and the production of grains for export were major economic endeavors. Rapid strides were also being made in industry and manufacturing, as well as mining one-seventh of the world's production of raw iron.

On the basis of the voyage of John Cabot to the North American mainland in 1497, England claimed the entire continent. France and Spain also claimed extensive territory in North America. At the end of the French and Indian War (1763), England acquired all of the territory east of the Mississippi River, including East and West Florida. During the colonial and Confederation period individual states each retained the right to issue money and did so. Independence from Great Britain was declared on July 4, 1776 and ratified in 1783 at the end of the American Revolution. The Constitution which organized and governs the present United States was ratified on Nov. 21, 1788 and became effective in 1789, removing from the states the right to issue money.

1775 Declaration of Independence; 1789 George Washington first president; 1861-1865 Civil War and defeat of the Confederate States by the Union. Originally 13 states, in 1959 Alaska joined the Union as 49th and Hawaii as 50th state.

MONETARY SYSTEM:
1 Dollar = 100 Cents

REPUBLIC

TREASURY

June 1812 - March 1861 The first paper money issued by the United States Government was not, as is often thought, the Interest Bearing Treasury Notes of 1861, the so-called "7-30's." Issued as a result of the Civil War, these 1861 notes were actually the last in a long series of Treasury notes that commenced in 1812 as a consequence of the financial condition of the nation during the War of 1812.

Paper Money Issued by the U.S. Government prior to the Civil War by Bruce W. Smith, unpublished manuscript, 1977.

Photos and notes from Larry Stevens, Eric P. Newman and Walter Breen.

ACT OF 30.6.1812
WAR OF 1812

5 2/5% interest bearing notes.

		VG	VF	UNC
1	**100 DOLLARS** 1812. Eagle on branch at upper r.	—	—	—
2	**1000 DOLLARS** 1812. Eagle on branch at upper l.	—	—	—

ACT OF 25.2.1813
5 2/5% interest bearing notes.

		VG	VF	UNC
3	**100 DOLLARS** 1813.	—	—	—

ACT OF 4.3.1814
5 2/5% interest bearing notes.

		VG	VF	UNC
4	**20 DOLLARS** 1814.	—	—	—
5	**50 DOLLARS** 1814.	—	—	—
6	**100 DOLLARS** 1814.	—	—	—

ACT OF 26.12.1814
5 2/5% interest bearing notes.

		VG	VF	UNC
7	**20 DOLLARS** 1814. Eagle on shield at upper l. Printer: MDF.	—	Rare	—
8	**50 DOLLARS** 1814.	—	—	—
9	**100 DOLLARS** 1814. Eagle on branch at upper r. Printer: MDF.	—	Rare	—

ACT OF 24.2.1815
Called "Small Treasury Notes". $3 to $50 notes without interest. $100 notes 5 2/5% interest bearing notes. This issue actually circulated as currency although not legal tender for all debts.

		VG	VF	UNC
10	**3 DOLLARS** 1815. U.S shield at upper ctr. Printer: MDF.			

		VG	VF	UNC
11	**5 DOLLARS** 1815. Eagle on branch at upper r. Printer: MDF.	—	—	—
12	**10 DOLLARS** 1815. Eagle on branch at upper l. Text in frame at r. Printer: MDF.	—	—	—

		VG	VF	UNC
13	**10 DOLLARS** 1815. Similar to #12 but *TEN DOLLARS* in frame at r.	—	—	—

		VG	VF	UNC
14	**20 DOLLARS** 1815. Eagle at upper l. Printer: MDF.			
15	**50 DOLLARS** 1815. Eagle on branch at upper r. Printer: MDF.			
16	**100 DOLLARS** 1815. Eagle at upper r., shield at lower ctr. Printer: MDF.			

ACT OF 12.10.1837
PANIC OF 1837 1 year notes issued at four different rates of interest - 1 mill, 2%, 5% or 6%, the rate written in ink at time of issue. The 1-mill rate, which was nominal, was used on notes intended to circulate as currency.

		VG	VF	UNC
17	**50 DOLLARS** 1837. Specimen.	—	—	—
18	**100 DOLLARS** 1837. Specimen.	—	—	—
19	**500 DOLLARS** 1837. Specimen.	—	—	—
20	**1000 DOLLARS** 1837. Specimen.	—	—	—

ACT OF 21.5.1838
1 Year notes at 6% interest.

		VG	VF	UNC
21	**50 DOLLARS** 1838.	—	—	—
22	**100 DOLLARS** 1838.	—	—	—
23	**500 DOLLARS** 1838.	—	—	—
24	**1000 DOLLARS** 1838.	—	—	—

ACT OF 2.3.1839
1 year notes at 2% or 6% interest.

		VG	VF	UNC
25	**50 DOLLARS** 1839.	—	—	—
26	**100 DOLLARS** 1839.	—	—	—
27	**500 DOLLARS** 1839.	—	—	—
28	**1000 DOLLARS** 1839.	—	—	—

ACT OF 31.3.1840
1 year notes at 2%, 5%, 5 2/5% or 6% interest, the rate being written in at time of issuance.

		VG	VF	UNC
29	**50 DOLLARS** 1840. Specimen.	—	—	—
30	**100 DOLLARS** 1840. Specimen.	—	—	—
31	**500 DOLLARS** 1840. Specimen.	—	—	—
32	**1000 DOLLARS** 1840. Specimen.	—	—	—
33	**10,000 DOLLARS** 1840. Specimen.	—	—	—

ACT OF 31.1.1842
1 year notes at 2% or 6% interest.

		VG	VF	UNC
34	**50 DOLLARS** 1842. Specimen.	—	—	—
35	**100 DOLLARS** 1842. Specimen.	—	—	—
36	**500 DOLLARS** 1842. Specimen.	—	—	—
37	**1000 DOLLARS** 1842. Specimen.	—	—	—

ACT OF 31.8.1842
1 year notes at 2% or 6% interest.

		VG	VF	UNC
38	**50 DOLLARS** 1842. Mercury at l., females at upper ctr., female at r. Printer: RW&H. Specimen only.	—	—	—
39	**100 DOLLARS** 1842. Specimen.	—	—	—
40	**500 DOLLARS** 1842. Specimen.	—	—	—
41	**1000 DOLLARS** 1842. Specimen.	—	—	—

ACT OF 3.3.1843
1 year notes at 1 mill or 4% interest.

NOTE: In 1887 there were only $83,425. outstanding in all Treasury Notes issued under acts prior to 1846!

		VG	VF	UNC
42	**50 DOLLARS** 1843. Female at l. eagle at upper ctr, female at r. Printer: RW&H.	—	—	—

ACT OF 22.7.1846
MEXICAN WAR

1 year notes at 1 mill or 5 2/5% interest.

		VG	VF	UNC
43	**50 DOLLARS** 1846. Specimen.	—	—	—
44	**100 DOLLARS** 1846. Specimen.	—	—	—
45	**500 DOLLARS** 1846. Specimen.	—	—	—
46	**1000 DOLLARS** 1846. Specimen.	—	—	—

ACT OF 28.1.1847
60 day or 1 or 2 year notes at 5 2/5% or 6% interest. Some notes were reissued.

		VG	VF	UNC
47	**50 DOLLARS** 1847. Specimen.	—	—	—
48	**100 DOLLARS** 1847. Specimen.	—	—	—
49	**500 DOLLARS** 1847. Specimen.	—	—	—
50	**1000 DOLLARS** 1847. Specimen.	—	—	—

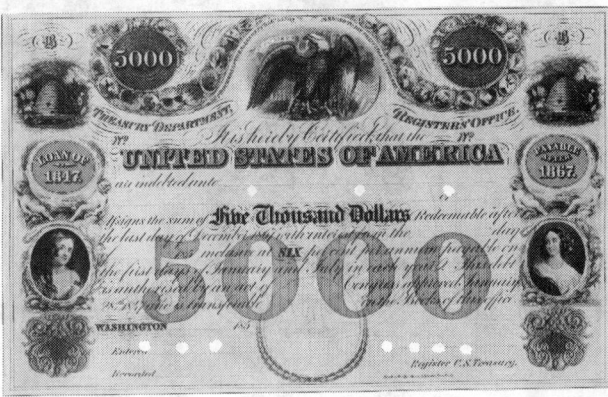

		VG	VF	UNC
51	**5000 DOLLARS** 1847. Girl at l. eagle at upper ctr. Lady at r. 2-year notes. Printer: RWH&E. Specimen.	Rare	—	—

		VG	VF	UNC
52	**5000 DOLLARS** 1847. Allegorical female w/sickle at l., eagle on branch and cameo of G. Washington at upper ctr., "Britannia"like female w/spear and shield at r. Printer:TCC. Specimen only.	—	—	—

ACT OF 23.12.1857
PANIC OF 1857

1 year notes at 3 to 6% interest.

		VG	VF	UNC
53	**100 DOLLARS** 1857. Printer: TCC.	—	—	—
54	**500 DOLLARS** 1857.	—	—	—
55	**1000 DOLLARS** 1857.	—	—	—

ACT OF 17.12.1860
1 year notes at 6% to 12% interest.

		VG	VF	UNC
56	**50 DOLLARS** 1860.	—	—	—
57	**100 DOLLARS** 1860.	—	—	—
58	**500 DOLLARS** 1860.	—	—	—
59	**1000 DOLLARS** 1860.	—	—	—

ACT OF 2.3.1861
1 or 2 year notes at 6% interest.

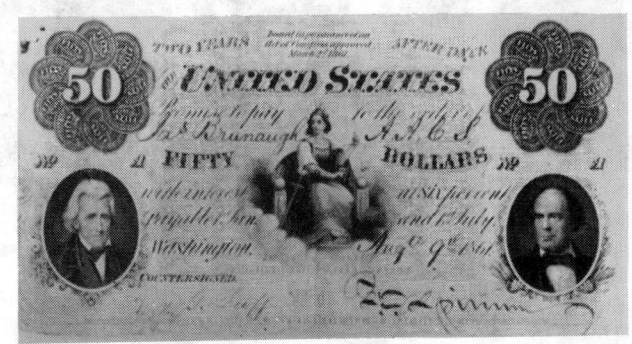

60 50 DOLLARS
1861. Black and orange. Portr. A. Jackson at l., Liberty seated at ctr., Portr. Webster at r. Back Blue. Printer: NBNC.

	VG	VF	UNC
	—	—	—

61 100 DOLLARS
1861. Black and orange. Seated Liberty at upper l., eagle at upper ctr. Back green.

	GOOD	FINE	XF
	1500.	2500.	

62 500 DOLLARS
1861. Black and green. Portr. Washington at lower l., females at upper ctr., eagle at lower right. Back brown. 60-day note. Printers: ABNC and RWH&E. Specimen.

	GOOD	FINE	XF
	—	—	—

63 500 DOLLARS
1861. Young male at lower l., Portr. Gen. Scott at upper ctr., male settler at lower r. 2-year note.

	GOOD	FINE	XF
	1500.	2500.	—

64 1000 DOLLARS
1861. Black and green. Portr. G. Washington at l., Liberty at ctr., Treasury bldg. at r. Back red-brown.

	GOOD	FINE	XF
	3000.	5000.	—

65 5000 DOLLARS
1861.

	—	—	—

FRACTIONAL CURRENCY
CIVIL WAR, 1861-65
1862 (FIRST) ISSUE - POSTAGE CURRENCY

97 5 CENTS
17.7.1862. Brown. Facsimile 5 Cent stamp w/Jefferson at ctr.

	VG	VF	UNC
a. Perforated edges; ABNC monogram on back.	12.50	15.50	120.00
b. Perforated edges; w/o ABNC monogram on back.	13.00	21.00	135.00
c. Straight edges; ABNC monogram on back.	12.00	13.00	40.00
d. Straight edges; w/o ABNC monogram on back.	13.00	20.00	150.00

98 10 CENTS
17.7.1862. Green. Facsimile 10 Cent stamp w/Washington at ctr.

	VG	VF	UNC
a. Perforated edges; ABNC monogram on back.	13.50	17.00	115.00
b. Perforated edges; w/o ABNC monogram on back.	14.00	30.00	130.00
c. Straight edges; ABNC monogram on back.	9.00	10.50	35.00
d. Straight edges; w/o ABNC monogram on back.	12.00	40.00	150.00

99 25 CENTS
17.7.1862. Brown. 5 facsimile 5 Cent stamps w/Jefferson.

	VG	VF	UNC
a. Perforated edges; ABNC monogram on back.	16.00	25.00	150.00
b. Perforated edges; w/o ABNC monogram on back.	16.00	60.00	275.00
c. Straight edges; ABNC monogram on back.	11.50	15.00	75.00
d. Straight edges; w/o ABNC monogram on back.	13.00	60.00	300.00

100 50 CENTS
17.7.1862. Green. 5 facsimile 10 Cent stamps w/Washington.

	VG	VF	UNC
a. 12 perforated edges; ABNC monogram on back.	24.00	30.00	250.00
b. 14 perforated edges; ABNC monogram on back.	—	Rare	—
c. Perforated edges; w/o ABNC monogram on back.	20.00	70.00	300.00
d. Straight edges; ABNC monogram on back.	13.00	16.00	100.00
e. Straight edges; w/o ABNC monogram on back.	20.00	75.00	300.00

1863 (SECOND) ISSUE
Many varieties. Back w/ or w/o ovpt. 1863 and letters; paper w or w/o fibers.

#101-104 oval bronze ovpt. on face around Washington at ctr. and bronze numerals on back.

				VG	VF	UNC
101	**5 CENTS**					
	3.3.1863.					
	a.	W/o ovpt. on back.		12.00	13.00	45.00
	b.	Ovpt: *18-63* on back.		12.00	13.00	50.00
	c.	Ovpt: *18-63* and *S* on back.		12.00	13.50	75.00
	d.	Ovpt: *18-63* on *R-1* on back.		16.00	25.00	200.00
102	**10 CENTS**					
	3.3.1863.					
	a.	W/o ovpt. on back.		10.00	15.00	50.00
	b.	Ovpt: *18-63* on back.		10.00	15.00	50.00
	c.	Ovpt: *18-63* and *S* on back.		10.00	17.00	65.00
	d.	Ovpt: *18-63* and *1* on back.		20.00	45.00	200.00
	e.	Ovpt: *O-63* on back.		500.00	1200.	2000.
	f.	Ovpt: *18-63* and *T-1* on back.		16.00	21.00	225.00
103	**25 CENTS**					
	3.3.1863.					
	a.	W/o ovpt. on back.		10.00	15.00	75.00
	b.	Ovpt: *18-63* on back.		10.00	22.00	85.00
	c.	Ovpt: *18-63* and *A* on back.		10.00	15.00	85.00
	d.	Ovpt: *18-63* and *S* on back.		10.00	15.00	85.00
	e.	Ovpt: *18-63* and *2* on back.		15.00	25.00	120.00
	f.	Ovpt: *18-63* and *T-1* on back.		15.00	18.00	250.00
	g.	Ovpt: *18-63* and *T-2* on back.		15.00	18.00	250.00
104	**50 CENTS**					
	3.3.1863.					
	a.	Ovpt: *18-63* on back.		15.00	35.00	150.00
	b.	Ovpt: *18-63* and *A* on back.		13.00	18.00	150.00
	c.	Ovpt: *18-63* and *I* on back.		13.00	18.00	150.00
	d.	Ovpt: *18-63* and *O-1* on back.		20.00	25.00	260.00
	e.	Ovpt: *18-63* and *R-2* on back.		15.00	22.00	260.00
	f.	Ovpt: *18-63* and *T-1* on back.		15.00	22.00	260.00

1863 (THIRD) ISSUE

				VG	VF	UNC
105	**3 CENTS**					
	3.3.1863. Washington at ctr.					
	a.	Portr. w/lt. background.		18.00	21.00	40.00
	b.	Portr. w/dk. background.		19.00	25.00	85.00

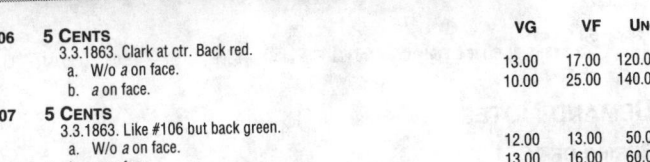

				VG	VF	UNC
106	**5 CENTS**					
	3.3.1863. Clark at ctr. Back red.					
	a.	W/o *a* on face.		13.00	17.00	120.00
	b.	*a* on face.		10.00	25.00	140.00
107	**5 CENTS**					
	3.3.1863. Like #106 but back green.					
	a.	W/o *a* on face.		12.00	13.00	50.00
	b.	*a* on face.		13.00	16.00	60.00

				VG	VF	UNC
108	**10 CENTS**					
	3.3.1863. Washington at ctr.; bronze 10's in each corner.					
	a.	Back red. Sm. sign: Colby-Spinner.		11.00	18.00	125.00
	b.	W/*1* on face.		12.00	25.00	150.00
	c.	Lg. sign: Colby-Spinner.		16.00	22.00	140.00
	d.	Lg. sign: Jeffries-Spinner.		20.00	50.00	250.00
	e.	Back green. Sm. sign: Colby-Spinner.		10.00	14.00	35.00
	f.	Lg. sign: Colby-Spinner.		—	Rare	—
	g.	Like d. W/*1* on face.		11.00	15.00	65.00

				VG	VF	UNC
109	**25 CENTS**					
	3.3.1863. Fessenden at ctr.					
	a.	Back red.		11.00	15.00	115.00
	b.	Sm. *a* on face.		11.00	15.00	150.00
	c.	Lg. *a* on face.		11.00	15.00	170.00

		VG	VF	UNC
d.	Back green.	10.00	12.00	80.00
e.	Sm. *a* on face.	10.00	12.00	80.00
f.	Lg. *a* on face.	10.00	12.00	80.00
g.	Ovpt: *M-2-6-5* on back.	16.00	25.00	200.00
h.	Ovpt: *a* on face. *M-2-6-5* on back.	18.00	50.00	250.00
i.	Solid bronze ornaments ovpt. on face.	250.00	450.00	1000.
j.	Solid bronze ornaments ovpt. and *a* on face.	400.00	800.00	1500.

			VG	VF	UNC
110	**50 CENTS**				
	3.3.1863. Spinner at ctr.				
	a.	Sm. sign: Colby-Spinner. Ovpt: *A-2-6-5* and multiple 50:s on red back.	38.00	60.00	275.00
	b.	*1* and *a* on face.	100.00	150.00	750.00
	c.	*1* on face.	38.00	70.00	325.00
	d.	*a* on face.	38.00	70.00	325.00
	e.	Lg. sign: Colby-Spinner.	37.50	70.00	325.00
	f.	Sign: Allison-Spinner.	37.50	75.00	350.00
	g.	Sign: Allison-New.	600.00	1250.	2000.
111	**50 CENTS**				
	3.3.1863. Like #110 but back green.				
			30.00	70.00	325.00
	a.	Issued note.	30.00	80.00	400.00
	b.	*1* and *a* on face.	30.00	70.00	325.00
	c.	*1* on face.	30.00	75.00	350.00
	d.	*a* on face.	37.50	75.00	325.00
	e.	Ovpt: *A-2-6-5* on back.	150.00	400.00	1750.
	f.	*1* and *a* on face.	40.00	80.00	325.00
	g.	*1* on face.	50.00	90.00	350.00
	h.	*a* on face.			
112	**50 CENTS**				
	3.3.1863. Like #111 but redesigned green back. *50* at ctr.				
			45.00	70.00	350.00
	a.	Issued note.	45.00	75.00	350.00
	b.	*1* and *a* on face.	45.00	80.00	350.00
	c.	*1* on face.	45.00	85.00	350.00
	d.	*a* on face.			

			VG	VF	UNC
113	**50 CENTS**				
	3.3.1863. Allegorical figure of Justice holding scales at ctr. Back red.				
	a.	Sm. sign.	45.00	95.00	500.00
	b.	*1* and *a* on face.	75.00	250.00	1500.
	c.	*1* on face.	45.00	95.00	500.00
	d.	*a* on face.	45.00	95.00	500.00
	e.	Ovpt: *A-2-6-5* on back.	45.00	95.00	500.00
	f.	*1* and *a* on face.	70.00	350.00	1500.
	g.	*1* on face.	70.00	90.00	475.00
	h.	*a* on face.	55.00	100.00	475.00
	i.	Sm. sign. Ovpt: *S-2-6-4* on back.	750.00	2000.	4000.
	j.	*1* and *a* on face. Fibre paper.	—	Rare	—
	k.	*1* on face. Fibre paper.	1000.	2750.	5000.
	l.	*a* on face. Fibre paper.	1250.	3000.	5500.
	m.	Back red. Lg. autograph sign.	45.00	60.00	450.00
	n.	Ovpt: *A-2-6-5* on back.	50.00	75.00	475.00
	o.	Ovpt: *S-2-6-4* on back.	60.00	200.00	825.00
114	**50 CENTS**				
	3.3.1863. Like #113 but back green.				
			45.00	75.00	425.00
	a.	Issued note.	100.00	250.00	950.00
	b.	*1* and *a* on face.	45.00	70.00	425.00
	c.	*1* on face.	45.00	75.00	425.00
	d.	*a* on face.	45.00	75.00	400.00
	e.	Ovpt: *A-2-6-5* on back compactly spaced.	100.00	225.00	850.00
	f.	*1* and *a* on face.	45.00	75.00	400.00
	g.	*1* on face.	50.00	80.00	485.00
	h.	*a* on face.	50.00	95.00	500.00
	i.	Ovpt: *A-2-6-5* on back widely spaced.	150.00	500.00	2000.
	j.	*1* and *a* on face.	55.00	110.00	550.00
	k.	*1* on face.	50.00	115.00	575.00
	l.	*a* on face.	45.00	75.00	600.00
	m.	Ovpt: *A-2-6-5* on back. Fibre paper.	100.00	500.00	1750.
	n.	*1* and *a* on face. Fibre paper.	45.00	75.00	575.00
	o.	*1* on face. Fibre paper.	60.00	90.00	600.00
	p.	*a* on face. Fibre paper.	1000.	2000.	3000.
	q.	Ovpt: *S-2-6-4* on back. Fibre paper.			

1863 (FOURTH) ISSUE

Many varieties of paper, of color and size of seal. Backs green.

115 10 CENTS

3.3.1863. Liberty at l. 40mm red seal.

	VG	VF	UNC
a. Wmk. paper w/pink silk fibres.	8.50	9.50	35.00
b. W/o wmk., paper w/pink silk fibres.	8.50	9.50	35.00
c. Bluish tint at r. side of face. Paper w/violet silk fibres.	9.00	20.00	65.00
d. 38mm red seal; bluish tint at r. side of face.	8.50	9.50	35.00

116 15 CENTS

3.3.1863. Columbia at l. 40mm red seal.

	VG	VF	UNC
a. Wmk. paper w/pink silk fibres.	28.00	34.00	125.00
b. W/o wmk., paper w/pink silk fibres.	28.00	34.00	145.00
c. Bluish tint at r. side of face. Paper w/violet silk fibres.	28.00	34.00	140.00
d. 38mm red seal; bluish tint at r. side of face.	28.00	34.00	125.00

118 25 CENTS

3.3.1863. Washington at l. 40mm red seal.

	VG	VF	UNC
a. Wmk. paper w/pink silk fibres.	9.00	10.00	45.00
b. W/o wmk., paper w/pink silk fibres.	9.00	10.00	45.00
c. Bluish tint at r. side of face. Paper w/violet silk fibres.	9.50	20.00	85.00
d. 38mm red seal; bluish tint at r. side of face.	9.00	10.00	45.00

119 50 CENTS

3.3.1863. Lincoln at r.

	VG	VF	UNC
a. Wmk. paper w/silk fibres.	28.00	50.00	275.00
b. W/o wmk., paper w/pink silk fibres.	30.00	60.00	300.00

120 50 CENTS

3.3.1863. E.M. Stanton at l.

	VG	VF	UNC
	12.00	16.00	125.00

121 50 CENTS

3.3.1863. Dexter at l.

	VG	VF	UNC
	12.00	15.00	90.00

1874-75 (FIFTH) ISSUE

Paper varieties. Values are for most common types of each denomination.

122 10 CENTS

3.3.1863; 30.6.1864. W. Meredith at l.

	VG	VF	UNC
a. Green seal w/long key.	8.00	10.00	50.00
b. Red seal w/long key.	8.00	10.00	18.00
c. Red seal w/short key.	8.00	10.00	18.00

123 25 CENTS

3.3.1863; 30.6.1864. Portr. R. Walker at l.

	VG	VF	UNC
a. Red seal w/long key.	8.00	10.00	25.00
b. Red seal w/short key.	8.00	10.00	25.00

124 50 CENTS

3.3.1863; 30.6.1864. Portr. Crawford at l. Pink or white paper.

	VG	VF	UNC
	12.00	15.00	35.00

DEMAND NOTES

SERIES OF 1861

#125-127 w/o seal. Printer: ABNC.

NOTE: Few Demand Notes of 1861 are known in better than VG condition.

125 5 DOLLARS

10.8.1861. Statue of Columbus at l., Hamilton at r.

	GOOD	FINE	XF
a. Payable at New York.	325.00	800.00	—
b. Payable at Philadelphia.	325.00	800.00	—
c. Payable at Boston.	325.00	800.00	—
d. Payable at Cincinnati.	5000.	11,000.	—
e. Payable at St. Louis.	5000.	11,000.	—

126	**10 DOLLARS**	**GOOD**	**FINE**	**XF**
	10.8.1861. Lincoln at l., allegorical female (Art) at r.	500.00	1200.	—
	a. Payable at New York.	500.00	1200.	—
	b. Payable at Philadelphia.	500.00	1200.	—
	c. Payable at Boston.	500.00	1200.	—
	d. Payable at Cincinnati.	7500.	17,500.	—
	e. Payable at St. Louis.	8000.	24,000.	—

127	**20 DOLLARS**	**GOOD**	**FINE**	**XF**
	10.8.1861. Liberty w/sword and shield at ctr.			
	a. Payable at New York.	5500.	12,000.	—
	b. Payable at Philadelphia.	5500.	12,000.	—
	c. Payable at Boston.	—	Rare	—
	d. Payable at Cincinnati.	—	Rare	—
	e. Deleted.	—	—	—

UNITED STATES NOTES

Varieties of red or brown seals. Prices are for most common types of each denomination.

SERIES OF 1862

NOTE: An example of #136 in Fine sold in 1974 for 10,000.00.

128	**1 DOLLAR**	**VG**	**VF**	**UNC**
	1862. Portr. Chase at l.	175.00	400.00	775.00

129	**2 DOLLARS**	**VG**	**VF**	**UNC**
	1862. Hamilton at l. ctr.	250.00	700.00	1750.

130	**5 DOLLARS**	**VG**	**VF**	**UNC**
	1862. Statue of Columbia at l.; Portr. Hamilton at r. Like #125 but w/o *On Demand* and w/seal.			
	a. First Obligation on back.	210.00	575.00	800.00
	b. Second Obligation on back.	200.00	550.00	775.00

131	**10 DOLLARS**	**VG**	**VF**	**UNC**
	1862. Lincoln at l., allegorical female (Art) at r. Like #126 but w/o *On Demand* and w/seal.			
	a. First Obligation on back.	525.00	1000.	2200.
	b. Second Obligation on back.	510.00	950.00	2100.

132	**20 DOLLARS**			
	1862. Liberty w/sword and shield at ctr. Like #123 but w/o *On Demand* and w/seal.			
	a. First Obligation on back.	1100.	1850.	3800.
	b. Second Obligation on back.	1100.	1800.	3800.

133	**50 DOLLARS**			
	1862. Hamilton at l. ctr.			
	a. First Obligation on back.	7000.	13,000.	—
	b. Second Obligation on back.	6500.	12,500.	—

134	**100 DOLLARS**	**VG**	**VF**	**UNC**
	1862. Heraldic eagle at l.			
	a. First Obligation on back.	8250.	15,000.	27,000.
	b. Second Obligation on back.	6500.	13,000.	27,500.

135	**500 DOLLARS**			
	1862. Gallatin at ctr.			
	a. First Obligation on back.	—	Rare	—
	b. Second Obligation on back.	—	Rare	—

136	**1000 DOLLARS**			
	1862. Morris at ctr.			
	a. First Obligation on back.	—	Rare	—
	b. Second Obligation on back. Uni que.	—	Rare	—

SERIES OF 1863

NOTE: An example of #142 in Fine sold in 1974 for $5000.00.

137	**5 DOLLARS**	**VG**	**VF**	**UNC**
	1863. Like #130b.	200.00	550.00	775.00

138	**10 DOLLARS**			
	1863. Like #131b.	510.00	950.00	2100.

		VG	VF	UNC
139	**20 DOLLARS** 1863. Like #132b.	1100.	1850.	3800.
140	**50 DOLLARS** 1863. Like #133b.	6500.	12,500.	—
141	**100 DOLLARS** 1863. Like #134b.	8250.	15,000.	30,000.
142	**500 DOLLARS** 1863. Like #135b. Possibly unique.	—	Rare	—
143	**1000 DOLLARS** 1863. Like #136b.	—	Rare	—

SERIES OF 1869

		VG	VF	UNC
144	**1 DOLLAR** 1869. Columbus sighting land at l., Washington at ctr. 1-ONE-DOLLAR at ctr. on back.	215.00	550.00	1100.

		VG	VF	UNC
145	**2 DOLLARS** 1869. Portr. Jefferson at upper l. Capitol at ctr. 2 at ctr. on back.	325.00	875.00	2275.

		VG	VF	UNC
146	**5 DOLLARS** 1869. Portr. Jackson at lower l., pioneer family at ctr. 5 at ctr. on back.	235.00	440.00	775.00

		VG	VF	UNC
147	**10 DOLLARS** 1869. Webster at lower l., presentation of Indian Princess at lower r. Text at ctr. on back.	365.00	825.00	1800.

		VG	VF	UNC
148	**20 DOLLARS** 1869. Portr. Hamilton at l., Victory w/sword and shield at r. Text at ctr. on back.	850.00	2600.	4500.

		VG	VF	UNC
149	**50 DOLLARS** 1869. Woman holding statue of Mercury at l., Clay at lower r.	6600.	24,000.	
150	**100 DOLLARS** 1869. Lincoln at upper l., allegorical female (Architecture) w/child at r. Text at ctr. on back.	8200.	15,000.	37,500.
151	**500 DOLLARS** 1869. Woman w/scales at l., Adams at r.	—	Rare	
152	**1000 DOLLARS** 1869. Columbus at l., Clinton at ctr. Text at ctr. on back.	—	Rare	

SERIES OF 1874

		VG	VF	UNC
153	**1 DOLLAR** 1874. Columbus sighting land at upper l., Washington at ctr. *UNITED STATES OF AMERICA* at ctr. on back.	60.00	170.00	500.00

		VG	VF	UNC
154	**2 DOLLARS** 1874. Jefferson at l., Capitol at ctr. *2* at ctr. and *2*s in all corners on back.	300.00	600.00	925.00

		VG	VF	UNC
155	**50 DOLLARS** 1874. Portr. Franklin at upper l., Columbia at r.	2850.	5600.	10,000.
156	**500 DOLLARS** 1874. Woman standing at l., Maj. Gen. Mansfield at r.	—	Rare	—

SERIES OF 1875

		VG	VF	UNC
157	**1 DOLLAR** 1875. Like #153. 2 sign. varieties.	55.00	125.00	425.00
	a. Series A.	110.00	200.00	550.00
	b. Series B.	100.00	200.00	500.00
	c. Series C.	120.00	275.00	700.00
	d. Series D.	200.00	400.00	700.00
	e. Series E.	250.00	400.00	900.00
158	**2 DOLLARS** 1875. Like #154. 2 sign. varieties.	300.00	475.00	825.00
	a. Series A.	300.00	525.00	1000.
	b. Series B.	155.00	400.00	975.00

		VG	VF	UNC
159	**5 DOLLARS** 1875. Jackson at l., pioneer family at ctr. Ornamental design at ctr. on back. 2 sign. varieties.	78.00	200.00	585.00
	a. Series A.	100.00	210.00	585.00
	b. Series B.	80.00	200.00	585.00
160	**10 DOLLARS** 1875. Webster at l., presentation of Indian Princess at r. Ornamental design at ctr w/text at r. on back.	450.00	1000.	2350.
	a. Series A.	450.00	1000.	2350.

		VG	VF	UNC
161	**20 DOLLARS** 1875. Portr. Hamilton at upper l., Victory w/sword and shield at r. Ornamental design at ctr. w/text at l. on back.	675.00	1275.	2650.
162	**50 DOLLARS** 1875. Like #155.	5850.	12,500.	—

		VG	VF	UNC
163	**100 DOLLARS** 1875. Lincoln at l., woman w/child at r. Ornamental design at ctr. on back. 2 sign. varieties.	5800.	12,000.	22,500.
164	**500 DOLLARS** 1875. Like #156. 2 sign. varieties.	—	Rare	—

SERIES OF 1878

		VG	VF	UNC
165	**1 DOLLAR** 1878. Like #153.	55.00	120.00	350.00
166	**2 DOLLARS** 1878. Like #154. 2 sign. varieties.	280.00	525.00	875.00
167	**5 DOLLARS** 1878. Like #159.	160.00	225.00	500.00
168	**10 DOLLARS** 1878. Like #160.	325.00	875.00	2200.
169	**20 DOLLARS** 1878. Like #161.	550.00	1000.	2350.
170	**50 DOLLARS** 1878. Like #155.	3000.	6250.	11,000.
171	**100 DOLLARS** 1878. Like #163.	4950.	15,000.	20,000.
172	**500 DOLLARS** 1878. Like #156.	—	Rare	—
173	**1000 DOLLARS** 1878. Columbus at l., Clinton at ctr. Text at l. on back.	—	Rare	—
174	**5000 DOLLARS** 1878. Madison at l. (All notes have been redeemed).	—	—	—
175	**10,000 DOLLARS** 1878. Jackson at l. (All notes have been redeemed).	—	—	—

SERIES OF 1880

		VG	VF	UNC
176	**1 DOLLAR** 1880. Like #153.			
	a. Seal at r.; red serial #; 3 sign. varieties.	70.00	110.00	350.00
	b. Red or brown seal at r.; blue serial #; 2 sign. varieties.	400.00	825.00	2100.
	c. Seal at l.; blue serial #; 2 sign. varieties.	42.00	80.00	310.00
177	**2 DOLLARS** 1880. Like #154.			
	a. Red serial #; 3 sign. varieties.	80.00	175.00	525.00
	b. Blue serial #; sm. or lg. red or brown seal; 3 sign. varieties.	440.00	1100.	3000.
178	**5 DOLLARS** 1880. Like #159.			
	a. Red serial #. 3 sign. varieties.	95.00	300.00	585.00
	b. Blue serial #. 4 varieties of seals; 8 sign. varieties.	55.00	115.00	350.00
179	**10 DOLLARS** 1880. Like #160.			
	a. Red serial #. 3 sign. varieties.	215.00	490.00	1000.
	b. Blue serial #. 4 varieties of seals; 8 sign. varieties.	260.00	450.00	825.00
180	**20 DOLLARS** 1880. Like #161.			
	a. Blue serial #. 4 varieties of seals; 12 sign. varieties.	220.00	575.00	1100.
	b. Red serial #. 2 sign. varieties.	195.00	540.00	900.00
181	**50 DOLLARS** 1880. Like #155. 4 varieties of seals; 8 sign. varieties.	1300.	4100.	10,500.
182	**100 DOLLARS** 1880. Like #163. 4 varieties of seals; 9 sign. varieties.	3900.	9000.	14,000.
183	**500 DOLLARS** 1880. Like #156. 4 varieties of seals; 10 sign. varieties.	—	Rare	—
184	**1000 DOLLARS** 1880. Like #173. 4 varieties of seals; 11 sign. varieties.	—	Rare	—

SERIES OF 1901

185	10 DOLLARS	VG	VF	UNC
	1901. Portr. Lewis at l., bison at ctr., Portr. Clark at r. 9 sign. varieties.	300.00	750.00	1500.

SERIES OF 1907

186	5 DOLLARS	VG	VF	UNC
	1907. Like #159. 10 sign. varieties.	45.00	90.00	190.00

SERIES OF 1917

187	1 DOLLAR	VG	VF	UNC
	1917. Like #153.	30.00	50.00	125.00
188	2 DOLLARS			
	1917. Like #154. 4 sign. varieties.	39.00	70.00	195.00

SERIES OF 1923

189	1 DOLLAR	VG	VF	UNC
	1923. Washington at ctr.	35.00	75.00	250.00

190	10 DOLLARS	VG	VF	UNC
	1923. Portr. Jackson at ctr.	525.00	1100.	3250.

GOLD CERTIFICATES

SERIES OF 1863

NOTE: Certain notes with listings incorporated in previous editions, encompassing various names of the actual bank of issue with national banks and national gold banks #191-244, 390-394A have been deleted from this section. The highly specialized *"Standard Catalog of National Bank Notes"* 1249 pages M 1990 released by Krause Publications is considered to be the ultimate reference for this colorful and rather extensive series of the chartered banks.

245	20 DOLLARS	VG	VF	UNC
	3.3.1863. Eagle w/shield at l.		Rare	
246	100 DOLLARS			
	3.3.1863. Eagle w/shield at l.	—	Rare	
247	100 DOLLARS			
	3.3.1863. Benton. Countersigned and dated or 1872 or 1872 by hand.	—		

248	500 DOLLARS	VG	VF	UNC
	3.3.1863. Eagle w/shield at l.	—	—	—
249	500 DOLLARS			
	3.3.1863. Lincoln. Countersigned and dated 1870 or 1872 by hand.	—	—	—
250	1000 DOLLARS			
	3.3.1863. Eagle w/shield at l.	—	—	—
251	1000 DOLLARS			
	3.3.1863. Hamilton. Countersigned and dated 1870 or 1872 by hand.	—	—	—
252	5000 DOLLARS			
	3.3.1863. Eagle w/shield at l.	—	—	—
253	5000 DOLLARS			
	3.3.1863. Madison. Countersigned and dated 1870 or 1871 by hand.	—	—	—
254	10,000 DOLLARS			
	3.3.1863. Eagle w/shield at l.	—	—	—
255	10,000 DOLLARS			
	3.3.1863. Jackson. Countersigned and dated 1870 or 1871 by hand.	—	—	—

SERIES OF 1875

256	100 DOLLARS	VG	VF	UNC
	1875. Benton at l.	—	Rare	—
257	500 DOLLARS			
	1875. Lincoln.	—	—	—
258	1000 DOLLARS			
	1875. Hamilton.	—	Rare	

SERIES OF 1882

259	20 DOLLARS	VG	VF	UNC
	1863. Pres. Garfield at r.			
	a. Countersigned sign.	—	Rare	—
	b. W/o countersigned sign. 3 seal varieties; 4 sign. varieties.	170.00	525.00	1100.

260	50 DOLLARS	VG	VF	UNC
	1882. Wright at l.			
	a. Countersigned sign.	—	Rare	—
	b. W/o countersigned sign. 4 seal; varieties; 9 sign. varieties.	525.00	1050.	4800.
261	100 DOLLARS			
	1882. Benton at l. (different than #256).			
	a. Countersigned sign.	—	Rare	—
	b. W/o countersigned sign. 4 seal varieties; 14 sign. varieties.	450.00	1300.	5500.
262	500 DOLLARS			
	1882. Lincoln at l.	—	Rare	
263	1000 DOLLARS			
	1882. Hamilton at r.	—	Rare	
264	5000 DOLLARS			
	1882. Madison at l.	—	Rare	
265	10,000 DOLLARS			
	1882. Jackson at l.	—	Rare	

SERIES OF 1888

266	5000 DOLLARS	VG	VF	UNC
	1888. Like #264.	—	Rare	—
267	10,000 DOLLARS			
	1888. Like #265.	—	Rare	

SERIES OF 1900

NOTE: During a fire at a treasury storage area in 1935 a number of cancelled notes were thrown into the street and were picked up by passers-by.

268	10,000 DOLLARS	VG	VF	UNC
	28.9.1916; 9.5.1917; 22.11.1916. Like #265. Uniface.			
	a. Issued note.	—	Rare	—
	b. Redeemed w/cancelling perforations.	400.00	750.00	

SERIES OF 1905

			VG	VF	UNC
269	**20 DOLLARS**		775.00	2800.	7300.
	1905. Washington at ctr. Red seal. 2 sign. varieties.				

SERIES OF 1906

			VG	VF	UNC
270	**20 DOLLARS**		80.00	225.00	575.00
	1906. Like #269 but gold seal. 6 sign. varieties.				

SERIES OF 1907

			VG	VF	UNC
271	**10 DOLLARS**		50.00	125.00	475.00
	1907. Hillegas at ctr. 6 sign. varieties.				
272	**1000 DOLLARS**		2500.	4500.	10,000.
	1907. Hamilton at ctr.				

SERIES OF 1913

			VG	VF	UNC
273	**50 DOLLARS**		385.00	800.00	1850.
	1913. Grant at ctr. 2 sign. varieties.				

SERIES OF 1922

			VG	VF	UNC
274	**10 DOLLARS**		50.00	125.00	475.00
	1922. Like #271.				
275	**20 DOLLARS**		72.00	195.00	450.00
	1922. Like #269.				
276	**50 DOLLARS**		300.00	700.00	1500.
	1922. Like #273.				

			VG	VF	UNC
277	**100 DOLLARS**		400.00	700.00	2500.
	1922. Like #261.				
278	**500 DOLLARS**		—	Rare	—
	1922. Like #262.				
279	**1000 DOLLARS**		—	Rare	—
	1922. Like #272.				

INTEREST BEARING NOTES

ACT OF 17.3.1861

			VG	VF	UNC
280	**50 DOLLARS**		—	Rare	—
	1861. Eagle at ctr. (7-3/10% interest for 3 years. 5 coupons).				

			VG	VF	UNC
281	**100 DOLLARS**		Unknown In Private Hands		
	1861. Portr. Gen. Scott at ctr. (7-3/10% interest for 3 years. 5 coupons).				
282	**500 DOLLARS**		Unknown In Private Hands		
	1861. Washington. (7-3/10% interest for 3 years. 5 coupons).				
283	**1000 DOLLARS**		Unknown In Private Hands		
	1861. Chase at ctr. (7-3/10% interest for 3 years. 5 coupons).				
284	**5000 DOLLARS**		Unknown In Private Hands		
	1861. Justice w/sword and scales at l., Indian woman w/shield and eagle at ctr. (7-3/10% interest for 3 years. 5 coupons).				

ACT OF 3.3.1863

			VG	VF	UNC
285	**10 DOLLARS**		3000.	6500.	—
	15.3.1864. Portr. Chase at lower l., eagle at ctr., allegorical woman at r. (5% interest for 1 year).				
286	**20 DOLLARS**		5000.	10,000.	—
	5.4.1864. Liberty at l., mortar at bottom ctr., Lincoln at r. (5% interest for 1 year).				
287	**50 DOLLARS**		—	Rare	—
	1864. Allegorical female at l., Hamilton at lower r. (5% interest for 1 year).				
288	**50 DOLLARS**		—	Rare	—
	1864. Allegorical female figure at ctr., at l. and r. (5% interest for 2 years).				
289	**100 DOLLARS**		—	Rare	—
	1864. Washington holding scroll at ctr. (5% interest for 1 year).				

290 **100 DOLLARS**
14.4.1864. 2 allegorical male figures (Science and Industry) seated at l., bldg. at upper ctr., coastal battery at lower r. (5% interest for 2 years).

	VG	VF	UNC
	—	Rare	

291 **500 DOLLARS**
1864. Ship "New Ironsides". (5% interest for 1 year). Unknown In Private Hands

292 **500 DOLLARS**
1864. Liberty and eagle. (5% interest for 2 years). Unknown In Private Hands

293 **1000 DOLLARS**
1864. Liberty and Justice. (5% interest for 1 year). Unknown In Private Hands

294 **1000 DOLLARS**
1864. Ships "Guerriere" and "Constitution". (5% interest for 2 years). Unknown In Private Hands

295 **5000 DOLLARS**
1864. Allegorical female. (5% interest for 1 year). Unknown In Private Hands

ACT OF 30.6.1864

296 **50 DOLLARS**
1864. Eagle at ctr. (7-3/10% interest for 3 years. 5 coupons).

	VG	VF	UNC
	—	Rare	

ACT OF 3.3.1865

297 **50 DOLLARS**
15.7.1865. Eagle l. looking r. at ctr. (7-3/10% interest for 3 years. 5 coupons).

	VG	VF	UNC
	—	Rare	

298 **100 DOLLARS**
1865. Gen. Scott at ctr. (7-3/10% interest for 3 years. 5 coupons). — Rare

299 **500 DOLLARS**
1865. (7-3/10% interest for 3 years. 5 coupons). Unknown In Private Hands

300 **1000 DOLLARS**
1865. Justice sitting w/scales and shield at ctr. (7-3/10% interest for 3 years. 5 coupons). Unknown In Private Hands

COMPOUND INTEREST TREASURY NOTES

ACT OF 3.3.1863 / 30.6.1864

#301-306 ovpt: *COMPOUND INTEREST TREASURY NOTE.*

301 **10 DOLLARS**
10.6.1864-15.12.1864. Like #285.

	VG	VF	UNC
	3000.	8000.	—

302 **20 DOLLARS**
14.7.1864-16.10.1865. Like #286.

	VG	VF	UNC
	4000.	9000.	—

303 **50 DOLLARS**
10.6.1864-1.9.1865. Like #287. — — —

304 **100 DOLLARS**
10.6.1864-1.9.1865. Like #289. — — —

305 **500 DOLLARS**
10.6.1864-1.10.1865. Like #291. Unknown In Private Hands

306 **1000 DOLLARS**
15.7.1864-15.9.1865. Like #293. Unknown In Private Hands

REFUNDING CERTIFICATES

ACT OF 26.2.1879

307 **10 DOLLARS**
1.4.1879. Franklin at upper l. l. *Payable to order* (4% interest).

	VG	VF	UNC
	—	Rare	

308 **10 DOLLARS**
1.4.1879. Like #307 but *Payable to bearer* (4% interest).

	VG	VF	UNC
	1050.	1800.	—

SILVER CERTIFICATES

Red or brown seal; and later blue.

SERIES OF 1878

309 **10 DOLLARS**
1878. Morris at l.

	F	XF	UNC
	7000.	Rare	—

310 **20 DOLLARS**
1878. Portr. Decatur at r.

	VG	VF	UNC
	—	—	—

311 **50 DOLLARS**
1878. *50* at upper l., vertical *Fifty* below it, Everett at r.

	VG	VF	UNC
	—	Rare	—

312 **100 DOLLARS**
1878. Monroe at l., *100* at lower r. — Rare —

313 **500 DOLLARS**
1878. Sumner at r. — Rare —

314 **1000 DOLLARS**
1878. Marcy at l. — Rare —

SERIES OF 1880

NOTE: 1878 and 1880 countersigned notes are normally available only in circulated grades.

315 **10 DOLLARS**
1880. Morris at l.

	VG	VF	UNC
a. Countersigned sign.	7000.	—	—
b. W/o countersigned sign. 2 seal varieties; 3 sign. varieties.	450.00	1000.	3000.

316 **20 DOLLARS**
1880. Decatur at r.

	VG	VF	UNC
a. Countersigned sign.	—	—	—
b. W/o countersigned sign. 2 seal varieties; 3 sign. varieties.	1250.	3600.	8500.

317 50 DOLLARS
1880. Like #311 but w/o countersigned sign. 3 seal varieties; 5 sign. varieties.

	VG	VF	UNC
	5200.	13,000.	24,000.

318 100 DOLLARS
1880. Like #312. 3 seal varieties; 3 sign. varieties.

	VG	VF	UNC
	6500.	20,000.	30,000.

319 500 DOLLARS
1880. Sumner at r. 3 sign. varieties.

—	Rare	—

320 1000 DOLLARS
1880. Marcy at l. 3 sign. varieties.

—	Rare	—

SERIES OF 1886

321 1 DOLLAR
1886. Martha Washington at l. 4 seal varieties; 4 sign. varieties.

	VG	VF	UNC
	175.00	400.00	800.00

322 2 DOLLARS
1886. Portr. Gen. Hancock at l. 2 seal varieties; 3 sign. varieties.

	VG	VF	UNC
	350.00	775.00	1200.

323 5 DOLLARS
1886. Grant at r. Illustration of 5 silver dollars on back. 4 seal varieties; 4 sign. varieties.

	VG	VF	UNC
	400.00	1300.	2750.

324 10 DOLLARS
1886. Hendricks at ctr. *UNITED STATES* w/text below at ctr. on back. 3 seal varieties; 4 sign. varieties.

	VG	VF	UNC
	450.00	900.00	2000.

325 20 DOLLARS
1886. Portr. Manning at ctr. *20* in 4 corners on back. 3 seal varieties; 3 sign. varieties.

	VG	VF	UNC
	2350.	6600.	11,000.

SERIES OF 1891

326	1 DOLLAR	VG	VF	UNC
	1891. Like #321 but different back. 2 sign. varieties.	130.00	325.00	700.00

327	2 DOLLARS	VG	VF	UNC
	1891. Portr. Windom at ctr. 2 sign. varieties.	240.00	800.00	1800.

328	5 DOLLARS	VG	VF	UNC
	1891. Grant at r. Like #323 but w/o illustration on back. 2 sign. varieties.	300.00	850.00	3000.

329	10 DOLLARS	VG	VF	UNC
	1891. Hendricks at ctr. UNITED STATES at ctr. on back. Red seal. 4 sign. varieties.	275.00	800.00	2150.

330	20 DOLLARS	VG	VF	UNC
	1891. Manning at ctr. XX at upper l. and lower r. on back. Red seal. 4 sign. varieties.	525.00	1250.	3000.
331	20 DOLLARS			
	1891. Like #330 but blue seal and lg. blue XX at l. 2 sign. varieties.	525.00	1250.	3000.

332	50 DOLLARS	VG	VF	UNC
	1891. Like #331 but FIFTY at upper l. Red seal.	1050.	2600.	7150.
332A	50 DOLLARS			
	1891. Like #332 but blue seal.	1100.	2750.	8000.

333	100 DOLLARS	VG	VF	UNC
	1891. Portr. Monroe at l. ctr., ONE HUNDRED around C at lower r. 2 sign. varieties.	4550.	7800.	14,000.
334	1000 DOLLARS			
	1891. Woman w/shield and sword at l., Marcy at r.	—	Unique	—

SERIES OF 1896
Educational Series

335	1 DOLLAR	VG	VF	UNC
	1896. Reclining woman w/youth at l. Border design w/names of famous Americans in wreaths. 2 sign. varieties.	160.00	400.00	750.00

336	**2 DOLLARS**	**VG**	**VF**	**UNC**
	1896. Group of 3 women w/2 children at ctr. 2 sign. varieties.	350.00	1075.	2150.

339	**2 DOLLARS**	**VG**	**VF**	**UNC**
	1899. Washington between allegorical figures of Commerce and Agriculture at ctr. 10 sign. varieties.	75.00	190.00	450.00

340	**5 DOLLARS**	**VG**	**VF**	**UNC**
	1899. Sioux Indian Chief Onepapa w/feather headdress at ctr. 11 sign. varieties.	165.00	425.00	900.00

SERIES OF 1908

341	**10 DOLLARS**	**VG**	**VF**	**UNC**
	1908. Like #329 but blue seal. Lg. blue X at l. 3 sign. varieties.	280.00	800.00	1700.

337	**5 DOLLARS**	**VG**	**VF**	**UNC**
	1896. Allegorical figures w/Electricity at ctr. 3 sign. varieties.	600.00	1800.	4200.

SERIES OF 1923

342	**1 DOLLAR**	**VG**	**VF**	**UNC**
	1923. Washington at ctr. 3 sign. varieties.	22.00	30.00	55.00

SERIES OF 1899

338	**1 DOLLAR**	**VG**	**VF**	**UNC**
	1899. Eagle w/flag over portr. of Lincoln at l. and portr. of Grant at ctr. r.			
a.	Series of 1899 above r. serial #.	40.00	70.00	175.00
b.	Series of 1899 below r. serial #. 3 sign. varieties.	35.00	65.00	175.00
c.	Series of 1899 vertical at r. 7 sign. varieties.	30.00	55.00	160.00

343   5 DOLLARS
1923. Lincoln at ctr.

	VG	VF	UNC
	190.00	450.00	1100.

TREASURY OR COIN NOTES

SERIES OF 1890

344   1 DOLLAR
1890. Stanton at upper l. ctr. Lg. *ONE* at ctr. on back. 2 seal varieties; 2 sign. varieties.

	VG	VF	UNC
	350.00	850.00	1450.

345   2 DOLLARS
1890. Gen. McPherson at r. Lg. *TWO* at ctr. on back. 2 seal varieties; 2 sign. varieties.

	VG	VF	UNC
	475.00	1650.	3900.

346   5 DOLLARS
1890. Portr. Gen. Thomas at ctr. Lg. *FIVE* at ctr. on back. 2 varieties of seals; 2 sign. varieties.

	VG	VF	UNC
	300.00	1050.	2150.

347   10 DOLLARS
1890. Gen. Sheridan at ctr. Lg. *TEN* at ctr. on back. 2 seal varieties; 2 sign. varieties.

	VG	VF	UNC
	590.00	1325.	3000.

348   20 DOLLARS
1890. Marshall at l. Lg. *TWENTY* at ctr. on back. 2 seal varieties; 2 sign. varieties.

	VG	VF	UNC
	2000.	5200.	11,000.

349   100 DOLLARS
1890. Commodore Farragut at r. Lg. *100* at ctr. on back.

	VG	VF	UNC
	12,000.	22,500.	—

---

350   1000 DOLLARS
1890. Gen. Meade at l. Lg. *1000* at ctr. on back. 2 seal varieties; 2 sign. varieties.

	VG	VF	UNC
	—	Rare	—

SERIES OF 1891

351   1 DOLLAR
1891. Stanton at l. Text at ctr. below sm. *ONE* on back. 3 sign. varieties.

	VG	VF	UNC
	80.00	170.00	425.00

352   2 DOLLARS
1891. Gen. McPherson at r. Ornament at ctr. on back. 3 sign. varieties.

	VG	VF	UNC
	195.00	475.00	925.00

353   5 DOLLARS
1891. Gen. Thomas at ctr. Ornament w/*Five Dollars* inside at ctr. on back. 4 sign. varieties.

	VG	VF	UNC
	190.00	400.00	700.00

354   10 DOLLARS
1891. Gen. Sheridan at ctr. Text at ctr. on back. 3 sign. varieties.

	VG	VF	UNC
	360.00	700.00	1650.

355   20 DOLLARS
1891. Marshall at l. Text at ctr. on back. 2 sign. varieties.

	VG	VF	UNC
	2750.	6750.	14,000.

356   50 DOLLARS
1891. Portr. Seward at ctr.

	VG	VF	UNC
	10,500.	22,500.	—

357   100 DOLLARS
1891. Commodore Farragut at r. Text at ctr. on back.

	VG	VF	UNC
	22,500.	35,000.	—

358   1000 DOLLARS
1891. Gen. Meade at l. Text at ctr. on back. 2 sign. varieties.

	VG	VF	UNC
	—	Rare	—

FEDERAL RESERVE NOTES

Imprinted letter, # and place name (in seal at l.) of 1 of the 12 Federal Reserve Banks:

1-A: Boston	7-G: Chicago
2-B: New York	8-H: St. Louis
3-C: Philadelphia	9-I: Minneapolis
4-D: Cleveland	10-J: Kansas City
5-E: Richmond	11-K: Dallas
6-F: Atlanta	12-L: San Francisco

NOTE: Market valuations are for the most common types.

SERIES OF 1914

359   5 DOLLARS
1914. Lincoln at ctr.

	VG	VF	UNC
a. Red seal.	40.00	100.00	350.00
b. Blue seal. 4 sign. varieties.	30.00	40.00	80.00

		VG	VF	UNC
360	**10 DOLLARS**			
	1914. Jackson at ctr.			
	a. Red seal.	50.00	140.00	500.00
	b. Blue seal. 4 sign. varieties.	30.00	45.00	100.00

		VG	VF	UNC
361	**20 DOLLARS**			
	1914. Portr. Cleveland at ctr.			
	a. Red seal.	80.00	390.00	1125.
	b. Blue seal. 4 sign. varieties.	45.00	60.00	150.00

		VG	VF	UNC
362	**50 DOLLARS**			
	1914. Grant at ctr.			
	a. Red seal.	325.00	750.00	2600.
	b. Blue seal. 4 sign. varieties.	115.00	205.00	975.00

		VG	VF	UNC
363	**100 DOLLARS**			
	1914. Franklin at ctr.			
	a. Red seal.	475.00	975.00	2850.
	b. Blue seal. 4 sign. varieties.	225.00	360.00	750.00

SERIES OF 1918

		VG	VF	UNC
364	**500 DOLLARS**			
	1918. Marshall at ctr.	—	Rare	—
365	**1000 DOLLARS**			
	1918. Hamilton at ctr.	—	Rare	—

		VG	VF	UNC
366	**5000 DOLLARS**			
	1918. Madison at ctr.	—	Rare	—
367	**10,000 DOLLARS**			
	1918. Chase at ctr.	—	Rare	—

NATIONAL CURRENCY

FEDERAL RESERVE BANK NOTES

Blue Treasury seal. Each note imprinted w/letter, # and place name of 1 of the 12 Federal Reserve Banks:

A-1: Boston	G-7: Chicago
B-2: New York	H-8: St. Louis
C-3: Philadelphia	I-9: Minneapolis
D-4: Cleveland	J-10: Kansas City
E-5: Richmond	K-11: Dallas
F-6: Atlanta	L-12: San Francisco

Sign. varieties. Market valuations are for the most common types.

SERIES OF 1915

		VG	VF	UNC
368	**5 DOLLARS**			
	1915. Lincoln at l. (only: F; G; J; K; L).	65.00	150.00	525.00
369	**10 DOLLARS**			
	1915. Jackson at l. (only: F; G; J; K).	225.00	550.00	1700.
370	**20 DOLLARS**			
	1915. Cleveland at l. (only: F; G; J; K).	425.00	900.00	2500.

SERIES OF 1918

		VG	VF	UNC
371	**1 DOLLAR**			
	1918. Portr. Washington at l. Eagle and flag at ctr. on back.	38.00	60.00	150.00

		VG	VF	UNC
372	**2 DOLLARS**			
	1918. Jefferson at l. Battleship at ctr. on back.	145.00	290.00	525.00
373	**5 DOLLARS**			
	1918. Lincoln at l. (all except E).	50.00	100.00	350.00

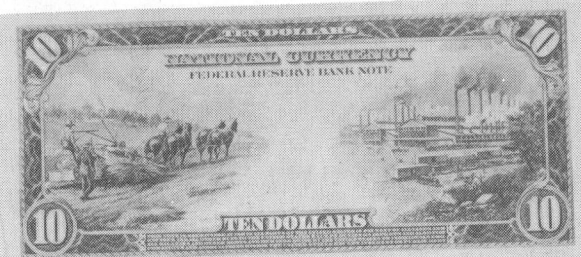

		VG	VF	UNC
374	**10 DOLLARS**			
	1918. Jackson at l. (only: B; F; G; H).	225.00	550.00	1700.
375	**20 DOLLARS**			
	1918. Cleveland at l. (only: F; H).	450.00	900.00	2500.

376	50 DOLLARS	VG	VF	UNC
	1918. Grant at l. (only: H).	2850.	4800.	9750.

United States Notes - Small Size

Red Treasury seal.

PORTRAITS

1 Dollar: George Washington	100 Dollars: Benjamin Franklin
2 Dollars: Thomas Jefferson	500 Dollars: William McKinley
5 Dollars: Abraham Lincoln	1000 Dollars: Grover Cleveland
10 Dollars: Alexander Hamilton	5000 Dollars: James Madison
20 Dollars: Andrew Jackson	10,000 Dollars: Salmon P. Chase
50 Dollars: U.S. Grant	100,000 Dollars: Woodrow Wilson

SERIES OF 1928

377	1 DOLLAR	VG	VF	UNC
	1928.	17.00	33.00	65.00
378	2 DOLLARS	VG	VF	UNC
	1928.	10.00	15.00	30.00
a.	1928A.	15.00	40.00	150.00
b.	1928B.	75.00	100.00	500.00
c.	1928C.	10.00	15.00	50.00
d.	1928D.	4.00	7.50	15.00
e.	1928E.	6.00	15.00	40.00
f.	1928F.	4.50	6.50	18.00
g.	1928G.	4.00	6.00	12.50
379	5 DOLLARS	VG	VF	UNC
	1928.	6.00	10.00	30.00
a.	1928A.	12.00	13.00	50.00
b.	1928B.	8.00	9.00	20.00
c.	1928C.	8.00	9.00	20.00
d.	1928D.	10.00	20.00	100.00
e.	1928E.	7.00	9.50	20.00
f.	1928F.	7.00	8.50	20.00

SERIES OF 1953

380	2 DOLLARS	VG	VF	UNC
	1953.	3.25	4.50	7.50
a.	1953A.	3.25	4.50	6.00
b.	1953B.	3.25	4.50	5.00
c.	1953C.	3.25	4.50	5.00
381	5 DOLLARS			
	1953.	7.00	8.50	15.00
a.	1953A.	6.50	8.00	12.50
b.	1953B.	6.50	7.50	12.50
c.	1953C.	6.50	8.00	12.50

National Currency

Federal Reserve Bank Notes

Brown Treasury seal.

Imprinted letter and name of 1 of the 12 Federal Reserve Banks.

1-A: Boston	7-G: Chicago
2-B: New York	8-H: St. Louis
3-C: Philadelphia	9-I: Minneapolis
4-D: Cleveland	10-J: Kansas City
5-E: Richmond	11-K: Dallas
6-F: Atlanta	12-L: San Fransisco

Market valuations are for the most common types of each denomination.

SERIES OF 1929

395	5 DOLLARS	VG	VF	UNC
	1929. (A-D; F-L).	FV	12.00	65.00

396	10 DOLLARS	VG	VF	UNC
	1929. (A-L).	FV	20.00	85.00
397	20 DOLLARS			
	1929. (A-L).	FV	35.00	60.00
398	50 DOLLARS			
	1929. (B; D; G; I-L).	FV	55.00	125.00
399	100 DOLLARS			
	1929. (B; D-E; G; I-K).	FV	125.00	200.00

Gold Certificates - Small Size

Gold Treasury seal.

SERIES OF 1928

400	10 DOLLARS	VG	VF	UNC
	1928.	25.00	40.00	200.00
a.	1928A. (Not issued).			

401	20 DOLLARS	VG	VF	UNC
	1928.	35.00	50.00	200.00
a.	1928A. (Not issued).		—	

402	50 DOLLARS	VG	VF	UNC
	1928.	100.00	175.00	550.00

403	**100 DOLLARS**	**VG**	**VF**	**UNC**
	1928.	160.00	250.00	875.00
	a. 1928A. (Not issued).	—	—	—

404	**500 DOLLARS**	**VG**	**VF**	**UNC**
	1928.	1000.	1500.	3600.
405	**1000 DOLLARS**			
	1928.	1800.	3000.	7000.
406	**5000 DOLLARS**			
	1928.	15,000.	20,000.	30,000.
407	**10,000 DOLLARS**			
	1928.	—	Rare	—

SERIES OF 1934

Issued for internal use within the Federal Reserve System. None were released for circulation.

		VG	**VF**	**UNC**
408	**100 DOLLARS**	—	—	—
	1934. Franklin.			
409	**1000 DOLLARS**	—	—	—
	1934. Cleveland.			
410	**10,000 DOLLARS**	—	—	—
	1934. Chase.			
411	**100,000 DOLLARS**	—	—	—
	1934. Wilson.			

SILVER CERTIFICATES - SMALL SIZE

Blue Treasury seal.

SERIES OF 1928

		VG	**VF**	**UNC**
412	**1 DOLLAR**	6.00	10.00	20.00
	1928. Lg. *ONE* across ctr. on back.	6.00	10.00	20.00
	a. 1928A.	6.00	10.00	20.00
	b. 1928B.	50.00	110.00	400.00
	c. 1928C.	30.00	80.00	275.00
	d. 1928D.	160.00	400.00	1075.
	e. 1928E.			

SERIES OF 1933

		VG	**VF**	**UNC**
413	**10 DOLLARS**	1200.	2250.	5000.
	1933.			
	a. 1933A. (No example known in collectors' hands).			

SERIES OF 1934

		VG	**VF**	**UNC**
414	**1 DOLLAR**	8.00	12.50	32.50
	1934.			
414A	**5 DOLLARS**	FV	8.00	20.00
	1934.	FV	8.00	15.00
	a. 1934A.	FV	10.00	35.00
	b. 1934B.	FV	8.00	18.00
	c. 1934C.	FV	8.00	14.00
	d. 1934D.			
414AY	**5 DOLLARS**	10.00	13.00	75.00
	1934A. Yellow seal. (Issued for military use in North Africa).			
415	**10 DOLLARS**	FV	18.00	40.00
	1934.	FV	18.00	45.00
	a. 1934A.	40.00	80.00	1000.
	b. 1934B.	FV	14.00	40.00
	c. 1934C.	FV	14.00	40.00
	d. 1934D.			
415Y	**10 DOLLARS**	700.00	1000.	5500.
	1934. Yellow seal. (Issued for military use in North Africa).	15.00	20.00	75.00
	a. 1934A.			

SERIES OF 1935

		VG	**VF**	**UNC**
416	**1 DOLLAR**	3.00	4.00	10.00
	1935.	FV	FV	4.00
	a. 1935A.			

416AR	**1 DOLLAR**	**VG**	**VF**	**UNC**
	1935A. Experimental issue w/red *R* at lower r.	14.00	35.00	175.00
416AS	**1 DOLLAR**	12.00	30.00	150.00
	1935A. Experimental issue w/red *S* at lower r.	FV	3.00	5.50
	b. 1935B.	FV	2.00	5.00
	c. 1935C.			

416AY	**1 DOLLAR**	**VG**	**VF**	**UNC**
	1935A. Yellow seal. (Issued for military use in North Africa).	8.50	13.50	40.00
416D1	**1 DOLLAR**	FV	FV	4.00
	1935D. Type I, wide margin.			
416D2	**1 DOLLAR**	FV	FV	5.00
	1935D. Type II, narrow design.	FV	FV	3.00
	e. 1935E.	FV	FV	3.50
	f. 1935F.			
416NM	**1 DOLLAR**	FV	FV	3.50
	1935G. W/o motto.			
416WM1	**1 DOLLAR**	FV	FV	15.00
	1935G. Motto: *In God We Trust* added on back.	FV	FV	5.00
	h. 1935H.			

SERIES OF 1953

		VG	**VF**	**UNC**
417	**5 DOLLARS**	FV	FV	12.50
	1953.	FV	FV	12.50
	a. 1953A.	FV	FV	12.50
	b. 1953B.			
418	**10 DOLLARS**	12.00	15.00	45.00
	1953.	12.00	15.00	80.00
	a. 1953A.	12.00	20.00	50.00
	b. 1953B.			

SERIES OF 1957

NOTE: For a full listing of all notes w/ovpt: *HAWAII* see Hawaii, #36-41.

		VG	**VF**	**UNC**
419	**1 DOLLAR**	FV	FV	2.50
	1957.	FV	FV	2.50
	a. 1957A.	FV	FV	2.50
	b. 1957B.			

FEDERAL RESERVE NOTES - SMALL SIZE

Green Treasury seal.

Imprinted #, letter and name (in seal at l.) of 1 of the 12 Federal Reserve Banks:

A-1: Boston	**G-7:** Chicago
B-2: New York	**H-8:** St. Louis
C-3: Philadelphia	**I-9:** Minneapolis
D-4: Cleveland	**J-10:** Kansas City
E-5: Richmond	**K-11:** Dallas
F-6: Atlanta	**L-12:** San Fransisco

SERIES OF 1928

		VG	**VF**	**UNC**
420	**5 DOLLARS**	FV	12.50	40.00
	1928. (A-L).	FV	12.50	40.00
	a. 1928A. (A-L).	FV	10.00	40.00
	b. 1928B. (A-L).	—	200.00	575.00
	c. 1928C. (A-L).	—	350.00	1000.
	d. 1928D. (F).			
421	**10 DOLLARS**	FV	FV	75.00
	1928. (A-L).	FV	FV	40.00
	a. 1928A. (A-L).	FV	FV	30.00
	b. 1928B. (A-L).	FV	30.00	90.00
	c. 1928C. (B-G).			

422	20 DOLLARS	VG	VF	UNC
	1928. (A-L).	FV	FV	50.00
a.	1928A. (A-H; J-K).	FV	FV	75.00
b.	1928B. (A-L).	FV	FV	45.00
c.	1928C. (G; L).	FV	125.00	500.00
423	50 DOLLARS			
	1928. (A-L).	FV	FV	150.00
a.	1928A. (A-L).	FV	FV	150.00
424	100 DOLLARS			
	1928. (A-L).	FV	FV	200.00
a.	1928A. (A-L).	FV	FV	200.00
425	500 DOLLARS			
	1928. (A-L).	FV	600.00	750.00
426	1000 DOLLARS			
	1928. (A-L).	FV	1150.	1400.
427	5000 DOLLARS			
	1928. (A-B; D-G; J-L).	FV	10,000.	15,000.
428	10,000 DOLLARS			
	1928. (A-B; D-L).	FV	18,000.	22,500.

SERIES OF 1934

429D	5 DOLLARS	VG	VF	UNC
	1934. Dk. green seal. (A-L).	FV	FV	20.00
a.	1934A. (A-H; L).	FV	FV	20.00
b.	1934B. (A-J; L).	FV	FV	30.00
c.	1934C. (A-L).	FV	FV	30.00
d.	1934D. (A-L).	FV	FV	30.00
429L	5 DOLLARS			
	1934. Lt. green seal.	FV	FV	20.00
430D	10 DOLLARS			
	1934. Dk. green seal. (A-L).	FV	FV	27.50
a.	1934A. (A-L).	FV	FV	25.00
b.	1934B. (A-L).	FV	FV	25.00
c.	1934C. (A-L).	FV	FV	20.00
d.	1934D. (A-L).	FV	FV	25.00
430L	10 DOLLARS			
	1934. Lt. green seal.	FV	FV	27.50
431D	20 DOLLARS			
	1934. Dk. green seal. (A-L).	FV	FV	40.00
a.	1934A. (A-L).	FV	FV	40.00
b.	1934B. (A-L).	FV	FV	40.00
c.	1934C. (A-L).	FV	FV	40.00
d.	1934D. (A-L).	FV	FV	35.00
431L	20 DOLLARS			
	1934. Lt. green seal.	FV	FV	40.00
432D	50 DOLLARS			
	1934. Dk. green seal. (A-L).	FV	FV	100.00
a.	1934A. (A-B; D-L).	FV	FV	100.00
b.	1934B. (C-L).	FV	FV	125.00
c.	1934C. (A-K).	FV	FV	85.00
d.	1934D. (A-C; E-G; K).	FV	FV	100.00
432L	50 DOLLARS			
	1934. Lt. green seal.	FV	FV	100.00
433D	100 DOLLARS			
	1934. Dk. green seal. (A-L).	FV	FV	175.00
a.	1934A. (A-L).	FV	FV	175.00
b.	1934B. (A; C-K).	FV	FV	175.00
c.	1934C. (A-D; F-L).	FV	FV	160.00
d.	1934D. (B-C; F-H, K).	FV	FV	175.00
433L	100 DOLLARS			
	1934. Lt. green seal.	FV	FV	175.00
434	500 DOLLARS			
	1934. (A-L).	FV	575.00	700.00
a.	1934A. (B-E; G-L).	FV	550.00	700.00
b.	1934B. (F).	FV	1500.	3500.
c.	1934C. (A-B).	FV	1250.	3500.
435	1000 DOLLARS			
	1934. (A-L).	FV	1075.	1350.
a.	1934A. (A-J; L).	FV	1075.	1350.
b.	1934C. (A-B).	FV	2000.	3750.
436	5000 DOLLARS			
	1934. (A-H; J-L).	FV	8500.	12,500.
a.	1934A. (H).	FV	9500.	14,000.
b.	1934B. (A-B).	FV	9500.	14,000.

437	10,000 DOLLARS	VG	VF	UNC
	1934. (A-H; J-L).	FV	16,000.	18,000.
a.	1934A. (G).	FV	17,000.	19,000.
b.	1934B. (B).	FV	22,000.	25,000.

SERIES OF 1950

438	5 DOLLARS	VG	VF	UNC
	1950. (A-L).	FV	FV	30.00
a.	1950A. (A-L).	FV	FV	16.00
b.	1950B. (A-L).	FV	FV	15.00
c.	1950C. (A-L).	FV	FV	15.00
d.	1950D. (A-L).	FV	FV	15.00
e.	1950E. (B; G; L).	FV	FV	20.00
439	10 DOLLARS			
	1950. (A-L).	FV	FV	25.00
a.	1950A. (A-L).	FV	FV	25.00
b.	1950B. (A-L).	FV	FV	25.00
c.	1950C. (A-L).	FV	FV	25.00
d.	1950D. (A-H; J-L).	FV	FV	25.00
e.	1950E. (B; G; L).	FV	FV	20.00
440	20 DOLLARS			
	1950. (A-L).	FV	FV	50.00
a.	1950A. (A-L).	FV	FV	40.00
b.	1950B. (A-L).	FV	FV	40.00
c.	1950C. (A-L).	FV	FV	40.00
d.	1950D. (A-L).	FV	FV	40.00
e.	1950E. (B; G; L).	FV	FV	60.00
441	50 DOLLARS			
	1950. (A-L).	FV	FV	90.00
a.	1950A. (A-H; J-L).	FV	FV	90.00
b.	1950B. (A-E; G-H; J-L).	FV	FV	85.00
c.	1950C. (A-E; G-L).	FV	FV	85.00
d.	1950D. (A-L).	FV	FV	80.00
e.	1950E. (B; G; L).	FV	FV	125.00
442	100 DOLLARS			
	1950. (A-L).	FV	FV	140.00
a.	1950A. (A-L).	FV	FV	130.00
b.	1950B. (A-L).	FV	FV	130.00
c.	1950C. (A-L).	FV	FV	135.00
d.	1950D. (A-L).	FV	FV	135.00
e.	1950E. (B; G; L).	FV	FV	135.00

MILITARY PAYMENT CERTIFICATES

Issued after World War II for use by American military and certain civilian personnel in 21 various occupied areas or military bases.

REPLACEMENT NOTES

Can be identified by serial # which will have a prefix letter but no suffix letter. All replacement notes are much scarcer than regular issues which have prefix and suffix letters.

SERIES 461

16.9.1946 to 10.3.1947.
#M1-M7 blue unpt., w/o pictorial designs.

M1	5 CENTS	VG	VF	UNC
	ND (1946).	.75	6.00	60.00
M2	10 CENTS			
	ND (1946). Like #M1.	.75	6.00	60.00
M3	25 CENTS			
	ND (1946). Like #M1.	1.25	10.00	95.00
M4	50 CENTS			
	ND (1946). Like #M1.	2.00	15.00	125.00

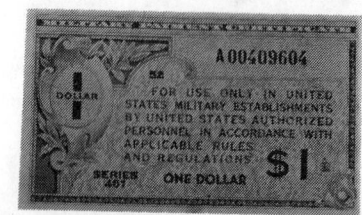

		VG	VF	UNC
M5 1 DOLLAR ND (1946).				
M6 5 DOLLARS ND (1946). Like #M7.		1.35 7.00 30.00	7.00	125.00 200.00

	VG	VF	UNC
M7 10 DOLLARS ND (1946).	5.00	25.00	150.00

SERIES 471
10.3.1947 to 22.3.1948.
#M8-M14 red and blue. Design like Series 461.

	VG	VF	UNC
M8 5 CENTS ND (1947).	1.60	9.00	75.00

	VG	VF	UNC
M9 10 CENTS ND (1947).	1.60	12.00	80.00
M10 25 CENTS ND (1947).	2.50	15.00	150.00
M11 50 CENTS ND (1947).	4.00	20.00	175.00

	VG	VF	UNC
M12 1 DOLLAR ND (1947).	4.00	25.00	200.00

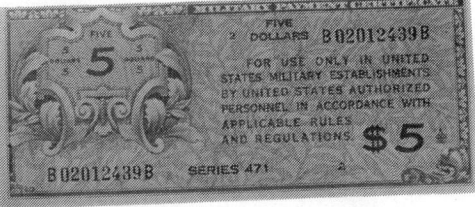

	VG	VF	UNC
M13 5 DOLLARS ND (1947).	200.00	600.00	5500.
M14 10 DOLLARS ND (1947).	37.50	200.00	2100.

SERIES 472
22.3.1948 to 20.6.1951.
#M15-M21 blue unpt. and seal of the United States at ctr.

	VG	VF	UNC
M15 5 CENTS ND (1948).	.15	.75	5.00

		VG	VF	UNC
M16 10 CENTS ND (1948). Like #M15.		.75	5.00	35.00
M17 25 CENTS ND (1948). Like #M15.		1.60	8.00	95.00
M18 50 CENTS ND (1948). Like #M15.		3.50	18.00	150.00

	VG	VF	UNC
M19 1 DOLLAR ND (1948).	3.50	15.00	165.00

	VG	VF	UNC
M20 5 DOLLARS ND (1948).	20.00	180.00	1900.
M21 10 DOLLARS ND (1948). Like #M20.	12.00	160.00	1100.

SERIES 481
20.6.1951 to 25.5.1954.
#M22-M28 lt. blue and brown unpt.
NOTE: #M26 exists w/position # at r. or l; the l. variety is worth 10 percent more.

	VG	VF	UNC
M22 5 CENTS ND (1951). Seated woman w/compasses and sphere at l.	.40	4.00	28.00

	VG	VF	UNC
M23 10 CENTS ND (1951). Like #M22.	.40	3.00	35.00
M24 25 CENTS ND (1951). Like #M22.	3.25	18.00	60.00
M25 50 CENTS ND (1951). Like #M22.	5.00	18.00	120.00

	VG	VF	UNC
M26 1 DOLLAR ND (1951). Women at upper l. and r.	8.00	55.00	220.00

M27 5 DOLLARS
ND (1951). Reclining youth w/sledge hammer at l.

	VG	VF	UNC
	20.00	140.00	1000.

M28 10 DOLLARS
ND (1951). Like #M27.

	5.00	50.00	850.00

SERIES 521
25.5.1954 to 27.5.1958.

M29 5 CENTS
ND (1954). Blue on green and yellow unpt. Woman w/helmet at l.

	VG	VF	UNC
	.40	6.00	25.00

M30 10 CENTS
ND (1954). Lilac on green and blue unpt. Like #M29.

	.40	6.00	30.00

M31 25 CENTS
ND (1954). Brown on green unpt. Like #M29.

	2.50	15.00	70.00

M32 50 CENTS
ND (1954). Green on lilac and blue unpt. Like #M29.

	3.25	25.00	125.00

M33 1 DOLLAR
ND (1954). Brown. Woman w/Liberty Cap at l.

	VG	VF	UNC
	3.25	18.00	110.00

M34 5 DOLLARS
ND (1954). Blue. Woman w/flower basket at ctr.

	VG	VF	UNC
	85.00	400.00	2500.

M35 10 DOLLARS
ND (1954). Brown-violet. Woman w/wreath at r.

	VG	VF	UNC
	40.00	250.00	1900.

SERIES 541
27.5.1958 to 26.5.1961.

M36 5 CENTS
ND (1958). Violet on green and yellow-green unpt. Woman w/wreath at l.

	VG	VF	UNC
	.40	1.50	6.00

M37 10 CENTS
ND (1958). Green on orange unpt. Like #M36.

	.80	3.00	15.00

M38 25 CENTS
ND (1958). Blue on lilac unpt. Like #M36.

	1.25	6.00	35.00

M39 50 CENTS
ND (1958). Brown on green and yellow unpt. Like #M36.

	1.25	10.00	80.00

M40 1 DOLLAR
ND (1958). Blue. Woman w/cap at ctr.

	VG	VF	UNC
	4.00	28.00	200.00

M41 5 DOLLARS
ND (1958). Lilac. Woman w/wreath at l.

	VG	VF	UNC
	225.00	700.00	4200.

M42 10 DOLLARS
ND (1958). Brown. Woman at ctr.

	VG	VF	UNC
	125.00	400.00	2500.

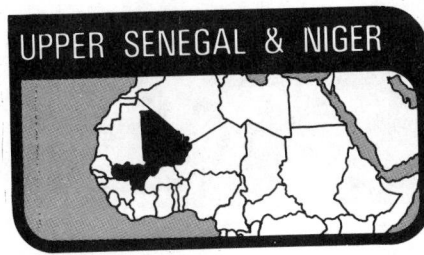

UPPER SENEGAL & NIGER

Once a part of the ancient Malinke Kingdom that controlled the area from the 11th to the 17th centuries. The upper course of the Senegal River runs through the western part of the area. The middle course of the Niger River has 1,000 miles of navigable waters within these boundaries. Legendary Tombouctou (Timbuktu) is a port on the Niger in the center of the country.

French dominance in the area occurred in the 1890s. The territories of Senegambia and Niger were formed into the colony of Upper Senegal and Niger in 1904. Following World War I the name of the area was changed to French Sudan.

RULERS:
French to 1960

MONETARY SYSTEM:
1 Franc = 100 Centimes

FRENCH INFLUENCE

GOUVERNEMENT GÉNÉRALDE L'AFRIQUE OCCIDENTALE FRANÇAISE (A.O.F.)

HAUT-SENEGAL-NIGER BRANCH

LAW OF 11.2.1917

		VG	VF	UNC
1	**0.50 FRANC** *L.1917.* Dk. brown on lt. brown. Reverse of 50 Centimes coin at l., obverse at r.	125.00	275.00	550.00
2	**1 FRANC** *L.1917.*		Reported Not Confirmed	
3	**2 FRANCS** *L.1917.*		Reported Not Confirmed	

URUGUAY

The Oriental Republic of Uruguay (so called because of its location on the east bank of the Uruguay River) is situated on the Atlantic coast of South America between Argentina and Brazil. This most advanced of South American countries has an area of 68,536 sq. mi. (176,220 sq. km.) and a population of 3.12 million. Capital: Montevideo. Uruguay's chief economic asset is its rich, rolling grassy plains. Meat, wool, hides and skins are exported.

Uruguay was discovered in 1516 by Juan Diaz de Solis, a Spaniard, but settled by the Portuguese who founded Colonia in 1680. Spain contested Portuguese possession and, after a long struggle, gained control of the country in 1778. During the general South American struggle for independence, Uruguay's first attempt was led by gaucho soldier José Gervasio Artigas leading the Banda Oriental which was quelled by Spanish and Portuguese forces in 1811. The armistice was soon broken and Argentine forces from Buenos Aires cast off the Spanish bond in the Plata region in 1814, only to be reconquered by the Portuguese from Brazil in the struggle of 1816-20. Revolt flared anew in 1825 and independence was reasserted in 1828 with the help of Argentina. The Uruguayan Republic was established in 1830.

MONETARY SYSTEM:
1 Patacón = 960 Reis
1 Peso = 8 Reales to 1860
1 Peso = 100 Centésimos, 1860-1975
1 Doblon = 10 Pesos 1860-1875
1 Nuevo Peso = 1000 Old Pesos, 1975-1993
1 Peso Uruguayo = 1000 Nuevos Pesos, 1993-

NOTE: Certain listings encompassing issues circulated by various bank and regional authorities are contained in Volume 1.

REPUBLIC

POLIZA DE DEUDA PUBLIC

PUBLIC DEBT DRAFTS

LEY DE 29 APRIL 1835

#A13-A17 black. National symbols of hill, scale, horse and bull in 4 corners, Montevideo Bay between cargo at l. and r. along bottom. Dated between 3-14.8.1835.

			GOOD	FINE	XF
A13	**400 PESOS** Aug. 1835.		—	—	—

			GOOD	FINE	XF
A14	**500 PESOS** Aug. 1835. a. Handwritten denomination. b. Printed denomination.		— 	— 	—
A16	**2000 PESOS** Aug. 1835.		—	—	—
A17	**5000 PESOS** Aug. 1835.		—	—	—

BANCO NACIONAL

LEY DE 23 DE JUNIO DE 1862

#A87-A98 printer: W&S. Sign. varieties.

Branch Ovpt.

#A87-A98 issues were ovpt. or perforated for the branches of:

Artigas	Florida	Rosario
Canelones	Maldonado	Salto
Carmelo	Minas	San Jose
Cerro Largo	Paysandu	Soriano
Colonia	Rio Negro	Tacuarembo
Durazno	Rivera	Treinta y Tres
Flores	Rocha	

A87	**10 CENTÉSIMOS**	GOOD	FINE	XF
	25.8.1887. Black on lt. blue unpt. Arms at l., cattle stampede at ctr. Back blue; seated woman at ctr.			
	a. Issued note w/o branch office perforation or ovpt.	4.00	15.00	40.00
	b. Cancelled w/perforation: *PAGADO 25.8.96.*	3.00	12.50	30.00
	c. Issued or cancelled w/branch office perforation or ovpt.	5.00	20.00	50.00

A92	**5 PESOS**	GOOD	FINE	XF
	25.8.1887. Black on gold and brown unpt. Arms at upper l., man at ctr. Back brown; bldgs. and street scene at ctr.			
	a. Issued note w/o branch office perforation or ovpt.	10.00	30.00	75.00
	b. Cancelled w/perforation: *PAGADO 25.8.96.*	6.00	20.00	50.00
	c. Issued or cancelled w/branch office perforation or ovpt.	15.00	40.00	90.00

A93	**10 PESOS**			
	25.8.1887. Black on green and orange unpt. Back orange.			
	a. Issued note w/o branch office perforation or ovpt.	15.00	40.00	90.00
	b. Cancelled w/perforation: *PAGADO 25.8.96.*	10.00	30.00	75.00
	c. Issued or cancelled w/branch office perforation or ovpt.	17.50	45.00	100.00

A88	**20 CENTÉSIMOS**	GOOD	FINE	XF
	25.8.1887. Black on pink unpt. Mercury seated at l., arms at r. Back green.			
	a. Issued note w/o branch office perforation or ovpt.	4.00	15.00	40.00
	b. Cancelled w/perforation: *PAGADO 25.8.96.*	3.00	12.50	30.00
	c. Issued or cancelled w/branch office perforation or ovpt.	6.00	20.00	50.00

A94	**20 PESOS**	GOOD	FINE	XF
	25.8.1887. Black on yellow and tan unpt. Man at l., arms at top l. ctr., bldg. at lower r. Back dk. blue; Liberty head at ctr.			
	a. Issued note w/o branch office perforation or ovpt.	15.00	40.00	90.00
	b. Cancelled w/perforation: *PAGADO 25.8.96.*	10.00	30.00	75.00
	c. Issued or cancelled w/branch office perforation or ovpt.	20.00	50.00	120.00

A89	**50 CENTÉSIMOS**	GOOD	FINE	XF
	25.8.1887. Black on yellow unpt. Arms at l., laureate woman's head at ctr. Back brown.			
	a. Issued note w/o branch office perforation or ovpt.	5.00	20.00	50.00
	b. Cancelled w/perforation: *PAGADO 25.8.96.*	4.00	15.00	40.00
	c. Issued or cancelled w/branch office perforation or ovpt.	6.00	20.00	50.00

A95	**50 PESOS**	GOOD	FINE	XF
	25.8.1887. Black on orange and green unpt. Man at l., church at ctr., arms at r. Back dk. orange; sheep at ctr.			
	a. Issued note w/o branch office perforation or ovpt.	20.00	50.00	120.00
	b. Cancelled w/perforation: *PAGADO 25.8.96.*	10.00	30.00	75.00
	c. Issued or cancelled w/branch office perforation or ovpt.	30.00	75.00	175.00

A90	**1 PESO**	GOOD	FINE	XF
	25.8.1887. Black on green and orange unpt. Arms at l., village at ctr. Back orange; seated woman at ctr.			
	a. Issued note w/o branch office perforation or ovpt.	8.00	25.00	60.00
	b. Cancelled w/perforation: *PAGADO 25.8.96.*	6.00	20.00	50.00
	c. Issued or cancelled w/branch office perforation or ovpt.	10.00	30.00	75.00

A96	**100 PESOS**	GOOD	FINE	XF
	25.8.1887. Black on green and pink unpt. Man at l., arms and cherubs at ctr., train at r. Back brown; woman at ctr.			
	a. Issued note.	40.00	90.00	200.00
	b. Cancelled w/perforation: *PAGADO 25.8.96.*	15.00	40.00	90.00

A97	**200 PESOS**			
	25.8.1887. Black on green and gold unpt. Arms at l., portr. at ctr., bldg. at r. Back green; street scene.			
	a. Issued note.	75.00	175.00	400.00
	b. Cancelled w/perforation: *PAGADO 25.8.96.*	50.00	125.00	275.00

A98	**500 PESOS**			
	25.8.1887. Black on pink unpt. Man at l., arms and cherubs at ctr., map at r. Back brown; group of men w/flag.			
	a. Issued note.			
	b. Cancelled w/perforation: *PAGADO 25.8.96.*	100.00	200.00	400.00

A91	**2 PESOS**	GOOD	FINE	XF
	25.8.1887. Black on rose and pastel blue unpt. Arms at upper l., bank at upper ctr. Back blue; woman at ctr.			
	a. Issued note.	8.00	25.00	60.00
	b. Cancelled w/perforation: *PAGADO 25.8.96.*	6.00	20.00	50.00
	c. Issued or cancelled w/branch office perforation or ovpt.	10.00	30.00	75.00

REPÚBLICA ORIENTAL DEL URUGUAY

RESERVE

COMISIÓN DE EXTINCIÓNDE BILLETES BRANCH

The purpose of this government agency was to redeem valueless or obsolete note issues, thus removing them from circulation.

1875 ISSUE

#A99-A107 w/ovpt: *Comisión de Extinción de Billetes* in rectangular frame on notes of La República Oriental del Uruguay. Printer: ABNC.

		Good	Fine	XF
A99	**20 CENTÉSIMOS** 27.3.1875. Black on brown unpt. Winged cherub at ctr. Uniface.	20.00	50.00	130.00

		Good	Fine	XF
A100	**50 CENTÉSIMOS** 27.3.1875. Black on green unpt., eagle at l; cows at upper ctr. Uniface.	25.00	60.00	150.00

		Good	Fine	XF
A101	**1 PESO** 27.3.1875. Black on pink unpt. Standing Columbia at l., sailor and anchor at ctr. Back reddish purple.	50.00	110.00	250.00

		Good	Fine	XF
A102	**2 PESOS** 27.3.1875. Black on brown unpt. Ostrich at lower l., horses at top ctr.; woman at lower r. Back brown.	75.00	200.00	—

		Good	Fine	XF
A103	**5 PESOS** 27.3.1875. Black on brown unpt. Arms at l., cow and calf at ctr., allegory of agriculture at r. Back brown.	—	—	—

		Good	Fine	XF
A104	**10 PESOS** 27.3.1875. Black on red-brown unpt. Arms at l., cattle at ctr., shepherd w/sheep at r. Back red-brown; steam locomotive at ctr.			

		Good	Fine	XF
A105	**20 PESOS** 27.3.1875. Black on orange unpt. Allegory of commerce at l., farm workers at ctr., arms at r. Steer's head at ctr. on orange back.	—	—	—

		Good	Fine	XF
A106	**50 PESOS** 27.3.1875. Black on red-orange unpt. "Columbia" at l., 3 farmers w/reaper at ctr., arms at r. Allegorical figures at ctr., ships at l. and r. on back.	—	—	—
A107	**100 PESOS** 27.3.1875.	—	—	—

JUNTA DE CRÉDITO PÚBLICO BRANCH

LEY 4.5.1870

#A108-A115 printer: BWC.

		Good	Fine	XF
A108	**20 CENTÉSIMOS** L.1870. Black on orange unpt. on yellow paper. Stallion at l. Uniface.	5.00	25.00	60.00

		Good	Fine	XF
A109	**50 CENTÉSIMOS** L.1870. Black on brown unpt. Cow at l., arms at upper ctr. r. Uniface.			
	a. Purple paper.	10.00	35.00	85.00
	b. White paper.	10.00	35.00	85.00

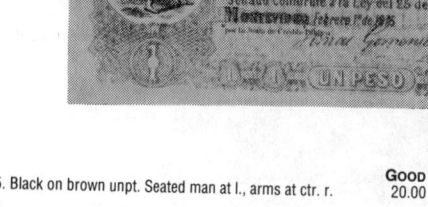

A110 1 PESO
L.1870. Black on dk. green unpt. on green paper. Winged Mercury
seated at l. Uniface.

	GOOD	FINE	XF
a. Dk. green paper.	20.00	60.00	135.00
b. Lt. green paper.	20.00	60.00	135.00

A118 1 PESO
1.2.1875. Black on brown unpt. Seated man at l., arms at ctr. r.

	GOOD	FINE	XF
	20.00	50.00	—

A118A 2 PESOS
1.2.1875. Black on orange unpt., green paper. Horse's head at l., arms
at ctr. Uniface.

A111 5 PESOS
L.1870. Blue. Ewe at l., arms at upper ctr. r. Uniface.

	GOOD	FINE	XF
	35.00	75.00	175.00

A112 10 PESOS
L.1870. Black and brown on orange paper. Woman standing w/sword
and shield at l., arms at upper ctr. r. Uniface.

	GOOD	FINE	XF
	25.00	70.00	160.00

A113 20 PESOS
L.1870. Brown on blue paper. Woman w/sheaf of wheat at l., arms at
upper ctr. r. Uniface.

	GOOD	FINE	XF
	35.00	80.00	185.00

A114 50 PESOS
L.1870. Green on brown paper. Justice at l.

	GOOD	FINE	XF
	—	—	—

A115 100 PESOS
L.1870. Blue on yellow paper. Woman w/horn of plenty.

	GOOD	FINE	XF
	—	—	—

A119 5 PESOS
1.2.1875. Black on green unpt. Boy holding 5 at l.

	GOOD	FINE	XF
	10.00	25.00	50.00

CAUTELA BRANCH

DECRETO 26 ABRIL 1875

A119E 100 PESOS
26.4.1875. Black on orange unpt. 2 women resting. Imprint: Litog. A.
Godel, Montevideo.

	GOOD	FINE	XF
	—	—	—

LEY 23.6.1875
#A119K and A119N printer: Lit. A. Godel, Montevideo.

EMISION NACIONAL BRANCH

LEY 25.1.1875
#A118-A119 imprint: Lit. Hequet y Cohas.

A116 20 CENTÉSIMOS
1.2.1875. Black on pink paper. Liberty standing at l. Uniface. Imprint:
Lit. Pena.

	GOOD	FINE	XF
	10.00	25.00	—

A119K 5 PESOS
1.9.1875. Black on blue unpt. Boy plowing at l., arms at ctr. r. Back
brown.

	GOOD	FINE	XF
	—	—	—

A119N 50 PESOS
1.10.1875. Black. Gaucho playing guitar w/girl at upper l., gaucho
w/sheep at lower l.

	GOOD	FINE	XF
	—	—	—

VALE DE TESORERÍA BRANCH

1855 ISSUE

A117 50 CENTÉSIMOS
1.2.1875. Black on blue unpt. Head of cow at l., arms at upper ctr.
Uniface. Imprint: Litografia A. Godel.

	GOOD	FINE	XF
	15.00	35.00	—

A120 2 REALES
12.7.1855.

	GOOD	FINE	XF
	50.00	100.00	—

A121	**4 REALES**		50.00	100.00	—
	12.7.1855.				
A122	**1 PESO**		60.00	125.00	—
	12.7.1855.				
A123	**5 PESOS**		75.00	150.00	—
	12.7.1855. 117 x 83mm.				

		GOOD	**FINE**	**XF**
A127C	**10 PESOS**	—	—	—

11.8.1886. Brown and black on ochre unpt. Minstrel, woman and dog in circle at l., reclining women and shield at upper ctr., vaquero and cows in circle at r. Back peach and blue.

REPÚBLICA (ORIENTAL) DEL URUGUAY

1868 EMERGENCY POSTAL SCRIP ISSUES

Uruguay suffered from a chronic shortage of small change during the 1860's. The apparent success of the U.S. Postage Currency issue of 1862 during the Civil War (U.S. #97-100) prompted the government of Uruguay to do much the same thing in 1868.

#A128-A132 exact copies of single current postage stamps at ctr., wide margins around. All uniface w/circular handstamp in purple or black w/issuing office and date.

		GOOD	**FINE**	**XF**
A124	**10 PESOS**	—	—	—

12.7.1855. Arms at upper ctr.

		GOOD	**FINE**	**XF**
A125	**25 PESOS**	—	—	—
	12.7.1855.			
A126	**50 PESOS**	—	—	—
	12.7.1855.			
A127	**100 PESOS**	—	—	—
	12.7.1855.			

VALES DEL TESORO BRANCH

LEY DE 13 DE JULIO 1886

#A127A and A127C imprint: Litografia Artistica - A. Godel - Montevideo.

		GOOD	**FINE**	**XF**
A127A	**1 PESO**	—	—	—

11.8.1886. Arms above seated woman w/sheaves of grain at l.

#A128   #A129

		GOOD	**FINE**	**XF**
A128	**1 CENTÉSIMO**	150.00	250.00	—
	1868. Black.			
A129	**5 CENTECIMOS**	200.00	300.00	—
	1868. Blue.			
A129A	**5 CENTECIMOS**	—	—	—
	1868. Green on pink paper.			
A130	**10 CENTÉSIMOS**	250.00	350.00	—
	1868. Blue.			
A131	**15 CENTÉSIMOS**	300.00	400.00	—
	1868. Orange on yellow paper.			
A132	**20 CENTÉSIMOS**	300.00	400.00	—
	1868. Red on green paper.			

BANCO DE LA REPÚBLICA ORIENTAL DEL URUGUAY

Authorized by law on 4.8.1896, this was to be one of the few authorized issuers of paper money in the country.

1896 PROVISIONAL ISSUE

NOTE: Most examples of #1 encountered are counterfeit.

		GOOD	**FINE**	**XF**
1 (1B)	**20 CENTÉSIMOS**			
	L.4.8.1896. J. G. Artigas at l. Printer: CSABB. (Not issued).			
1A (1)	**10 PESOS**	—	Rare	—
	1.10.1896. Green. Liberty head w/helmet at upper l., cherub w/shield at r. Imprint: CSABB.			
1B (1A)	**100 PESOS**			
	1.10.1896. (No examples known.)			

1896 ISSUE

#2-8 printer: G&D.

NOTE: For similar design issue but dated 1934, see #20-26.

2   50 CENTÉSIMOS
24.8.1896. Black on orange and green unpt. 2 men harvesting w/horses at lower l.

		GOOD	FINE	XF
a.	Imprint: G&D.	10.00	35.00	85.00
b.	Double imprint: Jacobo Peuser Buenos Aires; G&D.	15.00	40.00	90.00
c.	Dk. red ovpt: *Rosario* at upper r.	—	—	—

3   1 PESO
24.8.1896. Black on lilac and orange unpt. Portr. woman at ctr.

		GOOD	FINE	XF
a.	Imprint: G&D.	15.00	40.00	90.00
b.	Double imprint: Jacobo Peuser Buenos Aires; G&D.	20.00	50.00	115.00
c.	SALTO ovpt. on b.	—	—	—

4   5 PESOS
24.8.1896. Black on pink and lilac unpt. Man at l., arms at r.   50.00   125.00   250.00

5   10 PESOS
24.8.1896. Black on lt. blue and orange unpt. Sailor at l., woman and arms at r. Ships and train on back.   90.00   200.00   450.00

5A   10 PESOS
24.8.1896. Pres. Idiarte Borda at l. Proof. (Not issued).

	GOOD	FINE	XF
	—	—	—

6   50 PESOS
24.8.1896. Blue and orange. Women at l. and r.   —   —   —

7   100 PESOS
24.8.1896. Black on lilac and blue unpt. Man at l., woman w/sword at r.   —   —   —

8   500 PESOS
24.8.1896. Portr. man above arms between allegorical man and woman at ctr..

	GOOD	FINE	XF
	—	—	—

1899 ISSUE
NOTE: Most examples of #8A encountered are counterfeit.

8A   10 PESOS
1.7.1899. Black on pink and orange unpt. Woman leaning on column at l., arms at r. Back black on yellow and lilac unpt. Seated figure at ctr. Printer: BWC.

		GOOD	FINE	XF
a.	W/o branch ovpt.			
b.	Branch ovpt: *FLORIDA* at ctr.	—	Rare	
c.	Branch ovpt:*SORIANO*.	—	Rare	
x.	Counterfeit.	—	Rare	
		20.00	40.00	

LAW OF 4.8.1896 (1914 ISSUE)
#9-11 Portr. Artigas at ctr. w/engraved date: *Septiembre de 1914.* Sign. title varieties. Printer: W&S.
#12 and 13 Portr. J. G. Artigas at l. Arms on back. Printer: W&S.

9   1 PESO
Sept. 1914. Additional ovpt. dates 1924-35. Black on blue unpt. Back brown; arms at ctr. Issued 1915-36.

		GOOD	FINE	XF
a.	Series V-VIII. No added date. 3 sign.	3.00	8.00	35.00
b.	Series VIII-XI. Added date (diff. positions). 3 or 2 sign. 9.8.1924-14.11.1935.	2.50	6.00	30.00
c.	Series XI. Slightly modified portr., crosshatches on jacket.	2.00	5.00	25.00
d.	Series XI. No added date, and 2 sign.	2.00	5.00	25.00

10   5 PESOS
Sept. 1914. Additional ovpt. dates 1925-34. Brown on lt. red and lt. green unpt. Back green; arms at ctr. Issued 1915-34.

		GOOD	FINE	XF
a.	W/o ovpt. or additional dates.	5.00	20.00	65.00
b.	2 ovpt. on face: *CONVERTIBLE EN EMISION MAYOR. . .20 Feb. 1919* and *CONVERTIBLE EN PLATA.*	35.00	85.00	200.00
c.	Like b. but only the first ovpt. on face.	30.00	75.00	175.00
d.	Ovpt: *Certificado Metalico-Plata/Ley de 14 de Enero de 1916.* Issued 1927-28. No added dates.	15.00	50.00	95.00
e.	Added date (diff. positions). 4.8.1925-16.1.1934.	4.00	10.00	30.00

11   10 PESOS
Sept. 1914. Additional ovpt. dates 1925-35. Black on pale orange and pale green unpt. Back orange; arms at ctr. Issued 1915-35.

		GOOD	FINE	XF
a.	W/o additional ovpt. dates.	20.00	45.00	100.00
b.	Added date (diff. positions). 7.1.1925-19.3.1935.	20.00	45.00	100.00

12   100 PESOS
Sept. 1914. Black on brown unpt. Issued 1915-32.

		GOOD	FINE	XF
a.	W/o additional ovpt. date. 3 sign.	40.00	90.00	200.00
b.	Like a., but 2 sign.	40.00	90.00	190.00
c.	Additional ovpt. date 4.1.1932.	40.00	90.00	200.00

		GOOD	FINE	XF
13	**500 PESOS**	60.00	165.00	350.00
	Sept. 1914. Black on green unpt.			
	a. W/o additional ovpt. date.			
	b. Additional ovpt. date 6.12.1924.	100.00	200.00	400.00

1918 PROVISIONAL ISSUE

		GOOD	FINE	XF
14	**20 CENTÉSIMOS ON 1 PESO**	12.00	35.00	85.00
	Jan. 1918. Black on brown unpt. Portr. J. G. Artigas at l. 4 corners cut off, and black ovpt. lines w/new denomination on face and back. Red or black serial # (3 serial # varieties). Printer: C de M, Buenos Aires.			
15	**1 PESO**	—	—	—
	Jan. 1918. #14 w/o ovpt. (Not issued).			

1918 ISSUE

NOTE: Genuine examples of #16 have a true wmk. Counterfeits are made by putting 2 separate pieces of paper together with wmk. simulated by a drawing in between.

		GOOD	FINE	XF
16	**100 PESOS**			
	Jan. 1918. Purple on brown-orange unpt. Portr. J. G. Artigas at l. Similar to #14.			
	a. Issued note.	80.00	200.00	400.00
	x. Counterfeit.	40.00	100.00	—
16A	**500 PESOS**	—	—	—
	Jan. 1918. Black on green unpt. Similar to #16.			

1930 COMMEMORATIVE ISSUE

#17-19 Centennial of Uruguay 1830-1930. French printing. Wmk: Artigas.

		GOOD	FINE	XF
17	**1 PESO**	25.00	85.00	300.00
	18.7.1930. M/c. Woman w/helmet at ctr. Indians at l. and r., arms at upper ctr., sailboat at r. ctr. on back.			

		GOOD	FINE	XF
18	**5 PESOS**	175.00	550.00	—
	18.7.1930. M/c. Woman at ctr. Horseback riders and arms on back.			
19	**10 PESOS**	200.00	600.00	—
	18.7.1930. M/c. Woman at l. Arms and 4 allegorical women on back.			

LEY 4 AGOSTO DE 1896 (1931-34 ISSUE)

#20-26 reissued. Redesigned arms. Sign. and title varieties. Printer: G&D.

		VG	VF	UNC
20	**50 CENTÉSIMOS**			
	18.10.1934. Similar to #2.			
	a. 3 sign. Additional ovpt. dates 30.4.1935-22.9.1935.	4.00	20.00	75.00
	b. 2 sign. W/o additional ovpt. date.	4.00	20.00	75.00

		VG	VF	UNC
21	**1 PESO**	8.00	30.00	90.00
	9.8.1934. Similar to #3.			

		VG	VF	UNC
22	**5 PESOS**	20.00	60.00	150.00
	9.8.1934. Similar to #4.			
23	**10 PESOS**	25.00	80.00	200.00
	9.8.1934. Similar to #5.			

		VG	VF	UNC
26	**500 PESOS**	—	—	—
	25.8.1931. Similar to #8.			

DEPARTAMENTO DE EMISIÓN

LEY DE 14 DE AGOSTO DE 1935

#27-33 many sign., sign. title varieties and ovpt. Series A. Wmk: Artigas. Printer: TDLR.

Sign. titles in plate:

2 sign., *EL PRESIDENTE* and *EL DELEGADO DEL GOBIERNO.*

3 sign., *EL PRESIDENTE* or *EL VICE PRESIDENTE, EL SECRETARIO* or *SECRETARIO GENERAL*, and *GERENTE GENERAL.*

		VG	VF	UNC
27	**50 CENTÉSIMOS**			
	L.1935. Brown on orange and green unpt. Arms at ctr., man w/helmet at lower r. Back green; sailing ships. All notes have 2 sign. titles in plate.	1.50	5.00	15.00
	a. 2 sign.			
	b. 3 sign ovpt.			

		VG	VF	UNC
32	**500 PESOS**			
	L.1935. Violet and blue. "Industry" at l. Back brown; group of people w/symbols of agriculture.			
	a. 2 sign. titles in plate. 2 or 3 sign. ovpt.	30.00	60.00	200.00
	b. 3 sign. titles in plate. 3 sign. ovpt.	30.00	60.00	200.00
33	**1000 PESOS**			
	L.1935. Green. J. G. Artigas at r. Back blue and brown; horsemen.			
	a. 2 sign. titles in plate. 2 or 3 sign. ovpt.	90.00	175.00	—
	b. 3 sign. titles in plate. 3 sign. ovpt.	90.00	175.00	—

LEY DE 2 DE ENERO DE 1939

#35-41 w/a great many variations in sign. and sign. titles. No printed sign. titles are in plates. All notes have 2 or 3 sign. Printer: TDLR.

		VG	VF	UNC
28	**1 PESO**			
	L.1935. Orange-brown on green unpt. Indian w/spear at l., arms at ctr. r. Back blue; conquistadores fighting against Indians.			
	a. 2 sign. titles in plate. 2 or 3 sign. ovpt.	2.00	8.00	27.50
	b. W/o sign. titles in plate. 3 sign. ovpt.	2.00	8.00	27.50
	c. 3 sign. titles in plate. 3 sign. ovpt.	2.00	8.00	27.50

		VG	VF	UNC
29	**5 PESOS**			
	L.1935. Green on m/c unpt. Arms at upper l., old gaucho at lower r. Back red-brown; wagon drawn by oxen.			
	a. 2 sign. titles in plate. 2 or 3 sign. ovpt.	6.00	20.00	55.00
	b. W/o sign. titles in plate. 3 sign. ovpt.	6.00	20.00	55.00

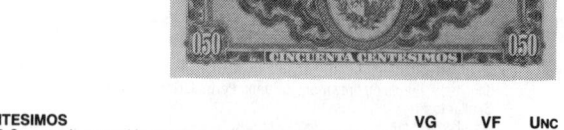

		VG	VF	UNC
34	**50 CENTESIMOS**			
	L.1939. Green on lt. tan and brown unpt. J. G. Artigas at ctr. Series A-T. Arms at ctr. on back. Imprint: Casa de Moneda de Chile.	.20	.50	2.00

		VG	VF	UNC
35	**1 PESO**			
	L.1939. Brown on m/c unpt. Arms at upper l., J. G. Artigas at ctr. Sailing ships on back.			
	a. Paper w/fibers. Series A; B.	.30	1.25	4.00
	b. Paper w/security thread. Series C.	.25	1.00	3.50
	c. Series D.	.20	.50	2.00

		VG	VF	UNC
30	**10 PESOS**			
	L.1935. Deep blue on m/c unpt. Warrior wearing helmet at l., arms at upper r. Back purple; group of men w/flag.			
	a. 2 sign. titles in plate. 2 or 3 sign. ovpt.	10.00	25.00	70.00
	b. W/o sign. titles in plate. 3 sign. ovpt.	10.00	25.00	70.00
31	**100 PESOS**			
	L.1935. Orange-brown and violet on m/c unpt. "Constitution" at l. Back orange-brown; crowd of people in town square.			
	a. 2 sign. titles in plate. 2 or 3 sign. ovpt.	12.00	35.00	90.00
	b. W/o sign. titles in plate. 3 sign. ovpt.	12.00	35.00	90.00

36	5 PESOS	VG	VF	UNC
	L.1939. Blue on m/c unpt. Arms at upper l., J. G. Artigas at r. Conquistadors fighting against Indians on back.			
	a. Paper w/fibers. Series A; B.	.75	2.50	7.00
	b. Paper w/security thread. Series C.	.40	1.00	3.50

37	10 PESOS	VG	VF	UNC
	L.1939. Purple on m/c unpt. Arms at upper l., J. G. Artigas at ctr. Farmer w/3-team ox-cart on back.	1.00	4.00	10.00
	a. Paper w/fibers. Series A.	.75	3.00	7.50
	b. As a. Series B.	.40	1.50	5.50
	c. Paper w/security thread. Series C.	.40	1.00	3.00
	d. Series D.			

38	50 PESOS	VG	VF	UNC
	L.1939. Blue and brown on m/c unpt. Arms at upper l., warrior wearing helmet at r. Group of men w/flag on back.			
	a. Paper w/fibers. Series A; B.	.75	3.00	9.00
	b. Paper w/security thread. Series C.	.40	1.50	5.00

39	100 PESOS	VG	VF	UNC
	L.1939. Red and brown. Arms at ctr., "Constitution" at r. People in town square on back.			
	a. Paper w/fibers. Series A; B.	2.00	6.00	20.00
	b. Paper w/security thread. Series C.	.75	3.00	8.00
	c. Series D.	.50	2.00	6.00

40	500 PESOS	VG	VF	UNC
	L.1939. Green and blue. Arms at upper l., "Industry" at r. People w/symbols of agriculture on back.	3.00	10.00	30.00
	a. Paper w/fibers. Series A; B.	1.00	4.00	10.00
	b. Paper w/security thread. Series C.	.75	2.00	7.00
	c. Series D.			

41	1000 PESOS	VG	VF	UNC
	L.1939. Purple and black. Arms at upper l., J. G. Artigas at r. Man on horseback at ctr. on back.	10.00	25.00	75.00
	a. Paper w/fibers. Series A; B.	3.00	10.00	25.00
	b. Paper w/security thread. Series C.	2.00	5.00	12.00
	c. Series D.			

UZBEKISTAN

The Republic of Uzbekistan (formerly the Uzbek S.S.R.), is bordered on the north by Kazakhstan, to the east by Kirghizia and Tajikistan, on the south by Afghanistan and on the west by Turkmenistan. The republic is comprised of the regions of Andizhan, Bukhara, Dzhizak, Ferghana, Kashkadar, Khorezm (Khiva), Namangan, Navoi, Samarkand, Surkhan-Darya, Syr-Darya, Tashkent and the Karakalpak Autonomous Republic. It has an area of 172,741 sq. mi. (447,400 sq. km.) and a population of 20.3 million. Capital: Tashkent.

Crude oil, natural gas, coal, copper and gold deposits make up the chief resources, while intensive farming, based on artificial irrigation, provides an abundance of cotton.

The original population was believed to be Iranian towards the north while the southern part hosted the satrapies of Sogdiana and Bactria, members of the Persian empire and once part of the empire of Alexander of Macedon. In the 2nd century B.C. they suffered an invasion by easterners referred to by the Chinese as Yue-chi and Hiung-nu. At the end of the 7th century and into the 8th century an Arab army under Emir Kotaiba ibu Muslim conquered Khiva (Khorezm) and Bukhara (Sogdiana). Persian influence developed from the Abbasid caliphs of Baghdad. About 874 the area was conquered by the Persian Saminids of Balkh.

In 999 a Turkic Karakhanid dynasty, the first to embrace Islam, supplanted the Samanids in Samarkand and Bukhara. At the beginning of the 11th century the Seljuk Turks passed through Transoxiana and appointed a hereditary governor at Khorezm. In 1141 another dynasty appeared in Transoxiana, the Kara Kitai from north China. Under the Seljuk shahs Khorezm remained a Moslem outpost.

The Mongol invasion of Jenghiz Khan in 1219-20 brought destruction and great ethnic changes among the population. The conquerors became assimilated and adopted the Turkic language "Chagatai." At the beginning of the 16th century Turkestan was conquered by another wave of Turkic nomads, the Uzbeks (Usbegs). The term Uzbek was used in the 15th century to indicate Moslem. In the 18th century Khokand made itself independent from the emirate of Bukhara, but was soon subject to China, which had conquered eastern Turkestan (now called Sinkiang). The khanate of Khiva, in 1688, became a vassal of Persia, but recovered its independence in 1747. While the Uzbek emirs and khans ruled central Turkestan, in the north were the Kazakhs, in the west lived the nomadic Turkmens, in the east dwelled the Kirghiz, and in the southeast was the homeland of the Persian-speaking Tajiks. In 1714-17 Peter the Great sent a military expedition against Khiva which ended in a disaster. In 1853 Ak-Mechet ("White Mosque," renamed Perovsk, later Kzyl Orda), was conquered by the Russians, and the following year the fortress of Vernoye (later Alma-Ata) was established. On July 29, 1867, Gen. C. P. Kaufmann was appointed governor general of Turkestan with headquarters in Tashkent. On July 5 Mozaffar ed-Din, emir of Bukhara, signed a treaty making his country a Russian vassal state with much-reduced territory. Khiva was conquered by Gen. N. N. Golovachev, and on Aug. 24, 1873, Khan Mohammed Rakhim Kuli had to become a vassal of Russia. Furthermore, all his possessions east of the Amu Darya were annexed to the Turkestan governor-generalship. The khanate of Khokand was suppressed and on March 3, 1876, became the Fergana province. On the eve of WW I Khiva and Bukhara were enclaves within a Russian Turkestan divided into five provinces or oblasti. The czarist government did not attempt to Russify the indigenous Turkic or Tajik populations, preferring to keep them backward and illiterate. The revolution of March 1917 created a confused situation in the area. In Tashkent there was a Turkestan committee of the provisional government; a Communist-controlled council of workers', soldiers' and peasants' deputies; also a Moslem Turkic movement, Shuro-i-Islamiya, and a Young-Turkestan or Jaddidi (Renovation) party. The last-named party claimed full political autonomy for Turkestan and the abolition of the emirate of Bukhara and the khanate of Khiva. After the Communist coup d'éin Petrograd, the council of people's commissars on Nov. 24 (Dec. 7), 1917, published an appeal to "all toiling Moslems in Russia and in the east" proclaiming their right to build their national life "freely and unhindered." In response, the Moslem and Jaddidi organizations in Dec. 1917 convoked a national congress in Khokand which appointed a provisional government headed by Mustafa Chokayev (or Chokaigolu; 1890-1941) and resolved to elect a constituent assembly to decide whether Turkestan should remain within a Russian federal state or proclaim its independence. In the spring of 1919 a Red army group defeated Kolchak and in September its commander, M.V. Frunze, arrived in Tashkent with V.V. Kuibyshev as political commissar. The Communists were still much too weak in Turkestan to proclaim the country part of Soviet Russia. Faizullah Khojayev organized a Young Bukhara movement, which on Sept. 14, 1920, proclaimed the dethronement of Emir Mir Alim. Bukhara was then made a S.S.R. In 1920 the Tashkent Communist government declared war on Junaid, who took to flight, and Khiva became another S.S.R. In Oct. 1921 Enver Pasha, the former leader of the Young Turks, appeared in Bukhara and assumed command of the Basmachi movement. In Aug. 1922 he was forced to retreat into Tajikistan and died on Aug. 4, in a battle near Baljuvan. Khiva concluded a treaty of alliance with the Russian S.F.S.R. in Sept. 1920, and Bukhara followed suit in March 1921. Theoretically, a Turkestan Autonomous Soviet Socialist Republic had existed since May 1, 1918; in 1920 this "Turkrepublic," as it was called, was proclaimed part of the R.S.F.S.R. On Sept. 18, 1924, the Uzbek and Turkmen peoples were authorized to form S.S.R.'s of their own, and the Kazakhs, Kirghiz and Tajiks to form autonomous S.S.R.'s. On Oct. 27, 1924, the Uzbek and Turkmen S.S.R. were officially constituted and the former was formally accepted on Jan. 15, 1925, as a member of the U.S.S.R. Tajikistan was an autonomous soviet republic within Uzbekistan until Dec. 5, 1929, when it became a S.S.R. On Dec. 5, 1936, Uzbekistan was territorially increased by incorporating into it the Kara-Kalpak A.S.S.R., which had belonged to Kazakhstan until 1930 and afterward had come under direct control of the R.S.F.S.R.

On June 20, 1990 the Uzbek Supreme Soviet adopted a declaration of sovereignty, and in Aug. 1991, following the unsuccessful coup, it declared itself independent as the 'Republic of Uzbekistan', which was confirmed by referendum in December. That same month Uzbekistan became a member of the CIS.

Monetary System:
1 ТЕНЬГА (Tenga) = 20 КОПЬЕКЪ (Kopeks)
5 ТЕНЬГОВЪ (Tengov) = 1 РЧБПЕЙ (Rublei)

BUKHARA, EMIRATE
RULER: Emir Sayyid Abdul Akhad Bahadu

TREASURY

1918 FIRST ISSUE
All notes in Persian script, w/only the denomination in Russian. Many printing, color and paper varieties.
Sign. seals for #1-10:

1	20 TENGAS	GOOD	FINE	XF
	AH1337 (1918). M/c.			
	a. Issued note.	80.00	150.00	—
	x. Misprint: back inverted on back.	100.00	170.00	—

Type I   Type II

2	60 TENGAS	GOOD	FINE	XF
	AH1337 (1918). M/c on white or yellowish paper.			
	a. Seals Type I.	100.00	160.00	—
	b. Seals Type II.	70.00	110.00	—
3	100 TENGAS			
	AH1337 (1918). M/c on white or yellowish paper.	25.00	60.00	—
4	200 TENGAS			
	AH1337 (1918). M/c on white or yellowish paper.	25.00	60.00	—

5	300 TENGAS	GOOD	FINE	XF
	AH1337 (1918). M/c.			
	a. Brownish paper.	50.00	85.00	—
	b. White paper. Green date on face.	120.00	200.00	—
	c. White paper. Red date on face.	20.00	40.00	—
6	500 TENGAS			
	AH1337 (1918). M/c on white or yellowish paper, thin or thick.	30.00	65.00	—

7	1000 TENGAS	GOOD	FINE	XF
	AH1337 (1918). White or yellowish paper.	40.00	70.00	—
8	2000 TENGAS			
	AH1337 (1918). M/c.	50.00	75.00	—
9	3000 TENGAS			
	AH1337 (1918). M/c.	50.00	80.00	—

10	5000 TENGAS	GOOD	FINE	XF
	AH1337 (1918). M/c on white or yellowish paper.			
	a. Dates 4 times.	40.00	100.00	—
	b. Like a., but inverted on back.	100.00	170.00	—
	c. Dates twice.	65.00	120.00	—

1918 SECOND ISSUE
Sign. seals for #11-18:

11	100 TENGAS	GOOD	FINE	XF
	AH1337 (1918). M/c.	25.00	45.00	—
12	200 TENGAS			
	AH1337 (1918). M/c.	40.00	70.00	—
13	300 TENGAS			
	AH1337 (1918). M/c.	25.00	45.00	—
14	500 TENGAS			
	AH1337 (1918). M/c.	25.00	45.00	—
15	1000 TENGAS			
	AH1337 (1918). M/c.	25.00	45.00	—
16	2000 TENGAS			
	AH1337 (1918). M/c.	25.00	45.00	—

17	3000 TENGAS	GOOD	FINE	XF
	AH1337 (1918). M/c.			
	a. Turquoise frame.	25.00	45.00	—
	b. Brown frame.	30.00	55.00	

18	5000 TENGAS	GOOD	FINE	XF
	AH1337 (1918).			
	a. Lt. green.	12.00	25.00	50.00
	b. Dk. green.	12.00	25.00	50.00
	c. Blue, on brownish paper.	10.00	20.00	40.00

1919 ISSUE
Sign. seal like #11-18 and #19-24.

19	50 TENGAS	GOOD	FINE	XF
	AH1338 (1919). M/c.	10.00	18.50	35.00

20	100 TENGAS	GOOD	FINE	XF
	AH1338 (1919). Olive.	10.00	20.00	50.00
21	200 TENGAS			
	AH1338 (1919). Dk. green.	12.00	25.00	60.00
22	500 TENGAS			
	AH1338 (1919). Blue, red, brown and green (color variations).	15.00	30.00	70.00

23	1000 TENGAS	GOOD	FINE	XF
	AH1338 (1919). M/c.	15.00	30.00	70.00

24	10,000 TENGAS	GOOD	FINE	XF
	AH1338 (1919). M/c. 3 sign. varieties. 267 x 125mm.	17.50	35.00	80.00

KHOREZM (KHIVA), KHANATE
RULER: Sayid Abdullah Khan

TREASURY

1918 ISSUE
Many varieties, especially in color, paper and printing.

25	200 TENGAS	GOOD	FINE	XF
	AH1337 (1918).			
	a. ТИНЬГОВЪ to be read from bottom to top Crescent at ctr. or top at r. on bac.	200.00	300.00	—
	b. ТИНЬГОВ to be read from top to bottom.	160.00	250.00	—
	c. ТИНЬГОВЪ to be read from top to bottom.	160.00	250.00	—
	d. ИНЬВО.	160.00	250.00	—
26	250 TENGAS			
	AH1337 (1918).			
	a. Russian wording at upper r.	160.00	250.00	—
	b. W/o Russian wording.	180.00	275.00	—
27	500 TENGAS			
	AH1337 (1918).			
	a. Text in the corners in ornaments.	120.00	200.00	—
	b. Text in squares, also Russian wording inverted.	100.00	175.00	—
	c. Text wording in the corners in circles.	100.00	175.00	—
28	1000 TENGAS			
	AH1337 (1918).			
	a. Text in the circle on 3 lines, also wording inverted.	120.00	200.00	—
	b. Text in the circle of 4 lines.	120.00	200.00	—
29	2500 TENGAS			
	AH1337 (1918).			
	a. 2 leaves below on back, also w/o 500 on back.	115.00	185.00	—
	b. Bush below on back, also wording inverted.	200.00	300.00	—

1042 UZBEKISTAN

1918 PAPER ISSUE

		GOOD	FINE	XF
30	**50 TENGAS = 10 RUBLES** AH1337 (1918). 6 different wmk., and w/o wmk.	80.00	145.00	225.00

1918 FIRST SILK ISSUE

		GOOD	FINE	XF
34	**200 TENGAS = 40 RUBLES** AH1337 (1919).	—	160.00	300.00
31	**500 TENGAS = 100 RUBLES** AH1337 (1919).	—	100.00	200.00
36	**500 TENGAS = 100 RUBLES** AH1338 (1919). Red-brown on yellow. Different printing errors in the denomination.	—	115.00	215.00
32	**1000 TENGAS = 200 RUBLES** AH1337 (1919).	—	120.00	225.00
37	**1000 TENGAS = 200 RUBLES** AH1338 (1919).	—	140.00	250.00
33	**2500 TENGAS = 500 RUBLES** AH1337 (1919).	—	200.00	325.00
38	**2500 TENGAS = 500 RUBLES** AH1338 (1919).	—	160.00	300.00

		GOOD	FINE	XF
41	**50 RUBLES** AH1338 (1920). Blue and red.	25.00	65.00	120.00
42	**100 RUBLES** AH1338 (1920).	35.00	85.00	170.00

1919 SILK ISSUE
Silk Notes in Ruble Currency

		GOOD	FINE	XF
39	**100 RUBLES** AH1338 (1919).	—	80.00	160.00

		GOOD	FINE	XF
40	**250 RUBLES** AH1338 (1919). Red-brown on lt. green.	—	80.00	160.00

1920 PAPER ISSUE
Paper Notes in Ruble Currency

The Republic of Venezuela ("Little Venice"), located on the northern coast of South America between Columbia and Guyana, has an area of 352,145 sq. mi. (912,050 sq. km.) and a population of *20.2 million. Capital: Caracas. Petroleum and mining provide 90 percent of Venezuela's exports although they employ less than 2 percent of the work force. Coffee, grown on 60,000 plantations, is the chief crop.

Columbus discovered Venezuela on his third voyage in 1498. Initial exploration did not reveal Venezuela to be a land of great wealth. An active pearl trade operated on the off-shore islands and slavers raided the interior in search of Indians to be sold into slavery, but no significant mainland settlements were made before 1567 when Caracas was founded. Venezuela, the home of Bolívar, was among the first South American colonies to revolt against Spain in 1810. Independence was attained in 1821 but not recognized by Spain until 1845. Together with Ecuador, Panama and Colombia, Venezuela was part of "Gran Colombia" until 1830 when it became a sovereign and independence state.

MONETARY SYSTEM:
1 Bolívar = 100 Centimos, 1879-
1 Venezolano = 100 Centavos to 1879.

NOTE: Certain listings encompassing issues circulated by various bank and regional authorities are contained in Volume 1.

ESTADOS UNIDOS DE VENEZUELA

UNITED STATES OF VENEZUELA

TREASURY

LAW OF 27.8.1811 FIRST ISSUE
#2 and 4 w/1 seal. Sign. varieties. Black on heavy white paper. Uniface.

		GOOD	FINE	XF
2	**2 REALES** L.1811.	—	Rare	—

		GOOD	FINE	XF
4	**1 PESO** L.1811. Un Peso at l. below center design.	400.00	800.00	—

LAW OF 27.8.1811 SECOND ISSUE

#5-8 w/2 seals. Sign. varieties. Black on heavy white paper. Uniface.

		GOOD	FINE	XF
4A	**1 PESO** L.1811. Un Peso at l. ctr. and not below design. 1 seal.	400.00	800.00	—
5	**2 PESOS** L.1811.	—	Rare	—

		GOOD	FINE	XF
6	**4 PESOS** L.1811.	1500.	3500.	—

		GOOD	FINE	XF
7	**8 PESOS** L.1811.	6500.	10,000.	—
8	**16 PESOS** L.1811.	Reported Not Confirmed		

BILLETE DE TESORERÍA

1849 ISSUE

		GOOD	FINE	XF
9	**5 PESOS** 19.1.1849. Black. Seated Liberty at l., arms at ctr., sailing ship at r.	—	—	—

REPUBLIC

REPÚBLICA DE VENEZUELA

DECREE OF 20.10.1859
#11-27 generally similar to #25.

		GOOD	FINE	XF
11	**5 PESOS** Black.	—	—	—
12	**10 PESOS** Black.	—	—	—
13	**50 PESOS** Black.	—	—	—
14	**100 PESOS** Black.	—	—	—
15	**500 PESOS** Black.	—	—	—
16	**1000 PESOS** Black.	—	—	—

DECREE OF 17.7.1860

		GOOD	FINE	XF
17	**5 PESOS** Black.	—	—	—
18	**10 PESOS** Black.	—	—	—
19	**50 PESOS** Black.	—	—	—

DECREE OF 2.8.1860

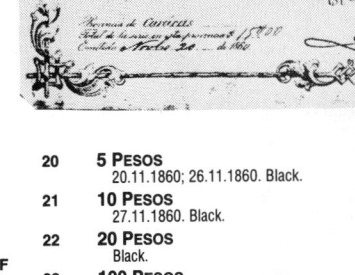

		GOOD	FINE	XF
20	**5 PESOS** 20.11.1860; 26.11.1860. Black.	—	—	—
21	**10 PESOS** 27.11.1860. Black.	—	—	—
22	**20 PESOS** Black.	—	—	—
23	**100 PESOS** Black.	—	—	—

DECREE OF 2.8.1860 AND RESOLUTION OF 18.9.1860

		GOOD	FINE	XF
24	**8 REALES** 30.8.1860. Black.	—	—	—

DECREE OF 15.1.1861

		GOOD	FINE	XF
25	**8 REALES** D.1861. Black. Guarantee text on back.	—	—	—
26	**20 PESOS** Black.	—	—	—
27	**100 PESOS** Black.	—	—	—

BANCO CENTRAL DE VENEZUELA

Issuing notes since 1940. Sign. and date varieties. Notes from 1940-53 bear the legend "E.E.U.U. de Venezuela" in the coat of arms and after 1953 "República de Venezuela." Many specimen notes were "liberated" about 1982. Up to 200 of each are known for many of the more common types which are now incorporated in these listings.

1940-45 ISSUES
#31-37 arms on back. Printer: ABNC.

		VG	VF	UNC
31	**10 BOLÍVARES** 19.7.1945-11.3.1960. Purple on m/c unpt. Portr. S. Bolívar at l., A. J. de Sucre at r. Arms at r. on back.			
	a. 1945-52.	4.00	16.00	50.00
	b. 1953-58.	3.00	12.00	37.50
	c. 1959-60.	2.00	8.00	25.00
32	**20 BOLÍVARES** 15.2.1941-18.6.1959. Dk. green on m/c unpt. Portr. S. Bolívar at r. Arms at l. on back.			
	a. 1941-52.	8.00	24.00	75.00
	b. 1952-59.	4.00	12.00	37.50
33	**50 BOLÍVARES** 12.12.1940-11.3.1960. Black on m/c unpt. Portr. S. Bolívar at l. Back orange.			
	a. 1940-52.	13.00	40.00	180.00
	b. 1953-58.	10.00	30.00	135.00
	c. 1959-60.	6.50	20.00	90.00
34	**100 BOLÍVARES** 11.12.1940-3.7.1962. Brown on m/c unpt. Portr. S. Bolívar at ctr. Arms at ctr. on back.			
	a. 1940-52.	20.00	60.00	200.00
	b. 1953-58.	15.00	45.00	150.00
	c. 1959-62.	10.00	30.00	100.00
35	**500 BOLÍVARES** 10.12.1940-23.12.1940. Blue on m/c unpt. Portr. S. Bolívar at r.	175.00	450.00	—
36	**500 BOLÍVARES** 21.1.1943-29.11.1946. Red on m/c unpt. Similar to #37.	145.00	375.00	—

1947 ISSUE

		VG	VF	UNC
37	**500 BOLÍVARES** 1947-71. Orange on m/c unpt.			
	a. 14.8.1947-17.1.1952.	60.00	150.00	—
	b. 23.7.1953-29.5.1958.	25.00	55.00	165.00
	c. 11.3.1960-9.11.1971.	20.00	50.00	135.00

1952-53 ISSUE
#38-41 cruder and differently etched portr. of S. Bolívar. Monument at ctr. on back. Printer: TDLR.

		VG	VF	UNC
38	**10 BOLÍVARES** 31.7.1952-23.7.1953. Purple on m/c unpt. Similar to #42. Arms at r. on back.	30.00	70.00	275.00
39	**20 BOLÍVARES** 21.8.1952. Similar to #43. Arms at l. on back.	35.00	75.00	350.00

		VG	VF	UNC
40	**50 BOLÍVARES** 26.2.1953; 23.7.1953. Bolívar at l., CINCUENTA BOLÍVARES at r.	50.00	135.00	425.00
41	**100 BOLÍVARES** 23.7.1953. Portr. S. Bolívar at r.	25.00	125.00	400.00

1960 ISSUE
#42-44 printer: TDLR.

		VG	VF	UNC
43	**20 BOLÍVARES** 11.3.1960-10.5.1966. Dk. green on m/c unpt. Portr. S. Bolívar at r., bank name in 1 line. Monument at ctr. on back.			
	a. Issued note.	4.00	12.00	30.00
	s. Specimen (varieties).	—	—	15.00

VIET NAM

The Socialist Republic of Viet Nam, located in Southeast Asia west of the South China Sea, has an area of 127,300 sq. mi. (329,560 sq. km.) and a population of *69.3 million million. Captial: Hanoi. Agricultural products, coal and mineral ores are exported.

The Vietnamese originated in North China, from where they were driven southward by the Han Chinese. They settled in the Red River Delta in northern Vietnam; by 208 BC, much of present-day southern China and northern Vietnam were incorporated into the independent kingdom of Nam Viet. China annexed Nam Viet in 111 BC and ruled it until 939, when independence was reestablished. The new state then expanded until it included much of Cambodia and southern Vietnam. Vietnam was reconquered by the Chinese in 1407; they were finally driven out, but the country was divided into two, not to be reunited until 1802.

During the latter half of the 19th century, the French gradually overran Vietnam. Cochin-China, an alluvial plain of the Mekong Delta, fell to the French in 1862-67. In 1884, France established protectorates over Annam, an historic kingdom on the east coast of Indochina, and Tonkin in the north. Cambodia, Cochin-China, Annam and Tonkin were incorporated into the Indo-Chinese Union in 1887.

Vietnamese nationalists never really acquiesced to French domination, but continued to resist through a number of clandestine extra-legal organizations. At the start of World War II, many nationalists, communist and non-communist alike, fled to China where Ho Chi Minh organized the League for the Independence of Vietnam ("Viet Minh") to free Vietnam from French rule. The Japanese occupied Vietnam during World War II. As the end of the war drew near, they ousted the Vichy French administration and granted Vietnam independence under a puppet government headed by Bao Dai, emperor of Annam. The Bao Dai government collapsed at the end of the war, and on Sept. 2, 1945, Ho Chi Minh proclaimed the existence of an independent Vietnam consisting of Cochin-China, Annam and Tonkin, and set up a provisional Communist government of the Democratic Republic of Vietnam. France recognized the new government as a free state, but later reneged and in 1949 reinstalled Bao Dai as ruler of Vietnam and extended the regime independence within the French Union. Ho Chi Minh led a guerrilla war, in the first Indochina war, against the French puppet state that raged on to the disastrous defeat of the French by the Viet Minh at Dien Bien Phu on May 7, 1954.

An agreement signed at Geneva on July 21, 1954, provided for a temporary division of Vietnam at the 17th parallel of latitude, with the Communist dominated Democratic Republic of Viet Nam (North Vietnam) to the north, and the US/French-supported Republic of Viet Nam (South Vietnam) to the south. In October 1955 South Vietnam deposed Bao Dai by referendum and authorized the establishment of a new republic with Ngo Dinh Diem as president. This Republic of Vietnam was proclaimed on October 26, 1955, and was recognized immediately by the Western powers.

The Democratic Republic of Viet Nam, working through Viet Cong guerrillas, instigated subversion in South Vietnam which led to US armed intervention and the second Indochina War. This war, from the viewpoint of the North merely a continuation of the first (anti-French) war, was a bitter, protracted military conflict which came to a brief halt in 1973 (when a cease-fire was arranged and US and its other allied forces withdrew), but did not end until April 30, 1975 when South Vietnam surrendered unconditionally. The National Liberation Front for South Viet Nam, the political arm of the Viet Cong, assumed governmental power when on July 2, 1976, North and South Vietnam were united as the Socialist Republic of Viet Nam with Hanoi as the capital.

*** This section has been renumbered. ***

MONETARY SYSTEM:
1 Hao = 10 Xu
1 Đồng = 100 Xu

NOTE: HCM - Ho Chi Minh

VIET NAM DAN CHU CONG HOA

GIAY BAC VIET NAM

VIETNAMESE BANKNOTE

Issues of the DRVN central treasury and, where indicated, the Nam-Bo Regional Administration.

1946 ND ISSUES

		Good	Fine	XF
1 (3A)	**1 ĐỒNG** ND (1946). Olive. Like #9. Wmk: Oval w/*Vietnam*.	—	Rare	—
2 (7A)	**5 ĐỒNG** ND (1946). Crude printing of #10.	10.00	20.00	40.00

		Good	Fine	XF
3 (9)	**5 ĐỒNG** ND (1946). Brown and green. Worker at l., factory in background. HCM at l. on back.			
	a. Wmk: *VNDCCH*.	4.00	15.00	50.00
	b. Wmk: Oval w/*Vietnam*.	4.00	15.00	50.00

		Good	Fine	XF
4 (10)	**5 ĐỒNG** ND (1946). Brown and gold. Like #3 but larger note. W/o wmk.	6.50	20.00	60.00

		Good	Fine	XF
5 (15)	**20 ĐỒNG** ND (1946). Brown and olive. Flag behind HCM at l. (25mm high). Farmer w/buffalo at l., female porter w/child at r. on back. 148 x 76mm.	7.50	25.00	80.00

		Good	Fine	XF
6 (16)	**20 ĐỒNG** ND (1946). Brown and olive. Like #5. HCM in oval frame (36mm high). 170 x 88mm.	7.50	25.00	75.00

		Good	Fine	XF
7 (17)	**20 ĐỒNG** ND (1946). Brown and yellow. Like #5 but HCM in frame (50mm high). 170 x 88mm.	5.00	20.00	60.00

8
(29) **100 DÔNG**
ND (1946). Green and olive. Like #12 but HCM different and smaller (57mm high).

	Good	Fine	XF
a. W/o wmk.	10.00	40.00	140.00
b. Wmk: Oval w/Vietnam.	5.00	20.00	85.00
c. Wmk: VNDCCH.	10.00	40.00	140.00

1947 ND ISSUE

9
(3) **1 DÔNG**
ND (1947). Lt. to dk. blue. HCM at ctr. Denomination numerals 1 in corners contain sm. circles. 2 workers in field w/unpt. of alternating x's and squares on back. White on brown paper.

	Good	Fine	XF
a. W/o wmk.	2.00	7.50	20.00
b. Wmk: VDCCH horizontal and vertical.	2.00	7.50	20.00
c. Wmk: Oval w/Vietnam.	2.00	7.50	20.00
d. Wmk: Circle w/star.	Reported Not Confirmed		

10
(7) **5 DÔNG**
ND (1947). Red-brown. HCM at top. Woman w/boy below on back. Vertical format.

	Good	Fine	XF
a. W/o wmk.	2.00	5.00	10.00
b. Sign. and sign. titles in clear unpt. area. Wmk: VDCCH.	2.00	5.00	10.00
c. As b but wmk: Oval w/Vietnam.	2.00	5.00	10.00
d. Sign. and sign. titles within wavy unpt. design. Wmk: VDCCH.	10.00	25.00	50.00
e. As d but wmk: Oval w/VIETNAM.	10.00	25.00	50.00

10A
(8) **5 DÔNG**
1947. Red-brown. Like #10 but year at lower l., KIEU THU II (second issue) at lower r. on back.

	Good	Fine	XF
a. W/o wmk.	5.00	15.00	35.00
b. Wmk: VDCCH.	10.00	30.00	60.00
c. Wmk: Oval w/Vietnam.	5.00	15.00	35.00

11
(23) **50 DÔNG**
ND (1947). Blue and brown. Portr. HCM at ctr. Worker and buffalo at ctr. on back. (Shade varieties).

	Good	Fine	XF
a. W/o wmk.	7.00	20.00	60.00
b. Wmk: VDCCH.	7.00	20.00	60.00
c. Wmk: Oval w/Vietnam.	7.00	20.00	60.00

12
(28) **100 DÔNG**
ND (1947). Blue and brown. Woman w/child at l. HCM (64mm high) at ctr., 3 workers at r. Agricultural workers w/buffalo on back. 207 x 102mm.

	Good	Fine	XF
a. W/o wmk.	20.00	50.00	150.00
b. Wmk: Oval w/Vietnam.	20.00	50.00	150.00

1948 ND ISSUE

NOTE: #16 and #17 exist in a great many color and shade varieties, such as brown face w/red back, green face w/brown back, blue-green face w/orange back, black face w/purple back, etc.

13
(1) **20 XU**
ND (1948). Red-brown. HCM at r. Soldier and woman on back.

	Good	Fine	XF
a. 5 sm. (1mm tall) stars at l. on back.	20.00	60.00	180.00
b. 5 lg. (2mm tall) stars at l. on back. Wmk: Star w/UN in circle.	20.00	60.00	180.00

14
(2) **50 XU**
ND (1948). Green. HCM at r. 2 people standing on back.

	Good	Fine	XF
a. Blue serial #.	30.00	70.00	190.00
b. Red serial #. Wmk: Star w/UN in circle.	20.00	60.00	180.00

15
(4) **1 DÔNG**
ND (1948). Dk. blue. Similar to #1 and 9 but corner numerals 1 on face w/o sm. circles. Back unpt. sun rays.

	Good	Fine	XF
	30.00	75.00	225.00

16
(5) **1 DÔNG**
ND (1948). Dk. blue. 2 women laborers in rice field at l., HCM at r. 5 armed women on back (Nam Bo).

	Good	Fine	XF
	2.00	7.50	20.00

17
(6) **5 DÔNG**
ND (1948). Green to gray. 2 men at ctr., water buffalo at r. Back brown; HCM in circle at l., man w/rifle at ctr. r. (Nam Bo).

	Good	Fine	XF
a. Issued note.	1.00	4.00	15.00
s. Uniface specimen (pair).	—	Unc	500.00

18
5 DÔNG
ND (1948). Green. Face similar to #19. Back red-brown; 2 peasants at l. and at r.

	Good	Fine	XF
a. Issued note.	5.00	15.00	35.00
s. Uniface specimen (face).	—	Unc	175.00

19
5 DÔNG
ND (1948). Dk. blue. HCM at r., peasants at l. Back red-brown; 2 peasants stacking grain sheaves at ctr. W/o wmk.

	Good	Fine	XF
	3.75	15.00	35.00

20
(11) **10 DÔNG**
ND (1948). Red-brown. Back green to black-green; soldier and worker at ctr., HCM at r. Blurred printing.

	Good	Fine	XF
a. W/o wmk.	4.00	12.50	35.00
b. Wmk: VDCCH.	4.00	12.50	35.00
c. Wmk: Oval w/Vietnam.	4.00	12.50	35.00
d. Wmk: Circle w/star.	4.00	12.50	35.00
e. Wmk: VND.	4.00	12.50	35.00

21
(11A) **10 DÔNG**
ND (1948). Like #20 but back brown.

	Good	Fine	XF
	20.00	60.00	125.00

22
(12)
10 ĐÔNG
ND (1948). Red-brown on green unpt. Like #20 but clear printing (Tonkin).

	GOOD	FINE	XF
a. W/o wmk.	4.00	12.50	40.00
b. Wmk: *VDCCH.*	4.00	12.50	40.00
c. Wmk: Oval w/*Vietnam.*	4.00	12.50	40.00
d. Wmk: Circle w/star.	4.00	12.50	40.00

23
(13)
10 ĐÔNG
ND (1948). Red-brown on green unpt. Like #20 w/red 4-line ovpt. on back (Trung-Bo).

	GOOD	FINE	XF
	5.00	15.00	45.00

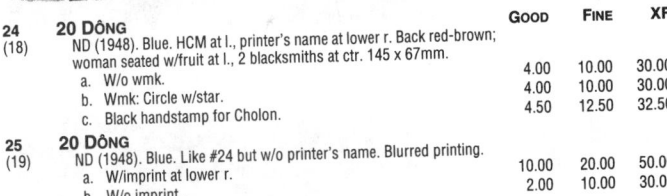

24
(18)
20 ĐÔNG
ND (1948). Blue. HCM at l., printer's name at lower r. Back red-brown; woman seated w/fruit at l., 2 blacksmiths at ctr. 145 x 67mm.

	GOOD	FINE	XF
a. W/o wmk.	4.00	10.00	30.00
b. Wmk: Circle w/star.	4.00	10.00	30.00
c. Black handstamp for Cholon.	4.50	12.50	32.50

25
(19)
20 ĐÔNG
ND (1948). Blue. Like #24 but w/o printer's name. Blurred printing.

	GOOD	FINE	XF
a. W/imprint at lower r.	10.00	20.00	50.00
b. W/o imprint.	2.00	10.00	30.00

26
(20)
20 ĐÔNG
ND (1948). Brown and olive. Soldiers at l., HCM at r. Back purple-black; farmers at work. 148 x 63mm (Nam-Bo).

	GOOD	FINE	XF
	5.00	15.00	45.00

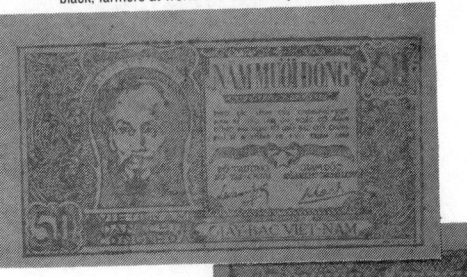

27
(22)
50 ĐÔNG
ND (1948-49). Dk. green. Portr. HCM at l. Back dk. green on red-brown unpt; woman, 2 children and 2 men at ctr.(Many varieties of printing and serial # sizes.)

	GOOD	FINE	XF
a. W/o wmk.	3.00	8.50	30.00
b. Wmk: Circle and star w/o writing.	3.00	8.50	30.00
c. Wmk: Circle and star, *VN* within.	3.00	8.50	30.00
d. Wmk: Circle and star, *ll.*	3.00	8.50	30.00
e. Black handstamp for Cholon.	3.00	8.50	30.00

28
(30)
100 ĐÔNG
ND (1948). Violet or brown on pink, orange or brown unpt. woman w/child and sm. flag at l., HCM at ctr., 3 workers at r. 2 seated women at l., soldier at ctr., agricultural worker at r. on back. 177 x 87mm. (Shade varieties).

	GOOD	FINE	XF
a. W/o wmk.	2.00	10.00	35.00
b. Wmk: Circle w/star.	2.00	10.00	35.00
c. Wmk: Oval w/ *Vietnam.*	2.00	10.00	35.00

1949 ISSUE

29
(31)
100 ĐÔNG
1949. Green. HCM at r. Back brown; 2 soldiers at l. 160 x 66mm.

	GOOD	FINE	XF
	3.00	10.00	30.00

30
(32)
100 ĐÔNG
1949. Like #29 but blue.

	GOOD	FINE	XF
a. Black serial #.	4.00	20.00	60.00
b. Red serial #.	4.00	20.00	60.00

31
(36)
500 ĐÔNG
1949. Dk. blue and brown. Man and woman w/torch at l., HCM at r. Soldiers at l., burning ship at r. on back.

	GOOD	FINE	XF
a. W/o wmk.	5.00	20.00	75.00
b. Wmk: Circle w/star.	5.00	20.00	75.00

1950 ND ISSUE

32
(26)
50 ĐÔNG
ND (1950). Black-green and yellow. HCM at ctr. Soldier w/flag at ctr. on back (Nam-Bo).

	GOOD	FINE	XF
	3.00	15.00	50.00

33
100 ĐÔNG
ND (1950). Blue and green. Agricultural scene at l., HCM at ctr., war scene at r. Back brown; star, worker and soldier at ctr. 170 x 98mm (Nam-Bo).

	GOOD	FINE	XF
	5.00	22.50	50.00

34 **200 Dông**   Good   Fine   XF
(35)   1950. Lilac-brown and dk. green. Shooting soldiers at l. and ctr., HCM at r. Soldier and 2 field workers on back. Color varieties.
   a. W/o wmk.   3.00   10.00   35.00
   b. Wmk: Circle w/star.   15.00   60.00   125.00

39 **50 Dông**   Good   Fine   XF
(24)   ND (1952). Violet and yellow. HCM at ctr. Back dull red; worker and   5.00   17.50   50.00
   woman at ctr. (Nam-Bo).

1951 ND Issue

35 **100 Dông**   Good   Fine   XF
(34)   ND (1951). Brown and green. HCM at l. overseeing lg. gathering. Back   10.00   30.00   65.00
   dk. brown and tan; 6 working women (Nam-Bo).

40 **100 Dông**   Good   Fine   XF
(27)   ND (1952). Violet on lt. brown-violet unpt. HCM at l. Back lilac;   50.00   125.00   250.00
   harvesting scene.

1952 ND Issue

1953 ND Issue

36 **5 Dông**   Good   Fine   XF
(10A)   ND (1952). Green. HCM at ctr. Back orange; 2 farmers planting at l.   20.00   60.00   150.00
   ctr.

41 **20 Dông**   Good   Fine   XF
(21A)   ND (1953). Black. HCM at ctr.   50.00   125.00   250.00

42 **50 Dông**   Good   Fine   XF
(25)   ND (1953). Brown and lt. green. HCM at l., rice harvesting at r. Back   5.00   20.00   60.00
   brown and purple; group of 10 people (Nam-Bo).

37 **10 Dông**   Good   Fine   XF
(14)   ND (1952). Red-brown and lt. green. 3 laborers at l., HCM at r.   10.00   20.00   50.00
   Soldiers and truck on back (Nam-Bo). White or brown paper.

Tin Phieu

Credit Note

1946-50 Issue

Issued for Trung Bo (1947-1951), w/*TIN PHIEU* indicated prominently.

38 **20 Dông**   Good   Fine   XF
(21)   ND (1952). Dk. brown and olive. Laborers at l. and r., HCM at ctr.   30.00   80.00   185.00
   Workers in factory on back (Nam-Bo).

43 (37)	**1 DÔNG** ND (1946). HCM at ctr. Man w/2 water buffalos on back.	GOOD	FINE	XF
	a. Black.	15.00	35.00	75.00
	b. Purple-brown.	15.00	35.00	75.00
44 (38)	**1 DÔNG** ND. Wine red. Like #43 but portr. and frame different. Back green.	15.00	35.00	75.00
45 (38A)	**1 DÔNG** ND (1946). Lt. blue. HCM at ctr. Farmer plowing w/2 oxen at l. ctr. on back.	15.00	35.00	75.00

46 (39)	**5 DÔNG** ND (1949-50). HCM at ctr. in oval wreath. Numeral *5* on back.	GOOD	FINE	XF
	a. Lilac-brown to brown.	6.00	15.00	40.00
	b. Blue-green.	6.50	16.50	42.50
47 (40)	**5 DÔNG** ND (1949-50). Like #46 but portr. w/o frame.			
	a. Brownish orange. Green back.	10.00	25.00	55.00
	b. Blue.	10.00	25.00	55.00
	c. Olive.	10.00	25.00	55.00
48 (41)	**20 DÔNG** ND (1948). Orange. *TIN PHIEU* and *HAI MUOI DONG* at ctr. Back green; work scenes at l. bottom and r., crude portr. of HCM in wreath at ctr. 133 x 77mm.			
	a. W/o wmk.	9.00	22.50	60.00
	b. Wmk: Circle w/star.	9.00	22.50	60.00

49 (41A)	**20 DÔNG** ND (1948). Like #48 but face and back brown on yellow unpt.	GOOD	FINE	XF
	a. W/o wmk.	9.00	22.50	65.00
	b. Wmk: Circle w/star.	9.00	22.50	65.00

50 (42)	**50 DÔNG** ND (1949-50). HCM in circle at lower ctr. Work scenes at l., r. and bottom. No unpt. on face. Men in sailboat on back. Brown or white paper.	GOOD	FINE	XF
	a. Face violet-brown, back blue. W/o wmk.	8.00	17.50	50.00
	b. Face orange, back gray-green. W/o wmk.	8.00	17.50	50.00
	c. Face and back gray. W/o wmk.	8.00	17.50	50.00
	d. Violet.	8.00	17.50	50.00
	e. Brown. Back gray-green.	8.00	17.50	50.00
	f. W/round handstamp and black sign. on back for Binh-Thuan Province.	8.00	17.50	55.00
	g. W/red circular handstamp on back for Cuc-Nam Province.	8.00	17.50	55.00

51 (43)	**50 DÔNG** ND (1949-50). Brown and green. Like #50 but unpt. at ctr. on face.	GOOD	FINE	XF
	a. White paper w/o wmk.	8.00	17.50	55.00
	b. Brown paper, Wmk: Circle w/star.	8.00	17.50	55.00
	c. As a w/2-line black Vietnamese ovpt. on back.	8.00	17.50	55.00

52 (44)	**50 DÔNG** 1951. Dk. brown. HCM at r. Back olive; soldier, worker and farmer at ctr.	GOOD	FINE	XF
	a. W/o wmk.	8.00	17.50	45.00
	b. Wmk: Circle w/star.	8.00	17.50	45.00
53 (45)	**100 DÔNG** ND (1950-51). Red or brown. HCM at l. Back green-gray; 2 workers and soldier.			
	a. W/o wmk.	6.00	12.50	40.00
	b. Wmk: Circle w/star.	6.00	12.50	40.00

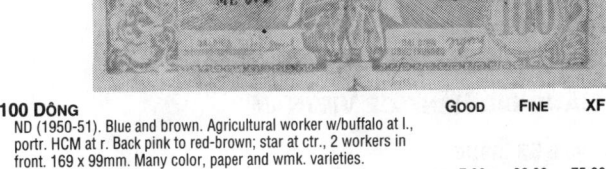

54 (46)	**100 DÔNG** ND (1950-51). Blue and brown. Agricultural worker w/buffalo at l., portr. HCM at r. Back pink to red-brown; star at ctr., 2 workers in front. 169 x 99mm. Many color, paper and wmk. varieties.	GOOD	FINE	XF
	a. W/o wmk.	7.00	20.00	75.00
	b. Wmk: Circle w/star.	7.00	20.00	75.00

55 (47)	**100 DÔNG** ND (1950-51). Green and gray. Back gray-brown; soldier, woman and children at ctr., HCM at r. 171 x 84mm.	GOOD	FINE	XF
	a. W/o wmk.	8.50	20.00	65.00
	b. Wmk: Circle w/star.	8.50	20.00	65.00

56 (48)	**100 DÔNG** ND (1950-51). Brownish red. HCM at r. Back blue-green and lt. brown; 2 soldiers at ctr.	**GOOD**	**FINE**	**XF**
	a. W/o wmk.	10.00	25.00	65.00
	b. Wmk: Circle w/star.	10.00	25.00	65.00

57 (49)	**500 DÔNG** ND (1950-51). Gray-blue. 2 workers at ctr., HCM at r. Back green; landscape and 3 people. Wmk: Star in circle.	**GOOD** 4.00	**FINE** 17.50	**XF** 45.00

62 (54)	**100 DÔNG** 1951. HCM at r. Bomb factory on back.	**VG**	**VF**	**UNC**
	a. Green.	8.00	40.00	125.00
	b. Blue.	5.00	15.00	50.00
	s. As a. Specimen.	—	—	150.00

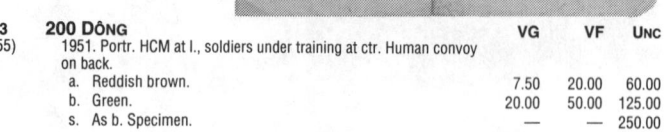

58 (50)	**1000 DÔNG** ND (1950-51). Red to brown. HCM at r. Soldiers and porters on back. Wmk: Star in circle.	**GOOD** 5.00	**FINE** 15.00	**XF** 35.00

63 (55)	**200 DÔNG** 1951. Portr. HCM at l., soldiers under training at ctr. Human convoy on back.	**VG**	**VF**	**UNC**
	a. Reddish brown.	7.50	20.00	60.00
	b. Green.	20.00	50.00	125.00
	s. As b. Specimen.	—	—	250.00

NGAN HANG QUOC GIA VIET NAM

NATIONAL BANK OF VIETNAM

1951-53 ISSUE

1 "New" Dong = 100 "Old" Dong

In 1952 all previously issued notes were withdrawn and demonetized. Notes in "new" Dong values, issue dated 1951 and later, were printed in Czechoslovakia and remained in circulation until 1958. Thus they were the last wartime notes issued during the fighting against the French, and they became the official currency of the post-1954 independent Democratic Republic of Viet Nam (North Vietnam). All notes w/HCM.

NOTE: For #59 w/ovpt. *1 XU* see #67.

#59-66 printer: CPF-Shanghai (w/o imprint).

59 (51)	**10 DÔNG** ND. Violet-brown. HCM at l. Farmers w/water buffalos on back.	**GOOD** —	**FINE** —	**XF** —

64 (56)	**500 DÔNG** 1951. Green. HCM at l., soldiers at a gun at r. Workers tilling field on back.	**VG**	**VF**	**UNC**
	a. Issued note.	10.00	20.00	80.00
	s. Specimen.	—	—	75.00

60 (52)	**20 DÔNG** 1951. Portr. HCM at l. Soldier and ships on back.	**GOOD**	**FINE**	**XF**
	a. Purple.	2.00	7.50	30.00
	b. Olive.	2.00	7.50	30.00
	s1. As a. Specimen.	—	—	50.00
	s2. As b. Specimen.	—	—	50.00

61 (53)	**50 DÔNG** 1951. Portr. HCM at r. Harvest work on back.			
		GOOD	**FINE**	**XF**
	a. Green.	2.00	8.50	40.00
	b. Brown.	2.00	7.50	30.00
	s1. As a. Specimen.	—	—	75.00
	s2. As b. Specimen.	—	—	85.00

65 (57)	**1000 DÔNG** 1951. Brown-orange. Portr. HCM at l., soldiers advancing at ctr. Soldier, worker and farmer on back.	**VG**	**VF**	**UNC**
	a. Issued note.	5.00	15.00	45.00
	s. Specimen.	—	—	85.00

66 **5000 Dông**
(58) 1953. Blue. HCM at l. Anti-aircraft artillery emplacements on back.

	VG	VF	UNC
a. Issued note.	30.00	110.00	325.00
s. Specimen.	—	—	550.00

NUOC VIET NAM DAN CHU CONG HOA

After the Geneva accords of 1954, which partitioned Vietnam at the 17th parallel, the Democratic Republic of Viet Nam (henceforth known unofficially as "North Vietnam") was physically identified with the former French colonial territories of Tonkin and northern Annam.

NGAN HANG QUOC GIA VIET NAM

NATIONAL BANK OF VIET NAM

1958 ND PROVISIONAL ISSUE
1 New Dong = 100 Old Dong (1951-53 series)

67 **1 Xu ON 10 Dông**
(A59) ND (1958). Ovpt. new denomination on #58 face and back.

	VG	VF	UNC
	—	300.00	600.00

DEMOCRATIC REPUBLIC OF VIET NAM

NGAN HANG QUOC GIA VIET NAM

NATIONAL BANK OF VIET NAM

1958 ISSUE
#68-72 printer: CPF-Shanghai (w/o imprint).

68 **1 HAO**
(59) 1958. Red on green unpt. Arms at ctr. Train on back.

	VG	VF	UNC
a. Issued note.	.50	1.50	5.00
b. Ovpt: *Cai Luu Hanj O Cua...* for circulation in Haiphong.	—	—	—
c. W/control handstamp: *DA THU*.	.75	2.25	7.50

69 **2 HAO**
(60) 1958. Green on tan unpt. Arms at ctr. Grazing animals near Coffer dam on back.

	VG	VF	UNC
a. Issued note.	1.00	3.00	10.00
b. W/control handstamp: *DA THU*.	1.50	4.50	15.00

70 **5 HAO**
(61) 1958. Brown on lt. green unpt. Arms at ctr. 4 women in spinning mill on back.

	VG	VF	UNC
a. Issued note.	1.50	4.50	15.00
b. W/control handstamp: *DA THU*.	2.00	6.50	20.00

71 **1 DÔNG**
(62) 1958. Brown on lt. green unpt. Arms at l., monument w/tower and flag at ctr. Work in rice paddies on back.

	VG	VF	UNC
a. Issued note.	1.00	3.00	10.00
b. W/control handstamp: *DA THU*.	1.50	4.50	15.00
x. US lithograph counterfeit w/propaganda message at l. 6 varieties: w/o code, Code 50, Code 4540 (2 text var.) Code 4543 (2 text var.).	1.00	2.50	10.00

72 **2 DÔNG**
(63) 1958. Blue on green unpt. Arms at l., 4 people w/flag at ctr. r. Boats and mountains on back.

	VG	VF	UNC
a. Issued note.	1.25	3.75	12.50
b. W/control handstamp: *DA THU*.	1.75	5.50	17.50
x. US lithograph counterfeit w/propaganda message at r. Code 4541.	1.00	3.00	9.00

73 **5 DÔNG**
(64) 1958. Brown on blue unpt. Arms at l., tractor at ctr., HCM at r. Road construction work on back.

	VG	VF	UNC
a. Issued note.	1.50	4.50	15.00
b. W/control handstamp: *DA THU*.	2.00	6.50	20.00
x. US lithograph counterfeit w/propaganda message at r. Code 4542.	2.00	5.00	20.00

74 **10 DÔNG**
(65) 1958. Red on blue and green unpt. Arms at ctr., HCM at r. Factory on back.

	VG	VF	UNC
a. Issued note.	1.75	5.50	17.50
b. W/control handstamp: *DA THU*.	2.50	7.50	22.50

REGIONAL

PHIEU TIEP TE

1949-50 ND EMERGENCY ISSUES
Issued by the various local (provincial and lower) administrations.

R1   5 CAC
ND (1949-50). Dk. blue. Farmers and oxen at l. ctr. Metal working on back.

R2   5 CAC
ND (1949-50). Red-brown. HCM at ctr. in oval wreath of corn. Soldier at l., seated man at r. on back (Soc-Trang).

	Good	Fine	XF
R1	15.00	30.00	60.00
R2	15.00	30.00	60.00

R3   1 DÔNG
ND (1949-50). Blue on brown. HCM at ctr. in oval formed of Laurel wreath. Soldier at l., star at r. on back (Soc-Trang).

	Good	Fine	XF
R3	12.50	25.00	50.00

R4   1 DÔNG
ND (1949-50). Red and yellow. Man and woman. 5 soldiers on back (Thu Dau Mot).

	Good	Fine	XF
a. Back w/text: *TINH-THU-DAU-MOT*.	10.00	25.00	50.00
b. Back w/text: *TINH THUDAUMOT*.	10.00	25.00	50.00
c. Back w/o either style of above legend.	10.00	25.00	50.00

R5   1 DÔNG
ND (1949-50). Red. 5 stars at l. and r. Woman carrying load on shoulder on back (Tay Ninh).

R6   1 DÔNG
ND (1949-50). Blue. HCM in rectangular frame. Man carrying load on head at l., man holding spear at r. on back (Soc Trang).

	Good	Fine	XF
R5	12.50	30.00	65.00
R6	12.50	30.00	65.00

R7   2 DÔNG
ND (1949-50). Dk. red. HCM at l. Lag. 2 at l., *HAI DONG* at r. on back.

	Good	Fine	XF
R7	12.50	30.00	60.00

R8   2 DÔNG
ND (1949-50). Brown. Mountains at r. Back green; man digging at l., blacksmith at r. (Ha Tien).

R10   2 DÔNG
23.12.1949. Blue. Soldiers at l. attacking burning village at r. Woman w/baskets on back (Can Tho).

	Good	Fine	XF
R8	15.00	35.00	75.00
a. Back w/text: *Tat Ca De.*	15.00	35.00	75.00
b. Back w/text: *Chuan Bi De.*	15.00	35.00	75.00

R10A   5 DÔNG
ND. HCM in spray at l.

	Good	Fine	XF
R10A	—	—	—

R10B   5 DÔNG
ND. Tower at ctr. Farmers and laborers on back.

	Good	Fine	XF
R10B	15.00	30.00	60.00

FANTASY

1949; 1950 DATED "ISSUES"
A series of very clever fantasy notes appeared on the market several years ago. These are easily identified as the serial # printed on each note were all done with the same font of type. Listed below are 4 examples.

R(6A)   1 DÔNG
1949(1983). HCM at l. (Modern fantasy).

	Good	Fine	XF
R(6A)	—	—	—

		GOOD	FINE	XF
R(9)	**1 DÔNG** 23.12.1949. Lt. brown. Woman at ctr. Star, swords and helmet on back (Can Tho). (Modern Fantasy).	—	—	—
R(10C)	**10 DÔNG** 9.5.1949. (Modern fantasy).	—	—	—

		GOOD	FINE	XF
R(10D)	**10 DÔNG** 1950. Value *10* in spray at l. Laborers on back. (Modern fantasy).			

VIET-MINH ADMINISTRATIVE COMMITTEES

1945 ND PROVISIONAL ISSUES

Beginning in 1945, various Viet-Minh administrative committees (provincial, city and military) hands-tamped notes of the Banque de l'Indochine for use in areas under Viet-Minh control.

		GOOD	FINE	XF
R10E (40A)	**5 DÔNG** ND. Star at ctr., fighters at sides. 3 workers at l. on back (Thu Bien). a. Red. Imprint on back at lower l. corner. b. Orange. W/imprint.	 15.00 18.00	 30.00 35.00	 75.00 85.00

		GOOD	FINE	XF
R11	**1 PIASTRE** ND. Red circular handstamp: *BIEN HOA* on French Indochina #54c.	7.00	20.00	—

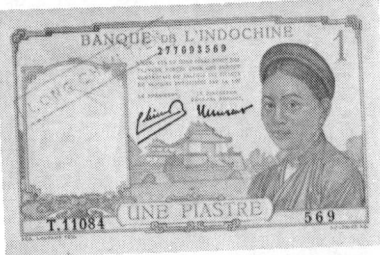

		GOOD	FINE	XF
R11A	**1 PIASTRE** ND. Red rectangular handstamp: *LONG CHAU TIEN* on French Indochina #54e for Long Xuyen, Chau Doc and Tien Giang provinces.	7.00	20.00	—
R11B	**1 PIASTRE** ND. Lg. circular handstamp: *THU BIEN* on French Indochina #48b. 2 sm. handstamps w/star in ctr. on back.	7.00	20.00	—

		GOOD	FINE	XF
R11C	**1 PIASTRE** ND. Lg. circular handstamp: *CHAO DOC* on French Indochina #105.	—	—	—
R12	**5 PIASTRES** ND. Red circular and rectangular handstamps: *BEN TRE* on Indochina #55.	7.00	20.00	—
R13	**5 PIASTRES** ND. Red circular handstamp: *CHO LON* on French Indochina #49.	7.00	20.00	—
R14	**5 PIASTRES** ND. Red circular handstamp: *CHO LON* on French Indochina #55.	7.00	20.00	—

		GOOD	FINE	XF
R15	**10 PIASTRES** ND. Black circular handstamps: *LONG PHUOC* on French Indochina #80.	20.00	—	—
R16	**20 PIASTRES** ND. Red circular handstamp: *CHO LON* on French Indochina #81.	10.00	25.00	—
R17	**100 PIASTRES** ND. Red circular handstamp: *RACH-GIA.* a. On French Indochina #66. b. On French Indochina #67. c. On French Indochina #73.	 10.00 10.00 10.00	 25.00 25.00 25.00	 — — —

		GOOD	FINE	XF
R18	**100 PIASTRES** ND. Red rectangular handstamp: *LONG CHAU HA* on French Indochina #66.	10.00	25.00	—
R19	**100 PIASTRES** ND. Red circular handstamp: *BEN-TRE* on French Indochina #66.	3.50	7.50	—

TRA VINH PROVINCE

1951 PROVISIONAL ISSUE

		GOOD	FINE	XF
R31	**100 DÔNG** 18.3.1951. Control ticket added w/red-violet handstamp: *TRA VINH* on #28.	125.00		

VIETNAM/South

South Vietnam (the former Republic of Viet Nam), located in Southeast Asia, bounded by North Vietnam on the north, Laos and Cambodia on the west, and the South China Sea on the east and south, had an area of 66,280 sq. mi. (171,665 sq. km.) and a population of 20 million. Capital: Saigon (now Ho Chi Minh City). The economy of the area is predominantly agricultural.

South Vietnam, the direct successor to the French-dominated Bao Dai regime (also known as the Republic of Vietnam), was created after the first Indochina War (between the French and the Viet-Minh) by the Geneva agreement of 1954 which divided Vietnam at the 17th parallel of latitude. The National Bank of Vietnam, with headquarters in the old Bank of Indochina building in Saigon, came into being on October 26, 1955. Elections which would have reunified North and South Vietnam in 1956 never took place, and the North continued the war for unification of Vietnam under the communist government of the Democratic Republic of Vietnam begun at the close of World War II. South Vietnam surrendered unconditionally on April 30, 1975. With the North dominating, there followed a short period of coexistence of the two Vietnamese states, the South being governed by the National Liberation Front. On July 2, 1976, South and North Vietnam joined to form the Socialist Republic of Vietnam.

Also see Viet Nam.

MONETARY SYSTEM
1 Dông = 100 Xu = 100 Su to 1975
1 New Dông = 500 Old Dông, 1975-76

VIET NAM - SOUTH

NGÂN-HÀNG QUÔC-GIA VIÊT-NAM

NATIONAL BANK OF VIETNAM

1955; 1956 ND FIRST ISSUE
#1-4 wmk: Tiger's head.

		VG	VF	UNC
1	**1 DÔNG**			
	ND (1956). Green on lilac unpt. Temple at r. Bldg. at l. on back.			
	a. Issued note.	.10	.30	1.00
	s. Specimen.	—	—	—
2	**5 DÔNG**			
	ND (1955). Green on gold and lilac unpt. Bird at ctr. Farmer w/water buffalo on back.			
	a. Issued note.	.20	.50	1.50
	s. Specimen.	—	—	—

		VG	VF	UNC
3	**10 DÔNG**			
	ND (1955). Deep red on blue and gray unpt. Fish at ctr. Coastal area w/boats on back.			
	a. Issued note.	.25	1.00	5.00
	s. Specimen.	—	—	—

		VG	VF	UNC
4	**20 DÔNG**			
	ND (1956). Green and m/c. Huts and boats at l., banana plants at r. Farmers and water buffalos on back.			
	a. Issued note.	2.00	10.00	40.00
	s. Specimen.	—		

		VG	VF	UNC
4A	**1000 DÔNG**			
	ND. M/c. Old man at l., temple at r. Sampan at lower l., young woman at r. on back. Specimen perforated: GIAY MAU.	—	—	1500.

1955-58 ND SECOND ISSUE

		VG	VF	UNC
7	**50 DÔNG**			
	ND (1956). Purple. Boy w/water buffalo at l. Sifting grain on back. Printer: SBNC.			
	a. Issued note.	2.00	10.00	75.00
	s. Specimen.	—		

8   100 DÔNG
ND (1955). Gray. Farmer on tractor at ctr. Stylized peacock on green
back. Printer: ABNC (w/o imprint).

	VG	VF	UNC
a. Issued note.	3.00	12.50	55.00
s. Specimen.	—	—	—

13   5 DÔNG
ND (1955). Dull red on peach unpt. Farmer w/water buffalo at l. River
scene w/house on back.

	VG	VF	UNC
a. Issued note.	.20	.75	2.50
s. Specimen.	—	—	—
x. Counterfeit. Propaganda on back.	—	—	—

9   200 DÔNG
ND (1958). Purple on green unpt. Bank at r. Fishing boats on back.
Printer: ABNC (w/o imprint).

	VG	VF	UNC
a. Issued note.	4.00	15.00	60.00
s. Specimen.	—	—	—

14   200 DÔNG
ND (1955). Green. Soldier at l. Girl w/sheaves in field on back.

	VG	VF	UNC
a. Issued note.	25.00	125.00	500.00
s. Specimen w/ovpt: *GIAY MAU*, punched hole cancelled.	—	—	—

14A   200 DÔNG
ND. Green. Like #14, but engraved. (Not issued.)

	VG	VF	UNC
s1. Specimen.	—	—	—
s2. Specimen. Uniface pair.	—	—	—

10   500 DÔNG
ND (1955). Blue. Pagoda at ctr. Back orange. Printer: ABNC (w/o
imprint).

	VG	VF	UNC
a. Issued note.	25.00	125.00	500.00
s. Specimen w/ovpt: *GIAY MAU*, punched hole cancelled.	—	—	—

1955 ND THIRD ISSUE
#11-14 printer: SBNC.

11   1 DÔNG
ND (1955). Gray. Woman farm worker threshing grain at l. Rice paddy
worker on back.

	VG	VF	UNC
a. Issued note.	.20	.75	5.00
s. Specimen.	—	—	—

12   2 DÔNG
ND (1955). Purplish blue. Boat at r. River scene on back.

	VG	VF	UNC
a. Issued note.	.20	.75	2.50
s. Specimen.	—	—	—

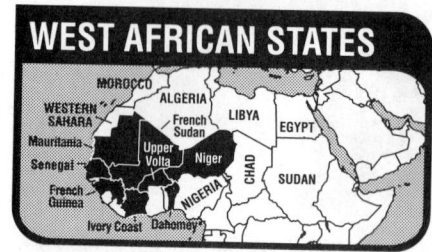

WEST AFRICAN STATES

The West African States, a former federation of eight French colonial territories on the northwest coast of Africa, had an area of 1,813,079 sq. mi. (4,742,495 sq. km.) and a population of about 17 million. Capital: Dakar. The constituent territories were Mauritania, Senegal, Dahomey, French Sudan, Ivory Coast, Upper Volta, Niger and French Guinea.

The members of the federation were overseas territories within the French Union until Sept. of 1958 when all but French Guinea approved the constitution of the Fifth French Republic, thereby electing to become autonomous members of the new French Community. French Guinea voted to become the fully independent Republic of Guinea. The other seven attained independence in 1960. The French West Africa territories were provided with a common currency, a practice which was continued as the monetary union of the West African States which provides a common currency to the autonomous republics of Dahomey (now Benin), Mali, Senegal, Upper Volta, Ivory Coast, Togo and Niger.

MONETARY SYSTEM:
1 Franc = 100 Centimes

DATING
The year of issue on the current 500, 1000 and 2500 Francs appears in the first 2 digits of the serial number, i.e. (19)91, (19)92, etc..

SIGNATURE VARIETIES

	LE PRÉSIDENT	LE DIRECTEUR GÉNÉRAL	Date
1	*(signature)*	R. *(signature)*	Various dates – 1959 20.3.1961
2	*(signature)*	R. *(signature)*	20.3.1961
3	*(signature)*	R. *(signature)*	2.12.1964
4	*(signature)*	R. *(signature)*	2.3.1965; ND
5	*(signature)*	R. *(signature)*	ND
6	*(signature)*	R. *(signature)*	ND
7	*(signature)*	R. *(signature)*	ND
8	*(signature)*	R. *(signature)*	ND
9	*(signature)*	R. *(signature)*	ND
	LE PRÉSIDENT DU CONSEIL DES MINISTRES	**LE GOUVERNEUR**	**Date**
10	*(signature)*	*(signature)*	ND
11	*(signature)*	*(signature)*	ND (1977); 1977
12	*(signature)*	*(signature)*	ND (1978); 1978; 1979
13	*(signature)*	*(signature)*	ND (1980); 1980

WEST AFRICAN STATES

NOTE: Begining with signatures #21 their postion has been reversed on the 500 Francs recorded herewith.

Banque Centrale des Etats de l'Afrique de l'Ouest

Notes of this bank were issued both w/and w/o code letters in the upper r. and lower l. corners. The code letter follows the control number and indicates which member country the note was issued for. Those w/o code letters are general issues. The code letters are as follows:

A	Ivory Coast	E	Mauritania (seceded in 1973)
B	Benin (formerly Dahomey)	F	Niger
C	Burkina Faso (formerly Upper Volta)	G	Senegal
D	Mali (seceded in 1962, rejoined 1984)	H	Togo

W/O BRANCH LETTER

1958; 1959 ND ISSUE
#1-5 w/o code letters to signify member countries.

		VG	VF	UNC
1	**50 FRANCS** ND (1958). Dk. brown, blue and m/c. Mask at l., woman w/headress at ctr. on back. Sign. 1.	10.00	40.00	110.00

		VG	VF	UNC
2	**100 FRANCS** 1959; ND. Dk. brown, orange and m/c. Mask at l., woman at r. Woman at l., carving at lower ctr. on back.			
	a. Sign. 1. 23.4.1959.	10.00	40.00	90.00
	b. Sign. 5. ND.	3.00	10.00	20.00
3	**500 FRANCS** 15.4.1959. Brown, green and m/c. Men doing field work at l., mask carving at r. Woman at l., farmer on tractor at r. on back. Sign. 1.	30.00	70.00	150.00
4	**1000 FRANCS** 17.9.1959. Brown, blue and m/c. Man and woman at ctr. Man w/rope suspension bridge in background and pineapples on back. Sign. 1.	20.00	50.00	125.00
5	**5000 FRANCS** 15.4.1959. Blue, brown and m/c. Bearded man at l., bldg. at ctr. Woman, corn grinders and huts on back. Sign. 1.	50.00	130.00	—

A FOR IVORY COAST

1959-65; ND ISSUE

		VG	VF	UNC
102A	**500 FRANCS** 1959-64; ND. Design like #3.			
	a. Engraved. Sign. 1. 15.4.1959.	25.00	55.00	100.00
	b. Sign. 1. 20.3.1961.	15.00	40.00	80.00
	c. Sign. 2. 20.3.1961.	15.00	40.00	80.00
	d. Sign. 3. 2.12.1964.	25.00	55.00	100.00
	f. Sign. 5. ND.	12.00	35.00	75.00
	g. Sign. 6. ND.	10.00	30.00	65.00
	h. Litho. Sign. 6. ND.	10.00	30.00	65.00
	i. Sign. 7. ND.	12.00	35.00	75.00
	j. Sign. 8. ND.	25.00	55.00	100.00
	k. Sign. 9. ND.	8.00	25.00	55.00
	l. Sign. 10. ND.	5.00	15.00	40.00
	m. Sign. 11. ND.	5.00	15.00	40.00
	n. Sign. 12. ND.	20.00	50.00	90.00
103A	**1000 FRANCS** 1959-65; ND. Design like #4.			
	a. Engraved. Sign. 1. 17.9.1959.	—	—	—
	b. Sign. 1. 20.3.1961.	15.00	45.00	100.00
	c. Sign. 2. 20.3.1961.	10.00	35.00	80.00
	d. Sign. 4. 2.3.1965.	30.00	70.00	—
	e. Sign. 5. ND.	8.00	25.00	60.00
	f. Sign. 6. ND.	8.00	25.00	60.00
	h. Litho. Sign. 6. ND.	8.00	35.00	60.00
	i. Sign. 7. ND.	10.00	35.00	70.00
	j. Sign. 8. ND.	12.00	40.00	90.00
	k. Sign. 9. ND.	5.00	20.00	50.00
	l. Sign. 10. ND.	5.00	15.00	40.00
	m. Sign. 11. ND.	5.00	15.00	40.00
	n. Sign. 12. ND.	5.00	15.00	40.00
	o. Sign. 13. ND.	5.00	15.00	40.00

B FOR BENIN (DAHOMEY) BRANCH

1959-65; ND ISSUE

#201B-209B have letter B for Benin.

203B	1000 FRANCS	VG	VF	UNC
	1961-65; ND. Like #4.			
	a. Engraved. Sign. 1. 17.9.1959.	35.00	75.00	—
	b. Sign. 2. 20.3.1961.	25.00	60.00	125.00
	e. Sign. 4. 2.3.1965.	25.00	60.00	125.00
	g. Sign. 6. ND.	8.00	30.00	65.00
	h. Litho. Sign. 6. ND.	7.00	25.00	60.00
	i. Sign. 7. ND.	20.00	55.00	110.00
	j. Sign. 8. ND.	10.00	35.00	70.00
	k. Sign. 9. ND.	10.00	35.00	70.00
	l. Sign. 10. ND.	5.00	15.00	45.00
	m. Sign. 11. ND.	5.00	15.00	45.00
	n. Sign. 12. ND.	5.00	15.00	45.00

D FOR MALI BRANCH

1959-61; ND ISSUE

402D	500 FRANCS	VG	VF	UNC
	1959; 1961. Like #3.			
	a. Sign. I. 15.4.1959.	90.00	175.00	—
	b. Sign. I. 20.3.1961.	—	—	—

403D	1000 FRANCS			
	1959; 1961. Like #4.			
	a. Sign. I. 17.9.1959.	75.00	150.00	—
	b. Sign. I. 20.3.1961.	75.00	150.00	—

E FOR MAURITANIA BRANCH

1959-64; ND ISSUE

502E	500 FRANCS	VG	VF	UNC
	1959-64; ND. Like #3.			
	a. Engraved. Sign. I. 15.4.1959.	55.00	120.00	—
	b. Sign. I. 20.3.1961.	45.00	100.00	—
	c. Sign. 2. 20.3.1961.	45.00	100.00	—
	e. Sign. 4. 2.3.1965.	45.00	100.00	—
	f. Sign. 5. ND.	45.00	100.00	—
	g. Sign. 6. ND.	45.00	100.00	—
	h. Litho. Sign. 6. ND.	45.00	100.00	—
	i. Sign. 7. ND.	45.00	100.00	—

H FOR NIGER BRANCH

1959-65; ND ISSUE

602H	500 FRANCS	VG	VF	UNC
	1959-65; ND. Like #3.			
	a. Engraved. Sign. 1. 15.4.1959.	25.00	65.00	130.00
	d. Sign. 3. 2.12.1964.	25.00	65.00	130.00
	e. Sign. 4. 2.3.1965.	25.00	65.00	130.00
	g. Sign. 6. ND.	15.00	40.00	85.00
	h. Litho Sign. 6. ND.	15.00	40.00	85.00
	i. Sign. 7. ND.	25.00	65.00	—
	j. Sign. 8. ND.	15.00	40.00	85.00
	k. Sign. 9. ND.	10.00	30.00	65.00
	m. Sign. 11. ND.	10.00	30.00	65.00

603H	1000 FRANCS			
	1959-65; ND. Like #4.			
	a. Sign. I. 17.9.1959.	—	—	—
	b. Sign. I. 20.3.1961.	30.00	65.00	150.00
	e. Sign. 4. 2.3.1965.	30.00	65.00	150.00
	f. Sign. 5. ND.	30.00	65.00	150.00
	g. Sign. 6. ND.	10.00	35.00	80.00
	h. Litho. Sign. 6. ND.	15.00	40.00	—
	i. Sign. 7. ND.	10.00	35.00	80.00
	j. Sign. 8. ND.	30.00	55.00	—
	k. Sign. 9. ND.	8.00	30.00	65.00
	l. Sign. 10. ND.	5.00	18.00	50.00
	m. Sign. 11. ND.	5.00	18.00	50.00
	n. Sign. 12. ND.	5.00	18.00	50.00
	o. Sign. 13. ND.	5.00	18.00	50.00

K FOR SENEGAL BRANCH

1959-65; ND ISSUE

702K	500 FRANCS	VG	VF	UNC
	1959-65; ND. Like #3.			
	a. Engraved. Sign. 1. 15.4.1959.	25.00	55.00	100.00
	b. Sign. 1. 20.3.1961.	15.00	40.00	80.00
	c. Sign. 2. 20.3.1961.	15.00	40.00	80.00
	d. Sign. 3. 2.12.1964.	15.00	40.00	80.00
	e. Sign. 4. 2.3.1965.	15.00	40.00	80.00
	f. Sign. 5. ND.	18.00	45.00	90.00
	g. Sign. 6. ND.	10.00	30.00	65.00
	h. Litho. Sign. 6. ND.	10.00	30.00	65.00
	i. Sign. 7. ND.	10.00	30.00	60.00
	j. Sign. 8. ND.	15.00	40.00	80.00
	k. Sign. 9. ND.	8.00	25.00	55.00
	l. Sign. 10. ND.	5.00	15.00	40.00
	m. Sign. 11. ND.	5.00	15.00	40.00
	n. Sign. 12. ND.	5.00	15.00	40.00

703K	1000 FRANCS			
	1959-65; ND. Like #4.			
	a. Engraved. Sign. I. 17.9.1959.	20.00	65.00	125.00
	b. Sign. I. 20.3.1961.	20.00	65.00	—
	c. Sign. 2. 20.3.1961.	10.00	50.00	100.00
	e. Sign. 4. 2.3.1965.	10.00	50.00	100.00
	f. Sign. 5. ND.	20.00	65.00	—
	g. Sign. 6. ND.	20.00	65.00	—
	h. Litho. Sign. 6. ND.	5.00	20.00	50.00
	i. Sign. 7. ND.	8.00	30.00	60.00
	j. Sign. 8. ND.	8.00	30.00	60.00
	k. Sign. 9. ND.	5.00	20.00	50.00
	l. Sign. 10. ND.	5.00	15.00	40.00
	m. Sign. 11. ND.	5.00	15.00	40.00
	n. Sign. 12. ND.	5.00	15.00	40.00
	o. Sign. 13. ND.	5.00	15.00	40.00

T FOR TOGO BRANCH

1959-65; ND ISSUE

802T	500 FRANCS	VG	VF	UNC
	1959-61; ND. Like #3.			
	a. Engraved. Sign. 1. 15.4.1959.	25.00	65.00	130.00
	b. Sign. 1. 20.3.1961.	25.00	65.00	—
	c. Sign. 2. 20.3.1961.	25.00	65.00	—
	f. Sign. 5. ND.	25.00	65.00	—
	g. Sign. 6. ND.	10.00	30.00	65.00
	i. Litho. Sign. 7. ND.	20.00	55.00	110.00
	j. Sign. 8. ND.	20.00	50.00	110.00
	k. Sign. 9. ND.	8.00	20.00	55.00
	l. Sign. 10. ND.	15.00	30.00	75.00
	m. Sign. 11. ND.	3.00	10.00	30.00

803T	1000 FRANCS			
	1959-65; ND. Like #4.			
	a. Engraved. Sign. 1. 17.9.1959.	30.00	70.00	—
	b. Sign. 1. 20.3.1961.	25.00	65.00	130.00
	c. Sign. 2. 20.3.1961.	25.00	65.00	—
	e. Sign. 4. 2.3.1965.	25.00	65.00	130.00
	f. Sign. 5. ND.	15.00	45.00	100.00
	g. Sign. 6. ND.	10.00	30.00	70.00
	h. Litho. Sign. 6. ND.	10.00	30.00	70.00
	i. Sign. 7. ND.	10.00	30.00	70.00
	j. Sign. 8. ND.	15.00	45.00	100.00
	k. Sign. 9. ND.	5.00	20.00	50.00
	l. Sign. 10. ND.	5.00	15.00	40.00
	m. Sign. 11. ND.	5.00	15.00	40.00
	n. Sign. 12. ND.	5.00	15.00	40.00
	o. Sign. 13. ND.	5.00	15.00	40.00

1058 WESTERN SAMOA

The Independent State of Western Samoa (formerly German Samoa), located in the Pacific Ocean 1,600 miles (2,574 km.) northeast of New Zealand, has an area of 1,097 sq. mi. (2,860 sq. km.) and a population of 157,000. Capital: Apia. The economy is based on agriculture, fishing and tourism. Copra, cocoa and bananas are exported.

The Samoan group of islands was discovered by Dutch navigator Jacob Roggeveen in 1772. Great Britain, the United States and Germany established consular representation at Apia in 1847, 1853 and 1861 respectively. The conflicting interests of the three powers produced the Berlin agreement of 1889 which declared Samoa neutral and had the effect of establishing a tripartite protectorate over the islands. A further agreement, 1899, recognized the rights of the United States in those islands east of 171 deg. west longitude (American Samoa) and of Germany in the other islands (Western Samoa). New Zealand occupied Western Samoa at the start of World War I and administered it as a League of Nations mandate and U.N. trusteeship until Jan. 1, 1962, when it became an independent state.

Western Samoa is a member of the Commonwealth of Nations. The Chief Executive is Chief of State. The prime minister is the Head of Government. The present Head of State, Malietoa Tanumafili II, holds his position for life. Future Heads of State will be elected by the Legislature Assembly for five-year terms.

RULERS:
British, 1914-1962
Malietoa Tanumafili II, 1962-

MONETARY SYSTEM:
1 Shilling = 12 Pence
1 Pound = 20 Shillings to 1967
1 Tala = 100 Sene, 1967-

NEW ZEALAND OCCUPATION - WWI

GOVERNMENT OF SAMOA

1920 ND PROVISIONAL ISSUE
#1, ovpt: *GOVERNMENT OF SAMOA, CURRENCY NOTE* on Bank of New Zealand 10 Shilling notes until 1921.
#2-6 *Deleted.*

		GOOD	FINE	XF
1	**10 SHILLINGS** (1920-old date 1917). M/c. Red ovpt. on face only on New Zealand #S223. Apia.	—	Rare	—

NEW ZEALAND ADMINISTRATION

TERRITORY OF WESTERN SAMOA

1920-22 TREASURY NOTE ISSUE
By Authority of New Zealand Government
#7-9 various date and sign. varieties. Printer: BWC.
#8 and 9 *STERLING* appears close beneath spelled out denominations at ctr. until about 1953.
NOTE: Some of these notes may appear to be ND, probably through error or washed out, faded or worn off hand-stamped dates.

		GOOD	FINE	XF
7	**10 SHILLINGS** 1922-61. Black on brown and green unpt. Palm trees along beach at ctr.			
	a. 3.3.1922.	—	Rare	—
	b. Sign. title: *MINISTER OF EXTERNAL AFFAIRS FOR NEW ZEALAND* at l. 24.4.1939-21.11.1949.	50.00	165.00	350.00
	c. Sign. title: *MINISTER OF ISLAND TERRITORIES FOR NEW ZEALAND* at l. 25.9.1953-27.5.1958.	75.00	250.00	600.00
	d. Sign. title: *HIGH COMMISSIONER* at l.20.3.1957-22.12.1959.	35.00	140.00	250.00

		GOOD	FINE	XF
8	**1 POUND** 1922-61. Purple on m/c unpt. Hut, palm trees at ctr.			
	a. 3.3.1922.	—	Rare	—
	b. Sign. title: *MINISTER OF EXTERNAL AFFAIRS FOR NEW ZEALAND* at l. 16.1.1939-12.1.1947.	65.00	175.00	450.00
	c. Sign. title: *MINISTER OF ISLAND TERRITORIES FOR NEW ZEALAND* at l. 21.6.1951-1.4.1958.	85.00	250.00	650.00
	d. Sign. title: *HIGH COMMISSIONER* at l. 20.4.1959; 10.12.1959; 1.5.1961.	50.00	135.00	350.00

		GOOD	FINE	XF
9	**5 POUNDS** 1920-59. Purple on m/c unpt. Boat at lower ctr.			
	a. (1920's).	—	Rare	—
	b. Sign. title: *MINISTER OF EXTERNAL AFFAIRS FOR NEW ZEALAND* at l. 1.11.1944.	700.00	1650.	—
	c. Sign. title: *MINISTER OF ISLAND TERRITORIES FOR NEW ZEALAND* at l. 11.4.1956.	400.00	1100.	—
	d. Sign. title: *HIGH COMMISSIONER* at l. 13.10.1958; 10.12.1959.	350.00	950.00	2100.

BANK OF WESTERN SAMOA

1960-61 PROVISIONAL ISSUE

#10-12 red ovpt: *Bank of Western Samoa, Legal Tender in Western Samoa by virtue of the Bank of Western Samoa Ordinance 1959* on older notes. Various date and sign. varieties.

10	**10 SHILLINGS**	**GOOD**	**FINE**	**XF**
	ND; 1960-61. Ovpt. on #7.			
	a. Sign. title: *HIGH COMMISSIONER* blocked out at lower l., w/*MINISTER OF FINANCE* below. 8.12.1960; 1.5.1961.	25.00	75.00	225.00
	b. ND. Sign. title: *MINISTER OF FINANCE* in plate w/o ovpt., at lower l. 1.5.1961.	25.00	75.00	225.00

11	**1 POUND**	**GOOD**	**FINE**	**XF**
	1960-61. Ovpt. on #8.			
	a. Sign. title: *HIGH COMMISSIONER* blocked out at lower l., w/*MINISTER OF FINANCE* below. 8.11.1960; 1.5.1961.	35.00	100.00	350.00
	b. Sign. title: *MINISTER OF FINANCE* in plate w/o ovpt., at lower l. 1.5.1961.	35.00	100.00	350.00

YUGOSLAVIA

The Federal Republic of Yugoslavia, a Balkan country located on the east shore of the Adriatic Sea. It has an area of 98,766 sq. mi. (255,804 sq. km.) and a population of *10.4 million. Capital: Belgrade. The chief industries are agriculture, mining, manufacturing and tourism. Machinery, nonferrous metals, meat and fabrics are exported.

Yugoslavia was proclaimed on Dec. 1, 1918, after the union of the Kingdom of Serbia, Montenegro and the South Slav territories of Austria-Hungary; and changed its official name from the Kingdom of the Serbs, Croats, and Slovenes to the Kingdom of Yugoslavia on Oct. 3, 1929. It was composed of six autonomous republics: Serbia, Croatia, Slovenia, Bosnia-Herzegovina, Macedonia and Montenegro with two autonomous provinces within Serbia: Kosovo-Melohija and Vojvodina. The Royal government of Yugoslavia attemped to remain neutral in World War II but, yielding to German pressure, aligned itself with the Axis powers in March of 1941; a few days later it was overthrown by revolutionary forces and its neutrality reasserted. The Nazis occupied the country on April 6, and throughout the remaining years were resisted by a number of guerrilla armies, notably that of Marshal Josip Broz Tito. After the defeat of the Axis powers, a leftist coalition headed by Tito abolished the monarchy and, on Jan. 31, 1946, established a "People's Republic".

The collapse of the Federal Republic during 1991-92 has resulted in the autonomous republics of Croatia, Slovenia, Bosnia-Herzegovina and Macedonia declaring their respective independence. Bosnia- Herzegovina is under military contest with the Serbian faction opposed to the Moslem populace. Besides the remainder of the older Serbian sectors, a Serbian enclave in Knin located in southern Croatia has emerged called REPUBLIKE SRPSKE KRAJINE or Serbian Republic-Krajina surrounding the city of Knin; it has also declared its independence in 1992.

Croatian forces overwhelmed this enclave in August 1995. In 1992 the Federal Republic of Yugoslavia, consisting of the former Republics of Serbia and Montenegro, was proclaimed.

* * * This section has been partially renumbered. * * *

RULERS:
Peter I, 1918-1921
Alexander I, 1921-1934
Peter II, 1934-1945

MONETARY SYSTEM:
1 Dinar = 100 Para
1 New Dinar = 100 Old Dinara, 1965-89
1 New Dinar = 10,000 Old Dinara, 1990-92
1 New Dinar = 10 Old Dinara, 1992-93
1 New Dinar = 1 Million "Old" Dinara, 1993
1 New Dinara = 1 Milliard "Old" Dinara, 1.1.1994

WATERMARK VARIETIES

Karageorge

Alexander I

КРАЉЕВСТВО СРБА ХРВАТА И СЛОВЕНАЦА

Kingdom of Serbs, Croats and Slovenes

МИНИСТАРСТВО ФИНАНСИЈА

MINISTRY OF FINANCE

Adhesive stamps affixed to old notes of the Austro-Hungarian Bank (including some already ovpt. in previous issue).

NOTE: Numerous local and government ovpt. (usually w/handstamp indicating redemption to Yugoslav currency), exist on notes of the Austro-Hungarian Bank and Serbian ovpt. on Bulgarian notes. As part of this second revalidation, special adhesive stamps were affixed to the notes. Wording on the 10, 20, and 50 Kronen stamps is tri-lingual (Serbian, Croatian, and Slovene), thus there is for lower denominations only one kind of stamp. Adhesive stamps affixed to 100 and 1000 Kronen notes have wording in only one language, Serbian (Cyrillic), Croatian or Slovene. Thus there are 3 different adhesive stamps for higher denominations.

1919 FIRST PROVISIONAL ISSUES

Black round ovpt. of inscription and eagle on old notes of the Austro-Hungarian Bank.

		GOOD	**FINE**	**XF**
1	**10 KRONEN** ND (1919 - old date 2.1.1915). Ovpt. on Austria #19.	8.00	20.00	50.00
2	**20 KRONEN** ND (1919 - old date 2.1.1913). Ovpt. on Austria #13.	40.00	100.00	200.00

3   50 KRONEN
ND (1919 - old date 2.1.1914). Ovpt. on Austria #15.

	Good	Fine	XF
	10.00	25.00	50.00

4   100 KRONEN
ND (1919 - old date 2.1.1912). Ovpt. on Austria #12.

	Good	Fine	XF
	8.00	20.00	50.00

5   1000 KRONEN
ND (1919 - old date 2.1.1902). Ovpt. on Austria #8.

	17.50	50.00	100.00

1919 SECOND PROVISIONAL ISSUES

NOTE: Descriptions for #6-10B relate only to the adhesive stamps affixed.

NOTE: #9, 9A, and 9B the adhesive stamp is either perforated or imperforate (straight edged).

6   10 KRONEN
ND (1919). Orange. Text in 3 languages; woman facing l.
  a. Adhesive stamp affixed to Austria #9 (-old date 2.1.1904).
  b. Adhesive stamp affixed to Austria #19 (-old date 2.1.1915).

	Good	Fine	XF
a.	3.00	8.00	20.00
b.	2.00	6.00	15.00

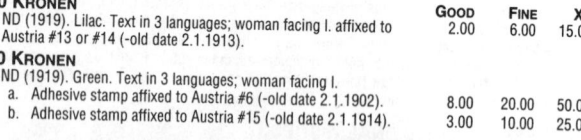

7   20 KRONEN
ND (1919). Lilac. Text in 3 languages; woman facing l. affixed to Austria #13 or #14 (-old date 2.1.1913).

	Good	Fine	XF
	2.00	6.00	15.00

8   50 KRONEN
ND (1919). Green. Text in 3 languages; woman facing l.
  a. Adhesive stamp affixed to Austria #6 (-old date 2.1.1902).
  b. Adhesive stamp affixed to Austria #15 (-old date 2.1.1914).

a.	8.00	20.00	50.00
b.	3.00	10.00	25.00

Slovenian text: KRALJESTVO • SRBOV • HRVATOV • SLOVENCEV

Croatian text: KRALJEVSTVO • SRBA • HRVATA • SLOVENACA

9   100 KRONEN
ND (1919-old date 2.1.1912). Brown. Text in Serbian (Cyrillic letters). Adhesive affixed to Austria #12.

	Good	Fine	XF
	4.00	12.00	30.00

9A   100 KRONEN
ND (1919-old date 2.1.1912). Brown. Text in Croatian. Adhesive stamp affixed to #12.

	3.00	10.00	25.00

9B   100 KRONEN
ND (1919-old date 2.1.1912). Text in Slovenian. Adhesive stamp affixed to Austria #12.

	4.00	12.00	30.00

10   1000 KRONEN
ND (1919-old date 2.1.1902). Blue, brown and orange. Text in Serbian (Cyrillic letters). Adhesive stamp affixed to Austria #8.

	4.00	12.00	30.00

10A   1000 KRONEN
ND (1919-old date 2.1.1902). Lt. blue, brown and orange. Text in Croatian. Adhesive stamp affixed to Austria #8.

	Good	Fine	XF
	3.00	10.00	25.00

10B   1000 KRONEN
ND (1919-old date 2.1.1902). Dk. blue, brown and orange. Text in Slovenian. Adhesive stamp affixed to Austria #8.

	5.00	12.00	30.00

1919 DINAR ISSUE

11   1/2 DINAR
1.2.1919. Brown and aqua on pink unpt. Arms at ctr. Back green and tan.

	VG	VF	UNC
	1.00	4.00	12.00

12   1 DINAR
ND (1919). Orange-brown on lt. tan unpt. Helmeted man at l.

	1.50	5.00	18.00

1921 ISSUE

13   25 PARA = 1/4 DINAR
21.3.1921. Blue on olive unpt. Girl at l. and r., bldg. at ctr. Back brown; church at l; equestrian statue at r.

	VG	VF	UNC
	1.00	5.00	15.00

1919 KRONE PROVISIONAL ISSUE

#14-20 ovpt. in Kronen-currency (Круна-Kruna-Kron). Color varieties of ovpt.

14   2 KRONEN ON 1/2 DINAR
ND (-old date 1.2.1919). Red ovpt. on #11.
  a. КРУНЕ (correct form).
  x. КУРНЕ (error).

	VG	VF	UNC
a.	2.00	6.00	18.00
x.	—	—	—

		VG	VF	UNC
15	**4 KRONEN ON 1 DINAR**	2.50	8.00	20.00
	ND (1919). Red ovpt. (always w/error *KYPHE*) on #12.			

		VG	VF	UNC
19	**400 KRONEN ON 100 DINARA**	60.00	150.00	500.00
	ND (1919). Lilac. Children at lower l. and r.			
20	**4000 KRONEN ON 1000 DINARA**	—	Rare	—
	ND (1919). Gray-violet. 3 allegorical figures at l. and r. Figures in ornamented circle at ctr., allegorical heads at l. and r. on back. Wmk: Helmeted man.			

		VG	VF	UNC
16	**20 KRONEN ON 5 DINARA**	2.00	10.00	40.00
	ND (1919). Lilac and brown on lt. blue unpt. Helmeted man at l. Caduceus w/wreath on back.			
	a. *KPYHA* (correct form).			
	x. *KYPHA* (error).			

НАПОДНА БАНКА КРАЉЕВИНЕ СРБА ХРВАТА И СЛОВЕНАЦА

NATIONAL BANK, KINGDOM OF SERBS, CROATS AND SLOVENES

1920 ISSUES

		VG	VF	UNC
17	**40 KRONEN ON 10 DINARA**	5.00	16.00	45.00
	1.2.1919. Blue w/black text. Blacksmith standing at l. Fruit baskets upper l. and r. on back.			

		VG	VF	UNC
21	**10 DINARA**	7.00	40.00	180.00
	1.11.1920. Blue on m/c unpt. "Progress" (man w/wheel) at l. Rocks and mountains on back. Printer: ABNC.			

		VG	VF	UNC
18	**80 KRONEN ON 20 DINARA**	6.00	25.00	80.00
	1.2.1919. Olive. Farmers plowing w/oxen. Back blue on red unpt.; wheat in field.			

22 100 DINARA
30.11.1920. Purple on yellow unpt. Boats in water at ctr., seated woman w/sword at r. Violet and m/c back; sailboats at ctr., man w/fruit leaning on shield w/arms at r.

	VG	VF	UNC
	10.00	50.00	250.00

23 1000 DINARA
30.11.1920. Brown and m/c. St. George slaying dragon at l., church at ctr. r. 5 city and farm scenes on back.

	VG	VF	UNC
a. Issued note.	—	Rare	—
x. Counterfeit (w/o wmk. or serial # and on thicker paper).	12.00	25.00	50.00

24 1000 DINARA
30.11.1920. Brown and m/c. Like #23 but blue ovpt. of male head (Karadjordjes) and inscription for Kingdom of Yugoslavia; colored rosette printing extending vertically through ctr.

	VG	VF	UNC
a. Issued note.	100.00	200.00	550.00
x1. Counterfeit on thicker paper and w/o wmk. or serial #.	—	—	—
x2. Counterfeit. Like x1 but w/rosette printing.	8.00	15.00	30.00

27 100 DINARA
1.12.1929. Purple on yellow unpt. Similar to #22.

	VG	VF	UNC
a. Wmk: Karageorge (lg. head, lt. moustache, top of collar shows).	5.00	12.00	30.00
b. Wmk: Alexander I (smaller head w/dk. moustache, full collar shows).	.35	1.00	4.00

1926 ISSUE

1931 ISSUE

25 10 DINARA
26.5.1926. Red-orange, blue and m/c. Woman at r. Arms at l. on back. Wmk: Woman's head. French printing.

	VG	VF	UNC
	10.00	30.00	140.00

КРАЉЕВИНЕ ЈУГОСЛАВИЈЕ

Kingdom of Yugoslavia

НАРОДНА БАНКА

NATIONAL BANK

1929 ISSUE

NOTE: For #27 w/ovpt. see Serbia #23.

28 50 DINARA
1.12.1931. Brown and m/c. Portr. Kg. Alexander I at l. Equestrian statue on back (issued in 1941 only as a Serbian note).

	VG	VF	UNC
	1.00	3.00	12.00

26 10 DINARA
1.12.1929. Red-orange, blue and m/c. Similar to #25.

	VG	VF	UNC
	20.00	70.00	225.00

29 **1000 DINARA**
1.12.1931. Blue-gray and brown. Qn. Marie at l., bird at r. Standing
women at l. and r. on back.

VG	VF	UNC
2.00	8.00	20.00

1934-36 ISSUE

30
(33) **20 DINARA**
6.9.1936. Brown on blue and m/c unpt. Kg. Peter II at ctr. Woman
w/wreath on back (issued in 1941 only as a Serbian note).

VG	VF	UNC
.50	1.00	7.00

31
(30) **100 DINARA**
15.7.1934. Blue and m/c. Woman seated w/boy at r. ctr. Shield
w/arms and 2 seated women on back. (Not issued).

VG	VF	UNC
10.00	25.00	60.00

32
(31) **500 DINARA**
6.9.1935. Green on lt. blue and pink unpt. Peter II at l. Women seated
w/sheaves of wheat on back.

VG	VF	UNC
3.00	8.00	20.00

33
(32) **1000 DINARA**
6.9.1935. M/c. Group of 6 people w/3 horses and lion. (Not issued).

VG	VF	UNC
20.00	80.00	225.00

34 **10,000 DINARA**
6.9.1936. Brown on m/c unpt. Kg. Peter II at l. (Not issued).

VG	VF	UNC
150.00	350.00	750.00

1939 ISSUE

35 **10 DINARA**
22.9.1939. Green. Kg. Peter II at l., bridge at ctr. Woman in national
costume at r. on back. Wmk: Older man in uniform.

VG	VF	UNC
2.00	8.00	20.00

1943 ISSUE

Kingdom in exile during WW II

#35A-35F portr. Kg. Peter II at ctr. English printing. (Not issued).

35A **5 DINARA**
ND (1943). Dk. green. Goats on hillside on back.
  a. Regular serial #.
  s. Specimen.

VG	VF	UNC
—	400.00	—
—	350.00	—

35B **10 DINARA**
ND (1943). Red and green. Landscape on back.
  a. Regular serial #.
  s. Specimen.

VG	VF	UNC
—	400.00	—
—	—	350.00

35C   25 DINARA
ND (1943). Blue and yellow. Monument on back.

	VG	VF	UNC
a. Regular serial #.	—	400.00	—
s. Specimen.	—	—	400.00

35D   100 DINARA
Sept. 1943. Green. Factory on back.

	VG	VF	UNC
a. Regular serial #.	—	400.00	—
s. Specimen.	—	—	350.00

35E   500 DINARA
Sept. 1943. Brown and green. Factory on back.

	VG	VF	UNC
a. Regular serial #.	—	500.00	—
s. Specimen.	—	—	500.00

35F   1000 DINARA
Sept. 1943. Black and green. Mountains and lake on back.

	VG	VF	UNC
a. Regular serial #.	—	500.00	—
s. Specimen.	—	—	500.00

DEMOKRATSKA FEDERATIVNA JUGOSLAVIJA

DEMOCRATIC FEDERATION OF YUGOSLAVIA

1944 ISSUE
#48-55 soldier w/rifle at r. Arms w/date *29.X1.1943* at l. on back.

48   1 DINAR
1944. Olive-brown.

	VG	VF	UNC
a. Thin paper.	.10	.20	1.50
b. Thick paper, w/o security thread.	.20	.40	1.00
c. Thick paper, thin security thread.	.25	.50	1.75

49   5 DINARA
1944. Blue. W/ or w/o security thread.

	VG	VF	UNC
a. Thin paper.	.10	1.50	3.50
b. Thick paper.	.20	2.00	5.00

50   10 DINARA
1944. Black on orange unpt.

	VG	VF	UNC
a. Unpt. yellow-orange.	.10	2.00	8.00
b. Unpt. deeper orange, wmk. paper.	.20	2.00	8.00
c. Vertical thread.	.30	3.00	15.00

51   20 DINARA
1944. Orange on lt. tan unpt.

	VG	VF	UNC
a. W/o security thread, w/lg. size numerals in serial #.	.20	2.00	10.00
b. Lg. size numerals in serial #, w/security thread.	.50	2.00	10.00
c. Sm. size numerals in serial #, w/o security thread.	.50	2.00	15.00

52   50 DINARA
ND (1944). Violet on gray unpt.

	VG	VF	UNC
a. Sm. size numerals in serial # (Russian print).	3.00	10.00	40.00
b. Lg. size numerals in serial # (Yugoslavian print).	5.00	15.00	45.00

53   100 DINARA
ND (1944). Dk. green on gray and lilac unpt.

	VG	VF	UNC
a. Like #52a.	2.00	4.00	25.00
b. Like #52b.	3.00	7.00	30.00

54   500 DINARA
1944. Brown on orange and lt. green unpt.

	VG	VF	UNC
a. Like #52a.	6.00	50.00	250.00
b. Like #52b.	7.00	60.00	300.00

55   1000 DINARA
1944. Dk. green on blue and tan unpt.

	VG	VF	UNC
a. Like #52a.	10.00	20.00	70.00
b. Like #52b.	5.00	12.50	60.00

FEDERATIVNE NARODNE REPUBLIKE JUGOSLAVIJE

NARODNA BANKA - NATIONAL BANK

1946 ISSUE

64   50 DINARA
1.5.1946. Brown on m/c unpt. Miner at l. Arms at l., woodchopper at ctr. on back.

	VG	VF	UNC
a. 1st issue: 8-digit serial #.	.75	2.50	15.00
b. 2nd issue: 9-digit serial #.	.75	1.50	12.00

65   100 DINARA

	VG	VF	UNC
1.5.1946. Brown on gold unpt. Blacksmith at l., arms at upper ctr., farmer at r. Fisherman on back.			
a. W/o security thread, sm. numerals in serial #.	.75	2.50	15.00
b. Horizontal thin security thread, lg. numerals in serial #.	.75	2.50	15.00
c. Like a., but error in Cyrillic: СУГОЧААВИСА (2 letter A's) instead of ЛА (L and A) at lower l.	4.00	15.00	30.00

66   500 DINARA

	VG	VF	UNC
1.5.1946. Brown on m/c unpt. Arms at l., soldier w/rifle at r. Farmers plowing w/horses on back.			
a. W/o security thread.	2.00	9.00	25.00
b. W/security thread.	2.00	8.00	22.00

67   1000 DINARA

	VG	VF	UNC
1.5.1946. Brown on m/c unpt. Arms at l., woman w/ears of corn at r. Waterfalls at l., standing woman w/sword at r. on back.			
a. W/o security thread.	1.00	7.00	18.00
b. W/horizontal security thread.	1.00	6.00	15.00
c. W/vertical security thread.	1.00	8.00	20.00

1949-51 ISSUE
#67I-67N (Not issued).

67I   10 DINARA

	VG	VF	UNC
1951. Brown.	—	—	450.00

67J   20 DINARA

	VG	VF	UNC
1951. Dk. blue.	—	—	600.00

67K   50 DINARA

	VG	VF	UNC
1.5.1950. Green. Partisan fighters at l. Women w/sheaves in field on back.	—	—	900.00

67L   100 DINARA

	VG	VF	UNC
1.5.1949. Blue and yellow. Similar to #68.	—	—	1000.

67M   1000 DINARA

	VG	VF	UNC
1.5.1949. Green. Farm workers at l. and r. Stonemasons at l., steel workers at r. on back.	—	—	800.00

		VG	VF	UNC
67X	**1000 DINARA**	—	1000.	1750.
(67G)	1950. Brown. Worker and woman at r.			
67Y	**5000 DINARA**	—	1000.	1750.
(67H)	1950. Green. 3 workers at r.			

1953 ISSUE

		VG	VF	UNC
67N	**5000 DINARA**	—	—	1350.
	1.11.1950. Blue and yellow. Cargo ship at dockside at l. Steel workers at ctr. r. on back.			

1950 ISSUE

#67P-67Y arms at l. on back. (Not issued.)

		VG	VF	UNC
67P	**1 DINAR**	—	—	120.00
(A67)	1950. Blue.			
67Q	**2 DINARA**	—	—	120.00
(B67)	1950. Red.			
67R	**5 DINARA**	—	—	100.00
(67A)	1950. Dk. brown.			

		VG	VF	UNC
67S	**10 DINARA**	—	—	100.00
(67B)	1950. Green. Portr. of young soldier at r.			
67T	**20 DINARA**	50.00	80.00	200.00
(67C)	1950. Brown. Boy at r.			

		VG	VF	UNC
67U	**50 DINARA**	100.00	125.00	250.00
(67D)	1950. Green. Farm woman w/sickle at r.			
67V	**100 DINARA**	100.00	125.00	250.00
(67E)	1950. Blue. Man w/hammer over shoulder at r.			

		VG	VF	UNC
67W	**500 DINARA**	250.00	350.00	450.00
(67F)	1950. Dk. blue. Soldier at r.			

		VG	VF	UNC
68	**100 DINARA**	10.00	30.00	80.00
	1.5.1953. Brown on m/c unpt. 4 workers at steam locomotive wheels. Farmers harvesting wheat on back.			

1955 ISSUE

		VG	VF	UNC
69	**100 DINARA**	.10	.25	1.50
	1.5.1955. Red on m/c unpt. Woman wearing national costume at l. Back m/c; view of Dubrovnik.			

		VG	VF	UNC
70	**500 DINARA**	.25	.75	5.00
	1.5.1955. Dk. green on m/c unpt. Farm woman w/sickle at l. 2 farm combines cutting wheat on back.			

71 1000 DINARA
1.5.1955. Dk. brown on m/c unpt. Male steel worker at l. Factory on
back.

	VG	VF	UNC
a. Plate #2 at lower r.	.50	1.00	6.00
b. W/o plate #.	2.00	10.00	35.00

72 5000 DINARA
1.5.1955. Blue-black on m/c unpt. Relief of Mestrovic at l. House of
Parliament bldg. in Belgrade at ctr. on back.

	VG	VF	UNC
a. Plate #2 at lower r.	12.00	40.00	100.00
b. W/o plate #.	13.50	60.00	180.00

REGIONAL

GOSPODARSKA BANKA ZA ISTRU, RIJEKU I SLOVENSKO PRIMORJE

STATE BANK FOR ISTRIA, FIUME AND SLOVENE COASTAL AREA

1945 ISSUE
#R1-R8 sailboat on back.

R1 1 LIRA
(56) 1945. Brown. Female soldier at l. on back.

VG 1.00 VF 3.00 UNC 30.00

R2 (57)	**5 LIRE** 1945. Green.	VG 1.00	VF 3.00	UNC 10.00
R3 (58)	**10 LIRE** 1945. Brown on green unpt.	1.00	4.00	10.00
R4 (59)	**20 LIRE** 1945. Purple on lt. green unpt.	VG	VF	UNC
	a. W/serial #.	1.50	4.00	15.00
	b. W/o serial #.	2.00	6.00	25.00
R5 (60)	**50 LIRE** 1945. Red-brown.			
	a. Red serial #.	10.00	20.00	60.00
	b. Black serial #.	30.00	60.00	350.00
	c. W/o serial #.	40.00	85.00	350.00
R6 (61)	**100 LIRE** 1945. Brown and blue.			
	a. W/serial #.	10.00	20.00	150.00
	b. W/o serial #.	8.00	15.00	130.00

R7 (62)	**500 LIRE** 1945. Gray on green unpt. Back brown on green unpt.	VG 12.00	VF 25.00	UNC 80.00
R8 (63)	**1000 LIRE** 1945. Purple and lt. brown. Farmer plowing w/ox on back.	8.00	15.00	65.00

HUNGARIAN OCCUPATION OF BACKA - WW II

HUNGARIAN ARMED FORCES

The western half of Vojvodina Province located in Northern Serbia.

1941 ISSUE

R9A 1000 DINARA
ND (1941). Revalidation adhesive stamp affixed to #29.

VG — VF — UNC —

ITALIAN OCCUPATION OF MONTENEGRO - WW II

ITALIAN ARMED FORCES

1941 ISSUE
#R10-R15 *VERIFICATO* handstamp on Yugoslav notes.

R10 10 DINARA
ND (1941 - old date 22.9.1939). Handstamp on #35.

GOOD 1.00 FINE 4.50 XF 15.00

R11	20 DINARA	GOOD	FINE	XF
	ND (1941 - old date 6.9.1936). Handstamp on #33.	1.00	4.50	15.00

R12	50 DINARA	GOOD	FINE	XF
	ND (1941 - old date 1.12.1931). Handstamp on #28.	1.00	3.50	12.50

R13	100 DINARA	GOOD	FINE	XF
	ND (1941 - old date 1.12.1929). Handstamp on #27.			
	a. Wmk: Karageorge.	2.00	8.00	20.00
	b. Wmk: Alexander.	.50	2.00	6.00
R13A	100 DINARA			
	ND (1941 - old date 30.11.1920). Handstamp on #22 in error.	—	Rare	—
R14	500 DINARA			
	ND (1941 - old date 3.9.1935). Handstamp on #31.	10.00	20.00	50.00

R15	1000 DINARA	GOOD	FINE	XF
	ND (1941 - old date 1.12.1931). Handstamp on #29.	10.00	20.00	50.00

ZANZIBAR

The British protectorate of Zanzibar and adjacent small islands, located in the Indian Ocean 22 miles (35 km.) off the coast of Tanganyika, comprised a portion of British East Africa. Zanzibar was also the name of a sultanate which included the Zanzibar and Kenya protectorates. Zanzibar has as area of 637 sq. mi. (1,651 sq. km.). Chief city: Zanzibar. The islands are noted for their cloves of which Zanzibar is the world's foremost producer.

Zanzibar came under Portuguese control in 1503, was conquered by the Omani Arabs in 1698, became independent of Oman in 1860, and (with Pemba) came under British control in 1890. Britain granted the protectorate self-government in 1961, and independence within the British Commonwealth on Dec. 19, 1963. On April 26, 1964, Tanganyika and Zanzibar (with Pemba) united to form the United Republic of Tanganyika and Zanzibar. The name of the country, which remained within the British Commonwealth, was changed to Tanzania on Oct. 29, 1964.

RULERS:
British to 1963

MONETARY SYSTEM:
1 Rupee = 100 Cents

BRITISH INFLUENCE

ZANZIBAR GOVERNMENT

1908-20 ISSUE

#1-7 dhow at lower l., group of 8 fruit pickers at lower r.

#2-4, 6 printer: W&S.

NOTE: From 1936 on notes of the East African Currency Board were in general use until notes of Tanzania were issued in 1966.

NOTE: Spink 10-96 100 Rupees #6 F-VF dated 1.8.1916 realized $7,360.

1	1 RUPEE	GOOD	FINE	XF
	1.9.1920. Lt. blue on green and brown. Uniface. Printer: TDLR.	600.00	1200.	2750.

2	5 RUPEES	GOOD	FINE	XF
	1.1.1908; 1.8.1916; 1.2.1928. Black on orange and green unpt. Uniface.	800.00	1500.	3750.

3	**10 RUPEES**	**GOOD**	**FINE**	**XF**
	1.1.1908; 1.8.1916; 1.9.1916; 1.2.1928. Red.	1000.	2500.	4750.

4	**20 RUPEES**	**GOOD**	**FINE**	**XF**
	1.1.1908; 1.8.1916; 1.2.1928. Lilac. Uniface.			
	a. Issued note.	—	Rare	—
	s. Specimen.	—	Rare	—
5	**50 RUPEES**			
	1.1.1908; 1.8.1916.	—	Unc	4000.

6	**100 RUPEES**	**GOOD**	**FINE**	**XF**
	1.1.1908; 1.8.1916. Dk. blue and red-brown.	—	Rare	—
7	**500 RUPEES**			
	1.9.1920.	—	Rare	—

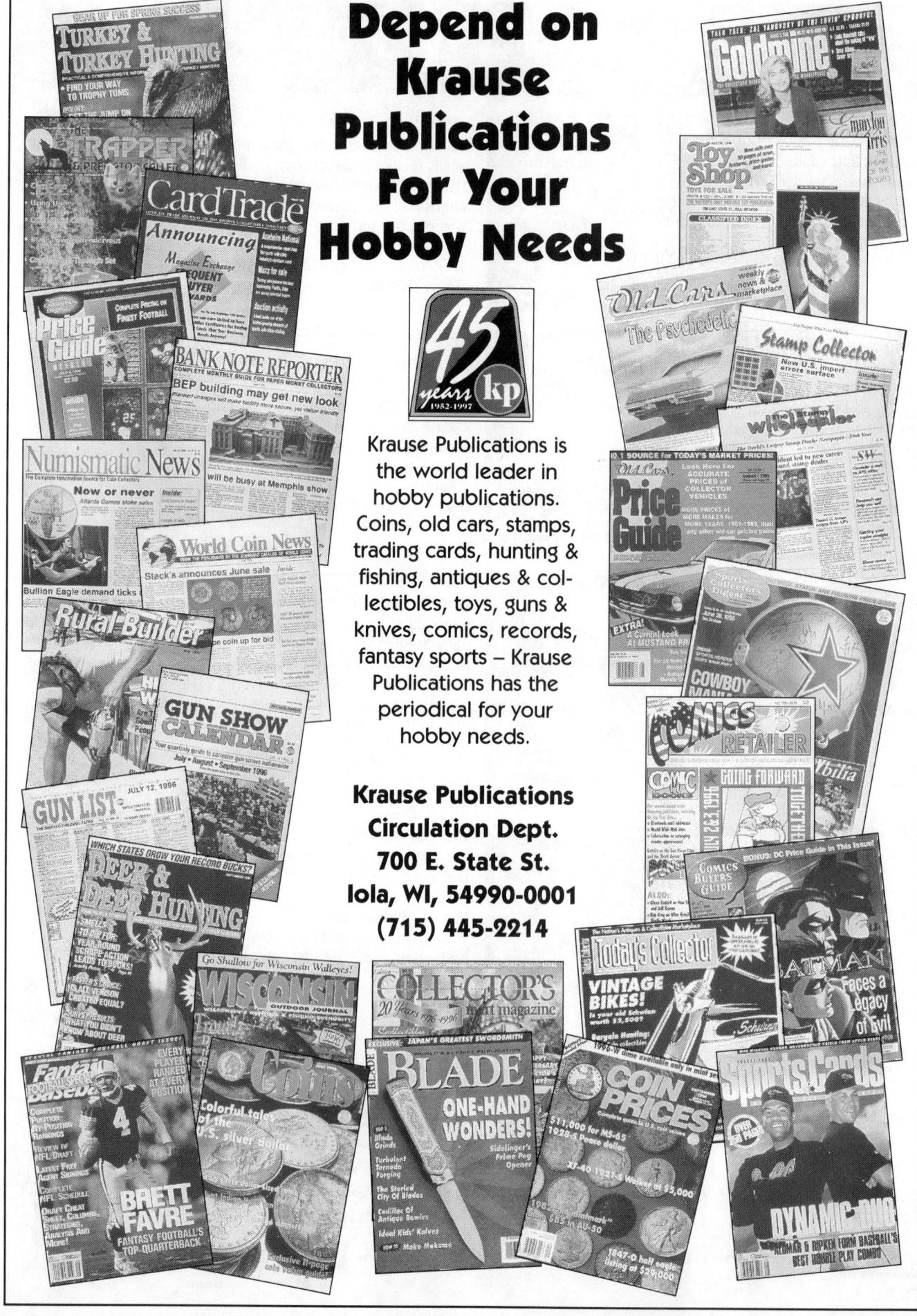